AIRLINE FLEETS 2010

Edited by Pete Webber

in collaboration with Colin Frost, Ken Marshall, Terry Smith, Barrie Towey, Tony Wheeler and John Wilkinson

Published by Air-Britain (Historians) Ltd

Sales Department — 41 Penshurst Road, Leigh, Tonbridge, Kent TN11 8HL

Membership Enquiries — 1 Rose Cottages, 179 Penn Road, Hazlemere,Bucks HP15 7NE

Further information is available on our website: http://www.air-britain.co.uk

PHOTO CAPTIONS

Front cover: Airbus A319 PR-MBU of TAM Linhas Aereas takes off towards the sea from Rio de Janeiro – Santos Dumont Airport. (Vito Cedrini)

Rear cover: *Top:* Arik Air Boeing 737-7GL 5N-MJE seen here at Abuja – Nnamdi Azikiwe International Airport, Nigeria on 24.6.09. (Juha Ritaranta/ABPic)
Centre: Saudi Arabian Airlines Embraer 170LR HZ-AEB on take-off from Dubai International, November 2009. (Tony Best)
Bottom: SAAB 340B JU-9905 of Eznis Airways taxies in at Ulan Bator – Buyant Ukhaa Airport, Mongolia on 13.5.09. (Juha Ritaranta/ABPic)

ISBN 978-0-85130-422-9 ISSN 0262-1657

Printed by Bell & Bain Ltd, Glasgow

INTRODUCTION

Information and Changes for the 2010 Edition

A second year as editor has allowed more time to take a look at the content of the book. I feel to have added less than the industry has taken away this year. A number of long term stored aircraft have gone to the axe. Space left in the various storage yards has quickly been filled however and tracking these changes has been a major undertaking this year.

Of late there has been some move towards some aircraft returning to service, only in small numbers so far but it may be the first small signs of some recovery in the health of the world's airlines.

The end of the year has seen a few more orders being placed after a noticable lull. Many aircraft have been deferred over the year and this has made it very difficult to present an accurate view of orders outstanding and expected delivery schedules. This has resulted in a change to the book for this year. I have removed all notes about outstanding orders, but those expected to be made in the next year are taken into account in the body of the fleets' listings, space being made available for the reader to add the details as aircraft are delivered.

It has also been a year of mergers, take-overs and some failures. The merger of Delta and Northwest is now complete and it has resulted in huge new combined fleets of both the mainline and commuter types. Others will no doubt follow suit over the next few years. Sadly every year a number of carriers find the game to be too hard and cease trading, those that have departed this year are shown with a full header entry followed by the date they ceased trading.

Airbus celebrated its 6000th aircraft delivery at the start of 2010 (an A380 to Emirates) plus the first flight of the A400M in December 2009.

The A320 'family' (A318,319,320,321) continues to sell well, the smaller models also booking regular sales in the corporate market. The 320 is due to be offered with winglets in the next year or so.

The A330 is still attracting orders and is profiting from the gap in time before the A350 and B787 become available. Production of the A330 is also boosted by military tanker orders and the soon to be in service A330F. The A340 is effectivly only made to special order now, though still available.

The A380 is now established in service, but production rates are still slow. Lufthansa will get their first aircraft in 2010 while Air France, Emirates, Qantas and Singapore Airlines will be expanding existing fleets.

Boeing has finally flown the B787 and still expecs to have the first aircraft in airline service in 2010. The 747-800 should fly around the time this book is launched and may also make it into service this year.

The 737 line goes on and on. Established operators continue to expand their fleets (though Ryanair have broken off negotiations for post-2013 orders). Older generation 737s are finding a good secondhand market in the former Soviet states.

The 747 line is now closed until the 800 series start to be delivered. Many aircraft have also been parked as a result of the slow trading in 2009.

The 767 line is continuing slowly, any change is likely to be driven by any new USAF tanker order should they ever be able to make a decision on which aircraft is bought, and stick to it!

The 777 is as strong as ever, added to this is the entry into service of the first 777F aircraft in 2009.

Embraer are finding strong sales for their 170 and 190 family aircraft. The smaller 145 line is mostly taken up with Legacy corporate aircraft, with new models being introduced to the existing strong line-up.

In Canada Bombardier is still busy with CRJ700 and CRJ900 production, the CRJ1000 programme is slipping however. Work on the new C Series is now very close to the final version. DHC are busy with the DHC-8-400 with regular deliveries worldwide and new orders.

The Russian industry continues to make a small number of new deliveries, the An148 making its entry into commercial service. Older types are going out of service quickly and I suspect they will be rare entries in the pages next year.

It is hoped that the Chinese ARJ21 will enter service in 2010, but this is far from certain at this time.

One interesting development this year is the number of new utility types being used. The PC-12 is finding a niche with carriers on thin routes, the C208 Caravan continues to sell well and new types such as the Quest Kodiak (in private and Missionary use at the moment) and PAC750XL are all finding work in the more remote areas of the world.

2010 will probably be a year of consolidation, better times will come and the airlines should benefit from changes made durring the hard times experienced of late.

Details included
Details are included for around 3000 operators in 200 countries – also included in the main text are those airlines whose fleets have been deleted this year, along with the reason. As a general guideline, the complete fleets of operators with an IATA two- or three-letter code are included (unless they only operate corporate flights), together with non-IATA coded operators of regular services where fleets are known. Many of the world's helicopter fleets down to Bell 206 size are included, with the large majority of all twin-engined aircraft and many single-engined aircraft down to Piper Cherokee Six that are also operated on passenger or express freight services.

The larger fleets are shown in type and registration order, with a space between types as they change. For reasons of saving space this is not done for smaller fleets with a large number of types, but only one or two aircraft of each type. These fleets are in registration order. This presentation is being developed all the time and I hope it has resulted in as clean a presentation of the data as is possible within sensible boundaries.

Civil registered jet and turboprop airliners in non-airline use, i.e. those owned and operated by the manufacturers or used as executive or special purpose, are again included in this year's edition. This section **does not** include details of the stored ex-airline aircraft.

The component parts of the US majors have again been grouped together under the airline heading and cross-referenced to the individual feeder carriers although this is becoming more difficult as more and more operators provide feeder services to a range of airlines Including, in some cases, regionals owned by one US major operating services for a competitor. As a result some of the feeders are listed separately for at least part of their fleets although they are cross-referenced to the majors as appropriate.

Credits
I am indebted to the following for contributions, corrections, assistance and the use of information, Ian Burnett, Colin Frost, Peter Gerhardt, Ken Marshall, Terry Smith, Chris Swan, Barrie Towey, John Wilkinson and all contributors to the Commercial Scene section of Air-Britain News edited by Tony Wheeler; Aviation Letter and the various Air-Britain publications as well as relevant web-sites.

On a personal note I must thank my long-suffering wife Tracey for all her understanding while I was working on the book over the winter. I am sure she was glad to see the back of me at first, but time sitting with the computer and not the family over Christmas and the New Year is hard to replace.

Update Information
For readers who are not already members of Air-Britain, this edition can be kept up to date by reading Commercial Scene and other sections of our regular publications. Details of the many benefits of membership are included at the end of this book.

Where possible, information received up to **30th January 2010** has been incorporated in the main text. Naturally, in a work of this complexity and scope, some errors and omissions will occur, and any reader who can add to, amend or correct the information included in this publication is invited to write to the address below.

Pete Webber, 20 Purbeck Close, Swindon, Wilts SN3 3RE pete.webber@air-britain.co.uk

EXPLANATORY NOTES

1 Noise Regulations

With effect from 01Jan85 FAR Part 36 Stage 2 regulations came into force with respect to four-engined aircraft. These prevented any further civil operations of Boeing 707/720 and DC-8 (except -70 series) aircraft to or from US airports unless they were fitted with hushkits so that they conformed to the new noise standards. Similar regulations applied in the UK from 01Jan88. Stage 3 requirements are now implemented with all non-compliant aircraft required to be hush-kitted or re-engined; this applies to 707s, 727s, 737s (srs-100/200s), DC-8/9s, 1-11s, Tu-134/154s and Il-62/76s. Many of these aircraft are being withdrawn from service as the economic situation makes it uneconomic to undertake the costly conversions (indeed some of the planned hush-kitting schemes have been abandoned). In the main text of the book reference is made, where known, to the type of hush-kit fitted to Boeing 707, 727, early 737s and Douglas DC-8s and 9s and whether it is Stage 2 or Stage 3 compliant. (For example, FedEx 3 means a 727 fitted with a Stage 3 compliant FedEx hush-kit). Stage 4 hush-kits are now available for MD-80 series and the first ones are included in this volume.

2 Chapter 11

In the US section of this book, reference is sometimes made to 'Chapter 11'. This refers to a section of the US bankruptcy code designed to give a company protection from its creditors while it attempts a financial reorganisation. Plans for such a reorganisation have to be submitted to and approved by the bankruptcy court. A Chapter 11 filing may or may not be accompanied by a cessation of operations. If operations do continue, then it is usually at a very much reduced level. If they are suspended, then it is possible that they may be restarted in some form at a future date. If the reorganisation plan fails, then an application for liquidation under Chapter 7 will be made.

Since a Chapter 11 filing does not automatically result in a permanent cessation of operations, airlines are only deleted from this book if at the time of writing it appears that resumption of operations in the near future is unlikely.

3 Boeing 747 Suffixes

An M suffix after Boeing 747-200s indicates that the aircraft is a Combi (Mixed) version fitted with a Side Cargo Door. While not used officially in national registers, the M suffix convention is used in Boeing official literature and is therefore adopted in this publication. Suffixes SCD and EUD indicate converted Side Cargo Door and Extended Upper Deck versions. SF indicates that the aircraft is a 'Special Freighter' conversion and BCF a Boeing Converted Freighter and BDSF is similar but converted by IAI without Boeing support (for 747-400 passenger to freight conversions).

4 Boeing 737 Test Registrations and Winglets

Several Boeing 737s complete their first flights from Renton (PAE) to Boeing Field (BFI) with the registration N1786B or other test registration and these are shown when known. In the book the suffix /W indicates the aircraft is fitted with Aviation Partner Boeing winglets.

5 German Spellings

German place names appear in anglicised form for operator bases but in the native German spelling for aircraft names (e.g. in the Lufthansa fleet).

6 Description of Entries

Countries are listed in alphabetical order of nationality prefix, with the airlines in each country also in alphabetical order. Fleets are listed in alphabetical order of aircraft manufacturer where five or more of the same type occur, otherwise they are listed in registration order. Aircraft type descriptions generally quote the manufacturer currently considered responsible for producing the aircraft. The immediate previous identity appears after the constructor's number and helps determine the source of newly acquired aircraft.

Each Country is identified in bold and italics and enclosed in a shadowed box; followed by airlines in alphabetical order, again enclosed in a box. The details listed for each airline are its name (and any trading or alternative name where appropriate); the two letter IATA designator and three-letter ICAO codes (where allocated and known); whether they are a member of IATA, and their main operating base(s), again with the recognised three letter code (where allocated). Also listed are the call-sign (as allocated by ICAO) and their IATA membership number (where known).

Each individual entry, from the left, lists current registration (or that known to be reserved and likely to be taken up with that operator in brackets), followed by type. This year Fokker 50 and 100 have been amended to reflect the actual designations. The next column lists the construction number, followed, for Boeing and McDonnell-Douglas types, by the line number separated by a slash (/). There then appears the immediate past identity (where known) followed by any fleet number or name. The final entry indicates any lease arrangements or other comments. Any three-letter designation refers to another airline. Aircraft on order are listed where either delivery is due in 2010 or where details of the aircraft are known. Otherwise details of aircraft on order for delivery in subsequent years are listed at the bottom of the aircraft type or airline entry; also listed there are any alliances, franchises or ownership details of interest.

Leased (lsd) aircraft will be found in the owner's fleet as well as that of the leasing airline. Where it is known that an aircraft is due to change operator during the currency of this book, it is shown in both fleets with a suitable note. Aircraft that have been withdrawn from service (wfs) are listed unless they are known to have been broken up or are beyond repair. Likewise, aircraft that have been involved in accidents but not confirmed as written off are still included.

7 Abbreviations

Abbreviations used in the text have the following meanings:

AOC	Air Operators Certificate
Avn	Aviation
c/s	colour scheme
dam	damaged
dbr	damaged beyond repair
fr	from
lsd	leased
Intl	International
Mgt	Management
o/o	on order (followed by date of delivery when known)
op	operate (d)
ops	operates/operations
resd	reserved
SPB	Seaplane Base
std	stored
svs	Services
wfs	withdrawn from service (i.e. unlikely to return to operational status with that operator)
w/o	written off

AP- PAKISTAN (Islamic Republic of Pakistan)

AIRBLUE — Pakblue (ED/ABQ) — Karachi (KHI)

	Type	c/n	Prev reg	Notes
☐ AP-BGV	Airbus A320-231	0443	ex G-CVYG	
☐ AP-BGZ	Airbus A320-232	0760	ex F-OHLO	
☐ AP-BIE	Airbus A319-112	3385	ex EI-DZY	
☐ AP-BIF	Airbus A319-112	3388	ex EI-DZZ	
☐ AP-BJA	Airbus A321-231	1199	ex D-ARFB	
☐ AP-BJB	Airbus A321-231	1218	ex D-ARFA	
☐ AP-BRJ	Airbus A321-231	1008	ex (TC-IEI)	
☐ AP-EDA	Airbus A320-200	3974	ex F-WWIT	on order

JS FOCUS AIR — JS Charters (JSJ) — Karachi (KHI)

	Type	c/n	Prev reg
☐ AP-BHZ	Fokker F.27 Friendship 500	10686	ex D-ADUP
☐ AP-BJC	Beech 1900C-1	UC-119	ex N119YV
☐ AP-BJD	Beech 1900C-1	UC-157	ex N157YV
☐ AP-BJS	Beech 1900C-1	UC-145	ex ZS-PCD

PAKISTAN INTERNATIONAL AIRLINES — Pakistan (PK/PIA) — Karachi (KHI)

	Type	c/n	Prev reg	Name	Notes
☐ AP-BDZ	Airbus A310-308	585	ex F-WWCH	City of Ziarat	
☐ AP-BEB	Airbus A310-308	587	ex F-WWCT	Thatta- Treasure of the Past	
☐ AP-BEC	Airbus A310-308	590	ex F-WWCX	Nowshera-The Defenders of the Land	
☐ AP-BEG	Airbus A310-308	653	ex F-WWCZ	Gilgit-The Silk Route	
☐ AP-BEQ	Airbus A310-308	656	ex F-WWCB		
☐ AP-BEU	Airbus A310-308	691	ex F-WWCD	Peshawar- Gateway to the East	
☐ AP-BGN	Airbus A310-324ET	676	ex F-WQTG	Taxila-The Exquisite Ghandara	
☐ AP-BGO	Airbus A310-324ET	678	ex F-WQTC	Gwadar-The New City Port	
☐ AP-BGP	Airbus A310-324ET	682	ex F-WQTF	Murree-Songs of the Pines	
☐ AP-BGQ	Airbus A310-325ET	660	ex F-OGYT	Sialkot-The Diligence of Industry	
☐ AP-BGR	Airbus A310-325ET	687	ex F-OGYU	Mohenjodaro-Indus Valley Civilisation	
☐ AP-BGS	Airbus A310-325ET	689	ex F-OGYV	Ziarat-The City of Flowers	
☐ AP-BHH	ATR 42-500	645	ex F-WWLE	Gwadar-The New Port City	
☐ AP-BHI	ATR 42-500	653	ex F-WWLK	Ziarat-The City of Flowers	
☐ AP-BHJ	ATR 42-500	657	ex F-WWLO	Mohenjodaro-IndusValley Civilisation	
☐ AP-BHM	ATR 42-500	659	ex F-WWLQ		
☐ AP-BHN	ATR 42-500	661	ex F-WWLS	Chitral-Mystery of the Kalash	
☐ AP-BHO	ATR 42-500	663	ex F-WWLU	The Gurdwara Glory	
☐ AP-BHP	ATR 42-500	665	ex F-WWLW		
☐ AP-BCA	Boeing 737-340	23294/1114			
☐ AP-BCB	Boeing 737-340	23295/1116			
☐ AP-BCC	Boeing 737-340	23296/1121		Quetta-Nature's Orchard	
☐ AP-BCD	Boeing 737-340	23297/1122			
☐ AP-BCF	Boeing 737-340	23299/1235			
☐ AP-BEH	Boeing 737-33A	25504/2341			
☐ AP-BFT	Boeing 737-340	23298/1123	ex AP-BCE		
☐ AP-BAK	Boeing 747-240M	21825/383		Thar-Colours of the Desert	
☐ AP-BAT	Boeing 747-240M	22077/429			stored
☐ AP-BFU	Boeing 747-367	23392/634	ex B-HIJ		
☐ AP-BFV	Boeing 747-367	23534/659	ex B-HIK		
☐ AP-BFW	Boeing 747-367	23221/615	ex B-HII	Lahore-Garden of the Mughal	
☐ AP-BFX	Boeing 747-367	23709/671	ex B-HOL	Karachi-Green Turtle Waters	stored
☐ AP-BFY	Boeing 747-367	23920/690	ex B-HOM		
☐ AP-BGG	Boeing 747-367	24215/709	ex B-HON	Kaghan	
☐ AP-BGJ	Boeing 777-240ER	33775/467			
☐ AP-BGK	Boeing 777-240ER	33776/469			
☐ AP-BGL	Boeing 777-240ER	33777/473			
☐ AP-BGY	Boeing 777-240LR	33781/504	ex N5022E		
☐ AP-BGZ	Boeing 777-240LR	33782/519	ex N6066Z		
☐ AP-BHV	Boeing 777-340ER	33778/601		Thar-Colours of the Desert	
☐ AP-BHW	Boeing 777-340ER	33779/611		Lahore-Garden of the Mughal	
☐ AP-BHX	Boeing 777-240ER	35296/613		Quetta-Nature's Orchard	
☐ AP-BID	Boeing 777-340ER	33780/705		Gilgit – The Silk Route	

RAYYAN AIR — Karachi (KHI)

	Type	c/n	Prev reg
☐ AP-BIB	Boeing 747-21AC	23652/669	ex N652AP

ROYAL AIRLINES — Royal Pakistan (R0/RPK) — Karachi (KHI)

	Type	c/n	Prev reg
☐ AP-BHS	Cessna 402C	402C0415	ex ZS-MNA

SHAHEEN AIR CARGO — Shaheen Cargo (SEE) — Islamabad (ISB)

Operate freight flights with Boeing 707-320Cs leased from Pakistan Air Force, and Ilyushin Il-76s leased from other operators, as required.

SHAHEEN AIR INTERNATIONAL — Shaheen Air (NL/SAI) — Karachi (KHI)

☐ AP-BHA	Boeing 737-277 (Nordam 3)	22645/768	ex N178AW	Yaz
☐ AP-BHB	Boeing 737-277 (Nordam 3)	22655/872	ex N188AW	Chundam
☐ AP-BHC	Boeing 737-291 (Nordam 3)	21509/521	ex EX-040	
☐ AP-BHG	Boeing 737-201 (Nordam 3)	21666/547	ex N224JT	
☐ AP-BIK	Boeing 737-2B7 (Nordam 3)	23114/997	ex N281AU	
☐ AP-BIP	Boeing 737-230 (Nordam 3)	22634/840	ex ZS-OIV	
☐ AP-BIQ	Boeing 737-258 (Nordam 3)	22857/919	ex ZS-OOD	
☐ AP-BIR	Boeing 737-228	23006/944	ex ZS-OVE	
☐ AP-BIT	Boeing 737-236	21803/677	ex ZS-OKD	
☐ AP-BIU	Boeing 737-236	21807/710	ex ZS-OKE	
☐ AP-BJH	Boeing 737-201 (Nordam 3)	22275/687	ex N235US	
☐ AP-BJI	Boeing 737-201 (Nordam 3)	22444/800	ex N242US	

STAR AIR AVIATION — (6S/URJ) — Karachi (KHI)

☐ AP-URJ	Boeing 727-224F	20660/985	ex N895AJ

VISION AIR INTERNATIONAL — (VIS) — Karachi (KHI)

☐ AP-BIA	Boeing 737-2H3	22625/776	ex UP-B7305

A2- BOTSWANA (Republic of Botswana)

AIR BOTSWANA — Botswana (BP/BOT) — Gaborone (GBE)

☐ A2-ABD	British Aerospace 146 Srs.100	E1101	ex (G-CBAE)		stored
☐ A2-ABN	ATR 42-500	507	ex F-WQNG	Chobe	
☐ A2-ABO	ATR 42-500	511	ex F-WQNC	Okavango	
☐ A2-ABP	ATR 42-500	512	ex F-WQNI	Makgadikgadi	
☐ A2-ABR	ATR 72-212A	786	ex F-WWEE		
☐ A2-ABS	ATR 72-212A	788	ex F-WWEG		
☐ A2-NAC	Beech 1900D	UE-325	ex ZS-OYM		Lsd fr NAC Executive

DELTA AIR — Maun (MUB)

☐ A2-AGR	Cessna U206F Stationair	U20601837	ex ZS-OCC
☐ A2-AHN	Cessna U206G Stationair 6 II	U20606432	ex ZS-LKX
☐ A2-AID	Cessna U206G Stationair 6 II	U20605755	ex N9353Z
☐ A2-AIW	Cessna 210N Centurion II	21064163	ex ZS-MYC
☐ A2-AJA	Britten-Norman BN-2A Islander	271	ex ZS-LKE
☐ A2-AJJ	Cessna 210L Centurion II	21061533	ex ZS-KPV

KALAHARI AIR SERVICES AND CHARTER — Gaborone (GBE)

☐ A2-AFK	Cessna 210N Centurion II	21064203	ex N5427Y
☐ A2-AHF	Beech 58 Baron	TH-859	ex N18405
☐ A2-AHZ	Beech 200 Super King Air	BB-95	ex ZS-JPD
☐ A2-DBH	Beech C90 King Air	LJ-988	ex ZS-LUU
☐ A2-KAB	Beech 1900C-1	UC-150	ex ZS-PCE
☐ A2-KAS	Beech 200 Super King Air	BB-614	ex ZS-LKA

MACK AIR — Maun (MUB)

☐ A2-AIC	Cessna U206G Stationair 6 II	U20606419	ex N9353Z
☐ A2-AJI	Cessna U206G Stationair 6 II	U20606842	ex ZS-NSS
☐ A2-AKB	Cessna U206F Stationair	U20601889	ex A2-ZHJ
☐ A2-AKI	Cessna 208B Caravan I	208B0552	ex 5Y-VIJ
☐ A2-FMD	Cessna U206G Stationair 6 II	U20606005	ex ZS-KSM
☐ A2-ZFF	Cessna U206D Super Skywagon	U206-1263	ex ZS-FPD
☐ A2-AJZ	Gippsland GA-8 Airvan	GA8-04-059	ex VH-CRQ
☐ A2-AKG	Cessna 208B Caravan I	208B0573	ex 3D-VIK
☐ A2-MAC	Cessna 210N Centurion II	21063337	ex V5-MRW
☐ A2-MEG	Cessna 208B Caravan I	208B0944	ex N4085S

MOREMI AIR SERVICES — Maun (MUB)

☐ A2-AEI	Cessna U206F Stationair	U20602470	ex ZS-LDJ
☐ A2-AFE	Cessna U206F Stationair	U20602452	ex ZS-IYD
☐ A2-AKD	Cessna 208B Caravan I	208B0582	ex ZS-JML
☐ A2-DOG	Cessna U206G Stationair 6 II	U20604819	ex A2-DOW
☐ A2-TEN	Cessna 210L Centurion II	21061141	ex A2-AIY
☐ A2-ZED	Britten-Norman BN-2A-21 Islander	736	ex ZS-XGF

NAC EXECUTIVE CHARTER — Gaborone (GBE)

☐ A2-AJO	Beech 58 Baron	TH-614	ex ZS-OGB	
☐ A2-MXI	Beech 200T Super King Air	BT-5	ex N205EC	
☐ A2-NAC	Beech 1900D	UE-325	ex ZS-OYM	Air Botswana colours

NORTHERN AIR — Maun (MUB)

☐ A2-ADK	Cessna U206G Stationair 6 II	U20606056	ex ZS-KUO
☐ A2-AER	Cessna U206G Stationair 6 II	U20606324	ex ZS-KXE
☐ A2-NAB	Cessna U206G Stationair 6 II	U20605439	ex ZS-KDA

SAFARI AIR — Maun (MUB)

☐ A2-AIX	Cessna U206F Stationair	U20601944	ex ZS-MAD
☐ A2-AJM	Britten-Norman BN-2B-21 Islander	862	ex ZS-KLK
☐ A2-AJQ	Gippsland GA-8 Airvan	GA8-02-023	ex VH-DTA
☐ A2-AJS	Gippsland GA-8 Airvan	GA8-04-047	ex VH-LED
☐ A2-CEX	Cessna 207 Skywagon	20700154	ex ZS-IDG
☐ A2-TAU	Britten-Norman BN-2B-20 Islander	2173	ex N999BR

SEFOFANE AIR CHARTER — Maun (MUB)

☐ A2-AIV	Cessna U206G Stationair 6 II	U20606410	ex ZS-LUA	
☐ A2-ANT	Cessna U206G Stationair 6 II	U20606237	ex ZS-ANT	
☐ A2-BEE	Cessna U206G Stationair 6 II	U20605665	ex ZS-KUL	
☐ A2-BUG	Cessna U206G Stationair 6 II	U20604700	ex N27MF	
☐ A2-FOX	Cessna U206G Stationair 6 II	U20604927	ex N735JM	
☐ A2-JET	Cessna 206H Stationair	20608027	ex ZS-OIA	
☐ A2-OWL	Cessna U206G Stationair 6 II	U20606978	ex ZS-NXR	
☐ A2-XIG	Cessna U206G Stationair 6 II	U20605528	ex ZS-NSU	
☐ A2-BUF	Cessna 208B Caravan I	208B0815	ex ZS-BUF	Kwatale
☐ A2-EGL	Cessna 208B Caravan I	208B1158	ex ZS-ABR	
☐ A2-GNU	Cessna 208B Caravan I	208B0848	ex N1287Y	
☐ A2-LEO	Cessna 208B Caravan I	208B0820	ex N1307A	
☐ A2-NAS	Cessna 208B Caravan I	208B0704	ex ZS-TSW	
☐ A2-ZEB	Cessna 208B Caravan I	208B0750	ex N750LK	
☐ A2-BVR	Cessna 310R	310R2134	ex ZS-KUY	

XUGANA AIR — Maun (MUB)

☐ A2-AKH	Cessna 208 Caravan I	20800288	ex C-FWTK
☐ A2-AKK	Cessna 208B Caravan I	208B0441	ex ZS-OAR
☐ A2-AKO	Cessna 208B Caravan I	208B0736	ex ZS-OWW

A3- TONGA (Kingdom of Tonga)

AIRLINES TONGA — Tongatapu-Fua'amotu International (TBU)

☐ DQ-FHC	Harbin Y-12 II	0056		Save our Oceans	Op by FAJ
☐ DQ-FHF	Harbin Y-12 II	0047	ex B-531L		Op by FAJ

PEAU VAVA'U AIR (30/PVU) — Tongatapu-Fua'amotu International (TBU)

☐ A3-AWP	Douglas DC-3C	16387/33135	ex ZK-AWP	Lucille	
☐ A3-FEW	Beech 65-80 Queen Air	LC-168	ex DQ-FEW		Queenaire 8800 conversion

A4O- OMAN (Sultanate of Oman)

OMANAIR — Khanjar (WY/OMA) — Muscat-Seeb Intl (MCT)

☐ A4O-DA	Airbus A330-243	1038	ex F-WWYM		
☐ A4O-DB	Airbus A330-243	1044	ex F-WWKA		
☐ A4O-DC	Airbus A330-243	1049	ex F-WWKL		
☐ A4O-DD	Airbus A330-243	1063	ex F-WWYN		
☐ A4O-DE	Airbus A330-243	1093	ex F-WW		on order
☐ A4O-DF	Airbus A330-243	1120	ex F-WW		on order
☐ A4O-BA	Boeing 737-8BK/W	29685/2457	ex N1786B	Fahud	
☐ A4O-BB	Boeing 737-8Q8/W	30721/2255			
☐ A4O-BC	Boeing 737-81M/W	35284/2738	ex N1786B	Ras Al Had	
☐ A4O-BD	Boeing 737-81M/W	35287/2804	ex N1786B		
☐ A4O-BE	Boeing 737-81M/W	37161/2919	ex N1786B		
☐ A4O-BF	Boeing 737-8FZ/W	29637/3051			
☐ A4O-BG	Boeing 737-8FZ/W	29664/3060	ex N1787B		
☐ A4O-BJ	Boeing 737-81M/W	34242/1674		803	
☐ A4O-BM	Boeing 737-8FZ/W	29682/2853			

☐ A4O-BN	Boeing 737-8Q8/W	30652/1018	ex N1795B	802 ; Muscat	
☐ A4O-BO	Boeing 737-71M	33103/1154	ex N6066Z	701	
☐ A4O-BP	Boeing 737-8Q8/W	35272/2537	ex N1786B		
☐ A4O-BR	Boeing 737-81M/W	33104/1337		801	
☐ A4O-BS	Boeing 737-7Q8	30649/1048		702	
☐ A4O-BU	Boeing 737-81M/W	35108/2554	ex N1786B		
☐ A4O-AS	ATR 42-500	574	ex VT-ADL		
☐ A4O-AT	ATR 42-500	576	ex F-WWEP		Lsd to DKN

A5- BHUTAN (Kingdom of Bhutan)

DRUKAIR — ***Royal Bhutan (KB/DRK)*** — ***Paro (PBH)***

☐ A5-RGF	Airbus A319-115	2306	ex D-AVYA
☐ A5-RGG	Airbus A319-115	2346	ex D-AVWO

A6- UNITED ARAB EMIRATES (Al Imarat al-Arabiya al-Muttahida)

ABU DHABI AVIATION — ***Abu Dhabi-Bateen (AZI)***

☐ A6-AWA	Agusta AW139	31044	ex I-EASJ	
☐ A6-AWB	Agusta AW139	31053		
☐ A6-AWC	Agusta AW139	31058		
☐ A6-AWF	Agusta AW139	31118		
☐ A6-AWH	Agusta AW139	41011		
☐ A6-AWK	Agusta AW139	31150		
☐ A6-AWL	Agusta AW139	31153		
☐ A6-BBB	Agusta AW139	31028	ex I-RAIP	Royal Jet colours
☐ A6-BCE	Bell 206B JetRanger III	2185		
☐ A6-BCF	Bell 206B JetRanger III	2423		
☐ A6-BCK	Bell 206B JetRanger III	2426		
☐ A6-BCL	Bell 206B JetRanger III	2720		
☐ A6-BAB	Bell 212	31227		
☐ A6-BAM	Bell 212	31165	ex C-GTHQ	
☐ A6-BBC	Bell 212	30777		
☐ A6-BBE	Bell 212	30783	ex N9937K	
☐ A6-BBK	Bell 212	30802		
☐ A6-BBL	Bell 212	30822		
☐ A6-BBO	Bell 212	30903		
☐ A6-BBP	Bell 212	30917		
☐ A6-BBQ	Bell 212	30942		
☐ A6-BBR	Bell 212	30976		
☐ A6-BBS	Bell 212	30977		
☐ A6-BBU	Bell 212	31183		
☐ A6-BBV	Bell 212	31189		
☐ A6-BBY	Bell 212	32125		
☐ A6-BBZ	Bell 212	32141		
☐ A6-	Bell 212	30891	ex C-FRUT	
☐ A6-BAE	Bell 412HP	36072		
☐ A6-BAF	Bell 412HP	36082		
☐ A6-BAH	Bell 412HP	36119	ex C-GBUP	
☐ A6-BAI	Bell 412HP	36122		
☐ A6-BAK	Bell 412HP	36123		
☐ A6-BAL	Bell 412HP	36150		
☐ A6-BAO	Bell 412HP	36152		
☐ A6-BAP	Bell 412HP	36189	ex N52091	
☐ A6-BAQ	Bell 412EP	36190		
☐ A6-BAS	Bell 412EP	36215		
☐ A6-BAT	Bell 412EP	36216		
☐ A6-BAV	Bell 412EP	36319	ex N70791	
☐ A6-BAZ	Bell 412	33107	ex PK-HMU	
☐ A6-HBM	Bell 412EP	36280	ex C-GJCO	
☐ A6-ADA	de Havilland DHC-8Q-202	471	ex C-GLOT	
☐ A6-ADB	de Havilland DHC-8Q-315	650	ex C-FLUJ	
☐ A6-ADC	de Havilland DHC-8Q-202	473	ex C-GFRP	
☐ A6-ADD	de Havilland DHC-8Q-315	627	ex V2-LGL	
☐ A6-ADE	de Havilland DHC-8Q-315	628	ex V2-LGM	
☐ A6-ADF	de Havilland DHC-8Q-315	610	ex V2-LGJ	
☐ A6-ADG	de Havilland DHC-8Q-315	624	ex V2-LGK	
☐ A6-ADK	de Havilland DHC-8-402Q	4222	ex C-FTIA	

AEROGULF SERVICES — ***Aerogulf*** — ***Dubai (DXB)***

☐ A6-ALO	Bell 206L-3 LongRanger III	51435	ex PT-YBK
☐ A6-ALP	Bell 206B JetRanger III	2495	ex (A6-BCJ)

Registration	Type	C/n	Previous identity	Name	Remarks
☐ A6-ALA	Bell 212	30664	ex N71AL		
☐ A6-ALC	Bell 212	30790	ex N2781A		
☐ A6-ALD	Bell 212	30809	ex N143AL		
☐ A6-ALU	Bell 212	30729	ex C-GBKC		
☐ A6-ALV	Bell 212	30703	ex A6-HMR		
☐ A6-ALW	Bell 212	35065	ex N62200		
☐ A6-ALX	Bell 212	30888	ex YV-191CP		

AIR ARABIA — *Arabia (G9/ABY)* — *Sharjah (SHJ)*

Registration	Type	C/n	Previous identity	Name	Remarks
☐ A6-ABA	Airbus A320-214	2158	ex F-WWDF	Al Bdee'a	
☐ A6-ABB	Airbus A320-214	2166	ex F-WWDR	Waset	
☐ A6-ABC	Airbus A320-214	2278	ex F-WWDM	Al Riqa'a	
☐ A6-ABD	Airbus A320-214	2349	ex F-WWBP	Sharjah	
☐ A6-ABE	Airbus A320-214	2712	ex F-WWBB	Al Heera	
☐ A6-ABF	Airbus A320-214	2764	ex F-WWBS	Al Mansura	
☐ A6-ABG	Airbus A320-214	2930	ex F-WWBU		
☐ A6-ABH	Airbus A320-214	2964	ex F-WWDA		
☐ A6-ABI	Airbus A320-214	3044	ex F-WWDP		
☐ A6-ABJ	Airbus A320-214	3218	ex F-WWBB	Kalba	
☐ A6-ABK	Airbus A320-214	3444	ex F-WWIF		
☐ A6-ABL	Airbus A320-214	3476	ex F-WWDG		
☐ A6-ABN	Airbus A320-214	3152	ex EC-KEZ		
☐ A6-ABO	Airbus A320-214	3626	ex F-WWIR		
☐ A6-ABP	Airbus A320-214	3802	ex F-WWBV		
☐ A6-ABQ	Airbus A320-214	3840	ex F-WWBM		
☐ A6-ABR	Airbus A320-214	3925	ex F-WWBP		
☐ A6-ABS	Airbus A320-214	4061	ex F-WWBE		
☐ A6-	Airbus A320-214	4243	ex		on order
☐ A6-	Airbus A320-214	4310	ex		on order
☐ A6-	Airbus A320-214		ex		on order
☐ A6-	Airbus A320-214		ex		on order
☐ A6-	Airbus A320-214		ex		on order
☐ A6-	Airbus A320-214		ex		on order

AVE.COM — *Phoenix Sharjah (2E/PHW)* — *Sharjah (SHJ)*

Registration	Type	C/n	Previous identity	Remarks
☐ A6-PHA	Boeing 737-2T4	23444/1154	ex EX-027	
☐ A6-PHC	Boeing 737-33A	23626/1284	ex EC-JJV	
☐ A6-PHD	Boeing 737-2T5 (Nordam 3)	22395/729	ex EX-048	
☐ A6-PHF	Boeing 737-219	21645/535	ex EX-012	
☐ A6-PHG	Boeing 737-3Q8	24986/2192	ex N431LF	
☐ A6-PHH	Boeing 737-3Q8	26314/2707	ex G-THOF	
☐ EX-077	Boeing 737-268	21277/469	ex HZ-AGJ	stored

DOLPHIN AIR — *Dolphin (ZD/FDN)* — *Sharjah (SHJ)*

Registration	Type	C/n	Previous identity	Remarks
☐ A6-ZYA	Boeing 737-2S2C	21926/597	ex N720A	stored RKT
☐ A6-ZYC	Boeing 737-2X2	22679/807	ex N719A	stored RKT

EASTERN SKYJETS — *(ESJ)* — *Dubai (DXB)*

Registration	Type	C/n	Previous identity
☐ A6-ESA	Douglas DC-9-51 (ABS 3)	48136/993	ex TG-JII
☐ A6-ESC	Douglas DC-9-32	48150/1014	ex TG-URY
☐ A6-ESK	British Aerospace Jetstream 41	41090	ex G-CEDS

EASTOK AVIA — *(EAA)* — *Sharjah (SHJ)*

Registration	Type	C/n	Previous identity	Remarks
☐ EX-532	Boeing 737-247 (Nordam 3)	23605/1371	ex N378DL	
☐ EX-734	Boeing 737-25A (Nordam 3)	23791/1486	ex 5N-BID	Lsd to East Air
☐ EX-736	Boeing 737-247 (Nordam 3)	23517/1261	ex N243WA	Lsd to KMF

EMIRATES — *Emirates (EK/UAE)* — *Dubai (DXB)*

Registration	Type	C/n	Previous identity
☐ A6-EAA*	Airbus A330-243	348	ex F-WWYK
☐ A6-EAB*	Airbus A330-243	365	ex F-WWKB
☐ A6-EAC*	Airbus A330-243	372	ex F-WWYQ
☐ A6-EAD+	Airbus A330-243	382	ex F-WWYR
☐ A6-EAE+	Airbus A330-243	384	ex F-WWYS
☐ A6-EAF+	Airbus A330-243	392	ex F-WWYX
☐ A6-EAG+	Airbus A330-243	396	ex F-WWKJ
☐ A6-EAH+	Airbus A330-243	409	ex F-WWKT
☐ A6-EAI+	Airbus A330-243	437	ex F-WWYI
☐ A6-EAJ+	Airbus A330-243	451	ex F-WWKE
☐ A6-EAK*	Airbus A330-243	452	ex F-WWKF
☐ A6-EAL*	Airbus A330-243	462	ex F-WWKK
☐ A6-EAM+	Airbus A330-243	491	ex F-WWYO
☐ A6-EAN+	Airbus A330-243	494	ex F-WWKJ
☐ A6-EAO+	Airbus A330-243	509	ex F-WWYX
☐ A6-EAP+	Airbus A330-243	525	ex F-WWKV
☐ A6-EAQ*	Airbus A330-243	518	ex F-WWKT

☐ A6-EAR+	Airbus A330-243	536	ex F-WWYF	
☐ A6-EAS*	Airbus A330-243	455	ex F-WWKH	
☐ A6-EKQ*	Airbus A330-243	248	ex F-WWYX	
☐ A6-EKR*	Airbus A330-243	251	ex F-WWKO	
☐ A6-EKS+	Airbus A330-243	283	ex F-WWKH	
☐ A6-EKT+	Airbus A330-243	293	ex F-WWKR	
☐ A6-EKU+	Airbus A330-243	295	ex F-WWYF	
☐ A6-EKV+	Airbus A330-243	314	ex F-WWYR	
☐ A6-EKW+	Airbus A330-243	316	ex F-WWYS	
☐ A6-EKX+	Airbus A330-243	326	ex F-WWYV	
☐ A6-EKY+	Airbus A330-243	328	ex F-WWYX	
☐ A6-EKZ*	Airbus A330-243	345	ex F-WWYI	
☐ A6-ERA+	Airbus A340-541	457	ex F-WWTI	
☐ A6-ERB+	Airbus A340-541	471	ex F-WWTK	
☐ A6-ERC+	Airbus A340-541	485	ex F-WWTL	
☐ A6-ERD+	Airbus A340-541	520	ex F-WWTS	
☐ A6-ERE+	Airbus A340-541	572	ex F-WWTV	
☐ A6-ERF+	Airbus A340-541	394	ex F-WWTE	
☐ A6-ERG+	Airbus A340-541	608	ex F-WWTX	
☐ A6-ERH+	Airbus A340-541	611	ex F-WWTY	
☐ A6-ERI+	Airbus A340-541	685	ex F-WWTP	
☐ A6-ERJ+	Airbus A340-541	694	ex F-WWTQ	
☐ A6-ERM+	Airbus A340-313X	236	ex D-AIFL	
☐ A6-ERN+	Airbus A340-313X	166	ex D-ASIC	
☐ A6-ERO+	Airbus A340-313X	163	ex D-ASIB	
☐ A6-ERP+	Airbus A340-313X	185	ex D-AGBM	
☐ A6-ERQ+	Airbus A340-313X	190	ex D-AJGP	
☐ A6-ERR+	Airbus A340-313X	202	ex D-ASID	
☐ A6-ERS+	Airbus A340-313X	139	ex D-ASIM	
☐ A6-ERT+	Airbus A340-313X	149	ex D-ASIN	
☐ A6-EDA	Airbus A380-861	011	ex D-AXXA	
☐ A6-EDB	Airbus A380-861	013	ex F-WWSJ	
☐ A6-EDC	Airbus A380-861	016	ex D-AXAC	
☐ A6-EDD	Airbus A380-861	020	ex F-WWSS	
☐ A6-EDE	Airbus A380-861	017	ex D-AXAE	
☐ A6-EDF	Airbus A380-861	007	ex F-WWJB	
☐ A6-EDG	Airbus A380-861	023	ex F-WWST	
☐ A6-EDH	Airbus A380-861	025	ex F-WWSV	
☐ A6-EDI	Airbus A380-861	009	ex F-WWSF	on order
☐ A6-EDJ	Airbus A380-861	028	ex F-WW	on order
☐ A6-EDK	Airbus A380-861	030	ex F-WW	on order
☐ A6-EDL	Airbus A380-861	046	ex F-WW	on order
☐ A6-EDM	Airbus A380-861	042	ex F-WW	on order
☐ A6-EDN	Airbus A380-861	056	ex F-WW	on order
☐ A6-EDO	Airbus A380-861	057	ex F-WW	on order
☐ A6-EDP	Airbus A380-861		ex F-WW	on order
☐ A6-EDR	Airbus A380-861		ex F-WW	on order
☐ A6-EDS	Airbus A380-861		ex F-WW	on order
☐ A6-EDT	Airbus A380-861		ex F-WW	on order
☐ A6-EDU	Airbus A380-861		ex F-WW	on order
☐ A6-EBA+	Boeing 777-31HER	32706/506		
☐ A6-EBB+	Boeing 777-36NER	32789/508		
☐ A6-EBC+	Boeing 777-36NER	32790/512		
☐ A6-EBD+	Boeing 777-31HER	33501/516	ex N5022E	
☐ A6-EBE+	Boeing 777-36NER	32788/532		
☐ A6-EBF*	Boeing 777-31HER	32708/536		
☐ A6-EBG+	Boeing 777-36NER	33862/535		
☐ A6-EBH*	Boeing 777-31HER	32707/539		
☐ A6-EBI+	Boeing 777-36NER	32785/540		
☐ A6-EBJ+	Boeing 777-36NER	32787/542		
☐ A6-EBK+	Boeing 777-31HER	34481/549	ex N5020K	
☐ A6-EBL+	Boeing 777-31HER	32709/551	ex N5017V	
☐ A6-EBM+	Boeing 777-31HER	34482/556		
☐ A6-EBN+	Boeing 777-36NER	32791/560		
☐ A6-EBO	Boeing 777-36NER	32792/568		
☐ A6-EBP+	Boeing 777-31HER	32710/569	ex N5017V	
☐ A6-EBQ	Boeing 777-36NER	33863/576	ex N5017V	
☐ A6-EBR+	Boeing 777-31HER	34483/578		
☐ A6-EBS+	Boeing 777-31HER	32715/582		
☐ A6-EBT+	Boeing 777-31HER	32730/585		
☐ A6-EBU	Boeing 777-31HER	34484/590		
☐ A6-EBV	Boeing 777-31HER	32728/594		
☐ A6-EBW	Boeing 777-36NER	32793/598		
☐ A6-EBX	Boeing 777-31HER	32729/619	ex N5017V	
☐ A6-EBY	Boeing 777-36NER	33864/622	ex N5017V	
☐ A6-EBZ	Boeing 777-31HER	32713/628		
☐ A6-ECA	Boeing 777-36NER	32794/632	ex N5017B	
☐ A6-ECB	Boeing 777-31HER	32714/641	ex N5016R	
☐ A6-ECC	Boeing 777-36NER	33865/664	ex N5020K	
☐ A6-ECD	Boeing 777-36NER	32795/669	ex N5017V	

	Registration	Type	c/n	Previous identity	Remarks
☐	A6-ECE	Boeing 777-31HER	35575/681		
☐	A6-ECF	Boeing 777-31HER	35574/690		
☐	A6-ECG	Boeing 777-31HER	35579/709		
☐	A6-ECH	Boeing 777-31HER	35581/714		
☐	A6-ECI	Boeing 777-31HER	35580/728	ex N1785B	
☐	A6-ECJ	Boeing 777-31HER	35583/734		
☐	A6-ECK	Boeing 777-31HER	35584/743		
☐	A6-ECL	Boeing 777-31HER	37704/748		
☐	A6-ECM	Boeing 777-31HER	37703/755	ex N5017V	
☐	A6-ECN	Boeing 777-31HER	37705/761		
☐	A6-ECO	Boeing 777-31HER	37706/765		
☐	A6-ECP	Boeing 777-31HER	37707/768		
☐	A6-ECQ	Boeing 777-31HER	35588/779		
☐	A6-ECR	Boeing 777-31HER	35592/794	ex N5017V	
☐	A6-ECS	Boeing 777-31HER	38980/803	ex N5017V	
☐	A6-ECT	Boeing 777-31HER	35591/808		
☐	A6-ECU	Boeing 777-31HER	35593/817		
☐	A6-ECV	Boeing 777-31HER	35594/824		
☐	A6-ECW	Boeing 777-31HER	38981/828		
☐	A6-ECX	Boeing 777-31HER	38982/830		
☐	A6-ECY	Boeing 777-31HER	35595/840		
☐	A6-ECZ	Boeing 777-31HER	38983/		on order
☐	A6-EFD	Boeing 777-F1H	35606/766		
☐	A6-EFE	Boeing 777-F1H	35607/788	ex N5017V	
☐	A6-	Boeing 777-F1H			on order
☐	A6-EGA	Boeing 777-31HER	38984/		on order
☐	A6-EMD*	Boeing 777-21H	27247/30		
☐	A6-EME*	Boeing 777-21H	27248/33		
☐	A6-EMF*	Boeing 777-21H	27249/42		
☐	A6-EMG+	Boeing 777-21HER	27252/63	ex N5020K	
☐	A6-EMH+	Boeing 777-21HER	27251/54		
☐	A6-EMI+	Boeing 777-21HER	27250/47	ex N5028Y	
☐	A6-EMJ+	Boeing 777-21HER	27253/91		
☐	A6-EMK+	Boeing 777-21HER	29324/171		
☐	A6-EML*	Boeing 777-21HER	29325/176		
☐	A6-EMM+	Boeing 777-31H	29062/256		
☐	A6-EMN*	Boeing 777-31H	29063/262		
☐	A6-EMO+	Boeing 777-31H	28680/300		
☐	A6-EMP*	Boeing 777-31H	29395/326	ex N50281	
☐	A6-EMQ*	Boeing 777-31H	32697/396		
☐	A6-EMR+	Boeing 777-31H	29396/402		
☐	A6-EMS+	Boeing 777-31H	29067/408	ex N50281	
☐	A6-EMT+	Boeing 777-31H	32699/414	ex N5014K	
☐	A6-EMU+	Boeing 777-31H	29064/418		
☐	A6-EMV+	Boeing 777-31H	28687/432		
☐	A6-EMW+	Boeing 777-31H	32700/434		
☐	A6-EMX+	Boeing 777-31H	32702/444		
☐	A6-EWA+	Boeing 777-21HLR	35572/654		
☐	A6-EWB+	Boeing 777-21HLR	35573/662	ex N5573S	
☐	A6-EWC+	Boeing 777-21HLR	35576/677		
☐	A6-EWD+	Boeing 777-21HLR	35577/688		
☐	A6-EWE+	Boeing 777-21HLR	35582/725		
☐	A6-EWF+	Boeing 777-21HLR	35586/739	ex N5017V	
☐	A6-EWG+	Boeing 777-21HLR	35578/741	ex N6018N	
☐	A6-EWH+	Boeing 777-21HLR	35587/747		
☐	A6-EWI+	Boeing 777-21HLR	35589/757	ex N5017V	
☐	A6-EWJ+	Boeing 777-21HLR	35590/775	ex N5017V	

*have 2-class configured cabins (high density)+ have 3-class cabins (low density)

	Registration	Type	c/n	Previous identity	Remarks
☐	A6-EFI	Boeing 747-81HF	37451		on order
☐	A6-	Boeing 747-81HF			on order
☐	OO-THC	Boeing 747-4HAERF	35235/1389	ex N50217	Lsd fr TAY
☐	OO-THD	Boeing 747-4HAERF	35236/1399		Lsd fr TAY

ETIHAD AIRWAYS | *Etihad (EY/ETD)* | *Abu Dhabi (AUH)*

	Registration	Type	c/n	Previous identity	Remarks
☐	A6-EID	Airbus A319-132	1947	ex D-APAA	
☐	A6-EIE	Airbus A319-132	1955	ex D-APAB	
☐	9H-AEP	Airbus A320-214	3056	ex F-WWDV	
☐	A6-EIA	Airbus A320-232	1944	ex PH-MPD	
☐	A6-EIB	Airbus A320-232	1945	ex PH-MPE	Abu Dhabi Grand Prix colours
☐	A6-EIC	Airbus A320-232	2167	ex PH-MPF	
☐	A6-EIF	Airbus A320-232	3004	ex EI-EAO	
☐	A6-EIG	Airbus A320-232	3050	ex EI-EAN	
☐	A6-EIH	Airbus A320-232	3693	ex F-WWBH	
☐	A6-EII	Airbus A320-232	3713	ex F-WWIX	
☐	A6-EIJ	Airbus A320-232	3902	ex F-WWIA	
☐	A6-EIK	Airbus A320-232	3676	ex VT-INW	
☐	A6-EIL	Airbus A320-232	4066	ex F-WWBH	
☐	A6-EIM	Airbus A320-232	4077	ex F-WWBO	
☐	A6-EIN	Airbus A320-232	4124	ex F-WWIN	
☐	A6-EIZ	Airbus A320-211	0350	ex 9H-AFE	Lsd fr AMC

☐ A6-AFA	Airbus A330-343E	1071	ex F-WWYP		
☐ A6-AFB	Airbus A330-343E	1081	ex F-WWYL		
☐ A6-	Airbus A330-343E		ex F-WW		on order
☐ A6-EYD	Airbus A330-243	658	ex F-WWYN		
☐ A6-EYE	Airbus A330-243	688	ex F-WWYJ		
☐ A6-EYF	Airbus A330-243	717	ex F-WWYN		
☐ A6-EYG	Airbus A330-243	724	ex F-WWKN		
☐ A6-EYH	Airbus A330-243	729	ex F-WWKR		
☐ A6-EYI	Airbus A330-243	730	ex F-WWKS		
☐ A6-EYJ	Airbus A330-243	737	ex F-WWYB		
☐ A6-EYK	Airbus A330-243	788	ex F-WWKM		
☐ A6-EYL	Airbus A330-243	809	ex F-WWYB		
☐ A6-EYM	Airbus A330-243	824	ex F-WWKD		
☐ A6-EYN	Airbus A330-243	832	ex F-WWKN		
☐ A6-EYO	Airbus A330-243	852	ex F-WWKT		
☐ A6-EYP	Airbus A330-243	854	ex F-WWYY		
☐ A6-EYQ	Airbus A330-243	868	ex F-WWYQ		
☐ A6-EYR	Airbus A330-243	975	ex F-WWKS		
☐ A6-EYS	Airbus A330-243	991	ex F-WWKM		
☐ A6-	Airbus A330-243F	1032	ex F-WWKG		on order
☐ A6-	Airbus A330-243F		ex F-WW		on order
☐ A6-EHA	Airbus A340-541	748	ex F-WWTS		
☐ A6-EHB	Airbus A340-541	757	ex F-WWTU		
☐ A6-EHC	Airbus A340-541	761	ex F-WWTV		
☐ A6-EHD	Airbus A340-541	783	ex F-WWTY		
☐ A6-EHE	Airbus A340-642HGW	829	ex F-WWCG		
☐ A6-EHF	Airbus A340-642HGW	837	ex F-WWCB		
☐ A6-EHH	Airbus A340-642HGW	870	ex F-WWCK		
☐ A6-EHI	Airbus A340-642HGW	929	ex F-WWCB		
☐ A6-EHJ	Airbus A340-642HGW	933	ex F-WWCF		
☐ A6-EHK	Airbus A340-642HGW	1030	ex F-WWCX		
☐ A6-EHL	Airbus A340-642HGW	1040	ex F-WWCH		
☐ A6-ETA	Boeing 777-3FXER	34597/538	ex N6018N		
☐ A6-ETB	Boeing 777-3FXER	34598/543	ex N5020K		
☐ A6-ETC	Boeing 777-3FXER	34599/544			
☐ A6-ETD	Boeing 777-3FXER	34600/547			
☐ A6-ETE	Boeing 777-3FXER	34601/548			
☐ A6-EYZ	Boeing 767-341ER	30341/768	ex A6-SUL		Lsd fr AUH
☐ TF-ELK	Airbus A300B4-622RF	557	ex EI-DGU	Crystal Cargo	Lsd fr ABD

FALCON EXPRESS CARGO AIRLINES *(FC/FVS)* *Dubai (DXB)*

☐ A6-FCA	Beech 1900C-1	UC-57	ex OY-GED
☐ A6-FCB	Beech 1900C-1	UC-66	ex OY-GEI
☐ A6-FCC	Beech 1900C-1	UC-68	ex OY-GEJ
☐ A6-FCD	Beech 1900C-1	UC-71	ex OY-GEK
☐ A6-FCZ	Fokker F.27 Friendship 500	10448	ex HB-ITY

FLYDUBAI *(FZ/FCB)*

☐ A6-FDA	Boeing 737-8GQ/W	35794/2794		
☐ A6-FDB	Boeing 737-8GQ/W	35795/2829		
☐ A6-FDC	Boeing 737-8KN/W	40233/2952	ex N1786B	
☐ A6-FDD	Boeing 737-8KN/W	40234/2966		
☐ A6-FDE	Boeing 737-8KN/W	40235/3053		
☐ A6-FDF	Boeing 737-8KN/W	40236/3110		
☐ A6-FDG	Boeing 737-8KN/W	29636		on order
☐ A6-	Boeing 737-8KN/W			on order

HEAVYLIFT INTERNATIONAL *(HVL)* *Sharjah (SHJ)*

☐ A6-HLA	Douglas DC-8-63AF (BAC 3)	46034/434	ex N868BX
☐ A6-HLB	Douglas DC-8-63F (BAC 3)	46035/438	ex N869BX
☐ A6-HLC	Douglas DC-8-63AF (BAC 3)	46126/524	ex N812AX
☐ A6-HLG	Boeing 737-3G7F	24710/1825	ex N308AW
☐ A6-HLH	Boeing 737-3G7F	24711/1843	ex N309AW

MAXIMUS AIR CARGO *Cargo Max (MXU)* *Abu Dhabi (AUH)*

☐ A6-MAC	Lockheed L-382G-44K-30 Hercules	5024	ex 1215	Lsd fr UAE AF	
☐ A6-MAX	Lockheed L-382G-44K-30 Hercules	4895	ex 1216	Lsd fr UAE AF	
☐ A6-MXA	Airbus A300B4-622RF	788	ex TF-ELA		Lsd fr ABD
☐ A6-MXB	Airbus A300B4-622RF	767	ex TF-ELE		Lsd fr ABD
☐ UR-ZYD	Antonov An-124 Ruslan	19530502843	ex UR-CCX		Lsd fr UAK
☐ UR-BXQ	Ilyushin Il-76TD	1023410360	ex EX-832		Lsd fr UKL
☐ UR-BXR	Ilyushin Il-76TD	1023411384	ex EX-411		Lsd fr UKL
☐ UR-BXS	Ilyushin Il-76TD	1023411368	ex EX-436		Lsd fr UKL

MIDEX AIRLINES		(MG/MIX)			Al Ain (AAN)
☐ A6-MDA	Airbus A300B4-203F	157	ex N371PC	Midex 1	
☐ A6-MDB	Airbus A300B4-203F	196	ex N372PC	Midex 2	
☐ A6-MDC	Airbus A300B4-203F	218	ex N373PC	Midex 3	
☐ A6-MDD	Airbus A300B4-203F	203	ex N473AS		
☐ A6-MDE	Airbus A300B4-203F	125	ex N472AS		
☐ A6-MDF	Airbus A300B4-203F	134	ex N370PC		
☐ A6-MDG	Boeing 747-228F	25266/878	ex PH-MCN		

RAK AIRLINES		Rakair (RT/RKM			Ras Al Khaimah (RKT)
☐ A6-AAM	Airbus A318-112	1599	ex D-AIJA		
☐ A6-RKA	Boeing 757-256	29311/940	ex EC-HIU		

SILVER AIR					
☐ A6-JUD	Boeing 737-306	23541/1309	ex PH-BDE		

SKYLINK ARABIA					Dubai (DXB)
☐ JY-TWB	Antonov An-26B-100				Op by TSJ
☐ ER-AZN	Antonov An-24RV	37308801	ex		
☐ RDPL-34157	Ilyushin Il-76T	093418556	ex ER-IBP		
☐ UP-I7610	Ilyushin Il-76TD	0053460832	ex UN-76030		
☐ UP-I7611	Ilyushin Il-76T	093418548	ex UN-76031		
☐ UP-I7630	Ilyushin Il-76T	0023441189	ex RA-76823		
☐ UP-AN203	Antonov An-12AP	00347408	ex UN-11021		
☐ ZS-MAD	Fokker F.28 Fellowship 4000	11225	ex 5H-ZAS		
☐ 4L-GLT	Antonov An-12BK	7345305	ex EX-130		

Also quoted as Skylink Airlines

A7- QATAR (State of Qatar)

GULF HELICOPTERS				Doha (DOH)
☐ A7-GHA	Agusta AW139	31132		
☐ A7-GHB	Agusta AW139	31140		
☐ A7-GHC	Agusta AW139	31225		
☐ A7-GHD	Agusta AW139	31233		
☐ A7-GHE	Agusta AW139	31235		
☐ A7-GHF	Agusta AW139	31242		
☐ A7-HBT	Agusta AW139	31068	ex I-EASO	
☐ A7-HBN	Bell 212	31130	ex VT-HGE	
☐ A7-HBO	Bell 212	30911	ex EP-HUE	
☐ A7-HAV	Bell 412SP	33205	ex D-HHNN	
☐ A7-HAW	Bell 412HP	36046	ex N9142N	
☐ A7-HAY	Bell 412EP	36126	ex N2045S	
☐ A7-HAZ	Bell 412HP	36041	ex N92801	
☐ A7-HBB	Bell 412EP	36259	ex N9026K	
☐ A7-HBC	Bell 412EP	36276	ex N9154J	
☐ A7-HBD	Bell 412EP	36088	ex N4324X	
☐ A7-HBH	Bell 412EP	36326	ex N8067Q	
☐ A7-HBI	Bell 412EP	36270	ex PP-MBE	
☐ A7-HBJ	Bell 412EP	36370	ex N43939	
☐ A7-HBL	Bell 412SP	33117	ex EP-HUC	
☐ A7-HBM	Bell 412EP	36400	ex N2116N	
☐ A7-HBP	Bell 412SP	36016	ex EP-HUF	
☐ A7-HBQ	Bell 412EP	36412	ex N7512Z	
☐ A7-HBR	Bell 412SP	36017	ex EP-HUG	
☐ A7-HBS	Bell 412SP	33116	ex A7-HBK	
☐ VT-HGF	Bell 412EP	36206	ex A7-HBE	Lsd to United Helicharters
☐ A7-HAO	Agusta-Bell 206B JetRanger II	8044	ex A4O-DC	
☐ A7-HBF	Bell 230	23015	ex N236X	
☐ A7-HHT	Sikorsky S-92A	920031	ex N7113U	

QATAR AIRWAYS		Qatari (QR/QTR)			Doha (DOH)
☐ A7-ABX	Airbus A300B4-622RF	554	ex HL7537	Al Dawha	
☐ A7-ABY	Airbus A300B4-622RF	560	ex HL7294	Fuwairit	
☐ A7-AFB	Airbus A300B4-622RF	614	ex HL7298	Al'ArishCargo titles	
☐ A7-CJA	Airbus A319-133LR	1656	ex D-AVYT	Al Hilal	
☐ A7-CJB	Airbus A319-133LR	2341	ex D-AVWK	Al Jasra	
☐ A7-	Airbus A319-133LR	4114	ex D-AV		on order
☐ A7-ADA	Airbus A320-232	1566	ex F-WWBG	Al Zubara	

	Registration	Type	c/n	Previous	Name	Notes
☐	A7-ADB	Airbus A320-232	1648	ex F-WWDU	Dukhan	
☐	A7-ADC	Airbus A320-232	1773	ex F-WWDG	Mesaieed	
☐	A7-ADD	Airbus A320-232	1895	ex F-WWBT	Halul	
☐	A7-ADE	Airbus A320-232	1957	ex F-WWIG	Al Gharafa	
☐	A7-ADF	Airbus A320-232	2097	ex F-WWIP	Al Wukeir	
☐	A7-ADG	Airbus A320-232	2121	ex F-WWIT	Al Ghuweriyah	
☐	A7-ADH	Airbus A320-232	2138	ex F-WWBI	Al Jumeilliyah	
☐	A7-ADI	Airbus A320-232	2161	ex F-WWBK	Al Khuraytiyat	
☐	A7-ADJ	Airbus A320-232	2288	ex F-WWBS	Al Samriya	
☐	A7-ADU	Airbus A320-232	3071	ex F-WWIM		
☐	A7-AHA	Airbus A320-232	4110	ex F-WWDT		
☐	A7-AHB	Airbus A320-232	4130	ex F-WWIR		
☐	A7-AHC	Airbus A320-232	4173	ex F-WW		
☐	A7-AHD	Airbus A320-232	4183	ex F-WW		
☐	A7-AHE	Airbus A320-232		ex F-WW		on order
☐	A7-AHF	Airbus A320-232		ex F-WW		on order
☐	A7-AHG	Airbus A320-232		ex F-WW		on order
☐	A7-AHH	Airbus A320-232		ex F-WW		on order
☐	A7-ADK	Airbus A321-231	1487	ex OE-LOS		
☐	A7-ADS	Airbus A321-231	1928	ex D-AVXA	Al Aaliyah	
☐	A7-ADT	Airbus A321-231	2107	ex D-AVXD	Al Saffiyah	
☐	A7-ADV	Airbus A321-231	3274	ex D-AVZM		
☐	A7-ADW	Airbus A321-231	3369	ex D-AVZJ		
☐	A7-ADX	Airbus A321-231	3397	ex D-AVZP		
☐	A7-ADY	Airbus A321-231	3636	ex D-AVZK		
☐	A7-ADZ	Airbus A321-231	3669	ex D-AVZY		
☐	A7-AIA	Airbus A321-231		ex D-		on order
☐	A7-AIB	Airbus A321-231		ex D-		on order
☐	A7-AIC	Airbus A321-231		ex D-		on order
☐	A7-ACA	Airbus A330-202	473	ex F-WWKR	Al Wajbah	
☐	A7-ACB	Airbus A330-202	489	ex F-WWYN	Al Majida	
☐	A7-ACC	Airbus A330-202	511	ex F-WWKR	Al Shahaniya	
☐	A7-ACD	Airbus A330-202	521	ex F-WWKU	Al Wuseil	
☐	A7-ACE	Airbus A330-202	571	ex F-WWKF	Al Dhakira	
☐	A7-ACF	Airbus A330-202	638	ex F-WWYQ	Al Kara'anah	
☐	A7-ACG	Airbus A330-202	743	ex F-WWKV	Al Wabra	
☐	A7-ACH	Airbus A330-202	441	ex F-WWYK	Al Mafjar	
☐	A7-ACI	Airbus A330-202	746	ex F-WWKV	Muathier	
☐	A7-ACJ	Airbus A330-202	760	ex F-WWYO	Zikreet	
☐	A7-ACK	Airbus A330-202	792	ex F-WWKP		
☐	A7-ACL	Airbus A330-202	820	ex F-WWKA		
☐	A7-ACM	Airbus A330-202	849	ex F-WWKP		
☐	A7-ACN	Airbus A330-202	893	ex F-WWYK		
☐	A7-AFL	Airbus A330-202	612	ex F-WWKZ	Al Messila	
☐	A7-AFM	Airbus A330-202	616	ex F-WWKT	Al-Udaid	
☐	A7-AFP	Airbus A330-202	684	ex F-WWYG	Al Shamal	
☐	A7-AEA	Airbus A330-302	623	ex F-WWYC	Al Muntazah	
☐	A7-AEB	Airbus A330-302	637	ex F-WWYP	Al Sayliyah	
☐	A7-AEC	Airbus A330-302	659	ex F-WWYX	Al Markhiya	
☐	A7-AED	Airbus A330-302	680	ex F-WWYD	Al Nu'uman	
☐	A7-AEE	Airbus A330-302	711	ex F-WWYK	Semaisma	
☐	A7-AEF	Airbus A330-302	721	ex F-WWKJ	Al Rumellah	
☐	A7-AEG	Airbus A330-302	734	ex F-WWYU	Al Duhell	
☐	A7-AEH	Airbus A330-302	789	ex F-WWKN		
☐	A7-AEI	Airbus A330-302	813	ex F-WWYI		
☐	A7-AEJ	Airbus A330-302	826	ex F-WWKF		
☐	A7-AEM	Airbus A330-302	893	ex F-WWYK		
☐	A7-AEN	Airbus A330-302	907	ex F-WWYE		
☐	A7-AEO	Airbus A330-302	918	ex F-WWYQ		
☐	A7-AGA	Airbus A340-642HGW	740	ex F-WWCP		
☐	A7-AGB	Airbus A340-642HGW	715	ex F-WWCR	Ras Dukhan	
☐	A7-AGC	Airbus A340-642HGW	766	ex F-WWCM	Ras Ushainij	
☐	A7-AGD	Airbus A340-642HGW	798	ex F-WWCL		
☐	A7-BBA	Boeing 777-2DZLR	36012/753	ex N1788B	Alhuwalla	
☐	A7-BBB	Boeing 777-2DZLR	36013/762	ex N50281	Gaz	
☐	A7-BBC	Boeing 777-2DZLR	36015/825	ex N5023Q		
☐	A7-BBD	Boeing 777-2DZLR	36016/831	ex N5573S		
☐	A7-BBE	Boeing 777-2DZLR	36017/837			
☐	A7-BBF	Boeing 777-2DZLR	36018/842			
☐	A7-BBG	Boeing 777-2DZLR	36101			on order
☐	A7-BBH	Boeing 777-2DZLR	36102			on order
☐	A7-BFA	Boeing 777-FDZ	36098			on order
☐	A7-BFB	Boeing 777-FDZ	36100			on order
☐	A7-BAA	Boeing 777-3DZER	36009/676			
☐	A7-BAB	Boeing 777-3DZER	36103/686		Um-Alamad	
☐	A7-BAC	Boeing 777-3DZER	36010/731	ex N5016R		
☐	A7-BAE	Boeing 777-3DZER	36104/769		Almas-Habia	

☐ A7-BAF	Boeing 777-3DZER	37661/815			
☐ A7-BAG	Boeing 777-3DZER	36014/819	ex N5017Q	Littoriya	
☐ A7-BAH	Boeing 777-3DZER	37662			on order
☐ A7-BAI	Boeing 777-3DZER	36095/742	ex N5028Y		
☐ A7-BAJ	Boeing 777-3DZER	36096			on order
☐ A7-BAK	Boeing 777-3DZER	36097			on order
☐ A7-BAL	Boeing 777-3DZER	38244			on order
☐ A7-BAO	Boeing 777-3DZER	36011/750			
☐ A7-	Boeing 777-3DZER				on order

A9C- BAHRAIN (State of Bahrain)

BAHRAIN AIR (2B/BAB) Bahrain (BAH)

☐ A9C-BAP	Airbus A320-214	3949	ex F-WWBE
☐ A9C-BAS	Airbus A320-214	3931	ex F-WWBT
☐ A9C-BAT	Airbus A320-214	3896	ex F-WWDI
☐ A9C-BAU	Airbus A320-214	4055	ex F-WWBB
☐ A9C-BAV	Airbus A320-214	3861	ex F-WWDP
☐ A9C-BAW	Airbus A319-111	2763	ex N946FR
☐ A9C-BAX	Airbus A319-111	2700	ex N944FR
☐ A9C-BAY	Airbus A320-212	0579	ex D-AKNY
☐ A9C-BAZ	Airbus A320-212	0645	ex D-AKNZ

DHL INTERNATIONAL AVIATION Dilmun (ES/DHX) Bahrain (BAH)

☐ A9C-DHB	Swearingen SA.227AT Merlin IVC	AT-434	ex HZ-SN8	Freighter SNAS c/s	
☐ HZ-SNA	Boeing 727-264F (FedEx 3)	20896/1051	ex EC-HLP	all-white	Joint ops with RSE
☐ HZ-SNB	Boeing 727-223F (FedEx 3)	21084/1199	ex EC-HAH	all-white	Joint ops with RSE
☐ HZ-SNC	Boeing 727-230F (FedEx 3)	20905/1091	ex EC-IVF		Joint ops with RSE
☐ HZ-SND	Boeing 727-223F (FedEx 3)	20994/1190	ex EC-IVE	all-white	Joint ops with RSE
☐ HZ-SNF	Boeing 727-277F (FedEx 3)	22643/1762	ex ZS-DPE		Joint ops with RSE

GULF AIR Gulf Air (GF/GFA) Bahrain (BAH)

☐ A9C-AA	Airbus A320-214	3706	ex F-WJKJ		
☐ A9C-AB	Airbus A320-214	4030	ex F-WWIB		
☐ A9C-AC	Airbus A320-214	4059	ex F-WWBD		
☐ A9C-AD	Airbus A320-214	4083	ex F-WWBT		
☐ A9C-AE	Airbus A320-214	4146	ex D-AVVG		
☐ A9C-AF	Airbus A320-214	4158	ex F-WWBQ		
☐ A9C-AG	Airbus A320-214	4188	ex F-WWIG		on order
☐ A9C-AH	Airbus A320-214	4218	ex		on order
☐ A9C-	Airbus A320-214		ex		on order
☐ A9C-	Airbus A320-214		ex		on order
☐ A9C-	Airbus A320-214		ex		on order
☐ A9C-	Airbus A320-214		ex		on order
☐ A9C-	Airbus A320-214		ex		on order
☐ A9C-	Airbus A320-214		ex		on order
☐ A9C-	Airbus A320-214		ex		on order
☐ A9C-EB	Airbus A320-212	0325	ex A4O-EB	802 Bahla	
☐ A9C-ED	Airbus A320-212	0375	ex A4O-ED	804 Sitra	
☐ A9C-EE	Airbus A320-212	0419	ex A4O-EE	805 Al-Rumaitha	
☐ A9C-EI	Airbus A320-212	0459	ex A4O-EI	809	
☐ A9C-EJ	Airbus A320-212	0466	ex A4O-EJ	810 50th anniversary colours	
☐ A9C-EL	Airbus A320-212	0497	ex A4O-EL	812	
☐ A9C-EN	Airbus A320-212	0537	ex A4O-EN	814	
☐ A9C-EO	Airbus A320-212	0409	ex A4O-EN	815	
☐ A9C-ES	Airbus A321-211	0675	ex F-OHGU		
☐ A9C-ET	Airbus A321-211	0761	ex F-GTAF		
☐ A9C-EU	Airbus A319-112	1884	ex C-GTDT		
☐ A9C-EV	Airbus A319-112	1901	ex C-GTDS		

☐ A9C-KA	Airbus A330-243	276	ex A4O-KA	501
☐ A9C-KB	Airbus A330-243	281	ex A4O-KB	502
☐ A9C-KC	Airbus A330-243	286	ex A4O-KC	503
☐ A9C-KD	Airbus A330-243	287	ex A4O-KD	504
☐ A9C-KE	Airbus A330-243	334	ex A4O-KE	505
☐ A9C-KF	Airbus A330-243	340	ex A4O-KF	506 Aldafra
☐ A9C-KG	Airbus A330-243	527	ex F-OMEA	
☐ A9C-KH	Airbus A330-243	529	ex F-OMEB	
☐ A9C-KI	Airbus A330-243	532	ex F-OMEC	
☐ A9C-KJ	Airbus A330-243	992	ex F-WWKN	

☐ A9C-LB	Airbus A340-312	039	ex A4O-LB	402 Al Fateh
☐ A9C-LC	Airbus A340-312	040	ex A4O-LC	403 Doha
☐ A9C-LD	Airbus A340-312	097	ex A4O-LD	404 Abu Dhabi
☐ A9C-LE	Airbus A340-312	103	ex A4O-LE	405
☐ A9C-LF	Airbus A340-312	133	ex A4O-LF	406
☐ A9C-LG	Airbus A340-313X	212	ex A4O-LG	407
☐ A9C-LH	Airbus A340-313X	215	ex A4O-LH	408

☐ A9C-LI	Airbus A340-313X	554	ex A4O-LI	409	
☐ A9C-LJ	Airbus A340-313X	282	ex A4O-LL	410	
☐ A9C-	Embraer 170-100IGW (170IGW)	17000278	ex PT-TQE		on order
☐ A9C-	Embraer 170-100IGW (170IGW)	17000293	ex PT-TQT		on order

B- CHINA (People's Republic Of China)

AIR CHINA — Air China (CA/CCA) — Beijing-Capital (PEK)

Member of Star Alliance

☐ B-2223	Airbus A319-111	1679	ex D-AVWI	
☐ B-2225	Airbus A319-111	1654	ex D-AVYS	
☐ B-2339	Airbus A319-111	1753	ex D-AVYJ	
☐ B-2364	Airbus A319-115	2499	ex D-AVWB	
☐ B-2404	Airbus A319-131	2454	ex D-AVWE	
☐ B-6004	Airbus A319-115	2508	ex D-AVWO	
☐ B-6014	Airbus A319-115	2525	ex D-AVWE	
☐ B-6022	Airbus A319-131	2000	ex D-AVYZ	
☐ B-6023	Airbus A319-131	2007	ex D-AVWM	
☐ B-6024	Airbus A319-131	2015	ex D-AVWT	
☐ B-6031	Airbus A319-131	2172	ex D-AVWW	
☐ B-6032	Airbus A319-131	2202	ex D-AVYF	
☐ B-6033	Airbus A319-131	2205	ex D-AVYJ	
☐ B-6034	Airbus A319-115	2237	ex D-AVWL	
☐ B-6035	Airbus A319-115	2269	ex D-AVWX	
☐ B-6036	Airbus A319-115	2285	ex D-AVYS	
☐ B-6037	Airbus A319-115	2293	ex D-AVYY	
☐ B-6038	Airbus A319-115	2298	ex D-AVWF	
☐ B-6044	Airbus A319-115	2532	ex D-AVWL	
☐ B-6046	Airbus A319-115	2545	ex D-AVWW	
☐ B-6047	Airbus A319-115	2551	ex D-AVYJ	
☐ B-6048	Airbus A319-131	2559	ex D-AVYU	
☐ B-6213	Airbus A319-131	2614	ex D-AVXS	
☐ B-6216	Airbus A319-131	2643	ex D-AVWO	
☐ B-6223	Airbus A319-115	2805	ex D-AVWV	
☐ B-6225	Airbus A319-115	2819	ex D-AVXB	
☐ B-6226	Airbus A319-115	2839	ex D-AVYI	
☐ B-6227	Airbus A319-115	2847	ex D-AVXG	
☐ B-6228	Airbus A319-115	2890	ex D-AVYI	
☐ B-6235	Airbus A319-131	3195	ex D-AVWC	
☐ B-6236	Airbus A319-131	3200	ex D-AVWG	
☐ B-6237	Airbus A319-131	3226	ex D-AVYJ	
☐ B-6238	Airbus A319-115	3250	ex D-AVWO	
☐ B-2210	Airbus A320-214	1296	ex F-WWBG	
☐ B-2354	Airbus A320-214	0707	ex F-WWIN	
☐ B-2355	Airbus A320-214	0724	ex F-WWBN	
☐ B-2376	Airbus A320-214	0876	ex F-WWIF	
☐ B-2377	Airbus A320-214	0921	ex F-WWDY	
☐ B-6606	Airbus A320-214	3337	ex B-6350	
☐ B-6607	Airbus A320-214	3461	ex B-6390	
☐ B-6608	Airbus A320-214	3601	ex B-6393	
☐ B-	Airbus A320-214		ex	on order
☐ B-	Airbus A320-214		ex	on order
☐ B-6326	Airbus A321-213	3329	ex D-AVZX	
☐ B-6327	Airbus A321-213	3307	ex D-AVZT	
☐ B-6361	Airbus A321-213	3523	ex D-AVZX	
☐ B-6362	Airbus A321-213	3623	ex D-AVZG	
☐ B-6363	Airbus A321-213	3653	ex D-AVZV	
☐ B-6365	Airbus A321-213	3655	ex D-AVZW	
☐ B-6382	Airbus A321-213	3665	ex D-AVZX	
☐ B-6383	Airbus A321-213	3678	ex D-AZAE	
☐ B-6385	Airbus A321-213	3722	ex D-AZAH	
☐ B-6386	Airbus A321-213	3725	ex D-AZVS	
☐ B-6555	Airbus A321-213	3766	ex D-AZAO	
☐ B-6556	Airbus A321-213	3806	ex D-AVZD	
☐ B-6593	Airbus A321-213	3973	ex D-AVZS	
☐ B-6595	Airbus A321-213	4022	ex D-AVZG	
☐ B-6596	Airbus A321-213	4031	ex D-AVZI	
☐ B-6597	Airbus A321-213	4062	ex D-AVZO	
☐ B-6599	Airbus A321-213	3940	ex D-AZAI	
☐ B-6603	Airbus A321-213	4131	ex D-AZAJ	
☐ B-6605	Airbus A321-213	4091	ex D-AVZX	
☐ B-6631	Airbus A321-213	4180	ex D-AZAM	
☐ B-	Airbus A321-213	4210	ex D-	on order
☐ B-	Airbus A321-213		ex D-	on order
☐ B-	Airbus A321-213		ex D-	on order
☐ B-	Airbus A321-213		ex D-	on order

Registration	Type	C/n	Previous identity	Notes	Remarks
☐ B-	Airbus A321-213		ex D-		on order
☐ B-	Airbus A321-213		ex D-		on order
☐ B-	Airbus A321-213		ex D-		on order
☐ B-6070	Airbus A330-243	750	ex F-WWKA		
☐ B-6071	Airbus A330-243	756	ex F-WWYQ		
☐ B-6072	Airbus A330-243	759	ex F-WWYK		
☐ B-6073	Airbus A330-243	780	ex F-WWKY		
☐ B-6075	Airbus A330-243	785	ex F-WWYY	Olympic Torch c/s	
☐ B-6076	Airbus A330-243	797	ex F-WWKU		
☐ B-6079	Airbus A330-243	810	ex F-WWYF		
☐ B-6080	Airbus A330-243	815	ex F-WWYL		
☐ B-6081	Airbus A330-243	839	ex F-WWYO		
☐ B-6090	Airbus A330-243	860	ex F-WWYN		
☐ B-6091	Airbus A330-243	867	ex F-WWYP	Star Alliance colours	
☐ B-6092	Airbus A330-243	873	ex F-WWKV		
☐ B-6093	Airbus A330-243	884	ex F-WWKO		
☐ B-6113	Airbus A330-243	890	ex F-WWYM		
☐ B-6115	Airbus A330-243	909	ex F-WWYG		
☐ B-6117	Airbus A330-243	903	ex F-WWKR		
☐ B-6130	Airbus A330-243	930	ex F-WWKS		
☐ B-6131	Airbus A330-243	941	ex F-WWKO		
☐ B-6132	Airbus A330-243	944	ex F-WWYT		
☐ B-6505	Airbus A330-243	957	ex F-WWYC		
☐ B-	Airbus A330-243	1087	ex F-WW		on order
☐ B-	Airbus A330-243		ex F-WW		on order
☐ B-	Airbus A330-243		ex F-WW		on order
☐ B-2385	Airbus A340-313X	192	ex B-HMX		
☐ B-2386	Airbus A340-313X	199	ex B-HMY		
☐ B-2387	Airbus A340-313X	201	ex B-HMZ		
☐ B-2388	Airbus A340-313X	242	ex F-WWJD		
☐ B-2389	Airbus A340-313X	243	ex F-WWJE		
☐ B-2390	Airbus A340-313X	264	ex F-WWJY		
☐ B-2504	Boeing 737-36M	28333/2810	ex N374PA		Lsd fr AFT Trust-Sub
☐ B-2522	Boeing 737-3Z0	23451/1240	ex N5573K		For Okair as freighter
☐ B-2530	Boeing 737-3Z0	27046/2252			
☐ B-2533	Boeing 737-3Z0	27138/2436			
☐ B-2535	Boeing 737-3J6	25078/2002			
☐ B-2580	Boeing 737-3J6	25080/2254			
☐ B-2581	Boeing 737-3J6	25081/2263			
☐ B-2584	Boeing 737-3J6	25891/2385			
☐ B-2585	Boeing 737-3J6	27045/2384			
☐ B-2586	Boeing 737-3Z0	27047/2357			
☐ B-2587	Boeing 737-3J6	25892/2396			
☐ B-2588	Boeing 737-3J6	25893/2489			
☐ B-2590	Boeing 737-3Z0	27126/2370			
☐ B-2597	Boeing 737-3Z0	27176/2495			
☐ B-2598	Boeing 737-3J6	27128/2493			
☐ B-2599	Boeing 737-3Z0	25896/2558			
☐ B-2600	Boeing 737-36N	28554/2835	ex G-ECAS		
☐ B-2614	Boeing 737-36N	28558/2876	ex G-OJTW		
☐ B-2627	Boeing 737-36E	26315/2706	ex N141LF		
☐ B-2630	Boeing 737-36E	26317/2719	ex N151LF		
☐ B-2905	Boeing 737-33A	25506/2360	ex N403AW		
☐ B-2906	Boeing 737-33A	25507/2373	ex N404AW		
☐ B-2907	Boeing 737-33A	25508/2414	ex N405AW		
☐ B-2947	Boeing 737-33A	25511/2599			
☐ B-2948	Boeing 737-3J6	27361/2631			
☐ B-2949	Boeing 737-3J6	27372/2650			
☐ B-2950	Boeing 737-3Z0	27374/2647			
☐ B-2951	Boeing 737-3Z0	27373/2658			
☐ B-2953	Boeing 737-3J6	27523/2710			
☐ B-2954	Boeing 737-3J6	27518/2768			
☐ B-2957	Boeing 737-3Z0	27521/2738			
☐ B-5035	Boeing 737-36N	28672/2976	ex F-GRFA		
☐ B-5036	Boeing 737-36N	28673/2995	ex F-GRFB		
☐ B-2161	Boeing 737-86N	28655/965	ex N1786B		
☐ B-2509	Boeing 737-8Z0	30072/466	ex N1787B		
☐ B-2510	Boeing 737-8Z0	30071/381	ex N1786B		
☐ B-2511	Boeing 737-8Z0	30073/487	ex N1786B		
☐ B-2612	Boeing 737-79L	33411/1538			
☐ B-2613	Boeing 737-79L	33412/1544	ex N1786B		
☐ B-2641	Boeing 737-89L	29876/337			
☐ B-2642	Boeing 737-89L	29877/359			
☐ B-2643	Boeing 737-89L	29878/379	ex N1786B		
☐ B-2645	Boeing 737-89L	29879/427	ex N1786B		
☐ B-2648	Boeing 737-89L	29880/511	ex N1786B		
☐ B-2649	Boeing 737-89L	30159/572	ex N1784B		
☐ B-2650	Boeing 737-89L	30160/594			
☐ B-2657	Boeing 737-89L	30517/1224			

☐ B-2670	Boeing 737-89L	30514/1055		
☐ B-2671	Boeing 737-89L	30515/1165		
☐ B-2672	Boeing 737-89L	30516/1168		
☐ B-2673	Boeing 737-86N	29888/1133	ex N1786B	
☐ B-2690	Boeing 737-86N	29889/1153		
☐ B-2700	Boeing 737-79L	33413/1560		
☐ B-5043	Boeing 737-79L	33408/1331		
☐ B-5044	Boeing 737-79L	33409/1351		
☐ B-5045	Boeing 737-79L	33410/1354		
☐ B-5063	Boeing 737-7BX	30736/658	ex G-STRC	
☐ B-5064	Boeing 737-7BX	30737/687	ex G-STRD	
☐ B-5167	Boeing 737-808	34701/1887	ex N1787B	
☐ B-5168	Boeing 737-808	34702/1917		
☐ B-5169	Boeing 737-808	34703/1941	ex N1795B	
☐ B-5170	Boeing 737-808	34705/1998		
☐ B-5171	Boeing 737-808	34706/2014	ex N1786B	
☐ B-5172	Boeing 737-8Q8	30704/1985		
☐ B-5173	Boeing 737-8Q8	30705/2001		
☐ B-5175	Boeing 737-86N	35209/2067		
☐ B-5176	Boeing 737-86N	34258/2096		Olympic mascot c/s
☐ B-5177	Boeing 737-86N	35210/2127		Olympic mascot c/s
☐ B-5178	Boeing 737-86N	32682/2117	ex N1787B	Olympic mascot c/s
☐ B-5179	Boeing 737-86N	35211/2146		
☐ B-5196	Boeing 737-86N	36810/2699		
☐ B-5197	Boeing 737-86N/W	36811/2777		
☐ B-5198	Boeing 737-89L/W	36491/2759		
☐ B-5201	Boeing 737-79L/W	34023/1795	ex N1786B	Olympic 2008 colours
☐ B-5202	Boeing 737-79L/W	34537/1837	ex N1786B	Olympic 2008 colours
☐ B-5203	Boeing 737-79L/W	34538/1853		
☐ B-5211	Boeing 737-79L	34019/1749		Olympic 2008 colours
☐ B-5213	Boeing 737-79L/W	34020/1769	ex N1786B	
☐ B-5214	Boeing 737-79L/W	34021/1774		
☐ B-5217	Boeing 737-79L/W	34022/1786		
☐ B-5220	Boeing 737-79L/W	34539/1856	ex (B-5204)	
☐ B-5226	Boeing 737-79L/W	34540/1877	ex N1787B	
☐ B-5227	Boeing 737-79L/W	34541/1937		
☐ B-5228	Boeing 737-79L/W	34542/1993		
☐ B-5229	Boeing 737-79L/W	34543/2006		
☐ B-5311	Boeing 737-8Q8	29373/2171		
☐ B-5312	Boeing 737-8Q8	29374/2203	ex N1786B	
☐ B-5313	Boeing 737-8Q8	30716/2210	ex N1786B	
☐ B-5325	Boeing 737-86N	32692/2275	ex N1786B	
☐ B-5326	Boeing 737-86N	35214/2308		
☐ B-5327	Boeing 737-86N	35219/2371	ex N1779B	
☐ B-5328	Boeing 737-86N	35221/2444	ex N1786B	
☐ B-5329	Boeing 737-86N	35222/2463		
☐ B-5341	Boeing 737-89L/W	36483/2403	ex N1786B	
☐ B-5342	Boeing 737-89L/W	36484/2441	ex N1786B	
☐ B-5343	Boeing 737-89L/W	36485/2470		
☐ B-5387	Boeing 737-89L/W	36492/2828		
☐ B-5390	Boeing 737-89L/W	36486/5390		
☐ B-5391	Boeing 737-89L/W	36487/2664		
☐ B-5392	Boeing 737-89L/W	36488/2674		
☐ B-5397	Boeing 737-89L/W	36489/2704	ex N1787B	
☐ B-5398	Boeing 737-89L/W	36490/2715		
☐ B-5422	Boeing 737-89L/W	36741/2845	ex N1787B	
☐ B-5423	Boeing 737-89L/W	36742/2877		
☐ B-5425	Boeing 737-89L/W	36743/2896		
☐ B-5426	Boeing 737-89L/W	36744/2969		
☐ B-5431	Boeing 737-86N	36812/2918	ex N1787B	
☐ B-5436	Boeing 737-86N	368132976		
☐ B-5437	Boeing 737-86N/W	36815/3020		
☐ B-5438	Boeing 737-86N/W	36816/3032		
☐ B-5442	Boeing 737-86N/W	36745/3049		
☐ B-5443	Boeing 737-86N/W	36746/3072	ex N1786B	
☐ B-5485	Boeing 737-89L/W	36747/3124	ex N1796B	
☐ B-5486	Boeing 737-89L/W	36748/3127	ex N1786B	
☐ B-5495	Boeing 737-89L/W	36749/3145		
☐ B-5496	Boeing 737-89L/W	36750/3155		
☐ B-5497	Boeing 737-89L/W	36751		on order
☐ B-5500	Boeing 737-89L/W	36752		on order
☐ B-	Boeing 737-89L/W			on order
☐ B-	Boeing 737-89L/W			on order
☐ B-	Boeing 737-89L/W			on order
☐ B-	Boeing 737-89L/W			on order
☐ B-	Boeing 737-89L/W			on order

☐ B-2443	Boeing 747-4J6	25881/957		
☐ B-2445	Boeing 747-4J6	25882/1021		
☐ B-2447	Boeing 747-4J6	25883/1054		
☐ B-2456	Boeing 747-4J6BCF	24346/743		
☐ B-2458	Boeing 747-4J6BCF	24347/775		
☐ B-2460	Boeing 747-4J6M	24348/792		

☐ B-2467	Boeing 747-4J6M	28754/1119		
☐ B-2468	Boeing 747-4J6M	28755/1128		
☐ B-2469	Boeing 747-4J6M	28756/1175		
☐ B-2470	Boeing 747-4J6M	29070/1181		
☐ B-2471	Boeing 747-4J6M	29071/1229		
☐ B-2472	Boeing 747-4J6	30158/1243		
☐ B-2820	Boeing 757-2Z0	25885/476		
☐ B-2821	Boeing 757-2Z0	25886/480		
☐ B-2826	Boeing 757-2Y0	26155/495		
☐ B-2832	Boeing 757-2Z0	25887/554		
☐ B-2836	Boeing 757-2Z0	27258/595		
☐ B-2837	Boeing 757-2Z0	27259/609		
☐ B-2839	Boeing 757-2Z0	27269/615		
☐ B-2840	Boeing 757-2Z0	27270/622		
☐ B-2841	Boeing 757-2Z0	27367/624		
☐ B-2844	Boeing 757-2Z0	27511/669		
☐ B-2845	Boeing 757-2Z0	27512/674		
☐ B-2855	Boeing 757-2Z0	29792/822		
☐ B-2856	Boeing 757-2Z0	29793/833		
☐ B-2496	Boeing 767-3Q8ER	30301/762	ex B-2494	
☐ B-2499	Boeing 767-332ER	30597/797	ex B-4025	
☐ B-2553	Boeing 767-2J6ER	23744/155	ex N60659	
☐ B-2557	Boeing 767-3J6	25875/429		
☐ B-2558	Boeing 767-3J6	25876/478		
☐ B-2559	Boeing 767-3J6	25877/530		
☐ B-2560	Boeing 767-3J6	25878/569		
☐ B-2059	Boeing 777-2J6	29153/168		
☐ B-2060	Boeing 777-2J6	29154/173		
☐ B-2061	Boeing 777-2J6	29155/179		
☐ B-2063	Boeing 777-2J6	29156/214		
☐ B-2064	Boeing 777-2J6	29157/240		
☐ B-2065	Boeing 777-2J6	29744/280		
☐ B-2066	Boeing 777-2J6	29745/290		
☐ B-2067	Boeing 777-2J6	29746/338		
☐ B-2068	Boeing 777-2J6	29747/344		
☐ B-2069	Boeing 777-2J6	29748/349		

AIR CHINA CARGO — *AirChina Freight (CA/CAO)* — *Beijing-Capital (PEK)*

☐ B-2409	Boeing 747-412 (SF)	26560/1052	ex 9V-SFC	Lsd fr SQC
☐ B-2462	Boeing 747-2J6F	24960/814		
☐ B-2475	Boeing 747-4FTF	34239/1367		
☐ B-2476	Boeing 747-4FTF	34240/1373		
☐ B-2477	Boeing 747-433BCF	24998/840	ex N998GP	
☐ B-2478	Boeing 747-433BCF	25075/868	ex N575GP	
☐ B-2871	Tupolev Tu-204-120SE	1450743664030		
☐ B-2872	Tupolev Tu-204-120SE	145074..64031		on order
☐ B-2873	Tupolev Tu-204-120SE	145074..64034		on order

CHANG AN AIRLINES — *Changan (HU/CGN)* — *Xi'an (SIA)*

☐ B-6210	Airbus A319-115	2557	ex D-AVYK	Lsd fr CHH
☐ B-6211	Airbus A319-115	2561	ex D-AVYO	Lsd fr CHH
☐ B-6212	Airbus A319-115	2581	ex D-AVXG	Lsd to DER
☐ B-6215	Airbus A319-112	2611	ex D-AVXR	Lsd to DER
☐ B-3444	AVIC I Y7-100C	09701		
☐ B-3445	AVIC I Y7-100C	09705		
☐ B-3475	AVIC I Y7-100C	06703		
☐ B-3707	AVIC I Y7-100C	12701		
☐ B-3708	AVIC I Y7-100C	11705		
☐ B-3720	AVIC I Y7-200A	200-0001		
☐ B-3721	AVIC I Y7-200A	200-0003		
☐ B-5092	Boeing 737-705	29092/260	ex VH-VBX	Lsd fr CHH
☐ B-5115	Boeing 737-8FH/W	29640/1649		Lsd fr CHH
☐ B-5116	Boeing 737-8FH/W	29672/1745	ex N1786B	Lsd fr CHH
☐ B-5180	Boeing 737-8FH/W	35089/2042		Lsd fr CHH
☐ B-5181	Boeing 737-8FH/W	35090/2073		Lsd fr CHH

CHINA CARGO AIRLINES — *Cargo King (CK/CKK)* — *Shanghai-Pu Dong Intl (PVG)*

☐ B-2076	Boeing 777-F6N	37711		on order
☐ B-2077	Boeing 777-F6N	37713		on order
☐ B-2078	Boeing 777-F6N	37714		on order
☐ B-2079	Boeing 777-F6N	37715		on order
☐ B-2170	McDonnell-Douglas MD-11F	48461/475		

☐ B-2171	McDonnell-Douglas MD-11F	48495/461		
☐ B-2172	McDonnell-Douglas MD-11F	48496/496		
☐ B-2173	McDonnell-Douglas MD-11F	48497/512		
☐ B-2174	McDonnell-Douglas MD-11F	48498/522		
☐ B-2175	McDonnell-Douglas MD-11F	48520/541	ex N9134D	
☐ B-2308	Airbus A300B4-605RF	532	ex F-WWAH	
☐ B-2425	Boeing 747-40BERF	35207/1377		
☐ B-2426	Boeing 747-40BERF	35208/1392		
☐ B-	Tupolev Tu-204-120SE	145074..64041		on order

CHINA EASTERN AIRLINES — **_China Eastern (MU/CES)_** — **_Shanghai-Pu Dong Intl (PVG)_**

☐ B-2306	Airbus A300B4-605RF	521	ex F-WWAF
☐ B-2307	Airbus A300B4-605RF	525	ex F-WWAJ
☐ B-2317	Airbus A300B4-605R	741	ex F-WWAY
☐ B-2318	Airbus A300B4-605R	707	ex F-WWAU
☐ B-2319	Airbus A300B4-605R	732	ex F-WWAT
☐ B-2324	Airbus A300B4-622R	725	ex F-WWAR
☐ B-2325	Airbus A300B4-605R	746	ex F-WWAA
☐ B-2326	Airbus A300B4-605R	754	ex F-WWAY
☐ B-2330	Airbus A300B4-605R	763	ex F-WWAH
☐ B-2215	Airbus A319-112	1541	ex D-AVWI
☐ B-2216	Airbus A319-112	1551	ex D-AVWN
☐ B-2217	Airbus A319-112	1601	ex D-AVWX
☐ B-2222	Airbus A319-112	1603	ex D-AVWY
☐ B-2226	Airbus A319-112	1786	ex D-AVYP
☐ B-2227	Airbus A319-112	1778	ex D-AVYE
☐ B-2331	Airbus A319-112	1285	ex D-AVYT
☐ B-2332	Airbus A319-112	1303	ex D-AVWN
☐ B-2333	Airbus A319-112	1377	ex D-AVWE
☐ B-2334	Airbus A319-112	1386	ex D-AVWC
☐ B-6167	Airbus A319-115	3168	ex D-AVWB
☐ B-6172	Airbus A319-115	3186	ex D-AVYG
☐ B-6217	Airbus A319-115	2693	ex D-AVXC
☐ B-6218	Airbus A319-115	2757	ex D-AVWH
☐ B-6231	Airbus A319-115	2825	ex D-AVXD
☐ B-6332	Airbus A319-115	3262	ex D-AVZB
☐ B-2201	Airbus A320-214	0914	ex F-WWDV
☐ B-2202	Airbus A320-214	0925	ex F-WWID
☐ B-2203	Airbus A320-214	1005	ex F-WWDL
☐ B-2205	Airbus A320-214	0984	ex F-WWDI
☐ B-2206	Airbus A320-214	0986	ex F-WWDJ
☐ B-2207	Airbus A320-214	1028	ex F-WWDG
☐ B-2208	Airbus A320-214	1070	ex F-WWBH
☐ B-2209	Airbus A320-214	1030	ex F-WWDU
☐ B-2211	Airbus A320-214	1041	ex F-WWID
☐ B-2212	Airbus A320-214	1316	ex F-WWDG
☐ B-2213	Airbus A320-214	1345	ex F-WWDX
☐ B-2219	Airbus A320-214	1532	ex F-WWIP
☐ B-2220	Airbus A320-214	1542	ex F-WWIV
☐ B-2221	Airbus A320-214	1639	ex F-WWDZ
☐ B-2228	Airbus A320-214	1906	ex F-WWDK
☐ B-2229	Airbus A320-214	1911	ex F-WWDT
☐ B-2230	Airbus A320-214	1964	ex F-WWDR
☐ B-2335	Airbus A320-214	1312	ex F-WWBZ
☐ B-2336	Airbus A320-214	1330	ex F-WWDV
☐ B-2337	Airbus A320-214	1357	ex F-WWBF
☐ B-2338	Airbus A320-214	1361	ex F-WWBU
☐ B-2356	Airbus A320-214	0665	ex F-WWBB
☐ B-2357	Airbus A320-214	0754	ex F-WWIY
☐ B-2358	Airbus A320-214	0838	ex F-WWBB
☐ B-2359	Airbus A320-214	0854	ex F-WWBK
☐ B-2360	Airbus A320-214	0772	ex F-WWDK
☐ B-2361	Airbus A320-214	0799	ex F-WWDI
☐ B-2362	Airbus A320-214	0828	ex F-WWIM
☐ B-2363	Airbus A320-214	0883	ex F-WWDC
☐ B-2372	Airbus A320-214	0897	ex F-WWDK
☐ B-2375	Airbus A320-214	0909	ex F-WWDS
☐ B-2378	Airbus A320-214	0939	ex F-WWIQ
☐ B-2379	Airbus A320-214	0967	ex F-WWBN
☐ B-2398	Airbus A320-214	1108	ex F-WWDH
☐ B-2399	Airbus A320-214	1093	ex F-WWIZ
☐ B-2400	Airbus A320-214	1072	ex F-WWBI
☐ B-2410	Airbus A320-214	2437	ex F-WWIX
☐ B-2411	Airbus A320-214	2451	ex F-WWDF
☐ B-2412	Airbus A320-214	2478	ex F-WWDV
☐ B-2413	Airbus A320-214	2493	ex F-WWDZ
☐ B-2415	Airbus A320-214	2498	ex F-WWIL
☐ B-6001	Airbus A320-214	1981	ex F-WWDL
☐ B-6002	Airbus A320-214	2022	ex F-WWDG

☐ B-6003	Airbus A320-214	2034	ex F-WWIF	
☐ B-6005	Airbus A320-214	2036	ex F-WWIZ	
☐ B-6006	Airbus A320-214	2068	ex F-WWIL	
☐ B-6007	Airbus A320-214	2056	ex F-WWIR	
☐ B-6008	Airbus A320-214	2049	ex F-WWII	
☐ B-6009	Airbus A320-214	2219	ex F-WWDN	
☐ B-6010	Airbus A320-214	2221	ex F-WWIU	
☐ B-6011	Airbus A320-214	2235	ex F-WWBY	
☐ B-6012	Airbus A320-214	2239	ex F-WWDP	
☐ B-6013	Airbus A320-214	2244	ex F-WWIR	
☐ B-6015	Airbus A320-214	2212	ex F-WWBF	
☐ B-6016	Airbus A320-214	2155	ex F-WWDU	
☐ B-6017	Airbus A320-214	2274	ex F-WWIJ	
☐ B-6028	Airbus A320-214	2171	ex F-WWDG	
☐ B-6029	Airbus A320-214	2182	ex F-WWIO	
☐ B-6030	Airbus A320-214	2199	ex F-WWDX	
☐ B-6259	Airbus A320-214	2562	ex F-WWIZ	
☐ B-6260	Airbus A320-214	2591	ex F-WWDT	
☐ B-6261	Airbus A320-214	2606	ex F-WWBR	
☐ B-6262	Airbus A320-214	2627	ex F-WWDV	
☐ B-6333	Airbus A320-214	3170	ex F-WWIN	
☐ B-6335	Airbus A320-214	3197	ex F-WWIX	
☐ B-6346	Airbus A320-232	3481	ex F-WWDL	
☐ B-6370	Airbus A320-214	3559	ex F-WWBF	
☐ B-6371	Airbus A320-214	3611	ex D-AVVF	
☐ B-6372	Airbus A320-232	3613	ex F-WWIH	
☐ B-6373	Airbus A320-232	3650	ex F-WWDP	
☐ B-6375	Airbus A320-232	3677	ex F-WWBC	
☐ B-6376	Airbus A320-232	3692	ex F-WWBF	
☐ B-6399	Airbus A320-232	3716	ex F-WWBJ	
☐ B-6558	Airbus A320-232	3793	ex F-WWBH	
☐ B-6559	Airbus A320-232	3904	ex F-WWIB	
☐ B-6560	Airbus A320-232	3937	ex F-WWDQ	
☐ B-6585	Airbus A320-232	3965	ex F-WWIE	
☐ B-6586	Airbus A320-232	3775	ex B-504L	
☐ B-6587	Airbus A320-232	3797	ex B-505L	
☐ B-6600	Airbus A320-232	3870	ex B-506L	
☐ B-6601	Airbus A320-232	4037	ex F-WWIL	
☐ B-6616	Airbus A320-232	3929	ex B-508L	
☐ B-6617	Airbus A320-232	4144	ex D-AVVC	
☐ B-6635	Airbus A320-232	4027	ex B-513L	
☐ B-	Airbus A320-232	4186	ex B-520L	on order
☐ B-	Airbus A320-232	4220	ex B-502L	on order
☐ B-	Airbus A320-232	4232	ex B-503L	on order
☐ B-	Airbus A320-232		ex	on order
☐ B-	Airbus A320-232		ex	on order
☐ B-	Airbus A320-232		ex	on order
☐ B-	Airbus A320-232		ex	on order
☐ B-	Airbus A320-232		ex	on order
☐ B-	Airbus A320-232		ex	on order

☐ B-2289	Airbus A321-211	2309	ex D-AVZD
☐ B-2290	Airbus A321-211	2315	ex D-AVZM
☐ B-2291	Airbus A321-211	2543	ex D-AVZF
☐ B-2292	Airbus A321-211	2549	ex D-AVZI
☐ B-2419	Airbus A321-211	2882	ex D-AVZJ
☐ B-2420	Airbus A321-211	2895	ex D-AVZA
☐ B-6329	Airbus A321-211	3233	ex D-AVZH
☐ B-6330	Airbus A321-211	3247	ex D-AVZK
☐ B-6331	Airbus A321-211	3249	ex D-AVZO
☐ B-6332	Airbus A321-211	3262	ex D-AVZB
☐ B-6366	Airbus A321-211	3593	ex D-AZAB
☐ B-6367	Airbus A321-211	3612	ex D-AZAD
☐ B-6368	Airbus A321-211	3639	ex D-AVZT
☐ B-6369	Airbus A321-211	3682	ex D-AVZJ

☐ B-6082	Airbus A330-243	821	ex F-WWKB
☐ B-6083	Airbus A330-343E	830	ex F-WWKK
☐ B-6085	Airbus A330-343E	836	ex F-WWYK
☐ B-6095	Airbus A330-343E	851	ex F-WWKR
☐ B-6096	Airbus A330-343E	862	ex F-WWYG
☐ B-6097	Airbus A330-343E	866	ex F-WWYL
☐ B-6099	Airbus A330-243	916	ex F-WWYP
☐ B-6100	Airbus A330-343E	928	ex F-WWKJ
☐ B-6119	Airbus A330-343	713	ex F-WWYI
☐ B-6120	Airbus A330-343	720	ex F-WWYZ
☐ B-6121	Airbus A330-243	728	ex F-WWKQ
☐ B-6122	Airbus A330-243	732	ex F-WWKT
☐ B-6123	Airbus A330-243	735	ex F-WWYA
☐ B-6125	Airbus A330-343	773	ex F-WWKF
☐ B-6126	Airbus A330-343	777	ex F-WWKK
☐ B-6127	Airbus A330-343	781	ex F-WWYT
☐ B-6128	Airbus A330-343	782	ex F-WWYV

☐ B-6129	Airbus A330-343	791	ex F-WWKO	
☐ B-6506	Airbus A330-343E	936	ex F-WWKG	
☐ B-6507	Airbus A330-343E	942	ex F-WWYK	
☐ B-2380	Airbus A340-313X	129	ex F-WWJQ	
☐ B-2381	Airbus A340-313X	131	ex F-WWJO	
☐ B-2382	Airbus A340-313X	141	ex F-WWJC	
☐ B-2383	Airbus A340-313X	161	ex F-WWJQ	
☐ B-2384	Airbus A340-313X	182	ex F-WWJM	
☐ B-6050	Airbus A340-642	468	ex F-WWCP	
☐ B-6051	Airbus A340-642	488	ex F-WWCT	
☐ B-6052	Airbus A340-642	514	ex F-WWCU	
☐ B-6053	Airbus A340-642	577	ex F-WWCM	
☐ B-6055	Airbus A340-642	586	ex F-WWCR	Expo 2010 colours
☐ B-2538	Boeing 737-3W0	25090/2040		
☐ B-2571	Boeing 737-39P	29410/3053		
☐ B-2572	Boeing 737-39P	29411/3071		
☐ B-2573	Boeing 737-39P	29412/3080	ex N1786B	
☐ B-2589	Boeing 737-3W0	27127/2377		
☐ B-2594	Boeing 737-341	26853/2275	ex (PP-VPB)	
☐ B-2955	Boeing 737-33A	27453/2687		
☐ B-2956	Boeing 737-33A	27907/2690		
☐ B-2958	Boeing 737-3W0	27522/2727		
☐ B-2966	Boeing 737-33A	27462/2765		
☐ B-2969	Boeing 737-36R	30102/3108	ex N1787B	
☐ B-2976	Boeing 737-3S3	29244/3059	ex N244SR	
☐ B-2981	Boeing 737-3W0	28972/2919		
☐ B-2983	Boeing 737-3W0	28973/2941		
☐ B-2985	Boeing 737-3W0	29068/2945		
☐ B-2986	Boeing 737-3W0	29069/2951		
☐ B-2988	Boeing 737-36R	29087/2970		
☐ B-2502	Boeing 737-7W0	30075/311		
☐ B-2503	Boeing 737-7W0	30074/292	ex N1786B	
☐ B-2639	Boeing 737-7W0	29912/140	ex N1787B	
☐ B-2640	Boeing 737-7W0	29913/148	ex N1800B	
☐ B-2665	Boeing 737-86R	30495/876		
☐ B-2680	Boeing 737-76Q	30282/1143	ex N706BA	
☐ B-2681	Boeing 737-79P	33037/1198		
☐ B-2682	Boeing 737-79P	33038/1219		
☐ B-2683	Boeing 737-79P	28253/1247		
☐ B-2684	Boeing 737-79P	33039/1227		
☐ B-2685	Boeing 737-79P	33040/1244		
☐ B-5030	Boeing 737-79P	30651/1267		
☐ B-5031	Boeing 737-79P	28255/1284		
☐ B-5032	Boeing 737-79P	30035/1288		
☐ B-5033	Boeing 737-79P	30657/1319		
☐ B-5034	Boeing 737-79P	30036/1336		
☐ B-5054	Boeing 737-79P	29365/1841	ex N1784B	
☐ B-5074	Boeing 737-79P	33008/1718	ex N1786B	
☐ B-5084	Boeing 737-79P	33009/1728	ex N1786B	
☐ B-5085	Boeing 737-89P/W	30691/1702		
☐ B-5086	Boeing 737-89P/W	32800/1681		
☐ B-5087	Boeing 737-89P/W	32802/1725		
☐ B-5093	Boeing 737-79P	29357/1630		
☐ B-5094	Boeing 737-79P	29358/1651		
☐ B-5095	Boeing 737-79P	29361/1694		
☐ B-5096	Boeing 737-79P	29362/1713		
☐ B-5097	Boeing 737-79P	29364/1823	ex N6067E	
☐ B-5100	Boeing 737-89P/W	30681/1645	ex N1786B	
☐ B-5101	Boeing 737-89P/W	30682/1673		
☐ B-5199	Boeing 737-89P/W	36272/2753		
☐ B-5208	Boeing 737-79P/W	33041/1902	ex N1787B	
☐ B-5209	Boeing 737-79P/W	33042/1947	ex N1779B	
☐ B-5210	Boeing 737-79P/W	33043/1976		
☐ B-5223	Boeing 737-79P/W	33044/1987		
☐ B-5225	Boeing 737-79P/W	33045/1999		
☐ B-5231	Boeing 737-79P/W	33046/2034		
☐ B-5242	Boeing 737-79P/W	36269/2357		
☐ B-5243	Boeing 737-79P/W	36270/2398		
☐ B-5245	Boeing 737-79P/W	36271/2697		
☐ B-5255	Boeing 737-79P/W	36757/2902	ex N1786B	
☐ B-5256	Boeing 737-79P/W	36758/2949		
☐ B-5257	Boeing 737-79P/W	33759/2968	ex N1786B	
☐ B-5258	Boeing 737-79P/W	36760/3009		
☐ B-5259	Boeing 737-79P/W	36762/3046		
☐ B-5262	Boeing 737-79P/W	36764/3067	ex N1787B	
☐ B-5263	Boeing 737-79P/W	36766/3086	ex N1796B	
☐ B-5376	Boeing 737-86N/W	35226/2641		
☐ B-5472	Boeing 737-79P/W	36761/3001	ex N1779B	
☐ B-5473	Boeing 737-79P/W	36763/3036	ex N1786B	
☐ B-5475	Boeing 737-79P/W	36765/3065		

☐ B-5492	Boeing 737-89P/W	29661/3083	ex N1787B
☐ B-5493	Boeing 737-89P/W	29652/3121	
☐ B-	Boeing 737-89P/W		on order
☐ B-	Boeing 737-89P/W		on order
☐ B-	Boeing 737-89P/W		on order
☐ B-	Boeing 737-89P/W		on order
☐ B-	Boeing 737-89P/W		on order
☐ B-	Boeing 737-89P/W		on order
☐ B-2568	Boeing 767-3W0ER	28148/620	
☐ B-2569	Boeing 767-3W0ER	28149/627	
☐ B-5001	Boeing 767-3W0ER	28264/644	
☐ B-3013	Canadair CL-600-2B19 (CRJ-200LR)	7571	ex C-FVAZ
☐ B-3019	Canadair CL-600-2B19 (CRJ-200LR)	7581	ex C-FMMX
☐ B-3021	Canadair CL-600-2B19 (CRJ-200LR)	7596	ex C-FMNW
☐ B-3070	Canadair CL-600-2B19 (CRJ-200LR)	7647	ex C-FMLB
☐ B-3071	Canadair CL-600-2B19 (CRJ-200LR)	7684	ex C-FMMT
☐ B-3049	Embraer EMB-145LI (ERJ-145LI)	14500839	ex PT-SOA
☐ B-3050	Embraer EMB-145LI (ERJ-145LI)	14500848	ex PT-SOB
☐ B-3051	Embraer EMB-145LI (ERJ-145LI)	14500898	ex PT-SOD
☐ B-3052	Embraer EMB-145LI (ERJ-145LI)	14500905	ex PT-SOE
☐ B-3053	Embraer EMB-145LI (ERJ-145LI)	14500882	ex PT-SOC
☐ B-3055	Embraer EMB-145LI (ERJ-145LI)	14500921	ex PT-S
☐ B-3056	Embraer EMB-145LI (ERJ-145LI)	14500928	ex PT-S
☐ B-3057	Embraer EMB-145LI (ERJ-145LI)	14500932	ex PT-S
☐ B-3058	Embraer EMB-145LI (ERJ-145LI)	14500958	
☐ B-3059	Embraer EMB-145LI (ERJ-145LI)	14500949	

CHINA EXPRESS AIRLINES — *China Express (G5/HXA)* — *Guiyang (KWE)*

☐ B-3001	Canadair CL-600-2B19 (CRJ-200LR)	7565	ex B-KBJ Lsd fr CDG
☐ B-3012	Canadair CL-600-2B19 (CRJ-200LR)	7557	ex C-FMLB Lsd fr CDG
☐ B-3016	Canadair CL-600-2B19 (CRJ-200LR)	7614	ex C-FMKV

CHINA FLYING DRAGON AVIATION CO — *Feilong (CFA)* — *Harbin - Ping Fang*

☐ B-7420	Aérospatiale AS350B2 Ecureuil	2522	ex F-WYMH
☐ B-7421	Aérospatiale AS350B2 Ecureuil	2523	ex F-WYMG
☐ B-7422	Aérospatiale AS350B2 Ecureuil	2534	ex F-WYMB
☐ B-7423	Aérospatiale AS350B2 Ecureuil	2538	ex F-WYMF
☐ B-7424	Aérospatiale AS350B2 Ecureuil	2547	ex F-WYME
☐ B-7425	Aérospatiale AS350B2 Ecureuil	2554	ex F-WYMF
☐ B-7427	Aérospatiale AS350B2 Ecureuil	2566	
☐ B-3201	AVIC II Y-11B	003	prototype, status?
☐ B-3862	AVIC II Y-11	(11)0407	
☐ B-3863	AVIC II Y-11	(11)0408	
☐ B-3864	AVIC II Y-11	(11)0409	
☐ B-3874	AVIC II Y-11	(11)0102	
☐ B-3875	AVIC II Y-11	(11)0105	
☐ B-3876	AVIC II Y-11	(11)0106	
☐ B-3877	AVIC II Y-11	(11)0107	
☐ B-3878	AVIC II Y-11	(11)0110	
☐ B-3879	AVIC II Y-11	(11)0201	
☐ B-3880	AVIC II Y-11	(11)0202	
☐ B-3881	AVIC II Y-11	(11)0203	
☐ B-3882	AVIC II Y-11	(11)0204	
☐ B-3883	AVIC II Y-11	(11)0205	
☐ B-3884	AVIC II Y-11	(11)0210	
☐ B-3801	Harbin Y-12 II	0006	Freighter
☐ B-3802	Harbin Y-12 II	0002	Surveyor
☐ B-3803	Harbin Y-12 II	0003	Surveyor
☐ B-3804	Harbin Y-12 II	0011	Surveyor
☐ B-3805	Harbin Y-12 II	0005	Surveyor
☐ B-3806	Harbin Y-12 II	0008	Freighter
☐ B-3807	Harbin Y-12 II	0016	Op for Maritime Service
☐ B-3808	Harbin Y-12 II	0017	Op for Maritime Service
☐ B-3819	Harbin Y-12 II	0004	Freighter
☐ B-7109	AVIC II Z-9A Haitun (SA365N)	045	Op for Ministry of Forestry
☐ B-7110	AVIC II Z-9A Haitun (SA365N)	047	Op for Ministry of Forestry
☐ B-7112	AVIC II Z-9A Haitun (SA365N)		

CHINA POSTAL AIRLINES — *China Post (8Y/CYZ)* — *Tianjin (TSN)*

☐ B-3101	AVIC II Y-8F-100	10(08)01	
☐ B-3102	AVIC II Y-8F-100	10(08)02	
☐ B-3103	AVIC II Y-8F-100	10(08)05	
☐ B-3109	AVIC II Y-8F-100	13(08)03	

☐ B-3110	AVIC II Y-8F-100	13(08)04		c/n not confirmed

☐ B-2135	Boeing 737-45R(SF)	29035/3046	ex N202BK	
☐ B-2526	Boeing 737-3Y0 (SF)	25172/2089		
☐ B-2527	Boeing 737-3Y0 (SF)	25173/2097		
☐ B-2528	Boeing 737-3Y0 (SF)	25174/2168		
☐ B-2656	Boeing 737-3Q8 (SF)	26292/2519	ex N141LF	
☐ B-2661	Boeing 737-3Q8 (SF)	26284/2418	ex N379BC	
☐ B-2662	Boeing 737-3Q8 (SF)	24988/2466	ex N441LF	
☐ B-2881	Boeing 737-45R (SF)	29032/2943	ex N651AC	
☐ B-2882	Boeing 737-45R (SF)	29033/2963	ex N652AC	
☐ B-2891	Boeing 737-46J (SF)	28334/2802	ex TF-BBB	
☐ B-2892	Boeing 737-46J (SF)	28271/2801	ex N211BF	
☐ B-5046	Boeing 737-341 (SF)	24276/1645	ex N276HE	
☐ B-5047	Boeing 737-341 (SF)	24278/1660	ex N278HE	
☐ B-5071	Boeing 737-341 (QC)	24277/1658	ex N277HE	
☐ B-5072	Boeing 737-341 (QC)	24279/1673	ex N279HE	
☐ B-	Boeing 737-45R (SF)	29034/3015	ex N653AC	on order

CHINA SOUTHERN AIRLINES — *China Southern (CZ/CSN)* — *Guangzhou (CAN)*

Member of Skyteam

☐ B-2315	Airbus A300B4-622RF	733	ex F-WWAU
☐ B-2316	Airbus A300B4-622R	734	ex F-WWAE
☐ B-2323	Airbus A300B4-622R	739	ex F-WWAB
☐ B-2327	Airbus A300B4-622R	750	ex HL7583
☐ B-2328	Airbus A300B4-622RF	756	ex HL7580

☐ B-2294	Airbus A319-132	2371	ex D-AVWL
☐ B-2295	Airbus A319-132	2408	ex D-AVWB
☐ B-2296	Airbus A319-132	2426	ex D-AVYZ
☐ B-2297	Airbus A319-132	2435	ex D-AVYH
☐ B-6018	Airbus A319-132	1971	ex D-AVYC
☐ B-6019	Airbus A319-132	1986	ex D-AVYJ
☐ B-6020	Airbus A319-133	2004	ex D-AVWB
☐ B-6021	Airbus A319-133	2008	ex D-AVWN
☐ B-6039	Airbus A319-132	2200	ex D-AVYE
☐ B-6040	Airbus A319-132	2203	ex D-AVYG
☐ B-6041	Airbus A319-132	2232	ex D-AVWI
☐ B-6042	Airbus A319-132	2273	ex D-AVWZ
☐ B-6158	Airbus A319-132	2901	ex D-AVWP
☐ B-6160	Airbus A319-132	2940	ex D-AVWW
☐ B-6161	Airbus A319-132	2948	ex D-AVXB
☐ B-6162	Airbus A319-132	2969	ex D-AVYT
☐ B-6168	Airbus A319-132	3020	ex D-AVXN
☐ B-6183	Airbus A319-115	3828	ex D-AVYK
☐ B-6187	Airbus A319-132	3903	ex D-AVWQ
☐ B-6190	Airbus A319-132	3860	ex D-AVWC
☐ B-6191	Airbus A319-132	3890	ex D-AVWJ
☐ B-6195	Airbus A319-112	3983	ex D-AVYF
☐ B-6200	Airbus A319-115	2519	ex D-AVYX
☐ B-6201	Airbus A319-115	2541	ex D-AVWV
☐ B-6202	Airbus A319-115	2546	ex D-AVWX
☐ B-6203	Airbus A319-112	2554	ex D-AVYS
☐ B-6205	Airbus A319-132	2505	ex D-AVWG
☐ B-6206	Airbus A319-132	2574	ex D-AVXD
☐ B-6207	Airbus A319-132	2579	ex D-AVXF
☐ B-6208	Airbus A319-112	2555	ex D-AVWU
☐ B-6209	Airbus A319-112	2558	ex D-AVYP
☐ B-6219	Airbus A319-132	2667	ex D-AVYG
☐ B-6220	Airbus A319-132	2815	ex D-AVWX
☐ B-6239	Airbus A319-132	3144	ex D-AVXT
☐ B-6240	Airbus A319-132	3258	ex D-AVXM
☐ B-6241	Airbus A319-132	3269	ex D-AVYA
☐ B-6242	Airbus A319-132	3311	ex D-AVYR
☐ B-6243	Airbus A319-132	3342	ex D-AVYJ
☐ B-6407	Airbus A319-132	4036	ex D-AVYK
☐ B-6408	Airbus A319-112	4038	ex D-AVYL
☐ B-6409	Airbus A319-132	4071	ex D-AVYU

☐ B-2347	Airbus A320-233	0705	ex F-WWIL
☐ B-2350	Airbus A320-232	0712	ex F-WWDI
☐ B-2351	Airbus A320-233	0718	ex F-WWBI
☐ B-2352	Airbus A320-232	0720	ex F-WWBU
☐ B-2353	Airbus A320-232	0722	ex F-WWBM
☐ B-2365	Airbus A320-232	0849	ex F-WWBI
☐ B-2366	Airbus A320-232	0859	ex F-WWBO
☐ B-2367	Airbus A320-232	0881	ex F-WWDB
☐ B-2368	Airbus A320-232	0895	ex F-WWDJ
☐ B-2369	Airbus A320-232	0900	ex F-WWDM
☐ B-2374	Airbus A320-232	2345	ex F-WWBC
☐ B-2391	Airbus A320-232	0950	ex F-WWIZ

☐ B-2392	Airbus A320-232	0966	ex F-WWBK	
☐ B-2393	Airbus A320-232	1035	ex F-WWDX	
☐ B-2395	Airbus A320-232	1039	ex F-WWDZ	
☐ B-2396	Airbus A320-232	1057	ex F-WWIO	
☐ B-2401	Airbus A320-232	0710	ex F-OHCY	
☐ B-2403	Airbus A320-232	2275	ex F-WWDL	
☐ B-2405	Airbus A320-232	2343	ex F-WWIV	
☐ B-2406	Airbus A320-214	2354	ex F-WWIP	
☐ B-2407	Airbus A320-232	2334	ex F-WWIM	
☐ B-2408	Airbus A320-214	2361	ex F-WWBM	
☐ B-2459	Airbus A320-214	0709	ex F-OHCX	
☐ B-6251	Airbus A320-214	2484	ex F-WWIO	
☐ B-6252	Airbus A320-214	2506	ex F-WWBP	
☐ B-6253	Airbus A320-214	2511	ex F-WWIT	
☐ B-6255	Airbus A320-214	2637	ex F-WWBX	
☐ B-6263	Airbus A320-214	2708	ex F-WWIU	
☐ B-6269	Airbus A320-232	2743	ex F-WWBK	
☐ B-6272	Airbus A320-214	2770	ex F-WWDM	
☐ B-6275	Airbus A320-232	2680	ex F-WWIY	
☐ B-6276	Airbus A320-232	2689	ex F-WWIG	
☐ B-6277	Airbus A320-232	2701	ex F-WWIR	
☐ B-6278	Airbus A320-231	2714	ex F-WWBD	
☐ B-6279	Airbus A320-232	2772	ex F-WWDR	
☐ B-6281	Airbus A320-214	2796	ex F-WWIC	
☐ B-6282	Airbus A320-214	2824	ex F-WWDF	
☐ B-6283	Airbus A320-214	2834	ex F-WWBP	
☐ B-6287	Airbus A320-214	2899	ex F-WWDB	
☐ B-6288	Airbus A320-214	2855	ex F-WWIS	
☐ B-6289	Airbus A320-214	2861	ex F-WWIY	
☐ B-6290	Airbus A320-214	2877	ex F-WWBK	
☐ B-6291	Airbus A320-214	2915	ex F-WWDM	
☐ B-6292	Airbus A320-214	2960	ex F-WWBN	
☐ B-6293	Airbus A320-214	2986	ex F-WWIG	
☐ B-6303	Airbus A320-214	2950	ex F-WWIL	
☐ B-6575	Airbus A320-214	3910	ex F-WWIS	
☐ B-6576	Airbus A320-214	3941	ex F-WWDS	
☐ B-6577	Airbus A320-214	3959	ex F-WWDJ	
☐ B-6582	Airbus A320-214	3999	ex F-WWDK	
☐ B-6583	Airbus A320-214	4003	ex F-WWDP	
☐ B-6588	Airbus A320-214	4017	ex F-WWBX	
☐ B-6620	Airbus A320-214	4172	ex F-WWDM	
☐ B-	Airbus A320-214	4140	ex B-518L	on order
☐ B-	Airbus A320-214		ex	on order
☐ B-	Airbus A320-214		ex	on order
☐ B-	Airbus A320-214		ex	on order
☐ B-	Airbus A320-214		ex	on order
☐ B-	Airbus A320-214		ex	on order
☐ B-	Airbus A320-214		ex	on order
☐ B-	Airbus A320-214		ex	on order
☐ B-	Airbus A320-214		ex	on order
☐ B-	Airbus A320-214		ex	on order
☐ B-	Airbus A320-214		ex	on order

☐ B-2280	Airbus A321-231	1596	ex D-AVZL	
☐ B-2281	Airbus A321-231	1614	ex D-AVZA	
☐ B-2282	Airbus A321-231	1776	ex D-AVZC	
☐ B-2283	Airbus A321-231	1788	ex D-AVZE	
☐ B-2284	Airbus A321-231	1974	ex D-AVZN	
☐ B-2285	Airbus A321-231	1995	ex D-AVZZ	
☐ B-2287	Airbus A321-231	2080	ex D-AVZW	
☐ B-2288	Airbus A321-231	2067	ex D-AVZP	
☐ B-2417	Airbus A321-231	2521	ex D-AVZC	
☐ B-2418	Airbus A321-231	2530	ex D-AVZD	
☐ B-6265	Airbus A321-231	2713	ex D-AVZI	
☐ B-6267	Airbus A321-231	2741	ex D-AVZK	
☐ B-6270	Airbus A321-231	2759	ex D-AVZL	
☐ B-6271	Airbus A321-231	2767	ex D-AVZM	
☐ B-6273	Airbus A321-231	2809	ex D-AVZC	
☐ B-6302	Airbus A321-231	2936	ex D-AVZT	
☐ B-6305	Airbus A321-231	2971	ex D-AVZM	
☐ B-6306	Airbus A321-231	3067	ex D-AVZJ	
☐ B-6307	Airbus A321-231	3075	ex D-AVZB	
☐ B-6308	Airbus A321-231	3112	ex D-AVZE	
☐ B-6317	Airbus A321-231	3217	ex D-AVZD	
☐ B-6318	Airbus A321-231	3251	ex D-AVZP	
☐ B-6319	Airbus A321-231	3241	ex D-AVZJ	
☐ B-6339	Airbus A321-231	3507	ex D-AVZJ	
☐ B-6342	Airbus A321-231	3459	ex D-AVZT	
☐ B-6343	Airbus A321-231	3493	ex D-AVZF	
☐ B-6345	Airbus A321-231	3471	ex D-AVZY	
☐ B-6353	Airbus A321-231	3552	ex D-AVZP	
☐ B-6355	Airbus A321-231	3566	ex D-AVZS	
☐ B-6356	Airbus A321-231	3587	ex D-AVZR	

☐ B-6378	Airbus A321-231	3645	ex D-AVZU	
☐ B-6379	Airbus A321-231	3681	ex D-AZAF	
☐ B-6389	Airbus A321-231	3764	ex D-AZAN	
☐ B-6397	Airbus A321-231	3784	ex D-AZAQ	
☐ B-6398	Airbus A321-231	3847	ex D-AVZH	
☐ B-6552	Airbus A321-231	3867	ex D-AVZL	
☐ B-6553	Airbus A321-231	3920	ex D-AZZY	
☐ B-6578	Airbus A321-231	3934	ex D-AZAE	
☐ B-6579	Airbus A321-231	3938	ex D-AZAH	
☐ B-6580	Airbus A321-231	3951	ex D-AZAT	
☐ B-6581	Airbus A321-231	3981	ex D-AZAM	
☐ B-	Airbus A321-231		ex	on order
☐ B-	Airbus A321-231		ex	on order
☐ B-	Airbus A321-231		ex	on order
☐ B-	Airbus A321-231		ex	on order
☐ B-	Airbus A321-231		ex	on order
☐ B-	Airbus A321-231		ex	on order
☐ B-	Airbus A321-231		ex	on order
☐ B-	Airbus A321-231		ex	on order
☐ B-	Airbus A321-231		ex	on order
☐ B-	Airbus A321-231		ex	on order
☐ B-6056	Airbus A330-243	649	ex F-WWKI	
☐ B-6057	Airbus A330-243	652	ex F-WWKL	
☐ B-6058	Airbus A330-243	656	ex F-WWYV	
☐ B-6059	Airbus A330-243	664	ex F-WWKP	
☐ B-6077	Airbus A330-243	818	ex F-WWYQ	
☐ B-6078	Airbus A330-243	840	ex F-WWYS	
☐ B-6086	Airbus A330-343E	879	ex F-WWKG	
☐ B-6087	Airbus A330-343E	889	ex F-WWKZ	
☐ B-6098	Airbus A330-343E	908	ex F-WWYF	
☐ B-6111	Airbus A330-343E	935	ex F-WWKF	
☐ B-6112	Airbus A330-343E	937	ex F-WWKI	
☐ B-6500	Airbus A330-343E	954	ex F-WWKT	
☐ B-6501	Airbus A330-343E	964	ex F-WWYK	
☐ B-6502	Airbus A330-343E	958	ex F-WWYD	
☐ B-	Airbus A330-343E	1096	ex F-WW	on order
☐ B-	Airbus A330-343E		ex F-WW	on order
☐ B-	Airbus A330-343E		ex F-WW	on order
☐ B-	Airbus A330-343E		ex F-WW	on order
☐ B-	Airbus A330-343E		ex F-WW	on order
☐ B-	Airbus A380-841	031	ex F-WWAM	on order
☐ B-	Airbus A380-841	036	ex F-WWAM	on order
☐ B-	Airbus A380-841	054	ex F-WWAX	on order
☐ B-3022	ATR 72-212A	521	ex F-WWED	
☐ B-3023	ATR 72-212A	531	ex F-WWLK	
☐ B-3025	ATR 72-212A	547	ex F-WWLO	
☐ B-3026	ATR 72-212A	552	ex F-WWLP	
☐ B-3027	ATR 72-212A	555	ex F-WWLL	
☐ B-2539	Boeing 737-3Y0	26068/2306		
☐ B-2574	Boeing 737-37K	29407/3100	ex N1786B	
☐ B-2575	Boeing 737-37K	29408/3104	ex N1800B	
☐ B-2582	Boeing 737-31B	25895/2499		
☐ B-2583	Boeing 737-31B	25897/2554		
☐ B-2596	Boeing 737-31B	27151/2437		
☐ B-2909	Boeing 737-3Y0	26082/2456		
☐ B-2910	Boeing 737-3Y0	26083/2459		
☐ B-2911	Boeing 737-3Y0	26084/2460		
☐ B-2920	Boeing 737-3Q8	27271/2523		
☐ B-2921	Boeing 737-3Q8	27286/2528		
☐ B-2922	Boeing 737-31B	27272/2555		
☐ B-2923	Boeing 737-31B	27275/2565		
☐ B-2924	Boeing 737-31B	27287/2575		
☐ B-2926	Boeing 737-31B	27289/2593		
☐ B-2927	Boeing 737-31B	27290/2595		
☐ B-2929	Boeing 737-31B	27343/2619		
☐ B-2930	Boeing 737-31L	27273/2556		
☐ B-2931	Boeing 737-31L	27276/2567		
☐ B-2935	Boeing 737-37K	27283/2547		
☐ B-2936	Boeing 737-37K	27335/2609		
☐ B-2941	Boeing 737-31B	27344/2622		
☐ B-2946	Boeing 737-37K	27375/2655		
☐ B-2952	Boeing 737-31B	27519/2678		
☐ B-2959	Boeing 737-31B	27520/2775		
☐ B-2162	Boeing 737-7K9	30041/909	ex N1786B	
☐ B-2163	Boeing 737-7K9	30042/931	ex N1786B	
☐ B-2169	Boeing 737-71B	32936/1531		
☐ B-2620	Boeing 737-71B	32937/1569		
☐ B-2622	Boeing 737-71B	32938/1603		

	Registration	Type	C/n	Previous identity	Status
☐	B-2693	Boeing 737-81B	32921/1187	ex N6065Y	
☐	B-2694	Boeing 737-81B	32922/1199		
☐	B-2695	Boeing 737-81B	32923/1213		
☐	B-2696	Boeing 737-81B	32924/1230		
☐	B-2697	Boeing 737-81B	32925/1250		
☐	B-2698	Boeing 737-76N	32583/994	ex N583SF	
☐	B-2699	Boeing 737-76N	32596/1028	ex N1786B	
☐	B-2916	Boeing 737-71B	32939/1607		
☐	B-2917	Boeing 737-71B	32940/1624		
☐	B-5020	Boeing 737-81B	32926/1268		
☐	B-5021	Boeing 737-81B	32927/1290		
☐	B-5022	Boeing 737-81B	32928/1323		
☐	B-5040	Boeing 737-81B	32929/1348		
☐	B-5041	Boeing 737-81B	32930/1355		
☐	B-5042	Boeing 737-81B	32931/1362		
☐	B-5067	Boeing 737-81B	32932/1395		
☐	B-5068	Boeing 737-71B	32933/1430		
☐	B-5069	Boeing 737-71B	32934/1465		
☐	B-5070	Boeing 737-71B	32935/1507		
☐	B-5107	Boeing 737-7K9	34320/1763		
☐	B-5108	Boeing 737-7K9	34321/1802	ex N1786B	
☐	B-5112	Boeing 737-86N	34248/1806		
☐	B-5113	Boeing 737-81B	34250/1784		
☐	B-5120	Boeing 737-83N/W	32580/1024	ex N313TZ	
☐	B-5121	Boeing 737-83N/W	32609/1059	ex N316TZ	
☐	B-5122	Boeing 737-83N/W	32610/1110	ex N320TZ	
☐	B-5123	Boeing 737-83N/W	32611/1135	ex N322TZ	
☐	B-5125	Boeing 737-83N/W	32612/1184	ex N326TZ	
☐	B-5126	Boeing 737-83N/W	32613/1197	ex N327TZ	
☐	B-5127	Boeing 737-83N/W	32615/1207	ex N329TZ	
☐	B-5128	Boeing 737-83N/W	32882/1163	ex N324TZ	
☐	B-5129	Boeing 737-83N/W	32884/1181	ex N325TZ	
☐	B-5133	Boeing 737-86N	34252/1851	ex N1787B	
☐	B-5147	Boeing 737-81B	30697/1915	ex N1786B	
☐	B-5149	Boeing 737-81B	30699/1933		
☐	B-5155	Boeing 737-8K5/W	30783/804	ex N307TA	
☐	B-5156	Boeing 737-81Q/W	30786/1138	ex N786TA	
☐	B-5157	Boeing 737-81Q/W	30787/1234	ex N787TM	
☐	B-5163	Boeing 737-81B	30708/2087		
☐	B-5165	Boeing 737-81B	30709/1961		
☐	B-5166	Boeing 737-81B	33006/1983		
☐	B-5189	Boeing 737-81B	35365/2191		
☐	B-5190	Boeing 737-81B	35366/2223		
☐	B-5191	Boeing 737-81B	35367/2237	ex N1786B	
☐	B-5192	Boeing 737-81B	35369/2272		
☐	B-5193	Boeing 737-81B	35370/2299		
☐	B-5195	Boeing 737-81B	35371/2302		
☐	B-5221	Boeing 737-71B	29366/1872	ex N1795B	
☐	B-5222	Boeing 737-71B	29367/1896	ex N1784B	
☐	B-5230	Boeing 737-71B	29371/2064		
☐	B-5232	Boeing 737-71B	35360/2051		
☐	B-5233	Boeing 737-71B	35361/2077		
☐	B-5235	Boeing 737-71B	29370/2137		
☐	B-5236	Boeing 737-71B	35362/2102		
☐	B-5237	Boeing 737-71B	29372/2131	ex N1786B	
☐	B-5238	Boeing 737-71B	35363/2066		
☐	B-5239	Boeing 737-71B	35364/2156		
☐	B-5240	Boeing 737-71B	35368/2264		
☐	B-5241	Boeing 737-71B	35372/2291		
☐	B-5247	Boeing 737-71B	35377/2980	ex N1786B	
☐	B-5250	Boeing 737-71B	35378/2346		
☐	B-5251	Boeing 737-71B	35384/2446		
☐	B-5252	Boeing 737-71B	35382/3034	ex N1786B	
☐	B-5253	Boeing 737-71B	35383/3005		
☐	B-5300	Boeing 737-81B	35375/2314		
☐	B-5310	Boeing 737-81B	35376/2329		
☐	B-5339	Boeing 737-81B	35380/2372	ex N1782B	
☐	B-5340	Boeing 737-81B	35381/2402		
☐	B-5356	Boeing 737-81B	35385/2486	ex N1787B	
☐	B-5419	Boeing 737-81B	35379/2957	ex N1787B	
☐	B-5420	Boeing 737-81B	35374/2940		
☐	B-5421	Boeing 737-81B	35373/2881		
☐	B-5445	Boeing 737-81B	35388/3154		
☐	B-5446	Boeing 737-8Q8	35389/3144		
☐	B-5468	Boeing 737-81B	35386/3068	ex N1786B	
☐	B-5469	Boeing 737-81B	35387/3041		
☐	B-	Boeing 737-8Q8			on order
☐	B-	Boeing 737-8Q8			on order
☐	B-2461	Boeing 747-41BF	32804/1312		
☐	B-2473	Boeing 747-41BF	32803/1306	ex N1788B	
☐	B-2812	Boeing 757-28S	32341/961		

Reg	Type	C/n	Previous	Name	Notes
☐ B-2813	Boeing 757-28S	32342/966			
☐ B-2816	Boeing 757-21B	25083/359			
☐ B-2817	Boeing 757-21B	25258/389			
☐ B-2818	Boeing 757-21B	25259/392			
☐ B-2822	Boeing 757-21B	25884/461			
☐ B-2823	Boeing 757-21B	25888/575			
☐ B-2824	Boeing 757-21B	25889/583			
☐ B-2825	Boeing 757-21B	25890/585			
☐ B-2827	Boeing 757-2Y0	26156/503			
☐ B-2830	Boeing 757-28S	32343/1015	ex N60668		
☐ B-2831	Boeing 757-2Y0	26153/482			
☐ B-2835	Boeing 757-236	25598/445	ex N5573P		
☐ B-2838	Boeing 757-2Z0	27260/613			
☐ B-2851	Boeing 757-28S	29215/797			
☐ B-2853	Boeing 757-28S	29216/811			
☐ B-2859	Boeing 757-28S	29217/868			
☐ B-2860	Boeing 757-236	29945/873	ex N546NA		
☐ B-2861	Boeing 757-236	29946/877	ex N547NA		

Reg	Type	C/n	Previous	Name	Notes
☐ B-2051	Boeing 777-21B	27357/20		Toyota Camry c/s	
☐ B-2052	Boeing 777-21B	27358/24	ex N5017V		
☐ B-2053	Boeing 777-21B	27359/46			
☐ B-2054	Boeing 777-21B	27360/48			
☐ B-2055	Boeing 777-21BER	27524/55			
☐ B-2056	Boeing 777-21BER	27525/66			
☐ B-2057	Boeing 777-21BER	27604/106	ex N5022E	Pearl of The South	
☐ B-2058	Boeing 777-21BER	27605/110	ex N5028Y		
☐ B-2062	Boeing 777-21BER	27606/121	ex N688CZ		
☐ B-2070	Boeing 777-21BER	32703/472			
☐ B-2071	Boeing 777-F1B	37309/760	ex N447BA		on order
☐ B-2072	Boeing 777-F1B	37310/770	ex N448BA		on order
☐ B-2073	Boeing 777-F1B	37311/811	ex N553BA		
☐ B-2075	Boeing 777-F1B	37310/820	ex N554BA		

Reg	Type	C/n	Previous	Name	Notes
☐ B-3060	Embraer EMB.145LI (ERJ-145LI)	145701	ex PT-SGF		
☐ B-3061	Embraer EMB.145LI (ERJ-145LI)	145755	ex PT-SNA		
☐ B-3062	Embraer EMB.145LI (ERJ-145LI)	145781	ex PT-SNB		
☐ B-3063	Embraer EMB.145LI (ERJ-145LI)	14500804	ex PT-S		
☐ B-3065	Embraer EMB.145LI (ERJ-145LI)	14500815	ex PT-S		
☐ B-3066	Embraer EMB.145LI (ERJ-145LI)	14500823	ex PT-SXL		

Reg	Type	C/n	Previous	Name	Notes
☐ B-2130	McDonnell-Douglas MD-82	49514/1589			SAIC c/n 15
☐ B-2132	McDonnell-Douglas MD-82	49516/1622			SAIC c/n 17
☐ B-2134	McDonnell-Douglas MD-82	49518/1647			SAIC c/n 19
☐ B-2136	McDonnell-Douglas MD-82	49520/1671			SAIC c/n 21
☐ B-2143	McDonnell-Douglas MD-82	49851/1807			SAIC c/n 28
☐ B-2145	McDonnell-Douglas MD-82	49853/1981			SAIC c/n 35
☐ B-2147	McDonnell-Douglas MD-82	53163/2025	ex N832AU		
☐ B-2152	McDonnell-Douglas MD-82	53164/2041	ex N833AU		stored HRB

Reg	Type	C/n	Previous	Name	Notes
☐ B-2100	McDonnell-Douglas MD-90-30	60001/4001		AVIC II assembled	
☐ B-2103	McDonnell-Douglas MD-90-30	60002/4002		AVIC II assembled	
☐ B-2250	McDonnell-Douglas MD-90-30	53523/2143			
☐ B-2251	McDonnell-Douglas MD-90-30	53524/2146			
☐ B-2252	McDonnell-Douglas MD-90-30	53525/2150			
☐ B-2253	McDonnell-Douglas MD-90-30	53526/2170			
☐ B-2254	McDonnell-Douglas MD-90-30	53527/2175			
☐ B-2255	McDonnell-Douglas MD-90-30	53528/2177			
☐ B-2259	McDonnell-Douglas MD-90-30	53529/2220			
☐ B-2260	McDonnell-Douglas MD-90-30	53530/2222			
☐ B-2261	McDonnell-Douglas MD-90-30	53531/2228			
☐ B-2266	McDonnell-Douglas MD-90-30	53532/2253			
☐ B-2267	McDonnell-Douglas MD-90-30	53533/2258			

Reg	Type	C/n	Previous	Name	Notes
☐ B-7303	Sikorsky S-76A	760289			
☐ B-7304	Sikorsky S-76A	760293			

Reg	Type	C/n	Previous	Name	Notes
☐ B-7306	Sikorsky S-76A	760106	ex VH-XHA		
☐ B-7307	Sikorsky S-76C+	760478			
☐ B-7308	Sikorsky S-76C+	760480			
☐ B-7311	Sikorsky S-76C+	760192			
☐ B-7320	Sikorsky S-76C+	760263			
☐ B-7331	Sikorsky S-76C++	760715	ex N2557H		

CHINA UNITED AIRLINES — *Lianhang (KN/CUA)* — *Beijing-Nanyuan (NAY)*

Reg	Type	C/n	Previous	Notes
☐ B-4008	Boeing 737-3T0	23839/1507	ex N19357	Op for Govt
☐ B-4009	Boeing 737-3T0	23840/1516	ex N27358	Op for Govt
☐ B-4018	Boeing 737-33A	25502/2310		Op for Govt
☐ B-4019	Boeing 737-33A	25503/2313		Op for Govt
☐ B-4020	Boeing 737-34N	28081/2746		Op for Govt
☐ B-4021	Boeing 737-34N	28082/2747		Op for Govt
☐ B-4052	Boeing 737-3Q8	24701/1957	ex PK-GWI	Op for Govt

☐ B-4053	Boeing 737-3Q8	24702/1994	ex PK-GWJ	Op for Govt
☐ B-2663	Boeing 737-7AD	28437/72	ex N701EW	Lsd fr CSH
☐ B-2997	Boeing 737-7Q8	28223/272		Lsd fr CSH
☐ B-4025	Boeing 737-76D	33470/1334	ex B-5048	Op for Govt
☐ B-4026	Boeing 737-76D	33472/1343	ex B-2689	Op for Govt
☐ B-5183	Boeing 737-8Q8/W	30711/2159	ex N1787B	Lsd fr CSH
☐ B-5323	Boeing 737-8Q8	30725/2292		Lsd fr CSH
☐ B-5399	Boeing 737-86N/W	35224/2617		Lsd fr CSH
☐ B-4005	Canadair CL-600-2B19 (CRJ-200LR)	7138	ex C-FZAT	Op for Govt
☐ B-4006	Canadair CL-600-2B19 (CRJ-200LR)	7149	ex C-FZIS	Op for Govt
☐ B-4007	Canadair CL-600-2B19 (CRJ-200LR)	7180	ex C-GATM	Op for Govt
☐ B-4010	Canadair CL-600-2B19 (CRJ-200LR)	7189	ex C-GATY	Op for Govt
☐ B-4011	Canadair CL-600-2B19 (CRJ-200LR)	7193	ex C-GBFR	Op for Govt
☐ B-4701	Canadair CL-600-2B19 (CRJ-200LR)	7639	ex C-GKAK	Op for China Maritime Service
☐ B-4702	Canadair CL-600-2B19 (CRJ-200LR)	7455	ex C-GHUT	Op for China Maritime Service
☐ B-4060	Canadair CL-600-2C10 (CRJ-701ER)	10164	ex C-FBNI	
☐ B-4061	Canadair CL-600-2C10 (CRJ-701ER)	10183	ex C-FCRA	
☐ B-4062	Canadair CL-600-2C10 (CRJ-701ER)	10187	ex C-FCRF	
☐ B-4063	Canadair CL-600-2C10 (CRJ-701ER)	10204	ex C-FEHT	
☐ B-4064	Canadair CL-600-2C10 (CRJ-701ER)	10206	ex C-FEHU	
☐ B-4016	Tupolev Tu-154M	91A-872		
☐ B-4017	Tupolev Tu-154M	91A-873		
☐ B-4028	Tupolev Tu-154M	93A-967		VIP
☐ B-4012	Yakovlev Yak-42D	4520424914375		Op for Chinese Navy
☐ B-4013	Yakovlev Yak-42D	45204249144..?		Op for Chinese Navy

CHINA XINHUA AIRLINES — *Xinhua (HU/CXH)* — *Tianjin (TSN)*

☐ B-2908	Boeing 737-341	26854/2303	ex PP-VPC	Lsd fr CHH
☐ B-2934	Boeing 737-39K	27274/2559		Lsd fr CHH
☐ B-2942	Boeing 737-332	25997/2506	ex N304DE	Lsd fr CHH
☐ B-2943	Boeing 737-332	25998/2510	ex N305DE	Lsd fr CHH
☐ B-2945	Boeing 737-39K	27362/2639		Lsd fr CHH
☐ B-2982	Boeing 737-36Q	28657/2859	ex N211BF	Lsd fr CHH
☐ B-2987	Boeing 737-46Q	28663/2922		Lsd fr CHH
☐ B-2989	Boeing 737-46Q	28758/2939		Lsd fr CHH
☐ B-2993	Boeing 737-46Q	28759/2981		Lsd fr CHH
☐ B-5080	Boeing 737-86N	28614/477	ex N614LS	Lsd fr CHH
☐ B-5081	Boeing 737-86N	30231/515	ex N302LS	Lsd fr CHH
☐ B-5138	Boeing 737-84P/W	32607/1832		Lsd fr CHH
☐ B-5139	Boeing 737-84P/W	32608/1855		Lsd fr CHH
☐ B-5141	Boeing 737-84P/W	34030/1800		Lsd fr CHH
☐ B-5153	Boeing 737-84P/W	34029/1921		Lsd fr CHH

CHONGQING AIRLINES — *Chongqing (OQ/CQN)* — *Chongqing (CKG)*

☐ B-2343	Airbus A320-233	0696	ex F-WWII	Lsd fr CSN
☐ B-2345	Airbus A320-233	0698	ex F-WWBT	Lsd fr CSN
☐ B-2346	Airbus A320-233	0704	ex F-WWDY	Lsd fr CSN
☐ B-6246	Airbus A319-133	3836	ex D-AVYO	
☐ B-6247	Airbus A319-133	3876	ex D-AVWG	
☐ B-6248	Airbus A319-133	3901	ex D-AVWP	

CITIC OFFSHORE HELICOPTERS — *China Helicopter (CHC)* — *Shenzhen Heliport*

☐ B-7127	Eurocopter EC225LP	2676	
☐ B-7128	Eurocopter EC225LP	2687	
☐ B-7951	Aérospatiale AS.332L	2165	ex F-WYMQ
☐ B-7956	Aérospatiale AS.332L1	2356	ex HL9202
☐ B-7957	Aérospatiale AS.332L1	9000	
☐ B-7958	Aérospatiale AS.332L1	9001	ex F-WQDT
☐ B-7959	Aérospatiale AS.332L1	2087	ex F-WYMR
☐ B-7961	Aérospatiale AS.332L1	2641	
☐ B-7962	Aérospatiale AS.332L1	2644	
☐ B-7005	Eurocopter EC155B	6639	
☐ B-7006	Eurocopter EC155B	6641	
☐ B-7007	Eurocopter EC135T2	0246	
☐ B-7008	Eurocopter EC155B	6623	
☐ B-7101	Aérospatiale AS365N	6012	
☐ B-7102	Aérospatiale AS365N	6013	
☐ B-7103	Aérospatiale AS365N	6041	
☐ B-7105	Aérospatiale AS365N	6046	
☐ B-7106	Aérospatiale AS365N	6047	
☐ B-7107	Aérospatiale AS365N	6027	
☐ B-7120	Eurocopter EC155B1	6717	ex F-WWOU

☐ B-7772	Agusta A.109E Power	11136		

DEER JET — Deer Jet (JD/DER) — Bejing-Capital (PEK)

☐ B-6156	Airbus A319-112	2849	ex D-AVXJ	Lsd fr CHH
☐ B-6157	Airbus A319-112	2891	ex D-AVYS	Lsd fr CHH
☐ B-6169	Airbus A319-112	2985	ex D-AVXJ	Lsd fr CHH
☐ B-6177	Airbus A319-112	3285	ex D-AVYY	Lsd fr CHH
☐ B-6178	Airbus A319-132	3548	ex D-AVWK	Lsd fr CHH
☐ B-6179	Airbus A319-132	3561	ex D-AVWR	Lsd fr CHH
☐ B-6180	Airbus A319-132	3578	ex D-AVYA	
☐ B-6181	Airbus A319-132	3580	ex D-AVYB	
☐ B-6182	Airbus A319-112	3520	ex D-AVWA	
☐ B-6192	Airbus A319-132	3768	ex D-AVXG	Lsd fr CHH
☐ B-6193	Airbus A319-133	3849	ex D-AVYV	
☐ B-6198	Airbus A319-112	2617	ex D-AVYI	
☐ B-6199	Airbus A319-112	2644	ex D-AVWP	
☐ B-6212	Airbus A319-115	2581	ex D-AVXG	Lsd fr CGN
☐ B-6215	Airbus A319-112	2611	ex D-AVXR	Lsd fr CGN
☐ B-6221	Airbus A319-112	2746	ex D-AVYL	
☐ B-6222	Airbus A319-112	2733	ex D-AVXL	
☐ B-6245	Airbus A319-133	3851	ex D-AVYW	
☐ B-6400	Airbus A319-132	3638	ex B-502L	
☐ B-6401	Airbus A319-133	3842	ex B-510L	
☐ B-6402	Airbus A319-132	3914	ex B-507L	
☐ B-6403	Airbus A319-132	3958	ex B-509L	
☐ B-6405	Airbus A319-132	3982	ex B-511L	
☐ B-	Airbus A319-133X	4042	ex F-WWDA	on order

☐ B-2112	Boeing 737-36N	28599/3115	ex EI-DRS	Lsd fr CHH
☐ B-2113	Boeing 737-36N	28602/3118	ex EI-DRY	Lsd fr CHH
☐ B-2115	Boeing 737-36N	28606/3124	ex EI-DRZ	Lsd fr CHH
☐ B-2608	Boeing 737-36Q	28662/2914	ex N305FA	Lsd fr CHH
☐ B-3000	Boeing 737-36Q	29326/3020	ex N932HA	Lsd fr CHH

DONGHAI AIRLINES — Donghai Air (J5/EPA) — Shenzhen (SXZ)

☐ B-2517	Boeing 737-3W0 (SF)	23396/1166	ex N5573K
☐ B-2518	Boeing 737-3W0 (SF)	23397/1193	ex N1791B

DONGHUA AIRLINES — Jinjiang (JJN)

☐ B-3889	AVIC II Y-11	(11)0305

EAST STAR AIRLINES — East Star (8C/DXH) — Wuhan (WUH)

Ceased operations 01 April 2009

GRAND CHINA AIRLINES — Grand China (CN/GDC) — Haikou (HAK)

☐ B-2637	Boeing 737-86N	28576/103	ex N576GE	
☐ B-2652	Boeing 737-84P	30475/731		Jin Sui Piao Xiangspecial c/s
☐ B-5337	Boeing 737-84P/W	35747/2433		Lsd fr CHH

GRANDSTAR CARGO INTERNATIONAL — (GD/GSC)

☐ B-2427	Boeing 747-4B5F	26401/1087	ex HL7497

GREAT WALL AIRLINES — G-W Air (IJ/GWL) — Shanghai-Pu Dong Intl (PVG)

☐ B-2428	Boeing 747-412F	28263/1094	ex 9V-SFE
☐ B-2430	Boeing 747-412BCF	27137/990	ex N137GP
☐ B-2433	Boeing 747-412F	28027/1256	ex 9V-SFI

HAINAN AIRLINES — Hainan (HU/CHH) — Haikou (HAK)

☐ B-6156	Airbus A319-112	2849	ex D-AVXJ	Lsd tp DER
☐ B-6157	Airbus A319-112	2891	ex D-AVYS	Lsd to DER
☐ B-6169	Airbus A319-112	2985	ex D-AVXJ	Lsd to DER
☐ B-6177	Airbus A319-112	3285	ex D-AVYY	Lsd to DER
☐ B-6178	Airbus A319-132	3548	ex D-AVWK	Lsd to DER
☐ B-6192	Airbus A319-132	3768	ex D-AVXG	Lsd to DER
☐ B-6210	Airbus A319-115	2557	ex D-AVYK	Op by CGN
☐ B-6211	Airbus A319-115	2561	ex D-AVYO	Op by CGN
☐ B-6212	Airbus A319-115	2581	ex D-AVXG	Op by CGN
☐ B-6215	Airbus A319-112	2611	ex D-AVXR	
☐ B-6221	Airbus A319-112	2746	ex D-AVYL	
☐ B-6222	Airbus A319-112	2733	ex D-AVXL	
☐ B-	Airbus A319-132		ex	on order
☐ B-	Airbus A319-132		ex	on order

	Registration	Type	c/n	Previous identity	Remarks	Notes
☐	B-	Airbus A319-132		ex		on order
☐	B-	Airbus A320-232		ex		on order
☐	B-	Airbus A320-232		ex		on order
☐	B-	Airbus A320-232		ex		on order
☐	B-6088	Airbus A330-243	906	ex F-WWYD		
☐	B-6089	Airbus A330-243	919	ex F-WWYS		
☐	B-6116	Airbus A330-243	875	ex F-WWKB		
☐	B-6118	Airbus A330-243	881	ex F-WWKI		
☐	B-6133	Airbus A330-243	982	ex F-WWYY		
☐	B-	Airbus A330-243		ex		on order
☐	B-	Airbus A330-243		ex		on order
☐	B-	Airbus A330-243		ex		on order
☐	B-6508	Airbus A340-642	436	ex B-HQA		
☐	B-6509	Airbus A340-642	453	ex B-HQB		
☐	B-6510	Airbus A340-642	475	ex B-HQC		
☐	B-2112	Boeing 737-36N	28599/3115	ex EI-DRS		Lsd to DER
☐	B-2113	Boeing 737-36N	28602/3118	ex EI-DRY		Lsd to DER
☐	B-2115	Boeing 737-36N	28606/3124	ex EI-DRZ		Lsd to DER
☐	B-2501	Boeing 737-44P	29914/3067	ex N1786B		
☐	B-2576	Boeing 737-44P	29915/3106	ex N1786B	special flower c/s	
☐	B-2578	Boeing 737-33A	25603/2333	ex N401AW	special flower c/s	
☐	B-2579	Boeing 737-33A	25505/2342	ex N402AW	special flower c/s	
☐	B-2608	Boeing 737-36Q	28662/2914	ex N305FA		Lsd to DER
☐	B-2934	Boeing 737-39K	27274/2559			Lsd to CXH
☐	B-2942	Boeing 737-332	25997/2506	ex N304DE		Lsd to CXH
☐	B-2943	Boeing 737-332	25998/2510	ex N305DE		Lsd to CXH
☐	B-2945	Boeing 737-39K	27362/2639			Lsd to CXH
☐	B-2960	Boeing 737-4Q8	24332/1866	ex N191LF		
☐	B-2963	Boeing 737-3Q8	26325/2772			
☐	B-2965	Boeing 737-4Q8	26334/2782			
☐	B-2967	Boeing 737-4Q8	26335/2793			
☐	B-2970	Boeing 737-4Q8	26337/2811			
☐	B-2987	Boeing 737-46Q	28663/2922			Lsd to CXH
☐	B-2989	Boeing 737-46Q	28758/2939			Lsd to CXH
☐	B-2993	Boeing 737-46Q	28759/2981			Lsd to CXH
☐	B-3000	Boeing 737-36Q	29326/3020	ex N932HA		Lsd to DER
☐	B-5053	Boeing 737-322F	24378/1704	ex N357UA		Lsd to YZR
☐	B-5055	Boeing 737-330 (QC)	24283/1677	ex N283A		Lsd to YZR
☐	B-5056	Boeing 737-330 (QC)	23836/1508	ex N836Y		Lsd to YZR
☐	B-5057	Boeing 737-330 (QC)	23837/1514	ex N837Y		Lsd to YZR
☐	B-5058	Boeing 737-330 (QC)	23835/1465	ex N835A		Lsd to YZR
☐	B-5059	Boeing 737-322F	24362/1696	ex N356UA		Lsd to YZR
☐	B-2157	Boeing 737-84P/W	32600/1015	ex N1786B		
☐	B-2158	Boeing 737-84P/W	32601/1033			
☐	B-2159	Boeing 737-84P/W	32599/972	ex N1787B		
☐	B-2636	Boeing 737-86N	28574/67	ex N574GE		
☐	B-2638	Boeing 737-8Q8	28220/212	ex N361LF	special palm c/s	
☐	B-2646	Boeing 737-8Q8	28056/273	ex N371LF	special orchid c/s	
☐	B-2647	Boeing 737-84P	29947/345	ex N1787B	special Happy Sea Wave c/s	
☐	B-2651	Boeing 737-84P	30474/607	ex N1787B		
☐	B-2675	Boeing 737-86Q/W	32885/1147			
☐	B-2676	Boeing 737-84P/W	32602/1170			
☐	B-2677	Boeing 737-84P/W	32604/1191			
☐	B-5060	Boeing 737-76N	28582/154	ex N582HE		Lsd to CXI
☐	B-5061	Boeing 737-76N	28583/163	ex N583HE		Lsd to CXI
☐	B-5062	Boeing 737-76N	28585/173	ex N585HE		Lsd to CXI
☐	B-5080	Boeing 737-86N	28614/477	ex N614LS		Lsd to CXH
☐	B-5081	Boeing 737-86N	30231/515	ex N302LS		Lsd to CXH
☐	B-5082	Boeing 737-883	30193/587	ex LN-RCS		Lsd to CXH
☐	B-5083	Boeing 737-883	28319/548	ex LN-RCO		
☐	B-5089	Boeing 737-883	28320/551	ex OY-KKU		
☐	B-5090	Boeing 737-883	28321/577	ex LN-RCR		
☐	B-5091	Boeing 737-705	29091/230	ex VH-VBW		Lsd to LKE
☐	B-5092	Boeing 737-705	29092/260	ex VH-VBX		Lsd to CGN
☐	B-5115	Boeing 737-8FH/W	29640/1649			Lsd to CGN
☐	B-5116	Boeing 737-8FH/W	29672/1745	ex N1786B		Lsd to CGN
☐	B-5135	Boeing 737-84P/W	32603/1766	ex N1786B		
☐	B-5136	Boeing 737-84P/W	32605/1796	ex B-KBE		
☐	B-5137	Boeing 737-84P/W	32606/1805	ex B-KBF		
☐	B-5138	Boeing 737-84P/W	32607/1832			Lsd to CXH
☐	B-5139	Boeing 737-84P/W	32608/1855			Lsd to CXH
☐	B-5141	Boeing 737-84P/W	34030/1800			Lsd to CXH
☐	B-5153	Boeing 737-84P/W	34029/1921			Lsd to CXH
☐	B-5180	Boeing 737-8FH/W	35089/2042			Lsd to CGN
☐	B-5181	Boeing 737-8FH/W	35090/2073			Lsd to CGN
☐	B-5182	Boeing 737-808/W	34708/2097			
☐	B-5248	Boeing 737-790/W	30626/1273	ex N629AS		Lsd to LKE
☐	B-5249	Boeing 737-790	33011/1291	ex N645AS		Lsd to LKE

☐ B-5337	Boeing 737-84P/W	35747/2433		Lsd to GDC
☐ B-5338	Boeing 737-84P/W	35749/2330		
☐ B-5346	Boeing 737-8BK/W	29673/2373	ex N1786B	
☐ B-5358	Boeing 737-84P/W	35077/2419	ex N1787B	
☐ B-5359	Boeing 737-8FH/W	35101/2459	ex N1786B	
☐ B-5371	Boeing 737-84P/W	35752/2556	ex N1787B	
☐ B-5372	Boeing 737-84P/W	35758/2593		
☐ B-5373	Boeing 737-84P/W	35754/2618	ex N1787B	
☐ B-5375	Boeing 737-84P/W	35762/2648		
☐ B-5403	Boeing 737-84P/W	35756/2691		
☐ B-5405	Boeing 737-84P/W	35759/2668		
☐ B-5406	Boeing 737-84P/W	35760/2678		
☐ B-5407	Boeing 737-808/W	34967/2239	ex B-HXF	
☐ B-5408	Boeing 737-84P/W	35764/2778	ex N1786B	
☐ B-5409	Boeing 737-808/W	34968/2265	ex B-KXG	
☐ B-5416	Boeing 737-84P/W	34031/2801	ex N1780B	
☐ B-5417	Boeing 737-86N/W	35639/2821		
☐ B-5418	Boeing 737-86N/W	36541/2769	ex N1786B	
☐ B-5427	Boeing 737-8Q8/W	35285/2772	ex N1787B	
☐ B-5428	Boeing 737-86N/W	36542/2806	ex N1796B	
☐ B-5429	Boeing 737-86N/W	36543/2831	ex N1796B	
☐ B-5430	Boeing 737-84P/W	34032/2827	ex N1787B	
☐ B-5439	Boeing 737-808/W	34707/2046	ex B-KBH	
☐ B-5449	Boeing 737-808/W	34971/2400	ex B-KXH	
☐ B-5462	Boeing 737-84P/W	36780/3095	ex N1796B	
☐ B-5465	Boeing 737-84P/W	34033/2854	ex N1787B	
☐ B-5466	Boeing 737-84P/W	34034/2912		
☐ B-5467	Boeing 737-84P/W	36779/2885		
☐ B-5478	Boeing 737-84P/W	35751/3038	ex N1786B	
☐ B-5479	Boeing 737-84P/W	35753/3066	ex N1786B	
☐ B-5480	Boeing 737-86N/W	35648/2973		
☐ B-5481	Boeing 737-86N/W	35649/2981		
☐ B-5482	Boeing 737-84P/W	35748/2938	ex N1786B	
☐ B-5483	Boeing 737-84P/W	35750/3007		
☐ B-	Boeing 737-84P/W			on order
☐ B-	Boeing 737-84P/W			on order
☐ B-	Boeing 737-84P/W			on order
☐ B-	Boeing 737-84P/W			on order
☐ B-	Boeing 737-84P/W			on order
☐ B-	Boeing 737-84P/W			on order
☐ B-	Boeing 737-84P/W			on order
☐ B-	Boeing 737-84P/W			on order
☐ B-	Boeing 737-84P/W			on order
☐ B-	Boeing 737-84P/W			on order
☐ B-	Boeing 737-84P/W			on order
☐ B-	Boeing 737-84P/W			on order
☐ B-KBI	Boeing 737-808/W	34709/2121	ex N1787B	Lsd to CRK
☐ B-KBK	Boeing 737-84P/W	35072/2155	ex N1786B	Lsd to CRK
☐ B-KBM	Boeing 737-84P/W	35076/2380		Lsd to CRK
☐ B-KBP	Boeing 737-8FH/W	35105/2501		Lsd to HKE
☐ B-KBQ	Boeing 737-84P/W	35274/2570		Lsd to HKE
☐ B-KBR	Boeing 737-84P/W	35276/2611		Lsd to HKE
☐ B-KXE	Boeing 737-808/W	34710/2144		Lsd to HKE
☐ B-2490	Boeing 767-34PER	33047/889		
☐ B-2491	Boeing 767-34PER	33048/891		
☐ B-2492	Boeing 767-34PER	33049/893		

JADE CARGO INTERNATIONAL — *Jade Cargo (JI/JAE)* — *Shenzhen (SZX)*

☐ B-2421	Boeing 747-4EVERF	35169/1391	ex N1794B
☐ B-2422	Boeing 747-4EVERF	35173/1387	
☐ B-2423	Boeing 747-4EVERF	35174/1398	
☐ B-2439	Boeing 747-4EVERF	35170/1376	
☐ B-2440	Boeing 747-4EVERF	35171/1380	
☐ B-2441	Boeing 747-4EVERF	35172/1383	

JIANGNAN UNIVERSAL AVIATION — *Changzhou-West Suburbs (CZX)*

☐ B-3865	AVIC II Y-11	(11)0410	
☐ B-3866	AVIC II Y-11	(11)0104	
☐ B-3867	AVIC II Y-11	(11)0206	
☐ B-3868	AVIC II Y-11	(11)0109	
☐ B-3821	Harbin Y-12 II	0032	ex (JU-1019)
☐ B-3823	Harbin Y-12 II	0068	ex (JU-1021)

JUNEYAO AIRLINES — *Air Juneyao (HO/DKH)* — *Shanghai-Hongqiao (SHA)*

☐ B-6232	Airbus A319-112	2879	ex D-AVXN
☐ B-6233	Airbus A319-112	2913	ex D-AVWZ
☐ B-6298	Airbus A320-214	2975	ex F-WWDO
☐ B-6311	Airbus A320-214	3027	ex F-WWBM

☐ B-6338	Airbus A320-214	3368	ex F-WWDE	
☐ B-6340	Airbus A320-214	3234	ex F-WWBH	
☐ B-6341	Airbus A320-214	3268	ex F-WWBU	
☐ B-6381	Airbus A320-214	3485	ex F-WWIG	
☐ B-6395	Airbus A320-214	3596	ex F-WWDI	
☐ B-6396	Airbus A320-214	3605	ex F-WWDN	
☐ B-6572	Airbus A320-214	3967	ex F-WWIF	
☐ B-6602	Airbus A320-214	3984	ex F-WWBJ	
☐ B-6618	Airbus A320-214	4102	ex F-WWDO	
☐ B-6619	Airbus A320-214	4154	ex F-WWBK	
☐ B-6640	Airbus A320-214	4064	ex B-515L	
☐ B-	Airbus A320-214	4276	ex	on order

KUNMING AIRLINES — *(KY/KNA)* — *Kunming (KMG)*

☐ B-2678	Boeing 737-76N	32244/895	ex N315ML
☐ B-2679	Boeing 737-76N	29893/710	ex N313ML

KUNPENG AIRLINES — *(VD/KPA)* — *Xian*

☐ B-7691	Canadair CL-600-2B19 (CRJ-200LR)	7218	ex N37218	
☐ B-	Canadair CL-600-2B19 (CRJ-200LR)	7191	ex N27191	on order
☐ B-3126	Embraer 190-100LR (190LR)	19000201	ex PT-SGJ	
☐ B-3130	Embraer 190-100LR (190LR)	19000223	ex PT-SHH	
☐ B-3131	Embraer 190-100LR (190LR)	19000220	ex PT-SIB	
☐ B-3132	Embraer 190-100LR (190LR)	19000263	ex PT-	
☐ B-3133	Embraer 190-100LR (190LR)	19000264	ex PT-TLE	

LUCKY AIRLINES — *Lucky Air (8L/LKE)* — *Dali City (DLU)*

☐ B-5060	Boeing 737-76N	28582/154	ex N582HE	Lsd fr CXI
☐ B-5061	Boeing 737-76N	28583/163	ex N583HE	Lsd fr CXI
☐ B-5091	Boeing 737-705	29091/230	ex VH-VBW	Lsd fr CHH
☐ B-5246	Boeing 737-7Q8/W	30674/1511	ex N751AL	
☐ B-5248	Boeing 737-790/W	30626/1273	ex N629AS	Lsd fr CHH
☐ B-5249	Boeing 737-790	33011/1291	ex N645AS	Lsd fr CHH

NORTHEAST AIRLINES — *(NS/DBH)* — *Shenyang*

☐ B-3040	Embraer EMB.145LR (ERJ-145LR)	145317	ex PT-SMI	Lsd fr CSC
☐ B-3041	Embraer EMB.145LR (ERJ-145LR)	145349	ex PT-SNP	Lsd fr CSC
☐ B-6170	Airbus A319-132	2396	ex N101LF	Lsd fr CSC

OKAIR — *Okayjet (BK/OKA)* — *Tianjin (TSN)*

☐ B-2117	Boeing 737-3Q8 (SF)	24961/2133	ex N141LF
☐ B-2519	Boeing 737-3Z0 (SF)	23448/1168	ex N5573P
☐ B-2522	Boeing 737-3Z0 (SF)	23451/1240	ex N5573K
☐ B-2863	Boeing 737-83N/W	30673/1500	ex N333TZ
☐ B-2865	Boeing 737-83N/W	30679/1404	ex N332TZ
☐ B-5366	Boeing 737-8GQ/W	35793/2428	ex N1787B
☐ B-5367	Boeing 737-8Q8/W	30733/2452	ex N1786B
☐ B-4071	AVIC II Y-8		
☐ B-4072	AVIC II Y-8		

RAINBOW JET — *Cai Hong (RBW)* — *Jinan (TNA)*

☐ B-3630	Cessna 208B Caravan I	208B0883	ex N12285	
☐ B-3631	Cessna 208 Caravan I	20800333	ex N1228V	Floatplane
☐ B-3632	Cessna 208 Caravan I	20800332	ex N1284F	Floatplane
☐ B-3636	Cessna 208 Caravan I	20800338	ex N1321L	Floatplane
☐ B-3639	Cessna 208 Caravan I	20800354	ex N5283U	Floatplane

SF AIRLINES

☐ B-2899	Boeing 757-21B(SF)	24401/232	ex N401AN

SHAN XI AIRLINES — *Shanxi (CXI)* — *Taiyuan-Wusu (TYN)*

☐ B-3701	AVIC I Y7-100C	12705		stored TYN
☐ B-3702	AVIC I Y7-100C	12707		stored TYN
☐ B-3703	AVIC I Y7-100C	12708		stored TYN
☐ B-5060	Boeing 737-76N	28582/154	ex N582HE	Lsd to LKE
☐ B-5061	Boeing 737-76N	28583/163	ex N583HE	Lsd to LKE
☐ B-5062	Boeing 737-76N	28585/173	ex N585HE	Lsd fr CHH

SHANDONG AIRLINES — Shandong (SC/CDG) — Jinan (TNA)

☐ B-2111	Boeing 737-36Q	29405/3047	ex N405GT		
☐ B-2877	Boeing 737-33V	29331/3062	ex G-EZYG		
☐ B-2878	Boeing 737-36Q	28760/2989	ex N307FL		
☐ B-2961	Boeing 737-35N	28156/2774			
☐ B-2962	Boeing 737-35N	28157/2778			
☐ B-2968	Boeing 737-35N	28158/2818			
☐ B-2995	Boeing 737-35N	29315/3054			
☐ B-2996	Boeing 737-35N	29316/3065			
☐ B-5065	Boeing 737-36Q	28664/2940	ex N287CH		
☐ B-5066	Boeing 737-36Q	28761/3011	ex N286CH		
☐ B-5098	Boeing 737-36Q	29140/3013	ex N914CH		
☐ B-5099	Boeing 737-36Q	29189/3057	ex N918CH		
☐ B-5111	Boeing 737-85N/W	33660/1752			
☐ B-5117	Boeing 737-85N/W	33661/1770			
☐ B-5118	Boeing 737-85N/W	33664/1726			
☐ B-5119	Boeing 737-85N/W	33665/1775	ex N1781B		
☐ B-5205	Boeing 737-75N/W	33654/1790			
☐ B-5206	Boeing 737-75N/W	33666/1742	ex N1779B		
☐ B-5207	Boeing 737-75N/W	33663/1838	ex N1787B		
☐ B-5321	Boeing 737-8AL/W	35073/2197			
☐ B-5331	Boeing 737-8AL/W	35075/2287			
☐ B-5332	Boeing 737-8FH/W	35095/2295			
☐ B-5333	Boeing 737-8FH/W	35096/2336	ex N1782B		
☐ B-5335	Boeing 737-8FH/W	35097/2345	ex N1787B		
☐ B-5336	Boeing 737-8FH/W	35098/2361			
☐ B-5347	Boeing 737-85N/W	36190/2429			
☐ B-5348	Boeing 737-85N/W	36191/2453	ex N1786B		
☐ B-5349	Boeing 737-85N/W	36192/2642			
☐ B-5350	Boeing 737-85N/W	36193/2669	ex N1786B		
☐ B-5351	Boeing 737-85N/W	36194/2684			
☐ B-5352	Boeing 737-85N/W	36195/2823			
☐ B-5450	Boeing 737-85N/W	36773/2874	ex N1786B		
☐ B-5451	Boeing 737-85N/W	36776/2998			
☐ B-5452	Boeing 737-85N/W	36777/3045	ex N1796B		
☐ B-5455	Boeing 737-85N/W	36774/2944			
☐ B-5457	Boeing 737-85N/W	36775/2951	ex N1787B		
☐ B-	Boeing 737-85N/W				on order
☐ B-	Boeing 737-85N/W				on order
☐ B-	Boeing 737-85N/W				on order
☐ B-3001	Canadair CL-600-2B19 (CRJ-200LR)	7565	ex C-FMNH	Lsd to HXA	
☐ B-3005	Canadair CL-600-2B19 (CRJ-200LR)	7435	ex C-FMKW		
☐ B-3006	Canadair CL-600-2B19 (CRJ-200LR)	7443	ex C-FMLV		
☐ B-3007	Canadair CL-600-2B19 (CRJ-200LR)	7498	ex C-FMLF		
☐ B-3008	Canadair CL-600-2B19 (CRJ-200LR)	7512	ex B-604L		
☐ B-3009	Canadair CL-600-2B19 (CRJ-200LR)	7522	ex C-FMMY		
☐ B-3012	Canadair CL-600-2B19 (CRJ-200LR)	7557	ex C-FMLB	Lsd to HXA	
☐ B-3079	Canadair CL-600-2C10 (CRJ-701ER)	10118	ex C-		
☐ B-3080	Canadair CL-600-2C10 (CRJ-701ER)	10120	ex C-		

SHANGHAI AIRLINES — Shanghai Air (FM/CSH) — Shanghai-Hongqiao (SHA)

Member of Star Alliance

☐ B-6591	Airbus A321-231	3969	ex D-AVZM	
☐ B-6592	Airbus A321-231	4045	ex D-AVZL	
☐ B-	Airbus A321-231		ex	on order
☐ B-	Airbus A321-231		ex	on order
☐ B-	Airbus A321-231		ex	on order
☐ B-2153	Boeing 737-8Q8	28242/942	ex N1786B	
☐ B-2167	Boeing 737-8Q8	30631/1047		
☐ B-2168	Boeing 737-8Q8	30632/1086		
☐ B-2577	Boeing 737-76D	30168/600	ex N1786B	
☐ B-2631	Boeing 737-7Q8	28212/35	ex N301LF	
☐ B-2632	Boeing 737-7Q8	28216/122	ex N1795B	
☐ B-2663	Boeing 737-7AD	28437/72	ex N701EW	Lsd to CUA
☐ B-2686	Boeing 737-8Q8	28251/1200		
☐ B-2688	Boeing 737-86D/W	33471/1192	ex N60668	
☐ B-2913	Boeing 737-76D	30167/550	ex N1786B	
☐ B-2997	Boeing 737-7Q8	28223/272	ex N1786B	Lsd to CUA
☐ B-5076	Boeing 737-86N	32739/1434		
☐ B-5077	Boeing 737-86N	32742/1464		
☐ B-5088	Boeing 737-82R	30666/1460	ex N171LF	
☐ B-5130	Boeing 737-8Q8	32801/1666		
☐ B-5131	Boeing 737-8Q8	30686/1704	ex N1784B	
☐ B-5132	Boeing 737-8Q8	30685/1789		
☐ B-5140	Boeing 737-8Q8	30698/1911		

Registration	Type	C/n	Previous identity	Notes
☐ B-5142	Boeing 737-8Q8	30700/1942	ex N1782B	
☐ B-5143	Boeing 737-86N/W	32691/2033		
☐ B-5145	Boeing 737-8Q8	33007/1986		
☐ B-5148	Boeing 737-86N/W	34254/1897		
☐ B-5183	Boeing 737-8Q8/W	30711/2159	ex N1787B	Lsd to CUA
☐ B-5185	Boeing 737-8Q8/W	30715/2230		
☐ B-5260	Boeing 737-76D/W	35777/3037		
☐ B-5261	Boeing 737-76D/W	35778/3064	ex N1786B	
☐ B-5315	Boeing 737-86D	35767/2316		
☐ B-5316	Boeing 737-86D	35768/2362		
☐ B-5320	Boeing 737-8Q8/W	30718/2251	ex N1786B	
☐ B-5323	Boeing 737-8Q8/W	30725/2292		Lsd to CUA
☐ B-5330	Boeing 737-86N/W	35212/2277	ex N1786B	
☐ B-5353	Boeing 737-8Q8	30728/2386		
☐ B-5368	Boeing 737-8Q8	35273/2567		
☐ B-5369	Boeing 737-8Q8/W	35281/2709		
☐ B-5370	Boeing 737-8Q8/W	35271/2551	ex N1786B	
☐ B-5393	Boeing 737-86D/W	35769/2632		
☐ B-5395	Boeing 737-86D/W	35770/2698	ex N1786B	
☐ B-5396	Boeing 737-86D/W	35771/2740	ex N1786B	
☐ B-5399	Boeing 737-86D/W	35224/2617		Lsd to CUA
☐ B-5460	Boeing 737-86D/W	35772/3047		
☐ B-5461	Boeing 737-86D/W	35773/2939	ex N1787B	
☐ B-5470	Boeing 737-86D/W	35774/3010	ex N1786B	
☐ B-5471	Boeing 737-86D/W	35775/3098	ex N1796B	
☐ B-	Boeing 737-86D/W			on order
☐ B-	Boeing 737-86D/W			on order
☐ B-	Boeing 737-76D/W			on order

Registration	Type	C/n	Previous identity	Notes
☐ B-2833	Boeing 757-26D	27152/560		
☐ B-2834	Boeing 757-26D	27183/576		
☐ B-2842	Boeing 757-26D	27342/626		
☐ B-2843	Boeing 757-26D	27681/684		
☐ B-2850	Boeing 757-231	30338/891	ex N725TW	
☐ B-2857	Boeing 757-26D	33959/1044		
☐ B-2858	Boeing 757-26D	33960/1045		
☐ B-2875	Boeing 757-26D	33966/1049	ex N1795B	
☐ B-2876	Boeing 757-26D	33967/1050		last 757 built
☐ B-2880	Boeing 757-26D	33961/1046	ex N1795B	

Registration	Type	C/n	Previous identity	Notes
☐ B-2498	Boeing 767-36D	27684/849		
☐ B-2500	Boeing 767-36DER	35155/946		
☐ B-2563	Boeing 767-36D	27309/546		
☐ B-2566	Boeing 767-36DER	35156/950		
☐ B-2567	Boeing 767-36D	27685/686		
☐ B-2570	Boeing 767-36D	27941/770		Star Alliance Colours
☐ B-5018	Boeing 767-3Q8ER	28207/695	ex N635TW	

Registration	Type	C/n	Previous identity	Notes
☐ B-3011	Canadair CL-600-2B19 (CRJ-200ER)	7556	ex C-FMKZ	
☐ B-3018	Canadair CL-600-2B19 (CRJ-200ER)	7453	ex C-FMNQ	
☐ B-3020	Canadair CL-600-2B19 (CRJ-200ER)	7459	ex C-FMMQ	
☐ B-3075	Canadair CL-600-2B19 (CRJ-200ER)	7226	ex G-DUOF	
☐ B-3090	Canadair CL-600-2B19 (CRJ-200ER)	7247	ex G-DUOG	

SHANGHAI AIRLINES CARGO INTERNATIONAL (F4/SHQ) — *Shanghai-Pu Dong Intl (PVG)*

Registration	Type	C/n	Previous identity	Notes
☐ B-2176	McDonnell-Douglas MD-11F	48415/576	ex N103EV	
☐ B-2177	McDonnell-Douglas MD-11F	48544/580	ex N105EV	
☐ B-2178	McDonnell-Douglas MD-11F	48543/572	ex N7821B	
☐ B-2179	McDonnell-Douglas MD-11F	48545/587	ex N106BV	
☐ B-2808	Boeing 757-26D (PCF)	24471/231	ex N1792B	freighter
☐ B-2809	Boeing 757-26D (PCF)	24472/235	ex N5573B	freighter

SHENZHEN AIRLINES — *Shenzhen Air (ZH/CSZ)* — *Shenzhen (SZX)*

Registration	Type	C/n	Previous identity	Notes
☐ B-6153	Airbus A319-115	2841	ex D-AVYM	
☐ B-6159	Airbus A319-115	2905	ex D-AVWQ	
☐ B-6165	Airbus A319-115X	2935	ex D-AVWM	VIP [CJ]
☐ B-6196	Airbus A319-115	2672	ex D-AVYK	
☐ B-6197	Airbus A319-115	2684	ex D-AVWM	
☐ B-	Airbus A319-115		ex D-AV	on order

Registration	Type	C/n	Previous identity	Notes
☐ B-2416	Airbus A320-214	0904	ex EC-HAB	
☐ B-6286	Airbus A320-214	2909	ex F-WWDU	
☐ B-6296	Airbus A320-214	2973	ex F-WWDN	
☐ B-6297	Airbus A320-214	2980	ex F-WWBP	
☐ B-6312	Airbus A320-214	3131	ex F-WWBK	
☐ B-6313	Airbus A320-214	3132	ex F-WWBP	
☐ B-6315	Airbus A320-214	3153	ex F-WWBZ	
☐ B-6316	Airbus A320-214	3206	ex F-WWII	
☐ B-6351	Airbus A320-214	3366	ex F-WWIU	
☐ B-6352	Airbus A320-214	3383	ex F-WWDN	

	Registration	Type	c/n	Previous identity	Name	Notes
☐	B-6357	Airbus A320-214	3440	ex F-WWDZ		
☐	B-6358	Airbus A320-214	3435	ex F-WWDV		
☐	B-6359	Airbus A320-214	3456	ex D-AVVA		
☐	B-6360	Airbus A320-214	3528	ex F-WWDV		
☐	B-6377	Airbus A320-214	3599	ex F-WWDK		
☐	B-6392	Airbus A320-214	3696	ex D-AVVA		
☐	B-6563	Airbus A320-214	3698	ex B-503L		
☐	B-6565	Airbus A320-214	3971	ex F-WWIO		
☐	B-6566	Airbus A320-214	3855	ex F-WWDK		
☐	B-6567	Airbus A320-214	3887	ex F-WWBS		
☐	B-6569	Airbus A320-214	3848	ex F-WWDE		
☐	B-6570	Airbus A320-214	4010	ex B-512L		
☐	B-6571	Airbus A320-214	3935	ex F-WWDO		
☐	B-6588	Airbus A320-214	3898	ex F-WWDN		
☐	B-6589	Airbus A320-214	4028	ex F-WWIA		
☐	B-6613	Airbus A320-214	4176	ex F-WWDY		
☐	B-6615	Airbus A320-214	4214	ex F-WWIM		on order
☐	B-6648	Airbus A320-214	4159	ex B-519L		on order
☐	B-	Airbus A320-214		ex		on order
☐	B-	Airbus A320-214		ex		on order
☐	B-	Airbus A320-214		ex		on order
☐	B-	Airbus A320-214		ex		on order
☐	B-	Airbus A320-214		ex		on order
☐	B-	Airbus A320-214		ex		on order
☐	B-	Airbus A320-214		ex		on order
☐	B-	Airbus A320-214		ex		on order
☐	B-2601	Boeing 737-36N	28559/2882	ex EI-CUL		
☐	B-2602	Boeing 737-36N	28573/3041	ex N573LS		
☐	B-2687	Boeing 737-36N	28555/2846	ex B-2610		
☐	B-2932	Boeing 737-3K9	25787/2302	ex N41069		
☐	B-2933	Boeing 737-3K9	25788/2331	ex N4113D		
☐	B-2939	Boeing 737-31L	27345/2625			
☐	B-2940	Boeing 737-31L	27346/2636			
☐	B-2971	Boeing 737-3Q8	25373/2290	ex N221LF		
☐	B-2972	Boeing 737-33A	27463/2831			
☐	B-2633	Boeing 737-79K	29190/110	ex N1786B		
☐	B-2635	Boeing 737-79K	29191/127	ex N1786B		
☐	B-2666	Boeing 737-78S	30169/631	ex N1786B		
☐	B-2667	Boeing 737-78S	30170/654			
☐	B-2668	Boeing 737-78S	30171/681	ex N1786B		
☐	B-2669	Boeing 737-77L	32722/1023	ex N1786B		
☐	B-2691	Boeing 737-8Q8	30628/808	ex N802SY		
☐	B-2692	Boeing 737-8Q8	28241/841	ex N803SY		
☐	B-5025	Boeing 737-7BX	30742/864	ex N366ML		
☐	B-5026	Boeing 737-7BX	30741/823	ex N367ML		
☐	B-5049	Boeing 737-86N	28639/772	ex N639SH		
☐	B-5050	Boeing 737-86N	28643/828	ex N643SH		
☐	B-5073	Boeing 737-8Q8	30680/1402			
☐	B-5075	Boeing 737-8Q8	30692/1410			
☐	B-5078	Boeing 737-8Q8	30690/1414	ex N1779B		
☐	B-5079	Boeing 737-8Q8	30693/1422			
☐	B-5102	Boeing 737-97L	33644/1750			
☐	B-5103	Boeing 737-97L	33645/1760			
☐	B-5105	Boeing 737-97L	33646/1764	ex N1784B		
☐	B-5106	Boeing 737-97L	33648/1722			
☐	B-5109	Boeing 737-97L	33649/1755			
☐	B-5186	Boeing 737-8BK	33020/2103			
☐	B-5187	Boeing 737-8BK	33828/2124			
☐	B-5317	Boeing 737-86N/W	32686/2175	ex N1781B		
☐	B-5322	Boeing 737-86N/W	32688/2218			
☐	B-5345	Boeing 737-86N/W	35215/2306	ex N1780B		
☐	B-5357	Boeing 737-8AL/W	35081/2519	ex N1787B		
☐	B-5360	Boeing 737-86J/W	30062/485	ex D-ABAW		Lsd fr BER
☐	B-5361	Boeing 737-86J/W	30063/517	ex D-ABAX		Lsd fr BER
☐	B-5362	Boeing 737-86J/W	30499/567	ex D-ABAY		Lsd fr BER
☐	B-5363	Boeing 737-86J/W	30500/593	ex D-ABAZ		Lsd fr BER
☐	B-5365	Boeing 737-86J/W	30501/619	ex D-ABAC		Lsd fr BER
☐	B-5377	Boeing 737-8AL/W	35079/2555	ex N1786B		
☐	B-5378	Boeing 737-8AL/W	35085/2563	ex N1787B		
☐	B-5379	Boeing 737-8AL/W	35087/2605	ex N1786B		
☐	B-5380	Boeing 737-87L/W	35527/2616			
☐	B-5381	Boeing 737-87L/W	35528/2631		City of Hohhot	
☐	B-5400	Boeing 737-87L/W	35529/2677			
☐	B-5401	Boeing 737-87L/W	35530/2703	ex N1786B		
☐	B-5402	Boeing 737-87L/W	35531/2726	ex N1786B		
☐	B-5410	Boeing 737-8AL/W	35088/2771			
☐	B-5411	Boeing 737-87L/W	35532/2851			
☐	B-5412	Boeing 737-87L/W	35533/2900			
☐	B-5413	Boeing 737-87L/W	35535/2895	ex N1786B		
☐	B-5440	Boeing 737-87L/W	35534/3003			
☐	B-5441	Boeing 737-87L/W	35536/3019	ex N1786B		

SHENZHEN DONGHAI AIRLINES — Shenzhen (SZX)

Reg	Type	C/n	Prev	Notes
☐ B-2897	Boeing 737-3B7F	24902/1973	ex N108KH	
☐ B-2898	Boeing 737-3Y0F	24916/2066	ex N106KH	

SHUANGYANG AVIATION — Shuangyang (CSY) — Anshun (AOG)

Reg	Type	C/n	Prev	Notes
☐ B-3811	Harbin Y-12 II	0012		Combi
☐ B-3812	Harbin Y-12 II	0024		Sprayer
☐ B-3813	Harbin Y-12 II	0025		Sprayer
☐ B-3814	Harbin Y-12 II	0026		Sprayer
☐ B-3895	AVIC II Y-11	(11)0401		
☐ B-3896	AVIC II Y-11	(11)0402		
☐ B-3897	AVIC II Y-11	(11)0403		
☐ B-3898	AVIC II Y-11	(11)0404		

SICHUAN AIRLINES — Chuanhang (3U/CSC) — Chengdu (CTU)

Reg	Type	C/n	Prev	Notes
☐ B-2298	Airbus A319-133	2534	ex D-AVYM	
☐ B-2299	Airbus A319-133	2597	ex D-AVXN	
☐ B-2300	Airbus A319-133	2639	ex D-AVWK	
☐ B-6043	Airbus A319-133	2313	ex D-AVYI	
☐ B-6045	Airbus A319-133	2348	ex D-AVYH	
☐ B-6054	Airbus A319-133	2510	ex D-AVWC	
☐ B-6170	Airbus A319-132	2396	ex N101LF	Lsd to Northeastern
☐ B-6171	Airbus A319-132	2431	ex N112CG	Lsd fr ACG
☐ B-6173	Airbus A319-133	3114	ex D-AYYA	
☐ B-6175	Airbus A319-133	3116	ex D-AYYB	
☐ B-6176	Airbus A319-133	3124	ex D-AYYC	
☐ B-6185	Airbus A319-133	3680	ex D-AVYY	
☐ B-6406	Airbus A319-133	3962	ex D-AVXP	
☐ B-6410	Airbus A319-133	4018	ex D-AVYG	
☐ B-2340	Airbus A320-233	0540	ex F-WWDK	
☐ B-2341	Airbus A320-232	0551	ex F-WWBI	
☐ B-2342	Airbus A320-232	0556	ex F-WWIL	
☐ B-2348	Airbus A320-233	0912	ex EI-TAA	
☐ B-2373	Airbus A320-233	0919	ex F-WWIC	
☐ B-2397	Airbus A320-233	1013	ex F-WWDP	
☐ B-6025	Airbus A320-232	0573	ex B-MAD	
☐ B-6026	Airbus A320-232	0582	ex B-MAE	stored TLS
☐ B-6027	Airbus A320-233	1007	ex N460TA	
☐ B-6049	Airbus A320-233	0902	ex (D-ANNI)	
☐ B-6256	Airbus A320-232	0872	ex N872CV	
☐ B-6257	Airbus A320-233	0874	ex EI-TAE	
☐ B-6295	Airbus A320-233	1500	ex N481TA	
☐ B-6321	Airbus A320-232	3210	ex F-WWIK	
☐ B-6322	Airbus A320-232	3158	ex F-WWDP	
☐ B-6323	Airbus A320-232	3167	ex F-WWIM	
☐ B-6325	Airbus A320-232	3196	ex F-WWIE	
☐ B-6347	Airbus A320-232	3386	ex F-WWDP	
☐ B-6348	Airbus A320-232	3449	ex F-WWIY	
☐ B-6388	Airbus A320-232	3591	ex B-501L	
☐ B-6621	Airbus A320-232	4068	ex F-WWBI	
☐ B-	Airbus A320-232		ex	on order
☐ B-	Airbus A320-232		ex	on order
☐ B-	Airbus A320-232		ex	on order
☐ B-	Airbus A320-232		ex	on order
☐ B-2286	Airbus A321-131	0550	ex N550BR	
☐ B-2293	Airbus A321-131	0591	ex N451LF	
☐ B-2370	Airbus A321-231	0878	ex D-AVZF	
☐ B-2371	Airbus A321-231	0915	ex D-AVZM	
☐ B-6285	Airbus A321-231	1060	ex HL7590	
☐ B-6300	Airbus A321-231	1293	ex HL7549	
☐ B-6387	Airbus A321-231	3583	ex D-AVZE	
☐ B-6551	Airbus A321-231	3730	ex D-AZAI	
☐ B-6590	Airbus A321-231	3893	ex D-AVZV	
☐ B-6598	Airbus A321-231	3996	ex D-AZAQ	
☐ B-	Airbus A321-231		ex	on order
☐ B-	Airbus A330-240	1082	ex F-WW	on order
☐ B-	Airbus A330-240		ex F-WW	on order
☐ B-3425	CAIC MA60	0101		
☐ B-3426	CAIC MA60			
☐ B-	CAIC MA60			on order
☐ B-	CAIC MA60			on order
☐ B-	CAIC MA60			on order
☐ B-3040	Embraer EMB.145LR (ERJ-145LR)	145317	ex PT-SMI	Lsd to Northeastern
☐ B-3041	Embraer EMB.145LR (ERJ-145LR)	145349	ex PT-SNP	Lsd to Northeastern

Registration	Type	c/n	Previous identity	Notes
☐ B-3042	Embraer EMB.145LR (ERJ-145LR)	145352	ex PT-SNR	
☐ B-3043	Embraer EMB.145LR (ERJ-145LR)	145377	ex PT-SQB	
☐ B-3045	Embraer EMB.145LR (ERJ-145LR)	145470	ex PT-SVP	

SICHUAN AOLIN GENERAL AVIATION — *Chengdu (CTU)*

Registration	Type	c/n	Previous identity	Notes
☐ B-3637	Cessna 208B Caravan I	208B0919	ex N1294D	
☐ B-3640	Cessna 208B Caravan I	208B0952	ex N1132X	
☐ B-3641	Cessna 208B Caravan I	208B0953	ex N1133B	

SPRING AIRLINES — *Air Spring (9S/CQH)* — *Shanghai-Hongqiao (SHA)*

Registration	Type	c/n	Previous identity	Notes
☐ B-6250	Airbus A320-214	1372	ex EI-DKS	
☐ B-6258	Airbus A320-214	0879	ex EC-GZD	
☐ B-6280	Airbus A320-214	1286	ex N120US	
☐ B-6301	Airbus A320-214	2939	ex F-WWIO	
☐ B-6309	Airbus A320-214	3014	ex F-WWBO	
☐ B-6310	Airbus A320-214	3023	ex F-WWBZ	
☐ B-6320	Airbus A320-214	1686	ex N686RL	
☐ B-6328	Airbus A320-214	0978	ex N888CQ	
☐ B-6349	Airbus A320-214	1852	ex I-EEZC	
☐ B-6380	Airbus A320-214	1769	ex EC-JDK	
☐ B-6561	Airbus A320-214	3819	ex F-WWIO	
☐ B-6562	Airbus A320-214	3747	ex F-WWIL	
☐ B-6573	Airbus A320-214	1920	ex I-EEZD	
☐ B-6612	Airbus A320-214	4072	ex F-WWBM	
☐ B-6645	Airbus A320-214	4168	ex D-AVVQ	
☐ B-6646	Airbus A320-214	4093	ex B-516L	on order
☐ B-	Airbus A320-214	4375	ex	on order

TIANJIN AIRLINES — *(GS/GCR)* — *Tianjin (TSN)*

Registration	Type	c/n	Previous identity	Notes
☐ B-3873	Dornier 328-300 (328JET)	3201	ex D-BAUU	
☐ B-3892	Dornier 328-300 (328JET)	3212	ex D-BGUU	
☐ B-3946	Dornier 328-300 (328JET)	3208	ex D-BDXI	
☐ B-3947	Dornier 328-300 (328JET)	3203	ex D-BXXX	
☐ B-3948	Dornier 328-300 (328JET)	3204	ex D-BDXT	
☐ B-3949	Dornier 328-300 (328JET)	3198	ex N328AB	
☐ B-3960	Dornier 328-300 (328JET)	3123	ex D-BDXJ	
☐ B-3961	Dornier 328-300 (328JET)	3128	ex D-BDXK	
☐ B-3962	Dornier 328-300 (328JET)	3143	ex D-BDXX	
☐ B-3963	Dornier 328-300 (328JET)	3138	ex D-BDXT	
☐ B-3965	Dornier 328-300 (328JET)	3140	ex D-BDXW	
☐ B-3966	Dornier 328-300 (328JET)	3135	ex D-BDXQ	
☐ B-3967	Dornier 328-300 (328JET)	3144	ex D-BDXB	
☐ B-3968	Dornier 328-300 (328JET)	3148	ex D-BDXE	
☐ B-3969	Dornier 328-300 (328JET)	3153	ex D-BDXN	
☐ B-3970	Dornier 328-300 (328JET)	3154	ex D-BDXP	
☐ B-3971	Dornier 328-300 (328JET)	3172	ex D-BDXJ	
☐ B-3972	Dornier 328-300 (328JET)	3175	ex D-BDXK	
☐ B-3973	Dornier 328-300 (328JET)	3158	ex D-BDXQ	
☐ B-3975	Dornier 328-300 (328JET)	3159	ex D-BDXU	
☐ B-3976	Dornier 328-300 (328JET)	3177	ex D-BDXY	
☐ B-3977	Dornier 328-300 (328JET)	3182	ex D-BDXD	
☐ B-3978	Dornier 328-300 (328JET)	3187	ex D-BDXP	
☐ B-3979	Dornier 328-300 (328JET)	3191	ex D-BDXJ	
☐ B-3982	Dornier 328-300 (328JET)	3195	ex D-BDXJ	
☐ B-3983	Dornier 328-300 (328JET)	3211	ex D-BEUU	
☐ B-3985	Dornier 328-300 (328JET)	3215	ex D-BHUU	
☐ B-3986	Dornier 328-300 (328JET)	3217	ex D-BJUU	
☐ B-3987	Dornier 328-300 (328JET)	3218	ex D-BKUU	

Registration	Type	c/n	Previous identity	Notes
☐ B-3030	Embraer EMB.145LI (ERJ-145LI)	14501009	ex PT-SOX	
☐ B-3031	Embraer EMB.145LI (ERJ-145LI)	14501013	ex PT-SOY	
☐ B-3032	Embraer EMB.145LI (ERJ-145LI)	14501019	ex PT-SOZ	
☐ B-3033	Embraer EMB.145LI (ERJ-145LI)	14501022	ex	
☐ B-3035	Embraer EMB.145LI (ERJ-145LI)	14500996	ex PT-SOU	
☐ B-3036	Embraer EMB.145LI (ERJ-145LI)	14501000	ex PT-S	
☐ B-3037	Embraer EMB.145LI (ERJ-145LI)	14501005	ex PT-S	
☐ B-3038	Embraer EMB.145LI (ERJ-145LI)	14501024	ex	
☐ B-3039	Embraer EMB.145LI (ERJ-145LI)	14500992	ex PT-SOT	
☐ B-3067	Embraer EMB.145LI (ERJ-145LI)	14501036	ex	
☐ B-3068	Embraer EMB.145LI (ERJ-145LI)	14501040	ex	
☐ B-3069	Embraer EMB.145LI (ERJ-145LI)	14501043	ex	
☐ B-3081	Embraer EMB.145LI (ERJ-145LI)	14501027	ex	
☐ B-3082	Embraer EMB.145LI (ERJ-145LI)	14501030	ex PT-SZP	
☐ B-3083	Embraer EMB.145LI (ERJ-145LI)	14501033	ex	
☐ B-3085	Embraer EMB.145LI (ERJ-145LI)	14501047	ex	
☐ B-	Embraer EMB.145LI (ERJ-145LI)	14501028	ex	on order
☐ B-	Embraer EMB.145LI (ERJ-145LI)	14501050	ex	on order
☐ B-	Embraer EMB.145LI (ERJ-145LI)	14501053	ex	on order
☐ B-	Embraer EMB.145LI (ERJ-145LI)	14501056	ex	on order

Reg	Type	C/n	Previous identity	Notes
☐ B-	Embraer EMB.145LI (ERJ-145LI)	14501059	ex	on order
☐ B-	Embraer EMB.145LI (ERJ-145LI)	14501063	ex	on order
☐ B-	Embraer EMB.145LI (ERJ-145LI)	14501068	ex	on order
☐ B-	Embraer EMB.145LI (ERJ-145LI)	14501070	ex	on order
☐ B-	Embraer EMB.145LI (ERJ-145LI)	14501073	ex	on order
☐ B-3120	Embraer 190-100	19000171	ex PT-SDG	
☐ B-3121	Embraer 190-100	19000181	ex PT-SDP	
☐ B-3122	Embraer 190-100	19000186	ex PT-S	
☐ B-3123	Embraer 190-100	19000192	ex PT-S	
☐ B-3125	Embraer 190-100	19000194	ex PT-SGC	
☐ B-3127	Embraer 190-100	19000207	ex PT-SGQ	
☐ B-3128	Embraer 190-100	19000229	ex PT-SIA	
☐ B-3129	Embraer 190-100	19000246	ex PT-SIR	
☐ B-3150	Embraer 190-100	19000253	ex PT-SIY	
☐ B-3151	Embraer 190-100	19000268	ex PT-	
☐ B-3152	Embraer 190-100	19000274	ex PT-	
☐ B-3153	Embraer 190-100	19000284	ex PT-	
☐ B-3155	Embraer 190-100	19000293	ex PT-TZH	
☐ B-3156	Embraer 190-100	19000299	ex PT-TZN	
☐ B-3157	Embraer 190-100	19000306	ex PT-TZU	
☐ B-3158	Embraer 190-100	19000313	ex PT-TXB	
☐ B-3159	Embraer 190-100	19000318	ex PT-	
☐ B-3160	Embraer 190-100	19000325	ex PT-TXL	
☐ B-3161	Embraer 190-100	19000328	ex PT-TXQ	
☐ B-	Embraer 190-100		ex	on order
☐ B-	Embraer 190-100		ex	on order
☐ B-	Embraer 190-100		ex	on order
☐ B-	Embraer 190-100		ex	on order
☐ B-	Embraer 190-100		ex	on order
☐ B-	Embraer 190-100		ex	on order
☐ B-	Embraer 190-100		ex	on order
☐ B-	Embraer 190-100		ex	on order

UNITED EAGLE AIRLINE — *United Eagle (EU/UEA)* — *Chengdu (CTU)*

Reg	Type	C/n	Previous identity	Notes
☐ B-6151	Airbus A319-112	1263	ex N739US	
☐ B-6152	Airbus A319-112	0946	ex N706US	
☐ B-6155	Airbus A319-112	0949	ex N707UW	
☐ B-6163	Airbus A319-112	3024	ex D-AVXR	
☐ B-6230	Airbus A319-112	2774	ex D-AVYF	

UNI-TOP AIRLINES — *(UW)*

Reg	Type	C/n	Previous identity	Notes
☐ B-2448	Boeing 747-2J6B (SF)	23461/628	ex N60668	stored WUH
☐ B-2450	Boeing 747-2J6B (SF)	23746/670	ex N6018N	stored PEK

WEST CHINA AIRLINES — *(PN/CHB)* — *Chongqing (CKG)*

Reg	Type	C/n	Previous identity	Notes
☐ B-2963	Boeing 737-3Q8	26325/2772		Lsd fr CHH

XIAMEN AIRLINES — *Xiamen Air (MF/CXA)* — *Xiamen (XMN)*

Reg	Type	C/n	Previous identity	Notes
☐ B-2656	Boeing 737-3Q8	26292/2519	ex B-2903	for CYZ
☐ B-2973	Boeing 737-505	26336/2805		
☐ B-2975	Boeing 737-505	26338/2822		
☐ B-2658	Boeing 737-75C	30512/637	ex N1786B	
☐ B-2659	Boeing 737-75C	30513/676		
☐ B-2991	Boeing 737-75C	29085/90		
☐ B-2992	Boeing 737-75C	29086/108	ex N1786B	
☐ B-2998	Boeing 737-75C	29042/73	ex N1786B	
☐ B-2999	Boeing 737-75C	29084/86	ex N1796B	
☐ B-5028	Boeing 737-75C	30034/1275		
☐ B-5029	Boeing 737-75C	30634/1229		
☐ B-5038	Boeing 737-7Q8	30656/1304	ex N1787B	
☐ B-5039	Boeing 737-75C	28258/1315		
☐ B-5146	Boeing 737-86N/W	34253/1866		
☐ B-5151	Boeing 737-86N/W	34255/1975		
☐ B-5152	Boeing 737-86N/W	34256/1990		
☐ B-5159	Boeing 737-85C/W	35044/2018	ex N1784B	
☐ B-5160	Boeing 737-85C/W	35045/2050		
☐ B-5161	Boeing 737-85C/W	35046/2105		
☐ B-5162	Boeing 737-85C/W	35047/2130	ex N1787B	
☐ B-5212	Boeing 737-75C	34024/1703		
☐ B-5215	Boeing 737-75C	34025/1724		
☐ B-5216	Boeing 737-75C	34026/1733		
☐ B-5218	Boeing 737-75C	34027/1767	ex N1786B	
☐ B-5219	Boeing 737-75C	34028/1771		
☐ B-5301	Boeing 737-85C/W	35048/2194		
☐ B-5302	Boeing 737-85C/W	35049/2271		
☐ B-5303	Boeing 737-85C/W	35050/2305	ex N1780B	

☐ B-5305	Boeing 737-85C/W	35051/2364		
☐ B-5306	Boeing 737-85C/W	35052/2418	ex N1786B	
☐ B-5307	Boeing 737-85C/W	35053/2447		
☐ B-5308	Boeing 737-86N/W	32687/2229		
☐ B-5309	Boeing 737-86N/W	32689/2254		
☐ B-5318	Boeing 737-85C/W	30723/2283		
☐ B-5319	Boeing 737-8FH/W	35102/2471	ex N1796B	
☐ B-5355	Boeing 737-8FH/W	35104/2495	ex N1780B	
☐ B-5382	Boeing 737-86N/W	36540/2681		
☐ B-5383	Boeing 737-86N/W	35631/2693		
☐ B-5385	Boeing 737-86N/W	35633/2741		
☐ B-5386	Boeing 737-86N/W	35634/2732		
☐ B-5388	Boeing 737-86N/W	35635/2764		
☐ B-5389	Boeing 737-86N/W	35636/2775	ex N1786B	
☐ B-5432	Boeing 737-86N/W	35641/2852		
☐ B-5433	Boeing 737-86N/W	35642/2855	ex N1796B	
☐ B-5435	Boeing 737-86N/W	35644/2922		
☐ B-5456	Boeing 737-85C/W	35054/2914	ex N1786B	
☐ B-5458	Boeing 737-85C/W	35055/3016	ex N1786B	
☐ B-5459	Boeing 737-85C/W	35057/2992		
☐ B-5476	Boeing 737-85C/W	35056/3091		
☐ B-5487	Boeing 737-85C/W	35058/3150		
☐ B-5488	Boeing 737-85C/W	37148/3104		
☐ B-5489	Boeing 737-85C/W	37149/3142		
☐ B-5498	Boeing 737-85C/W	37574/3160		
☐ B-5499	Boeing 737-85C/W	37575		
☐ B-	Boeing 737-85C/W			on order
☐ B-	Boeing 737-85C/W			on order
☐ B-	Boeing 737-85C/W			on order
☐ B-	Boeing 737-85C/W			on order
☐ B-	Boeing 737-85C/W			on order
☐ B-	Boeing 737-85C/W			on order
☐ B-	Boeing 737-85C/W			on order
☐ B-	Boeing 737-85C/W			on order
☐ B-	Boeing 737-85C/W			on order
☐ B-	Boeing 737-85C/W			on order
☐ B-2828	Boeing 757-25C	25899/565		
☐ B-2829	Boeing 757-25C	25900/574		
☐ B-2848	Boeing 757-25C	27513/685		
☐ B-2849	Boeing 757-25C	27517/698		
☐ B-2862	Boeing 757-25C	34008/1047		
☐ B-2866	Boeing 757-25C	34009/1048		
☐ B-2868	Boeing 757-25C	32941/993		
☐ B-2869	Boeing 757-25C	32942/1009		

XINJIANG GENERAL AVIATION — *Shihezi*

☐ B-3869	AVIC II Y-11	(11)0501		
☐ B-3870	AVIC II Y-11	(11)0502		
☐ B-3885	AVIC II Y-11	(11)0301		
☐ B-3887	AVIC II Y-11	(11)0303		
☐ B-3888	AVIC II Y-11	(11)0304		
☐ B-3890	AVIC II Y-11	(11)0306		
☐ B-3891	AVIC II Y-11	(11)0307		
☐ B-3894	AVIC II Y-11	(11)0310		
☐ B-3815	Harbin Y-12 II	0023		Geological survey
☐ B-3817	Harbin Y-12 II	0029		Photographic survey
☐ B-3818	Harbin Y-12 II	0030		Photographic survey

YANGTZE RIVER EXPRESS — *Yangtze River (Y8/YZR)* — *Shanghai-Hongqiao (SHA)*

☐ B-5053	Boeing 737-322F	24378/1704	ex N357UA	Lsd fr CHH
☐ B-5055	Boeing 737-330(QC)	24283/1677	ex N283A	Lsd fr CHH
☐ B-5056	Boeing 737-330(QC)	23836/1508	ex N836Y	Lsd fr CHH
☐ B-5057	Boeing 737-330(QC)	23837/1514	ex N837Y	Lsd fr CHH
☐ B-5058	Boeing 737-330(QC)	23835/1465	ex N835A	Lsd fr CHH
☐ B-5059	Boeing 737-322F	24362/1696	ex N356UA	Lsd fr CHH
☐ B-2431	Boeing 747-409F	30761/1254	ex N703CL	Lsd fr CAL
☐ B-2432	Boeing 747-481(SF)	28283/1142	ex N200FQ	
☐ B-2435	Boeing 747-481(SF)	28282/1133	ex N483YR	

ZHONGFEI AIRLINES — *Zhongfei (CFZ)* — *Xi'an-Yanliang*

☐ B-3820	Harbin Y-12 II	0031		
☐ B-4103	Cessna 550 Citation II	550-0301		Calibrator
☐ B-4104	Cessna 550 Citation II	550-0297		Calibrator
☐ B-4105	Cessna 550 Citation II	550-0305		Calibrator

B-H/K/L CHINA - HONG KONG

AIR HONG KONG — Air Hong Kong (LD/AHK) — Hong Kong (HKG)

☐ B-LDA	Airbus A300F4-605R	855	ex F-WWAN		
☐ B-LDB	Airbus A300F4-605R	856	ex F-WWAP		
☐ B-LDC	Airbus A300F4-605R	857	ex F-WWAQ		
☐ B-LDD	Airbus A300F4-605R	858	ex F-WWAR		
☐ B-LDE	Airbus A300F4-605R	859	ex F-WWAS		
☐ B-LDF	Airbus A300F4-605R	860	ex F-WWAT		
☐ B-LDG	Airbus A300F4-605R	870	ex F-WWAJ		
☐ B-LDH	Airbus A300F4-605R	871	ex F-WWAK		
☐ TC-AGK	Airbus A300B4-203F	117	ex G-CEXH	Siirt 5	Lsd fr KZU
☐ TC-KZU	Airbus A300B4-203	173	ex (TC-ORK)	Siirt 2	Lsd fr KZU

CATHAY PACIFIC AIRWAYS — Cathay (CX/CPA) — Hong Kong (HKG)

Member of Oneworld

☐ B-HLA	Airbus A330-342	071	ex VR-HLA		
☐ B-HLB	Airbus A330-342	083	ex VR-HLB		
☐ B-HLC	Airbus A330-342	099	ex VR-HLC		
☐ B-HLD	Airbus A330-342	102	ex VR-HLD		
☐ B-HLE	Airbus A330-342	109	ex VR-HLE		
☐ B-HLF	Airbus A330-342	113	ex VR-HLF		
☐ B-HLG	Airbus A330-342	118	ex VR-HLG		
☐ B-HLH	Airbus A330-342	121	ex VR-HLH		
☐ B-HLI	Airbus A330-342	155	ex VR-HLI		
☐ B-HLJ	Airbus A330-342	012	ex VR-HLJ		
☐ B-HLK	Airbus A330-342	017	ex VR-HLK		
☐ B-HLL	Airbus A330-342	244	ex F-WWKG		
☐ B-HLM	Airbus A330-343X	386	ex F-WWYT		
☐ B-HLN	Airbus A330-343X	389	ex F-WWYV		
☐ B-HLO	Airbus A330-343X	393	ex F-WWYY		
☐ B-HLP	Airbus A330-343X	418	ex F-WWKV		
☐ B-HLQ	Airbus A330-343X	420	ex F-WWYB		
☐ B-HLR	Airbus A330-343X	421	ex F-WWYC		
☐ B-HLS	Airbus A330-343X	423	ex F-WWYD		
☐ B-HLT	Airbus A330-343X	439	ex F-WWYJ		
☐ B-HLU	Airbus A330-343X	539	ex F-WWYG		
☐ B-HLV	Airbus A330-343X	548	ex F-WWYI		
☐ B-HLW	Airbus A330-343X	565	ex F-WWYR		
☐ B-LAA	Airbus A330-342E	669	ex F-WWKS	Asia's World City titles	
☐ B-LAB	Airbus A330-342E	673	ex F-WWKZ	Asia's World City titles	
☐ B-LAC	Airbus A330-342E	679	ex F-WWYC		
☐ B-LAD	Airbus A330-342E	776	ex F-WWKI	Progress Hong Kong c/s	
☐ B-LAE	Airbus A330-342E	850	ex F-WWKQ		
☐ B-LAF	Airbus A330-342E	855	ex F-WWYC		
☐ B-LAG	Airbus A330-342E	895	ex F-WWYV		
☐ B-LAH	Airbus A330-342E	915	ex F-WWYN		
☐ B-LAI	Airbus A330-342E	959	ex F-WWYE		

☐ B-HXA	Airbus A340-313X	136	ex VR-HXA		
☐ B-HXB	Airbus A340-313X	137	ex VR-HXB		
☐ B-HXC	Airbus A340-313X	142	ex VR-HXC		
☐ B-HXD	Airbus A340-313X	147	ex VR-HXD		
☐ B-HXE	Airbus A340-313X	157	ex VR-HXE		
☐ B-HXF	Airbus A340-313X	160	ex VR-HXF		
☐ B-HXG	Airbus A340-313X	208	ex F-WWJC		
☐ B-HXH	Airbus A340-313X	218	ex F-WWJT		
☐ B-HXI	Airbus A340-313X	220	ex F-WWJO		
☐ B-HXJ	Airbus A340-313X	227	ex F-WWJL		
☐ B-HXK	Airbus A340-313X	228	ex F-WWJI		
☐ B-HXL	Airbus A340-313X	381	ex F-WWJB		stored VCV
☐ B-HXM	Airbus A340-313X	123	ex 9V-SJA		stored VCV
☐ B-HXN	Airbus A340-313X	126	ex 9V-SJB		stored VCV
☐ B-HXO	Airbus A340-313X	128	ex 9V-SJC		stored VCV

☐ B-HKE	Boeing 747-412	25127/859	ex N127LC		
☐ B-HKF	Boeing 747-412	25128/860	ex 9V-SML		
☐ B-HKH	Boeing 747-412BCF	24227/831	ex 9V-SMH		
☐ B-HKJ	Boeing 747-412BCF	27133/962	ex 9V-SMR		
☐ B-HKS	Boeing 747-412BCF	27070/1049	ex 9V-SPC		
☐ B-HKT	Boeing 747-412	27132/955	ex 4X-ELS		
☐ B-HKU	Boeing 747-412	27069/1010	ex 9V-SMV		
☐ B-HKV	Boeing 747-412	26552/1056	ex 9V-SPD		
☐ B-HKX	Boeing 747-412BCF	26557/1101	ex 9V-SPL		
☐ B-HMD	Boeing 747-2L5B(SF)	22105/435	ex VR-HMD		stored VCV
☐ B-HME	Boeing 747-2L5B(SF)	22106/443	ex VR-HME		stored VCV
☐ B-HOO	Boeing 747-467	23814/705	ex VR-HOO		
☐ B-HOP	Boeing 747-467	23815/728	ex VR-HOP		

☐ B-HOR	Boeing 747-467	24631/771	ex VR-HOR		
☐ B-HOS	Boeing 747-467	24850/788	ex VR-HOS		
☐ B-HOT	Boeing 747-467	24851/813	ex VR-HOT		
☐ B-HOU	Boeing 747-467BCF	24925/834	ex VR-HOU		stored VCV
☐ B-HOV	Boeing 747-467	25082/849	ex VR-HOV		
☐ B-HOW	Boeing 747-467	25211/873	ex VR-HOW		
☐ B-HOX+	Boeing 747-467	24955/877	ex VR-HOX		
☐ B-HOY	Boeing 747-467	25351/887	ex VR-HOY	Asia's World City c/s	
☐ B-HOZ	Boeing 747-467BCF	25871/925	ex VR-HOZ		
☐ B-HUA	Boeing 747-467	25872/930	ex VR-HUA		stored VCV
☐ B-HUB	Boeing 747-467	25873/937	ex VR-HUB		
☐ B-HUD	Boeing 747-467	25874/949	ex VR-HUD		
☐ B-HUE	Boeing 747-467	27117/970	ex VR-HUE		
☐ B-HUF	Boeing 747-467	25869/993	ex VR-HUF		
☐ B-HUG	Boeing 747-467	25870/1007	ex VR-HUG		
☐ B-HUH	Boeing 747-467F	27175/1020	ex VR-HUH		
☐ B-HUI	Boeing 747-467	27230/1033	ex VR-HUI		
☐ B-HUJ	Boeing 747-467	27595/1061	ex VR-HUJ		
☐ B-HUK	Boeing 747-467F	27503/1065	ex VR-HUK		
☐ B-HUL	Boeing 747-467F	30804/1255			
☐ B-HUO	Boeing 747-467F	32571/1271	ex B-HUM		
☐ B-HUP	Boeing 747-467F	30805/1282	ex (B-HUN)		
☐ B-HUQ	Boeing 747-467F	34150/1356			
☐ B-HUR	Boeing 747-444BCF	24976/827	ex ZS-SAV		stored VCV
☐ B-HUS	Boeing 747-444BCF	25152/861	ex ZS-SAW		stored VCV
☐ B-HVX	Boeing 747-267F	24568/776	ex VR-HVX		stored VCV
☐ B-HVZ	Boeing 747-267F	23864/687	ex VR-HVZ		stored VCV
☐ B-KAA	Boeing 747-312M	23769/666	ex 9V-SKP		Freighter
☐ B-KAB	Boeing 747-312M	23409/637	ex 9V-SKM		stored VCV
☐ B-KAC	Boeing 747-3H6M	23600/650	ex N73741		stored VCV
☐ B-KAD	Boeing 747-209F	24308/752	ex B-18771		stored VCV
☐ B-KAE	Boeing 747-412BCF	25068/852	ex 9V-SMJ		stored VCV
☐ B-KAF	Boeing 747-412BCF	26547/921	ex 9V-SMM		stored VCV
☐ B-KAG	Boeing 747-412BCF	27067/953	ex 9V-SMP		
☐ B-KAH	Boeing 747-412BCF	27134/981	ex 9V-SMS		
☐ B-KAI	Boeing 747-412BCF	27217/1023	ex 9V-SMY		stored VCV
☐ B-LIA	Boeing 747-467ERF	37299/1404			
☐ B-LIB	Boeing 747-467ERF	36867/1409	ex N5014K		
☐ B-LIC	Boeing 747-467ERF	36868/1413	ex N5014K		
☐ B-LID	Boeing 747-467ERF	36869/1414			
☐ B-LIE	Boeing 747-467ERF	36870/1415	ex N5022E		
☐ B-LIF	Boeing 747-467ERF	36871/1417			
☐ B-LJA	Boeing 747-867F	39238			on order
☐ B-LJB	Boeing 747-867F	39239			on order
☐ B-LJC	Boeing 747-867F	39240			on order
☐ B-HNA	Boeing 777-267	27265/14	ex VR-HNA		
☐ B-HNB	Boeing 777-267	27266/18	ex VR-HNB		
☐ B-HNC	Boeing 777-267	27263/28	ex VR-HNC		
☐ B-HND	Boeing 777-267	27264/31	ex VR-HND		
☐ B-HNE	Boeing 777-367	27507/94	ex N5014K		
☐ B-HNF	Boeing 777-367	27506/102	ex N5016R		
☐ B-HNG	Boeing 777-367	27505/118	ex N5017V		
☐ B-HNH	Boeing 777-367	27504/136			
☐ B-HNI	Boeing 777-367	27508/204			
☐ B-HNJ	Boeing 777-367	27509/224			
☐ B-HNK	Boeing 777-367	27510/248			
☐ B-HNL	Boeing 777-267	27116/1	ex N7771		
☐ B-HNM	Boeing 777-367	33702/456			
☐ B-HNN	Boeing 777-367	33703/462			
☐ B-HNO	Boeing 777-367	33704/470			
☐ B-HNP	Boeing 777-367	34243/513			
☐ B-HNQ	Boeing 777-367	34244/567	ex N6009F		
☐ B-KPA	Boeing 777-367ER	36154/661	ex N1788B		
☐ B-KPB	Boeing 777-367ER	35299/670			
☐ B-KPC	Boeing 777-367ER	34432/674			
☐ B-KPD	Boeing 777-367ER	36155/680			
☐ B-KPE	Boeing 777-367ER	36156/685			
☐ B-KPF	Boeing 777-367ER	36832/692		Asia World City c/s	
☐ B-KPG	Boeing 777-367ER	35300/700			
☐ B-KPH	Boeing 777-367ER	35301/720	ex N50281		
☐ B-KPI	Boeing 777-367ER	36833/746			
☐ B-KPJ	Boeing 777-367ER	36157/754	ex N5016R		
☐ B-KPK	Boeing 777-367ER	36158/783	ex N5023Q		
☐ B-KPL	Boeing 777-367ER	36161/818			
☐ B-KPM	Boeing 777-367ER	36159/835			
☐ B-KPN	Boeing 777-367ER	36165/839			
☐ B-KPO	Boeing 777-367ER	36160/843			
☐ B-KPP	Boeing 777-367ER	36164			on order
☐ B-KPQ	Boeing 777-367ER	36162			on order
☐ B-KPR	Boeing 777-367ER	36163			on order

DRAGONAIR | **Dragon (KA/HDA)** | **Hong Kong (HKG)**

Reg	Type	C/n	Prev	Name	Notes
☐ B-HSD	Airbus A320-232	0756	ex F-WWBC		
☐ B-HSE	Airbus A320-232	0784	ex F-WWDL		
☐ B-HSG	Airbus A320-232	0812	ex B-22315		
☐ B-HSI	Airbus A320-232	0930	ex F-WWIE		
☐ B-HSJ	Airbus A320-232	1253	ex F-WWIU		
☐ B-HSK	Airbus A320-232	1721	ex F-WWDF		
☐ B-HSL	Airbus A320-232	2229	ex F-WWIE		
☐ B-HSM	Airbus A320-232	2238	ex F-WWDG		
☐ B-HSN	Airbus A320-232	2428	ex F-WWBI		
☐ B-HSO	Airbus A320-232	4023	ex F-WWDN		on order
☐ B-HSP	Airbus A320-232		ex		on order
☐ B-HTD	Airbus A321-231	0993	ex D-AVZF		
☐ B-HTE	Airbus A321-231	1024	ex D-AVZD		
☐ B-HTF	Airbus A321-231	0633	ex G-OZBC		
☐ B-HTG	Airbus A321-231	1695	ex D-AVZA		
☐ B-HTH	Airbus A321-231	1984	ex D-AVZX		
☐ B-HTI	Airbus A321-231	2021	ex D-AVXJ		
☐ B-HWF	Airbus A330-343	654	ex F-WWYM		
☐ B-HWG	Airbus A330-343	662	ex F-WWYZ	The Way of the Dragon	
☐ B-HWH	Airbus A330-343	692	ex F-WWYO		
☐ B-HWI	Airbus A330-343	716	ex F-WWYX		
☐ B-HWJ	Airbus A330-343	741	ex F-WWYE		
☐ B-HWK	Airbus A330-343	786	ex F-WWYZ		
☐ B-HYA	Airbus A330-342	098	ex VR-HYA		
☐ B-HYB	Airbus A330-342	106	ex VR-HYB		
☐ B-HYD	Airbus A330-342	132	ex VR-HYD		
☐ B-HYF	Airbus A330-342	234	ex F-WWKF		
☐ B-HYG	Airbus A330-343	405	ex F-WWKQ		
☐ B-HYI	Airbus A330-343	479	ex F-WWKU		
☐ B-HYJ	Airbus A330-343	512	ex F-WWYR		
☐ B-HYQ	Airbus A330-343	581	ex F-WWKK		

HONG KONG AIRLINES | **Bauhina (HX/CRK)** | **Hong Kong (HKG)**

Reg	Type	C/n	Prev	Notes
☐ B-KBI	Boeing 737-808/W	34709/2121	ex N1787B	Lsd fr CHH
☐ B-KBK	Boeing 737-84P/W	35072/2155	ex N1786B	Lsd fr CHH
☐ B-KBM	Boeing 737-84P/W	35076/2380		Lsd fr CHH

HONG KONG EXPRESS AIRWAYS | **Hong Kong Shuttle (UO/HKE)** | **Hong Kong (HKG)**

Reg	Type	C/n	Notes
☐ B-KBP	Boeing 737-8FH/W	35105/2501	Lsd fr CHH
☐ B-KBQ	Boeing 737-84P/W	35274/2570	Lsd fr CHH
☐ B-KBR	Boeing 737-84P/W	35276/2611	Lsd fr CHH
☐ B-KXE	Boeing 737-808/W	34710/2144	Lsd fr CHH

SKY SHUTTLE HELICOPTERS | **Heli Hong Kong (UO/HHK)** | **HK / Macau Heliport**

Reg	Type	C/n	Prev	Notes
☐ B-KHN	Agusta AW139	31243		
☐ B-MHI	Agusta AW139	31220		
☐ B-MHJ	Agusta AW139	31222	ex I-RIAI	
☐ B-MHK	Agusta AW139	31229		
☐ B-MHL	Agusta AW139	31230		
☐ B-	Agusta AW139			on order
☐ B-HJR	Sikorsky S-76C+	760497		
☐ B-KCC	Sikorsky S-76C+	760521	ex N9017M	
☐ B-MHF	Sikorsky S-76C+	760474	ex CS-MHF	
☐ B-MHG	Sikorsky S-76C+	760475	ex CS-MHG	
☐ B-MHH	Sikorsky S-76C+	760476	ex CS-MHH	

B-M CHINA - MACAU

AIR MACAU | **Air Macau (NX/AMU)** | **Macau (MFM)**

Reg	Type	C/n	Prev	Name
☐ B-MAS	Airbus A300B4-622RF	743	ex N221LF	Cargo titles
☐ B-MBJ	Airbus A300B4-622RF	677	ex TC-OAY	
☐ B-MAK	Airbus A319-132	1758	ex D-AVYF	Rio Yangtze
☐ B-MAL	Airbus A319-132	1790	ex D-AVYR	Rio Amarelo
☐ B-MAM	Airbus A319-112	1893	ex D-AVYJ	Lago Sul Lua
☐ B-MAN	Airbus A319-132	1912	ex D-AVWZ	Rio Huang Pu
☐ B-MAO	Airbus A319-132	1962	ex D-AVWU	Rio Yaluzangbu
☐ B-MAH	Airbus A320-232	0805	ex CS-MAH	Ilha da Madeira
☐ B-MAX	Airbus A320-232	0928	ex N928MD	

☐ B-MAB	Airbus A321-131	0557	ex VN-A341	Lotus
☐ B-MAF	Airbus A321-131	0620	ex CS-MAF	Acores
☐ B-MAG	Airbus A321-131	0631	ex CS-MAG	Ilha de Coloane
☐ B-MAJ	Airbus A321-231	0908	ex CS-MAJ	Farol da Guia
☐ B-MAP	Airbus A321-231	1850	ex D-AVZX	Rio das Perolas
☐ B-MAQ	Airbus A321-231	1926	ex D-AVZS	Lago Tai
☐ B-MAR	Airbus A321-131	0597	ex VN-A346	

VIVA MACAU *Jackpot (ZG/VVM)* *Macau (MFM)*

☐ B-MAV	Boeing 767-284ER	24716/297	ex N716AN
☐ B-MAW	Boeing 767-38EER	24798/331	ex N798AW
☐ B-MAY	Boeing 767-319ER	24875/371	ex N875AW

B- CHINA – TAIWAN (Republic of China)

CHINA AIRLINES *China Airlines/Dynasty (CI/CAL)* *Taipei-Chiang Kai Shek/Sung Shan (TPE/TSA)*

☐ B-18301	Airbus A330-302	602	ex F-WWYM		
☐ B-18302	Airbus A330-302	607	ex F-WWYY		
☐ B-18303	Airbus A330-302	641	ex F-WWYS		
☐ B-18305	Airbus A330-302	671	ex F-WWKN	orchid colours	
☐ B-18306	Airbus A330-302	675	ex F-WWYU		
☐ B-18307	Airbus A330-302	691	ex F-WWYL		
☐ B-18308	Airbus A330-302	699	ex F-WWKA		
☐ B-18309	Airbus A330-302	707	ex F-WWKI		
☐ B-18310	Airbus A330-302	714	ex F-WWYV		
☐ B-18311	Airbus A330-302	752	ex F-WWKZ	Taiwanese Fruits c/s	
☐ B-18312	Airbus A330-302	769	ex F-WWYS		
☐ B-18315	Airbus A330-302	823	ex F-WWKS		
☐ B-18316	Airbus A330-302	838	ex F-WWYM		
☐ B-18317	Airbus A330-302	861	ex F-WWYA		
☐ B-18351	Airbus A330-302	725	ex F-WWKO		
☐ B-18352	Airbus A330-302	805	ex F-WWYG		
☐ B-18353	Airbus A330-302	920	ex F-WWYU		
☐ B-18801	Airbus A340-313X	402	ex F-WWJC		
☐ B-18802	Airbus A340-313X	406	ex F-WWJK		
☐ B-18803	Airbus A340-313X	411	ex F-WWJL		
☐ B-18805	Airbus A340-313X	415	ex F-WWJO		
☐ B-18806	Airbus A340-313X	433	ex F-WWJS		
☐ B-18807	Airbus A340-313X	541	ex F-WWJK		
☐ B-18601	Boeing 737-809/W	28402/113	ex N1787B		
☐ B-18605	Boeing 737-809/W	28404/130	ex N1784B		
☐ B-18606	Boeing 737-809/W	28405/132			
☐ B-18607	Boeing 737-809/W	29104/139			
☐ B-18608	Boeing 737-809/W	28406/141			
☐ B-18609	Boeing 737-809/W	28407/161			
☐ B-18610	Boeing 737-809/W	29105/295			
☐ B-18612	Boeing 737-809/W	30173/695	ex N1785B		
☐ B-18615	Boeing 737-809/W	30174/1175	ex N6067E		
☐ B-16817	Boeing 737-809/W	29106/302	ex B-18611		
☐ B-18201	Boeing 747-409	28709/1114			
☐ B-18202	Boeing 747-409	28710/1132			
☐ B-18203	Boeing 747-409	28711/1136			
☐ B-18205	Boeing 747-409	28712/1137			
☐ B-18206	Boeing 747-409	29030/1145			
☐ B-18207	Boeing 747-409	29219/1176			
☐ B-18208	Boeing 747-409	29031/1186			
☐ B-18210	Boeing 747-409	33734/1353		Dreamliner c/s	
☐ B-18211	Boeing 747-409	33735/1354			
☐ B-18212	Boeing 747-409	33736/1357			
☐ B-18215	Boeing 747-409	33737/1358			
☐ B-18251	Boeing 747-409	27965/1063	ex B-16801		
☐ B-18701	Boeing 747-409F	30759/1249			
☐ B-18702	Boeing 747-409F	30760/1252			
☐ B-18705	Boeing 747-409F	30762/1263			
☐ B-18706	Boeing 747-409F	30763/1267			
☐ B-18707	Boeing 747-409F	30764/1269			
☐ B-18708	Boeing 747-409F	30765/1288			
☐ B-18709	Boeing 747-409F	30766/1294			
☐ B-18710	Boeing 747-409F	30767/1300		all-white	Lsd to HDA
☐ B-18711	Boeing 747-409F	30768/1314			
☐ B-18712	Boeing 747-409F	33729/1332			
☐ B-18715	Boeing 747-409F	33731/1334			
☐ B-18716	Boeing 747-409F	33732/1339			
☐ B-18717	Boeing 747-409F	30769/1346			
☐ B-18718	Boeing 747-409F	30770/1348			
☐ B-18719	Boeing 747-409F	33739/1355			

☐ B-18720	Boeing 747-409F	33733/1359			
☐ B-18721	Boeing 747-409F	33738/1362			
☐ B-18722	Boeing 747-409F	34265/1372		all-white	
☐ B-18723	Boeing 747-409F	34266/1379			
☐ B-18725	Boeing 747-409F	30771/1385			
☐ N168CL	Boeing 747-409	29906/1219	ex B-18209		

DAILY AIR — *Taipei-Sung Shan (TSA)*

☐ B-55561	Dornier 228-212	8215	ex B-12253
☐ B-55563	Dornier 228-212	8224	ex B-12259
☐ B-55565	Dornier 228-212	8234	ex B-11152
☐ B-55567	Dornier 228-212	8235	ex B-11156

EVA AIRWAYS — *Eva (BR/EVA)* — *Taipei-Chiang Kai Shek (TPE)*

☐ B-16301	Airbus A330-203	530	ex F-WWYA		
☐ B-16302	Airbus A330-203	535	ex F-WWYE		
☐ B-16303	Airbus A330-203	555	ex F-WWYL		
☐ B-16305	Airbus A330-203	573	ex F-WWYP		
☐ B-16306	Airbus A330-203	587	ex F-WWKL		
☐ B-16307	Airbus A330-203	634	ex F-WWYJ	Hello Kitty c/s	
☐ B-16308	Airbus A330-203	655	ex F-WWYT		
☐ B-16309	Airbus A330-203	661	ex F-WWYY	Hello Kitty c/s	
☐ B-16310	Airbus A330-203	678	ex F-WWYB		
☐ B-16311	Airbus A330-203	693	ex F-WWYP		
☐ B-16312	Airbus A330-203	755	ex F-WWYP		
☐ B-16401	Boeing 747-45E	27062/942			
☐ B-16402	Boeing 747-45EBDSF	27063/947			
☐ B-16403	Boeing 747-45EM	27141/976	ex N403EV		
☐ B-16405	Boeing 747-45EM	27142/982	ex N405EV		
☐ B-16406	Boeing 747-45EMBDSF	27898/1051	ex N406EV		
☐ B-16407	Boeing 747-45EM	27899/1053	ex N407EV		
☐ B-16408	Boeing 747-45EM	28092/1076	ex N408EV		
☐ B-16409	Boeing 747-45EM	28093/1077	ex N409EV		
☐ B-16410	Boeing 747-45E	29061/1140			
☐ B-16411	Boeing 747-45E	29111/1151			
☐ B-16412	Boeing 747-45E	29112/1159			
☐ B-16462	Boeing 747-45EMBDSF	27173/998			
☐ B-16463	Boeing 747-45EMBDSF	27174/1004			
☐ B-16481	Boeing 747-45EF	30607/1251			
☐ B-16482	Boeing 747-45EF	30608/1279			
☐ B-16483	Boeing 747-45EF	30609/1309			
☐ B-16701	Boeing 777-35EER	32639/524			
☐ B-16702	Boeing 777-35EER	32640/531			
☐ B-16703	Boeing 777-35EER	32643/572			
☐ B-16705	Boeing 777-35EER	32645/597	ex N6009F		
☐ B-16706	Boeing 777-35EER	33750/612			
☐ B-16707	Boeing 777-35EER	33751/634			
☐ B-16708	Boeing 777-35EER	33752/658			
☐ B-16709	Boeing 777-35EER	33753/683			
☐ B-16710	Boeing 777-35EER	32641/707			
☐ B-16711	Boeing 777-35EER	33754/721	ex N5028Y		
☐ B-16712	Boeing 777-35EER	33755/735			
☐ B-16713	Boeing 777-35EER	33756/758			
☐ B-16715	Boeing 777-35EER	33757/810			
☐ B-16716	Boeing 777-35EER	32642/822			
☐ B-16717	Boeing 777-35EER	32644			on order
☐ B-16101	McDonnell-Douglas MD-11F	48542/570			
☐ B-16107	McDonnell-Douglas MD-11F	48546/589			
☐ B-16108	McDonnell-Douglas MD-11F	48778/619			
☐ B-16109	McDonnell-Douglas MD-11F	48779/620			
☐ B-16110	McDonnell-Douglas MD-11F	48786/630			
☐ B-16111	McDonnell-Douglas MD-11F	48787/631			
☐ B-16112	McDonnell-Douglas MD-11F	48789/633	ex N90178		
☐ B-16113	McDonnell-Douglas MD-11F	48790/634	ex N9030Q		stored VCV
☐ B-17913	McDonnell-Douglas MD-90-30	53537/2162		Lsd fr UIA	
☐ B-17917	McDonnell-Douglas MD-90-30ER	53572/2217		Lsd fr UIA	
☐ B-17925	McDonnell-Douglas MD-90-30ER	53568/2171	ex B-16902	Lsd fr UIA	
☐ B-22310	Airbus A320-232	0791	ex F-WWDR		Lsd fr TNA

GREAT WING AIRLINES — *Taichung*

☐ B-69832	Britten-Norman BN-2A-26 Islander	2039	ex B-12232

MANDARIN AIRLINES — Mandarin Air (AE/MDA) — Taipei-Sung Shan (TSA)

☐ B-16821	Embraer 190-100AR (190AR)	19000087	ex PT-SNF	
☐ B-16822	Embraer 190-100AR (190AR)	19000091	ex PT-SNK	
☐ B-16823	Embraer 190-100AR (190AR)	19000099	ex PT-SNT	
☐ B-16825	Embraer 190-100AR (190AR)	19000167	ex PT-SAZ	
☐ B-16826	Embraer 190-100AR (190AR)	19000175	ex PT-SDK	
☐ B-16827	Embraer 190-100AR (190AR)	19000182	ex PT-SDQ	
☐ B-16828	Embraer 190-100AR (190AR)	19000190	ex PT-SDY	
☐ B-16829	Embraer 190-100AR (190AR)	19000302	ex PT-TZQ	

ROC AVIATION — Taipei-Sung Shan (TSA)

☐ B-68801	Britten-Norman BN-2B-26 Islander	2255	ex G-BTVI	
☐ B-68802	Britten-Norman BN-2B-20 Islander	2241	ex G-BSPU	

TRANSASIA AIRWAYS — Transasia (GE/TNA) — Taipei-Sung Shan (TSA)

☐ B-22310	Airbus A320-232	0791	ex F-WWDR		Lsd to EVA
☐ B-22311	Airbus A320-232	0822	ex F-WWBY		
☐ B-22601	Airbus A321-131	0538	ex F-WGYZ	Special colours	
☐ B-22602	Airbus A321-131	0555	ex F-WFYZ		
☐ B-22605	Airbus A321-131	0606	ex F-WGYY		
☐ B-22606	Airbus A321-131	0731	ex F-WQGL		
☐ B-22607	Airbus A321-131	0746	ex F-WQGM		

☐ B-22801	ATR 72-212A	517	ex F-WWLK	
☐ B-22802	ATR 72-212A	525	ex F-WWLB	
☐ B-22803	ATR 72-212A	527	ex F-WWLC	
☐ B-22805	ATR 72-212A	558	ex F-WQIU	
☐ B-22806	ATR 72-212A	560	ex F-WQIY	
☐ B-22807	ATR 72-212A	567	ex F-WQIZ	
☐ B-22810	ATR 72-212A	642	ex F-WQMF	
☐ B-22811	ATR 72-212A	749	ex F-WQNC	
☐ B-22812	ATR 72-212A	774	ex F-WWEM	

UNI AIR — Glory (B7/UIA) — Taipei-Sung Shan (TSA)

☐ B-15217	de Havilland DHC-8-311A	379	ex C-GEOA	
☐ B-15219	de Havilland DHC-8-311A	381	ex C-FDHD	
☐ B-15225	de Havilland DHC-8-311B	405	ex C-GFHZ	
☐ B-15231	de Havilland DHC-8-311B	414	ex C-GFBW	
☐ B-15233	de Havilland DHC-8-311B	402	ex C-GDFT	
☐ B-15235	de Havilland DHC-8Q-311B	443	ex C-FWBB	
☐ B-15237	de Havilland DHC-8Q-311B	467	ex C-GELN	
☐ B-15239	de Havilland DHC-8Q-311B	571	ex C-GEWI	

☐ B-17911	McDonnell-Douglas MD-90-30	53535/2158		
☐ B-17913	McDonnell-Douglas MD-90-30	53537/2162		Lsd to EVA
☐ B-17917	McDonnell-Douglas MD-90-30ER	53572/2217		Lsd to EVA
☐ B-17918	McDonnell-Douglas MD-90-30ER	53571/2193	ex B-16903	
☐ B-17919	McDonnell-Douglas MD-90-30	53569/2173	ex N6206F	
☐ B-17920	McDonnell-Douglas MD-90-30	53574/2186		
☐ B-17921	McDonnell-Douglas MD-90-30	53554/2166	ex SU-BNN	
☐ B-17922	McDonnell-Douglas MD-90-30	53601/2243	ex SU-BMT	
☐ B-17923	McDonnell-Douglas MD-90-30ER	53534/2153	ex B-16901	Lsd to EVA
☐ B-17925	McDonnell-Douglas MD-90-30ER	53568/2171	ex B-16902	Lsd to EVA
☐ B-17926	McDonnell-Douglas MD-90-30ER	53567/2169	ex B-15301	

C- CANADA

ABITIBI HELICOPTERS — La Sarre, QC/Calgary-Springbank, AB (SSQ/-)

☐ C-FHAK	Aérospatiale AS350BA+ AStar	1545	ex N517WW
☐ C-FHAP	Aérospatiale AS350B2 AStar	3292	
☐ C-FHAU	Aérospatiale AS350BA AStar	2778	
☐ C-FIYM	Aérospatiale AS350B1 AStar	1881	ex LN-OPT
☐ C-FNJY	Aérospatiale AS350BA AStar	2546	
☐ C-FSOZ	Aérospatiale AS350B2 AStar	2129	ex N141MB
☐ C-FSPE	Aérospatiale AS350BA AStar	2787	
☐ C-FXAH	Aérospatiale AS350BA AStar	2509	ex N905BK
☐ C-FXBP	Aérospatiale AS350BA AStar	1553	ex I-VBIT
☐ C-FXDM	Aérospatiale AS350BA AStar	1548	ex N798JH
☐ C-FXED	Aérospatiale AS350BA AStar	3087	
☐ C-FXEJ	Aérospatiale AS350BA AStar	1031	
☐ C-FXHP	Aérospatiale AS350BA AStar	3100	
☐ C-FXND	Aérospatiale AS350BA AStar	2168	ex G-COPT
☐ C-FXPM	Aérospatiale AS350BA AStar	1428	ex C-FBHX
☐ C-GAVQ	Aérospatiale AS350B2 AStar	2781	ex N350PD
☐ C-GHSM	Aérospatiale AS350BA+ AStar	1468	ex N700WW

Registration	Type	c/n	Previous identity		Notes
☐ C-GHUM	Bell 205A-1	30252	ex HI-733SP		

AC JETZ — Montreal-Mirabel/Montreal-Trudeau, QC (YMX/YUL)

Specialist sports charter and VIP division of Air Canada.

ADLAIR AVIATION — Cambridge Bay, NT/Yellowknife, NT (YCB/YZF)

Registration	Type	c/n	Previous identity		Notes
☐ C-FGYN	de Havilland DHC-2 Beaver	134	ex CF-GYN		Floatplane or skis
☐ C-GBFP	Learjet 25B	25B-167	ex N664CL	Ernie Lyall	EMS
☐ C-GBYN	Beech B200 Super King Air	BB-1232	ex N209CM		EMS
☐ C-GCYN	Beech 200 Super King Air	BB-710	ex C-GXHW		
☐ C-GFYN	de Havilland DHC-6 Twin Otter 200	209	ex N915SA	Wheels or skis	

ADLER AVIATION — Shockwave (SWH) — Kitchener-Waterloo, ON (YKF)

Registration	Type	c/n	Previous identity
☐ C-GBWB	Piper PA-31 Navajo C	31-7612025	ex N108DR
☐ C-GTGR	Cessna 421C Golden Eagle II	421C0061	ex N15LW

ADVENTURE AIR — Lac du Bonnet, MB (YAX)

Registration	Type	c/n	Previous identity		Notes
☐ CF-JFA	de Havilland DHC-2 Beaver	1581	ex N5563		Floatplane
☐ C-FKLR	Cessna 208 Caravan I	20800223	ex N899A		Floatplane
☐ C-FQZH	Piper PA-31-350 Chieftain	31-7952070	ex N105TT		
☐ C-FVQD	de Havilland DHC-3 Turbo Otter	466	ex CF-VQD	Floatplane	
☐ C-FXPC	de Havilland DHC-2 Beaver	1196	ex CF-XPC		Floatplane
☐ C-GAAX	Cessna 208B Caravan I	208B0348	ex N32JA		
☐ C-GGRJ	Cessna A185F Skywagon	18502745	ex (N1090F)		Floatplane
☐ C-GKYG	de Havilland DHC-3 Otter	261	ex N2750		Floatplane
☐ C-GMGV	de Havilland DHC-2 Beaver	432	ex N62278		Floatplane
☐ C-GSUV	de Havilland DHC-3 Otter	376	ex N445FD		Floatplane
☐ C-GUEH	Piper PA-31 Turbo Navajo C	31-7712057	ex N27255		
☐ C-GWQE	Cessna 337F Super Skymaster II	33701459	ex N1859M		

AERÓPRO — Aeropro (APO) — Montreal-Trudeau, QC (YUL)

Registration	Type	c/n	Previous identity
☐ C-FEON	Piper PA-31 Turbo Navajo B	31-7401249	
☐ C-GHRL	Piper PA-31-350 Chieftain	31-8052014	ex N3547A
☐ C-GPXW	Piper PA-31-350 Navajo Chieftain	31-7652134	
☐ C-GQAM	Piper PA-31 Navajo C	31-7912093	ex N3536Z
☐ C-GQZE	Piper PA-31 Navajo C	31-7912065	ex N3520E
☐ C-GRFJ	Piper PA-31 Navajo C	31-7812031	ex N27485
☐ C-GRYE	Piper PA-31-350 Chieftain	31-7852155	
☐ C-FCGN	Beech 65-A90 King Air	LJ-313	ex CF-CGN
☐ C-FGIN	Beech A100 King Air	B-164	ex N164RA
☐ C-FPLG	Beech A100 King Air	B-224	ex N16SM
☐ C-FZSN	Embraer EMB.110P1 Bandeirante	110407	ex VH-TLH
☐ C-GJBQ	Beech A100 King Air	B-191	ex N214CK
☐ C-GBYL	Embraer EMB.110P1 Bandeirante	110383	ex C-FPCX
☐ C-GLPG	Beech A100 King Air	B-159	ex N110KF

AEROSMITH — Gander, NL (YQX)

Registration	Type	c/n	Previous identity	Notes
☐ C-GAAM	Cessna A185F Skywagon	18502675	ex C-GMNM	Floatplane or wheels/skis
☐ C-GAAZ	Cessna A185F Skywagon	18502735	ex C-GAEH	Floatplane or wheels/skis
☐ C-GSND	Beech 80-A65 Queen Air	LC-299	ex N122Y	Queenaire 8200 conversion

AIR BRAVO — Thunder Bay, ON (YQT)

Registration	Type	c/n	Previous identity
☐ C-FAJV	Pilatus PC-12/45	234	ex HB-FRE
☐ C-FKPA	Pilatus PC-12/45	275	ex N275PC
☐ C-FKSL	Pilatus PC-12/45	324	ex N324PC
☐ C-FPCI	Pilatus PC-12/45	399	ex N399PB
☐ C-FPCN	Pilatus PC-12/45	258	ex N258WC
☐ C-GFIL	Pilatus PC-12/45	268	ex N268PC
☐ C-GVKC	Pilatus PC-12/45	207	ex ZS-OEV
☐ C-GBCM	Rockwell Commander 700	70027	ex N700DL
☐ C-GVWX	Rockwell Commander 700	70005	ex N9905S

AIR CAB — Vancouver-Coal Harbour, BC (CXH)

Registration	Type	c/n	Previous identity	Notes
☐ C-FBMO	Cessna A185E Skywagon	18501627	ex N1934U	Floatplane
☐ C-FQGZ	Cessna A185E Skywagon	18501691	ex N1967U	Floatplane
☐ C-FOES	de Havilland DHC-2 Turbo Beaver	1673/TB43	ex CF-OES	Floatplane
☐ C-FRJG	de Havilland DHC-2 Beaver	1550	ex CF-RJG	Floatplane
☐ C-GAXE	de Havilland DHC-2 Beaver	841	ex 54-1698	Floatplane
☐ C-GJGC	de Havilland DHC-2 Beaver	88	ex CF-GQM	Floatplane
☐ C-GJZE	de Havilland DHC-2 Beaver	1276	ex N87780	Floatplane

AIR CANADA	Air Canada (AC/ACA)	Montreal-Mirabel/Montreal-Trudeau, QC (YMX/YUL)

Member of Star Alliance

Registration	Type	C/n	Previous identity	Fleet no.	Notes
☐ C-FYIY	Airbus A319-114	0634	ex D-AVYP	252	
☐ C-FYJE	Airbus A319-114	0656	ex D-AVYZ	255	
☐ C-FYJG	Airbus A319-114	0670	ex D-AVYE	256	
☐ C-FYJH	Airbus A319-114	0672	ex D-AVYF	257	
☐ C-FYJI	Airbus A319-114	0682	ex D-AVYH	258	
☐ C-FYJP	Airbus A319-114	0688	ex D-AVYJ	259	
☐ C-FYKC	Airbus A319-114	0691	ex D-AVYP	260	
☐ C-FYKR	Airbus A319-114	0693	ex D-AVYQ	261	
☐ C-FYKW	Airbus A319-114	0695	ex D-AVYS	262	
☐ C-FYNS	Airbus A319-114	0572	ex D-AVYK	251	
☐ C-FZUG	Airbus A319-114	0697	ex D-AVYT	263	
☐ C-FZUH	Airbus A319-114	0711	ex D-AVYV	264	TCA retro c/s
☐ C-FZUJ	Airbus A319-114	0719	ex D-AVYW	265	
☐ C-FZUL	Airbus A319-114	0721	ex D-AVYY	266	
☐ C-GAPY	Airbus A319-114	0728	ex D-AVYE	267	
☐ C-GAQL	Airbus A319-114	0732	ex D-AVYX	268	
☐ C-GAQX	Airbus A319-114	0736	ex D-AVYG	269	
☐ C-GAQZ	Airbus A319-114	0740	ex D-AVYH	270	
☐ C-GARG	Airbus A319-114	0742	ex D-AVYM	271	
☐ C-GARJ	Airbus A319-114	0752	ex D-AVYP	272	
☐ C-GARO	Airbus A319-114	0757	ex D-AVYQ	273	
☐ C-GBHM	Airbus A319-114	0769	ex D-AVYB	274	
☐ C-GBHN	Airbus A319-114	0773	ex D-AVYK	275	
☐ C-GBHO	Airbus A319-114	0779	ex D-AVYT	276	
☐ C-GBHR	Airbus A319-114	0785	ex D-AVYU	277	
☐ C-GBHY	Airbus A319-114	0800	ex D-AVYE	278	
☐ C-GBHZ	Airbus A319-114	0813	ex D-AVYG	279	
☐ C-GBIA	Airbus A319-114	0817	ex D-AVYM	280	
☐ C-GBIJ	Airbus A319-114	0829	ex D-AVYH	281	
☐ C-GBIK	Airbus A319-114	0831	ex D-AVYI	282	
☐ C-GBIM	Airbus A319-114	0840	ex D-AVYQ	283	
☐ C-GBIN	Airbus A319-114	0845	ex D-AVYA	284	
☐ C-GBIP	Airbus A319-114	0546	ex D-AVYV	285	
☐ C-GITP	Airbus A319-112	1562	ex D-AVYR	286	
☐ C-GITR	Airbus A319-112	1577	ex D-AVWR	287	
☐ C-FDCA	Airbus A320-211	0232	ex F-WWIY	405	ACJetz
☐ C-FDQQ	Airbus A320-211	0059	ex F-WWDI	201	
☐ C-FDQV	Airbus A320-211	0068	ex F-WWDO	202	
☐ C-FDRH	Airbus A320-211	0073	ex F-WWDC	203	
☐ C-FDRK	Airbus A320-211	0084	ex F-WWDP	204	
☐ C-FDRP	Airbus A320-211	0122	ex F-WWIP	205	
☐ C-FDSN	Airbus A320-211	0126	ex F-WWIU	206	
☐ C-FDST	Airbus A320-211	0127	ex F-WWIV	207	
☐ C-FDSU	Airbus A320-211	0141	ex F-WWDH	208	
☐ C-FFWI	Airbus A320-211	0149	ex F-WWDP	209	
☐ C-FFWJ	Airbus A320-211	0150	ex F-WWDQ	210	
☐ C-FFWM	Airbus A320-211	0154	ex F-WWDY	211	
☐ C-FFWN	Airbus A320-211	0159	ex F-WWIG	212	65th colours
☐ C-FGYL	Airbus A320-211	0254	ex F-WWBF	218	
☐ C-FGYS	Airbus A320-211	0255	ex F-WWBG	219	
☐ C-FKCK	Airbus A320-211	0265	ex 'G-FKCK'	220	
☐ C-FKCO	Airbus A320-211	0277	ex F-WWDX	221	
☐ C-FKCR	Airbus A320-211	0290	ex F-WWBY	222	
☐ C-FKOJ	Airbus A320-211	0330	ex F-WWIB	226	
☐ C-FKPT	Airbus A320-211	0324	ex F-WWDC	225	
☐ C-FLSS	Airbus A320-211	0284	ex F-WWBU	408	
☐ C-FLSU	Airbus A320-211	0309	ex F-WWIJ	411	
☐ C-FMSX	Airbus A320-211	0378	ex 'C-FMSK'	232	
☐ C-FNVU	Airbus A320-211	0403	ex F-WWBO	415	
☐ C-FNVV	Airbus A320-211	0404	ex F-WWDF	416	
☐ C-FPDN	Airbus A320-211	0341	ex F-WWBR	228	
☐ C-FPWD	Airbus A320-211	0231	ex F-WWDV	404	AC Jetz
☐ C-FPWE	Airbus A320-211	0175	ex F-WWIN	402	AC Jetz
☐ C-FTJO	Airbus A320-211	0183	ex F-WWIX	213	
☐ C-FTJP	Airbus A320-211	0233	ex F-WWIQ	214	
☐ C-FTJQ	Airbus A320-211	0242	ex F-WWDJ	215	
☐ C-FTJR	Airbus A320-211	0248	ex F-WWDT	216	
☐ C-FTJS	Airbus A320-211	0253	ex F-WWBE	217	
☐ C-FXCD	Airbus A320-214	2018	ex F-WWBV	239	
☐ C-FZQS	Airbus A320-214	2145	ex F-WWDI	240	
☐ C-FZUB	Airbus A320-214	1940	ex F-WWIP	238	
☐ C-GJVT	Airbus A320-214	1719	ex F-WWBC	235	
☐ C-GKOD	Airbus A320-214	1864	ex F-WWIE	236	
☐ C-GKOE	Airbus A320-214	1874	ex F-WWBN	237	
☐ C-GPWG	Airbus A320-211	0174	ex F-WWIM	401	
☐ C-GQCA	Airbus A320-211	0210	ex F-WWIC	403	AC Jetz

☐ C-GITU	Airbus A321-211	1602	ex D-AMTA	451	
☐ C-GITY	Airbus A321-211	1611	ex D-AVAV	452	
☐ C-GIUB	Airbus A321-211	1623	ex D-AMTB	453	70th Anniversary colours
☐ C-GIUE	Airbus A321-211	1632	ex D-AMTC	454	
☐ C-GIUF	Airbus A321-211	1638	ex D-AMTD	455	
☐ C-GJVX	Airbus A321-211	1726	ex D-AVXC	456	
☐ C-GJWD	Airbus A321-211	1748	ex D-AVXE	457	
☐ C-GJWI	Airbus A321-211	1772	ex D-AVZA	458	
☐ C-GJWN	Airbus A321-211	1783	ex D-AVZD	459	
☐ C-GJWO	Airbus A321-211	1811	ex D-AVZI	460	
☐ C-GFAF	Airbus A330-343X	277	ex F-WWKO	931	
☐ C-GFAH	Airbus A330-343X	279	ex F-WWYB	932	
☐ C-GFAJ	Airbus A330-343X	284	ex F-WWYA	933	
☐ C-GFUR	Airbus A330-343X	344	ex F-WWYC	934	
☐ C-GHKR	Airbus A330-343X	400	ex F-WWKM	935	
☐ C-GHKW	Airbus A330-343X	408	ex F-WWKS	936	
☐ C-GHKX	Airbus A330-343X	412	ex F-WWKU	937	
☐ C-GHLM	Airbus A330-343X	419	ex F-WWYA	938	Star Alliance c/s
☐ C-FBEF	Boeing 767-233ER	24323/250	ex N6009F	617	stored ROW
☐ C-FBEG	Boeing 767-233ER	24324/252	ex N6009F	618	stored ROW
☐ C-FBEM	Boeing 767-233ER	24325/254	ex N6038E	619	stored ROW
☐ C-FCAB	Boeing 767-375ER	24082/213	ex N6055X	681	
☐ C-FCAE	Boeing 767-375ER	24083/215	ex N6046P	682	70th colours
☐ C-FCAF	Boeing 767-375ER	24084/219	ex N6038E	683	
☐ C-FCAG	Boeing 767-375ER	24085/220	ex N6009F	684	
☐ C-FMWP	Boeing 767-333ER	25583/508		631	
☐ C-FMWQ	Boeing 767-333ER	25584/596		632	
☐ C-FMWU	Boeing 767-333ER	25585/597		633	
☐ C-FMWV	Boeing 767-333ER	25586/599		634	
☐ C-FMWY	Boeing 767-333ER	25587/604		635	10 Year Star Alliance colours
☐ C-FMXC	Boeing 767-333ER	25588/606		636	
☐ C-FOCA	Boeing 767-375ER	24575/311		640	
☐ C-FPCA	Boeing 767-375ER	24306/258		637	
☐ C-FTCA	Boeing 767-375ER	24307/259		638	
☐ C-FVNM	Boeing 767-209ER	22681/18	ex ZK-NBF	621	stored ROW
☐ C-FXCA	Boeing 767-375ER	24574/302		639	
☐ C-GAUE	Boeing 767-233	22518/22		602	stored MZJ
☐ C-GAUH	Boeing 767-233	22519/40		603	stored MHV
☐ C-GAUN	Boeing 767-233	22520/47		604	stored MHV
☐ C-GAUS	Boeing 767-233	22522/75	ex N60659	606	stored MHV
☐ C-GAUU	Boeing 767-233	22523/87	ex N1784B	607	stored MHV
☐ C-GAUW	Boeing 767-233	22524/88	ex N6038E	608	stored MHV
☐ C-GAVC	Boeing 767-233ER	22527/102	ex N1783B	611	stored ROW
☐ C-GBZR	Boeing 767-38EER	25404/411	ex HL7267	645	Free Spirit c/s
☐ C-GDSP	Boeing 767-233ER	24142/229	ex N6009F	613	all-silver fuselage stored ROW
☐ C-GDSS	Boeing 767-233ER	24143/233	ex N6005C	614	stored MHZ
☐ C-GDSU	Boeing 767-233ER	24144/234	ex N6018N	615	stored ROW
☐ C-GDSY	Boeing 767-233ER	24145/236	ex N6005C	616	stored ROW
☐ C-GDUZ	Boeing 767-38EER	25347/399	ex HL7266	646	
☐ C-GEOQ	Boeing 767-375ER	30112/765		647	
☐ C-GEOU	Boeing 767-375ER	30108/771		648	
☐ C-GHLA	Boeing 767-35HER	26387/445	ex VH-BZL	656	
☐ C-GHLK	Boeing 767-35HER	26388/456	ex VH-BZM	657	
☐ C-GHLQ	Boeing 767-333ER	30846/832	ex N6009F	658	
☐ C-GHLT	Boeing 767-333ER	30850/835	ex N6018N	659	
☐ C-GHLU	Boeing 767-333ER	30851/836	ex N6046P	660	stored ROW
☐ C-GHLV	Boeing 767-333ER	30852/843	ex N6055X	661	
☐ C-GHOZ	Boeing 767-375ER	24087/249	ex N487CT	685	
☐ C-GHPD	Boeing 767-3Y0ER	24999/354	ex N25034	687	
☐ C-GHPF	Boeing 767-3Y0ER	26206/487	ex N226MT	689	
☐ C-GHPH	Boeing 767-3Y0ER	26207/503	ex N227MT	690	
☐ C-GLCA	Boeing 767-375ER	25120/361		641	
☐ C-GPWA	Boeing 767-275	22683/36		671	stored MHV
☐ C-GSCA	Boeing 767-375ER	25121/372	ex B-2564	642	
☐ C-FIUA	Boeing 777-233LR	35239/640		701	
☐ C-FIUF	Boeing 777-233LR	35243/651	ex N1788B	702	
☐ C-FIUJ	Boeing 777-233LR	35244/679		703	
☐ C-FIVK	Boeing 777-233LR	35245/689		704	
☐ C-FNND	Boeing 777-233LR	35246/695		705	
☐ C-FNNH	Boeing 777-233LR	35247/699		706	
☐ C-FITL	Boeing 777-333ER	35256/620		731	
☐ C-FITU	Boeing 777-333ER	35254/626		732	
☐ C-FITW	Boeing 777-333ER	35298/638		733	
☐ C-FIUL	Boeing 777-333ER	35255/642		734	
☐ C-FIUR	Boeing 777-333ER	35242/649		735	
☐ C-FIUV	Boeing 777-333ER	35248/702		736	
☐ C-FIUW	Boeing 777-333ER	35249/712		737	
☐ C-FIVM	Boeing 777-333ER	35251/717		738	
☐ C-FIVQ	Boeing 777-333ER	35240/749		740	

☐ C-FIVR Boeing 777-333ER 35241/763 741
☐ C-FIVS Boeing 777-333ER 35784/797 742
☐ C-FRAM Boeing 777-333ER 35250/726 739

☐ C-FEIQ Embraer 170-200SU (175SU) 17000083 ex PT-SZI 371
☐ C-FEIX Embraer 170-200SU (175SU) 17000085 ex PT-SZK 372
☐ C-FEJB Embraer 170-200SU (175SU) 17000086 ex PT-SZL 373
☐ C-FEJC Embraer 170-200SU (175SU) 17000089 ex PT-SZP 374
☐ C-FEJD Embraer 170-200SU (175SU) 17000090 ex PT-SZQ 375
☐ C-FEJF Embraer 170-200SU (175SU) 17000091 ex PT-SZR 376
☐ C-FEJL Embraer 170-200SU (175SU) 17000095 ex PT-SZV 377
☐ C-FEJP Embraer 170-200SU (175SU) 17000096 ex PT-SZW 378
☐ C-FEJY Embraer 170-200SU (175SU) 17000097 ex PT-SZX 379
☐ C-FEKD Embraer 170-200SU (175SU) 17000101 ex PT-SAC 380
☐ C-FEKH Embraer 170-200SU (175SU) 17000102 ex PT-SAH 381
☐ C-FEKI Embraer 170-200SU (175SU) 17000103 ex PT-SAI 382
☐ C-FEKJ Embraer 170-200SU (175SU) 17000109 ex PT-SAR 383
☐ C-FEKS Embraer 170-200SU (175SU) 17000110 ex PT-SAS 384
☐ C-FFYG Embraer 170-200SU (175SU) 17000116 ex PT-SDD 385

☐ C-FFYJ Embraer 190-100IGW (190AR) 19000013 ex PT-STM 302
☐ C-FFYM Embraer 190-100IGW (190AR) 19000015 ex PT-STP 303
☐ C-FFYT Embraer 190-100IGW (190AR) 19000018 ex PT-STS 304
☐ C-FGLW Embraer 190-100IGW (190AR) 19000022 ex PT-STW 306
☐ C-FGLX Embraer 190-100IGW (190AR) 19000024 ex PT-STY 307
☐ C-FGLY Embraer 190-100IGW (190AR) 19000028 ex PT-SGC 308
☐ C-FGMF Embraer 190-100IGW (190AR) 19000019 ex PT-STT 305
☐ C-FHIQ Embraer 190-100IGW (190AR) 19000031 ex PT-SGF 309
☐ C-FHIS Embraer 190-100IGW (190AR) 19000036 ex PT-SGK 310
☐ C-FHIU Embraer 190-100IGW (190AR) 19000037 ex PT-SGL 311
☐ C-FHJJ Embraer 190-100IGW (190AR) 19000041 ex PT-SGQ 312
☐ C-FHJT Embraer 190-100IGW (190AR) 19000043 ex PT-SGS 313
☐ C-FHJU Embraer 190-100IGW (190AR) 19000044 ex PT-SGT 314
☐ C-FHKA Embraer 190-100IGW (190AR) 19000046 ex PT-SGV 315
☐ C-FHKE Embraer 190-100IGW (190AR) 19000048 ex PT-SGX 316
☐ C-FHKI Embraer 190-100IGW (190AR) 19000052 ex PT-SIB 317
☐ C-FHKP Embraer 190-100IGW (190AR) 19000055 ex PT-SIE 318
☐ C-FHKS Embraer 190-100IGW (190AR) 19000064 ex PT-SJC 319
☐ C-FHLH Embraer 190-100IGW (190AR) 19000068 ex PT-SJH 320
☐ C-FHNL Embraer 190-100IGW (190AR) 19000070 ex PT-SJJ 321
☐ C-FHNP Embraer 190-100IGW (190AR) 19000071 ex PT-SJK 322
☐ C-FHNV Embraer 190-100IGW (190AR) 19000075 ex PT-SJP 323
☐ C-FHNW Embraer 190-100IGW (190AR) 19000077 ex PT-SJS 324
☐ C-FHNX Embraer 190-100IGW (190AR) 19000083 ex PT-SNA 325
☐ C-FHNY Embraer 190-100IGW (190AR) 19000085 ex PT-SND 326
☐ C-FHON Embraer 190-100IGW (190AR) 19000097 ex PT-SNR 330
☐ C-FHOS Embraer 190-100IGW (190AR) 19000101 ex PT-SNV 331
☐ C-FHOY Embraer 190-100IGW (190AR) 19000105 ex PT-SNZ 332
☐ C-FLWE Embraer 190-100IGW (190AR) 19000092 ex PT-SNL 327
☐ C-FLWH Embraer 190-100IGW (190AR) 19000094 ex PT-SNO 328
☐ C-FLWK Embraer 190-100IGW (190AR) 19000096 ex PT-SNQ 329
☐ C-FMYV Embraer 190-100IGW (190AR) 19000108 ex PT-SQC 333
☐ C-FMZB Embraer 190-100IGW (190AR) 19000111 ex PT-SQF 334
☐ C-FMZD Embraer 190-100IGW (190AR) 19000115 ex PT-SQJ 335
☐ C-FMZR Embraer 190-100IGW (190AR) 19000116 ex PT-SQK 336
☐ C-FMZU Embraer 190-100IGW (190AR) 19000118 ex PT-SQM 337
☐ C-FMZW Embraer 190-100IGW (190AR) 19000124 ex PT-SQT 338
☐ C-FNAI Embraer 190-100IGW (190AR) 19000132 ex PT-SYK 339
☐ C-FNAJ Embraer 190-100IGW (190AR) 19000134 ex PT-SYM 340
☐ C-FNAN Embraer 190-100IGW (190AR) 19000136 ex PT-SYO 341
☐ C-FNAP Embraer 190-100IGW (190AR) 19000142 ex PT-SYU 342
☐ C-FNAQ Embraer 190-100IGW (190AR) 19000146 ex PT-SYY 343
☐ C-FNAW Embraer 190-100IGW (190AR) 19000149 ex PT-SAC 344
☐ C-FNAX Embraer 190-100IGW (190AR) 19000151 ex PT-SAG 345
☐ C-GWEN Embraer 190-100IGW (190AR) 19000010 ex PT-STJ 301

☐ CF-TCC Lockheed L-10A 1116 ex N3749 Trans Canada Airlines colours

AIR CANADA JAZZ ***Jazz (QK/JZA)***
Halifax, NS/Calgary, AB/London, ON/Vancouver, BC (YHZ/YYC/YXU/YVR)

Note: Fleet is being repainted into mainline Air Canada c/s, colours will be replaced.....

☐ C-FDJA Canadair CL-600-2B19 (CRJ-200ER) 7979 ex C-FMLI 162 green
☐ C-FEJA Canadair CL-600-2B19 (CRJ-200ER) 7983 ex C-FMLV 163 yellow
☐ C-FFJA Canadair CL-600-2B19 (CRJ-200ER) 7985 ex C-FMNH 164 orange
☐ C-FIJA Canadair CL-600-2B19 (CRJ-200ER) 7987 ex C-FMNX 165 red
☐ C-FRIA Canadair CL-600-2B19 (CRJ-100ER) 7045 ex C-FMLQ 101 red
☐ C-FRIB Canadair CL-600-2B19 (CRJ-100ER) 7047 ex C-FMLT 102 green
☐ C-FRID Canadair CL-600-2B19 (CRJ-100ER) 7049 ex C-FMLV 103 yellow
☐ C-FSJF Canadair CL-600-2B19 (CRJ-100ER) 7054 ex C-FMMT 105 orange
☐ C-FSJJ Canadair CL-600-2B19 (CRJ-100ER) 7058 ex C-FMNB 106 orange

☐ C-FSJU	Canadair CL-600-2B19 (CRJ-100ER)	7060	ex C-FMNH	107 orange
☐ C-FSKE	Canadair CL-600-2B19 (CRJ-100ER)	7065	ex C-FMOI	108 red
☐ C-FSKM	Canadair CL-600-2B19 (CRJ-100ER)	7071	ex C-FMKZ	110 orange
☐ C-FVKM	Canadair CL-600-2B19 (CRJ-100ER)	7074	ex C-FMLI	111 green
☐ C-FVKN	Canadair CL-600-2B19 (CRJ-100ER)	7078	ex C-FMLU	112 orange
☐ C-FVKR	Canadair CL-600-2B19 (CRJ-100ER)	7083	ex C-FMNQ	114 green
☐ C-FVMD	Canadair CL-600-2B19 (CRJ-100ER)	7082		113 orange
☐ C-FWJB	Canadair CL-600-2B19 (CRJ-100ER)	7087		115 green
☐ C-FWJF	Canadair CL-600-2B19 (CRJ-100ER)	7095		116 orange
☐ C-FWJI	Canadair CL-600-2B19 (CRJ-100ER)	7096		117 red
☐ C-FWJS	Canadair CL-600-2B19 (CRJ-100ER)	7097		118 red
☐ C-FWJT	Canadair CL-600-2B19 (CRJ-100ER)	7098		119 green
☐ C-FWRR	Canadair CL-600-2B19 (CRJ-100ER)	7107		120 red
☐ C-FWRS	Canadair CL-600-2B19 (CRJ-100ER)	7112		121 red
☐ C-FWRT	Canadair CL-600-2B19 (CRJ-100ER)	7118		122 red
☐ C-FWSC	Canadair CL-600-2B19 (CRJ-100ER)	7120		123 green
☐ C-FXMY	Canadair CL-600-2B19 (CRJ-100ER)	7124		124 yellow
☐ C-FZAQ	Canadair CL-600-2B19 (CRJ-100ER)	7155	ex C-FMMB	151orange
☐ C-FZJA	Canadair CL-600-2B19 (CRJ-200ER)	7988	ex C-FMNY	166 green
☐ C-FZSI	Canadair CL-600-2B19 (CRJ-100ER)	7160	ex LV-WZU	126 yellow
☐ C-GGJA	Canadair CL-600-2B19 (CRJ-200ER)	8002	ex C-FMMY	167 yellow
☐ C-GJZA	Canadair CL-600-2B19 (CRJ-200ER)	7500	ex N658BR	153 yellow
☐ C-GJZB	Canadair CL-600-2B19 (CRJ-200ER)	7740	ex N691BR	160 red
☐ C-GJZD	Canadair CL-600-2B19 (CRJ-200ER)	7544	ex N668BR	155 green
☐ C-GJZF	Canadair CL-600-2B19 (CRJ-200ER)	7545	ex N669BR	156 yellow
☐ C-GJZG	Canadair CL-600-2B19 (CRJ-200ER)	7561	ex N670BR	158 orange
☐ C-GJZJ	Canadair CL-600-2B19 (CRJ-200ER)	7553	ex N706BR	157 orange
☐ C-GJZL	Canadair CL-600-2B19 (CRJ-200ER)	7572	ex N671BR	159 green
☐ C-GJZN	Canadair CL-600-2B19 (CRJ-200ER)	7520	ex N661BR	154 orange
☐ C-GJZZ	Canadair CL-600-2B19 (CRJ-200ER)	7978	ex C-FMLF	161 red
☐ C-GKEJ	Canadair CL-600-2B19 (CRJ-200ER)	7269	ex N577ML	180 red
☐ C-GKEK	Canadair CL-600-2B19 (CRJ-200ER)	7270	ex N578ML	181 green
☐ C-GKEM	Canadair CL-600-2B19 (CRJ-200ER)	7277	ex N579ML	182 yellow
☐ C-GKEP	Canadair CL-600-2B19 (CRJ-200ER)	7303	ex N581ML	183 orange
☐ C-GKER	Canadair CL-600-2B19 (CRJ-200ER)	7368	ex N588ML	184 red
☐ C-GKEU	Canadair CL-600-2B19 (CRJ-200ER)	7376	ex N589ML	185 green
☐ C-GKEW	Canadair CL-600-2B19 (CRJ-200ER)	7385	ex N590ML	186 yellow
☐ C-GKEZ	Canadair CL-600-2B19 (CRJ-200ER)	7327	ex N583ML	187 orange
☐ C-GKFR	Canadair CL-600-2B19 (CRJ-200ER)	7330	ex N584ML	188 red
☐ C-GKGC	Canadair CL-600-2B19 (CRJ-200ER)	7334	ex N585ML	189 green
☐ C-GMJA	Canadair CL-600-2B19 (CRJ-200ER)	8003	ex C-FMNB	168 orange
☐ C-GNJA	Canadair CL-600-2B19 (CRJ-200ER)	8004	ex C-FMKV	169 red
☐ C-GOJA	Canadair CL-600-2B19 (CRJ-200ER)	8009	ex C-FMLI	170 yellow
☐ C-GQJA	Canadair CL-600-2B19 (CRJ-200ER)	7963	ex C-FCGX	171 Star Alliance c/s
☐ C-GTJA	Canadair CL-600-2B19 (CRJ-200ER)	7966	ex C-FCLV	172 green
☐ C-GUJA	Canadair CL-600-2B19 (CRJ-200ER)	8011	ex C-FMLS	173 orange
☐ C-GXJA	Canadair CL-600-2B19 (CRJ-200ER)	8017	ex C-FMNX	174 yellow
☐ C-GZJA	Canadair CL-600-2B19 (CRJ-200ER)	8018	ex C-FMNY	175 orange
☐ C-FBJZ	Canadair CL-600-2D15 (CRJ-705ER)	15037		702 green
☐ C-FCJZ	Canadair CL-600-2D15 (CRJ-705ER)	15040		703 orange
☐ C-FDJZ	Canadair CL-600-2D15 (CRJ-705ER)	15041		704 yellow
☐ C-FJJZ	Canadair CL-600-2D15 (CRJ-705ER)	15043		705 red
☐ C-FKJZ	Canadair CL-600-2D15 (CRJ-705ER)	15044		706 green
☐ C-FLJZ	Canadair CL-600-2D15 (CRJ-705ER)	15045		707 yellow
☐ C-FNJZ	Canadair CL-600-2D15 (CRJ-705ER)	15046		708 orange
☐ C-FTJZ	Canadair CL-600-2D15 (CRJ-705ER)	15047		709 red
☐ C-FUJZ	Canadair CL-600-2D15 (CRJ-705ER)	15048		710 Star Alliance c/s
☐ C-GDJZ	Canadair CL-600-2D15 (CRJ-705ER)	15049		711 green
☐ C-GFJZ	Canadair CL-600-2D15 (CRJ-705ER)	15050		712 yellow
☐ C-GJAZ	Canadair CL-600-2D15 (CRJ-705ER)	15036		701 red
☐ C-GLJZ	Canadair CL-600-2D15 (CRJ-705ER)	15051		713 orange
☐ C-GNJZ	Canadair CL-600-2D15 (CRJ-705ER)	15052		714 red
☐ C-GOJZ	Canadair CL-600-2D15 (CRJ-705ER)	15053		715 green
☐ C-GPJZ	Canadair CL-600-2D15 (CRJ-705ER)	15055	ex C-FGND	716 red
☐ C-FABA	de Havilland DHC-8-102	92		805 orange
☐ C-FABN	de Havilland DHC-8-102	44		803 red
☐ C-FABT	de Havilland DHC-8-102	49		848 green
☐ C-FABW	de Havilland DHC-8-102	97		806 green
☐ C-FACD	de Havilland DHC-8-102	150		808 yellow
☐ C-FACF	de Havilland DHC-8-311A	259		308 yellow
☐ C-FACT	de Havilland DHC-8-311A	262		309 green
☐ C-FACV	de Havilland DHC-8-311A	278		311 red
☐ C-FADF	de Havilland DHC-8-311A	272	ex C-FACU	310 red
☐ C-FGQK	de Havilland DHC-8-102	193		819 yellow
☐ C-FGRC	de Havilland DHC-8-102	195		821 green
☐ C-FGRM	de Havilland DHC-8-102	199		820 red
☐ C-FGRP	de Havilland DHC-8-102	207		822 green
☐ C-FGRY	de Havilland DHC-8-102	212		844 red
☐ C-FJFM	de Havilland DHC-8-311A	240		324 yellow
☐ C-FJMG	de Havilland DHC-8-102A	255		824 orange
☐ C-FJVV	de Havilland DHC-8-311A	271		306 red

☐ C-FJXZ	de Havilland DHC-8-311A	264	ex C-FTAQ	326 red
☐ C-FMDW	de Havilland DHC-8-311A	269		305 green
☐ C-FPON	de Havilland DHC-8-102	171		836 orange
☐ C-FRUZ	de Havilland DHC-8-311	293	ex N2492B	327 red
☐ C-FSOU	de Havilland DHC-8-311A	342	ex LN-WFA	328 green
☐ C-FTAK	de Havilland DHC-8-311A	246		323 red
☐ C-GABF	de Havilland DHC-8-102	25		816 green
☐ C-GABO	de Havilland DHC-8-311A	248		312 orange
☐ C-GABP	de Havilland DHC-8-311A	257		307 green
☐ C-GANF	de Havilland DHC-8-102	42		802 orange
☐ C-GANI	de Havilland DHC-8-102	64		830 green
☐ C-GANK	de Havilland DHC-8-102	87		831 yellow
☐ C-GANQ	de Havilland DHC-8-102	96		833 yellow
☐ C-GANS	de Havilland DHC-8-102	57		828 green
☐ C-GCTC	de Havilland DHC-8-102	65	ex V2-LEE	846 orange
☐ C-GETA	de Havilland DHC-8-301	186		321 red
☐ C-GEWQ	de Havilland DHC-8-311A	202		325 red
☐ C-GHTA	de Havilland DHC-8-301	198		316 orange
☐ C-GION	de Havilland DHC-8-102	127		832 yellow
☐ C-GJIG	de Havilland DHC-8-102	68		826 orange
☐ C-GJMI	de Havilland DHC-8-102	77		825 yellow
☐ C-GJMO	de Havilland DHC-8-102	79		834 yellow
☐ C-GJSV	de Havilland DHC-8-102	85		814 green
☐ C-GJSX	de Havilland DHC-8-102	88		835 red
☐ C-GKON	de Havilland DHC-8-102	130		815 red
☐ C-GKTA	de Havilland DHC-8-301	124		317 green
☐ C-GLTA	de Havilland DHC-8-301	154		318 green
☐ C-GMON	de Havilland DHC-8-301	131		301 orange
☐ C-GMTA	de Havilland DHC-8-301	174		319 yellow
☐ C-GNON	de Havilland DHC-8-301	137		302 green
☐ C-GOND	de Havilland DHC-8-102	90		840 red
☐ C-GONJ	de Havilland DHC-8-102	95		839 orange
☐ C-GONN	de Havilland DHC-8-102	101		898 yellow
☐ C-GONO	de Havilland DHC-8-102	102		807 orange
☐ C-GONR	de Havilland DHC-8-102	109		841 green
☐ C-GONW	de Havilland DHC-8-102	112		843 green
☐ C-GONX	de Havilland DHC-8-102	118		829 red
☐ C-GONY	de Havilland DHC-8-102	115		827 yellow
☐ C-GSTA	de Havilland DHC-8-301	182		320 yellow
☐ C-GTAG	de Havilland DHC-8-301	200		315 orange
☐ C-GTAI	de Havilland DHC-8-102	78		853 yellow
☐ C-GTAQ	de Havilland DHC-8-301	180	ex C-FGVK	313 red
☐ C-GTAT	de Havilland DHC-8-301	188	ex C-FGVT	314 red
☐ C-GTBP	de Havilland DHC-8-102	66		855 green
☐ C-GUON	de Havilland DHC-8-301	143		303 green
☐ C-GVON	de Havilland DHC-8-301	149		304 orange
☐ C-GVTA	de Havilland DHC-8-301	190		322 red

AIR CREEBEC — *Cree (YN/CRQ)* — *Val d'Or, QC / Timmins, ON (YVO/YTS)*

☐ C-FCLS	de Havilland DHC-8-102	249	ex N841EX	
☐ C-FCSK	de Havilland DHC-8-102	122		
☐ C-FDWO	de Havilland DHC-8-106	277	ex N880CC	
☐ C-GAIS	de Havilland DHC-8-102	138	ex C-FCIZ	
☐ C-GJOP	de Havilland DHC-8-102	121	ex N381BC	
☐ C-GTCO	de Havilland DHC-8-102	119		
☐ C-GYWX	de Havilland DHC-8-102	175	ex N283BC	
☐ C-GZEW	de Havilland DHC-8-314	393	ex N801SA	
☐ C-FHGG	Beech A100 King Air	B-207	ex N727LE	
☐ C-FPCM	Embraer EMB.110P1 Bandeirante	110340	ex LN-TDI	
☐ C-FPCU	Embraer EMB.110P1 Bandeirante	110445	ex LN-TDA	
☐ C-FPJR	Hawker Siddeley HS.748 Srs.2A/244	1725	ex SE-LEK	Freighter
☐ C-FTQR	Beech 1900D	UE-129		
☐ C-FYRH	Embraer EMB.110P1 Bandeirante	110259	ex N91PB	
☐ C-GIZX	Beech A100 King Air	B-172	ex N753DB	

AIR-DALE FLYING SERVICE — *Ranger Lake SPB, ON/Wawa Hawk Junction SPB, ON*

☐ C-FGYT	de Havilland DHC-2 Beaver	182	ex CF-GYT	Floatplane
☐ CF-ODE	de Havilland DHC-2 Beaver	131		Floatplane
☐ C-GELP	de Havilland DHC-2 Beaver	780	ex N5318G	Floatplane
☐ C-GQXI	de Havilland DHC-2 Beaver	427	ex N1059	Floatplane

AIR GEORGIAN — *Georgian (ZX/GGN)* — *Toronto-Pearson Intl, ON (YYZ)*

☐ C-GAAR	Beech 1900D	UE-207	ex N10625	964 Baie-Saint Laurent
☐ C-GAAS	Beech 1900D	UE-209	ex N10659	965 Iles de la Madelaine
☐ C-GAAU	Beech 1900D	UE-232	ex N10705	904 Baie Comeau
☐ C-GAAV	Beech 1900D	UE-235	ex N10708	967
☐ C-GGGA	Beech 1900D	UE-291	ex N20704	951

	Registration	Type	C/n	Previous identity	Fleet no / Name	Notes
☐	C-GHGA	Beech 1900D	UE-293	ex N21063	953	
☐	C-GMGA	Beech 1900D	UE-315	ex N22890	956 Baie Comeau	
☐	C-GORA	Beech 1900D	UE-326	ex N23164	957	
☐	C-GORC	Beech 1900D	UE-320	ex N22976	959	
☐	C-GORF	Beech 1900D	UE-330	ex N23222	958	
☐	C-GORI	Beech 1900D	UE-47	ex N84502	970	
☐	C-GORZ	Beech 1900D	UE-134	ex N860CA	973	
☐	C-GVGA	Beech 1900D	UE-202	ex N20707	952	
☐	C-GWGA	Beech 1900D	UE-309	ex N22874	955	
☐	C-GZGA	Beech 1900D	UE-306	ex N22700	954	

AIR INUIT — *Air Inuit (3H/AIE)* — *Kuujjuaq, QC (YVP)*

	Registration	Type	C/n	Previous identity	Fleet no / Name	Notes
☐	C-FAIY	de Havilland DHC-6 Twin Otter 300	362	ex C-FASS		floats or wheels/skis
☐	C-FJFR	de Havilland DHC-6 Twin Otter 300	784	ex HK-2762		
☐	C-FTJJ	de Havilland DHC-6 Twin Otter 300	325	ex 8Q-MAJ		N93NC res
☐	C-GKCJ	de Havilland DHC-6 Twin Otter 300	698	ex A6-AMM		dbr 11Feb07?
☐	C-GMDC	de Havilland DHC-6 Twin Otter 300	763			
☐	C-GNDO	de Havilland DHC-6 Twin Otter 300	430			
☐	C-GTYX	de Havilland DHC-6 Twin Otter 300	631			
☐	C-FAIV	de Havilland DHC-8-102	235	ex N828EX		
☐	C-FCJD	de Havilland DHC-8-102	158			
☐	C-FDAO	de Havilland DHC-8-102	123			
☐	C-FDND	de Havilland DHC-8-102	129			
☐	C-GAII	de Havilland DHC-8-102	160	ex N831EX		
☐	C-GAIW	de Havilland DHC-8-102	155	ex N830EX		
☐	C-GRAI	de Havilland DHC-8Q-314	483	ex OE-LTK		
☐	C-GUAI	de Havilland DHC-8Q-314	423	ex OE-LTF		
☐	C-FAIO	Beech A100 King Air	B-132	ex C-GXHP		
☐	C-FAIP	Beech A100 King Air	B-193	ex F-GXAB		
☐	C-FDOX	Hawker Siddeley HS.748 Srs.2A/310LFD	1749	ex TJ-CCD		Freighter
☐	C-FGET	Hawker Siddeley HS.748 Srs.2A/244	1724	ex D-AFSG		
☐	C-GAIG	Boeing 737-2S2C	21928/603	ex A6-ZYB		
☐	C-GCUK	Hawker Siddeley HS.748 Srs.2A/343LFD	1762	ex V2-LAZ		Freighter
☐	C-GAIK	Beech A100 King Air	B-104	ex C-GCFD		
☐	C-GEGJ	Hawker Siddeley HS.748 Srs.2A/244	1711	ex TF-GMB		

AIR IVANHOE — *Foleyet-Ivanhoe Lake, ON*

	Registration	Type	C/n	Previous identity	Notes
☐	C-GERE	de Havilland DHC-2 Beaver	352	ex N62784	Floatplane
☐	C-GPUS	de Havilland DHC-2 Beaver	624	ex 53-2824	Floatplane

AIR KIPAWA — *Kipawa, QC*

	Registration	Type	C/n	Previous identity	Notes
☐	C-FODA	de Havilland DHC-2 Beaver	112	ex CF-ODA	Floatplane

AIR LABRADOR — *Lab Air (WJ/LAL)* — *Goose Bay, NL (YYR)*

	Registration	Type	C/n	Previous identity	Name	Notes
☐	C-FGON	de Havilland DHC-6 Twin Otter 300	369	ex CF-GON		Floatplane or wheels/skis
☐	C-GLAI	de Havilland DHC-6 Twin Otter 300	296	ex N5377G		Floatplane or wheels/skis
☐	C-GNQY	de Havilland DHC-6 Twin Otter 300	450	ex N965HA		Floatplane or wheels/skis
☐	C-FXON	de Havilland DHC-8-102	183	ex V2-LDZ		
☐	C-GAAN	de Havilland DHC-8-102	051		The Spirit of Flight	
☐	C-GLHO	Beech 1900D	UE-266	ex N10950		
☐	C-GLON	de Havilland DHC-8-102	133			
☐	C-GTMB	Beech 1900D	UE-345	ex N23388		
☐	C-GUYR	Cessna 208 Caravan I	20800031	ex N604MA		

AIR MECATINA — *La Romaine, QC*

	Registration	Type	C/n	Previous identity	Notes
☐	C-FJDP	Cessna A185E Skywagon	185-1425	ex CF-JDP	Floatplane
☐	C-FSKQ	Beech 200 Super King Air	BB-99	ex 5Y-SEL	
☐	C-GNBB	Beech 200 Super King Air	BB-479	ex N200UQ	
☐	C-GZIJ	Piper PA-31-350 Navajo Chieftain	31-7552041	ex N901FA	

AIR MELANCON — *St Anne-du-Lac, QC*

	Registration	Type	C/n	Previous identity	Notes
☐	C-FBPB	de Havilland DHC-2 Beaver	1434	ex VH-IDF	Floatplane or wheels/skis
☐	C-FQQD	de Havilland DHC-2 Beaver	1580	ex FAP 64-374	Floatplane or wheels/skis
☐	C-FZVP	de Havilland DHC-2 Beaver	1033	ex N5641	Floatplane or wheels/skis
☐	C-GQXH	de Havilland DHC-2 Beaver	536	ex N1579	Floatplane or wheels/skis

AIR MIKISEW — *Air Mikisew (V8)* — *Fort McMurray, AB (YMM)*

	Registration	Type	C/n	Previous identity	Notes
☐	C-FAMB	Beech B200 Super King Air	BB-1281	ex N865TC	
☐	C-FKAM	British Aerospace Jetstream 31	724	ex N852JS	
☐	C-FKEY	Cessna 208 Caravan I	20800307	ex N5264A	Floatplane
☐	C-FMCN	Beech 1900D	UE-2O	ex N220CJ	

☐ C-FUAM	British Aerospace Jetstream 31	746	ex N404UE
☐ C-FVGT	Piper PA-31-350 Navajo Chieftain	31-7405133	ex N74981
☐ C-GDIR	Cessna A185F Skylane	18503973	ex (N6552E)
☐ C-GFJN	Cessna 207A Stationair 7	20700592	ex (N73446)
☐ C-GURM	Piper PA-31-350 Navajo Chieftain	31-7752184	ex N273RH
☐ C-GVAM	Cessna U206G Stationair 6	U20606177	ex N918WJ
☐ C-GVQU	Cessna A185F Skylane	18503648	ex N8206Q
☐ C-GZAM	Beech 99A	U-116	ex N17AL

AIR MONT-LAURIER — Ste-Veronique, QC

☐ C-FGQA	de Havilland DHC-2 Beaver	72	ex CF-GQA	Floatplane
☐ C-FQQC	de Havilland DHC-2 Beaver	56	ex CF-QQC	Floatplane
☐ C-FSUB	de Havilland DHC-3 Otter	8	ex RCAF 3662	Floatplane
☐ C-FTUR	de Havilland DHC-2 Beaver	1529	ex CF-TUR	Floatplane
☐ C-GGSC	de Havilland DHC-3 Otter	366	ex N5072F	Floatplane
☐ C-GMGP	Cessna A185F Skywagon	18502077	ex N9054F	Floatplane
☐ C-GUML	de Havilland DHC-2 Beaver	307	ex N1402Z	Floatplane
☐ C-GVLK	Cessna U206G Stationair 6 II	U20604329	ex N756SW	Floatplane

AIR MONTMAGNY — Montmagny, QC

☐ C-GBFU	Britten-Norman BN-2A-27 Islander	535	ex N70JA
☐ C-GCTM	Cessna U206G Stationair	U20603794	ex N8920G
☐ C-GGJG	Britten-Norman BN-2B-26 Islander	2219	ex F-ODUP
☐ C-GTMQ	Cessna 206H Stationair	20608038	ex N7255B

AIR NOOTKA — Gold River, BC

☐ C-FIBR	Cessna 180K Skywagon	18052788	ex N818BR	Floatplane
☐ C-FOXD	de Havilland DHC-2 Beaver	807	ex N90723	Floatplane
☐ C-GIUR	Cessna A185F Skywagon	18503290	ex (N94214)	Floatplane
☐ C-GPVB	de Havilland DHC-2 Beaver	871	ex N9253Z	Floatplane

AIR NORTH — Air North (4N/ANT) — Whitehorse, YT (YXY)

☐ C-FAGI	Hawker Siddeley HS.748 Srs.2A/276	1699	ex G-11-6	
☐ C-FAID	de Havilland DHC-8Q-314	400	ex OE-LTD	
☐ C-FCSE	Hawker Siddeley HS.748 Srs 2A/269	1679	ex G-AYFL	
☐ C-FJLB	Boeing 737-201 (Nordam 3)	22273/680	ex N233US	
☐ C-FYDU	Hawker Siddeley HS.748 Srs.2A/273	1694	ex ZK-MCP	
☐ C-FYDY	Hawker Siddeley HS.748 Srs.2A/233	1661	ex ZK-MCJ	Freighter
☐ C-GANV	Boeing 737-2X6C	23122/1036	ex N816AL	
☐ C-GECN	de Havilland DHC-8-106	324	ex C-FSQY	Lsd fr TSH
☐ C-GLIZ	Cessna 206 Super Skywagon	206-0156	ex N5156U	
☐ C-GNAU	Boeing 737-201 (Nordam 3)	21817/602	ex N228US	

AIR NUNAVUT — Air Baffin(BFF) — Iqaluit, NT (YFB)

☐ C-FCGW	Beech 200 Super King Air	BB-207	ex N111WH	CatPass 200 conversion
☐ C-FZNQ	Beech 200 Super King Air	BB-264	ex N465CJ	CatPass 200 conversion
☐ C-GZYO	Beech 200 Super King Air	BB-383	ex N384DB	

AIR OPTIMA — Miramichi, NB (YCH)

☐ C-FIML	Cessna 310Q	310Q0758	ex CF-IML
☐ C-GABL	Cessna 310R II	310R0927	ex N3840G

AIR QUASAR — (QAT) — Montreal-St Hubert, QC (YHU)

☐ C-FCFC	Piper PA-23-150	23-312	ex CF-CFC
☐ C-FDTF	Cessna 210L Centurion II	21060291	ex N93168
☐ C-FVEI	Cessna 210L Centurion II	21059550	ex N4650Q
☐ C-GNEL	Cessna 210L Centurion II	21060004	ex N35636

AIR SAGUENAY — Lac St-Sebastien, QC

☐ C-FIUS	de Havilland DHC-2 Beaver	901	ex CF-IUS	Floatplane or wheels/skis
☐ C-FJAC	de Havilland DHC-2 Beaver	937	ex CF-JAC	Floatplane or wheels/skis
☐ C-FJKI	de Havilland DHC-2 Beaver	992	ex CF-JKI	Floatplane or wheels/skis
☐ C-FKRJ	de Havilland DHC-2 Beaver	1210	ex CF-KRJ	Floatplane or wheels/skis
☐ C-GAEF	de Havilland DHC-2 Beaver	372	ex 51-16830	Floatplane or wheels/skis
☐ C-GAXL	de Havilland DHC-2 Beaver	1032	ex 56-537	Floatplane or wheels/skis
☐ C-GPUO	de Havilland DHC-2 Beaver	810	ex 54-1677	Floatplane or wheels/skis
☐ C-GUJI	de Havilland DHC-2 Beaver	1141	ex N68013	Floatplane or wheels/skis

☐ C-FDAK	de Havilland DHC-3 Otter	157	ex CF-DAK	Floatplane or wheels/skis
☐ C-FMPX	de Havilland DHC-3 Otter	280	ex CF-MPX	Floatplane or wheels/skis
☐ C-FODT	de Havilland DHC-3 Otter	218	ex CF-ODT	Floatplane or wheels/skis
☐ C-GLFL	de Havilland DHC-3 Turbo Otter	329	ex 58-1712	Floatplane or wheels/skis
☐ C-GLMT	de Havilland DHC-3 Otter	216	ex IM-1716	Floatplane or wheels/skis

☐ C-GQDU	de Havilland DHC-3 Turbo Otter	43	ex N94472		Floatplane or wheels/skis
☐ C-GUTQ	de Havilland DHC-3 Otter	402	ex HK-3049X		Floatplane or wheels/skis
☐ C-FYAO	Cessna A185E Skywagon	18501472	ex (N2722J)		Floatplane or wheels/skis
☐ C-GTBY	Cessna 208 Caravan I	20800261	ex C-GFLN		Floatplane or wheels/skis

AIR SATELLITE — *Satellite (6O/ASJ)* — *Baie Comeau, QC (YBC)*

☐ C-GSSW	Piper PA-34-200 Seneca	34-7450046	ex N56995		

AIR-SPRAY — *Air Spray (ASB)* — *Edmonton-Municipal/Red Deer, AB (YEG/YQF)*

☐ CF-CBK	Douglas B-26C Invader	28940	ex N9996Z	11	
☐ CF-CUI	Douglas B-26C Invader	28803	ex N9401Z	12	
☐ C-FKBM	Douglas A-26B Invader	27415	ex N8017E	20	
☐ C-FOVC	Douglas B-26C Invader	28776	ex N3426G	56	
☐ C-FPGF	Douglas A-26B Invader	29154	ex 44-35875	1	
☐ CF-ZTC	Douglas B-26C Invader	29136	ex N9300R	13 Lucky Jack	
☐ C-GHZM	Douglas A-26B Invader	27400	ex N4805E	5 Fire Eater	
☐ C-GPTW	Douglas A-26B Invader	18800	ex N9402Z	26	
☐ C-GTOX	Douglas A-26B Invader	27802	ex N9174Z	14	
☐ C-FLJO	Lockheed L-188C Electra	1103	ex N429NA	82	
☐ C-FLXT	Lockheed L-188C Electra	1130	ex N308D		
☐ C-FVFH	Lockheed L-188A Electra	1006	ex PK-RLF	89	
☐ C-FVFI	Lockheed L-188C Electra	1082	ex PK-RLD		stored YQF
☐ C-FZCS	Lockheed L-188C Electra	1060	ex HR-SHN	87	
☐ C-GHZI	Lockheed L-188C Electra	2007	ex N1968R	84	
☐ C-GYVI	Lockheed L-188CF Electra	1112	ex N360Q	83	
☐ C-GZCF	Lockheed L-188CF Electra	1091	ex G-CEXS	90	
☐ C-GZVM	Lockheed L-188A Electra	1036	ex N351Q	85	
☐ C-GZYH	Lockheed L-188A Electra	1124	ex HR-AMM		stored YQF
☐ C-FAKP	Rockwell 690 Turbo Commander	11040	ex N690DC	56	
☐ C-FIIL	Rockwell 690A Turbo Commander	11167	ex N85AB		
☐ C-FMCX	Rockwell 690B Turbo Commander	11446	ex N137BW		
☐ C-FZRQ	Rockwell 690 Turbo Commander	11025	ex N100LS	51	
☐ C-GFPP	Rockwell 690 Turbo Commander	11032	ex N349AC	52	
☐ C-GJFO	Rockwell 690 Turbo Commander	11035	ex N15VZ	53	
☐ C-GKDZ	Rockwell 690 Turbo Commander	11016	ex N428SJ	54	
☐ C-GZON	Rockwell 690 Turbo Commander	11020	ex N14CV	55	
☐ C-FEHK	Ted Smith Aerostar 600A	60-0400-140	ex N17LH	307	
☐ C-FGWE	Cessna 310Q II	310Q0920	ex (N69686)	302	for sale
☐ C-FJCF	Ted Smith Aerostar 600A	60-0153-067	ex N37HA	308	
☐ C-GXJP	Cessna 310P	310P0073	ex N101QC	305	for sale
☐ C-GXXN	Cessna T310P	310P0002	ex N5702M	306	for sale

AIR TINDI — *Air Tindi (8T)* — *Yellowknife, NT (YZF)*

☐ C-FASG	de Havilland DHC-6 Twin Otter 300	373			Floatplane or wheels/skis
☐ C-FATM	de Havilland DHC-6 Twin Otter 300	265	ex PJ-ATL		Floatplane or wheels/skis
☐ C-FATN	de Havilland DHC-6 Twin Otter 300	226	ex N153BU		Floatplane or wheels/skis Lsd to Tli Cho Air
☐ C-FATO	de Havilland DHC-6 Twin Otter 310	674	ex A6-MRM		Floatplane or wheels/skis
☐ C-FATW	de Havilland DHC-6 Twin Otter 300	525	ex PK-BRA		Floatplane or wheels/skis
☐ C-GMAS	de Havilland DHC-6 Twin Otter 300	438	ex N546N		Floatplane or wheels/skis
☐ C-GNPS	de Havilland DHC-6 Twin Otter 300	558			Floatplane or wheels/skis
☐ C-FATA	Beech 200 Super King Air	BB-283	ex N283JP		
☐ C-FCGU	Beech 200B Super King Air	BB-301	ex N611SW		CatPass 200 conversion
☐ C-FKAY	Cessna 208B Caravan I	208B0470	ex N1294N		
☐ C-FWZV	de Havilland DHC-7-103	81	ex P2-ANP		
☐ C-FXUY	de Havilland DHC-3 Turbo Otter	142	ex N214L		Floatplane or wheels/skis
☐ C-FZDV	de Havilland DHC-3 Otter	349	ex N28NC		
☐ C-GATH	Cessna 208B Caravan I	208B1244	ex N5225K		
☐ C-GATV	Cessna 208B Caravan I	208B0308			
☐ C-GATY	Cessna 208 Caravan I	20800305	ex N52627		Floatplane or wheels/skis
☐ C-GCEV	de Havilland DHC-7-102	63	ex HB-IVY		
☐ C-GDPB	Beech 200C Super King Air	BL-44	ex N18379		EMS
☐ C-GFFL	de Havilland DHC-7-102	74	ex HB-IVY		
☐ C-GPHO	Cessna A185F Skywagon	18503099	ex (N80151)		Floatplane or wheels/skis
☐ C-GTUC	Beech 200 Super King Air	BB-268	ex N565RA		
☐ C-GWXI	Cessna A185F Skywagon	18502010	ex (N1290F)		Floatplane or wheels/skis
☐ C-GXHF	Beech 200 Super King Air	BB-1343	ex 5Y-ECO		Beech 1300 conversion
☐ C-GZIX	Cessna A185F Skywagon	18504182	ex N46CR		Floatplane or wheels/skis

AIR TRANSAT — *Transat (TS/TSC)* — *Montreal-Trudeau, QC (YUL)*

☐ C-FDAT	Airbus A310-308	658	ex A6-EKK	305	
☐ C-GFAT	Airbus A310-304	545	ex A6-EKG	301	
☐ C-GLAT	Airbus A310-308	588	ex A6-EKI	302	

☐ C-GPAT	Airbus A310-308	597	ex A6-EKJ	303
☐ C-GSAT	Airbus A310-308	600	ex 5Y-KQM	304
☐ C-GTSD	Airbus A310-304	547	ex D-AIDL	341
☐ C-GTSF	Airbus A310-304	472	ex CS-TEZ	345
☐ C-GTSH	Airbus A310-308	599	ex D-AIDN	343
☐ C-GTSK	Airbus A310-304	541	ex CS-TEW	
☐ C-GTSW	Airbus A310-304	483	ex CS-TEH	
☐ C-GTSX	Airbus A310-304	527	ex D-AIDH	346
☐ C-GTSY	Airbus A310-304	447	ex N447DN	344
☐ C-GVAT	Airbus A310-304	485	ex D-AIDC	321
☐ C-GCTS	Airbus A330-342	177	ex B-HYE	
☐ C-GGTS	Airbus A330-243	250	ex F-WWKK	101
☐ C-GITS	Airbus A330-243	271	ex F-WWKY	102
☐ C-GKTS	Airbus A330-342	111	ex B-HYC	100
☐ C-GPTS	Airbus A330-243	480	ex F-WWKV	103

AIR TUNILIK — *Schefferville-Squaw Lake, QC (YKL)*

☐ C-FLLX	de Havilland DHC-2 Beaver	1293	ex CF-LLX	Floatplane or wheels/skis
☐ C-GNKR	de Havilland DHC-2 Beaver	331	ex N5698	

AIRBORNE ENERGY SOLUTIONS — *Whitecourt, AB (YZU)*

☐ C-FPKM	Aérospatiale AS350B AStar	2426	ex JA6045
☐ C-FWKM	Aérospatiale AS350BA AStar	2427	ex JA6044
☐ C-GREV	Aérospatiale AS350BA AStar	1039	ex N98TV
☐ C-GTKM	Aérospatiale AS350BA AStar	2515	ex JA6095
☐ C-FARJ	Bell 206B JetRanger	741	ex N700BH
☐ C-FBKH	Bell 206B JetRanger	575	ex N100FW
☐ C-GJEL	Bell 206B JetRanger	116	ex N855NR
☐ C-GKRH	Bell 206B JetRanger II	2109	ex N354AC
☐ C-GTEZ	Bell 206B JetRanger	746	ex N2926W
☐ C-GTQU	Bell 206B JetRanger	766	ex N8199J
☐ C-GXAG	Bell 206B JetRanger	150	ex N6283N
☐ C-GXBY	Bell 206B JetRanger	477	ex N72HP
☐ C-FARQ	Cessna 208B Caravan I	208B0765	ex N5174W
☐ C-FHHA	Bell 206L-1 LongRanger	45662	ex C-GBPO
☐ C-FNCI	Piper PA-31 Navajo C	31-8112007	ex N9149Z
☐ C-FZGP	Bell 206B JetRanger II	940	ex N888LH
☐ C-FZHG	Piper PA-31 Turbo Navajo B	31-753	ex N103DE
☐ C-GAEO	Beech 300 Super King Air	FL-479	ex N3179V
☐ C-GEAH	Bell 205A-1	30096	ex LX-HAH
☐ C-GFYK	Cessna U206F Stationair II	U20603350	ex (N8492Q)
☐ C-GLRR	Piper PA-31-325 Navajo C/R	31-7812044	ex N824AB
☐ C-GQLG	Bell 205A-1	30008	ex A7-HAF

AIRCO AIRCRAFT CHARTERS — *Edmonton-Municipal, AB (YXD)*

☐ C-FTOW	Beech 1900D	UE-130	
☐ C-FWPG	Beech 100 King Air	B-67	ex N26KW
☐ C-FWYF	Beech 100 King Air	B-89	ex N169RA
☐ C-FWYN	Beech 100 King Air	B-47	ex C-GNAX
☐ C-FWYO	Beech 100 King Air	B-28	ex N27JJ
☐ C-GBMI	Piper PA-31-350 Chieftain	31-8352007	ex N23NP
☐ C-GZNB	Piper PA-31-350 Navajo Chieftain	31-7752079	ex N6654B

AIREXPRESS ONTARIO — *Oshawa, ON (YOO)*

☐ C-FSKX	Beech 200 Super King Air	BB-1126	ex N650JW
☐ C-FTIU	Beech 350 Super King Air	FL-584	ex N33984
☐ C-GBBS	Beech 200 Super King Air	BB-757	ex N948MB

AIRSPAN HELICOPTERS — *Sechelt, BC (YHS)*

☐ C-FBKS	Bell 206LR+ LongRanger	45033	ex N206ML
☐ C-FJPI	Aérospatiale AS350BA AStar	1260	ex N350NH
☐ C-FVSP	Bell 206B JetRanger	899	ex N83070
☐ C-GHHI	Bell 206L-3 LongRanger III	51037	ex N30EA
☐ C-GJKN	Bell 205A-1	30091	ex CS-HEA
☐ C-GVIW	Bell 206L-1 LongRanger III	45410	

ALBERTA CENTRAL AIRWAYS — *Lac la Biche, AB (YLB)*

☐ C-FJWU	Beech 65-E90 King Air	LW-332	ex N636GW	
☐ C-FNED	Beech 65-C90 King Air	LJ-680	ex N928RD	
☐ C-FTSU	de Havilland DHC-6 Twin Otter 300	451	ex C-FINM	
☐ C-FTWU	de Havilland DHC-6 Twin Otter 300	372	ex N17GL	
☐ C-FWPN	Beech 100 King Air	B-51	ex N16SW	
☐ C-GACA	Beech 200 Super King Air	BB-1309	ex N4277C	Beech 1300 conversion

☐ C-GACN	Beech 200 Super King Air	BB-1384	ex N575T	Beech 1300 conversion
☐ C-GEUA	Piper PA-31 Turbo Navajo	31-187	ex N64JK	
☐ C-GGBZ	Cessna U206G Stationair 6 II	U20605637		
☐ C-GUWO	Piper PA-31 Turbo Navajo	31-203	ex N9154Y	
☐ C-GWFF	Piper PA-31 Turbo Navajo C	31-7512063	ex N61390	
☐ C-GYUW	Cessna U206G Stationair 6	U20603738		

ALBERTA CITYLINK — *Alberta Citylink (ABK)* — *Calgary-Intl/Medicine Hat, AB (YYC/YXH)*

☐ C-FBID	British Aerospace Jetstream 31	802	ex G-31-802
☐ C-FIBD	British Aerospace Jetstream 31	943	ex N943AE
☐ C-FZVY	British Aerospace Jetstream 31	833	ex N833JX
☐ C-GZOS	British Aerospace Jetstream 31	796	ex N424UE

ALKAN AIR — *Alkan Air (AKN)* — *Whitehorse, YT (YXY)*

☐ C-FAKN	Beech 200 Super King Air	BB-216	ex LN-VIU
☐ C-FAKW	Beech 300 Super King Air	FA-183	ex N19NC
☐ C-FAKZ	Cessna 208B Caravan I	208B0666	ex N939JL
☐ C-FSKF	Cessna 208B Caravan I	208B0673	ex N5268M
☐ C-FTBI	Short SC.7 Skyvan	SH1847	ex N64HB
☐ C-GLCS	de Havilland DHC-3 Otter	428	ex N17685
☐ C-GMOC	Beech 200 Super King Air	BB-513	ex N513SA
☐ C-GSDT	Piper PA-31-350 Chieftain	31-8152102	ex N120FL
☐ C-GYTB	Cessna U206G Stationair	U20603685	ex (N7579N)

ALLEN AIRWAYS — *Sioux Lookout, ON (YXL)*

☐ C-FERZ	Cessna 180K	18053071	ex N2799K	Floatplane
☐ C-FYCK	Cessna A185E Skywagon	185-1478	ex CF-YCK	Floatplane or wheels/skis
☐ C-GQDO	Cessna A185F Skywagon	18503745	ex (N8585Q)	Floatplane or wheels/skis

ALPEN HELICOPTERS — *Langley, BC(YNJ)*

☐ C-GAHL	Bell 206B JetRanger III	2600	ex N8264U
☐ C-GJSG	Bell 206B JetRanger III	326	ex N1545V
☐ C-GPCX	Bell 206L-1 LongRanger II	45554	
☐ C-GRBO	Cessna A185F Skywagon	18503414	ex N903TH

ALPINE AVIATION — *Whitehorse, YT (YXY)*

☐ C-FGSI	Cessna U206F Stationair	U20602165	ex CF-GSI	
☐ C-GMGD	de Havilland DHC-2 Beaver	519	ex N67091	Floatplane

ALPINE HELICOPTERS — *Kelowna, BC (YLW)*

☐ C-FALU	Bell 206B JetRanger III	1072	
☐ C-FTED	Bell 206B JetRanger III	3556	
☐ C-GALR	Bell 206B JetRanger III	1892	ex N100YB
☐ C-GALX	Bell 206B JetRanger	1046	ex N58096
☐ C-FALC	Bell 206L-1 LongRanger	45500	ex N104UC
☐ C-FJCH	Bell 206L-1 LongRanger	45737	ex N144JD
☐ C-GALH	Bell 206L-3 LongRanger III	51297	ex N753HL
☐ C-GALJ	Bell 206L-3 LongRanger III	51010	ex N22654
☐ C-GALL	Bell 206L-3 LongRanger III	51015	ex N22660
☐ C-GRLK	Bell 206L-3 LongRanger III	51028	ex N42814
☐ C-FAHB	Bell 212	30794	ex A6-BBH
☐ C-FAHC	Bell 212	31246	ex N212HT
☐ C-FAHG	Bell 212	30940	ex N8530F
☐ C-FAHK	Bell 212	30852	ex XA-SSE
☐ C-FAHL	Bell 212	30588	ex XA-SSJ
☐ C-FAHP	Bell 212	30933	ex D-HELL
☐ C-FAHR	Bell 212	30789	ex A6-BBI
☐ C-FAHZ	Bell 212	30562	ex XA-SSI
☐ C-FALK	Bell 212	30982	ex N212EL
☐ C-FALV	Bell 212	30816	ex N74AL
☐ C-GAHO	Bell 212	30937	
☐ C-GAHV	Bell 212	30699	ex N90221
☐ C-GALI	Bell 212	30525	ex JA9510
☐ C-GIRZ	Bell 212	30622	ex RP-C1677
☐ C-GRNR	Bell 212	30999	
☐ C-FAHI	Bell 407	53016	ex N409KA
☐ C-FALA	Bell 407	53115	
☐ C-FALF	Bell 407	53271	ex CC-CWS
☐ C-FALM	Bell 407	53018	ex N409KA
☐ C-FNOB	Bell 407	53070	ex N57416
☐ C-GALG	Bell 407	53059	ex N409PH
☐ C-GYAA	Bell 407	53152	ex N407RH

ALTA FLIGHTS	***Alta Flights (ALZ)***	***Edmonton-Intl/Calgary-Intl/Fort McMurray, AB (YEG/YYC/YMM)***		
☐ C-FAFE	Beech B100 King Air	BE-72	ex ZS-MZS	
☐ C-FAFI	Swearingen SA.227DC Metro 23	DC-868B	ex ZK-JSV	Freighter
☐ C-FAFS	Beech B100 King Air	BE-31	ex N80DB	
☐ C-FTNY	Piper PA-31-350 Chieftain	31-7952245	ex N2169X	
☐ C-FVVS	Piper PA-31-350 Chieftain	31-7952199	ex N35347	
☐ C-GAAF	Swearingen SA.227DC Metro 23	DC-891B	ex B-3956	
☐ C-GSAF	Swearingen SA.227DC Metro 23	DC-866B	ex B-3951	
☐ C-GGKJ	Beech B100 King Air	BE-49	ex N400RK	

AMIGO AIRWAYS				***Nanaimo-Harbour SPB, BC***
☐ C-GGGF	Beech D18S	CA-267	ex N1042H	Floatplane

ARCTIC SUNWEST CHARTERS				***Yellowknife, NT (YZF)***
☐ C-FASC	de Havilland DHC-8-102	038	ex C-GJUZ	
☐ C-FASN	Beech B100 King Air	BE-17	ex N178NC	
☐ C-FASQ	de Havilland DHC-6 Twin Otter 100	78	ex C-FAKM	Floatplane or wheels/skis
☐ C-FASV	de Havilland DHC-5A Buffalo	95A	ex 5Y-GBA	
☐ C-FASY	de Havilland DHC-5A Buffalo	107A	ex 5Y-GAA	
☐ C-FKCL	Piper PA-31-350 Navajo Chieftain	31-7752134	ex C-GJET	
☐ C-FOEV	de Havilland DHC-2 Turbo Beaver III	1680/TB48	ex CF-OEV	Floatplane or wheels/skis
☐ C-FOPE	de Havilland DHC-2 Turbo Beaver III	1691/TB59	ex CF-OPE	Floatplane or wheels/skis
☐ C-FSWN	Piper PA-31-350 Chieftain	31-7952182	ex C-GREP	
☐ C-FTFX	de Havilland DHC-6 Twin Otter 300	340	ex CF-TFX	Floatplane or wheels/skis
☐ C-FTXQ	de Havilland DHC-6 Twin Otter 300	308	ex N776A	Lsd fr FAB
☐ C-GARW	de Havilland DHC-6 Twin Otter 300	367	ex N200DA	Floatplane or wheels/skis
☐ C-GASB	de Havilland DHC-8-102	013	ex N802MX	
☐ C-GASW	Beech 99	U-39	ex N99LP	
☐ C-GOZG	Piper PA-32-300 Cherokee Six	32-7540034		
☐ C-GRTA	Eurocopter EC120B Colibri	1076		
☐ C-GSDJ	Cessna A185F Skywagon	18504212	ex N31079	Floatplane or wheels/skis

ATIKOKAN AERO SERVICE				***Atikokan-Municipal, ON (YIB)***
☐ CF-IPL	de Havilland DHC-2 Beaver	132		Floatplane or wheels/skis
☐ C-GDZH	de Havilland DHC-2 Beaver	356	ex 51-16555	Floatplane or wheels/skis

ATLEO RIVER AIR SERVICE				***Tofino, BC (YTP)***
☐ C-GIYQ	Cessna A185F Skywagon II	18503618	ex (N7582Q)	Floatplane or wheels/skis
☐ C-GYJX	Cessna A185F Skywagon	18503187	ex (N93161)	Floatplane

ATLIN AIR CHARTERS				***Atlin, BC***
☐ C-GGEK	Cessna 207A Stationair 8 II	20700731	ex N63AK	
☐ C-GOZR	de Havilland DHC-2 Beaver	800	ex 54-1670	

AVIABEC				***La Tuque SPB, QC (YLQ)***
☐ C-FMPT	de Havilland DHC-2 Beaver	1260	ex CF-MPT	Floatplane
☐ C-GSJO	Cessna U206G Stationair 6	U20606827	ex (N9276R)	Floatplane

AVIATION COMMERCIAL AVIATION		***Access (CMS)***		***Hearst, ON (YHF)***
☐ C-FGSX	Piper PA-31T-2 Cheyenne II XL	31T-8166048	ex N600XL	
☐ C-GBFO	Piper PA-31T-2 Cheyenne II XL	31T-8166069	ex N511SC	

AVIATION MAURICIE				***Lac à la Tortue/Lac Sept-Iles, QC***
☐ C-FASO	Cessna U206F Stationair	U20602081	ex N70558	Floatplane or wheels/skis
☐ C-FIDG	de Havilland DHC-2 Beaver	718	ex N99872	Floatplane or wheels/skis
☐ C-FVDG+	Cessna U206B Super Skywagon	U206-0666	ex CF-VDG	Floatplane or wheels/skis
☐ C-GOER	de Havilland DHC-2 Beaver	514	ex N99830	Floatplane or wheels/skis
☐ C-GYXE	Cessna U206F Stationair	U20603801		Floatplane or wheels/skis

BAILEY HELICOPTERS				***Boundary Bay, BC (YDT)***
☐ C-FBHC	Aérospatiale AS350B2 AStar	2850	ex C-FWCH	
☐ C-FBHD	Aérospatiale AS350BA AStar	2166	ex PT-HSE	
☐ C-FBHN	Aérospatiale AS350B2 AStar	3763		
☐ C-FBHX	Aérospatiale AS350BA AStar	2311	ex N787KR	
☐ C-GAVL	Aérospatiale AS350BA AStar	2258	ex N350AH	
☐ C-GKKH	Aérospatiale AS350B AStar	2008	ex JA9481	
☐ C-FBYD	Bell 206B JetRanger III	2519	ex N5008L	
☐ C-FCQD	Bell 206B JetRanger III	534	ex N8146J	
☐ C-FHTM	Bell 206B JetRanger	1017	ex CF-HTM	
☐ C-FHTR	Bell 206B JetRanger	1036	ex CF-HTR	

☐ C-FKOD	Bell 206B JetRanger	1228	ex CF-DOK
☐ C-FPRB	Bell 206B JetRanger III	3232	ex N20EA
☐ C-FZWC	Bell 206B JetRanger II	2064	ex N16706
☐ C-GAXB	Bell 206B JetRanger III	3527	ex N226EC
☐ C-GBHB	Bell 206B JetRanger III	2415	ex N5001U
☐ C-GDRH	Bell 206B JetRanger II	2452	ex N37EA
☐ C-GHHE	Bell 206B JetRanger III	1979	ex N9906K
☐ C-GJXB	Bell 206B JetRanger II	2208	ex N220CH
☐ C-GPGF	Bell 206B JetRanger	1836	
☐ C-GTEK	Bell 206B JetRanger III	1684	ex N222ML
☐ C-FBHV	Bell 206LR+ LongRanger	45113	ex N403EH
☐ C-FBHW	Bell 205A-1	30286	ex N224HT
☐ C-GNMD	Bell 206LR+ LongRanger	45080	

BAKERS NARROWS AIR SERVICE — Flin Flon Athapapuskow Lake SPB, MN

☐ C-FNMN	Cessna U206G Stationair	U20604070	ex N756GB	Floatplane or wheels/skis`

BAMAJI AIR — Sioux Lookout, ON (YXL)

☐ C-FHEP	de Havilland DHC-2 Beaver	69	ex C-FIOB	Floatplane or wheels/skis
☐ C-FKAC	Found FBA-2C1 Bush Hawk XP	42		Floatplane or wheels/skis
☐ C-GAJU	de Havilland DHC-2 Beaver	1169	ex 56-0415	Floatplane or wheels/skis
☐ C-GBKA	Cessna A185F Skywagon	18502375	ex N53099	Floatplane or wheels/skis
☐ C-GFDS	de Havilland DHC-2 Beaver	1269	ex 31343	Floatplane or wheels/skis
☐ C-GIPR	Cessna 208 Caravan I	20800343		Floatplane or wheels/skis
☐ C-GZBS	de Havilland DHC-2 Beaver	975	ex N4703Z	Floatplane or wheels/skis

BAR XH AIR — Palliser (BXH) — Medicine Hat, AB (YXH)

☐ C-FCGB	Beech 200 Super King Air	BB-24	ex N183MC	035	CatPass 200 conversion EMS
☐ C-GXHD	Beech 200 Super King Air	BB-1338	ex N915YW		Beech 1300 conversion
☐ C-GXHG	Beech 200 Super King Air	BB-1383	ex N913YW		Beech 1300 conversion
☐ C-GXHN	Beech 200 Super King Air	BB-693	ex N245JS		
☐ C-GXHR	Beech 200 Super King Air	BB-1305	ex 5Y-EOB		Beech 1300 conversion
☐ C-GXHS	Beech 200 Super King Air	BB-1302	ex PP-WYY		Beech 1300 conversion
☐ C-FBHO	Piper PA-31-350 Navajo Chieftain	31-7405466	ex N61439		
☐ C-GMDF	Piper PA-31T Cheyenne	31T-7620019	ex N82000		
☐ C-GXHK	Piper PA-31-350 Navajo Chieftain	31-7752108	ex N115SC		

BC YUKON AIR SERVICE — Dease Lake, BC (YDL)

☐ C-FHGZ	de Havilland DHC-2 Beaver	759	ex CF-HGZ	Floatplane or wheels/skis

BEARSKIN AIRLINES — Bearskin (JV/BLS) — Sioux Lookout, ON (YXL)

☐ C-FAMC	Swearingen SA.227AC Metro III	AC-719B	ex N436MA		
☐ C-FFZN	Swearingen SA.227AC Metro III	AC-785B	ex N30019	Spirit of Service	
☐ C-FXUS	Swearingen SA.227CC Metro 23	CC-841B	ex N456LA		
☐ C-FYAC	Swearingen SA.227AC Metro III	AC-670B	ex N670VG	Spirit of Fort Frances	
☐ C-FYWG	Swearingen SA.227AC Metro III	AC-782B	ex N3000S	Spirit of Winnipeg	
☐ C-GAFQ	Swearingen SA.227DC Metro 23	DC-890B	ex N211SA		
☐ C-GJVB	Swearingen SA.227DC Metro 23	DC-902B	ex N902WB		
☐ C-GJVC	Swearingen SA.227DC Metro 23	DC-885B	ex N885ML		
☐ C-GJVH	Swearingen SA.227DC Metro 23	DC-898B	ex N898ML		
☐ C-GYHD	Swearingen SA.227AC Metro III	AC-739B	ex N227JH	Spirit of Dryden	
☐ C-GYQT	Swearingen SA.227AC Metro III	AC-644B	ex N644VG	Spirit of Thunder Bay	
☐ C-GYRL	Swearingen SA.227AC Metro III	AC-706B	ex G-BUKA		
☐ C-GYTL	Swearingen SA.227CC Metro 23	CC-829B	ex N30154	Spirit of Big Trout Lake	
☐ C-GYXL	Swearingen SA.227AC Metro III	AC-725B	ex N227FA		
☐ C-GEHY	Piper PA-23-250 Aztec C	27-3843	ex N6548Y		
☐ C-GFVY	Cessna A185F Skywagon	18503056	ex (N21379)		Floatplane or wheels/skis

BIG RIVER AIR — Fort Smith, NT/Yellowknife, NT (YSM/YZF)

☐ C-FDGW	Cessna 208 Caravan I	20800272	ex C-FCPW	
☐ C-FVVY	de Havilland DHC-3 Otter	410	ex RCAF 9427	Floatplane or wheels/skis
☐ C-GFZT	Cessna U206F Stationair II	U20603406	ex (N8550Q)	Floatplane or wheels/skis
☐ C-GJEM	Cessna 208 Caravan	20800152	ex N9728F	Floatplane or wheels
☐ C-GSMA	Cessna 310Q	310Q1008	ex N313SK	

BIG SALMON AIR — Whitehorse, YT (YXY)

☐ C-FZNL	Cessna A185E Skywagon	18501826	ex (N1602M)	Floatplane or wheels/skis
☐ C-GJSR	Cessna U206C Super Skywagon	U206-1106	ex N29136	Floatplane or wheels/skis
☐ C-GUAL	Cessna 207A Stationair 8	20700733	ex (N9806M)	Floatplane or wheels/skis

BLACK SHEEP AVIATION — Whitehorse, YT (YXY)

Reg	Type	c/n	Previous identity	Remarks
☐ C-GDJW	de Havilland DHC-3 Otter	10	ex C-FGTL	Floatplane or wheels/skis
☐ C-GMCW	de Havilland DHC-3 Otter	108	ex N5339G	Floatplane or wheels/skis
☐ C-GZTQ	Cessna A185F Skywagon II	18503491	ex (N1824Q)	Floatplane or wheels/skis

BLACK TUSK HELICOPTER — Squamish, BC (YSE)

Reg	Type	c/n	Previous identity
☐ C-FSAI	Aérospatiale AS350B2 AStar	2176	ex N121KR
☐ C-FWQU	Bell 214B-1	28029	ex N3999N
☐ C-FZVT	Bell 214B-1	28016	ex LN-OSG
☐ C-GLOG	Bell 206B JetRanger III	3186	ex N801H
☐ C-GSEE	Bell 206B JetRanger	451	ex N95SB

BLACKCOMB HELICOPTERS — Whistler Heliport, BC

Reg	Type	c/n	Previous identity
☐ C-FHRX	Cessna A185F Skywagon	18502185	ex CF-HRX
☐ C-FKKM	Bell 206B JetRanger II	883	ex N14854
☐ C-FXBC	Aérospatiale AS355F2 Twin Star	5274	ex C-FDNW
☐ C-GJPN	Aérospatiale AS350B2 AStar	4473	
☐ C-GJTH	Bell 205A-1	30036	ex PK-UHC
☐ C-GPGP	Bell 206B JetRanger	2244	
☐ C-GSKI	Aérospatiale AS350B2 AStar	3377	ex C-GILU
☐ C-GSRF	Aérospatiale AS350B2 AStar	2480	ex C-FLHA
☐ C-GYYR	Aérospatiale AS350BA AStar	1675	ex ZK-HBT

BLUE WATER AVIATION SERVICES — Silver Falls, MB

Reg	Type	c/n	Previous identity	Remarks
☐ C-FCUW	Cessna 337 Super Skymaster	337-0009	ex N2109X	
☐ C-GBTU	de Havilland DHC-3 Turbo Otter	209	ex IM-1711	Floatplane or wheels/skis
☐ C-GFVZ	Cessna A185F Skywagon	18503058	ex (N21451)	Floatplane or wheels/skis
☐ C-GGGD	Cessna TU206G Stationair 8	U20605664	ex (N5348X)	Floatplane or wheels/skis
☐ C-GHYB	de Havilland DHC-3 Otter	386	ex UB656	Floatplane or wheels/skis

BOLTON LAKE AIR SERVICES — Winnipeg-St Andrews, MB(YAV)

Reg	Type	c/n	Previous identity	Remarks
☐ C-GYXM	Cessna A185E Skywagon	185-1171	ex N4717Q	Floatplane

BRUCELANDAIR INTERNATIONAL — Wiarton, ON (YVV)

Reg	Type	c/n	Previous identity	Remarks
☐ C-FDME	Piper PA-31 Navajo C	31-7812107	ex N21PJ	
☐ C-GBTS	Socata TBM-700	19	ex N635DS	
☐ C-GGNA	Piper PA-23-250 Aztec C	27-3757	ex N6463Y	
☐ C-GPVN	Piper PA-31 Turbo Navajo B	31-7400979	ex TF-EGT	Photo/Survey

BUFFALO AIRWAYS — Buffalo (J4/BFL) — Hay River, NT/Yellowknife (YHY/YZF)

Reg	Type	c/n	Previous identity	Fleet no/Name	Remarks
☐ C-GBPD	Canadair CL-215-1A10 (CL-215)	1084		291	Op for NWT Govt
☐ C-GBYU	Canadair CL-215-1A10 (CL-215)	1083	ex C-GKEA	290	Op for NWT Govt
☐ C-GCSX	Canadair CL-215-1A10 (CL-215)	1088	ex c-GKEA	295	Op for NWT Govt
☐ C-GDHN	Canadair CL-215-1A10 (CL-215)	1089	ex C-GKEE	296	Op for NWT Govt
☐ C-FCUE	Douglas DC-3	12983	ex NC41407		
☐ C-FDTB	Douglas DC-3	12597	ex CF-TEC		stored YQF
☐ C-FDTH	Douglas DC-3	12591	ex CF-TEB		stored YQF
☐ C-FFAY	Douglas DC-3	4785	ex CF-FAY		stored YQF
☐ C-FLFR	Douglas DC-3	13155	ex CF-LFR		
☐ C-FROD	Douglas DC-3	13028	ex C-GPNW		
☐ C-GJKM	Douglas DC-3	13580	ex CAF 12946		
☐ C-GPNR	Douglas DC-3	13333	ex CAF 12932		
☐ C-GWIR	Douglas DC-3	9371	ex N18262		
☐ C-GWZS	Douglas DC-3	12327	ex CAF 12913		
☐ CF-BAA	Douglas C-54D-DC	10653	ex N4994H		
☐ C-FBAJ	Douglas C-54A-DC	3088	ex N11712	02	Tanker
☐ C-FBAK	Douglas C-54D-DC	10613	ex N62342		
☐ C-FBAM	Douglas C-54G-DC	36009	ex N4958M		
☐ C-FBAP	Douglas C-54A-DC	36089	ex N2742G		Tanker
☐ C-FIQM	Douglas C-54G-DC	36088	ex N4218S	57 Arctic Trader	Tanker
☐ C-GBAJ	Douglas C-54A-DC	27328	ex N62297		Tanker
☐ C-GBNV	Douglas C-54G-DC	35988	ex N3303F	56	Tanker
☐ C-GBPA	Douglas C-54D-DC	10673	ex N87591		
☐ C-GCTF	Douglas C-54E-DC	27281	ex N51819	58	Tanker
☐ C-GPSH	Douglas C-54A-DC	7458	ex N7171H	1 Arctic Distributor	
☐ C-GQIC	Douglas C-54E-DC	27343	ex N9756H		
☐ C-FAVO	Curtiss C-46D Commando	33242	ex N9891Z	Arctic Thunder	
☐ C-FBAQ	Lockheed L-188AF Electra	1039	ex OE-ILB		stored
☐ C-FCGE	Beech 65-A90 King Air	LJ-118	ex CF-CGE	Birddog 1	
☐ C-FCGH	Beech 65-A90 King Air	LJ-203	ex CF-CGH	Birddog 4	
☐ C-FNJE	Consolidated PBY-5A Catalina	CV-437	ex CF-NJE		

	Reg	Type	c/n	Previous identity	Fleet no	Remarks
☐	C-FPQM	Consolidated PBY-5A Catalina	CV-425	ex CF-GMS	714	
☐	CF-SAN	Noorduyn Norseman V	N29-29	ex CF-SAN		Floatplane
☐	C-FUAW	Consolidated PBY-5A Catalina	CV-201	ex (CF-NTK)	708	
☐	C-FULX	Beech 95-C55 Baron	TE-147	ex CF-ULX	Birddog 3	
☐	C-FUPT	Cessna A185E Skywagon	185-1075	ex (N4568F)	141	
☐	C-GBAU	Beech 95-D55 Baron	TE-701	ex N7907R		
☐	C-GIWJ	Beech 95 Travel Air	TD-32	ex N2707Y		
☐	C-GLDA	Lockheed L-100AF Electra	1145	ex OE-ILA		
☐	C-GTFC	Consolidated Vultee	279	ex N152PA		
☐	C-GTXW	Curtiss C-46A Commando	30386	ex 5Y-TXW		stored YZF
☐	C-GWCB	Beech B95 Travel Air	TD-369	ex N9914R		
☐	C-GYFM	Beech 95 Travel Air	TD-202	ex N654Q		

BUSHLAND AIRWAYS — *Moosonee, ON (YMO)*

	Reg	Type	c/n	Previous identity	Remarks
☐	C-FBGB	Cessna U206E Super Skywagon	U20601514	ex (N9114M)	Floatplane
☐	C-FYJR	Cessna A185E Skywagon	185-1520	ex (N2770J)	Floatplane
☐	C-GSNU	Cessna 207A Stationair 7	20700491	ex N6DF	
☐	C-GYWE	Piper PA-32-260 Cherokee Six	32-141	ex N3305W	

CALM AIR — *Calm Air (MO/CAV)* — *Thompson, MB (YTH)*

	Reg	Type	c/n	Previous identity	Fleet no	Remarks
☐	C-FCIJ	ATR 42-300	139	ex ZS-OSN		
☐	C-FJYV	ATR 42-300	216	ex N216AT	421	
☐	C-FJYW	ATR 42-300	235	ex N233RM	422	
☐	C-FMAK	ATR 42-300	142	ex N142GP		
☐	C-FULE	ATR 72-212	215	ex F-WNUE		
☐	C-FSKS	Cessna 208B Caravan I	208B0722	ex N5268M		
☐	C-GKRM	Cessna 208B Caravan I	208B0660	ex N73MM		
☐	C-FAMO	Hawker Siddeley HS.748 Srs.2A/258LFD	1669	ex CF-AMO	746	Freighter
☐	C-GDOP	Hawker Siddeley HS.748 Srs.2A/283	1745	ex F-ODQQ	744	stored YTH
☐	C-GEPB	Hawker Siddeley HS.748 Srs.2A/254	1686	ex 9G-ABX	743	stored YTH
☐	C-GHSC	Hawker Siddeley HS.748 Srs.2B/FAALFD	1790	ex G-BJTL	745	Freighter
☐	C-GSBF	Hawker Siddeley HS.748 Srs.2A/210	1662	ex G-BCDZ		
☐	C-FSPB	SAAB SF.340B	340B-351	ex B-3656	345	
☐	C-FTJV	SAAB SF.340B	340B-366	ex SE-C66	341	Combi
☐	C-FTJW	SAAB SF.340B	340B-377	ex SE-C77	342	Combi
☐	C-FTLW	SAAB SF.340B	340B-336	ex SE-C36	346	
☐	C-GMNM	SAAB SF.340B	340B-364	ex SE-LHO	344	
☐	C-GTJY	SAAB SF.340B	340B-166	ex N587MA	343	

CAMERON AIR SERVICE — *Toronto-City Centre, ON (YTZ)*

	Reg	Type	c/n	Previous identity
☐	C-FKCA	Cessna 208 Caravan I	20800211	ex N211PA
☐	C-FXWH	Cessna U206C Super Skywagon	U206-1170	ex CF-XWH
☐	C-GCGA	Cessna 208 Caravan I	20800242	ex (A6-CGA)
☐	C-GGSG	Cessna TU206G Stationair 6	U20605852	ex (N6281X)

CAMPBELL HELICOPTERS — *Abbotsford, BC (YXX)*

	Reg	Type	c/n	Previous identity
☐	C-FBEP	Bell 212	30746	ex 4X-BJN
☐	C-FJUR	Bell 212	30728	ex N8233V
☐	C-FJUT	Bell 212	30808	ex N8233V
☐	C-FJUU	Bell 212	30795	ex N8233V
☐	C-FMPZ	Bell 212	30528	ex HC-BOI
☐	C-GCVP	Bell 212	30542	ex G-BALZ
☐	C-GFDV	Bell 212	30842	ex N291B
☐	C-GFQN	Bell 212	30571	ex N554CR

CANADIAN AIR CRANE — *Delta, BC (DJN)*

	Reg	Type	c/n	Previous identity	Fleet no
☐	C-FCRN	Erickson/Sikorsky S-64E Skycrane	64061	ex N172AC	747
☐	C-GJZK	Erickson/Sikorsky S-64E Skycrane	64003	ex N176AC	

CANADIAN HELICOPTERS — *Canadian (CDN)* — *Montreal-Les Cedres, QC /Edmonton, AB*

	Reg	Type	c/n	Previous identity
☐	C-FCCA	Aérospatiale AS350BA AStar	2900	
☐	C-FCHN	Aérospatiale AS350BA AStar	2921	
☐	C-FETA	Aérospatiale AS350D AStar	1085	ex N137BH
☐	C-FFBU	Aérospatiale AS350BA AStar	1216	ex N3606B
☐	C-FHVH	Aérospatiale AS350BA AStar	1256	ex N36075
☐	C-FPBA	Aérospatiale AS350B2 AStar	2492	ex JA6091
☐	C-FPER	Aérospatiale AS350BA AStar	2552	ex F-WYMK
☐	C-FPLJ	Aérospatiale AS350D AStar	1060	ex C-FQNS
☐	C-FQNS	Aérospatiale AS350B2 AStar	1423	ex N5783Y
☐	C-FSHV	Aérospatiale AS350B AStar	1287	ex N5143R
☐	C-FSLB	Aérospatiale AS350B AStar	2142	ex JA9786
☐	C-FVVH	Aérospatiale AS350BA AStar	2612	
☐	C-FYCO	Aérospatiale AS350BA AStar	2899	

☐ C-GAHH	Aérospatiale AS350B AStar	1036	ex XA-...
☐ C-GAHI	Aérospatiale AS350B2 AStar	1086	
☐ C-GALD	Aérospatiale AS350BA AStar	1146	
☐ C-GALE	Aérospatiale AS350B AStar	1350	
☐ C-GATX	Aérospatiale AS350BA AStar	1221	
☐ C-GAYX	Aérospatiale AS350BA AStar	1179	
☐ C-GBCZ	Aérospatiale AS350B2 AStar	1159	ex N3600W
☐ C-GBPS	Aérospatiale AS350BA AStar	1277	ex N3610R
☐ C-GCEC	Aérospatiale AS350B AStar	1431	ex N666JK
☐ C-GCHH	Aérospatiale AS350B-2 AStar	2461	ex ZK-HND
☐ C-GCKP	Aérospatiale AS350D AStar	1138	ex N140BH
☐ C-GCWD	Aérospatiale AS350BA AStar	2047	ex N844BP
☐ C-GCWW	Aérospatiale AS350B2 AStar	1435	ex N340DF
☐ C-GDKD	Aérospatiale AS350BA AStar	1432	ex N5785H
☐ C-GDSX	Aérospatiale AS350BA AStar	1134	ex N35972
☐ C-GDUF	Aérospatiale AS350BA AStar	1309	
☐ C-GELC	Aérospatiale AS350B AStar	1162	ex VH-HRD
☐ C-GEPH	Aérospatiale AS350BA AStar	1193	ex ZK-HET
☐ C-GEVH	Aérospatiale AS350BA AStar	2620	ex F-WYMN
☐ C-GFHS	Aérospatiale AS350B AStar	1401	
☐ C-GGIE	Aérospatiale AS350B2 AStar	3280	
☐ C-GHVD	Aérospatiale AS350BA AStar	1236	ex N3606Y
☐ C-GLNE	Aérospatiale AS350BA AStar	1128	ex N3599N
☐ C-GLNK	Aérospatiale AS350D AStar	1261	ex N3608C
☐ C-GLNM	Aérospatiale AS350D AStar	1262	ex N3608D
☐ C-GLNO	Aérospatiale AS350D AStar	1264	ex N3608N
☐ C-GMEY	Aérospatiale AS350B AStar	1004	ex N350AS
☐ C-GMIZ	Aérospatiale AS350D AStar	1170	
☐ C-GNMN	Aérospatiale AS350BA AStar	1315	ex XA-SNA
☐ C-GOVH	Aérospatiale AS350BA AStar	1286	ex N224GA
☐ C-GRBT	Aérospatiale AS350D AStar	1246	ex N877JM
☐ C-GRGJ	Aérospatiale AS350B AStar	1171	ex N3600G
☐ C-GRGU	Aérospatiale AS350BA AStar	1213	ex N7172H
☐ C-GSLF	Aérospatiale AS350D AStar	1310	
☐ C-GTPF	Aérospatiale AS350BA AStar	2932	
☐ C-GTVH	Aérospatiale AS350BA AStar	2611	ex N600CH
☐ C-GVHC	Aérospatiale AS355F2 Twin Star	5195	ex N5801T
☐ C-GVHK	Aérospatiale AS355F1 Twin Star	5098	ex N60031
☐ C-FAHW	Bell 206B JetRanger II	785	ex CF-AHW
☐ C-FAJR	Bell 206B JetRanger II	123	ex CF-AJR
☐ C-FBQH	Bell 206B JetRanger II	745	ex CF-BQH
☐ C-FCQE	Bell 206B JetRanger II	535	ex N8147J
☐ C-FFVC	Bell 206B JetRanger II	934	ex CF-FVC
☐ C-FHTP	Bell 206B JetRanger II	1024	ex CF-HTP
☐ C-FHTS	Bell 206B JetRanger II	1037	ex CF-HTS
☐ C-FKNX	Bell 206B JetRanger III	2440	ex N5003X
☐ C-FOAN	Bell 206B JetRanger II	791	ex CF-OAN
☐ C-FPOD	Bell 206B JetRanger II	696	ex CF-POD
☐ C-GAHC	Bell 206B JetRanger II	468	ex N2959W
☐ C-GAHR	Bell 206B JetRanger II	873	ex N1488B
☐ C-GBHE	Bell 206B JetRanger II	1335	
☐ C-GBHI	Bell 206B JetRanger III	1758	ex N49584
☐ C-GCIR	Bell 206B JetRanger III	3029	
☐ C-GDBA	Bell 206B JetRanger III	2232	ex N16821
☐ C-GETF	Bell 206B JetRanger III	3036	
☐ C-GFQH	Bell 206B JetRanger II	1090	ex N100JG
☐ C-GHUQ	Bell 206B JetRanger II	1721	ex N3199G
☐ C-GIFY	Bell 206B JetRanger II	2008	
☐ C-GIXS	Bell 206B JetRanger III	2304	ex N272RM
☐ C-GMKT	Bell 206B JetRanger II	774	ex N101PN
☐ C-GNLD	Bell 206B JetRanger III	2357	ex N57PH
☐ C-GNLE	Bell 206B JetRanger III	2358	ex N56PH
☐ C-GNLG	Bell 206B JetRanger III	2360	
☐ C-GNPH	Bell 206B JetRanger III	2352	ex N58148
☐ C-GOKE	Bell 206B JetRanger III	1830	ex N49655
☐ C-GRGN	Bell 206B JetRanger II	1824	ex N333WW
☐ C-GSHP	Bell 206B JetRanger II	1259	ex N259CH
☐ C-GXHC	Bell 206B JetRanger II	395	ex N28956
☐ C-GYQH	Bell 206B JetRanger III	1394	ex N111BH
☐ C-GZQH	Bell 206B JetRanger II	1055	ex N58148
☐ C-FNYQ	Bell 206L LongRanger	45047	ex N20LT
☐ C-GGZQ	Bell 206L LongRanger	45006	ex N49637
☐ C-GLMV	Bell 206L-1 LongRanger II	45430	ex N454CH
☐ C-GLQY	Bell 206L LongRanger	45146	
☐ C-GMHS	Bell 206L LongRanger	45120	
☐ C-GMHT	Bell 206L LongRanger	45127	ex N16847
☐ C-GMHY	Bell 206L LongRanger	45145	ex N16924
☐ C-GNLC	Bell 206L LongRanger	45055	ex N9978K
☐ C-GNLK	Bell 206L LongRanger	46601	ex N16939
☐ C-GNMC	Bell 206L LongRanger	45067	

Reg	Type	C/n	Previous identity	Notes
☐ C-GNZR	Bell 206L LongRanger	45118	ex N16809	
☐ C-GQEZ	Bell 206L LongRanger	45038	ex N9942K	
☐ C-GTLB	Bell 206L LongRanger	45031	ex N9927K	
☐ C-GTOM	Bell 206L LongRanger	45010		
☐ C-GVHX	Bell 206L LongRanger	45138	ex N90AC	
☐ C-FBHF	Bell 212	30509	ex N7072J	
☐ C-FCAD	Bell 212	30923	ex HC-CFF	
☐ C-FNJJ	Bell 212	30944	ex N2093S	
☐ C-FOKV	Bell 212	30819	ex N16787	
☐ C-GAHD	Bell 212	30570	ex N7034J	
☐ C-GFQP	Bell 212	30578	ex N58120	
☐ C-GHVH	Bell 212	30877	ex N8555V	
☐ C-GICH	Bell 212	30950	ex N507EH	
☐ C-GKCH	Bell 212	31213	ex N360EH	
☐ C-GNCH	Bell 212	31113	ex N510EH	
☐ C-GOKG	Bell 212	30843		
☐ C-GOKL	Bell 212	30597	ex N2990W	
☐ C-GOKX	Bell 212	30680	ex VH-LHX	
☐ C-GOKY	Bell 212	30698	ex (5H-)	
☐ C-FFAB	Eurocopter EC120B	1486		
☐ C-FLCN	Eurocopter EC120B	1055		
☐ C-FOCH	Eurocopter EC120B	1547		
☐ C-FDCH	Sikorsky S-61N	61773	ex ZS-PWR	
☐ C-FIBN	Sikorsky S-61N	61811	ex PT-HPV	
☐ C-GIMN	Sikorsky S-76A	760110	ex G-BIAV	EMS
☐ C-GIMR	Sikorsky S-76A	760079	ex G-BHYB	
☐ C-GLFO	Sikorsky S-76A	760149	ex N76LA	

CANADIAN NORTH — *Norterra (5T/ANX)* — *Yellowknife, NT (YZF)*

Reg	Type	C/n	Previous identity	Notes
☐ C-GCNO	Boeing 737-25A	23790/1422	ex N790CC	
☐ C-GCNS	Boeing 737-275	23283/1109	ex C9-BAN	
☐ C-GCNV	Boeing 737-232	23074/993	ex N302DL	586
☐ C-GDPA	Boeing 737-2T2C (AvAero 3)	22056/655		584 Spirit of Yellowknife
☐ C-GFPW	Boeing 737-275C (AvAero 3)	21294/481		552
☐ C-GKCP	Boeing 737-217 (AvAero 3)	22729/915		523
☐ C-GNDU	Boeing 737-242C (AvAero 3)	22877/880		562
☐ C-GOPW	Boeing 737-275C (AvAero 3)	22160/688	ex N8288V	582 Spirit of Nunavut
☐ C-GSPW	Boeing 737-275C (AvAero 3)	22618/813		583
☐ C-FTAY	Fokker F.28 Fellowship 1000	11084	ex VH-ATG	158
☐ C-GECN	de Havilland DHC-8-106	324	ex C-FSQY	
☐ C-GRGI	de Havilland DHC-8-106	304	ex N829PH	
☐ C-GRGO	de Havilland DHC-8-102	258	ex N735AG	
☐ C-GXCN	de Havilland DHC-8-102	345	ex RA-67255	

CANJET — *Canjet (C6/CJA)* — *Halifax-Intl, NS (YHZ)*

Reg	Type	C/n	Previous identity	Notes
☐ C-FTCX	Boeing 737-8AS/W	29921/560	ex EI-CSF	801
☐ C-FTCZ	Boeing 737-8AS/W	29923/576	ex EI-CSH	802
☐ C-FXGG	Boeing 737-81Q/W	29051/479	ex N290AN	
☐ C-FYQN	Boeing 737-8AS/W	29933/1038	ex EI-CST	
☐ C-FYQO	Boeing 737-8AS/W	29934/1050	ex EI-CSV	

CAN-WEST CORPORATE AIR CHARTER — *Slave Lake, AB (YZH)*

Reg	Type	C/n	Previous identity
☐ C-FCWW	Piper PA-31-350 Chieftain	31-8152192	ex N4097L
☐ C-FKCW	Beech 200 Super King Air	BB-973	ex C-FEVC
☐ C-FOOS	Cessna U206E Stationair	U20601698	ex (N9498G)
☐ C-FSAO	Beech 200 Super King Air	BB-1610	ex N713TA
☐ C-FSAT	Beech 200 Super King Air	BB-1526	ex N417MC
☐ C-GAYZ	Cessna A185F Skywagon	18504040	ex (N6416E)
☐ C-GKOX	Beech 200 Super King Air	BB-389	ex C-GKOS
☐ C-GLGD	Cessna U206G Stationair 6	U20606261	ex (N6388Z)
☐ C-GNCW	Beech Baron 58	TH-1313	ex N6138C
☐ C-GSAZ	Piper PA-31 Navajo C	31-8112063	ex N4094Y
☐ C-GXNL	Cessna 210L Centurion II	21060909	ex N5327V
☐ C-GYDD	Cessna A185F Skywagon	18503124	ex (N80516)

CARAVAN AIRLINES — *Lloydminster, AD (YLL)*

Reg	Type	C/n	Previous identity	Notes
☐ C-GBIT	Cessna 208 Caravan I	20800135	ex N9706F	Floatplane or wheels

CARGAIR — *Ste Michel-des-Saints/Montreal-St.Hubert, QC (-/YHU)*

Reg	Type	C/n	Previous identity
☐ C-FDMP	Piper PA-23-250 Aztec C	27-3560	ex N6306Y
☐ C-FGQA	de Havilland DHC-2 Beaver	72	ex CF-GQA
☐ C-FTSJ	Piper PA-23-250 Aztec D	27-4387	ex N9652N

☐ C-GMRG	Piper PA-31 Navajo C	31-7812051	ex N27563	
☐ C-GSYH	Piper PA-23-250 Aztec D	27-4214	ex N28EA	

CARGOJET AIRWAYS — Cargojet (W8/CJT) — Winnipeg-Intl, MB/Toronto-Pearson Intl, QC (YWG/YYZ)

☐ C-FCJF	Boeing 727-223F (FedEx 3)	22011/1653	ex C-GACG	
☐ C-FCJI	Boeing 727-225F (FedEx 3)	22435/1674	ex N804MA	stored YHM
☐ C-FCJP	Boeing 727-223F (FedEx 3)	22012/1655	ex C-FUAC	
☐ C-FCJU	Boeing 727-260F (FedEx 3)	22759/1789	ex C-FACM	
☐ C-GCJB	Boeing 727-225F (FedEx 3)	21855/1535	ex N886MA	Lsd fr Flagship Intl
☐ C-GCJD	Boeing 727-231F (FedEx 3)	21988/1586	ex N808MA	Lsd fr Flagship Intl
☐ C-GCJN	Boeing 727-225F (FedEx 3)	21451/1310	ex N610PA	
☐ C-GCJQ	Boeing 727-225F (FedEx 3)	22437/1682	ex N806MA	Lsd fr Flagship Intl
☐ C-GCJY	Boeing 727-223F/W (Duganair 3)	22460/1746	ex N702NE	
☐ C-GCJZ	Boeing 727-225F (FedEx 3)	21854/1532	ex N889MA	
☐ C-GUJC	Boeing 727-260F (FedEx 3)	21979/1534	ex C-FACJ	
☐ C-FKCJ	Boeing 757-236F	24792/279	ex SE-DUO	
☐ C-FGAJ	Boeing 767-223F	22319/112	ex N317AA	
☐ C-FMCJ	Boeing 767-223F	22316/95	ex N313AA	

CARSON AIR — Kelowna, BC (YLW)

☐ C-FAFR	Swearingen SA.227AC Metro III	AC-684	ex N585MA		
☐ C-FBWQ	Swearingen SA.226TC Metro II	TC-379	ex N1011U		
☐ C-FCAW	Swearingen SA.26AT Merlin IIB	T26-172E	ex N135SR		
☐ C-FJKK	Swearingen SA.227AC Metro III	AC-713B	ex N2719H		
☐ C-FKKR	Swearingen SA.226TC Metro II	TC-308	ex N300GL		
☐ C-FTJC	Swearingen SA.226TC Metro II	TC-274	ex N7774H		
☐ C-FTSK	Swearingen SA.227AC Metro III	AC-674B	ex C-FAFM		Freighter
☐ C-GAMI	Swearingen SA.227AC Metro III	AC-587	ex N3115T		
☐ C-GCAU	Swearingen SA.226TC Metro II	TC-331E	ex N255AM		Freighter
☐ C-GCAW	Swearingen SA.226TC Metro II	TC-358	ex N1009R	no titles	
☐ C-GDLK	Swearingen SA.226TC Metro II	TC-302	ex N151SA		
☐ C-GKKC	Swearingen SA.226TC Metro II	TC-370	ex N125AV		
☐ C-GKLJ	Swearingen SA.226TC Metro II	TC-380	ex C-GMET		
☐ C-GKLN	Swearingen SA.226TC Metro II	TC-253	ex N328BA		
☐ C-GLSC	Swearingen SA.226TC Metro II	TC-325	ex N162SW		
☐ C-GSKC	Swearingen SA.226TC Metro II	TC-235	ex N235BA		
☐ C-FAFF	Beech B300 Super King Air	FL-112	ex N405J		
☐ C-FCAV	Piper PA-42 Cheyenne III	42-8001006	ex N131RC		
☐ C-FRLD	Beech B300 Super King Air	FL-33	ex N15WS		
☐ C-FVKC	Beech B300 Super King Air	FL-273	ex OY-JVL		
☐ C-FWPR	Beech B300 Super King Air	FL-125	ex N32KC		
☐ C-GJLK	Beech B300 Super King Air	FL-13	ex C-FWXR		EMS, for BC Ambulance Service

CC HELICOPTERS — Chilcotin (DES) — Lillooet, BC

☐ C-FGYQ	Bell 206B JetRanger III	1357	ex CF-GYQ
☐ C-FHTQ	Bell 206B JetRanger III	1030	ex CF-HTQ
☐ C-FUNF	Bell 407	53225	ex N80709
☐ C-FWCE	Bell 206L-1 LongRanger	45172	ex C-FHNN
☐ C-GPIH	Bell 407	53426	ex N407WS
☐ C-GSQM	Bell 212	31160	ex VH-LHL
☐ C-GTRH	Bell 212	30778	ex N9937K
☐ C-GWCF	Bell 206L-1 LongRanger	45448	ex N31LA

CENTRAL FLYWAY AIR — Thompson, MB (YTH)

☐ C-FBJA	Beech 95-B55 Baron	TC-71	ex N1238Z	
☐ C-FJOF	de Havilland DHC-2 Beaver	1053	ex CF-JOF	Floatplane
☐ C-FPEN	de Havilland DHC-3 Otter	439	ex CF-PEN	Floatplane
☐ C-FRHW	de Havilland DHC-3 Otter	445	ex 5N-ABN	Floatplane
☐ C-GICM	Beech 95-C55 Baron	TE-64	ex N171M	
☐ C-GYOK	de Havilland DHC-2 Beaver	677	ex N5152G	Floatplane

CENTRAL MOUNTAIN AIR — Glacier (9M/GLR) — Smithers, BC (YYD)

☐ C-FCMB	Beech 1900D	UE-278		916	
☐ C-FCME	Beech 1900D	UE-277		915	
☐ C-FCMN	Beech 1900D	UE-276		914	
☐ C-FCMO	Beech 1900D	UE-281		917	
☐ C-FCMP	Beech 1900D	UE-271	ex N11037	912	
☐ C-FCMR	Beech 1900D	UE-283	ex N21872	918	
☐ C-FCMU	Beech 1900D	UE-285		919	
☐ C-FCMV	Beech 1900D	UE-272	ex N11079	913	
☐ C-FDTR	Beech 1900D	UE-76	ex N76ZV		
☐ C-GCMA	Beech 1900D	UE-289		920	
☐ C-GCML	Beech 1900D	UE-243	ex N10879	925	
☐ C-GCMY	Beech 1900D	UE-287		921	Lsd to NTA
☐ C-GFSV	Beech 1900D	UE-346	ex N23424	922	

☐ C-GGBY	Beech 1900D	UE-351	ex N23517	923
☐ C-GGCA	Beech 1900D	UE-359	ex N31559	924
☐ C-FDYN	Dornier 328-110	3096	ex D-CMUC	
☐ C-FGQN	de Havilland DHC-2 Beaver	96		
☐ C-GWRN	Piper PA-31 Navajo Chieftain	31-7852062		

CHC HELICOPTERS INTERNATIONAL — Vancouver-International, BC (YVR)

☐ C-FYPO	Aérospatiale AS.332L	2077	ex LN-OMK	
☐ C-FYZD	Aérospatiale AS.332L	2007	ex OY-HEO	
☐ C-GOSA	Aérospatiale AS.332L	9008	ex F-WQEG	
☐ C-GOSE	Aérospatiale AS.332L	2048	ex C-GTCH	
☐ C-GOSI	Aérospatiale AS.332L	2074	ex C-GVCH	
☐ C-FYQC	Aérospatiale SA365N Dauphin 2	6419	ex 5N-BJF	
☐ C-FYRC	Aérospatiale SA365N Dauphin 3	6740	ex 5N-BJP	
☐ C-FRWF	Bell 212	30894	ex ZS-RXB	
☐ C-FUBW	Sikorsky S-61N	61764	ex OY-HGZ	
☐ PR-MEX	Sikorsky S-61N	61753	ex PH-NZG	
☐ C-	Sikorsky S-76A++	760032	ex HS-HTR	
☐ C-	Sikorsky S-76A++	760148	ex HS-HTI	
☐ C-FGDO	Sikorsky S-76C+	760602	ex 5N-BIV	
☐ C-FRHM	Sikorsky S-76C++	760689	ex N25042	
☐ C-FRSA	Sikorsky S-76C++	760691	ex 9M-AIS	
☐ C-FUVS	Sikorsky S-76C+	760547	ex ZS-RRX	
☐ C-FUVU	Sikorsky S-76C+	760548	ex ZS-RRY	
☐ C-FXXV	Sikorsky S-76C+	760468	ex 5N-BGN	
☐ C-FZSZ	Sikorsky S-76C++	760731	ex N781X	
☐ C-FZUT	Sikorsky S-76C++	760764	ex N764L	
☐ C-FZUY	Sikorsky S-76C++	760765	ex N765L	
☐ C-GBVZ	Sikorsky S-76A+	760183	ex G-BVCX	
☐ C-GBWC	Sikorsky S-76A+	760201	ex G-DRNT	
☐ C-GHRE	Sikorsky S-76C+	760575	ex N7100C	
☐ C-GIHO	Sikorsky S-76A++	760015	ex HS-HTO	
☐ C-GIMJ	Sikorsky S-76A++	760009	ex D2-EXZ	
☐ C-GIMQ	Sikorsky S-76A++	760102	ex HS-HTQ	
☐ C-GKWS	Sikorsky S-76A++	760297	ex EP-HCS	
☐ C-GKWT	Sikorsky S-76A++	760295	ex B-HZD	based Yangon
☐ C-GMNB	Sikorsky S-76C+	760490	ex VT-HGH	

CHIMO AIR SERVICE — Red Lake SPB, ON (YRL)

☐ CF-HZA	Beech D18S	A-111		Floatplane
☐ CF-JIN	Noorduyn Norseman V	CCF-55	ex CF-LFR	Floatplane
☐ CF-KAO	Noorduyn Norseman VI	636	ex 44-70371	Floatplane
☐ C-FODQ	de Havilland DHC-3 Otter	111	ex CF-ODQ	Floatplane

CLEARWATER AIRWAYS — Burditt Lake SPB, ON

☐ C-FGUE	Beech C-18S	8107	ex N480DB	Floatplane
☐ C-GESW	Beech C-18S	7911	ex N4858V	Floatplane

CLOUD AIR SERVICE — Lake Muskoka-Mortimer's Point SPB, ON

☐ C-FZXD	de Havilland DHC-2 Beaver 1	1336	ex YV-230C	Floatplane

COCHRANE AIR SERVICES — Cochrane-Lillabelle Lake, ON (YCN)

☐ C-FEYQ	de Havilland DHC-2 Beaver	465	ex CF-EYQ	Floatplane
☐ C-FGBF	de Havilland DHC-2 Beaver	168	ex CF-GBF	Floatplane

CONAIR AVIATION — Conair Canada (CRC) — Abbotsford, BC (YXX)

☐ C-FDHK	Air Tractor AT-802A	802A-0198		80
☐ C-FDHL	Air Tractor AT-802A	802A-0199		
☐ C-FDHN	Air Tractor AT-802A	802A-0200		
☐ C-FLSI	Air Tractor AT-802A	802A-0173		82
☐ C-FXVF	Air Tractor AT-802A	802A-0033		78
☐ C-FXVL	Air Tractor AT-802A	802A-0034		79
☐ C-GAAG	Air Tractor AT-802A	802A-0174		91
☐ C-GBWF	Air Tractor AT-802A	802A-0303		
☐ C-GSJB	Air Tractor AT-802A	802A-0148		06
☐ C-GWNL	Air Tractor AT-802A	802A-0299		
☐ C-FEFK	Conair Firecat	G-360/014	ex F-ZBEH	574
☐ C-FEFX	Conair Firecat	G-527/031	ex N425DF	575
☐ C-FJOH	Conair Firecat	G-254/034	ex N424DF	576
☐ C-FOPU	Conair Firecat	DHC-38/007	ex RCN1539	564

Registration	Type	C/n	Previous identity	Fleet no	Notes
☐ C-FOPV	Conair Firecat	DHC-34/006	ex RCN1535	566	
☐ C-FOPY	Conair Firecat	DHC-24/019	ex CF-IOF	569	
☐ C-GABC	Conair Firecat	DHC-90/011	ex RCAF12191		567
☐ C-GHDY	Conair Firecat	G-374/029	ex Bu136465	573	
☐ C-GHPJ	Conair Firecat	G-509/022	ex Bu136600	571	
☐ C-GWHK	Conair Firecat	DHC-37/016	ex CAF12138	2	Tanker
☐ C-GWUO	Conair Firecat	DHC-39/003	ex N99261	563	
☐ C-GWUP	Conair Firecat	DHC-19/012	ex RCN12120	568	
☐ C-FEKF	Convair 580	80	ex C-GEVB	445	Tanker 45
☐ C-FFKF	Convair 580	179	ex C-GEVC	444	Tanker 44
☐ C-FHKF	Convair 580	374	ex C-GEUZ	455	Tanker 55
☐ C-FJVD	Convair 580	478	ex N8099S		
☐ C-FKFA	Convair 580	100	ex C-FLVY	452	Tanker 52
☐ C-FKFB	Convair 580	57	ex N568JA	447	Tanker 47
☐ C-FKFL	Convair 580	465	ex C-FZQS	449	Tanker 49
☐ C-FKFM	Convair 580	70	ex N73133	454	Tanker 54
☐ C-FKFY	Convair 580	129	ex N5814	448	Tanker 48
☐ C-GKFO	Convair 580	78	ex N5815	453	Tanker 53
☐ C-GYXC	Convair 580	507	ex VH-PDV		
☐ C-GYXS	Convair 580	501	ex VH-PAL		
☐ C-FFIF	Piper PA-60 Aerostar 600A	60-0702-7961218	ex N6073K	122	
☐ C-GLVG	Piper PA-60 Aerostar 600A	60-0695-7961217	ex N6072U	111	
☐ C-GMGZ	Piper PA-60 Aerostar 600A	60-0708-7961220	ex N6075C	112	
☐ C-GOSX	Piper PA-60 Aerostar 600A	60-0863-8161246	ex N3647B	110	
☐ C-GRIK	Piper PA-60 Aerostar 600A	60-0563-7961183	ex N8040J	108	
☐ C-GSXX	Ted Smith Aerostar 600A	60-0430-146	ex N9795Q	109	
☐ C-GUHK	Piper PA-60 Aerostar 600A	60-0761-8061230	ex N8EA	119	
☐ C-GUSZ	Piper PA-60 Aerostar 600A	60-0894-8161253	ex N6893Q	118	
☐ C-FCZZ	Rockwell 690A Turbo Commander	11106	ex N57106	135	
☐ C-FNWD	Rockwell 690B Turbo Commander	11497	ex N81831		
☐ C-GAAL	Rockwell 690A Turbo Commander	11104	ex N690AZ	131	
☐ C-GDCL	Rockwell 690A Turbo Commander	11192	ex N57192	134	
☐ C-GHWF	Rockwell 690A Turbo Commander	11134	ex N45VT	132	
☐ C-GWEW	Rockwell 690 Turbo Commander	11057	ex N376TC	133	
☐ C-GFSK*	Canadair CL-215-1A10 (CL-215)	1085	ex C-GKDN	201	
☐ C-GFSL*	Canadair CL-215-1A10 (CL-215)	1086	ex C-GKDP	202	
☐ C-GFSM*	Canadair CL-215-1A10 (CL-215)	1098		203	
☐ C-GFSN*	Canadair CL-215-1A10 (CL-215)	1099		204	
☐ C-GHLY	Douglas DC-6B	45501/953	ex OO-VGE	446	Tanker
☐ C-GIBS	Douglas DC-6A/C	45531/1015	ex HB-IBS	451	Tanker
☐ C-GKUG	Douglas DC-6A/B	45177/859	ex N863TA	450	Tanker
☐ C-GSDG	Cessna 208B Caravan I	208B0376	ex N1118P	127	

CORILAIR CHARTERS — *Campbell River, BC*

Registration	Type	C/n	Previous identity	Notes
☐ C-FEWP	Cessna U206D Skylane	U206-1344	ex CF-EWP	
☐ C-FJPB	de Havilland DHC-2 Beaver	1319	ex N1019T	Floatplane
☐ C-FNEQ	Cessna U206G Stationair 6	U20605036	ex N4660U	
☐ C-GACK	de Havilland DHC-2 Beaver	711	ex 53-7903	Floatplane
☐ C-GTNE	Cessna A185E Skywagon	18501889	ex CF-QLN	Floatplane

CORPORATE EXPRESS AIRLINE — *Penta (CPB)* — *Calgary-Intl, AB (YYC)*

Registration	Type	C/n	Previous identity
☐ C-GEXI	Canadair CL-600-2B19 (CRJ-200)	7186	ex N621BR
☐ C-GEXM	Canadair CL-600-2B19 (CRJ-200)	7187	ex N622BR
☐ C-GPII	Piaggio P.180 Avanti	1133	ex N139PA
☐ C-GXPS	SAAB SF.340A	340A-075	ex N75UW

COUGAR HELICOPTERS — *Cougar (CHI)* — *Halifax-Waterfront Heliport, NS (YWF)*

Registration	Type	C/n	Previous identity
☐ C-GIHS	Sikorsky S-76A++	760150	ex HS-HTS
☐ C-GDKN	Sikorsky S-92A	920111	ex N21278
☐ C-GMCH	Sikorsky S-92A	920023	ex N8016B
☐ C-GQCH	Sikorsky S-92A	920074	ex N2581T
☐ C-GSCH	Sikorsky S-92A	920010	ex N7108J
☐ C-GTCH	Sikorsky S-92A	920061	ex N45160
☐ C-GVCH	Sikorsky S-92A	920080	ex N25837
☐ C-GZCH	Sikorsky S-92A	920048	ex N71143
☐ C-FHCH	Sikorsky S-61N	61761	ex N613RM
☐ C-FNCH	Sikorsky S-61N	61757	ex N461AL
☐ C-FTIG	Sikorsky S-61N	61491	ex N613RM
☐ C-GYCH	Sikorsky S-61N	61762	ex PH-NZI

COULSON AIRCRANE — Port Alberni, BC (YPB)

☐ C-FCLM	Sikorsky S-61N	61492	ex N265F		
☐ C-FDYK	Bell 206B JetRanger II	972	ex CF-DYK		
☐ C-FLYK	Martin JRM-3 Mars	76820	ex Bu76820	Philippine Mars	Tanker
☐ C-FLYL	Martin JRM-3 Mars	76823	ex Bu76823	Hawaii Mars	Tanker
☐ C-FMAY	Sikorsky S-61N	61363	ex N306V		
☐ C-FXEC	Sikorsky S-61N	61821	ex N264F		
☐ C-GXOH	Bell 206B JetRanger II	865	ex N14844		

COURTESY AIR — Buffalo Narrows, SK (YVT)

☐ C-FCAK	Beech A100 King Air	B-96	ex N116RJ
☐ C-FJDF	Beech 1900C	UB-68	ex N68GH
☐ C-FJMF	Beech 99	U-180	ex OY-PAG
☐ C-FLMF	Beech C99	U-189	ex N189AV
☐ C-FNMF	Beech C99	U-167	ex N167EE
☐ C-GDVD	Beech 58 Baron	TH-668	ex N4557S
☐ C-GKLO	Piper PA-31-350 Chieftain	31-8152118	ex N4505N
☐ C-GKNL	Piper PA-31-350 Chieftain	31-7852083	ex N27607
☐ C-GMFV	Cessna U206G Stationair 6 II	U20604714	ex N732RY
☐ C-GNRM	Piper PA-31-350 Navajo Chieftain	31-7752145	ex N27315

CUSTOM HELICOPTERS — Winnipeg-St Andrews, MB (YAV)

☐ C-FJMH	Bell 206B JetRanger II	1331	ex N70711
☐ C-FKBV	Bell 206B JetRanger II	364	ex N465CC
☐ C-FSVG	Bell 206B JetRanger III	2865	ex N1074G
☐ C-FZSJ	Bell 206B JetRanger II	648	ex CF-ZSJ
☐ C-GBWN	Bell 206B JetRanger II	2204	
☐ C-GFIV	Bell 206B JetRanger II	424	ex N1481W
☐ C-GGZS	Bell 206B JetRanger II	1885	
☐ C-GKBU	Bell 206B JetRanger II	386	ex N1448W
☐ C-GQQO	Bell 206B JetRanger II	1096	ex N83182
☐ C-GQQT	Bell 206B JetRanger II	1657	ex N90218
☐ C-GSHJ	Bell 206B JetRanger II	114	ex N125GW
☐ C-FYHN	Bell 206L LongRanger	45050	ex N600FB
☐ C-GAVH	Bell 206L-1 LongRanger III	45740	ex N385FP
☐ C-GCHG	Bell 206L-1 LongRanger II	51508	ex N8592X
☐ C-GCHI	Bell 206L-1 LongRanger II	45516	ex N141VG
☐ C-GCHZ	Bell 206L-1 LongRanger III	45314	ex N210AH
☐ C-GIPG	Bell 206L-1 LongRanger II	45592	ex N3895K
☐ C-FCHD	Bell 205A-1	30014	ex N5598M
☐ C-FCHE	Bell 205A-1	30167	ex XA-SSR
☐ C-FCHJ	Aérospatiale AS350B2 AStar	2603	ex XC-JAK
☐ C-GCHX	Aérospatiale AS350BA AStar	2517	ex CP-2335
☐ C-GRWK	Bell 205A-1	30005	ex N3764U

DELTA HELICOPTERS — High Level, AB (YOJ)

☐ C-FDHW	Aérospatiale AS350BA AStar	2211	ex ZK-HKZ
☐ C-FDKH	Aérospatiale AS350B-2 AStar	2226	ex ZK-HEE
☐ C-FKDS	Aérospatiale AS350BA AStar	2802	ex N6101U
☐ C-FRUQ	Aérospatiale AS350B-2 AStar	2596	ex EC-FUF
☐ C-FWCL	Aérospatiale AS350BA AStar	2869	ex C-FWAW
☐ C-GDLD	Aérospatiale AS350B AStar	1369	ex N5771C
☐ C-GUPH	Aérospatiale AS350B AStar	1368	ex N99PS
☐ C-GVIV	Aérospatiale AS350B2 AStar	3419	
☐ C-GVXA	Aérospatiale AS350BA AStar	1278	ex N78EW
☐ C-FAHO	Bell 204B	2060	ex CF-AHO
☐ C-GDUK	Bell 204B	2034	ex N636
☐ C-GJLV	Bell 204B	2064	ex Thai 918
☐ C-GRGA	Bell 204B	2026	ex N1177W
☐ C-GTNP	Bell 204B	2028	ex OY-HBS
☐ C-GVEX	Bell 204B	2031	ex OY-HBV
☐ C-FCQJ	Bell 206B JetRanger	540	ex N8152J
☐ C-FDYO	Bell 206B JetRanger	994	ex CF-DYO
☐ C-GDBN	Bell 206B JetRanger III	2467	ex C-GDEN
☐ C-GDJW	Bell 206B JetRanger III	2909	ex N353E
☐ C-GGOZ	Bell 206B JetRanger	443	ex N2162L
☐ C-GNMI	Bell 206B JetRanger III	2602	ex N5014F
☐ C-GPEZ	Bell 206B JetRanger	1130	ex N9JJ
☐ C-GSHN	Bell 206B JetRanger	616	ex N101TF
☐ C-GTIS	Bell 206B JetRanger	827	ex N3YE
☐ C-GWML	Bell 206B JetRanger	269	ex N30AL
☐ C-GEOM	Bell 206L-1 LongRanger II	45625	
☐ C-GERI	Bell 206L-1 LongRanger II	45668	

☐ C-GPGO	Bell 206L-1 LongRanger II	45475	ex N57416

DYNAMIC FLIGHT SERVICES — Calgary, AB (YYC)

☐ C-GTJJ	Piper PA-31 Navajo C	31-7712062	ex N27271
☐ C-GZOC	Piper PA-31 Navajo C	31-7512018	ex N59934

EAGLE AIR SERVICES — Port Hardy, BC (YZT)

☐ C-FEAZ	Piper PA-31-350 Navajo Chieftain	31-7652088	ex N88MG
☐ C-GITW	Piper PA-31-350 Navajo Chieftain	31-7652114	

EAGLE COPTERS — Calgary, AB (YYC)

☐ C-FBHY	Bell 212	31194	
☐ C-FBUA	Bell 212	30826	
☐ C-FDEF	Bell 205A	30038	ex CS-HET
☐ C-FNOS	Bell 212	30866	
☐ C-FNOU	Bell 212	30787	ex 5N-AXX
☐ C-FRWW	Eurocopter EC130B4	3855	ex N996PT
☐ C-FTIW	Sikorsky S-76A+	760186	
☐ C-FWZI	Bell 206L-1 LongRanger II	45447	ex N202EC
☐ C-FXXU	Bell 212	30803	
☐ C-FZXH	Bell 206B JetRanger II	622	
☐ C-GAHN	Bell 204B	2044	ex N120BX
☐ C-GBBP	Bell 212	30934	ex OB-1847P
☐ C-GBHF	Bell 206B JetRanger II	1028	
☐ C-GCZG	Bell 205A-1	30136	ex N58126
☐ C-GEAG	Bell 205A-1	30262	ex XC-CIC
☐ C-GIYO	Aérospatiale AS350BA AStar	2274	
☐ C-GQKU	Bell 206B JetRanger II	2173	

EAST-WEST TRANSPORTATION — Salmon Arm, BC (YSN)

☐ C-FXNI	Bell 214B-1	28022	ex N214GL

ELBOW RIVER HELICOPTERS — Calgary Springbank, AB (YBW)

☐ C-FGAV	Bell 206L-1 LongRanger II	45156	
☐ C-FPMR	Bell 212	31115	ex N48ZP
☐ C-GERB	Bell 206L-3 LongRanger III	51008	
☐ C-GERW	Bell 212	30814	ex C-FRWM
☐ C-GKCA	Bell 206L-3 LongRanger III	51341	
☐ C-GZAV	Bell 407	53002	

ENERJET — (ENJ)

☐ C-GBEJ	Boeing 737-7BD/W	34480/1900	ex N286AT	102
☐ C-GOEJ	Boeing 737-7BD/W	33920/1753	ex N268AT	101

ENTERPRISE AIR

☐ C-FCLO	Beech E-18S	BA-143	ex N31M	
☐ C-FCRR	Consolidated 28-5ACF Canso	21996	ex RCAF 9767	Princess des Etoiles

EXACT AIR — Chicoutimi-St Honore, QC

☐ C-FDOS	Beech A100 King Air	B-106	ex CF-DOS
☐ C-FLTS	Beech A100 King Air	B-149	ex N883CA
☐ C-FQQB	Piper PA-31 Turbo Navajo	31-310	ex N9239Y
☐ C-FTYZ	Beech 100 King Air	B-86	ex N53MD
☐ C-FUPQ	Beech A100 King Air	B-162	ex N224LB
☐ C-FVTL	Piper PA-31-325 Navajo C/R	31-7912091	ex N3532U
☐ C-FVYW	Piper PA-31-325 Navajo C/R	31-7612026	ex N22AU
☐ C-FXDE	Beech A100 King Air	B-176	ex N3076W
☐ C-GGTF	Cessna 310R	310R0550	ex N87409
☐ C-GIAS	Cessna 402B	402B0545	ex N678CM
☐ C-GPTU	Piper PA-31 Navajo C	31-7712005	ex N62986
☐ C-GURS	Cessna 402	402-0214	ex N26309
☐ C-GZAS	Cessna 402B	402B0626	ex N2083K

EXPLOITS VALLEY AIR SERVICES — Gander, NL (YQX)

☐ C-GAAT	Beech 1900D	UE-217	ex N1564J	963
☐ C-GZUZ	Beech A100 King Air	B-143	ex C-GNVB	

EXPRESS AIR — Expressair (WEW) — Ottawa, ON (YOW)

☐ C-FKAZ	Cessna 208 Caravan I	20800236		Floatplane
☐ C-GAWP	Pilatus PC-12/45	187	ex N187PC	

FAR WEST HELICOPTERS — Chilliwack, BC (YCW)

Reg	Type	C/n	Previous	Notes	Remarks
☐ C-FJSL	Bell 206B JetRanger III	1154	ex N59384		
☐ C-GCQT	Bell 206B JetRanger II	492	ex N15FD		
☐ C-GGQL	Bell 206B JetRanger II	2117	ex N16723		
☐ C-GVTM	Bell 206B JetRanger II	194	ex N4038G		

FAST AIR — Winnipeg-Intl, MB (YWG)

Reg	Type	C/n	Previous	Notes	Remarks
☐ C-FDEB	Beech 200 Super King Air	BB-55	ex N200BC		
☐ C-FFAR	Beech 200 Super King Air	BB-864	ex N847TS		
☐ C-GDHF	Beech B200 Super King Air	BB-1129	ex CS-DDF		CatPass 250 conversion
☐ C-GFAD	Beech B200 Super King Air	BB-1428	ex N660MW		
☐ C-GFSB	Beech 200 Super King Air	BB-84			
☐ C-GWGI	Beech B200 Super King Air	BB-1022	ex C-FDGP		
☐ C-FJAL	Piper PA-31-350 Navajo Chieftain	31-7752160	ex N19LA		
☐ C-GMDL	Piper PA-31-325 Navajo C/R	31-7512033	ex N775WM		
☐ C-GMOB	Piper PA-31-350 Chieftain	31-7852072	ex N27596		
☐ C-GNDI	Piper PA-31T Cheyenne	31T-7620036	ex N73TB		
☐ C-GPNP	Piper PA-31T Cheyenne	31T-7520024	ex N431AC		

FIREWEED HELICOPTERS — Whitehorse, YT (YXY)

Reg	Type	C/n	Previous	Notes	Remarks
☐ C-FAVT	Bell 206L-1 LongRanger II	45207	ex N302CK		
☐ C-FFWH	Bell 206B JetRanger III	2464	ex N1974T		
☐ C-GFWE	Bell 206L-4 LongRanger IV	52036	ex C-FMPK		
☐ C-GFWI	Bell 204C	2070	ex C-GEAI		
☐ C-GFWZ	Bell 206B JetRanger III	1900	ex C-GBJZ		
☐ C-GLAV	Bell 206L-1 LongRanger II	45414	ex C-GMPV		
☐ C-GMNW	Bell 206L-1 LongRanger II	45512			

FIRST AIR — Firstair (7F/FAB) — Carp, ON/Iqaluit, NT/Yellowknife, NT (YRP/YFB/YZF)

Reg	Type	C/n	Previous	Notes	Remarks
☐ C-FIQR	ATR 42-300 (QC)	133	ex F-WWEE		
☐ C-FIQU	ATR 42-300 (QC)	138	ex F-WWEK		
☐ C-FTCP	ATR 42-300 (QC)	143	ex F-WWEO		
☐ C-FTJB	ATR 42-300 (QC)	119	ex N423TE		
☐ C-GHCP	ATR 42-300 (QC)	123	ex F-WWET		
☐ C-GKLB	ATR 42-310	331	ex G-CDFF		
☐ C-GSRR	ATR 42-300 (QC)	125	ex OY-MUH		
☐ C-GULU	ATR 42-310	155	ex 5R-MJD		
☐ C-GUNO	ATR 42-310	132	ex 5R-MJC		
☐ C-FACP	Boeing 737-2L9 (AvAero 3)	22072/623	ex C2-RN9		
☐ C-FNVK	Boeing 737-2R4C	23130/1040	ex JY-JAF		Freighter
☐ C-FNVT	Boeing 737-248C (AvAero 3)	21011/411	ex F-GKTK	Snowy Owl c/s	
☐ C-GCPT	Boeing 737-217 (AvAero 3)	22258/770		Inukshuk tail logo	
☐ C-GNDC	Boeing 737-242C (AvAero 3)	21728/580			
☐ C-GNWN	Boeing 737-210C (AvAero 3)	21067/414	ex N4952W		
☐ C-FMOC	Douglas DC-3	12741	ex CF-MOC		
☐ C-FUFA	Boeing 727-233F (FedEx 3)	20941/1128	ex N727LS		
☐ C-GFNW	Hawker Siddeley HS.748 Srs.2A /335LFD	1758	ex 9Y-TFX		405
☐ C-GHPW	Lockheed L-382G-42C Hercules	4799		Capt Harry Sorenson	
☐ C-GKLY	Boeing 767-223 (SCD)	22314/73	ex N714AX		
☐ C-GUSI	Lockheed L-328G-31C Hercules	4600	ex ZS-RSI	EARL titles	
☐ C-GXFA	Boeing 727-233F (Raisbeck 3)	20938/1105	ex C-GAAG		

FLAIR AIRLINES — Flair (FLE) — Kelonwa, BC (YLW)

Reg	Type	C/n	Previous	Notes	Remarks
☐ C-FLEJ	Boeing 737-4B3	24751/2107	ex CN-RPB		
☐ C-FLEN	Boeing 737-4K5	24769/1839	ex OK-VGZ		
☐ C-FLER	Boeing 737-46B	24573/1844	ex N41XA		
☐ C-FLHR	Boeing 727-223/W (DuganAir 3)	21524/1473	ex C-FPKF	Leaving on a Jet Plane titles	

FNT FIRST NATIONS TRANSPORTATION — Gimili, MB (YGM)

Reg	Type	C/n	Previous	Notes	Remarks
☐ CF-FTR	Douglas DC-3	16095/32843	ex N142JR		
☐ C-FQHY	Douglas DC-3	14560/26005	ex CF-QHY	wears CF-QHY	
☐ C-GIBX	Curtiss C-46F Commando	22472	ex 5Y-IBX		
☐ C-GTPO	Curtiss C-46F Commando	22556	ex N519AC		

FORDE LAKE AIR SERVICES — Hearst, ON (YHF)

Reg	Type	C/n	Previous	Notes	Remarks
☐ C-FLUA	de Havilland DHC-2 Beaver	1318	ex CF-LUA		
☐ C-GGNM	Cessna A185F Skywagon	18502807	ex (N1283F)		Floatplane
☐ C-GRAP	de Havilland DHC-2 Beaver	829	ex 54-1690		Floatplane

FOREST PATROL — St John, NB (YSJ)

☐ C-FBEJ	Ayres S-2R	1768R	ex CF-BEJ		
☐ C-FZTE	Ayres S-2R	1578R	ex CF-ZTE		
☐ C-GMQA	Ayres S-2R-T34	T34-013DC	ex N4020H		
☐ C-GMQB	Ayres S-2R-T34	T34-014DC	ex N4020S		
☐ C-GMQC	Ayres S-2R-T34	T34-015DC	ex N4020U		
☐ C-FESS	Bell 407	53129			
☐ C-FXZU	Bell 206L-4 LongRanger IV	52164			
☐ C-GVDI	Cessna TU206G Stationair 6	U20606490	ex C-GJDI		

FOREST PROTECTION — Fredericton / Miramichi, NB (YFC/YCH)

☐ C-FFPL	Air Tractor AT-802	802-0110		620	Sprayer/Tanker
☐ C-FZPV	Air Tractor AT-802	802-0141	ex N8507T	622	Sprayer
☐ C-GJJK	Air Tractor AT-802	802-0120	ex N85071	621	Sprayer/Tanker
☐ C-GJJX	Air Tractor AT-802	802-0121		624	Tanker
☐ C-GZRH	Air Tractor AT-802	802-0143		623	Sprayer
☐ C-GZUE	Air Tractor AT-802	802-0147		625	Sprayer
☐ C-FIMR	Grumman TBM-3 Avenger	53610	ex RCN303	23	
☐ C-FIMY	Cessna A188B AgTruck	18801247T	ex CF-IMY		Sprayer
☐ C-GFPL	Grumman TBM-3E Avenger	86020	ex N7157C	22	stored YFC
☐ C-GJDF	Cessna 337G Super Skymaster	33701516	ex N72488		
☐ C-GLEL	Grumman TBM-3 Avenger	53200	ex N9010C	13	
☐ C-GLFA	Cessna A188B AgTruck	18802222T	ex (N9296R)		Sprayer
☐ C-GMEK	Cessna U206F Stationair II	U20603083	ex N3755C		
☐ C-GXJI	Cessna 210J Centurion II	21059155	ex N3355S		
☐ C-GXMA	Cessna 337G Super Skymaster	33701644	ex N53468		

FORT FRANCES SPORTSMEN AIRWAYS — Fort Frances, ON (YAG)

☐ C-GBQC	de Havilland DHC-3 Otter	401	ex RCAF 9420	Floatplane or wheels/skis
☐ C-GMDG	de Havilland DHC-3 Turbo Otter	302	ex N90575	Floatplane or wheels/skis
☐ C-GUTL	de Havilland DHC-3 Otter	365	ex HK-3048X	Floatplane or wheels/skis

FOUR SEASONS AVIATION — Toronto-Pearson International, ON (YYZ)

☐ C-FHNB	Aérospatiale AS355F1 Twin Star	5174	ex N5798B
☐ C-FWZZ	Aérospatiale AS350B2 AStar	3931	ex C-FFIQ
☐ C-GGAZ	Bell 206B JetRanger	2156	
☐ C-GHAQ	Aérospatiale AS350D AStar	1542	ex N515WW

FUGRO AVIATION CANADA — Ottawa-Rockcliffe, ON (YRO)

☐ C-FDKM	CASA 212 Srs 200	CC40-2-196	ex PR-FAB	Nose & tail magnetometer
☐ C-FYAU	Cessna 404 Titan II	404-0431	ex N408EX	Tail magnetometer
☐ C-FZLK	Cessna 208B Caravan I	208B0569	ex N1210N	Tail magnetometer
☐ C-GDPP	CASA 212 Srs 200	CC50-3-265	ex N430CA	Nose & tail magnetometer
☐ C-GFAV	Cessna 208 Caravan I	20800251	ex N1251V	Tail magnetometer
☐ C-GGRD	Cessna 208B Caravan I	208B1150	ex N208ML	
☐ C-GNCA	Cessna 208B Caravan I	208B0764	ex N208KC	Tail magnetometer

GATEWAY HELICOPTERS — North Bay, ON (YYB)

☐ C-FBTW	Aérospatiale AS350B2 AStar	3289	
☐ C-FDEV	Aérospatiale AS350B2 AStar	2970	ex TG-RAJ
☐ C-FGEO	Aérospatiale AS350B3 AStar	4368	
☐ C-GBGH	Aérospatiale AS350B2 AStar	4398	ex N398EC
☐ C-GEOY	Aérospatiale AS350B3 AStar	4316	
☐ C-GEOZ	Aérospatiale AS350B3 AStar	4223	ex F-GURR
☐ C-GCHB	Bell 206B JetRanger	1226	
☐ C-GENL	Bell 206B JetRanger III	2505	ex N5008F
☐ C-GINF	Bell 206B JetRanger III	3294	ex N39108
☐ C-GNBS	Bell 206B JetRanger	1138	ex N58134
☐ C-GTPG	Bell 206B JetRanger II	1233	ex C-FHZL
☐ C-GUIK	Bell 206B JetRanger II	1908	
☐ C-GDQH	Bell 206LR LongRanger	45046	ex N663JB
☐ C-GHUG	Bell 206LR+ LongRanger	45142	ex N286CP
☐ C-GKCW	Bell 206L LongRanger	45122	ex N6139U
☐ C-GKMJ	Bell 206LR+ LongRanger	45096	ex C-GJBC
☐ C-GMHK	Bell 206L-1 LongRanger II	45286	ex N29EA
☐ C-GRYS	Bell 206L LongRanger	45097	ex N16783
☐ C-GZCD	Bell 206L-1 LongRanger II	45688	ex N80KA
☐ C-GMVU	Cessna 185E Skywagon	18503432	ex N9373H
☐ C-GRGY	Bell 204B	2022	ex CF-OKZ

GEFFAIR CANADA — *Montreal-Trudeau, QC (YUL)*

☐ C-GMHZ	Piper PA-31 Turbo Navajo	31-434	ex N712NT	

GEMINI HELICOPTERS — *High Level/Footner Lake, AB (YOJ)*

☐ C-FETD	Aérospatiale AS350BA AStar	1025	ex N135BH	
☐ C-FXLD	Aérospatiale AS350B AStar	1438	ex N817CF	
☐ C-GAVA	Bell 205A-1	30187	ex N222HT	
☐ C-GEAP	Bell 204B	2063	ex Thai 917	
☐ C-GEMJ	Aérospatiale AS350B2 AStar	2064	ex N203TB	
☐ C-GEMK	Eurocopter EC120B	1427		
☐ C-GEMN	Eurocopter EC120B	1423		
☐ C-GEMU	Eurocopter EC120B	1057	ex VH-AZH	
☐ C-GVYI	Aérospatiale AS350D AStar	1041	ex F-WZFK	

GEOGRAPHIC AIR SURVEY — *Edmonton-City Centre, AL (YXD)*

☐ C-GEOG	Aero Commander 680F	1120-73	ex N444UB	Surveyor
☐ C-GEOS	Rockwell 690A Turbo Commander	11279	ex N57180	Surveyor

GEORGIAN BAY AIRWAYS — *Parry Sound, ON (YPD)*

☐ CF-IJG	Noorduyn Norseman VI	139		Floatplane

GILLAM AIR SERVICES — *Gillam, MB (YGX)*

☐ C-FSDY	de Havilland DHC-2 Beaver	897	ex N64273	
☐ C-GOXI	Piper PA-23-250 Aztec E	27-7405484		
☐ C-GPPP	Britten-Norman BN-2A-27 Islander	423	ex (N93JA)	
☐ C-GSAD	Britten-Norman BN-2A-26 Islander	7	ex N32JC	
☐ C-GXQV	Cessna A185F Skywagon	18503375		

GOGAL AIR SERVICES — *Snow Lake, MB*

☐ CF-ECG	Noorduyn Norseman V	N29-43		Floatplane or wheels/skis
☐ CF-GLI	Noorduyn Norseman VI	365	ex N88719	Floatplane or wheels/skis
☐ C-GBAO	Piper PA-31-350 Navajo Chieftain	31-7405234	ex N54309	
☐ C-GCWO	Cessna A185F Skywagon	18503207	ex N93275	Floatplane or wheels/skis

GOLDAK AIRBORNE SURVEYS — *Saskatoon, SK (YXE)*

☐ C-GJBA	Piper PA-31 Turbo Navajo	31-159	ex N9119Y	Surveyor, tail magnetometer
☐ C-GJBB	Piper PA-31 Turbo Navajo	31-519	ex N310DS	Surveyor
☐ C-GJBG	Piper PA-31 Navajo C	31-7612003	ex N59718	Surveyor
☐ C-GLDX	Cessna 208 Caravan I	20800366	ex C-FFCL	

GOVERNMENT OF QUEBEC — *Quebec (QUE)* — *Quebec, QC (YQB)*

☐ C-FASE	Canadair CL-215-6B11 (CL-215T)	1114	ex Greece 1114		238
☐ C-FAWQ	Canadair CL-215-6B11 (CL-215T)	1115	ex Greece 1115		239
☐ C-FTXG	Canadair CL-215-1A10 (CL-215)	1014	ex CF-TXG	228	
☐ C-FTXJ	Canadair CL-215-1A10 (CL-215)	1017	ex CF-TXJ	230	
☐ C-FTXK	Canadair CL-215-1A10 (CL-215)	1018	ex CF-TXK	231	
☐ C-GFQB	Canadair CL-215-1A10 (CL-215)	1092	ex C-GKDP	237	
☐ C-GQBA	Canadair CL-215-6B11 (CL-415)	2005	ex C-GKDN	240	
☐ C-GQBC	Canadair CL-215-6B11 (CL-415)	2012	ex C-GKET	241	
☐ C-GQBD	Canadair CL-215-6B11 (CL-415)	2016	ex C-GBPU	242	
☐ C-GQBE	Canadair CL-215-6B11 (CL-415)	2017	ex C-GKEA	243	
☐ C-GQBF	Canadair CL-215-6B11 (CL-415)	2019	ex C-FVKV	244	
☐ C-GQBG	Canadair CL-215-6B11 (CL-415)	2022	ex C-FVLW	245	
☐ C-GQBI	Canadair CL-215-6B11 (CL-415)	2023	ex C-FVLI	246	
☐ C-GQBK	Canadair CL-215-6B11 (CL-415)	2026	ex C-FVLY	247	
☐ C-FURG	Canadair CL-600-2A12 (Challenger 601)	3063	ex C-GLYH	EMS	
☐ C-GBPQ	Bell 206B JetRanger III	2897	ex YU-HLL		
☐ C-GQBQ	Canadair CL-600-2B16 (Challenger 604)	5051	ex N300KC	EMS	
☐ C-GQBT	de Havilland DHC-8Q-202	470	ex P2-ANL		EMS/VIP
☐ C-GSQA	Bell 206LT TwinRanger	52060			Police
☐ C-GSQL	Bell 412EP	36262	ex N6077U		

GREAT SLAVE HELICOPTERS — *Yellowknife, NT (YZF)*

☐ C-FGSC	Aérospatiale AS350BA AStar	3067		
☐ C-FHAF	Aérospatiale AS350BA AStar	1543	ex N516WW	
☐ C-FIDA	Aérospatiale AS350B3 AStar	4375		
☐ C-FQDA	Aérospatiale AS350BA AStar	4179		
☐ C-FYDA	Aérospatiale AS350B3 AStar	4157		
☐ C-FYKD	Aérospatiale AS350B2 AStar	4053	ex F-WQDE	
☐ C-FYZF	Aérospatiale AS350B2 AStar	3823		

☐ C-GABX	Aérospatiale AS350BA AStar	2438	ex HC-CBU
☐ C-GAVO	Aérospatiale AS350B3 AStar	3139	ex F-WWOG
☐ C-GBDA	Aérospatiale AS350B3 AStar	4065	ex PR-TDA
☐ C-GDCV	Aérospatiale AS350B2 AStar	4422	
☐ C-GFHN	Aérospatiale AS350B2 AStar	2128	ex EC-ELN
☐ C-GGSP	Aérospatiale AS350B1 AStar	2126	ex N213LA
☐ C-GGSW	Aérospatiale AS350B2 AStar	2675	
☐ C-GGSY	Aérospatiale AS350B2 AStar	3591	
☐ C-GHMZ	Aérospatiale AS350BA AStar	2325	
☐ C-GIUX	Aérospatiale AS350BA AStar	1240	ex C-GHRD
☐ C-GJGK	Aérospatiale AS350B2 AStar	2127	ex F-GHFJ
☐ C-GNGK	Aérospatiale AS350B2 AStar	2539	ex N392BK
☐ C-GRTM	Aérospatiale AS350BA AStar	1402	ex C-GAHE
☐ C-GYFS	Aérospatiale AS350B2 AStar	3868	
☐ C-FAFL	Bell 206B JetRanger	1256	
☐ C-FALP	Bell 206B JetRanger II	2090	ex N214EL
☐ C-FGSD	Bell 206B JetRanger	427	ex N83TA
☐ C-FHBH	Bell 206B JetRanger III	3258	ex N904R
☐ C-FHZP	Bell 206B JetRanger	1238	ex CF-HZP
☐ C-FMAD	Bell 206B JetRanger	408	ex N725BB
☐ C-FTWM	Bell 206B JetRanger	712	ex CF-TWM
☐ C-GAHP	Bell 206B JetRanger	805	ex N2959W
☐ C-GAHX	Bell 206B JetRanger	187	ex N4014G
☐ C-GGRC	Bell 206B JetRanger III	3623	
☐ C-GHPO	Bell 206B JetRanger II	2151	ex HR-AFT
☐ C-GOKA	Bell 206B JetRanger	156	ex N4052G
☐ C-GOMK	Bell 206B JetRanger	1889	
☐ C-GTYU	Bell 206B JetRanger II	2144	ex N16627
☐ C-GUYM	Bell 206B JetRanger	1687	ex N90191
☐ C-GVTK	Bell 206B JetRanger II	104	ex N6200N
☐ C-FBFH	Bell 206L-1 LongRanger II	45178	ex N5005G
☐ C-FGSG	Bell 206LR+ LongRanger	45115	ex N405EH
☐ C-GACG	Bell 206L-3 LongRanger III	51046	ex N53096
☐ C-GFEG	Bell 206L LongRanger	45150	ex N38Q
☐ C-GHBY	Bell 206LR+ LongRanger	45109	ex N402EH
☐ C-GHRR	Bell 206L-4 LongRanger IV	52017	ex C-GMPA
☐ C-GMSX	Bell 206L-3 LongRanger III	51474	ex N42489
☐ C-GRFZ	Bell 206L-1 LongRanger II	45610	
☐ C-GSHF	Bell 206L-3 LongRanger III	51349	ex C-GHHY
☐ C-GSHL	Bell 206L LongRanger	45092	ex N16751
☐ C-GSHQ	Bell 206L-4 LongRanger IV	52226	ex XC-LFC
☐ C-GSHW	Bell 206L-3 LongRanger III	51602	ex OK-XIS
☐ C-FBUC	Bell 212	30687	ex XA-TQG
☐ C-FJAD	Bell 212	30966	ex C-GZNA
☐ C-GEEC	Bell 212	30931	ex EC-GOR
☐ C-GEZO	Bell 212	30576	ex N4367Z
☐ C-GGSM	Bell 212	30741	ex N49676
☐ C-GKTL	Bell 212	32124	ex A6-BBX
☐ C-GJDA	Eurocopter EC130B4	4192	
☐ C-GRTN	Eurocopter EC120B Colibri	1058	
☐ C-GSDA	Eurocopter EC130B4	4041	ex F-WWXI
☐ C-GSHD	Bell 205A-1	30058	ex C-FNMQ
☐ C-GSHG	Bell 205A-1	30165	ex C-GENZ

GREEN AIRWAYS — *Red Lake, ON (YRL)*

☐ C-FLEA	de Havilland DHC-3 Otter	286	ex CF-LEA	Floatplane or wheels/skis
☐ C-FOBE	Noorduyn UC-64A Norseman	480	ex 43-35406	Floatplane or wheels/skis
☐ C-FODJ	de Havilland DHC-3 Otter	14	ex CF-ODJ	Floatplane or wheels/skis
☐ C-FVIA	de Havilland DHC-2 Beaver	714	ex N9047U	Floatplane or wheels/skis
☐ C-GEZU	de Havilland DHC-2 Beaver	647	ex 53-8159	Floatplane or wheels/skis
☐ C-GEZW	de Havilland DHC-2 Beaver	1217	ex 57-6138	Floatplane or wheels/skis
☐ C-GYUY	Cessna A185F Skywagon II	18503731	ex (N8550Q)	Floatplane or wheels/skis

GRONDAIR — *St Frederic du Beauce, QC*

☐ C-FNNM	Cessna TR182RG Skylane	R18200946	ex N738NR
☐ C-FQTA	Cessna R182RG Skylane	R18200324	ex N4107C
☐ C-FQTC	Cessna R182RG Skylane	R18201717	ex N4608T
☐ C-FRGN	Cessna R182RG Skylane	R18200394	ex N9083C
☐ C-FRYF	Cessna R182RG Skylane	R18201001	ex N65ET
☐ C-FRYP	Cessna R182RG Skylane	R18200479	ex N9879C
☐ C-FRZE	Cessna R182RG Skylane	R18200197	ex N2657C
☐ C-GCJA	Cessna R182RG Skylane	R18201219	ex (N757DM)
☐ C-GHVC	Cessna R182RG Skylane	R18201886	ex N5532T
☐ C-GRUA	Cessna R182RG Skylane	R18200077	ex N7325X
☐ C-GSCF	Cessna R182RG Skylane	R18201257	ex N757QM
☐ C-GVCV	Cessna R182RG Skylane	R18200030	ex N7343T

☐ C-FONY	Beech A100 King Air	B-154	ex N46JK
☐ C-GAST	Cessna 310R	310R0730	ex N5009J
☐ C-GBRC	Cessna 310R	310R1284	ex N6116X
☐ C-GIGB	Cessna 337G Super Skymaster II	33701599	ex N72478
☐ C-GJGW	Cessna 310R	310R0960	ex N37200
☐ C-GSRW	Piper PA-31 Turbo Navajo	31-262	ex N707FR
☐ C-GUMQ	Piper PA-31 Turbo Navajo	31-84	ex N777GS

GUARDIAN HELICOPTERS — Calgary-Springbank, AL/Fort Nelson, BC (YBW/YYE)

☐ C-FFJY	Bell 205A-1	30002	ex VH-NGM
☐ C-FJGK	Bell 206B JetRanger II	1940	ex N16HR
☐ C-FKNT	Bell 206L LongRanger	45028	ex N2494L
☐ C-FKOX	Bell 206B JetRanger	1261	ex CF-KOX
☐ C-FMGK	Bell 206L-1 LongRanger	45402	ex N723SH
☐ C-FOGK	Aérospatiale AS350BA Astar	1603	ex ZK-ICY
☐ C-FRDJ	Bell 206B JetRanger	63	ex N206WE
☐ C-FTGK	Bell 205A-1	30009	ex N4750R
☐ C-GLGK	Piper PA-31P Pressurised Navajo	31P-7300117	ex N777JP
☐ C-GLQI	Bell 206B JetRanger II	1964	ex N49694
☐ C-GRTL	Aérospatiale AS350BA AStar	1377	ex N577DL
☐ C-GTVA	Bell 206B JetRanger II	2133	
☐ C-GWGK	Aérospatiale AS350B3 AStar	3350	ex N335MB
☐ C-GXLE	Aérospatiale AS350BA AStar	1337	ex N2069B
☐ C-GZGK	Aérospatiale AS350BA AStar	2277	ex N391MA

HARBOUR AIR SEAPLANES — Harbour Air (H3) — Vancouver-Coal Harbour, BC (CXH)

☐ C-FAXI	de Havilland DHC-2 Beaver	1514	ex N6535D	205	Floatplane
☐ C-FFHQ	de Havilland DHC-2 Beaver	42	ex CF-FHQ	203	Floatplane
☐ C-FJFQ	de Havilland DHC-2 Beaver	963	ex CF-JFQ	206	Floatplane
☐ C-FMXS	de Havilland DHC-2 Beaver	1010	ex N43882	202	Floatplane
☐ C-FOCJ	de Havilland DHC-2 Beaver	39	ex CF-OCJ		Floatplane
☐ C-FOCN	de Havilland DHC-2 Beaver	44	ex CF-OCN	208	Floatplane
☐ C-FOCY	de Havilland DHC-2 Beaver	79	ex CF-OCY	204	Floatplane
☐ C-FOSP	de Havilland DHC-2 Beaver	1501	ex N2961	207	Floatplane
☐ C-GCYM	de Havilland DHC-2 Beaver	354	ex N63PS		Floatplane
☐ C-FHAA	de Havilland DHC-3 Turbo Otter	357	ex C-GIWT	309	Floatplane
☐ C-FHAD	de Havilland DHC-3 Turbo Otter	119	ex N81FW	315	Floatplane
☐ C-FHAX	de Havilland DHC-3 Turbo Otter	339	ex N41755	313	Floatplane
☐ C-FITF	de Havilland DHC-3 Turbo Otter	89	ex CF-ITF	303	Floatplane
☐ C-FIUZ	de Havilland DHC-3 Turbo Otter	135	ex F-OAKK	306	Floatplane
☐ C-FJHA	de Havilland DHC-3 Turbo Otter	393	ex 4R-ARB		Floatplane
☐ C-FODH	de Havilland DHC-3 Turbo Otter	3	ex CF-ODH	307	Floatplane
☐ C-FRNO	de Havilland DHC-3 Turbo Otter	21	ex N128F	301	Floatplane
☐ C-GHAR	de Havilland DHC-3 Turbo Otter	42	ex N234KA	308	Floatplane
☐ C-GHAS	de Havilland DHC-3 Turbo Otter	284	ex N84SF	310	Floatplane
☐ C-GHAZ	de Havilland DHC-3 Turbo Otter	19	ex C-FEYY		Floatplane
☐ C-GLCP	de Havilland DHC-3 Turbo Otter	422	ex N17682		Floatplane
☐ C-GOPP	de Havilland DHC-3 Turbo Otter	355	ex N53KA	305	Floatplane
☐ C-GUTW	de Havilland DHC-3 Turbo Otter	405	ex CAF 9423	302	Floatplane
☐ C-GVNL	de Havilland DHC-3 Turbo Otter	105	ex N5341G	304	Floatplane
☐ C-GCRE	Cessna A185F Skywagon	18502522	ex (N1807R)		Floatplane
☐ C-GZSH	Cessna A185F Skywagon	18503482	ex (N1463Q)		Floatplane

HAUTS-MONTS — Quebec, QC / Jackson, MS (YQB/JAN)

☐ C-GPSP	Cessna 441 Conquest II	441-0058	ex OY-BHM	Photo/survey
☐ C-GPSQ	Cessna 441 Conquest II	441-0076	ex N441RC	Photo/survey
☐ C-GPSR	Cessna 441 Conquest II	441-0143	ex N26PK	Photo/survey
☐ N454EA	Cessna 441 Conquest II	441-0054	ex C-GRSL	Photo/survey
☐ N8970N	Cessna 441 Conquest II	441-0092		Photo/survey
☐ C-GHMN	Piper PA-23-250 Aztec C	27-3893	ex N6590Y	Photo/survey
☐ C-GNZQ	Piper PA-23-250 Aztec E	27-7554067	ex N54755	Photo/survey
☐ C-GPSZ	Cessna 421C Golden Eagle II	421C0148	ex N303HC	Photo/survey

HAWK AIR — Wawa-Hawk Junction, ON (YXZ)

☐ C-FBBG	de Havilland DHC-2 Beaver	368 173	ex N2818D	Floatplane
☐ C-FQMN	de Havilland DHC-3 Otter	184	ex N2959W	Floatplane

HAWKAIR AVIATION SERVICE — Hawkair (BH) — Terrace, BC (YXT)

☐ C-FABG	de Havilland DHC-8-102	147	
☐ C-FCJE	de Havilland DHC-8-102	165	
☐ C-FDNG	de Havilland DHC-8-102	166	
☐ C-FIDL	de Havilland DHC-8-311	305	ex V2-LFW

HAYES HELICOPTER SERVICES — Duncan, BC (DUQ)

☐ C-FBHG	Bell 206B JetRanger II	713	ex CF-BHG
☐ C-FHHM	Sikorsky S-61N	61468	ex C-FZLU
☐ C-GHHF	Bell 206B JetRanger III	3311	ex C-FNHL
☐ C-GHHT	Bell 206B JetRanger III	2869	ex C-GFKD
☐ C-GPCT	Bell 206B JetRanger III	3085	

HEARST AIR SERVICE — Hearst, ON (YHF)

☐ C-FBTU	de Havilland DHC-2 Beaver	1564	ex CF-BTU	Floatplane or wheels/skis
☐ C-FDDX	de Havilland DHC-3 Turbo Otter	165	ex CF-DDX	Floatplane or wheels/skis
☐ C-FDPM	de Havilland DHC-2 Beaver	1247	ex N87878	Floatplane or wheels/skis

HELI-EXCEL — Sept-Iles, QC (YZV)

☐ C-FAEF	Aérospatiale AS350BA AStar	2152	ex N700YH
☐ C-FHEI	Aérospatiale AS350BA AStar	2969	
☐ C-FJYL	Aérospatiale AS350BA AStar	2959	
☐ C-FOZT	Aérospatiale AS350BA AStar	2644	
☐ C-FQHC	Aérospatiale AS350BA AStar	1011	ex N49561
☐ C-FSPF	Aérospatiale AS350BA AStar	2785	
☐ C-FVRT	Aérospatiale AS350BA AStar	2849	
☐ C-GAWV	Aérospatiale AS350B2 AStar	2998	
☐ C-GGPF	Aérospatiale AS350BA AStar	1313	ex N900BA
☐ C-GIEQ	Aérospatiale AS350B2 AStar	3349	ex N686CC
☐ C-GIYR	Aérospatiale AS350BA AStar	2299	ex JA9871
☐ C-GVEI	Aérospatiale AS350B2 AStar	2671	ex N682CC
☐ C-FBYU	Bell 205A-1	30168	ex LX-HFZ
☐ C-FDDG	Bell 205A-1	30019	ex LX-HRI
☐ C-FXKL	Aérospatiale AS355F2 Twin Star	5148	ex N5797P
☐ C-GLHE	Bell 205A-1	30092	ex F-GHHQ
☐ C-GLHH	Bell 205A-1	30223	ex F-GHHR

HELI-EXPRESS — Quebec, QC (YQB)

☐ C-FCCI	Aérospatiale AS350BA AStar	1303	ex N5768Y
☐ C-GDEH	Aérospatiale AS350BA AStar	1348	ex N905DB
☐ C-GHEX	Aérospatiale AS350B2 AStar	2867	ex CP-2392
☐ C-GIMG	Aérospatiale AS350D AStar	1382	ex ZK-HZZ
☐ C-GJPC	Aérospatiale AS350BA AStar	1398	ex N269JM
☐ C-GRDI	Aérospatiale AS350B2 AStar	2866	ex C-FWAU
☐ C-GVEM	Aérospatiale AS350BA AStar	2510	ex N752BH
☐ C-GADA	Bell 205A-1	30031	ex PK-UHJ

HELI-INTER — Val d'Or/Chicoutimi-St Honore, QC

☐ C-FMGB	Aérospatiale AS350BA+ AStar	1292	ex N350SS
☐ C-FMHI	Aérospatiale AS350BA AStar	9037	ex EI-MYO
☐ C-FMOZ	Aérospatiale AS350BA AStar	1374	ex F-GHFR
☐ C-FONZ	Aérospatiale AS350BA AStar	1400	ex HR-ANU
☐ C-FPOO	Aérospatiale AS350BA AStar	2508	ex N370WM
☐ C-FZSU	Aérospatiale AS350B2 AStar	2481	ex XA-TMJ
☐ C-FZXY	Aérospatiale AS350BA AStar	2082	ex N6102E
☐ C-GGHA	Aérospatiale AS350BA AStar	2624	ex F-GHYK
☐ C-GGIS	Aérospatiale AS350BA AStar	1110	ex N40445
☐ C-GILZ	Aérospatiale AS350B2 AStar	3386	
☐ C-GJPA	Aérospatiale AS350BA AStar	1075	ex C-FHAH
☐ C-GMQM	Aérospatiale AS350D AStar	1380	ex N108SH
☐ C-GZGM	Aérospatiale AS350B2 AStar	9056	
☐ C-FCNV	Bell 205A-1	30288	ex LX-HXU
☐ C-FSMI	Bell 205A-1	30263	ex (N205HT)
☐ C-GFHW	Bell 205A-1	30115	ex VH-NGI
☐ C-GHNQ	Bell 206L LongRanger	45014	ex N259MH
☐ C-GVHP	Bell 205A-1	30119	ex N688CC

HELI-LIFT INTERNATIONAL — Yorkton, SK (YQV)

☐ C-GHLE	Bell 205A-1	30195	ex HL9150
☐ C-GHLJ	Bell 206L-3 LongRanger III	51280	ex N60992
☐ C-GHLX	Aérospatiale AS350B AStar	1589	ex N85PB
☐ C-GIYN	Aérospatiale AS350BA AStar	1776	ex JA9368
☐ C-GMOR	Bell 205A-1	30159	ex LX-HOR
☐ C-GQCW	Aérospatiale AS350BA AStar	1255	ex N3607T
☐ C-GSHK	Bell 204B	2067	ex Thai 920

HELICOPTER TRANSPORT SERVICES — Carp, ON (YRP)

☐ C-FMIE	Aérospatiale AS350B2 AStar	4216	
☐ C-FVVQ	Aérospatiale AS350BA AStar	1210	ex N350LW
☐ C-FVVR	Aérospatiale AS350B AStar	1353	ex N9101N
☐ C-GHAV	Aérospatiale AS350B2 AStar	2758	
☐ C-GZCN	Aérospatiale AS350B1 AStar	2207	ex LN-OCD
☐ C-FCYW	Bell 204B	2004	ex N8588F
☐ C-FDZE	Bell 204B	2055	ex N7932S
☐ C-GFFY	Bell 205A-1	30123	ex N1084C
☐ C-GMHE	Bell 205A-1	30212	ex PT-HHZ
☐ C-GQLL	Bell 205A-1	30018	ex A7-HAG
☐ C-FMAO	Bell 206B JetRanger	407	ex CF-MAO
☐ C-FWGN	Bell 206B JetRanger	690	ex C-FCTV
☐ C-GQMR	Bell 206B JetRanger II	2207	
☐ C-GZPF	Bell 206B JetRanger	3490	ex N2168S
☐ C-GZPG	Bell 206B JetRanger	867	ex N28EE
☐ C-GZPH	Bell 206B JetRanger	3162	ex N70523
☐ C-GZRQ	Bell 206B JetRanger II	1981	ex N206YP
☐ C-FARV	Bell 206L LongRanger	45117	
☐ C-FKEP	Bell 206L LongRanger	45024	ex N111AL
☐ C-FLTX	Bell 206LR+ LongRanger	45043	ex N96AT
☐ C-FOVL	Bell 206L-3 LongRanger III	51041	ex N282BH
☐ C-FPOQ	Bell 206L-4 LongRanger IV	52363	
☐ C-GZPE	Bell 206L-4 LongRanger IV	52334	
☐ C-GZPI	Bell 206L-4 LongRanger IV	52351	
☐ C-GZPJ	Bell 206L-4 LongRanger IV	52353	
☐ C-GZRS	Bell 206L-3 LongRanger III	51146	ex N3193U
☐ C-FMLT	Bell 212	30889	ex JA9532
☐ C-GAHZ	Bell 212	30758	ex N5306T
☐ C-GHTK	Bell 212	30904	ex JA9538
☐ C-GXTF	Bell 212	30825	ex N212RT
☐ C-GPNC	Beech B300C Super King Air	FM-15	ex N415KA

HELICRAFT 2000 — Montreal-St.Hubert, QC (YHC)

☐ C-FHVV	Aérospatiale AS350BA AStar	1225	ex N215EH
☐ C-FIFL	Aérospatiale AS350D AStar	1453	ex F-GCTM
☐ C-FLIZ	Aérospatiale AS350BA AStar	2484	ex F-GHRD
☐ C-FLOO	Aérospatiale AS350BA AStar	2739	ex JA6133
☐ C-FPHY	Aérospatiale AS350BA AStar	1496	ex N5805B
☐ C-GIYJ	Aérospatiale AS350BA AStar	1407	ex JA9273
☐ C-GMAN	Aérospatiale AS350B2 AStar	3073	
☐ C-GMIM	Aérospatiale AS350BA AStar	1257	ex F-GCJC
☐ C-GMYG	Aérospatiale AS350D AStar	1201	ex N3604X
☐ C-GPHN	Aérospatiale AS350BA AStar	1251	
☐ C-FGDT	Bell 206B JetRanger	2993	ex N993RM
☐ C-FXHA	Aérospatiale AS355F2 Twin Star	5426	ex N684CC
☐ C-FXHE	Aérospatiale AS355F2 Twin Star	5074	ex N685CC
☐ C-GARE	Bell 206B JetRanger	1852	
☐ C-GKHX	Bell 206L-2 LongRanger	46612	ex N373MH
☐ C-GYHZ	Bell 206L LongRanger	45126	ex N16840

HELIFOR INDUSTRIES — Campbell River, BC (YBL)

☐ C-FHFB	Boeing Vertol 234UT Chinook	MJ-005	ex N238CH	Lsd fr WCO
☐ C-FHFW	Boeing Vertol 107 II	107	ex N188CH	Lsd fr WCO
☐ C-GHCD	Boeing Vertol 107 II	101	ex N6682D	Lsd fr WCO
☐ C-GHFF	Boeing Vertol 107 II	406	ex N195CH	Lsd fr WCO
☐ C-GHFY	Boeing Vertol 107 II	2002	ex N190CH	Lsd fr WCO

HELIJET INTERNATIONAL — Helijet (JB/JBA) — Vancouver-Intl, BC (YVR)

☐ C-GHJL	Sikorsky S-76A II	760214	ex N101PB	EMS
☐ C-GHJP	Sikorsky S-76A II	760065	ex (C-GHJT)	
☐ C-GHJT	Sikorsky S-76A	760052	ex VH-XHZ	
☐ C-GHJV	Sikorsky S-76A	760167	ex N5426U	
☐ C-GHJW	Sikorsky S-76A II	760074	ex N586C	
☐ C-GBSF	Sikorsky S-61N	61222	ex C-GROV	
☐ C-GHJJ	Learjet 31A	102	ex N681AF	EMS
☐ C-GHJU	Learjet 31A	120	ex N200TJ	EMS
☐ C-GLMX	Bell 206L-1 LongRanger	45439	ex N92ZT	
☐ C-GHJF	Beech 200 Super King Air	BB-1493	ex N3015Q	
☐ C-GXHJ	Bell 206L-1 LongRanger	45741	ex N3174P	

HELIQWEST AVIATION — Edmonton-Municipal, AB (YXD)

☐ C-FETK	Bell 205A-1	30299	ex OE-XEH
☐ C-FHQK	Bell 205A-1	30142	ex C-GXLF
☐ C-FIAN	Bell 206A JetRanger	32	ex CF-IAN
☐ C-FSXX	Bell 205A-1	30172	ex PP-EOU
☐ C-FXFT	Kaman K-1200 K-Max	A94-0007	ex N135KA
☐ C-FZQB	Bell 212	30629	ex PK-HCF
☐ C-GEAK	Bell 205A-1	30183	ex N393EH
☐ C-GEAT	Bell 205A-1	30088	ex G-BKGH

HICKS & LAWRENCE — St Thomas, ON (YQS)

☐ C-FBME	Cessna 337G Super Skymaster II	33701734	ex N146HA
☐ C-FBNX	Cessna 337G Super Skymaster II	33701738	ex N53614
☐ C-FBRG	Cessna 337G Super Skymaster II	33701695	ex N26286
☐ C-FBRH	Cessna 337G Super Skymaster II	33701662	ex N53496
☐ C-FBRK	Cessna 337H Super Skymaster II	33701884	ex N75BP
☐ C-FIGS	Cessna 337G Super Skymaster II	33701728	ex N714GP
☐ C-FIKM	Cessna 337G Super Skymaster	33701588	ex N72448
☐ C-FIXO	Cessna 337H Super Skymaster II	33701820	ex N1328L
☐ CF-JIP	Cessna 337G Super Skymaster	33701534	ex N72177
☐ C-FNHL	Cessna 337D Super Skymaster	337-1035	ex C-FPWB
☐ C-FSIW	Cessna 337G Super Skymaster	33701571	ex N72377
☐ C-FSIY	Cessna 337G Super Skymaster II	33701949	ex N959CC
☐ C-FSIZ	Cessna 337G Super Skymaster II	33701632	ex N53450
☐ C-GDQU	Cessna 337G Super Skymaster II	33701607	ex N53413
☐ C-GEOR	Cessna 337G Super Skymaster II	33701730	ex (N53595)
☐ C-GFSC	Cessna 337G Super Skymaster II	33701793	ex N53699
☐ C-GIOG	Cessna 337G Super Skymaster II	33701746	ex (N53638)
☐ C-GNRO	Cessna 337D Super Skymaster	337-1101	ex N68169
☐ C-GWDU	Cessna 337B Super Skymaster	337-0665	ex N2365S
☐ C-FMUM	Rockwell 500S Shrike Commander	3103	ex N37GW
☐ C-GAYR	Rockwell 500S Shrike Commander	3118	ex N9170N
☐ C-GETH	Rockwell 500S Shrike Commander	1800-15	ex N732
☐ C-GETJ	Rockwell 500S Shrike Commander	3275	ex N81450
☐ C-GIZV	Aero Commander 500B	1440-155	ex N678GH
☐ C-GJLO	Rockwell 500S Shrike Commander	1796-11	ex N5009E
☐ C-GJMA	Aero Commander 500B	1319-128	ex N330U
☐ C-FKJI	Beech 200 Super King Air	BB-105	ex N71TZ
☐ C-GJBZ	Piper PA-36-375 Pawnee Brave	36-7902036	ex N3989E
☐ C-GJLI	Beech 200 Super King Air	BB-347	ex N424CR
☐ C-GQNJ	Beech 200 Super King Air	BB-275	
☐ C-GTWW	Beech 65-C90 King Air	LJ-657	ex N9030R

HIGHLAND HELICOPTERS — Vancouver-Intl, BC (YVR)

☐ C-FHHC	Aérospatiale AS350B2 AStar	2569	ex N2PW
☐ C-FHHU	Aérospatiale AS350B2 AStar	2790	ex C-FSQY
☐ C-FHHY	Aérospatiale AS350BA AStar	1650	ex C-GSKI
☐ C-FJHH	Aérospatiale AS350B2 AStar	3279	
☐ C-FKHH	Aérospatiale AS350B2 AStar	2736	
☐ C-FYYA	Aérospatiale AS350BA AStar	2295	ex ZK-HOU
☐ C-GBHH	Aérospatiale AS350B2 AStar	3180	
☐ C-GDHH	Aérospatiale AS350B2 AStar	4103	
☐ C-GGTO	Aérospatiale AS350B2 AStar	4393	
☐ C-GHHH	Aérospatiale AS350B2 AStar	3270	
☐ C-GHHV	Aérospatiale AS350B2 AStar	2918	ex N4034Q
☐ C-GHHW	Aérospatiale AS350B2 AStar	3039	
☐ C-GHHZ	Aérospatiale AS350B2 AStar	3054	
☐ C-GNHH	Aérospatiale AS350B2 AStar	2737	ex N9446H
☐ C-GRHH	Aérospatiale AS350B2 AStar	3315	ex N37PT
☐ C-GRJO	Aérospatiale AS350B2 AStar	4277	
☐ C-GTIA	Aérospatiale AS350B2 AStar	4328	ex F-WWPZ
☐ C-GXHH	Aérospatiale AS350B2 AStar	4058	ex F-WQDF
☐ C-FCDL	Bell 206B JetRanger III	3852	ex N93AJ
☐ C-FCOY	Bell 206B JetRanger III	3280	ex N7023J
☐ C-FETC	Bell 206B JetRanger III	3515	ex C-GTIA
☐ C-FHHB	Bell 206B JetRanger	519	ex CF-HHB
☐ C-FHHI	Bell 206B JetRanger III	2310	ex N101CD
☐ C-GHHD	Bell 206B JetRanger	1566	ex N90003
☐ C-GHHG	Bell 206B JetRanger	1396	ex N918TR
☐ C-GHHM	Bell 206B JetRanger III	2712	
☐ C-GHHO	Bell 206B JetRanger	1690	
☐ C-GHHR	Bell 206B JetRanger II	1963	
☐ C-GHHX	Bell 206B JetRanger III	2714	
☐ C-GHXJ	Bell 206B JetRanger	1832	
☐ C-GIZO	Bell 206B JetRanger III	2715	
☐ C-GJJA	Bell 206B JetRanger II	2032	ex N9958K

	Registration	Type	c/n	Previous identity	Name	Notes
☐	C-GJMJ	Bell 206B JetRanger	620	ex N7112J		
☐	C-GKDG	Bell 206B JetRanger III	2969			
☐	C-GKGI	Bell 206B JetRanger	1790	ex N49629		
☐	C-GKJL	Bell 206B JetRanger III	3005			
☐	C-GMDQ	Bell 206B JetRanger III	3045			
☐	C-GMDX	Bell 206B JetRanger III	3032			
☐	C-GMZH	Bell 206B JetRanger III	3203			
☐	C-GNLT	Bell 206B JetRanger III	2973			
☐	C-GNSQ	Bell 206B JetRanger III	3274			
☐	C-GOPF	Bell 206B JetRanger III	3227			
☐	C-GOPK	Bell 206B JetRanger III	3247			
☐	C-FTHH	Bell 206L-3 LongRanger III	51369			
☐	C-GAXW	Bell 206L-3 LongRanger III	51395	ex N6501S		
☐	C-GFHH	Bell 206L-3 LongRanger III	51362	ex C-FPCL		

HORNE AIR — Hornepayne, ON (YHN)

	Registration	Type	c/n	Previous identity	Notes
☐	C-FFHP	de Havilland DHC-2 Beaver	57	ex CF-FHP	Floatplane
☐	C-FIDM	de Havilland DHC-2 Beaver	1323	ex N99871	Floatplane
☐	C-GEWG	de Havilland DHC-2 Beaver	842	ex N87572	Floatplane

HURON AIR AND OUTFITTERS — Armstrong, ON (YYW)

	Registration	Type	c/n	Previous identity	Notes
☐	C-FDPW	de Havilland DHC-2 Beaver	1339	ex 58-2011	Floatplane or wheels/skis
☐	C-FGSR	Noorduyn Norseman V	N29-47	ex CF-GSR	Floatplane
☐	C-FIOF	de Havilland DHC-3 Otter	24	ex LN-SUV	Floatplane or wheels/skis

HYDRO-QUEBEC (SERVICE TRANSPORT AERIEN) — Hydro (HYD) — Montreal-Trudeau, QC (YUL)

	Registration	Type	c/n	Previous identity	Notes
☐	C-GHQL	de Havilland DHC-8-402Q	4115		Op by AIE
☐	C-GHQP	de Havilland DHC-8-402Q	4004	ex C-GIHK	Op by AIE
☐	C-GJNL	de Havilland DHC-8-311	422	ex G-BXPZ	Op by AIE

ICARUS FLYING SERVICE — Ile de la Madelaine, QC (YGR)

	Registration	Type	c/n	Previous identity
☐	C-GFBF	Britten-Norman BN-2B-27 Islander	2125	ex VP-FBF

IGNACE AIRWAYS — Ignace/Thunder Bay, ON (ZUC/YQT)

	Registration	Type	c/n	Previous identity	Notes
☐	C-FAPR	de Havilland DHC-3 Otter	31	ex LN-LMM	Floatplane
☐	CF-TTL	Cessna U206C Super Skywagon	U206-1062	ex N29088	Floatplane
☐	C-GZBR	de Havilland DHC-2 Beaver	1272	ex N434GR	Floatplane

INFINITY FLIGHT SERVICES — Edmonton-Municipal, AB (YXD)

	Registration	Type	c/n	Previous identity
☐	C-GSWF	Beech B100 King Air	BE-129	ex LV-VCU

INLAND AIR CHARTERS — Prince Rupert, BC (YPR)

	Registration	Type	c/n	Previous identity	Notes
☐	C-FFRL	de Havilland DHC-2 Beaver	482	ex CF-FRL	Floatplane
☐	C-FGQC	de Havilland DHC-2 Beaver	75	ex CF-GQC	Floatplane
☐	C-FIAX	de Havilland DHC-2 Beaver	140	ex VH-AAD	Floatplane
☐	C-FJOM	de Havilland DHC-2 Beaver	1024	ex CF-JOM	Floatplane
☐	C-FJPX	de Havilland DHC-2 Beaver	1076	ex CF-JPX	Floatplane

INTEGRA AIR — Lethbridge, AB (YQL)

	Registration	Type	c/n	Previous identity
☐	C-FFIA	British Aerospace Jetstream 31	779	ex C-FSAS
☐	C-FFNV	Piper PA-31T Cheyenne	31T-7720058	ex N167DA
☐	C-GGIA	British Aerospace Jetstream 31	778	ex C-FMIP

JACKSON AIR SERVICES — Jackson (JCK) — Flin Flon, MB (YFO)

	Registration	Type	c/n	Previous identity	Notes
☐	C-FMAJ	de Havilland DHC-3 Otter	383	ex 4655	Floatplane or wheels/skis
☐	C-GDYR	Cessna A185F Skywagon	18503018		Floatplane or wheels/skis
☐	C-GISX	Cessna A185F Skywagon II	18503836	ex N4669E	Floatplane or wheels/skis
☐	C-GJMZ	Partenavia P.68B Observer	369-27/OB		

JOHNNY MAY'S AIR CHARTERS — Kuujjuaq, QC (YVP)

	Registration	Type	c/n	Previous identity	Name	Notes
☐	C-FCEE	de Havilland DHC-3 Otter	282	ex 57-6134		Floatplane or wheels/skis
☐	C-GMAY	de Havilland DHC-2 Beaver	1123	ex 56-0393	Pengo Palee	Floatplane or wheels/skis

KABEELO AIRWAYS — Confederation Lake, ON (YMY)

	Registration	Type	c/n	Previous identity	Notes
☐	C-GDYT	de Havilland DHC-2 Beaver	1109	ex 56-4403	Floatplane
☐	C-GLSA	de Havilland DHC-2 Beaver	1389	ex N94471	Floatplane

KALUSAIR — North Lancaster, ON

☐ C-FSYF	Piper PA-34-200	34-7450202	ex N44159	
☐ C-GKSB	Piper PA-31 Turbo Navajo	31-268	ex N370RC	
☐ C-GKSI	Piper PA-31-325 Navajo C/R	31-7912008	ex N27791	

KASABA AIR SERVICE — Kasba Lake, NT (YDU)

☐ CF-MAS	de Havilland DHC-2 Beaver	38	ex C-FMAS	Floatplane

KAYAIR — Ear Falls, ON (YMY)

☐ CF-TBH	Beech 3T	6226	43-35671	Floatplane

KD AIR — Kay Dee (XC/KDC) — Port Alberni, BC (YPB)

☐ C-GPCA	Piper PA-31 Turbo Navajo	31-42	ex N333DG	
☐ C-GXEY	Piper PA-31-350 Navajo Chieftain	31-7305044	ex N74910	

KECHIKA VALLEY AIR — Fort St John, BC (YXJ)

☐ C-GOSC	Cessna U206G Stationair 6	U20603757	ex (N5649G)	Floatplane or wheels/skis

KEEWATIN AIR — (FK) — Churchill, MB/Rankin Inlet, NU (YYQ /YRT)

☐ C-FBPK	Beech 1900D	UE-128	ex N128EU	
☐ C-FCGT	Beech 200 Super King Air	BB-159	ex N47FH	EMS
☐ C-FJXO	Beech 1900C	UC-124	ex N124CU	
☐ C-FRMV	Beech B200 Super King Air	BB-979	ex N22TP	
☐ C-FSKN	Beech B200 Super King Air	BB-1109	ex F-GLLH	
☐ C-FSKO	Beech B200 Super King Air	BB-1007	ex N514MA	EMS
☐ C-FZPW	Beech B200 Super King Air	BB-940	ex N519SA	EMS

KELOWNA FLIGHTCRAFT AIR CHARTER — Flightcraft (KW/KFA) — Kelowna, BC (YLW)

☐ C-GACU	Boeing 727-225F/W (Duganair 3)	20152/775	ex N8833E	710	Op for Purolator Courier
☐ C-GGKF	Boeing 727-223F (FedEx 3)	21523/1467	ex C-FMKF	718	Op for Purolator Courier
☐ C-GIKF	Boeing 727-227F (FedEx 3)	20772/982	ex N99763	721	Op for Purolator Courier
☐ C-GJKF	Boeing 727-227F (FedEx 3)	21042/1106	ex N10756	722	Op for Purolator Courier
☐ C-GKFJ	Boeing 727-281F (Raisbeck 3)	21455/1316	ex C-FLHJ		
☐ C-GKKF	Boeing 727-227F (FedEx 3)	21043/1113	ex N16758	723	Op for Purolator Courier
☐ C-GLKF	Boeing 727-227F (FedEx 3)	21118/1167	ex N14760	724	Op for Purolator Courier
☐ C-GMKF	Boeing 727-227F (FedEx 3)	21119/1175	ex N16761	725	Op for Purolator Courier
☐ C-GNKF	Boeing 727-227F (FedEx 3)	20839/1031	ex N88770		
☐ C-GQKF	Boeing 727-243F (FedEx 3)	21265/1226	ex N17402	720	Op for Purolator Courier
☐ C-GTKF	Boeing 727-225F (FedEx 3)	21580/1435	ex N8883Z	728	Op for Purolator Courier
☐ C-GWKF	Boeing 727-243F/W (Duganair 3)	21270/1231	ex N17407		
☐ C-GXKF	Boeing 727-243F/W (Duganair 3)	21663/1438	ex N17410		Op for Purolator Courier
☐ C-GYKF	Boeing 727-277F/W (Duganair 3)	20551/1054	ex VH-VLG		
☐ C-FKFZ	Convair 580	151	ex N11151	510	
☐ C-GKFF	Convair 580F	160	ex N9067R	511	Op for Purolator Courier
☐ C-GKFG	Convair 580	22	ex N32KA	516	stored YLW
☐ C-GKFU	Convair 580F	82	ex N90857	501	Op for Purolator Courier
☐ C-	Convair 580	34	ex N538JA		stored YLW as N538JA
☐ C-	Convair 580	69	ex N569JA		stored YLW as N569JA
☐ C-	Convair 340	238	ex N43938		
☐ C-GKFA	Douglas DC-10-30F	46921/214	ex N811SL	101	
☐ C-GKFB	Douglas DC-10-30F	46949/179	ex N949PL		
☐ C-	Douglas DC-10-30F	47928/192	ex N304WL		on order
☐ C-GJRH	Cessna 340	340-0058	ex N340BD		
☐ C-GKFX	Beech A60 Duke	P-235	ex N60GF		

KENN BOREK AIR — Borek Air (4K/KBA)
Calgary-Intl, AB/Edmonton-Intl, AB/ Iqaluit, NT/Resolute Bay, NT (YYC/YEG/YFB/YRB)

☐ C-FMKB	Basler BT-67TP	47/19560	ex N57NA	Freighter; dam Dec07
☐ C-GAWI	Basler BT-67	19227	ex N79017	Lidia; lsd to Alfred Wegener Institute
☐ C-GEAI	Basler BT-67	16305/33053	ex N200AN	
☐ C-GJKB	Basler BT-67	13383	ex N167BT	
☐ C-GVKB	Basler BT-67	12300	ex N907Z	
☐ C-FKBK	Beech 99	U-18	ex HP-1233APP	
☐ C-GKBA	Beech B99	U-164	ex SE-GRB	
☐ C-GKBB	Beech 65-C90 King Air	LJ-607	ex N48DA	
☐ C-GKKB	Beech B99	U-149	ex HP-1230APP	
☐ C-FAFD	Beech 100 King Air	B-42	ex LN-VIP	
☐ C-FHKB	Beech 100 King Air	B-63	ex N20880	

☐ C-FMWM	Beech A100 King Air	B-59	ex N702JL	
☐ C-FRKB	Beech 100 King Air	B-72	ex C-GTLF	
☐ C-FTUA	Beech 100 King Air	B-61	ex C-GSYN	
☐ C-GAVI	Beech A100 King Air	B-201	ex G-BBVM	
☐ C-GHOC	Beech A100 King Air	B-194	ex N57237	
☐ C-GKBQ	Beech 100 King Air	B-62	ex LN-NLB	
☐ C-GKBZ	Beech 100 King Air	B-85	ex LN-PAJ	
☐ C-GWWA	Beech 100 King Air	B-27	ex G-BOFN	

☐ C-FBCN	Beech 200 Super King Air	BB-7		
☐ C-FEKB	Beech 200 Super King Air	BB-468	ex N9UT	Beech 1300 conversion
☐ C-FKBU	Beech 200 Super King Air	BB-285	ex C-GQXF	
☐ C-GKBN	Beech 200 Super King Air	BB-29	ex LN-ASG	
☐ C-GKBP	Beech 200 Super King Air	BB-505	ex HP-1083P	

☐ C-FBBA	de Havilland DHC-6 Twin Otter 300	276	ex 8Q-MAK	
☐ C-FBBV	de Havilland DHC-6 Twin Otter 300	311	ex C-FMPC	
☐ C-FBBW	de Havilland DHC-6 Twin Otter 300	588	ex 8Q-KBA	
☐ C-FDHB	de Havilland DHC-6 Twin Otter 300	338	ex CF-DHB	
☐ C-FGOG	de Havilland DHC-6 Twin Otter 300	348	ex CF-GOG	Floatplane or wheels/skis
☐ C-FSJB	de Havilland DHC-6 Twin Otter 300	377	ex N4901D	
☐ C-FUGT	de Havilland DHC-6 Twin Otter 300	382	ex 8Q-MAR	
☐ C-GBPE	de Havilland DHC-6 Twin Otter 100	21	ex 8Q-QHC	
☐ C-GCKB	de Havilland DHC-6 Twin Otter 300	312	ex C-FMPF	
☐ C-GDHC	de Havilland DHC-6 Twin Otter 300	494		
☐ C-GIKB	de Havilland DHC-6 Twin Otter 100	64	ex 8Q-CSL	
☐ C-GKBC	de Havilland DHC-6 Twin Otter 300	650	ex N55921	
☐ C-GKBG	de Havilland DHC-6 Twin Otter 300	733		
☐ C-GKBH	de Havilland DHC-6 Twin Otter 300	732	ex 8Q-MAV	
☐ C-GKBO	de Havilland DHC-6 Twin Otter 300	725	ex HP-1273APP	
☐ C-GKBR	de Havilland DHC-6 Twin Otter 300	617	ex 8Q-MAU	
☐ C-GPAO	de Havilland DHC-6 Twin Otter 300	447	ex N5356A	
☐ C-GSKB	de Havilland DHC-6 Twin Otter 100	99	ex 8Q-QBU	
☐ C-GTKB	de Havilland DHC-6 Twin Otter 100	60	ex 8Q-MAC	
☐ C-GXXB	de Havilland DHC-6 Twin Otter 300	426	ex 8Q-MAN	
☐ C-GZVH	de Havilland DHC-6 Twin Otter 300	671	ex VP-CCB	

☐ C-FLKB	Embraer EMB.110P1 Bandeirante	110397	ex N903LE
☐ C-GANR	Embraer EMB.110P1 Bandeirante	110373	ex HP-931APP
☐ C-GBBR	Embraer EMB.110P1 Bandeirante	110444	ex HP-1177AP
☐ C-GFKB	Embraer EMB.110P1 Bandeirante	110400	ex 9N-AFF

KENORA AIR SERVICE — *Kenora SPB, ON (YQK)*

☐ CF-CBA	de Havilland DHC-3 Otter	230	ex C-FCBA	Floatplane
☐ CF-JEI	de Havilland DHC-2 Beaver	1020		Floatplane
☐ C-FNOT	de Havilland DHC-2 Beaver	1067	ex N4193A	Floatplane
☐ C-FODO	de Havilland DHC-2 Beaver	822	ex CF-ODO	Floatplane
☐ CF-TBX	Beech D18S	A-479	ex N841B	Floatplane
☐ C-FWDB	Cessna A185E Skywagon	185-1250	ex (N4783Q)	Floatplane
☐ C-FWMM	Cessna A185F Skywagon	18502238	ex N4361Q	Floatplane
☐ C-GAQJ	de Havilland DHC-2 Beaver	1130	ex 56-4411	Floatplane
☐ C-GEHX	Beech 3NM	CA-112	ex CF-ZNE	Floatplane
☐ C-GOTD	Cessna A185F Skywagon	18502445	ex (N1724R)	Floatplane
☐ C-GPVC	de Havilland DHC-2 Beaver	290	ex N9257Z	Floatplane
☐ C-GYJY	Cessna A185F Skywagon	18502468	ex N1748R	Floatplane

KEYSTONE AIR SERVICE — *Keystone (BZ/KEE)* — *Swan River, MB (YSE)*

☐ C-FAFT	Beech 200 Super King Air	BB-57	ex N121DA
☐ C-FPCD	Beech B99	U-151	ex C-FBRO
☐ C-FSPN	Beech 200 Super King Air	BB-745	ex N428P
☐ C-FXLO	Piper PA-31-350 Chieftain	31-8052022	ex N3547N
☐ C-GBDN	Piper PA-31-350 Navajo Chieftain	31-7652035	ex N59763
☐ C-GCJH	Piper PA-31-350 Chieftain	31-7952109	ex N42FL
☐ C-GFOL	Beech 200 Super King Air	BB-27	ex N120DP
☐ C-GGQU	Piper PA-31 Turbo Navajo	31-155	ex N9116Y
☐ C-GOSU	Piper PA-31-350 Navajo Chieftain	31-7752148	ex N27327

KISSISSING AIR — *Kississing Lake/Pine Falls, MB*

☐ C-FENB	Noorduyn UC-64A Norseman	324	ex 43-5384	Floatplane
☐ CF-FAQ	de Havilland DHC-2 Beaver	94	ex C-FFAQ	Floatplane
☐ C-FIDF	de Havilland DHC-2 Beaver	1321	ex N99870	Floatplane
☐ C-FIKP	de Havilland DHC-2 Beaver	890	ex CF-IKP	Floatplane
☐ C-FKIX	Cessna 185A Skywagon	18503794	ex N9866Q	Floatplane
☐ C-FOBR	Noorduyn Norseman V	N29-35	ex CF-OBR	Floatplane
☐ C-FYMV	de Havilland DHC-2 Beaver	1589	ex CF-YMV	Floatplane
☐ C-GADE	de Havilland DHC-2 Beaver	730	ex 53-7919	Floatplane
☐ C-GDLO	Cessna TU206B Super Skywagon	U206-0690	ex N4990F	Floatplane

KIVALLIQ AIR		**Kivalliq(FK)**	**Winnipeg-Intl, MB/Rankin Islet, NU (YWG/YRT)**	
☐ C-FJXL	Beech 1900C	UC-102	ex N15479	

KLUANE AIRWAYS				**Whitehorse, YT (YXY)**
☐ C-FMPS	de Havilland DHC-2 Beaver	1114	ex CF-MPS	Floatplane

L AND A AVIATION				**Hay River, NT (YHY)**
☐ C-FYFJ	Cessna A185F Skywagon II	18503797	ex N9913Q	Floatplane or wheels/skis
☐ CF-ZEB	Cessna 337F Super Skymaster	33701428	ex N1828M	
☐ C-GHYT	Beech A100 King Air	B-98	ex N998RC	
☐ C-GJHM	Cessna A185F Skywagon II	18504203		Floatplane or wheels/skis

LABRADOR AIR SAFARI				**Baie Comeau, QC (YBC)**
☐ C-FJGV	de Havilland DHC-2 Beaver	977	ex CF-JGV	Floatplane or wheels/skis
☐ C-FOCU	de Havilland DHC-2 Beaver	73	ex CF-OCU	Floatplane or wheels/skis
☐ C-FPQC	de Havilland DHC-2 Beaver	873	ex CF-IKQ	Floatplane or wheels/skis
☐ C-FUWJ	de Havilland DHC-2 Beaver	453	ex N7691	Floatplane or wheels/skis
☐ C-FYYT	de Havilland DHC-2 Beaver	1569	ex VH-IDZ	Floatplane or wheels/skis
☐ C-GUJU	de Havilland DHC-2 Beaver	1639	ex N4600Y	Floatplane or wheels/skis
☐ C-GWAE	de Havilland DHC-2 Beaver	1094	ex N93434	Floatplane or wheels/skis
☐ C-FAZW	de Havilland DHC-3 Otter	451	ex JW-9101	Floatplane or wheels/skis
☐ C-FJZN	de Havilland DHC-3 Otter	205	ex CF-JZN	Floatplane or wheels/skis
☐ C-GLCO	de Havilland DHC-3 Otter	420	ex N17681	Floatplane or wheels/skis
☐ C-GLJI	de Havilland DHC-3 Otter	150	ex 55-3297	Floatplane or wheels/skis
☐ C-GVNX	de Havilland DHC-3 Otter	353	ex N5335G	Floatplane or wheels/skis
☐ C-FTBC	Cessna U206F Stationair	U20602047	ex CF-TBC	Floatplane or wheels/skis
☐ C-GUBN	Cessna U206F Stationair II	U20602860	ex (N1185Q)	Floatplane or wheels/skis

Associated with Air Saguenay

LAC LA CROIX QUETICO AIR SERVICE				**Lac la Croix, ON/Crane Lake, MB**
☐ C-FHAN	de Havilland DHC-2 Beaver	316	ex N11255	Floatplane
☐ C-FVSF	Cessna A185E Skywagon	185-1223	ex CF-VSF	Floatplane
☐ C-GDZD	de Havilland DHC-2 Beaver	496	ex 52-6116	Floatplane
☐ C-GUEC	Cessna A185F Skywagon	18503986	ex N5513E	Floatplane

LAC SEUL AIRWAYS				**Ear Falls, ON (YMY)**
☐ CF-HXY	de Havilland DHC-3 Otter	67		Floatplane
☐ C-GLLO	Cessna U206F Stationair II	U20602913	ex N1602Q	Floatplane

LAKELAND AIRWAYS				**Temagami, ON**
☐ C-FJKT	de Havilland DHC-2 Beaver	1023	ex CF-JKT	
☐ C-GUFH	Cessna A185F Skywagon	18502857	ex (N1488F)	

LAKELSE AIR				**Terrace, BC (YXT)**
☐ C-FHQT	Bell 204B	2024	ex C-GEAV	
☐ C-FMGM	Kaman K-1200 K-MAX	A94-0013	ex N163KA	
☐ C-FNBR	Aérospatiale AS350B2 AStar	2565	ex N60618	
☐ C-GALU	Bell 206B JetRanger III	2511	ex N50071	
☐ C-GBCN	Aérospatiale AS350B2 AStar	2609	ex F-GLHP	
☐ C-GHQW	Bell 206B JetRanger III	1708		
☐ C-GJUP	Aérospatiale AS350B AStar	2155	ex JA9793	
☐ C-GPTC	Aérospatiale AS350B2 AStar	2092	ex OY-HDY	
☐ C-GWHO	Bell 206L LongRanger	45013	ex N3GH	

LAKES DISTRICT AIR SERVICES				**Burns Lake, BC (YPZ)**
☐ C-FFHS	de Havilland DHC-2 Beaver	51	ex CF-HHS	Floatplane or wheels/skis
☐ C-FVXQ	Cessna A185E Skywagon	185-1198	ex CF-XVQ	Floatplane or wheels/skis

LAUZON AVIATION				**Elliot Lake, ON (YEL)**
☐ C-FRUY	de Havilland DHC-2 Beaver	687	ex N74157	Floatplane

LAWRENCE BAY AIRWAYS				**Southend-Reindeer Lake, SK**
☐ C-GUJX	de Havilland DHC-2 Beaver	1132	ex 56-4412	Floatplane

LEUENBERGER AIR SERVICE — Nakina SPB, ON (YQN)

☐ C-FSOX	de Havilland DHC-3 Turbo Otter	437	ex CF-SOX		Floatplane
☐ C-GLCW	de Havilland DHC-3 Turbo Otter	172	ex 55-3310		Floatplane

LIARD AIR — Muncho Lake, BC

☐ C-CNNP	de Havilland DHC-3 Turbo Otter	465	ex N342KA		Floatplane
☐ C-GUDK	de Havilland DHC-2 Beaver	708	ex 53-7900		Floatplane
☐ C-GUGE	Cessna A185F Skywagon	18502904	ex N8730Z		Floatplane or wheels/skis

LITTLE RED AIR SERVICE — Little Red (LRA) — Fort Vermilion, AB

☐ C-FGWR	Beech B200 Super King Air	BB-1599	ex C-FGWD		
☐ C-FLRB	Beech A100 King Air	B-131	ex N102FG		
☐ C-FLRD	Beech A100 King Air	B-243	ex PT-OFZ		
☐ C-FLTC	Beech 65-C90 King Air	LJ-631	ex N103FG		
☐ C-FPQQ	Beech B200 Super King Air	BB-1304	ex N3173K		
☐ C-GGUH	Cessna 208B Caravan I	208B0827	ex N51478		
☐ C-GICJ	Cessna U206F Stationair	U20603044	ex N4318Q		
☐ C-GMIC	de Havilland DHC-2 Beaver	791	ex (N5218G)	604	
☐ C-GWVT	Cessna U206F Stationair	U20602918	ex (N1721Q)		

LOCKHART AIR SERVICES — Sioux Lookout, ON (YXL)

☐ C-FKQM	Cessna 404 Titan II	404-0108	ex N37102		
☐ G-GFIT	Cessna 310R	310R1865	ex (N3173M)		
☐ C-GIJF	Cessna 310R	310R1875	ex N3208M		
☐ C-GOGP	Cessna 402C	402C0516	ex N401SA		

MANITOBA GOVERNMENT AIR SERVICES — Winnipeg-Intl/Thompson, MB (YWG/YTH)

☐ C-FTUV	Canadair CL-215-1A10 (CL-215)	1020	ex CF-TUV	256	
☐ C-FTXI	Canadair CL-215-1A10 (CL-215)	1016	ex CF-TXI	255	
☐ C-GBOW	Canadair CL-215-1A10 (CL-215)	1087	ex C-GKDY	253	
☐ C-GMAF	Canadair CL-215-1A10 (CL-215)	1044	ex C-GUMW	250	
☐ C-GMAK	Canadair CL-215-1A10 (CL-215)	1107		254	
☐ C-GUMW	Canadair CL-215-1A10 (CL-215)	1065		251	
☐ C-GYJB	Canadair CL-215-1A10 (CL-215)	1068		252	
☐ C-FEMA	Cessna S550 Citation S/11	S550-0040			EMS
☐ C-FMAX	de Havilland DHC-3 Otter	267	ex CF-MAX		Floatplane or wheels/skis
☐ C-FODY	de Havilland DHC-3 Otter	429	ex CF-ODY		Floatplane or wheels/skis
☐ C-FWAH	de Havilland DHC-6 Twin Otter 300	240	ex CF-WAH		
☐ C-GBNX	Cessna 560 Citation V	0074	ex N593MD		EMS
☐ C-GDAT	Cessna 310R	310R1883	ex N315U		
☐ C-GMLN	Cessna 310R	310R1884	ex N316U		
☐ C-GRNE	Piper PA-31-350 Chieftain	31-7952224	ex N91834		
☐ C-GYNE	Cessna 310R	310R1367	ex N4086C		

MARITIME AIR CHARTER — Halifax, NS (YHZ)

☐ C-FCAI	Piper PA-31 Turbo Navajo	31-475	ex N22DC		
☐ C-FDOR	Beech A100 King Air	B-103	ex CF-DOR		
☐ C-FYKQ	Piper PA-31 Turbo Navajo	31-399	ex CF-YKQ		
☐ C-GILS	Britten-Norman BN-2A-21 Islander	0416	ex N92JA		
☐ C-GXUG	Piper PA-31 Turbo Navajo	31-665	ex N1GY		

MARTINI AVIATION — Fort Langley, BC

☐ C-GMNT	de Havilland DHC-2 Turbo Beaver	1653-TB30	ex N4478		
☐ C-GPLT	Pilatus PC-12/45	566	ex HB-FPX		
☐ C-GUWF	de Havilland DHC-2 Beaver	287	ex N91364		

MAX AVIATION — Max Aviation (MAX) — Montreal-St Hubert, QC (YHU)

☐ C-FOGP	Beech B100 King Air	BE-134	ex N363EA		
☐ C-FSIK	Beech B100 King Air	BE-39	ex N129CP		
☐ C-GPJL	Beech B100 King Air	BE-107	ex N3699B		
☐ C-GPRU	Beech B100 King Air	BE-26	ex N36WH		
☐ C-GSWG	Beech B100 King Air	BE-131	ex N6354H		
☐ C-GVIK	Beech A100 King Air	BE-7	ex N57HT		

Subsidiary of Cargair

McMURRAY AVIATION — Fort McMurray, AB (YMM)

☐ C-GHJB	Cessna U206E Stationair	U20601677	ex N9477G		
☐ C-GHGT	Cessna U206G Stationair	U20605874			
☐ C-GHLI	Cessna 208B Caravan I	208B0565	ex N5858J		
☐ C-GKOM	Cessna 208 Caravan	20800365	ex N675TF		
☐ C-GRKO	Cessna U206G Stationair	U20606617	ex N9707Z		

☐ C-GWKO	Cessna 208B Caravan I	208B1245	ex N52591	
☐ C-GZZD	Cessna U206F Stationair	U20601957	ex N50946	

MEADOW AIR — Meadow Lake, SK (YLJ)

☐ C-GBGR	Cessna 337 Super Skymaster	337-0398	ex N6398F
☐ C-GETG	Cessna 337 Super Skymaster	337-0921	ex N2621S
☐ C-GGFA	Cessna 337 Super Skymaster	337-1263	ex N1263M
☐ C-GYHW	Cessna 337 Super Skymaster	337-1111	ex N86204

MELAIRE — Fort Frances, ON (YAG)

☐ C-FOMJ	de Havilland DHC-2 Turbo Beaver	1683/TB51	ex CF-OMJ	Floatplane or wheels/skis

MINIPI AVIATION — Goose Bay, NL (YYR)

☐ C-FCOO	de Havilland DHC-2 Beaver	314	ex N377JW	Floatplane

MISSINIPPI AIRWAYS — The Pas, MB/Pukatawagan. MB (YQD/XPK)

☐ C-FIXS	Cessna 208B Caravan I	208B1209		
☐ C-FJKM	Piper PA-31-350 Chieftain	31-7952089	ex N764A	
☐ C-FMCB	Cessna 208B Caravan I	208B1114	ex N1274B	
☐ C-FTYO	Beech 200 Super King Air	BB-1222	ex N126KA	
☐ C-FWXI	Beech 200 Super King Air	BB-1224	ex C-GTLA	EMS
☐ C-GADW	Piper PA-31-350 Navajo Chieftain	31-7752078	ex N27191	
☐ C-GGGT	Cessna TU206G Stationair	U20604170	ex N756LF	
☐ C-GHQF	Piper PA-31-350 Chieftain	31-8052050	ex N633WA	
☐ C-GMKO	Piper PA-31-350 Chieftain	31-7952063	ex N932LA	
☐ C-GOCN	Cessna 208B Caravan I	208B0780	ex N308KC	
☐ C-GOGT	Beech B200 Super King Air	BB-535		
☐ C-GWHW	Piper PA-31-350 Chieftain	31-8052060	ex N223CH	
☐ C-GYQD	Piper PA-31-350 Chieftain	31-8152039	ex N4075T	

MISSIONAIR — Winnipeg-Intl, MB/Sachigo Lake, ON (YWG/ZPB)

☐ C-FSHA	Piper PA-31-350 Navajo Chieftain	31-7752062	ex PH-NTB
☐ C-GCJX	Piper PA-31-350 Navajo Chieftain	31-7552064	ex N4WE

MOLSON AIR — Wabowden, MB

☐ C-FBQY	de Havilland DHC-2 Beaver	1496	ex N147Q	Floatplane or wheels/skis
☐ C-GYBQ	Cessna A185F Skywagon	18503568	ex N4014Q	Floatplane or wheels/skis

MONTAIR AVIATION — Boundary Bay, BC (YDT)

☐ C-GRSL	Beech 65-90B King Air	LJ-609	ex Z-WSG
☐ C-GYPD	Piper PA-34-220T Seneca	34-7870025	ex N47991

MORGAN AIR SERVICES — Calgary-Intl, AB (YYC)

☐ C-FCCM	Piper PA-30-160 Twin Comanche	30-1632	ex CF-CCM
☐ C-FNRM	Gulfstream Commander 690C	11692	ex N152X
☐ C-FRQS	Piper PA-30-160 Twin Comanche	30-934	ex N7854Y
☐ C-GOMA	Beech 200 Super King Air	BB-262	ex EC-HHO
☐ C-GSQD	Cessna 401	401-0300	ex (176TC)

MORNINGSTAR AIR EXPRESS — Morningstar (MAL) — Edmonton-Intl, AB (YEG)

☐ C-FEXB	Cessna 208B Caravan I	208B0539	ex N758FX		Lsd fr/op for FDX
☐ C-FEXE	Cessna 208B Caravan I	208B0244	ex N750FE		Lsd fr/op for FDX
☐ C-FEXF	Cessna 208B Caravan I	208B0508	ex N749FX		Lsd fr/op for FDX
☐ C-FEXV	Cessna 208B Caravan I	208B0482	ex N738FX		Lsd fr/op for FDX
☐ C-FEXX	Cessna 208B Caravan I	208B0209	ex (N877FE)		Lsd fr/op for FDX
☐ C-FEXY	Cessna 208B Caravan I	208B0226	ex N896FE		Lsd fr/op for FDX
☐ C-FMEA	Boeing 727-247F (FedEx 3)	21329/1254	ex N235FE	Stephanie	Lsd fr/op for FDX
☐ C-FMEE	Boeing 727-247F (FedEx 3)	21330/1260	ex N236FE	Atima	Lsd fr/op for FDX
☐ C-FMEI	Boeing 727-247F (FedEx 3)	21327/1249	ex N233FE	Monika	Lsd fr/op for FDX
☐ C-FMES	Boeing 727-225F (FedEx 3)	22548/1734	ex N461FE	Carolina	Lsd fr/op for FDX
☐ C-FMEY	Boeing 727-247F (FedEx 3)	21328/1251	ex N234FE		Lsd fr/op for FDX
☐ C-GATK	ATR 42-310F	135	ex N923FX		Lsd fr/op for FDX

MUSTANG HELICOPTERS — Red Deer, AB (YQF)

☐ C-FAOV	Aérospatiale AS350B2 AStar	9066	
☐ C-FAOX	Aérospatiale AS350B2 AStar	9067	
☐ C-FAOZ	Aérospatiale AS350B2 AStar	9068	ex N68CQ
☐ C-FMNE	Aérospatiale AS350B2 AStar	9082	
☐ C-FNWE	Aérospatiale AS350B2 AStar	9086	

☐ C-FNYE	Aérospatiale AS350B2 AStar	9091		
☐ C-FNYF	Aérospatiale AS350B2 AStar	9092		
☐ C-FNYK	Aérospatiale AS350B2 AStar	9088		
☐ C-GJHC	Aérospatiale AS350B2 AStar	3412		
☐ C-GXTO	Aérospatiale AS350B2 AStar	9061	ex N681CC	
☐ C-GZGN	Aérospatiale AS350B2 AStar	9062	ex N680CC	
☐ C-FFHB	Bell 205A-1	30294	ex VH-HHW	
☐ C-GFRE	Bell 205A-1	30185	ex EC-FYX	
☐ C-GHUF	Bell 205A-1	30106	ex N687CC	
☐ C-GIVV	Bell 206B JetRanger III	2823	ex N2757C	
☐ C-GVHQ	Bell 205A-1	30110	ex N689CC	
☐ C-FUMN	Piper PA-31 Navajo C	31-8112076	ex N4095F	

NAKINA OUTPOST CAMPS AND AIR SERVICE (T2) — *Nakina, ON (YQN)*

☐ C-FDGV	de Havilland DHC-6 Twin Otter 200	154	ex TF-JMD	
☐ CF-MIQ	de Havilland DHC-3 Turbo Otter	336		Floatplane or wheels/skis
☐ C-FMPY	de Havilland DHC-3 Turbo Otter	324	ex CF-MPY	Floatplane or wheels/skis
☐ C-FNQB	Cessna 208 Caravan	20800387		
☐ C-FTIN	Cessna A185F Skywagon	18503362	ex N7325H	Floatplane or wheels/skis
☐ C-FUYC	Cessna 208B Caravan I	208B1204		
☐ C-FZRJ	Cessna 208B Caravan I	208B0597	ex N52609	
☐ C-GEOW	Pilatus PC-12/45	244	ex HB-FRO	
☐ C-GMVB	Cessna 208B Caravan I	208B0317		

NATIONAL HELICOPTERS — *Toronto, ON*

☐ C-FFUJ	Bell 206B JetRanger III	2982	ex N525W
☐ C-FLYC	Bell 206L-1 LongRanger II	45478	ex XA-SPN
☐ C-FNHB	Bell 206L-1 LongRanger II	45661	ex N166BH
☐ C-FNHG	Bell 206L-1 LongRanger II	45784	ex N220HC
☐ C-FTCH	Bell 206B JetRanger	860	ex N809JA
☐ C-GIGS	Bell 206B JetRanger	1434	ex N59474
☐ C-GMUR	Eurocopter EC120B	1438	
☐ C-GSZZ	Bell 206B JetRanger III	2319	ex XA-TCU

NESTOR FALLS FLY-IN OUTPOSTS — *Nestor Falls SPB, ON*

☐ C-FMDB	de Havilland DHC-2 Beaver	268	ex N2104X	Floatplane
☐ C-FODK	de Havilland DHC-3 Otter	13	ex CF-ODK	Floatplane
☐ C-FSOR	de Havilland DHC-3 Otter	239	ex IM 1725	Floatplane
☐ C-FWWV	Beech 3N	CA-18	ex RCAF 1443	Floatplane
☐ C-GDWB	Cessna U206G Stationair	U20604460	ex N756YJ	Floatplane
☐ C-GYGL	Cessna A185F Skywagon	18503298	ex (N94269)	Floatplane

NEWFOUNDLAND & LABRADOR AIR SERVICES — *St John's, NL (YYT)*

☐ C-FAYN	Canadair CL-215-1A10 (CL-215)	1105		282
☐ C-FAYU	Canadair CL-215-1A10 (CL-215)	1106		283
☐ C-FTXA	Canadair CL-215-1A10 (CL-215)	1006	ex CF-TXA	284
☐ C-FYWP	Canadair CL-215-1A10 (CL-215)	1002	ex CF-YWP	285
☐ C-GDKW	Canadair CL-215-1A10 (CL-215)	1095		280
☐ C-GDKY	Canadair CL-215-1A10 (CL-215)	1096		281
☐ C-GLFY	Cessna 337G Super Skymaster	33701700	ex (N53557)	
☐ C-GNLA	Beech B300 Super King Air	FL-26	ex N59TF	

NOLINOR AVIATION — *Nolinor (NRL)* — *Montreal-Trudeau, QC (YUL)*

☐ C-FAWV	Convair 580F	154	ex C-FMGB	Freighter
☐ C-FHNM	Convair 580F	454	ex N583P	Lsd to GV
☐ C-FTAP	Convair 580	334	ex N580N	
☐ C-GKFP	Convair 580	446	ex N589PL	
☐ C-GNRL	Convair 580F	375	ex CS-TMM	Freighter
☐ C-GQHB	Convair 580	376	ex ZS-KRX	
☐ C-GRLQ	Convair 580	347	ex N580TA	
☐ C-GNLN	Boeing 737-2B6C (Nordam 3)	23050/975	ex CN-RMN	Freighter
☐ C-GTUK	Boeing 737-2B6C (Nordam 3)	23049/951	ex CN-RMM	Freighter

NORDAIR QUEBEC 2000 — *La Grande Riviere, QC (YGL)*

☐ C-FGYK	de Havilland DHC-2 Beaver	123	ex CF-GYK	
☐ C-FKLC	de Havilland DHC-3 Otter	255	ex CF-KLC	Floatplane or wheels/skis
☐ C-FSVP	de Havilland DHC-3 Turbo Otter	28	ex N252KA	Floatplane or wheels/skis

NORDPLUS — Schefferville-Squaw Lake, QC (YKL)

☐ C-FLAP	de Havilland DHC-3 Otter	289	ex CF-LAP	Floatplane
☐ C-FODG	de Havilland DHC-2 Beaver	205		Floatplane
☐ C-FFYK	Cessna A185F Skywagon	18502174	ex CF-FYK	Floatplane
☐ C-GFUT	de Havilland DHC-3 Otter	404	ex CAF9422	Floatplane

NORTH CARIBOO AIR — North Caribou (NCB) — Fort St John, BC (YXJ)

☐ C-FDAM	Beech 100 King Air	B-8	ex N59T	
☐ C-FIDN	Beech 100 King Air	B-3	ex N128RC	
☐ C-FMXY	Beech 100 King Air	B-40	ex N923K	
☐ C-FSKA	Beech A100 King Air	B-239	ex N154TC	
☐ C-GBVX	Beech B100 King Air	BE-99	ex N524BA	
☐ C-GDFJ	Beech B100 King Air	BE-15	ex N300DG	
☐ C-GNCV	Beech 100 King Air	B-23	ex N701RJ	
☐ C-GPCB	Beech A100 King Air	B-45	ex N704S	
☐ C-GTLS	Beech 100 King Air	B-35	ex N178WM	
☐ C-FCGC	Beech 200 Super King Air	BB-236	ex N46KA	CatPass 200 conversion
☐ C-FCGM	Beech 200 Super King Air	BB-217	ex N200CD	CatPass 200 conversion
☐ C-FRRQ	Beech 200 Super King Air	BB-560	ex F-GTEF	
☐ C-GDFN	Beech 200 Super King Air	BB-359	ex N351MA	
☐ C-GDFT	Beech 200 Super King Air	BB-354	ex N221BG	
☐ C-GZRX	Beech 200 Super King Air	BB-574	ex N75WL	
☐ C-FCWP	de Havilland DHC-8-102	111	ex N925CA	
☐ C-FLSX	de Havilland DHC-8-102	285	ex N834EX	
☐ C-FMKD	Beech 65-B90 King Air	LJ-376	ex N300RV	
☐ C-FNCG	de Havilland DHC-8-102	211	ex C-GABH	
☐ C-FNCL	Beech 1900D	UE-11	ex C-FSKT	
☐ C-FNCP	Beech 1900D	UE-58	ex C-GSKY	
☐ C-FODL	de Havilland DHC-8-102	294	ex N881CC	
☐ C-GAQN	de Havilland DHC-8-311	548	ex 5N-BHW	
☐ C-GNPG	Beech 1900C	UB-71	ex N3069K	
☐ CF-QSX	Cessna A185F Skywagon	18502116	ex (N70334)	
☐ C-FVAX	Cessna 425 Conquest	425-0178	ex (N90GM)	
☐ C-GZTU	Beech 1900C-1	UC-103	ex N15031	
☐ C-GCFM	Beech 65-C90 King Air	LJ-886	ex N15SL	
☐ C-GELD	Piper PA-31 Turbo Navajo	31-555	ex N6621L	
☐ C-GIGK	de Havilland DHC-6 Twin Otter 300	492	ex N300BC	
☐ C-GLAC	Beech 58 Baron	TH-339	ex N6YC	
☐ C-GMWO	Piper PA-31 Navajo C	31-8112042	ex N4086Y	

NORTH PACIFIC SEAPLANES — Prince Rupert, BC (YPR)

☐ C-FIFQ	de Havilland DHC-2 Beaver	825	ex CF-IFQ	Floatplane
☐ C-FJOS	de Havilland DHC-2 Beaver	1030	ex CF-JOS	Floatplane
☐ C-FKDC	de Havilland DHC-2 Beaver	1080	ex CF-KDC	Floatplane
☐ C-FOCZ	de Havilland DHC-2 Beaver	100	ex N254BD	Floatplane
☐ C-FTCW	de Havilland DHC-2 Beaver	646	ex VH-SMH	Floatplane
☐ C-FHAS	de Havilland DHC-3 Turbo Otter	382	ex N382BH	Floatplane

NORTH WRIGHT AIRWAYS — Northwright (HW/NWL) — Norman Wells/Good Hope/Deline, NT (YVQ/YGH/YWJ)

☐ C-FBAX	Cessna 207 Skywagon	20700355	ex N1755U	
☐ C-FKHD	Beech 99	U-11	ex F-BRUN	
☐ C-FNWL	de Havilland DHC-6 Twin Otter 300	596	ex N16NG	
☐ C-FVCE	Beech 99A	U-118	ex N918BB	
☐ CF-WHP	Cessna 337C Super Skymaster	337-0895	ex (N2595S)	
☐ CF-ZIZ	Fairchild PC-6/B1-H2 Turbo Porter	2009	ex N353F	Floatplane
☐ C-GAAP	Pilatus PC-6/B1-H2 Turbo Porter	569	ex N2851T	Floatplane
☐ C-GALF	Cessna 207A Stationair 8 II	20700674	ex N9118M	
☐ C-GDBI	Cessna 207 Skywagon	20700039	ex N91052	
☐ C-GDLC	Cessna 208B Caravan I	208B0767	ex N5151D	
☐ C-GFCV	Cessna U206C Super Skywagon	U206-1213	ex N4345E	
☐ C-GHDT	Helio 295 Super Courier	1401	ex N6327V	
☐ C-GJGZ	Cessna A185F Skwagon II	18503856	ex (N4750E)	
☐ C-GMOK	Cessna 207A Stationair 8 II	20700673	ex N6373D	
☐ C-GNWA	Cessna A185F Skwagon II	18503345	ex C-GFJC	
☐ C-GRDD	de Havilland DHC-6 Twin Otter 100	54	ex N8081N	Floatplane or wheels/skis
☐ C-GWUY	Beech 200 Super King Air	BB-77	ex N300CP	
☐ C-GZGO	Britten-Norman BN-2A-26 Islander	2017	ex N59360	
☐ C-GZIZ	Cessna 208B Caravan I	208B0546	ex N5262W	
☐ C-GZVX	Cessna U206G Stationair 6	U20604110	ex (N756HT)	

NORTHERN AIR CARE — **Edmonton-City Centre, AB**

☐ C-GNAA	Beech 100 King Air	B-24	ex N382WC	

NORTHERN AIR CHARTER — **Peace River, AB (YPE)**

☐ C-GIRG	Cessna A185F Skywagon II	18504181	ex (N01424)	
☐ C-GNAC	Piper PA-31 Navajo C	31-7812106	ex N27707	
☐ C-GNAJ	Beech A100 King Air	B-107	ex LN-AAH	
☐ C-GNAK	Beech B200 Super King Air	BB-1376	ex HK-3990X	Catpass 200 conversion
☐ C-GNAM	Beech B200 Super King Air	BB-1339	ex N252AF	EMS, Beech 1300 conversion
☐ C-GNAP	Piper PA-23-250 Aztec F	27-8054002	ex C-GTGS	
☐ C-GNAR	Beech 1900D	UE-252	ex JA017A	
☐ C-GNAX	Beech B200 Super King Air	BB-1419	ex N146SB	

NORTHERN AIR SOLUTIONS — **Bracebridge, ON**

☐ C-FLDC	Cessna 208 Caravan I	20800319	ex N208JN	

NORTHERN LIGHTS AIR — **Lynn Lake SPB, MB (YYL)**

☐ C-GNLL	Cessna 206B Super Skywagon	206-0192	ex N5192U	Floatplane

NORTHSTAR AIR — **Pickle Lake, ON (YPL)**

☐ C-FLNB	Cessna 208B Caravan I	208B0799	ex N799B	
☐ C-FVPC	Pilatus PC-12/45	358	ex N358PC	
☐ C-GCQA	de Havilland DHC-3 Otter	77	ex N129JH	Floatplane or wheels/skis
☐ C-GJAS	Cessna 208 Caravan I	20800322	ex N51869	Floatplane or wheels/skis

NORTHWARD AIR — **Dawson Creek, BC (YDQ)**

☐ C-FOMF	Cessna A185A Skywagon	185-0423	ex (N1623Z)	
☐ CF-SLV	Cessna U206 Super Skywagon	U206-0412	ex N8012Z	

NORTHWAY AVIATION — **Northway (NAL)** — **Arnes, MB (YNR)**

☐ C-FBHP	Cessna 207A Stationair 8	20700647	ex N73857	
☐ C-FHDL	Cessna 180	18030430	ex N1730G	
☐ CF-ZZP	Cessna A185E Skywagon	18501843	ex (N1633M)	Floatplane or wheels/skis
☐ C-GNWD	Piper PA-31T Cheyenne	31T-7620029	ex C-GEBA	
☐ C-GNWG	Cessna 208 Caravan I	20800412	ex N52136	
☐ C-GNWV	Cessna 208B Caravan I	208B1115	ex N5093D	

NORTHWEST FLYING — **Nestor Falls SPB, ON**

☐ CF-NKL	Beech C-45H	AF-378	ex N9864Z	Floatplane
☐ C-GEBL	de Havilland DHC-2 Beaver	1068	ex N33466	Floatplane
☐ C-GYYS	de Havilland DHC-3 Otter	276	ex N1UW	Floatplane

NORTHWESTERN AIR — **Polaris (J3/PLR)** — **Fort Smith, NT (YSM)**

☐ C-FCPE	British Aerospace Jetstream 31	825	ex G-31-825	
☐ C-FNAE	British Aerospace Jetstream 31	881	ex N431AM	
☐ C-FNAF	British Aerospace Jetstream 31	789	ex N411UE	
☐ C-FNAM	British Aerospace Jetstream 31	767	ex N767JX	
☐ C-FNAY	British Aerospace Jetstream 31	768	ex N159PC	
☐ C-FNAZ	British Aerospace Jetstream 32	843	ex C-GEAZ	
☐ C-GNAQ	British Aerospace Jetstream 32EP	837	ex C-FZYB	
☐ C-GNGI	British Aerospace Jetstream 31	739	ex N855JS	
☐ C-FCGI	Beech 65-A90 King Air	LJ-220	ex CF-CGI	
☐ C-GNAH	Beech 99	U-107	ex N207BH	
☐ C-GNAL	Beech 99	U-57	ex TF-ELD	

NT AIR — **Thunderbird (NTA)** — **Prince George/Smithers, BC (YXS/YYD)**

☐ CF-GWM	Cessna U206F Stationair	U20601802	ex CF-BZO		Floatplane or wheels/skis
☐ C-FCPV	de Havilland DHC-6 Twin Otter 300	371	ex HC-CES		
☐ C-FEYT	Beech A100 King Air	B-210	ex N75GR		
☐ C-FHVX	Dornier 328-100	3094	ex D-CMTM		
☐ C-GAVY	Piper PA-31-350 Navajo Chieftain	31-7752165	ex N27409		
☐ C-GCMT	Beech 1900C-1	UC-120	ex N15683		
☐ C-GCMY	Beech 1900D	UE-287		921	Lsd fr GLR
☐ C-GCMZ	Beech 1900C-1	UC-61	ex N1568L	929	
☐ C-GCYA	Cessna A185F Skywagon	18502578	ex (N4515C)		Floatplane
☐ C-GDOX	Cessna 208B Caravan I	208B0541	ex N621BB		
☐ C-GEFA	Beech 1900C-1	UC-94	ex N80346	927	
☐ C-GJSU	Beech 100 King Air	B-88	ex N100ZM		
☐ C-GYIS	Cessna A185F Skywagon	18502895	ex N8679Z		Floatplane or wheels/skis

NUELTIN LAKE AIR SERVICE — Nueltin Lake, MB

☐ C-FDBR	Found FBA-2C1 Bush Hawk XP	34	ex C-GDWS	Floatplane
☐ C-FDCL	Cessna U206G Stationair	U20603542	ex N8790Q	Floatplane
☐ C-FSAP	Noorduyn Norseman VI	231	ex 43-5240	Floatplane
☐ C-GVDQ	Piper PA-31-350 Chieftain	31-8152119	ex N40869	

OMEGA AIR — Richmond, BC

☐ C-FMCL	Aérospatiale AS355F1 Twin Star	5255	ex C-FUHF
☐ C-GBFH	Bell 206B JetRanger	2171	
☐ C-GDHD	Eurocopter EC120B Colibri	1116	ex C-GOWC
☐ C-GHMH	Bell 206B JetRanger	1582	ex N116PC

ONTARIO MINISTRY OF NATURAL RESOURCES AVIATION SERVICES
Trillium (TRI) — Sault Ste Marie, ON (YAM)

☐ C-GOGD	Canadair CL-215-6B11 (CL-415)	2028	ex C-GAOI	270	
☐ C-GOGE	Canadair CL-215-6B11 (CL-415)	2031	ex C-GAUR	271	
☐ C-GOGF	Canadair CL-215-6B11 (CL-415)	2032	ex C-GBGE	272	
☐ C-GOGG	Canadair CL-215-6B11 (CL-415)	2033	ex C-GBFY	273	
☐ C-GOGH	Canadair CL-215-6B11 (CL-415)	2034	ex C-GCNO	274	
☐ C-GOGW	Canadair CL-215-6B11 (CL-415)	2037	ex C-GBPM	275	
☐ C-GOGX	Canadair CL-215-6B11 (CL-415)	2038	ex C-GBPU	276	
☐ C-GOGY	Canadair CL-215-6B11 (CL-415)	2040		277	
☐ C-GOGZ	Canadair CL-215-6B11 (CL-415)	2043		278	
☐ C-FOEH	de Havilland DHC-2 Turbo Beaver	1644/TB24	ex CF-OEH		Floatplane or wheels/skis
☐ C-FOER	de Havilland DHC-2 Turbo Beaver	1671/TB41	ex CF-OER		Floatplane or wheels/skis
☐ C-FOEU	de Havilland DHC-2 Turbo Beaver	1678/TB46	ex CF-OEU		Floatplane or wheels/skis
☐ C-FOEW	de Havilland DHC-2 Turbo Beaver	1682/TB50	ex CF-OEW		Floatplane or wheels/skis
☐ C-FOPA	de Havilland DHC-2 Turbo Beaver	1688/TB56	ex CF-OPA		Floatplane or wheels/skis
☐ C-FOPG	de Havilland DHC-6 Twin Otter 300	232	ex CF-OPG		Floatplane or wheels/skis
☐ C-FOPI	de Havilland DHC-6 Twin Otter 300	243	ex CF-OPI		Floatplane or wheels/skis
☐ C-FOPJ	de Havilland DHC-6 Twin Otter 300	344	ex CF-OPJ		Floatplane or wheels/skis
☐ C-GOGA	de Havilland DHC-6 Twin Otter 300	739			Floatplane or wheels/skis
☐ C-GOGB	de Havilland DHC-6 Twin Otter 300	761			Floatplane or wheels/skis
☐ C-GOGC	de Havilland DHC-6 Twin Otter 300	750			Floatplane or wheels/skis
☐ C-FATR	Eurocopter EC130B4	3759			
☐ C-FCHZ	Bell 206L-1 LongRanger II	45567	ex N313HL		
☐ C-FMNR	Eurocopter EC130B4	4391			
☐ C-GOFH	Bell 206L-1 LongRanger II	45359	ex N100U		
☐ C-GOFI	Bell 206L-1 LongRanger II	45342	ex N167CP		
☐ C-GOGJ	Aérospatiale AS350B2 AStar	2749			
☐ C-GOGL	Aérospatiale AS350B2 AStar	2738			
☐ C-GOGQ	Aérospatiale AS350B2 AStar	3196			
☐ C-GOGS	Beech B300 Super King Air	FL-269	ex N3169N		
☐ C-GOIC	Beech B300 Super King Air	FL-272	ex N3172N		
☐ C-GONT	Eurocopter EC130B4	4423			

OOTSA AIR — Burns Lake, BC (YPZ)

☐ C-FCDT	de Havilland DHC-2 Beaver	390	ex CF-CDT
☐ C-FYSI	Cessna A185E Skywagon	185-1524	ex CF-YSI
☐ C-GZXV	de Havilland DHC-2 Beaver	1079	ex N49771

ORCA AIR — Richmond, BC (YVR)

☐ C-FLRA	Piper PA-31-350 Navajo Chieftain	31-7752091	ex N52MS
☐ C-GPAK	Piper PA-31-350 Chieftain	31-8052070	ex N3558S
☐ C-GPMP	Piper PA-31-350 Chieftain	31-7852024	ex C-GWTT
☐ C-GPWP	Piper PA-31-350 Chieftain	31-7952090	ex N35164
☐ C-GWXL	Piper PA-31-350 Chieftain	31-7952036	ex C-GLYG
☐ C-GZBO	Piper PA-31-350 Chieftain	31-8252048	ex N430S

ORNGE

☐ C-	Agusta AW139			on order
☐ C-	Agusta AW139			on order
☐ C-	Agusta AW139			on order
☐ C-	Agusta AW139			on order
☐ C-	Agusta AW139			on order
☐ C-GRXA	Pilatus PC-12NG	1083	ex N983NG	EMS
☐ C-GRXB	Pilatus PC-12NG	1094	ex N994NG	EMS
☐ C-GRXD	Pilatus PC-12NG	1106	ex N106PC	EMS
☐ C-GRXE	Pilatus PC-12NG	1117	ex N117PZ	EMS
☐ C-GRXH	Pilatus PC-12NG	1163	ex N163NP	EMS
☐ C-GRXM	Pilatus PC-12NG	1169	ex N169NP	EMS

☐ C-FABH	Sikorsky S-76A II	760271	ex C-GHJV		EMS
☐ C-FSBH	Sikorsky S-76A	760168	ex N5427S		EMS
☐ C-GFFJ	Sikorsky S-76A	760138	ex VH-HUD		EMS
☐ C-GIMA	Sikorsky S-76A	760018	ex G-BZAC		EMS
☐ C-GIMB	Sikorsky S-76A	760111	ex G-BIAW		EMS
☐ C-GIMM	Sikorsky S-76A	760044	ex HS-HTM		EMS
☐ C-GIMT	Sikorsky S-76A	760130	ex N1548S		EMS
☐ C-GIMV	Sikorsky S-76A	760005	ex VH-WXE		EMS
☐ C-GIMW	Sikorsky S-76A	760226	ex N76FB		EMS
☐ C-GIMY	Sikorsky S-76A	760055	ex N376LL		EMS
☐ C-GIMZ	Sikorsky S-76A	760169	ex N399PK		EMS

OSNABURGH AIRWAYS — *Pickle Lake, ON (YPL)*

☐ C-FCZO	de Havilland DHC-3 Otter	71	ex CF-CZO		Floatplane or wheels/skis
☐ C-FFQX	Noorduyn Norseman VI	625	ex N51131		Floatplane or wheels/skis
☐ C-GMAU	de Havilland DHC-2 Beaver	1134	ex N775E		Floatplane or wheels/skis

OSPREY WINGS — *La Ronge, SK (YVC)*

☐ C-FTCT	de Havilland DHC-2 Beaver	962	ex FAP-0205		Floatplane or wheels/skis
☐ C-FZCO	de Havilland DHC-2 Beaver	1027	ex N8034J		Floatplane or wheels/skis
☐ C-GAIJ	de Havilland DHC-2 Beaver	1373	ex N5334G		Floatplane or wheels/skis
☐ C-GQKS	de Havilland DHC-2 Beaver	1096	ex N690		Floatplane or wheels/skis
☐ C-GUWL	de Havilland DHC-2 Beaver	1223	ex 67-6140		Floatplane or wheels/skis
☐ C-FASZ	de Havilland DHC-3 Otter	463	ex IM672		Floatplane or wheels/skis
☐ CF-DIZ	de Havilland DHC-3 Otter	460	ex JW-9107		Floatplane or wheels/skis
☐ C-FXRI	de Havilland DHC-3 Otter	258	ex VH-SBT		Floatplane or wheels/skis
☐ C-GPHD	de Havilland DHC-3 Otter	113	ex 55-3267		Floatplane or wheels/skis
☐ C-FLXP	de Havilland DHC-6 Twin Otter 200	217	ex N201EH		Floatplane or wheels/skis
☐ C-FVEG	de Havilland DHC-6 Twin Otter 300	260	ex OH-SLK		Floatplane or wheels/skis
☐ C-GCIM	Cessna A185F Skywagon II	18503953	ex (N5308E)		Floatplane or wheels/skis
☐ C-GQOQ	de Havilland DHC-6 Twin Otter 200	155	ex EC-BPE		Floatplane or wheels/skis

PACIFIC COASTAL AIRLINES — *Pasco (8P/PCO)* — *Port Hardy, BC (YZT)*

☐ C-FPCO	Beech 1900C	UB-52	ex C-GKHB		
☐ C-FPCV	Beech 1900C	UB-9	ex N189GA	302	
☐ C-FPCX	Beech 1900C	UB-66	ex OY-JRF		
☐ C-GBPC	Beech 1900C	UB-43	ex N565M		
☐ C-GIPC	Beech 1900C-1	UC-110	ex N210CU	Special colours	
☐ C-GPCY	Beech 1900C	UB-45	ex C-FYZD	301	
☐ C-FHUZ	Grumman G-21A Goose	B-83	ex BuA37830		
☐ C-FIOL	Grumman G-21A Goose	B-107	ex RCN 397		
☐ C-FUAZ	Grumman G-21A Goose	1077	ex N95400		
☐ C-GDDJ	Grumman G-21A Goose	1184	ex N1257A		
☐ C-GCPU	SAAB SF.340A	340A-140	ex N140CQ		
☐ C-GCPZ	SAAB SF.340A	340A-148	ex N148SD		
☐ C-GPCE	SAAB SF.340A	340A-004	ex N340SZ	Trawler c/s	
☐ C-GPCG	SAAB SF.340A	340A-094	ex N107EA		
☐ C-GPCJ	SAAB SF.340A	340A-006	ex N360SZ	Sailing boat c/s	
☐ C-GPCN	SAAB SF.340A	340A-027	ex N27XJ		on order
☐ C-GPCQ	SAAB SF.340A	340A-043	ex N43SZ		
☐ C-FDSG	de Havilland DHC-2 Beaver	892	ex 54-1737		Floatplane
☐ C-FMAZ	de Havilland DHC-2 Beaver	1413	ex CF-MAZ		Floatplane
☐ C-GASF	de Havilland DHC-2 Beaver	1202	ex 57-2561		Floatplane
☐ C-GPCF	Short SD.3-60	SH3620	ex (N366AC)	706	
☐ C-GPCP	Beech 200 Super King Air	BB-140		302	Catpass 200 conversion
☐ C-GPCW	Short SD.3-60	SH3622	ex 8Q-OCA	703	

PACIFIC EAGLE AVIATION — *Port McNeil, BC (YMP)*

☐ C-FEYN	de Havilland DHC-2 Beaver	508	ex N6167K		Floatplane
☐ C-FICK	de Havilland DHC-2 Beaver	796	ex CF-ICK		Floatplane
☐ C-FMXR	de Havilland DHC-2 Beaver	374	ex N7160C		Floatplane
☐ C-GIDE	Republic RC-3 Seabee	355	ex N6167K		Amphibian

PACIFIC WESTERN HELICOPTERS — *Prince George, BC (YXS)*

☐ C-GPWE	Aérospatiale AS350B2 AStar	3027	ex C-GBKV		
☐ C-GPWK	Aérospatiale AS350B AStar	1559	ex N29TV		
☐ C-GPWL	Aérospatiale AS350B2 AStar	2956	ex C-GVXT		
☐ C-GPWQ	Aérospatiale AS350B AStar	1099	ex N3596B		
☐ C-GPWV	Aérospatiale AS350B AStar	1637	ex ZK-HRQ		
☐ C-GPWZ	Aérospatiale AS350B2 AStar	2314	ex JA9863		

☐ C-GPGM	Bell 206B JetRanger III	3178	ex N38902	
☐ C-GPWH	Bell 206B JetRanger III	3131	ex N81AJ	
☐ C-GPWJ	Bell 206B JetRanger III	2240	ex C-GNMM	
☐ C-GPWR	Bell 206B JetRanger III	2989	ex N577AH	
☐ C-GPWY	Bell 206B JetRanger III	3790	ex C-GIYD	
☐ C-GTES	Bell 206B JetRanger III	2292	ex N16877	
☐ C-GPWC	Cessna TU206F Stationair II	U20602644	ex N59290	
☐ C-GPWT	Bell 205A-1	30231	ex N57954	
☐ C-GPWX	Bell 212	30535	ex C-FAHX	

PACIFIC WINGS AIRLINES — *Sechelt, BC (YLT)*

☐ C-GSUE	de Havilland DHC-2 Beaver	1199	ex N37AT	Floatplane

PANORAMA HELICOPTERS — *Alma, QC (YTF)*

☐ C-FDYS	Aérospatiale AS350B AStar	1057	ex N211TV	
☐ C-FETG	Aérospatiale AS350BA AStar	1378	ex N353LN	
☐ C-GOVD	Aérospatiale AS350D AStar	1621	ex N3604X	
☐ C-GRFM	Aérospatiale AS350B2 AStar	2601	ex N15234	
☐ C-GSOX	Aérospatiale AS350B2 AStar	9022	ex N301TH	
☐ C-GVED	Aérospatiale AS350BA AStar	1527	ex N597M	
☐ C-FOKY	Bell 204B	2043	ex CF-OKY	
☐ C-FSZX	Bell 206B JetRanger	2333	ex N206RM	
☐ C-GBKH	Bell 206L-3 LongRanger III	51261		
☐ C-GBKX	Bell 206B JetRanger III	2676		
☐ C-GSHC	Bell 206B JetRanger	1282	ex N65301	

PASCAN AVIATION — *Pascan (PSC)* — *Quebec, QC (YQB)*

☐ C-FHQA	British Aerospace Jetstream 32	876	ex N876CP	
☐ C-FHSC	Beech B100 King Air	BE-105	ex N87XX	
☐ C-FIDC	Beech B100 King Air	BE-27	ex N87JE	
☐ C-FKQA	British Aerospace Jetstream 32	877	ex N877CP	
☐ C-FODC	Beech B100 King Air	BE-59	ex N777DQ	
☐ C-FYUT	Pilatus PC-12/45	254	ex N254PC	
☐ C-GBTL	Pilatus PC-12/45	159	ex N159PB	
☐ C-GNSC	Beech B100 King Air	BE-102	ex N57TJ	
☐ C-GQJT	British Aerospace Jetstream 32EP	886	ex N886CP	
☐ C-GRDC	Pilatus PC-12/45	214	ex PT-XTG	
☐ C-GUSC	British Aerospace Jetstream 32	902	ex N242BM	

PELICAN NARROWS AIR SERVICES — *Pelican Narrows, SK*

☐ C-GFZA	Cessna A185F Skywagon	18503084		Floatplane or wheels/skis
☐ C-GTBC	de Havilland DHC-2 Beaver	1364	ex 58-2032	

PERIMETER AVIATION — *Perimeter (4B/PAG)* — *Winnipeg-Intl, MB (YWG)*

☐ C-FBTL	Swearingen SA.226TC Metro II	TC-385	ex XA-TGG	
☐ C-FFDB	Swearingen SA.226TC Metro II	TC-249	ex N327BA	
☐ C-FIHB	Swearingen SA.226TC Metro II	TC-361	ex N166SW	
☐ C-FIHE	Swearingen SA.226TC Metro II	TC-373	ex N1010Z	
☐ C-FIIA	Swearingen SA.226TC Metro II	TC-329	ex N236AM	
☐ C-FJNW	Swearingen SA.226TC Metro IIA	TC-352	ex N167MA	
☐ C-FSLZ	Swearingen SA.226TC Metro II	TC-222EE	ex N104GS	
☐ C-FSWT	Swearingen SA.226TC Metro II	TC-382	ex N1011N	
☐ C-FUZY	Swearingen SA.226TC Metro II	TC-343	ex VH-UZY	
☐ C-GIQF	Swearingen SA.226TC Metro II	TC-279	ex F-GFGE	
☐ C-GIQG	Swearingen SA.226TC Metro II	TC-285	ex F-GFGD	
☐ C-GIQK	Swearingen SA.226TC Metro II	TC-288	ex F-GFGF	
☐ C-GPCL	Swearingen SA.226AT Merlin IV	AT-017	ex N511M	Freighter
☐ C-GQAJ	Swearingen SA.226TC Metro II	TC-295	ex C-FUIF	EMS, Aeromed titles
☐ C-GQAP	Swearingen SA.226TC Metro II	TC-263	ex N103UR	
☐ C-GYRD	Swearingen SA.226TC Metro II	TC-278	ex N5493M	Jt ops with Dene Cree Air
☐ C-FFJM	Swearingen SA.227AC Metro III	AC-700	ex N459AM	
☐ C-FMAV	Swearingen SA.227AC Metro III	AC-616	ex VH-UUF	
☐ C-GFWX	Swearingen SA.227AC Metro III	AC-650B	ex N26863	
☐ C-GWVH	Swearingen SA.227AC Metro IIIA	AC-714	ex VH-UUQ	
☐ C-FAMF	Swearingen SA.226T Merlin IIIA	T-274	ex I-SWAA	
☐ C-FCMJ	Rockwell Commander 681B	6054	ex N21HC	
☐ C-FDMX	Beech D95A Travel Air	TD-587	ex N5663K	
☐ C-FEQK	Beech 95-B55 Baron	TC-1374	ex CF-EQK	
☐ C-FKMZ	Beech E95 Travel Air	TD-708	ex N6223V	
☐ C-FOFR	de Havilland DHC-8-106	317	ex N288DH	
☐ C-FRQI	Beech 99	U-124	ex TF-ELB	
☐ C-GEUJ	Beech B60 Duke	P-498	ex N36RR	
☐ C-GFQC	Beech B99	U-120	ex N47156	

☐ C-GQQC	Beech D95A Travel Air	TD-676	ex N7874L	
☐ C-GWPS	de Havilland DHC-8-102	120	ex N928HA	

PHOENIX HELI-FLIGHT — Fort McMurray, AB (YMM)

☐ C-FANK	Eurocopter EC120B Colibri	1498		
☐ C-FAVX	Aérospatiale AS350B2 AStar	4242		
☐ C-FHLF	Aérospatiale AS350D AStar	1074	ex N35934	
☐ C-FHLO	Aérospatiale AS350B3 AStar	4480		
☐ C-FNFU	Aérospatiale AS350B2 AStar	2467	ex C-GNIX	
☐ C-GFHF	Eurocopter EC120B Colibri	1417		
☐ C-GPHF	Eurocopter EC130B4	3862	ex F-WWXM	
☐ C-GTWN	Aérospatiale AS355N Twin Star	5673	ex 9M-JBG	
☐ C-GXNP	Aérospatiale AS355N Twin Star	5757	ex F-WWXA	

PORTER AIRLINES — (PD/POE) — Toronto-City Centre, ON (YTZ)

☐ C-GLQB	de Havilland DHC-8-402Q	4130		
☐ C-GLQC	de Havilland DHC-8-402Q	4134		
☐ C-GLQD	de Havilland DHC-8-402Q	4138		
☐ C-GLQE	de Havilland DHC-8-402Q	4140		
☐ C-GLQF	de Havilland DHC-8-402Q	4193		
☐ C-GLQG	de Havilland DHC-8-402Q	4194		
☐ C-GLQH	de Havilland DHC-8-402Q	4225		
☐ C-GLQJ	de Havilland DHC-8-402Q	4228		
☐ C-GLQK	de Havilland DHC-8-402Q	4247		
☐ C-GLQL	de Havilland DHC-8-402Q	4249		
☐ C-GLQM	de Havilland DHC-8-402Q	4252		
☐ C-GLQN	de Havilland DHC-8-402Q	4254		
☐ C-GLQO	de Havilland DHC-8-402Q	4270		
☐ C-GLQP	de Havilland DHC-8-402Q	4271		
☐ C-GLQQ	de Havilland DHC-8-402Q	4272		
☐ C-GLQR	de Havilland DHC-8-402Q	4278		
☐ C-GLQV	de Havilland DHC-8-402Q	4279		
☐ C-GLQX	de Havilland DHC-8-402Q	4282		
☐ C-	de Havilland DHC-8-402Q			on order
☐ C-	de Havilland DHC-8-402Q			on order

PRINCE EDWARD AIR — Comet (CME) — Charlottetown, PE (YYG)

☐ C-FKAX	Beech 1900C	UB-67	ex N3067X	Freighter
☐ C-GKGA	Beech 1900C-1	UC-117	ex N117ZR	Freighter
☐ C-GSKA	Beech 1900C	UB-32	ex N317BH	
☐ C-GSKG	Beech 1900C-1	UC-22	ex N19016	
☐ C-GSKM	Beech 1900C	UB-21	ex N61MK	
☐ C-GSKN	Beech 1900C-1	UC-54	ex N31729	
☐ C-GSKU	Beech 1900C	UB-35	ex N735GL	
☐ C-GSKW	Beech 1900C	UB-33	ex N318BH	
☐ C-GTGA	Beech 1900C-1	UC-62	ex N62YV	Freighter
☐ C-FFGA	Cessna 208B Caravan I	208B0662	ex N5264E	026
☐ C-FHGA	Cessna 208B Caravan I	208B0047	ex C-FESH	024
☐ C-GEGA	Cessna 208B Caravan I	208B0379	ex N1119A	
☐ C-GLGA	Cessna 208B Caravan I	208B0350	ex N64AP	
☐ C-GSKS	Cessna 208B Caravan I	208B0762	ex N52623	
☐ C-GSKV	Cessna 208B Caravan I	208B0847		
☐ C-FFFH	Piper PA-31-350 Navajo Chieftain	31-7552130	ex N54CG	
☐ C-GATD	Piper PA-31-350 Navajo Chieftain	31-7405143	ex N74986	
☐ C-GGQM	Piper PA-31-350 Navajo Chieftain	31-7952033	ex TF-EGU	
☐ C-GIIZ	Piper PA-31-350 Navajo Chieftain	31-7552099	ex N29TW	
☐ C-GILJ	Piper PA-31-350 Navajo Chieftain	31-7552010	ex N374SA	
☐ C-GRFA	Piper PA-31-350 Navajo Chieftain	31-7405228	ex N54292	
☐ C-GYYJ	Piper PA-31-350 Navajo Chieftain	31-7652086	ex N59833	
☐ C-FKCG	Beech 99	U-23	ex N218BH	
☐ C-FYSJ	Beech 99	U-73	ex N209BH	
☐ C-GHVI	Beech B99	U-153	ex N17RX	Lsd fr BLS
☐ C-GPEA	Beech 200 Super King Air	BB-170	ex N869MA	CatPass 250 conversion
☐ N340AQ	SAAB SF.340AF	340A-019	ex C-GYQM	

PROPAIR — Propair (PRO) — Rouyn-Noranda, QC (YUY)

☐ C-FDJX	Beech A100 King Air	B-165	ex N811CU	
☐ C-FDOU	Beech A100 King Air	B-112	ex CF-DOU	
☐ C-FPAJ	Beech A100 King Air	B-151	ex N324B	
☐ C-FWRM	Beech A100 King Air	B-125	ex N89JM	
☐ C-GJLJ	Beech A100 King Air	B-235	ex N23517	
☐ C-GJLP	Beech A100 King Air	B-148	ex N67V	
☐ C-FAWE	Grumman G.159 Gulfstream 1	188	ex HB-LDT	
☐ C-FLEO	de Havilland DHC-2 Beaver	1270	ex N8700R	Floatplane or wheels/skis

☐ C-FOGY	Beech 200 Super King Air	BB-168	ex N10VW	
☐ C-GLPJ	Beech 1900C-1	UC-139	ex N253RM	
☐ C-GLPM	de Havilland DHC-3 Turbo Otter	147	ex C-FJFJ	Floatplane or wheels/skis
☐ C-GQAB	Cessna A185F Skywagon	18502766	ex (N1203F)	Floatplane or wheels/skis
☐. C-GUGQ	de Havilland DHC-2 Beaver	400	ex 51-16485	Floatplane or wheels/skis

PROVINCE OF ALBERTA — Alberta (GOA) — Edmonton-Municipal, AB (YXD)

☐ C-GFSA	Beech B300 Super King Air	FL-174		Op by Air Transportation Services
☐ C-GFSD	Beech B200 Super King Air	BB-1962	ex N7162V	
☐ C-GFSE	Beech B200 Super King Air	BB-1963	ex N7063F	
☐ C-GFSJ	de Havilland DHC-8-103	017		Op by Air Transportation Services

PROVINCIAL AIRLINES — (PB/SPR) — St Johns, NL (YYT)

☐ C-FGFZ	Beech 200 Super King Air	BB-403	ex N147K	
☐ C-GGAO	Beech 200 Super King Air	BB-659	ex N77QX	
☐ C-GGJF	Beech B200 Super King Air	BB-939	ex N125KW	
☐ C-GMRS	Beech 200 Super King Air	BB-187	ex N630DB	Maritime Patrol
☐ C-GMWR	Beech 200 Super King Air	BB-68	ex N844N	Maritime Patrol
☐ C-GTJZ	Beech 200 Super King Air	BB-499	ex N499TT	
☐ C-FIZD	de Havilland DHC-6 Twin Otter 300	461	ex PK-NUX	Isd to Innu Mikun
☐ C-FUMY	de Havilland DHC-6 Twin Otter 300	675	ex PJ-TOD	
☐ C-FWLG	de Havilland DHC-6 Twin Otter 300	731	ex N915MA	
☐ C-GIED	de Havilland DHC-6 Twin Otter 300	600	ex N604NA	
☐ C-GJDE	de Havilland DHC-6 Twin Otter 300	471	ex C-GMPK	Floatplane or wheels/skis
☐ C-FHRC	de Havilland DHC-8-102	209	ex TR-LGL	
☐ C-GPAB*	de Havilland DHC-8-106MPA	275	ex N827PH	
☐ C-GPAL	de Havilland DHC-8-102	157	ex N824PH	
☐ C-GPAU	de Havilland DHC-8-106	282	ex N833EX	
☐ C-GRNN*	de Havilland DHC-8-106MPA	314	ex N830PH	
☐ C-FMPV	de Havilland DHC-2 Beaver	1304	ex CF-MPV	Floatplane
☐ C-FPAG	SAAB SF.340A	340A-028	ex N336BE	
☐ C-FPAI	SAAB SF.340A	340A-047	ex N337BE	
☐ C-GMEW	Swearingen SA.227AC Metro III	AC-668B	ex N668JS	
☐ C-GOFB	de Havilland DHC-3 Otter	39	ex 3681	

PROVINCIAL HELICOPTERS — Lac du Bonnet, MB

☐ C-FOGV	Bell 206L-3 LongRanger III	51121	ex V2-LGE
☐ C-FPHB	Bell 206B JetRanger	1213	ex N62SH
☐ C-FPMK	Bell 206B JetRanger III	3611	ex N8BG
☐ C-FXTO	Aérospatiale AS355F Twin Star	5087	ex N260MH
☐ C-FZYH	Bell 206B JetRanger II	1967	ex G-CRPS
☐ C-GSZY	Bell 206B JetRanger III	2313	ex V2-LFA

QUANTUM HELICOPTERS — Terrace, BC (YXT)

☐ C-FFHK	Bell 206B JetRanger	1065	ex CF-FHK
☐ C-FHKJ	Bell 206L LongRanger	45116	ex N222CD
☐ C-FNTR	Bell 205B	30297	ex OE-XBT
☐ C-FQHB	Bell 206L LongRanger	45095	ex 5N-AJC
☐ C-FRCL	Bell 206LR+ LongRanger	45019	ex SE-HUD
☐ C-FZXI	Bell 206B JetRanger	660	ex CF-ZXI
☐ C-GMQH	Bell 206L LongRanger	45103	ex PH-HXH
☐ C-GQNS	Bell 206LR+ LongRanger	45134	
☐ C-GSLV	Bell 206B JetRanger III	4199	ex N3202G
☐ C-GSML	Bell 206LR+ LongRanger	45056	ex ZK-HRA
☐ C-GTVL	Bell 206B JetRanger II	2166	

QWEST HELICOPTERS — Fort Nelson, BC (YYE)

☐ C-FMSZ	Aérospatiale AS350BA AStar	1101	ex N152AD
☐ C-FUOQ	Aérospatiale AS350BA AStar	2180	ex N102FX
☐ C-FSPR	Aérospatiale AS350B AStar	1814	ex ZK-HHY
☐ C-FWII	Aérospatiale AS350BA AStar	1746	ex N433EW
☐ C-GERL	Aérospatiale AS350B AStar	1645	ex JA9340
☐ C-GTHJ	Aérospatiale AS350B AStar	1540	ex N4454Y
☐ C-FMCH	Bell 206B-2 JetRanger	2132	ex N306CK
☐ C-GIOB	Bell 206B JetRanger III	603	ex N678KG
☐ C-GLCD	Bell 206B JetRanger	1284	
☐ C-GNMB	Bell 206B JetRanger	1631	ex N90171
☐ C-GNNH	Bell 206B JetRanger	1632	
☐ C-GTDQ	Bell 206B JetRanger	1503	ex C-GOXX
☐ C-GTVE	Bell 206B JetRanger	2163	

RAINBOW AIRWAYS — Dunchurch, ON

☐ C-GMOI	de Havilland DHC-2 Beaver	1236	ex N6083	Floatplane

RCMP - GRC AIR SERVICES — Ottawa, ON

☐ C-FGSB	Aérospatiale AS350B3 AStar	3796		
☐ C-FMPG	Aérospatiale AS350B3 AStar	3082		
☐ C-FMPH	Aérospatiale AS350B3 AStar	3683		
☐ C-FMPP	Aérospatiale AS350B3 AStar	4124		
☐ C-FRPQ	Aérospatiale AS350B3 AStar	3636	ex F-WQDZ	
☐ C-GMPF	Aérospatiale AS350B3 AStar	4229		
☐ C-GMPK	Aérospatiale AS350B3 AStar	3923		
☐ C-GMPN	Aérospatiale AS350B3 AStar	3072		
☐ C-FMPB	Pilatus PC-12/45	283	ex N283PC	
☐ C-FMPE	Pilatus PC-12/45	314	ex HB-FQZ	
☐ C-FMPF	Pilatus PC-12/45	768	ex HB-FSY	
☐ C-FMPN	Pilatus PC-12/45	296	ex HB-FQK	
☐ C-FMPO	Pilatus PC-12/45	229	ex HB-FRA	
☐ C-FMPW	Pilatus PC-12/45	315	ex HB-FRA	
☐ C-GFLA	Pilatus PC-12/45	293	ex N293PC	
☐ C-GMPI	Pilatus PC-12/45	239	ex HB-FRJ	
☐ C-GMPM	Pilatus PC-12/47E	1011	ex N911NG	
☐ C-GMPP	Pilatus PC-12/45	374	ex N374PC	
☐ C-GMPW	Pilatus PC-12/45	274	ex N274PC	
☐ C-GMPX	Pilatus PC-12/47E	1017		
☐ C-GMPY	Pilatus PC-12/45	311	ex N311PB	
☐ C-GMPZ	Pilatus PC-12/45	272	ex N272PC	
☐ C-FDGM	Cessna U206G Stationair 6 II	U20606864	ex N9450R	Soloy conversion
☐ C-FDTM	Cessna T206H Stationair 6	T20608476	ex (N6199U)	
☐ C-FMPL	de Havilland DHC-6 Twin Otter 300	320	ex CF-MPL	
☐ C-FMPQ	Eurocopter EC120B Colibri	1533		
☐ C-FRPH	Cessna 208B Caravan I	208B0377	ex N1118B	
☐ C-FSUJ	Cessna 208B Caravan I	208B0373	ex N973CC	
☐ C-FSWC	Cessna T206H Stationair	T20608438		
☐ C-GFOX	Piaggio P.180 Avanti	1065	ex N126PA	
☐ C-GMPJ	de Havilland DHC-6 Twin Otter 300	534		
☐ C-GMPR	Cessna 208 Caravan I	20800253	ex N208CF	
☐ C-GMPT	Eurocopter EC120B Colibri	1355		
☐ C-GTJN	Cessna T206H Stationair	T20608443		

RED SUCKER LAKE AIR SERVICES — Red Sucker Lake, MB

☐ C-FTHE	Piper PA-31 Navajo C	31-7512005	ex N121L	
☐ C-GMAM	de Havilland DHC-2 Beaver	1558	ex G-AZLU	Floatplane or wheels/skis

REGIONAL 1 AIRLINES — Transcanada (TSH) — Calgary-Intl, AB (YYC)

☐ C-FJFW	de Havilland DHC-8-311	315	ex N315SN
☐ C-FOVR	de Havilland DHC-8-102	105	ex RA-67253
☐ C-FYDH	de Havilland DHC-8-102	083	ex N809LR
☐ C-GRGK	de Havilland DHC-8Q-202	522	ex B-17201
☐ C-GZTC	de Havilland DHC-8-102	99	ex N923HA

REMOTE HELICOPTERS — Slave Lake, NT (YZH)

☐ C-GRHJ	Aérospatiale AS350BA AStar	2149	
☐ C-GRHK	Aérospatiale AS350B Ecureuil	2305	ex F-GGPE
☐ C-GRHL	Aérospatiale AS350B2 AStar	3018	ex C-GIRL
☐ C-GRHN	Aérospatiale AS350BA AStar	1683	ex N13TV
☐ C-GTAM	Aérospatiale AS350BA Ecureuil	1232	ex G-MAGI
☐ C-GRHA	Bell 212	30791	ex N82283I
☐ C-GRHS	Bell 212	30785	ex N8228R
☐ C-GRHW	Bell 204B	2056	ex N204FB
☐ C-GRHY	Bell 206B JetRanger	1087	ex C-FBJV
☐ C-GRHZ	Bell 206B JetRanger	2691	ex C-GSKX
☐ C-GRMH	Bell 206L-3 LongRanger III	51003	ex N2123X

RESOURCE HELICOPTERS — Vancouver-Intl, BC (YVR)

☐ C-FRSR	Bell 204B	2020	ex CF-RSR
☐ C-GSHB	Bell 204B	2038	ex 9Y-TDZ

RIVER AIR — Kenora/Menaki, ON (YQK/-)

☐ C-FAYM	Cessna U206E Skywagon	U20601541	ex (N9141M)	Floatplane
☐ C-FFYC	Cessna 208 Caravan I	20800111	ex N9647F	Floatplane
☐ C-FMAQ	de Havilland DHC-2 Beaver	14	ex CF-MAQ	Floatplane or wheels/skis

☐ C-FRSW	Beech 3NM	CA-105	ex CF-RSW	
☐ C-GIAT	Cessna A185F Skywagon	18502619	ex N4851C	Floatplane
☐ C-GPDS	de Havilland DHC-2 Beaver	1349	ex N62352	Floatplane
☐ C-GYKO	de Havilland DHC-3 Otter	287	ex N22UT	Floatplane

ROAD TRAILER RENTALS — *Toronto-Buttonville, ON (YKZ)*

☐ C-GLCE	Pilatus PC-12/45	475	ex N475PC	

ROSS AIR — *Clearwater Lake SPB, ON*

☐ CF-PFC	Beech C-45H	AF-199	ex N9942Z	
☐ C-GCIZ	Cessna A185F Skywagon	18503316	ex N1614H	Floatplane
☐ C-GDCN	de Havilland DHC-2 Turbo Beaver	1661/TB35	ex N8PE	Floatplane

ROSS AIR SERVICE — *Sandy Bay, SK*

☐ C-FWXV	Cessna A185E Skywagon	185-1355	ex CF-WXV	Floatplane or wheels/skis

RUSTY MYERS FLYING SERVICE — *Fort Frances,ON (YAG)*

☐ C-FERM	Beech 3N	CA-62	ex CAF 1487	Floatplane
☐ C-FKSJ	Cessna 208 Caravan I	20800035	ex N9382F	Floatplane
☐ C-FOBT	de Havilland DHC-2 Beaver	3	ex CF-OBT	Floatplane
☐ C-FOBY	de Havilland DHC-2 Beaver	13	ex CF-OBY	Floatplane
☐ C-FRPL	Beech 3NM	CA-225	ex CAF 2346	Floatplane
☐ C-FRVL	Beech 3T	7835	ex CAF 1396	Floatplane
☐ CF-ZRI	Beech D18S	A-940	ex N164U	Floatplane
☐ C-GAGK	Cessna 208 Caravan I	20800342	ex N51744	Floatplane

SABOURIN LAKE LODGE — *Sabourin Lake, MB*

☐ C-FSJX	de Havilland DHC-2 Beaver	1592	ex CF-SJX	Floatplane
☐ C-GYER	Cessna U206F Stationair	U20603503	ex N8750Q	Floatplane

SALTSPRING ISLAND AIR — *Saltspring Island, BC*

☐ C-FAOP	de Havilland DHC-2 Beaver	1249	ex CF-AOP	Floatplane
☐ C-FEGE	de Havilland DHC-2 Beaver	1539	ex CF-EGE	Floatplane
☐ C-FJFL	de Havilland DHC-2 Beaver	898	ex CF-JFL	Floatplane
☐ CF-ZZJ	de Havilland DHC-2 Beaver	1019	ex 5H-TCP	Floatplane

SALTWATER WEST ENTERPRISES — *Smithers, BC (YYD)*

☐ C-GFTZ	de Havilland DHC-3 Otter	174	ex N90574	

SANDY LAKE SEAPLANE SERVICE — *Sandy Lake, ON (ZSI)*

☐ C-GBBZ	Cessna U206G Stationair	U20605712	ex (N5396X)	Floatplane or wheels/skis
☐ C-GBGJ	Cessna U206G Stationair	U20605249	ex N5368U	Floatplane or wheels/skis
☐ C-GDYD	de Havilland DHC-2 Beaver	1461	ex VH-IMH	Floatplane or wheels/skis
☐ C-GEBZ	Cessna 207 Skywagon	20700303	ex N1703U	Floatplane or wheels/skis
☐ C-GTCC	Cessna U206F Stationair	U20602167	ex N7303Q	Floatplane or wheels/skis

SAPAWE AIR — *Eva Lake, QC*

☐ C-FEYR	de Havilland DHC-2 Beaver	497	ex CF-EYR	Floatplane
☐ C-FOCC	de Havilland DHC-2 Beaver	23	ex CF-OOC	Floatplane
☐ C-GKBW	de Havilland DHC-2 Beaver	310	ex N1441Z	Floatplane

SASAIR — *Quebec City, QC (YQB)*

☐ C-FADL	Cessna 310R II	310R1867	ex N44NC	
☐ C-FFJL	Cessna 310R II	310R1616	ex N2631A	
☐ C-GAWN	Cessna 310R II	310R0957	ex N37211	
☐ C-GAWT	Cessna 310R II	310R1600	ex N36846	
☐ C-GMCR	Cessna 310R II	310R1424	ex N5149C	
☐ C-GSVI	Cessna 310R II	310R0833	ex N58JB	
☐ C-GYOT	Cessna 310R II	310R0912		
☐ CF-DPQ	Cessna 337G Super Skymaster	33701519	ex N72091	
☐ C-GILW	Cessna 337G Super Skymaster II	33701781	ex 6Y-JNF	
☐ C-GJOD	Cessna 337G Super Skymaster II	33701694	ex N53551	
☐ C-GTEL	Cessna 337G Super Skymaster II	33701659	ex C-FKTN	
☐ C-GYOB	Cessna 337G Super Skymaster II	33701780		
☐ C-GZIS	Piper PA-31-300 Navajo	31-316	ex N9243Y	Floatplane or wheels/skis

SASKATCHEWAN GOVERNMENT NORTHERN AIR OPERATIONS
Saskatchewan (SGS) La Ronge/Saskatoon, SK (YVC/YXE)

☐ C-GNBA	Beech 95-B55 Baron	TC-1787			
☐ C-GPVD	Beech 95-B55 Baron	TC-1966			
☐ C-GSAO	Beech 95-B55 Baron	TC-2149	ex N4974M		
☐ C-GSPG	Beech 95-B55 Baron	TC-2213	ex N2064A		
☐ C-GVSE	Beech 95-B55 Baron	TC-2270	ex N717BC		
☐ C-FAFN	Canadair CL-215-1A10 (CL-215)	1093	ex C-GKDY	216	
☐ C-FAFO	Canadair CL-215-1A10 (CL-215)	1094	ex C-GKBO	217	
☐ C-FAFP	Canadair CL-215-1A10 (CL-215)	1100	ex C-GKEA	218	
☐ C-FAFQ	Canadair CL-215-1A10 (CL-215)	1101	ex C-GKEE	219	
☐ C-FYWO	Canadair CL-215-1A10 (CL-215)	1003	ex CF-YWO	214	
☐ C-FYXG	Canadair CL-215-1A10 (CL-215)	1009	ex CF-YXG	215	
☐ C-GEHP	Grumman CS2F-2 Tracker	DHC-97	ex CAF12198	1	Tanker
☐ C-GEHR	Grumman CS2F-2 Tracker	DHC-51	ex CAF12185	3	Tanker
☐ C-GEQC	Grumman CS2F-2 Tracker	DHC-53	ex CAF12187	4	Tanker
☐ C-GEQD	Grumman CS2F-2 Tracker	DHC-98	ex CAF12199	5	Tanker
☐ C-GEQE	Grumman CS2F-2 Tracker	DHC-92	ex CAF12193	6	Tanker
☐ C-FMFP	Rockwell 690A Turbo Commander	11307	ex N690TD		
☐ C-FNAO	Gulfstream Commander 690C	11731	ex N815BC		
☐ C-FSPM	Gulfstream Commander 690D	15002	ex N721ML		
☐ C-GEAS	Beech 350 Super King Air	FL-17	ex N56872		
☐ C-GLLS	Beech B200 Super King Air	BB-1601	ex N2303F		
☐ C-GOVT	Gulfstream Commander 695A	15020	ex N600CM		
☐ C-GSAE	Beech B200 Super King Air	BB-1748	ex N50848		EMS
☐ C-GSAH	Beech B200 Super King Air	BB-1972	ex N7022F		EMS
☐ C-GSAU	Beech B200 Super King Air	BB-1974	ex N7074N		EMS
☐ C-GSAV	Beech B200 Super King Air	BB-1790	ex N4470T		EMS
☐ C-GSKJ	Convair 580	202	ex N30EG		Tanker
☐ C-GSKR	Convair 580	509	ex N57RD	471	Tanker
☐ C-GSKQ	Convair 580	217	ex N723ES		Tanker
☐ C-GVSK	Convair 580	238	ex N43938		Tanker
☐ C-GYSK	Convair 580	234	ex N131SF		Tanker

SEAIR SEAPLANES
Vancouver-International SPB, BC

☐ C-FDHC	de Havilland DHC-2 Turbo Beaver	1677/TB45	ex N164WC	Floatplane
☐ C-FPCG	de Havilland DHC-2 Beaver	1000	ex N188JM	Floatplane
☐ C-FPMA	de Havilland DHC-2 Turbo Beaver	1625/TB15	ex N1454T	Floatplane
☐ C-GOBC	de Havilland DHC-2 Beaver	1560	ex N159M	Floatplane
☐ C-FJOE	Cessna 208 Caravan I	20800390	ex N5254Y	Floatplane
☐ C-FLAC	Cessna 208 Caravan I	20800357	ex N5267J	Floatplane
☐ C-GSAS	Cessna 208 Caravan I	20800341	ex N5154J	Floatplane
☐ C-GURL	Cessna 208 Caravan I	20800501		Floatplane
☐ C-GYIX	Cessna A185F Skywagon	18503162	ex (N93021)	Floatplane

SELKIRK AIR
Selkirk, MB

☐ C-GCKZ	Cessna A185F Skywagon	18502665	ex (N4949C)	Floatplane or wheels/skis
☐ C-GFIQ	de Havilland DHC-2 Beaver	632	ex N90525	Floatplane or wheels/skis
☐ C-GPHI	de Havilland DHC-2 Beaver	838	ex N67687	Floatplane or wheels/skis

SEQUOIA HELICOPTERS
Abbotsford, BC (YXX)

☐ C-GERH	Bell 212	30768	ex N42434
☐ C-GTHK	Bell 212	30641	ex N708H

SHARP WINGS
Williams Lake, BC

☐ C-FMQG	Cessna TU206G Turbo Skywagon	U206-1101	ex CF-MQG	
☐ C-GKMN	de Havilland DHC-2 Beaver	348	ex N9755Z	
☐ C-GWDW	de Havilland DHC-2 Beaver	306	ex N311N	Floatplane

SHOWALTER'S FLY-IN SERVICE
Ear Falls SPB, ON (YMY)

☐ C-FXUO	Beech D18S	CA-208	ex RCAF 2329	Floatplane
☐ C-FZNG	Beech D18S	CA-182	ex RCAF 2309	Floatplane
☐ C-FZYE	de Havilland DHC-2 Beaver	192	ex CF-ZYE	Floatplane

SIFTON AIR YUKON
Haines Junction, YK(YHT)

☐ C-FRKA	Cessna 206 Super Skywagon	206-0200	ex N5200U	Floatplane
☐ C-GEXT	Cessna U206F Stationair	U20603249	ex (N8338Q)	Floatplane
☐ C-GVCJ	Britten-Norman BN-2A Islander	90	ex N871JA	
☐ C-GVKJ	Cessna 205 (210-5)	205-0092	ex N1892Z	Floatplane

SIMPSON AIR COMMUTER CANADA — (NCS) — Fort Simpson, NT (YFS)

☐ CF-FHZ	de Havilland DHC-2 Beaver	66	ex C-FFHZ	
☐ C-FNML	Piper PA-23-250 Aztec	27-7554075	ex N8VV	
☐ C-GGHU	Cessna U206G Stationair 6 II	U20605723	ex (N5407X)	
☐ C-GPMS	Cessna U206G Stationair 6 II	U20604207	ex (N756MU)	

SIOUX AIR — Sioux Lookout, ON (YXL)

☐ C-GGRU	Cessna U206G Stationair 6 II	U20605838	ex N5373X	Floatplane or wheels/skis

SIOUX NARROWS AIRWAYS — Great Bear Lake, NT (DAS)

☐ CF-GTP	Noorduyn UC-64A Norseman	423	43-35349	
☐ CF-KOA	de Havilland DHC-3 Otter	130	ex N88753	Floatplane
☐ C-GBDW	de Havilland DHC-2 Beaver	954	ex C9-AGS	Floatplane
☐ C-GMXS	de Havilland DHC-2 Beaver	1213	ex N5382G	Floatplane
☐ C-GSMG	de Havilland DHC-3 Otter	363	ex CAF 9405	Floatplane
☐ C-GUJY	de Havilland DHC-2 Beaver	393	ex C-GVMH	Floatplane

SKYLINE HELICOPTERS — Kelowna, BC (YLW)

☐ C-GSLH	Bell 212	30565	ex N94W
☐ C-GSLI	Bell 212	30519	ex C-FNHB
☐ C-GSLJ	Agusta A.119 Koala	14526	ex N56TG
☐ C-GSLR	Agusta A.119 Koala	14511	ex N5UQ
☐ C-GSLT	Bell 212	30851	ex JA9527
☐ C-GSLZ	Bell 212	30975	ex JA9546

SKYNORTH AIR — Winnipeg International, MB (YWG)

☐ C-FSDA	Piper PA-31-350 Navajo Chieftain	31-7752167	ex N27413
☐ C-FSNA	Beech A100 King Air	B-227	ex N227BC
☐ C-GKAJ	Beech A100 King Air	B-232	ex N9192S
☐ C-GNAA	Beech 100 King Air	B-24	ex N382WC
☐ C-GRTG	Piper PA-31-350 Navajo Chieftain	31-7652004	ex N180RM
☐ C-GTZK	Piper PA-31 Turbo Navajo	31-381	ex N9SG
☐ C-GYQK	Beech A100 King Air	B-153	ex N120AS

SKYSERVICE AIRLINES — Skytour (5G/SSV) — Montreal-Trudeau, QC (YUL)

☐ C-FOJZ	Airbus A320-214	1965	ex G-DHJZ		Lsd fr TCX
☐ C-FRAA	Airbus A320-232	1411	ex G-TCAC		
☐ C-FZAZ	Airbus A320-214	2003	ex G-KKAZ		Lsd fr MYT
☐ C-GHRG	Airbus A320-214	1942	ex G-DHRG		Lsd fr TCX
☐ C-GTDG	Airbus A320-214	1571	ex G-OOPP		
☐ C-GTDH	Airbus A320-214	1605	ex G-OOAT	Signature Vacations	
☐ C-GTDP	Airbus A320-214	1780	ex OY-VKL	Sunquest	
☐ C-GUEW	Airbus A320-214	1961	ex G-SUEW		Lsd fr TCX
☐ C-FFAN	Boeing 757-21KER	28674/746	ex G-WJAN	Sunquest	
☐ C-FLEU	Boeing 757-236/W	29941/864	ex G-CPEU		Lsd fr TCX
☐ C-FFLA	Boeing 757-28A	27621/738	ex G-FCLA		
☐ C-FLOX	Boeing 757-236	26158/526	ex G-OOOX		Lsd fr TCX
☐ C-FOBH	Boeing 757-236/W	29944/872	ex G-OOBH		
☐ C-FULD	Boeing 757-25F	28718/752	ex G-FCLD		
☐ C-GMYH	Boeing 757-236/W	25053/358	ex N253CT	Maestro colours	
☐ C-GOEV	Boeing 757-236/W	29943/871	ex G-CPEV		Lsd fr TCX
☐ C-GOOZ	Boeing 757-236	25593/466	ex G-OOOZ		Lsd fr TCX
☐ C-GTBB	Boeing 757-28A/W	32447/951	ex G-OOBB		
☐ C-GTSJ	Boeing 757-236	24772/271	ex EC-JRT		
☐ C-GYBA	Boeing 757-28A/W	32446/950	ex G-OOBA		Lsd fr TCX

SLATE FALLS AIRWAYS — (SYJ) — Sioux Lookout, ON (YXL)

☐ CF-DIN	de Havilland DHC-2 Beaver	68		Floatplane or wheels/skis
☐ C-FCZP	de Havilland DHC-3 Otter	69	ex CF-CZP	Floatplane or wheels/skis
☐ C-FNWX	de Havilland DHC-3 Turbo Otter	412	ex CF-NWX	Floatplane or wheels/skis
☐ C-GGRW	Cessna U206G Stationair 6 II	U20605689	ex N5373X	Floatplane or wheels/skis
☐ C-GPCR	Cessna U206G Stationair 6 II	U20605082	ex N206JW	Floatplane or wheels/skis

SONTAIR — Sontair (STI) — Chatham, ON (XCM)

☐ C-GSKT	Cessna 208B Caravan I	208B0759	ex N5262W

SOUTH MORESBY AIR CHARTERS — Queen Charlotte, BC (ZQS)

☐ C-GHAO	Cessna A185F Skywagon	18502370	ex N53088	Floatplane or wheels/skis

SOUTHERN AVIATION — Regina, SK (YQR)

☐ C-GKKL	Cessna 414A Chancellor III	414A0301	ex N579CD	

STARLINK AVIATION — Avionair (ANU) — Montreal-Trudeau, QC (YUL)

☐ C-GCCN	British Aerospace Jetstream 31	704	ex N333PX	
☐ C-GCCZ	British Aerospace Jetstream 31	712	ex N335PX	
☐ C-GDFW	British Aerospace Jetstream 31	720	ex G-HDGS	
☐ C-GEMQ	British Aerospace Jetstream 31	747	ex N103XV	
☐ C-GNRG	British Aerospace Jetstream 31	791	ex N791JX	
☐ C-GOAD	Embraer EMB.120ER Brasilia	120086	ex N19704	GoAir Citylink colours

STRAIT AIR — L'Anse au Clair, NL

☐ C-FJJR	Britten-Norman BN-2A-27 Islander	424	ex OO-TOP	
☐ C-FVTQ	Piper PA-31-350 Chieftain	31-7853034	ex N300DT	
☐ C-GZBQ	de Havilland DHC-2 Beaver	919	ex 55-0697	

SUDBURY AVIATION — Whitewater Lake, ON

☐ C-FHVT	de Havilland DHC-2 Beaver I	284	ex VP-PAT	Floatplane or wheels/skis
☐ C-FIUU	de Havilland DHC-2 Beaver I	945	ex CF-IUU	Floatplane or wheels/skis
☐ C-GQVG	Cessna A185F Skywagon	18503818	ex N4619E	Floatplane or wheels/skis

SUMMIT AIR CHARTERS — Yellowknife, NT/Atlin, BC/Whitehorse, YT (YZF/YSQ/YXY)

☐ C-FEQV	Dornier 228-202	8126	ex P2-MBR	stored OBF
☐ C-FEQW	Dornier 228-202	8103	ex P2-MBQ	stored YZF
☐ C-FEQX	Dornier 228-202	8101	ex P2-MBP	stored OBF
☐ C-FPSA	Dornier 228-202	8122	ex D-CLUU	
☐ C-FPSH	Dornier 228-202	8071	ex N253MC	
☐ C-FUCN	Dornier 228-202	8109	ex N276MC	
☐ C-GJPY	Dornier 228-202	8088	ex 6Y-JQM	
☐ C-GSAX	Dornier 228-202	8153	ex P2-MBV	
☐ C-FYSQ	Short SC.7 Skyvan	SH1968	ex N491AS	Freighter
☐ C-GJGS	Short SC.7 Skyvan	SH1909	ex N56NS	Freighter
☐ C-GKOA	Short SC.7 Skyvan	SH1905	ex N52NS	Freighter

SUNWEST AVIATION — Chinook (CNK) — Calgary-Intl, AB (YYC)

☐ C-FAFJ	Cessna 208B Caravan I	208B0641	ex N52655	
☐ C-FDOI	Piper PA-31-350 Chieftain	31-8152150	ex N40901	
☐ C-FGEW	Swearingen SA.226TC Metro II	TC-347	ex N330BA	
☐ C-FJVR	Cessna 441 Conquest II	441-0096	ex N451WS	
☐ C-FNOC	Cessna 208 Caravan I	20800090	ex N9536F	
☐ C-FPCP	Beech B300 Super King Air	FL-317	ex N3217V	
☐ C-GHOP	Beech 200 Super King Air	BB-120	ex N6773S	
☐ C-GJFY	Beech 200 Super King Air	BB-812	ex C-GYUI	
☐ C-GMOZ	Piper PA-31-350 Chieftain	31-8052067	ex N3556B	
☐ C-GMWW	Swearingen SA.227DC Metro 23	DC-852B	ex N450LA	
☐ C-GOHO	Piper PA-31-350 Chieftain	31-8152167	ex N38SL	
☐ C-GRWN	Piper PA-31-350 Chieftain	31-8152044	ex N4076J	
☐ C-GSBC	Beech B200 Super King Air	BB-1780	ex N46TF	
☐ C-GSHV	Swearingen SA.227DC Metro 23	DC-900B	ex D-CJKO	
☐ C-GSHY	Swearingen SA.227DC Metro 23	DC-897B	ex N3051Q	
☐ C-GSHZ	Swearingen SA.227DC Metro 23	DC-887B	ex N3007C	
☐ C-GSLX	Beech 1900D	UE-264	ex C-GSLB	
☐ C-GSWB	Beech 1900D	UE-386	ex N847CA	
☐ C-GSWK	Swearingen SA.226TC Metro II	TC-368	ex F-GEBU	The Spirit of Medicine Hat
☐ C-GSWO	Cessna 208 Caravan I	20800153	ex N1016M	
☐ C-GSWV	Beech 1900D	UE-141	ex N17354	all-white
☐ C-GSWX	Beech 1900D	UE-63	ex N166K	
☐ C-GSWZ	Beech 1900D	UE-337	ex N23159	
☐ C-GVAG	Piper PA-31-350 Navajo Chieftain	31-7752166	ex N27411	

SUNWING AIRLINES — Sunwing (WG/SWG) — Toronto-Pearson Intl, ON (YYZ)

☐ C-FEAK	Boeing 737-86Q/W	30292/1451	ex N292AG	
☐ C-FLSW	Boeing 737-8HX/W	36552/2658		
☐ C-FTAH	Boeing 737-8Q8/W	29351/1471	ex OK-TVJ	
☐ C-FTDW	Boeing 737-808/W	34704/1958	ex N1786B	Joan Maria
☐ C-FTJH	Boeing 737-8BK	29642/2247	ex N1786B	
☐ C-FTOH	Boeing 737-8HX/W	29647/2865		
☐ C-FYLC	Boeing 737-8BK/W	33029/1945	ex G-OXLC	
☐ C-GDBX	Boeing 737-8Q8/W	33699/1309	ex 5B-DBX	Lsd fr ECA
☐ C-GLBW	Boeing 737-8Q8/W	30671/1307	ex 5B-DBW	Lsd fr ECA

SUPERIOR AIRWAYS — Sioux Lookout, ON (YXL)

☐ C-FVWY	Piper PA-31-350 Chieftain	31-8252063	ex N4110N	
☐ C-GAGT	Cessna T206H Stationair 6	T20608158	ex N1965	
☐ C-GAJT	Piper PA-31-350 Chieftain	31-8152012	ex N900SA	
☐ C-GAJW	Piper PA-31-350 Chieftain	31-8152157	ex N700TS	

SUPERIOR HELICOPTERS — Longlac, ON

☐ C-GSHF	Bell 206L-3 LongRanger III	51349	ex C-GHHY	
☐ C-GSHG	Bell 205A-1	30165	ex C-GENZ	
☐ C-GSHQ	Bell 206L-4 LongRanger IV	52226	ex XC-LFC	
☐ C-GSHW	Bell 206L-3 LongRanger III	51602	ex OK-XIS	

SUSTUT AIR — Smithers, BC (YYD)

☐ C-FAFV	Cessna 208B Caravan I	208B0528	ex N9510W	
☐ C-FUMC	Short SC.7 Skyvan	SH1844	ex N430NA	Freighter

SWANBERG AIR — Grande Prairie, AB (YQU)

☐ C-GCTH	Piper PA-31-350 Navajo Chieftain	31-7752063	ex N37620	
☐ C-GPSB	Piper PA-42 Cheyenne III	42-8001030	ex N855GA	
☐ C-GPSN	British Aerospace Jetstream 31	783	ex C-GHGI	
☐ C-GPSO	British Aerospace Jetstream 31	756	ex C-GJPX	
☐ C-GPSV	British Aerospace Jetstream 31	816	ex C-FBII	
☐ C-GPSW	British Aerospace Jetstream 31	735	ex N854JS	
☐ C-GPSX	Piper PA-31P Pressurised Navajo	31P-7300113	ex N100MC	

TASMAN HELICOPTERS — Vancouver-Intl, BC (YVR)

☐ C-FKGT	Bell 212	30901	ex HC-CBW	
☐ C-FTHD	Bell 407	53134	ex C-GFNR	
☐ C-FTVL	Bell 212	30551	ex XC-UHE	
☐ C-FVTS	Bell 212	30546	ex N2164Z	
☐ C-GFHA	Bell 205A-1	30086	ex VH-NHA	

THUNDER AIRLINES — Air Thunder (THU) — Thunder Bay, ON (YQT)

☐ C-FASB	Beech A100 King Air	B-163	ex SE-ING	
☐ C-FFFG	Mitsubishi MU-2L	662	ex N5191B	
☐ C-FJEL	Mitsubishi MU-2N	706SA	ex N866MA	
☐ C-FRWK	Mitsubishi MU-2L	1521SA	ex N437MA	
☐ C-FWVR	Cessna 208B Caravan I	208B0483	ex N51426	
☐ C-GAMC	Mitsubishi MU-2L	785SA	ex N273MA	
☐ C-GASI	Beech A100 King Air	B-126	ex N23BW	
☐ C-GNEX	Beech A100 King Air	B-211	ex N9194F	
☐ C-GUPP	Beech A100 King Air	B-157	ex N123CS	
☐ C-GZNS	Mitsubishi MU-2L	1550SA	ex N64WB	

THUNDERBIRD AVIATION — Stony Rapids, SK (YSF)

☐ CF-PEM	de Havilland DHC-3 Otter	438		Floatplane

TIMBERLAND HELICOPTERS — Courtenay, BC (YCA)

☐ C-FHDX	Aérospatiale AS.330J Puma	1355	ex JA9955	

TLI CHO AIR — Yellowknife, NT (YZF)

☐ C-FATN	de Havilland DHC-6 Twin Otter 300	226	ex N153BU	Floatplane or wheels/skis

TOFINO AIR LINES — Tofino, BC (YTP)

☐ C-FGCY	de Havilland DHC-2 Beaver	216	ex CF-GCY	Floatplane
☐ C-FHRT	de Havilland DHC-2 Beaver	1203	ex N64390	Floatplane
☐ C-FITS	de Havilland DHC-3 Otter	90	ex CF-ITS	Floatplane
☐ C-FJIM	de Havilland DHC-2 Beaver	461	ex N66035	Floatplane
☐ C-GFLT	de Havilland DHC-2 Beaver	279	ex N5149G	Floatplane
☐ C-GHBX	Cessna 180J	18052449	ex (N52029)	Floatplane
☐ C-GHZR	Cessna 180J	18052667	ex (N7542K)	Floatplane
☐ C-GIDX	Cessna 180J	18052709	ex (N7716K)	Floatplane
☐ C-GYFO	Cessna 180J	18052759	ex (N7825K)	Floatplane

TRANS CAPITAL AIR — Toronto-City Centre, ON (YTZ)

☐ C-FJHQ	de Havilland DHC-7-103	11	ex PK-TVS	Op for UN
☐ C-FWYU	de Havilland DHC-7-103	12	ex N678MA	Op for UN. UN-234
☐ C-GCPP	de Havilland DHC-7-102	87	ex HK-3111W	stored YTZ
☐ C-GGXS	de Havilland DHC-7-102	64	ex 4X-AHB	

☐ C-GVPP	de Havilland DHC-7-102	72	ex N272EP	Op for UN
☐ C-GVWD	de Havilland DHC-7-102	108	ex HK-3340W	Op for UN. UN-311

TRANS NORTH HELICOPTERS — *Trans North (TNT)* — *Whitehorse, YT (YXY)*

☐ C-FCHU	Bell 206B JetRanger III	2213	ex N70TT
☐ C-FDRZ	Bell 206B JetRanger II	764	ex CF-DRZ
☐ C-FGGC	Bell 206B JetRanger II	1080	ex N58113
☐ C-GMIG	Bell 206B JetRanger II	2186	
☐ C-GMYQ	Bell 206B JetRanger III	2628	ex N5016Q
☐ C-GPGH	Bell 206B JetRanger III	4022	
☐ C-GPWI	Bell 206B JetRanger III	2234	ex N347BB
☐ C-GTNY	Bell 206B JetRanger II	990	ex CF-KNY
☐ C-GTNT	Aérospatiale AS350B2 AStar	3327	
☐ C-GTNU	Aérospatiale AS350B2 AStar	3046	ex N318SA
☐ C-GTNV	Aérospatiale AS350B AStar	1655	ex N627LH

TRANSWEST AIR — *Athabaska(9T/ABS)* — *La Ronge/Stony Rapids, SK (YVC/YSF)*

☐ C-GALM	Cessna A185F Skywagon	18503711	ex N783A	Floatplane or wheels/skis
☐ C-GCJM	Cessna A185F Skywagon	18503955	ex (N5330E)	Floatplane or wheels/skis
☐ C-GXZA	Cessna A185F Skywagon	18503019	ex N5211R	Floatplane or wheels/skis
☐ C-GZVF	Cessna A185F Skywagon	18503202	ex N93256	Floatplane or wheels/skis
☐ C-FGHY	de Havilland DHC-2 Beaver	1344	ex 58-2015	Floatplane or wheels/skis
☐ C-FGQD	de Havilland DHC-2 Beaver	76	ex CF-QGD	Floatplane or wheels/skis
☐ C-FIFJ	de Havilland DHC-2 Beaver	831	ex CF-IFJ	Floatplane or wheels/skis
☐ C-FOED	de Havilland DHC-2 Turbo Beaver	1591/TB9	ex CF-OED	Floatplane or wheels/skis
☐ C-GAEB	de Havilland DHC-2 Beaver	703	ex 53-7895	Floatplane or wheels/skis
☐ C-GHGN	de Havilland DHC-2 Beaver	80	ex N115LA	Floatplane or wheels/skis
☐ C-GMAQ	de Havilland DHC-2 Beaver	234	ex 51-16784	Floatplane or wheels/skis
☐ C-FCCE	de Havilland DHC-6 Twin Otter 100	8	ex CF-CCE	Floatplane or wheels/skis
☐ C-FGLF	de Havilland DHC-6 Twin Otter 200	138	ex LV-APT	Floatplane or wheels/skis
☐ C-FPGE	de Havilland DHC-6 Twin Otter 200	197	ex CF-PGE	Floatplane or wheels/skis
☐ C-FSCA	de Havilland DHC-6 Twin Otter 100	17	ex CF-SCA	Floatplane or wheels/skis
☐ C-FVOG	de Havilland DHC-6 Twin Otter 100	35	ex CF-VOG	Floatplane or wheels/skis
☐ C-FAAF	Piper PA-31-350 Navajo Chieftain	31-7752096	ex N27229	
☐ C-FNVH	Piper PA-31-350 Navajo Chieftain	31-7305098	ex N98BJ	
☐ C-FQWP	Piper PA-31-325 Navajo C/R	31-7400990	ex N7082Y	
☐ C-FZPJ	Piper PA-31-350 Navajo Chieftain	31-7752185	ex N27359	
☐ C-GAYY	Piper PA-31 Navajo C	31-8012006		
☐ C-GCTG	Piper PA-31-350 Navajo Chieftain	31-7552087	ex N72ET	
☐ C-GGIQ	Piper PA-31-350 Navajo Chieftain	31-7552082	ex N59989	
☐ C-GNOV	Piper PA-31 Navajo C	31-7812087		
☐ C-GQHV	Piper PA-31-350 Navajo Chieftain	31-7405230	ex N54293	
☐ C-GQXX	Piper PA-31-350 Chieftain	31-7852009		
☐ C-GRQG	Piper PA-31-350 Chieftain	31-7952073		
☐ C-GUNP	Piper PA-31-350 Chieftain	31-8052048	ex N3554D	
☐ C-GWUM	Piper PA-31-350 Navajo Chieftain	31-7405404	ex N66878	
☐ C-FEYP	Beech A100 King Air	B-206	ex N86BM	
☐ C-FHPE	de Havilland DHC-3 Turbo Otter	273	ex Burma 4651	Floatplane or wheels/skis
☐ C-FJTG	Bell 205A-1	30104	ex N8138J	
☐ C-FOHG	Bell 407	53187	ex N478WN	
☐ C-FOKD	Bell 407	53193	ex N407NR	
☐ C-FSEW	British Aerospace Jetstream 31	764	ex N223JL	
☐ C-FSGD	de Havilland DHC-3 Turbo Otter	316	ex N521BK	Floatplane or wheels/skis
☐ C-FTMC	Bell 206L-4 LongRanger IV	52223	ex XC-CJS	
☐ C-FYID	Bell 206L-1 LongRanger II	45206	ex N78CF	
☐ C-GAON	Cessna 310R II	310R1627	ex N2632Y	
☐ C-GCNC	Bell 206B JetRanger II	1142	ex N58152	
☐ C-GELT	Bell 206B JetRanger III	2994	ex N5744V	
☐ C-GFSG	Beech 200 Super King Air	BB-671		
☐ C-GJHW	Beech A100 King Air	B-175	ex N92DL	
☐ C-GKCY	SAAB SF.340A	340A-133	ex SE-ISM	
☐ C-GPDC	British Aerospace Jetstream 31	766	ex N222JF	
☐ C-GPNO	Beech 95-B55 Baron	TC-734	ex N174E	
☐ C-GTJX	SAAB SF.340B	340B-165	ex N586MA	
☐ C-GTWG	Beech 1900D	UE-79	ex N79SK	
☐ C-GTWK	SAAB SF.340B	340B-190	ex XA-TUQ	
☐ C-GYHY	Bell 206B JetRanger III	2317	ex N16825	
☐ C-GZYJ	Cessna 310R II	310R1311	ex (N6174C)	

TRANSWEST HELICOPTERS — *Chilliwack, BC (YCW)*

☐ C-GIGG	Bell 206B JetRanger	155	ex N6295N
☐ C-GTWF	Bell 214B-1	28014	ex C-FQTJ
☐ C-GTWH	Bell 214B-1	28017	ex N214MV
☐ C-GTWI	Bell 214B-1	28011	ex LN-OSW

☐ C-GTWV	Bell 214B	28048	ex HB-XVZ	

TRIUMPH AIRWAYS — Oshawa, ON (YOO)

☐ C-FOOW	Douglas DC-3	13342	ex 8P-OOW	painted as CF-OOW

TSAYTA AVIATION — Fort St James, BC (YXJ)

☐ C-GHNH	Cessna A185F Skywagon	18502705	ex (N1048F)	Floatplane or wheels/skis
☐ C-GKAW	Britten-Norman BN-2A-8 Islander	128	ex N158MA	
☐ C-GWKX	Cessna A185E Skywagon	18502032	ex N70167	Floatplane or wheels/skis

TUDHOPE AIRWAYS — Hudson, ON

☐ C-FOCP	de Havilland DHC-2 Beaver	49	ex CF-OCP	Floatplane or wheels/skis
☐ C-FSDC	Found FBA-2C	17	ex CF-SDC	Floatplane or wheels/skis

TWEEDSMUIR AIR SERVICES — Nimpo Lake, BC

☐ C-FFHT	de Havilland DHC-2 Beaver	55	ex CF-FHT	Floatplane
☐ C-GFRJ	Cessna A185F Skywagon II	18504011		Floatplane
☐ C-GNPO	de Havilland DHC-2 Beaver	773	ex C-GMOJ	Floatplane

TYAX AIR SERVICE — Gold Bridge, BC

☐ C-GIYV	de Havilland DHC-2 Beaver	1488	ex XP823	Floatplane or wheels/skis

ULTRA HELICOPTERS — Grimshaw, AB

☐ C-FALE	Bell 206B JetRanger III	1074	ex N83160
☐ C-GBPB	Bell 206B JetRanger	321	ex N6285N
☐ C-GHHK	Bell 206B JetRanger	1588	
☐ C-GMXU	Bell 206B JetRanger	1520	ex N15DW
☐ C-GUHM	Bell 206B JetRanger	2439	ex C-GPQW

☐ C-FXMJ	Aérospatiale AS350BA AStar	1436	ex N816CF
☐ C-GAHM	Bell 205A-1	30215	ex N59607
☐ C-GAPJ	Bell 204B	2012	ex Thai 912
☐ C-GEWR	Bell 206L-1 LongRanger II	45594	ex N3892R
☐ C-GNMP	Aérospatiale AS350B AStar	1040	ex C-GSKI
☐ C-GUHB	Bell 206L-3 LongRanger III	51026	ex N5741X
☐ C-GUHZ	Bell 206L-3 LongRanger III	51014	ex N752HL

UNIVAIR AVIATION — Montreal-St Hubert, QC (YHU)

☐ C-FDCY	Piper PA-31 Navajo C	31-7912007	ex N27768
☐ C-GRTC	Piper PA-44-180 Seminole	44-7995077	ex N180TL

UNIVERSAL HELICOPTERS — Goose Bay, NL (YYR)

☐ C-FCNG	Bell 206L LongRanger	45149	ex C-GMPT
☐ C-FCWR	Bell 206L LongRanger	45086	ex C-GMPM
☐ C-FLIA	Bell 206L-4 LongRanger IV	52149	ex N9221U
☐ C-FPHO	Bell 206L LongRanger	45147	ex N3247K
☐ C-GAHS	Bell 206LR+ LongRanger	45048	ex D-HMHS
☐ C-GDCA	Bell 206LR+ LongRanger	45021	ex N31DM
☐ C-GIZY	Bell 206LR+ LongRanger	45027	ex N176KH
☐ C-GLSH	Bell 206LR+ LongRanger	45018	
☐ C-GQIX	Bell 206L LongRanger	45008	ex N8EL
☐ C-GVYM	Bell 206LR+ LongRanger	45143	ex N16992
☐ C-GVYO	Bell 206LR+ LongRanger	46609	ex N16950

☐ C-FAPN	Aérospatiale AS350BA AStar	2201	ex N891SA
☐ C-FHHH	Aérospatiale AS350BA AStar	1421	ex N5782X
☐ C-FXAL	Aérospatiale AS350B AStar	1816	ex SE-HNP
☐ C-GNAI	Aérospatiale AS350B AStar	1685	ex N380NA
☐ C-FTJU	Bell 407	53331	ex G-CEOA
☐ C-FXYF	Bell 407	53022	
☐ C-GEPA	Bell 407	53739	ex C-FLPA
☐ C-GOFL	Bell 407	53130	

VALHALLA HELICOPTERS — Kelowna, BC (YLW)

☐ C-FPSZ	Bell 205A-1	30230	ex N30091
☐ C-GLFT	Bell 212	30713	ex N20851

VALLEY HELICOPTERS — Hope & Merritt, BC

☐ C-FAVY	Bell 407	53120	ex N30EH
☐ C-FCHV	Bell 206B JetRanger	1541	ex N59620
☐ C-FHHJ	Bell 206L LongRanger III	51382	

☐ C-FVLY	Bell 407	53816	ex N234BH	
☐ C-GTTR	Bell 206B JetRanger	1538		
☐ C-GTYV	Bell 206B JetRanger II	1976	ex N49741	
☐ C-GXVS	Bell 206B JetRanger II	1893	ex N90266	

VANCOUVER ISLAND AIR — *Campbell River, BC (YBL)*

☐ C-FCSN	Beech D18S	CA-16	ex RCAF1441	Floatplane
☐ CF-GNR	Beech 3NM	CA-191	ex (CF-SIK)	Floatplane
☐ C-FIZB	Cessna 180J	18052409	ex N46262	Floatplane
☐ C-FSCM	de Havilland DHC-2 Beaver	1583	ex CF-SCM	Floatplane
☐ C-FUVQ	de Havilland DHC-2 Beaver	696	ex N34M	Floatplane
☐ C-FWCA	de Havilland DHC-2 Beaver	1285	ex C-GUDB	Floatplane
☐ C-GAIV	Beech TC-45G	AF-80	ex N711KP	Floatplane
☐ C-GHAG	de Havilland DHC-3 Turbo Otter	214	ex 4R-ARA	Floatplane

VIH HELICOPTERS — *Victoria, BC (YYJ)*

☐ C-FDUB	Aérospatiale AS350BA AStar	3041	ex N4073S
☐ C-FTDE	Aérospatiale AS350BA AStar	2796	
☐ C-FXHS	Aérospatiale AS350B1 AStar	2248	
☐ C-GEYN	Aérospatiale AS350B2 AStar	2732	ex VP-BBB
☐ C-GNME	Aérospatiale AS350B2 AStar	2826	ex N351WW
☐ C-GNMJ	Aérospatiale AS350BA AStar	2829	
☐ C-GOLV	Aérospatiale AS350BA AStar	1108	ex N3595N
☐ C-GPHM	Aérospatiale AS350B2 AStar	2488	
☐ C-GPHQ	Aérospatiale AS350B1 AStar	2017	ex N855NM
☐ C-GPHR	Aérospatiale AS350B1 AStar	2268	
☐ C-GPTL	Aérospatiale AS350B2 AStar	2103	ex OY-HEH
☐ C-GPWO	Aérospatiale AS350BA AStar	2236	ex N2BQ
☐ C-GVIA	Aérospatiale AS350B1 AStar	2297	ex N442BV
☐ C-FBVI	Bell 205A-1	30062	ex N204WW
☐ C-GAYB	Bell 205A-1	30295	
☐ C-GKVI	Bell 205A-1	30182	ex C-GOLE
☐ C-GLVI	Bell 205A-1	30209	ex C-GPET
☐ C-GVIE	Bell 205B	30188	ex JA9854
☐ C-GVIJ	Bell 205A-1	30105	ex C-FOAR
☐ C-FANC	Bell 206B JetRanger II	1283	
☐ C-FBER	Bell 206B JetRanger III	2648	ex N5018L
☐ C-FBHQ	Bell 206B JetRanger II	970	ex CF-BHQ
☐ C-FHSO	Bell 206B JetRanger	165	ex CF-HSO
☐ C-GHCQ	Bell 206B JetRanger II	1302	
☐ C-GISE	Bell 206B JetRanger II	839	ex N300FH
☐ C-GNMT	Bell 206B JetRanger III	2295	ex N722CH
☐ C-GORO	Bell 206B JetRanger II	2086	ex N15558
☐ C-GVIH	Bell 206B JetRanger II	1689	
☐ C-GWGS	Bell 206B JetRanger	447	ex N2230W
☐ C-FCTD	Bell 206L-1 LongRanger II	45159	ex N2943A
☐ C-FGSL	Bell 206L LongRanger	45759	ex N3174L
☐ C-FJTO	Bell 206L LongRanger	45085	ex SE-HOP
☐ C-FVIX	Bell 206L LongRanger	45139	ex SE-HTL
☐ C-GENT	Bell 206L LongRanger	45041	ex ZK-HYV
☐ C-GMJS	Bell 206L LongRanger	46608	ex N120RM
☐ C-GVIQ	Bell 206L-1 LongRanger II	45492	ex N83MT
☐ C-GVIZ	Bell 206L-1 LongRanger	45346	ex N26SH
☐ C-FNMD	Bell 212	30730	ex PT-HRK
☐ C-FVIK	Bell 212	30990	ex YV-O-CVG-8
☐ C-FWDV	Bell 212	30973	ex N2768N
☐ C-GGSO	Bell 212	30696	ex N90220
☐ C-GCVI	Bell 407	53854	
☐ C-GGVI	Bell 407	53834	
☐ C-GJVI	Bell 407	53866	
☐ C-GNVI	Bell 407	53847	
☐ C-GVIB	Bell 407	53826	ex C-FTLZ
☐ C-GVIU	Bell 407	53789	ex C-FPNX
☐ C-FIGR	Kamov Ka-32-IIBC	(31585)8707/05	ex B-77299
☐ C-FLIE	Eurocopter EC135P2+	0479	ex D-HECN
☐ C-FPZR	Sikorsky S-61L	61362	ex N305V
☐ C-FQNG	Sikorsky S-61N Helipro Short	61032	ex N301Y
☐ C-FTVI	Sikorsky S-61N Helipro Short	61818	ex N4240S
☐ C-FVIG	Aérospatiale AS350B2 AStar	2893	ex N333AS
☐ C-FVIT	Aérospatiale AS350B2 AStar	2890	ex N544AS
☐ C-GKHL	Kamov Ka-32-IIBC	(31594)8801/03	ex RA-31594
☐ C-GVIY	Bell 222UT	47562	ex JA9665

VILLERS AIR SERVICES — Fort Nelson, BC (YYE)

☐ C-FGAQ	Britten-Norman BN-2A-27 Islander	212	ex G-51-212
☐ C-FJBD	Beech 58 Baron	TH-260	ex N518SW
☐ C-FTUP	Piper PA-31-350 Navajo Chieftain	31-7652101	ex N76DE
☐ C-FTVP	Cessna 208B Caravan I	208B1264	ex N5090Y
☐ C-GEBH	Cessna U206E Stationair	U20601697	ex N8232Q
☐ C-GPMV	Piper PA-31 Navajo C	31-7712081	ex N273PE

VOYAGE AIR — Fort McMurray, AB (ZFM)

☐ C-GBNA	de Havilland DHC-3 Otter	125	ex N5368G	Floatplane or wheels/skis
☐ C-GDOB	de Havilland DHC-2 Beaver	774	ex C-GEZR	Floatplane or wheels/skis
☐ C-GOLB	Cessna A185F Skywagon	18503188	ex N93173	Floatplane or wheels/skis
☐ C-GOZP	Cessna A185F Skywagon	18503258	ex (N93874)	Floatplane or wheels/skis
☐ C-GQQJ	de Havilland DHC-2 Beaver	719	ex N202PS	Floatplane or wheels/skis
☐ C-GUJW	de Havilland DHC-2 Beaver	1657	ex 305	Floatplane or wheels/skis
☐ C-GZSI	de Havilland DHC-2 Beaver	1003	ex N5327	Floatplane or wheels/skis

VOYAGEUR AIRWAYS — Voyageur (VC/VAL) — Sudbury/North Bay, ON (YSB/YYB)

☐ C-FAPP	Beech A100 King Air	B-169	ex N305TZ	
☐ C-FBGS	Beech A100 King Air	B-204	ex N108JL	
☐ C-GDPI	Beech A100 King Air	B-156	ex N21RX	
☐ C-GISH	Beech A100 King Air	B-152	ex N67LC	
☐ C-GJBV	Beech A100 King Air	B-100	ex N100S	
☐ C-GJJF	Beech A100 King Air	B-123	ex N741EB	
☐ C-FZKM	de Havilland DHC-7-102	61	ex N903HA	
☐ C-GFOF	de Havilland DHC-7-102	37	ex N67RM	Op for United Nations
☐ C-GGUL	de Havilland DHC-7-102	70	ex N905HA	Op for RNethAF
☐ C-GGUN	de Havilland DHC-7-110	66	ex N66SU	stored YYB
☐ C-GJPI	de Havilland DHC-7-102	36	ex N702GW	Op for Fugro Airborne Surveys
☐ C-GLOL	de Havilland DHC-7-102	39	ex HB-IVW	Op for United Nations
☐ C-FEXZ	de Havilland DHC-8-314	319	ex G-BRYJ	
☐ C-FEYG	de Havilland DHC-8-311	320	ex N320BC	Op for UN
☐ C-FEZD	de Havilland DHC-8-311	385	ex LN-WFR	
☐ C-FIQT	de Havilland DHC-8-315	395	ex N342EN	
☐ C-FNCU	de Havilland DHC-8-311	517	ex G-NVSB	Op for UN?
☐ C-GHQZ	de Havilland DHC-8-314	370	ex OE-LLY	Op for UN
☐ C-FMCY	Canadair CL-600-2B19 (CRJ-200)	7064	ex D-ACLP	
☐ C-FMUV	Canadair CL-600-2B19 (CRJ-200)	7073	ex D-ACLQ	
☐ C-FTYS	Canadair CL-600-2B19 (CRJ-200LR)	7039	ex N653ML	
☐ C-FWWU	Canadair CL-600-2B19 (CRJ-200LR)	7299	ex N299BS	
☐ C-FXHC	Canadair CL-600-2B19 (CRJ-200ER)	7329	ex N329BS	
☐ C-FXLH	Canadair CL-600-2B19 (CRJ-200LR)	7283	ex G-MKSA	
☐ C-FZTU	Canadair CL-600-2D24 (CRJ-900ER)	15001	ex N529AP	
☐ C-FZVW	Beech 200 Super King Air	BB-787	ex N26G	
☐ C-FZVX	Beech 200 Super King Air	BB-231	ex N200FH	
☐ C-GIND	Beech 200C Super King Air B	BL-42	ex N819CD	
☐ C-GJJT	Beech 200 Super King Air	BB-828	ex N62GA	

WAASHESHKUN AIRWAYS — Baie du Poste (Mistassini Lake), ON

☐ C-FDIO	de Havilland DHC-3 Otter	452	ex TAF 9102	Floatplane or wheels/skis

WABAKIMI AIR — Armstrong, ON (YYW)

☐ CF-BJY	de Havilland DHC-2 Beaver	173	ex N4792C	Floatplane or wheels/skis
☐ C-FBPC	de Havilland DHC-2 Beaver	144	ex VH-AAS	Floatplane or wheels/skis
☐ C-FYLZ	de Havilland DHC-3 Otter	247	ex VH-SBR	Floatplane or wheels/skis

WABUSK AIR SERVICE — Moosonee, ON (YMO)

☐ C-GKMW	Piper PA-31 Turbo Navajo B	31-725	ex N231CD
☐ C-GLEW	Piper PA-31 Turbo Navajo	31-685	ex N6775L
☐ C-GMNX	Piper PA-31 Turbo Navajo	31-528	ex N6601L
☐ C-GWLW	Piper PA-31-350 Navajo Chieftain	31-7405221	ex N54277
☐ C-FDOY	Beech 100 King Air	B-120	ex CF-DOY

WAHKASH CONTRACTING — Campbell River, BC (YBL)

☐ C-FIGF	de Havilland DHC-2 Beaver	834	ex CF-IGF
☐ C-GVHT	de Havilland DHC-2 Beaver	257	ex 51-16797

WALSTEN AIR SERVICE		Walsten (WAS)			Kenora, ON (YQK)
☐ C-GFZQ	Cessna U206E Super Skywagon	U20601543	ex N9143M		Floatplane
☐ C-GJLI	Beech 200 Super King Air	BB-347	ex N424CR		

Current status uncertain

WAMAIR SERVICE & OUTFITTING					Matheson Island, MB
☐ C-FLXY	Cessna 208 Caravan I	20800297	ex N208LA		
☐ C-FWAM	Cessna 208B Caravan I	208B0561	ex SE-LPZ		
☐ C-FXOQ	Piper PA-31 Turbo Navajo	31-440	ex N6478L		
☐ C-GDCJ	de Havilland DHC-2 Beaver	1055	ex N4411F		Floatplane or wheels/skis
☐ C-GEIF	Cessna U206F Stationair 6	U20602938			Floatplane or wheels/skis
☐ C-GJPX	Cessna 208 Caravan I	20800302	ex N1284N		Amphibian
☐ C-GKCK	Cessna U206E Super Skywagon	U20601487	ex N1487M		Floatplane or wheels/skis
☐ C-GRNK	Piper PA-31-350 Navajo Chieftain	31-7652112	ex N59888		
☐ C-GWAB	Cessna A185F Skywagon	18502399	ex N1676R		Floatplane or wheels/skis

WASAYA AIRWAYS		Wasaya (WT/WSG)			Thunder Bay, ON (YQT)
☐ C-FKPI	Pilatus PC-12/45	250	ex N250PB		
☐ C-FKRB	Pilatus PC-12/45	233	ex HB-FRD		
☐ C-FKUL	Pilatus PC-12/45	204	ex ZS-PAY		
☐ C-FPCL	Pilatus PC-12/45	276	ex N276CN		
☐ C-FSRK	Pilatus PC-12/45	202	ex ZS-SRK		
☐ C-FWAV	Pilatus PC-12/45	280	ex N280PC		
☐ C-FYZS	Pilatus PC-12/45	227	ex N227PC		
☐ C-GBJV	Pilatus PC-12/45	237	ex HB-FRH		
☐ C-GBXW	Pilatus PC-12/45	170	ex N170PD		
☐ C-GKAY	Pilatus PC-12/45	178	ex N178PC		
☐ C-GPAI	Pilatus PC-12/45	491	ex N491VA		
☐ C-FFFS	Hawker Siddeley HS.748 Srs.2A/209LFD	1663	ex G-BHCJ	806	Freighter
☐ C-FTTW	Hawker Siddeley HS.748 Srs.2A/264	1681	ex G-AYIR	805	Freighter
☐ C-GLTC	Hawker Siddeley HS.748 Srs.2A/244LFD	1656	ex N57910	801	Super Tanker
☐ C-GMAA	Hawker Siddeley HS.748 Srs.2A/214LFD	1576	ex TR-LQY	807	Freighter
☐ C-FKAD	Cessna 208B Caravan I	208B0327			
☐ C-FKDL	Cessna 208B Caravan I	208B0240	ex (N5127B)		
☐ C-FPCC	Cessna 208B Caravan I	208B0840	ex N52623		
☐ C-FWAW	Cessna 208B Caravan I	208B0895	ex N5265B		
☐ C-FQWA	Beech 1900D	UE-75	ex N175MH		
☐ C-FWAU	Beech 1900D	UE-164	ex N861CA		
☐ C-FWAX	Beech 1900D	UE-297	ex N21679		
☐ C-FWZK	Beech 1900D	UE-8	ex D-CBSF		
☐ C-GSWA	Beech 1900D	UE-34	ex N83801		
☐ C-GZVJ	Beech 1900D	UE-223	ex N1123J		

WATSON'S SKYWAYS					Wawa-Hawk Junction, ON (YXZ)
☐ C-FAZQ	Cessna U206 Super Skywagon	U206-0337	ex CF-AZQ		Floatplane or wheels
☐ C-GIKP	Cessna 208 Caravan I	20800141	ex C-GHGV		Floatplane

WEAGAMOW AIR					Weagamow-Round Lake, ON (ZRJ)
☐ C-FLIN	Piper PA-31-350 Chieftain	31-8152013	ex N81TT		
☐ C-FOCD	de Havilland DHC-2 Beaver	24	ex CF-OCD		Floatplane or wheels/skis
☐ C-GNNO	Cessna A185F Skywagon	18502685	ex (N1016F)		Floatplane

WEST COAST AIR		(8O)			Vancouver-Coal Harbor, BC (CXH)
☐ C-FAWA	de Havilland DHC-2 Beaver	1430	ex VH-IDR		Floatplane
☐ C-FEBE	de Havilland DHC-2 Beaver	792	ex N9983B		Floatplane
☐ C-FJBP	de Havilland DHC-2 Beaver	942	ex CF-JBP		Floatplane
☐ C-FGQZ	de Havilland DHC-2 Beaver	118	ex CF-GQZ		Floatplane
☐ C-FWAC	de Havilland DHC-2 Beaver	1356	ex N68089		Floatplane
☐ C-GEZS	de Havilland DHC-2 Beaver	1277	ex 57-6170		Floatplane
☐ C-GFDI	de Havilland DHC-2 Beaver	606	ex 53-2810		Floatplane
☐ C-GHMI	de Havilland DHC-2 Beaver	1215	ex ZA-CAJ	205	Floatplane
☐ C-GMKP	de Havilland DHC-2 Beaver	1374	ex N87775		Floatplane
☐ C-GOLC	de Havilland DHC-2 Beaver	1392	ex N62354		Floatplane
☐ C-GTBQ	de Havilland DHC-2 Beaver	1316	ex N9036		Floatplane
☐ C-GVPB	de Havilland DHC-2 Beaver	1551	ex SE-KKR		Floatplane
☐ C-FGQE	de Havilland DHC-6 Twin Otter 100	40	ex CF-GQE	609	Floatplane
☐ C-FGQH	de Havilland DHC-6 Twin Otter 100	106	ex 8Q-MAF	604	Floatplane
☐ C-FMHR	de Havilland DHC-6 Twin Otter 100	51	ex CF-MHR	605	Floatplane
☐ C-FWTE	de Havilland DHC-6 Twin Otter 100	96	ex CF-WTE	603	Floatplane
☐ C-GJAW	de Havilland DHC-6 Twin Otter 200	176	ex N2261L	607	Floatplane
☐ C-GQKN	de Havilland DHC-6 Twin Otter 100	94	ex PZ-TAV	606	Floatplane

WEST COAST HELICOPTERS — Port McNeill, BC (YMP)

☐ C-FWCD	Aérospatiale AS350B AStar	1854	ex C-FQCD
☐ C-FWCH	Aérospatiale AS350B AStar	1696	ex C-FSUL
☐ C-FWCO	Aérospatiale AS350BA AStar	2868	ex C-FVTM
☐ C-FWCR	Aérospatiale AS350B2 AStar	2204	ex F-GMBZ
☐ C-FWCS	Aérospatiale AS350B2 AStar	1990	ex C-FSWH
☐ C-FWCW	Aérospatiale AS350B2 AStar	3651	
☐ C-FWEC	Aérospatiale AS350B2 AStar	3221	ex C-FWCN
☐ C-FYWC	Aérospatiale AS350B AStar	1356	ex C-FNTA
☐ C-GAVU	Aérospatiale AS350BA AStar	2533	ex PT-YAE
☐ C-GQSW	Aérospatiale AS350BA AStar	2091	ex JA9744
☐ C-GMEP	Bell 206B JetRanger III	3055	

WEST WIND AVIATION — Westwind (WEW) — Regina, SK (YQR)

☐ C-FCPD	British Aerospace Jetstream 31	822	ex G-31-822	
☐ C-FDAD	Cessna 401A	401A0058	ex N6601L	
☐ C-FWWF	Beech 200 Super King Air	BB-374	ex N111UR	
☐ C-FWWQ	Beech 200 Super King Air	BB-667	ex N667NA	
☐ C-FZJE	Cessna 401B	401B0032	ex (N7931Q)	
☐ C-GAXR	Cessna 401B	401B0050	ex N1250C	
☐ C-GEUY	Cessna 414 II	414-0821		
☐ C-GHGK	British Aerospace Jetstream 31	786	ex N786SC	
☐ C-GMAG	Beech 100A King Air	B-229	ex N100HC	
☐ C-GGPX	Cessna 402C II	402C0280	ex C-GGSN	
☐ C-GPRT	Beech 1900C	UC-140	ex N140YV	Pronto A/w colours
☐ C-GPRZ	Beech 1900C-1	UC-76	ex ZS-PJM	
☐ C-GRSY	Cessna 401	401-0248	ex N8400F	
☐ C-GWWB	Cessna 414	414-0514	ex N414DM	
☐ C-GWWC	ATR 42-300	209	ex N209AT	
☐ C-GWWD	ATR 42-300	211	ex N213AT	
☐ C-GWWN	Beech 200 Super King Air	BB-14	ex N418CS	
☐ C-GWWR	ATR 42-300	238	ex G-RHUM	
☐ C-GWWV	Beech 200 Super King Air	BB-287	ex N498AC	
☐ C-GWWX	Beech 1900C-1	UC-44	ex OY-JRI	
☐ C-GWWY	Beech 1900C-1	UC-63	ex ZS-PDI	

WESTAIR AVIATION — Northen Life (NLF) — Kamloops, BC (YKA)

☐ C-FRJE	Piper PA-31T Cheyenne II	31T-7820002	ex C-GCUL
☐ C-GPIM	Piper PA-31T Cheyenne II	31T-8020065	ex C-GNAM
☐ C-GVKA	Piper PA-31T Cheyenne II	31T-7920008	ex N9715N
☐ C-GWCA	Piper PA-42-720 Cheyenne IIIA	42-5501057	ex C-GSAA
☐ C-GXAJ	Cessna U206F Stationair II	U20602810	ex N35935

WESTJET — Westjet (WS/WJA) — Calgary-Intl, AB (YYC)

☐ C-FAWJ	Boeing 737-8CT/W	35502/2323		807
☐ C-FBWJ	Boeing 737-7CT/W	32767/1629	ex (C-GWSA)	230
☐ C-FBWS	Boeing 737-7CT/W	37088/3080	ex N1786B	
☐ C-FCWJ	Boeing 737-7CT/W	35086/2613		250
☐ C-FEWJ	Boeing 737-7CT/W	32769/1665		232
☐ C-FGWJ	Boeing 737-7CT/W	32764/1553		226
☐ C-FIWJ	Boeing 737-7CT/W	30712/2185		240
☐ C-FIWS	Boeing 737-76N/W	32404/851		001
☐ C-FJWS	Boeing 737-76N/W	28651/872		002
☐ C-FKWS	Boeing 737-76N/W	30134/905	ex N1787B	003
☐ C-FMWJ	Boeing 737-7CT/W	32771/1754		233
☐ C-FTWJ	Boeing 737-7CT/W	30713/2220	ex N1786B	241
☐ C-FUWS	Boeing 737-7CT/W	32765/1574		228
☐ C-FWAD	Boeing 737-7CT/W	32753/1222		201
☐ C-FWAF	Boeing 737-7CT/W	32747/1239		202
☐ C-FWAI	Boeing 737-7CT/W	33656/1246		203
☐ C-FWAO	Boeing 737-7CT/W	33657/1254		205
☐ C-FWAQ	Boeing 737-7CT/W	32748/1266		206
☐ C-FWBG	Boeing 737-7CT/W	32749/1281		207
☐ C-FWBL	Boeing 737-7CT/W	32750/1286		208
☐ C-FWBW	Boeing 737-7CT/W	33697/1303		209
☐ C-FWBX	Boeing 737-7CT/W	32751/1333		210
☐ C-FWCC	Boeing 737-7CT/W	32752/1339		211
☐ C-FWCN	Boeing 737-7CT/W	33698/1346		212
☐ C-FWSE	Boeing 737-8CT/W	36690/2987		811
☐ C-FWSF	Boeing 737-7CT/W	32758/1431		218
☐ C-FWSI	Boeing 737-7CT/W	36691/2983		253
☐ C-FWSK	Boeing 737-7CT/W	36420/2671		251
☐ C-FWSO	Boeing 737-7CT/W	32759/1445		219
☐ C-FWSV	Boeing 737-7CT/W	32760/1472		220
☐ C-FWSX	Boeing 737-7CT/W	32761/1493		221
☐ C-FWSY	Boeing 737-7CT/W	32762/1501		222
☐ C-FXWJ	Boeing 737-7CT/W	32768/1648	ex (C-GZWS)	231

Reg	Type	c/n	Previous identity	Fleet no	Notes
☐ C-FZWS	Boeing 737-76N/W	32731/1044		006	
☐ C-GBWS	Boeing 737-6CT	34288/1931		608	
☐ C-GCWJ	Boeing 737-7CT/W	33970/1556		227	
☐ C-GEWJ	Boeing 737-6CT	35571/2045		615	
☐ C-GGWJ	Boeing 737-7CT/W	35503/2334		242	
☐ C-GJWS	Boeing 737-8CT/W	34152/1714		802	
☐ C-GKWJ	Boeing 737-8CT/W	34151/1684		801	
☐ C-GLWS	Boeing 737-76N/W	32581/1009	ex N1787B	005	
☐ C-GMWJ	Boeing 737-7CT/W	35985/2135	ex N1779B	239	
☐ C-GPWS	Boeing 737-6CT	34284/1759		601	
☐ C-GQWJ	Boeing 737-7CT/W	35505/2436	ex N1786B	246	
☐ C-GRWS	Boeing 737-76N/W	32881/1155		007	
☐ C-GTWS	Boeing 737-76N/W	32883/1179		008	
☐ C-GUWJ	Boeing 737-7CT/W	36422/2497	ex N1786B	248	
☐ C-GUWS	Boeing 737-76N/W	33378/1206		009	
☐ C-GVWJ	Boeing 737-7CT/W	36421/2484	ex N1786B	247	
☐ C-GWAZ	Boeing 737-7CT/W	32763/1522		223	
☐ C-GWBF	Boeing 737-7CT/W	32757/1370		213	
☐ C-GWBJ	Boeing 737-7CT/W	32754/1385	ex N1787B	215	
☐ C-GWBL	Boeing 737-8CT	34154/1734		806	
☐ C-GWBN	Boeing 737-7CT/W	34155/1772		235	
☐ C-GWBT	Boeing 737-7CT/W	32755/1396		216	
☐ C-GWBX	Boeing 737-7CT/W	34156/1793		236	
☐ C-GWCM	Boeing 737-7CT/W	32756/1413		217	
☐ C-GWCN	Boeing 737-7CT/W	34157/1818	ex N1784B	237	
☐ C-GWCQ	Boeing 737-6CT	35111/2004		610	
☐ C-GWCT	Boeing 737-6CT	35112/2016		611	
☐ C-GWCY	Boeing 737-6CT	35113/2022		612	
☐ C-GWJE	Boeing 737-7CT/W	35078/2431		245	
☐ C-GWJF	Boeing 737-7CT/W	32766/1599		229	
☐ C-GWJG	Boeing 737-7CT/W	35504/2366	ex N1786B	243	
☐ C-GWJK	Boeing 737-7CT/W	35084/2564	ex N1786B	249	
☐ C-GWJO	Boeing 737-7CT/W	33969/1527		225	
☐ C-GWJU	Boeing 737-6CT	34289/1956		609	
☐ C-GWSA	Boeing 737-8CT/W	34153/1731		805	
☐ C-GWSB	Boeing 737-6CT	34285/1797		602	
☐ C-GWSE	Boeing 737-76N/W	33379/1216		010	
☐ C-GWSH	Boeing 737-76N/W	29886/1258		011	
☐ C-GWSI	Boeing 737-6CT	34286/1816		603	
☐ C-GWSJ	Boeing 737-6CT	34621/1862		605	
☐ C-GWSK	Boeing 737-6CT	34287/1912	ex N1787B	607	
☐ C-GWSL	Boeing 737-6CT	34633/1884		606	
☐ C-GWSN	Boeing 737-7CT/W	37089/3090	ex N1796B	256	
☐ C-GWSO	Boeing 737-7CT/W	37090/3092	ex N1796B	257	
☐ C-GWSP	Boeing 737-7CT/W	36693/3108		258	
☐ C-GWSQ	Boeing 737-7CT/W	37091/3134		259	
☐ C-GWSR	Boeing 737-8CT/W	35288/2802		809	
☐ C-GWSU	Boeing 737-7CT/W	36689/2860	ex N1787B	252	
☐ C-GWSV	Boeing 737-8CT/W	37158/2841		810	
☐ C-GWSY	Boeing 737-7CT/W	37421			on order
☐ C-GWSZ	Boeing 737-8CT/W	37092/3164			
☐ C-GWWJ	Boeing 737-8CT/W	35080/2524	ex N1786B	808	
☐ C-GXWJ	Boeing 737 6CT	35570/2032		613	
☐ C-GYWJ	Boeing 737-7CT/W	32772/1879		238	
☐ C-GZWS	Boeing 737-8CT/W	32770/1719		803	
☐ C-	Boeing 737-7CT/W				on order
☐ C-	Boeing 737-8CT/W				on order
☐ C-	Boeing 737-8CT/W				on order

WESTLAND HELICOPTERS — *Houston, BC*

Reg	Type	c/n
☐ C-GQKT	Bell 206 JetRanger II	2148

WHISTLER AIR SERVICES — *Whistler, BC (YWS)*

Reg	Type	c/n	Previous identity	Notes
☐ C-FSKZ	de Havilland DHC-2 Beaver	1594	ex CF-SKZ	Floatplane
☐ C-GEND	de Havilland DHC-3 Turbo Otter	371	ex N83U	Floatplane
☐ C-GSFA	Cessna 208 Caravan	20800212	ex 8Q-MAT	Floatplane

WHITE RIVER AIR — *White River, ON (YWR)*

Reg	Type	c/n	Previous identity
☐ CF-FHR	de Havilland DHC-2 Beaver	46	
☐ C-FWRA	de Havilland DHC-3 Otter	213	ex India IM1714

WILDCAT HELICOPTERS — *Penticton, BC (YYF)*

Reg	Type	c/n	Previous identity
☐ C-FCAN	Bell 212	30919	ex XA-IOW
☐ C-GGAT	Bell 212	30846	ex N16796
☐ C-GSGT	Bell 212	30771	ex C-FSAT
☐ C-GSRH	Bell 212	30895	ex N751HL

WILDERNESS AIR — Vermillion Bay, ON (YVG)

☐ C-FGMK	de Havilland DHC-2 Beaver	1329	ex 58-2003	Floatplane
☐ C-FODV	de Havilland DHC-3 Otter	411	ex CF-ODV	Floatplane
☐ C-GFZF	Cessna A185E Skywagon	18502002	ex N70118	Floatplane
☐ C-GLAB	de Havilland DHC-3 Otter	348	ex 59-2210	Floatplane
☐ C-GNFN	Cessna 208 Caravan	20800502		

WILDERNESS HELICOPTERS — Wawa-Hawk Junction, ON (YXZ)

☐ C-FALS	Bell 206L LongRanger	45061	ex N56DE
☐ C-GMCJ	Bell 206L-3 LongRanger III	51459	
☐ C-GWHA	Bell 206L-1 LongRanger II	45694	ex N82KA
☐ C-GWHM	Bell 206L-3 LongRanger III	51009	ex N22621

WILLISTON LAKE AIR SERVICES — Mackenzie, BC (YZY)

☐ C-FBAD	Piper PA-31-350 Navajo Chieftain	31-7752101	ex N6196C
☐ C-GRWP	Piper PA-31-350 Chieftain	31-7952095	

WINDWARD AIR SERVICES — Toronto, ON

☐ C-GAGE	Cessna 441 Conquest	441-0214	ex N792KC

WINGS OVER KISSISSING

☐ C-FFVZ	de Havilland DHC-3 Turbo Otter	145	ex N80944	Floatplane or wheels/skis
☐ C-FODW	de Havilland DHC-3 Turbo Otter	403	ex CF-ODW	Floatplane or wheels/skis
☐ C-FWEJ	de Havilland DHC-3 Turbo Otter	208	ex IM1710	Floatplane or wheels/skis
☐ C-GEWP	de Havilland DHC-2 Turbo Beaver	1543/TB2	ex ET-AKI	Floatplane
☐ C-GGOR	de Havilland DHC-3 Turbo Otter	97	ex TI-SPE	Floatplane

WOLVERINE AIR — Fort Simpson, NT (YFS)

☐ C-FTQB	Cessna A185F Skywagon	18501655	ex (N1948U)
☐ C-GHKB	Cessna 207 Skywagon	20700228	ex N1628U
☐ C-GIHF	Britten-Norman BN-2A-26 Islander	475	ex G-BDJU
☐ C-GQOA	Cessna U206G Stationair 6	U20604993	ex (N4600U)
☐ C-GTUG	Cessna U206G Stationair 6	U20606214	ex (N6282Z)

YELLOWHEAD HELICOPTERS — Valemount, BC

☐ C-FPQX	Bell 206B JetRanger	1330	
☐ C-FYHB	Bell 206B JetRanger	1655	ex C-GCHH
☐ C-FYHJ	Bell 206B JetRanger III	2900	ex N344P
☐ C-GDGH	Bell 206B JetRanger	2476	ex N352E
☐ C-GXYH	Bell 206B JetRanger III	2267	ex N130VG
☐ C-GYHL	Bell 206B JetRanger III	1702	
☐ C-GYHR	Bell 206B JetRanger III	2571	ex N5015A
☐ C-GYHT	Bell 206B JetRanger III	4104	ex HL9107

☐ C-FGYH	Bell 407	53641	
☐ C-FYHD	Bell 205A-1	30128	ex C-FNMO
☐ C-GJWC	Cessna T210L Turbo Centurion II	21060438	ex N93858
☐ C-GYHP	Bell 206L-1 LongRanger	45400	ex N2621
☐ C-GYHQ	Bell 206L-1 LongRanger	45419	ex N2629
☐ C-GYHX	Bell 206L-3 LongRanger III	51545	ex N206AC

ZIMMER AIR SERVICES — Blenheim, ON

☐ C-FIHC	Aérospatiale AS355F1 Twin Star	5191	ex N355TD
☐ C-GBCL	Bell 206B JetRanger II	3458	ex N2145R
☐ C-GFEC	Bell 206B JetRanger II	1611	
☐ C-GHSW	Aérospatiale AS350D AStar	1082	ex N4268V
☐ C-GMLO	Bell 206B JetRanger	957	ex N809JA

CC- CHILE (Republic of Chile)

AEROCARDAL

☐ CC-AAQ	Dornier 228	8119	ex CS-TGO

AEROLINEA PRINCIPAL CHILE (PCP) — Santiago-Benitez Intl (SCL)

☐ CC-CZK	Boeing 737-236	21804/686	ex G-BGDP
☐ CC-CZO	Boeing 737-236	22030/693	ex G-BGJI

AEROSERVICIO

Reg	Type	c/n	Previous identity	Notes
☐ CC-CEI	Cessna 421C Golden Eagle III	421C0655	ex CC-PFM	

AEROVIAS DAP — Dap (DAP) — Punta Arenas (PUQ)

Reg	Type	c/n	Previous identity	Notes
☐ CC-CHV	de Havilland DHC-6 Twin Otter 300	709	ex (G-BHUY)	
☐ CC-CLT	CASA C.212-100	A10-1-103	ex E-210	stored PUQ
☐ CC-CLV	Cessna 402C	402C0073	ex CC-CDU	
☐ CC-CLY	Beech 100 King Air	B-79	ex CC-PIE	
☐ CC-COV	Cessna 402C	402C0282	ex CC-CDS	
☐ CC-CZP	British Aerospace 146 Srs.200	E2042	ex G-FLTD	

BOSQUES ARAUCO

Reg	Type	c/n	Previous identity	Notes
☐ CC-CBB	Bell UH-1H	5162	ex N647F	
☐ CC-CBH	Bell UH-1H	5843	ex N49KP	
☐ CC-CBL	Bell UH-1H	9495	ex N97KP	
☐ CC-CBO	Bell UH-1H	4133	ex N3149N	
☐ CC-CBU	Bell UH-1H	4060	ex N768MC	
☐ CC-CBW	Bell UH-1H	10810	ex N45401	
☐ CC-CBY	Bell UH-1H	9445	ex N62615	
☐ CC-CBZ	Bell UH-1H	10091	ex N6259T	

COPTERS — Copters (KOP) — Rancagua (QRC)

Reg	Type	c/n	Previous identity	Notes
☐ CC-CLE	Bell UH-1H	8535	ex N46666	
☐ CC-CLI	Aérospatiale AS355N Ecureuil 2	5700	ex PR-YHE	
☐ CC-CLK	Bell UH-1H	4902	ex N38CF	

DAP HELICOPTEROS — HeliDap (DHE) — Punta Arenas (PUQ)

Reg	Type	c/n	Previous identity	Notes
☐ CC-CHK	MBB 105CB-4-2	S-687	ex H-62	EMS
☐ CC-CHM	MBB 105CB-4-2	S-688	ex H-63	EMS
☐ CC-CHN	MBB 105CB-4-2	S-689	ex H-64	EMS
☐ CC-CHQ	MBB 105CB-4-2	S-708	ex H-65	EMS
☐ CC-CHR	MBB 105CB-4-2	S-710	ex H-66	EMS
☐ CC-CCA	Eurocopter EC135T1	0122	ex N214TD	
☐ CC-CIB	Aérospatiale AS355F2 Twin Star	5371	ex XA-MDE	
☐ CC-CIK	Aérospatiale AS355F2 Twin Star	5413	ex N710KM	
☐ CC-CIN	Aérospatiale AS355F1 Twin Star	5147	ex N22TS	
☐ CC-CMV	Aérospatiale AS355F2 Twin Star	5372	ex N225CC	

EAGLE COPTERS

Reg	Type	c/n	Previous identity	Notes
☐ CC-CAF	Bell 204B	2010	ex CC-CLI	
☐ CC-CIS	Bell 212	30932	ex CS-HFY	Lsd to INAER
☐ CC-CIY	Bell 212	30685	ex CS-HFW	Lsd to INAER

EMPRESSA AERO - SERVICIOS PARRAGUE — Aspar (PRG) — Santiago

Reg	Type	c/n	Previous identity	Fleet no	Notes
☐ CC-CDT	Canadian Vickers PBY-5A Catalina	CV-332	ex F-YCHB	32	
☐ CC-CNP	Consolidated PBY-6A Catalina	2029	ex EC-FXN	35	

HELICOPTEROS DEL PACIFICO — Temuco

Reg	Type	c/n	Previous identity	Notes
☐ CC-CLO	Bell UH-1H	5057	ex EC-GOC	
☐ CC-COW	Bell UH-1H	5844	ex N7232K	
☐ CC-CPT	Garlick-Bell UH-1D	8001	ex 70+01	
☐ CC-CPU	Garlick-Bell UH-1D	8115	ex 70+55	
☐ CC-CPY	Garlick-Bell UH-1D	8205	ex 71+45	
☐ CC-CPZ	Garlick-Bell UH-1D	8221	ex 71+61	

HELICOPTERS CHILE — Machali Heliport

Reg	Type	c/n	Previous identity	Notes
☐ CC-CLB	Bell UH-1H	5892	ex N28BC	
☐ CC-CLF	Bell AH-1S	24060	ex N82277	

HELIWORKS — Heliworks (HLW) — Concepcion (CCP)

Reg	Type	c/n	Previous identity	Fleet no	Notes
☐ CC-CHU	Lockheed P2V-7S Neptune	726-7217	ex N703AU	03	

INAER HELICOPTER CHILE

Reg	Type	c/n	Previous identity	Notes
☐ CC-CIQ	Bell 205A-1	30134	ex EC-GAA	Lsd fr Helisureste
☐ CC-CIS	Bell 212	30932	ex CS-HFY	Lsd fr Eagle Copters
☐ CC-CIU	Bell 407	53727	ex C-FLFC	
☐ CC-CIY	Bell 212	30685	ex CS-HFW	Lsd fr Eagle Copters

LAN AIRLINES		LAN (LA/LAN)	Santiago-Benitez Intl (SCL)	

Member of Oneworld

☐ CC-CVA	Airbus A318-121	3001	ex D-AUAI	
☐ CC-CVB	Airbus A318-121	3030	ex D-AUAK	
☐ CC-CVF	Airbus A318-121	3062	ex D-AUAM	
☐ CC-CVH	Airbus A318-121	3214	ex D-AUAD	
☐ CC-CVN	Airbus A318-121	3216	ex D-AUAE	
☐ CC-CVP	Airbus A318-121	3371	ex D-AUAC	
☐ CC-CVR	Airbus A318-121	3390	ex D-AUAH	
☐ CC-CVS	Airbus A318-121	3438	ex D-AUAA	
☐ CC-CVU	Airbus A318-121	3469	ex D-AUAD	
☐ CC-CVV	Airbus A318-121	3509	ex D-AUAE	
☐ CC-CZJ	Airbus A318-121	3585	ex D-AUAB	
☐ CC-CZN	Airbus A318-121	3602	ex D-AUAF	
☐ CC-CZQ	Airbus A318-121	3606	ex D-AUAG	
☐ CC-CZR	Airbus A318-121	3635	ex D-AUAI	
☐ CC-CZS	Airbus A318-121	3642	ex D-AUAJ	
☐ CC-COU	Airbus A319-132	2089	ex D-AVWL	Lsd to LPE
☐ CC-COX	Airbus A319-132	2096	ex D-AVYN	Lsd to LPE
☐ CC-COY	Airbus A319-132	2295	ex D-AVWA	Lsd to LPE
☐ CC-COZ	Airbus A319-132	2304	ex D-AVWN	Lsd to LPE
☐ CC-CPE	Airbus A319-132	2321	ex D-AVYO	Lsd to LPE
☐ CC-CPF	Airbus A319-132	2572	ex D-AVXC	Lsd to LPE
☐ CC-CPI	Airbus A319-132	2585	ex D-AVXH	Lsd to LPE
☐ CC-CPJ	Airbus A319-132	2845	ex D-AVYX	
☐ CC-CPL	Airbus A319-132	2858	ex D-AVYB	
☐ CC-CPM	Airbus A319-132	2864	ex D-AVWC	Lsd to LPE
☐ CC-CPO	Airbus A319-132	2872	ex D-AVWJ	Lsd to LPE
☐ CC-CPQ	Airbus A319-132	2886	ex D-AVXP	Lsd to LPE
☐ CC-CPX	Airbus A319-132	2887	ex D-AVYF	Lsd to LPE
☐ CC-CQK	Airbus A319-132	2892	ex D-AVYV	Lsd to LPE
☐ CC-CQL	Airbus A319-132	2894	ex D-AVWE	Lsd to LPE
☐ CC-CYE	Airbus A319-132	3663	ex D-AVYV	
☐ CC-CYF	Airbus A319-132	3671	ex D-AVYW	
☐ CC-CYI	Airbus A319-132	3770	ex D-AVXE	
☐ CC-CYJ	Airbus A319-132	3772	ex D-AVXH	
☐ CC-CYL	Airbus A319-132	3779	ex D-AVXJ	
☐ CC-COF	Airbus A320-233	1355	ex F-WWBE	
☐ CC-COI	Airbus A320-233	1526	ex F-WWIM	
☐ CC-COL	Airbus A320-233	1568	ex VP-BCK	
☐ CC-COM	Airbus A320-233	1626	ex F-WWDL	
☐ CC-CQM	Airbus A320-233	3280	ex F-WWDM	Lsd to LPE
☐ CC-CQN	Airbus A320-233	3319	ex F-WWBC	
☐ CC-CQO	Airbus A320-233	3535	ex F-WWDZ	
☐ CC-CQP	Airbus A320-233	3556	ex F-WWBC	
☐ CC-	Airbus A320-233		ex	on order
☐ CC-	Airbus A320-233		ex	on order
☐ CC-	Airbus A320-233		ex	on order
☐ CC-	Airbus A320-233		ex	on order
☐ CC-	Airbus A320-233		ex	on order
☐ CC-	Airbus A320-233		ex	on order
☐ CC-CQA	Airbus A340-313X	359	ex F-WWJY	
☐ CC-CQC	Airbus A340-313X	363	ex F-WWJZ	
☐ CC-CQE	Airbus A340-313X	429	ex F-WWJQ	
☐ CC-CQF	Airbus A340-313X	442	ex F-WWJY	
☐ CC-CQG	Airbus A340-313X	167	ex C-FYLC	
☐ CC-CDM	Boeing 767-352ER	26261/575	ex VN-A763	
☐ CC-CDP	Boeing 767-316ER/W	27597/602		
☐ CC-CEB	Boeing 767-316ER	26327/621		
☐ CC-CRH	Boeing 767-375ER	25864/426	ex B-2562	
☐ CC-CRV	Boeing 767-316ER	27615/681	ex LV-BFU	
☐ CC-CWF	Boeing 767-316ER/W	34626/940		
☐ CC-CWG	Boeing 767-316ER/W	34629/944		
☐ CC-CWH	Boeing 767-316ER/W	34628/945		
☐ CC-CWN	Boeing 767-316ER/W	35229/949		
☐ CC-CWV	Boeing 767-316ER/W	35230/955		
☐ CC-CWY	Boeing 767-316ER/W	35231/961		
☐ CC-CXC	Boeing 767-316ER/W	36710/962		
☐ CC-CXD	Boeing 767-316ER/W	35697/967		
☐ CC-CXE	Boeing 767-316ER/W	35696/968		
☐ CC-CXF	Boeing 767-316ER/W	36711/970		
☐ CC-CXG	Boeing 767-316ER	36712/972	ex N5020K	
☐ CC-CXH	Boeing 767-316ER	35698/973		
☐ CC-CXI	Boeing 767-316ER	37800/984		
☐ CC-CXJ	Boeing 767-316ER	37801/985		
☐ CC-CXK	Boeing 767-316ER	37802		on order

☐ CC-CXL	Boeing 767-31BER	26265/570	ex LV-BFD	
☐ CC-CZT	Boeing 767-316ER	29228/699		
☐ CC-CZU	Boeing 767-316ER	29229/729		
☐ CC-CZW	Boeing 767-316ER/W	29227/698		

LAN CARGO — *LAN Cargo (UC/LCO)* — *Santiago-Benitez Intl (SCL)*

☐ CC-CSD	Boeing 737-204F	20417/255	ex TF-ABD	Lsd fr LAN
☐ CC-CZY	Boeing 767-316F/W	30780/806		
☐ CC-CZZ	Boeing 767-316F/W	25756/712		
☐ N314LA	Boeing 767-316F	32573/848		op by MAA
☐ N316LA	Boeing 767-316F	30842/860		op by FWL
☐ N420LA	Boeing 767-316F	34627/948		Lsd to MAA
☐ PR-ABD	Boeing 767-316F/W	34245/935		Lsd to TUS
☐ N772LA	Boeing 777-F6N	37708/774		
☐ N774LA	Boeing 777-F6N	37710/782		on order

LAN EXPRESS — *LANExpres (LU/LXP)* — *Santiago-Benitez Intl (SCL)*

99.4% owned subsidiary of LAN Airlines and operates aircraft leased from the parent.

LASSA - LINEAS DE AEROSERVICIOS — *(LSE)* — *Santiago-Tobalaba*

☐ CC-CIZ	Bell UH-1B	1124	ex EC-EOH	
☐ CC-CME	Bell UH-1H	8800	ex EC-GDO	
☐ CC-CMF	Bell UH-1H	5398	ex EC-GDM	
☐ CC-CNF	Bell UH-1H	5949	ex N1214B	
☐ CC-CNH	Bell UH-1H	10484	ex EC-GOH	
☐ CC-CNL	Garrick-Bell UH-1B	318	ex LV-WNR	
☐ CC-CNM	Bell UH-1H	4609	ex N1216Y	
☐ CC-CFY	Piper PA-31 Turbo Navajo	31-600	ex E-203	
☐ CC-CNW	Dornier 228-202K	8063	ex G-BMMR	

LINEA AEREA COSTA NORTE — *Costa Norte (NOT)* — *Iquique (IQQ)*

☐ CC-CAJ	Cessna 337H Super Skymaster II	33701860	ex N1368L	
☐ CC-CFU	Rockwell 500S Shrike Commander	3320	ex N348TT	
☐ CC-CFW	Rockwell 500S Shrike Commander	3230	ex N567PT	
☐ CC-CGB	Cessna 337H Super Skymaster II	33701941	ex N123YM	
☐ CC-CGK	Cessna 337H Super Skymaster II	33701818	ex N1326L	
☐ CC-CGX	Rockwell 500S Shrike Commander	3306	ex N10PP	Lsd fr S/A Aeropecsa
☐ CC-CHG	Rockwell 500S Shrike Commander	3293	ex N916AC	Lsd fr S/A Aeropecsa

PATAGONIA AIRLINES — *Puerto Montt (PMC)*

☐ CC-CDR	Cessna 208B Caravan I	208B1202	ex N13194	
☐ CC-CFF	Cessna 402C	402C0405	ex CC-CMI	
☐ CC-CTS	Cessna 208B Caravan I	208B1316	ex N21424	

SKY AIRLINE — *Aerosky (H2/SKU)* — *Santiago-Benitez Intl (SCL)*

☐ CC-CAP	Boeing 737-236	22027/654	ex CC-CZM	stored SCL
☐ CC-CDB	Boeing 737-230 (Nordam 3)	22120/715	ex N122NJ	
☐ CC-CTB	Boeing 737-2Q3	23481/1241	ex N381AC	
☐ CC-CTD	Boeing 737-2Q3	23117/1033	ex N380AC	
☐ CC-CTF	Boeing 737-230 (Nordam 3)	22122/721	ex LV-BCD	
☐ CC-CTH	Boeing 737-230 (Nordam 3)	22636/808	ex N271LR	stored SCL
☐ CC-CTJ	Boeing 737-296 (AvAero 3)	22276/665	ex N276AG	
☐ CC-CTK	Boeing 737-230 (Nordam 3)	22402/744	ex N261LR	
☐ CC-CTM	Boeing 737-230	22139/791	ex LV-BBO	
☐ CC-CTO	Boeing 737-230	22114/657	ex LV-BBI	
☐ CC-CTX	Boeing 737-2T4 (AvAero 3)	22698/823	ex N722WN	

TRANSPORTES AEREOS DON CARLOS — *Don Carlos (DCL)* — *Coyhaique-Teniente Vidal (GXQ)*

☐ CC-CCB	Cessna 402B	402B1089	ex N82930	
☐ CC-CCI	Beech 95-E55 Baron	TE-1008	ex CC-PDL	
☐ CC-CRU	Piper PA-23-250 Aztec C	27-3726	ex CC-PRX	

TRANSPORTES AEREOS SAN RAFAEL — *San Rafael (SRF)* — *Coyhaique-Teniente Vidal (GXQ)*

☐ CC-CEZ	Piper PA-31 Navajo C	31-7612035	ex CC-PVM	
☐ CC-CHI	Piper PA-23-250 Aztec F	27-8054054	ex N805BC	
☐ CC-CPN	Piper PA-31 Navajo C	31-7712052	ex CC-PVB	
☐ CC-CSE	Piper PA-31 Turbo Navajo B	31-731	ex CC-CKW	

CN- MOROCCO (Kingdom of Morocco)

AIR ARABIA MAROC — (3O/MAC)

☐ CN-NMA	Airbus A320-214	3809	ex F-WWDV	
☐ CN-NMB	Airbus A320-214	3833	ex D-ADBV	
☐ CN-NMC	Airbus A320-214	3246	ex A6-ABM	

ATLAS BLUE — Atlas Blue (8A/BMM) — Marrakech (RAK)

☐ CN-RMF	Boeing 737-4B6	24807/1880		Lsd fr RAM
☐ CN-RMG	Boeing 737-4B6	24808/1888		Lsd fr RAM
☐ CN-RMX	Boeing 737-4B6	26526/2219		Lsd fr RAM
☐ CN-RNA	Boeing 737-4B6	26531/2453		Lsd fr RAM
☐ CN-RNC	Boeing 737-4B6	26529/2584		Lsd fr RAM
☐ CN-RND	Boeing 737-4B6	26530/2588		Lsd fr RAM
☐ CN-RNX	Airbus A321-211	2064	ex D-AVZO	Lsd fr RAM
☐ CN-RNY	Airbus A321-211	2076	ex D-AVZS	Lsd fr RAM
☐ CN-ROM	Airbus A321-211	3070	ex D-AVZA	Lsd fr RAM

JET4YOU — Argan (8J/JFU) — Casablanca-Mohamed V (CMN)

☐ CN-RPA	Boeing 737-4B3	24750/1916	ex OO-TUM	Lsd fr CRL
☐ CN-RPC	Boeing 737-4K5	24125/1687	ex OO-TUI	
☐ CN-RPE	Boeing 737-8K5	27990/246	ex D-AHFJ	Lsd fr HLF
☐ CN-RPF	Boeing 737-8K5/W	34691/2246	ex G-FDZO	
☐ CN-RPG	Boeing 737-8K5/W	34692/2249	ex G-FDZP	
☐ CN-RPH	Boeing 737-46J	28867/2879	ex OO-JAM	

REGIONAL AIR LINES — Maroc Regional (FN/RGL) Casablanca-Anfa (CAS)

☐ CN-CDU	ATR 42-300	134	ex F-WWEF	Lsd fr RAM
☐ CN-CDV	ATR 42-300	137	ex F-WWEI	stored SBK
☐ CN-RLA	Beech 1900D	UE-259	ex N10863	
☐ CN-RLD	Beech 1900D	UE-267	ex N10999	
☐ CN-RLF	ATR 42-320	208	ex F-WQNL	
☐ CN-RLG	ATR 42-320	366	ex F-WQNM	

ROYAL AIR MAROC — Royalair Maroc (AT/RAM) — Casablanca-Mohamed V (CMN)

☐ CN-RNX	Airbus A321-211	2064	ex D-AVZO		Lsd to BMM
☐ CN-RNY	Airbus A321-211	2076	ex D-AVZS		Lsd to BMM
☐ CN-ROF	Airbus A321-211	2726	ex D-AVZO		
☐ CN-ROM	Airbus A321-211	3070	ex D-AVZA	all-white	Lsd to BMM
☐ CN-CDU	ATR 42-300	134	ex F-WWEF		Lsd to RGL
☐ CN-CDV	ATR 42-300	137	ex F-WWEI		Lsd to RGL
☐ CN-COA	ATR 72-201	441	ex F-WKVB		
☐ CN-COB	ATR 72-202	444	ex F-WKVD		
☐ CN-COC	ATR 72-201	470	ex F-WKVI		
☐ CN-COD	ATR 72-202	483	ex F-WKVC		
☐ CN-RMF	Boeing 737-4B6	24807/1880			Lsd BMM
☐ CN-RMG	Boeing 737-4B6	24808/1888			Lsd BMM
☐ CN-RMI	Boeing 737-2B6 (Nordam 3)	21214/449		El Ayoun	stored CAS
☐ CN-RMJ	Boeing 737-2B6 (Nordam 3)	21215/452		Oujda	stored CAS
☐ CN-RMK	Boeing 737-2B6 (Nordam 3)	21216/456		Smara	stored CAS
☐ CN-RML	Boeing 737-2B6 (Nordam 3)	22767/851	ex 6V-AHK		stored CMN
☐ CN-RMV	Boeing 737-5B6	25317/2157			
☐ CN-RMW	Boeing 737-5B6	25364/2166			
☐ CN-RMX	Boeing 737-4B6	26526/2219			Lsd to BMM
☐ CN-RMY	Boeing 737-5B6	26525/2209			
☐ CN-RNA	Boeing 737-4B6	26531/2453			Lsd to BMM
☐ CN-RNB	Boeing 737-5B6	26527/2472			
☐ CN-RNC	Boeing 737-4B6	26529/2584			Lsd to BMM
☐ CN-RND	Boeing 737-4B6	26530/2588			Lsd to BMM
☐ CN-RNG	Boeing 737-5B6	27679/2734	ex (CN-RNF)		
☐ CN-RNH	Boeing 737-5B6	27680/2855			
☐ CN-RNJ	Boeing 737-8B6/W	28980/55			
☐ CN-RNK	Boeing 737-8B6/W	28981/60			
☐ CN-RNL	Boeing 737-7B6/W	28982/236	ex N1786B		
☐ CN-RNM	Boeing 737-7B6/W	28984/294	ex N1786B		
☐ CN-RNP	Boeing 737-8B6/W	28983/492	ex N1786B		
☐ CN-RNQ	Boeing 737-7B6/W	28985/501	ex N1786B		
☐ CN-RNR	Boeing 737-7B6/W	28986/519	ex N1787B		
☐ CN-RNU	Boeing 737-8B6/W	28987/1095			
☐ CN-RNV	Boeing 737-7B6/W	28988/1261			
☐ CN-RNW	Boeing 737-8B6/W	33057/1347	ex N1787B		
☐ CN-RNZ	Boeing 737-8B6/W	33058/1432			
☐ CN-ROA	Boeing 737-8B6/W	33059/1457			

☐ CN-ROB	Boeing 737-8B6/W	33060/1646		
☐ CN-ROC	Boeing 737-8B6/W	33061/1661		
☐ CN-ROD	Boeing 737-7B6/W	33062/1883		
☐ CN-ROE	Boeing 737-8B6/W	33063/1913	ex N1781B	
☐ CN-ROH	Boeing 737-85P	33978/1957		
☐ CN-ROJ	Boeing 737-85P	33979/1963		
☐ CN-ROK	Boeing 737-8B6/W	33064/2180	ex N1786B	
☐ CN-ROL	Boeing 737-8B6/W	33065/2206	ex N1787B	
☐ CN-ROP	Boeing 737-8B6/W	33066/2506	ex N1782B	
☐ CN-ROR	Boeing 737-8B6/W	33067/2527	ex N1786B	
☐ CN-ROS	Boeing 737-8B6/W	37718/2773		
☐ CN-ROT	Boeing 737-8B6/W	33068/2883		
☐ CN-ROU	Boeing 737-8B6/W	33069/2911		
☐ CN-ROX	Boeing 737-3M8F	24020/1614	ex N240MT	
☐ CN-	Boeing 737-8B6/W			on order
☐ CN-	Boeing 737-8B6/W			on order
☐ CN-	Boeing 737-8B6/W			on order

☐ CN-RGA	Boeing 747-428	25629/956	ex F-OGTG	
☐ CN-RMT	Boeing 757-2B6	23686/103	ex N32831	
☐ CN-RMZ	Boeing 757-2B6	23687/106		
☐ CN-RNS	Boeing 767-36NER	30115/863		
☐ CN-RNT	Boeing 767-36NER	30843/867		
☐ CN-ROG	Boeing 767-328ER	27212/531	ex HL7200	
☐ CN-ROV	Boeing 767-3Q8ER	27686/793	ex N201LF	
☐ CN-ROW	Boeing 767-343ER	30008/743	ex N768MT	
☐ CN-CDF	Beech 200 Super King Air	BB-577		Trainer
☐ CN-CDN	Beech 200 Super King Air	BB-713	ex N36741	Trainer

CP- BOLIVIA (Republic of Bolivia)

AEROCON — *Aerocon (AEK)*

☐ CP-2176	Dornier Do.228-202K	8163	ex D-CIKI
☐ CP-2459	Swearingen SA.227DC Metro 23	DC-847B	ex N847LS
☐ CP-2477	Swearingen SA.227DC Metro 23	DC-830B	ex N1119K
☐ CP-2485	Swearingen SA.227DC Metro 23	DC-817B	ex VH-UUD
☐ CP-2500	Swearingen SA.227AC Metro III	AC-733B	ex N160MC
☐ CP-2527	Swearingen SA.227DC Metro 23	DC-824B	ex N471Z
☐ CP-2548	Swearingen SA.227BC Metro 23	BC-768B	ex N768ML
☐ CP-2563	Swearingen SA.227BC Metro 23	BC-783B	ex N783ML
☐ CP-2590	Swearingen SA.227BC Metro 23	BC-773B	ex N773US
☐ CP-2602	Swearingen SA.227BC Metro 23	BC-780B	ex N780AL
☐ CP-	Swearingen SA.227BC Metro 23	BC-781B	ex N781AL

AEROESTE — *Aeroeste (ROE)* — *Santa Cruz-El Trompillo (SRZ)*

☐ CP-2266	Rockwell 690B Turbo Commander	11395	ex N816PC
☐ CP-2328	LET L-410UVP-E20	912536	ex S9-TAY
☐ CP-2349	LET L-410UVP-E20	912530	ex S9-TBM
☐ CP-2382	LET L-410UVP-E9	861727	ex S9-TBH

AEROLINEAS SUD AMERICANAS

☐ CP-2499	Boeing 727-224 (FedEx 3)	22449/1756	ex N296SC

AEROSUR — *Aerosur (5L/RSU)* — *Santa Cruz-Viru Viru (VVI)*

☐ CP-2377	Boeing 727-23	20044/592	ex N1969	stored VVI
☐ CP-2422	Boeing 727-264 (FedEx 3)	21617/1416	ex XA-HON	
☐ CP-2423	Boeing 727-264 (FedEx 3)	21638/1457	ex XA-HOX	
☐ CP-2424	Boeing 727-264 (FedEx 3)	22156/1607	ex XA-MED	stored CCB
☐ CP-2431	Boeing 727-264 (FedEx 3)	22411/1696	ex XA-MEJ	stored VVI
☐ CP-2447	Boeing 727-264 (FedEx 3)	22409/1676	ex XA-MEH	
☐ CP-2455	Boeing 727-287 (FedEx 3)	22606/1812	ex N910PG	stored
☐ CP-2462	Boeing 727-264 (FedEx 3)	22158/1642	ex XA-MEF	
☐ CP-2498	Boeing 727-223 (FedEx 3)	22463/1755	ex CP-2463	
☐ CP-2438	Boeing 737-201 (Nordam 3)	21815/589	ex C-FNAX	
☐ CP-2476	Boeing 737-281 (AvAero 3)	21771/594	ex N751AA	
☐ CP-2484	Boeing 737-281	21768/586	ex N749AP	
☐ CP-2486	Boeing 737-281	21769/587	ex N752AP	
☐ CP-2515	Boeing 727-222	21904/1528	ex N346PA	
☐ CP-2521	Boeing 767-200ER	23107/93	ex CT-AIF	
☐ CP-2561	Boeing 737-2P6	21613/530	ex N835AL	
☐ CP-2595	Boeing 737-33A	24790/1955	ex N790AW	
☐ CP-2603	Boeing 747-443	32339/1275	ex G-VROM	

ALAS DEL SUR

☐ CP-2479	Fairchild F-27	99	ex CX-BRT	status?

AMASZONAS TRANSPORTES AEREOS		Amaszonas (Z8)		La Paz (LPB)
☐ CP-2413	Cessna 208B Caravan I	208B0838	ex N3039G	
☐ CP-2473	Swearingen SA.227DC Metro 23	DC-842B	ex N510FS	

BOLIVIANA DE AVIACION		(OB/BOV)		La Paz (LPB)
☐ CP-2550	Boeing 737-33A	25118/2065	ex N401LF	
☐ CP-2551	Boeing 737-382	24449/1857	ex N449AN	
☐ CP-2552	Boeing 737-3M8	25041/2024	ex D-ADIJ	

ECO EXPRESS				La Paz (LPB)
☐ CP-2026	Convair 340-70	249	ex 53-7797	

LAB AIRLINES		LloydAereo (LB/LLB)		Cochabamba (CBB)
☐ CP-1366	Boeing 727-2K3/W (Duganair 3)	21494/1373		
☐ CP-1367	Boeing 727-2K3/W (Duganair 3)	21495/1403		
☐ CP-2429	Boeing 727-259 (FedEx 3)	22475/1690	ex N289SC	
☐ CP-2555	Douglas DC-10-30F	46937/152	ex N833LA	
☐ CP-	Boeing 727-2S7 (FedEx 3)	22492/1729	ex N685CA	

LINEAS AEREAS CANEDO		(LCN)			Cochabamba (CBB)
☐ CP-744	Aero Commander 680	680341-34	ex OB-M-573	Juan Salvador Gaviota	
☐ CP-896	Aero Commander 680	680-548-216	ex N316E	Jose Fernando Gaviota	
☐ CP-973	Curtiss C-46C Commando	32941	ex N32227		
☐ CP-1080	Curtiss C-46A Commando	26771	ex TAM61		stored LPB
☐ CP-1093	Aero Commander 680F	680F-1035-51	ex N6197X		
☐ CP-1128	Douglas DC-3D	1998	ex N15M		stored CBB, on rebuild
☐ CP-1960	Douglas DC-3C	18993	ex PT-KVN		stored TDD
☐ CP-2421	Douglas C-117D	12979/43365	ex N545CT		Lsd to RSU

SAVE				Santa Cruz-El Trompillo (SRZ)
☐ CP-2405	British Aerospace Jetstream 31	676	ex N309PX	
☐ CP-2441	British Aerospace Jetstream 32EP	832	ex LV-WCZ	

TAB CARGO		Bol (BOL)		La Paz (LPB)
☐ CP-1376	Lockheed 382C-72D Hercules	4759	ex TAM-91	
☐ CP-2184	Lockheed 182A-2A Hercules	3228	ex TAM-69	
☐ CP-2489	Douglas DC-10-10F	46903/43	ex N68044	

TAM - TRANSPORTES AEREO MILITAR				La Paz (LPB)
☐ FAB-61	Lockheed 282-1B Hercules	3549	ex 58-0750	
☐ FAB-65	Lockheed 282-1B Hercules	3588	ex 59-1536	
☐ FAB-66	Lockheed 282-1B Hercules	3560	ex TAM-66	
☐ FAB-90	Fokker F.27M Troopship 400M	10578	ex TAM-90	
☐ FAB-93	Fokker F.27M Troopship 400M	10599	ex TAM-93	
☐ FAB-96	CAIC MA60	0411	ex B-850L	
☐ FAB-97	CAIC MA60	0412	ex B-858L	
☐ FAB-99	British Aerospace 146 Srs.100	E1081	ex N81HN	stored LPB
☐ FAB-100	British Aerospace 146 Srs.200	E2080	ex N290UE	
☐ FAB-101	British Aerospace 146 Srs.200	E2041	ex OY-RCZ	
☐ FAB-102	British Aerospace 146 Srs.200	E2023	ex G-CLHD	
☐ FAB-103	British Aerospace 146 Srs.200	E2040	ex EI-DJJ	
☐ FAB-104	British Aerospace 146 Srs.200	E2024	ex G-FLTB	

CS- PORTUGAL (Republic of Portugal)

AEROVIP				Cascais-Tires
☐ CS-AYT	Dornier 228-200	8084	ex VP-FBK	
☐ CS-TGG	Dornier 228-202K	8160	ex D-CORA	
☐ CS-TLJ	Short SD.3-60	SH3692	ex OY-MUD	std Cascais

EURO ATLANTIC AIRWAYS		EuroAtlantic (MM/MMZ)		Lisbon (LIS)	
☐ CS-TEB	Lockheed L-1011-500 Tristar	293A-1240	ex V2-LEO	Naughton Simao	
☐ CS-TFK	Boeing 757-2G5	23983/161	ex N983MQ		
☐ CS-TFM	Boeing 777-212ER	28513/144	ex 9V-SRA		Lsd to BBG
☐ CS-TFS	Boeing 767-3Y0ER	25411/408	ex S9-DBW		
☐ CS-TFT	Boeing 767-3Y0ER	26208/505	ex S9-DBY		
☐ CS-TLO	Boeing 767-383ER	24318/257	ex N318SR		
☐ CS-TLX	Boeing 757-2G5	24176/173	ex TC-OGD		
☐ CS-TLZ	Boeing 767-375ERF	24086/248	ex N240LD		

HELIBRAVO AVIACAO		HeliBravo (HIB)			Cascais-Tires
☐ CS-HED	Aérospatiale AS350B2 Ecureuil	2669	ex D-HJOE		
☐ CS-HFK	Aérospatiale AS350B2 Ecureuil	3223	ex LX-HDS		
☐ CS-HFM	Aérospatiale AS350B2 Ecureuil	1690	ex D-HFSF		
☐ CS-HFN	Aérospatiale AS350B2 Ecureuil	2437	ex D-HHWW		
☐ EC-	Aérospatiale AS350B2 Ecureuil	2097	ex I-FLAO		
☐ EC-JPM	Aérospatiale AS350B2 Ecureuil	3547	ex I-PAMR		
☐ CS-DIQ	Pilatus PC-12/45	625	ex HB-FPU		
☐ CS-HFQ	Eurocopter EC130B4	3541	ex HB-ZEY		
☐ SP-SSL	PZL Swidnik W-3A2 Sokol	370508	ex SP-PSL		Lsd fr PZL Swidnik
☐ SP-SWA	PZL Swidnik W-3A2 Sokol	310319	ex SP-SUP		Lsd fr PZL Swindik

HELIPORTUGAL		Heliportugal (HPL)			Cascais-Tires
☐ CS-HDK	Aérospatiale AS350B2 Ecureuil	1871	ex D-HHFZ		Lsd to CJR as 5N-BHS
☐ CS-HEL	Aérospatiale AS350B2 Ecureuil	2594	ex D-HEPB		
☐ CS-HEO	Aérospatiale AS350B2 Ecureuil	1222	ex RP-C8880		Lsd to CJR as 5N-BHT
☐ CS-HFI	Aérospatiale AS350B2 Ecureuil	1216	ex PT-YJC		
☐ CS-HFO	Aérospatiale AS350B2 Ecureuil	1824	ex F-GFDL		
☐ CS-HFX	Aérospatiale AS350B2 Ecureuil	4081	ex F-WWXD		
☐ CS-HGG	Aérospatiale AS350B2 Ecureuil	9085			
☐ CS-HFV	Aérospatiale SA365N Dauphin 2	6338	ex N661ME		
☐ CS-HGA	Aérospatiale SA365N Dauphin 2	6336	ex JA9978		
☐ CS-HGD	Aérospatiale SA365N Dauphin 2	6218	ex F-ONVU		
☐ CS-HGV	Aérospatiale SA365N Dauphin 2	6829			
☐ CS-HGW	Aérospatiale SA365N Dauphin 2	6830			
☐ F-OIBJ	Aérospatiale SA365N Dauphin 3	6089	ex N2XJ		
☐ F-OJTU	Aérospatiale SA365N Dauphin 2	6841			
☐ 5N-BIK	Aérospatiale SA365N Dauphin 3	6138	ex F-GNVS		Lsd to CJR
☐ CS-HEX	Eurocopter EC120B Colibri	1183	ex F-WQDV		
☐ CS-HFP	Eurocopter EC130B4	4033	ex F-WQDB		
☐ CS-HGQ	Agusta AW139	31057	ex N915DH		
☐ CS-HGU	Agusta AW139	31143			
☐ CS-HMF	Kamov Ka-32A11BC	9907			

HELISUL		Sul (HSU)			Cascais-Tires
☐ CS-HEN	Aérospatiale AS350BA Ecureuil	1845	ex LN-OPC		
☐ CS-HEZ	Bell 212	30557	ex EC-GHP		Lsd fr HSE
☐ CS-HFB	Bell 206B JetRanger III	3640	ex D-HSBA		
☐ CS-HFJ	Bell 212	30684	ex EC-IEM		
☐ EC-HFD	Bell 412EP	36183	ex N52247		EMS Lsd fr HSE
☐ EC-JLH	Bell 412EP	36374	ex N3119U		EMS Lsd fr HSE

HI FLY		Sky Flyer (5K/HFY)			Lisbon (LIS)
☐ CS-TEI	Airbus A310-304	495	ex F-WWCO		
☐ CS-TEX	Airbus A310-304	565	ex F-WWCC		
☐ CS-TFZ	Airbus A330-243	1008	ex F-WW		
☐ CS-TMT	Airbus A330-322	096	ex F-WQSA		Op for Belgium AF
☐ CS-TQM	Airbus A340-313X	117	ex A6-EYC		

HTA HELICOPTERES		Heliapra (AHT)			Loulé-Morgado de Apre
☐ CS-HEE	Aérospatiale AS355F1 Ecureuil 2	5006	ex F-WQEA		
☐ CS-HEY	Aérospatiale AS350B2 Ecureuil	9027	ex D-HXST		
☐ CS-HFR	Aérospatiale AS350B2 Ecureuil	9054	ex D-HHTA		
☐ CS-HFZ	Aérospatiale AS350B3 Ecureuil	9090	ex LN-OCR		

LUZAIR		Lisbon Jet (LUZ)			Lisbon (LIS)
☐ CS-TFY	Airbus A320-232	1868	ex N548JB		
☐ CS-TMP	Lockheed L-1011-500 Tristar	293A-1248	ex SE-DVI		
☐ CS-TMR	Lockheed L-1011-500 Tristar	293B-1241	ex SE-DVF		stored VCV
☐ CS-TQI	Boeing 767-3S1ER	25221/384	ex N237W		

OMNI - AVIACAO E TECNOLOGIA		Omni (OC/OAV)			Cascais-Tires
☐ CS-DDU	Beech 200 Super King Air	BB-640	ex N47CF		
☐ CS-HCO	Agusta-Bell 206B JetRanger III	8678	ex I-BDPL		
☐ CS-HDS	Bell 222	47028	ex G-META	EMS	
☐ CS-TLU	Airbus A319-133X	1256	ex F-GSVU		[CJ]
☐ CS-TMU	Beech 1900D	UE-335	ex N23269	Castor	Op for PGA Express
☐ CS-TMV	Beech 1900D	UE-341	ex N23309	Esquilio	Op for PGA Express
☐ CS-	Piper PA-31P-350 Mojave	31P-8414023	ex N684B		

ORBEST		Orbest (OBS)			Lisbon (LIS)
☐ CS-TRA	Airbus A330-243	461	ex EC-IDB		Lsd to NVR

PGA EXPRESS					Lisbon (LIS)
☐ CS-TMU	Beech 1900D	UE-335	ex N23269	Castor	Op by OAV
☐ CS-TMV	Beech 1900D	UE-341	ex N23309	Esquilio	Op by OAV

PORTUGALIA AIRLINES		Portugalia (NI/PGA)			Lisbon (LIS)
☐ CS-TPG	Embraer EMB.145EP (ERJ-145EP)	145014	ex PT-SYK	Melro	
☐ CS-TPH	Embraer EMB.145EP (ERJ-145EP)	145017	ex PT-SYN	Pardal	
☐ CS-TPI	Embraer EMB.145EP (ERJ-145EP)	145031	ex PT-SYZ	Cuco	
☐ CS-TPJ	Embraer EMB.145EP (ERJ-145EP)	145036	ex PT-SZC	Chapim	
☐ CS-TPK	Embraer EMB.145EP (ERJ-145EP)	145041	ex PT-SZG	Gaio	
☐ CS-TPL	Embraer EMB.145EP (ERJ-145EP)	145051	ex PT-SZQ	Pisco	
☐ CS-TPM	Embraer EMB.145EP (ERJ-145EP)	145095	ex PT-SBR	Rola	
☐ CS-TPN	Embraer EMB.145EP (ERJ-145EP)	145099	ex PT-SBV	Brigao	
☐ CS-TPA	Fokker F.28-0100 (Fokker 100)	11257	ex PH-LMF	Albatroz	
☐ CS-TPB	Fokker F.28-0100 (Fokker 100)	11262	ex PH-EZE	Pelicano	
☐ CS-TPC	Fokker F.28-0100 (Fokker 100)	11287	ex PH-LML	Flamingo	
☐ CS-TPD	Fokker F.28-0100 (Fokker 100)	11317	ex EP-IDK	Condor	
☐ CS-TPE	Fokker F.28-0100 (Fokker 100)	11342	ex PH-LNJ	Gaviao	
☐ CS-TPF	Fokker F.28-0100 (Fokker 100)	11258	ex PH-EZD	Grifo	

SATA AIR ACORES		SATA (SP/SAT)			Ponta Delgada (PDL)
☐ CS-TFJ	British Aerospace ATP	2018	ex (ES-NBB)	Açores	
☐ CS-TGL	British Aerospace ATP	2019	ex G-BRTG	Santa Mariastored	
☐ CS-TGN	British Aerospace ATP	2031	ex G-11-031	Flores	
☐ CS-TGY	British Aerospace ATP	2049	ex G-BTZJ		
☐ CS-TRB	de Havilland DHC-8Q-202	476	ex C-FXBX	Graciosa	
☐ CS-TRC	de Havilland DHC-8Q-202	480	ex C-FXBZ	Falal	
☐ CS-TRD	de Havilland DHC-8-402Q	4291	ex C-GAUA		
☐ CS-TRE	de Havilland DHC-8-402Q	4295	ex C-GBIY		
☐ CS-TRF	de Havilland DHC-8-402Q	4297	ex C-GBJE		
☐ CS-TRG	de Havilland DHC-8-402Q	4298	ex C-		

SATA INTERNACIONAL		Air Azores (S4/RZO)			Ponta Delgada (PDL)
☐ CS-TGU	Airbus A310-304	571	ex F-GJKQ	Terceira	
☐ CS-TGV	Airbus A310-304	651	ex F-WQKR	Sao Miguel	
☐ CS-TKJ	Airbus A320-212	0795	ex C-FTDA	Pico	
☐ CS-TKK	Airbus A320-214	2390	ex F-WWII	Corvo	
☐ CS-TKL	Airbus A320-214	2425	ex F-WWBH	Sao Jorge	
☐ CS-TKM	Airbus A310-304	661	ex JY-AGL	Autonomia	
☐ CS-TKN	Airbus A310-325ET	624	ex TF-ELR	Macaronesia	Lsd fr AUA
☐ CS-TKO	Airbus A320-214	3891	ex F-WWDC	Disapora	

TAP AIR PORTUGAL		Air Portugal (TP/TAP)			Lisbon (LIS)

Member of Star Alliance

☐ CS-TTA	Airbus A319-111	0750	ex D-AVYO	Vieira da Silva
☐ CS-TTB	Airbus A319-111	0755	ex D-AVYJ	Gago Coutinho
☐ CS-TTC	Airbus A319-111	0763	ex D-AVYS	Fernando Pessoa
☐ CS-TTD	Airbus A319-111	0790	ex D-AVYC	Amadeo de Souza-Cardoso
☐ CS-TTE	Airbus A319-111	0821	ex D-AVYN	Francisco d'Ollanda
☐ CS-TTF	Airbus A319-111	0837	ex D-AVYL	Calouste Gulbenkian
☐ CS-TTG	Airbus A319-111	0906	ex D-AVYN	Humberto Delgado
☐ CS-TTH	Airbus A319-111	0917	ex D-AVYJ	Antonio Sergio
☐ CS-TTI	Airbus A319-111	0933	ex D-AVYP	Eça de Queirós
☐ CS-TTJ	Airbus A319-111	0979	ex D-AVYM	Eusébio
☐ CS-TTK	Airbus A319-111	1034	ex D-AVYL	Miguel Torga
☐ CS-TTL	Airbus A319-111	1100	ex D-AVYX	Almeida Garrett
☐ CS-TTM	Airbus A319-111	1106	ex D-AVWR	Alexandre Herculano
☐ CS-TTN	Airbus A319-111	1120	ex D-AVYI	Camilo Castelo Branco
☐ CS-TTO	Airbus A319-111	1127	ex D-AVYH	Antero de Quental
☐ CS-TTP	Airbus A319-111	1165	ex D-AVWV	Josefa d'Obidos
☐ CS-TTQ	Airbus A319-112	0629	ex SU-LBF	Agostinho da Silva
☐ CS-TTR	Airbus A319-112	1756	ex C-GJWE	Soares dos Reis
☐ CS-TTS	Airbus A319-112	1765	ex C-GJWF	Guilhermina Suggia
☐ CS-TMW	Airbus A320-214	1667	ex F-WWII	Luisa Todi
☐ CS-TNA	Airbus A320-211	0185	ex F-WWDB	Grao Vasco
☐ CS-TNB	Airbus A320-211	0191	ex F-WWDH	Sophia de Mello Breyner
☐ CS-TNE	Airbus A320-211	0395	ex F-WWBJ	Sa de Miranda
☐ CS-TNG	Airbus A320-214	0945	ex F-WWIX	Monzinho de Silveira

☐ CS-TNH	Airbus A320-214	0960	ex F-WWBH	Almada Negreiros	
☐ CS-TNI	Airbus A320-214	0982	ex F-WWDF	Aquilino Ribeiro	
☐ CS-TNJ	Airbus A320-214	1181	ex F-WWDS	Florbela Espanca	
☐ CS-TNK	Airbus A320-214	1206	ex F-WWIL	Teofilo Braga	
☐ CS-TNL	Airbus A320-214	1231	ex F-WWIJ	Vitorino Nemésio	
☐ CS-TNM	Airbus A320-214	1799	ex F-WWIF	Natalia Correia	
☐ CS-TNN	Airbus A320-214	1816	ex F-WWID	Gil Vicente	
☐ CS-TNP	Airbus A320-214	2178	ex 9H-AER	Alexandre O'NeillStar Alliance c/s	
☐ CS-TNQ	Airbus A320-214	3769	ex F-WWDQ	José Regio	
☐ CS-TNR	Airbus A320-214	3883	ex F-WWIU	Luis De Freitas Branco	
☐ CS-TNS	Airbus A320-232	4021	ex F-WWDM	D Afonso Henriques	
☐ CS-TNT	Airbus A320-214	4095	ex F-WWDI		
☐ CS-TNU	Airbus A320-214	4106	ex F-WWDR	Columbano Bordalo Pinheiro	
☐ CS-TNV	Airbus A320-214	4145	ex F-WWIY		
☐ CS-TQD	Airbus A320-214	0870	ex HB-IJT	Eugénio de Andrade	
☐ CS-TJE	Airbus A321-211	1307	ex D-AVZM	Pero Vaz de Caminha	
☐ CS-TJF	Airbus A321-211	1399	ex D-AVZI	Luis Vaz de Camões	
☐ CS-TJG	Airbus A321-211	1713	ex D-AVZS	Amalia Rodrigues	
☐ CS-TOE	Airbus A330-223	305	ex D-AXEL	Pedro Alvares Cabral	
☐ CS-TOF	Airbus A330-223	308	ex D-ARND	Infante D Henrique	
☐ CS-TOG	Airbus A330-223	312	ex D-ARNO	Bartolomeu de Gusmão	
☐ CS-TOH	Airbus A330-223	181	ex OE-LAO	Nuno GonçalvesStar Alliance c/s	
☐ CS-TOI	Airbus A330-223	195	ex OE-LAN	Damião de Góis	
☐ CS-TOJ	Airbus A330-223	223	ex OE-LAM	D João II 'O Príncipe Perfeito'	
☐ CS-TOK	Airbus A330-223	317	ex OE-LAP	Padre António Vieira	
☐ CS-TOL	Airbus A330-223	877	ex F-WWKF	Joao Goncalves Zarco	
☐ CS-TOM	Airbus A330-202	899	ex F-WWKN	Vasco da Gama	
☐ CS-TON	Airbus A330-202	904	ex F-WWKT	Joao XXI	
☐ CS-TOO	Airbus A330-202	914	ex F-WWYL	Fernao de Magalhaes	
☐ CS-TOP	Airbus A330-202	934	ex F-WWKZ	Pedro Nunes	
☐ CS-TOA	Airbus A340-312	041	ex F-WWJB	Fernao Mendes Pinto	
☐ CS-TOB	Airbus A340-312	044	ex F-WWJN	D. Joao de Castro	
☐ CS-TOC	Airbus A340-312	079	ex F-WWJS	Wenceslau de Moraes	
☐ CS-TOD	Airbus A340-312	091	ex F-WWJA	D. Francisco de Almeida	

WHITE — *Young Sky (WHT)* — *Lisbon (LIS)*

☐ CS-TDI	Airbus A310-308	573	ex JY-AGK		
☐ CS-TEJ	Airbus A310-304	494			
☐ CS-TKI	Airbus A310-304	448	ex C-GRYA		
☐ CS-TQK	Airbus A320-232	2204	ex 9V-TAA	Flypurple	

CU- CUBA (Republic of Cuba)

AEROCARIBBEAN — *AeroCaribbean (7L/CRN)* — *Havana (HAV)*

☐ CU-T1509	ATR 42-300	009	ex CU-T1296		
☐ CU-T1512	ATR 42-300	136	ex CU-T1298		
☐ CU-T1544	ATR 72-212	472	ex F-WQNC		
☐ CU-T1545	ATR 72-212	473	ex F-WQNI		
☐ CU-T1547	ATR 72-212	485	ex F-WQNB		
☐ CU-T1549	ATR 72-212	459	ex F-WQND		
☐ CU-T1550	ATR 42-300	014	ex PP-PTE		Lsd fr Trip L/A
☐ CU-T1257	Antonov An-24RV	37309104	ex CU-T1536	no titles	
☐ CU-T1506	Antonov An-26	87306710	ex CU-T110		
☐ CU-C1515	Ilyushin Il-18GrM	188010805	ex CU-C132		Freighter
☐ CU-T1532	Ilyushin Il-18D	188010904	ex CU-T131		stored Holguin
☐ CU-T1534	Yakovlev Yak-40	9731754	ex CU-T1212		stored
☐ CU-T1537	Yakovlev Yak-40	9021360	ex CU-T1450		
☐ CU-T1538	Yakovlev Yak-40	9021260	ex CU-T1449		
☐ CU-T1546	Ilyushin Il-18D	186008802	ex RA-75598		
☐ CU-T1551	Embraer EMB.110P1 Bandeirante	110132	ex PT-GKV		

AEROGAVIOTA — *Gaviota (KG/GTV)* — *Havana (HAV)*

☐ CU-T1402	Antonov An-26B	12605	ex 14-02		
☐ CU-T1403	Antonov An-26B	12905	ex 14-03		
☐ CU-T1404	Antonov An-26B	12906	ex 14-04		
☐ CU-T1406	Antonov An-26B	13502	ex 14-06		
☐ CU-T1408	Antonov An-26	6903	ex 14-28		
☐ CU-T1417	Antonov An-26				
☐ CU-T1420	Antonov An-26	87306607	ex 14-20		
☐ CU-T1421	Antonov An-26	6610	ex 14-21		status uncertain
☐ CU-T1425	Antonov An-26	6904	ex 14-25		
☐ CU-T1426	Antonov An-26	5603	ex 14-26		
☐ CU-T1428	Antonov An-26B	11303	ex 14-28		
☐ CU-T1429	Antonov An-26	7006	ex 14-29		

☐ CU-T1432	Antonov An-26	7306	ex 14-32	status uncertain
☐ CU-T1433	Antonov An-26	7309	ex 14-33	status uncertain
☐ CU-T1434	Antonov An-26	7701	ex 14-34	
☐ CU-T1435	Antonov An-26	7702	ex 14-35	
☐ CU-T1240	ATR 42-500	617	ex F-WWLB	VIP lsd to/ op in CUB c/s
☐ CU-T1454	ATR 42-500	616	ex F-WWLA	
☐ CU-T1455	ATR 42-500	618	ex F-WWLC	
☐ CU-T1456	ATR 42-500	619	ex F-WWLD	
☐ CU-H1423	Mil Mi-8T			
☐ CU-H1424	Mil Mi-8P			
☐ CU-H1427	Mil Mi-8PS			
☐ CU-H1429	Mil Mi-17 (Mi-8MTV-1)			
☐ CU-H1430	Mil Mi-17 (Mi-8MTV-1)			
☐ CU-H1431	Mil Mi-8P			
☐ CU-H1436	Mil Mi-8T			

AEROTAXI — *Seraer (CNI)* — *Havana (HAV)*

☐ CU-T1540	Embraer EMB.110C Bandeirante	110091	ex CU-T1108	
☐ CU-T1541	Embraer EMB.110C Bandeirante	110116	ex CU-T1109	
☐ CU-T1542	Embraer EMB.110C Bandeirante	110136	ex PT-GKY	
☐ CU-T1558	Douglas DC-3	15916/32664	ex CU-T1058	Varadero
☐ CU-T1559	Douglas DC-3	11645	ex CU-T1059	

CUBANA DE AVIACION — *Cubana (CU/CUB)* — *Havana (HAV)*

☐ CU-T1214	Antonov An-24RV	47309404	ex CU-T923		
☐ CU-T1223	Antonov An-24RV	47309405	ex CU-T924		
☐ CU-T1236	Antonov An-24RV	27308102	ex ER-AWH		
☐ CU-T1244	Antonov An-24RV	57310301	ex JU-1011		
☐ CU-T1260	Antonov An-24RV	57310307	ex CCCP-47307		La Pinta
☐ CU-T1263	Antonov An-24RV	47309610	ex RA-46678		
☐ CU-T1267	Antonov An-24RV	47309907	ex CCCP-46696		
☐ CU-T1228	Antonov An-26B	12604	ex CU-T1401		
☐ CU-T1229	Antonov An-26B	13501	ex CU-T1405		
☐ CU-T1247	Yakovlev Yak-42D	4520424309017	ex UN-42712		
☐ CU-T1255	Yakovlev Yak-42D	4520424116664	ex RA-42443		
☐ CU-T1704	Yakovlev Yak-42D	4520424711397	ex CU-T1246		
☐ CU-T1705	Yakovlev Yak-42D	4520422014576	ex UR-42381		
☐ CU-T1240	ATR 42-500	617	ex F-WWLB		VIP Lsd fr/ op by GTV
☐ CU-T1250	Ilyushin Il-96-300	74393202015			
☐ CU-T1251	Ilyushin Il-96-300	74393202016			
☐ CU-T1254	Ilyushin Il-96-300	74393202017			
☐ CU-T1280	Ilyushin Il-62M	3749648		15 de Febrero	stored?
☐ CU-T1282	Ilyushin Il-62M	2052456			stored HAV
☐ CU-T1284	Ilyushin Il-62M	4053732			
☐ CU-C1700	Tupolev Tu-204-100SE	1450744664036	ex RA-64035		
☐ CU-T1701	Tupolev Tu-204-100E	1450743164035	ex RA-64035		
☐ CU-T1702	Tupolev Tu-204-100E	1450743164042	ex RA-64042		
☐ CU-C1703	Tupolev Tu-204-100SE	1450744664037			
☐ CU-	Ilyushin Il-96-300				on order
☐ XA-UBB	Boeing 737-291 (Nordam 3)	21750/574	ex N988UA		
☐ XA-UHY	Boeing 737-2C3	21016/406	ex XA-MAB		Lsd fr VLI
☐ YV287T	Boeing 737-217 (AvAero 3)	22728/911	ex N168WP		Lsd fr VNE

CX- URUGUAY (Republic of Uruguay)

AEROMAS — *Aeromas Express (MSM)* — *Montevideo-Carrasco (MVD)*

☐ CX-BDI	Piper PA-23-250 Aztec B	27-2265	ex N5217Y		
☐ CX-BRM	Beech A80 Queen Air	LD-200	ex N326JB	Excalibur Queenaire conv	stored MVD
☐ CX-MAS	Embraer EMB.110P1 Bandeirante	110393	ex N91DA		
☐ CX-MAX	Cessna 208A Caravan I	20800042	ex ZP-TYT		
☐ LV-LHO	Beech 65-B90 King Air	LJ-428	ex N74GR		

AIR CLASS — *Acla (QD/QCL)* — *Montevideo-Carrasco (MVD)*

☐ CX-CAF	British Aerospace Jetstream 41	41101	ex N333UE	
☐ CX-CLA	Swearingen SA.227AC Metro III	AC-736	ex N339LC	Op for DHL
☐ CX-CLS	Swearingen SA.227AC Metro III	AC-755B	ex N27465	
☐ CX-CSS	Swearingen SA.227AC Metro III	AC-642	ex N821BC	
☐ CX-LAS	Swearingen SA.227AC Metro III	AC-482	ex N784C	

PLUNA LINEAS AÉREAS URUGUAYAS — *Pluna (PU/PUA)* — *Montevideo-Carrasco (MVD)*

☐ CX-BON	Boeing 737-2A3	22737/830	ex PH-TSI	Gen Jose Artigas	stored MVD
☐ CX-BOO	Boeing 737-2A3	22738/834	ex PH-TSA	Brig Gen Juan A Lavalleja	stored MVD

☐ CX-BOP	Boeing 737-2A3	22739/844	ex PH-TSB	Gen Fructuoso Rivera	stored MVD
☐ CX-PUF	Boeing 737-230	22135/781	ex LV-BBM		
☐ CX-CRA	Canadair CL-600-2D24 (CRJ-900)	15165	ex C-FTMF		Blue c/s
☐ CX-CRB	Canadair CL-600-2D24 (CRJ-900)	15169	ex C-		Turquoise c/s
☐ CX-CRC	Canadair CL-600-2D24 (CRJ-900)	15175	ex C-		Red c/s
☐ CX-CRD	Canadair CL-600-2D24 (CRJ-900)	15180	ex C-		Purple c/s
☐ CX-CRE	Canadair CL-600-2D24 (CRJ-900)	15185	ex C-		Red c/s
☐ CX-CRF	Canadair CL-600-2D24 (CRJ-900)	15204	ex C-		Blue c/s

C2- NAURU (Republic of Nauru)

OUR AIRLINE — Air Nauru (ON/RON) — Brisbane, QLD (BNE)

☐ VH-INU	Boeing 737-3Y0	23684/1353	ex N323AW	Lsd fr Govt of Nauru

C3- ANDORRA (Principality of Andorra)

HELIAND — La Massana Heliport

☐ F-GYDJ	Aérospatiale AS350B3 Ecureuil	3719	ex N5219F	Lsd to/op by SHP

HELITRANS — Grau Roig Heliport

Leases Aérospatiale Ecureuil helicopters from Heliswiss Iberica when required

C5- GAMBIA (Republic of The Gambia)

MAHFOOZ AVIATION — Mahfooz (M2/MZS) — Banjul/Jeddah (BJL/JED)

☐ C5-SBM	Boeing 727-256	21609/1369	ex N903RF	all-white

SLOK AIR INTERNATIONAL — Slok Gambia (S0/OKS) — Banjul (BJL)

☐ C5-EUN	Boeing 737-201 (Nordam 3)	22798/924	ex 5N-EUN	Ibrahim Babangida	
☐ C5-IFY	Boeing 737-201 (Nordam 3)	22797/916	ex 5N-IFY	Olusegun Obasanjo	
☐ C5-NYA	Boeing 737-201 (Nordam 3)	22799/932	ex 5N-NYA	John Kuffour	stored PGF
☐ C5-OBJ	Boeing 737-201 (Nordam 3)	22795/912	ex N253AU	Atiku Abubakar	
☐ C5-OUK	Boeing 737-201 (Nordam 3)	22796/914	ex N254AU	Yahya Jammeh	
☐ C5-ZNA	Boeing 737-201 (Nordam 3)	22806/938	ex 5N-ZNA	Ahmadu Bello	

C6- BAHAMAS (Commonwealth of the Bahamas)

ABACO AIR — Marsh Harbour (MHH)

☐ C6-BAA	Britten-Norman BN-2A-21 Islander	214	ex N214TL
☐ C6-BFQ	Britten-Norman BN-2A-8 Islander	347	ex N69HA
☐ C6-BFR	Aero Commander 500	825	ex N840VK
☐ C6-BFS	Aero Commander 500	685	ex N6285B
☐ C6-BHH	Britten-Norman BN-2B-26 Islander	2021	ex N599MS
☐ C6-BHY	Aero Commander 500	834	ex N521SQ

BAHAMASAIR — Bahamas (UP/BHS) — Nassau (NAS)

☐ C6-BFG	de Havilland DHC-8-311A	288	ex C-GESR
☐ C6-BFH	de Havilland DHC-8-311A	291	ex C-GFOD
☐ C6-BFI	de Havilland DHC-8-311A	295	ex C-GFHZ
☐ C6-BFJ	de Havilland DHC-8Q-311	323	ex N583DS
☐ C6-BFN	de Havilland DHC-8-301	159	ex N801XV
☐ C6-BFO	de Havilland DHC-8-301	164	ex N802XV
☐ C6-BFP	de Havilland DHC-8Q-311	309	ex N994DC
☐ C6-BFM	Boeing 737-2K5 (Nordam 3)	22596/763	ex N231TA
☐ C6-BFW	Boeing 737-2K5 (Nordam 3)	22601/833	ex N233TA
☐ C6-BGK	Boeing 737-275	22086/667	ex C-GLPW
☐ C6-BGL	Boeing 737-275 (AvAero 3)	22087/673	ex C-GMPW

CAT ISLAND AIR — Nassau (NAS)

☐ C6-CAA	SAAB SF.340A	340A-122	ex N379KB	
☐ C6-CAH	Embraer EMB.110P1 Bandeirante	110249	ex C6-BHA	stored NAS
☐ C6-CAP	Embraer EMB.110P1 Bandeirante	110304	ex J8-VAZ	
☐ C6-CAT	Piper PA-23-250 Aztec E	27-7554083	ex N54779	

CHEROKEE AIR				Marsh Harbour (MHH)
☐ C6-BGS	Piper PA-23-250 Aztec F	27-7854067	ex N17MR	
☐ C6-NGS	Cessna 208B Caravan I	208B0994	ex N1239Z	
☐ C6-SBH	Cessna 208B Caravan I	208B0822	ex N822SA	

FLAMINGO AIR				Nassau (NAS)
☐ C6-BGI	Piper PA-23-250 Aztec E	27-7405469	ex N4443W	
☐ C6-BGZ	Piper PA-23-250 Aztec D	27-4246	ex C-FINU	

ISLAND WINGS				Stella Maris (SML)
☐ C6-FLY	Piper PA-23-250 Aztec E	27-4622	ex N140FR	
☐ C6-FOX	Piper PA-23-250 Aztec D	27-4535	ex N139BP	

LEAIR CHARTER SERVICES				Nassau (NAS)
☐ C6-BGJ	Cessna 402C II	402C0106	ex VQ-THC	
☐ C6-CAB	Embraer EMB.110P1 Bandeirante	110198	ex G-ONEW	Dam 25/02/2008
☐ C6-LEE	Piper PA-23-250 Aztec F	27-7654049	ex N62568	
☐ C6-PDX	Embraer EMB.110P1 Bandeirante	110288	ex OO-SKU	stored NAS

MAJOR'S AIR SERVICES				Freeport (FPO)
☐ C6-RRM	Beech C99	U-231	ex N141RM	

PINEAPPLE AIR		Pineapple (PNP)		Nassau (NAS)
☐ N60MJ	Beech 1900D	UE-60	ex N85445	
☐ N157PA	Beech 1900C	UB-56	ex N505RH	
☐ N381CR	Beech 1900C	UB-69	ex N331CR	
☐ C6-HAN	Beech C99	U-165	ex N42517	

REGIONAL AIIR				Nassau (NAS)
☐ C6-RAL	Cessna 208B Caravan I	208B0841	ex N1295G	
☐ C6-RAS	Cessna 208B Caravan I	208B0693	ex N90HE	

SALAMIS AVIATION				Nassau (NAS)
☐ N75X	Swearingen SA.227TT Merlin IIIC	TT-421	ex N90BJ	
☐ N81WS	Swearingen SA.227TT Merlin IIIC	TT-480	ex N500DB	

SEAIR AIRWAYS		Seair (DYL)		Nassau (NAS)
☐ C6-BGT	Piper PA-23-250 Aztec E	27-7305051	ex N89BB	
☐ C6-BUS	Britten-Norman BN-2A-26 Islander	2040	ex N23US	

SKY BAHAMAS		Sky Bahamas (SBM)		Nassau (NAS)
☐ C6-SBB	SAAB SF.340A	340A-149	ex N779SB	
☐ C6-SBC	SAAB SF.340A	340A-023	ex N778SB	
☐ C6-SBD	SAAB SF.340A	340A-021	ex N776SB	
☐ C6-	SAAB SF.340A	340A-099	ex N99VC	

SOUTHERN AIR CHARTER		Southern (PL/SOA)		Nassau (NAS)
☐ C6-BGY	Piper PA-23-250 Aztec E	27-7554044	ex N166PG	
☐ N70JL	Beech 100 King Air	B-87	ex N125DB	
☐ N376SA	Beech 1900C	UB-72	ex N504RH	
☐ N378SA	Beech 1900C	UB-31	ex N196GA	

STELLA MARIS AVIATION				Stella Maris (SML)
☐ C6-	Aero Commander 500B	500B-1520-184	ex N175AC	
☐ C6-	Piper PA-31-350 Chieftain	31-7952234	ex N750SC	

VISION AIR				Freeport (FPO)
☐ N888MX	Beech 1900C	UB-39	ex N502CG	

WESTERN AIR		(WST)		Freeport (FPO)
☐ C6-FPO	Swearingen SA.227AC Metro III	AC-652	ex N26877	
☐ C6-JER	Swearingen SA.227AC Metro III	AC-588	ex N892MA	
☐ C6-KER	Swearingen SA.227AC Metro III	AC-595	ex N385PH	
☐ C6-REX	Swearingen SA.227AC Metro III	AC-649	ex N26861	stored REX
☐ C6-SAD	Swearingen SA.227AC Metro III	AC-746B	ex N46NE	
☐ C6-SAR	Swearingen SA.227AC Metro III	AC-598	ex N3116Z	

☐ C6-HBW	SAAB SF.340A	340A-067	ex N712MG	
☐ C6-JAY	SAAB SF.340A	340A-120	ex N418MW	
☐ C6-RMW	SAAB SF.340A	340A-121	ex N121CQ	
☐ C6-VIP	SAAB SF.340A	340A-098	ex N98XJ	
☐ C6-WAL	Piper PA-31-350 Navajo Chieftain	31-7652129	ex N70FS	
☐ N900MX	Beech 1900C	UB-55	ex N155GA	

C9- MOZAMBIQUE (Republic of Mozambique)

LAM - LINHAS AEREAS DE MOCAMBIQUE — Mozambique (TM/LAM) — Maputo (MPM)

☐ C9-AUL	de Havilland DHC-8-402Q	4019	ex LN-RDC	
☐ C9-AUM	de Havilland DHC-8-402Q	4020	ex LN-RDE	
☐ C9-BAJ	Boeing 737-205	23464/1223	ex N464BA	Pemba
☐ C9-BAK	Boeing 737-2K9	23404/1176	ex N222TM	Bazaruto
☐ C9-BAO	Boeing 737-205 (Nordam 3)	23467/1245	ex XA-ABC	
☐ C9-EMA	Embraer 190-100	19000301	ex PT-TZP	Cobue
☐ C9-EMB	Embraer 190-100	19000309	ex PT-TZX	Chiloane

MOCAMBIQUE EXPRESSO — Mozambique Express (MXE) — Maputo / Beira (MPM/BEW)

☐ C9-ASV	Beech 200C Super King Air	BL-21	ex N3831T	
☐ C9-AUK	British Aerospace Jetstream 41	41044	ex ZS-NUO	
☐ ZS-AAB	Embraer EMB.120RT Brasilia	120228	ex N248CA	

STA - SOCIEDADE DE TRANSPORTS AÉREOS — Maputo (MPM)

Operates services with Islanders leased from sister company TTA and other aircraft as required

TRANSAIRWAYS — (TWM) — Maputo/Beira (MPM/BEW)

☐ 3D-BCI	Embraer EMB.120ER Brasilia	120139	ex N283UE	
☐ 3D-BEE	Beech 1900C-1	UC-148	ex N148YV	
☐ 3D-NVA	LET L-410UVP-E3	882035	ex 3D-ZZM	
☐ 3D-NVC	LET L-410UVP	831033	ex 5Y-BLC	Sluffy

TTA – SOCIEDADE DE TRANSPORTE E TRABALHO AEREO — Kanimanbo (TTA) — Maputo (MPM)

☐ C9-AMH	Piper PA-32-300 Cherokee Six C	32-40682	ex ZS-IGO	stored MPM
☐ C9-AOV	Britten-Norman BN-2A-3 Islander	624	ex G-AYJF	
☐ C9-APD	Britten-Norman BN-2A-9 Islander	683	ex G-AZXO	

D- GERMANY (Federal Republic of Germany)

ADVANCED AVIATION — Bad Saulgau / Bangui (-/BGF)

☐ D-CAAL	Dornier 228-202K	8152	ex CS-TGH	
☐ D-FINA	Cessna 208B Caravan I	208B0475	ex N1202D	
☐ D-FISH	Cessna 208 Caravan I	20800363	ex N41145	
☐ D-FLIP	Cessna 208B Caravan I	208B0331	ex N3331	
☐ D-IAAX	Dornier 228-202K	8159	ex CS-TGF	
☐ D-ISIS	Dornier 228-200	8007	ex RP-C2817	
☐ D4-CBK	Dornier 228-212	8222	ex 7Q-YKS	Op for Guardia Costiera
☐ SE-LDK	Short SC.7 Skyvan 3A	SH1870	ex SX-BBO	

AEROLINE — Sylt-Air (7E/AWU) — Westerland (GWT)

☐ D-GFPG	Partenavia P.68B	170		
☐ D-IOLB	Cessna 404 Titan II	404-0691	ex SE-IVG	

AEROLOGIC — (BOX) — Leipzig-Halle (LEJ)

☐ D-AALA	Boeing 777-FZN	36001/780		
☐ D-AALB	Boeing 777-FZN	36002/799	ex N5017Q	
☐ D-AALC	Boeing 777-FZN	36003/836		
☐ D-AALD	Boeing 777-FZN	36004/838		
☐ D-AALE	Boeing 777-FZN	36198		on order
☐ D-AALF	Boeing 777-FZN	36201		on order
☐ D-AALG	Boeing 777-FZN	36199		on order

AIR CARGO GERMANY — (6U/ACX)

☐ D-ACGA	Boeing 747-409(BDSF)	24311/869	ex N481AT	
☐ D-ACGB	Boeing 747-409(BDSF)	24312/954	ex N482AT	

AIR HAMBURG — Uetersen (QSM)

☐ D-IAEB	Britten-Norman BN-2A-6 Islander	218	ex OH-BNB	

AIR SERVICE BERLIN				Berlin-Schonefeld (SXF)
☐ D-CXXX	Douglas DC-3	16124/32872	ex G-AMPZ	Jack Bennett

AIR SERVICE WILDGRUBER				Friedrichshafen-Loewental (FDH)
☐ D-IEXE	Beech 99	U-46	ex LN-SAX	Op for Skydive Portugal

AIRBERLIN		AirBerlin (AB/BER)		Berlin-Tegel (TXL)
☐ D-ABGA	Airbus A319-132	2383	ex N807BR	
☐ D-ABGB	Airbus A319-132	2467	ex N814BR	
☐ D-ABGC	Airbus A319-132	2468	ex N815BR	
☐ D-ABGG	Airbus A319-112	3202	ex D-AVWJ	
☐ D-ABGH	Airbus A319-112	3245	ex D-AVWE	
☐ D-ABGI	Airbus A319-112	3346	ex D-AVYU	
☐ D-ABGJ	Airbus A319-112	3415	ex D-AVYI	
☐ D-ABGK	Airbus A319-112	3447	ex D-AVYS	
☐ D-ABGL	Airbus A319-112	3586	ex D-AVYF	
☐ D-ABGN	Airbus A319-112	3661	ex D-AVYU	
☐ D-ABGO	Airbus A319-112	3689	ex D-AVWF	
☐ D-ABGP	Airbus A319-112	3728	ex D-AVWF	
☐ D-ABGQ	Airbus A319-112	3700	ex D-AVWM	
☐ D-ABGR	Airbus A319-112	3704	ex D-AVWJ	
☐ D-ABGS	Airbus A319-112	3865	ex D-AVWD	
☐ D-ABDA	Airbus A320-214	2539	ex F-WWIR	
☐ D-ABDB	Airbus A320-214	2619	ex F-WWDK	
☐ D-ABDC	Airbus A320-214	2654	ex F-WWIN	
☐ D-ABDD	Airbus A320-214	2685	ex F-WWIB	
☐ D-ABDE	Airbus A320-214	2696	ex F-WWDI	
☐ D-ABDF	Airbus A320-214	2820	ex F-WWDA	
☐ D-ABDG	Airbus A320-214	2835	ex F-WWIB	
☐ D-ABDP	Airbus A320-214	3093	ex F-WWIT	
☐ D-ABDQ	Airbus A320-214	3121	ex F-WWBD	
☐ D-ABDR	Airbus A320-214	3242	ex F-WWBP	
☐ D-ABDS	Airbus A320-214	3289	ex F-WWDS	
☐ D-ABDT	Airbus A320-214	3422	ex F-WWIQ	
☐ D-ABDU	Airbus A320-214	3516	ex D-AVVC	
☐ D-ABDW	Airbus A320-214	3945	ex F-WWDX	
☐ D-ABDX	Airbus A320-214	3995	ex F-WWDG	
☐ D-ABDY	Airbus A320-214	4013	ex F-WWIG	
☐ D-ABFA	Airbus A320-214	4101	ex D-AVVK	
☐ D-ABFB	Airbus A320-214	4128	ex F-WWIQ	
☐ D-ABFC	Airbus A320-214	4161	ex D-AVVP	
☐ D-ABFD	Airbus A320-214	4187	ex D-AVVY	on order
☐ D-	Airbus A320-214		ex	on order
☐ D-	Airbus A320-214		ex	on order
☐ D-	Airbus A320-214		ex	on order
☐ D-	Airbus A320-214		ex	on order
☐ D-ALTB	Airbus A320-214	1385	ex F-WWIT	
☐ D-ALTC	Airbus A320-214	1441	ex F-WWBQ	
☐ D-ALTD	Airbus A320-214	1493	ex F-WWDY	
☐ D-ALTE	Airbus A320-214	1504	ex OE-LTU	
☐ D-ALTF	Airbus A320-214	1553	ex OE-LTV	
☐ D-ALTH	Airbus A320-214	1797	ex F-WWDV	
☐ D-ALTJ	Airbus A320-214	1838	ex F-WWBM	
☐ D-ALTK	Airbus A320-214	1931	ex F-WWIH	
☐ D-ALTL	Airbus A320-214	2009	ex F-WWBO	
☐ D-ABCA	Airbus A321-211	3708	ex D-AVZO	
☐ D-ABCB	Airbus A321-211	3749	ex D-AVZC	
☐ D-ABCF	Airbus A321-211	1966	ex N221LF	
☐ D-ABCG	Airbus A321-211	1988	ex N341LF	
☐ D-ALSA	Airbus A321-211	1629	ex D-AVZC	
☐ D-ALSB	Airbus A321-211	1994	ex D-AVZR	
☐ D-ALSC	Airbus A321-211	2005	ex D-AVXI	
☐ D-ALSD	Airbus A321-211	1607	ex I-PEKN	
☐ D-AERK	Airbus A330-322	120	ex F-WWKN	
☐ D-AERQ	Airbus A330-322	127	ex F-WWKO	
☐ D-AERS	Airbus A330-322	171	ex C-FRAV	
☐ D-ALPA	Airbus A330-223	403	ex F-WWKO	
☐ D-ALPB	Airbus A330-223	432	ex F-WWYG	
☐ D-ALPC	Airbus A330-223	444	ex F-WWKD	
☐ D-ALPD	Airbus A330-223	454	ex F-WWKG	
☐ D-ALPE	Airbus A330-223	469	ex F-WWKO	
☐ D-ALPF	Airbus A330-223	476	ex F-WWKT	
☐ D-ALPG	Airbus A330-223	493	ex F-WWKI	
☐ D-ALPH	Airbus A330-223	739	ex F-WWYD	
☐ D-ALPI	Airbus A330-223	828	ex F-WWKI	
☐ D-ALPJ	Airbus A330-223	911	ex F-WWYA	

☐ D-ADIH	Boeing 737-3Y0	23921/1513	ex N921NB	
☐ D-ADII	Boeing 737-329	23775/1412	ex N775AA	
☐ D-AGEB	Boeing 737-322	24320/1670	ex N352UA	Spirit of Hinrich Bischoff

☐ D-ABAA	Boeing 737-76Q	30271/740	ex N271CH	
☐ D-ABAB	Boeing 737-76Q	30277/947	ex N277CH	
☐ D-ABAF	Boeing 737-86J/W	30878/844	ex N1787B	
☐ D-ABAG	Boeing 737-86J/W	30879/871	ex N1786B	
☐ D-ABAP	Boeing 737-86J/W	28070/106		
☐ D-ABAQ	Boeing 737-86J/W	28071/133		
☐ D-ABAR	Boeing 737-86J/W	28072/147	ex N1786B	
☐ D-ABAS	Boeing 737-86J/W	28073/200	ex N1795B	
☐ D-ABAT	Boeing 737-86J/W	29120/202	ex N1786B	
☐ D-ABAU	Boeing 737-86J/W	29121/239	ex N1786B	
☐ D-ABAV	Boeing 737-86J/W	30498/450	ex N1787B	
☐ D-ABBA	Boeing 737-86J/W	30570/879	ex N1786B	
☐ D-ABBB	Boeing 737-86J/W	32624/961	ex N1798B	
☐ D-ABBC	Boeing 737-86J/W	32625/995	ex N1786B	
☐ D-ABBD	Boeing 737-86J/W	30880/1043		
☐ D-ABBE	Boeing 737-86J/W	30881/1067		
☐ D-ABBF	Boeing 737-86J/W	32917/1210		
☐ D-ABBG	Boeing 737-86J/W	32918/1255		
☐ D-ABBH	Boeing 737-86J/W	32919/1279		
☐ D-ABBI	Boeing 737-86J/W	32920/1293		
☐ D-ABBJ	Boeing 737-86Q/W	30286/1280	ex N1787B	
☐ D-ABBK	Boeing 737-8BK/W	33013/1317		
☐ D-ABBL	Boeing 737-85F	28821/151	ex F-GRNC	
☐ D-ABBM	Boeing 737-85F	28823/174	ex F-GRNA	
☐ D-ABBP	Boeing 737-86J/W	29641/1654		
☐ D-ABBQ	Boeing 737-86N/W	28608/410	ex EC-HHG	
☐ D-ABBR	Boeing 737-85F	28825/188	ex SE-DVU	
☐ D-ABBS	Boeing 737-76N/W	28654/986	ex N743AL	
☐ D-ABBT	Boeing 737-76N/W	32582/1013	ex N744AL	
☐ D-ABBU	Boeing 737-8Q8	30627/752	ex P4-BAS	
☐ D-ABBV	Boeing 737-7Q8	30629/1011	ex P4-CAS	
☐ D-ABBW	Boeing 737-7Q8	30642/1097	ex P4-DAS	
☐ D-ABBX	Boeing 737-808	34969/2293		
☐ D-ABBY	Boeing 737-808	34970/2379	ex N1787B	
☐ D-ABBZ	Boeing 737-85F	30478/997	ex TC-SKC	
☐ D-ABKA	Boeing 737-82R	29329/224	ex TC-APG	
☐ D-ABKD	Boeing 737-86J/W		37742/2796	
☐ D-ABKE	Boeing 737-86J/W	37743/2834	ex N1787B	
☐ D-ABKF	Boeing 737-86J/W	37745/3044	ex N1787B	
☐ D-ABKG	Boeing 737-86J/W	37746/3109	ex N1786B	
☐ D-ABKH	Boeing 737-86J/W	37747/3120	ex N1786B	
☐ D-ABKI	Boeing 737-86J/W	37748/3157		
☐ D-ABKJ	Boeing 737-86J/W	37749		on order
☐ D-	Boeing 737-86J/W			on order
☐ D-	Boeing 737-86J/W			on order
☐ D-	Boeing 737-86J/W			on order
☐ D-	Boeing 737-86J/W			on order
☐ D-	Boeing 737-86J/W			on order
☐ D-	Boeing 737-86J/W			on order
☐ D-	Boeing 737-86J/W			on order
☐ D-ABLA	Boeing 737-76J/W	36114/2421	ex N1786B	
☐ D-ABLB	Boeing 737-76J/W	36115/2692		
☐ D-ABLC	Boeing 737-76J/W	36116/2730		
☐ D-ABLD	Boeing 737-76J/W	36117/2776	ex N1787B	
☐ D-	Boeing 737-76J/W			on order
☐ D-	Boeing 737-76J/W			on order
☐ D-	Boeing 737-76J/W			on order
☐ D-	Boeing 737-76J/W			on order
☐ D-	Boeing 737-76J/W			on order
☐ D-	Boeing 737-76J/W			on order
☐ D-	Boeing 737-76J/W			on order

☐ D-AGEC	Boeing 737-76J/W	36118/2832	ex D-ABLE	Lsd to GMI
☐ D-AGEL	Boeing 737-75B	28110/5	ex N1791B	Lsd to GMI
☐ D-AGEN	Boeing 737-75B	28100/16	ex N1789B	Lsd to GMI
☐ D-AGEP	Boeing 737-75B	28102/18	ex N5573B	Lsd to GMI
☐ D-AGER	Boeing 737-75B	28107/27	ex N1002R	Lsd to GMI
☐ D-AGES	Boeing 737-75B	28108/28		Lsd to GMI
☐ D-AGEU	Boeing 737-75B	28104/39		Lsd to GMI

☐ D-ABQA	de Havilland DHC-8-402Q	4223	ex C-FTID
☐ D-ABQB	de Havilland DHC-8-402Q	4226	ex C-FTUM
☐ D-ABQC	de Havilland DHC-8-402Q	4231	ex C-FUCI
☐ D-ABQD	de Havilland DHC-8-402Q	4234	ex C-FUCS
☐ D-ABQE	de Havilland DHC-8-402Q	4239	ex C-FURQ
☐ D-ABQF	de Havilland DHC-8-402Q	4245	ex C-FVGV
☐ D-ABQG	de Havilland DHC-8-402Q	4250	ex C-FVUN
☐ D-ABQH	de Havilland DHC-8-402Q	4256	ex C-FWGO

☐ D-ABQI	de Havilland DHC-8-402Q	4264	ex C-FXIW
☐ D-ABQJ	de Havilland DHC-8-402Q	4274	ex C-FYGN

ARCUS AIR — ***Arcus Air (ZE/AZE)*** — ***Mannheim (MHG)***

☐ D-CAAM	Dornier 228-212	8205	ex D-CBDH
☐ D-CAAR	Dornier 228-212	8211	ex 57+02
☐ D-CAAZ	Dornier 228-212	8212	ex 57+03
☐ D-CUTT	Dornier 228-212	8200	ex D-CBDC

AUGSBURG AIRWAYS — ***Augsburg Air (IQ/AUB)*** — ***Munich (MUC)***

☐ D-BEBA	de Havilland DHC-8Q-314	543	ex C-GFVI	stored MUC
☐ D-BLEJ	de Havilland DHC-8Q-314	521	ex C-FDHU	stored MUC
☐ D-ADHA	de Havilland DHC-8-402Q	4028	ex C-GFBW	
☐ D-ADHB	de Havilland DHC-8-402Q	4029	ex C-GFCA	
☐ D-ADHC	de Havilland DHC-8-402Q	4045	ex C-GDIW	
☐ D-ADHD	de Havilland DHC-8-402Q	4056	ex C-GFYI	
☐ D-ADHE	de Havilland DHC-8-402Q	4066	ex C-GEOA	
☐ D-ADHP	de Havilland DHC-8-402Q	4003	ex C-FHUP	
☐ D-ADHQ	de Havilland DHC-8-402Q	4016	ex C-FSPV	
☐ D-ADHR	de Havilland DHC-8-402Q	4041	ex C-FRGT	
☐ D-ADHS	de Havilland DHC-8-402Q	4044	ex C-FRBO	
☐ D-ADHT	de Havilland DHC-8-402Q	4281	ex C-FYMQ	

AVANTI AIR — ***Euroexpress (EEX)*** — ***Frankfurt (FRA)***

☐ D-ANFC	ATR 72-202	237	ex F-WWEG
☐ D-BCRN	ATR 42-300	329	ex G-WLSH
☐ D-BCRO	ATR 42-300 (QC)	122	ex F-WWES
☐ D-BCRP	ATR 42-300 (QC)	158	ex F-WWEE

BINAIR — ***Binair (BID)*** — ***Munich (MUC)***

☐ D-CBIN	Swearingen SA.226AT Expediter IV	AT-440B	ex I-FSAD
☐ D-CCCC	Swearingen SA.227AT Merlin IVC	AT-511	ex N600N
☐ D-CKPP	Swearingen SA.227DC Metro 23	DC-805B	ex N715MQ
☐ D-CPSW	Swearingen SA.227AC Metro III	AC-757B	ex F-GJPN
☐ D-IBIN	Swearingen SA.226TC Metro II	TC-252	ex PH-RAZ
☐ D-ICRK	Swearingen SA.226TC Metro II	TC-333	ex 4X-CSD

BLUE WINGS — ***Blue Wings (QW/BWG)*** — ***Düsseldorf (DUS)***

Ceased operations 13/Jan/2010

BREMENFLY — ***Bremen (BRE)***

☐ D-ABRE	Boeing 737-46J	27826/2694	ex EI-DXO	stored CGN

BUSINESSWINGS — ***Kassel-Calden (KSF)***

☐ D-CUKT	Dornier 228-212	8192	ex LN-BER
☐ D-FALK	Cessna 208 Caravan I	20800023	ex N9354F
☐ D-FAST	Cessna 208 Caravan I	20800207	ex N208MC
☐ D-IROL	Dornier 228-100	7003	ex SE-KHL
☐ D-IVER	de Havilland DHC-6 Twin Otter 300	411	ex SE-IYP

CIRRUS AIRLINES — ***Cirrus (C9/RUS)*** — ***Saarbrücken-Ensheim (SCN)***

☐ D-BGAE	Dornier 328-300 (328JET)	3146	ex D-BDXC	
☐ D-BGAL	Dornier 328-300 (328JET)	3131	ex D-BDXN	
☐ D-BGAQ	Dornier 328-300 (328JET)	3130	ex D-BDXL	
☐ D-BGAS	Dornier 328-300 (328JET)	3139	ex D-BDXZ	
☐ D-CCIR	Dornier 328-130	3100	ex D-CDXA	
☐ D-CIRA	Dornier 328-120	3077	ex HB-AEJ	
☐ D-CIRB	Dornier 328-110	3017	ex HB-AEF	
☐ D-CIRC	Dornier 328-100	3041	ex HB-AEI	
☐ D-CIRD	Dornier 328-110	3011	ex HB-AEG	
☐ D-CIRE	Dornier 328-110	3058	ex N440JS	
☐ D-CIRG	Dornier 328-110	3040	ex N340LS	on order
☐ D-CIRI	Dornier 328-110	3005	ex TF-CSC	
☐ D-CIRJ	Dornier 328-110	3035	ex N335LS	on order
☐ D-CIRK	Dornier 328-110	3050	ex N350AD	
☐ D-CIRL	Dornier 328-110	3075	ex N461PS	
☐ D-CIRM	Dornier 328-110	3068	ex N458PS	on order
☐ D-CIRO	Dornier 328-110	3025	ex N328LS	on order
☐ D-CIRP	Dornier 328-110	3006	ex TF-CSD	
☐ D-CIRT	Dornier 328-110	3093	ex TF-CSB	
☐ D-CIRU	Dornier 328-110	3033	ex N424JS	on order
☐ D-CIRV	Dornier 328-110	3037	ex N425JS	on order
☐ D-CIRW	Dornier 328-110	3044	ex N430JS	on order

☐ D-COSA	Dornier 328-110	3085	ex D-CDXR		
☐ D-CPRP	Dornier 328-110	3066	ex D-CDXL	Maximillian	
☐ D-CPRW	Dornier 328-110	3097	ex D-CDXY		
☐ D-CTOB	Dornier 328-110	3107	ex OE-LKH		Damaged 19/3/2008
☐ D-ALIA	Embraer 170-100LR (170LR)	17000006	ex PT-SVD		
☐ D-ALIE	Embraer 170-100LR (170LR)	17000059	ex PT-SVI		

CONDOR — *Condor (DE/CFG)* — *Frankfurt (FRA)*

☐ D-ABOA	Boeing 757-330	29016/804	ex N757X	
☐ D-ABOB	Boeing 757-330	29017/810	ex N6067B	
☐ D-ABOC	Boeing 757-330	29015/818	ex N6069B	
☐ D-ABOE	Boeing 757-330/W	29012/839	ex N1012N	
☐ D-ABOF	Boeing 757-330	29013/846		
☐ D-ABOG	Boeing 757-330	29014/849		
☐ D-ABOH	Boeing 757-330/W	30030/855	ex N1787B	
☐ D-ABOI	Boeing 757-330	29018/909	ex N1002R	
☐ D-ABOJ	Boeing 757-330	29019/915		op for Apple Vacs
☐ D-ABOK	Boeing 757-330	29020/918	ex N1795B	
☐ D-ABOL	Boeing 757-330	29021/923		op for Apple Vacs
☐ D-ABOM	Boeing 757-330	29022/926		
☐ D-ABON	Boeing 757-330	29023/929	ex N1003M	
☐				
☐ D-ABUA	Boeing 767-330ER/W	26991/455		
☐ D-ABUB	Boeing 767-330ER/W	26987/466		
☐ D-ABUC	Boeing 767-330ER/W	26992/470		
☐ D-ABUD	Boeing 767-330ER/W	26983/471		
☐ D-ABUE	Boeing 767-330ER/W	26984/518	ex N1788B	
☐ D-ABUF	Boeing 767-330ER	26985/537		
☐ D-ABUH	Boeing 767-330ER	26986/553	ex N6046P	
☐ D-ABUI	Boeing 767-330ER	26988/562		
☐ D-ABUZ	Boeing 767-330ER/W	25209/382	ex (N634TW)	

CONDOR BERLIN — *Condor Berlin (CIB)* — *Berlin-Schönefeld (SXF)*

☐ D-AICA	Airbus A320-212	0774	ex F-WWDN
☐ D-AICC	Airbus A320-212	0809	ex F-WWIE
☐ D-AICD	Airbus A320-212	0884	ex F-WWDE
☐ D-AICE	Airbus A320-212	0894	ex F-WWDI
☐ D-AICF	Airbus A320-212	0905	ex F-WWDP
☐ D-AICG	Airbus A320-212	0957	ex F-WWBE
☐ D-AICH	Airbus A320-212	0971	ex F-WWBY
☐ D-AICI	Airbus A320-212	1381	ex F-WWIP
☐ D-AICJ	Airbus A320-212	1402	ex F-WWDB
☐ D-AICK	Airbus A320-212	1416	ex F-WWDZ
☐ D-AICL	Airbus A320-212	1437	ex F-WWBG
☐ D-AICN	Airbus A320-214	1968	ex G-TCKE

CONTACT AIR — *Contactair (KIS)* — *Stuttgart (STR)*

☐ D-BMMM	ATR 42-500	546	ex F-WWLE	Lsd fr EWG
☐ D-BPPP	ATR 42-500	581	ex F-WWLE	Lsd fr EWG
☐ D-BQQQ	ATR 42-500	584	ex F-WWEP	Lsd fr EWG
☐ D-BSSS	ATR 42-500	602	ex F-WWLA	Lsd fr EWG
☐ D-BTTT	ATR 42-500	603	ex F-WWLD	Lsd fr EWG
☐ D-AFKA	Fokker F.28-0100 (Fokker 100)	11517	ex B-12293	
☐ D-AFKB	Fokker F.28-0100 (Fokker 100)	11527	ex PH-MJL	
☐ D-AFKC	Fokker F.28-0100 (Fokker 100)	11496	ex PH-MJQ	
☐ D-AFKD	Fokker F.28-0100 (Fokker 100)	11500	ex PH-MJR	
☐ D-AFKE	Fokker F.28-0100 (Fokker 100)	11505	ex PH-MJP	
☐ D-AFKF	Fokker F.28-0100 (Fokker 100)	11470	ex PH-MJK	
☐ D-AGPH	Fokker F.28-0100 (Fokker 100)	11308	ex PH-CXH	
☐ D-AGPK	Fokker F.28-0100 (Fokker 100)	11313	ex PH-CXK	Lsd to SWR

EUROWINGS — *Eurowings (EW/EWG)* — *Dortmund/Nuremberg (DTM/NUE)*

☐ D-BLLL	ATR 42-500	549	ex F-WWLB	Lsd to CIM
☐ D-BMMM	ATR 42-500	546	ex F-WWLE	Lsd to KIS
☐ D-BPPP	ATR 42-500	581	ex F-WWLE	Lsd to KIS
☐ D-BQQQ	ATR 42-500	584	ex F-WWEP	Lsd to KIS
☐ D-BSSS	ATR 42-500	602	ex F-WWLA	Lsd to KIS
☐ D-BTTT	ATR 42-500	603	ex F-WWLD	Lsd to KIS
☐ D-ACFA	British Aerospace 146 Srs.200	E2200	ex G-BTVT	
☐ D-AEWF	British Aerospace 146 Srs.200	E2184	ex G-BTKC	
☐ D-AEWL	British Aerospace 146 Srs.300	E3123	ex G-UKHP	
☐ D-AEWQ	British Aerospace 146 Srs.300	E3203	ex G-BTTP	
☐ D-AHOI	British Aerospace 146 Srs.300	E3187	ex G-BSYT	stored EXE
☐ D-AQUA	British Aerospace 146 Srs.300	E3118	ex G-OAJF	

☐ D-ACRA	Canadair CL-600-2B19 (CRJ-200LR)	7567	ex C-FMNX		
☐ D-ACRB	Canadair CL-600-2B19 (CRJ-200LR)	7570	ex C-FMOW		
☐ D-ACRC	Canadair CL-600-2B19 (CRJ-200LR)	7573	ex C-FMNQ		
☐ D-ACRD	Canadair CL-600-2B19 (CRJ-200LR)	7583	ex C-FMNB		
☐ D-ACRE	Canadair CL-600-2B19 (CRJ-200LR)	7607	ex C-FMML		
☐ D-ACRF	Canadair CL-600-2B19 (CRJ-200LR)	7619	ex C-FMLI	Goch	
☐ D-ACRG	Canadair CL-600-2B19 (CRJ-200LR)	7630	ex C-FMOW		
☐ D-ACRH	Canadair CL-600-2B19 (CRJ-200LR)	7738	ex C-FMLF	Herzogenaurach	
☐ D-ACRI	Canadair CL-600-2B19 (CRJ-200ER)	7862	ex C-GZPA		
☐ D-ACRJ	Canadair CL-600-2B19 (CRJ-200LR)	7864	ex C-GZOZ		
☐ D-ACRK	Canadair CL-600-2B19 (CRJ-200LR)	7901	ex C-FVAZ		
☐ D-ACRL	Canadair CL-600-2B19 (CRJ-200LR)	7902	ex C-FMND		
☐ D-ACRM	Canadair CL-600-2B19 (CRJ-200LR)	7478	ex I-ADJA		
☐ D-ACRN	Canadair CL-600-2B19 (CRJ-200LR)	7486	ex I-ADJB		
☐ D-ACRO	Canadair CL-600-2B19 (CRJ-200LR)	7494	ex I-ADJC		
☐ D-ACRP	Canadair CL-600-2B19 (CRJ-200LR)	7625	ex I-ADJD		
☐ D-ACRQ	Canadair CL-600-2B19 (CRJ-200LR)	7629	ex I-ADJE		
☐ D-ACRR	Canadair CL-600-2B19 (CRJ-200LR)	7122	ex D-ACJA		
☐ D-ACSB	Canadair CL-600-2C10 (CRJ-701ER)	10028	ex G-DUOA		Lsd fr Maersk Air
☐ D-ACSC	Canadair CL-600-2C10 (CRJ-701ER)	10039	ex G-DUOC		Lsd fr Maersk Air

EXCELLENT AIR — *Excellent Air (GZA)* — *Münster-Osnabruck*

☐ D-IFUN	Beech 200 Super King Air	BB-575	ex D-ISJP	
☐ D-IICE	Beech 200 Super King Air	BB-269	ex N269D	EMS

FLM AVIATION — *FLM (FKI)* — *Hamburg/ Kiel/ Parchim (HAM/KEL/-)*

☐ D-CNAG	Swearingen SA.227DC Metro 23	DC-893B	ex N3032A	Op for Manx2
☐ D-CSAL	Swearingen SA.227AC Metro III	AC-601	ex I-FSAH	Op for Manx2
☐ D-GBRD	Partenavia P.68B	14	ex OY-DZR	
☐ D-IFFB	Beech 300LW Super King Air	FA-224	ex N56449	
☐ D-IHBL	Swearingen SA.227TT Merlin 300	TT-512A	ex N123GM	

FLUGDIENST FEHLHABER — *Witchcraft (FFG)* — *Cologne (CGN)*

☐ D-ISHY	Reims Cessna F406 Caravan II	F406-0027	ex PH-FWH	Freighter
☐ D-INUS	Reims Cessna F406 Caravan II	F406-0043	ex F-WQUD	Freighter

FRISIA LUFTVERKEHR — *Norden-Norddeich (NOE)*

☐ D-IFKU	Britten-Norman BN-2B-20 Islander	2290	ex G-BVXY	Norderney
☐ D-IFTI	Britten-Norman BN-2B-20 Islander	2299	ex G-BWYY	Norddeich
☐ D-IFUT	Britten-Norman BN-2B-20 Islander	2300	ex G-OBNG	Juist

GERMANIA — *Germania (ST/GMI)* — *Cologne (CGN)*

☐ D-AGEE	Boeing 737-35B	24238/1626	ex UR-GAG	Handel/Bach c/s	Lsd to HLX
☐ D-AGEG	Boeing 737-35B	24237/1624	ex UR-GAF		Lsd to HLX
☐ D-AGEJ	Boeing 737-3L9	24221/1604	ex OO-SEJ	Handel/Bach c/s	Lsd to HLF
☐ D-AGEK	Boeing 737-3M8	25015/1991	ex N799BB	Spirit of Peter Kiessling	
☐ D-AGEC	Boeing 737-76J/W	36118/2832	ex D-ABLE		Lsd fr BER
☐ D-AGEL	Boeing 737-75B	28110/5	ex N1791B		Lsd fr BER
☐ D-AGEN	Boeing 737-75B	28100/16	ex N1789B		Lsd fr BER
☐ D-AGEP	Boeing 737-75B	28102/18	ex N5573B		Lsd fr BER
☐ D-AGEQ	Boeing 737-75B	28103/23	ex N1787B		
☐ D-AGER	Boeing 737-75B	28107/27	ex N1002R		Lsd fr BER
☐ D-AGES	Boeing 737-75B	28108/28			Lsd fr BER
☐ D-AGET	Boeing 737-75B	28109/31			
☐ D-AGEU	Boeing 737-75B	28104/39			Lsd fr BER
☐ D-AGPB	Fokker F.28-0100 (Fokker 100)	11278	ex PH-CXB		stored WOE
☐ D-AGPC	Fokker F.28-0100 (Fokker 100)	11280	ex PH-CXC		stored WOE
☐ D-AGPD	Fokker F.28-0100 (Fokker 100)	11281	ex PH-CXD		stored WOE
☐ D-AGPE	Fokker F.28-0100 (Fokker 100)	11300	ex PH-CXE		stored WOE
☐ D-AGPG	Fokker F.28-0100 (Fokker 100)	11306	ex PH-CXG		stored WOE
☐ D-AGPL	Fokker F.28-0100 (Fokker 100)	11314	ex PH-CXL		stored WOE

GERMANWINGS — *German Wings (4U/GWI)* — *Cologne (CGN)*

☐ D-AGWA	Airbus A319-132	2813	ex D-AVWM
☐ D-AGWB	Airbus A319-132	2833	ex D-AVXI
☐ D-AGWC	Airbus A319-132	2976	ex D-AVYX
☐ D-AGWD	Airbus A319-132	3011	ex D-AVWB
☐ D-AGWE	Airbus A319-132	3128	ex D-AVXB
☐ D-AGWF	Airbus A319-132	3172	ex D-AVXG
☐ D-AGWG	Airbus A319-132	3193	ex D-AVYS
☐ D-AGWH	Airbus A319-132	3352	ex D-AVYX
☐ D-AGWI	Airbus A319-132	3358	ex D-AVYZ
☐ D-AGWJ	Airbus A319-132	3375	ex D-AVWB

☐ D-AGWK	Airbus A319-132	3500	ex D-AVYW	City of Rostock	
☐ D-AGWL	Airbus A319-132	3534	ex D-AVWB		
☐ D-AGWM	Airbus A319-132	3839	ex D-AVYQ		
☐ D-AGWN	Airbus A319-132	3841	ex D-AVYS		
☐ D-AGWO	Airbus A319-132	4166	ex D-AVWH		
☐ D-AGWP	Airbus A319-132		ex D-		on order
☐ D-AGWQ	Airbus A319-132		ex D-		on order
☐ D-AGWR	Airbus A319-132		ex D-		on order
☐ D-AKNK	Airbus A319-112	1077	ex N718UW		
☐ D-AKNL	Airbus A319-112	1084	ex N719US		
☐ D-AKNM	Airbus A319-112	1089	ex N720US	Baden-Wurttemberg colours	
☐ D-AKNN	Airbus A319-112	1136	ex N726US		
☐ D-AKNO	Airbus A319-112	1147	ex N727UW	Berlin Bearbus	
☐ D-AKNP	Airbus A319-112	1155	ex N728UW		
☐ D-AKNQ	Airbus A319-112	1170	ex N729US		
☐ D-AKNR	Airbus A319-112	1209	ex N736US	Spirit of T-Com	
☐ D-AKNS	Airbus A319-112	1277	ex N743UW	Insel Rugen	
☐ D-AKNT	Airbus A319-112	2607	ex D-AVXQ	City of Hamburg	
☐ D-AKNU	Airbus A319-112	2628	ex D-AVWB		
☐ D-AKNV	Airbus A319-112	2632	ex D-AVWE		

HAMBURG INTERNATIONAL — *Hamburg Jet (4R/HHI)* — *Hamburg (HAM)*

☐ D-AHIH	Airbus A319-111	3364	ex D-AVWA
☐ D-AHII	Airbus A319-111	3403	ex D-AVYA
☐ D-AHIJ	Airbus A319-112	3533	ex D-AVYV
☐ D-AHIK	Airbus A319-112	3560	ex D-AVWQ
☐ D-AHIL	Airbus A319-111	3589	ex D-AVYH
☐ D-AHIM	Airbus A319-111	3818	ex D-AVYG
☐ D-AHIN	Airbus A319-112	3853	ex D-AVYX
☐ D-AHIO	Airbus A319-112	3872	ex D-AVWE
☐ D-AHIA	Boeing 737-73S	29082/229	ex D-ASKH
☐ D-AHIC	Boeing 737-7BK	30617/812	ex N1787B

HELOG LUFTTRANSPORT — *Ainring / Salzburg*

☐ D-HAXH	Aérospatiale SA.330J Puma	1410		Op for United Nations
☐ D-HAXI	Aérospatiale SA.330J Puma	1429		Op for United Nations
☐ D-HAXK	Aérospatiale SA.330J Puma	1442		Op for United Nations
☐ D-HAXL	Aérospatiale SA.330J Puma	1454		Op for United Nations
☐ D-HAXR	Aérospatiale SA.330J Puma	1553		Op for United Nations
☐ D-HAXS	Aérospatiale SA.330J Puma	1573		Op for United Nations
☐ D-HAXW	Aérospatiale SA.330J Puma	1594		Op for United Nations
☐ D-HMAX	Kaman K-1200 K-Max	A94-0021	ex OE-XKM	

LGW - LUFTFAHRTGESELLSCHAFT WALTER — *Walter (HE/LGW)* — *Dortmund (DTM)*

☐ D-IKBA	Dornier 228-200	8066	ex D-CBDR
☐ D-ILKA	Dornier 228-100	7005	ex LN-HTB
☐ D-ILWB	Dornier 228-200	8035	ex D-CDIZ
☐ D-ILWD	Dornier 228-200	8069	ex D-CHOF
☐ D-ILWS	Dornier 228-200	8002	ex D-CBDU
☐ D-IMIK	Dornier 228-200	8058	ex D-CMIC

LUFTHANSA — *Lufthansa (LH/DLH)* — *Frankfurt (FRA)*

Member of Star Alliance

☐ D-AIAH	Airbus A300B4-603	380	ex F-WWAA	Lindau/Bodensee	stored DRS
☐ D-AIAK	Airbus A300B4-603	401	ex F-WWAO	Kronberg im Taunus	stored DRS
☐ D-AIAL	Airbus A300B4-603	405	ex F-WWAP	Stade	stored HAM
☐ D-AIAM	Airbus A300B4-603	408	ex F-WWAQ	Rosenheim	stored KBP
☐ D-AIAT	Airbus A300B4-603	618	ex F-WWAM	Bottrop	stored HAM
☐ D-AIAU	Airbus A300B4-603	623	ex F-WWAT	Bocholt	stored DRS
☐ D-AIAX	Airbus A300B4-605R	773	ex F-WWAO	Fürth	
☐ D-AIAZ	Airbus A300B4-605R	701	ex A6-EKM		
☐ D-AIBA	Airbus A319-114	4141	ex D-AVWG		
☐ D-A	Airbus A319-112		ex D-AV		on order
☐ D-A	Airbus A319-112		ex D-AV		on order
☐ D-A	Airbus A319-112		ex D-AV		on order
☐ D-A	Airbus A319-112		ex D-AV		on order
☐ D-AILA	Airbus A319-114	0609	ex D-AVYF	Frankfurt an der Oder	
☐ D-AILB	Airbus A319-114	0610	ex D-AVYG	Lutherstadt Wittenberg	
☐ D-AILC	Airbus A319-114	0616	ex D-AVYI	Rüsselsheim	
☐ D-AILD	Airbus A319-114	0623	ex D-AVYL	Dinkelsbühl	
☐ D-AILE	Airbus A319-114	0627	ex D-AVYO	Kelsterbach	
☐ D-AILF	Airbus A319-114	0636	ex D-AVYS	Trier	
☐ D-AILH	Airbus A319-114	0641	ex D-AVYV	Norderstedt	
☐ D-AILK	Airbus A319-114	0679	ex D-AVYG	Landshut	

☐ D-AILL	Airbus A319-114	0689	ex D-AVYL	Marburg	
☐ D-AILM	Airbus A319-114	0694	ex D-AVYR	Friedrichshafen	
☐ D-AILN	Airbus A319-114	0700	ex D-AVYU	Idar-Oberstein	
☐ D-AILP	Airbus A319-114	0717	ex D-AVYA	Tübingen	
☐ D-AILR	Airbus A319-114	0723	ex D-AVYD	Tegernsee	
☐ D-AILS	Airbus A319-114	0729	ex D-AVYF	Heide	
☐ D-AILT	Airbus A319-114	0738	ex D-AVYN	Straubing	
☐ D-AILU	Airbus A319-114	0744	ex D-AVYI	Verden	
☐ D-AILW	Airbus A319-114	0853	ex D-AVYO	Donaueschingen	
☐ D-AILX	Airbus A319-114	0860	ex D-AVYS	Fellbach	
☐ D-AILY	Airbus A319-114	0875	ex D-AVYC	Schweinfurt	
☐ D-AIPA	Airbus A320-211	0069	ex F-WWII	Buxtehude	
☐ D-AIPB	Airbus A320-211	0070	ex F-WWIJ	Heidelberg	
☐ D-AIPC	Airbus A320-211	0071	ex F-WWIO	Braunschweig	
☐ D-AIPD	Airbus A320-211	0072	ex F-WWIP	Freiburg	
☐ D-AIPE	Airbus A320-211	0078	ex F-WWIU	Kassel	
☐ D-AIPF	Airbus A320-211	0083	ex F-WWDE	Deggendorf	
☐ D-AIPH	Airbus A320-211	0086	ex F-WWDJ	Münster	
☐ D-AIPK	Airbus A320-211	0093	ex F-WWDQ		
☐ D-AIPL	Airbus A320-211	0094	ex 7T-VKO	Ludwigshafen am Rhein	
☐ D-AIPM	Airbus A320-211	0104	ex F-WWIG	Troisdorf	
☐ D-AIPP	Airbus A320-211	0110	ex F-WWID	Starnberg	
☐ D-AIPR	Airbus A320-211	0111	ex F-WWIE	Kaufbeuren	
☐ D-AIPS	Airbus A320-211	0116	ex F-WWIK	Augsburg	
☐ D-AIPT	Airbus A320-211	0117	ex F-WWIL	Cottbus	
☐ D-AIPU	Airbus A320-211	0135	ex F-WWDB		
☐ D-AIPW	Airbus A320-211	0137	ex F-WWDD	Schwerin	
☐ D-AIPX	Airbus A320-211	0147	ex F-WWDN	Mannheim	
☐ D-AIPY	Airbus A320-211	0161	ex F-WWIA	Magdeburg	
☐ D-AIPZ	Airbus A320-211	0162	ex F-WWDS		
☐ D-AIQA	Airbus A320-211	0172	ex F-WWIK		
☐ D-AIQB	Airbus A320-211	0200	ex F-WWDJ	Bielefeld	
☐ D-AIQC	Airbus A320-211	0201	ex F-WWDL	Zwickau	
☐ D-AIQD	Airbus A320-211	0202	ex F-WWDM	Jena	
☐ D-AIQE	Airbus A320-211	0209	ex F-WWDY	Gera	
☐ D-AIQF	Airbus A320-211	0216	ex F-WWDR	Halle a.d.Saale	
☐ D-AIQH	Airbus A320-211	0217	ex F-WWDS	Dessau	
☐ D-AIQK	Airbus A320-211	0218	ex F-WWDX	Rostock	
☐ D-AIQL	Airbus A320-211	0267	ex F-WWDY	Stralsund	
☐ D-AIQM	Airbus A320-211	0268	ex F-WWIB	Nordenham	
☐ D-AIQN	Airbus A320-211	0269	ex F-WWIC	Laupheim	
☐ D-AIQP	Airbus A320-211	0346	ex F-WWDX	Suhl	
☐ D-AIQR	Airbus A320-211	0382	ex F-WWIZ	Lahr/Schwarzwald	
☐ D-AIQS	Airbus A320-211	0401	ex F-WWBD	Eisenach	
☐ D-AIQT	Airbus A320-211	1337	ex F-WWDO	Gotha	
☐ D-AIQU	Airbus A320-211	1365	ex F-WWIG	Backnang	
☐ D-AIQW	Airbus A320-211	1367	ex F-WWIH	Kleve	
☐ D-AIZA	Airbus A320-214	4097	ex D-AVVF		
☐ D-AIZB	Airbus A320-214	4120	ex D-AVVV		
☐ D-AIZC	Airbus A320-214	4153	ex D-AVVL		
☐ D-AIZD	Airbus A320-214	4191	ex D-AVVD		on order
☐ D-AIZE	Airbus A320-214		ex		on order
☐ D-AIZF	Airbus A320-214		ex		on order
☐ D-AIZG	Airbus A320-214		ex		on order
☐ D-AIZH	Airbus A320-214		ex		on order
☐ D-AIZI	Airbus A320-214		ex		on order
☐ D-AIZJ	Airbus A320-214		ex		on order
☐ D-AIZK	Airbus A320-214		ex		on order
☐ D-AIRA	Airbus A321-131	0458	ex F-WWIQ	Finkenwerder	
☐ D-AIRB	Airbus A321-131	0468	ex F-WWIS	Baden-Baden	
☐ D-AIRC	Airbus A321-131	0473	ex D-AVZC	Erlangen	
☐ D-AIRD	Airbus A321-131	0474	ex D-AVZD	Coburg	
☐ D-AIRE	Airbus A321-131	0484	ex D-AVZF	Osnabrück	
☐ D-AIRF	Airbus A321-131	0493	ex D-AVZH	Kempten	
☐ D-AIRH	Airbus A321-131	0412	ex D-AVZA	Garmisch-Partenkirchen	
☐ D-AIRK	Airbus A321-131	0502	ex D-AVZL	Freudenstadt/Schwarzwald	
☐ D-AIRL	Airbus A321-131	0505	ex D-AVZM	Kulmbach	
☐ D-AIRM	Airbus A321-131	0518	ex D-AVZT	Darmstadt	
☐ D-AIRN	Airbus A321-131	0560	ex D-AVZK	Kaiserslautern	
☐ D-AIRO	Airbus A321-131	0563	ex D-AVZN	Konstanz	
☐ D-AIRP	Airbus A321-131	0564	ex D-AVZL	Lunenburg	
☐ D-AIRR	Airbus A321-131	0567	ex D-AVZM	Wismar	
☐ D-AIRS	Airbus A321-131	0595	ex D-AVZX	Husum	
☐ D-AIRT	Airbus A321-131	0652	ex D-AVZI	Regensburg	
☐ D-AIRU	Airbus A321-131	0692	ex D-AVZT	Würzburg	
☐ D-AIRW	Airbus A321-131	0699	ex D-AVZY	Heilbronn	
☐ D-AIRX	Airbus A321-131	0887	ex D-AVZI	Weimar	retro colours
☐ D-AIRY	Airbus A321-131	0901	ex D-AVZK	Flensburg	
☐ D-AISB	Airbus A321-231	1080	ex D-AVZP	Hameln	
☐ D-AISC	Airbus A321-231	1161	ex D-AVZG	Speyer	
☐ D-AISD	Airbus A321-231	1188	ex F-WWDD	Chemnitz	

	Registration	Type	c/n	Previous	Name	Notes
☐	D-AISE	Airbus A321-231	1214	ex D-AVZS	Neudstadt an der Weinstrasse	
☐	D-AISF	Airbus A321-231	1260	ex D-AVZI	Lippstadt	
☐	D-AISG	Airbus A321-231	1273	ex D-AVZU	Dormagen	
☐	D-AISH	Airbus A321-231	3265	ex D-AVZL		
☐	D-AISI	Airbus A321-231	3339	ex D-AVZD	Bergheim	
☐	D-AISJ	Airbus A321-231	3360	ex D-AVZF	Gutersloh	
☐	D-AISK	Airbus A321-231	3387	ex D-AVZO		
☐	D-AISL	Airbus A321-231	3434	ex D-AVZD	Arnsberg	
☐	D-AISN	Airbus A321-231	3592	ex D-AZAA	Goppingen	
☐	D-AISO	Airbus A321-231	3625	ex D-AVZH		
☐	D-AISP	Airbus A321-231	3864	ex D-AVZK		
☐	D-AISQ	Airbus A321-231	3936	ex D-AVAF	Lindau	
☐	D-AISR	Airbus A321-231	3987	ex D-AZAN		
☐	D-AIST	Airbus A321-231	4005	ex D-AVZD		
☐	D-AISU	Airbus A321-231	4016	ex D-AVZF	Nordlingen	
☐	D-AISV	Airbus A321-231	4047	ex D-AZAG	Bingen	
☐	D-AISW	Airbus A321-231	4054	ex D-AVAR	Stade	
☐	D-AISX	Airbus A321-231	4073	ex D-AVZR		
☐	D-AISZ	Airbus A321-231	4085	ex D-AVZW		
☐	D-AIKA	Airbus A330-343X	570	ex F-WWYV	Minden	
☐	D-AIKB	Airbus A330-343X	576	ex F-WWKN	Cuxhaven	
☐	D-AIKC	Airbus A330-343X	579	ex F-WWKG	Hamm	
☐	D-AIKD	Airbus A330-343X	629	ex F-WWYF	Siegen	
☐	D-AIKE	Airbus A330-343X	636	ex F-WWYL	Landshut	
☐	D-AIKF	Airbus A330-343X	642	ex F-WWKV	Witten	
☐	D-AIKG	Airbus A330-343X	645	ex F-WWKE	Ludwigsburg	
☐	D-AIKH	Airbus A330-343X	648	ex F-WWKG		
☐	D-AIKI	Airbus A330-343X	687	ex F-WWYI		
☐	D-AIKJ	Airbus A330-343X	701	ex F-WWKD		
☐	D-AIKK	Airbus A330-343X	896	ex F-WWYX		
☐	D-AIKL	Airbus A330-343X	905	ex F-WWYC		
☐	D-AIKM	Airbus A330-343X	913	ex F-WWYJ		
☐	D-AIKN	Airbus A330-343X	922	ex F-WWYY		
☐	D-AIKO	Airbus A330-343X	989	ex F-WWKJ		
☐	D-AIFA	Airbus A340-313X	352	ex F-WWJU	Dorsten	
☐	D-AIFB	Airbus A340-313X	355	ex F-WWJX	Gummersbach	
☐	D-AIFC	Airbus A340-313X	379	ex F-WWJJ	Gander & Halifax	
☐	D-AIFD	Airbus A340-313X	390	ex F-WWJE	Giessen	
☐	D-AIFE	Airbus A340-313X	434	ex F-WWJT	Passau	
☐	D-AIFF	Airbus A340-313X	447	ex F-WWJB	Delmenhorst	
☐	D-AIGA	Airbus A340-311	020	ex F-WWJK	Oldenburg	
☐	D-AIGB	Airbus A340-311	024	ex F-WWJO	Recklinghausen	
☐	D-AIGC	Airbus A340-311	027	ex F-WWJR	Wilhelmshaven	Star Alliance c/s
☐	D-AIGD	Airbus A340-311	028	ex F-WWJS	Remscheid	
☐	D-AIGF	Airbus A340-311	035	ex F-WWJV	Göttingen	
☐	D-AIGH	Airbus A340-311	052	ex F-WWJQ	Koblenz	
☐	D-AIGI	Airbus A340-311	053	ex F-WWJJ	Worms	
☐	D-AIGK	Airbus A340-311	056	ex F-WWJK	Bayreuth	
☐	D-AIGL	Airbus A340-313X	135	ex F-WWJS	Herne	
☐	D-AIGM	Airbus A340-313X	158	ex F-WWJN	Görlitz	
☐	D-AIGN	Airbus A340-313X	213	ex F-WWJM	Solingen	
☐	D-AIGO	Airbus A340-313X	233	ex F-WWJJ	Offenbach	
☐	D-AIGP	Airbus A340-313X	252	ex F-WWJM	Paderborn	
☐	D-AIGS	Airbus A340-313X	297	ex F-WWJK	Bergisch-Gladbach	
☐	D-AIGT	Airbus A340-313X	304	ex F-WWJY	Viersen	
☐	D-AIGU	Airbus A340-313X	321	ex F-WWJM	Castrop-Rauxel	
☐	D-AIGV	Airbus A340-313X	325	ex F-WWJN	Dinslaken	
☐	D-AIGW	Airbus A340-313X	327	ex F-WWJO	Gladbeck	
☐	D-AIGX	Airbus A340-313X	354	ex F-WWJV	Düren	
☐	D-AIGY	Airbus A340-313X	335	ex F-WWJS	Lünen	
☐	D-AIGZ	Airbus A340-313X	347	ex F-WWJT	Villingen-Schwenningen	
☐	D-AIHA	Airbus A340-642	482	ex F-WWCS	Nürnberg	Star Alliance c/s
☐	D-AIHB	Airbus A340-642	517	ex F-WWCR	Bremerhaven	
☐	D-AIHC	Airbus A340-642	523	ex F-WWCV	Essen	
☐	D-AIHD	Airbus A340-642	537	ex F-WWCZ	Stuttgart	
☐	D-AIHE	Airbus A340-642	540	ex F-WWCF	Leverkusen	
☐	D-AIHF	Airbus A340-642	543	ex F-WWCE	Lübeck	
☐	D-AIHH	Airbus A340-642	566	ex F-WWCJ	Wiesbaden	
☐	D-AIHI	Airbus A340-642	569	ex F-WWCB	Monchengladbach	
☐	D-AIHK	Airbus A340-642	580	ex F-WWCN	Mainz	
☐	D-AIHL	Airbus A340-642	583	ex F-WWCQ		
☐	D-AIHM	Airbus A340-642	762	ex F-WWCI	Wuppertal	
☐	D-AIHN	Airbus A340-642	763	ex F-WWCJ		
☐	D-AIHO	Airbus A340-642	767	ex F-WWCN		
☐	D-AIHP	Airbus A340-642	771	ex F-WWCQ		
☐	D-AIHQ	Airbus A340-642	790	ex F-WWCE		
☐	D-AIHR	Airbus A340-642	794	ex F-WWCF		
☐	D-AIHS	Airbus A340-642	812	ex F-WWCX		
☐	D-AIHT	Airbus A340-642	846	ex F-WWCH		
☐	D-AIHU	Airbus A340-642	848	ex F-WWCI		
☐	D-AIHV	Airbus A340-642	897	ex F-WWTI		

☐ D-AIHW	Airbus A340-642	972	ex F-WWCL		
☐ D-AIHX	Airbus A340-642	981	ex F-WWCN		
☐ D-AIHY	Airbus A340-642	987	ex F-WWCQ		
☐ D-AIHZ	Airbus A340-642	1005	ex F-WWCR		
☐ D-AIMA	Airbus A380-841	038	ex F-WWSH		on order
☐ D-AIMB	Airbus A380-841	041	ex F-WWAF		on order
☐ D-AIMC	Airbus A380-841	044	ex F-WWAJ		on order
☐ D-AIMD	Airbus A380-841	048	ex F-WW		on order
☐ D-AIME	Airbus A380-841	061	ex F-WW		on order
☐ D-AIMF	Airbus A380-841	066	ex F-WW		on order
☐ D-AIMG	Airbus A380-841	069	ex F-WW		on order
☐ D-AIMH	Airbus A380-841	076	ex F-WW		on order
☐ D-ABEA	Boeing 737-330	24565/1818		Saarbrucken	
☐ D-ABEB	Boeing 737-330	25148/2077		Xanten	
☐ D-ABEC	Boeing 737-330	25149/2081		Karlsruhe	
☐ D-ABED	Boeing 737-330	25215/2082		Hagen	
☐ D-ABEE	Boeing 737-330	25216/2084		Ulm	
☐ D-ABEF	Boeing 737-330	25217/2094		Weiden i.d.Opf	
☐ D-ABEH	Boeing 737-330	25242/2102		Bad Kissingen	
☐ D-ABEI	Boeing 737-330	25359/2158	ex (D-ABJK)	Bamberg	
☐ D-ABEK	Boeing 737-330	25414/2164	ex (D-ABJL)		
☐ D-ABEL	Boeing 737-330	25415/2175	ex (D-ABJM)	Pforzheim	
☐ D-ABEM	Boeing 737-330	25416/2182	ex (D-ABJN)	Eberswalde-Finow	
☐ D-ABEN	Boeing 737-330	26428/2196	ex (D-ABJP)	Neubrandenburg	
☐ D-ABEO	Boeing 737-330	26429/2207	ex (D-ABJR)	Plauen	
☐ D-ABEP	Boeing 737-330	26430/2216	ex (D-ABJS)	Naumburg/Saale	
☐ D-ABER	Boeing 737-330	26431/2242	ex TC-SUK	Merseburg	
☐ D-ABES	Boeing 737-330	26432/2247	ex (D-ABJU)	Köthen/Anhalt	
☐ D-ABET	Boeing 737-330	27903/2682		Gelsenkirchen	
☐ D-ABEU	Boeing 737-330	27904/2691		Goslar	
☐ D-ABEW	Boeing 737-330	27905/2705		Detmold	
☐ D-ABIA	Boeing 737-530	24815/1933	ex OK-SWY	Greifswald	
☐ D-ABIB	Boeing 737-530	24816/1958	ex OK-SWZ	Esslingen	
☐ D-ABIC	Boeing 737-530	24817/1967		Krefeld	
☐ D-ABID	Boeing 737-530	24818/1974		Aachen	
☐ D-ABIE	Boeing 737-530	24819/1979		Hildesheim	
☐ D-ABIF	Boeing 737-530	24820/1985		Landau	
☐ D-ABIH	Boeing 737-530	24821/1993		Bruchsal	
☐ D-ABII	Boeing 737-530	24822/1997		Lörrach	
☐ D-ABIK	Boeing 737-530	24823/2000		Rastatt	
☐ D-ABIL	Boeing 737-530	24824/2006		Memmingen	
☐ D-ABIM	Boeing 737-530	24937/2011		Salzgitter	
☐ D-ABIN	Boeing 737-530	24938/2023		Langenhagen	
☐ D-ABIO	Boeing 737-530	24939/2031		Wesel	
☐ D-ABIP	Boeing 737-530	24940/2034		Oberhausen	
☐ D-ABIR	Boeing 737-530	24941/2042		Anklam	
☐ D-ABIS	Boeing 737-530	24942/2048		Rendsburg	
☐ D-ABIT	Boeing 737-530	24943/2049		Neumünster	
☐ D-ABIU	Boeing 737-530	24944/2051		Limburg	
☐ D-ABIW	Boeing 737-530	24945/2063		Bad Nauheim	
☐ D-ABIX	Boeing 737-530	24946/2070		Iserlohn	
☐ D-ABIY	Boeing 737-530	25243/2086		Lingen	
☐ D-ABIZ	Boeing 737-530	25244/2098		Kirchheim unter Teck	
☐ D-ABJA	Boeing 737-530	25270/2116		Bad Segeberg	
☐ D-ABJB	Boeing 737-530	25271/2117		Rheine	
☐ D-ABJC	Boeing 737-530	25272/2118		Erding	
☐ D-ABJD	Boeing 737-530	25309/2122		Freising	
☐ D-ABJE	Boeing 737-530	25310/2126		Ingelheim am Rhein	
☐ D-ABJF	Boeing 737-530	25311/2128	ex LZ-BOI	Aalen	
☐ D-ABJH	Boeing 737-530	25357/2141		Heppenheim/Bergstrasse	
☐ D-ABJI	Boeing 737-530	25358/2151		Siegburg	
☐ D-ABWH	Boeing 737-330 (QC)	24284/1685		Rothenburg o.d. Tauber	
☐ D-ABXL	Boeing 737-330	23531/1307		Neuss	
☐ D-ABXM	Boeing 737-330	23871/1433		Herford	
☐ D-ABXN	Boeing 737-330	23872/1447		Böblingen	
☐ D-ABXO	Boeing 737-330	23873/1489		Schwäbisch Gmünd	
☐ D-ABXP	Boeing 737-330	23874/1495		Fulda	
☐ D-ABXR	Boeing 737-330	23875/1500		Celle	
☐ D-ABXS	Boeing 737-330	24280/1656		Sindelfingen	
☐ D-ABXT	Boeing 737-330	24281/1664		Reutlingen	
☐ D-ABXU	Boeing 737-330	24282/1671		Seeheim-Jugenheim	
☐ D-ABXW	Boeing 737-330	24561/1785		Hanau	
☐ D-ABXX	Boeing 737-330	24562/1787		Bad Homburg v d Höhe	
☐ D-ABXY	Boeing 737-330	24563/1801		Hof	
☐ D-ABXZ	Boeing 737-330	24564/1807		Bad Mergentheim	
☐ D-ABTA	Boeing 747-430M	24285/747		Sachsen	stored HAM
☐ D-ABTB	Boeing 747-430M	24286/749		Brandenburg	
☐ D-ABTC	Boeing 747-430M	24287/754		Mecklenburg-Vorpommern	
☐ D-ABTD	Boeing 747-430M	24715/785		Hamburg	
☐ D-ABTE	Boeing 747-430M	24966/846	ex N6046P	Sachsen-Anhalt	

☐ D-ABTF	Boeing 747-430M	24967/848		Thüringen	
☐ D-ABTH	Boeing 747-430M	25047/856		Duisburg	
☐ D-ABTK	Boeing 747-430	29871/1293	ex (D-ABVI)	Kiel	
☐ D-ABTL	Boeing 747-430	29872/1299	ex (D-ABVG)	Dresden	
☐ D-ABVA	Boeing 747-430	23816/723	ex N6055X	Berlin	
☐ D-ABVB	Boeing 747-430	23817/700	ex N5573S	Bonn	
☐ D-ABVC	Boeing 747-430	24288/757		Baden-Württemberg	
☐ D-ABVD	Boeing 747-430	24740/786	ex N60668	Bochum	
☐ D-ABVE	Boeing 747-430	24741/787		Potsdam	
☐ D-ABVF	Boeing 747-430	24761/796	ex N6018N	Frankfurt am Main	
☐ D-ABVH	Boeing 747-430	25045/845	ex N6018N	Düsseldorf	
☐ D-ABVK	Boeing 747-430	25046/847	ex N6009F	Hannover	
☐ D-ABVL	Boeing 747-430	26425/898	ex N60659	München	
☐ D-ABVM	Boeing 747-430	29101/1143	ex (V8-AC2)	Hessen	
☐ D-ABVN	Boeing 747-430	26427/915		Dortmund	
☐ D-ABVO	Boeing 747-430	28086/1080		Mülheim an der Ruhr	
☐ D-ABVP	Boeing 747-430	28284/1103		Bremen	
☐ D-ABVR	Boeing 747-430	28285/1106		Köln	
☐ D-ABVS	Boeing 747-430	28286/1109		Saarland	
☐ D-ABVT	Boeing 747-430	28287/1110		Rheinland-Pfalz	
☐ D-ABVU	Boeing 747-430	29492/1191		Bayern	
☐ D-ABVW	Boeing 747-430	29493/1205		Wolfsburg	
☐ D-ABVX	Boeing 747-430	29868/1237		Schleswig-Holstein	
☐ D-ABVY	Boeing 747-430	29869/1261		Nordrhein-Westfalen	
☐ D-ABVZ	Boeing 747-430	29870/1264		Niedersachsen	
☐ D-CDLH*	Junkers Ju52/3m g8e	130714	ex N52JU	Tempelhof	*Painted as D-AQUI

LUFTHANSA CARGO — *Lufthansa Cargo (LH/GEC)* — *Frankfurt (FRA)*

☐ D-ALCA	McDonnell-Douglas MD-11F	48781/625	ex N9020Q	Wilhelm Althen	
☐ D-ALCB	McDonnell-Douglas MD-11F	48782/626	ex N9166N		
☐ D-ALCC	McDonnell-Douglas MD-11F	48783/627		Karl-Ulrich Garnadt	
☐ D-ALCD	McDonnell-Douglas MD-11F	48784/628			
☐ D-ALCE	McDonnell-Douglas MD-11F	48785/629			
☐ D-ALCF	McDonnell-Douglas MD-11F	48798/637			
☐ D-ALCG	McDonnell-Douglas MD-11F	48799/639			
☐ D-ALCH	McDonnell-Douglas MD-11F	48801/640			
☐ D-ALCI	McDonnell-Douglas MD-11F	48800/641			
☐ D-ALCJ	McDonnell-Douglas MD-11F	48802/642			
☐ D-ALCK	McDonnell-Douglas MD-11F	48803/643	ex N9166N		
☐ D-ALCL	McDonnell-Douglas MD-11F	48804/644			
☐ D-ALCM	McDonnell-Douglas MD-11F	48805/645	ex N6069R		
☐ D-ALCN	McDonnell-Douglas MD-11F	48806/646			
☐ D-ALCO	McDonnell-Douglas MD-11F	48413/488	ex N413LT	light green	
☐ D-ALCP	McDonnell-Douglas MD-11F	48414/491	ex N414LT	purple	stored VCV
☐ D-ALCQ	McDonnell-Douglas MD-11F	48431/534	ex N431LT		
☐ D-ALCR	McDonnell-Douglas MD-11F	48581/565	ex N581LT	dark blue	stored VCV
☐ D-ALCS	McDonnell-Douglas MD-11F	48630/567	ex N630LT	orange	stored VCV

LUFTHANSA CITYLINE — *Hansaline (CL/CLH)* — *Frankfurt/Cologne (FRA/CGN)*

☐ D-AVRA	Avro 146-RJ85	E2256	ex G-6-256	
☐ D-AVRB	Avro 146-RJ85	E2253	ex G-BVWD	
☐ D-AVRC	Avro 146-RJ85	E2251	ex G-6-251	
☐ D-AVRD	Avro 146-RJ85	E2257	ex G-6-257	
☐ D-AVRE	Avro 146-RJ85	E2261	ex G-6-261	
☐ D-AVRF	Avro 146-RJ85	E2269	ex G-JAYV	
☐ D-AVRG	Avro 146-RJ85	E2266	ex G-6-266	
☐ D-AVRH	Avro 146-RJ85	E2268	ex G-OCLH	
☐ D-AVRI	Avro 146-RJ85	E2270	ex G-CLHX	
☐ D-AVRJ	Avro 146-RJ85	E2277	ex G-BWKY	
☐ D-AVRK	Avro 146-RJ85	E2278	ex G-6-278	
☐ D-AVRL	Avro 146-RJ85	E2285	ex G-6-285	
☐ D-AVRM	Avro 146-RJ85	E2288	ex G-6-288	
☐ D-AVRN	Avro 146-RJ85	E2293	ex G-6-293	
☐ D-AVRO	Avro 146-RJ85	E2246	ex G-6-246	
☐ D-AVRP	Avro 146-RJ85	E2303	ex G-6-303	
☐ D-AVRQ	Avro 146-RJ85	E2304	ex G-6-304	
☐ D-AVRR	Avro 146-RJ85	E2317	ex G-6-317	
☐ D-ACHA	Canadair CL-600-2B19 (CRJ-200LR)	7378	ex C-FMLF	Murrhardt
☐ D-ACHB	Canadair CL-600-2B19 (CRJ-200LR)	7391	ex C-GGKF	Meersburg
☐ D-ACHC	Canadair CL-600-2B19 (CRJ-200LR)	7394	ex C-GOKD	Füssen
☐ D-ACHD	Canadair CL-600-2B19 (CRJ-200LR)	7403	ex C-FMNB	Lutherstadt Eisleben
☐ D-ACHE	Canadair CL-600-2B19 (CRJ-200LR)	7407	ex C-FMLB	Meissen
☐ D-ACHF	Canadair CL-600-2B19 (CRJ-200LR)	7431	ex C-FMLI	Montabaur
☐ D-ACHI	Canadair CL-600-2B19 (CRJ-200LR)	7464	ex C-FMKV	Deidesheim
☐ D-ACHK	Canadair CL-600-2B19 (CRJ-200LR)	7499	ex C-FMLI	Schkeuditz
☐ D-ACJB	Canadair CL-600-2B19 (CRJ-200LR)	7128	ex C-FMMQ	
☐ D-ACJC	Canadair CL-600-2B19 (CRJ-200LR)	7130	ex C-FMMW	
☐ D-ACJD	Canadair CL-600-2B19 (CRJ-200LR)	7135	ex C-FMNH	

☐ D-ACJE	Canadair CL-600-2B19 (CRJ-200LR)	7165	ex C-FMNH		
☐ D-ACJF	Canadair CL-600-2B19 (CRJ-200LR)	7200	ex C-FMLQ		
☐ D-ACJG	Canadair CL-600-2B19 (CRJ-200LR)	7220	ex C-FMMW	Oberstdorf	
☐ D-ACJH	Canadair CL-600-2B19 (CRJ-200LR)	7266	ex C-FMNW		DLH 50th anniversary c/s
☐ D-ACLW	Canadair CL-600-2B19 (CRJ-200LR)	7114	ex C-FMMT		
☐ D-ACLY	Canadair CL-600-2B19 (CRJ-200LR)	7119	ex C-FMND		
☐ D-ACLZ	Canadair CL-600-2B19 (CRJ-200LR)	7121	ex C-FMNQ		
☐ D-ACPA	Canadair CL-600-2C10 (CRJ-701ER)	10012	ex C-GHZV	Westerland/Sylt	
☐ D-ACPB	Canadair CL-600-2C10 (CRJ-701ER)	10013	ex C-GHZY	Rüdesheim am Rhein	
☐ D-ACPC	Canadair CL-600-2C10 (CRJ-701ER)	10014	ex C-GISW	Espelkamp	
☐ D-ACPD	Canadair CL-600-2C10 (CRJ-701ER)	10015	ex C-GISZ	Vilshofen an der Donau	
☐ D-ACPE	Canadair CL-600-2C10 (CRJ-701ER)	10027	ex C-GIAZ	Belzig	
☐ D-ACPF	Canadair CL-600-2C10 (CRJ-701ER)	10030	ex C-GIBI	Uhingen	
☐ D-ACPG	Canadair CL-600-2C10 (CRJ-701ER)	10034	ex C-GIBO	Leinfelden-Echterdingen	
☐ D-ACPH	Canadair CL-600-2C10 (CRJ-701ER)	10043	ex C-GHZY	Eschwege	
☐ D-ACPI	Canadair CL-600-2C10 (CRJ-701ER)	10046	ex C-GIAE	Viernheim	
☐ D-ACPJ	Canadair CL-600-2C10 (CRJ-701ER)	10040	ex C-GKCO	Neumarkt in der Oberpfalz	
☐ D-ACPK	Canadair CL-600-2C10 (CRJ-701ER)	10063	ex C-GIBN	Besigheim	
☐ D-ACPL	Canadair CL-600-2C10 (CRJ-701ER)	10076	ex C-GIAE	Halberstadt	
☐ D-ACPM	Canadair CL-600-2C10 (CRJ-701ER)	10080	ex C-GIAO	Heidenheim an der Brenz	
☐ D-ACPN	Canadair CL-600-2C10 (CRJ-701ER)	10083	ex C-GIAU	Quedlinburg	
☐ D-ACPO	Canadair CL-600-2C10 (CRJ-701ER)	10085	ex C-FZYS	Spaichingen	
☐ D-ACPP	Canadair CL-600-2C10 (CRJ-701ER)	10086	ex C-GIGJ	Torgau	
☐ D-ACPQ	Canadair CL-600-2C10 (CRJ-701ER)	10091	ex C-GZJA	Lubbecke	Star Alliance c/s
☐ D-ACPR	Canadair CL-600-2C10 (CRJ-701ER)	10098	ex C-	Weinheim an der Bergstrasse	
☐ D-ACPS	Canadair CL-600-2C10 (CRJ-701ER)	10100	ex C-	Berchtesgaden	Star Alliance c/s
☐ D-ACPT	Canadair CL-600-2C10 (CRJ-701ER)	10103	ex C-GJLZ	Altötting	Star Alliance c/s
☐ D-ACKA	Canadair CL-600-2D24 (CRJ-900LR)	15072	ex C-	Pfaffenhofen a.d.Ilm	
☐ D-ACKB	Canadair CL-600-2D24 (CRJ-900LR)	15073	ex C-FJVT	Schliersee	
☐ D-ACKC	Canadair CL-600-2D24 (CRJ-900LR)	15078	ex C-	Mettman	
☐ D-ACKD	Canadair CL-600-2D24 (CRJ-900LR)	15080	ex C-	Wittlich	
☐ D-ACKE	Canadair CL-600-2D24 (CRJ-900LR)	15081	ex C-	Wernigerode	
☐ D-ACKF	Canadair CL-600-2D24 (CRJ-900LR)	15083	ex C-FJVR	Prenzlau	
☐ D-ACKG	Canadair CL-600-2D24 (CRJ-900LR)	15084	ex C-GIAO	Glücksburg	
☐ D-ACKH	Canadair CL-600-2D24 (CRJ-900LR)	15085	ex C-GICL	Radebeul	
☐ D-ACKI	Canadair CL-600-2D24 (CRJ-900LR)	15088	ex C-GIAP	Tuttlingen	
☐ D-ACKJ	Canadair CL-600-2D24 (CRJ-900LR)	15089	ex C-	Ilmenau	
☐ D-ACKK	Canadair CL-600-2D24 (CRJ-900LR)	15094	ex C-	Fürstenwalde	
☐ D-ACKL	Canadair CL-600-2D24 (CRJ-900LR)	15095	ex C-	Bad Bergzabern	
☐ D-ACNA	Canadair CL-600-2D24 (CRJ-900NG)	15229	ex C-GZQA	Amberg	
☐ D-ACNB	Canadair CL-600-2D24 (CRJ-900NG)	15230	ex C-GZQM	Wermelskirchen	
☐ D-ACNC	Canadair CL-600-2D24 (CRJ-900NG)	15236	ex C-GIBO		
☐ D-ACND	Canadair CL-600-2D24 (CRJ-900NG)	15238	ex C-GIBT		
☐ D-ACNE	Canadair CL-600-2D24 (CRJ-900NG)	15241	ex C-GICL		
☐ D-ACNF	Canadair CL-600-2D24 (CRJ-900NG)	15243	ex C-GIAU		
☐ D-ACNG	Canadair CL-600-2D24 (CRJ-900NG)	15245	ex C-GZQF		
☐ D-ACNH	Canadair CL-600-2D24 (CRJ-900NG)	15247	ex C-GZQK		
☐ D-ACNI	Canadair CL-600-2D24 (CRJ-900NG)	15248			
☐ D-ACNJ	Canadair CL-600-2D24 (CRJ-900NG)	15249			
☐ D-ACNK	Canadair CL-600-2D24 (CRJ-900NG)	15251			on order
☐ D-ACNL	Canadair CL-600-2D24 (CRJ-900NG)	15252			on order
☐ D-ACNM	Canadair CL-600-2D24 (CRJ-900NG)	15253			on order
☐ D-ACNN	Canadair CL-600-2D24 (CRJ-900NG)	15254			on order
☐ D-ACNO	Canadair CL-600-2D24 (CRJ-900NG)	15255			on order
☐ D-AEBA	Embraer E-190-200LR	19000314	ex PT-TXC		
☐ D-AEBB	Embraer E-190-200LR	19000316	ex PT-TXE		
☐ D-AEBC	Embraer E-190-200LR	19000320	ex PT-TXI		
☐ D-AEBD	Embraer E-190-200LR	19000324	ex PT-TXM		
☐ D-AECA	Embraer E-190-100LR	19000327	ex PT-TXP		
☐ D-AECB	Embraer E-190-100LR	19000332	ex PT-TXS		
☐ D-AECC	Embraer E-190-100LR	19000333	ex PT-TXT		
☐ D-AECD	Embraer E-190-100LR		ex PT-		on order
☐ D-AECE	Embraer E-190-100LR		ex PT-		on order
☐ D-AECF	Embraer E-190-100LR		ex PT-		on order
☐ D-AECG	Embraer E-190-100LR		ex PT-		on order
☐ D-AECH	Embraer E-190-100LR		ex PT-		on order
☐ D-AECI	Embraer E-190-100LR		ex PT-		on order
☐ D-AECJ	Embraer E-190-100LR		ex PT-		on order
☐ D-AECK	Embraer E-190-100LR		ex PT-		on order
☐ D-AECL	Embraer E-190-100LR		ex PT-		on order
☐ D-AEMA	Embraer E-190-100LR	19000290	ex PT-TZE		
☐ D-AEMB	Embraer E-190-100LR	19000297	ex PT-TZL		
☐ D-AEMC	Embraer E-190-100LR	19000300	ex PT-TZO		
☐ D-AEMD	Embraer E-190-100LR	19000305	ex PT-TZT		
☐ D-AEME	Embraer E-190-100LR	19000308	ex PT-TXH		
☐ D-AEMF	Embraer E-190-100LR	19000310	ex PT-TZY		

LUFTVERKEHR FRIESLAND HARLE					Harle
☐ D-IADE	Cessna 340A	340A0607	ex OE-FSK		
☐ D-ILFA	Britten-Norman BN-2B-26 Islander	2243	ex G-BSWO		
☐ D-ILFC	Britten-Norman BN-2B-20 Islander	2272	ex JA5321		
☐ D-ILFD	Britten-Norman BN-2B-20 Islander	2296	ex JA02TY		
☐ D-ILFH	Britten-Norman BN-2B-26 Islander	2212	ex G-BPXS		
☐ D-IORF	Britten-Norman BN-2A-26 Islander	2020	ex N100DA		Lsd fr Ostseeflug

NIGHTEXPRESS		Executive (EXT)			Frankfurt (FRA)
☐ D-CCAS	Short SD.3-60	SH3737	ex G-OLBA		
☐ D-CRAS	Short SD.3-60	SH3744	ex N825BE		
☐ D-IEXB	Beech 99	U-70	ex G-NUIT		

OCA INTERNATIONAL					Munster (FMO)
☐ D-COPS	SAAB SF.340A	340A-087	ex OK-CCB		Lsd fr CCB

OLT - OSTFRIESISCHE LUFTTRANSPORT		Oltra (OL/OLT)			Emden/Bremen (EME/BRE)
☐ D-AGPQ	Fokker F.28-0100 (Fokker 100)	11338	ex PH-CXQ		
☐ D-AOLB	SAAB 2000	2000-005	ex SE-005		
☐ D-AOLC	SAAB 2000	2000-016	ex SE-016		
☐ D-AOLT	SAAB 2000	2000-037	ex HB-IZU	Emden	
☐ D-AOLG	Fokker F.28-0100 (Fokker 100)	11452	ex PH-RRN	Toulouse	
☐ D-AOLH	Fokker F.28-0100 (Fokker 100)	11265	ex PH-SEM		
☐ D-CASB	SAAB SF.340B	340B-223	ex SE-KSI		
☐ D-CNAF	Swearingen SA.227AC Metro III	AC-505B	ex TF-BBG		Lsd fr REW
☐ D-COLB	Swearingen SA.227AC Metro III	AC-754B	ex N54NE		
☐ D-COLD	Swearingen SA.227AC Metro III	AC-421B	ex SE-LIM		
☐ D-COLE	SAAB SF.340A	340A-144	ex LV-WTF	Bremen	
☐ D-COLT	Swearingen SA.227AC Metro III	AC-690	ex N715C		
☐ D-ECDJ	Cessna 207 Skywagon	20700176	ex N1576U		
☐ D-EOLF	Gippsland GA-8 Airvan	GA8-05-080	ex VH-IMI	Borkum	
☐ D-FOLE	Cessna 208B Caravan I	208B0523	ex N5197A		
☐ D-IFBN	Britten-Norman BN-2B-26 Islander	2185	ex G-BLNF	Juist	
☐ D-IOLK	Britten-Norman BN-2B-26 Islander	2306	ex G-CEUB		
☐ D-IOLO	Britten-Norman BN-2B-26 Islander	2305	ex G-CEUA		

OSTSEEFLUG					Rostock-Laage (RLG)
☐ D-IORF	Britten-Norman BN-2A-26 Islander	2020	ex N100DA		Lsd to L Friesland Harle

PRIVATAIR		PrivatJet (PTG)			Düsseldorf (DUS)
☐ D-APAC	Airbus A319-132LR	1727	ex D-AVWQ		op for DLH
☐ D-APBB	Boeing 737-8Q8/W	35278/2625	ex N812SY		
☐ D-APBC	Boeing 737-8BK/W	33016/1588	ex N807SY		
☐ D-APBD	Boeing 737-8BK/W	33021/1667	ex N808SY		

PRIVATE WINGS		Private Wings (8W/PWF)			Berlin-Schönefeld (SXF)
☐ D-BIRD	Dornier 328-300 (328JET)	3180	ex N422FJ		
☐ D-BJET	Dornier 328-300 (328JET)	3207	ex N328FG		
☐ D-CATZ	Dornier 328-110	3090	ex N404SS		
☐ D-COCA	Beech 1900D	UE-224	ex N224YV		
☐ D-COLA	Beech B300 Super King Air	FL-75	ex HB-GJB		
☐ D-CPWF	Dornier 328-110	3112	ex D-CFWF		
☐ D-CREW	Dornier 328-110	3113	ex D-CGAO		Lsd to SUS

PTL LUFTFAHRTUNTERNEHMEN		King Star (KST)			Landshut (QLG)
☐ D-IBAD	Beech B200 Super King Air	BB-1229			

RAE REGIONAL AIR EXPRESS		Regional Wings (REW)			Münster-Osnabrück (FMO)
☐ D-CAVA	Swearingen SA.227AC Metro III	AC-758B	ex F-GPSN		
☐ D-CNAF	Swearingen SA.227AC Metro III	AC-505B	ex TF-BBG		Lsd to OLT
☐ D-CNAY	Swearingen SA.227AT Merlin IVC	AT-493	ex PH-RAX		
☐ D-CSWF	Swearingen SA.227DC Metro III	DC-896B	ex N3042E		

REGIO-AIR		German Link (RAG)			Trollenhagen
☐ D-IBIJ	Cessna 402B	402B0327	ex YU-BIJ		Lsd fr Goller
☐ D-IESS	Swearingen SA.226TC Metro II	TC-338	ex N90141		

TUIFLY		***Tuifly (X3/HLF, HLX)***			***Hanover (HAJ)***
☐ D-AGEE	Boeing 737-35B	24238/1626	ex UR-GAG	Handel/Bach c/s	Lsd fr GMI
☐ D-AGEG	Boeing 737-35B	24237/1624	ex UR-GAF		Lsd fr GMI
☐ D-AGEJ	Boeing 737-3L9	24221/1604	ex OO-SEJ	Handel/Bach c/s	Lsd fr GMI
☐ D-AGEQ	Boeing 737-75B	28103/23	ex N1787B		Lsd fr/op by GMI
☐ D-AGET	Boeing 737-75B	28109/31			Lsd fr/op by GMI
☐ D-AHXA	Boeing 737-7K5/W	30714/2202	ex N1786B		
☐ D-AHXB	Boeing 737-7K5/W	30717/2228		Robinson Club Granada	
☐ D-AHXC	Boeing 737-7K5/W	34693/2260		Robinson Club Alpffwang	
☐ D-AHXD	Boeing 737-7K5/W	30726/2298			
☐ D-AHXE	Boeing 737-7K5/W	35135/2451		Robinson Club Piz Buin	
☐ D-AHXF	Boeing 737-7K5/W	35136/2465		Robinson Club Arosa	
☐ D-AHXG	Boeing 737-7K5/W	35140/2575			
☐ D-AHXH	Boeing 737-7K5/W	35282/2585			
☐ D-AHXI	Boeing 737-7K5/W	35141/2603			
☐ D-AHXJ	Boeing 737-7K5/W	35277/2609			
☐ D-AHFA	Boeing 737-8K5/W	27981/7	ex N737BX	Robinson Club Pamfilya	
☐ D-AHFB	Boeing 737-8K5/W	27982/8	ex N35030	Robinson Club Nobilis	
☐ D-AHFC	Boeing 737-8K5/W	27977/9	ex N5573P	Robinson Club Sarigerme Park	
☐ D-AHFD	Boeing 737-8K5/W	27978/40	ex N35161	Robinson Club Daidalos	
☐ D-AHFE	Boeing 737-8K5/W	27979/44	ex N3502P	Robinson Club Playa Granada	
☐ D-AHFH	Boeing 737-8K5/W	27983/218	ex N1786B	Robinson Club Fleesensee	
☐ D-AHFI	Boeing 737-8K5/W	27984/220	ex N1787B		
☐ D-AHFK	Boeing 737-8K5/W	27991/248	ex HA-LKC		
☐ D-AHFL	Boeing 737-8K5/W	27985/470	ex HA-LKD		
☐ D-AHFM	Boeing 737-8K5/W	27986/474		Goldbair	
☐ D-AHFO	Boeing 737-8K5/W	27987/499			
☐ D-AHFP	Boeing 737-8K5/W	27988/508	ex N1786B		
☐ D-AHFQ	Boeing 737-8K5/W	27992/523	ex N1786B	Robinson Riad Zakaria	
☐ D-AHFR	Boeing 737-8K5/W	30593/528	ex N1787B	Robinson Club Agadir	
☐ D-AHFS	Boeing 737-8K5/W	28623/556			
☐ D-AHFT	Boeing 737-8K5/W	30413/636	ex N1015B		
☐ D-AHFU	Boeing 737-8K5/W	30414/703	ex N1787B	Robinson Club Soma Bay	
☐ D-AHFV	Boeing 737-8K5/W	30415/719	ex N1786B		
☐ D-AHFW	Boeing 737-8K5/W	30882/760	ex N1786B		
☐ D-AHFX	Boeing 737-8K5/W	30416/778	ex N1786B		
☐ D-AHFY	Boeing 737-8K5/W	30417/781	ex N1787B		
☐ D-AHFZ	Boeing 737-8K5/W	30883/783	ex N1786B	Robinson Club Cala Serena	
☐ D-AHLK	Boeing 737-8K5/W	35143/2763			
☐ D-AHLR	Boeing 737-8K5/W	32907/1117		Robinson Club Apulia	
☐ D-ATUC	Boeing 737-8K5/W	34684/1870	ex N1786B		
☐ D-ATUD	Boeing 737-8K5/W	34685/1901			
☐ D-ATUE	Boeing 737-8K5/W	34686/1903			
☐ D-ATUF	Boeing 737-8K5/W	34687/1907	ex N1786B		Retro c/s
☐ D-ATUG	Boeing 737-8K5/W	34688/1909			
☐ D-ATUH	Boeing 737-8K5/W	34689/1935			

WDL AVIATION		***WDL (WE/WDL)***			***Cologne (CGN)***
☐ D-ALIN	British Aerospace 146 Srs.300	E3142	ex EI-DEW		stored CGN
☐ D-AMAJ	British Aerospace 146 Srs.200	E2028	ex G-BZBA		
☐ D-AMGL	British Aerospace 146 Srs.200	E2055	ex G-CBFL	all-white	
☐ D-AWBA	British Aerospace 146 Srs.300A	E3134	ex ZK-NZF		Lsd to SAS
☐ D-AWDL	British Aerospace 146 Srs.100	E1011	ex G-UKJF		
☐ D-AWUE	British Aerospace 146 Srs.200	E2050	ex PK-PJP		
☐ D-	British Aerospace 146 Srs.300	E3157	ex EI-DEX		on order
☐ D-ADEP	Fokker F.27 Friendship 600	10318	ex OY-CCK		
☐ D-ADOP	Fokker F.27 Friendship 600	10316	ex OY-BVF	Babs	stored CGN
☐ D-AELG	Fokker F.27 Friendship 600	10338	ex VR-BLZ		stored CGN
☐ D-AELH	Fokker F.27 Friendship 400	10340	ex VR-BLX	Judestored CGN	
☐ D-AELJ	Fokker F.27 Friendship 600	10342	ex F-BYAB	Flying Dutchman	stored CGN
☐ D-AELK	Fokker F.27 Friendship 600	10361	ex F-GCJV	Petra	
☐ D-AELM	Fokker F.27 Friendship 600	10450	ex OY-CCL	Dietmar Rabe von Papenheim	str CGN
☐ D-AISY	Fokker F.27 Friendship 600	10391	ex OY-CCR		stored CGN
☐ D-BAKB	Fokker F.27 Friendship 600	10261	ex F-GHRC	Hully Gully	
☐ D-BAKC	Fokker F.27 Friendship 600	10195	ex F-GFJS		stored CGN
☐ D-BAKD	Fokker F.27 Friendship 600	10179	ex SP-FNF		stored CGN

XL AIRWAYS GERMANY		***(GV/GXL)***			***Frankfurt (FRA)***
☐ D-AXLD	Boeing 737-8FH/W	35093/2176	ex C-FYLD		
☐ D-AXLE	Boeing 737-8Q8/W	30724/2286			
☐ D-AXLF	Boeing 737-8Q8/W	28218/160	ex G-XLAB	Tinks	Lsd to NMB
☐ D-AXLG	Boeing 737-8Q8/W	28226/77	ex G-XLAA		

DQ- FIJI (Republic of Fiji)

AIR FIJI — *Fijiair (PC/FAJ)* — *Suva-Nausori (SUV)*

Reg	Type	C/n	Previous identity	Name / titles	Remarks
☐ DQ-AFR	AVIC II Y-12	013	ex B-744L		
☐ DQ-AFS	AVIC II Y-12	015	ex B-745L		
☐ DQ-FHC	Harbin Y-12 II	0056			Op for Airlines Tonga
☐ DQ-FHF	Harbin Y-12 II	0047	ex B-531L		Op for Airlines Tonga
☐ DQ-FSC	Harbin Y-12 II	0048	ex VH-LLK		Op for Airlines Tonga
☐ DQ-AFO	Embraer EMB.110P1 Bandeirante	110419	ex EI-BVX		
☐ DQ-FET	Britten-Norman BN-2A-21 Islander	661	ex ZK-NNE		stored SUV
☐ DQ-FIC	Britten-Norman BN-2A-21 Islander	511	ex ZK-KHB	Island Shuttle titles	
☐ DQ-MUM	Embraer EMB.120ER Brasilia	120079	ex VH-XFH	Pacific Link titles	
☐ DQ-TLC	Embraer EMB.110P1 Bandeirante	110417	ex VH-TLD		Op for Airlines Tonga
☐ DQ-YES	Embraer EMB.110P1 Bandeirante	110307	ex VH-FNR		
☐ DQ-	AVIC I MA-60				on order
☐ ZK-CIF	Convair 580	381	ex N566EA		Lsd fr CVA

AIR KATAFANGA — *Suva-Nausori (SUV)*

Reg	Type	C/n	Previous identity
☐ DQ-FIK	Piper PA-31-350 Navajo Chieftain	31-7752090	ex N7088C

AIR PACIFIC — *Pacific (FJ/FJI)* — *Nadi (NAN)*

Reg	Type	C/n	Previous identity	Name	Remarks
☐ DQ-FJC	Boeing 767-3X2ER	26260/552		Island of Taveuni	
☐ DQ-FJF	Boeing 737-7X2/W	28878/96	ex N1786B	Island of Koro	
☐ DQ-FJG	Boeing 737-8X2/W	29968/275	ex N1786B	Island of Kadavu	
☐ DQ-FJH	Boeing 737-8X2/W	29969/339	ex N1786B	Island of Gau	
☐ DQ-FJK	Boeing 747-412	24064/755	ex 9V-SMD	Island of Vanua Levu	Lsd fr SIA
☐ DQ-FJL	Boeing 747-412	24062/722	ex 9V-SMB	Island of Viti Levu	Lsd fr SIA

AIR WAKAYA — *Suva-Nausori (SUV)*

Reg	Type	C/n	Previous identity
☐ DQ-DHG	Cessna 208B Caravan I	208B1120	ex N1274X
☐ DQ-FHG	Britten-Norman BN-2B-26 Islander	2230	ex G-BSAC

NORTHERN AIR SERVICES — *Suva-Nausori (SUV)*

Reg	Type	C/n	Previous identity
☐ DQ-JJS	Britten-Norman BN-2A-26 Islander	856	ex VH-IFA

PACIFIC ISLAND AIR — *Nadi (NAN)*

Reg	Type	C/n	Previous identity	Remarks
☐ DQ-GEE	de Havilland DHC-2 Beaver	1358	ex C-GSKY	Floatplane
☐ DQ-GLL	de Havilland DHC-3 Turbo Otter	288	ex N68086	Floatplane
☐ DQ-SLM	Britten-Norman BN-2A-26 Islander	605	ex VH-XFI	
☐ DQ-YIR	Britten-Norman BN-2A-26 Islander	845	ex VH-FCOI	

PACIFIC SUN — *Sunflower (PI/SUF)* — *Nadi (NAN)*

Reg	Type	C/n	Previous identity	Name	Remarks
☐ DQ-FCX	Britten-Norman BN-2A-27 Islander	833	ex G-BEMJ	Adi Yasawa	
☐ DQ-FDV	Britten-Norman BN-2A-26 Islander	41	ex 9M-MDA	Bui Nigone	stored NAN
☐ DQ-FDW	Britten-Norman BN-2A-26 Islander	602	ex 9M-MDC	Adi Makutu	
☐ DQ-FEY	de Havilland DHC-6 Twin Otter 100	87	ex N64NB	Spirit of the North	
☐ DQ-FEZ	de Havilland DHC-6 Twin Otter 100	9	ex F-OCFJ	Spirit of the West	
☐ DQ-FIE	de Havilland DHC-6 Twin Otter 300	660	ex N933CL	Spirit of Nadi	
☐ DQ-FIN	Britten-Norman BN-2A-26 Islander	159	ex VH-ISA		
☐ DQ-PSA	ATR 42-500	554	ex 3B-NBB		
☐ DQ-PSB	ATR 42-500	534	ex 3B-NBA		

TURTLE AIRWAYS — *Turtle (TLT)* — *Nadi-Newtown Beach*

Reg	Type	C/n	Previous identity	Remarks
☐ DQ-FEX	Cessna U206G Stationair 6 II	U20605706	ex ZK-FHE	Floatplane
☐ DQ-TAL	de Havilland DHC-2 Beaver	1255	ex C-GLED	Floatplane
☐ DQ-TAM	de Havilland DHC-2 Beaver	1433	ex VH-IME	Floatplane
☐ DQ-TAN	Cessna U206G Stationair 6 II	U20605574	ex VH-HBX	Floatplane

D2- ANGOLA (Republic of Angola)

AEROJET — *Mabeco (MBC)* — *Luanda (LAD)*

Reg	Type	C/n	Previous identity
☐ D2-EDE	Embraer EMB.120ER Brasilia	120039	ex N188SW
☐ D2-EDF	Embraer EMB.120ER Brasilia	120037	ex N187SW
☐ D2-FDK	Embraer EMB.120ER Brasilia	120281	ex N215SW
☐ D2-FER	Yakovlev Yak-40	9541844	ex RA-87994

AIR 26 — *Air 26 (DCD)* — *Luanda (LAD)*

Reg	Type	C/n	Previous identity	Name
☐ D2-EYN	Embraer EMB.120ER Brasilia	120165	ex N264AS	Nova Erce
☐ D2-EYO	Embraer EMB.120RT Brasilia	120210	ex N269AS	

☐ D2-EYP	Embraer EMB.120RT Brasilia	120146	ex N262AS	
☐ D2-EYQ	Embraer EMB.120ER Brasilia	120062	ex F-GFEO	
☐ D2-EZC	Embraer EMB.120ER Brasilia	120200	ex N652CT	
☐ D2-EZZ	Embraer EMB.120FC Brasilia	120102	ex N126AM	Freighter

AIR GEMINI — *Twins (GLL)* — *Luanda (LAD)*

☐ D2-ERJ	Douglas DC-9-32 (ABS 3)	47765/900	ex N924LG	
☐ D2-ERL	Douglas DC-9-32 (ABS 3)	47788/901	ex N925LG	
☐ D2-ERN	Boeing 727-25C (FedEx 3)	19358/367	ex S9-BAU	
☐ D2-ERS	Douglas DC-9-32	47110/167	ex N923LG	
☐ D2-ERU	Boeing 727-2S7	22020/1592	ex N681CA	
☐ S9-BAR	Boeing 727-22C	19098/318	ex N832RV	stored LAD
☐ S9-BOE	Boeing 727-22C (FedEx 3)	19192/388	ex N706DH	stored LAD

ALADA — *Air Alada (RAD)* — *Luanda (LAD)*

☐ D2-FAM	Ilyushin Il-18V	184007401	ex UR-75475	
☐ D2-FAX	Antonov An-32A	1510	ex RA-48115 Kimoka	
☐ D2-FFR	Ilyushin Il-18D	0393607150	ex UR-75896	converted Il-22
☐ D2-FRB	Antonov An-32	2208	ex Hungary 208	

ANGOLA AIR CHARTER — *Angola Charter (AGO)* — *Luanda (LAD)*

☐ D2-FCO	Ilyushin Il-76MD	0043454615	ex ER-IBE
☐ D2-FCP	Boeing 727-77C (FedEx 3)	20370/821	ex N526PC
☐ D2-FDO	Embraer EMB.120RT Brasilia	120082	ex N102SK
☐ D2-FDT	Embraer EMB.120RT Brasilia	120081	ex N103SK
☐ D2-MBV	Antonov An-12BP	5343208	ex ER-AXH
☐ ZS-PCA	Beech 1900C-1	UC-138	ex N138GA

ANGOLAN AIRSERVICES — *Luanda (LAD)*

☐ ZS-NYK	British Aerospace Jetstream 4121	41095	G-4-095
☐ ZS-PCA	Beech 1900C-1	UC-138	ex N138GA
☐ D2-FHE	British Aerospace Jetstream 4101	41046	ex N146KM
☐ D2-FHF	British Aerospace Jetstream 4101	41049	ex N149KM

DIEXIM EXPRESS — *Luanda (LAD)*

☐ D2-FFE	Embraer EMB.120ER Brasilia	120242	ex N8078V		
☐ D2-FFI	Embraer EMB.120RT Brasilia	120035	ex N331JS	William Domingos	
☐ D2-FFO	Beech B300 Super King Air	FL-10	ex N350FH		
☐ D2-FFP	Embraer EMB.120RT Brasilia	120235	ex F-GJTF		
☐ D2-FFU	Embraer EMB.120ER Brasilia	120244	ex F-GTBH		id not confirmed
☐ D2-FFW	Embraer EMB.145MP (ERJ-145MP)	145360	ex F-OIJE		
☐ D2-	Embraer EMB.120RT Brasilia	120171	ex N221CR		

FLY540 ANGOLA

☐ D2-	ATR 72-212A	816	ex F-WWEF	on order
☐ D2-	ATR 72-212A	826	ex F-WWEU	on order
☐ D2-	ATR 72-212A	845	ex F-WWEK	on order

GIRA GLOBO — *Gira Globo (GGL)* — *Luanda (LAD)*

☐ D2-FCN	Ilyushin Il-76TD	0053462872	ex UR-76651		Op for Angolan Air Force, T-900
☐ D2-FDG	Antonov An-32B	2201	ex RA-48116	Mulanda	
☐ D2-FEM	Ilyushin Il-76TD	0063469062	ex UR-76688	Rei-Ekuikui	T-905
☐ D2-FEW	Ilyushin Il-76TD	0073475239	ex UR-76721		Op for Angolan Air Force, T-904

HM AIRWAYS — *Luanda (LAD)*

☐ D2-EYA	Bell 427	56037	ex N51804
☐ D2-EYB	Bell 427	56046	ex N427MM
☐ D2-EYC	Bell 427	56048	ex N804RM
☐ D2-EYD	Bell 427	56049	ex N88PQ
☐ D2-EYE	Bell 427	56050	ex N918RB
☐ D2-EYF	Bell 427	56051	ex N96EA
☐ D2-EYG	Bell 427	56052	ex N97EA
☐ D2-EYH	Bell 427	56053	ex N97TZ

☐ D2-EYI	Bell 430	49102	ex N41786
☐ D2-EYJ	Bell 430	49108	ex N767MM
☐ D2-EYK	Bell 430	49109	ex N825GB
☐ D2-EYL	de Havilland DHC-8-315	613	ex C-FDGW
☐ D2-EYM	de Havilland DHC-8-315	614	ex C-FDHE
☐ D2-EYU	de Havilland DHC-8-315	645	ex C-FLKI
☐ D2-EYV	Embraer EMB.120ER Brasilia	120145	ex N284UE

SAL - SOCIEDADE DE AVIACAO LIGEIRA — Luanda (LAD)

Reg	Type	C/n	Previous	Name	Notes
☐ D2-ECN	Cessna F406 Caravan II	F406-0002	ex PH-MNS		
☐ D2-ECO	Cessna F406 Caravan II	F406-0011	ex D-IDAA		
☐ D2-ECP	Cessna F406 Caravan II	F406-0016	ex PH-LAS		
☐ D2-ECQ	Cessna F406 Caravan II	F406-0019	ex G-CVAN		
☐ D2-ECW	Beech B300 Super King Air	FL-102	ex S9-TAP		
☐ D2-ECX	Beech B200 Super King Air	BB-1362	ex N1565F		
☐ D2-ECY	Beech B200C Super King Air	BL-135	ex S9-NAP		
☐ D2-EDA	Cessna 208B Caravan I	208B0568	ex N1215K		
☐ D2-EDB	Cessna 208B Caravan I	208B0665	ex N1256G		
☐ D2-EOD	Short SC.7 Skyvan 3	SH1938	ex CR-LOD		stored LAD

SONAIR — Sonair (SOR) — Luanda (LAD)

Reg	Type	C/n	Previous	Name	Notes
☐ D2-EQD	Aérospatiale SA365N2 Dauphin 2	6521	ex F-GJIA		
☐ D2-EQE	Aérospatiale SA365N2 Dauphin 2	6531	ex F-WQSR		
☐ D2-EUO	Aérospatiale SA365N Dauphin 2	9000			
☐ D2-EVE	Aérospatiale SA365N2 Dauphin 2	6418	ex F-WQSR		
☐ D2-EVF	Aérospatiale SA365N2 Dauphin 2	6410	ex F-GHRX		
☐ D2-EXX	Aérospatiale SA365N2 Dauphin 2	6439	ex F-WQSR		
☐ D2-ERQ	Beech 1900D	UE-274	ex N11015		
☐ D2-EVJ	Beech 1900D	UE-111	ex N3119U		
☐ D2-EVK	Beech 1900D	UE-121	ex N3221A		
☐ D2-EVL	Beech 1900D	UE-312	ex N312RC		
☐ D2-EVN	Beech 1900D	UE-370	ex N30539		
☐ D2-EVR	Beech 1900D	UE-280	ex N11284		
☐ D2-EVX	Beech 1900D	UE-340	ex N23317		
☐ D2-EVY	Beech 1900D	UE-249	ex N249GL		
☐ D2-EWW	Beech 1900D	UE-399	ex N854CA		
☐ D2-EWX	Beech 1900D	UE-405	ex N856CA		
☐ D2-EWY	Beech 1900D	UE-401	ex N840CA		
☐ D2-FFJ	Beech 1900D	UE-412	ex N44828		
☐ D2-EVA	de Havilland DHC-6 Twin Otter 310	728	ex V2-LDD		
☐ D2-EVB	de Havilland DHC-6 Twin Otter 310	810	ex V2-LDH		
☐ D2-EVC	de Havilland DHC-6 Twin Otter 310	809	ex V2-LDG		
☐ D2-EVH	de Havilland DHC-6 Twin Otter 300	511	ex HB-LOM		
☐ D2-FVM	de Havilland DHC-6 Twin Otter 310	794	ex HB-LRF		
☐ D2-FVN	de Havilland DHC-6 Twin Otter 310	817	ex N817L		
☐ D2-FVO	de Havilland DHC-6 Twin Otter 310	821	ex N821L		
☐ D2-FVP	de Havilland DHC-6 Twin Otter 310	743	ex 5Y-TMF		
☐ D2-FVQ	de Havilland DHC-6 Twin Otter 310	704	ex 5N-ASP		
☐ D2-EVS	Sikorsky S-76C	760603	ex C-GHRI		Lsd fr CHC Helicopters Intl
☐ D2-EXG	Sikorsky S-76A	760042	ex ZS-RKE		Lsd fr Heli-Union
☐ D2-EXH	Sikorsky S-76A	760268	ex ZS-RBE		Lsd fr CHC Helicopter (Africa)
☐ D2-EXK	Sikorsky S-76C	760525	ex N9017U		
☐ D2-EXL	Sikorsky S-76C	760526	ex N9007U		
☐ D2-EXO	Sikorsky S-76C	760543	ex N2040S		
☐ D2-EXP	Sikorsky S-76C	760544	ex N2048K		
☐ D2-ESN	Fokker F.27 Friendship 500	10610	ex PH-FTY	Kwanda	
☐ D2-ESR	Fokker F.27 Mk.050 (Fokker 50)	20240	ex PH-RPK	Lombo Este	
☐ D2-ESU	Boeing 727-23F	19431/372	ex N516FE		
☐ D2-ESW	Fokker F.27 Mk.050 (Fokker 50)	20241	ex PH-RRM		Lsd fr Golfo Intl
☐ D2-ESZ	Aérospatiale AS.332L2 II	2503	ex F-WQPA		
☐ D2-EVD	Boeing 727-29C	19403/435	ex CB-02		
☐ D2-EVG	Boeing 727-29C	19402/415	ex N70PA		
☐ D2-EVP	Aérospatiale AS.332L2 II	2398	ex F-WQEA		Lsd fr CHC Helicopter (Africa)
☐ D2-EVT	Eurocopter EC.225LP		ex F-WQDI		
☐ D2-EVW	Boeing 737-7HB	35954/2310			
☐ D2-EVZ	Boeing 737-7HBC/W	35955/2531			
☐ D2-EWS	Boeing 737-7HBC/W	35956/2536			
☐ D2-EXN	Aérospatiale AS.332L2 II	2590			
☐ D2-FSA	Boeing 727-29C	19987/634	ex HZ-HE4		Freighter
☐ S9-CAM	Beech B300 Super King Air	FL-163	ex N1057Q		Lsd fr Golfo Intl
☐ S9-CAN	Beech B300 Super King Air	FL-294	ex N3214J		Lsd fr Golfo Intl
☐ N262SG	Boeing 747-481	29262/1199	ex JA403A		stored KUL
☐ N263SG	Boeing 747-481	29263/1204	ex B-LFC		stored HKG
☐ N322SG	Boeing 747-481	30322/1250	ex B-LFD		stored HKG

TAAG ANGOLA AIRLINES — DTA (DT/DTA) — Luanda (LAD)

Reg	Type	C/n	Previous
☐ D2-TBC	Boeing 737-2M2C	21173/447	ex D2-TAB
☐ D2-TBF	Boeing 737-7M2/W	34559/2013	ex N1787B
☐ D2-TBG	Boeing 737-7M2/W	34560/2036	
☐ D2-TBH	Boeing 737-7M2/W	34561/2043	
☐ D2-TBJ	Boeing 737-7M2/W	34562/2149	

☐ D2-TBO	Boeing 737-2M2	22776/891	ex N1782B		stored BBU
☐ D2-TBX	Boeing 737-2M2	23351/1117			
☐ D2-TEA	Boeing 747-312M	23410/653	ex 9V-SKN	Cidade de Kuito	
☐ D2-TEB	Boeing 747-357M	23751/686	ex N375TC		
☐ D2-TED	Boeing 777-2M2ER	34565/581			
☐ D2-TEE	Boeing 777-2M2ER	34566/587		Kuitu Kuanavale	
☐ D2-TEF	Boeing 777-2M2ER	34567/687			

TRANSTECO — ***Transteco (TTC)*** — ***Luanda (LAD)***

☐ D2-FEI	Beech 200 King Air	BB-620	ex ZS-OGV

TROPICANA — ***Luanda (LAD)***

☐ D2-EBF	Beech B200 Super King Air	BB-836	ex S9-NAQ	
☐ D2-FFK	Beech B200 Super King Air	BB-1026	ex N153D	Aeronautica titles
☐ D2-FFL	Beech 200 Super King Air	BB-126	ex N777XZ	Capembe
☐ D2-FFM	Beech 1900D	UE-108	ex N118SK	Mavinga

D4- CAPE VERDE ISLANDS (Republic of Cape Verde)

CABO VERDE EXPRESS — ***(CVE)*** — ***Sal (SID)***

☐ D4-CBL	LET L-410UVP-E10	902511	ex 9Q-CUM	) D4-CBL, -CBR identities
☐ D4-CBR	LET L-410UVP-E20	912533	ex D-CLED	) may be reversed
☐ D4-JCA	LET L-410UVP-E20	912604	ex OY-PEY	

HALCYON AIR — ***Praia (RAI)***

☐ D4-CBQ	ATR 42-320	296	ex J5-GZZ	Santa Maria

TACV - TRANSPORTES AEREOS DE CABO VERDE / CAPE VERDE AIRLINES — ***Cabo Verde (VR/TCV)*** — ***Praia (RAI)***

☐ D4-CBP	Boeing 757-2Q8	30045/957	ex N301AM	Emigranti
☐ D4-CBT	ATR 72-212A	747	ex F-WWEH	Jorge Barbosa
☐ D4-CBU	ATR 72-212A	755	ex F-WWEP	Baltizar Lopes
☐ D4-CBV	ATR 42-512	669	ex F-WWLC	

D6- COMOROS (Federal Islamic Republic of the Comores)

COMORES AIR SERVICE — ***Moroni (YVA)***

☐ D6-CAM	LET L-410UVP	851336	ex D6-GDH
☐ D6-CAN	LET L-410UVP	841331	ex 9L-LCZ

COMORES AVIATION — ***Comores (KR/KMZ)*** — ***Moroni (YVA)***

☐ D6-BJH	British Aerospace 146 Srs.200	E2030	ex ZS-SFZ	
☐ D6-CAK	LET L-410UVP	841219	ex D2-TGH	dbr 09Apr07?
☐ D6-CAL	LET L-410UVP	800526	ex HA-LAB	

COMORES ISLAND AIRWAYS — ***Moroni (YVA)***

☐ D6-CAS	Airbus A320-214	3040	ex EC-KAX	
☐ D6-CAT	Airbus A320-214	3755	ex F-WWBU	on order

HERITAGE AVIATION — ***Moroni (YVA)***

☐ D6-CAQ LET L-410UVP
Status uncertain

EC- SPAIN (Kingdom of Spain)

AERONOVA — ***Aeronova (OVA)*** — ***Valencia (VLC)***

☐ EC-GVE	Swearingen SA.227AC Metro III	AC-669B	ex N2702Z
☐ EC-HCH	Swearingen SA.227AC Metro III	AC-658B	ex N2692P
☐ EC-HZH	Swearingen SA.227AC Metro III	AC-720	ex N2724S
☐ EC-IXL	Swearingen SA.227AC Metro III	AC-689B	ex D-COLC
☐ EC-JCU	Swearingen SA.227AC Metro III	AC-679B	ex N6UB

AIR COMET — ***Red Comet (A7/MPD)*** — ***Palma de Mallorca (PMI)***

Ceased operations 21/Dec/2009

AIR EUROPA — Europa (UX/AEA) — Palma de Mallorca (PMI)

Associate member of Skyteam

	Reg	Type	C/n	Previous identity	Name / Remarks
☐	EC-JPF	Airbus A330-202	733	ex F-WWKU	
☐	EC-JQG	Airbus A330-202	745	ex F-WWYG	Estepona-Costa del Sol
☐	EC-JQQ	Airbus A330-202	749	ex F-WWYJ	
☐	EC-JZL	Airbus A330-202	814	ex F-WWYJ	David Bisbal
☐	EC-KOM	Airbus A330-202	931	ex F-WWKU	
☐	EC-KTG	Airbus A330-202	950	ex F-WWKQ	
☐	EC-HBL	Boeing 737-85P	28381/250	ex N1787B	
☐	EC-HBM	Boeing 737-85P	28382/256	ex N1787B	
☐	EC-HBN	Boeing 737-85P	28383/266	ex N1786B	Llucmajor
☐	EC-HGO	Boeing 737-85P	28384/420	ex N1786B	
☐	EC-HGP	Boeing 737-85P	28385/421	ex N1786B	Marbella
☐	EC-HGQ	Boeing 737-85P	28386/426	ex N1786B	El Mundo titles
☐	EC-HJP	Boeing 737-85P	28535/480	ex N1800B	
☐	EC-HJQ	Boeing 737-85P	28387/522	ex N1786B	
☐	EC-HKQ	Boeing 737-85P/W	28388/533		San Pedro Alcantara
☐	EC-HKR	Boeing 737-85P/W	28536/540	ex N1787B	
☐	EC-HZS	Boeing 737-86Q/W	30276/920	ex N747BX	
☐	EC-IDA	Boeing 737-86Q/W	32773/1051	ex N73792	
☐	EC-IDT	Boeing 737-86Q/W	30281/1076	ex N73793	
☐	EC-III	Boeing 737-86Q/W	30284/1233		
☐	EC-ISE	Boeing 737-86Q/W	30290/1406	ex N1786B	
☐	EC-ISN	Boeing 737-86Q/W	30291/1435		
☐	EC-IVV	Boeing 737-883	28323/625	ex EI-CXU	Camino de Santiago
☐	EC-IYI	Boeing 737-883	30194/666	ex EI-CXW	
☐	EC-JAP	Boeing 737-85P/W	33971/1580		
☐	EC-JBJ	Boeing 737-85P/W	33972/1598		Salamanca
☐	EC-JBK	Boeing 737-85P/W	33973/1606		
☐	EC-JBL	Boeing 737-85P/W	33974/1610		
☐	EC-JHK	Boeing 737-85P/W	33975/1716	ex N1787B	
☐	EC-JHL	Boeing 737-85P/W	33976/1740		
☐	EC-JKZ	Boeing 737-86N/W	34251/1817		
☐	EC-JNF	Boeing 737-85P/W	33977/1878		Mutua Madrileqa
☐	EC-KBV	Boeing 737-85P/W	33980/2245	ex N1786B	
☐	EC-KCG	Boeing 737-85P/W	33981/2269		
☐	EC-KEO	Boeing 737-85P/W	33982/2338		
☐	EC-	Boeing 737-85P			on order
☐	EC-	Boeing 737-85P			on order
☐	EC-	Boeing 737-85P			on order
☐	EC-KRJ	Embraer 190-200LR (195LR)	19000196	ex PT-	
☐	EC-KXD	Embraer 190-200LR (195LR)	19000244	ex PT-SIP	
☐	EC-KYO	Embraer 190-200LR (195LR)	19000276	ex PT-	
☐	EC-KYP	Embraer 190-200LR (195LR)	19000281	ex PT-TLV	
☐	EC-LCQ	Embraer 190-200LR (195LR)	19000303	ex PT-TZR	on order
☐	EC-	Embraer 190-200LR (195LR)		ex	on order
☐	EC-	Embraer 190-200LR (195LR)		ex	on order
☐	EC-	Embraer 190-200LR (195LR)		ex	on order
☐	EC-HPU	Boeing 767-3Q8ER	30048/828		
☐	EC-HSV	Boeing 767-3Q8ER	29387/840		
☐	SP-LPF	Boeing 767-319ER	24876/413	ex ZK-NCF	Lsd fr LOT

AIR NOSTRUM — Nostrum Air (YW/ANE) — Valencia (VLC)

	Reg	Type	C/n	Previous identity	Name / Remarks
☐	EC-HBY	ATR 72-212A	578	ex F-WWEA	Abeto
☐	EC-HCG	ATR 72-212A	580	ex F-WWEC	Castano
☐	EC-HEI	ATR 72-212A	570	ex F-WWEG	Eucalipto
☐	EC-HEJ	ATR 72-212A	565	ex F-WWEE	Carrasca
☐	EC-HJI	ATR 72-212A	562	ex F-WWLZ	Sauce
☐	EC-GYI	Canadair CL-600-2B19 (CRJ-200ER)	7249	ex C-GDDM	Pinazo
☐	EC-GZA	Canadair CL-600-2B19 (CRJ-200ER)	7252	ex C-GDDO	Beniliure
☐	EC-HEK	Canadair CL-600-2B19 (CRJ-200ER)	7320	ex C-GFCN	Cecilio Pla
☐	EC-HHI	Canadair CL-600-2B19 (CRJ-200ER)	7343	ex C-GFKQ	Genaro Lahuerta Lopez
☐	EC-HHV	Canadair CL-600-2B19 (CRJ-200ER)	7350	ex C-GFKR	Sorolla
☐	EC-HPR	Canadair CL-600-2B19 (CRJ-200ER)	7430	ex C-GHDM	Mompo
☐	EC-HSH	Canadair CL-600-2B19 (CRJ-200ER)	7466	ex C-GHWD	J Michavilla
☐	EC-HTZ	Canadair CL-600-2B19 (CRJ-200ER)	7493	ex C-GIHJ	Ricardo Verde
☐	EC-HXM	Canadair CL-600-2B19 (CRJ-200ER)	7514	ex C-GIQL	Francisco Dominguez
☐	EC-HYG	Canadair CL-600-2B19 (CRJ-200ER)	7529	ex C-GIXG	E Sales Frances
☐	EC-HZR	Canadair CL-600-2B19 (CRJ-200ER)	7547	ex C-GJFR	José Ribera
☐	EC-IAA	Canadair CL-600-2B19 (CRJ-200ER)	7563	ex C-GJIZ	A Munoz Degrain
☐	EC-IBM	Canadair CL-600-2B19 (CRJ-200ER)	7591	ex C-GJQZ	J Navarro Llorens
☐	EC-IDC	Canadair CL-600-2B19 (CRJ-200ER)	7622	ex C-GJYV	Francisco Ribalta
☐	EC-IGO	Canadair CL-600-2B19 (CRJ-200ER)	7661	ex C-FVAZ	Juan de Juanes
☐	EC-IJE	Canadair CL-600-2B19 (CRJ-200ER)	7700	ex C-GZJZ	Josquin Agrasot
☐	EC-IJF	Canadair CL-600-2B19 (CRJ-200ER)	7705	ex C-GZKC	Vicente Magip

☐ EC-IJS	Canadair CL-600-2B19 (CRJ-200ER)	7706	ex C-GZKD	Manuel Benedito	
☐ EC-IKZ	Canadair CL-600-2B19 (CRJ-200ER)	7732	ex C-GZUR	Tomas Yepes	
☐ EC-ILF	Canadair CL-600-2B19 (CRJ-200ER)	7746	ex C-FZQR	Vincente Lopez	
☐ EC-INF	Canadair CL-600-2B19 (CRJ-200ER)	7785	ex C-GYVM	Pedro de Valencia	
☐ EC-IRI	Canadair CL-600-2B19 (CRJ-200ER)	7851	ex C-GZNF	Benjamin Palencia	
☐ EC-ITU	Canadair CL-600-2B19 (CRJ-200ER)	7866	ex C-GZSQ	Pons Arnau	
☐ EC-IVH	Canadair CL-600-2B19 (CRJ-200ER)	7915	ex C-FADU	José Mongrell	
☐ EC-IZP	Canadair CL-600-2B19 (CRJ-200ER)	7950	ex C-FBFI	Enriqe Martinez Cubells	
☐ EC-JCG	Canadair CL-600-2B19 (CRJ-200ER)	7973	ex C-FCEU	José Vergara	
☐ EC-JCL	Canadair CL-600-2B19 (CRJ-200ER)	7975	ex C-FCID		
☐ EC-JCM	Canadair CL-600-2B19 (CRJ-200ER)	7981	ex C-FCNN	Beato de Liebana	
☐ EC-JCO	Canadair CL-600-2B19 (CRJ-200ER)	7984	ex C-FCRX		
☐ EC-JEE	Canadair CL-600-2B19 (CRJ-200ER)	7989	ex C-FCZD	Juan Ignacio Pombo	
☐ EC-JEF	Canadair CL-600-2B19 (CRJ-200ER)	8008	ex C-FDKH	José Monleon	
☐ EC-JEN	Canadair CL-600-2B19 (CRJ-200ER)	7958	ex C-FBQO		
☐ EC-JNX	Canadair CL-600-2B19 (CRJ-200ER)	8058	ex C-FGEP	Catedral de Leon	
☐ EC-JOD	Canadair CL-600-2B19 (CRJ-200ER)	8061	ex C-FGYE		
☐ EC-JOY	Canadair CL-600-2B19 (CRJ-200ER)	8064	ex C-FHCW	Catedral de Leon	

☐ EC-JNB	Canadair CL-600-2D24 (CRJ-900ER)	15057	ex C-		
☐ EC-JTS	Canadair CL-600-2D24 (CRJ-900ER)	15071	ex C-FJTF		
☐ EC-JTT	Canadair CL-600-2D24 (CRJ-900ER)	15074	ex C-FJTJ		
☐ EC-JTU	Canadair CL-600-2D24 (CRJ-900ER)	15079	ex C-FJTE		
☐ EC-JXZ	Canadair CL-600-2D24 (CRJ-900ER)	15087	ex C-FLGI		
☐ EC-JYA	Canadair CL-600-2D24 (CRJ-900ER)	15090	ex C-FLIX		
☐ EC-JYV	Canadair CL-600-2D24 (CRJ-900ER)	15106	ex C-FLMJ		
☐ EC-JZS	Canadair CL-600-2D24 (CRJ-900ER)	15111	ex C-FLMK		
☐ EC-JZT	Canadair CL-600-2D24 (CRJ-900ER)	15113	ex C-FLMN		
☐ EC-JZU	Canadair CL-600-2D24 (CRJ-900ER)	15115	ex C-FLMQ		
☐ EC-JZV	Canadair CL-600-2D24 (CRJ-900ER)	15117	ex C-FLMS		
☐ EC-K	Canadair CL-600-2D24 (CRJ-900ER)		ex C-		on order
☐ EC-K	Canadair CL-600-2D24 (CRJ-900ER)		ex C-		on order
☐ EC-K	Canadair CL-600-2D24 (CRJ-900ER)		ex C-		on order
☐ EC-K	Canadair CL-600-2D24 (CRJ-900ER)		ex C-		on order
☐ EC-K	Canadair CL-600-2D24 (CRJ-900ER)		ex C-		on order

☐ EC-IBS	de Havilland DHC-8Q-315	560	ex PH-DME	Cerezo	
☐ EC-ICA	de Havilland DHC-8Q-315	562	ex PH-DML	Arce	
☐ EC-IGE	de Havilland DHC-8Q-315	576	ex PH-DMY	Alamo	
☐ EC-IIA	de Havilland DHC-8Q-315	587	ex C-GDIU	Palmera	
☐ EC-IIB	de Havilland DHC-8Q-315	588	ex C-GDIW	Nogal	
☐ EC-IOV	de Havilland DHC-8Q-315	581	ex PH-DEJ	Cedro	
☐ PH-DMQ	de Havilland DHC-8Q-315	567	ex C-GDOE	Almendro	Lsd fr/op by DNM
☐ PH-DMR	de Havilland DHC-8Q-315	569	ex C-GETI	Sabina	Lsd fr/op by DNM
☐ PH-DMU	de Havilland DHC-8Q-315	568	ex C-GERL	Olmo	Lsd fr/op by DNM
☐ PH-DMV	de Havilland DHC-8Q-315	570	ex C-GEVP	Haya	Lsd fr/op by DNM
☐ PH-DMW	de Havilland DHC-8Q-315	573	ex C-GFCF	Encina	Lsd fr/op by DNM
☐ PH-DXB	de Havilland DHC-8Q-315	589	ex EC-IJD	Nispero	Lsd fr/op by DNM
☐ PH-DXC	de Havilland DHC-8Q-315	590	ex EC-IKA		Lsd fr/op by DNM

ANDALUS LINEAS AEREAS — *Malaga*

☐ EC-KXQ	Embraer EMB.145EU (ERJ-145EU)	145219	ex G-EMBO
☐ EC-LCP	Embraer EMB.145MP (ERJ-145MP)	145408	ex EI-EEJ
☐ EC-LDB	Embraer EMB.145MP (ERJ-145MP)	145441	ex EI-EEK

AUDELI — *Audeli (ADI)* — *Madrid-Barajas (MAD)*

☐ EC-IDF	Airbus A340-313X	474	ex F-WWJG	Mariana Pineda
☐ EC-IIH	Airbus A340-313X	483	ex F-WWJI	Maria Barbara de Braganza
☐ EC-KCL	Airbus A340-311	005	ex F-GLZA	

BINTER CANARIAS — *(NT/IBB)* — *Las Palmas-Gran Canaria/Tenerife-Sur, Reine Sofia (LPA/TFS)*

☐ EC-GQF	ATR 72-202	489	ex F-WWLJ		Lsd fr/op for NAY
☐ EC-GRP	ATR 72-202	488	ex F-WWLI		Lsd fr/op for NAY
☐ EC-GRU	ATR 72-202	493	ex F-WWLN		Lsd fr/op for NAY
☐ EC-HEZ	ATR 72-212A	582	ex F-WWEL	Montana del Fuego	op for NAY
☐ EC-IYC	ATR 72-212A	709	ex F-WWEI		
☐ EC-IZO	ATR 72-212A	711	ex F-WWEK		
☐ EC-JAH	ATR 72-212A	712	ex F-WWEL		
☐ EC-JBI	ATR 72-212A	713	ex F-WWEM		
☐ EC-JCR	ATR 72-212A	468	ex OY-CIM	Fresno	
☐ EC-JEH	ATR 72-212A	716	ex F-WWEP		
☐ EC-JEV	ATR 72-212A	717	ex F-WWER		
☐ EC-JQL	ATR 72-212A	726	ex F-WWEG		
☐ EC-KGI	ATR 72-212A	752	ex F-WWEM		Lsd fr/op for NAY
☐ EC-KGJ	ATR 72-212A	753	ex F-WWEN		Lsd fr/op for NAY
☐ EC-KRY	ATR 72-212A	795	ex F-WWEV	Azero	Lsd fr/op for NAY
☐ EC-KSG	ATR 72-212A	796	ex F-WWEW	Malvasla Volcanica	Lsd fr/op for NAY
☐ EC-KYI	ATR 72-212A	850	ex F-WWET	Guarapo	Lsd fr/op for NAY
☐ EC-LAD	ATR 72-212A	864	ex F-WWEJ	Baifo	Lsd fr/op for NAY

☐ EC-IJO	Beech 1900D	UE-300	ex F-GRPM	Lsd fr/op by NAY

BKS AIR — *Cosmos (CKM)* — *Bilbao (BIO)*

☐ EC-JGB	Beech B200 Super King Air	BB-1478	ex D-IHAN	

CEGISA — *Salamanca-Matacan (SLM)*

☐ EC-GBP	Canadair CL-215-1A10 (CL-215)	1031	ex EC-957	Tanker op for DGCN
☐ EC-GBQ	Canadair CL-215-1A10 (CL-215)	1033	ex EC-958	Tanker op for DGCN
☐ EC-GBR	Canadair CL-215-1A10 (CL-215)	1051	ex EC-983	Tanker op for DGCN
☐ EC-GBS	Canadair CL-215-1A10 (CL-215)	1052	ex EC-984	Tanker op for DGCN
☐ EC-GBT	Canadair CL-215-1A10 (CL-215)	1054	ex EC-985	Tanker op for DGCN
☐ EC-HET	Canadair CL-215-1A10 (CL-215)	1034	ex I-SISB	Tanker op for Hisporavia
☐ EC-HEU	Canadair CL-215-1A10 (CL-215)	1038	ex I-SISC	Tanker op for Hisporavia
☐ EC-IQC	Air Tractor AT-802A	802A-0155	ex N8512Q	Tanker
☐ EC-IUJ	Air Tractor AT-802A	802A-0154	ex C-GYZB	Tanker

CLICKAIR

Merged with Vueling

CYGNUS AIR — *Cygnus Air (RGN)* — *Madrid-Barajas (MAD)*

☐ EC-FTR	Boeing 757-256 (PCF)	26239/553	ex EC-420	
☐ EC-IGZ	Douglas DC-8-73CF	46133/534	ex N961R	stored MAD
☐ EC-KLD	Boeing 757-256 (PCF)	24121/183	ex N28AT	

EURO CONTINENTAL AIR — *Euro Continental (ECN)* — *Barcelona (BCN)*

☐ EC-GPS	Swearingen SA.227AC Metro III	AC-722	ex N439MA	Freighter Lsd to/op for EAL
☐ EC-JIP	Swearingen SA.226TC Metro II	TC-301	ex N5FY	Viatauro titles
☐ EC-JQC	Swearingen SA.226AC Merlin IVA	AT-066	ex N5FY	

FAASA AVIACION — *FAASA (FAM)* — *Cordoba-Palma del Rio (ODB)*

☐ EC-HNJ	Air Tractor AT-802	802-0096	ex N9075U	
☐ EC-IVL	Air Tractor AT-802A	802A-0159	ex N85152	based Chile as CC-CII
☐ EC-JLD	Air Tractor AT-802A	802A-0210	ex N41810	
☐ EC-JTF	Air Tractor AT-802A	802A-0219		
☐ EC-JTG	Air Tractor AT-802A	802A-0220	ex N8522M	based Chile as CC-CIP
☐ EC-EOI	Bell UH-1B	408	ex N5023U	
☐ EC-EOX	Bell UH-1B	1214	ex N90632	
☐ EC-GAS	Bell 205A-1	30081	ex EC-844	based Chile as CC-CID
☐ EC-GIV	Bell UH-1H	12481	ex N11UH	based Chile as CC-CEN
☐ EC-GKY	Bell UH-1H	13274	ex HE.10B-37	
☐ EC-GKZ	Bell UH-1H	13275	ex HE.10B-38	
☐ EC-GOE	Bell UH-1H	5272	ex N19UH	based Chile as CC-CEL
☐ EC-GOG	Bell UH-1H	9960	ex N17UH	based Chile as CC-CEO
☐ EC-HDD	Bell UH-1H	13551	ex HE.10B-51	
☐ EC-IXU	Bell 412	33037	ex N177EH	
☐ EC-IXV	Bell 412	33068	ex N422EH	
☐ EC-JIM	Bell 412EP	36191	ex N70722	
☐ EC-JRY	Agusta-Bell 412HP	25803	ex SE-JIY	
☐ EC-JTD	Agusta-Bell 412HP	25801	ex SE-JIX	
☐ EC-DVR	Agusta A.109A	7231		EMS
☐ EC-FGL	Bell 206L-3 LongRanger III	51379	ex N65108	EMS
☐ EC-HBJ	Agusta A.109C	7646	ex D-HBRK	EMS
☐ EC-HFV	Bell 212	30818	ex N25UH	
☐ EC-HXL	Bell 222UT	47570	ex TC-HLS	
☐ EC-IFB	Bell 222UT	47572	ex TC-HKL	
☐ EC-IOM	Agusta-Bell 212	5504	ex D-HAFV	
☐ EC-KED	Agusta A.119 Koala	14015	ex N119LF	Lsd fr ERA Helicopters
☐ EC-KEF	Agusta A.119 Koala	14048	ex N325BC	
☐ EC-KEG	Agusta A.119 Koala	14520	ex N119JA	Lsd fr ERA Helicopters
☐ EC-KFZ	Kamov Ka.32A-11BC	9804		
☐ EC-KGA	Kamov Ka.32A-11BC	9805		

FLIGHTLINE — *Flight-Avia (FTL)* — *Barcelona (BCN)*

☐ EC-GFK	Swearingen SA.226AT Merlin IVA	AT-062	ex EC-125	
☐ EC-HBF	Swearingen SA.226AT Merlin IVA	AT-074	ex EC-GDR	MRW Courier titles
☐ EC-HHN	Embraer EMB.120RT Brasilia	120103	ex N127AM	all-white

FLYSUR — Cordoba-Palma del Rio (ODB)

Reg	Type	C/n	Previous identity	Notes
☐ EC-IDG	ATR 42-320	003	ex F-WQNE	Lsd fr TLY

HELI DUERO — Valladolid (VLL)

Reg	Type	C/n	Previous identity
☐ EC-HOX	Bell 212	32254	ex 4X-BCF
☐ EC-HOY	Bell 212	32225	ex 4X-BCN
☐ EC-HPJ	Bell 212	32217	ex 4X-BCJ
☐ EC-HXV	Bell 212	30647	ex FAP 74-614
☐ EC-HZG	Bell 212	32224	ex 4X-BCO
☐ EC-IXX	Bell 412	33043	ex N419EH

HELICSA HELICOPTEROS — Helicsa (HHH) — Albacete-Helicsa Heliport/Madrid

Reg	Type	C/n	Previous identity	Name	Notes
☐ EC-DXM	Aérospatiale SA365C2 Dauphin 2	5007	ex PH-SSL		
☐ EC-FOX	Aérospatiale SA365C2 Dauphin 2	5024	ex EC-136		EMS
☐ EC-GCZ	Aérospatiale SA365C2 Dauphin 2	5037	ex EC-887		EMS
☐ EC-GXY	Aérospatiale SA365N1 Dauphin 2	6242	ex N12AE		EMS
☐ EC-HCL	Aérospatiale AS365N2 Dauphin 2	6416	ex SE-JAE		SAR
☐ EC-HIM	Aérospatiale AS365N2 Dauphin 2	6478	ex SE-JCE		SAR
☐ EC-HRL	Aérospatiale AS365C2 Dauphin 2	5055	ex PH-SSY		EMS
☐ EC-IEL	Aérospatiale SA365C3 Dauphin 2	5017	ex F-GHXF		EMS
☐ EC-IGM	Aérospatiale SA365N3 Dauphin 2	6616	ex F-WQDA		Survey
☐ EC-ILN	Aérospatiale SA365N1 Dauphin 2	6234	ex LV-WLU		EMS
☐ EC-JDQ	Aérospatiale SA365N3 Dauphin 2	6679	ex EC-IZQ		Survey
☐ EC-JLV	Aérospatiale SA365N1 Dauphin 2	6264	ex LN-OPM		EMS
☐ EC-JLX	Aérospatiale SA365N1 Dauphin 2	6346	ex LN-OPL		EMS
☐ EC-JVG	Aérospatiale AS365N3 Dauphin 2	6718	ex F-WWOQ		
☐ EC-EEQ	Bell 212	30612	ex D-HOBB		EMS
☐ EC-FBM	Bell 212	30574	ex EC-552		SAR
☐ EC-GIC	Bell 212	30775	ex LN-OQD		SAR
☐ EC-GID	Bell 212	31150	ex OY-HCS		SAR
☐ EC-GLS	Bell 212	31155	ex OY-HCU		SAR
☐ EC-GVP	Bell 212	30572	ex LN-OQG		SAR
☐ EC-GXA	Bell 212	30812	ex LN-OQJ		SAR
☐ EC-HFX	Bell 212	30639	ex G-BCMC		SAR
☐ EC-HTJ	Bell 212	30648	ex PK-HMC		SAR
☐ EC-INN	Bell 212	31146	ex SE-JLP		
☐ EC-IKY	Eurocopter EC135T2	0255	ex D-HECO		EMS
☐ EC-ION	Eurocopter EC135T2	0272			EMS
☐ EC-ITJ	Eurocopter EC135T2	0306			EMS
☐ EC-IUN	Eurocopter EC135T2	0317			EMS
☐ EC-JDG	Eurocopter EC135T2	0354			EMS
☐ EC-JHT	Eurocopter EC135T2	0396			EMS
☐ EC-JUE	Eurocopter EC135T2	0345	ex EC-067		EMS
☐ EC-DVK	MBB Bo.105CB	S-630	ex D-HDSZ	Argos I	
☐ EC-DVL	MBB Bo.105CB	S-631	ex D-HDTA	Argos II	
☐ EC-ESX	MBB BK-117B-1	7176	ex D-HBHS		
☐ EC-FFV	MBB Bo.105CBS	S-852	ex D-HFHJ		
☐ EC-FMZ	Sikorsky S-61N	61361	ex LN-ORH		Op for SASEMAR
☐ EC-FTB	Sikorsky S-61N	61741	ex LN-OSY		Op for SASEMAR
☐ EC-FVO	Sikorsky S-61N	61756	ex EC-575		Op for SASEMAR
☐ EC-FZJ	Sikorsky S-61N	61758	ex EC-717		Op for SASEMAR
☐ EC-GHY	Aérospatiale AS355F1 Ecureuil 2	5089	ex EC-293		EMS
☐ EC-GSK	Bell 412	33092	ex SE-HVL		
☐ EC-HEE	Aérospatiale AS355N Ecureuil 2	5645	ex F-OHVD		
☐ EC-HXZ	Bell 412	33106	ex PK-HMT		EMS
☐ EC-JTO	Aérospatiale AS350B3 Ecureuil	3091	ex LN-OPK		
☐ EC-JTP	Aérospatiale AS350B3 Ecureuil	3445	ex SE-JHK		
☐ EC-JYE	Aérospatiale SA.330J Puma	1241	ex D-HAXC		
☐ EC-JYF	Aérospatiale SA.330J Puma	1285	ex D-HAXD		
☐ EC-KDO	Aérospatiale AS350B3 Ecureuil	3667	ex LN-OMA		
☐ EC-LCH	Agusta AW139	31257			

HELIMAR — Valencia-Heliport

Reg	Type	C/n	Previous identity	Notes
☐ EC-DNU	Aérospatiale AS350B Ecureuil	1475	ex F-WZFH	
☐ EC-DYK	Aérospatiale AS350B Ecureuil	1863		
☐ EC-FME	Aérospatiale AS350B2 Ecureuil	2448	ex F-GKLR	
☐ EC-GDL	Aérospatiale AS350B2 Ecureuil	2879		op for Policia Foral de Navarra
☐ EC-GDP	Aérospatiale AS350B2 Ecureuil	2886		op for Policia Foral de Navarra
☐ EC-GIY	Aérospatiale AS350B2 Ecureuil	2175	ex JA9809	
☐ EC-EVS	Bell UH-1B	893	ex EC-463	
☐ EC-EXO	Bell UH-1B	202	ex EC-436	
☐ EC-GIZ	Bell UH-1H	5631	ex EC-297	
☐ EC-GJA	Bell UH-1H	5387	ex EC-298	

☐ EC-GJB	Bell UH-1H	9262	ex EC-299		
☐ EC-GSP	Bell UH-1H	8853	ex N1206P		
☐ EC-IGP	Bell 212	30915	ex N5009N		
☐ EC-IGQ	Bell 212	30936	ex N5010F		

HELISURESTE	***Helisureste (UV/HSE)***	***Alicante-San Vincente Heliport***

☐ EC-DNM	Agusta A.109A	7222	ex N4210X		EMS
☐ EC-DZT	Agusta A.109A	7159	ex HB-XIU		EMS
☐ EC-FUY	Agusta A.109C	7670	ex EC-453		Fishery Patrol
☐ EC-GCQ	Agusta A.109C	7665	ex EC-895		Fishery Patrol
☐ EC-GRA	Agusta A.109C	7676	ex EC-GJD		
☐ EC-HAO	Agusta A.109C Max	7642	ex D-HAAC		EMS
☐ EC-HBQ	Agusta A.109A II	7399	ex I-SOCC		EMS
☐ EC-HHQ	Agusta A.109E Power	11058			EMS
☐ EC-IJR	Agusta A.109E Power	11137			EMS
☐ EC-IKN	Agusta A.109A II	7391	ex I-AGSL		EMS
☐ EC-ILA	Agusta A.109E Power	11028	ex F-GSMP		
☐ EC-IRQ	Agusta A.109E Power	11205			
☐ EC-IUS	Agusta A.109E Power	11229			
☐ EC-JGC	Agusta A.109E Power	11622			
☐ EC-JKP	Agusta A.109E Power	11637			Lsd to EDO
☐ EC-JPP	Agusta A.109S Grand	22005	ex I-RAIP		
☐ EC-JUS	Agusta A.109E Power	11675			
☐ EC-KJU	Agusta A.109S Grand	11709			
☐ I-REMS	Agusta A.109S Grand	22024			
☐ EC-JOU	Agusta AW139	31034	ex I-RAII		
☐ EC-KHV	Agusta AW139	31089			
☐ EC-KJT	Agusta AW139	31104	ex I-EASK		
☐ EC-KLM	Agusta AW139	31201	ex I-EASB	201	on order Op for SASEMAR
☐ EC-KLN	Agusta AW139	31202		202	Op for SASEMAR
☐ EC-KXE	Agusta AW139	31219			
☐ EC-KYR	Agusta AW139	31228			
☐ EC-LBM	Agusta AW139	31226			
☐ EC-EUT	Bell 206L-3 LongRanger III	51337	ex N8212U		
☐ EC-FCO	Bell 206L-3 LongRanger III	51179	ex N52CH		
☐ EC-FFQ	Bell 206L-3 LongRanger III	51463	ex N6635Y		
☐ EC-FOL	Bell 206L-3 LongRanger III	51417	ex N6605R		
☐ EC-FRY	Bell 206L-3 LongRanger III	51330	ex N43904		
☐ EC-GCU	Bell 206LT TwinRanger	52105	ex EC-843		EMS
☐ EC-JKG	Bell 206L-4 LongRanger IV	52068	ex OK-YIP		
☐ EC-FBL	Bell 212	30558	ex EC-553		
☐ EC-GXG	Bell 212	30759	ex N21601		
☐ EC-IFA	Bell 212	30689	ex N1074C		
☐ EC-IYO	Bell 212	30946	ex C-GZMZ		
☐ EC-IYP	Bell 212	30533	ex C-FZPX		
☐ EC-IMZ	Bell 407	53547	ex C-GLZA		
☐ EC-IYZ	Bell 407	53599			
☐ EC-IZB	Bell 407	53601			
☐ EC-JAR	Bell 407	53370	ex N54LM		
☐ EC-JBU	Bell 407	53241	ex I-FREC		
☐ EC-JBV	Bell 407	53613	ex C-FBXL		
☐ EC-JSD	Bell 407	53687	ex C-FHYS		
☐ EC-FEL	Agusta-Bell 412SP	25576	ex EC-607		
☐ EC-GOP	Bell 412HP	36031	ex N4603T		
☐ EC-GPA	Bell 412HP	36071	ex N7238Y		
☐ EC-HFD	Bell 412EP	36183	ex N52247		Lsd to HSU
☐ EC-HXX	Bell 412	33062	ex N4014U		
☐ EC-HYM	Bell 412	33045	ex C-FTDM		
☐ EC-HZD	Bell 412	33056	ex N4031F		
☐ EC-IPM	Bell 412	33050	ex C-GJKT		
☐ EC-JJE	Bell 412EP	33004	ex N164EH		
☐ EC-JJQ	Bell 412EP	36376	ex N46372		
☐ EC-JLH	Bell 412EP	36374	ex N3119U		Lsd to HSU
☐ EC-JXQ	Bell 412EP	36091	ex N5087V		
☐ EC-KBB	Bell 412EP	36426	ex N94479		
☐ EC-KBT	Bell 412EP	36423	ex C-FLOX		
☐ EC-KGZ	Bell 412EP	36434	ex C-FMQC		
☐ EC-KUV	Agusta-Bell 412	25602	ex I-MAGM		
☐ EC-LBL	Agusta-Bell 412SP	25600	ex I-CGCL		
☐ EC-JAK	Kamov Ka.32A-11BC	9624/8811/11			based Chile
☐ EC-JAL	Kamov Ka-32A-11BC	9625/8812/12			
☐ EC-JGV	Kamov Ka.32A-11BC	97-08/23			Based Chile
☐ EC-JGX	Kamov Ka.32A-11BC	97-09/24			Based Chile
☐ EC-JSP	Kamov Ka.32A-11BC	9710			
☐ EC-JSQ	Kamov Ka.32A-11BC	9712			

☐ EC-JUZ	Kamov Ka.32A-11BC	9713			
☐ EC-JVA	Kamov Ka.32A-11BC	9714			
☐ EC-JXG	Kamov Ka.32A-11BC	9715			
☐ EC-KFZ	Kamov Ka.32A-11BC	9804			
☐ EC-KGA	Kamov Ka.32A-11BC	9805			
☐ EC-KSH	Kamov Ka.32A-11BC	9814			

☐ EC-DYQ	Agusta-Bell 206B JetRanger III	8677	ex HB-XML		
☐ EC-KEL	CASA CN-235-300MPA	169	ex EC-027		Op for SASEMAR
☐ EC-KEM	CASA CN-235-300MPA	171	ex EC-021	103	Op for SASEMAR
☐ EC-KIJ	Eurocopter EC135T2i	0579			
☐ EC-KJP	Aérospatiale AS355NP Ecureuil 2	5752			

HELISWISS IBERICA — ***Iberswiss (HSW)*** — ***Barcelona-Sabadell / Baqueira-Beret***

☐ EC-FRU	Bell 206B JetRanger III	4268	ex EC-339		
☐ EC-GQH	Bell 206B JetRanger	578	ex HB-XDH		
☐ EC-IUO	Aérospatiale AS350B2 Ecureuil	2393	ex EC-HYV		
☐ EC-JFS	Aérospatiale AS350B3 Ecureuil	3785	ex N18HX		
☐ EC-JID	Aérospatiale AS350BA Ecureuil	1452	ex F-GKCF		

HOLA AIRLINES — ***Hola (H5/HOA)*** — ***Palma de Mallorca (PMI)***

☐ EC-HDS	Boeing 757-256	26252/900		Milagros Diaz	
☐ EC-ISY	Boeing 757-256	26241/572	ex N26ND		Lsd fr Bristol Assoc
☐ EC-KBO	Boeing 737-4Y0	23870/1647	ex OK-TVR		
☐ EC-LAV	Boeing 737-408	24352/1705	ex EC-KTM		

IBERIA LINEAS AEREAS DE ESPANA — ***Iberia (IB/IBE)*** — ***Madrid-Barajas (MAD)***

Member of Oneworld

☐ EC-HGR	Airbus A319-111	1154	ex D-AVYY	Ribeira Sacra	
☐ EC-HGS	Airbus A319-111	1180	ex D-AVWR	Bardenas Reales	
☐ EC-HGT	Airbus A319-111	1247	ex D-AVYV	Ignitas de Enciso	
☐ EC-HKO	Airbus A319-111	1362	ex D-AVWJ	Gorbea	
☐ EC-JAZ	Airbus A319-111	2264	ex D-AVWQ	Las Medulas	
☐ EC-JDL	Airbus A319-111	2365	ex D-AVYN	Los Llanos de Aridane	
☐ EC-JEI	Airbus A319-111	2311	ex D-AVYG	Xativa	
☐ EC-JVE	Airbus A319-111	2843	ex D-AVYT	Puerto de la Cruz	
☐ EC-JXA	Airbus A319-111	2870	ex D-AVWG	Ciudad de Ubeda	
☐ EC-JXJ	Airbus A319-111	2889	ex D-AVYH	Ciudad de Baeza	
☐ EC-JXV	Airbus A319-111	2897	ex D-AVWH	Concejo de Cabrales	
☐ EC-KBJ	Airbus A319-111	3054	ex D-AVYS	Lince Iberico	
☐ EC-KBX	Airbus A319-111	3078	ex D-AVYH	Oso Pardo	
☐ EC-KDI	Airbus A319-111	3102	ex D-AVYA	Cigüeña Negra	
☐ EC-KEV	Airbus A319-111	3169	ex D-AVXD	Urogallo	
☐ EC-KFT	Airbus A319-111	3179	ex D-AVXK	Nutria	
☐ EC-KHM	Airbus A319-111	3209	ex D-AVWL	Búho Real	
☐ EC-KJC	Airbus A319-111	3255	ex D-AVXL	Avutarda	
☐ EC-KKS	Airbus A319-111	3320	ex D-AVYF	Halcõn Peregrino	retro colours
☐ EC-KMD	Airbus A319-111	3380	ex D-AVWE		
☐ EC-KME	Airbus A319-111	3377	ex D-AVWC	Grulla	
☐ EC-KOY	Airbus A319-111	3443	ex D-AVYN		
☐ EC-KUB	Airbus A319-111	3651	ex D-AVYR		
☐ EC-K	Airbus A319-111	3744	ex D-AVWZ		on order

☐ EC-FCB	Airbus A320-211	0158	ex EC-579	Montana de Covadonga	
☐ EC-FDA	Airbus A320-211	0176	ex EC-581	Lagunas de Ruidera	
☐ EC-FDB	Airbus A320-211	0173	ex EC-580	Lago de Sanabria	
☐ EC-FGH	Airbus A320-211	0223	ex EC-585	Caldera de Taburiente	stored MAD
☐ EC-FGR	Airbus A320-211	0224	ex EC-586	Dehesa de Moncayo	stored MAD
☐ EC-FGV	Airbus A320-211	0207	ex EC-584	Monfrague	stored MAD
☐ EC-FLP	Airbus A320-211	0266	ex EC-881	Torcal de Antequera	stored MAD
☐ EC-FLQ	Airbus A320-211	0274	ex EC-882	Dunas de Liencres	stored MAD
☐ EC-FNR	Airbus A320-211	0323	ex EC-885	Monte el Valle	
☐ EC-FQY	Airbus A320-211	0356	ex EC-886	Juan Miro	
☐ EC-HAF	Airbus A320-214	1047	ex F-WWIE	Santiago de Compostela	
☐ EC-HAG	Airbus A320-214	1059	ex F-WWIP	Senorio de Bertiz	
☐ EC-HDK	Airbus A320-214	1067	ex F-WWBF	Mar Ortigola	
☐ EC-HDN	Airbus A320-214	1087	ex F-WWIY	Parque National de Somiedo	
☐ EC-HDO	Airbus A320-214	1099	ex F-WWDR	Formentera	
☐ EC-HDP	Airbus A320-214	1101	ex F-WWDB	Parque de Cabarceno	
☐ EC-HDT	Airbus A320-214	1119	ex F-WWBO	Museo Guggenheim Bilbao	
☐ EC-HGZ	Airbus A320-214	1208	ex F-WWIM	Boi Taull	
☐ EC-HQG	Airbus A320-214	1379	ex F-WWIO	Las Hurdes	stored MAD
☐ EC-HQK	Airbus A320-214	1454	ex F-WWBZ	Macarella	
☐ EC-HSF	Airbus A320-214	1255	ex EC-HHC	Mar Menor	
☐ EC-HTA	Airbus A320-214	1516	ex F-WWIK	Cadaques	
☐ EC-HTB	Airbus A320-214	1530	ex F-WWIO	Playa de las Americas	
☐ EC-HTC	Airbus A320-214	1540	ex F-WWIU	Alpujarra	For VLE
☐ EC-HUJ	Airbus A320-214	1292	ex EC-HKL	Getaria	

☐ EC-HUK Airbus A320-214 1318 ex EC-HKM Laguna Negra
☐ EC-HUL Airbus A320-214 1347 ex EC-HKN Monasterio de Rueda
☐ EC-HYC Airbus A320-214 1262 ex EC-HKI Ciudad de Ceuta
☐ EC-HYD Airbus A320-214 1288 ex EC-HKX Maspalomas
☐ EC-IEF Airbus A320-214 1655 ex F-WWDY Castillo de Loarre
☐ EC-IEG Airbus A320-214 1674 ex F-WWIL Costa Brava
☐ EC-IEI Airbus A320-214 1694 ex F-WWBT Monasterio de Valldigna
☐ EC-ILQ Airbus A320-214 1736 ex F-WWDJ La Padrera
☐ EC-ILR Airbus A320-214 1793 ex F-WWIM San Juan de la Pena
☐ EC-ILS Airbus A320-214 1809 ex F-WWBC Sierra de Cameros
☐ EC-IZH Airbus A320-214 2225 ex F-WWID San Pere de Roda
☐ EC-IZR Airbus A320-214 2242 ex F-WWDA Urkiola
☐ EC-JFG Airbus A320-214 2143 ex F-WWBV Valle de Ricote
☐ EC-JFH Airbus A320-214 2104 ex F-WWBE Trujillo
☐ EC-JFN Airbus A320-214 2391 ex F-WWDB Sierra de las Nieves
☐ EC-JSB Airbus A320-214 2776 ex F-WWDV Benalmadena
☐ EC-JSK Airbus A320-214 2807 ex F-WWIN Ciudad Encantada
☐ EC-KHJ Airbus A320-214 2347 ex XA-UDT Muralla de Lugo
☐ EC-KNM Airbus A320-214 1229 ex XA-MXD Hoces de Gabriel
☐ EC-KOH Airbus A320-214 2248 ex XA-UDU Fontibre
☐ EC- Airbus A320-214 ex on order
☐ EC- Airbus A320-214 ex on order
☐ EC- Airbus A320-214 ex on order
☐ EC- Airbus A320-214 ex on order
☐ EC- Airbus A320-214 ex on order

☐ EC-HUH Airbus A321-211 1021 ex EC-HAC Benidorm
☐ EC-HUI Airbus A321-211 1027 ex EC-HAE Comunidad Autonoma de la Rioja
☐ EC-IGK Airbus A321-211 1572 ex EC-HTF Costa Calida
☐ EC-IIG Airbus A321-211 1554 ex EC-HTE Ciudad de Siguenza
☐ EC-IJN Airbus A321-211 1836 ex D-AVZN Merida
☐ EC-ILO Airbus A321-211 1681 ex D-AVZW Cueva de Nerja
☐ EC-ILP Airbus A321-211 1716 ex D-AVZT Peniscola
☐ EC-ITN Airbus A321-211 2115 ex D-AVXG Empuries
☐ EC-IXD Airbus A321-211 2220 ex D-AVZR Valle de Aran
☐ EC-JDM Airbus A321-211 2357 ex D-AVZV Cantabria
☐ EC-JDR Airbus A321-211 2488 ex D-AVXD Sierra Cebollera
☐ EC-JEJ Airbus A321-211 2381 ex D-AVZI Riofrio
☐ EC-JGS Airbus A321-211 2472 ex D-AVXA Guadalupe
☐ EC-JLI Airbus A321-211 2563 ex D-AVZB Delta Del Llobregat
☐ EC-JMR Airbus A321-211 2599 ex D-AVZL Aranjuez
☐ EC-JNI Airbus A321-211 2270 ex D-AVZA Palmeral de Elche
☐ EC-JQZ Airbus A321-211 2736 ex D-AVZJ Generalife
☐ EC-JRE Airbus A321-211 2756 ex D-AVZA Villa de Uncastillo
☐ EC-JZM Airbus A321-211 2996 ex D-AVZP Aquila Imperial

☐ EC- Airbus A330-341 144 ex PK-GPD on order

☐ EC-GGS Airbus A340-313 125 ex EC-154 Concha Espina
☐ EC-GHX Airbus A340-313 134 ex EC-155 Rosalia de Castro
☐ EC-GJT Airbus A340-313 145 ex EC-156 Rosa Chacel
☐ EC-GLE Airbus A340-313 146 ex EC-157 Concepcion Arenal
☐ EC-GPB Airbus A340-313X 193 ex F-WWJR Teresa de Avila
☐ EC-GQK Airbus A340-313X 197 ex F-WWJL Emelia Pardo Bazan
☐ EC-GUP Airbus A340-313X 217 ex F-WWJG Agustina de Aragon
☐ EC-GUQ Airbus A340-313X 221 ex F-WWJA Beatriz Galindo
☐ EC-HDQ Airbus A340-313X 302 ex F-WWJU Sor Juana Ines de la Cruz
☐ EC-HGU Airbus A340-313X 318 ex F-WWJL Maria de Molina
☐ EC-HGV Airbus A340-313X 329 ex F-WWJP Maria Guerrero
☐ EC-HGX Airbus A340-313X 332 ex F-WWJR Maria Pita
☐ EC-HQF Airbus A340-313X 378 ex F-WWJI Maria de Zayas y Sotomayor
☐ EC-HQH Airbus A340-313X 387 ex F-WWJD Mariana de Silva
☐ EC-HQN Airbus A340-313X 414 ex F-WWJN Luisa Carvajal y Mendoza
☐ EC-ICF Airbus A340-313X 459 ex F-WWJU Maria Zambrano
☐ EC-IDF Airbus A340-313X 474 ex F-WWJG Mariana Pineda
☐ EC-IIH Airbus A340-313X 483 ex F-WWJI Maria Barbara de Braganza
☐ EC-KCL Airbus A340-311 005 ex F-GLZA
☐ EC-KOU Airbus A340-313 088 ex C-FTNQ
☐ EC-KSE Airbus A340-313X 170 ex C-FYLD

☐ EC-INO Airbus A340-642 431 ex F-WWCI Gaudi
☐ EC-IOB Airbus A340-642 440 ex F-WWCL Julio Romero de Torres
☐ EC-IQR Airbus A340-642 460 ex F-WWCO Salvador Dali
☐ EC-IZX Airbus A340-642 601 ex F-WWCS Mariano Benlliure
☐ EC-IZY Airbus A340-642 604 ex F-WWCH Ignacio de Zuloaga
☐ EC-JBA Airbus A340-642 606 ex F-WWCV Joaquin Rodrigo
☐ EC-JCY Airbus A340-642 617 ex F-WWCL Andres Segovia
☐ EC-JCZ Airbus A340-642 619 ex F-WWCP Vincente Aleixandre
☐ EC-JFX Airbus A340-642 672 ex F-WWCB Jacinto Benavente
☐ EC-JLE Airbus A340-642 702 ex F-WWCM Santiago Ramon y Cajal
☐ EC-JNQ Airbus A340-642 727 ex F-WWCV Antonio Machado
☐ EC-JPU Airbus A340-642 744 ex F-WWCF Pio Baroja
☐ EC- Airbus A340-642 960 ex F-WWCG Virgen de Montsserat stored LDE

☐ EC-KZI	Airbus A340-642	1017	ex F-WWCS		on order
☐ EC-LCZ	Airbus A340-642	993	ex F-WWCK		stored LDE
☐ EC-	Airbus A340-642	1079	ex F-WW		on order
☐ EC-	Airbus A340-642	1083	ex F-WW		on order

☐ EC-EXG	McDonnell-Douglas MD-87	49833/1706	ex EC-296	Ciudad de Almeria	
☐ EC-EXM	McDonnell-Douglas MD-87	49835/1717	ex EC-298	Ciudad de Zaragoza	stored MAD
☐ EC-FHD	McDonnell-Douglas MD-87	53212/1877	ex EC-638	Ciudad de Leon	
☐ EC-FIG	McDonnell-Douglas MD-88	53195/1929	ex EC-753	Penon de Ifach	stored MAD
☐ EC-FJE	McDonnell-Douglas MD-88	53197/1940	ex EC-755	Gibraltaro	stored MAD
☐ EC-FLN	McDonnell-Douglas MD-88	53303/1974	ex EC-945	Puerta de Tierra	
☐ EC-FOF	McDonnell-Douglas MD-88	53307/2015	ex EC-966	Puerta de Alcala	
☐ EC-FOZ	McDonnell-Douglas MD-88	53308/2022	ex EC-987	Montjuic	
☐ EC-FPD	McDonnell-Douglas MD-88	53309/2023	ex EC-988	Lago de Coradonga	stored MAD

IBERWORLD AIRLINES — Iberworld (TY/IWD) — Palma de Mallorca (PMI)

☐ EC-IMU	Airbus A320-214	1130	ex SE-RCD		
☐ EC-INZ	Airbus A320-214	2011	ex F-WWBR		
☐ EC-JQP	Airbus A320-214	2745	ex F-WWBO		
☐ EC-KYZ	Airbus A320-214	3758	ex F-WWBZ		
☐ EC-KZG	Airbus A320-214	3868	ex F-WWIC		
☐ EC-LAJ	Airbus A320-214	3889	ex F-WWBX		
☐ EC-LAQ	Airbus A320-214	3933	ex F-WWBU		

☐ EC-IJH	Airbus A330-322	072	ex D-AERG	Gloria Fluxa	
☐ EC-JHP	Airbus A330-343X	670	ex F-WWKU		
☐ EC-KCP	Airbus A330-343E	833	ex F-WWKO		

ISLAS AIRWAYS — Pintadera (IF/ISW) — Tenerife Norte (TNR)

☐ EC-IKQ	ATR 72-202	477	ex F-WQNM	La Palma	
☐ EC-JCD	ATR 72-202	452	ex F-WQND		retd?
☐ EC-KKZ	ATR 72-212	766	ex F-WWEE	Isla de Fuerteventura	
☐ EC-KNO	ATR 72-212	770	ex F-WWEI	Isla de Palma	
☐ EC-KUR	ATR 72-212A	808	ex F-WWES	Isla de Lanzarote	
☐ EC-	ATR 72-212		ex F-WW		on order
☐ EC-	ATR 72-212		ex F-WW		on order
☐ EC-	ATR 72-212		ex F-WW		on order

LANZAROTE AEROCARGO — Baraka (LZT) — Lanzarote-Arrecife (ACE)

☐ EC-IKM	Cessna 208B Caravan I	208B0948	ex D-FMCG		

MINT AIRWAYS

☐ EC-LBC	Boeing 757-28A	26276/704	ex TF-FIK	Tato Goya	

NAYSA AEROTAXIS — Naysa (ZN/NAY) — Las Palmas-Gran Canaria (LPA)

☐ EC-GQF	ATR 72-202	489	ex F-WWLJ		Lsd to/op for IBB
☐ EC-GRP	ATR 72-202	488	ex F-WWLI		Lsd to/op for IBB
☐ EC-GRU	ATR 72-202	493	ex F-WWLN		Lsd to/op for IBB
☐ EC-HEZ	ATR 72-212A	582	ex F-WWEL	Montana del Fuego	op for IBB
☐ EC-IJO	Beech 1900D	UE-300	ex F-GRPM	Garajonal	
☐ EC-IPJ	ATR 72-202	307	ex F-GKOC		Lsd to/op for IBB
☐ EC-KGI	ATR 72-212A	752	ex F-WWEM		Lsd to/op for IBB
☐ EC-KGJ	ATR 72-212A	753	ex F-WWEN		Lsd to/op for IBB
☐ EC-KRY	ATR 72-212A	795	ex F-WWEV	Azero	Lsd to/op for IBB
☐ EC-KSG	ATR 72-212A	796	ex F-WW		Lsd to/op for IBB
☐ EC-KYI	ATR 72-212A	850	ex F-WWET	Guarapo	Lsd to/op for IBB
☐ EC-LAD	ATR 72-212A	864	ex F-WWEJ	Baifo	Lsd to/op for IBB

PANAIR LINEAS AEREAS — Skyjet (PV/PNR) — Madrid-Barajas (MAD)

☐ EC-ELT	British Aerospace 146 Srs.200QT	E2102	ex EC-198		
☐ EC-FVY	British Aerospace 146 Srs.200QT	E2117	ex EC-615		
☐ EC-FZE	British Aerospace 146 Srs.200QT	E2105	ex EC-719		
☐ EC-GQO	British Aerospace 146 Srs.200QT	E2086	ex D-ADEI		
☐ EC-HDH	British Aerospace 146 Srs.200QT	E2056	ex G-TNTA		
☐ EC-HJH	British Aerospace 146 Srs.200QT	E2112	ex G-BOMK		

☐ EC-HQT	Airbus A300B4-103F	124	ex G-TNTS		stored MHV

PIRINAIR EXPRESS — Pirinair Express (PRN) — Zaragoza (ZAZ)

☐ EC-FZB	Swearingen SA.226TC Metro II	TC-221	ex EC-666		
☐ EC-JCV	Swearingen SA.226AT Merlin IVA	AT-038	ex SX-BGT		

PRONAIR AIRLINES — Valencia (VLC)

	Registration	Type	c/n	Previous identity	Name	Remarks
☐	EC-KJI	McDonnell-Douglas MD-87	49836/1721	ex EC-EXN	Ciudad de Torretallada	
☐	EC-KRP	Boeing 747-245F	20826/242	ex EC-KMR		
☐	EC-KRV	McDonnell-Douglas MD-87	49843/1771	ex EC-EZS		

PULLMANTUR AIR — Pullmantur (PLM) — Madrid-Barajas (MAD)

	Registration	Type	c/n	Previous identity	Name	Remarks
☐	EC-KQC	Boeing 747-412	26549/1030	ex 9V-SMZ		
☐	EC-KSM	Boeing 747-412	27178/1015	ex 9V-SMW		
☐	EC-KXN	Boeing 747-4H6	25703/1025	ex N703AC		

QUANTUM AIR — Palma de Mallorca (PMI)

	Registration	Type	c/n	Previous identity	Name	Remarks
☐	EC-HNY	Boeing 717-2CM	55059/5023	ex N6203U	Formentor	
☐	EC-HNZ	Boeing 717-2CM	55060/5026	ex N9010L	Espalmador	
☐	EC-HOA	Boeing 717-2CM	55061/5029		Macarella	
☐	EC-HUZ	Boeing 717-23S	55066/5054		Valdemossa	
☐	EC-JZX	Boeing 717-23S	55065/5048	ex SX-BOC	Es Vedra	stored PMI
☐	EC-KFR	Boeing 717-2K9	55056/5015	ex SX-BOA		
☐	EC-KHX	Boeing 717-2K9	55053/5016	ex SX-BOB		
☐	EC-KNE	Boeing 717-23S	55064/5037	ex HS-PGP		
☐	EC-KRO	Boeing 717-23S	55067/5059	ex HS-PGO		

RYJET — Malaga (AGP)

	Registration	Type	c/n	Previous identity	Name	Remarks
☐	EC-JHE	SAAB SF.340A	340A-018	ex SE-LMV		

SAESA — Saesa (SSS) — Madrid-Cuatro Vientos

	Registration	Type	c/n	Previous identity	Name	Remarks
☐	EC-IEU	Bell 205A-1	30083	ex PT-HCR		

SAICUS AIR — (FYA) — Palma de Mallorca (PMI)

	Registration	Type	c/n	Previous identity	Name	Remarks
☐	EC-JUV	Boeing 737-301 (SF)	23741/1498	ex N576US		
☐	EC-KKJ	Boeing 737-4B7 (SF)	24559/1847	ex N437US		stored PMI

SERAIR — Cargopress (SEV) — Las Palmas-Gran Canaria (LPA)

	Registration	Type	c/n	Previous identity	Name	Remarks
☐	EC-GTM	Beech 1900C	UB-30	ex N7210R		
☐	EC-GUD	Beech 1900C-1	UC-156	ex N156YV		
☐	EC-GZG	Beech 1900C-1	UC-161	ex N55635		
☐	EC-JDY	Beech 1900C-1	UC-91	ex N91YV		

SPANAIR — Spanair (JK/JKK) — Palma de Mallorca (PMI)

Member of Star Alliance

	Registration	Type	c/n	Previous identity	Name	Remarks
☐	EC-HPM	Airbus A321-231	1276	ex D-AVZO	Camilo Jose Cela	
☐	EC-HQZ	Airbus A321-231	1333	ex D-AVZB		
☐	EC-HRG	Airbus A321-231	1366	ex D-AVZC	Placido Domingo	
☐	EC-HRP	Airbus A320-232	1349	ex F-WWBD	Juan de Avalos	
☐	EC-HXA	Airbus A320-232	1497	ex F-WWID		
☐	EC-IAZ	Airbus A320-232	1631	ex F-WWDP		
☐	EC-ICL	Airbus A320-232	1682	ex F-WWBD		
☐	EC-IEJ	Airbus A320-232	1749	ex F-WWBO		
☐	EC-IIZ	Airbus A320-232	1862	ex F-WWDZ	Club Vacaciones titles	
☐	EC-IJU	Airbus A321-231	1843	ex D-AVZR		
☐	EC-ILH	Airbus A320-232	1914	ex F-WWDU		Star Alliance c/s
☐	EC-IMB	Airbus A320-232	1933	ex F-WWII	Vodafone Passport titles	
☐	EC-INB	Airbus A321-231	1946	ex D-AVXD	X TeNeRife titles	
☐	EC-INM	Airbus A320-232	1979	ex F-WWBE		Star Alliance c/s
☐	EC-IOH	Airbus A320-232	1998	ex F-WWIV		Star Alliance c/s
☐	EC-IPI	Airbus A320-232	2027	ex F-WWDP		Star Alliance c/s
☐	EC-IVG	Airbus A320-232	2168	ex F-WWDA		
☐	EC-IYG	Airbus A320-232	2210	ex F-WWBG		
☐	EC-IZK	Airbus A320-232	2223	ex F-WWDO	Reyno de Navarra titles	
☐	EC-JJD	Airbus A320-232	2479	ex F-WWIM	Costa Brava titles	
☐	EC-JNC	Airbus A320-232	2589	ex F-WWDP	Juan Antonio Samaranch	
☐	EC-KEC	Airbus A320-232	1183	ex G-MIDW		
☐	EC-KOX	Airbus A320-232	1383	ex G-MIDV		
☐	EC-KPX	Airbus A320-232	1407	ex G-MIDU		on order
☐	EC-FTS	McDonnell-Douglas MD-83	49621/1495	ex EC-479	Sunbird	
☐	EC-GCV	McDonnell-Douglas MD-82	53165/2042	ex EC-894	Sunburst	
☐	EC-GNY	McDonnell-Douglas MD-83	49396/1305	ex N396GE	Sunflash	
☐	EC-GOM	McDonnell-Douglas MD-83	49579/1465	ex EC-EIG	Sunlight	Star Alliance c/s
☐	EC-GQG	McDonnell-Douglas MD-83	49577/1454	ex EC-FSY		Star Alliance c/s
☐	EC-GVO	McDonnell-Douglas MD-83	49642/1421	ex N462GE	Sunspot	
☐	EC-GXU	McDonnell-Douglas MD-83	49622/1498	ex EC-FTT		Star Alliance c/s
☐	EC-HOV	McDonnell-Douglas MD-82	49416/1271	ex HL7543	Sunspeed	

☐ EC-JSU	McDonnell-Douglas MD-87	49610/1505	ex LN-RMK		Lsd fr SAS
☐ EC-KAZ	McDonnell-Douglas MD-87	49614/1556	ex OY-KHI	Star Alliance c/s	Lsd fr SAS
☐ EC-KCZ	McDonnell-Douglas MD-87	49609/1517	ex OY-KHF	Star Alliance c/s	Lsd fr SAS
☐ EC-KHA	McDonnell-Douglas MD-87	49611/1522	ex LN-RMG	Star Alliance c/s	Lsd fr SAS
☐ EC-KJE	McDonnell-Douglas MD-87	49606/1569	ex SE-DIF	Star Alliance c/s	Lsd fr SAS
☐ EC-KVA	McDonnell-Douglas MD-87	53208/1865	ex EC-FEY		stored MAD

SWIFTAIR — Swift (SWT) — Madrid-Barajas (MAD)

☐ EC-INV	ATR 72-201	274	ex N274AT	Freighter; for SWN
☐ EC-ISX	ATR 42-320	242	ex N242AT	Freighter; no titles
☐ EC-IVP	ATR 42-300	231	ex F-GKND	Freighter
☐ EC-IYH	ATR 72-212	330	ex F-WQUI	Freighter
☐ EC-JAD	ATR 42-300	321	ex F-GHPY	
☐ EC-JBN	ATR 42-300 (QC)	218	ex F-GHPK	all-white
☐ EC-JBX	ATR 42-300	254	ex N255AE	Freighter
☐ EC-JDX	ATR 72-201	234	ex F-GHPV	Freighter; all-white
☐ EC-JQF	ATR 72-201F	147	ex SE-LVK	
☐ EC-JRP	ATR 72-212	446	ex D-AEWK	
☐ EC-JXF	ATR 72-201F	150	ex OY-CIV	
☐ EC-KAD	ATR 72-202F	171	ex F-GKPC	
☐ EC-KAE	ATR 72-202F	192	ex F-GKPE	
☐ EC-KAI	ATR 42-300F	141	ex EI-FXF	
☐ EC-KIZ	ATR 72-202F	204	ex F-GPOA	Lsd fr FPO
☐ EC-KJA	ATR 72-202F	207	ex F-GPOB	Lsd fr FPO
☐ EC-KKQ	ATR 72-212A	763	ex F-WWEB	
☐ EC-KUL	ATR 72-212A	809	ex F-WWET	Lsd to AEE
☐ EC-KVI	ATR 72-212A	824	ex F-WWEM	Lsd to AEE
☐ EC-GQA	Embraer EMB-120ER Brasilia	120027	ex EC-GMT	Freighter
☐ EC-HAK	Embraer EMB-120ER Brasilia	120008	ex N212AS	Freighter
☐ EC-HCF	Embraer EMB.120ER Brasilia	120007	ex N211AS	Freighter
☐ EC-HFK	Embraer EMB.120ER Brasilia	120063	ex N7215U	Freighter
☐ EC-HMY	Embraer EMB.120ER Brasilia	120009	ex N214AS	Freighter, all-white
☐ EC-HTS	Embraer EMB.120ER Brasilia	120168	ex N168CA	Freighter
☐ EC-IMX	Embraer EMB.120ER Brasilia	120158	ex N312FV	Freighter
☐ EC-JBD	Embraer EMB.120ER Brasilia	120012	ex D-CAOB	Freighter
☐ EC-JBE	Embraer EMB.120ER Brasilia	120013	ex D-CAOA	Freighter
☐ EC-JKH	Embraer EMB.120ER Brasilia	120092	ex OM-SPY	
☐ EC-JJS	McDonnell-Douglas MD-83	49793/1656	ex N827NK	Lsd to United Nations
☐ EC-JQV	McDonnell-Douglas MD-83	49526/1342	ex N14879	Real Madrid c/s
☐ EC-JUF	McDonnell-Douglas MD-83	53168/2061	ex N802NK	Op for UN
☐ EC-JUG	McDonnell-Douglas MD-83	49847/1585	ex N834NK	Op for UN
☐ EC-KCX	McDonnell-Douglas MD-83	49619/1483	ex N814NK	
☐ EC-KSF	McDonnell-Douglas MD-87	53207/1862	ex EC-FEZ	
☐ EC-IMY	Boeing 727-225 (FedEx 3)	21293/1241	ex N8875Z	pax aircraft
☐ EC-JHU	Boeing 727-230F (FedEx 3)	21442/1326	ex N302FV	
☐ EC-KDY	Boeing 737-3S3F	23811/1445	ex N811AN	
☐ EC-KLR	Boeing 737-3Q8 (SF)	23766/1375	ex N237CP	
☐ EC-KRA	Boeing 737-3Y0F	24679/1897	ex SX-BGK	
☐ EC-KTZ	Boeing 737-375F	23708/1395	ex N111KH	
☐ EC-KVD	Boeing 737-306F	23538/1288	ex N102KH	
☐ EC-LAC	Boeing 737-3M8F	24022/1662	ex N107KH	

TAF HELICOPTERS — Helitaf (HET) — Barcelona (BCN)

☐ EC-DRG	Aérospatiale AS350B Ecureuil	1597			
☐ EC-ERD	Aérospatiale AS350B Ecureuil	1530	ex G-JORR		EMS
☐ EC-EZP	Aérospatiale AS350B Ecureuil	2413	ex EC-562		
☐ EC-FOA	Aérospatiale AS350BA Ecureuil	2626	ex EC-990		
☐ EC-FOQ	Aérospatiale AS350BA Ecureuil	2639	ex EC-906		
☐ EC-IHX	Aérospatiale AS350B3 Ecureuil	3587	ex F-WQRN	06	EMS
☐ EC-IOI	Aérospatiale AS350B3 Ecureuil	3640	ex F-WQDH		
☐ EC-IPC	Aérospatiale AS350B3 Ecureuil	3710			
☐ EC-JEA	Aérospatiale AS350B3 Ecureuil	3819	ex SE-JHX		
☐ EC-KFU	Aérospatiale AS350B3 Ecureuil	4251	ex SE-JJO		
☐ EC-KJF	Aérospatiale AS350B3 Ecureuil	4088	ex SE-JJJ		
☐ EC-IFU	Eurocopter EC135P2	0223			EMS
☐ EC-IQZ	Eurocopter EC135P2	0293			EMS
☐ EC-JJI	Eurocopter EC135P2	0383			
☐ EC-JVS	Eurocopter EC135P2	0436			
☐ EC-KDA	Eurocopter EC135P2+	0538			
☐ EC-DSU	MBB Bo.105CBS-5	S-623	ex D-HDSS	02	EMS
☐ EC-FYV	MBB Bo.105CBS-5	S-896	ex EC-705	01	EMS
☐ EC-HNT	MBB Bo.105CBS-4	S-414	ex D-HDMA		EMS
☐ EC-HPB	MBB Bo.105CBS-4	S-672	ex D-HEIM		EMS
☐ EC-IKO	MBB Bo.105CBS-4	S-661	ex D-HGYN		EMS
☐ EC-IKT	MBB Bo.105CBS	S-615	ex D-HEMS		EMS

☐ EC-GUH	Aérospatiale AS355F2 Twin Star	5474	ex N6040U		EMS
☐ EC-GUZ	Aérospatiale AS355F2 Twin Star	5454	ex N26ET		
☐ EC-IKV	Eurocopter EC130B4	3753			

TAS TRANSPORTES AEREOS DEL SUR					
☐ EC-KEK	CASA CN-235-300MPA	C166	ex EC-101		Op for SASEMA
☐ EC-KEL	CASA CN-235-300MPA	169	ex EC-027		Op for SASEMA
☐ EC-KEM	CASA CN-235-300MPA	171	ex EC-021		Op for SASEMA

TAVASA		***Tavasa (TVH)***			***Bilbao (BIO)***
☐ EC-EBB	Aérospatiale SA365C3 Dauphin 2	5013	ex F-GBOU		
☐ EC-EGV	Aérospatiale SA365C3 Dauphin 2	5032	ex F-GBTB		
☐ EC-ERY	Sikorsky S-76A+	760037	ex EC-364		
☐ EC-ERZ	Aérospatiale AS350B2 Ecureuil	2261			
☐ EC-GMZ	Eurocopter EC135T1	0016	ex D-HECG		
☐ EC-GNA	Eurocopter EC135T1	0017	ex D-HECH		

TOP-FLY		***Topfly (TLY)***			***Barcelona (BCN)***
☐ EC-EYV	Piper PA-34-220T Seneca III	34-8233109	ex OE-FYB		
☐ EC-GJM	Swearingen SA.227AC Metro III	BC-772B	ex N439MA		
☐ EC-HZM	Piper PA-34-200 Seneca	34-7250169	ex F-GFJE		
☐ EC-IDG	ATR 42-320	003	ex F-WQNE		all-white
☐ EC-IRS	Swearingen SA.227BC Metro III	BC-786B	ex N61AJ		
☐ EC-ITP	Swearingen SA.227BC Metro III	BC-789B	ex ZS-PDW		
☐ EC-JYJ	Aérospatiale AS355F2 Twin Star	5425	ex N225NR		

TRAGSA MEDIOS AEREOS		***Tragsa (TRG)***			***Madrid-Cuatro Vientos/Toledo***
☐ EC-HTV	Bell 212	30665	ex N212HS		
☐ EC-HTX	Bell 212	31151	ex N8169Q		
☐ EC-HUS	Bell 212	30655	ex D-HAFS		
☐ EC-HXR	Agusta-Bell 212	5522	ex D-HAFG		
☐ EC-IAV	Bell 212	30534	ex N7964J		
☐ EC-IGR	Bell 212	30989	ex N1074C		
☐ EC-ERK	Bell 204 (UH-1E)	6069	ex N151LC		
☐ EC-GSO	Bell UH-1H	5466	ex N1217A		
☐ EC-GUT	Bell UH-1H	13367	ex N21UH		
☐ EC-GXF	Bell UH-1H	12604	ex N22UH		

TRANPORTES AEREOS DEL SUR		***TAS (HSS)***			***Seville (SVQ)***
☐ EC-GHS	Partenavia P.68 Observer	329-20-OB	ex G-OBSV		
☐ EC-GSQ	Beech B300 Super King Air	FL-128	ex N128FL		
☐ EC-HAP	CASA C.212-300MPA	465	ex EC-011		Maritime Patrol
☐ EC-HTU	CASA C.212-300MPA	470			Maritime Patrol
☐ EC-IFL	Partenavia P.68C	412	ex N412VR		
☐ EC-ILE	Beech B200 Super King Air	BB-1792	ex N5092K	Muxtamel	EMS
☐ EC-INX	CASA C.212-300MPA	472			Maritime Patrol
☐ EC-IUX	Beech B200 Super King Air	BB-1840	ex N816LD		

VUELING AIRLINES		***Vueling (VY/VLG)***			***Barcelona (BCN)***
☐ EC-GRG	Airbus A320-211	0143	ex EC-FBS		
☐ EC-GRH	Airbus A320-211	0146	ex EC-FBR		
☐ EC-GRI	Airbus A320-211	0177	ex EC-FEO		
☐ EC-HHA	Airbus A320-214	1221	ex F-WWBF		
☐ EC-HQI	Airbus A320-214	1396	ex F-WWIX		
☐ EC-HQJ	Airbus A320-214	1430	ex F-WWBR		
☐ EC-HQL	Airbus A320-214	1461	ex F-WWDD	Click on Vueling	
☐ EC-HTD	Airbus A320-214	1550	ex F-WWDC	Unos vuelan, ostros Vueling	
☐ EC-ICQ	Airbus A320-211	0199	ex EC-FGU		
☐ EC-ICR	Airbus A320-211	0240	ex EC-FIA		
☐ EC-ICS	Airbus A320-211	0241	ex EC-FIC		
☐ EC-ICT	Airbus A320-211	0264	ex EC-FKD		
☐ EC-IZD	Airbus A320-214	2207	ex F-WWDS	Barceloning	
☐ EC-JAB	Airbus A320-214	2227	ex F-WWIG	Born to be Vueling	
☐ EC-JFF	Airbus A320-214	2388	ex F-WWIH	Vueling the world	
☐ EC-JGM	Airbus A320-214	2407	ex F-WWDC	The joy of Vueling	
☐ EC-JSY	Airbus A320-214	2785	ex F-WWBU	Connie Baraja	
☐ EC-JTQ	Airbus A320-214	2794	ex F-WWBN	Vueling, que es gerundio	
☐ EC-JTR	Airbus A320-214	2798	ex F-WWIF	no Vueling, no party	
☐ EC-JYX	Airbus A320-214	2962	ex F-WWDJ	Elisenda Masana	
☐ EC-JZI	Airbus A320-214	2988	ex F-WWII	Vueling in love	
☐ EC-JZQ	Airbus A320-214	0992	ex TC-JLE	I Want to Vueling	
☐ EC-KBU	Airbus A320-214	1413	ex TC-JLF	Be Vueling my friend	
☐ EC-KCU	Airbus A320-216	3109	ex F-WWIR	My name is Ling. Vue Ling	
☐ EC-KDG	Airbus A320-214	3095	ex F-WWIY		

	Reg	Type	c/n	Previous	Name / Notes
☐	EC-KDH	Airbus A320-214	3083	ex F-WWIX	Ain't no Vueling high enough
☐	EC-KDT	Airbus A320-216	3145	ex F-WWBM	Ready, steady, Vueling
☐	EC-KDX	Airbus A320-216	3151	ex F-WWBU	
☐	EC-KFI	Airbus A320-216	3174	ex F-WWIP	
☐	EC-KHN	Airbus A320-216	3203	ex F-WWIG	
☐	EC-KJD	Airbus A320-216	3237	ex F-WWBJ	
☐	EC-KKT	Airbus A320-214	3293	ex F-WWDU	Vueling Together
☐	EC-KLB	Airbus A320-214	3321	ex F-WWBY	Vuela y punto
☐	EC-KLT	Airbus A320-216	3376	ex F-WWDI	
☐	EC-KMI	Airbus A320-216	3400	ex F-WWBT	How are you? I'm Vueling!
☐	EC-KRH	Airbus A320-214	3529	ex D-AVVD	
☐	EC-LAA	Airbus A320-214	2678	ex A6-ABZ	
☐	EC-LAB	Airbus A320-214	2761	ex OE-LEV	

VUELOS MEDITERRANEO — *Vuelos Mediterraneo (VMM)* — *Valencia (VLC)*

	Reg	Type	c/n	Previous
☐	EC-FCC	Cessna 402B II	402B1013	ex EC-614
☐	EC-HCU	Swearingen SA.226TC Metro II	TC-390	ex N19WP

ZOREX — *Zorex (ORZ)* — *Madrid-Barajas (MAD)*

	Reg	Type	c/n	Previous
☐	EC-GPE	Swearingen SA.226TC Metro II	TC-273	ex OY-JER
☐	EC-HJC	Swearingen SA.226TC Metro II	TC-318	ex OY-JEO
☐	EC-JYC	Swearingen SA.226TC Metro II	TC-303	ex N117AR

EI- IRELAND (Eire)

AER ARANN — *Aer Arann (RE/REA)* — *Dublin (DUB)*

	Reg	Type	c/n	Previous	Notes
☐	EI-BYO	ATR 42-310	161	ex OY-CIS	
☐	EI-CBK	ATR 42-310	199	ex F-WWEM	
☐	EI-CPT	ATR 42-300	191	ex (SE-KCX)	
☐	EI-CVR	ATR 42-310	022	ex F-GGLK	
☐	EI-EHH	ATR 42-300	196	ex G-SSEA	
☐	EI-REH	ATR 72-202	260	ex OY-RTA	
☐	EI-REI	ATR 72-202	267	ex OY-RTB	
☐	EI-REL	ATR 72-212A	748	ex F-WWEI	
☐	EI-REM	ATR 72-212A	760	ex F-WWEW	Lsd to WBA
☐	EI-REO	ATR 72-212A	787	ex F-WWEF	
☐	EI-REP	ATR 72-212A	797	ex F-WWEZ	
☐	EI-RES	ATR 72-212A		ex F-WW	on order
☐	EI-RET	ATR 72-212A		ex F-WW	on order
☐	EI-REU	ATR 72-212A		ex F-WW	on order
☐	EI-REV	ATR 72-212A		ex F-WW	on order

AER ARANN ISLANDS — *Galway (GWY)*

	Reg	Type	c/n	Previous
☐	EI-AYN	Britten-Norman BN-2A-8 Islander	704	ex G-BBFJ
☐	EI-BCE	Britten-Norman BN-2A-26 Islander	519	ex G-BDUV
☐	EI-CUW	Britten-Norman BN-2B-26 Islander	2293	ex G-BWYW

AER LINGUS — *Shamrock (EI/EIN)* — *Dublin (DUB)*

	Reg	Type	c/n	Previous	Name
☐	EI-CVA	Airbus A320-214	1242	ex F-WWIT	St Schira/Scire
☐	EI-CVB	Airbus A320-214	1394	ex F-WWIV	St Mobhi/Mobhi
☐	EI-CVC	Airbus A320-214	1443	ex F-WWBS	St Kealin/Caolfhionn
☐	EI-CVD	Airbus A320-214	1467	ex F-WWDG	St Kevin/Caoimhin
☐	EI-DEA	Airbus A320-214	2191	ex F-WWBX	St Fidelma/Fiedeilme
☐	EI-DEB	Airbus A320-214	2206	ex F-WWBP	St Nathy/Naithi
☐	EI-DEC	Airbus A320-214	2217	ex F-WWBH	St Fergal/Fearghal
☐	EI-DEE	Airbus A320-214	2250	ex F-WWBE	St Ultan/Ultan
☐	EI-DEF	Airbus A320-214	2256	ex F-WWBK	St Declan/Deaglan
☐	EI-DEG	Airbus A320-214	2272	ex F-WWIB	St Fachtna/Fachtna
☐	EI-DEH	Airbus A320-214	2294	ex F-WWBX	St Conleth/Connlaodh
☐	EI-DEI	Airbus A320-214	2374	ex F-WWDU	St Oliver Plunkett/Oilibh Plunceid
☐	EI-DEJ	Airbus A320-214	2364	ex F-WWDI	St Kilian/Cillian
☐	EI-DEK	Airbus A320-214	2399	ex F-WWIZ	St Eunan/Eunan
☐	EI-DEL	Airbus A320-214	2409	ex F-WWDE	St Canice/Cainneach
☐	EI-DEM	Airbus A320-214	2411	ex F-WWDG	St Ibar/Ibhar
☐	EI-DEN	Airbus A320-214	2432	ex F-WWBK	St Kieran/Ciaran
☐	EI-DEO	Airbus A320-214	2486	ex F-WWIV	St Senan/Seanan
☐	EI-DEP	Airbus A320-214	2542	ex F-WWIU	St Eugene/Eoghan
☐	EI-DER	Airbus A320-214	2583	ex F-WWDE	St Mel/Mel
☐	EI-DES	Airbus A320-214	2635	ex F-WWDZ	St Pappin/Paipan
☐	EI-DET	Airbus A320-214	2810	ex F-WWIP	St Brendan/Breandan
☐	EI-DVE	Airbus A320-214	3129	ex F-WWBJ	St Aideen/Etaoin
☐	EI-DVF	Airbus A320-214	3136	ex F-WWDF	St Jarlath/Iarfhlaith
☐	EI-DVG	Airbus A320-214	3318	ex F-WWIV	St Flannan/Flannan
☐	EI-DVH	Airbus A320-214	3345	ex F-WWBP	
☐	EI-DVI	Airbus A320-214	3501	ex F-WWBQ	St Emer/Eimaer

Registration	Type	C/n	Previous identity	Name	Remarks
☐ EI-DVJ	Airbus A320-214	3857	ex F-WWDL	St Macarthan/Macarthain	
☐ EI-EDP	Airbus A320-214	3781	ex F-WWIR		
☐ EI-EDS	Airbus A320-214	3755	ex F-WWBU	St Malachy/Maolmhaodhog	
☐ EI-CPC	Airbus A321-211	0815	ex D-AVZT	St Fergus/Feargus	
☐ EI-CPD	Airbus A321-211	0841	ex D-AVZA	St Davnet/Damhnat	
☐ EI-CPE	Airbus A321-211	0926	ex D-AVZQ	St Enda/Eanna	
☐ EI-CPF	Airbus A321-211	0991	ex D-AVZE	St Ida/Ide	
☐ EI-CPG	Airbus A321-211	1023	ex D-AVZR	St Aidan/Aodhan	
☐ EI-CPH	Airbus A321-211	1094	ex F-WWDD	St Dervilla/Dearbhile	
☐ EI-DAA	Airbus A330-202	397	ex F-WWKK	St Keeva/Caoimhe	
☐ EI-DUO	Airbus A330-202	841	ex F-WWYT	St Columba/Colum	
☐ EI-DUZ	Airbus A330-302	847	ex F-WWKM	St Aoife/Aoife	
☐ EI-EAV	Airbus A330-302	985	ex F-WWKF	Ronan	
☐ EI-EDY	Airbus A330-302	1025	ex F-WWYU	Maincin	
☐ EI-LAX	Airbus A330-202	269	ex F-WWKV	St Mella/Mella	
☐ EI-ORD	Airbus A330-301	059	ex F-GMDD	St Maeve/Maedbh	
☐ EI-	Airbus A330-302	1120	ex F-WW		on order

AIR CONTRACTORS — *Contract / Rapex (AG/ABR)* — *Dublin (DUB)*

Registration	Type	C/n	Previous identity	Remarks
☐ EI-DHL	Airbus A300B4-203F	274	ex OO-DIB	
☐ EI-EAC	Airbus A300B4-203F	250	ex OO-DLT	
☐ EI-EAD	Airbus A300B4-203F	289	ex OO-DLU	
☐ EI-OZB	Airbus A300B4-103F	184	ex OO-DIH	
☐ EI-OZC	Airbus A300B4-103F	189	ex OO-DIJ	
☐ EI-OZD	Airbus A300B4-203F	236	ex OO-DLE	
☐ EI-OZF	Airbus A300B4-203F	259	ex OO-DLD	
☐ EI-OZH	Airbus A300B4-203F	234	ex OO-DLI	
☐ EI-SAF	Airbus A300B4-203F	220	ex OO-DIC	
☐ EI-FXA	ATR 42-320F	282	ex N282AT	Lsd fr/op for FDX
☐ EI-FXB	ATR 42-320F	243	ex (N924FX)	Lsd fr/op for FDX
☐ EI-FXC	ATR 42-320F	310	ex (N925FX)	Lsd fr/op for FDX
☐ EI-FXD	ATR 42-300F	273	ex (N927FX)	Lsd fr/op for FDX
☐ EI-FXE	ATR 42-320F	327	ex (N926FX)	Lsd fr/op for FDX
☐ EI-FXG	ATR 72-202F	224	ex (N814FX)	Lsd fr/op for FDX
☐ EI-FXH	ATR 72-202F	229	ex N815FX	Lsd fr/op for FDX
☐ EI-FXI	ATR 72-202F	294	ex N818FX	Lsd fr/op for FDX
☐ EI-FXJ	ATR 72-202F	292	ex N813FX	Lsd fr/op for FDX
☐ EI-FXK	ATR 72-202F	256	ex N817FX	Lsd fr/op for FDX
☐ EI-REJ	ATR 72-202F	126	ex ES-KRA	
☐ EI-SLA	ATR 42-300F	149	ex SE-LST	Lsd to MSA
☐ EI-SLC	ATR 42-300F	082	ex OY-CIE	Lsd to MSA
☐ EI-SLF	ATR 72-202F	210	ex OY-RUA	
☐ EI-SLG	ATR 72-202F	183	ex F-WQNI	
☐ EI-SLH	ATR 72-202F	157	ex OY-RTG	
☐ EI-SLJ	ATR 72-201	324	ex LY-PTK	
☐ EI-SLK	ATR 72-212	395	ex N642AS	
☐ EI-SLL	ATR 72-212	387	ex N641AS	
☐ EI-SLM	ATR 72-212	413	ex N643AS	
☐ EI-	ATR 72-212	405	ex N640AS	on order
☐ EI-JIV	Lockheed L-382G-35C Hercules	4673	ex ZS-JIV	Lsd fr SFR

CHC IRELAND — *Dublin (DUB)*

Registration	Type	C/n	Previous identity	Remarks
☐ EI-CXS	Sikorsky S-61N	61816	ex IAC 257	IMES Rescue based Sligo
☐ EI-CZN	Sikorsky S-61N	61740	ex G-CBWC	IMES Rescue standby
☐ EI-GCE	Sikorsky S-61N	61817	ex LN-ORC	IMES Rescue based Shannon
☐ EI-MES	Sikorsky S-61N	61776	ex G-BXAE	IMES Rescue based Dublin
☐ EI-RCG	Sikorsky S-61N	61807	ex G-87-1	IMES Rescue based Shannon
☐ EI-SAR	Sikorsky S-61N	61143	ex G-AYOM	IMES Rescue based Waterford
☐ EI-MIP	Aérospatiale SA365N2 Dauphin 2	6119	ex G-BLEY	

CITYJET — *City-Ireland (WX/BCY)* — *Dublin (DUB)*

Registration	Type	C/n	Previous identity	Name	Remarks
☐ EI-RJA	Avro 146-RJ85	E2329	ex G-CDYK	Rathlin Island	
☐ EI-RJB	Avro 146-RJ85	E2330	ex G-CEBS	Bere Island	
☐ EI-RJC	Avro 146-RJ85	E2333	ex G-CEHA	Achill Island	
☐ EI-RJD	Avro 146-RJ85	E2334	ex G-CEFL	Valentia Island	
☐ EI-RJE	Avro 146-RJ85	E2335	ex G-CEBU	St MacDara's Island	
☐ EI-RJF	Avro 146-RJ85	E2337	ex G-CEFN	Great Blasket Island	stored NWI
☐ EI-RJG	Avro 146-RJ85	E2344	ex G-CEHB	Sherkin Island	
☐ EI-RJH	Avro 146-RJ85	E2345	ex G-CEIC	Inishturkon order	
☐ EI-RJI	Avro 146-RJ85	E2346	ex (G-CDZP)	Skellig Michael	
☐ EI-RJJ	Avro 146-RJ85	E2347	ex G-CEIF	Hare Island	
☐ EI-RJK	Avro 146-RJ85	E2348	ex N523XJ	Collanmore Island	
☐ EI-RJN	Avro 146-RJ85	E2351	ex N526XJ	Lake Isle of Inisheer	CityJet c/s
☐ EI-RJO	Avro 146-RJ85	E2352	ex N527XJ	Inis Mor	

☐ EI-RJP	Avro 146-RJ85	E2363	ex N529XJ	Clare Island	
☐ EI-RJR	Avro 146-RJ85	E2364	ex N530XJ	Tory Island	
☐ EI-RJS	Avro 146-RJ85	E2365	ex N531XJ	Dursey Island	CityJet c/s
☐ EI-RJT	Avro 146-RJ85	E2366	ex N532XJ	Inishbofin	CityJet c/s
☐ EI-RJU	Avro 146-RJ85	E2367	ex N533XJ	Cape Clear	
☐ EI-RJV	Avro 146-RJ85	E2370	ex N534XJ	Lambay Island	
☐ EI-RJW	Avro 146-RJ85	E2371	ex N535XJ	Garinish Island	
☐ EI-RJX	Avro 146-RJ85	E2372	ex N536XJ	Scattery Island	
☐ EI-RJY	Avro 146-RJ85	E2307	ex N502XJ	Inishcealira	
☐ EI-RJZ	Avro 146-RJ85	E2326	ex N512XJ		
☐ EI-WXA	Avro 146-RJ85	E2310	ex N503XJ		
☐ EI-WXB	Avro 146-RJ85	E2311	ex N504XJ		stored NWI

Integrated services with VLM

IRISH HELICOPTERS — Dublin/Cork (DUB/ORK)

☐ EI-BLD	MBB Bo.105DB	S-381	ex D-HDLQ
☐ EI-LIT	MBB Bo.105CBS	S-434	ex A6-DBH
☐ EI-FAC	Aérospatiale AS350B1 Ecureuil	1991	ex G-BVJE

PREMIER HELICOPTERS — Dublin (DUB)

☐ EI-CGQ	Aérospatiale AS350B Ecureuil	2076	ex G-BUPK
☐ EI-ECA	Agusta A.109A II	7387	ex N109RP
☐ EI-LKS	Eurocopter EC130B4	3643	ex F-WQDQ
☐ EI-LNX	Eurocopter EC130B4	3498	ex N460AE
☐ EI-MLN	Agusta A.109E Power	11115	ex G-ECMM
☐ EI-MSG	Agusta A.109E Power	11692	
☐ EI-PKS	Bell 206B JetRanger III	4480	ex OE-XAC
☐ EI-SQG	Agusta A.109E Power	11084	
☐ EI-TWO	Agusta A.109E Power	11131	ex D-HARY

RYANAIR — Ryanair (FR/RYR) — Dublin (DUB)

☐ EI-DAC	Boeing 737-8AS/W	29938/1240		
☐ EI-DAD	Boeing 737-8AS/W	33544/1249		
☐ EI-DAE	Boeing 737-8AS/W	33545/1252		
☐ EI-DAF	Boeing 737-8AS/W	29939/1262		
☐ EI-DAG	Boeing 737-8AS/W	29940/1265		
☐ EI-DAH	Boeing 737-8AS/W	33546/1269		
☐ EI-DAI	Boeing 737-8AS/W	33547/1271		
☐ EI-DAJ	Boeing 737-8AS/W	33548/1274		
☐ EI-DAK	Boeing 737-8AS/W	33717/1310		
☐ EI-DAL	Boeing 737-8AS/W	33718/1311		
☐ EI-DAM	Boeing 737-8AS/W	33719/1312		
☐ EI-DAN	Boeing 737-8AS/W	33549/1361		
☐ EI-DAO	Boeing 737-8AS/W	33550/1366	ex N1800B	
☐ EI-DAP	Boeing 737-8AS/W	33551/1368	ex N6066U	
☐ EI-DAR	Boeing 737-8AS/W	33552/1371	ex EI-DAQ	
☐ EI-DAS	Boeing 737-8AS/W	33553/1372	ex EI-DAR	
☐ EI-DAT	Boeing 737-8AS/W	33554/1418		
☐ EI-DAV	Boeing 737-8AS/W	33555/1426		
☐ EI-DAW	Boeing 737-8AS/W	33556/1428		
☐ EI-DAX	Boeing 737-8AS/W	33557/1438		
☐ EI-DAY	Boeing 737-8AS/W	33558/1441		
☐ EI-DAZ	Boeing 737-8AS/W	33559/1443		
☐ EI-DCB	Boeing 737-8AS/W	33560/1447		
☐ EI-DCC	Boeing 737-8AS/W	33561/1463		
☐ EI-DCD	Boeing 737-8AS/W	33562/1466		
☐ EI-DCE	Boeing 737-8AS/W	33563/1473		
☐ EI-DCF	Boeing 737-8AS/W	33804/1529		
☐ EI-DCG	Boeing 737-8AS/W	33806/1530		
☐ EI-DCH	Boeing 737-8AS/W	33566/1546		
☐ EI-DCI	Boeing 737-8AS/W	33567/1547		
☐ EI-DCJ	Boeing 737-8AS/W	33564/1562		
☐ EI-DCK	Boeing 737-8AS/W	33565/1563		
☐ EI-DCL	Boeing 737-8AS/W	33806/1576	ex N1786B	Dreamliner colours
☐ EI-DCM	Boeing 737-8AS/W	33807/1578		
☐ EI-DCN	Boeing 737-8AS/W	33808/1590	ex N60436	
☐ EI-DCO	Boeing 737-8AS/W	33809/1592		
☐ EI-DCP	Boeing 737-8AS/W	33810/1595		
☐ EI-DCR	Boeing 737-8AS/W	33811/1613		
☐ EI-DCS	Boeing 737-8AS/W	33812/1615		
☐ EI-DCT	Boeing 737-8AS/W	33813/1617		
☐ EI-DCV	Boeing 737-8AS/W	33814/1618		
☐ EI-DCW	Boeing 737-8AS/W	33568/1631		
☐ EI-DCX	Boeing 737-8AS/W	33569/1635		
☐ EI-DCY	Boeing 737-8AS/W	33670/1637		
☐ EI-DCZ	Boeing 737-8AS/W	33815/1638		
☐ EI-DHA	Boeing 737-8AS/W	33571/1642		
☐ EI-DHB	Boeing 737-8AS/W	33572/1652		

☐	EI-DHC	Boeing 737-8AS/W	33573/1655	
☐	EI-DHD	Boeing 737-8AS/W	33816/1657	ex N1784B
☐	EI-DHE	Boeing 737-8AS/W	33574/1658	ex N1786B
☐	EI-DHF	Boeing 737-8AS/W	33575/1660	ex N1782B
☐	EI-DHG	Boeing 737-8AS/W	33576/1670	ex N1787B
☐	EI-DHH	Boeing 737-8AS/W	33817/1677	
☐	EI-DHI	Boeing 737-8AS/W	33818/1685	
☐	EI-DHJ	Boeing 737-8AS/W	33819/1691	
☐	EI-DHK	Boeing 737-8AS/W	33820/1696	
☐	EI-DHM	Boeing 737-8AS/W	33821/1698	
☐	EI-DHN	Boeing 737-8AS/W	33577/1782	
☐	EI-DHO	Boeing 737-8AS/W	33578/1792	ex N1786B
☐	EI-DHP	Boeing 737-8AS/W	33579/1794	
☐	EI-DHR	Boeing 737-8AS/W	33822/1798	
☐	EI-DHS	Boeing 737-8AS/W	33580/1807	
☐	EI-DHT	Boeing 737-8AS/W	33581/1809	
☐	EI-DHV	Boeing 737-8AS/W	33582/1811	
☐	EI-DHW	Boeing 737-8AS/W	33823/1819	ex N1786B
☐	EI-DHX	Boeing 737-8AS/W	33585/1824	ex N60436
☐	EI-DHY	Boeing 737-8AS/W	33824/1826	ex N1781B
☐	EI-DHZ	Boeing 737-8AS/W	33583/1834	
☐	EI-DLB	Boeing 737-8AS/W	33584/1836	ex N5573L
☐	EI-DLC	Boeing 737-8AS/W	33586/1844	ex N1786B
☐	EI-DLD	Boeing 737-8AS/W	33825/1847	
☐	EI-DLE	Boeing 737-8AS/W	33587/1864	
☐	EI-DLF	Boeing 737-8AS/W	33588/1867	
☐	EI-DLG	Boeing 737-8AS/W	33589/1869	ex N1786B
☐	EI-DLH	Boeing 737-8AS/W	33590/1886	
☐	EI-DLI	Boeing 737-8AS/W	33591/1894	ex N1786B
☐	EI-DLJ	Boeing 737-8AS/W	34177/1899	
☐	EI-DLK	Boeing 737-8AS/W	33592/1904	ex N1786B
☐	EI-DLL	Boeing 737-8AS/W	33593/1914	
☐	EI-DLM	Boeing 737-8AS/W	33694/1923	
☐	EI-DLN	Boeing 737-8AS/W	33595/1926	
☐	EI-DLO	Boeing 737-8AS/W	34178/1929	
☐	EI-DLR	Boeing 737-8AS/W	33596/2057	
☐	EI-DLS	Boeing 737-8AS/W	33621/2058	
☐	EI-DLT	Boeing 737-8AS/W	33597/2060	
☐	EI-DLV	Boeing 737-8AS/W	33598/2063	
☐	EI-DLW	Boeing 737-8AS/W	33599/2078	
☐	EI-DLX	Boeing 737-8AS/W	33600/2082	
☐	EI-DLY	Boeing 737-8AS/W	33601/2088	
☐	EI-DLZ	Boeing 737-8AS/W	33622/2101	
☐	EI-DPA	Boeing 737-8AS/W	33602/2109	
☐	EI-DPB	Boeing 737-8AS/W	33603/2112	ex N1787B
☐	EI-DPC	Boeing 737-8AS/W	33604/2120	ex N1786B
☐	EI-DPD	Boeing 737-8AS/W	33623/2123	ex N1786B
☐	EI-DPE	Boeing 737-8AS/W	33605/2140	ex N1787B
☐	EI-DPF	Boeing 737-8AS/W	33606/2158	
☐	EI-DPG	Boeing 737-8AS/W	33607/2163	
☐	EI-DPH	Boeing 737-8AS/W	33624/2168	
☐	EI-DPI	Boeing 737-8AS/W	33608/2173	
☐	EI-DPJ	Boeing 737-8AS/W	33609/2179	
☐	EI-DPK	Boeing 737-8AS/W	33610/2183	
☐	EI-DPL	Boeing 737-8AS/W	33611/2189	
☐	EI-DPM	Boeing 737-8AS/W	33640/2198	
☐	EI-DPN	Boeing 737-8AS/W	35549/2200	ex N1787B
☐	EI-DPO	Boeing 737-8AS/W	33612/2207	ex N1786B
☐	EI-DPP	Boeing 737-8AS/W	33613/2213	
☐	EI-DPR	Boeing 737-8AS/W	33614/2219	ex N1786B
☐	EI-DPS	Boeing 737-8AS/W	33641/2222	
☐	EI-DPT	Boeing 737-8AS/W	35550/2227	ex N1787B
☐	EI-DPV	Boeing 737-8AS/W	35551/2236	ex N1779B
☐	EI-DPW	Boeing 737-8AS/W	35552/2263	
☐	EI-DPX	Boeing 737-8AS/W	35553/2279	
☐	EI-DPY	Boeing 737-8AS/W	33615/2375	ex N1781B
☐	EI-DPZ	Boeing 737-8AS/W	33616/2376	
☐	EI-DWA	Boeing 737-8AS/W	33617/2377	
☐	EI-DWB	Boeing 737-8AS/W	36075/2382	
☐	EI-DWC	Boeing 737-8AS/W	36076/2384	
☐	EI-DWD	Boeing 737-8AS/W	33642/2389	ex N1781B
☐	EI-DWE	Boeing 737-8AS/W	36074/2391	
☐	EI-DWF	Boeing 737-8AS/W	33619/2396	
☐	EI-DWG	Boeing 737-8AS/W	33620/2397	
☐	EI-DWH	Boeing 737-8AS/W	33637/2408	ex N1787B
☐	EI-DWI	Boeing 737-8AS/W	33643/2410	
☐	EI-DWJ	Boeing 737-8AS/W	36077/2411	
☐	EI-DWK	Boeing 737-8AS/W	36078/2415	ex N1786B
☐	EI-DWL	Boeing 737-8AS/W	33618/2416	ex N1787B
☐	EI-DWM	Boeing 737-8AS/W	36080/2430	
☐	EI-DWO	Boeing 737-8AS/W	36079/2440	
☐	EI-DWP	Boeing 737-8AS/W	36082/2443	
☐	EI-DWR	Boeing 737-8AS/W	36081/2448	ex N1786B

☐ EI-DWS	Boeing 737-8AS/W	33625/2472	ex N1786B
☐ EI-DWT	Boeing 737-8AS/W	33626/2489	
☐ EI-DWV	Boeing 737-8AS/W	33627/2492	
☐ EI-DWW	Boeing 737-8AS/W	33629/2507	ex N1781B
☐ EI-DWX	Boeing 737-8AS/W	33630/2508	
☐ EI-DWY	Boeing 737-8AS/W	33638/2518	ex N1781B
☐ EI-DWZ	Boeing 737-8AS/W	33628/2520	ex N1796B
☐ EI-DYA	Boeing 737-8AS/W	33631/2529	ex N1786B
☐ EI-DYB	Boeing 737-8AS/W	33633/2542	
☐ EI-DYC	Boeing 737-8AS/W	36567/2543	ex N1787B
☐ EI-DYD	Boeing 737-8AS/W	33632/2544	ex N1786B
☐ EI-DYE	Boeing 737-8AS/W	36568/2548	
☐ EI-DYF	Boeing 737-8AS/W	36569/2549	ex N1786B
☐ EI-DYH	Boeing 737-8AS/W	36570/2573	
☐ EI-DYI	Boeing 737-8AS/W	36571/2574	
☐ EI-DYJ	Boeing 737-8AS/W	36572/2580	
☐ EI-DYK	Boeing 737-8AS/W	36573/2581	
☐ EI-DYL	Boeing 737-8AS/W	36574/2635	
☐ EI-DYM	Boeing 737-8AS/W	36575/2636	
☐ EI-DYN	Boeing 737-8AS/W	36576/2367	
☐ EI-DYO	Boeing 737-8AS/W	33636/2728	
☐ EI-DYP	Boeing 737-8AS/W	37515/2729	
☐ EI-DYR	Boeing 737-8AS/W	37513/2734	
☐ EI-DYS	Boeing 737-8AS/W	37514/2735	
☐ EI-DYT	Boeing 737-8AS/W	33634/2745	
☐ EI-DYV	Boeing 737-8AS/W	37512/2746	
☐ EI-DYW	Boeing 737-8AS/W	33635/2747	
☐ EI-DYX	Boeing 737-8AS/W	37517/2754	
☐ EI-DYY	Boeing 737-8AS/W	37521/2755	ex N1787B
☐ EI-DYZ	Boeing 737-8AS/W	37518/2760	
☐ EI-EBA	Boeing 737-8AS/W	37516/2761	
☐ EI-EBB	Boeing 737-8AS/W	37519/2779	ex N1787B
☐ EI-EBC	Boeing 737-8AS/W	37520/2780	ex N1795B
☐ EI-EBD	Boeing 737-8AS/W	37522/2781	ex N1796B
☐ EI-EBE	Boeing 737-8AS/W	37523/2788	
☐ EI-EBF	Boeing 737-8AS/W	37524/2791	ex N1796B
☐ EI-EBG	Boeing 737-8AS/W	37525/2792	
☐ EI-EBH	Boeing 737-8AS/W	37526/2797	
☐ EI-EBI	Boeing 737-8AS/W	37527/2798	
☐ EI-EBK	Boeing 737-8AS/W	37528/2807	
☐ EI-EBL	Boeing 737-8AS/W	37529/2808	ex N1796B
☐ EI-EBM	Boeing 737-8AS/W	35002/2839	ex N1787B
☐ EI-EBN	Boeing 737-8AS/W	35003/2840	
☐ EI-EBO	Boeing 737-8AS/W	35004/2843	ex N1796B
☐ EI-EBP	Boeing 737-8AS/W	37531/2844	
☐ EI-EBR	Boeing 737-8AS/W	37530/2856	ex N1779B
☐ EI-EBS	Boeing 737-8AS/W	35001/2857	ex N1786B
☐ EI-EBT	Boeing 737-8AS/W	35000/2858	
☐ EI-EBV	Boeing 737-8AS/W	35009/2872	
☐ EI-EBW	Boeing 737-8AS/W	35010/2873	
☐ EI-EBX	Boeing 737-8AS/W	35007/2882	
☐ EI-EBY	Boeing 737-8AS/W	35006/2886	
☐ EI-EBZ	Boeing 737-8AS/W	35008/2887	
☐ EI-EFA	Boeing 737-8AS/W	35005/2892	ex N1786B
☐ EI-EFB	Boeing 737-8AS/W	37532/2893	
☐ EI-EFC	Boeing 737-8AS/W	35015/2901	
☐ EI-EFD	Boeing 737-8AS/W	35011/2903	ex N1787B
☐ EI-EFE	Boeing 737-8AS/W	37533/2905	
☐ EI-EFF	Boeing 737-8AS/W	35016/2917	ex N1786B
☐ EI-EFG	Boeing 737-8AS/W	35014/2921	ex N1786B
☐ EI-EFH	Boeing 737-8AS/W	35012/2923	ex N1787B
☐ EI-EFI	Boeing 737-8AS/W	35013/2924	ex N1786B
☐ EI-EFJ	Boeing 737-8AS/W	37534/2936	ex N1786B
☐ EI-EFK	Boeing 737-8AS/W	37535/2948	ex N1786B
☐ EI-EFL	Boeing 737-8AS/W	37536/2958	
☐ EI-EFM	Boeing 737-8AS/W	37537/2960	ex N1787B
☐ EI-EFN	Boeing 737-8AS/W	37538/2967	ex N1787B
☐ EI-EFO	Boeing 737-8AS/W	37539/2978	
☐ EI-EFP	Boeing 737-8AS/W	37540/2979	
☐ EI-EFR	Boeing 737-8AS/W	37541/3012	ex N1786B
☐ EI-EFS	Boeing 737-8AS/W	37542/3021	
☐ EI-EFT	Boeing 737-8AS/W	37543/3023	ex N1787B
☐ EI-EFV	Boeing 737-8AS/W	35017/3052	ex N60659
☐ EI-EFW	Boeing 737-8AS/W	35018/3078	ex N1786B
☐ EI-EFX	Boeing 737-8AS/W	35019/3079	ex N1787B
☐ EI-EFY	Boeing 737-8AS/W	35020/3084	ex N1786B
☐ EI-EFZ	Boeing 737-8AS/W	38489/3089	ex N1787B
☐ EI-EGA	Boeing 737-8AS/W	38490/3096	ex N1787B
☐ EI-EGB	Boeing 737-8AS/W	38491/3097	ex N1787B
☐ EI-EGC	Boeing 737-8AS/W	38492/3099	ex N1786B
☐ EI-EKA	Boeing 737-8AS/W	35022/3139	
☐ EI-EKB	Boeing 737-8AS/W	38494/3141	
☐ EI-EKC	Boeing 737-8AS/W	38495/3143	

☐ EI-EKD	Boeing 737-8AS/W	35024/3146		
☐ EI-EKE	Boeing 737-8AS/W	35023/3148		
☐ EI-EKF	Boeing 737-8AS/W	35025/3152		
☐ EI-EKG	Boeing 737-8AS/W	35021/3161		
☐ EI-EKH	Boeing 737-8AS/W	38493/3162		
☐ EI-EKI	Boeing 737-8AS/W	38496		on order
☐ EI-EKJ	Boeing 737-8AS/W	38497		on order
☐ EI-EKK	Boeing 737-8AS/W	38500		on order
☐ EI-EKL	Boeing 737-8AS/W	38498		on order
☐ EI-EKM	Boeing 737-8AS/W	38499		on order
☐ EI-EKN	Boeing 737-8AS/W	35026		on order
☐ EI-EKO	Boeing 737-8AS/W	35027		on order
☐ EI-EKP	Boeing 737-8AS/W	35028		on order
☐ EI-EKR	Boeing 737-8AS/W	38503		on order
☐ EI-EKS	Boeing 737-8AS/W	38504		on order
☐ EI-EKT	Boeing 737-8AS/W	38505		on order
☐ EI-EKV	Boeing 737-8AS/W	38507		on order
☐ EI-EKW	Boeing 737-8AS/W	38506		on order
☐ EI-EKX	Boeing 737-8AS/W	35030		on order
☐ EI-	Boeing 737-8AS/W			on order
☐ EI-	Boeing 737-8AS/W			on order
☐ EI-	Boeing 737-8AS/W			on order
☐ EI-	Boeing 737-8AS/W			on order
☐ EI-	Boeing 737-8AS/W			on order
☐ EI-	Boeing 737-8AS/W			on order
☐ EI-	Boeing 737-8AS/W			on order
☐ EI-	Boeing 737-8AS/W			on order
☐ EI-	Boeing 737-8AS/W			on order
☐ EI-	Boeing 737-8AS/W			on order
☐ EI-	Boeing 737-8AS/W			on order
☐ EI-	Boeing 737-8AS/W			on order
☐ EI-	Boeing 737-8AS/W			on order
☐ EI-	Boeing 737-8AS/W			on order
☐ EI-	Boeing 737-8AS/W			on order
☐ EI-	Boeing 737-8AS/W			on order
☐ EI-	Boeing 737-8AS/W			on order
☐ EI-	Boeing 737-8AS/W			on order
☐ EI-	Boeing 737-8AS/W			on order
☐ EI-	Boeing 737-8AS/W			on order
☐ EI-	Boeing 737-8AS/W			on order

VISION AIR — *Vision (VAT)* — *Dublin (DUB)*

☐ EI-DIF	Piper PA-31-350 Navajo Chieftain	31-7752105	ex G-OAMT	

EK- ARMENIA (Republic of Armenia)

AIR ARMENIA — *Air Armenia (QN/ARR)* — *Yerevan-Zvartnots (EVN)*

☐ EK-11001	Antonov An-12TBK	8346107	ex CCCP-11244	
☐ EK-12104	Antonov An-12BK	8346104	ex CCCP-12110	Cargo titles
☐ EK-32500	Antonov An-32B	2009	ex 9L-LFP	
☐ EK-65848	Tupolev Tu-134A-3	23136	ex CCCP-65848	

AIR HIGHNESSES

☐ EK-12006	Antonov An-12B	01348006	ex UR-CGR
☐ EK-12908	Antonov An-12B	7344908	ex EK-11029
☐ EK-76300	Ilyushin Il-76TD	083410300	ex TN-AHT

ARARAT INTERNATIONAL AIRLINES

☐ EK-82852	McDonnell-Douglas MD-82	49852/1959	ex B-2151

ARMAVIA — *Armavia (U8/RNV)* — *Yerevan-Zvartnots (EVN)*

☐ EK-RA01	Airbus A319-132	0913	ex HZ-NAS		Op for Govt
☐ EK-32005	Airbus A320-211	3492	ex F-WWIU		
☐ EK-32007	Airbus A319-111	3834	ex D-AVYM	Victor Hambardzumyan	
☐ EK-32008	Airbus A320-211	0229	ex N229AN	Aram Khachatryan	
☐ EK-32011	Airbus A319-132	2277	ex N803BR	Mika	
☐ EK-32012	Airbus A319-132	2362	ex N806BR	Air Marshal S Khidiakov	
☐ EK-20014	Canadair CL-600-2B19 (CRJ-200LR)	7282	ex D-ACJI	Sergey Mergelyan	
☐ EK-20073	Canadair CL-600-2B19 (CRJ-200LR)	7373	ex 4L-TGS		
☐ EK-42362	Yakovlev Yak-42D	4520424811431	ex UR-CDU		
☐ EK-42417	Yakovlev Yak-42D	4520423219110	ex RA-42417	all-white	
☐ EK-65072	Tupolev Tu-134A-3	49972	ex CCCP-65072		Op for Govt
☐ EK-86118	Ilyushin Il-86	51483209086	ex CCCP-86118		
☐ 4L-TGL	Boeing 737-3B7	23859/1551	ex N524AU	all white	Lsd fr TGZ

ARMENIA AIR CARGO

□ EK-11810	Antonov An-12BP	5342908	ex UR-11810	

AYK AVIA — Yerevan-Zvartnots (EVN)

□ EK-32410	Antonov An-32	2416	ex 9L-LFU	
□ EK-74027	Antonov An-74-200	36547096920	ex RA-74027	
□ EK-74043	Antonov An-74-200	36547096923	ex RA-74043	

BLUE SKY — Blue Armenia (BLM) — Yerevan-Zvartnots (EVN)

□ EK-30044	Airbus A300B2K-3C	244	ex N142RF	Lsd to IRM
□ EK-30060	Airbus A300B2K-3C	160	ex N141RF	Lsd to IRM
□ EP-MNC	Boeing 747-422	26879/973	ex EK-74779	Lsd to IRM

CENTRAL AIRWAYS

□ EK-26443	Antonov An-26	17311705	ex ER-AFL	

MIAPET AVIA — Miapet (MPT) — Yerevan-Zvartnots (EVN)

□ EK-11660	Antonov An-12BP	5343209	ex RA-11660	dam PNR 25Jan08

NAVIGATOR AIRLINES

□ EK-26440	Antonov An-26	57303504	ex RA-26640	

PHOENIX AVIA — Phoenix Armenia (PHY) — Yerevan-Zvartnote (EVN)

□ EK-11007	Antonov An-12	5343506	ex RA-11995	
□ EK-12148	Antonov An-12BK	4341906	ex military	Vasili Pro Kho Renko titles
□ EK-12803	Antonov An-12B	01347803	ex XU-395	
□ EK-46419	Antonov An-24B	87303704	ex RA-46419	
□ EK-46741	Antonov An-12BK	8345408	ex RA-46741	White Bird
□ EK-46839	Antonov An-24T	7910201	ex RA-46839	Ali
□ EK-47835	Antonov An-24B	17307307	ex RA-47835	stored

SOUTH AIRLINES — South (STH) — Sharjah (SHJ)

□ EK-11112	Antonov An-12BP	5343307	ex EK-11132	
□ EK-11779	Antonov An-12BP	5343402	ex RA-11401	
□ EK-12122	Antonov An-12BP	5343507	ex RA-11786	
□ EK-12305	Antonov An-12BP	00347305	ex EK-12777	
□ EK-26441	Antonov An-26	57303009	ex ER-AZS	
□ EK-46507	Antonov An-24RV	37308403	ex RA-46507	
□ EK-46656	Antonov An-24RV	47309302	ex RA-46656	
□ EK-47828	Antonov An-24B	17307209	ex UN-47828	
□ EK-72101	Antonov An-72-100	36572040548	ex 4L-VAS	
□ EK-74045	Antonov An-74-200	36547098966	ex RA-74060	
□ EK-76707	Ilyushin Il-76TD	073410292	ex RA-76495	
□ EK-76717	Ilyushin Il-76TD	0043450484	ex UR-76581	
□ EK-76727	Ilyushin Il-76TD	0063467021	ex UR-76681	
□ EK-76737	Ilyushin Il-76MD	0083483502	ex UR-76778	
□ EK-85536	Tupolev Tu-154B-2	82A-536	ex CCCP-85536	Lsd to KES
□ EK-85566	Tupolev Tu-154B-2	82A-566	ex CCCP-85566	

TARON AVIA

□ EK-12005	Antonov An-12BP	5343005	ex XU-U4C	
□ EK-12704	Antonov An-12BP	01347704	ex EK-11102	
□ EK-12129	Antonov An-12BP	5342903	ex EK-11772	

VERTIR

□ EK-31095	Airbus A310-304	595	ex C-GTSI	

VETERAN AIRLINE — Veteran (RVT) — Yerevan-Zvartnots (EVN)

□ EK-46513	Antonov An-24RV	37308409	ex UR-46513	

YER AVIA — Yerevan-Avia (ERV) — Yerevan-Zvartnots (EVN)

□ EK-86724	Ilyushin Il-76M	073410284	ex EP-TPZ	
□ EK-86817	Ilyushin Il-76M	063407191	ex EP-TPO	

Operator Unknown

□ EK-76787	Ilyushin Il-76TD	0093495854	ex RA-76787	

EP- IRAN (Islamic Republic of Iran)

ARIA AIR — Aria (IRX) — Lar/Bandar Abbas (LRR/BND)

☐ EP-EAF	Fokker F.27 Mk.050 (Fokker 50)	20235	ex D-AFKP	
☐ EP-EAH	Fokker F.27 Mk.050 (Fokker 50)	20234	ex D-AFKO	

CASPIAN AIRLINES — Caspian (RV/CPN) — Rasht (RAS)

☐ EP-CPN	Tupolev Tu-154M	91A-898	ex EP-JAZ	
☐ EP-CPO	Tupolev Tu-154M	91A-899	ex EP-ARG	
☐ EP-CPS	Tupolev Tu-154M	93A-957	ex UN-85775	
☐ UR-BHJ	McDonnell-Douglas MD-83	53184/2088	ex TC-AKL	Lsd fr UKM

CHABAHAR AIR — Chabahar (IRU) — Tehran-Mehrabad (THR)

☐ EP-CFM	Fokker F.28-0100 (Fokker 100)	11394	ex PT-MQL	Lsd to IRA
☐ EP-CFN	Fokker F.28-0100 (Fokker 100)	11423	ex PT-MQO	Lsd to IRA
☐ EP-CFO	Fokker F.28-0100 (Fokker 100)	11389	ex PT-MQE	Lsd to IRA
☐ EP-CFP	Fokker F.28-0100 (Fokker 100)	11409	ex PT-MQN	Lsd to IRA
☐ EP-CFQ	Fokker F.28-0100 (Fokker 100)	11429	ex PT-MQT	Lsd to IRA
☐ EP-CFR	Fokker F.28-0100 (Fokker 100)	11383	ex PT-MQD	Lsd to IRA

ERAM AIR — Eram Air (YE/IRY) — Tabriz (TBZ)

☐ EP-EKA	Tupolev Tu-154M	92A-912	ex RA-85730	Lsd fr OMS
☐ EP-EKB	Tupolev Tu-154M	92A-946	ex RA-85763	Lsd fr OMS
☐ EP-EKC	Tupolev Tu-154M	89A-799	ex EP-MCE	
☐ EP-EKE	Tupolev Tu-154M	92A-940	ex EP-MCK	Lsd fr NKZ

FARS AIR

☐ EP-QFA	Yakovlev Yak-42D	4520422007018	ex ER-YCE	
☐ EP-QFB	Yakovlev Yak-42D	4520422003019	ex ER-YCF	

HELICOPTER SERVICES — Tehran

☐ EP-HEB	Aérospatiale AS350B2 Ecureuil	3050	ex F-WQDA	
☐ EP-HEC	Aérospatiale AS350B3 Ecureuil	3621	ex F-WQDD	
☐ EP-HED	Aérospatiale AS350B3 Ecureuil	3629	ex F-WQDJ	
☐ EP-HEE	Aérospatiale AS350B3 Ecureuil	3644	ex F-WQDK	
☐ EP-HEF	Aérospatiale AS350B3 Ecureuil	3655		
☐ EP-HEG	Aérospatiale AS350B3 Ecureuil	3658		
☐ EP-HEH	Aérospatiale AS350B3 Ecureuil	3668		
☐ EP-HBJ	Bell 212	30504	ex N8112J	
☐ EP-HDV	Aérospatiale AS365N2 Dauphin 2	6467	ex F-GLMZ	
☐ EP-HTN	Bell 212	30885	ex N5009K	
☐ EP-HTO	Bell 205A-1	30163	ex N64743	
☐ EP-HTQ	Bell 205A-1	30189	ex N90039	
☐ EP-HUA	Bell 212	31176	ex HB-XPO	

IRAN AIR — Iranair (IR/IRA) — Tehran-Mehrabad (THR)

☐ EP-IBA	Airbus A300B4-605R	723	ex F-WWAL	
☐ EP-IBB	Airbus A300B4-605R	727	ex F-WWAZ	
☐ EP-IBC	Airbus A300B4-605R	632	ex SX-BEK	
☐ EP-IBD	Airbus A300B4-605R	696	ex SX-BEL	
☐ EP-IBG	Airbus A300B4-203F	299	ex EP-MDA	
☐ EP-IBH	Airbus A300B4-203F	302	ex EP-MDB	
☐ EP-IBI	Airbus A300B4-2C	151	ex TC-FLK	
☐ EP-IBJ	Airbus A300B4-2C	256	ex TC-FLL	
☐ EP-IBS	Airbus A300B2-203	080	ex F-WZEO	
☐ EP-IBT	Airbus A300B2-203	185	ex F-WZMB	
☐ EP-IBV	Airbus A300B2-203	187	ex F-WZMD	
☐ EP-IBZ	Airbus A300B2-203	226	ex F-WZME	
☐ EP-ICE	Airbus A300B4-203F	139	ex TC-KZT	
☐ EP-IBK	Airbus A310-304	671	ex SU-MWB	
☐ EP-IBL	Airbus A310-304	436	ex A6-EKB	
☐ EP-IBM	Airbus A310-203	338	ex TC-JCL	
☐ EP-IBN	Airbus A310-203	375	ex TC-JCM	
☐ EP-IBO	Airbus A310-203	379	ex TC-JCN	stored THR
☐ EP-IBP	Airbus A310-203	370	ex TC-JCR	
☐ EP-IBQ	Airbus A310-203	389	ex TC-JCS	stored THR
☐ EP-IBX	Airbus A310-203	390	ex TC-JCU	stored THR
☐ EP-IEA	Airbus A320-232	0530	ex EP-MHK	
☐ EP-IEB	Airbus A320-232	0575	ex EP-MHN	
☐ EP-IEC	Airbus A320-232	0857	ex EP-MHJ	

☐ EP-IED	Airbus A320-212	0345	ex VP-CBZ		
☐ EP-IEE	Airbus A320-211	0303	ex EK-32303		
☐ EP-IEF	Airbus A320-211	0312	ex EK-32312		
☐ EP-IEG	Airbus A320-211	2054	ex EK-32054		
☐ EP-IRP	Boeing 727-286	20945/1048			
☐ EP-IRR	Boeing 727-286	20946/1052			
☐ EP-IRS	Boeing 727-286	20947/1070			
☐ EP-IRT	Boeing 727-286	21078/1114			
☐ EP-IAA	Boeing 747SP-86	20998/275			
☐ EP-IAB	Boeing 747SP-86	20999/278		Khorasan	
☐ EP-IAC	Boeing 747SP-86	21093/307		Fars	
☐ EP-IAD	Boeing 747SP-86	21758/371	ex N1800B	Khorasan	
☐ EP-IAG	Boeing 747-286M	21217/291		Azarabadegan	
☐ EP-IAH	Boeing 747-286M	21218/300		Khuzestan	
☐ EP-IAI	Boeing 747-230M	22670/550	ex EP-AUA		
☐ EP-IAM	Boeing 747-186B	21759/381	ex N5573P		
☐ EP-ICD	Boeing 747-21AC	24134/712	ex TC-AKZ		
☐ EP-AWZ	Fokker F.28-0100 (Fokker 100)	11497	ex PH-AFO		
☐ EP-CFD	Fokker F.28-0100 (Fokker 100)	11442	ex PT-MRI		
☐ EP-CFE	Fokker F.28-0100 (Fokker 100)	11422	ex F-GRMV		
☐ EP-CFH	Fokker F.28-0100 (Fokker 100)	11443	ex F-GSTG		
☐ EP-CFI	Fokker F.28-0100 (Fokker 100)	11511	ex PT-MRU		
☐ EP-CFJ	Fokker F.28-0100 (Fokker 100)	11516	ex PT-MRV		
☐ EP-CFK	Fokker F.28-0100 (Fokker 100)	11518	ex PT-MRW		
☐ EP-CFL	Fokker F.28-0100 (Fokker 100)	11343	ex PT-MRY		
☐ EP-CFM	Fokker F.28-0100 (Fokker 100)	11394	ex PT-MQL		Lsd fr IRU
☐ EP-CFN	Fokker F.28-0100 (Fokker 100)	11423	ex PT-MQO		Lsd fr IRU
☐ EP-CFO	Fokker F.28-0100 (Fokker 100)	11389	ex PT-MQE		Lsd fr IRU
☐ EP-CFP	Fokker F.28-0100 (Fokker 100)	11409	ex PT-MQN		Lsd fr IRU
☐ EP-CFQ	Fokker F.28-0100 (Fokker 100)	11429	ex PT-MQT		Lsd fr IRU
☐ EP-IDA	Fokker F.28-0100 (Fokker 100)	11292	ex PH-LMG		
☐ EP-IDD	Fokker F.28-0100 (Fokker 100)	11294	ex PH-LMM		
☐ EP-IDF	Fokker F.28-0100 (Fokker 100)	11298	ex PH-LMN		
☐ EP-IDG	Fokker F.28-0100 (Fokker 100)	11302	ex PH-LMW		
☐ UR-CHW	McDonnell-Douglas MD-82	49510/1514	ex S5-ACY		
☐ UR-CHX	McDonnell-Douglas MD-82	53162/2010	ex S5-ACZ		stored THR

IRAN AIR TOUR AIRLINE — *Iran Air Tour (B9/IRB) Tehran-Mehrabad/Mashad (THR/MHD)*

☐ EP-MBQ	Tupolev Tu-154M	92A-931	ex RA-85749	Lsd fr NKZ
☐ EP-MBT	Tupolev Tu-154M	92A-930	ex RA-85747	Lsd fr NKZ
☐ EP-MCJ	Tupolev Tu-154M	89A-800	ex EP-MBP	
☐ EP-MCL	Tupolev Tu-154M	91A-880	ex RA-85705	
☐ EP-MCM	Tupolev Tu-154M	90A-855	ex RA-85085	
☐ EP-MCN	Tupolev Tu-154M	88A-792	ex RA-85847	
☐ EP-MCO	Tupolev Tu-154M	88A-774	ex RA-85831	
☐ EP-MCP	Tupolev Tu-154M	85A-724	ex RA-85146	
☐ EP-MCS	Tupolev Tu-154M	88A-795	ex RA-85653	
☐ EP-MCT	Tupolev Tu-154M	90A-860	ex RA-85689	
☐ EP-MCU	Tupolev Tu-154M	93A-977	ex RA-85793	
☐ EP-MCV	Tupolev Tu-154M	85A-706	ex RA-85037	
☐ EP-MCX	Tupolev Tu-154M	85A-707	ex LZ-HMW	
☐ EP-	Tupolev Tu-204-100			on order
☐ EP-	Tupolev Tu-204-100			on order

IRAN ASEMAN AIRLINES — *(EP/IRC)* — *Tehran-Mehrabad (THR)*

☐ EP-ATA	ATR 72-212	334	ex F-WWLQ	
☐ EP-ATH	ATR 72-212	339	ex F-WWLU	
☐ EP-ATS	ATR 72-212	391	ex F-WWED	
☐ EP-ATU	ATR 72-212A	697	ex F-OIRA	
☐ EP-ATX	ATR 72-212A	573	ex F-OIRB	
☐ EP-ATZ	ATR 72-212	398	ex F-WWEK	
☐ EP-ASG	Fokker F.28-0100 (Fokker 100)	11438	ex HL7210	stored DNR
☐ EP-ASH	Fokker F.28-0100 (Fokker 100)	11439	ex HL7211	
☐ EP-ASI	Fokker F.28-0100 (Fokker 100)	11519	ex HL7215	
☐ EP-ASJ	Fokker F.28-0100 (Fokker 100)	11378	ex HL7206	
☐ EP-ASK	Fokker F.28-0100 (Fokker 100)	11388	ex HL7208	
☐ EP-ASL	Fokker F.28-0100 (Fokker 100)	11432	ex HL7209	stored
☐ EP-ASM	Fokker F.28-0100 (Fokker 100)	11433	ex F-GIOI	
☐ EP-ASO	Fokker F.28-0100 (Fokker 100)	11454	ex F-GIOJ	
☐ EP-ASP	Fokker F.28-0100 (Fokker 100)	11504	ex HL7213	
☐ EP-ASQ	Fokker F.28-0100 (Fokker 100)	11513	ex HL7214	
☐ EP-ASR	Fokker F.28-0100 (Fokker 100)	11522	ex HL7216	
☐ EP-AST	Fokker F.28-0100 (Fokker 100)	11523	ex HL7217	
☐ EP-ASU	Fokker F.28-0100 (Fokker 100)	11430	ex PT-MQP	

☐ EP-ASX	Fokker F.28-0100 (Fokker 100)	11431	ex PT-MQS	Lsd to IRK
☐ EP-ASZ	Fokker F.28-0100 (Fokker 100)	11421	ex PT-MQR	
☐ EP-ATB	Fokker F.28-0100 (Fokker 100)	11401	ex PT-MQF	
☐ EP-ASA	Boeing 727-228	22081/1594	ex LX-IRA	
☐ EP-ASB	Boeing 727-228	22082/1603	ex LX-IRB	
☐ EP-ASC	Boeing 727-228	22084/1638	ex LX-IRC	
☐ EP-ASD	Boeing 727-228	22085/1665	ex LX-IRD	
☐ EP-ASF	Fokker F.28 Fellowship 4000	11144	ex F-GDUZ	

KISH AIR — Kishair (Y9/IRK) — Tehran-Mehrabad (THR)

☐ EP-LBV	Fokker F.27 Mk.050 (Fokker 50)	20158	ex VP-CSE	
☐ EP-LCB	Fokker F.27 Mk.050 (Fokker 50)	20274	ex EC-GKV	
☐ EP-LCC	Fokker F.27 Mk.050 (Fokker 50)	20275	ex EC-GKX	
☐ EP-LCE	Fokker F.27 Mk.050 (Fokker 50)	20265	ex PH-LXF	
☐ EP-LCF	Fokker F.27 Mk.050 (Fokker 50)	20263	ex PH-LXE	
☐ EP-LCG	Fokker F.27 Mk.050 (Fokker 50)	20236	ex PH-JXL	
☐ EP-ASX	Fokker F.28-0100 (Fokker 100)	11431	ex PT-MQS	Lsd fr IRC
☐ EP-LCI	McDonnell-Douglas MD-83	49844/1579	ex UR-CHR	Lsd fr KHO
☐ UR-BXN	McDonnell-Douglas MD-83	49569/1405	ex LZ-LDV	Lsd fr KHO
☐ UR-CHS	McDonnell-Douglas MD-83	49572/1468	ex LZ-LDA	Lsd fr KHO
☐ EP-LBR	Tupolev Tu-154M	90A-838	ex RA-85089	
☐ EP-LBS	Tupolev Tu-154M	91A-901	ex UN-85719	

MAHAN AIR — Mahan Air (W5/IRM) — Kerman (KER)

☐ EK-30044	Airbus A300B2K-3C	244	ex N142RF	Lsd fr Blue Sky
☐ EK-30060	Airbus A300B2K-3C	160	ex N141RF	Lsd fr Blue Sky
☐ EP-MHF	Airbus A300B4-103	055	ex S7-AAZ	
☐ EP-MHG	Airbus A300B4-203	204	ex AP-BFL	
☐ EP-MHL	Airbus A300B4-203	175	ex SU-BMM	
☐ EP-MHM	Airbus A300B2K-3C	090	ex TC-SGA	Lsd fr SGX
☐ EP-MNQ	Airbus A300B4-603	553	ex EX-35010	
☐ EP-MNR	Airbus A300B4-603	411	ex EX-35009	
☐ EP-MNS	Airbus A300B4-603	414	ex EX-35008	
☐ EP-MNT	Airbus A300B4-603	546	ex EX-35007	
☐ EP-MNU	Airbus A300B4-605R	608	ex EX-35006	
☐ EK-35003	Airbus A310-304	567	ex OK-WAB	
☐ EP-MHO	Airbus A310-304	488	ex EK-31088	Lsd fr Blue Sky
☐ EP-MNX	Airbus A310-304	564	ex EX-35005	
☐ EX-301	Airbus A310-304	524	ex D-AIDF	Lsd fr KTC
☐ EX-35004	Airbus A310-308	620	ex D-AHLC	Lsd fr KTC
☐ F-OJHH	Airbus A310-304ER	586	ex EP-MHH	
☐ F-OJHI	Airbus A310-304ER	537	ex EP-MHI	
☐ EP-MNA	Boeing 747-422	24383/811	ex EK-74783	
☐ EP-MNB	Boeing 747-422	24363/740	ex EK-74763	Lsd fr Blue Sky
☐ EP-MNC	Boeing 747-422	26879/973	ex EK-74779	Lsd fr Blue Sky
☐ EP-MND	Boeing 747-3B3 (SCD)	23413/632	ex EK-74713	Lsd fr Blue Sky
☐ EP-MNE	Boeing 747-3B3 (SCD)	23480/641	ex EK-74780	
☐ EX-27000	British Aerospace 146 Srs.300	E3216	ex B-2717	
☐ EX-27001	British Aerospace 146 Srs.300	E3212	ex B-2712	

NAFT AIR — NAFT (IRG) — Ahwaz (AWZ)

☐ EP-GAS	Fokker F.27 Mk.050 (Fokker 50)	20224	ex PH-JXA
☐ EP-IOD	de Havilland DHC-6 Twin Otter 300	460	
☐ EP-IOE	de Havilland DHC-6 Twin Otter 300	425	
☐ EP-IOP	de Havilland DHC-6 Twin Otter 300	577	
☐ EP-MIS	Fokker F.28-0100 (Fokker 100)	11503	ex F-GPXI
☐ EP-NFT	Fokker F.27 Mk.050 (Fokker 50)	20220	ex PH-RRF
☐ EP-OIL	Fokker F.27 Mk.050 (Fokker 50)	20222	ex PH-LNZ
☐ EP-OPI	Fokker F.28-0100 (Fokker 100)	11509	ex F-GLIR
☐ EP-PET	Fokker F.27 Mk.050 (Fokker 50)	20283	ex PH-MXF
☐ EP-SUS	Fokker F.28-0100 (Fokker 100)	11487	ex F-GPXA

NAVID AIR — Navid (IRI) — Karaj-Payam (QKC)

☐ EP-NAA	Mil Mi-17I	59489602238	ex RA-25520	
☐ EP-NAB	Mil Mi-8MTV-1	95932	ex RA-27108	
☐ EP-NAC	Mil Mi-8T	99254442	ex RA-27024	
☐ EP-NAD	Mil Mi-8T	99254471	ex RA-27025	
☐ EP-NAF	Bell 212	31231	ex A6-BAC	Lsd fr Abu Dhabi Avn

PAYAM INTERNATIONAL AIR — Payamair (2F/IRP) — Karaj-Payam (QKC)

☐ EP-TPH	Embraer EMB.110P1A Bandeirante	110453	ex EP-TPM	Tehran
☐ EP-TPI	Embraer EMB.110P1 Bandeirante	110438	ex EP-TPA	Kerrian
☐ EP-TPJ	Embraer EMB.110P1 Bandeirante	110442	ex EP-TPT	Kashan

☐ EP-TPK	Embraer EMB.110P1 Bandeirante	110386	ex EP-TPG	Esfahan
☐ EP-TPL	Embraer EMB.110P1 Bandeirante	110423	ex EP-TPS	Semnan
☐ EP-TPC	Bell 212	30516	ex 6-9202	
☐ EP-TPN	Bell 212	30517	ex 6-9203	
☐ EP-	Boeing 727-222F (FedEx 3)	21920/1634	ex A6-RCA	
☐ EP-	Boeing 727-222F (FedEx 3)	21917/1616	ex A6-RCB	

QESHM AIR — *Faraz Air (IRQ)* — *Tehran-Mehrabad (THR)*

☐ JY-JRF	Boeing 767-233	22526/92	ex J2-KCN	
☐ JY-RFF	Boeing 737-4K5	27831/2677	ex OO-TUB	

SAFAT AIRLINES

☐ EP-SAJ	Antonov An-26	57314002	ex RA-26592	
☐ EP-SAK	Antonov An-26	57314001	ex RA-26591	

SAFIRAN AIRLINES — *Safiran (SFN)* — *Tehran-Mehrabad (THR)*

☐ EP-SFD	Ir.An-140	9001	ex HESA-01	
☐ EP-SFE	Ir.An-140	9002		Op by Police Avn
☐ EP-SFF	Ir.An-140	9003		Op by Police Avn as HESA 90-03
☐ EP-	Ir.An-140			on order

SAHA AIRLINE — *Saha (IRZ)* — *Tehran-Mehrabad (THR)*

☐ EP-CIF	Airbus A300B4-622R	762	ex ZS-TSA	on order
☐ EP-SHG	Boeing 707-3J9C	20830/876	ex 5-8301	
☐ EP-SHK	Boeing 707-3J9C	21128/917	ex 5-8312	
☐ EP-SHU	Boeing 707-3J9C	21126/914	ex 5-8310	stored THR
☐ EP-SHV	Boeing 707-3J9C	21125/912	ex 5-8309	

TABAN AIR — *Taban (TBM)* — *Mashad (MHD)*

☐ LZ-HBD	British Aerospace 146 Srs.300	E3141	ex N615AW	Lsd fr HMS
☐ LZ-HBZ	British Aerospace 146 Srs.300	E2103	ex G-JEAK	Lsd fr HMS
☐ EP-TBA	Tupolev Tu-154M	97A-1008	ex RA-85819	
☐ RA-85761	Tupolev Tu-154M	93A-944		Lsd fr KGL

TARA AIRLINES — *Tarair (IRR)* — *Bandar Abbas (BND)*

☐ EP-TRA	Kamov Ka-32	8902	ex RA-31071	
☐ EP-TRB	Agusta A.109E Power	11007	ex D-HOBM	
☐ EP-TRH	MBB Bo.105CB	S-66	ex A6-ALS	
☐ EP-TRK	Agusta A.109E Power	11023	ex I-MALL	
☐ EP-TRM	Kamov Ka-32	8604	ex RA-31582	
☐ EP-TRT	MBB Bo.105CB	S-100	ex A6-ALQ	
☐ EP-TRZ	Kamov Ka-32	8901	ex RA-31070	

YAS AIR — *Tehran-Mehrabad (THR)*

☐ EP-GOL	Ilyushin Il-76	1013409297	ex EP-PCC	
☐ EP-GOM	Ilyushin Il-76TD	1023409321	ex EP-PCB	
☐ EP-GOQ	Antonov An-74-200	365470991021	ex 15-2250	

ZAGROS AIRLINES — *(IZG)*

☐ SX-BTM	McDonnell-Douglas MD-83	49627/1580	ex TF-JXC	
☐ UR-CDQ	McDonnell-Douglas MD-82	49372/1252	ex SX-BSQ	Lsd fr KHO

ER- MOLDOVA (Republic of Moldova)

AERIANTUR-M AIRLINES — *Aerem (MBV)* — *Kishinev-Chisinau (KIV)*

☐ ER-AXI	Antonov An-12B	6344310	ex RA-11339	

AIR MOLDOVA — *Air Moldova (9U/MLD)* — *Kishinev-Chisinau (KIV)*

☐ ER-AXP	Airbus A320-233	0741	ex N452TA	
☐ ER-AXT	Airbus A320-231	0249	ex PR-MAF	
☐ ER-AXV	Airbus A320-211	0622	ex F-WQSG	
☐ ER-EMA	Embraer EMB.120RT Brasilia	120223	ex N246CA	Lsd to TDM
☐ ER-YGD	Yakovlev Yak-40D	9831458	ex RA-87970	Op for Govt
☐ ER-65140	Tupolev Tu-134A-3	60932	ex CCCP-65140	Op for Govt
☐ F-HBBB	Embraer EMB.120ER Brasilia	120209	ex EC-HUP	

AIRLINK ARABIA — *Kishinev-Chisinau (KIV)*

☐ ER-AZX	Antonov An-24RV	47309804	ex RA-46687	

GRIXONA				
☐ ER-ICS	Ilyushin IL-18D	187009903	ex UR-CEO	

MOLDAVIAN AIRLINES		Moldavian (2M/MDV)		Kishinev-Chisinau (KIV)
☐ ER-FZA	Fokker F.28-0100 (Fokker 100)	11395	ex F-WQVS	
☐ ER-SFA	SAAB 2000	2000-056	ex HB-IYA	Lsd fr SWR
☐ ER-SFB	SAAB 2000	2000-022	ex HB-IZL	

TANDEM-AERO		Tandem (TQ/TDM)		Kishinev-Chisinau (KIV)
☐ ER-46685	Antonov An-24RV	47309710	ex CCCP-46685	

TEPAVIA TRANS AIRLINE		Tepavia (TET)		Kishinev-Chisinau (KIV)
☐ ER-AJC	WSK-PZL/Antonov An-28	1AJ003-12	ex RA-28748	
☐ ER-AWM	Antonov An-32B	3009	ex HA-TCL	
☐ ER-AZW	Antonov An-32A	2109	ex S9-BOI	
☐ ER-LIC	LET L-410UVP	820904	ex EW-215KB	

Operator Unknown

☐ ER-ADP	Antonov An-12BK	8345702	ex UR-11346
☐ ER-AWD	Antonov An-24RV	17306907	ex RA-47805

ES- ESTONIA (Republic of Estonia)

AIREST		Elka (AIT)		Tallinn-Ylemiste (TLL)
☐ ES-LLB	LET L-410UVP-E20C	912608	ex OK-WDG	
☐ ES-LLC	LET L-410UVP-E20C	912609	ex OK-WDH	

AVIES AIR COMPANY		Avies (U3/AIA)		Tallinn-Ylemiste (TLL)
☐ ES-PAH	Piper PA-31-350 Navajo Chieftain	31-7405156	ex SE-GDI	
☐ ES-PJG	British Aerospace Jetstream 31	701	ex ES-LJD	Tooru
☐ ES-PJR	British Aerospace Jetstream 32EP	949	ex SE-LNU	
☐ ES-PLB	LET L-410UVP	851413	ex LY-AVY	
☐ LY-PCL	LET L-410UVP-E	892335	ex LY-AVV	

ENIMEX		Enimex (ENI)		Tallinn-Ylemiste (TLL)
☐ ES-NOB	Antonov An-72-100	36572070695	ex CCCP-72931	Lsd to United Nations as UNO-215
☐ ES-NOH	Antonov An-72-100	36572095909	ex EL-ALX	Op for UN
☐ ES-NOI	Antonov An-72-100	36572096914	ex 3C-QQO	
☐ ES-NOK	Antonov An-72-100	36572090780	ex RA-72939	Op for UN

ESTONIAN AIR		Estonian (OV/ELL)		Tallinn-Ylemiste (TLL)
☐ ES-ABH	Boeing 737-53S	29074/3086	ex F-GJNT	
☐ ES-ABJ	Boeing 737-33R	28873/2975	ex ZK-NGA	
☐ ES-ABK	Boeing 737-36N	28572/3031	ex G-STRE	Kalev
☐ ES-ABL	Boeing 737-5L9	28997/3008	ex OK-DGB	
☐ ES-ACB	Canadair CL-600-2D24 (CRJ-900)	15233	ex C-GZQI	on order
☐ ES-ACC	Canadair CL-600-2D24 (CRJ-900)	15234	ex C-GZQJ	on order

ESTONIAN AIR REGIONAL		Estonian (OV/ELL)		Tallinn-Ylemiste (TLL)
☐ ES-ASM	SAAB SF.340A	340A-132	ex SE-LMT	
☐ ES-ASN	SAAB SF.340A	340A-151	ex SE-KUU	

FLYLAL CHATERS EESTI				Tallinn-Ylemiste (TLL)
☐ ES-LBD	Boeing 737-35B	25069/2053	ex LY-AQV	

JP AIR CARGO				Tallinn-Ylemiste (TLL)
☐ ES-JFA	Swearingen SA.227AC Metro III	AC 657	ex SX-BBX	Jussi

ET- ETHIOPIA (Federal Democratic Republic of Ethiopia)

ABYSSINIAN FLIGHT SERVICES				Addis Ababa (ADD)
☐ ET-ALD	Cessna 208 Caravan I	208B00172	ex N9750F	
☐ ET-ALF	Cessna TU206F Turbo Stationair II	U20602598	ex N206AM	

ETHIOPIAN AIRLINES		Ethiopian (ET/ETH)		Addis Ababa (ADD)
☐ ET-ALK	Boeing 737-760/W	33764/1408		
☐ ET-ALM	Boeing 737-760/W	33765/1539		
☐ ET-ALN	Boeing 737-760/W	33766/1757		
☐ ET-ALQ	Boeing 737-76N/W	33420/1459		
☐ ET-ALU	Boeing 737-76N/W	32741/1487		
☐ ET-AMZ	Boeing 737-8BK/W	29646/2282	ex G-CEJP	
☐ ET-ANA	Boeing 737-86R/W	30494/786	ex B-2660	
☐ ET-ANG	Boeing 737-7K9/W	34401/2216	ex OY-MRP	
☐ ET-ANH	Boeing 737-7K9/W	34402/2270	ex OY-MRR	
☐ ET-AJS	Boeing 757-260PF	24845/300	ex N3519L	
☐ ET-AJX	Boeing 757-260 (PCF)	25014/348		
☐ ET-AKC	Boeing 757-260	25353/408		
☐ ET-AKE	Boeing 757-260ER	26057/444		
☐ ET-AKF	Boeing 757-260ER	26058/496		
☐ ET-ALY	Boeing 757-231	28480/750	ex N708TW	
☐ ET-ALZ	Boeing 757-231	30319/883	ex N720TW	
☐ ET-AMK	Boeing 757-23N	32449/974	ex C-GMYE	
☐ ET-AMT	Boeing 757-23N	27976/814	ex N520AT	
☐ ET-AMU	Boeing 757-23N	27975/779	ex N519AT	
☐ ET-ALC	Boeing 767-33AER	28043/734		
☐ ET-ALH	Boeing 767-3BGER	30565/802	ex HB-IHW	
☐ ET-ALJ	Boeing 767-360ER	33767/918	ex N5020K	
☐ ET-ALL	Boeing 767-3BGER	30564/798	ex OO-IHV	
☐ ET-ALO	Boeing 767-360ER	33768/922		
☐ ET-ALP	Boeing 767-360ER	33769/933		
☐ ET-AME	Boeing 767-306ER	27611/633	ex PH-BZH	
☐ ET-AMF	Boeing 767-3BGER	30563/786	ex B-2561	
☐ ET-AMG	Boeing 767-3BGER	30566/817	ex B-2562	
☐ ET-AMQ	Boeing 767-33AER	27909/591	ex PR-VAA	
☐ ET-	Boeing 777-260ER			on order
☐ ET-	Boeing 777-260LR			on order
☐ ET-AML	McDonnell-Douglas MD-11ERF	48758/615	ex N742BC	
☐ ET-AND	McDonnell-Douglas MD-11BCF	48780/624	ex N588BC	
☐ ET-	de Havilland DHC-8-402Q	4303		on order
☐ ET-	de Havilland DHC-8-402Q	4304		on order
☐ ET-	de Havilland DHC-8-402Q			on order
☐ ET-	de Havilland DHC-8-402Q			on order
☐ ET-	de Havilland DHC-8-402Q			on order
☐ ET-	de Havilland DHC-8-402Q			on order
☐ ET-AKR	Fokker F.27 Mk.050 (Fokker 50)	20313	ex PH-LOP	
☐ ET-AKS	Fokker F.27 Mk.050 (Fokker 50)	20328	ex PH-EXB all-white	
☐ ET-AKT	Fokker F.27 Mk.050 (Fokker 50)	20331	ex PH-EXC all-white	
☐ ET-AKU	Fokker F.27 Mk.050 (Fokker 50)	20333	ex PH-EXD all-white	
☐ ET-AKV	Fokker F.27 Mk.050 (Fokker 50)	20335	ex PH-EXE	
☐ ET-AIT	de Havilland DHC-6 Twin Otter 310	820	ex C-GDNG	
☐ ET-AIX	de Havilland DHC-6 Twin Otter 300	835	ex C-GDFT	

TRANS NATION AIRWAYS		Trans Nation (TNW)		Addis Ababa/Jeddah (ADD/JED)
☐ ET-AKZ	de Havilland DHC-8-202	469	ex C-GLOT	op for BBZ
☐ ET-ALX	de Havilland DHC-8-202	475	ex ZK-ECR	
☐ ET-AMR	Bell 222UT	47554	ex N111DS	

EW- BELARUS (Republic of Belarus)

BELAVIA BELARUSSIAN AIRLINES		Belarus Avia (B2/BRU)		Minsk 1 (MHP)
☐ EW-250PA	Boeing 737-524	26319/2748	ex N427LF	
☐ EW-251PA	Boeing 737-5Q8	27634/2889	ex PT-SSC	
☐ EW-252PA	Boeing 737-524	26340/2777	ex LY-AGZ	
☐ EW-253PA	Boeing 737-524	26339/2771	ex LY-AGQ	
☐ EW-254PA	Boeing 737-3Q8	26294/2550	ex N201LF	
☐ EW-282PA	Boeing 737-3Q8	26321/2764	ex B-5024	
☐ EW-283PA	Boeing 737-3Q8	26333/2786	ex B-2604	
☐ EW-290PA	Boeing 737-5Q8	27629/2834	ex N381LF	
☐ EW-001PA	Boeing 737-8EV/W	33079/1075	ex N375BC	Op for Govt BBJ2
☐ EW-100PJ	Canadair CL-600-2B19 (CRJ-200LR)	7309	ex N400MJ	
☐ EW-276PJ	Canadair CL-600-2B19 (CRJ-200ER)	7799	ex N698BR	
☐ EW-277PJ	Canadair CL-600-2B19 (CRJ-200ER)	7852	ex N710BR	
☐ EW-85703	Tupolev Tu-154M	91A-878	ex CCCP-85703	

☐ EW-85706	Tupolev Tu-154M	91A-881	ex CCCP-85706	
☐ EW-85741	Tupolev Tu-154M	91A-896	ex ES-LTC	
☐ EW-85748	Tupolev Tu-154M	92A-924		
☐ EW-85815	Tupolev Tu-154M	95A-1010		VIP
☐ EW-46615	Antonov An-24RV	37308702	ex CCCP-46615	
☐ EW-65106	Tupolev Tu-134A	60315	ex CCCP-65106	
☐ EW-65149	Tupolev Tu-134A-3	61033	ex CCCP-65149	
☐ EW-88187	Yakovlev Yak-40	9620748	ex CCCP-88187	Op for Govt

GENEX

☐ EW-246TG	Antonov An-26B	67314403	ex UR-26214	Op by Airest
☐ EW-259TG	Antonov An-26B	27312706	ex UR-26094	
☐ EW-278TG	Antonov An-26	13306	ex HA-TCZ	

GOMELAVIA — Gomel (YD/GOM) — Gomel (GME)

☐ EW-245TI	Antonov An-12BP	6344608	ex EX-096	
☐ EW-46250	Antonov An-24B	77303208	ex CCCP-46250	stored GME
☐ EW-46304	Antonov An-24B	97305304	ex CCCP-46304	stored GME
☐ EW-46631	Antonov An-24RV	37308810	ex CCCP-46631	
☐ EW-46835	Antonov An-24RV	17306802	ex CCCP-46835	
☐ EW-47697	Antonov An-24RV	27307604	ex CCCP-47697	

RUBYSTAR — RubyStar (RSB) — Minsk-Machulishchy

☐ EW-266TI	Antonov An-12B	6344610	ex LZ-VEC	
☐ EW-275TI	Antonov An-12BK	00347210	ex RA--13392	
☐ EW-47808	Antonov An-24RV	17306910	ex CCCP-47808	

TRANS AVIA EXPORT CARGO AIRLINES — Transexport (AL/TXC) — Minsk-Machulishchy

☐ EW-269TI	Antonov An-12BP	1340106	ex UN-11018	
☐ EW-76710	Ilyushin Il-76TD	0063473182	ex RA-76710	
☐ EW-76711	Ilyushin Il-76TD	0063473187	ex CCCP-76711	
☐ EW-76712	Ilyushin Il-76TD	0063473190	ex CCCP-76712	
☐ EW-76735	Ilyushin Il-76TD	0073476314	ex CCCP-76735	
☐ EW-76737	Ilyushin Il-76TD	0073477323	ex CCCP-76737	Lsd to AYZ
☐ EW-78769	Ilyushin Il-76MD	0083487607	ex CCCP-78769	
☐ EW-78779	Ilyushin Il-76TD	0083489662	ex CCCP-78779	Lsd to AYZ
☐ EW-78787	Ilyushin Il-76MD	0083490698	ex CCCP-78787	
☐ EW-78792	Ilyushin Il-76TD	0093490718	ex EP-CFA	all-white
☐ EW-78799	Ilyushin Il-76TD	0093491754	ex CCCP-78799	
☐ EW-78801	Ilyushin Il-76TD	0093492763	ex CCCP-78801	
☐ EW-78808	Ilyushin Il-76TD	0093493794	ex CCCP-78808	
☐ EW-78819	Ilyushin Il-76TD	0093495883	ex CCCP-78819	
☐ EW-78827	Ilyushin Il-76TD	1003499997	ex CCCP-78827	
☐ EW-78828	Ilyushin Il-76TD	1003401004	ex RA-78828	
☐ EW-78836	Ilyushin Il-76TD	0093499986	ex CCCP-78836	
☐ EW-78839	Ilyushin Il-76TD	1003402047	ex CCCP-78839	
☐ EW-78848	Ilyushin Il-76TD	1003405159	ex CCCP-78848	

Some are stored at any time

Operator Unknown

☐ EW-284TI	Antonov An-12BP	4342210	ex EK-11830	

EX- KYRGYZSTAN (Republic of Kyrgyzstan)

AEROVISTA AIRLINES — Aerovista Group (AAP) — Sharjah (SHJ)

☐ EX-87250	Yakovlev Yak-40	9310726	ex CCCP-87250	Lsd fr TLR
☐ EX-87664	Yakovlev Yak-40	9240825	ex CCCP-87664	Lsd to TLR
☐ EX-88207	Yakovlev Yak-40K	9631149	ex EY-87207	Lsd to TLR
☐ EX-88270	Yakovlev Yak-40	9720853	ex RA-88270	Lsd to TLR
☐ EX-011	Ilyushin Il-18D	182004804	ex ER-ICM	
☐ EX-019	Antonov An-24RV	77310710	ex ST-ING	
☐ EX-023	Antonov An-24RV	17307103	ex RA-47817	
☐ EX-417	LET L-410UVP	851417	ex CCCP-67513	stored KDH

AIR MANAS — Air Manas (MBB) — Bishkek-Manas (FRU)

☐ EX-00002	Tupolev Tu-154M	91A-904	ex RA-85722	VIP Op for Government

ANIKAY AIR — Anikay (AKF) — Bishkek-Manas/Sharjah (FRU/SHJ)

☐ EX-405	Ilyushin Il-18D	184007405	ex T9-ABB	no titles
☐ EX-601	Ilyushin Il-18E	185008601	ex EL-ALD	National Paints titles

AVIA TRAFFIC COMPANY — *Atomic (AVJ)* — *Bishkek-Manas (FRU)*

Reg	Type	C/n	Previous	Name	Notes
☐ EX-051	Antonov An-24RV	57310105	ex ER-AZG		
☐ EX-076	Boeing 737-268	20882/356	ex HZ-AGF		Lsd fr ESD
☐ EX-777	Boeing 737-268	21654/532	ex HZ-AGS		Lsd fr ESD

BOTIR-AVIA — *Botir-Avia (B8/BTR)* — *Bishkek-Manas (FRU)*

Reg	Type	C/n	Previous	Name	Notes
☐ EX-89616	Ilyushin Il-76T	0023438120	ex UR-86916		stored SHJ

BRITISH GULF INTERNATIONAL AIRLINES — *Gulf Inter (BGK)* — *Bishkek-Manas/Sharjah (FRU/SHJ)*

Reg	Type	C/n	Previous	Name	Notes
☐ S9-SAE	Antonov An-12B	402408	ex LZ-BRP		
☐ S9-SAH	Antonov An-12B	5343703	ex EX-164	Alex	
☐ S9-SAJ	Antonov An-12TB	401901	ex EX-160	Irenal	
☐ S9-SAM	Antonov An-12BP	3341408	ex EX-162	Akula	stored SHJ
☐ S9-SAP	Antonov An-12BP	5343305	ex EX-161	Fatima	
☐ S9-SAR	Antonov An-12TA	2340801	ex EX-085		
☐ S9-SAV	Antonov An-12AP	2340602	ex EX-045	Igor	

CLICK AIRWAYS — *Click (4C/CGK)* — *Sharjah (SHJ)*

Reg	Type	C/n	Previous	Name	Notes
☐ EK-11418	Antonov An-12BP	7344705	ex EX-166		Regd to Click Airways International
☐ EX-029	Antonov An-12BP	8345607	ex EX-12555		
☐ EX-169	Antonov An-12BP	01348005	ex EX-034		
☐ EX-401	Antonov An-12				
☐ EX-402	Antonov An-12				
☐ EX-403	Antonov An-12				
☐ EY-402	Antonov An-12B	8346006	ex EX-031	no titles	
☐ EK-76400	Ilyushin Il-76TD	1023413438	ex JY-JIB		
☐ EX-033	Ilyushin Il-76TD	0033446235	ex RA-76788		
☐ EX-035	Ilyushin Il-76TD	0093498962	ex RA-76795		
☐ EX-036	Ilyushin Il-76TD	0093495863	ex RA-76785		Lsd to Ababeel
☐ EY-604	Ilyushin Il-76TD	1023410355	ex ST-WTA		

ESSEN AIR — *Essen (ESD)*

Reg	Type	C/n	Previous	Name	Notes
☐ EX-076	Boeing 737-268	20882/356	ex HZ-AGF		Lsd to AVJ
☐ EX-777	Boeing 737-268	21654/532	ex HZ-AGS		Lsd to AVJ

GALAXY AIRLINES — *Kackar (GAL)* — *Bishkek-Manas (FRU)*

Reg	Type	C/n	Previous	Name	Notes
☐ EX-786	Ilyushin Il-18V	188011201	ex RA-74268		op by 'Osh Avia'
☐ EX-75466	Ilyushin Il-18	187010403	ex RA-75466	National Paints titles	

GARINCO AIRWAYS

Reg	Type	C/n	Previous	Name	Notes
☐ EX-87820	Yakovlev Yak-40	9231224	ex RA-87820		

INTAL AIR — *Intal (INL)* — *Bishkek-Manas/Sharjah (FRU/SHJ)*

Reg	Type	C/n	Previous	Name	Notes
☐ EX-050	Boeing 737-229C (Nordam 3)	21139/437	ex TJ-AIO		
☐ EX-061	Boeing 737-2S2C (Nordam 3)	21927/600	ex N806AL		
☐ EX-081	Boeing 737-268	21283/477	ex HZ-AGN		
☐ EX-201	Ilyushin Il-18D	188011201	ex EX-74268	no titles	
☐ EX-75905	Ilyushin Il-18E	186008905	ex LZ-ZAH	no titles	

ITEK AIR — *Itek Air (GI/IKA)* — *Bishkek-Manas (FRU)*

Reg	Type	C/n	Previous	Name	Notes
☐ EX-009	Boeing 737-219	22088/676	ex HP-1288CMP		
☐ EX-127	Boeing 737-275 (AvAero 3)	21819/627	ex AP-BHU		
☐ EX-311	Boeing 737-268	21276/468	ex EX-080		LSD to PIR
☐ EX-25003	Boeing 737-2T5	22632/847	ex UP-B3703		

KYRGHYZSTAN — *Altyn Avia (QH/LYN)* — *Bishkek-Manas (FRU)*

Reg	Type	C/n	Previous	Name	Notes
☐ EX-014	Antonov An-24RV	77310807	ex 4R-SEL		
☐ EX-020	Tupolev Tu-134A-3	61042	ex 4L-65750		
☐ EX-24805	Antonov An-24RV	77310805	ex S9-CBA	all-white	
☐ EX-85718	Tupolev Tu-154M	91A-900	ex CCCP-85718		

KYRGHYZSTAN AIRLINES — *Kyrgyz (R8/KGA)* — *Bishkek-Manas / Karakol / Osh (FRU/-/OSS)*

Reg	Type	C/n	Previous	Name	Notes
☐ EX-25004	Boeing 737-247 (Nordam 3)	23516/1257	ex EY-531		
☐ EX-65778	Tupolev Tu-134A-3	62590	ex CCCP-65778		
☐ EX-65779	Tupolev Tu-134A-3	62602	ex CCCP-65779		
☐ EX-65789	Tupolev Tu-134A-3	62850	ex CCCP-65789		
☐ EX-85257	Tupolev Tu-154B-2	78A-257	ex CCCP-85257		

Registration	Type	C/n	Previous identity	Notes
☐ EX-85259	Tupolev Tu-154B-1	78A-259	ex CCCP-85259	
☐ EX-85590	Tupolev Tu-154B-2	84A-590	ex CCCP-85590	
☐ EX-85762	Tupolev Tu-154M	92A-945	ex RA-85762	
☐ EX-87259	Yakovlev Yak-40	9311626	ex CCCP-87259	
☐ EX-87275	Yakovlev Yak-40	9311127	ex UN-87275	
☐ EX-87293	Yakovlev Yak-40	9320828	ex CCCP-87293	
☐ EX-87331	Yakovlev Yak-40	9510239	ex CCCP-87331	
☐ EX-87442	Yakovlev Yak-40	9431935	ex CCCP-87442	
☐ EX-87445	Yakovlev Yak-40	9430236	ex CCCP-87445	
☐ EX-87470	Yakovlev Yak-40	9441537	ex CCCP-87470	
☐ EX-87538	Yakovlev Yak-40	9530342	ex CCCP-87538	
☐ EX-87555	Yakovlev Yak-40	9210621	ex CCCP-87555	
☐ EX-87571	Yakovlev Yak-40	9221521	ex CCCP-87571	
☐ EX-87589	Yakovlev Yak-40	9220123	ex CCCP-87589	
☐ EX-87836	Yakovlev Yak-40	9240226	ex CCCP-87836	

KYRGYZ TRANS AIR — *Dinafra (KTC)* — *Bishkek-Manas (FRU)*

Registration	Type	C/n	Previous identity	Notes
☐ EX-301	Airbus A310-304	524	ex D-AIDF	Lsd to IRM
☐ EX-35004	Airbus A310-308	620	ex D-AHLC	Lsd to IRM

OSH AVIA

Registration	Type	C/n	Previous identity	Notes
☐ EX-112	Yakovlev Yak-40			Bintimak

REEM AIRLINES — *Reem Air (V4/REK)* — *Sharjah (SHJ)*

Registration	Type	C/n	Previous identity	Notes
☐ EX-049	Ilyushin Il-76T	083415453	ex RA-76514	

SKY WAY AIR — *Sky Worker (SAB)* — *Dubai (DXB)*

Registration	Type	C/n	Previous identity	Notes
☐ EX-016	Antonov An-26	17311207	ex RA-26065	
☐ EX-126	Antonov An-26B	11508	ex UN-26075	

TENIR AIRLINES — *Tenir Air (TEB)* — *Sharjah (SHJ)*

Registration	Type	C/n	Previous identity	Notes
☐ EK-11032	Antonov An-12V	7345004	ex 11032	
☐ EX-075	Ilyushin Il-76TD	0053463908	ex ER-IBL	all-white

TRANS AIR

Registration	Type	C/n	Previous identity	Notes
☐ EX-24103	Antonov An-24B	07306103	ex TN-AFL	

TRAST AERO — *Trast Aero (S5/TSJ)* — *Sharjah (SHJ)*

Registration	Type	C/n	Previous identity	Notes
☐ EK-46581	Antonov An-24B	97304910	ex RA-46581	
☐ EX-059	Ilyushin Il-18V	182004801	ex RA-75894	
☐ EX-103	ROMBAC One-Eleven 561RC	403	ex YR-BRC	
☐ JY-TWB	Antonov An-26B-100	27312610	ex EX-021	Op for Skylink Arabia
☐ TN-AGB	Antonov An-26B-100	87307210		
☐ 3C-OET	Antonov An-26B	4104	ex S9-KAV	
☐ 4L-BKA	Antonov An-26B	87306407	ex LZ-MNH	
☐ 4L-GAS	Boeing 707-379C	19821/718	ex EX-120	
☐ 4L-OVA	Antonov An-32	1408	ex 3X-GES	

Operator Unknown

Registration	Type	C/n	Previous identity	Notes
☐ EX-116	Antonov An-30	1303	ex RA-30072	
☐ EX-118	Antonov An-30	1301	ex RA-30070	
☐ EX-129	Antonov An-12BK	9346803	ex ER-ACN	

EY- TAJIKISTAN (Republic of Tajikistan)

EAST AIR

Registration	Type	C/n	Previous identity	Notes
☐ EY-532	Boeing 737-25A	23791/1486	ex EX-734	
☐ EY-538	Boeing 737-4Y0	23980/1667	ex N239DT	

RUS AVIATION

Registration	Type	C/n	Previous identity	Notes
☐ EY-403	Antonov An-12BP	00347107	ex EX-042	

SOMON AIR

Registration	Type	C/n	Previous identity	Notes
☐ EY-537	Boeing 737-4B7	24550/1793	ex N245DT	
☐ EY-777	Boeing 737-8GJ/W	34960/2765	ex N960BB	Sadriddin Ayni
☐ EY-787	Boeing 737-8GJ/W	34955/2512	ex N349FD	Ismoil Somoni

TAJIK AIR		Tajikistan (7J/TJK)		Dushanbe/Khudzhand (DYU/LBD)
☐ EY-46365	Antonov An-24B	07305906	ex CCCP-46365	
☐ EY-45595	Antonov An-24B	97305105	ex UR-45595	
☐ EY-47693	Antonov An-24RV	27307510	ex CCCP-47693	Lsd to DAO
☐ EY-47802	Antonov An-24RV	17306901	ex UN-47802	
☐ EY-24404	Mil Mi-8T	98625146	ex CCCP-24404	
☐ EY-25149	Mil Mi-8MTV-1	95190	ex CCCP-25149	
☐ EY-25167	Mil Mi-8MTV-1	95378	ex CCCP-25167	
☐ EY-25169	Mil Mi-8MTV-1	95380	ex CCCP-25169	Lsd to United Nations
☐ EY-25438	Mil Mi-8MTV-1	95549	ex CCCP-25438	
☐ EY-65003	Tupolev Tu-134A-3	44040	ex CCCP-65003	Lsd to AYZ
☐ EY-65022	Tupolev Tu-134A-3	48395	ex ES-AAE	
☐ EY-65763	Tupolev Tu-134A-3	62299	ex CCCP-65763	
☐ EY-65788	Tupolev Tu-134A-3	62835	ex CCCP-65788	
☐ EY-65835	Tupolev Tu-134A-3	17112	ex CCCP-65835	
☐ EY-65875	Tupolev Tu-134A-3	29317	ex CCCP-65875	
☐ EY-65895	Tupolev Tu-134A-3	40140	ex CCCP-65895	
☐ EY-85469	Tupolev Tu-154B-2	81A-469	ex CCCP-85469	
☐ EY-85487	Tupolev Tu-154B-2	81A-487	ex CCCP-85487	
☐ EY-85511	Tupolev Tu-154B-2	81A-511	ex CCCP-85511	
☐ EY-85651	Tupolev Tu-154M	88A-793	ex RA-85651	
☐ EY-85691	Tupolev Tu-154M	90A-864	ex EP-EAB	Lsd to IRX
☐ EY-85692	Tupolev Tu-154M	90A-865	ex EP-TUE	
☐ EY-85717	Tupolev Tu-154M	91A-897	ex EP-EAA	
☐ EY-87214	Yakovlev Yak-40K	9640851	ex HA-LJB	
☐ EY-87217	Yakovlev Yak-40	9510340	ex EP-EAL	
☐ EY-87434	Yakovlev Yak-40	9431035	ex EP-TUF	
☐ EY-87922	Yakovlev Yak-40K	9731355	ex EP-EAM	
☐ EY-87963	Yakovlev Yak-40K	9831058	ex EP-EAK	Lsd to KMF
☐ EY-87967	Yakovlev Yak-40K	9831158	ex EP-CPI	
☐ EY-88267	Yakovlev Yak-40K	9720553	ex CCP-66267	
☐ EX-536	Boeing 737-3B7	23700/1461	ex N514AU	
☐ LY-AWF	Boeing 737-522	26707/2512	ex C-FDCZ	
☐ LY-AWG	Boeing 737-522	26700/2490	ex C-FDCH	
☐ EY-751	Boeing 757-2Q8	24964/424	ex N926JS	
☐ EY-26205	Antonov An-26B	14107	ex CCCP-26205	
☐ EY-26658	Antonov An-26	7904	ex 26658	
☐ EY-28734	WSK-PZL/Antonov An-28	1AJ007-19	ex CCCP-28734	
☐ EY-28736	WSK-PZL/Antonov An-28	1AJ007-24	ex CCCP-28736	
☐ EY-28921	WSK-PZL/Antonov An-28	1AJ008-07	ex CCCP-28921	

EZ- TURKMENISTAN (Republic of Turkmenistan)

TURKMENISTAN AIRLINES		Turkmenistan (T5/TUA)		Askhabad (ASB)
☐ EZ-A101	Boeing 717-22K	55153/5072	ex N6202S	
☐ EZ-A102	Boeing 717-22K	55154/5078		
☐ EZ-A103	Boeing 717-22K	55155/5086		
☐ EZ-A104	Boeing 717-22K	55195/5130		
☐ EZ-A105	Boeing 717-22K	55196/5133		
☐ EZ-A106	Boeing 717-22K	55186/5146		
☐ EZ-A107	Boeing 717-22K	55187/5147		
☐ EZ-A001	Boeing 737-341	26855/2305	ex EK-A001	
☐ EZ-A002	Boeing 737-332	25994/2439	ex N301DE	
☐ EZ-A003	Boeing 737-332	25995/2455	ex N302DE	
☐ EZ-A004	Boeing 737-82K	36088/2181	ex N1795B	
☐ EZ-A005	Boeing 737-82K	36089/2233		
☐ EZ-A006	Boeing 737-7GL/W	37236/2986	ex N1786B	
☐ EZ-A007	Boeing 737-7GL/W	37234/2682		
☐ EZ-A008	Boeing 737-7GL/W	37237/2988	ex N1787B	
☐ EZ-A009	Boeing 737-7GL/W	37235/2993	ex N3134C	
☐ EZ-L482	Mil Mi-8MTV-1	96144		
☐ EZ-L483	Mil Mi-8MTV-1	96145		
☐ EZ-22763	Mil Mi-8T	9831150	ex CCCP-22763	
☐ EZ-24624	Mil Mi-8T	8253	ex CCCP-24624	
☐ EZ-24701	Mil Mi-8T	98103235	ex CCCP-24701	
☐ EZ-A010	Boeing 757-23A	25345/412	ex N58AW	
☐ EZ-A011	Boeing 757-22K	28336/725		
☐ EZ-A012	Boeing 757-22K	28337/726		
☐ EZ-A014	Boeing 757-22K	30863/952		
☐ EZ-A700	Boeing 767-32KER	33968/926		op for Govt

☐ EZ-F423	Ilyushin Il-76TD	1033418608			
☐ EZ-F426	Ilyushin Il-76TD	1033418609			
☐ EZ-F427	Ilyushin Il-76TD	1033418620			
☐ EZ-F428	Ilyushin Il-76TD	1043418624			
☐ EZ-P710	Aérospatiale AS.332L2	2577	ex F-WQDJ		op for Govt
☐ EZ-P711	Aérospatiale AS.332L2	2578	ex F-WWOU		op for Govt
☐ EZ-S701	Sikorsky S-76C+	760463			op for Govt
☐ EZ-S702	Sikorsky S-76C+	760461			
☐ EZ-S703	Sikorsky S-76A+	760294	ex VH-XHL		
☐ EZ-S720	Sikorsky S-92	920017	ex N7118Z		op for Govt
☐ EZ-S721	Sikorsky S-92	920026	ex N8103U		op for Govt

E3- ERITREA (State of Eritrea)

ERITREAN AIRLINES — *Eritrean (B8/ERT)* — *Asmara (ASM)*

☐ E3-AAQ	Boeing 767-238ER	23309/129	ex N771WD		

NAS AIR — *Asmara (ASM)*

☐ E3-NAS	Boeing 737-2T5	21960/642	ex EX-214	Dalia	

E5- COOK ISLANDS

AIR RAROTONGA — *Air Rarotonga (GZ)* — *Rarotonga (RAR)*

☐ E5-EFS	SAAB SF.340A	340A-049	ex ZK-EFS		
☐ E5-FTS	Embraer EMB.110P1 Bandeirante	110239	ex ZK-FTS		
☐ E5-TAK	Embraer EMB.110P1 Bandeirante	110448	ex ZK-TAK		

E7- BOSNIA-HERZEGOVINA (Republic of Bosnia-Herzegovina)

BH AIRLINES — *Air Bosna (JA/BON)* — *Banja Luka*

☐ E7-AAD	ATR 72-212	464	ex T9-AAD	Sarajevo	
☐ E7-AAE	ATR 72-212	465	ex T9-AAE	Mostar	
☐ TC-JDH	Boeing 737-4Y0	25184/2227		Amasra	Lsd fr THY

ICAR

☐ E7-AAK	LET L-410UVP-E	892321	ex T9-AAK		
☐ E7-BBA	Boeing 737-301	23937/1587	ex EY-535		

F- FRANCE (French Republic)

AERO SOTRAVIA — *Nangis les Loges*

☐ F-GCPO	Piper PA-34-200T Seneca II	34-8070358	ex N8266V		
☐ F-GDHD	Britten-Norman BN-2A-9 Islander	591	ex 9Q-CMJ		
☐ F-GMLJ	Cessna 414	414-0635	ex I-CCEE		

AIGLE AZUR — *Aigle Azur (ZI/AAF) Paris-Orly/Charles de Gaulle (ORY/CDG)*

☐ F-GXAG	Airbus A319-132	2296	ex N804BR		
☐ F-GXAH	Airbus A319-112	1846	ex C-GTDX		
☐ F-HBMI	Airbus A319-114	0639	ex N573SX		
☐ F-GJVF	Airbus A320-211	0244			
☐ F-HBAC	Airbus A320-214	0888	ex EC-GZE		
☐ F-HBII	Airbus A320-214	3852	ex F-WWDH		
☐ F-GUAA	Airbus A321-211	0808	ex G-JSJX		
☐ F-HBAB	Airbus A321-211	0823	ex F-WBAB		
☐ F-HBAF	Airbus A321-211	1006	ex EC-IXY		
☐ F-HCAI	Airbus A321-211	1451	ex TC-KTC		

AIR FRANCE — *Airfrans (AF/AFR) Paris Charles de Gaulle/Orly (CDG/ORY)*

Member of Skyteam

☐ F-GUGA	Airbus A318-111	2035	ex D-AUAD		
☐ F-GUGB	Airbus A318-111	2059	ex D-AUAF		
☐ F-GUGC	Airbus A318-111	2071	ex D-AUAG		
☐ F-GUGD	Airbus A318-111	2081	ex D-AUAH		
☐ F-GUGE	Airbus A318-111	2100	ex D-AUAI		
☐ F-GUGF	Airbus A318-111	2109	ex D-AUAJ		
☐ F-GUGG	Airbus A318-111	2317	ex D-AUAA		

	Reg	Type	c/n	Prev	Name	Remarks
☐	F-GUGH	Airbus A318-111	2344	ex D-AUAF		
☐	F-GUGI	Airbus A318-111	2350	ex D-AUAG		
☐	F-GUGJ	Airbus A318-111	2582	ex D-AUAE		
☐	F-GUGK	Airbus A318-111	2601	ex D-AUAF		
☐	F-GUGL	Airbus A318-111	2686	ex D-AUAA		
☐	F-GUGM	Airbus A318-111	2750	ex D-AUAB		
☐	F-GUGN	Airbus A318-111	2918	ex D-AUAB		
☐	F-GUGO	Airbus A318-111	2951	ex D-AUAD		
☐	F-GUGP	Airbus A318-111	2967	ex D-AUAF		
☐	F-GUGQ	Airbus A318-111	2972	ex D-AUAG		
☐	F-GUGR	Airbus A318-111	3009	ex D-AUAJ		
☐	F-GPMA	Airbus A319-113	0598	ex D-AVYD		
☐	F-GPMB	Airbus A319-113	0600	ex D-AVYC		
☐	F-GPMC	Airbus A319-113	0608	ex D-AVYE		
☐	F-GPMD	Airbus A319-113	0618	ex D-AVYJ		
☐	F-GPME	Airbus A319-113	0625	ex D-AVYQ		
☐	F-GPMF	Airbus A319-113	0637	ex D-AVYT		
☐	F-GRHA	Airbus A319-111	0938	ex D-AVYS		
☐	F-GRHB	Airbus A319-111	0985	ex D-AVYO		
☐	F-GRHC	Airbus A319-111	0998	ex D-AVYW		
☐	F-GRHD	Airbus A319-111	1000	ex D-AVYP		
☐	F-GRHE	Airbus A319-111	1020	ex D-AVYX		
☐	F-GRHF	Airbus A319-111	1025	ex D-AVYE		
☐	F-GRHG	Airbus A319-111	1036	ex D-AVYS		
☐	F-GRHH	Airbus A319-111	1151	ex D-AVWK		
☐	F-GRHI	Airbus A319-111	1169	ex D-AVYX		
☐	F-GRHJ	Airbus A319-111	1176	ex D-AVWN		
☐	F-GRHK	Airbus A319-111	1190	ex D-AVYQ		
☐	F-GRHL	Airbus A319-111	1201	ex D-AVWT		
☐	F-GRHM	Airbus A319-111	1216	ex D-AVYF		
☐	F-GRHN	Airbus A319-111	1267	ex D-AVWB		
☐	F-GRHO	Airbus A319-111	1271	ex D-AVWC		
☐	F-GRHP	Airbus A319-111	1344	ex D-AVYQ		
☐	F-GRHQ	Airbus A319-111	1404	ex D-AVYB		
☐	F-GRHR	Airbus A319-111	1415	ex D-AVYF		
☐	F-GRHS	Airbus A319-111	1444	ex D-AVWA		
☐	F-GRHT	Airbus A319-111	1449	ex D-AVWD		
☐	F-GRHU	Airbus A319-111	1471	ex D-AVYR		
☐	F-GRHV	Airbus A319-111	1505	ex D-AVYF		
☐	F-GRHX	Airbus A319-111	1524	ex D-AVWC		
☐	F-GRHY	Airbus A319-111	1616	ex D-AVWG		
☐	F-GRHZ	Airbus A319-111	1622	ex D-AVYO		
☐	F-GRXA	Airbus A319-111	1640	ex D-AVYJ		
☐	F-GRXB	Airbus A319-111	1645	ex D-AVYC		
☐	F-GRXC	Airbus A319-111	1677	ex D-AVWF		
☐	F-GRXD	Airbus A319-111	1699	ex D-AVYG		
☐	F-GRXE	Airbus A319-111	1733	ex D-AVWT		
☐	F-GRXF	Airbus A319-111	1938	ex D-AVWG		
☐	F-GRXG	Airbus A319-115LR	2213	ex D-AVYM	Dedicate	
☐	F-GRXH	Airbus A319-115LR	2228	ex D-AVWC	Dedicate	
☐	F-GRXI	Airbus A319-115LR	2279	ex D-AVYF	Dedicate	
☐	F-GRXJ	Airbus A319-115LR	2456	ex D-AVYX	Dedicate	
☐	F-GRXK	Airbus A319-115LR	2716	ex D-AVYX	Dedicate	
☐	F-GRXL	Airbus A319-111	2938	ex D-AVWV		
☐	F-GRXM	Airbus A319-111	2961	ex D-AVYI		
☐	F-GRXN	Airbus A319-115LR	3065	ex D-AVWP	Dedicate	
☐	F-GFKA	Airbus A320-111	0005	ex F-WWDI	Ville de Paris	
☐	F-GFKB	Airbus A320-111	0007	ex F-WWDJ	Ville de Rome	stored CDG
☐	F-GFKD	Airbus A320-111	0014	ex F-WWDO	Ville de Londres	
☐	F-GFKE	Airbus A320-111	0019		Ville de Bonn	stored ORY
☐	F-GFKH	Airbus A320-211	0061		Ville de Bruxelles	
☐	F-GFKI	Airbus A320-211	0062		Ville de Lisbonne	
☐	F-GFKJ	Airbus A320-211	0063		Ville de Copenhague	Retro c/s
☐	F-GFKM	Airbus A320-211	0102		Ville de Luxembourg	
☐	F-GFKN	Airbus A320-211	0128		Ville de Strasbourg	
☐	F-GFKR	Airbus A320-211	0186		Ville de Barcelonne	
☐	F-GFKS	Airbus A320-211	0187			
☐	F-GFKT	Airbus A320-211	0188		Ville de Lyon	
☐	F-GFKU	Airbus A320-211	0226		Ville de Manchester	
☐	F-GFKV	Airbus A320-211	0227		Ville de Bordeaux	
☐	F-GFKX	Airbus A320-211	0228		Ville de Francfort	
☐	F-GFKY	Airbus A320-211	0285		Ville de Toulouse	
☐	F-GFKZ	Airbus A320-211	0286		Ville de Turin	
☐	F-GGEB	Airbus A320-111	0012	ex F-WWDM		
☐	F-GGEE	Airbus A320-111	0016	ex F-WWDQ		
☐	F-GHQC	Airbus A320-211	0044	ex F-GGEH		
☐	F-GHQD	Airbus A320-211	0108			
☐	F-GHQE	Airbus A320-211	0115			
☐	F-GHQF	Airbus A320-211	0130			
☐	F-GHQG	Airbus A320-211	0155			
☐	F-GHQH	Airbus A320-211	0156			

Registration	Type	C/n	Previous identity	Name	Remarks
☐ F-GHQI	Airbus A320-211	0184			
☐ F-GHQJ	Airbus A320-211	0214			
☐ F-GHQK	Airbus A320-211	0236			
☐ F-GHQL	Airbus A320-211	0239			
☐ F-GHQM	Airbus A320-211	0237			
☐ F-GHQO	Airbus A320-211	0278			
☐ F-GHQP	Airbus A320-211	0337			
☐ F-GHQQ	Airbus A320-211	0352			
☐ F-GHQR	Airbus A320-211	0377			
☐ F-GJVA	Airbus A320-211	0144	ex F-WWDK		
☐ F-GJVB	Airbus A320-211	0145	ex F-WWDL		
☐ F-GJVG	Airbus A320-211	0270			
☐ F-GJVW	Airbus A320-211	0491			
☐ F-GKXA	Airbus A320-211	0287		Ville de Nantes	
☐ F-GKXB	Airbus A320-212	0235	ex F-OHFX		
☐ F-GKXC	Airbus A320-214	1502	ex F-WWIG		
☐ F-GKXD	Airbus A320-214	1873	ex F-WWDV		
☐ F-GKXE	Airbus A320-214	1879	ex F-WWDX		
☐ F-GKXF	Airbus A320-214	1885			
☐ F-GKXG	Airbus A320-214	1894	ex F-WWDV		
☐ F-GKXH	Airbus A320-214	1924			
☐ F-GKXI	Airbus A320-214	1949			
☐ F-GKXJ	Airbus A320-214	1900			
☐ F-GKXK	Airbus A320-214	2140	ex F-WWBR		
☐ F-GKXL	Airbus A320-214	2705			
☐ F-GKXM	Airbus A320-214	2721	ex F-WWXM		
☐ F-GKXN	Airbus A320-214	3008	ex F-WWBH		
☐ F-GKXO	Airbus A320-214	3420	ex F-WWIP		
☐ F-GKXP	Airbus A320-214	3470	ex F-WWBP		
☐ F-GKXQ	Airbus A320-214	3777	ex D-AVVH		
☐ F-GKXR	Airbus A320-214	3795	ex F-WWBM		
☐ F-GKXS	Airbus A320-214	3825	ex F-WWIV		
☐ F-GKXT	Airbus A320-214	3859	ex F-WWDM		
☐ F-GKXU	Airbus A320-214	4063	ex F-WWBF		
☐ F-GKXV	Airbus A320-214	4084	ex D-AVVA		
☐ F-GKXY	Airbus A320-214	4105	ex D-AVVR		
☐ F-GKXZ	Airbus A320-214	4137	ex F-WWIZ		
☐ F-HEPA	Airbus A320-214	4138	ex F-WWXZ		
☐ F-HEPB	Airbus A320-214	4241	ex		on order
☐ F-HEPC	Airbus A320-214	4267	ex		on order
☐ F-HEPD	Airbus A320-214		ex		on order
☐ F-HEPE	Airbus A320-214		ex		on order
☐ F-HEPF	Airbus A320-214		ex		on order

Registration	Type	C/n	Previous identity
☐ F-GMZA	Airbus A321-111	0498	ex D-AVZK
☐ F-GMZB	Airbus A321-111	0509	ex D-AVZN
☐ F-GMZC	Airbus A321-111	0521	ex D-AVZW
☐ F-GMZD	Airbus A321-111	0529	ex D-AVZA
☐ F-GMZE	Airbus A321-111	0544	ex D-AVZF
☐ F-GTAD	Airbus A321-211	0777	ex D-AVZI
☐ F-GTAE	Airbus A321-211	0796	ex D-AVZN
☐ F-GTAH	Airbus A321-211	1133	ex D-AVZD
☐ F-GTAI	Airbus A321-211	1299	ex D-AVZP
☐ F-GTAJ	Airbus A321-211	1476	ex D-AVZF
☐ F-GTAK	Airbus A321-211	1658	ex D-AVZP
☐ F-GTAL	Airbus A321-211	1691	ex D-AVZY
☐ F-GTAM	Airbus A321-211	1859	ex D-AVZY
☐ F-GTAN	Airbus A321-211	3051	ex D-AVZD
☐ F-GTAO	Airbus A321-211	3098	ex D-AVZQ
☐ F-GTAP	Airbus A321-211	3372	ex D-AVZK
☐ F-GTAQ	Airbus A321-211	3399	ex D-AVZQ
☐ F-GTAR	Airbus A321-211	3401	ex D-AVZR
☐ F-GTAS	Airbus A321-211	3419	ex D-AVZE
☐ F-GTAT	Airbus A321-211	3441	ex D-AVZH
☐ F-GTAU	Airbus A321-211	3814	ex D-AVZE
☐ F-GTAV	Airbus A321-211	3884	ex D-AVZU
☐ F-GTAX	Airbus A321-211	3930	ex D-AZAD

Registration	Type	C/n	Previous identity
☐ F-GZCA	Airbus A330-203	422	
☐ F-GZCB	Airbus A330-203	443	
☐ F-GZCC	Airbus A330-203	448	
☐ F-GZCD	Airbus A330-203	458	ex (F-WWJH)
☐ F-GZCE	Airbus A330-203	465	ex F-WWKM
☐ F-GZCF	Airbus A330-203	481	
☐ F-GZCG	Airbus A330-203	498	ex F-WWKI
☐ F-GZCH	Airbus A330-203	500	
☐ F-GZCI	Airbus A330-203	502	ex F-WWKJ
☐ F-GZCJ	Airbus A330-203	503	
☐ F-GZCK	Airbus A330-203	516	
☐ F-GZCL	Airbus A330-203	519	
☐ F-GZCM	Airbus A330-203	567	ex (F-WWYT)
☐ F-GZCN	Airbus A330-203	584	
☐ F-GZCO	Airbus A330-203	657	

	Registration	Type	c/n	Previous	Operator	Remarks
☐	F-GLZC	Airbus A340-311	029			
☐	F-GLZH	Airbus A340-311	078			
☐	F-GLZI	Airbus A340-311	084			
☐	F-GLZJ	Airbus A340-313X	186			
☐	F-GLZK	Airbus A340-313X	207			
☐	F-GLZL	Airbus A340-313X	210			
☐	F-GLZM	Airbus A340-313X	237			
☐	F-GLZN	Airbus A340-313X	245			
☐	F-GLZO	Airbus A340-313X	246			
☐	F-GLZP	Airbus A340-313X	260			
☐	F-GLZR	Airbus A340-313X	307			
☐	F-GLZS	Airbus A340-313X	310			
☐	F-GLZT	Airbus A340-313X	319			
☐	F-GLZU	Airbus A340-313X	377			
☐	F-GNIF	Airbus A340-313X	168			
☐	F-GNIG	Airbus A340-313X	174			
☐	F-GNIH	Airbus A340-313X	373			
☐	F-GNII	Airbus A340-313X	399			
☐	F-HPJA	Airbus A380-861	033	ex F-WWSB		
☐	F-HPJB	Airbus A380-861	040	ex F-WW		on order
☐	F-HPJC	Airbus A380-861	043	ex F-WWAB		on order
☐	F-HPJD	Airbus A380-861	049	ex F-WWAL		on order
☐	F-HPJE	Airbus A380-861	052	ex F-WWAN		on order
☐	F-HPJF	Airbus A380-861	064	ex F-WWAU		on order
☐	F-HPJG	Airbus A380-861	067	ex F-WW		on order
☐	F-HPJH	Airbus A380-861	077	ex F-WW		on order
☐	F-GCBG	Boeing 747-228F	22939/569	ex N4544F	Air France Cargo	stored Vatry
☐	F-GCBL	Boeing 747-228F	24735/772		Air France Cargo Asie	stored Vatry
☐	F-GCBM	Boeing 747-228F	24879/822		Air France Cargo	stored Vatry
☐	F-GEXA	Boeing 747-4B3	24154/741			
☐	F-GEXB	Boeing 747-4B3M	24155/864			
☐	F-GISA	Boeing 747-428MBCF	25238/872			stored CDG
☐	F-GISB	Boeing 747-428MBCF	25302/884			stored Vatry
☐	F-GISC	Boeing 747-428M	25599/899			stored Vatry
☐	F-GISD	Boeing 747-428M	25628/934			
☐	F-GISE	Boeing 747-428BCF	25630/960			stored Vatry
☐	F-GISF	Boeing 747-481BDSF	24801/805	ex TF-AMP		stored CDG
☐	F-GITA	Boeing 747-428	24969/836			
☐	F-GITB	Boeing 747-428	24990/843	ex N6009F		
☐	F-GITC	Boeing 747-428	25344/889			stored Vatry
☐	F-GITD	Boeing 747-428	25600/901			
☐	F-GITE	Boeing 747-428	25601/906			
☐	F-GITF	Boeing 747-428	25602/909			
☐	F-GITH	Boeing 747-428	32868/1325			
☐	F-GITI	Boeing 747-428	32869/1327			
☐	F-GITJ	Boeing 747-428	32871/1343			
☐	F-GIUA	Boeing 747-428ERF	32866/1315	ex N5017Q		
☐	F-GIUC	Boeing 747-428ERF	32867/1318			
☐	F-GIUD	Boeing 747-428ERF	32870/1344			
☐	F-GIUE	Boeing 747-428ERF	33097/1361			
☐	F-GSPA	Boeing 777-228ER	29002/129			
☐	F-GSPB	Boeing 777-228ER	29003/133			
☐	F-GSPC	Boeing 777-228ER	29004/138			
☐	F-GSPD	Boeing 777-228ER	29005/187			
☐	F-GSPE	Boeing 777-228ER	29006/189			
☐	F-GSPF	Boeing 777-228ER	29007/201			
☐	F-GSPG	Boeing 777-228ER	27609/195			
☐	F-GSPH	Boeing 777-228ER	28675/210			
☐	F-GSPI	Boeing 777-228ER	29008/258			
☐	F-GSPJ	Boeing 777-228ER	29009/263			
☐	F-GSPK	Boeing 777-228ER	29010/267			
☐	F-GSPL	Boeing 777-228ER	30457/284	ex N50281		
☐	F-GSPM	Boeing 777-228ER	30456/307			
☐	F-GSPN	Boeing 777-228ER	29011/314			
☐	F-GSPO	Boeing 777-228ER	30614/320			
☐	F-GSPP	Boeing 777-228ER	30615/327			
☐	F-GSPQ	Boeing 777-228ER	28682/331			
☐	F-GSPR	Boeing 777-228ER	28683/367			
☐	F-GSPS	Boeing 777-228ER	32306/370			
☐	F-GSPT	Boeing 777-228ER	32308/382			
☐	F-GSPU	Boeing 777-228ER	32309/383			
☐	F-GSPV	Boeing 777-228ER	28684/385			
☐	F-GSPX	Boeing 777-228ER	32698/392			
☐	F-GSPY	Boeing 777-228ER	32305/395			
☐	F-GSPZ	Boeing 777-228ER	32310/401			
☐	F-GSQA	Boeing 777-328ER	32723/466	ex N5017Q		
☐	F-GSQB	Boeing 777-328ER	32724/478			
☐	F-GSQC	Boeing 777-328ER	32727/480			
☐	F-GSQD	Boeing 777-328ER	32726/490			

	Registration	Type	C/n	Previous identity	Name/Colours	Remarks
☐	F-GSQE	Boeing 777-328ER	32851/492			
☐	F-GSQF	Boeing 777-328ER	32849/494	ex N50217		
☐	F-GSQG	Boeing 777-328ER	32850/500	ex N5028Y		
☐	F-GSQH	Boeing 777-328ER	32711/501			
☐	F-GSQI	Boeing 777-328ER	32725/502	ex N60697		
☐	F-GSQJ	Boeing 777-328ER	32852/510			
☐	F-GSQK	Boeing 777-328ER	32845/530	ex N5017Q		
☐	F-GSQL	Boeing 777-328ER	32853/545			
☐	F-GSQM	Boeing 777-328ER	32848/558			
☐	F-GSQN	Boeing 777-328ER	32960/565			
☐	F-GSQO	Boeing 777-328ER	32961/570			
☐	F-GSQP	Boeing 777-328ER	35676/573			
☐	F-GSQR	Boeing 777-328ER	35677/579			
☐	F-GSQS	Boeing 777-328ER	32962/608			
☐	F-GSQT	Boeing 777-328ER	32846/616			
☐	F-GSQU	Boeing 777-328ER	32847/624	ex N5022E		
☐	F-GSQV	Boeing 777-328ER	32854/636			
☐	F-GSQX	Boeing 777-328ER	32963/645	ex N5014X		
☐	F-GSQY	Boeing 777-328ER	35678/647			
☐	F-GUOA	Boeing 777-F28	32967/718	ex N453BA		
☐	F-GUOB	Boeing 777-F28	32965/732	ex N5023Q		
☐	F-GUOC	Boeing 777-F28	32966/752			
☐	F-GUOD	Boeing 777-F28	32969/827	ex N449BA		on order
☐	F-GZNA	Boeing 777-328ER	35297/671	ex N50217		
☐	F-GZNB	Boeing 777-328ER	32964/715			
☐	F-GZNC	Boeing 777-328ER	35542/723		Gille Dehove	
☐	F-GZND	Boeing 777-328ER	35543/777	ex N1785B		
☐	F-GZNE	Boeing 777-328ER	37432/790			
☐	F-GZNF	Boeing 777-328ER	37433/792	ex N50281		
☐	F-GZNG	Boeing 777-328ER	32968/795			

AIR FRANCE REGIONAL — *Various*

The majority of services are operated in full Air France colours with titles 'Air France by' the appropriate airline, Airlinair, Brit'Air, CCM Airlines, Regional and Cityjet.

AIR MEDITERRANÉE — *Mediterranée (BIE)* — *Tarbes (LDE)*

	Registration	Type	C/n	Previous identity	Name/Colours	Remarks
☐	F-GYAI	Airbus A320-211	0293	ex 9H-ABQ		
☐	F-GYAJ	Airbus A321-211	2707	ex D-AVZF		
☐	F-GYAN	Airbus A321-111	0535	ex F-WQQU		
☐	F-GYAO	Airbus A321-111	0642	ex F-WQQV		
☐	F-GYAP	Airbus A321-111	0517	ex HB-IOA		
☐	F-GYAQ	Airbus A321-211	0827	ex HB-IOI		
☐	F-GYAR	Airbus A321-211	0891	ex HB-IOJ	FRAM colours	
☐	F-GYAZ	Airbus A321-111	0519	ex D-ANJA		

AIRBUS TRANSPORT INTERNATIONAL — *Super Transport (4Y/BGA)* — *Toulouse-Blagnac (TLS)*

	Registration	Type	C/n	Previous identity	Name/Colours	Remarks
☐	F-GSTA	Airbus A300B4-608ST Beluga	655/001	ex F-WAST	Super Transporter 1	
☐	F-GSTB	Airbus A300B4-608ST Beluga	751/002	ex F-WSTB	Super Transporter 2	
☐	F-GSTC	Airbus A300B4-608ST Beluga	765/003	ex F-WSTC	Super Transporter 3	
☐	F-GSTD	Airbus A300B4-608ST Beluga	776/004	ex F-WSTD	Super Transporter 4	
☐	F-GSTF	Airbus A300B4-608ST Beluga	796/005	ex F-WSTF	Super Transporter 5	

AIRLEC AIR ESPACE — *AirLec (ARL)* — *Bordeaux (BOD)*

	Registration	Type	C/n	Previous identity	Name/Colours	Remarks
☐	F-GGRV	Piper PA-31T Cheyenne	31T-7720036	ex N41RC		
☐	F-GGVG	Swearingen SA.226T Merlin IIIB	T-293	ex D-IBBB		
☐	F-GLPT	Swearingen SA.226T Merlin IIIB	T-298	ex VH-AWU		
☐	F-GRNT	Swearingen SA.226T Merlin IIIB	T-312	ex N84GA		

AIRLINAIR — *Airlinair (A5/RLA)* — *Paris-Orly (ORY)*

	Registration	Type	C/n	Previous identity	Name/Colours	Remarks
☐	F-GKNB	ATR 42-300	226			
☐	F-GKNC	ATR 42-300	230			
☐	F-GKYN	ATR 42-300	095	ex F-ODUL		
☐	F-GPYA	ATR 42-500	457	ex F-WWET		
☐	F-GPYB	ATR 42-500	480	ex F-WWLZ		
☐	F-GPYC	ATR 42-500	484	ex F-WWEB		
☐	F-GPYD	ATR 42-500	490	ex F-WWLJ		
☐	F-GPYF	ATR 42-500	495	ex F-WWLM		op for AFR
☐	F-GPYK	ATR 42-500	537	ex F-WWLC		op for AFR
☐	F-GPYL	ATR 42-500	542	ex F-WWLH		op for AFR
☐	F-GPYM	ATR 42-500	520	ex F-WWLR		op for AFR
☐	F-GPYN	ATR 42-500	539	ex F-WWLO		op for AFR
☐	F-GPYO	ATR 42-500	544	ex F-WWLH		
☐	F-GVZB	ATR 42-500	524	ex F-OHQL		
☐	F-GVZJ	ATR 42-320	093	ex F-WQNO		
☐	F-GVZY	ATR 42-300	080	ex F-WVZY		Lsd to TLY
☐	F-GVZZ	ATR 42-300	055	ex F-WVZZ		
☐	F-GKPD	ATR 72-202	177	ex F-WWE	all-white	

☐ F-GPOC	ATR 72-202 (QC)	311	ex B-22707	op for AFR
☐ F-GPOD	ATR 72-202 (QC)	361	ex B-22711	op for AFR
☐ F-GVZF	ATR 72-212	461	ex F-OGXF	op for AFR
☐ F-GVZG	ATR 72-201	145	ex G-HERM	
☐ F-GVZL	ATR 72-212A	553	ex F-OHJO	
☐ F-GVZM	ATR 72-212A	590	ex F-OHJT	
☐ F-GVZN	ATR 72-212A	563	ex F-OHJU	

ALSAIR — ***Alsair (AL/LSR)*** — ***Colmar (CMR)***

☐ F-GEOU	Beech 65-C90 King Air	LJ-941	ex N3804C

ATLANTIQUE AIR ASSISTANCE — ***Triple A (TLB)*** — ***Nantes (NTE)***

☐ F-GIZB	Beech C90 King Air	LJ-955	ex N786SB
☐ F-GNBR	Beech 1900D	UE-327	ex N23154
☐ F-GPYY	Beech 1900C-1	UC-115	ex N115YV
☐ F-GTVA	Embraer EMB.120ER Brasilia	120253	ex F-GJTG
☐ F-HAAV	ATR 42-320	019	ex F-WKVB
☐ F-HBSO	ATR 42-320	066	ex D4-CBS

AXIS AIRWAYS — ***Axis (6V/AXY)*** — ***Marseille (MRS)***

Ceased operations 07/Dec/2009

BLUE LINE — ***Blue Berry (BLE)*** — ***Paris-Charles de Gaulle (CDG)***

☐ F-GMLI	McDonnell-Douglas MD-83	53014/1740	ex F-WMLI	VIP
☐ F-GMLK	McDonnell-Douglas MD-83	49672/1494	ex F-WMLK	
☐ F-GMLU	McDonnell-Douglas MD-83	49398/1332	ex N398MD	
☐ F-GMLX	McDonnell-Douglas MD-83	49823/1540	ex OE-LMI	
☐ F-GNLG	Fokker F.28-0100 (Fokker 100)	11363	ex D-ADFE	
☐ F-GNLH	Fokker F.28-0100 (Fokker 100)	11311	ex D-ADFB	Lsd to WIF
☐ F-HBOY	Airbus A310-325	650	ex F-WBOY	

BRIT'AIR — ***Brit Air (DB/BZH)*** — ***Morlaix (MXN)***

☐ F-GRJE	Canadair CL-600-2B19 (CRJ-100ER)	7106	ex C-FMNQ	
☐ F-GRJF	Canadair CL-600-2B19 (CRJ-100ER)	7108	ex C-FMLU	
☐ F-GRJG	Canadair CL-600-2B19 (CRJ-100ER)	7143	ex C-FMMQ	
☐ F-GRJI	Canadair CL-600-2B19 (CRJ-100ER)	7147	ex C-FZAL	
☐ F-GRJJ	Canadair CL-600-2B19 (CRJ-100ER)	7190	ex C-GBFF	
☐ F-GRJK	Canadair CL-600-2B19 (CRJ-100ER)	7219	ex C-FMMQ	
☐ F-GRJL	Canadair CL-600-2B19 (CRJ-100ER)	7221	ex C-FMNX	
☐ F-GRJM	Canadair CL-600-2B19 (CRJ-100ER)	7222	ex C-FMMY	
☐ F-GRJN	Canadair CL-600-2B19 (CRJ-100ER)	7262	ex C-FMLT	
☐ F-GRJO	Canadair CL-600-2B19 (CRJ-100ER)	7296	ex C-FMNW	
☐ F-GRJP	Canadair CL-600-2B19 (CRJ-100ER)	7301	ex C-FVAZ	
☐ F-GRJQ	Canadair CL-600-2B19 (CRJ-100ER)	7321	ex C-FMLS	
☐ F-GRJR	Canadair CL-600-2B19 (CRJ-100ER)	7375	ex C-FMKW	
☐ F-GRJT	Canadair CL-600-2B19 (CRJ-100ER)	7389	ex C-FMOS	

☐ F-GRZA	Canadair CL-600-2C10 (CRJ-701)	10006	ex C-GHCE	
☐ F-GRZB	Canadair CL-600-2C10 (CRJ-701)	10007	ex C-GHCF	
☐ F-GRZC	Canadair CL-600-2C10 (CRJ-701)	10008	ex C-GHCO	
☐ F-GRZD	Canadair CL-600-2C10 (CRJ-701)	10016	ex C-GJEZ	
☐ F-GRZE	Canadair CL-600-2C10 (CRJ-701)	10032	ex C-GIBL	
☐ F-GRZF	Canadair CL-600-2C10 (CRJ-701)	10036	ex C-GIBQ	
☐ F-GRZG	Canadair CL-600-2C10 (CRJ-701)	10037	ex C-GIBT	
☐ F-GRZH	Canadair CL-600-2C10 (CRJ-701)	10089	ex C-GIBI	
☐ F-GRZI	Canadair CL-600-2C10 (CRJ-701)	10093	ex C-	
☐ F-GRZJ	Canadair CL-600-2C10 (CRJ-701)	10096	ex C-	
☐ F-GRZK	Canadair CL-600-2C10 (CRJ-701)	10198	ex C-	
☐ F-GRZL	Canadair CL-600-2C10 (CRJ-701)	10245	ex C-	
☐ F-GRZM	Canadair CL-600-2C10 (CRJ-701)	10263	ex C-	
☐ F-GRZN	Canadair CL-600-2C10 (CRJ-701)	10264	ex C-	
☐ F-GRZO	Canadair CL-600-2C10 (CRJ-701)	10265	ex C-	

☐ F-GKHD	Fokker F.28-0100 (Fokker 100)	11381	ex HB-IVI	
☐ F-GKHE	Fokker F.28-0100 (Fokker 100)	11386	ex HB-IVK	
☐ F-GPXB	Fokker F.28-0100 (Fokker 100)	11492	ex PH-EZK	
☐ F-GPXC	Fokker F.28-0100 (Fokker 100)	11493	ex PH-EZY	
☐ F-GPXD	Fokker F.28-0100 (Fokker 100)	11494	ex PH-EZO	
☐ F-GPXE	Fokker F.28-0100 (Fokker 100)	11495	ex PH-EZP	
☐ F-GPXF	Fokker F.28-0100 (Fokker 100)	11330	ex F-WQJX	
☐ F-GPXG	Fokker F.28-0100 (Fokker 100)	11387	ex SX-BGL	
☐ F-GPXH	Fokker F.28-0100 (Fokker 100)	11476	ex SX-BGM	
☐ F-GPXJ	Fokker F.28-0100 (Fokker 100)	11323	ex EI-DBR	
☐ F-GPXK	Fokker F.28-0100 (Fokker 100)	11329	ex EI-DBE	
☐ F-GPXM	Fokker F.28-0100 (Fokker 100)	11296	ex EI-DFC	Op for RAE

CCM AIRLINES — Corsica (XK/CCM) — Ajaccio (AJA)

	Type	c/n	Previous	Notes
☐ F-GYFK	Airbus A320-214	0533	ex F-WQSY	
☐ F-GYFL	Airbus A320-214	0548	ex F-WQSZ	
☐ F-GYFM	Airbus A319-112	1068	ex F-WQRR	
☐ F-GYJM	Airbus A319-112	1145	ex F-WQRT	
☐ F-HBEV	Airbus A320-214	3952	ex F-WWBI	
☐ F-HBSA	Airbus A320-214	3882	ex F-WWIP	
☐ F-GRPI	ATR 42-500	722	ex F-WWEC	
☐ F-GRPJ	ATR 42-500	724	ex F-WWEI	
☐ F-GRPK	ATR 72-212A	727	ex F-WWEH	
☐ F-GRPX	ATR 72-212A	734	ex F-WWEO	
☐ F-GRPY	ATR 72-212A	742	ex F-WWEC	
☐ F-GRPZ	ATR 72-212A	745	ex F-WWEF	

CHALAIR AVIATION — Chalar (CLG) — Caen-Carpiquet (CFR)

	Type	c/n	Previous	Notes
☐ F-BXPY	Beech 65-C90 King Air	LJ-684		
☐ F-GHVV	Beech 200 Super King Air	BB-676	ex N1362B	
☐ F-GIJB	Beech 200 Super King Air	BB-13	ex N83MA	
☐ F-GOOB	Beech 1900C-1	UC-153	ex N153YV	
☐ F-GPAS	Beech 200 Super King Air	BB-209	ex D-IACS	
☐ F-HBCA	Beech 1900D	UE-188	ex SE-KXV	
☐ F-HBCB	Beech 1900D	UE-390	ex 3B-VTL	
☐ F-HBCC	Beech 1900D	UE-350	ex 3B-VIP	
☐ F-HBCE	Beech 1900D	UE-323	ex ZS-SHB	

CORSAIR — Corsair (SS/CRL) — Ajaccio (AJA)

	Type	c/n	Previous	Notes
☐ F-GTUI	Boeing 747-422	26875/931	ex N186UA	
☐ F-HKIS	Boeing 747-422	25380/913	ex F-WKIS	
☐ F-HSEA	Boeing 747-422	26877/944	ex F-WSEA	
☐ F-HSEX	Boeing 747-422	26878/966	ex F-WSEX	
☐ F-HSUN	Boeing 747-422	26880/984	ex F-WSUN	
☐ F-HLOV	Boeing 747-422	25379/911	ex F-WLOV	
☐ F-HBIL	Airbus A330-243	320		
☐ F-HCAT	Airbus A330-243	285	ex F-WWKB	

EAGLE AVIATION — French Eagle (EGN) — St Nazaire/Paris-Orly (SNR/ORY)

Ceased operations 02/Apr/2009

EUROPE AIRPOST — French Post (5O/FPO) — Paris-Charles de Gaulle (CDG)

	Type	c/n	Previous	Notes
☐ F-GFUE	Boeing 737-3B3 (QC)	24387/1693		
☐ F-GFUF	Boeing 737-3B3 (QC)	24388/1725		
☐ F-GIXB	Boeing 737-33A (QC)	24789/1953	ex F-OGSD	
☐ F-GIXC	Boeing 737-38B (QC)	25124/2047	ex F-OGSS	Saint-Louis
☐ F-GIXD	Boeing 737-33A (QC)	25744/2198	ex N3213T	
☐ F-GIXE	Boeing 737-3B3 (QC)	26850/2235	ex N854WT	
☐ F-GIXF	Boeing 737-3B3 (QC)	26851/2267	ex N4361V	
☐ F-GIXH	Boeing 737-3S3 (QC)	23788/1393	ex N271LF	
☐ F-GIXI	Boeing 737-348 (QC)	23809/1458	ex F-OGSY	
☐ F-GIXJ	Boeing 737-3Y0 (QC)	23685/1357	ex G-MONH	
☐ F-GIXL	Boeing 737-348 (QC)	23810/1474	ex F-OHCS	
☐ F-GIXO	Boeing 737-3Q8 (QC)	24132/1555	ex N241LF	
☐ F-GIXR	Boeing 737-3H6 (SF)	27125/2415	ex 9M-MZA	
☐ F-GIXS	Boeing 737-3H6 (SF)	27347/2615	ex 9M-MZB	
☐ F-GIXT	Boeing 737-39M (QC)	28898/2906	ex F-ODZZ	
☐ F-GZTA	Boeing 737-33V (QC)	29333/3084	ex HA-LKV	
☐ F-GZTB	Boeing 737-33VF	29336/3102	ex HA-LKU	
☐ F-GZTC	Boeing 737-73V	32414/1214	ex G-EZJS	
☐ F-GPOA	ATR 72-202 (QC)	204	ex F-ORAC	op by SWT
☐ F-GPOB	ATR 72-202 (QC)	207	ex F-ORAN	op by SWT
☐ F-GPOC	ATR 72-202 (QC)	311	ex B-22707	Lsd to RLA
☐ F-GPOD	ATR 72-202 (QC)	361	ex B-22711	Lsd to RLA

FINIST'AIR — Finistair (FTR) — Brest (BES)

	Type	c/n	Previous	Notes
☐ F-GHGZ	Cessna 208A Caravan I	20800188	ex (N9769F)	
☐ F-GJFI	Cessna 208B Caravan I	208B0230	ex N208GC	
☐ F-GNYR	Cessna 208B Caravan I	208B1039	ex D-FOXI	Op for Atlantic Air Lift

HELI-UNION — Heli Union (HLU) — Paris-Heliport/Toussus-le-Noble (JDP/TNF)

	Type	c/n	Previous	Notes
☐ F-GEPN	Aérospatiale SA365C3 Dauphin 2	5073	ex D-HELY	based PNR
☐ F-GERJ	Aérospatiale SA365N Dauphin 2	6066	ex F-ODRA	based Gabon
☐ F-GFCH	Aérospatiale SA365C2 Dauphin 2	5072	ex F-OCCD	

Reg	Type	c/n	Previous	Name	Notes
☐ F-GFEC	Aérospatiale SA365C2 Dauphin 2	5071	ex F-ODBV		
☐ F-GFPA	Aérospatiale SA365C2 Dauphin 2	5063	ex LV-AIE		
☐ F-GJPZ	Aérospatiale SA365N Dauphin 2	6115	ex LN-OLN		
☐ F-GKCU	Aérospatiale SA365N Dauphin 2	6011	ex PH-SEC		based PNR
☐ F-GMAY	Aérospatiale SA365N Dauphin 2	6137			
☐ F-GSYA	Aérospatiale SA365N Dauphin 2	6220	ex JA9913		
☐ F-GTCH	Aérospatiale AS365N3 Dauphin 2	6710	ex F-WWOR		
☐ F-GVGV	Aérospatiale AS365N3 Dauphin 2	6724	ex F-WWOL		
☐ F-HMLB	Aérospatiale AS365N3 Dauphin 2	6726	ex F-WWOS		
☐ TJ-SAH	Aérospatiale SA365N Dauphin 2	6037	ex F-GMHI		

Reg	Type	c/n	Previous	Name	Notes
☐ F-GHOY	Aérospatiale AS.332L1	9005	ex F-WQEB		
☐ F-GJTU	Aérospatiale AS350B3 Ecureuil	3449	ex EP-HEU		based Cayenne
☐ F-GYSH	Aérospatiale AS.332L1	9006	ex F-WQEE		on order

HEX'AIR — *Hex Airline (UD/HER)* — *Le Puy (LPY)*

Reg	Type	c/n	Previous	Name	Notes
☐ F-GOPE	Beech 1900D	UE-103	ex N82930		
☐ F-GUPE	Beech 1900D	UE-248	ex N10882		Lsd to PEA

OPENSKIES — *(BOS)* — *Paris-Orly (ORY)*

Reg	Type	c/n	Previous	Name	Notes
☐ F-HAVI	Boeing 757-26D/W	24473/301	ex N473AP	Violetta	
☐ F-HAVN	Boeing 757-230/W	25140/382	ex D-ABNF	Gloria	
☐ G-BPEJ	Boeing 757-236/W	25807/610		Penny	
☐ G-BPEK	Boeing 757-236/W	25808/665		Lauren	

PAN EUROPÉENE AIR SERVICE — *Pan Euro (PEA)* — *Chambéry (CMF)*

Reg	Type	c/n	Previous	Name	Notes
☐ F-GUPE	Beech 1900D	UE-248	ex N10882		Lsd fr HER
☐ F-GYPE	Embraer EMB.135LR (ERJ-135LR)	145492	ex PT-SXL	Savoie titles	
☐ F-GZPE	Piaggio P.180 Avanti	1064			
☐ F-HAPE	Beech 1900D	UE-367	ex N30515		
☐ F-HBPE	Embraer EMB.145LR (ERJ-145LR)	145106	ex PH-RXC		Lsd fr PEA

RÉGIONAL — *Régional Europe (YS/RAE)* — *Nantes (NTE)*

Reg	Type	c/n	Previous
☐ F-GOHA	Embraer EMB.135ER (ERJ-135ER)	145189	ex PT-SFM
☐ F-GOHB	Embraer EMB.135ER (ERJ-135ER)	145198	ex PT-SFQ
☐ F-GOHC	Embraer EMB.135ER (ERJ-135ER)	145243	ex PT-SJF
☐ F-GOHD	Embraer EMB.135ER (ERJ-135ER)	145252	ex PT-SJJ
☐ F-GOHE	Embraer EMB.135ER (ERJ-135ER)	145335	ex PT-SNB
☐ F-GOHF	Embraer EMB.135ER (ERJ-135ER)	145347	ex PT-SNN
☐ F-GRGP	Embraer EMB.135ER (ERJ-135ER)	145188	ex PT-SFL
☐ F-GRGQ	Embraer EMB.135ER (ERJ-135ER)	145233	ex PT-SJB
☐ F-GRGR	Embraer EMB.135ER (ERJ-135ER)	145236	ex PT-SJE

Reg	Type	c/n	Previous
☐ F-GRGA	Embraer EMB.145EP (ERJ-145EP)	145008	ex PT-SYE
☐ F-GRGB	Embraer EMB.145EP (ERJ-145EP)	145010	ex PT-SYG
☐ F-GRGC	Embraer EMB.145EP (ERJ-145EP)	145012	ex PT-SYI
☐ F-GRGD	Embraer EMB.145EP (ERJ-145EP)	145043	ex PT-SZI
☐ F-GRGE	Embraer EMB.145EP (ERJ-145EP)	145047	ex PT-SZM
☐ F-GRGF	Embraer EMB.145EP (ERJ-145EP)	145050	ex PT-SZP
☐ F-GRGG	Embraer EMB.145EP (ERJ-145EP)	145118	ex PT-SCT
☐ F-GRGH	Embraer EMB.145EP (ERJ-145EP)	145120	ex PT-SCW
☐ F-GRGI	Embraer EMB.145EP (ERJ-145EP)	145152	ex PT-SED
☐ F-GRGJ	Embraer EMB.145EP (ERJ-145EP)	145297	ex PT-SKO
☐ F-GRGK	Embraer EMB.145EP (ERJ-145EP)	145324	ex PT-SMQ
☐ F-GRGL	Embraer EMB.145EP (ERJ-145EP)	145375	ex PT-SOZ
☐ F-GRGM	Embraer EMB.145EP (ERJ-145EP)	145418	ex PT-STP
☐ F-GUAM	Embraer EMB.145MP (ERJ-145MP)	145266	ex PT-SIY
☐ F-GUBA	Embraer EMB.145MP (ERJ-145MP)	145398	ex PT-SQV
☐ F-GUBB	Embraer EMB.145MP (ERJ-145MP)	145419	ex PT-STQ
☐ F-GUBC	Embraer EMB.145MP (ERJ-145MP)	145556	ex PT-SZR
☐ F-GUBD	Embraer EMB.145MP (ERJ-145MP)	145333	ex PT-SMZ
☐ F-GUBE	Embraer EMB.145MP (ERJ-145MP)	145668	ex PT-SFC
☐ F-GUBF	Embraer EMB.145MP (ERJ-145MP)	145669	ex PT-SFD
☐ F-GUBG	Embraer EMB.145MP (ERJ-145MP)	14500890	ex PT-SYD
☐ F-GUEA	Embraer EMB.145MP (ERJ-145MP)	145342	ex PT-SNI
☐ F-GUFD	Embraer EMB.145MP (ERJ-145MP)	145197	ex PT-SGN
☐ F-GUJA	Embraer EMB.145MP (ERJ-145MP)	145407	ex PT-STE
☐ F-GUMA	Embraer EMB.145MP (ERJ-145MP)	145405	ex PT-STC
☐ F-GUPT	Embraer EMB.145MP (ERJ-145MP)	145294	ex PT-SKL
☐ F-GVGS	Embraer EMB.145MP (ERJ-145MP)	145385	ex PT-SQJ
☐ F-GVHD	Embraer EMB.145MP (ERJ-145MP)	145178	ex PT-SEZ

Reg	Type	c/n	Previous
☐ F-HBXA	Embraer 170-100 (170ST)	17000237	ex PT-SFN
☐ F-HBXB	Embraer 170-100 (170ST)	17000250	ex PT-SJB
☐ F-HBXC	Embraer 170-100 (170ST)	17000263	ex PT-SJR
☐ F-HBXD	Embraer 170-100 (170ST)	17000281	ex PT-TQH
☐ F-HBXE	Embraer 170-100 (170ST)	17000286	ex PT-TQM
☐ F-HBXF	Embraer 170-100 (170ST)	17000292	ex PT-TQS

☐ F-HBXG	Embraer 170-100 (170ST)	17000301	ex PT-XQA		on order
☐ F-	Embraer 170-100 (170ST)		ex PT-		on order
☐ F-	Embraer 170-100 (170ST)		ex PT-		on order
☐ F-	Embraer 170-100 (170ST)		ex PT-		on order
☐ F-HBLA	Embraer 190LR (190-100LR)	19000051	ex PT-SIA		
☐ F-HBLB	Embraer 190LR (190-100LR)	19000060	ex PT-SIN		
☐ F-HBLC	Embraer 190LR (190-100LR)	19000080	ex PT-SJW		
☐ F-HBLD	Embraer 190LR (190-100LR)	19000113	ex PT-SQH		
☐ F-HBLE	Embraer 190LR (190-100LR)	19000123	ex PT-SQS		
☐ F-HBLF	Embraer 190LR (190-100LR)	19000158	ex PT-SAO		
☐ F-HBLG	Embraer 190LR (190-100LR)	19000254	ex PT-SIZ		
☐ F-HBLH	Embraer 190LR (190-100LR)	19000266	ex PT-TLG		
☐ F-HBLI	Embraer 190LR (190-100LR)	19000298	ex PT-TZM		
☐ F-HBLJ	Embraer 190LR (190-100LR)	19000311	ex PT-		
☐ F-	Embraer 190LR (190-100LR)		ex PT-		on order
☐ F-	Embraer 190LR (190-100LR)		ex PT-		on order
☐ F-	Embraer 190LR (190-100LR)		ex PT-		on order
☐ F-GIOG	Fokker F.28-0100 (Fokker 100)	11364	ex PH-EZA		
☐ F-GNLI	Fokker F.28-0100 (Fokker 100)	11315	ex D-ADFC		
☐ F-GNLJ	Fokker F.28-0100 (Fokker 100)	11344	ex D-ADFD		
☐ F-GNLK	Fokker F.28-0100 (Fokker 100)	11307	ex D-ADFA		stored
☐ F-GPNK	Fokker F.28-0100 (Fokker 100)	11324	ex SE-DUC		stored WOE
☐ F-GPNL	Fokker F.28-0100 (Fokker 100)	11325	ex SE-DUD		
☐ F-GPXL	Fokker F.28-0100 (Fokker 100)	11290	ex EI-DFB		
☐ F-GPXM	Fokker F.28-0100 (Fokker 100)	11296	ex EI-DFC		Lsd fr BZH

REGOURD AVIATION

☐ F-GTSK	Embraer EMB.120RT Brasilia	120213	ex OO-MTD	no titles

SECURITÉ CIVILE — *Marseille (MRS)*

☐ F-ZBEO	Canadair CL-215-6B11 (CL-415)	2011	ex C-FWPD	P-36
☐ F-ZBEU	Canadair CL-215-6B11 (CL-415)	2024	ex C-FZDE	P-42
☐ F-ZBFN	Canadair CL-215-6B11 (CL-415)	2006	ex C-FVUK	P-33
☐ F-ZBFP	Canadair CL-215-6B11 (CL-415)	2002	ex C-FBET	P-31
☐ F-ZBFS	Canadair CL-215-6B11 (CL-415)	2001	ex C-GSCT	P-32
☐ F-ZBFV	Canadair CL-215-6B11 (CL-415)	2013	ex C-FWPE	P-37
☐ F-ZBFW	Canadair CL-215-6B11 (CL-415)	2014	ex C-FWZH	P-38
☐ F-ZBFX	Canadair CL-215-6B11 (CL-415)	2007	ex C-FVUJ	P-34
☐ F-ZBFY	Canadair CL-215-6B11 (CL-415)	2010	ex C-FVDY	P-35
☐ F-ZBME	Canadair CL-215-6B11 (CL-415)	2057	ex C-GILN	44
☐ F-ZBMF	Canadair CL-215-6B11 (CL-415)	2063	ex C-FGZT	
☐ F-ZBMG	Canadair CL-215-6B11 (CL-415)	2065	ex C-FLFW	
☐ F-ZBAA	Conair Turbo Firecat	456/027	ex F-WEOL	T-22
☐ F-ZBAP	Conair Turbo Firecat	567/026	ex F-ZBDA	T-12
☐ F-ZBAU	Conair Firecat	DHC-32/009	ex F-WZLQ	T-2
☐ F-ZBAZ	Conair Turbo Firecat	DHC-57/008	ex F-WEOL	T-01
☐ F-ZBCZ	Conair Turbo Firecat	DHC-94/036	ex F-ZBCA	T-23
☐ F-ZBEH	Conair Turbo Firecat	410/035	ex F-WEOJ	T-20
☐ F-ZBET	Conair Turbo Firecat	703/028	ex F-WEOJ	T-15
☐ F-ZBEW	Conair Turbo Firecat	621/025	ex F-WEOL	T-11
☐ F-ZBEY	Conair Turbo Firecat	400/017	ex F-WEOK	T-7
☐ F-ZBMA	Conair Turbo Firecat	461/021	ex C-GFZG	T-24
☐ F-ZBFJ	Beech B200 Super King Air	BB-1102	ex D-IWAN	B-98
☐ F-ZBFK	Beech B200 Super King Air	BB-876	ex F-GHSC	B-96
☐ F-ZBMB	Beech B200 Super King Air	BB-1379	ex F-GJFD	B-97
☐ F-ZBMC	de Havilland DHC-8-402QMRT	4040	ex C-FBAM	73
☐ F-ZBMD	de Havilland DHC-8-402QMRT	4043	ex C-FBSG	74

TAXI AIR FRET — *Paris-Le Bourget (LBG)*

☐ F-BTME	Beech 99	U-79	ex N551GP
☐ F-GFDJ	Beech 65-E90 King Air	LW-86	ex N410PB

TRANSAVIA FRANCE — *Transavia (TO/TVF)* — *Paris-Orly (ORY)*

☐ F-GZHA	Boeing 737-8GJ/W	34901/2267	ex (VT-SPN)
☐ F-GZHB	Boeing 737-8GJ/W	34902/2309	ex (VT-SPO)
☐ F-GZHC	Boeing 737-8K2/W	29651/2531	
☐ F-GZHD	Boeing 737-8K2/W	29650/2583	
☐ F-GZHE	Boeing 737-8K2/W	29678/2615	ex N1787B
☐ F-GZHN	Boeing 737-85H/W	29445/186	ex OY-SEI
☐ F-GZHV	Boeing 737-85H/W	29444/178	ex OY-SEH

TWIN JET — *Twin Jet (T7/TJT)* — *Marseille (MRS)*

☐ F-GLND	Beech 1900D	UE-196	ex N3234G	
☐ F-GLNE	Beech 1900D	UE-197	ex N3234U	
☐ F-GLNF	Beech 1900D	UE-69	ex YR-RLA	
☐ F-GLNH	Beech 1900D	UE-73	ex YR-BLB	
☐ F-GLNK	Beech 1900D	UE-269	ex N11017	
☐ F-GLPL	Beech 1900C-1	UC-92	ex N15382	
☐ F-GRYL	Beech 1900D	UE-301	ex N22161	
☐ F-GTKJ	Beech 1900D	UE-348	ex N23406	
☐ F-GTVC	Beech 1900D	UE-349	ex N23430	Op for Ministère de l'Interieur

XL AIRWAYS FRANCE — *Starway (SE/XLF)* — *Paris-Orly (ORY)*

☐ F-GKHK	Airbus A320-212	0343	ex OO-TCK
☐ F-GRSI	Airbus A320-214	0973	ex F-WWBR
☐ F-GRSQ	Airbus A330-243	501	ex F-WWKG
☐ F-GSEU	Airbus A330-243	635	ex F-WWYO
☐ F-GTHL	Airbus A320-212	0189	ex F-OHFR
☐ F-HAXL	Boeing 737-8Q8	35279	ex G-XLFR

F-O PACIFIC TERRITORIES (French Polynesia and New Caledonia)

AIR ARCHIPELS — *Archipels (RHL)* — *Papeete (PPT)*

☐ F-OIQK	Beech B200C Super King Air	BL-149	ex N36949
☐ F-OIQL	Beech B200C Super King Air	BL-148	ex N36948

AIR CALÉDONIE — *AirCal (TY/TPC)* — *Nouméa (NOU)*

☐ F-OIAQ	de Havilland DHC-6 Twin Otter 300	381	ex VH-RPZ
☐ F-OIPI	ATR 42-500	647	ex F-WWLE
☐ F-OIPN	ATR 72-212A	735	ex F-WWEP
☐ F-OIPS	ATR 72-212A	764	ex F-WWEC

AIR LOYAUTÉ — *Iazur (VZR)* — *Nouméa (NOU)*

☐ F-OIAY	de Havilland DHC-6 Twin Otter 300	507	ex P2-KSR

AIR MOOREA — *Air Moorea (QE/TAH)* — *Papeete (PPT)*

☐ F-ODBN	de Havilland DHC-6 Twin Otter 300	470	
☐ F-OHJG	de Havilland DHC-6 Twin Otter 300	603	ex Fr AF 603
☐ F-OIQF	de Havilland DHC-6 Twin Otter 300	815	ex N45KH
☐ F-OIQP	de Havilland DHC-6 Twin Otter 300	715	ex 5Y-SKL

AIR TAHITI — *Air Tahiti (VT/VTA)* — *Papeete (PPT)*

☐ F-OIQB	ATR 42-500	621	ex F-WWLB	
☐ F-OIQC	ATR 42-500	627	ex F-WWLH	
☐ F-OIQD	ATR 42-500	631	ex F-WWLL	
☐ F-O	ATR 42-500		ex F-WW	on order
☐ F-OHJS	ATR 72-212A	696	ex F-WWES	
☐ F-OIQN	ATR 72-212A	719	ex F-WWET	
☐ F-OIQO	ATR 72-212A	731	ex F-WWEL	
☐ F-OIQR	ATR 72-212A	862	ex F-WWEJ	
☐ F-OIQU	ATR 72-212A	751	ex F-WWEL	
☐ F-OIQT	ATR 72-212A	829	ex F-WWEW	
☐ F-OIQV	ATR 72-212A	806	ex F-WWER	

AIR TAHITI NUI — *Tahiti Airlines (TN/THT)* — *Papeete (PPT)*

☐ F-OJGF	Airbus A340-313X	385	ex F-WWJC	Mangareva
☐ F-OJTN	Airbus A340-313X	395	ex C-GZIA	Bora Bora
☐ F-OLOV	Airbus A340-313E	668	ex F-WWJD	Nuku Hiva
☐ F-OSEA	Airbus A340-313X	438	ex F-WWJV	Rangiroa
☐ F-OSUN	Airbus A340-313X	446	ex F-WWJA	Moorea

AIRCALIN — *AirCalin (SB/ACI)* — *Nouméa (NOU)*

☐ F-OCQZ	de Havilland DHC-6 Twin Otter 300	412	
☐ F-OHSD	Airbus A330-202	507	ex F-WWYS
☐ F-OJSB	Airbus A320-232	2152	
☐ F-OJSE	Airbus A330-202	510	ex F-WWYT

F-O ATLANTIC / INDIAN OCEAN TERRITORIES (St Pierre & Miquelon and Réunion)

AIR AUSTRAL — Réunion (UU/REU) — St Denis-Gilot (RUN)

☐ F-OHSF	ATR 72-212A	650	ex F-WWEC		
☐ F-OMRU	ATR 72-212A	855	ex F-WWEI		
☐ F-OZSF	ATR 72-212A	813	ex F-WWEC		
☐ F-ODZJ	Boeing 737-53A	24877/1943	ex F-GHXN		
☐ F-ODZY	Boeing 737-33A	27452/2679			
☐ F-OMAY	Boeing 777-2Q8ER	29402/517			
☐ F-ONOU	Boeing 777-3Q8ER	35783/786	ex N5573S	Leon Dierx	
☐ F-OPAR	Boeing 777-2Q8ER	29908/229	ex EI-CRS	Marcel Goulette	
☐ F-ORUN	Boeing 777-2Q8ER	28676/246	ex EI-CRT	Pierre Legourque	
☐ F-OSYD	Boeing 777-3Q8ER	35782/778	ex N5014K	C. Leconte de Lisle	

AIR ST-PIERRE — Saint-Pierre (PJ/SPM) — St-Pierre et Miquelon (FSP)

☐ F-OFSP	ATR 42-500	801	ex F-WWLT		
☐ F-OSPJ	Reims Cessna F406 Caravan II	F406-0091			

F-O FRENCH CARIBBEAN (Guadeloupe & Saint-Barthélemy, Martinique and French Guyana)

AIR ANTILLES EXPRESS — (3S) — Pointe-à-Pitre (PTP)

☐ F-GHPS	ATR 42-300	006	ex B-2206		Lsd fr GUY
☐ F-OIJB	ATR 42-500	579	ex F-WWLF		Lsd fr GUY
☐ F-OIXD	ATR 42-500	695	ex F-WWLQ		
☐ F-OIXE	ATR 42-500	807	ex F-WWLX		

AIR CARAIBES — French West (TX/FWI) — Pointe-à-Pitre/Fort-de-France/St Barthélemy/St Martin (PTP/FDF/SBH/SFG)

☐ F-OGOL	Dornier 228-202K	8139	ex D-CACC		Lsd to Take A/l
☐ F-OGVE	Dornier 228-212	8237	ex D-CBDD		Lsd to Take A/l
☐ F-OHQK	Dornier 228-212	8238	ex D-CBDH		
☐ F-OHQM	Cessna 208B Caravan I	208B0726			Lsd to Take A/l
☐ F-OHQN	Cessna 208B Caravan I	208B0715	ex N1285H		Lsd to Take A/l
☐ F-OHQU	Cessna 208B Caravan I	208B0725	ex N12326		Lsd to Take A/l
☐ F-OIJG	ATR 72-212A	654	ex F-WWEI		
☐ F-OIJH	ATR 72-212A	682	ex F-WWEE		
☐ F-OIJK	ATR 72-212A	736	ex F-WWEQ		
☐ F-OIJO	Cessna 208B Caravan I	208B0961	ex N4109K		Lsd to Take A/l
☐ F-OIXL	ATR 72-212A	888	ex F-WWES		
☐ F-OSUD	Embraer 190-100LR (190LR)	19000130	ex PT-SQZ		

AIR CARAIBES ATLANTIQUE — Car Line (TX/CAJ) — Pointe-à-Pitre (PTP)

☐ F-GOTO	Airbus A330-323E	1021	ex F-WWYN		
☐ F-OFDF	Airbus A330-223	253	ex HB-IQD		
☐ F-OONE	Airbus A330-323E	965	ex F-WWYL	Region Guyane	
☐ F-ORLY	Airbus A330-323X	758	ex F-WWYR		

AIR GUYANE EXPRESS — Green Bird (3S/GUY) — Cayenne (CAY)

☐ F-GHPS	ATR 42-300	006	ex B-2206		Lsd to Air Antilles Express
☐ F-OIJB	ATR 42-500	579	ex F-WWLF		Lsd to Air Antilles Express
☐ F-OIJI	de Havilland DHC-6 Twin Otter 300	277	ex HB-LSU		
☐ F-OIJL	de Havilland DHC-6 Twin Otter 300	281	ex HB-LSV		
☐ F-OIJY	de Havilland DHC-6 Twin Otter 300	797	ex D-IFLY		

AIRAWAK — Fort-de-France (FDF)

☐ F-OGXA	Britten-Norman BN-2A-26 Islander	788	ex D-IHUG		
☐ F-OIXB	Cessna 402B II	402B1220	ex V2-LEW		

ST BARTH COMMUTER — Black Fin (PV/SBU) — St Barthélemy (SBH)

☐ F-OCXB	Britten-Norman BN-2A-2 Islander	303	ex D-IHVH		stored
☐ F-OHQX	Britten-Norman BN-2A-26 Islander	3009	ex F-OHQW		
☐ F-OHQY	Britten-Norman BN-2B-20 Islander	2251	ex V2-LFE		
☐ F-OIJS	Britten-Norman BN-2B-20 Islander	2294	ex VH-CSS		
☐ F-OIJT	Piper PA-23-250 Aztec F	27-7854129	ex N6513A		

TAKE AIR LINES — Fort-de-France (FDF)

☐ F-OGOL	Dornier 228-202K	8139	ex D-CACC		
☐ F-OGVE	Dornier 228-212	8237	ex D-CBDD		Lsd fr FWI

☐ F-OHQM	Cessna 208B Caravan I	208B0726		Lsd fr FWI
☐ F-OHQN	Cessna 208B Caravan I	208B0715	ex N1285H	Lsd fr FWI
☐ F-OHQU	Cessna 208B Caravan I	208B0725	ex N12326	Lsd fr FWI
☐ F-OIJO	Cessna 208B Caravan I	208B0961	ex N4109K	Lsd fr FWI
☐ F-OTKE	LET L-410UVP-E	902409	ex OK-VDV	

G- UNITED KINGDOM (United Kingdom of Great Britain and Northern Ireland)

AIR ATLANTIQUE — *Atlantic (7M/AAG)* — *Coventry (CVT)*

☐ G-APSA	Douglas DC-6A	45497/995	ex 4W-ABQ	

AIR SOUTHWEST — *Swallow (WOW)* — *Plymouth (PLH)*

☐ G-WOWA	de Havilland DHC-8-311	296	ex C-GZOF	
☐ G-WOWB	de Havilland DHC-8-311	334	ex C-GZOU	
☐ G-WOWC	de Havilland DHC-8-311	311	ex N784BC	
☐ G-WOWD	de Havilland DHC-8-311	286	ex C-FDIY	
☐ G-WOWE	de Havilland DHC-8-311	256	ex C-FFBG	Cloud Surfer

ASTRAEUS — *Flystar (5W/AEU)* — *London-Gatwick (LGW)*

☐ G-STRP	Airbus A320-211	0136	ex EC-GRF	
☐ G-STRF	Boeing 737-76N/W	29885/1120	ex EI-CXD	
☐ G-STRI	Boeing 737-33A	25011/2012	ex OM-HLB	
☐ G-STRJ	Boeing 737-33A	25119/2069	ex OM-HLC	
☐ G-OJIB	Boeing 757-23AER	24292/219	ex G-OOOG	
☐ G-STRW	Boeing 757-28A	24543/286	ex C-GTSN	
☐ G-STRX	Boeing 757-2Q8	25621/457	ex N459AX	
☐ G-STRY	Boeing 757-2Q8	28161/723	ex N369AX	Lsd to BMI
☐ G-STRZ	Boeing 757-258	27622/745	ex 4X-EBI	Lsd to GHB

ATLANTIC RECONNAISSANCE — *Atlantic (AAG)* — *Coventry (CVT)*

☐ G-BCEN	Britten-Norman BN-2A-26 Islander	403	ex 4X-AYG	Maritime & Coastguard Agency
☐ G-EXEX	Cessna 404 Titan	404-0037	ex SE-GZF	Maritime & Coastguard Agency
☐ G-MIND	Cessna 404 Titan	404-0004	ex G-SKKC	Op for Enviroment Agency
☐ G-NOSE	Cessna 402B	402B0823	ex N98AR	Pollution control
☐ G-SOUL	Cessna 310R II	310R0140	ex N5020J	Op for OSRL
☐ G-TASK	Cessna 404 Titan	404-0829	ex PH-MPC	Maritime & Coastguard Agency
☐ G-TURF	Reims Cessna F406 Caravan II	F406-0020	ex PH-FWF	Maritime & Coastguard Agency

AURIGNY AIR SERVICES — *Ayline (GR/AUR)* — *Guernsey (GCI)*

☐ G-BWDB	ATR 72-202	449	ex F-WQNI	
☐ G-COBO	ATR 72-212A	852	ex F-WWEV	
☐ G-VZON	ATR 72-212A	853	ex F-WWEW	
☐ G-BDTO	Britten-Norman BN-2A Mk.III-2 Trislander	1027	ex G-RBSI	
☐ G-BEVT	Britten-Norman BN-2A Mk.III-2 Trislander	1057		
☐ G-FTSE	Britten-Norman BN-2A Mk.III-2 Trislander	1053	ex G-BEPI	
☐ G-JOEY	Britten-Norman BN-2A Mk.III-2 Trislander	1016	ex G-BDGG	Joey
☐ G-RBCI	Britten-Norman BN-2A Mk.III-2 Trislander	1035	ex G-BDWV	
☐ G-RLON	Britten-Norman BN-2A Mk.III-2 Trislander	1008	ex G-ITEX	Royal London Asset Mgt c/s
☐ G-XTOR	Britten-Norman BN-2A Mk.III-2 Trislander	359	ex G-BAXD	

BA CITYFLYER — *Flyer (CJ/CFE)* — *London City (LCY)*

☐ G-BXAS	Avro 146-RJ100	E3301	ex G-6-301	
☐ G-BZAU	Avro 146-RJ100	E3328	ex G-6-328	For NJS
☐ G-BZAY	Avro 146-RJ100	E3368	ex G-6-368	
☐ G-BZAZ	Avro 146-RJ100	E3369	ex G-6-369	
☐ G-CFAA	Avro 146-RJ100	E3373	ex G-6-373	
☐ G-LCYB	Avro 146-RJ85	E2383	ex OH-SAH	
☐ G-LCYC	Avro 146-RJ85	E2385	ex OH-SAI	
☐ G-LCYD	Embraer 170-100	17000294	ex PT-TQU	
☐ G-LCYE	Embraer 170-100	17000296	ex PT-TQW	
☐ G-LCYF	Embraer 170-100	17000298	ex PT-TQR	
☐ G-LCYG	Embraer 170-100	17000300	ex PT-TQZ	
☐ G-LCYH	Embraer 170-100	17000302	ex PT-XQB	
☐ G-LCYI	Embraer 170-100	17000305	ex PT-XQE	
☐ G-LCYJ	Embraer 190SR (190-100SR)		ex PT-	on order
☐ G-LCYK	Embraer 190SR (190-100SR)		ex PT-	on order
☐ G-LCYL	Embraer 190SR (190-100SR)		ex PT-	on order
☐ G-LCYM	Embraer 190SR (190-100SR)		ex PT-	on order
☐ G-LCYN	Embraer 190SR (190-100SR)		ex PT-	on order

BLUE ISLANDS — Blue Island (XA/BCI) — Jersey (JER)

☐ G-BEDP	Britten-Norman BN-2A Mk.III-2 Trislander	1039	ex ZS-SFG	
☐ G-BYHG	Dornier 328-110	3098	ex D-CDAE	Lsd fr SAY
☐ G-BYMK	Dornier 328-110	3062	ex LN-ASK	Lsd fr SAY
☐ G-DRFC	ATR 42-320	007	ex OY-CIB	
☐ G-ISLB	British Aerospace Jetstream 32	871	ex N871JX	
☐ G-ISLC	British Aerospace Jetstream 32	873	ex N873JX	
☐ G-ISLD	British Aerospace Jetstream 32EP	915	ex N915AE	
☐ G-LCOC	Britten-Norman BN-2A Mk.III-1 Trislander	366	ex G-BCCU	
☐ G-XAXA	Britten-Norman BN-2A-26 Islander	530	ex G-LOTO	
☐ LN-FAN	British Aerospace Jetstream 32	864	ex SE-LHK	Lsd fr HTA

BMI BRITISH MIDLAND INTERNATIONAL — Midland (BD/BMA)
East Midland-Nottingham/London-Heathrow (EMA/LHR)

Member of Star Alliance

☐ G-DBCA	Airbus A319-131	2098	ex D-AVYV	
☐ G-DBCB	Airbus A319-131	2188	ex D-AVYA	
☐ G-DBCC	Airbus A319-131	2194	ex D-AVYT	
☐ G-DBCD	Airbus A319-131	2389	ex D-AVYJ	
☐ G-DBCE	Airbus A319-131	2429	ex D-AVWG	
☐ G-DBCF	Airbus A319-131	2466	ex D-AVYA	
☐ G-DBCG	Airbus A319-131	2694	ex D-AVXD	
☐ G-DBCH	Airbus A319-131	2697	ex D-AVXE	
☐ G-DBCI	Airbus A319-131	2720	ex D-AVWC	
☐ G-DBCJ	Airbus A319-131	2981	ex D-AVXG	
☐ G-DBCK	Airbus A319-131	3049	ex D-AVYG	
☐ G-MEDE	Airbus A320-232	1194	ex F-WWDY	
☐ G-MEDH	Airbus A320-232	1922	ex F-WWBX	
☐ G-MEDK	Airbus A320-232	2441	ex F-WWBQ	
☐ G-MIDO	Airbus A320-232	1987	ex F-WWIR	
☐ G-MIDP	Airbus A320-232	1732	ex F-WWBK	
☐ G-MIDR	Airbus A320-232	1697	ex F-WWIQ	
☐ G-MIDS	Airbus A320-232	1424	ex F-WWBO	
☐ G-MIDT	Airbus A320-232	1418	ex F-WWBI	
☐ G-MIDX	Airbus A320-232	1177	ex F-WWDP	Star Alliance c/s
☐ G-MIDY	Airbus A320-232	1014	ex F-WWDQ	
☐ G-MEDF	Airbus A321-231	1690	ex D-AVZX	
☐ G-MEDG	Airbus A321-231	1711	ex D-AVZK	
☐ G-MEDJ	Airbus A321-231	2190	ex D-AVZD	
☐ G-MEDL	Airbus A321-231	2653	ex D-AVZC	
☐ G-MEDM	Airbus A321-231	2799	ex D-AVZP	
☐ G-MEDN	Airbus A321-231	3512	ex D-AVZK	
☐ G-MEDU	Airbus A321-231	3926	ex D-AZAB	
☐ G-	Airbus A321-231		ex	on order
☐ G-	Airbus A321-231		ex	on order
☐ G-	Airbus A321-231		ex	on order
☐ G-MIDC	Airbus A321-231	0835	ex D-AVZZ	
☐ G-MIDL	Airbus A321-231	1174	ex D-AVZH	Star Alliance c/s
☐ G-WWBB	Airbus A330-243	404	ex F-WWKP	
☐ G-WWBD	Airbus A330-243	401	ex F-WWKN	Star Alliance c/s
☐ G-WWBM	Airbus A330-243	398	ex F-WWKL	
☐ G-STRY	Boeing 757-2Q8	28161/723	ex N369AX	Lsd fr AEU

BMI REGIONAL — Granite (BD/BMR)
Aberdeen/East Midlands-Nottingham (ABZ/EMA)

☐ G-EMBI	Embraer EMB.145EP (ERJ-145EP)	145126	ex PT-SDG	
☐ G-EMBJ	Embraer EMB.145EU (ERJ-145EP)	145134	ex PT-SDL	
☐ G-EMBN	Embraer EMB.145EP (ERJ-145EP)	145201	ex PT-SGQ	
☐ G-RJXA	Embraer EMB.145EP (ERJ-145EP)	145136	ex PT-SDP	
☐ G-RJXB	Embraer EMB.145EP (ERJ-145EP)	145142	ex PT-SDS	
☐ G-RJXC	Embraer EMB.145EP (ERJ-145EP)	145153	ex PT-SEE	
☐ G-RJXD	Embraer EMB.145EP (ERJ-145EP)	145207	ex PT-SGX	
☐ G-RJXE	Embraer EMB.145EP (ERJ-145EP)	145245	ex PT-SIJ	
☐ G-RJXF	Embraer EMB.145EP (ERJ-145EP)	145280	ex PT-SJW	
☐ G-RJXG	Embraer EMB.145EP (ERJ-145EP)	145390	ex PT-SQO	
☐ G-RJXH	Embraer EMB.145EP (ERJ-145EP)	145442	ex PT-SUN	
☐ G-RJXI	Embraer EMB.145EP (ERJ-145EP)	145454	ex PT-SUZ	Star Alliance c/s
☐ G-RJXJ	Embraer EMB.135ER (ERJ-135ER)	145473	ex PT-SVS	
☐ G-RJXK	Embraer EMB.135ER (ERJ-135ER)	145494	ex PT-SXN	Star Alliance c/s
☐ G-RJXL	Embraer EMB.135ER (ERJ-135ER)	145376	ex PT-SQA	
☐ G-RJXM	Embraer EMB.145EP (ERJ-145MP)	145216	ex PH-RXA	
☐ G-RJXN	Embraer EMB.145MP (ERJ-145MP)	145336	ex SP-LGI	
☐ G-RJXO	Embraer EMB.145MP (ERJ-145MP)	145339	ex SP-LGK	

☐ G-RJXP	Embraer EMB.135ER (ERJ-135ER)	145431	ex G-CDFS	
☐ G-RJXR	Embraer EMB.145EP (ERJ-145EP)	145070	ex G-CCYH	

BMIBABY — Baby (WW/BMI) — East Midlands-Nottingham (EMA)

☐ G-BVKB	Boeing 737-59D	27268/2592	ex SE-DNM	foxy baby
☐ G-BVKD	Boeing 737-59D	26421/2279	ex SE-DNK	Ice Ice baby
☐ G-BVZE	Boeing 737-59D	26422/2412	ex SE-DNL	little costa baby
☐ G-OBMP	Boeing 737-3Q8	24963/2193		robin hood baby
☐ G-ODSK	Boeing 737-37Q	28537/2904		baby dragon fly
☐ G-OGBD	Boeing 737-3L9	27833/2688	ex OY-MAR	
☐ G-TOYA	Boeing 737-3Q8	26310/2680	ex G-BZZE	brummie baby
☐ G-TOYC	Boeing 737-3Q8	26312/2693	ex G-BZZG	
☐ G-TOYD	Boeing 737-3Q8	26307/2664	ex G-EZYT	
☐ G-TOYF	Boeing 737-36N	28557/2862	ex G-IGOO	Rainbow baby
☐ G-TOYG	Boeing 737-36N	28872/3082	ex G-IGOJ	Butterfly baby
☐ G-TOYH	Boeing 737-36N	28570/3010	ex G-IGOY	Baby of the north
☐ G-TOYI	Boeing 737-3Q8	28054/3016	ex YJ-AV18	Geordie baby
☐ G-TOYJ	Boeing 737-36M	28332/2809	ex PK-GGW	
☐ G-TOYK	Boeing 737-33R	28870/2899	ex N870GX	
☐ G-TOYM	Boeing 737-36Q	29141/3035	ex VT-SJD	Groovy baby

BOND AIR SERVICES — Red Head (RHD) — Gloucestershire (GLO)

☐ G-BZRS	Eurocopter EC135T2	0166	ex D-HECL	back-up
☐ G-DAAT	Eurocopter EC135T2	0312		EMS Devon
☐ G-DORS	Eurocopter EC135T2+	0517		EMS Dorset & Somerset
☐ G-EMAA	Eurocopter EC135T2	0448		EMS
☐ G-HBOB	Eurocopter EC135T2+	0664		Thames Valley Air Ambulance
☐ G-HWAA	Eurocopter EC135T2	0375		EMS
☐ G-KRNW	Eurocopter EC135T2	0175		EMS Cornwall Air Ambulance
☐ G-NWAA	Eurocopter EC135T2	0427		EMS North West Air Ambulance
☐ G-SASA	Eurocopter EC135T2	0147		EMS Scottish Ambulance Service
☐ G-SASB	Eurocopter EC135T2	0151		EMS Scottish Ambulance Service
☐ G-SPAO	Eurocopter EC135T2+	0546		Strathclyde Police
☐ G-SPHU	Eurocopter EC135T2	0245	ex D-HKBA	Great Western Air Ambulance
☐ G-SSXX	Eurocopter EC135T2	0270	ex G-SSSX	EMS Essex Air Ambulance
☐ G-WMAS	Eurocopter EC135T2	0174		EMS County Air Ambulance
☐ G-WONN	Eurocopter EC135T2+	0597		Strathclyde Police
☐ G-	Eurocopter EC135T2+			on order South & East Wales Police

☐ G-BATC	MBB Bo.105DB	S-45	ex D-HDAW	EMS North Wales Air Ambulance
☐ G-BTHV	MBB Bo.105DBS-4	S-855	ex D-HMBV	EMS
☐ G-BUXS	MBB Bo.105DBS-4	S-41/913	ex G-PASA	Northern Lighthouse
☐ G-CDBS	MBB Bo.105DBS-4	S-738	ex D-HDRZ	EMS
☐ G-NAAA	MBB Bo.105DBS-4	S-34/912	ex G-BUTN	EMS
☐ G-NAAB	MBB Bo.105DBS-4	S-416	ex D-HDMO	EMS
☐ G-NDAA	MBB Bo.105DBS-4	S-135/914	ex G-WMAA	EMS Devon Air Ambulance
☐ G-TVAM	MBB Bo.105DBS-4	S-392	ex G-SPOL	EMS Thames Valley Air Ambulance
☐ G-WAAS	MBB Bo.105DBS-4	S-138/911	ex G-ESAM	EMS Welsh Air Ambulance

BOND OFFSHORE HELICOPTERS — Bond (BND) — Gloucestershire/Aberdeen (GLO/ABZ)

☐ G-REDJ	Aérospatiale AS.332L2 II	2608	ex F-WWOJ	
☐ G-REDK	Aérospatiale AS.332L2 II	2610	ex F-WWOM	
☐ G-REDL	Aérospatiale AS.332L2 II	2612	ex F-WWOD	
☐ G-REDM	Aérospatiale AS.332L2 II	2614	ex F-WWOF	
☐ G-REDN	Aérospatiale AS.332L2 II	2616	ex F-WQDH	
☐ G-REDO	Aérospatiale AS.332L2 II	2622	ex F-WWOH	
☐ G-REDP	Aérospatiale AS.332L2 II	2634	ex F-WWOB	
☐ G-REDR	Eurocopter EC225LP	2699		
☐ G-REDT	Eurocopter EC225LP	2701		
☐ G-REDV	Eurocopter EC225LP	2732		
☐ G-REDW	Eurocopter EC225LP	2734		

BRISTOW HELICOPTERS — Bristow (BHL) — Redhill/Aberdeen (KRH/ABZ)

☐ G-BLXR	Aérospatiale AS.332L	2154		Cromarty
☐ G-BMCW	Aérospatiale AS.332L	2161	ex F-WYMG	Monifieth
☐ G-BMCX	Aérospatiale AS.332L	2164		Lossiemouth
☐ G-BWWI	Aérospatiale AS.332L	2040	ex OY-HMF	Johnshaven
☐ G-BWZX	Aérospatiale AS.332L	2120	ex F-WQDE	Muchalls
☐ G-TIGC	Aérospatiale AS.332L	2024	ex (G-BJYH)	Royal Burgh of Montrose
☐ G-TIGE	Aérospatiale AS.332L	2028	ex (G-BJYJ)	City of Dundee
☐ G-TIGF	Aérospatiale AS.332L	2030	ex F-WKQJ	Peterhead
☐ G-TIGG	Aérospatiale AS.332L	2032	ex F-WXFT	Macduff
☐ G-TIGJ	Aérospatiale AS.332L	2042	ex VH-BHT	Rosehearty
☐ G-TIGS	Aérospatiale AS.332L	2086		Findochty
☐ G-TIGV	Aérospatiale AS.332L	2099	ex LN-ONC	Burghead

☐ G-ZZSA	Eurocopter EC225LP	2603	ex F-WWOJ	
☐ G-ZZSB	Eurocopter EC225LP	2615	ex F-WWOG	

	Registration	Type	C/n	Previous	Name	Notes
☐	G-ZZSC	Eurocopter EC225LP	2654	ex F-WWOG		
☐	G-ZZSD	Eurocopter EC225LP	2658	ex F-WWOQ		
☐	G-ZZSE	Eurocopter EC225LP	2660	ex F-WWOJ		
☐	G-ZZSF	Eurocopter EC225LP	2662	ex F-WWOR		
☐	G-ZZSG	Eurocopter EC225LP	2714			
☐	G-ZZSI	Eurocopter EC225LP	2736	ex G-CGES		
☐	G-BDIJ	Sikorsky S-61N II	61751	ex 9M-AYF	Crathes	SAR
☐	G-BDOC	Sikorsky S-61N II	61765		Tolquhoun	SAR
☐	G-BIMU	Sikorsky S-61N II	61752	ex N8511Z	Stac Pollaidh	SAR
☐	G-BPWB	Sikorsky S-61N II	61822	ex EI-BHO	Portland Castle	SAR
☐	G-BIEJ	Sikorsky S-76A+	760097		Glen Lossie	
☐	G-BISZ	Sikorsky S-76A+	760156			
☐	G-BJFL	Sikorsky S-76A+	760056	ex EZ-S704		
☐	G-BJGX	Sikorsky S-76A+	760026	ex N103BH	Glen Elgin	
☐	G-CEYZ	Sikorsky S-76C++	760669	ex N4514R		
☐	G-CFDV	Sikorsky S-76C++	760666	ex N45140		
☐	G-CFJC	Sikorsky S-76C++	760708	ex N415Y		
☐	G-CFPZ	Sikorsky S-76C+	760744	ex N2039J		
☐	G-CFRD	Sikorsky S-76C+	760754	ex N754L		
☐	G-KAZA	Sikorsky S-76C+	760615	ex N81085		based Kazakhstan
☐	G-KAZB	Sikorsky S-76C+	760614	ex N8094S		based Kazakhstan
☐	G-IACA	Sikorsky S-92A	920050	ex N81254		
☐	G-IACB	Sikorsky S-92A	920062	ex N4516G		
☐	G-IACC	Sikorsky S-92A	920063	ex N45158		
☐	G-IACD	Sikorsky S-92A	920065	ex N4515G		
☐	G-IACE	Sikorsky S-92A	920066	ex N45148		
☐	G-IACF	Sikorsky S-92A	920068	ex N4509G		
☐	G-ISST	Eurocopter EC155 B1	6778			
☐	G-ISSU	Eurocopter EC155 B1	6762			
☐	G-ISSV	Eurocopter EC155 B1	6757			
☐	G-ISSW	Eurocopter EC155 B1	6755			

BRITISH AIRWAYS — *Speedbird & Shuttle (BA/BAW/SHT)*
London-Heathrow/Gatwick & Manchester (LHR/LGW/MAN)

Member of Oneworld

	Registration	Type	C/n	Previous
☐	G-EUNA	Airbus A318-121	4007	ex D-AUAC
☐	G-EUNB	Airbus A318-121	4039	ex D-AUAF
☐	G-EUOA	Airbus A319-131	1513	ex D-AVYE
☐	G-EUOB	Airbus A319-131	1529	ex D-AVWH
☐	G-EUOC	Airbus A319-131	1537	ex D-AVYP
☐	G-EUOD	Airbus A319-131	1558	ex D-AVYJ
☐	G-EUOE	Airbus A319-131	1574	ex D-AVWF
☐	G-EUOF	Airbus A319-131	1590	ex D-AVYW
☐	G-EUOG	Airbus A319-131	1594	ex D-AVWU
☐	G-EUOH	Airbus A319-131	1604	ex D-AVYM
☐	G-EUOI	Airbus A319-131	1606	ex D-AVYN
☐	G-EUPA	Airbus A319-131	1082	ex D-AVYK
☐	G-EUPB	Airbus A319-131	1115	ex D-AVYT
☐	G-EUPC	Airbus A319-131	1118	ex D-AVYU
☐	G-EUPD	Airbus A319-131	1142	ex D-AVWG
☐	G-EUPE	Airbus A319-131	1193	ex D-AVYT
☐	G-EUPF	Airbus A319-131	1197	ex D-AVWS
☐	G-EUPG	Airbus A319-131	1222	ex D-AVYG
☐	G-EUPH	Airbus A319-131	1225	ex D-AVYK
☐	G-EUPJ	Airbus A319-131	1232	ex D-AVYJ
☐	G-EUPK	Airbus A319-131	1236	ex D-AVYO
☐	G-EUPL	Airbus A319-131	1239	ex D-AVYP
☐	G-EUPM	Airbus A319-131	1258	ex D-AVYR
☐	G-EUPN	Airbus A319-131	1261	ex D-AVWA
☐	G-EUPO	Airbus A319-131	1279	ex D-AVYU
☐	G-EUPP	Airbus A319-131	1295	ex D-AVWU
☐	G-EUPR	Airbus A319-131	1329	ex D-AVYH
☐	G-EUPS	Airbus A319-131	1338	ex D-AVYM
☐	G-EUPT	Airbus A319-131	1380	ex D-AVWH
☐	G-EUPU	Airbus A319-131	1384	ex D-AVWP
☐	G-EUPV	Airbus A319-131	1423	ex D-AVYE
☐	G-EUPW	Airbus A319-131	1440	ex D-AVYP
☐	G-EUPX	Airbus A319-131	1445	ex D-AVWB
☐	G-EUPY	Airbus A319-131	1466	ex D-AVYU
☐	G-EUPZ	Airbus A319-131	1510	ex D-AVYY
☐	G-BUSH	Airbus A320-211	0042	ex F-WWDT
☐	G-BUSI	Airbus A320-211	0103	ex F-WWDB
☐	G-BUSJ	Airbus A320-211	0109	ex F-WWIC
☐	G-BUSK	Airbus A320-211	0120	ex F-WWIN

☐ G-EUUA	Airbus A320-232	1661	ex F-WWIH	
☐ G-EUUB	Airbus A320-232	1689	ex F-WWBE	
☐ G-EUUC	Airbus A320-232	1696	ex F-WWIO	
☐ G-EUUD	Airbus A320-232	1760	ex F-WWBN	
☐ G-EUUE	Airbus A320-232	1782	ex F-WWDO	
☐ G-EUUF	Airbus A320-232	1814	ex F-WWIY	
☐ G-EUUG	Airbus A320-232	1829	ex F-WWIU	
☐ G-EUUH	Airbus A320-232	1665	ex F-WWIG	
☐ G-EUUI	Airbus A320-232	1871	ex F-WWBI	
☐ G-EUUJ	Airbus A320-232	1883	ex F-WWBQ	
☐ G-EUUK	Airbus A320-232	1899	ex F-WWDO	
☐ G-EUUL	Airbus A320-232	1708	ex F-WWIV	
☐ G-EUUM	Airbus A320-232	1907	ex F-WWDN	
☐ G-EUUN	Airbus A320-232	1910	ex F-WWDP	
☐ G-EUUO	Airbus A320-232	1958	ex F-WWIT	
☐ G-EUUP	Airbus A320-232	2038	ex F-WWDB	
☐ G-EUUR	Airbus A320-232	2040	ex F-WWID	
☐ G-EUUS	Airbus A320-232	3301	ex F-WWIF	
☐ G-EUUT	Airbus A320-232	3314	ex F-WWIT	
☐ G-EUUU	Airbus A320-232	3351	ex F-WWID	
☐ G-EUUV	Airbus A320-232	3468	ex F-WWBO	
☐ G-EUUW	Airbus A320-232	3499	ex F-WWIN	
☐ G-EUUX	Airbus A320-232	3550	ex F-WWDM	
☐ G-EUUY	Airbus A320-232	3607	ex F-WWIC	
☐ G-EUUZ	Airbus A320-232	3649	ex F-WWDO	
☐ G-EUYA	Airbus A320-232	3697	ex F-WWBM	
☐ G-EUYB	Airbus A320-232	3703	ex F-WWBV	
☐ G-EUYC	Airbus A320-232	3721	ex F-WWBY	
☐ G-EUYD	Airbus A320-232	3726	ex F-WWDH	
☐ G-EUYE	Airbus A320-232	3912	ex F-WWBB	
☐ G-EUYF	Airbus A320-232	4185	ex F-WWIC	
☐ G-EUYG	Airbus A320-232	4238	ex	on order
☐ G-EUYH	Airbus A320-232		ex	on order
☐ G-EUYI	Airbus A320-232		ex	on order
☐ G-EUYJ	Airbus A320-232		ex	on order
☐ G-EUYK	Airbus A320-232		ex	on order
☐ G-EUYL	Airbus A320-232		ex	on order
☐ G-EUYM	Airbus A320-232		ex	on order
☐ G-EUYN	Airbus A320-232		ex	on order
☐ G-TTOB	Airbus A320-232	1687	ex F-WWIM	
☐ G-TTOE	Airbus A320-232	1754	ex F-WWDH	
☐ G-EUXC	Airbus A321-231	2305	ex D-AVZE	
☐ G-EUXD	Airbus A321-231	2320	ex D-AVZO	
☐ G-EUXE	Airbus A321-231	2323	ex D-AVZP	
☐ G-EUXF	Airbus A321-231	2324	ex D-AVZQ	
☐ G-EUXG	Airbus A321-231	2351	ex D-AVZU	
☐ G-EUXH	Airbus A321-231	2363	ex D-AVZW	
☐ G-EUXI	Airbus A321-231	2536	ex D-AVZE	
☐ G-EUXJ	Airbus A321-231	3081	ex D-AVZL	
☐ G-EUXK	Airbus A321-231	3235	ex D-AVZI	
☐ G-EUXL	Airbus A321-231	3254	ex D-AVZV	
☐ G-EUXM	Airbus A321-231	3290	ex D-AVZC	
☐ G-DOCA	Boeing 737-436	25267/2131		
☐ G-DOCB	Boeing 737-436	25304/2144		
☐ G-DOCE	Boeing 737-436	25350/2167		
☐ G-DOCF	Boeing 737-436	25407/2178		
☐ G-DOCG	Boeing 737-436	25408/2183		
☐ G-DOCH	Boeing 737-436	25428/2185		
☐ G-DOCL	Boeing 737-436	25842/2228		
☐ G-DOCN	Boeing 737-436	25848/2379		
☐ G-DOCO	Boeing 737-436	25849/2381		
☐ G-DOCS	Boeing 737-436	25852/2390		
☐ G-DOCT	Boeing 737-436	25853/2409		
☐ G-DOCU	Boeing 737-436	25854/2417		
☐ G-DOCV	Boeing 737-436	25855/2420		
☐ G-DOCW	Boeing 737-436	25856/2422		
☐ G-DOCX	Boeing 737-436	25857/2451		
☐ G-DOCY	Boeing 737-436	25844/2514	ex OO-LTQ	
☐ G-DOCZ	Boeing 737-436	25858/2522	ex EC-FXJ	
☐ G-GBTA	Boeing 737-436	25859/2532	ex G-BVHA	
☐ G-GBTB	Boeing 737-436	25860/2545	ex OO-LTS	
☐ G-BNLA	Boeing 747-436	23908/727	ex N60665	stored VCV
☐ G-BNLB	Boeing 747-436	23909/730		stored CWL
☐ G-BNLC	Boeing 747-436	23910/734		stored CWL
☐ G-BNLD	Boeing 747-436	23911/744	ex N6018N	
☐ G-BNLE	Boeing 747-436	24047/753		
☐ G-BNLF	Boeing 747-436	24048/773		
☐ G-BNLG	Boeing 747-436	24049/774		stored VCV
☐ G-BNLH	Boeing 747-436	24050/779	ex VH-NLH	stored VCV
☐ G-BNLI	Boeing 747-436	24051/784		

Registration	Type	c/n	Previous	Notes
☐ G-BNLJ	Boeing 747-436	24052/789	ex N60668	
☐ G-BNLK	Boeing 747-436	24053/790	ex N6009F	
☐ G-BNLL	Boeing 747-436	24054/794		
☐ G-BNLM	Boeing 747-436	24055/795	ex N6009F	
☐ G-BNLN	Boeing 747-436	24056/802		
☐ G-BNLO	Boeing 747-436	24057/817		
☐ G-BNLP	Boeing 747-436	24058/828		
☐ G-BNLR	Boeing 747-436	24447/829	ex N6005C	
☐ G-BNLS	Boeing 747-436	24629/841		
☐ G-BNLT	Boeing 747-436	24630/842		
☐ G-BNLU	Boeing 747-436	25406/895		stored VCV
☐ G-BNLV	Boeing 747-436	25427/900		stored VCV
☐ G-BNLW	Boeing 747-436	25432/903		
☐ G-BNLX	Boeing 747-436	25435/908		
☐ G-BNLY	Boeing 747-436	27090/959	ex N60659	
☐ G-BNLZ	Boeing 747-436	27091/964		
☐ G-BYGA	Boeing 747-436	28855/1190		
☐ G-BYGB	Boeing 747-436	28856/1194		
☐ G-BYGC	Boeing 747-436	25823/1195		
☐ G-BYGD	Boeing 747-436	28857/1196		
☐ G-BYGE	Boeing 747-436	28858/1198		
☐ G-BYGF	Boeing 747-436	25824/1200		
☐ G-BYGG	Boeing 747-436	28859/1212		
☐ G-CIVA	Boeing 747-436	27092/967		
☐ G-CIVB	Boeing 747-436	25811/1018		
☐ G-CIVC	Boeing 747-436	25812/1022		
☐ G-CIVD	Boeing 747-436	27349/1048		
☐ G-CIVE	Boeing 747-436	27350/1050		
☐ G-CIVF	Boeing 747-436	25434/1058	ex (G-BNLY)	
☐ G-CIVG	Boeing 747-436	25813/1059	ex N6009F	
☐ G-CIVH	Boeing 747-436	25809/1078		
☐ G-CIVI	Boeing 747-436	25814/1079		
☐ G-CIVJ	Boeing 747-436	25817/1102		
☐ G-CIVK	Boeing 747-436	25818/1104		
☐ G-CIVL	Boeing 747-436	27478/1108		
☐ G-CIVM	Boeing 747-436	28700/1116		
☐ G-CIVN	Boeing 747-436	28848/1129		
☐ G-CIVO	Boeing 747-436	28849/1135	ex N6046P	
☐ G-CIVP	Boeing 747-436	28850/1144		
☐ G-CIVR	Boeing 747-436	25820/1146		
☐ G-CIVS	Boeing 747-436	28851/1148		
☐ G-CIVT	Boeing 747-436	25821/1149		
☐ G-CIVU	Boeing 747-436	25810/1154		
☐ G-CIVV	Boeing 747-436	25819/1156	ex N6009F	
☐ G-CIVW	Boeing 747-436	25822/1157		
☐ G-CIVX	Boeing 747-436	28852/1172		
☐ G-CIVY	Boeing 747-436	28853/1178		
☐ G-CIVZ	Boeing 747-436	28854/1183		

Registration	Type	c/n	Previous	Notes
☐ G-BPEC	Boeing 757-236ER	24882/323		stored LHR
☐ G-BPED	Boeing 757-236ER	25059/363		stored LHR
☐ G-BPEE	Boeing 757-236ER	25060/364		stored LHR
☐ G-BPEI	Boeing 757-236	25806/601		stored LHR
☐ G-CPEL	Boeing 757-236	24398/224	ex N602DF	stored LHR
☐ G-CPEM	Boeing 757-236	28665/747		
☐ G-CPEN	Boeing 757-236	28666/751		
☐ G-CPEO	Boeing 757-236	28667/762		
☐ G-CPER	Boeing 757-236	29113/784		
☐ G-CPES	Boeing 757-236	29114/793		
☐ G-CPET	Boeing 757-236	29115/798		

Registration	Type	c/n	Previous	Notes
☐ G-BNWA	Boeing 767-336ER	24333/265	ex N6009F	
☐ G-BNWB	Boeing 767-336ER	24334/281	ex N6046P	
☐ G-BNWC	Boeing 767-336ER	24335/284		
☐ G-BNWD	Boeing 767-336ER	24336/286	ex N6018N	
☐ G-BNWH	Boeing 767-336ER	24340/335	ex N6005C	
☐ G-BNWI	Boeing 767-336ER	24341/342		
☐ G-BNWM	Boeing 767-336ER	25204/376		
☐ G-BNWN	Boeing 767-336ER	25444/398		
☐ G-BNWO	Boeing 767-336ER	25442/418		
☐ G-BNWR	Boeing 767-336ER	25732/421		
☐ G-BNWS	Boeing 767-336ER	25826/473	ex N6018N	
☐ G-BNWT	Boeing 767-336ER	25828/476		
☐ G-BNWU	Boeing 767-336ER	25829/483		
☐ G-BNWV	Boeing 767-336ER	27140/490		
☐ G-BNWW	Boeing 767-336ER	25831/526		
☐ G-BNWX	Boeing 767-336ER	25832/529		
☐ G-BNWY	Boeing 767-336ER	25834/608	ex N5005C	
☐ G-BNWZ	Boeing 767-336ER	25733/648		
☐ G-BZHA	Boeing 767-336ER	29230/702		
☐ G-BZHB	Boeing 767-336ER	29231/704		
☐ G-BZHC	Boeing 767-336ER	29232/708		

☐ G-RAES	Boeing 777-236ER	27491/76	ex (G-ZZZP)	
☐ G-VIIA	Boeing 777-236ER	27483/41	ex N5022E	
☐ G-VIIB	Boeing 777-236ER	27484/49	ex (G-ZZZG)	
☐ G-VIIC	Boeing 777-236ER	27485/53	ex (G-ZZZH)	
☐ G-VIID	Boeing 777-236ER	27486/56	ex (G-ZZZI)	
☐ G-VIIE	Boeing 777-236ER	27487/58	ex (G-ZZZJ)	
☐ G-VIIF	Boeing 777-236ER	27488/61	ex (G-ZZZK)	
☐ G-VIIG	Boeing 777-236ER	27489/65	ex (G-ZZZL)	
☐ G-VIIH	Boeing 777-236ER	27490/70	ex (G-ZZZM)	
☐ G-VIIJ	Boeing 777-236ER	27492/111	ex (G-ZZZN)	
☐ G-VIIK	Boeing 777-236ER	28840/117		
☐ G-VIIL	Boeing 777-236ER	27493/127		
☐ G-VIIM	Boeing 777-236ER	28841/130		
☐ G-VIIN	Boeing 777-236ER	29319/157		
☐ G-VIIO	Boeing 777-236ER	29320/182		
☐ G-VIIP	Boeing 777-236ER	29321/193		
☐ G-VIIR	Boeing 777-236ER	29322/203		
☐ G-VIIS	Boeing 777-236ER	29323/206		
☐ G-VIIT	Boeing 777-236ER	29962/217		
☐ G-VIIU	Boeing 777-236ER	29963/221		
☐ G-VIIV	Boeing 777-236ER	29964/228		
☐ G-VIIW	Boeing 777-236ER	29965/233		
☐ G-VIIX	Boeing 777-236ER	29966/236		
☐ G-VIIY	Boeing 777-236ER	29967/251		
☐ G-YMMA	Boeing 777-236ER	30302/242	ex N5017Q	
☐ G-YMMB	Boeing 777-236ER	30303/265		
☐ G-YMMC	Boeing 777-236ER	30304/268		
☐ G-YMMD	Boeing 777-236ER	30305/269		
☐ G-YMME	Boeing 777-236ER	30306/275		
☐ G-YMMF	Boeing 777-236ER	30307/281		
☐ G-YMMG	Boeing 777-236ER	30308/301		
☐ G-YMMH	Boeing 777-236ER	30309/303		
☐ G-YMMI	Boeing 777-236ER	30310/308		
☐ G-YMMJ	Boeing 777-236ER	30311/311		
☐ G-YMMK	Boeing 777-236ER	30312/312		
☐ G-YMML	Boeing 777-236ER	30313/334		
☐ G-YMMN	Boeing 777-236ER	30316/346		
☐ G-YMMO	Boeing 777-236ER	30317/361		
☐ G-YMMP	Boeing 777-236ER	30315/369		
☐ G-YMMR	Boeing 777-236ER	36516/771	ex N5014K	
☐ G-YMMS	Boeing 777-236ER	36517/784		
☐ G-YMMT	Boeing 777-236ER	36518/791		
☐ G-YMMU	Boeing 777-236ER	36519/796	ex N6009F	
☐ G-ZZZA	Boeing 777-236	27105/6	ex N77779	
☐ G-ZZZB	Boeing 777-236	27106/10	ex N77771	
☐ G-ZZZC	Boeing 777-236	27107/15	ex N5014K	
☐ G-STBA	Boeing 777-336ER	40542		on order
☐ G-STBB	Boeing 777-336ER	39286		on order
☐ G-STBC	Boeing 777-336ER	39287		on order

BRITISH GLOBAL — *Kruger Air (7G/MKA)* — *Ostend (OST)*

☐ G-MKAA	Boeing 747-2S4F	22169/472	ex 9G-MKQ	
☐ G-MKBA	Boeing 747-2B5F	22481/454	ex 9G-MKR	
☐ G-MKCA	Boeing 747-2B5B (SF)	22482/484	ex 9G-MKM	stored Kemble
☐ G-MKDA	Boeing 747-2B5F	22486/520	ex 9G-MKS	
☐ G-MKEA	Boeing 747-249F	22237/460	ex 9G-MKU	
☐ G-MKFA	Boeing 747-245F	21841/396	ex 9G-MKP	stored FZO
☐ G-MKHA	Boeing 747-2J6B (SF)	23071/591	ex B-2446	
☐ G-MKJA	Boeing 747-246F	22477/494	ex HS-ORB	
☐ G-MKKA	Boeing 747-212B (SF)	21940/547	ex HS-ORA	
☐ G-MKLA	Boeing 747-236B (SF)	23711/672	ex TF-ATX	
☐ 9G-MKH	Douglas DC-8-62AF (BAC 3)	46153/551	ex TF-MKH	stored FZO
☐ 9G-MKK	Douglas DC-8-62F (BAC 3)	46022/417	ex 9G-MKK	

BRITISH INTERNATIONAL — *Brintel (BS/VRA)* — *Cardiff, Penzance & Plymouth (CWL/PZE/PLH)*

☐ G-ATBJ	Sikorsky S-61N	61269	ex N10043		
☐ G-ATFM	Sikorsky S-61N	61270	ex CF-OKY		based Falklands Islands
☐ G-AYOY	Sikorsky S-61N	61476			
☐ G-BCEA	Sikorsky S-61N	61721			based Falklands Islands
☐ G-BCEB	Sikorsky S-61N	61454	ex N4023S	The Isles of Scilly	
☐ G-BFFJ	Sikorsky S-61N	61777	ex N6231	Tresco	
☐ G-BFRI	Sikorsky S-61N II	61809			
☐ G-BHOG	Sikorsky S-61N II	61825	ex PT-YEK		
☐ G-VIPZ	Sikorsky S-61N	61824	ex G-DAWS		

CHC SCOTIA HELICOPTERS		Helibus (SHZ)		Aberdeen (ABZ)
☐ G-BKZE	Aérospatiale AS.332L	2102	ex F-WKQE	Lsd fr Heliworld Lsg
☐ G-BKZG	Aérospatiale AS.332L	2106	ex HB-ZBT	
☐ G-BUZD	Aérospatiale AS.332L	2069	ex C-GSLJ	
☐ G-CHCF	Aérospatiale AS.332L2	2567		
☐ G-CHCG	Aérospatiale AS.332L2	2592		
☐ G-CHCH	Aérospatiale AS.332L2	2601		
☐ G-CHCI	Aérospatiale AS.322L	2395	ex LN-OHD	
☐ G-CHCL	Eurocopter EC225LP	2674		
☐ G-CHCM	Eurocopter EC225LP	2675		
☐ G-CHCN	Eurocopter EC225LP	2679		
☐ G-PUMA	Aérospatiale AS.332L	2038	ex F-WMHB	
☐ G-PUMB	Aérospatiale AS.332L	2075		
☐ G-PUME	Aérospatiale AS.332L	2091		
☐ G-PUMN	Aérospatiale AS.332L2	2484	ex LN-OHF	Lsd fr HKS
☐ G-PUMO	Aérospatiale AS.332L2	2467		
☐ G-PUMS	Aérospatiale AS.332L2	2504		
☐ G-BKXD	Aérospatiale SA365N Dauphin 2	6088	ex F-WMHD	
☐ G-BLEZ	Aérospatiale SA365N Dauphin 2	6131		
☐ G-BLUM	Aérospatiale SA365N Dauphin 2	6101		
☐ G-BTEU	Aérospatiale SA365N2 Dauphin 2	6392		
☐ G-BTNC	Aérospatiale SA365N2 Dauphin 2	6409		
☐ G-BTUX	Aérospatiale AS365N2 Dauphin 2	6424	ex LN-OLL	
☐ G-CHCO	Aérospatiale AS365N2 Dauphin 2	6358	ex LN-ODB	
☐ G-CGIJ	Agusta AW139	31203		Op for HM Coastguard
☐ G-CGWB	Agusta AW139	31209		Op for HM Coastguard
☐ G-CHCP	Agusta AW139	31046	ex PH-IEH	
☐ G-CHCT	Agusta AW139	31042	ex PH-TRH	
☐ G-CHCV	Agusta AW139	41005	ex N106AW	
☐ G-CHCW	Agusta AW139	31072	ex PH-EUA	
☐ G-JEZA	Agusta AW139	31255		
☐ G-SARD	Agusta AW139	31208		Op for HM Coastguard
☐ G-BMAL	Sikorsky S-76A+	760120	ex F-WZSA	
☐ G-CHCD	Sikorsky S-76A+	760101	ex (ZS-RNH)	
☐ G-SSSC	Sikorsky S-76C	760408		
☐ G-SSSD	Sikorsky S-76C	760415		
☐ G-SSSE	Sikorsky S-76C	760417		
☐ G-CGMU	Sikorsky S-92A	920034	ex N8010S	on order Op for HM Coastguard
☐ G-CGOC	Sikorsky S-92A	920051	ex N45165	
☐ G-CHCK	Sikorsky S-92A	920030	ex N8001N	
☐ G-SARB	Sikorsky S-92A	920045	ex N80562	Op for HM Coastguard
☐ G-SARC	Sikorsky S-92A	920052	ex N45168	on order Op for HM Coastguard

DHL AIR	World Express (D0/DHK)	East Midlands-Nottingham/Brussels (EMA/BRU)		
☐ G-BIKC	Boeing 757-236 (SF)	22174/11		
☐ G-BIKF	Boeing 757-236 (SF)	22177/16		
☐ G-BIKG	Boeing 757-236 (SF)	22178/23		
☐ G-BIKI	Boeing 757-236 (SF)	22180/25	ex OO-DLO	
☐ G-BIKJ	Boeing 757-236 (SF)	22181/29		
☐ G-BIKK	Boeing 757-236 (SF)	22182/30		
☐ G-BIKM	Boeing 757-236 (SF)	22184/33	ex N8293V	
☐ G-BIKN	Boeing 757-236 (SF)	22186/50		
☐ G-BIKO	Boeing 757-236 (SF)	22187/52		
☐ G-BIKP	Boeing 757-236 (SF)	22188/54		
☐ G-BIKS	Boeing 757-236 (SF)	22190/63		
☐ G-BIKU	Boeing 757-236 (SF)	23399/78		
☐ G-BIKV	Boeing 757-236 (SF)	23400/81		
☐ G-BIKZ	Boeing 757-236 (SF)	23532/98		
☐ G-BMRA	Boeing 757-236 (SF)	23710/123		
☐ G-BMRB	Boeing 757-236 (SF)	23975/145		
☐ G-BMRC	Boeing 757-236 (SF)	24072/160		
☐ G-BMRD	Boeing 757-236 (SF)	24073/166		
☐ G-BMRE	Boeing 757-236 (SF)	24074/168		
☐ G-BMRF	Boeing 757-236 (SF)	24101/175		
☐ G-BMRH	Boeing 757-236 (SF)	24266/210		
☐ G-BMRJ	Boeing 757-236 (SF)	24268/214		
☐ G-DHLE	Boeing 767-3JHF/W	37805/980		
☐ G-DHLF	Boeing 767-3JHF/W	37806/981		
☐ G-DHLG	Boeing 767-3JHF/W	37807/982		

DIRECTFLIGHT		Metman/Watchdog (DCT)		Cranfield/Exeter (-/EXT)
☐ G-LUXE	British Aerospace 146 Srs.301	E3001	ex G-5-300	Atmospheric Research, op for FAAM
☐ G-MAFA	Reims Cessna F406 Caravan II	F406-0036	ex G-DFLT	Op for DEFRA
☐ G-MAFB	Reims Cessna F406 Caravan II	F406-0080	ex F-WWSR	Op for DEFRA

☐ G-SICA	Britten-Norman BN-2B-20 Islander	2304	ex G-SLAP	Op for Shetland Islands Council
☐ G-SICB	Britten-Norman BN-2B-20 Islander	2260	ex G-NESU	Op for Shetland Islands Council

EASTERN AIRWAYS — Eastflight (T3/EZE) — Humberside (HUY)

☐ G-CDYI	British Aerospace Jetstream 41	41019	ex N305UE	
☐ G-MAJA	British Aerospace Jetstream 41	41032	ex G-4-032	
☐ G-MAJB	British Aerospace Jetstream 41	41018	ex G-BVKT	
☐ G-MAJC	British Aerospace Jetstream 41	41005	ex G-LOGJ	
☐ G-MAJD	British Aerospace Jetstream 41	41006	ex G-WAWR	
☐ G-MAJE	British Aerospace Jetstream 41	41007	ex G-LOGK	
☐ G-MAJF	British Aerospace Jetstream 41	41008	ex G-WAWL	
☐ G-MAJG	British Aerospace Jetstream 41	41009	ex G-LOGL	
☐ G-MAJH	British Aerospace Jetstream 41	41010	ex G-WAYR	
☐ G-MAJI	British Aerospace Jetstream 41	41011	ex G-WAND	
☐ G-MAJJ	British Aerospace Jetstream 41	41024	ex G-WAFT	
☐ G-MAJK	British Aerospace Jetstream 41	41070	ex G-4-070	
☐ G-MAJL	British Aerospace Jetstream 41	41087	ex G-4-087	
☐ G-MAJP	British Aerospace Jetstream 41	41039	ex N550HK	
☐ G-MAJT	British Aerospace Jetstream 41	41040	ex N551HK	
☐ G-MAJU	British Aerospace Jetstream 41	41071	ex N558HK	
☐ G-MAJV	British Aerospace Jetstream 41	41074	ex N557HK	
☐ G-MAJW	British Aerospace Jetstream 41	41015	ex N303UE	
☐ G-MAJX	British Aerospace Jetstream 41	41098	ex N330UE	
☐ G-MAJY	British Aerospace Jetstream 41	41099	ex N331UE	
☐ G-MAJZ	British Aerospace Jetstream 41	41100	ex N332UE	
☐ G-CDEA	SAAB 2000	2000-009	ex SE-009	
☐ G-CDEB	SAAB 2000	2000-036	ex SE-036	
☐ G-CDKA	SAAB 2000	2000-006	ex SE-006	Aberdeen City & Shire
☐ G-CDKB	SAAB 2000	2000-032	ex SE-032	
☐ G-CERY	SAAB 2000	2000-008	ex D-AOLA	
☐ G-CERZ	SAAB 2000	2000-042	ex SE-LSA	
☐ G-CFLU	SAAB 2000	2000-055	ex SE-LSG	
☐ G-CFLV	SAAB 2000	2000-023	ex SE-023	

EASYJET AIRLINES — Easy (U2/EZY) — London-Luton (LTN)

☐ G-EJAR	Airbus A319-111	2412	ex D-AVWH	
☐ G-EJJB	Airbus A319-111	2380	ex D-AVWV	
☐ G-EZAA	Airbus A319-111	2677	ex D-AVYU	
☐ G-EZAB	Airbus A319-111	2681	ex D-AVYY	
☐ G-EZAC	Airbus A319-111	2691	ex D-AVXB	
☐ G-EZAD	Airbus A319-111	2702	ex D-AVXI	
☐ G-EZAE	Airbus A319-111	2709	ex D-AVYI	
☐ G-EZAF	Airbus A319-111	2715	ex D-AVYT	
☐ G-EZAG	Airbus A319-111	2727	ex D-AVXG	
☐ G-EZAH	Airbus A319-111	2729	ex D-AVXK	
☐ G-EZAI	Airbus A319-111	2735	ex D-AVXM	
☐ G-EZAJ	Airbus A319-111	2742	ex D-AVXP	
☐ G-EZAK	Airbus A319-111	2744	ex D-AVXQ	
☐ G-EZAL	Airbus A319-111	2754	ex D-AVWG	
☐ G-EZAM	Airbus A319-111	2037	ex HB-JZA	
☐ G-EZAN	Airbus A319-111	2765	ex D-AVWL	
☐ G-EZAO	Airbus A319-111	2769	ex D-AVWO	
☐ G-EZAP	Airbus A319-111	2777	ex D-AVYG	
☐ G-EZAS	Airbus A319-111	2779	ex D-AVYH	
☐ G-EZAT	Airbus A319-111	2782	ex D-AVYO	
☐ G-EZAU	Airbus A319-111	2795	ex D-AVWQ	
☐ G-EZAV	Airbus A319-111	2803	ex D-AVWV	
☐ G-EZAW	Airbus A319-111	2812	ex D-AVYU	
☐ G-EZAX	Airbus A319-111	2818	ex D-AVXA	
☐ G-EZAY	Airbus A319-111	2827	ex D-AVXE	
☐ G-EZAZ	Airbus A319-111	2829	ex D-AVXF	
☐ G-EZBA	Airbus A319-111	2860	ex D-AVWB	
☐ G-EZBB	Airbus A319-111	2854	ex D-AVXM	
☐ G-EZBC	Airbus A319-111	2866	ex D-AVWD	
☐ G-EZBD	Airbus A319-111	2873	ex D-AVWK	
☐ G-EZBE	Airbus A319-111	2884	ex D-AVXO	
☐ G-EZBF	Airbus A319-111	2923	ex D-AVYK	
☐ G-EZBG	Airbus A319-111	2946	ex D-AVXA	
☐ G-EZBH	Airbus A319-111	2959	ex D-AVXH	
☐ G-EZBI	Airbus A319-111	3003	ex D-AVYB	Madrid
☐ G-EZBJ	Airbus A319-111	3036	ex D-AVWJ	
☐ G-EZBK	Airbus A319-111	3041	ex D-AVWK	
☐ G-EZBL	Airbus A319-111	3053	ex D-AVYJ	
☐ G-EZBM	Airbus A319-111	3059	ex D-AVWE	
☐ G-EZBN	Airbus A319-111	3061	ex D-AVWH	
☐ G-EZBO	Airbus A319-111	3082	ex D-AVYK	
☐ G-EZBR	Airbus A319-111	3088	ex D-AVYY	100th Airbus titles
☐ G-EZBT	Airbus A319-111	3090	ex D-AVWM	
☐ G-EZBU	Airbus A319-111	3118	ex D-AVWW	

☐	G-EZBV	Airbus A319-111	3122	ex D-AVWX	
☐	G-EZBW	Airbus A319-111	3134	ex D-AVXE	
☐	G-EZBX	Airbus A319-111	3137	ex D-AVXH	
☐	G-EZBY	Airbus A319-111	3176	ex D-AVXJ	
☐	G-EZBZ	Airbus A319-111	3184	ex D-AVYF	
☐	G-EZDA	Airbus A319-111	3413	ex D-AVYH	
☐	G-EZDB	Airbus A319-111	3411	ex D-AVYF	
☐	G-EZDC	Airbus A319-111	2043	ex HB-JZB	
☐	G-EZDD	Airbus A319-111	3442	ex D-AVYL	
☐	G-EZDE	Airbus A319-111	3426	ex D-AVYP	
☐	G-EZDF	Airbus A319-111	3432	ex D-AVYG	
☐	G-EZDH	Airbus A319-111	3466	ex D-AVWM	
☐	G-EZDI	Airbus A319-111	3537	ex D-AVWC	
☐	G-EZDJ	Airbus A319-111	3544	ex D-AVWJ	I Love Malpensa
☐	G-EZDK	Airbus A319-111	3555	ex D-AVWP	
☐	G-EZDL	Airbus A319-111	3569	ex D-AVWT	
☐	G-EZDM	Airbus A319-111	3571	ex D-AVWU	
☐	G-EZDN	Airbus A319-111	3608	ex D-AVYJ	
☐	G-EZDO	Airbus A319-111	3634	ex D-AVYP	
☐	G-EZDP	Airbus A319-111	3675	ex D-AVYX	
☐	G-EZDR	Airbus A319-111	3683	ex D-AVYZ	
☐	G-EZDS	Airbus A319-111	3702	ex D-AVWP	
☐	G-EZDT	Airbus A319-111	3720	ex D-AVWR	
☐	G-EZDU	Airbus A319-111	3735	ex D-AVWX	
☐	G-EZDV	Airbus A319-111	3742	ex D-AVWY	
☐	G-EZDW	Airbus A319-111	3746	ex D-AVXA	
☐	G-EZDX	Airbus A319-111	3754	ex D-AVXB	
☐	G-EZDY	Airbus A319-111	3763	ex D-AVXF	
☐	G-EZDZ	Airbus A319-111	3774	ex D-AVXI	
☐	G-EZEA	Airbus A319-111	2119	ex D-AVWZ	
☐	G-EZEB	Airbus A319-111	2120	ex D-AVYK	
☐	G-EZEC	Airbus A319-111	2129	ex D-AVWR	
☐	G-EZED	Airbus A319-111	2170	ex D-AVWT	
☐	G-EZEF	Airbus A319-111	2176	ex D-AVYS	
☐	G-EZEG	Airbus A319-111	2181	ex D-AVWF	
☐	G-EZEJ	Airbus A319-111	2214	ex D-AVYO	
☐	G-EZEK	Airbus A319-111	2224	ex D-AVYZ	
☐	G-EZEO	Airbus A319-111	2249	ex D-AVYN	
☐	G-EZEP	Airbus A319-111	2251	ex D-AVYQ	
☐	G-EZET	Airbus A319-111	2271	ex D-AVWY	
☐	G-EZEU	Airbus A319-111	2283	ex D-AVYP	
☐	G-EZEV	Airbus A319-111	2289	ex D-AVYV	
☐	G-EZEW	Airbus A319-111	2300	ex D-AVWH	
☐	G-EZEZ	Airbus A319-111	2360	ex D-AVWP	
☐	G-EZFA	Airbus A319-111	3788	ex D-AVXK	
☐	G-EZFB	Airbus A319-111	3799	ex D-AVXN	
☐	G-EZFC	Airbus A319-111	3808	ex D-AVYC	
☐	G-EZFD	Airbus A319-111	3810	ex D-AVYF	
☐	G-EZFE	Airbus A319-111	3824	ex D-AVYI	
☐	G-EZFF	Airbus A319-111	3844	ex D-AVYT	
☐	G-EZFG	Airbus A319-111	3845	ex D-AVYU	
☐	G-EZFH	Airbus A319-111	3854	ex D-AVWA	
☐	G-EZFI	Airbus A319-111	3888	ex D-AVWH	
☐	G-EZFJ	Airbus A319-111	4040	ex D-AVYM	
☐	G-EZFK	Airbus A319-111	4048	ex D-AVYP	
☐	G-EZFL	Airbus A319-111	4056	ex D-AVYS	
☐	G-EZFM	Airbus A319-111	4069	ex D-AVYT	
☐	G-EZFN	Airbus A319-111	4076	ex D-AVYV	
☐	G-EZFO	Airbus A319-111	4080	ex D-AVYW	
☐	G-EZFP	Airbus A319-111	4087	ex D-AVYX	
☐	G-EZFR	Airbus A319-111	4125	ex D-AVWC	
☐	G-EZFS	Airbus A319-111	4129	ex D-AVWE	
☐	G-EZFT	Airbus A319-111	4132	ex D-AVWF	
☐	G-	Airbus A319-111		ex D-AV	on order
☐	G-	Airbus A319-111		ex D-AV	on order
☐	G-	Airbus A319-111		ex D-AV	on order
☐	G-	Airbus A319-111		ex D-AV	on order
☐	G-	Airbus A319-111		ex D-AV	on order
☐	G-	Airbus A319-111		ex D-AV	on order
☐	G-	Airbus A319-111		ex D-AV	on order
☐	G-	Airbus A319-111		ex D-AV	on order
☐	G-	Airbus A319-111		ex D-AV	on order
☐	G-	Airbus A319-111		ex D-AV	on order
☐	G-	Airbus A319-111		ex D-AV	on order
☐	G-	Airbus A319-111		ex D-AV	on order
☐	G-	Airbus A319-111		ex D-AV	on order
☐	G-	Airbus A319-111		ex D-AV	on order
☐	G-	Airbus A319-111		ex D-AV	on order
☐	G-EZIA	Airbus A319-111	2420	ex D-AVYL	
☐	G-EZIC	Airbus A319-111	2436	ex D-AVWC	
☐	G-EZID	Airbus A319-111	2442	ex D-AVWT	'100' titles
☐	G-EZIE	Airbus A319-111	2446	ex D-AVWQ	
☐	G-EZIG	Airbus A319-111	2460	ex D-AVYM	

☐ G-EZIH	Airbus A319-111	2463	ex D-AVWV	
☐ G-EZII	Airbus A319-111	2471	ex D-AVYK	
☐ G-EZIJ	Airbus A319-111	2477	ex D-AVYU	
☐ G-EZIK	Airbus A319-111	2481	ex D-AVYV	
☐ G-EZIL	Airbus A319-111	2492	ex D-AVWM	
☐ G-EZIM	Airbus A319-111	2495	ex D-AVYO	
☐ G-EZIN	Airbus A319-111	2503	ex D-AVYZ	
☐ G-EZIO	Airbus A319-111	2512	ex D-AVWP	
☐ G-EZIP	Airbus A319-111	2514	ex D-AVWQ	
☐ G-EZIR	Airbus A319-111	2527	ex D-AVWK	
☐ G-EZIS	Airbus A319-111	2528	ex D-AVWJ	
☐ G-EZIT	Airbus A319-111	2538	ex D-AVYN	
☐ G-EZIU	Airbus A319-111	2548	ex D-AVYF	
☐ G-EZIV	Airbus A319-111	2565	ex D-AVYY	
☐ G-EZIW	Airbus A319-111	2578	ex D-AVXE	
☐ G-EZIX	Airbus A319-111	2605	ex D-AVXP	
☐ G-EZIY	Airbus A319-111	2636	ex D-AVWH	
☐ G-EZIZ	Airbus A319-111	2646	ex D-AVWQ	
☐ G-EZMH	Airbus A319-111	2053	ex HB-JZD	
☐ G-EZMS	Airbus A319-111	2378	ex D-AVWS	
☐ G-EZNC	Airbus A319-111	2050	ex HB-JZC	
☐ G-EZNM	Airbus A319-111	2402	ex D-AVYV	
☐ G-EZPG	Airbus A319-111	2385	ex D-AVYD	
☐ G-EZSM	Airbus A319-111	2062	ex HB-JZE	
☐ G-EZTA	Airbus A320-214	3805	ex D-AVVD	
☐ G-EZTB	Airbus A320-232	3843	ex F-WWBO	
☐ G-EZTC	Airbus A320-232	3871	ex F-WWIG	
☐ G-EZTD	Airbus A320-223	3909	ex D-AVVB	
☐ G-EZTE	Airbus A320-232	3913	ex D-AVYF	
☐ G-EZTF	Airbus A320-232	3922	ex D-AVVG	
☐ G-EZTG	Airbus A320-232	3946	ex D-AVVJ	
☐ G-EZTH	Airbus A320-232	3953	ex D-AVVM	
☐ G-EZTI	Airbus A320-232	3975	ex D-AVVN	
☐ G-EZTJ	Airbus A320-232	3979	ex D-AVVO	
☐ G-EZTK	Airbus A320-232	3991	ex D-AVVP	
☐ G-EZTL	Airbus A320-232	4012	ex D-AVVC	
☐ G-EZTM	Airbus A320-232	4014	ex D-AVVD	
☐ G-EZTN	Airbus A320-232	4006	ex F-WWDY	
☐ G-EZTP	Airbus A320-232	4157	ex D-AVVN	
☐ G-EZTR	Airbus A320-232	4179	ex D-AVVX	
☐ G-EZTS	Airbus A320-232	4196	ex D-AVVE	
☐ G-EZTT	Airbus A320-232	4219	ex D-AVVM	on order
☐ G-EZTU	Airbus A320-232	4233	ex F-WWBV	on order
☐ G-EZTV	Airbus A320-232	4234	ex	on order
☐ G-EZTW	Airbus A320-232		ex	on order
☐ G-TTOG	Airbus A320-232	1969	ex F-WWDZ	
☐ G-TTOH	Airbus A320-232	1993	ex F-WWDO	
☐ G-TTOI	Airbus A320-232	2137	ex F-WWBN	
☐ G-TTOJ	Airbus A320-232	2157	ex F-WWDE	
☐ G-TTIC	Airbus A321-231	1869	ex D-AVZZ	stored SNN
☐ G-TTID	Airbus A321-231	2462	ex D-AVZB	
☐ G-TTIE	Airbus A321-231	2682	ex D-AVZD	
☐ G-TTIF	Airbus A321-231	3106	ex D-AVZC	
☐ G-	Airbus A321-231	4155	ex D-AV	on order
☐ G-EZJU	Boeing 737-73V	32416/1270	ex N6046P	
☐ G-EZJV	Boeing 737-73V	32417/1285		
☐ G-EZJW	Boeing 737-73V	32418/1300		
☐ G-EZJX	Boeing 737-73V	32419/1321	ex N1787B	
☐ G-EZJY	Boeing 737-73V	32420/1341		
☐ G-EZJZ	Boeing 737-73V	32421/1357		Ray Webster
☐ G-EZKA	Boeing 737-73V	32422/1363	ex (G-ESYA)	
☐ G-EZKB	Boeing 737-73V	32423/1433	ex (G-ESYB)	
☐ G-EZKC	Boeing 737-73V	32424/1450	ex (G-ESYC)	
☐ G-EZKD	Boeing 737-73V	32425/1453	ex N1787B	
☐ G-EZKE	Boeing 737-73V	32426/1474	ex (G-ESYE)	Daniel Swaddle
☐ G-EZKF	Boeing 737-73V	32427/1489	ex (G-ESYF)	
☐ G-EZKG	Boeing 737-73V	32428/1495	ex (G-ESYG)	

FLYBE — *Jersey (BE/BEE)* — *Jersey/Exeter (JER/EXT)*

☐ G-ECOA	de Havilland DHC-8-402Q	4180	ex C-FMUE	
☐ G-ECOB	de Havilland DHC-8-402Q	4185	ex LN-WDT	
☐ G-ECOC	de Havilland DHC-8-402Q	4197	ex LN-WDU	
☐ G-ECOD	de Havilland DHC-8-402Q	4206	ex C-FPEX	
☐ G-ECOE	de Havilland DHC-8-402Q	4212	ex LN-WDV	Lsd to OAL
☐ G-ECOF	de Havilland DHC-8-402Q	4216	ex LN-WDW	Lsd to OAL
☐ G-ECOG	de Havilland DHC-8-402Q	4220	ex C-FSRQ	
☐ G-ECOH	de Havilland DHC-8-402Q	4221	ex C-FSRW	
☐ G-ECOI	de Havilland DHC-8-402Q	4224	ex C-FTIE	
☐ G-ECOJ	de Havilland DHC-8-402Q	4229	ex C-FTUS	

☐ G-ECOK	de Havilland DHC-8-402Q	4230	ex C-FTUT		
☐ G-ECOM	de Havilland DHC-8-402Q	4233	ex C-FUCR		
☐ G-ECOO	de Havilland DHC-8-402Q	4237	ex C-FUOG		
☐ G-ECOP	de Havilland DHC-8-402Q	4242	ex C-FUTG		
☐ G-ECOR	de Havilland DHC-8-402Q	4248	ex C-FVUJ		
☐ G-ECOT	de Havilland DHC-8-402Q	4251	ex C-FVUV		
☐ G-ECOV	de Havilland DHC-8-402Q	4033	ex LN-RDM		
☐ G-ECOW	de Havilland DHC-8-402Q	4021	ex LN-RDF		
☐ G-ECOY	de Havilland DHC-8-402Q	4022	ex LN-RDG		
☐ G-ECOZ	de Havilland DHC-8-402Q	4034	ex LN-RDR		
☐ G-FLBA	de Havilland DHC-8-402Q	4253	ex C-FVVB		
☐ G-FLBB	de Havilland DHC-8-402Q	4255	ex C-FWGE		
☐ G-FLBC	de Havilland DHC-8-402Q	4257	ex C-FWGY		
☐ G-FLBD	de Havilland DHC-8-402Q	4259	ex C-FWZN		Lsd to OAL
☐ G-FLBE	de Havilland DHC-8-402Q	4261	ex C-FXAB		Lsd to OAL
☐ G-	de Havilland DHC-8-402Q		ex C-		on order
☐ G-	de Havilland DHC-8-402Q		ex C-		on order
☐ G-	de Havilland DHC-8-402Q		ex C-		on order
☐ G-	de Havilland DHC-8-402Q		ex C-		on order
☐ G-JECE	de Havilland DHC-8-402Q	4094	ex C-FDHU		
☐ G-JECF	de Havilland DHC-8-402Q	4095	ex C-FDHV		
☐ G-JECG	de Havilland DHC-8-402Q	4098	ex C-FAQH		
☐ G-JECH	de Havilland DHC-8-402Q	4103	ex C-FCQC		
☐ G-JECI	de Havilland DHC-8-402Q	4105	ex C-FCQK		
☐ G-JECJ	de Havilland DHC-8-402Q	4110	ex C-FCVN		
☐ G-JECK	de Havilland DHC-8-402Q	4113	ex C-FDRL		
☐ G-JECL	de Havilland DHC-8-402Q	4114	ex C-FDRN	The George Best	
☐ G-JECM	de Havilland DHC-8-402Q	4118	ex C-FFCE		
☐ G-JECN	de Havilland DHC-8-402Q	4120	ex C-FFCL		
☐ G-JECO	de Havilland DHC-8-402Q	4126	ex C-FFPT		
☐ G-JECP	de Havilland DHC-8-402Q	4136	ex C-FHEL		
☐ G-JECR	de Havilland DHC-8-402Q	4139	ex C-FHQM		
☐ G-JECS	de Havilland DHC-8-402Q	4142	ex C-FHQV		
☐ G-JECT	de Havilland DHC-8-402Q	4144	ex C-FHQY	Matt le Tissier	
☐ G-JECU	de Havilland DHC-8-402Q	4146	ex C-FJKY		
☐ G-JECX	de Havilland DHC-8-402Q	4155	ex C-FLKO		
☐ G-JECY	de Havilland DHC-8-402Q	4157	ex C-FLKV		
☐ G-JECZ	de Havilland DHC-8-402Q	4179	ex C-FMTY		
☐ G-JEDI	de Havilland DHC-8-402Q	4052	ex C-GFOD		
☐ G-JEDJ	de Havilland DHC-8-402Q	4058	ex C-FDHZ		
☐ G-JEDK	de Havilland DHC-8-402Q	4065	ex C-GEMU	Vignoble de Bergerac	
☐ G-JEDL	de Havilland DHC-8-402Q	4067	ex C-GEOZ		
☐ G-JEDM	de Havilland DHC-8-402Q	4077	ex C-FGNP		
☐ G-JEDN	de Havilland DHC-8-402Q	4078	ex C-FNGB		
☐ G-JEDO	de Havilland DHC-8-402Q	4079	ex C-GDFT		
☐ G-JEDP	de Havilland DHC-8-402Q	4085	ex C-FDHO	Special colours	
☐ G-JEDR	de Havilland DHC-8-402Q	4087	ex C-FDHI		
☐ G-JEDT	de Havilland DHC-8-402Q	4088	ex C-FDHP		
☐ G-JEDU	de Havilland DHC-8-402Q	4089	ex C-GEMU	Pride of Exeter	
☐ G-JEDV	de Havilland DHC-8-402Q	4090	ex C-FDHX		
☐ G-JEDW	de Havilland DHC-8-402Q	4093	ex C-GFBW		
☐ G-KKEV	de Havilland DHC-8-402Q	4201	ex C-FOUU		

☐ G-FBEA	Embraer 190-200LR (195LR)	19000029	ex PT-SGD	Wings of the Community
☐ G-FBEB	Embraer 190-200LR (195LR)	19000057	ex PT-SII	
☐ G-FBEC	Embraer 190-200LR (195LR)	19000069	ex PT-SJI	
☐ G-FBED	Embraer 190-200LR (195LR)	19000084	ex PT-SNB	
☐ G-FBEE	Embraer 190-200LR (195LR)	19000093	ex PT-SNN	
☐ G-FBEF	Embraer 190-200LR (195LR)	19000104	ex PT-SNY	
☐ G-FBEG	Embraer 190-200LR (195LR)	19000120	ex PT-SQO	
☐ G-FBEH	Embraer 190-200LR (195LR)	19000128	ex PT-SQX	
☐ G-FBEI	Embraer 190-200LR (195LR)	19000143	ex PT-SYV	
☐ G-FBEJ	Embraer 190-200LR (195LR)	19000155	ex PT-SAK	
☐ G-FBEK	Embraer 190-200LR (195LR)	19000168	ex PT-SDC	
☐ G-FBEL	Embraer 190-200LR (195LR)	19000184	ex PT-SDS	
☐ G-FBEM	Embraer 190-200LR (195LR)	19000204	ex PT-SGN	
☐ G-FBEN	Embraer 190-200LR (195LR)	19000213	ex PT-SGW	

FLYGLOBESPAN.COM — *Globespan (Y2/GSM)* — *Prestwick/Edinburgh (PIK/EDI)*

Ceased operations 16/Dec/2009

GLOBAL SUPPLY SYSTEMS — *JetLift (GSS)* — *London-Stansted (STN)*

☐ G-GSSA	Boeing 747-47UF	29256/1213	ex N495MC		Lsd fr/op by GTI
☐ G-GSSB	Boeing 747-47UF	29252/1165	ex N491MC	Louise Jane	Lsd fr/op by GTI
☐ G-GSSC	Boeing 747-47UF	29255/1184	ex N494MC		Lsd fr/op by GTI

HD AIR — *(RPX)* — *Southend (SEN)*

☐ G-CLAS	Short SD.3-60	SH3635	ex EI-BEK

HEBRIDEAN AIR SERVICES

☐ G-BSPT	Britten-Norman BN-2B-20 Islander	2240	ex TF-VEG	
☐ G-HEBS	Britten-Norman BN-2B-26 Islander	2267	ex G-BUBJ	

HIGHLAND AIRWAYS — HiWay (8H/HWY) — Inverness (INV)

☐ G-BTXG	British Aerospace Jetstream 31	719	ex SE-FVP	
☐ G-CCPW	British Aerospace Jetstream 31	785	ex SE-LDI	
☐ G-EDAY	British Aerospace Jetstream 31	639	ex SE-LGB	
☐ G-EIGG	British Aerospace Jetstream 31	773	ex SE-LGH	
☐ G-FARA	British Aerospace Jetstream 31	740	ex LN-FAM	
☐ G-JURA	British Aerospace Jetstream 31	772	ex SE-LDH	City of Inverness
☐ G-LOVB	British Aerospace Jetstream 31	622	ex VH-HSW	
☐ G-NOSS	British Aerospace Jetstream 31	749	ex LN-FAZ	
☐ G-UIST	British Aerospace Jetstream 31	750	ex N190PC	
☐ G-CEGE	Swearingen SA.226TC Metro II	TC-258	ex OY-NPA	
☐ G-ISAY	British Aerospace Jetstream 41	41014	ex G-MAJN	
☐ G-LEAF	Reims Cessna F406 Caravan II	F406-0018	ex EI-CKY	
☐ G-SEIL	Britten-Norman BN-2B-26 Islander	2103	ex G-BIIP	
☐ G-TEXA	British Aerospace Jetstream 41	41041	ex N318UE	
☐ G-TMRA	Short SD.3-60	SH3686	ex G-SSWC	

ISLES OF SCILLY SKYBUS — Scillonia (5Y/IOS) — Lands End-St Just (LEQ)

☐ G-BIHO	de Havilland DHC-6 Twin Otter 310	738	ex A6-ADB	
☐ G-BUBN	Britten-Norman BN-2B-26 Islander	2270		
☐ G-CBML	de Havilland DHC-6 Twin Otter 310	695	ex C-FZSP	
☐ G-CEWM	de Havilland DHC-6 Twin Otter 300	656	ex N70551	
☐ G-SBUS	Britten-Norman BN-2A-26 Islander	3013	ex G-BMMH	
☐ G-SSKY	Britten-Norman BN-2B-26 Islander	2247	ex G-BSWT	

JANES AVIATION — Southend (SEN)

☐ G-AYIM	Hawker Siddeley HS.748 Srs.2A/270	1687	ex G-11-687	stored SEN
☐ G-OSOE	Hawker Siddeley HS.748 Srs.2A/270	1697	ex G-AYYG	stored SEN

JET2 — Channex (LS/EXS) Leeds-Bradford /Manchester (LBA/MAN)

☐ G-CELA	Boeing 737-377	23663/1323	ex VH-CZK	Jet2 Newcastle
☐ G-CELB	Boeing 737-377	23664/1326	ex VH-CZL	Jet2 Yorkshire
☐ G-CELC	Boeing 737-33A	23831/1471	ex N190FH	Jet2 Prague
☐ G-CELD	Boeing 737-33A	23832/1473	ex N191FH	Jet2 Espana
☐ G-CELE	Boeing 737-33A	24029/1601	ex VH-CZX	Jet2 Belfast
☐ G-CELF	Boeing 737-377	24302/1618	ex S7-ABB	Jet2 Valencia
☐ G-CELG	Boeing 737-377	24303/1620	ex S7-ABD	Jet2 London
☐ G-CELH	Boeing 737-330 (QC)	23525/1278	ex D-ABXD	Jet2 Faro
☐ G-CELI	Boeing 737-330	23526/1282	ex D-ABXE	Jet2 Manchester
☐ G-CELJ	Boeing 737-330	23529/1293	ex LZ-BOG	Jet2 Italia
☐ G-CELK	Boeing 737-330	23530/1297	ex LZ-BOH	Jet2 Edinburgh
☐ G-CELO	Boeing 737-33A (QC)	24028/1599	ex TF-ELO	
☐ G-CELP	Boeing 737-330 (QC)	23522/1246	ex TF-ELP	
☐ G-CELR	Boeing 737-330 (QC)	23523/1271	ex TF-ELR	
☐ G-CELS	Boeing 737-377	23660/1294	ex VH-CZH	Jet2 Leeds-Bradford
☐ G-CELU	Boeing 737-377	23657/1280	ex VH-CZE	Jet2 Barcelona
☐ G-CELV	Boeing 737-377	23661/1314	ex VH-CZI	Jet2 Amsterdam
☐ G-CELW	Boeing 737-377F	23659/1292	ex N659DG	
☐ G-CELX	Boeing 737-377	23654/1273	ex VH-CZB	Jet2 Malaga
☐ G-CELY	Boeing 737-377F	23662/1316	ex N622DG	Jet2 Ireland
☐ G-CELZ	Boeing 737-377F	23658/1281	ex VH-CZF	Jet2 Paris
☐ G-CGET	Boeing 737-33A	27455/2709	ex G-TOYE	
☐ G-GDFA	Boeing 737-3G7	24011/1608	ex OE-IAD	
☐ G-LSAA	Boeing 757-236	24122/187	ex N241CV	Jet2 Tenerife
☐ G-LSAB	Boeing 757-27B/W	24136/169	ex N136CV	Jet2 Menorca
☐ G-LSAC	Boeing 757-23A/W	25488/471	ex N254DG	Jet2 Lanzarote
☐ G-LSAD	Boeing 757-236	24397/221	ex SX-BLW	
☐ G-LSAE	Boeing 757-27B	24135/165	ex OM-SNA	Jet2 Murcia
☐ G-LSAG	Boeing 757-21B	24014/144	ex B-2801	
☐ G-LSAH	Boeing 757-21B	24015/148	ex B-2802	
☐ G-LSAI	Boeing 757-21B	24016/150	ex B-2803	
☐ G-LSAJ	Boeing 757-236	24793/292	ex G-CDUP	Jet2 New York
☐ G-LSAK	Boeing 757-23N	27973/735	ex N517AT	

LOCH LOMOND SEAPLANES — Luss

☐ G-MDJE	Cessna 208 Caravan I	20800336	ex N208FM	

LOGANAIR		***Logan (LOG)***			***Glasgow (GLA)***
☐ G-GNTB	SAAB SF.340A (QC)	340A-082	ex HB-AHL		
☐ G-GNTF	SAAB SF.340A (QC)	340A-113	ex SE-F13	all-white	
☐ G-LGNA	SAAB SF.340B	340B-199	ex N592MA		
☐ G-LGNB	SAAB SF.340B	340B-216	ex N595MA		
☐ G-LGNC	SAAB SF.340B	340B-318	ex SE-KXC		Flybe c/s
☐ G-LGND	SAAB SF.340B	340B-169	ex G-GNTH		
☐ G-LGNE	SAAB SF.340B	340B-172	ex G-GNTI		
☐ G-LGNF	SAAB SF.340B	340B-192	ex N192JE		
☐ G-LGNG	SAAB SF.340B	340B-327	ex SE-C27		
☐ G-LGNH	SAAB SF.340B	340B-333	ex SE-C33		
☐ G-LGNI	SAAB SF.340B	340B-160	ex SE-F60		
☐ G-LGNJ	SAAB SF.340B	340B-173	ex SE-F73	all-white	
☐ G-LGNK	SAAB SF.340B	340B-185	ex SE-F85		Flybe c/s
☐ G-LGNL	SAAB SF.340B	340B-246	ex SE-G46		
☐ G-LGNM	SAAB SF.340B	340B-187	ex SE-F47		
☐ G-LGNN	SAAB SF.340B	340B-197	ex SE-F97		
☐ G-BJOP	Britten-Norman BN-2B-26 Islander	2132		Capt EE Fresson	
☐ G-BLDV	Britten-Norman BN-2B-26 Islander	2179	ex D-INEY		
☐ G-BPCA	Britten-Norman BN-2B-26 Islander	2198	ex G-BLNX	Capt David Barclay MBE	
☐ G-BVVK	de Havilland DHC-6 Twin Otter 310	666	ex LN-BEZ		
☐ G-BZFP	de Havilland DHC-6 Twin Otter 310	696	ex C-GGNF		

LYDD AIR		***Lyddair (LYD)***		***Lydd (LYX)***
☐ G-LYDB	Piper PA-31-350 Chieftain	31-8052107	ex TI-PAI	
☐ G-LYDC	Piper PA-31-350 Navajo Chieftain	31-7652110	ex N210PM	
☐ G-LYDF	Piper PA-31-350 Chieftain	31-7952031	ex N12CD	
☐ G-OJAV	Britten-Norman BN-2A Mk.III-2 Trislander	1024	ex G-BDOS	

MANX2 AIRLINES		***Manx2 (MX)***			***Ronaldsway (IOM)***
☐ D-CNAG	Swearingen SA.227DC Metro 23	DC-893B	ex N3032A		Op by FKI
☐ D-CSAL	Swearingen SA.227AC Metro III	AC-601	ex I-FSAH	Failt Errin!	Op by FKI
☐ OK-RDA	LET L-410UVP-E9	861813	ex HA-YFG		Lsd fr/op by Van Air
☐ OK-TCA	LET L-410UVP-E	902431	ex SP-KPZ		Lsd fr/op by Van Air
☐ OK-UBA	LET L-410UVP-E	892319	ex SP-TXA		Lsd fr/op by Van Air
☐ D-CMNX	Dornier 228-202K	8065	ex TF-CSG		
☐ D-IFLM	Dornier 228-201	8046	ex TF-CSF		

MONARCH AIRLINES		***Monarch (ZB/MON)***		***London-Luton (LTN)***
☐ G-MONX	Airbus A320-212	0392	ex F-WWDR	
☐ G-MPCD	Airbus A320-212	0379	ex C-GZCD	
☐ G-MRJK	Airbus A320-214	1081	ex PH-BMC	
☐ G-OZBB	Airbus A320-212	0389	ex C-GZUM	
☐ G-OZBK	Airbus A320-214	1370	ex PH-BMD	
☐ G-MARA	Airbus A321-231	0983	ex D-AVZB	
☐ G-OJEG	Airbus A321-231	1015	ex D-AVZN	
☐ G-OZBE	Airbus A321-231	1707	ex D-AVZH	
☐ G-OZBF	Airbus A321-231	1763	ex D-AVZB	
☐ G-OZBG	Airbus A321-231	1941	ex D-AVXC	
☐ G-OZBH	Airbus A321-231	2105	ex D-AVXB	
☐ G-OZBI	Airbus A321-231	2234	ex D-AVZV	
☐ G-OZBL	Airbus A321-231	0864	ex G-MIDE	
☐ G-OZBM	Airbus A321-231	1045	ex G-MIDJ	
☐ G-OZBN	Airbus A321-231	1153	ex G-MIDK	
☐ G-OZBO	Airbus A321-231	1207	ex G-MIDM	
☐ G-OZBP	Airbus A321-231	1433	ex G-TTIB	
☐ G-OZBR	Airbus A321-231	1794	ex N586NK	
☐ G-OZBS	Airbus A321-231	1428	ex G-TTIA	
☐ G-OZBT	Airbus A321-231	3546	ex G-TTIH	
☐ G-OZBU	Airbus A321-231	3575	ex G-TTII	
☐ G-DAJB	Boeing 757-2T7ER	23770/125		
☐ G-MONJ	Boeing 757-2T7ER	24104/170		
☐ G-MONK	Boeing 757-2T7ER	24105/172		
☐ G-DIMB	Boeing 767-31KER	28865/657		Lsd fr MYT
☐ G-EOMA	Airbus A330-243	265	ex F-WWKU	
☐ G-MAJS	Airbus A300B4-605R	604	ex F-WWAX	
☐ G-MONR	Airbus A300B4-605R	540	ex VH-YMJ	
☐ G-MONS	Airbus A300B4-605R	556	ex VH-YMK	
☐ G-OJMR	Airbus A300B4-605R	605	ex F-WWAY	
☐ G-SMAN	Airbus A330-243	261	ex F-WWKR	

PALMAIR				Bournemouth (BOH)
☐ G-PJPJ	Boeing 737-5H6	27355/2646	ex G-GFFJ	

PDG HELICOPTERS		Osprey (PDG)		Inverness / Glasgow (INV/GLA)
☐ G-BXGA	Aérospatiale AS350B2 Ecureuil	2493	ex OO-RCH	
☐ G-PDGF	Aérospatiale AS350B2 Ecureuil	9024	ex G-FROH	
☐ G-PDGR	Aérospatiale AS350B2 Ecureuil	2559	ex G-RICC	
☐ G-PLMB	Aérospatiale AS350B Ecureuil	1207	ex G-BMMB	
☐ G-PLMH	Aérospatiale AS350B2 Ecureuil	2156	ex F-WQDJ	
☐ G-BPRJ	Aérospatiale AS355F1 Twin Star	5201	ex N368E	
☐ G-BVLG	Aérospatiale AS355F1 Twin Star	5011	ex N57745	
☐ G-NETR	Aérospatiale AS355F2 Ecureuil 2	5164	ex G-JARV	Op for Network Rail
☐ G-NTWK	Aérospatiale AS355F2 Ecureuil 2	5347	ex G-FTWO	Op for Network Rail
☐ G-PDGT	Aérospatiale AS355F2 Twin Star	5374	ex N325SC	
☐ G-HEMS	Aérospatiale AS365N Dauphin 2	6009	ex 8P-BHD	
☐ G-PDGN	Aérospatiale SA365N Dauphin 2	6074	ex PH-SSU	
☐ G-PLMI	Aérospatiale SA365C1 Dauphin 2	5001	ex F-GFYH	
☐ G-WAAN	MBB Bo.105DB	S-20	ex G-AZOR	Op for Great North Air Ambulance

POLICE AVIATION SERVICES		Special (PLC)		Gloucester (GLO)
☐ G-BXZK	MD Helicopters MD902 Explorer	900-00057	ex N9238T	Op for Dorset Police
☐ G-CEMS	MD Helicopters MD902 Explorer	900-00089	ex PK-OCR	Op for Yorkshire Air Ambulance
☐ G-GNAA	MD Helicopters MD902 Explorer	900-00079	ex PH-RVD	Op for Lincs & Notts Air Ambulance
☐ G-KAAT	MD Helicopters MD902 Explorer	900-00056	ex G-PASS	Op for Kent Air Ambulance
☐ G-KSSH	MD Helicopters MD902 Explorer	900-00062	ex G-WMID	Op for Surrey Air Ambulance
☐ G-LNAA	MD Helicopters MD902 Explorer	900-00074	ex G-76-074	Op for Lincs & Notts Air Ambulance
☐ G-SASH	MD Helicopters MD902 Explorer	900-00080	ex PH-SHF	Op for Yorkshire Air Ambulance
☐ G-SUSX	MD Helicopters MD902 Explorer	900-00065	ex N3065W	Op for Sussex Police
☐ G-WPAS	MD Helicopters MD902 Explorer	900-00053	ex N92237	Op for Wiltshire Police
☐ G-YPOL	MD Helicopters MD902 Explorer	900-00078	ex N7038S	Op for West Yorkshire Police
☐ G-CHEZ	Britten-Norman BN-2B-20 Islander	2234	ex 9M-TAM	Op for Cheshire Police
☐ G-PASV	Britten-Norman BN-2B-21 Islander	2157	ex G-BKJH	
☐ G-PASX	MBB Bo.105DBS-4	S-814	ex D-HDZX	
☐ G-WCAO	Eurocopter EC135T2	0204	ex D-HECU	Op for Western Counties Police
☐ G-WMAO	Eurocopter EC135P2+	0501		Op for West Midlands Police
☐ G-WYPA	MBB Bo.105DBS-4	S-815	ex D-HDZY	

PREMIAIR AVIATION SERVICES		Premiere (PGL)		Denham
☐ G-DANZ	Aérospatiale AS355N Ecureuil 2	5658		
☐ G-VONE	Aérospatiale AS355N Ecureuil 2	5572	ex G-LCON	
☐ G-VONF	Aérospatiale AS355F1 Ecureuil 2	5262	ex G-BXBT	
☐ G-VONG	Aérospatiale AS355F1 Ecureuil 2	5327	ex G-OILX	
☐ G-VONH	Aérospatiale AS355F1 Ecureuil 2	5303	ex G-BKUL	
☐ G-VONK	Aérospatiale AS355F1 Ecureuil 2	5325	ex G-BLRI	
☐ G-XOIL	Aérospatiale AS355N Ecureuil 2	5627	ex G-LOUN	
☐ G-BOYF	Sikorsky S-76B	760343		
☐ G-BURS	Sikorsky S-76A+	760040	ex G-OHTL	
☐ G-VONA	Sikorsky S-76A	760086	ex G-BUXB	
☐ G-VONB	Sikorsky S-76B	760339	ex G-POAH	
☐ G-VONC	Sikorsky S-76B	760354	ex N966PR	
☐ G-XXEA	Sikorsky S-76C+	760492		Op for Royal Travel Office
☐ VP-BIR	Sikorsky S-76B	760430	ex N9HM	
☐ G-CCAU	Eurocopter EC135T1	0040	ex G-79-01	Op for West Mercia Constabulary
☐ G-HAAT	MD Helicopters MD902 Explorer	900-00081	ex G-GMPS	Op for Hertfordshire Air Ambulance
☐ G-VOND	Bell 222	47041	ex G-OWCG	

SCOTAIRWAYS		Suckling (CB/SAY)		Cambridge (CBG)
☐ G-BWIR	Dornier 328-100	3023	ex D-CDXF	
☐ G-BWWT	Dornier 328-110	3022	ex D-CDXO	
☐ G-BYHG	Dornier 328-110	3098	ex D-CDAE	Lsd to BCI
☐ G-BYMK	Dornier 328-110	3062	ex LN-ASK	Lsd to BCI
☐ G-BZOG	Dornier 328-110	3088	ex D-CDXI	
☐ G-CCGS	Dornier 328-110	3101	ex D-CPRX	

SKYSOUTH		Skydrift (SDL)		Norwich (NWI)
☐ G-OETV	Piper PA-31-350 Chieftain	31-7852073	ex N27597	
☐ G-STHA	Piper PA-31-350 Chieftain	31-8052077	ex G-GLUG	
☐ G-TABS	Embraer EMB.110P1 Bandeirante	110212	ex G-PBAC	stored SEN

STERLING AVIATION		Silver (SVH)		Norwich (NWI)
☐ G-BFYA	MBB Bo.105DB	S-321	ex D-HJET	Op for Norfolk Police
☐ G-BMTC	Aérospatiale AS355F2 Ecureuil 2	5302	ex G-EPOL	
☐ G-BXNS	Bell 206B JetRanger III	2385	ex N16822	
☐ G-BXNT	Bell 206B JetRanger III	2398	ex N94CA	
☐ G-EYNL	MBB Bo.105DBS-5	S-382	ex LN-OTJ	Op for East Anglian Air Ambulance
☐ G-FFRI	Aérospatiale AS355F1 Ecureuil 2	5120	ex G-GLOW	
☐ G-OEMT	MBB BK-117C-1	7538	ex D-HMEC	Op for East Anglian Air Ambulance
☐ G-RESC	MBB BK-117C-1	7504	ex D-HELW	
☐ G-TOPS	Aérospatiale AS355F1 Ecureuil 2	5151	ex G-BPRH	

THOMAS COOK AIRLINES		Top Jet (MT/TCX)		Manchester (MAN)
☐ G-BYTH	Airbus A320-231	0429	ex C-GTDM	
☐ G-CRPH	Airbus A320-231	0424	ex C-GJUU	
☐ G-DHJZ	Airbus A320-214	1965	ex C-FOJZ	Lsd to SSV
☐ G-DHRG	Airbus A320-214	1942	ex C-GHRG	Lsd to SSV
☐ G-FTDF	Airbus A320-231	0437	ex C-FTDF	Lsd fr SSV
☐ G-GTDL	Airbus A320-231	0476	ex C-GTDL	
☐ G-KKAZ	Airbus A320-214	2003	ex C-FZAZ	Lsd to SSV
☐ G-OMYA	Airbus A320-214	0716	ex G-BXKB	
☐ G-SUEW	Airbus A320-214	1961	ex C-GUEW	Lsd to SSV
☐ G-TCAC	Airbus A320-232	1411	ex C-FRAA	
☐ G-TCAD	Airbus A320-214	2114	ex EC-JDO	
☐ G-DHJH	Airbus A321-211	1238	ex D-AVZL	
☐ G-NIKO	Airbus A321-211	1250	ex D-AVZF	
☐ G-OMYJ	Airbus A321-211	0677	ex G-OOAF	
☐ G-TCDA	Airbus A321-211	2060	ex TC-JMG	
☐ G-MDBD	Airbus A330-243	266	ex F-WWKG	
☐ G-MLJL	Airbus A330-243	254	ex F-WWKT	
☐ G-OJMB	Airbus A330-243	427	ex F-WWYH	
☐ G-OJMC	Airbus A330-243	456	ex F-WWKI	
☐ G-OMYT	Airbus A330-243	301	ex G-MOJO	
☐ G-TCXA	Airbus A330-243	795	ex F-WWKR	
☐ G-FCLA	Boeing 757-28A	27621/738	ex N1789B	
☐ G-FCLB	Boeing 757-28A	28164/749	ex N751NA	
☐ G-FCLC	Boeing 757-28A	28166/756		
☐ G-FCLD	Boeing 757-25F	28718/752	ex C-FULD	
☐ G-FCLE	Boeing 757-28A	28171/805		
☐ G-FCLF	Boeing 757-28A	28835/858	ex N1787B	
☐ G-FCLH	Boeing 757-28A	26274/676	ex N751LF	
☐ G-FCLI	Boeing 757-28A	26275/672	ex N161LF	
☐ G-FCLJ	Boeing 757-2Y0	26160/555	ex N160GE	
☐ G-FCLK	Boeing 757-2Y0	26161/557	ex EI-CJY	
☐ G-JMAA	Boeing 757-3CQ	32241/960	ex N5002K	
☐ G-JMAB	Boeing 757-3CQ	32242/963	ex N1795B	
☐ G-JMCD	Boeing 757-25F	30757/928	ex C-FCLD	
☐ G-JMCE	Boeing 757-25F	30758/932	ex XA-JPB	
☐ G-JMCF	Boeing 757-28A	24369/226	ex C-FMCF	
☐ G-JMCG	Boeing 757-2G5	26278/671	ex SX-BLV	
☐ G-TCBA	Boeing 757-28AER	28203/802	ex G-OOOY	
☐ G-DAJC	Boeing 767-31KER	27206/533	ex C-GJJC	
☐ G-DIMB	Boeing 767-31KER	28865/657		Lsd to MON
☐ G-TCCA	Boeing 767-31KER	27205/528	ex G-SJMC	

THOMSONFLY.COM		Thomson (BY/TOM)		London-Luton/Coventry (LTN/CVT)
☐ G-OOAR	Airbus A320-214	1320	ex F-WWDT	
☐ G-OOPP	Airbus A320-214	1571	ex C-GTDG	
☐ G-OOPU	Airbus A320-214	1637	ex G-OOAU	
☐ G-OOPX	Airbus A320-214	2180	ex G-OOAX	
☐ G-OOPE	Airbus A321-211	0852	ex G-OOAE	
☐ G-OOPH	Airbus A321-211	0781	ex G-OOAH	
☐ G-CDZH	Boeing 737-804	28227/452	ex SE-DZH	
☐ G-CDZI	Boeing 737-804	28229/478	ex SE-DZI	
☐ G-CDZL	Boeing 737-804	30465/502	ex D-ATUA	
☐ G-CDZM	Boeing 737-804	30466/505	ex D-ATUB	Lsd to BLX
☐ G-FDZA	Boeing 737-8K5/W	35134/2152		
☐ G-FDZB	Boeing 737-8K5/W	35131/2242		
☐ G-FDZD	Boeing 737-8K5/W	35132/2276		
☐ G-FDZE	Boeing 737-8K5/W	35137/2482	ex N1786B	
☐ G-FDZF	Boeing 737-8K5/W	35138/2499	ex N1786B	
☐ G-FDZG	Boeing 737-8K5/W	35139/2538		
☐ G-FDZJ	Boeing 737-8K5/W	34690/2184	ex D-ATUI	Lsd fr HLX
☐ G-FDZR	Boeing 737-8K5/W	35145/2849	ex N1786B	

☐ G-FDZS	Boeing 737-8K5/W	35147/2866	ex N1786B		
☐ G-THOG	Boeing 737-31S	29057/2942	ex D-ADBM		
☐ G-THOH	Boeing 737-31S	29058/2946	ex D-ADBN		
☐ G-THOL	Boeing 737-36N	28594/3107	ex G-IGOK		
☐ G-THON	Boeing 737-36N	28596/3112	ex G-IGOL		
☐ G-THOO	Boeing 737-33V	29335/3094	ex HA-LKT		
☐ G-THOP	Boeing 737-3U3	28740/3003	ex N335AW		
☐ C-GTBB	Boeing 757-28A/W	32447/951	ex G-OOBB		Lsd fm SSV
☐ G-BYAH	Boeing 757-204	26966/520			
☐ G-BYAI	Boeing 757-204	26967/522			
☐ G-BYAL	Boeing 757-204	25626/549			
☐ G-BYAO	Boeing 757-204	27235/598		Eric Morecombe	
☐ G-BYAP	Boeing 757-204	27236/600		John Lennon	
☐ G-BYAT	Boeing 757-204	27208/606		Becky Davey	
☐ G-BYAU	Boeing 757-204	27220/618			
☐ G-BYAW	Boeing 757-204	27234/663		Philip Stanley	
☐ G-BYAX	Boeing 757-204/W	28834/850			
☐ G-BYAY	Boeing 757-204/W	28836/861	ex N1786B		
☐ G-CPEP	Boeing 757-2Y0	25268/400	ex C-GTSU		
☐ G-CPEU	Boeing 757-236/W	29941/864	ex C-FLEU		
☐ G-CPEV	Boeing 757-236/W	29943/871	ex C-GOEV		
☐ G-OOBA	Boeing 757-28A/W	32446/950	ex C-GUBA		
☐ G-OOBC	Boeing 757-28A	33098/1026			
☐ G-OOBD	Boeing 757-28A	33099/1028			
☐ G-OOBE	Boeing 757-28A	33100/1029			
☐ G-OOBF	Boeing 757-28A/W	33101/1041			
☐ G-OOBG	Boeing 757-236/W	29942/867	ex C-FUBG		
☐ G-OOBH	Boeing 757-236/W	29944/872	ex C-FOBH		
☐ G-OOBI	Boeing 757-2B7	27146/551	ex N615AU		
☐ G-OOBJ	Boeing 757-2B7	27147/552	ex N616AU		
☐ G-OOOX	Boeing 757-2Y0ER	26158/526	ex C-FLOX		Lsd to SSV
☐ G-OOOZ	Boeing 757-236	25593/466	ex C-GOOZ		Lsd to SSV
☐ G-DBLA	Boeing 767-35EER	26063/434	ex B-16603		
☐ G-OOAN	Boeing 767-39HER	26256/484	ex G-UKLH	Caribbean Star	
☐ G-OOBK	Boeing 767-324ER/W	27392/568	ex VN-A762		
☐ G-OOBL	Boeing 767-324ER/W	27393/571	ex VN-A764		
☐ G-OOBM	Boeing 767-324ER/W	27568/593	ex VN-A765		
☐ G-OBYD	Boeing 767-304ER/W	28042/649	ex SE-DZG	Bill Travers	
☐ G-OBYE	Boeing 767-304ER	28979/691	ex D-AGYE		
☐ G-OBYF	Boeing 767-304ER/W	28208/705	ex D-AGYF		
☐ G-OBYG	Boeing 767-304ER	29137/733			
☐ G-OBYH	Boeing 767-304ER/W	28883/737	ex SE-DZO		
☐ G-OBYI	Boeing 767-304ER	29138/783			
☐ G-OBYJ	Boeing 767-304ER	29384/784			
☐ G-PJLO	Boeing 767-35EER	26064/438	ex B-16605		

TITAN AIRWAYS — *Zap (ZT/AWC)* — *London-Stansted (STN)*

☐ G-BUHB	British Aerospace 146 Srs.300	E3183	ex D-AEWB	
☐ G-POWB	Beech B300 Super King Air	FL-506	ex N7106L	
☐ G-POWC	Boeing 737-33A (QC)	25402/2159	ex SE-DPB	
☐ G-POWD	Boeing 767-36NER	30847/902	ex N308TL	
☐ G-WELY	Agusta A.109E Power	11710		
☐ G-ZAPK	British Aerospace 146 Srs.200 (QC)	E2148	ex G-BTIA	
☐ G-ZAPN	British Aerospace 146 Srs.200 (QC)	E2119	ex ZK-NZC	
☐ G-ZAPO	British Aerospace 146 Srs.200 (QC)	E2176	ex F-GMMP	
☐ G-ZAPR	British Aerospace 146 Srs.200QT	E2114	ex VH-JJZ	
☐ G-ZAPU	Boeing 757-2Y0	26151/472	ex EI-MON	all-white
☐ G-ZAPV	Boeing 737-3Y0 (SF)	24546/1811	ex G-IGOC	Royal Mail
☐ G-ZAPW	Boeing 737-3L9 (QC)	24219/1600	ex G-IGOX	Crystal Holidays
☐ G-ZAPX	Boeing 757-256	29309/936	ex EC-HIS	
☐ G-ZAPZ	Boeing 737-33A (QC)	25401/2067	ex SE-DPA	

VIRGIN ATLANTIC AIRWAYS — *Virgin (VS/VIR)* — *London-Gatwick/Heathrow (LGW/LHR)*

☐ G-VAIR	Airbus A340-313X	164	ex F-WWJA	Maiden Tokyo	
☐ G-VELD	Airbus A340-313X	214	ex F-WWJY	African Queen	
☐ G-VFAR	Airbus A340-313X	225	ex F-WWJZ	Diana	
☐ G-VHOL	Airbus A340-311	002	ex F-WWAS	Jetstreamer	
☐ G-VSEA	Airbus A340-311	003	ex F-WWDA	Plane Sailing	
☐ G-VSUN	Airbus A340-313	114	ex F-WWJI	Rainbow Lady	
☐ G-VATL	Airbus A340-642	376	ex F-WWCC	Miss Kitty	stored LDE
☐ G-VBLU	Airbus A340-642	723	ex F-WWCS	Soul Sister	
☐ G-VBUG	Airbus A340-642HGW	804	ex F-WWCV	Lady Bird	
☐ G-VEIL	Airbus A340-642	575	ex F-WWCK	Queen of the Skies	
☐ G-VFIT	Airbus A340-642	753	ex F-WWCG	Dancing Queen	
☐ G-VFIZ	Airbus A340-642	764	ex F-WWCB	Bubbles	
☐ G-VFOX	Airbus A340-642	449	ex F-WWCM	Silver Lady	

☐ G-VFUN	Airbus A340-642		ex F-WW	Party Girl	on order
☐ G-VGAS	Airbus A340-642	639	ex F-WWCI	Varga Girl	
☐ G-VGOA	Airbus A340-642	371	ex F-WWCB	Indian Princess	stored LDE
☐ G-VMEG	Airbus A340-642	391	ex F-WWCK	Mystic Maiden	
☐ G-VNAP	Airbus A340-642	622	ex F-WWCE	Sleeping Beauty	
☐ G-VOGE	Airbus A340-642	416	ex F-WWCF	Cover Girl	
☐ G-VRED	Airbus A340-642	768	ex F-WWCH	Scarlet Lady	
☐ G-VSHY	Airbus A340-642	383	ex F-WWCD	Madam Butterfly	
☐ G-VSSH	Airbus A340-642	615	ex F-WWCZ	Sweet Dreamer	
☐ G-VWEB	Airbus A340-642	787	ex F-WWCZ	Surfer Girl	
☐ G-VWIN	Airbus A340-642	736	ex F-WWCL	Lady Luck	
☐ G-VWKD	Airbus A340-642	706	ex F-WWCQ	Miss Behavin'	
☐ G-VYOU	Airbus A340-642	765	ex F-WWCK	Emmeline Heansy	
☐ G-VAST	Boeing 747-41R	28757/1117		Ladybird	
☐ G-VBIG	Boeing 747-4Q8	26255/1081		Tinker Belle	
☐ G-VFAB	Boeing 747-4Q8	24958/1028		Lady Penelope	
☐ G-VGAL	Boeing 747-443	32337/1272	ex (EI-CVH)	Jersey Girl	
☐ G-VHOT	Boeing 747-4Q8	26326/1043		Tubular Belle	
☐ G-VLIP	Boeing 747-443	32338/1274	ex (EI-CVI)	Hot Lips	
☐ G-VROC	Boeing 747-41R	32746/1336		Mustang Sally	
☐ G-VROS	Boeing 747-443	30885/1268	ex (EI-CVG)	English Rose	
☐ G-VROY	Boeing 747-443	32340/1277	ex (EI-CVK)	Pretty Woman	
☐ G-VTOP	Boeing 747-4Q8	28194/1100		Virginia Plain	
☐ G-VWOW	Boeing 747-41R	32745/1287		Cosmic Girl	
☐ G-VXLG	Boeing 747-41R	29406/1177		Ruby Tuesday	

WEST ATLANTIC — Neptune (NPT) — Coventry (CVT)

☐ G-BTPA	British Aerospace ATP (LFD)	2007	ex EC-HGC	
☐ G-BTPE	British Aerospace ATP (LFD)	2012	ex EC-HGE	
☐ G-BTPF	British Aerospace ATP (LFD)	2013	ex EC-HCY	
☐ G-BTPG	British Aerospace ATP (LFD)	2014	ex (G-JEMF)	stored CVT
☐ G-BTPH	British Aerospace ATP (LFD)	2015	ex (G-JEMF)	
☐ G-BTPJ	British Aerospace ATP (LFD)	2016	ex EC-HFR	stored CVT
☐ G-BTTO	British Aerospace ATP (LFD)	2033	ex EC-HNA	
☐ G-BUUP	British Aerospace ATP (LFD)	2008	ex G-MANU	
☐ G-BUUR	British Aerospace ATP (LFD)	2024	ex EC-GUX	
☐ G-MANH	British Aerospace ATP (LFD)	2017	ex G-LOGC	under conv
☐ G-OAAF	British Aerospace ATP	2029	ex G-JEMB	
☐ G-FIJR	Lockheed L-188PF Electra	1138	ex EI-HCF	
☐ G-FIZU	Lockheed L-188CF Electra	2014	ex EI-CHY	
☐ G-LOFB	Lockheed L-188CF Electra	1131	ex N667F	
☐ G-LOFC	Lockheed L-188CF Electra	1100	ex N665F	
☐ G-LOFD	Lockheed L-188AC Electra	1143	ex LN-FOG	
☐ G-LOFE	Lockheed L-188CF Electra	1144	ex EI-CET	
☐ G-JMCL	Boeing 737-322F	23951/1532	ex D-AGEA	

WOODGATE EXECUTIVE AIR SERVICES — Woodair (CWY) — Belfast-Aldergrove (BFS)

☐ G-JAJK	Piper PA-31-350 Chieftain	31-8152014	ex G-OLDB

HA- HUNGARY (Hungarian Republic)

ABC AIR HUNGARY — ABC Hungary (AHU) — Budapest (BUD)

☐ HA-LAD	LET L-410UVP-E	902516		
☐ HA-LAS	LET L-410UVP-E4	871924	ex 9A-BAL	
☐ HA-LAV	LET L-410UVP-E	892215	ex SP-KTA	Lsd fr BPS
☐ HA-LAZ	LET L-410UVP-E	902504	ex SP-KTZ	Lsd fr BPS

ATLANT HUNGARY — Atlant-Hungary (ATU) — Budapest (BUD)

☐ HA-TCG	Ilyushin Il-76TD	0023436048	ex RA-76382	
☐ HA-TCK	Ilyushin Il-76TD	1023409280	ex T-902	
☐ RA-64011	Tupolev Tu-204-100	1450741364011		Lsd fr VAZ

BUDAPEST AIR SERVICES — Base (BPS) — Budapest (BUD)

☐ HA-FAI	Embraer EMB.120ER Brasilia	120123	ex F-GTSI		
☐ HA-FAL	Embraer EMB.120RT Brasilia	120176	ex F-GTSJ		
☐ HA-LAF	LET L-410UVP-E8A	902518			Flight Inspection Services
☐ HA-LAV	LET L-410UVP-E	892215	ex SP-KTA		Lsd to AHU
☐ HA-LAZ	LET L-410UVP-E	902504	ex SP-KTZ	no titles	Lsd to AHU
☐ HA-TCT	Antonov An-26B	13505	ex UR-ELA		
☐ HA-TCY	Antonov An-26B	97308205	ex ER-AZR		Lsd fr MJL
☐ HA-YFD	LET L-410UVP-E17	892324			Op for Hungarian Air Ambulance

CITYLINE HUNGARY — Cityhun (ZM/CNB) — Budapest (BUD)

☐ HA-TCM	Antonov An-26	14009	ex UR-ELI		
☐ HA-TCN	Antonov An-26	7705	ex UR-26244	for sale	
☐ HA-TCO	Antonov An-26	2208	ex UR-CEP		Lsd fr Hegedus

FARNAIR HUNGARY — Blue Strip (FAH) — Budapest (BUD)

☐ HA-FAB	Fokker F.27 Friendship 500	10370	ex HB-ISY	no titles	
☐ HA-FAC	Fokker F.27 Friendship 500F	10341	ex PH-FLM		
☐ HA-FAD	Fokker F.27 Friendship 500	10449	ex PH-JLN		
☐ HA-FAE	Fokker F.27 Friendship 500	10425	ex HB-IVQ		stored BGY
☐ HA-FAF	Fokker F.27 Friendship 500F	10632	ex PH-FYC		
☐ HA-FAH	Fokker F.27 Friendship 500F	10634	ex PH-FHL		
☐ HA-FAJ	Beech 1900C-1	UC-79	ex A6-FCE		
☐ HA-FAM	Beech 1900D	UE-16	ex N16UE		
☐ HA-FAN	Embraer EMB.120ER Brasilia	120104	ex F-GTSH		
☐ HA-LAQ	LET L-410UVP-E4	841332	ex HAF-332		based UK for skydiving
☐ HA-YFC	LET L-410FG	851528			based UK for skydiving

FLEET AIR INTERNATIONAL

☐ HA-TAB	SAAB SF.340A	340A-083	ex EC-IUP
☐ HA-TAD	SAAB SF.340A	340A-126	ex SE-LSP

HEGEDUS

☐ HA-TCO	Antonov An-26	2208	ex UR-CEP	Lsd to CNB

MALEV – HUNGARIAN AIRLINES — Malev (MA/MAH) — Budapest (BUD)

Member of Oneworld

☐ HA-LOA	Boeing 737-7Q8	28254/1283			
☐ HA-LOB	Boeing 737-7Q8	29346/1264	ex N5573L		
☐ HA-LOC	Boeing 737-8Q8	32797/1287			
☐ HA-LOD	Boeing 737-6Q8	28259/1378			
☐ HA-LOE	Boeing 737-6Q8	28260/1400			
☐ HA-LOF	Boeing 737-6Q8	29348/1415			
☐ HA-LOG	Boeing 737-6Q8	28261/1437			
☐ HA-LOH	Boeing 737-8Q8	30667/1448			Lsd to LVG
☐ HA-LOI	Boeing 737-7Q8	29350/1452			
☐ HA-LOJ	Boeing 737-6Q8	29349/1455			
☐ HA-LOK	Boeing 737-8Q8	30669/1479			
☐ HA-LOL	Boeing 737-7Q8	29352/1491			
☐ HA-LOM	Boeing 737-8Q8	30672/1497		Charter Services	
☐ HA-LON	Boeing 737-6Q8	29353/1508			
☐ HA-LOP	Boeing 737-7Q8	29354/1581			
☐ HA-LOR	Boeing 737-7Q8	29355/1609			
☐ HA-LOS	Boeing 737-7Q8	29359/1659			
☐ HA-LOU	Boeing 737-8Q8	30684/1689	ex (HA-LOT)		
☐ HA-LMB	Fokker F.28-070 (Fokker 70)	11565	ex PH-EZX		
☐ HA-LMC	Fokker F.28-070 (Fokker 70)	11569	ex PH-EZA		
☐ HA-LME	Fokker F.28-070 (Fokker 70)	11575	ex PH-WXB		
☐ HA-LMF	Fokker F.28-070 (Fokker 70)	11571	ex PH-RVE		
☐ HA-LHB	Boeing 767-27GER	27049/482	ex N60668		stored BUD
☐ HA-LNA	Canadair CL-600-2B19 (CRJ-200ER)	7676	ex C-FMKZ		stored BUD
☐ HA-LQA	de Havilland DHC-8-402Q	4054	ex OY-KCD		
☐ HA-LQB	de Havilland DHC-8-402Q	4057	ex OY-KCE		
☐ HA-LQC	de Havilland DHC-8-402Q	4062	ex OY-KCF		
☐ HA-LQD	de Havilland DHC-8-402Q	4063	ex OY-KCG		

TRAVEL SERVICE HUNGARY — Traveller (TVL) — Budapest (BUD)

☐ HA-LKB	Boeing 737-86Q/W	30294/1469	ex OK-TVI

WIZZ AIR — (W6/WZZ) — Budapest (BUD)

☐ HA-LPA	Airbus A320-233	0839	ex EI-DFV
☐ HA-LPB	Airbus A320-233	1635	ex EI-DFT
☐ HA-LPC	Airbus A320-223	0892	ex EI-DGF
☐ HA-LPD	Airbus A320-233	1902	ex EI-DGB
☐ HA-LPE	Airbus A320-233	1892	ex EI-DFU
☐ HA-LPF	Airbus A320-223	1834	ex EI-DGC
☐ HA-LPH	Airbus A320-232	2688	ex F-WWIE
☐ HA-LPI	Airbus A320-232	2752	ex F-WWDE
☐ HA-LPJ	Airbus A320-232	3127	ex F-WWBH
☐ HA-LPK	Airbus A320-232	3143	ex F-WWBI
☐ HA-LPL	Airbus A320-232	3166	ex F-WWIL

☐ HA-LPM	Airbus A320-232	3177	ex F-WWDG		
☐ HA-LPN	Airbus A320-232	3354	ex F-WWIG		
☐ HA-LPO	Airbus A320-232	3384	ex F-WWDO		
☐ HA-LPQ	Airbus A320-232	3409	ex F-WWIC		
☐ HA-LPR	Airbus A320-232	3430	ex F-WWBC		
☐ HA-LPS	Airbus A320-232	3771	ex F-WWDS		
☐ HA-LPT	Airbus A320-232	3807	ex F-WWDR		
☐ HA-LPU	Airbus A320-232	3877	ex F-WWIJ		
☐ HA-LPV	Airbus A320-232	3927	ex F-WWBR		
☐ HA-LPW	Airbus A320-232	3947	ex F-WWBD		
☐ HA-LPX	Airbus A320-232	3968	ex F-WWIN		
☐ HA-LPY	Airbus A320-232	4109	ex D-AVVS		
☐ HA-LPZ	Airbus A320-232	4174	ex F-WWDU		
☐ HA-	Airbus A320-232		ex		on order
☐ HA-	Airbus A320-232		ex		on order
☐ HA-	Airbus A320-232		ex		on order
☐ HA-	Airbus A320-232		ex		on order
☐ HA-	Airbus A320-232		ex		on order
☐ HA-	Airbus A320-232		ex		on order
☐ HA-	Airbus A320-232		ex		on order

HB- SWITZERLAND & LIECHSTENSTEIN (Swiss Confederation)

AIR ENGIADINA — *St Moritz*

☐ HB-AEU	Dornier 328-310 (328JET)	3199	ex OE-HCM		Lsd fr/op by Swiss Jet

AIR GLACIERS — *Air Glaciers (7T/AGV)* — *Sion (SIR)*

☐ HB-CGW	Cessna U206G Stationair 6	U20604822	ex D-ELML		
☐ HB-FCT	Pilatus PC-6/B2-H2 Turbo Porter	637			
☐ HB-FDU	Pilatus PC-6/B1-H2 Turbo Porter	663			
☐ HB-FFW	Pilatus PC-6/B2-H2 Turbo Porter	735			
☐ HB-GIL	Beech 200 Super King Air	BB-194	ex N502EB		
☐ HB-GJI	Beech 200 Super King Air	BB-451	ex D-IBOW		
☐ HB-GJM	Beech 200 Super King Air	BB-255	ex N32KD		
☐ HB-ZCZ	Aérospatiale AS350B3 Ecureuil	3434	ex F-WQDG		
☐ HB-ZEP	Eurocopter EC120B Colibri	1336	ex F-WWPO		
☐ HB-ZFB	Eurocopter EC130B4	3536	ex F-GNLD		

AIR ZERMATT — *Air Zermatt (AZF)* — *Zermatt Heliport*

☐ HB-XSU	Aérospatiale AS350B2 Ecureuil	2115			
☐ HB-ZCC	Aérospatiale AS350B2 Ecureuil	2107	ex I-REGL		
☐ HB-ZCX	Aérospatiale AS350B2 Ecureuil	3105	ex I-AOLA		
☐ HB-ZEF	Eurocopter EC135T2	0259	ex D-HECA		

BELAIR AIRLINES — *Belair (4T/BHP)* — *Zurich (ZRH)*

☐ HB-IOR	Airbus A320-214	4033	ex D-ABDZ		
☐ HB-IOS	Airbus A320-214	2968	ex D-ABDK		
☐ HB-IOT	Airbus A320-214	2991	ex D-ABDL		
☐ HB-IOU	Airbus A320-214	3006	ex D-ABDM		
☐ HB-IOT	Airbus A320-214	3021	ex D-ABDN		
☐ HB-IOW	Airbus A320-214	3055	ex D-ABDO		
☐ HB-IOX	Airbus A319-112	3604	ex D-ABGM		
☐ HB-IHR	Boeing 757-2Q8ER	29379/919		Solemar	stored MUC
☐ HB-IHS	Boeing 757-2Q8ER	30394/922		Horizonte	stored MUC
☐ HB-ISE	Boeing 767-3Q8ER	27600/655	ex EI-CNS	RondoMondo	

DARWIN AIRLINE — *Darwin (0D/DWT)* — *Geneva (GVA)*

☐ HB-IYD	SAAB 2000	2000-059	ex VP-BPP		
☐ HB-IZG	SAAB 2000	2000-010	ex SE-010	Insubria	
☐ HB-IZH	SAAB 2000	2000-011	ex SE-011	Ticino	
☐ HB-IZJ	SAAB 2000	2000-015	ex (F-GOZJ)	Verbano	
☐ HB-IZZ	SAAB 2000	2000-048	ex SE-048	Ceresio	

EASYJET SWITZERLAND — *Topswiss (DS/EZS)* — *Geneva (GVA)*

☐ HB-JZF	Airbus A319-111	2184	ex G-EZEH		Lsd fr EZY
☐ HB-JZG	Airbus A319-111	2196	ex G-EZEI		Lsd fr EZY
☐ HB-JZH	Airbus A319-111	2230	ex G-EZEM		Lsd fr EZY
☐ HB-JZI	Airbus A319-111	2245	ex G-EZEN		Lsd fr EZY
☐ HB-JZJ	Airbus A319-111	2265	ex G-EZES		Lsd fr EZY
☐ HB-JZK	Airbus A319-111	2319	ex G-EZEX		Lsd fr EZY
☐ HB-JZL	Airbus A319-111	2353	ex G-EZEY		Lsd fr EZY
☐ HB-JZM	Airbus A319-111	2370	ex G-EZMK		Lsd fr EZY
☐ HB-JZN	Airbus A319-111	2387	ex G-EZBS		Lsd fr EZY
☐ HB-JZO	Airbus A319-111	2398	ex G-HMCC		Lsd fr EZY

☐ HB-JZP	Airbus A319-111	2427	ex G-EZIB		Lsd fr EZY
☐ HB-JZQ	Airbus A319-111	2450	ex G-EZIF		Lsd fr EZY
☐ HB-JZR	Airbus A320-232	4034	ex G-EZTO		Lsd fr EZY
☐ HB-JZS	Airbus A319-111	3084	ex G-EZBP		Lsd fr EZY

EDELWEISS AIR — *Edelweiss (WK/EDW)* — *Zurich (ZRH)*

☐ HB-IHX	Airbus A320-214	0942	ex F-WWIU	Calvaro	Lsd fr Alp Air
☐ HB-IHY	Airbus A320-214	0947	ex F-WWIY	Upali	Lsd fr Alp Air
☐ HB-IHZ	Airbus A320-214	1026	ex F-WWDD	Viktoria	
☐ HB-IQZ	Airbus A330-243	369	ex F-WWKG	Bahari	

FARNAIR SWITZERLAND — *Farner (FAT)* — *Basle (BSL)*

☐ HB-AFC	ATR 42-320F	087	ex F-WQLF		
☐ HB-AFD	ATR 42-320	121	ex F-WQNA	Starquest Expedition titles	
☐ HB-AFF	ATR 42-320	264	ex F-GOBK		
☐ HB-AFG	ATR 72-201F	108	ex F-WQNA		
☐ HB-AFH	ATR 72-202F	313	ex F-GJKP		
☐ HB-AFJ	ATR 72-202F	154	ex OY-RTE		
☐ HB-AFK	ATR 72-202F	232	ex F-GKOB		
☐ HB-AFL	ATR 72-202F	222	ex F-GKPF		
☐ HB-AFM	ATR 72-202F	364	ex B-22712		
☐ HB-AFN	ATR 72-202F	389	ex B-22716		
☐ HB-AFP	ATR 72-201F	381	ex B-22715		
☐ HB-AFR	ATR 72-201F	195	ex EC-JNK		
☐ HB-AFS	ATR 72-201F	198	ex F-WKVJ		

FLYBABOO — *Baboo (F7/BBO)* — *Geneva (GVA)*

☐ HB-JQA	de Havilland DHC-8-402Q	4017	ex C-FJJG		
☐ HB-JQB	de Havilland DHC-8-402Q	4175	ex C-FMKK		
☐ HB-JQE	Embraer 190LR (190LR)	19000163	ex PT-SAS		
☐ HB-JQF	Embraer 190LR (190LR)	19000178	ex PT-SDM		
☐ HB-JQG	Embraer 190LR (190LR)	19000189	ex PT-		

HELISWISS — *Heliswiss (HSI)* — *Bern (BRN)*

☐ HB-XKE	Kamov Ka-32A	8709/02	ex RA-31587		
☐ HB-ZFX	Kamov Ka-32A12	8809/09	ex RA-31599		

HELLO — *Fly Hello (HW/FHE)* — *Basle (BSL)*

☐ HB-JID	McDonnell-Douglas MD-90-30	53460/2142	ex OY-KIM		
☐ HB-JIE	McDonnell-Douglas MD-90-30	53461/2147	ex SE-DMG		
☐ HB-JIF	McDonnell-Douglas MD-90-30	53462/2149	ex LN-ROB		

HELOG — *Helog (HLG)* — *Küssnacht*

☐ HB-XVY	Aérospatiale AS.332C	2033	ex N5795P		Op for UN

HELVETIC AIRWAYS — *Helvetic (2L/OAW)* — *Zurich (ZRH)*

☐ HB-JVC	Fokker F.28-0100 (Fokker 100)	11501	ex N1468A		
☐ HB-JVE	Fokker F.28-0100 (Fokker 100)	11459	ex N1450A		
☐ HB-JVF	Fokker F.28-0100 (Fokker 100)	11466	ex N1454D		
☐ HB-JVG	Fokker F.28-0100 (Fokker 100)	11478	ex N1458H		

PRIVATAIR — *PrivatAir (PTI)* — *Geneva (GVA)*

☐ D-APBB	Boeing 737-8Q8/W	35278/2625	ex N812SY		
☐ HB-IEE	Boeing 757-23A/W	24527/249	ex HB-IHU		
☐ HB-IIQ	Boeing 737-7CN/W	30752/451	ex N1026G		[BBJ] stored AMM
☐ HB-IIR	Boeing 737-86Q/W	30295/1600			
☐ HB-JJA	Boeing 737-7AK/W	34303/1758	ex N1780B		[BBJ] Lsd to KLM
☐ HB-JJG	Boeing 767-306ER	30393/781	ex PH-BZO		

SKYWORK AIRLINES — *Skyfox (SRK)* — *Bern (BRP)*

☐ HB-AES	Dornier 328-110	3021	ex D-CHIC		
☐ HB-AEU	Dornier 328-310 (328JET)	3199	ex OE-HCM	Air Engiadina titles	Lsd fr AEC Intl
☐ HB-JGA	de Havilland DHC-8-402Q	4198	ex C-FOKB		

SWISS EUROPEAN AIR LINES — *Euroswiss (SWU)* — *Basle, Lugano, Geneva, Zurich (BSL/LUG/GVA/ZRH)*

☐ HB-IXN	Avro 146-RJ100	E3286	ex G-6-286	Balmhorn	
☐ HB-IXO	Avro 146-RJ100	E3284	ex G-6-284	Brisen	
☐ HB-IXP	Avro 146-RJ100	E3283	ex G-6-283	Chestenberg	
☐ HB-IXQ	Avro 146-RJ100	E3282	ex G-6-282	Corno Gries	
☐ HB-IXR	Avro 146-RJ100	E3281	ex G-6-281	Hohe Winde	

	Registration	Type	C/n	Previous identity	Name	Notes
☐	HB-IXS	Avro 146-RJ100	E3280	ex G-6-280	Mont Velan	
☐	HB-IXT	Avro 146-RJ100	E3259	ex G-BVYS	Ottenberg	
☐	HB-IXU	Avro 146-RJ100	E3276	ex G-6-276	Pfannenstiel	
☐	HB-IXV	Avro 146-RJ100	E3274	ex G-6-274	Saxer First	
☐	HB-IXW	Avro 146-RJ100	E3272	ex G-6-272	Schafarnisch	
☐	HB-IXX	Avro 146-RJ100	E3262	ex G-6-262	Siberen	
☐	HB-IYQ	Avro 146-RJ100	E3384	ex G-CFAH	Piz Bruin	
☐	HB-IYR	Avro 146-RJ100	E3382	ex G-CFAF	Vrenelisgärtli	
☐	HB-IYS	Avro 146-RJ100	E3381	ex G-CFAE	Churfirstenspecial c/s	
☐	HB-IYT	Avro 146-RJ100	E3380	ex G-CFAD	Bluemlisalp	
☐	HB-IYU	Avro 146-RJ100	E3379	ex G-CFAC	Rot TurmStar Alliance c/s	
☐	HB-IYV	Avro 146-RJ100	E3377	ex G-CFAB	Pizzo BaroneStar Alliance c/s	
☐	HB-IYW	Avro 146-RJ100	E3359	ex G-6-359	Spitzmeilen	
☐	HB-IYY	Avro 146-RJ100	E3339	ex G-6-339	Titlis	
☐	HB-IYZ	Avro 146-RJ100	E3338	ex G-6-338	Tour d'Ai	

SWISS INTERNATIONAL AIRLINES — *Swiss (LX/SWR)* — *Zurich (ZRH)*

Member of Star Alliance

	Registration	Type	C/n	Previous identity	Name	Notes
☐	HB-IPR	Airbus A319-112	1018	ex D-AVYQ	Piz Morteratsch	
☐	HB-IPS	Airbus A319-112	0734	ex D-AVYZ	Clariden	
☐	HB-IPT	Airbus A319-112	0727	ex D-AVYC	Rotsandnollen	
☐	HB-IPU	Airbus A319-112	0713	ex D-AVYB	Schrattenflue	
☐	HB-IPV	Airbus A319-112	0578	ex D-AVYA	Castelegns	
☐	HB-IPX	Airbus A319-112	0612	ex D-AVYH	Mont Racine	
☐	HB-IPY	Airbus A319-112	0621	ex D-AVYK	Les Ordons	
☐	HB-IJB	Airbus A320-214	0545	ex TC-JLA		
☐	HB-IJD	Airbus A320-214	0553	ex TC-JLH		
☐	HB-IJE	Airbus A320-214	0559	ex TC-JLI	Arosa	
☐	HB-IJF	Airbus A320-214	0562	ex TC-JLB		
☐	HB-IJH	Airbus A320-214	0574	ex TC-JLD		
☐	HB-IJI	Airbus A320-214	0577	ex F-WWDT	Basodino	
☐	HB-IJJ	Airbus A320-214	0585	ex F-WWIV	Les Diablerets	
☐	HB-IJK	Airbus A320-214	0596	ex F-WWBH	Wissigstock	
☐	HB-IJL	Airbus A320-214	0603	ex F-WWBK	Pizol	
☐	HB-IJM	Airbus A320-214	0635	ex F-WWDD	SchilthornEuro 2008 colours	
☐	HB-IJN	Airbus A320-214	0643	ex F-WWDI	Vanil Noir	
☐	HB-IJO	Airbus A320-214	0673	ex F-WWBF	Lisengrat	
☐	HB-IJP	Airbus A320-214	0681	ex F-WWBH	Nollen	
☐	HB-IJQ	Airbus A320-214	0701	ex F-WWDL	Locarno	
☐	HB-IJR	Airbus A320-214	0703	ex F-WWDS	Dammastock	
☐	HB-IJS	Airbus A320-214	0782	ex F-WWDS	Creux du Van	
☐	HB-IJU	Airbus A320-214	1951	ex F-WWIQ	Bietschhorn	
☐	HB-IJV	Airbus A320-214	2024	ex F-WWDK	Wildspitz	
☐	HB-IJW	Airbus A320-214	2134	ex F-WWBO	Bachtel	
☐	HB-IJX	Airbus A320-214	1762	ex D-ALTG	Davos	
☐	HB-IOC	Airbus A321-111	0520	ex D-AVZV	Eiger	
☐	HB-IOD	Airbus A321-111	0522	ex TC-JMA		
☐	HB-IOF	Airbus A321-111	0541	ex TC-JMB		
☐	HB-IOH	Airbus A321-111	0664	ex D-AVZL	Piz Palu	
☐	HB-IOK	Airbus A321-111	0987	ex D-AVZC	Biefertenstock	
☐	HB-IOL	Airbus A321-111	1144	ex D-AVZE	Kaiseregg	
☐	HB-IQA	Airbus A330-223	229	ex F-WWKS	Lauteraarhorn	
☐	HB-IQC	Airbus A330-223	249	ex F-WWKI	Breithorn	
☐	HB-IQH	Airbus A330-223	288	ex F-WWKX	Allainhorn	
☐	HB-IQI	Airbus A330-223	291	ex F-WWKS	Piz Bernina	
☐	HB-IQO	Airbus A330-223	343	ex F-WWYA	Weissmies	
☐	HB-IQQ	Airbus A330-223	322	ex D-AIMD	Bern	
☐	HB-JHA	Airbus A330-343E	1000	ex F-WWYX	Schwyz	
☐	HB-JHB	Airbus A330-343E	1018	ex F-WW		
☐	HB-JHC	Airbus A330-343E	1026	ex F-WWYY	Bellinzona	
☐	HB-JHD	Airbus A330-343E	1029	ex F-WWKE	St. Gallen	
☐	HB-JHE	Airbus A330-343E	1084	ex F-WWKE		
☐	HB-JHF	Airbus A330-343E	1089	ex F-WWKI		on order
☐	HB-JHG	Airbus A330-343E	1101	ex F-WW		on order
☐	HB-JHH	Airbus A330-343E	1145	ex F-WW		on order
☐	HB-JMA	Airbus A340-313X	538	ex F-WWJJ	Matterhorn	
☐	HB-JMB	Airbus A340-313X	545	ex F-WWJL	Zurich	
☐	HB-JMC	Airbus A340-313X	546	ex F-WWJM	Basel	
☐	HB-JMD	Airbus A340-313X	556	ex F-WWJN	Liestal	
☐	HB-JME	Airbus A340-313X	559	ex F-WWJP	Dom	
☐	HB-JMF	Airbus A340-313X	561	ex F-WWJQ	Liskamm	
☐	HB-JMG	Airbus A340-313X	562	ex F-WWJR	Luzern	
☐	HB-JMH	Airbus A340-313E	585	ex F-WWJV	Chur	
☐	HB-JMI	Airbus A340-313E	598	ex F-WWJX	Schaffhausen	
☐	HB-JMJ	Airbus A340-313X	150	ex C-FYKX	City of Basel	
☐	HB-JMK	Airbus A340-313X	169	ex OE-LAK		
☐	HB-JML	Airbus A340-313X	263	ex OE-LAI		Lsd fr AUA

☐ HB-JMM	Airbus A340-313X	154	ex C-FYKZ	
☐ HB-JMN	Airbus A340-313X	175	ex C-FYLG	
☐ HB-JMO	Airbus A340-313X	179	ex C-FYLU	
☐ HB-IIR	Boeing 737-86Q/W	1600/30295		Lsd fr PTI
☐ D-AGPK	Fokker F.28-0100 (Fokker 100)	11313	ex PH-CXK	Lsd fr KIS

ZIMEX AVIATION — Zimex (C4/IMX) — Zurich (ZRH)

☐ HB-LOK	de Havilland DHC-6 Twin Otter 300	658	ex D-IASL	
☐ HB-LQV	de Havilland DHC-6 Twin Otter 300	643	ex 5Y-LQV	
☐ HB-LRO	de Havilland DHC-6 Twin Otter 300	523	ex F-GKTO	
☐ HB-LRR	de Havilland DHC-6 Twin Otter 300	505	ex 5Y-KZT	
☐ HB-LTG	de Havilland DHC-6 Twin Otter 300	628	ex D-IFLY	
☐ HB-LTR	de Havilland DHC-6 Twin Otter 300	238	ex C-GHTO	
☐ HB-LUC	de Havilland DHC-6 Twin Otter 300	351	ex N353PM	
☐ HB-LUE	de Havilland DHC-6 Twin Otter 300	233	ex PK-LTX	
☐ HB-LUM	de Havilland DHC-6 Twin Otter 300	420	ex PK-TWG	
☐ ST-LRN	de Havilland DHC-6 Twin Otter 310	636	ex HB-LRN	
☐ HB-AEK	Beech 1900D	UE-296	ex D-CBCB	
☐ HB-AEL	Beech 1900D	UE-385	ex N839CA	Lsd fr Arab Wings
☐ HB-AEM	Beech 1900D	UE-379	ex F-HALS	
☐ HB-GJD	Beech 200C Super King Air	BL-7	ex F-GJBJ	
☐ HB-GJX	Beech B200 Super King Air	BB-932	ex SE-KKM	

HC- ECUADOR (Republic of Ecuador)

AEROGAL — Aerogal (2K/GLG) — Shell-Mera/Quito (-/UIO)

☐ HC-CDJ	Boeing 727-227	21246/1216	ex N14GA	Piquero
☐ HC-CED	Boeing 737-2B7 (Nordam 3)	22887/976	ex N275AU	
☐ HC-CEQ	Boeing 737-2Y5 (Nordam 3)	23848/1418	ex N342CA	Iguana
☐ HC-CER	Boeing 737-2Y5 (Nordam 3)	23847/1414	ex N341CA	
☐ HC-CFG	Boeing 737-281 (AvAero 3)	21770/588	ex N746AP	
☐ HC-CFH	Boeing 737-2T5 (Nordam 3)	22979/950	ex N120NJ	Nescafe titles
☐ HC-CFM	Boeing 737-244	22589/843	ex ZS-SIJ	
☐ HC-CFO	Boeing 737-2E3 (AvAero 3)	22703/811	ex N324JM	
☐ HC-CFR	Boeing 737-244	22581/796	ex ZS-SIB	
☐ HC-CGA	Boeing 737-247 (Nordam 3)	23188/1071	ex PK-KKL	
☐ HC-CHC	Boeing 757-236	25592/453	ex N521NA	
☐ HC-CIJ	Boeing 767-322ER	25287/449	ex N287AV	

AEROMASTER AIRWAYS — Quito (UIO)

☐ HC-BXT	Rockwell Commander 690C	11615	ex N811EC	
☐ HC-CBH	Bell 206L-1 LongRanger III	45354	ex N213HC	
☐ HC-CBT	Bell 427	56028	ex N40560	
☐ HC-	de Havilland DHC-6 Twin Otter 200	120	ex N120AA	on order stored FLL

AEROPACSA — Aeropacsa (RPC) — Guayaquil (GYE)

☐ HC-BDV	Cessna TU206F Turbo Stationair II	U20603439		
☐ HC-CBD	Dornier 28D-2 Skyservant	4182	ex HK-4004	
☐ HC-CDI	Dornier 28D-2 Skyservant	4152	ex 58+77	

ATESA — Atesa (TXU) — Quito (UIO)

☐ HC-BLP	Cessna TU206G Turbo Stationair 6 II	U20606449	ex N9383Z	

ATUR — (TUR) — Quito (UIO)

☐ HC-BYL	Cessna TU206G Turbo Centurion	U20606628	ex N9727Z	Soloy conv

EMETEBE TAXI AEREO — Emetebe (EMT) — Puerto Baquerizo Moreno

☐ HC-BDX	Britten-Norman BN-2A-27 Islander	51	ex F-OGEB	
☐ HC-BNE	Piper PA-23-250 Aztec D	27-3959	ex N6742Y	
☐ HC-BZF	Britten-Norman BN-2A-27 Islander	200	ex F-BTGO	

ICARO EXPRESS — Icaro (X8/ICD) — Quito (UIO)

☐ HC-CDK	Aérospatiale AS350B Ecureuil	3001	ex N444LH	
☐ HC-CDT	Fokker F.28 Fellowship 4000	11222	ex N475AU	
☐ HC-CDW	Fokker F.28 Fellowship 4000	11224	ex N476US	for sale
☐ HC-CEC	Aérospatiale AS350B Ecureuil	3009	ex N483AE	
☐ HC-CEN	Boeing Vertol 234UT Chinook	MJ-016	ex N241CH	Lsd fr WCO
☐ HC-CFD	Boeing 737-236 (Stage 3)	21801/669	ex ZS-SIS	Lsd fr SFR
☐ HC-CFL	Boeing 737-236	22026/644	ex ZS-SIU	Lsd fr SFR
☐ HC-CFY	Boeing 737-290QC	22577/760	ex N730AS	

LAN ECUADOR		Aerolane (XL/LNE)		Quito (UIO)	
☐ HC-CGZ	Boeing 767-3Q8ER/W	28206/694	ex CC-CML		
☐ HC-CHA	Boeing 767-316ER/W	27613/652	ex CC-CBJ		

SAEREO		Saereo (SRO)		Quito (UIO)	
☐ HC-BUD	Gulfstream Commander 690C	11669	ex N844MA		
☐ HC-BVN	Beech 1900C	UB-53	ex N814BE		
☐ HC-BYH	Cessna T207A Stationair 8 II	20700749	ex N9905M		
☐ HC-BZO	Bell 407	53302	ex N8226A		
☐ HC-CBC	Beech 1900D	UE-17	ex N17YV	stored UIO	
☐ HC-CDM	Embraer EMB.120ER Brasilia	120088	ex N193SW		
☐ HC-CEM	Embraer EMB.120ER Brasilia	120227	ex N198SW		

TAME		Tame (EQ/TAE)		Quito (UIO)	
☐ HC-CGT	Airbus A319-132	2659	ex N511NK	Ciudad de Esmeraldas	
☐ HC-CGW	Airbus A320-233	2084	ex N487TA	Ciudad de Quito	
☐ HC-CDY	Airbus A320-233	2014	ex F-WWBT		
☐ HC-CGJ	Airbus A320-214	0657	ex F-GRSE	Ciudad de Guayaquil	
☐ HC-CID	Airbus A320-232	0934	ex N934BV		
☐ HC-BHM	Boeing 727-2T3 (Raisbeck 3)	22078/1644	ex N1293E	Cotopaxi	Also FAE-078
☐ HC-BLE	Boeing 727-134	19691/487	ex RP-C1240	Manabistored LTX	Also FAE-691
☐ HC-BZS	Boeing 727-230 (Raisbeck 3)	21620/1419	ex TC-AFO	Imbabura	Also FAE-620
☐ HC-CEX	Embraer 170-100LR (170LR)	17000087	ex PT-SZM	Francisco de Orellana	
☐ HC-CEY	Embraer 170-100LR (170LR)	17000092	ex PT-SZS		
☐ HC-CEZ	Embraer 190-100LR (190LR)	19000027	ex PT-SGB	Cuidad de Cuenca	
☐ HC-CGF	Embraer 190-100LR (190LR)	19000137	ex PT-SYQ	Cuidad de Loja	
☐ HC-CGG	Embraer 190-100LR (190LR)	19000141	ex PT-SYT	Ciudad de Manta	
☐ HC-BZU	Fokker F.28 Fellowship 4000	11112	ex SE-DGE	Morona Santiago	Also FAE-112
☐ HC-CEH	Fokker F.28 Fellowship 4000	11228	ex N479AU	Ciudad de Loja	Also FAE-228

TRANS AM		Aero Transam (7T/RTM)		Guayaquil (GYE)	
☐ HC-CDX	ATR 42-300F	081	ex YV-914C	Op for DHL	

VIP-VUELOS INTERNOS PRIVADOS		Vipec (V6/VUR)		Quito (UIO)	
☐ HC-CFC	Dornier 328-110	3018	ex N422JS		
☐ HC-CFI	Dornier 328-110	3084	ex N462JS		
☐ HC-CFS	Dornier 328-110	3039	ex N427JS		

HH- HAITI (Republic of Haiti)

CARIBINTAIR		Caribintair (CRT)		Port-au-Prince (PAP)
☐ HH-CRB	LET L-410UVP	800413	ex HI-671CT	
☐ HH-CRT	LET L-410UVP-E	861721	ex 1721	
☐ HH-DMX	British Aerospace Jetstream 31	753	ex N842JS	

HANAIR			
☐ HH-	Britten-Norman BN-2A-26 Islander	150	ex 4X-CAH

NATION AIR			
☐ HH-NAT	LET L-410UVP	851439	ex HI-693CT

TORTUG'AIR				Port-au-Prince (PAP)
☐ HH-AET	LET L-410UVP-E3	871816	ex 3D-CCE	
☐ HH-BET	LET L-410UVP	851403	ex 3D-DSI	
☐ HH-JET	British Aerospace Jetstream 32	883	ex N883CH	
☐ HH-LOG	LET L-410UVP-E3	871827	ex S9-DIV	
☐ HH-TOR	LET L-410UVP-E	871930	ex S9-BAO	
☐ HH-YET	British Aerospace Jetstream 32	914	ex N914AE	

VISION AIR			
☐ HH-RPL	Britten-Norman BN-2A Mk.III-2 Trislander	1040	ex XA-TYU

HI- DOMINICAN REPUBLIC (Republica Dominicana)

ACSA — Santo Domingo-Herrara (HEX)

☐ HI-744CT	Cessna 401B	401B0214	ex N7995Q	
☐ HI-772CT	British Aerospace Jetstream 3101	660	ex N411MX	
☐ HI-816	British Aerospace Jetstream 31	694	ex N694AM	
☐ HI-840	British Aerospace Jetstream 32EP	819	ex N148JH	

AERODOMCA — Santo Domingo-Herrara (HEX)

☐ HI761	LET L-410UVP-E	871938	ex HI-761CT	

AIR DOMINICANA

☐ HI-864	Boeing 737-33A	23628/1304	ex EC-JSL	

AIR SANTO DOMINGO — Aero Domingo (EX/SDO) — Santo Domingo-Herrara (HEX)

☐ HI-657CT	Short SD.3-60	SH3672	ex 8P-SCD	
☐ HI-679CT	LET L-410UVP-E	882023	ex HI-679CA	
☐ HI-681CT	LET L-410UVP-E	882025	ex HI-681CA	Puerto Cana
☐ HI-688CT	LET L-410UVP-E	861616	ex HI-688CA	
☐ HI-695CT	LET L-410UVP-E	861615	ex HI-695CA	
☐ HI-760CT	Cessna 208B Caravan I	208B0802	ex N1326D	

CARIBAIR — Caribair (CBC) — Santo Domingo-Herrara (HEX)

☐ HI-569CT	Piper PA-31 Turbo Navajo B	31-700	ex HI-569CA	
☐ HI-585CA	Piper PA-31 Turbo Navajo B	31-850	ex N333GT	
☐ HI-653CA	Britten-Norman BN-2A-26 Islander	8	ex N28BN	
☐ HI-666CT	LET L-410UVP	851517	ex TG-TJV	
☐ HI-697CT	LET L-410UVP-E9A	882040	ex S9-TAV	
☐ HI-698CT	LET L-410UVP-E9A	882039	ex S9-TAU	status?
☐ HI-713CT	LET L-410UVP	851340	ex HI-713CA	
☐ HI-746CT	British Aerospace Jetstream 3101	692	ex HI-746CA	no titles
☐ HI-830	British Aerospace Jetstream 3101	780	ex HI-830CT	
☐ HI-848	SAAB SF.340A	340A-128	ex N128CH	
☐ HI-866	SAAB SF.340A	340A-138	ex N138SD	on order

PAN AM DOMINICA — (7Q) — Santo Domingo-Herrara (HEX)

☐ HI-817CT	British Aerospace Jetstream 31	673	ex N507PA	
☐ HI-841CT	British Aerospace Jetstream 31	674	ex N508PA	
☐ HI-	Douglas DC-9-32	47566/691	ex N949N	
☐ HI876	Douglas DC-9-32	47046/168	ex N602NE	
☐ HI	Douglas DC-9-31	47162/255	ex N919RW	
☐ N206ZT	Bell 206B JetRanger III	2906	ex N330B	

SAPAIR — Proservicios (5S/PSV) — Santo Domingo-Herrara (HEX)

☐ HI-690CT	LET L-410UVP	831106	ex S9-TAR	stored HEX
☐ HI-691CT	LET L-410UVP	831107	ex S9-TAW	
☐ HI-722CT	LET L-410UVP-E	861729	ex Russ AF 1729	stored HEX
☐ HI-723CT	LET L-410UVP-E	861730	ex LY-AZI	stored HEX
☐ HI-724CT	LET L-410UVP-E	882032	ex LY-AZN	
☐ HI-644	de Havilland DHC-6 Twin Otter 200	46	ex CS-TFG	
☐ HI-658CT	Short SD.3-60	SH3674	ex 8P-SCE	
☐ HI-720CT	Embraer EMB.120RT Brasilia	120038	ex N332JS	
☐ HI-819	British Aerospace Jetstream 31	811	ex TG-TAK	
☐ HI-851	British Aerospace Jetstream 32EP	940	ex N940AE	
☐ HI-856	British Aerospace Jetstream 32EP	919	ex N919AE	
☐ HI-858	British Aerospace Jetstream 32EP	938	ex N938AE	
☐ HI-	British Aerospace Jetstream 32EP	972	ex N972JX	

VOL AIR — Santo Domingo-Herrara (HEX)

☐ HI-785CT	Piper PA-31-350 Navajo Chieftain	31-7305066	ex N74923	
☐ HI-787CA	Britten-Norman BN-2A-8 Islander	5429	ex HI-787SP	
☐ HI-789CA	Britten-Norman BN-2A-21 Islander	849	ex HI-640CA	
☐ HI862	British Aerospace Jetstream 31	826	ex N16EX	

HK- COLOMBIA (Republic of Colombia)

ADA – AEROLINEAS DE ANTIOQUIA — Antioquia (ANQ) — Medellin-Olaya Herrera (MDE)

☐ HK-4364	British Aerospace Jetstream 32EP	897	ex N482UE	
☐ HK-4381	British Aerospace Jetstream 32EP	898	ex N483UE	

☐ HK-4398	British Aerospace Jetstream 32EP	828	ex N473UE	
☐ HK-4515	British Aerospace Jetstream 32EP	900	ex N496UE	
☐ HK-4548	British Aerospace Jetstream 32EP	893	ex N479UE	
☐ HK-4	British Aerospace Jetstream 32EP	890	ex N477UE	
☐ HK-2548	de Havilland DHC-6 Twin Otter 300	718	ex C-GDIW	
☐ HK-2603	de Havilland DHC-6 Twin Otter 300	749		
☐ HK-2669	de Havilland DHC-6 Twin Otter 300	760		Arcangel Rafael
☐ HK-3972	Dornier 28D-2 Skyservant	4156	ex YS-400P	
☐ HK-4000	Dornier 28D-2 Skyservant	4177	ex YS-404P	
☐ HK-4042	Cessna T303 Crusader	T30300155	ex N6421C	
☐ HK-4073	Dornier 28D-2 Skyservant	4114	ex N952	

ADES COLOMBIA — Villavicencio (VVC)

☐ HK-2279	Cessna U206G Stationair 6 II	U20604885	ex (N734WH)	
☐ HK-2430	Cessna TU206G Stationair 6 II	U20605166	ex (N4926U)	

AERCARIBE

☐ HK-4427	Antonov An-32	1909	ex HK-4427X	identity not confirmed
☐ HK-4257	Antonov An-32B	3203	ex OB-1699	

AEROLINEAS DE LA PAZ — Villavicencio (VVC)

☐ HK-1663	Cessna U206F Stationair	U20601962	ex N50961	
☐ HK-3035	Cessna T303 Crusader	T30300191		
☐ HK-4189	Douglas DC-3	4319	ex HK-3994	
☐ HK-4292X	Douglas DC-3	17061/34328	ex OB-1756	status?

AEROREPUBLICA COLOMBIA — Aerorepublica (P5/RPB) — Bogota-Eldorado (BOG)

☐ HK-4453X	Embraer 190-100LR (190LR)	19000063	ex PT-SJB	
☐ HK-4454X	Embraer 190-100LR (190LR)	19000061	ex PT-SIO	
☐ HK-4455X	Embraer 190-100LR (190LR)	19000076	ex PT-SJR	dam 17Jly07
☐ HK-4456X	Embraer 190-100LR (190LR)	19000074	ex PT-SJN	
☐ HK-4505X	Embraer 190-100LR (190LR)	19000114	ex PT-SQI	
☐ HK-4506X	Embraer 190-100LR (190LR)	19000110	ex PT-SQE	
☐ HK-4507X	Embraer 190-100LR (190LR)	19000122	ex PT-SQQ	
☐ HK-4508X	Embraer 190-100LR (190LR)	19000138	ex PT-SYR	
☐ HK-4559X	Embraer 190-100LR (190LR)	19000200	ex PT-SGI	
☐ HK-4560X	Embraer 190-100LR (190LR)	19000208	ex PT-SGR	
☐ HK-4599	Embraer 190-100LR (190LR)	19000269	ex PT-TLJ	
☐ HK-4601	Embraer 190-100LR (190LR)	19000251	ex PT-SIW	
☐ HP-1562CMP	Embraer 190-100IGW (190AR)	19000095	ex PT-SNP	Lsd fr CMP
☐ HK-4238X	McDonnell-Douglas MD-81	48009/985	ex N489NC	stored BOG
☐ HK-4259	McDonnell-Douglas MD-81	48005/957	ex N835F	stored
☐ HK-4265	McDonnell-Douglas MD-81	48002/938	ex N832F	
☐ HK-4408X	McDonnell-Douglas MD-83	53124/1991	ex N726BC	
☐ HK-3928X	Douglas DC-9-32	47311/398	ex N286AW	Miguel Angel
☐ HK-3963	Douglas DC-9-32	47437/544	ex I-RIZL	
☐ HK-4155	Douglas DC-9-32	47524/632	ex N27522	

AEROSUCRE — Aerosucre (6N/KRE) — Barranquilla (BAQ)

☐ HK-727	Boeing 727-59F	19127/243		
☐ HK-3985	Boeing 727-224F (FedEx 3)	20465/814	ex N32723	
☐ HK-4216	Boeing 737-230C (Nordam 3)	20253/223	ex HP-1408PVI	
☐ HK-4253X	Boeing 737-2H6C (Nordam 3)	21109/436	ex HP-1311CMP	
☐ HK-4328	Boeing 737-2S5C (Nordam 3)	22148/663	ex N802AL	
☐ HK-4465	Boeing 727-222F (FedEx 3)	19915/681	ex N7642U	
☐ HK-4504	Boeing 727-2J0F (FedEx 3)	21108/1174	ex N284KH	
☐ HK-4544	Boeing 727-2J0F (FedEx 3)	21105/1158	ex N281KH	

AEROVANGUARDIA — Villavicencio (VVC)

☐ HK-3199	Douglas DC-3	14599/26044	ex FAC1123	El Viejo

AERUPIA — Villavicencio (VVC)

☐ HK-2713	Piper PA-34-220T Seneca III	34-8133241		
☐ HK-2822	Britten-Norman BN-2B-27 Islander	2109	ex N2643X	

AIR COLOMBIA — Villavicencio (VVC)

☐ HK-3292	Douglas DC-3	19661	ex N9101S	
☐ HK-3293X	Douglas DC-3	9186	ex N46877	

AIRES — *Aires (4C/ARE)* — *Bogota-Eldorado (BOG)*

□ HK-3951	de Havilland DHC-8-301	184	ex N184CL	Gustavo Artunduaga	Lsd fr AGES
□ HK-3952	de Havilland DHC-8-301	169	ex N169CL		Lsd fr AGES
□ HK-4030	de Havilland DHC-8-301	100	ex N100CQ		Lsd fr AGES
□ HK-4107X	de Havilland DHC-8Q-311	224	ex D-BELT		Lsd fr AGES
□ HK-4345	de Havilland DHC-8-102	63	ex N820PH		Lsd fr AGES
□ HK-4432X	de Havilland DHC-8-201	428	ex N990HA		
□ HK-4473	de Havilland DHC-8Q-201	479	ex N985HA		id not confirmed
□ HK-4480	de Havilland DHC-8Q-201	509	ex N998HA		
□ HK-4491	de Havilland DHC-8Q-201	478	ex N983HA		
□ HK-4495	de Havilland DHC-8Q-201	497	ex N996HA		
□ HK-4509	de Havilland DHC-8Q-201	507	ex N997HA		
□ HK-4513X	de Havilland DHC-8Q-201	468	ex N969HA		
□ HK-4520	de Havilland DHC-8Q-201	465	ex N968HA		
□ HK-4539	de Havilland DHC-8Q-201	452	ex N966HA		
□ HK-4554X	de Havilland DHC-8Q-201	450	ex N965HA		
□ HK-4618	de Havilland DHC-8-201	432	ex HC-CFK		

□ HK-4608	Boeing 737-73S/W	29080/211	ex D-AHID
□ HK-4623	Boeing 737-73S/W	29081/215	ex D-AHIE
□ HK-4627	Boeing 737-73S/W	29078/187	ex OY-MLW
□ HK-4635	Boeing 737-73V/W	30249/1128	ex G-EZJN
□ HK-4641	Boeing 737-73V/W	30244/1148	ex G-EZJO
□ HK-4660X	Boeing 737-752/W	34296/1783	ex XA-WAM
□ HK-4675X	Boeing 737-73V/W	32415/1260	ex G-EZJT

ALIANSA — *Villavicencio (VVC)*

□ HK-122	Douglas DC-3	4414	ex C-122	Freighter
□ HK-2820	Douglas DC-3	20171	ex N151D	Freighter
□ HK-3215	Douglas DC-3	14666/26111	ex N124SF	Freighter status?

APSA - AEROEXPRESO BOGOTA — *Aeroexpreso (ABO)* — *Bogota-Guayamaral*

□ HK-3736X	Bell 212	31144	ex N3895P	Lsd fr Air Logistics
□ HK-3737X	Bell 212	31153	ex N3895U	
□ HK-4222X	Bell 212	30815	ex N24HL	Lsd fr Air Logistics
□ HK-4428X	Bell 212	30615	ex 9Y-TIF	
□ HK-4518X	Bell 212	30640	ex 9Y-TEY	

ARALL - AEROLINEAS LLANERAS — *Villavicencio (VVC)*

□ HK-1018	de Havilland DHC-2 Beaver	93	ex HK-240
□ HK-1231	Cessna TU206D Skywagon	U206-1391	ex (N72389)
□ HK-2257	Cessna U206G Stationair 6	U20604600	ex (N9950M)
□ HK-2373	de Havilland DHC-2 Beaver	61	ex HK-84
□ HK-2868	Cessna TU206G Stationair 6	U20606626	ex (N9724Z)

ARKAS

□ HK-4492X	ATR 42-300	015	ex PR-TTA
□ HK-4493X	ATR 42-300F	018	ex F-GPIA

AVIANCA — *Avianca (AV/AVA)* — *Bogota-Eldorado (BOG)*

□ HK-4553	Airbus A319-112	3467	ex D-AVWN	
□ HK-4552	Airbus A319-112	3518	ex D-AVYZ	
□ N647AV	Airbus A319-115	3647	ex D-AVYQ	
□ N691AV	Airbus A319-112	3691	ex D-AVWG	
□	Airbus A319-112		ex	on order
□	Airbus A319-112		ex	on order
□	Airbus A319-112		ex	on order
□	Airbus A319-112		ex	on order

□ HK-4549	Airbus A320-214	3408	ex F-WWBZ	
□ HK-4659	Airbus A320-214	4100	ex F-WWDK	
□ N398AV	Airbus A320-214	3988	ex F-WWBO	
□ N401AV	Airbus A320-214	4001	ex F-WWDL	
□ N411AV	Airbus A320-214	4011	ex F-WWIC	
□ N416AV	Airbus A320-214	4167	ex F-WWBY	
□ N426AV	Airbus A320-214	4026	ex F-WWDU	
□ N446AV	Airbus A320-214	4046	ex D-AVVI	
□ N451AV	Airbus A320-214	4051	ex F-WWIP	
□ N664AV	Airbus A320-214	3664	ex F-WWDX	
□ N961AV	Airbus A320-214	3961	ex F-WWDV	
□ N980AV	Airbus A320-214	3980	ex F-WWIZ	
□ N992AV	Airbus A320-214	3992	ex F-WWDE	
□	Airbus A320-214		ex	on order
□	Airbus A320-214		ex	on order
□	Airbus A320-214		ex	on order

☐		Airbus A320-214		ex	on order
☐		Airbus A320-214		ex	on order
☐		Airbus A320-214		ex	on order
☐		Airbus A320-214		ex	on order
☐		Airbus A320-214		ex	on order
☐	N948AC	Airbus A330-243	948	ex F-WWKN	
☐	N967CG	Airbus A330-243	967	ex F-WWYI	
☐	N968AV	Airbus A330-243	1009	ex F-WWYE	
☐	N969AV	Airbus A330-243	1016	ex F-WWYI	
☐	N973AV	Airbus A330-243	1073	ex F-WWKZ	
☐	EI-CEY	Boeing 757-2Y0ER	26152/478		
☐	EI-CEZ	Boeing 757-2Y0ER	26154/486		
☐	N635AV	Boeing 757-2K2/W	26635/608	ex PR-ONF	
☐	N802PG	Boeing 757-21B	24774/288	ex B-2815	
☐	N421AV	Boeing 767-2B1ER	25421/407	ex PT-TAK	
☐	N728CG	Boeing 767-283ER	24728/305	ex XA-TNS	special c/s
☐	N948AV	Boeing 767-3Y0ER	24948/380	ex 5Y-CCC	
☐	N984AN	Boeing 767-383ER	24357/262	ex LN-RCB	
☐	N986AN	Boeing 767-259ER	24835/321		Amerigo Vespucio
☐	HK-4467	Fokker F.27 Mk.050 (Fokker 50)	20301	ex PH-MXZ	
☐	HK-4468X	Fokker F.27 Mk.050 (Fokker 50)	20300	ex PH-MXT	Lsd to SAM
☐	HK-4469X	Fokker F.27 Mk.050 (Fokker 50)	20285	ex PH-AVJ	Lsd to SAM
☐	HK-4470	Fokker F.27 Mk.050 (Fokker 50)	20297	ex PH-AVO	
☐	HK-4487X	Fokker F.27 Mk.050 (Fokker 50)	20266	ex PH-LXW	Lsd to SAM
☐	HK-4496X	Fokker F.27 Mk.050 (Fokker 50)	20278	ex PH-AVG	
☐	HK-4497X	Fokker F.27 Mk.050 (Fokker 50)	20288	ex PH-MXJ	Lsd to SAM
☐	HK-4501X	Fokker F.27 Mk.050 (Fokker 50)	20299	ex PH-MXS	
☐	HK-4580	Fokker F.27 Mk.050 (Fokker 50)	20296	ex PR-OAX	
☐	HK-4581	Fokker F.27 Mk.050 (Fokker 50)	20281	ex PR-OAW	
☐	EI-CBY	McDonnell-Douglas MD-83	49944/1888		Ciudad de Barranquilla
☐	EI-CBZ	McDonnell-Douglas MD-83	49945/1889	ex N6206F	Ciudad de Santiago de Cali
☐	EI-CCE	McDonnell-Douglas MD-83	49947/1900		Ciudad de Medellin
☐	EI-CEP	McDonnell-Douglas MD-83	53122/1984		San Andres Isla
☐	EI-CEQ	McDonnell-Douglas MD-83	53123/1987		Ciudad de LeticiaJuan Valdez c/s
☐	EI-CFZ	McDonnell-Douglas MD-83	53120/1964	ex N6206F	Ciudad de San Juan de Pasto
☐	N632CT	McDonnell-Douglas MD-83	49632/1603	ex 9Y-THV	Retro c/s

AVIHECO — Bogota-Eldorado/Ibague (BOG/IBE)

☐	HK-3039	Bell 206L-2 LongRanger III	51052		
☐	HK-4142	LET L-410UVP-E	861703	ex N5957J	for sale
☐	HK-4267	Bell 206L-2 LongRanger III	51252	ex N37CA	
☐	HK-4306	Bell 206L-2 LongRanger III	51606	ex HC-BXA	
☐	HK-4334	Convair 580F	176	ex N631MB	Used by CIA/DAC

COSMOS AIR CARGO — Bogota-Eldorado (BOG)

☐	HK-4386X	Boeing 727-82C/W (FedEx 3)	19968/660	ex N709DH
☐	HK-4407X	Boeing 727-30C/W (Duganair 3)	19011/387	ex N701DH

EASYFLY

☐	HK-4502	British Aerospace Jetstream 4101	41091	ex N572HK	
☐	HK-4503	British Aerospace Jetstream 4101	41093	ex N574HK	
☐	HK-4521	British Aerospace Jetstream 4101	41092	ex N573HK	
☐	HK-4522	British Aerospace Jetstream 4101	41086	ex N568HK	
☐	HK-4551	British Aerospace Jetstream 4101	41089	ex N570HK	
☐	HK-4568	British Aerospace Jetstream 4101	41057	ex N552HK	
☐	HK-4584X	British Aerospace Jetstream 4101	41073	ex N556HK	stored BOG
☐	HK-4585X	British Aerospace Jetstream 4101	41067	ex N554HK	
☐	HK-4596X	British Aerospace Jetstream 4101	41079	ex N563HK	

HELIANDES — Medellin-Olaya Herrara (MDE)

☐	HK-3898X	Mil Mi-17 (Mi-8MTV-1)	96156	
☐	HK-4160X	Mil Mi-17 (Mi-8MTV-1)	95585	ex RA-25446
☐	HK-4164	Mil Mi-17 (Mi-8MTV-1)	95875	ex HK-3890X
☐	HK-4107X	LET L-410UVP-E	902132	ex HA-LAT
☐	HK-4223	Bell 206B JetRanger	303	ex HP-1321HC

HELICARGO — Medellin-Olaya Herrera (MDE)

☐	HK-2610	Aérospatiale AS350B Ecureuil	1339	ex F-WZFO
☐	HK-2967	Aérospatiale AS350B Ecureuil	1688	
☐	HK-3553	Bell 206L-3 LongRanger III	51177	ex N300WJ
☐	HK-3561	Rockwell Turbo Commander 690B	11365	ex LV-LZS
☐	HK-4215	Aérospatiale AS350BA Ecureuil	1495	ex N64050

☐ HK-4236	Beech 200 Super King Air	BB-135	ex N402RG		
☐ HK-4301	Aérospatiale AS355F2 Twin Star	5420	ex N1074P		
☐ HK-4370	Gulfstream Commander 695B	96080	ex N960AC		
☐ HK-4375	Aérospatiale AS355F2 Twin Star	5384	ex N9040V		

HELICOL ***Helicol (HEL)*** ***Bogota-Eldorado (BOG)***

☐ HK-3303X	Bell 212	30654	ex N59608		
☐ HK-3336X	Bell 212	31207	ex N2180J		
☐ HK-3340W	de Havilland DHC-7-102	108	ex C-GFBW		Op for Intercor/Carbocol
☐ HK-3578G	Bell 412	33203			
☐ HK-3633X	Bell 206L-1 LongRanger II	45510	ex N57497		
☐ HK-4031X	Bell 212	31203	ex HK-3184X		
☐ HK-4213G	Bell 407	53405	ex (N2382Z)		

HELITEC ***Cali (CLO)***

☐ HK-3341	Bell 212	31287	ex N3204H		
☐ HK-3742	Bell 212	30847			
☐ HK-4025	Bell 212	31143	ex HC-BSQ		
☐ HK-4231X	Kamov Ka-32S	9101	ex N40475		

HELIVALLE ***Palmira (QPI)***

☐ HK-3693	Piper PA-42 Cheyenne III	42-8001075	ex N4998M		
☐ HK-3978X	Bell 206L-3 LongRanger III	51446	ex N6643K		
☐ HK-4015X	Bell 206L-4 LongRanger IV	52092	ex N4268G		
☐ HK-4026X	Bell 212	35055	ex N4354J		
☐ HK-4129X	Bell 212	30926	ex N412AX		

LAP - LINEAS AÉREAS PETROLERAS ***LAP (APT)*** ***Bogota-Eldorado (BOG)***

☐ HK-2503	Piper PA-31 Navajo C	31-8012056			

LATINA DE AVIACION ***Villavicencio (VVC)***

☐ HK-4173X	Beech 1900C-1	UC-14	ex N38015		
☐ HK-2006	Douglas DC-3C	43086	ex N43A		

LINEAS AÉREAS SURAMERICANAS COLOMBIA ***Suramericano (LAU)*** ***Bogota-Eldorado (BOG)***

☐ HK-1271	Boeing 727-24C (Raisbeck 3)	19524/428	ex N1781B		
☐ HK-1273	Boeing 727-24C (Raisbeck 3)	19526/442	ex N8320	Voyager	
☐ HK-3814X	Boeing 727-25F (Raisbeck 3)	18270/79	ex N5111Y	Skipperstored	
☐ HK-4154	Boeing 727-51F (Raisbeck 3)	18804/162	ex N5607	Orion	
☐ HK-4261	Boeing 727-251F (FedEx 3)	21156/1170	ex N296AJ		Lsd fr Flying Cargo
☐ HK-4262	Boeing 727-2F9F/W (Duganair 3)	21427/1291	ex N299AJ		Lsd fr Flying Cargo
☐ HK-4354	Boeing 727-2X3F (FedEx 3)	22608/1727	ex N397AJ		Lsd fr Flying Cargo
☐ HK-4401	Boeing 727-2X3F (FedEx 3)	22609/1731	ex N797AJ		
☐ HK-4607	Boeing 727-259F (FedEx 3)	22476/1747	ex N901LF		
☐ HK-4636	Boeing 727-2S2F (FedEx 3)	22927/1821	ex N129FB		
☐ HK-4637	Boeing 727-2S2F (FedEx 3)	22928/1822	ex N131FB		

LAN CARGO COLOMBIA

☐ N312LA	Boeing 767-316F/W	32572/846			
☐ N418LA	Boeing 767-316F/W	34246/936			

SADELCA ***Sadelca (SDK)*** ***Neiva (NVA)***

☐ HK-1514	Douglas DC-3	11741	ex N100RW		
☐ HK-2494	Douglas DC-3	16357/33105	ex N87611		
☐ HK-2664	Douglas DC-3	19433	ex HK-2665	Angela Sofia	
☐ HK-3286	Douglas DC-3	6144	ex HP-86	Liliana	
☐ HK-4136X	Antonov An-32B	2509	ex (YV-1089CP)		

SADI ***Ibagué (IBE)***

☐ HK-3154	Cessna TU206G Stationair 6	U20606836	ex (N9330R)		
☐ HK-3829	Bell 222	47076	ex N50RX		
☐ HK-4013	LET L-410UVP-E	861601	ex TG-TJS		
☐ HK-4109	LET L-410UVP	912529	ex S9-TBB		
☐ HK-4226	Bell 206B JetRanger III	2684	ex N2753E		

SAEP ***SAEP (KSP)*** ***Bogota-Eldorado (BOG)***

☐ HK-4296X	Antonov An-32A	1704	ex ER-AXF		

SAM		SAM (MM/SAM)		Medellin-Olaya Herrara (MDE)
☐ EI-CBS	McDonnell-Douglas MD-83	49942/1799		Ciudad de Cucuta
☐ EI-CDY	McDonnell-Douglas MD-83	49948/1905		Ciudad de Santa Maria
☐ HK-4469X	Fokker F.27 Mk.050 (Fokker 50)	20285	ex PH-AVJ	
☐ HK-4487X	Fokker F.27 Mk.050 (Fokker 50)	20266	ex PH-LXW	
☐ HK-4497X	Fokker F.27 Mk.050 (Fokker 50)	20288	ex PH-MXJ	
☐ HK-4419	Fokker F.28-0100 (Fokker 100)	11457	ex N1448A	
☐ HK-4420	Fokker F.28-0100 (Fokker 100)	11482	ex N1462C	
☐ HK-4430	Fokker F.28-0100 (Fokker 100)	11465	ex N1453D	
☐ HK-4431	Fokker F.28-0100 (Fokker 100)	11506	ex N1470K	
☐ HK-4437	Fokker F.28-0100 (Fokker 100)	11469	ex N1457B	
☐ HK-4438	Fokker F.28-0100 (Fokker 100)	11514	ex N1472B	
☐ HK-4443	Fokker F.28-0100 (Fokker 100)	11479	ex N1459A	
☐ HK-4444	Fokker F.28-0100 (Fokker 100)	11458	ex N1449D	
☐ HK-4445	Fokker F.28-0100 (Fokker 100)	11449	ex N1446A	
☐ HK-4451	Fokker F.28-0100 (Fokker 100)	11464	ex N1452B	
☐ HK-4486	Fokker F.28-0100 (Fokker 100)	11414	ex OB-1831-P	
☐ HK-4488	Fokker F.28-0100 (Fokker 100)	11376	ex OB-1821-P	
☐ HK-4489	Fokker F.28-0100 (Fokker 100)	11377	ex OB-1816-P	
☐ HK-4578	Fokker F.28-0100 (Fokker 100)	11413	ex PR-OAH	
☐ HK-4579	Fokker F.28-0100 (Fokker 100)	11419	ex PR-OAV	

SARPA				
☐ HK-4099	Agusta-Bell 212	5630		
☐ HK-4100	Agusta-Bell 212	5631		
☐ HK-4124	Bell 212	30844	ex N405RA	
☐ HK-4232	Bell 212	30993	ex XA-SRZ	
☐ HK-4233	Bell 212	31164	ex XA-LAM	
☐ HK-4350	British Aerospace Jetstream 32EP	836	ex G-OEST	
☐ HK-4362	British Aerospace Jetstream 32EP	840	ex G-BYMA	
☐ HK-4394E	British Aerospace Jetstream 32EP	905	ex N486UE	EMS
☐ HK-4405E	British Aerospace Jetstream 32EP	849	ex N474UE	
☐ HK-4540X	British Aerospace Jetstream 32EP	933	ex N933CX	
☐ HK-4541	British Aerospace Jetstream 32EP	937	ex N937AE	

SATENA		Satena (9N/NSE)			Bogota-Eldorado (BOG)
☐ FAC-1160	Dornier 328-120	3079	ex D-CDXB	El Cafetero	
☐ FAC-1161	Dornier 328-120	3080	ex D-CDXH	La Macarena	
☐ FAC-1162	Dornier 328-120	3082	ex D-CDXP	Bahia Solano	
☐ FAC-1163	Dornier 328-120	3081	ex D-CDXM	El Antioqueño	
☐ FAC-1164	Dornier 328-120	3092	ex D-CDXO	El Casanereno	
☐ FAC-1165	Dornier 328-120	3103	ex D-CDXW	El Guambiano	
☐ FAC-1171	Embraer EMB.145LR (ERJ-145LR)	145774	ex PT-SME	Milenium I	
☐ FAC-1172	Embraer EMB.145LR (ERJ-145LR)	145776	ex PT-SMG	Milenium II	
☐ FAC-1173	Embraer EMB.145LR (ERJ-145LR)	14500879	ex PT-SXU		
☐ FAC-1176	Embraer EMB.145EP (ERJ-145EP)	145165	ex EI-DMV		
☐ FAC-1177	Embraer EMB.145EP (ERJ-145EP)	145227	ex EI-DMW		
☐ FAC-1103	LET L-410UVP-E	902420	ex HK-4224		Lsd fr/op by SRC
☐ FAC-1104	LET L-410UVP-E	861707	ex HK-4094X		Lsd to/op for NSE
☐ FAC-1180	Embraer 170-100LR (170LR)	17000151	ex PT-SEP		

SEARCA COLOMBIA		Searca (SRC)		Medellin-Olaya Herrara (MDE)
☐ HK-4266X	Beech 1900C-1	UC-64	ex N1568W	
☐ HK-4282	Beech 1900C-1	UC-60	ex N901SC	
☐ HK-4392	Beech 1900C-1	UC-38	ex N38SU	
☐ HK-4476	Beech 1900D	UE-123	ex N123YV	
☐ HK-4499	Beech 1900D	UE-110	ex N110YV	
☐ HK-4512	Beech 1900D	UE-105	ex N105YV	
☐ HK-4537	Beech 1900D	UE-95	ex N95YV	
☐ HK-4558	Beech 1900D	UE-156	ex N156E	
☐ HK-4563	Beech 1900D	UE-113	ex N113YV	
☐ HK-4598	Beech 1900D	UE-183	ex N48544	
☐ HK-4600	Beech 1900D	UE-99	ex N99YV	
☐ HK-4630	Beech 1900D	UE-93	ex N93ZV	
☐ HK-4673	Beech 1900D	UE-104	ex N104YV	
☐ HK-4681	Beech 1900D	UE-213	ex N3199Q	
☐ HK-4038X	LET L-410UVP	851323	ex TG-TJT	
☐ HK-4048	LET L-410UVP-E	912626	ex OM-111	
☐ HK-4105	LET L-410UVP-E	861613	ex N5957N	
☐ HK-4147	LET L-410UVP-E	892341	ex YV-986C	
☐ HK-4161	LET L-410UVP-E	861612	ex N6968L	
☐ HK-4196X	LET L-410UVP-E	861617	ex CCCP-67577	
☐ HK-4235	LET L-410UVP-E	902423	ex S9-BAD	

☐ FAC-1103	LET L-410UVP-E	902420	ex HK-4224	Lsd to/op for NSE
☐ FAC-1104	LET L-410UVP-E	861707	ex HK-4094X	Lsd to/op for NSE
☐ HK-4108X	Beech 200 Super King Air	BB-60	ex N530JA	

SELVA

☐ HK-4052	Antonov An-32	1805	ex	
☐ HK-4240	Antonov An-32B	3204	ex	
☐ HK-4295	Antonov An-26	67304702	ex	
☐ HK-4356	Antonov An-26B-100	77305109	ex	
☐ HK-4369	Antonov An-32	2510	ex	stored
☐ HK-4388	Antonov An-26B-100	27312402	ex	

TAMPA AIRLINES — *Tampa (QT/TPA)* — *Medellin-Olaya Herrara (MDE)*

☐ N767QT	Boeing 767-241ER (SF)	23804/178	ex PP-VNQ	Lsd fr 767 Leasing
☐ N768QT	Boeing 767-241ER (SF)	23803/161	ex N803HE	
☐ N769QT	Boeing 767-241ER (SF)	23801/170	ex PP-VNO	
☐ N770QT	Boeing 767-241ER (SF)	23802/172	ex PP-VNP	

TAP LINEAS AEREAS

☐ HK-	Boeing 727-151C	19868/529	ex N433EX

TAS - TRANSPORTE AEREO DE SANTANDER — *Bucaramanga (BGA)*

☐ HK-4102	Dornier 28D-2 Skyservant	4187	ex D-IDES
☐ HK-4104	Dornier 28D-2 Skyservant	4193	ex D-IDRV
☐ HK-4139	Dornier 28D-2 Skyservant	4153	ex D-IDRF
☐ HK-4290X	Cessna 402C	402C0427	ex N717A

TAXI AÉREO CUSIANA — *Bogota-Eldorado (BOG)*

☐ HK-2522	Cessna 402C II	402C0322	ex N2522P
☐ HK-3916	Cessna 208B Caravan I	208B0372	ex N1117P
☐ HK-4225X	LET L-410UVP	871929	ex S9-CBB
☐ HK-4367	LET L-410UVP-E20	851334	ex CP-2252

TRANS ORIENTE — *Villavicencio (VVC)*

☐ HK-3981	Dornier 28D-2 Skyservant	4162	ex D-IDND
☐ HK-3982	Dornier 28D-2 Skyservant	4169	ex D-IDNC
☐ HK-3991X	Dornier 28D-2 Skyservant	4148	ex D-IDNF
☐ HK-3992X	Dornier 28D-2 Skyservant	4161	ex D-IDNE
☐ HK-4053X	Dornier 28D-1 Skyservant	4105	ex D-IDNH

VERTICAL DE AVIACION — *Bogota-Guaymaral*

☐ HK-3730X	Mil Mi-8TV-1	95728	ex CCCP-25112
☐ HK-3731X	Mil Mi-8TV-1	95586	ex CCCP-25447
☐ HK-3732X	Mil Mi-8TV-1	95729	ex CCCP-25113
☐ HK-3758X	Mil Mi-8TV-1	95908	ex HC-BSG
☐ HK-3779X	Mil Mi-8TV-1	95645	ex CCCP-25500
☐ HK-3780X	Mil Mi-8TV-1	95909	ex RA-27068
☐ HK-3862	Mil Mi-8TV-1	95923	ex CCCP-27087
☐ HK-3863	Mil Mi-8TV-1	95894	ex CCCP-27060
☐ HK-3864	Mil Mi-8TV-1	95893	ex CCCP-27059
☐ HK-3865	Mil Mi-8TV-1	95892	ex CCCP-27058
☐ HK-3882X	Mil Mi-8TV-1	96018	
☐ HK-3888X	Mil Mi-8TV-1	95838	
☐ HK-3908X	Mil Mi-8TV-1	95823	
☐ HK-3910X	Mil Mi-8TV-1	96008	ex RA-27185
☐ HK-3911X	Mil Mi-8TV-1	96124	ex RA-25768
☐ HK-3250	Bell 212	31219	ex HC-BSI
☐ HK-3262	Bell 222UT	47556	
☐ HK-3723	Bell 212	32122	ex N1080V
☐ HK-4208X	Beech 1900C-1	UC-152	ex N152GL

VIARCO — *Villavicencio (VVC)*

☐ HK-1315	Douglas DC-3	4307	ex PP-ANG
☐ HK-1842	Cessna U206F Stationair II	U20603487	ex (N8734Q)
☐ HK-3349X	Douglas DC-3	11825	ex FAE 92066/HC-AVC

HL- SOUTH KOREA (Republic of Korea)

AIR BUSAN (BX/ABL)

Registration	Type	C/n	Previous identity	Notes
☐ HL7232	Boeing 737-58E	25767/2614		
☐ HL7233	Boeing 737-58E	25768/2724		
☐ HL7250	Boeing 737-58E	25769/2737		
☐ HL7510	Boeing 737-48E	25771/2816		
☐ HL7517	Boeing 737-48E	25774/2909		

ASIANA AIRLINES Asiana (OZ/AAR) Seoul-Incheon/Kimpo (ICN/SEL)

Member of Star Alliance

Registration	Type	C/n	Previous identity	Notes
☐ HL7737	Airbus A320-232	2397	ex F-WWIU	Unicef titles
☐ HL7738	Airbus A320-232	2459	ex F-WWDM	
☐ HL7744	Airbus A320-232	2808	ex F-WWIO	
☐ HL7745	Airbus A320-232	2840	ex F-WWIE	
☐ HL7753	Airbus A320-232	2943	ex F-WWIM	
☐ HL7762	Airbus A320-232	3244	ex F-WWBQ	
☐ HL7769	Airbus A320-232	3437	ex F-WWDX	
☐ HL7772	Airbus A320-232	3483	ex F-WWDN	
☐ HL7773	Airbus A320-232	3496	ex F-WWIL	
☐ HL7776	Airbus A320-232	3641	ex F-WWBS	
☐ HL7788	Airbus A320-232	3873	ex F-WWIH	
☐ HL7594	Airbus A321-231	1356	ex D-AVZA	
☐ HL7703	Airbus A321-231	1511	ex D-AVZA	
☐ HL7711	Airbus A321-231	1636	ex D-AVZG	
☐ HL7713	Airbus A321-231	1734	ex D-AVXD	
☐ HL7722	Airbus A321-231	2041	ex D-AVZA	
☐ HL7723	Airbus A321-231	2045	ex D-AVZC	
☐ HL7729	Airbus A321-231	2110	ex D-AVXF	
☐ HL7730	Airbus A321-231	2226	ex D-AVZU	
☐ HL7731	Airbus A321-231	2247	ex D-AVZG	
☐ HL7735	Airbus A321-231	2290	ex D-AVZB	
☐ HL7761	Airbus A321-231	1227	ex N127AG	
☐ HL7763	Airbus A321-231	3297	ex D-AVZR	
☐ HL7767	Airbus A321-231	0802	ex N802BV	
☐ HL7789	Airbus A321-231	4112	ex D-AZAE	
☐ HL7790	Airbus A321-231	4142	ex D-AVZM	
☐ HL7736	Airbus A330-323X	640	ex F-WWYR	
☐ HL7740	Airbus A330-323X	676	ex F-WWYA	
☐ HL7741	Airbus A330-323X	708	ex F-WWKL	
☐ HL7746	Airbus A330-323X	772	ex F-WWKE	
☐ HL7747	Airbus A330-323X	803	ex F-WWYE	Dae Jang Geum colours
☐ HL7754	Airbus A330-323X	845	ex F-WWYZ	
☐ HL7792	Airbus A330-323X	1001	ex F-WWKL	
☐ HL7793	Airbus A330-323X	1055	ex F-WWYD	
☐ HL	Airbus A330-323X	1151	ex	on order
☐ HL7508	Boeing 737-48E	25772/2791		
☐ HL7511	Boeing 737-48E	27630/2848		
☐ HL7513	Boeing 737-48E	25776/2860		
☐ HL7527	Boeing 737-4Q8	26299/2602	ex TC-JEK	Star Alliance c/s
☐ HL7592	Boeing 737-4Q8	26320/2563	ex TC-JEH	
☐ HL7413	Boeing 747-48EM (SF)	25405/880		
☐ HL7414	Boeing 747-48EM (SF)	25452/892		
☐ HL7415	Boeing 747-48EM (SF)	25777/946		
☐ HL7417	Boeing 747-48EM	25779/1006		
☐ HL7418	Boeing 747-48E	25780/1035	ex N6018N	
☐ HL7419	Boeing 747-48EF	25781/1044		
☐ HL7420	Boeing 747-48EF	25783/1064		
☐ HL7421	Boeing 747-48EM	25784/1086		
☐ HL7423	Boeing 747-48EM	25782/1115		
☐ HL7428	Boeing 747-48E	28552/1160	ex N6018N	
☐ HL7436	Boeing 747-48EF	29170/1305	ex N1785B	
☐ HL7604	Boeing 747-48EF	29907/1370		
☐ HL7247	Boeing 767-38E	25757/523		
☐ HL7248	Boeing 767-38E	25758/582		
☐ HL7506	Boeing 767-38E	25760/639		
☐ HL7507	Boeing 767-38EF	25761/616	ex N6005C	
☐ HL7514	Boeing 767-38E	25763/656		Tea Changum colours
☐ HL7515	Boeing 767-38E	25762/658	ex N6055X	
☐ HL7516	Boeing 767-38E	25759/668		Star Alliance colours
☐ HL7528	Boeing 767-38E	29129/693	ex N6005C	
☐ HL7500	Boeing 777-28EER	28685/400		

☐ HL7596	Boeing 777-28EER	28681/322		
☐ HL7597	Boeing 777-28EER	28686/359		
☐ HL7700	Boeing 777-28EER	30859/403	ex N5014K	
☐ HL7732	Boeing 777-28EER	29174/481		
☐ HL7739	Boeing 777-28EER	29175/526		
☐ HL7742	Boeing 777-28EER	29171/553		
☐ HL7755	Boeing 777-28EER	30861/646		
☐ HL7756	Boeing 777-28EER	30860/659		
☐ HL7775	Boeing 777-28EER	30862/738		
☐ HL7791	Boeing 777-28EER	35525		on order

EASTARJET *(ZE/ESR)*

☐ HL7781	Boeing 737-683	28302/243	ex G-CDKD
☐ HL7797	Boeing 737-73V	30240/974	ex G-EZJH
☐ HL8204	Boeing 737-73V	30248/1118	ex G-EZJM
☐ HL8205	Boeing 737-73V	32412/1151	ex G-EZJP
☐ HL8207	Boeing 737-73V	32413/1202	ex G-EZJR

JEJU AIR *(7C/JJA)* *Cheju International (CJU)*

☐ HL5251	de Havilland DHC-8-402Q	4119	ex C-FFCH
☐ HL5252	de Havilland DHC-8-402Q	4124	ex C-FFQF
☐ HL5254	de Havilland DHC-8-402Q	4129	ex C-FGAJ
☐ HL5255	de Havilland DHC-8-402Q	4137	ex C-FHQL
☐ HL5256	de Havilland DHC-8-402Q	4141	ex C-FHQQ
☐ HL7779	Boeing 737-85F	28824/180	ex VT-SPC
☐ HL7780	Boeing 737-85F	28827/467	ex VT-SPD
☐ HL7796	Boeing 737-86N/W	28628/573	ex N372LZ
☐ HL8206	Boeing 737-86J/W	30877/782	ex D-ABAE

JIN AIR *(LJ/JNA)* *Seoul-Incheon/Kimpo (ICN/SEL)*

☐ HL7555	Boeing 737-86N	30230/460	ex N1786B
☐ HL7558	Boeing 737-86N	28625/590	ex N1786B
☐ HL7564	Boeing 737-86N	28638/765	
☐ HL7798	Boeing 737-8Q8/W	28236/739	ex B-16802

KOREAN AIR *Koreanair (KE/KAL)* *Seoul-Incheon/Kimpo (ICN/SEL)*

Member of Skyteam

☐ HL7239	Airbus A300B4-622R	627	ex F-WWAD	
☐ HL7240	Airbus A300B4-622R	631	ex F-WWAB	
☐ HL7241	Airbus A300B4-622R	662	ex F-WWAT	
☐ HL7242	Airbus A300B4-622R	685	ex F-WWAG	Jeju colours
☐ HL7243	Airbus A300B4-622R	692	ex F-WWAR	
☐ HL7245	Airbus A300B4-622R	731	ex F-WWAK	
☐ HL7295	Airbus A300B4-622R	582	ex F-WWAM	
☐ HL7297	Airbus A300B4-622R	609	ex F-WWAE	

☐ HL7524	Airbus A330-322	206	ex HL7552
☐ HL7525	Airbus A330-322	219	ex F-WWKO
☐ HL7538	Airbus A330-223	222	ex F-WWKP
☐ HL7539	Airbus A330-223	226	ex F-WWKR
☐ HL7540	Airbus A330-322	241	ex F-WWKF
☐ HL7550	Airbus A330-322	162	ex F-WWKK
☐ HL7551	Airbus A330-322	172	ex F-WWKI
☐ HL7552	Airbus A330-223	258	ex F-WWKQ
☐ HL7553	Airbus A330-323X	267	ex F-WWKZ
☐ HL7554	Airbus A330-323X	256	ex F-WWKN
☐ HL7584	Airbus A330-323X	338	ex F-WWKP
☐ HL7585	Airbus A330-323X	350	ex F-WWYF
☐ HL7586	Airbus A330-323X	351	ex F-WWYH
☐ HL7587	Airbus A330-323X	368	ex F-WWKF
☐ HL7701	Airbus A330-323	425	ex F-WWYE
☐ HL7702	Airbus A330-323	428	ex F-WWYF
☐ HL7709	Airbus A330-323	484	ex F-WWKD
☐ HL7710	Airbus A330-323	490	ex F-WWKF
☐ HL7720	Airbus A330-323	550	ex F-WWKP

☐ HL	Airbus A380-861	035	ex F-WWAT	on order
☐ HL	Airbus A380-861	039	ex F-WWAZ	on order
☐ HL	Airbus A380-861		ex F-WW	on order
☐ HL	Airbus A380-861		ex F-WW	on order
☐ HL	Airbus A380-861		ex F-WW	on order

☐ HL7556	Boeing 737-86N	28615/482	ex N1787B
☐ HL7557	Boeing 737-86N	28622/562	ex N1786B
☐ HL7559	Boeing 737-86N	28626/611	
☐ HL7560	Boeing 737-8B5/W	29981/622	
☐ HL7561	Boeing 737-8B5/W	29982/663	

☐ HL7562	Boeing 737-8B5	29983/678	
☐ HL7563	Boeing 737-86N	28636/756	
☐ HL7565	Boeing 737-8B5/W	29984/848	
☐ HL7566	Boeing 737-8B5/W	29985/852	
☐ HL7567	Boeing 737-86N	28647/878	
☐ HL7568	Boeing 737-8B5/W	29986/891	
☐ HL7569	Boeing 737-9B5	29987/999	ex B-5110
☐ HL7599	Boeing 737-9B5	29988/1026	ex N1795B
☐ HL7704	Boeing 737-9B5	29989/1082	ex N1786B
☐ HL7705	Boeing 737-9B5	29990/1162	
☐ HL7706	Boeing 737-9B5	29991/1188	
☐ HL7707	Boeing 737-9B5	29992/1190	
☐ HL7708	Boeing 737-9B5	29993/1208	ex N60659
☐ HL7716	Boeing 737-9B5	29994/1320	
☐ HL7717	Boeing 737-9B5	29995/1332	
☐ HL7718	Boeing 737-9B5	29996/1338	
☐ HL7719	Boeing 737-9B5	29997/1416	
☐ HL7724	Boeing 737-9B5	29998/1494	
☐ HL7725	Boeing 737-9B5	29999/1512	
☐ HL7726	Boeing 737-9B5	30001/1729	ex N1786B
☐ HL7727	Boeing 737-9B5	30000/1536	ex N6066U
☐ HL7728	Boeing 737-9B5	30002/1620	
☐ HL7757	Boeing 737-8GQ/W	35790/2119	
☐ HL7758	Boeing 737-8GQ/W	35791/2150	
☐ HL7785	Boeing 737-8GQ/W	37162/2906	ex N1795B
☐ HL7786	Boeing 737-8GQ/W	37163/2955	ex N1786B

☐ HL7400	Boeing 747-4B5F	26414/1295	
☐ HL7402	Boeing 747-4B5	26407/1155	ex N6038E
☐ HL7403	Boeing 747-4B5F	26408/1163	ex N60659
☐ HL7404	Boeing 747-4B5	26409/1170	ex N6009F
☐ HL7412	Boeing 747-4B5BCF	24200/748	ex HL7479
☐ HL7434	Boeing 747-4B5F	32809/1316	
☐ HL7437	Boeing 747-4B5F	32808/1323	
☐ HL7438	Boeing 747-4B5ERF	33515/1329	ex N6005X
☐ HL7439	Boeing 747-4B5ERF	33516/1338	
☐ HL7443	Boeing 747-2B5B	21772/363	
☐ HL7448	Boeing 747-4B5F	26416/1246	
☐ HL7449	Boeing 747-4B5F	26411/1248	
☐ HL7460	Boeing 747-4B5	26404/1107	
☐ HL7461	Boeing 747-4B5	26405/1118	
☐ HL7462	Boeing 747-4B5F	26406/1123	
☐ HL7465	Boeing 747-4B5	26412/1284	
☐ HL7466	Boeing 747-4B5F	26413/1286	
☐ HL7467	Boeing 747-4B5F	27073/1291	
☐ HL7472	Boeing 747-4B5	26403/1095	
☐ HL7473	Boeing 747-4B5	28335/1098	
☐ HL7480	Boeing 747-4B5M	24619/793	ex N6009F
☐ HL7481	Boeing 747-4B5BCF	24621/830	ex VT-AID
☐ HL7482	Boeing 747-4B5BCF	25205/853	
☐ HL7483	Boeing 747-4B5BCF	25275/874	
☐ HL7484	Boeing 747-4B5	26392/893	
☐ HL7485	Boeing 747-4B5	26395/922	
☐ HL7486	Boeing 747-4B5	26396/951	
☐ HL7487	Boeing 747-4B5	26393/958	
☐ HL7488	Boeing 747-4B5	26394/986	
☐ HL7489	Boeing 747-4B5	27072/1013	
☐ HL7490	Boeing 747-4B5	27177/1019	
☐ HL7491	Boeing 747-4B5	27341/1037	
☐ HL7492	Boeing 747-4B5	26397/1055	
☐ HL7493	Boeing 747-4B5	26398/1057	
☐ HL7494	Boeing 747-4B5	27662/1067	
☐ HL7495	Boeing 747-4B5	28096/1073	
☐ HL7498	Boeing 747-4B5	26402/1092	
☐ HL7499	Boeing 747-4B5ERF	33517/1340	
☐ HL7600	Boeing 747-4B5ERF	33945/1347	
☐ HL7601	Boeing 747-4B5ERF	33946/1350	
☐ HL7602	Boeing 747-4B5ERF	34301/1365	
☐ HL7603	Boeing 747-4B5ERF	34302/1368	
☐ HL7605	Boeing 747-4B5ERF	35526/1375	
☐ HL7606	Boeing 747-4B5BCF	24199/739	ex VT-EVJ
☐ HL7607	Boeing 747-4B5	24198/729	ex VT-AIC
☐ HL7608	Boeing 747-4B5BCF	24521/830	ex VT-AID

☐ HL7526	Boeing 777-2B5ER	27947/148	ex N50217
☐ HL7530	Boeing 777-2B5ER	27945/59	
☐ HL7531	Boeing 777-2B5ER	27946/62	
☐ HL7532	Boeing 777-3B5	28371/162	
☐ HL7533	Boeing 777-3B5	27948/178	
☐ HL7534	Boeing 777-3B5	27950/120	ex N5020K
☐ HL7573	Boeing 777-3B5	27952/288	
☐ HL7574	Boeing 777-2B5ER	28444/305	
☐ HL7575	Boeing 777-2B5ER	28445/309	

☐ HL7598	Boeing 777-2B5ER	27949/356		
☐ HL7714	Boeing 777-2B5ER	27951/411		
☐ HL7715	Boeing 777-2B5ER	28372/416		
☐ HL7721	Boeing 777-2B5ER	33727/452		
☐ HL7733	Boeing 777-2B5ER	34206/520	ex N5023Q	
☐ HL7734	Boeing 777-2B5ER	34207/528		
☐ HL7743	Boeing 777-2B5ER	34208/584		
☐ HL7750	Boeing 777-2B5ER	34209/633		
☐ HL7751	Boeing 777-2B5ER	34210/657	ex N6018N	
☐ HL7752	Boeing 777-2B5ER	34211/682		
☐ HL7764	Boeing 777-2B5ER	34214/684	ex N50281	
☐ HL7765	Boeing 777-2B5ER	34212/711		
☐ HL7766	Boeing 777-2B5ER	34213/730		
☐ HL7782	Boeing 777-3B5ER	37643/785		
☐ HL7783	Boeing 777-3B5ER	37644/806	ex N5020K	
☐ HL7784	Boeing 777-3B5ER	37136/823		
☐ HL8208	Boeing 777-3B5ER	37645		on order
☐ HL8209	Boeing 777-3B5ER	37646		on order
☐ HL8210	Boeing 777-3B5ER	40377		on order

YEONGNAM AIR

☐ HL7774	Fokker F.28-0100 (Fokker 100)	11293	ex G-MAMH

HP- PANAMA (Republic of Panama)

AEROPERLAS — *Aeroperlas (WL/APP)* — *Panama City-Albrook (BLB)*

☐ HP-1251APP	Short SD.3-60	SH3610	ex N715NC	
☐ HP-1315APP	Short SD.3-60	SH3614	ex N363MQ	stored PAC
☐ HP-1319APP	Short SD.3-60	SH3607	ex N361MQ	
☐ HP-1326APP	Short SD.3-60	SH3631	ex N360MM	stored BLB
☐ HP-004APP	ATR 42-300	004	ex TG-IAX	Lsd fr ISV
☐ HP-1281APP	de Havilland DHC-6 Twin Otter 300	407	ex C-FVFK	
☐ HP-1283APP	de Havilland DHC-6 Twin Otter 300	269	ex C-GKBO	
☐ HP-1336APP	Beech A100 King Air	B-173	ex C-GAST	
☐ HP-1359APP	Cessna 208B Caravan I	208B0711	ex TI-BAO	
☐ HP-1445APP	Canadair CL-66B Cosmopolitan	CL66B-7	ex N4FY	
☐ TG-MYH	ATR 42-300	113	ex G-ZAPJ	Lsd fr TSP

AIR PANAMA — *Turismo Aereo (PST)* — *Panama City-Albrook (BLB)*

☐ HP-1542PST	Fokker F.27 Friendship 500F	10560	ex HP-1542PS	
☐ HP-1543PST	Fokker F.27 Friendship 400	10268	ex C-GWXC	
☐ HP-1604PST	Fokker F.27 Friendship 500F	10471	ex N716FE	Lsd fr NPTC
☐ HP-1631PST	Fokker F.27 Friendship 500	10658	ex N725FE	stored PAC
☐ HP-639PS	Britten-Norman BN-2A-8 Islander	60	ex HP-639KN	
☐ HP-1153PS	Britten-Norman BN-2A-26 Islander	672	ex HP-1153XI	
☐ HP-1345PS	Cessna 208B Caravan I	208B0380	ex HP-1354AR	
☐ HP-1494PS	Britten-Norman BN-2A-3 Islander	673	ex CN-TCC	
☐ HP-1507PS	de Havilland DHC-6 Twin Otter 300	532	ex C-GQKZ	
☐ HP-1509PS	de Havilland DHC-6 Twin Otter 300	360	ex HP-1509APP	
☐ HP-1625PST	de Havilland DHC-8-311	519	ex G-BRYY	
☐ HP-1670PST	SAAB SF.340B	340B-299	ex N299CJ	
☐ HP-1671PST	SAAB SF.340B	340B-294	ex N294CJ	

ARROW PANAMA — *Arrow Panama (8A/WAP)* — *Panama City-Tocumen Intl (PTY)*

☐ HP-441WAP	Douglas DC-8-63CF (BAC 3)	45988/416	ex N441J		
☐ HP-791WAP	Douglas DC-8-62F (BAC 3)	46150/539	ex N791AL	El Wapo	std MTY

COPA AIRLINES — *Copa (CM/CMP)* — *Panama City-Tocumen Intl (PTY)*

☐ HP-1369CMP	Boeing 737-71Q/W	29047/235	ex N8251R	669
☐ HP-1370CMP	Boeing 737-71Q/W	29048/288	ex N82521	670
☐ HP-1371CMP	Boeing 737-7V3/W	30049/388	ex N1787B	671
☐ HP-1372CMP	Boeing 737-7V3/W	28607/399		672
☐ HP-1373CMP	Boeing 737-7V3/W	30458/459		673
☐ HP-1374CMP	Boeing 737-7V3/W	30459/494	ex N1787B	674
☐ HP-1375CMP	Boeing 737-7V3/W	30460/558	ex N1787B	675
☐ HP-1376CMP	Boeing 737-7V3/W	30497/574		676
☐ HP-1377CMP	Boeing 737-7V3/W	30462/1161		677
☐ HP-1378CMP	Boeing 737-7V3/W	30461/1173		678
☐ HP-1379CMP	Boeing 737-7V3/W	30463/1221		679
☐ HP-1380CMP	Boeing 737-7V3/W	30464/1241		680
☐ HP-1520CMP	Boeing 737-7V3/W	33707/1376		681
☐ HP-1521CMP	Boeing 737-7V3/W	33708/1379		682
☐ HP-1522CMP	Boeing 737-8V3/W	33709/1387		480
☐ HP-1523CMP	Boeing 737-8V3/W	33710/1397		481

☐ HP-1524CMP	Boeing 737-7V3/W	33705/1505		683	
☐ HP-1525CMP	Boeing 737-7V3/W	33706/1518		684	
☐ HP-1526CMP	Boeing 737-8V3/W	34006/1585	ex N1782B	482	
☐ HP-1527CMP	Boeing 737-7V3/W	30676/1619		685	
☐ HP-1528CMP	Boeing 737-7V3/W	29360/1644		686	
☐ HP-1529CMP	Boeing 737-8V3/W	29670/1711		483	
☐ HP-1530CMP	Boeing 737-7V3/W	34535/1962		687	
☐ HP-1531CMP	Boeing 737-7V3/W	34536/1995		688	
☐ HP-1532CMP	Boeing 737-8V3/W	35068/2343		484	
☐ HP-1533CMP	Boeing 737-8V3/W	35067/2423		485	
☐ HP-1534CMP	Boeing 737-8V3/W	35125/2624		486	
☐ HP-1535CMP	Boeing 737-8V3/W	35126/2805	ex N1786B		
☐ HP-1536CMP	Boeing 737-8V3/W	35127/2963			
☐ HP-1537CMP	Boeing 737-8V3/W	36550/3114			
☐ HP-1538CMP	Boeing 737-8V3/W	36554/3130			
☐ HP-1539CMP	Boeing 737-8V3/W	29667/			

☐ HP-1540CMP	Embraer 190-100IGW (190AR	19000012	ex PT-STL	
☐ HP-1556CMP	Embraer 190-100IGW (190AR)	19000016	ex PT-STQ	
☐ HP-1557CMP	Embraer 190-100IGW (190AR)	19000034	ex PT-SGI	
☐ HP-1558CMP	Embraer 190-100IGW (190AR)	19000038	ex PT-SGN	
☐ HP-1559CMP	Embraer 190-100IGW (190AR)	19000053	ex PT-SIC	
☐ HP-1560CMP	Embraer 190-100IGW (190AR)	19000056	ex PT-SIF	
☐ HP-1561CMP	Embraer 190-100IGW (190AR)	19000089	ex PT-SNI	
☐ HP-1562CMP	Embraer 190-100IGW (190AR)	19000095	ex PT-SNP	Lsd to RMB
☐ HP-1563CMP	Embraer 190-100IGW (190AR)	19000098	ex PT-SNS	
☐ HP-1564CMP	Embraer 190-100IGW (190AR)	19000100	ex PT-SNU	
☐ HP-1565CMP	Embraer 190-100IGW (190AR)	19000126	ex PT-SQV	
☐ HP-1566CMP	Embraer 190-100IGW (190AR)	19000165	ex PT-SAX	
☐ HP-1567CMP	Embraer 190-100IGW (190AR)	19000174	ex PT-SDJ	
☐ HP-1568CMP	Embraer 190-100IGW (190AR)	19000212	ex PT-SGV	
☐ HP-1569CMP	Embraer 190-100IGW (190AR)	19000222	ex PT-SHG	

DHL AERO EXPRESSO — *Yellow (D5/DAE)* — *Panama City-Tocumen Intl (PTY)*

☐ HP-1310DAE	Boeing 727-264F (FedEx 3)	20894/1047	ex N9184X	El Gato	
☐ HP-1510DAE	Boeing 727-264F (FedEx 3)	20709/950	ex N624DH		stored ROW
☐ HP-1610DAE	Boeing 727-264F (FedEx 3)	20780/986	ex N625DH		
☐ HP-1710DAE	Boeing 727-2Q4F (FedEx 3)	22424/1683	ex OO-DHZ		

MAPIEX AERO — *Panama City-Albrook (BLB)*

☐ HP-1348MAM British Aerospace Jetstream 31

PANAIR CARGO — *Panama City-Tocumen Intl (PTY)*

☐ HP-1653CTW	Boeing 727-277F (FedEx 3)	21695/1481	ex N982JM

PANAVIA CARGO AIRLINES — *Panavia (6Z/PVI)* — *Panama City-Tocumen Intl (PTY)*

☐ HP-1261PVI	Boeing 727-25F/W (Duganair 3)	18965/205	ex N8141N	stored PTY
☐ HP-1585PVI	Boeing 727-224F (FedEx 3)	20662/1072	ex N334FV	

PARSA

☐ HP-1625PS de Havilland DHC-8-315
☐ HP-1626PS CASA C.212

HR- HONDURAS (Republic of Honduras)

AEROLINEAS SOSA — *Sosa (P4/VSO)* — *La Ceiba (LCE)*

☐ HR-AIH	Britten-Norman BN-2A-21 Islander	513	ex C-GVZY	
☐ HR-AQR	LET L-410UVP	851516	ex S9-TBD	
☐ HR-ARE	LET L-410UVP	841312	ex S9-TBL	
☐ HR-ARJ	Nord 262A-14	15	ex N417SA	stored
☐ HR-ARP	Nord 262A-27	33	ex N274A	stored
☐ HR-ARU	Nord 262A-21	21	ex TG-ANP	stored
☐ HR-ASI	LET L-410UVP-E	871925	ex N888LT	
☐ HR-ASR	Fairchild F-27F	84	ex 3C-QQA	
☐ HR-ASZ	LET L-410UVP	851530	ex HR-AQO	
☐ HR-ATA	British Aerospace Jetstream 31	725	ex N833JS	
☐ HR-ATB	British Aerospace Jetstream 31	726	ex N834JS	
☐ HR-ATE	British Aerospace Jetstream 31	757	ex N843JS	
☐ HR-AUE	LET L-410UVP			

ATLANTIC AIRLINES — *Atlantic Honduras (ZF/HHA)* — *La Ceiba (LCE)*

☐ HR-ASD	LET L-410UVP-E	882034	ex YS-15C
☐ HR-ASE	LET L-410UVP-E	861611	ex YS-10C

☐ HR-ASG	LET L-410UVP-E	861710	ex HR-AJG	
☐ HR-ASH	LET L-410UVP-E	861716	ex YS-14C	
☐ HR-ASJ	LET L-410UVP-E	861724	ex YS-12C	
☐ HR-ASM	LET L-410UVP-E	861711	ex YS-05C	
☐ HR-ASN	LET L-410UVP-E	861701	ex YS-06C	
☐ HR-ASW	LET L-410UVP-E	871910	ex CU-T1193	
☐ HR-ASX	LET L-410UVP-E	871915	ex CU-T1194	
☐ HR-ASK	Fairchild-Hiller FH-227B	542	ex N155JB	
☐ HR-ATC	Hawker Siddeley HS.748 Srs 2B/424	1801	ex C-GBCS	
☐ HR-ATI	Fairchild F-27F	95	ex N19FF	
☐ HR-ATL	Fokker F.27 Friendship 500F	10522	ex N283EA	
☐ HR-ATN	Boeing 737-2Y5 (Nordam 3)	23040/955	ex N118RW	

CENTRAL AMERICAN AIRWAYS — ***La Ceiba (LCE)***

☐ HR-AUQ	LET L-410UVP	912603	ex HH-AVP

ISLENA AIRLINES ***(WC/ISV)*** — ***La Ceiba (LCE)***

☐ HR-AUX	ATR 42-320 (QC)	394	ex 9A-CTU
☐ HR-AVA	ATR 42-320	388	ex F-WQNC
☐ HR-IAP	Short SD.3-60	SH3616	ex N345MV
☐ HR-IAW	Short SD.3-60	SH3669	ex N361PA
☐ HR-IAY	ATR 42-300	120	ex F-WQHM
☐ HR-IBH	Cessna 208B Caravan I		

ROTIS AIR

☐ HR-ASC	Yakovlev Yak-40	9332029	ex`RA-87321
☐ HR-	GAF N.22 Nomad		
☐ HR-	LET L-410UVP		

SETCO — ***Tegucigalpa (TGU)***

☐ HR-AFB	Rockwell 500S Shrike Commander	3268	ex HR-315		stored TGU
☐ HR-AFC	Rockwell 500S Shrike Commander	3271	ex HR-317		stored TGU
☐ HR-AJY	Douglas DC-3	6068	ex HP-685		stored TGU
☐ HR-AKM	Rockwell 500S Shrike Commander	3098	ex HR-CNA		
☐ HR-ALU	Douglas DC-3				stored TGU
☐ HR-ATH	Douglas DC-3	6102	ex HR-SAH	no titles	

HS- THAILAND (Kingdom of Thailand)

BANGKOK AIRWAYS ***Bangkok Air (PG/BKP)*** — ***Bangkok-Suvarnabhumi (BKK)***

☐ HS-PGN	Airbus A319-132	3759	ex D-AVXD		
☐ HS-PGT	Airbus A319-132	3421	ex D-AVYM		
☐ HS-PGX	Airbus A319-132	3424	ex D-AVYO		
☐ HS-PGY	Airbus A319-132	3454	ex D-AVWH	Angkor Wat	
☐ HS-PGZ	Airbus A319-132	3694	ex D-AVWH	Phnom Penh	
☐ HS-PPA	Airbus A319-132	3911	ex D-AVYN	Si Satchanali	
☐ HS-	Airbus A319-132	4101	ex		on order
☐ HS-PGU	Airbus A320-232	2254	ex F-WWDC	Guilin	
☐ HS-PGV	Airbus A320-232	2310	ex F-WWDS	Krabi	
☐ HS-PGW	Airbus A320-232	2509	ex F-WWIQ	Samui	
☐ HS-PGA	ATR 72-212A	710	ex F-WWEJ	Kut	
☐ HS-PGB	ATR 72-212A	708	ex F-WWEH	Phuket	
☐ HS-PGC	ATR 72-212A	715	ex F-WWEO	Nangyuan	
☐ HS-PGD	ATR 72-212A	833	ex F-WWEZ		
☐ HS-PGF	ATR 72-212A	700	ex F-WWEW	Hua Hin	
☐ HS-PGG	ATR 72-212A	692	ex F-WWEO	Chang	
☐ HS-PGK	ATR 72-212A	680	ex F-WWEV	Apsara	
☐ HS-PGM	ATR 72-212A	704	ex F-WWEC	Tao	

BUSINESS AIR — ***Bangkok-Suvarnabhumi (BKK)***

☐ HS-BIA	Boeing 767-222ER	21868/10	ex HS-SSC

DESTINATION AIR — ***Phuket (HKT)***

☐ HS-DAA	Cessna 208 Caravan I	20800321	ex N122KW	Floatplane
☐ HS-DAB	Cessna 206H Stationair 6	20608046	ex N2312V	Floatplane

HAPPY AIR — ***Phuket (HKT)***

☐ HS-HPY	SAAB SF.340A	340A-115	ex SE-F15

K-MILE AIR (8K/KMI) Bangkok-Suvarnabhumi (BKK)

	Reg	Type	C/n	Prev	Name	Notes
☐	HS-SCH	Boeing 727-247F (FedEx 3)	21700/1489	ex 9M-TGJ		Lsd fr TSE
☐	HS-SCJ	Boeing 727-247F (FedEx 3)	21392/1305	ex 9M-TGK		Lsd fr TSE

NOK AIR Nok Air (DD/NOK) Bangkok Don Muang (BMK)

	Reg	Type	C/n	Prev	Name	Notes
☐	HS-DDL	Boeing 737-4Y0	24917/2071	ex TC-JDF		
☐	HS-DDM	Boeing 737-4Y0	26065/2284	ex TC-JDY		
☐	HS-TDA	Boeing 737-4D7	24830/1899		Songkhla	
☐	HS-TDB	Boeing 737-4D7	24831/1922		Phuket	
☐	HS-TDE	Boeing 737-4D7	26612/2330		Surin	
☐	HS-	Boeing 737-800		ex	on order	
☐	HS-	Boeing 737-800		ex	on order	

ONE-TWO-GO Orient Express (OG/QTG) Bangkok-Suvarnabhumi (BKK)

	Reg	Type	C/n	Prev	Name	Notes
☐	HS-OMA	McDonnell-Douglas MD-82	49439/1318	ex N18835		stored DMK
☐	HS-OMB	McDonnell-Douglas MD-82	49441/1322	ex N35836		
☐	HS-OMC	McDonnell-Douglas MD-82	49479/1297	ex N819NY		stored DMK
☐	HS-OMD	McDonnell-Douglas MD-82	49485/1316	ex N72825		
☐	HS-OME	McDonnell-Douglas MD-82	49182/1128	ex N911TW		
☐	HS-OMI	McDonnell-Douglas MD-87	49464/1476	ex JA8278		stored DMK
☐	HS-OMJ	McDonnell-Douglas MD-87	49465/1604	ex JA8279		stored DMK
☐		McDonnell-Douglas MD-87	53040/1897	ex JA8372		on order
☐		McDonnell-Douglas MD-81	53297/2040	ex N821TH		on order
☐		McDonnell-Douglas MD-81	53298/2045	ex N822TH		on order
☐	HS-UTN	Boeing 747-346	23149/599	ex JA8163		

ORIENT THAI AIRLINES Orient Express (OX/OEA) Bangkok-Suvarnabhumi (BKK)

	Reg	Type	C/n	Prev	Name	Notes
☐	HS-UTD	Boeing 747-146A	21029/259	ex JA8128		Lsd to QTG
☐	HS-UTL	Boeing 747-3B5	22489/611	ex HL7469		
☐	HS-UTM	Boeing 747-346SR	23637/655	ex JA8176		
☐	HS-UTO	Boeing 747-346	23639/664	ex JA8178	all-white	
☐	HS-UTR	Boeing 747-246B	22479/496	ex JA8150		stored BKK
☐	HS-UTV	Boeing 747-346	23151/607	ex JA8166		
☐	HS-UTW	Boeing 747-346	23067/588	ex JA812J		

PHUKET AIRLINES Phuket (HKT)

	Reg	Type	C/n	Prev	Name	Notes
☐	HS-VAC	Boeing 747-306	23056/587	ex (HS-TSA)		
☐	HS-VAN	Boeing 747-312	23245/626	ex (HS-TSB)		

SGA AIRLINES (5E) Bangkok-Suvarnabhumi (BKK)

	Reg	Type	C/n	Prev	Name	Notes
☐	HS-GAA	Cessna 208B Caravan I	208B0643	ex N522GM		
☐	HS-GAB	Cessna 208B Caravan I	208B1196	ex N208WD		Ops in Nok Air colours
☐	HS-SKR	Cessna 208B Caravan I	208B1241	ex N208AE		

SKY EYES AVIATION Sky Eyes (I6/SEQ) Bangkok-Suvarnabhumi (BKK)

	Reg	Type	C/n	Prev	Name	Notes
☐	HS-SEC	Lockheed L-1011-200F Tristar	193N-1212	ex 9L-LDZ		stored FJR

SKYSTAR AIRWAYS (XT/SKT) Bangkok-Suvarnabhumi (BKK)

	Reg	Type	C/n	Prev	Name	Notes
☐	HS-SSA	Boeing 767-222ER	21871/15	ex N610UA	Pattana	stored ICN
☐	HS-SSB	Boeing 767-222ER	21872/20	ex N611UA	Suphahon	stored ICN
☐	HS-SSD	Boeing 767-222	21880/50	ex N620UA		stored CAN

SUVARNABHUMI AIRLINES Phuket (HKT)

	Reg	Type	C/n	Prev	Name	Notes
☐	HS-AKU	Boeing 737-2B7 (Nordam 3)	23115/998	ex N282AU	Kavida-Urawanstored CGK	

THAI AIRASIA (FD/AIQ) Bangkok-Suvarnabhumi (BKK)

	Reg	Type	C/n	Prev	Name	Notes
☐	HS-ABA	Airbus A320-216	3277	ex F-WWDH		
☐	HS-ABB	Airbus A320-216	3299	ex F-WWDZ		
☐	HS-ABC	Airbus A320-216	3338	ex F-WWBM		
☐	HS-ABD	Airbus A320-216	3394	ex F-WWBQ		
☐	HS-ABE	Airbus A320-216	3489	ex F-WWIR		
☐	HS-ABF	Airbus A320-216	3505	ex F-WWBS		
☐	HS-ABG	Airbus A320-216	3576	ex F-WWBN		
☐	HS-ABH	Airbus A320-216	3679	ex F-WWBD		
☐	HS-ABI	Airbus A320-216	3729	ex F-WWDK		
☐	HS-ABJ	Airbus A320-216	4019	ex F-WWDF		
☐	HS-ABK	Airbus A320-216	4088	ex F-WWBV		
☐	HS-ABL	Airbus A320-216	4126	ex F-WWIO		
☐	HS-AAI	Boeing 737-301	23510/1210	ex 9M-AAI	Amazing Thailand c/s	

☐ HS-AAJ	Boeing 737-301	23511/1268	ex 9M-AAJ	
☐ HS-AAO	Boeing 737-3T0	23365/1159	ex 9M-AAO	
☐ HS-AAP	Boeing 737-3T0	23367/1180	ex 9M-AAP	
☐ HS-AAQ	Boeing 737-3T0	23368/1181	ex 9M-AAQ	
☐ HS-AAR	Boeing 737-3T0	23358/1142	ex 9M-AAR	special colours
☐ HS-AAS	Boeing 737-3T0	23357/1141	ex 9M-AAS	
☐ HS-AAU	Boeing 737-3B7	22951/1007	ex N951WP	Scotch Bird's Nest Beverage

THAI AIRWAYS INTERNATIONAL — *Thai (TG/THA)* — *Bangkok-Suvarnabhumi (BKK)*

Member of Star Alliance

☐ HS-TAA	Airbus A300B4-601	368	ex F-WWAG	Suwannaphum	wfs UTP
☐ HS-TAF	Airbus A300B4-601	398	ex F-WWAN	Ratchasima	
☐ HS-TAG	Airbus A300B4-605R	464	ex F-WWAL	Srinapha	
☐ HS-TAH	Airbus A300B4-605R	518	ex F-WWAE	Napachinda	
☐ HS-TAK	Airbus A300B4-622R	566	ex F-WWAB	Phaya Thai	
☐ HS-TAL	Airbus A300B4-622R	569	ex F-WWAD	Sri Trang	
☐ HS-TAM	Airbus A300B4-622R	577	ex F-WWAG	Chiang Mai	
☐ HS-TAN	Airbus A300B4-622R	628	ex F-WWAE	Chiang Rai	
☐ HS-TAO	Airbus A300B4-622R	629	ex F-WWAF	Chanthaburi	Star Alliance c/s
☐ HS-TAP	Airbus A300B4-622R	635	ex F-WWAP	Pathum Thani	
☐ HS-TAR	Airbus A300B4-622R	681	ex F-WWAB	Yasothon	
☐ HS-TAS	Airbus A300B4-622R	705	ex F-WWAT	Yala	
☐ HS-TAT	Airbus A300B4-622R	782	ex F-WWAY	Srimuang	
☐ HS-TAW	Airbus A300B4-622R	784	ex F-WWAL	Suranaree	
☐ HS-TAX	Airbus A300B4-622R	785	ex F-WWAO	Thepsatri	
☐ HS-TAY	Airbus A300B4-622R	786	ex F-WWAQ	Srisoonthorn	
☐ HS-TAZ	Airbus A300B4-622R	787	ex F-WWAB	Srisubhan	
☐ HS-TEA	Airbus A330-321	050	ex F-WWKI	Manorom	
☐ HS-TEB	Airbus A330-321	060	ex F-WWKQ	Sri Sakhon	
☐ HS-TEC	Airbus A330-321	062	ex F-WWKR	Bang Rachan	
☐ HS-TED	Airbus A330-321	064	ex F-WWKS	Donchedi	
☐ HS-TEE	Airbus A330-321	065	ex F-WWKT	Kusuman	
☐ HS-TEF	Airbus A330-321	066	ex F-WWKJ	Song Dao	
☐ HS-TEG	Airbus A330-321	112	ex F-WWKM	Lam Plai Mat	
☐ HS-TEH	Airbus A330-321	122	ex F-WWKG	Sai Buri	
☐ HS-TEJ	Airbus A330-322	209	ex F-WWKN	Sudawadi	
☐ HS-TEK	Airbus A330-322	224	ex F-WWKD	Srichulalak	Royal Barge c/s
☐ HS-TEL	Airbus A330-322	231	ex F-WWKU	Thepamart	Star Alliance c/s
☐ HS-TEM	Airbus A330-323X	346	ex F-WWYE	Jiraprabha	
☐ HS-TEN	Airbus A330-343E	990	ex F-WWKK	Suchada	
☐ HS-TEO	Airbus A330-343E	1003	ex F-WWKR	Chutamas	
☐ HS-TEP	Airbus A330-343E	1035	ex F-WWKS	Srianocha	
☐ HS-TEQ	Airbus A330-343E	1037	ex F-WWYA	Si Ayutthaya	stored BOD
☐ HS-TER	Airbus A330-343E	1060	ex F-WWYQ	U Thong	stored BOD
☐ HS-TES	Airbus A330-343E	1074	ex F-WWKJ		stored BOD
☐ HS-TET	Airbus A330-343E	1086	ex F-WWYV		on order
☐ HS-TEU	Airbus A330-343E	1090	ex F-WWYB		on order
☐ HS-TLA	Airbus A340-541	624	ex F-WWTN	Chiang Kham	
☐ HS-TLB	Airbus A340-541	628	ex F-WWTO	Uttaradit	
☐ HS-TLC	Airbus A340-541	698	ex F-WWTR	Phitsanulok	
☐ HS-TLD	Airbus A340-541HGW	775	ex F-WWTX		
☐ HS-TNA	Airbus A340-642	677	ex F-WWCJ	Watthana Nakhon	
☐ HS-TNB	Airbus A340-642	681	ex F-WWCK	Saraburi	
☐ HS-TNC	Airbus A340-642	689	ex F-WWCN	Chon Buri	
☐ HS-TND	Airbus A340-642	710	ex F-WWCX	Phetchaburi	
☐ HS-TNE	Airbus A340-642	719	ex F-WWCH		
☐ HS-TNF	Airbus A340-642	953	ex F-WWCM	Mae Hong Son	
☐ HS-	Airbus A380-841	070	ex F-WW		on order
☐ HS-	Airbus A380-841	075	ex F-WW		on order
☐ HS-TDF	Boeing 737-4D7	26613/2338		Si Sa Ket	
☐ HS-TDG	Boeing 737-4D7	26614/2481		Kalasin	
☐ HS-TDH	Boeing 737-4D7	28703/2962		Lopburi	
☐ HS-TDJ	Boeing 737-4D7	28704/2968		Nakhon Chaisi	
☐ HS-TDK	Boeing 737-4D7	28701/2977		Sri Surat	
☐ HS-TYS	Boeing 737-8Z6/W	35478/1955	ex N369BJ	Also carries 55-555	BBJ2
☐ HS-TGA	Boeing 747-4D7	32369/1273		Srisuriyothai	
☐ HS-TGB	Boeing 747-4D7	32370/1278		Si Satchanalai	
☐ HS-TGF	Boeing 747-4D7	33770/1335		Sri Ubon	
☐ HS-TGG	Boeing 747-4D7	33771/1337		Pathoomawadi	
☐ HS-TGH	Boeing 747-4D7	24458/769		Chaiprakarn	
☐ HS-TGJ	Boeing 747-4D7	24459/777		Hariphunchai	
☐ HS-TGK	Boeing 747-4D7	24993/833		Alongkorn	
☐ HS-TGL	Boeing 747-4D7	25366/890		Theparat	
☐ HS-TGM	Boeing 747-4D7	27093/945		Chao Phraya	
☐ HS-TGN	Boeing 747-4D7	26615/950		Simongkhon	
☐ HS-TGO	Boeing 747-4D7	26609/1001		Bowonrangsi	

☐ HS-TGP	Boeing 747-4D7	26610/1047		Theppprasit
☐ HS-TGR	Boeing 747-4D7	27723/1071		Siriwatthna
☐ HS-TGT	Boeing 747-4D7	26616/1097		Watthanothai
☐ HS-TGW	Boeing 747-4D7	27724/1111		Visuthakasatriya
☐ HS-TGX	Boeing 747-4D7	27725/1134		Sirisobhakya
☐ HS-TGY	Boeing 747-4D7	28705/1164	ex N60697	Dararasmi
☐ HS-TGZ	Boeing 747-4D7	28706/1214		Phimara
☐ HS-TJA	Boeing 777-2D7	27726/25		Lamphun
☐ HS-TJB	Boeing 777-2D7	27727/32		U Thaithani
☐ HS-TJC	Boeing 777-2D7	27728/44		Nakhon Nayok
☐ HS-TJD	Boeing 777-2D7	27729/51		Mukdahan
☐ HS-TJE	Boeing 777-2D7	27730/89		Chaiyaphum
☐ HS-TJF	Boeing 777-2D7	27731/95		Phanom Sarakham
☐ HS-TJG	Boeing 777-2D7	27732/100		Pattani
☐ HS-TJH	Boeing 777-2D7	27733/113		Suphan Buri
☐ HS-TJR	Boeing 777-2D7ER	34586/588		Nakhon Sawan
☐ HS-TJS	Boeing 777-2D7ER	34587/595		Phra Nakhon
☐ HS-TJT	Boeing 777-2D7ER	34588/596		Pathum Wan
☐ HS-TJU	Boeing 777-2D7ER	34589/599		Phichit
☐ HS-TJV	Boeing 777-2D7ER	34590/665		Nakhon Pathom
☐ HS-TJW	Boeing 777-2D7ER	34591/672		Phetchabun
☐ HS-TKA	Boeing 777-3D7	29150/156	ex N5028Y	Sriwanna
☐ HS-TKB	Boeing 777-3D7	29151/170		Chainarai
☐ HS-TKC	Boeing 777-3D7	29211/250		Kwanmuang
☐ HS-TKD	Boeing 777-3D7	29212/260		Thepalai
☐ HS-TKE	Boeing 777-3D7	29213/304		Sukhirin
☐ HS-TKF	Boeing 777-3D7	29214/310		Chutamai
☐ HS-TRA	ATR 72-201	164	ex F-WWEO	Hummingbird/Lampang
☐ HS-TRB	ATR 72-201	167	ex F-WWEU	Chai Nat

THAI AVIATION SERVICES — **_Songkhla (SGZ)_**

☐ HS-HTE	Sikorsky S-76A++	760706	ex N2584R	Lsd fr CHC Helicopters
☐ HS-HTJ	Sikorsky S-76A++	760720	ex N720G	Lsd fr CHC Helicopters
☐ HS-HTK	Sikorsky S-76C+	760546	ex C-FCHC	Lsd fr CHC Helicopters
☐ HS-HTM	Sikorsky S-76C+	760537	ex VT-HGI	Lsd fr CHC Helicopters
☐ HS-HTP	Sikorsky S-76A++	760697	ex N25811	Lsd fr CHC Helicopters
☐ HS-HTU	Sikorsky S-76A++	760010	ex VH-HUB	Lsd fr CHC Helicopters
☐ HS-HTW	Sikorsky S-76C++	760724	ex C-FUWP	Lsd fr CHC Helicopters
☐ HS-HTY	Sikorsky S-76A	760011	ex C-GIHY	Lsd fr CHC Helicopters
☐ HS-HTZ	Sikorsky S-76C+	760561	ex C-GHRZ	Lsd fr CHC Helicopters
☐ HS-HTA	Sikorsky S-61N	61815	ex C-GOLH	Lsd fr CHC Helicopters Intl
☐ HS-HTC	Sikorsky S-61N	61722	ex C-GARC	Lsd fr CHC Helicopters Intl

THAI FLYING SERVICE — **_Thai Flying (TFT)_** — **_Bangkok-Don Muang (DMK)_**

☐ HS-ITD	Beech 200 350	FL-151	ex N10817
☐ HS-TFG	Rockwell Turbo Commander 690B	11482	ex N745T

HZ- SAUDI ARABIA (Kingdom of Saudi Arabia)

AL KHAYALA

Wholly owned by National Air Services and operates business class services between Jeddah and Riyadh

ALWAFEER AIR — **_(WFR)_**

☐ HZ-AWA1	Boeing 747-4H6	27672/1091	ex 9M-MPI
☐ HZ-AWA2	Boeing 747-4H6	28426/1130	ex 9M-MPJ
☐ HZ-AWA3	Boeing 747-4H6	25701/997	ex 9M-MPD

NAS AIR — **_(2N/KNE)_** — **_Jeddah (JED)_**

☐ F-OHJY	Airbus A319-112	1124	ex F-WIHG
☐ HZ-XY7	Airbus A320-214	2165	ex (VP-BBQ)
☐ VP-CAN	Airbus A319-112	1886	ex C-GKOC
☐ VP-CXR	Airbus A320-214	3894	ex F-WWDF
☐ VP-CXS	Airbus A320-214	3787	ex F-WWBB
☐ VP-CXT	Airbus A320-214	3817	ex F-WWIN
☐ VP-CXW	Airbus A320-214	3475	ex F-WWDF
☐ VP-CXX	Airbus A320-214	3425	ex F-WWIZ
☐ VP-CXY	Airbus A320-214	3396	ex F-WWBR
☐ VP-CXZ	Airbus A320-214	3361	ex F-WWIK
☐ VP-CQW	Embraer 190-200	19000232	ex PT-SID
☐ VP-CQX	Embraer 190-200	19000233	ex PT-SIE
☐ VP-CQY	Embraer 190-200	19000227	ex PT-SHQ
☐ VP-CQZ	Embraer 190-200	19000217	ex PT-SHA

☐	Embraer 190-200		ex PT-	on order
☐	Embraer 190-200		ex PT-	on order
☐	Embraer 190-200		ex PT-	on order

SAMA AIRLINES — *(ZS)* — *Jeddah (JED)*

☐ HZ-AMC	Boeing 737-3L9	24570/1800	ex N570LL	
☐ HZ-BBK	Boeing 737-3M8	25016/2004	ex ZK-FDM	
☐ HZ-CJB	Boeing 737-33A	24680/1927	ex N50881	
☐ HZ-DMO	Boeing 737-3Y0	24681/1929	ex N33341	
☐ HZ-DRW	Boeing 737-33A	25138/2153	ex N80054	
☐ HZ-NMA	Boeing 737-36N	28563/2921	ex N285MT	

SAUDI ARABIAN AIRLINES — *Saudia (SV/SVA)* — *Jeddah (JED)*

☐ HZ-ASA	Airbus A320-214	4081	ex F-WWSR	
☐ HZ-ASB	Airbus A320-214	4090	ex F-WWBZ	
☐ HZ-AS11	Airbus A320-214	4015	ex F-WWBS	
☐ HZ-AS12	Airbus A320-214	4057	ex F-WWBC	
☐ HZ-AS13	Airbus A320-214	4104	ex F-WWDQ	
☐ HZ-AS14	Airbus A320-214	4115	ex F-WWDX	
☐ HZ-AS15	Airbus A320-214	4122	ex F-WWIF	
☐ HZ-AS16	Airbus A320-214	4135	ex F-WWIU	
☐ HZ-AS31	Airbus A320-214	4092	ex F-WWDE	
☐ HZ-AS32	Airbus A320-214	4273	ex	on order
☐ HZ-	Airbus A320-214		ex	on order
☐ HZ-	Airbus A320-214		ex	on order
☐ HZ-	Airbus A320-214		ex	on order
☐ HZ-	Airbus A320-214		ex	on order
☐ HZ-	Airbus A320-214		ex	on order
☐ HZ-	Airbus A320-214		ex	on order
☐ HZ-	Airbus A320-214		ex	on order
☐ HZ-	Airbus A320-214		ex	on order
☐ HZ-	Airbus A320-214		ex	on order
☐ HZ-	Airbus A320-214		ex	on order
☐ HZ-	Airbus A320-214		ex	on order
☐ HZ-	Airbus A320-214		ex	on order

☐ HZ-	Airbus A330-343		ex	on order
☐ HZ-	Airbus A330-343		ex	on order
☐ HZ-	Airbus A330-343		ex	on order
☐ HZ-	Airbus A330-343		ex	on order
☐ HZ-	Airbus A330-343		ex	on order
☐ HZ-	Airbus A330-343		ex	on order
☐ TC-ETK	Airbus A330-223	358	ex I-EEZA	Lsd fr KKK
☐ TC-ETL	Airbus A330-223	364	ex I-EEZB	Lsd fr KKK

☐ HZ-AIB	Boeing 747-168B	22499/517		stored JED
☐ HZ-AIC	Boeing 747-168B	22500/522		
☐ HZ-AID	Boeing 747-168B	22501/525		
☐ HZ-AIE	Boeing 747-168B	22502/530	ex N8284V	
☐ HZ-AII	Boeing 747-168B	22749/557		
☐ HZ-AIK	Boeing 747-368	23262/616	ex N6005C	
☐ HZ-AIL	Boeing 747-368	23263/619	ex N6009F	
☐ HZ-AIM	Boeing 747-368	23264/620	ex N6046P	
☐ HZ-AIN	Boeing 747-368	23265/622	ex N6046P	
☐ HZ-AIP	Boeing 747-368	23267/630	ex N6055X	
☐ HZ-AIQ	Boeing 747-368	23268/631	ex N6005C	
☐ HZ-AIR	Boeing 747-368	23269/643	ex N6038E	
☐ HZ-AIS	Boeing 747-368	23270/645	ex N6046P	
☐ HZ-AIT	Boeing 747-368	23271/652	ex N6038N	
☐ HZ-AIU	Boeing 747-268F	24359/724	ex N6018N	
☐ HZ-AIV	Boeing 747-468	28339/1122	ex N6005C	
☐ HZ-AIW	Boeing 747-468	28340/1138		
☐ HZ-AIX	Boeing 747-468	28341/1182		
☐ HZ-AIY	Boeing 747-468	28342/1216	ex N6009F	
☐ TF-AMI	Boeing 747-412 (SF)	27066/940	ex N706RB	Lsd fr ABD
☐ TF-AMS	Boeing 747-481BCF	24920/832	ex JA8096	Lsd fr ABD
☐ TF-AMT	Boeing 747-481	25135/863	ex JA8097	Lsd fr ABD
☐ TF-AMU	Boeing 747-48EF	27603/1210	ex HL7426	Lsd fr ABD
☐ TF-AMV	Boeing 747-412	28022/1082	ex 9V-SPI	Lsd fr ABD
☐ TF-ATI	Boeing 747-341	24107/702	ex N824DS	Lsd fr ABD
☐ TF-ATJ	Boeing 747-341	24108/703	ex N420DS	Lsd fr ABD

☐ HZ-AKA	Boeing 777-268ER	28344/98	ex N50217	
☐ HZ-AKB	Boeing 777-268ER	28345/99	ex N5023Q	
☐ HZ-AKC	Boeing 777-268ER	28346/101		
☐ HZ-AKD	Boeing 777-268ER	28347/103		
☐ HZ-AKE	Boeing 777-268ER	28348/109		
☐ HZ-AKF	Boeing 777-268ER	28349/114		
☐ HZ-AKG	Boeing 777-268ER	28350/119		
☐ HZ-AKH	Boeing 777-268ER	28351/124		

☐ HZ-AKI	Boeing 777-268ER	28352/143		
☐ HZ-AKJ	Boeing 777-268ER	28353/147		
☐ HZ-AKK	Boeing 777-268ER	28354/154		
☐ HZ-AKL*	Boeing 777-268ER	28355/166		
☐ HZ-AKM*	Boeing 777-268ER	28356/175		
☐ HZ-AKN*	Boeing 777-268ER	28357/181		
☐ HZ-AKO*	Boeing 777-268ER	28358/186		
☐ HZ-AKP*	Boeing 777-268ER	28359/194		
☐ HZ-AKQ*	Boeing 777-268ER	28360/219	ex N5016R	
☐ HZ-AKR*	Boeing 777-268ER	28361/230	ex N5017V	
☐ HZ-AKS*	Boeing 777-268ER	28362/255		
☐ HZ-AKT*	Boeing 777-268ER	28363/298		
☐ HZ-AKU*	Boeing 777-268ER	28364/306		
☐ HZ-AKV*	Boeing 777-268ER	28365/323		
☐ HZ-AKW*	Boeing 777-268ER	28366/351		

*Operated on domestic services in F12C25Y250 configurationothers in F30C31Y183 for international routes

☐ HZ-AEA	Embraer 170-100LR (170LR)	17000108	ex PT-SAQ	
☐ HZ-AEB	Embraer 170-100LR (170LR)	17000114	ex PT-SAZ	
☐ HZ-AEC	Embraer 170-100LR (170LR)	17000118	ex PT-SDF	
☐ HZ-AED	Embraer 170-100LR (170LR)	17000119	ex PT-SDG	
☐ HZ-AEE	Embraer 170-100LR (170LR)	17000121	ex PT-SDJ	
☐ HZ-AEF	Embraer 170-100LR (170LR)	17000123	ex PT-SDM	
☐ HZ-AEG	Embraer 170-100LR (170LR)	17000124	ex PT-SDN	
☐ HZ-AEH	Embraer 170-100LR (170LR)	17000135	ex PT-SDY	
☐ HZ-AEI	Embraer 170-100LR (170LR)	17000142	ex PT-SEG	
☐ HZ-AEJ	Embraer 170-100LR (170LR)	17000145	ex PT-SEJ	
☐ HZ-AEK	Embraer 170-100LR (170LR)	17000149	ex PT-SEN	
☐ HZ-AEL	Embraer 170-100LR (170LR)	17000152	ex PT-SEQ	
☐ HZ-AEM	Embraer 170-100LR (170LR)	17000155	ex PT-SES	
☐ HZ-AEN	Embraer 170-100LR (170LR)	17000158	ex PT-SEW	
☐ HZ-AEO	Embraer 170-100LR (170LR)	17000161	ex PT-SMB	

☐ HZ-APA	McDonnell-Douglas MD-90-30	53491/2191		
☐ HZ-APB	McDonnell-Douglas MD-90-30	53492/2205	ex N9012S	
☐ HZ-APC	McDonnell-Douglas MD-90-30	53493/2209	ex N9014S	
☐ HZ-APD	McDonnell-Douglas MD-90-30	53494/2213	ex N9010L	
☐ HZ-APE	McDonnell-Douglas MD-90-30	53495/2215	ex N6203D	
☐ HZ-APF	McDonnell-Douglas MD-90-30	53496/2216	ex N9012S	
☐ HZ-APG	McDonnell-Douglas MD-90-30	53497/2219		
☐ HZ-APH	McDonnell-Douglas MD-90-30	53498/2221	ex N6202D	
☐ HZ-API	McDonnell-Douglas MD-90-30	53499/2223		
☐ HZ-APJ	McDonnell-Douglas MD-90-30	53500/2225		
☐ HZ-APK	McDonnell-Douglas MD-90-30	53501/2226		
☐ HZ-APL	McDonnell-Douglas MD-90-30	53502/2227		
☐ HZ-APM	McDonnell-Douglas MD-90-30	53503/2229		
☐ HZ-APN	McDonnell-Douglas MD-90-30	53504/2230		
☐ HZ-APO	McDonnell-Douglas MD-90-30	53505/2231	ex N9012S	
☐ HZ-APP	McDonnell-Douglas MD-90-30	53506/2232		
☐ HZ-APQ	McDonnell-Douglas MD-90-30	53507/2235		
☐ HZ-APR	McDonnell-Douglas MD-90-30	53508/2237		
☐ HZ-APS	McDonnell-Douglas MD-90-30	53509/2250	ex N6203D	
☐ HZ-APT	McDonnell-Douglas MD-90-30	53510/2251	ex N6203U	
☐ HZ-APU	McDonnell-Douglas MD-90-30	53511/2255		
☐ HZ-APV	McDonnell-Douglas MD-90-30	53512/2256		
☐ HZ-APX	McDonnell-Douglas MD-90-30	53514/2260	ex N6200N	
☐ HZ-APY	McDonnell-Douglas MD-90-30	53515/2262	ex N9014S	
☐ HZ-APZ	McDonnell-Douglas MD-90-30	53516/2263	ex N9075H	
☐ HZ-AP3	McDonnell-Douglas MD-90-30	53518/2289	ex N6203D	
☐ HZ-AP4	McDonnell-Douglas MD-90-30	53519/2290	ex N9075H	
☐ HZ-AP7	McDonnell-Douglas MD-90-30	53517/2288	ex HZ-AP2	

☐ HZ-ANA	McDonnell-Douglas MD-11F	48773/609	ex N90187	
☐ HZ-ANB	McDonnell-Douglas MD-11F	48775/616	ex N91566	
☐ HZ-ANC	McDonnell-Douglas MD-11F	48776/617	ex N91078	
☐ HZ-AND	McDonnell-Douglas MD-11F	48777/618	ex N9166N	

☐ HZ-AGG	Boeing 737-268	20883/366		
☐ TC-ETE	Boeing 757-2Q8	30044/954	ex TC-GLA	Lsd fr KKK
☐ TC-ETF	Airbus A321-231	1438	ex N585NK	Lsd fr KKK
☐ TC-ETG	Boeing 757-256	26254/905	ex EC-HDV	Lsd fr KKK
☐ TC-OGS	Boeing 757-256	29307/924	ex EC-HIQ	Lsd fr KKK
☐ TC-OGT	Boeing 757-256	29308/935	ex EC-HIR	Lsd fr KKK

SILVERWING

☐ HZ-AJW	Airbus A319-112	1494	ex N320NP

SNAS AVIATION — *Red Sea (RSE)* — *Riyadh/Bahrain (RUH/BAH)*

☐ HZ-SNA	Boeing 727-264F (FedEx 3)	20896/1051	ex EC-HLP	all-white
☐ HZ-SNB	Boeing 727-223F (FedEx 3)	21084/1199	ex EC-HAH	all-white

☐ HZ-SNC	Boeing 727-230F (FedEx 3)	20905/1091	ex EC-IVF		Lsd fr BCS
☐ HZ-SND	Boeing 727-223F (FedEx 3)	20994/1190	ex EC-IVE	all-white	Lsd fr BCS
☐ HZ-SNE	Boeing 727-230F (FedEx 3)	21619/1407	ex EC-JHC		

H4- SOLOMON ISLANDS

PACIFIC AIR EXPRESS — Solpac (PAQ) — Honiara / Brisbane, QLD (HIR/BNE)

Operates cargo flights using aircraft leased from HeavyLift Cargo as required

SOLOMONS — Solomon (IE/SOL) — Honiara (HIR)

☐ H4-AAI	Britten-Norman BN-2A-9 Islander	355	ex N355BN
☐ H4-HNP	de Havilland DHC-6 Twin Otter 300	491	ex YJ-RV1
☐ H4-SID	de Havilland DHC-6 Twin Otter 300	442	ex VH-XFE

I-ITALY (Italian Republic)

AIR DOLOMITI — Dolomiti (EN/DLA) — Trieste (TRS)

☐ I-ADLL	ATR 42-500	518	ex F-OHFP	La Rondine di Giacomo Puccini
☐ I-ADLP	ATR 42-500	604	ex F-WQKY	Falstaff di Giuseppe Verdi
☐ I-ADLQ	ATR 42-500	606	ex F-WQMA	L'Elisir d'Amore de Gaetano
☐ I-ADLU	ATR 42-500	609	ex F-WQMH	Luisa Miller di Giuseppe Verdi
☐ I-ADLV	ATR 42-500	610	ex F-OHJI	Don Carlos di Giuseppe Verdi Donizzetti
☐ I-ADLZ	ATR 42-500	611	ex F-WQMI	Lucia di Lammermoor di Gaetano
☐ I-ADCA	ATR 72-212A	658	ex D-ANFG	
☐ I-ADCB	ATR 72-212A	660	ex D-ANFH	
☐ I-ADCC	ATR 72-212A	662	ex D-ANFI	
☐ I-	ATR 72-212A	664	ex D-ANFJ	
☐ I-	ATR 72-212A	668	ex D-ANFL	
☐ I-ADLJ	ATR 72-212A	686	ex F-WQMO	Il Trovatore di Giuseppe Verdi
☐ I-ADLK	ATR 72-212A	706	ex F-WWEF	Il Barbiere de Siviglia di Gioacchino Rossini
☐ I-ADLM	ATR 72-212A	543	ex F-WWLB	Tosca de Giacomo Puccini
☐ I-ADLN	ATR 72-212A	557	ex F-WWLV	Turandot di Giacomo Puccini
☐ I-ADLO	ATR 72-212A	585	ex F-WQJH	La Bohème di Giacomo Puccini
☐ I-ADLS	ATR 72-212A	634	ex F-WQMB	Ernani di Giuseppe Verdi
☐ I-ADLT	ATR 72-212A	638	ex F-WQME	Otello di Giuseppe Verdi
☐ I-ADLW	ATR 72-212A	707	ex F-WWEG	La Gazza Ladra di Gioacchino Rossini
				Donizzetti
☐ I-ADJK	Embraer 190-200LR (195LR)	19000245	ex PT-SIQ	
☐ I-ADJL	Embraer 190-200LR (195LR)	19000256	ex PT-STE	
☐ I-ADJM	Embraer 190-200LR (195LR)	19000258	ex PT-STG	
☐ I-ADJN	Embraer 190-200LR (195LR)	19000270	ex PT-TQY	
☐ I-ADJO	Embraer 190-200LR (195LR)	19000280	ex PT-TLU	

AIR EUROPE ITALY — Air Europe (VA/VLE) — Milan-Malpensa (MXP)

Wholly owned subsidiary of Volare Group, parent of Volareweb

AIR ITALY — Air Italy (I9/AEY) — Milan-Malpensa (MXP)

☐ I-AIGG	Boeing 767-304ER	28041/614	ex G-OBYC
☐ I-AIGH	Boeing 767-23BER	23973/208	ex N252MY
☐ I-AIGI	Boeing 767-23BER	23974/214	ex N253MY
☐ I-AIGJ	Boeing 767-304ER	28039/610	ex N769NA
☐ I-AIGL	Boeing 737-33A	23636/1438	ex N636AN
☐ I-AIGM	Boeing 737-33A	24299/1598	ex SE-RCS
☐ I-AIGN	Boeing 737-84P/W	35074/2217	ex N574TC
☐ I-AIGP	Boeing 737-76N/W	37233/2578	ex OM-NGQ

AIR VALLÉE — Air Vallée (DO/RVL) — Aosta (AOT)

☐ I-AIRJ	Dornier 328-300 (328JET)	3186		
☐ I-AIRX	Dornier 328-300 (328JET)	3142	ex D-BDXS	Casino de la Vallée c/s

ALIDAUNIA — Lid (D4/LID) — Foggia (FOG)

☐ I-AGSE	Agusta A.109A II	7354		
☐ I-AGSH	Agusta A.109A II	7384		
☐ I-LIDC	MBB BK-117C-1	7529	ex D-HMB.	
☐ I-LIDD	Agusta A.109E Power	11107		
☐ I-MSTR	Agusta A.109A	7227	ex N4256P	
☐ I-RMDV	Sikorsky S-76A	760235	ex (N721CD)	
☐ I-	Agusta AW139			on order
☐ I-	Agusta AW139			on order

ALITALIA	***Alitalia (AZ/AZA)***	***Rome-Fiumicino (FCO)***

Member of Skyteam

☐ I-BIMA	Airbus A319-112	1722	ex D-AVWP	Isola d'Elba	
☐ I-BIMB	Airbus A319-112	2033	ex D-AVYP	Isola del Giglio	
☐ I-BIMC	Airbus A319-112	2057	ex D-AVYC	Isola di Lipari	
☐ I-BIMD	Airbus A319-112	2074	ex D-AVYM	Isola di Capri	
☐ I-BIME	Airbus A319-112	1740	ex D-AVWW	Isola di Panarea	
☐ I-BIMF	Airbus A319-112	2083	ex D-AVYZ	Isola Tremiti	
☐ I-BIMG	Airbus A319-112	2086	ex D-AVWD	Isola di Pantelleria	
☐ I-BIMH	Airbus A319-112	2101	ex D-AVYY	Isola di Ventotene	
☐ I-BIMI	Airbus A319-112	1745	ex D-AVWZ	Isola di Ponza	
☐ I-BIMJ	Airbus A319-112	1779	ex D-AVYG	Isola di Caprera	
☐ I-BIML	Airbus A319-112	2127	ex D-AVWN	Isola La Maddalena	
☐ I-BIMO	Airbus A319-112	1770	ex D-AVWC	Isola d'Ischia	
☐ EI-DSA	Airbus A320-216	2869	ex F-WWBE		
☐ EI-DSB	Airbus A320-216	2932	ex F-WWBX		
☐ EI-DSC	Airbus A320-216	2995	ex F-WWIY		
☐ EI-DSD	Airbus A320-216	3076	ex F-WWIP		
☐ EI-DSE	Airbus A320-216	3079	ex F-WWIL		
☐ EI-DSF	Airbus A320-216	3080	ex F-WWIV		
☐ EI-DSG	Airbus A320-216	3115	ex F-WWIZ		
☐ EI-DSH	Airbus A320-216	3178	ex F-WWDS		
☐ EI-DSI	Airbus A320-216	3213	ex F-WWIU		
☐ EI-DSJ	Airbus A320-216	3295	ex F-WWDV		
☐ EI-DSK	Airbus A320-216	3328	ex F-WWIX		
☐ EI-DSL	Airbus A320-216	3343	ex F-WWBO		
☐ EI-DSM	Airbus A320-216	3362	ex F-WWIR		
☐ EI-DSN	Airbus A320-216	3412	ex F-WWIL		
☐ EI-DSO	Airbus A320-216	3464	ex F-WWBO		
☐ EI-DSP	Airbus A320-216	3482	ex F-WWDM		
☐ EI-DSR	Airbus A320-216	3502	ex F-WWBR		
☐ EI-DSS	Airbus A320-216	3515	ex F-WWDP		
☐ EI-DST	Airbus A320-216	3532	ex F-WWDY		
☐ EI-DSU	Airbus A320-216	3563	ex F-WWBI		
☐ EI-DSV	Airbus A320-216	3598	ex F-WWDJ		
☐ EI-DSW	Airbus A320-216	3609	ex F-WWIE		
☐ EI-DSX	Airbus A320-216	3643	ex F-WWBT		
☐ EI-DSY	Airbus A320-216	3666	ex F-WWDY		
☐ EI-DSZ	Airbus A320-216	3695	ex F-WWBI		
☐ EI-DTA	Airbus A320-216	3732	ex F-WWDM		
☐ EI-DTB	Airbus A320-216	3815	ex F-WWIF	Giacomo Leopardi	
☐ EI-DTC	Airbus A320-216	3831	ex F-WWBD		
☐ EI-DTD	Airbus A320-216	3846	ex F-WWBY		
☐ EI-DTE	Airbus A320-216	3885	ex F-WWIY	Francesco Petrarca	
☐ EI-DTF	Airbus A320-216	3906	ex F-WWIM	Giovanni Boccaccio	
☐ EI-DTG	Airbus A320-216	3921	ex F-WWBK	Ludovico Ariosto	
☐ EI-DTH	Airbus A320-216	3956	ex F-WWBZ	Torquato Tasso	
☐ EI-DTI	Airbus A320-216	3976	ex F-WWIV	Niccolo Machiavelli	
☐ EI-DTJ	Airbus A320-216	3978	ex F-WWIX	Giovani Pascoli	
☐ EI-DTK	Airbus A320-216	4075	ex F-WWBN	Giovanni Verga	
☐ EI-DTL	Airbus A320-216	4108	ex F-WWDS		
☐ EI-DTM	Airbus A320-216	4119	ex F-WWIE		
☐ EI-DTN	Airbus A320-216	4143	ex F-WWBB		
☐ EI-DTO	Airbus A320-216	4152	ex F-WWBJ		
☐ EI-EIA	Airbus A320-216	4195	ex F-WWIL		on order
☐ EI-EIB	Airbus A320-216	4249	ex		on order
☐ EI-EIC	Airbus A320-216		ex		on order
☐ EI-EID	Airbus A320-216		ex		on order
☐ EI-EIE	Airbus A320-216		ex		on order
☐ EI-EIF	Airbus A320-216		ex		on order
☐ I-BIKA	Airbus A320-214	0951	ex F-WWBT	Johann Sebastian Bach	
☐ I-BIKB	Airbus A320-214	1226	ex F-WWIG	Wolfgang Amadeus Mozart	
☐ I-BIKC	Airbus A320-214	1448	ex F-WWBV	Torre di Pisa	
☐ I-BIKD	Airbus A320-214	1457	ex F-WWDE	Maschio Angioino Napoli	
☐ I-BIKE	Airbus A320-214	0999	ex F-WWBZ	Franz Liszt	
☐ I-BIKF	Airbus A320-214	1473	ex F-WWDP	Mole Antonelliana	
☐ I-BIKG	Airbus A320-214	1480	ex F-WWDT	Scirocco	
☐ I-BIKI	Airbus A320-214	1138	ex F-WWDJ	Girolamo Frescobaldi	
☐ I-BIKL	Airbus A320-214	1489	ex F-WWDN	Libeccio	
☐ I-BIKO	Airbus A320-214	1168	ex F-WWDL	George Bizet	
☐ I-BIKU	Airbus A320-214	1217	ex F-WWBD	Fryderyk Chopin	
☐ I-BIXA	Airbus A321-112	0477	ex D-AVZE	Piazza del Duomo-Milano	
☐ I-BIXB	Airbus A321-112	0524	ex D-AVZY	Piazza Castello-Torino	
☐ I-BIXC	Airbus A321-112	0526	ex D-AVZZ	Piazza del Campo-Siena	
☐ I-BIXD	Airbus A321-112	0532	ex D-AVZB	Piazza Pretoria-Palermo	
☐ I-BIXE	Airbus A321-112	0488	ex D-AVZG	Piazza di Spagna-Roma	
☐ I-BIXF	Airbus A321-112	0515	ex D-AVZQ	Piazza Maggiore-Bologna	
☐ I-BIXG	Airbus A321-112	0516	ex D-AVZR	Piazza del Miracoli-Pisa	

	Reg	Type	c/n	Previous identity	Name	Notes
☐	I-BIXH	Airbus A321-112	0940	ex D-AVZS	Piazza della Signoria-Gubbio	
☐	I-BIXI	Airbus A321-112	0494	ex D-AVZI	Piazza San Marco-Venezia	
☐	I-BIXJ	Airbus A321-112	0959	ex D-AVZP	Piazza del Municipio-Noto	
☐	I-BIXK	Airbus A321-112	1220	ex D-AVZC	Piazza Ducale Vigevano	
☐	I-BIXL	Airbus A321-112	0513	ex D-AVZO	Piazza del Duomo-Lecce	
☐	I-BIXM	Airbus A321-112	0514	ex D-AVZP	Piazza di San Francesco-Assisi	
☐	I-BIXN	Airbus A321-112	0576	ex D-AVZR	Piazza del Duomo-Catania	
☐	I-BIXO	Airbus A321-112	0495	ex D-AVZJ	Piazza Plebiscito-Napoli	
☐	I-BIXP	Airbus A321-112	0583	ex D-AVZT	Carlo Morelli	
☐	I-BIXQ	Airbus A321-112	0586	ex D-AVZU	Domenico Colapietro	
☐	I-BIXR	Airbus A321-112	0593	ex D-AVZW	Piazza del Campidoglio-Roma	
☐	I-BIXS	Airbus A321-112	0599	ex D-AVZZ	Piazza San Martino-Lucca	
☐	I-BIXT	Airbus A321-112	0765	ex D-AVZW	Piazza del Signori-Vicenza	
☐	I-BIXU	Airbus A321-112	0434	ex D-AVZB	Piazza della Signoria-Firenze	
☐	I-BIXV	Airbus A321-112	0819	ex D-AVZU	Piazza del Rinascimento-Urbino	
☐	I-BIXZ	Airbus A321-112	0848	ex D-AVZO	Piazza del Duomo Orvieto	
☐	EI-DIR	Airbus A330-202	272	ex A6-EYV		
☐	EI-DIP	Airbus A330-202	339	ex A6-EYW		
☐		Airbus A330-202	1123	ex		on order
☐		Airbus A330-202	1135	ex		on order
☐	D-AGMR	Boeing 737-430	27007/2367	ex TC-SUS		
☐	EI-COH	Boeing 737-430	27001/2316	ex D-ABKB		
☐	EI-COI	Boeing 737-430	27002/2323	ex D-ABKC		
☐	EI-COJ	Boeing 737-430	27005/2359	ex D-ABKK		
☐	EI-COK	Boeing 737-430	27003/2328	ex F-GRNZ		
☐	EI-CWE	Boeing 737-42C	24232/2060	ex N941PG		
☐	EI-CWF	Boeing 737-42C	24814/2270	ex PH-BPG		
☐	EI-CWW	Boeing 737-4Y0	24906/2009	ex EC-GAZ		
☐	EI-CWX	Boeing 737-4Y0	24912/2064	ex EC-GBN		
☐	EI-DMR	Boeing 737-436	25851/2387	ex G-DOCR		
☐	EI-DOH	Boeing 737-31S	29056/2928	ex VT-SAX		
☐	EI-DOS	Boeing 737-49R	28881/2833	ex PK-GWZ		
☐	EI-DOV	Boeing 737-48E	27632/2857	ex HL7512		
☐	EI-DXC	Boeing 737-4Q8	26300/2604	ex TC-JKA		
☐	EI-DXG	Boeing 737-4Q8	25376/2689	ex TC-JEN		
☐	F-GKTA	Boeing 737-3M8	24413/1884	ex (OO-LTH)		
☐	F-GKTB	Boeing 737-3M8	24414/1895	ex (OO-LTI)		
☐	I-JETA	Boeing 737-229 (Nordam 3)	21839/593	ex OO-SBS		
☐	I-JETD	Boeing 737-230 (Nordam 3)	23158/1089	ex D-ABMF		stored FCO
☐	SE-DJZ	Avro 146-RJ70	E1225	ex G-CDOF		Lsd fr TWE
☐	SP-KCA	ATR 42-300	085	ex F-WQNY	Freighter	Lsd fr WEA
☐	EI-CRD	Boeing 767-31BER	26259/534	ex B-2565		
☐	EI-CRF	Boeing 767-31BER	25170/542	ex B-2566		
☐	EI-CRM	Boeing 767-343ER	30009/746	ex (I-DEIB)	Amerigo Vespucci	
☐	EI-DBP	Boeing 767-35HER	26389/459	ex C-GGBJ	Duca degli Abruzzi	
☐	EI-DDW	Boeing 767-3S1ER	26608/559	ex N979PG	Sebastiano Caboto	
☐	I-DEIG	Boeing 767-33AER	27918/603	ex G-OITG	Francesco Agello	
☐	EI-DBK	Boeing 777-243ER	32783/455		Ostuni	
☐	EI-DBL	Boeing 777-243ER	32781/459		Sestriere	
☐	EI-DBM	Boeing 777-243ER	32782/463		Argentario	
☐	EI-DDH	Boeing 777-243ER	32784/477		Tropea	
☐	I-DISA	Boeing 777-243ER	32855/413		Taormina	
☐	I-DISB	Boeing 777-243ER	32859/426		Porto Rotondo	
☐	I-DISD	Boeing 777-243ER	32860/439		Cortina d'Ampezzo	
☐	I-DISE	Boeing 777-243ER	32856/421		Portofino	
☐	I-DISO	Boeing 777-243ER	32857/424	ex N5014K	Positano	
☐	I-DISU	Boeing 777-243ER	32858/425		Madonna de Campiglio	
☐	I-DACP	McDonnell-Douglas MD-82	49973/1762		Padova	stored FCO
☐	I-DACQ	McDonnell-Douglas MD-82	49974/1774		Taranto	stored FCO
☐	I-DACR	McDonnell-Douglas MD-82	49975/1775		Carrara	
☐	I-DACS	McDonnell-Douglas MD-82	53053/1806		Maratea	
☐	I-DACT	McDonnell-Douglas MD-82	53054/1856		Valtellina	
☐	I-DACU	McDonnell-Douglas MD-82	53055/1857		Brindisi	
☐	I-DACV	McDonnell-Douglas MD-82	53056/1880		Riccione	
☐	I-DACW	McDonnell-Douglas MD-82	53057/1894		Vieste	stored FCO
☐	I-DACX	McDonnell-Douglas MD-82	53060/1944		Piacenza	stored FCO
☐	I-DACY	McDonnell-Douglas MD-82	53059/1942		Novara	stored FCO
☐	I-DACZ	McDonnell-Douglas MD-82	53058/1927		Castelfidardo	
☐	I-DAND	McDonnell-Douglas MD-82	53061/1957		Trani	
☐	I-DANF	McDonnell-Douglas MD-82	53062/1960		Sassari	
☐	I-DANG	McDonnell-Douglas MD-82	53176/1972		Benevento	
☐	I-DANH	McDonnell-Douglas MD-82	53177/1973		Messina	
☐	I-DANL	McDonnell-Douglas MD-82	53178/1994		Cosenza	stored FCO
☐	I-DANM	McDonnell-Douglas MD-82	53179/1997		Vicenza	stored FCO
☐	I-DANP	McDonnell-Douglas MD-82	53180/2002		Fabriano	stored FCO
☐	I-DANQ	McDonnell-Douglas MD-82	53181/2005		Lecce	
☐	I-DANR	McDonnell-Douglas MD-82	53203/2007		Matera	stored FCO
☐	I-DANU	McDonnell-Douglas MD-82	53204/2009		Trapani	

☐ I-DANV	McDonnell-Douglas MD-82	53205/2028		Forte dei Marmi	stored FCO
☐ I-DANW	McDonnell-Douglas MD-82	53206/2034		Siena	
☐ I-DATA	McDonnell-Douglas MD-82	53216/2048		Gubbio	stored FCO
☐ I-DATB	McDonnell-Douglas MD-82	53221/2079		Bergamo	stored FCO
☐ I-DATC	McDonnell-Douglas MD-82	53222/2080		Foggia	
☐ I-DATD	McDonnell-Douglas MD-82	53223/2081		Savona	stored FCO
☐ I-DATE	McDonnell-Douglas MD-82	53217/2053		Grosseto	
☐ I-DATF	McDonnell-Douglas MD-82	53224/2084		Vittorio Veneto	stored FCO
☐ I-DATG	McDonnell-Douglas MD-82	53225/2086		Arezzo	
☐ I-DATH	McDonnell-Douglas MD-82	53226/2087		Pescara	stored FCO
☐ I-DATI	McDonnell-Douglas MD-82	53218/2060		Siracusa	
☐ I-DATJ	McDonnell-Douglas MD-82	53227/2103		Lunigiana	stored FCO
☐ I-DATK	McDonnell-Douglas MD-82	53228/2104		Ravenna	stored FCO
☐ I-DATL	McDonnell-Douglas MD-82	53229/2105		Alghero	
☐ I-DATM	McDonnell-Douglas MD-82	53230/2106		Cividale del Friuli	
☐ I-DATO	McDonnell-Douglas MD-82	53219/2062		Reggio Emilia	stored FCO
☐ I-DATQ	McDonnell-Douglas MD-82	53233/2110		Modena	
☐ I-DATR	McDonnell-Douglas MD-82	53234/2111		Livorno	stored FCO
☐ I-DATS	McDonnell-Douglas MD-82	53235/2113	ex N9021J	Foligno	stored FCO
☐ I-DATU	McDonnell-Douglas MD-82	53220/2073		Verona	
☐ I-DAVB	McDonnell-Douglas MD-82	49216/1262		Ferrara	
☐ I-DAVJ	McDonnell-Douglas MD-82	49431/1377		Parma	
☐ I-DAVR	McDonnell-Douglas MD-82	49550/1584		Pisa	stored FCO
☐ I-DAVT	McDonnell-Douglas MD-82	49552/1597		Como	
☐ I-DAVV	McDonnell-Douglas MD-82	49795/1639		Pavia	stored FCO

ALITALIA EXPRESS — *Ali Express (XM/SMX)* — *Rome-Fiumicino (FCO)*

☐ EI-DOT	Canadair CL-600-2D24 (CRJ-900ER)	15066	ex C-		
☐ EI-DOU	Canadair CL-600-2D24 (CRJ-900ER)	15068	ex C-		
☐ EI-DRI	Canadair CL-600-2D24 (CRJ-900ER)	15076	ex C-		
☐ EI-DRJ	Canadair CL-600-2D24 (CRJ-900ER)	15077	ex C-		
☐ EI-DRK	Canadair CL-600-2D24 (CRJ-900ER)	15075	ex C-		
☐ EI-DUK	Canadair CL-600-2D24 (CRJ-900ER)	15104	ex C-		
☐ EI-DVP	Canadair CL-600-2D24 (CRJ-900ER)	15116	ex C-		
☐ EI-DVR	Canadair CL-600-2D24 (CRJ-900ER)	15118	ex C-		
☐ EI-DVS	Canadair CL-600-2D24 (CRJ-900ER)	15119	ex C-		
☐ EI-DVT	Canadair CL-600-2D24 (CRJ-900ER)	15123	ex C-		
☐ EI-DFG	Embraer 170-100LR (170)	17000008	ex PT-SKA	Via Appia	
☐ EI-DFH	Embraer 170-100LR (170)	17000009	ex PT-SKB	Via Aurélia	
☐ EI-DFI	Embraer 170-100LR (170)	17000010	ex PT-SKC	Via Cassia	
☐ EI-DFJ	Embraer 170-100LR (170)	17000011	ex PT-SKD	Via Flaminia	
☐ EI-DFK	Embraer 170-100LR (170)	17000032	ex PT-SUA	Via Salaria	
☐ EI-DFL	Embraer 170-100LR (170)	17000036	ex PT-SUF	Via Tiburtina Valeria	

AQUA AIRLINES — *Como*

☐ I-SEAB	Cessna 208 Caravan I	20800225	ex N225WA		Floatplane

BLU EXPRESS.COM — *(BV/BPA)* — *Rome-Fiumicino (FCO)*

☐ EI-CUA	Boeing 737-4K5	24901/1854	ex D-AHLR		Lsd fr BPA
☐ EI-CUD	Boeing 737-4Q8	26298/2564	ex TC-JEI		Lsd fr BPA
☐ EI-CUN	Boeing 737-4K5	27074/2281	ex D-AHLS		Lsd fr BPA
☐ EI-DVY	Boeing 737-31S	29059/2967	ex LZ-BOM	Citta di Palermo	Lsd fr BPA
☐ EI-DXB	Boeing 737-31S	29060/2979	ex LZ-BON	Citta di Roma	Lsd fr BPA
☐ EI-EEW	Boeing 737-375	23808/1434	ex N238PL		
☐ I-LLAG	Boeing 767-330ER	25137/377	ex N691LF		

BLUE PANORAMA AIRLINES — *Blue Panorama (BV/BPA)* — *Rome-Fiumicino (FCO)*

☐ EI-CUA	Boeing 737-4K5	24901/1854	ex D-AHLR		
☐ EI-CUD	Boeing 737-4Q8	26298/2564	ex TC-JEI		
☐ EI-CUN	Boeing 737-4K5	27074/2281	ex D-AHLS		
☐ EI-DVY	Boeing 737-31S	29059/2967	ex LZ-BOM	Citta di Palermo	
☐ EI-DXB	Boeing 737-31S	29060/2979	ex LZ-BON	Citta di Roma	
☐ EI-DKL	Boeing 757-231	28482/770	ex N714P		
☐ EI-DNA	Boeing 757-231	28483/777	ex N715TW		
☐ EI-CXO	Boeing 767-3G5ER	28111/612	ex (I-BPAB)		
☐ EI-CZH	Boeing 767-3G5ER	29435/720	ex (I-BPAD)		
☐ EI-EED	Boeing 767-31AER	27619/595	ex N281LF		

CARGOITALIA — *White Pelican (2G/CRG)* — *Milan-Malpensa (MXP)*

☐ EI-UPI	McDonnell-Douglas MD-11C	48428/474	ex I-DUPI		
☐ I-CGIA	Douglas DC-10-30F	47843/335	ex N331FV	Amarone della Valpolicella	stored FNI

CARGOLUX ITALIA	***(C8 / ICV)***	***Milan-Malpensa (MXP)***

☐ LX-KCV	Boeing 747-4R7F	25868/1125		Dudelange	

CITYFLY	***City Fly (CII)***	***Rome-Urbe (ROM)***

☐ I-DEPE	Britten-Norman BN-2B-26 Islander	2253	ex G-BTLY		
☐ I-LACO	Britten-Norman BN-2A-6 Islander	17	ex G-AWBY		

CORPO FORESTALE DELLO STATO		***Rome-Ciampino (CIA)***

☐ I-CFAA	Agusta-Bell 412SP	25610		CFS-20	
☐ I-CFAB	Agusta-Bell 412SP	25614		CFS-21	
☐ I-CFAC	Agusta-Bell 412SP	25615		CFS-22	
☐ I-CFAD	Agusta-Bell 412SP	25618		CFS-23	
☐ I-CFAE	Agusta-Bell 412EP	25918		CFS-24	
☐ I-CFAF	Agusta-Bell 412EP	25919		CFS-25	
☐ I-CFAK	Agusta-Bell 412EP	25926		CFS-26	
☐ I-CFAL	Agusta-Bell 412EP	25978		CFS-27	
☐ I-CFSJ	Agusta-Bell 412	25561		CFS-14	
☐ I-CFSO	Agusta-Bell 412	25562		CFS-15	
☐ I-CFSP	Agusta-Bell 412	25563		CFS-16	
☐ I-CFSW	Agusta-Bell 412	25564		CFS-18	
☐ I-CFSX	Agusta-Bell 412	25572		CFS-19	
☐ I-CFAG	Erickson/Sikorsky S-64E Skycrane	64088	ex N213AC	CFS-100	Op by European Air-Crane
☐ I-CFAH	Erickson/Sikorsky S-64E Skycrane	64080	ex N174AC	CFS-101	Op by European Air-Crane
☐ I-CFAI	Erickson/Sikorsky S-64E Skycrane	64067	ex N197AC	CFS-102	Op by European Air-Crane
☐ I-CFAJ	Erickson/Sikorsky S-64E Skycrane	64078	ex N227AC	CFS-103	Op by European Air-Crane

ELBAFLY		***Elba-Island de Campo (EBA)***

☐ S5-BAF	LET L-410UVP-E8C	912540	ex OM-WDA	FedEx colours	Lsd fr/op by SOP

ELIDOLOMITI	***Elidolomiti (EDO)***	***Belluno (BLX)***

☐ EC-JKP	Agusta A.109E Power	11637			EMS Lsd fr HSE
☐ I-AGKL	Agusta A.109K2	10020			EMS
☐ I-REMJ	Agusta A.109S Grand	22041			EMS
☐ I-REMR	Agusta A.109E Power	11133			EMS
☐ I-REMV	Agusta A.109E Power	11119			EMS

ELIFRIULA	***Elifriula (EFG)***	***Trieste (TRS)***

☐ I-HBLU	Aérospatiale AS350B3 Ecureuil	3940	ex F-WWPE		
☐ I-HOLD	Aérospatiale AS350B3 Ecureuil	3566			
☐ I-HORT	Aérospatiale AS350B Ecureuil	3699			
☐ I-HPLC	Aérospatiale AS350B Ecureuil	3702			
☐ I-HALP	Eurocopter EC135T2	0469	ex D-HDOL		
☐ I-HIFI	Eurocopter EC135T1	0085			EMS
☐ I-HSAR	Agusta A.109E Power	11125			EMS
☐ I-ORAO	Aérospatiale AS355N Ecureuil 2	5583			

ELILARIO ITALIA	***Lario (ELH)***	***Colico/Bergamo-Orio al Serio(-/BGY)***

☐ I-EITB	Agusta-Bell 412SP	25972			
☐ I-MAGM	Agusta-Bell 412SP	25602	ex Fv11338		
☐ I-NUBJ	Agusta-Bell 412EP	25913			
☐ I-RMTI	Agusta-Bell 412EP	25923			
☐ I-RNBR	Agusta-Bell 412EP	25921			
☐ I-EITC	Agusta A.109S Grand	22007			
☐ I-ESUE	Agusta A.109E Power	11124			
☐ I-FLAK	Agusta A.109E Power	11076			
☐ I-GEMI	Agusta A.109E Power	11085			
☐ I-NIGI	Agusta A.109E Power	11619			
☐ I-RCPM	Agusta A.109E Power Elite	11172			
☐ I-AICO	MBB BK-117C-1	7542	ex D-HZBV		
☐ I-AVJF	MBB BK-117C-1	7525	ex D-HMBI		
☐ I-DENI	MBB BK-117C-1	7539			
☐ I-EITF	MBB BK-117C-1	9082	ex D-HMBI		
☐ I-EITG	MBB BK-117C-1	9086	ex D-HMBN		
☐ I-EITH	MBB BK-117C-1	9093	ex D-HMBB		
☐ I-HBHG	MBB BK-117B-2	7164	ex D-HBHG		
☐ I-HECD	MBB BK-117C-1	7500	ex D-HECD		EMS
☐ I-HVEN	MBB BK-117C-1	7526	ex D-HVEN		EMS
☐ I-MESO	MBB BK-117C-1	7532	ex D-HMB.		
☐ I-DAMS	Aérospatiale AS365N3 Dauphin 2	6700	ex F-WWQX		
☐ I-EITD	Agusta AW139	31054	ex I-RAIC		

☐ I-HMED	Aérospatiale EC.135T1	0082	ex D-HBYI	EMS
☐ I-LOBE	Aérospatiale AS365N3 Dauphin 2	6699	ex F-WWQX	
☐ I-ROCS	Agusta AW139	31005		EMS
☐ I-VRVR	Aérospatiale AS355F1 Ecureuil 2	5180		
☐ I-	Agusta AW139			on order

ELILOMBARDA (EQA) Calcinate del Pesce

☐ I-CEPA	Agusta AW139	31050		
☐ I-CESR	Agusta A.109S Grand	22033		
☐ I-HELO	Agusta A.109E Power	11605		
☐ I-MALF	Agusta-Bell 412EP	25975		EMS
☐ I-MECE	Agusta-Bell 412EP	25976		EMS
☐ I-PAXE	Agusta A.109E Power	11127		

EUROFLY Siriofly (GJ/EEZ) Milan-Malpensa (MXP)

☐ I-EEZE	Airbus A320-214	1937	ex F-WWIO	
☐ I-EEZF	Airbus A320-214	1983	ex F-WWDM	
☐ I-EEZG	Airbus A320-214	2001	ex F-WWBB	Domina titles
☐ I-EEZH	Airbus A320-214	0737	ex F-GRSG	
☐ I-EEZI	Airbus A320-214	0749	ex F-GRSH	
☐ I-EEZK	Airbus A320-214	1125	ex I-VLEA	
☐ I-EEZN	Airbus A320-232	1715	ex G-TTOC	
☐ I-EEZO	Airbus A320-232	1723	ex G-TTOD	
☐ I-EEZP	Airbus A320-233	2102	ex N489TA	
☐ EI-EZL	Airbus A330-223	802	ex I-EEZL	
☐ I-EEZJ	Airbus A330-223	665	ex F-WWKO	Campari titles
☐ I-EEZM	Airbus A330-223	822	ex 4X-ABE	

EUROPEAN AIR CRANE Florence (FLR)

European Air Crane is a subsidiary of Erikson Air Craneoperates Erickson/Sikorsky S-64E Skycranes for CFDS

HELI-ITALIA Helitalia (HIT) Florence (FLR)

☐ I-HBHA	Agusta A.109K2	10023	ex I-ECAM	EMS
☐ I-HBHB	Agusta A.109K2	10025	ex N109TA	EMS
☐ I-HDPR	Agusta A.109E	11625		EMS
☐ I-MAFP	Agusta A.109E Power	11121		EMS
☐ I-RRMM	Agusta A.109E Power	11667		EMS
☐ D-HDNO	MBB BK-117C-1	7548		EMS
☐ D-HDSR	MBB BK-117C-1	7545		EMS
☐ I-HBHC	MBB BK-117B-1	7251	ex D-HITZ	EMS
☐ I-HBMC	MBB BK-117C-1	7528	ex D-HBMC	EMS
☐ I-HBMS	MBB BK-117C-1	7531	ex D-HMBB	EMS
☐ I-HDBX	MBB BK-117C-1	7546	ex D-HDBX	EMS
☐ I-HDBZ	MBB BK-117C-1	7547	ex D-HDBZ	EMS
☐ I-HKAV	MBB BK-117C-1	7540	ex D-HKAV	EMS

ITALI AIRLINES Itali (9X/ACL) Pescara (PSR)

☐ I-ACLG	Dornier 328-310 (328JET)	3133	ex D-BGAG	
☐ I-ACLH	Dornier 328-310 (328JET)	3152	ex D-BGAR	
☐ I-BSTI	Swearingen SA.227AC Metro III	AC-470	ex N581BT	
☐ I-BSTS	Swearingen SA.227AC Metro III	AC-603	ex N3117S	
☐ I-DAVA	McDonnell-Douglas MD-82	49215/1253		
☐ I-DAWW	McDonnell-Douglas MD-82	49212/1233		
☐ I-DAWZ	McDonnell-Douglas MD-82	49214/1245		
☐ I-	ATR 72-		ex	on order

ITALIATOUR AIRLINES

☐ I-CLBA	Avro 146-RJ85	E2300	ex EI-CNJ	stored BSL

LIVINGSTON Livingston (LM/LVG) Milan-Malpensa (MXP)

☐ EI-LVA	Airbus A321-231	1950	ex I-LIVA	Capt Aldo Giannelli
☐ EI-LVB	Airbus A321-231	1970	ex I-LIVB	Jacaranda
☐ EI-LVD	Airbus A321-231	0792	ex I-LIVD	Boavista
☐ I-LIVL	Airbus A330-243	627	ex F-WWYE	Andilana
☐ I-LIVM	Airbus A330-243	551	ex F-WWKE	Playa Maroma
☐ I-LIVN	Airbus A330-243	597	ex F-WWKQ	Gran Dominicus

LUFTHANSA ITALIA

☐ D-AILI	Airbus A319-114	0651	ex D-AVYY	Roma
☐ D-AKNF	Airbus A319-112	0646	ex D-AVYB	Torino
☐ D-AKNG	Airbus A319-112	0654	ex D-AVYX	Varese

☐ D-AKNH	Airbus A319-112	0794	ex D-AVYD	Bologna	
☐ D-AKNI	Airbus A319-112	1016	ex D-AVYK	Genova	
☐ D-AKNJ	Airbus A319-112	1172	ex D-AVWF		

MERIDIANA		***Merair (IG/ISS)***			***Olbia (OLB)***
☐ EI-CIW	McDonnell-Douglas MD-83	49785/1628	ex HL7271	Isola Tremiti	
☐ EI-CKM	McDonnell-Douglas MD-83	49792/1655	ex TC-INC	Isola dell'Asinara	
☐ EI-CNR	McDonnell-Douglas MD-83	53199/1968	ex N531LS		
☐ EI-CRE	McDonnell-Douglas MD-83	49854/1601	ex D-ALLL	Tavolara-Punta Coda Cavallo	
☐ EI-CRH	McDonnell-Douglas MD-83	49935/1773	ex HB-IKM	Torre Guaceto	
☐ EI-CRW	McDonnell-Douglas MD-83	49951/1915	ex HB-IKN	Portofino	
☐ I-SMEB	McDonnell-Douglas MD-82	53064/1908	ex B-28001	Parco di Baia	
☐ I-SMEC	McDonnell-Douglas MD-83	49808/1836	ex N183NA	Porto Cesareo	
☐ I-SMED	McDonnell-Douglas MD-83	53182/2068	ex N875RA	Isole Ciclopi	
☐ I-SMEL	McDonnell-Douglas MD-82	49247/1151	ex HB-IKK	Parco Gaiola	
☐ I-SMEM	McDonnell-Douglas MD-82	49248/1152	ex HB-IKL	Penisola del sinis	
☐ I-SMEN	McDonnell-Douglas MD-83	53013/1738	ex EI-CRJ	Isole Egadi	
☐ I-SMEP	McDonnell-Douglas MD-82	49740/1618		Punta Campanella	
☐ I-SMER	McDonnell-Douglas MD-82	49901/1766	ex N6202S	Cinque Terre	
☐ I-SMES	McDonnell-Douglas MD-82	49902/1948		Isole Pelagie	
☐ I-SMET	McDonnell-Douglas MD-82	49531/1362		Miramere nel Golfo di Trieste	
☐ I-SMEV	McDonnell-Douglas MD-82	49669/1493		Isole di Ventotene e Santo Stefano	
☐ I-SMEZ	McDonnell-Douglas MD-82	49903/1949	ex PH-SEZ	Secche di Tor Patemo	
☐ EI-DEY	Airbus A319-112	1102	ex D-ANDA	Capo Rizzuto	
☐ EI-DEZ	Airbus A319-112	1283	ex F-WQQE	Capo Gallo	
☐ EI-DFA	Airbus A319-112	1305	ex D-ANDI	Capo Carbonara	
☐ EI-DFP	Airbus A319-112	1048	ex F-OHJV	Capo Caccia	

MINILINER		***Miniliner (MNL)***			***Bergamo-Orio al Serio (BGY)***
☐ I-MLGT	Fokker F.27 Friendship 500	10379	ex F-BPUG		
☐ I-MLHT	Fokker F.27 Friendship 500	10382	ex F-BPUH		
☐ I-MLQT	Fokker F.27 Friendship 400	10295	ex HB-ITQ		
☐ I-MLRT	Fokker F.27 Friendship 500	10377	ex F-BPUE		
☐ I-MLTT	Fokker F.27 Friendship 500	10378	ex F-BPUF		
☐ I-MLUT	Fokker F.27 Friendship 500	10369	ex F-BPUA		
☐ I-MLVT	Fokker F.27 Friendship 500	10373	ex F-BPUC		
☐ I-MLXT	Fokker F.27 Friendship 500	10374	ex F-BPUD		
☐ I-MLCT	Fokker F.27 Mk.050 (Fokker 50)	20191	ex PH-KVC	Freighter	
☐ I-MLDT	Fokker F.27 Mk.050 (Fokker 50)	20197	ex PH-KVD	Freighter	
☐ PH-LMA	Fokker F.27 Mk.050 (Fokker 50)	20118	ex (PH-LCA)	Freighter	Lsd to APF
☐ PH-LMB	Fokker F.27 Mk.050 (Fokker 50)	20119	ex (PH-LCD)	Freighter	Lsd to APF

MISTRAL AIR		***Airmerci (MSA)***			***Rome-Ciampino (CIA)***
☐ EI-DUS	Boeing 737-3M8 (QC)	24021/1630	ex TF-ELM	Maestrale	
☐ EI-DVA	Boeing 737-36E (QC)	25159/2068	ex F-GIXM		
☐ EI-DVC	Boeing 737-33A (QC)	25426/2172	ex SE-DPC	Libeccio	
☐ EI-SLA	ATR 42-300F	149	ex SE-LST		Lsd fr ABR
☐ EI-SLC	ATR 42-300F	082	ex OY-CIE		Lsd fr ABR

MYAIR		***(8I/MYW)***			***Bergamo-Orio al Serio (BGY)***
☐ EI-DJH	Airbus A320-212	0814	ex I-PEKW		
☐ EI-DOD	Airbus A320-231	0444	ex G-FHAJ		
☐ EI-DUM	Canadair CL-600-2D24 (CRJ-900)	15103	ex C-		
☐ EI-DUU	Canadair CL-600-2D24 (CRJ-900)	15102	ex C-		
☐ EI-DUX	Canadair CL-600-2D24 (CRJ-900)	15110	ex C-		
☐ EI-DUY	Canadair CL-600-2D24 (CRJ-900)	15112	ex C-		

NEOS		***Moonflower (NO/NOS)***			***Milan-Malpensa (MXP)***
☐ EI-DMJ	Boeing 767-306ER/W	27958/589	ex PH-BZB	Ciudad de la Habana	
☐ EI-DOF	Boeing 767-306ER	27610/605	ex PH-BZD		
☐ I-NEOS	Boeing 737-86N/W	32733/1078		Citta di Milano	
☐ I-NEOT	Boeing 737-86N/W	33004/1144		Citta di Torino	
☐ I-NEOU	Boeing 737-86N/W	29887/1263		Citta di Verona	
☐ I-NEOW	Boeing 737-86N/W	32685/2186	ex G-XLAN	Lago Maggiore	
☐ I-NEOX	Boeing 737-86N/W	33677/1486		Citta di Bologna	

SKYBRIDGE AIROPS					***Rome-Ciampano (CIA)***
☐ I-SKYB	Embraer EMB.120RT Brasilia	120087	ex F-GTSG		

SOREM			Rome-Ciampano/Urbe (CIA/ROM)	
☐ I-CFST	Canadair CL-215-1A10 (CL-215)	1072	ex MM62019	1
☐ I-SRMA	Canadair CL-215-1A10 (CL-215)	1004	ex I-SMRA	A1
☐ I-SRMC	Canadair CL-215-1A10 (CL-215)	1076	ex C-GBXQ	S2
☐ I-SRMD	Canadair CL-215-1A10 (CL-215)	1097	ex C-GOFN	S3
☐ I-SRME	Canadair CL-215-1A10 (CL-215)	1049	ex C-GUKM	S4
☐ I-DPCC	Canadair CL-215-6B11 (CL-415)	2066	ex C-FNLH	27
☐ I-DPCD	Canadair CL-215-6B11 (CL-415)	2003	ex C-FTUA	7
☐ I-DPCE	Canadair CL-215-6B11 (CL-415)	2004	ex C-FTUS	8
☐ I-DPCF	Canadair CL-215-6B11 (CL-415)	2059	ex C-GIWU	23
☐ I-DPCG	Canadair CL-215-6B11 (CL-415)	2060	ex C-GJHU	24
☐ I-DPCH	Canadair CL-215-6B11 (CL-415)	2062	ex C-GJLB	25
☐ I-DPCI	Canadair CL-215-6B11 (CL-415)	2058	ex C-GISM	26
☐ I-DPCN	Canadair CL-215-6B11 (CL-415)	2070	ex C-FUEP	28
☐ I-DPCO	Canadair CL-215-6B11 (CL-415)	2009	ex C-FVRA	10
☐ I-DPCP	Canadair CL-215-6B11 (CL-415)	2020	ex C-FYCY	11
☐ I-DPCQ	Canadair CL-215-6B11 (CL-415)	2021	ex C-FYDA	12
☐ I-DPCT	Canadair CL-215-6B11 (CL-415)	2029	ex C-FZYS	18
☐ I-DPCU	Canadair CL-215-6B11 (CL-415)	2030	ex C-GALV	14
☐ I-DPCV	Canadair CL-215-6B11 (CL-415)	2035	ex C-GCXG	15
☐ I-DPCW	Canadair CL-215-6B11 (CL-415)	2036	ex C-GDHW	6
☐ I-DPCY	Canadair CL-215-6B11 (CL-415)	2047	ex C-GFUS	20
☐ I-DPCZ	Canadair CL-215-6B11 (CL-415)	2048	ex C-GGCW	21
☐ I-DP	Canadair CL-215-6B11 (CL-415)	2073	ex C-FZEG	
☐ I-DP	Canadair CL-215-6B11 (CL-415)	2074	ex C-FZTY	

VOLAREWEB		Revola (VE/VLE)		Milan-Linate (LIN)
☐ I-WEBA	Airbus A320-214	3138	ex F-WWDI	
☐ I-WEBB	Airbus A320-214	3161	ex F-WWIC	Lsd

VOLIAMO			
☐ HA-LEW	Boeing 737-2K2C (AvAero 3)	20836/354	ex F-GIXA

WINDJET		Ghibli (IV/JET)	Catania (CTA)
☐ EI-DVD	Airbus A319-113	0647	ex F-GPMH
☐ EI-DVU	Airbus A319-113	0660	ex F-GPMI
☐ EI-ECX	Airbus A319-132	2698	ex N515NK
☐ EI-ECY	Airbus A319-132	2723	ex N519NK
☐ EI-EDM	Airbus A319-132	2424	ex N501NK
☐ EI-CUM	Airbus A320-232	0542	ex N721LF
☐ EI-DFO	Airbus A320-211	0371	ex A6-ABX
☐ EI-DNP	Airbus A320-212	0421	ex A4O-EF
☐ EI-DOE	Airbus A320-211	0215	ex F-GJVE
☐ EI-DOP	Airbus A320-232	0816	ex B-HSF
☐ EI-ELG	Airbus A320-232	0877	ex B-HSH
☐ F-GJVC	Airbus A320-211	0204	ex EI-DEN
☐ I-LINH	Airbus A320-231	0163	ex G-RDVE

JA JAPAN

AIR CENTRAL		(NV/CRF)		Nagoya-Chubu (NGO)
☐ JA841A	de Havilland DHC-8-402Q	4080	ex C-GDLK	
☐ JA853A	de Havilland DHC-8-402Q	4135	ex C-FGKN	Lsd to AKX
☐ JA854A	de Havilland DHC-8-402Q	4151	ex C-FJLH	Lsd to AKX

AIR DO		Air Do (HD/ADO)		Sapporo-New Chitose (CTS)
☐ JA01HD	Boeing 767-33AER	28159/689	ex OO-CTQ	
☐ JA98AD	Boeing 767-33AER	27476/687	ex N767AN	
☐ JA300K	Boeing 737-54K	27434/2872		Lsd fr ANA
☐ JA392K	Boeing 737-46M	28550/2847	ex N8550F	Lsd fr ANA
☐ JA8258	Boeing 767-381	23758/179	ex N6055X	Lsd fr ANA
☐ JA8404	Boeing 737-54K	27381/2708	ex N35108	Lsd fr ANA
☐ JA8595	Boeing 737-54K	28461/2850		

AIR DOLPHIN			Okinawa-Naha (OKA)
☐ JA21EG	Beech 65-C90A King Air	LJ-1591	ex N400TG
☐ JA3428	Cessna P206C Super Skylane	P206-0517	ex N1610C
☐ JA5320	Britten-Norman BN-2B-20 Islander	2269	ex G-BUBM

AIR JAPAN	*Air Japan (NQ/AJX)*	*Osaka-Itami/Kansi (ITM/KIX)*

Registration	Type	C/n	Previous identity	Notes	Lease
☐ JA55DZ	Cessna 208B Caravan I	208B0530	ex N164SA		

AIR NEXT	*Blue Dolphin (7A/NXA)*	*Fukuoka (FUK)*

Registration	Type	C/n	Previous identity	Notes	Lease
☐ JA302K	Boeing 737-54K	28990/3002	ex N1787B		Lsd fr ANA
☐ JA304K	Boeing 737-54K	28992/3030			Lsd fr ANA
☐ JA306K	Boeing 737-54K	29794/3109	ex N1786B		Lsd fr ANA
☐ JA307K	Boeing 737-54K	29795/3116	ex N60436		Lsd fr ANA
☐ JA351K	Boeing 737-5Y0	25189/2240	ex N189NK		Lsd fr ANA
☐ JA352K	Boeing 737-5Y0	26097/2534	ex N97NK		Lsd fr ANA
☐ JA353K	Boeing 737-5Y0	26104/2552	ex N104NK		Lsd fr ANA
☐ JA354K	Boeing 737-5Y0	26105/2553	ex N105NK		Lsd fr ANA
☐ JA359K	Boeing 737-5L9	28128/2817	ex N8128R		Lsd fr ANA

AIR NIPPON	*ANK Air (EL/ANK)*	*Tokyo-Haneda (HND)*

Registration	Type	C/n	Previous identity	Notes	Lease
☐ JA301K	Boeing 737-54K	27435/2875			Lsd fr ANA
☐ JA303K	Boeing 737-54K	28991/3017			Lsd fr ANA
☐ JA305K	Boeing 737-54K	28993/3075	ex N1781B		Lsd fr ANA
☐ JA355K	Boeing 737-5L9	28129/2823	ex N8129L		Lsd fr ANA
☐ JA356K	Boeing 737-5L9	28083/2784	ex N8083N		Lsd fr ANA
☐ JA357K	Boeing 737-5L9	28131/2828	ex N88131		Lsd fr ANA
☐ JA358K	Boeing 737-5L9	28130/2825	ex N8130J		Lsd fr ANA
☐ JA392K	Boeing 737-46M	28550/2847	ex N8550F		Lsd to ADO
☐ JA8195	Boeing 737-54K	27433/2815			Lsd fr ANA
☐ JA8196	Boeing 737-54K	27966/2824			Lsd fr ANA
☐ JA8404	Boeing 737-54K	27381/2708	ex N35108		Lsd to ADO
☐ JA8500	Boeing 737-54K	27431/2751			Lsd fr ANA
☐ JA8596	Boeing 737-54K	28462/2853			Lsd fr ANA
☐ JA01AN	Boeing 737-781/W	33916/1781	ex N6066U	Gold titles/cheatlines	Lsd fr ANA
☐ JA02AN	Boeing 737-781/W	33872/1850		Gold titles/cheatlines	Lsd fr ANA
☐ JA03AN	Boeing 737-781/W	33873/1871	ex N1787B		Lsd fr ANA
☐ JA04AN	Boeing 737-781/W	33874/1890	ex N1781B		Lsd fr ANA
☐ JA05AN	Boeing 737-781/W	33875/1971			Lsd fr ANA
☐ JA06AN	Boeing 737-781/W	33876/1992			Lsd fr ANA
☐ JA07AN	Boeing 737-781/W	33900/2071			Lsd fr ANA
☐ JA08AN	Boeing 737-781/W	33877/2086			Lsd fr ANA
☐ JA09AN	Boeing 737-781/W	33878/2145			Lsd fr ANA
☐ JA10AN	Boeing 737-781ER/W	33879/2157	ex N716BA	ANA Business Jet	Lsd fr ANA
☐ JA12AN	Boeing 737-781/W	33881/2301			Lsd fr ANA
☐ JA13AN	Boeing 737-781ER/W	33880/2232	ex N717BA	ANA Business Jet	Lsd fr ANA
☐ JA14AN	Boeing 737-781/W	33883/2370	ex N1787B		Lsd fr ANA
☐ JA15AN	Boeing 737-781/W	33888/2394	ex N6063S		Lsd fr ANA
☐ JA16AN	Boeing 737-781/W	33889/2488	ex N721BA	on order	Lsd fr ANA
☐ JA17AN	Boeing 737-781/W	33884/2513	ex N1779B		Lsd fr ANA
☐ JA18AN	Boeing 737-781/W	33885/2582			Lsd fr ANA
☐ JA52AN	Boeing 737-881/W	33887/2643			Lsd fr ANA
☐ JA53AN	Boeing 737-881/W	33891/2739			Lsd fr ANA
☐ JA54AN	Boeing 737-881/W	33890/2833			Lsd fr ANA
☐ JA55AN	Boeing 737-881/W	33892/2889			Lsd fr ANA
☐ JA56AN	Boeing 737-881/W	33893/2926			Lsd fr ANA
☐ JA57AN	Boeing 737-881/W	33894/2975	ex N1787B		Lsd fr ANA
☐ JA58AN	Boeing 737-881/W	33895/3029	ex N1796B		Lsd fr ANA
☐ JA59AN	Boeing 737-881/W	33886/3073			Lsd fr ANA
☐ JA60AN	Boeing 737-881/W	33897/3126			Lsd fr ANA
☐ JA61AN	Boeing 737-881/W	33906			on order
☐ JA801K	de Havilland DHC-8Q-314	565	ex C-GDFT		
☐ JA802K	de Havilland DHC-8Q-314	577	ex C-FDHD		
☐ JA803K	de Havilland DHC-8Q-314	583	ex C-FDHW		
☐ JA804K	de Havilland DHC-8Q-314	591	ex C-GFUM		
☐ JA805K	de Havilland DHC-8Q-314	592	ex C-GFYI		

AIR NIPPON NETWORK	*Alfa Wing (EH/ANA)*	*Sapporo-Okadama (OKD)*

Registration	Type	C/n	Previous identity	Notes	Lease
☐ JA801K	de Havilland DHC-8Q-314	565	ex C-GDFT	Tsubaki c/s	Lsd fr ANK
☐ JA802K	de Havilland DHC-8Q-314	577	ex C-FDHD	Himawari c/s	Lsd fr ANK
☐ JA803K	de Havilland DHC-8Q-314	583	ex C-FDHW	Suzuran c/s	Lsd fr ANK
☐ JA804K	de Havilland DHC-8Q-314	591	ex C-GFUM	Cosmos c/s	Lsd fr ANK
☐ JA805K	de Havilland DHC-8Q-314	592	ex C-GFYI	Hamanasu c/s	Lsd fr ANK
☐ JA841A	de Havilland DHC-8-402Q	4080	ex C-GDLK		Lsd fr ANA
☐ JA842A	de Havilland DHC-8-402Q	4082	ex C-GFOD		Lsd fr ANA
☐ JA843A	de Havilland DHC-8-402Q	4084	ex C-GFQL		Lsd fr ANA
☐ JA844A	de Havilland DHC-8-402Q	4091	ex C-GHRI		Lsd fr ANA
☐ JA845A	de Havilland DHC-8-402Q	4096	ex C-FAQB		Lsd fr ANA
☐ JA846A	de Havilland DHC-8-402Q	4097	ex C-FAQD		Lsd fr ANA
☐ JA847A	de Havilland DHC-8-402Q	4099	ex C-FAQK		Lsd fr ANA
☐ JA848A	de Havilland DHC-8-402Q	4102	ex C-FCQA		Lsd fr ANA
☐ JA849A	de Havilland DHC-8-402Q	4106	ex C-FCVE		Lsd fr ANA

☐ JA850A	de Havilland DHC-8-402Q	4108	ex C-FCVJ		Lsd fr ANA
☐ JA851A	de Havilland DHC-8-402Q	4109	ex C-FCVK		Lsd fr ANA
☐ JA852A	de Havilland DHC-8-402Q	4131	ex C-FGKC		Lsd fr ANA
☐ JA853A	de Havilland DHC-8-402Q	4135	ex C-FGKN		Lsd fr ANA
☐ JA854A	de Havilland DHC-8-402Q	4151	ex C-FJLH		Lsd fr ANA
☐ JA855A	de Havilland DHC-8-402Q	4292	ex C-GAUB		on order
☐ JA	de Havilland DHC-8-402Q		ex C-		on order
☐ JA	de Havilland DHC-8-402Q		ex C-		on order
☐ JA	de Havilland DHC-8-402Q		ex C-		on order

AMAKUSA AIRLINES ***(AHX)*** ***Kumamoto (KMJ)***

☐ JA81AM	de Havilland DHC-8Q-103	537	ex C-FCSG

ANA - ALL NIPPON AIRWAYS ***All Nippon (NH/ANA)*** ***Tokyo-Haneda (HND)***

Member of Star Alliance

☐ JA203A	Airbus A320-211	2061	ex F-WWDC		
☐ JA204A	Airbus A320-214	2998	ex F-WWIZ		
☐ JA205A	Airbus A320-214	3099	ex F-WWIE		
☐ JA206A	Airbus A320-214	3147	ex F-WWBQ		
☐ JA207A	Airbus A320-214	3148	ex F-WWBR		
☐ JA208A	Airbus A320-214	3189	ex F-WWDZ		
☐ JA8300	Airbus A320-211	0549	ex F-WWIT		
☐ JA8304	Airbus A320-211	0531	ex F-WWDY		
☐ JA8313	Airbus A320-211	0534	ex F-WWBC		
☐ JA8382	Airbus A320-211	0139	ex F-WWDF	wfs 30Nov07	
☐ JA8384	Airbus A320-211	0151	ex F-WWDR	D-ALLD resd	
☐ JA8385	Airbus A320-211	0167	ex F-WWIE	D-ALLE resd	
☐ JA8386	Airbus A320-211	0170	ex F-WWII		
☐ JA8387	Airbus A320-211	0196	ex F-WWDE		
☐ JA8388	Airbus A320-211	0212	ex F-WWIG		
☐ JA8389	Airbus A320-211	0219	ex F-WWDZ		
☐ JA8390	Airbus A320-211	0245	ex F-WWDE	D-ALLF resd	
☐ JA8391	Airbus A320-211	0300	ex F-WWDD	D-ALLG resd	
☐ JA8392	Airbus A320-211	0328	ex F-WWDR	D-ALLH resd	
☐ JA8393	Airbus A320-211	0365	ex F-WWBZ	D-ALLI resd	
☐ JA8394	Airbus A320-211	0383	ex F-WWBF		
☐ JA8395	Airbus A320-211	0413	ex F-WWIM		
☐ JA8396	Airbus A320-211	0482	ex F-WWIO	D-ALLJ resd	
☐ JA8400	Airbus A320-211	0554	ex F-WWIG		
☐ JA8609	Airbus A320-211	0501	ex F-WWIN		
☐ JA8654	Airbus A320-211	0507	ex F-WWBT		
☐ JA8946	Airbus A320-211	0669	ex F-WWBD		
☐ JA8947	Airbus A320-211	0685	ex F-WWDR		
☐ JA8997	Airbus A320-211	0658	ex F-WWIU		
☐ JA	Airbus A320-214		ex F-WW		on order
☐ JA	Airbus A320-214		ex F-WW		on order
☐ JA	Airbus A320-214		ex F-WW		on order

☐ JA300K	Boeing 737-54K	27434/2872		Lsd to ADO
☐ JA301K	Boeing 737-54K	27435/2875		Lsd to ANK
☐ JA302K	Boeing 737-54K	28990/3002	ex N1787B	Lsd to NXA
☐ JA303K	Boeing 737-54K	28991/3017		Lsd to ANK
☐ JA304K	Boeing 737-54K	28992/3030	ex N1786B	Lsd to NXA
☐ JA305K	Boeing 737-54K	28993/3075	ex N1781B	Lsd to ANK
☐ JA306K	Boeing 737-54K	29794/3109		Lsd to NXA
☐ JA307K	Boeing 737-54K	29795/3116	ex N60436	Lsd to NXA
☐ JA351K	Boeing 737-5Y0	25189/2240	ex N189NK	Lsd to NXA
☐ JA352K	Boeing 737-5Y0	26097/2534	ex N97NK	Lsd to NXA
☐ JA353K	Boeing 737-5Y0	26104/2552	ex N104NK	Lsd to NXA
☐ JA354K	Boeing 737-5Y0	26105/2553	ex N105NK	Lsd to NXA
☐ JA355K	Boeing 737-5L9	28129/2823	ex N8129L	Lsd to ANK
☐ JA356K	Boeing 737-5L9	28083/2784	ex N8083N	Lsd to ANK
☐ JA357K	Boeing 737-5L9	28131/2828	ex N88131	Lsd to ANK
☐ JA358K	Boeing 737-5L9	28130/2825	ex N8130J	Lsd to ANK
☐ JA359K	Boeing 737-5L9	28128/2817	ex N8128R	Lsd to NXA
☐ JA392K	Boeing 737-46M	28550/2847	ex N8550F	Lsd to ADO
☐ JA8195	Boeing 737-54K	27433/2815		Lsd to ANK
☐ JA8196	Boeing 737-54K	27966/2824		Lsd to ANK
☐ JA8404	Boeing 737-54K	27381/2708	ex N35108	Lsd to ANK
☐ JA8419	Boeing 737-54K	27430/2723		
☐ JA8500	Boeing 737-54K	27431/2751		Lsd to ANK
☐ JA8596	Boeing 737-54K	28462/2853		Lsd to ANK

☐ JA01AN	Boeing 737-781/W	33916/1781	ex N6066U	Lsd to ANK
☐ JA02AN	Boeing 737-781/W	33872/1850		Lsd to ANK
☐ JA03AN	Boeing 737-781/W	33873/1871	ex N1787B	Lsd to ANK
☐ JA04AN	Boeing 737-781/W	33874/1890	ex N1781B	Lsd to ANK
☐ JA05AN	Boeing 737-781/W	33875/1971		Lsd to ANK
☐ JA06AN	Boeing 737-781/W	33876/1992		Lsd to ANK

☐ JA07AN	Boeing 737-781/W	33900/2071		Lsd to ANK
☐ JA08AN	Boeing 737-781/W	33877/2086		Lsd to ANK
☐ JA09AN	Boeing 737-781/W	33878/2145		Lsd to ANK
☐ JA10AN	Boeing 737-781ER/W	33879/2157	ex N716BA	Lsd to ANK
☐ JA11AN	Boeing 737-781/W	33882/2268		Lsd to ANK
☐ JA12AN	Boeing 737-781/W	33881/2301		Lsd to ANK
☐ JA13AN	Boeing 737-781ER/W	33880/2232	ex N717BA	Lsd to ANK
☐ JA14AN	Boeing 737-781/W	33883/2370		Lsd to ANK
☐ JA15AN	Boeing 737-781/W	33888/2394		Lsd to ANK
☐ JA16AN	Boeing 737-781/W	33889/2488		Lsd to ANK
☐ JA17AN	Boeing 737-781/W	33884/2513		Lsd to ANK
☐ JA18AN	Boeing 737-781/W	33885/2582		Lsd to ANK
☐ JA51AN	Boeing 737-881/W	33886/2607	ex N1766B	Lsd to ANK
☐ JA52AN	Boeing 737-881/W	33887/2643		Lsd to ANK
☐ JA53AN	Boeing 737-881/W	33891/2739		Lsd to ANK
☐ JA54AN	Boeing 737-881/W	33890/2833		Lsd to ANK
☐ JA55AN	Boeing 737-881/W	33892/2889		Lsd to ANK
☐ JA56AN	Boeing 737-881/W	33893/2926		Lsd to ANK
☐ JA57AN	Boeing 737-881/W	33894/2975	ex N1787B	Lsd to ANK
☐ JA58AN	Boeing 737-881/W	33895/3029	ex N1796B	Lsd to ANK
☐ JA59AN	Boeing 737-881/W	33886/3073		Lsd to ANK
☐ JA60AN	Boeing 737-881/W	33897/3126		Lsd to ANK
☐ JA61AN	Boeing 737-881/W	33906		on order
☐ JA8098	Boeing 747-481	25207/870		
☐ JA8099	Boeing 747-481D	25292/891		
☐ JA8956	Boeing 747-481D	25640/920		Pocket Monsters 2004 colours
☐ JA8957	Boeing 747-481D	25642/927		Pocket Monsters colours
☐ JA8958	Boeing 747-481	25641/928	ex N6009F	
☐ JA8959	Boeing 747-481D	25646/952		
☐ JA8960	Boeing 747-481D	25643/972		
☐ JA8961	Boeing 747-481D	25644/975		
☐ JA8962	Boeing 747-481	25645/979		
☐ JA8963	Boeing 747-481D	25647/991	ex N6055X	
☐ JA8964	Boeing 747-481D	27163/996	ex N5573S	
☐ JA8965	Boeing 747-481D	27436/1060		
☐ JA8966	Boeing 747-481D	27442/1066		
☐ JA601A	Boeing 767-381	27943/669		
☐ JA601F	Boeing 767-381F	33404/885	ex N6055X	Lsd to AJV
☐ JA602A	Boeing 767-381	27944/684		
☐ JA602F	Boeing 767-381F	33509/937		Lsd to AJV
☐ JA603A*	Boeing 767-381ER	32972/877	ex N6046P	
☐ JA603F	Boeing 767-381F	33510/939		Lsd to AJV
☐ JA604A*	Boeing 767-381ER	32973/881		
☐ JA604F	Boeing 767-381F	35709/947		Lsd to AJV
☐ JA605A*	Boeing 767-381ER	32974/882		
☐ JA606A*	Boeing 767-381ER	32975/883		Fly Panda c/s
☐ JA607A*	Boeing 767-381ER	32976/884		
☐ JA608A*	Boeing 767-381ER	32977/886		
☐ JA609A*	Boeing 767-381ER	32978/888		
☐ JA610A*	Boeing 767-381ER	32979/895		
☐ JA611A*	Boeing 767-381ER	32980/914		Star Cluster
☐ JA612A*	Boeing 767-381ER	33506/920		
☐ JA613A*	Boeing 767-381ER	33507/924		
☐ JA614A	Boeing 767-381ER	33508/931		Star Alliance colours
☐ JA615A	Boeing 767-381ER	35877/951		
☐ JA616A	Boeing 767-381ER	35876/953		
☐ JA617A	Boeing 767-381ER	37719/971		
☐ JA618A	Boeing 767-381ER	37720/976		
☐ JA631A	Boeing 767-381F			on order
☐ JA632A	Boeing 767-381F			on order
☐ JA633A	Boeing 767-381F			on order
☐ JA8256	Boeing 767-381	23756/176	ex N6005C	
☐ JA8257	Boeing 767-381	23757/177	ex N6038E	
☐ JA8258	Boeing 767-381	23758/179	ex N6055X	Lsd to ADO
☐ JA8259	Boeing 767-381	23759/185	ex N6038E	
☐ JA8271	Boeing 767-381	24002/199	ex N60668	
☐ JA8272	Boeing 767-381	24003/212	ex N6038E	
☐ JA8273	Boeing 767-381	24004/218	ex N6055X	stored
☐ JA8274	Boeing 767-381	24005/222	ex N6046P	
☐ JA8275	Boeing 767-381	24006/223	ex N6018N	
☐ JA8285	Boeing 767-381	24350/245	ex N1789B	
☐ JA8286	Boeing 767-381BCF	24400/269		
☐ JA8287	Boeing 767-381	24351/271		
☐ JA8288	Boeing 767-381	24415/276		
☐ JA8289	Boeing 767-381	24416/280		
☐ JA8290	Boeing 767-381	24417/290		
☐ JA8291	Boeing 767-381	24755/295		
☐ JA8322	Boeing 767-381	25618/458		
☐ JA8323	Boeing 767-381ERBCF	25654/463		being converted
☐ JA8324	Boeing 767-381	25655/465		
☐ JA8342	Boeing 767-381	27445/573		Olympic c/s

Registration	Type	C/n	Previous identity	Notes	Remarks
☐ JA8356	Boeing 767-381ERBCF	25136/379			
☐ JA8357	Boeing 767-381	25293/401		ANA Woody Jet c/s	
☐ JA8358	Boeing 767-381ERBCF	25616/432		Yokoso Japan	
☐ JA8359	Boeing 767-381	25617/439			
☐ JA8360	Boeing 767-381	25055/352			
☐ JA8362	Boeing 767-381ERBCF	24632/285			being converted
☐ JA8363	Boeing 767-381	24756/300			
☐ JA8368	Boeing 767-381	24880/336			
☐ JA8567	Boeing 767-381	25656/510			
☐ JA8568	Boeing 767-381	25657/515			
☐ JA8569	Boeing 767-381	27050/516			
☐ JA8578	Boeing 767-381	25658/519			
☐ JA8579	Boeing 767-381	25659/520			
☐ JA8664	Boeing 767-381ER	27339/556			
☐ JA8669	Boeing 767-381	27444/567			
☐ JA8670	Boeing 767-381	25660/539			
☐ JA8674	Boeing 767-381	25661/543			
☐ JA8677	Boeing 767-381	25662/551			
☐ JA8970	Boeing 767-381ER	25619/645			
☐ JA8971	Boeing 767-381ER	27942/651			
☐ N742AX	Boeing 767-232 (SCD)	22217/27	ex N105DA		Lsd fr ABX
☐ N744AX	Boeing 767-232 (SCD)	22221/53	ex N109DL		Lsd fr ABX
☐ JA701A	Boeing 777-281	27938/77			
☐ JA702A	Boeing 777-281	27033/75			
☐ JA703A	Boeing 777-281	27034/81	ex N50217		
☐ JA704A	Boeing 777-281	27035/131			
☐ JA705A	Boeing 777-281	29029/137			
☐ JA706A	Boeing 777-281	27036/141			
☐ JA707A	Boeing 777-281ER	27037/247			
☐ JA708A	Boeing 777-281ER	28277/278			
☐ JA709A	Boeing 777-281ER	28278/286			
☐ JA710A	Boeing 777-281ER	28279/302			
☐ JA711A	Boeing 777-281	33406/482		Star Alliance c/s	
☐ JA712A	Boeing 777-281	33407/495		Star Alliance c/s	
☐ JA713A	Boeing 777-281	32647/509			
☐ JA714A	Boeing 777-281	28276/523			
☐ JA715A	Boeing 777-281ER	32646/563			
☐ JA716A	Boeing 777-281ER	33414/574			
☐ JA717A	Boeing 777-281ER	33415/580			
☐ JA	Boeing 777-281ER				on order
☐ JA	Boeing 777-281ER				on order
☐ JA	Boeing 777-281ER				on order
☐ JA	Boeing 777-281ER				on order
☐ JA731A	Boeing 777-381ER	28281/488	ex N240BA	Star Alliance colours	
☐ JA732A	Boeing 777-381ER	27038/511			
☐ JA733A	Boeing 777-381ER	32648/529	ex N5014K		
☐ JA734A	Boeing 777-381ER	32649/557			
☐ JA735A	Boeing 777-381ER	34892/571			
☐ JA736A	Boeing 777-381ER	34893/589			
☐ JA751A	Boeing 777-381	28272/142	ex N5017Q		
☐ JA752A	Boeing 777-381	28274/160			
☐ JA753A	Boeing 777-381	28273/132			Sky Blue
☐ JA754A	Boeing 777-381	27939/172			Sky Lark
☐ JA755A	Boeing 777-381	28275/104	ex N5017Q		
☐ JA756A	Boeing 777-381	27039/440			
☐ JA757A	Boeing 777-381	27040/442		Olympic colours	
☐ JA777A	Boeing 777-381ER	32650/593			
☐ JA778A	Boeing 777-381ER	32651/606			
☐ JA779A	Boeing 777-381ER	34894/631			
☐ JA780A	Boeing 777-381ER	34895/639			
☐ JA781A	Boeing 777-381ER	27041/667			
☐ JA782A	Boeing 777-381ER	33416/691			
☐ JA783A	Boeing 777-381ER	27940/737			
☐ JA784A	Boeing 777-381ER	37950/833			
☐ JA785A	Boeing 777-381ER	37951			on order
☐ JA786A	Boeing 777-381ER	37948			on order
☐ JA787A	Boeing 777-381ER	37949			on order
☐ JA8197	Boeing 777-281	27027/16	ex N5016R		
☐ JA8198	Boeing 777-281	27028/21			
☐ JA8199	Boeing 777-281	27029/29			
☐ JA8967	Boeing 777-281	27030/37			
☐ JA8968	Boeing 777-281	27031/38			
☐ JA8969	Boeing 777-281	27032/50			
☐ JA801A	Boeing 787-881	34485			on order
☐ JA802A	Boeing 787-881	34489			on order
☐ JA803A	Boeing 787-881	34486			on order
☐ JA804A	Boeing 787-881	34488			on order
☐ JA805A	Boeing 787-881	34497			on order
☐ JA842A	de Havilland DHC-8-402Q	4082	ex C-GFOD		
☐ JA843A	de Havilland DHC-8-402Q	4084	ex C-GFQL		

☐ JA844A	de Havilland DHC-8-402Q	4091	ex C-GHRI
☐ JA845A	de Havilland DHC-8-402Q	4096	ex C-FAQB
☐ JA846A	de Havilland DHC-8-402Q	4097	ex C-FAQD
☐ JA847A	de Havilland DHC-8-402Q	4099	ex C-FAQK
☐ JA848A	de Havilland DHC-8-402Q	4102	ex C-FCQA
☐ JA849A	de Havilland DHC-8-402Q	4106	ex C-FCVE
☐ JA850A	de Havilland DHC-8-402Q	4108	ex C-FCVJ
☐ JA851A	de Havilland DHC-8-402Q	4109	ex C-FCVK
☐ JA852A	de Havilland DHC-8-402Q	4131	ex C-FGKC

FUJI DREAM AIRLINES — *(JH / FDA)*

☐ JA01FJ	Embraer 170-100 (170ST)	17000271	ex PT-SNB
☐ JA02FJ	Embraer 170-100 (170ST)	17000289	ex PT-TQP
☐ JA03FJ	Embraer 170-100 (170ST)	17000304	ex PT-XQD

HOKKAIDO AIR SYSTEM — *North Air (NTH)* — *Sapporo-Chitose (CTS)*

☐ JA01HC	SAAB SF.340B	340B-432	ex SE-B32
☐ JA02HC	SAAB SF.340B	340B-440	ex SE-B40
☐ JA03HC	SAAB SF.340B	340B-458	ex SE-B58

HOKKAIDO INTERNATIONAL AIRLINES

☐ JA8504	Boeing 737-54K	27432/2783	

IBEX AIRLINES — *Fair (FW/IBX)* — *Sendai (SDJ)*

☐ JA01RJ	Canadair CL-600-2B19 (CRJ-100ER)	7052	ex OE-LRD
☐ JA02RJ	Canadair CL-600-2B19 (CRJ-100ER)	7033	ex OE-LRB
☐ JA03RJ	Canadair CL-600-2B19 (CRJ-200ER)	7624	ex C-GJZF
☐ JA04RJ	Canadair CL-600-2B19 (CRJ-200ER)	7798	ex C-FMLF
☐ JA05RJ	Canadair CL-600-2C10 (CRJ-702NG)	10279	ex C-FYDI

J-AIR — *(JL/JAL)* — *Nagoya-Komaki (NKM)*

☐ JA201J	Canadair CL-600-2B19 (CRJ-200ER)	7452	ex C-FMND
☐ JA202J	Canadair CL-600-2B19 (CRJ-200ER)	7484	ex C-FMLU
☐ JA203J	Canadair CL-600-2B19 (CRJ-200ER)	7626	ex C-FMNW
☐ JA204J	Canadair CL-600-2B19 (CRJ-200ER)	7643	ex C-FMNB
☐ JA205J	Canadair CL-600-2B19 (CRJ-200ER)	7767	ex C-FMLB
☐ JA206J	Canadair CL-600-2B19 (CRJ-200ER)	7834	ex C-FMMT
☐ JA207J	Canadair CL-600-2B19 (CRJ-200ER)	8050	ex C-FFVJ
☐ JA208J	Canadair CL-600-2B19 (CRJ-200ER)	8059	ex C-FMOW
☐ JA209J	Canadair CL-600-2B19 (CRJ-200ER)	8062	ex C-FMNQ

☐ JA211J	Embraer 170-100 (170ST)	17000251	ex PT-SJC
☐ JA212J	Embraer 170-100 (170ST)	17000268	ex PT-SJW
☐ JA213J	Embraer 170-100 (170ST)	17000285	ex PT-TQL
☐ JA214J	Embraer 170-100 (170ST)	17000295	ex PT-TQV
☐ JA215J	Embraer 170-100 (170ST)	17000297	ex PT-TQX
☐ JA216J	Embraer 170-100 (170ST)	17000299	ex PT-TQY

JAL EXPRESS — *Janex (JC/JEX)* — *Osaka-Kansai (KIX)*

☐ JA8991	Boeing 737-446	27916/2718		
☐ JA8992	Boeing 737-446	27917/2729	ex N1792B	
☐ JA8993	Boeing 737-446	28087/2812		Lsd fr JAL
☐ JA8994	Boeing 737-446	28097/2907	ex N1786B	Lsd fr JAL
☐ JA8995	Boeing 737-446	28831/2911		Lsd fr JAL
☐ JA8996	Boeing 737-446	28832/2953	ex N1786B	Lsd fr JAL
☐ JA8998	Boeing 737-446	28994/3044		Lsd fr JAL
☐ JA8999	Boeing 737-446	29864/3111	ex N1786B	Lsd fr JAL

☐ JA307J	Boeing 737-846/W	35336/2450		Lsd fr JAL
☐ JA308J	Boeing 737-846/W	35337/2479	ex N1786B	Lsd fr JAL
☐ JA309J	Boeing 737-846/W	35338/2522		Lsd fr JAL
☐ JA311J	Boeing 737-846/W	35340/2571		Lsd fr JAL
☐ JA313J	Boeing 737-846/W	35342/2633		Lsd fr JAL
☐ JA314J	Boeing 737-846/W	35343/2701		Lsd fr JAL
☐ JA316J	Boeing 737-846/W	35345/2762		Lsd fr JAL

☐ JA8262	McDonnell-Douglas MD-81	49463/1488		Lsd fr JAL
☐ JA8374	McDonnell-Douglas MD-81	53043/1982		Lsd fr JAL
☐ JA8556	McDonnell-Douglas MD-81	53301/2082		Lsd fr JAL

JAL WAYS — *Jalways (JO/JAZ)* — *Tokyo-Narita (NRT)*

Wholly owned by Japan Airlines and leases aircraft from the parent as required.

JAPAN AIR COMMUTER — Commuter (3X/JAC) — Amami (ASJ)

☐ JA841C	de Havilland DHC-8-402Q	4072	ex C-GEWI	
☐ JA842C	de Havilland DHC-8-402Q	4073	ex C-GFCA	
☐ JA843C	de Havilland DHC-8-402Q	4076	ex C-FDHZ	
☐ JA844C	de Havilland DHC-8-402Q	4092	ex C-GFEN	
☐ JA845C	de Havilland DHC-8-402Q	4101	ex C-FCPZ	
☐ JA846C	de Havilland DHC-8-402Q	4107	ex C-FCVI	
☐ JA847C	de Havilland DHC-8-402Q	4111	ex C-FCVS	
☐ JA848C	de Havilland DHC-8-402Q	4121	ex C-FFCO	
☐ JA849C	de Havilland DHC-8-402Q	4133	ex C-FGKJ	
☐ JA850C	de Havilland DHC-8-402Q	4158	ex C-FLKW	
☐ JA851C	de Havilland DHC-8-402Q	4177	ex C-FMTK	
☐ JA001C	SAAB SF.340B	340B-419	ex SE-B19	
☐ JA002C	SAAB SF.340B	340B-459	ex SE-B59	
☐ JA8594	SAAB SF.340B	340B-399	ex SE-C99	
☐ JA8642	SAAB SF.340B	340B-365	ex SE-C65	
☐ JA8649	SAAB SF.340B	340B-368	ex SE-C68	
☐ JA8703	SAAB SF.340B	340B-355	ex SE-C55	
☐ JA8704	SAAB SF.340B	340B-361	ex SE-C61	
☐ JA8886	SAAB SF.340B	340B-281	ex SE-G81	
☐ JA8887	SAAB SF.340B	340B-308	ex SE-C08	
☐ JA8888	SAAB SF.340B	340B-331	ex SE-C31	
☐ JA8900	SAAB SF.340B	340B-378	ex SE-C78	

JAPAN AIRLINES — Japanair (JL/JAL) — Tokyo-Haneda (HND)

Member of Oneworld

☐ JA011D	Airbus A300B4-622R	783	ex F-WWAA	
☐ JA012D	Airbus A300B4-622R	797	ex F-WWAQ	
☐ JA014D	Airbus A300B4-622R	836	ex F-WWAF	
☐ JA015D	Airbus A300B4-622R	837	ex F-WWAK	
☐ JA016D	Airbus A300B4-622R	838	ex F-WWAL	
☐ JA8375	Airbus A300B4-622R	602	ex F-WWAT	
☐ JA8376	Airbus A300B4-622R	617	ex F-WWAK	
☐ JA8377	Airbus A300B4-622R	621	ex F-WWAA	
☐ JA8527	Airbus A300B4-622R	724	ex F-WWAQ	
☐ JA8529	Airbus A300B4-622R	729	ex F-WWAM	
☐ JA8558	Airbus A300B4-622R	637	ex F-WWAX	
☐ JA8559	Airbus A300B4-622R	641	ex F-WWAM	
☐ JA8561	Airbus A300B4-622R	670	ex F-WWAD	
☐ JA8562	Airbus A300B4-622R	679	ex F-WWAL	
☐ JA8563	Airbus A300B4-622R	683	ex F-WWAJ	
☐ JA8564	Airbus A300B4-622R	703	ex F-WWAO	
☐ JA8565	Airbus A300B4-622R	711	ex F-WWAE	
☐ JA8566	Airbus A300B4-622R	730	ex F-WWAV	
☐ JA8573	Airbus A300B4-622R	737	ex F-WWAF	
☐ JA8574	Airbus A300B4-622R	740	ex F-WWAG	
☐ JA8657	Airbus A300B4-622R	753	ex F-WWAD	
☐ JA8659	Airbus A300B4-622R	770	ex F-WWAQ	
☐ JA8993	Boeing 737-446	28087/2812		Lsd to JEX
☐ JA8994	Boeing 737-446	28097/2907	ex N1786B	Lsd to JEX
☐ JA8995	Boeing 737-446	28831/2911		Lsd to JEX
☐ JA8996	Boeing 737-446	28832/2953	ex N1786B	Lsd to JEX
☐ JA8998	Boeing 737-446	28994/3044		Lsd to JEX
☐ JA8999	Boeing 737-446	29864/3111	ex N1786B	Lsd to JEX
☐ JA301J	Boeing 737-846/W	35330/2095		
☐ JA302J	Boeing 737-846/W	35331/2162		
☐ JA303J	Boeing 737-846/W	35332/2225	ex N6066U	
☐ JA304J	Boeing 737-846/W	35333/2253		
☐ JA305J	Boeing 737-846/W	35334/2289		
☐ JA306J	Boeing 737-846/W	35335/2395	ex N6065Y	
☐ JA307J	Boeing 737-846/W	35336/2450		Lsd to JEX
☐ JA308J	Boeing 737-846/W	35337/2479	ex N1786B	Lsd to JEX
☐ JA309J	Boeing 737-846/W	35338/2522		Lsd to JEX
☐ JA310J	Boeing 737-846/W	35339/2510		
☐ JA311J	Boeing 737-846/W	35340/2571		Lsd to JEX
☐ JA312J	Boeing 737-846/W	35341/2584	ex N1786B	
☐ JA313J	Boeing 737-846/W	35342/2633		Lsd to JEX
☐ JA314J	Boeing 737-846/W	35343/2701		Lsd to JEX
☐ JA315J	Boeing 737-846/W	35344/2731		
☐ JA316J	Boeing 737-846/W	35345/2762		Lsd to JEX
☐ JA317J	Boeing 737-846/W	35346/2824		
☐ JA318J	Boeing 737-846/W	35347/2830	ex N1784B	
☐ JA319J	Boeing 737-846/W	35348/2867	ex N1795B	
☐ JA320J	Boeing 737-846/W	35349/2953	ex N1786B	
☐ JA321J	Boeing 737-846/W	35350/2977		
☐ JA322J	Boeing 737-846/W	35351/3002		

☐ JA323J	Boeing 737-846/W	35352/3057	ex N1787B	
☐ JA324J	Boeing 737-846/W	35353/3105		
☐ JA325J	Boeing 737-846/W	35354/3117		
☐ JA326J	Boeing 737-846/W	35355		on order
☐ JA327J	Boeing 737-846/W	35356		on order
☐ JA328J	Boeing 737-846/W	35357		on order
☐ JA329J	Boeing 737-846/W	35358		on order
☐ JA330J	Boeing 737-846/W	35359		on order
☐ JA331J	Boeing 737-846/W	40346		on order
☐ JA401J	Boeing 747-446F	33748/1351	ex N5022E	JAL Cargo
☐ JA402J	Boeing 747-446F	33749/1352		JAL Cargo
☐ JA8071	Boeing 747-446	24423/758		stored NRT
☐ JA8073	Boeing 747-446	24425/767		
☐ JA8074	Boeing 747-446	24426/768		
☐ JA8075	Boeing 747-446	24427/780		
☐ JA8076	Boeing 747-446	24777/797	ex N6046P	
☐ JA8077	Boeing 747-446	24784/798		
☐ JA8078	Boeing 747-446	24870/821	ex N60697	
☐ JA8079	Boeing 747-446	24885/824	ex N6005C	
☐ JA8080	Boeing 747-446	24886/825		
☐ JA8081	Boeing 747-446	25064/851		
☐ JA8082	Boeing 747-446	25212/871		
☐ JA8083	Boeing 747-446D	25213/844	ex N60668	
☐ JA8084	Boeing 747-446D	25214/879		
☐ JA8085	Boeing 747-446	25260/876		
☐ JA8086	Boeing 747-446	25308/885		
☐ JA8087	Boeing 747-446	26346/897		
☐ JA8088	Boeing 747-446	26341/902		
☐ JA8089	Boeing 747-446	26342/905		Yokoso titles
☐ JA8090	Boeing 747-446D	26347/907		
☐ JA8901	Boeing 747-446	26343/918		
☐ JA8902	Boeing 747-446BCF	26344/929	ex N6018N	
☐ JA8903	Boeing 747-446D	26345/935		
☐ JA8904	Boeing 747-446D	26348/941		Tamagocchi colours
☐ JA8905	Boeing 747-446D	26349/948		Tamagocchi colours
☐ JA8906	Boeing 747-446BCF	26350/961		
☐ JA8907	Boeing 747-446D	26351/963		
☐ JA8908	Boeing 747-446D	26352/978		
☐ JA8909	Boeing 747-446BCF	26353/980		stored HND
☐ JA8910	Boeing 747-446	26355/1024		
☐ JA8911	Boeing 747-446BCF	26356/1026		
☐ JA8912	Boeing 747-446	27099/1031		
☐ JA8913	Boeing 747-446	26359/1153		
☐ JA8914	Boeing 747-446	26360/1166		
☐ JA8915	Boeing 747-446BCF	26361/1188		Yokoso Japan
☐ JA8916	Boeing 747-446	26362/1202		Yokoso Japan
☐ JA8917	Boeing 747-446	29899/1208	ex N6009F	
☐ JA8918	Boeing 747-446	27650/1234		
☐ JA8919	Boeing 747-446	27100/1236		Yokoso Japan
☐ JA8920	Boeing 747-446	27648/1253		
☐ JA8921	Boeing 747-446	27645/1262	ex N747BA	
☐ JA8922	Boeing 747-446	27646/1280	ex N747BJ	
☐ JA601J	Boeing 767-346ER	32886/875	ex N60697	
☐ JA602J	Boeing 767-346ER	32887/879		
☐ JA603J	Boeing 767-346ER	32888/880	ex N1794B	
☐ JA604J	Boeing 767-346ER	33493/905		
☐ JA605J	Boeing 767-346ER	33494/911		
☐ JA606J	Boeing 767-346ER	33495/915		
☐ JA607J	Boeing 767-346ER	33496/917		
☐ JA608J	Boeing 767-346ER	33497/919		
☐ JA609J	Boeing 767-346ER	33845/921		
☐ JA610J	Boeing 767-346ER	33846/925		
☐ JA611J	Boeing 767-346ER	33847/927		
☐ JA612J	Boeing 767-346ER	33848/929		
☐ JA613J	Boeing 767-346ER	33849/935		
☐ JA614J	Boeing 767-346ER	33851/938		
☐ JA615J	Boeing 767-346ER	33850/942	ex N50217	
☐ JA616J	Boeing 767-346ER	35813/954		
☐ JA617J	Boeing 767-346ER	35814/957	ex N5023Q	
☐ JA618J	Boeing 767-346ER	35815/964		
☐ JA619J	Boeing 767-346ER	37550/969		
☐ JA620J	Boeing 767-346ER	37547/974		
☐ JA621J	Boeing 767-346ER	37548/975		
☐ JA622J	Boeing 767-346ER	37549/977		
☐ JA623J	Boeing 767-346ER	36131/978	ex N1794B	
☐ JA631J	Boeing 767-346F	35816/956	ex N5028Y	
☐ JA632J	Boeing 767-346F	35817/959	ex N5017Q	
☐ JA633J	Boeing 767-346F	35818/960		
☐ JA634J	Boeing 767-346F			on order
☐ JA8231	Boeing 767-246	23212/117	ex N6046P	
☐ JA8232	Boeing 767-246	23213/118	ex N6038E	

Registration	Type	c/n	Previous identity	Remarks	Status
☐ JA8233	Boeing 767-246	23214/122	ex N6038E		
☐ JA8236	Boeing 767-346	23215/132	ex N767S		stored VCV
☐ JA8253	Boeing 767-346	23645/174	ex N6038E		
☐ JA8264	Boeing 767-346	23965/186	ex N6018N		
☐ JA8265	Boeing 767-346	23961/192	ex N6005C		
☐ JA8266	Boeing 767-346	23966/191	ex N6018N		
☐ JA8267	Boeing 767-346	23962/193	ex N6038E		
☐ JA8268	Boeing 767-346	23963/224	ex N6055X		
☐ JA8269	Boeing 767-346	23964/225	ex N6046P		
☐ JA8299	Boeing 767-346	24498/277	ex N6055X		
☐ JA8364	Boeing 767-346	24782/327			
☐ JA8365	Boeing 767-346	24783/329			
☐ JA8397	Boeing 767-346	27311/547			
☐ JA8398	Boeing 767-346	27312/548			
☐ JA8399	Boeing 767-346	27313/554			
☐ JA8975	Boeing 767-346	27658/581			
☐ JA8976	Boeing 767-346	27659/667			
☐ JA8980	Boeing 767-346	28837/673			
☐ JA8986	Boeing 767-346	28838/680			
☐ JA8987	Boeing 767-346	28553/688			
☐ JA8988	Boeing 767-346	29863/772			
☐ JA007D	Boeing 777-289	27639/134			
☐ JA008D	Boeing 777-289	27640/146			
☐ JA009D	Boeing 777-289	27641/159	ex N5017V		
☐ JA010D	Boeing 777-289	27642/213			
☐ JA701J	Boeing 777-246ER	32889/410	ex (JA8989)		
☐ JA702J	Boeing 777-246ER	32890/417	ex (JA8990)		
☐ JA703J	Boeing 777-246ER	32891/427	ex N5023Q		
☐ JA704J	Boeing 777-246ER	32892/435	ex N50281	oneworld c/s	
☐ JA705J	Boeing 777-246ER	32893/446			
☐ JA706J	Boeing 777-246ER	33394/464			
☐ JA707J	Boeing 777-246ER	32894/475			
☐ JA708J	Boeing 777-246ER	32895/483			
☐ JA709J	Boeing 777-246ER	32896/489			
☐ JA710J	Boeing 777-246ER	33395/525			
☐ JA711J	Boeing 777-246ER	33396/533			
☐ JA712J	Boeing 777-246ER	37879			on order
☐ JA713J	Boeing 777-246ER	37880			on order
☐ JA714J	Boeing 777-246ER	37881			on order
☐ JA715J	Boeing 777-246ER	37882			on order
☐ JA716J	Boeing 777-246ER	37883			on order
☐ JA731J	Boeing 777-346ER	32431/429	ex N5016R		
☐ JA732J	Boeing 777-346ER	32430/423	ex N5017V		
☐ JA733J	Boeing 777-346ER	32432/521			
☐ JA734J	Boeing 777-346ER	32433/527			
☐ JA735J	Boeing 777-346ER	32434/577			
☐ JA736J	Boeing 777-346ER	32435/583			
☐ JA737J	Boeing 777-346ER	36126/668			
☐ JA738J	Boeing 777-346ER	32436/724			
☐ JA739J	Boeing 777-346ER	32437/736			
☐ JA740J	Boeing 777-346ER	36127/744			
☐ JA741J	Boeing 777-346ER	36128/812	ex N50281		
☐ JA742J	Boeing 777-346ER	36129/816	ex N1788B		
☐ JA743J	Boeing 777-346ER	36130/821	ex N6009F		
☐ JA751J	Boeing 777-346	27654/458			
☐ JA752J	Boeing 777-346	27655/460			
☐ JA771J	Boeing 777-246	27656/437	ex (JA711J)		
☐ JA772J	Boeing 777-246	27657/507			
☐ JA773J	Boeing 777-246	27653/635			
☐ JA8941	Boeing 777-346	28393/152			
☐ JA8942	Boeing 777-346	28394/158	ex N50284		
☐ JA8943	Boeing 777-346	28395/196			
☐ JA8944	Boeing 777-346	28396/212			
☐ JA8945	Boeing 777-346	28397/238			
☐ JA8977	Boeing 777-289	27636/45			
☐ JA8978	Boeing 777-289	27637/79		Tamagotchi Jet colours	
☐ JA8979	Boeing 777-289	27638/107			
☐ JA8981	Boeing 777-246	27364/23	ex (JA8195)		
☐ JA8982	Boeing 777-246	27365/26	ex (JA8196)		
☐ JA8983	Boeing 777-246	27366/39			
☐ JA8984	Boeing 777-246	27651/68			
☐ JA8985	Boeing 777-246	27652/72			
☐ JA	Boeing 777-				on order
☐ JA8261	McDonnell-Douglas MD-81	49462/1477			
☐ JA8262	McDonnell-Douglas MD-81	49463/1488			Lsd to JEX
☐ JA8294	McDonnell-Douglas MD-81	49820/1598			
☐ JA8295	McDonnell-Douglas MD-81	49821/1615			
☐ JA8374	McDonnell-Douglas MD-81	53043/1982			Lsd to JEX
☐ JA8496	McDonnell-Douglas MD-81	49280/1194			
☐ JA8497	McDonnell-Douglas MD-81	49281/1200			
☐ JA8498	McDonnell-Douglas MD-81	49282/1282	ex N6202S		

Reg	Type	C/n		Notes
☐ JA8499	McDonnell-Douglas MD-81	49283/1299		
☐ JA8554	McDonnell-Douglas MD-81	53299/2075		
☐ JA8556	McDonnell-Douglas MD-81	53301/2082		Lsd to JEX
☐ JA8557	McDonnell-Douglas MD-81	53302/2085		

Reg	Type	C/n
☐ JA001D	McDonnell-Douglas MD-90-30	53555/2207
☐ JA002D	McDonnell-Douglas MD-90-30	53556/2210
☐ JA003D	McDonnell-Douglas MD-90-30	53557/2211
☐ JA004D	McDonnell-Douglas MD-90-30	53558/2212
☐ JA005D	McDonnell-Douglas MD-90-30	53559/2236
☐ JA006D	McDonnell-Douglas MD-90-30	53560/2245
☐ JA8004	McDonnell-Douglas MD-90-30	53359/2164
☐ JA8020	McDonnell-Douglas MD-90-30	53360/2190
☐ JA8029	McDonnell-Douglas MD-90-30	53361/2202
☐ JA8062	McDonnell-Douglas MD-90-30	53352/2098
☐ JA8063	McDonnell-Douglas MD-90-30	53353/2120
☐ JA8064	McDonnell-Douglas MD-90-30	53354/2125
☐ JA8065	McDonnell-Douglas MD-90-30	53355/2131
☐ JA8066	McDonnell-Douglas MD-90-30	53356/2157
☐ JA8069	McDonnell-Douglas MD-90-30	53357/2164
☐ JA8070	McDonnell-Douglas MD-90-30	53358/2179

JAPAN TRANSOCEAN AIR — *JAI Ocean (NU/JTA)* — *Okinawa-Naha (OKA)*

Reg	Type	C/n	Previous
☐ JA8523	Boeing 737-4Q3	26603/2618	
☐ JA8524	Boeing 737-4Q3	26604/2684	
☐ JA8525	Boeing 737-4Q3	26605/2752	
☐ JA8526	Boeing 737-4Q3	26606/2898	
☐ JA8597	Boeing 737-4Q3	27660/3043	
☐ JA8930	Boeing 737-4K5	27102/2394	ex D-AHLM
☐ JA8931	Boeing 737-429	25247/2106	ex N931NU
☐ JA8932	Boeing 737-429	25248/2120	ex N932NU
☐ JA8933	Boeing 737-429	25226/2104	ex N933NU
☐ JA8934	Boeing 737-4K5	27830/2670	ex N934NU
☐ JA8938	Boeing 737-4Q3	29485/3085	
☐ JA8939	Boeing 737-4Q3	29486/3088	ex N1800B
☐ JA8940	Boeing 737-4Q3	29487/3122	
☐ JA8953	Boeing 737-4K5	24129/1783	ex D-AHLP
☐ JA8954	Boeing 737-4K5	24130/1827	ex D-AHLQ

JP EXPRESS — *(9N/AJV)*

Reg	Type	C/n	Previous	Notes
☐ JA601F	Boeing 767-381F	33404/885	ex N6055X	Lsd fr ANA
☐ JA602F	Boeing 767-381F	33509/937		Lsd fr ANA
☐ JA603F	Boeing 767-381F	33510/939		Lsd fr ANA
☐ JA604F	Boeing 767-381F	35709/947		Lsd fr ANA

NEW CENTRAL AVIATION — *Tokyo-Chofu*

Reg	Type	C/n	Previous
☐ JA31CA	Dornier 228-212	8242	ex D-CBDO
☐ JA32CA	Dornier 228-212	8243	ex D-CBDP
☐ JA3453	Cessna TU206C Super Skywagon	U206-1218	ex N1775C
☐ JA3669	Cessna TU206F Turbo Stationair	U20601964	ex N1704C
☐ JA5305	Britten-Norman BN-2B-20 Islander	2239	ex G-BSPS
☐ JA5319	Britten-Norman BN-2B-20 Islander	2268	ex G-BUBK

NIPPON CARGO AIRLINES — *Nippon Cargo (KZ/NCA)* — *Tokyo-Narita (NRT)*

Reg	Type	C/n	Name	Notes
☐ JA01KZ	Boeing 747-481F	34016/1360	NCA Pleiades	
☐ JA02KZ	Boeing 747-481F	34017/1363	NCA Progress	
☐ JA03KZ	Boeing 747-4KZF	34018/1378	NCA Phoenix	
☐ JA04KZ	Boeing 747-4KZF	34283/1384		
☐ JA05KZ	Boeing 747-4KZF	36132/1394		
☐ JA06KZ	Boeing 747-4KZF	36133/1397	NCA Antares	
☐ JA07KZ	Boeing 747-4KZF	36134/1405	NCA Andromeda	
☐ JA08KZ	Boeing 747-4KZF	36135/1408	NCA Aries	
☐ JA11KZ	Boeing 747-8KZF	36136		on order
☐ JA12KZ	Boeing 747-8KZF	36137		on order
☐ JA13KZ	Boeing 747-6KZF	36138		on order

ORIENTAL AIR BRIDGE — *Oriental Bridge (NGK)* — *Nagasaki (NGS)*

Reg	Type	C/n	Previous
☐ JA801B	de Havilland DHC-8Q-201	566	ex C-GDNG
☐ JA802B	de Havilland DHC-8Q-201	579	ex C-FDHO

RYUKYU AIR COMMUTER — *(RAC)* — *Okinawa-Naha (OKA)*

Reg	Type	C/n	Previous
☐ JA5324	Britten-Norman BN-2B-20 Islander	2297	ex G-BWNG
☐ JA5325	Britten-Norman BN-2B-20 Islander	2298	ex G-BWYX
☐ JA8935	de Havilland DHC-8Q-103B	593	ex C-GSAH
☐ JA8936	de Havilland DHC-8Q-314	635	ex C-FIOX
☐ JA8972	de Havilland DHC-8Q-103	472	ex C-GDKL

☐ JA8973	de Havilland DHC-8Q-103	501	ex C-GDLD		
☐ JA8974	de Havilland DHC-8Q-103B	540	ex C-FDHP		

SKYMARK AIRLINES	***Skymark (BC/SKY)***	***Osaka-Itami (ITM)***

☐ JA737H	Boeing 737-86N	34247/1830	ex N1787B	
☐ JA737K	Boeing 737-86N	34249/1857	ex N1786B	
☐ JA737L	Boeing 737-86N	32694/1960		
☐ JA737M	Boeing 737-86N	32683/2136		
☐ JA737N	Boeing 737-8HX	36845/2339		
☐ JA737P	Boeing 737-8HX	29681/2493	ex N1795B	
☐ JA737Q	Boeing 737-86N/W	35228/2630		
☐ JA737R	Boeing 737-86N/W	35630/2666		
☐ JA737S	Boeing 737-8AL			on order
☐ JA737T	Boeing 737-8Q8/W	35290/2818		
☐ JA737U	Boeing 737-8FZ/W	29680/2888		
☐ JA737X	Boeing 737-8FZ/W	36692/3088	ex N1786B	
☐ JA737Y	Boeing 737-8FZ/W	29663		

SKYNET ASIA AIRWAYS	***Newsky (6J/SNJ)***	***Miyazaki (KMI)***

☐ JA391K	Boeing 737-4Y0	24545/1805	ex N545NK	
☐ JA737A	Boeing 737-46Q	29000/3033	ex N56CD	Miyazaki Intl c/s
☐ JA737B	Boeing 737-46Q	29001/3040	ex N89CD	
☐ JA737E	Boeing 737-4Y0	26069/2352	ex N869DC	
☐ JA737F	Boeing 737-43Q	28492/2837	ex N284CH	
☐ JA737G	Boeing 737-43Q	28491/2832	ex N491MT	
☐ JA737V	Boeing 737-4M0	29201/3018	ex N391LS	
☐ JA737W	Boeing 737-4M0	29202/3025	ex N392LS	

STARFLYER	***Starflyer (7G/SFJ)***	***Kitakyushu (KKJ)***

☐ JA01MC	Airbus A320-214	2620	ex F-WWDM	
☐ JA02MC	Airbus A320-214	2658	ex F-WWIP	
☐ JA03MC	Airbus A320-214	2695	ex F-WWII	
☐ JA04MC	Airbus A320-214	3025	ex F-WWBI	
☐ JA	Airbus A320-214	4077	ex	on order

JU - MONGOLIA (State of Mongolia)

AERO MONGOLIA	***Aero Mongolia (MNG)***	***Ulan Bator (ULN)***

☐ JU-8251	Fokker F.27 Mk.050 (Fokker 50)	20251	ex PH-WXH
☐ JU-8258	Fokker F.27 Mk.050 (Fokker 50)	20258	ex PH-KXU
☐ JU-8428	Fokker F.28-0100 (Fokker 100)	11428	ex C-GKZG
☐ JU-8452	Fokker F.28-0100 (Fokker 100)	11352	ex C-GKZB

CENTRAL MONGOLIAN AIRWAYS	***Central Mongolia (CEM)***	***Ulan Bator (ULN)***

☐ JU-5444	Mil Mi-8T	20409	ex JU-1024
☐ JU-5445	Mil Mi-8T	98103227	ex JU-1025
☐ JU-5446	Mil Mi-8T	20411	ex JU-1026

EZNIS AIRWAYS	***(EZA)***	***Ulan Bator (ULN)***

☐ JU-9901	SAAB SF.340B	340B-259	ex N259AE
☐ JU-9903	SAAB SF.340B	340B-297	ex N297AE
☐ JU-9905	SAAB SF.340B	340B-359	ex LY-ESK

HANGARD AIRLINES	***Hangard (HGD)***	***Ulan Bator (ULN)***

☐ RA-41902	Antonov An-38-120	4163847010002	Lsd fr NPO

MIAT - MONGOLIAN AIRLINES	***Mongol Air (OM/MGL)***	***Ulan Bator (ULN)***

☐ EI-CSG	Boeing 737-8AS/W	29922/571		Ogedei Khaan	
☐ EI-CXV	Boeing 737-8CX/W	32364/1166		Khubelai Khaan	
☐ JU-1004	Antonov An-24RV	17306807	ex MT-1004		stored ULN
☐ JU-1006	Antonov An-24RV	47309807	ex MT-1006		stored ULN
☐ JU-1009	Antonov An-24RV	57310104	ex MT-1009		stored ULN
☐ JU-1010	Airbus A310-304	526	ex F-OHPT	Chinggis Khan	
☐ JU-1014	Antonov An-26B-100	14101	ex MT-1014		

SKY HORSE AVIATION	***Sky Horse (TNL)***	***Ulan Bator (ULN)***

☐ JU-2030	LET L-410UVP-E1	861801	ex OK-RDE

JY- JORDAN (Hashemite Kingdom of Jordan)

BARQ AVIATION — Amman (AMM)

☐ N162AT	Lockheed L-1011-500 Tristar	193B-1220	ex JY-AGC		stored VCV
☐ N164AT	Lockheed L-1011-500 Tristar	193B-1238	ex JY-AGE		stored FJR
☐ N194AT	Lockheed L-1011-100 Tristar	193B-1230	ex N8034T		stored FJR

JORDAN AVIATION — Jordan Aviation (R5/JAV) — Amman (AMM)

☐ JY-JAB	Boeing 737-33A	23630/1312	ex N169AW	Noor	
☐ JY-JAC	Airbus A320-211	0029	ex N290SE		
☐ JY-JAD	Boeing 737-322	24662/1862	ex N387UA		
☐ JY-JAE	Boeing 727-2N4	21846/1549	ex 7O-ACX	hanaviation.jo titles	
☐ JY-JAG	Boeing 767-204ER	24757/299	ex G-SLVR		
☐ JY-JAH	Airbus A310-304	481	ex VT-EVH		
☐ JY-JAI	Boeing 767-204ER	24736/296	ex G-SILC		
☐ JY-JAL	Boeing 767-204ER	24239/243	ex G-BOPB		
☐ JY-JAN	Boeing 737-322	23956/1564	ex N324UA	Amman	
☐ JY-JAO	Boeing 737-322	24672/1915	ex N672RY		
☐ JY-JAP	Boeing 737-46B	24124/1679	ex SX-BGX		
☐ JY-JAV	Airbus A310-222	357	ex 3B-STK	Zuhair	op for UN
☐ JY-JAX	Boeing 737-322	23955/1550	ex N323UA		

JORDAN INTERNATIONAL AIR CARGO — (J4/JCI) — Amman (AMM)

☐ JY-JIA	Ilyushin Il-76TD	0023437093	ex EX-86911

ROYAL FALCON — Amman (AMM)

☐ JY-JRD	Boeing 767-3P6ER	26237/544	ex N90GZ	
☐ JY-JRF	Boeing 767-233	22526/92	ex J2-KCN	Lsd to IRQ
☐ JY-RFF	Boeing 737-4K5	27831/2677	ex OO-TUB	

ROYAL JORDANIAN — Jordanian (RJ/RJA) — Amman (AMM)

Member of Oneworld

☐ JY-AGM	Airbus A310-304	491	ex F-ODVH	Prince Hamzeh	
☐ JY-AGN	Airbus A310-304	531	ex F-ODVI	Princess Haya	
☐ JY-AGP	Airbus A310-304	416	ex 5Y-BEL		
☐ JY-AGQ	Airbus A310-304F	445	ex F-ODVF	Princess Raiyah	
☐ JY-AGR	Airbus A310-304F	490	ex F-ODVG	Prince Faisal	
☐ JY-AYL	Airbus A319-132	3428	ex D-AVYQ	Mafraq	
☐ JY-AYM	Airbus A319-132	3685	ex D-AVWC	Ma'an	
☐ JY-AYN	Airbus A319-132	3803	ex D-AVYB	Shobak	
☐ JY-AYP	Airbus A319-132	3832	ex D-AVYL	Ajloun	
☐ F-OHGV	Airbus A320-232	2649	ex F-WWIL	Irbid	
☐ F-OHGX	Airbus A320-231	2953	ex F-WWIX	Madaba	
☐ JY-AYD	Airbus A320-232	2598	ex F-WWBJ	Amman	
☐ JY-AYF	Airbus A320-232	2692	ex F-WWIH	Aqaba	
☐ JY-AYI	Airbus A320-212	0569	ex F-OGYC		Lsd to RWA
☐ JY-AYG	Airbus A321-231	2730	ex D-AVZB	As-Salt	
☐ JY-AYH	Airbus A321-231	2793	ex D-AVZN	Karak	
☐ JY-AYJ	Airbus A321-231	3458	ex D-AVZM	Ramtha	
☐ JY-AYK	Airbus A321-231	3522	ex D-AVZW	Tafila	
☐ JY-AY	Airbus A321-231		ex D-AV		on order
☐ JY-AIA	Airbus A340-212	038	ex F-GLZE	Prince Hussein bin Abdullah	
☐ JY-AIB	Airbus A340-212	043	ex F-GLZF	Princess Iman Bint Abdullah	
☐ JY-AIC	Airbus A340-212	014	ex F-OHLP	Princess Salma Bint Abdullah	
☐ JY-AID	Airbus A340-212	022	ex F-OHLQ	Queen Rania Alabdulah	
☐ ZS-JAV	Fokker F.28 Fellowship 4000	11161	ex N493US		Lsd fr AQU
☐ JY-EMA	Embraer 190-200IGW (195AR)	19000107	ex PT-SQB		
☐ JY-EMB	Embraer 190-200IGW (195AR)	19000131	ex PT-SYJ		
☐ JY-EMC	Embraer 170-200 (175)	17000223	ex PT-SCZ	Zay	
☐ JY-EME	Embraer 190-200IGW (195AR)	19000050	ex PT-SGZ	Jerash	
☐ JY-EMF	Embraer 190-200IGW (195AR)	19000067	ex PT-SJG		
☐ JY-EMG	Embraer 190-200IGW (195AR)	19000088	ex PT-SNG		
☐ JY-	Embraer 170-200 (175)		ex PT-S		on order

ROYAL JORDANIAN XPRESS — Amman (AMM)

Wholly owned subsidiary of Royal Jordanianleases aircraft from the parent as required.

ROYAL WINGS AIRLINES		Royal Wings (RY/RYW)			Amman (AMM)
☐ JY-AYI	Airbus A320-212	0569	ex F-OGYC		Lsd fr RJA
☐ JY-RWB	de Havilland DHC-8Q-315	401	ex N7985B		

SKYGATE INTERNATIONAL		Air Bishkek (SGD)			Amman/Sharjah (AMM/SHJ)
☐ (EX-058)	Lockheed L1011-250 Tristar	193C-1228	ex N737D		stored VCV
☐ JY-SGI	Lockheed L1011-250 Tristar	193C-1234	ex N1738D	Al Saafa	stored AMM

STARJET		(MBM)			Abu Dhabi (AUH)
☐ A6-BSM	Lockheed L-1011-500 Tristar	193G-1222	ex 9L-LED		stored CDG
☐ EX-088	Lockheed L-1011-500 Tristar	193G-1179	ex 9L-LDR	Saif	

TRANSWORLD AVIATION					Amman (AMM)
☐ JY-TWB	Antonov An-26				
☐ JY-TWC	Boeing 737-2T4C	23065/989	ex N110ER		

J2- DJIBOUTI (Republic of Djibouti)

DAALLO AIRLINES		Dalo Airlines (D3/DAO)			Djibouti/Dubai (JIB/DAB)
☐ (J2-KCV)	Boeing 747-212B	21938/436	ex N938GA		stored OPF, for IRA?
☐ J2-SHE	Antonov An-24RV	67310505	ex EK-47318		
☐ J2-SHF	Boeing 747SP-09	21300/304	ex 9Q-CWY		stored SHJ
☐ UP-I1802	Ilyushin Il-18E	185008603	ex UN-75002		Lsd fr MGK

DJIBOUTI AIRLINES		Djibouti Air (D8/DJB)			Djibouti (JIB)

Leases aircraft from other operators as required

SILVER AIR		(SVJ)			Djibouti / Dubai (JIB/DAB)
☐ J2-KCC	Boeing 737-268	20576/297	ex HZ-AGC		stored ADD
☐ J2-KCE	Boeing 737-268	21360/485	ex HZ-AGO		
☐ J2-SRH	Boeing 737-268	21280/471	ex HZ-AGK		
☐ J2-SRS	Boeing 737-268	21361/488	ex HZ-AGP		

TEEBAH AIRLINES		Teebah (TBN)			Amman (AMM)
☐ 9L-LEL	Boeing 727-247 (FedEx 3)	21483/1350	ex N831WA		Lsd to/op for IAW

J8- ST. VINCENT & GRENADINES (State of St. Vincent & Grenadines)

MUSTIQUE AIRWAYS		Mustique (MAW)			Mustique (MQS)
☐ J8-CIW	Britten-Norman BN-2B-26 Islander	2018	ex J8-VAH		
☐ J8-KIM	Rockwell 500S Shrike Commander	3253	ex J8-VBE		
☐ J8-MQS	Aero Commander 500B	1400-144	ex J8-SJK		
☐ J8-PUG	Aero Commander 500U	1670-18	ex J8-VBD		
☐ J6-SLU	Aero Commander 500B	1146-80	ex N6275X		
☐ J8-UVF	Britten-Norman BN-2B-26 Islander	2165	ex J8-VAM		

SVG AIR		Grenadines (SVD)			Kingston, St Vincent (SVD)
☐ J8-SUN	de Havilland DHC-6 Twin Otter 300	477	ex 8P-MLK	all-white	
☐ J8-VAQ	Cessna 402B II STOL	402B1038	ex N400XY		
☐ J8-VAY	Aero Commander 500U	1637-2	ex N6531V		
☐ J8-VBG	Aero Commander 500U	1660-13	ex C-FWPR		
☐ J8-VBI	Britten-Norman BN-2B-26 Islander	2025	ex J3-GAF		
☐ J8-VBJ	Britten-Norman BN-2A Islander	163	ex J3-GAG		
☐ J8-VBK	Britten-Norman BN-2A-26 Islander	570	ex J3-GAH		
☐ J8-VBL	Cessna 402C II	402C0640	ex N404MN		
☐ J8-VBQ	de Havilland DHC-6 Twin Otter 300	604	ex 8P-BGC	all-white	
☐ J8-VBS	de Havilland DHC-6 Twin Otter 300	249	ex 8P-ERK	Trans Island 2000 colours	

LN- NORWAY (Kingdom of Norway)

AIRLIFT					Foerde (FDE)
☐ LN-OCW	Aérospatiale AS350B3 Ecureuil	3942			
☐ LN-OMB	Aérospatiale AS350B2 Ecureuil	2514	ex F-WYMO		Lsd fr Offshore Helicopters
☐ LN-OPF	Aérospatiale AS350B3 Ecureuil	3679			
☐ LN-OPG	Aérospatiale AS350B3 Ecureuil	3712			
☐ LN-OPN	Aérospatiale AS350B3 Ecureuil	4116	ex F-WWXC		Lsd fr Offshore Helicopters

☐ LN-OPP	Aérospatiale AS350B2 Ecureuil	2020	ex SE-HRT		Lsd fr Offshore Helicopters
☐ LN-OPU	Aérospatiale AS350B3 Ecureuil	3563	ex SE-JGR		
☐ LN-OPV	Aérospatiale AS350B2 Ecureuil	2378	ex HB-XUS		Lsd fr Offshore Helicopters
☐ LN-OPW	Aérospatiale AS350B3 Ecureuil	4117	ex F-WWPH		Lsd fr Offshore Helicopters
☐ LN-OPZ	Aérospatiale AS350B3 Ecureuil	3064	ex SE-JCV		
☐ LN-OXA	Aérospatiale AS350B3 Ecureuil	4255			on order
☐ LN-OXB	Aérospatiale AS350B3 Ecureuil	4258	ex F-WWXP		on order
☐ LN-OXC	Aérospatiale AS350B3 Ecureuil	4260	ex F-WWXQ		on order
☐ LN-OXD	Aérospatiale AS350B3 Ecureuil	4278			on order
☐ LN-	Aérospatiale AS350B3 Ecureuil	4105	ex SE-JIM		on order
☐ LN-	Aérospatiale AS350B3 Ecureuil	4106	ex SE-JIO		on order
☐ LN-OBG	Aérospatiale AS355N Ecureuil 2	5681	ex F-WQDF		Lsd fr NOC
☐ LN-OBX	Aérospatiale AS.332C	2001	ex I-EMEB		
☐ LN-OCO	Aérospatiale AS365N Dauphin 2	6420	ex OY-HLL		
☐ LN-OMX	Aérospatiale AS.332L1	2351	ex G-BTNZ		
☐ LN-OPQ	Aérospatiale AS365N1 Dauphin 2	6319	ex 5N-BFP		

AIRWING — *Oslo-Gardermoen (OSL)*

☐ LN-ACY	Beech 65-E90 King Air	LW-309	ex N160TT
☐ LN-AWA	Beech A100 King Air	B-213	ex SE-LDL
☐ LN-AWB	Beech A100 King Air	B-217	ex N730EJ
☐ LN-AWD	Beech 350 Super King Air	FL-256	ex D-CSKF
☐ LN-AWE	Beech 200 Super King Air	BB-459	ex SE-KXM

BENAIR — *Scoop (HAX)* — *Oslo-Gardermoen (OSL)*

☐ LN-PBF	Cessna 208B Caravan I	208B0584	ex OY-PBF
☐ LN-PBK	Cessna 208B Caravan I	208B0914	ex N5196U
☐ LN-PBO	Cessna 208B Caravan I	208B1128	

BERGEN AIR TRANSPORT — *Bergen Air (BGT)* — *Bergen (BGO)*

☐ LN-BAA	Beech B200 Super King Air	BB-1327	ex N67SD
☐ LN-BAB	Beech 350 Super King Air	FL-590	ex N590EU
☐ LN-SEA	Cessna 208 Caravan I	20800383	ex N7890C
☐ LN-TWL	Beech B200 Super King Air	BB-1144	ex N120AJ

BRISTOW NORWAY — *Norske (NOR)* — *Stavanger (SVG)*

☐ LN-OBA	Aérospatiale AS.332L1	2384			
☐ LN-OMI	Aérospatiale AS.332L	2123	ex G-BLZJ		Lsd fr Airlog
☐ LN-ONH	Aérospatiale AS.332L2	2488	ex F-WQDB		Lsd fr Heliair
☐ LN-ONI	Aérospatiale AS.332L2	2500			Lsd fr Heliair
☐ LN-ONF	Eurocopter EC225LP 2	2750			
☐ LN-ONG	Eurocopter EC225LP 2	2755			
☐ LN-ONN	Sikorsky S-92	920011	ex N7107S	Mona Lisa	
☐ LN-ONO	Sikorsky S-92	920012	ex N7108Z	Madonna	
☐ LN-ONP	Sikorsky S-92A	920025	ex N8011N		
☐ LN-ONQ	Sikorsky S-92A	920032	ex N8036Q		
☐ LN-ONR	Sikorsky S-92A	920033	ex N8021R		
☐ LN-ONS	Sikorsky S-92A	920043	ex N8061E		
☐ LN-ONT	Sikorsky S-92A	920070	ex N4510G		
☐ LN-ONU	Sikorsky S-92A	920091	ex N2000Q		
☐ LN-ONV	Sikorsky S-92A	920092	ex N2010H		

CHC HELIKOPTER SERVICE — *Helibus (L5/HKS)* — *Stavanger/Bergen (SVG/BGO)*

☐ LN-OAW	Aérospatiale AS.332L	2053	ex VH-LHD	Lsd fr Heliwest
☐ LN-OHA	Aérospatiale AS.332L	2396	ex F-WYMS	
☐ LN-OHC	Aérospatiale AS.332L	2393		
☐ LN-OHE	Aérospatiale AS.332L2 2	2474		
☐ LN-OHG	Aérospatiale AS.332L2 2	2493		
☐ LN-OHI	Aérospatiale AS.332L2 2	2582	ex F-WW	
☐ LN-OHJ	Aérospatiale AS.332L2 2	2594		
☐ LN-OHK	Aérospatiale AS.332L2 2	2613		
☐ LN-OHL	Aérospatiale AS.332L2 2	2617		
☐ LN-OHM	Aérospatiale AS.332L2 2	2477	ex PR-HPG	
☐ LN-OHW	Eurocopter EC225LP 2	2715		
☐ LN-OHX	Eurocopter EC225LP 2	2707		
☐ LN-OHZ	Eurocopter EC225LP 2	2691		
☐ LN-OJA	Eurocopter EC225LP 2	2692		
☐ LN-OJB	Eurocopter EC225LP 2	2725		
☐ LN-OJE	Eurocopter EC225LP 2	2716		
☐ LN-OJF	Eurocopter EC225LP 2	2721		
☐ LN-OLB	Aérospatiale AS.332L	2082	ex OY-HMJ	Lsd fr Heliwest
☐ LN-OLD	Aérospatiale AS.332L	2103	ex OY-HMI	Lsd fr Heliwest
☐ LN-OME	Aérospatiale AS.332L	2139	ex C-GQCH	Lsd fr Heliwest
☐ LN-OMF	Aérospatiale AS.332L	2067	ex G-PUMK	

Reg	Type	C/n	Previous	Name	Notes
☐ LN-OMH	Aérospatiale AS.332L	2113	ex HZ-RH4		Lsd fr Heliwest
☐ LN-OPH	Aérospatiale AS.332L1	2347			
☐ LN-OPX	Aérospatiale AS.332L1	9009			
☐ LN-OQA	Sikorsky S-92A	920013	ex (LN-ONO)		
☐ LN-OQB	Sikorsky S-92A	920014	ex (LN-OQA)		
☐ LN-OQC	Sikorsky S-92A	920018	ex N7118N		
☐ LN-OQD	Sikorsky S-92A	920022	ex N8016T		
☐ LN-OQE	Sikorsky S-92A	920047	ex N80071		
☐ LN-OQF	Sikorsky S-92A	920056	ex N4502R		
☐ LN-OQG	Sikorsky S-92A	920095			
☐ LN-OQH	Sikorsky S-92A	920097	ex N2021Y		
☐ LN-OQI	Sikorsky S-92A	920098			
☐ LN-OQJ	Sikorsky S-92A	920110	ex N2126Z		
☐ LN-OQK	Sikorsky S-92A	920114			
☐ LN-OMM	Bell 214ST	28199	ex N3216U		Lsd fr Heliwest
☐ LN-OMN	Aérospatiale SA365N2 Dauphin 2	6423	ex F-GHXG		Lsd fr Heliwest

CLASSIC NORWAY AIR — **_Molde (MOL)_**

Reg	Type	C/n	Previous
☐ LN-SVZ	British Aerospace Jetstream 31	641	ex OY-SVZ

FONNAFLY — **_Fonna (NOF)_** — **_Rosendal / Bergen / Oslo-Gardermoen / Voss (-/BGN/OSL/-)_**

Reg	Type	C/n	Previous	Name	Notes
☐ LN-BWV	Cessna U206F Stationair	U20601994		Fonna 18	floatplane
☐ LN-FFF	Cessna U206G Stationair 6 II	U20604497	ex SE-GXB	Fonna 19	floatplane
☐ LN-HON	Cessna U206G Stationair 6 II	U20605475		Fonna 17	floatplane
☐ LN-HOO	Cessna TU206F Turbo Stationair 6 II	U20605490		Fonna 10	floatplane
☐ LN-IKA	Cessna TU206F Turbo Stationair 6 II	U20606251	ex N6356Z	Fonna 11	floatplane
☐ LN-MAG	Cessna U206G Stationair 6	U20603733	ex SE-GZY	Fonna 11	floatplane
☐ LN-TEP	Cessna U206G Stationair 6 II	U20605186	ex N5305U	Fonna 15	floatplane

HELITRANS — **_Scanbird (HTA)_** — **_Trondheim (TRD)_**

Reg	Type	C/n	Previous	Notes
☐ LN-OAK	Aérospatiale AS350B3 Ecureuil	3212		
☐ LN-OAU	Aérospatiale AS350BA Ecureuil	1533	ex SE-HRO	
☐ LN-OGL	Aérospatiale AS350B3 Ecureuil	3792	ex F-WQDD	Lsd fr Helicopter Network
☐ LN-OLG	Aérospatiale AS350B2 Ecureuil	2198		
☐ LN-OMD	Aérospatiale AS350B3 Ecureuil	3303	ex HB-ZCL	
☐ LN-OMY	Aérospatiale AS350BA Ecureuil	1017	ex SE-HIA	
☐ LN-OPA	Aérospatiale AS350B3 Ecureuil	3589		
☐ LN-OPE	Aérospatiale AS350B1 Ecureuil	2183		based Greenland
☐ LN-ABO	Cessna 185A Skywagon	185-0439	ex SE-EEM	
☐ LN-FAN	British Aerospace Jetstream 32	864	ex SE-LHK	Lsd to BCI
☐ LN-FAQ	British Aerospace Jetstream 32EP	953	ex UR-CET	
☐ LN-HTB	British Aerospace Jetstream 32EP	795	ex G-OAKJ	
☐ LN-HTD	Swearingen SA.226T Merlin III	T-294	ex PH-DYB	Op for Baltic Air Svs
☐ LN-OPO	Bell 214B	28053	ex N18091	Lsd fr Helitrans Heavylift
☐ LN-ORM	Bell 214B-1	28054	ex SE-HLE	

KATO AIRLINE — **_Kato-Air (6S/KAT)_** — **_Harstad (EVE)_**

Reg	Type	C/n	Previous
☐ LN-AAO	Dornier 228-201	8108	ex SE-LHD
☐ LN-KAT	Cessna 208B Caravan I	208B0970	ex N12295
☐ LN-KJK	Cessna 208B Caravan I	208B0554	ex N1267A

LUFTTRANSPORT — **_Luft Transport (L5/LTR)_** — **_Bardufoss (BDU)_**

Reg	Type	C/n	Previous	Name
☐ LN-OLE	Aérospatiale SA365N2 Dauphin 2	6405	ex VT-CKR	
☐ LN-OLM	Aérospatiale AS365N3 Dauphin 2	6725	ex F-WWOT	
☐ LN-OLN	Aérospatiale AS365N3 Dauphin 2	6721	ex F-WWOF	
☐ LN-OLF	Agusta AW139	31148		
☐ LN-OLO	Agusta AW139	31139		
☐ LN-OLS	Agusta AW139	31136		
☐ LN-OLU	Agusta AW139	31135		
☐ LN-OLV	Agusta AW139	31023	ex I-RAIB	Vaeroy
☐ LN-LTA	Beech B200 Super King Air	BB-1868	ex N954RM	
☐ LN-LTB	Beech B200 Super King Air	BB-2001	ex N3501D	
☐ LN-LTC	Beech B200 Super King Air	BB-2002	ex N60102	
☐ LN-LTD	Beech B200 Super King Air	BB-2006	ex N61806	
☐ LN-LTE	Beech B200 Super King Air	BB-2007	ex N63007	
☐ LN-LTG	Beech B200 Super King Air	BB-2009		
☐ LN-MOB	Beech 200 Super King Air	BB-584	ex (N490WP)	
☐ LN-MOC	Beech B200 Super King Air	BB-1449	ex N200KA	
☐ LN-MOD	Beech B200 Super King Air	BB-1459	ex N8163R	
☐ LN-MOE	Beech B200 Super King Air	BB-1460	ex N8164G	
☐ LN-MOF	Beech B200 Super King Air	BB-1461	ex N8261E	
☐ LN-MOG	Beech B200 Super King Air	BB-1465	ex N8214T	

☐ LN-MOH	Beech B200 Super King Air	BB-1466	ex N8216Z	
☐ LN-MOI	Beech B200 Super King Air	BB-1470	ex N8225Z	
☐ LN-MOJ	Beech B200 Super King Air	BB-1334	ex TC-SKO	
☐ LN-MOT	Beech B200 Super King Air	BB-1590	ex D-IHUT	
☐ LN-LYR	Dornier 228-202K	8166	ex D-CICA	Kings Bay
☐ LN-MOL	Dornier 228-202K	8156	ex TF-ELA	
☐ LN-OLA	Agusta A.109E Power	11117		
☐ LN-OLI	Agusta A.109E Power	11204		

NORSK LUFTAMBULANCE — ***Helidoc (DOC)*** — ***Oslo/Dröbak (OSL/-)***

☐ LN-OOC	Eurocopter EC135P2	0350	ex D-HECH	EMS
☐ LN-OOD	Eurocopter EC135P2	0356	ex D-HECL	EMS
☐ LN-OOE	Eurocopter EC135P2	0357	ex D-HECA	EMS
☐ LN-OOF	Eurocopter EC135P2	0390	ex D-HECH	EMS
☐ LN-OOG	Eurocopter EC135P2	0393	ex D-HECM	EMS
☐ LN-OOH	Eurocopter EC135P2	0399	ex D-HECG	EMS
☐ LN-OOI	Eurocopter EC135P2	0580		EMS
☐ LN-OOJ	Eurocopter EC135P2+	0588		EMS
☐ LN-OOK	Eurocopter EC135P2	0669	ex D-HTSH	EMS
☐ LN-OOM	MBB BK-117C-2	9074	ex D-HMBB	
☐ LN-OSI	MBB Bo.105CBS-4	S-609	ex N29144	EMS
☐ LN-OSZ	MBB Bo.105CBS-4	S-666	ex N4573A	EMS

NORWEGIAN — ***Nor Shuttle (DY/NAX)*** — ***Oslo-Gardermoen (OSL)***

☐ LN-DYA	Boeing 737-8JP/W	39162/2994	ex N1786B		
☐ LN-DYB	Boeing 737-8JP/W	39163/3054			
☐ LN-DYC	Boeing 737-8JP/W	39164			on order
☐ LN-DYD	Boeing 737-8JP/W	39002			on order
☐ LN-	Boeing 737-8JP/W				on order
☐ LN-	Boeing 737-8JP/W				on order
☐ LN-	Boeing 737-8JP/W				on order
☐ LN-	Boeing 737-8JP/W				on order
☐ LN-	Boeing 737-8JP/W				on order
☐ LN-	Boeing 737-8JP/W				on order
☐ LN-KHA	Boeing 737-31S/W	29100/2984	ex SX-BGY		
☐ LN-KHB	Boeing 737-31S	29264/3070	ex SX-BGW		
☐ LN-KHC	Boeing 737-31S/W	29265/3073	ex SX-BGZ		
☐ LN-KHD	Boeing 737-8BK/W	33022/1672	ex G-CDEG		
☐ LN-KKA	Boeing 737-33A	25033/2025	ex SX-BTO		
☐ LN-KKB	Boeing 737-33A	27457/2756	ex N457AN		
☐ LN-KKC	Boeing 737-3Y5	25615/2478	ex 9H-ABT		
☐ LN-KKD	Boeing 737-33V	29339/3119	ex 5N-VNB		
☐ LN-KKE	Boeing 737-33A	27285/2608	ex G-ZAPM		
☐ LN-KKF	Boeing 737-3K2	24326/1683	ex N730BC		
☐ LN-KKG	Boeing 737-3K2	24327/1712	ex PH-HVN	Gidsken Jakobsen	
☐ LN-KKH	Boeing 737-3K2	24328/1856	ex PH-HVT	Otto Sverdrup	
☐ LN-KKI	Boeing 737-3K2	24329/1858	ex PH-HVV	Helge Ingstad	
☐ LN-KKJ	Boeing 737-36N	28564/2936	ex N564SR	Sonja Henie	
☐ LN-KKL	Boeing 737-36N	28671/2955	ex N671SR	Roald Amundsen	
☐ LN-KKM	Boeing 737-3Y0	24676/1829	ex HA-LES	Thor Heyerdahl	
☐ LN-KKN	Boeing 737-3Y0	24910/2030	ex HA-LET	Sigrid Undset	
☐ LN-KKO	Boeing 737-3Y0	24909/2021	ex HA-LED	Henrik Ibsen	
☐ LN-KKP	Boeing 737-3M8	25040/2017	ex OO-SBX	Kirsten Flagstad	
☐ LN-KKQ	Boeing 737-36Q	28658/2865	ex EC-GMY	Alf Proysen	
☐ LN-KKR	Boeing 737-3Y0	24256/1629	ex OM-AAA		
☐ LN-KKS	Boeing 737-33A	24094/1729	ex ZK-PLU	Unicef colours	
☐ LN-KKT	Boeing 737-3L9	27336/2587	ex G-IGOS		
☐ LN-KKU	Boeing 737-3L9	27337/2594	ex G-IGOU		
☐ LN-KKV	Boeing 737-3Y5	25613/2446	ex 9H-ABR	Niels Henrik Abel	
☐ LN-KKW	Boeing 737-3K9	24213/1794	ex CS-TLL		
☐ LN-KKX	Boeing 737-33S/W	29072/3012	ex ZK-NGN		Networknorway c/s
☐ LN-KKY	Boeing 737-3S3	29245/3061	ex N292SZ		acta c/s
☐ LN-KKZ	Boeing 737-33A	27458/2959	ex N458AN		
☐ LN-NOB	Boeing 737-8FZ/W	34954/2483	ex N1786B	Edvard Grieg	
☐ LN-NOC	Boeing 737-81Q/W	30785/1007	ex EC-ICD		
☐ LN-NOD	Boeing 737-8Q8/W	35280/2629		Sonja Henie	
☐ LN-NOE	Boeing 737-8Q8/W	35283/2742	ex N1786B		
☐ LN-NOF	Boeing 737-86N/W	36809/2647			
☐ LN-NOG	Boeing 737-86N/W	35647/2927	ex N1786B		
☐ LN-NOH	Boeing 737-86N/W	35814/3015	ex N1796B		
☐ LN-NOJ	Boeing 737-86N/W	37884			on order
☐ LN-NOL	Boeing 737-8Q8/W	37159/2868			
☐ LN-NOM	Boeing 737-86N/W	28642/813	ex SE-RHA		
☐ LN-NON	Boeing 737-86N/W	28620/542	ex SE-RHB		
☐ LN-NOO	Boeing 737-86Q/W	30289/1399	ex N289CG		
☐ LN-NOP	Boeing 737-86N/W	32655/1662	ex EI-ECL		
☐ LN-NOQ	Boeing 737-86N/W	32658/1695	ex EI-ECM		
☐ LN-NOS	Boeing 737-8BK/W	33018/1488	ex EI-EDL		

☐ LN-NOT	Boeing 737-8JP/W	37816		on order
☐ LN-NOU	Boeing 737-8FZ/W	29674/3140		
☐ LN-NOV	Boeing 737-8FZ/W	31713		on order

SAS NORGE — *Scanor (SK/CNO)* — *Oslo-Gardermoen / Stavanger (OSL/SVG)*

Merged back into mainline SAS 01/Oct/2009

SCANDINAVIAN AIRLINE SYSTEM — *Scandinavian (SK/SAS)* — *Copenhagen-Kastrup (CPH)*

For details see under Sweden (SE-)

WIDERØE'S FLYVESELSKAP — *Widerøe (WF/WIF)* — *Bodo (BOO)*

☐ LN-ILS	de Havilland DHC-8-103	396	ex C-GHRI	
☐ LN-WDE	de Havilland DHC-8-402Q	4183	ex	
☐ LN-WDF	de Havilland DHC-8-402Q	4244	ex C-FUTZ	
☐ LN-WDG	de Havilland DHC-8-402Q	4266	ex C-FXJF	
☐ LN-WDH	de Havilland DHC-8-402Q	4273	ex C-FYGI	
☐ LN-WDI	de Havilland DHC-8-402Q	4286	ex C-FZFX	
☐ LN-WDJ	de Havilland DHC-8-402Q	4290	ex C-GARX	
☐ LN-WDK	de Havilland DHC-8-402Q		ex	on order
☐ LN-WFC	de Havilland DHC-8-311A	236	ex D-BEYT	
☐ LN-WFD	de Havilland DHC-8-311	407	ex C-FSIJ	
☐ LN-WFH	de Havilland DHC-8-311A	238	ex C-FZOH	all-white
☐ LN-WFO	de Havilland DHC-8Q-311	493	ex C-GERC	
☐ LN-WFP	de Havilland DHC-8Q-311	495	ex C-GFUM	Epledrikk colours
☐ LN-WFS	de Havilland DHC-8Q-311	535	ex C-GEWI	
☐ LN-WFT	de Havilland DHC-8Q-311	532	ex C-FATN	
☐ LN-WIA	de Havilland DHC-8-103B	359	ex C-GHRI	Nordland
☐ LN-WIB	de Havilland DHC-8-103B	360	ex C-GFBW	Finnmark
☐ LN-WIC	de Havilland DHC-8-103B	367	ex C-GDNG	Sogn og Fjordane
☐ LN-WID	de Havilland DHC-8-103B	369	ex C-FDHD	More og Romsdal
☐ LN-WIE	de Havilland DHC-8-103B	371	ex C-GFYI	Hordaland
☐ LN-WIF	de Havilland DHC-8-103B	372	ex C-GFOD	Nord-Tröndelag
☐ LN-WIG	de Havilland DHC-8-103B	382	ex C-GLOT	Troms
☐ LN-WIH	de Havilland DHC-8-103B	383	ex C-GFYI	Oslo
☐ LN-WII	de Havilland DHC-8-103B	384	ex C-GFOD	Nordkapp
☐ LN-WIJ	de Havilland DHC-8-103B	386	ex C-GFQL	Hammerfest
☐ LN-WIL	de Havilland DHC-8-103B	398	ex C-GFCF	Narvik
☐ LN-WIM	de Havilland DHC-8-103B	403	ex C-GDIU	Vesterälen
☐ LN-WIN	de Havilland DHC-8-103B	409	ex C-GDNG	Alstadhaug/Lofoten
☐ LN-WIO	de Havilland DHC-8-103B	417	ex C-GFQL	Rost/Akershus
☐ LN-WIP	de Havilland DHC-8-103A	239	ex C-FXNE	Alstahaug
☐ LN-WIR	de Havilland DHC-8-103A	273	ex C-FZNU	Nordkyn
☐ LN-WIT	de Havilland DHC-8-103	310	ex D-BIER	
☐ LN-WIU	de Havilland DHC-8-103	378	ex C-FZKQ	

LV- ARGENTINA (Republic of Argentina)

AEROCHACO

☐ LV-BSC	McDonnell-Douglas MD-87	49727/1621	ex N755RA
☐ LV-BZH	McDonnell-Douglas MD-87	49780/1674	ex N572SH
☐ LV-ZPZ	British Aerospace Jetstream 32EP	931	ex N931AE

AEROLINEAS ARGENTINAS — *Argentina (AR/ARG)* — *Buenos Aires-Ezeiza (EZE)*

☐ LV-BIT	Airbus A340-313	093	ex 9Y-TJN	
☐ LV-BMT	Airbus A340-312	048	ex C-FDRO	
☐ LV-ZPJ	Airbus A340-211	074	ex F-OHPG	
☐ LV-ZPO	Airbus A340-211	063	ex F-OHPF	
☐ LV-ZPX	Airbus A340-211	080	ex F-OHPH	
☐ LV-ZRA	Airbus A340-211	085	ex F-OHPI	stored EZE

☐ LV-AYE	Boeing 737-5H6	26456/2527	ex F-GJNY
☐ LV-AYI	Boeing 737-528	25234/2411	ex F-GJNI
☐ LV-AZU	Boeing 737-528	25235/2428	ex F-GJNJ
☐ LV-BAR	Boeing 737-528	26450/2503	ex F-GJNZ
☐ LV-BAT	Boeing 737-5H6	27356/2654	ex F-GJNP
☐ LV-BAX	Boeing 737-5H6	26448/2484	ex F-GJNL
☐ LV-BBN	Boeing 737-5H6	26454/2511	ex F-GJNX
☐ LV-BBW	Boeing 737-5Y0	24897/2003	ex B-2542
☐ LV-BDD	Boeing 737-5Y0	24899/2093	ex B-2544
☐ LV-BDV	Boeing 737-5Y0	24900/2095	ex B-2545
☐ LV-BEO	Boeing 737-5Y0	25176/2155	ex B-2547
☐ LV-BIH	Boeing 737-53A	24786/1898	ex N786AW
☐ LV-BIM	Boeing 737-53A	25425/2177	ex N425AN
☐ LV-BIX	Boeing 737-53A	24788/1921	ex N233BC
☐ LV-BNM	Boeing 737-5K5	24926/1966	ex D-AHLD
☐ LV-BNS	Boeing 737-5K5	24776/1848	ex D-AHLG

Registration	Type	c/n	Previous identity	Name	Remarks
☐ LV-BOT	Boeing 737-505	24652/1917	ex N650TC		
☐ LV-BYY	Boeing 737-7BD/W	33938/2863	ex N357AT		
☐ LV-BZA	Boeing 737-76N/W	32674/1952	ex OK-GCA		
☐ LV-BZO	Boeing 737-76N/W	32676/1974	ex OK-GCB		
☐ LV-CAD	Boeing 737-76N/W	32680/2089	ex OK-GCC		
☐ LV-CAM	Boeing 737-73V/W	30243/919	ex N243CL		
☐ LV-CAP	Boeing 737-76N/W	32695/1919	ex OK-GCD		
☐ LV-CAT	Boeing 737-73V/W	30235/672	ex N384DF		
☐ LV-CBF	Boeing 737-76N/W	32696/1922	ex OK-GCE		
☐ LV-CBG	Boeing 737-73V/W	30236/715	ex N385DF		
☐ LV-CBS	Boeing 737-73V/W	30237/730	ex N386DF		
☐ LV-CBT	Boeing 737-76N/W	34756/2208	ex OK-GCF		
☐ LV-GOO	Boeing 737-7BD	35962/2932	ex N358AT		
☐ LV-WSY	Boeing 737-281	20562/293	ex JA8416		Lsd to DLU
☐ LV-WTX	Boeing 737-281	20561/292	ex LV-PMI		stored
☐ LV-ZRO	Boeing 737-236	23164/1060	ex N925PG		stored EZE
☐ LV-ZSW	Boeing 737-236	23170/1086	ex N937PG		stored
☐ LV-ZTT	Boeing 737-236	21806/699	ex N947PG		stored EZE
☐ LV-ZTY	Boeing 737-236	23159/1047	ex N949PG		
☐ LV-ZXC	Boeing 737-236	23160/1053	ex N950PG		
☐ LV-ZXP	Boeing 737-228	23003/939	ex LV-PIV		stored EZE
☐ LV-ZXU	Boeing 737-236	23226/1105	ex N952PG		
☐ LV-ZYG	Boeing 737-236	21795/645	ex N954PG		stored EZE
☐ LV-ZYI	Boeing 737-228	23010/959	ex LV-PJC		
☐ LV-ZYN	Boeing 737-236	21794/643	ex N900PG		
☐ LV-ZZD	Boeing 737-228	23011/971	ex LV-PJD		
☐ LV-ZZI	Boeing 737-236	23166/1067	ex N956PG		
☐ LV-ALJ	Boeing 747-475	25422/912	ex N971PG		
☐ LV-AXF	Boeing 747-475	24895/837	ex N895NC		
☐ LV-BBU	Boeing 747-475	24883/823	ex N987PG		
☐ LV-MLP	Boeing 747-287B	21726/403			
☐ LV-MLR	Boeing 747-287B	21727/404			stored EZE
☐ LV-OEP	Boeing 747-287B	22297/487			
☐ LV-OPA	Boeing 747-287B	22593/552	ex EC-JJG		stored EZE
☐ LV-VBX	McDonnell-Douglas MD-88	53047/2016		Parque Nacional Lanin	
☐ LV-VBZ	McDonnell-Douglas MD-88	53049/2031		Parque Baritu	
☐ LV-VCB	McDonnell-Douglas MD-88	53351/2043	ex EC-JKC	Parque Iguazu	stored AEP
☐ LV-VGB	McDonnell-Douglas MD-88	53446/2046	ex EC-JOI	Parque Nahuel Huapi	stored AEP
☐ LV-VGC	McDonnell-Douglas MD-88	53447/2064		Parque Calilegua	stored AEP
☐ LV-AIV	Airbus A310-325	640	ex EC-IHV		stored EZE

AERO VIP ***(AOG)*** ***Buenos Aires-Aeroparque (AEP)***

Registration	Type	c/n	Previous identity
☐ LV-BYW	Canadair CL-600-2D24 (CRJ-900)	15209	ex CX-CRG

AIR TANGO ***Buenos Aires-Aeroparque (AEP)***

Registration	Type	c/n	Previous identity
☐ LV-WEO	Swearingen SA.226TC Metro II	TC-346	ex N52EA

AMERICAN JET ***Buenos Aires-Aeroparque (AEP)***

Registration	Type	c/n	Previous identity	Remarks
☐ LV-BYJ	Swearingen SA.227DC Metro 23	DC-889B	ex N889AJ	
☐ LV-BYL	Swearingen SA.227DC Metro 23	DC-819B	ex N819SK	
☐ LV-BYM	Swearingen SA.227DC Metro 23	DC-856B	ex N3027B	
☐ LV-BYN	Swearingen SA.227DC Metro 23	DC-888B	ex N332AJ	
☐ LV-WTD	Dornier 228-200	8094	ex D-CBDR	
☐ LV-WTV	Dornier 228-200	8093	ex N228AM	
☐ LV-ZXA	Swearingen SA.227DC Metro 23	DC-901B	ex LV-PIR	no titles

ANDES LINEAS AEREAS ***Aeroandes (ANS)*** ***Salta International (SLA)***

Registration	Type	c/n	Previous identity
☐ LV-BHF	McDonnell-Douglas MD-82	49508/1449	ex N821NK
☐ LV-BTH	McDonnell-Douglas MD-83	49952/1934	ex N995AC
☐ LV-BZR	McDonnell-Douglas MD-87	49706/1614	ex XA-TWT

AUSTRAL LINEAS AEREAS ***Austral (AU/AUT)*** ***Buenos Aires-Aeroparque (AEP)***

Registration	Type	c/n	Previous identity	Remarks
☐ LV-ZTE	Boeing 737-228	23349/1135	ex LV-PIJ	stored AEP
☐ LV-ZTX	Boeing 737-228	23504/1267	ex LV-PIP	stored EZE
☐ LV-ZXB	Boeing 737-228	23009/958	ex LV-PIS	
☐ LV-ZXH	Boeing 737-228	23503/1256	ex LV-PIU	stored AEP
☐ LV-ZXV	Boeing 737-228	23793/1426	ex LV-PIX	stored EZE
☐ LV-ARF	McDonnell-Douglas MD-83	49252/1169	ex LV-PJH	
☐ LV-AYD	McDonnell-Douglas MD-83	53015/1818	ex N824NK	stored Palomar
☐ LV-BAY	McDonnell-Douglas MD-83	49284/1209	ex LV-PJJ	
☐ LV-BDE	McDonnell-Douglas MD-83	49943/1887	ex N943MT	stored AEP
☐ LV-BDO	McDonnell-Douglas MD-83	49941/1793	ex N941MT	
☐ LV-BEG	McDonnell-Douglas MD-83	49630/1591	ex N320FV	stored AEP

☐ LV-BGV	McDonnell-Douglas MD-83	49904/1680	ex N960PG	stored AEP
☐ LV-BGZ	McDonnell-Douglas MD-82	49906/1786	ex EC-JZA	
☐ LV-BHH	McDonnell-Douglas MD-82	49741/1630	ex N959PG	
☐ LV-BHN	McDonnell-Douglas MD-83	53190/2148	ex N190AN	
☐ LV-VAG	McDonnell-Douglas MD-83	53117/1951	ex N6202D	
☐ LV-WFN	McDonnell-Douglas MD-81	48025/952	ex N10027	stored AEP
☐ LV-WGM	McDonnell-Douglas MD-83	49784/1627	ex N509MD	
☐ LV-WGN	McDonnell-Douglas MD-83	49934/1764	ex N907MD	
☐ LV-BOA	McDonnell-Douglas MD-88	53174/1854	ex N168PL	
☐ LV-BOH	McDonnell-Douglas MD-88	53175/1868	ex N169PL	
☐ LV-BOR	McDonnell-Douglas MD-88	49929/1741	ex XA-AMV	stored AEP
☐ LV-BTI	McDonnell-Douglas MD-88	49927/1716	ex XA-AMT	
☐ LV-BTW	McDonnell-Douglas MD-88	49926/1715	ex XA-AMS	
☐ LV-BXA	McDonnell-Douglas MD-88	49928/1732	ex XA-AMU	

BAIRES FLY — *Buenos Aires-Aeroparque (AEP)*

☐ LV-VDJ	Swearingen SA.227AC Metro III	AC-729	ex N27823
☐ LV-WHG	Swearingen SA.226TC Metro II	TC-344	ex N44CS
☐ LV-WJT	Swearingen SA.227AC Metro III	AC-776B	ex N776NE
☐ LV-WTE	Swearingen SA.227AC Metro III	AC-584	ex LV-PMF
☐ LV-ZMG	Swearingen SA.227AC Metro III	AC-425	ex N721MA

FLYING AMERICA — *Buenos Aires-Aeroparque (AEP)*

☐ LV-BGH	Swearingen SA.227AC Metro III	AC-467	ex TF-JMK
☐ LV-BGR	Swearingen SA.227AC Metro III	AC-461B	ex EC-HXY
☐ LV-YIC	Swearingen SA.227AC Metro III	AC-448	ex LV-PNF

HANGAR UNO — *Buenos Aires-Don Torcuato*

☐ LV-WFR	Britten-Norman BN-2B-26 Islander	2263	ex G-BUBF	Puerto Carmelo titles

HAWK AIR — *Air Hawk (HKR)* — *Buenos Aires-Aeroparque (AEP)*

☐ LV-WHX	Piper PA-31 Turbo Navajo	31-353	ex N716DR	
☐ LV-WIR	Swearingen SA.226T Merlin III	T-232	ex N56TA	Freighter
☐ LV-WNC	Swearingen SA.226AT Merlin IVA	AT-036	ex N642TS	Freighter
☐ LV-WXW	Swearingen SA.226TC Metro II	TC-419	ex N7205L	Freighter

LADE - LINEAS AEREAS DEL ESTADO — *Lade (5U/LDE)* — *Comodoro Rivadavia (CRD)*

☐ TC-91	Boeing 707-387B	21070/897	ex T-91	
☐ T-81	de Havilland DHC-6 Twin Otter 200	165		
☐ T-82	de Havilland DHC-6 Twin Otter 200	167		
☐ T-85	de Havilland DHC-6 Twin Otter 200	173		
☐ T-86	de Havilland DHC-6 Twin Otter 200	225		Antarctic red colours
☐ T-88	de Havilland DHC-6 Twin Otter 200	158	ex LV-JMP	
☐ T-89	de Havilland DHC-6 Twin Otter 200	185	ex LV-JPX	
☐ T-90	de Havilland DHC-6 Twin Otter 200	178	ex LV-JMR	
☐ T-44	Fokker F.27 Friendship 600	10454	ex PH-EXB	
☐ T-45	Fokker F.27 Friendship 600	10368	ex TC-79	
☐ TC-71	Fokker F.27 Friendship 400M	10403	ex PH-FOB	
☐ TC-74	Fokker F.27 Friendship 400M	10408	ex PH-FOG	
☐ TC-75	Fokker F.27 Friendship 500	10621	ex PH-EXM	
☐ TC-79	Fokker F.27 Friendship 400M	10575	ex PH-EXG	
☐ TC-52	Fokker F.28 Fellowship 1000C	11074	ex LV-RCS	stored El Palomar
☐ TC-53	Fokker F.28 Fellowship 1000C	11020	ex PH-EXX	
☐ TC-55	Fokker F.28 Fellowship 1000C	11024	ex PH-EXZ	stored
☐ T-31	SAAB SF.340B	340B-270	ex N284DC	
☐ T-32	SAAB SF.340B	340B-226	ex N285DC	
☐ T-33	SAAB SF.340B	340B-288	ex N288JJ	
☐ T-34	SAAB SF.340B	340B-217	ex N217JJ	

LAN ARGENTINA — *LAN Ar (4M/DSM)* — *Buenos Aires-Aeroparque (AEP)*

☐ LV-BET	Airbus A320-233	1854	ex CC-COO	Lsd fr LAN
☐ LV-BFO	Airbus A320-233	1877	ex CC-COQ	Lsd fr LAN
☐ LV-BFY	Airbus A320-233	1858	ex CC-COP	Lsd fr LAN
☐ LV-BGI	Airbus A320-233	1903	ex CC-COT	Lsd fr LAN
☐ LV-BHU	Airbus A320-233	1512	ex CC-COH	Lsd fr LAN
☐ LV-BOI	Airbus A320-233	1491	ex CC-COG	Lsd fr LAN
☐ LV-BRA	Airbus A320-233	1304	ex CC-COC	Lsd fr LAN
☐ LV-BRY	Airbus A320-233	1351	ex CC-COE	Lsd fr LAN
☐ LV-BSJ	Airbus A320-233	1332	ex CC-COD	Lsd fr LAN
☐ LV-BTA	Airbus A320-233	1548	ex CC-COK	Lsd fr LAN

☐ LV-BMR	Boeing 767-316ER	26329/641	ex CC-CEK	Lsd fr LAN
☐ LV-BTE	Boeing 767-375ER	25865/430	ex CC-CRG	Lsd fr LAN

MACAIR JET — *Buenos Aires-Aeroparque (AEP)*

☐ LV-ZOW	British Aerospace Jetstream 32EP	869	ex N869AE
☐ LV-ZPW	British Aerospace Jetstream 32EP	861	ex N861AE
☐ LV-ZRL	British Aerospace Jetstream 32EP	928	ex N928AE
☐ LV-ZSB	British Aerospace Jetstream 32EP	942	ex N942AE
☐ LV-ZST	British Aerospace Jetstream 32EP	941	ex N941AE

SOL LINEAS AEREAS — *Flight Sol (8R/OLS)* — *Rosario-Fisherton (ROS)*

☐ LV-BEW	SAAB SF.340A	340A-150	ex N150CN
☐ LV-BEX	SAAB SF.340A	340A-014	ex N14XS
☐ LV-BMD	SAAB SF.340A	340A-123	ex N123XS
☐ LV-BTP	SAAB SF.340A	340A-131	ex VH-KDI

TAPSA AVIACION — *Tapsa (TPS)* — *Buenos Aires-Aeroparque (AEP)*

☐ LV-LSI	de Havilland DHC-6 Twin Otter 300	456	ex LV-PTW

TRANSPORTES BRAGADO — *Buenos Aires-Aeroparque (AEP)*

☐ LV-MGD	Piper PA-31T Cheyenne	31T-7720059	ex LV-PXD
☐ LV-ZNU	Cessna 208B Caravan I	208B0718	ex LV-POC

LX- LUXEMBOURG (Grand Duchy of Luxembourg)

CARGOLUX AIRLINES INTERNATIONAL — *Cargolux (CV/CLX)* — *Luxembourg (LUX)*

☐ LX-ACV	Boeing 747-8R7F	35806/1423			on order
☐ LX-DCV	Boeing 747-8R7F	35807/1424			on order
☐ LX-ECV	Boeing 747-8R7F	35808/1420			on order
☐ LX-GCV	Boeing 747-4R7F	25867/1008		Esch/Alzette	
☐ LX-LCV	Boeing 747-4R7F	29053/1139		Grevenmacher	
☐ LX-MCV	Boeing 747-4R7F	29729/1189		Echternach	
☐ LX-NCV	Boeing 747-4R7F	29730/1203		Vianden	
☐ LX-OCV	Boeing 747-4R7F	29731/1222		Differdange	
☐ LX-PCV	Boeing 747-4R7F	29732/1231		Diekirch	
☐ LX-RCV	Boeing 747-4R7F	30400/1235		Schengen	
☐ LX-SCV	Boeing 747-4R7F	29733/1281		Niederanven	
☐ LX-TCV	Boeing 747-4R7F	30401/1311	ex N6046P	Sandweiler	
☐ LX-UCV	Boeing 747-4R7F	33827/1345		Bertrange	
☐ LX-VCV	Boeing 747-4R7F	34235/1366		Walferdange	
☐ LX-WCV	Boeing 747-4R7F	35804/1390	ex N5022E	Pétange	
☐ LX-YCV	Boeing 747-4R7F	35805/1407		City of Contern	

LUXAIR — *Luxair (LG/LGL)* — *Luxembourg (LUX)*

☐ LX-LGP	Boeing 737-5C9	26439/2444		Chateau de Bourglinster	
☐ LX-LGQ	Boeing 737-7C9/W	33802/1442		Chateau de Berg	
☐ LX-LGR	Boeing 737-7C9/W	33803/1468		Chateau de Fischbach	
☐ LX-LGS	Boeing 737-7C9/W	33956/1634		Chateau de Senningen	
☐ LX-LGT	Boeing 737-8K5/W	28228/484	ex D-AHFN		
☐ LX-LGA	de Havilland DHC-8-402Q	4159	ex C-FLKX		
☐ LX-LGC	de Havilland DHC-8-402Q	4162	ex C-FLTY		
☐ LX-LGD	de Havilland DHC-8-402Q	4171	ex C-FMJC		
☐ LX-LGE	de Havilland DHC-8-402Q	4284	ex C-FXYV		
☐ LX-	de Havilland DHC-8-402Q		ex C-		on order
☐ LX-LGI	Embraer EMB.145LU (ERJ-145LU)	145369	ex PT-SOU		
☐ LX-LGJ	Embraer EMB.145LU (ERJ-145LU)	145395	ex PT-SQS		
☐ LX-LGK	Embraer EMB.135LR (ERJ-135LR)	14500886	ex PT-SXY		
☐ LX-LGL	Embraer EMB.135LR (ERJ-135LR)	14500893	ex PT-SYF	900th titles	
☐ LX-LGW	Embraer EMB.145LU (ERJ-145LU)	145135	ex PT-SDM		
☐ LX-LGX	Embraer EMB.145LU (ERJ-145LU)	145147	ex PT-SDX		
☐ LX-LGY	Embraer EMB.145LU (ERJ-145LU)	145242	ex PT-SIH		
☐ LX-LGZ	Embraer EMB.145LU (ERJ-145LU)	145258	ex PT-SIR		

WEST AIR EUROPE — *West Lux (WLX)* — *Luxembourg (LUX)*

☐ LX-WAL	British Aerospace ATPF	2059	ex SE-LHZ	Lsd fr SWN
☐ LX-WAO	British Aerospace ATP (LFD)	2043	ex SE-LPS	Lsd fr SWN
☐ LX-WAP	British Aerospace ATPF	2057	ex SE-LPR	Lsd fr SWN
☐ LX-WAS	British Aerospace ATP	2058	ex SE-LPT	Lsd fr SWN
☐ LX-WAT	British Aerospace ATP (LFD)	2011	ex SE-MAO	Lsd fr SWN
☐ LX-WAV	British Aerospace ATP (LFD)	2041	ex SE-LPV	Lsd fr SWN
☐ LX-WAW	British Aerospace ATP (LFD)	2021	ex SE-LGZ	

☐ LX-WAB	ATR 72-201F	227	ex OY-RUC	

LY- LITHUANIA (Republic of Lithuania)

APATAS — Apatas (LYT) — Kaunus-Karmelava (KUN)

☐ LY-AVA	LET L-410UVP-E3	882036	ex Soviet AF 2036	
☐ LY-AVP	LET L-410UVP	851514	ex RA-67547	
☐ LY-AVT	LET L-410UVP-E3	882033	ex Soviet AF 2033	

AURELA — Aurela (LSK) — Vilnius (VNO)

☐ LY-SKA	Boeing 737-35B	23972/1537	ex N223DZ	
☐ LY-SKJ	Boeing 757-23N	30735/931	ex EI-LTY	
☐ LY-SKR	Boeing 757-23N	30233/895	ex EI-LTU	
☐ LY-SKT	Boeing 737-400			
☐ LY-SKW	Boeing 737-382	25162/2241	ex N161LF	

AVIAVILSA — Aviavilsa (LVR) — Vilnius (VNO)

☐ LY-APK	Antonov An-26B	27312201	ex RA-26114	Lsd fr GZP
☐ LY-APN	Antonov An-26B	27312010	ex UR-BXF	
☐ LY-ETM	ATR 42-300F	067	ex (SE-MAS)	

AVION EXPRESS

☐ LY-ISA	SAAB SF.340A	340A-056	ex SE-LMX	

DANU ORO TRANSPORTAS — Danu (R6/DNU) — Vilnius (VNO)

☐ LY-ARI	ATR 42-300	012A	ex F-WQBT	
☐ LY-DOT	ATR 42-300	176	ex OY-MUK	
☐ LY-LWH	ATR 42-300	148	ex LN-FAO	
☐ LY-OOV	ATR 42-300F	005	ex EI-SLD	
☐ LY-RUM	ATR 42-300	010	ex OY-RUM	Lsd fr DTR
☐ LY-RUN	SAAB SF.340A	340A-086	ex G-RUNG	Lsd fr DTR
☐ LY-RUS	SAAB SF.340A	340A-074	ex SE-LTO	

FLYLAL — Lithuania Air (TE/LIL) — Vilnius (VNO)

☐ LY-AWD	Boeing 737-522	26739/2494	ex C-FDCU	
☐ LY-AWE	Boeing 737-522	26684/2388	ex C-FCFR	
☐ LY-BSD	Boeing 737-2T4	22701/886	ex N4569N	Steponas Dariusstored VNO
☐ LY-FLC	Boeing 737-31S	29055/2923	ex EI-DNX	
☐ LY-FLD	Boeing 737-322	24664/1877	ex ES-LBC	
☐ LY-FLA	Boeing 757-29J/W	27203/588	ex N703AM	
☐ LY-FLG	Boeing 757-204	27237/602	ex G-BYAR	

NORDIC SOLUTIONS AIR SERVICES — Nordvind (N9/NVD) — Vilnius (VNO)

☐ LY-NSA	SAAB SF.340AF	340A-055	ex SE-KPE	
☐ LY-NSB	SAAB SF.340AF	340A-045	ex SE-ISV	
☐ LY-NSC	SAAB SF.340AF	340A-037	ex SE-KPD	

STAR1 AIRLINES — (HCW) — Vilnius (VNO)

☐ LY-STG	Boeing 737-73S	29083/392	ex D-AHIB	

LZ- BULGARIA (Republic of Bulgaria)

AIR MAX — Aeromax (RMX) — Plovdiv (PDV)

☐ LZ-RMK	LET L-410UVP	851406	ex UR-67502	
☐ LZ-RMW	LET L-410UVP-E	902517	ex HA-LAE	

AIR SCORPIO — Scorpio Univers (SCU) — Sofia (SOF)

☐ LZ-CCB	Cessna 402B	402B0581	ex EC-HDF	
☐ LZ-MNR	Antonov An-26	87307504	ex LZ-NHC	
☐ LZ-MNT	Antonov An-26	2209	ex HAF-209	
☐ LZ-RMC	LET L-410UVP-E12	882207	ex LZ-LSC	

BH AIR		Balkan Holidays (BGH)		Sofia (SOF)
☐ LZ-BHB	Airbus A320-212	0294	ex OY-CNP	
☐ LZ-BHC	Airbus A320-212	0349	ex OY-CNR	
☐ LZ-BHD	Airbus A320-212	0221	ex CS-TQE	
☐ LZ-BHE	Airbus A320-211	0305	ex EI-DNK	
☐ TC-OAN	Airbus A321-231	1421	ex D-ALAP	Lsd fr OHY

BULGARIA AIR		Flying Bulgaria (FB/LZB)		Sofia (SOF)
☐ LZ-FBE	Airbus A320-214	3780	ex D-AVVI	
☐ LZ-FBF	Airbus A319-111	3028	ex N950FR	
☐ LZ-BOP	Boeing 737-522	26704/2508	ex N956UA	
☐ LZ-BOQ	Boeing 737-522	26687/2402	ex N946UA	
☐ LZ-BOU	Boeing 737-3L9	23717/1365	ex N231DN	
☐ LZ-BOV	Boeing 737-330	23833/1439	ex N241DL	
☐ LZ-BOW	Boeing 737-330	23834/1454	ex N242DL	
☐ LZ-HVB	Boeing 737-3S1	24834/1896	ex N371TA	Lsd fr HMS

BULGARIAN AIR CHARTER		Bulgarian Charter (BUC)		Sofia (SOF)
☐ LZ-LDC	McDonnell-Douglas MD-82	49217/1268	ex I-DAVC	
☐ LZ-LDF	McDonnell-Douglas MD-82	49219/1310	ex I-DAVF	
☐ LZ-LDG	McDonnell-Douglas MD-83	53149/1817	ex TC-FLN	
☐ LZ-LDH	McDonnell-Douglas MD-83	53150/1831	ex TC-FLO	
☐ LZ-LDK	McDonnell-Douglas MD-82	49432/1378	ex I-DAVK	
☐ LZ-LDR	McDonnell-Douglas MD-82	49277/1181	ex HB-INR	
☐ LZ-LDY	McDonnell-Douglas MD-82	49213/1243	ex I-DAWY	
☐ LZ-LDZ	McDonnell-Douglas MD-83	49930/1720	ex HB-ISZ	
☐ LZ-	McDonnell-Douglas MD-82	49523/1724	ex B-2139	
☐ LZ-	McDonnell-Douglas MD-82	49524/1746	ex B-2140	

CARGO AIR		Vega Airlines (VEA)		Sofia (SOF)
☐ LZ-CGO	Boeing 737-301F	23237/1222	ex N503UW	

HELI AIR		Heli Bulgaria (HLR)		Sofia (SOF)
☐ LZ-CBG	Antonov An-12A	2340804	ex RA-11370	stored SOF
☐ LZ-CCE	LET L-410UVP-E	871816	ex 1816	
☐ LZ-CCF	LET L-410UVP-E	861722	ex 1722	Op for UN
☐ LZ-CCG	LET L-410UVP-E	902503	ex S5-BAE	
☐ LZ-CCP	LET L-410UVP-E20	912540	ex OK-WDA	
☐ LZ-CCR	LET L-410UVP-E10	892301	ex SP-FTX	
☐ LZ-CCS	LET L-410UVP-E	902425	ex 3D-EER	Op for UN
☐ LZ-CCT	LET L-410UVP-E10	912528	ex ST-DND	Op for UN
☐ LZ-LSB	LET L-410UVP-E2	861802	no titles	Op for UN

HEMUS AIR		Hemus Air (DU/HMS)		Sofia (SOF)
☐ LZ-HBA	British Aerospace 146 Srs.200	E2072	ex VH-NJQ	
☐ LZ-HBB	British Aerospace 146 Srs.200	E2073	ex VH-NJU	
☐ LZ-HBC	British Aerospace 146 Srs.200	E2093	ex VH-JJS	
☐ LZ-HBD	British Aerospace 146 Srs.300	E3141	ex N615AW	Lsd to TBM
☐ LZ-HBE	British Aerospace 146 Srs.300	E3131	ex EI-CLG	
☐ LZ-HBF	British Aerospace 146 Srs.300	E3159	ex EI-CLI	
☐ LZ-HBG	British Aerospace 146 Srs.300	E3146	ex EI-CLH	
☐ LZ-HBZ	British Aerospace 146 Srs.300	E2103	ex G-JEAK	Lsd to TBM
☐ LZ-TIM	Avro 146-RJ70	E1258	ex EI-CPJ	Op for Bulgarian Govt
☐ LZ-FBA	Airbus A319-112	3564	ex D-AVWS	
☐ LZ-FBB	Airbus A319-112	3309	ex EI-DZW	
☐ LZ-FBC	Airbus A320-214	2540	ex EC-JMB	
☐ LZ-FBD	Airbus A320-214	2596	ex EC-JNA	
☐ LZ-HVB	Boeing 737-3S1	24834/1896	ex N371TA	Lsd to LZB
☐ LZ-ATR	ATR 42-300	151	ex F-WQNC	Lsd to LBY
☐ LZ-ATS	ATR 42-300	130	ex F-WQNO	

VIA - AIR VIA		(VL/VIM)		Varna (VAR)
☐ LZ-MDA	Airbus A320-232	2732	ex F-WWBE	
☐ LZ-MDB	Airbus A320-232	3125	ex F-WWBF	
☐ LZ-MDM	Airbus A320-232	2804	ex F-WWIM	
☐ LZ-MDT	Airbus A320-232	2108	ex D-ARFD	

WIZZ AIR BULGARIA AIRLINES		(8Z/WVL)		Sofia (SOF)
☐ LZ-WZA	Airbus A320-232	2571	ex HA-LPG	Lsd fr WZZ
☐ LZ-WZB	Airbus A320-232	3562	ex F-WWBH	Lsd fr WZZ

N UNITED STATES OF AMERICA

ABX AIR — Abex (GB/ABX) — Wilmington-Airborne Airpark, OH (ILN)

Registration	Type	c/n	Previous identity	Colours	Remarks
☐ N312AA	Boeing 767-223SF	22315/94			
☐ N702AX	Boeing 767-231ER	22566/29	ex N603TW		
☐ N707AX	Boeing 767-231ER	22570/63	ex N607TW		
☐ N708AX	Boeing 767-231ER	22571/64	ex N608TW		
☐ N709AX	Boeing 767-231ER	22572/65	ex N609TW		
☐ N713AX	Boeing 767-205ER	23058/101	ex N651TW		
☐ N739AX	Boeing 767-232 (SCD)	22216/26	ex N104DA		
☐ N740AX	Boeing 767-232 (SCD)	22213/6	ex N101DA		
☐ N741AX	Boeing 767-232 (SCD)	22215/17	ex N103DA		for conv to freighter
☐ N742AX	Boeing 767-232 (SCD)	22217/27	ex N105DA		Lsd to ANA
☐ N743AX	Boeing 767-232 (SCD)	22218/31	ex N106DA		
☐ N744AX	Boeing 767-232 (SCD)	22221/53	ex N109DL		Lsd to ANA
☐ N745AX	Boeing 767-232 (SCD)	22222/56	ex N110DL		
☐ N746AX	Boeing 767-232 (SCD)	22223/74	ex N111DN		
☐ N747AX	Boeing 767-232 (SCD)	22224/56	ex N112DL		
☐ N748AX	Boeing 767-232 (SCD)	22225/77	ex N113DA		
☐ N749AX	Boeing 767-232	22226/78	ex N114DL		for conv to freighter
☐ N750AX	Boeing 767-232 (SCD)	22227/83	ex N115DA		
☐ N752AX	Boeing 767-281	23434/171	ex JA8255		
☐ N767AX	Boeing 767-281	22785/51	ex JA8479		
☐ N768AX	Boeing 767-281	22786/54	ex JA8480		
☐ N769AX	Boeing 767-281	22787/58	ex JA8481		
☐ N773AX	Boeing 767-281	22788/61	ex JA8482		
☐ N774AX	Boeing 767-281	22789/67	ex JA8483		
☐ N775AX	Boeing 767-281	22790/69	ex JA8484		
☐ N783AX	Boeing 767-281	23016/80	ex JA8485		
☐ N784AX	Boeing 767-281	23017/82	ex JA8486		
☐ N785AX	Boeing 767-281	23018/84	ex JA8487		
☐ N786AX	Boeing 767-281	23019/85	ex JA8488		
☐ N787AX	Boeing 767-281F	23020/96	ex JA8489		
☐ N788AX	Boeing 767-281	23021/103	ex JA8490		
☐ N789AX	Boeing 767-281	23022/104	ex JA8491		
☐ N790AX	Boeing 767-281	23140/106	ex JA8238		
☐ N791AX	Boeing 767-281	23141/108	ex JA8239		
☐ N792AX	Boeing 767-281 (SCD)	23142/110	ex JA8240		
☐ N793AX	Boeing 767-281	23143/114	ex JA8241		
☐ N794AX	Boeing 767-281	23144/115	ex JA8242		
☐ N795AX	Boeing 767-281F	23145/116	ex JA8243		
☐ N796AX	Boeing 767-281	23146/121	ex JA8244		
☐ N797AX	Boeing 767-281	23147/123	ex JA8245		
☐ N798AX	Boeing 767-281 (SCD)	23431/143	ex JA8251	DHL colours	
☐ N847AX	Douglas DC-8-61F (BAC 2)	46031/435	ex N28UA		stored CVG
☐ N900AX	Douglas DC-9-32 (ABS 3)	47380/514	ex N1284L		
☐ N903AX	Douglas DC-9-32 (ABS 3)	47427/573	ex N1287L		stored ROW
☐ N904AX	Douglas DC-9-32CF (ABS 3)	47040/172	ex N931F		stored ROW
☐ N924AX	Douglas DC-9-31 (ABS 3)	47403/507	ex N8987E		stored ROW
☐ N928AX	Douglas DC-9-33RC (ABS 3)	47392/447	ex YU-AJB		stored ROW
☐ N929AX	Douglas DC-9-31 (ABS 3)	45874/351	ex N965ML	DHL colours	stored ROW
☐ N930AX	Douglas DC-9-33RC (ABS 3)	47363/445	ex N502MD		
☐ N932AX	Douglas DC-9-33RC (ABS 3)	47465/584	ex N7465B		
☐ N933AX	Douglas DC-9-33RC (ABS 3)	47291/343	ex N94454		
☐ N934AX	Douglas DC-9-33RC (ABS 3)	47462/564	ex N32UA		stored CVG
☐ N935AX	Douglas DC-9-33F (ABS 3)	47413/521	ex N939F		
☐ N937AX	Douglas DC-9-31 (ABS 3)	47074/376	ex N973ML		stored ROW
☐ N939AX	Douglas DC-9-32 (ABS 3)	47201/459	ex EC-ECU		stored ROW
☐ N943AX	Douglas DC-9-31 (ABS 3)	47528/617	ex VH-TJR		stored ROW
☐ N944AX	Douglas DC-9-31 (ABS 3)	47550/623	ex VH-TJS		
☐ N949AX	Douglas DC-9-31 (ABS 3)	47325/515	ex N540MD		stored MZJ
☐ N951AX	Douglas DC-9-41 (ABS 3)	47616/749	ex JA8433		
☐ N952AX	Douglas DC-9-41 (ABS 3)	47615/751	ex JA8432		
☐ N953AX	Douglas DC-9-41 (ABS 3)	47608/732	ex JA8427		
☐ N954AX	Douglas DC-9-41 (ABS 3)	47612/736	ex JA8428		
☐ N955AX	Douglas DC-9-41 (ABS 3)	47619/768	ex JA8436	DHL colours	
☐ N956AX	Douglas DC-9-41 (ABS 3)	47620/777	ex JA8437	DHL colours	
☐ N957AX	Douglas DC-9-41 (ABS 3)	47759/871	ex JA8439		
☐ N959AX	Douglas DC-9-41 (ABS 3)	47761/875	ex JA8441		
☐ N960AX	Douglas DC-9-41 (ABS 3)	47762/876	ex JA8442		
☐ N962AX	Douglas DC-9-41 (ABS 3)	47768/887	ex JA8449		
☐ N963AX	Douglas DC-9-41 (ABS 3)	47780/894	ex JA8450		
☐ N965AX	Douglas DC-9-41 (ABS 3)	47498/566	ex SE-DAL		
☐ N966AX	Douglas DC-9-41 (ABS 3)	47510/645	ex OY-KGK		
☐ N967AX	Douglas DC-9-41 (ABS 3)	47509/643	ex SE-DAO		
☐ N968AX	Douglas DC-9-41 (ABS 3)	47499/568	ex SE-DAM		
☐ N969AX	Douglas DC-9-41 (ABS 3)	47464/575	ex SE-DAN	DHL colours	

☐ N972AX	Douglas DC-9-41 (ABS 3)	47631/743	ex SE-DAX		
☐ N973AX	Douglas DC-9-41 (ABS 3)	47511/677	ex LN-RLU		
☐ N974AX	Douglas DC-9-41 (ABS 3)	47623/728	ex LN-RLS		
☐ N975AX	Douglas DC-9-41 (ABS 3)	47512/678	ex SE-DAP		
☐ N976AX	Douglas DC-9-41 (ABS 3)	47596/714	ex SE-DAR		
☐ N977AX	Douglas DC-9-41 (ABS 3)	47513/679	ex LN-RLX		
☐ N978AX	Douglas DC-9-41 (ABS 3)	47628/740	ex OY-KGN		
☐ N979AX	Douglas DC-9-41 (ABS 3)	47492/559	ex SE-DAK		
☐ N981AX	Douglas DC-9-32 (ABS 3)	47273/347	ex N3337L		stored ROW
☐ N983AX	Douglas DC-9-32 (ABS 3)	47257/386	ex N1262L		stored CVG
☐ N984AX	Douglas DC-9-32 (ABS 3)	47258/387	ex N1263L		stored ROW
☐ N986AX	Douglas DC-9-32 (ABS 3)	47543/654	ex EC-BYG	DHL colours	
☐ N989AX	Douglas DC-9-32 (ABS 3)	47314/279	ex EC-BIU		stored CVG
☐ N990AX	Douglas DC-9-41 (ABS 3)	47493/562	ex SE-DLC		

ACADEMY AIRLINES — *Academy (ACD)* — *Hampton-Clayton Co/Tara Field, GA*

☐ N17WT	Beech 65-90 King Air	LJ-86	ex N60RJ	Lsd fr Jeffair

ACTION AIRLINES — *Action Air (AXQ)* — *Groton-New London, CT (GON)*

☐ N660RA	Piper PA-34-200T Seneca II	34-7870354	ex N36708	Lsd fr Griswold Air Service

ADIRONDACK FLYING SERVICE — *Lake Placid, NY (LKP)*

☐ N83D	Cessna 414A Chancellor II	414A0615	ex C-FACF
☐ N8091Q	Cessna 402B	402B0369	ex F-OGFL
☐ N33247	Cessna U206F Stationair	U20602692	

ADVANCED AIRWAYS — *West Palm Beach-Lantana County Park, FL (LNA)*

☐ N89M	Aero Commander 500	500-659	ex N4300S	dbr Oct05?
☐ N312EC	Aero Commander 500	500-782	ex N123RK	
☐ N3836C	Aero Commander 500	500-791	ex N8447C	
☐ N3841C	Aero Commander 500	500-707		

AERO CHARTER — *Char Tran (CTA)* — *Albuquerque-International Sunport, NM (ABQ)*

☐ N38CJ	Cessna 402C II	402C0023	ex N38CC
☐ N593DM	Cessna 402B II	402B1228	ex N25BH
☐ N596DM	Cessna 402C II	402C0255	ex N7011X
☐ N598DM	Cessna 402C II	402C0114	ex N81970
☐ N635MA	Cessna 402C II	402C0634	ex 5H-TGA
☐ N775RC	Cessna 402C II	402C0311	ex 5Y-BKK
☐ N588DM	Cessna 310Q	310Q0624	ex C-GYLZ
☐ N589DM	Cessna 310Q II	310Q1048	ex C-GONG
☐ N590DM	Cessna 310Q	310Q0059	ex N212TA

AERO FLITE — *Kingman, AZ (IGM)*

☐ N262NR	Canadair CL-215-1A10 (CL-215)	1081	ex C-GDRS	262	op for Minnesota DNR
☐ N263NR	Canadair CL-215-1A10 (CL-215)	1082	ex C-GENU	263	Lsd fr/op for Minnesota DNR
☐ N264V	Canadair CL-215-1A10 (CL-215)	1090	ex C-GOFM	264	
☐ N266NR	Canadair CL-215-1A10 (CL-215)	1102	ex C-GOFO	266	Lsd fr/op for Minnesota DNR
☐ N267V	Canadair CL-215-1A10 (CL-215)	1103	ex C-GOFP	267	

AERO INDUSTRIES — *Wabash (WAB)* — *Richmond, VA (RIC)*

☐ N3521S	Piper PA-31-350 Chieftain	31-7952107
☐ N27508	Piper PA-31-350 Chieftain	31-7852031

AERO UNION — *Chico-Municipal, CA (CIC)*

☐ N900AU	Lockheed P-3A Orion	185-5104	ex N406TP	00	Tanker
☐ N920AU	Lockheed P-3A Orion	185-5039	ex Bu150513	20	Tanker
☐ N921AU	Lockheed P-3A Orion	185-5098	ex Bu151385	21	Tanker
☐ N922AU	Lockheed P-3A Orion	185-5100	ex N181AU	22	Tanker
☐ N923AU	Lockheed P-3A Orion	185-5085	ex N185AU	23	Tanker
☐ N925AU	Lockheed P-3A Orion	185-5074	ex N183AU	25	Tanker
☐ N927AU	Lockheed P-3A Orion	185-5082	ex N182AU	27	Tanker
☐ N4096W	Piper PA-32-300 Cherokee Six	32-40159			
☐ N5938Y	Piper PA-23-250 Aztec C	27-3103			

AEX AIR — *Desert (DST)* — *Phoenix-Sky Harbor, AZ/La Verne, CA (PHX/POC)*

☐ N14FB	Piper PA-31 Turbo Navajo	31-351	ex N93H
☐ N57AS	Piper PA-31 Turbo Navajo	31-113	ex N585HW
☐ N300WA	Piper PA-31 Turbo Navajo	31-294	ex N9227Y
☐ N49SA	Piper PA-34-200 Seneca	34-7350057	ex C-FDRW

☐ N86PP	Piper PA-34-200 Seneca	34-7250358	ex N15054	
☐ N1080U	Piper PA-34-200 Seneca	34-7250083		
☐ N1656H	Piper PA-34-200T Seneca II	34-7770131		
☐ N2817T	Piper PA-34-200 Seneca	34-7250170		
☐ N4581T	Piper PA-34-200 Seneca	34-7250139		
☐ N41298	Piper PA-34-200 Seneca	34-7450106		
☐ N55549	Piper PA-34-200 Seneca	34-7350228		
☐ N56795	Piper PA-34-200 Seneca	34-7450032		
☐ N56974	Piper PA-34-200 Seneca	34-7450044		
☐ N57368	Piper PA-34-200 Seneca	34-7450054		
☐ N75053	Piper PA-34-200T Seneca II	34-7670233		

AIR AMERICA — San Juan –Luis Munoz Marin Intl, PR (SJU)

☐ N21WW	Piper PA-23-250 Aztec E	27-7554066	ex N54754	
☐ N30PT	Cessna 421C Golden Eagle	421C0157	ex N5284J	
☐ N2395Z	Piper PA-23-250 Aztec F	27-7954107	ex (AN-LAS)	
☐ N7049T	Britten-Norman BN-2A-21 Islander	643	ex C-GPAB	
☐ N62749	Piper PA-23-250 Aztec F	27-7654198		

AIR ARCTIC — Fairbanks-Intl, AK (FAI)

☐ N234CE	Piper PA-31-350 Chieftain	31-8052203		Lsd fr Northern Alaska
☐ N820FS	Piper PA-31-350 Chieftain	31-7952185	ex TF-VLA	
☐ N7164D	Piper PA-31-350 Chieftain	31-8052013	ex C-GBGI	
☐ N3589B	Piper PA-31-350 Chieftain	31-8052134		
☐ N59826	Piper PA-31-350 Navajo Chieftain	31-7652077		

AIR CARGO CARRIERS — Night Cargo (2Q/SNC) — Milwaukee-General Mitchell Intl, WI (MKE)

☐ N58DD	Short SD.3-30	SH3008	ex TG-TJA	
☐ N167RC	Short SD.3-30	SH3038	ex N690RA	
☐ N330AC	Short SD.3-30	SH3007	ex C-GSKW	
☐ N334AC	Short SD.3-30	SH3029	ex VH-LSI	special colours
☐ N336MV	Short SD.3-30	SH3018	ex PJ-DDB	
☐ N390GA	Short SD.3-30	SH3077	ex 4X-CSP	
☐ N936MA	Short SD.3-30	SH3036	ex G-BGNI	
☐ N2629P	Short SD.3-30	SH3079	ex G-BJLL	
☐ N124CA	Short SD.3-60	SH3652	ex G-BLJS	
☐ N136LR	Short SD.3-60	SH3752	ex VH-SUL	all-white
☐ N151CA	Short SD.3-60	SH3653	ex G-BLJT	
☐ N360AB	Short SD.3-60	SH3756	ex G-BPKZ	
☐ N360RW	Short SD.3-60	SH3613	ex C-FCRB	
☐ N360SA	Short SD.3-60	SH3601	ex G-WIDE	
☐ N367AC	Short SD.3-60	SH3626	ex VH-MVW	
☐ N368AC	Short SD.3-60	SH3651	ex VH-BWO	
☐ N376AC	Short SD.3-60	SH3736	ex G-VBAC	
☐ N601CA	Short SD.3-60	SH3623	ex G-BKWM	
☐ N617FB	Short SD.3-60	SH3617	ex G-BKUF	
☐ N688AN	Short SD.3-60	SH3633	ex C-GPCJ	
☐ N701A	Short SD.3-60	SH3627	ex G-BKZP	
☐ N742CC	Short SD.3-60	SH3742	ex D-CFXH	
☐ N764JR	Short SD.3-60	SH3764	ex VH-SUF	
☐ N972AA	Short SD.3-60	SH3754	ex N263GA	
☐ N973AA	Short SD.3-60	SH3749	ex N749JT	
☐ N3732X	Short SD.3-60	SH3732	ex PK-DSN	
☐ N4498Y	Short SD.3-60	SH3625	ex G-BKZN	
☐ N960AA	AMD Falcon 20C	144	ex N385AC	
☐ N961AA	AMD Falcon 20D	205	ex N585AC	

AIR CHOICE ONE — Weber (WBR) — Farmington Regional, MD (FAM)

☐ N86SJ	Beech Baron 58	TH-656	ex N4184S	
☐ N45038	Piper PA-31-350 Chieftain	31-8052202		

AIR DIRECT — Rhinelander-Oneida County, WI (RHI)

☐ N213JD	Cessna 310R II	310R0136	ex N102CT	
☐ N800L	Piper PA-31 Turbo Navajo	31-426	ex C-GSGA	
☐ N87395	Cessna 310R	310R0543		

AIR EVAC

☐ N12AE	Bell 206L-1 LongRanger	45649	ex N46SG	
☐ N19AE	Bell 206L-1 LongRanger	45691	ex N2025V	
☐ N24AE	Bell 206L-1 LongRanger	45646	ex N2124Z	
☐ N27AE	Bell 206L-1 LongRanger	45192	ex N5007Y	
☐ N28AE	Bell 206L-3 LongRanger III	51077	ex N10UB	
☐ N29AE	Bell 206L-3 LongRanger III	51191	ex N804SB	
☐ N32AE	Bell 206L-1 LongRanger	45327	ex N1067C	

☐ N43AE	Bell 206L-1 LongRanger	45187	ex N5007Q
☐ N48AE	Bell 206L-1 LongRanger	45562	ex N206AH
☐ N51AE	Bell 206L-1 LongRanger	45165	ex N119SD
☐ N52AE	Bell 206L-1 LongRanger	45758	ex N2253E
☐ N53AE	Bell 206L-1 LongRanger	45300	ex N27702
☐ N54AE	Bell 206L-1 LongRanger	45157	ex N16938
☐ N59AE	Bell 206L-1 LongRanger	45291	ex N522MT
☐ N61AE	Bell 206L-1 LongRanger	45470	ex N9900M
☐ N62AE	Bell 206L-1 LongRanger	45169	ex N50034
☐ N63AE	Bell 206L-1 LongRanger	45499	ex N5748Q
☐ N68AE	Bell 206L-1 LongRanger	45647	ex N21240
☐ N74AE	Bell 206L-1 LongRanger	45765	ex N3178K
☐ N79AE	Bell 206L-1 LongRanger	45436	ex N1068S
☐ N83AE	Bell 206L-1 LongRanger	45272	ex N2759U
☐ N88AE	Bell 206L-1 LongRanger	45263	ex N119TA
☐ N89AE	Bell 206L-1 LongRanger	45433	ex N1084Y
☐ N96AE	Bell 206L-1 LongRanger	45751	ex N2245Y
☐ N101AE	Bell 206L-1 LongRanger	45454	ex N5737T
☐ N103AE	Bell 206L-1 LongRanger	45597	ex N3904L
☐ N105AE	Bell 206L-1 LongRanger	45297	ex N2275A
☐ N106AE	Bell 206L-1 LongRanger	45566	ex N677M
☐ N108AE	Bell 206L-1 LongRanger	45730	ex N2070Z
☐ N113AE	Bell 206L-1 LongRanger	45371	ex N719RR
☐ N114AE	Bell 206L-1 LongRanger	45507	ex HK-3823X
☐ N116AE	Bell 206L-1 LongRanger	45632	ex HK-3619X
☐ N117AE	Bell 206L-1 LongRanger	45627	ex HK-3581
☐ N118AE	Bell 206L-1 LongRanger	45724	ex HK-3582
☐ N119AE	Bell 206L-3 LongRanger III	51201	ex HK-3725X
☐ N121AE	Bell 206L-1 LongRanger	45690	ex N2025G
☐ N122AE	Bell 206L-1 LongRanger	45276	ex N60WJ
☐ N124AE	Bell 206L-3 LongRanger III	51591	ex HK-3754X
☐ N127AE	Bell 206L-3 LongRanger III	51592	ex HK-3972P
☐ N129AE	Bell 206L-1 LongRanger	45547	ex N4753T
☐ N130AE	Bell 206L-1 LongRanger	45467	ex N5741Y
☐ N132AE	Bell 206L-1 LongRanger	45491	ex N5745S
☐ N133AE	Bell 206L-1 LongRanger	45280	ex N2762D
☐ N134AE	Bell 206L-1 LongRanger	45593	ex N38958
☐ N138AE	Bell 206L-1 LongRanger	45782	ex N3197V
☐ N139AE	Bell 206L-1 LongRanger	45546	ex N5756N
☐ N176AE	Bell 206L-1 LongRanger	45224	ex N911QC
☐ N192AE	Bell 206L-1 LongRanger	45660	ex N194H
☐ N209S	Bell 206B JetRanger III	3511	ex N713TV
☐ N216S	Bell 206L-1 LongRanger	45669	ex C-FJRG
☐ N225AE	Bell 206L-1 LongRanger	45577	ex N577E
☐ N228AE	Bell 206L-1 LongRanger	45697	ex XA-TKU
☐ N229AE	Bell 206L-1 LongRanger	45256	ex N2756A
☐ N230AE	Bell 206L-3 LongRanger III	51331	ex N941SL
☐ N233AE	Bell 206L-3 LongRanger III	51453	ex N6643T
☐ N239AE	Bell 206L-1 LongRanger	45367	ex 5N-BAS
☐ N242AE	Bell 206L-1 LongRanger	45506	ex 5N-AQB
☐ N248AE	Bell 206L-3 LongRanger III	51129	ex N206AH
☐ N249AE	Bell 206L-1 LongRanger	45459	ex N5740L
☐ N258AE	Bell 206L-1 LongRanger	45578	ex N805KA
☐ N267AE	Bell 206L-1 LongRanger	45582	ex C-GKCX
☐ N269AE	Bell 206L-3 LongRanger III	51530	ex N3116P
☐ N271AE	Bell 206L-3 LongRanger III	51351	ex N792CA
☐ N274AE	Bell 206L-1 LongRanger	45762	ex N676M
☐ N275AE	Bell 206L-3 LongRanger III	51186	ex N708M
☐ N277AE	Bell 206L-3 LongRanger III	51421	ex N9107G
☐ N279AE	Bell 206L-1 LongRanger	45682	ex N258LH
☐ N281AE	Bell 206L-3 LongRanger III	51451	ex N719H
☐ N282AE	Bell 206L-3 LongRanger III	51452	ex N722H
☐ N285AE	Bell 206L-3 LongRanger III	51550	ex N727H
☐ N287AE	Bell 206L-3 LongRanger III	51404	ex N6251V
☐ N288AE	Bell 206L-3 LongRanger III	51327	ex N165SB
☐ N290AE	Bell 206L-3 LongRanger III	51192	ex N805SB
☐ N292AE	Bell 206L-1 LongRanger	45780	ex N3192P
☐ N293AE	Bell 206L-3 LongRanger III	51476	ex N793CA
☐ N295AE	Bell 206L-3 LongRanger III	51455	ex N791CA
☐ N296AE	Bell 206L-1 LongRanger	45398	ex N1078G
☐ N299AE	Bell 206L-1 LongRanger	45621	ex N911WA
☐ N302AE	Bell 206L-1 LongRanger	45435	ex N1067D
☐ N303AE	Bell 206L-1 LongRanger	45348	ex N1075P
☐ N311AE	Bell 206L-1 LongRanger	45572	ex N87TV
☐ N314AE	Bell 206L-4 LongRanger IV	52222	ex XC-CUU
☐ N315AE	Bell 206L-1 LongRanger	45482	ex N2654
☐ N318AE	Bell 206L-3 LongRanger III	51160	ex N911NS
☐ N319AE	Bell 206L-4 LongRanger IV	52040	ex N96AP
☐ N322AE	Bell 206L-3 LongRanger III	51387	ex P2-HLT
☐ N325AE	Bell 206L-4 LongRanger IV	52009	ex N203UT
☐ N327AE	Bell 206L-3 LongRanger III	51365	ex N203M
☐ N334AE	Bell 206L-3 LongRanger III	51326	ex N401CJ
☐ N395AE	Bell 206L-1 LongRanger	45551	ex N5749J

☐ N402AE	Bell 206L-4 LongRanger IV	52393		
☐ N406LS	Bell 407	53275	ex N405S	
☐ N407LS	Bell 407	53363	ex N4001B	
☐ N408LS	Bell 407	53328	ex N407DD	
☐ N595AE	Bell 206L-1 LongRanger	45244	ex N5019F	
☐ N600CE	Bell 407	53347		
☐ N911SA	Bell 206L-1 LongRanger	45383	ex N1080A	
☐ N162GC	Beech B200	BB-1238	ex N212JB	
☐ N300MT	Beech E-90	LW-143	ex N300BA	

AIR FLAMENCO — *San Juan-Fernando Luis Ribas Dominici, PR (SIG)*

☐ N821RR	Britten-Norman BN-2A-9 Islander	338	ex N146A	
☐ N901GD	Britten-Norman BN-2A-26 Islander	855	ex XA-JEK	The Spirit of Culebra
☐ N903GD	Britten-Norman BN-2A-6 Islander	625	ex HI-636CT	
☐ N904GD	Britten-Norman BN-2B-26 Islander	2128	ex N902VL	
☐ N905GD	Britten-Norman BN-2A-9 Islander	339	ex C-FTAM	
☐ N906GD	Britten-Norman BN-2A-26 Islander	3008	ex VP-AAB	
☐ N907GD	Britten-Norman BN-2A-9 Islander	340	ex N161A	
☐ N908GD	Britten-Norman BN-2A-26 Islander	2040	ex C6-BUS	
☐ N909GD	Britten-Norman BN-2A-6 Islander	239	ex N143BW	

AIR GRAND CANYON — *Grand Canyon-National Park, AZ (GCN)*

☐ N803AN	Cessna T207A Stationair 7	20700570	ex N73204	
☐ N6308H	Cessna T207A Stationair 7	20700476		
☐ N6491H	Cessna T207A Stationair 7	20700543		
☐ N7311U	Cessna T207A Turbo Skywagon	20700395		
☐ N7351U	Cessna T207A Stationair 7	20700415		

AIR LOGISTICS — *Airlog (ALG)* — *New Iberia-Air Logistics Heliport, LA (-)*

☐ N139TZ	Agusta AW139	41202		
☐	Agusta AW139			on order
☐ N206XS	Bell 206B JetRanger III	3040		Op by Bristow Academy
☐ N5008N	Bell 206B JetRanger III	2518		Op by Bristow Academy
☐ N8WH	Bell 206L-1 LongRanger	45318	ex N2775D	
☐ N69AL	Bell 206L-4 LongRanger IV	52139	ex PT-YBH	
☐ N76AL	Bell 206L-4 LongRanger IV	52165	ex N15EW	
☐ N133AL	Bell 206L-3 LongRanger III	51133		based Alaska
☐ N176AL	Bell 206L-4 LongRanger IV	52146	ex C-FOFE	
☐ N177AL	Bell 206L-4 LongRanger IV	52157	ex C-GLZU	
☐ N182AL	Bell 206L-3 LongRanger III	52057	ex D-HSDA	
☐ N188AL	Bell 206L-4 LongRanger IV	52082	ex N84TV	
☐ N189AL	Bell 206L-4 LongRanger IV	52340		
☐ N192AL	Bell 206L-4 LongRanger IV	52342		
☐ N193AL	Bell 206L-4 LongRanger IV	52344		
☐ N194AL	Bell 206L-4 LongRanger IV	52148	ex XA-TFI	
☐ N196AL	Bell 206L-4 LongRanger IV	52380	ex N218K	
☐ N206DB	Bell 206L-4 LongRanger IV	52127		
☐ N265AL	Bell 206L-4 LongRanger IV	52280	ex C-GFNY	
☐ N266AL	Bell 206L-4 LongRanger IV	52281		
☐ N267AL	Bell 206L-4 LongRanger IV	52282	ex C-GAXE	
☐ N268AL	Bell 206L-4 LongRanger IV	52283		
☐ N269AL	Bell 206L-4 LongRanger IV	52284		
☐ N271AL	Bell 206L-4 LongRanger IV	52287		
☐ N272AL	Bell 206L-4 LongRanger IV	52288		
☐ N272M	Bell 206L-1 LongRanger III	45365	ex RP-C173	
☐ N275AL	Bell 206L-4 LongRanger IV	52285		
☐ N276AL	Bell 206L-4 LongRanger IV	52312		
☐ N278AL	Bell 206L-4 LongRanger IV	52313		
☐ N279AL	Bell 206L-4 LongRanger IV	52314	ex C-GAEP	
☐ N280AL	Bell 206L-4 LongRanger IV	52315		
☐ N281AL	Bell 206L-4 LongRanger IV	52319		
☐ N330P	Bell 206L-3 LongRanger III	51295		
☐ N346AL	Bell 206L-3 LongRanger III	51378		based Alaska
☐ N358AL	Bell 206L-3 LongRanger III	51460		based Alaska
☐ N360AL	Bell 206L-3 LongRanger III	51462		based Alaska
☐ N363AL	Bell 206L-3 LongRanger III	51472	ex C-GLZE	based Alaska
☐ N3174Y	Bell 206L-3 LongRanger III	51038		
☐ N403AL	Bell 407	53478	ex N4041F	
☐ N404AL	Bell 407	53479	ex N40410	
☐ N405AL	Bell 407	53480	ex N40414	
☐ N406AL	Bell 407	53481	ex N6146J	
☐ N407AL	Bell 407	53044		
☐ N407TZ	Bell 407	53204	ex N487AL	
☐ N408AL	Bell 407	53491	ex N6148U	
☐ N409AL	Bell 407	53494	ex N9182V	

☐ N410AL	Bell 407	53982	ex N388RT	
☐ N415AL	Bell 407	53182	ex N415AG	
☐ N417AL	Bell 407	53054		
☐ N431AL	Bell 407	53923	ex C-FYPN	
☐ N436AL	Bell 407	53069	ex N58236	
☐ N437AL	Bell 407	53141		
☐ N447AL	Bell 407	53126	ex PT-YNM	
☐ N457AL	Bell 407	53151		
☐ N477AL	Bell 407	53203		
☐ N497AL	Bell 407	53172		
☐ N507AL	Bell 407	53103	ex N407ST	
☐ N527AL	Bell 407	53211		
☐ N537AL	Bell 407	53230		
☐ N547AL	Bell 407	53240		
☐ N557AL	Bell 407	53243		
☐ N577AL	Bell 407	53247		
☐ N587AL	Bell 407	53248		
☐ N597AL	Bell 407	53091	ex N427AL	
☐ N607AL	Bell 407	53264		
☐ N617AL	Bell 407	53265		
☐ N627AL	Bell 407	53284		
☐ N637AL	Bell 407	53293	ex PT-YUW	
☐ N647AL	Bell 407	53357	ex N60321	
☐ N657AL	Bell 407	53413	ex N155ZS	
☐ N667AL	Bell 407	53624	ex XA-SKY	
☐ N687AL	Bell 407	53366	ex N6302B	
☐ N697AL	Bell 407	53374	ex N6112Q	
☐ N727AL	Bell 407	53227	ex N298RS	
☐ N796RV	Bell 407	53037	ex RP-C2468	
☐ N847AL	Bell 407	53150	ex N407XS	
☐ N937AL	Bell 407	53383	ex N63894	
☐ N535AL	Eurocopter EC135P2+	0716		
☐ N635AL	Eurocopter EC135P2+	0758		
☐ N935AL	Eurocopter EC135P2+	0817		
☐ N76TZ	Sikorsky S-76C	760656	ex N45049	
☐ N519AL	Sikorsky S-76A	760058	ex G-EWEL	
☐ N522AL	Sikorsky S-76A	760236	ex N202SR	
☐ N701AL	Sikorsky S-76A	760238		
☐ N702AL	Sikorsky S-76A	760243		
☐ N707AL	Sikorsky S-76A	760189	ex N989QS	
☐ N709AL	Sikorsky S-76A	760278		
☐ N717AL	Sikorsky S-76A	760221	ex G-BWIM	
☐ N741SW	Sikorsky S-76A	760070	ex N721SW	
☐ N768L	Sikorsky S-76C+	760768		
☐ N773L	Sikorsky S-76C+	760773		
☐ N774L	Sikorsky S-76C+	760774		
☐ N775L	Sikorsky S-76C+	760775		
☐ N777LQ	Sikorsky S-76C+	760777		
☐ N778T	Sikorsky S-76C+	760778		
☐ N860AL	Sikorsky S-76C+	760527	ex N9024W	
☐ N861AL	Sikorsky S-76C+	760529	ex N2032W	
☐ N862AL	Sikorsky S-76C+	760531	ex N2021W	
☐ N863AL	Sikorsky S-76C+	760536	ex N5009K	
☐ N864AL	Sikorsky S-76C+	760557	ex N50093	
☐ N865AL	Sikorsky S-76C	760564	ex N70089	
☐ N866AL	Sikorsky S-76C	760562	ex N50085	
☐ N867AL	Sikorsky S-76C	760579	ex N7104Q	
☐ N868AL	Sikorsky S-76C+	760580	ex N7102S	
☐ N870AL	Sikorsky S-76C+	760606	ex N8119N	
☐ N871AL	Sikorsky S-76C+	760627	ex N80907	
☐ N873AL	Sikorsky S-76C+	760639		
☐ N877AL	Sikorsky S-76C+	760618	ex N81081	
☐ N879AL	Sikorsky S-76C+	760652	ex 9M-SPU	
☐ N881AL	Sikorsky S-76C+	760673	ex N4512G	
☐ N883AL	Sikorsky S-76C	760677	ex N4514G	
☐ N884AL	Sikorsky S-76C	760721		
☐ N20868	Sikorsky S-76C+	760780		
☐ N31211	Sikorsky S-76A	760225		
☐ N920AL	Sikorsky S-92A	920088	ex N2577X	
☐ N921AL	Sikorsky S-92A	920090	ex N2563T	
☐ N922AL	Sikorsky S-92A	920093	ex N20128	
☐ N2082Q	Sikorsky S-92A	920105		
☐ N29AL	Bell 212	30569		based Alaska
☐ N368AL	Bell 412EP	36256	ex SU-CBK	
☐ N390AL	Bell 214ST	28198		
☐ N392AL	Bell 214ST	28114	ex G-BKJD	
☐ N393AL	Bell 214ST	28117	ex N214EV	
☐ N397AL	Bell 412	36012	ex XA-TLO	
☐ N492HL	MBB Bo.105CBS-4	S-803	ex N124PW	based Alaska

☐ N494HL	MBB Bo.105CBS-4	S-813	ex N494HL	

AIR METHODS — **Denver-International, CO (DEN)**

Reg	Type	C/n	Previous	Remarks
☐ N94LG	Aérospatiale AS350B2 AStar	2728	ex N60928	EMS
☐ N97LG	Aérospatiale AS350B2 AStar	2917	ex N4030W	EMS
☐ N103HN	Aérospatiale AS350B2 AStar	2575	ex N92LG	EMS
☐ N108LN	Aérospatiale AS350B3 AStar	3959		
☐ N111LN	Aérospatiale AS350B AStar	1602	ex N58045	
☐ N152AC	Aérospatiale AS350B2 AStar	3574	ex N471AE	
☐ N220CF	Aérospatiale AS350B2 AStar	3411	ex N436AE	
☐ N350AM	Aérospatiale AS350B3 AStar	3996	ex N203AE	
☐ N350RM	Aérospatiale AS350D AStar	1024		
☐ N379AM	Aérospatiale AS350B2 AStar	3474	ex N779LF	
☐ N392LG	Aérospatiale AS350B3 AStar	3252	ex N5229Y	EMS
☐ N394LG	Aérospatiale AS350B3 AStar	3134	ex N104LG	EMS
☐ N396LG	Aérospatiale AS350B3 AStar	3336	ex N415AE	
☐ N397LG	Aérospatiale AS350B3 AStar	3268	ex N404AE	EMS
☐ N781LF	Aérospatiale AS350B AStar	1178	ex N1113H	
☐ N792LF	Aérospatiale AS350B AStar	1035	ex N9004M	
☐ N852HW	Aérospatiale AS350B2 AStar	2630	ex N352HW	
☐ N902CF	Aérospatiale AS350B3 AStar	3630	ex N477AE	
☐ N903CF	Aérospatiale AS350B3 AStar	3645	ex N481AE	
☐ N904CF	Aérospatiale AS350B3 AStar	3676	ex N484AE	
☐ N916AM	Aérospatiale AS350B2 AStar	2404	ex N911LM	EMS
☐ N937AM	Aérospatiale AS350B2 AStar	2654	ex N93LG	EMS
☐ N5797T	Aérospatiale AS350D AStar	1472	ex N3944S	
☐ N206AL	Bell 206L-1 LongRanger II	45446	ex N5735M	
☐ N206UH	Bell 206L-3 LongRanger III	51167		
☐ N220LL	Bell 206L-3 LongRanger III	51039	ex N3175R	EMS
☐ N222AM	Bell 222U	47547	ex N221HX	
☐ N222LL	Bell 222	47060	ex N222LG	EMS
☐ N226LL	Bell 222UT	47537	ex N781SA	EMS
☐ N227AM	Bell 222U	47542	ex N820AM	
☐ N404EM	Bell 222U	47514	ex N7XM	
☐ N911NM	Bell 222U	47569	ex N4181X	
☐ N247SM	Bell 407	53176	ex N911WB	
☐ N406LL	Bell 407	53279	ex N407CX	EMS
☐ N407AM	Bell 407	53309		EMS Lsd fr/op for Guardian Air
☐ N407LL	Bell 407	53561	ex N386T	EMS
☐ N407UH	Bell 407	53345		EMS
☐ N407VV	Bell 407	53476		EMS Lsd fr/op for Guardian Air
☐ N408AM	Bell 407	53445	ex N61002	
☐ N408GA	Bell 407	53392		EMS Guardian Air titles
☐ N772AL	Bell 407	53040		EMS
☐ N773AL	Bell 407	53160	ex N176PA	EMS
☐ N905HA	Bell 407	53497	ex N200LN	
☐ N911AL	Bell 407	53144	ex N70829	EMS
☐ N101HN	Eurocopter EC135P1	0162	ex N427AE	EMS
☐ N102HN	Eurocopter EC135P1	0159	ex N426AE	EMS
☐ N135DH	Eurocopter EC135P1	0133	ex N5233N	EMS
☐ N135ED	Eurocopter EC135P2	0335		
☐ N135LN	Eurocopter EC135P2	0322	ex N135BF	
☐ N135N	Eurocopter EC135P1	0086	ex N52268	EMS Lsd fr Memorial Mission H/c
☐ N135SJ	Eurocopter EC135P1	0054	ex N4056V	
☐ N137LN	Eurocopter EC135P2	0339		
☐ N138LN	Eurocopter EC135P2	0352	ex N135BF	
☐ N101VU	MBB BK-117C-2	9039		EMS
☐ N102VU	MBB BK-117C-2	9044		EMS
☐ N117AM	MBB BK-117B-1	7140	ex N90620	
☐ N117CW	MBB BK-117A-4	7125	ex N9021D	
☐ N117MV	MBB BK-117A-3	7089	ex N492MB	
☐ N118NY	MBB BK-117A-4	7115	ex N202HN	
☐ N125EC	MBB BK-117A-4	7065	ex N155SC	
☐ N138HH	MBB BK-117A-3	7060	ex N127HH	
☐ N156AM	MBB BK-117A-3	7173	ex N155SC	
☐ N158BK	MBB BK-117A-3	7058	ex D-HBNF	
☐ N163BK	MBB BK-117A-3	7063	ex D-HBNK	
☐ N164AM	MBB BK-117B-2	7229	ex N104VU	
☐ N335AM	MBB BK-117B-1	7143	ex N105VU	EMS
☐ N420MB	MBB BK-117A-3	7077	ex D-HBNY	
☐ N424MB	MBB BK-117A-4	7082	ex D-HBPC	
☐ N485UH	MBB BK-117A-1	7036	ex N128HH	
☐ N485UM	MBB BK-117A-1	7129	ex N586BH	
☐ N528SF	MBB BK-117A-3	7104	ex N528MB	
☐ N612AM	MBB BK-117B-1	7230	ex N61LF	
☐ N911BY	MBB BK-117A-4	7127	ex N11UM	
☐ N990SL	MBB BK-117B-2	7057	ex N911KD	

☐ N299AM	Pilatus PC-12/45	236	ex HB-FRG	EMS
☐ N399AM	Pilatus PC-12/45	249	ex HB-FRT	EMS
☐ N852AL	Pilatus PC-12/45	213	ex N213WA	EMS
☐ N853AL	Pilatus PC-12/45	168	ex N168WA	EMS
☐ N854AL	Pilatus PC-12/45	397	ex N397WA	EMS
☐ N912NM	Pilatus PC-12/45	169	ex N661DT	EMS

☐ N28MS	Beech 65-E90 King Air	LW-100	ex N31FN	
☐ N30LG	Aérospatiale AS355F1 Twin Star	5065	ex N5787B	
☐ N92DV	Beech 65-E90 King Air	LW-292	ex N7MA	EMS Air 4 Lsd fr/op for Guardian Air
☐ N105LC	MBB Bo.105CBS-4	S-789	ex N5414F	Op for LEC Medical Center
☐ N151AC	Eurocopter EC130B4	3732		
☐ N206CM	Bell 430	49041	ex N430RX	EMS
☐ N208CM	Bell 430	49010	ex N151MH	EMS
☐ N220TB	Beech B200 Super King Air	BB-1057	ex F-GILY	
☐ N412LG	Bell 412SP	33209		
☐ N430Q	Bell 430	49002	ex N430U	
☐ N430UH	Bell 430	49056	ex N430UM	EMS
☐ N554AL	Bell 412	33017	ex N20703	
☐ N778AM	Bell 412	33033	ex N565AC	
☐ N791DC	Beech B200 Super King Air	BB-1402	ex N91CD	EMS
☐ N793DC	Beech B200 Super King Air	BB-1404	ex N93CD	EMS
☐ N825LF	MBB Bo.105CBS-4	S-796	ex N5417E	
☐ N910U	Eurocopter EC130B4	3470	ex N452AE	
☐ N920U	Eurocopter EC130B4	3453	ex N451AE	
☐ N15460	Sikorsky S-76C+	760477	ex N176AE	

AIR MIDWEST — *Air Midwest (ZV/AMW)* — *Wichita-Mid Continent, KS (ICT)*

☐ N135YV	Beech 1900D	UE-135	Mesa Airlines	Lsd fr ASH
☐ N138YV	Beech 1900D	UE-138	Mesa Airlines	Lsd fr ASH
☐ N142ZV	Beech 1900D	UE-142	all-white	Lsd fr ASH
☐ N146ZV	Beech 1900D	UE-146	Mesa Airlines	Lsd fr ASH
☐ N159YV	Beech 1900D	UE-159	all-white	Lsd fr ASH
☐ N10675	Beech 1900D	UE-229	Mesa Airlines	Lsd fr ASH

AIR ST THOMAS — *Paradise (ZP/STT)* — *St Thomas-Cyril E King, VI (STT)*

☐ N5623Y	Piper PA-23-250 Aztec C	27-2733		Lsd fr Virgin Air
☐ N6389Y	Piper PA-23-250 Aztec C	27-3675		
☐ N8125F	Cessna 402	402-0231	ex LV-PLC	

AIR SUNSHINE — *Air Sunshine (YI/RSI)* — *Fort Lauderdale-Hollywood Intl, FL (FLL)*

☐ N122TA	Cessna 402C	402C0122	ex N2712P	
☐ N220RS	Cessna 402C	402C0220	ex N2716L	
☐ N347AB	Cessna 402C	402C0347	ex N26548	
☐ N351AB	Cessna 402C	402C0351	ex N26629	
☐ N402RS	Cessna 402C	402C0402	ex N2663N	
☐ N603AB	Cessna 402C	402C0603	ex N84PB	

☐ N123HY	Embraer EMB.110P1 Bandeirante	110321	ex N619KC	
☐ N744BA	SAAB SF.340A	340A-105	ex SE-F05	stored FLL

AIR TAHOMA — *Tahoma (5C/HMA)* — *Columbus-Rickenbacker, OH (LCK)*

☐ N581P	Convair 580	29	ex C-FBHW		
☐ N582P	Convair 580	475	ex N969N		stored LCK
☐ N584E	Convair 580	24	ex C-FAUF		
☐ N585P	Convair 580	163	ex N718RA		
☐ N587X	Convair 580	361	ex HZ-SN14		
☐ N588X	Convair 580	52	ex EC-HLD		
☐ N590X	Convair 580	130	ex EC-GSJ		stored LCK
☐ N150PA	Convair 240-27	278	ex N99377	no titles	Lsd fr Cool Air
☐ N156PA	Convair 240-27	324	ex N9016L		stored LCK Lsd fr Cool Air
☐ N99380	Convair 240-27 (T-29B)	249	ex 51-5118		Lsd fr Cool Air

AIR TEJAS — *Gainesville-Municipal, TX (GLE)*

☐ N141JR	Douglas DC-3	19366	ex CF-CUC	
☐ N472AF	Douglas DC-3	13485	ex XA-SYN	
☐ N941AT	Douglas DC-3	12907	ex N6666A	Vera Lynn II

AIR WISCONSIN — *Air Wisconsin (ZW/AWI)* — *Appleton-Outagamie Co, WI (ATW)*

Operates Canadair CL-600-2B19 (CRJ-200LR)s for US Airways Express, for details see that listing

AIRBORNE SUPPORT				**Houma-Terrebonne, LA (HUM)**
☐ N38WA	Rockwell 690A Turbo Commander	11169	ex XB-FLF	
☐ N64766	Douglas DC-3	27218	ex CAF12910	Sprayer
☐ N64767	Douglas DC-3	10199	ex CAF12941	Sprayer
☐ N67024	Douglas DC-4	10550	ex Bu50871	Sprayer

AIRNET SYSTEMS — ***Star Check (USC)***
Columbus-Port Columbus Intl, OH / Dallas-Love Field, TX (CMH/DAL)

☐ N4AW	Beech 58 Baron	TH-450	ex N228TA
☐ N21ES	Beech 58 Baron	TH-1123	ex N6744V
☐ N26CC	Beech 58 Baron	TH-136	
☐ N27MT	Beech 58 Baron	TH-1120	ex F-GDJY
☐ N33DK	Beech 58 Baron	TH-372	ex N2CF
☐ N33WC	Beech 58 Baron	TH-170	
☐ N58WA	Beech 58 Baron	TH-201	ex N58TC
☐ N65FS	Beech 58 Baron	TH-1084	ex N6681Y
☐ N78DM	Beech 58 Baron	TH-281	ex N78MM
☐ N78RE	Beech 58 Baron	TH-371	ex N904AJ
☐ N95BB	Beech 58 Baron	TH-333	ex N95BD
☐ N140S	Beech 58 Baron	TH-1155	ex N3677N
☐ N297AT	Beech 58 Baron	TH-1349	ex F-GOGA
☐ N367S	Beech 58 Baron	TH-1393	ex N158EB
☐ N400RP	Beech 58 Baron	TH-319	ex N1036W
☐ N456WW	Beech 58 Baron	TH-444	ex N444TE
☐ N525GW	Beech 58 Baron	TH-557	ex N52WP
☐ N696BD	Beech 58 Baron	TH-352	ex N43HK
☐ N858LG	Beech 58 Baron	TH-518	ex N555GP
☐ N882MT	Beech 58 Baron	TH-1343	ex F-WQFG
☐ N1653W	Beech 58 Baron	TH-252	
☐ N1814W	Beech 58 Baron	TH-287	
☐ N1847F	Beech 58 Baron	TH-1291	
☐ N1859K	Beech 58 Baron	TH-1299	
☐ N2027V	Beech 58 Baron	TH-965	
☐ N2064V	Beech 58 Baron	TH-1004	
☐ N2892W	Beech 58 Baron	TH-389	
☐ N3695V	Beech 58 Baron	TH-1183	
☐ N3703Q	Beech 58 Baron	TH-1189	
☐ N4098S	Beech 58 Baron	TH-600	
☐ N6573K	Beech 58 Baron	TH-1369	
☐ N6650D	Beech 58 Baron	TH-1375	
☐ N6758C	Beech 58 Baron	TH-1080	
☐ N7383R	Beech 58 Baron	TH-502	
☐ N9044V	Beech 58 Baron	TH-216	
☐ N9189Q	Beech 58 Baron	TH-148	
☐ N9367Q	Beech 58 Baron	TH-192	
☐ N17708	Beech 58 Baron	TH-813	
☐ N36673	Beech 58 Baron	TH-1143	
☐ N36901	Beech 58 Baron	TH-1173	
☐ N62500	Beech 58 Baron	TH-1347	
☐ N3RY	Cessna 208B Caravan I	208B0436	ex C-GSKR
☐ N102AN	Cessna 208B Caravan I	208B0906	ex N51666
☐ N103AN	Cessna 208B Caravan I	208B0928	
☐ N104AN	Cessna 208B Caravan I	208B0918	
☐ N105AN	Cessna 208B Caravan I	208B0956	
☐ N106AN	Cessna 208B Caravan I	208B0917	ex N5207V
☐ N107AN	Cessna 208B Caravan I	208B0993	
☐ N108AN	Cessna 208B Caravan I	208B0975	
☐ N1026V	Cessna 208B Caravan I	208B0319	
☐ N1115M	Cessna 208B Caravan I	208B0356	
☐ N9514F	Cessna 208 Caravan I	20800079	
☐ N9539F	Cessna 208 Caravan I	20800092	
☐ N9642F	Cessna 208 Caravan I	20800110	
☐ N3597G	Cessna 310R	310R0875	
☐ N5238J	Cessna 310R	310R0810	
☐ N6121C	Cessna 310R	310R1288	
☐ N6122C	Cessna 310R	310R1290	
☐ N6160X	Cessna 310R	310R1305	
☐ N8521G	Cessna 310R	310R0931	
☐ N37223	Cessna 310R	310R0963	
☐ N37575	Cessna 310R	310R1207	
☐ N15WH	Learjet 35A	35A-085	
☐ N25AN	Learjet 35A	35A-259	ex HK-3983X
☐ N27BL	Learjet 35A	35A-163	ex YV-173CP
☐ N27TT	Learjet 35A	35A-122	ex OE-GMP
☐ N31WR	Learjet 35A	35A-313	ex TR-LZI
☐ N39DK	Learjet 35A	35A-480	ex (N35FH)
☐ N51LC	Learjet 35A	35A-302	ex N631CW

☐ N56EM	Learjet 35A	35A-144	ex N56HF
☐ N64CP	Learjet 35A	35A-264	ex VR-CDI
☐ N72JF	Learjet 35A	35A-088	ex OE-GBR
☐ N81FR	Learjet 35A	35A-081	ex N118DA
☐ N88BG	Learjet 35A	35A-090	ex I-FIMI
☐ N98LC	Learjet 35A	35A-077	ex ZS-NRZ
☐ N122JW	Learjet 35A	35A-217	ex N111RF
☐ N130F	Learjet 35	35-044	ex N44VW
☐ N400JE	Learjet 35A	35A-120	
☐ N684HA	Learjet 35A	35A-113	ex N684LA
☐ N700SJ	Learjet 35A	35A-082	ex N700GB
☐ N701AS	Learjet 35A	35A-047	ex N13MJ
☐ N813AS	Learjet 35A	35A-167	ex N725P
☐ N900JC	Learjet 35	35-178	ex N35GG
☐ N959SA	Learjet 35A	35A-076	
☐ N1140A	Learjet 35	35-045	ex N304AT
☐ N8040A	Learjet 35	35-048	ex F-GHMP

☐ N2KC	Piper PA-31-350 Chieftain	31-7952217	ex N3540X
☐ N4UE	Piper PA-31-350 Chieftain	31-8152061	ex N4U
☐ N42HD	Piper PA-31-350 Chieftain	31-8152031	ex N42ND
☐ N106TG	Piper PA-31-350 Chieftain	31-8052002	ex N106FC
☐ N225TM	Piper PA-31-350 Chieftain	31-8152165	ex XA-MAU
☐ N525AA	Piper PA-31-350 Chieftain	31-8052111	ex N3583U
☐ N711LH	Piper PA-31-350 Chieftain	31-8152174	ex N711BH
☐ N3547C	Piper PA-31-350 Chieftain	31-8052018	
☐ N3587P	Piper PA-31-350 Chieftain	31-8052120	
☐ N3590D	Piper PA-31-350 Chieftain	31-8052144	
☐ N4079Y	Piper PA-31-350 Chieftain	31-8152079	ex (N479MG)
☐ N22427	Piper PA-31-350 Chieftain	31-8152065	ex (N4078S)
☐ N35453	Piper PA-31-350 Chieftain	31-8052006	ex (N900GF)
☐ N35551	Piper PA-31-350 Chieftain	31-8052063	
☐ N35584	Piper PA-31-350 Chieftain	31-8052076	
☐ N35871	Piper PA-31-350 Chieftain	31-8052123	ex (N191VF)
☐ N40919	Piper PA-31-350 Chieftain	31-8152162	
☐ N6892R	Piper PA-60	60-0887-8161251	

All are freighters.

AIRNOW — *Sky Courier (RLR)* — *Burlington-Intl, VT (BTV)*

☐ N804TH	Cessna 208B Caravan I	208B0421	ex N9551F
☐ N805TH	Cessna 208B Caravan I	208B0609	ex N9551F
☐ N929TG	Cessna 208B Caravan I	208B0371	ex N207TA
☐ N9339B	Cessna 208B Caravan I	208B0057	
☐ N9612B	Cessna 208B Caravan I	208B0136	

☐ N24AN	Embraer EMB.110P1 Bandeirante	110318	ex F-GBRM
☐ N31AN	Embraer EMB.110P1 Bandeirante	110372	ex C-FSXR
☐ N36AN	Embraer EMB.110P1 Bandeirante	110451	ex C-GDCQ
☐ N42AN	Embraer EMB.110P1 Bandeirante	110456	ex C-GHCA
☐ N51BA	Embraer EMB.110P1 Bandeirante	110404	ex N903FB
☐ N62CZ	Embraer EMB.110P1 Bandeirante	110388	ex PT-SFF
☐ N64CZ	Embraer EMB.110P1 Bandeirante	110399	ex PT-SFQ
☐ N83BA	Embraer EMB.110P1 Bandeirante	110351	ex N405AS
☐ N97BA	Embraer EMB.110P1 Bandeirante	110322	ex N403AS
☐ N101TN	Embraer EMB.110P1 Bandeirante	110271	ex PT-SBI
☐ N621KC	Embraer EMB.110P1 Bandeirante	110335	ex PT-SDL
☐ N710NH	Embraer EMB.110P1 Bandeirante	110250	ex PT-SAQ
☐ N830AC	Embraer EMB.110P1 Bandeirante	110205	ex N524MW

AIRPAC AIRLINES — *Airpac (APC)* — *Seattle-Boeing Field, WA (BFI)*

☐ N36PB	Piper PA-31-350 Navajo Chieftain	31-7405128	
☐ N627HA	Piper PA-31-350 Chieftain	31-7952241	
☐ N777KT	Piper PA-31-350 Navajo Chieftain	31-7552053	ex N1TW
☐ N3582X	Piper PA-31-350 Chieftain	31-8052105	
☐ N27594	Piper PA-31-350 Chieftain	31-7852070	

☐ N41SA	Cessna 404 Titan	404-0023	ex N5271J
☐ N2117V	Piper PA-34-200T Seneca II	34-7970160	
☐ N2880A	Beech 99	U-109	
☐ N4490F	Piper PA-34-200T Seneca II	34-7670339	
☐ N5278J	Cessna 404 Titan	404-0635	
☐ N8107D	Piper PA-34-200T Seneca II	34-8070010	
☐ N36319	Piper PA-34-200T Seneca II	34-7870318	

AIRSERV INTERNATIONAL — *Warrenton, VA*

☐ N8HZ	Cessna 208B Caravan I	208B0980
☐ N715BT	Cessna 208B Caravan I	208B0835
☐ N718BT	Cessna 208B Caravan I	208B0881
☐ N719BT	Cessna 208B Caravan I	208B0898

☐ N899AS	de Havilland DHC-6 Twin Otter 300	347	ex LN-FKB		Op for United Nations
☐ N970AS	de Havilland DHC-6 Twin Otter 300	838	ex ZS-PNS		

AIRTRAN AIRWAYS — ***Citrus (FL/TRS)***
Orlando-Intl, FL/Atlanta-Hartsfield Intl, GA (MCO/ATL)

☐ N603AT	Boeing 717-22A	55127/5074	ex N482HA	771
☐ N717JL	Boeing 717-2BD	55042/5115	ex N983AT	740
☐ N891AT	Boeing 717-2BD	55043/5131	ex (N984AT)	741
☐ N892AT	Boeing 717-2BD	55044/5134	ex N7071U	742
☐ N893AT	Boeing 717-2BD	55045/5136		743
☐ N894AT	Boeing 717-2BD	55046/5137		744
☐ N895AT	Boeing 717-2BD	55047/5139		745
☐ N896AT	Boeing 717-2BD	55048/5141		746
☐ N899AT	Boeing 717-2BD	55049/5143		747
☐ N906AT	Boeing 717-231	55087/5060	ex N420TW	795
☐ N910AT	Boeing 717-231	55086/5056	ex N2419C	794
☐ N915AT	Boeing 717-231	55085/5055	ex N418TW	793
☐ N919AT	Boeing 717-231	55084/5052	ex N2417F	792
☐ N920AT	Boeing 717-231	55083/5049	ex N416TW	791
☐ N921AT	Boeing 717-231	55082/5046	ex N415TW	790
☐ N922AT	Boeing 717-2BD	55050/5144		748
☐ N923AT	Boeing 717-2BD	55051/5148		749
☐ N924AT	Boeing 717-231	55080/5043	ex N413TW	789
☐ N925AT	Boeing 717-231	55079/5042	ex N412TW	788
☐ N926AT	Boeing 717-231	55078/5039	ex N411TW	787
☐ N927AT	Boeing 717-231	55077/5038	ex N2410W	786
☐ N928AT	Boeing 717-231	55076/5035	ex N409TW	785
☐ N929AT	Boeing 717-231	55075/5032	ex N408TW	784
☐ N930AT	Boeing 717-231	55072/5025	ex N405TW	782
☐ N932AT	Boeing 717-231	55073/5028	ex N406TW	783
☐ N933AT	Boeing 717-231	55071/5024	ex N2404A	781
☐ N934AT	Boeing 717-231	55070/5022	ex N403TW	780
☐ N935AT	Boeing 717-231	55069/5019	ex N402TW	779
☐ N936AT	Boeing 717-231	55058/5017	ex N401TW	778
☐ N937AT	Boeing 717-231	55091/5075	ex N424TW	799
☐ N938AT	Boeing 717-2BD	55098/5155		751
☐ N939AT	Boeing 717-2BD	55099/5156		752
☐ N940AT	Boeing 717-2BD	55004/5005	ex N717XE	702
☐ N942AT	Boeing 717-2BD	55005/5006		703
☐ N943AT	Boeing 717-2BD	55006/5007		704
☐ N944AT	Boeing 717-2BD	55007/5008		705
☐ N945AT	Boeing 717-2BD	55008/5009		706
☐ N946AT	Boeing 717-2BD	55009/5010		707
☐ N947AT	Boeing 717-2BD	55010/5011		708
☐ N948AT	Boeing 717-2BD	55011/5012		709
☐ N949AT	Boeing 717-2BD	55003/5004	ex N717XD	701
☐ N950AT	Boeing 717-2BD	55012/5018		710
☐ N951AT	Boeing 717-2BD	55013/5021		711
☐ N952AT	Boeing 717-2BD	55014/5027		712
☐ N953AT	Boeing 717-2BD	55015/5033		713
☐ N954AT	Boeing 717-2BD	55016/5036		714
☐ N955AT	Boeing 717-2BD	55017/5040		715
☐ N956AT	Boeing 717-2BD	55018/5044		716
☐ N957AT	Boeing 717-2BD	55019/5047		717
☐ N958AT	Boeing 717-2BD	55020/5051		718
☐ N959AT	Boeing 717-2BD	55021/5057		719
☐ N960AT	Boeing 717-2BD	55022/5058		720
☐ N961AT	Boeing 717-2BD	55023/5062		721
☐ N963AT	Boeing 717-2BD	55024/5066		722
☐ N964AT	Boeing 717-2BD	55025/5071		723
☐ N965AT	Boeing 717-2BD	55026/5076		724
☐ N966AT	Boeing 717-2BD	55027/5081		725
☐ N967AT	Boeing 717-2BD	55028/5082		726
☐ N968AT	Boeing 717-2BD	55029/5091		727
☐ N969AT	Boeing 717-2BD	55030/5094		728
☐ N970AT	Boeing 717-2BD	55031/5096		729
☐ N971AT	Boeing 717-2BD	55032/5097		730
☐ N972AT	Boeing 717-2BD	55033/5099		731
☐ N974AT	Boeing 717-2BD	55034/5101		732
☐ N975AT	Boeing 717-2BD	55035/5102		733
☐ N977AT	Boeing 717-2BD	55036/5106		734
☐ N978AT	Boeing 717-2BD	55037/5108		735
☐ N979AT	Boeing 717-2BD	55038/5109		736
☐ N980AT	Boeing 717-2BD	55039/5111		737
☐ N981AT	Boeing 717-2BD	55040/5113		738
☐ N982AT	Boeing 717-2BD	55041/5114		739
☐ N983AT	Boeing 717-2BD	55052/5150		750
☐ N985AT	Boeing 717-231	55090/5068	ex N423TW	798
☐ N986AT	Boeing 717-231	55089/5067	ex N422TW	797
☐ N987AT	Boeing 717-231	55088/5063	ex N2421A	796
☐ N988AT	Boeing 717-23S	55068/5065	ex (EI-CWJ)	760

☐ N989AT	Boeing 717-23S	55152/5085	ex (EI-CWK)	761
☐ N990AT	Boeing 717-23S	55134/5088	ex (EI-CWM)	762
☐ N991AT	Boeing 717-23S	55135/5090	ex N6202S	763
☐ N992AT	Boeing 717-2BD	55136/5100	ex N6202D	764
☐ N993AT	Boeing 717-2BD	55137/5103		765
☐ N994AT	Boeing 717-2BD	55138/5104	ex N6206F	766
☐ N995AT	Boeing 717-2BD	55139/5105		767
☐ N996AT	Boeing 717-2BD	55140/5107		768
☐ N997AT	Boeing 717-2BD	55141/5110		769
☐ N998AT	Boeing 717-2BD	55142/5112		770

☐ N126AT	Boeing 737-76N/W	32679/1514		300
☐ N149AT	Boeing 737-76N/W	32681/1526		301
☐ N166AT	Boeing 737-7BD/W	33917/1550		302
☐ N167AT	Boeing 737-7BD/W	33918/1572		304
☐ N168AT	Boeing 737-76N/W	32653/1566		303
☐ N169AT	Boeing 737-76N/W	32744/1584		305
☐ N173AT	Boeing 737-76N/W	32661/1593		306
☐ N174AT	Boeing 737-76N/W	32667/1623	ex N1787B	307
☐ N175AT	Boeing 737-76N/W	32652/1627		308
☐ N176AT	Boeing 737-76N/W	32654/1641		309
☐ N184AT	Boeing 737-76N/W	32656/1671		310
☐ N240AT	Boeing 737-76N/W	32657/1687		311
☐ N261AT	Boeing 737-76N/W	32660/1710		312
☐ N267AT	Boeing 737-7BD/W	33919/1730		313
☐ N272AT	Boeing 737-7BD/W	33921/1778	ex N1784B	315
☐ N273AT	Boeing 737-76N/W	32662/1788		316
☐ N276AT	Boeing 737-76N/W	32664/1804		317
☐ N278AT	Boeing 737-76N/W	32665/1827		318
☐ N279AT	Boeing 737-76N/W	32666/1833		319
☐ N281AT	Boeing 737-7BD/W	33922/1845		320
☐ N283AT	Boeing 737-7BD/W	34479/1874		321
☐ N284AT	Boeing 737-76N/W	32668/1876		322
☐ N285AT	Boeing 737-76N/W	32670/1898	ex N5573L	323
☐ N287AT	Boeing 737-76N/W	32671/1925		325
☐ N288AT	Boeing 737-7BD/W	33924/1940		326
☐ N289AT	Boeing 737-76N/W	32673/1943	ex N1787B	327
☐ N290AT	Boeing 737-7BD/W	33925/1967		328
☐ N291AT	Boeing 737-76N/W	32675/1970		329
☐ N292AT	Boeing 737-7BD/W	33926/1997		330
☐ N295AT	Boeing 737-76N/W	32677/2002		331
☐ N296AT	Boeing 737-7BD/W	34861/2041		332
☐ N299AT	Boeing 737-76N/W	32678/2055		333
☐ N300AT	Boeing 737-7BD/W	33923/2083		334
☐ N307AT	Boeing 737-7BD/W	34862/2094		335
☐ N308AT	Boeing 737-7BD/W	35109/2126	ex N1787B	336
☐ N309AT	Boeing 737-7BD/W	33929/2129		337
☐ N311AT	Boeing 737-7BD/W	33930/2143		338
☐ N312AT	Boeing 737-7BD/W	35110/2147		339
☐ N313AT	Boeing 737-7BD/W	33927/2169		340
☐ N315AT	Boeing 737-7BD/W	35788/2178		341
☐ N316AT	Boeing 737-7BD/W	33928/2190		342
☐ N318AT	Boeing 737-7BD/W	33931/2214		344
☐ N326AT	Boeing 737-7BD/W	33933/2278	ex N1786B	345
☐ N328AT	Boeing 737-7BD/W	33934/2296		346
☐ N329AT	Boeing 737-7BD/W	36091/2304		347
☐ N330AT	Boeing 737-7BD/W	36399/2312		348
☐ N336AT	Boeing 737-7BD/W	36716/2505	ex N1787B	350
☐ N337AT	Boeing 737-7BD/W	36717/2526	ex N1786B	351
☐ N338AT	Boeing 737-7BD/W	33943/2552		352
☐ N344AT	Boeing 737-7BD/W	36718/2568	ex N1786B	353
☐ N353AT	Boeing 737-7BD/W	36724/2813	ex N1787B	
☐ N354AT	Boeing 737-7BD/W	36725/2815	ex N1787B	

AK AIR — *Anchorage Intl, AK / Palmer Municipal, AK (ANC/PAQ)*

☐ N90KH	Beech 65-C90 King Air	LJ-542	ex N9442Q	
☐ N98UP	Aero Commander 680FL	680FL-1475	ex N30321	previously c/n 680FLP-1475-4
☐ N210HD	Aero Commander 500S Shrike	1841-33	ex N9016N	
☐ N222ME	Rockwell 690A Turbo Commander	11338	ex N46906	
☐ N340AH	Cessna 340	340-0100	ex N123S	
☐ N634CT	Rockwell 500S Shrike Commander	3121	ex N803AC	
☐ N9116N	Rockwell 500S Shrike Commander	3086		

ALASKA AIRLINES — *Alaska (AS/ASA)* — *Seattle-Tacoma Intl, WA (SEA)*

☐ N703AS	Boeing 737-490	28893/3039	ex (N747AS)	
☐ N705AS	Boeing 737-490	29318/3042	ex (N748AS)	
☐ N706AS	Boeing 737-490	28894/3050	ex (N749AS)	Disneyworld titles
☐ N708AS	Boeing 737-490	28895/3098		
☐ N709AS	Boeing 737-490 (SF)	28896/3099	ex N1787B	
☐ N713AS	Boeing 737-490	30161/3110	ex N1787B	

☐ N754AS	Boeing 737-4Q8	25095/2265		Spirit of Alaska	
☐ N755AS	Boeing 737-4Q8	25096/2278			
☐ N756AS	Boeing 737-4Q8	25097/2299			
☐ N760AS	Boeing 737-4Q8	25098/2320			
☐ N762AS	Boeing 737-4Q8F	25099/2334			
☐ N763AS	Boeing 737-4Q8F	25100/2346			
☐ N764AS	Boeing 737-4Q8F	25101/2348			
☐ N765AS	Boeing 737-4Q8F	25102/2350			
☐ N767AS	Boeing 737-490	27081/2354			
☐ N768AS	Boeing 737-490F	27082/2356			
☐ N769AS	Boeing 737-4Q8	25103/2452			
☐ N771AS	Boeing 737-4Q8	25104/2476			
☐ N772AS	Boeing 737-4Q8	25105/2505			
☐ N773AS	Boeing 737-4Q8	25106/2518			
☐ N778AS	Boeing 737-4Q8	25110/2586			
☐ N779AS	Boeing 737-4Q8	25111/2605			
☐ N784AS	Boeing 737-4Q8	28199/2826		Spirit of Disneyland c/s	
☐ N785AS	Boeing 737-4Q8	27628/2858			
☐ N786AS	Boeing 737-4S3	24795/1870	ex TF-FIE		
☐ N788AS	Boeing 737-490	28885/2891			
☐ N791AS	Boeing 737-490	28886/2902			
☐ N792AS	Boeing 737-490	28887/2903		Salmon Thirty Seven	
☐ N793AS	Boeing 737-490	28888/2990			
☐ N794AS	Boeing 737-490	28889/3000			
☐ N795AS	Boeing 737-490	28890/3006			
☐ N796AS	Boeing 737-490	28891/3027			
☐ N797AS	Boeing 737-490	28892/3036			
☐ N799AS	Boeing 737-490	29270/3038			

☐ N607AS	Boeing 737-790/W	29751/313			
☐ N609AS	Boeing 737-790/W	29752/350			
☐ N611AS	Boeing 737-790/W	29753/385			
☐ N612AS	Boeing 737-790/W	30162/406	ex N1787B		
☐ N613AS	Boeing 737-790/W	30163/430			
☐ N614AS	Boeing 737-790/W	30343/439			
☐ N615AS	Boeing 737-790/W	30344/472	ex N1787B		
☐ N617AS	Boeing 737-790/W	30542/532			
☐ N618AS	Boeing 737-790/W	30543/536	ex N1787B		
☐ N619AS	Boeing 737-790/W	30164/597			
☐ N622AS	Boeing 737-790/W	30165/661			
☐ N623AS	Boeing 737-790/W	30166/700			
☐ N624AS	Boeing 737-790/W	30778/724			
☐ N625AS	Boeing 737-790/W	30792/754	ex N1795B		
☐ N626AS	Boeing 737-790/W	30793/763			
☐ N627AS	Boeing 737-790/W	30794/796	ex N1787B		
☐ N644AS	Boeing 737-790/W	30795/1277			
☐ N648AS	Boeing 737-790/W	30662/1382			
☐ N649AS	Boeing 737-790/W	30663/1386			
☐ N506AS	Boeing 737-890/W	35690/2627			
☐ N508AS	Boeing 737-890/W	35691/2662	ex N1786B		
☐ N512AS	Boeing 737-890/W	39043/2711			
☐ N513AS	Boeing 737-890/W	35192/2721	ex N1786B		
☐ N514AS	Boeing 737-890/W	35193/2727	ex N1786B		
☐ N516AS	Boeing 737-890/W	39044/2751			
☐ N517AS	Boeing 737-890/W	35197/2770			
☐ N518AS	Boeing 737-890/W	35693/2785			
☐ N519AS	Boeing 737-890/W	36482/2800	ex N1795B		
☐ N520AS	Boeing 737-890/W	36481/2812	ex N1786B		
☐ N523AS	Boeing 737-890/W	35194/2816			
☐ N524AS	Boeing 737-890/W	35195/2850	ex N1796B		
☐ N525AS	Boeing 737-890/W	35692/2859	ex N1786B		
☐ N526AS	Boeing 737-890/W	35196/2862	ex N1796B		
☐ N527AS	Boeing 737-890/W	35694/2913	ex N1796B		
☐ N528AS	Boeing 737-890/W	35695/2930			
☐ N529AS	Boeing 737-890/W	35198			
☐ N530AS	Boeing 737-890/W	36578			
☐ N531AS	Boeing 737-890/W	35199			
☐ N	Boeing 737-890/W				on order
☐ N	Boeing 737-890/W				on order
☐ N	Boeing 737-890/W				on order
☐ N	Boeing 737-890/W				on order
☐ N546AS	Boeing 737-890/W	30022/1640			
☐ N548AS	Boeing 737-890/W	30020/1738			
☐ N549AS	Boeing 737-8FH/W	30824/1664			
☐ N551AS	Boeing 737-890/W	34593/1860			
☐ N552AS	Boeing 737-890/W	34595/1882	ex N1795B		
☐ N553AS	Boeing 737-890/W	34594/1906			
☐ N556AS	Boeing 737-890/W	35175/1980			
☐ N557AS	Boeing 737-890/W	35176/2010			
☐ N558AS	Boeing 737-890/W	35177/2031			
☐ N559AS	Boeing 737-890/W	35178/2026	ex N6067E	ETOPS test aircraft	
☐ N560AS	Boeing 737-890/W	35179/2072			
☐ N562AS	Boeing 737-890/W	35091/2084			

☐ N563AS	Boeing 737-890/W	35180/2090		
☐ N564AS	Boeing 737-890/W	35103/2099		
☐ N565AS	Boeing 737-890/W	35181/2134		
☐ N566AS	Boeing 737-890/W	35182/2164		
☐ N568AS	Boeing 737-890/W	35183/2166		
☐ N569AS	Boeing 737-890/W	35184/2192		75th anniversary colours
☐ N570AS	Boeing 737-890/W	35185/2212		
☐ N577AS	Boeing 737-890/W	35186/2221	ex N1787B	
☐ N579AS	Boeing 737-890/W	35187/2226		
☐ N581AS	Boeing 737-890/W	35188/2259		
☐ N583AS	Boeing 737-890/W	35681/2333		
☐ N584AS	Boeing 737-890/W	35682/2365		
☐ N585AS	Boeing 737-890/W	35683/2385		
☐ N586AS	Boeing 737-890/W	35189/2393		
☐ N587AS	Boeing 737-890/W	35684/2422	ex N1786B	
☐ N588AS	Boeing 737-890/W	35685/2454	ex N1786B	
☐ N589AS	Boeing 737-890/W	35686/2458	ex N1786B	
☐ N590AS	Boeing 737-890/W	35687/2478		
☐ N592AS	Boeing 737-890/W	35190/2511	ex N1786B	
☐ N593AS	Boeing 737-890/W	35107/2545	ex N1786B	
☐ N594AS	Boeing 737-890/W	35191/2560	ex N1786B	
☐ N596AS	Boeing 737-890/W	35688/2587		
☐ N597AS	Boeing 737-890/W	35689/2601		

☐ N302AS	Boeing 737-990/W	30017/596	ex N737X
☐ N303AS	Boeing 737-990/W	30016/683	ex N672AS
☐ N305AS	Boeing 737-990/W	30013/774	ex (N673AS)
☐ N306AS	Boeing 737-990/W	30014/802	ex (N674AS)
☐ N307AS	Boeing 737-990/W	30015/838	ex N1786B
☐ N309AS	Boeing 737-990/W	30857/902	ex N1786B
☐ N315AS	Boeing 737-990/W	30019/1218	
☐ N317AS	Boeing 737-990/W	30856/1296	ex N1786B
☐ N318AS	Boeing 737-990/W	30018/1326	
☐ N319AS	Boeing 737-990/W	33679/1344	
☐ N320AS	Boeing 737-990/W	33680/1380	
☐ N323AS	Boeing 737-990/W	30021/1454	

ALASKA CENTRAL EXPRESS — *Ace Air (KO/AER)* — *Anchorage-Intl, AK (ANC)*

☐ N111AX	Beech 1900C-1	UC-81	ex N5632C
☐ N113AX	Beech 1900C-1	UC-41	ex N41UE
☐ N114AX	Beech 1900C-1	UC-36	ex N1566C
☐ N115AX	Beech 1900C-1	UC-2	ex N19NG

☐ N9874M	Cessna 207A Stationair 8 II	20700745
☐ N9957M	Cessna 207A Stationair 8 II	20700764

ALASKA SEAPLANE SERVICE — *(J5)* — *Juneau-Int'l, AK (JNU)*

☐ N777DH	de Havilland DHC-2 Beaver	47	ex CF-FHN	Floatplane
☐ N4794C	de Havilland DHC-2 Beaver	342	ex 51-16545	Floatplane
☐ N60077	de Havilland DHC-2 Beaver	1419	ex LV-GLJ	Floatplane

ALASKA WEST AIR — *Kenai Island Lake, AK (ENA)*

☐ N49AW	de Havilland DHC-3 Otter	310	ex N21PG	
☐ N87AW	de Havilland DHC-3 Otter	52	ex C-FMPO	
☐ N222RL	de Havilland DHC-2 Turbo Beaver	1570/TB5	ex C-FOEB	Floatplane
☐ N1432Z	de Havilland DHC-2 Beaver	797	ex 54-1668	Floatplane

ALLEGIANT AIR — *Allegiant (G4/AAY)* — *Las Vegas-McCarran Int'l, NV (LAS)*

☐ N399NV	McDonnell-Douglas MD-87	49413/1681	ex XA-TXH	stored MHV
☐ N401NV	McDonnell-Douglas MD-88	49761/1623	ex N158PL	
☐ N402NV	McDonnell-Douglas MD-88	49763/1626	ex N160PL	
☐ N403NV	McDonnell-Douglas MD-88	49764/1632	ex N161PL	
☐ N404NV	McDonnell-Douglas MD-88	49765/1645	ex N162PL	
☐ N405NV	McDonnell-Douglas MD-83	49623/1499	ex SE-RFA	
☐ N406NV	McDonnell-Douglas MD-82	49900/1765	ex SE-RFC	
☐ N407NV	McDonnell-Douglas MD-82	53244/1901	ex SE-RFD	
☐ N408NV	McDonnell-Douglas MD-82	53246/1918	ex SE-RFB	
☐ N409NV	McDonnell-Douglas MD-83	49574/1413	ex SE-RDV	
☐ N410NV	McDonnell-Douglas MD-83	49965/2044	ex SE-DLV	
☐ N411NV	McDonnell-Douglas MD-82	53245/1978	ex HK-4413	
☐ N412NV	McDonnell-Douglas MD-88	49759/1607	ex N822ME	
☐ N414NV	McDonnell-Douglas MD-88	49766/1657	ex N823ME	
☐ N860GA	McDonnell-Douglas MD-83	49786/1631	ex 9Y-THW	
☐ N861GA	McDonnell-Douglas MD-83	49557/1436	ex SE-DPI	
☐ N862GA	McDonnell-Douglas MD-83	49556/1415	ex LN-RMF	
☐ N863GA	McDonnell-Douglas MD-83	49911/1653	ex OY-KHL	
☐ N864GA	McDonnell-Douglas MD-83	49912/1659	ex LN-RMJ	
☐ N865GA	McDonnell-Douglas MD-83	49998/1800	ex SE-DIX	

☐ N866GA	McDonnell-Douglas MD-83	49910/1638	ex OY-KHK	
☐ N868GA	McDonnell-Douglas MD-83	49554/1379	ex LN-RMA	
☐ N869GA	McDonnell-Douglas MD-83	53294/1917	ex SE-DIZ	
☐ N871GA	McDonnell-Douglas MD-83	53296/1937	ex OY-KHT	
☐ N872GA	McDonnell-Douglas MD-83	53295/1922	ex LN-RMN	
☐ N873GA	McDonnell-Douglas MD-83	49658/1461	ex N946AS	
☐ N874GA	McDonnell-Douglas MD-83	49643/1423	ex N945AS	
☐ N875GA	McDonnell-Douglas MD-83	53468/2130	ex C-GKLN	
☐ N876GA	McDonnell-Douglas MD-83	53469/2116	ex C-GKLR	
☐ N877GA	McDonnell-Douglas MD-83	53467/2102	ex C-GKLJ	
☐ N878GA	McDonnell-Douglas MD-83	53487/2132	ex C-GKLQ	
☐ N879GA	McDonnell-Douglas MD-83	53486/2130	ex C-GKLN	
☐ N880GA	McDonnell-Douglas MD-83	49625/1503	ex OH-LMG	all-white
☐ N881GA	McDonnell-Douglas MD-83	49708/1561	ex SE-RGO	
☐ N883GA	McDonnell-Douglas MD-83	49710/1547	ex SE-RGP	all-white
☐ N884GA	McDonnell-Douglas MD-83	49401/1357	ex SE-RDS	
☐ N886GA	McDonnell-Douglas MD-82	49931/1754	ex N829NK	
☐ N887GA	McDonnell-Douglas MD-82	49932/1756	ex N830NK	
☐ N891GA	McDonnell-Douglas MD-83	49423/1283	ex LN-RLG	
☐ N892GA	McDonnell-Douglas MD-83	49826/1578	ex N861LF	
☐ N893GA	McDonnell-Douglas MD-83	53051/1718	ex N881LF	
☐ N894GA	McDonnell-Douglas MD-82	49660/1445	ex EI-BTX	
☐ N895GA	McDonnell-Douglas MD-82	49667/1466	ex EI-BTY	
☐ N945MA	McDonnell-Douglas MD-87	49725/1552	ex VP-BOP	
☐ N948MA	McDonnell-Douglas MD-87	49778/1646	ex VP-BOO	
☐ N949MA	McDonnell-Douglas MD-87	49779/1670	ex N751RA	
☐ N952MA	McDonnell-Douglas MD-87	49673/1508	ex N673HC	

ALLWEST FREIGHT — *Kenai-Municipal, AK (ENA)*

☐ N549WB	Short SC.7 Skyvan	SH1911	ex XA-SRD	Freighter

ALOHA AIR CARGO — *Honolulu-Intl, HI (HNL)*

☐ N826AL	Boeing 737-282C	23051/1002	ex CS-TEQ
☐ N834AL	Boeing 737-210C	20917/344	ex XA-ABX
☐ N840AL	Boeing 737-2X6C	23124/1046	ex N747AS
☐ N841AL	Boeing 737-2X6C	23123/1042	ex N746AS
☐ N842AL	Boeing 737-290QC	23136/1032	ex N742AS

ALPINE AIR EXPRESS — *Alpine Air (5A/AIP)* — *Provo-Municipal, UT (PVU)*

☐ N14MV	Beech 99	U-59	ex C-FGJT	
☐ N24BH	Beech 99	U-67	ex C-GVNQ	
☐ N95WA	Beech 99	U-6	ex N19RA	
☐ N99CA	Beech 99A	U-127	ex N22AT	
☐ N99GH	Beech 99A	U-112	ex N86569	
☐ N216CS	Beech C99	U-216	ex C-GGPP	based HNL
☐ N236AL	Beech C99	U-236	ex RP-C2317	based HNL
☐ N237SL	Beech C99	U-237	ex RP-C2370	based HNL
☐ N238AL	Beech C99	U-238	ex RP-C2380	based HNL
☐ N239AL	Beech C99	U-239	ex RP-C2390	based HNL
☐ N326CA	Beech B99	U-135	ex N10RA	
☐ N950AA	Beech B99	U-159	ex C-FCBU	
☐ N955AA	Beech 99A	U-128	ex J6-AAE	
☐ N4381Y	Beech 99	U-71	ex N216BH	

☐ N17ZV	Beech 1900C-1	UC-17	ex CC-COK	
☐ N125BA	Beech 1900C	UB-6	ex N125GP	
☐ N127BA	Beech 1900C	UB-7	ex N126GP	
☐ N153GA	Beech 1900C	UB-34	ex N734GL	based HNL
☐ N154GA	Beech 1900C	UB-25	ex N315BH	
☐ N155CJ	Beech 1900D	UE-55	ex N85230	
☐ N172GA	Beech 1900C	UB-11	ex N11ZR	
☐ N190GA	Beech 1900C	UB-1	ex N1YW	
☐ N192GA	Beech 1900C	UB-17	ex N17ZR	based HNL
☐ N194GA	Beech 1900C	UB-8	ex CC-CAF	
☐ N197GA	Beech 1900C	UB-16	ex N16ZR	
☐ N198GA	Beech 1900C	UB-5	ex CC-CAS	

AMERICAN AIRLINES — *American (AA/AAL)* — *Dallas-Fort Worth, TX (DFW)*

Member of Oneworld

☐ N800NN	Boeing 737-823/W	29564/2964	3DY
☐ N801NN	Boeing 737-823/W	29565/2972	3EA
☐ N802NN	Boeing 737-823/W	31073/2982	3EB
☐ N803NN	Boeing 737-823/W	29566/2995	3EC
☐ N804NN	Boeing 737-823/W	29567/3004	3ED
☐ N805NN	Boeing 737-823/W	31075/3013	3EE
☐ N806NN	Boeing 737-823/W	29561/3028	3EF
☐ N807NN	Boeing 737-823/W	31077/3035	3EF

	Registration	Type	C/n	Previous	Fleet no.	Remarks
☐	N808NN	Boeing 737-823/W	33206/3042		3EH	
☐	N809NN	Boeing 737-823/W	33519/3050		3EJ	
☐	N810NN	Boeing 737-823/W	33207/3056		3EK	
☐	N811NN	Boeing 737-823/W	31079/3063		3EL	
☐	N812NN	Boeing 737-823/W	33520/3070		3EM	
☐	N813NN	Boeing 737-823/W	30918/3077		3EN	
☐	N814NN	Boeing 737-823/W	29562/3085		3EP	
☐	N815NN	Boeing 737-823/W	33208/3094		3ER	
☐	N816NN	Boeing 737-823/W	31081/3102		3ES	
☐	N817NN	Boeing 737-823/W	29558/3107		3ET	
☐	N818NN	Boeing 737-823/W	30910/3112		3EU	
☐	N819NN	Boeing 737-823/W	31083/3118		3EV	
☐	N820NN	Boeing 737-823/W	29559/3125		3EW	
☐	N821NN	Boeing 737-823/W	30912/3137		3EX	
☐	N822NN	Boeing 737-823/W	31085/3149			
☐	N823NN	Boeing 737-823/W	29560/3156			
☐	N824NN	Boeing 737-823/W	30916			on order
☐	N825NN	Boeing 737-823/W	31087			on order
☐	N826NN	Boeing 737-823/W	31089			on order
☐	N827NN	Boeing 737-823/W	33209			on order
☐	N829NN	Boeing 737-823/W	33210			on order
☐	N830NN	Boeing 737-823/W	31091			on order
☐	N831NN	Boeing 737-823/W	33211			on order
☐	N832NN	Boeing 737-823/W	33521			on order
☐	N833NN	Boeing 737-823/W	31093			on order
☐	N834NN	Boeing 737-823/W	29576			on order
☐	N835NN	Boeing 737-823/W	29577			on order
☐	N836NN	Boeing 737-823/W	31095			on order
☐	N837NN	Boeing 737-823/W	30908			on order
☐	N838NN	Boeing 737-823/W	31097			on order
☐	N839NN	Boeing 737-823/W	29557			on order
☐	N840NN	Boeing 737-823/W	33518			on order
☐	N841NN	Boeing 737-823/W	30914			on order
☐	N842NN	Boeing 737-823/W	31099			on order
☐	N843NN	Boeing 737-823/W	30906			on order
☐	N844NN	Boeing 737-823/W	33212			on order
☐	N845NN	Boeing 737-823/W	40579			on order
☐	N846NN	Boeing 737-823/W	31101			on order
☐		Boeing 737-823/W				on order
☐		Boeing 737-823/W				on order
☐		Boeing 737-823/W				on order
☐		Boeing 737-823/W				on order
☐		Boeing 737-823/W				on order
☐		Boeing 737-823/W				on order
☐		Boeing 737-823/W				on order
☐		Boeing 737-823/W				on order
☐		Boeing 737-823/W				on order
☐		Boeing 737-823/W				on order
☐		Boeing 737-823/W				on order
☐		Boeing 737-823/W				on order
☐		Boeing 737-823/W				on order
☐		Boeing 737-823/W				on order
☐		Boeing 737-823/W				on order
☐		Boeing 737-823/W				on order
☐	N901AN	Boeing 737-823/W	29503/184		3AA	
☐	N902AN	Boeing 737-823/W	29504/190		3AB	
☐	N903AN	Boeing 737-823/W	29505/196		3AC	
☐	N904AN	Boeing 737-823/W	29506/207		3AD	
☐	N905AN	Boeing 737-823/W	29507/231		3AE	
☐	N906AN	Boeing 737-823/W	29508/240		3AF	
☐	N907AN	Boeing 737-823/W	29509/254		3AG	
☐	N908AN	Boeing 737-823/W	29510/263		3AH	
☐	N909AN	Boeing 737-823/W	29511/267	ex (N909AM)	3AJ	
☐	N910AN	Boeing 737-823/W	29512/271		3AK	
☐	N912AN	Boeing 737-823/W	29513/289		3AL	
☐	N913AN	Boeing 737-823/W	29514/293		3AM	
☐	N914AN	Boeing 737-823/W	29515/316		3AN	
☐	N915AN	Boeing 737-823/W	29516/322		3AP	
☐	N916AN	Boeing 737-823/W	29517/332		3AR	
☐	N917AN	Boeing 737-823/W	29518/344		3AS	
☐	N918AN	Boeing 737-823/W	29519/353		3AT	
☐	N919AN	Boeing 737-823/W	29520/363		3AU	
☐	N920AN	Boeing 737-823/W	29521/378		3AV	
☐	N921AN	Boeing 737-823/W	29522/383		3AW	
☐	N922AN	Boeing 737-823/W	29523/398		3AX	
☐	N923AN	Boeing 737-823/W	29524/405		3AY	
☐	N924AN	Boeing 737-823/W	29525/434		3BA	
☐	N925AN	Boeing 737-823/W	29526/440		3BB	
☐	N926AN	Boeing 737-823/W	29527/453		3BC	
☐	N927AN	Boeing 737-823/W	30077/462		3BD	
☐	N928AN	Boeing 737-823/W	29528/473		3BE	
☐	N929AN	Boeing 737-823/W	30078/488		3BF	
☐	N930AN	Boeing 737-823/W	29529/503		3BG	

	Registration	Type	c/n	Previous	Code	Remarks
☐	N931AN	Boeing 737-823/W	30079/509		3BH	
☐	N932AN	Boeing 737-823/W	29530/527		3BJ	
☐	N933AN	Boeing 737-823/W	30080/531		3BK	
☐	N934AN	Boeing 737-823/W	29531/553		3BL	
☐	N935AN	Boeing 737-823/W	30081/559		3BM	
☐	N936AN	Boeing 737-823/W	29532/575		3BN	
☐	N937AN	Boeing 737-823/W	30082/579		3BP	
☐	N938AN	Boeing 737-823/W	29533/608		3BR	
☐	N939AN	Boeing 737-823/W	30083/612		3BS	
☐	N940AN	Boeing 737-823/W	30598/616		3BT	
☐	N941AN	Boeing 737-823/W	29534/624		3BU	
☐	N942AN	Boeing 737-823/W	30084/629		3BV	
☐	N943AN	Boeing 737-823/W	30599/635		3BW	
☐	N944AN	Boeing 737-823/W	29535/645		3BX	
☐	N945AN	Boeing 737-823/W	30085/649		3BY	
☐	N946AN	Boeing 737-823/W	30600/655		3CA	
☐	N947AN	Boeing 737-823/W	29536/671	ex (N2292Z)	3CB	
☐	N948AN	Boeing 737-823/W	30086/679	ex (N2294B)	3CC	
☐	N949AN	Boeing 737-823/W	29537/699		3CD	
☐	N950AN	Boeing 737-823/W	30087/704		3CE	
☐	N951AA	Boeing 737-823/W	29538/720		3CF	Astrojet c/s
☐	N952AA	Boeing 737-823/W	30088/726		3CG	
☐	N953AN	Boeing 737-823/W	29539/741		3CH	
☐	N954AN	Boeing 737-823/W	30089/745		3CJ	
☐	N955AN	Boeing 737-823/W	29540/762		3CK	
☐	N956AN	Boeing 737-823/W	30090/764		3CL	
☐	N957AN	Boeing 737-823/W	29541/788		3CM	
☐	N958AN	Boeing 737-823/W	30091/797		3CN	
☐	N959AN	Boeing 737-823/W	30828/801		3CP	
☐	N960AN	Boeing 737-823/W	29542/818		3CR	
☐	N961AN	Boeing 737-823/W	30092/822		3CS	
☐	N962AN	Boeing 737-823/W	30858/825		3CT	
☐	N963AN	Boeing 737-823/W	29543/834		3CU	
☐	N964AN	Boeing 737-823/W	30093/837		3CV	
☐	N965AN	Boeing 737-823/W	29544/860		3CW	
☐	N966AN	Boeing 737-823/W	30094/863		3CX	
☐	N967AN	Boeing 737-823/W	29545/883		3CY	
☐	N968AN	Boeing 737-823/W	30095/886		3DA	
☐	N969AN	Boeing 737-823/W	29546/910		3DB	
☐	N970AN	Boeing 737-823/W	30096/915		3DC	
☐	N971AN	Boeing 737-823/W	29547/937		3DD	
☐	N972AN	Boeing 737-823/W	30097/941		3DE	
☐	N973AN	Boeing 737-823/W	29548/971		3DF	
☐	N974AN	Boeing 737-823/W	30098/977		3DG	
☐	N975AN	Boeing 737-823/W	29549/992		3DH	
☐	N976AN	Boeing 737-823/W	30099/1001		3DJ	
☐	N978AN	Boeing 737-823/W	30100/1022		3DL	
☐	N979AN	Boeing 737-823/W	29568/2838		3DM	
☐	N980AN	Boeing 737-823/W	33203/2846		3DN	
☐	N981AN	Boeing 737-823/W	29569/2870		3DP	
☐	N982AN	Boeing 737-823/W	31067/2876		3DR	
☐	N983AN	Boeing 737-823/W	29570/2899		3DS	
☐	N987AN	Boeing 737-823/W	31060/2907		3DT	
☐	N989AN	Boeing 737-823/W	33205/2915		3DU	
☐	N990AN	Boeing 737-823/W	29563/2935		3DV	
☐	N991AN	Boeing 737-823/W	30920/2945		3DW	
☐	N992AN	Boeing 737-823/W	31071/2954		3DX	
☐	N172AJ	Boeing 757-223/W	32400/1012		5FT	
☐	N173AN	Boeing 757-223/W	32399/1005		5FS	
☐	N174AA	Boeing 757-223/W	31308/998		5FR	
☐	N175AN	Boeing 757-223/W	32394/992		5FK	
☐	N176AA	Boeing 757-223/W	32395/994		5FL	
☐	N177AN	Boeing 757-223/W	32396/996		5FM	
☐	N178AA	Boeing 757-223/W	32398/1002	ex (N20171)	5FN	
☐	N179AA	Boeing 757-223/W	32397/1000	ex (N20140)	5FP	
☐	N181AN	Boeing 757-223/W	29591/852	ex N5573L	5EN	
☐	N182AN	Boeing 757-223/W	29592/853		5EP	
☐	N183AN	Boeing 757-223ER/W	29593/862		5ER	
☐	N184AN	Boeing 757-223ER/W	29594/866	ex N1787B	5ES	
☐	N185AN	Boeing 757-223/W	32379/962		5ET	
☐	N186AN	Boeing 757-223/W	32380/964		5EU	
☐	N187AN	Boeing 757-223/W	32381/965		5EV	
☐	N188AN	Boeing 757-223/W	32382/969		5EW	
☐	N189AN	Boeing 757-223/W	32383/970		5EX	
☐	N190AA	Boeing 757-223/W	32384/973		5EY	
☐	N191AN	Boeing 757-223/W	32385/977		5FA	
☐	N192AN	Boeing 757-223/W	32386/979		5FB	
☐	N193AN	Boeing 757-223/W	32387/981		5FC	
☐	N194AA	Boeing 757-223/W	32388/983		5FD	
☐	N195AN	Boeing 757-223/W	32389/984		5FE	
☐	N196AA	Boeing 757-223/W	32390/986		5FF	
☐	N197AN	Boeing 757-223/W	32391/988		5FG	

☐ N198AA	Boeing 757-223/W	32392/989		5FH	
☐ N199AN	Boeing 757-223/W	32393/991		5FJ	
☐ N601AN	Boeing 757-223/W	27052/661		5DU	
☐ N602AN	Boeing 757-223/W	27053/664		5DV	
☐ N603AA	Boeing 757-223/W	27054/670		5DW	
☐ N604AA	Boeing 757-223/W	27055/677		5DX	
☐ N605AA	Boeing 757-223/W	27056/680		5DY	
☐ N606AA	Boeing 757-223/W	27057/707		5EA	
☐ N607AM	Boeing 757-223/W	27058/712		5EB	
☐ N608AA	Boeing 757-223ER/W	27446/720		5EC	
☐ N609AA	Boeing 757-223ER/W	27447/722		5ED	
☐ N610AA	Boeing 757-223//W	24486/234		610	
☐ N611AM	Boeing 757-223/W	24487/236		611	
☐ N612AA	Boeing 757-223/W	24488/240		612	
☐ N613AA	Boeing 757-223/W	24489/242		613	
☐ N614AA	Boeing 757-223/W	24490/243		614	
☐ N615AM	Boeing 757-223/W	24491/245		615	
☐ N616AA	Boeing 757-223/W	24524/248		616	
☐ N617AM	Boeing 757-223/W	24525/253		617	
☐ N618AA	Boeing 757-223/W	24526/260		618	
☐ N619AA	Boeing 757-223/W	24577/269		619	
☐ N620AA	Boeing 757-223/W	24578/276		620	
☐ N621AM	Boeing 757-223/W	24579/283		621	
☐ N622AA	Boeing 757-223/W	24580/289		622	
☐ N623AA	Boeing 757-223/W	24581/296		623	
☐ N624AA	Boeing 757-223/W	24582/297		624	
☐ N625AA	Boeing 757-223/W	24583/303		625	
☐ N626AA	Boeing 757-223/W	24584/304		626	
☐ N627AA	Boeing 757-223/W	24585/308		627	
☐ N628AA	Boeing 757-223/W	24586/309		628	
☐ N629AA	Boeing 757-223/W	24587/315		629	
☐ N630AA	Boeing 757-223/W	24588/316		630	
☐ N631AA	Boeing 757-223/W	24589/317		631	
☐ N632AA	Boeing 757-223/W	24590/321		632	
☐ N633AA	Boeing 757-223/W	24591/324		633	
☐ N634AA	Boeing 757-223/W	24592/327		634	
☐ N635AA	Boeing 757-223/W	24593/328		635	
☐ N636AM	Boeing 757-223/W	24594/336		636	
☐ N637AM	Boeing 757-223/W	24595/337		637	
☐ N638AA	Boeing 757-223/W	24596/344		638	
☐ N639AA	Boeing 757-223/W	24597/345		639	
☐ N640A	Boeing 757-223/W	24598/350		640	
☐ N641AA	Boeing 757-223/W	24599/351		641	
☐ N642AA	Boeing 757-223/W	24600/357		642	
☐ N643AA	Boeing 757-223/W	24601/360		643	
☐ N645AA	Boeing 757-223/W	24603/370		5BR	
☐ N646AA	Boeing 757-223/W	24604/375		5BS	
☐ N647AM	Boeing 757-223/W	24605/378		5BT	
☐ N648AA	Boeing 757-223/W	24606/379		5BU	
☐ N649AA	Boeing 757-223/W	24607/383		5BV	
☐ N650AA	Boeing 757-223/W	24608/384		5BW	
☐ N652AA	Boeing 757-223/W	24610/391		5BY	
☐ N653A	Boeing 757-223/W	24611/397		5CA	
☐ N654A	Boeing 757-223/W	24612/398		5CB	
☐ N655AA	Boeing 757-223/W	24613/402		5CC	
☐ N656AA	Boeing 757-223/W	24614/404		5CD	
☐ N657AM	Boeing 757-223/W	24615/409		5CE	
☐ N658AA	Boeing 757-223/W	24616/410		5CF	
☐ N659AA	Boeing 757-223/W	24617/417		5CG Pride of American	
☐ N660AM	Boeing 757-223/W	25294/418		5CH	
☐ N661AA	Boeing 757-223/W	25295/423		5CJ	
☐ N662AA	Boeing 757-223/W	25296/425		5CK	
☐ N663AM	Boeing 757-223/W	25297/432		5CL	
☐ N664AA	Boeing 757-223/W	25298/433		5CM	
☐ N665AA	Boeing 757-223/W	25299/436		5CN	
☐ N666A	Boeing 757-223/W	25300/451		5CP	
☐ N668AA	Boeing 757-223/W	25333/460		5CS	
☐ N669AA	Boeing 757-223/W	25334/463		5CT	
☐ N670AA	Boeing 757-223/W	25335/468		5CU	
☐ N671AA	Boeing 757-223/W	25336/473		5CV	
☐ N672AA	Boeing 757-223/W	25337/474		5CW	
☐ N673AN	Boeing 757-223/W	29423/812		5EE	
☐ N674AN	Boeing 757-223/W	29424/816		5EF	
☐ N675AN	Boeing 757-223/W	29425/817		5EG	
☐ N676AN	Boeing 757-223/W	29426/827	ex N1798B	5EH	
☐ N677AN	Boeing 757-223/W	29427/828		5EJ	
☐ N678AN	Boeing 757-223/W	29428/837	ex N1787B	5EK	
☐ N679AN	Boeing 757-223/W	29589/842	ex N1800B	5EL	Astrojet c/s
☐ N680AN	Boeing 757-223/W	29590/847		5EM	
☐ N681AA	Boeing 757-223/W	25338/483		5CX	
☐ N682AA	Boeing 757-223/W	25339/484		5CY	
☐ N683A	Boeing 757-223/W	25340/491		5DA	
☐ N684AA	Boeing 757-223/W	25341/504		5DB	

	Registration	Type	c/n	Fleet no.
☐	N685AA	Boeing 757-223/W	25342/507	5DC
☐	N686AA	Boeing 757-223/W	25343/509	5DD
☐	N687AA	Boeing 757-223ER/W	25695/536	5DE
☐	N688AA	Boeing 757-223ER/W	25730/548	5DF
☐	N689AA	Boeing 757-223ER/W	25731/562	5DG
☐	N690AA	Boeing 757-223ER/W	25696/566	5DH
☐	N691AA	Boeing 757-223ER/W	25697/568	5DJ
☐	N692AA	Boeing 757-223/W	26072/678	5DK
☐	N693AA	Boeing 757-223/W	26973/580	5DL
☐	N694AN	Boeing 757-223/W	26974/582	5DM
☐	N695AN	Boeing 757-223/W	26975/621	5DN
☐	N696AN	Boeing 757-223/W	26976/627	5DP
☐	N697AN	Boeing 757-223/W	26977/633	5DR
☐	N698AN	Boeing 757-223/W	26980/635	5DS
☐	N699AN	Boeing 757-223/W	27051/660	5DT
☐	N7667A	Boeing 757-223/W	25301/459	5CR
☐	N319AA	Boeing 767-223ER	22320/128	319
☐	N320AA	Boeing 767-223ER	22321/130	320
☐	N321AA	Boeing 767-223ER	22322/139	321
☐	N322AA	Boeing 767-223ER	22323/140	322
☐	N323AA	Boeing 767-223ER	22324/146	323
☐	N324AA	Boeing 767-223ER	22325/147	324
☐	N325AA	Boeing 767-223ER	22326/157	325
☐	N327AA	Boeing 767-223ER	22327/159	327
☐	N328AA	Boeing 767-223ER	22328/160	328
☐	N329AA	Boeing 767-223ER	22329/164	329
☐	N332AA	Boeing 767-223ER	22331/168	332
☐	N335AA	Boeing 767-223ER	22333/194	335
☐	N336AA	Boeing 767-223ER	22334/195	336
☐	N338AA	Boeing 767-223ER	22335/196	338
☐	N339AA	Boeing 767-223ER	22336/198	339
☐	N342AN	Boeing 767-323ER	33081/896	342
☐	N343AN	Boeing 767-323ER	33082/899	343
☐	N344AN	Boeing 767-323ER	33083/900	344
☐	N345AN	Boeing 767-323ER/W	33084/906	345
☐	N346AN	Boeing 767-323ER	33085/907	346
☐	N347AN	Boeing 767-323ER	33086/908	347
☐	N348AN	Boeing 767-323ER	33087/910	348
☐	N349AN	Boeing 767-323ER	33088/913	349
☐	N350AN	Boeing 767-323ER	33089/916	350
☐	N351AA	Boeing 767-323ER	24032/202	351
☐	N352AA	Boeing 767-323ER	24033/205	352
☐	N353AA	Boeing 767-323ER	24034/206	353
☐	N354AA	Boeing 767-323ER	24035/211	354
☐	N355AA	Boeing 767-323ER	24036/221	355
☐	N357AA	Boeing 767-323ER	24038/227	357
☐	N358AA	Boeing 767-323ER	24039/228	358
☐	N359AA	Boeing 767-323ER	24040/230	359
☐	N360AA	Boeing 767-323ER	24041/232	360
☐	N361AA	Boeing 767-323ER	24042/235	361
☐	N362AA	Boeing 767-323ER	24043/237	362
☐	N363AA	Boeing 767-323ER	24044/238	363
☐	N366AA	Boeing 767-323ER	25193/388	366
☐	N368AA	Boeing 767-323ER	25195/404	368
☐	N369AA	Boeing 767-323ER	25196/422	369
☐	N370AA	Boeing 767-323ER	25197/425	370
☐	N371AA	Boeing 767-323ER	25198/431	371
☐	N372AA	Boeing 767-323ER	25199/433	372
☐	N373AA	Boeing 767-323ER/W	25200/435	373
☐	N374AA	Boeing 767-323ER	25201/437	374
☐	N376AN	Boeing 767-323ER	25445/447	376
☐	N377AN	Boeing 767-323ER/W	25446/453	377
☐	N378AN	Boeing 767-323ER	25447/469	378
☐	N379AA	Boeing 767-323ER	25448/481	379
☐	N380AN	Boeing 767-323ER/W	25449/489	380
☐	N381AN	Boeing 767-323ER/W	25450/495	381
☐	N382AN	Boeing 767-323ER	25451/498	382
☐	N383AN	Boeing 767-323ER	26995/500	383
☐	N384AA	Boeing 767-323ER	26996/512	384
☐	N385AM	Boeing 767-323ER	27059/536	385
☐	N386AA	Boeing 767-323ER	27060/540	386
☐	N387AM	Boeing 767-323ER	27184/541	387
☐	N388AA	Boeing 767-323ER	27448/563	388
☐	N389AA	Boeing 767-323ER/W	27449/564	389
☐	N390AA	Boeing 767-323ER	27450/565	390
☐	N391AA	Boeing 767-323ER	27451/566	391
☐	N392AN	Boeing 767-323ER	29429/700	392
☐	N393AN	Boeing 767-323ER	29430/701	393
☐	N394AN	Boeing 767-323ER	29431/703	394
☐	N395AN	Boeing 767-323ER	29432/709	395
☐	N396AN	Boeing 767-323ER	29603/739	396
☐	N397AN	Boeing 767-323ER	29604/744	397

	Registration	Type	C/n	Previous identity	Fleet no.	Notes
☐	N398AN	Boeing 767-323ER	29605/748		398	
☐	N399AN	Boeing 767-323ER/W	29606/752		399	
☐	N7375A	Boeing 767-323ER	25202/441		375	
☐	N39356	Boeing 767-323ER	24037/226		356	
☐	N39364	Boeing 767-323ER	24045/240		364	
☐	N39365	Boeing 767-323ER	24046/241		365	
☐	N39367	Boeing 767-323ER	25194/394		367	
☐	N750AN	Boeing 777-223ER	30259/332	ex (N798AN)	7BJ	
☐	N751AN	Boeing 777-223ER	30798/333		7BK	
☐	N752AN	Boeing 777-223ER	30260/339	ex (N799AN)	7BL	
☐	N753AN	Boeing 777-223ER	30261/341	ex (N750AN)	7BM	
☐	N754AN	Boeing 777-223ER	30262/345		7BN	
☐	N755AN	Boeing 777-223ER	30263/354		7BP	
☐	N756AM	Boeing 777-223ER	30264/358		7BR	
☐	N757AN	Boeing 777-223ER	32636/363		7BS	
☐	N758AN	Boeing 777-223ER	32637/371		7BT	
☐	N759AN	Boeing 777-223ER	32638/376		7BU	Pink Ribbon c/s
☐	N760AN	Boeing 777-223ER	31477/379		7BV	
☐	N761AJ	Boeing 777-223ER	31478/393		7BW	
☐	N762AN	Boeing 777-223ER	31479/399		7BX	
☐	N765AN	Boeing 777-223ER	32879/433		7BY	
☐	N766AN	Boeing 777-223ER	32880/445		7CA	
☐	N767AJ	Boeing 777-223ER	33539/555		7CB	
☐	N768AA	Boeing 777-223ER	33540/566		7CC	
☐	N770AN	Boeing 777-223ER	29578/185		7AA	
☐	N771AN	Boeing 777-223ER	29579/190		7AB	
☐	N772AN	Boeing 777-223ER	29580/198		7AC	
☐	N773AN	Boeing 777-223ER	29583/199		7AD	
☐	N774AN	Boeing 777-223ER	29581/208		7AE	
☐	N775AN	Boeing 777-223ER	29584/209		7AF	
☐	N776AN	Boeing 777-223ER	29582/215		7AG	
☐	N777AN	Boeing 777-223ER	29585/218		7AH	
☐	N778AN	Boeing 777-223ER	29587/223		7AJ	
☐	N779AN	Boeing 777-223ER	29955/225		7AK	
☐	N780AN	Boeing 777-223ER	29956/241	ex N6055X	7AL	
☐	N781AN	Boeing 777-223ER	29586/266		7AM	
☐	N782AN	Boeing 777-223ER	30003/270		7AN	
☐	N783AN	Boeing 777-223ER	30004/271		7AP	
☐	N784AN	Boeing 777-223ER	29588/272		7AR	
☐	N785AN	Boeing 777-223ER	30005/274		7AS	
☐	N786AN	Boeing 777-223ER	30250/276		7AT	
☐	N787AL	Boeing 777-223ER	30010/277		7AU	
☐	N788AN	Boeing 777-223ER	30011/283		7AV	
☐	N789AN	Boeing 777-223ER	30252/285		7AW	
☐	N790AN	Boeing 777-223ER	30251/287		7AX	
☐	N791AN	Boeing 777-223ER	30254/289		7AY	
☐	N792AN	Boeing 777-223ER	30253/292		7BA	
☐	N793AN	Boeing 777-223ER	30255/299		7BB	
☐	N794AN	Boeing 777-223ER	30256/313		7BC	
☐	N795AN	Boeing 777-223ER	30257/315		7BD	
☐	N796AN	Boeing 777-223ER	30796/316		7BE	
☐	N797AN	Boeing 777-223ER	30012/321	ex (N796AN)	7BF American Spirit	
☐	N798AN	Boeing 777-223ER	30797/324		7BG	
☐	N799AN	Boeing 777-223ER	30258/328	ex (N797AN)	7BH	
☐	N110HM	McDonnell-Douglas MD-83	49787/1636	ex HL7274	4WU	
☐	N208AA	McDonnell-Douglas MD-82	49159/1107		208	
☐	N218AA	McDonnell-Douglas MD-82	49168/1100		218	stored ROW
☐	N219AA	McDonnell-Douglas MD-82	49171/1112		219	stored ROW
☐	N223AA	McDonnell-Douglas MD-82	49173/1114		223	stored ROW
☐	N227AA	McDonnell-Douglas MD-82	49177/1121		227	
☐	N232AA	McDonnell-Douglas MD-82	49179/1123		232	stored ROW
☐	N233AA	McDonnell-Douglas MD-82	49180/1124		233	stored ROW
☐	N234AA	McDonnell-Douglas MD-82	49181/1125		234	stored MIA
☐	N245AA	McDonnell-Douglas MD-82	49257/1160		245	
☐	N249AA	McDonnell-Douglas MD-82	49269/1164		249	
☐	N251AA	McDonnell-Douglas MD-82	49270/1165		251	
☐	N253AA	McDonnell-Douglas MD-82	49286/1175		253	
☐	N255AA	McDonnell-Douglas MD-82	49287/1176		255	
☐	N258AA	McDonnell-Douglas MD-82	49288/1187		258	
☐	N259AA	McDonnell-Douglas MD-82	49289/1193		269	
☐	N262AA	McDonnell-Douglas MD-82	49290/1195		262	
☐	N266AA	McDonnell-Douglas MD-82	49291/1210		266	
☐	N271AA	McDonnell-Douglas MD-82	49293/1212		271	
☐	N274AA	McDonnell-Douglas MD-82	49271/1166		274	
☐	N278AA	McDonnell-Douglas MD-82	49294/1213		278	
☐	N279AA	McDonnell-Douglas MD-82	49295/1214		279	stored ROW
☐	N283AA	McDonnell-Douglas MD-82	49296/1215		283	stored ROW
☐	N287AA	McDonnell-Douglas MD-82	49299/1218		287	stored ROW
☐	N290AA	McDonnell-Douglas MD-82	49302/1221		290	
☐	N291AA	McDonnell-Douglas MD-82	49303/1222		291	
☐	N292AA	McDonnell-Douglas MD-82	49304/1223		292	

☐ N293AA	McDonnell-Douglas MD-82	49305/1226	293	
☐ N298AA	McDonnell-Douglas MD-82	49310/1247	298	
☐ N403A	McDonnell-Douglas MD-82	49314/1256	403	
☐ N408AA	McDonnell-Douglas MD-82	49319/1266	408	stored ROW
☐ N410AA	McDonnell-Douglas MD-82	49321/1273	410	stored ROW
☐ N411AA	McDonnell-Douglas MD-82	49322/1280	411	stored ROW
☐ N412AA	McDonnell-Douglas MD-82	49323/1281	412	
☐ N413AA	McDonnell-Douglas MD-82	49324/1289	413	stored ROW
☐ N415AA	McDonnell-Douglas MD-82	49326/1295	415	stored ROW
☐ N416AA	McDonnell-Douglas MD-82	49327/1296	416	stored ROW
☐ N417AA	McDonnell-Douglas MD-82	49328/1301	417	stored ROW
☐ N418AA	McDonnell-Douglas MD-82	49329/1302	418	stored ROW
☐ N419AA	McDonnell-Douglas MD-82	49331/1306	419	stored ROW
☐ N420AA	McDonnell-Douglas MD-82	49332/1307	420	
☐ N422AA	McDonnell-Douglas MD-82	49334/1312	422	
☐ N423AA	McDonnell-Douglas MD-82	49335/1320	423	
☐ N424AA	McDonnell-Douglas MD-82	49336/1321	424	
☐ N426AA	McDonnell-Douglas MD-82	49338/1327	426	
☐ N427AA	McDonnell-Douglas MD-82	49339/1328	427	stored ROW
☐ N429AA	McDonnell-Douglas MD-82	49341/1336	429	stored ROW
☐ N430AA	McDonnell-Douglas MD-82	49342/1337	430	stored ROW
☐ N431AA	McDonnell-Douglas MD-82	49343/1339	431	
☐ N432AA	McDonnell-Douglas MD-82	49350/1376	432	
☐ N433AA	McDonnell-Douglas MD-83	49451/1388	433	
☐ N434AA	McDonnell-Douglas MD-83	49452/1389	434	
☐ N435AA	McDonnell-Douglas MD-83	49453/1390	435	
☐ N436AA	McDonnell-Douglas MD-83	49454/1391	436	
☐ N437AA	McDonnell-Douglas MD-83	49455/1392	437	
☐ N438AA	McDonnell-Douglas MD-83	49456/1393	438	
☐ N439AA	McDonnell-Douglas MD-83	49457/1398	439	
☐ N440AA	McDonnell-Douglas MD-82	49459/1407	440	
☐ N441AA	McDonnell-Douglas MD-82	49460/1408	441	
☐ N442AA	McDonnell-Douglas MD-82	49468/1409	442	
☐ N443AA	McDonnell-Douglas MD-82	49469/1410	443	
☐ N445AA	McDonnell-Douglas MD-82	49471/1418	445	
☐ N446AA	McDonnell-Douglas MD-82	49472/1426	446	
☐ N447AA	McDonnell-Douglas MD-82	49473/1427	447	
☐ N448AA	McDonnell-Douglas MD-82	49474/1431	448	
☐ N449AA	McDonnell-Douglas MD-82	49475/1432	449	
☐ N450AA	McDonnell-Douglas MD-82	49476/1439	450	
☐ N451AA	McDonnell-Douglas MD-82	49477/1441	451	
☐ N452AA	McDonnell-Douglas MD-82	49553/1450	452	
☐ N453AA	McDonnell-Douglas MD-82	49558/1451	453	
☐ N454AA	McDonnell-Douglas MD-82	49559/1460	454	
☐ N455AA	McDonnell-Douglas MD-82	49560/1462	455	
☐ N456AA	McDonnell-Douglas MD-82	49561/1474	456	
☐ N457AA	McDonnell-Douglas MD-82	49562/1475	457	
☐ N458AA	McDonnell-Douglas MD-82	49563/1485	458	
☐ N459AA	McDonnell-Douglas MD-82	49564/1486	459	
☐ N460AA	McDonnell-Douglas MD-82	49565/1496	460	
☐ N461AA	McDonnell-Douglas MD-82	49566/1497	461	
☐ N462AA	McDonnell-Douglas MD-82	49592/1505	462	
☐ N463AA	McDonnell-Douglas MD-82	49593/1506	463	
☐ N464AA	McDonnell-Douglas MD-82	49594/1507	464	
☐ N465A	McDonnell-Douglas MD-82	49595/1509	465	
☐ N466AA	McDonnell-Douglas MD-82	49596/1510	466	
☐ N467AA	McDonnell-Douglas MD-82	49597/1511	467	
☐ N468AA	McDonnell-Douglas MD-82	49598/1513	468	
☐ N469AA	McDonnell-Douglas MD-82	49599/1515	469	
☐ N470AA	McDonnell-Douglas MD-82	49600/1516	470	
☐ N471AA	McDonnell-Douglas MD-82	49601/1518	471	
☐ N472AA	McDonnell-Douglas MD-82	49647/1520	472	
☐ N473AA	McDonnell-Douglas MD-82	49648/1521	473	
☐ N474	McDonnell-Douglas MD-82	49649/1526	474	
☐ N475AA	McDonnell-Douglas MD-82	49650/1527	475	
☐ N476AA	McDonnell-Douglas MD-82	49651/1528	476	
☐ N477AA	McDonnell-Douglas MD-82	49652/1529	477	
☐ N478AA	McDonnell-Douglas MD-82	49653/1534	478	
☐ N479AA	McDonnell-Douglas MD-82	49654/1535	479	
☐ N480AA	McDonnell-Douglas MD-82	49655/1536	480	
☐ N481AA	McDonnell-Douglas MD-82	49656/1545	481	
☐ N482AA	McDonnell-Douglas MD-82	49675/1546	482	
☐ N483A	McDonnell-Douglas MD-82	49676/1550	483	
☐ N484AA	McDonnell-Douglas MD-82	49677/1551	484	
☐ N485AA	McDonnell-Douglas MD-82	49678/1555	485	
☐ N486AA	McDonnell-Douglas MD-82	49679/1557	486	
☐ N487AA	McDonnell-Douglas MD-82	49680/1558	487	
☐ N488AA	McDonnell-Douglas MD-82	49681/1560	488	
☐ N489AA	McDonnell-Douglas MD-82	49682/1562	489	
☐ N490AA	McDonnell-Douglas MD-82	49683/1563	490	
☐ N491AA	McDonnell-Douglas MD-82	49684/1564	491	
☐ N492AA	McDonnell-Douglas MD-82	49730/1565	492	
☐ N493AA	McDonnell-Douglas MD-82	49731/1566	493	

☐ N494AA	McDonnell-Douglas MD-82	49732/1567		494		
☐ N495AA	McDonnell-Douglas MD-82	49733/1607		495		
☐ N496AA	McDonnell-Douglas MD-82	49734/1619		496		
☐ N497AA	McDonnell-Douglas MD-82	49735/1635		497		
☐ N498AA	McDonnell-Douglas MD-82	49736/1640		498		
☐ N499AA	McDonnell-Douglas MD-82	49737/1641		499		
☐ N501AA	McDonnell-Douglas MD-82	49738/1648		501		
☐ N505AA	McDonnell-Douglas MD-82	49799/1652		505		
☐ N510AM	McDonnell-Douglas MD-82	49804/1669		510		
☐ N513AA	McDonnell-Douglas MD-82	49890/1686		513		
☐ N516AM	McDonnell-Douglas MD-82	49893/1696		516		
☐ N552AA	McDonnell-Douglas MD-82	53034/1826		552		
☐ N553AA	McDonnell-Douglas MD-82	53083/1828		553		
☐ N554AA	McDonnell-Douglas MD-82	53084/1830		554		
☐ N555AN	McDonnell-Douglas MD-82	53085/1839		555		
☐ N556AA	McDonnell-Douglas MD-82	53086/1840		556		
☐ N557AN	McDonnell-Douglas MD-82	53087/1841		557		
☐ N558AA	McDonnell-Douglas MD-82	53088/1852		558		
☐ N559AA	McDonnell-Douglas MD-82	53089/1853		559		
☐ N560AA	McDonnell-Douglas MD-82	53090/1858		560		
☐ N561AA	McDonnell-Douglas MD-82	53091/1863		561		
☐ N562AA	McDonnell-Douglas MD-83	49344/1370		562		
☐ N563AA	McDonnell-Douglas MD-83	49345/1371		563		
☐ N564AA	McDonnell-Douglas MD-83	49346/1372		564		
☐ N565AA	McDonnell-Douglas MD-83	49347/1373		565		
☐ N566AA	McDonnell-Douglas MD-83	49348/1374		566		
☐ N567AM	McDonnell-Douglas MD-83	53293/2021		567		
☐ N568AA	McDonnell-Douglas MD-83	49349/1375		568		
☐ N569AA	McDonnell-Douglas MD-83	49351/1385		569		
☐ N570AA	McDonnell-Douglas MD-83	49352/1386		570		
☐ N571AA	McDonnell-Douglas MD-83	49353/1387		571		
☐ N572AA	McDonnell-Douglas MD-83	49458/1406		572		
☐ N573AA	McDonnell-Douglas MD-82	53092/1864		573		
☐ N574AA	McDonnell-Douglas MD-82	53151/1866		574		
☐ N575AM	McDonnell-Douglas MD-82	53152/1875		575		
☐ N576AA	McDonnell-Douglas MD-82	53153/1876		576		
☐ N577AA	McDonnell-Douglas MD-82	53154/1878		577		
☐ N578AA	McDonnell-Douglas MD-82	53155/1883		578		
☐ N579AA	McDonnell-Douglas MD-82	53156/1884		579		
☐ N580AA	McDonnell-Douglas MD-82	53157/1885		580		
☐ N581AA	McDonnell-Douglas MD-82	53158/1891		581		
☐ N582AA	McDonnell-Douglas MD-82	53159/1892		582		
☐ N583AA	McDonnell-Douglas MD-82	53160/1893		583		
☐ N584AA	McDonnell-Douglas MD-82	53247/1902		584		
☐ N585AA	McDonnell-Douglas MD-82	53248/1903		585		
☐ N586AA	McDonnell-Douglas MD-82	53249/1904		586		
☐ N587AA	McDonnell-Douglas MD-82	53250/1907		587		
☐ N588AA	McDonnell-Douglas MD-83	53251/1909		588		
☐ N589AA	McDonnell-Douglas MD-83	53252/1910		589		
☐ N590AA	McDonnell-Douglas MD-83	53253/1919		590		
☐ N591AA	McDonnell-Douglas MD-83	53254/1920		591		
☐ N592AA	McDonnell-Douglas MD-83	53255/1932		592		
☐ N593AA	McDonnell-Douglas MD-83	53256/1933		593		
☐ N594AA	McDonnell-Douglas MD-83	53284/1966		594		
☐ N595AA	McDonnell-Douglas MD-83	53285/1989		595		
☐ N596AA	McDonnell-Douglas MD-83	53286/2000		596		
☐ N597AA	McDonnell-Douglas MD-83	53287/2006		597		
☐ N598AA	McDonnell-Douglas MD-83	53288/2011		598		
☐ N599AA	McDonnell-Douglas MD-83	53289/2012		599		
☐ N919TW	McDonnell-Douglas MD-82	49368/1198		4TU		stored ROW
☐ N923TW	McDonnell-Douglas MD-82	49379/1205	ex D-ALLS	4UN		stored ROW
☐ N931TW	McDonnell-Douglas MD-82	49527/1382		4WA		
☐ N940AS	McDonnell-Douglas MD-83	49825/1577		4UJ		stored ROW
☐ N941AS	McDonnell-Douglas MD-83	49925/1616		4UK		stored ROW
☐ N948TW	McDonnell-Douglas MD-83	49575/1414	ex EI-BWD	4WS	Wings of Pride	
☐ N951TW	McDonnell-Douglas MD-83	53470/2135	ex N978AS	4XA		
☐ N953U	McDonnell-Douglas MD-82	49267/1239		4UA		stored ROW
☐ N954U	McDonnell-Douglas MD-82	49426/1399	ex N786JA	4UB		
☐ N955U	McDonnell-Douglas MD-82	49427/1401	ex N787JA	4UC		
☐ N961TW	McDonnell-Douglas MD-83	53611/2264		4XT		
☐ N962TW	McDonnell-Douglas MD-83	53612/2265		4XU		
☐ N963TW	McDonnell-Douglas MD-83	53613/2266		4XV		
☐ N964TW	McDonnell-Douglas MD-83	53614/2267		4XW		
☐ N965TW	McDonnell-Douglas MD-83	53615/2268		4XX		
☐ N966TW	McDonnell-Douglas MD-83	53616/2269		4XY		
☐ N967TW	McDonnell-Douglas MD-83	53617/2270		4YA		
☐ N968TW	McDonnell-Douglas MD-83	53618/2271		4YB		
☐ N969TW	McDonnell-Douglas MD-83	53619/2272		4YC		
☐ N970TW	McDonnell-Douglas MD-83	53620/2273		4YD		stored TUL
☐ N971TW	McDonnell-Douglas MD-83	53621/2274		4YE		stored TUL
☐ N972TW	McDonnell-Douglas MD-83	53622/2275		4YF		
☐ N973TW	McDonnell-Douglas MD-83	53623/2276		4YG		
☐ N974TW	McDonnell-Douglas MD-83	53624/2277		4YH		

	Reg	Type	C/n	Previous	Fleet no	Remarks
☐	N975TW	McDonnell-Douglas MD-83	53625/2278		4YJ	
☐	N976TW	McDonnell-Douglas MD-83	53626/2279		4YK	
☐	N978TW	McDonnell-Douglas MD-83	53628/2281		4YM	
☐	N979TW	McDonnell-Douglas MD-83	53629/2282		4YN	
☐	N980TW	McDonnell-Douglas MD-83	53630/2283		4YP	
☐	N982TW	McDonnell-Douglas MD-83	53632/2285		4YR	
☐	N983TW	McDonnell-Douglas MD-83	53633/2286		4YS	
☐	N984TW+	McDonnell-Douglas MD-83	53634/2287		4YT	Spirit of Long Beach
☐	N3507A	McDonnell-Douglas MD-82	49801/1661		507	
☐	N3515	McDonnell-Douglas MD-82	49892/1695		515	
☐	N7506	McDonnell-Douglas MD-82	49800/1660		506	
☐	N7508	McDonnell-Douglas MD-82	49802/1662		508	
☐	N7509	McDonnell-Douglas MD-82	49803/1663		509	
☐	N7512A	McDonnell-Douglas MD-82	49806/1673		512	
☐	N7514A	McDonnell-Douglas MD-82	49891/1694		514	
☐	N7517A	McDonnell-Douglas MD-82	49894/1697		517	
☐	N7518A	McDonnell-Douglas MD-82	49895/1698		518	
☐	N7519A	McDonnell-Douglas MD-82	49896/1707		519	
☐	N7520A	McDonnell-Douglas MD-82	49897/1708		520	
☐	N7521A	McDonnell-Douglas MD-82	49898/1709		521	
☐	N7522A	McDonnell-Douglas MD-82	49899/1722		522	
☐	N7525A	McDonnell-Douglas MD-82	49917/1735		525	
☐	N7526A	McDonnell-Douglas MD-82	49918/1743		526	
☐	N7527A	McDonnell-Douglas MD-82	49919/1744		527	
☐	N7528A	McDonnell-Douglas MD-82	49920/1750		528	
☐	N7530	McDonnell-Douglas MD-82	49922/1753		530	
☐	N7531A	McDonnell-Douglas MD-82	49923/1758		531	
☐	N7532A	McDonnell-Douglas MD-82	49924/1759		532	
☐	N7533A	McDonnell-Douglas MD-82	49987/1760		533	
☐	N7534A	McDonnell-Douglas MD-82	49988/1768		534	
☐	N7535A	McDonnell-Douglas MD-82	49989/1769		535	
☐	N7536A	McDonnell-Douglas MD-82	49990/1770		536	
☐	N7537A	McDonnell-Douglas MD-82	49991/1780		537	
☐	N7538A	McDonnell-Douglas MD-82	49992/1781		538	
☐	N7539A	McDonnell-Douglas MD-82	49993/1782		539	
☐	N7540A	McDonnell-Douglas MD-82	49994/1790		540	
☐	N7541A	McDonnell-Douglas MD-82	49995/1791		541	
☐	N7542A	McDonnell-Douglas MD-82	49996/1792		542	
☐	N7543A	McDonnell-Douglas MD-82	53025/1802		543	
☐	N7544A	McDonnell-Douglas MD-82	53026/1804		544	
☐	N7546A	McDonnell-Douglas MD-82	53028/1813		546	
☐	N7547A	McDonnell-Douglas MD-82	53029/1814		547	
☐	N7548A	McDonnell-Douglas MD-82	53030/1816		548	
☐	N7549A	McDonnell-Douglas MD-82	53031/1819		549	
☐	N7550	McDonnell-Douglas MD-82	53032/1820		550	
☐	N9302B	McDonnell-Douglas MD-83	49528/1383		4WB	
☐	N9304C	McDonnell-Douglas MD-83	49530/1397		4WD	
☐	N9307R	McDonnell-Douglas MD-83	49663/1437	ex SE-DPH	4WG	stored ROW
☐	N9401W	McDonnell-Douglas MD-83	53137/1872	ex N9001L	4WJ	
☐	N9402W	McDonnell-Douglas MD-83	53138/1886	ex N9001D	4WK	
☐	N9403W	McDonnell-Douglas MD-83	53139/1899	ex N9035C	4WL	
☐	N9404V	McDonnell-Douglas MD-83	53140/1923	ex N9075H	4WM	
☐	N9405T	McDonnell-Douglas MD-83	53141/1935		4WN	
☐	N9406W	McDonnell-Douglas MD-83	53126/2026	ex N6203U	4WP	
☐	N9407R	McDonnell-Douglas MD-83	49400/1356	ex EI-CKB	4WR	
☐	N9409F	McDonnell-Douglas MD-83	53121/1971	ex N532MD	4WT	
☐	N9412W	McDonnell-Douglas MD-83	53187/2118		4WU	
☐	N9413T	McDonnell-Douglas MD-83	53188/2119		4WW	
☐	N9414W	McDonnell-Douglas MD-83	53189/2121		4WX	
☐	N9420D	McDonnell-Douglas MD-83	49824/1554	ex 9Y-THU	4WY	
☐	N9615W	McDonnell-Douglas MD-83	53562/2192		4XB	
☐	N9616G	McDonnell-Douglas MD-83	53563/2196		4XC	
☐	N9617R	McDonnell-Douglas MD-83	53564/2199		4XD	
☐	N9618A	McDonnell-Douglas MD-83	53565/2201		4XE	
☐	N9619V	McDonnell-Douglas MD-83	53566/2206		4XF	
☐	N9620D	McDonnell-Douglas MD-83	53591/2208		4XG	
☐	N9621A	McDonnell-Douglas MD-83	53592/2234		4XH	
☐	N9622A	McDonnell-Douglas MD-83	53593/2239		4XJ	
☐	N9624T	McDonnell-Douglas MD-83	53594/2241		4XK	
☐	N9625W	McDonnell-Douglas MD-83	53595/2244		4XL	
☐	N9626F	McDonnell-Douglas MD-83	53596//2247		4XM	
☐	N9627R	McDonnell-Douglas MD-83	53597/2249		4XN	
☐	N9628W	McDonnell-Douglas MD-83	53598/2252		4XP	
☐	N9629H	McDonnell-Douglas MD-83	53599/2254		4XR	
☐	N9630A	McDonnell-Douglas MD-83	53561/2174	ex N90126	4XS	
☐	N9677W	McDonnell-Douglas MD-83	53627/2280		4YL	
☐	N9681B	McDonnell-Douglas MD-83	53631/2284	ex (N981TW)	4XT	
☐	N14551	McDonnell-Douglas MD-82	53033/1822		551	
☐	N16545	McDonnell-Douglas MD-82	53027/1805		545	
☐	N33414	McDonnell-Douglas MD-82	49325/1290		414	
☐	N33502	McDonnell-Douglas MD-82	49739/1649		502	
☐	N44503	McDonnell-Douglas MD-82	49797/1650		503	
☐	N59523	McDonnell-Douglas MD-82	49915/1723		523	

☐ N70401	McDonnell-Douglas MD-82	49312/1249	401
☐ N70425	McDonnell-Douglas MD-82	49337/1325	425
☐ N70504	McDonnell-Douglas MD-82	49798/1651	504
☐ N70524	McDonnell-Douglas MD-82	49916/1729	524
☐ N70529	McDonnell-Douglas MD-82	49921/1752	529
☐ N73444	McDonnell-Douglas MD-82	49470/1417	444 Working Together titles
☐ N76200	McDonnell-Douglas MD-83	53290/2013	200
☐ N76201	McDonnell-Douglas MD-83	53291/2019	201
☐ N76202	McDonnell-Douglas MD-83	53292/2020	202
☐ N77421	McDonnell-Douglas MD-82	49333/1311	421
☐ N90511	McDonnell-Douglas MD-82	49805/1672	511

AMERICAN CONNECTION *Waterski (AX/LOF)* *Indianapolis, IN/St Louis-Lambert Intl, MO (IND/STL)*

☐ N295SK	Embraer EMB.135KL (ERJ-140LR)	145513	ex PT-SYF	Chautauqua
☐ N297SK	Embraer EMB.135KL (ERJ-140LR)	145522	ex PT-SYN	Chautauqua
☐ N299SK	Embraer EMB.135KL (ERJ-140LR)	145532	ex PT-STW	Chautauqua
☐ N371SK	Embraer EMB.135KL (ERJ-140LR)	145535	ex PT-STZ	Chautauqua
☐ N372SK	Embraer EMB.135KL (ERJ-140LR)	145538	ex PT-SZC	Chautauqua
☐ N373SK	Embraer EMB.135KL (ERJ-140LR)	145543	ex PT-SZG	Chautauqua
☐ N374SK	Embraer EMB.135KL (ERJ-140LR)	145544	ex PT-SZH	Chautauqua
☐ N375SK	Embraer EMB.135KL (ERJ-140LR)	145569	ex PT-SBF	Chautauqua
☐ N376SK	Embraer EMB.135KL (ERJ-140LR)	145578	ex PT-SBO	Chautauqua
☐ N377SK	Embraer EMB.135KL (ERJ-140LR)	145579	ex PT-SBP	Chautauqua
☐ N378SK	Embraer EMB.135KL (ERJ-140LR)	145593	ex PT-SCC	Chautauqua
☐ N379SK	Embraer EMB.135KL (ERJ-140LR)	145606	ex PT-SCP	Chautauqua
☐ N380SK	Embraer EMB.135KL (ERJ-140LR)	145613	ex PT-SCX	Chautauqua
☐ N381SK	Embraer EMB.135KL (ERJ-140LR)	145619	ex PT-SDH	Chautauqua
☐ N382SK	Embraer EMB.135KL (ERJ-140LR)	145624	ex PT-SDM	Chautauqua
☐ N811HK	Embraer EMB.145ER (ERJ-145ER)	145256	ex PT-SIQ	Trans State

AMERICAN EAGLE *Eagle Flight (MQ/EGF)* *Dallas-Fort Worth, TX (DFW)*

☐ N4AE	ATR 72-212	244	ex N244AT
☐ N260AE	ATR 72-201	263	ex N263AT
☐ N270AT	ATR 72-212	270	ex F-WWEL
☐ N288AM	ATR 72-212	288	ex F-WWLP
☐ N308AE	ATR 72-212	309	ex N309AM
☐ N322AC	ATR 72-212	320	ex N320AT
☐ N342AT	ATR 72-212	345	ex N345AT
☐ N348AE	ATR 72-212	349	ex N349AT
☐ N355AT	ATR 72-212	355	ex F-WWEQ
☐ N369AT	ATR 72-212	369	ex F-WWEC
☐ N377AT	ATR 72-212	377	ex F-WWLA
☐ N399AT	ATR 72-212	399	ex F-WWLK
☐ N407AT	ATR 72-212	407	ex F-WWEL
☐ N408AT	ATR 72-212	408	ex F-WWEM
☐ N410AT	ATR 72-212	410	ex F-WWLS
☐ N414WF	ATR 72-212	414	ex F-WWLD
☐ N417AT	ATR 72-212	417	ex F-WWIT
☐ N420AT	ATR 72-212	420	ex F-WWLY
☐ N425MJ	ATR 72-212	425	ex F-WWEC
☐ N426AT	ATR 72-212	426	ex F-WWED
☐ N429AT	ATR 72-212	429	ex F-WWEH
☐ N431AT	ATR 72-212	431	ex F-WWEI
☐ N434AT	ATR 72-212	434	ex F-WWEM
☐ N440AM	ATR 72-212	440	ex F-WWEP
☐ N447AM	ATR 72-212	447	ex F-WWEC
☐ N448AM	ATR 72-212	448	ex F-WWED
☐ N451AT	ATR 72-212	451	ex F-WWES
☐ N494AE	ATR 72-212A	494	ex F-WWLS
☐ N498AT	ATR 72-212A	498	ex F-WWLW
☐ N499AT	ATR 72-212A	499	ex F-WWLY
☐ N529AM	ATR 72-212A	529	ex F-WWLR
☐ N533AT	ATR 72-212A	533	ex F-WWLO
☐ N536AT	ATR 72-212A	536	ex F-WWLZ
☐ N538AT	ATR 72-212A	538	ex F-WWEA
☐ N540AM	ATR 72-212A	540	ex F-WWLJ
☐ N541AT	ATR 72-212	541	ex F-WWLA
☐ N545AT	ATR 72-212A	545	ex F-WWLE
☐ N548AT	ATR 72-212A	548	ex F-WWLI
☐ N550LL	ATR 72-212A	550	ex F-WWLK
☐ N500AE	Canadair CL-600-2C10 (CRJ-701ER)	10025	ex C-GJEX
☐ N501BG	Canadair CL-600-2C10 (CRJ-701ER)	10017	ex C-GIAH
☐ N502AE	Canadair CL-600-2C10 (CRJ-701ER)	10018	ex C-GJUI
☐ N503AE	Canadair CL-600-2C10 (CRJ-701ER)	10021	ex C-GIAP
☐ N504AE	Canadair CL-600-2C10 (CRJ-701ER)	10044	ex C-GHZZ
☐ N505AE	Canadair CL-600-2C10 (CRJ-701ER)	10053	ex C-GIAU
☐ N506AE	Canadair CL-600-2C10 (CRJ-701ER)	10056	ex C-GIAX
☐ N507AE	Canadair CL-600-2C10 (CRJ-701ER)	10059	ex C-GIBH

	Registration	Type	C/n	Previous identity	Remarks	Status
☐	N508AE	Canadair CL-600-2C10 (CRJ-701ER)	10072	ex C-GHZV		
☐	N509AE	Canadair CL-600-2C10 (CRJ-701ER)	10078	ex C-GZUC		
☐	N510AE	Canadair CL-600-2C10 (CRJ-701ER)	10105	ex C-		
☐	N511AE	Canadair CL-600-2C10 (CRJ-701ER)	10107	ex C-		
☐	N512AE	Canadair CL-600-2C10 (CRJ-701ER)	10110	ex C-		
☐	N513AE	Canadair CL-600-2C10 (CRJ-701ER)	10114	ex C-		
☐	N514AE	Canadair CL-600-2C10 (CRJ-701ER)	10119	ex C-		
☐	N515AE	Canadair CL-600-2C10 (CRJ-701ER)	10121	ex C-		
☐	N516AE	Canadair CL-600-2C10 (CRJ-701ER)	10123	ex C-		
☐	N517AE	Canadair CL-600-2C10 (CRJ-701ER)	10124	ex C-		
☐	N518AE	Canadair CL-600-2C10 (CRJ-701ER)	10126	ex C-		
☐	N519AE	Canadair CL-600-2C10 (CRJ-701ER)	10131	ex C-		
☐	N520DC	Canadair CL-600-2C10 (CRJ-701ER)	10140	ex C-		
☐	N521AE	Canadair CL-600-2C10 (CRJ-701ER)	10142	ex C-		
☐	N522AE	Canadair CL-600-2C10 (CRJ-701ER)	10147	ex C-		
☐	N523AE	Canadair CL-600-2C10 (CRJ-701ER)	10152	ex C-		
☐	N524AE	Canadair CL-600-2C10 (CRJ-701ER)	10154	ex C-		
☐		Canadair CL-600-2C10 (CRJ-701ER)		ex C-		on order
☐		Canadair CL-600-2C10 (CRJ-701ER)		ex C-		on order
☐		Canadair CL-600-2C10 (CRJ-701ER)		ex C-		on order
☐		Canadair CL-600-2C10 (CRJ-701ER)		ex C-		on order
☐		Canadair CL-600-2C10 (CRJ-701ER)		ex C-		on order
☐		Canadair CL-600-2C10 (CRJ-701ER)		ex C-		on order
☐		Canadair CL-600-2C10 (CRJ-701ER)		ex C-		on order
☐		Canadair CL-600-2C10 (CRJ-701ER)		ex C-		on order
☐	N700LE	Embraer EMB.135LR (ERJ-135LR)	145156	ex PT-SFC		
☐	N701MH	Embraer EMB.135LR (ERJ-135LR)	145162	ex PT-SFD		
☐	N702AE	Embraer EMB.135LR (ERJ-135LR)	145164	ex PT-SFE		stored IGM
☐	N703MR	Embraer EMB.135LR (ERJ-135LR)	145173	ex PT-SFG		stored IGM
☐	N704PG	Embraer EMB.135LR (ERJ-135LR)	145174	ex PT-SFH		stored IGM
☐	N705AE	Embraer EMB.135LR (ERJ-135LR)	145184	ex PT-SFJ		stored IGM
☐	N706RG	Embraer EMB.135LR (ERJ-135LR)	145194	ex PT-SFO		stored IGM
☐	N707EB	Embraer EMB.135LR (ERJ-135LR)	145195	ex PT-SFP		stored CMI
☐	N708AE	Embraer EMB.135LR (ERJ-135LR)	145205	ex PT-SFR		
☐	N709GB	Embraer EMB.135LR (ERJ-135LR)	145211	ex PT-SFV		stored IGM
☐	N710TB	Embraer EMB.135LR (ERJ-135LR)	145224	ex PT-SFZ		stored IGM
☐	N711PH	Embraer EMB.135LR (ERJ-135LR)	145235	ex PT-SJC		
☐	N712AE	Embraer EMB.135LR (ERJ-135LR)	145247	ex PT-SJG		
☐	N713AE	Embraer EMB.135LR (ERJ-135LR)	145249	ex PT-SJH		
☐	N715AE	Embraer EMB.135LR (ERJ-135LR)	145262	ex PT-SIV		stored IGM
☐	N716AE	Embraer EMB.135LR (ERJ-135LR)	145264	ex PT-SIW		
☐	N717AE	Embraer EMB.135LR (ERJ-135LR)	145272	ex PT-SJO		
☐	N718AE	Embraer EMB.135LR (ERJ-135LR)	145275	ex PT-SJR		stored IGM
☐	N719AE	Embraer EMB.135LR (ERJ-135LR)	145276	ex PT-SJS		
☐	N720AE	Embraer EMB.135LR (ERJ-135LR)	145279	ex PT-SJV		
☐	N721HS	Embraer EMB.135LR (ERJ-135LR)	145283	ex PT-S JZ		
☐	N722AE	Embraer EMB.135LR (ERJ-135LR)	145287	ex PT-SKE		
☐	N723AE	Embraer EMB.135LR (ERJ-135LR)	145288	ex PT-SKF		
☐	N724AE	Embraer EMB.135LR (ERJ-135LR)	145301	ex PT-SKS		
☐	N725AE	Embraer EMB.135LR (ERJ-135LR)	145312	ex PT-SMD		
☐	N726AE	Embraer EMB.135LR (ERJ-135LR)	145314	ex PT-SMF		stored IGM
☐	N727AE	Embraer EMB.135LR (ERJ-135LR)	145326	ex PT-SMS		stored IGM
☐	N728AE	Embraer EMB.135LR (ERJ-135LR)	145328	ex PT-SMU		
☐	N729AE	Embraer EMB.135LR (ERJ-135LR)	145343	ex PT-SNJ		stored IGM
☐	N730KW	Embraer EMB.135LR (ERJ-135LR)	145346	ex PT-SNM		
☐	N731BE	Embraer EMB.135LR (ERJ-135LR)	145356	ex PT-SNV		stored IGM
☐	N732DH	Embraer EMB.135LR (ERJ-135LR)	145358	ex PT-SNX		stored ABI
☐	N733KR	Embraer EMB.135LR (ERJ-135LR)	145368	ex PT-SOT		
☐	N734EK	Embraer EMB.135LR (ERJ-135LR)	145371	ex PT-SOW		
☐	N735TS	Embraer EMB.135LR (ERJ-135LR)	145386	ex PT-SQK		
☐	N736DT	Embraer EMB.135LR (ERJ-135LR)	145388	ex PT-SQM		
☐	N737MW	Embraer EMB.135LR (ERJ-135LR)	145396	ex PT-SQT		
☐	N738NR	Embraer EMB.135LR (ERJ-135LR)	145401	ex PT-SQY		
☐	N739AE	Embraer EMB.135LR (ERJ-135LR)	145402	ex PT-SQZ		
☐	N800AE	Embraer EMB.135KL (ERJ-140LR)	145425	ex PT-XGF		
☐	N801AE	Embraer EMB.135KL (ERJ-140LR)	145469	ex PT-SVO		
☐	N802AE	Embraer EMB.135KL (ERJ-140LR)	145471	ex PT-SVQ		
☐	N803AE	Embraer EMB.135KL (ERJ-140LR)	145483	ex PT-SXC	100th RJ Spirit of Eagle titles	
☐	N804AE	Embraer EMB.135KL (ERJ-140LR)	145487	ex PT-SXG		
☐	N805AE	Embraer EMB.135KL (ERJ-140LR)	145489	ex PT-SXI		
☐	N806AE	Embraer EMB.135KL (ERJ-140LR)	145503	ex PT-SXW		
☐	N807AE	Embraer EMB.135KL (ERJ-140LR)	145506	ex PT-SXZ	Make A Wish colours	
☐	N808AE	Embraer EMB.135KL (ERJ-140LR)	145519	ex PT-SYK		
☐	N809AE	Embraer EMB.135KL (ERJ-140LR)	145521	ex PT-SYM		
☐	N810AE	Embraer EMB.135KL (ERJ-140LR)	145525	ex PT-SYQ		
☐	N811AE	Embraer EMB.135KL (ERJ-140LR)	145529	ex PT-STT		
☐	N812AE	Embraer EMB.135KL (ERJ-140LR)	145531	ex PT-STV		
☐	N813AE	Embraer EMB.135KL (ERJ-140LR)	145539	ex PT-SZD		
☐	N814AE	Embraer EMB.135KL (ERJ-140LR)	145541	ex PT-SZF		
☐	N815AE	Embraer EMB.135KL (ERJ-140LR)	145545	ex PT-SZI		
☐	N816AE	Embraer EMB.135KL (ERJ-140LR)	145552	ex PT-SZO		

☐ N817AE	Embraer EMB.135KL (ERJ-140LR)	145554	ex PT-SZQ	
☐ N818AE	Embraer EMB.135KL (ERJ-140LR)	145561	ex PT-SZW	
☐ N819AE	Embraer EMB.135KL (ERJ-140LR)	145566	ex PT-SBC	
☐ N820AE	Embraer EMB.135KL (ERJ-140LR)	145576	ex PT-SBM	
☐ N821AE	Embraer EMB.135KL (ERJ-140LR)	145577	ex PT-SBN	
☐ N822AE	Embraer EMB.135KL (ERJ-140LR)	145581	ex PT-SBS	
☐ N823AE	Embraer EMB.135KL (ERJ-140LR)	145582	ex PT-SBT	
☐ N824AE	Embraer EMB.135KL (ERJ-140LR)	145584	ex PT-SBV	
☐ N825AE	Embraer EMB.135KL (ERJ-140LR)	145589	ex PT-SBZ	
☐ N826AE	Embraer EMB.135KL (ERJ-140LR)	145592	ex PT-SCA	
☐ N827AE	Embraer EMB.135KL (ERJ-140LR)	145602	ex PT-SCL	
☐ N828AE	Embraer EMB.135KL (ERJ-140LR)	145604	ex PT-SCN	
☐ N829AE	Embraer EMB.135KL (ERJ-140LR)	145609	ex PT-SCS	
☐ N830AE	Embraer EMB.135KL (ERJ-140LR)	145615	ex PT-SDD	
☐ N831AE	Embraer EMB.135KL (ERJ-140LR)	145616	ex PT-SDE	
☐ N832AE	Embraer EMB.135KL (ERJ-140LR)	145627	ex PT-SDP	
☐ N833AE	Embraer EMB.135KL (ERJ-140LR)	145629	ex PT-SDR	
☐ N834AE	Embraer EMB.135KL (ERJ-140LR)	145631	ex PT-SDT	
☐ N835AE	Embraer EMB.135KL (ERJ-140LR)	145634	ex PT-SDW	
☐ N836AE	Embraer EMB.135KL (ERJ-140LR)	145635	ex PT-SDX	
☐ N837AE	Embraer EMB.135KL (ERJ-140LR)	145647	ex PT-SEH	
☐ N838AE	Embraer EMB.135KL (ERJ-140LR)	145651	ex PT-SEL	
☐ N839AE	Embraer EMB.135KL (ERJ-140LR)	145653	ex PT-SEN	
☐ N840AE	Embraer EMB.135KL (ERJ-140LR)	145656	ex PT-SEQ	
☐ N841AE	Embraer EMB.135KL (ERJ-140LR)	145667	ex PT-SFB	
☐ N842AE	Embraer EMB.135KL (ERJ-140LR)	145673	ex PT-SFG	
☐ N843AE	Embraer EMB.135KL (ERJ-140LR)	145680	ex PT-SFM	
☐ N844AE	Embraer EMB.135KL (ERJ-140LR)	145682	ex PT-SFO	
☐ N845AE	Embraer EMB.135KL (ERJ-140LR)	145685	ex PT-SFR	
☐ N846AE	Embraer EMB.135KL (ERJ-140LR)	145692	ex PT-SFY	
☐ N847AE	Embraer EMB.135KL (ERJ-140LR)	145707	ex PT-SGK	
☐ N848AE	Embraer EMB.135KL (ERJ-140LR)	145710	ex PT-SGO	
☐ N849AE	Embraer EMB.135KL (ERJ-140LR)	145716	ex PT-SGT	
☐ N850AE	Embraer EMB.135KL (ERJ-140LR)	145722	ex PT-SGY	
☐ N851AE	Embraer EMB.135KL (ERJ-140LR)	145734	ex PT-SHK	
☐ N852AE	Embraer EMB.135KL (ERJ-140LR)	145736	ex PT-SHM	
☐ N853AE	Embraer EMB.135KL (ERJ-140LR)	145742	ex PT-SJB	
☐ N854AE	Embraer EMB.135KL (ERJ-140LR)	145743	ex PT-SJC	
☐ N855AE	Embraer EMB.135KL (ERJ-140LR)	145747	ex PT-SJG	
☐ N856AE	Embraer EMB.135KL (ERJ-140LR)	145748	ex PT-SJH	
☐ N857AE	Embraer EMB.135KL (ERJ-140LR)	145752	ex PT-SJL	
☐ N858AE	Embraer EMB.135KL (ERJ-140LR)	145754	ex PT-SJN	
☐ N600BP	Embraer EMB.145LR (ERJ-145LR)	145044	ex N813HK	
☐ N601DW	Embraer EMB.145LR (ERJ-145LR)	145046	ex N814HK	
☐ N602AE	Embraer EMB.145LR (ERJ-145LR)	145048	ex N815HK	stored IGM
☐ N603KC	Embraer EMB.145LR (ERJ-145LR)	145055	ex N816HK	
☐ N604AE	Embraer EMB.145LR (ERJ-145LR)	145058	ex N604DG	
☐ N605KS	Embraer EMB.145LR (ERJ-145LR)	145059	ex N818HK	
☐ N606AE	Embraer EMB.145LR (ERJ-145LR)	145062	ex N819HK	
☐ N607AE	Embraer EMB.145LR (ERJ-145LR)	145064	ex N820HK	
☐ N608LM	Embraer EMB.145LR (ERJ-145LR)	145068	ex N821HK	
☐ N609DP	Embraer EMB.145LR (ERJ-145LR)	145069	ex N822HK	
☐ N610AE	Embraer EMB.145LR (ERJ-145LR)	145073	ex PT-SAR	
☐ N611AE	Embraer EMB.145LR (ERJ-145LR)	145074	ex PT-SAS	
☐ N612AE	Embraer EMB.145LR (ERJ-145LR)	145079	ex PT-SAX	
☐ N613AE	Embraer EMB.145LR (ERJ-145LR)	145081	ex PT-S	
☐ N614AE	Embraer EMB.145LR (ERJ-145LR)	145086	ex PT-S	
☐ N615AE	Embraer EMB.145LR (ERJ-145LR)	145087	ex PT-S	
☐ N616AE	Embraer EMB.145LR (ERJ-145LR)	145092	ex PT-S	
☐ N617AE	Embraer EMB.145LR (ERJ-145LR)	145093	ex PT-SBP	
☐ N618AE	Embraer EMB.145LR (ERJ-145LR)	145097	ex PT-SBT	
☐ N619AE	Embraer EMB.145LR (ERJ-145LR)	145101	ex PT-S	
☐ N620AE	Embraer EMB.145LR (ERJ-145LR)	145102	ex PT-S	
☐ N621AE	Embraer EMB.145LR (ERJ-145LR)	145105	ex PT-S	
☐ N622AE	Embraer EMB.145LR (ERJ-145LR)	145108	ex PT-S	
☐ N623AE	Embraer EMB.145LR (ERJ-145LR)	145109	ex PT-S	
☐ N624AE	Embraer EMB.145LR (ERJ-145LR)	145111	ex PT-S	
☐ N625AE	Embraer EMB.145LR (ERJ-145LR)	145115	ex PT-SCR	
☐ N626AE	Embraer EMB.145LR (ERJ-145LR)	145117	ex PT-SCT	
☐ N627AE	Embraer EMB.145LR (ERJ-145LR)	145121	ex PT-SCX	
☐ N628AE	Embraer EMB.145LR (ERJ-145LR)	145124	ex PT-SDA	
☐ N629AE	Embraer EMB.145LR (ERJ-145LR)	145130	ex PT-SDH	
☐ N630AE	Embraer EMB.145LR (ERJ-145LR)	145132	ex PT-SDJ	
☐ N631AE	Embraer EMB.145LR (ERJ-145LR)	145139	ex PT-SDQ	
☐ N632AE	Embraer EMB.145LR (ERJ-145LR)	145143	ex PT-SDT	
☐ N633AE	Embraer EMB.145LR (ERJ-145LR)	145148	ex PT-SDY	
☐ N634AE	Embraer EMB.145LR (ERJ-145LR)	145150	ex PT-SEB	
☐ N635AE	Embraer EMB.145LR (ERJ-145LR)	145158	ex PT-S	
☐ N636AE	Embraer EMB.145LR (ERJ-145LR)	145160	ex PT-S	
☐ N637AE	Embraer EMB.145LR (ERJ-145LR)	145170	ex PT-S	
☐ N638AE	Embraer EMB.145LR (ERJ-145LR)	145172	ex PT-S	
☐ N639AE	Embraer EMB.145LR (ERJ-145LR)	145182	ex PT-SGE	

☐ N640AE	Embraer EMB.145LR (ERJ-145LR)	145183	ex PT-SGF	
☐ N641AE	Embraer EMB.145LR (ERJ-145LR)	145191	ex PT-SGJ	
☐ N642AE	Embraer EMB.145LR (ERJ-145LR)	145193	ex PT-SGK	
☐ N643AE	Embraer EMB.145LR (ERJ-145LR)	145200	ex PT-S	200th titles
☐ N644AE	Embraer EMB.145LR (ERJ-145LR)	145204	ex PT-SGW	
☐ N645AE	Embraer EMB.145LR (ERJ-145LR)	145212	ex PT-SGZ	
☐ N646AE	Embraer EMB.145LR (ERJ-145LR)	145213	ex PT-SHA	
☐ N647AE	Embraer EMB.145LR (ERJ-145LR)	145222	ex PT-SHH	
☐ N648AE	Embraer EMB.145LR (ERJ-145LR)	145225	ex PT-SHJ	
☐ N649PP	Embraer EMB.145LR (ERJ-145LR)	145234	ex PT-SIB	
☐ N650AE	Embraer EMB.145LR (ERJ-145LR)	145417	ex PT-STO	
☐ N651AE	Embraer EMB.145LR (ERJ-145LR)	145422	ex PT-STT	
☐ N652RS	Embraer EMB.145LR (ERJ-145LR)	145432	ex PT-SUD	
☐ N653AE	Embraer EMB.145LR (ERJ-145LR)	145433	ex PT-SUE	
☐ N654AE	Embraer EMB.145LR (ERJ-145LR)	145437	ex PT-SUI	
☐ N655AE	Embraer EMB.145LR (ERJ-145LR)	145452	ex PT-SUX	
☐ N656AE	Embraer EMB.145LR (ERJ-145LR)	145740	ex PT-SHV	
☐ N657AE	Embraer EMB.145LR (ERJ-145LR)	145744	ex PT-SJD	
☐ N658AE	Embraer EMB.145LR (ERJ-145LR)	145760	ex PT-SJO	
☐ N659AE	Embraer EMB.145LR (ERJ-145LR)	145762	ex PT-SJT	
☐ N660CL	Embraer EMB.145LR (ERJ-145LR)	145764	ex PT-SJV	
☐ N661JA	Embraer EMB.145LR (ERJ-145LR)	145766	ex PT-SJX	
☐ N662EH	Embraer EMB.145LR (ERJ-145LR)	145777	ex PT-SMG	
☐ N663AR	Embraer EMB.145LR (ERJ-145LR)	145778	ex PT-SMH	
☐ N664MS	Embraer EMB.145LR (ERJ-145LR)	145779	ex PT-SMI	
☐ N665BC	Embraer EMB.145LR (ERJ-145LR)	145783	ex PT-SMK	
☐ N667GB	Embraer EMB.145LR (ERJ-145LR)	145784	ex PT-SML	
☐ N668HH	Embraer EMB.145LR (ERJ-145LR)	145785	ex PT-SMM	
☐ N669MB	Embraer EMB.145LR (ERJ-145LR)	145788	ex PT-SMQ	
☐ N670AE	Embraer EMB.145LR (ERJ-145LR)	145790	ex PT-SMR	
☐ N671AE	Embraer EMB.145LR (ERJ-145LR)	145793	ex PT-SMU	
☐ N672AE	Embraer EMB.145LR (ERJ-145LR)	145794	ex PT-SMV	
☐ N673AE	Embraer EMB.145LR (ERJ-145LR)	145797	ex PT-SMX	
☐ N674RJ	Embraer EMB.145LR (ERJ-145LR)	14500801	ex PT-SNF	
☐ N675AE	Embraer EMB.145LR (ERJ-145LR)	14500806	ex PT-SNI	
☐ N676AE	Embraer EMB.145LR (ERJ-145LR)	14500807	ex PT-SNJ	
☐ N677AE	Embraer EMB.145LR (ERJ-145LR)	14500810	ex PT-SNL	
☐ N678AE	Embraer EMB.145LR (ERJ-145LR)	14500813	ex PT-SNP	
☐ N679AE	Embraer EMB.145LR (ERJ-145LR)	14500814	ex PT-SNQ	
☐ N680AE	Embraer EMB.145LR (ERJ-145LR)	14500820	ex PT-SNU	
☐ N681AE	Embraer EMB.145LR (ERJ-145LR)	14500824	ex PT-SNX	
☐ N682AE	Embraer EMB.145LR (ERJ-145LR)	14500826	ex PT-SNY	
☐ N683AE	Embraer EMB.145LR (ERJ-145LR)	14500833	ex PT-SQF	
☐ N684JW	Embraer EMB.145LR (ERJ-145LR)	14500835	ex PT-SQH	
☐ N685AE	Embraer EMB.145LR (ERJ-145LR)	14500836	ex PT-SQI	
☐ N686AE	Embraer EMB.145LR (ERJ-145LR)	14500843	ex PT-SQN	
☐ N687JS	Embraer EMB.145LR (ERJ-145LR)	14500846	ex PT-SQQ	
☐ N688AE	Embraer EMB.145LR (ERJ-145LR)	14500849	ex PT-SQS	
☐ N689EC	Embraer EMB.145LR (ERJ-145LR)	14500853	ex PT-SQV	
☐ N690AE	Embraer EMB.145LR (ERJ-145LR)	14500858	ex PT-SXM	
☐ N691AE	Embraer EMB.145LR (ERJ-145LR)	14500860	ex PT-SXA	
☐ N692AE	Embraer EMB.145LR (ERJ-145LR)	14500866	ex PT-SXF	
☐ N693AE	Embraer EMB.145LR (ERJ-145LR)	14500868	ex PT-SXG	
☐ N694AE	Embraer EMB.145LR (ERJ-145LR)	14500869	ex PT-SXN	
☐ N695AE	Embraer EMB.145LR (ERJ-145LR)	14500870	ex PT-SXH	
☐ N696AE	Embraer EMB.145LR (ERJ-145LR)	14500874	ex PT-SXO	
☐ N697AB	Embraer EMB.145LR (ERJ-145LR)	14500875	ex PT-SXQ	
☐ N698CB	Embraer EMB.145LR (ERJ-145LR)	14500877	ex PT-SXS	
☐ N699AE	Embraer EMB.145LR (ERJ-145LR)	14500883	ex PT-SXW	
☐ N900AE	Embraer EMB.145LR (ERJ-145LR)	14500885	ex PT-SXX	
☐ N902BC	Embraer EMB.145LR (ERJ-145LR)	14500887	ex PT-SXZ	
☐ N905JH	Embraer EMB.145LR (ERJ-145LR)	14500892	ex PT-SYE	
☐ N906AE	Embraer EMB.145LR (ERJ-145LR)	14500894	ex PT-SYG	
☐ N907AE	Embraer EMB.145LR (ERJ-145LR)	14500895	ex PT-SYH	
☐ N908AE	Embraer EMB.145LR (ERJ-145LR)	14500897	ex PT-SYJ	
☐ N909AE	Embraer EMB.145LR (ERJ-145LR)	14500899	ex PT-SYK	
☐ N918AE	Embraer EMB.145LR (ERJ-145LR)	14500902	ex PT-SYM	
☐ N922AE	Embraer EMB.145LR (ERJ-145LR)	14500906	ex PT-SYO	
☐ N923AE	Embraer EMB.145LR (ERJ-145LR)	14500907	ex PT-SYQ	
☐ N925AE	Embraer EMB.145LR (ERJ-145LR)	14500908	ex PT-SYR	
☐ N928AE	Embraer EMB.145LR (ERJ-145LR)	14500911	ex PT-SYT	
☐ N931AE	Embraer EMB.145LR (ERJ-145LR)	14500912	ex PT-SYU	
☐ N932AE	Embraer EMB.145LR (ERJ-145LR)	14500915	ex PT-SYW	
☐ N933JN	Embraer EMB.145LR (ERJ-145LR)	14500918	ex PT-SYY	
☐ N935AE	Embraer EMB.145LR (ERJ-145LR)	14500920	ex PT-SYZ	
☐ N939AE	Embraer EMB.145LR (ERJ-145LR)	14500923	ex PT-SOU	
☐ N941LT	Embraer EMB.145LR (ERJ-145LR)	14500926	ex PT-SOW	
☐ N942LL	Embraer EMB.145LR (ERJ-145LR)	14500930	ex PT-SOZ	

AMERIFLIGHT ***Ameriflight (AMF)*** ***Burbank Glendale-Pasadena, CA (BUR)***

☐ N20FW	Beech 99A	U-111
☐ N21FW	Beech 99A	U-117

	Registration	Type	c/n	Previous identity
☐	N34AK	Beech 99A	U-105	ex N4099A
☐	N51RP	Beech C99	U-212	
☐	N52RP	Beech C99	U-210	ex N66305
☐	N53RP	Beech C99	U-195	ex N64997
☐	N55RP	Beech C99	U-198	ex N64002
☐	N68TA	Beech C99	U-177	ex N177EE
☐	N96AV	Beech C99	U-201	
☐	N102GP	Beech C99	U-208	ex N6628K
☐	N104BE	Beech C99	U-221	ex N7203L
☐	N106SX	Beech C99	U-166	
☐	N107SX	Beech C99	U-176	
☐	N108SX	Beech C99	U-184	ex N6787P
☐	N130GP	Beech C99	U-222	ex N818FL
☐	N134PM	Beech B99	U-34	ex N852SA
☐	N164HA	Beech B99	U-60	ex N72TC
☐	N174AV	Beech C99	U-174	ex N99CJ
☐	N191AV	Beech C99	U-191	ex VR-CIB
☐	N193SU	Beech C99	U-193	ex C-GFAT
☐	N199AF	Beech B99	U-161	ex N12AK
☐	N204AF	Beech C99	U-204	ex N575W
☐	N213AV	Beech C99	U-213	ex N6656N
☐	N221BH	Beech C99	U-168	ex N18AK
☐	N223BH	Beech C99	U-173	ex N6460D
☐	N225BH	Beech C99	U-181	ex N62936
☐	N226BH	Beech C99	U-182	ex N6263D
☐	N228BH	Beech C99	U-229	ex N3067L
☐	N235AV	Beech C99	U-235	ex N235BH
☐	N261SW	Beech C99	U-202	
☐	N802BA	Beech 99	U-29	ex N800BE
☐	N805BA	Beech 99A	U-147	ex N803BE
☐	N949K	Beech 99A	U-36	
☐	N990AF	Beech C99	U-211	ex N113GP
☐	N991AF	Beech C99	U-214	ex N112GP
☐	N992AF	Beech C99	U-203	ex N541JC
☐	N997SB	Beech C99	U-192	ex N6534A
☐	N1924T	Beech 99A	U-115	ex N24AT
☐	N4199C	Beech C99	U-50	ex N7940
☐	N4299A	Beech B99	U-146	
☐	N6199D	Beech C99	U-169	
☐	N6724D	Beech C99	U-215	
☐	N7200Z	Beech C99	U-219	
☐	N7209W	Beech C99	U-224	
☐	N7862R	Beech 99A	U-85	
☐	N8226Z	Beech C99	U-190	ex 6Y-JVB
☐	N8227P	Beech C99	U-194	ex 6Y-JVA
☐	N62989	Beech C99	U-183	
☐	N63978	Beech C99	U-171	
☐	N81820	Beech C99	U-232	ex N232BH

	Registration	Type	c/n	Previous identity
☐	N19RZ	Beech 1900C-1	UC-75	ex JA190C
☐	N26RZ	Beech 1900C-1	UC-134	ex JA190D
☐	N34RZ	Beech 1900C-1	UC-151	ex JA190A
☐	N49UC	Beech 1900C-1	UC-49	ex C-GCMJ
☐	N111YV	Beech 1900C-1	UC-111	ex F-GPYX
☐	N112YV	Beech 1900C-1	UC-112	ex VH-AFR
☐	N330AF	Beech 1900C	UB-38	ex N805BE
☐	N331AF	Beech 1900C	UB-44	ex N807BE
☐	N1568G	Beech 1900C-1	UC-58	ex F-GNAD
☐	N2049K	Beech 1900C-1	UC-164	ex J6-AAJ
☐	N3052K	Beech 1900C	UB-70	
☐	N3071A	Beech 1900C	UB-46	ex N10RA
☐	N3229A	Beech 1900C	UB-51	
☐	N7203C	Beech 1900C	UB-28	
☐	N31701	Beech 1900C	UB-2	ex N121CZ
☐	N31702	Beech 1900C	UB-3	ex N122CZ
☐	N31703	Beech 1900C	UB-10	ex N123CZ
☐	N31704	Beech 1900C	UB-12	ex N124CZ
☐	N31705	Beech 1900C	UB-60	

	Registration	Type	c/n	Previous identity
☐	N179CA	Embraer EMB.120ER Brasilia	120179	ex PT-SQR
☐	N189CA	Embraer EMB.120ER Brasilia	120189	ex PT-SRC
☐	N201YW	Embraer EMB.120RT Brasilia	120201	ex N142EB
☐	N246AS	Embraer EMB.120ER Brasilia	120100	ex PP-SMS
☐	N247CA	Embraer EMB.120ER Brasilia	120225	ex PT-SSU
☐	N257AS	Embraer EMB.120ER Brasilia	120126	ex PT-SNS
☐	N258AS	Embraer EMB.120ER Brasilia	120131	ex PT-SNX

	Registration	Type	c/n	Previous identity
☐	N94AF	Learjet 35A	35A-094	ex (N35PF)
☐	N128CA	Learjet 35A	35A-248	ex C-GBFA
☐	N237AF	Learjet 35A	35A-262	ex N237GA
☐	N535AF	Learjet 35A	35A-191	ex N35SE
☐	N754WS	Learjet 35A	35A-197	ex N754GL

☐ N199DS	Piper PA-31 Turbo Navajo B	31-7400980	ex N7588L
☐ N500CF	Piper PA-31 Turbo Navajo	31-425	ex N6467L
☐ N6480L	Piper PA-31 Turbo Navajo	31-443	
☐ N6733L	Piper PA-31 Turbo Navajo	31-636	
☐ N6759L	Piper PA-31 Turbo Navajo	31-661	ex N479SJ
☐ N7434L	Piper PA-31 Turbo Navajo B	31-822	
☐ N7441L	Piper PA-31 Turbo Navajo B	31-844	
☐ N9132Y	Piper PA-31 Turbo Navajo	31-178	
☐ N27275	Piper PA-31 Navajo C	31-7712066	
☐ N3BT	Piper PA-31-350 Navajo Chieftain	31-7752172	ex N27422
☐ N29UM	Piper PA-31-350 Navajo Chieftain	31-7652127	ex N29JM
☐ N555RG	Piper PA-31-350 Navajo Chieftain	31-7305103	ex N555RC
☐ N600TS	Piper PA-31-350 Navajo Chieftain	31-7305047	ex N537N
☐ N777MP	Piper PA-31-350 Navajo Chieftain	31-7552072	ex N59983
☐ N961CA	Piper PA-31-350 Navajo Chieftain	31-7652014	ex N961PS
☐ N3525G	Piper PA-31-350 Chieftain	31-7952123	
☐ N3527D	Piper PA-31-350 Chieftain	31-7952137	
☐ N3540N	Piper PA-31-350 Chieftain	31-7952214	
☐ N3548B	Piper PA-31-350 Chieftain	31-8052025	
☐ N3553F	Piper PA-31-350 Chieftain	31-8052044	
☐ N3555D	Piper PA-31-350 Chieftain	31-8052059	
☐ N4044P	Piper PA-31-350 Chieftain	31-8152004	
☐ N4078B	Piper PA-31-350 Chieftain	31-8152055	
☐ N4087J	Piper PA-31-350 Chieftain	31-8152128	
☐ N4098A	Piper PA-31-350 Chieftain	31-8152200	
☐ N4502Y	Piper PA-31-350 Chieftain	31-8052189	
☐ N27426	Piper PA-31-350 Navajo Chieftain	31-7752175	
☐ N27579	Piper PA-31-350 Chieftain	31-7852063	
☐ N27677	Piper PA-31-350 Chieftain	31-7852101	
☐ N35336	Piper PA-31-350 Chieftain	31-7952189	
☐ N35805	Piper PA-31-350 Chieftain	31-8052090	
☐ N42076	Piper PA-31-350 Navajo Chieftain	31-7405209	ex G-OSPT
☐ N42079	Piper PA-31-350 Navajo Chieftain	31-7405488	ex G-BCOD
☐ N45004	Piper PA-31-350 Chieftain	31-8052163	
☐ N45014	Piper PA-31-350 Chieftain	31-8052171	
☐ N59820	Piper PA-31-350 Navajo Chieftain	31-7652073	
☐ N59973	Piper PA-31-350 Navajo Chieftain	31-7552079	
☐ N62858	Piper PA-31-350 Navajo Chieftain	31-7652115	
☐ N62959	Piper PA-31-350 Navajo Chieftain	31-7752008	
☐ N66859	Piper PA-31-350 Navajo Chieftain	31-7405168	
☐ N123KC	Piper PA-32R-300 Lance	32R-7680431	
☐ N188SP	Piper PA-32R-300 Lance	32R-7780309	
☐ N1333H	Piper PA-32R-300 Lance	32R-7780154	
☐ N4588F	Piper PA-32R-300 Lance	32R-7680462	
☐ N5363F	Piper PA-32R-300 Lance	32R-7680510	
☐ N7612F	Piper PA-32R-300 Lance	32R-7780063	
☐ N7838C	Piper PA-32R-300 Lance	32R-7680064	
☐ N8456F	Piper PA-32R-300 Lance	32R-7780100	
☐ N9226K	Piper PA-32R-300 Lance	32R-7680199	
☐ N75195	Piper PA-32R-300 Lance	32R-7680277	
☐ N75397	Piper PA-32R-300 Lance	32R-7680301	
☐ N152AF	Swearingen SA.227AC Metro III	AC-520	ex TG-DHL
☐ N155AF	Swearingen SA.227AC Metro III	AC-455	ex N356AE
☐ N191AF	Swearingen SA.227AC Metro III	AC-491	ex N209CA
☐ N240DH	Swearingen SA.227AT Expediter	AT-602B	ex N3117P
☐ N241DH	Swearingen SA.227AT Expediter	AT-607B	ex N3118A
☐ N242DH	Swearingen SA.227AT Expediter	AT-608B	ex N3118G
☐ N243DH	Swearingen SA.227AT Expediter	AT-609B	ex N3118H
☐ N244DH	Swearingen SA.227AT Expediter	AT-618B	
☐ N245DH	Swearingen SA.227AT Expediter	AT-624B	
☐ N246DH	Swearingen SA.227AT Expediter	AT-625B	
☐ N247DH	Swearingen SA.227AT Expediter	AT-626B	
☐ N248DH	Swearingen SA.227AT Expediter	AT-630B	
☐ N249DH	Swearingen SA.227AT Expediter	AT-631B	
☐ N360AE	Swearingen SA.227AC Metro III	AC-675	
☐ N362AE	Swearingen SA.227AC Metro III	AC-677B	
☐ N377PH	Swearingen SA.227AC Metro III	AC-574	ex (D-CABG)
☐ N421MA	Swearingen SA.227AC Metro III	AC-634	ex N3119Q
☐ N422MA	Swearingen SA.227AC Metro III	AC-635	ex N3119T
☐ N423MA	Swearingen SA.227AC Metro III	AC-636	ex N26823
☐ N424MA	Swearingen SA.227AC Metro III	AC-639	
☐ N426MA	Swearingen SA.227AC Metro III	AC-645	
☐ N428MA	Swearingen SA.227AC Metro III	AC-646	
☐ N443AF	Swearingen SA.227AC Metro III	AC-443	ex N443NE
☐ N473AF	Swearingen SA.227AC Metro III	AC-473	ex N473NE
☐ N475AF	Swearingen SA.227AC Metro III	AC-475	ex N475NE
☐ N476AF	Swearingen SA.227AC Metro III	AC-476	ex N476NE
☐ N488AF	Swearingen SA.227AC Metro III	AC-488	ex N488NE
☐ N529AF	Swearingen SA.227AC Metro III	AC-752	ex XA-TML
☐ N544UP	Swearingen SA.227AT Expediter	AT-544	ex N68TA
☐ N548UP	Swearingen SA.227AT Expediter	AT-548	ex N548SA

☐ N556UP	Swearingen SA.227AT Expediter	AT-556	ex N3113B	
☐ N560UP	Swearingen SA.227AT Expediter	AT-560	ex N3113A	
☐ N561UP	Swearingen SA.227AT Expediter	AT-561	ex N3113F	
☐ N566UP	Swearingen SA.227AT Expediter	AT-566	ex N3113N	
☐ N569UP	Swearingen SA.227AT Expediter	AT-569	ex N31134	
☐ N573G	Swearingen SA.227AT Merlin IVC	AT-446B	ex N3008L	
☐ N578AF	Swearingen SA.227AC Metro III	AC-578	ex C-FJLE	
☐ N671AV	Swearingen SA.227AC Metro III	AC-671		
☐ N672AV	Swearingen SA.227AC Metro III	AC-672		
☐ N673AV	Swearingen SA.227AC Metro III	AC-673		
☐ N698AF	Swearingen SA.227AC Metro III	AC-698	ex N698FA	
☐ N801AF	Swearingen SA.227AC Metro III	AC-701	ex C-GWXZ	
☐ N807M	Swearingen SA.227AT Merlin IVC	AT-454B	ex N3013T	
☐ N838AF	Swearingen SA.227AC Metro III	AC-738	ex C-GWXX	
☐ N200AF	Beech 200 Super King Air	BB-102	ex N997MA	

AMERIJET INTERNATIONAL ***Amerijet (M6/AJT)*** ***Fort Lauderdale-Hollywood Intl, FL (FLL)***

☐ N199AJ	Boeing 727-2F9F/W (Duganair 3)	21426/1285	ex N83428	
☐ N395AJ	Boeing 727-233F/W (Duganair 3)	21100/1148	ex N727SN	
☐ N495AJ	Boeing 727-233F/W (Duganair 3)	20937/1103	ex C-GAAD	
☐ N598AJ	Boeing 727-212F/W (Duganair 3)	21947/1506	ex N86430	
☐ N794AJ	Boeing 727-227F/W (Duganair 3)	21243/1197	ex N567PE	Nogravity.com 'G-Force-One'
☐ N804AJ	Boeing 727-2D3F/W (Super 27)	21021/1082	ex N8883Z	stored GYR
☐ N905AJ	Boeing 727-231F/W (Super 27)	21989/1590	ex N84357	
☐ N909PG	Boeing 727-2K5F (FedEx 3)	21852/1553	ex XA-SXL	
☐ N994AJ	Boeing 727-233F/W (Duganair 3)	20942/1130	ex N727JH	

AMERISTAR JET CHARTER ***Ameristar (AJI)*** ***Dallas-Addison, TX (ADS)***

☐ N148TW	AMD Falcon 20C	148	ex N148WC	
☐ N158TW	AMD Falcon 20C	158	ex N450MA	
☐ N204TW	AMD Falcon 20DC	204	ex EC-EGM	
☐ N221TW	AMD Falcon 20DC	221	ex EC-EIV	
☐ N223TW	AMD Falcon 20C	123	ex N45MR	
☐ N232TW	AMD Falcon 20C	32	ex F-GIVT	
☐ N236TW	AMD Falcon 20D	236	ex N936NW	
☐ N240TW	AMD Falcon 20C	40	ex C-GSKQ	
☐ N285TW	AMD Falcon 20EF	285	ex N285AP	
☐ N295TW	AMD Falcon 20C	5	ex F-GJPR	
☐ N314TW	AMD Falcon 20E	314	ex F-GDLU	
☐ N699TW	AMD Falcon 20DC	50	ex EC-EDO	
☐ N977TW	AMD Falcon 20C	13	ex F-BTCY	
☐ N147TW	Learjet 25	25-023	ex N767SC	
☐ N157TW	Learjet 24	24-157	ex N659AT	
☐ N222TW	Learjet 24	24-161	ex N24KF	
☐ N233TW	Learjet 24B	24B-221	ex N59JG	
☐ N237TW	Learjet 24D	24D-237	ex N825DM	
☐ N265TW	Learjet 25D	25D-265	ex N69GF	
☐ N266TW	Learjet 24D	24D-266	ex N266BS	
☐ N277TW	Learjet 24D	24D-277	ex N57BC	
☐ N299TW	Learjet 24D	24D-299	ex XB-GJS	
☐ N324TW	Learjet 24D	24D-324	ex XA-SCY	
☐ N330TW	Learjet 24E	24E-330	ex N511AT	
☐ N333TW	Learjet 24	24-168	ex N155BT	
☐ N525TW	Learjet 25	25-011	ex N108GA	
☐ N888TW	Learjet 24D	24D-292	ex N800PC	
☐ N176TW	Beech 65-E90 King Air	LW-76	ex ZS-LJF	
☐ N732TW	Boeing 737-2H4 (AvAero 3)	22731/864	ex N82SW	stored ELP
☐ N733TW	Boeing 737-2H4 (AvAero 3)	22732/877	ex N83SW	
☐ N783TW	Douglas DC-9-15F (ABS 3)	47010/97	ex N916R	
☐ N784TW	Douglas DC-9-15F (ABS 3)	47014/141	ex N923R	
☐ N785TW	Douglas DC-9-15F (ABS 3)	47015/156	ex N5373G	

ANDREW AIRWAYS ***Kodiak-Municipal, AK (KDK)***

☐ N1544	de Havilland DHC-2 Beaver	1230	ex N67686	Floatplane or wheels/skis
☐ N1545	de Havilland DHC-2 Beaver	1493	ex N123UA	Floatplane or wheels/skis
☐ N5303X	Cessna U206G Stationair 6 II	U20605622		Floatplane or wheels/skis

ANOKA AIR CHARTER ***Red Zone (RZZ)*** ***Minneapolis-Anoka County / Blaine, MN (-/BWS)***

☐ N200VW	Piper PA-31-350 Chieftain	31-8052011	ex N200NC	
☐ N633D	Piper PA-31-350 Chieftain	31-7852098	ex N63ND	
☐ N646DR	Beech 200 Super King Air	BB-646	ex N646BM	
☐ N700RF	Beech 65-C90A King Air	LJ-1262	ex N200HV	

ARCTIC CIRCLE AIR SERVICE — **Air Arctic (5F/CIR)** — **Aniak/Bethel/Dillingham-Municipal/Fairbanks-Intl, AK (ANI/BET/DLG/FAI)**

☐ N300SN	Cessna 402C II	402C0060	ex N5871C	
☐ N402ET	Cessna 402C II	402C0054	ex C-GTKJ	
☐ N4630N	Cessna 402C II	402C0001		
☐ N168LM	Short SD.3-30	SH3104	ex N174Z	Freighter
☐ N261AG	Short SD.3-30	SH3117	ex 84-0470	Freighter
☐ N7721C	Piper PA-32R-300 Lance	32R-7680060		

ARCTIC TRANSPORTATION SERVICES — **Arctic Transport (7S/RCT)** — **Unalakleet-Municipal, AK (UNK)**

☐ N19TA	Cessna 207A Stationair 7	20700468	ex N6289H	
☐ N26TA	Cessna 207A Stationair 8	20700725	ex N9759M	
☐ N624DR	Cessna 207A Stationair 7 II	20700517	ex N917AC	
☐ N624ER	Cessna 207A Stationair 8 II	20700752	ex N9936M	
☐ N7305U	Cessna 207A Skywagon	20700392		
☐ N7605U	Cessna 207A Stationair 7	20700443		
☐ N9475M	Cessna 207A Stationair 8	20700695		
☐ N9736M	Cessna 207A Stationair 8	20700722		
☐ N9829M	Cessna 207A Stationair 8	20700741		
☐ N9956M	Cessna 207A Stationair 8	20700763		
☐ N73217	Cessna 207A Stationair 8	20700572		
☐ N73467	Cessna 207A Stationair 8 II	20700594		
☐ N73503	Cessna 207A Stationair 8	20700599		
☐ N73789	Cessna 207A Stationair 8	20700629		
☐ N424CA	CASA 212-200	CC20-7-242		
☐ N437RA	CASA 212-200	CC21-2-166	ex N437CA	
☐ N439RA	CASA 212-200	CC50-9-287	ex N287MA	
☐ N440RA	CASA 212-200	CC20-6-174	ex N687MA	Freighter
☐ N1906	Short SC.7 Skyvan 3A	SH1906	ex HS-DCC	Freighter
☐ N2719A	Cessna 402C	402C0233		

ARIS HELICOPTERS — **San Jose-Intl, CA (SJC)**

☐ N58AH	Sikorsky S-58ET	58-328	ex N39790	

ARROW CARGO — **Big A (JW/APW)** — **Miami-Intl, FL (MIA)**

☐ N688GX	Boeing 757-225 (PCF)	22688/115	ex TC-OGH	
☐ N689GX	Boeing 757-225 (PCF)	22689/117	ex PR-LGK	
☐ N822PB	Boeing 757-28APCF	23822/130	ex G-OOOB	
☐ N868AN	Boeing 757-23APF	24868/314	ex B-27201	stored MZJ
☐ N906R	Douglas DC-8-63F (BAC 3)	46087/454	ex N774FT	
☐ N142WE	Douglas DC-10-40F	46966/262	ex VP-BDH	
☐ N450ML	Douglas DC-10-30F	47831/327	ex 5X-JCR	
☐ N478CT	Douglas DC-10-30F	47819/314	ex PR-BME	
☐ N524MD	Douglas DC-10-30F	46999/289	ex S2-ADA	
☐ N526MD	Douglas DC-10-30F	46998/267	ex OO-LRM	
☐ N68041	Douglas DC-10-10F	46900/34		

ASIA PACIFIC AIRLINES — **Magellan (MGE)** — **Guam (GUM)**

☐ N319NE	Boeing 727-212F/W (Duganair 3)	21349/1289	ex N591DB	
☐ N705AA	Boeing 727-223F/W (Super 27)	22462/1751		
☐ N86425	Boeing 727-212F/W (Duganair 3)	21459/1329	ex N296AS	

ASPEN HELICOPTERS — **Aspen (AHF)** — **Oxnard, CA (OXR)**

☐ N212AH	Bell 212	30959	ex C-FYMJ	
☐ N383SH	Bell 206L-3 LongRanger III	51073	ex N333SH	
☐ N1085T	Bell 206L-1 LongRanger III	45376		
☐ N3832K	Partenavia P.68C	272		
☐ N5006Y	Bell 206B JetRanger III	2485		
☐ N5012F	Bell 206B JetRanger III	2559		
☐ N6602L	Partenavia P.68 Observer	326-19-OB	ex VH-OBS	
☐ N8131	Piper PA-31-350 Chieftain	31-8152032	ex LN-REM	
☐ N39049	Bell 206B JetRanger III	3101		
☐ N49643	Bell 206B JetRanger	1813		

ASTAR AIR CARGO — **DHL (ER/DHL)** — **Cincinnati-Northern Kentucky Intl, OH (CVG)**

☐ N362DH	Airbus A300B4-103F	084	ex HS-THP	stored IGM
☐ N363DH	Airbus A300B4-103F	085	ex HS-THR	stored IGM
☐ N364DH	Airbus A300B4-203F	141	ex HS-THT	stored IGM
☐ N365DH	Airbus A300B4-203F	149	ex HS-THW	stored IGM
☐ N366DH	Airbus A300B4-203F	249	ex F-WIHZ	stored IGM

☐ N367DH	Airbus A300B4-203F	265	ex F-WIHY		stored IGM
☐ N740DH	Boeing 727-2Q9F (FedEx 3)	21930/1508	ex N200AV		stored IGM
☐ N741DH	Boeing 727-2Q9F (FedEx 3)	21931/1531	ex N202AV		stored IGM
☐ N742DH	Boeing 727-225F (FedEx 3)	21290/1238	ex N8872Z		stored IGM
☐ N745DH	Boeing 727-224F (FedEx 3)	20665/1149	ex N69736		stored IGM
☐ N747DH	Boeing 727-224F (FedEx 3)	22253/1702	ex N79744		stored IGM
☐ N748DH	Boeing 727-225F (FedEx 3)	22440/1692	ex XA-TCX		stored IGM
☐ N749DH	Boeing 727-223F (FedEx 3)	22013/1659	ex N897AA		stored IGM
☐ N750DH	Boeing 727-2M7 (FedEx 3)	21951/1680	ex A7-ABC		stored IGM
☐ N751DH	Boeing 727-264 (FedEx 3)	22982/1802	ex A7-ABD		stored IGM
☐ N752DH	Boeing 727-223F (FedEx 3)	22466/1763	ex N709AA		stored IGM
☐ N753DH	Boeing 727-223F (FedEx 3)	22468/1766	ex N712AA		stored IGM
☐ N754DH	Boeing 727-223F (FedEx 3)	22008/1646	ex N892AA		stored IGM
☐ N760AT	Boeing 727-2B7F (FedEx 3)	21954/1525	ex N760US		stored IGM
☐ N762AT	Boeing 727-2B7F (FedEx 3)	22162/1717	ex N762US		stored IGM
☐ N763AT	Boeing 727-264F (FedEx 3)	22983/1806	ex N763US		stored IGM
☐ N764AT	Boeing 727-264F (FedEx 3)	22984/1813	ex N764US		stored IGM
☐ N765AT	Boeing 727-264F (FedEx 3)	23014/1816	ex N765US		stored IGM
☐ N770AT	Boeing 727-2B7F (FedEx 3)	21953/1516	ex N755US		stored IGM
☐ N780DH	Boeing 727-223F (FedEx 3)	22006/1636	ex N890AA		stored IGM
☐ N782DH	Boeing 727-227F (FedEx 3)	21998/1577	ex N769AT		stored IGM
☐ N783DH	Boeing 727-227F (FedEx 3)	21999/1581	ex N766AT		stored IGM
☐ N784DH	Boeing 727-227F (FedEx 3)	22001/1585	ex N767AT		stored IGM
☐ N785AT	Boeing 727-214F (FedEx 3)	21691/1480	ex N752US		stored IGM
☐ N786AT	Boeing 727-214F (FedEx 3)	21692/1482	ex N753US		stored IGM
☐ N788AT	Boeing 727-214F (FedEx 3)	21958/1533	ex N754US		stored IGM
☐ N793DH	Boeing 727-247F (FedEx 3)	21393/1307	ex N784AT		stored IGM
☐ N801DH	Douglas DC-8-73AF	46033/431	ex C-FTIK		
☐ N802DH	Douglas DC-8-73AF	46076/451	ex C-FTIO		
☐ N804DH	Douglas DC-8-73AF	46124/511	ex C-FTIR		
☐ N805DH	Douglas DC-8-73AF	46125/515	ex C-FTIS		
☐ N806DH	Douglas DC-8-73CF	46002/394	ex N815UP		
☐ N807DH	Douglas DC-8-73CF	45990/375	ex N816UP		
☐ N873SJ	Douglas DC-8-73F	46091/519	ex F-GESM	Billy J Benson	

ATI-AIR TRANSPORT INTERNATIONAL — *Air Transport (8C/ATN)* — *Little Rock-Adams Field, AR (LIT)*

☐ N21CX	Douglas DC-8-62F (BAC 3)	45955/365	ex N163CA		
☐ N41CX	Douglas DC-8-62CF (BAC 3)	46129/523	ex N798AL		
☐ N71CX	Douglas DC-8-62F (BAC 3)	45961/361	ex N818CK		
☐ N602AL	Douglas DC-8-73F	45991/380	ex D-ADUI		
☐ N603AL	Douglas DC-8-73F	46003/401	ex D-ADUA		
☐ N604BX	Douglas DC-8-73CF	46046/444	ex N792FT		
☐ N605AL	Douglas DC-8-73F	46106/490	ex D-ADUC		
☐ N606AL	Douglas DC-8-73F	46044/432	ex D-ADUE		
☐ N721CX	Douglas DC-8-72CF	46013/427	ex 46013		
☐ N722CX	Douglas DC-8-72CF	46130/542	ex 46130		
☐ N728PL	Douglas DC-8-62F (BAC 3)	45918/353	ex F-BOLF	Jerry 'Pete' Zerkel	
☐ N761CX	Boeing 767-223 (SCD)	22318/111	ex N316AA		
☐ N799AL	Douglas DC-8-62F (BAC 3)	45922/335	ex RTAF 60112		Lsd fr BAX Global
☐ N820BX+	Douglas DC-8-71F	46065/460	ex N8098U	Larry LJ Johnston'	
☐ N821BX	Douglas DC-8-71F	45811/262	ex N8071U		
☐ N822BX	Douglas DC-8-71F	45813/284	ex N8073U		
☐ N823BX	Douglas DC-8-71F	46064/459	ex N8097U		
☐ N825BX	Douglas DC-8-71F	45978/381	ex N8088U		
☐ N826BX	Douglas DC-8-71F	45998/399	ex N8094U		stored ROW
☐ N828BX	Douglas DC-8-71F	45993/392	ex N8089U		
☐ N829BX	Douglas DC-8-71F	45994/387	ex N501SR		stored MHV
☐ N830BX	Douglas DC-8-71F	45973/358	ex N783UP		

ATLANTIC AIR CARGO — *Miami-Intl, FL (MIA)*

☐ N437GB	Douglas DC-3	19999	ex HR-LAD	Freighter
☐ N705GB	Douglas DC-3	13854	ex TG-SAA	Freighter

ATLANTIC SOUTHEAST AIRLINES — *Candler(EV/CAA)* — *Atlanta-Hartsfield Intl, GA/Orlando-Intl, FL (ATL/MCO)*

Wholly owned subsidiary of SkyWest Airlines, and operates as Delta Connection

ATLAS AIR — *Giant (5Y/GTI)* — *New York-JFK Intl, NY (JFK)*

☐ N355MC	Boeing 747-341 (SF)	23395/629	ex PP-VNI	Lsd to PAC
☐ N408MC	Boeing 747-47UF	29261/1192	ex (N495MC)	Op for UAE
☐ N409MC	Boeing 747-47UF	30558/1242		
☐ N412MC	Boeing 747-47UF	30559/1244		
☐ N415MC	Boeing 747-47UF	32837/1304		Op for UAE
☐ N416MC	Boeing 747-47UF	32838/1307		Lsd to PAC
☐ N418MC	Boeing 747-47UF	32840/1319		
☐ N419MC	Boeing 747-48EF	28367/1096	ex TF-AMO	

☐ N429MC	Boeing 747-481BCF	24833/812	ex JA8095		
☐ N492MC	Boeing 747-47UF	29253/1169			
☐ N493MC	Boeing 747-47UF	29254/1179			
☐ N496MC	Boeing 747-47UF	29257/1217			
☐ N497MC	Boeing 747-47UF	29258/1220			Op for UAE
☐ N498MC	Boeing 747-47UF	29259/1227			Op for UAE
☐ N499MC	Boeing 747-47UF	29260/1240			
☐ N505MC	Boeing 747-2D3M	21251/206	ex F-GFUK		stored ROW
☐ N506MC	Boeing 747-2D3M	21252/297	ex LX-ZCV	all-white	stored ROW
☐ N508MC	Boeing 747-230M	21644/256	ex D-ABYS		stored
☐ N512MC	Boeing 747-230M	21220/294	ex D-ABYJ		stored ROW
☐ N516MC	Boeing 747-243M	22507/497	ex I-DEMD		stored ROW
☐ N517MC	Boeing 747-243B (SF)	23300/613	ex I-DEMT		
☐ N522MC	Boeing 747-2D7B (SF)	21783/417	ex HS-TGB		
☐ N523MC	Boeing 747-2D7B (SF)	21782/402	ex N323MC		
☐ N524MC	Boeing 747-2D7B (SF)	21784/424	ex HS-TGC		
☐ N526MC	Boeing 747-2D7B (SF)	22337/479	ex HS-TGF	all-white	
☐ N528MC	Boeing 747-2D7B (SF)	22472/597	ex HS-TGS		stored ROW
☐ N537MC	Boeing 747-271C	22403/524	ex LX-BCV	all-white	stored ROW
☐ N540MC	Boeing 747-243M	22508/499	ex I-DEMF		
☐ N809MC	Boeing 747-228F	20887/245	ex LX-DCV		
☐ N850GT	Boeing 747-87UF	37562			on order

BAKER AVIATION — *Baker Aviation (8Q/BAJ)* — *Kotzebue-Wien Memorial, AK (OTZ)*

☐ N6908M	Cessna 207A Stationair 8	20700672	
☐ N9942M	Cessna 207A Stationair 8	20700756	

BALD MOUNTAIN AIR SERVICE — *Homer, AK*

☐ N104BM	de Havilland DHC-3 Turbo Otter	118	ex CF-BEP	Floatplane or wheels/skis
☐ N413JP	de Havilland DHC-3 Otter	314	ex C-GCDX	Floatplane or wheels/skis
☐ N564DH	de Havilland DHC-6 Twin Otter 300	564	ex B-3504	
☐ N716JP	de Havilland DHC-6 Twin Otter 300	527	ex TI-AZV	

BANKAIR — *Bankair (B4/BKA)* — *Columbia-Owens Field, SC (CUB)*

☐ N33PT	Learjet 25D	25D-240	ex N83EA
☐ N58EM	Learjet 35	35-046	ex VH-LJL
☐ N58HC	Learjet 25D	25D-341	ex XA-SAE
☐ N67PA	Learjet 35A	35A-208	ex (N39DJ)
☐ N90WR	Learjet 35	35-022	ex OY-BLG
☐ N135AG	Learjet 35A	35A-132	ex N37TJ
☐ N155AM	Learjet 35A	35A-131	ex N26GD
☐ N326DD	Learjet 35A	35A-173	ex YU-BPY
☐ N369BA	Learjet 35A	35A-312	ex LV-OFV
☐ N399BA	Learjet 35A	35A-371	ex LV-ALF
☐ N465NW	Learjet 35A	35A-465	
☐ N500ED	Learjet 35A	35A-241	ex N500EX
☐ N900BJ	Learjet 35A	35A-123	ex N900JE
☐ N21CJ	Mitsubishi MU-2L	789SA	ex N278MA
☐ N21JA	Mitsubishi MU-2J	614	ex N998CA
☐ N44KU	Mitsubishi MU-2J	647	ex N44KS
☐ N174MA	Mitsubishi MU-2B	753SA	ex N100BY
☐ N334EB	Mitsubishi MU-2J	568	ex N99SL
☐ N535WM	Mitsubishi MU-2J	655	ex N535MA
☐ N610CA	Mitsubishi MU-2B	788SA	ex N277MA
☐ N637WG	Mitsubishi MU-2J	637	ex N951MS
☐ N942ST	Mitsubishi MU-2B	745SA	ex N942MA

BARON AVIATION SERVICES — *Show-Me (BVN)* — *Rolla-Vichy-National, MO (VIH)*

Operates Cessna 208/208B Caravans on behalf of Federal Express

BASLER AIRLINES — *Basler (BFC)* — *Oshkosh-Wittman Regional, WI (OSH)*

☐ N300BF	Basler BT-67	15299/26744	ex N300TX	Turbo-Express

BAY AIR — *Dillingham & Shannons Pond SPB, AK (DLG/-)*

☐ N364RA	de Havilland DHC-2 Beaver	364	ex N62300	Floatplane

BEMIDJI AIRLINES — *Bemidji (CH/BMJ)* — *Bemidji, MN (BJI)*

☐ N55SA	Beech 65-A80 Queen Air	LD-243	ex N794A	Queenaire 8800 conversion
☐ N80RR	Beech 65-B80 Queen Air	LD-296		Queenaire 8800 conversion
☐ N95LL	Beech 65-A80 Queen Air	LD-235	ex N33TX	Queenaire 8800 conversion
☐ N103BA	Beech 65-B80 Queen Air	LD-435	ex N103EE	Queenaire 8800 conversion
☐ N104BA	Beech 65-B80 Queen Air	LD-411	ex N4258S	
☐ N106BA	Beech 65-B80 Queen Air	LD-409	ex N1338T	Queenaire 8800 conversion

Registration	Type	C/n	Previous identity	Remarks
☐ N107BA	Beech 65-B80 Queen Air	LD-358	ex N7838L	Queenaire 8800 conversion
☐ N110BA	Beech 65-B80 Queen Air	LD-279	ex N102KK	Queenaire 8800 conversion
☐ N111AR	Beech 65-80 Queen Air	LF-68	ex 62-3780	
☐ N131BA	Beech 65-B80 Queen Air	LD-297	ex N1555M	Queenaire 8800 conversion
☐ N132BA	Beech 65-B80 Queen Air	LD-331	ex C-GRID	Queenaire 8800 conversion
☐ N134BA	Beech 65-A80 Queen Air	LD-202	ex N848S	Queenaire 8800 conversion
☐ N135BA	Beech 65-80 Queen Air	LD-68	ex N29RG	Queenaire 8800 conversion
☐ N138BA	Beech 65-80 Queen Air	LD-361	ex N3344Z	
☐ N306D	Beech 65-80 Queen Air	LD-439	ex N4258S	
☐ N5078E	Beech 65-80 Queen Air	LF-76	ex 63-13637	
☐ N5078N	Beech 65-80 Queen Air	LF-16	ex 60-3467	
☐ N5078U	Beech 65-80 Queen Air	LF-32	ex 62-3834	
☐ N5079E	Beech 65-80 Queen Air	LF-52	ex 62-3854	
☐ N5080L	Beech 65-80 Queen Air	LF-59	ex 62-3861	
☐ N5080H	Beech 65-80 Queen Air	LF-27		

Registration	Type	C/n	Previous identity	Remarks
☐ N70NP	Beech 99	U-14	ex N914Y	
☐ N108BA	Beech 99	U-40	ex C-GQFD	
☐ N125DP	Beech 99	U-12	ex C-GPCE	
☐ N130BA	Beech 99A	U-80	ex N51PA	Freighter
☐ N137BA	Beech 99	U-137	ex C-GAWW	
☐ N172EE	Beech C99	U-172	ex N993SB	
☐ N175EE	Beech C99	U-175	ex N994SB	
☐ N223CA	Beech C99	U-200	ex SE-IZX	Freighter
☐ N6645K	Beech C99	U-209		
☐ N7207E	Beech C99	U-223		
☐ N7212P	Beech C-99	U-220		

Registration	Type	C/n	Previous identity	Remarks
☐ N60BA	Beech 65-E90 King Air	LW-79	ex N12AK	
☐ N70DD	Beech 58 Baron	TH-370	ex N25660	
☐ N4016A	Beech 58 Baron	TH-9		

BERING AIR — *Bering Air (8E/BRG)* — *Nome, AK (OME)*

Registration	Type	C/n	Previous identity	Remarks
☐ N205BA	Cessna 208B Caravan I	208B0890		
☐ N806BA	Cessna 208B Caravan I	208B0943		
☐ N1128L	Cessna 208B Caravan I	208B0536		

Registration	Type	C/n	Previous identity	Remarks
☐ N141ME	Piper PA-31-350 Chieftain	31-8152117	ex N4086L	
☐ N4112D	Piper PA-31-350 T-1020	31-8353004		
☐ N4112E	Piper PA-31-350 T-1020	31-8353005		
☐ N4118G	Piper PA-31-350 T-1020	31-8453001		
☐ N41189	Piper PA-31-350 T-1020	31-8553002		
☐ N45052	Piper PA-31-350 Chieftain	31-8152063		

Registration	Type	C/n	Previous identity	Remarks
☐ N15GA	Beech 1900D	UE-37	ex F-HCHA	
☐ N79CF	Beech 200 Super King Air	BB-441		CatPass 250 conversion
☐ N148SK	Beech 1900D	UE-148		
☐ N326KW	Beech 200 Super King Air	BB-1360	ex HK-3703X	CatPass 250 conversion
☐ N349TA	CASA 212-200	CC60-9-349	ex N316CA	Freighter
☐ N9964M	Cessna 207A Stationair 8	20700766		
☐ N9988M	Cessna 207A Stationair 8	20700776		

BERRY AVIATION — *Berry (BYA)* — *San Marcos-Municipal, TX (HYI)*

Registration	Type	C/n	Previous identity	Remarks
☐ N335PH	Dornier 328-100	3013	ex D-CALT	
☐ N900LH	Dornier 328-100	3014	ex N336PH	
☐ N339PH	Dornier 328-100	3015	ex D-CARR	
☐ N473PS	Dornier 328-100	3010	ex HB-AEG	

Registration	Type	C/n	Previous identity	Remarks
☐ N373PH	Swearingen SA.227AC Metro III	AC-538	ex N732C	
☐ N589BA	Swearingen SA.227AC Metro III	AC-589	ex XA-TSF	stored HYI
☐ N590BA	Swearingen SA.227AC Metro III	AC-590	ex XA-TSG	stored HYI
☐ N680AX	Swearingen SA.227AC Metro III	AC-680	ex N365AE	
☐ N691AX	Swearingen SA.227AC Metro III	AC-691	ex N367AE	
☐ N697AX	Swearingen SA.227AC Metro III	AC-697	ex N730C	
☐ N729C	Swearingen SA.227AC Metro III	AC-571	ex N374PH	
☐ N789C	Swearingen SA.227AC Metro III	AC-540	ex N389PH	
☐ N26959	Swearingen SA.227AC Metro III	AC-662B		
☐ N27442	Swearingen SA.227AC Metro III	AC-750B		

Registration	Type	C/n	Previous identity	Remarks
☐ N165BA	Swearingen SA.226TC Metro II	TC-215	ex N911HF	
☐ N226BA	Swearingen SA.226TC Metro II	TC-321	ex N105UR	
☐ N323BA	Swearingen SA.226TC Metro II	TC-280	ex N303TL	Freighter

BIG ISLAND AIR — *Big Isle (BIG)* — *Kailua-Keahole Kona Intl, HI (KOA)*

Registration	Type	C/n	Previous identity	Remarks
☐ N281A	Cessna 208 Caravan I	20800271	ex LV-WYX	

BIGHORN AIRWAYS — **Bighorn Air (BHR)** — **Sheridan-County, WY/Casper-Natrona Co, WY (SHR/CPR)**

Registration	Type	C/n	Previous identity		
☐ N107BH	CASA C.212-200	CC20-4-165	ex N212TH		
☐ N112BH	CASA C.212-200	CC50-11-292	ex N311ST		
☐ N114BH	Cessna 340A	340A1230	ex N6228X		
☐ N115BH	Cessna 340A	340A1531	ex N2688Q		
☐ N117BH	CASA C.212-200	CC23-1-171	ex N349CA		
☐ N118BH	Cessna 340A	340A0003	ex N5168J		
☐ N257MC	Dornier 228-202	8102	ex YV-648C		
☐ N263MC	Dornier 228-202	8141	ex N116DN		
☐ N266MC	Dornier 228-202	8150	ex D-CBDL		
☐ N414PG	Cessna 414A Chancellor III	414A0811	ex D-ICAC		
☐ N543CC	Bell 206B JetRanger III	3593	ex N2295W		
☐ N700WJ	Cessna 425 Conquest I	425-0036	ex F-GCQN		
☐ N6266C	Cessna T210N Turbo Centurion II	21063849			

BIMINI ISLAND AIR — **(BMY)** — **Fort Lauderdale-Executive, FL (FXE)**

Registration	Type	C/n	Previous identity		
☐ N46ZP	Cessna 402B II	402B1004	ex N87159		
☐ N325SV	SAAB SF.340A	340A-072	ex N72VN		
☐ N460BA	SAAB SF.340A	340A-033	ex N441EA		

BORINQUEN AIR — **San Juan-Munoz Marin Intl, PR (SJU)**

Registration	Type	C/n	Previous identity		
☐ N1019B	Beech E-18S	BA-254			Freighter
☐ N86553	Douglas DC-3	4715	ex 41-18590		Freighter

BOSTON-MAINE AIRWAYS — **Clipper Express (E9/CXS)** — **Portsmouth-Pease Intl, NH (PSM)**

Registration	Type	C/n	Previous identity		
☐ N342PA	Boeing 727-222 (FedEx 3)	21893/1503	ex N7298U	Clipper Guilford	
☐ N348PA	Boeing 727-222 (FedEx 3)	21921/1639	ex N7467U	Clipper Ed Bali	stored BQK
☐ N525PA	British Aerospace Jetstream 31	666	ex N305PX	Clipper Tay	
☐ N529PA	British Aerospace Jetstream 31	771	ex N846JS	Clipper Shenandoah	
☐ N530PA	British Aerospace Jetstream 31	732	ex N836JS	Clipper Allagash	
☐ N531PA	British Aerospace Jetstream 31	748	ex N839JS	Clipper Missouri	
☐ N538PA	British Aerospace Jetstream 31	751	ex N841JS	Clipper Isar	
☐ N539PA	British Aerospace Jetstream 31	741	ex N838JS		

BRAVO AIRLINES — **Miami-Opa Locka, FL (OPF)**

Registration	Type	C/n	Previous identity		
☐ N701AU	Lockheed P2V-7 Neptune Firestar	726-7190	ex N920AU	01	Tanker
☐ N716AU	Lockheed P2V-7 Neptune Firestar	726-7065	ex N90YY	16	Tanker
☐ N718AU	Lockheed P2V-7 Neptune Firestar	726-7214	ex N964L	18	Tanker

BROOKS AVIATION — **Douglas-Municipal, GA (DQH)**

Registration	Type	C/n	Previous identity		
☐ N99FS	Douglas DC-3	12425	ex (N89BF)		

BROOKS FUEL — **Fairbanks-Intl, AK (FAI)**

Registration	Type	C/n	Previous identity		
☐ N708Z	Douglas C-54G	36067	ex USCG 5614		
☐ N3054V	Douglas DC-4	10547	ex N76AU	162	Tanker
☐ N51802	Douglas C-54G	35930	ex 45-0477		stored FAI
☐ N96358	Douglas C-54E	27284	ex Bu90398		

BUSINESS AVIATION COURIER — **Dakota (DKT)** — **Sioux Falls-Joe Foss Field, SD (FSD)**

Registration	Type	C/n	Previous identity		
☐ N76MD	Cessna 402B II	402B1055	ex N987PF		
☐ N402BP	Cessna 402B	402B0353	ex N5419M		
☐ N402SS	Cessna 402B	402B0562	ex N402CC		
☐ N624CA	Cessna 402B	402B0876	ex D-IJOS		
☐ N780MB	Cessna 402B	402B0249	ex N402RT		
☐ N1048	Cessna 402B	402B0628	ex N104WM		
☐ N3729C	Cessna 402B	402B0589	ex XB-EAC		
☐ N3796C	Cessna 402B	402B0803			
☐ N3813	Cessna 402B	402B0807	ex PK-VCE		
☐ N366AE	Swearingen SA.227AC Metro III	AC-681B			
☐ N371PH	Swearingen SA.227AC Metro III	AC-576	ex N3119W		
☐ N387PH	Swearingen SA.227AC Metro III	AC-531	ex N31094		
☐ N685BA	Swearingen SA.227AC Metro III	AC-685	ex N685AV		
☐ N3108B	Swearingen SA.227AC Metro III	AC-509	ex XA-TAK		
☐ N3116N	Swearingen SA.227AC Metro III	AC-596			
☐ N80BS	Cessna 404 Titan II	404-0048	ex G-ZAPB		
☐ N500FS	Cessna 310R II	310R0630			
☐ N1533T	Cessna 310R II	310R0111			
☐ N3482G	Cessna 310R II	310R0850			

BUTLER AIRCRAFT — Redmond, OR (RDM)

☐ N401US	Douglas DC-7	45145/767	ex N6331C	62	Tanker
☐ N531BA	Lockheed 182-1A Hercules (C-130A)	3139	ex 56-0531	67	Tanker
☐ N838D	Douglas DC-7	45347/936		66	Tanker
☐ N6353C	Douglas DC-7	45486/964		60	Tanker
☐ N60018	Cessna TU206F Stationair	U20602002			

C&M AIRWAYS — Red Wing (RWG) — El Paso-Intl, TX (ELP)

☐ N640CM	Convair 640	104	ex C-GCWY	stored ELP
☐ N640R	Convair 640	332	ex PH-MAL	stored ELP
☐ N3420	Convair 640	64		stored ELP
☐ N563PC	Douglas DC-9-15RC (ABS 3)	47055/194	ex N1305T	

CAPE AIR — Cair (9K/KAP) — Hyannis-Barnstable Municipal, MA/Naples-Municipal, FL (HYA/APF)

☐ N69SC	Cessna 402C II	402C0041	ex N5778C	
☐ N83PB	Cessna 402C II	402C0350	ex N26627	
☐ N106CA	Cessna 402C III	402C1020	ex TJ-AHQ	
☐ N120PC	Cessna 402C II	402C0079	ex N2612L	
☐ N121PB	Cessna 402C II	402C0507	ex N6874X	
☐ N161TA	Cessna 402C II	402C0070	ex N2611A	
☐ N223PB	Cessna 402C II	402C0105	ex N261PB	
☐ N247GS	Cessna 402C II	402C0637	ex N404BK	
☐ N401TJ	Cessna 402C II	402C0109	ex TJ-AFV	
☐ N402VN	Cessna 402C II	402C0488	ex (N6840D)	
☐ N406GA	Cessna 402C II	402C0329	ex N2642D	
☐ N494BC	Cessna 402C II	402C0308	ex N67PB	
☐ N514NC	Cessna 402C II	402C0514	ex N125PB	
☐ N524CA	Cessna 402C II	402C0522	ex C-GSKG	
☐ N525RH	Cessna 402C II	402C0525	ex N68761	
☐ N548GA	Cessna 402C II	402C0653	ex N6773T	
☐ N618CA	Cessna 402C II	402C0620	ex VH-RGK	
☐ N660CA	Cessna 402C II	402C0406	ex C-GHMI	
☐ N747WS	Cessna 402C II	402C0080	ex C-GHYZ	
☐ N762EA	Cessna 402C II	402C0061	ex N5872C	
☐ N763EA	Cessna 402C II	402C0497	ex N763AN	
☐ N764EA	Cessna 402C II	402C0237	ex N2719T	
☐ N769EA	Cessna 402C II	402C0303	ex N3283M	
☐ N770CA	Cessna 402C II	402C0432	ex C-GIBL	
☐ N771EA	Cessna 402C II	402C0046	ex N5809C	
☐ N781EA	Cessna 402C II	402C0310	ex N822AN	
☐ N812AN	Cessna 402C II	402C0229	ex N2718P	
☐ N818AN	Cessna 402C II	402C0501	ex N6842Q	
☐ N991AA	Cessna 402C II	402C0317	ex N36916	
☐ N1361G	Cessna 402C II	402C0270		
☐ N1376G	Cessna 402C II	402C0271	ex N156PB	special landscape c/s
☐ N2611X	Cessna 402C II	402C0072		
☐ N2615G	Cessna 402C II	402C0101	ex C-GHGM	
☐ N2649Z	Cessna 402C II	402C0333		
☐ N2651S	Cessna 402C II	402C0342		
☐ N2714B	Cessna 402C II	402C0210		
☐ N2714M	Cessna 402C II	402C0211		
☐ N3292M	Cessna 402C II	402C0304		
☐ N4652N	Cessna 402C II	402C0011		
☐ N6813J	Cessna 402C II	402C0641		
☐ N6875D	Cessna 402C II	402C0511		special Flagship Whalers c/s
☐ N6879R	Cessna 402C II	402C0611	ex C-GJVC	
☐ N7037E	Cessna 402C II	402C0471	ex C-GGXH	
☐ N26156	Cessna 402C II	402C0112		
☐ N26514	Cessna 402C II	402C0344		
☐ N26632	Cessna 402C II	402C0404		
☐ N36911	Cessna 402C II	402C0314		
☐ N67786	Cessna 402C II	402C0631		special Key West Express c/s
☐ N67886	Cessna 402C II	402C0435		
☐ N68391	Cessna 402C II	402C0483		
☐ N68752	Cessna 402C II	402C0518		
☐ N88833	Cessna 402C II	402C0265		special flowers c/s

CAPITAL CARGO INTERNATIONAL AIRLINES — Cappy (PT/CCI) — Orlando-Intl, FL (MCO)

☐ N286SC	Boeing 727-2A1F (FedEx 3)	21601/1694	ex N328AS	Beth
☐ N287SC	Boeing 727-2A1F (FedEx 3)	21345/1673	ex N327AS	Florence
☐ N308AS	Boeing 727-227F (FedEx 3)	22002/1627	ex N479BN	Eloise
☐ N357KP	Boeing 727-230F (FedEx 3)	20675/924	ex G-BPNY	Princess Kendall
☐ N708AA	Boeing 727-223F (FedEx 3)	22465/1761		
☐ N713AA	Boeing 727-223F (FedEx 3)	22469/1769		Jessica
☐ N715AA	Boeing 727-223F (FedEx 3)	22470/1771		

☐ N755DH	Boeing 727-225F (FedEx 3)	21857/1539	ex N887MA	
☐ N801EA	Boeing 727-225F (FedEx 3)	22432/1658		Miss Ashley
☐ N808EA	Boeing 727-225F(FedEx 3)	22439/1689	ex TC-DEL	Yvonnestd JAX
☐ N815EA	Boeing 727-225F (FedEx 3)	22552/1773		Gudrund
☐ N898AA	Boeing 727-223F (FedEx 3)	22014/1663		Roberta
☐ N899AA	Boeing 727-223F (FedEx 3)	22015/1666		Angie
☐ N89427	Boeing 727-227F (FedEx 3)	21365/1273	ex N323AS	Carol
☐ N605DL	Boeing 757-232F	22812/46		
☐ N620DL	Boeing 757-232F	22910/111		
☐ N315AA	Boeing 767-223F	22317/109		

CAPITAL CITY AIR CARRIER — *Cap City (CCQ)* — *Pierre-Regional, SD (PIR)*

☐ N300VF	Piper PA-31-350 Chieftain	31-7852050	ex N27532
☐ N305SK	Piper PA-31-350 Navajo Chieftain	31-7652039	ex N59769
☐ N400RA	Piper PA-31-350 Navajo Chieftain	31-7405167	ex N22AE
☐ N777ZM	Piper PA-31-350 Chieftain	31-8052193	ex N45027
☐ N984PA	Piper PA-31-350 Navajo Chieftain	31-7305104	ex N74995
☐ N27537	Piper PA-31-350 Chieftain	31-7852053	
☐ N13PB	Piper PA-34-200T Seneca II	34-7870003	
☐ N6597F	Piper PA-34-200T Seneca II	34-7770032	
☐ N8017C	Piper PA-34-220T Seneca III	34-8133200	
☐ N8180G	Piper PA-34-200T Seneca II	34-8070174	
☐ N9638K	Piper PA-34-200T Seneca II	34-7670212	
☐ N36369	Piper PA-34-200T Seneca II	34-7870323	
☐ N126BP	Cessna 414A Chancellor	414A0214	ex N5660C
☐ N402RM	Cessna 402B	402B0607	ex C-FEAG
☐ N75156	Piper PA-32R-300 Lance	32R-7680272	

CARIBBEAN SUN AIRLINES

☐ N802WA	McDonnell-Douglas MD-83	53052/1731	ex N751LF

CARSON HELICOPTERS — *Perkasie-Heliport, PA/Jackonsville Heliport, OR*

☐ N103WF	Sikorsky S-61N	61766	ex 9M-AVO	
☐ N116AZ	Sikorsky S-61N	61242	ex VH-BHO	
☐ N302Y	Sikorsky S-61N	61472	ex YV-323C	
☐ N349FC	Sikorsky S-61 (UH-3H)	61239		
☐ N349RH	Sikorsky S-61 (UH-3H)	61117	ex Bu149702	
☐ N350DA	Sikorsky S-61 (SH-3H)	61187		
☐ N352DH	Sikorsky S-61 (SH-3H)	61161	ex N1048Y	
☐ N364DZ	Sikorsky S-61N II	61819	ex G-BGWJ	
☐ N364FH	Sikorsky S-61N II	61718	ex G-BBVA	
☐ N364HH	Sikorsky S-61N II	61712	ex G-BBHL	
☐ N410GH	Sikorsky S-61N	61749	ex V8-BSP	
☐ N502SC	Sikorsky S-61N	61737	ex G-BCLC	
☐ N561EH	Sikorsky S-61N	61471	ex ZS-RAX	
☐ N561SC	Sikorsky S-61A	61272	ex N81661	
☐ N612RM	Sikorsky S-61N	61744	ex C-FSYH	
☐ N617HM	Sikorsky S-61N	61754	ex C-GSBL	
☐ N618PA	Sikorsky S-61L	61426	ex	
☐ N725JH	Sikorsky S-61N	61775	ex V8-SAV	
☐ N905AL	Sikorsky S-61N	61717	ex V8-UDZ	
☐ N3173U	Sikorsky S-61A	61186	ex 149916	
☐ N4263A	Sikorsky S-61R	61551	ex 65-5700	
☐ N4263F	Sikorsky S-61R	61533	ex 64-14230	
☐ N4503E	Sikorsky S-61N	61220	ex G-ASNL	
☐ N6981R	Sikorsky S-61N	61453	ex	
☐ N7011M	Sikorsky S-61N	61216	ex G-AWFX	
☐ N8167B	Sikorsky S-61A	61137	ex Bu149720	
☐ N8170V	Sikorsky S-61A	61232	ex	
☐ N8174J	Sikorsky S-61R	61584	ex 66-13286	stored
☐ N9260A	Sikorsky S-61D	61442	ex Bu156496	
☐ N9271A	Sikorsky S-61D	61449	ex Bu156486	
☐ N13491	Sikorsky S-61A	61129		
☐ N42626	Sikorsky S-61R	61522	ex 63-9690	
☐ N81664	Sikorsky S-61A	61063	ex Bu148989	
☐ N81692	Sikorsky S-61A	61074	ex Bu149000	
☐ N81701	Sikorsky S-61R	61529	ex 64-14226	stored
☐ N81702	Sikorsky S-61R	61608	ex 64-14706	stored
☐ N81743	Sikorsky S-61R	61575	ex 65-12800	stored
☐ N82702	Sikorsky S-61D	61432	ex N92592	
☐ N92590	Sikorsky S-61D	61351	ex Bu152691	
☐ N239Z	de Havilland DHC-6 Twin Otter 300	239	ex N15239	Based Argentina
☐ N920R	de Havilland DHC-6 Twin Otter 100	45	ex HC-BYK	Based Argentina

CASCADE AIR — Ephrata-Municipal, WA (EPH)

☐ N272R	Douglas DC-3	13678	ex NC88824	
☐ N91314	Douglas DC-3	4538	ex NC17884	

CASTLE AVIATION — Castle (CSJ) — Akron-Canton Regional, OH (CAK)

☐ N24MG	Cessna 208B Caravan I	208B0850	ex N5261R	Freighter
☐ N27MG	Cessna 208B Caravan I	208B0650	ex N5262Z	Freighter
☐ N29MG	Cessna 208B Caravan I	208B0812	ex N52229	Freighter
☐ N31MG	Cessna 208B Caravan I	208B1065		Freighter
☐ N1029Y	Cessna 208B Caravan I	208B0325		Freighter
☐ N49MG	Piper PA-60 Aerostar 600	60-0634-7961201	ex N8232J	
☐ N52MG	Ted Smith Aerostar 600A	60-0530-172	ex N8047J	

CATALINA FLYING BOATS — Catalina Air (CBT) — Long Beach-Daugherty Field, CA (LGB)

☐ N18R	Beech E-18S	BA-312		Lsd to PPG
☐ N103AF	Beech G-18S	BA-526	ex N277S	Lsd to PPG
☐ N166H	Beech E-18S	BA-253		
☐ N403JB	Douglas DC-3	16943/34202	ex N17778	
☐ N2298C	Douglas DC-3	16453/33201	ex (N352SA)	
☐ N9375Y	Beech G-18S	BA-564		Lsd to PPG
☐ N9680B	Cessna 208B Caravan I	208B0150		

CDF AVIATION — Sacramento-Mather, CA (MHR)

☐ N481DF	Bell UH-1H	13318	ex 72-21019	104	
☐ N489DF	Bell UH-1H	12224	ex 69-15936	901	standby
☐ N490DF	Bell UH-1H	12375	ex 70-15765	205	
☐ N491DF	Bell UH-1H	12146	ex 69-15858	301	
☐ N492DF	Bell UH-1H	11433	ex 69-15145		standby
☐ N493DF	Bell UH-1H	12001	ex 69-15713		standby
☐ N494DF	Bell UH-1H	11303	ex 69-15015	404	
☐ N495DF	Bell UH-1H	12218	ex 69-15930	106	
☐ N496DF	Bell UH-1H	11964	ex 69-15676	102	
☐ N497DF	Bell UH-1H	11553	ex 69-15265	202	
☐ N498DF	Bell UH-1H	12153	ex 69-15865	406	
☐ N499DF	Bell UH-1H	12846	ex 71-20022	101	
☐ N417DF	Grumman S-2A Tracker	061	ex Bu133090	76	
☐ N443DF	Grumman S-2A Tracker	195	ex Bu133224	72	
☐ N422DF	Marsh S-2T Turbo Tracker	286C	ex N518DF	82	
☐ N424DF	Marsh S-2T Turbo Tracker	289C	ex N519DF	83	
☐ N425DF	Marsh S-2T Turbo Tracker	294C	ex N522DF	89	
☐ N426DF	Marsh S-2T Turbo Tracker	293C	ex N520DF	88	
☐ N427DF	Marsh S-2T Turbo Tracker	326C	ex N524DF	70	
☐ N428DF	Marsh S-2T Turbo Tracker	137C	ex N511DF	91	
☐ N431DF	Marsh S-2T Turbo Tracker	109C	ex N504DF	78	
☐ N432DF	Marsh S-2T Turbo Tracker	112C	ex N505DF	71	
☐ N433DF	Marsh S-2T Turbo Tracker	130C	ex N510DF	86	
☐ N434DF	Marsh S-2T Turbo Tracker	335C	ex N527DF	90	
☐ N435DF	Marsh S-2T Turbo Tracker	329C	ex N526DF	76	
☐ N437DF	Marsh S-2T Turbo Tracker	123C	ex N507DF	73	
☐ N438DF	Marsh S-2T Turbo Tracker	173C	ex N513DF	85	
☐ N439DF	Marsh S-2T Turbo Tracker	129C	ex N509DF	74	
☐ N440DF	Marsh S-2T Turbo Tracker	148C	ex N512DF	96	
☐ N441DF	Marsh S-2T Turbo Tracker	277C	ex N517DF	100	
☐ N442DF	Marsh S-2T Turbo Tracker	295C	ex Bu152826	94	
☐ N444DF	Marsh S-2T Turbo Tracker	187C	ex N515DF	75	
☐ N445DF	Marsh S-2T Turbo Tracker	232C	ex N516DF	80	
☐ N449DF	Marsh S-2T Turbo Tracker	307C	ex N523DF	81	
☐ N450DF	Marsh S-2T Turbo Tracker	228C	ex Bu152341		
☐ N400DF	Rockwell OV-10A Bronco	305-122M-65	ex Bu155454	440	
☐ N401DF	Rockwell OV-10A Bronco	305-128M-68	ex Bu155457	310	standby
☐ N402DF	Rockwell OV-10A Bronco	305-132M-70	ex Bu155459	210	
☐ N403DF	Rockwell OV-10A Bronco	305-148M-78	ex Bu155467	240	standby
☐ N407DF	Rockwell OV-10A Bronco	305-164M-86	ex Bu155475	430	
☐ N408DF	Rockwell OV-10A Bronco	305-178M-90	ex Bu155480	230	
☐ N409DF	Rockwell OV-10A Bronco	305-18M-12	ex Bu155401	330	
☐ N410DF	Rockwell OV-10A Bronco	305-158M-82	ex Bu155471	110	
☐ N413DF	Rockwell OV-10A Bronco	305-20M-13	ex Bu155402	120	
☐ N414DF	Rockwell OV-10A Bronco	305-26M-16	ex Bu155415	140	
☐ N415DF	Rockwell OV-10A Bronco	305-68M-38	ex Bu155427	460	
☐ N418DF	Rockwell OV-10A Bronco	305-70M-39	ex Bu155428	340	
☐ N421DF	Rockwell OV-10A Bronco	305-206M-107	ex Bu155496	240	
☐ N429DF	Rockwell OV-10A Bronco	305A-17M-11	ex Bu155400	310	

CENTRAL AIR SOUTHWEST — Central Commuter (CTL) — Kansas City-Downtown, KS/Cushing-Municipal, OK (MKC/CUH)

Reg	Type	C/n	Previous identity
☐ N23BQ	Aero Commander 500B	1065-46	ex N6196X
☐ N30MB	Aero Commander 500B	1453-160	ex N6376U
☐ N107DF	Aero Commander 500B	1191-97	ex N88PC
☐ N127KH	Aero Commander 500B	1027-38	ex N801TC
☐ N261ER	Aero Commander 500B	1362-133	ex N780SP
☐ N272CA	Aero Commander 500B	1409-146	ex N635BC
☐ N304JT	Aero Commander 500B	1494-175	ex N222AV
☐ N324RR	Aero Commander 500B	1386-139	ex N471A
☐ N411ET	Aero Commander 500B	1621-214	ex N445CA
☐ N411JF	Aero Commander 500B	1014-35	ex N6178X
☐ N411JT	Rockwell 500S Shrike Commander	3097	ex N9134N
☐ N411PT	Aero Commander 500B	1207-99	ex N291CA
☐ N415BH	Aero Commander 500B	918-5	ex N6129X
☐ N443WA	Aero Commander 500B	1315-124	ex N553RA
☐ N444CA	Aero Commander 500B	1458-162	ex N6326U
☐ N444CB	Aero Commander 500B	1119-69	ex N6229X
☐ N446AE	Aero Commander 500B	1613-211	ex N724LH
☐ N477CC	Aero Commander 500B	1480-172	ex N477CA
☐ N516DT	Aero Commander 500B	1574-200	ex N134X
☐ N518TM	Aero Commander 500B	995-26	ex N6156X
☐ N524HW	Aero Commander 500B	1533-191	ex N324MA
☐ N607MM	Aero Commander 500U Shrike	1712-25	ex N252LD
☐ N610BW	Aero Commander 500B	1523-185	ex N159BM
☐ N615MT	Aero Commander 500B	911-2	ex N193CA
☐ N626DS	Aero Commander 500B	1460-163	ex N315TG
☐ N630KC	Aero Commander 500B	997-28	ex N6163X
☐ N662MW	Aero Commander 500B	1235-106	ex N106CA
☐ N667CA	Aero Commander 500B	1468-166	ex C-FRJU
☐ N690RR	Aero Commander 500B	1169-88	ex N6289X
☐ N716TC	Aero Commander 500B	1225-102	ex N192CA
☐ N777CM	Aero Commander 500B	1412-147	ex N120EL
☐ N888CA	Aero Commander 500B	1318-127	ex N621RM
☐ N917GT	Aero Commander 500B	1137-77	ex N177CA
☐ N922BS	Aero Commander 500B	1598-207	ex N1193Z
☐ N6154X	Aero Commander 500B	983-24	
☐ N6324U	Aero Commander 500B	1363-134	
☐ N690AT	Rockwell 690A Turbo Commander	11202	ex N600PB

CENTURION II AIR CARGO — Challenge Cargo (WE/CWC) — Miami-Intl, FL (MIA)

Reg	Type	C/n	Previous identity	Name	Notes
☐ N279AX	Douglas DC-10-30F	47816/316	ex N47816	Wings of Miami	stored SFB
☐ N612GC	Douglas DC-10-30F	47840/337	ex G-BHDJ		
☐ N701GC	McDonnell-Douglas MD-11F	48434/476	ex PP-VOP		
☐ N984AR	McDonnell-Douglas MD-11BCF	48429/500	ex N429AN		
☐ N47888	Douglas DC-10-30F	47888/291	ex G-MULL		

CHAMPLAIN AIR — Plattsburg-Clinton County, NY (PLB)

Reg	Type	C/n	Previous identity	Name
☐ N59NA	Douglas DC-3	9043	ex G-AKNB	
☐ N700CA	Douglas DC-3	12438	ex N107AD	Mary Ann

CHANNEL ISLANDS AVIATION — Channel (CHN) — Camarillo, CA (CMA)

Reg	Type	C/n	Previous identity
☐ N55JA	Britten-Norman BN-2A-8 Islander	295	ex G-51-295
☐ N2722D	Cessna 441 Conquest II	441-0168	
☐ N6844D	Cessna 425 Conquest I	425-0062	

CHAUTAUQUA AIRLINES — Chautauqua (RP/CHQ) — Indianapolis-Intl, IN (IND)

Operates as US Airways Express from Boston, ME, Indianapolis, IN, Pittsburgh, PA and New York-La Guardia, NY. Also operates as American Connection from St Louis, MO, as Delta Connection from Orlando, FL, as United Express from Chicago, IL and Washington, DC and as Continental Express from Cleveland, OH, Houston, TX and Newark, NJ.
Wholly owned subsidiary of Republic Airways Holdings.

CHERRY-AIR — Cherry (CCY) — Dallas-Addison, TX (ADS)

Reg	Type	C/n	Previous identity	Notes
☐ N207CA	AMD Falcon 20D	153	ex N70MD	
☐ N209CA	AMD Falcon 20C	71	ex N195AS	
☐ N216CA	AMD Falcon 20C	11	ex N983AJ	
☐ N217CA	AMD Falcon 20C	75	ex UR-EFB	
☐ N218CA	AMD Falcon 20D	218	ex EC-EEU	
☐ N219CA	AMD Falcon 20D	193	ex 9Q-CTT	
☐ N220CA	AMD Falcon 20D	220	ex EC-EDL	
☐ N234CA	AMD Falcon 20C	17	ex N55TH	
☐ N235CA	AMD Falcon 20C	139	ex N900WB	
☐ N140CA	Learjet 25	25B-140	ex N403AC	stored ADS

☐ N151WW	Learjet 24	24-170	ex N200DH	
☐ N213CA	Learjet 25D	25D-241	ex N713LJ	stored ADS
☐ N233CA	Learjet 25B	25B-133	ex XA-RZY	
☐ N236CA	Learjet 25B	25B-161	ex N61EW	stored ADS
☐ N238CA	Learjet 25	25-040	ex N23FN	
☐ N343CA	Learjet 25B	25B-202	ex YU-BRA	

CIMARRON AIRE — *Cimmaron Aire (CMN)* — *McAlester-Regional, OK (MLC)*

☐ N737SW	Beech E-18S	BA-402	ex N388W	Freighter

COASTAL AIR TRANSPORT — *Coastal (DQ/CXT)* — *St Croix-Alexander Hamilton, VI (STX)*

☐ N676MF	Cessna 402B	402B0106	ex N7856Q	Cruzan Queen
☐ N677MF	Cessna 404 Titan	404-0421	ex N96889	

COASTAL HELICOPTER — *Juneau-Intl, AK (JNU)*

☐ N178CH	Aérospatiale AS350B2 AStar	2042	ex N910TV
☐ N203CH	Aérospatiale AS350BA AStar	1430	ex N57843
☐ N204CH	Aérospatiale AS350B1 AStar	2054	ex N6080D
☐ N205CH	Aérospatiale AS350BA AStar	1254	ex N3607S
☐ N207CH	Aérospatiale AS350B1 AStar	2027	ex C-FUAM
☐ N209CH	Aérospatiale AS350BA AStar	2494	ex N532BH
☐ N216CH	Aérospatiale AS350B2 AStar	3619	ex N67PT
☐ N655TV	Aérospatiale AS350B AStar	1590	ex N38TH
☐ N57717	Aérospatiale AS350A+ AStar	1334	ex N112SH
☐ N53AG	Bell UH-1H	13827	ex 72-21588
☐ N371AH	Bell 206B JetRanger	1660	ex N450AS
☐ N496CH	Bell 206B JetRanger	1905	ex N49686

COLGAN AIR — *Colgan (9L/CJC)* — *Manassas-Regional, VA (MNZ)*

☐ N202SR	SAAB SF.340B	340B-202	ex N305CE
☐ N210CJ	SAAB SF.340B	340B-210	ex N308CE
☐ N251CJ	SAAB SF.340B	340B-251	ex XA-TQO

United Express, also at Washington-Dulles, DC.

COLUMBIA HELICOPTERS — *Columbia Heli (WCO)* — *Aurora-State, OR/Lake Charles-Regional, LA (UAO/LCH)*

☐ C-FHFW	Boeing Vertol 107 II	107	ex N188CH	Lsd to Helifor
☐ C-GHFF	Boeing Vertol 107 II	406	ex N195CH	Lsd to Helifor
☐ C-GHFY	Boeing Vertol 107 II	2002	ex N190CH	
☐ N184CH	Kawasaki KV107-II	4001	ex Thai 4001	
☐ N185CH	Kawasaki KV107-II	4003	ex Thai 4003	
☐ N186CH	Kawasaki KV107-II	4005	ex P2-CHA	
☐ N187CH	Kawasaki KV107-II	4012	ex HC-BZP	
☐ N191CH	Boeing Vertol 107 II	2003	ex P2-CHD	
☐ N192CH	Kawasaki KV107-II	4011	ex JA9505	
☐ N194CH	Boeing Vertol 107 II	404	ex 04454	
☐ N6672D	Boeing Vertol 107 II	2		
☐ N6674D	Boeing Vertol 107 II	4	ex C-FHFV	
☐ N6676D	Boeing Vertol 107 II	6		
☐ C-FHFB	Boeing Vertol 234UT Chinook	MJ-005	ex N238CH	Lsd to Helifor
☐ HC-CEN	Boeing Vertol 234UT Chinook	MJ-016	ex N241CH	Lsd to Icaro
☐ N235CH	Boeing Vertol 234UT Chinook	MJ-002	ex G-BISO	
☐ N239CH	Boeing Vertol 234UT Chinook	MJ-006	ex C-FHFJ	
☐ N242CH	Boeing Vertol 234UT Chinook	MJ-023	ex HC-BYF	
☐ N245CH	Boeing Vertol 234UT Chinook	MJ-022	ex P2-CHJ	
☐ N246CH	Boeing Vertol 234UT Chinook	MJ-017	ex LN-OMK	
☐ P2-CHI	Boeing Vertol 234UT Chinook	MJ-003	ex N237CH	Lsd to TOK
☐ N111NS	Beech 200C Super King Air	BL-36		
☐ N3697F	Beech 200C Super King Air	BL-14		

COMAIR — *Comair (OH/COM)* — *Cincinnati-Northern Kentucky Intl, OH (CVG)*

Wholly owned subsidiary of Delta Air Lines operates as Delta Connection in full colours and using DL flight numbers from Cincinnati, OH and Orlando, FL.

COMMUTAIR — *Commutair (C5/UCA)* — *Plattsburgh-Clinton County, NY (PLB)*

Operates as Continental Connection in full colours and using CO flight numbers. Commutair is a trading name of Champlain Enterprises. Lease sixteen de Havilland DHC-8Q-200s from Horizon Airlines for service from Cleveland.

COMPASS AIRLINES — *(CP/CPZ)* — *Washington-Dulles-Intl, DC (IAD)*

Wholly owned subsidiary of Northwest Airlines (nwa) and operates as nwa airlink (Northwest Airlink).

CONTINENTAL AIRLINES	***Continental (CO/COA)*** ***Cleveland, OH/Houston-Intercontinental, TX/Newark, NJ (CLE/IAH/EWR)***

Member of Star Alliance

Fleets are listed in last three order

	Registration	Type	C/n	Previous identity	Fleet no.	Notes
☐	N63305	Boeing 737-3T0	23356/1133		305	
☐	N14308	Boeing 737-3T0	23359/1144		308	stored ARG
☐	N16310	Boeing 737-3T0	23361/1150		310	stored VCV
☐	N69311	Boeing 737-3T0	23362/1152		311	stored VCV
☐	N12318	Boeing 737-3T0	23369/1188		318	
☐	N12319	Boeing 737-3T0	23370/1190		319	stored HOU
☐	N14320	Boeing 737-3T0	23371/1191		320	stored GYR
☐	N12322	Boeing 737-3T0/W	23373/1202		322	stored ARG
☐	N10323	Boeing 737-3T0/W	23374/1204		323	stored GYR
☐	N14324	Boeing 737-3T0/W	23375/1207		324	
☐	N14325	Boeing 737-3T0	23455/1228		325	
☐	N17326	Boeing 737-3T0	23456/1230		326	stored GWO
☐	N12327	Boeing 737-3T0	23457/1238		327	stored GWO
☐	N17329	Boeing 737-3T0	23459/1247		329	
☐	N70330	Boeing 737-3T0	23460/1253		330	stored Walnut Ridge
☐	N14334	Boeing 737-3T0	23572/1296		334	stored ARG
☐	N14336	Boeing 737-3T0/W	23574/1328		336	
☐	N16339	Boeing 737-3T0	23577/1340		339	stored GYR
☐	N17344	Boeing 737-3T0/W	23582/1383		344	stored GYR
☐	N70353	Boeing 737-3T0	23591/1472		353	
☐	N76355	Boeing 737-3T0	23593/1478		355	stored GYR
☐	N17356	Boeing 737-3T0	23942/1522	ex N320AW	356	stored ARG
☐	N19357	Boeing 737-3T0	23841/1518	ex N301AL	357	stored GYR
☐	N14604	Boeing 737-524/W	27317/2576		604	stored GYR
☐	N58606	Boeing 737-524/W	27319/2590		606	stored GYR
☐	N27610	Boeing 737-524/W	27323/2616		610	stored GYR
☐	N11612	Boeing 737-524/W	27325/2630		612	stored GYR
☐	N14613	Boeing 737-524/W	27326/2633		613	stored GYR
☐	N17614	Boeing 737-524/W	27327/2634		614	stored GYR
☐	N16617	Boeing 737-524/W	27330/2648		617	
☐	N17619	Boeing 737-524/W	27332/2659		619	
☐	N17620	Boeing 737-524/W	27333/2660	ex N1790B	620	
☐	N19621	Boeing 737-524/W	27334/2661		621	
☐	N18622	Boeing 737-524/W	27526/2669		622	
☐	N19623	Boeing 737-524/W	27527/2672		623	
☐	N13624	Boeing 737-524/W	27528/2675		624	
☐	N46625	Boeing 737-524/W	27529/2683		625	
☐	N32626	Boeing 737-524/W	27530/2686		626	
☐	N17627	Boeing 737-524/W	27531/2700		627	
☐	N14628	Boeing 737-524/W	27532/2712		628	
☐	N14629	Boeing 737-524/W	27533/2725		629	
☐	N59630	Boeing 737-524/W	27534/2726		630	
☐	N62631	Boeing 737-524/W	27535/2728		631	
☐	N16632	Boeing 737-524/W	27900/2736		632	
☐	N24633	Boeing 737-524/W	27901/2743		633	
☐	N19638	Boeing 737-524/W	28899/2912		638	
☐	N14639	Boeing 737-524/W	28900/2913		639	
☐	N17640	Boeing 737-524/W	28901/2924		640	
☐	N11641	Boeing 737-524/W	28902/2926		641	
☐	N16642	Boeing 737-524/W	28903/2927		642	
☐	N17644	Boeing 737-524/W	28905/2934	ex N1786B	644	
☐	N14645	Boeing 737-524/W	28906/2935	ex N1786B	645	
☐	N16646	Boeing 737-524/W	28907/2956	ex N1786B	646	
☐	N16647	Boeing 737-524/W	28908/2958		647	
☐	N16648	Boeing 737-524/W	28909/2960		648	
☐	N16649	Boeing 737-524/W	28910/2972		649	
☐	N16650	Boeing 737-524/W	28911/2973		650	
☐	N11651	Boeing 737-524/W	28912/2980	ex (N16651)	651	
☐	N14652	Boeing 737-524/W	28913/2985		652	
☐	N14653	Boeing 737-524/W	28914/2986		653	
☐	N14654	Boeing 737-524/W	28915/2993		654	stored GYR
☐	N14655	Boeing 737-524/W	28916/2994		655	stored GYR
☐	N16701	Boeing 737-724/W	28762/29	ex N1786B	701	
☐	N24702	Boeing 737-724/W	28763/32		702	
☐	N16703	Boeing 737-724/W	28764/37		703	
☐	N14704	Boeing 737-724/W	28765/43		704	
☐	N25705	Boeing 737-724/W	28766/46		705	
☐	N24706	Boeing 737-724/W	28767/47		706	
☐	N23707	Boeing 737-724/W	28768/48	ex N1787B	707	
☐	N23708	Boeing 737-724/W	28769/52		708	
☐	N16709	Boeing 737-724/W	28779/93		709	
☐	N15710	Boeing 737-724/W	28780/94		710	
☐	N54711	Boeing 737-724/W	28782/97	ex N1786B	711	
☐	N15712	Boeing 737-724/W	28783/105	ex N1786B	712	
☐	N16713	Boeing 737-724/W	28784/107	ex N1786B	713	

☐ N33714	Boeing 737-724/W	28785/119	ex N1786B	714		
☐ N24715	Boeing 737-724/W	28786/125	ex N1795B	715		
☐ N13716	Boeing 737-724/W	28787/156	ex N1782B	716		
☐ N29717	Boeing 737-724/W	28936/182	ex N1786B	717		
☐ N13718	Boeing 737-724/W	28937/185	ex N1786B	718		
☐ N17719	Boeing 737-724/W	28938/195	ex N1786B	719		
☐ N13720	Boeing 737-724/W	28939/214	ex N1786B	720		
☐ N23721	Boeing 737-724/W	28940/219		721		
☐ N27722	Boeing 737-724/W	28789/247	ex N1786B	722		
☐ N21723	Boeing 737-724/W	28790/253	ex N1787B	723		
☐ N27724	Boeing 737-724/W	28791/283	ex N1787B	724		
☐ N49725	Boeing 737-724/W			725		on order
☐ N39726	Boeing 737-724/W	28796/315	ex N1787B	726		
☐ N38727	Boeing 737-724/W	28797/317	ex N1786B	727		
☐ N39728	Boeing 737-724/W	28944/321	ex N1786B	728		
☐ N24729	Boeing 737-724/W	28945/325	ex N1784B	729		
☐ N17730	Boeing 737-724/W	28798/338	ex N1786B	730		
☐ N14731	Boeing 737-724/W	28799/346	ex N1786B	731		
☐ N16732	Boeing 737-724/W	28948/352	ex N60436	732		
☐ N27733	Boeing 737-724/W	28800/364	ex N1786B	733	Sir Samuel J LeFrak	
☐ N27734	Boeing 737-724/W	28949/371	ex N1786B	734		
☐ N14735	Boeing 737-724/W	28950/376	ex N1786B	735		
☐ N24736	Boeing 737-724/W	28803/380	ex N1786B	736		
☐ N13738	Boeing 737-724/W			738		on order
☐ N17739	Boeing 737-724/W			739		on order
☐ N15740	Boeing 737-724/W			740		on order
☐ N14741	Boeing 737-724/W			741		on order
☐ N15742	Boeing 737-724/W			742		on order
☐ N19743	Boeing 737-724/W			743		on order
☐ N13744	Boeing 737-724/W			744		on order
☐ N19745	Boeing 737-724/W			745		on order
☐ N12746	Boeing 737-724/W			746		on order
☐ N15747	Boeing 737-724/W			747		on order
☐ N23748	Boeing 737-724/W			748		on order
☐ N13750	Boeing 737-724/W	28941/286		750		

☐ N25201	Boeing 737-824/W	28958/443	ex N1786B	201
☐ N24202	Boeing 737-824/W	30429/581	ex N1786B	202
☐ N33203	Boeing 737-824/W	30613/591	ex N1786B	203
☐ N35204	Boeing 737-824/W	30576/606	ex N1795B	204
☐ N27205	Boeing 737-824/W	30577/615	ex N1786B	205
☐ N11206	Boeing 737-824/W	30578/618	ex N1786B	206
☐ N36207	Boeing 737-824/W	30579/627	ex N1786B	207
☐ N26208	Boeing 737-824/W	30580/644	ex N1786B	208
☐ N33209	Boeing 737-824/W	30581/647	ex N1786B	209
☐ N26210	Boeing 737-824/W	28770/56		210
☐ N24211	Boeing 737-824/W	28771/58		211
☐ N24212	Boeing 737-824/W	28772/63		212
☐ N27213	Boeing 737-824/W	28773/65		213
☐ N14214	Boeing 737-824/W	28774/74		214
☐ N26215	Boeing 737-824/W	28775/76		215
☐ N12216	Boeing 737-824/W	28776/79		216
☐ N16217	Boeing 737-824/W	28777/81		217
☐ N12218	Boeing 737-824/W	28778/84		218
☐ N14219	Boeing 737-824/W	28781/88		219
☐ N18220	Boeing 737-824/W	28929/134	ex N60436	220
☐ N12221	Boeing 737-824/W	28930/153	ex N1796B	221
☐ N34222	Boeing 737-824/W	28931/159		222
☐ N18223	Boeing 737-824/W	28932/162	ex N1786B	223
☐ N24224	Boeing 737-824/W	28933/165	ex N1782B	224
☐ N12225	Boeing 737-824/W	28934/168	ex N1782B	225
☐ N26226	Boeing 737-824/W	28935/171	ex N1787B	226
☐ N13227	Boeing 737-824/W	28788/262	ex N1787B	227
☐ N14228	Boeing 737-824/W	28792/281	ex N1787B	228
☐ N17229	Boeing 737-824/W	28793/287	ex N1786B	229
☐ N14230	Boeing 737-824/W	28794/296	ex N1787B	230
☐ N14231	Boeing 737-824/W	28795/300	ex N1787B	231
☐ N26232	Boeing 737-824/W	28942/304		232
☐ N17233	Boeing 737-824/W	28943/328	ex N1787B	233
☐ N16234	Boeing 737-824/W	28946/334	ex N1787B	234
☐ N14235	Boeing 737-824/W	28947/342		235
☐ N35236	Boeing 737-824/W	28801/367	ex N1786B	236
☐ N14237	Boeing 737-824/W	28802/374		237
☐ N12238	Boeing 737-824/W	28804/386	ex N1786B	238
☐ N27239	Boeing 737-824/W	28951/391	ex N1787B	239
☐ N14240	Boeing 737-824/W	28952/394	ex N1786B	240
☐ N54241	Boeing 737-824/W	28953/395	ex N1787B	241
☐ N14242	Boeing 737-824/W	28805/402	ex N1786B	242
☐ N18243	Boeing 737-824/W	28806/403	ex N1786B	243
☐ N17244	Boeing 737-824/W	28954/409	ex N1787B	244
☐ N17245	Boeing 737-824/W	28955/411	ex N1786B	245
☐ N27246	Boeing 737-824/W	28956/413	ex N1786B	246
☐ N36247	Boeing 737-824/W	28807/431	ex N1786B	247

	Reg	Type	C/n	Previous	Fleet no	Remarks
☐	N13248	Boeing 737-824/W	28808/435	ex N1786B	248	
☐	N14249	Boeing 737-824/W	28809/438	ex N1786B	249	
☐	N14250	Boeing 737-824/W	28957/441	ex N1786B	250	
☐	N73251	Boeing 737-824/W	30582/650	ex N1786B	251	
☐	N37252	Boeing 737-824/W	30583/656	ex N1787B	252	
☐	N37253	Boeing 737-824/W	30584/660		253	
☐	N76254	Boeing 737-824/W	30779/667	ex N1786B	254	
☐	N37255	Boeing 737-824/W	30610/686	ex N1787B	255	
☐	N73256	Boeing 737-824/W	30611/692	ex N1787B	256	
☐	N38257	Boeing 737-824/W	30612/706	ex N1786B	257	
☐	N77258	Boeing 737-824/W	30802/708	ex N1786B	258	
☐	N73259	Boeing 737-824/W	30803/854	ex N1786B	259	
☐	N35260	Boeing 737-824/W	30855/862	ex N1786B	260	
☐	N77261	Boeing 737-824/W	31582/897	ex N1786B	261	
☐	N33262	Boeing 737-824/W	32402/901	ex N1786B	262	
☐	N37263	Boeing 737-824/W	31583/906	ex N1786B	263	
☐	N33264	Boeing 737-824/W	31584/916	ex N1786B	264	
☐	N76265	Boeing 737-824/W	31585/928	ex N1786B	265	
☐	N33266	Boeing 737-824/W	32403/930		266	
☐	N37267	Boeing 737-824/W	31586/939	ex N1786B	267	
☐	N38268	Boeing 737-824/W	31587/957	ex N1786B	268	
☐	N76269	Boeing 737-824/W	31588/966	ex N1786B	269	
☐	N73270	Boeing 737-824/W	31632/970	ex N1787B	270	
☐	N35271	Boeing 737-824/W	31589/982	ex N1786B	271	
☐	N36272	Boeing 737-824/W	31590/987	ex N1795B	272	
☐	N37273	Boeing 737-824/W	31591/1012	ex N1787B	273	
☐	N37274	Boeing 737-824/W	31592/1062		274	
☐	N73275	Boeing 737-824/W	31593/1077		275	
☐	N73276	Boeing 737-824/W	31594/1079		276	
☐	N37277	Boeing 737-824/W	31595/1099		277	
☐	N73278	Boeing 737-824/W	31596/1390		278	
☐	N79279	Boeing 737-824/W	31597/1411	ex N1787B	279	
☐	N36280	Boeing 737-824/W	31598/1423		280	
☐	N37281	Boeing 737-824/W	31599/1425		281	
☐	N34282	Boeing 737-824/W	31634/1440		282	
☐	N73283	Boeing 737-824/W	31606/1456		283	
☐	N33284	Boeing 737-824/W	31635/1475		284	
☐	N78285	Boeing 737-824/W	33452/1540		285	
☐	N33286	Boeing 737-824/W	31600/1506		286	
☐	N37287	Boeing 737-824/W	31636/1509		287	
☐	N76288	Boeing 737-824/W	33451/1516		288	
☐	N33289	Boeing 737-824/W	31607/1542	ex N1786B	289	
☐	N37290	Boeing 737-824/W	31601/1567		290	
☐	N73291	Boeing 737-824/W	33454/1611		291	
☐	N33292	Boeing 737-824/W	33455/1622		292	
☐	N37293	Boeing 737-824/W	33453/1743		293	
☐	N33294	Boeing 737-824/W	34000/1762		294	
☐	N77295	Boeing 737-824/W	34001/1779		295	
☐	N77296	Boeing 737-824/W	34002/1787		296	
☐	N39297	Boeing 737-824/W	34003/1791		297	
☐	N37298	Boeing 737-824/W	34004/1813		298	
☐	N73299	Boeing 737-824/W	34005/1821	ex N1786B	299	
☐	N78501	Boeing 737-824/W	31602/1994	ex N1786B	501	
☐	N76502	Boeing 737-824/W	31603/2017		502	
☐	N76503	Boeing 737-824/W	33461/2023		503	
☐	N76504	Boeing 737-824/W	31604/2035		504	
☐	N76505	Boeing 737-824/W	32834/2048	ex N1786B	505	
☐	N78506	Boeing 737-824/W	32832/2065		506	
☐	N87507	Boeing 737-824/W	31637/2487	ex N1786B	507	
☐	N76508	Boeing 737-824/W	31639/2514		508	
☐	N78509	Boeing 737-824/W	31638/2523	ex N1787B	509	
☐	N77510	Boeing 737-824/W	32828/2579		510	
☐	N78511	Boeing 737-824/W	33459/2598		511	
☐	N87512	Boeing 737-824/W	33458/2602		512	
☐	N87513	Boeing 737-824/W	31621/2655		513	
☐	N76514	Boeing 737-824/W	31626/2680		514	
☐	N76515	Boeing 737-824/W	31623/2713		515	
☐	N76516	Boeing 737-824/W	37096/2718		516	
☐	N76517	Boeing 737-824/W	31628/2723		518	
☐	N77518	Boeing 737-824/W	31605/2768		518	
☐	N76519	Boeing 737-824/W	30132/3138		519	on order
☐	N77520	Boeing 737-824/W	31658/3158		520	on order
☐	N79521	Boeing 737-824/W	31662		521	on order
☐	N76522	Boeing 737-824/W	31660		522	on order
☐	N76523	Boeing 737-824/W	37101		523	on order
☐	N78524	Boeing 737-824/W	31642		524	on order
☐	N77525	Boeing 737-824/W	31659		525	on order
☐		Boeing 737-824/W				on order
☐		Boeing 737-824/W				on order
☐	N30401	Boeing 737-924/W	30118/820		401	
☐	N79402	Boeing 737-924/W	30119/857		402	
☐	N38403	Boeing 737-924/W	30120/884	ex N1786B	403	

☐ N32404	Boeing 737-924/W	30121/893	ex N1787B	404
☐ N72405	Boeing 737-924/W	30122/911	ex N1786B	405
☐ N73406	Boeing 737-924/W	30123/943	ex N1786B	406
☐ N35407	Boeing 737-924/W	30124/951	ex N1786B	407
☐ N37408	Boeing 737-924/W	30125/962	ex N1787B	408
☐ N37409	Boeing 737-924/W	30126/1004	ex N1787B	409
☐ N75410	Boeing 737-924/W	30127/1021	ex N1786B	410
☐ N71411	Boeing 737-924/W	30128/1052		411
☐ N31412	Boeing 737-924/W	30129/1112		412
☐ N37413	Boeing 737-924ER/W	31664/2474		413
☐ N47414	Boeing 737-924ER/W	32827/2490	ex N1787B	414
☐ N39415	Boeing 737-924ER/W	32826/2516		415
☐ N39416	Boeing 737-924ER/W	37093/2528		416
☐ N38417	Boeing 737-924ER/W	31665/2541		417
☐ N39418	Boeing 737-924ER/W	33456/2547		418
☐ N37419	Boeing 737-924ER/W	31666/2553		419
☐ N37420	Boeing 737-924ER/W	33457/2565		420
☐ N27421	Boeing 737-924ER/W	37094/2577		421
☐ N37422	Boeing 737-924ER/W	31620/2614		422
☐ N39423	Boeing 737-924ER/W	32829/2645		423
☐ N38424	Boeing 737-924ER/W	37095/2651		424
☐ N75425	Boeing 737-924ER/W	33460/2657		425
☐ N75426	Boeing 737-924ER/W	31622/2676		426
☐ N37427	Boeing 737-924ER/W	37097/2707		427
☐ N75428	Boeing 737-924ER/W	31633/2737		428
☐ N75429	Boeing 737-924ER/W	30130/2750		429
☐ N77430	Boeing 737-924ER/W	37098/2774	ex N1786B	430
☐ N77431	Boeing 737-924ER/W	32833/2787		431
☐ N75432	Boeing 737-924ER/W	32835/2817		432
☐ N75433	Boeing 737-924ER/W	33527/2842		433
☐ N37434	Boeing 737-924ER/W	33528/2891		434
☐ N75435	Boeing 737-924ER/W	33529/2916		435
☐ N75436	Boeing 737-924ER/W	33531/2947		436
☐ N37437	Boeing 737-924ER/W	33532/2959		437
☐ N78438	Boeing 737-924ER/W	33533/2971		438
☐ N57439	Boeing 737-924ER/W	33534/2990	ex N1786B	439
☐ N45440	Boeing 737-924ER/W	33535/2996		440
☐ N53441	Boeing 737-924ER/W	30131/3014	ex N1787B	441
☐ N53442	Boeing 737-924ER/W	33536/3027		442
☐ N58101	Boeing 757-224/W	27291/614		101
☐ N14102	Boeing 757-224/W	27292/619		102
☐ N33103	Boeing 757-224/W	27293/623		103
☐ N17104	Boeing 757-224/W	27294/629		104
☐ N17105	Boeing 757-224/W	27295/632		105
☐ N14106	Boeing 757-224/W	27296/637		106 Sam E Ashmore
☐ N14107	Boeing 757-224/W	27297/641		107
☐ N21108	Boeing 757-224/W	27298/645		108
☐ N12109	Boeing 757-224/W	27299/648		109
☐ N13110	Boeing 757-224/W	27300/650		110
☐ N57111	Boeing 757-224/W	27301/652		111
☐ N18112	Boeing 757-224/W	27302/653		112
☐ N13113	Boeing 757-224/W	27555/668		113
☐ N12114	Boeing 757-224/W	27556/682		114
☐ N14115	Boeing 757-224/W	27557/686		115
☐ N12116	Boeing 757-224/W	27558/702		116
☐ N19117	Boeing 757-224/W	27559/706		117
☐ N14118	Boeing 757-224/W	27560/748	ex (N19118)	118
☐ N18119	Boeing 757-224/W	27561/753		119
☐ N14120	Boeing 757-224/W	27562/761		120
☐ N14121	Boeing 757-224/W	27563/766		121
☐ N17122	Boeing 757-224/W	27564/768		122
☐ N26123	Boeing 757-224/W	28966/781		123
☐ N29124	Boeing 757-224/W	27565/786		124
☐ N12125	Boeing 757-224/W	28967/788	ex N1787B	125
☐ N17126	Boeing 757-224/W	27566/790		126
☐ N48127	Boeing 757-224/W	28968/791		127
☐ N17128	Boeing 757-224/W	27567/795		128
☐ N29129	Boeing 757-224/W	28969/796		129
☐ N19130	Boeing 757-224/W	28970/799		130
☐ N34131	Boeing 757-224/W	28971/806		131
☐ N33132	Boeing 757-224/W	29281/809		132
☐ N17133	Boeing 757-224/W	29282/840		133
☐ N67134	Boeing 757-224/W	29283/848	ex N1800B	134
☐ N41135	Boeing 757-224/W	29284/851		135
☐ N19136	Boeing 757-224/W	29285/856		136
☐ N34137	Boeing 757-224/W	30229/899		137
☐ N13138	Boeing 757-224/W	30351/903	ex N1795B	138
☐ N17139	Boeing 757-224/W	30352/911		139
☐ N41140	Boeing 757-224/W	30353/913		140
☐ N19141	Boeing 757-224/W	30354/933		141
☐ N75851	Boeing 757-324/W	32810/990		851

☐ N57852 Boeing 757-324 32811/995 852
☐ N75853 Boeing 757-324 32812/997 853
☐ N75854 Boeing 757-324/W 32813/999 854
☐ N57855 Boeing 757-324 32814/1038 855
☐ N74856 Boeing 757-324 32815/1039 856
☐ N57857 Boeing 757-324/W 32816/1040 857
☐ N75858 Boeing 757-324/W 32817/1042 858
☐ N56859 Boeing 757-324/W 32818/1043 859 last 757-300 built
☐ N73860 Boeing 757-33N/W 32584/972 ex N550TZ 860
☐ N75861 Boeing 757-33N/W 32585/976 ex N551TZ 861
☐ N57862 Boeing 757-33N/W 32586/978 ex N552TZ 863
☐ N57863 Boeing 757-33N 32587/980 ex N553TZ 863
☐ N57864 Boeing 757-33N/W 32588/985 ex N554TZ 864
☐ N77865 Boeing 757-33N/W 32589/1003 ex N555TZ 865
☐ N78866 Boeing 757-33N 32591/1007 ex N557TZ 866
☐ N77867 Boeing 757-33N/W 32592/1008 ex N558TZ 867
☐ N57868 Boeing 757-33N 32590/1017 ex N556TZ 868
☐ N57869 Boeing 757-33N 32593/1018 ex N559TZ 869
☐ N57870 Boeing 757-33N 33525/1031 ex N560TZ 870
☐ N77871 Boeing 757-33N/W 33526/1032 ex N561TZ 871

☐ N76151 Boeing 767-224ER 30430/811 ex (N37165) 151
☐ N73152 Boeing 767-224ER 30431/815 ex (N37166) 152
☐ N76153 Boeing 767-224ER 30432/819 ex (N37167) 153
☐ N69154 Boeing 767-224ER 30433/823 ex (N37168) 154
☐ N68155 Boeing 767-224ER 30434/825 ex (N37169) 155
☐ N76156 Boeing 767-224ER 30435/827 ex (N37170) 156
☐ N67157 Boeing 767-224ER 30436/833 157
☐ N67158 Boeing 767-224ER 30437/839 158
☐ N68159 Boeing 767-224ER 30438/845 159
☐ N68160 Boeing 767-224ER 30439/851 160

☐ N66051 Boeing 767-424ER 29446/799 ex (N76401) 051
☐ N67052 Boeing 767-424ER 29447/805 ex (N87402) 052
☐ N59053 Boeing 767-424ER 29448/809 ex (N47403) 053
☐ N76054 Boeing 767-424ER 29449/816 ex (N87404) 054
☐ N76055 Boeing 767-424ER 29450/826 055
☐ N66056 Boeing 767-424ER 29451/842 056
☐ N66057 Boeing 767-424ER 29452/859 057
☐ N67058 Boeing 767-424ER 29453/862 058
☐ N69059 Boeing 767-424ER 29454/864 059
☐ N78060 Boeing 767-424ER 29455/866 060
☐ N68061 Boeing 767-424ER 29456/868 061
☐ N76062 Boeing 767-424ER 29457/869 062
☐ N69063 Boeing 767-424ER 29458/872 063
☐ N76064 Boeing 767-424ER 29459/873 064
☐ N76065 Boeing 767-424ER 29460/876 065
☐ N77066 Boeing 767-424ER 29461/878 066

☐ N78001 Boeing 777-224ER 27577/161 001 Gordon M Bethune
☐ N78002 Boeing 777-224ER 27578/165 002
☐ N78003 Boeing 777-224ER 27579/167 003
☐ N78004 Boeing 777-224ER 27580/169 004
☐ N78005 Boeing 777-224ER 27581/177 005
☐ N77006 Boeing 777-224ER 29476/183 006 Robert F Six
☐ N74007 Boeing 777-224ER 29477/197 007
☐ N78008 Boeing 777-224ER 29478/200 008
☐ N78009 Boeing 777-224ER 29479/211 009
☐ N76010 Boeing 777-224ER 29480/220 010
☐ N79011 Boeing 777-224ER 29859/227 011
☐ N77012 Boeing 777-224ER 29860/234 012
☐ N78013 Boeing 777-224ER 29861/243 013
☐ N77014 Boeing 777-224ER 29862/253 014
☐ N27015 Boeing 777-224ER 28678/273 015
☐ N57016 Boeing 777-224ER 28679/279 016
☐ N78017 Boeing 777-224ER 31679/391 017
☐ N37018 Boeing 777-224ER 31680/397 018
☐ N77019 Boeing 777-224ER 35547/617 019
☐ N69020 Boeing 777-224ER 31687/625 020
☐ N76021 Boeing 777-224ER 39776 021 on order
☐ N77022 Boeing 777-224ER 39777 022 on order

CONTINENTAQL CONNECTION (CO/COA)
Miami Intl, FL/ Guam/ Plattsburg, NY/Houston Intl, TX, Fort Lauderdale. FL (MIA/GUM/PLB/IAH/FLL)

☐ N14834 ATR 42-320 193 ex F-WWEG Cape Air
☐ N42836 ATR 42-320 200 ex F-WWEN 836 Cape Air
☐ N81533 Beech 1900D UE-137 ex N137ZV Gulfstream Intl
☐ N81535 Beech 1900D UE-147 Gulfstream Intl
☐ N81536 Beech 1900D UE-152 Gulfstream Intl
☐ N38537 Beech 1900D UE-158 Gulfstream Intl
☐ N81538 Beech 1900D UE-199 Gulfstream Intl

☐ N82539	Beech 1900D	UE-168			Gulfstream Intl
☐ N16540	Beech 1900D	UE-172			Gulfstream Intl
☐ N17541	Beech 1900D	UE-203			Gulfstream Intl
☐ N47542	Beech 1900D	UE-198			Gulfstream Intl
☐ N49543	Beech 1900D	UE-181			Gulfstream Intl
☐ N53545	Beech 1900D	UE-185			Gulfstream Intl
☐ N81546	Beech 1900D	UE-187			Gulfstream Intl
☐ N69547	Beech 1900D	UE-189			Gulfstream Intl
☐ N69549	Beech 1900D	UE-194			Gulfstream Intl
☐ N87550	Beech 1900D	UE-205			Gulfstream Intl
☐ N87551	Beech 1900D	UE-206			Gulfstream Intl
☐ N87552	Beech 1900D	UE-216			Gulfstream Intl
☐ N87554	Beech 1900D	UE-227			Gulfstream Intl
☐ N87555	Beech 1900D	UE-234			Gulfstream Intl
☐ N81556	Beech 1900D	UE-239			Gulfstream Intl
☐ N87557	Beech 1900D	UE-246			Gulfstream Intl

☐ N351PH	de Havilland DHC-8Q-202	490	ex C-GFUM	763	Commutair Lsd fr QXE
☐ N359PH	de Havilland DHC-8Q-202	514	ex C-GEOA	764	Commutair Lsd fr QXE
☐ N360PH	de Havilland DHC-8Q-202	515	ex C-GEWI	762	Commutair Lsd fr QXE
☐ N361PH	de Havilland DHC-8Q-202	516	ex C-GFOD	767	Commutair Lsd fr QXE
☐ N362PH	de Havilland DHC-8Q-202	518	ex C-FDHI	766	Commutair Lsd fr QXE
☐ N363PH	de Havilland DHC-8Q-202	520	ex C-FDHP	760	Commutair Lsd fr QXE
☐ N364PH	de Havilland DHC-8Q-202	524	ex C-FDHX	765	Commutair Lsd fr QXE
☐ N366PH	de Havilland DHC-8Q-202	510	ex C-GELN	769	Commutair Lsd fr QXE
☐ N368PH	de Havilland DHC-8Q-202	512	ex C-GDFT	768	Commutair Lsd fr QXE
☐ N375PH	de Havilland DHC-8Q-202	529	ex C-GDKL	761	Commutair Lsd fr QXE
☐ N187WQ	de Havilland DHC-8-402Q	4187	ex C-FNQG	777	Colgan Air
☐ N188WQ	de Havilland DHC-8-402Q	4188	ex C-FNQH	778	Colgan Air
☐ N190WQ	de Havilland DHC-8-402Q	4190	ex C-FNQN	779	Colgan Air
☐ N191WQ	de Havilland DHC-8-402Q	4191	ex C-FNQQ	780	Colgan Air
☐ N195WQ	de Havilland DHC-8-402Q	4195	ex C-FOJM	781	Colgan Air
☐ N196WQ	de Havilland DHC-8-402Q	4196	ex C-FOJT	782	Colgan Air
☐ N199WQ	de Havilland DHC-8-402Q	4199	ex C-FOUD	783	Colgan Air
☐ N202WQ	de Havilland DHC-8-402Q	4202	ex C-FOUY	785	Colgan Air
☐ N203WQ	de Havilland DHC-8-402Q	4203	ex C-FPDY	786	Colgan Air
☐ N204WQ	de Havilland DHC-8-402Q	4204	ex C-FPEF	787	Colgan Air
☐ N208WQ	de Havilland DHC-8-402Q	4208	ex C-FPPW	788	Colgan Air
☐ N209WQ	de Havilland DHC-8-402Q	4209	ex C-FPQA	789	Colgan Air
☐ N213WQ	de Havilland DHC-8-402Q	4213	ex C-FQXO		Colgan Air
☐ N214WQ	de Havilland DHC-8-402Q	4214	ex C-FQXP		Colgan Air

☐ N184CJ	SAAB SF.340B	340B-184	ex N300CE		Colgan Air
☐ N191MJ	SAAB SF.340B	340B-191	ex N301AE		Colgan Air
☐ N193CJ	SAAB SF.340B	340B-193	ex N302CE		Colgan Air
☐ N194CJ	SAAB SF.340B	340B-194	ex N303CE		Colgan Air
☐ N198CJ	SAAB SF.340B	340B-198	ex N304CE		Colgan Air
☐ N204CJ	SAAB SF.340B	340B-204	ex N307CE		Colgan Air
☐ N314CE	SAAB SF.340B	340B-335	ex N335AE		Colgan Air
☐ N334CJ	SAAB SF.340B	340B-334	ex N312CE		Colgan Air
☐ N343CJ	SAAB SF.340B	340B-343	ex N315CE		Colgan Air
☐ N352CJ	SAAB SF.340B	340B-352	ex N317CE		Colgan Air
☐ N356CJ	SAAB SF.340B	340B-356	ex N356SB		Colgan Air

CONTINENTAL EXPRESS — *Jet Link(CO/BTA)*

Cleveland, OH/Houston Intercontinental, TX, Newark, NJ (CLE/IAH/EWR)

☐ N473CA	Canadair CL-600-2B19 (CRJ-200ER)	7668	ex C-FMMN	472	Chautauqua
☐ N642BR	Canadair CL-600-2B19 (CRJ-200ER)	7356	ex C-FMNW		Chautauqua
☐ N645BR	Canadair CL-600-2B19 (CRJ-200ER)	7383	ex C-FMLV	462	Chautauqua
☐ N647BR	Canadair CL-600-2B19 (CRJ-200ER)	7399	ex C-FMNQ	463	Chautauqua
☐ N648BR	Canadair CL-600-2B19 (CRJ-200ER)	7406	ex C-FMKZ		Chautauqua
☐ N652BR	Canadair CL-600-2B19 (CRJ-200ER)	7429	ex C-FMMQ	458	Chautauqua
☐ N653BR	Canadair CL-600-2B19 (CRJ-200ER)	7438	ex C-FMLF	460	Chautauqua
☐ N667BR	Canadair CL-600-2B19 (CRJ-200ER)	7535	ex C-FMNH	461	Chautauqua
☐ N702BR	Canadair CL-600-2B19 (CRJ-200ER)	7462	ex N851FJ	459	Chautauqua

☐ N16501	Embraer EMB.135ER (ERJ-135ER)	145145	ex PT-SDV	501	stored IGM
☐ N16502	Embraer EMB.135ER (ERJ-135ER)	145166	ex PT-SFF	502	stored IGM
☐ N19503	Embraer EMB.135ER (ERJ-135ER)	145176	ex PT-SFI	503	stored IGM
☐ N25504	Embraer EMB.135ER (ERJ-135ER)	145186	ex PT-SFK	504	stored CLE
☐ N14505	Embraer EMB.135ER (ERJ-135ER)	145192	ex PT-SFN	505	stored IGM
☐ N27506	Embraer EMB.135ER (ERJ-135ER)	145206	ex PT-SFT	506	stored IGM
☐ N17507	Embraer EMB.135ER (ERJ-135ER)	145215	ex PT-SFW	507	stored IGM
☐ N14508	Embraer EMB.135ER (ERJ-135ER)	145220	ex PT-SFY	508	stored IGM
☐ N15509	Embraer EMB.135ER (ERJ-135ER)	145238	ex PT-SID	509	stored IGM
☐ N16510	Embraer EMB.135ER (ERJ-135ER)	145251	ex PT-SJI	510	stored IGM
☐ N16511	Embraer EMB.135ER (ERJ-135ER)	145267	ex PT-SIZ	511	stored IGM
☐ N27512	Embraer EMB.135ER (ERJ-135ER)	145274	ex PT-SJQ	512	stored IGM
☐ N17513	Embraer EMB.135LR (ERJ-135LR)	145292	ex PT-SKJ	513	stored IGM
☐ N14514	Embraer EMB.135LR (ERJ-135LR)	145303	ex PT-SKU	514	stored IGM
☐ N29515	Embraer EMB.135LR (ERJ-135LR)	145309	ex PT-SMA	515	stored IGM

☐	N14516	Embraer EMB.135LR (ERJ-135LR)	145323	ex PT-SMP	516	stored IGM
☐	N24517	Embraer EMB.135LR (ERJ-135LR)	145332	ex PT-SMY	517	stored IGM
☐	N28518	Embraer EMB.135LR (ERJ-135LR)	145334	ex PT-SNA	518	stored IGM
☐	N12519	Embraer EMB.135LR (ERJ-135LR)	145366	ex PT-SOQ	519	stored IGM
☐	N16520	Embraer EMB.135LR (ERJ-135LR)	145372	ex PT-SOX	520	stored IGM
☐	N17521	Embraer EMB.135LR (ERJ-135LR)	145378	ex PT-SQC	521	stored IGM
☐	N14522	Embraer EMB.135LR (ERJ-135LR)	145383	ex PT-SQH	522	stored IGM
☐	N27523	Embraer EMB.135LR (ERJ-135LR)	145389	ex PT-SQN	523	stored IGM
☐	N17524	Embraer EMB.135LR (ERJ-135LR)	145399	ex PT-SQW	524	stored IGM
☐	N16525	Embraer EMB.135LR (ERJ-135LR)	145403	ex PT-STA	525	stored IGM
☐	N11526	Embraer EMB.135LR (ERJ-135LR)	145410	ex PT-STH	526	Republic
☐	N15527	Embraer EMB.135LR (ERJ-135LR)	145413	ex PT-STJ	527	Republic
☐	N12528	Embraer EMB.135LR (ERJ-135LR)	145504	ex PT-SXX	528	Republic
☐	N28529	Embraer EMB.135LR (ERJ-135LR)	145512	ex PT-SYE	529	Republic
☐	N12530	Embraer EMB.135LR (ERJ-135LR)	145533	ex PT-STX	530	Republic
☐	N261SK	Embraer EMB.145LR (ERJ-145LR)	145144	ex PT-SDU		Chautauqua
☐	N264SK	Embraer EMB.145LR (ERJ-145LR)	145221	ex PT-SHG	434	Chautauqua
☐	N265SK	Embraer EMB.145LR (ERJ-145LR)	145226	ex PT-SHL		Chautauqua
☐	N266SK	Embraer EMB.145LR (ERJ-145LR)	145241	ex PT-SIG	436	Chautauqua
☐	N267SK	Embraer EMB.145LR (ERJ-145LR)	145260	ex PT-SJK	437	Chautauqua
☐	N268SK	Embraer EMB.145LR (ERJ-145LR)	145270	ex PT-SJM		Chautauqua
☐	N275SK	Embraer EMB.145LR (ERJ-145LR)	145345	ex PT-SNL	439	Chautauqua
☐	N276SK	Embraer EMB.145LR (ERJ-145LR)	145348	ex PT-SNO		Chautauqua
☐	N277SK	Embraer EMB.145LR (ERJ-145LR)	145355	ex PT-SNU	440	Chautauqua
☐	N278SK	Embraer EMB.145LR (ERJ-145LR)	145370	ex PT-		Chautauqua
☐	N279SK	Embraer EMB.145LR (ERJ-145LR)	145379	ex PT-SQD		Chautauqua
☐	N281SK	Embraer EMB.145LR (ERJ-145LR)	145391	ex PT-		Chautauqua
☐	N283SK	Embraer EMB.145LR (ERJ-145LR)	145424	ex PT-STV	442	Chautauqua
☐	N284SK	Embraer EMB.145LR (ERJ-145LR)	145427	ex PT-STY		Chautauqua
☐	N285SK	Embraer EMB.145LR (ERJ-145LR)	145435	ex PT-SUG	444	Chautauqua
☐	N286SK	Embraer EMB.145LR (ERJ-145LR)	145443	ex PT-SUO		Chautauqua
☐	N287SK	Embraer EMB.145LR (ERJ-145LR)	145460	ex PT-SVF		Chautauqua
☐	N288SK	Embraer EMB.145LR (ERJ-145LR)	145461	ex PT-SVG		Chautauqua
☐	N289SK	Embraer EMB.145LR (ERJ-145LR)	145463	ex PT-SVI		Chautauqua
☐	N296SK	Embraer EMB.145LR (ERJ-145LR)	145514	ex PT-SYG		Chautauqua
☐	N11535	Embraer EMB.145LR (ERJ-145LR)	145518	ex PT-SYJ	535	ExpressJet
☐	N11536	Embraer EMB.145LR (ERJ-145LR)	145520	ex PT-SYL	536	ExpressJet
☐	N21537	Embraer EMB.145LR (ERJ-145LR)	145523	ex PT-SYO	537	ExpressJet
☐	N13538	Embraer EMB.145LR (ERJ-145LR)	145527	ex PT-STS	538	ExpressJet
☐	N11539	Embraer EMB.145LR (ERJ-145LR)	145536	ex PT-SZA	539	ExpressJet
☐	N12540	Embraer EMB.145LR (ERJ-145LR)	145537	ex PT-SZB	540	ExpressJet
☐	N16541	Embraer EMB.145LR (ERJ-145LR)	145542	ex PT-SZF	541	ExpressJet
☐	N14542	Embraer EMB.145LR (ERJ-145LR)	145547	ex PT-SZK	542	ExpressJet
☐	N14543	Embraer EMB.145LR (ERJ-145LR)	145553	ex PT-SZP	543	ExpressJet
☐	N26545	Embraer EMB.145LR (ERJ-145LR)	145558	ex PT-SZT	545	ExpressJet
☐	N16546	Embraer EMB.145LR (ERJ-145LR)	145562	ex PT-SZX	546	ExpressJet
☐	N11547	Embraer EMB.145LR (ERJ-145LR)	145563	ex PT-SZY	547	ExpressJet
☐	N11548	Embraer EMB.145LR (ERJ-145LR)	145565	ex PT-SBB	548	ExpressJet
☐	N26549	Embraer EMB.145LR (ERJ-145LR)	145571	ex PT-SBH	549	ExpressJet
☐	N13550	Embraer EMB.145LR (ERJ-145LR)	145575	ex PT-SBL	550	ExpressJet
☐	N12552	Embraer EMB.145LR (ERJ-145LR)	145583	ex PT-SBU	552	ExpressJet
☐	N13553	Embraer EMB.145LR (ERJ-145LR)	145585	ex PT-SBW	553	ExpressJet
☐	N15555	Embraer EMB.145LR (ERJ-145LR)	145594	ex PT- (SCD)	555	ExpressJet
☐	N18556	Embraer EMB.145LR (ERJ-145LR)	145595	ex PT-SCE	556	ExpressJet
☐	N14558	Embraer EMB.145LR (ERJ-145LR)	145598	ex PT-SCG	558	ExpressJet
☐	N16559	Embraer EMB.145LR (ERJ-145LR)	145603	ex PT-SCM	559	ExpressJet
☐	N17560	Embraer EMB.145LR (ERJ-145LR)	145605	ex PT-SCO	560	ExpressJet
☐	N16561	Embraer EMB.145LR (ERJ-145LR)	145610	ex PT-SCT	561	ExpressJet
☐	N14562	Embraer EMB.145LR (ERJ-145LR)	145611	ex PT-SCV	562	ExpressJet
☐	N12563	Embraer EMB.145LR (ERJ-145LR)	145612	ex PT-SCW	563	ExpressJet
☐	N12564	Embraer EMB.145LR (ERJ-145LR)	145618	ex PT-SDG	564	ExpressJet
☐	N11565	Embraer EMB.145LR (ERJ-145LR)	145621	ex PT-SDJ	565	ExpressJet
☐	N13566	Embraer EMB.145LR (ERJ-145LR)	145622	ex PT-SDK	566	ExpressJet
☐	N12567	Embraer EMB.145LR (ERJ-145LR)	145623	ex PT-SDL	567	ExpressJet
☐	N14568	Embraer EMB.145LR (ERJ-145LR)	145628	ex PT-SDQ	568	ExpressJet
☐	N16571	Embraer EMB.145LR (ERJ-145LR)	145633	ex PT-SDV	571	ExpressJet
☐	N15572	Embraer EMB.145LR (ERJ-145LR)	145636	ex PT-SDY	572	ExpressJet
☐	N14573	Embraer EMB.145LR (ERJ-145LR)	145638	ex PT-SDZ	573	ExpressJet
☐	N15574	Embraer EMB.145LR (ERJ-145LR)	145639	ex PT-SEB	574	ExpressJet
☐	N12900	Embraer EMB.145LR (ERJ-145LR)	145511	ex PT-SYD	900	ExpressJet
☐	N48901	Embraer EMB.145LR (ERJ-145LR)	145501	ex PT-SXU	901	ExpressJet
☐	N14902	Embraer EMB.145LR (ERJ-145LR)	145496	ex PT-SXO	902	ExpressJet
☐	N13903	Embraer EMB.145LR (ERJ-145LR)	145479	ex PT-SVY	903	ExpressJet
☐	N14904	Embraer EMB.145LR (ERJ-145LR)	145477	ex PT-SVW	904	ExpressJet
☐	N14905	Embraer EMB.145LR (ERJ-145LR)	145476	ex PT-SVV	905	ExpressJet
☐	N29906	Embraer EMB.145LR (ERJ-145LR)	145472	ex PT-SVR	906	ExpressJet
☐	N13908	Embraer EMB.145LR (ERJ-145LR)	145465	ex PT-SVK	908	ExpressJet
☐	N15910	Embraer EMB.145LR (ERJ-145LR)	145455	ex PT-SVA	910	ExpressJet
☐	N16911	Embraer EMB.145LR (ERJ-145LR)	145446	ex PT-SUR	911	ExpressJet
☐	N15912	Embraer EMB.145LR (ERJ-145LR)	145439	ex PT-SUK	912	ExpressJet
☐	N13913	Embraer EMB.145LR (ERJ-145LR)	145438	ex PT-SUJ	913	ExpressJet
☐	N13914	Embraer EMB.145LR (ERJ-145LR)	145430	ex PT-SUB	914	ExpressJet

	Registration	Type	c/n	Previous identity	Fleet no		Operator
☐	N36915	Embraer EMB.145LR (ERJ-145LR)	145421	ex PT-STS	915		ExpressJet
☐	N14916	Embraer EMB.145LR (ERJ-145LR)	145415	ex PT-STL	916		ExpressJet
☐	N29917	Embraer EMB.145LR (ERJ-145LR)	145414	ex PT-STK	917		ExpressJet
☐	N16918	Embraer EMB.145LR (ERJ-145LR)	145397	ex PT-SQU	918		ExpressJet
☐	N16919	Embraer EMB.145LR (ERJ-145LR)	145393	ex PT-SQQ	919		ExpressJet
☐	N14920	Embraer EMB.145LR (ERJ-145LR)	145380	ex PT-SQE	920		ExpressJet
☐	N12921	Embraer EMB.145LR (ERJ-145LR)	145354	ex PT-SNT	921		ExpressJet
☐	N12922	Embraer EMB.145LR (ERJ-145LR)	145338	ex PT-SNE	922		ExpressJet
☐	N14923	Embraer EMB.145LR (ERJ-145LR)	145318	ex PT-SMJ	923		ExpressJet
☐	N12924	Embraer EMB.145LR (ERJ-145LR)	145311	ex PT-SMC	924		ExpressJet
☐	N14925	Embraer EMB.145EP (ERJ-145EP)	145004	ex PT-SYA	925		ExpressJet
☐	N15926	Embraer EMB.145EP (ERJ-145EP)	145005	ex PT-SYB	926		ExpressJet
☐	N16927	Embraer EMB.145EP (ERJ-145EP)	145006	ex PT-SYC	927		ExpressJet
☐	N17928	Embraer EMB.145EP (ERJ-145EP)	145007	ex PT-SYD	928		ExpressJet
☐	N13929	Embraer EMB.145EP (ERJ-145EP)	145009	ex PT-SYF	929		ExpressJet
☐	N14930	Embraer EMB.145EP (ERJ-145EP)	145011	ex PT-SYH	930		ExpressJet
☐	N15932	Embraer EMB.145EP (ERJ-145EP)	145015	ex PT-SYL	932		ExpressJet
☐	N14933	Embraer EMB.145EP (ERJ-145EP)	145018	ex PT-SYO	933		ExpressJet
☐	N12934	Embraer EMB.145EP (ERJ-145EP)	145019	ex PT-SYP	934		ExpressJet
☐	N13935	Embraer EMB.145EP (ERJ-145EP)	145022	ex PT-SYS	935		ExpressJet
☐	N13936	Embraer EMB.145EP (ERJ-145EP)	145025	ex PT-SYV	936		ExpressJet
☐	N14937	Embraer EMB.145EP (ERJ-145EP)	145026	ex PT-SYW	937		ExpressJet
☐	N14938	Embraer EMB.145EP (ERJ-145EP)	145029	ex PT-SYX	938		ExpressJet
☐	N14939	Embraer EMB.145EP (ERJ-145EP)	145030	ex PT-SYY	939		ExpressJet
☐	N14940	Embraer EMB.145EP (ERJ-145EP)	145033	ex PT-SZA	940		ExpressJet
☐	N15941	Embraer EMB.145EP (ERJ-145EP)	145035	ex PT-SZB	941		ExpressJet
☐	N14942	Embraer EMB.145EP (ERJ-145EP)	145037	ex PT-SZD	942		ExpressJet
☐	N14943	Embraer EMB.145EP (ERJ-145EP)	145040	ex PT-SZF	943		ExpressJet
☐	N16944	Embraer EMB.145EP (ERJ-145EP)	145045	ex PT-SZK	944		ExpressJet
☐	N14945	Embraer EMB.145EP (ERJ-145EP)	145049	ex PT-SZO	945		ExpressJet
☐	N12946	Embraer EMB.145EP (ERJ-145EP)	145052	ex PT-SZR	946		ExpressJet
☐	N14947	Embraer EMB.145EP (ERJ-145EP)	145054	ex PT-SZT	947		ExpressJet
☐	N15948	Embraer EMB.145EP (ERJ-145EP)	145056	ex PT-SZV	948		ExpressJet
☐	N13949	Embraer EMB.145LR (ERJ-145LR)	145057	ex PT-SZW	949		ExpressJet
☐	N14950	Embraer EMB.145LR (ERJ-145LR)	145061	ex PT-SAE	950		ExpressJet
☐	N16951	Embraer EMB.145LR (ERJ-145LR)	145063	ex PT-SAG	951		ExpressJet
☐	N14952	Embraer EMB.145LR (ERJ-145LR)	145067	ex PT-SAL	952		ExpressJet
☐	N14953	Embraer EMB.145LR (ERJ-145LR)	145071	ex PT-SAP	953		ExpressJet
☐	N16954	Embraer EMB.145LR (ERJ-145LR)	145072	ex PT-SAQ	954		ExpressJet
☐	N13955	Embraer EMB.145LR (ERJ-145LR)	145075	ex PT-SAT	955		ExpressJet
☐	N13956	Embraer EMB.145LR (ERJ-145LR)	145078	ex PT-S	956		ExpressJet
☐	N12957	Embraer EMB.145LR (ERJ-145LR)	145080	ex PT-S	957		ExpressJet
☐	N13958	Embraer EMB.145LR (ERJ-145LR)	145085	ex PT-S	958		ExpressJet
☐	N14959	Embraer EMB.145LR (ERJ-145LR)	145091	ex PT-S	959		ExpressJet
☐	N14960	Embraer EMB.145LR (ERJ-145LR)	145100	ex PT-SBW	960	100th c/s	ExpressJet
☐	N16961	Embraer EMB.145LR (ERJ-145LR)	145103	ex PT-S	961		ExpressJet
☐	N27962	Embraer EMB.145LR (ERJ-145LR)	145110	ex PT-S	962		ExpressJet
☐	N16963	Embraer EMB.145LR (ERJ-145LR)	145116	ex PT-SCS	963		ExpressJet
☐	N13964	Embraer EMB.145LR (ERJ-145LR)	145123	ex PT-SCZ	964		ExpressJet
☐	N13965	Embraer EMB.145LR (ERJ-145LR)	145125	ex PT-SDC	965		ExpressJet
☐	N19966	Embraer EMB.145LR (ERJ-145LR)	145131	ex PT-SDI	966		ExpressJet
☐	N12967	Embraer EMB.145LR (ERJ-145LR)	145133	ex PT-SDK	967		ExpressJet
☐	N13968	Embraer EMB.145LR (ERJ-145LR)	145138	ex PT-SDP	968		ExpressJet
☐	N13969	Embraer EMB.145LR (ERJ-145LR)	145141	ex PT-SDR	969		ExpressJet
☐	N13970	Embraer EMB.145LR (ERJ-145LR)	145146	ex PT-SDW	970		ExpressJet
☐	N22971	Embraer EMB.145LR (ERJ-145LR)	145149	ex PT-SDZ	971		ExpressJet
☐	N14972	Embraer EMB.145LR (ERJ-145LR)	145151	ex PT-SEC	972		ExpressJet
☐	N15973	Embraer EMB.145LR (ERJ-145LR)	145159	ex PT-S	973		ExpressJet
☐	N14974	Embraer EMB.145LR (ERJ-145LR)	145161	ex PT-S	974		ExpressJet
☐	N13975	Embraer EMB.145LR (ERJ-145LR)	145163	ex PT-S	975		ExpressJet
☐	N16976	Embraer EMB.145LR (ERJ-145LR)	145171	ex PT-SEV	976		ExpressJet
☐	N14977	Embraer EMB.145LR (ERJ-145LR)	145175	ex PT-SEX	977		ExpressJet
☐	N13978	Embraer EMB.145LR (ERJ-145LR)	145180	ex PT-SGC	978		ExpressJet
☐	N13979	Embraer EMB.145LR (ERJ-145LR)	145181	ex PT-SGD	979		ExpressJet
☐	N15980	Embraer EMB.145LR (ERJ-145LR)	145202	ex PT-SGT	980		ExpressJet
☐	N16981	Embraer EMB.145LR (ERJ-145LR)	145208	ex PT-SGY	981		ExpressJet
☐	N18982	Embraer EMB.145LR (ERJ-145LR)	145223	ex PT-SHI	982		ExpressJet
☐	N15983	Embraer EMB.145LR (ERJ-145LR)	145239	ex PT-SIE	983		ExpressJet
☐	N17984	Embraer EMB.145LR (ERJ-145LR)	145246	ex PT-SIK	984		ExpressJet
☐	N15985	Embraer EMB.145LR (ERJ-145LR)	145248	ex PT-SIL	985		ExpressJet
☐	N15986	Embraer EMB.145LR (ERJ-145LR)	145254	ex PT-SIO	986		ExpressJet
☐	N16987	Embraer EMB.145LR (ERJ-145LR)	145261	ex PT-SIU	987		ExpressJet
☐	N13988	Embraer EMB.145LR (ERJ-145LR)	145265	ex PT-SIX	988		ExpressJet
☐	N13989	Embraer EMB.145LR (ERJ-145LR)	145271	ex PT-SJN	989		ExpressJet
☐	N13990	Embraer EMB.145LR (ERJ-145LR)	145277	ex PT-SJT	990		ExpressJet
☐	N14991	Embraer EMB.145LR (ERJ-145LR)	145278	ex PT-SJU	991		ExpressJet
☐	N13992	Embraer EMB.145LR (ERJ-145LR)	145284	ex PT-SKB	992		ExpressJet
☐	N14993	Embraer EMB.145LR (ERJ-145LR)	145289	ex PT-SKG	993		ExpressJet
☐	N13994	Embraer EMB.145LR (ERJ-145LR)	145291	ex PT-SKI	994		ExpressJet
☐	N13995	Embraer EMB.145LR (ERJ-145LR)	145295	ex PT-SKM	995		ExpressJet
☐	N12996	Embraer EMB.145LR (ERJ-145LR)	145296	ex PT-SKN	996		ExpressJet
☐	N13997	Embraer EMB.145LR (ERJ-145LR)	145298	ex PT-SKP	997		ExpressJet
☐	N14998	Embraer EMB.145LR (ERJ-145LR)	145302	ex PT-SKT	998		ExpressJet

☐ N16999	Embraer EMB.145LR (ERJ-145LR)	145307	ex PT-SKY	999	ExpressJet
☐ N18101	Embraer EMB.145XR (ERJ-145XR)	145590	ex PT-SDC	101	ExpressJet
☐ N18102	Embraer EMB.145XR (ERJ-145XR)	145643	ex PT-SEE	102	ExpressJet
☐ N24103	Embraer EMB.145XR (ERJ-145XR)	145645	ex PT-SEF	103	ExpressJet
☐ N41104	Embraer EMB.145XR (ERJ-145XR)	145646	ex PT-SEG	104	ExpressJet
☐ N14105	Embraer EMB.145XR (ERJ-145XR)	145649	ex PT-SEJ	105	ExpressJet
☐ N11106	Embraer EMB.145XR (ERJ-145XR)	145650	ex PT-SEK	106	ExpressJet
☐ N11107	Embraer EMB.145XR (ERJ-145XR)	145654	ex PT-SEO	107	ExpressJet
☐ N17108	Embraer EMB.145XR (ERJ-145XR)	145655	ex PT-SEP	108	ExpressJet
☐ N11109	Embraer EMB.145XR (ERJ-145XR)	145657	ex PT-SER	109	ExpressJet
☐ N34110	Embraer EMB.145XR (ERJ-145XR)	145658	ex PT-SES	110	ExpressJet
☐ N34111	Embraer EMB.145XR (ERJ-145XR)	145659	ex PT-SET	111	ExpressJet
☐ N16112	Embraer EMB.145XR (ERJ-145XR)	145660	ex PT-SEU	112	ExpressJet
☐ N11113	Embraer EMB.145XR (ERJ-145XR)	145662	ex PT-SEW	113	ExpressJet
☐ N18114	Embraer EMB.145XR (ERJ-145XR)	145664	ex PT-SEY	114	ExpressJet
☐ N17115	Embraer EMB.145XR (ERJ-145XR)	145666	ex PT-SFA	115	ExpressJet
☐ N14116	Embraer EMB.145XR (ERJ-145XR)	145672	ex PT-SFF	116	ExpressJet
☐ N14117	Embraer EMB.145XR (ERJ-145XR)	145674	ex PT-SFH	117	ExpressJet
☐ N13118	Embraer EMB.145XR (ERJ-145XR)	145675	ex PT-SFI	118	ExpressJet
☐ N11119	Embraer EMB.145XR (ERJ-145XR)	145677	ex PT-SFK	119	ExpressJet
☐ N18120	Embraer EMB.145XR (ERJ-145XR)	145681	ex PT-SFN	120	ExpressJet
☐ N11121	Embraer EMB.145XR (ERJ-145XR)	145683	ex PT-SFP	121	ExpressJet
☐ N12122	Embraer EMB.145XR (ERJ-145XR)	145684	ex PT-SFQ	122	ExpressJet
☐ N13123	Embraer EMB.145XR (ERJ-145XR)	145688	ex PT-SFU	123	ExpressJet
☐ N13124	Embraer EMB.145XR (ERJ-145XR)	145689	ex PT-SFV	124	ExpressJet
☐ N14125	Embraer EMB.145XR (ERJ-145XR)	145690	ex PT-SFW	125	ExpressJet
☐ N12126	Embraer EMB.145XR (ERJ-145XR)	145693	ex PT-SFZ	126	ExpressJet
☐ N11127	Embraer EMB.145XR (ERJ-145XR)	145697	ex PT-SGC	127	ExpressJet
☐ N24128	Embraer EMB.145XR (ERJ-145XR)	145700	ex PT-SGE	128	ExpressJet
☐ N21129	Embraer EMB.145XR (ERJ-145XR)	145703	ex PT-SGH	129	ExpressJet
☐ N21130	Embraer EMB.145XR (ERJ-145XR)	145704	ex PT-SGI	130	ExpressJet
☐ N31131	Embraer EMB.145XR (ERJ-145XR)	145705	ex PT-SGJ	131	ExpressJet
☐ N13132	Embraer EMB.145XR (ERJ-145XR)	145708	ex PT-SGL	132	ExpressJet
☐ N13133	Embraer EMB.145XR (ERJ-145XR)	145712	ex PT-SGP	133	ExpressJet
☐ N25134	Embraer EMB.145XR (ERJ-145XR)	145714	ex PT-SGR	134	ExpressJet
☐ N12135	Embraer EMB.145XR (ERJ-145XR)	145718	ex PT-SGU	135	ExpressJet
☐ N12136	Embraer EMB.145XR (ERJ-145XR)	145719	ex PT-SGV	136	ExpressJet
☐ N17138	Embraer EMB.145XR (ERJ-145XR)	145727	ex PT-SHD	138	ExpressJet
☐ N23139	Embraer EMB.145XR (ERJ-145XR)	145731	ex PT-SHH	139	ExpressJet
☐ N11140	Embraer EMB.145XR (ERJ-145XR)	145732	ex PT-SHI	140	ExpressJet
☐ N26141	Embraer EMB.145XR (ERJ-145XR)	145733	ex PT-SHJ	141	ExpressJet
☐ N12142	Embraer EMB.145XR (ERJ-145XR)	145735	ex PT-SHL	142	ExpressJet
☐ N14143	Embraer EMB.145XR (ERJ-145XR)	145739	ex PT-SHT	143	ExpressJet
☐ N21144	Embraer EMB.145XR (ERJ-145XR)	145741	ex PT-SJA	144	ExpressJet
☐ N12145	Embraer EMB.145XR (ERJ-145XR)	145745	ex PT-SJE	145	ExpressJet
☐ N17146	Embraer EMB.145XR (ERJ-145XR)	145746	ex PT-SJF	146	ExpressJet
☐ N16147	Embraer EMB.145XR (ERJ-145XR)	145749	ex PT-SJI	147	ExpressJet
☐ N14148	Embraer EMB.145XR (ERJ-145XR)	145751	ex PT-SJK	148	ExpressJet
☐ N16149	Embraer EMB.145XR (ERJ-145XR)	145753	ex PT-SJM	149	ExpressJet
☐ N11150	Embraer EMB.145XR (ERJ-145XR)	145756	ex PT-SJP	150	ExpressJet
☐ N16151	Embraer EMB.145XR (ERJ-145XR)	145758	ex PT-SJQ	151	ExpressJet
☐ N27152	Embraer EMB.145XR (ERJ-145XR)	145759	ex PT-SJR	152	ExpressJet
☐ N14153	Embraer EMB.145XR (ERJ-145XR)	145761	ex PT-SJS	153	ExpressJet
☐ N21154	Embraer EMB.145XR (ERJ-145XR)	145772	ex PT-SMC	154	ExpressJet
☐ N11155	Embraer EMB.145XR (ERJ-145XR)	145782	ex PT-SMJ	155	ExpressJet
☐ N10156	Embraer EMB.145XR (ERJ-145XR)	145786	ex PT-SMN	156	ExpressJet
☐ N12157	Embraer EMB.145XR (ERJ-145XR)	145787	ex PT-SMP	157	ExpressJet
☐ N14158	Embraer EMB.145XR (ERJ-145XR)	145791	ex PT-SMS	158	ExpressJet
☐ N17159	Embraer EMB.145XR (ERJ-145XR)	145792	ex PT-SMT	159	ExpressJet
☐ N12160	Embraer EMB.145XR (ERJ-145XR)	145799	ex PT-SMZ	160	ExpressJet
☐ N13161	Embraer EMB.145XR (ERJ-145XR)	14500805	ex PT-SNH	161	ExpressJet
☐ N11164	Embraer EMB.145XR (ERJ-145XR)	14500817	ex PT-SNS	164	ExpressJet
☐ N12166	Embraer EMB.145XR (ERJ-145XR)	14500831	ex PT-SQE	166	ExpressJet
☐ N17169	Embraer EMB.145XR (ERJ-145XR)	14500844	ex PT-SQO	169	ExpressJet
☐ N12172	Embraer EMB.145XR (ERJ-145XR)	14500864	ex PT-SXD	172	ExpressJet
☐ N14177	Embraer EMB.145XR (ERJ-145XR)	14500888	ex PT-SYA	177	ExpressJet
☐ N14180	Embraer EMB.145XR (ERJ-145XR)	14500900	ex PT-SYL	180	ExpressJet
☐ N17185	Embraer EMB.145XR (ERJ-145XR)	14500922	ex PT-SOT	185	ExpressJet
☐ N14186	Embraer EMB.145XR (ERJ-145XR)	14500924	ex PT-SOV	186	ExpressJet
☐ N11187	Embraer EMB.145XR (ERJ-145XR)	14500927	ex PT-SOX	187	ExpressJet
☐ N27190	Embraer EMB.145XR (ERJ-145XR)	14500934	ex PT-SCC	190	ExpressJet
☐ N11191	Embraer EMB.145XR (ERJ-145XR)	14500935	ex PT-SCH	191	ExpressJet
☐ N11194	Embraer EMB.145XR (ERJ-145XR)	14500940	ex PT-SCL		ExpressJet
☐ N12195	Embraer EMB.145XR (ERJ-145XR)	14500943	ex PT-SCO	195	ExpressJet
☐ N17196	Embraer EMB.145XR (ERJ-145XR)	14500945	ex PT-SCQ	196	ExpressJet
☐ N21197	Embraer EMB.145XR (ERJ-145XR)	14500947	ex PT-SCS	197	ExpressJet
☐ N27200	Embraer EMB.145XR (ERJ-145XR)	14500956	ex PT-SFE	200	ExpressJet
☐ N13202	Embraer EMB.145XR (ERJ-145XR)	14500962	ex PT-SFJ	202	ExpressJet
☐ N14203	Embraer EMB.145XR (ERJ-145XR)	14500964	ex PT-SFL	203	ExpressJet
☐ N14204	Embraer EMB.145XR (ERJ-145XR)	14500968	ex PT-	204	ExpressJet

CONTINENTAL MICRONESIA	Air Mike (CS/CMI)	Guam, GU (GUM)

A wholly owned subsidiary of Continental Airlines and operates 10 Boeing 737-824/Ws and 757's leased from the parent

CORPJET	Beewee (CPJ)	Baltimore-Martin State, MD (MTN)

☐ N208HF	Cessna 208 Caravan I	20800116	ex C-GMPR	
☐ N716BT	Cessna 208B Caravan I	208B0843	ex N5260Y	Freighter
☐ N718BT	Cessna 208B Caravan I	208B0881		Freighter
☐ N801TH	Cessna 208 Caravan I	20800123	ex N9680F	
☐ N801FL	Cessna 208B Caravan I	208B0809	ex N5264E	
☐ N5YV	Beech 1900D	UE-5		

CORPORATE AIR	Air Spur (CPT)	Billings-Logan Intl, MT (BIL)

☐ N210AS	Embraer EMB.120FC Brasilia	120006	ex PT-SIA	Freighter
☐ N223AS	Embraer EMB.120FC Brasilia	120021	ex PT-SIQ	stored OPF
☐ N319BH	Beech 1900C	UB-36	ex N19RA	Freighter
☐ N330SB	Short SD.3-30	SH3013	ex N241CA	Freighter
☐ N331SB	Short SD.3-30	SH3015	ex N331CA	Freighter; stored HNL
☐ N7254R	Beech 1900C	UB-22		Freighter

CORPORATE FLIGHT MANAGEMENT	Volunteer (VTE)	Smyrna, TN (MQY)

☐ N10UP	British Aerospace Jetstream 31	635	ex N635JX
☐ N643JX	British Aerospace Jetstream 31	643	ex N421MX
☐ N657BA	British Aerospace Jetstream 31	657	ex N412MX

CSA AIR	Iron Air (IRO)	Iron Mountain--Ford, MI (IMT)

Operates Cessna Caravans leased from and on behalf of Federal Express

CUSTOM AIR TRANSPORT	Catt (5R/CTT)	Fort Lauderdale-Hollywood Intl, FL (FLL)

☐ N511PE	Boeing 727-232F (FedEx 3)	20634/917	ex N452DA	
☐ N902PG	Boeing 727-281F (FedEx 3)	20725/958	ex OY-TNT	stored ROW
☐ N7635U	Boeing 727-222F (FedEx 3)	19908/653		
☐ N7644U	Boeing 727-222F (FedEx 3)	20038/716		stored ROW
☐ N7645U	Boeing 727-222F (FedEx 3)	20039/720		
☐ N24343	Boeing 727-231F (Super 27)	21630/1458		

DELTA AIR LINES	Delta (DL/DAL)	Atlanta-Hartsfield Intl, GA (ATL)

Member of Skyteam

☐ N301NB	Airbus A319-114	1058	ex D-AVYP	3101	City of Duluth
☐ N302NB	Airbus A319-114	1062	ex D-AVWA	3102	
☐ N314NB	Airbus A319-114	1191	ex D-AVWO	3114	
☐ N315NB	Airbus A319-114	1230	ex D-AVYM	3115	
☐ N316NB	Airbus A319-114	1249	ex D-AVYW	3116	
☐ N317NB	Airbus A319-114	1324	ex D-AVWT	3117	
☐ N318NB	Airbus A319-114	1325	ex D-AVYF	3118	
☐ N319NB	Airbus A319-114	1346	ex D-AVYR	3119	
☐ N320NB	Airbus A319-114	1392	ex D-AVYT	3120	
☐ N321NB	Airbus A319-114	1414	ex D-AVYL	3121	
☐ N322NB	Airbus A319-114	1434	ex D-AVYO	3122	
☐ N323NB	Airbus A319-114	1453	ex D-AVWE	3123	
☐ N324NB	Airbus A319-114	1456	ex D-AVWF	3124	
☐ N325NB	Airbus A319-114	1483	ex D-AVYU	3125	
☐ N326NB	Airbus A319-114	1498	ex D-AVYC	3126	
☐ N327NB	Airbus A319-114	1501	ex D-AVYD	3127	
☐ N328NB	Airbus A319-114	1520	ex D-AVYN	3128	
☐ N329NB	Airbus A319-114	1543	ex D-AVWJ	3129	
☐ N330NB	Airbus A319-114	1549	ex D-AVWM	3130	
☐ N331NB	Airbus A319-114	1567	ex D-AVYU	3131	
☐ N332NB	Airbus A319-114	1570	ex D-AVWD	3132	
☐ N333NB	Airbus A319-114	1582	ex D-AVYA	3133	
☐ N334NB	Airbus A319-114	1659	ex D-AVYU	3134	
☐ N335NB	Airbus A319-114	1662	ex D-AVYW	3135	
☐ N336NB	Airbus A319-114	1683	ex D-AVWJ	3136	
☐ N337NB	Airbus A319-114	1685	ex D-AVWL	3137	
☐ N338NB	Airbus A319-114	1693	ex D-AVYD	3138	
☐ N339NB	Airbus A319-114	1709	ex D-AVWG	3139	
☐ N340NB	Airbus A319-114	1714	ex D-AVWN	3140	
☐ N341NB	Airbus A319-114	1738	ex D-AVWV	3141	
☐ N342NB	Airbus A319-114	1746	ex D-AVYA	3142	
☐ N343NB	Airbus A319-114	1752	ex D-AVYH	3143	
☐ N344NB	Airbus A319-114	1766	ex D-AVYU	3144	
☐ N345NB	Airbus A319-114	1774	ex D-AVYD	3145	
☐ N346NB	Airbus A319-114	1796	ex D-AVYX	3146	
☐ N347NB	Airbus A319-114	1800	ex D-AVYZ	3147	

☐	N348NB	Airbus A319-114	1810	ex D-AVWH	3148	
☐	N349NB	Airbus A319-114	1815	ex D-AVWI	3149	
☐	N351NB	Airbus A319-114	1820	ex D-AVWL	3151	
☐	N352NB	Airbus A319-114	1824	ex D-AVWM	3152	
☐	N353NB	Airbus A319-114	1828	ex D-AVWO	3153	
☐	N354NB	Airbus A319-114	1833	ex D-AVWS	3154	
☐	N355NB	Airbus A319-114	1839	ex D-AVWA	3155	
☐	N357NB	Airbus A319-114	1875	ex D-AVYH	3157	
☐	N358NB	Airbus A319-114	1897	ex D-AVYK	3158	
☐	N359NB	Airbus A319-114	1923	ex D-AVWC	3159	
☐	N360NB	Airbus A319-114	1959	ex D-AVWL	3160	
☐	N361NB	Airbus A319-114	1976	ex D-AVYB	3161	
☐	N362NB	Airbus A319-114	1982	ex D-AVYF	3162	
☐	N363NB	Airbus A319-114	1990	ex D-AVYL	3163	
☐	N364NB	Airbus A319-114	2002	ex D-AVWA	3164	
☐	N365NB	Airbus A319-114	2013	ex D-AVWS	3165	
☐	N366NB	Airbus A319-114	2026	ex D-AVWX	3166	
☐	N368NB	Airbus A319-114	2039	ex D-AVYT	3168	
☐	N369NB	Airbus A319-114	2047	ex D-AVWC	3169	
☐	N370NB	Airbus A319-114	2087	ex D-AVWI	3170	
☐	N371NB	Airbus A319-114	2095	ex D-AVYI	3171	
☐	N309US	Airbus A320-211	0118	ex F-WWIM	3209	
☐	N310NW	Airbus A320-211	0121	ex F-WWIO	3210	
☐	N311US	Airbus A320-211	0125	ex F-WWIT	3211	
☐	N312US	Airbus A320-211	0152	ex F-WWDT	3212	
☐	N313US	Airbus A320-211	0153	ex F-WWDX	3213	
☐	N314US	Airbus A320-211	0160	ex F-WWDZ	3214	Delta c/s
☐	N315US	Airbus A320-211	0171	ex F-WWIJ	3215	
☐	N316US	Airbus A320-211	0192	ex F-WWIY	3216	
☐	N317US	Airbus A320-211	0197	ex F-WWDF	3217	
☐	N318US	Airbus A320-211	0206	ex F-WWDK	3218	
☐	N319US	Airbus A320-211	0208	ex F-WWDT	3219	
☐	N320US	Airbus A320-211	0213	ex F-WWIB	3220	
☐	N321US	Airbus A320-211	0262	ex F-WWDI	3221	
☐	N322US	Airbus A320-211	0263	ex F-WWDQ	3222	
☐	N323US	Airbus A320-211	0272	ex F-WWBP	3223	
☐	N324US	Airbus A320-211	0273	ex F-WWDS	3224	
☐	N325US	Airbus A320-211	0281	ex F-WWBS	3225	
☐	N326US	Airbus A320-211	0282	ex F-WWIA	3226	
☐	N327NW	Airbus A320-211	0297	ex F-WWIO	3227	
☐	N328NW	Airbus A320-211	0298	ex F-WWIP	3228	
☐	N329NW	Airbus A320-211	0306	ex F-WWDG	3229	
☐	N330NW	Airbus A320-211	0307	ex F-WWDJ	3230	
☐	N331NW	Airbus A320-211	0318	ex F-WWBF	3231	
☐	N332NW	Airbus A320-211	0319	ex F-WWBG	3232	
☐	N333NW	Airbus A320-211	0329	ex F-WWDY	3233	
☐	N334NW	Airbus A320-212	0339	ex F-WWBP	3234	
☐	N335NW	Airbus A320-212	0340	ex F-WWBQ	3235	
☐	N336NW	Airbus A320-212	0355	ex F-WWIE	3236	
☐	N337NW	Airbus A320-212	0358	ex F-WWIO	3237	
☐	N338NW	Airbus A320-212	0360	ex F-WWBY	3238	
☐	N339NW	Airbus A320-212	0367	ex F-WWDG	3239	
☐	N340NW	Airbus A320-212	0372	ex F-WWIX	3240	
☐	N341NW	Airbus A320-212	0380	ex F-WWIS	3241	
☐	N342NW	Airbus A320-212	0381	ex F-WWIJ	3242	
☐	N343NW	Airbus A320-212	0387	ex F-WWBV	3243	
☐	N344NW	Airbus A320-212	0388	ex F-WWDC	3244	
☐	N345NW	Airbus A320-212	0399	ex F-WWIG	3245	
☐	N347NW	Airbus A320-212	0408	ex F-WWDN	3247	
☐	N348NW	Airbus A320-212	0410	ex F-WWDV	3248	
☐	N349NW	Airbus A320-212	0417	ex F-WWBR	3249	
☐	N350NA	Airbus A320-212	0418	ex F-WWDG	3250	
☐	N351NW	Airbus A320-212	0766	ex F-WWDG	3251	
☐	N352NW	Airbus A320-212	0778	ex F-WWDO	3252	
☐	N353NW	Airbus A320-212	0786	ex F-WWDP	3253	
☐	N354NW	Airbus A320-212	0801	ex F-WWDY	3254	
☐	N355NW	Airbus A320-212	0807	ex F-WWIC	3255	
☐	N356NW	Airbus A320-212	0818	ex F-WWBD	3256	
☐	N357NW	Airbus A320-212	0830	ex F-WWIN	3257	
☐	N358NW	Airbus A320-212	0832	ex F-WWIO	3258	
☐	N359NW	Airbus A320-212	0846	ex F-WWBH	3259	
☐	N360NW	Airbus A320-212	0903	ex F-WWDO	3260	
☐	N361NW	Airbus A320-212	0907	ex F-WWDQ	3261	
☐	N362NW	Airbus A320-212	0911	ex F-WWDT	3262	
☐	N363NW	Airbus A320-212	0923	ex F-WWDZ	3263	
☐	N364NW	Airbus A320-212	0962	ex F-WWBF	3264	
☐	N365NW	Airbus A320-212	0964	ex F-WWBJ	3265	
☐	N366NW	Airbus A320-212	0981	ex F-WWDE	3266	
☐	N367NW	Airbus A320-212	0988	ex F-WWIH	3267	
☐	N368NW	Airbus A320-212	0996	ex F-WWBV	3268	
☐	N369NW	Airbus A320-212	1011	ex F-WWDO	3269	
☐	N370NW	Airbus A320-212	1037	ex F-WWDY	3270	

☐ N371NW	Airbus A320-212	1535	ex F-WWIS	3271	
☐ N372NW	Airbus A320-212	1633	ex F-WWDO	3272	
☐ N373NW	Airbus A320-212	1641	ex F-WWIR	3273	
☐ N374NW	Airbus A320-212	1646	ex F-WWDS	3274	
☐ N375NC	Airbus A320-212	1789	ex F-WWDU	3275	
☐ N376NW	Airbus A320-212	1812	ex F-WWBB	3276	
☐ N377NW	Airbus A320-212	2082	ex F-WWIU	3277	
☐ N378NW	Airbus A320-212	2092	ex F-WWBP	3278	
☐ N801NW	Airbus A330-323E	524	ex F-WWYZ	3301	
☐ N802NW	Airbus A330-323E	533	ex F-WWYD	3302	
☐ N803NW	Airbus A330-323E	542	ex F-WWYH	3303	
☐ N804NW	Airbus A330-323E	549	ex F-WWYJ	3304	
☐ N805NW	Airbus A330-323E	552	ex F-WWKQ	3305	
☐ N806NW	Airbus A330-323E	578	ex F-WWKD	3306	
☐ N807NW	Airbus A330-323E	588	ex F-WWKM	3307	
☐ N808NW	Airbus A330-323E	591	ex F-WWKO	3308	
☐ N809NW	Airbus A330-323E	663	ex F-WWKM	3309	
☐ N810NW	Airbus A330-323E	674	ex F-WWKT	3310	
☐ N811NW	Airbus A330-323E	690	ex F-WWKV	3311	
☐ N812NW	Airbus A330-323E	784	ex F-WWYX	3312	
☐ N813NW	Airbus A330-323E	799	ex F-WWKV	3313	
☐ N814NW	Airbus A330-323E	806	ex F-WWYN	3314	
☐ N815NW	Airbus A330-323E	817	ex F-WWYP	3315	
☐ N816NW	Airbus A330-323E	827	ex F-WWKG	3316	
☐ N817NW	Airbus A330-323E	843	ex F-WWYX	3317	
☐ N818NW	Airbus A330-323E	857	ex F-WWYD	3318	
☐ N819NW	Airbus A330-323E	858	ex F-WWYE	3319	
☐ N820NW	Airbus A330-323E	859	ex F-WWYF	3320	
☐ N821NW	Airbus A330-323E	865	ex F-WWYJ	3321	
☐ N851NW	Airbus A330-223	609	ex F-WWYZ	3351	
☐ N852NW	Airbus A330-223	614	ex F-WWKU	3352	
☐ N853NW	Airbus A330-223	618	ex F-WWKN	3353	
☐ N854NW	Airbus A330-223	620	ex F-WWYA	3354	
☐ N855NW	Airbus A330-223	621	ex F-WWYB	3355	
☐ N856NW	Airbus A330-223	631	ex F-WWYG	3356	
☐ N857NW	Airbus A330-223	633	ex F-WWYI	3357	
☐ N858NW	Airbus A330-223	718	ex F-WWYY	3358	
☐ N859NW	Airbus A330-223	722	ex F-WWKM	3359	
☐ N860NW	Airbus A330-223	778	ex F-WWKL	3360	
☐ N861NW	Airbus A330-223	796	ex F-WWKT	3361	
☐ N301DQ	Boeing 737-732/W	29687/2667	ex N1795B		
☐ N302DQ	Boeing 737-732/W	29648/2683			
☐ N303DQ	Boeing 737-732/W	29688/2720	ex N1786B		
☐ N304DQ	Boeing 737-732/W	29683/2724	ex N1787B		
☐ N305DQ	Boeing 737-732/W	29645/2743			
☐ N306DQ	Boeing 737-732/W	29633/2758			
☐ N307DQ	Boeing 737-732/W	29679/2767			
☐ N308DE	Boeing 737-732/W	29656/3022	ex N1786B		
☐ N309DE	Boeing 737-732/W	29634/3031	ex N1796B		
☐ N310DE	Boeing 737-732/W	29665/3058	ex N1786B		
☐ N371DA	Boeing 737-832	29619/115	ex N1787B	3701	
☐ N372DA	Boeing 737-832	29620/118	ex N1782B	3702	
☐ N373DA	Boeing 737-832	29621/123	ex N1800B	3703	
☐ N374DA	Boeing 737-832/W	29622/128	ex N1787B	3704	
☐ N375DA	Boeing 737-832	29623/145		3705	
☐ N376DA	Boeing 737-832	29624/176		3706	
☐ N377DA	Boeing 737-832/W	29625/264		3707	
☐ N378DA	Boeing 737-832	30265/340		3708	
☐ N379DA	Boeing 737-832	30349/351		3709	
☐ N380DA	Boeing 737-832	30266/361		3710	
☐ N381DN	Boeing 737-832/W	30350/365	ex (N381DA)	3711	
☐ N382DA	Boeing 737-832/W	30345/389		3712	
☐ N383DN	Boeing 737-832/W	30346/393	ex (N383DA)	3713	
☐ N384DA	Boeing 737-832/W	30347/412		3714	
☐ N385DN	Boeing 737-832	30348/418		3715	
☐ N386DA	Boeing 737-832/W	30373/446	ex N1780B	3716	
☐ N387DA	Boeing 737-832/W	30374/457	ex N1795B	3717	
☐ N388DA	Boeing 737-832	30375/469		3718	
☐ N389DA	Boeing 737-832/W	30376/513	ex N1787B	3719	
☐ N390DA	Boeing 737-832/W	30536/518	ex N6063S	3720	
☐ N391DA	Boeing 737-832/W	30560/535	ex N1787B	3721	
☐ N392DA	Boeing 737-832	30561/564		3722	
☐ N393DA	Boeing 737-832/W	30377/584	ex N1782B	3723	
☐ N394DA	Boeing 737-832/W	30562/589		3724	
☐ N395DN	Boeing 737-832/W	30773/604		3725	
☐ N396DA	Boeing 737-832	30378/632	ex N1795B	3726	Delta Shuttle
☐ N397DA	Boeing 737-832/W	30537/638		3727	Delta Shuttle
☐ N398DA	Boeing 737-832/W	30774/641		3728	Delta Shuttle
☐ N399DA	Boeing 737-832/W	30379/657		3729	Delta Shuttle

☐ N3730B	Boeing 737-832	30538/662		3730		Delta Shuttle
☐ N3731T	Boeing 737-832/W	30775/665		3731		Delta Shuttle
☐ N3732J	Boeing 737-832/W	30380/674		3732		Delta Shuttle
☐ N3733Z	Boeing 737-832	30539/685		3733		Delta Shuttle
☐ N3734B	Boeing 737-832/W	30776/689		3734		Delta Shuttle
☐ N3735D	Boeing 737-832/W	30381/694	ex (N3735J)	3735		Delta Shuttle
☐ N3736C	Boeing 737-832	30540/709		3736		Delta Shuttle
☐ N3737C	Boeing 737-832/W	30799/712		3737		
☐ N3738B	Boeing 737-832	30382/723		3738		
☐ N3739P	Boeing 737-832/W	30541/729		3739		
☐ N3740C	Boeing 737-832/W	30800/732		3740		
☐ N3741S	Boeing 737-832	30487/750		3741		
☐ N3742C	Boeing 737-832/W	30835/755	ex N1781B	3742		
☐ N3743H	Boeing 737-832/W	30836/770	ex N1795B	3743		
☐ N3744F	Boeing 737-832/W	30837/805		3744		
☐ N3745B	Boeing 737-832/W	32373/831		3745		
☐ N3746H	Boeing 737-832/W	30488/842		3746		
☐ N3747D	Boeing 737-832/W	32374/846	ex N1787B	3747		
☐ N3748Y	Boeing 737-832/W	30489/865		3748		
☐ N3749D	Boeing 737-832/W	30490/867		3749		
☐ N3750D	Boeing 737-832/W	32375/870	ex N1787B	3750		
☐ N3751B	Boeing 737-832/W	30491/892		3751		
☐ N3752	Boeing 737-832/W	30492/894		3752		
☐ N3753	Boeing 737-832/W	32626/899		3753		
☐ N3754A	Boeing 737-832/W	29626/907		3754		
☐ N3755D	Boeing 737-832/W	29627/914		3755		
☐ N3756	Boeing 737-832/W	30493/917	ex N1799B	3756		
☐ N3757D	Boeing 737-832/W	30813/921		3757		
☐ N3758Y	Boeing 737-832/W	30814/923		3758		
☐ N3759	Boeing 737-832/W	30815/949		3759		
☐ N3760C	Boeing 737-832/W	30816/952	ex N1787B	3760		
☐ N3761R	Boeing 737-832/W	29628/964	ex N1784B	3761		
☐ N3762Y	Boeing 737-832/W	30817/968		3762		
☐ N3763D	Boeing 737-832/W	29629/1003	ex N1787B	3763		
☐ N3764D	Boeing 737-832/W	30818/1006		3764		
☐ N3765	Boeing 737-832/W	30819/1008	ex N1795B	3765		
☐ N3766	Boeing 737-832/W	30820/1029		3766		
☐ N3767	Boeing 737-832/W	30821/1031		3767		
☐ N3768	Boeing 737-832/W	29630/1053		3768		
☐ N3769L	Boeing 737-832/W	30822/1057		3769		
☐ N3771K	Boeing 737-832/W	29632/1103		3771		
☐ N37700	Boeing 737-832/W	29631/1074		3770		

☐ N616US	Boeing 747-251F	21120/258		6716		stored MZJ
☐ N619US	Boeing 747-251F	21321/308		6719		stored MZJ
☐ N623US	Boeing 747-251B	21705/374		6623		stored VCV
☐ N624US	Boeing 747-251B	21706/377		6624		stored MZJ
☐ N629US	Boeing 747-251F	22388/444		6729		stored MZJ
☐ N630US	Boeing 747-2J9F	21668/400	ex N1288E	6730		stored MZJ
☐ N631NW	Boeing 747-251B (SF)	23111/594	ex N631US	6631		
☐ N632NW	Boeing 747-251B (SF)	23112/595	ex N632US	6632		
☐ N639US	Boeing 747-251F	23887/680		6739		
☐ N640US	Boeing 747-251F	23888/682		6740		stored MZJ
☐ N643NW	Boeing 747-249F	22245/458	ex N9401	6743		
☐ N644NW^	Boeing 747-212F	24177/710	ex ZS-SBJ	6744		
☐ N645NW	Boeing 747-222B (SF)	23736/673	ex N151UA	6745		stored MZJ
☐ N646NW	Boeing 747-222B (SF)	23737/675	ex N152UA	6746		stored MZJ
☐ N661US	Boeing 747-451	23719/696	ex N401PW	6301		
☐ N662US	Boeing 747-451	23720/708	ex (N302US)	6302		
☐ N663US	Boeing 747-451	23818/715	ex (N303US)	6303		
☐ N664US	Boeing 747-451	23819/721	ex (N304US)	6304	The Spirit of Beijing	
☐ N665US	Boeing 747-451	23820/726	ex (N305US)	6305		Delta c/s
☐ N666US	Boeing 747-451	23821/742	ex (N306US)	6306		
☐ N667US	Boeing 747-451	24222/799	ex (N307US)	6307		
☐ N668US	Boeing 747-451	24223/800	ex (N308US)	6308		
☐ N669US	Boeing 747-451	24224/803	ex (N309US)	6309		
☐ N670US	Boeing 747-451	24225/804	ex (N311US)	6310	Alliance Spirit	
☐ N671US	Boeing 747-451	26477/1206		6311		
☐ N672US	Boeing 747-451	30267/1223		6312		
☐ N673US	Boeing 747-451	30268/1226		6313		
☐ N674US	Boeing 747-451	30269/1232		6314		
☐ N675NW	Boeing 747-451	33001/1297		6315	N	
☐ N676NW	Boeing 747-451	33002/1303		6316		

☐ N501US	Boeing 757-251	23190/53		5501	St Paul	
☐ N502US	Boeing 757-251	23191/55		5502	Minneapolis	
☐ N503US	Boeing 757-251	23192/59		5503	Detroit	
☐ N507US	Boeing 757-251	23196/68		5507	Seattle	
☐ N508US	Boeing 757-251	23197/69		5508	Washington DC	stored MZJ
☐ N513US	Boeing 757-251	23201/83		5513	Orlando	stored MZJ
☐ N514US	Boeing 757-251	23202/86		5514	San Francisco	
☐ N516US	Boeing 757-251	23204/104		5516	San Diego	
☐ N517US	Boeing 757-251	23205/105		5517	Portland	

Registration	Type	C/n	Previous identity	Fleet no	Name	Notes
☐ N518US	Boeing 757-251	23206/107		5518	Milwaukee	
☐ N519US	Boeing 757-251	23207/108		5519	Cleveland	
☐ N520US	Boeing 757-251	23208/109		5520	Philadelphia	
☐ N521US	Boeing 757-251	23209/110		5521	Denver	
☐ N522US	Boeing 757-251	23616/119		5522		stored MZJ
☐ N523US	Boeing 757-251	23617/121		5523	Dallas	
☐ N525US	Boeing 757-251	23619/124		5525	Miami	stored MZJ
☐ N526US	Boeing 757-251	23620/131		5526	Memphis	
☐ N528US	Boeing 757-251	23843/137		5528		
☐ N529US	Boeing 757-251	23844/140		5529	New Orleans	
☐ N530US	Boeing 757-251	23845/188		5530	Omaha	
☐ N531US	Boeing 757-251	23846/190		5531	Newark	
☐ N532US	Boeing 757-251	24263/192		5532	Fort Myers	stored MZJ
☐ N533US	Boeing 757-251	24264/194		5533	Orange County	
☐ N534US	Boeing 757-251	24265/196		5534	Winnipeg	
☐ N535US	Boeing 757-251/W	26482/693		5635		
☐ N536US	Boeing 757-251/W	26483/695		5636		
☐ N537US	Boeing 757-251/W	26484/697		5637		
☐ N538US	Boeing 757-251/W	26485/699		5638		
☐ N539US	Boeing 757-251/W	26486/700		5639		Delta c/s
☐ N540US	Boeing 757-251/W	26487/701		5640		
☐ N541US	Boeing 757-251	26488/703		5641		
☐ N542US	Boeing 757-251	26489/705		5642		
☐ N543US	Boeing 757-251	26490/709		5643		
☐ N544US	Boeing 757-251/W	26491/710		5644		
☐ N545US	Boeing 757-251/W	26492/711		5645		
☐ N546US	Boeing 757-251/W	26493/713		5646		
☐ N547US	Boeing 757-251/W	26494/714		5647		
☐ N548US	Boeing 757-251/W	26495/715		5648		
☐ N549US	Boeing 757-251/W	26496/716		5649		
☐ N550NW	Boeing 757-251	26497/968		5550		
☐ N551NW	Boeing 757-251	26498/971		5551		
☐ N552NW	Boeing 757-251	26499/975		5552		
☐ N553NW	Boeing 757-251/W	26500/982		5553		
☐ N554NW	Boeing 757-251/W	26501/987		5554		
☐ N555NW	Boeing 757-251/W	33391/1011		5555		
☐ N556NW	Boeing 757-251/W	33392/1013		5556		
☐ N557NW	Boeing 757-251/W	33393/1016		5557		

names prefixed 'City of'

Registration	Type	C/n	Previous identity	Fleet no	Name	Notes
☐ N581NW	Boeing 757-351	32982/1001	ex N753JM	5801		
☐ N582NW	Boeing 757-351	32981/1014		5802,	The Bernie Epple	
☐ N583NW	Boeing 757-351	32983/1019		5803		
☐ N584NW	Boeing 757-351	32984/1020		5804		
☐ N585NW	Boeing 757-351	32985/1021		5805		
☐ N586NW	Boeing 757-351	32987/1022		5806		
☐ N587NW	Boeing 757-351	32986/1023		5807		
☐ N588NW	Boeing 757-351	32988/1024		5808		
☐ N589NW	Boeing 757-351	32989/1025		5809		
☐ N590NW	Boeing 757-351	32990/1027	ex N1795B	5810		
☐ N591NW	Boeing 757-351	32991/1030		5811		
☐ N592NW	Boeing 757-351	32992/1033		5812		
☐ N593NW	Boeing 757-351	32993/1034	ex N1795B	5813		
☐ N594NW	Boeing 757-351	32994/1035		5814		
☐ N595NW	Boeing 757-351	32995/1036	ex N1795B	5815		
☐ N596NW	Boeing 757-351	32996/1037		5816		

Registration	Type	C/n	Previous identity	Fleet no	Name	Notes
☐ N602DL	Boeing 757-232	22809/39		602		
☐ N603DL	Boeing 757-232	22810/41		603		
☐ N604DL	Boeing 757-232	22811/43		604		
☐ N608DA	Boeing 757-232	22815/64		608		
☐ N609DL	Boeing 757-232	22816/65		609		
☐ N610DL	Boeing 757-232	22817/66		610		pink c/s
☐ N612DL	Boeing 757-232	22819/73		612		
☐ N613DL	Boeing 757-232	22820/84		613		
☐ N614DL	Boeing 757-232	22821/85		614		
☐ N615DL	Boeing 757-232	22822/87		615		
☐ N616DL	Boeing 757-232	22823/91		616		stored SAT
☐ N617DL	Boeing 757-232	22907/92		617		stored MZJ
☐ N618DL	Boeing 757-232	22908/95		618		stored MZJ
☐ N619DL	Boeing 757-232	22909/101		619		
☐ N620DL	Boeing 757-232	22910/111		620		for CCI
☐ N621DL	Boeing 757-232	22911/112		621		
☐ N622DL	Boeing 757-232	22912/113		622		stored MZJ
☐ N623DL	Boeing 757-232	22913/118		623		
☐ N624DL	Boeing 757-232	22914/120		624		
☐ N625DL	Boeing 757-232	22915/126		625		
☐ N626DL	Boeing 757-232	22916/128		626		
☐ N627DL	Boeing 757-232	22917/129		627		
☐ N628DL	Boeing 757-232	22918/133		628		
☐ N629DL	Boeing 757-232	22919/134		629		
☐ N630DL	Boeing 757-232	22920/135		630		
☐ N631DL	Boeing 757-232	23612/138		631		

☐ N632DL	Boeing 757-232	23613/154		632	
☐ N633DL	Boeing 757-232	23614/157		633	
☐ N634DL	Boeing 757-232	23615/158		634	
☐ N635DL	Boeing 757-232	23762/159	ex 'N635DA'	635	
☐ N636DL	Boeing 757-232	23763/164		636	
☐ N637DL	Boeing 757-232	23760/171		637	
☐ N638DL	Boeing 757-232	23761/177		638	
☐ N639DL	Boeing 757-232	23993/198		639	
☐ N640DL	Boeing 757-232	23994/201		640	
☐ N641DL	Boeing 757-232	23995/202		641	
☐ N642DL	Boeing 757-232	23996/205		642	
☐ N643DL	Boeing 757-232	23997/206		643	
☐ N644DL	Boeing 757-232	23998/207		644	
☐ N645DL	Boeing 757-232	24216/216		645	
☐ N646DL	Boeing 757-232	24217/217		646	stored VCV
☐ N647DL	Boeing 757-232	24218/222		647	
☐ N648DL	Boeing 757-232/W	24372/223		648	
☐ N649DL	Boeing 757-232/W	24389/229		649	
☐ N650DL	Boeing 757-232/W	24390/230		650	
☐ N651DL	Boeing 757-232	24391/238		651	
☐ N652DL	Boeing 757-232	24392/239		652	
☐ N653DL	Boeing 757-232	24393/261		653	
☐ N654DL	Boeing 757-232	24394/264		654	
☐ N655DL	Boeing 757-232	24395/265		655	
☐ N656DL	Boeing 757-232	24396/266		656	
☐ N657DL	Boeing 757-232	24419/286		657	
☐ N658DL	Boeing 757-232	24420/287		658	stored MZJ
☐ N659DL	Boeing 757-232	24421/293		659	stored MZJ
☐ N660DL	Boeing 757-232	24422/294		660	
☐ N661DN	Boeing 757-232	24972/335		661	stored MZJ
☐ N662DN	Boeing 757-232	24991/342		662	
☐ N663DN	Boeing 757-232	24992/343		663	
☐ N664DN	Boeing 757-232	25012/347		664	
☐ N665DN	Boeing 757-232	25013/349		665	
☐ N666DN	Boeing 757-232	25034/354		666	
☐ N667DN	Boeing 757-232	25035/355		667	
☐ N668DN	Boeing 757-232	25141/376		668	
☐ N669DN	Boeing 757-232	25142/377		669	
☐ N670DN	Boeing 757-232	25331/415		670	
☐ N671DN	Boeing 757-232	25332/416		671	
☐ N672DL	Boeing 757-232	25977/429		672	
☐ N673DL	Boeing 757-232	25978/430		673	
☐ N674DL	Boeing 757-232	25979/439		674	
☐ N675DL	Boeing 757-232	25980/448		675	
☐ N676DL	Boeing 757-232	25981/455		676	
☐ N677DL	Boeing 757-232	25982/456		677	
☐ N678DL	Boeing 757-232	25983/465		678	
☐ N679DA	Boeing 757-232	26955/500		679	
☐ N680DA	Boeing 757-232	26956/502		680	
☐ N681DA	Boeing 757-232	26957/516		681	
☐ N682DA	Boeing 757-232	26958/518		682	
☐ N683DA	Boeing 757-232	27103/533		683	
☐ N684DA	Boeing 757-232	27104/535		684	
☐ N685DA	Boeing 757-232	27588/667		685	
☐ N686DA	Boeing 757-232	27589/689		686	
☐ N687DL	Boeing 757-232	27586/800		687	
☐ N688DL	Boeing 757-232	27587/803		688	
☐ N689DL	Boeing 757-232	27172/807		689	
☐ N690DL	Boeing 757-232	27585/808		690	
☐ N692DL	Boeing 757-232	29724/820	ex N1799B	692	
☐ N693DL	Boeing 757-232	29725/826	ex N1799B	693	
☐ N694DL	Boeing 757-232	29726/831		694	
☐ N695DL	Boeing 757-232	29727/838	ex N1795B	695	
☐ N696DL	Boeing 757-232	29728/845	ex N1795B	696	
☐ N697DL	Boeing 757-232	30318/880	ex N1795B	697	
☐ N698DL	Boeing 757-232	29911/885		698	
☐ N699DL	Boeing 757-232	29970/887	ex N1795B	699	
☐ N702TW	Boeing 757-2Q8/W	28162/732		6801	
☐ N703TW	Boeing 757-2Q8ER/W	27620/736		6802	
☐ N704X	Boeing 757-2Q8/W	28163/741		6803	
☐ N705TW	Boeing 757-231/W	28479/742		6811	
☐ N706TW	Boeing 757-2Q8/W	28165/743		6804	
☐ N707TW	Boeing 757-2Q8ER/W	27625/744		6805	
☐ N709TW	Boeing 757-2Q8/W	28168/754		6806	
☐ N710TW	Boeing 757-2Q8/W	28169/757		6807	
☐ N711ZX	Boeing 757-231/W	28481/758		6814	
☐ N712TW	Boeing 757-2Q8ER/W	27624/760		6808	
☐ N713TW	Boeing 757-2Q8/W	28173/764		6809	
☐ N717TW	Boeing 757-231/W	28485/854		6812	
☐ N718TW	Boeing 757-231/W	28486/869		6815	
☐ N721TW	Boeing 757-231/W	29954/874		6810	
☐ N722TW	Boeing 757-231/W	29385/893	ex N1795B	6816	
☐ N723TW	Boeing 757-231/W	29378/907		6817	

☐ N727TW	Boeing 757-231/W	30340/901		6813	
☐ N750AT	Boeing 757-212ER	23126/45	ex 9V-SGL	6902	
☐ N751AT	Boeing 757-212ER	23125/44	ex 9V-SGK	6901	
☐ N752AT	Boeing 757-212ER	23128/48	ex 9V-SGN	6904	
☐ N757AT	Boeing 757-212ER	23127/47	ex 9V-SGM	6903	
☐ N900PC	Boeing 757-26D	28446/740		691	
☐ N6700	Boeing 757-232	30337/890		6700	
☐ N6701	Boeing 757-232	30187/892		6701	
☐ N6702	Boeing 757-232	30188/898		6702	
☐ N6703D	Boeing 757-232	30234/908	ex N1795B	6703	
☐ N6704Z	Boeing 757-232	30396/914	ex N1795B	6704	
☐ N6705Y	Boeing 757-232	30397/917		6705	
☐ N6706Q	Boeing 757-232	30422/921		6706	
☐ N6707A	Boeing 757-232	30395/927		6707	
☐ N6708D	Boeing 757-232	30480/934		6708	
☐ N6709	Boeing 757-232	30481/937		6709	
☐ N6710E	Boeing 757-232	30482/939		6710	
☐ N6711M	Boeing 757-232	30483/941		6711	
☐ N6712B	Boeing 757-232	30484/942		6712	
☐ N6713Y	Boeing 757-232	30777/944		6713	
☐ N6714Q	Boeing 757-232	30485/949		6714	
☐ N6715C	Boeing 757-232	30486/953		6715	
☐ N6716C	Boeing 757-232	30838/955		6716	
☐ N67171	Boeing 757-232	30839/959		6717	

☐ N121DE	Boeing 767-332	23435/162		121	stored VCV
☐ N124DE	Boeing 767-332	23438/189		124	stored VCV
☐ N125DL	Boeing 767-332	24075/200		125	
☐ N126DL	Boeing 767-332	24076/201		126	
☐ N127DL	Boeing 767-332	24077/203		127	
☐ N128DL	Boeing 767-332	24078/207		128	
☐ N129DL	Boeing 767-332	24079/209		129	
☐ N130DL	Boeing 767-332	24080/216		130	
☐ N131DN	Boeing 767-332	24852/320		131	stored MZJ
☐ N132DN	Boeing 767-332	24981/345		132	stored VCV
☐ N133DN	Boeing 767-332	24982/348		133	stored VCV
☐ N134DL	Boeing 767-332	25123/353		134	stored VCV
☐ N135DL	Boeing 767-332	25145/356		135	stored VCV
☐ N136DL	Boeing 767-332	25146/374		136	
☐ N137DL	Boeing 767-332	25306/392		137	
☐ N138DL	Boeing 767-332	25409/410		138	
☐ N139DL	Boeing 767-332	25984/427		139	
☐ N140LL	Boeing 767-332	25988/499		1401	
☐ N143DA	Boeing 767-332	25991/721		1403	
☐ N144DA	Boeing 767-332	27584/751		1404	
☐ N152DL	Boeing 767-3P6ER	24984/339	ex A4O-GM	1502	
☐ N153DL	Boeing 767-3P6ER	24985/340	ex A4O-GN	1503	
☐ N154DL	Boeing 767-3P6ER	25241/389	ex A4O-GO	1504	
☐ N155DL	Boeing 767-3P6ER	25269/390	ex A4O-GP	1505	
☐ N156DL	Boeing 767-3P6ER	25354/406	ex A4O-GR	1506	
☐ N169DZ	Boeing 767-332ER	29689/706		1601	
☐ N171DN	Boeing 767-332ER	24759/304		171	
☐ N171DZ	Boeing 767-332ER	29690/717		1701	Habitat for Humanity c/s
☐ N172DN	Boeing 767-332ER	24775/312		172	stored VCV
☐ N172DZ	Boeing 767-332ER	29691/719		1702	
☐ N173DN	Boeing 767-332ER	24800/313		173	stored VCV
☐ N173DZ	Boeing 767-332ER	29692/723		1703	
☐ N174DN	Boeing 767-332ER	24802/317		174	
☐ N174DZ	Boeing 767-332ER	29693/725		1704	
☐ N175DN	Boeing 767-332ER	24803/318		175	
☐ N175DZ	Boeing 767-332ER	29696/740		1705	
☐ N176DN	Boeing 767-332ER	25061/341		176	
☐ N176DZ	Boeing 767-332ER	29697/745		1706	
☐ N177DN	Boeing 767-332ER	25122/346		177	
☐ N177DZ	Boeing 767-332ER	29698/750		1707	
☐ N178DN	Boeing 767-332ER	25143/349		178	
☐ N178DZ	Boeing 767-332ER	30596/795		1708	
☐ N179DN	Boeing 767-332ER	25144/350		179	
☐ N180DN	Boeing 767-332ER	25985/428		180	
☐ N181DN	Boeing 767-332ER	25986/446		181	
☐ N182DN	Boeing 767-332ER	25987/461		182	
☐ N183DN	Boeing 767-332ER	27110/492		183	
☐ N184DN	Boeing 767-332ER	27111/496		184	
☐ N185DN	Boeing 767-332ER/W	27961/576		185	
☐ N186DN	Boeing 767-332ER	27962/585		186	stored MZJ
☐ N187DN	Boeing 767-332ER	27582/617		187	
☐ N188DN	Boeing 767-332ER	27583/631		188	
☐ N189DN	Boeing 767-332ER	25990/646		189	
☐ N190DN	Boeing 767-332ER	28447/653		190	
☐ N191DN	Boeing 767-332ER/W	28448/654		191	
☐ N192DN	Boeing 767-332ER/W	28449/664		192	
☐ N193DN	Boeing 767-332ER	28450/671		193	
☐ N194DN	Boeing 767-332ER	28451/675		194	stored MZJ

☐ N195DN	Boeing 767-332ER	28452/676		195	
☐ N196DN	Boeing 767-332ER	28453/679		196	
☐ N197DN	Boeing 767-332ER	28454/683		197	
☐ N198DN	Boeing 767-332ER	28455/685		198	
☐ N199DN	Boeing 767-332ER	28456/690		199	
☐ N394DL	Boeing 767-324ER	27394/572	ex HL7505	1521	
☐ N1200K	Boeing 767-332ER	28457/696		1200	
☐ N1201P	Boeing 767-332ER	28458/697		1201	
☐ N1402A	Boeing 767-332	25989/506		1402	
☐ N1501P	Boeing 767-3P6ER	24983/334	ex A4O-GL	1501	
☐ N1602	Boeing 767-332ER	29694/735		1602	
☐ N1603	Boeing 767-332ER	29695/736		1603	
☐ N1604R	Boeing 767-332ER	30180/749		1604	
☐ N1605	Boeing 767-332ER	30198/753		1605	
☐ N1607B	Boeing 767-332ER/W	30388/787		1607	
☐ N1608	Boeing 767-332ER/W	30573/788		1608	
☐ N1609	Boeing 767-332ER/W	30574/789		1609	
☐ N1610D	Boeing 767-332ER/W	30594/790		1610	
☐ N1611B	Boeing 767-332ER	30595/794		1611	
☐ N1612T	Boeing 767-332ER/W	30575/838		1612	
☐ N1613B	Boeing 767-332ER/W	32776/847		1613	
☐ N16065	Boeing 767-332ER	30199/755		1606	
☐ N825MH	Boeing 767-432ER	29703/758	ex N6067U	1801	
☐ N826MH	Boeing 767-432ER	29713/769		1802	
☐ N827MH	Boeing 767-432ER	29705/773	ex N76400	1803	
☐ N828MH	Boeing 767-432ER	29699/791		1804	
☐ N829MH	Boeing 767-432ER	29700/801		1805	
☐ N830MH	Boeing 767-432ER	29701/803		1806	
☐ N831MH	Boeing 767-432ER	29702/804		1807	
☐ N832MH	Boeing 767-432ER	29704/807		1808	
☐ N833MH	Boeing 767-432ER	29706/810		1809	
☐ N834MH	Boeing 767-432ER	29707/813		1810	
☐ N835MH	Boeing 767-432ER	29708/814		1811	
☐ N836MH	Boeing 767-432ER	29709/818		1812	
☐ N837MH	Boeing 767-432ER	29710/820		1813	
☐ N838MH	Boeing 767-432ER	29711/821		1814	
☐ N839MH	Boeing 767-432ER	29712/824		1815	
☐ N840MH	Boeing 767-432ER	29718/830		1816	
☐ N841MH	Boeing 767-432ER	29714/855		1817	
☐ N842MH	Boeing 767-432ER	29715/856		1818	
☐ N843MH	Boeing 767-432ER	29716/865		1819	
☐ N844MH	Boeing 767-432ER	29717/871		1820	
☐ N845MH	Boeing 767-432ER	29719/874		1821	
☐ N701DN	Boeing 777-232LR	29740/697	ex N5016R	7101	
☐ N702DN	Boeing 777-232LR	29741/704		7102	
☐ N703DN	Boeing 777-232LR	32222/767		7103	
☐ N704DK	Boeing 777-232LR	29739/772	ex N5016R		
☐ N705DN	Boeing 777-232LR	29742/773			
☐ N706DN	Boeing 777-232LR	30440/776	ex N5023Q		
☐ N707DN	Boeing 777-232LR	39091/782			
☐ N708DN	Boeing 777-232LR	39254/789			
☐ N709DN	Boeing 777-232LR	40559			on order
☐ N710DN	Boeing 777-232LR	40560			on order
☐ N860DA	Boeing 777-232ER	29951/202		7001	
☐ N861DA	Boeing 777-232ER	29952/207		7002	
☐ N862DA	Boeing 777-232ER	29734/235	ex N5022E	7003	
☐ N863DA	Boeing 777-232ER	29735/245	ex N5014K	7004	
☐ N864DA	Boeing 777-232ER	29736/249	ex N50217	7005	
☐ N865DA	Boeing 777-232ER	29737/257		7006	
☐ N866DA	Boeing 777-232ER	29738/261		7007	
☐ N867DA	Boeing 777-232ER	29743/387		7008	
☐ N89S	Douglas DC-9-31	47042/486		9930	
☐ N90S	Douglas DC-9-31	47244/498		9931	stored MZJ
☐ N401EA	Douglas DC-9-51	47682/788	ex N920VJ	9885	
☐ N600TR	Douglas DC-9-51	47783/899	ex YV-40C	9886	
☐ N613NW	Douglas DC-9-32	47438/545	ex I-RIFP	9613	
☐ N616NW	Douglas DC-9-32	47229/356	ex I-RIFS	9616	stored MZJ
☐ N618NW	Douglas DC-9-32	47433/526	ex I-RIFU	9618	stored MZJ
☐ N621NW	Douglas DC-9-32	47544/676	ex I-RIFM	9621	stored MZJ
☐ N623NW	Douglas DC-9-32	47591/706	ex I-RIFT	9623	stored MZJ
☐ N670MC	Douglas DC-9-51	47659/807	ex HB-ISP	9882	
☐ N671MC	Douglas DC-9-51	47660/818	ex HB-ISR	9883	
☐ N675MC	Douglas DC-9-51	47651/780	ex OE-LDK	9880	stored MZJ
☐ N676MC	Douglas DC-9-51	47652/798	ex OE-LDL	9881	
☐ N677MC	Douglas DC-9-51	47756/873	ex OE-LDO	9884	
☐ N750NW	Douglas DC-9-41	47114/218	ex SE-DBX	9750	stored MZJ
☐ N751NW	Douglas DC-9-41	47115/261	ex OY-KGA	9751	
☐ N752NW	Douglas DC-9-41	47116/308	ex LN-RLK	9752	
☐ N753NW	Douglas DC-9-41	47117/319	ex SE-DBW	9753	stored MZJ
☐ N754NW	Douglas DC-9-41	47178/323	ex OY-KGB	9754	stored MZJ

☐ N755NW	Douglas DC-9-41	47179/335	ex LN-RLC	9755	
☐ N756NW	Douglas DC-9-41	47180/354	ex SE-DBU	9756	stored MZJ
☐ N758NW	Douglas DC-9-41	47286/359	ex OY-KGC	9758	stored MZJ
☐ N759NW	Douglas DC-9-41	47287/364	ex LN-RLJ	9759	
☐ N760NC	Douglas DC-9-51	47708/813		9851	
☐ N760NW	Douglas DC-9-41	47288/369	ex SE-DBT	9760	
☐ N761NC	Douglas DC-9-51	47709/814		9852	
☐ N762NC	Douglas DC-9-51	47710/818		9853	
☐ N762NW	Douglas DC-9-41	47395/555	ex OY-KGG	9762	
☐ N763NW	Douglas DC-9-41	47396/557	ex LN-RLD	9763	
☐ N764NC	Douglas DC-9-51	47717/833		9855	
☐ N765NC	Douglas DC-9-51	47718/834		9856	
☐ N766NC	Douglas DC-9-51	47739/852		9857	
☐ N767NC	Douglas DC-9-51	47724/853		9858	
☐ N768NC	Douglas DC-9-51	47729/854		9859	
☐ N769NC	Douglas DC-9-51	47757/877		9860	
☐ N770NC	Douglas DC-9-51	47758/880		9861	
☐ N771NC	Douglas DC-9-51	47769/881		9862	
☐ N772NC	Douglas DC-9-51	47774/884		9863	
☐ N773NC	Douglas DC-9-51	47775/888		9864	
☐ N774NC	Douglas DC-9-51	47776/889		9865	
☐ N775NC	Douglas DC-9-51	47785/904		9866	
☐ N776NC	Douglas DC-9-51	47786/905		9867	Delta c/s
☐ N777NC	Douglas DC-9-51	47787/912		9868	
☐ N778NC	Douglas DC-9-51	48100/927		9869	
☐ N779NC	Douglas DC-9-51	48101/931		9870	
☐ N780NC	Douglas DC-9-51	48102/932		9871	
☐ N781NC	Douglas DC-9-51	48121/935		9872	
☐ N782NC	Douglas DC-9-51	48107/936		9873	
☐ N783NC	Douglas DC-9-51	48108/937		9874	
☐ N784NC	Douglas DC-9-51	48109/939		9875	
☐ N785NC	Douglas DC-9-51	48110/945		9876	
☐ N786NC	Douglas DC-9-51	48148/984		9877	
☐ N787NC	Douglas DC-9-51	48149/990		9878	
☐ N914RW	Douglas DC-9-31	47362/492	ex N907H	9962	stored MZJ
☐ N915RW	Douglas DC-9-31	47139/169	ex N8930E	9957	
☐ N916RW	Douglas DC-9-31	47144/239	ex N8935E	9952	stored MZJ
☐ N917RW	Douglas DC-9-31	47145/247	ex N8936E	9958	stored MZJ
☐ N920RW	Douglas DC-9-31	47163/256	ex N8940E	9960	stored MZJ
☐ N921RW	Douglas DC-9-31	47164/259	ex N8941E	9954	stored MZJ
☐ N923RW	Douglas DC-9-31	47183/272	ex N8947E	9956	
☐ N925US	Douglas DC-9-32	47472/596	ex YU-AHO	9925	
☐ N926NW	Douglas DC-9-32	47425/589	ex YU-AHL	9926	
☐ N940N	Douglas DC-9-32	47572/708		9918	stored MZJ
☐ N943N	Douglas DC-9-32	47647/773		9921	stored MZJ
☐ N945N	Douglas DC-9-32	47664/775		9922	
☐ N956N	Douglas DC-9-31	47252/294		9906	stored MZJ
☐ N959N	Douglas DC-9-31	47255/310		9909	stored MZJ
☐ N964N	Douglas DC-9-31	47416/512		9914	stored MZJ
☐ N965N	Douglas DC-9-31	47417/518		9915	stored MZJ
☐ N967N	Douglas DC-9-32	47573/694		9917	
☐ N984US	Douglas DC-9-32	47383/538	ex HB-IFV	9984	stored MZJ
☐ N987US	Douglas DC-9-32	47458/646	ex OE-LDF	9987	stored MZJ
☐ N994Z	Douglas DC-9-32	47097/193	ex N979NE	9981	stored MZJ
☐ N1309T	Douglas DC-9-31	47316/439		9944	
☐ N1332U	Douglas DC-9-31	47404/554		9935	
☐ N1334U	Douglas DC-9-31	47280/597		9933	
☐ N1799U	Douglas DC-9-31	47370/551		9936	stored MZJ
☐ N3322L	Douglas DC-9-32	47031/187	ex YV-68C	9940	stored MZJ
☐ N3324L	Douglas DC-9-32	47103/205	ex YV-70C	9941	stored MZJ
☐ N8920E	Douglas DC-9-31	45835/95		9927	
☐ N8921E	Douglas DC-9-31	45836/96		9928	stored MZJ
☐ N8923E	Douglas DC-9-31	45838/104		9929	
☐ N8925E	Douglas DC-9-31	45840/117		9945	
☐ N8926E	Douglas DC-9-31	45863/124		9946	
☐ N8928E	Douglas DC-9-31	45865/137		9949	
☐ N8929E	Douglas DC-9-31	45866/138		9948	stored MZJ
☐ N8932E	Douglas DC-9-31	47141/227		9996	
☐ N8933E	Douglas DC-9-31	47142/232		9997	
☐ N8938E	Douglas DC-9-31	47161/249	ex 5N-GIN	9947	
☐ N8944E	Douglas DC-9-31	47167/266		9988	
☐ N8945E	Douglas DC-9-31	47181/267		9989	
☐ N8960E	Douglas DC-9-31	45869/331		9992	
☐ N8978E	Douglas DC-9-31	47327/391		9993	
☐ N8986E	Douglas DC-9-31	47402/482	ex 5N-INZ	9993	
☐ N9330	Douglas DC-9-31	47138/318		9966	stored MZJ
☐ N9332	Douglas DC-9-31	47264/329	ex (N9107)	9968	stored MZJ
☐ N9333	Douglas DC-9-31	47246/292		9969	stored MZJ
☐ N9338	Douglas DC-9-31	47347/478		9974	
☐ N9341	Douglas DC-9-31	47390/490		9977	stored MZJ
☐ N9343	Douglas DC-9-31	47439/501		9979	stored MZJ
☐ N9344	Douglas DC-9-31	47440/502		9980	stored MZJ
☐ N9346	Douglas DC-9-32	47376/517	ex N394PA	9950	

	Reg	Type	c/n	Previous	Fleet no	Notes
☐	N9347	Douglas DC-9-32	45827/135	ex HL7201	9951	stored MZJ
☐	N900DE	McDonnell-Douglas MD-88	53372/1970		9000	
☐	N901DE	McDonnell-Douglas MD-88	53378/1980		9001	
☐	N902DE	McDonnell-Douglas MD-88	53379/1983		9002	
☐	N903DE	McDonnell-Douglas MD-88	53380/1986		9003	
☐	N904DE	McDonnell-Douglas MD-88	53409/1990		9004	
☐	N904DL	McDonnell-Douglas MD-88	49535/1347		904	
☐	N905DE	McDonnell-Douglas MD-88	53410/1992		9005	
☐	N905DL	McDonnell-Douglas MD-88	49536/1348		905	
☐	N906DE	McDonnell-Douglas MD-88	53415/2027		9006	
☐	N906DL	McDonnell-Douglas MD-88	49537/1355		906	
☐	N907DE	McDonnell-Douglas MD-88	53416/2029		9007	
☐	N907DL	McDonnell-Douglas MD-88	49538/1365		907	
☐	N908DE	McDonnell-Douglas MD-88	53417/2032		9008	
☐	N908DL	McDonnell-Douglas MD-88	49539/1366		908	
☐	N909DE	McDonnell-Douglas MD-88	53418/2033		9009	
☐	N909DL	McDonnell-Douglas MD-88	49540/1395		909	
☐	N910DE	McDonnell-Douglas MD-88	53419/2036		9010	
☐	N910DL	McDonnell-Douglas MD-88	49541/1416		910	
☐	N911DE	McDonnell-Douglas MD-88	49967/2037		9011	
☐	N911DL	McDonnell-Douglas MD-88	49542/1433		911	
☐	N912DE	McDonnell-Douglas MD-88	49997/2038		9012	
☐	N912DL	McDonnell-Douglas MD-88	49543/1434		912	
☐	N913DE	McDonnell-Douglas MD-88	49956/2039		9013	
☐	N913DL	McDonnell-Douglas MD-88	49544/1443		913	
☐	N914DE	McDonnell-Douglas MD-88	49957/2049		9014	
☐	N914DL	McDonnell-Douglas MD-88	49545/1444		914	
☐	N915DE	McDonnell-Douglas MD-88	53420/2050		9015	Delta Shuttle
☐	N915DL	McDonnell-Douglas MD-88	49546/1447		915	
☐	N916DE	McDonnell-Douglas MD-88	53421/2051		9016	
☐	N916DL	McDonnell-Douglas MD-88	49591/1448		916	
☐	N917DE	McDonnell-Douglas MD-88	49958/2054		9017	
☐	N917DL	McDonnell-Douglas MD-88	49573/1469		917	
☐	N918DE	McDonnell-Douglas MD-88	49959/2055		9018	
☐	N918DL	McDonnell-Douglas MD-88	49583/1470		918	stored VCV
☐	N919DE	McDonnell-Douglas MD-88	53422/2058		9019	
☐	N919DL	McDonnell-Douglas MD-88	49584/1471		919	
☐	N920DE	McDonnell-Douglas MD-88	53423/2059		9020	
☐	N920DL	McDonnell-Douglas MD-88	49644/1473		920	
☐	N921DL	McDonnell-Douglas MD-88	49645/1480		921	
☐	N922DL	McDonnell-Douglas MD-88	49646/1481		922	
☐	N923DL	McDonnell-Douglas MD-88	49705/1491		923	
☐	N924DL	McDonnell-Douglas MD-88	49711/1492		924	stored VCV
☐	N925DL	McDonnell-Douglas MD-88	49712/1500		925	
☐	N926DL	McDonnell-Douglas MD-88	49713/1523		926	
☐	N927DA	McDonnell-Douglas MD-88	49714/1524		927	
☐	N928DL	McDonnell-Douglas MD-88	49715/1530		928	
☐	N929DL	McDonnell-Douglas MD-88	49716/1531		929	
☐	N930DL	McDonnell-Douglas MD-88	49717/1532		930	
☐	N931DL	McDonnell-Douglas MD-88	49718/1533		931	
☐	N932DL	McDonnell-Douglas MD-88	49719/1570		932	
☐	N933DL	McDonnell-Douglas MD-88	49720/1571		933	
☐	N934DL	McDonnell-Douglas MD-88	49721/1574		934	
☐	N935DL	McDonnell-Douglas MD-88	49722/1575		935	
☐	N936DL	McDonnell-Douglas MD-88	49723/1576		936	
☐	N937DL	McDonnell-Douglas MD-88	49810/1588		937	
☐	N938DL	McDonnell-Douglas MD-88	49811/1590		938	
☐	N939DL	McDonnell-Douglas MD-88	49812/1593		939	
☐	N940DL	McDonnell-Douglas MD-88	49813/1599		940	
☐	N941DL	McDonnell-Douglas MD-88	49814/1602		941	
☐	N942DL	McDonnell-Douglas MD-88	49815/1605		942	
☐	N943DL	McDonnell-Douglas MD-88	49816/1608		943	
☐	N944DL	McDonnell-Douglas MD-88	49817/1612		944	
☐	N945DL	McDonnell-Douglas MD-88	49818/1613		945	
☐	N946DL	McDonnell-Douglas MD-88	49819/1629		946	
☐	N947DL	McDonnell-Douglas MD-88	49878/1664		947	
☐	N948DL	McDonnell-Douglas MD-88	49879/1666		948	
☐	N949DL	McDonnell-Douglas MD-88	49880/1676		949	
☐	N950DL	McDonnell-Douglas MD-88	49881/1677		950	
☐	N951DL	McDonnell-Douglas MD-88	49882/1679		951	
☐	N952DL	McDonnell-Douglas MD-88	49883/1683		952	
☐	N953DL	McDonnell-Douglas MD-88	49884/1685		953	
☐	N954DL	McDonnell-Douglas MD-88	49885/1689		954	
☐	N955DL	McDonnell-Douglas MD-88	49886/1691		955	
☐	N956DL	McDonnell-Douglas MD-88	49887/1699		956	
☐	N957DL	McDonnell-Douglas MD-88	49976/1700		957	
☐	N958DL	McDonnell-Douglas MD-88	49977/1701		958	
☐	N959DL	McDonnell-Douglas MD-88	49978/1710		959	
☐	N960DL	McDonnell-Douglas MD-88	49979/1711		960	
☐	N961DL	McDonnell-Douglas MD-88	49980/1712		961	
☐	N962DL	McDonnell-Douglas MD-88	49981/1725		962	
☐	N963DL	McDonnell-Douglas MD-88	49982/1726		963	

Registration	Type	C/n	Previous identity	Fleet no.	Notes
☐ N964DL	McDonnell-Douglas MD-88	49983/1747		964	
☐ N965DL	McDonnell-Douglas MD-88	49984/1748		965	
☐ N966DL	McDonnell-Douglas MD-88	53115/1795		966	
☐ N967DL	McDonnell-Douglas MD-88	53116/1796		967	
☐ N968DL	McDonnell-Douglas MD-88	53161/1808		968	
☐ N969DL	McDonnell-Douglas MD-88	53172/1810		969	
☐ N970DL	McDonnell-Douglas MD-88	53173/1811		970	
☐ N971DL	McDonnell-Douglas MD-88	53214/1823		971	
☐ N972DL	McDonnell-Douglas MD-88	53215/1824		972	
☐ N973DL	McDonnell-Douglas MD-88	53241/1832		973	
☐ N974DL	McDonnell-Douglas MD-88	53242/1833		974	
☐ N975DL	McDonnell-Douglas MD-88	53243/1834		975	
☐ N976DL	McDonnell-Douglas MD-88	53257/1845		976	
☐ N977DL	McDonnell-Douglas MD-88	53258/1848		977	
☐ N978DL	McDonnell-Douglas MD-88	53259/1849		978	
☐ N979DL	McDonnell-Douglas MD-88	53266/1859		979	
☐ N980DL	McDonnell-Douglas MD-88	53267/1860		980	
☐ N981DL	McDonnell-Douglas MD-88	53268/1861		981	
☐ N982DL	McDonnell-Douglas MD-88	53273/1870		982	
☐ N983DL	McDonnell-Douglas MD-88	53274/1873		983	
☐ N984DL	McDonnell-Douglas MD-88	53311/1912		984	
☐ N985DL	McDonnell-Douglas MD-88	53312/1914		985	
☐ N986DL	McDonnell-Douglas MD-88	53313/1924		986	
☐ N987DL	McDonnell-Douglas MD-88	53338/1926		987	
☐ N988DL	McDonnell-Douglas MD-88	53339/1928		988	
☐ N989DL	McDonnell-Douglas MD-88	53341/1936		989	
☐ N990DL	McDonnell-Douglas MD-88	53342/1939		990	
☐ N991DL	McDonnell-Douglas MD-88	53343/1941		991	
☐ N992DL	McDonnell-Douglas MD-88	53344/1943		992	
☐ N993DL	McDonnell-Douglas MD-88	53345/1950		993	
☐ N994DL	McDonnell-Douglas MD-88	53346/1952		994	
☐ N995DL	McDonnell-Douglas MD-88	53362/1955		995	
☐ N996DL	McDonnell-Douglas MD-88	53363/1958		996	
☐ N997DL	McDonnell-Douglas MD-88	53364/1961		997	
☐ N998DL	McDonnell-Douglas MD-88	53370/1963		998	
☐ N999DN	McDonnell-Douglas MD-88	53371/1965		999	

Registration	Type	C/n	Previous identity	Fleet no.	Notes
☐ N901DA	McDonnell-Douglas MD-90-30	53381/2100	ex N902DC	9201	
☐ N902DA	McDonnell-Douglas MD-90-30	53382/2094		9202	
☐ N903DA	McDonnell-Douglas MD-90-30	53383/2095		9203	
☐ N904DA	McDonnell-Douglas MD-90-30	53384/2096		9204	
☐ N905DA	McDonnell-Douglas MD-90-30	53385/2097		9205	
☐ N906DA	McDonnell-Douglas MD-90-30	53386/2099		9206	
☐ N907DA	McDonnell-Douglas MD-90-30	53387/2115		9207	
☐ N908DA	McDonnell-Douglas MD-90-30	53388/2117		9208	
☐ N909DA	McDonnell-Douglas MD-90-30	53389/2122		9209	
☐ N910DN	McDonnell-Douglas MD-90-30	53390/2123		9210	
☐ N911DA	McDonnell-Douglas MD-90-30	53391/2126		9211	
☐ N912DN	McDonnell-Douglas MD-90-30	53392/2136		9212	
☐ N913DN	McDonnell-Douglas MD-90-30	53393/2154		9213	
☐ N914DN	McDonnell-Douglas MD-90-30	53394/2156		9214	
☐ N915DN	McDonnell-Douglas MD-90-30	53395/2159		9215	
☐ N916DN	McDonnell-Douglas MD-90-30	53396/2161		9216	
☐ N917DN	McDonnell-Douglas MD-90-30	53552/2163	ex N593BC		
☐ N918DH	McDonnell-Douglas MD-90-30	53553/2165	ex HB-JIB		
☐ N919DN	McDonnell-Douglas MD-90-30ER	53576/2195	ex HB-JIC		
☐ N	McDonnell-Douglas MD-90-30	53582/2198	ex B-2256		on order
☐ N	McDonnell-Douglas MD-90-30	53583/2200	ex B-2257		on order
☐ N	McDonnell-Douglas MD-90-30	53584/2203	ex B-2258		on order
☐ N	McDonnell-Douglas MD-90-30	53585/2224	ex B-2262		on order
☐ N	McDonnell-Douglas MD-90-30	53586/2233	ex B-2263		on order
☐ N	McDonnell-Douglas MD-90-30	53587/2240	ex B-2265		on order
☐ N	McDonnell-Douglas MD-90-30	53588/2248	ex B-2268		on order
☐ N	McDonnell-Douglas MD-90-30	53589/2259	ex B-2269		on order
☐ N	McDonnell-Douglas MD-90-30	53590/2261	ex B-2270		on order

DELTA CONNECTION (DL/DAL)

Cincinnati-Northern Kentucky Intl, OH/Atlanta-Hartsfield Intl, GA/Orlando-Intl, FL (CVG/ATL/MCO)

Registration	Type	C/n	Previous identity	Fleet no.	Notes
☐ N630AS	ATR 72-212	336	ex F-WWLS		Atlantic Southeast
☐ N631AS	ATR 72-212	362	ex F-WWEZ		Atlantic Southeast
☐ N632AS	ATR 72-212	338	ex F-WWLT		Atlantic Southeast
☐ N633AS	ATR 72-212	344	ex F-WWLC		Atlantic Southeast
☐ N634AS	ATR 72-212	370	ex F-WWEF		Atlantic Southeast
☐ N635AS	ATR 72-212	372	ex F-WWEP		Atlantic Southeast
☐ N636AS	ATR 72-212	375	ex F-WWLW		Atlantic Southeast
☐ N637AS	ATR 72-212	383	ex F-WWEB		Atlantic Southeast

Registration	Type	C/n	Previous identity	Fleet no.	Notes
☐ N403CA	Canadair CL-600-2B19 (CRJ-200ER)	7428	ex N896AS	7428	stored VCV
☐ N405SW	Canadair CL-600-2B19 (CRJ-200ER)	7029	ex C-FMND	7029	SkyWest
☐ N406SW	Canadair CL-600-2B19 (CRJ-200ER)	7030	ex C-FMNH	7030	SkyWest
☐ N408CA	Canadair CL-600-2B19 (CRJ-200ER)	7440	ex C-FMLQ	7440	Comair

☐	N408SW	Canadair CL-600-2B19 (CRJ-200ER)	7055	ex C-FMMW	7055	SkyWest
☐	N409CA	Canadair CL-600-2B19 (CRJ-200ER)	7441	ex C-FMLS	7441	Comair
☐	N409SW	Canadair CL-600-2B19 (CRJ-200ER)	7056	ex C-FMMX	7056	SkyWest
☐	N410SW	Canadair CL-600-2B19 (CRJ-200ER)	7066	ex C-FMOL	7066	SkyWest
☐	N411SW	Canadair CL-600-2B19 (CRJ-200ER)	7067	ex C-FMOS	7067	SkyWest
☐	N412SW	Canadair CL-600-2B19 (CRJ-200ER)	7101	ex C-FMMX	7101	SkyWest
					SkyWest 30th anniversary c/s	
☐	N416SW	Canadair CL-600-2B19 (CRJ-200ER)	7089	ex N60SR	7089	SkyWest
☐	N417SW	Canadair CL-600-2B19 (CRJ-200ER)	7400	ex C-FMMW	7400	SkyWest
☐	N418SW	Canadair CL-600-2B19 (CRJ-200ER)	7446	ex C-FMNW	7446	SkyWest
☐	N420CA	Canadair CL-600-2B19 (CRJ-200ER)	7451	ex C-FVAZ	7451	Comair
☐	N423SW	Canadair CL-600-2B19 (CRJ-200ER)	7456	ex C-FMMB	7456	SkyWest
☐	N426SW	Canadair CL-600-2B19 (CRJ-200ER)	7468	ex C-FMLF	7468	SkyWest
☐	N427CA	Canadair CL-600-2B19 (CRJ-200ER)	7460	ex N897AS	7460	Comair
☐	N427SW	Canadair CL-600-2B19 (CRJ-200ER)	7497	ex C-FMLB	7497	SkyWest
☐	N429SW	Canadair CL-600-2B19 (CRJ-200ER)	7518	ex C-FMMN	7518	SkyWest
☐	N430CA	Canadair CL-600-2B19 (CRJ-200ER)	7461	ex N898AS	7461	Comair
☐	N430SW	Canadair CL-600-2B19 (CRJ-200ER)	7523	ex C-FMNB	7523	SkyWest
☐	N431SW	Canadair CL-600-2B19 (CRJ-200ER)	7536	ex C-FMNW	7536	SkyWest
☐	N432SW	Canadair CL-600-2B19 (CRJ-200ER)	7548	ex C-GJFG	7548	SkyWest
☐	N433SW	Canadair CL-600-2B19 (CRJ-200ER)	7550	ex C-GJFH	7550	SkyWest
☐	N435CA	Canadair CL-600-2B19 (CRJ-200ER)	7473	ex N496SW	7473	Comair
☐	N435SW	Canadair CL-600-2B19 (CRJ-200ER)	7555	ex C-GJHK	7555	SkyWest
☐	N436CA	Canadair CL-600-2B19 (CRJ-200ER)	7482	ex N497SW	7482	Comair
☐	N437SW	Canadair CL-600-2B19 (CRJ-200ER)	7564	ex C-GJIA	7564	SkyWest
☐	N438SW	Canadair CL-600-2B19 (CRJ-200ER)	7574	ex C-FMLU	7574	SkyWest
☐	N439SW	Canadair CL-600-2B19 (CRJ-200ER)	7578	ex C-FMMN	7578	SkyWest
☐	N440SW	Canadair CL-600-2B19 (CRJ-200ER)	7589	ex C-FMLI	7589	SkyWest
☐	N441SW	Canadair CL-600-2B19 (CRJ-200ER)	7602	ex C-FMND	7602	SkyWest
☐	N442CA	Canadair CL-600-2B19 (CRJ-200ER)	7483	ex N498SW	7483	Comair
☐	N442SW	Canadair CL-600-2B19 (CRJ-200ER)	7609	ex C-FMMQ	7609	SkyWest
☐	N443CA	Canadair CL-600-2B19 (CRJ-200ER)	7539	ex C-GJJH	7539	Comair
☐	N443SW	Canadair CL-600-2B19 (CRJ-200ER)	7638	ex C-FMMN	7638	SkyWest
			SkyWest 30th anniversary c/s			
☐	N445SW	Canadair CL-600-2B19 (CRJ-200ER)	7651	ex C-FMLS	7651	SkyWest
☐	N446CA	Canadair CL-600-2B19 (CRJ-200ER)	7546	ex C-GJLH	7546	Comair
☐	N446SW	Canadair CL-600-2B19 (CRJ-200ER)	7666	ex C-FMMB	7666	SkyWest
☐	N447CA	Canadair CL-600-2B19 (CRJ-200ER)	7552	ex C-GJLL	7552	Comair
☐	N447SW	Canadair CL-600-2B19 (CRJ-200ER)	7677	ex C-FMLB	7677	SkyWest
☐	N448SW	Canadair CL-600-2B19 (CRJ-200ER)	7678	ex C-FMLF	7678	SkyWest
☐	N449SW	Canadair CL-600-2B19 (CRJ-200ER)	7699	ex C-FMMQ	7699	SkyWest
☐	N451CA	Canadair CL-600-2B19 (CRJ-200ER)	7562	ex C-GJVH	7562	Comair
			Comair 25th anniversary c/s			
☐	N452SW	Canadair CL-600-2B19 (CRJ-200ER)	7716	ex C-FMNW	7716	SkyWest
☐	N453SW	Canadair CL-600-2B19 (CRJ-200ER)	7743	ex C-FMLV	7743	SkyWest
☐	N454SW	Canadair CL-600-2B19 (CRJ-200ER)	7749	ex C-FMOS	7749	SkyWest
☐	N455CA	Canadair CL-600-2B19 (CRJ-200ER)	7592	ex C-FMLT	7592	Pinnacle
☐	N455SW	Canadair CL-600-2B19 (CRJ-200ER)	7760	ex C-FMMW	7760	SkyWest
☐	N457SW	Canadair CL-600-2B19 (CRJ-200ER)	7773	ex C-FMLV	7773	SkyWest
☐	N459SW	Canadair CL-600-2B19 (CRJ-200ER)	7782	ex C-FMND	7782	SkyWest
☐	N460SW	Canadair CL-600-2B19 (CRJ-200ER)	7803	ex C-FMLV	7803	SkyWest
☐	N461SW	Canadair CL-600-2B19 (CRJ-200ER)	7811	ex C-FVAZ	7811	SkyWest
☐	N463SW	Canadair CL-600-2B19 (CRJ-200ER)	7820	ex C-FMMW	7820	SkyWest
☐	N464SW	Canadair CL-600-2B19 (CRJ-200ER)	7827	ex C-FMLB	7827	SkyWest
☐	N465SW	Canadair CL-600-2B19 (CRJ-200ER)	7845	ex C-FMOI	7845	SkyWest
☐	N466SW	Canadair CL-600-2B19 (CRJ-200ER)	7856	ex C-FMKZ	7856	SkyWest
☐	N477CA	Canadair CL-600-2B19 (CRJ-200ER)	7670	ex C-FMMW	7670	Mesaba
☐	N487CA	Canadair CL-600-2B19 (CRJ-200ER)	7729	ex C-FMMQ	7729	Mesaba
☐	N492SW	Canadair CL-600-2B19 (CRJ-100ER)	7168	ex N982CA	7168	SkyWest
☐	N528CA	Canadair CL-600-2B19 (CRJ-200ER)	7841	ex C-FVAZ	7841	Comair
☐	N587SW	Canadair CL-600-2B19 (CRJ-100ER)	7062	ex N943CA	7062	SkyWest
☐	N588SW	Canadair CL-600-2B19 (CRJ-100ER)	7069	ex N945CA	7069	Comair
☐	N589SW	Canadair CL-600-2B19 (CRJ-100ER)	7072	ex N946CA	7072	Comair
☐	N590SW	Canadair CL-600-2B19 (CRJ-100ER)	7077	ex N947CA	7077	Comair
☐	N591SW	Canadair CL-600-2B19 (CRJ-100ER)	7079	ex N948CA	7079	SkyWest
☐	N594SW	Canadair CL-600-2B19 (CRJ-100ER)	7285	ex N767CA	7285	Comair Lsd fr DAL
☐	N595SW	Canadair CL-600-2B19 (CRJ-100ER)	7292	ex N769CA	7292	Comair Lsd fr DAL
☐	N597SW	Canadair CL-600-2B19 (CRJ-100ER)	7293	ex N776CA	7293	Comair Lsd fr DAL
☐	N601XJ	Canadair CL-600-2B19 (CRJ-200LR)	8044	ex C-FFHW		
☐	N602XJ	Canadair CL-600-2B19 (CRJ-200LR)	8045	ex C-FMKZ		
☐	N629BR	Canadair CL-600-2B19 (CRJ-200ER)	7251	ex (N533CA)	7251	Comair
☐	N659BR	Canadair CL-600-2B19 (CRJ-200ER)	7509	ex C-FMOS	7509	Comair
☐	N675BR	Canadair CL-600-2B19 (CRJ-200ER)	7635	ex (N536CA)	7635	Comair
☐	N680BR	Canadair CL-600-2B19 (CRJ-200ER)	7679	ex C-FMLI		Atlantic Southeast
☐	N681BR	Canadair CL-600-2B19 (CRJ-200ER)	7680	ex C-FMLQ		Atlantic Southeast
☐	N683BR	Canadair CL-600-2B19 (CRJ-200ER)	7692	ex C-FMND		Atlantic Southeast
☐	N684BR	Canadair CL-600-2B19 (CRJ-200ER)	7708	ex C-FMLF		Atlantic Southeast
☐	N685BR	Canadair CL-600-2B19 (CRJ-200ER)	7712	ex (N532CA)	7712	Comair
☐	N686BR	Canadair CL-600-2B19 (CRJ-200ER)	7715	ex C-FMNH		Atlantic Southeast
☐	N710CA	Canadair CL-600-2B19 (CRJ-100ER)	7241	ex C-FVAZ	7241	Comair
☐	N712CA	Canadair CL-600-2B19 (CRJ-100ER)	7244	ex C-FMLU	7244	Comair
☐	N713CA	Canadair CL-600-2B19 (CRJ-100ER)	7245	ex C-FMOI	7245	Comair
☐	N716CA	Canadair CL-600-2B19 (CRJ-100ER)	7250	ex C-FMMW	7250	Comair

☐ N720SW	Canadair CL-600-2B19 (CRJ-200ER)	7297	ex N778CA	7297	SkyWest Lsd fr DAL
☐ N721CA	Canadair CL-600-2B19 (CRJ-100ER)	7259	ex C-FMLI	7259	Comair
☐ N739CA	Canadair CL-600-2B19 (CRJ-100ER)	7273	ex C-FMNQ	7273	Comair
☐ N779CA	Canadair CL-600-2B19 (CRJ-100ER)	7306	ex C-FMMB	7306	Comair
☐ N781CA	Canadair CL-600-2B19 (CRJ-100ER)	7312	ex C-FMMY	7312	Comair
☐ N783CA	Canadair CL-600-2B19 (CRJ-100ER)	7315	ex C-FMKW	7315	Comair
☐ N784CA	Canadair CL-600-2B19 (CRJ-100ER)	7319	ex C-FMLI	7319	Comair
☐ N785CA	Canadair CL-600-2B19 (CRJ-100ER)	7326	ex C-FMNW	7326	Comair
☐ N786CA	Canadair CL-600-2B19 (CRJ-100ER)	7333	ex C-FMNQ	7333	Comair
☐ N797CA	Canadair CL-600-2B19 (CRJ-100ER)	7344	ex C-FMKV	7344	Comair
☐ N800AY	Canadair CL-600-2B19 (CRJ-200LR)	8000	ex C-FMMW	8000	
☐ N801AY	Canadair CL-600-2B19 (CRJ-200LR)	8001	ex C-FMMX	8001	
☐ N804CA	Canadair CL-600-2B19 (CRJ-100ER)	7352	ex C-FMLT	7352	Comair
☐ N805AY	Canadair CL-600-2B19 (CRJ-200LR)	8005	ex C-FDQP	8005	
☐ N807CA	Canadair CL-600-2B19 (CRJ-100ER)	7364	ex C-FMLU	7364	Comair
☐ N809CA	Canadair CL-600-2B19 (CRJ-100ER)	7366	ex C-FMMB	7366	Comair
☐ N810CA	Canadair CL-600-2B19 (CRJ-200ER)	7370	ex C-FMMW	7370	Comair
☐ N811CA	Canadair CL-600-2B19 (CRJ-200ER)	7380	ex C-FMLQ	7380	Comair
☐ N812AY	Canadair CL-600-2B19 (CRJ-200LR)	8012	ex C-	8012	
☐ N812CA	Canadair CL-600-2B19 (CRJ-200ER)	7381	ex C-FMLS	7381	Comair
☐ N813AY	Canadair CL-600-2B19 (CRJ-200LR)	8013	ex C-	8013	
☐ N814CA	Canadair CL-600-2B19 (CRJ-200ER)	7387	ex C-GFVM	7387	Comair
☐ N815CA	Canadair CL-600-2B19 (CRJ-200ER)	7397	ex C-FMML	7397	Comair
☐ N818CA	Canadair CL-600-2B19 (CRJ-200ER)	7408	ex C-FMLF	7408	Comair
☐ N819AY	Canadair CL-600-2B19 (CRJ-200LR)	8019	ex C-FMLQ	8019	
☐ N819CA	Canadair CL-600-2B19 (CRJ-200ER)	7415	ex C-FMNH	7415	Comair
☐ N820AS	Canadair CL-600-2B19 (CRJ-200ER)	7188	ex C-FMMQ	820	Atlantic Southeast
☐ N820AY	Canadair CL-600-2B19 (CRJ-200LR)	8020	ex C-FMLS	8020	
☐ N821AS	Canadair CL-600-2B19 (CRJ-200ER)	7194	ex C-FMKV	821	Atlantic Southeast
☐ N821AY	Canadair CL-600-2B19 (CRJ-200LR)	8021	ex C-FMLT	8021	
☐ N821CA	Canadair CL-600-2B19 (CRJ-200ER)	7420	ex C-FMOW	7420	stored VCV
☐ N823AS	Canadair CL-600-2B19 (CRJ-200ER)	7196	ex C-FMKZ	823	Atlantic Southeast
☐ N823AY	Canadair CL-600-2B19 (CRJ-200LR)	8023	ex C-FMMT	8023	
☐ N824AS	Canadair CL-600-2B19 (CRJ-200ER)	7203	ex C-FMLB	824	Atlantic Southeast
☐ N824AY	Canadair CL-600-2B19 (CRJ-200LR)	8024	ex C-FMNH	8024	
☐ N825AS	Canadair CL-600-2B19 (CRJ-200ER)	7207	ex C-FMNX	825	Atlantic Southeast
☐ N825AY	Canadair CL-600-2B19 (CRJ-200LR)	8025	ex C-FMNW	8025	
☐ N826AS	Canadair CL-600-2B19 (CRJ-200ER)	7210	ex C-FMOW	826	Atlantic Southeast
☐ N826AY	Canadair CL-600-2B19 (CRJ-200LR)	8026	ex C-FMNX	8026	
☐ N827AS	Canadair CL-600-2B19 (CRJ-200ER)	7212	ex C-FMND	827	Atlantic Southeast
☐ N827AY	Canadair CL-600-2B19 (CRJ-200LR)	8027	ex C-FMNY	8027	
☐ N828AS	Canadair CL-600-2B19 (CRJ-200ER)	7213	ex C-FMNQ	828	Atlantic Southeast
☐ N829AS	Canadair CL-600-2B19 (CRJ-200ER)	7232	ex C-FMLT	829	Atlantic Southeast
☐ N829AY	Canadair CL-600-2B19 (CRJ-200LR)	8029	ex C-FMOW	8029	
☐ N830AS	Canadair CL-600-2B19 (CRJ-200ER)	7236	ex C-FMNW	830	Atlantic Southeast
☐ N830AY	Canadair CL-600-2B19 (CRJ-200LR)	8030	ex C-FVAZ	8030	
☐ N831AY	Canadair CL-600-2B19 (CRJ-200LR)	8031	ex C-FETZ	8031	
☐ N832AS	Canadair CL-600-2B19 (CRJ-200ER)	7243	ex C-FMNQ	832	Atlantic Southeast
☐ N832AY	Canadair CL-600-2B19 (CRJ-200LR)	8032	ex C-FMNQ	8032	
☐ N833AS	Canadair CL-600-2B19 (CRJ-200ER)	7246	ex C-FMMB	833	Atlantic Southeast
☐ N833AY	Canadair CL-600-2B19 (CRJ-200LR)	8033	ex C-FMLU	8033	
☐ N834AS	Canadair CL-600-2B19 (CRJ-200ER)	7254	ex C-FMKV	834	Atlantic Southeast
☐ N834AY	Canadair CL-600-2B19 (CRJ-200LR)	8034	ex C-FEXV	8034	
☐ N835AS	Canadair CL-600-2B19 (CRJ-200ER)	7258	ex C-FMLF	835	Atlantic Southeast
☐ N835AY	Canadair CL-600-2B19 (CRJ-200LR)	8035	ex C-FMMB	8035	
☐ N836AS	Canadair CL-600-2B19 (CRJ-200ER)	7263	ex C-FMLU	836	Atlantic Southeast
☐ N836AY	Canadair CL-600-2B19 (CRJ-200LR)	8036	ex C-FMML	8036	
☐ N837AS	Canadair CL-600-2B19 (CRJ-200ER)	7271	ex C-FVAZ	837	Atlantic Southeast
☐ N838AS	Canadair CL-600-2B19 (CRJ-200ER)	7276	ex C-FMMB	838	Atlantic Southeast
☐ N839AS	Canadair CL-600-2B19 (CRJ-200ER)	7284	ex C-FMKV	839	Atlantic Southeast
☐ N839AY	Canadair CL-600-2B19 (CRJ-200LR)	8039	ex C-FMMW	8039	
☐ N840AS	Canadair CL-600-2B19 (CRJ-200ER)	7290	ex C-FMLQ	840	Atlantic Southeast
☐ N840AY	Canadair CL-600-2B19 (CRJ-200LR)	8040	ex C-FEZX	8040	
☐ N841AS	Canadair CL-600-2B19 (CRJ-200ER)	7300	ex C-FMOW	841	Atlantic Southeast
☐ N841AY	Canadair CL-600-2B19 (CRJ-200LR)	8041	ex C-FMMY	8041	
☐ N842AS	Canadair CL-600-2B19 (CRJ-200ER)	7304	ex C-FMLU	842	Atlantic Southeast
☐ N843AS	Canadair CL-600-2B19 (CRJ-200ER)	7310	ex C-FMMW	843	Atlantic Southeast
☐ N844AS	Canadair CL-600-2B19 (CRJ-200ER)	7317	ex C-FMLB	844	Atlantic Southeast
☐ N845AS	Canadair CL-600-2B19 (CRJ-200ER)	7324	ex C-FMMT	845	Atlantic Southeast
☐ N846AS	Canadair CL-600-2B19 (CRJ-200ER)	7328	ex C-FMNY	846	Atlantic Southeast
☐ N847AS	Canadair CL-600-2B19 (CRJ-200ER)	7335	ex C-FMOI	847	Atlantic Southeast
☐ N848AS	Canadair CL-600-2B19 (CRJ-200ER)	7339	ex C-FMMQ	848	Atlantic Southeast
☐ N849AS	Canadair CL-600-2B19 (CRJ-200ER)	7347	ex C-FMLB	849	Atlantic Southeast
	Special 20th Anniversary c/s, City of Atlanta				
☐ N850AS	Canadair CL-600-2B19 (CRJ-200ER)	7355	ex C-FMNH	850	Atlantic Southeast
☐ N851AS	Canadair CL-600-2B19 (CRJ-200ER)	7360	ex C-FMOW	851	Atlantic Southeast
☐ N852AS	Canadair CL-600-2B19 (CRJ-200ER)	7369	ex C-FMMQ	852	Atlantic Southeast
☐ N853AS	Canadair CL-600-2B19 (CRJ-200ER)	7374	ex C-FMKV	853	Atlantic Southeast
☐ N854AS	Canadair CL-600-2B19 (CRJ-200ER)	7382	ex C-FMLT	854	Atlantic Southeast
☐ N855AS	Canadair CL-600-2B19 (CRJ-200ER)	7395	ex C-GGKY	855	Atlantic Southeast
☐ N856AS	Canadair CL-600-2B19 (CRJ-200ER)	7404	ex C-FMKV	856	Atlantic Southeast
☐ N857AS	Canadair CL-600-2B19 (CRJ-200ER)	7411	ex C-FMLS	857	Atlantic Southeast
☐ N858AS	Canadair CL-600-2B19 (CRJ-200ER)	7417	ex C-FMNX	858	Atlantic Southeast

☐ N859AS	Canadair CL-600-2B19 (CRJ-200ER)	7421	ex C-FVAZ	859	Atlantic Southeast
☐ N860AS	Canadair CL-600-2B19 (CRJ-200ER)	7433	ex C-FMNB	860	Atlantic Southeast
☐ N861AS	Canadair CL-600-2B19 (CRJ-200ER)	7445	ex C-FMNH	861	Atlantic Southeast
☐ N862AS	Canadair CL-600-2B19 (CRJ-200ER)	7476	ex C-FMNW	7476	SkyWest
☐ N863AS	Canadair CL-600-2B19 (CRJ-200ER)	7487	ex C-FMML	7487	SkyWest
☐ N864AS	Canadair CL-600-2B19 (CRJ-200ER)	7502	ex C-FMLT	864	SkyWest
☐ N865AS	Canadair CL-600-2B19 (CRJ-200ER)	7507	ex C-FMNX	865	Comair
☐ N866AS	Canadair CL-600-2B19 (CRJ-200ER)	7517	ex C-FMML	7517	SkyWest
☐ N867AS	Canadair CL-600-2B19 (CRJ-200ER)	7463	ex C-FMNB	867	Atlantic Southeast
☐ N868AS	Canadair CL-600-2B19 (CRJ-200ER)	7474	ex C-FMMT	868	Atlantic Southeast
		Texas Bluebonnet c/s			
☐ N868CA	Canadair CL-600-2B19 (CRJ-200ER)	7427	ex C-FMML	7427	Comair
☐ N869AS	Canadair CL-600-2B19 (CRJ-200ER)	7479	ex C-FMOS	869	SkyWest
☐ N870AS	Canadair CL-600-2B19 (CRJ-200ER)	7530	ex C-FMLQ	870	Atlantic Southeast
☐ N871AS	Canadair CL-600-2B19 (CRJ-200ER)	7537	ex C-FMNX	871	Atlantic Southeast
☐ N872AS	Canadair CL-600-2B19 (CRJ-200ER)	7542	ex C-FMND	872	Atlantic Southeast
☐ N873AS	Canadair CL-600-2B19 (CRJ-200ER)	7549	ex C-GJLI	873	Atlantic Southeast
☐ N874AS	Canadair CL-600-2B19 (CRJ-200ER)	7551	ex C-GJLK	874	Atlantic Southeast
☐ N875AS	Canadair CL-600-2B19 (CRJ-200ER)	7559	ex C-GJLQ	875	Atlantic Southeast
☐ N876AS	Canadair CL-600-2B19 (CRJ-200ER)	7576	ex C-FMMB	876	Atlantic Southeast
☐ N877AS	Canadair CL-600-2B19 (CRJ-200ER)	7579	ex C-FMMQ	877	Atlantic Southeast
☐ N878AS	Canadair CL-600-2B19 (CRJ-200ER)	7590	ex C-FMLQ	878	Atlantic Southeast
☐ N879AS	Canadair CL-600-2B19 (CRJ-200ER)	7600	ex C-FMOW	879	Atlantic Southeast
☐ N880AS	Canadair CL-600-2B19 (CRJ-200ER)	7606	ex C-FMMB	880	Atlantic Southeast
☐ N881AS	Canadair CL-600-2B19 (CRJ-200ER)	7496	ex C-GIXF	881	Atlantic Southeast
☐ N882AS	Canadair CL-600-2B19 (CRJ-200ER)	7503	ex C-GJAO	882	Atlantic Southeast
☐ N883AS	Canadair CL-600-2B19 (CRJ-200ER)	7504	ex C-GIZD	883	Atlantic Southeast
☐ N884AS	Canadair CL-600-2B19 (CRJ-200ER)	7513	ex C-GIZF	884	Atlantic Southeast
☐ N885AS	Canadair CL-600-2B19 (CRJ-200ER)	7521	ex C-GJDX	885	Atlantic Southeast
☐ N886AS	Canadair CL-600-2B19 (CRJ-200ER)	7531	ex C-GJJC	886	Atlantic Southeast
☐ N889AS	Canadair CL-600-2B19 (CRJ-200ER)	7538	ex C-GJJG	889	Atlantic Southeast
☐ N900EV	Canadair CL-600-2B19 (CRJ-200ER)	7608	ex C-FMMN	900	Atlantic Southeast
☐ N901EV	Canadair CL-600-2B19 (CRJ-200ER)	7616	ex C-FMKZ	901	Atlantic Southeast
☐ N902EV	Canadair CL-600-2B19 (CRJ-200ER)	7620	ex C-FMLQ	902	Atlantic Southeast
☐ N903EV	Canadair CL-600-2B19 (CRJ-200ER)	7621	ex C-FMLS	903	Atlantic Southeast
☐ N904EV	Canadair CL-600-2B19 (CRJ-200ER)	7628	ex C-FMNY	904	Atlantic Southeast
☐ N905EV	Canadair CL-600-2B19 (CRJ-200ER)	7632	ex C-FMND	905	Atlantic Southeast
☐ N906EV	Canadair CL-600-2B19 (CRJ-200ER)	7642	ex C-FMMY	906	Atlantic Southeast
☐ N907EV	Canadair CL-600-2B19 (CRJ-200ER)	7648	ex C-FMLF	907	Atlantic Southeast
☐ N908EV	Canadair CL-600-2B19 (CRJ-200ER)	7654	ex C-FMMT	908	Atlantic Southeast
☐ N909EV	Canadair CL-600-2B19 (CRJ-200ER)	7658	ex C-FMNY	909	Atlantic Southeast
☐ N910EV	Canadair CL-600-2B19 (CRJ-200ER)	7727	ex C-FMML	7727	SkyWest
☐ N912CA	Canadair CL-600-2B19 (CRJ-100ER)	7011	ex C-FMKZ	7011	Comair
☐ N912EV	Canadair CL-600-2B19 (CRJ-200ER)	7728	ex C-FMMN	7728	SkyWest
☐ N913EV	Canadair CL-600-2B19 (CRJ-200ER)	7731	ex C-FMMX	7731	SkyWest
☐ N914CA	Canadair CL-600-2B19 (CRJ-100ER)	7012	ex C-FMLB	7012	Comair
☐ N914EV	Canadair CL-600-2B19 (CRJ-200ER)	7752	ex C-FMND	914	Atlantic Southeast
☐ N915CA	Canadair CL-600-2B19 (CRJ-100ER)	7013	ex C-FMLQ	7013	Comair
☐ N915EV	Canadair CL-600-2B19 (CRJ-200ER)	7754	ex C-FMLU	7754	SkyWest
☐ N916CA	Canadair CL-600-2B19 (CRJ-100ER)	7014	ex C-FMLI	7014	Comair
☐ N916EV	Canadair CL-600-2B19 (CRJ-200ER)	7757	ex C-FMML	916	Atlantic Southeast
☐ N917CA	Canadair CL-600-2B19 (CRJ-100ER)	7017	ex C-FMLT	7017	Comair
☐ N917EV	Canadair CL-600-2B19 (CRJ-200ER)	7769	ex C-FMLI	917	Atlantic Southeast
☐ N918CA	Canadair CL-600-2B19 (CRJ-100ER)	7018	ex C-FMLU	7018	Comair
☐ N919EV	Canadair CL-600-2B19 (CRJ-200ER)	7780	ex C-FMOW	919	Atlantic Southeast
☐ N920CA	Canadair CL-600-2B19 (CRJ-100ER)	7022	ex C-FMMN	7022	Comair
☐ N920EV	Canadair CL-600-2B19 (CRJ-200ER)	7810	ex C-FMOW	920	Atlantic Southeast
☐ N921EV	Canadair CL-600-2B19 (CRJ-200ER)	7819	ex C-FMMQ	921	Atlantic Southeast
☐ N922EV	Canadair CL-600-2B19 (CRJ-200ER)	7822	ex C-FMMY	922	Atlantic Southeast
☐ N923EV	Canadair CL-600-2B19 (CRJ-200ER)	7826	ex C-FMKZ	923	Atlantic Southeast
☐ N924CA	Canadair CL-600-2B19 (CRJ-100ER)	7026	ex C-FMMX	7026	Comair
☐ N924EV	Canadair CL-600-2B19 (CRJ-200ER)	7830	ex C-FMLQ	924	Atlantic Southeast
☐ N925EV	Canadair CL-600-2B19 (CRJ-200ER)	7831	ex C-FMLS	925	Atlantic Southeast
☐ N926CA	Canadair CL-600-2B19 (CRJ-100ER)	7027	ex C-FMMY	7027	Comair
☐ N926EV	Canadair CL-600-2B19 (CRJ-200ER)	7843	ex C-FMNQ	926	Atlantic Southeast
☐ N927CA	Canadair CL-600-2B19 (CRJ-100ER)	7031	ex C-FMNQ	7031	Comair
☐ N927EV	Canadair CL-600-2B19 (CRJ-200ER)	7844	ex C-FMLU	927	Atlantic Southeast
☐ N928EV	Canadair CL-600-2B19 (CRJ-200ER)	8006	ex C-FMMB	928	Atlantic Southeast Lsd fr DAL
☐ N929CA	Canadair CL-600-2B19 (CRJ-100ER)	7035	ex C-FMOI	7035	Comair
☐ N929EV	Canadair CL-600-2B19 (CRJ-200ER)	8007	ex C-FMMN	929	Atlantic Southeast Lsd fr DAL
☐ N930EV	Canadair CL-600-2B19 (CRJ-200ER)	8014	ex C-FMKW	930	Atlantic Southeast Lsd fr DAL
☐ N931CA	Canadair CL-600-2B19 (CRJ-100ER)	7037	ex C-FMOS	7037	Comair
☐ N931EV	Canadair CL-600-2B19 (CRJ-200ER)	8015	ex C-FMKZ	931	Atlantic Southeast Lsd fr DAL
☐ N932CA	Canadair CL-600-2B19 (CRJ-100ER)	7038	ex C-FMOW	7038	Comair
☐ N932EV	Canadair CL-600-2B19 (CRJ-200ER)	8016	ex C-FMLB	932	Atlantic Southeast Lsd fr DAL
☐ N933CA	Canadair CL-600-2B19 (CRJ-100ER)	7040	ex C-FMKW	7040	Comair
☐ N933EV	Canadair CL-600-2B19 (CRJ-200ER)	8022	ex C-FEHV	933	Atlantic Southeast Lsd fr DAL
☐ N934CA	Canadair CL-600-2B19 (CRJ-100ER)	7042	ex C-FMLB	7042	Comair
☐ N934EV	Canadair CL-600-2B19 (CRJ-200ER)	8028	ex C-FMOS	934	Atlantic Southeast Lsd fr DAL
☐ N935EV	Canadair CL-600-2B19 (CRJ-200ER)	8037	ex C-FMMN	935	Atlantic Southeast Lsd fr DAL
☐ N936CA	Canadair CL-600-2B19 (CRJ-100ER)	7043	ex C-FMLF	7043	Comair
☐ N936EV	Canadair CL-600-2B19 (CRJ-200ER)	8038	ex C-FEZT	936	Atlantic Southeast Lsd fr DAL
☐ N937CA	Canadair CL-600-2B19 (CRJ-100ER)	7044	ex C-FMLI	7044	Comair

	Registration	Type	C/n	Previous identity	Fleet no	Remarks
☐	N937EV	Canadair CL-600-2B19 (CRJ-200ER)	8042	ex C-FFAB	937	Atlantic Southeast Lsd fr DAL
☐	N938CA	Canadair CL-600-2B19 (CRJ-100ER)	7046	ex C-FMLS	7046	Comair
☐	N940CA	Canadair CL-600-2B19 (CRJ-100ER)	7048	ex C-FMLU	7048	Comair
☐	N941CA	Canadair CL-600-2B19 (CRJ-100ER)	7050	ex C-FMMB	7050	Comair
☐	N954CA	Canadair CL-600-2B19 (CRJ-100ER)	7100	ex C-FXFB	7100	Comair Lsd fr DAL
☐	N956CA	Canadair CL-600-2B19 (CRJ-100ER)	7105	ex C-FMNH	7105	Comair Lsd fr DAL
☐	N957CA	Canadair CL-600-2B19 (CRJ-100ER)	7109	ex C-FMLV	7109	Comair Lsd fr DAL
☐	N958CA	Canadair CL-600-2B19 (CRJ-100ER)	7111	ex C-FMML	7111	Comair Lsd fr DAL
☐	N959CA	Canadair CL-600-2B19 (CRJ-100ER)	7116	ex C-FMMX	7116	Comair Lsd fr DAL
☐	N960CA	Canadair CL-600-2B19 (CRJ-100ER)	7117	ex C-FMMY	7117	Comair
☐	N962CA	Canadair CL-600-2B19 (CRJ-100ER)	7123	ex C-FMLU	7123	Comair
☐	N963CA	Canadair CL-600-2B19 (CRJ-100ER)	7127	ex C-FMMN	7127	Comair
☐	N964CA	Canadair CL-600-2B19 (CRJ-100ER)	7129	ex C-FMMT	7129	Comair Lsd fr DAL
☐	N965CA	Canadair CL-600-2B19 (CRJ-100ER)	7131	ex C-FMMX	7131	Comair stored
☐	N966CA	Canadair CL-600-2B19 (CRJ-100ER)	7132	ex C-FMMY	7132	Comair Lsd fr DAL
☐	N967CA	Canadair CL-600-2B19 (CRJ-100ER)	7134	ex C-FMND	7134	Comair
☐	N969CA	Canadair CL-600-2B19 (CRJ-100ER)	7141	ex C-FMML	7141	Comair
☐	N970EV	Canadair CL-600-2B19 (CRJ-200ER)	7527	ex N663BR	970	Atlantic Southeast Lsd fr DAL
☐	N971CA	Canadair CL-600-2B19 (CRJ-100ER)	7145	ex C-FMMW	7145	Comair
☐	N971EV	Canadair CL-600-2B19 (CRJ-200ER)	7528	ex N664BR	971	Atlantic Southeast Lsd fr DAL
☐	N972EV	Canadair CL-600-2B19 (CRJ-200ER)	7534	ex N665BR	972	Atlantic Southeast Lsd fr DAL
☐	N973CA	Canadair CL-600-2B19 (CRJ-100ER)	7146	ex C-FMMX	7146	Comair
☐	N973EV	Canadair CL-600-2B19 (CRJ-200ER)	7575	ex N708BR	973	Atlantic Southeast Lsd fr DAL
☐	N974EV	Canadair CL-600-2B19 (CRJ-200ER)	7594	ex N672BR	974	Atlantic Southeast Lsd fr DAL
☐	N975EV	Canadair CL-600-2B19 (CRJ-200ER)	7599	ex N673BR	975	Atlantic Southeast Lsd fr DAL
☐	N976EV	Canadair CL-600-2B19 (CRJ-200ER)	7601	ex N674BR	976	Atlantic Southeast Lsd fr DAL
☐	N977EV	Canadair CL-600-2B19 (CRJ-200ER)	7720	ex N687BR	977	Atlantic Southeast Lsd fr DAL
☐	N978EV	Canadair CL-600-2B19 (CRJ-200ER)	7723	ex N688BR	978	Atlantic Southeast Lsd fr DAL
☐	N979EV	Canadair CL-600-2B19 (CRJ-200ER)	7737	ex N689BR	979	Atlantic Southeast Lsd fr DAL
☐	N980EV	Canadair CL-600-2B19 (CRJ-200ER)	7759	ex N692BR	980	Atlantic Southeast Lsd fr DAL
☐	N981EV	Canadair CL-600-2B19 (CRJ-200ER)	7768	ex N694BR	981	Atlantic Southeast Lsd fr DAL
☐	N989CA	Canadair CL-600-2B19 (CRJ-100ER)	7215	ex C-FMOI	7215	Comair Lsd fr DAL
☐	N8390A	Canadair CL-600-2B19 (CRJ-200LR)	7390	ex C-FMOW	8390	Spirit of 'Memphis Belle'
☐	N8409N	Canadair CL-600-2B19 (CRJ-200LR)	7409	ex C-FMLI	8409	
☐	N8412F	Canadair CL-600-2B19 (CRJ-200LR)	7412	ex C-FMLT	8412	
☐	N8416B	Canadair CL-600-2B19 (CRJ-200LR)	7416	ex C-FMNW	8416	
☐	N8423C	Canadair CL-600-2B19 (CRJ-200LR)	7423	ex C-FMNQ	8423	
☐	N8432A	Canadair CL-600-2B19 (CRJ-200LR)	7432	ex C-GHRR	8432	
☐	N8444F	Canadair CL-600-2B19 (CRJ-200LR)	7444	ex C-FMMT	8444	
☐	N8458A	Canadair CL-600-2B19 (CRJ-200LR)	7458	ex C-FMMN	8458	
☐	N8475B	Canadair CL-600-2B19 (CRJ-200LR)	7475	ex C-FMNH	8475	
☐	N8477R	Canadair CL-600-2B19 (CRJ-200LR)	7477	ex C-FMNX	8477	
☐	N8488D	Canadair CL-600-2B19 (CRJ-200LR)	7488	ex C-FMMN	8488	
☐	N8492C	Canadair CL-600-2B19 (CRJ-200LR)	7492	ex C-FMMY	8492	
☐	N8495B	Canadair CL-600-2B19 (CRJ-200LR)	7495	ex C-FMKW	8495	
☐	N8501F	Canadair CL-600-2B19 (CRJ-200LR)	7501	ex C-FMLS	8501	
☐	N8505Q	Canadair CL-600-2B19 (CRJ-200LR)	7505	ex C-FMNH	8505	
☐	N8506C	Canadair CL-600-2B19 (CRJ-200LR)	7506	ex C-FMNW	8506	
☐	N8515F	Canadair CL-600-2B19 (CRJ-200LR)	7515	ex C-FMOI	8515	
☐	N8516C	Canadair CL-600-2B19 (CRJ-200LR)	7516	ex C-FMMB	8516	
☐	N8524A	Canadair CL-600-2B19 (CRJ-200LR)	7524	ex C-FMKV	8524	
☐	N8525B	Canadair CL-600-2B19 (CRJ-200LR)	7525	ex C-FMKW	8525	
☐	N8532G	Canadair CL-600-2B19 (CRJ-200LR)	7532	ex C-FMLT	8532	
☐	N8533D	Canadair CL-600-2B19 (CRJ-200LR)	7533	ex C-FMLV	8533	
☐	N8541D	Canadair CL-600-2B19 (CRJ-200LR)	7541	ex C-FVAZ	8541	
☐	N8543F	Canadair CL-600-2B19 (CRJ-200LR)	7543	ex C-FMNQ	8543	
☐	N8554A	Canadair CL-600-2B19 (CRJ-200LR)	7554	ex C-FMKV	8554	
☐	N8560F	Canadair CL-600-2B19 (CRJ-200LR)	7560	ex C-FMLQ	8560	
☐	N8577D	Canadair CL-600-2B19 (CRJ-200LR)	7577	ex C-FMML	8577	
☐	N8580A	Canadair CL-600-2B19 (CRJ-200LR)	7580	ex C-FMMW	8580	
☐	N8587E	Canadair CL-600-2B19 (CRJ-200LR)	7587	ex C-FMLB	8587	
☐	N8588D	Canadair CL-600-2B19 (CRJ-200LR)	7588	ex C-GJSZ	8588	
☐	N8598B	Canadair CL-600-2B19 (CRJ-200LR)	7598	ex C-FMNY	8598	
☐	N8604C	Canadair CL-600-2B19 (CRJ-200LR)	7604	ex C-FMLU	8604	
☐	N8611A	Canadair CL-600-2B19 (CRJ-200LR)	7611	ex C-FMMX	8611	
☐	N8623A	Canadair CL-600-2B19 (CRJ-200LR)	7623	ex C-FMLV	8623	
☐	N8631E	Canadair CL-600-2B19 (CRJ-200LR)	7631	ex C-FVAZ	8631	
☐	N8646A	Canadair CL-600-2B19 (CRJ-200LR)	7646	ex C-FMKZ	8646	
☐	N8659B	Canadair CL-600-2B19 (CRJ-200LR)	7659	ex C-FMOS	8659	
☐	N8665A	Canadair CL-600-2B19 (CRJ-200LR)	7665	ex C-FMOI	8665	
☐	N8672A	Canadair CL-600-2B19 (CRJ-200LR)	7672	ex C-FMMY	8672	
☐	N8673D	Canadair CL-600-2B19 (CRJ-200LR)	7673	ex C-FMNB	8673	
☐	N8674A	Canadair CL-600-2B19 (CRJ-200LR)	7674	ex C-FMKV	8674	
☐	N8683B	Canadair CL-600-2B19 (CRJ-200LR)	7683	ex C-FMLV	8683	
☐	N8688C	Canadair CL-600-2B19 (CRJ-200LR)	7688	ex C-FMNY	6888	
☐	N8694A	Canadair CL-600-2B19 (CRJ-200LR)	7694	ex C-FMLU	8694	
☐	N8696C	Canadair CL-600-2B19 (CRJ-200LR)	7696	ex C-FMMB	8696	
☐	N8698A	Canadair CL-600-2B19 (CRJ-200LR)	7698	ex C-FMMN	8698	
☐	N8709A	Canadair CL-600-2B19 (CRJ-200LR)	7709	ex C-FMLI	8709	
☐	N8710A	Canadair CL-600-2B19 (CRJ-200LR)	7710	ex C-FMLQ	8710	
☐	N8718E	Canadair CL-600-2B19 (CRJ-200LR)	7718	ex C-FMNY	8718	
☐	N8721B	Canadair CL-600-2B19 (CRJ-200LR)	7721	ex C-FVAZ	8721	
☐	N8733G	Canadair CL-600-2B19 (CRJ-200LR)	7733	ex C-FMNB	8733	

	Registration	Type	c/n	Previous identity	Fleet no	Remarks
☐	N8736A	Canadair CL-600-2B19 (CRJ-200LR)	7736	ex C-FMKZ	8736	
☐	N8745B	Canadair CL-600-2B19 (CRJ-200LR)	7745	ex C-FMNH	8745	
☐	N8747B	Canadair CL-600-2B19 (CRJ-200LR)	7747	ex C-FMNX	8747	
☐	N8751D	Canadair CL-600-2B19 (CRJ-200LR)	7751	ex C-FVAZ	8751	
☐	N8758D	Canadair CL-600-2B19 (CRJ-200LR)	7758	ex C-FMMN	8758	
☐	N8771A	Canadair CL-600-2B19 (CRJ-200LR)	7771	ex C-FMLS	8771	
☐	N8775A	Canadair CL-600-2B19 (CRJ-200LR)	7775	ex C-FMNH	8775	
☐	N8783E	Canadair CL-600-2B19 (CRJ-200LR)	7783	ex C-FMNQ	8783	
☐	N8790A	Canadair CL-600-2B19 (CRJ-200LR)	7790	ex C-FMMW	8790	
☐	N8794B	Canadair CL-600-2B19 (CRJ-200LR)	7794	ex C-FMKV	8794	
☐	N8797A	Canadair CL-600-2B19 (CRJ-200LR)	7797	ex C-FMLB	8797	
☐	N8800G	Canadair CL-600-2B19 (CRJ-200LR)	7800	ex C-FMLQ	8800	
☐	N8808H	Canadair CL-600-2B19 (CRJ-200LR)	7808	ex C-FMNY	8808	
☐	N8828D	Canadair CL-600-2B19 (CRJ-200LR)	7828	ex C-FMLF	8828	
☐	N8836A	Canadair CL-600-2B19 (CRJ-200LR)	7836	ex C-FMNW	8836	
☐	N8837B	Canadair CL-600-2B19 (CRJ-200LR)	7837	ex C-FMNX	8837	
☐	N8839E	Canadair CL-600-2B19 (CRJ-200LR)	7839	ex C-FMOS	8839	
☐	N8847A	Canadair CL-600-2B19 (CRJ-200LR)	7847	ex C-FMML	8847	
☐	N8855A	Canadair CL-600-2B19 (CRJ-200LR)	7855	ex C-FMKW	8855	
☐	N8869B	Canadair CL-600-2B19 (CRJ-200LR)	7869	ex C-FMOS	8869	
☐	N8877A	Canadair CL-600-2B19 (CRJ-200LR)	7877	ex C-FMML	8877	
☐	N8883E	Canadair CL-600-2B19 (CRJ-200LR)	7883	ex C-FMNB	8883	
☐	N8884E	Canadair CL-600-2B19 (CRJ-200LR)	7884	ex C-FMKV	8884	
☐	N8886A	Canadair CL-600-2B19 (CRJ-200LR)	7886	ex C-FMKZ	8886	
☐	N8888D	Canadair CL-600-2B19 (CRJ-200LR)	7888	ex C-FMLF	8888	
☐	N8891A	Canadair CL-600-2B19 (CRJ-200LR)	7891	ex C-FMLS	8891	
☐	N8894A	Canadair CL-600-2B19 (CRJ-200LR)	7894	ex C-FMMT	8894	
☐	N8896A	Canadair CL-600-2B19 (CRJ-200LR)	7896	ex C-FMNW	8896	
☐	N8903A	Canadair CL-600-2B19 (CRJ-200LR)	7903	ex C-FMNQ	8903	
☐	N8907A	Canadair CL-600-2B19 (CRJ-200LR)	7907	ex C-FMML	8907	
☐	N8908D	Canadair CL-600-2B19 (CRJ-200LR)	7908	ex C-FMMN	8908	
☐	N8913A	Canadair CL-600-2B19 (CRJ-200LR)	7913	ex C-FMNB	8913	
☐	N8914A	Canadair CL-600-2B19 (CRJ-200LR)	7914	ex C-FMKV	8914	
☐	N8918B	Canadair CL-600-2B19 (CRJ-200LR)	7918	ex C-FMLF	8918	
☐	N8921B	Canadair CL-600-2B19 (CRJ-200LR)	7921	ex C-FMLS	8921	
☐	N8923A	Canadair CL-600-2B19 (CRJ-200LR)	7923	ex C-FMLV	8923	
☐	N8924B	Canadair CL-600-2B19 (CRJ-200LR)	7924	ex C-FMMT	8924	
☐	N8928A	Canadair CL-600-2B19 (CRJ-200LR)	7928	ex C-FMNY	8928	
☐	N8930E	Canadair CL-600-2B19 (CRJ-200LR)	7930	ex C-FMOW	8930	
☐	N8932C	Canadair CL-600-2B19 (CRJ-200LR)	7932	ex C-FMND	8932	
☐	N8933B	Canadair CL-600-2B19 (CRJ-200LR)	7933	ex C-FMNQ	8933	
☐	N8936A	Canadair CL-600-2B19 (CRJ-200LR)	7936	ex C-FMMB	8936	
☐	N8938A	Canadair CL-600-2B19 (CRJ-200LR)	7938	ex C-FMMN	8938	
☐	N8940E	Canadair CL-600-2B19 (CRJ-200LR)	7940	ex C-FMMW	8940	
☐	N8942A	Canadair CL-600-2B19 (CRJ-200LR)	7942	ex C-FMMY	8942	
☐	N8943A	Canadair CL-600-2B19 (CRJ-200LR)	7943	ex C-FMNB	8943	
☐	N8944B	Canadair CL-600-2B19 (CRJ-200LR)	7944	ex C-FMKV	8944	Spirit of Beale St
☐	N8946A	Canadair CL-600-2B19 (CRJ-200LR)	7946	ex C-FMKZ	8946	
☐	N8948B	Canadair CL-600-2B19 (CRJ-200LR)	7948	ex C-FMLF	8948	
☐	N8960A	Canadair CL-600-2B19 (CRJ-200LR)	7960	ex C-FMOW	8960	
☐	N8964E	Canadair CL-600-2B19 (CRJ-200LR)	7964	ex C-FMLU	8964	
☐	N8965E"	Canadair CL-600-2B19 (CRJ-200LR)	7965	ex C-FMOI	8965	
☐	N8968E	Canadair CL-600-2B19 (CRJ-200LR)	7968	ex C-FMMN	8968	
☐	N8969A	Canadair CL-600-2B19 (CRJ-200LR)	7969	ex C-FMMQ	8969	
☐	N8970D	Canadair CL-600-2B19 (CRJ-200LR)	7970	ex C-FMMW	8970	
☐	N8971A	Canadair CL-600-2B19 (CRJ-200LR)	7971	ex C-FMMX	8971	
☐	N8972E	Canadair CL-600-2B19 (CRJ-200LR)	7972	ex C-FMMY	8972	
☐	N8974C"	Canadair CL-600-2B19 (CRJ-200LR)	7974	ex C-FMKV	8974	
☐	N8976E"	Canadair CL-600-2B19 (CRJ-200LR)	7976	ex C-FMKZ	8976	
☐	N8977A	Canadair CL-600-2B19 (CRJ-200LR)	7977	ex C-FMLB	8977	
☐	N8980A	Canadair CL-600-2B19 (CRJ-200LR)	7980	ex C-FMLQ	8980	
☐	N8982A	Canadair CL-600-2B19 (CRJ-200LR)	7982	ex C-FMLT	8982	
☐	N8986B	Canadair CL-600-2B19 (CRJ-200LR)	7986	ex C-FMNW	8986	

Operated by Pinnacle Airlines except those marked " which are operated by Mesaba.

	Registration	Type	c/n	Previous identity	Fleet no	Remarks
☐	N317CA	Canadair CL-600-2C10 (CRJ-701ER)	10055	ex C-GZXI	10055	Atlantic Southeast Lsd fr DAL
☐	N331CA	Canadair CL-600-2C10 (CRJ-701ER)	10061	ex C-GIBJ	10061	SkyWest Lsd fr DAL
☐	N340CA	Canadair CL-600-2C10 (CRJ-701ER)	10062	ex C-GIBL	10062	SkyWest Lsd fr DAL
☐	N354CA	Canadair CL-600-2C10 (CRJ-701ER)	10064	ex C-GIBO	10064	Atlantic Southeast Lsd fr DAL
☐	N355CA	Canadair CL-600-2C10 (CRJ-701ER)	10067	ex C-GIBT	10067	Atlantic Southeast Lsd fr DAL
☐	N367CA	Canadair CL-600-2C10 (CRJ-701ER)	10069	ex C-GICL	10069	SkyWest Lsd fr DAL
☐	N368CA	Canadair CL-600-2C10 (CRJ-701ER)	10075	ex C-GIAD	10075	SkyWest Lsd fr DAL
☐	N369CA	Canadair CL-600-2C10 (CRJ-701ER)	10079	ex C-GZUD	10079	Comair
☐	N371CA	Canadair CL-600-2C10 (CRJ-701ER)	10082	ex C-GIAR	10082	Comair
☐	N374CA	Canadair CL-600-2C10 (CRJ-701ER)	10090	ex C-	10090	Comair stored CVG
☐	N376CA	Canadair CL-600-2C10 (CRJ-701ER)	10092	ex C-	10092	Atlantic Southeast Lsd fr DAL
☐	N378CA	Canadair CL-600-2C10 (CRJ-701ER)	10097	ex C-GIAJ	10097	Comair stored CVG
☐	N379CA	Canadair CL-600-2C10 (CRJ-701ER)	10102	ex C-	10102	Atlantic Southeast Lsd fr DAL
☐	N390CA	Canadair CL-600-2C10 (CRJ-701ER)	10106	ex C-	10106	Atlantic Southeast Lsd fr DAL
☐	N391CA	Canadair CL-600-2C10 (CRJ-701ER)	10108	ex C-	10108	Comair
☐	N398CA	Canadair CL-600-2C10 (CRJ-701ER)	10112	ex C-	10112	Comair
☐	N603SK	Canadair CL-600-2C10 (CRJ-702ER)	10248	ex C-FHUC	10248	SkyWest
☐	N604SK	Canadair CL-600-2C10 (CRJ-702ER)	10249	ex C-	10239	SkyWest

☐ N606SK	Canadair CL-600-2C10 (CRJ-702ER)	10250	ex C-	10250	SkyWest
☐ N607SK	Canadair CL-600-2C10 (CRJ-702ER)	10251	ex C-FIBQ	10251	SkyWest
☐ N608SK	Canadair CL-600-2C10 (CRJ-702ER)	10252	ex C-	10252	SkyWest
☐ N609SK	Canadair CL-600-2C10 (CRJ-701ER)	10020	ex N701EV	10020	SkyWest
☐ N611SK	Canadair CL-600-2C10 (CRJ-701ER)	10035	ex N702EV	10035	SkyWest
☐ N613SK	Canadair CL-600-2C10 (CRJ-701ER)	10038	ex N703EV	10038	SkyWest
☐ N614SK	Canadair CL-600-2C10 (CRJ-701ER)	10051	ex N705EV	10051	SkyWest
☐ N625CA	Canadair CL-600-2C10 (CRJ-701ER)	10113	ex C-	10113	Comair
☐ N641CA	Canadair CL-600-2C10 (CRJ-701ER)	10122	ex C-	10122	Comair
☐ N642CA	Canadair CL-600-2C10 (CRJ-701ER)	10125	ex C-	10125	Comair
☐ N653CA	Canadair CL-600-2C10 (CRJ-701ER)	10129	ex C-GZUC	10129	Comair
☐ N655CA	Canadair CL-600-2C10 (CRJ-701ER)	10134	ex C-	10134	Comair
☐ N656CA	Canadair CL-600-2C10 (CRJ-701ER)	10143	ex C-GIAU	10143	Comair
☐ N658CA	Canadair CL-600-2C10 (CRJ-701ER)	10148	ex C-GIAU	10148	Comair
☐ N659CA	Canadair CL-600-2C10 (CRJ-701ER)	10153	ex C-	10153	Atlantic Southeast Lsd fr DAL
☐ N668CA	Canadair CL-600-2C10 (CRJ-701ER)	10162	ex C-	10162	SkyWest Lsd fr DAL
☐ N669CA	Canadair CL-600-2C10 (CRJ-701ER)	10176	ex C-	10176	Comair
☐ N690CA	Canadair CL-600-2C10 (CRJ-701ER)	10182	ex C-	10182	Comair on order
☐ N706EV	Canadair CL-600-2C10 (CRJ-701ER)	10054	ex C-GIAV		Atlantic Southeast
☐ N707EV	Canadair CL-600-2C10 (CRJ-701ER)	10057	ex C-GIAZ		Atlantic Southeast
☐ N708EV	Canadair CL-600-2C10 (CRJ-701ER)	10060	ex C-GIBI		Atlantic Southeast
☐ N709EV	Canadair CL-600-2C10 (CRJ-701ER)	10068	ex C-GICB		Atlantic Southeast
☐ N710EV	Canadair CL-600-2C10 (CRJ-701ER)	10071	ex C-GICP		Atlantic Southeast
☐ N712EV	Canadair CL-600-2C10 (CRJ-701ER)	10074	ex C-GHZZ		Atlantic Southeast
☐ N713EV	Canadair CL-600-2C10 (CRJ-701ER)	10081	ex C-GIAP		Atlantic Southeast
☐ N716EV	Canadair CL-600-2C10 (CRJ-701ER)	10084	ex C-GIAV		Atlantic Southeast
☐ N717EV	Canadair CL-600-2C10 (CRJ-701ER)	10088	ex C-GIBH		Atlantic Southeast
☐ N718EV	Canadair CL-600-2C10 (CRJ-701ER)	10095	ex C-		Atlantic Southeast
☐ N719EV	Canadair CL-600-2C10 (CRJ-701ER)	10099	ex C-GICL		Atlantic Southeast
☐ N720EV	Canadair CL-600-2C10 (CRJ-701ER)	10115	ex C-GIAW		Atlantic Southeast
☐ N722EV	Canadair CL-600-2C10 (CRJ-701ER)	10127	ex C-		Atlantic Southeast
☐ N723EV	Canadair CL-600-2C10 (CRJ-701ER)	10132	ex C-		Atlantic Southeast
☐ N724EV	Canadair CL-600-2C10 (CRJ-701ER)	10138	ex C-GIBT		Atlantic Southeast
☐ N730EV	Canadair CL-600-2C10 (CRJ-701ER)	10141	ex C-GIAP		Atlantic Southeast
☐ N738EV	Canadair CL-600-2C10 (CRJ-701ER)	10146	ex C-		Atlantic Southeast
		ASA 25th Anniversary c/s			
☐ N740EV	Canadair CL-600-2C10 (CRJ-701ER)	10151	ex C-		Atlantic Southeast
☐ N741EV	Canadair CL-600-2C10 (CRJ-701ER)	10155	ex C-FBQS		Atlantic Southeast
☐ N744EV	Canadair CL-600-2C10 (CRJ-701ER)	10157	ex C-		Atlantic Southeast
☐ N748EV	Canadair CL-600-2C10 (CRJ-701ER)	10158	ex C-		Atlantic Southeast
☐ N750EV	Canadair CL-600-2C10 (CRJ-701ER)	10161	ex C-		Atlantic Southeast
☐ N751EV	Canadair CL-600-2C10 (CRJ-701ER)	10163	ex C-		Atlantic Southeast
☐ N752EV	Canadair CL-600-2C10 (CRJ-701ER)	10166	ex C-		Atlantic Southeast
☐ N753EV	Canadair CL-600-2C10 (CRJ-701ER)	10169	ex C-		Atlantic Southeast
☐ N754EV	Canadair CL-600-2C10 (CRJ-701ER)	10173	ex C-FCRJ		Atlantic Southeast
☐ N755EV	Canadair CL-600-2C10 (CRJ-701ER)	10185	ex C-		Atlantic Southeast
☐ N758EV	Canadair CL-600-2C10 (CRJ-701ER)	10210	ex C-		Atlantic Southeast
☐ N759EV	Canadair CL-600-2C10 (CRJ-701ER)	10211	ex C-		Atlantic Southeast
☐ N760EV	Canadair CL-600-2C10 (CRJ-701ER)	10212	ex C-		Atlantic Southeast
☐ N761ND	Canadair CL-600-2C10 (CRJ-701ER)	10213	ex C-		Atlantic Southeast

☐ N131EV	Canadair CL-600-2D24 (CRJ-900ER)	15217	ex C-		Atlantic Southeast
☐ N132EV	Canadair CL-600-2D24 (CRJ-900ER)	15219	ex C-		Atlantic Southeast
☐ N133EV	Canadair CL-600-2D24 (CRJ-900ER)	15222	ex C-		Atlantic Southeast
☐ N134EV	Canadair CL-600-2D24 (CRJ-900ER)	15223	ex C-		Atlantic Southeast
☐ N135EV	Canadair CL-600-2D24 (CRJ-900ER)	15225	ex C-GIBI		Atlantic Southeast
☐ N136EV	Canadair CL-600-2D24 (CRJ-900ER)	15226	ex C-		Atlantic Southeast
☐ N137EV	Canadair CL-600-2D24 (CRJ-900ER)	15227	ex C-		Atlantic Southeast
☐ N138EV	Canadair CL-600-2D24 (CRJ-900ER)	15235	ex C-GZQW		Atlantic Southeast
☐ N146PQ	Canadair CL-600-2D24 (CRJ-900ER)	15146	ex C-		Pinnacle
☐ N147PQ	Canadair CL-600-2D24 (CRJ-900ER)	15147	ex C-		Pinnacle
☐ N153PQ	Canadair CL-600-2D24 (CRJ-900ER)	15153	ex C-		Pinnacle
☐ N161PQ	Canadair CL-600-2D24 (CRJ-900ER)	15161	ex C-		Pinnacle
☐ N162PQ	Canadair CL-600-2D24 (CRJ-900ER)	15162	ex C-		Pinnacle
☐ N166PQ	Canadair CL-600-2D24 (CRJ-900ER)	15166	ex C-		Pinnacle
☐ N170PQ	Canadair CL-600-2D24 (CRJ-900ER)	15170	ex C-		Pinnacle
☐ N176PQ	Canadair CL-600-2D24 (CRJ-900ER)	15176	ex C-		Pinnacle
☐ N181PQ	Canadair CL-600-2D24 (CRJ-900ER)	15181	ex C-		Pinnacle
☐ N186PQ	Canadair CL-600-2D24 (CRJ-900ER)	15186	ex C-		Pinnacle
☐ N187PQ	Canadair CL-600-2D24 (CRJ-900ER)	15187	ex C-		Pinnacle
☐ N195PQ	Canadair CL-600-2D24 (CRJ-900ER)	15195	ex C-FVWD		Pinnacle
☐ N197PQ	Canadair CL-600-2D24 (CRJ-900ER)	15197	ex C-GZQV		Pinnacle
☐ N200PQ	Canadair CL-600-2D24 (CRJ-900ER)	15200	ex C-GWVU		Pinnacle
☐ N228PQ	Canadair CL-600-2D24 (CRJ-900ER)	15228	ex C-		Pinnacle
☐ N232PQ	Canadair CL-600-2D24 (CRJ-900ER)	15232	ex C-GZQR		Pinnacle
☐ N538CA	Canadair CL-600-2D24 (CRJ-900ER)	15157	ex C-		Comair Lsd fr DAL
☐ N548CA	Canadair CL-600-2D24 (CRJ-900ER)	15159	ex C-		Comair
☐ N549CA	Canadair CL-600-2D24 (CRJ-900ER)	15164	ex C-		Comair
☐ N554CA	Canadair CL-600-2D24 (CRJ-900ER)	15168	ex C-		Comair
☐ N582CA	Canadair CL-600-2D24 (CRJ-900ER)	15171	ex C-		Comair
☐ N600LR	Canadair CL-600-2D24 (CRJ-900ER)	15142	ex C-		Mesaba
☐ N601LR	Canadair CL-600-2D24 (CRJ-900ER)	15145	ex C-		Mesaba
☐ N602LR	Canadair CL-600-2D24 (CRJ-900ER)	15151	ex C-		Mesaba

☐ N604LR	Canadair CL-600-2D24 (CRJ-900ER)	15152	ex C-		Mesaba Lsd fr DAL
☐ N605LR	Canadair CL-600-2D24 (CRJ-900ER)	15160	ex C-		Mesaba Lsd fr DAL
☐ N606LR	Canadair CL-600-2D24 (CRJ-900ER)	15173	ex C-		Pinnacle Lsd fr DAL
☐ N607LR	Canadair CL-600-2D24 (CRJ-900ER)	15178	ex C-		Atlantic Southeast Lsd fr DAL
☐ N676CA	Canadair CL-600-2D24 (CRJ-900ER)	15127	ex C-		Comair
☐ N678CA	Canadair CL-600-2D24 (CRJ-900ER)	15125	ex C-		Comair
☐ N679CA	Canadair CL-600-2D24 (CRJ-900ER)	15132	ex C-		Comair
☐ N689CA	Canadair CL-600-2D24 (CRJ-900ER)	15133	ex C-		Comair
☐ N691CA	Canadair CL-600-2D24 (CRJ-900ER)	15136	ex C-		Comair
☐ N692CA	Canadair CL-600-2D24 (CRJ-900ER)	15092	ex C-		Comair
☐ N693CA	Canadair CL-600-2D24 (CRJ-900ER)	15096	ex C-		Comair
☐ N695CA	Canadair CL-600-2D24 (CRJ-900ER)	15097	ex C-	30th Anniversary c/s	Comair
☐ N800SK	Canadair CL-600-2D24 (CRJ-900ER)	15060	ex C-		SkyWest
☐ N802SK	Canadair CL-600-2D24 (CRJ-900ER)	15061	ex C-		SkyWest
☐ N803SK	Canadair CL-600-2D24 (CRJ-900ER)	15062	ex C-FJTQ		SkyWest
☐ N804SK	Canadair CL-600-2D24 (CRJ-900ER)	15067	ex C-		SkyWest
☐ N805SK	Canadair CL-600-2D24 (CRJ-900ER)	15069	ex C-GZQT		SkyWest
☐ N806SK	Canadair CL-600-2D24 (CRJ-900ER)	15070	ex C-GZQV		SkyWest
☐ N807SK	Canadair CL-600-2D24 (CRJ-900ER)	15082	ex C-		SkyWest
☐ N809SK	Canadair CL-600-2D24 (CRJ-900ER)	15086	ex C-FLCX		SkyWest
☐ N810SK	Canadair CL-600-2D24 (CRJ-900ER)	15093	ex C-		SkyWest
☐ N812SK	Canadair CL-600-2D24 (CRJ-900ER)	15098	ex C-		SkyWest
☐ N813SK	Canadair CL-600-2D24 (CRJ-900ER)	15099	ex C-		SkyWest
☐ N814SK	Canadair CL-600-2D24 (CRJ-900ER)	15100	ex C-		SkyWest
☐ N815SK	Canadair CL-600-2D24 (CRJ-900ER)	15101	ex C-		SkyWest
☐ N816SK	Canadair CL-600-2D24 (CRJ-900ER)	15105	ex C-		SkyWest
☐ N817SK	Canadair CL-600-2D24 (CRJ-900ER)	15107	ex C-		SkyWest
☐ N820SK	Canadair CL-600-2D24 (CRJ-900ER)	15108	ex C-		SkyWest
☐ N821SK	Canadair CL-600-2D24 (CRJ-900ER)	15109	ex C-	35th anniversary c/s	SkyWest
☐ N822SK	Canadair CL-600-2D24 (CRJ-900ER)	15203	ex C-		SkyWest
☐ N823SK	Canadair CL-600-2D24 (CRJ-900ER)	15205	ex C-		SkyWest
☐ N824SK	Canadair CL-600-2D24 (CRJ-900ER)	15208	ex C-		SkyWest
☐ N825SK	Canadair CL-600-2D24 (CRJ-900ER)	15212	ex C-		SkyWest
☐ N901XJ	Canadair CL-600-2D24 (CRJ-900)	15130	ex C-		Mesaba
☐ N902XJ	Canadair CL-600-2D24 (CRJ-900)	15131	ex C-FNWB		Mesaba
☐ N903XJ	Canadair CL-600-2D24 (CRJ-900)	15134	ex C-FOFO		Mesaba
☐ N904XJ	Canadair CL-600-2D24 (CRJ-900)	15135	ex C-		Mesaba
☐ N905XJ	Canadair CL-600-2D24 (CRJ-900)	15137	ex C-		Mesaba
☐ N906XJ	Canadair CL-600-2D24 (CRJ-900)	15138	ex C-		Mesaba
☐ N907XJ	Canadair CL-600-2D24 (CRJ-900)	15139	ex C-FOVM		Mesaba
☐ N908XJ	Canadair CL-600-2D24 (CRJ-900)	15140	ex C-FOWF		Mesaba
☐ N909XJ	Canadair CL-600-2D24 (CRJ-900)	15141	ex C-		Mesaba
☐ N910XJ	Canadair CL-600-2D24 (CRJ-900)	15143	ex C-		Mesaba
☐ N912XJ	Canadair CL-600-2D24 (CRJ-900)	15144	ex C-		Mesaba
☐ N913XJ	Canadair CL-600-2D24 (CRJ-900)	15148	ex C-FQYX		Mesaba
☐ N914XJ	Canadair CL-600-2D24 (CRJ-900)	15149	ex C-		Mesaba
☐ N915XJ	Canadair CL-600-2D24 (CRJ-900)	15150	ex C-		Mesaba
☐ N916XJ	Canadair CL-600-2D24 (CRJ-900)	15154	ex C-		Mesaba
☐ N917XJ	Canadair CL-600-2D24 (CRJ-900)	15155	ex C-		Mesaba
☐ N918XJ	Canadair CL-600-2D24 (CRJ-900)	15156	ex C-		Mesaba
☐ N919XJ	Canadair CL-600-2D24 (CRJ-900)	15163	ex C-		Mesaba
☐ N920XJ	Canadair CL-600-2D24 (CRJ-900)	15167	ex C-		Mesaba
☐ N921XJ	Canadair CL-600-2D24 (CRJ-900)	15172	ex C-		Mesaba
☐ N922XJ	Canadair CL-600-2D24 (CRJ-900)	15174	ex C-FTTY		Mesaba
☐ N923XJ	Canadair CL-600-2D24 (CRJ-900)	15177	ex C-		Mesaba
☐ N924XJ	Canadair CL-600-2D24 (CRJ-900)	15179	ex C-		Mesaba
☐ N925XJ	Canadair CL-600-2D24 (CRJ-900)	15183	ex C-		Mesaba
☐ N926XJ	Canadair CL-600-2D24 (CRJ-900)	15184	ex C-		Mesaba
☐ N927XJ	Canadair CL-600-2D24 (CRJ-900)	15188	ex C-		Mesaba
☐ N928XJ	Canadair CL-600-2D24 (CRJ-900)	15190	ex C-		Mesaba
☐ N929XJ	Canadair CL-600-2D24 (CRJ-900)	15191	ex C-		Mesaba
☐ N930XJ	Canadair CL-600-2D24 (CRJ-900)	15192	ex C-		Mesaba
☐ N931XJ	Canadair CL-600-2D24 (CRJ-900)	15193	ex C-		Mesaba
☐ N932XJ	Canadair CL-600-2D24 (CRJ-900)	15194	ex C-		Mesaba
☐ N933XJ	Canadair CL-600-2D24 (CRJ-900)	15196	ex C-		Mesaba
☐ N934XJ	Canadair CL-600-2D24 (CRJ-900)	15198	ex C-		Mesaba
☐ N935XJ	Canadair CL-600-2D24 (CRJ-900)	15199	ex C-		Mesaba
☐ N936XJ	Canadair CL-600-2D24 (CRJ-900)	15201	ex C-		Mesaba
☐ N937XJ	Canadair CL-600-2D24 (CRJ-900)	15210	ex C-		Mesaba

☐ N272SK	Embraer EMB.145LR (ERJ-145LR)	145306	ex PT-SKX	8272	Chautauqua
☐ N273SK	Embraer EMB.145LR (ERJ-145LR)	145331	ex PT-SMX	8273	Chautauqua
☐ N274SK	Embraer EMB.145LR (ERJ-145LR)	145344	ex PT-SNK	8274	Chautauqua
☐ N561RP	Embraer EMB.145LR (ERJ-145LR)	145447	ex PT-SUS	8561	Chautauqua
☐ N562RP	Embraer EMB.145LR (ERJ-145LR)	145451	ex PT-SUW	8562	Chautauqua
☐ N563RP	Embraer EMB.145LR (ERJ-145LR)	145509	ex PT-SYB	8563	Chautauqua
☐ N564RP	Embraer EMB.145LR (ERJ-145LR)	145524	ex PT-SYP	8564	Chautauqua
☐ N565RP	Embraer EMB.145LR (ERJ-145LR)	145679	ex PT-SFL	8565	Chautauqua
☐ N566RP	Embraer EMB.145LR (ERJ-145LR)	145691	ex PT-SFX	8566	Chautauqua
☐ N567RP	Embraer EMB.145LR (ERJ-145LR)	145698	ex PT-SGD	8567	Chautauqua
☐ N568RP	Embraer EMB.145LR (ERJ-145LR)	145800	ex PT-SNE	8568	Chautauqua
☐ N569RP	Embraer EMB.145LR (ERJ-145LR)	14500816	ex PT-SNR	8569	Chautauqua
☐ N570RP	Embraer EMB.145LR (ERJ-145LR)	14500821	ex PT-SNV	8570	Chautauqua

☐ N571RP	Embraer EMB.145LR (ERJ-145LR)	14500827	ex PT-SNZ	8571	Chautauqua
☐ N572RP	Embraer EMB.145LR (ERJ-145LR)	14500828	ex PT-SQB	8572	Chautauqua
☐ N573RP	Embraer EMB.145LR (ERJ-145LR)	14500837	ex PT-SQJ	8573	Chautauqua
☐ N574RP	Embraer EMB.145LR (ERJ-145LR)	14500845	ex PT-SQP	8574	Chautauqua
☐ N575RP	Embraer EMB.145LR (ERJ-145LR)	14500847	ex PT-SQR	8575	Chautauqua
☐ N576RP	Embraer EMB.145LR (ERJ-145LR)	14500856	ex PT-SQX	8576	Chautauqua
☐ N577RP	Embraer EMB.145LR (ERJ-145LR)	14500862	ex PT-SXC	8577	Chautauqua
☐ N578RP	Embraer EMB.145LR (ERJ-145LR)	14500865	ex PT-SXE	8578	Chautauqua
☐ N579RP	Embraer EMB.145LR (ERJ-145LR)	14500871	ex PT-SXI	8579	Chautauqua
☐ N825MJ	Embraer EMB.145LR (ERJ-145LR)	145179	ex PT-SGB		Mesa
☐ N826MJ	Embraer EMB.145LR (ERJ-145LR)	145214	ex PT-SHB		Freedom
☐ N827MJ	Embraer EMB.145LR (ERJ-145LR)	145217	ex PT-SHD		Mesa
☐ N828MJ	Embraer EMB.145LR (ERJ-145LR)	145218	ex PT-SHE		Mesa
☐ N829MJ	Embraer EMB.145LR (ERJ-145LR)	145228	ex PT-SHQ		Freedom
☐ N830MJ	Embraer EMB.145LR (ERJ-145LR)	145259	ex PT-SIS		Freedom
☐ N831MJ	Embraer EMB.145LR (ERJ-145LR)	145273	ex PT-SJP		Mesa
☐ N832MJ	Embraer EMB.145LR (ERJ-145LR)	145310	ex PT-SMB		Freedom
☐ N833MJ	Embraer EMB.145LR (ERJ-145LR)	145327	ex PT-SMT		Mesa
☐ N836MJ	Embraer EMB.145LR (ERJ-145LR)	145359	ex PT-SNY		Freedom
☐ N837MJ	Embraer EMB.145LR (ERJ-145LR)	145367	ex PT-SOR		Freedom
☐ N838MJ	Embraer EMB.145LR (ERJ-145LR)	145384	ex PT-SQI		Freedom
☐ N841MJ	Embraer EMB.145LR (ERJ-145LR)	145448	ex PT-SUT		Mesa
☐ N842MJ	Embraer EMB.145LR (ERJ-145LR)	145457	ex PT-SVC		Freedom
☐ N844MJ	Embraer EMB.145LR (ERJ-145LR)	145481	ex PT-SXA		Mesa
☐ N845MJ	Embraer EMB.145LR (ERJ-145LR)	145502	ex PT-SXV		Freedom
☐ N847MJ	Embraer EMB.145LR (ERJ-145LR)	145517	ex PT-SYI		Mesa
☐ N848MJ	Embraer EMB.145LR (ERJ-145LR)	145530	ex PT-STU		Mesa
☐ N849MJ	Embraer EMB.145LR (ERJ-145LR)	145534	ex PT-STY		Mesa
☐ N850MJ	Embraer EMB.145LR (ERJ-145LR)	145568	ex PT-SBE		Mesa
☐ N851MJ	Embraer EMB.145LR (ERJ-145LR)	145572	ex PT-SBI		Freedom
☐ N852MJ	Embraer EMB.145LR (ERJ-145LR)	145567	ex PT-SBD		Mesa
☐ N853MJ	Embraer EMB.145LR (ERJ-145LR)	145464	ex PT-SVJ		Freedom
☐ N854MJ	Embraer EMB.145LR (ERJ-145LR)	145490	ex PT-SXJ		Mesa
☐ N855MJ	Embraer EMB.145LR (ERJ-145LR)	145614	ex PT-SCZ		Mesa
☐ N856MJ	Embraer EMB.145LR (ERJ-145LR)	145626	ex PT-SDO		Freedom
☐ N857MJ	Embraer EMB.145LR (ERJ-145LR)	145765	ex PT-SJW		Mesa
☐ N860MJ	Embraer EMB.145LR (ERJ-145LR)	145773	ex PT-SMD		Mesa
☐ N12569	Embraer EMB.145LR (ERJ-145LR)	145630	ex PT-SDS		ExpressJet
☐ N14570	Embraer EMB.145LR (ERJ-145LR)	145632	ex PT-SDU		ExpressJet
☐ N10575	Embraer EMB.145LR (ERJ-145LR)	145640	ex PT-SEC		ExpressJet
☐ N22909	Embraer EMB.145LR (ERJ-145LR)	145459	ex PT-SVE		ExpressJet
☐ N11137	Embraer EMB.145XR (ERJ-145XR)	145721	ex PT-SGX		ExpressJet
☐ N11165	Embraer EMB.145XR (ERJ-145XR)	14500819	ex PT-SNT		ExpressJet
☐ N11176	Embraer EMB.145XR (ERJ-145XR)	14500881	ex PT-SXV		ExpressJet
☐ N11181	Embraer EMB.145XR (ERJ-145XR)	14500904	ex PT-SYN		ExpressJet
☐ N11184	Embraer EMB.145XR (ERJ-145XR)	14500917	ex PT-SVX		ExpressJet
☐ N11193	Embraer EMB.145XR (ERJ-145XR)	14500938	ex PT-SCJ		ExpressJet
☐ N12167	Embraer EMB.145XR (ERJ-145XR)	14500834	ex PT-SQG		ExpressJet
☐ N14168	Embraer EMB.145XR (ERJ-145XR)	14500840	ex PT-SQL		ExpressJet
☐ N14171	Embraer EMB.145XR (ERJ-145XR)	14500859	ex PT-SQZ		ExpressJet
☐ N14173	Embraer EMB.145XR (ERJ-145XR)	14500872	ex PT-SXK		ExpressJet
☐ N14179	Embraer EMB.145XR (ERJ-145XR)	14500896	ex PT-SYI		ExpressJet
☐ N16170	Embraer EMB.145XR (ERJ-145XR)	14500850	ex PT-SQT		ExpressJet
☐ N16183	Embraer EMB.145XR (ERJ-145XR)	14500914	ex PT-SYV		ExpressJet
☐ N33182	Embraer EMB.145XR (ERJ-145XR)	14500909	ex PT-SYS		ExpressJet
☐ N201JQ	Embraer 170-200LR (175LR)	17000235	ex PT-SFL		Shuttle America
☐ N202JQ	Embraer 170-200LR (175LR)	17000240	ex PT-SFQ		Shuttle America
☐ N203JQ	Embraer 170-200LR (175LR)	17000242	ex PT-SFT		Shuttle America
☐ N204JQ	Embraer 170-200LR (175LR)	17000243	ex PT-SFU		Shuttle America
☐ N206JQ	Embraer 170-200LR (175LR)	17000249	ex PT-SJA		Shuttle America
☐ N207JQ	Embraer 170-200LR (175LR)	17000254	ex PT-SJG		Shuttle America
☐ N208JQ	Embraer 170-200LR (175LR)	17000257	ex PT-SJJ		Shuttle America
☐ N209JQ	Embraer 170-200LR (175LR)	17000258	ex PT-SJK		Shuttle America
☐ N210JQ	Embraer 170-200LR (175LR)	17000260	ex PT-SJN		Shuttle America
☐ N211JQ	Embraer 170-200LR (175LR)	17000261	ex PT-SJO		Shuttle America
☐ N212JQ	Embraer 170-200LR (175LR)	17000264	ex PT-SJS		Shuttle America
☐ N213JQ	Embraer 170-200LR (175LR)	17000265	ex PT-SJT		Shuttle America
☐ N214JQ	Embraer 170-200LR (175LR)	17000267	ex PT-SJV		Shuttle America
☐ N215JQ	Embraer 170-200LR (175LR)	17000270	ex PT-SNA		Shuttle America
☐ N216JQ	Embraer 170-200LR (175LR)	17000273	ex PT-SNH		Shuttle America
☐ N602CZ	Embraer 170-200LR (175LR)	17000171	ex PT-SMN		Compass
☐ N603CZ	Embraer 170-200LR (175LR)	17000176	ex PT-SMT		Compass
☐ N604CZ	Embraer 170-200LR (175LR)	17000181	ex PT-SMY		Compass
☐ N605CZ	Embraer 170-200LR (175LR)	17000186	ex PT-SUD		Compass
☐ N606CZ	Embraer 170-200LR (175LR)	17000188	ex PT-SUH		Compass
☐ N607CZ	Embraer 170-200LR (175LR)	17000192	ex PT-SUT		Compass
☐ N608CZ	Embraer 170-200LR (175LR)	17000195	ex PT-SXA		Compass
☐ N609CZ	Embraer 170-200LR (175LR)	17000197	ex PT-SXJ		Compass
☐ N610CZ	Embraer 170-200LR (175LR)	17000198	ex PT-SXK		Compass
☐ N612CZ	Embraer 170-200LR (175LR)	17000201	ex PT-SXQ		Compass
☐ N613CZ	Embraer 170-200AR (175AR)	17000203	ex PT-SXS		Compass

☐ N614CZ	Embraer 170-200AR (175AR)	17000205	ex PT-SCA		Compass
☐ N615CZ	Embraer 170-200LR (175LR)	17000207	ex PT-SCC		Compass
☐ N616CZ	Embraer 170-200LR (175LR)	17000209	ex PT-SCG		Compass
☐ N617CZ	Embraer 170-200LR (175LR)	17000210	ex PT-SCH		Compass
☐ N619CZ	Embraer 170-200LR (175LR)	17000213	ex PT-SCK		Compass
☐ N620CZ	Embraer 170-200LR (175LR)	17000214	ex PT-SCL		Compass
☐ N621CZ	Embraer 170-200LR (175LR)	17000218	ex PT-SCP		Compass
☐ N622CZ	Embraer 170-200LR (175LR)	17000219	ex PT-SCQ		Compass
☐ N623CZ	Embraer 170-200LR (175LR)	17000221	ex PT-SCT		Compass
☐ N624CZ	Embraer 170-200LR (175LR)	17000222	ex PT-SCX		Compass
☐ N625CZ	Embraer 170-200AR (175AR)	17000225	ex PT-SFB		Compass
☐ N626CZ	Embraer 170-200AR (175AR)	17000226	ex PT-SFC		Compass
☐ N627CZ	Embraer 170-200AR (175AR)	17000229	ex PT-SFF		Compass
☐ N628CZ	Embraer 170-200AR (175AR)	17000233	ex PT-SFJ		Compass
☐ N629CZ	Embraer 170-200AR (175AR)	17000236	ex PT-SFM		Compass
☐ N630CZ	Embraer 170-200AR (175AR)	17000238	ex PT-SFO		Compass
☐ N631CZ	Embraer 170-200AR (175AR)	17000239	ex PT-SFP		Compass
☐ N632CZ	Embraer 170-200AR (175AR)	17000244	ex PT-SFV		Compass
☐ N633CZ	Embraer 170-200AR (175AR)	17000245	ex PT-SFW		Compass
☐ N634CZ	Embraer 170-200AR (175AR)	17000246	ex PT-SFX		Compass
☐ N635CZ	Embraer 170-200AR (175AR)	17000252	ex PT-SJD		Compass
☐ N636CZ	Embraer 170-200AR (175AR)	17000253	ex PT-SJE		Compass
☐ N637CZ	Embraer 170-200AR (175AR)	17000256	ex PT-SJI		Compass
☐ N638CZ	Embraer 170-200AR (175AR)	17000259	ex PT-SJL		Compass
☐ N639CZ	Embraer 170-200AR (175AR)	17000262	ex PT-SJP		Compass
☐ N855RW	Embraer 170-100SE (170SE)	17000077	ex PT-SZC		Shuttle America
☐ N859RW	Embraer 170-100SE (170SE)	17000082	ex PT-SZH		Shuttle America
☐ N860RW	Embraer 170-100SE (170SE)	17000084	ex PT-SZJ		Shuttle America
☐ N862RW	Embraer 170-100SE (170SE)	17000098	ex PT-SZY		Shuttle America
☐ N866RW	Embraer 170-100SE (170SE)	17000129	ex PT-SDS		Republic
☐ N867RW	Embraer 170-100SE (170SE)	17000130	ex PT-SDT		Shuttle America
☐ N868RW	Embraer 170-100SU (170SU)	17000131	ex PT-SDU		Republic
☐ N869RW	Embraer 170-100SE (170SE)	17000133	ex PT-SDW		Shuttle America
☐ N870RW	Embraer 170-100SE (170SE)	17000138	ex PT-SEC		Republic
☐ N958WH	Embraer 170-200LR (175LR)	17000248	ex PT-SFZ	8205	Shuttle America

☐ N365PX	SAAB SF.340B	340B-265	ex SE-G65		Mesaba; stored BGR
☐ N408XJ	SAAB SF.340B	340B-408	ex SE-B08		Mesaba
☐ N410XJ	SAAB SF.340B	340B-410	ex SE-B10		Mesaba
☐ N411XJ	SAAB SF.340B	340B-411	ex SE-B11		Mesaba
☐ N412XJ	SAAB SF.340B	340B-412	ex SE-B12		Mesaba
☐ N413XJ	SAAB SF.340B	340B-413	ex SE-B13		Mesaba
☐ N414XJ	SAAB SF.340B	340B-414	ex SE-B14		Mesaba
☐ N415XJ	SAAB SF.340B	340B-415	ex SE-B15		Mesaba
☐ N416XJ	SAAB SF.340B	340B-416	ex SE-B16		Mesaba
☐ N417XJ	SAAB SF.340B	340B-417	ex SE-B17		Mesaba
☐ N418XJ	SAAB SF.340B	340B-418	ex SE-B18		Mesaba
☐ N420XJ	SAAB SF.340B	340B-420	ex SE-B20		Mesaba
☐ N421XJ	SAAB SF.340B	340B-421	ex SE-B21		Mesaba
☐ N422XJ	SAAB SF.340B	340B-422	ex SE-B22		Mesaba
☐ N423XJ	SAAB SF.340B	340B-423	ex SE-B23		Mesaba
☐ N424XJ	SAAB SF.340B	340B-424	ex SE-B24		Mesaba
☐ N425XJ	SAAB SF.340B	340B-425	ex SE-B25		Mesaba
☐ N426XJ	SAAB SF.340B	340B-426	ex SE-B26		Mesaba
☐ N427XJ	SAAB SF.340B	340B-427	ex SE-B27		Mesaba
☐ N428XJ	SAAB SF.340B	340B-428	ex SE-B28		Mesaba
☐ N429XJ	SAAB SF.340B	340B-429	ex SE-B29		Mesaba
☐ N430XJ	SAAB SF.340B	340B-430	ex SE-B30		Mesaba
☐ N433XJ	SAAB SF.340B	340B-433	ex SE-B33		Mesaba
☐ N434XJ	SAAB SF.340B	340B-434	ex SE-B34		Mesaba
☐ N435XJ	SAAB SF.340B	340B-435	ex SE-B35		Mesaba
☐ N436XJ	SAAB SF.340B	340B-436	ex SE-B36		Mesaba
☐ N437XJ	SAAB SF.340B	340B-437	ex SE-B37		Mesaba
☐ N438XJ	SAAB SF.340B	340B-438	ex SE-B38		Mesaba
☐ N439XJ	SAAB SF.340B	340B-439	ex SE-B39		Mesaba
☐ N441XJ	SAAB SF.340B	340B-441	ex SE-B41	25th Anniversary c/s	Mesaba
☐ N442XJ	SAAB SF.340B	340B-442	ex SE-B42		Mesaba
☐ N443XJ	SAAB SF.340B	340B-443	ex SE-B43		Mesaba
☐ N444XJ	SAAB SF.340B	340B-444	ex SE-B44		Mesaba
☐ N445XJ	SAAB SF.340B	340B-445	ex SE-B45		Mesaba
☐ N446XJ	SAAB SF.340B	340B-446	ex SE-B46		Mesaba
☐ N447XJ	SAAB SF.340B	340B-447	ex SE-B47		Mesaba
☐ N448XJ	SAAB SF.340B	340B-448	ex SE-B48		Mesaba
☐ N449XJ	SAAB SF.340B	340B-449	ex SE-B49		Mesaba
☐ N450XJ	SAAB SF.340B	340B-450	ex SE-B50		Mesaba
☐ N451XJ	SAAB SF.340B	340B-451	ex SE-B51		Mesaba
☐ N452XJ	SAAB SF.340B	340B-452	ex SE-B52		Mesaba
☐ N453XJ	SAAB SF.340B	340B-453	ex SE-B53		Mesaba
☐ N454XJ	SAAB SF.340B	340B-454	ex SE-B54		Mesaba
☐ N456XJ	SAAB SF.340B	340B-456	ex SE-B56		Mesaba
☐ N457XJ	SAAB SF.340B	340B-457	ex SE-B57		Mesaba

DESERT AIR — Anchorage, AK (ANC)

Registration	Type	c/n	Previous identity	Notes
☐ N105CA	Douglas DC-3	14275/25720	ex N85FA	stored CLK
☐ N153PA	Convair 240-27	304	ex 51-7892	
☐ N19906	Douglas DC-3	4747	ex 41-38644	stored ANC
☐ N44587	Douglas DC-3	12857	ex N353SA	stored ANC

DODITA AIR CARGO — San Juan-Munoz Marin Intl, PR (SJU)

Registration	Type	c/n	Previous identity	Notes
☐ N912AL	Convair 440-78	353	ex PZ-TGA	stored SJU
☐ N31325	Convair 240-52	52-8	ex 52-1183	stored SJU

EASTERN CARIBBEAN AIR — (JI) — San Juan-Munoz Marin Intl, PR (SJU)

Registration	Type	c/n	Previous identity
☐ N288RA	Beech 100 King Air	B-5	ex N280RA

EDWARDS JET CENTER OF MONTANA — Edwards (EDJ) — Billings-Logan Intl, MT (BIL)

Registration	Type	c/n	Previous identity
☐ N90EJ	Beech C90 King Air	LJ-749	ex N552R
☐ N102LF	Beech 100 King Air	B-65	ex N102RS
☐ N265EJ	Beech 200 Super King Air	BB-911	ex N411CC
☐ N2703U	Cessna 340A	340A0914	
☐ N6316X	Cessna 340A	340A0487	
☐ N9781S	Cessna 414A Chancellor III	414A0515	ex D-IFLO

EG & G

Registration	Type	c/n	Previous identity
☐ N20RA	Beech 1900C	UB-42	
☐ N623RA	Beech 1900C-1	UC-163	ex N3043L

Registration	Type	c/n	Previous identity
☐ N273RH	Boeing 737-66N	29890/1276	ex N824SR
☐ N288DP	Boeing 737-66N	29892/1305	ex N892SR
☐ N319BD	Boeing 737-66N	28649/887	ex N649MT
☐ N365SR	Boeing 737-66N	29891/1294	ex N891RD
☐ N859WP	Boeing 737-66N	28652/938	ex N645DM
☐ N869HH	Boeing 737-66N	28650/932	ex N628SR

EMPIRE AIRLINES — Empire Air (EM/CFS) — Coeur d'Alene, ID/Spokane-Intl, WA (COE/GEG)

Operates Cessna 208 Caravans and ATR 42/72s plus Fokker F.27 Friendship 500s leased from, and operated on behalf of, FedEx

EPPS AVIATION CHARTER — Epps Air (EPS) — Atlanta-De Kalb-Peachtree, GA (PDK)

Registration	Type	c/n	Previous identity
☐ N10HT	Mitsubishi MU-2B-60	778SA	ex N264MA
☐ N46AK	Mitsubishi MU-2B-60	754SA	ex N942ST
☐ N888RH	Mitsubishi MU-2B-60	737SA	ex N315MA
☐ N888SE	Mitsubishi MU-2B-60	1549SA	ex N475MA
☐ N941MA	Mitsubishi MU-2B-60	744SA	
☐ N984RE	Mitsubishi MU-2B-60	787SA	ex N267PC
☐ N1164F	Mitsubishi MU-2B-60	1562SA	ex D-ICDG
☐ N8083A	Mitsubishi MU-2B-60	739SA	ex N707EZ

All Cavanaugh (SCD) conversions

Registration	Type	c/n	Previous identity
☐ N23WJ	Beech 200 Super King Air	BB-1297	ex N21VF
☐ N57GA	Beech 200 Super King Air	BB-477	ex F-GILB
☐ N109DT	Beech 65-C90A King Air	LJ-1102	ex N682TA
☐ N795CA	Beech 200 Super King Air	BB-559	ex N559BM

ERA AVIATION — Erah (7H/ERH) — Anchorage-Intl South, AK (ANC)

Registration	Type	c/n	Previous identity
☐ N881EA	de Havilland DHC-8-106	233	ex C-GFOD
☐ N882EA	de Havilland DHC-8-103	98	ex D-BERT
☐ N883EA	de Havilland DHC-8-106	260	ex C-GGEW
☐ N971EA	Beech 1900D	UE-387	ex N848CA
☐ N972EA	Beech 1900D	UE-389	ex N852CA
☐ N973EA	Beech 1900D	UE-391	ex N841CA

ERA HELICOPTERS — Anchorage-Intl South, AK/Lake Charles-Regional, LA (ANC/LCH)

Registration	Type	c/n	Previous identity
☐ N108TA	Aérospatiale AS350BA AStar	3080	
☐ N109TA	Aérospatiale AS350B2 AStar	3103	
☐ N118TA	Aérospatiale AS350B2 AStar	3110	
☐ N147BH	Aérospatiale AS350BA AStar	1273	ex N3610G
☐ N152TA	Aérospatiale AS350B1 AStar	2241	ex N60321
☐ N159JK	Aérospatiale AS350B2 AStar	3253	
☐ N161EH	Aérospatiale AS350B2 AStar	2144	
☐ N162EH	Aérospatiale AS350B2 AStar	2147	
☐ N165EH	Aérospatiale AS350B1 AStar	2185	
☐ N166EH	Aérospatiale AS350B2 AStar	2194	

☐ N178EH	Aérospatiale AS350B2 AStar	2264		
☐ N181EH	Aérospatiale AS350B2 AStar	2680		
☐ N182EH	Aérospatiale AS350B2 AStar	2681		
☐ N183EH	Aérospatiale AS350B2 AStar	2752		
☐ N185EH	Aérospatiale AS350B2 AStar	2823		
☐ N186EH	Aérospatiale AS350B2 AStar	2844		
☐ N187EH	Aérospatiale AS350B2 AStar	2839		
☐ N188EH	Aérospatiale AS350B2 AStar	2954		
☐ N190EH	Aérospatiale AS350B2 AStar	2974		
☐ N191EH	Aérospatiale AS350B2 AStar	2505		
☐ N192EH	Aérospatiale AS350B2 AStar	2582		
☐ N193EH	Aérospatiale AS350B2 AStar	2599		
☐ N194EH	Aérospatiale AS350B2 AStar	2608		
☐ N195EH	Aérospatiale AS350B2 AStar	2615		
☐ N196EH	Aérospatiale AS350B2 AStar	2976		
☐ N212EH	Aérospatiale AS350B2 AStar	3151		
☐ N214EH	Aérospatiale AS350B2 AStar	3163		
☐ N215EH	Aérospatiale AS350B2 AStar	3172		
☐ N216EH	Aérospatiale AS350B2 AStar	3184		
☐ N217EH	Aérospatiale AS350B2 AStar	3197		
☐ N217FD	Aérospatiale AS350B2 AStar	4221	ex N646PT	
☐ N328BF	Aérospatiale AS350B2 AStar	4284		
☐ N420JA	Aérospatiale AS350B2 AStar	4212		
☐ N603WB	Aérospatiale AS350B2 AStar	4225		
☐ N747WB	Aérospatiale AS350B2 AStar	2768		
☐ N906BA	Aérospatiale AS350B AStar	1479	ex N5786Y	
☐ N4061G	Aérospatiale AS350BA AStar	3051	ex F-OHVB	
☐ N40584	Aérospatiale AS350B2 AStar	2924	ex F-OHNT	
☐ N18EA	Agusta A.109E Power	11210	ex N261CF	
☐ N530KS	Agusta A.109E Power	11694		
☐ N820FT	Agusta A.109E Power	11701		
☐ N903RW	Agusta A.109E Power	11601	ex N3ZJ	
☐ N910LB	Agusta A.109E Power	11682		
☐ N108AG	Agusta A.119 Koala	14053	ex N911AM	
☐ N126RD	Agusta A.119 Koala	14504	ex N6QY	
☐ N149JM	Agusta A.119 Koala	14533		
☐ N203JP	Agusta A.119 Koala	14535		
☐ N330JN	Agusta A.119 Koala	14510		
☐ N514RE	Agusta A.119 Koala II	14701		
☐ N602FB	Agusta A.119 Koala	14528		
☐ N626JP	Agusta A.119 Koala II	14716		
☐ N628RL	Agusta A.119 Koala II	14713		
☐ N709CG	Agusta A.119 Koala	14052	ex N18YC	
☐ N715RT	Agusta A.119 Koala	14516		
☐ N802SM	Agusta A.119 Koala II	14711		
☐ N803EB	Agusta A.119 Koala	14033	ex N7KN	
☐ N822MM	Agusta A.119 Koala	14055	ex N6QX	
☐ N907AG	Agusta A.119 Koala	14045	ex N119MW	
☐ N915BE	Agusta A.119 Koala	14519		
☐ N927JK	Agusta A.119 Koala	14517		
☐ N149DH	Agusta AW139	41004		
☐ N156JS	Agusta AW139	41003	ex I-EASH	
☐ N339DF	Agusta AW139	41021		
☐ N339JR	Agusta AW139	41015		
☐ N428NE	Agusta AW139	41001	ex I-EASJ	
☐ N725TF	Agusta AW139	31074		
☐ N813DG	Agusta AW139	31032		
☐ N	Agusta AW139			on order
☐ N	Agusta AW139			on order
☐ N	Agusta AW139			on order
☐ N125TA	Bell 206B JetRanger III	1315	ex N302SH	
☐ N297CA	Bell 206B JetRanger III	1453	ex N117V	
☐ N707HJ	Bell 206B JetRanger III	3173	ex N707TV	
☐ N39114	Bell 206B JetRanger III	3293		
☐ N59582	Bell 206B JetRanger III	1460		
☐ N357EH	Bell 212	31209		
☐ N358EH	Bell 212	31211		
☐ N359EH	Bell 212	31212	ex C-GRVN	
☐ N361EH	Bell 212	30554	ex XA-TRY	
☐ N362EH	Bell 212	30853	ex XA-TRX	
☐ N370EH	Bell 212	30624		
☐ N399EH	Bell 212	30810	ex XA-AAM	
☐ N500EH	Bell 212	30945		
☐ N508EH	Bell 212	30908		
☐ N509EH	Bell 212	30925		
☐ N511EH	Bell 212	31118		
☐ N522EH	Bell 212	31199	ex XA-TRZ	
☐ N523EH	Bell 212	31214	ex C-GRWX	

☐ N167EH	Bell 412	33089	ex VH-NSO
☐ N168EH	Bell 412	33058	ex VH-NSI
☐ N169EH	Bell 412	33064	ex XA-BDD
☐ N417EH	Bell 412	33031	ex N3911E
☐ N421EH	Bell 412	33067	ex N57413

☐ N116KG	Eurocopter EC120B Colibri	1152	ex N413AE
☐ N120GB	Eurocopter EC120B Colibri	1063	
☐ N120TX	Eurocopter EC120B Colibri	1029	
☐ N131MB	Eurocopter EC120B Colibri	1070	
☐ N517SS	Eurocopter EC120B Colibri	1080	ex N5234N

☐ N89EM	Eurocopter EC135P1	0049	ex N94387
☐ N320TV	Eurocopter EC135P2	0467	
☐ N357TC	Eurocopter EC135P2+	0626	
☐ N551BA	Eurocopter EC135P2	0188	
☐ N605SS	Eurocopter EC135P2	0461	
☐ N611LS	Eurocopter EC135P2	0472	
☐ N812LV	Eurocopter EC135P2+	0614	

☐ N124EH	MBB Bo.105CBS	S-559	ex 9Y-TJE
☐ N125EH	MBB Bo.105CBS	S-562	ex N9376Y
☐ N129EH	MBB Bo.105CBS	S-580	ex N29077
☐ N130EH	MBB Bo.105CBS	S-588	ex N2910H
☐ N131EH	MBB Bo.105CBS	S-595	ex N3129U
☐ N135EH	MBB Bo.105CBS	S-675	ex N4573D
☐ N149EH	MBB Bo.105CBS	S-705	ex N968MB
☐ N152EH	MBB Bo.105CBS	S-701	ex N954MB
☐ N153EH	MBB Bo.105CBS	S-702	ex PH-NZY
☐ N290EH	MBB Bo.105CBS-4	S-850	ex N6554Y
☐ N291EH	MBB Bo.105CBS-4	S-842	ex N65962
☐ N293EH	MBB Bo.105CBS-4	S-844	ex N6612K
☐ N294EH	MBB Bo.105CBS-4	S-846	ex N6559A
☐ N296EH	MBB Bo.105CBS-4	S-849	ex N65385
☐ N298EH	MBB Bo.105CBS-4	S-845	ex N4186F
☐ N423EH	MBB Bo.105CBS	S-543	ex N42018
☐ N424EH	MBB Bo.105CBS	S-548	ex N42001
☐ N426EH	MBB Bo.105CBS	S-552	ex N93173
☐ N427EH	MBB Bo.105CBS	S-554	ex N93205

☐ N562EH	Sikorsky S-61N	61257	ex PH-NZA
☐ N564EH	Sikorsky S-61N	61365	ex C-GBSF

☐ N547WM	Sikorsky S-76C++	760722	ex N2579P
☐ N573EH	Sikorsky S-76A++	760373	ex B-
☐ N574EH	Sikorsky S-76A++	760369	ex N369AG
☐ N575EH	Sikorsky S-76A++	760366	ex N621LH
☐ N576EH	Sikorsky S-76A++	760212	ex N15458
☐ N577EH	Sikorsky S-76A++	760222	ex N15459
☐ N578EH	Sikorsky S-76A++	760099	ex N223BF
☐ N761EH	Sikorsky S-76C++	760736	ex N20302
☐ N905RD	Sikorsky S-76C+	760610	ex N8109K

ERICKSON AIR CRANE — *Central Point, OR*

☐ N154AC	Erickson/Sikorsky S-64E Skycrane	64037	ex 68-18435	733 Georgia Peach	
☐ N158AC	Erickson/Sikorsky S-64F Skycrane	64081	ex HL9260	744 Goliath	
☐ N159AC	Erickson/Sikorsky S-64F Skycrane	64084	ex 68-18476	741	
☐ N163AC	Erickson/Sikorsky S-64E Skycrane	64093	ex 70-18485	738 Hurricane Bubba	
☐ N164AC	Erickson/Sikorsky S-64E Skycrane	64034	ex C-FCRN	730 The Incredible Hulk	
☐ N171AC	Erickson/Sikorsky S-64F Skycrane	64090	ex 69-18482		stored Central Point
☐ N173AC	Erickson/Sikorsky S-64E Skycrane	64015	ex 68-18413	736 Christina	
☐ N178AC	Erickson/Sikorsky S-64E Skycrane	64097	ex 70-18489	748 Isabelle	
☐ N179AC	Erickson/Sikorsky S-64E Skycrane	64091	ex C-GFAH	733 Elvis	
☐ N194AC	Erickson/Sikorsky S-64E Skycrane	64017	ex C-GFLH	746	
☐ N217AC	Erickson/Sikorsky S-64E Skycrane	64064	ex N542SB	732 Malcolm	
☐ N218AC	Erickson/Sikorsky S-64E Skycrane	64033	ex N545SB	749 Elsie	
☐ N229AC	Erickson/Sikorsky S-64E Skycrane	64018	ex N4099Y	743 Tug	
☐ N237AC	Erickson/Sikorsky S-64E Skycrane	64095	ex 69-18487		stored Central Point
☐ N243AC	Erickson/Sikorsky S-64E Skycrane	64022	ex N544CH		stored Central Point
☐ N247AC	Erickson/Sikorsky S-64E Skycrane	64052	ex N2270B		stored Central Point
☐ N543CH	Erickson/Sikorsky S-64E Skycrane	64016	ex N4409U		stored Central Point
☐ N957AC	Erickson/Sikorsky S-64E Skycrane	64065	ex C-GESG	745	
☐ N4099M	Erickson/Sikorsky S-64E Skycrane	64028	ex 67-18426		stored Central Point
☐ N6962R	Erickson/Sikorsky S-64E Skycrane	64058	ex HC-CAT	741 Olga	
☐ N7073C	Erickson/Sikorsky S-64E Skycrane	64042	ex 68-18440		stored Central Point

EVERGREEN HELICOPTERS *(7E)*
McMinnville, OR/Anchorage-Merrill, AK/ Galveston, TX (RNC/MRI/GLS)

☐ N351EV	Aérospatiale AS350B2 AStar	2930	ex SE-JCX	Lsd fr GC Air

☐ N352EV	Aérospatiale AS350B2 AStar	2555	ex JA6112	
☐ N353EV	Aérospatiale AS350B2 AStar	2444	ex C-GJVG	
☐ N354EV	Aérospatiale AS350B3 AStar	3664	ex SE-JHG	
☐ N355EV	Aérospatiale AS350B3 AStar	3550	ex F-GYDE	
☐ N356EV	Aérospatiale AS350B3 AStar	3649	ex SE-JHF	
☐ N359EV	Aérospatiale AS350B3 AStar	3797	ex I-BALO	
☐ N917JT	Aérospatiale AS350B2 AStar	2759	ex N6096P	
☐ N33AZ	Bell 206L-3 LongRanger III	51110		
☐ N85TC	Bell 206L-3 LongRanger III	51143		
☐ N206EV	Bell 206L-4 LongRanger IV	52311	ex N46340	
☐ N3195S	Bell 206L-3 LongRanger III	51136		
☐ N5007F	Bell 206L-1 LongRanger III	45186		
☐ N212EV	Bell 212	30881	ex HK-4064X	
☐ N241LG	Bell 212	30930	ex N5017H	
☐ N398EH	Bell 212	30766	ex HK-4059X	
☐ N5410N	Bell 212	31206	ex VH-CUZ	
☐ N16973	Bell 212	30882	ex VH-CRO	
☐ N59633	Bell 212	30676		
☐ N22MS	Learjet 35A	35A-209	ex N711DS	
☐ N60EV	Sikorsky S-61 (H-3E)	61642	ex 69-5799	
☐ N61EV	Sikorsky S-61 (H-3E)	61566	ex 65-12791	
☐ N62EV	Sikorsky S-61 (HH-3F)	61670	ex USCG 1493	
☐ N63EV	Sikorsky S-61 (HH-3F)	61674	ex USCG 1497	
☐ N70DB	Bell 206B JetRanger	1730		
☐ N134WJ	Beech B200C Super King Air	BL-134	ex SE-LMP	
☐ N191EV	Beech 1900D	UE-114	ex N114YV	
☐ N202EV	Lockheed P2V-5 Neptune	726-5387	ex Bu131502 141	Tanker
☐ N204BB	MBB B0.105C	S-57	ex D-HDBH	
☐ N330J	Aérospatiale SA.330J Puma	1647	ex XA-SKT	
☐ N348CA	CASA C.212-200	CC20-7-175		
☐ N352CA	CASA C.212-200	CC40-1-190		Lsd to US Air Force
☐ N352HS	Learjet 35A	35A-596	ex N826CP	
☐ N405PC	Learjet 35A	35A-651	ex HB-VJK	
☐ N405R	Aérospatiale SA.330J Puma	1475	ex PP-MGB	
☐ N413EV	Bell 412EP	36381	ex N91755	
☐ N416EV	Bell 412EP	36424	ex C-FCLP	
☐ N419EV	Bell 412EP	36464	ex C-FSOD	
☐ N422CA	CASA C.212-200	CC40-5-238		
☐ N423CA	CASA C.212-200	S1-1-240		Lsd to US Air Force
☐ N500KM	MBB Bo.105C	S-76	ex N500KV	
☐ N6979R	Sikorsky S-64E	64079		
☐ N9688G	Cessna U206F Stationair	U20601888		
☐ N10729	Bell 206B JetRanger III	2876		

EVERGREEN INTERNATIONAL AIRLINES — *Evergreen (EZ/EIA)* — *McMinnville, OR/Marana-Pinal Airpark, AZ (RNC/MZJ)*

☐ N470EV	Boeing 747-273C	20653/237	ex N749WA	947 Super Tanker	
☐ N471EV	Boeing 747-273C	20651/209	ex N747WR		
☐ N477EV	Boeing 747SR-46 (SCD)	20784/231	ex N688UP		stored MZJ
☐ N478EV	Boeing 747SR-46 (SCD)	21033/254	ex PT-TDE		stored MZJ
☐ N479EV	Boeing 747-132 (SCD)	19898/94	ex N725PA		Water Bomber 979
☐ N480EV	Boeing 747-121 (SCD)	20348/106	ex N690UP		stored MZJ
☐ N481EV	Boeing 747-132 (SCD)	19896/72	ex N902PA		
☐ N482EV	Boeing 747-212B (SCD)	20713/219	ex N729PA		
☐ N485EV	Boeing 747-212B (SCD)	20712/218	ex N728PA		
☐ N486EV	Boeing 747-212B (SCD)	20888/240	ex N745SJ		
☐ N487EV	Boeing 747-230B (SCD)	23286/614	ex TF-AMF		
☐ N488EV	Boeing 747-230B (SCD)	23287/617	ex D-ABZA		
☐ N489EV	Boeing 747-230B (SF)	23393/633	ex TF-AMH		
☐ N490EV	Boeing 747-230F	24138/706	ex TF-ARV		
☐ N249BA	Boeing 747-409LCF	24309/766	ex B-18271		Op for Boeing
☐ N718BA	Boeing 747-4H6LCF	27042/932	ex N74713	on order	Op for Boeing
☐ N747BC	Boeing 747-4J6LCF	25879/904	ex B-2464		Op for Boeing
☐ N780BA	Boeing 747-409LCF	24310/778	ex B-18272		Op for Boeing
☐ N915F	Douglas DC-9-15RC (ABS 3)	47061/207	ex EC-EYS		stored MZJ
☐ N916F	Douglas DC-9-15RC (ABS 3)	47044/265	ex OH-LYH		stored MZJ
☐ N933F	Douglas DC-9-33RC (ABS 3)	47191/280	ex N33UA		stored MZJ
☐ N941F	Douglas DC-9-33F (ABS 3)	47193/311	ex VH-IPC		stored MZJ
☐ N944F	Douglas DC-9-33RC (ABS 3)	47194/324	ex PH-DNP		stored MZJ

EVERTS AIR ALASKA — *Everts (3Z/VTS)* — *Fairbanks-Intl, AK (FAI)*

☐ N108NS	Piper PA-32R-300 Lance	32R-7680288
☐ N148RF	Piper PA-32R-300 Lance	32R-7680076

☐ N575JD	Cessna 208B Caravan I	208B0595	ex N5268V	
☐ N1063H	Piper PA-32R-300 Lance	32R-7780129		
☐ N6969J	Piper PA-32R-300 Lance	32R-7680398		

EVERTS AIR CARGO — *Everts (3K/VTS)* — *Fairbanks-Intl, AK (FAI)*

☐ N151	Douglas DC-6B	45496/992	ex C-GICD	
☐ N251CE	Douglas C-118A	44612/532	ex Bu153693	
☐ N351CE	Douglas C-118A	44599/505	ex 53-3228	
☐ N400UA	Douglas DC-6A	44258/467	ex YV-296C	
☐ N555SQ	Douglas DC-6B	45137/830	ex N37585	
☐ N1036F	Douglas C-118A	43581/295		stored FAI
☐ N1377K	Douglas C-118A	44596/499		stored FAI
☐ N6174C	Douglas DC-6A	44075/451	ex C-GBYN	
☐ N6586C	Douglas DC-6BF	45222/849		
☐ N9056R	Douglas DC-6A/B	45498/1005	ex C-FCZZ	
☐ N99330	Douglas C-118A	43576/275	ex C-GPEG	stored FAI
☐ N1105G	Embraer EMB.120FC Brasilia	120105	ex PT-SMX	
☐ N1110J	Embraer EMB.120FC Brasilia	120110	ex PT-SNC	
☐ N7848B	Curtiss C-46R Commando	273	ex HP-238	Dumbo
☐ N12703	Embraer EMB.120FC Brasilia	120084	ex PT-SMB	stored FAI
☐ N54514	Curtiss C-46D Commando	33285	ex 51-1122	Maid in Japan

EVERTS AIR FUEL — *Fairbanks-Intl, AK (FAI)*

☐ N444CE	Douglas DC-6B	45478/962	ex C-GHLZ	Spirit of America
☐ N451CE	Douglas C-118B	43712/358	ex N840CS	
☐ N747CE	Douglas C-118A	44661/628	ex N223HP	
☐ N801FA	Curtiss C-46F Commando	22600	ex CF-NAU	
☐ N1822M	Curtiss C-46F Commando	22521	ex 44-18698	Salmon Ella
☐ N1837M	Curtiss C-46F Commando	22388	ex CF-FNC	Hot Stuff
☐ N7780B	Douglas DC-6A	45372/875		
☐ N51599	Douglas C-118A	44662/629	ex 53-3291	

EXECUTIVE AIRLINES — *Executive Eagle (OW/EXK)*
San Juan-Luis Munoz Marin Intl, PR / Miami Intl, FL (SJU/MIA)

A wholly owned subsidiary of American Eagle Airlines and operates as American Eagle

EXPRESSJET AIRLINES — *Jet Link (CO/BTA)*
Cleveland, OH/Houston- Intercontinental, TX/Newark, NJ (CLE/IAH/EWR)

☐ N11544	Embraer EMB.145LR (ERJ-145LR)	145557	ex PT-SZS
☐ N11551	Embraer EMB.145LR (ERJ-145LR)	145411	ex PT-STI
☐ N18557	Embraer EMB.145LR (ERJ-145LR)	145596	ex PT-SCF
☐ N19554	Embraer EMB.145LR (ERJ-145LR)	145587	ex PT-SBX
☐ N14907	Embraer EMB.145LR (ERJ-145LR)	145468	ex PT-SVN
☐ N11189	Embraer EMB.145XR (ERJ-145XR)	14500931	ex PT-SCA
☐ N11192	Embraer EMB.145XR (ERJ-145XR)	14500936	ex PT-SCI
☐ N11199	Embraer EMB.145XR (ERJ-145XR)	14500953	ex PT-SFA
☐ N12163	Embraer EMB.145XR (ERJ-145XR)	14500811	ex PT-SNN
☐ N12175	Embraer EMB.145XR (ERJ-145XR)	14500878	ex PT-SXT
☐ N12201	Embraer EMB.145XR (ERJ-145XR)	14500959	ex PT-SFG
☐ N14162	Embraer EMB.145XR (ERJ-145XR)	14500808	ex PT-SNK
☐ N14174	Embraer EMB.145XR (ERJ-145XR)	14500876	ex PT-SXR
☐ N14188	Embraer EMB.145XR (ERJ-145XR)	14500929	ex PT-SOY
☐ N14198	Embraer EMB.145XR (ERJ-145XR)	14500951	ex PT-SCZ
☐ N16178	Embraer EMB.145XR (ERJ-145XR)	14500889	ex PT-SYC

FEDERICO HELICOPTERS — *(FDE)*
Fresno-Air Terminal, CA/Mariposa-Yosemite, CA (FAT/OYS)

☐ N205JG	Bell UH-1H (205)	9884	ex 67-17686
☐ N752A	Sikorsky S-55A	55981	ex C-GRXA
☐ N1386L	Bell UH-1B (204)	652	ex 62-4592

FEDEX EXPRESS — *FedEx (FX/FDX)* — *Memphis-Intl, TN (MEM)*

☐ N650FE	Airbus A300F4-605R	726	ex F-WWAP	Molly Mickler
☐ N651FE	Airbus A300F4-605R	728	ex F-WWAJ	Diane Kathleen
☐ N652FE	Airbus A300F4-605R	735	ex F-WWAN	Rachel Patricia
☐ N653FE	Airbus A300F4-605R	736	ex F-WWAD	Samantha Massey
☐ N654FE	Airbus A300F4-605R	738	ex F-WWAX	Richard
☐ N655FE	Airbus A300F4-605R	742	ex F-WWAJ	Dion
☐ N656FE	Airbus A300F4-605R	745	ex F-WWAP	Devin
☐ N657FE	Airbus A300F4-605R	748	ex F-WWAM	Lizzie
☐ N658FE	Airbus A300F4-605R	752	ex F-WWAE	Tristian
☐ N659FE	Airbus A300F4-605R	757	ex F-WWAF	Calvin
☐ N660FE	Airbus A300F4-605R	759	ex F-WWAG	Zack

☐ N661FE	Airbus A300F4-605R	760	ex F-WWAL	Whitney	
☐ N662FE	Airbus A300F4-605R	761	ex F-WWAK	Tessa	
☐ N663FE	Airbus A300F4-605R	766	ex F-WWAO	Domenick	
☐ N664FE	Airbus A300F4-605R	768	ex F-WWAA	Amanda	
☐ N665FE	Airbus A300F4-605R	769	ex F-WWAM	Ethan	
☐ N667FE	Airbus A300F4-605R	771	ex F-WWAF	Sean	
☐ N668FE	Airbus A300F4-605R	772	ex F-WWAP	Tianna	
☐ N669FE	Airbus A300F4-605R	774	ex F-WWAE	Kaitlyn	
☐ N670FE	Airbus A300F4-605R	777	ex F-WWAQ	Amrit	
☐ N671FE	Airbus A300F4-605R	778	ex F-WWAV	Drew	
☐ N672FE	Airbus A300F4-605R	779	ex F-WWAZ	Young Joe	
☐ N673FE	Airbus A300F4-605R	780	ex F-WWAU	Mark	
☐ N674FE	Airbus A300F4-605R	781	ex F-WWAN	Thea	
☐ N675FE	Airbus A300F4-605R	789	ex F-WWAZ	Byron	
☐ N676FE	Airbus A300F4-605R	790	ex F-WWAV	Jade	
☐ N677FE	Airbus A300F4-605R	791	ex F-WWAD	Clifford	
☐ N678FE	Airbus A300F4-605R	792	ex F-WWAF	Allison	
☐ N679FE	Airbus A300F4-605R	793	ex F-WWAG	Ty	
☐ N680FE	Airbus A300F4-605R	794	ex F-WWAH	Tierney	
☐ N681FE	Airbus A300F4-605R	799	ex F-WWAJ	Kaci	
☐ N682FE	Airbus A300F4-605R	800	ex F-WWAK	Gabrial	
☐ N683FE	Airbus A300F4-605R	801	ex F-WWAL	Xenophon	
☐ N684FE	Airbus A300F4-605R	802	ex F-WWAM	Daniel	
☐ N685FE	Airbus A300F4-605R	803	ex F-WWAB	Landon Ostlie	
☐ N686FE	Airbus A300F4-605R	804	ex F-WWAO	Alex	
☐ N687FE	Airbus A300F4-605R	873	ex F-WWAO		
☐ N688FE	Airbus A300F4-605R	874	ex F-WWAP		
☐ N689FE	Airbus A300F4-605R	875	ex F-WWAQ		
☐ N690FE	Airbus A300F4-605R	876	ex F-WWAR		
☐ N691FE	Airbus A300F4-605R	877	ex F-WWAS		
☐ N692FE	Airbus A300F4-605R	878	ex F-WWAT	Gabriel	
☐ N716FD	Airbus A300B4-622F	358	ex HL7287	Halle	
☐ N717FD	Airbus A300B4-622F	361	ex HL7280	Roben	
☐ N718FD	Airbus A300B4-622F	365	ex HL7281	Anna	
☐ N719FD	Airbus A300B4-622F	388	ex HL7290	Cale	
☐ N720FD	Airbus A300B4-622F	417	ex HL7291	Kristin Marie	
☐ N721FD	Airbus A300B4-622RF	477	ex D-ASAE	Kathryn	
☐ N722FD	Airbus A300B4-622RF	479	ex HL7535	Terry	
☐ N723FD	Airbus A300B4-622RF	543	ex HL7536	Cody	
☐ N724FD	Airbus A300B4-622RF	530	ex F-OIHA	Anacarina	
☐ N725FD	Airbus A300B4-622RF	572	ex SU-GAT	Zebradedra	
☐ N726FD	Airbus A300B4-622RF	575	ex SU-GAU		
☐ N727FD	Airbus A300B4-622RF	579	ex SU-GAV	Mira	
☐ N728FD	Airbus A300B4-622RF	581	ex SU-GAW	Cassie	
☐ N729FD	Airbus A300B4-622RF	657	ex TF-ELU	Kaylee	
☐ N730FD	Airbus A300B4-622RF	659	ex TF-ELB	Kailey	
☐ N731FD	Airbus A300B4-605RF	709	ex B-2320		
☐ N732FD	Airbus A300B4-605RF	713	ex B-2321		
☐ N733FD	Airbus A300B4-605RF	715	ex B-2322		
☐ N740FD	Airbus A300B4-622RF	559	ex F-WQTD		
☐ N741FD	Airbus A300B4-622RF	611	ex A7-AFC		
☐ N742FD	Airbus A300B4-622RF	613	ex A7-AFD		
☐ N743FD	Airbus A300B4-622RF	630	ex A7-AFA		
☐ N744FD	Airbus A300B4-622RF	664	ex A7-ABN		
☐ N745FD	Airbus A300B4-622RF	668	ex A7-ABO		
☐ N746FD	Airbus A300B4-622RF	688	ex A7-ABW		
☐ N748FD	Airbus A300B4-622RF	633	ex N633AN		
☐ N749FD	Airbus A300B4-622RF	536	ex TF-ELD		
☐ N750FD	Airbus A300B4-622RF	555	ex F-HEEE		
☐ N751FD	Airbus A300B4-622RF	625	ex F-HDDD		
☐ N401FE	Airbus A310-203F	191	ex D-AICA	David	stored VCV
☐ N402FE	Airbus A310-203F	201	ex D-AICB	Carlye	
☐ N403FE	Airbus A310-203F	230	ex D-AICC	Maddison	
☐ N404FE	Airbus A310-203F	233	ex D-AICD	Collin	
☐ N405FE	Airbus A310-203F	237	ex D-AICF	Mariah	
☐ N407FE	Airbus A310-203F	254	ex D-AICH	Stacey Denise	stored VCV
☐ N408FE	Airbus A310-203F	257	ex D-AICK	Kealoha	stored VCV
☐ N409FE	Airbus A310-203F	273	ex D-AICL	Jake	stored VCV
☐ N410FE	Airbus A310-203F	356	ex D-AICM	Carolyn	stored VCV
☐ N411FE	Airbus A310-203F	359	ex D-AICN	Barbra	stored VCV
☐ N412FE	Airbus A310-203F	360	ex D-AICP	Corina	stored VCV
☐ N413FE	Airbus A310-203F	397	ex D-AICR	Skip Moyer	stored VCV
☐ N414FE	Airbus A310-203F	400	ex D-AICS	Tanner	stored VCV
☐ N416FE	Airbus A310-222F	288	ex F-WGYR	Patrick	stored VCV
☐ N417FE	Airbus A310-222F	333	ex N802PA	Kyle	
☐ N418FE	Airbus A310-222F	343	ex N803PA	Rachel	
☐ N419FE	Airbus A310-222F	345	ex N804PA	Krystle	stored VCV
☐ N421FE	Airbus A310-222F	342	ex N806PA	Caitlin	
☐ N423FE	Airbus A310-203F	281	ex PH-MCA	Trey	
☐ N424FE	Airbus A310-203F	241	ex PH-AGA	Kendall	stored VCV
☐ N425FE	Airbus A310-203F	264	ex PH-AGD	Jerome	
☐ N426FE	Airbus A310-203F	245	ex PH-AGB	Shana	

Registration	Type	C/n	Previous identity	Name	Remarks
☐ N427FE	Airbus A310-203F	362	ex PH-AGH	Zackary	
☐ N428FE	Airbus A310-203F	248	ex PH-AGC	Kristina	
☐ N429FE	Airbus A310-203F	364	ex PH-AGI	Conner	
☐ N430FE	Airbus A310-203F	394	ex PH-AGK	Kelleen	
☐ N431FE	Airbus A310-203F	316	ex F-WWAD	Asumi	
☐ N432FE	Airbus A310-203F	326	ex F-GEMB	Tatsuva	stored VCV
☐ N435FE	Airbus A310-203F	369	ex F-GEME	Ceara	
☐ N436FE	Airbus A310-203F	454	ex F-GEMG	Gillian	
☐ N443FE	Airbus A310-203F	283	ex PH-AGE	Katelin	
☐ N445FE	Airbus A310-203F	297	ex PH-AGF	Nicholas	
☐ N446FE	Airbus A310-222F	224	ex HB-IPA	Makenna	
☐ N447FE	Airbus A310-222F	251	ex HB-IPB	Shaunna	
☐ N448FE	Airbus A310-222F	260	ex HB-IPD	Augustine	
☐ N449FE	Airbus A310-222F	217	ex F-GOCJ	Treydn	stored VCV
☐ N450FE	Airbus A310-222F	162	ex F-GPDJ	Selna	
☐ N451FE	Airbus A310-222F	303	ex OO-SCA	Reis	
☐ N453FE	Airbus A310-222F	267	ex D-ASAL	Rush	
☐ N454FE	Airbus A310-222F	278	ex D-ASAK	Marissa	
☐ N455FE	Airbus A310-222F	331	ex F-WWAH	Sara	
☐ N456FE	Airbus A310-222F	318	ex F-OHPQ	Simon	
☐ N801FD	Airbus A310-324F	539	ex D-ASAD	Amos	
☐ N802FD	Airbus A310-324F	542	ex D-ASAD	Saeed	
☐ N803FD	Airbus A310-324F	378	ex N853CH	Rylan	
☐ N804FD	Airbus A310-324F	549	ex N101MP	Paige	
☐ N805FD	Airbus A310-324F	456	ex F-OGYR	Fernando	
☐ N806FD	Airbus A310-324F	458	ex F-OGYN	Addisyn	
☐ N807FD	Airbus A310-324F	492	ex F-WQTA	Joshua	
☐ N808FD	Airbus A310-324F	439	ex F-OHPU	Berkeley	
☐ N809FD	Airbus A310-324F	449	ex F-OHPV	Gavin	
☐ N810FD	Airbus A310-324F	452	ex F-OHPY	Sebastian	
☐ N811FD	Airbus A310-324F	457	ex F-OGYM		
☐ N812FD	Airbus A310-324F	467	ex F-OGYS	Agyei	
☐ N813FD	Airbus A310-324F	500	ex N501RR		
☐ N814FD	Airbus A310-324F	534	ex N534RR		
☐ N815FD	Airbus A310-324F	638	ex F-OJAF	Tommy	
☐ N816FD	Airbus A310-304F	593	ex F-OGQR		
☐ N817FD	Airbus A310-304F	552	ex TF-ELS		
☐ N68096	Airbus A310-324	589	ex N285BA		stored VCV
☐ C-GATK	ATR 42-310F	135	ex N923FX		Lsd to MAL
☐ EC-KAI	ATR 42-300F	141	ex EI-FXF		Lsd to SWT
☐ N900FX	ATR 42-320F	170	ex N14825		Op by CFS
☐ N901FX	ATR 42-320F	172	ex N26826		Op by CFS
☐ N903FX	ATR 42-320F	179	ex N14828		Op by CFS
☐ N906FX	ATR 42-320F	280	ex N97841		Op by MTN
☐ N907FX	ATR 42-320F	286	ex N86842		Op by MTN
☐ N908FX	ATR 42-300F	023	ex N972NA		Op by CFS
☐ N909FX	ATR 42-300F	275	ex N275BC		Op by MTN
☐ N910FX	ATR 42-300F	277	ex N277AT		Op by MTN
☐ N911FX	ATR 42-300F	045	ex N424MQ		Op by CFS
☐ N912FX	ATR 42-300F	047	ex N47AE		Op by CFS
☐ N913FX	ATR 42-320F	250	ex N251AE		Op by CFS
☐ N914FX	ATR 42-300F	293	ex N293AT		Op by CFS
☐ N915FX	ATR 42-320F	269	ex N269AT		Op by MTN
☐ N916FX	ATR 42-300F	314	ex N314AM		Op by MTN
☐ N917FX	ATR 42-320F	354	ex N351AT		Op by CFS
☐ N918FX	ATR 42-300F	262	ex N262AT		Op by MTN
☐ N919FX	ATR 42-320F	266	ex N265AE		Op by CFS
☐ N920FX	ATR 42-320F	325	ex N325AT		Op by MTN
☐ N921FX	ATR 42-300F	319	ex N319AM		Op by CFS
☐ EI-FXG	ATR 72-202F	224	ex (N814FX)		Lsd to ABR
☐ EI-FXH	ATR 72-202F	229	ex N815FX		Lsd to ABR
☐ EI-FXI	ATR 72-202F	294	ex N818FX		Lsd to ABR
☐ EI-FXJ	ATR 72-202F	292	ex N813FX		Lsd to ABR
☐ EI-FXK	ATR 72-202F	256	ex N817FX		Lsd to ABR
☐ N809FX	ATR 72-202F	217	ex N721TE		Op by MTN
☐ N810FX	ATR 72-202F	220	ex N722TE		Op by MTN stored COE
☐ N811FX	ATR 72-202F	283	ex N723TE		Op by MTN
☐ N812FX	ATR 72-212F	404	ex D-AEWI		Op by CFS
☐ N816FX	ATR 72-212F	347	ex D-AEWG		Op by CFS
☐ N819FX	ATR 72-212F	359	ex D-AEWH		Op by CFS
☐ N820FX	ATR 72-212F	248	ex N248AT		
☐ N821FX	ATR 72-212F	253	ex N252AM		
☐ C-FMEA	Boeing 727-247F (FedEx 3)	21329/1254	ex N235FE		Lsd to MAL
☐ C-FMEE	Boeing 727-247F (FedEx 3)	21330/1260	ex N236FE		Lsd to MAL
☐ C-FMEI	Boeing 727-247F (FedEx 3)	21327/1249	ex N233FE		Lsd to MAL
☐ N203FE	Boeing 727-2S2F (FedEx 3)	22925/1819		Jonathan	
☐ N204FE	Boeing 727-2S2F (FedEx 3)	22926/1820		Rebecca	
☐ N207FE	Boeing 727-2S2F (Super 27)	22929/1823		Vivian	
☐ N211FE	Boeing 727-2S2F (FedEx 3)	22933/1827		Bobby	
☐ N213FE	Boeing 727-2S2F (FedEx 3)	22935/1829		Cagen	

☐ N215FE	Boeing 727-2S2F (Super 27)	22936/1830		Billy	
☐ N216FE	Boeing 727-2S2F (Super 27)	22937/1831		Wade	
☐ N217FE	Boeing 727-2S2F (Super 27)	22938/1832		Sonja	
☐ N218FE	Boeing 727-233F (FedEx 3)	21101/1150	ex C-GAAM	Christin	
☐ N220FE	Boeing 727-233F (FedEx 3)	20934/1074	ex C-GAAC	Emily	
☐ N221FE	Boeing 727-233F (FedEx 3)	20932/1069	ex C-GAAA	Megan Nicole	
☐ N222FE	Boeing 727-233F (FedEx 3)	20933/1071	ex C-GAAB	Michael	stored VCV
☐ N223FE	Boeing 727-233F (FedEx 3)	20935/1076	ex C-GAAD	Dustin	
☐ N237FE	Boeing 727-247F (FedEx 3)	21331/1266	ex N2826W	Tristan	
☐ N240FE	Boeing 727-277F (FedEx 3)	20978/1083	ex VH-RMY	Baron	
☐ N241FE	Boeing 727-277F (FedEx 3)	20979/1098	ex VH-RMZ	Jill	
☐ N243FE	Boeing 727-277F (FedEx 3)	21480/1352	ex VH-RML	Braden	stored VCV
☐ N244FE	Boeing 727-277F (FedEx 3)	21647/1436	ex VH-RMM	Crystal	
☐ N245FE	Boeing 727-277F (FedEx 3)	22016/1566	ex VH-RMO	Kelsey	
☐ N254FE	Boeing 727-233F (FedEx 3)	20936/1078	ex C-GAAE	Courtney	
☐ N257FE	Boeing 727-233F (FedEx 3)	20939/1112	ex C-GAAH	Felicia	
☐ N258FE	Boeing 727-233F (FedEx 3)	20940/1120	ex C-GAAI	Lacey	
☐ N262FE	Boeing 727-233F (FedEx 3)	21624/1468	ex C-GAAO	Betsy	
☐ N263FE	Boeing 727-233F (FedEx 3)	21625/1470	ex C-GAAP	Marc	
☐ N264FE	Boeing 727-233F (FedEx 3)	21626/1472	ex C-GAAQ	Brennan	
☐ N265FE	Boeing 727-233F (FedEx 3)	21671/1523	ex C-GBZB	Paul	
☐ N266FE	Boeing 727-233F (FedEx 3)	21672/1538	ex C-GAAS	Steven	
☐ N267FE	Boeing 727-233F (FedEx 3)	21673/1541	ex C-GMSX	Jolene	
☐ N268FE	Boeing 727-233F (FedEx 3)	21674/1543	ex C-GAAU	Ginger	
☐ N269FE	Boeing 727-233F (FedEx 3)	21675/1555	ex C-GAAV	Alexander	
☐ N271FE	Boeing 727-233F (FedEx 3)	22036/1596	ex C-GAAX	Andrew	
☐ N273FE	Boeing 727-233F (FedEx 3)	22038/1612	ex C-GAAZ	Samantha	
☐ N274FE	Boeing 727-233F (FedEx 3)	22039/1614	ex C-GYNA	Jessica	
☐ N275FE	Boeing 727-233F (FedEx 3)	22040/1626	ex C-GYNB	Skylar	
☐ N276FE	Boeing 727-233F (FedEx 3)	22041/1628	ex C-GYNC	Devan	
☐ N277FE	Boeing 727-233F (FedEx 3)	22042/1630	ex C-GYND	Hutch	
☐ N278FE	Boeing 727-233F (FedEx 3)	22345/1699	ex C-GYNE	Jeffrey	
☐ N279FE	Boeing 727-233F (FedEx 3)	22346/1704	ex C-GYNF	Ryan	
☐ N280FE	Boeing 727-223F (FedEx 3)	22347/1708	ex C-GYNG	Chad	
☐ N281FE	Boeing 727-233F (FedEx 3)	22348/1714	ex C-GYNH	Ivie	
☐ N282FE	Boeing 727-233F (FedEx 3)	22349/1722	ex C-GYNI	Dominique	
☐ N283FE	Boeing 727-233F (FedEx 3)	22350/1745	ex C-GYNJ	Randall	
☐ N284FE	Boeing 727-233F (FedEx 3)	22621/1791	ex C-GYNK	Victoria	
☐ N285FE	Boeing 727-233F (FedEx 3)	22622/1792	ex C-GYNL	Jordann	
☐ N286FE	Boeing 727-233F (FedEx 3)	22623/1803	ex C-GYNM	Charlsi	
☐ N287FE	Boeing 727-2D4F (FedEx 3)	21849/1527	ex N361PA	Alexa	
☐ N288FE	Boeing 727-2D4F (FedEx 3)	21850/1536	ex N362PA	Michelle	
☐ N462FE	Boeing 727-225F (FedEx 3)	22550/1739	ex N813EA	Daven	
☐ N463FE	Boeing 727-225F (FedEx 3)	22551/1744	ex N814EA	Tonga	
☐ N464FE	Boeing 727-225F (FedEx 3)	21288/1234	ex N8870Z	Blake	
☐ N465FE	Boeing 727-225F (FedEx 3)	21289/1235	ex N8871Z	Nathan	
☐ N466FE	Boeing 727-225F (FedEx 3)	21292/1240	ex N8874Z	Gideon	
☐ N467FE	Boeing 727-225F (FedEx 3)	21449/1306	ex N8876Z	Joy	
☐ N468FE	Boeing 727-225F (FedEx 3)	21452/1312	ex N8879Z	Chad	
☐ N469FE	Boeing 727-225F (FedEx 3)	21581/1437	ex N8884Z	Ray	
☐ N479FE	Boeing 727-227F (FedEx 3)	21461/1337	ex N455BN	Norah	
☐ N480FE	Boeing 727-227F (FedEx 3)	21462/1342	ex N456BN	Warren	stored VCV
☐ N481FE	Boeing 727-227F (FedEx 3)	21463/1353	ex N457BN	Tiffany	
☐ N482FE	Boeing 727-227F (FedEx 3)	21464/1355	ex N458BN	Natalie	
☐ N483FE	Boeing 727-227F (FedEx 3)	21465/1363	ex N459BN	David	
☐ N484FE	Boeing 727-227F (FedEx 3)	21466/1372	ex N460BN	Hallie	
☐ N485FE	Boeing 727-227F (FedEx 3)	21488/1388	ex N461BN	Kristen	
☐ N486FE	Boeing 727-227F (FedEx 3)	21489/1390	ex N462BN	Hunter	
☐ N487FE	Boeing 727-227F (FedEx 3)	21490/1396	ex N463BN	Britney	
☐ N488FE	Boeing 727-227F (FedEx 3)	21491/1402	ex N464BN	Olivia	
☐ N489FE	Boeing 727-227F (FedEx 3)	21492/1440	ex N465BN	Timothy	
☐ N490FE	Boeing 727-227F (FedEx 3)	21493/1442	ex N466BN	Chase	
☐ N491FE	Boeing 727-227F (FedEx 3)	21529/1444	ex N467BN	Noel	
☐ N492FE	Boeing 727-227F (FedEx 3)	21530/1446	ex N468BN	Two Bears	
☐ N493FE	Boeing 727-227F (FedEx 3)	21531/1450	ex N469BN	Maxx	
☐ N494FE	Boeing 727-227F (FedEx 3)	21532/1453	ex N470BN	Ebony	
☐ N495FE	Boeing 727-227F (FedEx 3)	21669/1484	ex N471BN	Leslie	
☐ N498FE	Boeing 727-232F (FedEx 3)	20867/1068	ex CS-TCI	Aidan	
☐ N499FE	Boeing 727-232F (FedEx 3)	21018/1095	ex CS-TCJ	Sierra	

☐ N226CL	Boeing 757-225	22612/114	ex G-VKND	stored VCV
☐ N240MQ	Boeing 757-2Y0	25240/388	ex XA-MTY	stored VCV
☐ N513NA	Boeing 757-2T7	23895/132	ex G-BYAM	stored VCV
☐ N901FD	Boeing 757-2B7F	27122/526	ex N610AU	
☐ N902FD	Boeing 757-2B7SF	27123/534	ex N927UW	
☐ N903FD	Boeing 757-2B7SF	27124/540	ex N928UW	
☐ N904FD	Boeing 757-2B7	27144/544	ex N929UW	
☐ N905FD	Boeing 757-2B7	27145/546	ex N930UW	stored VCV
☐ N906FD	Boeing 757-2B7SF	27148/564	ex N931UW	
☐ N907FD	Boeing 757-2B7	27198/584	ex N932UW	stored VCV
☐ N908FD	Boeing 757-2B7	27199/586	ex N933UW	stored
☐ N909FD	Boeing 757-2B7	27200/589	ex N934UW	stored VCV
☐ N910FD	Boeing 757-236SF	25054/362	ex G-OOOK	under conv

Reg	Type	C/n	Previous	Name	Notes
☐ N912FD	Boeing 757-28ASF	24260/204	ex N517NA		
☐ N913FD	Boeing 757-28ASF	24017/162	ex C-FTDV		under conv
☐ N914FD	Boeing 757-28A	24367/208	ex C-FCLG		under conv
☐ N915FD	Boeing 757-236SF	24120/174	ex 4X-EBO		under conv
☐ N916FD	Boeing 757-27BSF	24137/178	ex 4X-EBY		
☐ N917FD	Boeing 757-23A	24291/215	ex CX-PUD		under conv
☐ N918FD	Boeing 757-23AER	24290/212	ex N290AN		under conv
☐ N919FD	Boeing 757-23ASF	24636/259	ex G-FJEA		
☐ N920FD	Boeing 757-23AER	24289/209	ex G-OAVB		under conv
☐ N921FD	Boeing 757-204	24924/333	ex N924AW		stored VCV
☐ N922FD	Boeing 757-23A	24293/220	ex N293AW		stored VCV
☐ N923FD	Boeing 757-204F	26266/514	ex G-BYAF		
☐ N924FD	Boeing 757-204	26267/538	ex G-BYAK		stored VCV
☐ N925FD	Boeing 757-204	27238/604	ex G-BYAS		stored VCV
☐ N933FD	Boeing 757-21BSF	24330/200	ex B-2804		
☐ N934FD	Boeing 757-21B	24331/203	ex B-2805		stored HKG
☐ N935FD	Boeing 757-2T7ER	22780/15	ex G-MONB		under conv
☐ N936FD	Boeing 757-2T7ER	23293/56	ex G-MONE		stored VCV
☐ N941FD	Boeing 757-225	22691/155	ex TF-LLY		stored VCV
☐ N993FD	Boeing 757-2Q8	24965/438	ex SU-BPY		stored VCV
☐ N994FD	Boeing 757-23A	25490/510	ex N490AN		stored VCV
☐ N850FD	Boeing 777-FS2	37721/813		Saad	
☐ N851FD	Boeing 777-FS2	37722			
☐ N852FD	Boeing 777-FS2	37723			
☐ N853FD	Boeing 777-FS2	37724/829		Talon	
☐ N854FD	Boeing 777-FS2	37725			
☐ N855FD	Boeing 777-FS2	37726			
☐ N856FD	Boeing 777-FS2	37727			
☐ N857FD	Boeing 777-FS2	37728			
☐ C-FEXB	Cessna 208B Caravan I	208B0539	ex N758FX		Lsd to MAL
☐ C-FEXF	Cessna 208B Caravan I	208B0508	ex N749FX		Lsd to MAL
☐ C-FEXV	Cessna 208B Caravan I	208B0482	ex N738FX		Lsd to MAL
☐ C-FEXY	Cessna 208B Caravan I	208B0226	ex N896FE		Lsd to MAL
☐ N700FX	Cessna 208B Caravan I	208B0419			Op by CFS
☐ N701FX	Cessna 208B Caravan I	208B0420			Op by WIG
☐ N702FX	Cessna 208B Caravan I	208B0422			Op by BVN
☐ N703FX	Cessna 208B Caravan I	208B0423			Op by IRO
☐ N705FX	Cessna 208B Caravan I	208B0425			Op by CFS
☐ N706FX	Cessna 208B Caravan I	208B0426			Op by IRO
☐ N707FX	Cessna 208B Caravan I	208B0427			Op by PCM
☐ N708FX	Cessna 208B Caravan I	208B0429			Op by MTN
☐ N709FX	Cessna 208B Caravan I	208B0430			Op by CFS
☐ N710FX	Cessna 208B Caravan I	208B0431			Op by CPT
☐ N711FX	Cessna 208B Caravan I	208B0433			Op by CFS
☐ N712FX	Cessna 208B Caravan I	208B0435			Op by IRO
☐ N713FX	Cessna 208B Caravan I	208B0438			Op by PCM
☐ N715FX	Cessna 208B Caravan I	208B0440			Op by MTN
☐ N716FX	Cessna 208B Caravan I	208B0442			Op by CPT
☐ N717FX	Cessna 208B Caravan I	208B0445			Op by IRO
☐ N718FX	Cessna 208B Caravan I	208B0448			Op by BVN
☐ N719FX	Cessna 208B Caravan I	208B0450			Op by BVN
☐ N720FX	Cessna 208B Caravan I	208B0452			Op by CFS
☐ N721FX	Cessna 208B Caravan I	208B0453			Op by MTN
☐ N722FX	Cessna 208B Caravan I	208B0454			Op by PCM
☐ N723FX	Cessna 208B Caravan I	208B0456			Op by BVN
☐ N724FX	Cessna 208B Caravan I	208B0458			Op by CPT
☐ N725FX	Cessna 208B Caravan I	208B0460			Op by WIG
☐ N726FX	Cessna 208B Caravan I	208B0465			Op by PCM
☐ N727FX	Cessna 208B Caravan I	208B0468			Op by IRO
☐ N728FX	Cessna 208B Caravan I	208B0471			Op by CFS
☐ N729FX	Cessna 208B Caravan I	208B0474			Op by MTN
☐ N730FX	Cessna 208B Caravan I	208B0477			Op by CPT
☐ N731FX	Cessna 208B Caravan I	208B0480			Op by WIG
☐ N740FX	Cessna 208B Caravan I	208B0484			Op by MTN
☐ N741FX	Cessna 208B Caravan I	208B0486			Op by BVN
☐ N742FX	Cessna 208B Caravan I	208B0489			Op by MTN
☐ N744FX	Cessna 208B Caravan I	208B0492			Op by PCM
☐ N745FX	Cessna 208B Caravan I	208B0495			Op by BVN
☐ N746FX	Cessna 208B Caravan I	208B0498			Op by CFS
☐ N747FE	Cessna 208B Caravan I	208B0238			Op by MTN
☐ N747FX	Cessna 208B Caravan I	208B0501			Op by MTN
☐ N748FE	Cessna 208B Caravan I	208B0241			Op by WIG
☐ N748FX	Cessna 208B Caravan I	208B0503			Op by PCM
☐ N749FE	Cessna 208B Caravan I	208B0242			Op by BVN
☐ N750FX	Cessna 208B Caravan I	208B0511			Op by PCM
☐ N751FE	Cessna 208B Caravan I	208B0245			Op by CPT
☐ N751FX	Cessna 208B Caravan I	208B0514			Op by BVN
☐ N752FE	Cessna 208B Caravan I	208B0247			Op by IRO
☐ N752FX	Cessna 208B Caravan I	208B0517			Op by CFS
☐ N753FX	Cessna 208B Caravan I	208B0520			Op by BVN
☐ N754FX	Cessna 208B Caravan I	208B0526			Op by PCM

	Registration	Type	c/n	Previous identity	Operator
☐	N755FE	Cessna 208B Caravan I	208B0250		Op by MTN
☐	N755FX	Cessna 208B Caravan I	208B0529		Op by WIG
☐	N756FE	Cessna 208B Caravan I	208B0251		Op by BVN
☐	N756FX	Cessna 208B Caravan I	208B0532		Op by CFS
☐	N757FX	Cessna 208B Caravan I	208B0535		Op by WIG
☐	N760FE*	Cessna 208B Caravan I	208B0252		Op by CPT
☐	N761FE	Cessna 208B Caravan I	208B0254		Op by IRO
☐	N762FE	Cessna 208B Caravan I	208B0255		Op by PCM
☐	N763FE	Cessna 208B Caravan I	208B0256		Op by PCM
☐	N764FE	Cessna 208B Caravan I	208B0258		Op by MTN
☐	N765FE	Cessna 208B Caravan I	208B0259		Op by BVN
☐	N766FE*	Cessna 208B Caravan I	208B0260		Op by CPT
☐	N767FE	Cessna 208B Caravan I	208B0262		Op by IRO
☐	N768FE	Cessna 208B Caravan I	208B0263		Op by PCM
☐	N769FE	Cessna 208B Caravan I	208B0264		Op by MTN
☐	N770FE	Cessna 208B Caravan I	208B0265		Op by BVN
☐	N771FE	Cessna 208B Caravan I	208B0267		Op by PCM
☐	N772FE	Cessna 208B Caravan I	208B0268		Op by PCM
☐	N773FE	Cessna 208B Caravan I	208B0269		Op by BVN
☐	N774FE	Cessna 208B Caravan I	208B0271		Op by BVN
☐	N775FE	Cessna 208B Caravan I	208B0272		Op by CFS
☐	N776FE	Cessna 208B Caravan I	208B0273		Op by MTN
☐	N778FE	Cessna 208B Caravan I	208B0275		Op by CFS
☐	N779FE	Cessna 208B Caravan I	208B0276		Op by CFS
☐	N780FE	Cessna 208B Caravan I	208B0277		Op by WIG
☐	N781FE	Cessna 208B Caravan I	208B0278		Op by PCM
☐	N782FE	Cessna 208B Caravan I	208B0280		Op by PCM
☐	N783FE	Cessna 208B Caravan I	208B0281		Op by WIG
☐	N784FE	Cessna 208B Caravan I	208B0282		Op by IRO
☐	N785FE	Cessna 208B Caravan I	208B0283		Op by PCM
☐	N786FE	Cessna 208B Caravan I	208B0284		Op by BVN
☐	N787FE	Cessna 208B Caravan I	208B0285		Op by MTN
☐	N788FE	Cessna 208B Caravan I	208B0286		Op by CFS
☐	N789FE	Cessna 208B Caravan I	208B0287		Op by WIG
☐	N790FE	Cessna 208B Caravan I	208B0288		Op by PCM
☐	N792FE	Cessna 208B Caravan I	208B0290		Op by MTN
☐	N793FE	Cessna 208B Caravan I	208B0291		Op by BVN
☐	N794FE	Cessna 208B Caravan I	208B0292		Op by CPT
☐	N795FE	Cessna 208B Caravan I	208B0293		Op by IRO
☐	N796FE	Cessna 208B Caravan I	208B0212	ex C-FEXY	Op by CPT
☐	N797FE	Cessna 208B Caravan I	208B0042	ex C-FEXH	Op by CPT
☐	N798FE	Cessna 208B Caravan I	208B0174	ex C-FEDY	Op by CPT
☐	N799FE	Cessna 208A Caravan I	20800065	ex C-FEXF	Op by CPT
☐	N800FE	Cessna 208A Caravan I	20800007	ex (N9300F)	Op by CPT
☐	N801FE	Cessna 208A Caravan I	20800009	ex (N9305F)	Op by MTN
☐	N804FE	Cessna 208B Caravan I	208B0039	ex F-GETN	Op by WIG
☐	N807FE	Cessna 208B Caravan I	208B0041	ex F-GETO	Op by WIG
☐	N812FE	Cessna 208A Caravan I	20800040	ex (N9401F)	Op by CPT
☐	N819FE	Cessna 208A Caravan I	20800056	ex (N9451F)	Op by MTN
☐	N820FE	Cessna 208B Caravan I	208B0111	ex F-GHHC	Op by MTN
☐	N827FE	Cessna 208A Caravan I	20800072	ex (N9491F)	Op by CPT
☐	N828FE	Cessna 208B Caravan I	208B0122	ex F-GHHD	Op by IRO
☐	N830FE	Cessna 208A Caravan I	20800075	ex (N9502F)	Op by IRO
☐	N831FE	Cessna 208B Caravan I	208B0225	ex F-GHHE	Op by MTN
☐	N832FE	Cessna 208 Caravan I	20800081	ex (N9518F)	Op by BVN
☐	N833FE	Cessna 208A Caravan I	20800084	ex EI-FDX	Op by CFS
☐	N835FE	Cessna 208A Caravan I	20800016	ex EI-FEX	Op by WIG
☐	N841FE	Cessna 208B Caravan I	208B0144		Op by BVN
☐	N842FE	Cessna 208B Caravan I	208B0146		Op by MTN
☐	N843FE	Cessna 208B Caravan I	208B0147		Op by IRO
☐	N844FE	Cessna 208B Caravan I	208B0149		Op by PCM
☐	N845FE	Cessna 208B Caravan I	208B0152		Op by BVN
☐	N846FE	Cessna 208B Caravan I	208B0154		Op by CPT
☐	N847FE	Cessna 208B Caravan I	208B0156		Op by MTN
☐	N848FE	Cessna 208B Caravan I	208B0158		Op by MTN
☐	N849FE	Cessna 208B Caravan I	208B0162		Op by MTN
☐	N850FE	Cessna 208B Caravan I	208B0164		Op by CFS
☐	N851FE	Cessna 208B Caravan I	208B0166		Op by CPT
☐	N852FE	Cessna 208B Caravan I	208B0168		Op by MTN
☐	N853FE	Cessna 208B Caravan I	208B0170		Op by MTN
☐	N855FE	Cessna 208B Caravan I	208B0203		Op by MTN
☐	N856FE	Cessna 208B Caravan I	208B0176		Op by CFS
☐	N857FE	Cessna 208B Caravan I	208B0177		Op by PCM
☐	N858FE	Cessna 208B Caravan I	208B0178		Op by IRO
☐	N859FE	Cessna 208B Caravan I	208B0181		Op by CFS
☐	N860FE*	Cessna 208B Caravan I	208B0182		Op by CPT
☐	N861FE	Cessna 208B Caravan I	208B0183		Op by BVN
☐	N862FE	Cessna 208B Caravan I	208B0184		Op by MTN
☐	N863FE	Cessna 208B Caravan I	208B0186		Op by CPT
☐	N864FE	Cessna 208B Caravan I	208B0187		Op by CPT
☐	N865FE	Cessna 208B Caravan I	208B0188		Op by WIG
☐	N866FE	Cessna 208B Caravan I	208B0189	ex HK-3924X	Op by BVN
☐	N867FE	Cessna 208B Caravan I	208B0191		Op by CPT

☐ N869FE	Cessna 208B Caravan I	208B0195		Op by MTN
☐ N870FE	Cessna 208B Caravan I	208B0196		Op by WIG
☐ N871FE	Cessna 208B Caravan I	208B0198		Op by IRO
☐ N872FE	Cessna 208B Caravan I	208B0200		Op by PCM
☐ N873FE	Cessna 208B Caravan I	208B0202		Op by CFS
☐ N874FE	Cessna 208B Caravan I	208B0205		Op by MTN
☐ N875FE	Cessna 208B Caravan I	208B0206		Op by CFS
☐ N876FE	Cessna 208B Caravan I	208B0207		Op by CFS
☐ N877FE	Cessna 208B Caravan I	208B0232		Op by CPT
☐ N878FE	Cessna 208B Caravan I	208B0211		Op by MTN
☐ N879FE	Cessna 208B Caravan I	208B0213		Op by PCM
☐ N880FE	Cessna 208B Caravan I	208B0215		Op by CFS
☐ N881FE	Cessna 208B Caravan I	208B0204		Op by MTN
☐ N882FE	Cessna 208B Caravan I	208B0208		Op by CFS
☐ N883FE	Cessna 208B Caravan I	208B0210		Op by IRO
☐ N884FE	Cessna 208B Caravan I	208B0233		Op by IRO
☐ N885FE	Cessna 208B Caravan I	208B0185		Op by CPT
☐ N886FE	Cessna 208B Caravan I	208B0190		Op by PCM
☐ N887FE	Cessna 208B Caravan I	208B0216		Op by MTN
☐ N888FE	Cessna 208B Caravan I	208B0217		Op by WIG
☐ N889FE	Cessna 208B Caravan I	208B0218		Op by BVN
☐ N890FE	Cessna 208B Caravan I	208B0219		Op by CPT
☐ N891FE	Cessna 208B Caravan I	208B0221		Op by PCM
☐ N892FE	Cessna 208B Caravan I	208B0222		Op by PCM
☐ N894FE	Cessna 208B Caravan I	208B0224		Op by BVN
☐ N895FE	Cessna 208B Caravan I	208B0015	ex C-FEXG	Op by CFS
☐ N897FE	Cessna 208B Caravan I	208B0227		Op by CFS
☐ N898FE	Cessna 208B Caravan I	208B0228		Op by WIG
☐ N899FE	Cessna 208B Caravan I	208B0235		Op by CFS
☐ N900FE	Cessna 208B Caravan I	208B0054	ex SE-KLX	Op by BVN
☐ N901FE	Cessna 208B Caravan I	208B0001	ex N9767F	Op by WIG
☐ N902FE	Cessna 208B Caravan I	208B0002		Op by BVN
☐ N903FE	Cessna 208B Caravan I	208B0003		Op by CPT
☐ N904FE	Cessna 208B Caravan I	208B0004		Op by CPT
☐ N905FE	Cessna 208B Caravan I	208B0005		Op by MTN
☐ N906FE	Cessna 208B Caravan I	208B0006		Op by IRO
☐ N907FE	Cessna 208B Caravan I	208B0007		Op by IRO
☐ N908FE	Cessna 208B Caravan I	208B0008		Op by PCM
☐ N909FE	Cessna 208B Caravan I	208B0009		Op by WIG
☐ N910FE	Cessna 208B Caravan I	208B0010		Op by CPT
☐ N911FE	Cessna 208B Caravan I	208B0011		Op by WIG
☐ N912FE	Cessna 208B Caravan I	208B0012		Op by BVN
☐ N914FE	Cessna 208B Caravan I	208B0014		Op by IRO
☐ N916FE	Cessna 208B Caravan I	208B0016		Op by CPT
☐ N917FE	Cessna 208B Caravan I	208B0017		Op by MTN
☐ N918FE	Cessna 208B Caravan I	208B0018		Op by CFS
☐ N919FE	Cessna 208B Caravan I	208B0019		Op by WIG
☐ N920FE	Cessna 208B Caravan I	208B0020		Op by PCM
☐ N921FE	Cessna 208B Caravan I	208B0021		Op by MTN
☐ N922FE	Cessna 208B Caravan I	208B0022		Op by BVN
☐ N923FE	Cessna 208B Caravan I	208B0023		Op by IRO
☐ N924FE	Cessna 208B Caravan I	208B0024		Op by CPT
☐ N925FE	Cessna 208B Caravan I	208B0025		Op by IRO
☐ N926FE	Cessna 208B Caravan I	208B0026		Op by CPT
☐ N927FE	Cessna 208B Caravan I	208B0027		Op by IRO
☐ N928FE	Cessna 208B Caravan I	208B0028		Op by BVN
☐ N929FE	Cessna 208B Caravan I	208B0029		Op by BVN
☐ N930FE	Cessna 208B Caravan I	208B0030		Op by PCM
☐ N931FE	Cessna 208B Caravan I	208B0031		Op by WIG
☐ N933FE	Cessna 208B Caravan I	208B0033		Op by CPT
☐ N934FE	Cessna 208B Caravan I	208B0034		Op by BVN
☐ N935FE	Cessna 208B Caravan I	208B0035		Op by WIG
☐ N936FE	Cessna 208B Caravan I	208B0036		Op by CPT
☐ N937FE	Cessna 208B Caravan I	208B0037		Op by WIG
☐ N938FE	Cessna 208B Caravan I	208B0038		Op by MTN
☐ N939FE	Cessna 208B Caravan I	208B0180		Op by BVN
☐ N940FE	Cessna 208B Caravan I	208B0040		Op by CFS
☐ N943FE	Cessna 208B Caravan I	208B0043		Op by MTN
☐ N946FE	Cessna 208B Caravan I	208B0048	ex (N948FE)	Op by IRO
☐ N947FE	Cessna 208B Caravan I	208B0050	ex (N950FE)	Op by WIG
☐ N950FE	Cessna 208B Caravan I	208B0056	ex (N956FE)	Op by BVN
☐ N952FE	Cessna 208B Caravan I	208B0060	ex (N960FE)	Op by CPT
☐ N953FE	Cessna 208B Caravan I	208B0062	ex (N962FE)	Op by CFS
☐ N954FE	Cessna 208B Caravan I	208B0064	ex (N964FE)	Op by IRO
☐ N955FE	Cessna 208B Caravan I	208B0066	ex (N966FE)	Op by MTN
☐ N956FE	Cessna 208B Caravan I	208B0068	ex (N968FE)	Op by CFS
☐ N957FE	Cessna 208B Caravan I	208B0070	ex (N970FE)	Op by BVN
☐ N958FE	Cessna 208B Caravan I	208B0071		Op by WIG
☐ N959FE	Cessna 208B Caravan I	208B0073		Op by WIG
☐ N960FE	Cessna 208B Caravan I	208B0075		Op by CFS
☐ N961FE	Cessna 208B Caravan I	208B0077		Op by BVN
☐ N962FE	Cessna 208B Caravan I	208B0078		Op by MTN
☐ N963FE	Cessna 208B Caravan I	208B0080		Op by WIG

☐ N964FE	Cessna 208B Caravan I	208B0083		Op by CPT
☐ N965FE	Cessna 208B Caravan I	208B0084		Op by CFS
☐ N966FE	Cessna 208B Caravan I	208B0086		Op by WIG
☐ N967FE	Cessna 208B Caravan I	208B0088		Op by MTN
☐ N968FE	Cessna 208B Caravan I	208B0090		Op by PCM
☐ N969FE	Cessna 208B Caravan I	208B0092		Op by PCM
☐ N970FE	Cessna 208B Caravan I	208B0093		Op by BVN
☐ N971FE	Cessna 208B Caravan I	208B0094		Op by CPT
☐ N972FE	Cessna 208B Caravan I	208B0096		Op by CPT
☐ N973FE	Cessna 208B Caravan I	208B0098		Op by MTN
☐ N975FE	Cessna 208B Caravan I	208B0101		Op by MTN
☐ N976FE	Cessna 208B Caravan I	208B0103		Op by CFS
☐ N977FE	Cessna 208B Caravan I	208B0104		Op by CPT
☐ N979FE	Cessna 208B Caravan I	208B0106		Op by MTN
☐ N980FE	Cessna 208B Caravan I	208B0108		Op by CPT
☐ N981FE	Cessna 208B Caravan I	208B0110		Op by WIG
☐ N983FE	Cessna 208B Caravan I	208B0113		Op by CFS
☐ N984FE	Cessna 208B Caravan I	208B0115		Op by PCM
☐ N985FE	Cessna 208B Caravan I	208B0117		Op by PCM
☐ N986FE	Cessna 208B Caravan I	208B0194		Op by IRO
☐ N987FE	Cessna 208B Caravan I	208B0201		Op by PCM
☐ N989FE	Cessna 208B Caravan I	208B0124		Op by WIG
☐ N990FE	Cessna 208B Caravan I	208B0125		Op by CPT
☐ N991FE	Cessna 208B Caravan I	208B0127		Op by CPT
☐ N992FE	Cessna 208B Caravan I	208B0128		Op by CFS
☐ N993FE	Cessna 208B Caravan I	208B0130		Op by IRO
☐ N994FE	Cessna 208B Caravan I	208B0132		Op by BVN
☐ N995FE	Cessna 208B Caravan I	208B0133		Op by PCM
☐ N996FE	Cessna 208B Caravan I	208B0135		Op by WIG
☐ N997FE	Cessna 208B Caravan I	208B0197		Op by CPT
☐ N998FE	Cessna 208B Caravan I	208B0139		Op by WIG
☐ N999FE	Cessna 208B Caravan I	208B0231		Op by MTN
☐ N301FE	McDonnell-Douglas MD-10-30CF	46800/96	ex N101TV	Braun
☐ N302FE	McDonnell-Douglas MD-10-30CF	46801/103	ex N102TV	Cori
☐ N303FE	McDonnell-Douglas MD-10-30CF	46802/110	ex N103TV	Amanda
☐ N304FE	McDonnell-Douglas MD-10-30CF	46992/257	ex EC-DSF	Claire
☐ N306FE	McDonnell-Douglas MD-10-30F	48287/409		John
☐ N307FE	McDonnell-Douglas MD-10-30F	48291/412		Erin Lee
☐ N308FE	McDonnell-Douglas MD-10-30F	48297/416		Ann
☐ N311FE	McDonnell-Douglas MD-10-30CF	46871/219	ex LN-RKB	Abraham
☐ N312FE	McDonnell-Douglas MD-10-30CF	48300/433		Angela
☐ N313FE	McDonnell-Douglas MD-10-30F	48311/440		Ameyali
☐ N314FE	McDonnell-Douglas MD-10-30F	48312/442		Caitlan
☐ N315FE	McDonnell-Douglas MD-10-30F	48313/443		Kevin stored VCE
☐ N316FE	McDonnell-Douglas MD-10-30F	48314/444		Brandon
☐ N317FE	McDonnell-Douglas MD-10-30CF	46835/277	ex N106WA	Madison
☐ N318FE	McDonnell-Douglas MD-10-30CF	46837/282	ex N108WA	Mason
☐ N319FE	McDonnell-Douglas MD-10-30CF	47820/317	ex N112WA	Sheridan
☐ N320FE	McDonnell-Douglas MD-10-30F	47835/326	ex OO-SLD	Maura stored VCV
☐ N321FE	McDonnell-Douglas MD-10-30F	47836/330	ex OO-SLE	Athena
☐ N357FE	McDonnell-Douglas MD-10-10F	46939/203	ex N1849U	Channelle
☐ N358FE	McDonnell-Douglas MD-10-10F	46633/297	ex N1839U	Kurt
☐ N359FE	McDonnell-Douglas MD-10-10F	46635/307	ex N1842U	Michaela
☐ N360FE	McDonnell-Douglas MD-10-10F	46636/309	ex N1843U	Phillip
☐ N361FE	McDonnell-Douglas MD-10-10F	48260/344	ex N1844U	Lucas
☐ N362FE	McDonnell-Douglas MD-10-10F	48261/347	ex N1845U	Cole
☐ N363FE	McDonnell-Douglas MD-10-10F	48263/353	ex N1847U	Carter
☐ N365FE	McDonnell-Douglas MD-10-10F	46601/6	ex N1802U	Joey stored VCV
☐ N366FE	McDonnell-Douglas MD-10-10F	46602/8	ex N1803U	Gretchen
☐ N367FE	McDonnell-Douglas MD-10-10F	46605/15	ex N1806U	Lathan
☐ N368FE	McDonnell-Douglas MD-10-10F	46606/17	ex N1807U	Cindy
☐ N369FE	McDonnell-Douglas MD-10-10F	46607/25	ex N1808U	Jessie
☐ N370FE	McDonnell-Douglas MD-10-10F	46608/26	ex N1809U	Jay stored VCV
☐ N371FE	McDonnell-Douglas MD-10-10F	46609/27	ex N1810U	Vincent
☐ N372FE	McDonnell-Douglas MD-10-10F	46610/32	ex N1811U	Gus
☐ N373FE	McDonnell-Douglas MD-10-10F	46611/35	ex N1812U	
☐ N374FE	McDonnell-Douglas MD-10-10F	46612/39	ex N1813U	Brittnie stored VCV
☐ N375FE	McDonnell-Douglas MD-10-10F	46613/42	ex N1814U	
☐ N377FE	McDonnell-Douglas MD-10-10F	47965/59	ex N1833U	Shelby stored VCV
☐ N381FE	McDonnell-Douglas MD-10-10F	46615/76	ex N1816U	Duval stored VCV
☐ N383FE	McDonnell-Douglas MD-10-10F	46616/86	ex N1817U	Cody
☐ N384FE	McDonnell-Douglas MD-10-10F	46617/89	ex N1818U	Kelly
☐ N385FE	McDonnell-Douglas MD-10-10F	46619/119	ex N1820U	Lindsay
☐ N386FE	McDonnell-Douglas MD-10-10F	46620/138	ex N1821U	TJ first MD-10 conversion
☐ N387FE	McDonnell-Douglas MD-10-10F	46621/140	ex N1822U	Joel
☐ N388FE	McDonnell-Douglas MD-10-10F	46622/144	ex N1823U	Izzul
☐ N389FE	McDonnell-Douglas MD-10-10F	46623/154	ex N1824U	Kayla
☐ N390FE	McDonnell-Douglas MD-10-10F	46624/155	ex N1825U	Rasik
☐ N392FE	McDonnell-Douglas MD-10-10F	46626/198	ex N1827U	Axton
☐ N394FE	McDonnell-Douglas MD-10-10F	46628/207	ex N1829U	Parker
☐ N395FE	McDonnell-Douglas MD-10-10F	46629/208	ex N1830U	Audreon
☐ N396FE	McDonnell-Douglas MD-10-10F	46630/209	ex N1831U	Adrienne

☐ N397FE	McDonnell-Douglas MD-10-10F	46631/210	ex N1832U	Stefani
☐ N398FE	McDonnell-Douglas MD-10-10F	46634/298	ex N1841U	Kacie
☐ N399FE	McDonnell-Douglas MD-10-10F	48262/351	ex N1846U	Tariq
☐ N550FE	McDonnell-Douglas MD-10-10F	46521/55	ex N121AA	Adam
☐ N554FE	McDonnell-Douglas MD-10-10F	46708/62	ex N153AA	
☐ N556FE	McDonnell-Douglas MD-10-10F	46710/70	ex N160AA	Kirsten
☐ N559FE	McDonnell-Douglas MD-10-10F	46930/112	ex N167AA	Francesca
☐ N560FE	McDonnell-Douglas MD-10-10F	46938/153	ex N168AA	Deonna
☐ N562FE	McDonnell-Douglas MD-10-10F	46947/247	ex N126AA	Janai
☐ N563FE	McDonnell-Douglas MD-10-10F	46948/249	ex N127AA	Kristine
☐ N564FE	McDonnell-Douglas MD-10-10F	46984/250	ex N128AA	Ava
☐ N566FE	McDonnell-Douglas MD-10-10F	46989/271	ex N130AA	Ben
☐ N567FE	McDonnell-Douglas MD-10-10F	46994/273	ex N131AA	
☐ N569FE	McDonnell-Douglas MD-10-10F	47828/319	ex N133AA	Stas
☐ N570FE	McDonnell-Douglas MD-10-10F	47829/321	ex N134AA	Joelle
☐ N571FE	McDonnell-Douglas MD-10-10F	47830/323	ex N135AA	Ella
☐ N10060	McDonnell-Douglas MD-10-10F	46970/269	ex N581LF	Haylee
☐ N40061	McDonnell-Douglas MD-10-10F	46973/272	ex N591LF	Garrett
☐ N68049	McDonnell-Douglas MD-10-10CF	47803/139		Dusty
☐ N68050	McDonnell-Douglas MD-10-10CF	47804/142		Merideth Allison
☐ N68051	McDonnell-Douglas MD-10-10CF	47805/145		Todd
☐ N68052	McDonnell-Douglas MD-10-10CF	47806/148		Brock
☐ N68053	McDonnell-Douglas MD-10-10CF	47807/173		Chayne
☐ N68054	McDonnell-Douglas MD-10-10CF	47808/177		Eren
☐ N68057	McDonnell-Douglas MD-10-10CF	48264/379	ex N1848U	Nelson
☐ N68059	McDonnell-Douglas MD-10-10F	46907/78	ex TC-JAY	Mary Rea
☐ N521FE	McDonnell-Douglas MD-11F	48478/514	ex N807DE	
☐ N522FE	McDonnell-Douglas MD-11F	48476/510	ex N805DE	
☐ N523FE	McDonnell-Douglas MD-11F	48479/536	ex N808DE	
☐ N524FE	McDonnell-Douglas MD-11F	48480/538	ex N809DE	
☐ N525FE	McDonnell-Douglas MD-11F	48565/542	ex N810DE	
☐ N526FE	McDonnell-Douglas MD-11F	48600/560	ex N813DE	
☐ N527FE	McDonnell-Douglas MD-11F	48601/562	ex N812DE	
☐ N528FE	McDonnell-Douglas MD-11F	48623/605	ex N814DE	
☐ N529FE	McDonnell-Douglas MD-11F	48624/622	ex N815DE	
☐ N572FE	McDonnell-Douglas MD-11ER	48755/613	ex N730BC	
☐ N573FE	McDonnell-Douglas MD-11BCF	48769/603	ex N746BC	
☐ N574FE	McDonnell-Douglas MD-11F	48499/486	ex N499HE	
☐ N575FE	McDonnell-Douglas MD-11F	48500/493	ex N485LS	Sonni
☐ N576FE	McDonnell-Douglas MD-11F	48501/513	ex N501FR	Keeley
☐ N577FE	McDonnell-Douglas MD-11F	48469/519	ex B-18172	Tobias
☐ N578FE	McDonnell-Douglas MD-11F	48458/449	ex N489GX	Stephen
☐ N579FE	McDonnell-Douglas MD-11F	48470/546	ex B-18151	Nash
☐ N580FE	McDonnell-Douglas MD-11F	48471/558	ex B-18152	Ashton
☐ N582FE	McDonnell-Douglas MD-11F	48420/451	ex N1751A	Jamie
☐ N583FE	McDonnell-Douglas MD-11F	48421/452	ex N1752K	Nnacy
☐ N584FE	McDonnell-Douglas MD-11F	48436/483	ex N1768D	Jeffrey Wellington
☐ N585FE	McDonnell-Douglas MD-11F	48481/482	ex N1759	Katherine
☐ N586FE	McDonnell-Douglas MD-11F	48487/469	ex N1753	Dylan
☐ N587FE	McDonnell-Douglas MD-11F	48489/492	ex N1754	Jeanno
☐ N588FE	McDonnell-Douglas MD-11F	48490/499	ex N1755	Kendra
☐ N589FE	McDonnell-Douglas MD-11F	48491/503	ex N1756	Shaun
☐ N590FE	McDonnell-Douglas MD-11F	48505/462	ex N1757A	Stan
☐ N591FE	McDonnell-Douglas MD-11F	48527/504	ex N1758B	Giovanni
☐ N592FE	McDonnell-Douglas MD-11F	48550/526	ex N1760A	Joshua
☐ N593FE	McDonnell-Douglas MD-11F	48551/527	ex N1761R	Harrison
☐ N594FE	McDonnell-Douglas MD-11F	48552/530	ex N1762B	Derek
☐ N595FE	McDonnell-Douglas MD-11F	48553/531	ex N1763	Avery
☐ N596FE	McDonnell-Douglas MD-11F	48554/535	ex N1764B	Peyton
☐ N597FE	McDonnell-Douglas MD-11F	48596/537	ex N1765B	Corbin
☐ N598FE	McDonnell-Douglas MD-11F	48597/540	ex N1766A	Kate
☐ N599FE	McDonnell-Douglas MD-11F	48598/550	ex N1767A	Mariana
☐ N601FE	McDonnell-Douglas MD-11F	48401/447	ex N111MD	Jim Riedmeyer
☐ N602FE	McDonnell-Douglas MD-11F	48402/448	ex N211MD	Malcolm Baldrige 1990
☐ N603FE	McDonnell-Douglas MD-11F	48459/470		Elizabeth
☐ N604FE	McDonnell-Douglas MD-11F	48460/497		Hollis
☐ N605FE	McDonnell-Douglas MD-11F	48514/515		April Star
☐ N606FE	McDonnell-Douglas MD-11F	48602/549		Charles & Teresa
☐ N607FE	McDonnell-Douglas MD-11F	48547/517		Christina
☐ N608FE	McDonnell-Douglas MD-11F	48548/521		Colton
☐ N609FE	McDonnell-Douglas MD-11F	48549/545		Scott
☐ N610FE	McDonnell-Douglas MD-11F	48603/551		Marisa
☐ N612FE	McDonnell-Douglas MD-11F	48605/555		Alyssa
☐ N613FE	McDonnell-Douglas MD-11F	48749/598		Krista
☐ N614FE	McDonnell-Douglas MD-11F	48528/507		Cristy
☐ N615FE	McDonnell-Douglas MD-11F	48767/602		Max
☐ N616FE	McDonnell-Douglas MD-11F	48747/594		Shanita
☐ N617FE	McDonnell-Douglas MD-11F	48748/595		Travis
☐ N618FE	McDonnell-Douglas MD-11F	48754/604		Justin
☐ N619FE	McDonnell-Douglas MD-11F	48770/607		Lyndon
☐ N620FE	McDonnell-Douglas MD-11F	48791/635		Grady
☐ N621FE	McDonnell-Douglas MD-11F	48792/636		Connor
☐ N623FE	McDonnell-Douglas MD-11F	48794/638		Meghan

☐ N624FE	McDonnell-Douglas MD-11F	48443/458	ex HB-IWA	Corinne
☐ N628FE	McDonnell-Douglas MD-11F	48447/464	ex HB-IWE	Noah
☐ N631FE	McDonnell-Douglas MD-11F	48454/477	ex HB-IWI	

FLIGHT ALASKA — *Tundra (4Y/UYA)* — *Dillingham-Memorial, AK (DLG)*

☐ N755AB	Cessna 207A Stationair 8 II	20700622	ex HP-916
☐ N1704U	Cessna 207 Skywagon	20700304	
☐ N6470H	Cessna 207A Stationair 7 II	20700534	
☐ N7336U	Cessna 207A Skywagon	20700405	

FLIGHT EXPRESS — *Flight Express (FLX)* — *Orlando-Executive, FL (ORL)*

☐ N6BW	Beech 58 Baron	TH-292	
☐ N31T	Beech 58 Baron	TH-121	ex N9146Q
☐ N46US	Beech 58 Baron	TH-294	ex N220DC
☐ N80AC	Beech 58 Baron	TH-56	ex N949SR
☐ N103GA	Beech 58 Baron	TH-213	ex N72TM
☐ N112BS	Beech 58 Baron	TH-628	ex N4075S
☐ N112KB	Beech 58 Baron	TH-1007	ex N20663
☐ N159TH	Beech 58 Baron	TH-159	ex N270K
☐ N225TA	Beech 58 Baron	TH-64	ex N225TC
☐ N258TJ	Beech 58 Baron	TH-988	ex N12WZ
☐ N329H	Beech 58 Baron	TH-219	ex N1529W
☐ N703MC	Beech 95-E55 Baron	TE-974	ex N18BL
☐ N752P	Beech 58 Baron	TH-422	ex YV-52P
☐ N796Q	Beech 58 Baron	TH-43	
☐ N950JP	Beech 58 Baron	TH-432	ex (N982DC)
☐ N955HE	Beech 58 Baron	TH-230	ex N955HF
☐ N1888W	Beech 58 Baron	TH-340	
☐ N4099S	Beech 95-E55 Baron	TE-1037	
☐ N4174S	Beech 58 Baron	TH-621	
☐ N4492F	Beech 95-E55 Baron	TE-1097	ex YV-1229P
☐ N4626A	Beech 58 Baron	TH-39	
☐ N4675S	Beech 58 Baron	TH-689	
☐ N8195R	Beech 58 Baron	TH-529	
☐ N9098Q	Beech 58 Baron	TH-109	
☐ N18447	Beech 58 Baron	TH-883	

☐ N8WE	Cessna 210L Centurion II	21060766	ex N1745X
☐ N70TC	Cessna 210M Centurion II	21061707	
☐ N102CR	Cessna T210N Turbo Centurion II	21064745	
☐ N210CT	Cessna 210L Centurion II	21060356	
☐ N221AT	Cessna 210N Centurion II	21064567	ex N9637V
☐ N274CS	Cessna 210L Centurion II	21060148	
☐ N300EW	Cessna 210L Centurion II	21061219	
☐ N318JP	Cessna 210L Centurion II	21060770	
☐ N732CQ	Cessna 210L Centurion II	21061413	
☐ N732HN	Cessna T210L Turbo Centurion II	21061527	
☐ N732LW	Cessna 210M Centurion II	21061606	
☐ N732ST	Cessna 210M Centurion II	21061744	
☐ N732YA	Cessna 210M Centurion II	21061870	
☐ N761AT	Cessna 210M Centurion II	21062100	
☐ N761AY	Cessna 210M Centurion II	21062113	
☐ N761BQ	Cessna 210M Centurion II	21062129	
☐ N761DW	Cessna T210M Turbo Centurion II	21062183	
☐ N777BK	Cessna 210L Centurion II	21060560	
☐ N778VK	Cessna 210M Centurion II	21062895	
☐ N965B	Cessna 210M Centurion II	21061580	ex N732KU
☐ N1666X	Cessna 210L Centurion II	21060701	
☐ N2013S	Cessna 210L Centurion II	21060981	
☐ N2110S	Cessna 210L Centurion II	21061074	
☐ N2137S	Cessna 210L Centurion II	21061098	
☐ N2145U	Cessna T210N Turbo Centurion II	21064776	
☐ N2255S	Cessna 210L Centurion II	21061199	
☐ N2263S	Cessna 210L Centurion II	21061207	
☐ N2280S	Cessna 210L Centurion II	21061223	
☐ N2437S	Cessna 210L Centurion II	21061281	
☐ N2495S	Cessna 210L Centurion II	21061304	
☐ N2667S	Cessna 210L Centurion II	21061347	
☐ N4637Y	Cessna 210N Centurion II	21063965	
☐ N4673C	Cessna 210N Centurion II	21063586	
☐ N4702C	Cessna T210N Turbo Centurion II	21063591	
☐ N4781C	Cessna 210N Centurion II	21063624	
☐ N5171V	Cessna 210L Centurion II	21060846	
☐ N5229A	Cessna 210N Centurion II	21063320	
☐ N5307A	Cessna 210N Centurion II	21063360	
☐ N5489V	Cessna 210L Centurion II	21060961	
☐ N6149B	Cessna T210M Turbo Centurion II	21062694	
☐ N6195N	Cessna 210N Centurion II	21062966	
☐ N6490N	Cessna 210N Centurion II	21063064	
☐ N6598Y	Cessna T210N Turbo Centurion II	21064451	

☐ N6611C	Cessna T210N Turbo Centurion II	21063930	
☐ N6622N	Cessna 210N Centurion II	21063125	
☐ N7398M	Cessna 210M Centurion II	21062018	
☐ N7660E	Cessna 210M Centurion II	21062692	
☐ N7874J	Cessna 210L Centurion II	21060597	ex YV-644CP
☐ N8427M	Cessna 210M Centurion II	21062043	
☐ N9073M	Cessna 210M Centurion II	21062058	
☐ N9489M	Cessna 210M Centurion II	21062081	
☐ N29209	Cessna 210L Centurion II	21059832	
☐ N29278	Cessna 210L Centurion II	21059852	
☐ N30326	Cessna 210L Centurion II	21059914	
☐ N59130	Cessna 210L Centurion II	21060110	
☐ N59141	Cessna 210L Centurion II	21060118	
☐ N59240	Cessna 210L Centurion II	21060174	
☐ N59299	Cessna 210L Centurion II	21060199	
☐ N93111	Cessna 210L Centurion II	21060266	
☐ N93887	Cessna 210L Centurion II	21060445	

FLIGHT INTERNATIONAL AVIATION — *Flight International (FNT)* — *Newport News-Williamsburg Intl, VA (PHF)*

☐ N10FN	Learjet 36	36-015	ex N14CF
☐ N12FN	Learjet 36	36-016	ex N616DJ
☐ N16FN	Learjet 36A	36A-027	ex N27MJ
☐ N26FN	Learjet 36	36-011	ex N26MJ
☐ N39FN	Learjet 35	35-006	ex N39DM
☐ N50FN	Learjet 35A	35A-070	ex N543PA
☐ N51FN	Learjet 35A	35A-069	ex N48GP
☐ N52FN	Learjet 35A	35A-424	ex N508GP
☐ N54FN	Learjet 25C	25C-083	ex N200MH
☐ N55FN	Learjet 35A	35A-202	ex D-CGPD
☐ N83FN	Learjet 36	36-007	ex N83DM
☐ N84FN	Learjet 36	36-002	ex N84DM
☐ N96FN	Learjet 35A	35A-186	ex (N317JD)
☐ N118FN	Learjet 35A	35A-118	ex N88JA
☐ N710GS	Learjet 35	35-032	ex N711MA

☐ N175SW	Swearingen SA.227AC Metro III	AC-621B	
☐ N766C	Swearingen SA.227AC Metro III	AC-559	ex N170SW
☐ N781C	Swearingen SA.227AC Metro III	AC-535	ex N3110J
☐ N782C	Swearingen SA.227AC Metro III	AC-525	ex N31078
☐ N26974	Swearingen SA.227AC Metro III	AC-664	

☐ N707ML	Piper PA-31T Cheyenne	31T-7520017	ex N502RH

FLIGHT LINE — *American Check (ACT)* — *Denver-Centennial, CO/Salt Lake City, UT (DEN/SLC)*

☐ N6KF	Mitsubishi MU-2B-36	659	ex N5JE
☐ N34AL	Mitsubishi MU-2B-60	792SA	ex N66LA
☐ N35RR	Mitsubishi MU-2B-60	1525SA	ex N442MA
☐ N60FL	Mitsubishi MU-2B-60	1512SA	ex HB-LQB
☐ N132BK	Mitsubishi MU-2B-60	1529SA	ex N818R
☐ N157CA	Mitsubishi MU-2B-60	1558SA	ex N5PQ
☐ N361JA	Mitsubishi MU-2B-36	681	ex C-GJWM
☐ N740PB	Mitsubishi MU-2B-36	657	ex N740PC

☐ N103BU	Piper PA-31-350 Navajo Chieftain	31-7405202	ex N999DW
☐ N350FL	Piper PA-31-350 Navajo Chieftain	31-7752182	ex N5SL

FLORIDA AIR CARGO — *Miami-Opa Locka, FL (OPF)*

☐ N15MA	Douglas DC-3	19286	ex F-WSGV	no titles	
☐ N123DZ	Douglas DC-3	12004	ex N337AF	no titles	
☐ N130D	Douglas DC-3	19800	ex NC55115	Animal Crackers	stored damaged

FLORIDA AIR TRANSPORT — *Fort Lauderdale-Executive, FL (FXE)*

☐ N70BF	Douglas C-118B	43720/373	ex XA-SCZ	dam June 2007
☐ N381AA	Douglas DC-7BF	44921/666	ex N101LM	stored OPF Jt ops with Turks Air
☐ N406WA	Douglas C-54G	35944	ex N460WA	stored OPF

FLORIDA COASTAL AIRLINES — *Florida Coastal (PA/FCL)* — *Fort Pierce-St Lucie, FL (FPR)*

☐ N77FC	Cessna 402C II	402C0044	ex N440RC
☐ N78FC	Cessna 402C II	402C0496	ex C-FFCH
☐ N79FC	Cessna 402C II	402C0421	ex N6787V
☐ N567JS	Cessna 402B II	402B1090	ex N87216
☐ N856D	Cessna 402B II	402B1339	ex N40EM

FLORIDA WEST INTERNATIONAL AIRLINES — Flo West (RF/FWL) — Miami-Intl, FL (MIA)

☐ N316LA	Boeing 767-316ERF	30842/860		Lsd fr LCO

FOCUS AIR — Focus (F2/FKS) — Fort Lauderdale-Hollywood Intl, FL (FLL)

Focus Air is a subsidiary of Omega Air Holdings

40 MILE AIR — Mile-Air (Q5/MLA) — Tok-Junction, AK (TKJ)

☐ N87TS	Piper PA-31 Turbo Navajo B	31-7300969	ex N4426Y
☐ N207DG	Cessna T207 Turbo Skywagon	20700070	ex N91902
☐ N734GW	Cessna U206G Stationair 6	U20604832	
☐ N1541F	Cessna 185D Skywagon	185-0896	

FOUR STAR AIR CARGO — Four Star (HK/FSC) — St Thomas-Cyril E King, VI (STT)

☐ N131FS	Douglas DC-3	16172/32920	ex N67PA	Freighter
☐ N132FS	Douglas DC-3	14333/25778	ex N333EF	Freighter
☐ N133FS	Douglas DC-3	15757/27202	ex N53NA	Freighter
☐ N135FS	Douglas DC-3	20063	ex NC63107	Freighter
☐ N138FS	Douglas DC-3	9967	ex N303SF	Freighter

FREEDOM AIR — Freedom (FP/FRE) — Guam, GU (GUM)

☐ N4168R	Piper PA-32-300 Cherokee Six C	32-40484	
☐ N4171R	Piper PA-32-300 Cherokee Six C	32-40504	
☐ N8628N	Piper PA-32-300 Cherokee Six	32-7140021	
☐ N8938N	Piper PA-32-300 Cherokee Six C	32-40736	
☐ N8969N	Piper PA-32-300 Cherokee Six	32-40769	
☐ N44FA	Cessna 207A Stationair 8	20700659	ex N75975
☐ N72FA	Piper PA-31 Navajo C	31-7812023	ex JA5278
☐ N74NF	Short SD.3-60	SH3721	ex N121PC
☐ N131FA	Piper PA-23-250 Aztec D	27-4097	ex N234SP
☐ N330FA	Short SD.3-30	SH3112	ex N188LM
☐ N2843F	Short SD.3-60	SH3739	ex SX-BFW

FREEDOM AIRLINES — (FRL) — New York-JFK, NY/Orlando, FL (JFK/MCO)

A division of Mesa Airlines; provides Delta Connection services from Orlando-MCO, FL and New York, NY

FREIGHT RUNNERS EXPRESS — Freight Runners (FRG) — Milwaukee-General Mitchell Intl, WI (MKE)

☐ N199CZ	Beech 99	U-30	ex N3RP	Freighter
☐ N299CZ	Beech 99	U-74	ex C-FCVJ	Freighter
☐ N399CZ	Beech B99	U-91	ex N195WA	Freighter
☐ N499CZ	Beech 99A	U-81	ex N36AK	Freighter
☐ N599CZ	Beech B99	U-89	ex 5Y-BJW	Freighter
☐ N699CZ	Beech B99	U-133	ex N27AL	Freighter dbr 24Jan07?
☐ N799CZ	Beech 99	U-68	ex N196WA	Freighter dbr 23Dec06?
☐ N899CZ	Beech 99A	U-96	ex N199CA	Freighter
☐ N75GB	Cessna 402B	402B0912		
☐ N191CZ	Beech 1900C	UB-59	ex D-CARA	
☐ N727CA	Cessna 402A	402A0102	ex N7802Q	Freighter
☐ N1517U	Cessna 207 Skywagon	20700117		Freighter
☐ N1518U	Cessna 207 Skywagon	20700118		Freighter
☐ N4504B	Cessna 402B	402B1370	ex C-GSMN	

FRONTIER AIRLINES — Frontier Flight (F9/FFT) — Denver-International, CO (DEN)

☐ N801FR	Airbus A318-111	1939	ex D-AUAA	Grizzly Bear
☐ N802FR	Airbus A318-111	1991	ex D-AUAB	Elk
☐ N803FR	Airbus A318-111	2017	ex D-AUAC	Hare 'Bugs'
☐ N804FR	Airbus A318-111	2051	ex D-AUAE	Kit Fox Pups
☐ N805FR	Airbus A318-111	1660	ex D-AUAA	Great Grey Owl
☐ N806FR	Airbus A318-111	2218	ex D-AUAB	American Bison
☐ N807FR	Airbus A318-111	2276	ex D-AUAC	Cougar
☐ N810FR	Airbus A318-111	3110	ex D-AUAA	Green Sea Turtle
☐ N812FR	Airbus A318-111	3163	ex D-AUAC	Grizzly Bear
☐ N902FR	Airbus A319-111	1515	ex D-AVYM	
☐ N904FR	Airbus A319-111	1579	ex D-AVWS	Trumpeter Swan
☐ N905FR	Airbus A319-111	1583	ex D-AVYC	Seal
☐ N906FR	Airbus A319-111	1684	ex D-AVWK	Pronghorn Antelope
☐ N908FR	Airbus A319-111	1759	ex D-AVYL	Blue Heron
☐ N910FR	Airbus A319-112	1781	ex D-AVYK	Cougar
☐ N912FR	Airbus A319-111	1803	ex D-AVWE	Red Fox Pup
☐ N914FR	Airbus A319-111	1841	ex D-AVWT	Great Egret
☐ N918FR	Airbus A319-111	1943	ex D-AVWH	Whitetail Deer

☐ N919FR	Airbus A319-111	1980	ex D-AVYD	Ocelot	
☐ N920FR	Airbus A319-111	1997	ex D-AVYO	Coyote	
☐ N921FR	Airbus A319-111	2010	ex D-AVWO	Mountain Goat	
☐ N922FR	Airbus A319-111	2012	ex D-AVWR	Red Fox	
☐ N923FR	Airbus A319-111	2019	ex D-AVWV	Racoon	
☐ N924FR	Airbus A319-111	2030	ex D-AVYG	Polar Bear Cubs	
☐ N925FR	Airbus A319-111	2103	ex D-AVWH	Dall's Sheep	
☐ N926FR	Airbus A319-111	2198	ex D-AVYD	Black-tailed Deer Fawn	
☐ N927FR	Airbus A319-111	2209	ex D-AVYL	Bottle-nosed Dolphin	
☐ N928FR	Airbus A319-111	2236	ex D-AVWK	Bobcat	
☐ N929FR	Airbus A319-111	2240	ex D-AVWP	Lynx	
☐ N930FR	Airbus A319-111	2241	ex D-AVWU	Cougar & cub	
☐ N931FR	Airbus A319-111	2253	ex D-AVYR	Bear cub	
☐ N932FR	Airbus A319-111	2258	ex D-AVYK	Bald Eagle	
☐ N933FR	Airbus A319-111	2260	ex D-AVYX	Hawk	
☐ N934FR	Airbus A319-111	2287	ex D-AVYU	Lynx pup	
☐ N935FR	Airbus A319-111	2318	ex D-AVYJ	Sea Otter	
☐ N936FR	Airbus A319-111	2392	ex D-AVYK	Walrus	
☐ N937FR	Airbus A319-111	2400	ex D-AVYU	Blue crowned conure	
☐ N938FR	Airbus A319-111	2406	ex D-AVWA	Arctic Fox	
☐ N939FR	Airbus A319-111	2448	ex D-AVWL	Emperor Penguins	
☐ N940FR	Airbus A319-111	2465	ex D-AVWW	Snow Hare	
☐ N941FR	Airbus A319-112	2483	ex D-AVYY	Gray Wolf	
☐ N942FR	Airbus A319-111	2497	ex D-AVYT	Bighorn	
☐ N943FR	Airbus A319-112	2518	ex D-AVWT	Fawn	
☐ N945FR	Airbus A319-112	2751	ex D-AVWD	Bull Moose	
☐ N947FR	Airbus A319-111	2806	ex D-AVYK	Leopard	
☐ N948FR	Airbus A319-112	2836	ex D-AVXR	Pelican	
☐ N949FR	Airbus A319-112	2857	ex D-AVYL	White Ermine	
☐ N201FR	Airbus A320-214	3389	ex F-WWDQ	Elk	
☐ N202FR	Airbus A320-214	3431	ex F-WWDT	Named 'Colorado'	
☐ N203FR	Airbus A320-214	1806	ex D-ALTI		
☐ N204FR	Airbus A320-214	2325	ex N270AV		
☐ N205FR	Airbus A320-214	4253	ex D-AXAB		on order
☐ N206FR	Airbus A320-214	4272	ex		on order
☐ N207FR	Airbus A320-214	4307	ex		on order
☐ N501LX	de Havilland DHC-8-402Q	4165	ex C-FMFG	Lynx Cub	
☐ N502LX	de Havilland DHC-8-402Q	4168	ex C-FMIU	Wolf Cubs	
☐ N503LX	de Havilland DHC-8-402Q	4170	ex C-FMIX	Mountain Lion Cubs	
☐ N504LX	de Havilland DHC-8-402Q	4172	ex C-FMJN	Elk	
☐ N505LX	de Havilland DHC-8-402Q	4174	ex C-FMKH	Fox	
☐ N506LX	de Havilland DHC-8-402Q	4176	ex C-FMKN	Raccoon	
☐ N507LX	de Havilland DHC-8-402Q	4181	ex C-FMUF	Bull	
☐ N508LX	de Havilland DHC-8-402Q	4182	ex C-FMUH	Toucan	
☐ N509LX	de Havilland DHC-8-402Q	4184	ex C-FNEI	Elk	
☐ N510LX	de Havilland DHC-8-402Q	4186	ex C-FNER	Bobcat	
☐ N511LX	de Havilland DHC-8-402Q	4265	ex C-FXJC	Snowy Owl	
☐ N	de Havilland DHC-8-402Q	4299	ex		on order

FRONTIER FLYING SERVICE — *Frontier-Air (2F/FTA)* — *Fairbanks-Intl, AK (FAI)*

☐ N575A	Beech 1900C-1	UC-83	ex N80334
☐ N575F	Beech 1900C-1	UC-99	ex N80598
☐ N575G	Beech 1900C-1	UC-155	ex N155YV
☐ N575P	Beech 1900C-1	UC-95	ex N80532
☐ N575Q	Beech 1900C-1	UC-160	ex N160AM
☐ N575X	Beech 1900C-1	UC-149	ex N149YV
☐ N575Y	Beech 1900C-1	UC-162	ex N162YV
☐ N575Z	Beech 1900C-1	UC-136	ex N21493
☐ N44AC	Piper PA-31-350 Chieftain	31-8052147	ex N3590M
☐ N137CS	Piper PA-31-350 Chieftain	31-8152137	ex C-GVPP
☐ N200AK	Piper PA-31-350 Chieftain	31-8052180	ex N8529T
☐ N3516A	Piper PA-31-350 Chieftain	31-7952106	
☐ N3535F	Piper PA-31-350 Chieftain	31-7952200	
☐ N3536B	Piper PA-31-350 Chieftain	31-7952205	
☐ N4112K	Piper PA-31-350 T-1020	31-8353006	
☐ N4301C	Piper PA-31-350 T-1020	31-8353001	ex C-FKGX
☐ N4501B	Piper PA-31-350 Chieftain	31-8052168	
☐ N4585U	Piper PA-31-350 Chieftain	31-8052198	ex C-GPIJ
☐ N190WA	Beech C99	U-207	ex N207CS
☐ N196WA	Beech C99	U-179	ex N995SB
☐ N9620M	Cessna 207A Stationair 8	20700711	
☐ N73100	Cessna 207A Stationair 7	20700559	

GALLUP FLYING SERVICES — *Gallup-Municipal, NM (GUP)*

☐ N41BG	Cessna 340A	340A0305	ex N4134G
☐ N986GM	Cessna 414A Chancellor	414A0089	ex N612CB

☐ N6640C	Cessna 414A Chancellor	414A0044		
☐ N7909Q	Cessna T310Q	310Q0620		
☐ N8840K	Cessna 414A Chancellor	414A0236		
☐ N9700M	Cessna U206G Stationair 6 II	U20604557		
☐ N29359	Cessna 210L Centurion II	21059858		
☐ N68149	Cessna 414A Chancellor	414A0642		

GB AIRLINK *Island Tiger (GBX) Fort Lauderdale-Hollywood Intl, FL (FLL)*

☐ N80GB	Short SC.7 Skyvan 3	SH1888	ex LX-ABC	Freighter
☐ N911E	Beech E-18S	BA-10	ex N501J	Freighter

GEO AIR *Fort Lauderdale-Hollywood Intl, FL (FLL)*

☐ N905GA	Convair 580F	121	ex C-FMGC

GO! *Honolulu-Intl, HI (HNL)*

☐ N591ML	Canadair CL-600-2B19 (CRJ-200LR)	7388	ex B-7699
☐ N27318	Canadair CL-600-2B19 (CRJ-200LR)	7318	ex C-FMLF
☐ N37342	Canadair CL-600-2B19 (CRJ-200LR)	7342	ex C-FMMY
☐ N77278	Canadair CL-600-2B19 (CRJ-200LR)	7278	ex C-FMMN
☐ N77302	Canadair CL-600-2B19 (CRJ-200LR)	7302	ex C-FMND
☐ N87353	Canadair CL-600-2B19 (CRJ-200LR)	7353	ex C-FMLV

GO! EXPRESS *Honolulu-Intl, HI (HNL)*

Operated by Mokulele Airlines.

GOJET AIRLINES *Gateway (G7/GJS) St Louis-Lambert Intl, MO (STL)*

GoJet Airlines is a wholly owned subsidiary of Trans State Airlines and operates feeder services for United Express.

GRAND CANYON AIRLINES *Canyon View (CVU) Grand Canyon-National Park, AZ/Valle-J Robidoux, AZ (GCN/VLE)*

☐ N72GC	de Havilland DHC-6 Twin Otter 300	264	ex N264Z
☐ N74GC	de Havilland DHC-6 Twin Otter 300	559	ex J6-AAK
☐ N171GC	de Havilland DHC-6 Twin Otter 300	406	ex J8-VBR
☐ N173GC	de Havilland DHC-6 Twin Otter 300	295	ex C-GLAZ
☐ N177GC	de Havilland DHC-6 Twin Otter 300	263	ex N102AC
☐ N178GC	de Havilland DHC-6 Twin Otter 300	697	ex TI-AZD
☐ N414H	Ford 5-AT-C Trimotor	74	ex TG-AFA

GRANT AVIATION *(GV/GUN) Emmonak, AK (EMK)*

☐ N8NZ	Cessna 207A Stationair 7 II	20700421	ex VH-XXL
☐ N48CF	Cessna T207A Turbo Skywagon	20700366	
☐ N54GV	Cessna 207A Stationair 7 II	20700447	
☐ N207DF	Cessna 207A Stationair 8 II	20700728	ex ZK-EAL
☐ N562CT	Cessna 207A Stationair 7 II	20700487	ex HI-562CT
☐ N2162C	Cessna 207A Stationair 8 II	20700575	ex HI-346
☐ N9651M	Cessna 207A Stationair 8 II	20700715	
☐ N9728M	Cessna 207A Stationair 8 II	20700721	
☐ N9973M	Cessna 207A Stationair 8 II	20700771	
☐ N77HV	Piper PA-31-350 Chieftain	31-8152193	ex C-GLCN
☐ N78GA	Piper PA-31-350 Chieftain	31-8352030	ex XA-DAM
☐ N90PB	Beech 200 Super King Air	BB-125	ex TG-UGA
☐ N162GA	Cessna 208B Caravan I	208B0667	ex C-FPNG
☐ N417PM	Piper PA-31-350 Chieftain	31-8052051	ex N357CT
☐ N454SF	Cessna 208B Caravan I	208B0797	ex N5180C
☐ N4105D	Piper PA-31-350 Chieftain	31-8252027	
☐ N27739	Piper PA-31-350 Chieftain	31-7852135	ex SE-KKS

GREAT LAKES AIRLINES *Lakes Air (ZK/GLA) Cheyenne, WY (CYS)*

☐ N92SK	Beech 1900D	UE-92		
☐ N100UX	Beech 1900D	UE-100		Fly Telluride
☐ N122UX	Beech 1900D	UE-122	ex N122YV	
☐ N153GL	Beech 1900D	UE-153	ex N153ZV	
☐ N154GL	Beech 1900D	UE-154	ex N154ZV	Sierra Vista
☐ N169GL	Beech 1900D	UE-169		
☐ N170GL	Beech 1900D	UE-170	ex N170YV	Garden City, NE
☐ N173YV	Beech 1900D	UE-173		
☐ N182YV	Beech 1900D	UE-182		
☐ N184UX	Beech 1900D	UE-184	ex N184YV	
☐ N192GL	Beech 1900D	UE-192	ex N192YV	Telluride, CO
☐ N195GL	Beech 1900D	UE-195	ex N195YV	Denver International
☐ N201GL	Beech 1900D	UE-201	ex N201YQ	Ponca City, OK

☐ N202UX	Beech 1900D	UE-202	ex (N202GV)	
☐ N208GL	Beech 1900D	UE-208	ex N208YV	Fly Telluride
☐ N210GL	Beech 1900D	UE-210	ex N210UX	
☐ N211GL	Beech 1900D	UE-211	ex N211UX	Laramie, WY
☐ N218YV	Beech 1900D	UE-218		
☐ N219GL	Beech 1900D	UE-219	ex N219YV	
☐ N220GL	Beech 1900D	UE-220	ex N220UX	Hays, KS
☐ N231YV	Beech 1900D	UE-231		
☐ N237YV	Beech 1900D	UE-237		
☐ N240GL	Beech 1900D	UE-240	ex N240YV	Devil's Tower, WY
☐ N245GL	Beech 1900D	UE-245	ex N245YV	Show Low, AZ
☐ N247GL	Beech 1900D	UE-247	ex N247YV	
☐ N251GL	Beech 1900D	UE-251	ex N251ZV	Grand Tetons
☐ N253GL	Beech 1900D	UE-253	ex N253YV	
☐ N254GL	Beech 1900D	UE-254	ex N10840	Grand Island, NE
☐ N255GL	Beech 1900D	UE-255	ex N10860	
☐ N257GL	Beech 1900D	UE-257	ex N257YV	
☐ N261GL	Beech 1900D	UE-261	ex N261YV	Scotts Bluff, NE

☐ N71GL	Embraer EMB.120ER Brasilia	120071	ex N267UE
☐ N96ZK	Embraer EMB.120ER Brasilia	120096	ex N452UE
☐ N108UX	Embraer EMB.120ER Brasilia	120108	ex N451UE
☐ N293UX	Embraer EMB.120ER Brasilia	120293	ex PT-SVN
☐ N297UX	Embraer EMB.120ER Brasilia	120297	ex PT-SVQ
☐ N299UX	Embraer EMB.120ER Brasilia	120299	ex PT-SVT

GREAT NORTHERN AIR — Anchorage-Lake Hood SPB, AK (LHD)

☐ N36GB	Cessna U206F Stationair	U20601854	ex N9654G	Floatplane

GRIFFING FLYING SERVICE — Sandusky-Griffing, OH (SKY)

☐ N426S	Piper PA-31-350 Chieftain	31-8152190	ex N426SC
☐ N428S	Piper PA-32-301 Saratoga	32-8106021	
☐ N442S	Britten-Norman BN-2A-20 Islander	770	ex N6863G

GRIZZLY MOUNTAIN AVIATION — Prineville Heliport, OR

☐ N22753	Bell UH-1B	1109	ex 64-13985

GUARDIAN AIR — Flagstaff, AZ / Bullhead City, AZ (FLG/IFP)

☐ N62GA	Pilatus PC-12/45	259	ex N259WA	EMS	op by Air Methods
☐ N92DV	Beech 65-E90 King Air	LW-292	ex N7MA	EMS Air 4	op by Air Methods
☐ N407AM	Bell 407	53309		EMS	op by Air Methods
☐ N407VV	Bell 407	53476		EMS	op by Air Methods
☐ N408GA	Bell 407	53392		EMS	op by Air Methods
☐ N987GM	Beech 65-E90 King Air	LW-65	ex N3065W	EMS Air 2	op by Air Methods

GULF AND CARIBBEAN AIR — Trans Auto (TSU) — Fort Lauderdale-Hollywood Intl, FL (FLL)

☐ N471FL	AMD Falcon 20	163	ex N258PE
☐ N481FL	AMD Falcon 20C-5	27	ex N326VW
☐ N511FL	AMD Falcon 20C-5	122	ex N302TT
☐ N521FL	AMD Falcon 20C-5	68	ex N458SW
☐ N531FL	AMD Falcon 20	113	ex N22WJ
☐ N541FL	AMD Falcon 20	48	ex N23ND

☐ N221FL	Boeing 727-22C (FedEx 3)	19805/543	ex C-GKFW	709
☐ N281FL	Boeing 727-225F/W (Duganair 3)	20153/779	ex C-GKFH	711

☐ N131FL	Convair 580	155	ex N5804	13	Freighter
☐ N141FL	Convair 580	111	ex N302K	14	Freighter
☐ N151FL	Convair 580	51	ex N5810	15	Freighter
☐ N171FL	Convair 580	318	ex N300K	17	Freighter
☐ N181FL	Convair 580	387	ex N301K	18	Freighter
☐ N191FL	Convair 580	326	ex N923DR	19	Freighter
☐ N361FL	Convair 5800	343	ex C-FKFS		
☐ N371FL	Convair 5800	309	ex C-FMKF		Freighter
☐ N381FL	Convair 5800	276	ex C-FKFS		Freighter
☐ N391FL	Convair 5800	278	ex C-GKFD		Freighter
☐ N991FL	Convair 580	508	ex C-GTTG		Freighter
☐ N7813B	Convair 340-70	265	ex 53-7813		stored

GULFSTREAM INTERNATIONAL — Gulf Flight (3M/GFT) — Fort Lauderdale-Hollwood, FL (FLL)

☐ N45AR	Beech 1900D	UE-12	ex N138MA		Lsd fm CSC
☐ N46AR	Beech 1900D	UE-27			Lsd fm CSC
☐ N266AS	Embraer EMB.120ER Brasilia	120188	ex PT-SRB	201	stored SGF
☐ N614HR	Piper PA-31-350 Navajo Chieftain	31-7305121	ex N74HP		Lsd to Gulfstream Air Charter
☐ N27319	Piper PA-31-350 Chieftain	31-7852137			Lsd to Gulfstream Air Charter

HAGELAND AVIATION SERVICES		Hageland (H6/HAG)		St Mary's, Bethel, AK (KSM)
☐ N17GN	Cessna 207A Stationair 8 II	20700693	ex C-GDFK	
☐ N104K	Cessna 207 Skywagon	20700122	ex C-GUHZ	
☐ N327CT	Cessna 207A Stationair 7 II	20700535	ex N6475H	
☐ N747SQ	Cessna 207A Skywagon	20700387	ex N1787U	
☐ N1668U	Cessna 207 Skywagon	20700268		
☐ N5277J	Cessna 207A Stationair 8 II	20700772	ex N9975M	
☐ N6207H	Cessna 207A Stationair 7 II	20700551	ex C-FSEE	
☐ N6314H	Cessna 207A Stationair 7 II	20700478		
☐ N7320U	Cessna 207A Skywagon	20700397		
☐ N7384U	Cessna 207A Stationair 7 II	20700431		
☐ N7389U	Cessna 207A Stationair 7 II	20700432		
☐ N9399M	Cessna 207A Stationair 8 II	20700652	ex VH-UAA	
☐ N9400M	Cessna 207A Stationair 8 II	20700687		
☐ N9869M	Cessna 207A Stationair 8 II	20700744		
☐ N9996M	Cessna 207A Stationair 8 II	20700779		
☐ N73067	Cessna 207A Stationair 7 II	20700558		
☐ N126AR	Cessna 208B Caravan I	208B1004	ex N5163K	
☐ N169LJ	Cessna 208B Caravan I	208B0599	ex N169BJ	
☐ N208SD	Cessna 208B Caravan I	208B0491		
☐ N215MC	Cessna 208B Caravan I	208B0730	ex N12328	
☐ N303GV	Cessna 208B Caravan I	208B0581		
☐ N407GV	Cessna 208B Caravan I	208B0616	ex N5262X	
☐ N410GV	Cessna 208B Caravan I	208B0632	ex N5264U	
☐ N411GV	Cessna 208B Caravan I	208B0672		
☐ N715HE	Cessna 208B Caravan I	208B0603	ex N715HL	
☐ N717PA	Cessna 208B Caravan I	208B0804	ex N12890	
☐ N1232Y	Cessna 208B Caravan I	208B0566	ex N5246Z	
☐ N1275N	Cessna 208B Caravan I	208B0756		
☐ N12373	Cessna 208B Caravan I	208B0697	ex N5268Z	
☐ N404GV	Beech 1900C-1	UC-154	ex N154YV	
☐ N406GV	Reims Cessna F406 Caravan II	F406-0049	ex 9M-PMS	
☐ N1553C	Beech 1900C-1	UC-24	ex N31226	
☐ N6590Y	Reims Cessna F406 Caravan II	F406-0052		
☐ N6591R	Reims Cessna F406 Caravan II	F406-0054		
☐ N9575G	Cessna U206F Stationair	U20601775		
☐ N91361	Cessna 180H	180-52045		
☐ N15503	Beech 1900C-1	UC-72		

HAWAIIAN AIRLINES		Hawaiian (HA/HAL)			Honolulu-Intl, HI (HNL)
☐ N	Airbus A330-243	1104	ex		on order
☐ N	Airbus A330-243		ex		on order
☐ N	Airbus A330-243		ex		on order
☐ N475HA	Boeing 717-22A	55121/5050		I'Iwi	
☐ N476HA	Boeing 717-22A	55118/5053		Elepaio	
☐ N477HA	Boeing 717-22A	55122/5061		Apapane	
☐ N478HA	Boeing 717-22A	55123/5064		Amakihi	
☐ N479HA	Boeing 717-22A	55124/5069		Akepa	
☐ N480HA	Boeing 717-22A	55125/5070		Pueo	
☐ N481HA	Boeing 717-22A	55126/5073		Alauahio	
☐ N483HA	Boeing 717-22A	55128/5079	ex N604AT		
☐ N484HA	Boeing 717-22A	55129/5080		Oma'o	
☐ N485HA	Boeing 717-22A	55130/5089		Palila	
☐ N486HA	Boeing 717-22A	55131/5092		Akiki	
☐ N487HA	Boeing 717-22A	55132/5098		Lo	
☐ N488HA	Boeing 717-23S	55001/5002	ex VH-NXF		
☐ N489HA	Boeing 717-23S	55002/5003	ex VH-NXB		
☐ N490HA	Boeing 717-23S	55151/5041	ex VH-NXC		
☐ N580HA	Boeing 767-33AER/W	28140/850		Kolea	
☐ N581HA	Boeing 767-33AER/W	28141/853		Manu o Ku	
☐ N582HA	Boeing 767-33AER/W	28139/857		Ake Ake	
☐ N583HA	Boeing 767-33AER	25531/423	ex D-AMUP	A	
☐ N584HA	Boeing 767-3G5ER	24258/255	ex D-AMUS	Kioea	
☐ N585HA	Boeing 767-3G5ER	24257/251	ex D-AMUR	Noio	
☐ N586HA	Boeing 767-3G5ER	24259/268	ex D-AMUN	Ou	
☐ N587HA	Boeing 767-33AER/W	33421/887		Pakalakala	
☐ N588HA	Boeing 767-3CBER	33466/890		Iwa	
☐ N589HA	Boeing 767-33AER	33422/892		Moli	
☐ N590HA	Boeing 767-3CBER	33467/894		Koa'e Ula	
☐ N591HA	Boeing 767-33AER	33423/897		Ake keke	
☐ N592HA	Boeing 767-3CBER	33468/898		Hunakai	
☐ N593HA	Boeing 767-33AER	33424/901		Nene	
☐ N594HA	Boeing 767-332	23275/136	ex N116DL		
☐ N596HA	Boeing 767-332	23276/151	ex N117DL		
☐ N597HA	Boeing 767-332	23277/152	ex N118DL		
☐ N598HA	Boeing 767-332	23278/153	ex N119DL		

HEARTLAND AVIATION		Night Chase (NTC)	Eau Claire-Chippewa Valley Regional, WI (EAU)		
☐ N310JZ	Cessna 310R II	310R1623	ex N310JD		
☐ N3286M	Cessna 310R II	310R1894			

HEAVY LIFT HELICOPTERS			Apple Valley, CA/Ketchikan, AK (APV/KTN)	
☐ N53HL	Sikorsky CH-53D Fire Stallion		ex 156668	
☐ N68HL	Sikorsky CH-53D Fire Stallion		ex 156674	
☐ N6156U	Sikorsky S-64 Skycrane	64012	ex 66-18410	790 Pegasus
☐ N44094	Sikorsky S-64 Skycrane	64023	ex 67-18421	794

HELI-FLITE			Corona-Municipal, CA (AJO)
☐ N1078Q	Bell 206B JetRanger III	2425	ex N5002X
☐ N9043N	Sikorsky S-58F (SH-34G)	58761	ex Bu143957
☐ N87717	Sikorsky S-58F (SH-34J)	581269	ex Bu148011

HELI-JET			Eugene-Private Heliport, OR
☐ N28HJ	Bell 205A-1	30006	ex PK-UHI
☐ N58HJ	Bell 205A-1	30314	
☐ N66HJ	Bell 205A-1	30239	ex N49766
☐ N73HJ	Bell 212	30552	ex XC-EDM
☐ N97HJ	Bell 205A-1	30173	ex C-GFHG

HELICOPTER TRANSPORT SERVICES			Baltimore-Martin State, MD (MTN)	
☐ N715HT	Sikorsky S-64F Skycrane	64077	ex N470KG	715
☐ N716HT	Sikorsky S-64F Skycrane	64092	ex N484KG	716
☐ N718HT	Sikorsky S-64F Skycrane	64074	ex N467KG	718
☐ N719HT	Sikorsky S-64F Skycrane	64076	ex N469KG	719
☐ N720HT	Sikorsky S-64F Skycrane	64070	ex N463KG	720
☐ N721HT	Sikorsky S-64F Skycrane	64073	ex N466KG	721
☐ N722HT	Sikorsky S-64F Skycrane	64075	ex N468KG	722
☐ N47B	Sikorsky S-58BT	58-530	ex EC-CYJ	
☐ N72B	Sikorsky S-58ET	58-1626	ex EC-DJN	
☐ N664Y	Sikorsky S-61R	61501		
☐ N724HT	Bell 214ST	28123	ex FAP634	
☐ N725HT	Bell 214ST	28128	ex N241WJ	
☐ N91158	Sikorsky S-61N Helipro Short	61424	ex G-AZDC	

HELIFLIGHT			Fort Lauderdale-Executive, FL (FLE)
☐ N58HF	Sikorsky S-58J		ex 57-1692

HOMER AIR			Homer, AK (HOM)
☐ N206DC	Cessna U206F Stationair II	U20603198	ex N8337Q
☐ N522HA	Cessna U206B Super Skywagon	U206-0755	ex N3455L
☐ N7138Q	Cessna U206F Stationair II	U20603074	
☐ N9815M	Cessna U206G Stationair 6 II	U20604572	

HORIZON AIR		Horizon Air (QX/QXE)		Seattle-Tacoma Intl, WA (SEA)	
☐ N600QX	Canadair CL-600-2C10 (CRJ-701)	10005	ex C-GCRA	600	
☐ N601QX	Canadair CL-600-2C10 (CRJ-701)	10009	ex C-GHCS	601	
☐ N603QX	Canadair CL-600-2C10 (CRJ-701)	10011	ex C-GHCZ	603	
☐ N604QX	Canadair CL-600-2C10 (CRJ-701)	10019	ex C-GIAJ	604	
☐ N605QX	Canadair CL-600-2C10 (CRJ-701)	10022	ex C-GIAR	605	
☐ N606QX	Canadair CL-600-2C10 (CRJ-701)	10023	ex C-GISU	606	
☐ N608QX	Canadair CL-600-2C10 (CRJ-701)	10026	ex C-GIAX	608	
☐ N609QX	Canadair CL-600-2C10 (CRJ-701)	10031	ex C-GIBJ	609	
☐ N610QX	Canadair CL-600-2C10 (CRJ-701)	10033	ex C-GIBN	610	
☐ N611QX	Canadair CL-600-2C10 (CRJ-701)	10041	ex C-GICP	611	
☐ N612QX	Canadair CL-600-2C10 (CRJ-701)	10042	ex C-GHZV	612	
☐ N613QX	Canadair CL-600-2C10 (CRJ-701)	10045	ex C-GIAD	613	
☐ N614QX	Canadair CL-600-2C10 (CRJ-701)	10049	ex C-GIAJ	614	
☐ N615QX	Canadair CL-600-2C10 (CRJ-701)	10065	ex C-GIBQ	615	
☐ N616QX	Canadair CL-600-2C10 (CRJ-701)	10128	ex C-	616	WSU Cougars c/s
☐ N617QX	Canadair CL-600-2C10 (CRJ-701)	10130	ex C-	617	
☐ N618QX	Canadair CL-600-2C10 (CRJ-701)	10205	ex C-	618	
☐ N619QX	Canadair CL-600-2C10 (CRJ-701)	10246	ex C-	619	
☐ N353PH	de Havilland DHC-8Q-202	496	ex C-GFRP		
☐ N354PH	de Havilland DHC-8Q-202	498	ex C-FCSG	City of North Bend/Coos Bay	
☐ N358PH	de Havilland DHC-8Q-202	506	ex C-FWBB		
☐ N359PH	de Havilland DHC-8Q-202	514	ex C-GEOA	City of Kelowna	Lsd to UCA
☐ N360PH	de Havilland DHC-8Q-202	515	ex C-GEWI	City of Medford	Lsd to UCA

☐ N361PH	de Havilland DHC-8Q-202	516	ex C-GFOD	City of Sun Valley	Lsd to UCA
☐ N362PH	de Havilland DHC-8Q-202	518	ex C-FDHI		Lsd to UCA
☐ N363PH	de Havilland DHC-8Q-202	520	ex C-FDHP	City of Boise	Lsd to UCA
☐ N364PH	de Havilland DHC-8Q-202	524	ex C-FDHX	Cities of Seattle/Tacoma	Lsd to UCA
☐ N365PH	de Havilland DHC-8Q-202	526	ex C-FDHZ	City of Pocatello	Lsd to UCA
☐ N366PH	de Havilland DHC-8Q-202	510	ex C-GELN	City of Redding	Lsd to UCA
☐ N367PH	de Havilland DHC-8Q-202	511	ex C-GDLD		Lsd to UCA
☐ N368PH	de Havilland DHC-8Q-202	512	ex C-GDFT	City of Idaho Falls	Lsd to UCA
☐ N369PH	de Havilland DHC-8Q-202	513	ex C-FWBB		
☐ N374PH	de Havilland DHC-8Q-202	528	ex C-GDIU		
☐ N375PH	de Havilland DHC-8Q-202	529	ex C-GDKL		Lsd to UCA
☐ N379PH	de Havilland DHC-8Q-202	530	ex C-GDLK		Lsd to UCA

☐ N400QX	de Havilland DHC-8-402Q	4030	ex C-GFCF	
☐ N401QX	de Havilland DHC-8-402Q	4031	ex C-GFCW	
☐ N402QX	de Havilland DHC-8-402Q	4032	ex C-GFOD	
☐ N403QX	de Havilland DHC-8-402Q	4037	ex C-FDHP	
☐ N404QX	de Havilland DHC-8-402Q	4046	ex C-GDKL	
☐ N405QX	de Havilland DHC-8-402Q	4047	ex C-GDLD	
☐ N406QX	de Havilland DHC-8-402Q	4048	ex C-GDLK	
☐ N407QX	de Havilland DHC-8-402Q	4049	ex C-GDNK	
☐ N408QX	de Havilland DHC-8-402Q	4050	ex C-GFCA	
☐ N409QX	de Havilland DHC-8-402Q	4051	ex C-GFCW	
☐ N410QX	de Havilland DHC-8-402Q	4053	ex C-GFQL	
☐ N411QX	de Havilland DHC-8-402Q	4055	ex C-GFUM	
☐ N412QX	de Havilland DHC-8-402Q	4059	ex C-FGNP	
☐ N413QX	de Havilland DHC-8-402Q	4060	ex C-FNGB	
☐ N414QX	de Havilland DHC-8-402Q	4061	ex C-GDFT	
☐ N415QX	de Havilland DHC-8-402Q	4081	ex C-GELN	
☐ N416QX	de Havilland DHC-8-402Q	4083	ex C-GDNK	
☐ N417QX	de Havilland DHC-8-402Q	4086	ex C-FCSG	
☐ N418QX	de Havilland DHC-8-402Q	4143	ex C-FHQX	
☐ N419QX	de Havilland DHC-8-402Q	4145	ex C-FHRD	
☐ N420QX	de Havilland DHC-8-402Q	4147	ex C-FJLA	
☐ N421QX	de Havilland DHC-8-402Q	4149	ex C-FJLF	
☐ N422QX	de Havilland DHC-8-402Q	4150	ex C-FJLG	
☐ N423QX	de Havilland DHC-8-402Q	4153	ex C-FJLO	
☐ N424QX	de Havilland DHC-8-402Q	4006	ex B-3568	
☐ N425QX	de Havilland DHC-8-402Q	4039	ex B-3569	25 Years Jubilee c/s
☐ N426QX	de Havilland DHC-8-402Q	4154	ex C-FJLX	
☐ N427QX	de Havilland DHC-8-402Q	4156	ex C-FLKU	
☐ N428QX	de Havilland DHC-8-402Q	4160	ex C-FLTL	
☐ N429QX	de Havilland DHC-8-402Q	4161	ex C-FLTT	
☐ N430QX	de Havilland DHC-8-402Q	4163	ex C-FMES	
☐ N431QX	de Havilland DHC-8-402Q	4164	ex C-FMEU	
☐ N432QX	de Havilland DHC-8-402Q	4166	ex C-FMFH	
☐ N433QX	de Havilland DHC-8-402Q	4210	ex C-FPQB	
☐ N434MK	de Havilland DHC-8-402Q	4227	ex C-FTUQ	Milton G Koult II
☐ N435QX	de Havilland DHC-8-402Q	4232	ex C-FUCO	
☐ N436QX	de Havilland DHC-8-402Q	4236	ex C-FUOF	
☐ N437QX	de Havilland DHC-8-402Q	4240	ex C-FUSM	
☐ N438QX	de Havilland DHC-8-402Q	4243	ex C-FUTP	
☐ N439QX	de Havilland DHC-8-402Q	4246	ex C-FVGY	

HOWE BROS ENTERPRISES — *Punta Gorda-Charlotte Co, FL (PGD)*

☐ N213GB	Douglas DC-3	16484/33232	ex (N2007J)	Freighter
☐ N231GB	Douglas DC-3	14663/26108	ex N2002J	Freighter

IBC AIRWAYS — *Chasqui (II/CSQ)* — *Miami-Intl, FL (MIA)*

☐ N431BC	SAAB SF.340B	340B-260	ex N363PX	
☐ N481BC	SAAB SF.340B	340B-274	ex N368PX	
☐ N541BC	SAAB SF.340A	340A-029	ex N184K	
☐ N611BC	SAAB SF.340A	340A-060	ex N403BH	Freighter
☐ N631BC	SAAB SF.340A	340A-061	ex N404BH	Freighter
☐ N641BC	SAAB SF.340A	340A-069	ex N340SL	Freighter
☐ N651BC	SAAB SF.340A	340A-076	ex N76XJ	Freighter
☐ N661BC	SAAB SF.340A	340A-125	ex N125CH	Freighter
☐ N671BC	SAAB SF.340A	340A-084	ex N163PW	Freighter
☐ N691BC	SAAB SF.340A	340A-041	ex XA-BML	Freighter

☐ N831BC	Swearingen SA.227AC Metro III	AC-654B	ex N26906
☐ N841BC	Swearingen SA.227TC Metro II	TC-282	ex N240AM
☐ N851BC	Swearingen SA.227AT Merlin IVC	AT-495B	ex N9UA
☐ N861BC	Swearingen SA.227AC Metro III	AC-487B	ex N550TD
☐ N871BC	Swearingen SA.227AC Metro III	AC-659B	ex N2693C
☐ N891BC	Swearingen SA.227AC Metro III	AC-709B	ex N2708D

ILIAMNA AIR TAXI — Iliamna Air (V8/IAR) — Iliamna, AK (ILI)

☐ N38KC	Piper PA-31-350 Chieftain	31-8352033	ex N35AT	
☐ N715HL	Pilatus PC-12/45	292	ex N292PB	
☐ N715TL	Pilatus PC-12/45	548	ex HB-FST	
☐ N3682Z	Beech 58 Baron	TH-1159		
☐ N1748U	Cessna 207 Skywagon	20700348		
☐ N7379U	Cessna 207A Stationair 7 II	20700427		
☐ N9720M	Cessna 207A Stationair 8 II	20700720		
☐ N62230	de Havilland DHC-2 Beaver	707	ex 53-7899	Floatplane
☐ N68088	de Havilland DHC-2 Beaver	1197	ex 56-4447	Floatplane

INLAND AVIATION SERVICES — (7N) — Aniak, AK (ANI)

☐ N1673U	Cessna 207 Skywagon	20700273
☐ N1701U	Cessna 207 Skywagon	20700301
☐ N1754U	Cessna T207 Turbo Skywagon	20700354
☐ N91002	Cessna 207 Skywagon	20700003
☐ N91099	Cessna 207 Skywagon	20700073

INTER ISLAND AIR — Pago Pago International (PPG)

☐ N27BN	Britten-Norman BN-2B-26 Islander	2220	ex ZK-JOC	
☐ N228ST	Dornier 228-212	8240	ex D-CBDJ	Islands of Manu'a

INTERMOUNTAIN HELICOPTERS — Columbia, CA (COA)

☐ N9122Z	Bell 212	30716	ex C-GFRS

INTERNATIONAL AIR RESPONSE — Coolidge-Municipal, AZ

☐ N117TG	Lockheed C-130A-1A Hercules	3018	ex 54-1631	31 Iron Butterfly	
☐ N118TG	Lockheed C-130A-1A Hercules	3219	ex 57-0512	32	
☐ N119TG	Lockheed C-130A Hercules	3227	ex N138FF		stored CHD
☐ N121TG	Lockheed C-130A Hercules	3119	ex N132FF		
☐ N125TG	Lockheed C-130A Hercules	3138	ex N131FF		stored CHD
☐ N131HP	Lockheed C-130A-1A Hercules	3142	ex N132FF		
☐ N133HP	Lockheed C-130A-1A Hercules	3189	ex N8026J		
☐ N797AL	Douglas DC-8-63F (BAC 3)	46163/556	ex SE-DBL		stored VCV
☐ N995CF	Douglas DC-8-62F (BAC 3)	46024/428	ex N815ZA		stored VCV
☐ N4887C	Douglas DC-7B	45351/903		33	

ISLAND AIR — Moku (WP/MKU — Honolulu-Intl, HI (HNL)

☐ N805WP	de Havilland DHC-8-103	353	ex N853MA
☐ N806WP	de Havilland DHC-8-103	357	ex N854MA
☐ N808WP	de Havilland DHC-8-103	026	ex N812PH
☐ N809WP	de Havilland DHC-8-103	032	ex N813SN
☐ N829EX	de Havilland DHC-8-103	146	ex N805AW
☐ N979HA	de Havilland DHC-8-103	373	ex C-GFQL

ISLAND AIR CHARTERS — Barracuda (ILF) — Fort Lauderdale-Hollywood Intl, FL (FLL)

☐ N138LW	Britten-Norman BN-2A-27 Islander	138	ex YR-BNF
☐ N779KS	Britten-Norman BN-2A-27 Islander	779	ex YR-BNE

ISLAND AIR SERVICE — (2O) — Kodiak-Municipal, AK (ADQ)

☐ N27MR	Britten-Norman BN-2A-26 Islander	884	ex XC-DUN	dam 18Jun07
☐ N1162W	Beech B80 Queen Air	LD-350		
☐ N2233Z	Britten-Norman BN-2A-26 Islander	23	ex C-FXYK	
☐ N3941W	Piper PA-32-260 Cherokee Six	32-890		
☐ N4875X	Cessna U206G Stationair 6 II	U20605559		Floatplane or wheels
☐ N5891V	Britten-Norman BN-2A-26 Islander	3011	ex J8-VAN	
☐ N8152Z	Piper PA-32-301 Saratoga	32-8006004		

ISLAND AIRLINES — Island (IS/ISA) — Nantucket-Memorial, MA (ACK)

☐ N401BK	Cessna 402C II	402C0297	ex N3252M
☐ N402BK	Cessna 402C II	689	ex N550CQ
☐ N403BK	Cessna 402C II	402C0330	ex N26436
☐ N406BK	Cessna 402C III	402C0807	ex N1235A
☐ N407BK	Cessna 402C II	402C0238	ex N279CB
☐ N409BK	Cessna 402C II	402C0651	ex N67220
☐ N410BK	Cessna 402C II	402C1006	ex N175TT

ISLAND AIRWAYS — Charlevoix-Municipal, MI (CVX)

☐ N19WA	Britten-Norman BN-2A-8 Islander	524	ex N307SK
☐ N80KM	Britten-Norman BN-2A Islander	80	ex G-BNXA

☐ N95BN	Britten-Norman BN-2A-8 Islander	95	ex G-AXKB	
☐ N137MW	Britten-Norman BN-2A Islander	137	ex G-AXWH	
☐ N866JA	Britten-Norman BN-2A-6 islander	185	ex G-31-185	

ISLAND SEAPLANE SERVICE — Honolulu-Keehi Lagoon SPB, HI

☐ N110AW	de Havilland DHC-2 Beaver	690	ex N11015	Fantasy Islands c/sfloatplane

ISLAND WINGS AIR SERVICE — Ketchikan-Waterfront SPB, AK (WFB)

☐ N1117F	de Havilland DHC-2 Beaver	1369	ex N6783L	Floatplane

JETBLUE AIRWAYS — JetBlue (B6/JBU) — New York-JFK Intl, NY (JFK)

☐ N503JB^	Airbus A320-232	1123	ex F-WWBR	Blue Bird
☐ N504JB*	Airbus A320-232	1156	ex F-WWBV	Shades Of Blue
☐ N505JB+	Airbus A320-232	1173	ex F-WWDN	Blue Skies
☐ N506JB*	Airbus A320-232	1235	ex F-WWIN	Wild Blue Yonder
☐ N509JB*	Airbus A320-232	1270	ex F-WWDF	True Blue
☐ N510JB+	Airbus A320-232	1280	ex F-WWBA	Out Of The Blue
☐ N516JB*	Airbus A320-232	1302	ex F-WWBQ	Royal Blue
☐ N517JB^	Airbus A320-232	1327	ex F-WWDU	Blue Moon
☐ N519JB*	Airbus A320-232	1398	ex F-WWIY	It Had To Be Blue
☐ N520JB+	Airbus A320-232	1446	ex F-WWBT	Blue Velvet
☐ N521JB^	Airbus A320-232	1452	ex F-WWBY	Baby Blue
☐ N523JB+	Airbus A320-232	1506	ex F-WWII	Born To Be Blue
☐ N524JB^	Airbus A320-232	1528	ex F-WWIN	Blue Belle
☐ N529JB*	Airbus A320-232	1610	ex F-WWDE	Ole Blue Eyes
☐ N534JB>	Airbus A320-232	1705	ex F-WWIU	Bada Bing, Bada Blue
☐ N535JB>	Airbus A320-232	1739	ex F-WWBQ	Estrella Azul
☐ N536JB>	Airbus A320-232	1784	ex F-WWDS	Canyon Blue
☐ N547JB>	Airbus A320-232	1849	ex F-WWDF	Forever Blue
☐ N552JB>	Airbus A320-232	1861	ex F-WWDM	Blue Jay
☐ N554JB>	Airbus A320-232	1898	ex F-WWBK	Sacre' Bleu!
☐ N556JB>	Airbus A320-232	1904	ex F-WWDD	Betty Blue
☐ N558JB"	Airbus A320-232	1915	ex F-WWIF	Song Sung Blue
☐ N559JB"	Airbus A320-232	1917	ex F-WWIR	Here's Looking At Blue, Kid
☐ N561JB"	Airbus A320-232	1927	ex F-WWIC	La Vie En Blue
☐ N562JB"	Airbus A320-232	1948	ex F-WWDF	The Name Is Blue, jetBlue
☐ N563JB"	Airbus A320-232	2006	ex F-WWBY	Blue Chip
☐ N564JB"	Airbus A320-232	2020	ex F-WWBZ	Absolute Blue
☐ N565JB"	Airbus A320-232	2031	ex F-WWDT	Bippity Boppity Blue
☐ N566JB"	Airbus A320-232	2042	ex F-WWDU	Blue Suede Shoes
☐ N568JB"	Airbus A320-232	2063	ex F-WWDE	Blue Sapphire
☐ N569JB"	Airbus A320-232	2075	ex F-WWDF	Blues Brothers
☐ N570JB"	Airbus A320-232	2099	ex F-WWBD	Devil With A Blue Dress On
☐ N571JB"	Airbus A320-232	2125	ex F-WWIX	Blue Monday
☐ N579JB"	Airbus A320-232	2132	ex F-WWDB	Can't Stop Lovin' Blue
☐ N580JB"	Airbus A320-232	2136	ex F-WWBB	Mo Better Blue
☐ N583JB"	Airbus A320-232	2150	ex F-WWII	Bluesville
☐ N584JB"	Airbus A320-232	2149	ex F-WWID	Blue Fox
☐ N585JB<	Airbus A320-232	2159	ex F-WWIC	I Got Blue Babe
☐ N586JB<	Airbus A320-232	2160	ex F-WWIN	Blue Flight Special
☐ N587JB<	Airbus A320-232	2177	ex F-WWIL	Blue Kid In Town
☐ N588JB<	Airbus A320-232	2201	ex F-WWIT	Hopelessly Devoted To Blue
☐ N589JB<	Airbus A320-232	2215	ex F-WWBJ	Blue Skies Ahead
☐ N590JB<	Airbus A320-232	2231	ex F-WWIH	Liberty Blue
☐ N591JB<	Airbus A320-232	2246	ex F-WWIS	Tale Of Blue Cities
☐ N592JB<	Airbus A320-232	2259	ex F-WWBI	American Blue
☐ N593JB<	Airbus A320-232	2280	ex F-WWDT	I Only Have Eyes For Blue
☐ N594JB<	Airbus A320-232	2284	ex F-WWBQ	Whole Lotta Blue
☐ N595JB<	Airbus A320-232	2286	ex F-WWBR	Rhythm & Blues
☐ N597JB<	Airbus A320-232	2307	ex F-WWIC	For The Love Of Blue
☐ N598JB<	Airbus A320-232	2314	ex F-WWDK	Me & You & A Plane Named Blue
☐ N599JB<	Airbus A320-232	2336	ex F-WWIN	If The Blue Fits
☐ N603JB	Airbus A320-232	2352	ex F-WWIL	Viva La Blue
☐ N605JB#	Airbus A320-232	2368	ex F-WWDO	Blue Yorker
☐ N606JB#	Airbus A320-232	2384	ex F-WWIE	Idlewild Blue
☐ N607JB#	Airbus A320-232	2386	ex F-WWIG	Beantown Blue
☐ N608JB#	Airbus A320-232	2415	ex F-WWDP	..And Along Came Blue
☐ N612JB#	Airbus A320-232	2447	ex F-WWBU	Blue Look Maaahvelous
☐ N613JB#	Airbus A320-232	2449	ex F-WWBX	Bahama Blue
☐ N615JB#	Airbus A320-232	2461	ex F-WWDR	I Love Blue
☐ N618JB#	Airbus A320-232	2489	ex F-WWDX	Can't Get Enough Of Blue
☐ N621JB#	Airbus A320-232	2491	ex F-WWDY	Do-be-do-be Blue
☐ N623JB#	Airbus A320-232	2504	ex F-WWBM	All We Need Is Blue
☐ N624JB#	Airbus A320-232	2520	ex F-WWBN	Blue-T-Ful
☐ N625JB#	Airbus A320-232	2535	ex F-WWII	CompanyBlue
☐ N627JB#	Airbus A320-232	2577	ex F-WWDB	A Friend Like Blue
☐ N629JB#	Airbus A320-232	2580	ex F-WWBH	Bright Lights, Blue City
☐ N630JB#	Airbus A320-232	2640	ex F-WWBY	Honk If You love Blue
☐ N632JB#	Airbus A320-232	2647	ex F-WWIF	Clear Blue Sky

☐ N633JB^	Airbus A320-232	2671	ex F-WWDF	Major Blue
☐ N634JB^	Airbus A320-232	2710	ex F-WWIZ	B*L*U*E
☐ N635JB^	Airbus A320-232	2725	ex F-WWDQ	All Because of Blue
☐ N636JB^	Airbus A320-232	2755	ex F-WWDL	All Wrapped Up In Blue
☐ N637JB^	Airbus A320-232	2781	ex F-WWDY	Big Blue Bus
☐ N638JB^	Airbus A320-232	2802	ex F-WWIL	Blue begins with you
☐ N639JB^	Airbus A320-232	2814	ex F-WWIV	A Little Blue Will Do
☐ N640JB^	Airbus A320-232	2832	ex F-WWBD	Blue Better Believe It
☐ N641JB*	Airbus A320-232	2848	ex F-WWIK	Blue Come Back Now Ya Hear
☐ N643JB*	Airbus A320-232	2871	ex F-WWBF	Blue Jersey
☐ N644JB*	Airbus A320-232	2880	ex F-WWBO	Blue Loves Ya, Baby
☐ N645JB	Airbus A320-232	2900	ex F-WWDE	Blues Have More Fun
☐ N646JB	Airbus A320-232	2945	ex F-WWIP	Bravo Lima Uniform Echo
☐ N648JB*	Airbus A320-232	2970	ex F-WWDI	That's What I Like About Blue
☐ N649JB	Airbus A320-232	2977	ex F-WWBD	Fancy Meeting Blue Here
☐ N651JB*	Airbus A320-232	2992	ex F-WWIS	BetaBlue
☐ N652JB+	Airbus A320-232	3029	ex F-WWBT	Out With The Old, In With The Blue
☐ N653JB	Airbus A320-232	3039	ex F-WWDH	Breath of Fresh Blue
☐ N655JB	Airbus A320-232	3072	ex F-WWIN	special colours, Blue 100
☐ N656JB	Airbus A320-232	3091	ex F-WWIQ	California Blue
☐ N657JB	Airbus A320-232	3119	ex F-WWBC	Denim Blue
☐ N658JB	Airbus A320-232	3150	ex F-WWBT	Woo-Hoo JetBlue
☐ N659JB	Airbus A320-232	3190	ex F-WWIQ	Simply Blue
☐ N661JB	Airbus A320-232	3228	ex F-WWBD	Let the Blue Times Roll
☐ N662JB	Airbus A320-232	3263	ex F-WWDO	Glad to be Blue
☐ N663JB	Airbus A320-232	3287	ex F-WWDG	Paint the town blue
☐ N665JB	Airbus A320-232	3348	ex F-WWBV	Something about blue
☐ N703JB	Airbus A320-232	3381	ex F-WWDM	It's up to blue, New York, New York
☐ N705JB	Airbus A320-232	3416	ex F-WWIN	Big Blue People Seater
☐ N706JB	Airbus A320-232	3451	ex F-WWBE	As blue as it gets
☐ N708JB	Airbus A320-232	3479	ex F-WWDJ	All that and a bag of blue chips
☐ N709JB	Airbus A320-232	3488	ex F-WWIK	Brand Spanking Blue
☐ N712JB	Airbus A320-232	3517	ex F-WWDQ	Enough about me..Let's talk about Blue
☐ N715JB	Airbus A320-232	3554	ex F-WWBB	How's My Flying? Call 1-800-JetBlue
☐ N729JB	Airbus A320-232	3572	ex F-WWBJ	If You Can Read This, Your Blue Close
☐ N746JB	Airbus A320-232	3622	ex F-WWIL	Some Like It Blue
☐ N760JB	Airbus A320-232	3659	ex F-WWDU	The Blues Were Made For Flying
☐ N763JB	Airbus A320-232	3707	ex F-WWIQ	Unforgetably blue
☐ N766JB	Airbus A320-232	3724	ex F-WWDG	Etjay LueJay
☐ N768JB	Airbus A320-232	3760	ex F-WWDC	Blue Crew
☐ N775JB	Airbus A320-232	3800	ex F-WWBT	Canard Bleu
☐ N779JB	Airbus A320-232	3811	ex F-WWID	Real Blue

☐ N178JB#	Embraer 190-100IGW (190AR)	19000004	ex PT-STD	It's A Blue Thing
☐ N179JB^	Embraer 190-100IGW (190AR)	19000006	ex PT-STF	Come Fly With Blue
☐ N183JB*	Embraer 190-100IGW (190AR)	19000007	ex PT-STG	Azul Brasileiro
☐ N184JB+	Embraer 190-100IGW (190AR)	19000008	ex PT-STH	Outta the Blue
☐ N187JB"	Embraer 190-100IGW (190AR)	19000009	ex PT-STI	Dream Come Blue
☐ N190JB#	Embraer 190-100IGW (190AR)	19000011	ex PT-STK	Luiz F Kahl
☐ N192JB^	Embraer 190-100IGW (190AR)	19000014	ex PT-STO	Yes, I'm A Natural Blue
☐ N193JB	Embraer 190-100IGW (190AR)	19000017	ex PT-STR	Peek-a-Blue
☐ N197JB"	Embraer 190-100IGW (190AR)	19000020	ex PT-STU	Color Me Blue
☐ N198JB	Embraer 190-100IGW (190AR)	19000021	ex PT-STV	Big Apple Blue
☐ N203JB	Embraer 190-100IGW (190AR)	19000023	ex PT-STX	Look at Blue now
☐ N206JB#	Embraer 190-100IGW (190AR)	19000025	ex PT-STZ	Blue-It's the New Black
☐ N216JB^	Embraer 190-100IGW (190AR)	19000026	ex PT-SGA	Blue Getaway
☐ N228JB*	Embraer 190-100IGW (190AR)	19000030	ex PT-SGE	Blue 4 You
☐ N229JB	Embraer 190-100IGW (190AR)	19000032	ex PT-SGG	Blue Amigo
☐ N231JB	Embraer 190-100IGW (190AR)	19000033	ex PT-SGH	Blue Bonnet
☐ N236JB	Embraer 190-100IGW (190AR)	19000035	ex PT-SGJ	Blue by Design
☐ N238JB	Embraer 190-100IGW (190AR)	19000039	ex PT-SGO	Blue Clipper
☐ N239JB	Embraer 190-100IGW (190AR)	19000040	ex PT-SGP	Blissfully Blue
☐ N247JB	Embraer 190-100IGW (190AR)	19000042	ex PT-SGR	Blue is so You
☐ N249JB	Embraer 190-100IGW (190AR)	19000045	ex PT-SGU	Blueprint
☐ N258JB	Embraer 190-100IGW (190AR)	19000047	ex PT-SGW	Blue Send Me
☐ N265JB	Embraer 190-100IGW (190AR)	19000049	ex PT-SGY	Blue Streak
☐ N266JB	Embraer 190-100IGW (190AR)	19000054	ex PT-SID	Blue Sweet Blue
☐ N267JB	Embraer 190-100IGW (190AR)	19000065	ex PT-SJD	Bluesmobile
☐ N273JB	Embraer 190-100IGW (190AR)	19000073	ex PT-SJM	Carribean Blue
☐ N274JB	Embraer 190-100IGW (190AR)	19000082	ex PT-SJY	Good, Better, Blue
☐ N279JB	Embraer 190-100IGW (190AR)	19000090	ex PT-SNJ	Indigo Blue
☐ N281JB	Embraer 190-100IGW (190AR)	19000103	ex PT-SNX	Lady in Blue
☐ N283JB	Embraer 190-100IGW (190AR)	19000125	ex PT-SQU	Pretty in Blue
☐ N284JB	Embraer 190-100IGW (190AR)	19000144	ex PT-SVY	Sincerely Blue
☐ N289JB	Embraer 190-100IGW (190AR)	19000002	ex PT-XMB	Blue Complete Me
☐ N292JB	Embraer 190-100IGW (190AR)	19000179	ex PT-SDN	Parlez-Blue?
☐ N294JB	Embraer 190-100IGW (190AR)	19000185	ex PT-SDT	Room with a blue
☐ N296JB	Embraer 190-100IGW (190AR)	19000219	ex PT-SHC	Blue's your daddy
☐ N298JB	Embraer 190-100IGW (190AR)	19000249	ex PT-SIT	Cool Blue
☐ N304JB	Embraer 190-100IGW (190AR)	19000257	ex PT-STF	
☐ N306JB	Embraer 190-100IGW (190AR)	19000272	ex PT-TLM	Mi Corazon Azul
☐ N307JB	Embraer 190-100IGW (190AR)	19000286	ex PT-TZA	
☐ N309JB	Embraer 190-100IGW (190AR)	19000289	ex PT-TZD	

☐ N316JB	Embraer 190-100IGW (190AR)	19000292	ex PT-TZG	Usto Schulz	
☐ N	Embraer 190-100IGW (190AR)		ex PT-		on order
☐ N	Embraer 190-100IGW (190AR)		ex PT-		on order
☐ N	Embraer 190-100IGW (190AR)		ex PT-		on order
☐ N	Embraer 190-100IGW (190AR)		ex PT-		on order

Have differing tail colour schemes, namely Harlequin*, Blue Dots+, Stripes^, Super Dots ”, Plaid<, Squares > and Mosaic #, all on a blue background. 19% owned by Lufthansa.

JIM HANKINS AIR SERVICE — Hankins (HKN) — Jackson-Hawkins Field, MS (JAN)

☐ N22BR	Beech H-18	BA-729	ex N402AP	Freighter
☐ N81CK	Volpar Turboliner	BA-509	ex F-ODHJ	Freighter
☐ N231SK	Volpar Turboliner	AF-856	ex N346V	Freighter
☐ N404CK	Volpar Turboliner	AF-297	ex N404TH	Freighter
☐ N4209V	Volpar Turboliner	AF-884	ex HB-GFX	Freighter
☐ N92756	Beech H-18	BA-728	ex JA5133	Freighter

☐ N3BA	Douglas DC-3	12172	ex N94530	Freighter
☐ N40XL	Beech 58 Baron	TH-400	ex N80LM	
☐ N366MQ	Short SD.3-60	SH3639	ex G-BLEH	
☐ N899DD	Beech 58 Baron	TH-899	ex VH-BWJ	
☐ N958JH	Beech 65-C90A King Air	LJ-1108	ex N438SP	
☐ N3106W	Beech 58 Baron	TH-408		
☐ N6652A	Beech 58 Baron	TH-1045		
☐ N8061A	Douglas DC-3	6085	ex (N351SA)	Freighter

KACHINA AVIATION — Boise-Air Terminal, ID (BOI)

☐ N171KA	Bell 206L-1 LongRanger III	45607	ex C-GZPZ
☐ N212KA	Bell 212	30776	ex C-FAHI
☐ N213KA	Bell 212	31172	ex C-FNOB
☐ N214KA	Bell 212	30827	ex C-FAHC
☐ N215KA	Bell 212	30651	ex C-FAHZ

KALITTA AIR — Connie (K4/CKS) — Detroit-Willow Run, MI (YIP)

☐ N700CK	Boeing 747-246B (SF)	22990/579	ex JA8161	
☐ N701CK	Boeing 747-259B (SCD)	21730/372	ex N924FT	
☐ N703CK	Boeing 747-212B (SF)	21939/449	ex N319FV	
☐ N704CK	Boeing 747-246F	23391/654	ex JA8171	stored OSC
☐ N705CK	Boeing 747-246B (SCD)	21034/243	ex JA8123	
☐ N706CK	Boeing 747-249F	21827/406	ex N806FT	
☐ N707CK	Boeing 747-246F	21681/382	ex JA8132	
☐ N708CK	Boeing 747-212B (SF)	21937/419	ex N526UP	stored OSC
☐ N709CK	Boeing 747-132 (SCD)	20247/159	ex N625PL	
☐ N710CK	Boeing 747-2B4M	21097/262	ex N204AE	
☐ N712CK	Boeing 747-122 (SCD)	19754/60	ex N854FT	
☐ N713CK	Boeing 747-2B4M	21099/264	ex OD-AGH	
☐ N715CK	Boeing 747-209B (SF)	22447/556	ex B-18755	
☐ N716CK	Boeing 747-122 (SCD)	19753/52	ex N853FT	
☐ N717CK	Boeing 747-123 (SCD)	20325/125	ex N673UP	
☐ N740CK	Boeing 747-4H6FCF	24405/745	ex N73714	
☐ N741CK	Boeing 747-4H6FCF	24315/738	ex N73713	
☐ N742CK	Boeing 747-446BCF	24424/760	ex JA8072	
☐ N746CK	Boeing 747-246F	22989/571	ex JA811J	
☐ N748CK	Boeing 747-221F	21744/392	ex JA8160	
☐ N768CK	Boeing 747-346	23969/691	ex JA8185	stored OSC

KALITTA CHARTERS II — Kalitta (KFS) — Detroit-Willow Run, MI (YIP)

☐ N720CK	Boeing 727-2B6F (Raisbeck 3)	21298/1246	ex N721SK
☐ N722CK	Boeing 727-2H3F (Raisbeck 3)	20948/1084	ex N722SK
☐ N723CK	Boeing 727-2H3F (Raisbeck 3)	20545/877	ex N723SK
☐ N724CK	Boeing 727-225F (Raisbeck 3)	20383/831	ex N8840E
☐ N725CK	Boeing 727-224F (Raisbeck 3)	22252/1697	ex N746DH
☐ N915CK	Douglas DC-9-15RC	47086/219	ex N915R

KALITTA FLYING SERVICES — Kalitta (KFS) — Detroit-Willow Run, MI/Morristown, TN/El Paso, TX (YIP/MRX/ESP)

☐ N70CK	AMD Falcon 20C	128	ex N228CK	
☐ N108R	AMD Falcon 20DC	108	ex N101ZE	
☐ N192CK	AMD Falcon 20C	192	ex N192R	
☐ N212R	AMD Falcon 20DC	212	ex N31FE	
☐ N226CK	AMD Falcon 20DC	226	ex N226R	
☐ N227CK	AMD Falcon 20DC	227	ex N227R	
☐ N229CK	AMD Falcon 20DC	229	ex N229R	
☐ N230RA	AMD Falcon 20DC	230	ex N26EV	
☐ N240CK	AMD Falcon 20C-5	24	ex N240TJ	
☐ N301R	AMD Falcon 20C	3	ex N92MH	
☐ N560RA	AMD Falcon 20C	56	ex N388AJ	stored YIP
☐ N810RA	AMD Falcon 20C	81	ex N93RS	

Reg	Type	c/n	Previous		
☐ N995CK	AMD Falcon 20C	95	ex N950RA		
☐ N998CK	AMD Falcon 20C	98	ex N980R		
☐ N39CK	Learjet 25	25-005	ex XA-SDQ		
☐ N50CK	Learjet 25B	25B-157	ex N57CK		
☐ N71CK	Learjet 36A	36A-035	ex VH-BIB		
☐ N72CK	Learjet 35A	35A-165	ex N16BJ		
☐ N73CK	Learjet 35A	35A-092	ex N39WA		
☐ N75CK	Learjet 25D	25D-256	ex N6LL		
☐ N76CK	Learjet 25	25-020	ex N500JS		
☐ N83CK	Learjet 25B	25B-183	ex N5LL		
☐ N130CK	Learjet 25	25-038	ex N813JW		
☐ N150CK	Learjet 25D	25D-150	ex N251JA		
☐ N222B	Learjet 25	25-047			
☐ N248CK	Learjet 25D	25D-248	ex (N248LJ)		
☐ N536KN	Learjet 35A	35A-073	ex N610GA		
☐ N588CG	Learjet 24D	24D-304	ex N500CG		
☐ N818CK	Learjet 25B	25B-118	ex N118MB		
☐ N905CK	Learjet 36	36-005	ex N9108Z		
☐ N913CK	Learjet 35	35-013	ex N535TA		

All freighters. A sister company of Kalitta Charters II

KAMAKA AIR — *Honolulu-Intl, HI (HNL)*

Reg	Type	c/n	Previous
☐ N231H	Beech E-18S	BA-281	ex N23Y
☐ N933T	Beech Super H-18	BA-665	
☐ N9796N	Douglas C-117D	43375	ex C-FLED

KATMAI AIR — *King Salmon, AK / Anchorage-Lake Hood SPB, AK (AKN/LHD)*

Reg	Type	c/n	Previous	Remarks
☐ N31TN	Beech B99	U-49	ex N98RZ	
☐ N491K	de Havilland DHC-3 Otter	434	ex N49KA	Floatplane
☐ N492K	Piper PA-31-350 Chieftain	31-8052176	ex C-GAWL	
☐ N495K	Cessna U206F Stationair II	U20602549	ex N1274V	Floatplane
☐ N496K	Cessna U206G Stationair	U20603953	ex N756BE	Floatplane
☐ N498K	Cessna T207A Stationair 8	20700624	ex N73762	Floatplane
☐ N499K	Cessna T207A Stationair 8	20700632	ex N73835	Floatplane
☐ N9644G	Cessna U206F Stationair	U20601844		Floatplane

KENMORE AIR — *Kenmore (M5/KEN)* — *Kenmore SPB, WA (KEH)*

Reg	Type	c/n	Previous	Notes	Remarks
☐ N74KA	Cessna 208B Caravan I	208B0770	ex N36SJ		Floatplane
☐ N426KM	Cessna 208 Caravan I	20800306	ex N12656		Floatplane
☐ N518KM	Cessna 208 Caravan I	20800279	ex C-FWCS		Floatplane
☐ N694MA	Cessna 208B Caravan I	208B0694			Floatplane
☐ N41F	de Havilland DHC-2 Beaver	1352	ex 58-2022		Floatplane
☐ N900KA	de Havilland DHC-2 Beaver	1676	ex LN-BFH	Maggie Evening Magazine	Floatplane
☐ N1018F	de Havilland DHC-2 Beaver	710	ex N62SJ		Floatplane
☐ N1455T	de Havilland DHC-2 Turbo Beaver III	1647/TB26	ex CF-OEI		Floatplane
☐ N6781L	de Havilland DHC-2 Beaver	788	ex N10LU		Floatplane
☐ N9744T	de Havilland DHC-2 Turbo Beaver III	1692/TB60	ex N1944		Floatplane
☐ N9766Z	de Havilland DHC-2 Beaver	504	ex N13454		Floatplane
☐ N17598	de Havilland DHC-2 Beaver	1129	ex VP-FAH		Floatplane
☐ N57576	de Havilland DHC-2 Beaver	1168	ex C-GNPQ		Floatplane
☐ N72355	de Havilland DHC-2 Beaver	1164	ex N62355		Floatplane
☐ N50KA	de Havilland DHC-3 Turbo Otter	221	ex C-GLMT	K5 Evening c/s	Floatplane
☐ N58JH	de Havilland DHC-3 Turbo Otter	131	ex N8510Q		Floatplane
☐ N87KA	de Havilland DHC-3 Turbo Otter	11	ex N8262V		Floatplane
☐ N606KA	de Havilland DHC-3 Turbo Otter	37	ex N8260L		Floatplane
☐ N707KA	de Havilland DHC-3 Turbo Otter	106	ex N888KA		Floatplane
☐ N3125S	de Havilland DHC-3 Turbo Otter Floatplane	407	ex RCAF 9424		Seattle Hospital c/s
☐ N90422	de Havilland DHC-3 Turbo Otter	152	ex 55-3296	Expedia.com titles	Floatplane

KEY LIME AIR — *Key Lime (LYM)* — *Denver-International, CO (DEN)*

Reg	Type	c/n	Previous
☐ N313RA	Piper PA-31-350 Chieftain	31-8052069	ex N333BM
☐ N411BJ	Piper PA-31-350 Chieftain	31-7952043	ex C-GPQR
☐ N3549X	Piper PA-31-350 Chieftain	31-8052034	ex C-FAWT
☐ N9247L	Piper PA-31-350 Chieftain	31-8152160	ex G-BWAS
☐ N27989	Piper PA-31-350 Chieftain	31-7952077	
☐ N66906	Piper PA-31-350 Navajo Chieftain	31-7405197	
☐ N74952	Piper PA-31-350 Navajo Chieftain	31-7305100	
☐ N184SW	Swearingen SA.227AC Metro III	AC-647	ex CX-TAA
☐ N340AE	Swearingen SA.227AC Metro III	AC-510	ex N3108E
☐ N425MA	Swearingen SA.227AC Metro III	AC-640	
☐ N508FA	Swearingen SA.227AC Metro III	AC-508	ex ZK-NSW
☐ N542FA	Swearingen SA.227AC Metro III	AC-542	ex ZK-NSX
☐ N765FA	Swearingen SA.227AC Metro III	AC-765	ex ZK-NSI

☐ N769KL	Swearingen SA.227AC Metro III	AC-769B	ex HZ-SN10	
☐ N779BC	Swearingen SA.227AC Metro III	BC-779B	ex XA-RXW	
☐ N787KL	Swearingen SA.227BC Metro III	BC-787B	ex XA-SAQ	
☐ N882DC	Swearingen SA.227DC Metro 23	DC-882B	ex C-GAFQ	
☐ N2691W	Swearingen SA.227AC Metro III	AC-655B		
☐ N2728G	Swearingen SA.227AC Metro III	AC-731		

☐ N27BJ	Learjet 24B	24B-227	ex N28AT	
☐ N62Z	Swearingen SA.226TC Metro II	TC-237	ex N5437M	
☐ N404MG	Cessna 404 Titan	404-0813	ex 3X-GCF	
☐ N509SS	Swearingen SA.226TC Metro II	TC-206	ex N261S	
☐ N770S	Swearingen SA.226TC Metro II	TC-248		
☐ N37127	Cessna 404 Titan	404-0114		
☐ N81418	Swearingen SA.226TC Metro II	TC-223	ex EC-GNM	

KING AIRELINES — *Las Vegas-Henderson Executive, NV (HSH)*

☐ N8564Q	Cessna U206F Stationair	U20603420		
☐ N1570U	Cessna 207 Skywagon	20700170	ex N67TA	
☐ N3156X	Cessna T207 Turbo Skywagon	20700376		
☐ N3728B	Cessna T207 Turbo Skywagon	20700298	ex JA3728	
☐ N70437	Cessna 207A Stationair 7	20700552		
☐ N73320	Cessna T207A Stationair 7	20700577		

☐ N57SA	Cessna 402A	402A0101	ex N7801Q	
☐ N69PB	Cessna 402B II	402B1248		
☐ N82TA	Cessna 402	402-0156	ex N402DK	
☐ N402SW	Cessna 402	402-0036	ex N8236Q	
☐ N2966Q	Cessna 402B	402B0321	ex RP-C1998	
☐ N5098G	Cessna 402A	402A0056	ex C-FPDH	
☐ N9901F	Cessna 402B	402B0402	ex C-GXHC	

KING FLYING SERVICE — *Naknek, AK (NNK)*

☐ N38186	Piper PA-32-300 Cherokee Six	32-7740077		
☐ N44851	Piper PA-32-300 Cherokee Six	32-7740107		

KITTY HAWK AIRCARGO — *Air Kittyhawk (KR/KHA)* — *Fort Wayne-International, IN (FWA)*

☐ N90AX	Boeing 727-222F (FedEx 3)	20040/729	ex N7646U	stored ROW
☐ N855AA	Boeing 727-223F (FedEx 3)	20996/1193		stored ROW
☐ N858AA	Boeing 727-223F (FedEx 3)	21085/1200		stored ROW
☐ N6808	Boeing 727-223F (FedEx 3)	19483/558	ex (N744CK)	stored ROW
☐ N6809	Boeing 727-223F (FedEx 3)	19484/560		stored ROW
☐ N6827	Boeing 727-223F (FedEx 3)	20180/698		stored ROW
☐ N6831	Boeing 727-223F (FedEx 3)	20184/707		stored ROW
☐ N6833	Boeing 727-223F (FedEx 3)	20186/721		stored ROW
☐ N69740	Boeing 727-224F (FedEx 3)	20668/1154		stored ROW
☐ N77780	Boeing 727-232F (FedEx 3)	20635/918	ex N13780	store

Filed Chapter 11 bankruptcy protection 15Oct07, operations continued for a short period but then they terminated scheduled operations and returned some of the fleet to lessors. Plans to continue to fly cargo charters but current status uncertain.

KOLOB CANYONS AIR SERVICES — *Cedar City, UT (CDC)*

☐ N2BZ	Aero Commander 500S Shrike	3227	ex N57150	
☐ N57RS	Rockwell 690A Turbo Commander	11149	ex N5KW	
☐ N66GW	Rockwell 690A Turbo Commander	11174	ex N6B	
☐ N90AT	Rockwell 690A Turbo Commander	11272	ex N888PB	
☐ N98PJ	Rockwell 690A Turbo Commander	11320	ex N220HC	
☐ N900DT	Aero Commander 500S Shrike	3056	ex N9008N	

☐ N481UE	British Aerospace Jetstream 32	895	ex G-31-895	
☐ N894KA	British Aerospace Jetstream 32	894	ex N480UE	Cargo conversion

K2 AVIATION — *Talkeetna, AK (TKA)*

☐ N121KT	de Havilland DHC-2 Beaver	1407	ex N692F	Wheels or skis
☐ N122KT	Piper PA-32-300 Cherokee Six	32-7940190	ex N2898W	
☐ N125KT	Cessna A185F Skywagon II	18503494	ex N1855Q	Wheels or skis
☐ N323KT	de Havilland DHC-2 Beaver	1022	ex N10RM	Wheels or skis
☐ N727KT	de Havilland DHC-3 Turbo Otter	419	ex N427PM	Wheels or skis
☐ N828KT	Piper PA-32-350 Chieftain	31-8052098	ex SE-KDB	
☐ M929KT	de Havilland DHC-3 Turbo Otter	461	ex N271PA	Wheels or skis
☐ N1292F	Cessna A185F Skywagon	18502668	ex N3263C	Wheels or skis

LAB FLYING SERVICE — *LAB (JF/LAB)* — *Juneau-Intl, AK/Haines-Municipal, AK (JNU/HNS)*

☐ N54KA	Piper PA-32-300 Cherokee Six	32-7840197		
☐ N666EB	Piper PA-32-300 Six	32-7940115	ex N2116G	
☐ N2181Z	Piper PA-32-300 Six	32-7940104		
☐ N2897X	Piper PA-32-300 Six	32-7940187		
☐ N2930Q	Piper PA-32R-300 Lance	32R-7780269		

☐ N3957X	Piper PA-32-300 Cherokee Six	32-7640003		
☐ N4485X	Piper PA-32-300 Cherokee Six	32-7640026		
☐ N5686V	Piper PA-32R-300 Lance	32R-7780361		
☐ N6117J	Piper PA-32-300 Cherokee Six	32-7640095		
☐ N6968J	Piper PA-32R-300 Lance	32R-7680397		
☐ N7718C	Piper PA-32-300 Cherokee Six	32-7640049		
☐ N8127Q	Piper PA-32-300 Six	32-7940269		
☐ N8493C	Piper PA-32R-300 Lance	32R-7680118		
☐ N9795C	Piper PA-32-300 Cherokee Six	32-7840118		
☐ N39636	Piper PA-32-300 Cherokee Six	32-7840172		
☐ N3523Y	Piper PA-31-350 Chieftain	31-7952115		
☐ N3835Z	Britten-Norman BN-2A-26 Islander	2010	ex G-BEJW	
☐ N6314V	Helio H-295 Courier II	2534		
☐ N7333L	Piper PA-34-200T Seneca II	34-7670099		
☐ N27513	Piper PA-31-350 Chieftain	31-7852033		
☐ N29884	Britten-Norman BN-2A-26 Islander	847	ex G-HMCG	
☐ N54732	Piper PA-31-350 Navajo Chieftain	31-7405254		

LAKE & PENINSULA AIRLINES — *Port Alsworth, AK (PTA)*

☐ N756BW	Cessna U206G Stationair	U20603969		Floatplane/Wheels or skis
☐ N9530F	Cessna 208 Caravan I	20800088		
☐ N9602F	Cessna 208 Caravan I	20800103		
☐ N9909Z	Cessna U206G Stationair 6	U20606740		Floatplane/Wheels or skis

LAKE CLARK AIR — *Port Alsworth, AK (PTA)*

☐ N76RA	Piper PA-31-350 Navajo Chieftain	31-7752089	ex N27212	
☐ N200VF	Piper PA-31-350 Navajo Chieftain	31-7405445	ex N61402	
☐ N733KD	Cessna U206G Stationair 6 II	U20604772		Floatplane
☐ N991AK	Beech 99	U-28	ex N33TN	
☐ N8300Q	Cessna U206F Stationair II	U20603161		Floatplane
☐ N27231	Piper PA-31-350 Navajo Chieftain	31-7752106		
☐ N70076	Cessna 207A Stationair 7 II	20700547		
☐ N91028	Cessna 207 Skywagon	20700019		

LAS VEGAS HELICOPTERS — *Las Vegas NV (LAS)*

☐ N700LV	Aérospatiale AS350D	1289	ex N91GT	
☐ N701LV	Aérospatiale AS350BA	1546	ex N73MH	
☐ N702LV	Eurocopter EC130B4	3845	ex N325MP	
☐ N703LV	Aérospatiale AS350BA	2896	ex XA-AUR	
☐ N705LV	Aérospatiale AS350BA	1878		
☐ N707LV	Eurocopter EC130B4	4388	ex N578AM	

LINDSAY AVIATION — *Lindsay Air (LSY)* — *Buffalo-Intl, NY (BUF)*

☐ N85DS	Cessna 310Q	310Q0080	ex N7580Q	
☐ N3376G	Cessna 310R II	310R0818		
☐ N8669G	Cessna 310R II	310R0948		

LOGISTIC AIR — *Reno, NV (RNO)*

☐ N303TW	Boeing 747-257B	20116/112	ex LV-YSB	stored MZJ
☐ N741LA	Boeing 747-246B	19824/122	ex TF-ATB	stored MZJ
☐ 5U-ACE	Boeing 747-230B	20527/179	ex N745LA	stored ROW
☐ 5U-ACF	Boeing 747-146B	23150/601	ex (CP-2480)	
☐ 5U-ACG	Boeing 747-146B	22067/427	ex N553SW	
☐ N735LA	Boeing 737-268	20574/294	ex HZ-AGA	stored RKT
☐ N2409N	Boeing 737-242C (AvAero 3)	20496/268	ex C-FNAP	stored QUE
☐ N24089	Boeing 737-242C (AvAero 3)	20455/254	ex C-FNAQ	stored MZJ

LYNDEN AIR CARGO — *Lynden (L2/LYC)* — *Anchorage-Intl, AK (ANC)*

☐ N401LC	Lockheed L-382G-31C Hercules	4606	ex ZS-RSJ	
☐ N402LC	Lockheed L-382G-35C Hercules	4698	ex ZS-JJA	
☐ N403LC	Lockheed L-382G-31C Hercules	4590	ex N903SJ	
☐ N404LC	Lockheed L-382G-38C Hercules	4763	ex N909SJ	
☐ N405LC	Lockheed L-382G-69C Hercules	5025	ex ZS-OLG	
☐ N406LC	Lockheed L-382G-35C Hercules	4676	ex ZS-JVL	

LYNX AIR INTERNATIONAL — *Lynx Flight (LXF)* — *Fort Lauderdale-Executive, FL (FXE)*

☐ N60NE	Swearingen SA.227AC Metro III	AC-760B	ex N307NE	
☐ N61NE	Swearingen SA.227AC Metro III	AC-761B		
☐ N158SD	SAAB SF.340A	340A-158	ex N158CQ	stored FLL

LYNX AVIATION	(SHA)	Denver, CO (DEN)

Operates de Havilland DHC-8-402Qs on behalf of Frontier Airlines, of which it is a wholly owned subsidiary.

M & N AVIATION	(W4)	San Juan-Munoz Marin Intl, PR (SJU)

☐ N409MN	Cessna 208B Caravan I	208B0846	ex N51666
☐ N410MN	Beech 1900C	UC-167	ex N167GL
☐ N787RA	Cessna 208B Caravan I	208B1019	ex N52144
☐ N1131G	Cessna 208B Caravan I	208B0661	
☐ N1241X	Cessna 208B Caravan I	208B0657	ex N52601

MARTINAIRE	Martex (MRA)	Dallas-Addison, TX (ADS)

☐ N78SA	Cessna 208B Caravan I	208B0467	ex N5058J
☐ N162SA	Cessna 208B Caravan I	208B0548	ex N1219N
☐ N854BF	Cessna 208B Caravan I	208B0854	
☐ N1031P	Cessna 208B Caravan I	208B0404	
☐ N1037N	Cessna 208B Caravan I	208B0334	ex (C-GWFN)
☐ N1116W	Cessna 208B Caravan I	208B0411	
☐ N1119V	Cessna 208B Caravan I	208B0383	
☐ N1120N	Cessna 208B Caravan I	208B0386	
☐ N1120W	Cessna 208B Caravan I	208B0388	
☐ N1324G	Cessna 208B Caravan I	208B0777	ex N5262Z
☐ N4591B	Cessna 208B Caravan I	208B0137	ex (N997FE)
☐ N4602B	Cessna 208B Caravan I	208B0140	ex (N999FE)
☐ N4625B	Cessna 208B Caravan I	208B0159	
☐ N4655B	Cessna 208B Caravan I	208B0160	
☐ N4662B	Cessna 208B Caravan I	208B0161	
☐ N4687B	Cessna 208B Caravan I	208B0167	
☐ N4698B	Cessna 208B Caravan I	208B0175	
☐ N7580B	Cessna 208B Caravan I	208B0051	ex (N951FE)
☐ N9331B	Cessna 208B Caravan I	208B0055	ex (N995FE)
☐ N9471B	Cessna 208B Caravan I	208B0081	
☐ N9505B	Cessna 208B Caravan I	208B0085	
☐ N9525B	Cessna 208B Caravan I	208B0087	
☐ N9546B	Cessna 208B Caravan I	208B0126	
☐ N9594B	Cessna 208B Caravan I	208B0131	
☐ N9623B	Cessna 208B Caravan I	208B0138	
☐ N9634B	Cessna 208B Caravan I	208B0141	
☐ N9714B	Cessna 208B Caravan I	208B0153	
☐ N9738B	Cessna 208B Caravan I	208B0097	
☐ N9760B	Cessna 208B Caravan I	208B0102	
☐ N9761B	Cessna 208B Caravan I	208B0107	
☐ N9762B	Cessna 208B Caravan I	208B0109	
☐ N9766B	Cessna 208B Caravan I	208B0112	
☐ N9829B	Cessna 208B Caravan I	208B0116	
☐ N9956B	Cessna 208B Caravan I	208B0119	
☐ N354AE	Swearingen SA.227AC Metro III	AC-633	ex N3113C
☐ N370AE	Swearingen SA.227AC Metro III	AC-506	ex N87FM
☐ N592BA	Swearingen SA.227AC Metro III	AC-592	ex N384PH
☐ N26932	Swearingen SA.227AC Metro III	AC-660	ex (N660AV)

MAVERICK HELICOPTERS	Las Vegas-McCarran Intl / Grand Canyon-National Park (LAS/GCN)

☐ N801MH	Eurocopter EC130B4	3654
☐ N802MH	Eurocopter EC130B4	3707
☐ N803MH	Eurocopter EC130B4	3735
☐ N804MH	Eurocopter EC130B4	3750
☐ N805MH	Eurocopter EC130B4	3799
☐ N806MH	Eurocopter EC130B4	3833
☐ N807MH	Eurocopter EC130B4	3912
☐ N808MH	Eurocopter EC130B4	3914
☐ N809MH	Eurocopter EC130B4	3927
☐ N810MH	Eurocopter EC130B4	3949
☐ N812MH	Eurocopter EC130B4	3956
☐ N813MH	Eurocopter EC130B4	3967
☐ N814MH	Eurocopter EC130B4	4020
☐ N815MH	Eurocopter EC130B4	4022
☐ N816MH	Eurocopter EC130B4	4038
☐ N817MH	Eurocopter EC130B4	4125
☐ N818MH	Eurocopter EC130B4	4131
☐ N821MH	Eurocopter EC130B4	4134
☐ N822MH	Eurocopter EC130B4	4142
☐ N823MH	Eurocopter EC130B4	4158
☐ N824MH	Eurocopter EC130B4	4173
☐ N846MH	Eurocopter EC130B4	4248
☐ N847MH	Eurocopter EC130B4	4266
☐ N848MH	Eurocopter EC130B4	4290
☐ N849MH	Eurocopter EC130B4	4313
☐ N850MH	Eurocopter EC130B4	4327

☐ N851MH	Eurocopter EC130B4	4340		
☐ N852MH	Eurocopter EC130B4	4356		
☐ N853MH	Eurocopter EC130B4	4417		
☐ N854MH	Eurocopter EC130B4	4433		
☐ N856MH	Eurocopter EC130B4	4437		
☐ N857MH	Eurocopter EC130B4	4457		
☐ N858MH	Eurocopter EC130B4	4503		
☐ N862MH	Eurocopter EC130B4	4545		
☐ N567MA	Beech 1900D	UE-67	ex N67YV	
☐ N886MA	Beech 1900D	UE-86	ex N86YV	

MCCALL AVIATION — *McCall, ID (MYL)*

☐ N848MA	Britten-Norman BN-2B-20 Islander	2210	ex 8P-TAJ
☐ N7520N	Cessna TU206G Stationair	U20603663	

MCNEELY CHARTER SERVICE — *Mid-South (MDS)* — *West Memphis-Municipal, AR/Malden, MO (AWM/MAW)*

☐ N106GA	Beech Baron 58	TH-437	ex N4379W
☐ N120SC	Swearingen SA.226TC Merlin IVA	AT-067	ex C-FJTL
☐ N212SA	Cessna 208B Caravan I	208B0466	
☐ N262AG	Short SD.3-30	SH3120	ex 84-0473
☐ N700RH	Cessna 208B Caravan I	208B0700	
☐ N866D	Mitsubishi MU-2B-36 (MU-2L)	656	ex N666D
☐ N2699Y	Swearingen SA.227AC Metro III	AC-666	

MESA AIRLINES — *Air Shuttle (YV/ASH)* — *Phoenix-Sky Harbor Intl, AZ/Albuquerque-Intl, NM (PHX/ABQ)*

☐ N126YV	Beech 1900D	UE-126		stored
☐ N133YV	Beech 1900D	UE-133		Lsd to AMW
☐ N135YV	Beech 1900D	UE-135		Lsd to AMW
☐ N138YV	Beech 1900D	UE-138		Lsd to AMW
☐ N139ZV	Beech 1900D	UE-139		Lsd to BSY
☐ N142ZV	Beech 1900D	UE-142		Lsd to AMW
☐ N143YV	Beech 1900D	UE-143		Lsd to AMW
☐ N144ZV	Beech 1900D	UE-144		Lsd to AMW
☐ N146ZV	Beech 1900D	UE-146		Lsd to AMW
☐ N155ZV	Beech 1900D	UE-155		Lsd to AMW
☐ N159YV	Beech 1900D	UE-159		Lsd to AMW
☐ N161YV	Beech 1900D	UE-161		Lsd to AMW
☐ N162ZV	Beech 1900D	UE-162		Lsd to AMW
☐ N163YV	Beech 1900D	UE-163		Lsd to AMW
☐ N165YV	Beech 1900D	UE-165		Lsd to BSY
☐ N166YV	Beech 1900D	UE-166		Lsd to AMW
☐ N167YV	Beech 1900D	UE-167		Lsd to AMW
☐ N171ZV	Beech 1900D	UE-171		Lsd to BSY
☐ N174YV	Beech 1900D	UE-174	ex N17541	stored ABQ
☐ N176YV	Beech 1900D	UE-176		Lsd to AMW
☐ N237YV	Beech 1900D	UE-237		Lsd to BSY
☐ N242YV	Beech 1900D	UE-242		Lsd to AMW
☐ N244YV	Beech 1900D	UE-244		Lsd to AMW
☐ N10675	Beech 1900D	UE-229		Lsd to AMW

MESABA AIRLINES — *Mesaba (XJ/MES)* — *Minneapolis-St Paul Intl, MN (MSP)*

Operates services as part of the Delta Connection network, using flight numbers in the range 3000-3439.

MIAMI AIR INTERNATIONAL — *Biscayne (LL/BSK)* — *Miami-Intl, FL (MIA)*

☐ N732MA	Boeing 737-81Q/W	30618/830	ex G-OXLC	
☐ N733MA	Boeing 737-81Q/W	30619/856	ex G-OXLA	
☐ N734MA	Boeing 737-8Q8/W	30039/701	ex 5W-SAM	Billie
☐ N737KA	Boeing 737-7BX	30740/776	ex VH-VBT	
☐ N738MA	Boeing 737-8Q8/W	32799/1467		Diane
☐ N739MA	Boeing 737-8Q8/W	30670/1481		Ely
☐ N740EH	Boeing 737-8DC/W	34596/1875		
☐ N742MA	Boeing 737-83N/W	30675/898	ex N304TZ	
☐ N752MA	Boeing 737-48E	28198/2806	ex HL7509	
☐ N753MA	Boeing 737-48E	28053/2954	ex HL7518	Miami Heat c/s

MIAMI AIR LEASE — *Miami-Opa Locka, FL (OPF)*

☐ N41527	Convair 440-72	346	ex C-FPUM

MID-ATLANTIC FREIGHT — *(MDC)* — *Greensboro-Piedmont Triad Intl, NC (GSO)*

☐ N1041L	Cessna 208B Caravan I	208B0337	
☐ N4698B	Cessna 208B Caravan I	208B0175	ex XC-AA35
☐ N9525B	Cessna 208B Caravan I	208B0087	

MIDWEST AIRLINES	**Midex (YX/MEP)**	**Appleton-Outagamie County, WI/Milwaukee -General Mitchell Intl, WI (ATW/MKE)**		
☐ N907ME	Boeing 717-2BL	55171/5121		stored VCV
☐ N908ME	Boeing 717-2BL	55172/5122		stored VCV
☐ N912ME	Boeing 717-2BL	55175/5125		stored VCV
☐ N922ME	Boeing 717-2BL	55184/5142		stored VCV
☐ N927ME	Boeing 717-2BL	55193/5153		
☐ N601ME	McDonnell-Douglas MD-88	49762/1624	ex (N159PL)	stored BYH
☐ N701ME	McDonnell-Douglas MD-88	49760/1620	ex (N157PL)	stored BYH
☐ N804ME	McDonnell-Douglas MD-81	48030/962	ex JA8459	stored BYH
☐ N808ME	McDonnell-Douglas MD-82	48070/999	ex JA8468	
☐ N809ME	McDonnell-Douglas MD-82	48071/1004	ex JA8469	stored BYH
☐ N810ME	McDonnell-Douglas MD-82	48072/1011	ex JA8470	stored BYH
☐ N812ME	McDonnell-Douglas MD-81	48006/966	ex OY-KIG	stored BYH
☐ N813ME	McDonnell-Douglas MD-81	48007/971	ex OY-KIH	stored GSP
☐ N814ME	McDonnell-Douglas MD-81	48010/992	ex SE-DMY	stored BYH

MIDWEST AVIATION	**Midwest (MWT)**	**Marshall-Ryan Field, MN (MML)**	
☐ N185MV	Beech 200 Super King Air	BB-1034	ex N185MC
☐ N382JM	Piper PA-32R-301T Saratoga SP	32R-8229026	ex D-EHJE
☐ N727SC	Piper PA-31-350 Navajo Chieftain	31-7305110	ex G-BBZB
☐ N3558X	Piper PA-31-350 Chieftain	31-8052073	
☐ N6894G	Piper PA-60 Aerostar 600	60-0905-8161256	
☐ N43305	Piper PA-32R-301 Saratoga	32R-8413002	

MIDWEST CONNECT	**Skyway-Ex (AL/SYX)**	**Milwaukee-General Mitchell Intl, WI (MKE)**		
☐ N881SK	Beech 1900D	UE-88		Skyway
☐ N403SW	Canadair CL-600-2B19 (CRJ-200ER)	7028	ex C-FMNB	SkyWest
☐ N407SW	Canadair CL-600-2B19 (CRJ-200ER)	7034	ex C-FMNY	SkyWest
☐ N468CA	Canadair CL-600-2B19 (CRJ-200ER)	7649	ex C-FMLI	SkyWest
☐ N471CA	Canadair CL-600-2B19 (CRJ-200ER)	7655	ex C-FMNH	SkyWest
☐ N472CA	Canadair CL-600-2B19 (CRJ-200ER)	7667	ex C-FMML	SkyWest
☐ N479CA	Canadair CL-600-2B19 (CRJ-200ER)	7675	ex C-FMKW	SkyWest
☐ N494CA	Canadair CL-600-2B19 (CRJ-200ER)	7765	ex C-FMKW	SkyWest
☐ N495CA	Canadair CL-600-2B19 (CRJ-200ER)	7774	ex C-FMMT	SkyWest
☐ N496CA	Canadair CL-600-2B19 (CRJ-200ER)	7791	ex C-FMMX	SkyWest
☐ N498CA	Canadair CL-600-2B19 (CRJ-200ER)	7792	ex C-FMMY	SkyWest
☐ N506CA	Canadair CL-600-2B19 (CRJ-200ER)	7793	ex C-FMNB	SkyWest
☐ N507CA	Canadair CL-600-2B19 (CRJ-200ER)	7796	ex C-GZFC	SkyWest
☐ N699BR	Canadair CL-600-2B19 (CRJ-200ER)	7801	ex C-FMLS	SkyWest
☐ N709BR	Canadair CL-600-2B19 (CRJ-200ER)	7850	ex C-FMMW	SkyWest
☐ N983CA	Canadair CL-600-2B19 (CRJ-100ER)	7169	ex C-FMNX	SkyWest
☐ N984CA	Canadair CL-600-2B16 (CRJ-100ER)	7171	ex C-FMML	SkyWest
☐ N986CA	Canadair CL-600-2B19 (CRJ-100ER)	7174	ex C-FMNX	SkyWest
☐ N988CA	Canadair CL-600-2B16 (CRJ-100ER)	7204	ex C-FMMT	SkyWest
☐ N836RP	Embraer EMB.135LR (ERJ 135LR)	145713	ex PT-SCQ	Chautauqua
☐ N810MD	Embraer 170-100SU (170SU)	17000026	ex PT-SKT	Republic
☐ N813MA	Embraer 170-100SU (170SU)	17000031	ex PT-SKZ	Republic
☐ N815MD	Embraer 170-100SU (170SU)	17000034	ex PT-SUD	Republic
☐ N818MD	Embraer 170-100SU (170SU)	17000039	ex PT-SUI	Republic
☐ N821MD	Embraer 170-100SU (170SU)	17000042	ex PT-SUL	Republic
☐ N823MD	Embraer 170-100SU (170SU)	17000044	ex PT-SUO	Republic
☐ N824MD	Embraer 170-100SU (170SU)	17000045	ex PT-SUO	Republic
☐ N826MD	Embraer 170-100SU (170SU)	17000046	ex PT-SUP	Republic
☐ N871RW	Embraer 170-100SU (170SU)	17000140	ex PT-SEE	Republic
☐ N872RW	Embraer 170-100SE (170SU)	17000143	ex PT-SEH	Republic
☐ N873RW	Embraer 170-100SE (170SU)	17000144	ex PT-SEI	Republic
☐ N874RW	Embraer 170-100SE (170SU)	17000148	ex PT-SEM	Republic
☐ N161HL	Embraer 190-100IGW (190AR)	19000154	ex N161HQ	Republic
☐ N162HL	Embraer 190-100IGW (190AR)	19000231	ex N162HQ	Republic
☐ N163HQ	Embraer 190-100IGW (190AR)	19000255	ex PT-STD	Republic
☐ N164HQ	Embraer 190-100IGW (190AR)	19000275	ex PT-TLP	Republic
☐ N165HQ	Embraer 190-100IGW (190AR)	19000291	ex PT-TZF	Republic
☐ N166HQ	Embraer 190-100IGW (190AR)	19000166	ex N959UW	Republic
☐ N167HQ	Embraer 190-100IGW (190AR)	19000173	ex N960UW	Republic
☐ N168HQ	Embraer 190-100IGW (190AR)	19000183	ex N961UW	Republic
☐ N169HQ	Embraer 190-100IGW (190AR)	19000188	ex N962UW	Republic
☐ N170HQ	Embraer 190-100IGW (190AR)	19000191	ex N963UW	Republic
☐ N171HQ	Embraer 190-100IGW (190AR)	19000197	ex N964UW	Republic
☐ N172HQ	Embraer 190-100IGW (190AR)	19000198	ex N965UW	Republic
☐ N173HQ	Embraer 190-100IGW (190AR)	19000206	ex N966UW	Republic
☐ N174HQ	Embraer 190-100IGW (190AR)	19000211	ex N967UW	Republic
☐ N175HQ	Embraer 190-100IGW (190AR)	19000216	ex N968UW	Republic

MIDWEST HELICOPTER AIRWAYS				Hinsdale-Midwest Heliport, IL
☐ N129NH	Sikorsky S-58ET	58555	ex N47781	
☐ N827MW	Sikorsky S-58ET	58827	ex C-GLOG	
☐ N2256Z	Sikorsky S-58JT	58867	ex 57-1707	
☐ N4247V	Sikorsky S-58ET	581547		
☐ N90561	Sikorsky S-58JT	581332	ex Bu148777	

MINDEN AIR					Minden, NV (MEV)
☐ N446MA	British Aerospace 146 Srs.200	E2111	ex C-FBAO		Tanker
☐ N355MA	Lockheed P2V-7 Neptune (P-2H)	726-7229	ex 148344	55	Tanker - red colours
☐ N4692A	Lockheed P2V-7 Neptune (P-2H)	726-7247	ex 148357	48	Tanker - yellow colours

MOKULELE AIRLINES				Kailua/Kona-Keahole-Kona Intl, HI (KOA)
☐ N861MA	Cessna 208B Caravan I	208B0825	ex N98RR	
☐ N862MA	Cessna 208B Caravan I	208B1138	ex N115KW	
☐ N863MA	Cessna 208B Caravan I	208B1049	ex N208LR	
☐ N864MA	Cessna 208B Caravan I	208B1275	ex N4115J	

MOUNTAIN AIR CARGO		Mountain (MTN)		Kinston-Regional Jetport, NC (ISO)
☐ N2679U	Short SD.3-30	SH3071	ex (N330AE)	
☐ N26288	Short SD.3-30	SH3074	ex G-BIYF	

MOUNTAIN WEST HELICOPTERS				Provo-Municipal, UT (PVU)
☐ N317KA	Kaman K-1200 K-Max	A94-0025		

MURRAY AIR		Murray Air (5M/MUA)		Detroit-Willow Run, MI (YIP)
☐ N290MA	British Aerospace Jetstream 32EP	800	ex N370MT	
☐ N339TE	British Aerospace Jetstream 32	935	ex G-31-935	
☐ N343TE	British Aerospace Jetstream 32	955	ex G-31-955	
☐ N695MA	British Aerospace Jetstream 31	695	ex N169PC	
☐ N743PE	British Aerospace Jetstream 31	755	ex N755SP	
☐ N155CA	Douglas DC-8-73CF	46073/485	ex N803UP	
☐ N865F	Douglas DC-8-63F (BAC 3)	46088/464	ex TF-FLC	
☐ N872SJ	Douglas DC-8-71F	46040/449	ex HK-4294	
☐ N921R	Douglas DC-8-63F (BAC 3)	46145/548	ex N806WA	

NATIVE AMERICAN AIR SERVICES				Phoenix-Williams Gateway, AZ (CHD)
☐ N617LH	Aérospatiale AS350B2 AStar	2140		EMS
☐ N827NA	Aérospatiale AS350B3 AStar	3144		EMS
☐ N3819	Aérospatiale AS350B3 AStar	3877		EMS
☐ N41299	Aérospatiale AS350B3 AStar	3806		EMS
☐ N44925	Aérospatiale AS350B3 AStar	3838		EMS
☐ N317NA	Pilatus PC-12/45	223	ex N223PD	Air Ambulance
☐ N562NA	Pilatus PC-12/45	174	ex N174PC	Air Ambulance
☐ N613NA	Pilatus PC-12/45	197	ex N197PC	Air Ambulance
☐ N970NA	Pilatus PC-12/45	226	ex N308NA	Air Ambulance

NAVAIR				Minneapolis-Flying Cloud, MN (FCM)
☐ N16U	Beech E-18S	BA-394	ex N5660D	Freighter

NEPTUNE AVIATION SERVICES					Missoula-Intl, MT (MSO)
☐ N122HP	Lockheed P2V-7 Neptune	726-7226	ex Bu148341		
☐ N128HP	Lockheed P2V-7 Neptune	726-7074	ex Bu140972		
☐ N443NA	Lockheed P2V-7 Neptune	726-7168	ex N139HP		
☐ N445NA	Lockheed P2V-7 Neptune	726-7102	ex N140HP		
☐ N807NA	Lockheed P2V-5 Neptune	426-5305	ex N1386K	07	
☐ N1386C	Lockheed P2V-5 Neptune	426-5268	ex Bu128422	44	
☐ N4235N	Lockheed SP-2H Neptune	726-7158	ex Bu144681	10	
☐ N2216S	Lockheed P2V-7 Neptune	726-7231	ex Bu148346		
☐ N2218E	Lockheed P2V-7 Neptune	726-7246	ex Bu148356		
☐ N2218Q	Lockheed P2V-7 Neptune	726-7255	ex Bu148359		
☐ N9855F	Lockheed P2V-5 Neptune	426-5326	ex Bu131445	06	
☐ N14447	Lockheed P2V-7 Neptune	826-8010	ex RCAF 24110		11
☐ N96264	Lockheed P2V-5 Neptune	426-5192	ex Bu128346	12	
☐ N96278	Lockheed P2V-5 Neptune	426-5340	ex Bu131459	05	

NEW ENGLAND AIRLINES		New England (EJ/NEA)		Westerly-State, RI (WST)
☐ N123NE	Britten-Norman BN-2A-26 Islander	46	ex G-BJSA	
☐ N404WB	Britten-Norman BN-2A-26 Islander	564	ex N304SK	
☐ N345CS	Piper PA-32-300 Cherokee Six	32-7640043	ex N345ES	
☐ N406WB	Piper PA-32-300 Cherokee Six	32-7640058	ex N8303C	

☐ N408WB	Piper PA-32-300 Cherokee Six	32-7240092	ex N4885T	
☐ N598JA	Britten-Norman BN-2A Islander	66		

NEW MEXICO AIRLINES

☐ N306PW	Cessna 208B Caravan I	208B1240	ex N208TD	

NORD AVIATION — Santa Teresa-Dona Ana County, NM (EPZ)

☐ N321L	Douglas C-117D	43345	ex N307SF	Freighter
☐ N620NA	Douglas DC-6A	44677/527	ex N32RU	freighter
☐ N738WB	Beech D50C Twin Bonanza	DH-286		Freighter
☐ N57626	Douglas DC-3	4564	ex NC57626	Freighter

NORTH AMERICAN AIRLINES — North American (NA/NAO) — New York-JFK Intl, NY (JFK)

☐ N750NA	Boeing 757-28A	26277/658		Deidre Stiehm
☐ N752NA	Boeing 757-28A	28174/865	ex N1795B	Alisa Ferrara
☐ N754NA	Boeing 757-28A	29381/958		
☐ N755NA	Boeing 757-28A	30043/925	ex N523NA	John Plueger
☐ N756NA	Boeing 757-28A	32448/967		Claudette Abrahams
☐ N760NA	Boeing 767-39HER	26257/488	ex N164LF	Tom Cygan
☐ N764NA	Boeing 767-328ER	27135/493	ex N135EL	
☐ N765NA	Boeing 767-306ER	28098/607	ex PH-BZE	
☐ N767NA	Boeing 767-324ER	27569/601	ex N569NB	Janice M
☐ N768NA	Boeing 767-36NER	29898/754	ex N898GE	Lisa Caroline

NORTH STAR AIR CARGO — Sky Box (SBX) — Milwaukee-General Mitchell Intl, WI (MKE)

☐ N50NS	Short SC.7 Skyvan	SH1856	ex N50GA	Freighter
☐ N51NS	Short SC.7 Skyvan	SH1843	ex N20DA	Freighter
☐ N101WA	Short SC.7 Skyvan 3	SH1859	ex (PH-DAF)	Freighter
☐ N731E	Short SC.7 Skyvan	SH1853	ex N80JJ	Freighter

NORTH STAR AVIATION — Boca Raton, FL (BCT)

☐ N153KM	British Aerospace Jetstream 4101	41053	ex ZK-JSN
☐ N308UE	British Aerospace Jetstream 4101	41023	ex G-4-023
☐ N679AS	British Aerospace Jetstream 4101	41056	ex N156KM
☐ N680AS	British Aerospace Jetstream 4101	41030	ex N410JA

NORTHERN AIR CARGO — Yukon (NC/NAC) — Anchorage-Intl, AK (ANC)

☐ N779TA	Douglas DC-6A	45529/1035	ex PP-LFC	stored FAI
☐ N2907F	Douglas C-118A	44636/574	ex 53-3265	stored FAI
☐ N43872	Douglas C-118A	44665/632	ex 53-3294	stored ANC
☐ N320DL	Boeing 737-232F (Nordam 3)	23092/1023		Lsd fr JetGlobal
☐ N321DL	Boeing 737-232F (Nordam 3)	23093/1024		Lsd fr JetGlobal
☐ N322DL	Boeing 737-232F (Nordam 3)	23094/1026		Lsd fr JetGlobal

NORTHWEST AIRLINES – NWA — Northwest (NW/NWA)

Fleet merged with Delta Airlines

NORTHWEST AIRLINK – NWA AIRLINK — Northwest (NW)

Fleet now shown under Delta Connection

NORTHWEST HELICOPTERS — Olympia, WA (OLM)

☐ N64NH	Bell UH-1H	4379	ex 64-13672
☐ N65NH	Bell UH-1H	5078	ex 65-10034
☐ N66NH	Bell UH-1H	5624	ex 66-1141
☐ N67NH	Bell UH-1H	9486	ex 67-17282
☐ N71NH	Bell UH-1H	11682	ex 69-16267
☐ N78NW	Bell UH-1H	9266	ex N342WN
☐ N79NW	Bell UH-1H	4417	ex 64-13710
☐ N111DR	Bell UH-1H	4406	ex N83NW
☐ N114DR	Bell UH-1H	5275	ex N85NW
☐ N117DR	Bell UH-1H	5204	ex N95NW
☐ N166DR	Bell UH-1H	9143	ex N86NW
☐ N175SF	Bell EH-1H	12290	ex 69-16713
☐ N176SF	Bell EH-1H	11757	ex 69-15469
☐ N313B	Bell UH-1H	4057	ex 63-08765
☐ N602WA	Bell UH-1H	4746	ex 65-9702
☐ N5517N	Bell UH-1H	9589	ex 67-17391
☐ N6165X	Bell UH-1K	6307	ex 157183
☐ N7515S	Bell UH-1H		ex 69-15328
☐ N7515Z	Bell UH-1H		ex 70-16336

☐ N8833D	Bell UH-1H	9021	ex 66-16827

NORTHWEST SEAPLANES — Mariner (2G/MRR) — Seattle-Lake Union, WA/Seattle-Renton (LKS/RNT)

☐ N90YC	de Havilland DHC-2 Beaver	1338	ex N127WA	Floatplane
☐ N67681	de Havilland DHC-2 Beaver	1158	ex N215LU	Floatplane
☐ N67684	de Havilland DHC-2 Beaver	1208	ex N67894	Floatplane
☐ N67685	de Havilland DHC-2 Beaver	1250	ex N128WA	Floatplane
☐ N67689	de Havilland DHC-2 Beaver	1242	ex N67675	Floatplane

OMNI AIR INTERNATIONAL — Omni (OY/OAE) — Tulsa-Intl, OK (TUL)

☐ N549AX	Boeing 757-23A	24528/250	ex XU-123	
☐ N558AX	Boeing 757-23N	27971/690	ex N514AT	
☐ N639AX	Boeing 757-28A	24368/213	ex N368CG	
☐ N342AX	Boeing 767-328ER	27136/497	ex N225LF	
☐ N351AX	Boeing 767-33AER	27908/578	ex I-DEIF	
☐ N378AX	Boeing 767-33AER	28147/622	ex I-DEIL	
☐ N108AX	Douglas MD-10-30	47927/190	ex N49082	
☐ N270AX	Douglas DC-10-30	48318/446	ex N353WL	
☐ N522AX	Douglas DC-10-30ER	48315/436	ex N243NW	
☐ N531AX	Douglas DC-10-30ERF	48316/437	ex N244NW	
☐ N540AX	Douglas DC-10-30	46595/299	ex D-ADPO	stored VCV
☐ N603AX	Douglas DC-10-30	48267/434	ex N238NW	
☐ N612AX	Douglas DC-10-30ER	48290/435	ex N239NW	
☐ N621AX	Douglas DC-10-30ER	48319/438	ex N240NW	
☐ N630AX	Douglas DC-10-30	46596/301	ex D-ADQO	stored VCV
☐ N720AX	Douglas DC-10-30	48252/342	ex D-ADSO	
☐ N810AX	Douglas DC-10-30ER	48265/345	ex F-GPVC	
☐ N59083	Douglas DC-10-30	47926/170	ex OO-SLG	stored VCV

OMNIFLIGHT HELICOPTERS — Dallas-Addison, TX (ADS)

☐ N93CH	Bell 206L-3 LongRanger III	51314		
☐ N94CH	Bell 206L-4 LongRanger IV	52070		
☐ N95CH	Bell 206L-4 LongRanger IV	52195		
☐ N154MW	Bell 206L-4 LongRanger IV	52154	ex PT-YBQ	
☐ N206AZ	Bell 206L-3 LongRanger III	51007	ex N725RE	
☐ N206MH	Bell 206L-1 LongRanger III	45426	ex N518EH	EMS
☐ N224LF	Bell 206L-1 LongRanger II	45199	ex N5013Y	EMS
☐ N314LS	Bell 206L-3 LongRanger III	51006	ex N2210H	EMS
☐ N112LL	MBB BK-117A-3	7038	ex N4493X	
☐ N113LL	MBB BK-117B-1	7013	ex N117LF	
☐ N117AP	MBB BK-117B-1	7144	ex N311LS	
☐ N117M	MBB BK-117A-3	7023	ex N39251	EMS
☐ N117MH	MBB BK-117A-3	7112	ex N627MB	EMS
☐ N117MK	MBB BK-117B-2	7196	ex N117BK	EMS
☐ N117NG	MBB BK-117A-4	7083	ex N312LF	EMS
☐ N117UC	MBB BK-117B-1	7206	ex N214AE	EMS
☐ N117VU	MBB BK-117B-1	7211	ex N8194S	
☐ N118LL	MBB BK-117A-3	7097	ex N117SJ	
☐ N170MC	MBB BK-117B-1	7217	ex N7161S	
☐ N171MU	MBB BK-117A-4	7138	ex N313LF	
☐ N217MC	MBB BK-117B-1	7195	ex N54113	EMS Op for Mayo Foundation
☐ N317MC	MBB BK-117C-1	7505	ex N117AE	EMS Op for Mayo Foundation
☐ N460H	MBB BK-117B-1	7142	ex N90266	EMS
☐ N504LH	MBB BK-117A-3	7061	ex N312LS	
☐ N527MB	MBB BK-117A-3	7103	ex D-HBPX	
☐ N711FC	MBB BK-117A-4	7070	ex N311LF	EMS
☐ N911MZ	MBB BK-117A-3	7098	ex N117UC	
☐ N1140H	MBB BK-117A-3	7078	ex N212AE	
☐ N75LV	Beech B200 Super King Air	BB-1075	ex C-GTDY	EMS
☐ N222HX	Bell 222UT	47533	ex N3201W	
☐ N277LF	Bell 222UT	47520	ex N911LW	EMS
☐ N350AZ	Aérospatiale AS350B2 AStar	3127	ex N4073A	
☐ N350GR	Aérospatiale AS350B AStar	3140	ex N911GF	EMS
☐ N40751	Aérospatiale AS350B2 AStar	3154		

PACE AIRLINES — Pace (Y5/PCE) — Winston-Salem/Smith Reynolds, NC (INT)

☐ N373PA	Boeing 737-3Y0	23749/1389	ex N749AP	The Steffie Pacemaker
☐ N583CC	Boeing 737-291 (Nordam 3)	21069/415	ex N15255	
☐ N737DX	Boeing 737-408	24804/1851	ex TF-FIC	
☐ N801DM	Boeing 757-256	26240/561	ex N286CD	Op for Dallas Mavericks

PACIFIC AIRWAYS (3F) Ketchikan-Harbor SPB, AK (WFB)

	Registration	Type	C/n	Previous identity	Notes
☐	N12UA	de Havilland DHC-2 Beaver	700	ex C-GSIN	Floatplane
☐	N96DG	de Havilland DHC-2 Beaver	702	ex N99132	Floatplane
☐	N264P	de Havilland DHC-2 Beaver	464	ex N23RF	Floatplane
☐	N5595M	de Havilland DHC-2 Beaver	1571	ex 105	Floatplane
☐	N9290Z	de Havilland DHC-2 Beaver	1387	ex 58-2055	Floatplane
☐	N9294Z	de Havilland DHC-2 Beaver	1379	ex 58-2047	Floatplane

PACIFIC HELICOPTERS Kahului-International, HI (OGG)

	Registration	Type	C/n	Previous identity
☐	N1076C	Bell TH-1F	6436	ex N64F
☐	N4963F	Bell TH-1L	6404	ex Bu157809
☐	N6131P	Bell UH-1H	5787	ex 66-16093
☐	N6226H	Bell UH-1B	3115	ex 66-14420
☐	N8079E	Bell UH-1H	4762	ex 65-9718
☐	N80780	Bell UH-1H	4527	ex 64-13820
☐	N64F	Bell 204B	2027	ex N103CR
☐	N261F	Sikorsky S-61N	61771	ex G-BEOO
☐	N262F	Sikorsky S-61N	61364	ex V8-UDU
☐	N263F	Sikorsky S-61N	61488	ex V8-UDQ
☐	N503AH	Bell 206B JetRanger	686	ex C-FAOL
☐	N622F	Bell 222U	47543	ex C-GIVU
☐	N866JH	Ted Smith Aerostar 601	61-0042-83	ex N7471S
☐	N5743H	Bell 206B JetRanger III	3042	
☐	N6651H	Bell 206L-1 LongRanger II	45211	
☐	N8649Z	Cessna TP206C Super Skylane	P206-0449	
☐	N38993	Bell 206L-1 LongRanger III	45601	

PACIFIC WINGS Tsunami (LW/NMI) Kahului-Intl, HI (OGG)

	Registration	Type	C/n	Previous identity
☐	N301PW	Cessna 208B Caravan I	208B0983	
☐	N302PW	Cessna 208B Caravan I	208B0984	
☐	N303PW	Cessna 208B Caravan I	208B0985	
☐	N304PW	Cessna 208B Caravan I	208B0833	ex N699BA
☐	N305PW	Cessna 208B Caravan I	208B0828	ex N297DF

PAPILLON GRAND CANYON AIRWAYS (HI) Grand Canyon-National Park, AZ, (GCN)

	Registration	Type	C/n	Previous identity	Fleet no.
☐	N197AE	Aérospatiale AS350B2 AStar	3909		36
☐	N425EH	Aérospatiale AS350B2 AStar	4197		35
☐	N453NW	Aérospatiale AS350B2 AStar	2475	ex HB-XYC	26
☐	N890PA	Aérospatiale AS350B2 AStar	4554		37
☐	N891PA	Aérospatiale AS350B2 AStar	4557		33
☐	N6093R	Aérospatiale AS350B2 AStar	2415		25
☐	N177PA	Bell 206L-1 LongRanger III	45194	ex N992PA	17
☐	N178PA	Bell 206L-1 LongRanger III	45319	ex F-ODUB	8
☐	N333ER	Bell 206L-1 LongRanger III	45203		12
☐	N1075S	Bell 206L-1 LongRanger III	45366		10
☐	N1076T	Bell 206L-1 LongRanger II	45373		30
☐	N2070U	Bell 206L-1 LongRanger II	45706		5
☐	N2072M	Bell 206L-1 LongRanger II	45720		2
☐	N3893U	Bell 206L-3 LongRanger III	51020		9
☐	N3895D	Bell 206L-1 LongRanger II	45590		1
☐	N4227E	Bell 206L-1 LongRanger III	45702	ex N725RE	18
☐	N5743C	Bell 206L-1 LongRanger II	45474		23
☐	N5745Y	Bell 206L-1 LongRanger III	45531		11
☐	N10761	Bell 206L-1 LongRanger II	45381		27
☐	N20316	Bell 206L-1 LongRanger II	45687		21
☐	N22425	Bell 206L-1 LongRanger II	45743		29
☐	N27694	Bell 206L-1 LongRanger II	45282		4
☐	N38885	Bell 206L-1 LongRanger II	45726		20
☐	N50046	Bell 206L-1 LongRanger II	45173		28
☐	N57491	Bell 206L-1 LongRanger II	45505		15
☐	N130GC	Eurocopter EC130B4	3562		41
☐	N130PH	Eurocopter EC130B4	3670		38
☐	N132GC	Eurocopter EC130B4	3756		43
☐	N133GC	Eurocopter EC130B4	3883		48
☐	N133PH	Eurocopter EC130B4	3939		49
☐	N135PH	Eurocopter EC130B4	[illegible]		30
☐	N136PH	Eurocopter EC130B4	3896		46
☐	N137PH	Eurocopter EC130B4	3775		40
☐	N138PH	Eurocopter EC130B4	3790		44
☐	N151GC	Eurocopter EC130B4	4402		51
☐	N152GC	Eurocopter EC130B4	4448		52
☐	N175PA	Bell 407	53154		
☐	N368PA	MD Helicopters MD900 Explorer	900-00012	ex N901CF	
☐	N407PA	Bell 407	53567	ex N16FR	

☐ N616AC	Bell 407	53354	ex N407BR	

PARAGON AIR EXPRESS | **Paragon Express (PGX)** | **Nashville-Intl, TN (BNA)**

☐ N703PA	Cessna 208B Caravan I	208B0776	ex N5262B	Freighter

PARAMOUNT JET | **Little Rock-Adams Field, AR (LIT)**

☐ N406BN	Boeing 727-291F (Raisbeck 3)	19991/521	ex HI-630CA	no titles

PENAIR | **Peninsula(KS/PEN)** | **Anchorage-Intl, AK (ANC)**

☐ N4327P	Piper PA-32-301 Saratoga	32-8406002		
☐ N8212H	Piper PA-32-301 Saratoga	32-8006046		
☐ N8259V	Piper PA-32-301 Saratoga	32-8006097		
☐ N8305H	Piper PA-32-301 Saratoga	32-8106017		
☐ N8402S	Piper PA-32-301 Saratoga	32-8106075		
☐ N8470Y	Piper PA-32-301 Saratoga	32-8206012		
☐ N81052	Piper PA-32-301 Saratoga	32-8206023		
☐ N81844	Piper PA-32-301 Saratoga	32-8006012		
☐ N82455	Piper PA-32-301 Saratoga	32-8006079		
☐ N109XJ	SAAB SF.340A	340A-109	ex N109AE	
☐ N110XJ	SAAB SF.340A	340A-110	ex N110MQ	
☐ N665PA	SAAB SF.340B	340B-181	ex N590MA	
☐ N675PA	SAAB SF.340B	340B-206	ex N593MA	Spirit of Bristol Bay
☐ N676PA	SAAB SF.340B	340B-316	ex VH-LIH	
☐ N677PA	SAAB SF.340B	340B-328	ex VH-XDZ	
☐ N679PA	SAAB SF.340B	340B-345	ex N345CV	
☐ N685PA	SAAB SF.340B	340B-212	ex N594MA	Spirit of the Aleutians
☐ N41NE	Swearingen SA.227AC Metro III	AC-741B	ex C-FNAM	
☐ N640PA	Swearingen SA.227AC Metro III	AC-759B	ex N306NE	Spirit of the Aleutians
☐ N892DC	Swearingen SA.227DC Metro 23	DC-892B	ex C-GAFO	
☐ N15PR	Piper PA-31-350 Chieftain	31-8352011	ex SE-KPC	
☐ N28KE	Piper PA-31-350 Chieftain	31-8152049	ex C-GVSX	
☐ N700RD	Piper PA-31T3 T-1040	31T-5575001	ex HP-1101P	
☐ N741	Grumman G-21A Goose	B-97		
☐ N750PA	Cessna 208B Caravan I	208B0628		
☐ N7811	Grumman G-21A Goose	B-122		
☐ N9304F	Cessna 208 Caravan I	20800008		
☐ N9481F	Cessna 208 Caravan I	20800070		
☐ N22932	Grumman G-21A Goose	B-139	ex CF-WCP	

PHI - PETROLEUM HELICOPTERS | **Petroleum (PHM)** | **Lafayette-Regional, LA (LFT)**

☐ N151AE	Aérospatiale AS350B3 AStar	3814		
☐ N153AE	Aérospatiale AS350B3 AStar	3829		
☐ N350LG	Aérospatiale AS350B3 AStar	3690	ex N499AE	
☐ N351LG	Aérospatiale AS350B3 AStar	3722	ex N580AE	
☐ N352LG	Aérospatiale AS350B3 AStar	3777	ex N142AE	
☐ N353P	Aérospatiale AS350B2 AStar	3885	ex N194AE	
☐ N354P	Aérospatiale AS350B2 AStar	3886	ex N196AE	
☐ N498AE	Aérospatiale AS350B3 AStar	3687		
☐ N585AE	Aérospatiale AS350B3 AStar	3736		
☐ N587AE	Aérospatiale AS350B3 AStar	3730		
☐ N590AE	Aérospatiale AS350B3 AStar	3733		
☐ N732AE	Aérospatiale AS350B2 AStar	2873	ex N4000L	EMS
☐ N946AE	Aérospatiale AS350B2 AStar	3351	ex N855PH	EMS
☐ N945AE	Aérospatiale AS350B2 AStar	3004	ex N40466	EMS
☐ N954AE	Aérospatiale AS350B2 AStar	3248	ex N854PH	EMS
☐ N956AE	Aérospatiale AS350B2 AStar	3352	ex N856PH	
☐ N972AE	Aérospatiale AS350B3 AStar	3234		EMS
☐ N973AE	Aérospatiale AS350B3 AStar	3229	ex C-GFIH	EMS
☐ N974AE	Aérospatiale AS350B2 AStar	2653	ex N350BZ	
☐ N975AE	Aérospatiale AS350B2 AStar	2777	ex N6095S	
☐ N4031L	Aérospatiale AS350B2 AStar	2907		Based Antarctica
☐ N4036H	Aérospatiale AS350B2 AStar	2919		Based Antarctica
☐ N30KH	Bell 206L-3 LongRanger III	51527	ex HK-3726X	
☐ N45RP	Bell 206L-1 LongRanger II	45521	ex HC-BXS	
☐ N49EA	Bell 206L-3 LongRanger III	51507	ex D-HHSG	
☐ N92MT	Bell 206L-3 LongRanger III	51175	ex CC-ETG	
☐ N108PH	Bell 206L-3 LongRanger III	51334	ex C-FPUB	
☐ N202PH	Bell 206L-3 LongRanger III	51076	ex N31821	
☐ N203PH	Bell 206L-3 LongRanger III	51520	ex N31077	
☐ N204PH	Bell 206L-3 LongRanger III	51465	ex N41791	
☐ N205FC	Bell 206L-3 LongRanger III	51130		
☐ N206FS	Bell 206L-3 LongRanger III	51506	ex C-FLNW	
☐ N214PH	Bell 206L-3 LongRanger III	51131	ex N4835	
☐ N215PH	Bell 206L-3 LongRanger III	51575	ex N53119	

☐ N219PH	Bell 206L-3 LongRanger III	51509	ex N8593X	
☐ N266P	Bell 206L-4 LongRanger IV	52271	ex N3020J	
☐ N269AE	Bell 206L-3 LongRanger III	51530	ex N3116P	
☐ N306PH	Bell 206L-1 LongRanger II	45411	ex N11027	
☐ N363BH	Bell 206L-3 LongRanger III	51345	ex N997PT	
☐ N436PH	Bell 206L-3 LongRanger III	51436	ex EI-CIO	
☐ N530PR	Bell 206L-3 LongRanger III	51419	ex N6610Y	
☐ N593AE	Bell 206L-2 LongRanger II	45421	ex N513EH	
☐ N595AE	Bell 206L-1 LongRanger II	45244	ex N5019F	EMS
☐ N668PH	Bell 206L-3 LongRanger III	51487	ex N8589X	
☐ N979BH	Bell 206L-3 LongRanger III	51403	ex N998PT	
☐ N2249Z	Bell 206L-1 LongRanger II	45753		
☐ N3107N	Bell 206L-3 LongRanger III	51512		
☐ N3108E	Bell 206L-3 LongRanger III	51498		
☐ N3116L	Bell 206L-3 LongRanger III	51529		
☐ N3207Q	Bell 206L-3 LongRanger III	51540	ex C-FLYD	
☐ N4180F	Bell 206L-3 LongRanger III	51469		
☐ N4282Z	Bell 206L-3 LongRanger III	51499		
☐ N5014V	Bell 206L-1 LongRanger II	45217		
☐ N6160Y	Bell 206L-3 LongRanger III	51609	ex C-FOYN	
☐ N6160Z	Bell 206L-3 LongRanger III	51610		
☐ N6251Y	Bell 206L-3 LongRanger III	51556	ex C-FLYG	
☐ N6603X	Bell 206L-3 LongRanger III	51412		
☐ N6610C	Bell 206L-3 LongRanger III	51425		
☐ N6748D	Bell 206L-3 LongRanger III	51106	ex HC-BVB	
☐ N7074W	Bell 206L-4 LongRanger IV	52033		
☐ N7077F	Bell 206L-4 LongRanger IV	52038		
☐ N8587X	Bell 206L-3 LongRanger III	51464		
☐ N8588X	Bell 206L-3 LongRanger III	51486		
☐ N8590X	Bell 206L-3 LongRanger III	51494		
☐ N8591X	Bell 206L-3 LongRanger III	51495		
☐ N8594X	Bell 206L-3 LongRanger III	51531		
☐ N21497	Bell 206L-3 LongRanger III	51518		
☐ N32041	Bell 206L-3 LongRanger III	51539	ex C-FLXL	
☐ N54641	Bell 206L-3 LongRanger III	51184	ex JA9471	
☐ N62127	Bell 206L-4 LongRanger IV	52023		
☐ N401PH	Bell 407	53615	ex N407MD	
☐ N402PH	Bell 407	53159		
☐ N403PH	Bell 407	53267	ex N8595X	
☐ N404PH	Bell 407	53188		
☐ N406PH	Bell 407	53198		
☐ N407H	Bell 407	53464	ex N407XM	
☐ N407PH	Bell 407	53003	ex C-FWRD	
☐ N408PH	Bell 407	53228		
☐ N409PH	Bell 407	53626	ex N45655	
☐ N410PH	Bell 407	53636	ex C-FDXK	
☐ N411PH	Bell 407	53637		
☐ N415PH	Bell 407	53390	ex N492PH	
☐ N416PH	Bell 407	53276	ex N3193E	
☐ N417PH	Bell 407	53038		
☐ N418PH	Bell 407	53640	ex N418PH	
☐ N420PH	Bell 407	53747	ex C-FLZR	
☐ N421PH	Bell 407	53749	ex C-FLZP	
☐ N422PH	Bell 407	53675		
☐ N424PH	Bell 407	53682		
☐ N426PH	Bell 407	53751		
☐ N428PH	Bell 407	53754		
☐ N429PH	Bell 407	53772		
☐ N432PH	Bell 407	53681	ex N431P	
☐ N433PH	Bell 407	53679	ex N433P	
☐ N434PH	Bell 407	53773		
☐ N447PH	Bell 407	53114		
☐ N467PH	Bell 407	53142		
☐ N490PH	Bell 407	53378	ex N6387C	
☐ N491PH	Bell 407	53386	ex N6390Y	
☐ N493PH	Bell 407	53393		
☐ N494PH	Bell 407	53396		
☐ N495PH	Bell 407	53397		
☐ N496PH	Bell 407	53398		
☐ N498PH	Bell 407	53399		
☐ N501PH	Bell 407	53401		
☐ N510PH	Bell 407	53209		
☐ N612PH	Bell 407	53199		
☐ N719PH	Bell 407	53266		
☐ N720PH	Bell 407	53277		
☐ N721PH	Bell 407	53278		
☐ N722PH	Bell 407	53288		
☐ N723PH	Bell 407	53283		
☐ N724PH	Bell 407	53327		
☐ N740PH	Bell 407	53435	ex N6077V	
☐ N741PH	Bell 407	53457		
☐ N742PH	Bell 407	53461		

Registration	Type	C/n	Previous identity	Notes
☐ N807PH	Bell 407	53656	ex C-FFQS	
☐ N4999	Bell 407	53323		
☐ N107X	Bell 412SP	33113		
☐ N108X	Bell 412SP	33115		
☐ N126PA	Bell 412	33168		
☐ N142PH	Bell 412SP	33150	ex HL9236	
☐ N143PH	Bell 412SP	33134	ex N800Y	
☐ N412SM	Bell 412EP	36213	ex N426DR	EMS
☐ N412UM	Bell 412SP	33023	ex N3911L	
☐ N413UM	Bell 412	33012	ex N3893P	
☐ N1202T	Bell 412SP	33112	ex D-HHOF	
☐ N2014K	Bell 412	33020	ex YV-922C	
☐ N2148K	Bell 412SP	36001		
☐ N2149S	Bell 412SP	36002		
☐ N2258F	Bell 412	33073	ex YV-1030C	
☐ N2261D	Bell 412SP	33076		
☐ N2298Z	Bell 412	33077		
☐ N3893L	Bell 412	33006	ex C-FOQL	
☐ N3893N	Bell 412	33010		
☐ N6559Z	Bell 412SP	36019		
☐ N7128R	Bell 412SP	36007		
☐ N21498	Bell 412SP	36003		
☐ N22347	Bell 412SP	36005	ex XA-RSL	
☐ N22608	Bell 412	33075		
☐ N33008	Bell 412SP	36004		
☐ N301PH	Eurocopter EC135P2	0355		
☐ N302PH	Eurocopter EC135P2	0364	EMS	
☐ N303PH	Eurocopter EC135P2	0372		
☐ N304PH	Eurocopter EC135P2	0386		
☐ N305PH	Eurocopter EC135P2	0395		
☐ N307PH	Eurocopter EC135P2	0398		
☐ N308PH	Eurocopter EC135P2	0401		
☐ N309PH	Eurocopter EC135P2	0403		
☐ N311PH	Eurocopter EC135P2	0413		
☐ N312PH	Eurocopter EC135P2	0404		PHi Air Medical
☐ N314PH	Eurocopter EC135P2	0409		
☐ N317PH	Eurocopter EC135P2	0423		
☐ N320PH	Eurocopter EC135P2	0430		
☐ N323PH	Eurocopter EC135P2	0434		
☐ N324PH	Eurocopter EC135P2	0571		
☐ N327PH	Eurocopter EC135P2	0445	ex D-HECB	
☐ N328PH	Eurocopter EC135P2	0450	ex D-HECG	
☐ N330PH	Eurocopter EC135P2	0514		
☐ N332PH	Eurocopter EC135P2	0519		
☐ N343PH	Eurocopter EC135P2	0456		
☐ N344PH	Eurocopter EC135P2	0459		
☐ N376PH	Eurocopter EC135P2	0523		
☐ N380PH	Eurocopter EC135P2	0593		
☐ N381PH	Eurocopter EC135P2	0611		
☐ N382PH	Eurocopter EC135P2	0618		
☐ N383PH	Eurocopter EC135P2	0622		
☐ N800PH	MBB Bo.105CBS-4	S-800	ex N133AE	
☐ N838PH	MBB Bo.105CBS-4	S-838	ex N135AE	
☐ N851PH	MBB Bo.105CBS-4	S-851	ex N137AE	
☐ N868PH	MBB Bo.105CB	S-668	ex N205UC	
☐ N4573B	MBB Bo.105S	S-673		
☐ N5421E	MBB Bo.105CBS-4	S-806		
☐ N6607K	MBB Bo.105CBS-4	S-841		
☐ N8199J	MBB Bo.105CBS-4	S-826		
☐ N9190Y	MBB Bo.105CB	S-669		
☐ N54191	MBB Bo.105CBS-4	S-804		
☐ N81832	MBB Bo.105CBS-4	S-828		
☐ N81992	MBB Bo.105CBS-4	S-827		
☐ N89H	Sikorsky S-76C	760406		
☐ N127FH	Sikorsky S-76A	760063	ex N402M	
☐ N274X	Sikorsky S-76C+	760440	ex N278X	
☐ N276X	Sikorsky S-76C	760405		
☐ N478X	Sikorsky S-76C	760493		
☐ N709P	Sikorsky S-76C-2	760716		
☐ N718P	Sikorsky S-76C-2	760686		
☐ N725P	Sikorsky S-76C-2	760688		
☐ N734P	Sikorsky S-76C	760600	ex N70936	
☐ N738P	Sikorsky S-76C-2	760668		
☐ N745P	Sikorsky S-76C	760619		
☐ N746P	Sikorsky S-76C	760623		
☐ N759P	Sikorsky S-76C-2	760690		
☐ N760PH	Sikorsky S-76A	760078	ex VH-BJR	
☐ N761PH	Sikorsky S-76A	760224	ex VH-BJS	
☐ N762P	Sikorsky S-76A	760060	ex N76NY	

Reg	Type	C/n	Previous	Notes
☐ N763P	Sikorsky S-76A	760166	ex C-GHJT	
☐ N764P	Sikorsky S-76A	760276	ex N913UK	
☐ N766P	Sikorsky S-76C	760594		
☐ N767P	Sikorsky S-76C++	760599		
☐ N769P	Sikorsky S-76C	760671		
☐ N776P	Sikorsky S-76A	760275	ex N911UK	
☐ N776PH	Sikorsky S-76C	760505	ex N505PH	
☐ N778P	Sikorsky S-76A	760035	ex N4253S	
☐ N779P	Sikorsky S-76C+	760655	ex N4501G	
☐ N784P	Sikorsky S-76C	760634		
☐ N785P	Sikorsky S-76C	760635		
☐ N786P	Sikorsky S-76C	760643		
☐ N787P	Sikorsky S-76C-2	760692		
☐ N790P	Sikorsky S-76C	760675	ex N45138	
☐ N792P	Sikorsky S-76A	760193	ex N792CH	
☐ N796P	Sikorsky S-76C-2	760681		
☐ N798P	Sikorsky S-76C-2	760685		
☐ N911MJ	Sikorsky S-76A	760231	ex N3122D	
☐ N1545K	Sikorsky S-76A	760047		
☐ N1545X	Sikorsky S-76A	760050		
☐ N1546G	Sikorsky S-76A	760076		
☐ N1546K	Sikorsky S-76A	760082		
☐ N5435V	Sikorsky S-76A	760158		
☐ PP-MCS	Sikorsky S-76A	760077	ex N1547D	Based Brazil
☐ PR-CHG	Sikorsky S-76C+	760658	ex N658A	Based Brazil
☐ PR-CHI	Sikorsky S-76C+	760670	ex N4514K	Based Brazil

Reg	Type	C/n	Previous	Notes
☐ N192PH	Sikorsky S-92	920006		
☐ N292PH	Sikorsky S-92	920008		
☐ N392PH	Sikorsky S-92	920015		
☐ N492PH	Sikorsky S-92	920016	ex N592PH	
☐ N592PH	Sikorsky S-92A	920027		
☐ N692PH	Sikorsky S-92A	920028		
☐ N925PH	Sikorsky S-92A	920118		
☐ N992PH	Sikorsky S-92A	920055	ex N4502G	

Reg	Type	C/n	Previous	Notes
☐ N14UH	Bell 230	23028	ex XA-IKA	Op for Univ of Mississippi
☐ N217AE	MBB BK-117B-2	7152	ex N217UC	
☐ N217PH	MBB BK-117A-4	7092	ex N911RZ	
☐ N226PH	Bell 212	31106	ex N27805	
☐ N230H	Bell 230	23004	ex N500HG	
☐ N241PH	Beech B200 Super King Air	BB-1182	ex N416CS	
☐ N430X	Bell 430	49058		
☐ N430XM	Bell 430	49073	ex N9125G	
☐ N911TL	MBB BK-117B-1	7198	ex N911AF	
☐ N2275Y	Bell 206B JetRanger III	3626		
☐ N2753F	Bell 206B JetRanger III	2729		
☐ N3131S	Bell 212	30953	ex N2763Y	
☐ N3208H	Bell 212	31304		
☐ N3897N	Bell 214ST	28106		
☐ N5736J	Bell 212	31140		
☐ N5748M	Bell 214ST	28102	ex VH-LHU	
☐ N6992	Bell 222U	47521	ex N911WY	
☐ N8045T	Bell 214ST	28101	ex VH-LHQ	
☐ N8765J	MBB BK-117A-3	7054	ex ZS-HRP	
☐ N59806	Bell 214ST	28140	ex B-7723	

PHILLIPS AIR CHARTER — *Beachball (BCH)* — *Del Rio Intl, TX (DRT)*

Reg	Type	C/n	Previous	Notes
☐ N666AK	Beech E-18S	BA-18	ex N3602B	Freighter

PHOENIX AIR — *Gray Bird (PHA)* — *Cartersville, GA (VPC)*

Reg	Type	C/n	Previous	Notes
☐ N164PA	Grumman G-159 Gulfstream I	54	ex N26AJ	
☐ N167PA	Grumman G-159 Gulfstream I	199	ex N183PA	
☐ N171PA	Grumman G-159 Gulfstream I	192	ex YV-76CP	
☐ N185PA	Grumman G-159 Gulfstream I	26	ex YV-82CP	
☐ N190PA	Grumman G-159 Gulfstream I (LFD)	195	ex N1900W	Freighter
☐ N192PA	Grumman G-159 Gulfstream I	149	ex N684FM	stored VPC
☐ N193PA	Grumman G-159 Gulfstream I (LFD)	125	ex N5NA	Freighter
☐ N195PA	Grumman G-159C Gulfstream I	88	ex C-GPTN	
☐ N196PA	Grumman G-159 Gulfstream I	139	ex C-FRTU	
☐ N198PA	Grumman G-159C Gulfstream I	27	ex N415CA	

Reg	Type	C/n	Previous	Notes
☐ N32PA	Learjet 36A	36A-025	ex N800BL	
☐ N56PA	Learjet 36A	36A-023	ex N6YY	
☐ N62PG	Learjet 36A	36A-031	ex N20UG	
☐ N71PG	Learjet 36	36-013	ex D-CBRD	
☐ N80PG	Learjet 35	35-063	ex N663CA	
☐ N524PA	Learjet 35	35-033	ex N31FN	
☐ N527PA	Learjet 36A	36A-019	ex N540PA	
☐ N541PA	Learjet 35	35-053	ex N53FN	

☐ N542PA	Learjet 35	35-030	ex C-GKPE		
☐ N544PA	Learjet 35A	35A-247	ex N523PA	coded NY	
☐ N545PA	Learjet 36A	36A-028	ex N75TD	coded HI	
☐ N547PA	Learjet 36	36-012	ex N712JE	coded AK	
☐ N549PA	Learjet 35A	35A-119	ex (N64DH)	coded GA	
☐ N568PA	Learjet 35A	35A-205	ex N59FN		
☐ N163PA	Gulfstream G-1159A Gulfstream III-SMA	249	ex F-249		
☐ N173PA	Gulfstream G-1159A Gulfstream III-SMA	313	ex F-313		

PHOENIX AIRTRANSPORT — *Papago (PPG)* — *Phoenix-Sky Harbor Intl, AZ (PHX)*

☐ N18R	Beech E-18S	BA-312		Lsd fr CBT
☐ N103AF	Beech G-18S	BA-526	ex N277S	Lsd fr CBT

PIEDMONT AIRLINES — *Piedmont (US/PDT)* — *Salisbury-Wicomico Regional, MD (SBY)*

A wholly owned subsidiary of US Airways and uses US Airways Express flight numbers in the range US3000-3399.

PINNACLE AIRLINES — *Flagship (9E/FLG)* — *Memphis-Intl, TN/Minneapolis-St Paul Intl, MN (MEM/MSP)*

Operates for Delta Connection: Colgan Air is a wholly owned subsidiary.

PLANEMASTERS — *Planemaster (PMS)* — *Chicago-Du Page, IL (DPA)*

☐ N274PM	Cessna 208B Caravan I	208B0705		
☐ N279PM	Cessna 208B Caravan I	208B0623	ex N104VE	Freighter
☐ N281PM	Cessna 208B Caravan I	208B0902		
☐ N282PM	Cessna 208B Caravan I	208B0981		
☐ N286PM	Cessna 208B Caravan I	208B0631		
☐ N1114A	Cessna 208B Caravan I	208B0309		Freighter
☐ N1256P	Cessna 208B Caravan I	208B0564		

PLATINUM AIRLINES — *Miami-Opa Locka, FL (OPF)*

☐ N727PL	Boeing 727-232 (Raisbeck 3)	20643/951	ex N17789	Poliana, std OPF

PLAYERS AIR — *Players Air (PYZ)* — *Atlanta-de Kalb Peachtree, GA (PDK)*

☐ N650CT	Embraer EMB.120RT	120198	ex N267AS
☐ N651CT	Embraer EMB.120RT	120197	ex N58733
☐ N653CT	Embraer EMB.120ER	120243	ex N204SW

POLAR AIR CARGO — *Polar (PO/PAC)* — *New York-JFK Intl, NY (JFK)*

☐ N355MC	Boeing 747-341 (SF)	23395/629	ex PP-VNI		Lsd fr GTI
☐ N416MC	Boeing 747-47UF	32838/1307			Lsd fr GTI
☐ N450PA	Boeing 747-46NF	30808/1257		The Spirit of Long Beach	
☐ N451PA	Boeing 747-46NF	30809/1259		Wings of Change	
☐ N452PA	Boeing 747-46NF	30810/1260		Polar Spirit	
☐ N453PA	Boeing 747-46NF	30811/1283			
☐ N454PA	Boeing 747-46NF	30812/1310			

PONDEROSA AIRLINES — *Taylor, AZ (TYZ)*

☐ N3UV	Rockwell 500S Shrike Commander	3146	ex N3U
☐ N4QS	Aero Commander 500S Shrike	1755-1	ex N4GS
☐ N17DL	Aero Commander 500S Shrike	1866-42	ex N9029N
☐ N40TC	Rockwell 500S Shrike Commander	3091	ex SE-EWH
☐ N88CB	Rockwell 500S Shrike Commander	3067	ex N9081N
☐ N519WA	Rockwell 500S Shrike Commander	3081	ex N222GS
☐ N999GB	Aero Commander 500U Shrike	1717-27	ex CF-YGP

PRESIDENTIAL AIRWAYS — *Melbourne-Intl, FL (MLB)*

☐ N961BW	CASA C.212-200	CC40-8-248	ex N202FN	
☐ N962BW	CASA C.212-200	CC44-1-290	ex N439CA	
☐ N963BW	CASA C.212-200	CC60-3-320	ex N204FN	
☐ N966BW	CASA C.212-200	CC50-10-289	ex N316ST	
☐ N967BW	CASA C.212-200	CD51-2-304	ex N203PA	
☐ N969BW	CASA C.212-200	CC50-1-262	ex N262MA	Freighter
☐ N2357G	CASA C.212-200	CD51-2-309	ex N968BW	
☐ N4399T	CASA C.212-300	DF-1-393	ex N965BW	
☐ N6369C	CASA C.212-200	MS03-08-379	ex M964BW	
☐ N150RN	de Havilland DHC-8-103	086	ex N986BW	
☐ N955BW	Swearingen SA.227DC Metro 23	DC-821B	ex N821JB	
☐ N956BW	Swearingen SA.227DC Metro 23	DC-864B	ex C-GKAF	
☐ N982BW	CASA CN-235-100	010	ex ZS-OGE	stored JNB as ZS-OGE

PRIORITY AIR — New Orleans-Lakefront, LA (NEW)

Registration	Type	C/n	Previous identity	Notes
☐ N46SA	Swearingen SA.226T Merlin III	T-231	ex N20QN	EMS

PRIORITY AIR CHARTER — Priority Air (PRY) — Kidron-Stolzfus Airfield, OH

Registration	Type	C/n	Previous identity	Notes
☐ N208TF	Cessna 208B Caravan I	208B0592		
☐ N218PA	Cessna 208B Caravan I	208B0306	ex N218PF	
☐ N228PA	Cessna 208B Caravan I	208B0930	ex N2418W	
☐ N248PA	Cessna 208B Caravan I	208B0134	ex N208JL	
☐ N719BT	Cessna 208B Caravan I	208B0898		
☐ N820B	Cessna 340A II	340A0328	ex YV-1268P	

PROFESSIONAL AIR CHARTER — Fort Lauderdale Executive, FL (FXE)

Registration	Type	C/n	Previous identity	Notes
☐ N100RN	Piper PA-31-350 Chieftain	31-8152080	ex G-BYRN	
☐ N4633P	Beech 95-B55 Baron	TC-1560		
☐ N27888	Piper PA-31-350 Chieftain	31-7952025		

PROMECH AIR — (Z3) — Ketchikan-Harbor SPB, AK (WFB)

Registration	Type	C/n	Previous identity	Notes
☐ N1108Q	de Havilland DHC-2 Beaver	416	ex 51-16851	Floatplane
☐ N4787C	de Havilland DHC-2 Beaver	1330	ex C-FGMK	Floatplane
☐ N64393	de Havilland DHC-2 Beaver	845	ex 54-1701	Floatplane
☐ N64397	de Havilland DHC-2 Beaver	760	ex 53-7943	Floatplane
☐ N270PA	de Havilland DHC-3 Turbo Otter	270	ex N51KA	Floatplane
☐ N409PA	de Havilland DHC-3 Turbo Otter	409	ex C-FLDD	Floatplane
☐ N435B	de Havilland DHC-3 Turbo Otter	183	ex C-GIGZ	Floatplane
☐ N959PA	de Havilland DHC-3 Turbo Otter	159	ex N67KA	Floatplane
☐ N3952B	de Havilland DHC-3 Turbo Otter	225	ex C-GGON	Floatplane
☐ N444BA	Cessna A185E Skywagon	185-1433		Floatplane
☐ N531H	Cessna A185E Skywagon	185-1348		Floatplane

PSA AIRLINES — Blue Streak (JIA) — Dayton-Cox Intl, OH (DAY)

A wholly owned subsidiary of US Airways, operates services as a US Airways Express commuter using US flight numbers in the range 4000-4299. All aircraft officially leased to US Airways from AFS Investments and sub-leased to PSA Airlines.

PUERTO RICO AIR MANAGEMENT SERVICES(2P) — Sun Juan-Luis Munoz Marin Intl, PR (SJU)

Registration	Type	C/n	Previous identity	Notes
☐ N75LA	Beech 100 King Air	B-75	ex C-F (SCD)	

QUICK AIR — Danville-Vermillion County, IL (DNV)

Registration	Type	C/n	Previous identity	Notes
☐ N16BE	Beech Baron 58	TH-946		
☐ N233H	Beech G-18S	BA-481	ex (N584MS)	Freighter

RAM AIR FREIGHT — RAM Express (REX) — Raleigh-Durham-Intl, NC (RDU)

Registration	Type	C/n	Previous identity	Notes
☐ N958MC	Beech 58 Baron	TH-552		
☐ N7351R	Beech 58 Baron	TH-481		
☐ N401NA	Cessna 402B	402B0035	ex SE-FXI	
☐ N884RC	Cessna 402B	402B0884	ex TF-JVC	
☐ N6350X	Cessna 402B	402B1317		
☐ N130BW	Piper PA-32-300 Cherokee Six	32-40963	ex D-EBOK	
☐ N169BW	Piper PA-32RT-300 Lance II	32R-7885080	ex N30006	
☐ N221MC	Piper PA-32RT-300 Lance II	32R-7885032		
☐ N333TG	Piper PA-32R-300 Lance	32R-7680320	ex N202SW	
☐ N631BW	Piper PA-32-300 Cherokee Six	32-7340041	ex N4GQ	
☐ N833WC	Piper PA-32-300 Cherokee Six	32-7640059		
☐ N1061Q	Piper PA-32-260 Cherokee Six E	32-7200015	ex SE-FLD	
☐ N4498F	Piper PA-32R-300 Lance	32R-7680453		
☐ N4817S	Piper PA-32-260 Cherokee Six	32-1277		
☐ N5454F	Piper PA-32R-300 Lance	32R-7780012		
☐ N6291J	Piper PA-32R-300 Lance	32R-7680350		
☐ N6934J	Piper PA-32R-300 Lance	32R-7680389		
☐ N8209C	Piper PA-32R-300 Lance	32R-7680082		
☐ N8954C	Piper PA-32R-300 Lance	32R-7680146		
☐ N8985C	Piper PA-32R-300 Lance	32R-7680147		
☐ N9392K	Piper PA-32R-300 Lance	32R-7680219		
☐ N38305	Piper PA-32R-300 Lance	32R-7780413		
☐ N87619	Piper PA-32-300 Cherokee Six C	32-40752		
☐ N48LJ	Piper PA-34-200T Seneca II	34-7770030	ex C-GQET	
☐ N86BW	Piper PA-34-200T Seneca II	34-7770340	ex C-GZAQ	
☐ N88WA	Piper PA-34-200T Seneca II	34-7570274		
☐ N286BW	Piper PA-34-200T Seneca II	34-7970182	ex N341DK	

☐ N553DM	Piper PA-34-200T Seneca II	34-7670330	ex C-GXHY
☐ N1063X	Piper PA-34-200T Seneca II	34-7570198	
☐ N3570M	Piper PA-34-200T Seneca II	34-7870117	
☐ N4358X	Piper PA-34-200T Seneca II	34-7670027	
☐ N6935C	Piper PA-34-200T Seneca II	34-7870167	
☐ N7633C	Piper PA-34-200T Seneca II	34-7670098	
☐ N8076N	Piper PA-34-200T Seneca II	34-7970487	
☐ N8793E	Piper PA-34-200T Seneca II	34-7670180	
☐ N21407	Piper PA-34-200T Seneca II	34-7870435	
☐ N39545	Piper PA-34-200T Seneca II	34-7870389	ex C-FWFJ

RAM AIR SERVICES

☐ N702RS	SAAB SF.340B	340B-233	ex N233CJ
☐ N703RS	SAAB SF.340B	340B-252	ex N252CJ

RAMP 66 — *Pelican (PPK) North Myrtle Beach-Grand Strand, NC (CRE)*

☐ N6656C	Beech 58 Baron	TH-1060

RAPID AIR — *Grand Rapids-Kent County Intl, MI (GRR)*

☐ N4084L	Cessna 310Q	310Q0493

REDDING AERO ENTERPRISES — *Boxer (BXR)* — *Redding-Municipal, CA (RDD)*

☐ N2610G	Cessna 402C II	402C0064	
☐ N2613B	Cessna 402C II	402C0083	
☐ N2712F	Cessna 402C II	402C0121	
☐ N5826C	Cessna 402C II	402C0050	
☐ N5849C	Cessna 402C II	402C0052	
☐ N36908	Cessna 402C II	402C0313	
☐ N48SA	Cessna 404A Titan II	404-0417	ex C-GSPG
☐ N932C	Cessna 208B Caravan I	208B0032	ex N932FE
☐ N6072V	Piper Aerostar 601P	61P-0696-7963332	

REPUBLIC AIRWAYS — *Brickyard (RW/RPA)* — *Chicago-O'Hare, IL/Washington-Dulles, DC (ORD/DUL)*

Operates Embraer 170/175s for US Airways Express from Chicago and Washington although headquarters are in Indianapolis, IN.

RHOADES INTERNATIONAL — *Rhoades Express (RDS)* — *Columbus-Municipal, IN (CLU)*

☐ N132JR	Cessna 402B	402B1363	ex (N4606N)	
☐ N134JR	Cessna 310R	310R2117	ex N6831X	Freighter
☐ N376AS	AMI Turbo DC-3-65TP	15602/27047	ex ZS-OBU	Freighter
☐ N587CA	Convair 640	463	ex C-FPWO	Freighter

ROBLEX AVIATION — *Roblex (ROX)* — *Isla Grande, PR (SIG)*

☐ N151PR	Short SD.3-60	SH3725	ex N162DD	The Warrior
☐ N165DD	Short SD.3-60	SH3740	ex D-CFXF	
☐ N377AR	Short SD.3-60	SH3755	ex SE-LHY	
☐ N411ER	Short SD.3-60	SH3726	ex G-BNMW	
☐ N875RR	Short SD.3-60	SH3741	ex G-ZAPD	
☐ N948RR	Short SD.3-60	SH3751	ex G-BVMX	
☐ N821RR	Britten-Norman BN-2A-9 Islander	338	ex N146A	El Beb

ROGERS HELICOPTERS — *Fresno, CA*

☐ N505WW	Aérospatiale AS350B2 AStar	2442	ex JA6046
☐ N910VR	Aérospatiale AS350B2 AStar	3213	ex I-VINO
☐ N911EW	Aérospatiale AS350B2 AStar	2657	ex I-MUSY
☐ N912KW	Aérospatiale AS350B2 AStar	2260	ex EC-ESA
☐ N3609J	Aérospatiale AS350D AStar	1245	
☐ N2292W	Bell 206B JetRanger III	505	
☐ N2762P	Bell 206B JetRanger III	2711	
☐ N2763M	Bell 206B JetRanger III	2646	
☐ N16832	Bell 206B JetRanger III	2243	
☐ N20395	Bell 206B JetRanger III	3301	
☐ N58140	Bell 206B JetRanger III	1108	
☐ N59564	Bell 206B JetRanger III	1389	
☐ N59571	Bell 206B JetRanger III	1433	ex XA-SVF
☐ N91AL	Bell 212	30821	
☐ N212HL	Bell 212	30621	ex XA-VVM
☐ N811KA	Bell 212	30656	ex N59630
☐ N873HL	Bell 212	30873	ex N910KW
☐ N911HW	Bell 212	31101	ex N703H
☐ N911KW	Bell 212	30592	ex N50EW

☐ N911VR	Bell 212	30998	ex N701H	
☐ N24GT	Rockwell 690A Turbo Commander	11254	ex XA-RMZ	
☐ N101MZ	Aérospatiale AS355F1 Twin Star	5045		
☐ N102UM	Aérospatiale AS355F1 Twin Star	5075	ex N130US	
☐ N313DH	Bell 206L LongRanger II	45630	ex A6-CAC	
☐ N700PQ	Rockwell 690B Turbo Commander	11389	ex N700PC	
☐ N712M	Bell 206L-3 LongRanger III	51072		
☐ N896SB	Beech A100 King Air	B-160	ex OY-CCS	
☐ N912VR	Agusta A.109K2	10028	ex JA111D	EMS
☐ N10864	Bell 206L-1 LongRanger III	45434		
☐ N27472	Piper PA-31-350 Chieftain	31-7852019		
☐ N29176	Cessna T210L Turbo Centurion II	21059828		

ROSS AVIATION — *Energy (NRG)* — *Albuquerque-Kirkland AFB, NM*

☐ N148DE	de Havilland DHC-6 Twin Otter 300	493	ex N72348
☐ N162DE	de Havilland DHC-6 Twin Otter 300	429	ex N35062
☐ N166DE	Douglas DC-9-15RC (ABS 3)	47152/170	ex N66AF
☐ N229DE	Douglas DC-9-15RC (ABS 3)	45826/79	ex N29AF
☐ N7232R	Beech B200C Super King Air	BL-69	ex N2811B

ROTORCRAFT — *Broussard-Heliport, LA / Patterson-HPW Memorial, LA (-/PTN)*

☐ N3RL	Bell 206B JetRanger	396	ex N99NW
☐ N21RT	Bell 206B JetRanger III	2659	ex C-GFSE
☐ N37AJ	Bell 206B JetRanger	1877	ex N999GC
☐ N65DD	Bell 206B JetRanger	1235	ex N66677
☐ N72Z	Bell 206B JetRanger III	3537	ex N22181
☐ N113RL	Bell 206B JetRanger III	3306	ex N97BL
☐ N203RL	Bell 206B JetRanger III	3337	ex N2033J
☐ N275RL	Bell 206B JetRanger	1601	ex N90115
☐ N277RL	Bell 206B JetRanger III	3277	ex N181AA
☐ N314RT	Bell 206B JetRanger III	3014	ex N223HA
☐ N496RL	Bell 206B JetRanger III	3496	ex N2163Y
☐ N742RT	Bell 206B JetRanger III	2742	ex N921RB
☐ N913RL	Bell 206B JetRanger III	2913	ex B-66061
☐ N969RL	Bell 206B JetRanger III	3969	ex N187AA
☐ N2043B	Bell 206B JetRanger III	3355	
☐ N3187D	Bell 206B JetRanger	1326	ex C-GOKC
☐ N104RT	Bell 206L-3 LongRanger III	51364	ex LV-WCF
☐ N157H	Bell 206L-4 LongRanger IV	52320	
☐ N204RL	Bell 206L-1 LongRanger II	45204	ex N73FA
☐ N207RT	Bell 206L-4 LongRanger IV	52207	ex HC-BYQ
☐ N283RL	Bell 206L-1 LongRanger II	45283	ex N2761X
☐ N303RL	Bell 206L-3 LongRanger III	51202	ex N303MP
☐ N317RL	Bell 206L-4 LongRanger IV	52317	ex C-FFRB
☐ N318RL	Bell 206L-4 LongRanger IV	52318	
☐ N322RL	Bell 206L-4 LongRanger IV	52322	
☐ N370RL	Bell 206L-1 LongRanger II	45370	ex N618DE
☐ N396RL	Bell 206L-1 LongRanger II	45396	ex N396RT
☐ N397RL	Bell 206L-1 LongRanger II	45397	ex N1078D
☐ N405RL	Bell 206L-3 LongRanger III	51405	ex N253EV
☐ N410RL	Bell 206L-4 LongRanger IV	52310	
☐ N468RL	Bell 206L-3 LongRanger III	51155	ex N468AG
☐ N473RT	Bell 206L-3 LongRanger III	51473	ex CX-SCX
☐ N505RL	Bell 206L-1 LongRanger II	45176	ex N5005F
☐ N510RT	Bell 206L-3 LongRanger II	51078	ex N946L
☐ N514RL	Bell 206L-3 LongRanger III	51514	ex N206MY
☐ N516EH	Bell 206L-1 LongRanger II	45416	
☐ N518RL	Bell 206L-1 LongRanger II	45183	ex N406EH
☐ N520RL	Bell 206L-4 LongRanger IV	52052	ex N802D
☐ N523RL	Bell 206L-4 LongRanger IV	52321	ex N194H
☐ N598RL	Bell 206L-1 LongRanger II	45598	ex N264AA
☐ N709RL	Bell 206L-3 LongRanger III	51101	ex N709M
☐ N720RL	Bell 206L-4 LongRanger IV	52027	ex XA-FJM
☐ N772RL	Bell 206L-1 LongRanger II	45311	ex N2772A
☐ N801RL	Bell 206L-3 LongRanger III	51081	ex N704M
☐ N5019G	Bell 206L-1 LongRanger II	45247	
☐ N5750Y	Bell 206L-1 LongRanger II	45517	
☐ N52192	Bell 206L-4 LongRanger IV	52192	
☐ N163RL	Bell 407	53163	ex N972AA
☐ N164RL	Bell 407	53140	ex N407MT
☐ N167RL	Bell 407	53167	ex N973AA
☐ N309RL	Bell 407	53092	ex N407HX
☐ N594RL	Bell 407	53594	ex C-GAFF
☐ N595RL	Bell 407	53595	ex C-GAFI
☐ N83T	Sikorsky S-76A	760117	
☐ N293CA	Bell 412	33005	ex N3912Y

☐ N4125C	Bell 412	33103	ex N412AC	

ROYAL AIR FREIGHT — Air Royal (RAX) — Pontiac-Oakland, MI (PTK)

☐ N120RA	AMD Falcon 20DC	211	ex N764LA	
☐ N123RA	AMD Falcon 20C	30	ex N514SA	
☐ N277RA	AMD Falcon 20C	8	ex N612GA	
☐ N299RA	AMD Falcon 20C	146	ex N345FH	
☐ N900RA	AMD Falcon 20C	59	ex N159MV	
☐ N22DM	Cessna 310R	310R0069	ex N7593Q	
☐ N22LE	Cessna 310R	310R0033	ex N1398G	
☐ N310KS	Cessna 310R	310R1501		
☐ N1591T	Cessna 310R	310R0112		
☐ N2643D	Cessna 310R	310R1686		
☐ N87309	Cessna 310R	310R0510		
☐ N87341	Cessna 310R	310R0520		
☐ N34A	Embraer EMB.110P1 Bandeirante	110350	ex N4361Q	
☐ N49RA	Embraer EMB.110P1 Bandeirante	110424	ex C-GPRV	
☐ N64DA	Embraer EMB.110P1 Bandeirante	110385	ex PT-SFC	
☐ N72RA	Embraer EMB.110P1 Bandeirante	110377	ex C-GHOV	stored PTK
☐ N73RA	Embraer EMB.110P1 Bandeirante	110413	ex C-GPNW	
☐ N9RA	Learjet 25D	25D-277	ex N81MW	
☐ N16KK	Learjet 25B	25B-174	ex N412SP	
☐ N25FM	Learjet 25	25-063	ex N24LT	
☐ N25MD	Learjet 25	25-054	ex N509G	
☐ N48L	Learjet 24A	24A-107		
☐ N110RA	Learjet 25	25-025	ex (N111LM)	
☐ N688GS	Learjet 25B	25B-123	ex N906SU	
☐ N710TV	Learjet 24	24-159	ex N66MR	N269AL resd
☐ N876MC	Learjet 24B	24B-217	ex C-FZHT	
☐ N2094L	Learjet 25B	25B-095	ex C-GRCO	
☐ N160PB	Cessna 402C	402C0493	ex N6841M	
☐ N200AJ	Beech A100 King Air	B-146	ex N410SB	
☐ N305CW	Mitsubishi MU-2B-36 (MU-2L)	667	ex N300CW	
☐ N688RA	Mitsubishi MU-2B-36 (MU-2L)	688	ex N688MA	
☐ N717PS	Mitsubishi MU-2B-36 (MU-2L)	686	ex N23RA	
☐ N5279J	Cessna 402B	402B1202	ex N6841M	
☐ N5373J	Cessna 402B	402B0367	ex C-GCXI	

RUSTS FLYING SERVICE — Anchorage-Lake Hood SPB, AK (LHD)

☐ N626KT	Cessna U206G Stationair 6 II	U20604426	ex N756WY	Floatplane
☐ N2740X	de Havilland DHC-2 Beaver	579	ex C-GIJO	Floatplane
☐ N2899J	de Havilland DHC-3 Turbo Otter	425	ex C-GLCR	Floatplane
☐ N4444Z	de Havilland DHC-2 Beaver	1307	ex N123PG	Floatplane
☐ N4596U	Cessna U206G Stationair 6 II	U20604990		Floatplane
☐ N4661Z	Cessna U206G Stationair 6 II	U20605998		Floatplane
☐ N4891Z	Cessna U206G Stationair 6 II	U20606044		Floatplane
☐ N68083	de Havilland DHC-2 Beaver	1254	ex 57-2580	Floatplane

RYAN INTERNATIONAL AIRLINES — Ryan International (RD/RYN) — Wichita-Mid Continent, KS (ICT)

☐ N120DL	Boeing 767-332	23279/154		Lsd to LAV
☐ N123DN	Boeing 767-332	23437/188		
☐ N125RD	Boeing 767-383ER	24849/330	ex XA-MIR	
☐ N151GX	Boeing 757-2G5	24451/227	ex OB-1788-P	stored ROW
☐ N526NA	Boeing 757-236	24794/278	ex EC-HDG	
☐ N637TW	Boeing 767-33AER	25403/409	ex PR-BRW	
☐ N763BK	Boeing 767-3Z9ER	23765/165	ex G-VKNG	
☐ N764RD	Boeing 767-3Y0ER	26204/464	ex PR-VAD	
☐ N932RD	McDonnell-Douglas MD-83	49233/1203	ex N932AS	
☐ N964AS	McDonnell-Douglas MD-83	53078/1996		
☐ N969NS	McDonnell-Douglas MD-83	53063/1851	ex N969AS	
☐ N976AS	McDonnell-Douglas MD-83	53452/2109		

SAFEWING AVIATION — Swiftwing (SFF) — Kansas City-Downtown, MO (MKC)

☐ N7197F	Piper PA-32R-300 Lance	32R-7780058		
☐ N8304C	Piper PA-32R-300 Lance	32R-7680091		
☐ N33MP	Piper PA-23-250 Aztec F	27-7654194	ex N62746	
☐ N63798	Piper PA-23-250 Aztec F	27-7754124		

SAINT LOUIS HELICOPTER — Chesterfield-Spirit of St Louis, MO (SUS)

☐ N1078T	Sikorsky S-58HT	581016	ex C-FOHA	
☐ N6488	Sikorsky S-58D	581573		
☐ N45726	Sikorsky S-58 (H-34A)	58675	ex 56-4037	

SALMON AIR — Mountain Bird (S6/MBI) — Salmon-Lemhi County, ID (SMN)

☐ N80GV	Piper PA-31-350 Navajo Chieftain	31-7552003	ex N61487	
☐ N3528Y	Piper PA-31-350 Chieftain	31-7952149		
☐ N4237D	Piper PA-31-350 Navajo Chieftain	31-7305055	ex N800MW	
☐ N31932	Piper PA-31-350 Navajo Chieftain	31-7405144	ex N888TV	
☐ N84859	Piper PA-31-350 Navajo Chieftain	31-7305043	ex N804PC	
☐ N6561B	Britten-Norman BN-2A-20 Islander	520	ex YV-0-GSF-6	dam 15Jly07
☐ N7067Z	Cessna T210M Turbo Centurion II	21062572	ex C-GPTX	
☐ N8514C	Piper PA-34-200T Seneca II	34-7670147		

SAN JUAN AIRLINES — West Isle Air (2G/MRR) — Anacortes, WA (OTS)

☐ N63SJ	Cessna U206F Stationair	U20603521	ex N8768Q
☐ N1584U	Cessna 207 Skywagon	20700184	
☐ N7405	Cessna T207 Turbo Skywagon	20700147	exV3-HNO

SAPPHIRE AVIATION — Sapphire (SPP) — West Palm Beach, FL (LNA)

☐ N57EB	Aero Commander 500A	500A-1245-71	ex N357TK
☐ N78343	Aero Commander 500A	500A-1264-87	

SB AIR — S-Bar (SBF) — Albuquerque-Intl Sunport, NM/Dallas-Love Field, TX (ABQ/DAL)

☐ N17NM	Beech 65-E90 King Air	LW-237	ex N5NM	EMS
☐ N21NM	Beech 65-E90 King Air	LW-336	ex N675J	EMS
☐ N44GK	Beech 65-E90 King Air	LW-298	ex N2029X	EMS N118SB resd
☐ N304LG	Beech 65-E90 King Air	LW-231	ex N4954S	EMS
☐ N11692	Beech 65-C90 King Air	LJ-772	ex F-GFBO	EMS
☐ N114SB	Beech 200 Super King Air	BB-161	ex N131PA	

SCENIC AIRLINES — Scenic (YR/SCE) — Las Vegas-North, NV/Page, AZ (VGT/PGA)

☐ N140SA	de Havilland DHC-6 Twin Otter 300	267	ex N387EX
☐ N142SA	de Havilland DHC-6 Twin Otter 300	241	ex N385EX
☐ N146SA	de Havilland DHC-6 Twin Otter 300	514	ex N27RA
☐ N148SA	de Havilland DHC-6 Twin Otter 300	409	ex N548N
☐ N226SA	de Havilland DHC-6 Twin Otter 300	585	ex Chile 934
☐ N227SA	de Havilland DHC-6 Twin Otter 300	517	ex N43SP
☐ N228SA	de Havilland DHC-6 Twin Otter 300	253	ex N103AC
☐ N241SA	de Havilland DHC-6 Twin Otter 300	556	ex N97RA
☐ N297SA	de Havilland DHC-6 Twin Otter 300	297	ex N852TB
☐ N359AR	de Havilland DHC-6 Twin Otter 300	359	ex N148SA
☐ N692AR	de Havilland DHC-6 Twin Otter 300	692	ex N230SA

SCENIC AVIATION — Blanding Municipal, UT (BDG)

☐ N13GZ	Beech 65-C90B King Air	LJ-1590	ex PT-WXH
☐ N588SA	Beech 65-C90B King Air	LJ-1588	
☐ N590GM	Beech 65-C90B King Air	LJ-1594	
☐ N1083S	Beech 65-C90B King Air	LJ-1443	
☐ N47744	Piper PA-34-200T Seneca II	34-7870026	

SEABORNE AIRLINES — Seaborne (BB) — St Thomas-SPB, VI (SPB)

☐ N224SA	de Havilland DHC-6 Twin Otter 300	247	ex C-GOES	VistaLiner
☐ N288SA	de Havilland DHC-6 Twin Otter 300	389	ex V2-LEY	VistaLiner
☐ N562CP	de Havilland DHC-6 Twin Otter 300	562	ex TI-BAL	
☐ N573SA	de Havilland DHC-6 Twin Otter 300	573	ex N41991	
☐ N888PV	de Havilland DHC-6 Twin Otter 300	620	ex CF-TWW	

SEAPLANES OF KEY WEST — Key West-Intl, FL (EYW)

☐ N200KW	Cessna U206F Stationair	U20602785	ex N108SM	Floatplane

SERVANT AIR(8D) — Kodiak-Municipal, AK (KDK)

☐ N1658U	Cessna 207 Skywagon	20700258
☐ N1750U	Cessna 207 Skywagon	20700350
☐ N75311	Piper PA-32R-300 Lance	32R-7680291

SHUTTLE AMERICA — Shuttlecraft (S5/TCF) — Wilmington-Newcastle, DE/Windsor Locks-Bradley Intl, CT (ILG/BDL)

Operates aircraft for Delta Connection and United Express in full colours. Wholly owned by Republic Airlines.

SIERRA PACIFIC AIRLINES — Sierra Pacific (SI/SPA) — Tucson-Intl, AZ (TUS)

☐ N703S	Boeing 737-2T4 (AvAero 3)	22529/750	ex N703ML	
☐ N712S	Boeing 737-2Y5 (AvAero 3)	23038/949	ex ZK-NAF	

SIERRA WEST AIRLINES — Platinum West (PKW) — Oakdale, CA (SCK)

☐ N63NE	Swearingen SA.227AC Metro III	AC-763B		Freighter
☐ N221TR	Learjet 35A	35A-221	ex VH-FSY	Freighter
☐ N242DR	Learjet 35A	35A-242	ex VH-FSZ	Freighter
☐ N283SA	AMD Falcon 20	83	ex (N82SR)	Freighter
☐ N681TR	Swearingen SA.227AC Metro III	AC-682	ex N921BC	Freighter
☐ N8897Y	Swearingen SA.226AT Merlin IVC	AT-492	ex C-FJTA	Freighter

SILLER AVIATION — Yuba City-Sutter County, CA (MYV)

☐ N4196Z	Sikorsky S-61R	61567	ex 65-12792
☐ N4197R	Sikorsky S-61R	61571	ex 65-12796
☐ N5193J	Sikorsky S-61A	61014	ex Bu148036
☐ N8170V	Sikorsky S-61A	61232	
☐ N15456	Sikorsky S-61N	61826	
☐ N45917	Sikorsky S-61V-1	61271	
☐ N51953	Sikorsky S-61A	61172	ex Bu149903
☐ N429C	Sikorsky CH-54A	64031	ex 67-18429
☐ N2268L	Sikorsky CH-54A	64013	ex 66-18411
☐ N4035S	Sikorsky S-64E Skycrane	64099	ex 70-18491
☐ N4037S	Sikorsky S-64E Skycrane	64101	ex 70-18493
☐ N7095B	Sikorsky CH-54A	64032	ex 67-18430
☐ N9125M	Sikorsky CH-54A	64057	ex 68-18455

SKAGWAY AIR SERVICE — Skagway Air (N5/SGY) — Skagway, AK (SGY)

☐ N1132Q	Piper PA-32-300 Cherokee Six	32-7740046
☐ N2884M	Piper PA-32-300 Cherokee Six	32-7840058
☐ N8127K	Piper PA-32-300 Six	32-7940268
☐ N31589	Piper PA-32-300 Cherokee Six	32-7840135
☐ N40698	Piper PA-32-300 Cherokee Six	32-7440056
☐ N8216T	Piper PA-32-301 Saratoga	32-8206037
☐ N9540K	Piper PA-34-200T Seneca II	34-7670208

SKY CASTLE AVIATION — New Castle-Henry County, IN (MIE)

☐ N38W	Beech H18	BA-580	ex N616T	Freighter
☐ N4231V	Piper PA-31-350 Navajo Chieftain	31-7652162	ex C-GBHM	
☐ N6685S	Beech 58 Baron	TH-718		

SKY KING — Songbird (F3/SGB) — Sacramento-Metropolitan, CA (SMF)

☐ N147AW	Boeing 737-297 (Nordam 3)	22630/860	ex N729AL	no titles
☐ N249TR	Boeing 737-2K5 (Nordam 3)	22598/792	ex F-GFLX	
☐ N252TR	Boeing 737-228 (Nordam 3)	23001/936	ex F-GBYB	Boni Belle
☐ N464AT	Boeing 737-2L9 (AvAero 3)	21278/479	ex N358AS	no titles
☐ N465AT	Boeing 737-2L9 (AvAero 3)	21528/517	ex N359AS	no titles
☐ N916SK	Boeing 737-4Q8	24706/1996	ex SP-LLI	
☐ N977UA	Boeing 737-2L9 (AvAero 3)	21508/518	ex N7391F	no titles

SKYWAY ENTERPRISES — Skyway Inc (SKZ) — Orlando-Kissimmee, FL/Detroit-Willow Run, IL (ISM/YIP)

☐ N366MQ	Short SD.3-60	SH3639	ex G-14-3639
☐ N367MQ	Short SD.3-60	SH3640	ex G-BLGA
☐ N377MQ	Short SD.3-60	SH3699	ex G-BMUY
☐ N378MQ	Short SD.3-60	SH3700	ex G-BMXP
☐ N380MQ	Short SD.3-60	SH3702	ex (G-BMXS)
☐ N381MQ	Short SD.3-60	SH3703	ex G-14-3703
☐ N383MQ	Short SD.3-60	SH3706	ex (G-BNBB)
☐ N384MQ	Short SD.3-60	SH3711	ex G-BNBG
☐ N385MQ	Short SD.3-60	SH3707	ex G-BNBC
☐ N387MQ	Short SD.3-60	SH3710	ex G-BNBF
☐ N112PS	Douglas DC-9-15F (ABS 3)	47013/129	ex N557AS
☐ N118SW	Short SD.3-30	SH3100	ex 83-0512

SKYWEST AIRLINES — SkyWest (OO/SKW) — Salt Lake City-Intl, UT/Los Angeles-Intl, CA (SLC/LAX)

☐ N947SW	Canadair CL-600-2B19 (CRJ-200ER)	7786	ex C-FMMB	7786
☐ N216SW	Embraer EMB.120ER Brasilia	120285	ex PT-SVF	
☐ N217SW	Embraer EMB.120ER Brasilia	120286	ex PT-SVG	
☐ N224SW	Embraer EMB.120ER Brasilia	120294	ex PT-SVO	

☐ N271YV	Embraer EMB.120ER Brasilia	120271	ex PT-SUS	
☐ N296SW	Embraer EMB.120ER Brasilia	120325	ex PT-SXR	
☐ N299SW	Embraer EMB.120ER Brasilia	120329	ex PT-SXV	
☐ N301YV	Embraer EMB.120ER Brasilia	120301	ex PT-SVV	
☐ N576SW	Embraer EMB.120ER Brasilia	120345	ex PT-SBZ	

Operates for Delta Air Lines (as Delta Connection [231 CRJs, 13 EMB.120s and 12 ATRs]), including some code-shared with Continental Airlines, plus United Air Lines as United Express [171 CRJs and 48 EMB.120s] from points on the West Coast and Nevada and Midwest Connect services (19 CRJs) from Milwaukee and Kansas City. Note some are in SkyWest colours.
Atlantic Southeast Airlines is a wholly owned subsidiary of SkyWest Inc

SMITHAIR — *Smithair (SMH)* — *Hampton-Clayton County, GA*

☐ N351N	Learjet 23	23-054	ex N351NR	Freighter
☐ N900NA	Learjet 24A	24A-111	ex N44WD	EMS
☐ N7200K	Learjet 23	23-099		Freighter

SMOKEY BAY AIR — *(2E)* — *Homer, AK (HOM)*

☐ N35860	Cessna U206G Super Skywagon	U20602764
☐ N72067	Cessna U206D Super Skywagon	U206-1273

SNOW AVIATION — *Columbus-Rickenbacker, OH (LCK)*

☐ N130SA	Lockheed C-130A Hercules	3035	ex N2127W	Development aircraft
☐ N307SA	Lockheed C-130E Hercules	3688	ex N131EV	Development aircraft

SOUTH AERO — *Albuquerque-Intl Sunport, NM (ABQ)*

☐ N42MG	Cessna 402C II	402C0320	ex N36992
☐ N57PB	Cessna 402C II	402C0300	ex N3628M
☐ N305AT	Cessna 402C II	402C0030	ex C-GZVM
☐ N402MQ	Cessna 402C II	402C0095	ex N81PB
☐ N2711X	Cessna 402C II	402C0116	
☐ N2713X	Cessna 402C II	402C0207	
☐ N4643N	Cessna 402C II	402C0006	ex C-GIKA
☐ N5820C	Cessna 402C II	402C0047	
☐ N6880A	Cessna 402C II	402C0616	
☐ N54ZP	Cessna 404 Titan II	404-0694	ex N6764X
☐ N165SA	Cessna 404 Titan II	404-0622	
☐ N5388J	Cessna 404 Titan II	404-0666	
☐ N6479N	Cessna T210N Turbo Centurion II	21063053	
☐ N7213N	Cessna T210N Turbo Centurion II	21063207	

SOUTH PACIFIC EXPRESS — *Pago Pago International (PPG)*

☐ N711MP	Short SD.3-60	SH3698	ex G-BMUX

SOUTHEAST AVIATION — *Ketchikan-SPB, AK (WFB)*

☐ N82SF	de Havilland DHC-2 Beaver	839	ex N44CD	Floatplane
☐ N9279Z	de Havilland DHC-2 Beaver	345	ex 51-16821	Floatplane

SOUTHERN AIR — *Southern Air (9S/SOO)* — *Columbus-Rickenbacker, OH (LCK)*

☐ N704SA	Boeing 747-2B5F	24195/718	ex N298JD		
☐ N708SA	Boeing 747-2B5F	24196/720	ex N299JD		
☐ N723SA	Boeing 747-246F	23641/684	ex JA8180		stored MHV
☐ N740SA	Boeing 747-230B (SF)	21380/320	ex N507MC		stored MHV
☐ N746SA	Boeing 747-206M (EUD)	21111/276	ex PH-BUI	Wilbur Wright	
☐ N748SA	Boeing 747-206M (EUD/(SF))	21110/271	ex PH-BUH		stored MHV
☐ N749SA	Boeing 747-2B5F	24194/713	ex N301JD		
☐ N751SA	Boeing 747-228F	22678/535	ex F-GCBE		stored CGK
☐ N752SA	Boeing 747-228F	21255/295	ex F-BPVR	William Neff	
☐ N753SA	Boeing 747-228F	21787/398	ex F-BPVZ	Southern Dreams	
☐ N754SA	Boeing 747-228F	21576/334	ex N536MC		
☐ N758SA	Boeing 747-281F	23138/604	ex JA8167		
☐ N760SA	Boeing 747-230M	21221/299	ex N509MC		
☐ N761SA	Boeing 747-2F6SF	21832/421	ex N534MC		
☐ N765SA	Boeing 747-2F6B (SCD)	21833/423	ex N535FC		
☐ N783SA	Boeing 747-281F	23919/689	ex JA8188		
☐ N789SA	Boeing 747-341 (SF)	23394/627	ex N354FC		
☐ N795SA	Boeing 747-243M	22506/492	ex VP-BIB		
☐ N798SA	Boeing 747-246B (SF)	23389/635	ex JA8169		stored MHV
☐ N815SA	Boeing 747-2L5B(SF)	22107/469	ex B-HMF		stored MHV
☐ N818SA	Boeing 747-346	23068/589	ex JA813J		stored VCV

SOUTHERN SEAPLANE — *Southern Skies (SSC)* — *Belle Chase-Southern Seaplane SPB, LA (BCS)*

☐ N2272X	Cessna U206E Skywagon	U20601556		Floatplane
☐ N21058	de Havilland DHC-2 Beaver	630	ex CF-HOE	Floatplane

☐ N61301	Cessna A185F Skywagon	18504144		Floatplane
☐ N61441	Cessna A185F Skywagon	18504191		Floatplane
☐ N70822	Cessna U206F Stationair	U20602099		Floatplane

SOUTHWEST AIRLINES — Southwest (WN/SWA) — Dallas-Love Field, TX (DAL)

☐ N300SW	Boeing 737-3H4	22940/1037		The Spirit of Kitty Hawk
☐ N302SW	Boeing 737-3H4	22942/1052		The Spirit of Kitty Hawk
☐ N303SW	Boeing 737-3H4	22943/1101		
☐ N304SW	Boeing 737-3H4	22944/1138		
☐ N305SW	Boeing 737-3H4	22945/1139		
☐ N306SW	Boeing 737-3H4	22946/1148		
☐ N307SW	Boeing 737-3H4	22947/1156		
☐ N308SA	Boeing 737-3Y0	23498/1233	ex G-EZYA	
☐ N309SW	Boeing 737-3H4	22948/1160		
☐ N310SW	Boeing 737-3H4	22949/1161		
☐ N311SW	Boeing 737-3H4	23333/1183		
☐ N312SW	Boeing 737-3H4	23334/1185		
☐ N313SW	Boeing 737-3H4	23335/1201		
☐ N314SW	Boeing 737-3H4	23336/1229		
☐ N315SW	Boeing 737-3H4	23337/1231		
☐ N316SW	Boeing 737-3H4	23338/1232		
☐ N317WN	Boeing 737-3Q8	24068/1506	ex G-EZYE	
☐ N318SW	Boeing 737-3H4	23339/1255		
☐ N323SW	Boeing 737-3H4	23344/1378		
☐ N325SW	Boeing 737-3H4	23689/1398		
☐ N326SW	Boeing 737-3H4	23690/1400		
☐ N327SW	Boeing 737-3H4	23691/1407		
☐ N328SW	Boeing 737-3H4	23692/1521		
☐ N329SW	Boeing 737-3H4	23693/1525		
☐ N330SW	Boeing 737-3H4	23694/1529		
☐ N331SW	Boeing 737-3H4	23695/1536		
☐ N332SW	Boeing 737-3H4	23696/1545		
☐ N333SW	Boeing 737-3H4	23697/1547		
☐ N334SW	Boeing 737-3H4	23938/1549		Shamu
☐ N335SW	Boeing 737-3H4	23939/1553		
☐ N336SW	Boeing 737-3H4	23940/1557		
☐ N337SW	Boeing 737-3H4	23959/1567		
☐ N338SW	Boeing 737-3H4	23960/1571		
☐ N339SW	Boeing 737-3H4	24090/1591		
☐ N340LV	Boeing 737-3K2	23738/1360	ex PH-HVJ	
☐ N341SW	Boeing 737-3H4	24091/1593		
☐ N342SW	Boeing 737-3H4	24133/1682		
☐ N343SW	Boeing 737-3H4	24151/1686		
☐ N344SW	Boeing 737-3H4	24152/1688		
☐ N345SA	Boeing 737-3K2	23786/1386	ex PH-HVK	
☐ N346SW	Boeing 737-3H4	24153/1690		
☐ N347SW	Boeing 737-3H4	24374/1708		
☐ N348SW	Boeing 737-3H4	24375/1710		
☐ N349SW	Boeing 737-3H4	24408/1734		
☐ N350SW	Boeing 737-3H4	24409/1748		
☐ N351SW	Boeing 737-3H4	24572/1790		
☐ N352SW	Boeing 737-3H4	24888/1942		Lone Star One
☐ N353SW	Boeing 737-3H4	24889/1947		
☐ N354SW	Boeing 737-3H4	25219/2092		
☐ N355SW	Boeing 737-3H4	25250/2103		
☐ N356SW	Boeing 737-3H4	25251/2105		
☐ N357SW	Boeing 737-3H4	26594/2294		
☐ N358SW	Boeing 737-3H4	26595/2295		
☐ N359SW	Boeing 737-3H4/W	26596/2297		
☐ N360SW	Boeing 737-3H4/W	26571/2307		
☐ N361SW	Boeing 737-3H4/W	26572/2309		
☐ N362SW	Boeing 737-3H4/W	26573/2322		
☐ N363SW	Boeing 737-3H4/W	26574/2429		Heroes of the Heart
☐ N364SW	Boeing 737-3H4/W	26575/2430		
☐ N365SW	Boeing 737-3H4/W	26576/2433		
☐ N366SW	Boeing 737-3H4/W	26577/2469		
☐ N367SW	Boeing 737-3H4/W	26578/2470		
☐ N368SW	Boeing 737-3H4/W	26579/2473		
☐ N369SW	Boeing 737-3H4/W	26580/2477		
☐ N370SW	Boeing 737-3H4/W	26597/2497		
☐ N371SW	Boeing 737-3H4/W	26598/2500		
☐ N372SW	Boeing 737-3H4/W	26599/2504		
☐ N373SW	Boeing 737-3H4/W	26581/2509		
☐ N374SW	Boeing 737-3H4/W	26582/2515		
☐ N375SW	Boeing 737-3H4/W	26583/2520		
☐ N376SW	Boeing 737-3H4/W	26584/2570		
☐ N378SW	Boeing 737-3H4/W	26585/2579		
☐ N379SW	Boeing 737-3H4/W	26586/2580		
☐ N380SW	Boeing 737-3H4/W	26587/2610		
☐ N382SW	Boeing 737-3H4/W	26588/2611		
☐ N383SW	Boeing 737-3H4/W	26589/2612		Arizona One
☐ N384SW	Boeing 737-3H4	26590/2613		

☐ N385SW	Boeing 737-3H4	26600/2617		
☐ N386SW	Boeing 737-3H4	26601/2626		
☐ N387SW	Boeing 737-3H4	26602/2627		
☐ N388SW	Boeing 737-3H4	26591/2628		
☐ N389SW	Boeing 737-3H4	26592/2629		
☐ N390SW	Boeing 737-3H4/W	26593/2642		
☐ N391SW	Boeing 737-3H4/W	27378/2643		
☐ N392SW	Boeing 737-3H4/W	27379/2644		
☐ N394SW	Boeing 737-3H4/W	27380/2645		
☐ N395SW	Boeing 737-3H4/W	27689/2667		
☐ N396SW	Boeing 737-3H4/W	27690/2668		
☐ N397SW	Boeing 737-3H4/W	27691/2695		
☐ N398SW	Boeing 737-3H4/W	27692/2696		
☐ N399WN	Boeing 737-3H4/W	27693/2697		
☐ N600WN	Boeing 737-3H4	27694/2699		
☐ N601WN	Boeing 737-3H4/W	27695/2702		Jack Vidal
☐ N602SW	Boeing 737-3H4/W	27953/2713		
☐ N603SW	Boeing 737-3H4/W	27954/2714		
☐ N604SW	Boeing 737-3H4/W	27955/2715		
☐ N605SW	Boeing 737-3H4	27956/2716		
☐ N606SW	Boeing 737-3H4/W	27926/2740		
☐ N607SW	Boeing 737-3H4/W	27927/2741		June M Morris
☐ N608SW	Boeing 737-3H4/W	27928/2742		
☐ N609SW	Boeing 737-3H4	27929/2744		California One
☐ N610WN	Boeing 737-3H4/W	27696/2745		
☐ N611SW	Boeing 737-3H4/W	27697/2750		
☐ N612SW	Boeing 737-3H4/W	27930/2753		
☐ N613SW	Boeing 737-3H4	27931/2754		
☐ N614SW	Boeing 737-3H4/W	28033/2755		
☐ N615SW	Boeing 737-3H4/W	27698/2757		
☐ N616SW	Boeing 737-3H4/W	27699/2758		
☐ N617SW	Boeing 737-3H4/W	27700/2759	ex N1786B	
☐ N618WN	Boeing 737-3H4	28034/2761		
☐ N619SW	Boeing 737-3H4/W	28035/2762		
☐ N620SW	Boeing 737-3H4/W	28036/2766		
☐ N621SW	Boeing 737-3H4	28037/2767		
☐ N622SW	Boeing 737-3H4/W	27932/2779		
☐ N623SW	Boeing 737-3H4/W	27933/2780		
☐ N624SW	Boeing 737-3H4/W	27934/2781		
☐ N625SW	Boeing 737-3H4/W	27701/2787		
☐ N626SW	Boeing 737-3H4/W	27702/2789		
☐ N627SW	Boeing 737-3H4/W	27935/2790		
☐ N628SW	Boeing 737-3H4/W	27703/2795		
☐ N629SW	Boeing 737-3H4/W	27704/2796		25 Silver One
☐ N630WN	Boeing 737-3H4/W	27705/2797		
☐ N631SW	Boeing 737-3H4/W	27706/2798		
☐ N632SW	Boeing 737-3H4/W	27707/2799		
☐ N633SW	Boeing 737-3H4/W	27936/2807		
☐ N634SW	Boeing 737-3H4/W	27937/2808		
☐ N635SW	Boeing 737-3H4/W	27708/2813		
☐ N636WN	Boeing 737-3H4/W	27709/2814		
☐ N637SW	Boeing 737-3H4/W	27710/2819		
☐ N638SW	Boeing 737-3H4/W	27711/2820		
☐ N639SW	Boeing 737-3H4/W	27712/2821		
☐ N640SW	Boeing 737-3H4/W	27713/2840		
☐ N641SW	Boeing 737-3H4/W	27714/2841		
☐ N642WN	Boeing 737-3H4/W	27715/2842		
☐ N643SW	Boeing 737-3H4/W	27716/2843		
☐ N644SW	Boeing 737-3H4/W	28329/2869		
☐ N645SW	Boeing 737-3H4/W	28330/2870		
☐ N646SW	Boeing 737-3H4/W	28331/2871		
☐ N647SW	Boeing 737-3H4/W	27717/2892		Triple Crown c/s
☐ N648SW	Boeing 737-3H4/W	27718/2893		
☐ N649SW	Boeing 737-3H4/W	27719/2894		
☐ N650SW	Boeing 737-3H4/W	27720/2901		
☐ N651SW	Boeing 737-3H4	27721/2915		
☐ N652SW	Boeing 737-3H4/W	27722/2916		
☐ N653SW	Boeing 737-3H4/W	28398/2917		
☐ N654SW	Boeing 737-3H4/W	28399/2918		
☐ N655WN	Boeing 737-3H4/W	28400/2931		
☐ N656SW	Boeing 737-3H4/W	28401/2932		
☐ N657SW	Boeing 737-3L9	23331/1111	ex N960WP	
☐ N658SW	Boeing 737-3L9	23332/1118	ex N961WP	
☐ N659SW	Boeing 737-301	23229/1112	ex N950WP	
☐ N660SW	Boeing 737-301	23230/1115	ex N949WP	
☐ N661SW	Boeing 737-317	23173/1098	ex N946WP	
☐ N662SW	Boeing 737-3Q8	23255/1125	ex N327US	
☐ N663SW	Boeing 737-3Q8	23256/1128	ex N329US	
☐ N664WN	Boeing 737-3Y0	23495/1206	ex EC-FVT	
☐ N665WN	Boeing 737-3Y0	23497/1227	ex G-MONF	
☐ N669SW	Boeing 737-3A4	23752/1484	ex N758MA	
☐ N670SW	Boeing 737-3G7	23784/1533	ex N779MA	
☐ N671SW	Boeing 737-3G7	23785/1535	ex N778MA	

	Registration	Type	C/n	Previous identity	Name
☐	N675AA	Boeing 737-3A4	23253/1096	ex (TF-AIC)	
☐	N676SW	Boeing 737-3A4	23288/1100	ex N742MA	
☐	N679AA	Boeing 737-3A4	23291/1211	ex N306AC	
☐	N680AA	Boeing 737-3A4	23505/1318	ex N310AC	
☐	N682SW	Boeing 737-3Y0	23496/1217	ex N67AB	
☐	N683SW	Boeing 737-3G7	24008/1576	ex N301AW	
☐	N684WN	Boeing 737-3T0	23941/1520	ex EC-EID	
☐	N685SW	Boeing 737-3Q8	23401/1209	ex G-BOWR	
☐	N686SW	Boeing 737-317	23175/1110	ex EI-CHU	
☐	N687SW	Boeing 737-3Q8	23388/1187	ex N103GU	
☐	N688SW	Boeing 737-3Q8	23254/1107	ex N780MA	
☐	N689SW	Boeing 737-3Q8	23387/1163	ex N734MA	
☐	N690SW	Boeing 737-3G7	23783/1531	ex N785MA	
☐	N691WN	Boeing 737-3G7	23781/1494	ex N784MA	
☐	N692SW	Boeing 737-3T5	23062/1083	ex N733MA	
☐	N693SW	Boeing 737-317	23174/1104	ex N775MA	
☐	N694SW	Boeing 737-3T5	23061/1080	ex N744MA	
☐	N697SW	Boeing 737-3T0	23838/1505	ex N764MA	
☐	N698SW	Boeing 737-317	23176/1213	ex EI-CHD	
☐	N699SW	Boeing 737-3Y0	23826/1372	ex EI-CHE	
☐	N501SW	Boeing 737-5H4	24178/1718	ex N73700	
☐	N502SW	Boeing 737-5H4	24179/1744		
☐	N503SW	Boeing 737-5H4	24180/1766		
☐	N504SW	Boeing 737-5H4	24181/1804		
☐	N505SW	Boeing 737-5H4	24182/1826		
☐	N506SW	Boeing 737-5H4	24183/1852		
☐	N507SW	Boeing 737-5H4	24184/1864		
☐	N508SW	Boeing 737-5H4	24185/1932		
☐	N509SW	Boeing 737-5H4	24186/1934		
☐	N510SW	Boeing 737-5H4	24187/1940		
☐	N511SW	Boeing 737-5H4	24188/2029		
☐	N512SW	Boeing 737-5H4	24189/2056		
☐	N513SW	Boeing 737-5H4	24190/2058		
☐	N514SW	Boeing 737-5H4	25153/2078		
☐	N515SW	Boeing 737-5H4	25154/2080		
☐	N519SW	Boeing 737-5H4	25318/2121		
☐	N520SW	Boeing 737-5H4	25319/2134		
☐	N521SW	Boeing 737-5H4	25320/2136		
☐	N522SW	Boeing 737-5H4	26564/2202		
☐	N523SW	Boeing 737-5H4	26565/2204		
☐	N524SW	Boeing 737-5H4	26566/2224		
☐	N525SW	Boeing 737-5H4	26567/2283		
☐	N526SW	Boeing 737-5H4	26568/2285		
☐	N527SW	Boeing 737-5H4	26569/2287		
☐	N528SW	Boeing 737-5H4	26570/2292		
☐	N200WN	Boeing 737-7H4/W	32482/1638	ex N1795B	
☐	N201LV	Boeing 737-7H4/W	29854/1650		Fred J Jones
☐	N202WN	Boeing 737-7H4/W	33999/1653		
☐	N203WN	Boeing 737-7H4/W	32483/1656		
☐	N204WN	Boeing 737-7H4/W	29855/1663		
☐	N205WN	Boeing 737-7H4/W	34010/1668	ex N1784B	
☐	N206WN	Boeing 737-7H4/W	34011/1675		
☐	N207WN	Boeing 737-7H4/W	34012/1678		
☐	N208WN	Boeing 737-7H4/W	29856/1679		
☐	N209WN	Boeing 737-7H4/W	32484/1683	ex N1787B	
☐	N210WN	Boeing 737-7H4/W	34162/1690		
☐	N211WN	Boeing 737-7H4/W	34163/1699		
☐	N212WN	Boeing 737-7H4/W	32485/1708		
☐	N213WN	Boeing 737-7H4/W	34217/1717		
☐	N214WN	Boeing 737-7H4/W	32486/1721		Maryland One
☐	N215WN	Boeing 737-7H4/W	32487/1723		Ron Chapman
☐	N216WR	Boeing 737-7H4/W	32488/1735	ex N1784B	
☐	N217JC	Boeing 737-7H4/W	34232/1737	ex (N217WN)	
☐	N218WN	Boeing 737-7H4/W	32489/1741		
☐	N219WN	Boeing 737-7H4/W	32490/1744	ex N1786B	
☐	N220WN	Boeing 737-7H4/W	32491/1756		
☐	N221WN	Boeing 737-7H4/W	34259/1776	ex N1786B	
☐	N222WN	Boeing 737-7H4/W	34290/1780		
☐	N223WN	Boeing 737-7H4/W	32492/1799	ex N1795B	
☐	N224WN	Boeing 737-7H4/W	32493/1801	ex N1786B	Slam Dunk One
☐	N225WN	Boeing 737-7H4/W	34333/1820		
☐	N226WN	Boeing 737-7H4/W	32494/1822	ex N1786B	
☐	N227WN	Boeing 737-7H4/W	34450/1831	ex N1786B	
☐	N228WN	Boeing 737-7H4/W	32496/1835	ex N1780B	
☐	N229WN	Boeing 737-7H4/W	32498/1858		
☐	N230WN	Boeing 737-7H4/W	34592/1868		5000th 737 built
☐	N231WN	Boeing 737-7H4/W	32499/1881	ex N1787B	
☐	N232WN	Boeing 737-7H4/W	32500/1888		
☐	N233LV	Boeing 737-7H4/W	32501/1893		
☐	N234WN	Boeing 737-7H4/W	32502/1905		
☐	N235WN	Boeing 737-7H4/W	34630/1916	ex N1787B	

☐ N236WN	Boeing 737-7H4/W	34631/1928	ex N1786B	
☐ N237WN	Boeing 737-7H4/W	34632/1930		
☐ N238WN	Boeing 737-7H4/W	34713/1950		Spreading the LUV
☐ N239WN	Boeing 737-7H4/W	34714/1954	ex N1786B	
☐ N240WN	Boeing 737-7H4/W	32503/1959	ex N1786B	
☐ N241WN	Boeing 737-7H4/W	32504/1965		
☐ N242WN	Boeing 737-7H4/W	32505/1969		
☐ N243WN	Boeing 737-7H4/W	34863/1973		
☐ N244WN	Boeing 737-7H4/W	34864/1977		
☐ N245WN	Boeing 737-7H4/W	32506/1982		
☐ N246LV	Boeing 737-7H4/W	32507/1984	ex N1786B	
☐ N247WN	Boeing 737-7H4/W	32508/1989		
☐ N248WN	Boeing 737-7H4/W	32509/2000		
☐ N249WN	Boeing 737-7H4/W	34951/2005		
☐ N250WN	Boeing 737-7H4/W	34972/2019		
☐ N251WN	Boeing 737-7H4/W	32510/2025		
☐ N252WN	Boeing 737-7H4/W	34973/2027		
☐ N253WN	Boeing 737-7H4/W	32511/2038		
☐ N254WN	Boeing 737-7H4/W	32512/2040		
☐ N255WN	Boeing 737-7H4/W	32513/2049		
☐ N256WN	Boeing 737-7H4/W	32514/2059		
☐ N257WN	Boeing 737-7H4/W	32515/2062		
☐ N258WN	Boeing 737-7H4/W	32516/2076		
☐ N259WN	Boeing 737-7H4/W	35554/2092		
☐ N260WN	Boeing 737-7H4/W	32518/2114	ex N1786B	
☐ N261WN	Boeing 737-7H4/W	32517/2133	ex N1787B	
☐ N262WN	Boeing 737-7H4/W	32519/2139	ex N1786B	
☐ N263WN	Boeing 737-7H4/W	32520/2153		
☐ N264LV	Boeing 737-7H4/W	32521/2161		
☐ N265WN	Boeing 737-7H4/W	32522/2174		
☐ N266WN	Boeing 737-7H4/W	32523/2182	ex N1787B	Colleen Barrett
☐ N267WN	Boeing 737-7H4/W	32525/2193		
☐ N268WN	Boeing 737-7H4/W	32524/2199		
☐ N269WN	Boeing 737-7H4/W	32526/2204		
☐ N270WN	Boeing 737-705/W	29089/83	ex VP-BBT	
☐ N271LV	Boeing 737-705/W	29090/109	ex VP-BBU	
☐ N272WN	Boeing 737-7H4/W	32527/2224	ex N1786B	
☐ N273WN	Boeing 737-7H4/W	32528/2238		
☐ N274WN	Boeing 737-7H4/W	32529/2244		
☐ N275WN	Boeing 737-7H4/W	36153/2256		
☐ N276WN	Boeing 737-7H4/W	32530/2262		
☐ N277WN	Boeing 737-7H4/W	32531/2274		
☐ N278WN	Boeing 737-7H4/W	36441/2281	ex N1787B	
☐ N279WN	Boeing 737-7H4/W	32532/2284	ex N1786B	
☐ N280WN	Boeing 737-7H4/W	32533/2294		
☐ N281WN	Boeing 737-7H4/W	36528/2307		Southwest's 500th Boeing 737
☐ N282WN	Boeing 737-7H4/W	32534/2318		
☐ N283WN	Boeing 737-7H4/W	36610/2322		
☐ N284WN	Boeing 737-7H4/W	32535/2328	ex N1786B	
☐ N285WN	Boeing 737-7H4/W	32536/2337		
☐ N286WN	Boeing 737-7H4/W	32471/1535	ex N471WN	
☐ N287WN	Boeing 737-7H4/W	32537/2344	ex N1786B	
☐ N288WN	Boeing 737-7H4/W	36611/2350	ex N1786B	
☐ N289CT	Boeing 737-7H4/W	36633/2354	ex N1786B	
☐ N290WN	Boeing 737-7H4/W	36632/2363		
☐ N291WN	Boeing 737-7H4/W	32539/2378		
☐ N292WN	Boeing 737-7H4/W	32538/2383		
☐ N293WN	Boeing 737-7H4/W	36612/2387		
☐ N294WN	Boeing 737-7H4/W	32540/2390	ex N1786B	
☐ N295WN	Boeing 737-7H4/W	32541/2409		
☐ N296WN	Boeing 737-7H4/W	36613/2413		
☐ N297WN	Boeing 737-7H4/W	32542/2417		
☐ N298WN	Boeing 737-7H4/W	32543/2438		
☐ N299WN	Boeing 737-7H4/W	36614/2442		
☐ N400WN	Boeing 737-7H4/W	27891/806		
☐ N401WN	Boeing 737-7H4/W	29813/810		
☐ N402WN	Boeing 737-7H4/W	29814/811	ex N1786B	
☐ N403WN	Boeing 737-7H4/W	29815/821	ex N1786B	
☐ N404WN	Boeing 737-7H4/W	27892/880	ex N1787B	
☐ N405WN	Boeing 737-7H4/W	27893/881	ex N1786B	
☐ N406WN	Boeing 737-7H4/W	27894/885	ex N1786B	
☐ N407WN	Boeing 737-7H4/W	29817/903	ex N1786B	
☐ N408WN	Boeing 737-7H4/W	27895/934	ex N1786B	
☐ N409WN	Boeing 737-7H4/W	27896/945	ex N1787B	
☐ N410WN	Boeing 737-7H4/W	27897/946	ex N1786B	
☐ N411WN	Boeing 737-7H4/W	29821/950	ex N1786B	
☐ N412WN	Boeing 737-7H4/W	29818/956	ex N1795B	
☐ N413WN	Boeing 737-7H4/W	29819/960		
☐ N414WN	Boeing 737-7H4/W	29820/967	ex N1795B	
☐ N415WN	Boeing 737-7H4/W	29836/980	ex N1787B	
☐ N416WN	Boeing 737-7H4/W	32453/990	ex N1786B	
☐ N417WN	Boeing 737-7H4/W	29822/993	ex N1786B	The Rollin W King
☐ N418WN	Boeing 737-7H4/W	29823/1000		The Winning Spirit

☐ N419WN	Boeing 737-7H4/W	29824/1017	ex N1786B	
☐ N420WN	Boeing 737-7H4/W	29825/1039		
☐ N421LV	Boeing 737-7H4/W	32452/1040		
☐ N422WN	Boeing 737-7H4/W	29826/1093		
☐ N423WN	Boeing 737-7H4/W	29827/1101		
☐ N424WN	Boeing 737-7H4/W	29828/1105		
☐ N425LV	Boeing 737-7H4/W	29829/1109		
☐ N426WN	Boeing 737-7H4/W	29830/1114		
☐ N427WN	Boeing 737-7H4/W	29831/1119		
☐ N428WN	Boeing 737-7H4/W	29844/1243		
☐ N429WN	Boeing 737-7H4/W	33658/1256		
☐ N430WN	Boeing 737-7H4/W	33659/1257		
☐ N431WN	Boeing 737-7H4/W	29845/1259		
☐ N432WN	Boeing 737-7H4/W	33715/1297	ex N1786B	
☐ N433LV	Boeing 737-7H4/W	33716/1301		
☐ N434WN	Boeing 737-7H4/W	32454/1313		
☐ N435WN	Boeing 737-7H4/W	32455/1328		
☐ N436WN	Boeing 737-7H4/W	32456/1342		
☐ N437WN	Boeing 737-7H4/W	29832/1349		
☐ N438WN	Boeing 737-7H4/W	29833/1353		
☐ N439WN	Boeing 737-7H4/W	29834/1356		The Donald G Ogden
☐ N440LV	Boeing 737-7H4/W	29835/1358		
☐ N441WN	Boeing 737-7H4/W	29837/1360		
☐ N442WN	Boeing 737-7H4/W	32459/1365	ex (N442LV)	
☐ N443WN	Boeing 737-7H4/W	29838/1369		The Spirit of Hope
☐ N444WN	Boeing 737-7H4/W	29839/1374	ex N1786B	
☐ N445WN	Boeing 737-7H4/W	29841/1388		
☐ N446WN	Boeing 737-7H4/W	29842/1401	ex N1787B	
☐ N447WN	Boeing 737-7H4/W	33720/1405		
☐ N448WN	Boeing 737-7H4/W	33721/1409		The Spirit of Kitty Hawk
☐ N449WN	Boeing 737-7H4/W	32469/1427		
☐ N450WN	Boeing 737-7H4/W	32470/1429	ex N60668	
☐ N451WN	Boeing 737-7H4/W	32495/1458		
☐ N452WN	Boeing 737-7H4/W	29846/1461		
☐ N453WN	Boeing 737-7H4/W	29847/1476		
☐ N454WN	Boeing 737-7H4/W	29851/1477		
☐ N455WN	Boeing 737-7H4/W	32462/1480		
☐ N456WN	Boeing 737-7H4/W	32463/1484		
☐ N457WN	Boeing 737-7H4/W	33856/1485		
☐ N458WN	Boeing 737-7H4/W	33857/1490		
☐ N459WN	Boeing 737-7H4/W	32497/1492		
☐ N460WN	Boeing 737-7H4/W	32464/1499		
☐ N461WN	Boeing 737-7H4/W	32465/1510		
☐ N462WN	Boeing 737-7H4/W	32466/1513		
☐ N463WN	Boeing 737-7H4/W	32467/1515		
☐ N464WN	Boeing 737-7H4/W	32468/1517		
☐ N465WN	Boeing 737-7H4/W	33829/1519		
☐ N466WN	Boeing 737-7H4/W	30677/1520		
☐ N467WN	Boeing 737-7H4/W	33830/1521		
☐ N468WN	Boeing 737-7H4/W	33858/1523		
☐ N469WN	Boeing 737-7H4/W	33859/1525		
☐ N470WN	Boeing 737-7H4/W	33860/1528		
☐ N472WN	Boeing 737-7H4/W	33831/1537		
☐ N473WN	Boeing 737-7H4/W	33832/1541		
☐ N474WN	Boeing 737-7H4/W	33861/1543	ex N1786B	
☐ N475WN	Boeing 737-7H4/W	32474/1545		
☐ N476WN	Boeing 737-7H4/W	32475/1549		
☐ N477WN	Boeing 737-7H4/W	33988/1552		
☐ N478WN	Boeing 737-7H4/W	33989/1555		
☐ N479WN	Boeing 737-7H4/W	33990/1558		
☐ N480WN	Boeing 737-7H4/W	33998/1561		
☐ N481WN	Boeing 737-7H4/W	29853/1564		
☐ N482WN	Boeing 737-7H4/W	29852/1568		
☐ N483WN	Boeing 737-7H4/W	32472/1570		
☐ N484WN	Boeing 737-7H4/W	33841/1575	ex N1786B	
☐ N485WN	Boeing 737-7H4/W	32473/1577	ex N1786B	
☐ N486WN	Boeing 737-7H4/W	33852/1579		
☐ N487WN	Boeing 737-7H4/W	33854/1583		
☐ N488WN	Boeing 737-7H4/W	33853/1587		
☐ N489WN	Boeing 737-7H4/W	33855/1589	ex N1780B	
☐ N490WN	Boeing 737-7H4/W	32476/1591		100 H-E-B titles
☐ N491WN	Boeing 737-7H4/W	33867/1598		
☐ N492WN	Boeing 737-7H4/W	33866/1605		
☐ N493WN	Boeing 737-7H4/W	32477/1616		
☐ N494WN	Boeing 737-7H4/W	33868/1621		
☐ N495WN	Boeing 737-7H4/W	33869/1625		
☐ N496WN	Boeing 737-7H4/W	32478/1626		
☐ N497WN	Boeing 737-7H4/W	32479/1628		
☐ N498WN	Boeing 737-7H4/W	32480/1633		
☐ N499WN	Boeing 737-7H4/W	32481/1636		
☐ N550WN	Boeing 737-76Q/W	30279/1010	ex VT-SIR	
☐ N551WN	Boeing 737-76Q/W	30280/1025	ex VT-SIS	
☐ N700GS	Boeing 737-7H4/W	27835/4		

	Reg	Type	C/n	Previous	Notes
☐	N701GS	Boeing 737-7H4/W	27836/6	ex N35108	
☐	N703SW	Boeing 737-7H4/W	27837/12	ex N1792B	
☐	N704SW	Boeing 737-7H4/W	27838/15		
☐	N705SW	Boeing 737-7H4/W	27839/20		
☐	N706SW	Boeing 737-7H4/W	27840/24		
☐	N707SA	Boeing 737-7H4/W	27841/1	ex N737X	
☐	N708SW	Boeing 737-7H4/W	27842/2		
☐	N709SW	Boeing 737-7H4/W	27843/3		
☐	N710SW	Boeing 737-7H4/W	27844/34	ex N1787B	
☐	N711HK	Boeing 737-7H4/W	27845/38		The Herbert D Kelleher
☐	N712SW	Boeing 737-7H4/W	27846/53		
☐	N713SW	Boeing 737-7H4/W	27847/54		Shamu c/s
☐	N714CB	Boeing 737-7H4/W	27848/61		Southwest Classic colours
☐	N715SW	Boeing 737-7H4/W	27849/62		Shamu c/s
☐	N716SW	Boeing 737-7H4/W	27850/64		
☐	N717SA	Boeing 737-7H4/W	27851/70	ex N1799B	
☐	N718SW	Boeing 737-7H4/W	27852/71	ex N3134C	
☐	N719SW	Boeing 737-7H4/W	27853/82		
☐	N720WN	Boeing 737-7H4/W	27854/121	ex N1787B	
☐	N723SW	Boeing 737-7H4/W	27855/199	ex N1787B	
☐	N724SW	Boeing 737-7H4/W	27856/201	ex N1787B	
☐	N725SW	Boeing 737-7H4/W	27857/208	ex N1786B	
☐	N726SW	Boeing 737-7H4/W	27858/213		
☐	N727SW	Boeing 737-7H4/W	27859/274	ex N1786B	Nevada One c/s
☐	N728SW	Boeing 737-7H4/W	27860/276	ex N1787B	
☐	N729SW	Boeing 737-7H4/W	27861/278	ex N1786B	
☐	N730SW	Boeing 737-7H4/W	27862/284	ex N1795B	
☐	N731SA	Boeing 737-7H4/W	27863/318	ex N1786B	
☐	N732SW	Boeing 737-7H4/W	27864/319	ex N1787B	
☐	N733SA	Boeing 737-7H4/W	27865/320	ex N1787B	
☐	N734SA	Boeing 737-7H4/W	27866/324	ex N1795B	
☐	N735SA	Boeing 737-7H4/W	27867/354	ex N1786B	
☐	N736SA	Boeing 737-7H4/W	27868/357	ex N1786B	
☐	N737JW	Boeing 737-7H4/W	27869/358		
☐	N738CB	Boeing 737-7H4/W	27870/360	ex N1786B	
☐	N739GB	Boeing 737-7H4/W	29275/144	ex N1786B	
☐	N740SW	Boeing 737-7H4/W	29276/155		
☐	N741SA	Boeing 737-7H4/W	29277/157		
☐	N742SW	Boeing 737-7H4/W	29278/172		Nolan Ryan Express
☐	N743SW	Boeing 737-7H4/W	29279/175	ex N60436	
☐	N744SW	Boeing 737-7H4/W	29490/232	ex N1781B	
☐	N745SW	Boeing 737-7H4/W	29491/237	ex "N728SW"	
☐	N746SW	Boeing 737-7H4/W	29798/299	ex N1786B	
☐	N747SA	Boeing 737-7H4/W	29799/306		
☐	N748SW	Boeing 737-7H4/W	29800/331	ex N1786B	
☐	N749SW	Boeing 737-7H4/W	29801/343	ex N1786B	
☐	N750SA	Boeing 737-7H4/W	29802/366		
☐	N751SW	Boeing 737-7H4/W	29803/373	ex N1786B	
☐	N752SW	Boeing 737-7H4/W	29804/387		
☐	N753SW	Boeing 737-7H4/W	29848/400	ex N1787B	
☐	N754SW	Boeing 737-7H4/W	29849/416	ex N1787B	
☐	N755SA	Boeing 737-7H4/W	27871/419	ex N1787B	
☐	N756SA	Boeing 737-7H4/W	27872/422	ex N1786B	
☐	N757LV	Boeing 737-7H4/W	29850/425	ex N1786B	
☐	N758SW	Boeing 737-7H4/W	27873/437	ex N1786B	
☐	N759GS	Boeing 737-7H4/W	30544/448	ex N1786B	
☐	N760SW	Boeing 737-7H4/W	27874/468	ex N1786B	
☐	N761RR	Boeing 737-7H4/W	27875/495		
☐	N762SW	Boeing 737-7H4/W	27876/512	ex N1786B	
☐	N763SW	Boeing 737-7H4/W	27877/520	ex N1786B	
☐	N764SW	Boeing 737-7H4/W	27878/521	ex N1787B	
☐	N765SW	Boeing 737-7H4/W	29805/525	ex N1786B	
☐	N766SW	Boeing 737-7H4/W	29806/537	ex N1786B	
☐	N767SW	Boeing 737-7H4/W	29807/541	ex N1787B	
☐	N768SW	Boeing 737-7H4/W	30587/580	ex N1002R	
☐	N769SW	Boeing 737-7H4/W	30588/592		
☐	N770SA	Boeing 737-7H4/W	30589/595		
☐	N771SA	Boeing 737-7H4/W	27879/599		
☐	N772SW	Boeing 737-7H4/W	27880/601		
☐	N773SA	Boeing 737-7H4/W	27881/603	ex N1786B	
☐	N774SW	Boeing 737-7H4/W	27882/609	ex N1786B	
☐	N775SW	Boeing 737-7H4/W	30590/617	ex N1786B	
☐	N776WN	Boeing 737-7H4/W	30591/620	ex N1786B	
☐	N777QC	Boeing 737-7H4/W	30592/621	ex N1786B	
☐	N778SW	Boeing 737-7H4/W	27883/626	ex N1786B	
☐	N779SW	Boeing 737-7H4/W	27884/628	ex N1786B	
☐	N780SW	Boeing 737-7H4/W	27885/643	ex N1786B	
☐	N781WN	Boeing 737-7H4/W	30601/646		New Mexico One
☐	N782SA	Boeing 737-7H4/W	29808/670	ex N1787B	
☐	N783SW	Boeing 737-7H4/W	29809/675	ex N1785B	
☐	N784SW	Boeing 737-7H4/W	29810/677	ex N1786B	
☐	N785SW	Boeing 737-7H4/W	30602/693	ex N1786B	
☐	N786SW	Boeing 737-7H4/W	29811/698	ex N1787B	

☐ N787SA	Boeing 737-7H4/W	29812/705	ex N1786B	
☐ N788SA	Boeing 737-7H4/W	30603/707	ex N1786B	
☐ N789SW	Boeing 737-7H4/W	29816/718	ex N1786B	
☐ N790SW	Boeing 737-7H4/W	30604/721	ex N1786B	
☐ N791SW	Boeing 737-7H4/W	27886/736	ex N1786B	
☐ N792SW	Boeing 737-7H4/W	27887/737		
☐ N793SA	Boeing 737-7H4/W	27888/744	ex N1786B	Spirit One
☐ N794SW	Boeing 737-7H4/W	30605/748	ex N1781B	
☐ N795SW	Boeing 737-7H4/W	30606/780	ex N1786B	
☐ N796SW	Boeing 737-7H4/W	27889/784	ex N1786B	
☐ N797MX	Boeing 737-7H4/W	27890/803		
☐ N798SW	Boeing 737-7AD/W	28436/41	ex N700EW	
☐ N799SW	Boeing 737-7Q8/W	28209/14	ex 9Y-TJI	
☐ N900WN	Boeing 737-7H4/W	32544/2460		
☐ N901WN	Boeing 737-7H4/W	32545/2462		
☐ N902WN	Boeing 737-7H4/W	36615/2469		
☐ N903WN	Boeing 737-7H4/W	32457/2473		
☐ N904WN	Boeing 737-7H4/W	36616/2480	ex N1780B	
☐ N905WN	Boeing 737-7H4/W	36617/2491	ex N1786B	
☐ N906WN	Boeing 737-7H4/W	36887/2494		
☐ N907WN	Boeing 737-7H4/W	36619/2500		
☐ N908WN	Boeing 737-7H4/W	36620/2509	ex N1786B	
☐ N909WN	Boeing 737-7H4/W	32458/2517		
☐ N910WN	Boeing 737-7H4/W	36618/2521	ex N1786B	
☐ N912WN	Boeing 737-7H4/W	36621/2532	ex N1786B	
☐ N913WN	Boeing 737-7H4/W	29840/2536	ex N1787B	
☐ N914WN	Boeing 737-7H4/W	36622/2540	ex N1787B	
☐ N915WN	Boeing 737-7H4/W	36888/2546		
☐ N916WN	Boeing 737-7H4/W	36623/2558		
☐ N917WN	Boeing 737-7H4/W	36624/2562	ex N1787B	
☐ N918WN	Boeing 737-7H4/W	29843/2572		
☐ N919WN	Boeing 737-7H4/W	36625/2591		
☐ N920WN	Boeing 737-7H4/W	32460/2597	ex N1796B	
☐ N921WN	Boeing 737-7H4/W	36626/2600		
☐ N922WN	Boeing 737-7H4/W	32461/2620		
☐ N923WN	Boeing 737-7H4/W	36627/2634		
☐ N924WN	Boeing 737-7H4/W	36628/2640		
☐ N925WN	Boeing 737-7H4/W	36630/2656	ex N1786B	
☐ N926WN	Boeing 737-7H4/W	36629/2663	ex N1786B	
☐ N927WN	Boeing 737-7H4/W	36889/2679		
☐ N928WN	Boeing 737-7H4/W	36890/2687		
☐ N929WN	Boeing 737-7H4/W	36631/2689		
☐ N930WN	Boeing 737-7H4/W	36636/2784	ex N1786B	
☐ N931WN	Boeing 737-7H4/W	36637/2799	ex N1799B	
☐ N932WN	Boeing 737-7H4/W	36639/2837	ex N1786B	
☐ N933WN	Boeing 737-7H4/W	36640/2847		
☐ N934WN	Boeing 737-7H4/W	36642/2878		
☐ N935WN	Boeing 737-7H4/W	36641/2894		
☐ N936WN	Boeing 737-7H4/W	36643/2909	ex N1787B	
☐ N937WN	Boeing 737-7H4/W	36644/2925	ex N1787B	
☐ N938WN	Boeing 737-7H4/W	36645/2929	ex N1786B	
☐ N939WN	Boeing 737-7H4/W	36646/2933	ex N1787B	
☐ N940WN	Boeing 737-7H4/W	36900/2943	ex N1786B	
☐ N941WN	Boeing 737-7H4/W	36647/2961	ex N1796B	
☐ N942WN	Boeing 737-7H4/W	36648/2985	ex N1787B	
☐ N943WN	Boeing 737-7H4/W	36913		on order
☐ N944WN	Boeing 737-7H4/W	36659		on order
☐ N945WN	Boeing 737-7H4/W	36660		on order
☐	Boeing 737-7H4/W			on order
☐	Boeing 737-7H4/W			on order
☐	Boeing 737-7H4/W			on order
☐	Boeing 737-7H4/W			on order
☐	Boeing 737-7H4/W			on order
☐	Boeing 737-7H4/W			on order
☐	Boeing 737-7H4/W			on order

SPERNAK AIRWAYS — *Anchorage-Merrill, AK (MRI)*

☐ N29CF	Cessna 207 Skywagon	20700353	
☐ N6492H	Cessna 207A Stationair 7 II	20700544	
☐ N7392U	Cessna 207A Stationair 7 II	20700435	
☐ N73047	Cessna 207A Stationair 7 II	20700556	ex XB-EXR

SPIRIT AIRLINES — *Spirit Wings (NK/NKS)* — *Fort Lauderdale-Hollywood Intl, FL (FLL)*

☐ N502NK	Airbus A319-132	2433	ex D-AVWX	St Maarten/St Martin
☐ N503NK	Airbus A319-132	2470	ex D-AVYJ	The Caribbean
☐ N504NK	Airbus A319-132	2473	ex D-AVYP	The Bahamas
☐ N505NK	Airbus A319-132	2485	ex D-AVYI	
☐ N506NK	Airbus A319-132	2490	ex D-AVWH	
☐ N507NK	Airbus A319-132	2560	ex D-AVYV	
☐ N508NK	Airbus A319-132	2567	ex D-AVWM	

☐ N509NK	Airbus A319-132	2603	ex D-AVXO	
☐ N510NK	Airbus A319-132	2622	ex D-AVYT	Fort Lauderdale
☐ N512NK	Airbus A319-132	2673	ex D-AVYO	Turks & Caicos Islands
☐ N514NK	Airbus A319-132	2679	ex D-AVYV	Cayman Islands
☐ N516NK	Airbus A319-132	2704	ex D-AVXJ	Cancun
☐ N517NK	Airbus A319-132	2711	ex D-AVYM	Orlando
☐ N522NK	Airbus A319-132	2893	ex D-AVYY	Las Vegas
☐ N523NK	Airbus A319-132	2898	ex D-AVWN	Tampa
☐ N524NK	Airbus A319-132	2929	ex D-AVYU	Suncatcher
☐ N525NK	Airbus A319-132	2942	ex D-AVWX	The Americas
☐ N526NK	Airbus A319-132	2963	ex D-AVYM	
☐ N527NK	Airbus A319-132	2978	ex D-AVXD	
☐ N528NK	Airbus A319-132	2983	ex D-AVXI	
☐ N529NK	Airbus A319-132	3007	ex D-AVYL	
☐ N530NK	Airbus A319-132	3017	ex D-AVXL	
☐ N531NK	Airbus A319-132	3026	ex D-AVWC	
☐ N532NK	Airbus A319-132	3165	ex D-AVYX	
☐ N533NK	Airbus A319-132	3393	ex D-AVWJ	
☐ N534NK	Airbus A319-132	3395	ex D-AVWK	

All names prefixed 'Spirit of'

☐ N587NK	Airbus A321-231	2476	ex D-AVXB	Jamaica
☐ N588NK	Airbus A321-231	2590	ex D-AVZK	

SPRINGFIELD AIR CHARTER — *Springfield, MO (SGF)*

☐ N935MA	SAAB SF.340A	340A-073	ex SE-E73

SPUR AVIATION — *Twin Falls, ID (TWF)*

☐ N531SA	Rockwell 500S Shrike Commander	3059	ex N9027N
☐ N532SA	Aero Commander 500S Shrike	1868-44	ex N9032N
☐ N533SA	Aero Commander 500S Shrike	1786-9	ex N4664E
☐ N534SA	Aero Commander 500S Shrike	1816-22	ex N8485P
☐ N535SA	Rockwell 500S Shrike Commander	3138	ex N1BK
☐ N536SA	Rockwell 500S Shrike Commander	3169	ex N54LW
☐ N50655	Rockwell Turbo Commander 680V	1714-88	ex XB-CED
☐ N54163	Rockwell Turbo Commander 680W	1774-12	ex N5416

STARS AND STRIPES AIR TOURS — *Boulder City, AZ*

☐ N208WF	Cessna 208B Caravan I	208B1042	ex N208JF
☐ N1242Y	Cessna 208B Caravan I	208B0939	ex N124LA

Helicopter flights operated by Las Vegas Helicopters

SUBURBAN AIR FREIGHT — *Sub Air (SUB)* — *Omaha-Eppley Airfield, NE (OMA)*

☐ N114MN	Aero Commander 680FL	1553-107	ex (N2611L)
☐ N290MP	Aero Commander 680FL	1535-104	
☐ N309VS	Aero Commander 680FL	1659-128	ex N6626V
☐ N2828S	Aero Commander 680FL	1329-14	
☐ N4983S	Aero Commander 680FL	1427-70	ex CF-LAC
☐ N5035E	Aero Commander 680FL	1764-147	
☐ N9011N	Aero Commander 680FL	1836-153	

☐ N118SF	Beech C99	U-32	ex C-FESU
☐ N124GP	Beech 1900C	UB-23	ex N23VK
☐ N128SF	Beech 99	U-87	ex N59CA
☐ N147SF	Beech 99	U-47	ex N204BH
☐ N208QC	Cessna 208B Caravan I	208B0774	ex N5261R
☐ N398A	Cessna 208B Caravan I	208B0390	ex LN-TWE
☐ N719GL	Beech 1900C	UB-19	ex N314BH
☐ N864SF	Cessna 208B Caravan I	208B0864	
☐ N895SF	Cessna 208B Caravan I	208B0095	ex N9662B
☐ N7994R	Beech C99	U-103	
☐ N31764	Beech 1900C-1	UC-53	ex LV-WPH

SUN COUNTRY AIRLINES — *Sun Country (SY/SCX)* — *Minneapolis/St Paul Intl, MN (MSP)*

☐ N710SY	Boeing 737-73V	30241/1034	ex N241CL	
☐ N711SY	Boeing 737-73V	30245/1058	ex G-EZJJ	
☐ N801SY	Boeing 737-8Q8/W	30332/777	ex N1787B	The Phoenix
☐ N804SY	Boeing 737-8Q8/W	30689/908		Laughlin Luck
☐ N805SY	Boeing 737-8Q8/W	30032/985	ex N1781B	The Spirit of Minnesota
☐ N806SY	Boeing 737-8Q8/W	28215/75	ex N800NA	
☐ N809SY	Boeing 737-8Q8/W	30683/1669		
☐ N811SY	Boeing 737-8BK/W	29660/2355	ex N1787B	
☐ N813SY	Boeing 737-8Q8	28237/769	ex OY-SED	

SUPERIOR AVIATION		Spend Air (SO/HKA)		Iron Mountain-Kingsford, MI (IMT)
☐ N6851X	Cessna 441 Conquest II	441-0212		

SUPERIOR HELICOPTERS				Glendale-Heliport, OR
☐ N161KA	Kaman K-1200 K-Max	A94-0016		
☐ N312KA	Kaman K-1200 K-Max	A94-0024		

TALKEETNA AIR TAXI				Talkeetna, AK (TKA)
☐ N144Q	de Havilland DHC-2 Beaver	1465		Wheels or skis
☐ N185FK	Cessna A185F Skywagon	18502513	ex N1796R	Wheels or skis
☐ N561TA	de Havilland DHC-2 Beaver	581	ex CF-HGV	Wheels or skis
☐ N565TA	de Havilland DHC-3 Otter	46	ex C-FQOQ	Wheels or skis
☐ N1694M	Cessna A185F Skywagon	18501879		Wheels or skis
☐ N8190Y	de Havilland DHC-2 Beaver	824	ex C-GPUP	Wheels or skis

TANANA AIR SERVICE		Tan Air (4E/TNR)		Ruby, AK (RBY)
☐ N97CR	Piper PA-32R-300 Lance	32R-7780078	ex JA3776	
☐ N4352F	Piper PA-32R-300 Lance	32R-7680441		
☐ N4803S	Piper PA-32-260 Cherokee Six B	32-1188		
☐ N31606	Piper PA-32-260 Cherokee Six E	32-7840137		
☐ N75387	Piper PA-32R-300 Lance	32R-7680298		
☐ N101LJ	Piper PA-31 Turbo Navajo	31-267	ex N9204Y	

TAQUAN AIR SERVICE	Taquan (K3)	Metlakatla/Ketchikan-Waterfront SPB, AK (MTM/WFB)		
☐ N1018A	de Havilland DHC-2 Beaver	178	ex N52409	Floatplane
☐ N5160G	de Havilland DHC-2 Beaver	236	ex 51-16483	Floatplane
☐ N37756	de Havilland DHC-2 Beaver	1456	ex G-203	Floatplane
☐ N67673	de Havilland DHC-2 Beaver	1284	ex 57-2586	Floatplane
☐ N67676	de Havilland DHC-2 Beaver	809	ex N93AK	Floatplane
☐ N68010	de Havilland DHC-2 Beaver	1243	ex 57-6150	Floatplane

TBM		Tulare-Mefford Field, CA/Visalia-Municipal, CA (TLR/VIS)			
☐ N466TM	Lockheed C-130A-1A Hercules	3173	ex 57-0466	64	Tanker
☐ N473TM	Lockheed C-130A-1A Hercules	3081	ex 56-0473	63	Tanker stored TLR

TELESIS TRANSAIR		Telesis (TLX)		Dallas-Love Field, TX (DAL)
☐ N403TE	Cessna 401	401-0008	ex N4080Q	
☐ N405TE	Cessna 401	401-0121	ex N3208Q	
☐ N408TE	Cessna 401	401-0269	ex N4021Q	
☐ N409TE	Cessna 401A	401A0118	ex N217BA	
☐ N3220Q	Cessna 401	401-0020		
☐ N301TE	Piper PA-32-300 Cherokee Six	32-40216	ex N4146W	
☐ N406TE	Cessna 402B	402B1366	ex N110KS	
☐ N602TE	Piper PA-60-601P Aerostar	61P-0583-7962134	ex N942TJ	
☐ N603TE	Ted Smith Aerostar 600	60-0320-118	ex N90609	
☐ N604TE	Ted Smith Aerostar 600	60-0206-091	ex N7544S	

TEMSCO HELICOPTERS		Temsco (TMS)		Ketchikan-Temsco Heliport, AK
☐ N94TH	Aérospatiale AS350B AStar	2548		
☐ N141TH	Aérospatiale AS350B2 AStar	1167	ex N98MB	
☐ N143TH	Aérospatiale AS350B2 AStar	9043		
☐ N145TH	Aérospatiale AS350B2 AStar	9060		
☐ N147TH	Aérospatiale AS350B2 AStar	9070		
☐ N149TH	Aérospatiale AS350B2 AStar	9071		
☐ N403AE	Aérospatiale AS350B3 AStar	3281		
☐ N405AE	Aérospatiale AS350B3 AStar	3286		
☐ N802TH	Aérospatiale AS350B2 AStar	9023		
☐ N911CV	Aérospatiale AS350B3 AStar	3142	ex N40729	
☐ N913LP	Aérospatiale AS350B2 AStar	2383		
☐ N970TH	Aérospatiale AS350BA AStar	9011		
☐ N4022D	Aérospatiale AS350B2 AStar	2891		
☐ N6015S	Aérospatiale AS350BA AStar	1884		
☐ N6080R	Aérospatiale AS350BA AStar	2685		
☐ N6094E	Aérospatiale AS350BA AStar	2750		
☐ N6094U	Aérospatiale AS350BA AStar	2751		
☐ N6302Y	Aérospatiale AS350B2 AStar	9007		
☐ N57954	Aérospatiale AS350B AStar	1127	ex N35977	
☐ N57958	Aérospatiale AS350B AStar	1512		
☐ N214TH	Bell 214B-1	28031	ex N4374D	
☐ N502TH	Bell 205A-1	30030	ex C-FKHQ	

☐ N16920	Bell 212	30865		
☐ N83230	Bell 212	30560		

TEPPER AVIATION — **Crestview-Bob Sikes, FL (CEW)**

☐ N2679C	Lockheed L-382G-69C Hercules	4796	ex N8183J	
☐ N2731G	Lockheed L-382G-30C Hercules	4582	ex N2189M	
☐ N3796B	Lockheed L-382G-39C Hercules	5027	ex N4557C	

Operates for various US Government agencies

TIGER CONTRACT CARGO — **Gainsville-Municipal, TX (-)**

☐ N973AT	Convair 340-70	257	ex N92102	Freighter

TIMBERLINE AIR SERVICE — **Alpine Heliport, OR**

☐ N154TL	Bell UH-IE	6155	ex Bu154770	
☐ N155TL	Bell UH-IE	6164	ex Bu154779	
☐ N457CC	Bell UH-IL	6401	ex N204FW	

TOLAIR SERVICES — **Tol Air (TI/TOL)** — **San Juan-Munoz Marin Intl, PR (SJU)**

☐ N728T	Beech E-18S	BA-130	ex N28V	Freighter
☐ N732T	Beech E-18S	BA-114	ex N52A	Freighter
☐ N748T	Beech E-18S	BA-329	ex N398B	Freighter
☐ N749T	Beech E-18S	BA-55	ex N4641A	Freighter
☐ N779T	Beech H-18	BA-618	ex N220WH	Freighter
☐ N87T	Douglas DC-3	6148	ex N31MC	Freighter
☐ N147JR	Convair 240-57 (T-29C)	403	ex N154PA	stored OPF
☐ N783T	Douglas DC-3	4219	ex N783V	Freighter
☐ N840T	Cessna 402B	402B1099	ex N87280	

TRADEWINDS CARGO — **Tradewinds Express (WI/TDX)** — **Greensboro-Piedmont Triad Intl, NC (GSO)**

☐ N501TR	Airbus A300B4-203F	053	ex N6254X	
☐ N504TA	Airbus A300B4-203F	216	ex N861PA	
☐ N821SC	Airbus A300B4-203F	211	ex TC-ALU	
☐ N985AR	McDonnell-Douglas MD-11C	48430/508	ex EI-UPU	
☐ N986AR	McDonnell-Douglas MD-11C	48426/468	ex EI-UPA	

TRANS NORTH AVIATION — **(HX)** — **Eagle River, WI (EGV)**

☐ N4599F	Cessna 340A	340A0652		
☐ N59773	Piper PA-31-350 Navajo Chieftain	31-7652044		

TRANS STATES AIRLINES — **Waterski (AX/LOF)** — **St Louis-Lambert Intl, MO (STL)**

Operates commuter services for American Airlines as American Connection, US Airways as US Airways Express and United Air Lines as United Express from St Louis, MO, Baltimore-Washington, MD, Newark, NJ, Chicago, IL and Pittsburgh, PA.
Go Jet Airlines is a wholly owned subsidiary based in St Louis, MO operating CRJ-700s for United Express.

TRANSAIR — **Maui (P6/MUI)** — **Honolulu-Intl, HI (HNL)**

☐ N221LM	Short SD.3-60	SH3722	ex N722PC	
☐ N351TA	Short SD.3-60	SH3759	ex N159CC	
☐ N729PC	Short SD.3-60	SH3729	ex 6Y-JMY	
☐ N808KR	Short SD.3-60	SH3734	ex D-CFAO	Freighter
☐ N808TR	Short SD.3-60	SH3718	ex VQ-TSK	Freighter
☐ N827BE	Short SD.3-60	SH3746	ex N746SA	Freighter
☐ N4476F	Short SD.3-60	SH3731	ex 5N-BFT	

TRANSNORTHERN AVIATION — **Transnorthern (TNV)** — **Talkeetna / Fairbanks, AK (TKA/FAI)**

☐ N30TN	Douglas C-117D	43159	ex N53315	Passenger
☐ N39TN	Beech 99	U-2	ex TI-AYM	
☐ N3114G	Swearingen SA.227AC Metro III	AC-583		
☐ N99857	Douglas C-117D	43332	ex N456WL	

TRICOASTAL AIR — **Grand Express (GAE)** — **Toledo Express, OH (TOL)**

☐ N168GA	Swearingen SA.226TC Metro	TC-207	ex N501AB	
☐ N309TC	Learjet 24D	24D-309	ex N80TC	
☐ N589DC	AMD Falcon 20	45	ex N175GA	stored TOL

TROPIC AIR CHARTERS — **Fort Lauderdale Executive, FL (FXE)**

☐ N131JL	Britten-Norman BN-2A-6 Islander	225	ex G-51-225	
☐ N200MU	Britten-Norman BN-2A-27 Islander	78	ex 6Y-JSX	
☐ N296TA	Britten-Norman BN-2A-26 Islander	384	ex J8-VBN	
☐ N297TA	Britten-Norman BN-2A-26 Islander	741	ex N196TA	

TWIN CITIES AIR SERVICE — *Twin City (TCY)* — *Auburn-Lewiston Municipal, ME (LEW)*

☐ N18VV	Cessna 402C	402C0619	ex N180PB	
☐ N196TC	Cessna 310R	310R1801		
☐ N401SX	Cessna 402C	402C0447	ex 9A-BPV	
☐ N402SX	Cessna 402C	402C0606	ex 9A-BPX	
☐ N3249M	Cessna 402C	402C0296		

UFLY AIRWAYS — *(6F/FAO)* — *Miami, FL (MIA)*

☐ N836NK	McDonnell-Douglas MD-83	53045/1777	ex N833RA	
☐ N836RA	McDonnell-Douglas MD-83	53046/1794	ex YV-44C	

UNION FLIGHTS — *Union Flights (UNF)* — *Dayton-Carson City, NV (CSN)*

☐ N127HA	Cessna 208B Caravan I	208B0148		
☐ N208N	Cessna 208B Caravan I	208B0279	ex F-OGRU	
☐ N1116N	Cessna 208B Caravan I	208B0417		
☐ N9655B	Cessna 208B Caravan I	208B0145		
☐ N6654Z	Piper PA-31-350 Navajo Chieftain	31-7752143	ex C-GSUY	Freighter

UNITED AIR LINES — *United (UA/UAL)* — *Chicago-O'Hare Intl, IL/San Francisco-Intl, CA (ORD/SFO)*

Member of Star Alliance

☐ N801UA	Airbus A319-131	0686	ex D-AVYI	4001
☐ N802UA	Airbus A319-131	0690	ex D-AVYO	4002
☐ N803UA	Airbus A319-131	0748	ex D-AVYL	4003
☐ N804UA	Airbus A319-131	0759	ex D-AVYR	4004
☐ N805UA	Airbus A319-131	0783	ex D-AVYY	4005
☐ N806UA	Airbus A319-131	0788	ex D-AVYW	4006
☐ N807UA	Airbus A319-131	0798	ex D-AVYX	4007
☐ N808UA	Airbus A319-131	0804	ex D-AVYF	4008
☐ N809UA	Airbus A319-131	0825	ex D-AVYZ	4009
☐ N810UA	Airbus A319-131	0843	ex D-AVYR	4010
☐ N811UA	Airbus A319-131	0847	ex D-AVYB	4011
☐ N812UA	Airbus A319-131	0850	ex D-AVYK	4012
☐ N813UA	Airbus A319-131	0858	ex D-AVYP	4013
☐ N814UA	Airbus A319-131	0862	ex D-AVYT	4014
☐ N815UA	Airbus A319-131	0867	ex D-AVYU	4015
☐ N816UA	Airbus A319-131	0871	ex D-AVYY	4016
☐ N817UA	Airbus A319-131	0873	ex D-AVYX	4017
☐ N818UA	Airbus A319-131	0882	ex D-AVYE	4018
☐ N819UA	Airbus A319-131	0893	ex D-AVYV	4019
☐ N820UA	Airbus A319-131	0898	ex D-AVYZ	4020
☐ N821UA	Airbus A319-131	0944	ex D-AVYC	4021
☐ N822UA	Airbus A319-131	0948	ex D-AVYE	4022
☐ N823UA	Airbus A319-131	0952	ex D-AVYF	4023
☐ N824UA	Airbus A319-131	0965	ex D-AVYH	4024
☐ N825UA	Airbus A319-131	0980	ex D-AVYN	4025
☐ N826UA	Airbus A319-131	0989	ex D-AVYU	4026
☐ N827UA	Airbus A319-131	1022	ex D-AVYD	4027
☐ N828UA	Airbus A319-131	1031	ex D-AVYF	4028
☐ N829UA	Airbus A319-131	1211	ex D-AVYC	4029
☐ N830UA	Airbus A319-131	1243	ex D-AVWI	4030
☐ N831UA	Airbus A319-131	1291	ex D-AVWF	4031
☐ N832UA	Airbus A319-131	1321	ex D-AVWQ	4032
☐ N833UA	Airbus A319-131	1401	ex D-AVYA	4033
☐ N834UA	Airbus A319-131	1420	ex D-AVYM	4034
☐ N835UA	Airbus A319-131	1426	ex D-AVYN	4035
☐ N836UA	Airbus A319-131	1460	ex D-AVYI	4036
☐ N837UA	Airbus A319-131	1474	ex D-AVYS	4037
☐ N838UA	Airbus A319-131	1477	ex D-AVYG	4038
☐ N839UA	Airbus A319-131	1507	ex D-AVYX	4039
☐ N840UA	Airbus A319-131	1522	ex D-AVYZ	4040
☐ N841UA	Airbus A319-131	1545	ex D-AVWK	4041
☐ N842UA	Airbus A319-131	1569	ex D-AVWA	4042
☐ N843UA	Airbus A319-131	1573	ex D-AVWE	4043
☐ N844UA	Airbus A319-131	1581	ex D-AVWT	4044
☐ N845UA	Airbus A319-131	1585	ex D-AVYD	4045
☐ N846UA	Airbus A319-131	1600	ex D-AVWW	4046
☐ N847UA	Airbus A319-131	1627	ex D-AVYB	4047
☐ N848UA	Airbus A319-131	1647	ex D-AVYK	4048
☐ N849UA	Airbus A319-131	1649	ex D-AVYP	4049
☐ N850UA	Airbus A319-131	1653	ex D-AVYR	4050
☐ N851UA	Airbus A319-131	1664	ex D-AVYX	4051
☐ N852UA	Airbus A319-131	1671	ex D-AVWD	4052
☐ N853UA	Airbus A319-131	1688	ex D-AVWM	4053
☐ N854UA	Airbus A319-131	1731	ex D-AVWS	4054
☐ N855UA	Airbus A319-131	1737	ex D-AVWU	4055

☐ N401UA	Airbus A320-232	0435	ex F-WWDD	4501

	Reg	Type	c/n	Previous identity	Fleet no	Name
☐	N402UA	Airbus A320-232	0439	ex F-WWIJ	4502	
☐	N403UA	Airbus A320-232	0442	ex F-WWIY	4703	
☐	N404UA	Airbus A320-232	0450	ex F-WWII	4704	
☐	N405UA	Airbus A320-232	0452	ex F-WWBF	4705	
☐	N406UA	Airbus A320-232	0454	ex F-WWBJ	4506	
☐	N407UA	Airbus A320-232	0456	ex F-WWDB	4507	
☐	N408UA	Airbus A320-232	0457	ex F-WWDG	4508	
☐	N409UA	Airbus A320-232	0462	ex F-WWDQ	4709	
☐	N410UA	Airbus A320-232	0463	ex F-WWDV	4910	
☐	N411UA	Airbus A320-232	0464	ex F-WWDX	4711	
☐	N412UA	Airbus A320-232	0465	ex F-WWIM	4712	
☐	N413UA	Airbus A320-232	0470	ex F-WWBM	4713	
☐	N414UA	Airbus A320-232	0472	ex F-WWIU	4814	
☐	N415UA	Airbus A320-232	0475	ex F-WWBP	4615	
☐	N416UA	Airbus A320-232	0479	ex F-WWDH	4616	
☐	N417UA	Airbus A320-232	0483	ex F-WWIT	4617	
☐	N418UA	Airbus A320-232	0485	ex F-WWIZ	4618	
☐	N419UA	Airbus A320-232	0487	ex F-WWDJ	4619	
☐	N420UA	Airbus A320-232	0489	ex F-WWDM	4620	
☐	N421UA	Airbus A320-232	0500	ex F-WWDZ	4621	
☐	N422UA	Airbus A320-232	0503	ex F-WWIV	4622	
☐	N423UA	Airbus A320-232	0504	ex F-WWBO	4623	
☐	N424UA	Airbus A320-232	0506	ex F-WWBQ	4624	
☐	N425UA	Airbus A320-232	0508	ex F-WWBY	4625	
☐	N426UA	Airbus A320-232	0510	ex F-WWBZ	4626	
☐	N427UA	Airbus A320-232	0512	ex F-WWDD	4627	
☐	N428UA	Airbus A320-232	0523	ex F-WWDE	4628	
☐	N429UA	Airbus A320-232	0539	ex F-WWIX	4629	
☐	N430UA	Airbus A320-232	0568	ex F-WWDC	4630	
☐	N431UA	Airbus A320-232	0571	ex F-WWDH	4631	
☐	N432UA	Airbus A320-232	0587	ex F-WWBB	4632	
☐	N433UA	Airbus A320-232	0589	ex F-WWBD	4633	
☐	N434UA	Airbus A320-232	0592	ex F-WWBF	4634	
☐	N435UA	Airbus A320-232	0613	ex F-WWBQ	4635	
☐	N436UA	Airbus A320-232	0638	ex F-WWDE	4636	
☐	N437UA	Airbus A320-232	0655	ex F-WWIK	4637	
☐	N438UA	Airbus A320-232	0678	ex F-WWBJ	4838	
☐	N439UA	Airbus A320-232	0683	ex F-WWDQ	4839	
☐	N440UA	Airbus A320-232	0702	ex F-WWDP	4840	
☐	N441UA	Airbus A320-232	0751	ex F-WWIU	4841	
☐	N442UA	Airbus A320-232	0780	ex F-WWDQ	4842	
☐	N443UA	Airbus A320-232	0820	ex F-WWBT	4643	
☐	N444UA	Airbus A320-232	0824	ex F-WWBZ	4844	
☐	N445UA	Airbus A320-232	0826	ex F-WWIL	4845	
☐	N446UA	Airbus A320-232	0834	ex F-WWIP	4846	
☐	N447UA	Airbus A320-232	0836	ex F-WWIR	4847	
☐	N448UA	Airbus A320-232	0842	ex F-WWBF	4848	
☐	N449UA	Airbus A320-232	0851	ex F-WWBJ	4849	
☐	N451UA	Airbus A320-232	0865	ex F-WWBR	4851	
☐	N452UA	Airbus A320-232	0955	ex F-WWBD	4852	
☐	N453UA	Airbus A320-232	1001	ex F-WWBH	4853	
☐	N454UA	Airbus A320-232	1104	ex F-WWDC	4654	
☐	N455UA	Airbus A320-232	1105	ex F-WWDE	4655	
☐	N456UA	Airbus A320-232	1128	ex F-WWIJ	4656	
☐	N457UA	Airbus A320-232	1146	ex F-WWBM	4857	
☐	N458UA	Airbus A320-232	1163	ex F-WWDK	4858	
☐	N459UA	Airbus A320-232	1192	ex F-WWDX	4859	
☐	N460UA	Airbus A320-232	1248	ex F-WWIS	4860	
☐	N461UA	Airbus A320-232	1266	ex F-WWDC	4661	
☐	N462UA	Airbus A320-232	1272	ex F-WWDI	4962	
☐	N463UA	Airbus A320-232	1282	ex F-WWBJ	4663	Jim Briggs
☐	N464UA	Airbus A320-232	1290	ex F-WWBR	4664	
☐	N465UA	Airbus A320-232	1341	ex F-WWDP	4865	
☐	N466UA	Airbus A320-232	1343	ex F-WWDQ	4666	
☐	N467UA	Airbus A320-232	1359	ex F-WWBH	4867	
☐	N468UA	Airbus A320-232	1363	ex F-WWIE	4668	
☐	N469UA	Airbus A320-232	1409	ex F-WWDF	4869	
☐	N470UA	Airbus A320-232	1427	ex F-WWBN	4870	
☐	N471UA	Airbus A320-232	1432	ex F-WWBA	4871	
☐	N472UA	Airbus A320-232	1435	ex F-WWBC	4872	
☐	N473UA	Airbus A320-232	1469	ex F-WWDL	4873	
☐	N474UA	Airbus A320-232	1475	ex F-WWDQ	4874	
☐	N475UA	Airbus A320-232	1495	ex F-WWIC	4875	
☐	N476UA	Airbus A320-232	1508	ex F-WWBB	4876	
☐	N477UA	Airbus A320-232	1514	ex F-WWBF	4877	
☐	N478UA	Airbus A320-232	1533	ex F-WWIQ	4878	
☐	N479UA	Airbus A320-232	1538	ex F-WWIT	4879	
☐	N480UA	Airbus A320-232	1555	ex F-WWBP	4880	
☐	N481UA	Airbus A320-232	1559	ex F-WWDH	4881	
☐	N482UA	Airbus A320-232	1584	ex F-WWBN	4882	
☐	N483UA	Airbus A320-232	1586	ex F-WWBR	4883	
☐	N484UA	Airbus A320-232	1609	ex F-WWBZ	4884	
☐	N485UA	Airbus A320-232	1617	ex F-WWDD	4885	

☐ N486UA	Airbus A320-232	1620	ex F-WWDG	4886	
☐ N487UA	Airbus A320-232	1669	ex F-WWIJ	4887	
☐ N488UA	Airbus A320-232	1680	ex F-WWBF	4888	
☐ N489UA	Airbus A320-232	1702	ex F-WWIT	4889	
☐ N490UA	Airbus A320-232	1728	ex F-WWBI	4890	
☐ N491UA	Airbus A320-232	1741	ex F-WWBU	4891	
☐ N492UA	Airbus A320-232	1755	ex F-WWDZ	4892	
☐ N493UA	Airbus A320-232	1821	ex F-WWIO	4893	
☐ N494UA	Airbus A320-232	1840	ex F-WWDC	4894	
☐ N495UA	Airbus A320-232	1842	ex F-WWBP	4895	
☐ N496UA	Airbus A320-232	1845	ex F-WWDR	4896	
☐ N497UA	Airbus A320-232	1847	ex F-WWDE	4897	
☐ N498UA	Airbus A320-232	1865	ex F-WWIK	4898	
☐ N104UA	Boeing 747-422	26902/1141		8104	
☐ N105UA	Boeing 747-451	26473/985	ex N60659	8105	
☐ N107UA	Boeing 747-422	26900/1168		8107	
☐ N116UA	Boeing 747-422	26908/1193		8116	
☐ N117UA	Boeing 747-422	28810/1197		8117	
☐ N118UA	Boeing 747-422	28811/1201		8118	
☐ N119UA	Boeing 747-422	28812/1207		8119	
☐ N120UA	Boeing 747-422	29166/1209		8120	
☐ N121UA	Boeing 747-422	29167/1211		8121	
☐ N122UA	Boeing 747-422	29168/1218		8122	
☐ N127UA	Boeing 747-422	28813/1221		8127	
☐ N128UA	Boeing 747-422	30023/1245		8128	
☐ N171UA	Boeing 747-422	24322/733		8171	
☐ N173UA	Boeing 747-422	24380/759		8173	
☐ N174UA	Boeing 747-422	24381/762		8174	
☐ N175UA	Boeing 747-422	24382/806		8175	
☐ N177UA	Boeing 747-422	24384/819		8177	
☐ N178UA	Boeing 747-422	24385/820		8178	
☐ N179UA	Boeing 747-422	25158/866		8179	
☐ N180UA	Boeing 747-422	25224/867		8180	
☐ N181UA	Boeing 747-422	25278/881	ex N6005C	8181	
☐ N182UA	Boeing 747-422	25279/882		8182	
☐ N187UA	Boeing 747-422	26876/939		8187	
☐ N193UA	Boeing 747-422	26890/1085		8193	stored VCV
☐ N194UA	Boeing 747-422	26892/1088		8194	stored VCV
☐ N195UA	Boeing 747-422	26899/1113		8195	stored VCV
☐ N196UA	Boeing 747-422	28715/1120		8196	stored VCV
☐ N197UA	Boeing 747-422	26901/1121		8197	
☐ N198UA	Boeing 747-422	28716/1124		8198	stored VCV
☐ N199UA	Boeing 747-422	28717/1126		8199	
☐ N501UA	Boeing 757-222	24622/241		5401	
☐ N502UA	Boeing 757-222/W	24623/246		5702	
☐ N503UA	Boeing 757-222	24624/247		5403	
☐ N504UA	Boeing 757-222	24625/251		5404	
☐ N505UA	Boeing 757-222	24626/254		5705	
☐ N506UA	Boeing 757-222	24627/263		5406	
☐ N507UA	Boeing 757-222	24743/270		5407	
☐ N508UA	Boeing 757-222	24744/277		5708	
☐ N509UA	Boeing 757-222	24763/284		5409	
☐ N510UA	Boeing 757-222/W	24780/290		5710	
☐ N511UA	Boeing 757-222	24799/291		5411	
☐ N512UA	Boeing 757-222/W	24809/298		5712	
☐ N513UA	Boeing 757-222	24810/299		5413	
☐ N514UA	Boeing 757-222	24839/305		5414	
☐ N515UA	Boeing 757-222	24840/306		5415	
☐ N516UA	Boeing 757-222	24860/307		5416	
☐ N517UA	Boeing 757-222/W	24861/310		5717	
☐ N518UA	Boeing 757-222/W	24871/311		5718	
☐ N519UA	Boeing 757-222	24872/312		5419	
☐ N520UA	Boeing 757-222	24890/313		5420	
☐ N521UA	Boeing 757-222	24891/319		5421	
☐ N522UA	Boeing 757-222	24931/320		5422	
☐ N523UA	Boeing 757-222	24932/329		5423	
☐ N524UA	Boeing 757-222	24977/331		5424	
☐ N525UA	Boeing 757-222/W	24978/338		5725	
☐ N526UA	Boeing 757-222	24994/339		5426	
☐ N527UA	Boeing 757-222	24995/341		5427	
☐ N528UA	Boeing 757-222	25018/346		5428	
☐ N529UA	Boeing 757-222	25019/352		5429	
☐ N530UA	Boeing 757-222	25043/353		5430	
☐ N532UA	Boeing 757-222/W	25072/366		5732	
☐ N533UA	Boeing 757-222	25073/367		5433	
☐ N534UA	Boeing 757-222	25129/372		5434	
☐ N535UA	Boeing 757-222	25130/373		5435	
☐ N536UA	Boeing 757-222	25156/380		5436	
☐ N537UA	Boeing 757-222	25157/381		5437	
☐ N538UA	Boeing 757-222	25222/385		5438	
☐ N539UA	Boeing 757-222	25223/386		5439	

	Registration	Type	C/n	Previous identity	Fleet no	Notes	Status
☐	N540UA	Boeing 757-222	25252/393		5440		
☐	N541UA	Boeing 757-222	25253/394		5441		
☐	N542UA	Boeing 757-222	25276/396		5442		
☐	N543UA	Boeing 757-222ER/W	25698/401		5543		
☐	N544UA	Boeing 757-222ER/W	25322/405		5544		
☐	N545UA	Boeing 757-222ER/W	25323/406		5545		
☐	N546UA	Boeing 757-222ER/W	25367/413		5546		
☐	N547UA	Boeing 757-222ER	25368/414		5547		
☐	N548UA	Boeing 757-222ER	25396/420		5548		
☐	N549UA	Boeing 757-222ER/W	25397/421		5549		
☐	N550UA	Boeing 757-222ER	25398/426		5550		
☐	N551UA	Boeing 757-222ER	25399/427		5551		
☐	N552UA	Boeing 757-222ER	26641/431		5552		
☐	N553UA	Boeing 757-222	25277/434		5453		
☐	N554UA	Boeing 757-222/W	26644/435		5754		
☐	N555UA	Boeing 757-222/W	26647/442		5755		
☐	N556UA	Boeing 757-222	26650/447		5456		
☐	N557UA	Boeing 757-222	26653/454		5757		
☐	N558UA	Boeing 757-222	26654/462		5458		
☐	N559UA	Boeing 757-222	26657/467		5459		
☐	N560UA	Boeing 757-222	26660/469		5760		
☐	N561UA	Boeing 757-222	26661/479		5461		
☐	N562UA	Boeing 757-222	26664/487		5462		
☐	N563UA	Boeing 757-222	26665/488		5463		
☐	N564UA	Boeing 757-222	26666/490		5464		
☐	N565UA	Boeing 757-222	26669/492		5465		
☐	N566UA	Boeing 757-222	26670/494		5466		
☐	N567UA	Boeing 757-222	26673/497		5467		
☐	N568UA	Boeing 757-222	26674/498		5468		
☐	N569UA	Boeing 757-222	26677/499		5469		
☐	N570UA	Boeing 757-222	26678/501		5470		
☐	N571UA	Boeing 757-222	26681/506		5471		
☐	N572UA	Boeing 757-222	26682/508		5472		
☐	N573UA	Boeing 757-222	26685/512		5473		
☐	N574UA	Boeing 757-222	26686/513		5474		
☐	N575UA	Boeing 757-222	26689/515		5475		
☐	N576UA	Boeing 757-222	26690/524		5676		
☐	N577UA	Boeing 757-222	26693/527		5677		
☐	N578UA	Boeing 757-222	26694/531		5678		
☐	N579UA	Boeing 757-222	26697/539		5679		
☐	N580UA	Boeing 757-222	26698/542		5680		
☐	N581UA	Boeing 757-222	26701/543		5681		
☐	N582UA	Boeing 757-222	26702/550		5682		
☐	N583UA	Boeing 757-222	26705/556		5683		
☐	N584UA	Boeing 757-222	26706/559		5684		
☐	N585UA	Boeing 757-222	26709/563		5685		
☐	N586UA	Boeing 757-222	26710/567		5686		
☐	N587UA	Boeing 757-222	26713/570		5687		
☐	N588UA	Boeing 757-222	26717/571		5688		
☐	N589UA	Boeing 757-222ER	28707/773	ex N3509J	5589		
☐	N590UA	Boeing 757-222ER	28708/785		5590		
☐	N592UA	Boeing 757-222	28143/719		5492	Richard Damron, Captain	
☐	N593UA	Boeing 757-222	28144/724		5493		
☐	N594UA	Boeing 757-222	28145/727		5494		
☐	N595UA	Boeing 757-222ER	28748/789		5595		
☐	N596UA	Boeing 757-222ER	28749/794		5596		
☐	N597UA	Boeing 757-222ER	28750/841		5597		
☐	N598UA	Boeing 757-222ER	28751/844	ex N1787B	5598		
☐	N641UA	Boeing 767-322ER	25091/360		6341		
☐	N642UA	Boeing 767-322ER	25092/367		6342		
☐	N643UA	Boeing 767-322ER	25093/368		6343		
☐	N644UA	Boeing 767-322ER	25094/369		6344		
☐	N646UA	Boeing 767-322ER	25283/420		6346		
☐	N647UA	Boeing 767-322ER	25284/424		6347		
☐	N648UA	Boeing 767-322ER	25285/443		6348		stored MZJ
☐	N649UA	Boeing 767-322ER	25286/444		6349		
☐	N651UA	Boeing 767-322ER	25389/452		6351		
☐	N652UA	Boeing 767-322ER	25390/457		6352		
☐	N653UA	Boeing 767-322ER	25391/460		6353	Star Alliance c/s	
☐	N654UA	Boeing 767-322ER	25392/462		6354		
☐	N655UA	Boeing 767-322ER	25393/468		6355		
☐	N656UA	Boeing 767-322ER	25394/472		6356		
☐	N657UA	Boeing 767-322ER	27112/479		6357		
☐	N658UA	Boeing 767-322ER	27113/400		6358		
☐	N659UA	Boeing 767-322ER	27114/485		6359		
☐	N660UA	Boeing 767-322ER	27115/494		6360		
☐	N661UA	Boeing 767-322ER	27158/507		6361		
☐	N662UA	Boeing 767-322ER	27159/513		6362		
☐	N663UA	Boeing 767-322ER	27160/514		6363		
☐	N664UA	Boeing 767-322ER	29236/707		6764		
☐	N665UA	Boeing 767-322ER	29237/711		6765		
☐	N666UA	Boeing 767-322ER	29238/715		6766		

	Registration	Type	C/n	Previous identity	Fleet no	Notes
☐	N667UA	Boeing 767-322ER	29239/716		6767	
☐	N668UA	Boeing 767-322ER	30024/742		6768	
☐	N669UA	Boeing 767-322ER	30025/757		6769	
☐	N670UA	Boeing 767-322ER	29240/763		6770	
☐	N671UA	Boeing 767-322ER	30026/766		6771	
☐	N672UA	Boeing 767-322ER	30027/773		6772	
☐	N673UA	Boeing 767-322ER	29241/779		6773	
☐	N674UA	Boeing 767-322ER	29242/782		6774	
☐	N675UA	Boeing 767-322ER	29243/800		6775	
☐	N676UA	Boeing 767-322ER	30028/834		6776	
☐	N677UA	Boeing 767-322ER	30029/852		6777	

	Registration	Type	C/n	Previous identity	Fleet no	Notes
☐	N204UA	Boeing 777-222ER	28713/191		2904	
☐	N206UA	Boeing 777-222ER	30212/216		2906	
☐	N209UA	Boeing 777-222ER	30215/259		2609	
☐	N210UA	Boeing 777-222ER	30216/264		2510	
☐	N211UA	Boeing 777-222	30217/282		2511	
☐	N212UA	Boeing 777-222	30218/293		2512	
☐	N213UA	Boeing 777-222	30219/295		2513	
☐	N214UA	Boeing 777-222	30220/296		2514	
☐	N215UA	Boeing 777-222	30221/297		2515	
☐	N216UA	Boeing 777-222ER	30549/291		2616	
☐	N217UA	Boeing 777-222ER	30550/294		2617	
☐	N218UA	Boeing 777-222ER	30222/317		2618	10 Years Star Alliance c/s
☐	N219UA	Boeing 777-222ER	30551/318		2619	
☐	N220UA	Boeing 777-222ER	30223/340		2620	
☐	N221UA	Boeing 777-222ER	30552/347		2621	
☐	N222UA	Boeing 777-222ER	30553/352		2622	
☐	N223UA	Boeing 777-222ER	30224/357		2623	
☐	N224UA	Boeing 777-222ER	30225/375		2624	
☐	N225UA	Boeing 777-222ER	30554/377		2625	Spirit of United
☐	N226UA	Boeing 777-222ER	30226/380		2626	
☐	N227UA	Boeing 777-222ER	30555/381		2627	
☐	N228UA	Boeing 777-222ER	30556/384		2628	
☐	N229UA	Boeing 777-222ER	30557/388		2629	
☐	N768UA	Boeing 777-222	26919/11		2368	
☐	N769UA	Boeing 777-222	26921/12		2369	
☐	N771UA	Boeing 777-222	26932/3	ex N7773	2371	
☐	N772UA	Boeing 777-222	26930/5	ex (N77775)	2372	
☐	N773UA	Boeing 777-222	26929/4	ex N7774	2373	Richard H Leung, Customer
☐	N774UA	Boeing 777-222	26936/2	ex N7772	2374	
☐	N775UA	Boeing 777-222	26947/22		2375	
☐	N776UA	Boeing 777-222	26937/27		2376	
☐	N777UA	Boeing 777-222	26916/7		2377	
☐	N778UA	Boeing 777-222	26940/34		2378	
☐	N779UA	Boeing 777-222	26941/35		2379	
☐	N780UA	Boeing 777-222	26944/36		2380	
☐	N781UA	Boeing 777-222	26945/40		2381	
☐	N782UA	Boeing 777-222ER	26948/57		2982	
☐	N783UA	Boeing 777-222ER	26950/60		2983	
☐	N784UA	Boeing 777-222ER	26951/69		2984	
☐	N785UA	Boeing 777-222ER	26954/73		2985	
☐	N786UA	Boeing 777-222ER	26938/52		2986	
☐	N787UA	Boeing 777-222ER	26939/43		2987	
☐	N788UA	Boeing 777-222ER	26942/82		2988	
☐	N791UA	Boeing 777-222ER	26933/93		2991	
☐	N792UA	Boeing 777-222ER	26934/96		2992	
☐	N793UA	Boeing 777-222ER	26946/97		2993	
☐	N794UA	Boeing 777-222ER	26953/105		2994	
☐	N795UA	Boeing 777-222ER	26927/108		2995	
☐	N796UA	Boeing 777-222ER	26931/112		2996	
☐	N797UA	Boeing 777-222ER	26924/116		2997	
☐	N798UA	Boeing 777-222ER	26928/123		2998	
☐	N799UA	Boeing 777-222ER	26926/139		2999	

UNITED EXPRESS — ***United (UA)***

Chicago-O'Hare Intl, IL/San Francisco-Intl, CA/Denver, CO (ORD/SFO/DEN)

	Registration	Type	C/n	Previous identity	Fleet no	Operator
☐	N154SF	Canadair CL-600-2B19 (CRJ-200LR)	7154	ex LV-WSB	154	Mesa
☐	N571ML	Canadair CL-600-2B19 (CRJ-200LR)	7209	ex C-GBNW		Mesa
☐	N592ML	Canadair CL-600-2B19 (CRJ-200LR)	7410	ex C-FMLQ		Mesa
☐	N650ML	Canadair CL-600-2B19 (CRJ-200LR)	7137	ex N261BD		Mesa
☐	N715SF	Canadair CL-600-2B19 (CRJ-200LR)	7115	ex LV-WPF		Mesa
☐	N903SW	Canadair CL-600-2B19 (CRJ-200ER)	7425	ex C-FMOI	7425	SkyWest
☐	N905SW	Canadair CL-600-2B19 (CRJ-200ER)	7437	ex C-FMLB	7437	SkyWest
☐	N906SW	Canadair CL-600-2B19 (CRJ-200ER)	7510	ex C-FMOW	7510	SkyWest
☐	N907SW	Canadair CL-600-2B19 (CRJ-200ER)	7511	ex C-FVAZ	7511	SkyWest
☐	N908SW	Canadair CL-600-2B19 (CRJ-200ER)	7540	ex C-FMOW	7540	SkyWest
☐	N909SW	Canadair CL-600-2B19 (CRJ-200ER)	7558	ex C-GJHL	7558	SkyWest
☐	N910SW	Canadair CL-600-2B19 (CRJ-200ER)	7566	ex C-GJHY	7566	SkyWest
☐	N912SW	Canadair CL-600-2B19 (CRJ-200ER)	7595	ex C-FMNH	7595	SkyWest
☐	N913SW	Canadair CL-600-2B19 (CRJ-200ER)	7597	ex C-FMNX	7597	SkyWest

☐ N915SW	Canadair CL-600-2B19 (CRJ-200ER)	7615	ex C-GKJQ	7615	SkyWest
☐ N916SW	Canadair CL-600-2B19 (CRJ-200ER)	7634	ex C-FMLU	7634	SkyWest
☐ N917SW	Canadair CL-600-2B19 (CRJ-200ER)	7641	ex C-FMMX	7641	SkyWest
☐ N918SW	Canadair CL-600-2B19 (CRJ-200ER)	7645	ex C-FMKW	7645	SkyWest
☐ N919SW	Canadair CL-600-2B19 (CRJ-200ER)	7657	ex C-FMNX	7657	SkyWest
☐ N920SW	Canadair CL-600-2B19 (CRJ-200ER)	7660	ex C-FMOW	7660	SkyWest
☐ N923SW	Canadair CL-600-2B19 (CRJ-200ER)	7664	ex C-FMLU	7664	SkyWest
☐ N924SW	Canadair CL-600-2B19 (CRJ-200ER)	7681	ex C-FMLS	7681	SkyWest
☐ N925SW	Canadair CL-600-2B19 (CRJ-200ER)	7682	ex C-FMLI	7682	SkyWest
☐ N926SW	Canadair CL-600-2B19 (CRJ-200ER)	7687	ex C-FMNX	7687	SkyWest
☐ N927SW	Canadair CL-600-2B19 (CRJ-200ER)	7693	ex C-FMNQ	7693	SkyWest
☐ N928SW	Canadair CL-600-2B19 (CRJ-200ER)	7701	ex C-FMMX	7701	SkyWest
☐ N929SW	Canadair CL-600-2B19 (CRJ-200ER)	7703	ex C-FMNB	7703	SkyWest
☐ N930SW	Canadair CL-600-2B19 (CRJ-200ER)	7713	ex C-FMLV	7713	SkyWest
☐ N932SW	Canadair CL-600-2B19 (CRJ-200ER)	7714	ex C-FMMT	7714	SkyWest
☐ N934SW	Canadair CL-600-2B19 (CRJ-200ER)	7722	ex C-FMND	7722	SkyWest
☐ N935SW	Canadair CL-600-2B19 (CRJ-200ER)	7725	ex C-FMOI	7725	SkyWest
☐ N936SW	Canadair CL-600-2B19 (CRJ-200ER)	7726	ex C-FMMB	7726	SkyWest
☐ N937SW	Canadair CL-600-2B19 (CRJ-200ER)	7735	ex C-FMKW	7735	SkyWest
☐ N938SW	Canadair CL-600-2B19 (CRJ-200ER)	7741	ex C-FMLS	7741	SkyWest
☐ N939SW	Canadair CL-600-2B19 (CRJ-200ER)	7742	ex C-FMLT	7742	SkyWest
☐ N941SW	Canadair CL-600-2B19 (CRJ-200ER)	7750	ex C-FMOW	7750	SkyWest
☐ N943SW	Canadair CL-600-2B19 (CRJ-200ER)	7762	ex C-FMMY	7762	SkyWest
☐ N944SW	Canadair CL-600-2B19 (CRJ-200ER)	7764	ex C-FMKV	7764	SkyWest
☐ N945SW	Canadair CL-600-2B19 (CRJ-200ER)	7770	ex C-FMLQ	7770	SkyWest
☐ N946SW	Canadair CL-600-2B19 (CRJ-200ER)	7776	ex C-FMNW	7776	SkyWest
☐ N948SW	Canadair CL-600-2B19 (CRJ-200ER)	7789	ex C-GXTU	7789	SkyWest
☐ N951SW	Canadair CL-600-2B19 (CRJ-200ER)	7795	ex C-FMKW	7795 30th anniversary c/s	SkyWest
☐ N952SW	Canadair CL-600-2B19 (CRJ-200ER)	7805	ex C-FMNH	7805	SkyWest
☐ N953SW	Canadair CL-600-2B19 (CRJ-200ER)	7813	ex C-GZGP	7813	SkyWest
☐ N954SW	Canadair CL-600-2B19 (CRJ-200ER)	7815	ex C-FMOI	7815	SkyWest
☐ N955SW	Canadair CL-600-2B19 (CRJ-200ER)	7817	ex C-FMML	7817	SkyWest
☐ N956SW	Canadair CL-600-2B19 (CRJ-200ER)	7825	ex C-FMKW	7825	SkyWest
☐ N957SW	Canadair CL-600-2B19 (CRJ-200ER)	7829	ex C-FMLI	7829	SkyWest
☐ N958SW	Canadair CL-600-2B19 (CRJ-200ER)	7833	ex C-FMLV	7833	SkyWest
☐ N959SW	Canadair CL-600-2B19 (CRJ-200ER)	7840	ex C-FMOW	7840	SkyWest
☐ N960SW	Canadair CL-600-2B19 (CRJ-200ER)	7853	ex C-FMNB	7853	SkyWest
☐ N961SW	Canadair CL-600-2B19 (CRJ-200ER)	7857	ex C-FMLB	7857	SkyWest
☐ N962SW	Canadair CL-600-2B19 (CRJ-200ER)	7859	ex C-FMLI	7859	SkyWest
☐ N963SW	Canadair CL-600-2B19 (CRJ-200ER)	7865	ex C-FMNH	7865	SkyWest
☐ N964SW	Canadair CL-600-2B19 (CRJ-200ER)	7868	ex C-GZTD	7867	SkyWest
☐ N965SW	Canadair CL-600-2B19 (CRJ-200ER)	7871	ex C-FVAZ	7871	SkyWest
☐ N967SW	Canadair CL-600-2B19 (CRJ-200ER)	7872	ex C-FMND	7872	SkyWest
☐ N969SW	Canadair CL-600-2B19 (CRJ-200ER)	7876	ex C-FMMB	7876	SkyWest
☐ N970SW	Canadair CL-600-2B19 (CRJ-200ER)	7881	ex C-GZUJ	7881	SkyWest
☐ N971SW	Canadair CL-600-2B19 (CRJ-200ER)	7947	ex C-FMLB	7947	SkyWest
☐ N973SW	Canadair CL-600-2B19 (CRJ-200ER)	7949	ex C-FMLI	7949	SkyWest
☐ N975SW	Canadair CL-600-2B19 (CRJ-200ER)	7951	ex C-FMLS	7951	SkyWest
☐ N976SW	Canadair CL-600-2B19 (CRJ-200ER)	7952	ex C-FMLT	7952	SkyWest
☐ N978SW	Canadair CL-600-2B19 (CRJ-200ER)	7953	ex C-FMLV	7953	SkyWest
☐ N979SW	Canadair CL-600-2B19 (CRJ-200ER)	7954	ex C-FMMT	7954	SkyWest
☐ N980SW	Canadair CL-600-2B19 (CRJ-200ER)	7955	ex C-FMNH	7955	SkyWest
☐ N982SW	Canadair CL-600-2B19 (CRJ-200ER)	7956	ex C-FMNW	7956	SkyWest
☐ N983SW	Canadair CL-600-2B19 (CRJ-200ER)	7961	ex C-FVAZ	7961	SkyWest
☐ N986SW	Canadair CL-600-2B19 (CRJ-200ER)	7967	ex C-FMML	7967	SkyWest
☐ N17156	Canadair CL-600-2B19 (CRJ-200LR)	7156	ex C-FZSC		Mesa
☐ N17175	Canadair CL-600-2B19 (CRJ-200LR)	7175	ex LV-WXB		Mesa
☐ N27172	Canadair CL-600-2B19 (CRJ-200LR)	7172	ex C-FMMN		Mesa
☐ N27185	Canadair CL-600-2B19 (CRJ-200LR)	7185	ex C-FMMB		Mesa
☐ N37208	Canadair CL-600-2B19 (CRJ-200LR)	7208	ex C-FMNY		Mesa
☐ N37228	Canadair CL-600-2B19 (CRJ-200LR)	7228	ex B-7692		Mesa
☐ N47202	Canadair CL-600-2B19 (CRJ-200LR)	7202	ex C-FMLT		Mesa
☐ N75987	Canadair CL-600-2B19 (CRJ-200LR)	7405	ex C-FZSZ		Mesa
☐ N75991	Canadair CL-600-2B19 (CRJ-200LR)	7422	ex C-FZSY		Mesa
☐ N75992	Canadair CL-600-2B19 (CRJ-200LR)	7401	ex C-FZTH		Mesa
☐ N75993	Canadair CL-600-2B19 (CRJ-200LR)	7372	ex C-FZTT		Mesa
☐ N75994	Canadair CL-600-2B19 (CRJ-200LR)	7367	ex C-FZTY		Mesa
☐ N75995	Canadair CL-600-2B19 (CRJ-200LR)	7361	ex C-FZTW		Mesa
☐ N75998	Canadair CL-600-2B19 (CRJ-200LR)	7336	ex C-FZTU		Mesa
☐ N77181	Canadair CL-600-2B19 (CRJ-200LR)	7181	ex C-FMNQ		Mesa

☐ N151GJ	Canadair CL-600-2C10 (CRJ-702ER)	10216	ex C-		GoJet
☐ N152GJ	Canadair CL-600-2C10 (CRJ-702ER)	10218	ex C-		GoJet
☐ N153GJ	Canadair CL-600-2C10 (CRJ-702ER)	10219	ex C-		GoJet
☐ N154GJ	Canadair CL-600-2C10 (CRJ-702ER)	10224	ex C-		GoJet
☐ N155GJ	Canadair CL-600-2C10 (CRJ-702ER)	10225	ex C-		GoJet
☐ N156GJ	Canadair CL-600-2C10 (CRJ-702ER)	10227	ex C-		GoJet
☐ N157GJ	Canadair CL-600-2C10 (CRJ-702ER)	10230	ex C-		GoJet
☐ N158GJ	Canadair CL-600-2C10 (CRJ-702ER)	10237	ex C-		GoJet
☐ N159GJ	Canadair CL-600-2C10 (CRJ-702ER)	10238	ex C-		GoJet
☐ N160GJ	Canadair CL-600-2C10 (CRJ-702ER)	10239	ex C-		GoJet
☐ N161GJ	Canadair CL-600-2C10 (CRJ-702ER)	10253	ex C-		GoJet
☐ N162GJ	Canadair CL-600-2C10 (CRJ-702ER)	10254	ex C-		GoJet

Reg	Type	C/n	Previous identity	Fleet no	Operator
☐ N163GJ	Canadair CL-600-2C10 (CRJ-702ER)	10255	ex C-		GoJet
☐ N164GJ	Canadair CL-600-2C10 (CRJ-702ER)	10256	ex C-		GoJet
☐ N165GJ	Canadair CL-600-2C10 (CRJ-702ER)	10257	ex C-		GoJet
☐ N166GJ	Canadair CL-600-2C10 (CRJ-702ER)	10266	ex C-		GoJet
☐ N167GJ	Canadair CL-600-2C10 (CRJ-702ER)	10269	ex C-		GoJet
☐ N168GJ	Canadair CL-600-2C10 (CRJ-702ER)	10272	ex C-GHZZ		GoJet
☐ N169GJ	Canadair CL-600-2C10 (CRJ-702ER)	10273	ex C-		GoJet
☐ N170GJ	Canadair CL-600-2C10 (CRJ-702ER)	10280	ex C-GICN		GoJet
☐ N171GJ	Canadair CL-600-2C10 (CRJ-702ER)	10282	ex C-GIAR		GoJet
☐ N172GJ	Canadair CL-600-2C10 (CRJ-702ER)	10283	ex C-		GoJet
☐ N173GJ	Canadair CL-600-2C10 (CRJ-702ER)	10287	ex C-		GoJet
☐ N174GJ	Canadair CL-600-2C10 (CRJ-702ER)	10296	ex C-		GoJet
☐ N175GJ	Canadair CL-600-2C10 (CRJ-702ER)	10297	ex C-		GoJet
☐ N501MJ	Canadair CL-600-2C10 (CRJ-701ER)	10047	ex C-FZVM		Mesa
☐ N502MJ	Canadair CL-600-2C10 (CRJ-701ER)	10050	ex C-GIAI		Mesa
☐ N503MJ	Canadair CL-600-2C10 (CRJ-701ER)	10058	ex C-GIBG		Mesa
☐ N504MJ	Canadair CL-600-2C10 (CRJ-701ER)	10066	ex C-GIBR		Mesa
☐ N505MJ	Canadair CL-600-2C10 (CRJ-701ER)	10070	ex C-GICN		Mesa
☐ N506MJ	Canadair CL-600-2C10 (CRJ-701ER)	10073	ex C-GHZY		Mesa
☐ N507MJ	Canadair CL-600-2C10 (CRJ-701ER)	10077	ex C-GIAH		Mesa
☐ N508MJ	Canadair CL-600-2C10 (CRJ-701ER)	10087	ex C-FZZE		Mesa
☐ N509MJ	Canadair CL-600-2C10 (CRJ-701ER)	10094	ex C-		Mesa
☐ N510MJ	Canadair CL-600-2C10 (CRJ-701ER)	10101	ex C-		Mesa
☐ N511MJ	Canadair CL-600-2C10 (CRJ-701ER)	10104	ex C-		Mesa
☐ N512MJ	Canadair CL-600-2C10 (CRJ-701ER)	10109	ex C-		Mesa
☐ N513MJ	Canadair CL-600-2C10 (CRJ-701ER)	10111	ex C-		Mesa
☐ N514MJ	Canadair CL-600-2C10 (CRJ-701ER)	10116	ex C-		Mesa
☐ N515MJ	Canadair CL-600-2C10 (CRJ-701ER)	10117	ex C-		Mesa
☐ N516LR	Canadair CL-600-2C10 (CRJ-701ER)	10258	ex C-		Mesa
☐ N518LR	Canadair CL-600-2C10 (CRJ-701ER)	10259	ex C-		Mesa
☐ N519LR	Canadair CL-600-2C10 (CRJ-701ER)	10260	ex C-FLGD		Mesa
☐ N521LR	Canadair CL-600-2C10 (CRJ-701ER)	10261	ex C-FMHJ		Mesa
☐ N522LR	Canadair CL-600-2C10 (CRJ-701ER)	10262	ex C-		Mesa
☐ N701SK	Canadair CL-600-2C10 (CRJ-701ER)	10133	ex C-	10133	SkyWest
☐ N702SK	Canadair CL-600-2C10 (CRJ-701ER)	10136	ex C-	10136	SkyWest
☐ N703SK	Canadair CL-600-2C10 (CRJ-701ER)	10139	ex C-	10139	SkyWest
☐ N705SK	Canadair CL-600-2C10 (CRJ-701ER)	10145	ex C-	10145	SkyWest
☐ N706SK	Canadair CL-600-2C10 (CRJ-701ER)	10149	ex C-	10149	SkyWest
☐ N707SK	Canadair CL-600-2C10 (CRJ-701ER)	10003	ex C-FBKA	10003	SkyWest
☐ N708SK	Canadair CL-600-2C10 (CRJ-701ER)	10156	ex C-	10156	SkyWest
☐ N709SK	Canadair CL-600-2C10 (CRJ-701ER)	10159	ex C-	10159	SkyWest
☐ N710SK	Canadair CL-600-2C10 (CRJ-701ER)	10170	ex C-	10170	SkyWest
☐ N712SK	Canadair CL-600-2C10 (CRJ-701ER)	10172	ex C-GIAR	10172	SkyWest
☐ N713SK	Canadair CL-600-2C10 (CRJ-701ER)	10174	ex C-	10174	SkyWest
☐ N715SK	Canadair CL-600-2C10 (CRJ-701ER)	10179	ex C-	10179	SkyWest
☐ N716SK	Canadair CL-600-2C10 (CRJ-701ER)	10180	ex C-	10180	SkyWest
☐ N718SK	Canadair CL-600-2C10 (CRJ-701ER)	10184	ex C-	10184	SkyWest
☐ N719SK	Canadair CL-600-2C10 (CRJ-701ER)	10188	ex C-	10188	SkyWest
☐ N724SK	Canadair CL-600-2C10 (CRJ-701ER)	10189	ex C-	10189	SkyWest
☐ N726SK	Canadair CL-600-2C10 (CRJ-701ER)	10190	ex C-	10190	SkyWest
☐ N727SK	Canadair CL-600-2C10 (CRJ-701ER)	10191	ex C-	10191	SkyWest
☐ N728SK	Canadair CL-600-2C10 (CRJ-701ER)	10192	ex C-	10192	SkyWest
☐ N730SK	Canadair CL-600-2C10 (CRJ-701ER)	10193	ex C-	10193	SkyWest
☐ N732SK	Canadair CL-600-2C10 (CRJ-701ER)	10194	ex C-	10194	SkyWest
☐ N738SK	Canadair CL-600-2C10 (CRJ-701ER)	10195	ex C-	10195	SkyWVst
☐ N740SK	Canadair CL-600-2C10 (CRJ-701ER)	10196	ex C-	10196	SkyWest
☐ N742SK	Canadair CL-600-2C10 (CRJ-701ER)	10197	ex C-	10197	SkyWest
☐ N743SK	Canadair CL-600-2C10 (CRJ-701ER)	10199	ex C-	10199	SkyWest
☐ N744SK	Canadair CL-600-2C10 (CRJ-701ER)	10200	ex C-	10200	SkyWest
☐ N745SK	Canadair CL-600-2C10 (CRJ-701ER)	10201	ex C-	10201	SkyWest
☐ N746SK	Canadair CL-600-2C10 (CRJ-701ER)	10202	ex C-FEUP	10202	SkyWest
☐ N748SK	Canadair CL-600-2C10 (CRJ-701ER)	10203	ex C-	10203	SkyWest
☐ N750SK	Canadair CL-600-2C10 (CRJ-701ER)	10207	ex C-	10207	SkyWest
☐ N751SK	Canadair CL-600-2C10 (CRJ-701ER)	10208	ex C-	10208	SkyWest
☐ N752SK	Canadair CL-600-2C10 (CRJ-701ER)	10209	ex C-	10209	SkyWest
☐ N753SK	Canadair CL-600-2C10 (CRJ-701ER)	10214	ex C-FEVZ	10214	SkyWest
☐ N754SK	Canadair CL-600-2C10 (CRJ-701ER)	10215	ex C-	10215	SkyWest
☐ N755SK	Canadair CL-600-2C10 (CRJ-701ER)	10220	ex C-FFVZ	10220	SkyWest
☐ N756SK	Canadair CL-600-2C10 (CRJ-701ER)	10221	ex C-	10221	SkyWest
☐ N758SK	Canadair CL-600-2C10 (CRJ-701ER)	10222	ex C-	10222	SkyWest
☐ N760SK	Canadair CL-600-2C10 (CRJ-701ER)	10223	ex C-	10223	SkyWest
☐ N762SK	Canadair CL-600-2C10 (CRJ-702ER)	10226	ex C-	10226	SkyWest
☐ N763SK	Canadair CL-600-2C10 (CRJ-702ER)	10228	ex C-	10228	SkyWest
☐ N764SK	Canadair CL-600-2C10 (CRJ-702ER)	10229	ex C-FGRE	10229	SkyWest
☐ N765SK	Canadair CL-600-2C10 (CRJ-702ER)	10231	ex C-	10231	SkyWest
☐ N766SK	Canadair CL-600-2C10 (CRJ-702ER)	10232	ex C-	10232	SkyWest
☐ N767SK	Canadair CL-600-2C10 (CRJ-702ER)	10233	ex C-	10233	SkyWest
☐ N768SK	Canadair CL-600-2C10 (CRJ-702ER)	10234	ex C-	10234	SkyWest
☐ N770SK	Canadair CL-600-2C10 (CRJ-702ER)	10243	ex C-	10243	SkyWest
☐ N771SK	Canadair CL-600-2C10 (CRJ-702ER)	10244	ex C-	10244	SkyWest
☐ N772SK	Canadair CL-600-2C10 (CRJ-702ER)	10235	ex C-	10235	SkyWest
☐ N773SK	Canadair CL-600-2C10 (CRJ-702ER)	10236	ex C-	10236	SkyWest
☐ N774SK	Canadair CL-600-2C10 (CRJ-702ER)	10240	ex C-	10240	SkyWest

	Reg	Type	c/n	Previous		Operator
☐	N778SK	Canadair CL-600-2C10 (CRJ-702ER)	10242	ex C-	10242	SkyWest
☐	N779SK	Canadair CL-600-2C10 (CRJ-702ER)	10276	ex C-	10276	SkyWest
☐	N780SK	Canadair CL-600-2C10 (CRJ-702ER)	10277	ex C-	10277	SkyWest
☐	N782SK	Canadair CL-600-2C10 (CRJ-702ER)	10278	ex C-	10278	SkyWest
☐	N783SK	Canadair CL-600-2C10 (CRJ-702ER)	10281	ex C-GICP	10281	SkyWest
☐	N784SK	Canadair CL-600-2C10 (CRJ-702ER)	10284	ex C-	10284	SkyWest
☐	N785SK	Canadair CL-600-2C10 (CRJ-702ER)	10285	ex C-	10285	SkyWest
☐	N786SK	Canadair CL-600-2C10 (CRJ-702ER)	10286	ex C-	10286	SkyWest
☐	N787SK	Canadair CL-600-2C10 (CRJ-702ER)	10288	ex C-	10288	SkyWest
☐	N788SK	Canadair CL-600-2C10 (CRJ-702ER)	10290	ex C-	10290	SkyWest
☐	N789SK	Canadair CL-600-2C10 (CRJ-702ER)	10291	ex C-	10291	SkyWest
☐	N790SK	Canadair CL-600-2C10 (CRJ-702ER)	10292	ex C-	10292	SkyWest
☐	N791SK	Canadair CL-600-2C10 (CRJ-702ER)	10293	ex C-	10293	SkyWest
☐	N792SK	Canadair CL-600-2C10 (CRJ-702ER)	10294	ex C-	10294	SkyWest
☐	N793SK	Canadair CL-600-2C10 (CRJ-702ER)	10295	ex C-	10295	SkyWest
☐	N794SK	Canadair CL-600-2C10 (CRJ-702ER)	10298	ex C-	10298	SkyWest
☐	N795SK	Canadair CL-600-2C10 (CRJ-702ER)	10299	ex C-	10299	SkyWest
☐	N796SK	Canadair CL-600-2C10 (CRJ-702ER)	10300	ex C-	10300	SkyWest
☐	N	Canadair CL-600-2C10 (CRJ-702ER)		ex C-		SkyWest
☐	N	Canadair CL-600-2C10 (CRJ-702ER)		ex C-		SkyWest
☐	N	Canadair CL-600-2C10 (CRJ-702ER)		ex C-		SkyWest
☐	N	Canadair CL-600-2C10 (CRJ-702ER)		ex C-		SkyWest
☐	N	Canadair CL-600-2C10 (CRJ-702ER)		ex C-		SkyWest
☐	N	Canadair CL-600-2C10 (CRJ-702ER)		ex C-		SkyWest
☐	N	Canadair CL-600-2C10 (CRJ-702ER)		ex C-		SkyWest
☐	N	Canadair CL-600-2C10 (CRJ-702ER)		ex C-		SkyWest
☐	N	Canadair CL-600-2C10 (CRJ-702ER)		ex C-		SkyWest
☐	N	Canadair CL-600-2C10 (CRJ-702ER)		ex C-		SkyWest
☐	N	Canadair CL-600-2C10 (CRJ-702ER)		ex C-		SkyWest
☐	N	Canadair CL-600-2C10 (CRJ-702ER)		ex C-		SkyWest
☐	N	Canadair CL-600-2C10 (CRJ-702ER)		ex C-		SkyWest
☐	N	Canadair CL-600-2C10 (CRJ-702ER)		ex C-		SkyWest
☐	N	Canadair CL-600-2C10 (CRJ-702ER)		ex C-		SkyWest
☐	N	Canadair CL-600-2C10 (CRJ-702ER)		ex C-		SkyWest
☐	N	Canadair CL-600-2C10 (CRJ-702ER)		ex C-		SkyWest
☐	N	Canadair CL-600-2C10 (CRJ-702ER)		ex C-		SkyWest
☐	N	Canadair CL-600-2C10 (CRJ-702ER)		ex C-		SkyWest
☐	N	Canadair CL-600-2C10 (CRJ-702ER)		ex C-		SkyWest
☐	N	Canadair CL-600-2C10 (CRJ-702ER)		ex C-		SkyWest
☐	N	Canadair CL-600-2C10 (CRJ-702ER)		ex C-		SkyWest
☐	N	Canadair CL-600-2C10 (CRJ-702ER)		ex C-		SkyWest
☐	N	Canadair CL-600-2C10 (CRJ-702ER)		ex C-		SkyWest
☐	N	Canadair CL-600-2C10 (CRJ-702ER)		ex C-		SkyWest
☐	N436YV	de Havilland DHC-8-202	436	ex C-GDNG		Mesa
☐	N444YV	de Havilland DHC-8Q-202	444	ex C-GFRP	all-white	Mesa
☐	N445YV	de Havilland DHC-8Q-202	445	ex C-GFEN		Mesa
☐	N446YV	de Havilland DHC-8Q-202	446	ex C-GEOA		Mesa
☐	N448YV	de Havilland DHC-8Q-202	448	ex C-GLOT		Mesa
☐	N454YV	de Havilland DHC-8Q-202	454	ex C-GEOA		Mesa
☐	N455YV	de Havilland DHC-8Q-202	455	ex C-GFRP		Mesa
☐	N456YV	de Havilland DHC-8Q-202	456	ex C-GFOD		Mesa
☐	N218SW	Embraer EMB.120ER Brasilia	120287	ex PT-SVH		SkyWest
☐	N221SW	Embraer EMB.120ER Brasilia	120290	ex PT-SVK		SkyWest
☐	N223SW	Embraer EMB.120ER Brasilia	120291	ex PT-SVL		SkyWest
☐	N226SW	Embraer EMB.120ER Brasilia	120296	ex PT-SVQ		SkyWest
☐	N229SW	Embraer EMB.120ER Brasilia	120305	ex PT-SVX		SkyWest
☐	N233SW	Embraer EMB.120ER Brasilia	120307	ex PT-SVZ		SkyWest
☐	N234SW	Embraer EMB.120ER Brasilia	120308	ex PT-SXA		SkyWest
☐	N235SW	Embraer EMB.120ER Brasilia	120310	ex PT-SXC		SkyWest
☐	N236SW	Embraer EMB.120ER Brasilia	120312	ex PT-SXE		SkyWest
☐	N237SW	Embraer EMB.120ER Brasilia	120314	ex PT-SXG		SkyWest
☐	N251YV	Embraer EMB.120ER Brasilia	120251	ex PT-STX		SkyWest
☐	N270YV	Embraer EMB.120ER Brasilia	120270	ex PT-SUR		SkyWest
☐	N284YV	Embraer EMB.120ER Brasilia	120284	ex PT-SVE		SkyWest
☐	N288SW	Embraer EMB.120ER Brasilia	120316	ex PT-SXI		SkyWest
☐	N290SW	Embraer EMB.120ER Brasilia	120317	ex PT-SXJ		SkyWest
☐	N291SW	Embraer EMB.120ER Brasilia	120318	ex PT-SXK		SkyWest
☐	N292SW	Embraer EMB.120ER Brasilia	120319	ex PT-SXL		SkyWest
☐	N292UX	Embraer EMB.120ER Brasilia	120292	ex PT-SVM		SkyWest
☐	N294SW	Embraer EMB.120ER Brasilia	120321	ex PT-SXN		SkyWest
☐	N295SW	Embraer EMB.120ER Brasilia	120322	ex PT-SXO		SkyWest
☐	N295UX	Embraer EMB.120ER Brasilia	120295	ex PT-SVP		SkyWest
☐	N297SW	Embraer EMB.120ER Brasilia	120327	ex PT-SXT		SkyWest
☐	N298SW	Embraer EMB.120ER Brasilia	120328	ex PT-SXU		SkyWest
☐	N308SW	Embraer EMB.120ER Brasilia	120326	ex PT-SXS		SkyWest
☐	N393SW	Embraer EMB.120ER Brasilia	120330	ex PT-SXW		SkyWest
☐	N560SW	Embraer EMB.120ER Brasilia	120334	ex PT-SXX		SkyWest
☐	N561SW	Embraer EMB.120ER Brasilia	120335	ex PT-SXY		SkyWest
☐	N562SW	Embraer EMB.120ER Brasilia	120336	ex PT-SXZ		SkyWest
☐	N564SW	Embraer EMB.120ER Brasilia	120339	ex PT-SAC		SkyWest
☐	N565SW	Embraer EMB.120ER Brasilia	120340	ex PT-SAI		SkyWest

	Registration	Type	c/n	Previous identity	Operator
☐	N566SW	Embraer EMB.120ER Brasilia	120341	ex PT-SAF	SkyWest
☐	N567SW	Embraer EMB.120ER Brasilia	120342	ex PT-SAL	SkyWest
☐	N568SW	Embraer EMB.120ER Brasilia	120343	ex PT-SAZ	SkyWest
☐	N569SW	Embraer EMB.120ER Brasilia	120344	ex PT-SBY	SkyWest
☐	N578SW	Embraer EMB.120ER Brasilia	120346	ex PT-SCA	SkyWest
☐	N579SW	Embraer EMB.120ER Brasilia	120347	ex PT-SCB	SkyWest
☐	N580SW	Embraer EMB.120ER Brasilia	120348	ex PT-SCC	SkyWest
☐	N581SW	Embraer EMB.120ER Brasilia	120349	ex PT-SCZ	SkyWest
☐	N582SW	Embraer EMB.120ER Brasilia	120350	ex PT-SDC	SkyWest
☐	N583SW	Embraer EMB.120ER Brasilia	120351	ex PT-SEF	SkyWest
☐	N584SW	Embraer EMB.120ER Brasilia	120352	ex PT-SEG	SkyWest
☐	N585SW	Embraer EMB.120ER Brasilia	120353	ex PT-SEH	SkyWest
☐	N586SW	Embraer EMB.120ER Brasilia	120354	ex PT-SEJ	SkyWest
☐	N269SK	Embraer EMB.145LR (ERJ-145LR)	145293	ex PT-SYG	Chautauqua
☐	N270SK	Embraer EMB.145LR (ERJ-145LR)	145304	ex PT-SKV	Chautauqua
☐	N271SK	Embraer EMB.145LR (ERJ-145LR)	145305	ex PT-SKW	Chautauqua
☐	N290SK	Embraer EMB.145LR (ERJ-145LR)	145474	ex PT-SVT	Chautauqua
☐	N292SK	Embraer EMB.145LR (ERJ-145LR)	145488	ex PT-SXH	Chautauqua
☐	N294SK	Embraer EMB.145LR (ERJ-145LR)	145497	ex PT-SXQ	Chautauqua
☐	N806HK	Embraer EMB.145ER (ERJ-145ER)	145112	ex PT-SCO	Trans State
☐	N807HK	Embraer EMB.145ER (ERJ-145ER)	145119	ex PT-SCV	Trans State
☐	N810HK	Embraer EMB.145LR (ERJ-145LR)	145231	ex PT-SHV	Trans State
☐	N829HK	Embraer EMB.145LR (ERJ-145LR)	145281	ex HB-JAE	Trans State
☐	N833HK	Embraer EMB-145LR (ERJ-145LR)	145240	ex HB-JAB	Trans State
☐	N834HK	Embraer EMB.145LR (ERJ-145LR)	145269	ex HB-JAD	Trans State
☐	N835HK	Embraer EMB.145LR (ERJ-145LR)	145670	ex PT-SFE	Trans Stare
☐	N836HK	Embraer EMB.145LR (ERJ-145LR)	145695	ex PT-SGA	Trans State
☐	N838HK	Embraer EMB.145LR (ERJ-145LR)	145321	ex HB-JAG	Trans State
☐	N839HK	Embraer EMB-145LR (ERJ-145LR)	14500829	ex PT-SQC	Trans State
☐	N840HK	Embraer EMB.145LR (ERJ-145LR)	145341	ex HB-JAH	Trans State
☐	N841HK	Embraer EMB.145LR (ERJ-145LR)	145382	ex HB-JAJ	Trans State
☐	N842HK	Embraer EMB-145LR (ERJ-145LR)	14500830	ex PT-SQD	Trans State
☐	N843HK	Embraer EMB-145LR (ERJ-145LR)	14500822	ex PT-SNW	Trans State
☐	N844HK	Embraer EMB.145LR (ERJ-145LR)	14500838	ex PT-SQK	Trans State
☐	N845HK	Embraer EMB.145LR (ERJ-145LR)	14500842	ex PT-SQM	Trans State
☐	N846HK	Embraer EMB.145LR (ERJ-145LR)	14500855	ex PT-SQW	Trans State
☐	N847HK	Embraer EMB.145LR (ERJ-145LR)	14500857	ex PT-SQY	Trans State
☐	N851HK	Embraer EMB.145LR (ERJ-145LR)	145340	ex N834MJ	Trans State
☐	N852HK	Embraer EMB.145LR (ERJ-145LR)	145353	ex N835MJ	Trans State
☐	N859MJ	Embraer EMB.145LR (ERJ-145LR)	145769	ex PT-SMA	Mesa
☐	N858MJ	Embraer EMB.145LR (ERJ-145LR)	145767	ex PT-SJY	Mesa
☐	N631RW	Embraer 170-100SE (170SE)	17000007	ex PT-SKX	Shuttle America
☐	N632RW	Embraer 170-100SE (170SE)	17000050	ex PT-SUU	Shuttle America
☐	N633RW	Embraer 170-100SE (170SE)	17000054	ex PT-SUZ	Shuttle America
☐	N634RW	Embraer 170-100SE (170SE)	17000055	ex PT-SVE	Shuttle America
☐	N635RW	Embraer 170-100SE (170SE)	17000056	ex PT-SVF	Shuttle America
☐	N636RW	Embraer 170-100SE (170SE)	17000052	ex PT-SVK	Shuttle America
☐	N637RW	Embraer 170-100SE (170SE)	17000051	ex PT-SUV	Shuttle America
☐	N638RW	Embraer 170-100SE (170SE)	17000053	ex PT-SUY	Shuttle America
☐	N639RW	Embraer 170-100SE (170SE)	17000057	ex PT-SVG	Shuttle America
☐	N640RW	Embraer 170-100SE (170SE)	17000058	ex PT-SVH	Shuttle America
☐	N641RW	Embraer 170-100SE (170SE)	17000062	ex PT-SVN	Shuttle America
☐	N642RW	Embraer 170-100SE (170SE)	17000063	ex PT-SVO	Shuttle America
☐	N643RW	Embraer 170-100SE (170SE)	17000060	ex PT-SVL	Shuttle America
☐	N644RW	Embraer 170-100SE (170SE)	17000061	ex PT-SVM	Shuttle America
☐	N645RW	Embraer 170-100SE (170SE)	17000064	ex PT-SVP	Shuttle America
☐	N646RW	Embraer 170-100SE (170SE)	17000066	ex PT-SVR	Shuttle America
☐	N647RW	Embraer 170-100SE (170SE)	17000067	ex PT-SVS	Shuttle America
☐	N648RW	Embraer 170-100SE (170SE)	17000068	ex PT-SVT	Shuttle America
☐	N649RW	Embraer 170-100SE (170SE)	17000070	ex PT-SVV	Shuttle America
☐	N650RW	Embraer 170-100SE (170SE)	17000071	ex PT-SVW	Shuttle America
☐	N651RW	Embraer 170-100SE (170SE)	17000072	ex PT-SVX	Shuttle America
☐	N652RW	Embraer 170-100SE (170SE)	17000075	ex PT-SZA	Shuttle America
☐	N653RW	Embraer 170-100SE (170SE)	17000076	ex PT-SZB	Shuttle America
☐	N654RW	Embraer 170-100SE (170SE)	17000104	ex PT-SAK	Shuttle America
☐	N655RW	Embraer 170-100SE (170SE)	17000105	ex PT-SAM	Shuttle America
☐	N656RW	Embraer 170-100SE (170SE)	17000113	ex PT-SAY	Shuttle America
☐	N657RW	Embraer 170-100SE (170SE)	17000115	ex PT-SDC	Shuttle America
☐	N856RW	Embraer 170-100SE (170SE)	17000078	ex PT-SZD	Shuttle America
☐	N857RW	Embraer 170-100SE (170SE)	17000079	ex PT-SZE	Shuttle America
☐	N858RW	Embraer 170-100SE (170SE)	17000080	ex PT-SZF	Shuttle America
☐	N861RW	Embraer 170-100SE (170SE)	17000094	ex PT-SZU	Shuttle America
☐	N863RW	Embraer 170-100SE (170SE)	17000100	ex PT-SAB	Shuttle America
☐	N864RW	Embraer 170-100SE (170SE)	17000117	ex PT-SDE	Shuttle America
☐	N865RW	Embraer 170-100SE (170SE)	17000122	ex PT-SDK	Shuttle America
☐	N196CJ	SAAB SF.340B	340B-196	ex N196JW	Colgan Air
☐	N220MJ	SAAB SF.340B	340B-220	ex N360PX	Colgan Air
☐	N237MJ	SAAB SF.340B	340B-237	ex N351BE	Colgan Air
☐	N239CJ	SAAB SF.340B	340B-239	ex N352BE	Colgan Air
☐	N242CJ	SAAB SF.340B	340B-242	ex N353BE	Colgan Air

Registration	Type	C/n	Previous	Remarks	Operator/Status
☐ N277MJ	SAAB SF.340B	340B-277	ex N357BE		Colgan Air
☐ N309CE	SAAB SF.340B	340B-201	ex N201AE		Colgan Air
☐ N311CE	SAAB SF.340B	340B-214	ex SE-G14		Colgan Air

UNIVERSAL AIRLINES — Pacific Northern (PNA) — Victoria-Regional, TX (VCT)

Registration	Type	C/n	Previous
☐ N170UA	Douglas DC-6A	45518/998	ex N870TA
☐ N500UA	Douglas DC-6A	44597/501	ex N766WC
☐ N600UA	Douglas DC-6BF	44894/651	ex N37570

UPS AIRLINES — UPS (5X/UPS) — Louisville-Intl, KY (SDF)

Registration	Type	C/n	Previous
☐ N120UP	Airbus A300F4-622R	805	ex F-WWAR
☐ N121UP	Airbus A300F4-622R	806	ex F-WWAP
☐ N122UP	Airbus A300F4-622R	807	ex F-WWAX
☐ N124UP	Airbus A300F4-622R	808	ex F-WWAT
☐ N125UP	Airbus A300F4-622R	809	ex F-WWAU
☐ N126UP	Airbus A300F4-622R	810	ex F-WWAB
☐ N127UP	Airbus A300F4-622R	811	ex F-WWAD
☐ N128UP	Airbus A300F4-622R	812	ex F-WWAE
☐ N129UP	Airbus A300F4-622R	813	ex F-WWAF
☐ N130UP	Airbus A300F4-622R	814	ex F-WWAG
☐ N131UP	Airbus A300F4-622R	815	ex F-WWAH
☐ N133UP	Airbus A300F4-622R	816	ex F-WWAJ
☐ N134UP	Airbus A300F4-622R	817	ex F-WWAL
☐ N135UP	Airbus A300F4-622R	818	ex F-WWAM
☐ N136UP	Airbus A300F4-622R	819	ex F-WWAN
☐ N137UP	Airbus A300F4-622R	820	ex F-WWAO
☐ N138UP	Airbus A300F4-622R	821	ex F-WWAQ
☐ N139UP	Airbus A300F4-622R	822	ex F-WWAS
☐ N140UP	Airbus A300F4-622R	823	ex F-WWAV
☐ N141UP	Airbus A300F4-622R	824	ex F-WWAY
☐ N142UP	Airbus A300F4-622R	825	ex F-WWAA
☐ N143UP	Airbus A300F4-622R	826	ex F-WWAB
☐ N144UP	Airbus A300F4-622R	827	ex F-WWAD
☐ N145UP	Airbus A300F4-622R	828	ex F-WWAE
☐ N146UP	Airbus A300F4-622R	829	ex F-WWAG
☐ N147UP	Airbus A300F4-622R	830	ex F-WWAJ
☐ N148UP	Airbus A300F4-622R	831	ex F-WWAM
☐ N149UP	Airbus A300F4-622R	832	ex F-WWAN
☐ N150UP	Airbus A300F4-622R	833	ex F-WWAO
☐ N151UP	Airbus A300F4-622R	834	ex F-WWAP
☐ N152UP	Airbus A300F4-622R	835	ex F-WWAQ
☐ N153UP	Airbus A300F4-622R	839	ex F-WWAR
☐ N154UP	Airbus A300F4-622R	840	ex F-WWAS
☐ N155UP	Airbus A300F4-622R	841	ex F-WWAT
☐ N156UP	Airbus A300F4-622R	845	ex F-WWAU
☐ N157UP	Airbus A300F4-622R	846	ex F-WWAV
☐ N158UP	Airbus A300F4-622R	847	ex F-WWAX
☐ N159UP	Airbus A300F4-622R	848	ex F-WWAZ
☐ N160UP	Airbus A300F4-622R	849	ex F-WWAF
☐ N161UP	Airbus A300F4-622R	850	ex F-WWAG
☐ N162UP	Airbus A300F4-622R	851	ex F-WWAJ
☐ N163UP	Airbus A300F4-622R	852	ex F-WWAK
☐ N164UP	Airbus A300F4-622R	853	ex F-WWAL
☐ N165UP	Airbus A300F4-622R	854	ex F-WWAM
☐ N166UP	Airbus A300F4-622R	861	ex F-WWAU
☐ N167UP	Airbus A300F4-622R	862	ex F-WWAH
☐ N168UP	Airbus A300F4-622R	863	ex F-WWAV
☐ N169UP	Airbus A300F4-622R	864	ex F-WWAX
☐ N170UP	Airbus A300F4-622R	865	ex F-WWAZ
☐ N171UP	Airbus A300F4-622R	866	ex F-WWAE
☐ N172UP	Airbus A300F4-622R	867	ex F-WWAF
☐ N173UP	Airbus A300F4-622R	868	ex F-WWAG
☐ N174UP	Airbus A300F4-622R	869	ex F-WWAN

Registration	Type	C/n	Previous	Remarks	Status
☐ N520UP	Boeing 747-212B (SF)	21943/475	ex RP-C5746		stored ROW
☐ N521UP	Boeing 747-212B (SF)	21944/510	ex 9V-SQS	Olympic c/s	stored ROW
☐ N522UP	Boeing 747-212B (SF)	21936/401	ex VT-ENQ		stored ROW
☐ N523UP	Boeing 747-283B (SF)	22381/500	ex N155FW		stored ROW
☐ N672UP	Boeing 747-123 (SF)	20324/119	ex N9672		stored ROW
☐ N675UP	Boeing 747-123 (SF)	20390/136	ex N9675		stored ROW
☐ N676UP	Boeing 747-123 (SF)	20101/57	ex N9676		stored ROW
☐ N677UP	Boeing 747-123 (SF)	20391/143	ex N629FE		stored ROW
☐ N681UP	Boeing 747-121 (SF)	19661/70	ex N628FE		stored ROW
☐ N682UP	Boeing 747-121 (SF)	20349/110	ex N626FE		stored ROW
☐ N683UP	Boeing 747-121 (SF)	20353/131	ex N627FE	United Way titles	
☐ N570UP	Boeing 747-44AF	35667/1388			
☐ N571UP	Boeing 747-44AF	35668/1393			
☐ N572UP	Boeing 747-44AF	35669/1396			
☐ N573UP	Boeing 747-44AF	35662/1401			
☐ N574UP	Boeing 747-44AF	35663/1403			

	Registration	Type	C/n	Previous identity
☐	N575UP	Boeing 747-44AF	35664/1406	
☐	N576UP	Boeing 747-44AF	35665/1410	
☐	N577UP	Boeing 747-44AF	35666/1412	
☐	N578UP	Boeing 747-45EM	27154/994	ex B-16461
☐	N579UP	Boeing 747-45EM	26062/1016	ex B-16465
☐	N580UP	Boeing 747-428F	25632/968	ex LX-ICV
☐	N581UP	Boeing 747-4R7F	25866/1002	ex LX-FCV

	Registration	Type	C/n	Previous identity
☐	N401UP	Boeing 757-24APF	23723/139	
☐	N402UP	Boeing 757-24APF	23724/141	
☐	N403UP	Boeing 757-24APF	23725/143	
☐	N404UP	Boeing 757-24APF	23726/147	
☐	N405UP	Boeing 757-24APF	23727/149	
☐	N406UP	Boeing 757-24APF	23728/176	
☐	N407UP	Boeing 757-24APF	23729/181	
☐	N408UP	Boeing 757-24APF	23730/184	
☐	N409UP	Boeing 757-24APF	23731/186	
☐	N410UP	Boeing 757-24APF	23732/189	
☐	N411UP	Boeing 757-24APF	23851/191	
☐	N412UP	Boeing 757-24APF	23852/193	
☐	N413UP	Boeing 757-24APF	23853/195	
☐	N414UP	Boeing 757-24APF	23854/197	
☐	N415UP	Boeing 757-24APF	23855/199	
☐	N416UP	Boeing 757-24APF	23903/318	
☐	N417UP	Boeing 757-24APF	23904/322	
☐	N418UP	Boeing 757-24APF	23905/326	
☐	N419UP	Boeing 757-24APF	23906/330	
☐	N420UP	Boeing 757-24APF	23907/334	
☐	N421UP	Boeing 757-24APF	25281/395	
☐	N422UP	Boeing 757-24APF	25324/399	
☐	N423UP	Boeing 757-24APF	25325/403	
☐	N424UP	Boeing 757-24APF	25369/407	
☐	N425UP	Boeing 757-24APF	25370/411	
☐	N426UP	Boeing 757-24APF	25457/477	
☐	N427UP	Boeing 757-24APF	25458/481	
☐	N428UP	Boeing 757-24APF	25459/485	
☐	N429UP	Boeing 757-24APF	25460/489	
☐	N430UP	Boeing 757-24APF	25461/493	
☐	N431UP	Boeing 757-24APF	25462/569	ex OY-USA
☐	N432UP	Boeing 757-24APF	25463/573	ex OY-USB
☐	N433UP	Boeing 757-24APF	25464/577	ex OY-USC
☐	N434UP	Boeing 757-24APF	25465/579	ex OY-USD
☐	N435UP	Boeing 757-24APF	25466/581	
☐	N436UP	Boeing 757-24APF	25467/625	
☐	N437UP	Boeing 757-24APF	25468/628	
☐	N438UP	Boeing 757-24APF	25469/631	
☐	N439UP	Boeing 757-24APF	25470/634	
☐	N440UP	Boeing 757-24APF	25471/636	
☐	N441UP	Boeing 757-24APF	27386/638	
☐	N442UP	Boeing 757-24APF	27387/640	
☐	N443UP	Boeing 757-24APF	27388/642	
☐	N444UP	Boeing 757-24APF	27389/644	
☐	N445UP	Boeing 757-24APF	27390/646	
☐	N446UP	Boeing 757-24APF	27735/649	
☐	N447UP	Boeing 757-24APF	27736/651	
☐	N448UP	Boeing 757-24APF	27737/654	
☐	N449UP	Boeing 757-24APF	27738/656	
☐	N450UP	Boeing 757-24APF	25472/659	
☐	N451UP	Boeing 757-24APF	27739/675	
☐	N452UP	Boeing 757-24APF	25473/679	
☐	N453UP	Boeing 757-24APF	25474/683	
☐	N454UP	Boeing 757-24APF	25475/687	
☐	N455UP	Boeing 757-24APF	25476/691	
☐	N456UP	Boeing 757-24APF	25477/728	
☐	N457UP	Boeing 757-24APF	25478/729	
☐	N458UP	Boeing 757-24APF	25479/730	
☐	N459UP	Boeing 757-24APF	25480/733	
☐	N460UP	Boeing 757-24APF	25481/734	
☐	N461UP	Boeing 757-24APF	28265/755	
☐	N462UP	Boeing 757-24APF	28266/759	
☐	N463UP	Boeing 757-24APF	28267/763	
☐	N464UP	Boeing 757-24APF	28268/765	
☐	N465UP	Boeing 757-24APF	28269/767	
☐	N466UP	Boeing 757-24APF	25482/769	
☐	N467UP	Boeing 757-24APF	25483/771	
☐	N468UP	Boeing 757-24APF	25484/774	
☐	N469UP	Boeing 757-24APF	25485/776	
☐	N470UP	Boeing 757-24APF	25486/778	
☐	N471UP	Boeing 757-24APF	28842/813	
☐	N472UP	Boeing 757-24APF	28843/815	
☐	N473UP	Boeing 757-24APF	28846/823	ex N5573L
☐	N474UP	Boeing 757-24APF	28844/879	
☐	N475UP	Boeing 757-24APF	28845/882	

☐ N301UP	Boeing 767-34AF	27239/580			
☐ N302UP	Boeing 767-34AF	27240/590			
☐ N303UP	Boeing 767-34AF	27241/594			
☐ N304UP	Boeing 767-34AF	27242/598			
☐ N305UP	Boeing 767-34AF	27243/600			
☐ N306UP	Boeing 767-34AF	27759/622			
☐ N307UP	Boeing 767-34AF	27760/624			
☐ N308UP	Boeing 767-34AF	27761/626			
☐ N309UP	Boeing 767-34AF	27740/628			
☐ N310UP	Boeing 767-34AF	27762/630			
☐ N311UP	Boeing 767-34AF	27741/632			
☐ N312UP	Boeing 767-34AF	27763/634			
☐ N313UP	Boeing 767-34AF	27764/636			
☐ N314UP	Boeing 767-34AF	27742/638			
☐ N315UP	Boeing 767-34AF	27743/640			
☐ N316UP	Boeing 767-34AF	27744/660			
☐ N317UP	Boeing 767-34AF	27745/666			
☐ N318UP	Boeing 767-34AF	27746/670			
☐ N319UP	Boeing 767-34AF	27758/672			
☐ N320UP	Boeing 767-34AF	27747/674			
☐ N322UP	Boeing 767-34AF	27748/678			
☐ N323UP	Boeing 767-34AF	27749/682			
☐ N324UP	Boeing 767-34AF	27750/724			
☐ N325UP	Boeing 767-34AF	27751/726			
☐ N326UP	Boeing 767-34AF	27752/728			
☐ N327UP	Boeing 767-34AF	27753/730			
☐ N328UP	Boeing 767-34AF	27754/732			
☐ N329UP	Boeing 767-34AF	27755/756			
☐ N330UP	Boeing 767-34AF	27756/760			
☐ N331UP	Boeing 767-34AF	27757/764			
☐ N332UP	Boeing 767-34AF	32843/854			
☐ N334UP	Boeing 767-34AF	32844/858			
☐ N335UP	Boeing 767-34AF	37856/979	ex N5023Q		
☐ N336UP	Boeing 767-34AF	37857/983			
☐ N337UP	Boeing 767-34AF	37858			on order
☐ N338UP	Boeing 767-34AF	37944			on order
☐ N339UP	Boeing 767-34AF	37859			on order
☐ N340UP	Boeing 767-34AF	37860			on order
☐ N341UP	Boeing 767-34AF	37861			on order
☐ N700UP	Douglas DC-8-71CF	45900/316	ex N861FT		stored ROW
☐ N701UP	Douglas DC-8-71CF	45938/331	ex N860FT		stored ROW
☐ N702UP	Douglas DC-8-71CF	45902/294	ex N810EV		
☐ N703UP	Douglas DC-8-71CF	45939/351	ex N867FT		
☐ N705UP	Douglas DC-8-71CF	45949/329	ex N863FT		stored ROW
☐ N706UP	Douglas DC-8-71F	46056/495	ex N1307L		
☐ N708UP	Douglas DC-8-71F	46048/450	ex N1304L		stored ROW
☐ N709UP	Douglas DC-8-71F	45914/292	ex N823E		stored ROW
☐ N715UP	Douglas DC-8-71F	45915/295	ex N824E		stored ROW
☐ N718UP	Douglas DC-8-71F	46018/420	ex N1301L		stored ROW
☐ N729UP	Douglas DC-8-71F	46029/425	ex N1302L		
☐ N730UP	Douglas DC-8-71F	46030/426	ex N1303L		stored ROW
☐ N744UP	Douglas DC-8-71F	45944/326	ex N825E		stored ROW
☐ N750UP	Douglas DC-8-71CF	45950/354	ex N868FT		stored ROW
☐ N752UP	Douglas DC-8-71CF	45952/338	ex N864FT		stored ROW
☐ N755UP	Douglas DC-8-71F	46055/492	ex N1306L		stored ROW
☐ N772UP	Douglas DC-8-71F	46072/477	ex N1305L		
☐ N779UP	Douglas DC-8-71F	45979/363	ex N826E		stored ROW
☐ N798UP	Douglas DC-8-71CF	45898/320	ex N8787R		stored ROW
☐ N801UP	Douglas DC-8-73CF	46101/389	ex N8630		
☐ N802UP	Douglas DC-8-73AF	46100/502	ex C-FTIP		stored ROW
☐ N804UP	Douglas DC-8-73AF	46004/403	ex N784FT		stored ROW
☐ N805UP	Douglas DC-8-73CF	46117/525	ex N401FE		stored ROW
☐ N806UP	Douglas DC-8-73AF	46006/413	ex N786FT		stored ROW
☐ N807UP	Douglas DC-8-73AF	46007/422	ex N787FT		stored ROW
☐ N808UP	Douglas DC-8-73AF	46008/423	ex N788FT		
☐ N809UP	Douglas DC-8-73CF	46109/493	ex N772FT		stored ROW
☐ N810UP	Douglas DC-8-73CF	46001/395	ex N404FE		
☐ N811UP	Douglas DC-8-73CF	46089/501	ex N407FE		stored ROW
☐ N812UP	Douglas DC-8-73CF	46112/520	ex N776FT		stored ROW
☐ N813UP	Douglas DC-8-73CF	46059/456	ex N703FT	Spirit of Manila	stored ROW
☐ N814UP	Douglas DC-8-73CF	46090/504	ex N405FE		stored ROW
☐ N818UP	Douglas DC-8-73CF	46108/522	ex N798FT		stored ROW
☐ N819UP	Douglas DC-8-73F	46019/411	ex TF-VLY		
☐ N840UP	Douglas DC-8-73CF	46140/528	ex N797FT		
☐ N851UP	Douglas DC-8-73CF	46051/440	ex N811EV		stored ROW
☐ N852UP	Douglas DC-8-73CF	46052/442	ex N31EK		
☐ N866UP	Douglas DC-8-73CF	45966/393	ex N773FT		stored ROW
☐ N867UP	Douglas DC-8-73CF	45967/385	ex N907CL		stored ROW
☐ N868UP	Douglas DC-8-73CF	45968/389	ex N871TV		stored ROW
☐ N874UP	Douglas DC-8-73PF	46074/468	ex HB-IDZ		stored ROW
☐ N880UP	Douglas DC-8-73F	46080/466	ex TF-VLZ		

☐ N894UP	Douglas DC-8-73CF	46094/482	ex N910CL	stored ROW

☐ N250UP	McDonnell-Douglas MD-11F	48745/596	ex N798BA
☐ N251UP	McDonnell-Douglas MD-11F	48744/592	ex N797BA
☐ N252UP	McDonnell-Douglas MD-11F	48768/601	ex PP-SFA
☐ N253UP	McDonnell-Douglas MD-11F	48439/554	ex PP-VPM
☐ N254UP	McDonnell-Douglas MD-11F	48406/547	ex PP-VPL
☐ N255UP	McDonnell-Douglas MD-11F	48404/523	ex PP-VPJ
☐ N256UP	McDonnell-Douglas MD-11F	48405/524	ex PP-VPK
☐ N257UP	McDonnell-Douglas MD-11F	48451/505	ex HS-TMG
☐ N258UP	McDonnell-Douglas MD-11F	48416/466	ex HS-TMD
☐ N259UP	McDonnell-Douglas MD-11F	48417/467	ex HS-TME
☐ N260UP	McDonnell-Douglas MD-11F	48418/501	ex HS-TMF
☐ N270UP	McDonnell-Douglas MD-11F	48576/574	ex JA8585
☐ N271UP	McDonnell-Douglas MD-11F	48572/556	ex JA8581
☐ N272UP	McDonnell-Douglas MD-11F	48571/552	ex JA8580
☐ N273UP	McDonnell-Douglas MD-11F	48574/566	ex JA8583
☐ N274UP	McDonnell-Douglas MD-11F	48575/568	ex JA8584
☐ N275UP	McDonnell-Douglas MD-11F	48774/610	ex JA8589
☐ N276UP	McDonnell-Douglas MD-11F	48579/599	ex JA8588
☐ N277UP	McDonnell-Douglas MD-11F	48578/588	ex JA8587
☐ N278UP	McDonnell-Douglas MD-11F	48577/583	ex JA8586
☐ N279UP	McDonnell-Douglas MD-11F	48573/559	ex JA8582
☐ N280UP	McDonnell-Douglas MD-11F	48634/614	ex N38WF
☐ N281UP	McDonnell-Douglas MD-11F	48538/533	ex N48WF
☐ N282UP	McDonnell-Douglas MD-11F	48452/472	ex N74WF
☐ N283UP	McDonnell-Douglas MD-11F	48484/484	ex V5-NMC
☐ N284UP	McDonnell-Douglas MD-11F	48541/621	ex PP-VTU
☐ N285UP	McDonnell-Douglas MD-11F	48457/498	ex PP-VTH
☐ N286UP	McDonnell-Douglas MD-11F	48453/473	ex V5-NMD
☐ N287UP	McDonnell-Douglas MD-11	48539/571	ex PP-VTP
☐ N288UP	McDonnell-Douglas MD-11F	48540/611	ex PP-VTK
☐ N289UP	McDonnell-Douglas MD-11	48455/487	ex PP-VTJ
☐ N290UP	McDonnell-Douglas MD-11F	48456/494	ex PP-VTI
☐ N291UP	McDonnell-Douglas MD-11F	48477/511	ex N806DE
☐ N292UP	McDonnell-Douglas MD-11F	48566/543	ex N811DE
☐ N293UP	McDonnell-Douglas MD-11F	48473/481	ex N802DE
☐ N294UP	McDonnell-Douglas MD-11F	48472/480	ex N801DE
☐ N295UP	McDonnell-Douglas MD-11F	48475/489	ex N804DE
☐ N296UP	McDonnell-Douglas MD-11F	48474/485	ex N803DE

US AIRWAYS — *U S Air (US/USA)*
Pittsburgh-Greater Pittsburgh Intl, PA/Phoenix-Sky Harbor Intl, AZ (PIT/PHX)

Member of Star Alliance

☐ N700UW	Airbus A319-112	0885	ex D-AVYF	Star Alliance c/s
☐ N701UW	Airbus A319-112	0890	ex D-AVYG	Star Alliance c/s
☐ N702UW	Airbus A319-112	0896	ex D-AVYH	Star Alliance c/s
☐ N703UW	Airbus A319-112	0904	ex D-AVYI	Star Alliance c/s
☐ N704US	Airbus A319-112	0922	ex D-AVYQ	
☐ N705UW	Airbus A319-112	0929	ex D-AVYA	
☐ N708UW	Airbus A319-112	0972	ex D-AVYT	
☐ N709UW	Airbus A319-112	0997	ex D-AVYV	Philadelphia Eagles c/s
☐ N710UW	Airbus A319-112	1019	ex D-AVYR	
☐ N711UW	Airbus A319-112	1033	ex D-AVYG	
☐ N712US	Airbus A319-112	1038	ex D-AVYW	
☐ N713UW	Airbus A319-112	1040	ex D-AVYH	
☐ N714US	Airbus A319-112	1046	ex D-AVYZ	
☐ N715UW	Airbus A319-112	1051	ex D-AVYV	
☐ N716UW	Airbus A319-112	1055	ex D-AVYM	
☐ N717UW	Airbus A319-112	1069	ex D-AVWC	Carolina Panthers c/s
☐ N721UW	Airbus A319-112	1095	ex D-AVYQ	
☐ N722US	Airbus A319-112	1097	ex D-AVYS	
☐ N723UW	Airbus A319-112	1109	ex D-AVWP	
☐ N724UW	Airbus A319-112	1122	ex D-AVYA	
☐ N725UW	Airbus A319-112	1135	ex D-AVWC	
☐ N730US	Airbus A319-112	1182	ex D-AVYD	
☐ N732US	Airbus A319-112	1203	ex D-AVYA	
☐ N733UW	Airbus A319-112	1205	ex D-AVYB	Pittsburgh Steelers c/s
☐ N737US	Airbus A319-112	1245	ex D-AVYN	
☐ N738US	Airbus A319-112	1254	ex D-AVYQ	
☐ N740UW	Airbus A319-112	1265	ex D-AVWO	
☐ N741UW	Airbus A319-112	1269	ex D-AVWP	
☐ N742PS	Airbus A319-112	1275	ex N742US	PSA c/s
☐ N744P	Airbus A319-112	1287	ex N744US	Piedmont c/s
☐ N745VJ	Airbus A319-112	1289	ex N745UW	Allegheny c/s 'Vistajet'
☐ N746UW	Airbus A319-112	1297	ex D-AVWV	
☐ N747UW	Airbus A319-112	1301	ex D-AVWM	
☐ N748UW	Airbus A319-112	1311	ex D-AVYA	
☐ N749US	Airbus A319-112	1313	ex D-AVWG	
☐ N750UW	Airbus A319-112	1315	ex D-AVWH	

☐ N751UW	Airbus A319-112	1317	ex D-AVWK		
☐ N752US	Airbus A319-112	1319	ex D-AVWS		
☐ N753US	Airbus A319-112	1326	ex D-AVYG		
☐ N754UW	Airbus A319-112	1328	ex D-AVYJ		
☐ N755US	Airbus A319-112	1331	ex D-AVYN		
☐ N756US	Airbus A319-112	1340	ex D-AVYO		
☐ N757UW	Airbus A319-112	1342	ex D-AVYP		
☐ N758US	Airbus A319-112	1348	ex D-AVYS		
☐ N760US	Airbus A319-112	1354	ex D-AVWI		
☐ N762US	Airbus A319-112	1358	ex D-AVWD		
☐ N763US	Airbus A319-112	1360	ex D-AVWF		
☐ N764US	Airbus A319-112	1369	ex D-AVWM		
☐ N765US	Airbus A319-112	1371	ex D-AVWO		
☐ N766US	Airbus A319-112	1378	ex D-AVWG		
☐ N767UW	Airbus A319-112	1382	ex D-AVWN		
☐ N768US	Airbus A319-112	1389	ex D-AVYI		
☐ N769US	Airbus A319-112	1391	ex D-AVYJ		
☐ N770UW	Airbus A319-112	1393	ex D-AVYU		
☐ N801AW	Airbus A319-132	0889	ex D-AVYM		
☐ N802AW	Airbus A319-132	0924	ex D-AVYR		
☐ N803AW	Airbus A319-132	0931	ex D-AVYK		
☐ N804AW	Airbus A319-132	1043	ex D-AVYY		
☐ N805AW	Airbus A319-132	1049	ex D-AVYU		
☐ N806AW	Airbus A319-132	1056	ex D-AVYO		
☐ N807AW	Airbus A319-132	1064	ex D-AVWB		
☐ N808AW	Airbus A319-132	1088	ex D-AVWM		
☐ N809AW	Airbus A319-132	1111	ex D-AVWT		
☐ N810AW	Airbus A319-132	1116	ex D-AVWV		
☐ N812AW	Airbus A319-132	1178	ex D-AVWP		
☐ N813AW	Airbus A319-132	1223	ex D-AVYH		
☐ N814AW	Airbus A319-132	1281	ex D-AVYC		
☐ N815AW	Airbus A319-132	1323	ex D-AVWW		
☐ N816AW	Airbus A319-132	1350	ex D-AVYV		
☐ N817AW	Airbus A319-132	1373	ex D-AVWA		
☐ N818AW	Airbus A319-132	1375	ex D-AVWB		
☐ N819AW	Airbus A319-132	1395	ex D-AVYX		
☐ N820AW	Airbus A319-132	1397	ex D-AVWQ		
☐ N821AW	Airbus A319-132	1406	ex D-AVYC		
☐ N822AW	Airbus A319-132	1410	ex D-AVYD	Nevada flag c/s	
☐ N823AW	Airbus A319-132	1463	ex D-AVYJ		
☐ N824AW	Airbus A319-132	1490	ex D-AVYA		
☐ N825AW	Airbus A319-132	1527	ex D-AVWG		
☐ N826AW	Airbus A319-132	1534	ex D-AVYO	Arizona flag c/s	
☐ N827AW	Airbus A319-132	1547	ex D-AVWL		
☐ N828AW	Airbus A319-132	1552	ex D-AVWO	America West Heritage c/s	
☐ N829AW	Airbus A319-132	1563	ex D-AVYS		
☐ N830AW	Airbus A319-132	1565	ex D-AVYT		
☐ N831AW	Airbus A319-132	1576	ex D-AVWQ		
☐ N832AW	Airbus A319-132	1643	ex D-AVYA		
☐ N833AW	Airbus A319-132	1844	ex D-AVWV		
☐ N834AW	Airbus A319-132	2302	ex D-AVWM		
☐ N835AW	Airbus A319-132	2458	ex D-AVYN		
☐ N836AW	Airbus A319-132	2570	ex D-AVXB		
☐ N837AW	Airbus A319-132	2595	ex D-AVXM	Arizona Cardinals c/s	
☐ N838AW	Airbus A319-132	2615	ex D-AVXT	America West Heritage c/s	
☐ N839AW	Airbus A319-132	2669	ex D-AVYH	dam	
☐ N840AW	Airbus A319-132	2690	ex D-AVXA		
☐ N102UW	Airbus A320-214	0844	ex F-WWBG		
☐ N103US	Airbus A320-214	0861	ex F-WWBP		
☐ N104UW	Airbus A320-214	0863	ex F-WWBQ		
☐ N105UW	Airbus A320-214	0868	ex F-WWBU		
☐ N107US	Airbus A320-214	1052	ex F-WWIM		
☐ N108UW	Airbus A320-214	1061	ex F-WWBB		
☐ N109UW	Airbus A320-214	1065	ex F-WWBD		
☐ N110UW	Airbus A320-214	1112	ex F-WWBJ		
☐ N111US	Airbus A320-214	1114	ex F-WWBK		
☐ N112US	Airbus A320-214	1134	ex F-WWIV		
☐ N113UW	Airbus A320-214	1141	ex F-WWBC		
☐ N114UW	Airbus A320-214	1148	ex F-WWBQ		
☐ N117UW	Airbus A320-214	1224	ex F-WWBH		
☐ N118US	Airbus A320-214	1264	ex F-WWDE		
☐ N119US	Airbus A320-214	1268	ex F-WWDH		
☐ N121UW	Airbus A320-214	1294	ex F-WWBC		
☐ N122US	Airbus A320-214	1298	ex F-WWBM		
☐ N123UW	Airbus A320-214	1310	ex F-WWBX		
☐ N124US	Airbus A320-214	1314	ex F-WWDJ		
☐ N125UW	Airbus A320-232	4086	ex F-WWBU		
☐ N126UW	Airbus A320-232	4149	ex D-AVVJ		on order
☐	Airbus A320-232		ex		on order
☐	Airbus A320-232		ex		on order
☐ N601AW	Airbus A320-232	1935	ex D-ALAU		
☐ N604AW	Airbus A320-232	1196	ex F-WWDZ		

	Registration	Type	c/n	Previous identity	Notes	
☐	N620AW	Airbus A320-231	0052	ex N901BN		
☐	N621AW	Airbus A320-231	0053	ex N902BN		
☐	N622AW	Airbus A320-231	0054	ex N903BN		
☐	N624AW	Airbus A320-231	0055	ex N904BN		
☐	N625AW	Airbus A320-231	0064	ex N905BN		
☐	N626AW	Airbus A320-231	0065	ex N906BN		
☐	N627AW	Airbus A320-231	0066	ex N907GP		
☐	N628AW	Airbus A320-231	0067	ex N908GP		
☐	N629AW	Airbus A320-231	0076	ex N910GP		
☐	N631AW	Airbus A320-231	0077	ex N911GP		
☐	N632AW	Airbus A320-231	0081	ex N912GP		
☐	N633AW	Airbus A320-231	0082	ex N913GP		
☐	N637AW	Airbus A320-231	0099	ex N917GP	Arizona Cardinals c/s	
☐	N640AW	Airbus A320-232	0448	ex N931LF		
☐	N642AW	Airbus A320-232	0584	ex F-WWDZ		
☐	N644AW	Airbus A320-231	0317	ex N300ML		
☐	N647AW	Airbus A320-232	0762	ex F-WWDE		
☐	N648AW	Airbus A320-232	0770	ex F-WWDJ		
☐	N649AW	Airbus A320-232	0803	ex F-WWDZ		
☐	N650AW	Airbus A320-232	0856	ex F-WWBM		
☐	N651AW	Airbus A320-232	0866	ex F-WWBS		
☐	N652AW	Airbus A320-232	0953	ex F-WWDR		
☐	N653AW	Airbus A320-232	1003	ex F-WWDK		
☐	N654AW	Airbus A320-232	1050	ex F-WWIL		
☐	N655AW	Airbus A320-232	1075	ex F-WWIG		
☐	N656AW	Airbus A320-232	1079	ex F-WWIQ		
☐	N657AW	Airbus A320-232	1083	ex F-WWIU		
☐	N658AW	Airbus A320-232	1110	ex F-WWDI		
☐	N659AW	Airbus A320-232	1166	ex F-WWDG		
☐	N660AW	Airbus A320-232	1234	ex F-WWIO		
☐	N661AW	Airbus A320-232	1284	ex F-WWBK		
☐	N662AW	Airbus A320-232	1274	ex F-WWDR		
☐	N663AW	Airbus A320-232	1419	ex F-WWBJ		
☐	N664AW	Airbus A320-232	1621	ex F-WWDK		
☐	N665AW	Airbus A320-232	1644	ex F-WWDN		
☐	N667AW	Airbus A320-232	1710	ex F-WWIX		
☐	N668AW	Airbus A320-232	1764	ex F-WWBZ		
☐	N669AW	Airbus A320-232	1792	ex F-WWDX		
☐	N672AW	Airbus A320-232	2193	ex F-WWDZ		
☐	N673AW	Airbus A320-232	2312	ex F-WWDJ		
☐	N674AW	Airbus A320-232	2359	ex F-WWIT		
☐	N675AW	Airbus A320-232	2405	ex F-WWDA		N233UW resd
☐	N676AW	Airbus A320-232	2422	ex F-WWBB		
☐	N677AW	Airbus A320-232	2430	ex F-WWBJ		
☐	N678AW	Airbus A320-232	2482	ex F-WWIN		N236UW resd
☐	N679AW	Airbus A320-232	2613	ex F-WWIX		
☐	N680AW	Airbus A320-232	2630	ex F-WWDX		
☐	N161UW	Airbus A321-211	1403	ex D-AVZD		
☐	N162UW	Airbus A321-211	1412	ex D-AVZF		
☐	N163US	Airbus A321-211	1417	ex D-AVZG		
☐	N165US	Airbus A321-211	1431	ex D-AVZB		
☐	N167US	Airbus A321-211	1442	ex D-AVXA		
☐	N169UW	Airbus A321-211	1455	ex D-AVXD		
☐	N170US	Airbus A321-211	1462	ex D-AVZM		
☐	N171US	Airbus A321-211	1465	ex D-AVZN		
☐	N172US	Airbus A321-211	1472	ex D-AVZO		
☐	N173US	Airbus A321-211	1481	ex D-AVZI		
☐	N174US	Airbus A321-211	1492	ex D-AVZR		
☐	N176UW	Airbus A321-211	1499	ex D-AVZT		
☐	N177US	Airbus A321-211	1517	ex D-AVZF		
☐	N178US	Airbus A321-211	1519	ex D-AVZH		
☐	N179UW	Airbus A321-211	1521	ex D-AVZJ		
☐	N180US	Airbus A321-211	1525	ex D-AVZV		
☐	N181UW	Airbus A321-211	1531	ex D-AVZW		
☐	N182UW	Airbus A321-211	1536	ex D-AVZB		
☐	N183UW	Airbus A321-211	1539	ex D-AVZC		
☐	N184US	Airbus A321-211	1651	ex D-AVZQ		
☐	N185UW	Airbus A321-211	1666	ex D-AVZI		
☐	N186US	Airbus A321-211	1701	ex D-AVZD		
☐	N187US	Airbus A321-211	1704	ex D-AVZE		
☐	N188US	Airbus A321-211	1724	ex D-AVXB		
☐	N189UW	Airbus A321-211	1425	ex N164UW		
☐	N190UW	Airbus A321-211	1436	ex N166US		
☐	N191UW	Airbus A321-211	1447	ex N168US		
☐	N192UW	Airbus A321-211	1496	ex N175US		
☐	N193UW	Airbus A321-231	3584	ex D-AVZL		
☐	N194UW	Airbus A321-231	3629	ex D-AVZI		
☐	N195UW	Airbus A321-231	3633	ex D-AVZJ		
☐	N196UW	Airbus A321-231	3879	ex D-AVZR		
☐	N197UW	Airbus A321-231	3928	ex D-AZAC		
☐	N507AY	Airbus A321-231	3712	ex D-AVZP		
☐	N508AY	Airbus A321-231	3740	ex D-AZAL		

☐ N509AY	Airbus A321-231	3796	ex D-AZAS	
☐ N510UW	Airbus A321-231	3858	ex D-AVZI	
☐ N519UW	Airbus A321-231	3881	ex D-AVZT	
☐ N520UW	Airbus A321-231	3924	ex D-AZAA	
☐ N521UW	Airbus A321-231	3944	ex D-AZAJ	
☐ N523UW	Airbus A321-231	3960	ex D-AZAV	
☐ N524UW	Airbus A321-231	3977	ex F-WWIX	
☐ N534UW	Airbus A321-231	3989	ex D-AZAO	
☐ N535UW	Airbus A321-231	3993	ex D-AZAP	
☐ N536UW	Airbus A321-231	4025	ex D-AVZH	
☐ N537UW	Airbus A321-231	4041	ex D-AVZJ	
☐ N538UW	Airbus A321-231	4050	ex D-AZAK	
☐ N539UW	Airbus A321-231	4082	ex D-AVZV	
☐ N540UW	Airbus A321-231	4107	ex D-AZAD	
☐ N541UW	Airbus A321-231	4123	ex D-AZAI	
☐ N542UW	Airbus A321-231	4134	ex D-AZAL	
☐ N270AY	Airbus A330-323X	315	ex N670UW	
☐ N271AY	Airbus A330-323X	323	ex N671UW	
☐ N272AY	Airbus A330-323X	333	ex N672UW	
☐ N273AY	Airbus A330-323X	337	ex N673UW	
☐ N274AY	Airbus A330-323X	342	ex N674UW	
☐ N275AY	Airbus A330-323X	370	ex N675US	
☐ N276AY	Airbus A330-323X	375	ex N676UW	
☐ N277AY	Airbus A330-323X	380	ex N677UW	
☐ N278AY	Airbus A330-323X	388	ex N678US	
☐ N279AY	Airbus A330-223	1011	ex F-WWYG	
☐ N280AY	Airbus A330-223	1022	ex F-WWYP	
☐ N281AY	Airbus A330-223	1041	ex F-WWYT	
☐ N282AY	Airbus A330-223	1069	ex F-WWYG	
☐ N283AY	Airbus A330-223	1076	ex F-WWKP	
☐ N284AY	Airbus A330-223	1095	ex F-WWYS	
☐ N285AY	Airbus A330-223	1100	ex F-WW	on order
☐ N154AW	Boeing 737-3G7	23776/1417		
☐ N155AW	Boeing 737-3G7	23777/1419		
☐ N156AW	Boeing 737-3G7	23778/1455		
☐ N157AW	Boeing 737-3G7	23779/1457		
☐ N158AW	Boeing 737-3G7	23780/1459		
☐ N166AW	Boeing 737-33A	23627/1302	ex (N3281Y)	N338AW resd
☐ N168AW	Boeing 737-33A	23629/1311	ex (N3282N)	N339AW resd
☐ N302AW	Boeing 737-3G7	24009/1578		
☐ N303AW	Boeing 737-3G7	24010/1606		
☐ N305AW	Boeing 737-3G7	24012/1612		
☐ N313AW	Boeing 737-3S3	23712/1336	ex EC-EBZ	
☐ N314AW	Boeing 737-3S3	23733/1345	ex G-BMTG	
☐ N315AW	Boeing 737-3S3	23734/1359	ex G-BMTH	
☐ N316AW	Boeing 737-3S3	23713/1341	ex G-BMTF	
☐ N332AW	Boeing 737-3B7	23384/1427	ex N953WP	
☐ N334AW	Boeing 737-3Y0	23748/1381	ex N962WP	
☐ N504AU	Boeing 737-3B7	23379/1362	ex N373AU	
☐ N505AU	Boeing 737-3B7	23380/1366	ex N374AU	
☐ N506AU	Boeing 737-3B7	23381/1394	ex N375AU	
☐ N516AU	Boeing 737-3B7	23702/1475	ex N385AU	
☐ N529AU	Boeing 737-3B7	24411/1713		
☐ N530AU	Boeing 737-3B7	24412/1735		
☐ N531AU	Boeing 737-3B7	24478/1743		
☐ N532AU	Boeing 737-3B7	24479/1745		
☐ N533AU	Boeing 737-3B7	24515/1767		
☐ N574US	Boeing 737-301	23739/1469	ex N358US	
☐ N588US	Boeing 737-301	23933/1559	ex (N360P)	stored GYR
☐ N404US	Boeing 737-401	23886/1487	ex (N402P)	
☐ N405US	Boeing 737-401	23885/1512	ex (N403P)	
☐ N406US	Boeing 737-401	23876/1528	ex (N404P)	
☐ N409US	Boeing 737-401	23879/1573	ex (N407P)	
☐ N417US	Boeing 737-401	23984/1674		
☐ N418US	Boeing 737-401	23985/1676		
☐ N419US	Boeing 737-401	23986/1684		
☐ N420US	Boeing 737-401	23987/1698		
☐ N421US	Boeing 737-401	23988/1714		
☐ N422US	Boeing 737-401	23989/1716		
☐ N423US	Boeing 737-401	23990/1732		
☐ N424US	Boeing 737-401	23991/1746		
☐ N425US	Boeing 737-401	23992/1764		
☐ N426US	Boeing 737-4B7	24548/1789		
☐ N427US	Boeing 737-4B7	24549/1791		
☐ N430US	Boeing 737-4B7	24552/1797		
☐ N432US	Boeing 737-4B7	24554/1817		
☐ N433US	Boeing 737-4B7	24555/1819		
☐ N434US	Boeing 737-4B7	24556/1821		
☐ N435US	Boeing 737-4B7	24557/1835		
☐ N438US	Boeing 737-4B7	24560/1849		

☐ N439US	Boeing 737-4B7	24781/1874			
☐ N440US	Boeing 737-4B7	24811/1890			stored
☐ N441US	Boeing 737-4B7	24812/1892			
☐ N442US	Boeing 737-4B7	24841/1906			
☐ N443US	Boeing 737-4B7	24842/1908			
☐ N444US	Boeing 737-4B7	24862/1910			
☐ N445US	Boeing 737-4B7	24863/1914			
☐ N449US	Boeing 737-4B7	24893/1946			
☐ N450UW	Boeing 737-4B7	24933/1954	ex N775AU		
☐ N451UW	Boeing 737-4B7	24934/1956	ex N776AU		
☐ N452UW	Boeing 737-4B7	24979/1980	ex N777AU		
☐ N453UW	Boeing 737-4B7	24980/1982	ex N778AU		
☐ N454UW	Boeing 737-4B7	24996/1986	ex N779AU		
☐ N455UW	Boeing 737-4B7	24997/1990	ex N780AU		
☐ N456UW	Boeing 737-4B7	25020/1992	ex N781AU		
☐ N457UW	Boeing 737-4B7	25021/1995	ex N782AU		
☐ N458UW	Boeing 737-4B7	25022/2010	ex N783AU		
☐ N459UW	Boeing 737-4B7	25023/2020	ex N784AU		
☐ N460UW	Boeing 737-4B7	25024/2026	ex N785AU		

☐ N200UU	Boeing 757-2B7/W	27809/673	ex N631AU		
☐ N201UU	Boeing 757-2B7/W	27810/678	ex N632AU		
☐ N202UW	Boeing 757-2B7/W	27811/681	ex N633AU		
☐ N203UW	Boeing 757-23N/W	30548/930	ex N642UW		
☐ N204UW	Boeing 757-23N/W	30886/945	ex N643UW		
☐ N205UW	Boeing 757-23N/W	30887/946	ex N644UW		
☐ N206UW	Boeing 757-2B7/W	27808/666	ex N630AU		
☐ N901AW	Boeing 757-2S7	23321/76	ex N601RC		
☐ N902AW	Boeing 757-2S7	23322/79	ex N602RC		
☐ N903AW	Boeing 757-2S7	23323/80	ex N603RC		
☐ N904AW	Boeing 757-2S7	23566/96	ex N604RC		
☐ N905AW	Boeing 757-2S7	23567/97	ex N605RC		
☐ N906AW	Boeing 757-2S7	23568/99	ex N606RC		
☐ N908AW	Boeing 757-2G7/W	24233/244			
☐ N909AW	Boeing 757-2G7/W	24522/252			
☐ N910AW	Boeing 757-2G7/W	24523/256			
☐ N916UW	Boeing 757-225	22192/3	ex N600AU		
☐ N918UW	Boeing 757-225	22196/7	ex N602AU		
☐ N920UW	Boeing 757-225	22199/17	ex N604AU		
☐ N923UW	Boeing 757-225	22203/26	ex N607AU		stored VCV
☐ N924UW	Boeing 757-225	22204/27	ex N608AU		
☐ N925UW	Boeing 757-225	22205/28	ex N609AU		
☐ N935UW	Boeing 757-2B7/W	27201/605	ex N622AU	Star Alliance c/s	
☐ N936UW	Boeing 757-2B7	27244/607	ex N623AU		
☐ N937UW	Boeing 757-2B7/W	27245/630	ex N624AU		
☐ N938UW	Boeing 757-2B7/W	27246/643	ex N625VJ		
☐ N939UW	Boeing 757-2B7/W	27303/647	ex N626AU		
☐ N940UW	Boeing 757-2B7/W	27805/655	ex N627AU		
☐ N941UW	Boeing 757-2B7/W	27806/657	ex N628AU		
☐ N942UW	Boeing 757-2B7/W	27807/662	ex N629AU		

☐ N245AY	Boeing 767-201ER	23897/173	ex N645US
☐ N246AY	Boeing 767-201ER	23898/175	ex N646US
☐ N248AY	Boeing 767-201ER	23900/190	ex N648UA
☐ N249AU	Boeing 767-201ER	23901/197	ex N649US
☐ N250AY	Boeing 767-201ER	23902/217	ex N650US
☐ N251AY	Boeing 767-2B7ER	24764/306	ex N651US
☐ N252AU	Boeing 767-2B7ER	24765/308	ex N652US
☐ N253AY	Boeing 767-2B7ER	24894/338	ex N653US
☐ N255AY	Boeing 767-2B7ER	25257/383	ex N655US
☐ N256AY	Boeing 767-2B7ER	26847/486	ex N656US

US AIRWAYS EXPRESS ***Air Express (USX)***
Charlotte, NC,/Philadelphia. PA/Pittsburgh, PA (CLT/PHL/PIT)

☐ N124CJ	Beech 1900D	UE-24	ex N575D	LVA	Colgan Air
☐ N152MJ	Beech 1900D	UE-52	ex N84703	LVV	Colgan Air
☐ N171CJ	Beech 1900D	UE-71	ex N85704	LVU	Colgan Air
☐ N172MJ	Beech 1900D	UE-72	ex N85804	LVI	Colgan Air
☐ N191CJ	Beech 1900D	UE-19	ex N83005	LVW	Colgan Air
☐ N221CJ	Beech 1900D	UE-221		LVG	Colgan Air

☐ N202PS	Canadair CL-600-2B19 (CRJ-200ER)	7858	ex C-FMLF	202	PSA Airlines
☐ N206PS	Canadair CL-600-2B19 (CRJ-200ER)	7860	ex C-FMLQ	206	PSA Airlines
☐ N207PS	Canadair CL-600-2B19 (CRJ-200ER)	7873	ex C-FMNQ	207	PSA Airlines
☐ N209PS	Canadair CL-600-2B19 (CRJ-200ER)	7874	ex C-FMLU	209	PSA Airlines
☐ N213PS	Canadair CL-600-2B19 (CRJ-200ER)	7879	ex C-FMMQ	213	PSA Airlines
☐ N215PS	Canadair CL-600-2B19 (CRJ-200ER)	7880	ex C-FMMW	215	PSA Airlines
☐ N216PS	Canadair CL-600-2B19 (CRJ-200ER)	7882	ex C-FMMY	216	PSA Airlines
☐ N218PS	Canadair CL-600-2B19 (CRJ-200ER)	7885	ex C-FMKW	218	PSA Airlines
☐ N220PS	Canadair CL-600-2B19 (CRJ-200ER)	7887	ex C-FMLB	220	PSA Airlines
☐ N221PS	Canadair CL-600-2B19 (CRJ-200ER)	7889	ex C-FMLI	221	PSA Airlines

☐ N223JS	Canadair CL-600-2B19 (CRJ-200ER)	7892	ex C-FMLT	223	PSA Airlines
☐ N226JS	Canadair CL-600-2B19 (CRJ-200ER)	7895	ex C-FMNH	226	PSA Airlines
☐ N228PS	Canadair CL-600-2B19 (CRJ-200ER)	7897	ex C-FMNX	228	PSA Airlines
☐ N229PS	Canadair CL-600-2B19 (CRJ-200ER)	7898	ex C-FMNY	229	PSA Airlines
☐ N230PS	Canadair CL-600-2B19 (CRJ-200ER)	7904	ex C-FMLU	230	PSA Airlines
☐ N237PS	Canadair CL-600-2B19 (CRJ-200ER)	7906	ex C-FMMB	237	PSA Airlines
☐ N241PS	Canadair CL-600-2B19 (CRJ-200ER)	7909	ex C-FMMQ	241	PSA Airlines
☐ N242JS	Canadair CL-600-2B19 (CRJ-200ER)	7911	ex C-FMMX	242	PSA Airlines
☐ N244PS	Canadair CL-600-2B19 (CRJ-200ER)	7912	ex C-FMMY	244	PSA Airlines
☐ N245PS	Canadair CL-600-2B19 (CRJ-200ER)	7919	ex C-FMLI	245	PSA Airlines
☐ N246PS	Canadair CL-600-2B19 (CRJ-200ER)	7920	ex C-FMLQ	246	PSA Airlines
☐ N247JS	Canadair CL-600-2B19 (CRJ-200ER)	7922	ex C-FMLT	247	PSA Airlines
☐ N248PS	Canadair CL-600-2B19 (CRJ-200ER)	7925	ex C-FMNH	248	PSA Airlines
☐ N249PS	Canadair CL-600-2B19 (CRJ-200ER)	7926	ex C-FMNW	249	PSA Airlines
☐ N250PS	Canadair CL-600-2B19 (CRJ-200ER)	7929	ex C-FMOS	250	PSA Airlines
☐ N251PS	Canadair CL-600-2B19 (CRJ-200ER)	7931	ex C-FVAZ	251	PSA Airlines
☐ N253PS	Canadair CL-600-2B19 (CRJ-200ER)	7934	ex C-FMLU	253	PSA Airlines
☐ N254PS	Canadair CL-600-2B19 (CRJ-200ER)	7935	ex C-FMOI	254	PSA Airlines
☐ N256PS	Canadair CL-600-2B19 (CRJ-200ER)	7937	ex C-FMML	256	PSA Airlines
☐ N257PS	Canadair CL-600-2B19 (CRJ-200ER)	7939	ex C-FMMQ	257	PSA Airlines
☐ N258PS	Canadair CL-600-2B19 (CRJ-200ER)	7941	ex C-FMMX	258	PSA Airlines
☐ N259PS	Canadair CL-600-2B19 (CRJ-200ER)	7945	ex C-FMKW	259	PSA Airlines
☐ N260JS	Canadair CL-600-2B19 (CRJ-200ER)	7957	ex C-FMNX	260	PSA Airlines
☐ N261PS	Canadair CL-600-2B19 (CRJ-200ER)	7959	ex C-FMOS	261	PSA Airlines
☐ N262PS	Canadair CL-600-2B19 (CRJ-200ER)	7962	ex C-FMND	262	PSA Airlines
☐ N401AW	Canadair CL-600-2B19 (CRJ-200LR)	7280	ex C-FMLQ	401	Air Wisconsin
☐ N403AW	Canadair CL-600-2B19 (CRJ-200LR)	7288	ex C-FMLF	403	Air Wisconsin
☐ N404AW	Canadair CL-600-2B19 (CRJ-200LR)	7294	ex C-FMMT	404	Air Wisconsin
☐ N405AW	Canadair CL-600-2B19 (CRJ-200LR)	7362	ex C-FMND	405	Air Wisconsin
☐ N406AW	Canadair CL-600-2B19 (CRJ-200LR)	7402	ex C-FMMY	406	Air Wisconsin
☐ N407AW	Canadair CL-600-2B19 (CRJ-200LR)	7424	ex C-FMLU	407	Air Wisconsin
☐ N408AW	Canadair CL-600-2B19 (CRJ-200LR)	7568	ex C-FMNY	408	Air Wisconsin
☐ N409AW	Canadair CL-600-2B19 (CRJ-200LR)	7447	ex C-FMNX	409	Air Wisconsin
☐ N410AW	Canadair CL-600-2B19 (CRJ-200LR)	7490	ex C-FMMW	410	Air Wisconsin
☐ N411ZW	Canadair CL-600-2B19 (CRJ-200LR)	7569	ex C-FMNZ	411	Air Wisconsin
☐ N412AW	Canadair CL-600-2B19 (CRJ-200LR)	7582	ex C-FMMY	412	Air Wisconsin
☐ N413AW	Canadair CL-600-2B19 (CRJ-200LR)	7585	ex C-FMKW	413	Air Wisconsin
☐ N414ZW	Canadair CL-600-2B19 (CRJ-200LR)	7586	ex C-FMKZ	414	Air Wisconsin
☐ N415AW	Canadair CL-600-2B19 (CRJ-200LR)	7593	ex C-FMLV	415	Air Wisconsin
☐ N416AW	Canadair CL-600-2B19 (CRJ-200LR)	7603	ex C-FMNQ	416	Air Wisconsin
☐ N417AW	Canadair CL-600-2B19 (CRJ-200LR)	7610	ex C-FMMW	417	Air Wisconsin
☐ N418AW	Canadair CL-600-2B19 (CRJ-200LR)	7618	ex C-FMLF	418	Air Wisconsin
☐ N419AW	Canadair CL-600-2B19 (CRJ-200LR)	7633	ex C-FMNQ	419	Air Wisconsin
☐ N420AW	Canadair CL-600-2B19 (CRJ-200LR)	7640	ex C-FMMW	420	Air Wisconsin
☐ N421ZW	Canadair CL-600-2B19 (CRJ-200LR)	7346	ex N587ML	421	Air Wisconsin
☐ N422AW	Canadair CL-600-2B19 (CRJ-200LR)	7341	ex N586ML	422	Air Wisconsin
☐ N423AW	Canadair CL-600-2B19 (CRJ-200LR)	7636	ex C-FMMB	423	Air Wisconsin
☐ N424AW	Canadair CL-600-2B19 (CRJ-200LR)	7656	ex C-FMNW	424	Air Wisconsin
☐ N425AW	Canadair CL-600-2B19 (CRJ-200LR)	7663	ex C-FMNQ	425	Air Wisconsin
☐ N426AW	Canadair CL-600-2B19 (CRJ-200LR)	7669	ex C-FMMQ	426	Air Wisconsin
☐ N427ZW	Canadair CL-600-2B19 (CRJ-200LR)	7685	ex C-FMNH	427	Air Wisconsin
☐ N428AW	Canadair CL-600-2B19 (CRJ-200LR)	7695	ex C-FMOI	428	Air Wisconsin
☐ N429AW	Canadair CL-600-2B19 (CRJ-200LR)	7711	ex CFMLS	429	Air Wisconsin
☐ N430AW	Canadair CL-600-2B19 (CRJ-200LR)	7719	ex C-FMOS	430	Air Wisconsin
☐ N431AW	Canadair CL-600-2B19 (CRJ-200LR)	7256	ex N575ML	431	Air Wisconsin
☐ N432AW	Canadair CL-600-2B19 (CRJ-200LR)	7257	ex N576ML	432	Air Wisconsin
☐ N433AW	Canadair CL-600-2B19 (CRJ-200LR)	7289	ex N580ML	433	Air Wisconsin
☐ N434AW	Canadair CL-600-2B19 (CRJ-200LR)	7322	ex N582ML	434	Air Wisconsin
☐ N435AW	Canadair CL-600-2B19 (CRJ-200LR)	7724	ex C-FMLU	435	Air Wisconsin
☐ N436AW	Canadair CL-600-2B19 (CRJ-200LR)	7734	ex C-FMKV	436	Air Wisconsin
☐ N437AW	Canadair CL-600-2B19 (CRJ-200LR)	7744	ex C-FMMT	437	Air Wisconsin
☐ N438AW	Canadair CL-600-2B19 (CRJ-200LR)	7748	ex C-GFAX	438	Air Wisconsin
☐ N439AW	Canadair CL-600-2B19 (CRJ-200LR)	7753	ex C-FZZO	439	Air Wisconsin
☐ N440AW	Canadair CL-600-2B19 (CRJ-200LR)	7766	ex C-FMKZ	440	Air Wisconsin
☐ N441ZW	Canadair CL-600-2B19 (CRJ-200LR)	7777	ex C-FMNX	441	Air Wisconsin
☐ N442AW	Canadair CL-600-2B19 (CRJ-200LR)	7778	ex C-FMNY	442	Air Wisconsin
☐ N443AW	Canadair CL-600-2B19 (CRJ-200LR)	7781	ex C-FVAZ	443	Air Wisconsin
☐ N444ZW	Canadair CL-600-2B19 (CRJ-200LR)	7788	ex C-FMMN	444	Air Wisconsin
☐ N445AW	Canadair CL-600-2B19 (CRJ-200LR)	7804	ex C-FMMT	445	Air Wisconsin
☐ N446AW	Canadair CL-600-2B19 (CRJ-200LR)	7806	ex C-FMNW	446	Air Wisconsin
☐ N447AW	Canadair CL-600-2B19 (CRJ-200LR)	7812	ex C-FMND	447	Air Wisconsin
☐ N448AW	Canadair CL-600-2B19 (CRJ-200LR)	7814	ex C-FMLU	448	Air Wisconsin
☐ N449AW	Canadair CL-600-2B19 (CRJ-200LR)	7818	ex C-FMMN	449	Air Wisconsin
☐ N450AW	Canadair CL-600-2B19 (CRJ-200LR)	7823	ex C-FMNB	450	Air Wisconsin
☐ N451AW	Canadair CL-600-2B19 (CRJ-200LR)	7832	ex C-FMLT	451	Air Wisconsin
☐ N452AW	Canadair CL-600-2B19 (CRJ-200LR)	7835	ex C-FMNH	452	Air Wisconsin
☐ N453AW	Canadair CL-600-2B19 (CRJ-200LR)	7838	ex C-FMNY	453	Air Wisconsin
☐ N454AW	Canadair CL-600-2B19 (CRJ-200LR)	7842	ex C-FMND	454	Air Wisconsin
☐ N455AW	Canadair CL-600-2B19 (CRJ-200LR)	7848	ex C-FMMN	455	Air Wisconsin
☐ N456ZW	Canadair CL-600-2B19 (CRJ-200LR)	7849	ex C-FMMQ	456	Air Wisconsin
☐ N457AW	Canadair CL-600-2B19 (CRJ-200LR)	7854	ex C-FMKV	457	Air Wisconsin
☐ N458AW	Canadair CL-600-2B19 (CRJ-200LR)	7861	ex C-FMLS	458	Air Wisconsin
☐ N459AW	Canadair CL-600-2B19 (CRJ-200LR)	7863	ex C-FMLV	459	Air Wisconsin

☐ N460AW	Canadair CL-600-2B19 (CRJ-200LR)	7867	ex C-GZTD	460		Air Wisconsin
☐ N461AW	Canadair CL-600-2B19 (CRJ-200LR)	7870	ex C-FMOW	461		Air Wisconsin
☐ N462AW	Canadair CL-600-2B19 (CRJ-200LR)	7875	ex C-FMOI	462		Air Wisconsin
☐ N463AW	Canadair CL-600-2B19 (CRJ-200LR)	7878	ex C-FMMN	463		Air Wisconsin
☐ N464AW	Canadair CL-600-2B19 (CRJ-200LR)	7890	ex C-FMLQ	464		Air Wisconsin
☐ N465AW	Canadair CL-600-2B19 (CRJ-200LR)	7893	ex C-FMLV	465		Air Wisconsin
☐ N466AW	Canadair CL-600-2B19 (CRJ-200LR)	7899	ex C-FMOS	466		Air Wisconsin
☐ N467AW	Canadair CL-600-2B19 (CRJ-200LR)	7900	ex C-FMOW	467		Air Wisconsin
☐ N468AW	Canadair CL-600-2B19 (CRJ-200LR)	7916	ex C-FMKZ	468		Air Wisconsin
☐ N469AW	Canadair CL-600-2B19 (CRJ-200LR)	7917	ex C-FMLB	469		Air Wisconsin
☐ N470ZW	Canadair CL-600-2B19 (CRJ-200LR)	7927	ex C-FMNX	470		Air Wisconsin, dam Dec07
☐ N570ML	Canadair CL-600-2B19 (CRJ-200LR)	7206	ex C-GBNO	YJX		Mesa
☐ N651ML	Canadair CL-600-2B19 (CRJ-200LR)	7139	ex N787BC	YCD		Mesa
☐ N7264V	Canadair CL-600-2B19 (CRJ-200LR)	7264	ex C-FMMT			Mesa
☐ N7291Z	Canadair CL-600-2B19 (CRJ-200LR)	7291	ex C-FMLS			Mesa
☐ N7305V	Canadair CL-600-2B19 (CRJ-200LR)	7305	ex C-F			Mesa
☐ N17231	Canadair CL-600-2B19 (CRJ-200LR)	7231	ex C-FMLS			Mesa
☐ N17275	Canadair CL-600-2B19 (CRJ-200LR)	7275	ex C-FMOI			Mesa
☐ N17337	Canadair CL-600-2B19 (CRJ-200LR)	7337	ex C-FMML			Mesa
☐ N17358	Canadair CL-600-2B19 (CRJ-200LR)	7358	ex C-FMNY			Mesa
☐ N27173	Canadair CL-600-2B19 (CRJ-200LR)	7173	ex C-FMMQ			Mesa
☐ N27314	Canadair CL-600-2B19 (CRJ-200LR)	7314	ex C-FMKV			Mesa
☐ N37178	Canadair CL-600-2B19 (CRJ-200LR)	7178	ex C-GAVO			Mesa
☐ N75984	Canadair CL-600-2B19 (CRJ-200LR)	7489	ex C-GZGX	YJW		Mesa
☐ N75996	Canadair CL-600-2B19 (CRJ-200LR)	7357	ex C-FZTZ	YJP		Mesa
☐ N77195	Canadair CL-600-2B19 (CRJ-200LR)	7195	ex C-FMKW	all-white		Mesa
☐ N77260	Canadair CL-600-2B19 (CRJ-200LR)	7260	ex C-FMLQ			Mesa
☐ N77286	Canadair CL-600-2B19 (CRJ-200LR)	7286	ex C-FMKZ			Mesa
☐ N97325	Canadair CL-600-2B19 (CRJ-200LR)	7325	ex C-FMNH			Mesa

☐ N702PS	Canadair CL-600-2C10 (CRJ-701ER)	10135	ex C-	702		PSA Airlines
☐ N703PS	Canadair CL-600-2C10 (CRJ-701ER)	10137	ex C-	703		PSA Airlines
☐ N705PS	Canadair CL-600-2C10 (CRJ-701ER)	10144	ex C-	705		PSA Airlines
☐ N706PS	Canadair CL-600-2C10 (CRJ-701ER)	10150	ex C-FBLQ	706		PSA Airlines
☐ N708PS	Canadair CL-600-2C10 (CRJ-701ER)	10160	ex C-	708	Star Alliance c/s	PSA Airlines
☐ N709PS	Canadair CL-600-2C10 (CRJ-701ER)	10165	ex N165MD	709		PSA Airlines
☐ N710PS	Canadair CL-600-2C10 (CRJ-701ER)	10167	ex N167MD	710		PSA Airlines
☐ N712PS	Canadair CL-600-2C10 (CRJ-701ER)	10168	ex N168MD	712		PSA Airlines
☐ N716PS	Canadair CL-600-2C10 (CRJ-701ER)	10171	ex N171MD	716		PSA Airlines
☐ N718PS	Canadair CL-600-2C10 (CRJ-701ER)	10175	ex C-FCQX	718		PSA Airlines
☐ N719PS	Canadair CL-600-2C10 (CRJ-701ER)	10177	ex N177MD	719		PSA Airlines
☐ N720PS	Canadair CL-600-2C10 (CRJ-701ER)	10178	ex N175MD	720		PSA Airlines
☐ N723PS	Canadair CL-600-2C10 (CRJ-701ER)	10181	ex C-FCRE	723		PSA Airlines
☐ N725PS	Canadair CL-600-2C10 (CRJ-701ER)	10186	ex C-	725		PSA Airlines
☐ N726PS	Canadair CL-600-2C10 (CRJ-701ER)		ex C-	726	on order	PSA Airlines
☐ N728PS	Canadair CL-600-2C10 (CRJ-701ER)		ex C-	728	on order	PSA Airlines
☐ N729PS	Canadair CL-600-2C10 (CRJ-701ER)		ex C-	729	on order	PSA Airlines
☐ N730PS	Canadair CL-600-2C10 (CRJ-701ER)		ex C-	730	on order	PSA Airlines
☐ N736PS	Canadair CL-600-2C10 (CRJ-701ER)		ex C-	736	on order	PSA Airlines
☐ N740PS	Canadair CL-600-2C10 (CRJ-701ER)		ex C-	740	on order	PSA Airlines
☐ N741PS	Canadair CL-600-2C10 (CRJ-701ER)		ex C-	741	on order	PSA Airlines
☐ N743PS	Canadair CL-600-2C10 (CRJ-701ER)		ex C-	743	on order	PSA Airlines
☐ N744PS	Canadair CL-600-2C10 (CRJ-701ER)		ex C-		on order	PSA Airlines
☐ N745PS	Canadair CL-600-2C10 (CRJ-701ER)		ex C-		on order	PSA Airlines
☐ N746PS	Canadair CL-600-2C10 (CRJ-701ER)		ex C-		on order	PSA Airlines
☐ N748PS	Canadair CL-600-2C10 (CRJ-701ER)		ex C-		on order	PSA Airlines
☐ N749PS	Canadair CL-600-2C10 (CRJ-701ER)		ex C-		on order	PSA Airlines
☐ N750PS	Canadair CL-600-2C10 (CRJ-701ER)		ex C-		on order	PSA Airlines
☐ N751PS	Canadair CL-600-2C10 (CRJ-701ER)		ex C-		on order	PSA Airlines
☐ N752PS	Canadair CL-600-2C10 (CRJ-701ER)		ex C-		on order	PSA Airlines
☐ N753PS	Canadair CL-600-2C10 (CRJ-701ER)		ex C-		on order	PSA Airlines
☐ N754PS	Canadair CL-600-2C10 (CRJ-701ER)		ex C-		on order	PSA Airlines
☐ N755PS	Canadair CL-600-2C10 (CRJ-701ER)		ex C-		on order	PSA Airlines
☐ N756PS	Canadair CL-600-2C10 (CRJ-701ER)		ex C-		on order	PSA Airlines
☐ N	Canadair CL-600-2C10 (CRJ-701ER)		ex C-		on order	PSA Airlines
☐ N	Canadair CL-600-2C10 (CRJ-701ER)		ex C-		on order	Mesa
☐ N	Canadair CL-600-2C10 (CRJ-701ER)		ex C-		on order	Mesa
☐ N	Canadair CL-600-2C10 (CRJ-701ER)		ex C-		on order	Mesa
☐ N	Canadair CL-600-2C10 (CRJ-701ER)		ex C-		on order	Mesa
☐ N	Canadair CL-600-2C10 (CRJ-701ER)		ex C-		on order	Mesa
☐ N	Canadair CL-600-2C10 (CRJ-701ER)		ex C-		on order	Mesa
☐ N	Canadair CL-600-2C10 (CRJ-701ER)		ex C-		on order	Mesa
☐ N	Canadair CL-600-2C10 (CRJ-701ER)		ex C-		on order	Mesa
☐ N	Canadair CL-600-2C10 (CRJ-701ER)		ex C-		on order	Mesa
☐ N	Canadair CL-600-2C10 (CRJ-701ER)		ex C-		on order	Mesa

☐ N902FJ	Canadair CL-600-2D24 (CRJ-900ER)	15002	ex C-GDNH			Mesa
☐ N903FJ	Canadair CL-600-2D24 (CRJ-900ER)	15003	ex C-GZQA			Mesa
☐ N904FJ	Canadair CL-600-2D24 (CRJ-900ER)	15004	ex C-GZQB			Mesa
☐ N905J	Canadair CL-600-2D24 (CRJ-900ER)	15005	ex C-GZQC			Mesa
☐ N906FJ	Canadair CL-600-2D24 (CRJ-900ER)	15006	ex C-GZQE			Mesa
☐ N907FJ	Canadair CL-600-2D24 (CRJ-900ER)	15007	ex C-GZQF			Mesa
☐ N908FJ	Canadair CL-600-2D24 (CRJ-900ER)	15008	ex C-GZQG			Mesa

	Registration	Type	c/n	Previous	Code	Operator
☐	N909FJ	Canadair CL-600-2D24 (CRJ-900ER)	15009	ex C-GZQI		Mesa
☐	N910FJ	Canadair CL-600-2D24 (CRJ-900ER)	15010	ex C-GZQJ		Mesa
☐	N911FJ	Canadair CL-600-2D24 (CRJ-900ER)	15011	ex C-GZQK		Mesa
☐	N912FJ	Canadair CL-600-2D24 (CRJ-900ER)	15012	ex C-GZQL		Mesa
☐	N913FJ	Canadair CL-600-2D24 (CRJ-900ER)	15013	ex C-GZQM		Mesa
☐	N914FJ	Canadair CL-600-2D24 (CRJ-900ER)	15014	ex C-GZQO		Mesa
☐	N915FJ	Canadair CL-600-2D24 (CRJ-900ER)	15015	ex C-GZQP		Mesa
☐	N916FJ	Canadair CL-600-2D24 (CRJ-900ER)	15016	ex C-GZQQ		Mesa
☐	N917FJ	Canadair CL-600-2D24 (CRJ-900ER)	15017	ex C-GZQR		Mesa
☐	N918FJ	Canadair CL-600-2D24 (CRJ-900ER)	15018	ex C-		Mesa
☐	N919FJ	Canadair CL-600-2D24 (CRJ-900ER)	15019	ex C-		Mesa
☐	N920FJ	Canadair CL-600-2D24 (CRJ-900ER)	15020	ex C-		Mesa
☐	N921FJ	Canadair CL-600-2D24 (CRJ-900ER)	15021	ex C-		Mesa
☐	N922FJ	Canadair CL-600-2D24 (CRJ-900ER)	15022	ex C-		Mesa
☐	N923FJ	Canadair CL-600-2D24 (CRJ-900ER)	15023	ex C-		Mesa
☐	N924FJ	Canadair CL-600-2D24 (CRJ-900ER)	15024	ex C-		Mesa
☐	N925FJ	Canadair CL-600-2D24 (CRJ-900ER)	15025	ex C-		Mesa
☐	N926LR	Canadair CL-600-2D24 (CRJ-900ER)	15026	ex C-		Mesa
☐	N927LR	Canadair CL-600-2D24 (CRJ-900ER)	15027	ex C-		Mesa
☐	N928LR	Canadair CL-600-2D24 (CRJ-900ER)	15028	ex C-		Mesa
☐	N929LR	Canadair CL-600-2D24 (CRJ-900ER)	15029	ex C-		Mesa
☐	N930LR	Canadair CL-600-2D24 (CRJ-900ER)	15030	ex C-		Mesa
☐	N931LR	Canadair CL-600-2D24 (CRJ-900ER)	15031	ex C-		Mesa
☐	N932LR	Canadair CL-600-2D24 (CRJ-900ER)	15032	ex C-		Mesa
☐	N933LR	Canadair CL-600-2D24 (CRJ-900ER)	15033	ex C-		Mesa
☐	N934FJ	Canadair CL-600-2D24 (CRJ-900ER)	15034	ex C-		Mesa
☐	N935LR	Canadair CL-600-2D24 (CRJ-900ER)	15035	ex C-		Mesa
☐	N938LR	Canadair CL-600-2D24 (CRJ-900ER)	15038	ex C-		Mesa
☐	N939LR	Canadair CL-600-2D24 (CRJ-900ER)	15039	ex C-		Mesa
☐	N942LR	Canadair CL-600-2D24 (CRJ-900ER)	15042	ex C-		Mesa
☐	N956LR	Canadair CL-600-2D24 (CRJ-900ER)	15056	ex C-		Mesa
☐	N326EN	de Havilland DHC-8-311	234	ex N386DC	HDF	Piedmont
☐	N327EN	de Havilland DHC-8-311A	261	ex N379DC	HDD	Piedmont
☐	N328EN	de Havilland DHC-8-311A	281	ex N380DC	HDC	Piedmont
☐	N329EN	de Havilland DHC-8-311	290	ex SU-UAD	HDG	Piedmont
☐	N330EN	de Havilland DHC-8-311A	274	ex N805SA	HDI	Piedmont
☐	N331EN	de Havilland DHC-8-311A	279	ex N806SA	HDJ	Piedmont
☐	N333EN	de Havilland DHC-8-311	221	ex N803SA	HDK	Piedmont
☐	N335EN	de Havilland DHC-8-311	375	ex N804SA	HDN	Piedmont
☐	N336EN	de Havilland DHC-8-311A	336	ex N284BC	HAD	Piedmont
☐	N337EN	de Havilland DHC-8-311A	284	ex SU-UAE	HDH	Piedmont
☐	N343EN	de Havilland DHC-8-311A	340	ex OE-LLZ	HDE	Piedmont
☐	N437YV	de Havilland DHC-8-202	437	ex C-FDHD		Mesa
☐	N447YV	de Havilland DHC-8Q-202	447	ex C-GFYI		Mesa
☐	N449YV	de Havilland DHC-8Q-202	449	ex C-GFHZ		Mesa
☐	N804EX	de Havilland DHC-8-102A	227	ex C-GFYI	ESA	Piedmont
☐	N805EX	de Havilland DHC-8-102A	228	ex C-GLOT	ESB	Piedmont
☐	N806EX	de Havilland DHC-8-102A	263	ex C-GEVP	ESC	Piedmont
☐	N807EX	de Havilland DHC-8-102A	292	ex C-GFQL	ESD	Piedmont
☐	N808EX	de Havilland DHC-8-102A	299	ex C-GDKL	ESE	Piedmont
☐	N809EX	de Havilland DHC-8-102A	302	ex PT-MFI	ESF	Piedmont
☐	N810EX	de Havilland DHC-8-102A	308	ex C-GDKL	ESG	Piedmont
☐	N812EX	de Havilland DHC-8-102A	312	ex C-GDNG	ESH	Piedmont
☐	N814EX	de Havilland DHC-8-102A	318	ex C-GDNG	ESI	Piedmont
☐	N815EX	de Havilland DHC-8-102A	321	ex C-GDFT	ESJ	Piedmont
☐	N816EX	de Havilland DHC-8-102A	329	ex C-GEVP	ESK	Piedmont
☐	N825EX	de Havilland DHC-8-102A	388	ex G-GHRI	EST	stored SBY
☐	N827EX	de Havilland DHC-8-102A	390	ex C-GEOA	ESV	Piedmont
☐	N837EX	de Havilland DHC-8-102A	217	ex N976HA	ERH	Piedmont
☐	N838EX	de Havilland DHC-8-102A	220	ex N977HA	ERK	Piedmont
☐	N845EX	de Havilland DHC-8-102	344	ex N846MA	EBB	Piedmont
☐	N846EX	de Havilland DHC-8-102	326	ex N960HA	EBC	stored SBY
☐	N906HA	de Havilland DHC-8-102	9	ex C-GHRI	HAS	Piedmont
☐	N907HA	de Havilland DHC-8-102	11	ex C-GESR	HSB	Piedmont
☐	N908HA	de Havilland DHC-8-102	15	ex C-GIBQ	HSC	Piedmont
☐	N911HA	de Havilland DHC-8-102	34	ex C-GEOA	HSF	Piedmont
☐	N912HA	de Havilland DHC-8-102	40	ex C-GEOA	HSG	Piedmont
☐	N914HA	de Havilland DHC-8-102	53	ex C-GETI	HSH	Piedmont
☐	N930HA	de Havilland DHC-8-102	126	ex C-GFQL	HSW	Piedmont
☐	N931HA	de Havilland DHC-8-102	132	ex C-GFOD	HSZ	Piedmont
☐	N933HA	de Havilland DHC-8-102	134	ex C-GFUM	HBA	Piedmont
☐	N934HA	de Havilland DHC-8-102	139	ex C-GETI	HBB	Piedmont
☐	N935HA	de Havilland DHC-8-102	142	ex C-GLOT	HBC	Piedmont
☐	N936HA	de Havilland DHC-8-102	145	ex C-GFQL	HRA	Piedmont
☐	N937HA	de Havilland DHC-8-102	148	ex C-GLOT	HRB	Piedmont
☐	N938HA	de Havilland DHC-8-102	152	ex C-GFUM	HRC	Piedmont
☐	N940HA	de Havilland DHC-8-102	156	ex C-GLOT	HRE	Piedmont
☐	N941HA	de Havilland DHC-8-102	161	ex C-GETI	HRF	Piedmont
☐	N942HA	de Havilland DHC-8-102	163	ex C-GFUM	HRG	Piedmont
☐	N943HA	de Havilland DHC-8-102	167	ex C-GFOD	HRH	Piedmont
☐	N987HA	de Havilland DHC-8-201	425	ex C-GFHZ		Mesa
☐	N988HA	de Havilland DHC-8-201	426	ex C-FDHD		Mesa

	Registration	Type	c/n	Previous identity	Fleet no.	Operator
☐	N989HA	de Havilland DHC-8-201	427	ex C-GFEN		Mesa
☐	N991HA	de Havilland DHC-8-201	431	ex C-GLOT		Mesa
☐	N257JQ	Embraer EMB.145LR (ERJ-145LR)	14500812	ex PT-SNO	JBJ	Chautauqua
☐	N258JQ	Embraer EMB.145LR (ERJ-145LR)	145768	ex PT-SJZ	JBI	Chautauqua
☐	N259JQ	Embraer EMB.145LR (ERJ-145LR)	145763	ex PT-SJU	JBH	Chautauqua
☐	N280SK	Embraer EMB.145LR (ERJ-145LR)	145381	ex PT-SQF	JRM	Chautauqua
☐	N291SK	Embraer EMB.145LR (ERJ-145LR)	145486	ex PT-SXF	JRX	Chautauqua
☐	N293SK	Embraer EMB.145LR (ERJ-145LR)	145500	ex PT-SXT	JRY	Chautauqua
☐	N298SK	Embraer EMB.145LR (ERJ-145LR)	145508	ex PT-SYA	JRZ	Chautauqua
☐	N370SK	Embraer EMB.145LR (ERJ-145LR)	145515	ex PT-SYH	JBA	Chautauqua
☐	N801HK	Embraer EMB.145ER (ERJ-145ER)	145053	ex PT-SZS	TRK	Trans State
☐	N802HK	Embraer EMB.145ER (ERJ-145ER)	145066	ex PT-SAJ	TRL	Trans State
☐	N803HK	Embraer EMB.145ER (ERJ-145ER)	145077	ex PT-S	TRM	Trans State
☐	N804HK	Embraer EMB.145ER (ERJ-145ER)	145082	ex PT-S	TRA	Trans State
☐	N805HK	Embraer EMB.145ER (ERJ-145ER)	145096	ex PT-SBS	TRB	Trans State
☐	N808HK	Embraer EMB.145ER (ERJ-145ER)	145157	ex PT-SEK	TRD	Trans State
☐	N809HK	Embraer EMB.145ER (ERJ-145ER)	145187	ex PT-SGH	TRE	Trans State
☐	N812HK	Embraer EMB.145ER (ERJ-145ER)	145373	ex PT-SOY	TRG	Trans State
☐	N839MJ	Embraer EMB.145LR (ERJ-145LR)	145416	ex PT-STM	YRO	Mesa
☐	N840MJ	Embraer EMB.145LR (ERJ-145LR)	145429	ex PT-SUA	YRP	Mesa
☐	N843MJ	Embraer EMB.145LR (ERJ-145LR)	145478	ex PT-SVX	YRT	Mesa
☐	N846MJ	Embraer EMB.145LR (ERJ-145LR)	145507	ex PT-SXZ	YRW	Mesa
☐	N977RP	Embraer EMB.145EP (ERJ-145MP	145185	ex SE-DZD	JBH	Chautauqua Lsd fr SKX
☐	N978RP	Embraer EMB.145LR (ERJ-145LR)	145169	ex G-CCLD	JBX	Chautauqua Lsd fr SKX
☐	N656RW	Embraer 170-100SE (170SE)	17000113	ex PT-SAY		Shuttle America
☐	N657RW	Embraer 170-100SE (170SE)	17000115	ex PT-SDC		Shuttle America
☐	N801MA	Embraer 170-100SU (170SU)	17000012	ex PT-SKE	801	Republic
☐	N802MD	Embraer 170-100SU (170SU)	17000013	ex PT-SKF	802	Republic
☐	N803MD	Embraer 170-100SU (170SU)	17000015	ex PT-SKI	803	Republic
☐	N805MD	Embraer 170-100SU (170SU)	17000018	ex PT-SKL	805	Republic
☐	N806MD	Embraer 170-100SU (170SU)	17000019	ex PT-SKM	806	Republic
☐	N807MD	Embraer 170-100SU (170SU)	17000020	ex PT-SKN	807	Republic
☐	N808MD	Embraer 170-100SU (170SU)	17000021	ex PT-SKO	808	Republic
☐	N809MD	Embraer 170-100SU (170SU)	17000022	ex PT-SKP	809	Republic
☐	N811MD	Embraer 170-100SU (170SU)	17000028	ex PT-SKV	811	Republic
☐	N812MD	Embraer 170-100SU (170SU)	17000030	ex PT-SKY	812	Republic
☐	N814MD	Embraer 170-100SU (170SU)	17000033	ex PT-SUB	814	Republic
☐	N816MA	Embraer 170-100SU (170SU)	17000037	ex PT-SUG	816	Republic
☐	N817MD	Embraer 170-100SU (170SU)	17000038	ex PT-SUH	817	Republic
☐	N819MD	Embraer 170-100SU (170SU)	17000040	ex PT-SUJ	819	Republic
☐	N820MD	Embraer 170-100SU (170SU)	17000041	ex PT-SUK	820	Republic
☐	N822MD	Embraer 170-100SU (170SU)	17000043	ex PT-SUM	822	Republic
☐	N827MD	Embraer 170-100SU (170SU)	17000047	ex PT-SUQ	827	Republic
☐	N828MD	Embraer 170-100SU (170SU)	17000048	ex PT-SUR	828	Republic
☐	N829MD	Embraer 170-100SU (170SU)	17000049	ex PT-SUT	829	Republic
☐	N101HQ	Embraer 170-200LR (175LR)	17000156	ex PT-SEU		Republic
☐	N102HQ	Embraer 170-200LR (175LR)	17000157	ex PT-SEV		Republic
☐	N103HQ	Embraer 170-200LR (175LR)	17000159	ex PT-SEX		Republic
☐	N104HQ	Embraer 170-200LR (175LR)	17000160	ex PT-SMA		Republic
☐	N105HQ	Embraer 170-200LR (175LR)	17000163	ex PT-SMF		Republic
☐	N106HQ	Embraer 170-200LR (175LR)	17000164	ex PT-SMG		Republic
☐	N107HQ	Embraer 170-200LR (175LR)	17000165	ex PT-SMH		Republic
☐	N108HQ	Embraer 170-200LR (175LR)	17000166	ex PT-SMI		Republic
☐	N109HQ	Embraer 170-200LR (175LR)	17000168	ex PT-SMK		Republic
☐	N110HQ	Embraer 170-200LR (175LR)	17000172	ex PT-SMP		Republic
☐	N111HQ	Embraer 170-200LR (175LR)	17000173	ex PT-SMQ		Republic
☐	N112HQ	Embraer 170-200LR (175LR)	17000174	ex PT-SMR		Republic
☐	N113HQ	Embraer 170-200LR (175LR)	17000177	ex PT-SMU		Republic
☐	N114HQ	Embraer 170-200LR (175LR)	17000179	ex PT-SMW		Republic
☐	N115HQ	Embraer 170-200LR (175LR)	17000182	ex PT-SMZ		Republic
☐	N116HQ	Embraer 170-200LR (175LR)	17000183	ex PT-SUA		Republic
☐	N117HQ	Embraer 170-200LR (175LR)	17000184	ex PT-SUB		Republic
☐	N118HQ	Embraer 170-200LR (175LR)	17000189	ex PT-SUI		Republic
☐	N119HQ	Embraer 170-200LR (175LR)	17000190	ex PT-SUQ		Republic
☐	N120HQ	Embraer 170-200LR (175LR)	17000193	ex PT-SUV		Republic
☐	N121HQ	Embraer 170-200LR (175LR)	17000194	ex PT-SUY		Republic
☐	N122HQ	Embraer 170-200LR (175LR)	17000196	ex PT-SXF		Republic
☐	N123HQ	Embraer 170-200LR (175LR)	17000199	ex PT-SXM		Republic
☐	N124HQ	Embraer 170-200LR (175LR)	17000200	ex PT-SXO		Republic
☐	N125HQ	Embraer 170-200LR (175LR)	17000202	ex PT-SXR		Republic
☐	N126HQ	Embraer 170-200LR (175LR)	17000204	ex PT-SXU		Republic
☐	N127HQ	Embraer 170-200LR (175LR)	17000206	ex PT-SCB		Republic
☐	N128HQ	Embraer 170-200LR (175LR)	17000208	ex PT-SCF		Republic
☐	N129HQ	Embraer 170-200LR (175LR)	17000211	ex PT-SCI		Republic
☐	N130HQ	Embraer 170-200LR (175LR)	17000212	ex PT-SCJ		Republic
☐	N131HQ	Embraer 170-200LR (175LR)	17000215	ex PT-SCM		Republic
☐	N132HQ	Embraer 170-200LR (175LR)	17000216	ex PT-SCN		Republic
☐	N133HQ	Embraer 170-200LR (175LR)	17000217	ex PT-SCO		Republic
☐	N134HQ	Embraer 170-200LR (175LR)	17000220	ex PT-SCS		Republic
☐	N135HQ	Embraer 170-200LR (175LR)	17000224	ex PT-SFA		Republic

Registration	Type	C/n	Previous identity	Code	Operator
☐ N136HQ	Embraer 170-100SU (170LR)	17000228	ex PT-SFE		Republic
☐ N137HQ	Embraer 170-100SU (170LR)	17000231	ex PT-SFH		Republic
☐ N138HQ	Embraer 170-100SU (170LR)	17000234	ex PT-SFK		Republic
☐ N139HQ	Embraer 170-100SU (170LR)		ex PT-S		Republic on order
☐ N140HQ	Embraer 170-100SU (170LR)		ex PT-S		Republic on order
☐ N141HQ	Embraer 170-100SU (170LR)		ex PT-S		Republic on order
☐ N142HQ	Embraer 170-100SU (170LR)		ex PT-S		Republic on order
☐ N143HQ	Embraer 170-100SU (170LR)		ex PT-S		Republic on order
☐ N144HQ	Embraer 170-100SU (170LR)		ex PT-S		Republic on order
☐ N145HQ	Embraer 170-100SU (170LR)		ex PT-S		Republic on order
☐ N146HQ	Embraer 170-100SU (170LR)		ex PT-S		Republic on order
☐ N147HQ	Embraer 170-100SU (170LR)		ex PT-S		Republic on order
☐ N148HQ	Embraer 170-100SU (170LR)		ex PT-S		Republic on order
☐ N149HQ	Embraer 170-100SU (170LR)		ex PT-S		Republic on order
☐ N150HQ	Embraer 170-100SU (170LR)		ex PT-S		Republic on order
☐ N151HQ	Embraer 170-100SU (170LR)		ex PT-S		Republic on order
☐ N152HQ	Embraer 170-100SU (170LR)		ex PT-S		Republic on order
☐ N153HQ	Embraer 170-100SU (170LR)		ex PT-S		Republic on order
☐ N154HQ	Embraer 170-100SU (170LR)		ex PT-S		Republic on order
☐ N155HQ	Embraer 170-100SU (170LR)		ex PT-S		Republic on order
☐ N944UW	Embraer 190-100IGW (190AR)	19000058	ex PT-SIL		Republic
☐ N945UW	Embraer 190-100IGW (190AR)	19000062	ex PT-SJA		Republic
☐ N946UW	Embraer 190-100IGW (190AR)	19000072	ex PT-SJL		Republic
☐ N947UW	Embraer 190-100IGW (190AR)	19000078	ex PT-SJU		Republic
☐ N948UW	Embraer 190-100IGW (190AR)	19000081	ex PT-SJX		Republic
☐ N949UW	Embraer 190-100IGW (190AR)	19000102	ex PT-SNW		Republic
☐ N950UW	Embraer 190-100IGW (190AR)	19000106	ex PT-SQA		Republic
☐ N951UW	Embraer 190-100IGW (190AR)	19000112	ex PT-SQG		Republic
☐ N952UW	Embraer 190-100IGW (190AR)	19000119	ex PT-SQN		Republic
☐ N953UW	Embraer 190-100IGW (190AR)	19000133	ex PT-		Republic
☐ N954UW	Embraer 190-100IGW (190AR)	19000139	ex PT-SYS		Republic
☐ N955UW	Embraer 190-100IGW (190AR)	19000152	ex PT-SAH		Republic
☐ N956UW	Embraer 190-100IGW (190AR)	19000156	ex PT-SAM		
☐ N957UW	Embraer 190-100IGW (190AR)	19000161	ex PT-SAQ		
☐ N958UW	Embraer 190-100IGW (190AR)	19000164	ex PT-SAT		
☐ N9CJ	SAAB SF.340B	340B-224	ex N224TH	LVE	Colgan Air
☐ N203CJ	SAAB SF.340B	340B-203	ex N306CE	LNI	Colgan Air
☐ N249CJ	SAAB SF.340B	340B-249	ex N361PX		Colgan Air
☐ N321CJ	SAAB SF.340B	340B-321	ex XA-TQX	LVH	Colgan Air
☐ N338CJ	SAAB SF.340B	340B-338	ex N338SB	LNG	Colgan Air
☐ N339CJ	SAAB SF.340B	340B-339	ex N339SB	LNA	Colgan Air
☐ N341CJ	SAAB SF.340B	340B-341	ex N341SB	LND	Colgan Air
☐ N344CJ	SAAB SF.340B	340B-344	ex N344SB	LNF	Colgan Air
☐ N346CJ	SAAB SF.340B	340B-346	ex N346SB	LNB	Colgan Air
☐ N347CJ	SAAB SF.340B	340B-347	ex N347SB	LNH	Colgan Air
☐ N350CJ	SAAB SF.340B	340B-350	ex N350CF	LNE	Colgan Air
☐ N362PX	SAAB SF.340B	340B-258	ex SE-G58		ColganAir

US FOREST SERVICE — *Boise, ID (BOI)*

Registration	Type	C/n	Previous identity
☐ N106Z	Bell 206B JetRanger	508	ex N950NS
☐ N109Z	Bell UH-I (CobraLifter)	20854	ex 69-16422
☐ N111Z	Cessna TU206F Stationair	U20602919	
☐ N115Z	Basler Turbo-67 (DC-3TP)	16819/33567	ex N146Z
☐ N126Z	Cessna TU206F Stationair	U20602367	ex N2399U
☐ N127Z	Beech A100 King Air	B-179	ex N20EG
☐ N136Z	Cessna TU206G Stationair 6	U20606923	ex N9659R
☐ N141Z	de Havilland DHC-6 Twin Otter 300	803	ex C-GDNG
☐ N142Z	Basler Turbo-67 (DC-3TP)	20494	ex N100Z
☐ N143Z	de Havilland DHC-6 Twin Otter 300	437	ex 87-0802
☐ N144Z	Cessna 550 Citation Bravo	550-0926	ex N100Z
☐ N147Z	Aero Commander 500B	1432-152	
☐ N148Z	Beech 65-B90 King Air	LJ-472	ex N104Z
☐ N149Z	Beech B200C Super King Air	BL-124	ex N107Z
☐ N173Z	Short SD.3-30	SH3116	ex 84-0469
☐ N175Z	Short SD.3-30	SH3115	ex 84-0468
☐ N178Z	Short SD.3-30	SH3119	ex 84-0472
☐ N179Z	Short SD.3-30	SH3109	ex 84-0462
☐ N181Z	Beech 65-E90 King Air	LW-52	ex N74171
☐ N182Z	Beech 200 Super King Air	BB-402	ex N318W
☐ N191Z	de Havilland DHC-2 Beaver	1006	
☐ N192Z	de Havilland DHC-2 Beaver	1347	
☐ N193Z	de Havilland DHC-2 Beaver	11627	ex N197Z

US HELICOPTERS — *Wingate-US Heliport, NC*

Registration	Type	C/n	Previous identity
☐ N36TV	Aérospatiale AS350B AStar	1858	ex N69TL
☐ N129TV	Aérospatiale AS350BA AStar	2897	
☐ N311TV	Aérospatiale AS350BA AStar	2922	
☐ N355TV	Aérospatiale AS350B AStar	2647	ex TG-JBG

☐ N357TV	Aérospatiale AS350B AStar	2376	ex N795WC	
☐ N915HD	Aérospatiale AS350B2 AStar	3583	ex N311SJ	
☐ N73DP	Bell 206B JetRanger II	2513		
☐ N79TV	Bell 206L-1 LongRanger III	45718	ex N84PC	
☐ N116TV	Bell 206L-3 LongRanger III	51199	ex N45MH	
☐ N141TV	Bell 206B JetRanger III	4148	ex N748M	
☐ N188TV	Bell 206B JetRanger III	2704		
☐ N212TV	Bell 206B JetRanger II	2048	ex N97CW	

USA 3000 AIRLINES — *Getaway (U5/GWY)* — *Philadelphia-Intl, PA (PHL)*

☐ N260AV	Airbus A320-214	1564	ex D-AXLC	
☐ N261AV	Airbus A320-214	1615	ex F-WWDR	
☐ N262AV	Airbus A320-214	1725	ex F-WWBP	Miss Doreen
☐ N263AV	Airbus A320-214	1860	ex D-AXLB	Chicago
☐ N264AV	Airbus A320-214	1867	ex F-WWIL	Bermuda
☐ N266AV	Airbus A320-214	1152	ex I-PEKO	
☐ N267AV	Airbus A320-214	1198	ex I-PEKP	La Romana
☐ N271AV	Airbus A320-214	2327	ex F-WWDX	Punra Cana

USA JET AIRLINES — *Jet USA (JUS)* — *Detroit-Willow Run, MI (YIP)*

☐ N505AJ	AMD Falcon 20C	89	ex N71CP	stored YIP
☐ N822AA	AMD Falcon 20D	195	ex N195MP	
☐ N823AA	AMD Falcon 20D	228	ex OE-GRU	
☐ N826AA	AMD Falcon 20C	67	ex N821AA	
☐ N827AA	AMD Falcon 20E	298	ex OE-GNN	
☐ N192US	Douglas DC-9-15RC	47156/228	ex N9357	VIP
☐ N194US	Douglas DC-9-15RC (ABS 3)	47016/173	ex N9349	stored YIP
☐ N195US	Douglas DC-9-15RC (ABS 3)	47017/186	ex N9352	VIP
☐ N205US	Douglas DC-9-32CF	47690/843	ex N724HB	
☐ N208US	Douglas DC-9-32F (ABS 3)	47220/296	ex N935F	stored YIP
☐ N215US	Douglas DC-9-32 (ABS 3)	47480/607	ex N986US	
☐ N231US	Douglas DC-9-32 (ABS 3)	48114/919	ex XA-TXG	
☐ N327US	Douglas DC-9-33F (ABS 3)	47414/536	ex N940F	
☐ N829AA	LearJet 25B	25B-100	ex N25TK	

VIEQUES AIR LINK — *Vieques (VES)* — *Vieques, PR (VQS)*

☐ N663VL	Britten-Norman BN-2B-26 Islander	2110	ex N663J	
☐ N861VL	Britten-Norman BN-2B-26 Islander	2155	ex N861JA	
☐ N902VL	Britten-Norman BN-2A-20 Islander	685	ex N148ES	
☐ N903VL	Britten-Norman BN-2A-26 Islander	2019	ex N2159X	
☐ N904VL	Britten-Norman BN-2A-26 Islander	3014	ex HK-3813	no titles
☐ N335VL	Cessna 208B Caravan I	208B0964	ex N5260Y	
☐ N741VL	Cessna 208B Caravan I	208B1091	ex N1272N	
☐ N742VL	Cessna 208B Caravan I	208B1100	ex N12727	
☐ N905VL	Britten-Norman BN-2A Mk.III-2 Trislander	1048	ex N905GD	
☐ N906VL	Britten-Norman BN-2A Mk.III-2 Trislander	1060	ex N906GD	

VINTAGE PROPS AND JETS — *(VQ)* — *New Smyrna Beach-Municipal, FL*

☐ N211VP	Beech 100 King Air	B-2	ex N11JJ	
☐ N219VP	Beech 1900C	UB-14	ex N188GA	
☐ N431R	Beech 100 King Air	B-71	ex N431CH	
☐ N577D	Beech 100 King Air	B-22	ex N577L	
☐ N5727	Beech 100 King Air	B-48	ex N572	

VIRGIN AMERICA — *(VX/VRD)* — *San Francisco, CA (SFO)*

☐ N521VA	Airbus A319-112	2773	ex D-AVWZ	let there be flight
☐ N522VA	Airbus A319-112	2811	ex D-AVYP	Nationwide Insurance c/s
☐ N523VA	Airbus A319-112	3181	ex D-AVYB	
☐ N524VA	Airbus A319-112	3204	ex D-AVWK	dark horse
☐ N525VA	Airbus A319-112	3324	ex D-AVYG	
☐ N526VA	Airbus A319-112	3347	ex D-AVYW	
☐ N527VA	Airbus A319-112	3417	ex D-AVYK	tubular belle
☐ N528VA	Airbus A319-112	3445	ex D-AVYR	log cutter
☐ N529VA	Airbus A319-112	3684	ex D-AVWB	moodlights, camera, action
☐ N530VA	Airbus A319-112	3686	ex D-AVWD	gogo dancer
☐ N621VA	Airbus A320-214	2616	ex F-WWDJ	air colbert
☐ N622VA	Airbus A320-214	2674	ex F-WWID	California Dreaming
☐ N623VA	Airbus A320-214	2740	ex PR-MHH	three if by air
☐ N624VA	Airbus A320-214	2778	ex F-WWDX	red, white & blue
☐ N625VA	Airbus A320-214	2800	ex F-WWIJ	Jefferson Airplane
☐ N626VA	Airbus A320-214	2830	ex F-WWDO	unicorn chaser
☐ N627VA	Airbus A320-214	2851	ex F-WWIQ	

☐ N628VA	Airbus A320-214	2993	ex F-WWIT	
☐ N629VA	Airbus A320-214	3037	ex PR-MHL	Midnight Ride
☐ N630VA	Airbus A320-214	3101	ex F-WWIG	superfly
☐ N631VA	Airbus A320-214	3135	ex F-WWDL	chic mobile
☐ N632VA	Airbus A320-214	3155	ex F-WWDH	youtube air
☐ N633VA	Airbus A320-214	3230	ex F-WWBE	the tim clark express
☐ N634VA	Airbus A320-214	3359	ex F-WWII	mach daddy
☐ N635VA	Airbus A320-214	3308	ex F-WWBS	my other ride's a spaceship
☐ N636VA	Airbus A320-214	3460	ex F-WWBJ	
☐ N637VA	Airbus A320-214	3465	ex F-WWBN	an airplane named desire
☐ N638VA	Airbus A320-214	3503	ex D-AVVB	san francisco pride

VISION AIR — *Las Vegas North, NV (VGT)*

☐ N402VA	Dornier 228-202K	8085	ex G-BWEX	
☐ N403VA	Dornier 228-202K	8171	ex 9M-BAS	
☐ N404VA	Dornier 228-203F	8120	ex N279MC	
☐ N405VA	Dornier 228-203F	8144	ex N264MC	
☐ N409VA	Dornier 228-201	8097	ex N228ME	
☐ N38VP	Dornier 328-310 (328JET)	3174	ex N417FJ	
☐ N328DA	Dornier 328-310 (328JET)	3171	ex N416FJ	stored VGT
☐ N329MX	Dornier 328-100	3049	ex D-CAOS	
☐ N330MX	Dornier 328-100	3067	ex D-CDXN	
☐ N331MX	Dornier 328-100	3074	ex D-CDXA	
☐ N431JS	Dornier 328-110	3028	ex D-CDHN	on order
☐ N905HB	Dornier 328-310 (328JET)	3178	ex N420FJ	stored VGT
☐ N906HB	Dornier 328-310 (328JET)	3179	ex N421FJ	
☐ N732VA	Boeing 737-3T0	23366/1174	ex N34315	
☐ N742VA	Boeing 737-448	24773/1850	ex TC-MNH	
☐ N743VA	Boeing 737-4B6	25262/2088	ex N252MQ	
☐ N744VA	Boeing 737-4Q8	24704/1855	ex SX-BKI	
☐ N781VA	Boeing 737-8Q8/W	28214/78	ex OY-SEB	
☐ N766VA	Boeing 767-2Q8ER	24448/272	ex EI-DMP	
☐ N767VA	Boeing 767-222ER	21870/13	ex N609UA	
☐ N768VA	Boeing 767-222ER	21869/11	ex N608UA	
☐ N769VA	Boeing 767-222ER	21866/7	ex N605UA	

WARBELOW'S AIR — *Ventaire (4W/WAV)* — *Fairbanks-Intl, AK (FAI)*

☐ N42WP	Piper PA-31-350 Chieftain	31-8252038	ex N41063	
☐ N300ED	Piper PA-31-350 Chieftain	31-7852008	ex N27457	
☐ N3527U	Piper PA-31-350 Chieftain	31-7952141		
☐ N3582P	Piper PA-31-350 Chieftain	31-8052103		
☐ N4082T	Piper PA-31-350 Chieftain	31-8152089		
☐ N4434D	Piper PA-31-350 Navajo Chieftain	31-7552020	ex PH-ASC	
☐ N27755	Piper PA-31-350 Chieftain	31-7852148		
☐ N59764	Piper PA-31-350 Navajo Chieftain	31-7652037		
☐ N59829	Piper PA-31-350 Navajo Chieftain	31-7652081		
☐ N121WV	Beech 1900C-1	UC-78	ex N503RH	
☐ N756DJ	Cessna U206G Stationair	U20604005		
☐ N767DM	Piper PA-31-T2 Cheyenne II XL	31T-8166042	ex N500XL	
☐ N5200X	Cessna U206G Stationair 6 II	U20605591		
☐ N7380U	Cessna 207A Stationair 7	20700428		

WARD AIR — *Juneau-Intl, AK (JNU)*

☐ N767RR	Cessna 310Q	310Q0455		
☐ N8295Q	Cessna U206F Stationair II	U20603156		Floatplane
☐ N62353	de Havilland DHC-2 Beaver	1363	ex 58-2031	Floatplane
☐ N62355	de Havilland DHC-2 Beaver	1045	ex N67897	Floatplane
☐ N62357	de Havilland DHC-2 Beaver	1145	ex N64391	Floatplane
☐ N63354	de Havilland DHC-3 Otter	30	ex C-FWAF	Floatplane
☐ N93025	Cessna A185F Skywagon	18503163		Floatplane
☐ N93356	de Havilland DHC-3 Otter	144	ex N62KA	Floatplane

WEST AIR — *PAC Valley (PCM)* — *Fresno-Air Terminal, CA / Chico-Municipal, CA (FAT/CIC)*

Operates Cessna Caravans leased from, and operated on behalf of, FedEx

WESTERN AIR EXPRESS — *Western Express (WAE)* — *Boise, ID (BOI)*

☐ N167WA	Cessna 402B II	402B1044	ex N98680	
☐ N6367X	Cessna 402B II	402B1330		
☐ N7947Q	Cessna 402B	402B0397		
☐ N158WA	Swearingen SA.226TC Metro II	TC-411	ex N5974V	
☐ N159WA	Swearingen SA.226TC Metro II	TC-334	ex N341PL	
☐ N160WA	Swearingen SA.226TC Metro IIA	TC-399	ex N56EA	
☐ N162WA	Swearingen SA.226TC Metro IIA	TC-418	ex C-GRET	

☐ N163WA	Swearingen SA.227AC Metro III	AC-565	ex HZ-SN7

WESTERN AIR EXPRESS — Lubbock-Intl, TX (LBB)

☐ N6AQ	Beech 65-A80 Queen Air	LD-214	ex N699WW	Freighter
☐ N20NP	Beech 65-B80 Queen Air	LD-433	ex N3289A	Freighter
☐ N5376M	Beech 65-B80 Queen Air	LD-301	ex CF-HOA	Freighter
☐ N7817L	Beech 65-B80 Queen Air	LD-340		Freighter
☐ N8071R	Beech 65-B80 Queen Air	LD-420		Freighter

WESTERN AVIATORS — Westavia (WTV) — Grand Junction-Walker Field, CO (GJT)

☐ N106RE	Piper PA-31-350 Navajo Chieftain	31-7752056	
☐ N159SW	Piper PA-31-350 Navajo Chieftain	31-7405229	ex N400AA
☐ N494SC	Piper PA-31-350 Navajo Chieftain	31-7752099	ex N27199
☐ N495SC	Piper PA-31-350 Chieftain	31-8052062	ex N3555Y

WESTWIND AVIATION — Phoenix-Deer Valley, AZ (DVT)

☐ N9317M	Cessna T207A Stationair 8 II	20700680	
☐ N9482M	Cessna T207A Stationair 8 II	20700698	
☐ N122JB	Cessna 208B Caravan I	208B1025	ex N5090V
☐ N208WW	Cessna 208B Caravan I	208B0721	
☐ N785WW	Cessna 208B Caravan I	208B0792	ex N5267T
☐ N786WW	Cessna 208B Caravan I	208B1099	ex N12744
☐ N1129G	Cessna 208B Caravan I	208B0924	ex N5262X

WIGGINS AIRWAYS — Wiggins (WIG) — Norwood-Memorial, MA (OWD)

☐ N190WA	Beech C99	U-207	ex N207CS
☐ N191WA	Beech C99	U-136	ex C-GCPF
☐ N192WA	Beech C99	U-152	ex C-GEOI
☐ N193WA	Beech 99	U-17	ex N10MV
☐ N194WA	Beech 99	U-64	ex C-FAWX
☐ N195WA	Beech 99	U-38	ex N202BH
☐ N196WA	Beech C99	U-179	ex N995SB
☐ N197WA	Beech 99A	U-130	ex C-FOZU
☐ N198WA	Beech 99A	U-142	ex N133BA
☐ N199WA	Beech B99	U-154	ex N99CH
☐ N91RK	Beech A100 King Air	B-226	ex N9126S

WILLOW AIR — Willow-Lake SPB, AK (WOW)

☐ N98JH	de Havilland DHC-2 Beaver	953	ex 5-3 RNAF	Floatplane

WINGS OF ALASKA — Wings Alaska (K5/WAK) — Juneau-Intl, AK (JNU)

☐ N335AK	de Havilland DHC-3 Turbo Otter	263	ex C-FOMS	Floatplane
☐ N336AK	de Havilland DHC-3 Turbo Otter	333	ex N567KA	Floatplane
☐ N337AK	de Havilland DHC-3 Turbo Otter	418	ex N2783J	Floatplane
☐ N338AK	de Havilland DHC-3 Turbo Otter	262	ex N62355	Floatplane
☐ N339AK	de Havilland DHC-3 Turbo Otter	454	ex N28TH	Floatplane
☐ N753AK	de Havilland DHC-3 Turbo Otter	7	ex N342AK	Floatplane
☐ N39AK	Cessna 207A Stationair 8 II	20700597	ex N73482	Floatplane or wheels/skis
☐ N62AK	Cessna 207A Stationair 8 II	20700780	ex N9997M	Floatplane or wheels/skis
☐ N72KA	Cessna 208B Caravan I	208B0326	ex N1030N	Floatplane
☐ N92AK	de Havilland DHC-2 Beaver	1031	ex C-GFNR	Floatplane or wheels/skis
☐ N96AK	Cessna 207A Stationair 8 II	20700782	ex N1347Q	Floatplane or wheels/skis
☐ N331AK	Cessna 208B Caravan I	208B0739	ex N5264S	
☐ N332AK	Cessna 208B Caravan I	208B0779	ex N5264S	Floatplane or wheels/skis

WORLD AIRWAYS — World (WO/WOA) — Charleston-Intl, SC (CHS)

☐ N136WA	Douglas DC-10-30	47844/336	ex N237NW		
☐ N137WA	Douglas DC-10-30	48282/355	ex N241NW		
☐ N138WA	Douglas DC-10-30	47845/356	ex N242NW		
☐ N223NW	Douglas DC-10-30	46580/183	ex HB-IHF		stored MZJ
☐ N224NW	Douglas DC-10-30	46581/184	ex HB-IHG		stored MZJ
☐ N303WL	Douglas DC-10-30F	46917/211	ex N13086	303	stored MZJ
☐ N702TZ	Douglas DC-10-30	46912/188	ex N234NW		stored MZJ
☐ N705TZ	Douglas DC-10-30	46915/199	ex N235NW		
☐ N706TZ	Douglas DC-10-30	46582/187	ex N225NW		stored MZJ
☐ N14075	Douglas DC-10-30	46922/221	ex EC-CSJ	351	stored MZJ
☐ N270WA	McDonnell-Douglas MD-11	48449/455	ex OH-LGA		
☐ N271WA	McDonnell-Douglas MD-11	48518/525		271	
☐ N272WA	McDonnell-Douglas MD-11	48437/506		272	
☐ N273WA	McDonnell-Douglas MD-11	48519/539		273	

☐ N274WA	McDonnell-Douglas MD-11F	48633/563		274	
☐ N275WA	McDonnell-Douglas MD-11CF	48631/579		275	
☐ N276WA	McDonnell-Douglas MD-11CF	48632/582		276	
☐ N277WA	McDonnell-Douglas MD-11ER	48743/590	ex N6203D	277	
☐ N278WA	McDonnell-Douglas MD-11ER	48746/597	ex N9020Q	278	
☐ N279WA	McDonnell-Douglas MD-11F	48756/623	ex P4-TKA	279	
☐ N380WA	McDonnell-Douglas MD-11F	48407/456	ex HL7371	380	stored MZJ
☐ N381WA	McDonnell-Douglas MD-11F	48523/516	ex HL7375	381	
☐ N382WA	McDonnell-Douglas MD-11F	48411/453	ex N703GC		
☐ N383WA	McDonnell-Douglas MD-11F	48412/454	ex N705GC		
☐ N384WA	McDonnell-Douglas MD-11F	48435/478	ex N702GC		
☐ N740WA	Boeing 747-4H6 (BDSF)	25700/974	ex 9V-SPS		
☐ N741WA	Boeing 747-4H6 (BDSF)	25702/999	ex 9V-SPR		

WRIGHT AIR SERVICE — *Wright Air (8V/WRT)* — *Fairbanks-Intl, AK (FAI)*

☐ N32WA	Cessna 208B Caravan I	208B0234	ex C-FKEL
☐ N540ME	Cessna 208B Caravan I	208B0540	
☐ N900WA	Cessna 208B Caravan I	208B0659	ex N52613
☐ N976E	Cessna 208B Caravan I	208B0976	ex N5263D
☐ N1323R	Cessna 208B Caravan I	208B0745	
☐ N4365U	Cessna 208B Caravan I	208B0253	ex N208CC
☐ N9FW	Piper PA-31-350 Navajo Chieftain	31-7405468	ex N61441
☐ N54WA	Piper PA-31-350 Navajo Chieftain	31-7652067	ex N942LU
☐ N7426L	Piper PA-31 Turbo Navajo B	31-812	
☐ N91027	Cessna 207 Skywagon	20700018	

XTRA AIRWAYS — *Casino Express (XP/CXP)* — *Elko-JC Harris Field, NV (EKO)*

☐ N42XA	Boeing 737-429	25729/2217	ex TF-ELP
☐ N43XA	Boeing 737-4S3	24796/1887	ex TF-ELV

YUKON AVIATION — *Bethel, AK (BET)*

☐ N150HH	Bell 206B JetRanger III	701	
☐ N205WA	Bell UH-1H	12261	ex 69-16663
☐ N1322F	Cessna A185F Skywagon	18502825	
☐ N1653U	Cessna 207 Super Skywagon	20700253	
☐ N4237V	Bell 204 (UH-1B)	261	ex 60-0315
☐ N7318U	Cessna 207A Skywagon	20700396	
☐ N24165	Beech Baron 58TC	TK-78	
☐ N29970	Cessna A185F Skywagon II	18504292	ex (C-GMTU)
☐ N91060	Cessna T207 Turbo Skywagon	20700047	

OB- PERU (Republic of Peru)

AERO TRANSPORTE — *ATSA (AMP)* — *Lima-Jorge Chavez Intl (LIM)*

☐ OB-1029	Piper PA-42 Cheyenne III	42-8001067	ex N183CC
☐ OB-1630	Piper PA-42 Cheyenne III	42-8001022	ex N145CA
☐ OB-1633	Piper PA-42 Cheyenne III	42-7801003	ex N134KM
☐ OB-1687	Piper PA-42 Cheyenne III	42-8001016	ex N69PC
☐ OB-1803	Piper PA-42 Cheyenne III	42-7800002	ex N911VJ
☐ OB-1667-P	Beech 1900C	UB-54	ex N815BE
☐ OB-1778-P	Antonov An-26B-100	14205	ex OB-1777-T
☐ OB-1869-T	Antonov An-32B	3305	ex ER-AFM
☐ OB-1875	Beech 1900D	UE-68	ex N168AZ

AEROCONDOR — *Condor (Q6/CDP)* — *Lima-Jorge Chavez Intl (LIM)*

☐ OB-1192	Cessna U206G Stationair 6	U20605538		
☐ OB-1204	Cessna U206G Stationair 6	U20605800		
☐ OB-1297	Beech 65-B90 King Air	LJ-326	ex N7702	Fray GregorioTaurus conversion
☐ OB-1594	Beech 65-B90 King Air	LJ-322	ex N45SC	Taurus conversion
☐ OB-1616	Cessna U206B Super Skywagon	U206-0878	ex N3878G	
☐ OB-1627	Fokker F.27 Friendship 100	10116	ex YV-929C	
☐ OB-1650-P	Antonov An-24RV	37308802	ex OB-1562	
☐ OB-1693-P	Fokker F.27 Friendship 200	10181	ex N863MA	stored LIM
☐ OB-1740-P	Cessna 208B Caravan I	208B0735	ex N12652	
☐ OB-1741	Cessna 208B Caravan I	208B0670	ex N1132D	
☐ OB-1770-P	Fokker F.27 Mk.050 (Fokker 50)	20280	ex PH-LXU	
☐ OB-1793-P	Boeing 737-2H6 (Nordam 3)	20583/303	ex N121GU	
☐ OB-1797-P	Cessna 208B Caravan I	208B1068	ex OB-1797-T	
☐ OB-1815-P	Cessna 208B Caravan I	208B1129	ex N1282M	
☐ OB-1828	Antonov An-26	87307409	ex RA-26647	
☐ OB-1829-P	Fokker F.27 Mk.050 (Fokker 50)	20260	ex SE-LLN	

AIR MAJORO

☐ OB-1920-P	Cessna 402C II	402C0442	ex N6790B
☐ OB-1921-P	Cessna 402C II	402C0419	ex N419RC

AMAZON SKY — *Lima-Jorge Chavez Intl (LIM)*

☐ OB-1859-P	Antonov An-26B-100	6209	ex UR-VYV

AVIASUR — *Iquitos (IQT)*

☐ OB-1663	Mil Mi-17 (Mi-8MTV-1)	94704	ex OB-1725
☐ OB-1760	Mil Mi-17 (Mi-8MTV-1)	93823	
☐ OB-1761	Mil Mi-17 (Mi-8MTV-1)	93477	

CIELOS AIRLINES — *Cielos (A2/CIU)* — *Lima-Jorge Chavez Intl (LIM)*

☐ N609GC	Douglas DC-10-30F	46932/158	ex G-NIUK	Petete VIII
☐ N614GC	Douglas DC-10-30F	46931/137	ex N832LA	Petete V
☐ OB-1749	Douglas DC-10-30CF	46891/127	ex N105AM	Petete
☐ OB-1812-P	Douglas DC-10-30CF	46975/248	ex N1856U	

HELICOPTEROS MERCOSUR — *Lima*

☐ OB-1856-P	Bell 212	31225	ex 9Y-BPT

HELISUR — *Iquitos (IQT)*

☐ OB-1584	Mil Mi-17 (Mi-8MTV-1)	95432	ex CCCP-70879
☐ OB-1585	Mil Mi-17 (Mi-8MTV-1)	223M103	ex RA-70951
☐ OB-1586	Mil Mi-17 (Mi-8MTV-1)	223M104	
☐ OB-1691	Mil Mi-17 (Mi-8MTV-1)	96153	ex RA-27193
☐ OB-1826	Mil Mi-8MTV-1	93281	

HELITAXI SERVICES

☐ OB-1842P	Mil Mi-8T	9785572	ex RA-27099

LAN PERU — *Linea Peru (LP/LPE)* — *Lima-Jorge Chavez Intl (LIM)*

☐ CC-COU	Airbus A319-132	2089	ex D-AVWL	Lsd fr LAN
☐ CC-COX	Airbus A319-132	2096	ex D-AVYN	Lsd fr LAN
☐ CC-COY	Airbus A319-132	2295	ex D-AVWA	Lsd fr LAN
☐ CC-COZ	Airbus A319-132	2304	ex D-AVWN	Lsd fr LAN
☐ CC-CPE	Airbus A319-132	2321	ex D-AVYO	Lsd fr LAN
☐ CC-CPF	Airbus A319-132	2572	ex D-AVXC	Lsd fr LAN
☐ CC-CPI	Airbus A319-132	2585	ex D-AVXH	Lsd fr LAN
☐ CC-CPM	Airbus A319-132	2864	ex D-AVWC	Lsd fr LAN
☐ CC-CPO	Airbus A319-132	2872	ex D-AVWJ	Lsd fr LAN
☐ CC-CPQ	Airbus A319-132	2886	ex D-AVXP	Lsd fr LAN
☐ CC-CPX	Airbus A319-132	2887	ex D-AVYF	Lsd fr LAN
☐ CC-CQK	Airbus A319-132	2892	ex D-AVYV	Lsd fr LAN
☐ CC-CQL	Airbus A319-132	2894	ex D-AVWE	Lsd fr LAN
☐ CC-CQM	Airbus A320-233	3280	ex F-WWDM	Lsd fr LAN

LC BUSRE — *Busre (LCB)* — *Lima-Jorge Chavez Intl (LIM)*

☐ N139LC	Swearingen SA.227TC Metro III	AC-732	ex XA-ACT	
☐ N239LC	Swearingen SA.227TC Metro III	AC-735	ex N523WA	Lsd fr Pacific Coast Grp
☐ N386PH	Swearingen SA.227TC Metro III	AC-597	ex N3116T	

PERUVIAN AIRLINES

☐ OB-	Boeing 737-217	21716/560	ex N716SH

SERVICIOS AEREOS DE LOS ANDES

☐ OB-1864	de Havilland DHC-6 Twin Otter 200	282	ex CC-PCI
☐ OB-1866	Bell 204B	2197	ex C-GVEL
☐ OB-1897-P	de Havilland DHC-6 Twin Otter 300	521	ex C-FSXF
☐ OB-1910-P	Bell 212	30798	ex C-GSLL
☐ OB-1912-P	Bell 212	30820	ex C-GZMQ
☐ OB-1913-P	de Havilland DHC-6 Twin Otter 300	391	ex C-GHVV

STAR PERU — *Star Up (2I/SRU)* — *Lima-Jorge Chavez Intl (LIM)*

☐ OB-1794-P	Boeing 737-2Y5 (Nordam 3)	23039/954	ex HR-ATM	Best of Peru colours
☐ OB-1800-P	Boeing 737-291 (Nordam 3)	21641/537	ex HR-ATR	Machu Picchu colours
☐ OB-1823-P	Boeing 737-2T2 (Nordam 3)	22793/892	ex LY-BSG	Lord of Sipan colours
☐ OB-1839-P	Boeing 737-204	22640/867	ex N640AD	

☐ OB-1841-P	Boeing 737-204	22058/629	ex N58AD		
☐ OB-1851-P	Boeing 737-230 (Nordam 3)	22133/772	ex N133AD		
☐ OB-1051-P	Cessna 208B Caravan I				
☐ OB-1717	Antonov An-24RV	27308010	ex ER-AFU	Anna	
☐ OB-1734-P	Antonov An-24RV	17307006	ex ER-AFC		
☐ OB-1769	Antonov An-24RV	57310110	ex ER-AWX	Leonid	
☐ OB-1772-P	Antonov An-26B 100	10704	ex UR-26216		
☐ OB-1877-P	British Aerospace 146 Srs.100	E1199	ex A5-RGE		
☐ OB-1879-P	British Aerospace 146 Srs.100	E1095	ex A5-RGD		
☐ OB-1885-P	British Aerospace 146 Srs.200	E2087	ex N292UE		
☐ OB-1914-P	British Aerospace 146 Srs.300	E3181	ex G-JEBE		
☐ OB-1923-P	British Aerospace 146 Srs.300	E3185	ex G-JEBB		
☐ OB-	British Aerospace 146 Srs.200	E2201	ex D-AJET		

TACA PERU — *Trans Peru (T0/TPU)* — *Lima-Jorge Chavez Intl (LIM)*

☐ N471TA	Airbus A319-132	1066	ex D-AVWE	Lsd fr TAI
☐ N472TA	Airbus A319-132	1113	ex D-AVWU	Lsd fr TAI

TRANSPORTES AEREOS CIELOS ANDINOS — *(NDN)* — *Lima-Jorge Chavez Intl (LIM)*

☐ OB-1651	Antonov An-24RV	27308303	ex OB-1571
☐ OB-1859-P	Antonov An-26		
☐ OB-1876-T	Antonov An-26B-100	17311506	ex EX-063
☐ OB-1887-P	Antonov An-26-100	87306606	ex UR-VIG
☐ OB-1893-P	Antonov An-26-100	8401	

OD- LEBANON (Republic of Lebanon)

BERYTOS AIRWAYS — *(BYR)* — *Beirut (BEY)*

Operates charter flights with Airbus A320 and Douglas DC-9-51 aircraft wet leased from UM Air as required

CIRRUS MIDDLE EAST — *Beirut (BEY)*

☐ OD-NOR	Boeing 737-247 (Nordam 3)	22754/870	ex N247US

FLYING CARPET AIR TRANSPORT SERVICES — *Flying Carpet (7Y/FCR)* — *Beirut (BEY)*

☐ OD-AMB	Boeing 737-2H4 (AvAero 3)	23109/1016	ex N103SW
☐ OD-LMB	Boeing 737-232	23082/1006	ex N310DA
☐ OD-MAB	Swearingen SA.227AC Metro III	AC-604	ex C-FNAL

MENAJET — *Menajet (IM/MNJ)* — *Beirut (BEY)*

☐ F-OKRM	Airbus A320-211	0615	ex F-WQSD

MIDDLE EAST AIRLINES — *Cedar Jet (ME/MEA)* — *Beirut (BEY)*

☐ OD-MRR	Airbus A320-232	3837	ex F-WWBJ	
☐ OD-MRS	Airbus A320-232	3804	ex F-WWDJ	
☐ OD-MRT	Airbus A320-232	3736	ex F-ORMK	
☐ OD-	Airbus A320-232		ex	on order
☐ OD-	Airbus A320-232		ex	on order
☐ F-ORME	Airbus A321-231	1878	ex D-AVZA	
☐ F-ORMF	Airbus A321-231	1953	ex D-AVXF	
☐ F-ORMG	Airbus A321-231	1956	ex D-AVZE	
☐ F-ORMH	Airbus A321-231	1967	ex D-AVZI	
☐ F-ORMI	Airbus A321-231	1977	ex D-AVZU	
☐ F-ORMJ	Airbus A321-231	2055	ex D-AVZE	
☐ F-ORMA	Airbus A330-243	926	ex F-WWKD	
☐ OD-MEA	Airbus A330-243	984	ex F-WWKE	
☐ OD-MEB	Airbus A330-243	995	ex F-WWKQ	
☐ OD-MEC	Airbus A330-243	998	ex F-WWKQ	

WINGS OF LEBANON AVIATION — *Wings Lebanon (WLB)* — *Beirut (BEY)*

☐ OD-HAJ	Boeing 737-3Q8	26313/2704	ex G-THOE	
☐ OD-WOL	Boeing 737-232 (AvAero 3)	23083/1008	ex N311DL	Lsd to THE

OE- AUSTRIA (Republic of Austria)

AIR ALPS AVIATION — *Alpav (A6/LPV)* — *Innsbruck (INN)*

☐ OE-LKA	Dornier 328-110	3110	ex D-COXI	Igls-Innsbruck
☐ OE-LKB	Dornier 328-110	3036	ex HB-AEH	Sudtirol colours

☐ OE-LKC	Dornier 328-110	3119	ex D-CDXK	Regio Bodensee	
☐ OE-LKD	Dornier 328-110	3072	ex HS-PBB	Riviera di Rimini	
☐ OE-LKE	Dornier 328-110	3063	ex D-CALP		

AMERER AIR	***Amer Air (AMK)***	***Linz (LNZ)***

☐ OE-ILW	Fokker F.27 Friendship 500	10681	ex N505AW	Sissy	freighter

AUSTRIAN AIRLINES	***Austrian (OS/AUA)***	***Vienna-Schwechat (VIE)***

Member of Star Alliance

☐ OE-LDA	Airbus A319-112	2131	ex D-AVWS	Sofia	
☐ OE-LDB	Airbus A319-112	2174	ex D-AVYP	Bucharest	
☐ OE-LDC	Airbus A319-112	2262	ex D-AVWE	Kiev	
☐ OE-LDD	Airbus A319-112	2416	ex D-AVWN	Moscow	
☐ OE-LDE	Airbus A319-112	2494	ex D-AVYL	Baku	
☐ OE-LDF	Airbus A319-112	2547	ex D-AVYA	Sarajevo	
☐ OE-LDG	Airbus A319-112	2652	ex D-AVYF	Tbilisi	
☐ OE-LBN	Airbus A320-214	0768	ex F-WWDH		
☐ OE-LBO	Airbus A320-214	0776	ex F-WWDM	Pyhrn-Eisenwürzen	
☐ OE-LBP	Airbus A320-214	0797	ex F-WWDV	Neusiedlersee	Retro c/s
☐ OE-LBQ	Airbus A320-214	1137	ex F-WWDF	Ray Charles	
☐ OE-LBR	Airbus A320-214	1150	ex F-WWBP	Frida Kahlo	
☐ OE-LBS	Airbus A320-214	1189	ex F-WWDV	Waldviertel	
☐ OE-LBT	Airbus A320-214	1387	ex F-WWIS	Wörthersee	
☐ OE-LBU	Airbus A320-214	1478	ex F-WWDS	Mühlvierter	stored VIE
☐ OE-LBA	Airbus A321-111	0552	ex D-AVZH	Salzkammergut	
☐ OE-LBB	Airbus A321-111	0570	ex D-AVZQ	Pinzgau	
☐ OE-LBC	Airbus A321-111	0581	ex D-AVZS	Südtirol	stored VIE
☐ OE-LBD	Airbus A321-211	0920	ex D-AVZN	Steirisches Weinland	
☐ OE-LBE	Airbus A321-211	0935	ex D-AVZR	Wachau	
☐ OE-LBF	Airbus A321-211	1458	ex D-AVXE	Wien	
☐ OE-LNJ	Boeing 737-8Z9/W	28177/69		Falco	
☐ OE-LNK	Boeing 737-8Z9/W	28178/222			
☐ OE-LNL	Boeing 737-6Z9	30137/526	ex N743NV		
☐ OE-LNM	Boeing 737-6Z9	30138/546	ex N1795B	Albert Einstein	
☐ OE-LNN	Boeing 737-7Z9/W	30418/815		Maria Callas	
☐ OE-LNO	Boeing 737-7Z9/W	30419/874		Greta Garbo	
☐ OE-LNP	Boeing 737-8Z9/W	30420/1100		George Harrison	
☐ OE-LNQ	Boeing 737-8Z9/W	30421/1345		Gregory Peck	
☐ OE-LNR	Boeing 737-8Z9/W	33833/1680		Frank Zappa	
☐ OE-LNS	Boeing 737-8Z9/W	34262/1720		Miles Davis	
☐ OE-LNT	Boeing 737-8Z9/W	33834/1938		Kurt Cobain	
☐ OE-LAE	Boeing 767-3Z9ER/W	30383/812		Wiener Sangerknaben	
☐ OE-LAT	Boeing 767-31AER	25273/393	ex PH-MCK		Star Alliance c/s
☐ OE-LAW	Boeing 767-3Z9ER	26417/448		China	
☐ OE-LAX	Boeing 767-3Z9ER/W	27095/467		Thailand	
☐ OE-LAY	Boeing 767-3Z9ER/W	29867/731	ex D-ABUV	Japan	Star Alliance c/s
☐ OE-LAZ	Boeing 767-3Z9ER/W	30331/759	ex D-ABUW	India	Star Alliance c/s
☐ OE-LPA	Boeing 777-2Z9ER	28698/87	ex N5022E	Melbourne	
☐ OE-LPB	Boeing 777-2Z9ER	28699/163		Sydney	
☐ OE-LPC	Boeing 777-2Z9ER	29313/386		Don Bradman	
☐ OE-LPD	Boeing 777-2Z9ER	35960/607		America	

AUSTRIAN ARROWS	***Vienna-Schwechat (VIE)***

☐ OE-LCF	Canadair CL-600-2B19 (CRJ-200LR)	7094	ex C-FMLV	Stadt Düsseldorf	stored LJU
☐ OE-LCG	Canadair CL-600-2B19 (CRJ-200LR)	7103	ex C-FMNB	Stadt Köln	stored LJU
☐ OE-LCH	Canadair CL-600-2B19 (CRJ-200LR)	7110	ex C-FMMB	Stadt Amsterdam	stored VIE
☐ OE-LCI	Canadair CL-600-2B19 (CRJ-200LR)	7133	ex C-FMNB	Stadt Zürich	
☐ OE-LCJ	Canadair CL-600-2B19 (CRJ-200LR)	7142	ex B-3017	Stadt Hannover	
☐ OE-LCK	Canadair CL-600-2B19 (CRJ-200LR)	7148	ex C-FMNB	Stadt Brüssel	
☐ OE-LCL	Canadair CL-600-2B19 (CRJ-200LR)	7167	ex B-3015	Stadt Oslo	
☐ OE-LCM	Canadair CL-600-2B19 (CRJ-200LR)	7205	ex C-FMNH	Stadt Bologna	
☐ OE-LCN	Canadair CL-600-2B19 (CRJ-200LR)	7365	ex C-FMOI	Stadt Bremen	
☐ OE-LCO	Canadair CL-600-2B19 (CRJ-200LR)	7371	ex C-FMMX	Stadt Göteborg	
☐ OE-LCP	Canadair CL-600-2B19 (CRJ-200LR)	7480	ex C-FMOW	Stadt Hamburg	
☐ OE-LCQ	Canadair CL-600-2B19 (CRJ-200LR)	7605	ex C-FMOI	Stadt Strassburg	
☐ OE-LCR	Canadair CL-600-2B19 (CRJ-200LR)	7910	ex C-FMMW	Stadt Baden	
☐ OE-LGA	de Havilland DHC-8-402Q	4014	ex C-GDNG	Kärnten	
☐ OE-LGB	de Havilland DHC-8-402Q	4015	ex C-GDOE	Tirol	
☐ OE-LGC	de Havilland DHC-8-402Q	4026	ex C-GEVP	Salzburg	
☐ OE-LGD	de Havilland DHC-8-402Q	4027	ex C-GEWI	Land Steiermark	
☐ OE-LGE	de Havilland DHC-8-402Q	4042	ex C-FNGB	Land Oberösterreich	
☐ OE-LGF	de Havilland DHC-8-402Q	4068	ex C-GERC	Land Niederösterreich	

☐ OE-LGG	de Havilland DHC-8-402Q	4074	ex C-GFCF	Stadt Budapest
☐ OE-LGH	de Havilland DHC-8-402Q	4075	ex C-GFCW	Vorarlberg
☐ OE-LGI	de Havilland DHC-8-402Q	4100	ex C-FAQR	Eisenstadt
☐ OE-LGJ	de Havilland DHC-8-402Q	4104	ex C-FCQH	St Pölten
☐ OE-LGK	de Havilland DHC-8-402Q	4280	ex C-FYMK	
☐ OE-LTG	de Havilland DHC-8Q-314	438	ex C-GDFT	Hall in Tirol
☐ OE-LTH	de Havilland DHC-8Q-314	442	ex C-GFUM	Stadt Kitzbühel
☐ OE-LTI	de Havilland DHC-8Q-314	466	ex C-GFQL	Bregenz
☐ OE-LTJ	de Havilland DHC-8Q-314	481	ex C-GDOE	Seefeld
☐ OE-LTL	de Havilland DHC-8Q-314	485	ex C-GFYI	Stubaital
☐ OE-LTM	de Havilland DHC-8Q-314	527	ex C-FDHW	Achensee
☐ OE-LTN	de Havilland DHC-8Q-314	531	ex C-GDNK	St Anton am Arlberg
☐ OE-LTO	de Havilland DHC-8Q-314	553	ex C-FWBB	Kufstein
☐ OE-LTP	de Havilland DHC-8Q-314	554	ex C-GDLK	Lienz
☐ OE-LFG	Fokker F.28-070 (Fokker 70)	11549	ex PH-EZW	Innsbruck
☐ OE-LFH	Fokker F.28-070 (Fokker 70)	11554	ex PH-EZN	Stadt Salzburg
☐ OE-LFI	Fokker F.28-070 (Fokker 70)	11529	ex PH-WXF	Stadt Klagenfurt
☐ OE-LFJ	Fokker F.28-070 (Fokker 70)	11532	ex PH-WXG	Stadt Graz
☐ OE-LFK	Fokker F.28-070 (Fokker 70)	11555	ex PH-EZP	Krems
☐ OE-LFL	Fokker F.28-070 (Fokker 70)	11573	ex PH-WXE	Stadt Linz
☐ OE-LFP	Fokker F.28-070 (Fokker 70)	11560	ex PH-EZW	Wels
☐ OE-LFQ	Fokker F.28-070 (Fokker 70)	11568	ex PH-EZC	Dornbirn
☐ OE-LFR	Fokker F.28-070 (Fokker 70)	11572	ex PH-EZD	Steyr
☐ OE-LVA	Fokker F.28-0100 (Fokker 100)	11490	ex PH-ZFB	Riga
☐ OE-LVB	Fokker F.28-0100 (Fokker 100)	11502	ex PH-ZFE	Vilnius
☐ OE-LVC	Fokker F.28-0100 (Fokker 100)	11446	ex PH-ZFF	Tirana
☐ OE-LVD	Fokker F.28-0100 (Fokker 100)	11515	ex PH-ZFG	Skopje
☐ OE-LVE	Fokker F.28-0100 (Fokker 100)	11499	ex PH-ZFH	Zagreb
☐ OE-LVF	Fokker F.28-0100 (Fokker 100)	11483	ex PH-ZFI	Yerevan
☐ OE-LVG	Fokker F.28-0100 (Fokker 100)	11520	ex PH-ZFJ	Krakow Star Alliance c/s
☐ OE-LVH	Fokker F.28-0100 (Fokker 100)	11456	ex PH-ZFK	Minsk
☐ OE-LVI	Fokker F.28-0100 (Fokker 100)	11468	ex PH-ZFL	Prague
☐ OE-LVJ	Fokker F.28-0100 (Fokker 100)	11359	ex PH-ZFM	Bratislava
☐ OE-LVK	Fokker F.28-0100 (Fokker 100)	11397	ex PH-ZFQ	Timisoara Euro 2008 titles
☐ OE-LVL	Fokker F.28-0100 (Fokker 100)	11404	ex PH-ZFR	Odessa
☐ OE-LVM	Fokker F.28-0100 (Fokker 100)	11361	ex PH-ZFN	Krasnodar
☐ OE-LVN	Fokker F.28-0100 (Fokker 100)	11367	ex PH-ZFO	
☐ OE-LVO	Fokker F.28-0100 (Fokker 100)	11460	ex PH-ZFS	

FLYING BULLS — *Salzburg (SZG)*

☐ OE-EDM	Cessna 208 Caravan I	20800257	ex N666CS	Amphibian
☐ N996DM	Douglas DC-6B	45563/1034	ex V5-NCF	Red Bull
☐ N6123C	North American B-25J Mitchell	108-47647	ex 44-86893A	

Operate some pleasure flights as well as airshow appearances

GROSSMANN AIR TRANSPORT — *Grossman (HTG)* — *Vienna-Schwechat (VIE)*

☐ OE-HTG	Dornier 328-300 (Envoy 3)	3162	ex D-BDXG

INTERSKY — *Intersky (3L/ISK)* — *Freidrichschafen-Lowental (FDH)*

☐ OE-LIA	de Havilland DHC-8Q-311	505	ex D-BHAT	
☐ OE-LIC	de Havilland DHC-8Q-314	503	ex D-BHAS	
☐ OE-LIE	de Havilland DHC-8Q-315	546	ex HB-JEJ	
☐ OE-LSB	de Havilland DHC-8Q-314	525	ex C-FDHY	Espace Mittelland

LAUDA AIR — *Lauda Air (NG/LDA)* — *Vienna-Schwechat (VIE)*

Operates leisure services for Austrian Airlines using OS/AUA designators as 'Lauda Air-the Austrian way to holidays'. Leases aircraft as required from Austrian. Member of Star Alliance.

MAPJET — *MapJet (MPJ)* — *Vienna-Schwechat (VIE)*

☐ OE-IKB	McDonnell-Douglas MD-83	49448/1313	ex N990PG		
☐ OE-LOG	McDonnell-Douglas MD-83	49359/1349	ex HB-INV		
☐ OE-LRW	McDonnell-Douglas MD-83	49629/1583	ex EC-HBP	all-white	
☐ OE-LMP	Airbus A310-322	410	ex N410AN		stored BRU

NIKI — *FlyNiki (HG/NLY)* — *Vienna-Schwecat (VIE)*

☐ OE-LEA	Airbus A320-214	2529	ex F-WWID	Rock'n Roll
☐ OE-LED	Airbus A319-132	3407	ex D-AVYC	
☐ OE-LEE	Airbus A320-214	2749	ex F-WWDB	
☐ OE-LEK	Airbus A319-132	3019	ex D-AVXM	Tango
☐ OE-LEO	Airbus A320-214	2668	ex F-WWBP	Soul
☐ OE-LES	Airbus A321-231	3504	ex D-AVZI	Boogie Woogie
☐ OE-LET	Airbus A321-211	3830	ex D-AVZD	Heavy Metal
☐ OE-LEU	Airbus A320-214	2902	ex F-WWDH	

☐ OE-LEX	Airbus A320-214	2867	ex F-WWBC	Jazz	
☐ OE-	Airbus A320-214		ex		on order
☐ OE-IHA	Embraer 190-100	19000285	ex PT-TLZ		
☐ OE-IHB	Embraer 190-100	19000294	ex PT-TZI		
☐ OE-	Embraer 190-100		ex PT-		on order
☐ OE-	Embraer 190-100		ex PT-		on order

ROBIN HOOD AVIATION — *(RH/RHA)* — *Graz (GRZ)*

☐ OE-GIR	SAAB SF.340A	340A-134	ex SE-F34	Graz-Zurich titles
☐ OE-GOD	SAAB SF.340A	340A-153	ex ZK-NLO	

TYROLEAN AIRWAYS — *Tyrolean (VO/TYR)* — *Innsbruck (INN)*

Wholly owned by Austrian Airlines. Operates scheduled services as 'Austrian Arrows, operated by Tyrolean' using OS/ AUA designators in 5000 range and in full Austrian colours.

TYROLEAN JET SERVICE — *Tyroljet (TJS)* — *Innsbruck (INN)*

☐ OE-HMS	Dornier 328-300 (328JET)	3121	ex D-BDXI
☐ OE-HTJ	Dornier 328-300 (328JET)	3114	ex D-BDXA

WELCOME AIR — *Welcomeair (2W/WLC)* — *Innsbruck (INN)*

☐ OE-GBB	Dornier 328-110	3078	ex D-CDXG	Rotterdam
☐ OE-HRJ	Dornier 328-310 (328JET)	3206	ex N328EF	
☐ OE-LIR	Dornier 328-110	3115	ex D-CDXG	Phőnix
☐ OE-LJR	Dornier 328-310 (328JET)	3213	ex D-BDX.	Aurora

OH- FINLAND (Republic of Finland)

AIR ALAND — *Mariehamn (MHQ)*

☐ LY-RIK	SAAB SF.340A	340A-112	ex SE-F12

AIR FINLAND — *Air Finland (OF/FIF)* — *Helsinki-Vantaa (HEL)*

☐ OH-AFI	Boeing 757-2K2/W	26330/717	ex PH-TKD
☐ OH-AFJ	Boeing 757-28A	26269/612	ex N321LF
☐ OH-AFK	Boeing 757-28A	25622/530	ex N364LF

BLUE1 — *Bluefin (KF/BLF)* — *Helsinki-Vantaa (HEL)*

Member of Star Alliance

☐ OH-SAJ	Avro 146-RJ85	E2388	ex G-6-388	Pyhaselka	
☐ OH-SAK	Avro 146-RJ85	E2389	ex G-6-389	Nasijarvi	
☐ OH-SAL	Avro 146-RJ85	E2392	ex G-6-390	Orivesi	
☐ OH-SAO	Avro 146-RJ85	E2393	ex G-CBMG	Oulujärvi	
☐ OH-SAP	Avro 146-RJ85	E2394	ex G-CBMH	Pielinen	
☐ OH-SAQ	Avro 146-RJ85	E2349	ex EI-RJL	Inarijavi	Lsd fr BCY
☐ OH-SAR	Avro 146-RJ85	E2350	ex EI-RJM		Lsd fr BCY
☐ OH-BLC	McDonnell-Douglas MD-90-30	53459/2141	ex LN-ROA	Lappajärvi	Lsd fr SAS
☐ OH-BLD	McDonnell-Douglas MD-90-30	53544/2197	ex OY-KIN	Kallavesi	Lsd fr SAS
☐ OH-BLE	McDonnell-Douglas MD-90-30	53457/2138	ex SE-DMF		Lsd fr SAS
☐ OH-BLF	McDonnell-Douglas MD-90-30	53543/2194	ex SE-DMH	Star Alliance c/s	Lsd fr SAS
☐ OH-BLU	McDonnell-Douglas MD-90-30	53458/2140	ex OY-KIL		Lsd fr SAS

COPTERLINE — *Copterline (AAQ)* — *Helsinki-Malmi (HEM)*

☐ OH-HCH	Eurocopter EC135P1	0008	ex D-HPOZ
☐ OH-HCK	Eurocopter EC135P2	0378	
☐ OH-HCL	Eurocopter EC135P2	0379	
☐ OH-HCM	Eurocopter EC135P2	0414	
☐ OH-HCN	Eurocopter EC135P2	0415	
☐ OH-HCO	Eurocopter EC135P2	0418	ex D-HECT
☐ OH-HCP	Eurocopter EC135P2	0419	
☐ OH-HCD	MBB Bo.105CBS-4	S-547	ex AB-7
☐ OH-HKI	MBB Bo.105CBS-4	S-731	ex D-HECB

FINNAIR — *Finnair (AY/FIN)* — *Helsinki-Vantaa (HEL)*

Member of Oneworld

☐ OH-LVA	Airbus A319-112	1073	ex F-WWID
☐ OH-LVB	Airbus A319-112	1107	ex D-AVWS
☐ OH-LVC	Airbus A319-112	1309	ex D-AVWY

☐ OH-LVD	Airbus A319-112	1352	ex D-AVYW	
☐ OH-LVE	Airbus A319-112	1791	ex D-AVYS	Retro c/s
☐ OH-LVF	Airbus A319-112	1808	ex D-AVWG	
☐ OH-LVG	Airbus A319-112	1916	ex D-AVYG	
☐ OH-LVH	Airbus A319-112	1184	ex EI-CZE	
☐ OH-LVI	Airbus A319-112	1364	ex F-WQQZ	
☐ OH-LVK	Airbus A319-112	2124	ex D-AVWB	
☐ OH-LVL	Airbus A319-112	2266	ex D-AVWS	
☐ OH-LXA	Airbus A320-214	1405	ex F-WWDH	
☐ OH-LXB	Airbus A320-214	1470	ex F-WWDO	
☐ OH-LXC	Airbus A320-214	1544	ex F-WWIX	
☐ OH-LXD	Airbus A320-214	1588	ex F-WWBQ	
☐ OH-LXE	Airbus A320-214	1678	ex F-WWIF	
☐ OH-LXF	Airbus A320-214	1712	ex F-WWIY	
☐ OH-LXG	Airbus A320-214	1735	ex F-WWBM	
☐ OH-LXH	Airbus A320-214	1913	ex F-WWIZ	
☐ OH-LXI	Airbus A320-214	1989	ex F-WWDN	
☐ OH-LXK	Airbus A320-214	2065	ex F-WWIQ	
☐ OH-LXL	Airbus A320-214	2146	ex F-WWDN	
☐ OH-LXM	Airbus A320-214	2154	ex F-WWDP	
☐ OH-LZA	Airbus A321-211	0941	ex D-AVZT	
☐ OH-LZB	Airbus A321-211	0961	ex D-AVZU	
☐ OH-LZC	Airbus A321-211	1185	ex D-AVZI	
☐ OH-LZD	Airbus A321-211	1241	ex D-AVZG	
☐ OH-LZE	Airbus A321-211	1978	ex D-AVZV	
☐ OH-LZF	Airbus A321-211	2208	ex D-AVZI	
☐ OH-LTM	Airbus A330-302E	994	ex F-WWKO	
☐ OH-LTN	Airbus A330-302E	1007	ex F-WWYC	
☐ OH-LTO	Airbus A330-302E	1013	ex F-WW	
☐ OH-LTP	Airbus A330-302E	1023	ex F-WW	
☐ OH-LTR	Airbus A330-302E	1067	ex F-WWKY	
☐ OH-LTS	Airbus A330-302E	1078	ex F-WWYU	on order
☐ OH-LTT	Airbus A330-302E	1088	ex F-WWKH	on order
☐ OH-LTU	Airbus A330-302E		ex F-	on order
☐ OH-LQA	Airbus A340-311	058	ex G-VFLY	
☐ OH-LQB	Airbus A340-313E	835	ex F-WWJG	
☐ OH-LQC	Airbus A340-313E	844	ex F-WWJI	
☐ OH-LQD	Airbus A340-313E	921	ex F-WWJK	
☐ OH-LQE	Airbus A340-313E	938	ex F-WWJL	
☐ OH-LBO	Boeing 757-2Q8/W	28172/772	ex N1789B	
☐ OH-LBR	Boeing 757-2Q8/W	28167/775		
☐ OH-LBS	Boeing 757-2Q8/W	27623/792	ex N5573K	
☐ OH-LBT	Boeing 757-2Q8/W	28170/801		
☐ OH-LBU	Boeing 757-2Q8/W	29377/857		
☐ OH-LBV	Boeing 757-2Q8/W	30046/1006	ex N60659	
☐ OH-LBX	Boeing 757-2Q8/W	29382/1010	ex N60668	
☐ OH-LEE	Embraer 170-100STD (170LR)	17000093	ex PT-SZT	
☐ OH-LEF	Embraer 170-100STD (170LR)	17000106	ex PT-SAO	
☐ OH-LEG	Embraer 170-100STD (170LR)	17000107	ex PT-SAP	
☐ OH-LEH	Embraer 170-100STD (170LR)	17000112	ex PT-SAX	
☐ OH-LEI	Embraer 170-100STD (170LR)	17000120	ex PT-SDI	
☐ OH-LEK	Embraer 170-100STD (170LR)	17000127	ex PT-SDQ	
☐ OH-LEL	Embraer 170-100STD (170LR)	17000139	ex PT-SED	
☐ OH-LEM	Embraer 170-100STD (170LR)	17000141	ex PT-SEF	
☐ OH-LEN	Embraer 170-100STD (170LR)	17000146	ex PT-SEK	
☐ OH-LEO	Embraer 170-100STD (170LR)	17000150	ex PT-SEO	
☐ OH-LKE	Embraer 190-100LR (190LR)	19000059	ex PT-SEW	
☐ OH-LKF	Embraer 190-100LR (190LR)	19000066	ex PT-SJE	
☐ OH-LKG	Embraer 190-100LR (190LR)	19000079	ex PT-SJV	
☐ OH-LKH	Embraer 190-100LR (190LR)	19000086	ex PT-SNE	
☐ OH-LKI	Embraer 190-100LR (190LR)	19000117	ex PT-SQL	
☐ OH-LKK	Embraer 190-100LR (190LR)	19000127	ex PT-SQW	
☐ OH-LKL	Embraer 190-100LR (190LR)	19000153	ex PT-SAI	
☐ OH-LKM	Embraer 190-100LR (190LR)	19000160	ex PT-SAP	
☐ OH-LKN	Embraer 190-100LR (190LR)	19000252	ex PT-SIX	
☐ OH-LKO	Embraer 190-100LR (190LR)	19000267	ex PT-	
☐ OH-	Embraer 190-100LR (190LR)		ex PT-S	on order
☐ OH-LGB	McDonnell-Douglas MD-11	48450/479		Moomin c/s
☐ OH-LGD	McDonnell-Douglas MD-11	48513/564		stored HEL
☐ OH-LGF	McDonnell-Douglas MD-11	48766/600	ex P4-BDL	Moomin c/s
☐ OH-LGG	McDonnell-Douglas MD-11ER	48753/608	ex PP-VQI	

FINNCOMM AIRLINES		Westbird (FC/WBA)		Helsinki-Vantaa (HEL)
☐ EI-REM	ATR 72-212A	760	ex F-WWEW	Lsd fm REA
☐ OH-ATA	ATR 42-500	641	ex F-WWLV	
☐ OH-ATB	ATR 42-500	643	ex F-WWLA	
☐ OH-ATC	ATR 42-500	651	ex F-WWLI	
☐ OH-ATD	ATR 42-500	655	ex F-WWLM	
☐ OH-ATE	ATR 72-212A	741	ex F-WWEB	
☐ OH-ATF	ATR 72-212A	744	ex F-WWEE	
☐ OH-ATG	ATR 72-212A	757	ex F-WWER	
☐ OH-ATH	ATR 72-212A	769	ex F-WWEH	
☐ OH-ATI	ATR 72-212A	783	ex F-WWEB	
☐ OH-ATJ	ATR 72-212A	792	ex F-WWEM	
☐ OH-ATK	ATR 72-212A	848	ex F-WWEN	
☐ OH-ATL	ATR 72-212A	851	ex F-WWEU	
☐ OH-EBE	Embraer EMB.145LU (ERJ-145LU)	145351	ex HB-JAI	for PTB
☐ OH-EBF	Embraer EMB.145LU (ERJ-145LU)	145387	ex HB-JAK	for PTB

SCANWINGS		Skywings (ABF)		Helsinki-Vantaa (HEL)
☐ OH-BAX	Beech 65-C90 King Air	LJ-948	ex N4495U	
☐ OH-BEX	Beech 65-C90 King Air	LJ-978	ex N725KR	

TURKU AIR				Turku (TKU)
☐ OH-KYC	Piper PA-31-350 Chieftain	31-8052186	ex SE-KYC	
☐ OH-PNU	Piper PA-31-350 Navajo Chieftain	31-7752027	ex N62993	
☐ OH-PNX	Piper PA-31-350 Chieftain	31-8052040	ex ES-PAG	
☐ OH-PNY	Piper PA-31-350 Navajo Chieftain	31-7652079	ex LN-SAB	

UTIN LENTO				Utti
☐ OH-SIS	Cessna 208 Caravan I	20800105	ex LN-PBD	
☐ OH-USI	Cessna 208 Caravan I	20800275	ex N52639	

OK- CZECH REPUBLIC

CENTRAL CONNECT AIRLINES		(3B/CCG)		Ostrava (OSR)
☐ OK-CCC	SAAB SF.340B	340B-208	ex YR-VGM	
☐ OK-CCD	SAAB SF.340B	340A-161	ex SE-KXH	
☐ OK-CCE	SAAB SF.340A	340A-108	ex N108CQ	Freighter; Op for UPS
☐ OK-CCF	SAAB SF.340A	340A-101	ex N101CN	Freighter; Op for UPS
☐ OK-CCG	SAAB SF.340A	340A-104	ex N104CQ	Freighter; Op for UPS
☐ OK-CCK	SAAB SF.340A	340A-078	ex SE-LSR	
☐ OK-CCL	SAAB SF.340A	340A-159	ex LY-NSD	Freighter
☐ OK-CCN	SAAB SF.340B	340B-230	ex SE-KTE	
☐ OK-CCO	SAAB SF.340B	340B-188	ex XA-TJI	

CSA CZECH AIRLINES		CSA Lines (OK/CSA)			Prague-Ruzyne (PRG)
Member of Skyteam					
☐ OK-YAC	Airbus A310-325	672	ex F-OHPX	Zlin	
☐ OK-YAD	Airbus A310-325	674	ex F-OIHS	Frydek-Mistek	Lsd to AIC
☐ OK-MEK	Airbus A319-112	3043	ex D-AVWL		
☐ OK-MEL	Airbus A319-112	3094	ex D-AVWN		
☐ OK-NEM	Airbus A319-112	3406	ex D-AVYB		
☐ OK-NEN	Airbus A319-112	3436	ex D-AVYJ		
☐ OK-NEO	Airbus A319-112	3452	ex D-AVYY		
☐ OK-NEP	Airbus A319-112	3660	ex D-AVYT		
☐ OK-OER	Airbus A319-112	3892	ex D-AVYT		
☐ OK-	Airbus A319-112		ex D		on order
☐ OK-GEA	Airbus A320-214	1439	ex CS-TQA	Roznov pod Radhostem	
☐ OK-GEB	Airbus A320-214	1450	ex CS-TQB	Strakonice	
☐ OK-LEE	Airbus A320-214	2719	ex F-WWDC		
☐ OK-LEF	Airbus A320-214	2758	ex F-WWDP		
☐ OK-LEG	Airbus A320-214	2789	ex F-WWBX		
☐ OK-MEH	Airbus A320-214	3031	ex F-WWBU		
☐ OK-MEI	Airbus A320-214	3060	ex F-WWDY		
☐ OK-MEJ	Airbus A320-214	3097	ex F-WWID		
☐ OK-CEC	Airbus A321-211	0674	ex C-GKOH	Nove mesto nad Metuji	
☐ OK-CED	Airbus A321-211	0684	ex C-GKOJ	Havlickuv Brod	
☐ OK-JFJ	ATR 42-500	623	ex F-WWLD	Namest nad Oslavou	
☐ OK-JFK	ATR 42-500	625	ex F-WWLF	Slavkov u Brna	

☐ OK-JFL	ATR 42-500	629	ex F-WWLJ	Susice
☐ OK-KFM	ATR 42-500	635	ex F-WWLP	Benesov
☐ OK-KFN	ATR 42-500	637	ex F-WWLR	Prerov
☐ OK-KFO	ATR 42-500	633	ex F-WWLN	Sokolov
☐ OK-KFP	ATR 42-500	639	ex F-WWLT	Svitavy
☐ OK-VFI	ATR 42-320	173	ex F-WQNE	Nebesky jezdec/Sky Rider
☐ OK-XFA	ATR 72-202	285	ex F-WWLO	Cesky Krumlov
☐ OK-XFB	ATR 72-202	297	ex F-WWLW	Znojmo
☐ OK-XFC	ATR 72-202	299	ex F-WWLX	Nitra
☐ OK-XFD	ATR 72-202	303	ex F-WWLB	Mlada Boleslav
☐ OK-CGH	Boeing 737-55S	28469/2849		Usit nad Labem
☐ OK-CGJ	Boeing 737-55S	28470/2861		Hradec Kralove
☐ OK-CGK	Boeing 737-55S	28471/2885		Pardubice
☐ OK-CGT	Boeing 737-46M	28549/2844	ex OO-VEC	Pisek
☐ OK-DGL	Boeing 737-55S	28472/3004		Tabor
☐ OK-DGM	Boeing 737-45S	28473/3014		
☐ OK-DGN	Boeing 737-45S	28474/3028		Trebic
☐ OK-EGO	Boeing 737-55S	28475/3096		Jindrichuv Hradec
☐ OK-EGP	Boeing 737-45S	28476/3103		Kladno
☐ OK-FGR	Boeing 737-45S	28477/3131		Ostrava
☐ OK-FGS	Boeing 737-45S	28478/3132		Brno
☐ OK-WGX	Boeing 737-436	25349/2156	ex G-DOCD	Unicov
☐ OK-WGY	Boeing 737-436	25839/2188	ex G-DOCI	Roudnice nad Labem
☐ OK-XGA	Boeing 737-55S	26539/2300	ex (OO-SYL)	Plzen
☐ OK-XGB	Boeing 737-55S	26540/2317	ex (OO-SYM)	Olomouc
☐ OK-XGC	Boeing 737-55S	26541/2319	ex (OO-SYN)	Ceske Budejovice
☐ OK-XGD	Boeing 737-55S	26542/2337	ex (OO-SYO)	Poprad
☐ OK-XGE	Boeing 737-55S	26543/2339	ex (OO-SYP)	Kosice

LR AIRLINES — *Lady Racine (LRB)* — *Ostrava (OSR)*

☐ OK-LRA	LET L-410UVP-E	892216	ex CCCP-67605	Lady Racine

SILVER AIR — *Solid (SLD)* — *Prague-Ruzyne (PRG)*

☐ OK-SLD	LET L-410UVP-E9	022634		Ceska Posta titles
☐ OK-WDC	LET L-410UVP-E	912531		
☐ OK-WDT	LET L-410UVP-E	912615	ex CCCP-67684	DHL c/s

SKYDIVE & AIR SERVICE — *Pribram-Dlouha Lhota*

☐ OK-ASA	LET L-410UVP-E	902439	ex RA-67646	
☐ OK-SAS	LET L-410UVP	831040	ex RA-67412	
☐ OK-SKY	LET L-410UVP	851418	ex UR-67514	Lsd fr Aeronautical Research

SMARTWINGS — *Skytravel (QS/TVS)* — *Prague-Ruzyne (PRG)*

☐ OK-SWU	Boeing 737-522	26703/2498	ex N955UA
☐ OK-SWV	Boeing 737-522	26696/2440	ex N951UA

TIME AIR

☐ OK-GTJ	Beech 300 Super King Air	FA-223	ex D-IHHB	
☐ OK-SUR	Cessna 421C Golden Eagle III	421C0861	ex D-IOAA	Op for Pony Express

TRAVEL SERVICE AIRLINES — *Skytravel (QS/TVS)* — *Prague-Ruzyne (PRG)*

☐ OK-TVA	Boeing 737-86N/W	32243/869	ex N1786B	
☐ OK-TVB	Boeing 737-8CX/W	32362/1125		
☐ OK-TVC	Boeing 737-86Q/W	30278/963	ex N289CD	O2 c/s
☐ OK-TVD	Boeing 737-86N	28595/285	ex CN-RNO	Prague Airport
☐ OK-TVF	Boeing 737-8FH/W	29669/1692		
☐ OK-TVG	Boeing 737-8Q8/W	30719/2257		
☐ OK-TVH	Boeing 737-8Q8/W	35275/2604		
☐ OK-TVK	Boeing 737-86N/W	32740/1444	ex N977RY	
☐ OK-TVL	Boeing 737-8FN/W	37076/3147		
☐ OK-TVM	Boeing 737-8FN/W	37077/3163		

VAN AIR EUROPE — *(6Z/VAA)* — *Brno-Turany*

☐ OK-RDA	LET L-410UVP-E9	861813	ex HA-YFG	Op for Manx2
☐ OK-TCA	LET L-410UVP-E	902431	ex SP-KPZ	Op for Manx2
☐ OK-UBA	LET L-410UVP-E19	892319	ex SP-TXA	Op for Manx2

OM- SLOVAKIA (Slovak Republic)

AIR SLOVAKIA — Slovakia (GM/SVK) — Bratislava-MR Stefanik (BTS)

Reg	Type	c/n	Previous	Notes
☐ OM-ASC	Boeing 737-3Z9	23601/1254	ex OE-ILF	
☐ OM-ASD	Boeing 737-306	23542/1317	ex PH-BDG	
☐ OM-ASE	Boeing 737-306	23545/1343	ex PH-BDK	
☐ OM-ASF	Boeing 737-306	23544/1335	ex PH-BDI	
☐ OM-ASG	Boeing 757-28A	24544/280	ex N241LF	
☐ OM-RAN	Boeing 737-230 (Nordam 3)	23156/1082	ex N621AC	

DANUBE WINGS — (V5) — Bratislava-MR Stefanik (BTS)

Reg	Type	c/n	Previous	Notes
☐ OM-VRA	ATR 72-201	373	ex F-WAGR	
☐ OM-VRB	ATR 72-202	367	ex EI-REG	
☐ OM-VRC	ATR 72-202	307	ex F-WKVB	
☐ OK-WGY	Boeing 737-436	25839/2188	ex G-DOCI	Roudnice nad Labem

DUBNICA AIR — Slavnica

Reg	Type	c/n	Previous	Notes
☐ OM-ODQ	LET L-410UVP	841320	ex OK-ODQ	
☐ OM-PGA	LET L-410UVP-T	820909	ex OM-DAA	
☐ OM-SAB	LET L-410MA	750405	ex 0405 Slovak AF	

SEAGLE AIR — Seagle (CGL) — Trencin

Reg	Type	c/n	Previous	Notes
☐ OM-CGL	LET L-410UVP-E3	871914	ex OM-HLB	

SKYEUROPE AIRLINES

Ceased operation 10/09/2009

SLOVAK GOVERNMENT FLYING SERVICE — Slovak Government (SSG) — Bratislava-MR Stefanik (BTS)

Reg	Type	c/n	Previous	Notes
☐ OM-BYE	Yakovlev Yak-40	9440338	ex OK-BYE	IP
☐ OM-BYL	Yakovlev Yak-40	9940560	ex OK-BYL	IP
☐ OM-BYO	Tupolev Tu-154M	89A-803	ex OK-BYO	
☐ OM-BYR	Tupolev Tu-154M	98A-1012		IP

OO- BELGIUM (Kingdom of Belgium)

AIR SERVICE LIEGE — Liege (LGG)

Reg	Type	c/n	Previous	Notes
☐ OO-ASL	Beech B200C Super King Air	BL-49	ex OK-LFB	
☐ OO-GMJ	Beech B300 Super King Air	FL-460	ex D-CGMJ	
☐ OO-LET	Beech B200 Super King Air	BB-1473	ex N8210X	
☐ OO-PHB	Beech 1900D	UE-106	ex N106UE	Mr Blue Sky

AIRVENTURE — Venture Liner (RVE) — Antwerp-Deurne (ANR)

Reg	Type	c/n	Previous	Notes
☐ OO-SXC	Embraer EMB.121A Xingu	121042	ex PT-MBJ	MS

BRUSSELS AIRLINES — Estail (TV/DAT) — Brussels-National (BRU)

Member of Star Alliance

Reg	Type	c/n	Previous	Notes
☐ OO-SSG	Airbus A319-112	1160	ex EI-CZF	
☐ OO-SSK	Airbus A319-112	1336	ex F-WQRU	
☐ OO-SSM	Airbus A319-112	1388	ex F-WQRV	
☐ OO-SSP	Airbus A319-113	0644	ex F-GPMG	
☐ OO-SFM	Airbus A330-301	030	ex F-GMDA	
☐ OO-SFN	Airbus A330-301	037	ex F-GMDB	
☐ OO-SFO	Airbus A330-301	045	ex F-GMDC	
☐ OO-SFW	Airbus A330-322	082	ex EI-DVB	
☐ OO-	Airbus A330-322	095	ex 9M-MKR	on order
☐ OO-DJK	Avro 146-RJ85	E2271	ex G-6-271	
☐ OO-DJL	Avro 146-RJ85	E2273	ex G-6-273	
☐ OO-DJN	Avro 146-RJ85	E2275	ex G-6-275	
☐ OO-DJO	Avro 146-RJ85	E2279	ex G-6-279	
☐ OO-DJP	Avro 146-RJ85	E2287	ex G-6-287	
☐ OO-DJQ	Avro 146-RJ85	E2289	ex G-6-289	
☐ OO-DJR	Avro 146-RJ85	E2290	ex G-6-290	
☐ OO-DJS	Avro 146-RJ85	E2292	ex G-6-292	
☐ OO-DJT	Avro 146-RJ85	E2294	ex G-6-294	
☐ OO-DJV	Avro 146-RJ85	E2295	ex G-6-295	
☐ OO-DJW	Avro 146-RJ85	E2296	ex G-6-296	
☐ OO-DJX	Avro 146-RJ85	E2297	ex G-6-297	

☐ OO-DJY	Avro 146-RJ85	E2302	ex G-6-302		
☐ OO-DJZ	Avro 146-RJ85	E2305	ex G-6-305		
☐ OO-DWA	Avro 146-RJ100	E3308	ex G-BXEU		
☐ OO-DWB	Avro 146-RJ100	E3315	ex G-6-315		
☐ OO-DWC	Avro 146-RJ100	E3322	ex G-6-322		
☐ OO-DWD	Avro 146-RJ100	E3324	ex G-6-324		
☐ OO-DWE	Avro 146-RJ100	E3327	ex G-6-327		
☐ OO-DWF	Avro 146-RJ100	E3332	ex G-6-332		
☐ OO-DWG	Avro 146-RJ100	E3336	ex G-6-336		
☐ OO-DWH	Avro 146-RJ100	E3340	ex G-6-340		
☐ OO-DWI	Avro 146-RJ100	E3342	ex G-6-342		
☐ OO-DWJ	Avro 146-RJ100	E3355	ex G-6-355		
☐ OO-DWK	Avro 146-RJ100	E3360	ex G-6-360		
☐ OO-DWL	Avro 146-RJ100	E3361	ex G-6-361		
☐ OO-LTM	Boeing 737-3M8	25070/2037	ex F-GMTM		
☐ OO-VBR	Boeing 737-4Y0	24314/1680	ex F-GMBR	all-white	
☐ OO-VEG	Boeing 737-36N/W	28568/2987	ex EI-TVQ		
☐ OO-VEH	Boeing 737-36N/W	28571/3022	ex EI-TVR		
☐ OO-VEJ	Boeing 737-405	24271/1738	ex LN-BRB		
☐ OO-VEK	Boeing 737-405	24270/1726	ex LN-BRA		
☐ OO-VEN	Boeing 737-36N	28586/3090	ex EI-TVN		
☐ OO-VEP	Boeing 737-43Q	28489/2827	ex VH-VGA		
☐ OO-VES	Boeing 737-43Q	28493/2838	ex VH-VGE		
☐ OO-VET	Boeing 737-4Q8	28202/3009	ex VT-SJB		
☐ OO-VEX	Boeing 737-36N/W	28670/2948	ex EI-TVS		
☐ OO-DJE	British Aerospace 146 Srs.200	E2164	ex G-6-164		stored BRU
☐ OO-DJF	British Aerospace 146 Srs.200	E2167	ex G-6-167		stored BRU
☐ OO-DJG	British Aerospace 146 Srs.200	E2180	ex G-BSZZ		stored BRU
☐ OO-DJJ	British Aerospace 146 Srs.200	E2196	ex SE-DRM		stored BRU
☐ OO-MJE	British Aerospace 146 Srs.200	E2192	ex G-6-192		stored BRU

CARGO B AIRLINES — *(CBB)* — *Brussels-National (BRU)*

Ceased operations 30/Jun/2009

EUROPEAN AIR TRANSPORT — *Eurotrans (QY/BCS)* — *Brussels-National (BRU)*

☐ OO-DLC	Airbus A300B4-203F	152	ex D-ASAD	
☐ OO-DLG	Airbus A300B4-203F	208	ex N212PA	
☐ OO-DLR	Airbus A300B4-203F	095	ex EC-JHO	stored LEJ
☐ OO-DLV	Airbus A300B4-203F	150	ex EI-EAA	stored LEJ
☐ OO-DLW	Airbus A300B4-203F	199	ex EI-EAB	stored LEJ
☐ OO-DLZ	Airbus A300B4-203F	219	ex N474AS	stored LEJ
☐ OO-DLJ	Boeing 757-23APF	24971/340	ex N573CA	
☐ OO-DLN	Boeing 757-236 (SF)	22172/9	ex G-BIKA	
☐ OO-DLP	Boeing 757-236 (SF)	22179/24	ex G-BIKH	
☐ OO-DLQ	Boeing 757-236 (SF)	22175/13	ex G-BIKD	
☐ OO-DPB	Boeing 757-236 (SF)	22183/32	ex G-BIKL	
☐ OO-DPF	Boeing 757-236 (SF)	22173/10	ex G-BIKB	
☐ OO-DPJ	Boeing 757-236 (SF)	23493/90	ex G-BIKX	
☐ OO-DPK	Boeing 757-236 (SF)	23492/89	ex G-BIKW	
☐ OO-DPM	Boeing 757-236 (SF)	22189/58	ex G-BIKR	
☐ OO-DPN	Boeing 757-236 (SF)	23533/93	ex G-BIKY	
☐ OO-DPO	Boeing 757-236 (SF)	23398/77	ex G-BIKT	

JETAIRFLY — *Beauty (TB/JAF)* — *Brussels-National (BRU)*

☐ OO-JAF	Boeing 737-8K5	35133/2313	ex N1780B	Smile
☐ OO-JAN	Boeing 737-76N/W	28609/417	ex VT-JNT	Revelation
☐ OO-JAQ	Boeing 737-8K5/W	35148/2790	ex N1786B	Vision
☐ OO-JAP	Boeing 767-38EER	30840/829	ex N308MT	Crystal
☐ OO-JAR	Boeing 737-7K5/W	35150/2825		Enjoy
☐ OO-JAS	Boeing 737-7K5/W	35144/2652	ex D-AHXK	
☐ OO-JAT	Boeing 737-5K5	24927/1968	ex D-AHLF	
☐ OO-JBG	Boeing 737-8K5/W	35142/2660		Gerard Brackx
☐ OO-TUA	Boeing 737-4K5	24127/1707	ex D-AHLL	Passion
☐ OO-VAC	Boeing 737-8BK/W	33014/1367	ex N334CT	Rising Sun
☐ OO-VAS	Boeing 737-86Q/W	30285/1237	ex N712BA	Welcome
☐ OO-TUC	Boeing 767-341ER	24844/324	ex N484TC	Discover

NOORDZEE HELIKOPTERS VLAANDEREN — *Ostend /Antwerp-Deurne/Kortrijk-Wevelgem (OST/ANR/KJK)*

☐ OO-NHE	Aérospatiale AS365N3 Dauphin 2	6843		
☐ OO-NHG	Aérospatiale AS365N3 Dauphin 2	6881		
☐ OO-NHH	Aérospatiale AS365N3 Dauphin 2	6891		
☐ OO-NHK	Aérospatiale AS365N3 Dauphin 2	6876		
☐ OO-NHU	Aérospatiale AS365SR Dauphin	6665	ex F-WWOS	Flipper 2
☐ OO-NHX	Aérospatiale AS365N3 Dauphin 2	6706	ex OY-HMO	

☐ OO-NHY	Aérospatiale AS365N3 Dauphin 2	6754			
☐ OO-NHZ	Aérospatiale AS365N2 Dauphin 2	6450	ex N4H	Flipper 3	EMS
☐ OO-ECB	Eurocopter EC120B Colibri	1096	ex F-WQDK		
☐ OO-EMS	MD Helicopters MD900 Explorer	900-00020	ex SE-JCG		EMS
☐ OO-NHB	Eurocopter EC145B	9083	ex D-HMBG		EMS
☐ OO-NHF	MD Helicopters MD900 Explorer	900-00015	ex N9015P		EMS

SKY SERVICE — *Sky Service (SKS)* — *Kortrijk-Wevelgem (KJK)*

☐ OO-LAC	Beech 200C Super King Air	BL-16	ex F-GLTX
☐ OO-SKL	Beech B200 Super King Air	BB-1348	ex D2-EST
☐ OO-SKM	Beech B200 Super King Air	BB-1407	ex D2-ESQ
☐ OO-VHV	Beech 65-E90 King Air	LW-316	ex N77WZ

THOMAS COOK AIRLINES BELGIUM — *Thomas Cook (FQ/TCW)* — *Brussels-National (BRU)*

☐ OO-TCH	Airbus A320-214	1929	ex D-AICM	Experience
☐ OO-TCI	Airbus A320-214	1975	ex EI-DBD	Mega Mindy
☐ OO-TCJ	Airbus A320-214	1787	ex EI-DBC	inspire
☐ OO-TCN	Airbus A320-232	0425	ex SX-BVA	
☐ OO-TCO	Airbus A320-214	1306	ex G-OOAP	sensation
☐ OO-TCP	Airbus A320-214	0653	ex F-GRSD	

TNT AIRWAYS — *Quality (3V/TAY)* — *Liege (LGG)*

☐ EC-HQT	Airbus A300B4-203F	124	ex G-TNTS		stored MHV
☐ OO-TZB	Airbus A300B4-203F	261	ex N229KW		
☐ OO-TNA	Boeing 737-3T0 (SF)	23569/1258	ex N13331		
☐ OO-TNB	Boeing 737-3T0 (SF)	23578/1358	ex N39340		
☐ OO-TNC	Boeing 737-301 (SF)	23513/1327	ex N559AU		
☐ OO-TNE	Boeing 737-3Q8 (SF)	23535/1301	ex TF-ELQ		
☐ OO-TNF	Boeing 737-3Q8 (QC)	24131/1541	ex N241MT		
☐ OO-TNG	Boeing 737-3Y0 (QC)	24255/1625	ex N255CF		
☐ OO-TNH	Boeing 737-301 (SF)	23930/1539	ex N585US		
☐ OO-TNI	Boeing 737-301 (SF)	23512/1291	ex N94417		
☐ OO-TNJ	Boeing 737-301 (SF)	23260/1146	ex N325AW		
☐ OO-TNK	Boeing 737-301 (SF)	23258/1126	ex N326AW		
☐ OO-THA	Boeing 747-4HAERF	35232/1381		Peter Abeles 1924-1999	
☐ OO-THB	Boeing 747-4HAERF	35234/1386		Ken Thomas 1913-1997	
☐ OO-THC	Boeing 747-4HAERF	35235/1389	ex N50217		op for UAE
☐ OO-THD	Boeing 747-4HAERF	35236/1399			op for UAE
☐ G-BNPJ	British Aerospace 146 Srs.200QT	E2078	ex I-TNTC		
☐ G-TNTD	British Aerospace 146 Srs.200QT	E2109	ex I-MSAA		
☐ OO-TAA	British Aerospace 146 Srs.300QT	E3151	ex G-TNTR		
☐ OO-TAD	British Aerospace 146 Srs.300QT	E3166	ex G-TNTM		
☐ OO-TAE	British Aerospace 146 Srs.300QT	E3182	ex G-TNTG		
☐ OO-TAF	British Aerospace 146 Srs.300QT	E3186	ex G-TNTK		
☐ OO-TAH	British Aerospace 146 Srs.300QT	E3168	ex G-TNTL		
☐ OO-TAJ	British Aerospace 146 Srs.300QT	E3153	ex G-TNTE		
☐ OO-TAK	British Aerospace 146 Srs.300QT	E3150	ex G-TJPM		
☐ OO-TAR	British Aerospace 146 Srs.200QT	E2067	ex G-TNTB		
☐ OO-TAS	British Aerospace 146 Srs.300QT	E3154	ex EC-FFY		
☐ OO-TAU	British Aerospace 146 Srs.200QT	E2100	ex EC-GQP		
☐ OO-TAW	British Aerospace 146 Srs.200QT	E2089	ex EC-EPA		
☐ OO-TAY	British Aerospace 146 Srs.200 (QC)	E2211	ex F-GOMA		
☐ OO-TAZ	British Aerospace 146 Srs.200 (QC)	E2188	ex F-GLNI		

VLM AIRLINES — *Rubens (VG/VLM)* — *Antwerp-Deurne (ANR)*

☐ OO-VLE	Fokker F.27 Mk.050 (Fokker 50)	20132	ex PH-ARG	City of Southampton
☐ OO-VLF	Fokker F.27 Mk.050 (Fokker 50)	20208	ex PH-DMT	Panamarenko
☐ OO-VLI	Fokker F.27 Mk.050 (Fokker 50)	20226	ex PH-JXC	
☐ OO-VLJ	Fokker F.27 Mk.050 (Fokker 50)	20105	ex PH-ARE	Isle of Man
☐ OO-VLK	Fokker F.27 Mk.050 (Fokker 50)	20122	ex PH-FZF	City of Antwerp
☐ OO-VLL	Fokker F.27 Mk.050 (Fokker 50)	20144	ex TF-JMG	City of Groningen
☐ OO-VLM	Fokker F.27 Mk.050 (Fokker 50)	20135	ex PH-VLM	Ville de Nantes
☐ OO-VLN	Fokker F.27 Mk.050 (Fokker 50)	20145	ex PH-VLN	City of Reenstar
☐ OO-VLO	Fokker F.27 Mk.050 (Fokker 50)	20127	ex ES-AFL	Angela Dirkin
☐ OO-VLP	Fokker F.27 Mk.050 (Fokker 50)	20209	ex PH-DMS	
☐ OO-VLQ	Fokker F.27 Mk.050 (Fokker 50)	20159	ex EC-GBH	City of Manchester
☐ OO-VLR	Fokker F.27 Mk.050 (Fokker 50)	20121	ex PH-ARF	City of Brussels
☐ OO-VLS	Fokker F.27 Mk.050 (Fokker 50)	20109	ex EC-GBG	City of Hamburg
☐ OO-VLT	Fokker F.27 Mk.050 (Fokker 50)	20237	ex PH-JXM	City of Eindhoven
☐ OO-VLV	Fokker F.27 Mk.050 (Fokker 50)	20160	ex EC-GDD	Island of Jersey
☐ OO-VLX	Fokker F.27 Mk.050 (Fokker 50)	20177	ex PH-ZFD	City of Luxembourg
☐ OO-VLY	Fokker F.27 Mk.050 (Fokker 50)	20181	ex PH-ZFC	City of Liverpool
☐ OO-VLZ	Fokker F.27 Mk.050 (Fokker 50)	20264	ex TF-JMU	City of Rotterdam

Integrated services with CityJet

OY- DENMARK (Kingdom of Denmark)

AIR ALPHA GREENLAND — Air Alpha (GD/AHA) — Nuuk-Godthaab (GOH)

Reg	Type	C/n	Previous	Notes
☐ OY-HIC	Bell 222U	47522	ex PT-HXC	
☐ OY-HIG	Bell 222B	47132	ex N222LB	

AIR GREENLAND — Greenlandair (GL/GRL) — Nuuk-Godthaab (GOH)

Reg	Type	C/n	Previous	Notes
☐ OY-HGA	Aérospatiale AS350B2 Ecureuil	2600		
☐ OY-HGK	Aérospatiale AS350B2 Ecureuil	2570	ex C-FNJW	
☐ OY-HGO	Aérospatiale AS350B3 Ecureuil	3919		
☐ OY-HGP	Aérospatiale AS350B3 Ecureuil	4062		
☐ OY-HGR	Aérospatiale AS350B3 Ecureuil	4089		
☐ OY-HGS	Aérospatiale AS350B3 Ecureuil	4226		
☐ OY-HIZ	Aérospatiale AS350B3 Ecureuil	3727	ex LN-ODM	
☐ OY-CBT	de Havilland DHC-7-103	10	ex C-GRQB-X	Papikkaaq
☐ OY-CBU	de Havilland DHC-7-103	20		Nipiki
☐ OY-CTC	de Havilland DHC-7-102	101	ex G-BNDC	Minniki
☐ OY-GRD	de Havilland DHC-7-103	9	ex A6-ALM	Sapangaq
☐ OY-GRE	de Havilland DHC-7-103	106	ex N54026	Taateraaq
☐ OY-GRF	de Havilland DHC-7-102	113	ex OE-LLU	Sululik
☐ OY-ATY	de Havilland DHC-6 Twin Otter 300	561	ex C-GRZH	Naaja
☐ OY-GRL	Boeing 757-236	25620/449	ex TF-GRL	Kunuunnguaq
☐ OY-GRN	Airbus A330-223	230	ex F-WIHL	Norsaq
☐ OY-HAF	Sikorsky S-61N	61267	ex N10045	Nattoralik
☐ OY-HAG	Sikorsky S-61N	61268	ex N10046	Kussak
☐ OY-HCY	Bell 212	31166		Piseeq 2
☐ OY-HDM	Bell 212	31142	ex N57545	
☐ OY-HDN	Bell 212	31136	ex N5752K	Miteq
☐ OY-HIA	Bell 222UT	47529	ex TC-HCS	
☐ OY-HID	Bell 222U	47548	ex D-HCAN	
☐ OY-HIE	Bell 222U	47501	ex D-HUKM	
☐ OY-HIF	Bell 222UT	47512	ex N256SP	
☐ OY-HMD	Bell 212	31125	ex LN-ORI	
☐ OY-PCL	Beech 200 Super King Air	BB-1675	ex N2355Z	
☐ OY-POF	de Havilland DHC-6 Twin Otter 300	235	ex N6868	

ATLANTIC AIRWAYS — Faroeline (RC/FLI) — Vagar (FAE)

Reg	Type	C/n	Previous	Notes
☐ OY-HMB	Bell 212	30686	ex LN-OSR	
☐ OY-HSJ	Bell 412	36069	ex N412SX	
☐ OY-HSR	Bell 412EP	36133	ex N62734	
☐ OY-RCA	British Aerospace 146 Srs.200A	E2045	ex G-CLHE	
☐ OY-RCB	British Aerospace 146 Srs.200	E2094	ex SE-DRD	
☐ OY-RCC	Avro 146-RJ100	E3357	ex HB-IYX	
☐ OY-RCD	Avro 146-RJ85	E2235	ex HB-IXK	
☐ OY-RCE	Avro 146-RJ85	E2233	ex HB-IXH	

BEL AIR — Holsted

Reg	Type	C/n	Previous	Notes
☐ OY-HJL	Agusta AW139	31245		

BENAIR AIR SERVICE — Birdie (BDI) — Stauning (STA)

Reg	Type	C/n	Previous	Notes
☐ OY-ARJ	Cessna 414	414-0614	ex D-IAWM	
☐ OY-BJP	Swearingen SA.227AC Metro III	AC-499	ex F-GHVG	
☐ OY-HDD	Bell 206B JetRanger III	3649	ex N130S	
☐ OY-MUG	Short SD.3-60	SH3716	ex G-BNDM	all-white
☐ OY-PBH	LET L-410UVP-E20	972736	ex OK-EDA	
☐ OY-PBI	LET L-410UVP-E20	871936	ex OK-SDM	
☐ OY-PBV	Short SD.3-60	SH3747	ex G-GPBV	
☐ OY-PBW	Short SD.3-60	SH3760	ex VH-SEG	

CHC DENMARK — Helibird (HBI) — Esbjerg (EBJ)

Reg	Type	C/n	Previous	Notes
☐ OY-HDT	Aérospatiale AS.332L	2017	ex G-BWHN	Lsd fr CHC Helicopters Intl
☐ OY-HHC	Aérospatiale AS.332L	2179	ex G-BOZK	Lsd fr CHC Scotia
☐ OY-HKA	Sikorsky S-92A	920046	ex N8052Z	
☐ OY-HKB	Sikorsky S-92A	920058	ex N4502X	
☐ OY-HKC	Sikorsky S-92A	920060	ex N4503U	

CIMBER AIR — Cimber (QI/CIM) — Sonderborg (SGD)

Reg	Type	C/n	Previous	Notes
☐ OY-CIJ	ATR 42-500	497	ex F-WWLR	
☐ OY-CIK	ATR 42-500	501	ex F-WWEE	Lsd to OMA
☐ OY-CIL	ATR 42-500	514	ex F-WWLO	

☐ OY-CIN	ATR 72-212A	568	ex F-WWEH	
☐ OY-CIO	ATR 72-212A	595	ex EC-JCF	Lsd to MAU
☐ OY-RTC	ATR 72-202	508	ex F-WQNK	
☐ OY-RTD	ATR 72-211	509	ex F-OHFQ	
☐ OY-RTF	ATR 72-202	496	ex F-WQNL	
☐ OY-RTH	ATR 42-500	549	ex D-BLLL	Lsd fr EWG

☐ OY-MBI	Canadair CL-600-2B19 (CRJ-200LR)	7436	ex G-MSKT		
☐ OY-MBJ	Canadair CL-600-2B19 (CRJ-200LR)	7442	ex G-MSKU		
☐ OY-MBT	Canadair CL-600-2B19 (CRJ-200LR)	7617	ex C-GKDI		
☐ OY-RJA	Canadair CL-600-2B19 (CRJ-200LR)	7413	ex D-ACIM		
☐ OY-RJB	Canadair CL-600-2B19 (CRJ-200LR)	7419	ex D-ACIN	all-white	Op for Air France
☐ OY-RJC	Canadair CL-600-2B19 (CRJ-200LR)	7015	ex D-ACLF		
☐ OY-RJD	Canadair CL-600-2B19 (CRJ-200LR)	7007	ex D-ACLH		
☐ OY-RJE	Canadair CL-600-2B19 (CRJ-200LR)	7009	ex C-FMUQ		
☐ OY-RJF	Canadair CL-600-2B19 (CRJ-200LR)	7019	ex C-FMUR		
☐ OY-RJG	Canadair CL-600-2B19 (CRJ-200LR)	7104	ex D-ACLU		
☐ OY-RJH	Canadair CL-600-2B19 (CRJ-200LR)	7090	ex D-ACLS		
☐ OY-RJI	Canadair CL-600-2B19 (CRJ-200LR)	7093	ex D-ACLT		
☐ OY-RJJ	Canadair CL-600-2B19 (CRJ-200ER)	7784	ex HA-LNC		

CIMBER STERLING

☐ OY-MRE	Boeing 737-7L9/W	28008/203	
☐ OY-MRF	Boeing 737-7L9/W	28009/221	
☐ OY-MRG	Boeing 737-7L9/W	28010/396	
☐ OY-MRH	Boeing 737-7L9/W	28013/682	
☐ OY-MRS	Boeing 737-76N/W	32737/1130	ex G-STRH
☐ OY-MRU	Boeing 737-73S	29079/194	

COPENHAGEN AIRTAXI — *Aircat (CAT)* — *Copenhagen-Roskilde (RKE)*

☐ OY-CAC	Partenavia P.68B	179	
☐ OY-CAT	Britten-Norman BN-2B-26 Islander	2224	ex EC-FFZ
☐ OY-CDC	Partenavia P.68C	211	ex D-GEMD

DANCOPTER — *Holsted Heliport & Esbjerg (-/EBJ)*

☐ OY-HJA	Eurocopter EC155B1	6828	
☐ OY-HJP	Eurocopter EC155B1	6655	ex F-WWOI
☐ OY-HSK	Eurocopter EC155B1	6660	ex N155EW
☐ OY-HSL	Eurocopter EC155B1	6658	

DANISH AIR TRANSPORT — *Danish (DX/DTR)* — *Kolding-Vamdrup*

☐ LY-RUM	ATR 42-300	010	ex OY-RUM	Lsd to DNU
☐ OY-CIR	ATR 42-310	107	ex F-GHPX	
☐ OY-CIU	ATR 42-310	112	ex C-FIQB	
☐ OY-JRJ	ATR 42-320	036	ex F-WQIS	based BSG
☐ OY-JRY	ATR 42-300	063	ex F-WQOC	
☐ OY-RUB	ATR 72-202	301	ex F-WQNS	
☐ OY-RUD	ATR 72-201	162	ex LY-ATR	
☐ OY-JRU	McDonnell-Douglas MD-87	49403/1404	ex SE-RBA	
☐ OY-RUE	McDonnell-Douglas MD-83	49936/1778	ex YR-HBZ	

JETTIME — *Jettime (JTG)* — *Copenhagen-Kastrup (CPH)*

☐ OY-JTA	Boeing 737-33A	23631/1337	ex N371FA
☐ OY-JTB	Boeing 737-3Y0	24464/1753	ex RP-C4010
☐ OY-JTC	Boeing 737-3L9/W	23718/1402	ex 9M-AAB
☐ OY-JTD	Boeing 737-3Y0/W	24678/1853	ex 9M-AAY
☐ OY-JTE	Boeing 737-3L9	27834/2692	ex G-OGBE

NORTH FLYING — *North Flying (M3/NFA)* — *Aalborg (AAL)*

☐ OY-DLY	Piper PA-31 Turbo Navajo	31-229	ex G-AWOW	
☐ OY-FRE	Piper PA-31 Turbo Navajo	31-632	ex G-AXYA	
☐ OY-NPB	Swearingen SA.227AC Metro III	AC-420	ex N67TC	Lsd to Air Norway
☐ OY-NPD	Swearingen SA.227DC Metro 23	DC-865B	ex 9M-BCH	
☐ OY-NPE	Swearingen SA.227DC Metro 23	DC-867B	ex N23VJ	
☐ OY-NPF	Swearingen SA.227DC Metro 23	DC-880B	ex TF-JME	

PRIMERA AIR SCANDINAVIA — *(PF)*

☐ OY-PSA	Boeing 737-8Q8/W	30688/2280	ex TF-JXD
☐ OY-PSB	Boeing 737-8Q8/W	30722/2261	ex TF-JXE
☐ OY-PSC	Boeing 737-86N/W	33419/1251	ex TF-JXF
☐ OY-PSD	Boeing 737-86N/W	28618/514	ex TF-JXH
☐ OY-PSE	Boeing 737-8Q8/W	30664/743	ex TF-JXI
☐ OY-PSF	Boeing 737-7Q8/W	28210/22	ex TF-JXG

SCANDINAVIAN AIRLINE SYSTEM	Scandinavian (SK/SAS)	Copenhagen-Kastrup (CPH)

For details see under Sweden (SE-)

STAR AIR	Whitestar (S6/SRR)	Copenhagen-Kastrup (CPH)

☐ OY-SRF	Boeing 767-219ER (SF)	23327/134	ex N327MR
☐ OY-SRG	Boeing 767-219ER (SF)	23328/149	ex N328MT
☐ OY-SRH	Boeing 767-204ER (SF)	24457/256	ex N457GE
☐ OY-SRI	Boeing 767-25E (SF)	27193/527	ex N622EV
☐ OY-SRJ	Boeing 767-25E (SF)	27195/535	ex N625EV
☐ OY-SRK	Boeing 767-204ER (SF)	23072/107	ex N307MT
☐ OY-SRL	Boeing 767-232 (SF)	22219/37	ex N107DL
☐ OY-SRM	Boeing 767-25E (SF)	27192/524	ex N621EV
☐ OY-SRN	Boeing 767-219ER (SF)	23326/124	ex N326MR
☐ OY-SRO	Boeing 767-25E (SF)	27194/532	ex N623EV
☐ OY-SRP	Boeing 767-232 (SF)	22220/38	ex N108DL

STENBERG AVIATION		Thisted (TED)

☐ OY-ASY	Embraer EMB.110P1 Bandeirante	110308	ex EI-BPI	flying.dk titles	Op by Flyvsmart
☐ OY-BHT	Embraer EMB.110P2 Bandeirante	110161	ex N4942S	flying dk titles	Op by Flyvsmart

SUN-AIR OF SCANDINAVIA	Sunscan (EZ/SUS)	Billund (BLL)

☐ OY-NCA	Dornier 328-110	3047	ex N433JS		
☐ OY-NCC	Dornier 328-110	3083	ex D-CIAC	all-white	
☐ OY-NCD	Dornier 328-120	3104	ex D-CIAA		
☐ OY-NCE	Dornier 328-110	3106	ex D-CPRY		
☐ OY-NCG	Dornier 328-110	3055	ex N437JS		
☐ OY-NCK	Dornier 328-110	3061	ex N460PS		
☐ OY-NCL	Dornier 328-300 (328JET)	3192	ex N427FJ		
☐ OY-NCM	Dornier 328-310 (328JET)	3190	ex N426FJ		
☐ OY-NCN	Dornier 328-310 (328JET)	3193	ex N428FJ		
☐ OY-NCO	Dornier 328-310 (328JET)	3210	ex OE-HAB		
☐ OY-NCS	Dornier 328-110	3070	ex N459PS		
☐ OY-	Dornier 328-310 (328JET)	3132	ex N328AC		on order
☐ OY-SVB	British Aerospace Jetstream 31	985	ex JA8591		
☐ OY-SVF	British Aerospace Jetstream 31	686	ex G-BSFG	Skien	

THOMAS COOK SCANDINAVIA	(DK/VKG)	Copenhagen-Kastrup (CPH)

☐ OY-VKA	Airbus A321-211	1881	ex D-AVZO	
☐ OY-VKB	Airbus A321-211	1921	ex D-AVZQ	
☐ OY-VKC	Airbus A321-211	1932	ex D-AVXB	
☐ OY-VKD	Airbus A321-211	1960	ex G-EFPA	Lsd fr MYT
☐ OY-VKE	Airbus A321-211	1887	ex G-CTLA	Lsd fr MYT
☐ OY-VKM	Airbus A320-214	1889	ex F-WWBV	
☐ OY-VKS	Airbus A320-214	1954	ex G-YLBM	
☐ OY-VKT	Airbus A321-211	1972	ex G-SMTJ	
☐ OY-VKF	Airbus A330-243	309	ex G-CSJS	
☐ OY-VKG	Airbus A330-343X	349	ex F-WWYG	
☐ OY-VKH	Airbus A330-343X	356	ex F-WWYJ	
☐ OY-VKI	Airbus A330-343X	357	ex C-GVKI	

TRANSAVIA DENMARK	(PH/TDK)

☐ OY-TDA	Boeing 737-8K2/W	30646/1122	ex PH-HZY
☐ OY-TDB	Boeing 737-8K2/W	30650/1158	ex PH-HZV
☐ OY-TDZ	Boeing 737-7K2/W	29347/1318	ex PH-XRC

P- KOREA (Democratic People's Republic of Korea)

AIR KORYO	Air Koryo (JS/KOR)	Pyongyang (FNJ)

☐ P-527	Antonov An-24B	67302207			
☐ P-532	Antonov An-24RV	47309707			
☐ P-533	Antonov An-24RV	47309708			
☐ P-534	Antonov An-24RV	47309802			
☐ P-537	Antonov An-24B	67302408			
☐ P-551	Tupolev Tu-154B	75A-129	ex 551		
☐ P-552	Tupolev Tu-154B	76A-143	ex 552		
☐ P-553	Tupolev Tu-154B	77A-191	ex 553		
☐ P-561	Tupolev Tu-154B-2	83A-573			
☐ P-618	Ilyushin Il-62M	2546624		no titles	Op for Govt
☐ P-632	Tupolev Tu-204-300	1450742364012	ex RA-64012		
☐ P-813	Tupolev Tu-134B-3	66215			

☐ P-814	Tupolev Tu-134B-3	66368			
☐ P-835	Ilyushin Il-18D	188011205	ex 835		
☐ P-836	Ilyushin Il-18V	185008204	ex 836		
☐ P-881	Ilyushin Il-62M	3647853			
☐ P-882	Ilyushin Il-62M	2850236		no titles	Op for Govt
☐ P-885	Ilyushin Il-62M	3933913	ex 885		
☐ P-912	Ilyushin Il-76MD	1003403104			
☐ P-913	Ilyushin Il-76MD	1003404126			
☐ P-914	Ilyushin Il-76MD	1003404146			
☐ P-	Tupolev Tu-204-300				on order

PH- NETHERLANDS (Kingdom of the Netherlands)

AMSTERDAM AIRLINES — *Amsterdam-Schiphol (AMS)*

☐ PH-AAX	Airbus A320-231	0430	ex XA-TXT
☐ PH-AAY	Airbus A320-232	0527	ex N619AW
☐ PH-AAZ	Airbus A320-232	0565	ex N602AW

ARKEFLY/ TUI NETHERLANDS — *(OR/TFL)* — *Amsterdam-Schiphol (AMS)*

☐ PH-AHQ	Boeing 767-383ER	24477/337	ex OY-KDL	
☐ PH-AHX	Boeing 767-383ER	24847/315	ex LN-RCD	
☐ PH-AHY	Boeing 767-383ER	24848/325	ex OY-KDN	
☐ PH-TFA	Boeing 737-8FH/W	35100/2424	ex N1786B	Ferdinand Fransen
☐ PH-TFB	Boeing 737-8K5/W	35149/2820	ex N1781B	
☐ PH-TFC	Boeing 737-8K5/W	35146/2875	ex N1787B	

CHC AIRWAYS — *Schreiner (AW/SCH)* — *Rotterdam (RTM)*

☐ 5A-DLX	de Havilland DHC-8-311A	254	ex PH-SDK	Op for Waha Oil

CHC HELICOPTERS NETHERLANDS — *den Helder (DHR)*

☐ PH-NZS	Sikorsky S-76B	760325	ex G-UKLS
☐ PH-NZT	Sikorsky S-76B	760326	ex G-UKLT
☐ PH-NZU	Sikorsky S-76B	760329	ex G-UKLU
☐ PH-NZV	Sikorsky S-76B	760336	ex G-UKLM
☐ PH-NZW	Sikorsky S-76B	760381	ex G-OKLE
☐ PH-NZZ	Sikorsky S-76B	760316	ex N373G
☐ PH-NZD	Sikorsky S-61N	61489	ex EI-CTK
☐ PH-EAA	Agusta AW139	31141	
☐ PH-SHK	Agusta AW139	31030	ex I-RAIA
☐ PH-SHL	Agusta AW139	31041	
☐ PH-SHN	Eurocopter EC155B1	6755	ex F-WQVV
☐ PH-SHO	Eurocopter EC155B1	6739	ex F-WWOV
☐ PH-SHP	Agusta AW139	31099	

DENIM AIR — *Denim (3D/DNM)* — *Amsterdam-Schiphol (AMS)*

☐ PH-DMQ	de Havilland DHC-8Q-315	567	ex C-GDOE		
☐ PH-DMR	de Havilland DHC-8Q-315	569	ex C-GETI		
☐ PH-DMU	de Havilland DHC-8Q-315	568	ex C-GERL		
☐ PH-DMV	de Havilland DHC-8Q-315	570	ex C-GEVP		
☐ PH-DMW	de Havilland DHC-8Q-315	573	ex C-GFCF	Francisco Domingo	
☐ PH-DMX	de Havilland DHC-8Q-315	574	ex EC-IFK		Lsd to ARA
☐ PH-DMZ	de Havilland DHC-8Q-315	582	ex EC-IJP		Lsd to ARA
☐ PH-DXA	de Havilland DHC-8Q-315	586	ex EC-IGS		Lsd to ARA
☐ PH-DXB	de Havilland DHC-8Q-315	589	ex EC-IJD		
☐ PH-DXC	de Havilland DHC-8Q-315	590	ex EC-IKA		
☐ PH-FZG	Fokker F.27 Mk.050 (Fokker 50)	20202			Lsd to ARA
☐ PH-FZH	Fokker F.27 Mk.050 (Fokker 50)	20210	ex EC-IAD	Olivostatus?	
☐ PH-JXJ	Fokker F.27 Mk.050 (Fokker 50)	20232	ex PT-SLJ		Lsd to ARA
☐ PH-JXK	Fokker F.27 Mk.050 (Fokker 50)	20233	ex PT-SLK	all-white	Lsd to ARA
☐ PH-JXM	Fokker F.27 Mk.050 (Fokker 50)	20237	ex PK-PFH		OO-VLT reserved for VLM
☐ PH-JXN	Fokker F.27 Mk.050 (Fokker 50)	20239	ex EC-GFP		
☐ PH-KXM	Fokker F.27 Mk.050 (Fokker 50)	20252	ex PT-SLO		Lsd to ARA
☐ PH-LMT	Fokker F.27 Mk.050 (Fokker 50)	20192	ex EC-HYJ		Lsd to ARA
☐ PH-LNE	Fokker F.28-0100 (Fokker 100)	11322	ex EC-JDN		

INTERSTATE AIRLINES — *Freewayair (I4/FWA)* — *Maastricht (MST)*

☐ PH-ISA	ATR 42-500	532	ex D-BKKK	all-white	stored MST

KLM CITYHOPPER		City (WA/KLC)			Amsterdam-Schiphol (AMS)
☐ PH-EZA	Embraer 190-100 (190AR)	19000224	ex PT-SHI		
☐ PH-EZB	Embraer 190-100 (190AR)	19000235	ex PT-SIG		
☐ PH-EZC	Embraer 190-100 (190AR)	19000250	ex PT-SIU		
☐ PH-EZD	Embraer 190-100 (190AR)	19000279	ex PT-TLT		
☐ PH-EZE	Embraer 190-100 (190AR)	19000288	ex PT-TZC		
☐ PH-EZF	Embraer 190-100 (190AR)	19000304	ex PT-TZS		
☐ PH-EZG	Embraer 190-100 (190AR)	19000315	ex PT-		
☐ PH-EZH	Embraer 190-100 (190AR)	19000319	ex PT-		
☐ PH-EZI	Embraer 190-100 (190AR)	19000322	ex PT-TXK		
☐ PH-EZK	Embraer 190-100 (190AR)	19000326	ex PT-TXO		
☐ PH-EZL	Embraer 190-100 (190AR)	19000334	ex PT-		on order
☐ PH-EZM	Embraer 190-100 (190AR)	19000338	ex PT-		on order
☐ PH-EZN	Embraer 190-100 (190AR)	19000342	ex PT-		on order
☐ PH-EZO	Embraer 190-100 (190AR)	19000347	ex PT-		on order
☐ PH-EZP	Embraer 190-100 (190AR)	19000348	ex PT-		on order
☐ PH-	Embraer 190-100 (190AR)		ex PT-		on order
☐ PH-	Embraer 190-100 (190AR)		ex PT-		on order
☐ PH-KVG	Fokker F.27 Mk.050 (Fokker 50)	20211		City of Stuttgart	
☐ PH-KVH	Fokker F.27 Mk.050 (Fokker 50)	20217		City of Hanover	
☐ PH-KVI	Fokker F.27 Mk.050 (Fokker 50)	20218		City of Bordeaux	
☐ PH-KVK	Fokker F.27 Mk.050 (Fokker 50)	20219		City of London	
☐ PH-LXJ	Fokker F.27 Mk.050 (Fokker 50)	20270	ex G-UKTE	City of Hull	
☐ PH-LXP	Fokker F.27 Mk.050 (Fokker 50)	20276	ex G-UKTG	City of Durham	
☐ PH-LXR	Fokker F.27 Mk.050 (Fokker 50)	20277	ex G-UKTH	City of Amsterdam	
☐ PH-LXT	Fokker F.27 Mk.050 (Fokker 50)	20279	ex G-UKTI	City of Stavanger	stored AMS
☐ PH-JCH	Fokker F.28-070 (Fokker 70)	11528	ex OE-LFS		
☐ PH-JCT	Fokker F.28-070 (Fokker 70)	11537	ex OE-LFT		
☐ PH-KBX	Fokker F.28-070 (Fokker 70)	11547			
☐ PH-KZA	Fokker F.28-070 (Fokker 70)	11567			
☐ PH-KZB	Fokker F.28-070 (Fokker 70)	11562			
☐ PH-KZC	Fokker F.28-070 (Fokker 70)	11566			
☐ PH-KZD	Fokker F.28-070 (Fokker 70)	11582			
☐ PH-KZE	Fokker F.28-070 (Fokker 70)	11576			
☐ PH-KZF	Fokker F.28-070 (Fokker 70)	11577	ex (G-BVTH)		
☐ PH-KZG	Fokker F.28-070 (Fokker 70)	11578	ex (G-BWTI)		
☐ PH-KZH	Fokker F.28-070 (Fokker 70)	11583			
☐ PH-KZI	Fokker F.28-070 (Fokker 70)	11579	ex (I-REJC)		
☐ PH-KZK	Fokker F.28-070 (Fokker 70)	11581	ex (I-REJD)		
☐ PH-KZL	Fokker F.28-070 (Fokker 70)	11536	ex 9V-SLK		
☐ PH-KZM	Fokker F.28-070 (Fokker 70)	11561	ex 9V-SLL		
☐ PH-KZN	Fokker F.28-070 (Fokker 70)	11553	ex PK-PFE		
☐ PH-KZO	Fokker F.28-070 (Fokker 70)	11538	ex G-BVTE		
☐ PH-KZP	Fokker F.28-070 (Fokker 70)	11539	ex G-BVTF		
☐ PH-KZR	Fokker F.28-070 (Fokker 70)	11551	ex G-BVTG		
☐ PH-KZS	Fokker F.28-070 (Fokker 70)	11540	ex F-GLIS		
☐ PH-KZT	Fokker F.28-070 (Fokker 70)	11541	ex F-GLIT		
☐ PH-KZU	Fokker F.28-070 (Fokker 70)	11543	ex F-GLIU		
☐ PH-KZV	Fokker F.28-070 (Fokker 70)	11556	ex F-GLIV		
☐ PH-KZW	Fokker F.28-070 (Fokker 70)	11558	ex F-GLIX		
☐ PH-WXA	Fokker F.28-070 (Fokker 70)	11570	ex I-REJO		
☐ PH-WXC	Fokker F.28-070 (Fokker 70)	11574	ex I-REJI		
☐ PH-WXD	Fokker F.28-070 (Fokker 70)	11563	ex HA-LMD		
☐ PH-KLD	Fokker F.28-0100 (Fokker 100)	11269	ex G-UKFM		stored WOE
☐ PH-KLI	Fokker F.28-0100 (Fokker 100)	11273	ex G-UKFR		stored WOE
☐ PH-OFA	Fokker F.28-0100 (Fokker 100)	11246	ex G-UKFA		stored AMS
☐ PH-OFB	Fokker F.28-0100 (Fokker 100)	11247	ex G-UKFB		stored AMS
☐ PH-OFC	Fokker F.28-0100 (Fokker 100)	11263	ex G-UKFC		stored WOE
☐ PH-OFD	Fokker F.28-0100 (Fokker 100)	11259	ex G-UKFD		
☐ PH-OFE	Fokker F.28-0100 (Fokker 100)	11260	ex G-UKFE		
☐ PH-OFF	Fokker F.28-0100 (Fokker 100)	11274	ex G-UKFF		stored WOE
☐ PH-OFG	Fokker F.28-0100 (Fokker 100)	11275	ex G-UKFG		stored AMS
☐ PH-OFH	Fokker F.28-0100 (Fokker 100)	11277	ex G-UKFH		stored WOE
☐ PH-OFI	Fokker F.28-0100 (Fokker 100)	11279	ex G-UKFI		
☐ PH-OFJ	Fokker F.28-0100 (Fokker 100)	11248	ex G-UKFJ		stored NWI
☐ PH-OFL	Fokker F.28-0100 (Fokker 100)	11444	ex F-OORG		
☐ PH-OFM	Fokker F.28-0100 (Fokker 100)	11475	ex F-OFRG		
☐ PH-OFN	Fokker F.28-0100 (Fokker 100)	11477	ex F-OHXA		
☐ PH-OFO	Fokker F.28-0100 (Fokker 100)	11462	ex PT-MRS		
☐ PH-OFP	Fokker F.28-0100 (Fokker 100)	11472	ex PT-MRP		

KLM ROYAL DUTCH AIRLINES		KLM (KL/KLM)		Amsterdam-Schiphol (AMS)

Member of Skyteam

☐ PH-AOA	Airbus A330-203	682	ex F-WWYE	dam-Amsterdam
☐ PH-AOB	Airbus A330-203	686	ex F-WWYH	Potsdamer Platz-Berlin
☐ PH-AOC	Airbus A330-203	703	ex F-WWKE	Place de la Concorde-Paris

Reg	Type	c/n	ex	Name	Notes
☐ PH-AOD	Airbus A330-203	738	ex F-WWYC	Piazza del Duomo-Milano	
☐ PH-AOE	Airbus A330-203	770	ex F-WWKD	Parliament Square-Edinburgh	
☐ PH-AOF	Airbus A330-203	801	ex F-WWYC	Federation Square-Melbourne	
☐ PH-AOH	Airbus A330-203	811	ex F-WWYH	Senaatintori/Senate Square-Helsinki	
☐ PH-AOI	Airbus A330-203	819	ex F-WWYR	Plaza de la Independencia-Madrid	
☐ PH-AOK	Airbus A330-203	834	ex F-WWKZ	Radhuspladsen-Kobenhavn	
☐ PH-AOL	Airbus A330-203	900	ex F-WWKP		
☐ PH-AOM	Airbus A330-203		ex		on order

Reg	Type	c/n	ex	Name	Notes
☐ PH-BDN	Boeing 737-306	24261/1640		Willem van Ruysbroeck	
☐ PH-BDO	Boeing 737-306	24262/1642		Jacob van Heemskerck	
☐ PH-BDP	Boeing 737-306	24404/1681		Jacob Roggeveen	
☐ PH-BDT	Boeing 737-406	24530/1772		Gerrit de Veer	
☐ PH-BDW	Boeing 737-406	24858/1903		Leifur Eiriksson	
☐ PH-BDZ	Boeing 737-406	25355/2132		Christophorus Columbus	
☐ PH-BPB	Boeing 737-4Y0	24344/1723	ex G-UKLB	Jan Tinbergen	
☐ PH-BPC	Boeing 737-4Y0	24468/1747	ex G-UKLE	Ernest Hemingway	
☐ PH-BTA	Boeing 737-406	25412/2161		Fernao de Magelhaes	
☐ PH-BTB	Boeing 737-406	25423/2184		Henry Hudson	
☐ PH-BTD	Boeing 737-306	27420/2406		James Cook	
☐ PH-BTE	Boeing 737-306	27421/2438		Roald Amundsen	
☐ PH-BTF	Boeing 737-406	27232/2591		Alexander von Humboldt	
☐ PH-BTG	Boeing 737-406	27233/2601		Sir Henry Morton Stanley	
☐ PH-BTH	Boeing 737-306	28719/2930		Heike Kamerling-Onnes	
☐ PH-BTI	Boeing 737-306	28720/2957	ex N1786B	Niels Bohr	

Reg	Type	c/n	ex	Name	Notes
☐ HB-JJA+	Boeing 737-7AK/W	34303/1758	ex N1780B		[BBJ] Lsd fr PTI
☐ PH-BGA	Boeing 737-8K2/W	37593/2569	ex N1786B		
☐ PH-BGB	Boeing 737-8K2/W	37594/2594		Whimbiel/Regenwulp	
☐ PH-BGC	Boeing 737-8K2/W	30361/2619		Pintail/Pijlstaart	
☐ PH-BGD	Boeing 737-706/W	30366/2675		Goldcrest/Goadhaantje	
☐ PH-BGE	Boeing 737-706/W	30371/2705		Ortolan Bunting/Ortolaan	
☐ PH-BGF	Boeing 737-706/W	30365/2714		Great White Heron/Grote Ziverreiger	
☐ PH-BGG	Boeing 737-706/W	30367/2835		King Eider/Koening Seider	
☐ PH-BGH	Boeing 737-7K2/W	38053/3119			
☐ PH-BGI	Boeing 737-7K2/W	30364			on order
☐ PH-BGK	Boeing 737-7K2/W	38054			on order
☐ PH-BGL	Boeing 737-7K2/W	30369			on order
☐ PH-BXA	Boeing 737-8K2/W	29131/198	ex N1786B	Zwann/Swan	Retro c/s
☐ PH-BXB	Boeing 737-8K2/W	29132/261	ex N1786B	Valk/Falcon	
☐ PH-BXC	Boeing 737-8K2/W	29133/305		Karhoen/Grouse	
☐ PH-BXD	Boeing 737-8K2/W	29134/355	ex N1784B	Arend/Eagle	
☐ PH-BXE	Boeing 737-8K2/W	29595/552	ex N1787B	Havik/Hawk	
☐ PH-BXF	Boeing 737-8K2/W	29596/583	ex N1787B	Zwalluw/Swallow	
☐ PH-BXG	Boeing 737-8K2/W	30357/605	ex N1787B	Kraanvogel/Crane	
☐ PH-BXH	Boeing 737-8K2/W	29597/630	ex N1786B	Gans/Goose	
☐ PH-BXI	Boeing 737-8K2/W	30358/633	ex N1787B	Zilvermeeuw/Herring Gull	
☐ PH-BXK	Boeing 737-8K2/W	29598/639	ex N1015G	Gierzwalluw/Swift	
☐ PH-BXL	Boeing 737-8K2/W	30359/659		Sperwer/Sparrow Hawk	
☐ PH-BXM	Boeing 737-8K2/W	30355/714	ex N1786B	Kluut/Avocet	
☐ PH-BXN	Boeing 737-8K2/W	30356/728	ex N1787B	Merel/Blackbird	
☐ PH-BXO	Boeing 737-9K2/W	29599/866	ex N1786B	Plevier/Plover	
☐ PH-BXP	Boeing 737-9K2/W	29600/924	ex N1786B	Merkroet/Crested Coot	
☐ PH-BXR	Boeing 737-9K2/W	29601/959	ex N1786B	Nachtegaal/Nightingale	
☐ PH-BXS	Boeing 737-9K2/W	29602/981	ex N1786B	Buizard/Buzzard	
☐ PH-BXT	Boeing 737-9K2/W	32944/1498		Zeestern/Sea Tern	
☐ PH-BXU	Boeing 737-8BK/W	33028/1936		Albatross	
☐ PH-BXV	Boeing 737-8K2/W	30370/2205	ex N1786B	Roodborstje/Robin	
☐ PH-BXW	Boeing 737-8K2/W	30360/2467	ex N1784B	Partridge	
☐ PH-BXY	Boeing 737-8K2/W	30372/2503		Grebe/Fuut	
☐ PH-BXZ	Boeing 737-8K2/W	30368/2533	ex N1786B		

Reg	Type	c/n	ex	Name	Notes
☐ PH-BFA	Boeing 747-406	23999/725	ex N6018N	City of Atlanta	
☐ PH-BFB	Boeing 747-406	24000/732		City of Bangkok	
☐ PH-BFC*	Boeing 747-406M	23982/735	ex N6038E	City of Calgary	
☐ PH-BFD*	Boeing 747-406M	24001/737		City of Dubai/Doebai	
☐ PH-BFE	Boeing 747-406M	24201/763	ex N6046P	City of Melbourne	Lsd ORIX
☐ PH-BFF*	Boeing 747-406M	24202/770	ex N6046P	City of Freetown	Lsd ORIX
☐ PH-BFG	Boeing 747-406	24517/782		City of Guayaquil	
☐ PH-BFH*	Boeing 747-406M	24518/783	ex N60668	City of Hong Kong	
☐ PH-BFI	Boeing 747-406M	25086/850		City of Jakarta	
☐ PH-BFK	Boeing 747-406	25087/854		City of Karachi	
☐ PH-BFL	Boeing 747-406	25356/888		City of Lima	
☐ PH-BFM*	Boeing 747-406M	26373/896		City of Mexico	
☐ PH-BFN	Boeing 747-406	26372/969		City of Nairobi	
☐ PH-BFO	Boeing 747-406M	25413/938		City of Orlando	
☐ PH-BFP*	Boeing 747-406M	26374/992		City of Paramaribo	
☐ PH-BFR	Boeing 747-406M	27202/1014		City of Rio de Janeiro	
☐ PH-BFS	Boeing 747-406	28195/1090		City of Seoul	
☐ PH-BFT	Boeing 747-406	28459/1112		City of Tokyo	
☐ PH-BFU	Boeing 747-406	28196/1127		City of Beijing	
☐ PH-BFV	Boeing 747-406	28460/1225		City of Vancouver	
☐ PH-BFW	Boeing 747-406	30454/1258		City of Shanghai	

☐ PH-BFY	Boeing 747-406	30455/1302		City of Johannesburg	
☐ PH-CKA	Boeing 747-406ERF	33694/1326		EendrachtKLM Cargo	
☐ PH-CKB	Boeing 747-406ERF	33695/1328		LeeuwinKLM Cargo	
☐ PH-CKC	Boeing 747-406ERF	33696/1341		OranjeKLM Cargo	
☐ PH-CKD	Boeing 747-406ERF	35233/1382			
☐ PH-BQA	Boeing 777-206ER	33711/454	ex N5014K	Albert Plesman	
☐ PH-BQB	Boeing 777-206ER	33712/457		Borobudur	
☐ PH-BQC	Boeing 777-206ER	29397/461		Chichen-Itza	
☐ PH-BQD	Boeing 777-206ER	33713/465		Darjeeling Highway	
☐ PH-BQE	Boeing 777-206ER	28691/468		Epidaurus	
☐ PH-BQF	Boeing 777-206ER	29398/474		Ferrara City	
☐ PH-BQG	Boeing 777-206ER	32704/476		Galapagos Islands	
☐ PH-BQH	Boeing 777-206ER	32705/493	ex N5016R	Hadrian's Wall	
☐ PH-BQI	Boeing 777-206ER	33714/497		Iguazu Falls	
☐ PH-BQK	Boeing 777-206ER	29399/499		Mount Kilimanjaro	
☐ PH-BQL	Boeing 777-206ER	34711/552		Litomyšl Castle	
☐ PH-BQM	Boeing 777-206ER	34712/559		Machu Picchu	
☐ PH-BQN	Boeing 777-206ER	32720/561		Nahanni National Park	
☐ PH-BQO	Boeing 777-206ER	35295/609		Old Rauma	
☐ PH-BQP	Boeing 777-206ER	32721/630		Pont du Gard	
☐ PH-BVA	Boeing 777-306ER	35671/694	(ex PH-BQR)	De Hoge Veluwe National Park	
☐ PH-BVB	Boeing 777-306ER	36145/706		Fulufjallet National Park	
☐ PH-BVC	Boeing 777-306ER	37582/787		Sian Ka'an National Park	
☐ PH-BVD	Boeing 777-306ER	35979/807		National Park Amboseli	
☐ PH-BVE	Boeing 777-306ER	35947			on order
☐ PH-KCA	McDonnell-Douglas MD-11	48555/557	ex N6202D	Amy Johnson	
☐ PH-KCB	McDonnell-Douglas MD-11	48556/561		Maria Montessori	
☐ PH-KCC	McDonnell-Douglas MD-11	48557/569		Marie Curie	
☐ PH-KCD	McDonnell-Douglas MD-11	48558/573		Florence Nightingale	
☐ PH-KCE	McDonnell-Douglas MD-11	48559/575	ex N91566	Audrey Hepburn	
☐ PH-KCF	McDonnell-Douglas MD-11	48560/578		Annie Romein	
☐ PH-KCG	McDonnell-Douglas MD-11	48561/585		Maria Callas	
☐ PH-KCH	McDonnell-Douglas MD-11	48562/591		Anna Pavlova	
☐ PH-KCI	McDonnell-Douglas MD-11	48563/593	ex PP-SPM	Mother Theresa	
☐ PH-KCK	McDonnell-Douglas MD-11	48564/612		Ingrid Bergman	

MARTINAIR — *Martinair (MP/MPH)* — *Amsterdam-Schiphol (AMS)*

☐ PH-MPP	Boeing 747-412BCF	24061/717	ex N733BA		stored MZJ
☐ PH-MPQ	Boeing 747-412BCF	24975/838	ex N223BA		stored MZJ
☐ PH-MPR	Boeing 747-412BCF	24226/809	ex N242BA		
☐ PH-MPS	Boeing 747-412BCF	24066/791	ex N728BA		stored MZJ
☐ PH-MCI	Boeing 767-31AER	25312/400		Prins Pieter-Christiaan	
☐ PH-MCJ	Boeing 767-33AER	25535/491	ex CS-TLM		
☐ PH-MCL	Boeing 767-31AER	26469/415		Koningin Beatrix	Retro c/s
☐ PH-MCM	Boeing 767-31AER	26470/416		Prins Floris	
☐ PH-MCP	McDonnell-Douglas MD-11CF	48616/577	ex N90187		
☐ PH-MCR	McDonnell-Douglas MD-11CF	48617/581		Cargo	
☐ PH-MCS	McDonnell-Douglas MD-11CF	48618/584			
☐ PH-MCT	McDonnell-Douglas MD-11CF	48629/486			
☐ PH-MCU	McDonnell-Douglas MD-11F	48757/606		Prinses Maxima	
☐ PH-MCW	McDonnell-Douglas MD-11CF	48788/632			
☐ PH-MCY	McDonnell-Douglas MD-11F	48445/460	ex N626FE		

ORANGE AIRCRAFT LEASING — *Orange (RNG)* — *Lelystad (LEY)*

☐ PH-RAQ	ATR 42-300	139	ex ZS-OSN		stored MST
☐ PH-RNG	Beech 1900D	UE-70	ex ZS-PZH		

QUICK AIRWAYS — *Quick (QAH)* — *Groningen-Eelde (GRQ)*

☐ PH-PTC	Piper PA-31-350 Chieftain	31-7852052	ex G-CLAN		

TRANSAVIA AIRLINES — *Transavia (HV/TRA)* — *Amsterdam-Schiphol (AMS)*

☐ PH-HSA	Boeing 737-8K2/W	34171/2950	ex N1786B		
☐ PH-HSB	Boeing 737-8K2/W	34172			on order
☐ PH-HSC	Boeing 737-8K2/W	34173			on order
☐ PH-HSW	Boeing 737-8K2/W	37160/2880			
☐ PH-HZB	Boeing 737-8K2/W	28374/57			
☐ PH-HZC	Boeing 737-8K2/W	28375/85	ex C-GHZC	City of Rotterdam	
☐ PH-HZD	Boeing 737-8K2/W	28376/252	ex N1786B		
☐ PH-HZE	Boeing 737-8K2/W	28377/277	ex N1786B	City of Rhodos	
☐ PH-HZF	Boeing 737-8K2/W	28378/291	ex N1796B		
☐ PH-HZG	Boeing 737-8K2/W	28379/498	ex N1786B		
☐ PH-HZI	Boeing 737-8K2/W	28380/524			
☐ PH-HZJ	Boeing 737-8K2/W	30389/549	ex N1796B		
☐ PH-HZK	Boeing 737-8K2/W	30390/555	ex N1786B		

☐ PH-HZL	Boeing 737-8K2/W	30391/814	ex N1786B		
☐ PH-HZM	Boeing 737-8K2/W	30392/833	ex N1786B		
☐ PH-HZN	Boeing 737-8K2/W	32943/1478			
☐ PH-HZO	Boeing 737-8K2/W	34169/2243			
☐ PH-HZW	Boeing 737-8K2/W	29345/1132	ex VT-SPZ	Jumbo Supermarket	
☐ PH-HZX	Boeing 737-8K2/W	28248/1126			
☐ PH-XRA	Boeing 737-7K2/W	30784/873	ex N1786B	Leontien van Moorsel	
☐ PH-XRB	Boeing 737-7K2/W	28256/1298			
☐ PH-XRD	Boeing 737-7K2/W	30659/1329			
☐ PH-XRE	Boeing 737-7K2/W	30668/1482			
☐ PH-XRV	Boeing 737-7K2/W	34170/1701			
☐ PH-XRW	Boeing 737-7K2/W	33465/1316			
☐ PH-XRX	Boeing 737-7K2/W	33464/1299		Stadprins Akkedeer	
☐ PH-XRY	Boeing 737-7K2/W	33463/1292			
☐ PH-XRZ	Boeing 737-7K2/W	33462/1278			
☐ PH-ZOM	Boeing 737-8HX/W	29677/2946	ex N1779B		

PJ- NETHERLANDS ANTILLES

DIVI DIVI AIR — *Divi divi (DVR)* — *Curacao (CUR)*

☐ PJ-BMV	Cessna 402B	402B0865	ex C-GCKB		
☐ PJ-DVA	Dornier 228-202	8100	ex ZK-VIR		
☐ PJ-SEA	Britten-Norman BN-2A-26 Islander	311	ex C-FFXS	FlyDivi.com titles	
☐ PJ-SKY	Britten-Norman BN-2A-26 Islander	885	ex C-FDYT		

DUTCH ANTILLES AIRLINES — *Curacao (CUR)*

☐ PJ-DAA	Fokker F.28-0100 (Fokker 100)	11310	ex D-AGPI	FlyDAE titles	
☐ PJ-DAB	Fokker F.28-0100 (Fokker 100)	11331	ex D-AGPM		

DUTCH ANTILLES EXPRESS — *BonExpress (9H/DNL)* — *Kralendijk (BON)*

☐ PJ-SLH	ATR 42-320	090	ex F-WQNN	all-white	
☐ PJ-XLM	ATR 42-320	378	ex PH-XLM		
☐ PJ-XLN	ATR 42-500	513	ex PH-XLN		

INSEL AIR INTERNATIONAL — *Inselair (7I/INC)* — *Curacao (CUR)*

☐ PJ-MDA	McDonnell-Douglas MD-83	49449/1354	ex 9A-CBJ		
☐ PJ-MDB	McDonnell-Douglas MD-82	48021/1078	ex N812NK	kulula colours	Lsd fr SFR
☐ PJ-MDC	McDonnell-Douglas MD-82	49434/1446	ex N434AG		
☐ PJ-MDD	McDonnell-Douglas MD-82	49972/1757	ex N972AG		
☐ PJ-	McDonnell-Douglas MD-82	49194/1130	ex N431LF		On Order
☐ PJ-VIA	Embraer EMB.110P1 Bandeirante	110387	ex E5-TAI		
☐ PJ-VIP	Embraer EMB.110P1 Bandeirante	110382	ex YV-249C	Curacao	

WINAIR — *Windward (WM/WIA)* — *St. Maarten (SXM)*

☐ PJ-AIW	Britten-Norman BN-2A-26 Islander	2038	ex C-GZKG		
☐ PJ-CIW	Britten-Norman BN-2B-26 Islander	876	ex C-GZTP		
☐ N181CS	de Havilland DHC-6 Twin Otter 200		181 ex 5Y-BEK		
☐ PJ-WIH	de Havilland DHC-6 Twin Otter 300	766	ex N304CH		
☐ PJ-WIL	de Havilland DHC-6 Twin Otter 300	358	ex C-FCSY		
☐ PJ-WIN	de Havilland DHC-6 Twin Otter 300	518	ex 5Y-SKA		

WINDWARD EXPRESS AIRWAYS — *St Maarten (SXM)*

☐ PJ-WEA	Britten-Norman BN-2A-27 Islander	659	ex N659CM		
☐ PJ-WEB	Britten-Norman BN-2A-26 Islander	2208	ex 8P-TAG		

PK- INDONESIA (Republic of Indonesia)

AIR MALEO

☐ PK-VKD	British Aerospace 146 Srs.100	E1104	ex RP-C5255		stored Clark
☐ PK-	British Aerospace 146 Srs.200	E2031	ex N66LN		on order

AIR MARK INDONESIA AVIATION — *Jakarta-Halim (HLP)*

☐ EW-262TK	Antonov An-32A	2103	ex ER-AWY		
☐ PK-AIY	Fokker F.27 Mk.050F (Fokker 50)	20227	ex OY-EBG		

AIRFAST INDONESIA — *Airfast (AFE)* — *Balikpapan/Jayapura (BPN/DJJ)*

☐ PK-OAT	Agusta-Bell 204B	3169	ex PK-LBC		
☐ PK-OAW	Beech 65-B80 Queen Air	LD-308	ex PK-JBF		
☐ PK-OAZ	Douglas DC-3	19623	ex PK-GDF		stored HLP

☐	PK-OBA	Bell 204B	2050	ex VH-UTW	
☐	PK-OCA	ITPN Bell 412	34009/NB09	ex PK-XFJ	
☐	PK-OCB	ITPN Bell 412	34007/NB07	ex PK-XFH	
☐	PK-OCC	CASA-Nurtanio C.212	50N/CC4-2-210	ex PK-NZJ	
☐	PK-OCE	Bell 212	30981	ex PK-VBZ	
☐	PK-OCJ	de Havilland DHC-6 Twin Otter 300	522	ex A6-MBM	
☐	PK-OCK	de Havilland DHC-6 Twin Otter 310	616	ex 9Q-CLE	all-white
☐	PK-OCI	de Havilland DHC-6 Twin Otter 300	689	ex N689WJ	Santigi
☐	PK-OCP	Boeing 737-27A	23794/1424	ex B-2625	
☐	PK-OCT	McDonnell-Douglas MD-82	49889/1761	ex N823RA	
☐	PK-OCU	McDonnell-Douglas MD-82	53017/1797	ex N824RA	
☐	PK-OCY	Beech 1900D	UE-393	ex N830CA	
☐	PK-OSP	British Aerospace 146 Srs.100	E1124	ex G-CBXY	Op for Metro TV

AVIASI UPATA RAKSA INDONESIA — *Jakarta-Halim (HLP)*

☐	PK-AFE	Pilatus PC-6/B2-H2 Turbo Porter	799	ex ST-0604
☐	PK-AGD	Cessna 402B	402B0398	ex VH-WNE
☐	PK-AGE	Cessna 402B	402B0046	ex L-4021
☐	PK-AGF	Cessna 402B	402B0047	ex L-4022

AVIASTAR MANDIRI — *Banjarmasin (BDJ)*

☐	PK-BRE	British Aerospace 146 Srs.200	E2139	ex C-GRNU	
☐	PK-BRF	British Aerospace 146 Srs.200	E2210	ex PK-LNJ	
☐	PK-BRM	CASA-Nurtanio C.212	91N/411	ex PK-VSD	
☐	PK-BRN	CASA-Nurtanio C.212	90N/410	ex PK-VSC	dam 11Jan07
☐	PK-BRP	de Havilland DHC-6 Twin Otter 300	356	ex N972SW	
☐	PK-BRQ	de Havilland DHC-6 Twin Otter 300	702	ex N702PV	
☐	PK-BRS	de Havilland DHC-6 Twin Otter 300	756	ex C-FOIJ	
☐	PK-BRT	de Havilland DHC-6 Twin Otter 300	380	ex C-GHBP	

BATAVIA AIR — *Batavia (7P/BTV)* — *Jakarta-Soekarno Hatta (CGK)*

☐	PK-YVA	Airbus A319-132	2648	ex D-AVWT	
☐	PK-YVC	Airbus A319-132	2660	ex D-AVWU	
☐	PK-	Airbus A319-132		ex D-AV	on order
☐	PK-YVD	Airbus A320-231	0449	ex G-JOEM	
☐	PK-YVE	Airbus A320-231	0441	ex B-22306	
☐	PK-YVF	Airbus A320-233	1676	ex N206CT	
☐	PK-YVG	Airbus A320-231	0168	ex N168BN	
☐	PK-YVI	Airbus A330-202	330	ex EI-EWR	
☐	PK-YVJ	Airbus A330-202	205	ex N271LF	
☐	PK-	Airbus A330-202	211	ex N272LF	on order
☐	PK-	ATR 72-212A		ex F-WW	on order
☐	PK-	ATR 72-212A		ex F-WW	on order
☐	PK-RIT	Boeing 737-4Y0	23979/1661	ex F-GLXK	
☐	PK-YTA	Boeing 737-266	21192/451	ex N201YT	
☐	PK-YTC	Boeing 737-2M8	22090/664	ex N220LS	
☐	PK-YTD	Boeing 737-2T4	22802/901	ex N203YT	stored CGK
☐	PK-YTE	Boeing 737-405	25303/2137	ex LN-BRP	
☐	PK-YTG	Boeing 737-2Q8	22453/748	ex N453LS	stored CGK
☐	PK-YTH	Boeing 737-204	20806/338	ex N806YT	stored CGK
☐	PK-YTI	Boeing 737-2L9	22407/698	ex N30AU	stored CGK
☐	PK-YTJ	Boeing 737-204	21693/541	ex N693YT	
☐	PK-YTK	Boeing 737-4Y0	24687/1865	ex TC-APT	
☐	PK-YTL	Boeing 737-2P5	23113/1010	ex N113YT	stored CGK
☐	PK-YTM	Boeing 737-3B7	22957/1127	ex N384US	stored CGK
☐	PK-YTN	Boeing 737-217 (AvAero 3)	22659/874	ex N986PG	
☐	PK-YTP	Boeing 737-4Y0	24345/1731	ex TC-APC	
☐	PK-YTQ	Boeing 737-281 (AvAero 3)	21767/585	ex N745AP	stored CGK
☐	PK-YTR	Boeing 737-281 (AvAero 3)	21766/583	ex N738AP	
☐	PK-YTS	Boeing 737-2T4 (AvAero 3)	22055/633	ex N739AA	stored
☐	PK-YTU	Boeing 737-3Y9	25604/2405	ex N999CZ	
☐	PK-YTV	Boeing 737-2M8 (AvAero 3)	21955/659	ex N742AP	
☐	PK-YTW	Boeing 737-3B7	23318/1234	ex N396US	stored CGK
☐	PK-YTX	Boeing 737-3B7	22953/1022	ex N374US	
☐	PK-YTY	Boeing 737-3B7	22955/1043	ex N376US	stored CGK
☐	PK-YTZ	Boeing 737-4Y0	23869/1639	ex N869AP	stored CGK
☐	PK-YVK	Boeing 737-301	23233/1200	ex N232AP	
☐	PK-YVL	Boeing 737-322	24638/1784	ex N373UA	
☐	PK-YVM	Boeing 737-322	24253/1650	ex N349UA	
☐	PK-YVN	Boeing 737-48E	25766/2543	ex N766SJ	
☐	PK-YVO	Boeing 737-4Y0	23868/1616	ex PK-RIH	
☐	PK-YVQ	Boeing 737-4S3	25594/2223	ex N594AB	
☐	PK-YVR	Boeing 737-4Y0	24494/1757	ex N494AC	
☐	PK-YVS	Boeing 737-4H6	27352/2624	ex HS-DDJ	
☐	PK-YVT	Boeing 737-4H6	27191/2676	ex HS-DDH	

☐ PK-YVU	Boeing 737-33A	24097/1741	ex N497AN		
☐ PK-YVV	Boeing 737-3B7	23316/1212	ex N394US		
☐ PK-YVW	Boeing 737-3B7	23319/1250	ex N397US		
☐ PK-YVX	Boeing 737-33A	24093/1727	ex N493AN		
☐ PK-YVY	Boeing 737-3B7	22952/1015	ex N373US		stored CGK
☐ PK-YVZ	Boeing 737-3B7	23317/1221	ex N395US		
☐ PK-YCM	Fokker F.28 Fellowship 4000	11168	ex PK-KFD		stored CGK

CARDIG AIR

☐ PK-BBA	Boeing 737-347SF	23597/1287	ex N311WA
☐ PK-BBB	Boeing 737-347SF	23598/1289	ex N312WA

CITILINK — Jakarta-Halim (HLP)

☐ PK-GHV	Boeing 737-3Y0	24914/2054	ex HA-LEF	stored CGK

DERAYA AIR TAXI — Deraya (DRY) — Jakarta-Halim (HLP)

☐ PK-DCC	Cessna 402C II	402C0250	ex N444DS	
☐ PK-DCJ	Cessna 402B	402B0615	ex N3759C	
☐ PK-DCO	CASA-Nurtanio C.212-A4	13N/A4-11-93	ex PK-XCL	stored HLP
☐ PK-DCP	CASA-Nurtanio C.212-A4	14N/A4-11-101	ex PK-XCM	
☐ PK-DCQ	CASA-Nurtanio C.212-A4	16N/A4-13-112	ex PK-XCO	
☐ PK-DCZ	Cessna 402B	402B0890	ex N5203J	
☐ PK-DGA	British Aerospace ATP(F)	2026	ex G-JEMD	
☐ PK-DGI	British Aerospace ATP(F)	2027	ex G-JEME	
☐ PK-DSB	Short SD.3-30	SH3056	ex DQ-SUN	
☐ PK-DSF	Short SC.7 Skyvan 3	SH1881	ex AF-702	
☐ PK-DSH	Short SD.3-60	SH3757	ex N350TA	
☐ PK-DSR	Short SD.3-30	SH3060	ex DQ-FIJ	
☐ PK-DSS	Short SD.3-60	SH3743	ex N743RW	
☐ PK-DYR	Piper PA-31T Cheyenne II	31T-7820054	ex VH-MWT	
☐ PK-LPN	Cessna U206F Stationair II	U20602789	ex PK-UFO	

DIRGANTARA AIR SERVICE — Dirgantara (AW/DIR) — Jakarta-Halim/Bandarmasin/Pontianak (HLP/BDJ/PNK)

☐ PK-VIB	Britten-Norman BN-2A-21 Islander	545	ex PK-TRC
☐ PK-VIM	Britten-Norman BN-2A-3 Islander	634	ex 9V-BEB
☐ PK-VIN	Britten-Norman BN-2A-3 Islander	351	ex G-BBJA
☐ PK-VIS	Britten-Norman BN-2A-21 Islander	485	ex G-BEGB
☐ PK-VIU	Britten-Norman BN-2A-21 Islander	781	ex PK-KNH
☐ PK-VIW	Britten-Norman BN-2A-21 Islander	2026	ex G-BIPD
☐ PK-VIX	Britten-Norman BN-2A-21 Islander	2027	ex G-BIUF
☐ PK-VIY	Britten-Norman BN-2A-21 Islander	2133	ex G-BJOR
☐ PK-VSA	CASA-Nurtanio C.212	87N/CC4-38-282	ex PK-HJA
☐ PK-VSB	CASA-Nurtanio C.212	88N/CC4-39-283	ex PK-HJB
☐ PK-VSE	CASA-Nurtanio C.212	92N/4-412	ex PK-HJE
☐ PK-VSF	CASA Nurtanio C.212	93N/4-413	ex PK-HJI
☐ PK-VSN	CASA-Nurtanio C.212	22N/A4-19-136	ex PK-XCU
☐ PK-VMB	Gippsland GA-8 Airvan	GA8-03-031	ex VH-BOI
☐ PK-VMC	Gippsland GA-8 Airvan	GA8-03-033	ex VH-BNL
☐ PK-VMD	Gippsland GA-8 Airvan	GA8-03-041	ex VH-FDR
☐ PK-VME	Gippsland GA-8 Airvan	GA8-03-042	ex VH-JYN

EASTINDO — Jakarta-Halim (HLP)

☐ PK-RGA	Beech 1900D	UE-376	ex N31425
☐ PK-RGE	Fokker F.28-0100 (Fokker 100)	11445	ex F-WQVP
☐ PK-RGI	Beech B200 Super King Air	BB-1732	ex N23268
☐ PK-RGP	Britten-Norman BN-2B-20 Islander	2249	ex PK-HNG

GADING SARI AVIATION SERVICES

☐ 9M-PMM	Boeing 737-205C	20458/278	ex RP-C2906	Freighter	Lsd fr TSE

GARUDA INDONESIA — Indonesia (GA/GIA) — Jakarta-Soekarno Hatta (CGK)

☐ PK-GPA	Airbus A330-341	138	ex F-WWKH	
☐ PK-GPC	Airbus A330-341	140	ex F-WWKU	
☐ PK-GPD	Airbus A330-341	144	ex F-WWKG	for IBE
☐ PK-GPE	Airbus A330-341	148	ex F-WWKD	
☐ PK-GPF	Airbus A330-341	153	ex F-WWKY	
☐ PK-GPG	Airbus A330-341	165	ex F-WWKL	
☐ PK-GPH	Airbus A330-243	1020	ex F-WWYL	
☐ PK-GPI	Airbus A330-243	1052	ex F-WWKQ	
☐ PK-GPJ	Airbus A330-243	988	ex F-WWKI	

☐ PK-GPK	Airbus A330-243	1028	ex F-WWYZ	
☐ PK-GCA	Boeing 737-3L9	24569/1775	ex N569AG	
☐ PK-GCC	Boeing 737-3Q8	28200/2854	ex 9M-AAC	
☐ PK-GEE	Boeing 737-8CX/W	32361/1098	ex TC-IEA	
☐ PK-GEF	Boeing 737-8CX/W	32363/1139	ex N236GX	
☐ PK-GEG	Boeing 737-83N/W	30033/1149	ex N323TZ	
☐ PK-GEH	Boeing 737-83N/W	30643/1106	ex N319TZ	
☐ PK-GEI	Boeing 737-86N/W	29883/1083	ex N29883	
☐ PK-GEJ	Boeing 737-86N/W	33003/1121	ex G-XLAG	
☐ PK-GEK	Boeing 737-86J/W	30568/793	ex N568MQ	
☐ PK-GEL	Boeing 737-8AS/W	29927/727	ex EI-CSN	
☐ PK-GEM	Boeing 737-8AS/W	29928/735	ex EI-CSO	
☐ PK-GEN	Boeing 737-8AS/W	29929/753	ex EI-CSP	
☐ PK-GEO	Boeing 737-8AS/W	29930/757	ex EI-CSQ	
☐ PK-GEP	Boeing 737-8AS/W	29931/1020	ex EI-CSR	
☐ PK-GEQ	Boeing 737-86N/W	32659/1709	ex EC-JEX	
☐ PK-GER	Boeing 737-86J/W	30876/759	ex D-ABAD	
☐ PK-GGA	Boeing 737-5U3	28726/2920		
☐ PK-GGC	Boeing 737-5U3	28727/2937	ex N1786B	
☐ PK-GGD	Boeing 737-5U3	28728/2938	ex N1786B	
☐ PK-GGE	Boeing 737-5U3	28729/2950	ex N60436	
☐ PK-GGF	Boeing 737-5U3	28730/2952		
☐ PK-GGG	Boeing 737-3U3	28731/2949		
☐ PK-GGN	Boeing 737-3U3	28735/3029	ex N5573K	
☐ PK-GGO	Boeing 737-3U3	28736/3032	ex N3134C	
☐ PK-GGP	Boeing 737-3U3	28737/3037	ex N1020L	
☐ PK-GGQ	Boeing 737-3U3	28739/3064	ex N1024A	
☐ PK-GGR	Boeing 737-3U3	28741/3079	ex N1026G	
☐ PK-GGV	Boeing 737-3Q8	26293/2541	ex N318FL	
☐ PK-GHQ	Boeing 737-34S	29108/2983	ex (PK-GHA)	
☐ PK-GHR	Boeing 737-34S	29109/3001	ex (PK-GHC)	
☐ PK-GHW	Boeing 737-3M8	25039/2007	ex N303FL	
☐ PK-GHX	Boeing 737-3L9	26440/2234		
☐ PK-GMA	Boeing 737-8U3/W	30151/2942	ex N1784B	
☐ PK-GMC	Boeing 737-8U3/W	30155/3081	ex N1786B	
☐ PK-GMD	Boeing 737-8U3/W	30156/3100		
☐ PK-GME	Boeing 737-8U3/W	30157/3123		
☐ PK-GMF	Boeing 737-8U3/W	30140/3129		
☐ PK-GMG	Boeing 737-8U3/W	30141/3166		on order
☐ PK-GMH	Boeing 737-8U3/W	30142		on order
☐ PK-GMI	Boeing 737-8U3/W	31763		on order
☐ PK-GMJ	Boeing 737-8U3/W	30144		on order
☐ PK-GMK	Boeing 737-8U3/W	30145		on order
☐ PK-GML	Boeing 737-8U3/W	30146		on order
☐ PK-GMM	Boeing 737-8U3/W	30147		on order
☐ PK-GWK	Boeing 737-4U3	25713/2531		
☐ PK-GWL	Boeing 737-4U3	25714/2535	ex N6067B	
☐ PK-GWM	Boeing 737-4U3	25715/2537		
☐ PK-GWN	Boeing 737-4U3	25716/2540		
☐ PK-GWO	Boeing 737-4U3	25717/2546		
☐ PK-GWP	Boeing 737-4U3	25718/2548		
☐ PK-GWQ	Boeing 737-4U3	25719/2549		
☐ PK-GWT	Boeing 737-4K5	26316/2711	ex D-AHLG	
☐ PK-GWU	Boeing 737-4Q8	24708/2076	ex N708KS	
☐ PK-GZA	Boeing 737-497	25663/2382	ex N663AL	
☐ PK-GZH	Boeing 737-4M0	29203/3049	ex VP-BAJ	
☐ PK-GZI	Boeing 737-4M0	29204/3051	ex VP-BAL	
☐ PK-GZJ	Boeing 737-4M0	29205/3056	ex VP-BAM	
☐ PK-GZK	Boeing 737-4M0	29206/3058	ex VP-BAN	
☐ PK-GZL	Boeing 737-4M0	29207/3078	ex VP-BAO	
☐ PK-GZM	Boeing 737-4M0	29208/3081	ex VP-BAP	
☐ PK-GZN	Boeing 737-4M0	29209/3087	ex VP-BAQ	
☐ PK-GZO	Boeing 737-4M0	29210/3091	ex VP-BAR	
☐ PK-GZP	Boeing 737-46Q	28661/2910	ex EI-CXI	
☐ PK-GZQ	Boeing 737-4S3	25134/2083	ex N534AG	
☐ PK-GSG	Boeing 747-4U3	25704/1011		
☐ PK-GSH	Boeing 747-4U3	25705/1029	ex N6038E	
☐ PK-GSI	Boeing 747-441	24956/917	ex N791LF	
☐ PK-	Boeing 777-3U3ER			on order
☐ PK-	Boeing 777-3U3ER			on order
☐ PK-	Boeing 777-3U3ER			on order
☐ PK-	Boeing 777-3U3ER			on order

GATARI AIR SERVICE — *Gatari (GHS)* — *Jakarta-Halim (HLP)*

☐ PK-HMB	Bell 212	30502	ex PK-DBY	
☐ PK-HMM	Bell 212	30958	ex PK-PGF	
☐ PK-HNH	Fokker F.28 Fellowship 4000	11218	ex PK-GQB	
☐ PK-HNJ	Fokker F.28 Fellowship 3000RC	11134	ex PK-GFW	stored HLP
☐ PK-HNN	Fokker F.28 Fellowship 3000R	11119	ex PK-GFS	stored HLP

☐ PK-HNP	Fokker F.28 Fellowship 4000	11216	ex PK-GKZ		stored HLP
☐ PK-HNS	ATR 42-500	601	ex PK-TSQ		
☐ PK-HNY	Kawasaki/MBB BK-117B-1	1052	ex JA6614		

GT AIR — **Jakarta-Halim (HLP)**

☐ PK-LTP	Fokker F.27 Friendship 500	10398	ex PH-FNW	Syaloomstored HLP	
☐ PK-LTQ	Fokker F.27 Friendship 500	10389/10528	ex HB-ILQ	stored HLP	
☐ PK-LTT	Dornier 28D-1 Skyservant	4031	ex PK-VRB		
☐ PK-LTU	Dornier 28D-1 Skyservant	4026	ex PK-VRA		
☐ PK-LTY	de Havilland DHC-6 Twin Otter 300	831	ex B-3512	Anugrah	

INDONESIA AIR TRANSPORT — **Intra (IDA)** — **Jakarta-Halim (HLP)**

☐ PK-TRD	Aérospatiale SA365C Dauphin 2	5058	ex N3606Q		
☐ PK-TRE	Aérospatiale SA365C Dauphin 2	5004	ex N3604G		
☐ PK-TSH	Aérospatiale SA365N Dauphin 2	6008	ex N801BA		
☐ PK-TSI	Aérospatiale SA365N Dauphin 2	6026	ex N87SV		
☐ PK-TSW	Aérospatiale AS365N2 Dauphin 2	6470	ex HL9204		
☐ PK-TSX	Aérospatiale AS365N2 Dauphin 2	6472	ex HL9206		
☐ PK-TRU	BAC One-Eleven 492GM	262	ex G-BLDH		stored AOR
☐ PK-TRW	Beech 1900D	UE-177	ex N3237H		
☐ PK-TRX	Beech 1900D	UE-186	ex N3233J		
☐ PK-TSF	Bell 212	30974	ex N27664		
☐ PK-TSG	Bell 212	30753	ex N81FC		
☐ PK-TSJ	Fokker F.27 Friendship 500RFC	10525	ex N702A		
☐ PK-TSO	Fokker F.27 Mk.050 (Fokker 50)	20186	ex PH-ZDB		
☐ PK-TSP	Fokker F.27 Mk.050 (Fokker 50)	20316	ex PK-TWJ		
☐ PK-TST	BAC One-Eleven 423ET	118	ex G-BEJM		VIP stored AOR
☐ PK-TSY	ATR 42-300	118	ex LY-ARY		
☐ PK-TSZ	ATR 42-300	059	ex LY-ARJ		

INDONESIA AIRASIA — **Wagon Air (QZ/AWQ)** — **Jakarta-Soekarno Hatta (CGK)**

☐ PK-AXA	Airbus A320-216	3610	ex F-WWIG		
☐ PK-AXC	Airbus A320-216	3648	ex F-WWBZ		
☐ PK-AXE	Airbus A320-216	3715	ex F-WWIZ		
☐ PK-AXF	Airbus A320-216	3765	ex F-WWDO		
☐ PK-AXG	Airbus A320-216	3813	ex F-WWIE		
☐ PK-AXH	Airbus A320-216	3875	ex F-WWII		
☐ PK-AXI	Airbus A320-216	3963	ex F-WWID		
☐ PK-AXJ	Airbus A320-214	4035	ex F-WWIJ		
☐ PK-AXK	Airbus A320-214	4147	ex F-WWBC		
☐ PK-AWG	Boeing 737-3L9	27061/2347	ex 9M-AAG		Lsd fr AXM
☐ PK-AWN	Boeing 737-3L9	26442/2277	ex 9M-AED		
☐ PK-AWO	Boeing 737-322	24659/1836	ex 9M-AEA		
☐ PK-AWP	Boeing 737-3Y0	24905/2001	ex 9M-AAD		
☐ PK-AWQ	Boeing 737-3B7	23376/1308	ex N947WP		Lsd fr AXM
☐ PK-AWT	Boeing 737-3B7	23345/1170	ex N304WA		Lsd fr AXM
☐ PK-AWU	Boeing 737-301	23257/1124	ex 9M-AAU		
☐ PK-AWX	Boeing 737-3Y0	24547/1813	ex 9M-AEC		

ISLAND SEAPLANES — **Bali-Benoa Harbour**

☐ PK-SDL	de Havilland DHC-2 Beaver	413	ex C-GIPL	Floatplane	

JATAYU AIR — **Jatayu (VJ/JTY)** — **Jakarta-Soekarno Hatta (CGK)**

☐ PK-JAC	Boeing 727-232 (FedEx 3)	21587/1492	ex PK-RIZ		stored CGK
☐ PK-JAG	Boeing 727-232 (FedEx 3)	21306/1270	ex PK-MBW		
☐ PK-JGN	Boeing 727-223 (Raisbeck 3)	21384/1328	ex N872AA		stored CGK
☐ PK-JGP	Boeing 737-204 (Nordam 3)	22364/696	ex PK-AIG		stored CGK
☐ PK-JGS	Boeing 737-222	19949/197	ex N199NA		stored PCB
☐ PK-JGW	Boeing 737-2N7	21226/458	ex N119SW		stored MES
☐ PK-LIA	Boeing 737-2P5	21440/502	ex N440GB		stored CGK

KALSTAR — **Serpong**

☐ PK-KSE	ATR 42-320	415	ex N415AN		
☐ PK-KSI	ATR 42-320	348	ex N38AN		

KARTIKA AIRLINES — **Kartika (3Y/KAE)** — **Jakarta-Soekarno Hatta (CGK)**

☐ PK-KAD	Boeing 737-284	22338/691	ex PK-IJQ		
☐ PK-KAO	Boeing 737-284	22339/692	ex PK-IJP		Lsd fr Aero Nusantara

KURA KURA AVIATION — Semarang (SRG)

☐ PK-WLW	Cessna 402B	402B0555	ex VH-ASL
☐ PK-WLX	Cessna 402B	402B0549	ex VH-AAP
☐ PK-WLY	Cessna 402B	402B0541	ex VH-PEK

LION AIRLINES — Lion Inter (JT/LNI) — Jakarta-Soekarno Hatta (CGK)

☐ PK-LIF	Boeing 737-4Y0	24467/1733	ex PK-MBL	
☐ PK-LIG	Boeing 737-4Y0	24513/1779	ex PK-MBM	stored CGK
☐ PK-LIH	Boeing 737-4Y0	24520/1803	ex HL7260	
☐ PK-LII	Boeing 737-46B	24123/1663	ex EC-GRX	
☐ PK-LIQ	Boeing 737-4Y0	24911/2033	ex OK-TVS	
☐ PK-LIR	Boeing 737-4Y0	24692/1963	ex EC-IRA	
☐ PK-LIS	Boeing 737-4Y0	24693/1972	ex OK-WGG	
☐ PK-LIT	Boeing 737-4Y0	24512/1777	ex PK-GWV	
☐ PK-LIU	Boeing 737-3G7	23218/1076	ex N380WL	
☐ PK-LIV	Boeing 737-3G7	23219/1090	ex N390WL	
☐ PK-LIW	Boeing 737-4Y0	24684/1841	ex EI-CVN	
☐ PK-LFF	Boeing 737-9GPER/W	35679/2093	ex N6055X	
☐ PK-LFG	Boeing 737-9GPER/W	35680/1981	ex N900ER	
☐ PK-LFH	Boeing 737-9GPER/W	35710/2285	ex N1786B	
☐ PK-LFI	Boeing 737-9GPER/W	35711/2319	ex N1780B	
☐ PK-LFJ	Boeing 737-9GPER/W	35712/2349	ex (PK-LAJ)	
☐ PK-LFK	Boeing 737-9GPER/W	35713/2437	ex N1781B	
☐ PK-LFL	Boeing 737-9GPER/W	35714/2461	ex (PK-LAL)	
☐ PK-LFM	Boeing 737-9GPER/W	35715/2485	ex N1786B	
☐ PK-LFO	Boeing 737-9GPER/W	35716/2504	ex N1786B	
☐ PK-LFP	Boeing 737-9GPER/W	35717/2455		
☐ PK-LFQ	Boeing 737-9GPER/W	35718/2670		
☐ PK-LFR	Boeing 737-9GPER/W	35719/2694		
☐ PK-LFS	Boeing 737-9GPER/W	35720/2756		
☐ PK-LFT	Boeing 737-9GPER/W	35721/2793		
☐ PK-LFU	Boeing 737-9GPER/W	35722/2836	ex N1784B	
☐ PK-LFV	Boeing 737-9GPER/W	35723/2848	ex N1787B	
☐ PK-LFW	Boeing 737-9GPER/W	35724/2879		
☐ PK-LFY	Boeing 737-9GPER/W	35725/2897	ex N1786B	
☐ PK-LFZ	Boeing 737-9GPER/W	35726/2904		
☐ PK-LGF	Boeing 737-96NER/W	35223/2559	ex N223MT	
☐ PK-LGG	Boeing 737-96NER/W	35225/2590	ex N225MT	
☐ PK-LGH	Boeing 737-96NER/W	35227/2621	ex G-XLAR	
☐ PK-LGI	Boeing 737-96NER/W	36539/2596	ex G-XLAP	
☐ PK-LGJ	Boeing 737-9GPER/W	35727/2934	ex N1796B	
☐ PK-LGK	Boeing 737-9GPER/W	35728/2984	ex N1786B	
☐ PK-LGL	Boeing 737-9GPER/W	35729/3008		
☐ PK-LGM	Boeing 737-9GPER/W	35730/3075		
☐ PK-LGO	Boeing 737-9GPER/W	35731/3093		
☐ PK-LGP	Boeing 737-9GPER/W	35732/3111		
☐ PK-LGQ	Boeing 737-9GPER/W	35733/3135		
☐ PK-LGR	Boeing 737-9GPER/W	35734/3153		
☐ PK-LGS	Boeing 737-9GPER/W	35735		on order
☐ PK-LGT	Boeing 737-9GPER/W	35736		on order
☐ PK-LGU	Boeing 737-9GPER/W	35737		on order
☐ PK-LGV	Boeing 737-9GPER/W	37268		on order
☐ PK-LGW	Boeing 737-9GPER/W	37269		on order
☐ PK-LGY	Boeing 737-9GPER/W	37270		on order
☐ PK-LGZ	Boeing 737-9GPER/W	37271		on order
☐ PK-	Boeing 737-9GPER/W			on order
☐ PK-	Boeing 737-9GPER/W			on order
☐ PK-	Boeing 737-9GPER/W			on order
☐ PK-	Boeing 737-9GPER/W			on order
☐ PK-	Boeing 737-9GPER/W			on order
☐ PK-LHF	Boeing 747-412	24063/736	ex N240BA	
☐ PK-LHG	Boeing 747-412	24065/761	ex N465BB	
☐ PK-LMI	McDonnell-Douglas MD-82	49263/1163	ex N809NY	
☐ PK-LMM	McDonnell-Douglas MD-82	48069/1032	ex N480CT	stored CGK
☐ PK-LMO	McDonnell-Douglas MD-82	49373/1201	ex N493AP	
☐ PK-LMR	McDonnell-Douglas MD-82	49116/1061	ex N16887	stored CGK
☐ PK-LMW	McDonnell-Douglas MD-82	49443/1291	ex N830US	dbr 04Mar06?
☐ PK-LMY	McDonnell-Douglas MD-82	49250/1188	ex N17812	Lsd UBA
☐ PK-LIK	McDonnell-Douglas MD-90-30	53570/2181	ex N904RA	
☐ PK-LIL	McDonnell-Douglas MD-90-30	53573/2182	ex N905RA	
☐ PK-LIM	McDonnell-Douglas MD-90-30	53489/2129	ex N901RA	
☐ PK-LIO	McDonnell-Douglas MD-90-30	53490/2133	ex N902RA	
☐ PK-LIP	McDonnell-Douglas MD-90-30	53551/2144	ex N903RA	

MANDALA AIRLINES — Mandala (RI/MDL) — Jakarta-Soekarno Hatta (CGK)

	Type	c/n	Previous		Notes
☐ PK-RMH	Airbus A319-132	2797	ex N521NK		
☐ PK-RMI	Airbus A319-132	2784	ex N520NK		
☐ PK-RMJ	Airbus A319-132	1492	ex VT-WAC		
☐ PK-RMA	Airbus A320-211	0279	ex EI-DOZ		
☐ PK-RMC	Airbus A320-212	0391	ex EI-DIJ		
☐ PK-RME	Airbus A320-232	3264	ex F-WWBR		
☐ PK-RMG	Airbus A320-232	3330	ex F-WWIY		
☐ PK-RMK	Airbus A320-232	3524	ex VT-DNU		
☐ PK-RML	Airbus A320-232	3543	ex VT-DNT		
☐ PK-RIA	Boeing 737-2P6	21357/497	ex LV-WFX		
☐ PK-RII	Boeing 737-2E7	22876/922	ex G-BLDE	gold colours	stored SUB
☐ PK-RIJ	Boeing 737-210	21820/578	ex G-BKNH		stored
☐ PK-RIL	Boeing 737-230	22137/788	ex D-ABHL		
☐ PK-RIN	Boeing 737-2H6	21732/559	ex PK-KJM		stored CGK
☐ PK-RIQ	Boeing 737-291	23023/957	ex TF-ABI		stored CGK
☐ PK-RIY	Boeing 727-232 (FedEx 3)	21585/1479	ex N525DA		

MANUNGGAL AIR — Jakarta-Halim (HLP)

	Type	c/n	Previous	Notes
☐ PK-VTA	British Aerospace 146 Srs.100	E1015	ex N146AP	
☐ PK-VTM	British Aerospace 146 Srs.100	E1009	ex RP-C2999	
☐ PK-VTR	Aérospatiale/MBB Transall C-160NG	233	ex PK-PTO	stored HLP
☐ PK-VTS	Aérospatiale/MBB Transall C-160P	207	ex PK-PTY	stored HLP

MEGANTARA AIR — (MKE) — Jakarta-Soekarno Hatta (CGK)

	Type	c/n	Previous
☐ PK-TMA	Boeing 727-247F (FedEx 3)	21697/1471	ex 9M-TGE
☐ PK-TME	Boeing 737-209F (AvAero 3)	24197/1581	ex 9M-PMW

MERPATI NUSANTARA AIRLINES — Merpati (MZ/MNA) — Jakarta-Soekarno Hatta/Surabaya (CGK/SUB)

	Type	c/n	Previous	Name	Notes
☐ PK-MZA	CAIC MA60	0407			
☐ PK-MZB	CAIC MA60	0406			
☐ PK-MZC	CAIC MA60	0409			
☐ PK-MZD	CAIC MA60	0410			on order
☐ PK-MZE	CAIC MA60	0501			on order
☐ PK-MZF	CAIC MA60	0502			on order
☐ PK-MZG	CAIC MA60	0505			on order
☐ PK-MZI	CAIC MA60	0506			on order
☐ PK-MZJ	CAIC MA60	0601			on order
☐ PK-MZK	CAIC MA60	0602			on order
☐ PK-MZL	CAIC MA60	0603			on order
☐ PK-MZM	CAIC MA60	0604			on order
☐ PK-MBC	Boeing 737-230	22129/754	ex D-ABFY		stored SUB
☐ PK-MBE	Boeing 737-230	22142/797	ex D-ABHS	Batanta	
☐ PK-MBH	Boeing 737-2S3	22279/650	ex N279AD		
☐ PK-MBJ	Boeing 737-2U4	22576/761	ex N576DF		
☐ PK-MBN	Boeing 737-377	24304/1622	ex S2-AEA		
☐ PK-MBO	Boeing 737-377	24305/1641	ex S2-AEB		
☐ PK-MBP	Boeing 737-33A	23632/1344	ex N173AW		
☐ PK-MBQ	Boeing 737-217 (AvAero 3)	22260/784	ex N285TR		
☐ PK-MBS	Boeing 737-217 (AvAero 3)	22342/810	ex N288TR		stored SUB
☐ PK-MBU	Boeing 737-217 (AvAero 3)	22259/771	ex N284TR		stored SUB
☐ PK-MBX	Boeing 737-228 (Nordam 3)	23005/943	ex N253TR		stored SUB
☐ PK-MBY	Boeing 737-228 (Nordam 3)	23004/941	ex N234TR		stored SUB
☐ PK-MBZ	Boeing 737-228 (Nordam 3)	23007/948	ex N237TR		stored SUB
☐ PK-MDC	Boeing 737-2L9	21685	ex PK-RIF		
☐ PK-MDD	Boeing 737-2S3	22278/646	ex PK-RIC		
☐ PK-MDF	Boeing 737-3S1	24856/1911	ex PK-AWS		
☐ PK-MDG	Boeing 737-3Q8	26296/2581	ex N296AG		
☐ PK-MDH	Boeing 737-301	23932/1554	ex N587US		
☐ PK-MDJ	Boeing 737-301	23931/1552	ex N586US		
☐ PK-MDK	Boeing 737-3B7	23858/1509	ex N140CT		
☐ PK-MDO	Boeing 737-4Q8	24069/1635	ex N240AD		
☐ PK-MDQ	Boeing 737-3Q8	24300/1666	ex N243AD		
☐ PK-MDZ	Boeing 737-4Q8	26280/2239	ex N129AC		
☐ PK-	Boeing 737-322	24660/1838	ex N385UA		
☐ PK-NCH	CASA-Nurtanio C.212-AB4	30N/AB4-2-173	ex PK-XAD	Weh	
☐ PK-NCN	CASA-Nurtanio C.212-AB4	36N/AB4-8-191	ex PK-XAJ	Seribu	
☐ PK-NCU	CASA-Nurtanio C.212-C4	74N/CC4-24-254	ex PK-XDW	Pantar	
☐ PK-NCV	CASA-Nurtanio C.212-C4	75N/CC4-26-255	ex PK-XDX	Misool	
☐ PK-NCX	CASA-Nurtanio C.212-C4	77N/CC4-28-257	ex PK-XDZ	Batudata	
☐ PK-NCZ	CASA-Nurtanio C.212-C4	79N/CC4-30-274	ex PK-XEC	Tanah Massa	
☐ PK-MNC	CASA-Nurtanio CN-235	5/N002	ex PK-XND	Wokam	

☐ PK-MND	CASA-Nurtanio CN-235	7/N003	ex PK-XNE	Sermata	stored SUB
☐ PK-MNE	CASA-Nurtanio CN-235	9/N004	ex PK-XNF	Letiall-white	
☐ PK-MNF	CASA-Nurtanio CN-235-200	10/N005	ex PK-XNG	Wowoni	stored SUB
☐ PK-MNG	CASA-Nurtanio CN-235	14/N006	ex PK-XNH	Timorall-white	
☐ PK-MNI	CASA-Nurtanio CN-235	16/N007	ex PK-XNI	Babarall-white	
☐ PK-MNJ	CASA-Nurtanio CN-235	19/N009	ex PK-XNK	Damar	stored SUB
☐ PK-MNK	CASA-Nurtanio CN-235	20/N010	ex PK-XNL	Kobroor	
☐ PK-MNM	CASA-Nurtanio CN-235	26/N012	ex PK-XNN	Moa	
☐ PK-MNP	CASA-Nurtanio CN-235	30/N015	ex PK-XNQ	Kaledupo	
☐ PK-NUH	de Havilland DHC-6 Twin Otter 300	383		Natuna	
☐ PK-NUO	de Havilland DHC-6 Twin Otter 300	487		Singkep	stored BIK
☐ PK-NUR	de Havilland DHC-6 Twin Otter 300	484		Muna	stored BIK
☐ PK-NUS	de Havilland DHC-6 Twin Otter 300	481		Peleng	
☐ PK-NUV	de Havilland DHC-6 Twin Otter 300	472		Tanimbar	
☐ PK-NUZ	de Havilland DHC-6 Twin Otter 300	443	ex PK-NUM	Alor	
☐ PK-NVA	de Havilland DHC-6 Twin Otter 300	551	ex VH-UQY		
☐ PK-MFF	Fokker F.27 Friendship 500	10551	ex ZK-NFA	Tanah Bela	stored SUB
☐ PK-MFG	Fokker F.27 Friendship 500	10552	ex ZK-NFB	Lingga	stored SUB
☐ PK-MFJ	Fokker F.27 Friendship 500	10598	ex ZK-NFE	Adonara	stored SUB
☐ PK-MFK	Fokker F.27 Friendship 500	10607	ex ZK-NFF	Wangi-Wangi	stored SUB
☐ PK-MFQ	Fokker F.27 Friendship 500	10623	ex PK-GRF	Bintan	stored SUB
☐ PK-MFV	Fokker F.27 Friendship 500	10625	ex PK-GRH	Kabia	stored SUB
☐ PK-MFW	Fokker F.27 Friendship 500	10626	ex PK-GRI	Maja	stored SUB
☐ PK-MFY	Fokker F.27 Friendship 500	10629	ex PK-GRK	Halmahera	
☐ PK-MJA	Fokker F.28-0100 (Fokker 100)	11453	ex PH-MXO	Bawal	stored SUB
☐ PK-MJC	Fokker F.28-0100 (Fokker 100)	11463	ex PH-EZV	Sabu	
☐ PK-MJD	Fokker F.28-0100 (Fokker 100)	11474	ex PH-EZW	Rupat	

NUSANTARA AIR CHARTER — *Jakarta-Halim (HLP)*

☐ PK-JKC	British Aerospace 146 Srs.200	E2113	ex SE-DRN
☐ PK-JKM	Fokker F.28 Fellowship 4000	11116	ex PK-YHK
☐ PK-JKW	British Aerospace 146 Srs.200	E2204	ex PK-LNI

PELITA AIR — *Pelita (6D/PAS)* — *Jakarta-Halim/Pondok Cabe (HLP/PCB)*

☐ PK-PDT	Aérospatiale SA.330G Puma	1264	ex F-WTNB		
☐ PK-PDY	Aérospatiale SA.330G Puma	1160			
☐ PK-PEI	Aérospatiale SA.330J Puma	1299			
☐ PK-PEK	Aérospatiale SA.330G Puma	1283			
☐ PK-PEO	Aérospatiale SA.330J Puma	1261			
☐ PK-PHW	Aérospatiale SA.330G Puma	1082	ex F-OCRQ		
☐ PK-PUG	Aérospatiale AS.332C	NSP2/2020	ex PK-XSB		
☐ PK-PUH	Aérospatiale AS.332C	NSP3/2021	ex PK-XSC		
☐ PK-PCN	CASA-Nurtanio C.212-A4	56N/CC4-8-216	ex PK-XDE		stored PCB
☐ PK-PCO	CASA-Nurtanio C.212-A4	55N/CC4-8-215	ex PK-XDD		
☐ PK-PCP	CASA-Nurtanio C.212-A4	48N/AB4-20-208	ex PK-XAV		
☐ PK-PCQ	CASA-Nurtanio C.212-A4	47N/AB4-18-207	ex PK-XDE		stored PCB
☐ PK-PCR	CASA-Nurtanio C.212-A4	46N/AB4-18-206	ex PK-XAT		
☐ PK-PCS	CASA-Nurtanio C.212-A4	45N/AB4-17-205	ex PK-XAS		
☐ PK-PCT	CASA-Nurtanio C.212-A4	44N/AB4-16-204	ex PK-XAR		
☐ PK-PCU	CASA-Nurtanio C.212-A4	43N/AB4-15-203	ex PK-XAQ		
☐ PK-PKT	de Havilland DHC-7-110	54	ex C-FYXV		
☐ PK-PSV	de Havilland DHC-7-103	105	ex C-GFOD		
☐ PK-PSW	de Havilland DHC-7-103	100	ex C-GFCF		
☐ PK-PSX	de Havilland DHC-7-103	94	ex C-GFYI		
☐ PK-PSY	de Havilland DHC-7-103	86	ex C-GFUM		
☐ PK-PSZ	de Havilland DHC-7-103	75	ex C-GFCF		
☐ PK-PFZ	Fokker F.28-0100 (Fokker 100)	11486	ex PH-ZFA		
☐ PK-PJK	Fokker F.28 Fellowship 4000	11192	ex PH-EXW	Lengguru	stored PCB
☐ PK-PJL	Fokker F.28 Fellowship 4000	11111	ex PH-EZA	Kurau	
☐ PK-PJM	Fokker F.28 Fellowship 4000	11178	ex PH-EXW	Matak	stored PCB
☐ PK-PJN	Fokker F.28-0100 (Fokker 100)	11288	ex PH-LMU	Minas	
☐ PK-PJY	Fokker F.28 Fellowship 4000	11146	ex PH-EXN	Aceh	
☐ PK-PGQ	Nurtanio/MBB Bo.105CB	N60/S-458			
☐ PK-PGR	Nurtanio/MBB Bo.105CB	N62/S-460			
☐ PK-PGU	Nurtanio/MBB Bo.105C	N12/S-218	ex PK-XZJ		
☐ PK-PGZ	Nurtanio/MBB Bo.105CB	N65/S-553			
☐ PK-PIH	Nurtanio/MBB Bo.105CB	N68/S-556			
☐ PK-PIJ	Nurtanio/MBB Bo.105CB	N70/S-558	ex PK-XYN		
☐ PK-PIM	Nurtanio/MBB Bo.105CB	N72/S-560	ex PK-XYP		
☐ PK-PJJ	Avro 146-RJ85	E2239	ex G-6-239	Wamena	
☐ PK-PUA	Sikorsky S-76A	76-0179	ex N5446U		Lsd to Travira
☐ PK-PUD	Sikorsky S-76A	76-0195	ex N3121A		Lsd to Travira

Registration	Type	C/n	Previous identity	Name	Notes
☐ PK-PUE	Sikorsky S-76A	76-0200			Lsd to Travira
☐ PK-PUJ	Bell 412EP	36282	ex N2012Y		
☐ PK-PUK	Bell 412EP	36288	ex N2028L		
☐ PK-PUL	Bell 430	49088	ex N3005J		

PENAS — *Penas (PNS)* — *Jakarta-Halim (HLP)*

Registration	Type	C/n	Previous identity	Name	Notes
☐ PK-VCD	Cessna 402B	402B0024	ex N5242M		

PREMIAIR — *Jakarta-Halim (HLP)*

Registration	Type	C/n	Previous identity	Name	Notes
☐ PK-RJC	Embraer EMB.120ER Brasilia	120214	ex VH-ANV		
☐ PK-RJI	Fokker F.28-0100 (Fokker 100)	11328	ex G-BXWF	Imanuel	VIP

RIAU AIRLINES — *Riau (RIU)* — *Pekanbaru (PKU)*

Registration	Type	C/n	Previous identity	Name	Notes
☐ PK-RAL	Fokker F.27 Mk.050 (Fokker 50)	20282	ex PH-MXE	Bengkalis	
☐ PK-RAS	Fokker F.27 Mk.050 (Fokker 50)	20261	ex PT-SRA	Kampat	
☐ PK-RAY	Avro 146-RJ100	E3243	ex G-CEFW		
☐ PK-RAZ	Avro 146-RJ100	E3265	ex G-CDRK		

RPX AIRLINES — *Public Express (RH/RPH)* — *Jakarta-Soekarno Hatta (CGK)*

Registration	Type	C/n	Previous identity	Name	Notes
☐ PK-RPH	Boeing 737-2K2C (AvAero 3)	20943/405	ex F-GGVP		
☐ PK-RPI	Boeing 737-2K2C (AvAero 3)	20944/408	ex F-GGVQ		

SABANG MERAUKE RAYA AIR CHARTER — *Samer (SMC)* — *Medan (MES)*

Registration	Type	C/n	Previous identity	Name	Notes
☐ PK-ZAE	Britten-Norman BN-2A-21 Islander	565	ex G-BEGH		
☐ PK-ZAF	Fokker F27 Friendship 200	10222	ex PK-MFA		
☐ PK-ZAK	Piper PA-31 Turbo Navajo	31-407	ex PK-FJA		
☐ PK-ZAN	CASA-Nurtanio C.212-A4	5N/A4-3-60	ex A-2102		
☐ PK-ZAO	CASA-Nurtanio C.212-A4	6N/A4-3-64	ex A-2101		
☐ PK-ZAQ	CASA-Nurtanio C.212-A4	82N/277	ex PK-JSR		
☐ PK-ZAV	CASA-Nurtanio C.212-A4	81N/276	ex PK-JSS		
☐ PK-ZAY	Fokker F27 Friendship 200	10223	ex PK-CFY		

SRIWIJAYA AIR — *Sriwijaya (SJ/SJY)* — *Jakarta-Soekarno Hatta (CGK)*

Registration	Type	C/n	Previous identity	Name	Notes
☐ PK-CJA	Boeing 737-284	22301/683	ex PK-IJS	Brenda	
☐ PK-CJC	Boeing 737-33A	24025/1556	ex SE-RCP		I
☐ PK-CJD	Boeing 737-204 (Nordam 3)	22057/621	ex 9L-LFI	Emilio	
☐ PK-CJE	Boeing 737-2T4	23446/1165	ex ET-ALE	Citra	
☐ PK-CJF	Boeing 737-284	22343/695	ex SX-BCI		
☐ PK-CJG	Boeing 737-2H6	23320/1120	ex PK-ALC	Serumpun Sebalai	
☐ PK-CJH	Boeing 737-2B7 (Nordam 3)	22883/935	ex N271AU		
☐ PK-CJI	Boeing 737-2B7 (Nordam 3)	23135/1054	ex PK-ALV	Membalong	stored CGK
☐ PK-CJJ	Boeing 737-2B7 (Nordam 3)	22880/927	ex N268AU		
☐ PK-CJK	Boeing 737-236	22032/742	ex PK-ALK		
☐ PK-CJL	Boeing 737-284	21301/474	ex PK-TXE		
☐ PK-CJM	Boeing 737-2B7 (Nordam 3)	22884/956	ex PK-TXC		
☐ PK-CJN	Boeing 737-2B7 (Nordam 3)	23134/1050	ex PK-TXA	Sherly	stored CGK
☐ PK-CJO	Boeing 737-284	22300/674	ex PK-IJR	Lomasasta	
☐ PK-CJP	Boeing 737-2B7 (Nordam 3)	23132/1044	ex PK-ALN	Lenggang	stored CGK
☐ PK-CJR	Boeing 737-284	21225/464	ex SX-BCB	Perkasa	
☐ PK-CJS	Boeing 737-3L9	27925/2763	ex N104VR		
☐ PK-CJT	Boeing 737-33A	24791/1984	ex N791AW		
☐ PK-CJU	Boeing 737-4Q8	24234/1627	ex N234AN		
☐ PK-CJV	Boeing 737-4Y0	24689/1883	ex N689MD		
☐ PK-CJW	Boeing 737-4Y0	24690/1885	ex N690MD		
☐ PK-CKA	Boeing 737-4Q8	25169/2237	ex N483JC		
☐ PK-CKC	Boeing 737-4Q8	26285/2416	ex N587BC		
☐ PK-CKD	Boeing 737-4Y0	25180/2201	ex N251MD		
☐ PK-GHS	Boeing 737-3Q8	24698/1846	ex G-IGOF		
☐ PK-	Boeing 737-3Q8	24987/2268	ex N596BC		

SUSI AIR — *Medan (MES)*

Registration	Type	C/n	Previous identity	Name	Notes
☐ PK-BVA	Cessna 208B Caravan I	208B2126	ex N61905		
☐ PK-BVD	Cessna 208B Caravan I	208B2141	ex N61932		
☐ PK-BVE	Cessna 208B Caravan I	208B2142	ex N6194X		
☐ PK-BVF	Cessna 208B Caravan I	208B2143	ex N61983		
☐ PK-BVG	Cessna 208B Caravan I	208B2146	ex N6203C		
☐ PK-BVH	Cessna 208B Caravan I	208B2151	ex N6204C		
☐ PK-VVA	Cessna 208B Caravan I	208B1066	ex N12690		
☐ PK-VVB	Cessna 208B Caravan I	208B1285	ex N4117B		
☐ PK-VVD	Cessna 208B Caravan I	208B1303	ex N20722		
☐ PK-VVE	Cessna 208B Caravan I	208B1287	ex N41176		
☐ PK-VVF	Cessna 208B Caravan I	208B1177	ex OB-1844-T		
☐ PK-VVG	Cessna 208B Caravan I	208B1308	ex N20840		
☐ PK-VVH	Cessna 208B Caravan I	208B1078	ex N278ST		

Registration	Type	C/n	Previous identity	Notes
☐ PK-VVI	Cessna 208B Caravan I	208B1205	ex RP-C2929	
☐ PK-VVJ	Cessna 208B Caravan I	208B2086	ex N2232Y	
☐ PK-VVM	Cessna 208B Caravan I	208B2093	ex N2154L	
☐ PK-VVO	Cessna 208B Caravan I	208B2111	ex N61611	
☐ PK-VVR	Cessna 208B Caravan I	208B1085	ex N12722	
☐ PK-VVS	Cessna 208B Caravan I	208B1117	ex N12775	
☐ PK-VVT	Cessna 208B Caravan I	208B2068	ex N61413	
☐ PK-VVK	Pilatus PC-6/B2-H4 Turbo Porter	958		
☐ PK-VVP	Pilatus PC-6/B2-H4 Turbo Porter	957		
☐ PK-VVQ	Pilatus PC-6/B2-H4 Turbo Porter	965		
☐ PK-VVU	Pilatus PC-6/B2-H4 Turbo Porter	967		

TIMAX CARGO AIRLINES

Registration	Type	C/n	Previous identity	Notes
☐ PK-YGZ	Boeing 727-31F (FedEx 3)	20112/700	ex OO-DHO	Lsd fr TMG

TRANSWISATA AIR — *Jakarta-Halim (HLP)*

Registration	Type	C/n	Previous identity	Notes
☐ PK-TWA	Fokker F.28 Fellowship 4000	11234	ex N484US	
☐ PK-TWC	Fokker F.27 Mk.050 (Fokker 50)	20272	ex D-AFFI	
☐ PK-TWF	Fokker F.27 Mk.050 (Fokker 50)	20142	ex D-AFFX	
☐ PK-TWM	Fokker F.28 Fellowship 4000	11183	ex ZS-JAV	
☐ PK-TWN	Fokker F.28-0100 (Fokker 100)	11335	ex PH-SXI	on order
☐ PK-TWR	Fokker F.27 Mk.050 (Fokker 50)	20317	ex B-12279	

TRAVIRA AIR — *Denpasar (DPS)*

Registration	Type	C/n	Previous identity	Notes
☐ PK-TVE	Beech 1900D	UE-338	ex N338RH	
☐ PK-TVH	Beech 1900D	UE-364	ex N30469	
☐ PK-TVJ	Beech 1900D	UE-352	ex N352RA	
☐ PK-TVK	Beech 1900D	UE-375	ex PK-TVK	Air Ambulance
☐ PK-TVL	Beech 1900D	UE-360	ex VH-FOZ	
☐ PK-PUA	Sikorsky S-76A	760179	ex N5446U	Lsd fr PAS
☐ PK-PUD	Sikorsky S-76A	760195	ex N3121A	Lsd fr PAS
☐ PK-PUE	Sikorsky S-76A	760200		Lsd fr PAS
☐ PK-TVF	Sikorsky S-76A	760154	ex VH-CPH	
☐ PK-TVP	Sikorsky S-76C	760421	ex N899KK	
☐ PK-TVQ	Sikorsky S-76A	760286	ex N30DJ	
☐ PK-TVP	Sikorsky S-76C	760436	ex N476X	
☐ PK-TVU	Sikorsky S-76C	760298	ex N520AL	
☐ PK-NZU	IPTN/MBB Bo.105CB	N121/S-719	ex PK-IWJ	
☐ PK-TVA	IPTN/MBB Bo.105CB	N1/S-124	ex PK-PEE	
☐ PK-TVB	IPTN/MBB Bo.105CB	N6/S-177	ex PK-PGV	
☐ PK-TVI	Cessna 208 Caravan I	20800313	ex C-FAMB	Floatplane
☐ PK-TVN	Cessna 208 Caravan I	20800358	ex N1229N	Floatplane
☐ PK-TVW	Cessna 208 Caravan I	20800418	ex N20869	
☐ PK-TVX	Cessna 208 Caravan I	20800421	ex N2098U	
☐ PK-TVY	de Havilland DHC-8-315	549	ex VH-AAY	
☐ PK-TVZ	Boeing 737-5L9	28996/2998	ex N737RH	VIP

TRIGANA AIR SERVICE — *Trigana (TGN)* — *Jakarta-Halim (HLP)*

Registration	Type	C/n	Previous identity	Notes
☐ PK-YRE	ATR 42-300	027	ex F-GPZB	Lsd fr Martinique Aero Lease
☐ PK-YRH	ATR 42-300	097	ex F-ODGN	
☐ PK-YRI	ATR 72-202	326	ex F-WQUF	
☐ PK-YRK	ATR 42-300	106	ex N422TE	
☐ PK-YRN	ATR 42-300	102	ex N421TE	
☐ PK-YRP	ATR 42-300	050	ex ZS-DHL	
☐ PK-YRR	ATR 42-310	214	ex F-GHPI	
☐ PK-YRV	ATR 42-300	190	ex G-BYHA	
☐ PK-YRX	ATR 72-202	342	ex F-WQRY	
☐ PK-YRY	ATR 72-202	201	ex F-WQAL	
☐ PK-YPX	de Havilland DHC-6 Twin Otter 300	684	ex HB-LTF	
☐ PK-YRA	Fokker F.27 Friendship 500	10506	ex HB-ISQ	
☐ PK-YRC	Cessna TU206D Skywagon	U206-1269	ex PK-MCA	
☐ PK-YRF	de Havilland DHC-6 Twin Otter 300	462	ex D-ISKY	
☐ PK-YRG	Fokker F.27 Friendship 500	10397	ex PH-FNV	
☐ PK-YRJ	de Havilland DHC-4A Caribou	27	ex N666NC	
☐ PK-YRO	de Havilland DHC-4A Caribou	24	ex N90NC	
☐ PK-YRQ	Bell 206L-4 LongRanger IV	52069	ex F-GPOC	
☐ PK-YRT	Boeing 737-2K5	22599/814	ex PK-KJN	
☐ PK-YRU	de Havilland DHC-6 Twin Otter 300	685	ex VH-VHP	

TRI-MG INTRA-ASIA AIRLINES — *Trilines (GY/TMG)* — *Jakarta-Halim (HLP)*

Registration	Type	C/n	Previous identity	Name	Notes
☐ PK-YGL	LET L-410UVP-E	892342	ex RP-C748		
☐ PK-YGR	Boeing 727-223F (FedEx 3)	20893/1189	ex N117JB	Zenith	
☐ PK-YGZ	Boeing 727-31F (FedEx 3)	20112/700	ex OO-DHO	Noble Witness	Lsd to Timax Cargo

WINGS AIR		**Wings Abadi (IW/WON)**		**Jakarta-Soekarno Hatta (CGK)**
☐ PK-WFF	ATR 72-212A	869	ex F-WWET	
☐ PK-WFG	ATR 72-212A	882	ex F-WWEL	
☐ PK-WFH	ATR 72-212A	883	ex F-WWEM	
☐ PK-WF	ATR 72-212A	871	ex F-WWEV	
☐ PK-WIA	de Havilland DHC-8-301	194	ex N194TY	
☐ PK-WID	de Havilland DHC-8-301	116	ex N116TY	
☐ PK-WIE	de Havilland DHC-8-301	108	ex N108TY	
☐ PK-LMG	McDonnell-Douglas MD-82	49417/1278	ex N417GE	stored CGK, Lsd fr LNI
☐ PK-LMP	McDonnell-Douglas MD-82	49117/1063	ex N35888	Lsd fr LNI
☐ PK-LMS	McDonnell-Douglas MD-82	49114/1066	ex N14890	stored CGK, Lsd fr LNI
☐ PK-LMT	McDonnell-Douglas MD-82	49118/1065	ex N14889	Lsd fr LNI
☐ PK-LMU	McDonnell-Douglas MD-82	49429/1242	ex N829US	stored CGK, Lsd fr LNI
☐ PK-WIF	McDonnell-Douglas MD-82	49481/1308	ex N72821	Lsd fr LNI
☐ PK-WIG	McDonnell-Douglas MD-82	49489/1351	ex N72829	stored CGK, Lsd fr LNI
☐ PK-WIH	McDonnell-Douglas MD-82	49582/1411	ex N57837	Lsd fr LNI
☐ PK-WIK	McDonnell-Douglas MD-82	49788/1637	ex PK-LMK	Lsd fr LNI
☐ PK-WIL	McDonnell-Douglas MD-82	48083/1043	ex PK-LML	Lsd fr LNI
☐ PK-WIO	McDonnell-Douglas MD-82	49102/1076	ex PK-LMQ	stored CGK, Lsd fr LNI
☐ PK-WIP	McDonnell-Douglas MD-82	49190/1180	ex PK-LMV	stored CGK, Lsd fr LNI

XPRESS AIR		**(XN/XAR)**		**Ujung Pandang**
☐ PK-TXD	Boeing 737-284	22400/766	ex SX-BCK	Grace
☐ PK-TXF	Boeing 737-284	21302/475	ex SX-BCD	
☐ PK-TXG	Boeing 737-5L9	25066/2038	ex OY-MAE	
☐ PK-TXM	Dornier 328-110	3032	ex N423JS	
☐ PK-TXN	Dornier 328-110	3030	ex N328CH	
☐ PK-TXP	Dornier 328-110	3043	ex N429JS	
☐ PK-TXQ	Dornier 328-110	3038	ex N426JS	
☐ PK-YGN	LET L-410UVP-E	902434	ex RP-C728	

PP-, PR-, PT- BRAZIL (Federative Republic of Brazil)

ABAETE AEROTAXI				**Salvador, BA (SSA)**
☐ PT-OGK	Cessna 208A Caravan I	20800078	ex N65575	
☐ PT-OGP	Cessna 208A Caravan I	20800050	ex N817FE	
☐ PT-OGR	Cessna 208A Caravan I	20800100	ex N838FE	
☐ PT-OGS	Cessna 208A Caravan I	20800034	ex N811FE	
☐ PT-OGT	Cessna 208A Caravan I	20800038	ex N815FE	
☐ PT-OGU	Cessna 208A Caravan I	20800066	ex N826FE	
☐ PT-OZA	Cessna 208B Caravan I	208B0157	ex N4615B	
☐ PP-ATT	Cessna 402B	402B0631	ex N3786C	
☐ PT-JBD	Cessna 402B	402B0404		
☐ PT-JRT	Cessna 402B	402B0552	ex N1634T	
☐ PT-JTZ	Cessna 402B	402B0532		
☐ PT-LKZ	Cessna 402B	402B1074	ex N1554G	
☐ PT-RGV	Embraer EMB.821 Caraja	820136	ex PT-ZNA	
☐ PT-VCH	Embraer EMB.821 Caraja	821012		
☐ PT-VCI	Embraer EMB.821 Caraja	820144		
☐ PT-VKD	Embraer EMB.821 Caraja	820159		
☐ PT-WFL	Embraer EMB.821 Caraja	820150		
☐ PT-ACM	Embraer EMB.121A Xingu	121021	ex PT-MAN	
☐ PT-MCA	Embraer EMB.121A1 Xingu	121058		

ABAETE LINHAS AEREAS		**(ABJ)**		**Salvador, BA (SSA)**
☐ PT-GKO	Embraer EMB.110P Bandeirante	110119		
☐ PT-MFO	Embraer EMB.110C Bandeirante	110058	ex FAB2158	
☐ PT-MFP	Embraer EMB.110C Bandeirante	110105	ex FAB2181	
☐ PT-MFQ	Embraer EMB.110C Bandeirante	110121	ex FAB2188	
☐ PT-MFS	Embraer EMB.110C Bandeirante	110054	ex FAB2160	

ABSA CARGO		**Absa Cargo (M3/TUS)**		**Sao Paulo-Viracopos, SP (VCP)**
☐ PR-ABB	Boeing 767-316F	29881/778	ex CC-CZX	Lsd fr LAN
☐ PR-ABD	Boeing 767-316F/W	34245/934		Lsd fr LAN

AEB TAXI AERO				**Porto Alegre, RS (POA)**
☐ PT-EVP	Embraer EMB.810C Seneca II	810250		
☐ PT-IUD	Piper PA-31-350 Navajo Chieftain	31-7305037	ex N74915	

☐ PT-JEH	Piper PA-31-350 Navajo Chieftain	31-7305057	ex N74928

AERO STAR TAXI AEREO — Salvador, BA (SSA)

☐ PT-EDF	Embraer EMB-820C Navajo	820014	
☐ PT-EZN	Embraer EMB-820C Navajo	820106	
☐ PT-KRO	Britten-Norman BN-2A-21 Islander	742	ex G-BCVL
☐ PT-KTR	Britten-Norman BN-2A-27 Islander	495	ex G-BDNN

AEROLEO TAXI AERO — Rio de Janeiro-Santos Dumont, RJ / Macae & Sao Tome, RJ (SDU/MEA)

☐ PR-FNT	Aérospatiale AS.332L1	2468	ex LN-OMT	
☐ PR-GDR	Aérospatiale AS.332L1	2381	ex LN-OBF	
☐ PP-MNL	Sikorsky S-61N	61745	ex G-BFMY	Lsd fr BHL
☐ PR-AEL	Sikorsky S-61N	61808	ex N563EH	
☐ PR-CHL	Sikorsky S-76A++	760160	ex D2-EXF	
☐ PR-CHP	Sikorsky S-76C+	760743	ex C-FYDD	
☐ PR-EDA	Sikorsky S-76A	760279	ex N710AL	Lsd fr Airlog Intl
☐ PR-GPC	Sikorsky S-76A	760266	ex N703AL	Lsd fr Airlog Intl
☐ PR-LBA	Sikorsky S-76C+	760705	ex N2584Q	Lsd fr Airlog Intl
☐ PR-LCT	Sikorsky S-76C+	760723	ex N723Y	Lsd fr Airlog Intl
☐ PR-LCL	Sikorsky S-76A	760280	ex N712AL	Lsd fr Airlog Intl
☐ PR-LCV	Sikorsky S-76C+	760672	ex N4508N	Lsd fr Airlog Intl
☐ PR-LCX	Sikorsky S-76C+	760704	ex N231Y	Lsd fr Airlog Intl
☐ PR-LCZ	Sikorsky S-76C+	760707	ex N415Y	Lsd fr Airlog Intl
☐ PR-LDA	Sikorsky S-76C+	760756	ex N756N	Lsd fr Airlog Intl
☐ PR-LDB	Sikorsky S-76C+	760759	ex N759L	Lsd fr Airlog Intl
☐ PR-LDD	Sikorsky S-76C+	760679	ex N882AL	Lsd fr Airlog Intl
☐ PR-NLF	Sikorsky S-76A	760085	ex N1547K	Lsd fr Airlog Intl
☐ PT-HOR	Sikorsky S-76A	760003	ex N476AL	Lsd fr Airlog Intl
☐ PT-YAY	Sikorsky S-76A	760277	ex N708AL	Lsd fr Airlog Intl
☐ PR-JAA	Sikorsky S-92A	920092	ex N2059J	

AIR BRASIL CARGO — (BSL) — Sao Paulo-Guarulhos, SP (GRU)

☐ PR-AIB	Boeing 727-227F (FedEx 3)	21363/1258	ex N79754	Lsd fr Flightstar Group

AIR MINAS — (6M) — Belo Horizonte, MG (CNF)

☐ PR-GDC	Embraer EMB.120ER Brasilia	120150	ex N789TX
☐ PR-MDP	Embraer EMB.120ER Brasilia	120250	ex N250YV
☐ PR-MGE	Embraer EMB.120RT Brasilia	120130	ex N130G
☐ PR-TUH	Embraer EMB.120ER Brasilia	120276	ex N212SW
☐ PR-UHT	Embraer EMB.120ER Brasilia	120280	ex N214SW

AMAZONAVES TAXI AEREO — Tefe / Manaus, AM (-/MAO)

☐ PP-ITZ	Cessna 208B Caravan I	208B0499	ex N5188N
☐ PT-EUS	Embraer EMB.810C Seneca	810230	
☐ PT-MET	Cessna 208B Caravan I	208B0509	ex N5073G
☐ PT-OLJ	Embraer EMB.810C Seneca	810330	
☐ PT-WIG	Embraer EMB.810C Seneca	810433	

AMERICAN AIR TAXI AEREO — Sorocab, SP (SOB)

☐ PR-OAN	Embraer EMB.120RT Brasilia	120051	ex N237AS

APUI TAXI AEREO — Manaus-Ponta Pelada, AM (PLL)

☐ PT-GKX	Embraer EMB.110P Bandeirante	110129	
☐ PT-LRR	Embraer EMB.110P1 Bandeirante	110315	
☐ PT-ODJ	Embraer EMB.110 Bandeirante	110034	ex FAB 2144
☐ PT-ODY	Embraer EMB.110 Bandeirante	110039	ex FAB 2147
☐ PT-RCV	Embraer EMB.810C Seneca	810333	

ATA BRASIL — ATA Brasil (ABZ) — Fortaleza, CE (FOR)

☐ PR-GMA	Boeing 727-224F (FedEx 3)	20659/979	ex OY-SEY	stored GYN
☐ PR-LSW	Boeing 737-248C	20219/208	ex CC-CEI	
☐ PR-MGA	Boeing 737-204C	20282/245	ex N282AD	

AZUL — (AZU)

☐ PR-AYA	Embraer 190-200LR (195LR)	19000237	ex PT-SIK	Azul e Brasil
☐ PR-AYB	Embraer 190-200LR (195LR)	19000239	ex PT-	Tudo Azul
☐ PR-AYC	Embraer 190-200LR (195LR)	19000240	ex PT-	A Liberdade e Azul
☐ PR-AYD	Embraer 190-200LR (195LR)	19000247	ex PT-	Azalou
☐ PR-AYE	Embraer 190-200LR (195LR)	19000260	ex PT-STI	

☐ PR-AYF	Embraer 190-200LR (195LR)		ex PT-	on order
☐ PR-	Embraer 190-200LR (195LR)		ex PT-	on order
☐ PR-	Embraer 190-200LR (195LR)		ex PT-	on order
☐ PR-	Embraer 190-200LR (195LR)		ex PT-	on order
☐ PR-	Embraer 190-200LR (195LR)		ex PT-	on order
☐ PR-	Embraer 190-200LR (195LR)		ex PT-	on order
☐ PR-	Embraer 190-200LR (195LR)		ex PT-	on order
☐ PR-	Embraer 190-200LR (195LR)		ex PT-	on order
☐ PR-	Embraer 190-200LR (195LR)		ex PT-	on order
☐ PR-	Embraer 190-200LR (195LR)		ex PT-	on order
☐ PR-	Embraer 190-200LR (195LR)		ex PT-	on order
☐ PR-	Embraer 190-200LR (195LR)		ex PT-	on order
☐ PR-	Embraer 190-200LR (195LR)		ex PT-	on order
☐ PR-AZA	Embraer 190-100IGW (190AR)	19000150	ex N290JB	Azulville
☐ PR-AZB	Embraer 190-100IGW (190AR)	19000241	ex N840JE	Azul Paulista
☐ PR-AZC	Embraer 190-100IGW (190AR)	19000242	ex N841JS	Ceu Azul
☐ PR-AZD	Embraer 190-100IGW (190AR)	19000271	ex PT-TLL	
☐ PR-AZE	Embraer 190-100IGW (190AR)	19000282	ex PT-TLW	Verda, Amarelo e Azul
☐ PR-AZF	Embraer 190-100IGW (190AR)	19000295	ex PT-	Voce que e Feilo de Azul
☐ PR-AZG	Embraer 190-100IGW (190AR)	19000329	ex PT-	
☐ PR-AZH	Embraer 190-100IGW (190AR)	19000330	ex PT-	
☐ PR-AZL	Embraer 190-100IGW (190AR)	19000147	ex N288JB	O Rio de Janeiro continua Azul

BAHIA TAXI AEREO – BATA — *Salvador, BA (SSA)*

☐ PT-EPY	Embraer EMB.820C Navajo	820077		

BETA CARGO AIR — *Beta Cargo (BET)* — *Sao Paulo-Guarulhos, SP (GRU)*

☐ PP-BEL	Douglas DC-8-73AF	46047/447	ex N809DH	
☐ PP-BEM	Douglas DC-8-73F	46086/478	ex N870TV	
☐ PP-BET	Douglas DC-8-73CF	46103/483	ex N795FT	
☐ PP-BEX	Douglas DC-8-73F	46104/488	ex N796FT	
☐ PP-BRG	Boeing 707-323C (Comtran 2)	19586/670	ex CP-1698	stored VCP
☐ PP-BRI	Boeing 707-351C (Comtran 2)	19776/732	ex N8091J	stored
☐ PP-BRR	Boeing 707-323C (Comtran 2)	20088/727	ex PT-TCN	stored GRU

BHS - BRAZILIAN HELICOPTER SERVICES TAXI AEREO
Sao Paulo-Marte, SP, Farol de Sao Tome, SP, Macae& Sao Tome, RJ

☐ PP-MEM	Sikorsky S-76A+	760092	ex N176PA	
☐ PP-MET	Sikorsky S-76A	760229	ex N31217	
☐ PP-MHM	Sikorsky S-76C	760376	ex N776AB	
☐ PP-MPM	Sikorsky S-76C	760375	ex N775AB	
☐ PR-CHA	Sikorsky S-76C+	760625	ex C-GBQE	
☐ PR-CHB	Sikorsky S-76A++	760004	ex C-GIME	
☐ PR-CHC	Sikorsky S-76C+	760632	ex C-GBQF	
☐ PR-CHD	Sikorsky S-76C+	760636	ex C-GBQG	
☐ PR-CHE	Sikorsky S-76C+	760642	ex C-GBQH	
☐ PR-CHF	Sikorsky S-76C+	760657	ex N4505G	
☐ PR-CHK	Sikorsky S-76C+	760687	ex C-FRHF	Lsd fr CHC Helicopters Intl
☐ PR-CJK	Sikorsky S-76C+	760674	ex N4513G	Lsd fr CHC Helicopters Intl
☐ PR-CHN	Sikorsky S-76A++	760187	ex C-FIHD	
☐ PR-CHP	Sikorsky S-76C++	760743	ex C-FYDD	
☐ PR-CHQ	Sikorsky S-76C++	760734	ex C-FXFK	
☐ PR-MCH	Sikorsky S-76A++	760213	ex C-GIMX	
☐ PT-YGM	Sikorsky S-76A	760067	ex ZS-RJK	Lsd fr CHC Helicopters Africa
☐ PT-YIM	Sikorsky S-76A	760144	ex XA-SRS	
☐ PT-YQM	Sikorsky S-76A	760051	ex ZS-RGZ	Lsd fr CHC Helicopters Africa
☐ PR-CHR	Sikorsky S-92A	920112	ex C-FRWL	
☐ PR-CHS	Sikorsky S-92A	920113	ex C-FPKW	
☐ PP-MTM	Aérospatiale AS.332L2	2599		
☐ PP-MZM	Aérospatiale AS.332L2	2572	ex F-WQDJ	
☐ PR-CHW	Eurocopter EC225LP	2740	ex G-DRIT	
☐ PR-CHX	Eurocopter EC225LP	2729	ex G-CLAR	
☐ PR-CHY	Eurocopter EC225LP	2722	ex G-LJAM	
☐ PR-CHZ	Aérospatiale AS.332L	2015	ex OY-HHA	Lsd fr CHC Helicopters Intl
☐ PR-PLL	Eurocopter EC225LP	2680	ex N225EH	
☐ PR-VLL	Eurocopter EC225LP	2685	ex N247CF	
☐ PR-YCL	Eurocopter EC225LP 2	2708	ex LN-OHY	
☐ PR-MEK	Aérospatiale SA365N Dauphin 2	6030	ex PH-SSX	
☐ PT-HNZ	Helibras HS.350B Esquilo	B-1151-2486		

BRA - BRASIL RODO AEREO — *Brasair (7R/BRB)* — *Sao Paulo-Congonhas, SP (CGH)*

Ceased operations 15/Jan/2010

CRUISER TAXI AEREO BRASIL (J6) Curitiba, PR (CWB)

☐ PR-CRA	LET L-410UVP-E20	902514	ex OK-VDP	
☐ PR-CRX	LET L-410UVP-E20	912617	ex OK-2617	
☐ PT-WBR	Embraer EMB.110C Bandeirante	110045	ex FAB 2153	

GENSA Gensa Brasil (GEN) Campo Grande, MS (CGR)

☐ PR-GSA	Embraer EMB.120ER Brasilia	120119	ex 5N-TCE	
☐ PR-GSB	Embraer EMB.120ER Brasilia	120127	ex 5N-LCE	
☐ PT-SHN	Embraer EMB.110P1A Bandeirante	110460		
☐ PT-SOG	Embraer EMB.110P1 Bandeirante	110490		

GIRASSOL AEROTAXI Manaus-Eduardo Gomes, AM (MAO)

☐ PT-DKO	Beech 95-B55 Baron	TC-1335		
☐ PT-EAA	Embraer EMB.810C Seneca	810001		
☐ PT-EBN	Embraer EMB.820C Navajo	820001		
☐ PT-JBT	Piper PA-31-350 Navajo Chieftain	31-7305101	ex N74953	
☐ PT-KXV	Rockwell 500S Shrike Commander	3104	ex PT-FRA	
☐ PT-LYH	Piper PA-31-350 Navajo Chieftain	31-7305124	ex PP-EFS	

GOL TRANSPORTES AEREOS Gol Transporte (G3/GLO) Sao Paulo-Congonhas, SP (CGH)

☐ PR-GLE	Boeing 737-322	24249/1638	ex N345UA	
☐ PR-GLN	Boeing 737-322	24379/1724	ex N358UA	
☐ PR-GLO	Boeing 737-322	23952/1534	ex N320UA	
☐ PR-GLQ	Boeing 737-322	24247/1634	ex N343UA	

☐ PR-GEA	Boeing 737-7EH/W	37595/3026		
☐ PR-GGA	Boeing 737-8EH/W	35063/2476	ex N1787B	
☐ PR-GGB	Boeing 737-8EH/W	35064/2498		
☐ PR-GGK	Boeing 737-8EH/W	35065/2561		
☐ PR-GGD	Boeing 737-8EH/W	34275/2588		
☐ PR-GGE	Boeing 737-8EH/W	35824/2665	ex N1786B	
☐ PR-GGF	Boeing 737-8EH/W	35826/2749		
☐ PR-GGG	Boeing 737-8EH/W	36566/2809		
☐ PR-GGH	Boeing 737-8EH/W	36147/2864	ex N1787B	
☐ PR-GGJ	Boeing 737-8EH/W	35825/2786	ex N1796B	
☐ PR-GGK	Boeing 737-8EH/W	35065/2561		
☐ PR-GGL	Boeing 737-8EH/W	36148/2890		
☐ PR-GGM	Boeing 737-8EH/W	36149/2920	ex N1786B	
☐ PR-GGN	Boeing 737-8EH/W	35827/2991	ex N1786B	
☐ PR-GGO	Boeing 737-8EH/W	35828/3025		
☐ PR-GGP	Boeing 737-8EH/W	35829/3076	ex N1787B	
☐ PR-GGQ	Boeing 737-8EH/W	37596/3103	ex N1786B	
☐ PR-GGR	Boeing 737-8EH/W	36150/3106	ex N1787B	
☐ PR-GGT	Boeing 737-8EH/W	35830/3115		
☐ PR-GGU	Boeing 737-8EH/W	37597/3133		
☐ PR-GGV	Boeing 737-8EH/W	37598/3136		
☐ PR-GGW	Boeing 737-8EH/W	35831/3165		on order
☐ PR-GGX	Boeing 737-8EH/W	36596		on order
☐ PR-GGY	Boeing 737-8EH/W	36599		on order
☐ PR-GGZ	Boeing 737-8EH/W	36600		on order
☐ PR-	Boeing 737-8EH/W			on order
☐ PR-	Boeing 737-8EH/W			on order
☐ PR-	Boeing 737-8EH/W			on order
☐ PR-GIB	Boeing 737-83N/W	32348/933	ex PH-HSS	
☐ PR-GIC	Boeing 737-83N/W	32576/875	ex PH-HST	
☐ PR-GID	Boeing 737-76N/W	29904/347	ex N745AL	
☐ PR-GIE	Boeing 737-8BK/W	33027/1918	ex N1786B	
☐ PR-GIF	Boeing 737-73S	29076/98	ex OY-MLY	
☐ PR-GIG	Boeing 737-73S	29077/104	ex OY-MLZ	
☐ PR-GIH	Boeing 737-76N/W	32743/1503	ex N750AL	
☐ PR-GII	Boeing 737-7L9	28011/1203	ex OY-MRL	
☐ PR-GIJ	Boeing 737-7L9	28012/1092	ex OY-MRK	Lsd to SNB
☐ PR-GIK	Boeing 737-7Q8	28224/369	ex N161LF	
☐ PR-GIL	Boeing 737-7Q8	30635/713	ex N151LF	
☐ PR-GIM	Boeing 737-73V	30238/913	ex G-EZJE	
☐ PR-GIN	Boeing 737-73V	30242/690	ex G-EZJD	
☐ PR-GIO	Boeing 737-85F/W	30477/976	ex N477GX	
☐ PR-GIP	Boeing 737-85F/W	30571/936	ex N571GX	
☐ PR-GIQ	Boeing 737-86N/W	28616/483	ex TC-SUC	
☐ PR-GIR	Boeing 737-8Q8	28213/50	ex OY-SEA	
☐ PR-GIT	Boeing 737-809	28403/117	ex TC-APM	
☐ PR-GIU	Boeing 737-809	29103/129	ex TC-APZ	
☐ PR-GIV	Boeing 737-86N/W	28578/89	ex VT-JNA	
☐ PR-GIW	Boeing 737-86N/W	28575/91	ex VT-JNB	
☐ PR-GIX	Boeing 737-8Q8	30636/768	ex N330LF	
☐ PR-GOA	Boeing 737-7L9	28005/11	ex OY-MRB	special c/s
☐ PR-GOB	Boeing 737-75B	28099/13	ex D-AGEM	
☐ PR-GOC	Boeing 737-75B	28101/17	ex D-AGEO	

☐ PR-GOD	Boeing 737-75B	28105/66	ex D-AGEV	
☐ PR-GOE	Boeing 737-75B	28106/68	ex D-AGEW	
☐ PR-GOF	Boeing 737-76Q	30273/843	ex N1786B	Aurea
☐ PR-GOG	Boeing 737-76Q	30275/900	ex N795BA	
☐ PR-GOH	Boeing 737-76N	32440/954	ex N1786B	
☐ PR-GOI	Boeing 737-76N	32574/983	ex N1786B	
☐ PR-GOJ	Boeing 737-8CX	32359/1041		stored PTY
☐ PR-GOL	Boeing 737-7L9	28004/10	ex OY-MRA	
☐ PR-GOM	Boeing 737-76N	28613/463	ex N312ML	
☐ PR-GON	Boeing 737-76N	30051/436	ex N311ML	
☐ PR-GOO	Boeing 737-76N	30135/1068	ex N135SF	
☐ PR-GOP	Boeing 737-8BK	30621/1194	ex N461LF	Victoria
☐ PR-GOQ	Boeing 737-76N	33417/1215		
☐ PR-GOR	Boeing 737-76N	33380/1231		
☐ PR-GOT	Boeing 737-8BK	30625/1248		
☐ PR-GOU	Boeing 737-7Q8	28219/183	ex N331LF	
☐ PR-GOV	Boeing 737-76N	28580/135	ex N580HE	
☐ PR-GOW	Boeing 737-76N	28584/170	ex N584SR	
☐ PR-GOX	Boeing 737-7K9	28088/19	ex N100UN	
☐ PR-GOY	Boeing 737-7K9	28089/25	ex N101UN	
☐ PR-GOZ	Boeing 737-83N/W	28648/888	ex N303TZ	
☐ PR-GTA	Boeing 737-8EH/W	34474/1843	ex N6067U	
☐ PR-GTB	Boeing 737-8EH/W	34475/2020		
☐ PR-GTC	Boeing 737-8EH/W	34277/2028	ex N1786B	
☐ PR-GTE	Boeing 737-8EH/W	34278/2052		
☐ PR-GTF	Boeing 737-8EH/W	34279/2061		
☐ PR-GTG	Boeing 737-8EH/W	34654/2075		
☐ PR-GTH	Boeing 737-8EH/W	34655/2091		
☐ PR-GTI	Boeing 737-8EH/W	34280/2100		
☐ PR-GTJ	Boeing 737-8EH/W	34656/2110		
☐ PR-GTK	Boeing 737-8EH/W	34281/2116		
☐ PR-GTL	Boeing 737-8EH/W	34962/2215	ex N1786B	
☐ PR-GTM	Boeing 737-8EH/W	34963/2240		
☐ PR-GTN	Boeing 737-8EH/W	34267/2311		
☐ PR-GTO	Boeing 737-8EH/W	34964/2332		
☐ PR-GTP	Boeing 737-8EH/W	34965/2341		
☐ PR-GTQ	Boeing 737-8EH/W	36146/2358		
☐ PR-GTR	Boeing 737-8EH/W	34966/2367		
☐ PR-GTT	Boeing 737-8EH/W	34268/2407		
☐ PR-GTU	Boeing 737-8EH/W	34269/2412	ex N1786B	
☐ PR-GTV	Boeing 737-8EH/W	34270/2420		
☐ PR-GTY	Boeing 737-8EH/W	34273/2464		
☐ PR-GTZ	Boeing 737-8EH/W	34274/2468	ex N1795B	
☐ PR-VBH	Boeing 737-73V	30239/944	ex N239CG	
☐ PR-VBI	Boeing 737-73V	30246/1064	ex N346CL	
☐ PR-VBO	Boeing 737-73V	30247/1066	ex G-EZJL	
☐ PR-VBW	Boeing 737-7BX	30739/758	ex 6V-AHO	
☐ PR-VBY	Boeing 737-73A/W	28499/390	ex N738AL	
☐ PR-VBZ	Boeing 737-73A/W	28500/414	ex N739AL	

HELISUL TAXI AEREO — *Foz do Iguaçu, PR*

☐ PR-HTA	Helibras HS.350B2 Esquilo	AS3523	
☐ PT-HGB	Bell 206B JetRanger III	4298	ex C-FRIN
☐ PT-HMI	Helibras HS.350B Esquilo	1639/HB1046	
☐ PT-HML	Helibras HS.350B Esquilo	1642/HB1049	
☐ PT-HOY	Bell 206B JetRanger III	4171	ex N4171J
☐ PT-HTC	Bell 206B JetRanger III	3449	ex N2113Z
☐ PT-YAP	Bell 206B JetRanger III	3481	ex N215RG
☐ PT-YEL	Bell 206L-4 LongRanger IV	52198	ex N6593X

HELIVIA AERO TAXI — *Manaus-Ponta Pelada, AM (PLL)*

☐ PT-HVA	MBB Bo.105CBS-4	S-795	ex N5416X
☐ PT-HVB	MBB Bo.105CBS-4	S-792	ex N7062W
☐ PT-HXK	MBB Bo.105CBS-4	S-785	ex N54125
☐ PT-YAW	Aérospatiale SA.330J Puma	1590	ex F-GEQI

INTERAVIA TAXI AEREO

☐ PR-JAT	Cessna 208B Caravan I	208B1193	ex N13189

LITORANEA

☐ PR-VLA	LET L-410UVP-E20	882101	ex OK-TDA

MANAUS AERO TAXI — *Manaus-Ponta Pelada, AM (PLL)*

☐ PR-MPE	Cessna 208 Caravan I	20800510	ex N13189

META - MESQUITA TRANSPORTES AEREO — Meta (MSQ) — Boa Vista, RR (BVB)

Reg	Type	C/n	Previous	Notes
☐ PT-FLY	Embraer EMB.120ER Brasilia	120044	ex PT-SLI	
☐ PT-LMZ	Cessna U206F Stationair	U20602184		
☐ PT-LNW	Embraer EMB.110P1 Bandeirante	110346	ex N697RA	
☐ PT-LXN	Embraer EMB.120ER Brasilia	120052	ex D-CEMG	
☐ PT-OND	Cessna U206G Stationair 6	U20606542	ex N9529Z	

MTA CARGO — Master (MST) — Sao Paulo-Viracopos, SP (VCP)

Reg	Type	C/n	Previous	Notes
☐ PP-MTA	Douglas DC-10-30CF	47908/215	ex N322FE	Petete IV
☐ PR-MTC	Douglas DC-10-30F	46540/268	ex N304SP	

NHR TAXI AEREO — Sorocaba, SP (SOD)

Reg	Type	C/n	Previous	Notes
☐ PR-ELT	Embraer EMB.110P1 Bandeirante	110412	ex P2-IAL	
☐ PR-KIN	Embraer EMB.110P1 Bandeirante	110254	ex P2-IAJ	
☐ PR-NHR	Embraer EMB.110P1 Bandeirante	110394	ex P2-IAK	
☐ PT-MAL	Embraer EMB.121A1 Xingu	121019		
☐ PT-SHY	Embraer EMB.110P1 Bandeirante	110470		
☐ PT-WAW	Embraer EMB.110 Bandeirante	110122	ex FAB 2189	
☐ PT-WCM	Embraer EMB.110 Bandeirante	110041	ex FAB 2148	

NHT LINHAS AEREAS — (NHG) — Sorocaba, SP (SOD)

Reg	Type	C/n	Previous	Notes
☐ PR-NHA	LET L-410UVP-E20	062636		
☐ PR-NHB	LET L-410UVP-E20	062637		
☐ PR-NHC	LET L-410UVP-E20	072639		
☐ PR-NHD	LET L-410UVP-E20	072640		
☐ PR-NHE	LET L-410UVP-E20	082714	ex OK-2714	
☐ PR-	LET L-410UVP-E20			

OCEANAIR LINHAS AEREAS — Oceanair (ONE) — Rio de Janeiro-Santos Dumont, RJ (SDU)

Reg	Type	C/n	Previous	Notes
☐ PR-OAO	Embraer EMB.120RT Brasilia	120057	ex N239AS	Grey c/s
☐ PR-OAP	Embraer EMB.120RT Brasilia	120060	ex N240AS	Magenta c/s
☐ PT-SLC	Embraer EMB.120ER Brasilia	120094	ex PT-SML	Red c/s
☐ PT-SRF	Embraer EMB.120ER Brasilia	120192		White c/s
☐ PR-OAD	Fokker F.28-0100 (Fokker 100)	11370	ex N1412A	
☐ PR-OAE	Fokker F.28-0100 (Fokker 100)	11426	ex N1436A	
☐ PR-OAF	Fokker F.28-0100 (Fokker 100)	11415	ex N1430D	
☐ PR-OAG	Fokker F.28-0100 (Fokker 100)	11412	ex N1427A	
☐ PR-OAI	Fokker F.28-0100 (Fokker 100)	11417	ex N1432A	
☐ PR-OAJ	Fokker F.28-0100 (Fokker 100)	11418	ex N1433B	
☐ PR-OAK	Fokker F.28-0100 (Fokker 100)	11425	ex N1435D	
☐ PR-OAL	Fokker F.28-0100 (Fokker 100)	11435	ex N1440A	
☐ PR-OAM	Fokker F.28-0100 (Fokker 100)	11436	ex N1441A	
☐ PR-OAQ	Fokker F.28-0100 (Fokker 100)	11467	ex N1455K	
☐ PR-OAR	Fokker F.28-0100 (Fokker 100)	11481	ex N1461C	
☐ PR-OAS	Fokker F.28-0100 (Fokker 100)	11405	ex N1422J	
☐ PR-OAT	Fokker F.28-0100 (Fokker 100)	11411	ex N1420A	
☐ PR-OAU	Fokker F.28-0100 (Fokker 100)	11427	ex N1437B	
☐ PR-BRB	Boeing 737-3Q4	24210/1577	ex PT-TEH	
☐ PR-BRD	Boeing 737-3M8	24376/1717	ex EC-GGO	
☐ PR-BRK	Boeing 737-3S3	23787/1374	ex PP-VQW	

PANTANAL — Pantanal (P8/PTN) — Sao Paulo-Congonhas, SP (CGH)

Reg	Type	C/n	Previous	Notes
☐ PT-MFJ	ATR 42-320	343	ex F-WQHV	
☐ PT-MFM	ATR 42-300	376	ex F-GKNH	
☐ PT-MFT	ATR 42-320	306	ex G-BXEH	
☐ PT-MFU	ATR 42-310	070	ex F-GHJE	
☐ PT-MFV	ATR 42-300	043	ex F-GGLR	

PASSAREDO TRANSPORTES AEREOS — (PTB) — Ribeirao Preto, SP (RAO)

Reg	Type	C/n	Previous	Notes
☐ PP-PSA	Embraer EMB.120ER Brasilia	120302		
☐ PP-PSB	Embraer EMB.120ER Brasilia	120303		
☐ PR-PSD	Embraer EMB.120ER Brasilia	120118	ex N507DM	
☐ PT-SLD	Embraer EMB.120ER Brasilia	120147		
☐ PT-SLE	Embraer EMB.120ER Brasilia	120181		
☐ PR-PSF	Embraer EMB.145EP (ERJ-145EP)	145016	ex N826HK	
☐ PR-PSG	Embraer EMB.145EP (ERJ-145EP)	145021	ex N827HK	
☐ PR-PSH	Embraer EMB.145LR (ERJ-145LR)	145597	ex N559MD	
☐ PR-PSI	Embraer EMB.145LR (ERJ-145LR)	145607	ex N607MD	
☐ PR-PSJ	Embraer EMB.145LU (ERJ-145LU)	145351	ex OH-EBE	on order
☐ PR-PSK	Embraer EMB.145LU (ERJ-145LU)	145387	ex OH-EBF	on order

PENTA - PENA TRANSPORTES AEREOS | Aero Pena (5P/PEP) | Santarem, PA (STM)

☐ PP-ISE	Embraer EMB.120ER Brasilia	120246	ex N6222Z	
☐ PT-LLC	Embraer EMB.110P1 Bandeirante	110427	ex N302EB	
☐ PT-MPB	Cessna 208B Caravan I	208B0630	ex N5263A	
☐ PT-MPD	Cessna 208B Caravan I	208B0644	ex N5267T	
☐ PT-MPG	Cessna 208B Caravan I	208B0645	ex N5268A	
☐ PT-OSG	Cessna 208B Caravan I	208B0300	ex N5516B	
☐ PT-SOF	Embraer EMB.110P1A Bandeirante	110486		

PLATINUM AIR LINHAS AEREAS | (PLJ) | Sao Jose dos Campos (SJK)

☐ PR-PLH	Boeing 727-225 (Super 27)	22434/1671	ex N770PL	
☐ PR-PLQ	Boeing 727-231F (Super 27)	21984/1574	ex N984RT	on order

PUMA AIR LINHAS AEREAS | Puma Brasil (PLY) | Belem, PA (BEL)

☐ PP-PTB	Embraer EMB.120RT Brasilia	120080	ex F-GFEP	dbr 24Nov06?
☐ PR-PMC	Cessna 208B Caravan I	208B0909	ex N12826	
☐ PT-STN	Embraer EMB.120ER Brasilia	120241		

RICO LINHAS AEREAS | Rico (C7/RLE) | Manaus-Eduardo Gomez, AM (MAO)

☐ PR-RLA	Boeing 737-241	21009/417	ex PP-VMN	stored MAO
☐ (PR-RLB)	Boeing 737-241	21008/402	ex PP-VMM	stored MAO
☐ (PR-RLC)	Boeing 737-241	21000/378	ex PP-VME	
☐ PR-RLJ	Boeing 727-214F	21513/1365	ex N751US	
☐ PT-WDB	Embraer EMB.110C Bandeirante	110051	ex FAB2159	
☐ PT-WJA	Embraer EMB.110P1 Bandeirante	110265	ex PT-OHF	
☐ PT-WJG	Embraer EMB.120ER Brasilia	120064	ex PT-PCA	
☐ PT-WRU	Cessna 208 Caravan I	20800284		Floatplane
☐ PT-WZM	Embraer EMB.120ER Brasilia	120041	ex PP-IAD	
☐	Antonov An-32			on order
☐	Antonov An-32			on order

RICO TAXI AEREO | | Manaus-Eduardo Gomez, AM (MAO)

☐ PT-GJC	Embraer EMB.110E Bandeirante	110055		
☐ PT-MAA	Embraer EMB.121A Xingu II	121001	ex PT-ZCT	

SETE TAXI AEREO | Sete | Goiania, GO (GYN)

☐ PR-MEG	Cessna 208B Caravan I	208B0352	ex N1114N	
☐ PR-MEH	Cessna 208B Caravan I	208B0354	ex N1114W	
☐ PR-MEI	Cessna 208B Caravan I	208B0358	ex N1115P	
☐ PT-MEK	Cessna 208B Caravan I	208B0360	ex N1115W	
☐ PT-MEL	Cessna 208B Caravan I	208B0361	ex N1116G	
☐ PT-EHE	Embraer EMB.820C Navajo	820041		
☐ PT-LHH	Mitsubishi MU-2B-60 Marquise	1508SA	ex N618RT	
☐ PT-WST	Mitsubishi MU-2B-36A	711SA	ex N171CA	
☐ PT-WYT	Mitsubishi MU-2B-36A	722SA	ex N722MU	

SKYLIFT TAXI AEREO | | Campinhas, SP (CPQ)

☐ PT-PQD	Short SC.7 Skyvan 3	SH1951	ex C-FSDZ	

SKYMASTER AIRLINES | Skymaster Air (SKC) | Manaus-Eduardo Gomes, AM/Sao Paulo-Viracopos, SP (MAO/VCP)

☐ PR-SKC	Douglas DC-8-63F (BAC 3)	46143/547	ex N959R	
☐ PR-SKI	Douglas DC-8-62F (BAC 3)	46154/554	ex N997CF	
☐ PR-SKM	Douglas DC-8-63F (BAC 3)	46137/527	ex N957R	
☐ PT-MTE	Boeing 707-321C (Comtran 2)	20017/753	ex OB-1716	
☐ PT-MTR	Boeing 707-369C (Comtran 2)	20084/758	ex OB-1699	
☐ PT-WSZ	Boeing 707-338C (Comtran 2)	18808/404	ex HK-3030	
☐ PT-WUS	Boeing 707-324C (Comtran 2)	19352/576	ex HK-3604X	stored GRU

TAF LINHAS AEREAS | Tafi (TSD) | Fortaleza, CE (FOR)

☐ PP-SBF	Embraer EMB.110C Bandeirante	110023			stored FOR
☐ PR-MTD	Boeing 727-227F (Raisbeck 3)	21248/1218	ex N76752		
☐ PR-MTG	Boeing 737-217 (AvAero 3)	22255/666	ex N5JY	Gracinha	
☐ PR-MTH	Boeing 737-232 (Nordam 3)	23102/1045	ex N330DL		
☐ PR-MTJ	Boeing 727-2M7F (FedEx 3)	21952/1693	ex N742RW		
☐ PR-MTK	Boeing 737-222F	20037/701	ex N7643U		
☐ PR-MTL	Boeing 727-2J7F	20879/1033	ex N128NA		
☐ PT-GJD	Embraer EMB.110EJ Bandeirante	110056			
☐ PT-LBU	Embraer EMB.110C Bandeirante	110033	ex PT-FAE		stored FOR
☐ PT-MTC	Boeing 727-228F (FedEx 3)	20409/845	ex N726DH	Comte Dilsonr	
☐ PT-MTF	Boeing 737-241	21007/400	ex PP-VML		

☐ PT-OGG	Cessna 208A Caravan I	20800041	ex N813FE	
☐ PT-OGL	Cessna 208A Caravan I	20800102	ex N839FE	
☐ PT-OGV	Cessna 208A Caravan I	20800019	ex N805FE	
☐ PT-OQT	Cessna 208B Grand Caravan	208B0314	ex N1018X	
☐ PT-YTF	Helibras AS350B2 Esquilo	AS.3149		

TAM LINHAS AEREAS — *TAM (JJ/TAM)* — *Sao Paulo-Congonhas, SP (GGH)*

☐ PR-MAH	Airbus A319-132	1608	ex D-AIJO		
☐ PR-MAI	Airbus A319-132	1703	ex D-AIMM		
☐ PR-MAL	Airbus A319-132	1801	ex D-AVWD		
☐ PR-MAM	Airbus A319-132	1826	ex D-AVWN		
☐ PR-MAN	Airbus A319-132	1831	ex D-AVWR		
☐ PR-MAO	Airbus A319-132	1837	ex D-AVYQ		
☐ PR-MAQ	Airbus A319-132	1855	ex D-AVYA		
☐ PR-MBI	Airbus A319-132	1575	ex N475TA		
☐ PR-MBN	Airbus A319-132	3032	ex D-AVWG		
☐ PR-MBU	Airbus A319-132	3588	ex D-AVYG		
☐ PR-MBV	Airbus A319-132	3595	ex D-AVYC		
☐ PR-MBW	Airbus A319-132	3710	ex D-AVWQ		on order
☐ PR-MYB	Airbus A319-112	3727	ex D-AVWT		
☐ PR-MYC	Airbus A319-112	3733	ex D-AVWW		
☐ PT-MZA	Airbus A319-132	0976	ex D-AVYI		
☐ PT-MZB	Airbus A319-132	1010	ex D-AVYA		
☐ PT-MZC	Airbus A319-132	1092	ex D-AVYD		
☐ PT-MZD	Airbus A319-132	1096	ex D-AVYR		
☐ PT-MZE	Airbus A319-132	1103	ex D-AVWD		
☐ PT-MZF	Airbus A319-132	1139	ex D-AVYO		
☐ PT-TMA	Airbus A319-132	4000	ex D-AVYA		
☐ PT-TMB	Airbus A319-132	4163	ex D-AVYF		on order
☐ PT-TMC	Airbus A319-132	4171	ex D-AVWJ		on order
☐ PT-TMD	Airbus A319-132	4194	ex D-AV		on order
☐ PT-TME	Airbus A319-132		ex D-AV		on order

☐ PR-MAA	Airbus A320-232	1595	ex F-WWBU	
☐ PR-MAB	Airbus A320-232	1663	ex F-WWIE	
☐ PR-MAC	Airbus A320-232	1672	ex F-WWIK	450 anos
☐ PR-MAD	Airbus A320-232	1771	ex F-WWDD	
☐ PR-MAE	Airbus A320-232	1804	ex F-WWII	
☐ PR-MAG	Airbus A320-232	1832	ex F-WWBD	Sao Paulo 450 Anos
☐ PR-MAJ	Airbus A320-232	1818	ex F-WWIN	
☐ PR-MAK	Airbus A320-232	1825	ex F-WWIX	
☐ PR-MAP	Airbus A320-232	1857	ex F-WWBZ	
☐ PR-MAR	Airbus A320-232	1888	ex F-WWBS	
☐ PR-MAS	Airbus A320-232	2372	ex F-WWDQ	
☐ PR-MAV	Airbus A320-232	2393	ex F-WWIR	
☐ PR-MAW	Airbus A320-232	2417	ex F-WWDT	
☐ PR-MAX	Airbus A320-232	2602	ex F-WWBO	
☐ PR-MAY	Airbus A320-232	2661	ex F-WWIV	
☐ PR-MAZ	Airbus A320-232	2513	ex F-WWIY	
☐ PR-MBA	Airbus A320-232	2734	ex F-WWBF	
☐ PR-MBB	Airbus A320-232	2737	ex F-WWBH	
☐ PR-MBC	Airbus A320-232	2783	ex F-WWDZ	
☐ PR-MBD	Airbus A320-232	2838	ex F-WWID	
☐ PR-MBE	Airbus A320-232	2859	ex F-WWIU	
☐ PR-MBF	Airbus A320-232	2896	ex F-WWBZ	
☐ PR-MBG	Airbus A320-232	1459	ex OE-LOR	
☐ PR-MBH	Airbus A320-232	2904	ex F-WWDP	
☐ PR-MBJ	Airbus A320-232	2445	ex ZK-OJK	
☐ PR-MBL	Airbus A320-233	2044	ex HC-CDZ	
☐ PR-MBM	Airbus A320-233	1339	ex N463TA	
☐ PR-MBO	Airbus A320-232	3156	ex F-WWDK	
☐ PR-MBP	Airbus A320-232	1215	ex G-TTOA	
☐ PR-MBQ	Airbus A320-232	1652	ex N533JB	
☐ PR-MBR	Airbus A320-232	1802	ex N542JB	
☐ PR-MBS	Airbus A320-232	1835	ex N544JB	
☐ PR-MBX	Airbus A320-232	1591	ex N528JB	
☐ PR-MBY	Airbus A320-232	1891	ex N550JB	
☐ PR-MBZ	Airbus A320-232	1827	ex N546JB	
☐ PR-MHA	Airbus A320-214	2924	ex F-WWDV	
☐ PR-MHB	Airbus A320-214	1692	ex F-GRSN	
☐ PR-MHC	Airbus A320-214	1717	ex EC-ICN	
☐ PR-MHD	Airbus A320-214	1775	ex EC-JHJ	
☐ PR-MHE	Airbus A320-214	3111	ex F-WWIS	
☐ PR-MHF	Airbus A320-214	3180	ex F-WWDT	
☐ PR-MHG	Airbus A320-214	3002	ex F-WWBB	
☐ PR-MHI	Airbus A320-214	3035	ex F-WWDE	
☐ PR-MHJ	Airbus A320-214	3047	ex F-WWDQ	
☐ PR-MHK	Airbus A320-214	3058	ex F-WWDX	
☐ PR-MHM	Airbus A320-214	3211	ex F-WWIR	
☐ PR-MHN	Airbus A320-214	3240	ex F-WWBM	
☐ PR-MHO	Airbus A320-214	3278	ex F-WWDK	
☐ PR-MHP	Airbus A320-214	3266	ex F-WWBS	

☐ PR-MHQ	Airbus A320-214	3284	ex F-WWDQ	
☐ PR-MHR	Airbus A320-214	3313	ex F-WWIQ	
☐ PR-MHS	Airbus A320-214	3325	ex F-WWBF	
☐ PR-MHT	Airbus A320-214	1757	ex EI-DJI	
☐ PR-MHU	Airbus A320-214	3391	ex F-WWDR	
☐ PR-MHV	Airbus A320-214	3540	ex F-WWIO	
☐ PR-MHW	Airbus A320-214	3630	ex F-WWBQ	
☐ PR-MHX	Airbus A320-214	3565	ex F-WWBM	
☐ PR-MHY	Airbus A320-214	3594	ex F-WWDG	
☐ PR-MHZ	Airbus A320-214	3658	ex F-WWDT	
☐ PR-MYA	Airbus A320-214	3662	ex F-WWDV	
☐ PR-MYD	Airbus A320-214	3750	ex F-WWBR	
☐ PR-MYE	Airbus A320-214	3908	ex F-WWIR	
☐ PR-MYF	Airbus A320-214	3972	ex F-WWIQ	
☐ PR-MYI	Airbus A320-214	4169	ex	on order
☐ PR-	Airbus A320-214		ex	on order
☐ PR-	Airbus A320-214		ex	on order
☐ PR-	Airbus A320-214		ex	on order
☐ PR-	Airbus A320-214		ex	on order
☐ PR-	Airbus A320-214		ex	on order
☐ PR-	Airbus A320-214		ex	on order
☐ PR-	Airbus A320-214		ex	on order
☐ PR-	Airbus A320-214		ex	on order
☐ PR-	Airbus A320-214		ex	on order
☐ PT-MZG	Airbus A320-232	1143	ex F-WWBG	
☐ PT-MZH	Airbus A320-232	1158	ex F-WWBY	
☐ PT-MZI	Airbus A320-232	1246	ex F-WWIR	
☐ PT-MZJ	Airbus A320-232	1251	ex F-WWIV	
☐ PT-MZK	Airbus A320-232	1368	ex F-WWIJ	
☐ PT-MZL	Airbus A320-232	1376	ex F-WWIN	
☐ PT-MZN	Airbus A320-231	0440	ex ZS-SHG	
☐ PT-MZO	Airbus A320-231	0250	ex ZS-SHC	
☐ PT-MZQ	Airbus A320-231	0335	ex ZS-SHF	
☐ PT-MZR	Airbus A320-231	0334	ex ZS-SHE	
☐ PT-MZT	Airbus A320-232	1486	ex F-WWDV	
☐ PT-MZU	Airbus A320-232	1518	ex F-WWIJ	
☐ PT-MZV	Airbus A320-232	0758	ex N758SL	
☐ PT-MZW	Airbus A320-232	1580	ex F-WWBK	
☐ PT-MZX	Airbus A320-232	1613	ex F-WWDI	
☐ PT-MZY	Airbus A320-232	1628	ex F-WWDO	
☐ PT-MZZ	Airbus A320-232	1593	ex F-WWBT	
☐ PT-MXA	Airbus A321-231	3222	ex D-AVZF	
☐ PT-MXB	Airbus A321-231	3229	ex D-AVZG	
☐ PT-MXC	Airbus A321-231	3294	ex D-AVZE	
☐ PT-MXD	Airbus A321-231	3761	ex D-AZAP	
☐ PT-MXE	Airbus A321-231	3816	ex D-AVZB	
☐ PT-MVA	Airbus A330-223	232	ex A6-EYX	
☐ PT-MVB	Airbus A330-223	238	ex A6-EYY	
☐ PT-MVC	Airbus A330-223	247	ex F-WWKH	
☐ PT-MVD	Airbus A330-223	259	ex A6-EYB	
☐ PT-MVE	Airbus A330-223	361	ex A6-EYA	
☐ PT-MVF	Airbus A330-203	466	ex F-WWKP	
☐ PT-MVG	Airbus A330-203	472	ex F-WWKQ	
☐ PT-MVH	Airbus A330-203	477	ex F-WWKS	
☐ PT-MVK	Airbus A330-203	486	ex F-WWYL	
☐ PT-MVL	Airbus A330-203	700	ex F-WWKB	
☐ PT-MVM	Airbus A330-223	869	ex F-WWYR	
☐ PT-MVN	Airbus A330-223	876	ex F-WWKE	
☐ PT-MVO	Airbus A330-223	949	ex F-WWKP	
☐ PT-MVP	Airbus A330-223	961	ex F-WWYF	
☐ PT-MVQ	Airbus A330-223	968	ex F-WWYN	
☐ PT-MVR	Airbus A330-223	977	ex F-WWKV	
☐ PT-MSL	Airbus A340-541	464	ex C-GKOM	
☐ PT-MSN	Airbus A340-541	445	ex C-GKOL	
☐ PT-MSR	Boeing 767-33AER	27377/561	ex I-DEIC	on order
☐ PT-MSQ	Boeing 767-33AER	27468/584	ex I-DEID	
☐ PT-MSU	Boeing 767-33AER	27376/560	ex PR-VAG	
☐ PT-MUA	Boeing 777-32WER	37664/727		
☐ PT-MUB	Boeing 777-32WER	37665/733	ex N6009F	
☐ PT-MUC	Boeing 777-32WER	37666/740		
☐ PT-MUD	Boeing 777-32WER	37667/751		
☐ PT-MQC	Fokker F.28-0100 (Fokker 100)	11371	ex PH-JXP	
☐ PT-MRE	Fokker F.28-0100 (Fokker 100)	11348	ex PH-LNM	

TAM - TAXI AEREO MARILIA — Sao Paulo-Congonhas, SP (GGH)

☐ PP-ITY	Cessna 208B Caravan I	208B0560	ex N1301B
☐ PR-MAU	Cessna 208B Caravan I	208B0621	ex ZP-CAD
☐ PT-MEA	Cessna 208B Caravan I	208B0333	ex N1037L
☐ PT-MEB	Cessna 208B Caravan I	208B0335	ex N1038G
☐ PT-MEC	Cessna 208B Caravan I	208B0342	ex N1045C
☐ PT-MED	Cessna 208B Caravan I	208B0343	ex N1052C
☐ PT-MEJ	Cessna 208B Caravan I	208B0359	ex N1115V
☐ PT-MEM	Cessna 208B Caravan I	208B0405	
☐ PT-MEN	Cessna 208B Caravan I	208B0408	
☐ PT-MEO	Cessna 208B Caravan I	208B0412	
☐ PT-MES	Cessna 208B Caravan I	208B0507	
☐ PT-MEX	Cessna 208B Caravan I	208B0515	ex N50280
☐ PT-MHC	Cessna 208B Caravan I	208B0543	

TASUL - TAXI AEREO SUL — Porto Alegre-Salgado Filho, RS (PQA)

☐ PT-JJB	Cessna 402B	402B0399	ex N8063Q
☐ PT-KDA	Cessna 310Q	310Q1087	

TAVAJ LINHAS AEREAS — Tavaj (4U/TVJ) — Rio Branco, AC (RBR)

☐ PT-GJP	Embraer EMB.110EJ Bandeirante	110065	
☐ PT-LRB	Embraer EMB.110P1 Bandeirante	110409	ex N720RA
☐ PT-LRJ	Embraer EMB.110P1 Bandeirante	110384	ex N699RA
☐ PT-LTN	Embraer EMB.110P1 Bandeirante	110418	ex N860AC
☐ PT-OCX	Embraer EMB.110P1 Bandeirante	110316	ex N94PB
☐ PT-LAG	Fokker F.27 Friendship 600	10197	ex PH-FDM
☐ PT-LAH	Fokker F.27 Friendship 600	10178	ex PH-FCS

TAXI AEREO ITAITUBA — Santarem, PA (STM)

☐ PT-GJR	Embraer EMB.110EJ Bandeirante	110070	
☐ PT-GKE	Embraer EMB.110B1 Bandeirante	110096	ex PP-ZKE

TAXI AEREO WEISS — Curitiba, PR (CWB)

☐ PT-EFU	Embraer EMB.820C Navajo	820031	
☐ PT-ELY	Embraer EMB.820C Navajo	820063	
☐ PT-GKQ	Embraer EMB.110P Bandeirante	110125	
☐ PT-TAW	Embraer EMB.110P1 Bandeirante	110258	ex CX-VIP

TEAM AIRLINES – TEAM TRANSPORTES AEREOS — Team Brasil (TIM) — Rio de Janeiro-Santos Dumont, RJ (SDU)

☐ PR-AIA	LET L-410UVP-E	912611	ex CCCP-67680
☐ PR-IMO	LET L-410UVP-E20	922701	ex OK-XDJ

TRIP LINHAS AEREAS — (8R) — Sao Paulo-Viracopos, SP (VCP)

☐ PP-ATV	ATR 42-300	298	ex F-WQHA	
☐ PP-PTC	ATR 42-300	035	ex F-ODUD	
☐ PP-PTD	ATR 42-320	091	ex F-WQNS	
☐ PP-PTF	ATR 42-300	072	ex LV-ZNV	
☐ PP-PTG	ATR 42-320	128	ex F-WQNA	
☐ PP-PTI	ATR 42-320	374	ex F-WQNP	
☐ PP-PTJ	ATR 42-320	284	ex CX-PUC	
☐ PP-PTV	ATR 42-500	503	ex F-WNUA	
☐ PP-PTW	ATR 42-500	510	ex F-WNUB	
☐ PR-TTE	ATR 42-300	400	ex F-WQNG	
☐ PR-TTF	ATR 42-300	021	ex F-WQNS	
☐ PR-TTG	ATR 42-320	020	ex F-OHOT	
☐ PR-TTH	ATR 42-500	506	ex F-WQNL	
☐ PR-TTK	ATR 42-500	504	ex F-WQNK	
☐ PR-TTM	ATR 42-500	551	ex D-BNNN	
☐ PT-MFE	ATR 42-300	295	ex F-WWLU	
☐ PT-TTL	ATR 42-320	380	ex N988MA	
☐ PP-PTH	ATR 72-202	365	ex F-GMGK	
☐ PP-PTK	ATR 72-202	352	ex F-GKPH	
☐ PP-PTL	ATR 72-212A	773	ex F-WWEL	
☐ PP-PTM	ATR 72-212A	798	ex F-WWEO	
☐ PP-PTN	ATR 72-212A	832	ex F-WWEI	
☐ PP-PTO	ATR 72-212A	837	ex F-WWEO	
☐ PP-PTP	ATR 72-212A	865	ex F-WWEO	
☐ PP-PTQ	ATR 72-212A	874	ex F-WWEZ	
☐ PP-PTR	ATR 72-212A	785	ex F-WWED	on order
☐ PR-TTI	ATR 72-212	454	ex N531AS	
☐ PR-TTJ	ATR 72-212	463	ex N534AS	

☐ PR-TTB	Boeing 727-223 (FedEx 3)	22007/1643	ex N891AA	
☐ PR-TTO	Boeing 727-2M7F (FedEx 3)	21200/1206	ex N721RW	
☐ PR-TTP	Boeing 727-2M7F (FedEx 3)	1339/21502	ex N998PG	
☐ PT-MTQ	Boeing 727-243F	22053/1620	ex N198PC	
☐ PT-MTT	Boeing 727-243F	22167/1752	ex N270PC	
☐ PP-PJA	Embraer 170-200LR (175LR)	17000272	ex PT-SNF	
☐ PP-PJB	Embraer 170-200LR (175LR)	17000277	ex PT-TQD	
☐ PP-PJC	Embraer 170-200LR (175LR)	17000287	ex PT-TQN	
☐ PP-PJD	Embraer 170-200LR (175LR)	17000017	ex D-ALIB	
☐ PP-PJE	Embraer 170-200LR (175LR)	17000291		on order
☐ PP-PJF	Embraer 170-200LR (175LR)	17000309	ex PT-	on order

VARIG *Varig (RG/VRN)* *Rio de Janeiro-Galeao, RJ/Porto Alegre-Canoas, RS (GIG/POA)*

☐ PP-VNT	Boeing 737-33A	23828/1446		
☐ PP-VNY	Boeing 737-3K9	24864/1918		
☐ PP-VNZ	Boeing 737-3K9	24869/1926		
☐ PP-VQN	Boeing 737-33A	24098/1783	ex N98NG	
☐ PP-VQO	Boeing 737-3M8	24377/1719	ex N77NG	stored GYR
☐ PP-VTA	Boeing 737-3K9	23797/1416	ex PT-TEU	stored ROW
☐ PP-VTB	Boeing 737-3K9	23798/1429	ex PT-TEV	
☐ PR-VBA	Boeing 737-8AS/W	29916/210	ex EI-CSA	
☐ PR-VBB	Boeing 737-8AS/W	29917/298	ex EI-CSB	
☐ PR-VBC	Boeing 737-8AS/W	29918/307	ex EI-CSC	
☐ PR-VBD	Boeing 737-8AS/W	29919/341	ex EI-CSD	
☐ PR-VBE	Boeing 737-8AS/W	29920/362	ex EI-CSE	
☐ PR-VBF	Boeing 737-8EH/W	34276/2716		
☐ PR-VBG	Boeing 737-8EH/W	35066/2700		
☐ PR-VBJ	Boeing 737-86N/W	36434/2706		
☐ PR-VBK	Boeing 737-8EH/W	34271/2445	ex PR-GTX	Lsd fr GLO
☐ PR-VBL	Boeing 737-8EH/W	34272/2449	ex PR-GTW	Lsd fr GLO
☐ PR-VBM	Boeing 737-7EA	32406/859	ex N815PG	
☐ PR-VBN	Boeing 737-76N	28577/124	ex N966PG	
☐ PR-VBP	Boeing 737-7EA	32407/904	ex N160CK	
☐ PR-VBU	Boeing 737-76N/W	29905/372	ex N746AL	
☐ PR-VBV	Boeing 737-76N/W	30050/429	ex N748AL	
☐ PR-VBX	Boeing 737-7BX	30738/716	ex 6V-AHN	
☐ PR-VAB	Boeing 767-33AER	27477/337	ex B-2497	stored VNF
☐ PR-VAF	Boeing 767-38EER	25132/417	ex CC-CIO	stored GYR
☐ PR-VAN	Boeing 767-328ER	27427/579	ex N801PG	stored GIG

VARIG LOG *(LC/VLO)* *Sao Paulo-Guarulhos, SP/ (GRU)*

☐ PP-VQV	Boeing 727-243F	22166/1725	ex PP-SFE		
☐ PR-LGC	Boeing 727-2A1F (FedEx 3)	21342/1256	ex N214UP	Leandra	Lsd fr Platinum Air
☐ PR-LGF	Boeing 757-28A (PCF)	24235/180	ex N235SC		
☐ PR-LGH	Boeing 757-225 (PCF)	22211/74	ex N314ST		
☐ PR-LGJ	Boeing 757-225 (PCF)	22210/42	ex N930RD		

WEBJET LINHAS AEREAS *(WEB)* *Curitiba (CWB)*

☐ PR-WJA	Boeing 737-322	24663/1875	ex N401TZ
☐ PR-WJB	Boeing 737-341	25050/2125	ex PR-BRG
☐ PR-WJC	Boeing 737-341	25051/2127	ex PR-BRF
☐ PR-WJD	Boeing 737-3Y0	23922/1538	ex PT-SSK
☐ PR-WJE	Boeing 737-33A	25057/2046	ex PT-MNJ
☐ PR-WJF	Boeing 737-341	24936/1951	ex PP-VOO
☐ PR-WJG	Boeing 737-322	24452/1728	ex N359UA
☐ PR-WJH	Boeing 737-341	26856/2321	ex PP-VPB
☐ PR-WJI	Boeing 737-341	26857/2326	ex PP-VPC
☐ PR-WJJ	Boeing 737-341	24935/1935	ex PP-VON
☐ PR-WJK	Boeing 737-33A	23830/1462	ex N238MQ
☐ PR-WJL	Boeing 737-36N	28590/3097	ex SP-LME
☐ PR-WJM	Boeing 737-36Q	28660/2883	ex G-THOK
☐ PR-WJN	Boeing 737-36Q	29327/3023	ex G-THOI
☐ PR-WJO	Boeing 737-3Q8	26295/2557	ex N295AH
☐ PR-WJP	Boeing 737-3Q8	26309/2674	ex N309AN
☐ PR-WJQ	Boeing 737-3U3	28742/2992	ex ZK-FRE
☐ PR-WJR	Boeing 737-36N	28566/2964	ex PK-GGT
☐ PR-WJS	Boeing 737-3Y0	24465/1755	ex N465BV
☐ PR-WJT	Boeing 737-3Y0	24908/2015	ex N908BV

PZ- SURINAME (Republic of Suriname)

BLUE WINGS AIRLINES — Paramaribo-Zorg en Hoop (ORG)

☐ PZ-TGQ	Cessna U206G Stationair 6	U20605917	ex PZ-TAO	
☐ PZ-TLV	Cessna U206G Stationair 6	U20606951		
☐ PZ-TSB	Cessna 208 Caravan I	20000090	ex N207RM	
☐ PZ-TSD	de Havilland DHC-6 Twin Otter 200	117	ex VH-JEA	
☐ PZ-TSH	de Havilland DHC-6 Twin Otter 200	145	ex VH-TZR	
☐ PZ-	Reims Cessna F406 Caravan II	F406-0033	ex VH-JVN	
☐ PZ-TSA	WSK/PZL Antonov An-28	1AJ007-21	ex PZ-TGW	
☐ PZ-TSN	WSK/PZL Antonov An-28	1AJ007-20	ex YV-528C	
☐ PZ-TSV	WSK/PZL Antonov An-28	1AJ007-10	ex SP-FHS	

GUM AIR — (GUM) — Paramaribo-Zorg en Hoop (ORG)

☐ PZ-TBD	Cessna U206G Stationair	U20603786	ex N8286G	
☐ PZ-TBE	Cessna U206G Stationair 6	U20606776	ex N9959Z	
☐ PZ-TBG	Cessna U206B Super Skywagon	U206-0832	ex N3832G	
☐ PZ-TBH	Cessna 208B Caravan I	208B0923	ex N1132W	Spirit of Pike
☐ PZ-TBL	Britten-Norman BN-2B-26 Islander	2153	ex N633BB	
☐ PZ-TBW	de Havilland DHC-6 Twin Otter 300	601	ex N28SP	
☐ PZ-TBY	de Havilland DHC-6 Twin Otter 300	646	ex N7015A	
☐ PZ-TVC	Cessna 404 Titan	404-0243	ex YV-236CP	
☐ PZ-TVU	Cessna TU206G Stationair 6	U20604783	ex PZ-PVU	

SURINAM AIRWAYS — Surinam (PY/SLM) — Paramaribo-Zanderij International/Zorg en Hoop (PBM/ORG)

☐ PZ-TCM	Boeing 747-306M	23508/657	ex PH-BUW	Ronald Elwin Kappel
☐ PZ-TCN	Boeing 737-36N	28668/2890	ex N668AN	
☐ PZ-TCO	Boeing 737-36N	28669/2897	ex N669AN	
☐ PZ-TCP	Airbus A340-311	049	ex F-GLZG	

P2- PAPUA NEW GUINEA (Independent State of Papua New Guinea)

AIR NIUGINI — Niugini (PX/ANG) — Port Moresby (POM)

☐ P2-ANK	de Havilland DHC-8Q-202	461	ex C-GFBW		
☐ P2-ANL	de Havilland DHC-8-102	153	ex D-BOBO		
☐ P2-ANM	de Havilland DHC-8Q-314	523	ex D-BPAD		
☐ P2-ANN	de Havilland DHC-8-315	401	ex JY-RWB		
☐ P2-ANO	de Havilland DHC-8-311A	252	ex D-BOBU		
☐ P2-ANP	de Havilland DHC-8-102	177	ex D-BOBY		
☐ P2-ANX	de Havilland DHC-8Q-202	463	ex D-BHAL		
☐ P2-ANZ	de Havilland DHC-8Q-201	421	ex N986HA		
☐ P2-	de Havilland DHC-8-402Q				
☐ P2-	de Havilland DHC-8-402Q				
☐ P2-ANC	Fokker F.28-0100 (Fokker 100)	11471	ex PH-MXW		
☐ P2-AND	Fokker F.28-0100 (Fokker 100)	11473	ex PT-MRQ		
☐ P2-ANE	Fokker F.28-0100 (Fokker 100)	11264	ex PH-THY		
☐ P2-ANF	Fokker F.28-0100 (Fokker 100)	11351	ex PH-FDI		
☐ P2-ANH	Fokker F.28-0100 (Fokker 100)	11301	ex C-GPNL		
☐ P2-ANQ	Fokker F.28-0100 (Fokker 100)	11451	ex PH-ZDJ		
☐ P2-ANI	Fokker F.28 Fellowship 4000	11223	ex PH-RRB		stored POM
☐ P2-ANJ	Fokker F.28 Fellowship 4000	11219	ex PH-RRA		stored POM
☐ P2-ANR	Fokker F.28 Fellowship 4000	11207	ex VH-EWC	W/Cmdr RH (Bobby) Gibbes	stored KUL
☐ P2-ANS	Fokker F.28 Fellowship 4000	11195	ex VH-EWA		stored POM
☐ P2-ANA	Boeing 767-366ER	24541/275	ex TF-LLA		Lsd fr ICE
☐ P2-ANB	Boeing 757-256	29312/943	ex TF-FIY		Lsd fr ICE

AIRLINES OF PAPUA NEW GUINEA — (CG/TOK) — Port Moresby (POM)

☐ P2-MCC	de Havilland DHC-6 Twin Otter 200	218	ex VH-IPD
☐ P2-MCD	de Havilland DHC-6 Twin Otter 300	592	ex C-GOVG
☐ P2-MCE	de Havilland DHC-6 Twin Otter 300	673	ex C-GHRB
☐ P2-MCF	de Havilland DHC-6 Twin Otter 300	741	ex C-GRBY
☐ P2-MCR	de Havilland DHC-6 Twin Otter 300	219	ex P2-MFY
☐ P2-MCS	de Havilland DHC-6 Twin Otter 310	516	ex 5W-PAH
☐ P2-MCG	de Havilland DHC-8-102	6	ex C-GJCB
☐ P2-MCH	de Havilland DHC-8-102	12	ex C-GPYD
☐ P2-MCI	de Havilland DHC-8-102	197	ex ZK-NET
☐ P2-MCJ	de Havilland DHC-8-102	125	ex ZK-NES
☐ P2-MCL	de Havilland DHC-8-102	27	ex VH-WZJ
☐ P2-MCP	de Havilland DHC-8-102	33	ex VH-QQH

☐ P2-MCQ	de Havilland DHC-8-103A	243	ex VH-TNW	
☐ P2-MCT	de Havilland DHC-8-102	135	ex VH-QQH	
☐ P2-MCU	de Havilland DHC-8-102	208	ex VH-QQJ	
☐ P2-CHI	Boeing Vertol 234UT Chinook	MJ-003	ex N237CH	Lsd fr WCO

ASIA PACIFIC AIRLINES — *Tabubil (TBG)*

☐ P2-NAX	de Havilland DHC-8-103	229	ex VH-JSI		Lsd fr NJS
☐ P2-NAZ	de Havilland DHC-8-106	316	ex C-GFUM	Spirit of Tabubil	Lsd fr NJS

CENTRAL AIR TRANSPORT — *Port Moresby (POM)*

☐ P2-ALM	Britten-Norman BN-2A-26 Islander	124	ex P2-NAA

EMERALD AIR

☐ P2-EMO	de Havilland DHC-6 Twin Otter 300	726	ex N726JM

HELI NIUGINI — *Madang/Mount Hagen (MAG/HGU)*

☐ P2-HBC	Bell 206L-3 LongRanger III	51396	ex VH-SBC	
☐ P2-HBH	Bell 206L-3 LongRanger III	51012	ex SE-HOR	
☐ P2-HBJ	Bell 206L-3 LongRanger III	51373	ex VH-CKP	
☐ P2-HBM	Bell 206L-1 LongRanger III	45241	ex VH-HJL	
☐ P2-HBN	Bell 206L-1 LongRanger III	45487	ex VH-CKU	
☐ P2-HBP	Bell 206L-1 LongRanger III	51042	ex VH-CKI	
☐ P2-JND	Bell 206L-1 LongRanger III	45645	ex VH-MQA	
☐ P2-HBK	Kawasaki/MBB BK-117B-2	1046	ex ZK-HBK	
☐ P2-HBL	Kawasaki/MBB BK-117B-2	1021	ex ZK-HLU	
☐ P2-HBQ	Kawasaki/MBB BK-117B-2	1075	ex ZK-HLI	
☐ P2-RAA	Kamov Ka-32S	8705	ex RA-31583	Lsd fr VLK
☐ RA-25503	Mil Mi-8MTV-1	95651	ex CCCP-25503	Lsd fr VLK
☐ RA-27101	Mil Mi-8AMT	59489605182		Lsd fr VLK
☐ RA-27158	Mil Mi-8AMT	59489611156	ex RA-25755	Lsd fr VLK
☐ RA-31031	Kamov Ka-32S/T	6106	ex CCCP-31031	Lsd fr VLK
☐ RA-31032	Kamov Ka-32S	6107	ex CCCP-31032	Lsd fr VLK
☐ RA-31036	Kamov Ka-32T	6111	ex CCCP-31036	Lsd fr VLK

HEVI-LIFT — *(IU)* — *Mount Hagen/Cairns (HGU/CNS)*

☐ P2-HCA	Bell 206L-1 LongRanger II	45337	ex VH-BJX
☐ P2-HCB	Bell 206L-1 LongRanger II	45404	ex VH-HHS
☐ P2-HCC	Bell 206L-1 LongRanger III	45427	ex N5019T
☐ P2-HCD	Bell 206L-1 LongRanger III	45528	ex C-GGHZ
☐ P2-HCM	Bell 206L-1 LongRanger III	45608	ex P2-NHE
☐ P2-HCO	Bell 206L-3 LongRanger III	51178	ex N3204K
☐ P2-HCU	Bell 206L-3 LongRanger III	51416	ex N254EV
☐ P2-HLT	Bell 206L-3 LongRanger III	51387	ex VH-HQT
☐ P2-HCJ	Bell 212	30799	ex VH-EMJ
☐ P2-HCK	Bell 212	30583	ex N212SX
☐ P2-HCQ	Bell 212	30860	ex JA9528
☐ P2-HCW	Bell 212	30520	ex PK-EBO
☐ P2-HLV	Bell 212	30508	ex VH-SYV
☐ ER-MHL	Mil Mi-8MTV-1	95721	ex RA-25105
☐ ER-MHM	Mil Mi-8MTV-1	95881	ex RA-27047
☐ P2-HCL	Aérospatiale AS350B2 Ecureuil	3374	ex SE-JFO
☐ P2-HCN	Beech 200C Super King Air	BL-22	ex P2-PJV
☐ P2-HCS	Bell 412HP	33160	ex VH-HQQ
☐ P2-HCY	Aérospatiale AS350B3 Ecureuil	3242	ex JA6292
☐ P2-HCZ	Aérospatiale AS350B3 Ecureuil	3634	ex ZK-HRD
☐ P2-KSF	de Havilland DHC-6 Twin Otter 300	528	ex PK-HCF

ISLAND AIRWAYS — *Madang (MAG)*

☐ P2-CBC	Cessna 402B	402B0909	ex VH-LCF

ISLANDS NATIONAIR — *(CN)* — *Port Moresby (POM)*

☐ P2-IHA	Bell 206L-1 LongRanger II	45333	ex VH-BLV
☐ P2-IHE	Bell 206L-1 LongRanger III	45238	ex N140VG
☐ P2-IHH	Bell 206L-3 LongRanger III	45255	ex P2-NHD

KIUNGA AVIATION — *Lae (LAE)*

☐ P2-KAA	Cessna 402C	402C0247	ex N2748X

NORTH COAST AVIATION (N9/AOH) Madang (MAG)

☐ P2-DWA	Britten-Norman BN-2A-26 Islander	113	ex VH-EQE	
☐ P2-IAC	Britten-Norman BN-2A-21 Islander	425	ex P2-KAF	
☐ P2-ISA	Britten-Norman BN-2A-20 Islander	758	ex P2-SWB	
☐ P2-ISB	Britten-Norman BN-2A-20 Islander	709	ex P2-MKW	stored
☐ P2-ISL	Britten-Norman BN-2A-20 Islander	806	ex G-BDYT	
☐ P2-ISM	Britten-Norman BN-2A-20 Islander	227	ex VH-EDI	
☐ P2-NCE	Britten-Norman BN-2A-20 Islander	768	ex P2-IAD	
☐ P2-SAC	Britten-Norman BN-2A-20 Islander	94	ex P2-DNY	
☐ P2-DQU	Cessna U206B Super Skywagon	U206-0892	ex VH-DQU	
☐ P2-GKB	Cessna 402	402-0141	ex VH-GKB	
☐ P2-IDK	Cessna U206G Super Skywagon	U206-1418	ex P2-TNK	
☐ P2-IDM	Cessna U206F Stationair	U20603126	ex P2-SIA	
☐ P2-NCD	Cessna 402B	402B1027	ex VH-USV	
☐ P2-OHS	Cessna P206B Super Skylane	P206-0392	ex P2-HCM	

PACIFIC HELICOPTERS Goroka (GKA)

☐ P2-PHA	Aérospatiale AS350BA Ecureuil	1181	ex P2-PHU	
☐ P2-PHD	Aérospatiale AS350BA Ecureuil	1067	ex 9N-ACQ	
☐ P2-PHH	Aérospatiale AS350BA Ecureuil	1608	ex VH-CHO	
☐ P2-PHK	Aérospatiale AS350B2 Ecureuil			
☐ P2-PHX	Aérospatiale AS350BA Ecureuil	1817		
☐ P2-PAU	Bell 212	30793	ex A6-BBG	
☐ P2-PAV	Bell 212	30913	ex G-GLEN	
☐ P2-PAX	Bell 212	30786	ex A6-BBF	
☐ P2-PBA	Bell 206L-1 LongRanger III	45642	ex VH-SCV	
☐ P2-PBB	Bell 206L-3 LongRanger III	51400	ex N86CE	
☐ P2-PBC	Bell 206L-1 LongRanger III	45349	ex N1077N	
☐ P2-PBD	Bell 206L-3 LongRanger III	51275	ex VH-CKI	

REGIONAL AIR (QT) Madang (MAG)

☐ P2-KSA	Beech 200 Super King Air	BB-1527	ex N170W	
☐ P2-KSB	de Havilland DHC-6 Twin Otter 300	485	ex VH-RPU	
☐ P2-KSS	de Havilland DHC-6 Twin Otter 300	578	ex N578SA	id not confirmed
☐ P2-KST	de Havilland DHC-6 Twin Otter 300	520	ex YJ-RV5	

SIL AVIATION Aiyura (AYU)

☐ P2-SIA	Beech B200C Super King Air	BL-39	ex VH-FDR	
☐ P2-SIG	Cessna TU206G Stationair 6	U20606029	ex VH-XAA	Robertson STOL conversion
☐ P2-SIJ	Cessna TU206G Stationair 6	U20605805	ex N5491X	Robertson STOL conversion
☐ P2-SIL	Bell 206B JetRanger III	3498	ex ZK-HTF	
☐ P2-SIT	Cessna TU206G Stationair 6	U20606158	ex N181PK	Robertson STOL conversion
☐ P2-SIV	Britten-Norman BN-2T Islander	2138	ex 9M-TIR	

SOUTHWEST AIR Mendi (MDU)

☐ P2-SHA	Bell 206L-3 LongRanger III	51533	ex VH-IRE	
☐ P2-SWE	de Havilland DHC-6 Twin Otter 300	480	ex P2-RDL	
☐ P2-SWF	Embraer EMB.110P1 Bandeirante	110237	ex N691RA	stored BNE

TRANSNIUGINI AIRWAYS Port Moresby (POM)

☐ P2-TND	Britten-Norman BN-2A-21 Islander	813	ex P2-COD	

TROPICAIR Port Moresby (POM)

☐ P2-AMH	Cessna 208B Caravan I	208B0785	ex N785SC	
☐ P2-BEN	Cessna 208B Caravan I	208B0424	ex VH-LSA	
☐ P2-SAH	Cessna 208B Caravan I	208B1263	ex N41149	
☐ P2-SMA	Cessna U206G Stationair 6	U20604227	ex P2-AAC	

VAN AIR Vanimo (VAI)

☐ P2-VAB	Britten-Norman BN-2A-20 Islander	759	ex P2-MFZ	

P4- ARUBA

TIARA AIR (3P/TNM) Aruba (AUA)

☐ P4-TIA	Short SD.3-60	SH3619	ex C-GPCG	
☐ P4-TIB	Short SD.3-60	SH3621	ex C-GPCN	stored OPF

RA- RUSSIA (Russian Federation)

ABAKAN-AVIA — Abakan-Avia (ABG) — Abakan (ABA)

	Registration	Type	c/n	Previous identity	Notes
☐	RA-76457	Ilyushin Il-76T	093421621	ex CCCP-76457	
☐	RA-76504	Ilyushin Il-76T	073411330	ex CCCP-76504	
☐	RA-76509	Ilyushin Il-76T	083413415	ex CCCP-76509	all-white
☐	RA-76780	Ilyushin Il-76T	0013430901	ex CCCP-76780	all-white

AERO RENT — Aeromaster (NRO) — Moscow-Vnukovo (VKO)

	Registration	Type	c/n	Previous identity	Notes
☐	RA-21506	Yakovlev Yak-40KD	9840259	ex CCCP-21506	VIP
☐	RA-42434	Yakovlev Yak-42D	4520424305017		
☐	RA-65557	Tupolev Tu-134A	66380	ex 65557	VIPop for Itera
☐	RA-65790	Tupolev Tu-134A-3	63100	ex UR-65790	VIPop for Stroytransgaz
☐	RA-87397	Yakovlev Yak-40	9410933	ex CCCP-87397	
☐	RA-88306	Yakovlev Yak-40KD	9640651	ex OK-GEL	VIPop for Stroytransgaz

AERO-KAMOV — Aerafkam (MSV) — Moscow-Lyubersty

	Registration	Type	c/n	Previous identity	Notes
☐	RA-31005	Kamov Ka-32T	5701	ex CCCP-31005	
☐	RA-31027	Kamov Ka-32S	6102	ex CCCP-31027	
☐	RA-31065	Kamov Ka-32A	300048607	ex CCCP-31065	
☐	RA-31091	Kamov Ka-32T	8807		
☐	RA-31584	Kamov Ka-32S	8706	ex CCCP-31584	Op for Moscow Firebrigade
☐	RA-31592	Kamov Ka-32T	8717		

AEROBRATSK — Aerobra (BRP) — Bratsk (BTK)

	Registration	Type	c/n	Previous identity	Notes
☐	RA-22856	Mil Mi-8T	98415350	ex CCCP-22856	
☐	RA-24261	Mil Mi-8T	98734147	ex CCCP-24261	
☐	RA-88205	Yakovlev Yak-40	9630749	ex CCCP-88205	
☐	RA-88215	Yakovlev Yak-40K	9630150	ex CCCP-88215	

AEROFLOT CARGO — Aeroflot Cargo (SU/RCF) — Hahn/Mosvow-Sheremetyevo (HHN/SVO)

Merged back into Aeroflot

AEROFLOT PLUS — (PLS) — Moscow-Sheremetyevo (SVO)

	Registration	Type	c/n	Previous identity	Notes
☐	RA-65559	Tupolev Tu-134A	7349909	ex CCCP-65559	VIP
☐	RA-65694	Tupolev Tu-134B-3	63235	ex UN-65694	VIP
☐	RA-65790	Tupolev Tu-134A-3	63100	ex UR-65790	VIP

AEROFLOT RUSSIAN AIRLINES — Aeroflot (SU/AFL) — Moscow-Sheremetyevo (SVO)

Member of Skyteam

	Registration	Type	c/n	Previous identity	Name
☐	VP-BDM	Airbus A319-111	2069	ex D-AVYJ	A Borodin
☐	VP-BDN	Airbus A319-111	2072	ex D-AVYL	A Dargomyzhsky
☐	VP-BDO	Airbus A319-111	2091	ex D-AVWU	I Stravinsky
☐	VP-BUK	Airbus A319-111	3281	ex D-AVYP	YU Senkevich
☐	VP-BUN	Airbus A319-111	3298	ex D-AVYI	
☐	VP-BUO	Airbus A319-111	3336	ex D-AVYS	
☐	VP-BWA	Airbus A319-111	2052	ex D-AVYA	S Prokofiev
☐	VP-BWG	Airbus A319-111	2093	ex D-AVYE	A Aleksandrov
☐	VP-BWJ	Airbus A319-111	2179	ex D-AVYU	A Shnitke
☐	VP-BWK	Airbus A319-111	2222	ex D-AVYI	S Taneyev
☐	VP-BWL	Airbus A319-111	2243	ex D-AVWV	A Grechaninov
☐	VQ-BBA	Airbus A319-111	3794	ex D-AVXM	S Cheliuskin
☐	VQ-BBD	Airbus A319-111	3838	ex D-AVYP	V Golovnin
☐	VQ-BCO	Airbus A319-111	3942	ex D-AVWR	A Hachaturian
☐	VQ-BCP	Airbus A319-111	3998	ex D-AVYZ	D Mendeleev
☐	VP-BDK	Airbus A320-214	2106	ex F-WWDR	G Sviridov
☐	VP-BKC	Airbus A320-214	3545	ex F-WWIT	I Kruzenshtern
☐	VP-BKX	Airbus A320-214	3410	ex F-WWIJ	
☐	VP-BKY	Airbus A320-214	3511	ex F-WWBZ	
☐	VP-BME	Airbus A320-214	3699	ex F-WWBO	N Mikluho-Maklay
☐	VP-BMF	Airbus A320-214	3711	ex F-WWIV	G Shelihov
☐	VP-BQP	Airbus A320-214	2875	ex F-WWBJ	A Rublev
☐	VP-BQU	Airbus A320-214	3373	ex F-WWDG	
☐	VP-BQV	Airbus A320-214	2920	ex F-WWDY	V Vasnetsov
☐	VP-BQW	Airbus A320-214	2947	ex F-WWBV	V Vereschchagin
☐	VP-BRX	Airbus A320-214	3063	ex F-WWDZ	V Surikov
☐	VP-BRY	Airbus A320-214	3052	ex F-WWDT	K Brulloff
☐	VP-BRZ	Airbus A320-214	3157	ex F-WWDM	V Serov
☐	VP-BWD	Airbus A320-214	2116	ex F-WWDY	A Aliabiev
☐	VP-BWE	Airbus A320-214	2133	ex F-WWDX	N Rimsky-Korsakov

☐ VP-BWF	Airbus A320-214	2144	ex F-WWBY	D Shostakovich	
☐ VP-BWH	Airbus A320-214	2151	ex F-WWIR	M Balakirev	
☐ VP-BWI	Airbus A320-214	2163	ex F-WWBD	A Glazunov	
☐ VP-BWM	Airbus A320-214	2233	ex F-WWII	S Rackhmaninov	
☐ VP-BZO	Airbus A320-214	3574	ex F-WWBK	V Bering	
☐ VP-BZP	Airbus A320-214	3631	ex D-AVYG	E Haborov	
☐ VP-BZQ	Airbus A320-214	3627	ex F-WWIS	Yu. Lisiansky	
☐ VP-BZR	Airbus A320-214	3640	ex F-WWBR	F Bellinghausen	
☐ VP-BZS	Airbus A320-214	3644	ex F-WWBU	M Lazarev	
☐ VQ-BAX	Airbus A320-214	3778	ex F-WWIM	G Nevelskoy	
☐ VQ-BAY	Airbus A320-214	3786	ex D-AVVL	S Krasheninnikov	
☐ VQ-BAZ	Airbus A320-214	3789	ex F-WWBC	V Obruchev	
☐ VQ-BBB	Airbus A320-214	3823	ex F-WWIT	Yu Gagarin	
☐ VQ-BBC	Airbus A320-214	3835	ex F-WWBI	N Przhevalsky	
☐ VQ-BCM	Airbus A320-214	3923	ex F-WWBN	G Titov	
☐ VQ-BCN	Airbus A320-214	3954	ex F-WWBV	V Chelomey	
☐ VQ-BEH	Airbus A320-214	4133	ex F-WWIS	I Pavlov	
☐ VQ-BEJ	Airbus A320-214	4160	ex D-AVVO		
☐ VP-BQR	Airbus A321-211	2903	ex D-AVZD	I Repin	
☐ VP-BQS	Airbus A321-211	2912	ex D-AVZL	I Kramskoi	
☐ VP-BQT	Airbus A321-211	2965	ex D-AVZE	I Shishkin	
☐ VP-BQX	Airbus A321-211	2957	ex D-AVZU	I Ayvazovsky	
☐ VP-BRW	Airbus A321-211	3191	ex D-AVZW	N Rerih	
☐ VP-BUM	Airbus A321-211	3267	ex D-AVZQ		
☐ VP-BUP	Airbus A321-211	3334	ex D-AVZY		
☐ VP-BWN	Airbus A321-211	2330	ex D-AVZR	A Skriabin	
☐ VP-BWO	Airbus A321-211	2337	ex D-AVZS	P Chaikovsky	
☐ VP-BWP	Airbus A321-211	2342	ex D-AVZT	M Musorgsky	
☐ VQ-BEA	Airbus A321-211	4058	ex D-AZAS	I Michurin	
☐ VQ-BED	Airbus A321-211	4074	ex D-AVZT	N Pirogov	
☐ VQ-BEE	Airbus A321-211	4099	ex D-AZAA		
☐ VQ-BEF	Airbus A321-211	4103	ex D-AZAC		
☐ VQ-BEG	Airbus A321-211	4116	ex D-AZAF		
☐ VQ-BEI	Airbus A321-211	4148	ex D-AVZS		
☐ VQ-	Airbus A321-211		ex D-		on order
☐ VQ-	Airbus A321-211		ex D-		on order
☐ VP-BLX	Airbus A330-243	963	ex F-WWYJ	E. Sveetlanov	
☐ VP-BLY	Airbus A330-243	973	ex F-WWKA	V Vysctsky	
☐ VQ-BBE	Airbus A330-243	1014	ex F-WWKU	I Brodsky	
☐ VQ-BBF	Airbus A330-243	1045	ex F-WWYB	A Griboedov	
☐ VQ-BBG	Airbus A330-243	1047	ex F-WWKD	N Gogol	
☐ VQ-BCQ	Airbus A330-343E	1058	ex F-WWYX		
☐ VQ-BCU	Airbus A330-343E	1065	ex F-WWYJ	V Mayakovsky	
☐ VQ-BCV	Airbus A330-343E	1072	ex F-WWYK	B Pasternak	
☐ VQ-BEK	Airbus A330-343E	1077	ex F-WWKN		
☐	Airbus A330-343E	1103	ex F-WW		on order
☐ VQ-	Airbus A330-223	343	ex HB-IQO		on order
☐ VP-BAV	Boeing 767-36NER	30107/761		L Tolstoy	
☐ VP-BAX	Boeing 767-36NER	30109/767		F Dostoevsky	
☐ VP-BAY	Boeing 767-36NER	30110/775		I Turgenev	
☐ VP-BAZ	Boeing 767-36NER	30111/776		N Nekrasov	
☐ VP-BDI	Boeing 767-38AER	29618/792	ex N618SH	A Pushkin	
☐ VP-BWQ	Boeing 767-341ER	30342/774	ex EI-CTW	M Lermontov	
☐ VP-BWT	Boeing 767-38AER	29617/741	ex G-OOAL	A Checkov	
☐ VP-BWU	Boeing 767-3T7ER	25076/366	ex N601EV	I Bunin	
☐ VP-BWV	Boeing 767-3T7ER	25117/370	ex N602EV	A Kuprin	
☐ VP-BWW	Boeing 767-306ER	27959/609	ex PH-BZF		
☐ VP-BWX	Boeing 767-306ER	27960/625	ex PH-BZG		
☐ RA-96005	Ilyushin Il-96-300	74393201002	ex CCCP-96005	V Chkalov	
☐ RA-96007	Ilyushin Il-96-300	74393201004		A Mayorov	
☐ RA-96008	Ilyushin Il-96-300	74393201005		IA Moiseyev	
☐ RA-96010	Ilyushin Il-96-300	74393201007		Nikolaj Karpajev	
☐ RA-96011	Ilyushin Il-96-300	74393201008		K Kokkinaki	
☐ RA-96015	Ilyushin Il-96-300	74393201012		M Gromov	
☐ RA-	Ilyushin Il-96-300				on order
☐ RA-	Ilyushin Il-96-300				on order
☐ RA-	Ilyushin Il-96-300				on order
☐ RA-	Ilyushin Il-96-300				on order
☐ RA-	Ilyushin Il-96-300				on order
☐ RA-	Ilyushin Il-96-300				on order
☐ VP-BDP	McDonnell-Douglas MD-11F	48502/520	ex N774BC		
☐ VP-BDQ	McDonnell-Douglas MD-11F	48504/548	ex N702BC		
☐ VP-BDR	McDonnell-Douglas MD-11F	48503/528	ex N725BC		
☐ N512SU	McDonnell-Douglas MD-11F	48512/529	ex OH-LGC		on order
☐ RA-85135	Tupolev Tu-154M	92A-922	ex B-2628		
☐ RA-85627	Tupolev Tu-154M	87A-756	ex CCCP-85627		
☐ RA-85637	Tupolev Tu-154M	87A-767	ex CCCP-85637		

	Registration	Type	c/n	Previous identity	Notes
☐	RA-85639	Tupolev Tu-154M	88A-771	ex CCCP-85639	
☐	RA-85641	Tupolev Tu-154M	88A-773	ex CCCP-85641	stored VKO
☐	RA-85642	Tupolev Tu-154M	88A-778	ex CCCP-85642	
☐	RA-85643	Tupolev Tu-154M	88A-779	ex CCCP-86643	
☐	RA-85644	Tupolev Tu-154M	88A-780	ex MPR-85644	
☐	RA-85646	Tupolev Tu-154M	88A-784	ex CCCP-85646	
☐	RA-85648	Tupolev Tu-154M	88A-786	ex CCCP-85648	
☐	RA-85649	Tupolev Tu-154M	88A-787	ex CCCP-85649	
☐	RA-85661	Tupolev Tu-154M	89A-811	ex CCCP-85661	
☐	RA-85662	Tupolev Tu-154M	89A-816	ex CCCP-85662	stored VKO
☐	RA-85663	Tupolev Tu-154M	89A-817	ex CCCP-85663	
☐	RA-85665	Tupolev Tu-154M	89A-819	ex CCCP-85665	
☐	RA-85668	Tupolev Tu-154M	89A-826	ex CCCP-85668	
☐	RA-85670	Tupolev Tu-154M	89A-828	ex CCCP-85670	stored VKO
☐	RA-85735	Tupolev Tu-154M	92A-917	ex B-2627	
☐	RA-85760	Tupolev Tu-154M	92A-942	ex EW-85760	
☐	RA-85765	Tupolev Tu-154M	90A-832	ex LZ-HMN	
☐	RA-85810	Tupolev Tu-154M	89A-824	ex SP-LCM	
☐	RA-85811	Tupolev Tu-154M	89A-831	ex SP-LCN	

AEROKUZBASS — ***Novokuznetsk (NKZ)*** — ***Novokuznetsk (NOZ)***

	Registration	Type	c/n	Previous identity	Notes
☐	RA-85392	Tupolev Tu-154B-2	80A-392	ex CCCP-85392	
☐	RA-85471	Tupolev Tu-154B-2	81A-471	ex CCCP-85471	
☐	RA-85747	Tupolev Tu-154M	92A-930	ex EP-EAD	Lsd to IRB as EP-MBT
☐	RA-85749	Tupolev Tu-154M	92A-931	ex EP-MBM	Lsd to IRB as EP-MBQ
☐	RA-22725	Mil Mi-8T	98308700	ex CCCP-22725	
☐	RA-24140	Mil Mi-8T	98841391	ex CCCP-24140	
☐	RA-24430	Mil Mi-8T	98625661	ex CCCP-24430	

AIR BASHKORTOSTAN — ***(BBT)*** — ***Ufa (UFA)***

	Registration	Type	c/n	Previous identity	Notes
☐	RA-73015	Boeing 757-230	25901/464	ex D-ABNO	Lsd fr MOV

AIRBRIDGE CARGO — ***Volga Dnepr (RU/ABW)*** — ***MoscowSheremetyevo(SVO)***

	Registration	Type	c/n	Previous identity	Notes
☐	VP-BIC	Boeing 747-329 (SF)	24837/810	ex TF-ARY	
☐	VP-BIG	Boeing 747-46NERF	35420/1395	ex N5022E	
☐	VP-BII	Boeing 747-281F	24576/818	ex JA8191	
☐	VP-BIJ	Boeing 747-281F	25171/886	ex JA8194	
☐	VP-BIK	Boeing 747-46NERF	35421/1400		
☐	VP-BIM	Boeing 747-4HAERF	35237/1402		
☐	VQ-BFX	Boeing 747-428ERF	33096/1317	ex F-GIUB	
☐	RA-64051	Tupolev Tu-204-120C	64051		on order
☐	RA-64052	Tupolev Tu-204-120C	64052		on order

AIRSTARS AIRWAYS — ***Morozov (PL/ASE)*** — ***Moscow-Domodedovo (DME)***

	Registration	Type	c/n	Previous identity	Notes
☐	RA-76476	Ilyushin Il-76TD	0043451528	ex CCCP-76476	
☐	RA-76750	Ilyushin Il-76TD	0083485561	ex CCCP-76750	
☐	RA-86523	Ilyushin Il-62M	2241647	ex CCCP-86523	
☐	RA-86568	Ilyushin Il-62M	4256223		stored DME
☐	RA-96002	Ilyushin Il-96-300	74393201001		

ALANIA AIRLINE — ***Alania (2D/OST)*** — ***Vladikavkaz (OGZ)***

	Registration	Type	c/n	Previous identity	Notes
☐	RA-42435	Yakovlev Yak-42D	4520424306017	ex ER-YCA	
☐	RA-65613	Tupolev Tu-134A	3352106	ex 65613	

ALPHA AIRLINES

	Registration	Type	c/n	Previous identity	Notes
☐	RA-86597	Ilyushin Il-62M	2932748	ex OK-JBI	Uliya

Current status uncertain

ALROSA AVIA — ***Alrosa (LRO)*** — ***Moscow-Zhukovsky / Vnukovo***

	Registration	Type	c/n	Previous identity	Notes
☐	RA-65693	Tupolev Tu-134B-3	63221	ex YL-LBC	Executive
☐	RA-65907	Tupolev Tu-134A	63996	ex CCCP-65907	Executive

ALROSA AVIATION — ***Mirny (6R/DRU)*** — ***Mirny (MJZ)***

	Registration	Type	c/n	Previous identity	Notes
☐	RA-22394	Mil Mi-8T	7296	ex CCCP-22394	
☐	RA-22570	Mil Mi-8T	7816	ex CCCP-22570	
☐	RA-22571	Mil Mi-8T	7817	ex CCCP-22571	
☐	RA-22731	Mil Mi-8T	98308847	ex CCCP-22731	
☐	RA-22744	Mil Mi-8T	98311127	ex CCCP-22744	
☐	RA-22879	Mil Mi-8T	98415832	ex CCCP-22879	
☐	RA-22899	Mil Mi-8T	98417179	ex CCCP-22899	
☐	RA-22902	Mil Mi-8T	98420099	ex CCCP-22902	

☐ RA-24256	Mil Mi-8T	98734114	ex CCCP-24256	
☐ RA-24257	Mil Mi-8T	98734121	ex CCCP-24257	
☐ RA-24435	Mil Mi-8T	98625845	ex CCCP-24435	
☐ RA-24451	Mil Mi-8T	98628263	ex CCCP-24451	
☐ RA-24506	Mil Mi-8T	98520843	ex CCCP-24506	
☐ RA-24536	Mil Mi-8T	98522588	ex CCCP-24536	
☐ RA-24741	Mil Mi-8T	98417837	ex CCCP-24741	
☐ RA-25220	Mil Mi-8T	7763	ex CCCP-25228	
☐ RA-25313	Mil Mi-8T	98203720	ex CCCP-25313	
☐ RA-25333	Mil Mi-8T	98206010	ex CCCP-25333	
☐ RA-25376	Mil Mi-8T	98209062	ex CCCP-25376	
☐ RA-25606	Mil Mi-8T	99150564	ex CCCP-25606	
☐ RA-85654	Tupolev Tu-154M	89A-796	ex CCCP-86654	
☐ RA-85675	Tupolev Tu-154M	90A-835	ex CCCP-85675	
☐ RA-85684	Tupolev Tu-154M	90A-851	ex CCCP-85684	
☐ RA-85728	Tupolev Tu-154M	92A-910	ex CCCP-85728	
☐ RA-85757	Tupolev Tu-154M	92A-939	ex EP-MHX	
☐ RA-85782	Tupolev Tu-154M	93A-966	ex UN-85782	
☐ RA-06036	Mil Mi-26	34001212426	ex CCCP-06036	
☐ RA-06081	Mil Mi-26	34001212471	ex CCCP-06081	
☐ RA-26552	Antonov An-26	3107	ex CCCP-26552	stored YKS
☐ RA-26668	Antonov An-26B-100	8201	ex CCCP-26668	
☐ RA-41904	Antonov An-38-100	4163839010004		
☐ RA-41907	Antonov An-38-100	4163820010007		
☐ RA-46488	Antonov An-24RV	27308106	ex CCCP-46488	
☐ RA-46621	Antonov An-24RV	37308708	ex CCCP-46621	
☐ RA-47272	Antonov An-24B	07306402	ex CCCP-47272	
☐ RA-47694	Antonov An-24B	27307601	ex CCCP-47694	
☐ RA-65101	Tupolev Tu-134A-3	60260	ex CCCP-65101	Lsd fr ORB
☐ RA-65146	Tupolev Tu-134B-3	61000	ex YL-LBA	
☐ RA-65715	Tupolev Tu-134B-3	63536	ex 4L-AAC	
☐ RA-76357	Ilyushin Il-76TD	1023414467		
☐ RA-76360	Ilyushin Il-76TD	1033414492		
☐ RA-76373	Ilyushin Il-76TD	1033415507		
☐ RA-76420	Ilyushin Il-76TD	1023413446		Jt ops with TIS

AMUR ARTEL STARATELEI AVIAKOMPANIA — *Khabarovsk-Novy (KHV)*

☐ RA-26001	Antonov An-26	9705	ex CCCP-26001
☐ RA-26048	Antonov An-26B	10901	ex CCCP-26048

AMURSKIE AVIALINII

☐ RA-87395	Yakovlev Yak-40	9410733	
☐ RA-87452	Yakovlev Yak-40	9430936	ex CCCP-87452
☐ RA-87938	Yakovlev Yak-40K	9710153	ex CCCP-87936

ANGARA AIRLINES — *Sarma (AGU)* — *Irkutsk-One (IKT)*

☐ RA-26511	Antonov An-26-100	6808	ex CCCP-26511
☐ RA-26655	Antonov An-26-100	7802	ex CCCP-26655
☐ RA-46625	Antonov An-24RV	37308804	ex CCCP-46625
☐ RA-46662	Antonov An-24RV	47309410	ex CCCP-46662
☐ RA-46697	Antonov An-24RV	47309908	ex CCCP-46697
☐ RA-46712	Antonov An-24RV	57310408	ex EK-24408
☐ RA-47818	Antonov An-24RV	17307107	ex CCCP-47818
☐ RA-47848	Antonov An-24B	17307410	ex CCCP-47848

ARKHANGELSK 2ND AVIATION ENT'PRISE — *Dvina (5N/OAO)* — *Arkhangelsk-Vaslearo*

☐ RA-67553	LET L-410UVP-E	851430	ex CCCP-67553
☐ RA-67562	LET L-410UVP-E	851602	ex CCCP-67562
☐ RA-67563	LET L-410UVP-E	861603	ex CCCP-67563
☐ RA-67564	LET L-410UVP-E	851604	ex CCCP-67564
☐ RA-67565	LET L-410UVP-E	851605	ex CCCP-67565
☐ RA-67567	LET L-410UVP-E	861607	ex CCCP-67567
☐ RA-67569	LET L-410UVP-E	861609	ex CCCP-67569
☐ RA-22341	Mil Mi-8T	7166	ex CCCP-22341
☐ RA-22762	Mil Mi-8T	98311485	ex CCCP-22762
☐ RA-24012	Mil Mi-8MTV-1	95713	ex CCCP-24012
☐ RA-24485	Mil Mi-8T	98628927	ex CCCP-24485
☐ RA-06039	Mil Mi-26T	34001212429	ex CCCP-06039
☐ RA-06042	Mil Mi-26T	34001212432	ex CCCP-06042
☐ RA-06044	Mil Mi-26T	34001212434	ex CCCP-06044
☐ RA-21077	Mil Mi-6T	7065302B	ex CCCP-21077
☐ RA-21161	Mil Mi-6T	0533	ex CCCP-21161

ARKHANGELSK AIRLINES — Arkhangelsk-Vaslearo

☐ RA-46667	Antonov An-24RV	47309508	ex CCCP-46667	

ASTAIR

☐ RA-85031	Tupolev Tu-154M	87A-751	ex EX-087	

ATLANT-SOYUZ AIRLINES — Atlant-Soyuz (3G/AYZ) — Moscow-Domodedovo (DME)

☐ VP-BBL	Boeing 737-347	23183/1108	ex N303WA	
☐ VP-BBM	Boeing 737-347	23442/1239	ex N309WA	
☐ VP-BMI	Boeing 737-81Q	29052/557	ex G-XLAD	
☐ VQ-BBR	Boeing 737-8AS/W	32778/1140	ex EI-CSX	on order
☐ VQ-BBS	Boeing 737-8AS/W	32779/1167	ex EI-CSY	on order
☐ VQ-BCH	Boeing 737-8AS/W	32780/1178	ex EI-CSZ	on order
☐ VQ-BDU	Boeing 737-8AS/W	29936/1236	ex EI-CTA	
☐ VQ-BDV	Boeing 737-8AS/W	29937/1238	ex EI-CTB	
☐	Boeing 737-700			on order
☐	Boeing 737-700			on order
☐	Boeing 737-700			on order
☐	Boeing 737-700			on order
☐ RA-	Embraer EMB.120ER Brasilia	120172	ex N365AS	
☐ RA-	Embraer EMB.120ER Brasilia	120133	ex N366AS	
☐ RA-02581	Embraer EMB.120ER Brasilia	120125	ex N363AS	
☐ RA-02582	Embraer EMB.120ER Brasilia	120128	ex N364AS	
☐ RA-02854	Embraer EMB.120ER Brasilia	120136	ex N367AS	
☐ RA-02856	Embraer EMB.120ER Brasilia	120240	ex N203SW	
☐ RA-86109	Ilyushin Il-86	51483208077	ex CCCP-86109	
☐ RA-86123	Ilyushin Il-86	51483210091	ex CCCP-86123	
☐ RA-86125	Ilyushin Il-86	51483210093	ex UR-86125	
☐ RA-86136	Ilyushin Il-86	51483210094		
☐ RA-86138	Ilyushin Il-86	51483210096		
☐ EW-78779	Ilyushin Il-76TD	0083489662	ex CCCP-78779	Lsd fr TXC
☐ RA-76401	Ilyushin Il-76TD	1023412399	ex CCCP-76401	Lsd fr UHS
☐ RA-76783	Ilyushin Il-76TD	0093498974	ex CCCP-76783	Lsd fr UHS
☐ RA-76817	Ilyushin Il-76TD	1023412387	ex CCCP-76817	Lsd fr ESL
☐ RA-85140	Tupolev Tu-154M	85A-716	ex UN-85835	
☐ RA-85709	Tupolev Tu-154M	91A-884	ex EP-MAK	
☐ RA-85740	Tupolev Tu-154M	91A-895	ex 9XR-DU	VIP
☐ RA-85841	Tupolev Tu-154M	90A-858	ex EP-MBG	Jt ops with OMS
☐ RA-85849	Tupolev Tu-154M	89A-815	ex B-2620	

ATRAN - AVIATRANS CARGO AIRLINES — Atran (V8/VAS) — Moscow-Domodedovo / Myachkovo (DME/-)

☐ RA-11868	Antonov An-12B	9346310	ex OB-1448	
☐ RA-12990	Antonov An-12B	00347304	ex OB-1449	
☐ RA-26218	Antonov An-26B	5408	ex FAP 363	stored Myachkovo
☐ RA-93913	Antonov An-12B	4342609	ex CCCP-93913	
☐ RA-93916	Antonov An-26	9105	ex CCCP-93916	

AVIACON ZITOTRANS — Zitotrans (ZR/AZS) — Ekaterinburg-Koltsovo (SVX)

☐ RA-76352	Ilyushin Il-76TD	1023411378	ex EP-SFB	Op for UN WFP
☐ RA-76386	Ilyushin Il-76TD	1033418600	ex UK-76386	
☐ RA-76807	Ilyushin Il-76TD	1013405176	ex CCCP-76807	Op for UN WFP
☐ RA-76842	Ilyushin Il-76TD	1033418616		

AVIAENERGO — Aviaenergo (7U/ERG) — Moscow-Sheremetyevo (SVO)

☐ RA-65962	Tupolev Tu-134A-3	3351901	ex CCCP-65962	VIP
☐ RA-85809	Tupolev Tu-154M	94A-985		
☐ RA-86583	Ilyushin Il-62M	1356851	ex CCCP-86583	VIP

AVIAL AVIATION CO — New Avial (NVI) — Moscow-Domodedovo (DME)

☐ RA-11113	Antonov An-12TB	01347908	ex CCCP-11113	
☐ RA-11115	Antonov An-12BP	01348003	ex CCCP-11115	
☐ RA-11372	Antonov An-12BP	401912	ex EW-252TI	
☐ RA-11906	Antonov An-12BP	2340802	ex CCCP-11906	
☐ RA-69314	Antonov An-12BP	5343004	ex CCCP-69314	

AVIALESOOKHRANA VLADIMIR AIR ENTERPRISE (FFA) — Vladimir

☐ RA-26002	Antonov An-26	07309706	ex CCCP-26002	
☐ RA-26005	Antonov An-26	9809	ex CCCP-26005	
☐ RA-26011	Antonov An-26B	9908	ex CCCP-26011	
☐ RA-26040	Antonov An-26B	10703	ex CCCP-26040	stored IKT

☐ RA-26532	Antonov An-26	7410	ex CCCP-26532	
☐ RA-46480	Antonov An-24RV	27308008	ex CCCP-46480	

AVIANOVA (AO)

☐ EI-EEI	Airbus A320-232	0661	ex N603AW	
☐ EI-EEL	Airbus A320-232	0543	ex N605AW	
☐ EI-ELD	Airbus A320-232	1918	ex G-TTOF	

AVIAST AIR — Ialsi (6I/VVA) — Moscow-Vnukovo (VKO)

☐ RA-11756	Antonov An-12BP	4342208	ex CCCP-11756	Lsd to SHU
☐ RA-11962	Antonov An-12BP	5343007	ex CCCP-11962	
☐ RA-76843	Ilyushin Il-76TD	1013408269		Op for United Nations WFP
☐ RA-76849	Ilyushin Il-76TD	0023440161	ex UR-86921	stored BKA

AVIASTAR – TUPOLEV — Tupolev Air (4B/TUP) — Moscow-Zhukovsky / Domodedovo (-/DME)

☐ RA-64011	Tupolev Tu-204-100	1450743164011		
☐ RA-64021	Tupolev Tu-204-100C	1450743164021		
☐ RA-64024	Tupolev Tu-204-100C	1450743164024	ex LY-AGT	DHL Colours
☐ RA-64032	Tupolev Tu-204-100C	1450743164032		

BARKOL AVIAKOMPANIA — Moscow-Byokovo/Volgograd-Gurmak (BKA/VOG)

☐ RA-87280	Yakovlev Yak-40	9322025	ex CCCP-87280	Executive
☐ RA-87372	Yakovlev Yak-40	9340332	ex CCCP-87372	Executive
☐ RA-87957	Yakovlev Yak-40K	9821857	ex CCCP-87957	Executive
☐ RA-88229	Yakovlev Yak-40	9641850	ex CCCP-88229	Executive

BUGULMA AIR ENTERPRISE — Bugavia (BGM) — Bugulma (UUA)

☐ RA-87209	Yakovlev Yak-40K	9810657	ex CCCP-87209	all-white
☐ RA-87227	Yakovlev Yak-40K	9810559	ex CCCP-87227	all-white
☐ RA-87239	Yakovlev Yak-40	9530643	ex CCCP-87239	
☐ RA-87247	Yakovlev Yak-40	9531543	ex CCCP-87247	
☐ RA-87342	Yakovlev Yak-40	9511139	ex CCCP-87342	Op in Tatneft coloursVIP
☐ RA-87447	Yakovlev Yak-40	9430436	ex CCCP-87447	AK Bars Bank titlesVIP
☐ RA-87462	Yakovlev Yak-40	9430137	ex CCCP-87462	
☐ RA-87505	Yakovlev Yak-40	9510740	ex CCCP-87505	
☐ RA-87517	Yakovlev Yak-40	9521940	ex CCCP-87517	VIP
☐ RA-87588	Yakovlev Yak-40	9222022	ex CCCP-87588	
☐ RA-87849	Yakovlev Yak-40	9331830	ex CCCP-87849	
☐ RA-88156	Yakovlev Yak-40	9611046	ex CCCP-88156	Op in Tatarstan colours
☐ RA-88165	Yakovlev Yak-40	9611946	ex CCCP-88165	
☐ RA-88176	Yakovlev Yak-40	9621447	ex CCCP-88176	Op in Tatneft colours
☐ RA-88182	Yakovlev Yak-40	9620248	ex CCCP-88182	Op in Tatneft colours

BURAL — Bural (BUN) — Ulan Ude-Mukhino (UUD)

☐ RA-46408	Antonov An-24B	77304003	ex CCCP-46408	
☐ RA-46614	Antonov An-24RV	37308701	ex CCCP-46614	

BUSINESS AERO

☐ RA-42344	Yakovlev Yak-42	4520422708295	ex LY-AAQ	

BYLINA — Bylina (BYL) — Moscow-Vnukovo (VKO)

☐ RA-88263	Yakovlev Yak-40	9711852	ex CCCP-88263	VIP
☐ RA-88274	Yakovlev Yak-40	9721253	ex CCCP-88274	VIP

CENTER-SOUTH AIRLINES — Center-South (CTS) — Belgorod (EGO)

☐ RA-87276	Yakovlev Yak-40	9311227	ex UR-87276	
☐ RA-87655	Yakovlev Yak-40	9211820	ex CCCP-87655	
☐ RA-87921	Yakovlev Yak-40	9731155	ex UR-CLA	VIP
☐ RA-87966	Yakovlev Yak-40	9820958	ex CCCP-87966	
☐ RA-88236	Yakovlev Yak-40	9640551	ex CCCP-88236	

CENTRE-AVIA AIRLINES — Aviacentre (J7/CVC) — Moscow-Bykovo (BKA)

☐ RA-42325	Yakovlev Yak-42D	4520424402148	ex CCCP-42325	
☐ RA-42341	Yakovlev Yak-42D	4520421706292	ex CCCP-42341	
☐ RA-42353	Yakovlev Yak-42D	4520424711396	ex LY-AAT	
☐ RA-42385	Yakovlev Yak-42D	4520423016309	ex ER-YCC	
☐ RA-42423	Yakovlev Yak-42	4520424216606	ex CCCP-42423	VIP
☐ RA-42542	Yakovlev Yak-42D	11140804	ex CCCP-42542	
☐ RA-87507	Yakovlev Yak-40	9520940	ex LY-AAB	

CHUKOTAVIA			Anadyr (DYR)
☐ RA-26099 Antonov An-26B-100	11905	ex CCCP-26099	
☐ RA-26128 Antonov An-26B	12702	ex CCCP-26128	
☐ RA-26590 Antonov An-26B	13910	ex CCCP-26590	
☐ RA-46616 Antonov An-24RV	37308703	ex CCCP-46616	
☐ RA-47159 Antonov An-24B	89901701	ex CCCP-47159	
☐ RA-22728 Mil Mi-8T	98308799	ex CCCP-22728	
☐ RA-24199 Mil Mi-8T	98943825	ex CCCP-24199	
☐ RA-24422 Mil Mi-8T	98625391	ex CCCP-24422	
☐ RA-24497 Mil Mi-8T	98734707	ex CCCP-24497	
☐ RA-24498 Mil Mi-8T	98734729	ex CCCP-24498	
☐ RA-24503 Mil Mi-8T	96520730	ex CCCP-24503	
☐ RA-24531 Mil Mi-8T	98522401	ex CCCP-24531	
☐ RA-24719 Mil Mi-8T	98417340	ex CCCP-24719	
☐ RA-24738 Mil Mi-8T	98417759	ex CCCP-24738	
☐ RA-25158 Mil Mi-8T	99047875	ex CCCP-25158	
☐ RA-25189 Mil Mi-8T	98943829	ex CCCP-25189	
☐ RA-25470 Mil Mi-8MTV-1	95614	ex CCCP-25470	
☐ RA-25988 Mil Mi-8T	7520	ex CCCP-25988	
☐ RA-27014 Mil Mi-8MTV-1	96352		
☐ RA-27025 Mil Mi-8PS	8730		

CONTINENTAL AIRWAYS	Contair (PC/PVV)		Moscow-Sheremetyevo (SVO)
☐ RA-85696 Tupolev Tu-154M	91A-869	ex CCCP-85696	
☐ RA-85773 Tupolev Tu-154M	93A-955	ex EP-TUB	
☐ RA-85777 Tupolev Tu-154M	93A-959	ex EP-TUA	

DAGHESTAN AIRLINES	Dagal (N2/DAG)		Makhachkala (MCX)
☐ RA-22859 Mil Mi-8T	98415435	ex CCCP-22859	
☐ RA-25760 Mil Mi-8MTV-1	96123		EMS
☐ RA-46654 Antonov An-24RV	47309209	ex CCCP-46654	
☐ RA-65569 Tupolev Tu-134B-3	63340	ex 4L-AAB	
☐ RA-65570 Tupolev Tu-134A-3	66550	ex RA-64451	
☐ RA-65579 Tupolev Tu-134B-3	63295	ex 4L-AAD	
☐ RA-85495 Tupolev Tu-154B-2	81A-495	ex CCCP-85495	
☐ RA-85756 Tupolev Tu-154M	92A-938		
☐ RA-85828 Tupolev Tu-154M	97A-1009	Rasul Gamzatov	
☐ RA-85840 Tupolev Tu-154M	98A-1011		

DALAVIA	Khabarovsk Air (H8/KHB)		Khabarovsk-Novy (KHV)
☐ RA-46474 Antonov An-24RV	27308002	ex CCCP-46474	
☐ RA-46522 Antonov An-24RV	47310001	ex CCCP-46522	
☐ RA-46529 Antonov An-24RV	57310008	ex CCCP-46529	
☐ RA-46643 Antonov An-24RV	37309001	ex CCCP-46643	
☐ RA-47354 Antonov An-24RV	67310603	ex CCCP-47354	
☐ RA-47367 Antonov An-24RV	77310806	ex CCCP-47367	
☐ RA-86128 Ilyushin Il-62M	2255719	ex CCCP-86128	
☐ RA-86131 Ilyushin Il-62M	4255244	ex CCCP-86131	
☐ RA-86479 Ilyushin Il-62M	4728118	ex CCCP-86479	
☐ RA-86493 Ilyushin Il-62M	4140748	ex CU-T1248	
☐ RA-86503 Ilyushin Il-62M	4934512	ex CU-T1245	
☐ RA-86525 Ilyushin Il-62M	4851612	ex CCCP-86525	
☐ RA-86560 Ilyushin Il-62M	2153347	ex CCCP-86560	
☐ RA-85114 Tupolev Tu-154M	89A-814	ex EP-EAC	
☐ RA-85341 Tupolev Tu-154B-2	79A-341	ex CCCP-85341	stored KHV
☐ RA-85477 Tupolev Tu-154B-2	81A-477	ex CCCP-85477	
☐ RA-85607 Tupolev Tu-154M	85A-702	ex EK-85607	stored KHV
☐ RA-85734 Tupolev Tu-154M	86A-734	ex B-2608	
☐ RA-85752 Tupolev Tu-154M	92A-934	ex EP-MAT	
☐ RA-85797 Tupolev Tu-154M	93A-981		
☐ RA-85802 Tupolev Tu-154M	93A-961	ex EP-MAN	stored
☐ RA-64502 Tupolev Tu-214	42625002	Yuri Vorob'yoy	
☐ RA-64503 Tupolev Tu-214	43103003		
☐ RA-64507 Tupolev Tu-214	42305007		
☐ RA-64510 Tupolev Tu-214	42305010		
☐ RA-64512 Tupolev Tu-214	42305012		
☐ RA-26000 Antonov An-26	7309604	ex CCCP-26000	
☐ RA-26058 Antonov An-26B	11101	ex CCCP-26058	

DAURIA			Chita-Kadala (HTA)
☐ RA-26053 Antonov An-26B	17310909	ex CCCP-26053	

Registration	Type	C/n	Previous identity	Notes
☐ RA-26543	Antonov An-26	5732709	ex CCCP-26543	stored IKT
☐ RA-47268	Antonov An-24B	07306306	ex CCCP-47268	
☐ RA-47838	Antonov An-24B	17307310	ex CCCP-47838	Avialinii Zabaikalaya titles

DOMODEDOVO AIRLINES — *Domodedovo (E3/DMO)* — *Moscow-Domodedovo (DME)*

Registration	Type	C/n	Previous identity	Notes
☐ RA-86127	Ilyushin Il-62M	1254851	ex CCCP-86127	stored DME
☐ RA-86519	Ilyushin Il-62M	4140212	ex CCCP-86519	
☐ RA-76799	Ilyushin Il-76TD	1003403075	ex CCCP-76799	Lsd to ESL
☐ RA-76806	Ilyushin Il-76TD	1003403121	ex CCCP-76806	stored DME Lsd to ESL
☐ RA-85745	Tupolev Tu-154M	92A-928	ex EP-MHR	stored DME Jt ops with OMS
☐ RA-96006	Ilyushin Il-96-300	74393201003	ex CCCP-96006	
☐ RA-96009	Ilyushin Il-96-300	74393201006		stored DME
☐ RA-96013	Ilyushin Il-96-300	74393202013		stored DME

DONAVIA — *Donavia (D9/DNV)* — *Rostov-on-Don (ROV)*

Registration	Type	C/n	Previous identity	Notes
☐ VP-BLF	Boeing 737-528	25232/2231	ex F-GJNG	
☐ VP-BLG	Boeing 737-528	25233/2251	ex F-GJNH	
☐ VP-BVU	Boeing 737-5Q8	25166/2129	ex G-BVZH	
☐ VP-BWY	Boeing 737-528	27305/2574	ex F-GJNO	
☐ VP-BWZ	Boeing 737-528	27304/2572	ex F-GJNN	
☐ VP-BYU	Boeing 737-5Q8	25167/2173	ex G-BVZI	
☐ VP-BYV	Boeing 737-5Q8	25160/2114	ex G-BVZG	
☐ VQ-BAN	Boeing 737-4Q8	25113/2656	ex N782AS	
☐ VQ-BAO	Boeing 737-4Q8	25114/2666	ex N783AS	
☐ VQ-BCS	Boeing 737-43Q	28494/2839	ex SX-BTN	
☐ RA-85149	Tupolev Tu-154M	89A-797	ex B-609L	Lsd fr VARZ
☐ RA-85409	Tupolev Tu-154B-2	80A-409	ex CCCP-85409	
☐ RA-85626	Tupolev Tu-154M	87A-753	ex CCCP-85626	
☐ RA-85630	Tupolev Tu-154M	87A-759	ex CCCP-85630	
☐ RA-85640	Tupolev Tu-154M	87A-772	ex CCCP-85640	
☐ RA-85726	Tupolev Tu-154M	86A-725	ex EP-TQD	
☐ RA-65566	Tupolev Tu-134A	63952	ex 11+11 GAF	
☐ RA-65771	Tupolev Tu-134A-3	62445	ex CCCP-65771	
☐ RA-86113	Ilyushin Il-86	51483209081	ex CCCP-86113	stored SVO
☐ RA-86124	Ilyushin Il-86	51483210092	ex CCCP-86124	stored SVO
☐ RA-86140	Ilyushin Il-86	51483211102	ex CCCP-86140	
☐ RA-86141	Ilyushin Il-86	51483211103		

ELBRUS AVIA — *Elavia (NLK)* — *Nalchik (NAL)*

Registration	Type	C/n	Previous identity	Notes
☐ RA-42346	Yakovlev Yak-42D	4520423708311	ex CCCP-42346	Lsd fr Aviatechnologia Lsg
☐ RA-42371	Yakovlev Yak-42D	4520422914225	ex CCCP-42371	
☐ RA-42422	Yakovlev Yak-42D	4520424304017	ex ER-YCB	Lsd fr Aviatechnologia Lsg

EVENKIA AVIA — *Tura*

Registration	Type	C/n	Previous identity	Notes
☐ RA-26008	Antonov An-26B-100	9902	ex CCCP-26008	
☐ RA-26118	Antonov An-26B-100	12207	ex CCCP-26118	
☐ RA-69354	Antonov An-32	1606	ex CCCP-69354	
☐ RA-87900	Yakovlev Yak-40K	9720254	ex CCCP-87900	VIP

FLIGHT INSPECTIONS & SYSTEMS — *Aviaspec (LTS)* — *Moscow-Bykovo/Khabarovsk-Novy (BKA/KHV)*

Registration	Type	C/n	Previous identity	Notes
☐ RA-26571	Antonov An-26	67303909	ex CCCP-26571	Calibrator/Flying laboratory
☐ RA-26631	Antonov An-26ASLK	77305503	ex CCCP-26631	Calibrator/Flying laboratory
☐ RA-26673	Antonov An-26ASLK	97308408	ex CCCP-26673	Calibrator/Flying laboratory
☐ RA-46395	Antonov An-24ALK	07306209	ex CCCP-46395	Calibrator/Flying laboratory

GAZPROMAVIA — *Gazprom (4G/GZP)* — *Moscow-Ostafyevo/Moscow-Vnukovo (-/VKO)*

Registration	Type	C/n	Previous identity	Notes
☐ RA-74005	Antonov An-74TK-100C	36547095892	ex CCCP-74005	EMS
☐ RA-74008	Antonov An-74TK-100	36547095900	ex UR-74008	
☐ RA-74012	Antonov An-74D	36547098959	ex UR-74055	VIP, stored
☐ RA-74016	Antonov An-74TK-200	365470991034		
☐ RA-74032	Antonov An-74TK-100	36547098962	ex UR-74032	
☐ RA-74035	Antonov An-74TK-100	36547098963		
☐ RA-74036	Antonov An-74-200	36547098965		
☐ RA-74044	Antonov An-74-200	36547097936	ex UN 74044	
☐ RA-74056	Antonov An-74-200	36547098951		
☐ RA-74058	Antonov An-74-200	36547098956		
☐ RA-21505	Yakovlev Yak-40K	9830159	ex CCCP-21505	
☐ RA-87511	Yakovlev Yak-40	9521340	ex CCCP-87511	
☐ RA-88186	Yakovlev Yak-40K	9620648	ex CCCP-88186	
☐ RA-88300	Yakovlev Yak-40K	9641451	ex OK-GEO	
☐ RA-98113	Yakovlev Yak-40	9710253	ex CCCP-98113	VIP
☐ RA-42436	Yakovlev Yak-42D	4520421605018		

☐ RA-42437	Yakovlev Yak-42D	4520423606018		
☐ RA-42438	Yakovlev Yak-42D	4520423609018		VIP
☐ RA-42439	Yakovlev Yak-42D	4520423904019		
☐ RA-42442	Yakovlev Yak-42D	4520421402019		VIP
☐ RA-42451	Yakovlev Yak-42D	4520422708018		VIP
☐ RA-42452	Yakovlev Yak-42D	409016	ex RA-42431	
☐ RA-65045	Tupolev Tu-134A-3	49500	ex CCCP-65045	VIP Lsd to KGL
☐ RA-73000	Boeing 737-76N	28630/664	ex VT-JNP	
☐ RA-73004	Boeing 737-76N	28635/734	ex VT-JNQ	
☐ RA-76370	Ilyushin Il-76TD	1033414458		Lsd to VDA
☐ RA-76402	Ilyushin Il-76TD	1023413430		Lsd to VDA
☐ RA-76445	Ilyushin Il-76TD	1023410330	ex EK-76445	Lsd to VDA
☐ RA-76446	Ilyushin Il-76TD	1023412418	ex EK-76446	Lsd to VDA
☐ RA-85625	Tupolev Tu-154M	87A-752	ex CCCP-85625	stored
☐ RA-85751	Tupolev Tu-154M	92A-933		stored VKO
☐ RA-85774	Tupolev Tu-154M	93A-956		
☐ RA-85778	Tupolev Tu-154M	93A-962		

GEODYNAMICA CENTRE — *Geo Centre (CGS)* — *Moscow-Myachkovo*

☐ RA-30001	Antonov An-30	1402	ex CCCP-30001	Photo/survey
☐ RA-30006	Antonov An-30	1407	ex CCCP-30006	Photo/survey
☐ RA-30039	Antonov An-30	0710	ex CCCP-30039	Photo/survey

GLOBUS — *(GLP)*

☐ RA-85611	Tupolev Tu-154M	85A-715	ex CCCP-85611	
☐ RA-85623	Tupolev Tu-154M	87A-749	ex CCCP-85623	stored DME
☐ VP-BAN	Boeing 737-4Y0	26071/2361	ex N314PW	
☐ VP-BND	Boeing 737-83N/W	28245/1054	ex N315TZ	
☐ VP-BNG	Boeing 737-83N/W	30640/1035	ex N314TZ	
☐ VP-BQD	Boeing 737-83N/W	28239/847	ex N301TZ	
☐ VP-BQF	Boeing 737-83N/W	28243/984	ex N310TZ	
☐ VP-BQG	Boeing 737-46J	27171/2465	ex EI-DGL	
☐ VP-BTA	Boeing 737-4Q8	25168/2210	ex TF-ELY	
☐ VP-BTH	Boeing 737-42C	24231/1871	ex N60669	

GROZNYYAVIA — *Grozny (GRV)*

☐ RA-42418	Yakovlev Yak-42D	4520423219118	ex CCCP-42418
☐ RA-42379	Yakovlev Yak-42D	4520421014543	ex EP-YAE

IFLY

☐ EI-DUA	Boeing 757-256	26247/860	ex N241LF
☐ EI-DUC	Boeing 757-256	26248/863	ex N263LF
☐ EI-DUD	Boeing 757-256	26249/881	ex N271LF

IKAR — *Magadan-Sokol (GDX)*

☐ RA-28723	WSK-PZL/Antonov An-28	1AJ007-08	ex CCCP-26105
☐ RA-26726	WSK-PZL/Antonov An-28	1AJ007-11	ex CCCP-26105

ILIN AVIAKOMPANIA — *Yakutsk-Magan*

☐ RA-67623	LET L-410UVP-E	902405	ex CCCP-67623
☐ RA-67664	LET L-410UVP-E	902526	ex CCCP-67664

INTERAVIA AIRLINES — *Astair (8D/SUW)* — *Moscow-Domodedovo (DME)*

☐ RA-86533	Ilyushin Il-62M	1343123	ex CCCP-86533	Novowilov
☐ RA-86567	Ilyushin Il-62M	4256314		
☐ RA-86575	Ilyushin Il-62M	1647928	ex UK-86575	
☐ RA-86577	Ilyushin Il-62M	2748552	ex UK-86577	
☐ RA-42356	Yakovlev Yak-42D	4520422811400	ex CCCP-42356	
☐ RA-42339	Yakovlev Yak-42D	4520424606267	ex LY-AAO	
☐ RA-42359	Yakovlev Yak-42D	4520424811417	ex LY-AAW	

IRAERO — *Irkutsk-One (IKT)*

☐ RA-26051	Antonov An-26B	10906	ex CCCP-26051
☐ RA-26130	Antonov An-26B	12704	ex CCCP-26130
☐ RA-26131	Antonov An-26B	12707	ex CCCP-26131
☐ RA-26692	Antonov An-26	9409	ex CCCP-26692
☐ RA-46846	Antonov An-24RV	27307504	ex ER-AWC
☐ RA-47321	Antonov An-24RV	67310507	ex TC-TOP
☐ RA-47804	Antonov An-24RV	17306903	ex CCCP-47804

IZHAVIA — Izhavia (IZA) — Izhevsk (IJK)

☐ RA-26529	Antonov An-26-100	7401	ex CCCP-26529	
☐ RA-26683	Antonov An-26	8707	ex CCCP-26683	
☐ RA-42450	Yakovlev Yak-42	4520424601019		
☐ RA-42524	Yakovlev Yak-42D	11030603	ex CCCP-42524	
☐ RA-46620	Antonov An-24RV	37308707	ex CCCP-46620	
☐ RA-46637	Antonov An-24RV	37308903	ex CCCP-46637	
☐ RA-47315	Antonov An-24RV	67310502	ex CCCP-47315	
☐ RA-65056	Tupolev Tu-134A-3	49860	ex CCCP-65056	
☐ RA-65141	Tupolev Tu-134A-3	60945	ex CCCP-65141	

JET 2000

☐ RA-87216	Yakovlev Yak-40	9510440	ex CCCP-87216	

JET AIR GROUP — Sistema (JSI) — Moscow-Sheremetyevo (SME)

☐ P4-AIR	McDonnell-Douglas MD-87ER	49412/1424	ex N871DP	Op for Siviera
☐ RA-65701	Tupolev Tu-134B-3	63365	ex YL-LBI	stored
☐ RA-65723	Tupolev Tu-134A-3M	66440	ex CCCP-65723	Executive
☐ RA-65930	Tupolev Tu-134A-3M	66500	ex CCCP-65930	Executive

KAPO — Kazavia (KAO) — Kazan-Bonsoglebskow (KZN)

☐ RA-26597	Antonov An-26B	13310	ex CCCP-26597	
☐ RA-86126	Ilyushin Il-62MF	4154535		
☐ RA-86576	Ilyushin Il-62MF	4546257	ex UK-86576	Freighter
☐ RA-86579	Ilyushin Il-62MF	2951636	ex UK-86579	Freighter Govt of Amur Region
☐ RA-86945	Ilyushin Il-62M	3850145	ex OK-BYV	VIP Govt of Amur Region

KATEKAVIA — Katekavia (KTK) — Sharypovo/Krasnoyarsk-Yernelyanovo (-/KJA)

☐ RA-46491	Antonov An-24RV	27308204	ex 3X-GEB	
☐ RA-46493	Antonov An-24RV	27308206	ex CCCP-46493	
☐ RA-46497	Antonov An-24RV	27308210	ex CCCP-46497	
☐ RA-46520	Antonov An-24RV	37308506	ex CCCP-46520	no titles
☐ RA-46524	Antonov An-24RV	47310003	ex CCCP-46524	
☐ RA-46604	Antonov An-24RV	37308601	ex CCCP-46604	
☐ RA-46683	Antonov An-24RV	47309706	ex CCCP-46683	
☐ RA-46689	Antonov An-24RV	47309806	ex CCCP-46689	
☐ RA-46693	Antonov An-24RV	47309904	ex CCCP-46693	
☐ RA-47351	Antonov An-24RV	67310510	ex YL-LCI	
☐ RA-47358	Antonov An-24RV	67310607	ex CCCP-47358	
☐ RA-48102	Antonov An-24RT	1911804	ex CCCP-48102	

KAZAN AIR ENTERPRISES — Kazan Osnovnoi / Khanty Mansisk (KZN/-)

☐ RA-67142	LET L-410UVP	800408	ex CCCP-67142	
☐ RA-67171	LET L-410UVP	790207	ex CCCP-67171	stored Kazan
☐ RA-67672	LET L-410UVP-E	872013	ex 2013 no titles	
☐ RA-67675	LET L-410UVP-E	882027	ex 2027	stored Kazan
☐ RA-67693	LET L-410UVP-E	952624	ex OK-ADT	stored Kazan
☐ RA-67694	LET L-410UVP-E	952625		stored Kazan
☐ RA-06171	Mil Mi-8T	98420128	ex CCCP-06171	
☐ RA-22674	Mil Mi-8T	8127	ex CCCP-22674	
☐ RA-22679	Mil Mi-8T	8133	ex CCCP-22679	
☐ RA-22734	Mil Mi-8T	98308901	ex CCCP-22734	
☐ RA-22873	Mil Mi-8T	98415711	ex CCCP-22873	
☐ RA-25408	Mil Mi-8T	98233135	ex CCCP-25408	
☐ RA-25519	Mil Mi-8T	9775214	ex CCCP-25519	
☐ RA-25599	Mil Mi-8T	99150362	ex CCCP-25599	
☐ RA-27023	Mil Mi-8T	9754622	ex CCCP-27023	
☐ RA-27176	Mil Mi-8PS	8710	ex TC-HSA	

KD AVIA — Kaliningrad Air (KD/KNI) — Kaliningrad-Khrabovo (KGD)

Ceased operations 14/Sep/2009

KHABAROVSK AIRLINES — Nikolaevsk-na-Amure

☐ RA-24532	Mil Mi-8T	98522422	ex CCCP-24532	
☐ RA-24722	Mil Mi-8T	98417398	ex CCCP-24722	
☐ RA-25196	Mil Mi-8T	99047381	ex CCCP-25196	
☐ RA-26174	Antonov An-26B-100	97308304	ex CCCP-26174	
☐ RA-87651	Yakovlev Yak-40	9141220	ex CCCP-87651	Nikolaevsk titles
☐ RA-88251	Yakovlev Yak-40K	9710552	ex CCCP-88251	

KIROV AVIA ENTERPRISE		***Vyatka-Avia (KTA)***		***Kirov (KVX)***
☐ RA-46230	Antonov An-24B	77303110	ex CCCP-46230	
☐ RA-46660	Antonov An-24RV	47309307	ex CCCP-46660	
☐ RA-47295	Antonov An-24RV	07306608	ex CCCP-47295	Op as UNO 030
☐ RA-26086	Antonov An-26B	12302	ex CCCP-26086	
☐ RA-26101	Antonov An-26B	11908	ex CCCP-26101	
☐ RA-26664	Antonov An-26B	97307905	ex CCCP-26664	Op for UN
☐ RA-26677	Antonov An-26B	8603	ex CCCP-26677	

KMV MINERALNYE VODY AIRLINES		***Air Minvody (KV/MVD)***		***Mineralnye Vody (MRV)***
☐ RA-85307	Tupolev Tu-154B-2	78A-307	ex CCCP-85307	
☐ RA-85371	Tupolev Tu-154B-2	79A-371	ex CCCP-85371	
☐ RA-85380	Tupolev Tu-154B-2	79A-380	ex CCCP-85380	
☐ RA-85382	Tupolev Tu-154B-2	79A-382	ex CCCP-85382	
☐ RA-85457	Tupolev Tu-154B-2	80A-457	ex CCCP-85457	
☐ RA-85494	Tupolev Tu-154B-2	81A-494	ex CCCP-85494	
☐ RA-85715	Tupolev Tu-154M	91A-891	ex EP-MAX	
☐ RA-85746	Tupolev Tu-154M	92A-929	ex EP-MAV	
☐ RA-85826	Tupolev Tu-154M	89A-812	ex SP-LCL	
☐ RA-64016	Tupolev Tu-204-100	1450742364016	Alexej Tupolev	
☐ RA-64022	Tupolev Tu-204-100	1450743164022		
☐ RA-	Tupolev Tu-204-300			on order
☐ RA-	Tupolev Tu-204-300			on order

KNAAPO		***Knaapo (KNM)***		***Komsomolsk na Amur (KXK)***
☐ RA-11125	Antonov An-12BP	3341006	ex CCCP-11125	
☐ RA-11371	Antonov An-12BP	00347406	ex 22 red	
☐ RA-11789	Antonov An-12BP	6343905	ex LZ-BFB	

KOLAVIA		***Kogalym (7K/KGL)***		***Kogalym (KGP)***
☐ RA-22501	Mil Mi-8T	99357415		
☐ RA-26641	Mil Mi-8T	8026	ex CCCP-22641	
☐ RA-22980	Mil Mi-8AMT	59489607603	ex RA-22509	
☐ RA-24588	Mil Mi-8T	98839385	ex CCCP-24588	
☐ RA-25328	Mil Mi-8T	98203998	ex CCCP-25328	
☐ RA-25342	Mil Mi-8T	98206652	ex CCCP-25342	
☐ RA-25761	Mil Mi-8MTV-1	96073		
☐ RA-27066	Mil Mi-8MTV-1	95902	ex CCCP-27066	
☐ TC-KLA	Airbus A320-232	2029	ex N615SA	
☐ TC-KLB	Airbus A320-232	2077	ex N607SA	
☐ RA-65045	Tupolev Tu-134A-3	49500	ex CCCP-65045	VIP Lsd fr GZP
☐ RA-65131	Tupolev Tu-134A-3	60637	ex CCCP-65131	
☐ RA-65861	Tupolev Tu-134A	1351407	ex EW-65861	
☐ RA-65942	Tupolev Tu-134A-3	17103	ex (EW-65942)	
☐ RA-65943	Tupolev Tu-134A-3	63580	ex (EW-65943)	
☐ RA-65944	Tupolev Tu-134A-3	12096	ex (EW-65944)	
☐ RA-85427	Tupolev Tu-154B-2	80A-427	ex CCCP-85427	
☐ RA-85481	Tupolev Tu-154B-2	81A-481	ex CCCP-85481	
☐ RA-85522	Tupolev Tu-154B-2	82A-522	ex CCCP-85522	
☐ RA-85588	Tupolev Tu-154B-2	83A-588	ex CCCP-85588	
☐ RA-85632	Tupolev Tu-154M	87A-761	ex CCCP-85632	
☐ RA-85761	Tupolev Tu-154M	93A-944		Lsd to TBM
☐ RA-85784	Tupolev Tu-154M	93A-968		
☐ RA-85786	Tupolev Tu-154M	93A-970		
☐ RA-85829	Tupolev Tu-154M	87A-755	ex SP-LCD	

KORYAKAVIA				***Tilichiki***
☐ RA-74039	Antonov An-74	36547097931		
☐ RA-74050	Antonov An-74	36547181011		
☐ RA-28713	WSK-PZL/Antonov An-28	1AJ006-23	ex CCCP-28713	
☐ RA-28714	WSK-PZL/Antonov An-28	1AJ006-24	ex CCCP-28714	
☐ RA-28715	WSK-PZL/Antonov An-28	1AJ006-25	ex CCCP-28715	
☐ RA-28716	WSK-PZL/Antonov An-28	1AJ007-01	ex CCCP-28716	
☐ RA-28722	WSK-PZL/Antonov An-28	1AJ007-07	ex CCCP-28722	

KOSMOS AIRLINES		***Kosmos (KSM)***		***Moscow-Vnukovo (VKO)***
☐ RA-11025	Antonov An-12TB	6344103	ex CCCP-11025	
☐ RA-12957	Antonov An-12B	8345508	ex CCCP-12957	
☐ RA-65010	Tupolev Tu-134A	46130	ex CCCP-65010	Yelena

☐ RA-65097	Tupolev Tu-134AK	60540	ex CCCP-65097	
☐ RA-65719	Tupolev Tu-134AK	63637	ex CCCP-65719	VIP
☐ RA-65726	Tupolev Tu-134AK	63720	ex CCCP-65726	VIP
☐ RA-65727	Tupolev Tu-134B-3	03564820	ex CCCP-65727	VIP,Bank Moscovski Kapital
☐ RA-65805	Tupolev Tu-134B-3	64775	ex 57	
☐ RA-65935	Tupolev Tu-134A-3	66180	ex CCCP-65935	VIP
☐ RA-65956	Tupolev Tu-134AK	2351709	ex CCCP-65956	VIP

KOSTROMA AIR ENTERPRISE — Kostroma (KMW)

☐ RA-26595	Antonov An-26	47313401	ex CCCP-26595	
☐ RA-27210	Antonov An-26-100	5410	ex CCCP-27210	Marshal Novikov
☐ RA-67647	LET L-410UVP	902440	ex CCCP-67467	

KUBAN AIRLINES — Air Kuban (GW/KIL) — Krasnodar-Pashkovskaya (KRR)

☐ VQ-	Boeing 737-3Q8	26311/2681	ex G-TOYB	
☐ RA-42331	Yakovlev Yak-42	4520424505128	ex CCCP-42331	
☐ RA-42336	Yakovlev Yak-42	4250422606220	ex CCCP-42336	stored
☐ RA-42342	Yakovlev Yak-42	4520421706302	ex EK-42342	
☐ RA-42350	Yakovlev Yak-42	4520424711372	ex CCCP-42350	
☐ RA-42363	Yakovlev Yak-42D	4520424811438	ex CCCP-42363	
☐ RA-42367	Yakovlev Yak-42D	4520421914133	ex CCCP-42367	
☐ RA-42375	Yakovlev Yak-42D	4520424914410	ex CCCP-42375	
☐ RA-42386	Yakovlev Yak-42D	4520424016310	ex CCCP-42386	
☐ RA-42421	Yakovlev Yak-42D	4520422303017	ex CCCP-42421	
☐ RA-42541	Yakovlev Yak-42	11140704	ex CCCP-42541	

KVZ - KAZANSKY VERTOLETNY ZAVOD — KAMA (KPH) — Kazan-Osnovnoi (KZN)

☐ RA-47715	Antonov An-24B	69900505	ex CCCP-47715

LIPETSK AVIA

☐ RA-87372	Yakovlev Yak-40	9340332	ex CCCP-87372

Current status uncertain

LUKIAVIATRANS — Velikie Luki/Pskov-Kresty (VLU/PKV)

☐ RA-30042	Antonov An-30	0901	ex CCCP-30042	no titles
☐ RA-30053	Antonov An-30D	1008	ex CCCP-30053	
☐ RA-30067	Antonov An-30	1208	ex CCCP-30067	
☐ RA-46632	Antonov An-30	0201	ex CCCP-46632	

MCHS ROSSII — Sumes (SUM) — Moscow-Zhukovsky

☐ RF-32765	Beriev Be-200ES	768200010101	ex RA-21515		
☐ RF-32766	Beriev Be-200ES	768200010102	ex RA-21516		
☐ RF-32767	Beriev Be-200ES	76820002501	ex RA-21517		
☐ RF-32768	Beriev Be-200ES				
☐ RF-	Beriev Be-200ES				on order
☐ RA-76362	Ilyushin Il-76TD	1033416533		Anatoliy Lyapidevskiy	
☐ RA-76363	Ilyushin Il-76TD	1033417540		Vasiliy Molokov	
☐ RA-76429	Ilyushin Il-76TD	1043419639			
☐ RA-76840	Ilyushin Il-76TD	1033417553		Nikolay Kamanin	
☐ RA-76841	Ilyushin Il-76TD	1033418601		Mavrikiy Slepnev	
☐ RA-76845	Ilyushin Il-76TDP	1043420696		Mikhail Vodop'yanov	
☐ RA-06075	Mil Mi-26T	34001212465			
☐ RA-06278	Mil Mi-26T	34001212522			
☐ RA-06279	Mil Mi-26T	34001212603			

Above three now believed to be RF-31110, RF-31124 and RF-32821 but order unknown

☐ RF-31122	Antonov An-74P	36547136012	ex RA-74034	Alexander Belyakov	
☐ RF-31350	Antonov An-74P	36547097940	ex RF-31112	Georgl Baidukov	
☐ RA-42441	Yakovlev Yak-42D	4520421402018	ex EP-LAN	Velerij Chkalov	VIP
☐ RA-42446	Yakovlev Yak-42D	4520423308017	ex UN-42446	Vladimir Kokkinaki	
☐ RA-86570	Ilyushin Il-62M	1356344		Mikhail Gromov	
☐ RA-87482	Yakovlev Yak-40	9441038	ex CCCP-87482		

MORDOVIA AIR — Saransk (SKX)

☐ RA-26247	Antonov An-26B-100	4103	ex CCCP-26247	
☐ RA-46505	Antonov An-24RV	37308309	ex CCCP-46505	
☐ RA-46640	Antonov An-24RV	37308908	ex CCCP-46640	Lsd to KMV

MOSKOVIA — Gromov Airline (3R/GAI) — Moscow-Zhukovsky

☐ RA-11309	Antonov An-12BP	00347510	ex CCCP-11309	Op for Irkut
☐ RA-11310	Antonov An-12BP	4342601	ex CCCP-11310	Op for Irkut

☐ RA-12162	Antonov An-12BP	3341509	ex CCCP-12162	Op for Irkut
☐ RA-30028	Antonov An-30	0510	ex CCCP-30028	
☐ VQ-BDI	Boeing 737-73A	28497/216	ex N497TF	
☐ VQ-BER	Boeing 737-7L9/W	28006/26	ex N280AG	
☐ VQ-BFR	Boeing 737-883	30468/668	ex SE-DTP	
☐ VQ-BFU	Boeing 737-883	30467/634	ex SE-DTN	
☐ RA-65606	Tupolev Tu-134A-3	46300	ex D-AOBR	Op for Tupolev Design
☐ RA-85615	Tupolev Tu-154M	86A-731	ex CCCP-85615	
☐ RA-85736	Tupolev Tu-154M	92A-918	ex CCCP-85736	Yuri Morozov
☐ RA-85743	Tupolev Tu-154M	92A-926	ex CCCP-85743	Yuri Sheffer

NAPO AVIATRANS — *Novsib (NPO)* — *Novosibirsk-Yeltsovka*

☐ RA-12193	Antonov An-12BK	9346805	ex CCCP-12193	
☐ RA-12194	Antonov An-12BK	00347203	ex CCCP-12194	
☐ RA-12195	Antonov An-12BK	00347410	ex CCCP-12195	
☐ RA-41900	Antonov An-38-120	4160381607003		Lsd to LAY
☐ RA-41902	Antonov An-38-120	4163847010002		Lsd to VTK

NORDAVIA REGIONAL AIRLINES — *Dvina (5N/AUL)* — *Arkhangelsk-Talegi (ARH)*

☐ VP-BKP	Boeing 737-59D	25065/2028	ex OK-WGD	
☐ VP-BKT	Boeing 737-33R	28871/2900	ex PP-VPY	
☐ VP-BKU	Boeing 737-505	25789/2229	ex G-GFFB	
☐ VP-BKV	Boeing 737-505	27155/2449	ex N215BV	
☐ VP-BOH	Boeing 737-59D	25038/1969	ex G-GFFA	
☐ VP-BOI	Boeing 737-505	24650/1792	ex G-GFFG	
☐ VP-BOQ	Boeing 737-505	27153/2516	ex N153BV	
☐ VP-BQI	Boeing 737-5Y0	25186/2236	ex OM-SEA	
☐ VP-BQL	Boeing 737-5Y0	25185/2220	ex OM-SEF	
☐ VP-BRE	Boeing 737-53C	24827/2243	ex OM-SEE	
☐ VP-BRG	Boeing 737-53C	24826/2041	ex OM-SED	
☐ VP-BRI	Boeing 737-5Y0	25289/2288	ex OM-SEG	Lsd to AFL
☐ VP-BRK	Boeing 737-5Y0	25288/2286	ex OM-SEC	
☐ VP-BRN	Boeing 737-5Y0	25191/2260	ex OM-SEB	
☐ VP-BRP	Boeing 737-505	24651/1842	ex LN-BRD	
☐ VP-BXM	Boeing 737-59D	24695/1872	ex G-THOD	
☐ VP-BXN	Boeing 737-53A	24754/1868	ex G-GFFF	
☐ VQ-	Boeing 737-382	24450/1873	ex G-LGTF	on order
☐ RA-65034	Tupolev Tu-134A-3	48565	ex CCCP-65034	
☐ RA-65043	Tupolev Tu-134A-3	49400	ex CCCP-65043	stored
☐ RA-65052	Tupolev Tu-134A-3	49825	ex CCCP-65052	white coloursstored
☐ RA-65062	Tupolev Tu-134A-3	49875	ex CCCP-65062	
☐ RA-65066	Tupolev Tu-134A-3	49898	ex CCCP-65066	stored
☐ RA-65083	Tupolev Tu-134A-3	60090	ex CCCP-65083	Lsd to UTA
☐ RA-65084	Tupolev Tu-134A-3	60115	ex CCCP-65084	stored
☐ RA-65096	Tupolev Tu-134A-3	60257	ex CCCP-65096	
☐ RA-65103	Tupolev Tu-134A-3	60297	ex CCCP-65103	
☐ RA-65108	Tupolev Tu-134A-3	60332	ex EW-65108	Lsd to UTA
☐ RA-65116	Tupolev Tu-134A-3	60420	ex CCCP-65116	
☐ RA-65564	Tupolev Tu-134A-3	63165	ex CCCP-65564	
☐ RA-26104	Antonov An-26BRL	27312002	ex CCCP-26104	Arctica titles
☐ RA-26135	Antonov An-26B	12806	ex CCCP-26135	
☐ RA-46528	Antonov An-24RV	47310007	ex CCCP-46528	
☐ RA-46651	Antonov An-24RV	47309202	ex CCCP-46651	

NORDSTAR

☐ VQ-BDN	Boeing 737-8K5/W	32905/1046	ex D-AHLP
☐ VQ-BDO	Boeing 737-8K5/W	32906/1087	ex D-AHLQ
☐ VQ-BDP	Boeing 737-8Q8/W	28221/226	ex N282AG

NORDWIND

☐ VQ-BAK	Boeing 757-2Q8	26332/688	ex N401JS
☐ VQ-BAL	Boeing 757-2Q8	27351/639	ex N403JS
☐ VQ-BBT	Boeing 757-2Q8	29443/821	ex N763MX
☐ VQ-BBU	Boeing 757-2Q8	29442/819	ex N762MX
☐ VQ-BJK	Boeing 757-2Q8	29380/836	ex N380RM

NOVOSIBIRSK AIR ENTERPRISE — *Nakair (NBE)* — *Novosibirsk-Severny*

☐ RA-46642	Antonov An-24RV	37308910	ex CCCP-46642
☐ RA-46659	Antonov An-24RV	47309306	ex CCCP-46659
☐ RA-46682	Antonov An-24RV	47309704	ex CCCP-46682
☐ RA-47306	Antonov An-24RV	57310306	ex CCCP-47306
☐ RA-30007	Antonov An-30D	1408	ex CCCP-30007

ORENAIR — Orenburg (R2/ORB) — Orenburg-Tsentralny (REN)

☐ VP-BEW	Boeing 737-505	26297/2578	ex N371LF		
☐ VP-BGP	Boeing 737-4Y0	24691/1904	ex N691GE		
☐ VP-BGQ	Boeing 737-4Y0	24683/1901	ex N683GE		
☐ VP-BGR	Boeing 737-505	25790/2245	ex ES-ABG		
☐ VP-BPE	Boeing 737-5H6	26445/2327	ex OK-XGV	Aleksandr Kukishev	
☐ VP-BPF	Boeing 737-5H6	26446/2358	ex OK-XGW		
☐ VP-BPG	Boeing 737-8AS/W	29924/578	ex EI-CSI		
☐ VP-BPI	Boeing 737-83N/W	28244/958	ex N308TZ		
☐ VP-BPY	Boeing 737-83N/W	28247/1091	ex N318TZ		
☐ VQ-BCJ	Boeing 737-8AS/W	29932/1030	ex EI-CSS		
☐ VQ-BEM	Boeing 737-85R/W	29036/164	ex N636AC	Michael	
☐ VQ-BEN	Boeing 737-85R/W	29037/177	ex N637AC		
☐ RA-65049	Tupolev Tu-134A-3	49755	ex EW-65049		
☐ RA-65054	Tupolev Tu-134A	49840	ex CCCP-65054		
☐ RA-65090	Tupolev Tu-134A	60185	ex CCCP-65090		Lsd to SVR
☐ RA-65101	Tupolev Tu-134A-3	60260	ex CCCP-65101		Lsd to DRU
☐ RA-65110	Tupolev Tu-134A-3	60343	ex (HA-LBT)		
☐ RA-65117	Tupolev Tu-134A-3	60450	ex (HA-LBU)		
☐ RA-65136	Tupolev Tu-134A-3	60885	ex CCCP-65136		Lsd to UTA
☐ RA-46315	Antonov An-24B	97305401	ex CCCP-46315		
☐ RA-85603	Tupolev Tu-154B-2	84A-603	ex CCCP-85603		no titles
☐ RA-85604	Tupolev Tu-154B-2	85A-604	ex CCCP-85604		
☐ RA-85768	Tupolev Tu-154M	94A-949		Konstantine Brexos	
☐ RA-87272	Yakovlev Yak-40	9330827	ex CCCP-87272		stored REN
☐ RA-87352	Yakovlev Yak-40	9330131	ex CCCP-87352		stored REN
☐ RA-87471	Yakovlev Yak-40	9441637	ex UN-87471		stored REN

PERM AIRLINES — Perm Air (P9/PGP) — Perm-Bolshoe Savina (PEE)

☐ RA-26520	Antonov An-26-100	87307101	ex CCCP-26520	
☐ RA-26636	Antonov An-26-100	87306306	ex EP-TQB	
☐ RA-47152	Antonov An-24B	89901604	ex CCCP-47152	
☐ RA-47756	Antonov An-24B	79901209	ex CCCP-47756	
☐ RA-65064	Tupolev Tu-134A-3	49886	ex CCCP-65064	
☐ RA-65751	Tupolev Tu-134A-3	61066	ex CCCP-65751	Sverbank titles
☐ RA-65775	Tupolev Tu-134A-3	62530	ex CCCP-65775	
☐ RA-85287	Tupolev Tu-154B-1	78A-287	ex CCCP-85287	stored PEE

PETROPAVLOVSK-KAMCHATSKY AIR ENTERPRISE — Petrokam (PTK) — Petropavlovsk Kamchatsky-Yelixovo (PKC)

☐ RA-87385	Yakovlev Yak-40K	9411632	ex CCCP-87385	stored
☐ RA-87947	Yakovlev Yak-40K	9621145	ex CCCP-87947	
☐ RA-87949	Yakovlev Yak-40K	9621345	ex CCCP-87949	
☐ RA-87988	Yakovlev Yak-40	9541244	ex CCCP-87988	
☐ RA-88241	Yakovlev Yak-40K	9641351	ex CCCP-88241	
☐ RA-26122	Antonov An-26B	12401	ex CCCP-26122	
☐ RA-26251	Antonov An-26-100	9109		
☐ RA-67645	LET L-410UVP-E	902438	ex CCCP-67645	
☐ RA-67662	LET L-410UVP-E	902520	ex CCCP-67662	

POLAR AIRLINES — Batagai

☐ RA-11130	Antonov An-12BP	02348205	ex CCCP-11130
☐ RA-46333	Antonov An-24B	97305510	ex CCCP-46333
☐ RA-46374	Antonov An-24B	07306005	ex CCCP-46374
☐ RA-47158	Antonov An-24B	89901610	ex CCCP-47158
☐ RA-47161	Antonov An-24B	89901703	ex CCCP-47161
☐ RA-47260	Antonov An-24B	27307802	ex CCCP-47260
☐ RA-26030	Antonov An-26B	10501	ex CCCP-26030
☐ RA-26061	Antonov An-26B	11108	ex CCCP-26061
☐ RA-26538	Antonov An-26-100	47302102	ex CCCP-26538
☐ RA-26635	Antonov An-26	6305	ex CCCP-26635
☐ RA-26674	Antonov An-26	8506	ex CCCP-26674
☐ RA-26685	Antonov An-26	1307	ex CCCP-26685

POLET AVIAKOMPANIA — Polet (YQ/POT) — Voronezh (VOZ)

☐ RA-82010	Antonov An-124-100 Ruslan	9773053616017	ex CCCP-82010		
☐ RA-82014	Antonov An-124-100 Ruslan	9773054732039	ex CCCP-82014		
☐ RA-82024	Antonov An-124 Ruslan	19530502033	ex CCCP-82024		stored ULY
☐ RA-82026	Antonov An-124 Ruslan	19530502127	ex 10 black		stored ULY
☐ RA-82068	Antonov An-124-100 Ruslan	9773051359127	ex RA-82070		
☐ RA-82075	Antonov An-124-100 Ruslan	9773053459147		Boris Naginski	
☐ RA-82077	Antonov An-124-100 Ruslan	9773054459151			

☐ RA-82080	Antonov An-124-100 Ruslan	9773051462161		
☐ RA-96101	Ilyushin Il-96-400T	74393201001		Freighter
☐ RA-96102	Ilyushin Il-96-400T	73439201002		Freighter
☐ RA-96103	Ilyushin Il-96-400T	97693201003		Freighter, on order
☐ VP-BPL	SAAB 2000	2000-029	ex HB-IZO	
☐ VP-BPM	SAAB 2000	2000-057	ex HB-IYB	
☐ VP-BPN	SAAB 2000	2000-058	ex HB-IYC	
☐ VP-BPQ	SAAB 2000	2000-060	ex HB-IYE	
☐ VP-BPR	SAAB 2000	2000-061	ex HB-IYF	
☐ RA-30024	Antonov An-30	0502	ex CCCP-30024	
☐ RA-30048	Antonov An-30	0910	ex CCCP-30048	
☐ RA-46676	Antonov An-24RV	47309608	ex CCCP-46676	
☐ RA-46690	Antonov An-24RV	47309901	ex CCCP-46690	Nikolai Pribilov
☐ RA-48096	Antonov An-24RV	57310406	ex CCCP-48096	
☐ RA-88304	Yakovlev Yak-40S2	9510439	ex ST-YAK	

POLYARNYA AVIA — Yakutsk (YKS)

☐ RA-46834	Antonov An-24RV	17306801		

PROGRESS AVIAKOMPANIA — Progress (PSS) — Samara-Bezymyanka (KUF)

☐ RA-26180	Antonov An-26	9737810	ex CCCP-26180	
☐ RA-26192	Antonov An-24RT	1911805	ex CCCP-26192	

PSKOVAVIA — Pskovavia (PSW) — Pskov-Kresty (PKV)

☐ RA-26107	Antonov An-26B	27312008	ex LY-LVR	
☐ RA-26120	Antonov An-26B	27312304	ex CCCP-26120	
☐ RA-26134	Antonov An-26B	12805	ex CCCP-26134	
☐ RA-26142	Antonov An-26B	37312904	ex CCCP-26142	

RED WINGS — Remont Air (VAZ) — Moscow-Vnukovo (VKO)

☐ RA-64018	Tupolev Tu-204-100	1450741964018		
☐ RA-64019	Tupolev Tu-204-100	1450741064019		
☐ RA-64020	Tupolev Tu-204-100	1450743164020		
☐ RA-64043	Tupolev Tu-204-100	64043		on order
☐ RA-64046	Tupolev Tu-204-100	64046		
☐ RA-64047	Tupolev Tu-204-100	64047		
☐ RA-64048	Tupolev Tu-204-100	64048		
☐ RA-64049	Tupolev Tu-204-100	64049		
☐ RA-64050	Tupolev Tu-204-100	64050		
☐ RA-64051	Tupolev Tu-204-100	1450743164051		on order
☐ RA-64053	Tupolev Tu-204-100	1450743164053		on order

REGIONAL AIRLINES

☐ VQ-BBX	Embraer EMB.120ER Brasilia	120205	ex N205CA	
☐ VQ-BBY	Embraer EMB.120ER Brasilia	120265	ex N285AS	
☐ VQ-BCB	Embraer EMB.120ER Brasilia	120231	ex N280AS	
☐ VQ-BCL	Embraer EMB.120ER Brasilia	120304	ex N227SW	
☐ VQ-	Embraer EMB.120ER Brasilia	120141	ex N261AS	on order
☐ VQ-	Embraer EMB.120ER Brasilia	120202	ex N268AS	on order
☐ VQ-	Embraer EMB.120ER Brasilia	120226	ex N282AS	on order
☐ VQ-	Embraer EMB.120ER Brasilia	120236	ex N283AS	on order
☐ RA-28728	WSK-PZL/Antonov An-28	1AJ-007-13	ex CCCP-28728	
☐ RA-28900	WSK/PZL Antonov An-28	1AJ-007-14	ex EX-28729	
☐ RA-28901	WSK/PZL Antonov An-28	1AJ008-01	ex EX-28738	
☐ RA-28903	WSK-PZL/Antonov An-28	1AJ009-19	ex RA-28953	

ROSNEFT-BALTIKA — Rosbalt (RNB) — St Petersburg-Pulkovo (LED)

☐ RA-21500	Yakovlev Yak-40K	9741356	ex CCCP-21500	
☐ RA-87244	Yakovlev Yak-40	9531243	ex CCCP-87244	

ROSSIYA RUSSIAN AIRLINES — Russia (FV/SDM) — Moscow-Vnukovo/St Petersburg-Pulkovo (VKO/LED)

☐ VP-BIQ	Airbus A319-111	1890	ex N917FR	
☐ VP-BIT	Airbus A319-112	1761	ex N909FR	
☐ VP-BIU	Airbus A319-114	0649	ex N574SX	
☐ VP-BTQ	Airbus A319-114	1149	ex N310NB	Lsd fr SBI
☐ VP-BTS	Airbus A319-114	1164	ex N311NB	Lsd fr SBI
☐ VQ-BAQ	Airbus A319-111	1560	ex N903FR	
☐ VQ-BAR	Airbus A319-111	1488	ex N901FR	
☐ VQ-BAS	Airbus A319-111	1863	ex N913FR	

	Registration	Type	c/n	Previous identity	Notes
☐	VQ-BAT	Airbus A319-112	1876	ex N916FR	
☐	VQ-BAU	Airbus A319-112	1851	ex N915FR	
☐	VQ-BAV	Airbus A319-111	1743	ex N907FR	
☐	EI-DXY	Airbus A320-212	0525	ex D-AKNX	
☐	EI-DZR	Airbus A320-212	0427	ex N265AV	
☐	VQ-BBM	Airbus A320-214	1578	ex EC-HZU	
☐	VQ-BDQ	Airbus A320-214	1767	ex EC-KDD	
☐	VQ-BDY	Airbus A320-214	1657	ex EC-KBQ	
☐	EI-CDD	Boeing 737-548	24989/1989	ex EI-BXH	
☐	EI-CDE	Boeing 737-548	25115/2050	ex PT-SLM	
☐	EI-CDF	Boeing 737-548	25737/2232		
☐	EI-CDG	Boeing 737-548	25738/2261		
☐	EI-CDH	Boeing 737-548	25739/2271		
☐	EI-DZH	Boeing 767-3Q8ER	29390/870	ex N101LF	
☐	EI-EAR	Boeing 767-3Q8ER	27616/714	ex N364LF	
☐	EI-ECB	Boeing 767-3Q8ER	27617/722	ex N151LF	
☐	RA-86094	Ilyushin Il-86	51483207065	ex CCCP-86094	
☐	RA-86106	Ilyushin Il-86	51483208074	ex CCCP-86106	
☐	RA-86466	Ilyushin Il-62M	2749316	ex CCCP-86466	
☐	RA-86467	Ilyushin Il-62M	3749733	ex CCCP-86467	VIP
☐	RA-86468	Ilyushin Il-62M	4749857	ex CCCP-86468	VIP
☐	RA-86536	Ilyushin Il-62M	4445948	ex CCCP-86536	
☐	RA-86540	Ilyushin Il-62M	3546548	ex CCCP-86540	VIP
☐	RA-86559	Ilyushin Il-62M	2153258	ex CCCP-86559	VIP
☐	RA-86561	Ilyushin Il-62M	4154842	ex CCCP-86561	VIP
☐	RA-86710	Ilyushin Il-62M	2647646	ex CCCP-86710	
☐	RA-86712	Ilyushin Il-62M	4648339	ex CCCP-86712	VIP
☐	RA-65093	Tupolev Tu-134A-3	60215	ex UR-65093	
☐	RA-65109	Tupolev Tu-134A-3	60339	ex UR-65109	stored LED
☐	RA-65113	Tupolev Tu-134A-3	60380	ex ES-AAM	
☐	RA-65553	Tupolev Tu-134A-3	66300	ex CCCP-65553	
☐	RA-65555	Tupolev Tu-134A-3	66350	ex CCCP-65555	VIP
☐	RA-65759	Tupolev Tu-134A-3	62239	ex ES-AAO	
☐	RA-65912	Tupolev Tu-134A-3	63985	ex CCCP-65912	
☐	RA-65921	Tupolev Tu-134A-3	63997	ex CCCP-65921	
☐	RA-85171	Tupolev Tu-154M	92A-893	ex B-2625	
☐	RA-85187	Tupolev Tu-154M	91A-919	ex B-2629	
☐	RA-85204	Tupolev Tu-154M	91A-886	ex B-2624	
☐	RA-85552	Tupolev Tu-154B-2	82A-552	ex CCCP-85552	stored LED
☐	RA-85629	Tupolev Tu-154M	87A-758	ex CCCP-85629	
☐	RA-85645	Tupolev Tu-154M	88A-782	ex CCCP-85645	
☐	RA-85658	Tupolev Tu-154M	89A-808	ex CCCP-85658	
☐	RA-85659	Tupolev Tu-154M	89A-809	ex CCCP-85659	VIP
☐	RA-85695	Tupolev Tu-154M	91A-868	ex CCCP-85695	
☐	RA-85739	Tupolev Tu-154M	92A-925	ex HA-LGD	
☐	RA-85753	Tupolev Tu-154M	92A-935		
☐	RA-85767	Tupolev Tu-154M	93A-948		
☐	RA-85769	Tupolev Tu-154M	93A-951		
☐	RA-85770	Tupolev Tu-154M	93A-952		
☐	RA-85771	Tupolev Tu-154M	93A-953		
☐	RA-85779	Tupolev Tu-154M	93A-963		
☐	RA-85785	Tupolev Tu-154M	93A-969		
☐	RA-85800	Tupolev Tu-154M	94A-984		
☐	RA-85832	Tupolev Tu-154M	92A-908	ex RA-85726	
☐	RA-85834	Tupolev Tu-154M	98A-1014	ex OM-AAA	
☐	RA-85835	Tupolev Tu-154M	98A-1015	ex OM-AAB	
☐	RA-85836	Tupolev Tu-154M	98A-1018	ex OM-AAC	
☐	RA-85843	Tupolev Tu-154M	95A-991	ex RA-85811	
☐	RA-64504	Tupolev Tu-214	41203004		
☐	RA-64505	Tupolev Tu-214	42204005		
☐	RA-64506	Tupolev Tu-214	44204006		
☐	RA-64515	Tupolev Tu-214	42305015		
☐	RA-64516	Tupolev Tu-214	42709016		
☐	RA-87203	Yakovlev Yak-40	9741456	ex CCCP-87203	VIP
☐	RA-87969	Yakovlev Yak-40	9831358	ex CCCP-87969	VIP
☐	RA-87971	Yakovlev Yak-40D	9831558	ex CCCP-87971	VIP
☐	RA-88200	Yakovlev Yak-40	9630149	ex CCCP-88200	
☐	RA-96012	Ilyushin Il-96-300	74393201009		Presidential a/c
☐	RA-96016	Ilyushin Il-96-300PU	74393202010	ex (RA-96013)	Presidential a/c
☐	RA-96018	Ilyushin Il-96-300PU	74393202018		VIP
☐	RA-61701	Antonov An-148-100B	40-03		
☐	RA-61702	Antonov An-148-100B	40-04		on order
☐	RA-61703	Antonov An-148-100B	40-06		on order
☐	RA-61704	Antonov An-148-100B	40-07		on order
☐	RA-61705	Antonov An-148-100B	40-09		on order

RUSAIR		CGI-Rusair (CGI)	Moscow-Sheremetyevo (SVO)	
☐ RA-65087	Tupolev Tu-134A-3	60155	ex CCCP-65087	VIP
☐ RA-65124	Tupolev Tu-134A	60560	ex ES-AAN	VIP
☐ RA-65908	Tupolev Tu-134A	63870	ex CCCP-65908	VIP Op for VAP Avn Grp
☐ RA-87311	Yakovlev Yak-40	9320629	ex CCCP-87311	VIP, APP titles & logo
☐ RA-87494	Yakovlev Yak-40	9541745	ex CCCP-87494	VIP
☐ RA-87502	Yakovlev Yak-40	9510140	ex CCCP-87502	VIP

RUSJET			Moscow-Vnukovo (VKO)	
☐ RA-42365	Yakovlev Yak-42D	4520424811447	ex CCCP-42365	
☐ RA-42411	Yakovlev Yak-42D	4520421219043	ex CCCP-42411	VIP
☐ RA-42444	Yakovlev Yak-42D	4520424116677	ex CU-T1249	
☐ RA-65737	Tupolev Tu-134B-3	64195	ex CCCP-65737	converted Tu-134UBL
☐ RA-87418	Yakovlev Yak-40	9421034	ex CCCP-87418	VIP
☐ RA-88240	Yakovlev Yak-40K	9641151	ex CCCP-88240	Executive

RUSLINE AIR		Rusline Air (RLU)	Moscow-Sheremetyevo (SVO)	
☐ RA-65756	Tupolev Tu-134A	62179	ex CCCP-65756	
☐ RA-65903	Tupolev Tu-134A	63750	ex CCCP-65903	
☐ RA-65934	Tupolev Tu-134A	66143	ex CCCP-65934	
☐ RA-65941	Tupolev Tu-134A-3	60642	ex LZ-TUS	
☐ RA-87248	Yakovlev Yak-40K	9540144	ex CCCP-87248	
☐ RA-87380	Yakovlev Yak-40	9421225	ex 5N-MAR	
☐ RA-87828	Yakovlev Yak-40	9242024	ex CCCP-87828	
☐ RA-87981	Yakovlev Yak-40K	9540444	ex ER-YGA	stored
☐ RA-88308	Yakovlev Yak-40	9230224	ex SP-GEA	
☐ VP-BAO	Canadair CL-600-2B19 (CRJ-100)	7177	ex F-GPTB	
☐ VQ-BBV	Canadair CL-600-2B19 (CRJ-200)	7454	ex N654BR	
☐ VQ-BBW	Canadair CL-600-2B19 (CRJ-200)	7426	ex N651BR	

RUSSIAN SKY AIRLINES		Ruduga (P7/ESL)	Moscow-Domodedovo (DME)	
☐ RA-76799	Ilyushin Il-76TD	10034030375	ex CCCP-76799	Lsd fr DMO
☐ RA-76817	Ilyushin Il-76TD	1023412387	ex CCCP-76817	Lsd to AYZ

RYAZANAVIA TRANS		Ryazan Air (RYZ)	Ryazan (RZN)	
☐ RA-47359	Antonov An-24RV	67310608	ex UR-47359	
☐ RA-47362	Antonov An-24RV	67310706	ex UR-47362	

S-AIR		S-Air (RLS)	Ermolino	
☐ RA-65550	Tupolev Tu-134A-3	66200	ex CCCP-65550	
☐ RA-65692	Tupolev Tu-134A-3	63215	ex YL-LBB	
☐ RA-65721	Tupolev Tu-134A-3M	66130	ex CCCP-65721	
☐ RA-65926	Tupolev Tu-134A-3	66101	ex CCCP-65926	
☐ RA-65932	Tupolev Tu-134A-3	66405	ex 65932	
☐ RA-42402	Yakovlev Yak-42D	4520422116583	ex CCCP-42402	
☐ RA-42427	Yakovlev Yak-42D	4520422305016		Marco Group

S7 AIRLINES		Siberia Airlines (S7/SBI)	Novosibirsk-Tolmachevo (OVB)	
☐ VP-BTJ	Airbus A310-304	520	ex D-AHLA	
☐ VP-BTL	Airbus A310-204	487	ex D-AHLX	
☐ VP-BTM	Airbus A310-204	486	ex F-GYYY	
☐ VP-BHF	Airbus A319-114	1819	ex N350NB	
☐ VP-BHG	Airbus A319-114	1870	ex N356NB	
☐ VP-BHI	Airbus A319-114	2028	ex N367NB	
☐ VP-BHJ	Airbus A319-114	2369	ex N372NB	
☐ VP-BHK	Airbus A319-114	2373	ex N373NB	
☐ VP-BHL	Airbus A319-114	2464	ex N374NB	
☐ VP-BHP	Airbus A319-114	2618	ex N376NB	
☐ VP-BHQ	Airbus A319-114	2641	ex N377NB	
☐ VP-BHV	Airbus A319-114	2474	ex N375NB	
☐ VP-BTN	Airbus A319-114	1126	ex N307NB	
☐ VP-BTO	Airbus A319-114	1129	ex N308NB	
☐ VP-BTP	Airbus A319-114	1131	ex N309NB	
☐ VP-BTQ	Airbus A319-114	1149	ex N310NB	Lsd to SDM
☐ VP-BTS	Airbus A319-114	1164	ex N311NB	Lsd to SDM
☐ VP-BTT	Airbus A319-114	1167	ex N312NB	
☐ VP-BTU	Airbus A319-114	1071	ex N303NB	
☐ VP-BTV	Airbus A319-114	1078	ex N304NB	
☐ VP-BTW	Airbus A319-114	1090	ex N305NB	
☐ VP-BTX	Airbus A319-114	1091	ex N306NB	

☐ VP-BCZ	Airbus A320-214	3446	ex F-WWIT	
☐ VP-BCP	Airbus A320-214	3473	ex F-WWBY	
☐ VP-BCS	Airbus A320-214	3490	ex F-WWIS	
☐ VP-BDT	Airbus A320-214	3494	ex F-WWIC	
☐ VQ-BCI	Airbus A320-214	2623	ex EC-JNT	
☐ VQ-BDE	Airbus A320-214	3866	ex F-WW	
☐ VQ-BDF	Airbus A320-214	3880	ex F-WWIL	
☐ VQ-BES	Airbus A320-214	4032	ex F-WWIH	
☐ VQ-BET	Airbus A320-214	4150	ex F-WWBG	
☐ VQ-	Airbus A320-214		ex	on order
☐ VQ-	Airbus A320-214		ex	on order
☐ VQ-	Airbus A320-214		ex	on order
☐ VQ-	Airbus A320-214		ex	on order
☐ VQ-	Airbus A320-214		ex	on order
☐ VQ-	Airbus A320-214		ex	on order
☐ VQ-	Airbus A320-214		ex	on order
☐ VQ-	Airbus A320-214		ex	on order
☐ VQ-	Boeing 737-800		ex	on order
☐ VQ-	Boeing 737-800		ex	on order
☐ VQ-	Boeing 737-800		ex	on order
☐ VQ-	Boeing 737-800		ex	on order
☐ VQ-	Boeing 737-800		ex	on order
☐ VP-BVH	Boeing 767-33AER	28495/643	ex N495AN	
☐ VQ-BBI	Boeing 767-328ER	27428/586	ex EC-JJJ	on order
☐ RA-86084	Ilyushin Il-86	51483206055	ex CCCP-86084	stored
☐ RA-86085	Ilyushin Il-86	51483208056	ex CCCP-86085	
☐ RA-86089	Ilyushin Il-86	51483207060	ex CCCP-86089	
☐ RA-86091	Ilyushin Il-86	51483207062	ex CCCP-86091	
☐ RA-86097	Ilyushin Il-86	51483207068	ex CCCP-86097	
☐ RA-86104	Ilyushin Il-86	51483208072	ex CCCP-86104	
☐ RA-86105	Ilyushin Il-86	51483208073	ex CCCP-86105	stored OVB
☐ RA-86107	Ilyushin Il-86	51483208075	ex CCCP-86107	
☐ RA-86108	Ilyushin Il-86	51483208076	ex CCCP-86108	
☐ RA-85610	Tupolev Tu-154M	84A-705	ex CCCP-85610	stored OVB
☐ RA-85612	Tupolev Tu-154M	86A-721	ex CCCP-85612	
☐ RA-85613	Tupolev Tu-154M	86A-722	ex CCCP-85613	
☐ RA-85618	Tupolev Tu-154M	86A-737	ex CCCP-85618	SPSR Ekspress titles
☐ RA-85619	Tupolev Tu-154M	86A-738	ex CCCP-85619	Yulia Fomina
☐ RA-85620	Tupolev Tu-154M	86A-739	ex TC-ACT	stored OVB
☐ RA-85622	Tupolev Tu-154M	87A-746	ex CCCP-85622	
☐ RA-85624	Tupolev Tu-154M	87A-750	ex CCCP-85624	
☐ RA-85628	Tupolev Tu-154M	87A-757	ex CCCP-85628	stored OVB
☐ RA-85633	Tupolev Tu-154M	87A-762	ex CCCP-85633	
☐ RA-85635	Tupolev Tu-154M	87A-764	ex CCCP-85635	
☐ RA-85652	Tupolev Tu-154M	88A-794	ex LZ-LTF	stored OVB
☐ RA-85674	Tupolev Tu-154M	90A-834	ex TC-ACI	
☐ RA-85687	Tupolev Tu-154M	90A-857	ex EP-MAZ	
☐ RA-85688	Tupolev Tu-154M	90A-859	ex OM-VEA	
☐ RA-85690	Tupolev Tu-154M	90A-861	ex CCCP-85690	
☐ RA-85697	Tupolev Tu-154M	91A-870	ex EP-MAQ	stored DME
☐ RA-85699	Tupolev Tu-154M	91A-874	ex EP-ITC	
☐ RA-85724	Tupolev Tu-154M	92A-906	ex EP-MHD	
☐ RA-85827	Tupolev Tu-154M	87A-745	ex SP-LCC	stored OVB
☐ RA-85848	Tupolev Tu-154M	89A-804	ex OK-UCE	

SAKHA AVIATION SCHOOL — *Moscow-Bykovo (BKA)*

☐ RA-74003	Antonov An-74	36547070690	ex CCCP-74003
☐ RA-88177	Yakovlev Yak-40	9621747	ex CCCP-88177

Current status uncertain

SAMARA AIRLINES — *Beryoza (E5/BRZ)* — *Samara-Kurumotch (KUF)*

☐ RA-65105	Tupolev Tu-134A	60308	ex LY-ABH	
☐ RA-65122	Tupolev Tu-134A-3	60518	ex CCCP-65122	
☐ RA-65753	Tupolev Tu-134A-3	61099	ex CCCP-65753	
☐ RA-65758	Tupolev Tu-134A-3	62230	ex CCCP-65758	
☐ RA-65792	Tupolev Tu-134A-3	63121	ex CCCP-65792	
☐ RA-65797	Tupolev Tu-134A-3	63173	ex CCCP-65797	
☐ RA-85057	Tupolev Tu-154M	..A-1001		on order Op for Samara Oblast
☐ RA-85332	Tupolev Tu-154B-2	79A-332	ex ER-85585	
☐ RA-85585	Tupolev Tu-154B-2	83A-585	ex CCCP-85585	
☐ RA-85601	Tupolev Tu-154B-2	84A-601	ex 85601	Op for Samara Oblast
☐ RA-85707	Tupolev Tu-154M	91A-882	ex UR-85707	
☐ RA-85716	Tupolev Tu-154M	91A-892	ex EP-MCI	
☐ RA-85723	Tupolev Tu-154M	92A-905	ex HA-LGB	

☐ RA-85731	Tupolev Tu-154M	92A-913	ex EP-LBH		
☐ RA-85792	Tupolev Tu-154M	93A-976	ex EP-LAZ		
☐ RA-85817	Tupolev Tu-154M	95A-1007	ex EP-LBM		Lsd to KJC
☐ RA-85818	Tupolev Tu-154M	85A-719	ex EP-MAJ	AiRUnion colours	
☐ RA-85821	Tupolev Tu-154M	89A-805	ex SP-LCI	AiRUnion colours	
☐ RA-85822	Tupolev Tu-154M	89A-806	ex HA-LGC		
☐ RA-85823	Tupolev Tu-154M	88A-775	ex HA-LGA		
☐ RA-76475	Ilyushin Il-76TD	0043451523	ex EP-TPV		stored KUF as EP-TPV
☐ RA-76791	Ilyushin Il-76TD	0093497936	ex EP-TPU		stored KUF as EP-TPU

SARATOV AIRLINES — *Saratov Air (6W/SOV)* — *Saratov-Tsentralny (RTW)*

☐ RA-42316	Yakovlev Yak-42	4520422202030	ex CCCP-42316		stored RTW
☐ RA-42326	Yakovlev Yak-42D	4520424402154	ex CCCP-42326		
☐ RA-42328	Yakovlev Yak-42	4520421505058	ex CCCP-42328		
☐ RA-42361	Yakovlev Yak-42D	4520423811427	ex CCCP-42361		stored RTW
☐ RA-42378	Yakovlev Yak-42D	4520421014494	ex TC-FAR		
☐ RA-42389	Yakovlev Yak-42D	4520424016542	ex CCCP-42389		
☐ RA-42432	Yakovlev Yak-42D	4520424410016	ex TC-ALY	no titles	
☐ RA-42550	Yakovlev Yak-42D	11140205	ex CCCP-42550		stored
☐ RA-42551	Yakovlev Yak-42	11140305	ex CCCP-42551		
☐ RA-87844	Yakovlev Yak-40	9331330	ex CCCP-87844		

SAT AIRLINES — *Satair (HZ/SHU)* — *Yuzhno-Sakhalinsk Khomutovo (UUZ)*

☐ RA-46530	Antonov An-24B	57310009	ex CCCP-46530	
☐ RA-46618	Antonov An-24RV	37308705	ex CCCP-46618	
☐ RA-46639	Antonov An-24RV	37308905	ex CCCP-46639	
☐ RA-47198	Antonov An-24RV	27307702	ex CCCP-47198	
☐ RA-47317	Antonov An-24RV	67310504	ex CCCP-47317	
☐ RA-47366	Antonov An-24RV	77310804	ex CCCP-47366	
☐ RA-67251	de Havilland DHC-8-311	533	ex C-FWFH	
☐ RA-67257	de Havilland DHC-8-201	457	ex C-FJFW	Op for Exxon Neftegas
☐ RA-67259	de Havilland DHC-8-201	459	ex C-FNOP	Op for Exxon Neftegas
☐ RA-67261	de Havilland DHC-8-102	460	ex C-FNOQ	
☐ RA-11364	Antonov An-12V	347601	ex CCCP-11364	
☐ RA-11376	Antonov An-12BP	2348206	ex 02 red, Russian AF	
☐ RA-12988	Antonov An-12B	00347206	ex CCCP-12988	
☐ RA-26132	Antonov An-26B	37312708	ex CCCP-26132	
☐ RA-26138	Antonov An-26B	12810	ex CCCP-26138	
☐ RA-48984	Antonov An-12BP	402913	ex UR-48984	
☐ RA-73003	Boeing 737-2J8 (Nordam 3)	22859/890	ex N235WA	
☐ RA-73005	Boeing 737-232 (Nordam 3)	23100/1038	ex N328DL	
☐ RA-73013	Boeing 737-5L9	28721/2856	ex OY-APH	

SATURN AVIAKOMPANIA — *Rybmotors (RMO)* — *Rybinsk-Starosel'ye (RYB)*

☐ RA-87225	Yakovlev Yak-40K	9841359	ex CCCP-87225
☐ RA-87936	Yakovlev Yak-40K	9740756	ex CCCP-87936
☐ RA-88289	Antonov An-26B	11804	ex CCCP-88289

SEVERSTAL AIRCOMPANY — *Severstal (D2/SSF)* — *Cherepovets (CEE)*

☐ RA-87224	Yakovlev Yak-40K	9841259	ex CCCP-87224	VIP Op for Yava Group
☐ RA-87586	Yakovlev Yak-40	9221822	ex CCCP-87586	
☐ RA-87954	Yakovlev Yak-40	9811357	ex CCCP-87954	
☐ RA-88180	Yakovlev Yak-40	9622047	ex CCCP-88180	
☐ RA-88188	Yakovlev Yak-40	9620848	ex CCCP-88188	
☐ RA-88296	Yakovlev Yak-40	9421634	ex VN-A445	VIP

SHAR INK — *Sharink (UGP)* — *Moscow-Ostafyevo*

☐ RA-74001	Antonov An-74TK-100	36547070655	ex CCCP-74001	
☐ RA-74014	Antonov An-74-200	36547098968	ex ST-BDA	
☐ RA-74015	Antonov An-74-200	36547098969		
☐ RA-74020	Antonov An-74TK-100	36547195014		
☐ RA-74047	Antonov An-74-200	36547097941		on rebuild
☐ RA-25770	Mil Mi-8PS-11	8709	ex CCCP-25770	VIP

SIBAVIATRANS — *Sibavia (5M/SIB)* — *Krasnoyarsk-Yemelyanovo (KJA)*

☐ RA-46674	Antonov An-24RV	47309606	ex CCCP-46674		Lsd fr OMS
☐ RA-49278	Antonov An-24RV	47309808	ex YR-AMJ		
☐ RA-49279	Antonov An-24RV	17306905	ex YR-AMB	AiRUnion colours	
☐ RA-49287	Antonov An-24RV	27307607	ex YR-AME		
☐ RA-65571	Tupolev Tu-134AK	63955	ex EW-63955		

☐ RA-65605	Tupolev Tu-134A	09070	ex EW-65605	
☐ RA-65615	Tupolev Tu-134A-3	4352205	ex D-AOBE	
☐ RA-65881	Tupolev Tu-134A-3	35220	ex CCCP-65881	
☐ RA-65694	Tupolev Tu-134B-3	63235	ex UN-65694	AiRUnion colours
☐ RA-21503	Yakovlev Yak-40K	9820358	ex CCCP-21503	
☐ RA-48113	Antonov An-32	1709	ex CCCP-48113	
☐ RA-87916	Yakovlev Yak-40K	9730655	ex CCCP-87916	

SIRIUS AERO		***Sirius Aero (CIG)***		***Moscow-Vnukovo (VKO)***
☐ RA-65079	Tupolev Tu-134A-3	60054	ex LY-ASK	VIP
☐ RA-65099	Tupolev Tu-134A-3	63700	ex CCCP-65099	VIP
☐ RA-65604	Tupolev Tu-134AK	62561	ex CCCP-65604	VIP
☐ RA-65722	Tupolev Tu-134A-3M	66420	ex CCCP-65722	VIP
☐ RA-65928	Tupolev Tu-134A-3M	66491	ex CCCP-65928	VIP
☐ RA-65978	Tupolev Tu-134A-3	63357	ex CCCP-65978	Svetlana VIP

SKOL AVIAKOMPANIA		***(CDV)***		***Surgut (SGC)***
☐ RA-06033	Mil Mi-26T	34001212423	ex CCCP-06033	
☐ RA-06394	Mil Mi-26T	34001212123		
☐ RA-46848	Antonov An-24RV	27307506	ex CCCP-46848	
☐ RA-87240	Yakovlev Yak-40	9530743	ex CCCP-87240	
☐ RA-87940	Yakovlev Yak-40	9540444	ex CCCP-87940	
☐ RA-88226	Yakovlev Yak-40	9641350	ex CCCP-88226	

SKYEXPRESS		***(XW/SXR)***		***Moscow-Vnukovo (VNO)***
☐ VP-BET	Boeing 737-53C	24825/1894	ex D-ACIN	
☐ VP-BFB	Boeing 737-5Y0	26067/2304	ex N606TA	
☐ VP-BFJ	Boeing 737-53A	24859/1919	ex G-THOA	
☐ VP-BFK	Boeing 737-5L9	24928/1961	ex G-THOB	
☐ VP-BFM	Boeing 737-53A	24921/1962	ex N921AW	
☐ VP-BFN	Boeing 737-53A	24922/1964	ex N922AV	
☐ VP-BHA	Boeing 737-529	26538/2298	ex C-GAHB	
☐ VP-BOT	Boeing 737-341	25048/2085	ex N728BC	
☐ VP-BOU	Boeing 737-341	25049/2091	ex N729BC	

SOKOL		***Aerosokol (PIV)***		***Novotitarovskaya Heliport***
☐ RA-06025	Mil Mi-26T	34001212401	ex CCCP-06025	
☐ RA-06072	Mil Mi-26T	34001212491	ex CCCP-06072	
☐ RA-06087	Mil Mi-26T	340012112480		
☐ RA-22788	Mil Mi-8T	6201	ex CCCP-22788	

SVERDLOVSK 2ND AIR ENTERPRISE		***Pyshma (UKU)***		***Yekaterinburg-Koltsovo (SVX)***
☐ RA-74004	Antonov An-74	36547094890	ex CCCP-74004	VIP
☐ RA-74006	Antonov An-74	36547095896	ex CCCP-74006	
☐ RA-74048	Antonov An-74D	36547098943	all-white, no titles	VIP
☐ RA-87253	Yakovlev Yak-40	9321026	ex CCCP-87253	all-whiteVIP
☐ RA-87503	Yakovlev Yak-40AT	9520240	ex CCCP-87503	VIP. op for Kolsto Ural
☐ RA-87524	Yakovlev Yak-40	9520641	ex CCCP-87524	VIP
☐ RA-87974	Yakovlev Yak-40K	9621346	ex CCCP-87974	no titlesVIP
☐ RA-88159	Yakovlev Yak-40	9621346	ex CCCP-88159	all-whiteVIP
☐ RA-88234	Yakovlev Yak-40	9640351	ex CCCP-82834	

TATARSTAN AIR		***Air Tatarstan (U9/TAK)***		***Kazan-Osnovnoi (KZN)***
☐ VQ-BAP	Boeing 737-322	24665/1889	ex LZ-BOT	
☐ VQ-BBN	Boeing 737-53A	24785/1882	ex LZ-BOY	
☐ VQ-BBO	Boeing 737-548	25165/2463	ex LZ-BOR	
☐ VQ-BDB	Boeing 737-4D7	28702/2978	ex HS-TDL	
☐ VQ-BDC	Boeing 737-341	26852/2273	ex LZ-BOO	
☐ RA-86142	Ilyushin Il-86	51483210097	ex B-2016	stored DME
☐ RA-86143	Ilyushin Il-86	51483210099	ex B-2018	
☐ RA-86926	Ilyushin Il-86	51463210100	ex B-2019	
☐ RA-65065	Tupolev Tu-134A-3	49890	ex CCCP-65065	
☐ RA-65102	Tupolev Tu-134A-3	60267	ex CCCP-65102	
☐ RA-65691	Tupolev Tu-134A	63195	ex CCCP-65691	
☐ RA-65970	Tupolev Tu-134A	3351910	ex CCCP-65970	
☐ RA-65973	Tupolev Tu-134A	3352003	ex LY-ABA	
☐ RA-85101	Tupolev Tu-154M	88A-783	ex B-608L	
☐ RA-85109	Tupolev Tu-154M	88A-790	ex B-609L	
☐ RA-85136	Tupolev Tu-154M	88A-791	ex B-607L	
☐ RA-85798	Tupolev Tu-154M	93A-982	ex EP-MBO	
☐ RA-85799	Tupolev Tu-154M	94A-983		

☐ RA-42332	Yakovlev Yak-42	4520424505135	ex CCCP-42332	
☐ RA-42333	Yakovlev Yak-42	4520422606156	ex CCCP-42333	
☐ RA-42335	Yakovlev Yak-42	4520422606204	ex CU-T1274	
☐ RA-42347	Yakovlev Yak-42	4520423711322	ex CCCP-42347	
☐ RA-42357	Yakovlev Yak-42	4520422811408	ex CCCP-42357	stored KZN
☐ RA-42374	Yakovlev Yak-42D	4520423914340	ex CU-T1273	
☐ RA-42380	Yakovlev Yak-42D	4520422014549	ex CU-T1242	
☐ RA-42413	Yakovlev Yak-42D	4520422219066	ex EP-YAB	
☐ RA-42433	Yakovlev Yak-42D	4520421301017		
☐ RA-88287	Yakovlev Yak-40K	9940360	ex CCCP-88287	VIP op for Tatarstan Govt

TESIS — *Tesis (UZ/TIS)* — *Moscow-Domodedovo (DME)*

☐ VP-BXC	Boeing 747-258B (SCD)	22254/418	ex 4X-AXH

TOMSKAVIA — *Tomsk Avia (TSK)* — *Tomsk (TOF)*

☐ RA-26039	Antonov An-26B	10702	ex CCCP-26039
☐ RA-46627	Antonov An-24RV	37308806	ex CCCP-46627
☐ RA-46679	Antonov An-24RV	47309701	ex CCCP-46679
☐ RA-47254	Antonov An-24RV	27307706	ex CCCP-47254
☐ RA-47355	Antonov An-24RV	67310604	ex CCCP-47355

TRANSAERO AIRLINES — *Transoviet (UN/TSO)* — *Moscow-Domodedovo (DME)*

☐ EI-CXK	Boeing 737-4S3	25596/2255	ex G-OGBA	
☐ EI-CXN	Boeing 737-329	23772/1432	ex OO-SDW	
☐ EI-CXR	Boeing 737-329	24355/1709	ex OO-SYA	
☐ EI-CZK	Boeing 737-4Y0	24519/1781	ex N519AP	
☐ EI-DDK	Boeing 737-4S3	24165/1720	ex N758BC	
☐ EI-DDY	Boeing 737-4Y0	24904/1988	ex HA-LEV	
☐ EI-DNM	Boeing 737-4S3	24166/1722	ex EC-JHX	
☐ EI-DTU	Boeing 737-5Y0	25175/2150	ex B-2546	
☐ EI-DTV	Boeing 737-5Y0	25183/2218	ex B-2549	
☐ EI-DTW	Boeing 737-5Y0	25188/2238	ex B-2550	
☐ EI-DTX	Boeing 737-5Q8	28052/2965	ex LY-AZX	
☐ EI-EDZ	Boeing 737-8K5/W	27980/45	ex D-AHFF	
☐ EI-EEA	Boeing 737-8K5/W	27989/59	ex D-AHFG	
☐ VP-BPA	Boeing 737-5K5	25037/2022	ex D-AHLI	
☐ VP-BPD	Boeing 737-5K5	25062/2044	ex D-AHLN	
☐ VP-BYI	Boeing 737-524	28921/3052	ex N14660	
☐ VP-BYJ	Boeing 737-524	28923/3060	ex N14662	
☐ VP-BYT	Boeing 737-524	28928/3077	ex N14668	
☐ VQ-	Boeing 737-524	28919/3045	ex N18658	on order
☐ VQ-	Boeing 737-524	28922/3055	ex N23661	on order
☐ VQ-	Boeing 737-524	28924/3063	ex N17663	on order
☐ N747ZZ	Boeing 747-338	23222/602	ex VH-EBT	stored Rome, NY
☐ N749UN	Boeing 747-246B	22991/581	ex JA8162	
☐ VP-BGU	Boeing 747-346	23482/640	ex N740UN	
☐ VP-BGW	Boeing 747-346	24019/695	ex N742UN	
☐ VP-BGX	Boeing 747-346	24156/716	ex N741UN	
☐ VP-BGY	Boeing 747-346	23640/668	ex N743UN	
☐ VP-BKJ	Boeing 747-444	26638/995	ex N7716Q	
☐ VP-BKL	Boeing 747-444	28468/1162	ex N3508M	
☐ VP-BPX	Boeing 747-267B	22872/566	ex N747VC	
☐ VP-BQA	Boeing 747-219B	22723/527	ex N723TA	
☐ VP-BQB	Boeing 747-219B	22724/528	ex N703TA	
☐ VP-BQC	Boeing 747-219B	22725/563	ex N705TA	
☐ VP-BQE	Boeing 747-219B	22722/523	ex N702TA	
☐ VP-BQH	Boeing 747-219B	22791/568	ex N701TA	
☐ VP-BVR	Boeing 747-444	26637/943	ex (VP-BKG)	
☐ EI-CXZ	Boeing 767-216ER	24973/347	ex N502GX	
☐ EI-CZD	Boeing 767-216ER	23623/142	ex N762TA	
☐ EI-DBF	Boeing 767-3Q8ER	24745/355	ex F-GHGF	
☐ EI-DBG	Boeing 767-3Q8ER	24746/378	ex F-GHGG	
☐ EI-DBU	Boeing 767-37EER	25077/385	ex F-GHGH	
☐ EI-DBW	Boeing 767-201ER	23899/182	ex N647US	
☐ EI-DFS	Boeing 767-33AER	25346/403	ex ET-AKW	
☐ EI-UNA	Boeing 767-3P6ER	26233/501	ex A4O-GU	
☐ EI-UNB	Boeing 767-3P6ER	26234/538	ex A4O-GY	
☐ EI-UND	Boeing 767-3P6ER	26236/436	ex A4O-GX	
☐ EI-UNF	Boeing 767-3P6ER	26238/440	ex A4O-GT	
☐ EI-UNW	Boeing 777-222ER	30214/254	ex N208UA	
☐ EI-UNX	Boeing 777-222ER	30213/232	ex N207UA	
☐ EI-UNZ	Boeing 777-222	26925/13	ex N770UA	on order Lsd fr VTB
☐ RA-64509	Tupolev Tu-214	42305009		
☐ RA-64516	Tupolev Tu-214	42709016		

☐ RA-64517	Tupolev Tu-214	42305017		
☐ RA-64518	Tupolev Tu-214	42305018		
☐ RA-64549	Tupolev Tu-214	42305013	ex RA-64513	

TRANSAVIA GARANTIA — *Arkhangelsk-Talagi (ARH)*

☐ RA-26024	Antonov An-26B-100	10306	ex CCCP-26024	
☐ RA-26081	Antonov An-26B-100	11703	ex UR-BXU	
☐ RA-26089	Antonov An-26B-100	12203	ex UR-26089	
☐ RA-26682	Antonov An-26B-100	97308706	ex CCCP-26682	Freighter
☐ RA-26687	Antonov An-26B-100	8902	ex CCCP-26687	
☐ RA-87235	Yakovlev Yak-40	9530143	ex CCCP-87235	
☐ RA-87336	Yakovlev Yak-40	9610539	ex CCCP-87336	

TULPAR AIR — *(TUL)* — *Kazan-Osnovnoi / Orenburg-Tsentralny (KZN/REN)*

☐ RA-21504	Yakovlev Yak-40K	9831758	ex CCCP-21504	Executive
☐ RA-87496	Yakovlev Yak-40	9541945	ex CCCP-87496	op for Nizhykamsk Petrol
☐ RA-87535	Yakovlev Yak-40	9521941	ex CCCP-87535	Vasili Nesterov
☐ RA-87977	Yakovlev Yak-40	9321128	ex OK-BYH	
☐ RA-88269	Yakovlev Yak-40	9720753	ex LY-AAY	Kamaz titles
☐ RA-42330	Yakovlev Yak-42D	4520422505122	ex UR-42330	
☐ RA-42415	Yakovlev Yak-42D	4520422219089	ex CCCP-42415	
☐ RA-42440	Yakovlev Yak-42D	4520424210018	ex 9L-LDT	all-white

TUVA AIRLINES — *Kyzyl (KYZ)*

☐ RA-87425	Yakovlev Yak-40	9420135	ex CCCP-87425
☐ RA-87925	Yakovlev Yak-40	9731655	ex CCCP-87925
☐ RA-88212	Yakovlev Yak-40	9631849	ex CCCP-88212

TYUMENSPECAVIA — *(TUM)* — *Tyumen-Roshchino (TJM)*

☐ RA-26088	Antonov An-26	17311209	ex CCCP-26088	
☐ RA-26102	Antonov An-26	17311909	ex CCCP-26102	
☐ RA-26662	Antonov An-26	97308101	ex CCCP-26102	all-white

URAL AIRLINES — *Sverdlovsk Air (U6/SVR)* — *Yekaterinburg-Koltsovo (SVX)*

☐ VP-BFZ	Airbus A320-214	0735	ex G-BXKD	
☐ VP-BPU	Airbus A320-211	0220	ex F-GLGH	
☐ VP-BPV	Airbus A320-211	0203	ex F-GLGG	
☐ VP-BQY	Airbus A320-211	0140	ex TS-ING	
☐ VP-BQZ	Airbus A320-211	0157	ex TS-INH	
☐ VQ-BAG	Airbus A320-214	1063	ex EC-KLU	
☐ VQ-BCY	Airbus A320-214	1484	ex EC-HQM	
☐ VQ-BCZ	Airbus A320-214	1777	ex G-OOPW	
☐ VQ-BCX	Airbus A321-211	1720	ex G-OOAV	
☐ VQ-BDA	Airbus A321-211	1012	ex TC-KTY	
☐ VQ-BDJ	Airbus A320-214	2175	ex N268AV	
☐ VQ-BDM	Airbus A320-214	2187	ex N269AV	
☐ RA-46532	Antonov An-24RV	57310101	ex CCCP-46532	
☐ RA-47182	Antonov An-24B	99901907	ex CCCP-47182	
☐ RA-47187	Antonov An-24B	99902002	ex CCCP-47187	
☐ RA-86078	Ilyushin Il-86	51483205049	ex CCCP-86078	
☐ RA-86093	Ilyushin Il-86	51483207064	ex CCCP-86093	
☐ RA-86114	Ilyushin Il-86	51483209082	ex CCCP-86114	
☐ RA-86120	Ilyushin Il-86	51483209088	ex CCCP-86120	
☐ RA-65090	Tupolev Tu-134A	60185	ex CCCP-65090	Lsd fr ORB
☐ RA-85219	Tupolev Tu-154B-2	77A-219	ex CCCP-85219	
☐ RA-85319	Tupolev Tu-154B-2	78A-319	ex CCCP-85319	
☐ RA-85337	Tupolev Tu-154B-2	79A-337	ex UN-85337	
☐ RA-85357	Tupolev Tu-154B-2	79A-357	ex CCCP-85357	
☐ RA-85374	Tupolev Tu-154B-2	79A-374	ex CCCP-85374	
☐ RA-85375	Tupolev Tu-154B-2	79A-375	ex CCCP-85375	
☐ RA-85432	Tupolev Tu-154B-2	80A-432	ex CCCP-85432	
☐ RA-85459	Tupolev Tu-154B-2	80A-459	ex CCCP-85459	
☐ RA-85508	Tupolev Tu-154B-2	81A-508	ex CCCP-85508	
☐ RA-85807	Tupolev Tu-154M	94A-988		
☐ RA-85814	Tupolev Tu-154M	95A-994		
☐ RA-85833	Tupolev Tu-154M	01A-1020		
☐ RA-85844	Tupolev Tu-154M	03A-992		

UTAIR AIRLINES — *UTair (UT/UTA)* — *Tyumen-Roshchino (TJM)*

☐ RA-46267	Antonov An-24B	77303510	ex CCCP-46267
☐ RA-46362	Antonov An-24B	07305903	ex CCCP-46362
☐ RA-46388	Antonov An-24B	07306201	ex CCCP-46388

	Registration	Type	c/n	Previous identity	Remarks
☐	RA-46481	Antonov An-24RV	27308009	ex CCCP-46481	
☐	RA-46509	Antonov An-24RV	37308405	ex CCCP-46509	
☐	RA-46609	Antonov An-24RV	37308606	ex CCCP-46609	
☐	RA-46619	Antonov An-24RV	37308706	ex CCCP-46619	
☐	RA-46828	Antonov An-24B	17306705	ex CCCP-46828	
☐	RA-47271	Antonov An-24RV	07306401	ex BNMAU-47271	
☐	RA-47273	Antonov An-24B	07306403	ex CCCP-47273	
☐	RA-47289	Antonov An-24B	07306509	ex CCCP-47289	
☐	RA-47357	Antonov An-24RV	67310606	ex CCCP-47357	
☐	RA-47827	Antonov An-24B	17307208	ex CCCP-47827	stored
☐	RA-47829	Antonov An-24B	17307210	ex CCCP-47829	
☐	VP-BCA	ATR 42-300	051	ex I-NOWA	
☐	VP-BCB	ATR 42-300	054	ex I-NOWT	
☐	VP-BCD	ATR 42-300	042	ex I-ATRG	
☐	VP-BCF	ATR 42-300	068	ex I-ATRL	
☐	VP-BCG	ATR 42-300	057	ex I-ATRJ	
☐	VP-BLI	ATR 42-300	233	ex D-BCRQ	
☐	VP-BLJ	ATR 42-300	255	ex D-BCRR	
☐	VP-BLN	ATR 42-300	278	ex D-BJJJ	
☐	VP-BLO	ATR 42-300	289	ex D-BCRT	
☐	VP-BLU	ATR 42-300	287	ex D-BCRS	
☐	VP-BPJ	ATR 42-300	165	ex N15823	
☐	VP-BPK	ATR 42-300	166	ex N16824	
☐	VP-BYW	ATR 72-201	174	ex ES-KRE	
☐	VP-BYX	ATR 72-201	251	ex ES-KRK	
☐	VP-BYZ	ATR 72-201	332	ex ES-KRL	
☐	VP-BVL	Boeing 737-524	28926/3069	ex N13665	
☐	VP-BVZ	Boeing 737-524	28925/3066	ex N14664	
☐	VP-BXO	Boeing 737-524/W	27314/2566	ex N14601	
☐	VP-BXQ	Boeing 737-524/W	27315/2571	ex N69602	
☐	VP-BXR	Boeing 737-524/W	27316/2573	ex N69603	
☐	VP-BXU	Boeing 737-524/W	27318/2582	ex N14605	
☐	VP-BXV	Boeing 737-524/W	27322/2607	ex N14609	
☐	VP-BXY	Boeing 737-524/W	27328/2640	ex N37615	
☐	VP-BXZ	Boeing 737-524/W	27329/2641	exN52616	
☐	VP-BYK	Boeing 737-524	28918/3026	ex N23657	
☐	VP-BYL	Boeing 737-524	28920/3048	ex N15659	
☐	VP-BYM	Boeing 737-524	28917/3019	ex N11656	
☐	VP-BYP	Boeing 737-524	28927/3074	ex N14667	
☐	VQ-BAC	Boeing 737-524/W	27321/2597	ex N33608	
☐	VQ-BAD	Boeing 737-524/W	27331/2652	ex N16618	
☐	VQ-BAE	Boeing 737-524/W	27320/2596	ex N16607	
☐	RA-65005	Tupolev Tu-134A-3	44065	ex CCCP-65005	
☐	RA-65024	Tupolev Tu-134A	48420	ex CCCP-65024	
☐	RA-65033	Tupolev Tu-134A-3	48540	ex CCCP-65033	
☐	RA-65055	Tupolev Tu-134A	49856	ex CCCP-65055	
☐	RA-65059	Tupolev Tu-134A-3	49870	ex CCCP-65059	
☐	RA-65127	Tupolev Tu-134A-3	60627	ex EY-65127	
☐	RA-65136	Tupolev Tu-134A-3	60885	ex CCCP-65136	
☐	RA-65148	Tupolev Tu-134A-3	61025	ex CCCP-65148	
☐	RA-65560	Tupolev Tu-134A	60321	ex YU-AJW	
☐	RA-65565	Tupolev Tu-134A-1	63998	ex CCCP-65565	
☐	RA-65572	Tupolev Tu-134AK-3	63960	ex UR-CCG	
☐	RA-65607	Tupolev Tu-134A	48560	ex CCCP-65607	VIP
☐	RA-65608	Tupolev Tu-134A	38040	ex CCCP-65608	VIP
☐	RA-65609	Tupolev Tu-134A-3	46155	ex CCCP-65609	
☐	RA-65611	Tupolev Tu-134A-3	3351903	ex CCCP-65611	
☐	RA-65614	Tupolev Tu-134A	4352207	ex CCCP-65614	
☐	RA-65616	Tupolev Tu-134A-3	4352206	ex CCCP-65616	
☐	RA-65618	Tupolev Tu-134A-3	12095	ex CCCP-65618	
☐	RA-65620	Tupolev Tu-134A-3	35180	ex CCCP-65620	
☐	RA-65621	Tupolev Tu-134A-3	48320	ex CCCP-65621	
☐	RA-65622	Tupolev Tu-134A-3	60495	ex CCCP-65622	
☐	RA-65716	Tupolev Tu-134B-3	63595	ex CCCP-65716	
☐	RA-65728	Tupolev Tu-134B-3	49858	ex LZ-TUG	
☐	RA-65755	Tupolev Tu-134A-3	62165	ex CCCP-65755	
☐	RA-65777	Tupolev Tu-134A-3	62552	ex CCCP-65777	
☐	RA-65780	Tupolev Tu-134A-3	62622	ex CCCP-65780	
☐	RA-65793	Tupolev Tu-134A-3	63128	ex CCCP-65793	
☐	RA-65847	Tupolev Tu-134A-3	23135	ex CCCP-85847	
☐	RA-65901	Tupolev Tu-134A-3	63731	ex CCCP-65901	
☐	RA-65902	Tupolev Tu-134A-3	63742	ex CCCP-65902	
☐	RA-65916	Tupolev Tu-134A-3	66152	ex CCCP-65916	
☐	RA-65960	Tupolev Tu-134A	3351806	ex CCCP-65960	stored
☐	RA-65977	Tupolev Tu-134A	63245	ex CCCP-65977	
☐	RA-85013	Tupolev Tu-154M	90A-840	ex LZ-MIG	
☐	RA-85016	Tupolev Tu-154M	90A-844	ex LZ-MIH	
☐	RA-85018	Tupolev Tu-154M	90A-852	ex LZ-MIR	
☐	RA-85056	Tupolev Tu-154M	90A-845	ex LZ-MIL	

☐ RA-85069	Tupolev Tu-154M	90A-863	ex LZ-MIS		
☐ RA-85504	Tupolev Tu-154B-2	81A-504	ex CCCP-85504		
☐ RA-85595	Tupolev Tu-154B-2	84A-595	ex CCCP-85595		
☐ RA-85602	Tupolev Tu-154B-2	84A-602	ex CCCP-85602		
☐ RA-85681	Tupolev Tu-154M	90A-848	ex LZ-LTE	Abakan	stored
☐ RA-85727	Tupolev Tu-154M	92A-909	ex ES-LTP		
☐ RA-85733	Tupolev Tu-154M	92A-915	ex EP-MAL	Antonina Grigoreva	
☐ RA-85755	Tupolev Tu-154M	92A-937		Vasilij Bachilov	
☐ RA-85788	Tupolev Tu-154M	93A-972	ex EP-ITS		
☐ RA-85789	Tupolev Tu-154M	93A-973			
☐ RA-85796	Tupolev Tu-154M	94A-980		Victor Muravlenko	
☐ RA-85805	Tupolev Tu-154M	94A-986		Farman Salmanov	
☐ RA-85806	Tupolev Tu-154M	94A-987			
☐ RA-85808	Tupolev Tu-154M	94A-989		Shetr Panov	
☐ RA-85813	Tupolev Tu-154M	95A-990			
☐ RA-85820	Tupolev Tu-154M	98A-995		Roman Marchenko	
☐ RA-87292	Yakovlev Yak-40	9320728	ex CCCP-87292		
☐ RA-87348	Yakovlev Yak-40	9511739	ex CCCP-87348		
☐ RA-87907	Yakovlev Yak-40	9731254	ex CCCP-87907		
☐ RA-87941	Yakovlev Yak-40	9540545	ex CCCP-87941		
☐ RA-87942	Yakovlev Yak-40K	9540645	ex CCCP-87942		
☐ RA-87997	Yakovlev Yak-40	9540145	ex CCCP-87997		
☐ RA-88209	Yakovlev Yak-40K	9730353	ex CCCP-88209		
☐ RA-88210	Yakovlev Yak-40	9631649	ex CCCP-88210		
☐ RA-88213	Yakovlev Yak-40	9631949	ex CCCP-88213		
☐ RA-88227	Yakovlev Yak-40	9641550	ex CCCP-88227		VIP
☐ RA-88244	Yakovlev Yak-40	9641751	ex CCCP-88244		
☐ RA-88280	Yakovlev Yak-40	9820658	ex CCCP-88280		

UTAIR EXPRESS — *Komiinter (UR/KMV)* — *Syktyvkar (SCW)*

☐ RA-13344	Antonov An-24RV	37308310	ex CCCP-13344	
☐ RA-46468	Antonov An-24RV	27307906	ex CCCP-46468	
☐ RA-46494	Antonov An-24RV	27308207	ex CCCP-46494	
☐ RA-46603	Antonov An-24RV	37308510	ex CCCP-46603	
☐ RA-46610	Antonov An-24RV	37308607	ex CCCP-46610	
☐ RA-46640	Antonov An-24RV	37308908	ex CCCP-46640	
☐ RA-46692	Antonov An-24RV	47309903	ex CCCP-46692	
☐ RA-47820	Antonov An-24RV	17307201	ex CCCP-47820	

UVAUGA — *Pilot Air (UHS)* — *Ulyanovsk-Tsentralny (ULY)*

☐ RA-26025	Antonov An-26B	10308	ex CCCP-26025	
☐ RA-26503	Antonov An-26	6310	ex CCCP-26503	
☐ RA-26513	Antonov An-26	6810	ex CCCP-26513	
☐ RA-26544	Antonov An-26	2710	ex CCCP-26544	
☐ RA-76401	Ilyushin Il-76TD	1023412399	ex CCCP-76401	Lsd to AYZ
☐ RA-76783	Ilyushin Il-76TD	0093498974	ex CCCP-76783	Lsd to AYZ
☐ RA-86062	Ilyushin Il-86	51483203029	ex EW-86062	
☐ RA-85470	Tupolev Tu-154B-2	81A-470	ex CCCP-85470	
☐ RA-85609	Tupolev Tu-154M	84A-704	ex CCCP-85609	no titles
☐ RA-85636	Tupolev Tu-154M	87A-766	ex CCCP-85636	
☐ RA-87315	Yakovlev Yak-40	9331429	ex CCCP-87315	
☐ RA-87580	Yakovlev Yak-40	9221222	ex CCCP-87580	
☐ RA-87653	Yakovlev Yak-40	9211620	ex CCCP-87653	VIP
☐ RA-42528	Yakovlev Yak-42D	11041003	ex CCCP-42528	stored ULY
☐ RA-42539	Yakovlev Yak-42D	11140504	ex CCCP-42539	stored ULY
☐ RA-42543	Yakovlev Yak-42D	11250904	ex CCCP-42543	

V GRIZODUBOVA AIR — *Grizodubova Air (GZD)* — *Moscow-Zhukovsky*

☐ RA-76490	Ilyushin Il-76T	093416506	ex YI-AKO	Lsd to ASE

VASO AIRLINES — *Vaso (2Z/VSO)* — *Voronezh-Chertovitskoye (VOZ)*

☐ RA-86115	Ilyushin Il-86	51483209083	ex CCCP-86115

VIM AIRLINES — *MovAir (NN/MOV)* — *Moscow-Domodedovo (DME)*

☐ RA-73007	Boeing 757-230	24749/295	ex D-ABNE		
☐ RA-73008	Boeing 757-230	25436/419	ex D-ABNH		
☐ RA-73009	Boeing 757-230	25437/422	ex D-ABNI		Op as UN152
☐ RA-73010	Boeing 757-230	25438/428	ex D-ABNK		
☐ RA-73011	Boeing 757-230	25439/437	ex D-ABNL		
☐ RA-73012	Boeing 757-230	25440/443	ex D-ABNM		
☐ RA-73014	Boeing 757-230	25441/446	ex D-ABNN		
☐ RA-73015	Boeing 757-230	25901/464	ex D-ABNO		Lsd to BBT
☐ RA-73016	Boeing 757-230	26433/521	ex D-ABNP	returned?	

☐ RA-73017	Boeing 757-230	26434/532	ex D-ABNR	
☐ RA-73018	Boeing 757-230	26435/537	ex D-ABNS	
☐ RA-73019	Boeing 757-230	26436/588	ex D-ABNT	stored DME
☐ RA-42329	Yakovlev Yak-42D	4520422505093	ex CCCP-42329	
☐ RA-42340	Yakovlev Yak-42D	4520424606270	ex CCCP-42340	
☐ RA-42343	Yakovlev Yak-42	4520421708285	ex UR-42343	
☐ RA-42345	Yakovlev Yak-42D	4520422708304	ex EK-42345	
☐ RA-42370	Yakovlev Yak-42D	4520422914203	ex CCCP-42370	
☐ RA-42408	Yakovlev Yak-42D	4520422216698	ex EP-YAC	
☐ RA-42425	Yakovlev Yak-42D	4520423303016	ex CU-T1243	

VLADIVOSTOK AIR — Vladair (XF/VLK) — Vladivostok-Knevichi (VVO)

☐ VP-BEQ	Airbus A320-212	0422	ex 6Y-JMB	
☐ VP-BRB	Airbus A320-212	0528	ex 6Y-JMA	
☐ VP-BFX	Airbus A320-214	0714	ex G-BXKA	
☐ VP-BFY	Airbus A320-214	0730	ex G-BXKC	
☐ VQ-BCG	Airbus A320-214	1200	ex EC-HGY	
☐ VQ-BCW	Airbus A330-301	070	ex EI-CRK	
☐ VQ-BEQ	Airbus A330-301	086	ex EI-JFK	
☐ VQ-	Airbus A330-301	055	ex EI-DUB	on order
☐ RA-85562	Tupolev Tu-154B-2	82A-562	ex CCCP-85562	Dalnerechenskstored
☐ RA-85596	Tupolev Tu-154B-2	84A-596	ex CCCP-85596	
☐ RA-85676	Tupolev Tu-154M	90A-836	ex EP-MAM Sayanogorsk	
☐ RA-85685	Tupolev Tu-154M	90A-853	ex CCCP-85685	Nakhodkastored
☐ RA-85710	Tupolev Tu-154M	91A-885	ex UR-85710 Vladivostok	
☐ RA-85766	Tupolev Tu-154M	92A-923	ex EP-MAP	
☐ RA-85803	Tupolev Tu-154M	89A-822	ex EK-85803 Spassk-Dalny	
☐ RA-85837	Tupolev Tu-154M	91A-876	ex UR-85701 Khakasia	
☐ RA-64026	Tupolev Tu-204-300	1450743164026		
☐ RA-64038	Tupolev Tu-204-300	1450744464038	Sberbank Rossii titles	
☐ RA-64039	Tupolev Tu-204-300	1450741564039	Sberbank Rossii titles	
☐ RA-64040	Tupolev Tu-204-300	1450744565040		
☐ RA-64044	Tupolev Tu-204-300	1450744564044		
☐ RA-64045	Tupolev Tu-204-300	1450744564045		
☐ RA-87273	Yakovlev Yak-40	9310927	ex CCCP-87273	
☐ RA-87958	Yakovlev Yak-40K	9821957	ex CCCP-87958	
☐ RA-88172	Yakovlev Yak-40K	9611047	ex CCCP-88172	
☐ RA-88216	Yakovlev Yak-40	9630250	ex CCCP-88216	Dveuk
☐ RA-88232	Yakovlev Yak-40K	9640151	ex CCCP-88232	

VOLGA AVIAEXPRESS — Goumrak (WLG) — Volgograd-Goomrak (VOG)

☐ RA-42364	Yakovlev Yak-42D	4520424811442	ex CU-T1272	
☐ RA-42384	Yakovlev Yak-42D	4520423016230	ex CCCP-42384	
☐ RA-42406	Yakovlev Yak-42D	4520424116683	ex CCCP-42406	stored
☐ RA-42549	Yakovlev Yak-42D	11040105	ex ER-YCD Yevgeni Kucher	
☐ RA-65019	Tupolev Tu-134A	48375	ex CCCP-65019	
☐ RA-65086	Tupolev Tu-134A-3	60130	ex CCCP-65086	
☐ RA-76484	Ilyushin Il-76TD	0063469081	ex CCCP-76484	
☐ RA-88171	Yakovlev Yak-40	9620947	ex EP-LBK	
☐ RA-88228	Yakovlev Yak-40	9641750	ex CCCP-88228	
☐ VP-BMN	Canadair CL-600-2B19 (CRJ-200)	7179	ex N620BR	
☐ VP-BMR	Canadair CL-600-2B19 (CRJ-200)	7192	ex N623BR	
☐ VQ-BFA	Canadair CL-600-2B19 (CRJ-200ER)	7627	ex N466CA	
☐ VQ-BFB	Canadair CL-600-2B19 (CRJ-200ER)	7637	ex N467CA	
☐ VQ-BFF	Canadair CL-600-2B19 (CRJ-200LR)	7470	ex N705BR	
☐ VQ-BFI	Canadair CL-600-2B19 (CRJ-200ER)	7671	ex N478CA	

VOLGA-DNEPR AIRLINES — Volga Dnepr (VI/VDA) — Ulyanovsk-Vostochniy East

☐ RA-82042	Antonov An-124-100	9773054055093	ex CCCP-82042	
☐ RA-82043	Antonov An-124-100	9773054155101	ex CCCP-82043	
☐ RA-82044	Antonov An-124-100	9773054155109	ex CCCP-82044	
☐ RA-82045	Antonov An-124-100	9773052255113	ex CCCP-82045	
☐ RA-82046	Antonov An-124-100	9773052255117	ex RA-82067	
☐ RA-82047	Antonov An-124-100	9773053259121		
☐ RA-82074	Antonov An-124-100	9773051459142		
☐ RA-82078	Antonov An-124-100	9773054559153		
☐ RA-82079	Antonov An-124-100	9773052062157		
☐ RA-82081	Antonov An-124-100M	9773051462165		
☐ EW-76734	Ilyushin Il-76TD	0073476312	ex RA-76734	
☐ EW-78843	Ilyushin Il-76TD	1003403082	ex CCCP-78843	
☐ RA-76370	Ilyushin Il-76TD	1033414458		Lsd fr GZP
☐ RA-76402	Ilyushin Il-76TD	1023413430		Lsd fr GZP
☐ RA-76445	Ilyushin Il-76TD	1023410330	ex EK-76445	Lsd fr GZP

☐ RA-76446	Ilyushin Il-76TD	1023412418	ex EK-76446		Lsd fr GZP
☐ RA-76483	Ilyushin Il-76TD	0063468042	ex CCCP-76483		
☐ RA-76493	Ilyushin Il-76TD	0043456700			dam 10Jun07
☐ RA-76950	Ilyushin Il-76-90VD	2053420697	Vladimir Kokkinaki		
☐ RA-76951	Ilyushin Il-76-90VD	2073421704			
☐ RA-87357	Yakovlev Yak-40	9340631	ex CCCP-87357		VIP
☐ RA-87400	Yakovlev Yak-40	9421233	ex CCCP-87400		
☐ RA-87484	Yakovlev Yak-40	9441238	ex CCCP-87484		Lsd fr VGV
☐ RA-87842	Yakovlev Yak-40	9321030	ex CCCP-87842		
☐ RA-88231	Yakovlev Yak-40K	9642050	ex CCCP-88231		

VOLOGDA AIR ENTERPRISE — *Vologda Air (VGV)* — *Vologda-Grishino (VGD)*

☐ RA-87284	Yakovlev Yak-40	9311927	ex CCCP-87277	
☐ RA-87484	Yakovlev Yak-40	9441238	ex CCCP-87484	
☐ RA-87665	Yakovlev Yak-40	9240925	ex CCCP-87665	no titles
☐ RA-87669	Yakovlev Yak-40	9021760	ex CCCP-87665	no titles
☐ RA-88247	Yakovlev Yak-40	9642051	ex EP-LBJ	

VOSTOK AIRLINES — *Vostok (VTK)* — *Khabarovsk-Novy (KHV)*

☐ RA-67634	LET L-410UVP-E	902427	ex CCCP-67634		
☐ RA-67635	LET L-410UVP-E	902428	ex CCCP-67635		
☐ RA-67636	LET L-410UVP-E	902429	ex CCCP-67636		
☐ RA-28920	WSK/PZL Antonov An-28	1AJ008-06	ex CCCP-28920		stored KHV
☐ RA-28929	WSK/PZL Antonov An-28	1AJ008-16	ex CCCP-28929		
☐ RA-28931	WSK/PZL Antonov An-28	1AJ008-18	ex CCCP-28931		no titles
☐ RA-28933	WSK/PZL Antonov An-28	1AJ008-20	ex CCCP-28933		
☐ RA-28941	WSK/PZL Antonov An-28	1AJ009-07	ex CCCP-28941		
☐ RA-28942	WSK/PZL Antonov An-28	1AJ009-08	ex CCCP-28942		stored KHV
☐ RA-41901	Antonov An-38-100	4163847010001		Vera	
☐ RA-41903	Antonov An-38-100	4163838010003		Lyubov	

VYBORG AIRLINES — *Vyborg Air (VBG)* — *St Petersburg-Pulkovo (LED)*

☐ RA-91011	Ilyushin Il-114		
☐ RA-91015	Ilyushin Il-114	1033828025	ex UK-91015

YAK SERVICE — *Yak-Service (AKY)* — *Moscow-Bykovo (BKA)*

☐ RA-42368	Yakovlev Yak-42D	4520422914166	ex EP-LBT	
☐ RA-42387	Yakovlev Yak-42	4520423016436	ex CCCP-42387	
☐ RA-42412	Yakovlev Yak-42D	4520422219055	ex EP-YAA	
☐ RA-87648	Yakovlev Yak-40	9140920	ex CCCP-87648	VIP
☐ RA-87659	Yakovlev Yak-40	9240325	ex CCCP-87659	VIP
☐ RA-88294	Yakovlev Yak-40	9331029	ex UN-88294	VIP
☐ RA-88295	Yakovlev Yak-40	9331329	ex 035	VIP

YAKUTIA AIRLINES — *Air Yakutia (K7/SYL)* — *Yakutsk (YKS)*

☐ RA-46510	Antonov An-24RV	37308406	ex CCCCP-46510		
☐ RA-46496	Antonov An-24RV	27308209	ex CCCP-47496		
☐ RA-46665	Antonov An-24RV	47309506	ex CCCP-46665		
☐ RA-47352	Antonov An-24RV	67310601	ex CCCP-47352		
☐ RA-47353	Antonov An-24RV	67310602	ex CCCP-47353		
☐ RA-47360	Antonov An-24RV	67310704	ex CCCP-47360		
☐ RA-47819	Antonov An-24RV	17307108	ex CCCP-47819		
☐ RA-47830	Antonov An-24RV	17307301	ex CCCP-47830		stored YKS
☐ RA-47845	Antonov An-24RV	17307407	ex CCCP-47845		stored YKS
☐ RA-85007	Tupolev Tu-154M	88A-777	ex LZ-HMF		
☐ RA-85520	Tupolev Tu-154B-2	81A-520	ex CCCP-85520		
☐ RA-85577	Tupolev Tu-154B-2	83A-577	ex CCCP-85577		stored YKS
☐ RA-85700	Tupolev Tu-154M	91A-875	ex LZ-HMY		
☐ RA-85790	Tupolev Tu-154M	93A-974	ex EP-CPL	Valery Kuzmin	
☐ RA-85791	Tupolev Tu-154M	93A-975	ex EP-MBR		
☐ RA-85794	Tupolev Tu-154M	93A-978			
☐ RA-85812	Tupolev Tu-154M	94A-1005		AirUnion colours	
☐ RA-11354	Antonov An-12BP	401812	ex CCCP-11354		stored YKS
☐ RA-11767	Antonov An-12BP	401909	ex CCCP-11767		stored YKS
☐ RA-11884	Antonov An-12BP	401710	ex CCCP-11884		stored YKS
☐ RA-26037	Antonov An-26	10608	ex CCCP-26037		stored YKS
☐ RA-26105	Antonov An-26B-100	12003	ex CCCP-26105		
☐ RA-26516	Antonov An-26	7001	ex CCCP-26516		stored YKS
☐ RA-26660	Antonov An-26-100	97308008	ex CCCP-26660		
☐ RA-87205	Yakovlev Yak-40	9810257	ex CCCP-87205		
☐ RA-87903	Yakovlev Yak-40K	9720654	ex CCCP-87903		no titles
☐ RA-88166	Yakovlev Yak-40	9612046	ex CCCP-88166		

☐ RA-88261	Yakovlev Yak-40	9711652	ex CCCP-88261	
☐ RA-41250	Antonov An-140-100	05A001		stored
☐ RA-41251	Antonov An-140-100	07A012		
☐ RA-41252	Antonov An-140-100	09A014		
☐ VQ-BEO	Boeing 737-76Q/W	30293/1496	ex D-ABBN	
☐ VP-BFG	Boeing 757-256/W	26244/616	ex TF-FIT	
☐ VP-BFI	Boeing 757-27B	24838/302	ex TF-FIW	
☐ VQ-BCF	Boeing 757-23N/W	27974/737	ex N518AT	
☐ VQ-BCK	Boeing 757-256/W	26245/617	ex TF-FIS	

YAMAL AIRLINES — *Yamal (YL/LLM)* — *Salekhard-Nepalkovo (SLY)*

☐ VP-BRQ	Boeing 737-528	25230/2191	ex F-GJNE	
☐ VP-BRS	Boeing 737-528	25231/2208	ex F-GJNF	
☐ VP-BRU	Boeing 737-528	25206/2099	ex F-GJNA	
☐ VP-BRV	Boeing 737-528	25227/2108	ex F-GJNB	
☐ VQ-BAB	Boeing 737-56N	28565/2944	ex N565LS	
☐ RA-65132	Tupolev Tu-134A-3	60639	ex CCCP-65132	
☐ RA-65143	Tupolev Tu-134A	60967	ex CCCP-65143	
☐ RA-65552	Tupolev Tu-134A-3	66270	ex CCCP-65552	
☐ RA-65554	Tupolev Tu-134A-3	66320	ex CCCP-65554	
☐ RA-65906	Tupolev Tu-134A	66175	ex CCCP-65906	Salekhard
☐ RA-65914	Tupolev Tu-134A-3	66109	ex CCCP-65914	
☐ RA-65915	Tupolev Tu-134A-3	66120	ex TC-GRE	
☐ RA-65919	Tupolev Tu-134A-3	66168	ex CCCP-65919	
☐ RA-65983	Tupolev Tu-134A-3	63350	ex CCCP-65983	
☐ RA-87222	Yakovlev Yak-40K	9832058	ex CCCP-87222	
☐ RA-87340	Yakovlev Yak-40	9510939	ex YL-TRA	
☐ RA-87381	Yakovlev Yak-40	9411232	ex CCCP-87381	
☐ RA-87416	Yakovlev Yak-40	9420834	ex CCCP-87416	
☐ RA-88264	Yakovlev Yak-40K	9711952	ex CCCP-88264	
☐ RA-26133	Antonov An-26B	37312709	ex CCCP-26133	
☐ RA-46694	Antonov An-24RV	47309905	ex CCCP-46694	
☐ RA-46695	Antonov An-24RV	47309906	ex UN 46695	
☐ RA-72918	Antonov An-72	36572040548	ex CCCP-72918	
☐ RA-74052	Antonov An-74-200	36547098944		
☐ RA-85842	Tupolev Tu-154B-2	80A-420	ex 0420 Slovak AFVIP	

ZAPOLYARYE AVIAKOMPANIA — *Norlisk-Alykel (NSK)*

☐ RA-11363	Antonov An-12B	00347505	ex CCCP-11363
☐ RA-26620	Antonov An-26-100	5104	ex CCCP-26620
☐ RA-85725	Tupolev Tu-154M	92A-907	ex EP-MHB

RDPL- LAOS (Lao People's Democratic Republic

LAO AIRLINES — *Lao (QV/LAO)* — *Vientiane (VTE)*

☐ RDPL-34129	AVIC II Y-12	0085	
☐ RDPL-34131	AVIC II Y-12	0087	
☐ RDPL-34132	ATR 72-202	396	ex F-OLAO
☐ RDPL-34137	ATR 72-202	316	ex F-OHOB
☐ RDPL-34173	ATR 72-202	870	ex F-WNUD
☐ RDPL-34174	ATR 72-202	878	ex F-WWEG
☐ RDPL-34144	Cessna 208B Caravan I	208B0967	ex VH-KCV
☐ RDPL-34149	Cessna 208B Caravan I	208B1159	ex N12879
☐ RDPL-34168	CAIC MA60	0402	ex B-761L
☐ RDPL-34169	CAIC MA60	0403	
☐ RDPL-34171	CAIC MA60	0507	
☐ RDPL-341712	CAIC MA60	0508	

LAO AVIATION — *Lavie (LLL)* — *Vientiane (VTE)*

☐ RDPL-34139	Mil Mi-17 (Mi-8MTV-1)	95946	ex CCCP-27114
☐ RDPL-34140	Mil Mi-17 (Mi-8MTV-1)	95984	ex CCCP-27121
☐ RDPL-34145	Aérospatiale AS350BA Ecureuil	2532	ex D-HLEA
☐ RDPL-34156	Antonov An-12BP	402001	ex LZ-VEF

LAO CAPRICORN AIR

☐ RDPL-34153	Antonov An-12TB	01347907	ex ER-AXA

RP- PHILIPPINES (Republic of the Philippines)

2GO (BOI) Manila-Ninoy Aquino Intl (MNL)

☐ RP-C2253	NAMC YS-11-100	2020	ex RP-C1936	stored MNL
☐ RP-C2677	NAMC YS-11A-500	2092	ex JA8717	stored MNL
☐ RP-C2739	NAMC YS-11A-500	2090	ex JA8710	stored MNL
☐ RP-C3389	NAMC YS-11A-213	2078	ex JA8722	stored ?
☐ RP-C3585	NAMC YS-11A-227	2149	ex JA8771	

AIR LINK INTERNATIONAL AIRWAYS Manila-Sangley Point (SGL)

☐ RP-C180	Cessna 414	414-0402	ex RP.180
☐ RP-C1102	Beech 88 Queen Air	LP-44	ex RP-94
☐ RP-C2252	NAMC YS-11A-500	2079	ex RP-C1931

AIR PHILIPPINES Orient Pacific (2P/GAP) Manila-Ninoy Aquino Intl (MNL)

☐ RP-C2025	Boeing 737-222	19077/103	ex N9039U	stored
☐ RP-C3011	Boeing 737-2H4	21533/524	ex N52SW	
☐ RP-C3012	Boeing 737-2H4	21448/509	ex N51SW	
☐ RP-C3015	Boeing 737-2H4	21534/526	ex N53SW	
☐ RP-C8001	Boeing 737-2B7 (Nordam 3)	23116/999	ex N283AU	stored MNL
☐ RP-C8002	Boeing 737-2B7 (Nordam 3)	22886/974	ex N274AU	stored MNL
☐ RP-C8003	Boeing 737-2B7 (Nordam 3)	22888/979	ex N276US	stored MNL
☐ RP-C8007	Boeing 737-2B7 (Nordam 3)	22878/921	ex N266AU	
☐ RP-C8009	Boeing 737-201 (Nordam 3)	22879/926	ex N267AU	stored MNL
☐ RP-C8011	Boeing 737-247 (Nordam 3)	23606/1379	ex N379DL	
☐ RP-C8022	Boeing 737-247 (Nordam 3)	23607/1387	ex N380DL	stored MNL
☐ RP-C4007	Boeing 737-332	25996/2488	ex RP-C2000	Lsd fr PAL
☐ RP-C4011	Boeing 737-3Y0	24770/1941	ex EI-BZN	Lsd fr PAL
☐ RP-C3016	de Havilland DHC-8Q-311	653	ex C-FNEA	
☐ RP-C3017	de Havilland DHC-8Q-314	657	ex C-FOUN	
☐ RP-C3018	de Havilland DHC-8Q-314	658	ex C-FPDR	on order
☐ RP-C3030	de Havilland DHC-8-402Q	4064	ex LN-WDD	on order
☐ RP-C3031	de Havilland DHC-8-402Q	4069	ex LN-WDA	
☐ RP-C3032	de Havilland DHC-8-402Q	4070	ex LN-WDB	
☐ RP-C3033	de Havilland DHC-8-402Q	4071	ex LN-WDC	
☐ RP-C3035	de Havilland DHC-8-402Q	4012	ex LN-RDP	
☐ RP-C3036	de Havilland DHC-8-402Q	4023	ex LN-RDH	

CEBU PACIFIC AIR Cebu Air (5J/CEB) Manila-Sangley Point (SGL)

☐ RP-C3189	Airbus A319-111	2556	ex D-AVYG
☐ RP-C3190	Airbus A319-111	2586	ex D-AVXI
☐ RP-C3191	Airbus A319-111	2625	ex D-AVYZ
☐ RP-C3192	Airbus A319-111	2638	ex D-AVWJ
☐ RP-C3193	Airbus A319-111	2786	ex D-AVYV
☐ RP-C3194	Airbus A319-111	2790	ex D-AVWN
☐ RP-C3195	Airbus A319-111	2831	ex D-AVXH
☐ RP-C3196	Airbus A319-111	2821	ex D-AVXC
☐ RP-C3197	Airbus A319-111	2852	ex D-AVXL
☐ RP-C3198	Airbus A319-111	2876	ex D-AVWL
☐ RP-C3240	Airbus A320-214	2419	ex F-WWID
☐ RP-C3241	Airbus A320-214	2439	ex F-WWBO
☐ RP-C3242	Airbus A320-214	2994	ex F-WWIU
☐ RP-C3243	Airbus A320-214	3048	ex F-WWDR
☐ RP-C3244	Airbus A320-214	3272	ex F-WWBZ
☐ RP-C3245	Airbus A320-214	3433	ex F-WWDU
☐ RP-C3246	Airbus A320-214	3472	ex F-WWBV
☐ RP-C3247	Airbus A320-214	3487	ex F-WWII
☐ RP-C3248	Airbus A320-214	3646	ex F-WWBX
☐ RP-C3249	Airbus A320-214	3762	ex F-WWDI
☐ RP-C3250	Airbus A320-214	3767	ex F-WWDP
☐ RP-C7250	ATR 72-212A	779	ex F-WWER
☐ RP-C7251	ATR 72-212A	784	ex F-WWEC
☐ RP-C7252	ATR 72-212A	820	ex F-WWEJ
☐ RP-C7253	ATR 72-212A	828	ex F-WWEV
☐ RP-C7254	ATR 72-212A	838	ex F-WWEP
☐ RP-C7255	ATR 72-212A	842	ex F-WWEH
☐ RP-C7256	ATR 72-212A	847	ex F-WWEI
☐ RP-C7257	ATR 72-212A	857	ex F-WWEB

CHEMTRAD AVIATION Manila-Sangley Point (SGL)

☐ RP-C28	Britten-Norman BN-2A-21 Islander	409	ex G-BCLF
☐ RP-C764	Britten-Norman BN-2A-26 Islander	318	ex G-BANL
☐ RP-C1262	Britten-Norman BN-2A-21 Islander	408	ex G-BCLE

☐ RP-C2207 Britten-Norman BN-2A-26 Islander 718 ex G-BCAF

CORPORATE AIR — Subic Bay-Intl (SFS)

☐ RP-C2801 Cessna 208B Caravan I 208B1057 ex N4088Z

INTERISLAND AIRLINES — (ISN) — Manila-Ninoy Aquino Intl (MNL)

☐ RP-C2639	Antonov An-26	77305509	ex EK-26227	
☐ RP-C2695	Yakovlev Yak-40A	9522041	ex EK-87536	dbr 01Nov06?
☐ RP-C2803	Yakovlev Yak-40	9430537	ex 4L-AVD	
☐ RP-C2805	Yakovlev Yak-40	9342031	ex 4L-AVC	
☐ RP-C6868	LET L-410UVP-E	871926	ex 5V-TTG	

ISLAND AVIATION — Soriano (SOY) — Manila-Sangley Point (SGL)

☐ RP-C2282	Dornier 228-202K	8173	ex N23UA
☐ RP-C2283	Dornier 228-202K	8077	ex F-ODZH
☐ RP-C22837	Dornier 228-202K	8174	ex VH-YJD

ISLAND TRANSVOYAGER — Manila-Sangley Point (SGL)

☐ RP-C1008	Dornier 228-212	8193	ex D-CARD
☐ RP-C2289	Dornier 228-212	8177	ex B-11150

JANS HELICOPTERS — Guam (GUM)

☐ RP-C2733	Beech 95-B55 Baron	TC-1770	ex N8770R	Freighter
☐ RP-C2324	Learjet 24B	24B-182	ex N155J	Freighter
☐ RP-C2424	Learjet 24B	24B-226	ex N335RY	Freighter
☐ RP-C2702	de Havilland DHC-4A Caribou	98	ex N800NC	Freighter

LIONAIR

☐ RP-C3988 LET-410UVP-E10 892317 ex 3D-FTY

NORTH SOUTH AIRLINES — Manila-Ninoy Aquino Intl (MNL)

☐ RP-C8258 LET L-410UVP-E 882038 ex 3D-RTV

PACIFIC EAST ASIA CARGO AIRLINES — Pac-East Cargo (Q8/PEC) — Manila-Ninoy Aquino Intl (MNL)

☐ RP-C5353	Boeing 727-23F	19131/218	ex ZS-NPX	
☐ RP-C5354	Learjet 35A	35A-185	ex ZS-SES	
☐ RP-C5355	Boeing 727-223F (FedEx 3)	20185/710	ex PK-YGT	Lsg fr TMG

PACIFIC PEARL AIRWAYS

☐ RP-C8777 Boeing 737-232 (AvAero 3) 23088/1018 ex N316DL

PACIFICAIR — Pacific West (GX/PFR) — Manila-Sangley Point (SGL)

☐ RP-C1320	Britten-Norman BN-2A-21 Islander	569	ex PAF-569
☐ RP-C1321	Britten-Norman BN-2A-21 Islander	547	ex PAF-547
☐ RP-C1324	Britten-Norman BN-2A-21 Islander	539	ex PAF 538
☐ RP-C1801	Britten-Norman BN-2A-21 Islander	739	ex G-BCNI
☐ RP-C2132	Britten-Norman BN-2A-21 Islander	422	ex G-BCSG
☐ RP-C2137	Britten-Norman BN-2A-21 Islander	443	ex G-BCZU
☐ RP-C2138	Britten-Norman BN-2A-21 Islander	445	ex G-BCZW
☐ RP-C1103	Beech H-18	BA-660	ex N638CZ
☐ RP-C1358	Beech H-18 Tri-Gear	BA-750	ex RP-C1986
☐ RP-C1611	Cessna 421C Golden Eagle	421C0155	ex N5282J

PHILIPPINE AIRLINES — Philippine (PR/PAL) — Manila-Ninoy Aquino Intl (MNL)

☐ RP-C3221	Airbus A320-214	0706	ex F-WWIM
☐ RP-C3223	Airbus A320-214	0745	ex F-WWIR
☐ RP-C3227	Airbus A320-214	2183	ex OY-VKP
☐ RP-C3228	Airbus A320-214	2162	ex RP-C3226
☐ RP-C3229	Airbus A320-214	0936	ex N101UW
☐ RP-C3230	Airbus A320-214	1171	ex N115US
☐ RP-C3231	Airbus A320-214	1210	ex N116US
☐ RP-C8600	Airbus A319-112	2878	ex D-AVWO
☐ RP-C8601	Airbus A319-112	2925	ex D-AVYP
☐ RP-C8602	Airbus A319-112	2954	ex D-AVXE
☐ RP-C8603	Airbus A319-112	3108	ex D-AVYM
☐ RP-C8604	Airbus A320-214	3087	ex F-WWBV
☐ RP-C8605	Airbus A320-214	3107	ex F-WWIK
☐ RP-C8606	Airbus A320-214	3187	ex F-WWDY
☐ RP-C8607	Airbus A320-214	3205	ex F-WWIH

☐ RP-C8609	Airbus A320-214	3273	ex F-WWIC
☐ RP-C8610	Airbus A320-214	3310	ex F-WWIO
☐ RP-C8611	Airbus A320-214	3455	ex F-WWBH
☐ RP-C8612	Airbus A320-214	3553	ex F-WWIZ
☐ RP-C8613	Airbus A320-214	3579	ex F-WWBY
☐ RP-C8614	Airbus A320-214	3652	ex F-WWDQ
☐ RP-C8615	Airbus A320-214	3731	ex F-WWDL

☐ RP-C3330	Airbus A330-301	183	ex F-OHZM
☐ RP-C3331	Airbus A330-301	184	ex F-OHZN
☐ RP-C3332	Airbus A330-301	188	ex F-OHZO
☐ RP-C3333	Airbus A330-301	191	ex F-OHZP
☐ RP-C3335	Airbus A330-301	189	ex F-OHZQ
☐ RP-C3336	Airbus A330-301	198	ex F-OHZR
☐ RP-C3337	Airbus A330-301	200	ex F-OHZS
☐ RP-C3340	Airbus A330-301	203	ex F-OHZT

☐ RP-C3430	Airbus A340-313X	173	ex F-OHPJ
☐ RP-C3431	Airbus A340-313X	176	ex F-OHPK
☐ RP-C3432	Airbus A340-313X	187	ex F-OHPL
☐ RP-C3434	Airbus A340-313X	196	ex F-OHPM

☐ RP-C4007	Boeing 737-332	25996/2488	ex RP-C2000	Lsd to GAP
☐ RP-C4011	Boeing 737-3Y0	24770/1941	ex EI-BZN	Lsd to GAP

☐ N751PR	Boeing 747-4F6	27261/1005	ex (RP-C5751)
☐ N752PR	Boeing 747-4F6	27262/1012	ex (RP-C5752)
☐ RP-C7573	Boeing 747-4F6	27828/1039	ex N753PR
☐ RP-C7475	Boeing 747-469M	27663/1068	ex N754PR
☐ RP-C8168	Boeing 747-4F6	27827/1038	ex C-FGHZ

☐ RP-C7776	Boeing 777-36NER	37712/841	
☐ RP-C7777	Boeing 777-36NER	37709/826	

ROYAL STAR AVIATION — *Manila-Sangley Point (SGL)*

☐ RP-C2812	British Aerospace Jetstream 3217	923	ex N93BA
☐ RP-C8298	British Aerospace Jetstream 4101	41013	ex N302UE
☐ RP-C8299	British Aerospace Jetstream 4101	41080	ex N327UE
☐ RP-C8328	Dornier 328-300 (328JET)	3136	ex N360SK

SOUTH EAST ASIAN AIRLINES — *Seair (DG/SRQ)*
Manila- Ninoy Aquino Intl/Diosdado Macapagal Intl (MNL/CRK)

☐ RP-C2128	LET L-410UVP-E	882102	ex S9-BOX
☐ RP-C2328	LET L-410UVP-E3	872004	ex S9-BOY
☐ RP-C2428	LET L-410UVP-E3	871909	ex 3D-DAM
☐ RP-C2628	LET L-410UVP-E	871931	ex Russ AF 1931
☐ RP-C2728	LET L-410UVP-E	861708	ex RA-67588 jungle c/s
☐ RP-C2928	LET L-410UVP-E	871821	ex Russ AF 1821
☐ RP-C3328	LET L-410UVP-E	872003	ex RP-C528

☐ RP-C1170	Dornier 28D-2 Skyservant	4127	ex D-IDRH
☐ RP-C2403	Dornier 24ATT	5345	ex D-CATD Amphibian
☐ RP-C2814	Dornier 228-200	8019	ex JA8836
☐ RP-C4328	Dornier 328-120	3042	ex D-CPRT
☐ RP-C5328	Dornier 328-110	3046	ex D-CPRS
☐ RP-C6328	Dornier 328-110	3027	ex N653JC
☐ RP-C7328	Dornier 328-110	3069	ex G-BYML
☐ RP-C9328	Dornier 328-110	3003	ex D-CDOL all-white

SPIRIT OF MANILA AIRLINES

☐ RP-C7701	Boeing 737-301	23234/1208	ex HS-AAN
☐ RP-C7702	McDonnell-Douglas MD-83	49939/1787	ex N939MD
☐ RP-C7703	McDonnell-Douglas MD-83	49946/1898	ex N964MD

TRANSGLOBAL AIRWAYS — *Diosdado Macapagal IntL (CRK)*

☐ RP-C8015	Boeing 737-2B1C	20536/289	ex C9-BAC
☐ RP-C8018	McDonnell-Douglas MD-83	49985/1838	ex PK-ALF

VICTORIA AIR — *Manila-Sangley Point (SGL)*

☐ RP-C535	Douglas DC-3	15571/27016	ex RP-C95

ZEST AIRWAYS — *(6K/RIT)* — *Manila-Sangley Point (SGL)*

☐ RP-C2895	de Havilland DHC-7-102	035	ex 7O-ADB
☐ RP-C2915	de Havilland DHC-7-102	092	ex C-GELY
☐ RP-C2955	de Havilland DHC-7-102	090	ex SX-BNA

☐ RP-C2978	de Havilland DHC-7-102	079	ex N67DA	
☐ RP-C2988	de Havilland DHC-7-102	078	ex N60RA	stored MNL
☐ RP-C2996	de Havilland DHC-7-102	018	ex N701AC	
☐ RP-C3338	NAMC YS-11A-227	2142	ex JA8766	
☐ RP-C3339	NAMC YS-11A-222	2147	ex JA8768	
☐ RP-C3588	NAMC YS-11A-213	2168	ex JA8787	stored MNL
☐ RP-C3592	NAMC YS-11A-213	2108	ex JA8735	dam 02Jan08
☐ RP-C2918	LET L-410UVP	902510	ex 9A-BNZ	Fleuris titles
☐ RP-C3880	LET L-410UVP-E	892228	ex RA-67601	Fleuris titles
☐ RP-C3889	LET L-410UVP-E	851511	ex RA-67544	Fleuris titles
☐ RP-C4000	ITPN CASA CN-235	N020	ex PK-XNV	
☐ RP-C5000	ITPN CASA CN-235	N001	ex PK-MNA	
☐ RP-C8892	CAIC MA60	0703	ex B-956L	dam 25Jun09
☐ RP-C8894	CAIC MA60	0710	ex B-956L	
☐ RP-C8895	CAIC MA60	0711	ex B-963L	
☐ RP-C8896	CAIC MA60	0712	ex B-964L	
☐ RP-C8897	Airbus A320-232	2141	ex N581JB	
☐ RP-C8988	Airbus A320-232	2147	ex RP-C8898	
☐ RP-C8989	Airbus A320-232	3621	ex F-WWIK	

SE- SWEDEN (Kingdom of Sweden)

AMAPOLA FLYG — *Amapola (APF)* — *Stockholm-Arlanda (ARN)*

☐ PH-LMA	Fokker F.27 Mk.050 (Fokker 50)	20118	ex OY-EBB	Lsd fr MNL
☐ SE-KTC	Fokker F.27 Mk.050 (Fokker 50)	20124	ex OY-MMG	
☐ SE-KTD	Fokker F.27 Mk.050 (Fokker 50)	20125	ex OY-MMH	
☐ SE-LIP	Fokker F.27 Mk.050 (Fokker 50)	20147	ex PH-PRD	
☐ SE-LJG	Fokker F.27 Mk.050 (Fokker 50)	20168	ex LX-LGC	
☐ SE-LJH	Fokker F.27 Mk.050 (Fokker 50)	20171	ex LX-LGD	
☐ SE-LJI	Fokker F.27 Mk.050 (Fokker 50)	20180	ex LX-LGE	
☐ SE-LJV	Fokker F.27 Mk.050 (Fokker 50)	20103	ex VT-CAA	
☐ SE-LJY	Fokker F.27 Mk.050 (Fokker 50)	20259	ex OY-PAA	

AVITRANS NORDIC — *Extrans (2Q/ETS)* — *Nyköping (NYO)*

☐ SE-ISR	SAAB SF.340A	340A-017	ex LY-ISR
☐ SE-ISY	SAAB SF.340A	340A-080	ex SE-E80
☐ SE-KCS	SAAB SF.340A (QC)	340A-066	ex (SP-KPH)
☐ SE-KCT	SAAB SF.340A (QC)	340A-070	ex OH-FAC
☐ SE-KXE	SAAB SF.340A	340A-111	ex LY-KXE
☐ SE-KXI	SAAB SF.340B	340B-176	ex XA-AFR
☐ SE-LJK	SAAB SF.340A	340A-089	ex N89XJ
☐ SE-LJL	SAAB SF.340A	340A-091	ex N991XK
☐ SE-LJR	SAAB SF.340B	340B-168	ex D-CDAU
☐ SE-LJS	SAAB SF.340B	340B-215	ex D-CDEO
☐ SE-LJT	SAAB SF.340B	340B-221	ex D-CASD

BARENTS AIRLINK — *Nordflight (8N/NKF)* — *Lulea (LLA)*

☐ SE-IUX	Beech 200 Super King Air	BB-675	ex N26SD
☐ SE-KEC	Piper PA-31-350 Chieftain	31-7952098	ex LN-FAM
☐ SE-LTL	Beech 200 Super King Air	BB-582	ex LN-MOA

CITY AIRLINE — *Swedestar (CF/SDR)* — *Gothenburg-Landvetter (GOT)*

☐ SE-DZB	Embraer EMB.145EP (ERJ-145EP)	145113	ex PT-SCP
☐ SE-RAA	Embraer EMB.135ER (ERJ-135ER)	145210	ex PT-SFU
☐ SE-RAB	Embraer EMB.135LR (ERJ-135LR)	145453	ex PT-SUY
☐ SE-RAC	Embraer EMB.145LR (ERJ-145LR)	145098	ex N285CD
☐ SE-RIA	Embraer EMB.145MP (ERJ-145MP)	145320	ex PH-RXB

DIREKTFLYG — *Skyreg (HS/HSV)* — *Borlänge (BLE)*

☐ SE-LHB	British Aerospace Jetstream 32EP	844	ex N844JX
☐ SE-LHC	British Aerospace Jetstream 32EP	846	ex N846JX
☐ SE-LHE	British Aerospace Jetstream 32EP	854	ex N854JX
☐ SE-LHF	British Aerospace Jetstream 32EP	855	ex N855JX
☐ SE-LHG	British Aerospace Jetstream 32EP	857	ex N857JX
☐ SE-LHH	British Aerospace Jetstream 32EP	848	ex N848JX
☐ SE-LHI	British Aerospace Jetstream 32EP	841	ex N841JX
☐ SE-LXD	British Aerospace Jetstream 32	977	ex G-BUVD
☐ SE-LXE	British Aerospace Jetstream 32	970	ex G-BUVC

FLY LOGIC SWEDEN — *Logic (LOD)* — *Malmö-Sturup (MMX)*

☐ SE-GIN	Piper PA-31 Navajo C	31-7512039	
☐ SE-IDR	Piper PA-31 Navajo C	31-7712085	ex LN-DAB

☐ SE-IKV	Piper PA-31-350 Navajo Chieftain	31-7405148	ex G-BDFN
☐ SE-KCP	Swearingen SA.226TC Merlin	TC-330	ex N7217N

FLYGCENTRUM — **_(LIQ)_** — **_Stockholm-Bromma (BMA)_**

☐ SE-ILY	Piper PA-31-350 Chieftain	31-7852051	ex G-FTTA

FLYNORDIC — **_Nordic (LF/NDC)_** — **_Stockholm-Arlanda/Umeå (ARN/UME)_**

☐ SE-RBE	McDonnell-Douglas MD-82	49152/1089	ex OH-LMP
☐ SE-RDR	McDonnell-Douglas MD-82	49151/1088	ex N619DB

GOLDEN AIR — **_Golden (DC/GAO)_** — **_Trollhattan (THN)_**

☐ OH-FAF	SAAB SF.340B	340B-167	ex SE-F67	Lsd fr WBA
☐ SE-ISE	SAAB SF.340A	340A-156	ex YL-BAP	
☐ SE-ISG	SAAB SF.340B	340B-162	ex SE-F62	
☐ SE-KTK	SAAB SF.340B	340B-276	ex F-GHVT	
☐ SE-KXG	SAAB SF.340B	340A-164	ex XA-AAO	
☐ SE-LES	SAAB SF.340A	340A-129	ex B-12299	
☐ SE-LMR	SAAB SF.340A	340A-141	ex OK-UFO	Lsd to NTJ
☐ SE-KXK	SAAB 2000	2000-012	ex F-GOZI	Lsd to KRP
☐ SE-LOM	SAAB 2000	2000-035	ex LY-SBK	
☐ SE-LTU	SAAB 2000	2000-062	ex HB-IYG	
☐ SE-LTV	SAAB 2000	2000-063	ex HB-IYH	
☐ SE-LTX	SAAB 2000	2000-024	ex HB-IZM	
☐ SE-LXH	SAAB 2000	2000-007	ex LY-SBQ	
☐ SE-MDA	ATR 72-212A	778	ex EI-REN	
☐ SE-MDB	ATR 72-212A	822	ex EI-RER	
☐ SE-MDC	ATR 72-212A	894	ex F-WWED	
☐ SE-MDB	ATR 72-212A	822	ex EI-RER	

INTERNATIONAL BUSINESS AIR — **_Interbiz (6I/IBZ)_** — **_Stockholm-Bromma (BMA)_**

☐ SE-LEF	Swearingen SA.227AC Metro III	AC-451B	ex VH-NEM
☐ SE-LIL	Swearingen SA.227AC Metro III	AC-432B	ex F-GLPE
☐ SE-LKC	Embraer EMB.120ER Brasilia	120046	ex N273UE

JONAIR — **_Umea (UME)_**

☐ SE-GLE	Piper PA-31 Navajo C	31-7512056	

MALMÖ AVIATION — **_Scanwing (TF/SCW)_** — **_Stockholm-Arlanda/Malmö-Sturup (ARN/MMX)_**

☐ SE-DSO	Avro 146-RJ100	E3221	ex N504MM
☐ SE-DSP	Avro 146-RJ100	E3242	ex N505MM
☐ SE-DSR	Avro 146-RJ100	E3244	ex N506MM
☐ SE-DSS	Avro 146-RJ100	E3245	ex N507MM
☐ SE-DST	Avro 146-RJ100	E3247	ex N508MM
☐ SE-DSU	Avro 146-RJ100	E3248	ex N509MM
☐ SE-DSV	Avro 146-RJ100	E3250	ex N510MM
☐ SE-DSX	Avro 146-RJ100	E3255	ex N511MM
☐ SE-DSY	Avro 146-RJ100	E3263	ex N512MM

MCA AIRLINES AB — **_Luna (AEQ)_** — **_Stockholm-Arlanda (ARN)_**

☐ SE-DUU	Fokker F.28-0100 (Fokker 100)	11286	ex G-FMAH

NEXTJET — **_Nextjet (2N/NTJ)_** — **_Stockholm-Bromma (BMA)_**

☐ SE-KXY	Beech 1900D	UE-236	ex SX-BST	
☐ SE-LEP	SAAB SF.340A	340A-127	ex B-12200	
☐ SE-LJN	SAAB SF.340A	340A-114	ex LY-DIG	
☐ SE-LLO	British Aerospace ATP	2023	ex G-MANP	
☐ SE-LMR	SAAB SF.340A	340A-141	ex OK-UFO	Lsd fr GAO
☐ SE-LCX	Beech 1900D	UE-275	ex N11189	
☐ SE-MAK	British Aerospace ATP	2040	ex G-MANF	Lsd fr SWN
☐ SE-MAL	British Aerospace ATP	2045	ex G-MANE	

NORD-FLYG — **_Nordex (NEF)_** — **_Eskilstuna (EKT)_**

☐ SE-GBO	Piper PA-31 Turbo Navajo B	31-7400983		
☐ SE-KYI	Cessna 208B Caravan I	208B0629	ex N52639	
☐ SE-LSK	Cessna 208B Caravan I	208B1012	ex N5236L	
☐ SE-LSL	Cessna 208B Caravan I	208B0810	ex OY-TPG	
☐ SE-LSM	de Havilland DHC-8-402PF	4008	ex LN-RDQ	
☐ SE-LSN	de Havilland DHC-8-402PF	4024	ex LN-RDI	On Order

NORDIC AIRWAYS — Northrider (6N/NRD) — Stockholm-Arlanda/Umeå (ARN/UME)

☐ SE-DMT	McDonnell-Douglas MD-81	48003/944	ex N480LT	

NORRLANDSFLYG — Lifeguard Sweden (HMF) — Gallivare/Kiruna (GEV/KRN)

☐ SE-HAJ	Sikorsky S-76C	760510	ex OH-HCJ	SAR
☐ SE-HAV	Sikorsky S-76C	760377	ex N50KH	SAR
☐ SE-HEJ	Sikorsky S-76C+	760604	ex N71141	SAR
☐ SE-HOJ	Sikorsky S-76C+	760605	ex N8125H	SAR
☐ SE-JEZ	Sikorsky S-76A	760215	ex N72WW	EMS
☐ SE-JUC	Sikorsky S-76A	760219	ex N18KH	EMS
☐ SE-JUS	Sikorsky S-76A	760172	ex N876TC	EMS
☐ SE-JUY	Sikorsky S-76C	760407	ex N154AE	SAR
☐ SE-JUZ	Sikorsky S-76A++	760282	ex N92RR	SAR

NOVAIR — Navigator (1I/NVR) — Stockholm-Arlanda (ARN)

☐ CS-TRA	Airbus A330-243	461	ex EC-IDB	Lsd fr OBS
☐ SE-RDN	Airbus A321-231	2211	ex D-AVZK	
☐ SE-RDO	Airbus A321-231	2216	ex D-AVZN	
☐ SE-RDP	Airbus A321-231	2410	ex D-AVZK	

ÖREBRO AVIATION — Bluelight (BUE) — Örebro-Bofors (ORB)

☐ SE-FNE	Piper PA-31-350 Navajo Chieftain	31-7405434	ex N54306	
☐ SE-GBS	Piper PA-31-310 Navajo	31-7400984	ex OH-MRS	

SCANDINAVIAN AIRLINES SYSTEM — Scandinavian (SK/SAS) — Copenhagen-Kastrup/Oslo-Gardermoen/Stockholm-Arlanda (CPH/OSL/ARN)

Member of Star Alliance

☐ OY-KBO	Airbus A319-132	2850	ex D-AVXK	Christian Valdemar Viking	retro c/s
☐ OY-KBP	Airbus A319-132	2888	ex D-AVYG	Viger Viking	
☐ OY-KBR	Airbus A319-131	3231	ex D-AVYV	Sten Viking	
☐ OY-KBT	Airbus A319-131	3292	ex D-AVYC	Ragnvald Viking	
☐ LN-RKI	Airbus A321-232	1817	ex D-AVZK	Gunnhild Viking	
☐ LN-RKK	Airbus A321-232	1848	ex SE-REG	Svipdag Viking	
☐ OY-KBB	Airbus A321-232	1642	ex D-AVZN	Hjörulf Viking	
☐ OY-KBE	Airbus A321-232	1798	ex D-AVZG	Emma Viking	
☐ OY-KBF	Airbus A321-232	1807	ex D-AVZH	Skapti Viking	
☐ OY-KBH	Airbus A321-232	1675	ex D-AVZV	Sulke Viking	
☐ OY-KBK	Airbus A321-232	1587	ex D-AVZK	Arne Viking	
☐ OY-KBL	Airbus A321-232	1619	ex D-AVZB	Gunnbjörn Viking	
☐ LN-RKH	Airbus A330-343X	497	ex F-WWYP	Emund Viking	
☐ OY-KBN	Airbus A330-343X	496	ex F-WWKK	Eystein Viking	
☐ SE-REE	Airbus A330-343X	515	ex F-WWYY	Sigrid Viking	
☐ SE-REF	Airbus A330-343X	568	ex F-WWYS	Erik Viking	Star Alliance c/s
☐ LN-RKF	Airbus A340-313X	413	ex SE-REA	Godfred Viking	stored LDE
☐ LN-RKG	Airbus A340-313X	424	ex SE-REB	Gudrod Viking	
☐ OY-KBA	Airbus A340-313X	435	ex F-WWJU	Adalstein Viking	
☐ OY-KBC	Airbus A340-313X	467	ex F-WWJE	Freydis Viking	
☐ OY-KBD	Airbus A340-313X	470	ex F-WWJF	Toste Viking	
☐ OY-KBI	Airbus A340-313X	430	ex F-WWJR	Rurik Viking	
☐ LN-BRE	Boeing 737-405	24643/1860		Hakon V Magnusson	
☐ LN-BRH	Boeing 737-505	24828/1925	ex D-ACBB	Haakon den Gode	
☐ LN-BRI	Boeing 737-405	24644/1938	ex 9M-MLL	Harald Hårfagre	
☐ LN-BRJ	Boeing 737-505	24273/2018	ex YL-BBB	Olav Tryggvason	
☐ LN-BRK	Boeing 737-505	24274/2035		Magnus Barfot	
☐ LN-BRM	Boeing 737-505	24645/2072		Olav den Hellige	
☐ LN-BRO	Boeing 737-505	24647/2143		Magnus Haraldsson	
☐ LN-BRQ	Boeing 737-405	25348/2148		Harald Gråfell	
☐ LN-BRS	Boeing 737-505	24649/2225		Olav Kyrre	stored SNN
☐ LN-BRV	Boeing 737-505	25791/2351		Hakon Sverresson	
☐ LN-BRX	Boeing 737-505	25797/2434		Sigurd Munn	
☐ LN-BUC	Boeing 737-505	26304/2649		Magnus Erlingsson	
☐ LN-BUD	Boeing 737-505	25794/2803		Inge Krokrygg	stored KRS
☐ LN-BUE	Boeing 737-505	27627/2800		Erling Skjalgsson	
☐ LN-BUF	Boeing 737-405	25795/2867		Magnus den Gode	
☐ LN-BUG	Boeing 737-505	27631/2866		Øystein Haraldsson	
☐ LN-RCN+>	Boeing 737-883	28318/529	ex SE-DTK	Hedrun Viking	
☐ LN-RCT*>	Boeing 737-683	30189/303	ex OY-KKF	Fridlev Viking	
☐ LN-RCU*>	Boeing 737-683	30190/335	ex SE-DNZ	Sigfrid Viking	
☐ LN-RCW*>	Boeing 737-683	28308/333	ex SE-DNY	Yngvar Viking	
☐ LN-RCX*>	Boeing 737-883	30196/733	ex SE-DYH	Höttur Viking	

	Registration	Type	c/n	Previous identity	Name	Notes
☐	LN-RCY*>	Boeing 737-883	28324/767	ex SE-DTT	Eylime Viking	
☐	LN-RCZ+>	Boeing 737-883	30197/798	ex SE-DTS	Glitne Viking	
☐	LN-RNN+>	Boeing 737-783	28315/464	ex OY-KKI	Borgny Viking	
☐	LN-RNO+>	Boeing 737-783	28316/476	ex OY-KKR	Gjuke Viking	
☐	LN-RNW	Boeing 737-783/W	34549			on order
☐	LN-RPA*	Boeing 737-683	28290/100	ex N5002K	Amljot Viking	
☐	LN-RPB*	Boeing 737-683	28294/137	ex N1787B	Bure Viking	
☐	LN-RPE*>	Boeing 737-683	28306/329	ex SE-DOT	Edla Viking	
☐	LN-RPF*>	Boeing 737-683	28307/330	ex N1784B	Frede Viking	
☐	LN-RPG*	Boeing 737-683	28310/255	ex N1787B	Geirmund Viking	
☐	LN-RPH*>	Boeing 737-683	28605/375		Hamder Viking	
☐	LN-RPJ+>	Boeing 737-783	30192/486	ex N1786B	Grimhild Viking	
☐	LN-RPK+>	Boeing 737-783	28317/500	ex N1786B	Heimer Viking	
☐	LN-RPL+>	Boeing 737-883	30469/673	ex (SE-DYC)	Svanevit Viking	
☐	LN-RPM*>	Boeing 737-883	30195/696	ex (SE-DYD)	Frigg Viking	
☐	LN-RPN+	Boeing 737-883	30470/717	ex (SE-DYG)	Bergfora Viking	
☐	LN-RPS+	Boeing 737-683	28298/191	ex OY-KKC	Gautrek Viking	
☐	LN-RPT+	Boeing 737-683	28299/193	ex OY-KKD	Ellida Viking	
☐	LN-RPU*>	Boeing 737-683	28312/407	ex OY-KKP	Ragna Viking	
☐	LN-RPW*	Boeing 737-683	28289/92	ex OY-KKA	Alvid Viking	
☐	LN-RPX*>	Boeing 737-683	28291/112	ex SE-DNN	Nanna Viking	
☐	LN-RPY*	Boeing 737-683	28292/116	ex SE-DNO	Olof Viking	
☐	LN-RPZ*>	Boeing 737-683	28293/120	ex OY-KKB	Bera Viking	
☐	LN-RRA*>	Boeing 737-783/W	30471/2288	ex (SE-DYD)	Steinar Viking	
☐	LN-RRB*>	Boeing 737-783/W	32276/2331		Dag Viking	
☐	LN-RRC+	Boeing 737-683	28300/209	ex OY-KKG	Sindre Viking	
☐	LN-RRD+	Boeing 737-683	28301/227	ex OY-KKH	Embla Viking	
☐	LN-RRE	Boeing 737-85P/W	35706/2586		Knut Viking	
☐	LN-RRF	Boeing 737-85P/W	35707/2610		Froydis Viking	
☐	LN-RRG	Boeing 737-85P/W	35708/2653			
☐	LN-RRH	Boeing 737-883/W	34546/2898	ex N1786B	Freja Viking	
☐	LN-RRJ	Boeing 737-883/W	34547/2956	ex N5573L	Frida Viking	
☐	LN-RRK+	Boeing 737-883/W	32278/1169	ex SE-DYG	Gerud Viking	
☐	LN-RRL+>	Boeing 737-883/W	28328/1424	ex SE-DYT	Jarlabanke Viking	Star Alliance c/s
☐	LN-RRM+>	Boeing 737-783	28314/458	ex SE-DTI	Erland Viking	
☐	LN-RRN+>	Boeing 737-783	30191/404	ex SE-DTG	Solveig Viking	
☐	LN-RRO*	Boeing 737-683	28288/49	ex SE-DNM	Bernt Viking	
☐	LN-RRP*	Boeing 737-683	28311/382	ex SE-DTU	Vilborg Viking	
☐	LN-RRR*	Boeing 737-683	28309/368	ex SE-DTF	Torbjörn Viking	
☐	LN-RRS+	Boeing 737-883	28325/1014	ex (SE-DYM)	Ymer Viking	
☐	LN-RRT+>	Boeing 737-883	28326/1036	ex (SE-DYN)	Lodyn Viking	
☐	LN-RRU+>	Boeing 737-883	28327/1070	ex (SE-DYP)	Vingolf Viking	
☐	LN-RRW+	Boeing 737-883	32277/1554	ex SE-DTR	Saga Viking	
☐	LN-RRX*	Boeing 737-683	28296/21	ex SE-DNR	Ragnfast Viking	
☐	LN-RRY>	Boeing 737-683	28297/30	ex SE-DNS	Signe Viking	
☐	LN-RRZ*>	Boeing 737-683	28295/149	ex SE-DNP	Gisla Viking	
☐	LN-TUA>	Boeing 737-705	28211/33		Ingeborg Eriksdatter	
☐	LN-TUD	Boeing 737-705	28217/142		Magrete Skulesdatter	
☐	LN-TUF	Boeing 737-705	28222/245		Tyra Haraldsdatter	
☐	LN-TUH>	Boeing 737-705	29093/471		Margrete Ingesdatter	
☐	LN-TUI>	Boeing 737-705	29094/507	ex N1787B	Kristin Knudsdatter	
☐	LN-TUJ>	Boeing 737-705	29095/773		Eirik Blodöks	
☐	LN-TUK>	Boeing 737-705	29096/794		Inge Bärdsson	
☐	LN-TUL>	Boeing 737-705	29097/1072	ex N1786B	Hakon IV Hakonsson	
☐	LN-TUM>	Boeing 737-705	29098/1116		Øystein Magnusson	
☐	OY-KKS+	Boeing 737-683	28322/614	ex LN-RPC	Ramveig Viking	
☐	SE-DNX	Boeing 737-683	28304/270	ex G-CDRA		
☐	SE-DOR	Boeing 737-683	28305/290	ex G-CDRB		
☐	SE-DTH*	Boeing 737-683	28313/447	ex (OY-KKI)	Vile Viking	

*Indicates Euro version and + means domestic version with regards to seating configuration.

	Registration	Type	c/n	Previous identity	Name	Notes
☐	LN-RNL	Canadair CL-600-2D24 (CRJ-900)	15250	ex C-		
☐	OY-KFA	Canadair CL-600-2D24 (CRJ-900)	15206	ex C-GIAW	Johan Viking	
☐	OY-KFB	Canadair CL-600-2D24 (CRJ-900)	15211	ex C-	Allhid Viking	
☐	OY-KFC	Canadair CL-600-2D24 (CRJ-900)	15218	ex C-	Bertil Viking	
☐	OY-KFD	Canadair CL-600-2D24 (CRJ-900)	15221	ex C-	Estrid Viking	
☐	OY-KFE	Canadair CL-600-2D24 (CRJ-900)	15224	ex C-	Ingemar Viking	
☐	OY-KFF	Canadair CL-600-2D24 (CRJ-900)	15231	ex C-GZQO	Karl Viking	
☐	OY-KFG	Canadair CL-600-2D24 (CRJ-900)	15237	ex C-	Maria Viking	
☐	OY-KFH	Canadair CL-600-2D24 (CRJ-900)	15240	ex C-GZQU	Ella Viking	
☐	OY-KFI	Canadair CL-600-2D24 (CRJ-900)	15242	ex C-GIAP	Rolf Viking	
☐	OY-KFK	Canadair CL-600-2D24 (CRJ-900)	15244	ex C-GIAW	Hardenknud Viking	
☐	OY-KFL	Canadair CL-600-2D24 (CRJ-900)	15246	ex C-	Regin Viking	

	Registration	Type	c/n	Previous identity	Name	Notes
☐	LN-RDA	de Havilland DHC-8-402Q	4013	ex C-GDFT		stored NYO
☐	LN-RDD	de Havilland DHC-8-402Q	4009	ex C-GFQL		stored NYO
☐	LN-RDI	de Havilland DHC-8-402Q	4024			stored CPH
☐	LN-RDJ	de Havilland DHC-8-402Q	4010	ex N480DC		stored CPH
☐	LN-RDO	de Havilland DHC-8-402Q	4036	ex C-FDHD		stored CPH
☐	LN-RDP	de Havilland DHC-8-402Q	4012	ex OY-KCA		stored NYO
☐	LN-RDT	de Havilland DHC-8-402Q	4038	ex N382BC		stored NYO

	Registration	Type	c/n	Previous identity	Name	Notes
☐	LN-RNC	Fokker F.27 Mk.050 (Fokker 50)	20176	ex PH-EXY	Eivind Viking	

☐ LN-RND	Fokker F.27 Mk.050 (Fokker 50)	20178	ex PH-EXZ	Inge Viking	
☐ LN-RNE	Fokker F.27 Mk.050 (Fokker 50)	20179	ex PH-EXE	Ebbe Viking	
☐ LN-RNF	Fokker F.27 Mk.050 (Fokker 50)	20183	ex PH-EXI	Leif Viking	
☐ LN-RNG	Fokker F.27 Mk.050 (Fokker 50)	20184	ex PH-EXJ	Gudrid Viking	
☐ LN-RLE	McDonnell-Douglas MD-82	49382/1232		Kettil Viking	
☐ LN-RLF	McDonnell-Douglas MD-82	49383/1236	ex VH-LNJ	Finn Viking	
☐ LN-RLR	McDonnell-Douglas MD-82	49437/1345	ex VH-LNL	Vegard Viking	
☐ LN-RMC	McDonnell-Douglas MD-82	49909/1625	ex TF-JXB	Sigtrygg Viking	
☐ LN-RMH	McDonnell-Douglas MD-87	49612/1827	ex EC-JRR		stored PMI
☐ LN-RMK	McDonnell-Douglas MD-87	49610/1705		Ragnhild Viking	Sublsd to JKK
☐ LN-RML	McDonnell-Douglas MD-82	53002/1835		Aud Viking	
☐ LN-RMM	McDonnell-Douglas MD-82	53005/1855		Blenda Viking	
☐ LN-RMO	McDonnell-Douglas MD-82	53315/1947		Bergljot Viking	
☐ LN-RMP	McDonnell-Douglas MD-87	53337/1962		Reidun Viking	stored LDE
☐ LN-RMR	McDonnell-Douglas MD-82	53365/1998		Olav Viking	
☐ LN-RMS	McDonnell-Douglas MD-82	53368/2003		Nial Viking	
☐ LN-RMT	McDonnell-Douglas MD-82	53001/1815	ex OY-KHS	Jarl Viking	
☐ LN-RMU	McDonnell-Douglas MD-87	53340/1967	ex SE-DMC	Grim Viking	stored ARN
☐ LN-ROM	McDonnell-Douglas MD-82	53008/1895	ex SE-DIY	Albin Viking	
☐ LN-RON	McDonnell-Douglas MD-82	53347/1979	ex SE-DMD	Holmfrid Viking	stored OSL
☐ LN-ROO	McDonnell-Douglas MD-82	53366/1999	ex SE-DME	Kristin Viking	stored LDE
☐ LN-ROP	McDonnell-Douglas MD-82	49384/1237	ex SE-DFS	Bjorn Viking	
☐ LN-ROR	McDonnell-Douglas MD-82	49385/1244	ex SE-DFT	Assur Viking	stored OSL
☐ LN-ROS	McDonnell-Douglas MD-82	49421/1263	ex SE-DFU	Isulv Viking	
☐ LN-ROT	McDonnell-Douglas MD-82	49422/1264	ex SE-DFR	Ingjald Viking	
☐ LN-ROU	McDonnell-Douglas MD-82	49424/1284	ex SE-DFX	Ring Viking	
☐ LN-ROW	McDonnell-Douglas MD-82	49438/1353	ex SE-DFY	Ottar Viking	stored LDE
☐ LN-ROX	McDonnell-Douglas MD-82	49603/1442	ex SE-DIA	Ulvrik Viking	
☐ LN-ROY	McDonnell-Douglas MD-82	49615/1543	ex SE-DID	Spjute Viking	
☐ LN-ROZ	McDonnell-Douglas MD-87	49608/1572	ex EC-KET		stored PMI
☐ OY-KGT	McDonnell-Douglas MD-82	49380/1225	ex N845RA	Hake Viking	
☐ OY-KGY	McDonnell-Douglas MD-82	49420/1254		Rollo Viking	stored OSL
☐ OY-KGZ	McDonnell-Douglas MD-82	49381/1231		Hagbard Viking	stored LDE
☐ OY-KHC	McDonnell-Douglas MD-82	49436/1303		Faste Viking	
☐ OY-KHE	McDonnell-Douglas MD-82	49604/1456	ex N842RA	Saxo Viking	Star Alliance c/s
☐ OY-KHG	McDonnell-Douglas MD-82	49613/1519		Alle Viking	
☐ OY-KHM	McDonnell-Douglas MD-82	49914/1693		Mette Viking	
☐ OY-KHN	McDonnell-Douglas MD-82	53000/1812		Dan Viking	
☐ OY-KHP	McDonnell-Douglas MD-82	53007/1882		Arild Viking	Star Alliance c/s
☐ OY-KHR	McDonnell-Douglas MD-82	53275/1896		Torkild Viking	stored ARN
☐ OY-KHU	McDonnell-Douglas MD-87	53336/1953		Ravn Viking	stored LDE
☐ OY-KHW	McDonnell-Douglas MD-87	53348/1985	ex EC-JTK		stored PMI
☐ SE-DIC	McDonnell-Douglas MD-87	49607/1512		Grane Viking	stored LDE
☐ SE-DIK	McDonnell-Douglas MD-82	49728/1553	ex (SE-DIE)	Stenkil Viking	
☐ SE-DIL	McDonnell-Douglas MD-82	49913/1665		Tord Viking	
☐ SE-DIN	McDonnell-Douglas MD-82	49999/1803		Eskil Viking	
☐ SE-DIO	McDonnell-Douglas MD-82	49555/1402	ex LN-RMD	Fenge Viking	
☐ SE-DIP	McDonnell-Douglas MD-87	53010/1921	ex N6202D	Margret Viking	
☐ SE-DIR	McDonnell-Douglas MD-82	53004/1846		Nora Viking	
☐ SE-DIS	McDonnell-Douglas MD-82	53006/1869		Adis Viking	
☐ SE-DIU	McDonnell-Douglas MD-87	53011/1931		Torsten Viking	
☐ SE-DMB	McDonnell-Douglas MD-82	53314/1946		Bjarne Viking	
☐ D-AWBA	British Aerospace 146 Srs.300A	E3134	ex ZK-NZF		Lsd fr WDL
☐ SE-DJO	Avro 146-RJ85	E2226	ex HB-IXF		Lsd fr TWE
☐ SE-DJX	Avro 146-RJ70	E1223	ex G-BZFA		Lsd fr TWE

SKYWAYS EXPRESS — *Sky Express (JZ/SKX)* — *Jönköping /Stockholm-Arlanda (JKG/ARN)*

☐ SE-LEA	Fokker F.27 Mk.050 (Fokker 50)	20116	ex PH-GHK	Dalarna
☐ SE-LEC	Fokker F.27 Mk.050 (Fokker 50)	20112	ex VH-FNG	Västerbotten
☐ SE-LED	Fokker F.27 Mk.050 (Fokker 50)	20111	ex VH-FNF	Södermanland
☐ SE-LEH	Fokker F.27 Mk.050 (Fokker 50)	20108	ex VH-FNC	
☐ SE-LEL	Fokker F.27 Mk.050 (Fokker 50)	20110	ex VH-FNE	
☐ SE-LEU	Fokker F.27 Mk.050 (Fokker 50)	20115	ex 9M-MGZ	
☐ SE-LEZ	Fokker F.27 Mk.050 (Fokker 50)	20128	ex PH-PRA	
☐ SE-LIO	Fokker F.27 Mk.050 (Fokker 50)	20146	ex PH-PRC	
☐ SE-LIR	Fokker F.27 Mk.050 (Fokker 50)	20151	ex PH-PRE	
☐ SE-LIS	Fokker F.27 Mk.050 (Fokker 50)	20152	ex PH-PRF	
☐ SE-LIT	Fokker F.27 Mk.050 (Fokker 50)	20194	ex PH-ZDF	

TOR AIR

☐ SE-RJA	Boeing 737-4Q8	26302/2620	ex EI-CXM	Lsd to IAW

TRANSWEDE — *Transwede (5T/TWE)* — *Gothenburg-Landvetter (GOT)*

☐ SE-DJN	Avro 146-RJ85	E2231	ex HB-IXG	
☐ SE-DJO	Avro 146-RJ85	E2226	ex HB-IXF	Op for CNO
☐ SE-DJP	Avro 146-RJ70	E1254	ex EI-COQ	Op for CNO

TUIFLY NORDIC		Bluescan (6B/BLX)		Stockholm-Arlanda (ARN)
☐ SE-DZK	Boeing 737-804/W	28231/538		
☐ SE-DZN	Boeing 737-804/W	32903/1127	ex PH-AAW	
☐ SE-DZV	Boeing 737-804/W	32904/1302		
☐ SE-RFO	Boeing 757-28AER/W	25623/528	ex G-BYAJ	
☐ SE-RFP	Boeing 757-204/W	27219/596	ex G-BYAN	
☐ SE-RFS	Boeing 767-304ER/W	28040/613	ex G-OBYB	

VIKING AIRLINES		Swedjet (4P/VIK)		Athens/Heraklion (ATH/HER)
☐ SE-RHR	Boeing 737-8Q8	30637/800	ex N171LF	
☐ SE-RHS	Boeing 737-86N/W	28617/504	ex PH-ILK	
☐ SE-RHT	Boeing 737-3Q8	24962/2139	ex G-BYZJ	
☐ SE-RHU	Boeing 737-36N	28560/2888	ex B-2977	
☐ SE-RHV	Boeing 737-36N	28567/2971	ex PK-GGU	
☐ SE-RHX	Boeing 737-86N/W	28592/258	ex EI-DJT	
☐ SX-BTG	McDonnell-Douglas MD-83	49856/1675	ex SE-RDG	

WALTAIR EUROPE		Gothic (GOT)		Norrköping (NRK)
☐ SE-KOL	Beech 300LW Super King Air	FA-189	ex N7241V	

WEST AIR EUROPE		Air Sweden (PT/SWN)		Lidköping (LDK)
☐ SE-KXP	British Aerospace ATP (LFD)	2056	ex G-MANA	
☐ SE-LGU	British Aerospace ATP	2022	ex N853AW	
☐ SE-LGV	British Aerospace ATP	2034	ex N857AW	
☐ SE-LGX	British Aerospace ATP	2036	ex N859AW	
☐ SE-LGY	British Aerospace ATP	2035	ex N858AW	
☐ SE-LHX	British Aerospace ATP	2020	ex LX-WAN	
☐ SE-LNX	British Aerospace ATP	2061	ex OY-SVI	
☐ SE-LNY	British Aerospace ATP	2062	ex OY-SVT	Op for Posten Norge
☐ SE-LPU	British Aerospace ATP	2060	ex LX-WAM	
☐ SE-LPX	British Aerospace ATP	2063	ex OY-SVU	
☐ SE-MAF	British Aerospace ATP	2002	ex G-MAUD	
☐ SE-MAH	British Aerospace ATP	2004	ex G-MANJ	
☐ SE-MAI	British Aerospace ATP (LFD)	2010	ex G-BTPC	Lsd fr Capital Bank Lsg
☐ SE-MAJ	British Aerospace ATP (LFD)	2038	ex G-BTNI	
☐ SE-MAN	British Aerospace ATP (LFD)	2006	ex G-MANO	
☐ SE-MAP	British Aerospace ATP (LFD)	2037	ex G-CORP	
☐ SE-MAR	British Aerospace ATP	2053	ex G-OBWR	
☐ SE-DUX	Canadair CL-600-2B19F (CRJ-200F)	7010	ex C-FJGI	freighter
☐ SE-DUY	Canadair CL-600-2B19F (CRJ-200F)	7023	ex C-FJGK	freighter
☐ SE-	ATR 72-201	274	ex EC-INV	on order

SP- POLAND (Republic of Poland)

AIR ITALY POLSKA		Polish Bird (4Q/AEI)		Warsaw-Okecie (WAW)
☐ EI-IGC	Boeing 757-230	24747/275	ex I-AIGC	

CENTRALWINGS		(C0/CLW)		Warsaw-Okecie (WAW)
☐ SP-LLE	Boeing 737-45D	27914/2804	ex N1786B	Lsd fr LOT
☐ SP-LLF	Boeing 737-45D	28752/2874		Lsd fr LOT
☐ SP-LLK	Boeing 737-4Q8	25740/2461	ex EI-CZG	
☐ SP-LLL	Boeing 737-4Q8	25164/2447	ex EI-CXJ	

EUROLOT		Eurolot (K2/ELO)		Warsaw-Okecie (WAW)
☐ SP-EDA	ATR 42-500	516	ex F-GPYG	
☐ SP-EDB	ATR 42-500	522	ex F-GPYH	
☐ SP-EDC	ATR 42-500	526	ex F-GPYI	
☐ SP-EDD	ATR 42-500	530	ex F-GPYJ	
☐ SP-EDE	ATR 42-500	443	ex F-WWEZ	
☐ SP-EDF	ATR 42-500	559	ex D-BOOO	
☐ SP-LFA	ATR 72-202	246	ex F-WWEM	
☐ SP-LFB	ATR 72-202	265	ex F-WWEI	
☐ SP-LFC	ATR 72-202	272	ex F-WWEN	
☐ SP-LFD	ATR 72-202	279	ex F-WWLD	
☐ SP-LFE	ATR 72-202	328	ex F-WWLJ	
☐ SP-LFF	ATR 72-202	402	ex F-WWLM	
☐ SP-LFG	ATR 72-202	411	ex F-WWEO	
☐ SP-LFH	ATR 72-202	478	ex F-WWEK	

EXIN		Exin (EXN)			Katowice-Muchoeiec (KTW)
☐ SP-FDO	Antonov An-26B	10503	ex RA-26031		
☐ SP-FDP	Antonov An-26B	11903	ex RA-26098	DHL colours	
☐ SP-FDR	Antonov An-26B	11305	ex RA-26067	DHL colours	
☐ SP-FDS	Antonov An-26B	12205	ex RA-26116		
☐ SP-FDT	Antonov An-26B	12102	ex RA-26110		

JET AIR		Jeta (O2/JEA)			Warsaw-Okecie (WAW)
☐ SP-KTR	ATR 42-300	092	ex D-BAAA		
☐ SP-KWD	British Aerospace Jetstream 3202	847	ex G-BYRM		op for LOT
☐ SP-KWE	British Aerospace Jetstream 3201	842	ex G-CBCS		op for LOT
☐ SP-KWF	British Aerospace Jetstream 3201	845	ex G-BYRA		op for LOT
☐ SP-KWN	British Aerospace Jetstream 3201	856	ex LN-FAC		

LOT - POLISH AIRLINES		LOT (LO/LOT)			Warsaw-Okecie (WAW)
Member of Star Alliance					
☐ SP-LKA	Boeing 737-55D	27416/2389			
☐ SP-LKB	Boeing 737-55D	27417/2392			
☐ SP-LKC	Boeing 737-55D	27418/2397			
☐ SP-LKD	Boeing 737-55D	27419/2401			
☐ SP-LKE	Boeing 737-55D	27130/2448		Star Alliance c/s	
☐ SP-LKF	Boeing 737-55D	27368/2603			
☐ SP-LLA	Boeing 737-45D	27131/2458			
☐ SP-LLB	Boeing 737-45D	27156/2492	ex UR-VVH		
☐ SP-LLC	Boeing 737-45D	27157/2502			
☐ SP-LLD	Boeing 737-45D	27256/2589			
☐ SP-LLE	Boeing 737-45D	27914/2804			
☐ SP-LLF	Boeing 737-45D	28752/2874			
☐ SP-LLG	Boeing 737-45D	28753/2895	ex SX-BGN		
☐ SP-LPA	Boeing 767-35DER	24865/322		Warszawa	
☐ SP-LPB	Boeing 767-35DER	27902/577		Gdansk	
☐ SP-LPC	Boeing 767-35DER	28656/659		Poznan	
☐ SP-LPE	Boeing 767-341ER	24843/314	ex N483TC	Star Alliance c/s	
☐ SP-LPF	Boeing 767-319ER	24876/413	ex ZK-NCF		Lsd to AEA
☐ SP-LPG	Boeing 767-306ER	26263/592	ex N261LF		
☐ SP-LGD	Embraer EMB.145MP (ERJ-145MP)	145244	ex PT-SII		
☐ SP-LGE	Embraer EMB.145MP (ERJ-145MP)	145285	ex PT-SKC		
☐ SP-LGF	Embraer EMB.145MP (ERJ-145MP)	145308	ex PT-SKZ		
☐ SP-LGG	Embraer EMB.145MP (ERJ-145MP)	145319	ex PT-SMK		
☐ SP-LGH	Embraer EMB.145MP (ERJ-145MP)	145329	ex PT-SMV		
☐ SP-LGO	Embraer EMB.145MP (ERJ-145MP)	145560	ex PT-SZV	Pomocy logo	
☐ SP-LDA	Embraer 170-100STD (170STD)	17000023	ex PT-SKQ		
☐ SP-LDB	Embraer 170-100STD (170STD)	17000024	ex PT-SKR		
☐ SP-LDC	Embraer 170-100STD (170STD)	17000025	ex PT-SKS	Star Alliance c/s	
☐ SP-LDD	Embraer 170-100STD (170STD)	17000027	ex PT-SKU		
☐ SP-LDE	Embraer 170-100LR (170LR)	17000029	ex PT-SKW		
☐ SP-LDF	Embraer 170-100LR (170LR)	17000035	ex PT-SUE		
☐ SP-LDG	Embraer 170-100LR (170LR)	17000065	ex PT-SVQ		
☐ SP-LDH	Embraer 170-100LR (170LR)	17000069	ex PT-SVU		
☐ SP-LDI	Embraer 170-100LR (170LR)	17000073	ex PT-SVY		
☐ SP-LDK	Embraer 170-100LR (170LR)	17000074	ex PT-SVZ		
☐ SP-LIA	Embraer 170-200STD (175STD)	17000125	ex PT-SDO		
☐ SP-LIB	Embraer 170-200STD (175STD)	17000132	ex PT-SDV		
☐ SP-LIC	Embraer 170-200STD (175STD)	17000134	ex PT-SDX		
☐ SP-LID	Embraer 170-200STD (175STD)	17000136	ex PT-SDZ		
☐ SP-LIE	Embraer 170-200LR (175LR)	17000153	ex EI-DVW		
☐ SP-LIF	Embraer 170-200LR (175LR)	17000154	ex EI-DVV		
☐ SP-LIG	Embraer 170-200STD (175STD)	17000283	ex PT-TQJ		
☐ SP-LIH	Embraer 170-200STD (175STD)	17000288	ex PT-TQO		
☐ SP-LII	Embraer 170-200STD (175STD)	17000290	ex PT-TQQ		
☐ SP-LIK	Embraer 170-200STD (175STD)	17000303	ex PT-XQB		
☐ SP-LIL	Embraer 170-200STD (175STD)	17000306	ex PT-		on order
☐ SP-LIM	Embraer 170-200STD (175STD)		ex PT-		on order
☐ SP-LIN	Embraer 170-200STD (175STD)		ex PT-		on order
☐ SP-LILO	Embraer 170-200STD (175STD)		ex PT-		on order

SKY TAXI		Iguana (IGA)			Wroclaw (WRO)
☐ SP-MRB	SAAB SF.340A (QC)	340A-100	ex OE-GIF	all white	
☐ SP-MRC	SAAB SF.340A	340A-143	ex EC-IRR		

SPRINT AIR — (SXP) — Warsaw-Okecie (WAW)

	Registration	Type	C/n	Previous		Notes
☐	SP-KPE	SAAB SF.340A (QC)	340A-130	ex SE-ISL		
☐	SP-KPF	SAAB SF.340A (QC)	340A-135	ex SE-KCU		
☐	SP-KPG	SAAB SF.340A (QC)	340A-065	ex SE-KCR		
☐	SP-KPH	SAAB SF.340A (QC)	340A-015	ex SE-ISP		Op for Farnair
☐	SP-KPK	SAAB SF.340AF	340A-026	ex VH-ZLY		
☐	SP-KPL	SAAB SF.340A	340A-038	ex VH-ZRX		
☐	SP-KPN	SAAB SF.340A	340A-118	ex SE-F18		
☐	SP-KPO	SAAB SF.340A (QC)	340A-010	ex SE-LTI		
☐	SP-KPR	SAAB SF.340A (QC)	340A-139	ex OH-FAE		
☐	SP-KPU	SAAB SF.340AF	340A-145	ex SE-ISD		
☐	SP-KPV	SAAB SF.340A	340A-071	ex SE-LGS		Lsd to Direct Fly

WHITE EAGLE GENERAL AVIATION — White Eagle (WEA) — Warsaw-Okecie (WAW)

	Registration	Type	C/n	Previous		Notes
☐	SP-FES	Mil Mi-8T	99150472	ex UR-25603		
☐	SP-FNS	Beech B300 Super King Air	FL-134	ex N3252V		
☐	SP-KCA	ATR 42-300	085	ex F-WQNY		Freighter
☐	SP-KTR	ATR 42-300	092	ex D-BAAA		Op for Globus

ST- SUDAN (Republic of the Sudan)

ABABEEL AVIATION — Khartoum (KRT)

	Registration	Type	C/n	Previous		Notes
☐	EX-036	Ilyushin Il-76TD	0093495863	ex RA-76785		Lsd fr CKW
☐	ST-ARL	Antonov An-26	2606	ex EK-13399		
☐	ST-AWT	Antonov An-26				
☐	ST-WTB	Ilyushin Il-76TD	100349994	ex UN-76009		
☐	ST-WTS	Antonov An-74-200	36547098960	ex UR-74057		

AIR TAXI & CARGO — (WAM) — Khartoum (KRT)

	Registration	Type	C/n	Previous		Notes
☐	ST-TKO	Antonov An-32B	3110	ex ER-AWL	Deena	Lsd fr PXA

AIR WEST CARGO — (AWZ) — Sharjah (SHJ)

	Registration	Type	C/n	Previous		Notes
☐	ST-AWH	WSK-PZL/Antonov An-28	1AJ004-07	ex ER-AJH		
☐	ST-AWN	WSK-PZL/Antonov An-28	1AJ004-06	ex ER-AIP		
☐	ST-AWR	Ilyushin Il-76TD	0033447365	ex RDPL-11308		stored FJR
☐	ST-EWC	Ilyushin Il-76TD	0023438129	ex EX-86919		
☐	ST-EWD	Ilyushin Il-76TD	0063466989	ex UR-CAP		
☐	ST-EWX	Ilyushin Il-76TD	1013409282	ex UN-76810		
☐	ST-SDA	Boeing 737-2T4	23274/1099	ex B-2508		Lsd to Nova Air
☐	ST-SDB	Boeing 737-2T4	23273/1097	ex B-2507		Lsd to MSL

ALMAJARA AVIATION — (MJA)

	Registration	Type	C/n	Previous		Notes
☐	ST-ATH	Ilyushin Il-76MD	0063472158	ex EK-76705		
☐	ST-ATI	Ilyushin Il-76MD	1033418596	ex RA-76831		

AYR AVIATION

	Registration	Type	C/n	Previous		Notes
☐	ST-SMZ	Antonov An-32	3205	ex ER-AFI	AMIS titles	

AZZA AIR TRANSPORT — Azza Transport (AZZ) — Khartoum (KRT)

	Registration	Type	C/n	Previous		Notes
☐	ST-APS	Ilyushin Il-76TD	1023409316	ex RA-76837		
☐	ST-AQB	Ilyushin Il-76TD	0053460795	ex EP-ALA		
☐	ST-ARV	Antonov An-12BP	8345310	ex EK-11028		status?
☐	ST-ASA	Antonov An-12	402010	ex RA-11374		
☐	ST-AZN	Antonov An-12	9346808	ex UR-CFC		
☐	ST-AZZ	Ilyushin Il-76TD	1023408265	ex XT-FCB		
☐	ST-DAS	Antonov An-12	7345209	ex ER-AXC		
☐	ST-JAC	Antonov An-26B-100	10203	ex EX-003		
☐	ST-JCC	Boeing 707-384C (Comtran 2)	18948/495	ex P4-JCC		stored KRT

BADR AIRLINES — Badr Air (BDR) — Khartoum (KRT)

	Registration	Type	C/n	Previous		Notes
☐	ST-BDE	Ilyushin Il-76TD	1013408252	ex RA-76809		
☐	ST-BDK	Antonov An-72	36547060642	ex 4L-SAS	AMIS titles	
☐	ST-BDN	Ilyushin Il-76TD	1023413443	ex UK-76448		
☐	ST-BDR	Antonov An-74				
☐	ST-BDT	Antonov An-72	36547097935	ex RA-74046	AMIS titles	
☐	ST-BDX	Antonov An-74-200	36547096924	ex RA-7401	AMIS titles	
☐	ST-SAL	Antonov An-26B	17311907	ex RA-26100		

BENTIU AIR TRANSPORT		Bentiu Air (BNT)		Sharjah/Khartoum (SHJ/KRT)
☐ ST-BEN	Antonov An-26	87306907	ex UR-26514	
☐ ST-NDC	Antonov An-26	17310908	ex RA-26052	
☐ ST-SRA	Antonov An-26	17311807	ex RA-08827	

BLUE BIRD AIRLINES				Khartoum (KRT)
☐ ST-AFP	de Havilland DHC-6 Twin Otter 300	479	ex C-GDUN-X	
☐ ST-AHV	de Havilland DHC-6 Twin Otter 300	765		
☐ ZS-TIL	Beech 1900D	UE-21	ex 5Y-RAE	

EL MAGAL AVIATION		El Magal (MGG)		Khartoum (KRT)
☐ ST-APJ	Antonov An-12BP	2400701	ex RA-11308	
☐ ST-EIB	Antonov An-32B	2903	ex D2-FAP	
☐ ST-ISG	WSK-PZL/Antonov An-28	1AJ005-01	ex EK-28501	
☐ ST-MGD	Ilyushin Il-76TD	1013407230	ex RA-76812	
☐ ST-NSP	Antonov An-32	2109	ex ER-AZW	
☐ S9-PSE	Antonov An-32	2803	ex UR-48053	Lsd fr GLE

FEEDER AIRLINES		(FDD)		
☐ ST-NEW	Fokker F.27 Mk.050 (Fokker 50)	20138	ex PH-PRB	

IMAATONG SOUTH SUDAN AIRLINES				
☐ 5Y-BTD	Fokker F.27 Friendship 300M	10154	ex TR-LGH	stored WIL

JET				Khartoum (KRT)
☐ ST-AWH	WSK/PZL Antonov An-28	1AJ004-07	ex ER-AJH	also reported as operated by TFT

JUBA AIR CARGO		Juba (JUC)		Khartoum/Sharjah (KRT/SHJ)
☐ ST-ARN	Antonov An-12BK	8346010	ex EK-11011	

KATA TRANSPORTATION COMPANY				Khartoum (KRT)
☐ ST-AZL	Antonov An-32	3009	ex ER-AWM	
☐ ST-AZM	Antonov An-12BK	00346907	ex 05 red	
☐ ST-HIS	Antonov An-26B	07310310	ex UN-26026	

MARSLAND AVIATION		Marslandair (M7/MSL)		Khartoum (KRT)
☐ ST-ARJ	Antonov An-26	5602	ex ER-AZC	
☐ ST-ARP	Antonov An-24RV	37308809	ex EK-46630	
☐ ST-MRL	Yakovlev Yak-42	4520424116690	ex UN-43703	
☐ ST-MRS	Tupolev Tu-134B-3	63333	ex YL-LBG	stored FJR
☐ ST-SDB	Boeing 737-2T4	23273/1097	ex B-2507	Lsd fr AWZ

MID AIRLINES		Nile (7Y/NYL)		Khartoum (KRT)
☐ ST-ARG	Fokker F.27 Mk.050 (Fokker 50)	20130	ex LN-BBA	
☐ ST-ARH	Fokker F.27 Mk.050 (Fokker 50)	20131	ex LN-BBB	
☐ ST-ARZ	Fokker F.27 Mk.050 (Fokker 50)	20134	ex LN-BBC	

NOVA AIRLINES				Khartoum (KRT)
☐ ST-NVA	Fokker F.27 Mk.050 (Fokker 50)	20227	ex PK-AIY	stored MST
☐ ST-NVB	Canadair CL-600-2B19 (CRJ-200ER)	7807	ex HA-LND	
☐ ST-NVC	Canadair CL-600-2B19 (CRJ-200ER)	7686	ex HA-LNB	
☐ ST-SDA	Boeing 737-2T4	23274/1099	ex B-2508	Lsd fr AWZ

SACSO AIR LINES				Khartoum (KRT)
☐ ST-ARJ	Antonov An-26	77305602		
☐ ST-ARQ	Antonov An-24B	07305910	ex ST-RAS	

SUDAN AIRWAYS		Sudanair (SD/SUD)			Khartoum (KRT)
☐ ST-ASD	Fokker F.27 Mk.050 (Fokker 50)	20201	ex PH-PRI		
☐ ST-ASF	Fokker F.27 Mk.050 (Fokker 50)	20155	ex PH-PRG		
☐ ST-ASI	Fokker F.27 Mk.050 (Fokker 50)	20247	ex G-UKTB		
☐ ST-ASJ	Fokker F.27 Mk.050 (Fokker 50)	20246	ex G-UKTA		
☐ ST-ASO	Fokker F.27 Mk.050 (Fokker 50)	20256	ex G-UKTD		
☐ ST-AFA	Boeing 707-3J8C	20897/885		Blue Nile	
☐ ST-ASS	Airbus A300B4-622	252	ex F-ODTK		stored CHR
☐ ST-AST	Airbus A310-322	437	ex SU-BOW		

☐ ST-ATA	Airbus A300B4-622R	775	ex TF-ELC	Alqaswa	Lsd fr ABD
☐ ST-ATB	Airbus A300B4-622R	666	ex TF-ELB	Elburag	

SUDANESE STATES AVIATION — Khartoum (KRT)

☐ ST-AQW	Boeing 707-320C	20517/854	ex 3D-GFG

TRANS ATTICO — Tranattico Sudan (ML/ETC) — Khartoum / Sharjah (KRT/SHJ)

☐ ST-AQM	Antonov An-26	1404	ex RA-48099	no titles
☐ ST-AQR	Ilyushin Il-76TD	0043453575	ex 9L-LCX	
☐ ST-AQU	Antonov An-32B	2009	ex RA-69344	
☐ ST-ASX	Ilyushin Il-76	0073479392	ex 5A-DMQ	
☐ ST-CAT	LET L-410UVP-E	902527	ex SP-FGM	
☐ ST-CAU	LET L-410UVP-E	892340	ex RA-67612	

SU- EGYPT (Arab Republic of Egypt)

AIR CAIRO — (MSC) — Cairo-Intl (CAI)

☐ SU-BPU	Airbus A320-214	2937	ex F-WWIJ
☐ SU-BPV	Airbus A320-214	2966	ex F-WWDC
☐ SU-BPW	Airbus A320-214	3282	ex F-WWDP
☐ SU-BPX	Airbus A320-214	3323	ex F-WWBE

AIR MEMPHIS — Air Memphis (MHS) — Cairo-Intl (CAI)

☐ SU-BME	McDonnell-Douglas MD-83	49628/1582	ex F-GRML
☐ SU-PBG	Airbus A320-233	1353	ex N464TA
☐ SU-BPH	Airbus A320-233	1300	ex N461TA
☐ SU-PBO	Douglas DC-9-31 (ABS 3)	48131/940	ex N928VJ
☐ SU-TCA	Airbus A320-232	0932	ex VT-ADX

AIR SINAI — Air Sinai (4D/ASD) — Cairo-Intl (CAI)

A wholly owned subsidiary of Egyptair; operates services with aircraft leased from the parent

ALEXANDRIA AIRLINES — (ZR/KHH) — Alexandria

☐ SU-KHM	Boeing 737-5C9	26438/2413	ex JY-JA1	Lsd fr JAV

ALMASRIA UNIVERSAL AIRLINES — AMC (UJ/LMU) — Cairo-Intl (CAI)

☐ SU-TCB	Airbus A320-232	0943	ex VT-ADY

AMC AIRLINES — AMC (YJ/AMV) — Cairo-Intl (CAI)

☐ SU-AYK	Boeing 737-266	21194/455		stored CAI
☐ SU-BOZ	McDonnell-Douglas MD-83	53192/2155	ex N192AJ	Lsd to Sham Wings
☐ SU-BPG	Boeing 737-86N/W	32669/1895		
☐ SU-BPH	Boeing 737-86N/W	34257/2024		
☐ SU-BPZ	Boeing 737-86N/W	35213/2300		
☐ SU-BQA	Boeing 737-86N/W	35220/2406		

CAIRO AVIATION — Cairo Air (CCE) — Cairo-Intl (CAI)

☐ SU-EAF	Tupolev Tu-204-120	1450742764027	ex RA-64027		
☐ SU-EAG	Tupolev Tu-204-120S	1450744764028	ex RA-64028	TNT c/s	stored CAI
☐ SU-EAH	Tupolev Tu-204-120	1450744864023			stored CAI
☐ SU-EAI	Tupolev Tu-204-120	1450744964025			
☐ SU-EAJ	Tupolev Tu-204-120S	1450742264029	ex RA-64029	TNT c/s	stored CAI

EGYPTAIR — Egyptair (MS/MSR) — Cairo-Intl (CAI)

Member of Star Alliance

☐ SU-BDG	Airbus A300B4-203F	200	ex F-WZMN	Toshki
☐ SU-GAC	Airbus A300B4-203F	255	ex F-WZMY	New Valley
☐ SU-GAS	Airbus A300B4-622RF	561	ex F-WWAN	Cheops
☐ SU-GAY	Airbus A300B4-622RF	607	ex F-WWAB	Seti 1

☐ SU-GBA	Airbus A320-231	0165	ex F-WWDV	Aswan
☐ SU-GBB	Airbus A320-231	0166	ex F-WWID	Luxor
☐ SU-GBC	Airbus A320-231	0178	ex F-WWIQ	Hurghada
☐ SU-GBD	Airbus A320-231	0194	ex F-WWIZ	Taba
☐ SU-GBE	Airbus A320-231	0198	ex F-WWDG	El Alamein
☐ SU-GBF	Airbus A320-231	0351	ex F-WWDM	Sharm El Sheikh
☐ SU-GBG	Airbus A320-231	0366	ex F-WWDD	Saint Catherine
☐ SU-GBZ	Airbus A320-232	2070	ex F-WWDJ	
☐ SU-GCA	Airbus A320-232	2073	ex F-WWIO	

☐ SU-GCB	Airbus A320-232	2079	ex F-WWDV		
☐ SU-GCC	Airbus A320-232	2088	ex F-WWBH		
☐ SU-GCD	Airbus A320-232	2094	ex F-WWBX		
☐ SU-GCL	Airbus A320-231	0322	ex SU-RAA		Lsd to MSC
☐ SU-GBT	Airbus A321-231	0680	ex D-AVZB	Red Sea	
☐ SU-GBU	Airbus A321-231	0687	ex D-AVZR	Sinai	
☐ SU-GBV	Airbus A321-231	0715	ex D-AVZX	Mediterranean	
☐ SU-GBW	Airbus A321-231	0725	ex D-AVZA	The Nileno titles	
☐ SU-GCE	Airbus A330-243	600	ex F-WWYK		
☐ SU-GCF	Airbus A330-243	610	ex F-WWKS		
☐ SU-GCG	Airbus A330-243	666	ex F-WWKQ		
☐ SU-GCH	Airbus A330-243	683	ex F-WWYF		
☐ SU-GCI	Airbus A330-243	696	ex F-WWYR		
☐ SU-GCJ	Airbus A330-243	709	ex F-WWKK		
☐ SU-GCK	Airbus A330-243	726	ex F-WWKP		
☐ SU-	Airbus A330-243		ex F-		on order
☐ SU-	Airbus A330-243		ex F-		on order
☐ SU-GBM	Airbus A340-212	156	ex F-WWJK	Osiris Express	
☐ SU-GBN	Airbus A340-212	159	ex F-WWJV	Cleo Express	
☐ SU-GBO	Airbus A340-212	178	ex F-WWJD	Hathor Express	
☐ SU-GBH	Boeing 737-566	25084/2019		Karnakno titles	
☐ SU-GBJ	Boeing 737-566	25352/2169		Philae	
☐ SU-GBK	Boeing 737-566	26052/2276		Kalabshano titles	
☐ SU-GBL	Boeing 737-566	26051/2282		Ramesseum	
☐ SU-GCM	Boeing 737-866/W	35558/2054			
☐ SU-GCN	Boeing 737-866/W	35559/2113	ex N1795B		
☐ SU-GCO	Boeing 737-866/W	35561/2369	ex N1795B		
☐ SU-GCP	Boeing 737-866/W	35560/2434	ex N1786B		
☐ SU-GCR	Boeing 737-866/W	35562/2826	ex N1786B		
☐ SU-GCS	Boeing 737-866/W	35563/2695			
☐ SU-GCZ	Boeing 737-866/W	35568/2795			
☐ SU-GDA	Boeing 737-866/W	35565/2999	ex N1796B		
☐ SU-GDB	Boeing 737-866/W	35567/3017	ex N1786B		
☐ SU-GDC	Boeing 737-866/W	35564/3040	ex N1779B		
☐ SU-GDD	Boeing 737-866/W	35566/3061			
☐ SU-GDE	Boeing 737-866/W	35569/3043	ex N1786B		
☐ SU-	Boeing 737-866/W		ex		on order
☐ SU-	Boeing 737-866/W		ex		on order
☐ SU-	Boeing 737-866/W		ex		on order
☐ SU-	Boeing 737-866/W		ex		on order
☐ SU-GBP	Boeing 777-266	28423/71		Nefertiti	
☐ SU-GBR	Boeing 777-266	28424/80		Nefertari	
☐ SU-GBS	Boeing 777-266	28425/85		Tiye	
☐ SU-GBX	Boeing 777-266ER	32629/362		Neit	
☐ SU-GBY	Boeing 777-266ER	32630/368			
☐ SU-GDL	Boeing 777-36NER	38284			on order
☐ SU-GDM	Boeing 777-36NER	38285			on order
☐ SU-	Boeing 777-36NER				on order

EGYPTAIR EXPRESS *(MSE)* *Cairo-Intl (CAI)*

☐ SU-GCT	Embraer 170-100LR (170LR)	17000167	ex PT-SMJ
☐ SU-GCU	Embraer 170-100LR (170LR)	17000169	ex PT-SML
☐ SU-GCV	Embraer 170-100LR (170LR)	17000170	ex PT-SMM
☐ SU-GCW	Embraer 170-100LR (170LR)	17000175	ex PT-SMR
☐ SU-GCX	Embraer 170-100LR (170LR)	17000178	ex PT-SMV
☐ SU-GCY	Embraer 170-100LR (170LR)	17000185	ex PT-SUC
☐ SU-GDF	Embraer 170-100LR (170LR)	17000266	ex PT-SJU
☐ SU-GDG	Embraer 170-100LR (170LR)	17000269	ex PT-SJZ
☐ SU-GDH	Embraer 170-100LR (170LR)	17000274	ex PT-TQA
☐ SU-GDI	Embraer 170-100LR (170LR)	17000276	ex PT-TQC
☐ SU-GDJ	Embraer 170-100LR (170LR)	17000282	ex PT-TQI
☐ SU-GDK	Embraer 170-100LR (170LR)	17000284	ex PT-TQK

FAST LINK *Cairo Intl (CAI)*

☐ SU-FLE	SAAB SF.340A	340A-146	ex N146SD

KORAL BLUE *(KBR)* *Sharm el Sheikh (SSH)*

☐ SU-KBA	Airbus A320-212	0937	ex SU-LBC
☐ SU-KBB	Airbus A319-112	3171	ex EI-EAF
☐ SU-KBC	Airbus A320-214	2123	ex EI-EDO
☐ SU-KBD	Airbus A320-214	1597	ex TS-INP

LOTUS AIR		Lotus Flower (TAS)		Cairo-Intl (CAI)
☐ SU-LBG	Airbus A320-233	0743	ex 9V-VLD	Lsd to AAW
☐ SU-LBH	Airbus A320-233	0739	ex 9V-VLC	Lsd to AAW
☐ SU-LBI	Airbus A320-232	0667	ex OE-LOF	
☐ SU-LBJ	Airbus A320-214	1054	ex TC-JLG	

MIDWEST AIRLINES EGYPT		(MY/MWA)		Cairo-Intl (CAI)
☐ SU-MWC	Boeing 737-683	28303/257	ex G-CDKT	

NILE AIR		(NIA)		
☐ SU-BOA	Airbus A320-232	3183	ex N621SA	
☐ SU-BQC	Airbus A320-232	3219	ex N623SA	

PETROLEUM AIR SERVICES				Al Arish / Hurghada (AAC/HRG)
☐ SU-CAC	Bell 206L-3 LongRanger III	51004		
☐ SU-CAE	Bell 206L-3 LongRanger III	51030		
☐ SU-CAF	Bell 206L-3 LongRanger III	51031		
☐ SU-CAG	Bell 206B JetRanger III	3574		
☐ SU-CAH	Bell 206B JetRanger III	3581		
☐ SU-CAI	Bell 206L-3 LongRanger III	51018		
☐ SU-CAB	Bell 212	31223		
☐ SU-CAJ	Bell 212	31247		
☐ SU-CAL	Bell 212	31215	ex N3889A	
☐ SU-CAM	Bell 212	31249		
☐ SU-CAN	Bell 212	31250		
☐ SU-CAO	Bell 212	31260		
☐ SU-CAQ	Bell 212	31262		
☐ SU-CAR	Bell 212	31263		
☐ SU-CAS	Bell 212	31264		
☐ SU-CAU	Bell 212	35036		
☐ SU-CAV	Bell 412HP	36037	ex XA-TNO	
☐ SU-CAX	Bell 412HP	36081	ex N2156S	
☐ SU-CAY	Bell 412EP	36158	ex N6489P	
☐ SU-CAZ	Bell 412EP	36184	ex N55248	
☐ SU-CBI	Bell 412EP	36353	ex C-FCSC	
☐ SU-CBL	Bell 412EP	36377	ex C-FENJ	
☐ SU-CBM	Bell 412EP	36379	ex C-FEON	
☐ SU-CBO	Bell 412EP	36410	ex C-FIRW	
☐ SU-CBR	Bell 412EP	36432	ex C-FMQV	
☐ SU-CBS	Bell 412EP	36468	ex C-FTCJ	
☐ SU-CBT	Bell 412EP	36492	ex C-FVDY	
☐ SU-CBA	de Havilland DHC-7-102	93	ex C-GFYI	
☐ SU-CBB	de Havilland DHC-7-102	96	ex C-GEWQ	stored CAI
☐ SU-CBC	de Havilland DHC-7-102	97	ex C-GFQL	
☐ SU-CBD	de Havilland DHC-7-102	98	ex C-GEWQ	
☐ SU-CBE	de Havilland DHC-7-102	99	ex C-GFBW	
☐ SU-CBF	de Havilland DHC-8Q-315	584	ex C-FDHX	
☐ SU-CBG	de Havilland DHC-8Q-315	585	ex C-FDHY	
☐ SU-CBH	de Havilland DHC-8Q-315	594	ex C-FPJH	
☐ SU-CBJ	de Havilland DHC-8Q-315	607	ex C-FBNT	
☐ SU-CBN	de Havilland DHC-8Q-315	632	ex C-FIOY	
☐ SU-CBP	Eurocopter EC135P2+	0604		
☐ SU-CBQ	Eurocopter EC135P2+	0607		

TRISTAR AIR		Triple Star (TSY)		Cairo-Intl (CAI)
☐ SU-BMZ	Airbus A300B4-203F	129	ex N825SC	

SU-Y PALESTINE

PALESTINIAN AIRLINES		Palestine (PF/PNW)		Gaza-Yasser Arafat Intl (GZA)
☐ SU-YAH	Fokker F.27 Mk.050 (Fokker 50)	20123	ex PH-FZJ	stored AMM?
☐ SU-YAI	Fokker F.27 Mk.050 (Fokker 50)	20143	ex PH-FZI	stored WOE?

Airline non-operative; Gaza Airport closed.

SX- GREECE (Hellenic Republic)

AEGEAN AIRLINES — Aegean (A3/AEE) — Athens-Eleftherios Venizelos Intl (ATH)

	Registration	Type	C/n	Previous	Name	Notes
☐	SX-DGB	Airbus A320-232	4165	ex F-WWBX		
☐	SX-	Airbus A320-232		ex		on order
☐	SX-	Airbus A320-232		ex		on order
☐	SX-	Airbus A320-232		ex		on order
☐	SX-	Airbus A320-232		ex		on order
☐	SX-	Airbus A320-232		ex		on order
☐	SX-DVG	Airbus A320-232	3033	ex F-WWBX	Eethos	
☐	SX-DVH	Airbus A320-232	3066	ex F-WWIF	Nostos	
☐	SX-DVI	Airbus A320-232	3074	ex F-WWIO	Kinesis	
☐	SX-DVJ	Airbus A320-232	3365	ex F-WWIS	Exelixis	
☐	SX-DVK	Airbus A320-232	3392	ex F-WWDS		
☐	SX-DVL	Airbus A320-232	3423	ex F-WWIV		
☐	SX-DVM	Airbus A320-232	3439	ex F-WWDY		
☐	SX-DVN	Airbus A320-232	3478	ex F-WWDI		
☐	SX-DVQ	Airbus A320-232	3526	ex F-WWDU		
☐	SX-DVR	Airbus A320-232	3714	ex D-AVVB		
☐	SX-DVS	Airbus A320-232	3709	ex F-WWIT		
☐	SX-DVT	Airbus A320-232	3745	ex F-WWIJ		
☐	SX-DVU	Airbus A320-232	3753	ex F-WWBS		
☐	SX-DVV	Airbus A320-232	3773	ex F-WWDT		
☐	SX-DVW	Airbus A320-232	3785	ex F-WWIU		
☐	SX-DVX	Airbus A320-232	3829	ex F-WWIZ		
☐	SX-DVY	Airbus A320-232	3850	ex F-WWDG		
☐	SX-DGA	Airbus A321-231	3878	ex D-AVZP		
☐	SX-DVO	Airbus A321-231	3462	ex D-AVZU	Philoxenia	
☐	SX-DVP	Airbus A321-231	3527	ex D-AVZZ		
☐	SX-DVZ	Airbus A321-231	3820	ex D-AVZF		
☐	SX-DVA	Avro 146-RJ100	E3341	ex G-6-341		
☐	SX-DVB	Avro 146-RJ100	E3343	ex G-6-343		
☐	SX-DVC	Avro 146-RJ100	E3358	ex G-6-358		
☐	SX-DVD	Avro 146-RJ100	E3362	ex G-6-362		
☐	SX-DVE	Avro 146-RJ100	E3374	ex G-6-374		
☐	SX-DVF	Avro 146-RJ100	E3375	ex G-6-375		
☐	SX-BBU	Boeing 737-33A	25743/2206	ex EC-FMP	Joanna	
☐	SX-BGJ	Boeing 737-4S3	25595/2233	ex N280CD		
☐	SX-BGQ	Boeing 737-4Y0	25177/2176	ex F-GLXJ		stored SNN
☐	SX-BGV	Boeing 737-4Q8	26308/2665	ex HL7235		
☐	SX-BLM	Boeing 737-42C	24813/2062	ex PH-BPF		
☐	EC-KUL	ATR 72-212A	809	ex F-WWET		Lsd fr SWT
☐	EC-KVI	ATR 72-212A	824	ex F-WWEM		Lsd fr SWT

AEROLAND AIRWAYS — (3S/AEN) — Athens-Eleftherios Venizelos Intl (ATH)

	Registration	Type	C/n	Previous	Name
☐	SX-ARU	Cessna 208B Caravan I	208B1146	ex N1293Z	Isle of Tinos
☐	SX-ARW	Cessna 208B Caravan I	208B1174	ex N13080	
☐	SX-ARX	Cessna 208B Caravan I	208B1182	ex N1300G	
☐	SX-ARY	Cessna 208B Caravan I	208B1301	ex N2028N	
☐	SX-BVE	de Havilland DHC-8-106	351	ex C-FRIY	Island of Mykonos

AIRGO AIRLINES

	Registration	Type	C/n	Previous	Name
☐	SX-BPS	British Aerospace ATP (LFD)	2005	ex SE-MAM	Eleonora

AIRSEA LINES — Pegaviation (PEV) — Corfu-Gouvia Marina SPB

	Registration	Type	C/n	Previous	Name	Notes
☐	SX-BMG	de Havilland DHC-6 Twin Otter 300	375	ex C-GHAZ	Floatplane	op for UN
☐	SX-BVP	de Havilland DHC-6 Twin Otter 300	283	ex HB-LSY	Floatplane	

ASTRA AIRLINES

	Registration	Type	C/n	Previous
☐	SX-DIX	British Aerospace 146 Srs.300	E3193	ex I-ADJF
☐	SX-DIZ	British Aerospace 146 Srs.300	E3206	ex G-JEBE

ATHENS AIRWAYS

	Registration	Type	C/n	Previous
☐	SX-CMA	Embraer EMB.145EU (ERJ-145EU)	145107	ex G-EMBH
☐	SX-CMB	Embraer EMB.145EU (ERJ-145EU)	145167	ex G-EMBK
☐	SX-CMC	Embraer EMB.145EU (ERJ-145EU)	145177	ex G-EMBL
☐	SX-CMD	Embraer EMB.145EU (ERJ-145EU)	145196	ex G-EMBM

AVIATOR AIRWAYS — Aviator (AVW) — Athens-Eleftherios Venizelos Intl (ATH)

	Reg	Type	C/n	Prev	Name	Remarks
☐	SX-APJ	Beech 200 Super King Air	BB-401	ex OY-JAO		
☐	SX-BSR	British Aerospace Jetstream 31	718	ex G-OAKI		

EUROAIR — Eurostar (6I/EUP) — Athens-Eleftherios Venizelos Intl (ATH)

	Reg	Type	C/n	Prev	Name	Remarks
☐	SX-APP	Piper PA-31-350 Chieftain	31-8152171	ex N4093G		
☐	SX-BFL	Piper PA-31-350 Chieftain	31-7952171	ex N64TT		
☐	SX-BMS	Piper PA-31-350 Navajo Chieftain	31-7752122	ex HP-1049PS		

GAINJET — Athens-Eleftherios Venizelos Intl (ATH)

	Reg	Type	C/n	Prev	Name	Remarks
☐	SX-RFA	Boeing 757-23N/W	30232/888	ex EI-LTO		

HELLAS JET — Hellas Jet (HJ/HEJ) — Athens-Eleftherios Venizelos Intl (ATH)

	Reg	Type	C/n	Prev	Name	Remarks
☐	SX-BVK	Airbus A320-211	0088	ex N9070N	Orion	
☐	SX-BVL	Airbus A320-211	0087	ex N5015G	Pegasus	

HELLENIC IMPERIAL AIRWAYS — (IMP) — Athens-Eleftherios Venizelos Intl (ATH)

	Reg	Type	C/n	Prev	Name	Remarks
☐	SX-TIB	Boeing 747-230B	23622/665	ex JY-AUB		
☐	SX-TIC	Boeing 747-281B	23501/648	ex AP-BIC		
☐	SX-TID	Boeing 747-281B	23502/649	ex (SX-DID)		
☐	SX-TIE	Boeing 747-230M	23509/663	ex 5T-AUE		Lsd fr UVS

OLYMPIC AIRLINES — Olympic (OA/OAL) — Athens-Eleftherios Venizelos Intl (ATH)

	Reg	Type	C/n	Prev	Name	Remarks
☐	SX-OAF	Airbus A319-111	3895	ex D-AHIP		
☐	SX-OAG	Airbus A319-112	3950	ex D-AHIQ		
☐	SX-OAJ	Airbus A319-112	3905	ex D-AVWS		
☐	SX-OAK	Airbus A319-132	3317	ex M-ABCK		
☐	SX-OAL	Airbus A319-132	3252	ex M-ABCJ		
☐	SX-OAN	Airbus A319-133	1727	ex D-APAC		
☐	SX-OAO	Airbus A319-133	1880	ex D-APAD		
☐	SX-OAV	Airbus A319-132	3142	ex M-ABCL		
☐	SX-OAH	Airbus A320-232	3316	ex VT-DNV		
☐	SX-OAI	Airbus A320-232	3162	ex VT-DNY		
☐	SX-OAM	Airbus A320-232	3990	ex F-WWBY		
☐	SX-OAP	Airbus A320-232	4065	ex D-AVVL		
☐	SX-OAQ	Airbus A320-232	3748	ex F-WWBQ		
☐	SX-OAR	Airbus A320-232	3812	ex D-AVVE		
☐	SX-OAS	Airbus A320-232	4094	ex D-AVVB		
☐	SX-OAT	Airbus A320-232	4190	ex F-WWII		
☐	SX-OAU	Airbus A320-232	4193	ex F-WWIJ		
☐	SX-BIO	de Havilland DHC-8-102	330	ex C-GZQZ	Katerina Thanou	
☐	SX-BIP	de Havilland DHC-8-102	347	ex C-GZRA	Voula Patoulidou	
☐	SX-BIQ	de Havilland DHC-8-102	361	ex C-GZRD	Kahi Kahiasvili	
☐	SX-BIR	de Havilland DHC-8-102	304	ex C-GZRF	Kostas Kontoris	
☐	SX-BIW	de Havilland DHC-8-102	289	ex OE-HWG		
☐	G-ECOE	de Havilland DHC-8-402Q	4212	ex LN-WDV		Lsd fr BEE
☐	G-ECOF	de Havilland DHC-8-402Q	4216	ex LN-WDW		Lsd fr BEE
☐	G-FLBD	de Havilland DHC-8-402Q	4259	ex C-FWZN		Lsd fr BEE
☐	G-FLBE	de Havilland DHC-8-402Q	4261	ex C-FXAB		Lsd fr BEE
☐	SX-BIT	de Havilland DHC-8-402Q	4148	ex G-JECV		
☐	SX-BIU	de Havilland DHC-8-402Q	4152	ex G-JECW		
☐	SX-OBA	de Havilland DHC-8-402Q	4267	ex G-PTHA		
☐	SX-OBB	de Havilland DHC-8-402Q	4268	ex G-PTHB		
☐	SX-OBC	de Havilland DHC-8-402Q	4276	ex G-PTHC		
☐	SX-DFA	Airbus A340-313X	235	ex F-WWJN	Olympia	stored ATH
☐	SX-DFB	Airbus A340-313X	239	ex F-WWJC	Delphi	stored ATH
☐	SX-DFC	Airbus A340-313X	280	ex F-WWJJ	Marathon	stored ATH
☐	SX-DFD	Airbus A340-313X	292	ex F-WWJB	Epidaurus	stored ATH
☐	SX-BIA	ATR 42-320	169	ex F-WWEW	Plato	stored ATH
☐	SX-BIB	ATR 42-320	182	ex F-WWER	Socrates	stored ATH
☐	SX-BIC	ATR 42-320	197	ex F-WWEE	Aristotle	stored ATH
☐	SX-BID	ATR 42-320	219	ex F-WWEG	Pythagoras	stored ATH
☐	SX-BIE	ATR 72-202	239	ex F-WWED	Thales	stored ATH
☐	SX-BIF	ATR 72-202	241	ex F-WWEA	Democritus	stored ATH
☐	SX-BIG	ATR 72-202	290	ex F-WWLQ	Homer	stored ATH
☐	SX-BIH	ATR 72-202	305	ex F-WWLC	Herodotus	stored ATH
☐	SX-BII	ATR 72-202	353	ex F-WWEK	Hipocrates	stored ATH
☐	SX-BIK	ATR 72-202	350	ex F-WWEG	Archimedes	stored ATH
☐	SX-BIL	ATR 72-202	437	ex F-WWLC	Melina-Eliada	stored ATH
☐	SX-BIM	ATR 42-320	337	ex F-WQNQ	Kostas Tsiklitiras	stored ATH

☐ SX-BIN	ATR 42-320	291	ex F-WQNZ	Spyros Louis	stored ATH
☐ SX-BPA	ATR 42-300	033	EI-CVS		stored ATH
☐ SX-BKA	Boeing 737-484	25313/2109		Vergina	stored ATH
☐ SX-BKB	Boeing 737-484	25314/2124		Olynthos	stored ATH
☐ SX-BKC	Boeing 737-484	25361/2130		Philippi	stored ATH
☐ SX-BKD	Boeing 737-484	25362/2142		Amphipoli	stored ATH
☐ SX-BKE	Boeing 737-484	25417/2160		Stagira	stored ATH
☐ SX-BKF	Boeing 737-484	25430/2174		Dion	stored ATH
☐ SX-BKH	Boeing 737-4Q8	24703/1828	ex N407KW		stored ATH
☐ SX-BKT	Boeing 737-4Q8	25377/2717	ex TC-JEO		stored ATH
☐ SX-BKX	Boeing 737-430	27000/2311	ex EI-DGD		stored ATH
☐ SX-BLC	Boeing 737-3Q8	26303/2635	ex (G-JKID)	all-white	stored ATH
☐ SX-BLD	Boeing 737-3M8	25071/2039	ex 9M-AAT		stored ATH
☐ SX-BMC	Boeing 737-42J	27143/2457	ex N734AB	City of Alexandroupolis	stored ATH

SKY EXPRESS — *Air Crete (G3/SEH)* — *Heraklion (HER)*

☐ SX-BLL	McDonnell-Douglas MD-83	49933/1837	ex JY-JRC
☐ SX-BPP	McDonnell-Douglas MD-83	53377/2057	ex JY-JRB
☐ SX-IDI	British Aerospace Jetstream 32	947	ex N149JH
☐ SX-ROD	British Aerospace Jetstream 41	41076	ex G-CEYW

SKY WINGS AIRLINES — *(GSW)* — *Heraklion (HER)*

☐ SX-BTF	McDonnell-Douglas MD-83	49857/1687	ex SE-RDE
☐ SX-BTG	McDonnell-Douglas MD-83	49856/1675	ex SE-RDG
☐ SX-BTH	Boeing 757-29J	27204/591	ex N410JR

SWIFTAIR HELLAS — *Med-Freight (MDF)* — *Athens-Eleftherios Venizelos Intl (ATH)*

☐ SX-BGU	Swearingen SA.227AC Metro III	AC-615B	ex EC-HJO
☐ SX-BKZ	Swearingen SA.227AC Metro III	AC-694B	ex SX-BKW
☐ SX-BMT	Swearingen SA.227AC Metro III	AC-699B	ex EC-GYB

VER-AVIA — *Night Rider (GRV)* — *Athens-Eleftherios Venizelos Intl (ATH)*

☐ SX-BMM	Swearingen SA.227AC Metro III	BC-774B	ex N774MW
☐ SX-BNN	Swearingen SA.227AC Metro III	BC-771B	ex N771MW

VIKING HELLAS AIRLINES

☐ SX-SMS	McDonnell-Douglas MD-83	49631/1596	ex SE-RDI
☐ SX-BRM	Fokker F.27 Mk.050 (Fokker 50)	20207	ex PH-KVF
☐ SX-BRS	Fokker F.27 Mk.050 (Fokker 50)	20206	ex PH-KVE
☐ SX-BRT	Fokker F.27 Mk.050 (Fokker 50)	20230	ex 5B-DCB
☐ SX-BRV	Fokker F.27 Mk.050 (Fokker 50)	20199	ex PH-ZDI

S2- BANGLADESH (People's Republic of Bangladesh)

BEST AIR — *Best Air (5Q/BEA)* — *Dhaka (DAC)*

☐ S2-AAT	Hawker Siddeley HS.748 Srs.2A/351	1770	ex ZS-XGE	Freighter
☐ S2-ABE	Hawker Siddeley HS.748 Srs.2A/245	1658	ex F-GODD	Freighter
☐ S2-AEE	Hawker Siddeley HS.748 Srs 2A/242	1647	ex G-ORCP	Freighter

BIMAN BANGLADESH AIRLINES — *Bangladesh (BG/BBC)* — *Dhaka (DAC)*

☐ S2-ADF	Airbus A310-325	700	ex F-WWCB	City of Chittagong	
☐ S2-ADK	Airbus A310-325	594	ex N594RC		
☐ TC-API	Boeing 737-86N/W	32732/1056			Lsd fr PGT
☐ S2-AFM	Boeing 737-83N/W	28653/948	ex PR-GIA		
☐ CS-TFM	Boeing 777-212ER	28513/144	ex 9V-SRA		Lsd fr MMZ
☐ S2-ACO	Douglas DC-10-30	46993/263	ex 9V-SDB	City of Hazrat Shah Makhdoom (RA)	
☐ S2-ACP	Douglas DC-10-30	46995/275	ex 9V-SDD	City of Dhaka	
☐ S2-ACQ	Douglas DC-10-30	47817/300	ex 9V-SDF	City of Hazrat Shah Jalal (RA)	
☐ S2-ACR	Douglas DC-10-30	48317/445		The New Era	
☐ S2-ACV	Fokker F.28 Fellowship 4000	11124	ex PK-YPV		
☐ S2-ACW	Fokker F.28 Fellowship 4000	11148	ex PK-YPJ		
☐ S2-ADY	Fokker F.28 Fellowship 4000	11120	ex HS-PBC		
☐ S2-ADZ	Fokker F.28 Fellowship 4000	11123	ex HS-PBA		stored DAC

BISMILLAH AIRLINES — *Bismillah (5Z/BML)* — *Dhaka/Sharjah (DAC/SHJ)*

☐ S2-ADW	Hawker Siddeley HS.748 Srs 2A/347	1766	ex G-BGMN	Freighter
☐ S2-AEK	Douglas DC-8-61F	45888/290	ex N30UA	stored OPF

EASY FLY — Dhaka (DAC)

☐ S2-AAX	Hawker Siddeley HS.748 Srs.2A/242	1767	ex G-BGMO	stored DAK

GMG AIRLINES — (Z5) — Dhaka (DAC)

☐ S2-AAA	de Havilland DHC-8-102	245	ex N802MA	In memory of Bangabondu
☐ S2-ACT	de Havilland DHC-8-311	307	ex OE-LRW	
☐ S2-ADJ	de Havilland DHC-8-102	54	ex N816PH	
☐ S2-ADM	McDonnell-Douglas MD-82	53147/2069	ex PK-LMF	stored BKK Lsd fr LNI
☐ S2-ADO	McDonnell-Douglas MD-82	53481/2145	ex S7-ASK	
☐ S2-ADP	McDonnell-Douglas MD-83	53044/1776	ex N835NK	
☐ S2-ADX	de Havilland DHC-8Q-311A	464	ex G-BRYZ	In memory of HZT Saha Jalal

ROYAL BENGAL AIRLINES

☐ S2-AEL	de Havilland DHC-8-102A	225	ex D-BOBL

UNITED AIRWAYS — (4H)

☐ S2-AER	de Havilland DHC-8-102	366	ex N811WP
☐ S2-AES	de Havilland DHC-8-103	363	ex N810WP
☐ S2-AEU	McDonnell-Douglas MD-83	49790/1643	ex G-FLTL

VOYAGER AIRLINES — Voyager Air (V6/VOG) — Dhaka (DAC)

Operates charter flights using aircraft leased from other operators as required

YOUNGONE

☐ S2-ACU	Cessna 208B Caravan I	208B0612	ex N1215A

ZOOM AIRWAYS — Zed Air (3Z/ZAW) — Dhaka (DAC)

☐ S2-AET	Lockheed L-1011-1F Tristar	193-1012	ex HS-AXF

S5- SLOVENIA (Republic of Slovenia)

ADRIA AIRWAYS — Adria (JP/ADR) — Ljubljana (LJU)

Member of Star Alliance

☐ S5-AAD	Canadair CL-600-2B19 (CRJ-200LR)	7166	ex C-FZWS	retd?
☐ S5-AAE	Canadair CL-600-2B19 (CRJ-200LR)	7170	ex C-GAIK	
☐ S5-AAF	Canadair CL-600-2B19 (CRJ-200LR)	7272	ex C-FMND	
☐ S5-AAG	Canadair CL-600-2B19 (CRJ-200LR)	7384	ex C-FMMT	Star Alliance colours
☐ S5-AAH	Canadair CL-600-2B19 (CRJ-200LR)	7032	ex HA-LNX	
☐ S5-AAI	Canadair CL-600-2B19 (CRJ-200LR)	7248	ex G-DUOH	
☐ S5-AAJ	Canadair CL-600-2B19 (CRJ-200LR)	8010	ex C-	

☐ S5-AAA	Airbus A320-231	0043	ex SX-BAS	Lsd to AAW
☐ S5-AAB	Airbus A320-231	0113	ex SX-BAT	
☐ S5-AAK	Canadair CL-600-2D24 (CRJ-900ER)	15128	ex C-	
☐ S5-AAL	Canadair CL-600-2D24 (CRJ-900ER)	15129	ex C-	
☐ S5-AAN	Canadair CL-600-2D24 (CRJ-900ER)	15207	ex C-	
☐ S5-AAO	Canadair CL-600-2D24 (CRJ-900ER)	15215	ex C-	
☐ S5-	Canadair CL-600-2E25 (CRJ-1000ER)		ex C-	on order
☐ UR-GAT	Boeing 737-528/W	25237/2464	ex F-GJNM	Lsd fr AUI

AURORA AIRLINES — (URR) — Ljubljana (LJU)

☐ S5-ACC	McDonnell-Douglas MD-82	48095/1055	ex ZA-ARB	
☐ S5-ACD	McDonnell-Douglas MD-82	49143/1095	ex 9A-CBC	stored IST

SOLINAIR — Solinair (SOP) — Portoroz (POW)

☐ S5-ABS	Airbus A300B4-203F	126	ex TC-MNN		Lsd fr MNG
☐ S5-BAF	LET L-410UVP-E8C	912540	ex OM-WDA	FedEx colours	Lsd fr/op for ADR
☐ S5-BAM	SAAB SF.340AF	340A-020	ex G-GNTC		
☐ S5-BAO	SAAB SF.340AF	340A-011	ex VH-KEQ		
☐ S5-BAT	SAAB SF.340AF	340A-007	ex S5-BAN		

S7- SEYCHELLES (Republic of Seychelles)

AIR SEYCHELLES — Seychelles (HM/SEY) — Mahe (SEZ)

☐ S7-AAA	Britten-Norman BN-2A-27 Islander	540	ex G-BDZP	Isle of Remire	stored
☐ S7-AAF	de Havilland DHC-6 Twin Otter 300	623	ex S7-AAO	Isle of Praslin	

☐ S7-AAJ	de Havilland DHC-6 Twin Otter 310	499	ex PH-STB	Isle of Desroches	
☐ S7-AAR	de Havilland DHC-6 Twin Otter 300	539	ex PH-STF	Isle of Farquhar	
☐ S7-AHM	Boeing 767-37DER	26328/637	ex (S7-AAZ)	Vailee de Mai	
☐ S7-ASY	Boeing 767-3Q8ER	29386/831		Aldabra	
☐ S7-FCS	Boeing 767-306ER	28884/738	ex HA-LHC		
☐ S7-ILF	Boeing 767-205	23057/81	ex N260MY		
☐ S7-PAL	Short SD.3-60	SH3758	ex G-KBAC	Isle de Palme	
☐ S7-PRI	Short SD.3-60	SH3724	ex G-BNMU	Isle of La Digue	
☐ S7-SEZ	Boeing 767-219ER	24150/2	ex N263LF		

IDC AIRCRAFT — Mahe (SEZ)

☐ S7-AAI	Reims Cessna F406 Caravan II	F406-0051	ex N7148P	
☐ S7-AAU	Britten-Norman BN-2A-21 Islander	589	ex A2-01M	Op for Coast Guard
☐ S7-IDC	Beech 1900D	UE-212	ex N3217U	

S9- SAO TOME (Democratic Republic of São Tomé & Principe)

GOLFO INTERNATIONAL — São Tomé/Luanda (TMS/LAD)

☐ S9-BAJ	Beech 1900D	UE-357	ex N23598
☐ S9-BAK	Beech 1900D	UE-358	ex N23610

GOLIAF AIR — Goliaf Air (GLE) — São Tomé (TMS)

☐ S9-BOH	Antonov An-32	2108	ex T-256		
☐ S9-BOZ	Antonov An-12A	2340803	ex RA-122375		Lsd to Africa West
☐ S9-CAH	WSK-PZL/Antonov An-28	1AJ005-12	ex ER-AJK		
☐ S9-DAB	Douglas DC-9-32	47313/268	ex LV-YAB	Calypso	
☐ S9-DAF	Antonov An-12A	2340606	ex RA-12971	Principe	
☐ S9-DBA	Antonov An-12AP	2400802	ex UR-11326		
☐ S9-GAR	Lockheed L-1011-200 Tristar	193U-1201	ex EX-102		
☐ S9-PSB	WSK-PZL/Antonov An-28	1AJ003-07	ex ER-AJA		
☐ S9-PSE	Antonov An-32	2803	ex UR-48053		Lsd to MGG
☐ S9-PSO	Antonov An-12BP	5343109	ex EW-11365		
☐ S9-PSV	WSK/PZL Antonov An-28	1AJ008-13	ex ER-AKO		Op for Dallex Air

TRANSAFRIK INTERNATIONAL — (TFK) — São Tomé/Luanda (TMS/LAD)

☐ S9-BAE	Boeing 727-31F	18903/147	ex N210NE		
☐ S9-BAG	Boeing 727-30C	19313/411	ex PP-ITP	all-white	stored UTN
☐ S9-BAV	Boeing 727-223 (Raisbeck 3)	21383/1324	ex N871AA	Tanker	
☐ S9-BOC	Boeing 727-23F	18447/127	ex ZS-NMY	all-white	stored UTN
☐ S9-BOD	Boeing 727-25F	18968/223	ex PP-ITA	all-white	stored UTN
☐ S9-BOG	Boeing 727-90C	19170/332	ex N270AX	all-white	stored UTN
☐ S9-CAA	Boeing 727-95F	19836/494	ex HR-AMR		
☐ S9-PAC	Boeing 727-44C (FedEx 3)	20475/854	ex C-GVFA		
☐ S9-TAO	Boeing 727-23F	19390/350	ex N931FT		
☐ 5X-PST	Boeing 727-171C	19859/559	ex S9-PST		
☐ S9-BAT	Lockheed L-382G-3C Hercules	4134	ex N916SJ		
☐ S9-BOF	Lockheed L-382G-32C Hercules	4586	ex N921SJ		
☐ S9-BOR	Lockheed L-382E-20C Hercules	4362	ex N522SJ		
☐ S9-CAV	Lockheed L-382G-11C Hercules	4301	ex N923SJ		
☐ S9-CAW	Lockheed L-382G-13C Hercules	4300	ex N908SJ		
☐ S9-NAL	Lockheed L-382E-25C Hercules	4385	ex 9Q-CHZ		

TRANSLIZ AVIATION — São Tomé (TMS)

☐ S9-KHC	Antonov An-12B	00347306	ex ER-ACY
☐ S9-KHD	Antonov An-12B	01347908	ex ER-ACQ
☐ S9-KHF	Antonov An-12V	00347109	ex ER-ADG
☐ S9-KHL	Antonov An-12B	00347401	ex ER-ACS

Operator Unknown

☐ S9-DBP	Antonov An-12BP	8346201	ex 4K-AZ23
☐ S9-DBS	Antonov An-26	07309504	ex EX-091

TC- TURKEY (Republic of Turkey)

ACT AIRLINES — (9T/RUN) — Istanbul-Ataturk (IST)

☐ TC-ACB	Airbus A300B4-203F	121	ex G-CEXI	
☐ TC-ACC	Airbus A300B4-203F	147	ex N318FV	
☐ TC-ACD	Airbus A300B4-203F	075	ex N502TA	Op for Empost
☐ TC-ACE	Airbus A300B4-203F	154	ex N320SC	
☐ TC-ACU	Airbus A300B4-203F	183	ex N512TA	
☐ TC-ACY	Airbus A300B4-203F	107	ex N59107	

☐ TC-ACZ	Airbus A300B4-203F	105	ex N317FV		

ANADOLU JET — Ankara/Esenboga International (ESB)

☐ TC-JDT	Boeing 737-4Y0	25261/2258	ex N600SK	Alanya	
☐ TC-JEY	Boeing 737-4Y0	26086/2475		Side	
☐ TC-JEZ	Boeing 737-4Y0	26088/2487		Bergama	
☐ TC-JHG	Boeing 737-8GJ/W	34958/2688	ex VT-SGD	Pamukkale	
☐ TC-JHH	Boeing 737-8GJ/W	34959/2719		Kemer	
☐ TC-JHI	Boeing 737-8FH/W	35092/2160	ex G-XLAK	Hendek	
☐ TC-JKF	Boeing 737-76N/W	32684/1889	ex EI-EDT		
☐ TC-JKG	Boeing 737-76N/W	34754/2172	ex OM-NGH	Mugla	
☐ TC-JKH	Boeing 737-76N/W	34757/2241	ex OM-NGL	Ihlara	
☐ TC-JKI	Boeing 737-76N/W	34758/2266	ex EI-EDU	Abant	
☐ TC-JKJ	Boeing 737-752/W	34297/1808	ex N297MD		
☐ TC-JKK	Boeing 737-752/W	34298/1812	ex N298MD		
☐ TC-JKL	Boeing 737-76N/W	34753/2165	ex OM-NGG	Anamur	
☐ TC-JKM	Boeing 737-76N/W	34755/2187	ex OM-NGJ		
☐ TC-	Boeing 737-752/W	34299/1829	ex XA-LUN		
☐ TC-	Boeing 737-752/W	34300/1848	ex N343CT		

ANKA AIR

☐ TC-AKN	McDonnell-Douglas MD-83	53186/2092	ex TC-FBD		stored IST

ATLASJET INTERNATIONAL — Atlasjet (KK/KKK) — Antalya (AYT)

☐ TC-ETF	Airbus A321-231	1438	ex N585NK		Lsd to SVA
☐ TC-ETH	Airbus A321-231	0968	ex TC-IEF		
☐ TC-ETM	Airbus A321-131	0604	ex TC-TUB		
☐ TC-ETN	Airbus A321-131	0614	ex TC-TUC		
☐ TC-OGI	Airbus A320-232	0640	ex N381LF		
☐ TC-OGJ	Airbus A320-232	0676	ex N391LF		
☐ TC-ETK	Airbus A330-223	358	ex I-EEZA		Lsd to SVA
☐ TC-ETL	Airbus A330-223	364	ex I-EEZB		Lsd to SVA
☐ TC-ETE	Boeing 757-2Q8	30044/954	ex TC-GLA		Lsd to SVA
☐ TC-ETG	Boeing 757-256	26254/905	ex EC-HDV		Lsd to SVA
☐ TC-OGS	Boeing 757-256	29307/924	ex EC-HIQ		Lsd to SVA
☐ TC-OGT	Boeing 757-256	29308/935	ex EC-HIR		Lsd to SVA

BEST AIR — (5F/BST) — Istanbul-Ataturk (IST)

☐ TC-TUA	McDonnell-Douglas MD-82	49138/1090	ex TC-MNO	Tamcelik	

BORAJET

☐ TC-YAB	ATR 72-212A	588	ex G-CGFT		
☐ TC-YAC	ATR 72-212A	701	ex OY-EDC		
☐ TC-YAD	ATR 72-212A	702	ex OY-EDD		

CORENDON AIR — Corendon (7H/CAI) — Istanbul-Sabiha Gokcen Int'l (SAW)

☐ TC-TJB	Boeing 737-3Q8	27633/2878	ex N304FL	Ayhan Saracoglu	
☐ TC-TJC	Boeing 737-4Q8	25374/2562	ex TC-MNL		
☐ TC-TJD	Boeing 737-4Q8	25375/2598	ex TC-MNM		
☐ TC-TJE	Boeing 737-4Y0	26073/2375	ex TC-JER		
☐ TC-TJF	Boeing 737-4Y0	26078/2431	ex TC-JEU		

FREEBIRD AIRLINES — Free Turk (FHY) — Istanbul-Ataturk (IST)

☐ TC-FBE	Airbus A320-212	0132	ex SE-RCG		
☐ TC-FBF	Airbus A320-212	0288	ex 9H-AED		
☐ TC-FBG	Airbus A321-231	0771	ex HL7588		
☐ TC-FBJ	Airbus A320-232	0580	ex N580CG		
☐ TC-FBR	Airbus A320-232	2524	ex VT-DKZ		
☐ TC-FBT	Airbus A321-231	0855	ex HL7589		

IZMIR AIRLINES — Izmir (4I/IZM) — Izmir (ADB)

☐ TC-IZA	Airbus A320-233	2118	ex N488TA		
☐ TC-IZH	Airbus A319-132	2452	ex N812BR	Goztepe	
☐ TC-IZL	Airbus A320-233	1730	ex N486TA	Cesme	
☐ TC-IZM	Airbus A319-132	2404	ex N809BR	Alsancak	
☐ TC-IZR	Airbus A319-132	2414	ex N810BR	Karsiyaka	

KTHY CYPRUS TURKISH AIRLINES — Airkibris (YK/KYV) — Ercan (ECN)

☐ TC-JYK	Airbus A310-203	172	ex F-GEMF	Erenköy	stored IST
☐ TC-TCC	Airbus A320-232	3259	ex VT-INM		

☐ TC-KTD	Airbus A321-211	2117	ex D-AVZB	Iskele	
☐ TC-CTA	Boeing 737-86N	35643/2884	ex N1786B	Mesarya	
☐ TC-MAO	Boeing 737-86N	28645/840	ex N1795B	Karpaz	
☐ TC-MSO	Boeing 737-8S3	29246/475	ex N1787B	Magusa	
☐ TC-MZZ	Boeing 737-8S3	29247/493		Guzelyurt	

KUZU CARGO AIRLINES — ***Kuzu Cargo (GO/KZU)*** — ***Istanbul-Ataturk (IST)***

☐ TC-ABK	Airbus A300B4-203	101	ex N59101	Adiyaman	
☐ TC-AGK	Airbus A300B4-203F	117	ex G-CEXH	Siirt 5	Lsd to AHK
☐ TC-KZU	Airbus A300B4-203	173	ex (TC-ORK)	Siirt 2	Lsd to AHK
☐ TC-KZV	Airbus A300B4-103F	041	ex PH-EAN	Siirt 4	
☐ TC-KZY	Airbus A300B4-103F	044	ex PH-CLA	Siirt 3	
☐ TC-LER	Airbus A310-304F	646	ex A6-EFA		
☐ TC-SGM	Airbus A310-304F	592	ex A6-EFB		
☐ TC-VEL	Airbus A310-304F	622	ex A6-EFC		

MARIN AIR — ***Antalya / Bodrum-Marina / Marmaris-Marina (AYT/-/-)***

☐ TC-KEU	Cessna 208 Caravan I	20800317	ex N52234	Floatplane	

MNG CARGO AIRLINES — ***Black Sea (MB/MNB)*** — ***Istanbul-Ataturk (IST)***

☐ TC-MCB	Airbus A300B4-203F	304	ex N308FV		
☐ TC-MNA	Airbus A300B4-203F	019	ex N742SC		
☐ TC-MNB	Airbus A300B4-203F	292	ex HL7279		
☐ TC-MNC	Airbus A300B4-203F	277	ex HL7278		
☐ TC-MND	Airbus A300C4-203F	212	ex ZS-SDG		Lsd to Ceiba Cargo
☐ TC-MNJ	Airbus A300B4-203F	123	ex PH-JLH		
☐ TC-MNU	Airbus A300B4-203F	047	ex N740SC		
☐ TC-MNV	Airbus A300C4-605R	758	ex TF-ELG		
☐ TC-	Boeing 737-4K5SF	24126/1697	ex EC-KRD		
☐ TC-MBA	Fokker F.27 Friendship 500	10654	ex G-CEXE		
☐ TC-MBF	Fokker F.27 Friendship 600	10405	ex G-BNIZ		
☐ TC-MBH	Fokker F.27 Friendship 500	10550	ex G-CEXB		

ONUR AIR — ***Onur Air (8Q/OHY)*** — ***Istanbul-Ataturk (IST)***

☐ TC-OAA	Airbus A300B4-605R	744	ex F-WQRD		
☐ TC-OAB	Airbus A300B4-605R	749	ex F-WQRC	Safuan 1	
☐ TC-OAG	Airbus A300B4-605R	747	ex F-OHLN		
☐ TC-OAH	Airbus A300B4-605R	584	ex S7-RGO		
☐ TC-OAO	Airbus A300B4-605R	764	ex D-AIAW		
☐ TC-OAZ	Airbus A300B4-605R	603	ex SX-BEM		
☐ TC-ONT	Airbus A300B4-203	138	ex ZS-SDE	Kaptan Bilal Basar	
☐ TC-ONU	Airbus A300B4-203	192	ex ZS-SDF	B Basar	
☐ TC-OBD	Airbus A320-232	0455	ex N11112		
☐ TC-OBE	Airbus A320-232	0471	ex VT-WAB		
☐ TC-OAE	Airbus A321-231	0663	ex F-OHMP		
☐ TC-OAF	Airbus A321-231	0668	ex F-OHMQ		
☐ TC-OAI	Airbus A321-231	0787	ex D-AVZL		
☐ TC-OAK	Airbus A321-231	0954	ex D-ALAI		
☐ TC-OAL	Airbus A321-231	1004	ex D-ALAK		
☐ TC-OAN	Airbus A321-231	1421	ex D-ALAP		Lsd to BGH
☐ TC-OBF	Airbus A321-231	0963	ex OE-IAA		on order
☐ TC-ONJ	Airbus A321-131	0385	ex D-AVZG	Kaptan Koray Sahin	
☐ TC-ONS	Airbus A321-131	0364	ex D-AVZD	Funda	
☐ TC-OAS	McDonnell-Douglas MD-83	53465/2093	ex N162BS		
☐ TC-OAT	McDonnell-Douglas MD-83	53466/2101	ex N163BS		
☐ TC-OAU	McDonnell-Douglas MD-83	53488/2134	ex N164BS		
☐ TC-ONM	McDonnell-Douglas MD-88	53546/2167		Yasemin	
☐ TC-ONN	McDonnell-Douglas MD-88	53547/2176		Ece	
☐ TC-ONO	McDonnell-Douglas MD-88	53548/2180		Yonca	
☐ TC-ONP	McDonnell-Douglas MD-88	53549/2185		Esra	
☐ TC-ONR	McDonnell-Douglas MD-88	53550/2187		Evren	

PEGASUS AIRLINES — ***Sunturk (1I/PGT)*** — ***Istanbul-Ataturk (IST)***

☐ TC-AAD	Boeing 737-5Q8	28201/2999	ex PT-SSF		
☐ TC-AAF	Boeing 737-58E	29122/2991	ex N291SZ		
☐ TC-AAG	Boeing 737-5L9	29234/3068	ex ES-ABI		
☐ TC-APD	Boeing 737-42R	29107/2997			
☐ TC-APR	Boeing 737-4Y0	24685/1859	ex EC-GXR		
☐ TC-AAE	Boeing 737-82R/W	35700/2435		Hayirli	
☐ TC-AAH	Boeing 737-82R/W	35701/2496		Hanim	
☐ TC-AAI	Boeing 737-82R/W	35699/2712			

☐ TC-AAJ	Boeing 737-82R/W	35702/2810	ex N1787B	Ece	
☐ TC-AAK	Boeing 737-8FH/W	35094/2195			
☐ TC-AAL	Boeing 737-82R/W	35984/2937	ex N1786B		
☐ TC-AAN	Boeing 737-82R/W	38173/3011			
☐ TC-AAO	Boeing 737-86N/W	28619/534	ex EI-DJU		
☐ TC-AAP	Boeing 737-86N/W	32736/1113			
☐ TC-AAR	Boeing 737-86N/W	28624/585	ex EI-DGZ		
☐ TC-APH	Boeing 737-8S3/W	29250/792	ex N1787B		
☐ TC-API	Boeing 737-86N/W	32732/1056			Lsd to BBC
☐ TC-APJ	Boeing 737-86N/W	32735/1104			
☐ TC-APU	Boeing 737-82R	29344/849	ex N1786B		

REDSTAR AVIATION — ***Istanbul-Sabiha Gokcen (SAW)***

☐ TC-RSA	British Aerospace Jetstream 32EP	986	ex G-CBDA		

SAGA AIRLINES — ***(SGX)*** — ***Istanbul-Ataturk (IST)***

☐ TC-SGA	Airbus A300B2K-3C	090	ex JA8466	Kemal Kolot	Lsd to IRM
☐ TC-SGB	Airbus A310-304	562	ex N351LF	Akçaabat	
☐ TC-SGC	Airbus A310-304	519	ex VT-EVI	Fethiya Kolot	
☐ TC-SGD	Boeing 737-48E	25773/2905	ex VT-JAM		
☐ TC-SGE	Boeing 737-48E	25775/2925	ex VT-JAN	Kalrel Alodolou	
☐ TC-SGF	Boeing 737-83N/W	28249/1123	ex N321TZ		
☐ TC-SGG	Boeing 737-83N/W	30706/929	ex N305TZ		
☐ TC-SGH	Boeing 737-86J/W	28068/36	ex D-ABAN	Vakfikebir	
☐ TC-SGJ	Airbus A330-343	407	ex B-HYH		

SKY AIRLINES — ***Antalya Bird (SHY)*** — ***Antalya (AYT)***

☐ TC-SKB	Boeing 737-430	27004/2344	ex EI-CPU	StarAdam+Eve	
☐ TC-SKD	Boeing 737-4Q8	25372/2280	ex TC-JDI	Black Eagle	Lsd DAH
☐ TC-SKE	Boeing 737-4Q8	25163/2264	ex VH-TJV	Milky Way	
☐ TC-SKF	Boeing 737-4Q8	26291/2513	ex HL7591	Sugar	
☐ TC-SKG	Boeing 737-4Q8	25371/2195	ex SX-BKK	Gold	
☐ TC-SKH	Boeing 737-8BK	29644/2231	ex N1786B	Rainbow	
☐ TC-SKI	Airbus A321-231	0811	ex D-ALAA	Antalya	
☐ TC-SKJ	Airbus A320-211	0138	ex N138LC	Jupiter	
☐ TC-SKK	Airbus A320-211	0148	ex N148LC	Side	
☐ TC-SKL	Airbus A321-231	1670	ex HL7712		
☐ TC-SKM	Boeing 737-49R	28882/2845	ex OK-CGI		
☐ TC-SKN	Boeing 737-94XER/W	36086/2910	ex N1787B	Alanya Smile in the Sky	
☐ TC-SKP	Boeing 737-94XER/W	36087/2928	ex N1786B	Kapadokya	

SUNEXPRESS — ***Sunexpress (XQ/SXS)*** — ***Antalya (AYT)***

☐ TC-SNE	Boeing 737-8HX/W	29684/2539	ex N1786B
☐ TC-SNF	Boeing 737-8HC/W	36529/2566	ex N1787B
☐ TC-SNG	Boeing 737-8HC/W	36530/2622	ex N1786B
☐ TC-SNH	Boeing 737-8FH/W	30826/1732	ex EI-ECD
☐ TC-SNI	Boeing 737-8FH/W	29671/1700	ex EI-DMZ
☐ TC-SNJ	Boeing 737-86J/W	30827/1632	ex D-ABBO
☐ TC-SUG	Boeing 737-8CX/W	32365/1209	
☐ TC-SUH	Boeing 737-8CX/W	32366/1235	
☐ TC-SUI	Boeing 737-8CX/W	32367/1253	
☐ TC-SUJ	Boeing 737-8CX/W	32368/1289	
☐ TC-SUL	Boeing 737-85F/W	28822/166	ex SE-DVO
☐ TC-SUM	Boeing 737-85F/W	28826/238	ex SE-DVR
☐ TC-SUO	Boeing 737-86Q/W	30272/824	ex VH-VOE
☐ TC-SUU	Boeing 737-86Q/W	30274/845	ex VH-VOF
☐ TC-SUV	Boeing 737-86N/W	30807/829	ex N50089
☐ TC-SUY	Boeing 737-86N/W	30806/790	ex G-OXLB
☐ TC-SUZ	Boeing 737-8HXS/W	29649/2515	ex N1786B
☐ TC-SNB	Boeing 757-2Q8/W	26271/592	ex N804AM
☐ TC-SNC	Boeing 757-2Q8/W	26273/597	ex N806AM
☐ TC-SND	Boeing 757-2Q8/W	26268/590	ex N803AM

TAILWIND AIRLINES

☐ TC-TLA	Boeing 737-4Q8	25107/2526	ex N774AS	
☐ TC-TLB	Boeing 737-4Q8	25108/2551	ex N775AS	
☐ TC-TLC	Boeing 737-4Q8	25112/2638	ex N780AS	Capt Z Kllic

TARHAN AIR — ***(TTH)*** — ***Istanbul-Ataturk (IST)***

☐ TC-TTA	McDonnell-Douglas MD-83	48096/1057	ex TC-MNT	Surmeli	stored IST
☐ TC-TTB	McDonnell-Douglas MD-82	49144/1096	ex N800NK	Ufuk	stored IST

THK-TURK HAVA KURUMU — Hur Kus (THK) — Ankara (ANK)

☐ TC-CAU	Cessna 208 Caravan I	20800248	ex N1123X	
☐ TC-CAV	Cessna 208 Caravan I	20800256	ex N1249T	
☐ TC-CAY	Cessna 402B	402B1073	ex 10007	
☐ TC-CAZ	Cessna 421C Golden Eagle II	421C0089	ex 10006	
☐ TC-FAH	Piper PA-42-720 Cheyenne IIIA	42-5501033		
☐ TC-THK	Piper PA-42-720 Cheyenne IIIA	42-5501031	ex TC-FAG	
☐ TC-ZTP	Cessna 402B	402B0412	ex N69289	
☐ TC-ZVJ	Cessna 402B	402B1084	ex N1906G	

TURKISH AIRLINES — Turkair (TK/THY) — Istanbul-Ataturk (IST)

Member of Star Alliance

☐ TC-JCT	Airbus A310-304F	502	ex TF-ELE	Samsun
☐ TC-JCV	Airbus A310-304F	476	ex F-WWCT	Aras
☐ TC-JCY	Airbus A310-304F	478	ex F-WWCX	Coruh
☐ TC-JCZ	Airbus A310-304F	480	ex F-WWCZ	Ergene
☐ TC-JLJ	Airbus A320-232	1856	ex EI-DIV	Sirnak
☐ TC-JLK	Airbus A320-232	1909	ex EI-DIW	Kirklareli
☐ TC-JLL	Airbus A320-232	1956	ex EI-DIX	Duzce
☐ TC-JLM	Airbus A319-132	2738	ex D-AVXN	Sinop
☐ TC-JLN	Airbus A319-132	2739	ex D-AVXO	Karabuk
☐ TC-JLO	Airbus A319-132	2631	ex TC-OGU	
☐ TC-JLP	Airbus A319-132	2655	ex TC-OGV	Koycegiz
☐ TC-JPA	Airbus A320-232	2609	ex F-WWBU	Mus
☐ TC-JPB	Airbus A320-232	2626	ex F-WWDS	Rize
☐ TC-JPC	Airbus A320-232	2928	ex F-WWDZ	Erzurum
☐ TC-JPD	Airbus A320-232	2934	ex F-WWIC	Isparta
☐ TC-JPE	Airbus A320-232	2941	ex F-WWIF	Gumushane
☐ TC-JPF	Airbus A320-232	2984	ex F-WWIE	Yozgat
☐ TC-JPG	Airbus A320-232	3010	ex F-WWBJ	Osmaniye
☐ TC-JPH	Airbus A320-232	3185	ex F-WWDX	Kars
☐ TC-JPI	Airbus A320-232	3208	ex F-WWIS	Dogubevazit
☐ TC-JPJ	Airbus A320-232	3239	ex F-WWBK	Edremit
☐ TC-JPK	Airbus A320-232	3257	ex F-WWDI	Erdek
☐ TC-JPL	Airbus A320-232	3303	ex F-WWIJ	Göreme
☐ TC-JPM	Airbus A320-232	3341	ex F-WWBN	
☐ TC-JPN	Airbus A320-232	3558	ex F-WWBE	Sarikamis
☐ TC-JPO	Airbus A320-232	3567	ex F-WWBP	Kemer
☐ TC-JPP	Airbus A320-232	3603	ex F-WWDL	Harran
☐ TC-JPR	Airbus A320-232	3654	ex F-WWDR	Kusadasi
☐ TC-JPS	Airbus A320-232	3718	ex F-WWBK	
☐ TC-JPT	Airbus A320-232	3719	ex D-AVVC	Urgup
☐ TC-JMC	Airbus A321-231	0806	ex G-MIDA	Aksaray
☐ TC-JMD	Airbus A321-231	0810	ex G-MIDF	Cankiri
☐ TC-JME	Airbus A321-211	1219	ex EC-IMA	Burdur
☐ TC-JMF	Airbus A321-211	1233	ex EC-ILG	Bingol
☐ TC-JMH	Airbus A321-231	3637	ex D-AVZM	Didim
☐ TC-JMI	Airbus A321-231	3673	ex D-AVZZ	Milas
☐ TC-JMJ	Airbus A321-231	3688	ex D-AZAG	Tekirdag
☐ TC-JMK	Airbus A321-231	3738	ex D-AZAK	Uskudar
☐ TC-JML	Airbus A321-231	3382	ex G-TTIG	Eminonu
☐ TC-JRA	Airbus A321-231	2823	ex D-AVZE	
☐ TC-JRB	Airbus A321-231	2868	ex D-AVZI	Sanliurfa
☐ TC-JRC	Airbus A321-231	2999	ex D-AVZV	Sakarya
☐ TC-JRD	Airbus A321-231	3015	ex D-AVZX	Balikesir
☐ TC-JRE	Airbus A321-231	3126	ex D-AVZS	Trabzon
☐ TC-JRF	Airbus A321-231	3207	ex D-AVZY	Fethiye
☐ TC-JRG	Airbus A321-231	3283	ex D-AVZZ	Finike
☐ TC-JRH	Airbus A321-231	3350	ex D-AVZI	
☐ TC-JRI	Airbus A321-231	3405	ex D-AVZS	
☐ TC-JRJ	Airbus A321-231	3429	ex D-AVZC	
☐ TC-JRK	Airbus A321-231	3525	ex D-AVZY	
☐ TC-JRL	Airbus A321-231	3539	ex D-AVZB	Tarsus
☐ TC-JNA	Airbus A330-203	697	ex F-WWYS	Gaziantep
☐ TC-JNB	Airbus A330-203	704	ex F-WWKF	Konya
☐ TC-JNC	Airbus A330-203	742	ex F-WWYF	Bursa
☐ TC-JND	Airbus A330-203	754	ex F-WWYL	Antalya
☐ TC-JNE	Airbus A330-203	774	ex F-WWKG	Kayseri
☐ TC-JNF	Airbus A330-202	463	ex A7-AFN	Canakkale
☐ TC-JNG	Airbus A330-202	504	ex A7-AFO	Esklsehir
☐ TC-JDJ	Airbus A340-311	023	ex F-WWJN	Istanbul
☐ TC-JDK	Airbus A340-311	025	ex F-WWJP	Isparta
☐ TC-JDL	Airbus A340-311	057	ex F-WWJF	Ankara
☐ TC-JDM	Airbus A340-311	115	ex F-WWJN	Izmir
☐ TC-JDN	Airbus A340-313X	180	ex F-WWJU	Adana

☐ TC-JIH	Airbus A340-313X	270	ex F-WWJP	Hakkari	
☐ TC-JII	Airbus A340-313X	331	ex F-WWJQ	Aydin	
☐ TC-JIJ	Airbus A340-313X	216	ex 6Y-JMM	Selcuk	
☐ TC-JIK	Airbus A340-313X	257	ex 6Y-JMP	Kas	
☐ TC-	Airbus A340-313X		ex F-WW		on order
☐ TC-	Airbus A340-313X		ex F-WW		on order
☐ TC-JDG	Boeing 737-4Y0	25181/2203		Marmaris	
☐ TC-JDH	Boeing 737-4Y0	25184/2227		Amasra	Lsd to BON
☐ TC-JFC	Boeing 737-8F2/W	29765/80		Diyarbakir	
☐ TC-JFD	Boeing 737-8F2/W	29766/87		Artvin	
☐ TC-JFE	Boeing 737-8F2/W	29767/95	ex N1786B	Hatay	
☐ TC-JFF	Boeing 737-8F2/W	29768/99	ex N1786B	Afyonkarahisar	
☐ TC-JFG	Boeing 737-8F2/W	29769/102	ex N1787B	Mardin	
☐ TC-JFH	Boeing 737-8F2/W	29770/114	ex N1787B	Igdir	
☐ TC-JFI	Boeing 737-8F2/W	29771/228	ex N1795B	Sivas	
☐ TC-JFJ	Boeing 737-8F2/W	29772/242	ex N1786B	Agri	
☐ TC-JFK	Boeing 737-8F2/W	29773/259	ex N1786B	Zonguldak	
☐ TC-JFL	Boeing 737-8F2/W	29774/269	ex N1786B	Ordu	
☐ TC-JFM	Boeing 737-8F2/W	29775/279	ex N1786B	Nigde	
☐ TC-JFN	Boeing 737-8F2/W	29776/308		Bitlis	
☐ TC-JFO	Boeing 737-8F2/W	29777/309		Batman	
☐ TC-JFP	Boeing 737-8F2/W	29778/349	ex N1787B	Amasya	
☐ TC-JFR	Boeing 737-8F2/W	29779/370	ex N1786B	Giresun	
☐ TC-JFT	Boeing 737-8F2/W	29780/454	ex N1787B	Kastamonu	
☐ TC-JFU	Boeing 737-8F2/W	29781/461	ex N1795B	Elazig	
☐ TC-JFV	Boeing 737-8F2/W	29782/490	ex N1786B	Tuncell	
☐ TC-JFY	Boeing 737-8F2/W	29783/497	ex N1786B	Manisa	
☐ TC-JFZ	Boeing 737-8F2/W	29784/539		Bolu	
☐ TC-JGA	Boeing 737-8F2/W	29785/544	ex N1786B	Malatya	
☐ TC-JGB	Boeing 737-8F2/W	29786/566	ex N1786B	Foca	
☐ TC-JGC	Boeing 737-8F2/W	29787/771	ex N1786B	Kocaeli	
☐ TC-JGD	Boeing 737-8F2/W	29788/791	ex N1787B	Nevsehir	
☐ TC-JGF	Boeing 737-8F2/W	29790/1088	ex N1786B	Ardahan	
☐ TC-JGG	Boeing 737-8F2/W	34405/1828		Erzincan	
☐ TC-JGH	Boeing 737-8F2/W	34406/1852		Tokat	
☐ TC-JGI	Boeing 737-8F2/W	34407/1873		Siirt	
☐ TC-JGJ	Boeing 737-8F2/W	34408/1880		Aydin	
☐ TC-JGK	Boeing 737-8F2	34409/1924	ex N1786B	Kirsehir	
☐ TC-JGL	Boeing 737-8F2	34410/1927	ex N1787B	Karaman	
☐ TC-JGM	Boeing 737-8F2/W	34411/1944		Hakkari	
☐ TC-JGN	Boeing 737-8F2/W	34412/1949		Bilecik	
☐ TC-JGO	Boeing 737-8F2/W	34413/1972	ex N1786B	Kilis	
☐ TC-JGP	Boeing 737-8F2/W	34414/1978	ex N1786B	Bartin	
☐ TC-JGR	Boeing 737-8F2/W	34415/1988	ex N1786B	Usak	
☐ TC-JGS	Boeing 737-8F2/W	34416/1996		Kahramanmaras	
☐ TC-JGT	Boeing 737-8F2/W	34417/2009		Avanos	
☐ TC-JGU	Boeing 737-8F2/W	34418/2012			
☐ TC-JGV	Boeing 737-8F2/W	34419/2021	ex N60668		
☐ TC-JGY	Boeing 737-8F2/W	35738/2592		Manavgat	
☐ TC-JGZ	Boeing 737-8F2/W	35739/2654		Midyat	
☐ TC-JHA	Boeing 737-8F2/W	35740/2673		Mudanya	
☐ TC-JHB	Boeing 737-8F2/W	35741/2685		Safranbolu	
☐ TC-JHC	Boeing 737-8F2/W	35742/2708		Iskenderun	
☐ TC-JHD	Boeing 737-8F2/W	35743/2717		Serik	
☐ TC-JHE	Boeing 737-8F2/W	357442733	ex N1786B	Burhanlye	
☐ TC-JHF	Boeing 737-8F2/W	35745/2748		Ayvalik	
☐ TC-JJA	Boeing 777-35RER	35160/653	ex VT-JED	Akdeniz	
☐ TC-JJB	Boeing 777-35RER	35162/666	ex VT-JEF		
☐ TC-JJC	Boeing 777-35RER	35164/660	ex VT-JEE	Karadeniz	
☐ TC-JJD	Boeing 777-35RER	35159/650	ex VT-JEC		

TURKUAZ AIR — *Istanbul-Ataturk (IST)*

☐ TC-TCD	Airbus A320-232	3308	ex VT-INN
☐ TC-TCE	Airbus A321-211	0666	ex 6Y-JMD
☐ TC-TCF	Airbus A321-211	0775	ex 6Y-JME
☐ TC-TCG	Airbus A321-211	1905	ex N361LF
☐ TC-TCH	Airbus A320-214	2048	ex N351LF

UENSPED PAKET SERVISI/ UPS — *Unsped (UNS)* — *Istanbul-Ataturk (IST)*

☐ TC-APS	Cessna 340A	340A0247	ex N3964G		
☐ TC-UPS	Swearingen SA.226TC Merlin IVA	AT-044	ex TC-BPS	Beril	Op for UPS

TF- ICELAND (Republic of Iceland)

AIR ATLANTA — *Atlanta (CC/ABD)* — *Keflavik (KEF)*

	Registration	Type	c/n	Previous	Name	Remarks
☐	TF-ELF	Airbus A300B4-622RF	529	ex EI-DJN		
☐	TF-ELK	Airbus A300B4-622RF	557	ex EI-DGU		op for ETD
☐	TF-ELW	Airbus A300C4-605R	755	ex D-ABFH		Lsd to MAS
☐	TF-AAA	Boeing 747-236B (SCD)	22442/526	ex N361FC		Lsd to MAS
☐	TF-AMD	Boeing 747-243M	23476/647	ex N518MC		
☐	TF-AME	Boeing 747-312	23032/603	ex F-GSEA		
☐	TF-AMI	Boeing 747-412 (SF)	27066/940	ex N706RB		Lsd to SVA
☐	TF-AMJ	Boeing 747-312	23030/593	ex CP-2525		
☐	TF-AMK	Boeing 747-312	23028/584	ex F-GSEX		Lsd to GMG A/I
☐	TF-AMS	Boeing 747-481BCF	24920/832	ex JA8096		Lsd to SVA
☐	TF-AMT	Boeing 747-481	25135/863	ex JA8097		Lsd to SVA
☐	TF-AMU	Boeing 747-48EF	27603/1210	ex HL7426		Lsd to SVA
☐	TF-AMV	Boeing 747-412	28022/1082	ex 9V-SPI		Lsd to SVA
☐	TF-ARH	Boeing 747-230M (SF)	22669/549	ex N531TA		
☐	TF-ARJ	Boeing 747-236M	23735/674	ex G-BDXN		Lsd to MAS
☐	TF-ARL	Boeing 747-230B (SF)	22671/574	ex VP-BXE		
☐	TF-ARM	Boeing 747-230B (SF)	22363/490	ex N744SA		
☐	TF-ARN	Boeing 747-2F6B (SF)	22382/498	ex N745SA		Lsd to MAS
☐	TF-ARP	Boeing 747-230F	23348/625	ex VP-BXD		
☐	TF-ARU	Boeing 747-344	22970/577	ex ZS-SAT		
☐	TF-ATI	Boeing 747-341	24107/702	ex N824DS		Lsd to SVA
☐	TF-ATJ	Boeing 747-341	24108/703	ex N420DS		Lsd to SVA
☐	TF-ATZ	Boeing 747-236B (SF)	24088/697	ex G-BDXP		
☐	TF-	Boeing 747-481BCF		ex JA		on order
☐	TF-	Boeing 747-481BCF		ex JA		on order

AIR ICELAND — *Iceland (NY/FXI)* — *Akureyri/Reykjavik (AEY/REK)*

	Registration	Type	c/n	Previous	Name	Remarks
☐	TF-JMM	Fokker F.27 Mk.050 (Fokker 50)	20214	ex D-AFKM		
☐	TF-JMN	Fokker F.27 Mk.050 (Fokker 50)	20223	ex D-AFKN		
☐	TF-JMO	Fokker F.27 Mk.050 (Fokker 50)	20205	ex D-AFKK		
☐	TF-JMR	Fokker F.27 Mk.050 (Fokker 50)	20243	ex TF-FIR	Asdis	
☐	TF-JMS	Fokker F.27 Mk.050 (Fokker 50)	20244	ex TF-FIS	Sigdis	
☐	TF-JMT	Fokker F.27 Mk.050 (Fokker 50)	20250	ex TF-FIT	Freydis	
☐	TF-JMA	de Havilland DHC-8-106	335	ex C-FIZE		
☐	TF-JMB	de Havilland DHC-8-106	337	ex C-FHYQ		
☐	TF-JMC	de Havilland DHC-6 Twin Otter 300	413	ex C-GIZR		
☐	TF-JMD	de Havilland DHC-6 Twin Otter 300	475	ex C-GDAA		

BLUEBIRD CARGO — *Blue Cargo (BF/BBD)* — *Keflavik (KEF)*

	Registration	Type	c/n	Previous
☐	TF-BBD	Boeing 737-3Y0 (SF)	24463/1701	ex OY-SEE
☐	TF-BBE	Boeing 737-36E (SF)	25256/2123	ex N314FL
☐	TF-BBF	Boeing 737-36E (SF)	25264/2194	ex N316FL
☐	TF-BBG	Boeing 737-36E (SF)	25263/2187	ex N317FL
☐	TF-BBH	Boeing 737-4Y0F	23865/1582	ex N865FC

ERNIR AIR — *Artic Eagle (FEI)* — *Reykjavik (REK)*

	Registration	Type	c/n	Previous
☐	TF-ORA	British Aerospace Jetstream 32	925	ex OY-SVR
☐	TF-ORB	Cessna 207A Stationair 8 II	20700781	ex OY-SUC
☐	TF-ORC	British Aerospace Jetstream 3212	981	ex OY-SVY
☐	TF-ORD	Reims Cessna F406 Caravan II	F406-0047	ex D-IAAD
☐	TF-ORF	Cessna 441 Conquest II	441-0057	ex N441AK

ICEJET — *Icejet (ICJ)*

	Registration	Type	c/n	Previous
☐	TF-MIK	Dornier 328-300 (328JET)	3147	ex N402FJ
☐	TF-MIL	Dornier 328-300 (328JET)	3149	ex N403FJ
☐	TF-MIO	Dornier 328-300 (328JET)	3181	ex N423FJ
☐	TF-NPA	Dornier 328-300 (328JET)	3220	ex D-BDXC
☐	TF-NPB	Dornier 328-300 (328JET)	3161	ex TF-MIM

ICELANDAIR — *Iceair (FI/ICE)* — *Keflavik/Reykjavik (KEF/REK)*

	Registration	Type	c/n	Previous	Name	Remarks
☐	TF-CIB	Boeing 757-204 (PCF)	26962/440	ex N512NA		
☐	TF-FIA	Boeing 757-256/W	29310/938	ex EC-HIT	Herdubreid	
☐	TF-FID	Boeing 757-23A (PCF)	24567/257	ex N757NA		TNT c/s
☐	TF-FIE	Boeing 757-23A (PCF)	24566/255	ex N566AN		
☐	TF-FIG	Boeing 757-23APF	24456/237	ex N571CA		
☐	TF-FIH	Boeing 757-208 (PCF)	24739/273		Hafdis	
☐	TF-FII	Boeing 757-208	24760/281		Fanndis	
☐	TF-FIJ	Boeing 757-208/W	25085/368	ex G-BTEJ	Surtsey	
☐	TF-FIN	Boeing 757-208/W	28989/780	ex N1790B	Edborg	

☐ TF-FIO	Boeing 757-208/W	29436/859		Krafla
☐ TF-FIP	Boeing 757-208/W	30423/916	ex N1006K	Leifur Eriksson
☐ TF-FIR	Boeing 757-256/W	26242/593	ex EC-FYJ	
☐ TF-FIU	Boeing 757-256/W	26243/603	ex PH-ITA	Hekla
☐ TF-FIV	Boeing 757-208/W	30424/956		Katla
☐ TF-FIX	Boeing 757-308	29434/1004	ex N60659	Henglil
☐ TF-FIZ	Boeing 757-256/W	30052/948	ex EC-HIX	Keilir
☐ TF-FIB	Boeing 767-383ER	25365/395	ex N365SR	

ICELAND EXPRESS — *Reykjavik (REK)*

☐ G-STRF	Boeing 737-76N/W	29885/1120	ex EI-CXD
☐ G-STRN	Boeing 737-7L9	28007/136	ex D-AABH

LOFTLEIDIR ICELANDIC

Operates charter flights and ACMI leases using the AOC of its parent, Icelandair, from whom the aircraft are leased

MYFLUG — *Myflug (MYA)* — *Myvatn (MVA)*

☐ TF-MYF	Cessna U206G Stationair 6 II	U20606614	ex TC-FAE	
☐ TF-MYX	Beech 200 Super King Air	BB-1136	ex LN-VIZ	
☐ TF-MYY	Cessna U206F Stationair	U20602831	ex N35960	
☐ TF-SEA	Cessna 208 Caravan I	20800118	ex N9678F	Floatplane

WESTMANN ISLANDS AIRLINES — *Reykjavik (REK)*

☐ TF-VEJ	Britten-Norman BN-2B-26 Islander	2209	ex G-BPLR
☐ TF-VEV	Piper PA-31-350 Chieftain	31-8152007	ex N4051Q
☐ TF-VEY	Partenavia P.68B	109	ex G-JVMR

TG- GUATEMALA (Republic of Guatemala)

AEREO RUTA MAYA — *Guatemala City-La Aurora (GUA)*

☐ TG-ARM	Cessna 208B Caravan I	208B0768	ex N5152X
☐ TG-JCA	de Havilland DHC-6 Twin Otter 300	647	ex N300WH
☐ TG-JCB	Cessna 208B Caravan I	20800325	ex N5212M
☐ TG-JCC	Embraer EMB.110P2 Bandeirante	110348	ex N57DA
☐ TG-JCO	Embraer EMB.110P2 Bandeirante	110350	ex N102EB
☐ TG-JCS	Cessna 208B Caravan I	20800327	ex N5268E
☐ TG-TJG	LET L-410UVP-E	902419	ex CCCP-67626
☐ TG-TJH	LET L-410UVP-E	902418	ex CCCP-67625

Possibly also trades as Jungle Flying

AVIATECA — *Guatemala City-La Aurora (GUA)*

☐ TG-TRA	ATR 42-300 (QC)	312	ex 9A-CTS
☐ TG-TRB	ATR 42-300 (QC)	317	ex 9A-CTT

AVCOM — *Guatemala City-La Aurora (GUA)*

☐ TG-JAB	Rockwell 500S Shrike Commander	3303		
☐ TG-JAD	Rockwell 500S Shrike Commander	3123	ex N500MT	
☐ TG-JAM	Aero Commander 500B	1594-205	ex TG-HIA	
☐ TG-JAY	de Havilland DHC-7-102	46	ex C-FYMK	Mundo Maya
☐ TG-JWC	Rockwell 500S Shrike Commander	3209		

DHL DE GUATEMELA — *(L3/JOS)* — *Guatemala City-La Aurora (GUA)*

☐ TG-DHP	ATR 42-300	052	ex YV-876C

Operates in DHL colours

INTER - TRANSPORTES AEREOS INTER — *Transpo-Inter (9O/TSP)* — *Guatemala City-La Aurora (GUA)*

☐ TG-MYH	ATR 42-300	113	ex G-ZAPJ	Lsd to APP
☐ TG-RMM	Cessna 208B Caravan I	208B0614	ex TI-LRV	

JUNGLE FLYING — *Guatemala City-La Aurora (GUA)*

☐ TG-AGY	LET L-410UVP	851404	ex HR-IBC
☐ TG-JFT	Cessna 208B Caravan I	208B0622	ex N52601

RACSA (RUTAS AEREAS CENTRO AMERICANOS) — *(R6)* — *Guatemala City-La Aurora (GUA)*

☐ TG-JSG	Nord 262	37	ex HK-3878X

TRANSPORTES AEREOS GUATEMALTECOS (GUM)			Guatemala City-La Aurora (GUA)
☐ TG-BJO	SAAB SF.340A	340A-142	ex N142XJ	
☐ TG-TAA	Piper PA-23-250 Aztec E	27-7304965	ex TG-PYM	
☐ TG-TAB	Bell 206L LongRanger I	45315	ex N2775G	
☐ TG-TAJ	LET L-410UVP	800527	ex N26RZ	
☐ TG-TAT	Piper PA-31 Turbo Najavo B	31-826	ex N7438L	
☐ TG-TAG	Embraer EMB.110P1 Bandeirante	110441	ex VH-LNB	
☐ TG-TAK	Embraer EMB.110P1 Bandeirante	110405	ex C-FPCO	
☐ TG-TAM	Embraer EMB.110P1 Bandeirante	110220	ex N101RA	
☐ TG-TAN	Embraer EMB.110P1 Bandeirante	110342	ex C-GPCQ	
☐ TG-TAY	Embraer EMB.110P1 Bandeirante	110218	ex N127JM	

TI- COSTA RICA (Republic of Costa Rica)

AEROBELL AIR CHARTER — San José-Tobias Bolanos (SYQ)

☐ TI-BAD	Bell 407	53403	ex N501TH	
☐ TI-BAJ	Cessna 208B Caravan I	208B1180	ex N5058J	
☐ TI-BAY	Cessna 208B Caravan I	208B1218		

AVIONES TAXI AEREO — San José-Juan Santamaria (SJO)

☐ TI-ABA	Piper PA-23-250 Aztec D	27-4229	ex TI-1089C	stored
☐ TI-ACA	Piper PA-23-250 Aztec C	27-3515	ex TI-1058C	
☐ TI-AST	Piper PA-23-250 Aztec E	27-7554074	ex N54763	
☐ TI-ATZ	de Havilland DHC-6 Twin Otter 200	169	ex N931MA	

NATUREAIR (5C/NRR) — San José-Tobias Bolanos (SYQ)

☐ TI-AYQ	de Havilland DHC-6 Twin Otter 300	422	ex F-OGJV	
☐ TI-AZC	de Havilland DHC-6 Twin Otter 300	433	ex N239SA	VistaLiner
☐ TI-BBF	de Havilland DHC-6 Twin Otter 300	683	ex N237SA	VistaLiner
☐ TI-BBQ	de Havilland DHC-6 Twin Otter 300	537	ex N147SA	VistaLiner
☐ TI-	de Havilland DHC-6 Twin Otter 300	285	ex N190GC	
☐ TI-BBN	Beech 65-E90 King Air	LW-250	ex N321DM	

PARADISE AIR — San José-Tobias Bolanos (SYQ)

☐ N13AV	Gippsland GA-8 Airvan	GA8-03-028	ex VH-ARW	
☐ TI-AZY	Gippsland GA-8 Airvan	GA8-02-021	ex N530AV	
☐ TI-BBC	Cessna 208B Caravan I	208B1210	ex N1320U	

SANSA REGIONAL — Sansa (RZ/LRS) — San José-Juan Santamaria (SJO)

☐ TI-BAK	Cessna 208B Caravan I	208B0681	ex HP-1355APP	
☐ TI-BAN	Cessna 208B Caravan I	208B0710	ex HP-1358APP	
☐ TI-BAP	Cessna 208B Caravan I	208B0789	ex HP-1402APP	
☐ TI-BAQ	Cessna 208B Caravan I	208B0790	ex HP-1403APP	
☐ TI-BCU	Cessna 208B Caravan I	208B2045	ex N5166U	
☐ TI-BCV	Cessna 208B Caravan I	208B2050	ex N5148B	
☐ TI-BCX	Cessna 208B Caravan I	208B2058	ex N5040E	
☐ TI-BCY	Cessna 208B Caravan I	208B2064	ex N5214L	
☐ TG-RYM	ATR 42-300	109	ex G-BUPS	

TACA COSTA RICA — TACA CostaRica (TI/TAT) — San José-Juan Santamaria (SJO)

☐ TI-BCF	Embraer 190-100IGW (190AR)	19000205	ex PT-SGO	
☐ TI-BCG	Embraer 190-100IGW (190AR)	19000215	ex PT-SGY	
☐ TI-BCH	Embraer 190-100IGW (190AR)	19000221	ex PT-SHE	
☐ TI-BCI	Embraer 190-100IGW (190AR)	19000228	ex PT-SHS	
☐ TI-	Embraer 190-100IGW (190AR)		ex PT-	on order
☐ TI-	Embraer 190-100IGW (190AR)		ex PT-	on order
☐ TI-	Embraer 190-100IGW (190AR)		ex PT-	on order
☐ TI-	Embraer 190-100IGW (190AR)		ex PT-	on order
☐ TI-	Embraer 190-100IGW (190AR)		ex PT-	on order
☐ TI-	Embraer 190-100IGW (190AR)		ex PT-	on order
☐ TI-	Embraer 190-100IGW (190AR)		ex PT-	on order

TACSA — San José-Tobias Bolanos (SYQ)

☐ TI-ADK	Piper PA-23-250 Aztec C	27-3209	ex TI-1087C	
☐ TI-ADT	Piper PA-31 Turbo Navajo	31-403	ex F-OCOE	
☐ TI-AML	Cessna TU206G Turbo Stationair 6 II	U20605181		
☐ TI-AOW	Piper PA-34-200 Seneca II	34-7670124	ex N8312C	
☐ TI-ATM	Piper PA-23-250 Aztec E	27-7405413	ex N89SL	
☐ TI-ATN	Cessna U206G Stationair 6 II	U20604231	ex N756NU	
☐ TI-ATT	Piper PA-31 Navajo C	31-7512030	ex N500PM	
☐ TI-ATU	Piper PA-31 Navajo C	31-7512011	ex N111MM	
☐ TI-ATX	Piper PA-34-200 Seneca II	34-7970150	ex HP-1013JO	

☐ TI-AVF	Piper PA-31 Turbo Navajo [Panther conv]	31-582	ex N6644L		

TJ- CAMEROON (Republic of Cameroon)

AFRICAN LINES — Douala (DLA)

☐ TJ-ALD	Fokker F.28 Fellowship 4000	11226	ex N477AU		

Status uncertain

CAMEROON AIRLINES — Cam-Air (UY/UYC) — Douala (DLA)

☐ TJ-CAC	Boeing 767-33AER	28138/822		Le Dja	stored YAO
☐ TJ-CAD	Boeing 767-231ER	22564/14	ex N601TW		
☐ TJ-CCG	Hawker Siddeley HS.748 Srs.2B/435	1805	ex G-11-11	Menchum	stored DLA

CHC CAMEROON — Douala (DLA)

☐ TJ-ALL	de Havilland DHC-6 Twin Otter 300	572	ex 5N-AKY		
☐ TJ-CQD	Aérospatiale SA365N Dauphin 2	6062	ex 5N-ARM		
☐ TJ-CQE	de Havilland DHC-6 Twin Otter 300	662	ex 5N-EVS		
☐ TJ-SAB	de Havilland DHC-8-311A	276	ex PH-SDT		
☐ TJ-SAY	Aérospatiale AS365N3 Dauphin 2	6571	ex PH-SLW		

ELYSIAN AIRLINES

☐ ZS-OEN	Embraer EMB.120RT Brasilia	120200	ex N200CD		Lsd fr NRK

NATIONAL AIRWAYS CAMEROON — (9O) — Yaounde (YAO)

☐ ZS-NTT	Beech 200 Super King Air	BB-350	ex N125MS		
☐ ZS-OLY	Beech 1900D	UE-39	ex N39ZV	all-white	

TL- CENTRAL AFRICAN REPUBLIC

AFRICA WEST — Ougadougou (OUA)

☐ S9-BOZ	Antonov An-12A	2340803	ex RA-122375	São Tomé	Lsd fr GLE
☐ UN-11376	Antonov An-12BK	8345805	ex ER-AXQ		

CENTRAFRIQUE AIR EXPRESS

☐ TL-ADR	Boeing 737-268	21281/472	ex HZ-AGL		
☐ TL-ADY	Boeing 727-223 (Raisbeck 3)	21385/1331	ex YK-DGL		

LOBAYE AIRWAYS — (LB) — Bangui (BGF)

☐ TL-ADU	Boeing 737-247 (Nordam 3)	23518/1265	ex N244WA		

MINAIR — Ormine (OMR) — Bangui (BGF)

☐ ZS-TAS	Cessna 208B Caravan I	208B0378	ex N208SA		

PRIVILEGE JET AIRLINES — Bangui (BGF)

☐ TL-ADW	Lockheed L-1011-500 Tristar	293B-1242	ex YK-DLC		

TN- CONGO BRAZZAVILLE (People's Republic of Congo)

AERO FRET BUSINESS — Brazzaville (BZV)

☐ EX-124	Antonov An-12BK	7345403	ex TN-AGZ		
☐ TN-AHH	Antonov An-24RV	47309705	ex 9XR-DB		

AEROSERVICE — Congoserv (BF/RSR) — Brazzaville/Pointe Noire (BZV/PNR)

☐ ER-AZP	Antonov An-24RV	17307002	ex RA-47810		Lsd fr PXA
☐ TN-ACY	Cessna 402B	402B0810	ex TR-LTN		
☐ TN-ADN	Britten-Norman BN-2A-9 Islander	647	ex TL-AAQ		
☐ TN-ADY	Britten-Norman BN-2A-9 Islander	704	ex TR-LWL		
☐ TN-AEK	Cessna 404 Titan II	404-0132	ex TR-LXI		
☐ TN-AFA	CASA C.212-100	CB13-1-151	ex HB-LKX		
☐ TN-AFD	CASA C.212-300	DF72-2-398	ex D4-CBB		

AIR CONGO INTERNATIONAL — Brazzaville (BZV)

☐ TN-AHL	AVIC 1 MA-60	0405	ex B-762L		
☐ TN-AHN	AVIC 1 MA-60	0406	ex B-800L		

☐ TN-AHO	AVIC 1 MA-60	0408	ex B-800L	
☐ TN-AHX	British Aerospace 146 Srs.200	E2051	ex ZS-PZY	
☐ TN-AIB	British Aerospace 146 Srs.200	E2046	ex ZS-SDX	
☐ TN-AIC	British Aerospace 146 Srs.200	E2044	ex TN-AIE	
☐ ZS-AAG	Embraer EMB.120ER Brasilia	120252	ex TN-AHV	

BRAZZA AIRWAYS — Point Noire (PNR)

☐ TN-AHZ	Antonov An-12B	8345507	ex 4R-EXC

CANADIAN AIRWAYS CONGO — Point Noire (PNR)

☐ EX-008	Antonov An-24RV	37308307	ex RA-46502

COMP AIR MOUENE

☐ TN-AHF	LET L-410UVP	830922	ex UR-67366

Status uncertain

EQUAFLIGHT SERVICE — Brazzaville (BZV)

☐ F-GLPJ	Beech 1900C-1	UC-40	ex OY-BVG
☐ F-GVBR	Embraer EMB.120ER Brasilia	120014	ex (F-HAOC)

TRANSAIR CONGO — Trans-Congo (Q8/TSG) — Brazzaville/Pointe Noire (BZV/PNR)

☐ EX-041	Antonov An-24B	99901908	ex TN-AHB	all-white	
☐ TN-AFZ	Boeing 727-23	19839/542	ex D2-FLZ		Lsd fr Kirra
☐ TN-AGD	LET L-410MU	781116	ex RA-02155		
☐ TN-AGK	Antonov An-12BP	402006	ex RA-11991		
☐ TN-AHI	Boeing 737-247 (Nordam 3)	23609/1403	ex N328DL		
☐ TN-AIN	Boeing 737-236	23172/1091	ex N843AL		
☐ ZS-XGV	Fokker F.28 Fellowship 4000	11128	ex SE-DGM		

TR- GABON (Gabonese Republic)

AIR AFFAIRES GABON — Nouvelle Affaires (NVS) — Libreville (LBV)

☐ PH-JXK	Fokker F.27 Mk.050 (Fokker 50)	20233	ex PT-SLK	Lsd fr DNM
☐ TR-LCB	de Havilland DHC-8Q-314	545	ex D-BDTM	
☐ TR-LEM	Cessna 208B Caravan I	208B0585	ex N1205M	
☐ TR-LFO	Beech 1900D	UE-313	ex ZS-OCW	
☐ TR-LFX	Cessna 208B Caravan I	208B0796	ex N99FX	
☐ TR-LGQ	Fokker F.28-0100 (Fokker 100)	11424	ex F-GIOH	

AIR SERVICE GABON — (X7/AGB) — Libreville (LBV)

☐ TR-LFJ	de Havilland DHC-8-311	332	ex N106AV
☐ TR-LGC	de Havilland DHC-8-102	241	ex PH-TTB
☐ TR-LGR	de Havilland DHC-8-102	237	ex PH-TTA
☐ TR-LGS	de Havilland DHC-6 Twin Otter 300	288	ex ZS-OVD
☐ TR-LGU	de Havilland DHC-6 Twin Otter 300	242	ex C-FNAN
☐ TR-LHF	de Havilland DHC-8-102	206	ex C-FHRA

AVIREX — Avirex-Gabon (G2/AVX) — Libreville (LBV)

☐ TR-LEB	Cessna 402B	402B1078	ex TN-AEZ
☐ TR-LEI	Piper PA-31 Turbo Navajo B	31-7300904	ex N4330B
☐ TR-LEQ	Reims Cessna F406 Caravan II	F406-0007	ex LX-LMS
☐ TR-LFG	Cessna 404 Titan II	404-0844	ex TJ-AHY
☐ TR-LGP	Fokker F.28 Fellowship 4000	11126	ex SE-DGL
☐ TR-LHG	Douglas DC-9-32	47198/302	ex 3D-JES
☐ TR-LVR	Cessna 207 Skywagon	20700310	ex N1710U

GABON AIRLINES — (GY/GBK) — Libreville (LBV)

☐ TF-FII	Boeing 757-208	24760/281		Fanndis	Lsd fr ICE
☐ TR-LHP	Boeing 767-222	21877/46	ex N617UA		
☐ TR-LHQ	Boeing 767-222	21878/48	ex N618UA		stored VCV

LA NATIONALE — Libreville (LBV)

☐ ZS-DOC	Dornier 228-202	8104	ex MAAW-R1
☐ ZS-PMS	SAAB SF.340A	340A-059	ex N327PX

SCD AVIATION

☐ TR-NRT	Embraer EMB.120ER Brasilia	120184	ex SX-BHW

SCORPION AIR

☐ TR-LID	Antonov An-26	47302203	ex LZ-MNS		
☐ TR-LIE	Antonov An-26				

SKY GABON SA (GV)

☐ C-FIINM	Convair 580F	454	ex N583P		Lsd fr NRL

TS- TUNISIA

KARTHAGO AIRLINES Karthago (5R/KAJ) Tunis-Carthage/Djerba-Zarzis (TUN/DJE)

☐ TS-IEC	Boeing 737-33A	25010/2008	ex OO-LTW		
☐ TS-IED	Boeing 737-33A	25032/2014	ex OO-LTP		
☐ TS-IEG	Boeing 737-31S	29116/3005	ex D-ADBS		
☐ TS-IEJ	Boeing 737-322	24655/1814	ex N380UA		

NOUVELAIR Nouvelair (BJ/LBT) Monastir (MIB)

☐ TS-INA	Airbus A320-214	1121	ex F-WWBT	Dora	
☐ TS-INB	Airbus A320-214	1175	ex F-WWDO		
☐ TS-INC	Airbus A320-214	1744	ex F-WWBS	Youssef	
☐ TS-IND	Airbus A320-212	0348	ex OY-CNN		Lsd to LAA
☐ TS-INE	Airbus A320-212	0222	ex OY-CNC		Lsd to LAA
☐ TS-INF	Airbus A320-212	0299	ex G-JDFW		
☐ TS-INI	Airbus A320-212	0301	ex OY-CNM		
☐ TS-INK	Airbus A320-211	0112	ex A6-ABY		
☐ TS-INL	Airbus A320-212	0400	ex N346NW		
☐ TS-INM	Airbus A320-211	0246	ex EC-GRJ		
☐ TS-INN	Airbus A320-212	0793	ex D-AICB		
☐ TS-INO	Airbus A320-214	3480	ex F-WWDK		
☐ TS-IQA	Airbus A321-211	0970	ex OO-SUA		
☐ TS-IQB	Airbus A321-211	0995	ex OO-SUB		

SEVENAIR (UG/TUI) Tunis-Carthage (TUN)

☐ TS-ISA	Canadair CL-600-2D24 (CRJ-900)	15091	ex C-	Didon	
☐ TS-	Canadair CL-600-2D24 (CRJ-900)		ex C-		on order
☐ TS-LBA	ATR 42-300	245	ex G-BXBV	Alyssa	
☐ TS-LBC	ATR 72-202	281	ex F-WWLK	Tahar Haddad	
☐ TS-LBD	ATR 72-202	756	ex F-WWEQ	HasdrubalF	
☐ TS-LBE	ATR 72-202	794	ex F-WWEU		
☐ ZS-PYU	Beech 1900D	UE-107	ex N107YV		

TUNISAIR Tunair (TU/TAR) Tunis-Carthage (TUN)

☐ TS-IPA	Airbus A300B4-605R	558	ex A6-EKD	Sidi Bou Said	
☐ TS-IPB	Airbus A300B4-605R	563	ex A6-EKE	Tunis	
☐ TS-IPC	Airbus A300B4-605R	505	ex F-OIHB	Amilcar	
☐ TS-IMB	Airbus A320-211	0119	ex F-WWIJ	Fahrat Hached	
☐ TS-IMC	Airbus A320-211	0124	ex F-WWIS	7 Novembre	
☐ TS-IMD	Airbus A320-211	0205	ex F-WWDO	Khereddine	
☐ TS-IME	Airbus A320-211	0123	ex F-OGYC	Tabarka	
☐ TS-IMF	Airbus A320-211	0370	ex F-WWIP	Djerba	
☐ TS-IMG	Airbus A320-211	0390	ex F-WWDL	Abou el Kacem Chebbi	
☐ TS-IMH	Airbus A320-211	0402	ex F-WWBN	Ali Belhaouane	Lsd to Mauritania AW
☐ TS-IMI	Airbus A320-211	0511	ex F-WWDC	Jughurta	
☐ TS-IMJ	Airbus A319-114	0869	ex D-AVYW	El Kantaoui	
☐ TS-IMK	Airbus A319-114	0880	ex D-AVYD	Kerkenah	
☐ TS-IML	Airbus A320-211	0958	ex F-WWBI	Gafsa El Ksar	
☐ TS-IMM	Airbus A320-211	0975	ex F-WWIR	Le Bardo	
☐ TS-IMN	Airbus A320-211	1187	ex F-WWDU	Ibn Khaldoun	
☐ TS-IMO	Airbus A319-114	1479	ex D-AVYT	Hannibal	
☐ TS-IMP	Airbus A320-211	1700	ex F-WWIS	La Galite	
☐ TS-IMQ	Airbus A319-112	3096	ex D-AVWZ	Alyssa	
☐ TS-IOG	Boeing 737-5H3	26639/2253		Sfax	
☐ TS-IOH	Boeing 737-5H3	26640/2474		Hammamet	
☐ TS-IOI	Boeing 737-5H3	27257/2583		Mahdia	
☐ TS-IOJ	Boeing 737-5H3	27912/2701		Monastir	
☐ TS-IOK	Boeing 737-6H3	29496/268	ex N1786B	Kairouan	
☐ TS-IOL	Boeing 737-6H3	29497/282	ex N1786B	Tozeur Nefta	
☐ TS-IOM	Boeing 737-6H3	29498/310	ex N1786B	Carthage	
☐ TS-ION	Boeing 737-6H3	29499/510	ex N1786B	Utique	
☐ TS-IOP	Boeing 737-6H3	29500/543		El Jem	
☐ TS-IOQ	Boeing 737-6H3	29501/563	ex N1787B	Bizerte	
☐ TS-IOR	Boeing 737-6H3	29502/816	ex N1786B	Tahar Haddad	

TUNISAVIA | *Tunisavia (TAJ)* | *Tunis-Carthage (TUN)*

☐ TS-HSD	Aérospatiale SA365N Dauphin 2	6117	ex F-WXFC
☐ TS-HSE	Aérospatiale SA365N Dauphin 2	6150	ex F-WYMN
☐ TS-LIB	de Havilland DHC-6 Twin Otter 300	716	ex TS-DIB
☐ TS-LSF	de Havilland DHC-6 Twin Otter 300	575	ex TS-DSF

TT- TCHAD (Republic of Chad)

AIR HORIZON AFRIQUE | *Tchad-Horizon (TPK)* | *N'Djamena (NDJ)*

Operates cargo flights with Antonov An-12 freighters leased from other operators as required

AMW TCHAD | *(MCW)* | *N'Djamena (NDJ)*

☐ TT-DAE	Lockheed L-1011-100 Tristar	193N-1101	ex EX-072
☐ TT-DWE	Lockheed L-1011-100 Tristar	193N-1093	ex A8-AAB

MID EXPRESS TCHAD | *N'Djamena (NDJ)*

☐ TT-DAX	Boeing 707-3K1C	20803/878	ex S2-ADU

TOUMAI AIR CHAD | *Toumai Air (9D/THE)* | *N'Djamena (NDJ)*

☐ OD-WOL	Boeing 737-232 (AvAero 3)	23083/1008	ex N311DL	Lsd fr WLB
☐ TT-EAS	Fokker F.28 Fellowship 4000	11173	ex TJ-ALC	

TU- IVORY COAST (Republic of the Ivory Coast)

AIR INTER IVOIRE | *Inter Ivoire (NTV)* | *Abidjan (ABJ)*

☐ TU-TDC	Fairchild FH-227B	558	ex 5N-BCB	
☐ TU-TDM	Grumman G.159 Gulfstream I	20	ex TJ-WIN	stored MAD
☐ TU-TGF	Piper PA-31-350 Navajo Chieftain	31-7305072	ex N74930	
☐ TU-TJF	Piper PA-23-250 Aztec F	27-7654072	ex N62594	
☐ TU-TJN	Beech 58 Baron	TH-776	ex HB-GGE	

AIR IVOIRE | *Air Ivoire (VU/VUN)* | *Abidjan (ABJ)*

☐ F-OIVU	Airbus A321-211	1017	ex G-OOAJ	
☐ TU-TIW	Fokker F.28 Fellowship 4000	11233	ex N483US	all-white
☐ TU-TIX	Fokker F.28 Fellowship 4000	11237	ex N486US	
☐ TU-TSC	Boeing 737-522	25001/1948	ex N394RM	
☐ TU-TSD	Boeing 737-522	25008/1987	ex N384RM	
☐ TU-TSE	Boeing 737-522	25009/1999	ex N374RM	

SOPHIA AIRLINES

☐ TU-TBG	LET L-410UVP	851423	ex 3D-GAM
☐ TU-TBS	LET L-410UVP	810724	ex 3D-BHK

TY- BENIN (Republic of Benin)

AERO BENIN | *AeroBen (EM/AEB)* | *Cotonou (COO)*

Operates services with Boeing 727 and Boeing 737 aircraft leased from Interair or Aero Africa when required

BENIN GOLF AIR | *Benin Golf (A8/BGL)* | *Cotonou (COO)*

☐ XU-RKA	Boeing 737-2H4 (AvAero 3)	22061/639	ex N63SW	Lsd fr RKH
☐ XU-RKC	Boeing 737-2H4 (AvAero 3)	22903/905	ex (PK-RIP)	Lsd fr RKH
☐ XU-RKG	Boeing 727-223F	19475/511	ex N316NE	
☐ 3D-BGA	Boeing 737-2H4	21722/568	ex OM-ERA	Lsd fr RFC

ROYAL AIR

☐ TY-KEC	Lockheed L-1011-1 Tristar	193C-1225	ex YK-KEC
☐ TY-KEQ	Lockheed L-1011-1 Tristar	193C-1199	ex YK-KEQ
☐ TY-KEU	Lockheed L-1011-1 Tristar	193C-1226	ex YK-KEU

TRANS AIR BENIN | *Trans-Benin (N4/TNB)* | *Cotonou (COO)*

Operates services with aircraft leased from Airquarius Aviation or TransAir Congo as required

TZ- MALI (Republic of Mali)

ASKARI AVIATION

☐ TZ-SGI	Lockheed L1011-250 Tristar	193C-1245	ex EX-044
☐ TZ-SPA	Lockheed L1011-250 Tristar	193C-1237	ex EX-056

COMPAGNIE AÉRIENNE DU MALI — Bamako (BKO)

☐ TZ-RMA	McDonnell-Douglas MD-87	49832/1703	ex I-AFRB
☐ TZ-RMB	McDonnell-Douglas MD-87	49841/1751	ex EC-EYZ
☐ TZ-RMK	McDonnell-Douglas MD-83	53463/2089	ex N160BS
☐ ZS-PML	SAAB SF.340A	340A-034	ex N338BE

MALI AIR EXPRESS — Avion Express (VXP) — Bamako (BKO)

☐ 3X-GDK	LET L-410UVP	800419	ex RA-67153
☐ 3X-GDL	LET L-410UVP	800420	ex RA-67154
☐ 3X-GED	SAAB SF.340A	340A-051	ex ZS-PMN
☐ 3X-GEJ	SAAB SF.340A	340A-136	ex ZK-NLN

MALI AIR TRANSPORT — Bamako (BKO)

☐ TZ-NBA	Boeing 727-2K5/W (Duganair 3)	21853/1640	ex P4-JLI

T3- KIRIBATI (Republic of Kiribati)

AIR KIRIBATI — (4A) — Tarawa-Bonriki Intl (TRW)

☐ T3-ATI	Harbin Y-12 II	0077	
☐ T3-ATJ	CASA C.212-200	CD67-01-356	ex N398FL

CORAL SUN AIRWAYS

☐ T3-JMR	Britten-Norman BN-2A-21 Islander	494	ex VH-SQS
☐ T3-VIN	Britten-Norman BN-2B-26 Islander	2154	ex VH-YIE

UK- UZBEKISTAN (Republic of Uzbekistan)

AVIALEASING — Twinarrow (EC/TWN) — Tashkent-Vostochny/Miami-Opa Locka, FL (TAS/OPF)

☐ N5057E	Antonov An-26	6101	ex 57 red		based OPF
☐ N8038Y	Antonov An-26	07309104	ex UK-26002		stored OPF
☐ UK-11418	Antonov An-12B	402504	ex RA-11996		based OPF
☐ UK-12002	Antonov An-12B	402002	ex RA-11373		
☐ UK-26001	Antonov An-26B	67314402	ex UK-26213		stored OPF
☐ UK-26003	Antonov An-26	07310406	ex S9-BOW	The Sky's the Limit	based OPF

Those based at Opa Locka, FL operate cargo flights for Bahamasair and DHL

QANOT SHARQ — Qanot Sharq (QNT) — Tashkent-Vostochny (TAS)

☐ UK-76353	Ilyushin Il-76TD	102314454	ex 76353

SAMARKAND AIRWAYS — Sogdiana (C7/UZS) — Tashkent-Vostochny (TAS)

Operates services with Antonov An-12/26 and Ilyushin Il-76 aircraft leased from other operators as required

TAPO-AVIA — Cortas (4C/CTP) — Tashkent-Vostochny (TAS)

☐ UK-11807	Antonov An-12BK	00346910	ex CCCP-11807	
☐ UK-58644	Antonov An-12BP	2340303	ex CCCP-58644	
☐ UK-76375	Ilyushin Il-76TD	1033414496		
☐ UK-76427	Ilyushin Il-76TD	1013406207	ex 06207	stored
☐ UK-76821	Ilyushin Il-76TD	0023441200	ex 4K-AZ62	
☐ UK-76831	Ilyushin Il-76TD	1013409287	ex CCCP-76831	status not confirmed

UZBEKISTAN AIRWAYS — Uzbek (HY/UZB) — Tashkent-Vostochny/Samarkand (TAS/SKD)

☐ UK-31004	Airbus A300B4-622RF	717	ex HL7299	
☐ UK-31005	Airbus A300B4-622RF	722	ex HL7244	
☐ UK-31001	Airbus A310-324	574	ex F-OGQY	Tashkent
☐ UK-31002	Airbus A310-324	576	ex F-OGQZ	Fergana
☐ UK-31003	Airbus A310-324	706	ex F-WWCM	Bukhara
☐ UK-46223	Antonov An-24B	77303102	ex CCCP-46223	
☐ UK-46360	Antonov An-24B	07305901	ex RA-46360	

☐ UK-46373	Antonov An-24B	07306004	ex CCCP-46373	
☐ UK-46387	Antonov An-24B	07306110	ex 46387	
☐ UK-46392	Antonov An-24B	07306205	ex CCCP-46392	
☐ UK-46573	Antonov An-24B	87304807	ex CCCP-46573	
☐ UK-46594	Antonov An-24B	97305104	ex CCCP-46594	
☐ UK-46623	Antonov An-24RV	37308710	ex CCCP-46623	
☐ UK-46658	Antonov An-24RV	47309304	ex CCCP-46658	
☐ UK-47274	Antonov An-24B	07306404	ex CCCP-47274	
☐ UK-80001	Avro 146-RJ85	E2312	ex G-6-312	VIP a/cop for Govt
☐ UK-80002	Avro 146-RJ85	E2309	ex G-6-309	
☐ UK-80003	Avro 146-RJ85	E2319	ex G-6-319	
☐ UK-75700	Boeing 757-23P	28338/731		Op for Govt
☐ VP-BUB*	Boeing 757-23P	30060/875	ex UK-75701 Urgench	
☐ VP-BUD*	Boeing 757-23P	30061/886	ex N6066Z Shahrisabz	
☐ VP-BUH	Boeing 757-231	30339/896	ex N726TW	
☐ VP-BUI	Boeing 757-231	28487/878	ex N719TW	
☐ VP-BUJ	Boeing 757-231	28488/884	ex N724TW	
☐ UK-67000	Boeing 767-33PER	35796/958	ex N5014K	VIP a/c op for Govt
☐ UK-67001	Boeing 767-33PER	28370/635	ex VP-BUA Samarkand	
☐ VP-BUE	Boeing 767-3CBER	33469/904	ex N594HA	
☐ VP-BUF	Boeing 767-33PER	33078/928		
☐ VP-BUZ	Boeing 767-33PER	28392/650	ex (UK-76702)	Khiva
☐ UK-76351	Ilyushin Il-76TD	1013408240	ex RA-76351	stored TAS
☐ UK-76358	Ilyushin Il-76TD	1023410339		
☐ UK-76359	Ilyushin Il-76TD	1033414483		
☐ UK-76426	Ilyushin Il-76TD	1043419644		
☐ UK-76428	Ilyushin Il-76TD	1043419648	ex 76428	
☐ UK-76449	Ilyushin Il-76TD	1023403058	ex 76449	
☐ UK-76782	Ilyushin Il-76TD	0093498971	ex CCCP-76782	
☐ UK-76793	Ilyushin Il-76TD	0093498951	ex CCCP-76793	
☐ UK-76794	Ilyushin Il-76TD	0093498954	ex CCCP-76794	stored TAS
☐ UK-76805	Ilyushin Il-76TD	1003403109	ex CCCP-76805	
☐ UK-76811	Ilyushin Il-76TD	1013407223	ex 76811	stored TAS
☐ UK-76813	Ilyushin Il-76TD	1013408246	ex CCCP-76813	stored TAS
☐ UK-76824	Ilyushin Il-76TD	1023410327	ex CCCP-76824	stored TAS
☐ UK-86056	Ilyushin Il-86	51483203023	ex CCCP-86056	stored TAS
☐ UK-86064	Ilyushin Il-86	51483203031	ex CCCP-86064	stored TAS
☐ UK-86090	Ilyushin Il-86	51483207061	ex CCCP-86090	stored TAS
☐ UK-91102	Ilyushin Il-114-100	109380202	ex UK-91009	
☐ UK-91104	Ilyushin Il-114-100	0204		
☐ UK-91105	Ilyushin Il-114-100	2063800205	ex 91105	
☐ UK-91106	Ilyushin Il-114-100	2083800206	ex 91106	
☐ UK-85575	Tupolev Tu-154B-2	83A-575	ex 85575	
☐ UK-85578	Tupolev Tu-154B-2	83A-578	ex 85578	
☐ UK-85600	Tupolev Tu-154B-2	84A-600	ex 85600	VIP
☐ UK-85711	Tupolev Tu-154M	91A-887	ex 85711	
☐ UK-85764	Tupolev Tu-154M	93A-947	ex RA-85764	stored
☐ UK-85776	Tupolev Tu-154M	93A-958		
☐ UK-87923	Yakovlev Yak-40	9741455	ex CCCP-87923	VIP
☐ UK-87989	Yakovlev Yak-40	9541344	ex CCCP-8789	
☐ UK-87996	Yakovlev Yak-40	9542044	ex CCCP-87996	
☐ UK-88194	Yakovlev Yak-40	9621448	ex CCCP-88194	
☐ UK-88217	Yakovlev Yak-40	9630350	ex CCCP-88217	VIP

UP- KAZAKHSTAN (Republic of Kazakhstan)

AEROTRANS — *Bachyt (ATG)* — *Taraz (DMB)*

☐ UN-85521	Tupolev Tu-154B-2	81A-521	ex CCCP-85521
☐ UN-85569	Tupolev Tu-154B-2	82A-569	ex LZ-BTV

AEROTUR AIR — *Diasa (RAI)* — *Astana (TSE)*

☐ UP-T5407	Tupolev Tu-154M	87A-754	ex UN-85570

AIR ALMATY — *Agleb (LMY)* — *Almaty (ALA)*

☐ UP-AN215	Antonov An-12BP	6344305	ex UN-11650
☐ UP-I7601	Ilyushin Il-76TD	1013409295	ex YL-LAJ
☐ UP-I7602	Ilyushin Il-76T	0003427796	ex UN-76034
☐ UP-I7603	Ilyushin Il-76	083414432	ex UN-76023
☐ UP-I7633	Ilyushin Il-76T	093420594	ex RA-76518

AIR AKTOBE | Aktobe

Registration	Type	C/n	Previous identity	Notes
☐ UP-L4101	LET L-410UVP	841229	ex UN-67464	

AIR ASTANA | Astanaline(KC/KZR) | Astana/Almaty(TSE/ALA)

Registration	Type	C/n	Previous identity	Notes
☐ P4-NAS	Airbus A321-231	1042	ex N104AQ	
☐ P4-OAS	Airbus A321-231	1204	ex N120ED	
☐ P4-PAS	Airbus A320-232	2128	ex D-ARFF	
☐ P4-SAS	Airbus A320-232	2016	ex SX-BVC	
☐ P4-TAS	Airbus A320-232	2828	ex F-WWDN	
☐ P4-UAS	Airbus A320-232	2987	ex F-WWIH	
☐ P4-VAS	Airbus A320-232	3141	ex F-WWDO	
☐ P4-WAS	Airbus A320-232	3484	ex F-WWIE	
☐ P4-XAS	Airbus A319-132	3519	ex F-WWDR	on order
☐ P4-YAS	Airbus A319-132	3614	ex D-AVYL	
☐ P4-HAS	Fokker F.27 Mk.050 (Fokker 50)	20198	ex PH-ZDH	
☐ P4-IAS	Fokker F.27 Mk.050 (Fokker 50)	20188	ex PH-ZDD	
☐ P4-JAS	Fokker F.27 Mk.050 (Fokker 50)	20195	ex PH-ZDG	
☐ P4-KAS	Fokker F.27 Mk.050 (Fokker 50)	20187	ex PH-ZDC	
☐ P4-LAS	Fokker F.27 Mk.050 (Fokker 50)	20193	ex PH-ZDE	
☐ P4-EAS	Boeing 757-2G5/W	29488/830	ex D-AMUG	
☐ P4-FAS	Boeing 757-2G5/W	29489/834	ex D-AMUH	
☐ P4-GAS	Boeing 757-2G5/W	28112/708	ex D-AMUI	
☐ P4-MAS	Boeing 757-2Q8/W	28833/782	ex B-2852	
☐ P4-KCA	Boeing 767-306ER	27612/647	ex PH-BZI	
☐ P4-KCB	Boeing 767-306ER	27614/661	ex PH-BZK	

ASIA CONTINENTAL AIRLINES | Acid (CID) | Almaty (ALA)

Registration	Type	C/n	Previous identity	Notes
☐ UP-I7617	Ilyushin Il-76TD	0013430890	ex UN-76021	
☐ UP-I7618	Ilyushin Il-76T	0013428831	ex UN-76022	
☐ UP-I7627	Ilyushin Il-76T	0003423699	ex ER-IBV	
☐ UP-I7639	Ilyushin Il-76TD	1023410344	ex EW-244TH	

ATMA | (AMA)

Registration	Type	C/n	Previous identity	Notes
☐ UP-AN211	Antonov An-12B	02348207	ex UN-11017	
☐ UP-AN212	Antonov An-12TB	01347701	ex UN-11019	
☐ UP-AN213	Antonov An-12BP	2340806	ex UN-11015	
☐ UN-76499	Ilyushin Il-76TD	0023441186	ex RA-76499	

ATYRAU AIR WAYS | Edil (IP/JOL) | Atyrau (GUW)

Registration	Type	C/n	Previous identity	Notes
☐ UP-T3406	Tupolev Tu-134A	40150	ex UN-65610 Bayterek	
☐ UP-T3405	Tupolev Tu-134A	31218	ex UN-65619 Venera	VIP
☐ UP-T5406	Tupolev Tu-154M	93A-965	ex UN-85781	
☐ UN-25358	Mil Mi-8T	00206781	ex CCCP-25388	Jt ops with KAW
☐ UN-27055	Mil Mi-8MTV-1	95889	ex CCCP-27055	
☐ UN-65069	Tupolev Tu-134A-3	49908	ex RA-65069 Kashagan	
☐ UN-65070	Tupolev Tu-134A-3	49912	ex RA-65070 Tungysh	

AVIA JAYNAR | Tobol (SAP) | Kostanay (KSN)

Registration	Type	C/n	Previous identity	Notes
☐ UP-AN401	Antonov An-24B	88901605	ex UN-47153	

BEIBARS

Registration	Type	C/n	Previous identity	Notes
☐ UP-I7625	Ilyushin Il-76TD	0033446350	ex UN-76472	
☐ UP-I7626	Ilyushin Il-76M	1013409303	ex YU-AMJ	

BERKUT AIR | Berkut (BEK) | Almaty (ALA)

Registration	Type	C/n	Previous identity	Notes
☐ UP-Y4003	Yakovlev Yak-40	9632048	ex UN-88198	
☐ UP-Y4023	Yakovlev Yak-40	9411533	ex UN-87403	
☐ UN-87306	Yakovlev Yak-40	9302229	ex CCCP-87306	
☐ UN-88191	Yakovlev Yak-40	9621148	ex CCCP-88191	VIP
☐ UN-88260	Yakovlev Yak-40	9711552	ex CCCP-88260	VIP

BERKUT STATE AIR COMPANY | (BEC) | Almaty (ALA)

Registration	Type	C/n	Previous identity	Notes
☐ UP-AN205	Antonov An-12BP	02348304	ex UN-11373	
☐ UP-B6701	Boeing 767-2DXER	32954/861	ex UN-B7601	VIP
☐ UP-I7604	Ilyushin Il-76TD	1033414485	ex UN-76371	
☐ UP-I7605	Ilyushin Il-76TD	1033416520	ex UN-76374	
☐ UP-MI702	Mil Mi-172 (Mi-8MTV-3)	398C01	ex UN-17201	VIP
☐ UP-MI814	Mil Mi-8MTV-1	96275	ex UN-25401	VIP

☐ UP-T5401	Tupolev Tu-154M	91A-889	ex UN-85713	
☐ UN-A1901	Airbus A319-115X	2592	ex HB-IPO	VIP [CJ]
☐ UN-B5701	Boeing 757-2M6ER	23454/102	ex P4-NSN	VIP
☐ UN-85464	Tupolev Tu-154B-2	80A-464	ex 85464	VIP

DETA AIR — ***Almaty (ALA)***

☐ UP-DC101	Douglas DC-10-40F	47823/306	ex VP-BDE	
☐ UP-DC102	Douglas DC-10-40F	47855/349	ex VP-BDF	
☐ UP-I6206	Ilyushin Il-62M	3242321	ex UN-86524 Galina	
☐ UP-I6207	Ilyushin Il-62M	1545951	ex UN-86935	
☐ UP-I6209	Ilyushin Il-62M	3139956	ex RA-86518	

DON AVIA — ***Donsebai (DVB)*** — ***Almaty (ALA)***

☐ UN-87271	Yakovlev Yak-40	9310727	ex CCCP-87271	VIP

EAST KAZAKHSTAN REGION AIR ENTERPRISE — ***Galeta (UCK)*** — ***Ust-Kamenogorsk (UKK)***

☐ UP-Y4204	Yakovlev Yak-42D	4520423408016	ex UN-42430

EAST WING — ***E Wing (EWZ)*** — ***Taraz / Fujairah, UAE (DMB/FJR)***

☐ UP-I7621	Ilyushin Il-76TD	0013434018	ex UN-76008
☐ UP-I7622	Ilyushin Il-76T	0003426765	ex UN-76011
☐ UP-I7623	Ilyushin Il-76TD	0033448404	ex UN-76010
☐ UP-I7624	Ilyushin Il-76TD	0023442218	ex UN-76033
☐ UN-76497	Ilyushin Il-76T	043402039	ex 3C-QRA
☐ UN-B1110	BAC One-Eleven 401AK	078	ex UN-B1111 East Wing titles
☐ UN-11006	Antonov An-12BP	01347909	ex 3C-QRI
☐ UN-11008	Antonov An-12B	4342505	ex 18 RED
☐ UN-11009	Antonov An-12B	53403408	ex 3C-MIR
☐ UN-11010	Antonov An-12B	53403606	
☐ UN-26087	Antonov An-26	27312601	ex 4L-26087

EASTERN EXPRESS

☐ UP-I7606	Ilyushin Il-76T	0033446325	ex UN-76026
☐ UP-I7607	Ilyushin Il-76TD	0033447364	ex UN-76027
☐ UP-I7612	Ilyushin Il-76T	0003425746	ex UN-76032
☐ UP-I7628	Ilyushin Il-76TD	0053460790	ex EW-264TH
☐ UP-I7629	Ilyushin Il-76TD	1013408257	ex HA-TCB
☐ UN-76029	Ilyushin Il-76TD	1013406294	ex ER-IAS
☐ UN-11020	Antonov An-12		
☐ UP-AN203	Antonov An-12BK	00347408	ex ER-ACV
☐ UN-11021	Antonov An-12		

EURO-ASIA INTERNATIONAL — ***Eakaz (5B/EAK)*** — ***Almaty/Sharjah (ALA/SHJ)***

☐ UP-Y4026	Yakovlev Yak-40	9510639	ex UN-87337 Aibike titles	VIP
☐ UP-Y4027	Yakovlev Yak-40K	9741856	ex UN-87935	VIP
☐ UP-Y4028	Yakovlev Yak-40K	9710453	ex UN-88266	
☐ UP-Y4029	Yakovlev Yak-40	9621147	ex UN-88173	
☐ UP-Y4030	Yakovlev Yak-40	9541444	ex UN-87990	

EXCELLENT GLIDE

☐ UP-Y4208	Yakovlev Yak-42D	4520423116650	ex UN-42642

INVESTAVIA — ***(TLG)*** — ***Almaty (ALA)***

☐ UP-I6210	Ilyushin Il-62M	3255333	ex UN-86130 NRG titles

KAZ AIR TRANS

☐ UP-B3704	Boeing 737-2H3	22624/758	ex A6-AVE

KAZAIR WEST — ***Kazwest (KAW)*** — ***Atyrau (GUW)***

☐ UP-L4104	LET L-410UVP-E	861606	ex UN-67566	
☐ UP-T3402	Tupolev Tu-134B-3	63187	ex YL-LBN	VIP
☐ UP-Y4015	Yakovlev Yak-40K	9831958	ex UN-87221	
☐ UN-25358	Mil Mi-8T	98206781	ex CCCP-25358	Jt ops with JOL
☐ UN-25517	Mil Mi-8PS-9	8687	ex CCCP-25517	
☐ UN-67611	LET L-410UVP-E	892339	ex OM-UDX	

KAZAKHMYS

☐ UP-L4102	LET L-410UVP-E	902512	ex UR-SVI	
☐ UP-Y4012	Yakovlev Yak-40K	9741755	ex UN-87926	VIP
☐ UP-Y4014	Yakovlev Yak-40K	9732054	ex UN-87912	

KAZZINC

☐ UP-Y4006	Yakovlev Yak-40K	9740556	ex UN-87934	
☐ UP-Y4204	Yakovlev Yak-42	45204223408016	ex UN-42430	VIP

KHOZU AVIA — Khozavia (OZU) — Almaty (ALA)

☐ UP-Y4201	Yakovlev Yak-42D	4520423302017	ex UN-42641	VIPop for Govt
☐ UP-Y4202	Yakovlev Yak-42D	4520423402116	ex UN-42323	VIP
☐ UP-C8501	Canadair CL-600-2B19 (CRJ-200ER)	8054	ex C-FHTO	
☐ UP-C8502	Canadair CL-600-2B19 (CRJ-200ER)	8049	ex C-FHGK	

KOKSHETAU AIRLINES — Kokta (KRT) — Kokchetav (KOV)

☐ UN-86505	Ilyushin Il-62M	1748445	ex UR-86135 no titles	stored ALA
☐ UN-86506	Ilyushin Il-62M	1138234	ex UR-86133	stored ALA
☐ UN-87913	Yakovlev Yak-40	9730255	ex CCCP-87913	
☐ UN-88221	Yakovlev Yak-40	9630750	ex CCCP-88221	
☐ UN-88277	Yakovlev Yak-40	9721953	ex CCCP-88277	

MAK AIR — (AKM) — Almaty (ALA)

☐ UP-T5405	Tupolev Tu-154M	89A-823	ex UN-85855	

MEGA AIRCOMPANY — Mega (MGK) — Almaty (ALA)

☐ UP-B2701	Boeing 727-232 (FedEx 3)	22045/1602	ex UN-B2701	
☐ UP-B2702	Boeing 727-232 (FedEx 3)	21861/1554	ex UN-B2702	
☐ UP-B2703	Boeing 727-232 (FedEx 3)	21584/1478	ex UN-B2703	
☐ UP-I1801	Ilyushin Il-18D	187010204	ex UN-75005	
☐ UP-I1802	Ilyushin Il-18E	185008603	ex UN-75002	
☐ UP-I1803	Ilyushin Il-18V	184006903	ex UN-75003	
☐ UP-I1804	Ilyushin Il-18GrM	186009202	ex UN-75004	
☐ UN-26517	Antonov An-26	7002	ex CCCP-26517	

MIRAS AIR — Miras (MIF) — Almaty (ALA)

☐ UP-AN201	Antonov An-12BP	01348007	ex YU-AIA	

SAMAL AIR — (SAV) — Almaty (ALA)

☐ UP-T3401	Tupolev Tu-134AK-3	63684	ex UN-65900	stored ALA
☐ UN-86507	Ilyushin Il-62M	4242654	ex RA-86507 Ivan	

SAT AIRLINES — Satco (SOZ) — Almaty (ALA)

☐ UP-T3403	Tupolev Tu-134A-3	62545	ex UN-65776	VIP
☐ UP-T3404	Tupolev Tu-134A-3	66212	ex UN-65551	VIP
☐ UN-65720	Tupolev Tu-134B-3	62820	ex CCCP-65720	VIP

SAYAKHAT — Sayakhat (W7/SAH) — Almaty (ALA)

☐ UP-I7613	Ilyushin Il-76	1023412395	ex UN-76434	
☐ UP-I7615	Ilyushin Il-76TD	1003401015	ex UN-76384	
☐ UP-I7616	Ilyushin Il-76TD	1033416515	ex UN-76385	
☐ UP-T5402	Tupolev Tu-154M	86A-726	ex UN-85852	
☐ UP-T5403	Tupolev Tu-154M	86A-728	ex UN-85853	
☐ UP-T5404	Tupolev Tu-154M	86A-729	ex UN-85854	Lsd to SXA

SAYAT AIR — (SYM) — Almaty (ALA)

☐ UP-I6204	Ilyushin Il-62M	4255152	ex UN-86566	
☐ UP-I6205	Ilyushin Il-62M	3357947	ex UN-86586	

SCAT AIRCOMPANY — Vlasta (DV/VSV) — Shymkent

☐ UP-AN202	Antonov An-12BP	3341201	ex UN-11367	
☐ UP-AN404	Antonov An-24B	17307303	ex UN-26196	
☐ UP-AN405	Antonov An-24B	77303508	ex UN-46265	
☐ UP-AN406	Antonov An-24B	77303604	ex UN-46271	
☐ UP-AN407	Antonov An-24B	87305305	ex UN-46310	
☐ UP-AN408	Antonov An-24B	97305608	ex UN-46340	
☐ UP-AN409	Antonov An-24B	07305909	ex UN-46368	

Registration	Type	Serial	Previous	Notes
☐ UP-AN410	Antonov An-24B	07306104	ex UN-46381	
☐ UP-AN411	Antonov An-24B	87304106	ex UN-46421	
☐ UP-AN412	Antonov An-24B	87304309	ex UN-46438	
☐ UP-AN413	Antonov An-24RV	37309305	ex UN-46500	
☐ UP-AN414	Antonov An-24RV	37308305	ex UN-46626	
☐ UP-AN415	Antonov An-24RV	47309505	ex UN-46664	
☐ UP-AN416	Antonov An-24RV	47309604	ex UN-46672	
☐ UP-AN417	Antonov An-24RV	47309910	ex UN-46699	
☐ UP-AN418	Antonov An-24B	89901810	ex UN-47176	
☐ UP-AN419	Antonov An-24RV	27307609	ex UN-47258	
☐ UP-AN420	Antonov An-24B	07306308	ex UN-47270	
☐ UP-AN421	Antonov An-24B	07306407	ex UN-47277	
☐ UP-AN422	Antonov An-24B	07306504	ex UN-47284	
☐ UP-AN423	Antonov An-24RV	67310509	ex UN-47350	
☐ UP-AN424	Antonov An-24RV	27307509	ex UN-47692	
☐ UP-AN425	Antonov An-24B	79901307	ex UN-47763	
☐ UP-AN426	Antonov An-24B	17307406	ex UN-47844	
☐ UP-AN601	Antonov An-26	0503	ex UN-26027	
☐ LY-FLB	Boeing 737-322/W	24667/1893	ex ES-LBA	
☐ UP-B3701	Boeing 737-230 (Nordam 3)	22123/726	ex N123AQ	
☐ UP-B3702	Boeing 737-277 (Nordam 3)	22650/806	ex YA-GAB	
☐ LY-FLG	Boeing 757-204	27237/602	ex G-BYAR	
☐ UP-Y4203	Yakovlev Yak-42D	4250421116567	ex UN-42401	
☐ UP-Y4205	Yakovlev Yak-42D	4520421219029	ex UN-42410	Lsd fr MSI
☐ UP-Y4210	Yakovlev Yak-42D	4520422306016	ex UN-42428	

SEMEYAVIA — *Ertis (SMK)* — *Semipalatinsk (PLX)*

Registration	Type	Serial	Previous
☐ UP-Y4016	Yakovlev Yak-40K	9810557	ex UN-87208
☐ UN-87204	Yakovlev Yak-40K	9810157	ex CCCP-87204
☐ UN-88259	Yakovlev Yak-40K	9711452	ex CCCP-88259

SKY CARGO — *Sharjah (SHJ)*

Registration	Type	Serial	Previous
☐ UP-B2702	Boeing 727-225F (FedEx 3)	21861/1554	ex UN-B2702

Status uncertain

SKYJET

Registration	Type	Serial	Previous
☐ UP-I6203	Ilyushin Il-62M	1052128	ex UN-86558 no titles

STARLINE KZ

Registration	Type	Serial	Previous
☐ UP-B2704	Boeing 727-225F (FedEx 3)	22046/1604	ex A6-RSA

TULPAR AIR SERVICE — *Tulpa (2T/TUX)* — *Qaraghandy-Sary Arka (KGF)*

Registration	Type	Serial	Previous	Notes
☐ UP-AN427	Antonov An-24B	97305001	ex UN -46582	
☐ UN-46253	Antonov An-24B	77303305	ex CCCP-46253	stored
☐ UN-46448	Antonov An-24B	87304410	ex CCCP-46448	
☐ UN-46492	Antonov An-24RV	27305001	ex CCCP-46492	
☐ UN-46611	Antonov An-24RV	37308608	ex CCCP-46611	
☐ UN-26579	Antonov An-26B	13404	ex CCCP-26579	

YUZHNAYA AIRCOMPANY — *Pluton (UGN)* — *Almaty (ALA)*

Registration	Type	Serial	Previous
☐ UN-75001	Ilyushin Il-18D	187009904	ex YR-IMM
☐ UN-85478	Tupolev Tu-154B-2	81A-478	ex EX-017

ZHETYSU AVIA — *Zhetysu Avia (JTU)* — *Almaty (ALA)*

Registration	Type	Serial	Previous
☐ UP-Y4019	Yakovlev Yak-40K	9741855	ex UN-87927
☐ UN-87931	Yakovlev Yak-40	9740256	ex CCCP-87931

ZHEZHAIR — *Ulutau (KZH)* — *Zhezkazgan (DZN)*

Registration	Type	Serial	Previous
☐ UP-Y4012	Yakovlev Yak-40	9742055	ex UN-87929 KCC titles
☐ UP-Y4013	Yakovlev Yak-40	9731055	ex UN-87920 KCC titles
☐ UN-24143	Mil Mi-8T	98841441	ex RA-24143
☐ UN-24262	Mil Mi-8T	98734158	ex CCCP-24262
☐ UN-67407	LET L-410UVP	831035	ex CCCP-67407
☐ UN-67491	LET L-410UVP	841316	ex CCCP-67491

UR- UKRAINE

AERO-CHARTER UKRAINE — *Charter Ukraine (DW/UCR)* — *Kiev-Borispol (KBP)*

Registration	Type	Serial	Previous
☐ UR-DWA	Antonov An-26	47313905	ex HA-TCS
☐ UR-DWB	Antonov An-26B	6207	ex UR-BXB

☐ UR-DWD	Antonov An-26B	10103	ex ER-AFF	
☐ UR-DWF	Antonov An-12BK	8345802	ex LZ-MNK	
☐ UR-DWG	Antonov An-12BP	8345710	ex LZ-MNP	
☐ UR-CDW	Yakovlev Yak-40	9610546	ex UR-88151	
☐ UR-DAP	Yakovlev Yak-40	9521241	ex RA-87530	
☐ UR-DWC	Yakovlev Yak-40	9541144	ex UR-87987	
☐ UR-DWE	Yakovlev Yak-40	9240326	ex RA-87837 all-white	
☐ UR-LRZ	Yakovlev Yak-40K	9641851	ex LY-ARZ	
☐ UR-88290	Yakovlev Yak-40K	9840459	ex CCCP-88290	

AEROMOST KHARKOV — *Aeromist (HT/AHW)* — *Kharkov-Osnova (HRK)*

☐ UR-14002	Antonov An-140	36525302006		

AEROSTAR — *Aerostar (UAR)* — *Kiev-Zhulyany/Kiev-Borispol (IEV/KBP)*

☐ UR-AIS	Yakovlev Yak-40	9211821	ex UR-87566	
☐ UR-BWH	Yakovlev Yak-40	9640951	ex RA-88238	
☐ UR-MIG	Yakovlev Yak-40	9641250	ex RA-88225 Keramist titles	
☐ UR-SAN	Yakovlev Yak-40	9542043	ex 9L-LDI	
☐ UR-87961	Yakovlev Yak-40K	9820458	ex CCCP-87961	
☐ UR-87998	Yakovlev Yak-40	9540245	ex CCCP-87998	airtaxi.ua titles

AEROSVIT AIRLINES — *Aerosvit (VV/AEW)* — *Kiev-Borispol (KBP)*

☐ UR-46514	Antonov An-24RV	37308410	ex RA-46514	Lsd fr LHS
☐ UR-46677	Antonov An-24RV	47309609	ex RA-46677	
☐ UR-47294	Antonov An-24RV	07306604	ex RA-47294	Lsd fr URP
☐ UR-47296	Antonov An-24RV	07306609	ex CCCP-47296	
☐ UR-47312	Antonov An-24RV	57310403	ex RA-47312 all-white	
☐ UR-	Antonov An-148-100B			on order
☐ UR-	Antonov An-148-100B			on order
☐ UR-	Antonov An-148-100B			on order
☐ UR-BVY	Boeing 737-2Q8	22760/852	ex F-GEXJ	
☐ UR-VVA	Boeing 737-3Q8	24492/1808	ex N492GD	
☐ UR-VVB	Boeing 737-529	26537/2296	ex OO-SYJ	
☐ UR-VVD	Boeing 737-529	25419/2165	ex UR-GAP	
☐ UR-VVE	Boeing 737-448	24521/1788	ex EI-BXB	
☐ UR-VVL	Boeing 737-448	25052/2036	ex EI-BXI	
☐ UR-VVM	Boeing 737-448	25736/2269	ex EI-BXK	
☐ UR-VVN	Boeing 737-4Y0	24903/1978	ex OK-WGF	
☐ UR-VVP	Boeing 737-4Q8	26290/2482	ex OK-YGA	
☐ UR-VVQ	Boeing 737-5L9	29235/3076	ex OK-DGC	
☐ UR-VVR	Boeing 737-3Q8	24699/1886	ex TC-TJA	
☐ UR-VVS	Boeing 737-5Q8	26324/2735	ex ES-ABC	
☐ UR-VVU	Boeing 737-5Q8	26323/2770	ex ES-ABD	
☐ UR-VVF	Boeing 767-383ER	24476/274	ex N4476F	
☐ UR-VVO	Boeing 767-383ER	24475/273	ex XA-MXB	
☐ UR-VVT	Boeing 767-3Q8ER	28132/692	ex B-2493	

AEROVIS AIRLINES — *Aeroviz (VIZ)* — *Rivnu (RWN)*

☐ UR-CBF	Antonov An-12BP	2340507	ex LZ-SFW	
☐ UR-CBG	Antonov An-12BP	6343705	ex UR-11302	
☐ UR-CCP	Antonov An-12A	2340505	ex LZ-CBM	
☐ UR-CEX	Antonov An-12B	4342103	ex RA-93915	
☐ UR-CEZ	Antonov An-12B	6344304	ex RA-98118	
☐ UR-CFB	Antonov An-12BP	6343802	ex 02 red	
☐ UR-CGU	Antonov An-12BK	7345203	ex 09 red	

AIR URGA — *Urga (3N/URG)* — *Kirovograd-Khmelyovoye (KGO)*

☐ UR-CFU	Antonov An-24RV		ex	
☐ UR-ELC	Antonov An-24RV	57310410	ex UR-47313	Op for United Nations
☐ UR-ELK	Antonov An-24RV	57310203	ex UR-47300 all-white	
☐ UR-ELL	Antonov An-24RV	67310503	ex UR-47316	
☐ UR-ELM	Antonov An-24RV	67310506	ex UR-47319	
☐ UR-ELN	Antonov An-24B	89901607	ex UR-47155	Op for UN as UN-967
☐ UR-ELO	Antonov An-24RV	47309507	ex UR-46666	Op for UNA as UN-628
☐ UR-ELT	Antonov An-24RV	27307809	ex XU-054	Op for UN
☐ UR-ELW	Antonov An-24RV	57310109	ex XU-375	stored
☐ UR-46311	Antonov An-24B	97305307	ex LZ-MND	Op for UN as UN-969
☐ UR-46464	Antonov An-24RV	27307810	ex ER-46464	Op for United Nations
☐ UR-46577	Antonov An-24B	87304902	ex CCCP-46577	
☐ UR-ELB	Antonov An-26B	14005	ex UR-26201	
☐ UR-ELD	Antonov An-26B	14010	ex UR-26203	
☐ UR-ELE	Antonov An-26B	12108	ex UR-26111	Op for United Nations

☐ UR-ELF	Antonov An-26B	12204	ex UR-26115	
☐ UR-ELG	Antonov An-26B	12902	ex UR-26140	Op for United Nations as UN-698
☐ UR-ELH	Antonov An-26B	12908	ex UR-26143	Lsd to / op for Air Boyoma
☐ UR-ELP	Antonov An-26B	47313408	ex UR-26580	
☐ UR-ELR	Antonov An-26B	9807	ex UR-26004	Op for United Nations as UNO-967

ANTONOV AIRLINES — *Antonov Bureau (ADB)* — *Kiev-Gostomel*

☐ UR-82007	Antonov An-124-100	19530501005	ex CCCP-82007	
☐ UR-82008	Antonov An-124-100M-150	19530501006	ex CCCP-82008	
☐ UR-82009	Antonov An-124-100	19530501007	ex CCCP-82009	
☐ UR-82027	Antonov An-124-100	19530502288	ex CCCP-82027	
☐ UR-82029	Antonov An-124-100	19530502630	ex CCCP-82029	
☐ UR-82072	Antonov An-124-100	9773053359136	ex RA-82072	
☐ UR-82073	Antonov An-124-100	9773054359139	ex RA-82073	
☐ UR-09307	Antonov An-22A	043481244	ex CCCP-09307	
☐ UR-11315	Antonov An-12BP	4342307	ex RA-11315	
☐ UR-21510	Antonov An-12AP	0901404	ex 88 red Soviet AF	
☐ UR-74010	Antonov An-74T	36547030450	ex CCCP-74010	VIP
☐ UR-82060	Antonov An-225 Mriya	19530503763	ex CCCP-82060	

ARP 410 AIRLINES — *Air-Arp (URP)* — *Kiev-Zhulyany (IEV)*

☐ UR-CDY	Antonov An-24RV	47309305	ex ST-SHE	
☐ UR-PWA	Antonov An-24RV	67302608	ex RA-46820	
☐ UR-47256	Antonov An-24RV	27307708	ex TC-MOB	
☐ UR-47278	Antonov An-24B	07306408	ex CCCP-47278	
☐ UR-47294	Antonov An-24RV	07306604	ex RA-47294	Lsd to AEW
☐ UR-47297	Antonov An-24RV	07306610	ex CCCP-47297	
☐ UR-BWZ	Antonov An-26B	12208	ex UR-26119	
☐ UR-CBJ	Antonov An-26B	11401	ex UR-26069	
☐ UR-26581	Antonov An-26B	57313503	ex RA-26581	

ARTEM AVIA — *Artem Avia (ABA)* — *Kiev-Zhulyany (IEV)*

☐ UR-26094	Antonov An-26B	12706	ex CCCP-26094

AS AVIAKOMPANIA — *Kiev-Borispol (KBP)*

☐ UR-30036	Antonov An-30	0703	ex CCCP-30036

AVIAEXPRESS AIRCOMPANY — *Expressavia (VXX)* — *Kiev-Zhulyany (IEV)*

☐ UR-LAA	LET L-410UVP	851425	ex YL-KAA
☐ UR-67199	LET L-410UVP	790305	ex CCCP-67199

AVIANT — *Aviation Plant (UAK)* — *Kiev-Gostomel*

☐ UR-ZYD	Antonov An-124-100	19530502843	ex UR-CCX	Lsd to MXU
☐ UR-26175	Antonov An-24RV	77310810A	ex CCCP-26175	
☐ UR-48023	Antonov An-32B	3409	ex HK-4006X	
☐ UR-48086	Antonov An-32P	2901	ex CCCP-48086	
☐ UR-48087	Antonov An-32B	2904	ex CCCP-48087	
☐ UR-69312	Antonov An-26	2906	ex CCCP-69312	
☐ UR-79165	Antonov An-26	5409	ex CCCP-26219	

AVIATRANS K — *Kiev-Borispol (IEV)*

☐ UR-11332	Antonov An-12BP	4342202	ex T9-CAD

AZOV-AVIA — *Azov Avia (AZV)* — *Melitopol*

☐ UR-ZVB	Ilyushin Il-76MD	0053463902	ex UR-76658	Op for UN/WFP
☐ UR-ZVC	Ilyushin Il-76TD	0053463891	ex UR-76656	

CHALLENGE AERO — *Sky Challenger (5U/CHG)* — *Kiev-Zhulyany (IEV)*

☐ UR-CLB	Yakovlev Yak-40K	9731555	ex RA-87924
☐ UR-ECL	Yakovlev Yak-40K	9932059	ex RA-87219
☐ UR-87965	Yakovlev Yak-40	9820858	ex RA-87965
☐ UR-88309	Yakovlev Yak-40	9840859	ex 5R-MUA
☐ UR-88310	Yakovlev Yak-40	9940760	ex 5R-MUB

CONSTANTA AIRLINES — *Constanta (UZA)* — *Zaporozhye (OZH)*

☐ UR-ETG	Yakovlev Yak-40	9531143	ex RA-87243	VIP
☐ UR-FRU	Yakovlev Yak-40	9440737	ex RA-87211	VIPop for Sumy Frunze
☐ UR-ZPR	Yakovlev Yak-40	9240426	ex RA-87838	VIP

☐ UR-87389	Yakovlev Yak-40	9410133	ex CCCP-87389	
☐ UR-87463	Yakovlev Yak-40	9430237	ex CCCP-87463	
☐ UR-87512	Yakovlev Yak-40	9521440	ex CCCP-87512	
☐ UR-87547	Yakovlev Yak-40	9531242	ex CCCP-87547	VIP
☐ UR-87806	Yakovlev Yak-40	9231223	ex CCCP-87806	

DNEPR-AIR — ***Dniepro (Z6/UDN)*** — ***Dnepropetrovsk-Kodaki (DNK)***

☐ UR-IVK	Boeing 737-3L9	24571/1815	ex G-IGOT	
☐ UR-KIV	Boeing 737-4Y0	24686/1861	ex F-GQQJ	
☐ UR-DNC	Boeing 737-5L9	28995/2947	ex OY-APK	
☐ UR-DND	Boeing 737-5L9	28722/2868	ex OY-API	
☐ UR-DNH	Boeing 737-5Y0	24696/1960	ex N246ST	
☐ UR-DNJ	Boeing 737-36Q	28659/2680	ex G-THOJ	
☐ UR-DNM	Boeing 767-322ER	25280/391	ex N202AC	
☐ UR-DNA	Embraer EMB.145EU (ERJ-145EU)	145088	ex G-EMBF	
☐ UR-DNB	Embraer EMB.145EU (ERJ-145EU)	145094	ex G-EMBG	
☐ UR-DNE	Embraer EMB.145EU (ERJ-145EU)	145357	ex G-EMBS	
☐ UR-DNF	Embraer EMB.145EU (ERJ-145EU)	145404	ex G-EMBT	
☐ UR-DNG	Embraer EMB.145EP (ERJ-145EP)	145394	ex G-ERJG	
☐ UR-DNI	Embraer EMB.145EP (ERJ-145EP)	145325	ex G-ERJF	
☐ UR-DNK	Embraer EMB.145EU (ERJ-145EU)	145039	ex G-EMBD	
☐ UR-DNL	Embraer EMB.145EU (ERJ-145EU)	145042	ex G-EMBE	
☐ UR-DNO	Embraer EMB.145EP (ERJ-145EP)	145237	ex G-ERJB	
☐ UR-DNP	Embraer EMB.145EP (ERJ-145EP)	145290	ex G-ERJD	
☐ UR-DNQ	Embraer EMB.145EP (ERJ-145EP)	145315	ex G-ERJE	
☐ UR-BWE	Yakovlev Yak-40	9530943	ex RA-87241	VIP
☐ UR-BWF	Yakovlev Yak-40	9711352	ex RA-88258	VIPop for Privatbank
☐ UR-LEV	Yakovlev Yak-40	9720154	ex LY-AAA	VIP
☐ UR-PIT	Yakovlev Yak-40	9610647	ex RA-88168	VIP
☐ UR-88237	Yakovlev Yak-40	9640751	ex CCCP-88237	
☐ UR-42376	Yakovlev Yak-42D	4520424914477	ex EP-CPK	
☐ UR-42405	Yakovlev Yak-42D	4520423116624	ex CCCP-42405	
☐ UR-42409	Yakovlev Yak-42D	4520421216709	ex ER-42409	
☐ UR-42426	Yakovlev Yak-42D	4520421304016	ex TC-IYI	
☐ UR-42449	Yakovlev Yak-42D	4520421401018	ex EP-CPC	

DONBASSAERO — ***Donbassaero (7D/UDC)*** — ***Donetsk (DOK)***

☐ UR-DAA	Airbus A320-211	0085	ex EI-CTD		
☐ UR-DAB	Airbus A320-231	0230	ex G-SSAS		
☐ UR-DAC	Airbus A320-233	0733	ex N451TA		
☐ UR-DAD	Airbus A320-233	0747	ex N453TA		
☐ UR-46302	Antonov An-24B	97305202	ex CCCP-46302		
☐ UR-46585	Antonov An-24B	97305004	ex CCCP-46585		
☐ UR-46586	Antonov An-24B	97305006	ex CCCP-46586		
☐ UR-46647	Antonov An-24RV	37309107	ex CCCP-46647		
☐ UR-47846	Antonov An-24B	17307408	ex CCCP-47846		
☐ UR-42308	Yakovlev Yak-42	11040303	ex CCCP-42308		
☐ UR-42318	Yakovlev Yak-42	4520423402051	ex RA-42318		
☐ UR-42319	Yakovlev Yak-42	4520423402062	ex CCCP-42319		
☐ UR-42327	Yakovlev Yak-42	4520424402161	ex T9-ABF		
☐ UR-42366	Yakovlev Yak-42	4520424814047	ex T9-ABH	no titles	
☐ UR-42372	Yakovlev Yak-42D	4520423914266	ex CCCP-42372		no titles
☐ UR-42377	Yakovlev Yak-42D	4520421014479	ex CCCP-42377		
☐ UR-42383	Yakovlev Yak-42D	4520422016201	ex T9-ABD		
☐ UR-42530	Yakovlev Yak-42	11120204	ex CCCP-42530		

GORLITSA AIRLINES — ***Gorlitsa (GOR)*** — ***Kiev-Zhulyany (IEV)***

☐ UR-BXU	Antonov An-26B-100	17311703	ex UR-26077	
☐ UR-BXV	Antonov An-26B-100	12110	ex UR-26113	
☐ UR-GLS	Antonov An-26B	07310109	ex RA-26017	Lsd to TWN
☐ UR-YMR	Antonov An-12BK	9346302	ex UR-11349	non-airworthy; Lsd to VPB

ILYICH AVIA — ***Marlupol (MPW)***

☐ UR-MMK	Yakovlev Yak-40	9521540	ex RA-87513	Ilyichevets 3	VIP
☐ UR-14007	Antonov An-140-100	36525305029		Ilyichevets 4	stored
☐ UR-14008	Antonov An-140-100	36525305032		Ilyichevets 2	stored
☐ UR-87440	Yakovlev Yak-40	9431635	ex RA-87440	Ilyichevets 1	

ISD AVIA — ***Isdavia (ISD)*** — ***Donetsk (DOK)***

☐ UR-CAR	Yakovlev Yak-40K	9741756	ex RA-21501	VIP
☐ UR-ISD	Yakovlev Yak-40	9530541	ex RA-88291	VIP stored

KHARKOV AVIATION PRODUCTION ASSOCIATION — West-Kharkov (WKH) — Kharkov-Osnova (HRK)

☐ UR-NPO	LET L-410UVP-E	871932	ex FLARF-01833	
☐ UR-67472	LET L-410UVP	841237	ex CCCP-67472	

KHORS AIR — Aircompany Khors (X9/KHO) — Kiev-Borispol (KBP)

☐ UR-CBV	Douglas DC-9-51 (ABS 3)	47772/890	ex OH-LYV	
☐ UR-CBY	Douglas DC-9-51 (ABS 3)	47773/891	ex OH-LYW	Lsd to UKM
☐ UR-CCR	Douglas DC-9-51 (ABS 3)	47736/827	ex OH-LYR	Lsd to UKM
☐ UR-CCT	Douglas DC-9-51 (ABS 3)	47696/808	ex OH-LYP	Lsd to UKM
☐ UR-BXI	McDonnell-Douglas MD-82	53170/2065	ex G-CEPJ	
☐ UR-BXL	McDonnell-Douglas MD-82	49512/1548	ex G-CEPG	
☐ UR-BXN	McDonnell-Douglas MD-83	49569/1405	ex LZ-LDV	Lsd to IRK
☐ UR-CBN	McDonnell-Douglas MD-82	49490/1352	ex N72830	
☐ UR-CBO	McDonnell-Douglas MD-82	49483/1314	ex RP-C2986	
☐ UR-CDN	McDonnell-Douglas MD-83	53520/2137	ex TC-OAV	
☐ UR-CDP	McDonnell-Douglas MD-83	49769/1559	ex SE-RDF	
☐ UR-CDR	McDonnell-Douglas MD-83	49949/1906	ex SX-BSW	
☐ UR-CDQ	McDonnell-Douglas MD-82	49372/1252	ex SX-BSQ	Lsd to IZG
☐ UR-CHJ	McDonnell-Douglas MD-82	53066/1938	ex N482JC	
☐ UR-CHK	McDonnell-Douglas MD-82	49188/1172	ex N501AM	
☐ UR-CHS	McDonnell-Douglas MD-83	49572/1468	ex LZ-LDA	Lsd to IRK
☐ UR-CHZ	McDonnell-Douglas MD-82	53169/2063	ex G-CEPI	

KIROVOHRADAVIA — Air Kirovograd (KAD) — Kirovograd-Khmelyovoye (KGO)

☐ UR-XYZ	Yakovlev Yak-40	9610946	ex RA-88155	VIP
☐ UR-87245	Yakovlev Yak-40	9531343	ex RA-87245	Lsd to UCR
☐ UR-87405	Yakovlev Yak-40	9421733	ex RA-87405	stored
☐ UR-87435	Yakovlev Yak-40	9431135	ex CCCP-87435	VIP
☐ UR-87479	Yakovlev Yak-40	9441838	ex CCCP-87479	
☐ UR-87562	Yakovlev Yak-40	9211321	ex CCCP-87562	
☐ UR-87814	Yakovlev Yak-40	9230524	ex RA-87814	VIP Also reported as Air Kirovograd

KRYM — Crimea Air (KYM) — Simferopol-Zavodstoye (SIP)

☐ UR-46833	Antonov An-24RV	17306710	ex CCCP-46833	stored SIP
☐ UR-47265	Antonov An-24RV	27307807	ex CCCP-47265	

LIZINGTEKHTRANS

☐ UR-NTA	Antonov An-148	0101		

LUGANSK AVIATION ENTERPRISE — Enterprise Lugansk (LE/LHS) — Lugansk (VSG)

☐ UR-46475	Antonov An-24RV	27308003	ex CCCP-46475	
☐ UR-46514	Antonov An-24RV	37308410	ex RA-46514	Lsd to AEW
☐ UR-46517	Antonov An-24RV	37308503	ex CCCP-46517	

LVIV AIRLINES — Ukraine West (5V/UKW) — Lviv-Snilow (LWO)

☐ UR-CFN	Antonov An-24RV	47309607	ex UR-46675	
☐ UR-46301	Antonov An-24B	97305201	ex CCCP-46301	
☐ UR-BXD	Ilyushin Il-18D	172011401	ex Soviet AF	
☐ UR-42317	Yakovlev Yak-42	4520422202039	ex 42317	
☐ UR-42358	Yakovlev Yak-42D	4520422811413	ex CCCP-42358	
☐ UR-42369	Yakovlev Yak-42D	4520422914190	ex CCCP-42369	all-white
☐ UR-42403	Yakovlev Yak-42D	4520422116588	ex CCCP-42403	no titles Lsd to SAI
☐ UR-42527	Yakovlev Yak-42	11040903	ex CCCP-42527	
☐ UR-42540	Yakovlev Yak-42	11140604	ex T9-ABC (2)	
☐ UR-42544	Yakovlev Yak-42	11151004	ex T9-ABC (1)	

MERIDIAN — (MEM) — Poltava (PLV)

☐ UR-CAG	Antonov An-12BK	9346904	ex ER-AXY	
☐ UR-CAH	Antonov An-12BK	8345604	ex ER-AXX	
☐ UR-CAJ	Antonov An-12BK	8346106	ex ER-AXZ	
☐ UR-CAK	Antonov An-12BP	6343707	ex ER-ACI	id not confirmed
☐ UR-CGW	Antonov An-12B	402410	ex EW-265TI	
☐ UR-CHF	Antonov An-26B	2706	ex Romanian 706	
☐ UR-CHT	Antonov An-26B	77305901	ex UR-VIV	
☐ UR-MDA	Antonov An-26-100	87307108		
☐ UR-67449	LET L-410UVP	841214	ex CCCP-67449	Avia Soyuz titles

MOTOR SICH AIRLINES		Motor Sich (M9/MSI)		Zaporozhye (OZH)
☐ UR-BXC	Antonov An-24RV	37308902	ex UR-46636	
☐ UR-MSI	Antonov An-24RV	27307608	ex UR-47699	
☐ UR-06130	Mil Mi-8T	22686		
☐ UR-06131	Mil-Mi-8T	22688		
☐ UR-11316	Antonov An-12BK	9346810	ex RA-11316	
☐ UR-11819	Antonov An-12B	6344009	ex CCCP-11819	no titles
☐ UR-14005	Antonov An-140	36525305021		
☐ UR-14006	Antonov An-140K	36525305025		
☐ UR-74026	Antonov An-74TK-200	36547096919	ex HK-3810X	Op for UN
☐ UR-87215	Yakovlev Yak-40	9510540	ex OK-FEJ	
☐ UR-88219	Yakovlev Yak-40K	9630550	ex CCCP-88219	

MRK AIRLINES		(6V)		Kiev-Borispol (KBP)
☐ UR-CGQ	SAAB SF.340A	340A-097	ex N771DF	

ODESSA AIRLINES		Odessa Air (5K/ODS)		Odessa-Tsentralny (ODS)
☐ UR-87327	Yakovlev Yak-40	9330630	ex CCCP-87327	
☐ UR-87421	Yakovlev Yak-40	9421734	ex CCCP-87421	
☐ UR-87469	Yakovlev Yak-40	9441437	ex CCCP-87469	
☐ UR-88299	Yakovlev Yak-40	9321028	ex OK-BYI	
☐ UR-14001	Antonov An-140	36535391003	ex UR-PWO	

PODILIA AVIA		Podilia (PDA)		Khmelnitsky-Ruzuchaya (HMJ)
☐ UR-26199	Antonov An-26-100	5806	ex LZ-MNO	stored IEV
☐ UR-46397	Antonov An-24B	07306301	ex RA-46397	Op for Istanbul Sabiha Cokcan

RIVNE UNIVERSAL AVIA		Rivne Universal (UNR)		Rivnu (RWN)
☐ UR-67084	LET L-410UVP	810721	ex UR-SKD	
☐ UR-67085	LET L-410UVP	810722	ex CCCP-67085	
☐ UR-67102	LET L-410UVP	841328	ex HA-LAP	
☐ UR-67439	LET L-410UVP	841204	ex YL-KAH	based UK
☐ UR-67504	LET L-410UVP	851408	ex HA-LAN	
☐ UR-67524	LET L-410UVP	851431	ex CCCP-67524	stored RWN
☐ UR-67663	LET L-410UVP-E	902525	ex CCCP-67663	

SEVASTOPOL AVIA		Sevavia (SVL)		Sevastopol
☐ UR-TMD	Ilyushin Il-18D	187009903	ex ER-ICL	

SHOVKOVLY SHLYAH		Way Aero (S8/SWW)		Kiev-Zhulyany (IEV)
☐ UR-CAF	Antonov An-12BP	3341209	ex 4K-AZ56	
☐ UR-CBU	Antonov An-12TBK	9346308	ex 4K-AZ18	
☐ UR-CGX	Antonov An-12BP	5343510	ex 4K-AZ60	

SHUTTLE BIRD				Kiev-Borispol (KBP)
☐ UR-SEV	LET L-410UVP	851507	ex LY-KAJ	

SOUTH AIRLINES		Southline (YG/OTL)		Odessa-Tsentralny (ODS)
☐ UR-MLD	LET L-410UVP	820830	ex UR-87330	
☐ UR-SEV	LET L-410UVP	851507	ex YL-KAJ Shuttle Bird titles	
☐ UR-TVA	LET L-410UVP	851438	ex ES-PLI	
☐ UR-YAM	LET L-410UVP-E	902513	ex UR-67659	
☐ UR-67368	LET L-410UVP	830936	ex CCCP-67368	
☐ UR-BZY	Tupolev Tu-134A-3	6348565	ex ER-TCH	
☐ UR-CFA	Yakovlev Yak-42D	4520423016269	ex LY-SKC	
☐ UR-CFH	Yakovlev Yak-42D	4520423606235	ex UR-42337	
☐ UR-EEE	Yakovlev Yak-40	9340632	ex 5N-DAN	
☐ UR-IMX	SAAB SF.340B	340B-225	ex YR-VGR	
☐ UR-SAL	Tupolev Tu-134A-3	62315	ex UR-65765	
☐ UR-47308	Antonov An-24RV	57310308	ex CCCP-47308	
☐ UR-47311	Antonov An-24RV	57310402	ex CCCP-47311	
☐ UR-87818	Yakovlev Yak-40	9230924	ex CCCP-87818	all-white

TAVREY AIRCOMPANY		Tavrey (T6/TVR)		Odessa-Tsentralny (ODS)
☐ UR-CER	Yakovlev Yak-42D	4520423914323	ex UN-42640	

UES AVIA	Aviasystem (UES)		Dnepropetrovsk-Kodaki (DNK)
☐ UR-UES Tupolev Tu-134A-3M	66472	ex RA-65725	
☐ UR-87590 Yakovlev Yak-40K	9741156	ex OK-HER	
☐ UR-87591 Yakovlev Yak-40K	9741056	ex OK-HEQ	

UKRAINE AIR ALLIANCE	Ukraine Airalliance (UKL)		Kiev-Borispol (KBP)
☐ UR-BXQ Ilyushin Il-76TD	1023410360	ex EX-832	Lsd to MXU
☐ UR-BXR Ilyushin Il-76TD	1023411384	ex EX-411	Lsd to MXU
☐ UR-BXS Ilyushin Il-76TD	1023411368	ex EX-436	Lsd to MXU
☐ UR-CAI Antonov An-26B	7010	ex UR-26519	Lsd to TAC
☐ UR-CAT Ilyushin Il-76TD	0053464922	ex UR-76663	
☐ UR-CID Ilyushin Il-76TD	0063465956	ex UP-I7640	
☐ UR-26650 Antonov An-26B	87307507	ex UN-26650	all-white
☐ UR-48083 Antonov An-32B	3001	ex CCCP-48083	stored
☐ UR- Antonov An-24B	27307903	ex LZ-ASZ	

UKRAINE AIR ENTERPRISE	Enterprise Ukraine (UKN)		Kiev-Borispol (KBP)
☐ UR-YVA Antonov An-74TK-300	36547098984	ex UR-LDK	
☐ UR-65556 Tupolev Tu-134A-3	66372	ex 65556	
☐ UR-65718 Tupolev Tu-134A-3	63668	ex 65718	
☐ UR-65782 Tupolev Tu-134A-3	62672	ex CCCP-65782	
☐ UR-86527 Ilyushin Il-62M	4037758	ex 86527	
☐ UR-86528 Ilyushin Il-62M	4038111	ex 86528	

UKRAINE FLIGHT STATE ACADEMY	Flight Academy (UFA)		Kirovograd-Khmelyovoye (KGO)
☐ UR-47179 Antonov An-24B	99901904	ex CCCP-47179	
☐ UR-47702 Antonov An-24B	59900203	ex CCCP-47702	
☐ UR-47705 Antonov An-24B	59900303	ex CCCP-47705	
☐ UR-47711 Antonov An-24B	69900501	ex CCCP-47711	
☐ UR-47743 Antonov An-24B	79901106	ex CCCP-47743	
☐ UR-47791 Antonov An-24B	67303004	ex LZ-MNF	
☐ UR-67357 LET L-410UVP	820917	ex CCCP-67357	
☐ UR-67392 LET L-410UVP	831020	ex CCCP-67392	
☐ UR-67395 LET L-410UVP	831023	ex CCCP-67395	
☐ UR-67411 LET L-410UVP	831039	ex CCCP-67411	
☐ UR-67417 LET L-410UVP	831108	ex CCCP-67417	
☐ UR-67526 LET L-410UVP	851433	ex CCCP-67526	
☐ UR-67527 LET L-410UVP	851434	ex CCCP-67527	
☐ UR-67543 LET L-410UVP	851510	ex LZ-MNB	
☐ UR-67555 LET L-410UVP	851519	ex LZ-MNC	

UKRAINE INTERNATIONAL AIRLINES	Ukraine International (PS/AUI)		Kiev-Borispol (KBP)
☐ UR-GAH Boeing 737-32Q/W	29130/3105	ex N1779B Mayrni	
☐ UR-GAJ Boeing 737-5Y0	25192/2262	ex PT-SSA	
☐ UR-GAK Boeing 737-5Y0/W	26075/2374	ex PT-SLN	
☐ UR-GAM Boeing 737-4Y0	25190/2256	ex HA-LEU	
☐ UR-GAN Boeing 737-36N/W	28569/2996	ex F-GRFC	
☐ UR-GAO Boeing 737-4Z9	25147/2043	ex OE-LNH	
☐ UR-GAP Boeing 737-4Z9	27094/2432	ex OE-LNI	
☐ UR-GAQ Boeing 737-33R/W	28869/2887	ex SX-BLA	
☐ UR-GAR Boeing 737-4Y0	26081/2442	ex EI-CVP	
☐ UR-GAS Boeing 737-528/W	25236/2443	ex S5-AAM	
☐ UR-GAT Boeing 737-528/W	25237/2464	ex F-GJNM	Lsd ADR
☐ UR-GAU Boeing 737-5Y0/W	25182/2211	ex N182GE	
☐ UR-GAV Boeing 737-4C9	26437/2249	ex EI-DGM	
☐ UR-GAW Boeing 737-5Y0	24898/2079	ex N898ED	
☐ UR-GAX Boeing 737-4Y0	26066/2301	ex LZ-HVA	
☐ UR-PSA Boeing 737-8HX/W	29658/2970	ex N1787B	
☐ UR-PSB Boeing 737-8HX/W	29654/3018		

UKRAINIAN CARGO AIRWAYS	Cargotrans (6Z/UKS)		Zaporozhye (OZH)
☐ UR-UCA Ilyushin Il-76TD	0073479394	ex UR-76715	
☐ UR-UCC Ilyushin Il-76MD	0083489647	ex UR-78775	Op for United Nations
☐ UR-UCO Ilyushin Il-76MD	0053458749	ex UR-76630	Op for United Nations
☐ UR-UCQ Ilyushin Il-76MD	0063465963	ex UR-76671	
☐ UR-UCT Ilyushin Il-76TD	0063470089	ex UR-76691	Op for United Nations
☐ UR-UCU Ilyushin Il-76MD	0073476275	ex UR-76729	
☐ UR-UCX Ilyushin Il-76MD	0063470112	ex UR-76695	
☐ UR-UCK Antonov An-12BK	0346905	ex 11304	
☐ UR-UCN Antonov An-12BK	00347604	ex UR-11303	
☐ UR-UCZ Tupolev Tu-154B-2	82A-561	ex UR-85561	Operates as UC Airways
☐ UR-UDM Antonov An-26	0909	ex UR-26241	
☐ UR-UDS Antonov An-26	97307808		

☐ UR-UWA	Mil Mi-8MTV-1	93151	ex LZ-MOT	
☐ UR-UWC	Mil Mi-8MTV-1	95236	ex UR-MOR	
☐ UR-UWD	Mil Mi-8MTV-1	95235	ex UR-MOQ	

UKRAINIAN PILOT SCHOOL — Pilot School (UPL) — Kiev-Chaika

☐ UR-VTV	LET L-410UVP	810705	ex UR-67069	based UK for para flights
☐ UR-28721	WSK/PZL Antonov An-28	1AJ007-06	ex RA-28721	

UKTRANSLIZING

☐ UR-14004	Antonov An-140	3652530211

UM AIR — Mediterranee Ukraine (UF/UKM) — Kiev-Borispol (KBP)

☐ UR-CBY	Douglas DC-9-51 (ABS 3)	47773/891	ex OH-LYW		Lsd fr KHO
☐ UR-CCR	Douglas DC-9-51 (ABS 3)	47736/827	ex OH-LYR		Lsd fr KHO
☐ UR-CCS	Douglas DC-9-51 (ABS 3)	47737/829	ex OH-LYS		Lsd fr KHO
☐ UR-CCT	Douglas DC-9-51 (ABS 3)	47696/808	ex OH-LYP	Diana	Lsd fr KHO
☐ UR-CDS	Antonov An-24RV	57310209	ex JU-1010		
☐ UR-BHJ	McDonnell-Douglas MD-83	53184/2088	ex TC-AKL		Lsd to CPN
☐ UR-CFF	McDonnell-Douglas MD-83	49845/1573	ex N989PG		
☐ UR-CFG	McDonnell-Douglas MD-82	49370/1206	ex N14816		
☐ UR-CHY	McDonnell-Douglas MD-82	53171/2067	ex G-CEPK		

UTAIR UKRAINE

☐ UR-UTA	ATR 42-320	382	ex VP-BLP
☐ UR-UTB	ATR 42-320	386	ex VP-BLQ

VETERAN AIRLINES — Veteran (VPB) — Simferopol-Zavodstoye (SIP)

☐ UR-CBZ	Antonov An-12BP	402707	ex RA-11117	all-white	
☐ UR-CCY	Antonov An-12B	02348106	ex RA-11124		Lsd to ACP
☐ UR-CDB	Antonov An-12BP	401605	ex RA-11766	all-white	
☐ UR-CEM	Antonov An-12BP	3340908	ex RA-11813		Lsd to ACP
☐ UR-CEN	Antonov An-12BP	02348203	ex RA-11128	all-white	stored
☐ UR-PAS	Antonov An-12AP	2401105		all-white	op for SDR
☐ UR-YMR	Antonov An-12BK	9346302	ex UR-11349		Lsd fr GOR

VOLARE AVIATION ENTERPRISE — Ukraine Volare (VRE) — Rivne/Frankfurt-Hahn (RWN/HHN)

☐ UR-BWM	Antonov An-12BK	00347004	ex 20 blue
☐ UR-LMI	Antonov An-12BK	6344605	ex 73 blue
☐ UR-LTG	Antonov An-12BP	00347201	ex RA-12986
☐ UR-SMA	Antonov An-12BK	7345208	ex UR-11348
☐ UR-76628	Ilyushin Il-76TD	0053458741	ex CCCP-76628
☐ UR-76687	Ilyushin Il-76TD	0063469051	ex CCCP-76687

WIND ROSE — Wind Rose 7W/WRC — Kiev-Borispol (BPL)

☐ UR-WRA	Antonov An-24RV	37308709	ex UR-VIK		
☐ UR-WRF	Embraer 190-200	19000169	ex HZ-NQB		
☐ UR-WRG	Embraer 190-200	19000157	ex HZ-NQA	Sophia Kylvska Ukraine	
☐ UR-CDI	McDonnell-Douglas MD-82	49279/1230	ex SX-BMP		Lsd to IRK
☐ UR-CDX	McDonnell-Douglas MD-82	53119/1956	ex N481JC		
☐ UR-CEW	McDonnell-Douglas MD-82	49634/1419	ex N34838		
☐ UR-WRB	McDonnell-Douglas MD-82	49364/1276	ex N937AS		
☐ UR-WRE	McDonnell-Douglas MD-82	49278/1183	ex UR-CDA		

WIZZ AIR UKRAINE — Wizzair Ukraine (WU/WUA) — Kiev-Borispol (BPL)

☐ UR-WUA	Airbus A320-232	3531	ex F-WWDX
☐ UR-WUB	Airbus A319-132	3741	ex F-WWIB

YAVSON

☐ UR-MAY	Yakovlev Yak-40

YUZMASHAVIA — Yuzmash (2N/UMK) — Dnepropetrovsk-Kodakı (DNK)

☐ UR-78785	Ilyushin Il-76MD	0083489691	ex RA-78785	
☐ UR-78786	Ilyushin Il-76TD	0083490693	ex CCCP-78786	
☐ UR-87298	Yakovlev Yak-40	9241325	ex CCCP-87298	VIP, Dnepropetrosvk Insurance Grp
☐ UR-87508	Yakovlev Yak-40	9521040	ex CCCP-87508	
☐ UR-87951	Yakovlev Yak-40K	9810957	ex CCCP-87951	

VH- AUSTRALIA (Commonwealth of Australia)

AD-ASTRAL — Perth International, WA (PER)

☐ VH-FWA	Beech 1900C	UB-61	ex N818BE

AEROLINK AIR SERVICES — Sydney-Bankstown, NSA (BWU)

☐ VH-LJF	Cessna 310R	310R0691	ex N41TV
☐ VH-OZF	Embraer EMB.110P1 Bandeirante	110201	ex G-EIIO
☐ VH-XMA	Cessna 310R	310R0628	ex N31HS

AEROPELICAN AIR SERVICES — Aeropelican (OT/PEL) — Newcastle-Belmont, NSW (BEO)

☐ VH-OTA	British Aerospace Jetstream 3202	868	ex VH-TQM	
☐ VH-OTD	British Aerospace Jetstream 3202	978	ex G-BZYP	City of Newcastle
☐ VH-OTE	British Aerospace Jetstream 3202	980	ex G-CBEP	City of Port Stephens
☐ VH-OTF	British Aerospace Jetstream 3202	982	ex G-CBER	Narrabri Shire
☐ VH-OTP	British Aerospace Jetstream 3202	974	ex G-BURU	Pride of Mudgee
☐ VH-OTQ	British Aerospace Jetstream 3202	975	ex G-BUTW	
☐ VH-OTR	British Aerospace Jetstream 3202	976	ex G-BUUZ	
☐ VH-HAN	Swearingen SA.227DC Metro 23	DC-822B	ex N822MM	

AIR FRASER ISLAND — Maryborough, QLD (MBH)

☐ VH-BFS	Gippsland GA-8 Airvan	GA8-03-035
☐ VH-BNX	Gippsland GA-8 Airvan	GA8-03-032

AIR FRONTIER — Darwin, NT (DRW)

☐ VH-CMH	Beech Baron 58	TH-108	ex VH-HWQ
☐ VH-DMD	Beech Baron 58	TH-1294	ex N1839Y
☐ VH-JBH	Beech 65-B80 Queen Air	LD-443	ex VH-AMQ
☐ VH-JMD	Piper PA-31 Turbo Navajo B	31-7401260	ex VH-SOW
☐ VH-LHE	Piper PA-31-350 Chieftain	31-7305028	ex N2GG
☐ VH-MCE	Cessna 210M	21062633	ex N761YV
☐ VH-MRH	Beech 65-B80 Queen Air	LD-456	ex VH-BQA
☐ VH-OBI	de Havilland DH.104 Dove 8	04525	ex G-LIDD
☐ VH-PRH	Beech Baron 58	TH-380	ex N3103W
☐ VH-SWP	Beech 65-B80 Queen Air	LD-472	ex VH-MWK

AIR LINK — (ZL) — Dubbo, NSW (DBO)

☐ VH-DVR	Piper PA-31-350 Chieftain	31-7952052	ex N27936
☐ VH-DVW	Piper PA-31-350 Chieftain	31-7952011	ex VH-LHH
☐ VH-MWP	Piper PA-31-350 Chieftain	31-8352005	ex N4109C
☐ VH-MZF	Piper PA-31-350 Chieftain	31-8252039	ex N41064

☐ VH-BWQ	Cessna 310R	310R1401	ex N4915A
☐ VH-HSL	Cessna 310R	310R0946	ex N8643G
☐ VH-JMP	Cessna 310R	310R1270	ex N125SP
☐ VH-RUE	Beech 1900D	UE-53	ex ZK-JNG
☐ VH-RUI	Beech 1900D	UE-395	ex N831CA
☐ VH-TDL	Piper PA-39 Twin Comanche C/R	39-152	ex VH-NHC

AIR SOUTH REGIONAL — Adelaide, SA (ADL)

☐ VH-EMP	Beech Baron 58	TH-1491	ex VH-FEK
☐ VH-ENT	Cessna 404 Titan II	404-0818	ex ZK-ECP
☐ VH-EQB	Embraer EMB.110P1 Bandeirante	110214	ex ZK-MAS
☐ VH-SKC	Cessna 404 Titan II	404-0404	ex VH-TWZ
☐ VH-SZP	Cessna 404 Titan II	404-0637	ex ZS-OVU
☐ VH-TMP	Cessna 404 Titan II	404-0125	ex N37182
☐ VH-ZOA	Beech 1900D	UE-85	ex ZS-SER

AIR WHITSUNDAY SEAPLANES — (RWS) — Whitsunday/Airlie Beach, QLD (WSY)

☐ VH-AQV	de Havilland DHC-2 Beaver	1257	ex N67685	Floatplane stored
☐ VH-AWD	de Havilland DHC-2 Beaver	1066	ex VH-AYS	Floatplane
☐ VH-AWI	de Havilland DHC-2 Beaver	298	ex VH-HQE	Floatplane
☐ VH-AWY	de Havilland DHC-2 Beaver	1444	ex VH-SSG	Floatplane

☐ VH-PGA	Cessna 208 Caravan I	20800312	ex N1127W	Floatplane
☐ VH-PGB	Cessna 208 Caravan I	20800346	ex N209E	Floatplane
☐ VH-PGT	Cessna 208 Caravan I	20800345	ex N208E	Floatplane

AIRLINES OF TASMANIA — Airtas (FO/ATM) — Hobart, TAS (HBA)

☐ VH-ATO	GAF N22C Nomad	108	ex F-ODMX
☐ VH-ATZ	Dornier 228-212	8198	ex F-OHAA

☐ VH-BTD	Piper PA-31 Navajo C	31-7912041	ex VH-ATG		
☐ VH-BTI	Piper PA-31 Navajo C	31-8212003	ex ZK-VNA		
☐ VH-BTN	Aero Commander 680FL	1695-35	ex D-IBME		
☐ VH-CCN	Cessna 404 Titan II	404-0801	ex VH-WZK		
☐ VH-LAD	Cessna 404 Titan II	404-0224	ex 9V-BMT		
☐ VH-LAM	Cessna 404 Titan II	404-0627	ex VH-ANN		
☐ VH-LCD	Cessna U206G Stationair 6	20604523	ex N673AA		
☐ VH-MYS	Cessna U206G Stationair 6	20605162	ex N4921U		
☐ VH-OBL	Britten-Norman BN-2A-20 Islander	2035	ex ZK-OBL		
☐ VH-RQW	Britten-Norman BN-2A-26 Islander	73	ex P2-ALI		
☐ VH-RTP	Britten-Norman BN-2A-6 Islander	79	ex G-AXIN		
☐ VH-SGA	Piper PA-31P Pressurised Navajo	31P-7300166	ex N66804		
☐ VH-WZM	Cessna 404 Titan II	404-0837	ex N68075		

AIRNORTH REGIONAL — ***Topend (TL/ANO)*** — ***Darwin, NT***

☐ VH-ANB	Embraer EMB.120ER Brasilia	120116	ex VH-XFX		
☐ VH-ANJ	Embraer EMB.120ER Brasilia	120163	ex N455UE		
☐ VH-ANK	Embraer EMB.120ER Brasilia	120155	ex VH-YDD		
☐ VH-ANN	Embraer EMB.120ER Brasilia	120203	ex VH-BRP		
☐ VH-ANZ	Embraer EMB.120RT Brasilia	120135	ex VH-XFR		
☐ VH-DIL	Embraer EMB.120ER Brasilia	120153	ex N285UE		
☐ VH-ANA	Swearingen SA.227DC Metro 23	DC-871B	ex VH-HCB		
☐ VH-ANO	Embraer 170-100LR (170LR)	17000099	ex B-KXB	Savannah	
☐ VH-ANV	Embraer 170-100LR (170LR)	17000280	ex PT-TQG		
☐ VH-ANW	Swearingen SA.227DC Metro 23	DC-873B	ex N3031Q		
☐ VH-ANY	Swearingen SA.227DC Metro 23	DC-840B	ex N3022L		

ALLIANCE AIRLINES — ***Alli (QQ/UTY)*** — ***Brisbane-International, QLD (BNE)***

☐ VH-AHX	Fokker F.27 Mk.050 (Fokker 50)	20161	ex 9M-MGC		stored ADL
☐ VH-FKV	Fokker F.27 Mk.050 (Fokker 50)	20303	ex B-12273		
☐ VH-FKW	Fokker F.27 Mk.050 (Fokker 50)	20306	ex B-12275		
☐ VH-FKX	Fokker F.27 Mk.050 (Fokker 50)	20312	ex B-12276		
☐ VH-FKY	Fokker F.27 Mk.050 (Fokker 50)	20284	ex B-12271		
☐ VH-FKZ	Fokker F.27 Mk.050 (Fokker 50)	20286	ex B-12272		
☐ VH-FKA	Fokker F.28-0100 (Fokker 100)	11345	ex N885US		
☐ VH-FKC	Fokker F.28-0100 (Fokker 100)	11349	ex N887US		
☐ VH-FKD	Fokker F.28-0100 (Fokker 100)	11357	ex N888AU		
☐ VH-FKE	Fokker F.28-0100 (Fokker 100)	11358	ex P2-ANA		stored BNE
☐ VH-FKF	Fokker F.28-0100 (Fokker 100)	11365	ex N890US		
☐ VH-FKG	Fokker F.28-0100 (Fokker 100)	11366	ex N891US		
☐ VH-FKJ	Fokker F.28-0100 (Fokker 100)	11372	ex N892US		
☐ VH-FKK	Fokker F.28-0100 (Fokker 100)	11379	ex N894US		
☐ VH-FKL	Fokker F.28-0100 (Fokker 100)	11380	ex N895US		
☐ VH-FWH	Fokker F.28-0100 (Fokker 100)	11316	ex G-BXNF	City of Townsville	based PER
☐ VH-FWI	Fokker F.28-0100 (Fokker 100)	11318	ex G-FIOR	City of Rockhampton	based PER

ALLIGATOR AIRWAYS — ***Kununurra, WA (KNX)***

☐ VH-RAS	Cessna 207 Skywagon	20700158	ex N1558U
☐ VH-WOT	Cessna 207 Skywagon	20700267	ex ZK-DEW
☐ VH-WOU	Cessna 207 Skywagon	20700099	ex N91164
☐ VH-WOX	Cessna 207 Skywagon	20700130	ex VH-DMS
☐ VH-WOY	Cessna 207A Stationair 8	20700707	ex N9592M
☐ VH-WOG	Gippsland GA-8 Airvan	GA8-02-012	
☐ VH-WOP	Gippsland GA-8 Airvan	GA8-00-004	ex VH-RYT
☐ VH-WOQ	Gippsland GA-8 Airvan	GA8-00-127	
☐ VH-WOS	Gippsland GA-8 Airvan	GA8-00-099	ex VH-AFJ
☐ VH-WOV	Gippsland GA-8 Airvan	GA8-01-006	
☐ VH-EDE	Cessna 210L Centurion II	21060517	ex (N94140)
☐ VH-IXE	Partenavia P.68B	178	
☐ VH-KWP	Piper PA-34-220T Seneca	34-8133024	ex ZS-KWN
☐ VH-PQJ	Cessna U206F Stationair	U20602245	ex N1537U
☐ VH-RDA	Piper PA-31-350 Navajo Chieftain	31-7305032	ex N74903
☐ VH-WNI	Cessna 210M Centurion II	21062462	ex N761RR

ARNHEM LAND COMMUNITY AIRLINE — ***Cairns, QLD (CNS)***

☐ VH-ASJ	Cessna U206G Stationair 6	U20605867	ex N6402X
☐ VH-KBN	Cessna U206G Stationair 6	U20606630	ex N9731Z
☐ VH-LHQ	Cessna U206G Stationair	U20603773	ex VH-LGN
☐ VH-LHX	Cessna U206G Stationair	U20603555	ex VH-STK
☐ VH-SOP	Cessna U206G Stationair 6 II	U20606216	ex N6284Z
☐ VH-WOC	Cessna U206F Stationair	U20603464	ex N1948C
☐ VH-LHC	Gippsland GA-8 Airvan	GA8-04-057	ex VH-LHH
☐ VH-LHD	Gippsland GA-8 Airvan	GA8-04-051	ex VH-SFX

☐ VH-LHV	Gippsland GA-8 Airvan	GA8-04-045	ex VH-UAF
☐ VH-MFI	Gippsland GA-8 Airvan	GA8-04-065	ex P2-MFI
☐ VH-MFX	Gippsland GA-8 Airvan	GA8-04-053	ex VH-TMN
☐ VH-MTR	Gippsland GA-8 Airvan	GA8-05-073	ex PK-MPK
☐ VH-WRA	Gippsland GA-8 Airvan	GA8-01-007	
☐ VH-WRU	Gippsland GA-8 Airvan	GA8-04-048	ex VH-MEX
☐ VH-LHL	Cessna 210N Centurion II	21063739	ex VH-UBO
☐ VH-UBL	Cessna 210N Centurion II	21064712	ex N8148G

AUSTRALIAN AIR EXPRESS (XM/XME) Melbourne-Tullamarine, VIC (MEL)

☐ VH-EEP	Swearingen SA.227AT Expediter	AT-567	ex N565UP	Op by QWA
☐ VH-NJF	British Aerospace 146 Srs.300QT	E3198	ex G-BTLD	Op by NJS
☐ VH-NJM	British Aerospace 146 Srs.300QT	E3194	ex G-BTHT	Op by NJS
☐ VH-NJV	British Aerospace 146 Srs.100QT	E1002	ex G-BSTA	Op by NJS
☐ VH-XMB	Boeing 737-376 (SF)	23478/1251	ex ZK-JNG	Op by EFA
☐ VH-XML	Boeing 737-376 (SF)	23486/1286	ex ZK-JNF	Op by EFA
☐ VH-XMO	Boeing 737-376 (SF)	23488/1352	ex ZK-JNH	Op by EFA
☐ VH-XMR	Boeing 737-376 (SF)	23490/1390	ex ZK-JNA	Op by EFA

AVTEX AVIATION Sydney-Bankstown, NSW (BWU)

☐ VH-HJE	Piper PA-31-350 Chieftain	31-7852074	ex N5038X
☐ VH-HJK	Piper PA-31-350 Chieftain	31-8052153	ex VH-JNX
☐ VH-HJS	Piper PA-31-350 Navajo Chieftain	31-7652091	ex VH-TWB
☐ VH-IGK	Piper PA-31-350 Navajo Chieftain	31-7752190	ex N711WE
☐ VH-IGW	Piper PA-31P-350 Mojave	31P-8414019	ex N9223Y
☐ VH-MKK	Piper PA-31-350 Navajo Chieftain	31-7652068	ex VH-OZQ
☐ VH-OGW	Piper PA-31P-350 Mojave	31P-8414044	ex VH-HFD
☐ VH-OZG	Piper PA-31-350 Chieftain	31-7952053	ex VH-LGI
☐ VH-OZP	Piper PA-31-350 Navajo Chieftain	31-7752050	ex VH-MBP
☐ VH-PGW	Piper PA-31P-350 Mojave	31P-8414036	ex N855MH
☐ VH-TWU	Piper PA-31-350 Navajo Chieftain	31-7552110	ex N61387
☐ VH-XGW	Piper PA-31P-350 Mojave	31P-8414001	ex N9087P
☐ VH-AVS	Ted Smith Aerostar 601	60-0604-7961194	ex N8204J
☐ VH-IGN	Piper PA-61 Aerostar 601P	61-0682-7962142	ex N60700
☐ VH-OZN	Swearingen SA.227AC Metro III	AC-665	ex N2698C
☐ VH-OZV	Swearingen SA.227AC Metro III	AC-610B	ex VH-TGQ
☐ VH-PDN	Piper PA-31 Turbo Navajo	31-177	ex N9131Y
☐ VH-PWY	Ted Smith Aerostar 601P	61P-0378-123	ex N9785Q

BARRIER AVIATION Cairns, QLD (CNS)

☐ VH-JOH	Cessna 402C	4020486	ex VH-JOC
☐ VH-JOV	Cessna 402C	4020087	ex VH-JOC
☐ VH-LKC	Cessna 402C	4020625	ex N6386X
☐ VH-THX	Cessna 402C	4020250	ex PK-DCC
☐ VH-UCM	Cessna 402C	4020472	ex N6838D
☐ VH-VDK	Cessna 402C III	402C0801	ex PK-DCY
☐ VH-BSO	Britten-Norman BN-2B-26 Islander	2129	ex JA5282
☐ VH-BWO	Britten-Norman BN-2A-26 Islander	2042	ex T8A-103
☐ VH-CIR	Cessna 310R II	310R1813	ex G-BPYC
☐ VH-FTM	Cessna 210L Centurion	310R0021	ex ZS-JBL
☐ VH-HGO	Cessna 310R II	21061159	ex N2198S
☐ VH-IEK	Piper PA-31 Navajo	31-759	ex VH-TFK
☐ VH-MDU	Cessna 210M Centurion	21061634	ex (N732NB)
☐ VH-MHL	Cessna 207 Skywagon	20700059	ex N91076
☐ VH-URJ	Britten-Norman BN-2A-21 Islander	402	ex VH-OIA

BRINDABELLA AIRLINES (FQ) Canberra, ACT (CBR)

☐ VH-SEF	Swearingen SA.227AC Metro III	AC-641	ex ZK-SDA	
☐ VH-TAG	Swearingen SA.227AC Metro III	AC-705	ex ZK-NSU	
☐ VH-TAH	British Aerospace Jetstream 41	41084	ex N566HK	
☐ VH-WAL	Piper PA-31 Turbo Navajo B	31-7300943	ex N71TC	
☐ VH-	British Aerospace Jetstream 41		ex N	on order

Operates services for Qantas

BRISTOW HELICOPTERS (AUSTRALIA)
Perth-Jandakot/Karratha/Barrow Island, WA / Darwin, NT (-/KTA/BWB/DRW)

☐ G-BMCX	Aérospatiale AS.332L	2164		
☐ VH-BHH	Aérospatiale AS.332L	2059	ex G-TIGW	Nairn
☐ VH-BHK	Aérospatiale AS.332L	2096	ex G-TIGU	
☐ VH-BHX	Aérospatiale AS.332L	2079	ex G-BRWE	City of Albany
☐ VH-BHY	Aérospatiale AS.332L	2129	ex B-HZY	
☐ VH-BWJ	Aérospatiale AS.332L	2023	ex G-TIGB	
☐ VH-BXZ	Aérospatiale AS.332L	2078	ex G-TIGT	
☐ VH-BYT	Aérospatiale AS.332L	2083	ex G-CEYJ	

☐ VH-BYV	Aérospatiale AS.332L	2061	ex G-TIGO
☐ VH-BZB	Aérospatiale AS.332L	2157	ex LN-OND
☐ VH-BZC	Aérospatiale AS.332L	2036	ex 9M-BEM
☐ VH-BZF	Aérospatiale AS.332L	2064	ex G-TIGP
☐ VH-BZU	Aérospatiale AS.332L	2045	ex G-TIGM
☐ VH-TZD	Aérospatiale AS.332L	2122	ex G-BLPM
☐ VH-ZFB	Eurocopter EC225LP	2695	ex G-ZZSO
☐ VH-ZFC	Eurocopter EC225LP	2709	ex G-ZZSP
☐ VH-ZFD	Eurocopter EC225LP	2724	ex G-CFZE
☐ VH-ZFE	Eurocopter EC225LP	2726	ex G-CFZY
☐ VH-ZFH	Eurocopter EC225LP	2723	ex G-ZZSH
☐ VH-BHI	Sikorsky S-76A+	760118	ex G-BVKS
☐ VH-BHL	Sikorsky S-76A+	760046	ex G-BHLY
☐ VH-BHM	Sikorsky S-76A+	760107	ex G-BVKO
☐ VH-BHQ	Sikorsky S-76A++	760090	ex G-BVKN
☐ VH-BZR	Sikorsky S-76A++	760132	ex EZ-S704
☐ VH-BZW	Sikorsky S-76A+	760157	ex G-BITR
☐ VH-TZK	Sikorsky S-76A++	760718	ex N2577C
☐ VH-TZL	Sikorsky S-76C+	760735	ex G-CFPY
☐ VH-TZN	Sikorsky S-76A	760116	ex G-BVKR
☐ VH-ZFJ	Sikorsky S-76C+	760733	ex G-CFPV
☐ VH-BHO	Bell 206L-3 LongRanger	51354	ex JA9893
☐ VH-BKK	Kawasaki/MBB BK-117B-1	1044	ex JA9993

Subsidiary of Bristow Group

BROOME AVIATION — *Broome, WA (BME)*

☐ VH-CRN	Cessna 208 Caravan I	20800428	ex VH-URT
☐ VH-MOX	Cessna 208 Caravan I	20800227	ex VH-NGD
☐ VH-NGS	Cessna 208B Caravan I	208B0416	ex N1114W
☐ VH-NTC	Cessna 208B Caravan I	208B0418	ex VH-DEX
☐ VH-TLD	Cessna 208B Caravan I	208B0339	ex P2-TSJ
☐ VH-TWX	Cessna 208B Caravan I	208B0648	ex VH-UZF
☐ VH-DZH	Cessna 210L Centurion II	21061247	ex VH-SJQ
☐ VH-EGB	Cessna 210M Centurion	21062858	ex N6969B
☐ VH-KDM	Cessna 210N Centurion II	21063041	ex N6467N
☐ VH-KJL	Cessna 210L Centurion II	21060776	ex N1765C
☐ VH-RLP	Cessna 210-5 (205)	21050213	ex (N8213Z)
☐ VH-SKQ	Cessna 210L Centurion II	21061243	ex N1629C
☐ VH-TCI	Cessna 210L Centurion II	21060548	ex N94225
☐ VH-WTX	Cessna 210L Centurion II	21060222	ex (N93025)
☐ VH-BBU	Cessna U206G Stationair	20604109	ex N756HS
☐ VH-DAW	Cessna 310R II	310R0148	ex N5028J
☐ VH-DLF	Cessna 404	404-0683	ex N6763K
☐ VH-JOR	Cessna 404	404-0642	ex D-IEEE
☐ VH-SHZ	Cessna U206G Stationair	20603726	ex (N9909N)

CAIRNS SEAPLANES — *Cairns, QLD (CNS)*

☐ VH-CXS	de Havilland DHC-2 Beaver	1360	ex N211AW	Floatplane
☐ VH-PCF	de Havilland DHC-2 Beaver	1348	ex VH-CZS	Floatplane

CASAIR — *Perth International, WA (PER)*

☐ VH-AKG	Beech Baron 58	TH-1011	ex N2070D
☐ VH-KGX	Swearingen SA.226TC Metro II	TC-326	ex VH-UUK
☐ VH-NGX	Swearingen SA.226TC Metro II	TC-287	ex VH-WGV
☐ VH-OGX	Swearingen SA.226TC Metro II	TC-395	ex VH-TFQ
☐ VH-WGX	Swearingen SA.226TC Metro II	TC-312	ex N1015B

CENTRAL AIRLINES — *Emerald, QLD (EMD)*

☐ VH-BCQ	Piper PA-31-350 Chieftain	31-7952134	ex N35265
☐ VH-FLZ	Beech Baron 58	TH-274	ex VH-OTP
☐ VH-FWJ	Piper PA-31 Navajo C	31-7712092	ex ZK-PNX
☐ VH-LWW	Piper PA-31 Navajo C	31-8112034	ex VH-NMT
☐ VH-NWN	Piper PA-31-350 Chieftain	31-8152197	ex VH-SAQ
☐ VH-TQC	Cessna 210N Centurion	21063325	ex N44ZP
☐ VH-VJE	Dornier Do.228-202	8041	ex 5N-DOC

CHARTAIR — *(TL)* — *Alice Springs, NT (ASP)*

☐ VH-BYK	Cessna 210L Centurion	21060435	ex N2691W
☐ VH-IDZ	Cessna 210M Centurion II	21062530	ex N761UN
☐ VH-JLC	Cessna 210N Centurion II	21063490	ex VH-OKH
☐ VH-KST	Cessna 210M Centurion II	21062521	ex ZK-KLG
☐ VH-LTB	Cessna 210N Centurion II	21064679	ex N670A
☐ VH-NQP	Cessna 210N Centurion II	21064572	ex N9678Y

☐ VH-OKJ	Cessna 210M Centurion II	21061602	ex VH-FZO	
☐ VH-PZO	Cessna 210L Centurion	21060298	ex (N93185)	
☐ VH-RDH	Cessna 210N Centurion II	21065374	ex N5427Y	
☐ VH-TFF	Cessna 210N Centurion II	21064277	ex N6169Y	
☐ VH-TFT	Cessna 210N Centurion II	21063448		
☐ VH-TIJ	Cessna 210L Centurion	21060591	ex N60105	
☐ VH-TWP	Cessna 210M Centurion II	21061841	ex N1636C	
☐ VH-WMP	Cessna 210M Centurion II	21062731	ex N6278B	
☐ VH-CAJ	Cessna 402C II	402C0026	ex N5717C	
☐ VH-COQ	Cessna 310R	310R1643	ex N2635Y	
☐ VH-FTW	Beech 95-B55 Baron	TC-2123	ex N24097	
☐ VH-JJN	Beech Baron 58	TH-1276	ex N3837M	
☐ VH-LGX	Piper PA-31-350 Chieftain	31-8452001	ex N41160	
☐ VH-NGC	Cessna 208	208B0916	ex VH-SMH	
☐ VH-NGK	Cessna 208B Caravan I	208B1203	ex HB-CZE	
☐ VH-PBI	Cessna 310R	310R0831	ex N3423G	
☐ VH-SKN	Cessna 310R	310R1681	ex ZK-ETM	
☐ VH-SMW	Beech Baron 58	TH-694	ex N6076S	
☐ VH-SWT	Beech Baron 58	TH-560	ex N9380S	
☐ VH-TFM	Cessna 402C II	402C0067	ex N2610Y	
☐ VH-TZH	Cessna 402C II	402C0617	ex N6880Y	
☐ VH-UCD	Cessna 402C II	402C0049	ex N5825C	
☐ VH-WZT	Beech Baron 58	TH-642	ex VH-TYR	

CHC HELICOPTERS (AUSTRALIA) — *Hems (HEM)* — *Adelaide, SA (ADL)*

☐ VH-LAF	Aérospatiale SA.332L1	2319	ex LN-OBT	Lsd fr CHC Scotia
☐ VH-LAG	Aérospatiale SA.332L1	2352	ex LN-OBU	Lsd fr CHC Scotia
☐ VH-LHG	Aérospatiale SA.332L1	2317	ex LN-OBR	
☐ VH-LHH	Aérospatiale AS.332L1	2407	ex 9M-STU	Lsd fr CHC Helicopters Intl
☐ VH-LHJ	Aérospatiale AS.332L	2063	ex G-BSOI	
☐ VH-LHK	Aérospatiale AS.332L	2107	ex G-BKZH	Lsd fr CHC Scotia
☐ VH-LOF	Aérospatiale AS.332L	2058	ex G-CDSV	Lsd fr CHC Intl
☐ VH-BZH	Bell 412	33044	ex N18098	
☐ VH-EPH	Bell 412EP	36419	ex N3070R	Op for NSW Air Ambulance
☐ VH-EPK	Bell 412EP	36100	ex N412HH	Op for NSW Air Ambulance
☐ VH-EWA	Bell 412EP	36312	ex C-GUOP	
☐ VH-NSC	Bell 412	33029	ex VH-CRQ	EMS, based CBR
☐ VH-NSP	Bell 412	33091	ex N22976	EMS
☐ VH-NSV	Bell 412	33084	ex VH-AHH	EMS, based MKY
☐ VH-VAA	Bell 412EP	36274	ex C-GLZM	Op for Metropolitan Ambulance Sve
☐ VH-VAB	Bell 412EP	36275		Op for Metropolitan Ambulance Sve
☐ VH-HRP	Sikorsky S-76A+	760122	ex N176CH	based East Sale op for RAAF
☐ VH-LAH	Sikorsky S-76A+	760089	ex RJAF 725	based NTL
☐ VH-LAI	Sikorsky S-76A+	760103	ex RJAF 727	
☐ VH-LHN	Sikorsky S-76A++	760300	ex B-HZE	
☐ VH-LHY	Sikorsky S-76A+	760105	ex RJAF 729	based Pearce
☐ VH-LHZ	Sikorsky S-76A+	760113	ex RJAF 732	RAAF rescue
☐ VH-LYO	Sikorsky S-76A++	760017	ex C-GIML	
☐ VH-LOH	Sikorsky S-92D	920036	ex N8068D	
☐ VH-PVA	Aérospatiale SA365C1 Dauphin 2	5025	ex F-WYMH	based MEN
☐ VH-PVD	Aérospatiale AS365N3 Dauphin 2	6846		
☐ VH-PVE	Eurocopter EC135T2	0834		based MEN
☐ VH-PVH	Aérospatiale AS365N3 Dauphin 2	6604	ex F-WQDC	based MEN
☐ VH-PVM	Aérospatiale AS350B Ecureuil	2058	ex JA9705	based MEN
☐ VH-SYB	Eurocopter EC145	9203		Op for NSW Air Ambulance
☐ VH-SYG	Eurocopter EC145	9235		Op for NSW Air Ambulance
☐ VH-SYJ	Agusta AW139	31114		Op for NSW Air Ambulance
☐ VH-SYV	Agusta AW139	31126		Op for NSW Air Ambulance
☐ VH-SYZ	Agusta AW139	31155		Op for NSW Air Ambulance

COBHAM AVIATION SERVICES AUSTRALIA — *National Jet (NC/NJS)* — *Adelaide-International, SA (ADL)*

☐ VH-NJC	British Aerospace 146 Srs.100	E1013	ex G-6-013	
☐ VH-NJF	British Aerospace 146 Srs.300QT	E3198	ex G-BTLD	
☐ VH-NJG	British Aerospace 146 Srs.200	E2170	ex G-BSOH	
☐ VH-NJL	British Aerospace 146 Srs.300	E3213	ex G-BVPE	
☐ VH-NJM	British Aerospace 146 Srs.300QT	E3194	ex G-BTHT	
☐ VH-NJN	British Aerospace 146 Srs.300	E3217	ex G-BUHW	
☐ VH-NJR	British Aerospace 146 Srs.100	E1152	ex G-BRLN	
☐ VH-NJT	Avro 146-RJ70A	E1228	ex G-OLXX	
☐ VH-NJV	British Aerospace 146 Srs.100QT	E1002	ex G-BSTA	
☐ VH-NJX	British Aerospace 146 Srs.100	E1003	ex EI-CPY	stored ADL
☐ VH-YAD	British Aerospace 146 Srs.200	E2097	ex N293UE	
☐ VH-YAE	British Aerospace 146 Srs.200	E2107	ex N294UE	
☐ VH-	Avro 146-RJ100	E3328	ex G-BZAU	on order
☐ VH-	Avro 146-RJ100	E3354	ex G-BZAW	on order

☐ VH-JSJ	de Havilland DHC-8-103	170	ex VH-NJD	
☐ VH-LCL	de Havilland DHC-8Q-202	492	ex C-GEOA	Op for RAN
☐ VH-SBJ	de Havilland DHC-8Q-315	578	ex C-FDHI	
☐ VH-ZZA	de Havilland DHC-8-202MPA	419	ex C-FWWU	Op for Custom Coastwatch
☐ VH-ZZB	de Havilland DHC-8-202MPA	424	ex C-FXBC	Op for Custom Coastwatch
☐ VH-ZZC	de Havilland DHC-8-202MPA	433	ex C-FXFK	Op for Custom Coastwatch
☐ VH-ZZE	de Havilland DHC-8Q-315MPA	640	ex C-FHQG	Op for Custom Coastwatch
☐ VH-ZZF	de Havilland DHC-8Q-315MPA	643	ex C-FJKS	Op for Custom Coastwatch
☐ VH-ZZG	de Havilland DHC-8Q-315MPA	644	ex C-FJKU	Op for Custom Coastwatch
☐ VH-ZZI	de Havilland DHC-8-202MPA	550	ex C-GDLD	Op for Custom Coastwatch
☐ VH-ZZJ	de Havilland DHC-8-202MPA	551	ex C-FDHI	Op for Custom Coastwatch
☐ VH-ZZN	de Havilland DHC-8-315	399	ex VH-JSQ	Op for Custom Coastwatch
☐ VH-ZZP	de Havilland DHC-8-202	411	ex VH-JSH	
☐ VH-YZE	Reims Cessna F406 Vigilant	F406-0076	ex VH-ZZE	Op for Custom Coastwatch
☐ VH-YZF	Reims Cessna F406 Vigilant	F406-0078	ex VH-ZZF	stored ADL
☐ VH-YZG	Reims Cessna F406 Vigilant	F406-0079	ex VH-ZZG	stored ADL

CORPORATE AIR — *Canberra, ACT (CBR)*

☐ VH-VED	Cessna 441 Conquest II	441-0272	ex N394G
☐ VH-VEH	Cessna 441 Conquest II	441-0238	ex N3NC
☐ VH-VEJ	Cessna 441 Conquest II	441-0249	ex N911ER
☐ VH-VEM	Cessna 441 Conquest II	441-0174	ex VH-IJG
☐ VH-VEW	Cessna 441 Conquest II	441-0254	ex C-FWCP
☐ VH-VEY	Cessna 441 Conquest II	441-0295	ex N181MD
☐ VH-VEZ	Cessna 441 Conquest II	441-0182	ex VH-AZB
☐ VH-VEA	Cessna 404 Titan II	404-0219	ex VH-ARQ
☐ VH-VEB	Beech Baron 58	TH-399	ex VH-CYT
☐ VH-VEC	Cessna 404 Titan II	404-0217	ex VH-CSV
☐ VH-VEG	Beech Baron 58	TH-822	ex VH-WIM
☐ VH-VEK	Swearingen SA.227DC Metro 23	DC-845B	ex VH-KED
☐ VH-VEU	Swearingen SA.227TC Metro 23	DC-797B	ex VH-KDJ

DE BRUIN AIR — *Mount Gambier, SA (MGB)*

☐ VH-OAA	Cessna 441 Conquest	441-0102	ex N4246Z
☐ VH-OAB	British Aerospace Jetstream 32EP	853	ex N853JX
☐ VH-OAE	British Aerospace Jetstream 32EP	851	ex N851JX
☐ VH-OAM	British Aerospace Jetstream 32EP	859	ex N859AE

DENIS BEAHAN AVIATION — *Charters Towers, QLD*

☐ VH-AMD	Beech 65-B80 Queen Air	LD-504	ex TR-LUU	
☐ VH-BOZ	Cessna 402A	402A0065	ex ZK-DHW	
☐ VH-BPZ	Cessna 402	402-0103	ex N4003Q	
☐ VH-BQL	Beech 65-B80 Queen Air	LD-288	ex DQ-FCQ	
☐ VH-BUS	Cessna 402	402-0198	ex N991SA	
☐ VH-RUU	Beech 65-B80 Queen Air	LC-311	ex N7643N	Excalibur Queenaire 8200 conv

Current status uncertain

DIRECT AIR SERVICES

☐ VH-BPI	Cessna 310R	310R0936	ex N8556G
☐ VH-TAO	Swearingen SA.227AC Metro III	AC-513	ex N513FA

EASTERN AUSTRALIA AIRLINES — *(EAQ)* — *Sydney-Kingsford Smith, NSW (SYD)*

A wholly-owned subsidiary of Qantas and operates scheduled services in full colours as QantasLink

EXPRESS FREIGHTERS AUSTRALIA — *(EFA)* — *Sydney-Kingsford Smith, NSW (SYD)*

☐ VH-XMB	Boeing 737-376 (SF)	23478/1251	ex ZK-JNG	Op for XME
☐ VH-XML	Boeing 737-376 (SF)	23486/1286	ex ZK-JNF	Op for XME
☐ VH-XMO	Boeing 737-376 (SF)	23488/1352	ex ZK-JNH	Op for XME
☐ VH-XMR	Boeing 737-376 (SF)	23490/1390	ex ZK-JNA	Op for XME

GAM SERVICES — *Melbourne-Essendon, VIC (MEB)*

☐ VH-DZC	Rockwell 500S Shrike Commander	3226	ex G-BDAL
☐ VH-KAK	Rockwell 500S Shrike Commander	3269	ex N57163
☐ VH-LET	Rockwell 500S Shrike Commander	3264	ex N70343
☐ VH-LTP	Rockwell 500S Shrike Commander	3323	ex N12RS
☐ VH-MDW	Rockwell 500S Shrike Commander	3158	ex N801AC
☐ VH-MEH	Rockwell 500S Shrike Commander	3258	ex N57213
☐ VH-PAR	Rockwell 500S Shrike Commander	3311	ex N84SA
☐ VH-UJE	Rockwell 500S Shrike Commander	3120	ex VH-BGE
☐ VH-UJI	Rockwell 500S Shrike Commander	3301	ex VH-TWS
☐ VH-UJL	Rockwell 500S Shrike Commander	3088	ex N9120N
☐ VH-UJM	Rockwell 500S Shrike Commander	3117	ex N5007H

☐ VH-UJN	Rockwell 500S Shrike Commander	3151	ex ZS-NRO
☐ VH-UJR	Rockwell 500S Shrike Commander	3311	ex VH-PAR
☐ VH-UJS	Rockwell 500S Shrike Commander	1797-12	ex VH-EXF
☐ VH-UJU	Rockwell 500S Shrike Commander	3055	ex VH-PWO
☐ VH-UJV	Rockwell 500S Shrike Commander	3161	ex N712PC
☐ VH-UJX	Aero Commander 500S Shrike	1839-31	ex VH-EXI
☐ VH-UJY	Rockwell 500S Shrike Commander	3170	ex VH-TSS
☐ VH-YJC	Rockwell 500S Shrike Commander	3176	ex VH-ACZ
☐ VH-YJE	Rockwell 500S Shrike Commander	3053	ex VH-EXE
☐ VH-YJI	Rockwell 500S Shrike Commander	3130	ex VH-BAJ
☐ VH-YJJ	Rockwell 500S Shrike Commander	3178	ex VH-ACJ
☐ VH-YJL	Aero Commander 500S Shrike	1875-48	ex VH-ACL
☐ VH-YJM	Rockwell 500S Shrike Commander	3186	ex RP-C1268
☐ VH-YJO	Aero Commander 500B	1506-180	ex VH-WRU
☐ VH-YJR	Rockwell 500S Shrike Commander	3231	ex VH-PCO
☐ VH-YJS	Rockwell 500S Shrike Commander	3315	ex VH-FGS
☐ VH-YJU	Aero Commander 500U Shrike	1765-49	ex F-ODHD
☐ VH-AAG	Rockwell 690 Turbo Commander	11101	ex N57101
☐ VH-NBT	Rockwell Commander 681B	6047	ex VH-NYE
☐ VH-NYC	Rockwell 690 Turbo Commander	11026	ex N9226N
☐ VH-PCV	Rockwell 690ATurbo Commander	11283	ex N57228
☐ VH-UJA	Aero Commander 680FL	1521-100	ex PK-MAG
☐ VH-UJG	Rockwell 690 Turbo Commander	11062	ex VH-NEY
☐ VH-YJA	Aero Commander 680FL	1734-140	ex RP-C699
☐ VH-YJF	Aero Commander 680FL	1642-122	ex N1414S
☐ VH-YJG	Rockwell 690A Turbo Commander	11308	ex N99WC
☐ VH-YJP	Rockwell 690A Turbo Commander	11173	ex N950M
☐ VH-VJD	Dornier 228-202K	8157	ex D2-EBT
☐ VH-VJE	Dornier 228-202	8041	ex 5N-DOC
☐ VH-VJF	Dornier 228-202	8047	ex 5N-ARF
☐ VH-VJJ	Dornier 228-202	8025	ex 5N-DOA
☐ VH-VJN	Dornier 228-202	8040	ex VH-VJB
☐ VH-IHA	Piper PA-31 Turbo Navajo	31-136	ex N9099Y
☐ VH-YJZ	Beech 95-B55 Baron	TC-1933	ex VH-ARL

GOLD COAST SEAPLANES — *Coolangatta, QLD (OOL)*

☐ VH-IDO	de Havilland DHC-2 Beaver	1545		Floatplane

GOLDEN EAGLE AIRLINES — *Port Hedland, WA (PHE)*

☐ VH-AEC	Britten-Norman BN-2B-26 Islander	2164	ex G-BKJO
☐ VH-AEU	Britten-Norman BN-2B-26 Islander	2130	ex G-BJON
☐ VH-AEX	Cessna U206G Stationair 6 II	U20606587	ex N9635Z
☐ VH-EGE	Britten-Norman BN-2A-26 Islander	3015	ex VH-WRM
☐ VH-FML	Piper PA-31 Navajo C	31-8112015	ex N40540
☐ VH-KTS	Piper PA-31 Navajo C	31-7912014	ex N27833
☐ VH-LCK	Piper PA-34-200 Seneca	34-7350236	ex N55663
☐ VH-NMK	Piper PA-31-350 Chieftain	31-8152163	ex P2-RHA
☐ VH-NPA	Piper PA-31-350 Chieftain	31-8452016	ex N41171
☐ VH-PJY	Cessna U206G Stationair 6 II	U20605120	ex N4829U
☐ VH-UPK	Cessna U206G Stationair 6 II	U20605477	ex (N6399U)

GOLDFIELDS AIR SERVICES — *(GOS)* — *Kalgoorlie, WA (KGI)*

☐ VH-ANP	Cessna 404	404-0054	ex N404MP
☐ VH-CYT	Cessna 402	402-0293	ex VH-OKZ
☐ VH-HOR	Cessna 402C	402C0108	ex P2-KSR
☐ VH-LAE	Cessna 402C	402C0097	ex N2614Z
☐ VH-LCO	Cessna 310R	310R1216	ex N1386G
☐ VH-LNX	Cessna 402	402-0295	ex ZS-LNX
☐ VH-LWA	Cessna 208B Caravan I	208B1173	ex N208JJ
☐ VH-MFF	Cessna 402B	402B0874	ex N5187J
☐ VH-OOT	Cessna 310R	310R1635	ex VH-PEE

GREAT WESTERN AVIATION — *Brisbane-International, QLD (BNE)*

☐ VH-DEH	Piper PA-31 Navajo C	31-7812123	ex N27792
☐ VH-FMO	Piper PA-31 Navajo C	31-8012052	ex N35574
☐ VH-FMU	Piper PA-31 Navajo C	31-8212015	ex N41033
☐ VH-KTU	Piper PA-31 Navajo C	31-7912079	ex N35301
☐ VH-NAD	Piper PA-31 Navajo C	31-8212004	ex N4099T
☐ VH-OMM	Piper PA-31-350 Chieftain	31-8152153	ex N4091B
☐ VH-SGV	Beech 200 Super King Air	BB-718	ex N6728N

HARDY AVIATION — Darwin, NT (DRW)

☐ VH-ANM	Cessna 404 Titan II	404-0010	ex VH-BPM
☐ VH-ANS	Cessna 210M Centurion II	21062784	ex N784ED
☐ VH-ARJ	Cessna 402B	402B0629	ex N3784C
☐ VH-ASN	Embraer EMB.120RT Brasilia	120056	ex N334JS
☐ VH-AZW	Cessna 441 Conquest II	441-0028	ex VH-FWA
☐ VH-BEM	Cessna 402B	404B0590	ex N402HA
☐ VH-HAZ	Cessna 404 Titan II	404-0046	ex G-BYLR
☐ VH-HMA	Cessna 404 Titan II	404-0122	ex N37158
☐ VH-HPA	Cessna U206G Stationair 6	U20605002	ex VH-WIW
☐ VH-HVH	Swearingen SA.227DC Metro 23	DC-886B	ex N3006M
☐ VH-HVR	Cessna 404 Titan II	404-0673	ex N404MT
☐ VH-JVB	Cessna 441 Conquest	441-0231	ex N441YA
☐ VH-JVL	Cessna 441 Conquest	441-0352	ex AP-BCQ
☐ VH-JZL	Cessna TU206G Stationair 6	U20604721	ex N732TS
☐ VH-MJN	Cessna 210M Centurion	21061888	ex N732YU
☐ VH-MKS	Swearingen SA.226TC Metro II	TC-262	ex N49GW
☐ VH-NOK	Cessna 210M Centurion II	21062063	ex N9127M
☐ VH-RAP	Cessna U206F Stationair	U20602989	ex VH-DXU
☐ VH-RUY	Cessna 402C	402C0273	ex N1774G
☐ VH-SGO	Beech 58 Baron	TH-1185	ex N3702D
☐ VH-SMO	Cessna 441 Conquest	441-0132	ex VH-ANJ
☐ VH-SQL	Cessna 402C II	402C0326	ex VH-OAS
☐ VH-TQD	Swearingen SA.227AC Metro III	AC-667B	ex C-FAFS
☐ VH-UOP	Cessna 404 Titan II	404-0636	ex N5280J
☐ VH-XSM	Beech E55 Baron	TE-804	ex P2-COE

HEAVYLIFT CARGO AIRLINES — HeavyCargo (HN/HVY) — Brisbane-International, QLD (BNE)

☐ RP-C8016	Boeing 727-51C (FedEx 3)	19288/389	ex 9L-LEK
☐ RP-C8017	Boeing 727-51C (FedEx 3)	19289/403	ex 9L-LFJ
☐ RP-C8019	Boeing 727-227F (Raisbeck 3)	21249/1219	ex N76753
☐ RP-C8020	Short SC.5 Belfast	SH1819	ex 9L-LDQ

HINTERLAND AVIATION — Cairns, QLD (CNS)

☐ VH-CVN	Cessna 208B Caravan I	208B0676	ex N12372
☐ VH-HLJ	Beech 200B Super King Air	BB-945	ex RP-C11577
☐ VH-HLL	Cessna 208B Caravan I	208B0615	ex VH-AGS
☐ VH-JOB	Cessna 310R	310R1236	ex G-BOAT
☐ VH-MRZ	Cessna 208B Caravan I	208B1048	ex N1266V
☐ VH-SKH	Cessna 310R	310R1221	
☐ VH-TFC	Cessna U206G Stationair	U20604576	ex VH-CMT
☐ VH-TFK	Cessna 402C III	402C1011	ex VH-PVU
☐ VH-TFO	Cessna 404 Titan II	404-0076	ex N32L
☐ VH-TFQ	Cessna 208B Caravan I	208B1216	ex N84BP
☐ VH-TFS	Cessna 208B Caravan I	208B1006	ex N1247N
☐ VH-TFU	Cessna 404 Titan	404-0834	ex VH-SZO
☐ VH-TFY	Rockwell 500S Shrike Commander	3057	ex VH-IBY
☐ VH-TFZ	Cessna 402C II	402C0408	ex VH-RMI
☐ VH-TSI	Cessna 402C	402C0492	ex N6841L

ISLAND AIR TAXIS — Hamilton Island, QLD (HTI)

☐ VH-BVA	de Havilland DHC-2 Beaver	245	ex N77WK
☐ VH-LNI	Cessna 208 Caravan I	20800298	ex N94MS
☐ VH-PNP	Partenavia P.68B	51	

JETSTAR AIRWAYS — Jetstar (JQ/JST) — Melbourne-Tullamarine, VIC (MEL)

☐ VH-JQG	Airbus A320-232	2169	ex F-WWDQ	
☐ VH-JQL	Airbus A320-232	2185	ex F-WWDB	
☐ VH-JQW	Airbus A320-232	2423	ex TC-OGO	
☐ VH-JQX	Airbus A320-232	2197	ex F-WWDH	
☐ VH-	Airbus A320-232	4229	ex F-WWBU	on order
☐ VH-	Airbus A320-232		ex	on order
☐ VH-	Airbus A320-232		ex	on order
☐ VH-	Airbus A320-232		ex	on order
☐ VH-	Airbus A320-232		ex	on order
☐ VH-	Airbus A320-232		ex	on order
☐ VH-	Airbus A320-232		ex	on order
☐ VH-	Airbus A320-232		ex	on order
☐ VH-	Airbus A320-232		ex	on order
☐ VH-VGT	Airbus A320-232	4178	ex	on order
☐ VH-VGZ	Airbus A320-232	3917	ex F-WWBF	
☐ VH-VQA	Airbus A320-232	3783	ex F-WWIS	
☐ VH-VQB	Airbus A320-232	3743	ex F-WWII	
☐ VH-VQC	Airbus A320-232	3668	ex F-WWID	
☐ VH-VQD	Airbus A320-232	3547	ex F-WWIV	
☐ VH-VQE	Airbus A320-232	3495	ex F-WWIJ	

☐ VH-VQF	Airbus A320-232	3474	ex F-WWDE	
☐ VH-VQG	Airbus A320-232	2787	ex F-WWBV	
☐ VH-VQH	Airbus A320-232	2766	ex F-WWDG	
☐ VH-VQI	Airbus A320-232	2717	ex F-WWBG	
☐ VH-VQJ	Airbus A320-232	2703	ex F-WWIS	
☐ VH-VQK	Airbus A320-232	2651	ex F-WWIM	
☐ VH-VQL	Airbus A320-232	2642	ex F-WWBZ	
☐ VH-VQM	Airbus A320-232	2608	ex F-WWBS	
☐ VH-VQN	Airbus A320-232	2600	ex F-WWBK	
☐ VH-VQO	Airbus A320-232	2587	ex F-WWDL	
☐ VH-VQP	Airbus A320-232	2573	ex F-WWBD	Gold Coast Titans c/s
☐ VH-VQQ	Airbus A320-232	2537	ex F-WWIJ	
☐ VH-VQR	Airbus A320-232	2526	ex F-WWDQ	
☐ VH-VQS	Airbus A320-232	2515	ex F-WWIE	
☐ VH-VQT	Airbus A320-232	2475	ex F-WWDS	
☐ VH-VQU	Airbus A320-232	2455	ex F-WWDJ	
☐ VH-VQV	Airbus A320-232	2338	ex F-WWIO	
☐ VH-VQW	Airbus A320-232	2329	ex F-WWDZ	
☐ VH-VQX	Airbus A320-232	2322	ex 9V-VQX	
☐ VH-VQY	Airbus A320-232	2299	ex F-WWBV	
☐ VH-VQZ	Airbus A320-232	2292	ex 9V-VQZ	
☐ VH-VWT	Airbus A321-231	3717	ex D-AVZQ	
☐ VH-VWU	Airbus A321-231	3948	ex D-AZAL	
☐ VH-VWW	Airbus A321-231	3916	ex D-AVZX	
☐ VH-VWX	Airbus A321-231	3899	ex D-AVZW	
☐ VH-VWY	Airbus A321-231	1408	ex N584NK	
☐ VH-VWZ	Airbus A321-231	1195	ex N583NK	
☐ VH-EBA	Airbus A330-202	508	ex F-WWKM	
☐ VH-EBB	Airbus A330-202	522	ex F-WWYQ	
☐ VH-EBC	Airbus A330-202	506	ex F-WWYU	
☐ VH-EBD	Airbus A330-202	513	ex F-WWYV	
☐ VH-EBE	Airbus A330-202	842	ex F-WWYV	
☐ VH-EBF	Airbus A330-202	853	ex F-WWYU	
☐ VH-EBK	Airbus A330-202	945	ex F-WWYV	Savannah Way

KAKADU AIR SERVICES — *Jabiru, NT (JAB)*

☐ VH-KNA	Gippsland GA-8 Airvan	GA8-04-044	ex VH-IXN
☐ VH-KNB	Gippsland GA-8 Airvan	GA8-07-109	
☐ VH-KNE	Gippsland GA-8 Airvan	GA8-08-133	
☐ VH-KNP	Gippsland GA-8 Airvan	GA8-04-063	ex VH-YAH
☐ VH-LFU	Cessna 207 Skywagon	20700296	ex ZK-DXT
☐ VH-UBW	Cessna 207 Skywagon	20700137	ex N1537U

KARRATHA FLYING SERVICES — *Karratha, WA (KTA)*

☐ VH-KFE	Beech B200 Super King Air	BB-1172	ex VH-FDG
☐ VH-KFF	Piper PA-31-350 Chieftain	31-7952125	ex VH-UOT
☐ VH-KFG	Beech 65-C90 King Air	LJ-777	ex N9AN
☐ VH-KFM	Beech 58 Baron	TH-1339	ex VH-MOS
☐ VH-KFQ	Piper PA-31 Turbo Navajo B	31-7401250	ex VH-SRZ
☐ VH-KFW	Piper PA-31 Turbo Navajo	31-366	ex VH-WGU
☐ VH-KFX	Beech B200 Super King Air	BB-1862	ex N225WC
☐ VH-ZKF	de Havilland DHC-6 Twin Otter 100	43	ex VH-TZL

KING ISLAND AIRLINES — *Melbourne-Moorabbin, VIC (MBW)*

☐ VH-KGQ	Embraer EMB.110P1 Bandeirante	110221	ex VH-XFD
☐ VH-KIB	Piper PA-31-350 Navajo Chieftain	31-7305035	ex VH-TXD
☐ VH-KIG	Piper PA-31-350 Chieftain	31-7852146	ex VH-HRL
☐ VH-KIO	Piper PA-31-350 Navajo Chieftain	31-7405487	ex VH-DMV
☐ VH-KIY	Piper PA-31-350 Chieftain	31-7952061	ex VH-KGN

MACAIR AIRLINES — *(CC/MCK)* — *Townsville, QLD (TSV)*

Ceased operations 30/Jan/2009.

MAROOMBA AIRLINES — *(KN)* — *Perth-International, WA (PER)*

☐ VH-ITA	Beech B200 Super King Air	BB-1244	ex F-OINC	
☐ VH-LOA	Beech B200 Super King Air	BB-1463	ex ZS-PLK	
☐ VH-MQZ	Beech B200 Super King Air	BB-1961	ex N74061	
☐ VH-QQA	de Havilland DHC-8-102	005	ex P2-MCN	Lsd fr Skytrans
☐ VH-QQB	de Havilland DHC-8-102	004	ex VH-TQO	Lsd fr Skytrans

MILITARY SUPPORT SERVICES — *Brisbane (BNE)*

☐ VH-MQD	CASA C.212-200	CC50-7-272	ex N433CA
☐ VH-MQE	CASA C.212-200	CD51-6-318	ex N7241E

NGAANYATJARRA AIR				**Alice Springs, NT (ASP)**
☐ VH-HXH	Cessna 210N Centurion	21063847	ex N6260C	

NETWORK AVIATION AUSTRALIA				**Perth-International, WA (PER)**
☐ VH-NHA	Embraer EMB.120ER Brasilia	120269	ex N209SW	
☐ VH-NHC	Embraer EMB.120ER Brasilia	120152	ex VH-TLZ	
☐ VH-NHZ	Embraer EMB.120ER Brasilia	120034	ex N186SW	
☐ VH-NIF	Embraer EMB.120ER Brasilia	120054	ex VH-FNQ	
☐ VH-TWF	Embraer EMB.120ER Brasilia	120186	ex N197SW	
☐ VH-TWZ	Embraer EMB.120ER Brasilia	120266	ex N207SW	
☐ VH-NHF	Fokker F.28-0100 (Fokker 100)	11398	ex N898US	
☐ VH-NHO	Fokker F.28-0100 (Fokker 100)	11312	ex D-AGPJ	
☐ VH-NHP	Fokker F.28-0100 (Fokker 100)	11399	ex D-AGPS	

NORFOLK AIR				**Norfolk Island, NSW(NLK)**
☐ VH-NLK	Boeing 737-33A	23635/1436	ex N635AN	

OUR AIRLINE				
☐ VH-NLK	Boeing 737-33A	23635/1436	ex N635AN	

OZJET AIRLINES	**AusJet (O7/OZJ)**	**Melbourne-Tullamarine, VIC (MEL)**

Ceased operations 20/May/2009

PEARL AVIATION				**Perth-International, WA (PER)**
☐ VH-FII	Beech 200 Super King Air	BB-653	ex VH-MXK	Op for Flight Inspection Alliance
☐ VH-NTE	Beech 200 Super King Air	BB-529	ex VH-SWP	Op for NT Aerial Medical Services
☐ VH-NTG	Beech 200C Super King Air	BL-9	ex VH-KZL	Op for NT Aerial Medical Services
☐ VH-NTH	Beech 200C Super King Air	BL-12	ex VH-SWO	Op for NT Aerial Medical Services
☐ VH-NTS	Beech 200C Super King Air	BL-30	ex VH-TNQ	Op for NT Aerial Medical Services
☐ VH-OYA	Beech 200 Super King Air	BB-365	ex P2-SML	Lsd to RAAF
☐ VH-OYD	Beech 200 Super King Air	BB-1041	ex N200BK	EMS
☐ VH-OYE	Beech 200 Super King Air	BB-355	ex VH-SMB	EMS
☐ VH-OYH	Beech 200 Super King Air	BB-148	ex VH-WNH	Op for Granites Gold Mines
☐ VH-OYT*	Beech 200T Super King Air	BT-6/BB-489	ex VH-PPJ	
☐ VH-TLX	Beech 200 Super King Air	BB-550	ex P2-MBM	EMS
☐ VH-PPF	Dornier 328-110	3057	ex N439JS	based PER
☐ VH-PPG	Dornier 328-110	3053	ex D-CIAB	based DRW
☐ VH-PPJ	Dornier 328-110	3059	ex D-CCAD	based CNS
☐ VH-PPQ	Dornier 328-110	3051	ex D-CEAD	based MEB
☐ VH-PPV	Dornier 328-110	3052	ex D-CDAD	based BNE
☐ VH-FIX	Beech 300 Super King Air	FL-90	ex D-CKRA	Calibrator
☐ VH-OYB	Swearingen SA.227DC Metro 23	DC-848B	ex N452LA	
☐ VH-OYG	Swearingen SA.227DC Metro 23	DC-875B	ex VH-SWM	
☐ VH-OYI	Swearingen SA.227DC Metro 23	DC-839B	ex VH-DMI	
☐ VH-OYN	Swearingen SA.227DC Metro 23	DC-870B	ex VH-DMO	

PEL-AIR	**Questair (QWA)**	**Sydney Kingsford-Smith, NSW / Brisbane, QLD (SYD/BNE)**		
☐ VH-AJG	IAI 1124 Westwind	281	ex N1124F	EMS/Freighter
☐ VH-AJJ	IAI 1124 Westwind	248	ex N25RE	EMS/Freighter
☐ VH-AJK	IAI 1124 Westwind	256	ex 4X-CNB	EMS/Freighter
☐ VH-AJP	IAI 1124 Westwind	238	ex 4X-CMJ	EMS/Freighter
☐ VH-AJV	IAI 1124 Westwind	282	ex N186G	EMS/Freighter
☐ VH-KNR	IAI 1124A Westwind II	340	ex N118MP	Freighter
☐ VH-KNS	IAI 1124 Westwind	323	ex N816H	Freighter
☐ VH-KNU	IAI 1124 Westwind	317	ex VH-UUZ	EMS/Freighter
☐ VH-EEJ	Swearingen SA.227AC Metro III	AC-617	ex VH-SSV	Combi
☐ VH-EEN	Swearingen SA.227AT Expediter	AT-563	ex N563UP	Freighter Jt ops with XME
☐ VH-EEO	Swearingen SA.227AT Expediter	AT-564	ex N564UP	Freighter Jt ops with XME
☐ VH-EEP	Swearingen SA.227AT Expediter	AT-567	ex N565UP	stored WGA
☐ VH-EER	Swearingen SA.227AC Metro III	AC-632	ex VH-SSW	stored WGA
☐ VH-EES	Swearingen SA.227AC Metro III	AC-614	ex VH-SSZ	stored WGA
☐ VH-EET	Swearingen SA.227AC Metro III	AC-404	ex VH-SSM	Combi Op for TNT
☐ VH-EEU	Swearingen SA.227AC Metro III	AC-619B	ex VH-OYC	
☐ VH-EEX	Swearingen SA.227AC Metro III	AC-611B	ex VH-NEL	
☐ VH-KAN	Swearingen SA.227DC Metro 23	DC-838B	ex N3021U	
☐ VH-KDO	Swearingen SA.227DC Metro 23	DC-837B	ex N3021N	
☐ VH-KEU	Swearingen SA.227DC Metro 23	DC-846B	ex N30236	
☐ VH-KEX	Swearingen SA.227DC Metro 23	DC-872B	ex N3030X	
☐ VH-EEB	Embraer EMB.120FC Brasilia	120117	ex N1117H	stored WGA

☐ VH-EKT	SAAB SF.340AF	340A-085	ex F-GGBJ	Freighter
☐ VH-KDB	SAAB SF.340AF	340A-008	ex PH-KJK	Freighter
☐ VH-KDK	SAAB SF.340AF	340A-016	ex SE-E16	Freighter
☐ VH-SLD	Learjet 35A	35A-145	ex (N166AG)	Freighter
☐ VH-SLE	Learjet 35A	35A-428	ex N17LH	
☐ VH-SLF	Learjet 36A	36A-049	ex N136ST	
☐ VH-SLJ	Learjet 36	36-014	ex N200Y	Freighter

PIONAIR AUSTRALIA — *Sydney-Bankstown, NSW (BWU)*

☐ VH-PDL	Convair 580	137	ex N631MW
☐ VH-PDW	Convair 580F	86	ex C-GKFQ
☐ VH-PDX	Convair 580F	126	ex C-FIWN

POLAR AVIATION — *Port Hedland, WA (PHE)*

☐ VH-BIV	Cessna 210N Centurion II	21063398	ex N5373A
☐ VH-BLW	Beech Baron 58	TH-490	ex N1349K
☐ VH-ILD	Beech 95-E55 Baron	TE-788	ex N4055A
☐ VH-NSM	Beech 58 Baron	TH-1798	ex N1098C
☐ VH-NWT	Cessna 208B Caravan I	208B0733	ex N1269N
☐ VH-YOT	Cessna U206G Stationair	20605045	ex VH-TEO
☐ VH-YSS	Beech 58 Baron	TH-1583	ex N56569

QANTAS AIRWAYS — *Qantas (QF/QFA)* — *Sydney-Kingsford Smith, NSW (SYD)*

Member of Oneworld

☐ VH-EBG	Airbus A330-202	887	ex F-WWKD	Barossa Valley	
☐ VH-EBH	Airbus A330-202	892	ex F-WWYT	Hunter Valley	
☐ VH-EBI	Airbus A330-202	898	ex F-WWKM		
☐ VH-EBJ	Airbus A330-202	940	ex F-WWKL	Margaret River	
☐ VH-EBL	Airbus A330-202	976	ex F-WWKU	Whitsundays	
☐ VH-EBM	Airbus A330-202	1061	ex F-WWKU	Tamar Valley	
☐ VH-EBN	Airbus A330-202	1094	ex F-WWKM		on order
☐ VH-	Airbus A330-202		ex F-WW		on order
☐ VH-QPA	Airbus A330-303	553	ex F-WWKS	Kununurra	
☐ VH-QPB	Airbus A330-303	558	ex F-WWYO	Freycinet Peninsula	
☐ VH-QPC	Airbus A330-303	564	ex F-WWYQ	Broken Hill	
☐ VH-QPD	Airbus A330-303	574	ex F-WWYU	Port Macquarie	
☐ VH-QPE	Airbus A330-303	593	ex F-WWKP	Port Lincoln	
☐ VH-QPF	Airbus A330-303	595	ex F-WWKR	Esperance	
☐ VH-QPG	Airbus A330-303	603	ex F-WWYN	Mount Gambier	
☐ VH-QPH	Airbus A330-303	695	ex F-WWYQ	Noosa	
☐ VH-QPI	Airbus A330-303	705	ex F-WWKG	Cairns	
☐ VH-QPJ	Airbus A330-303	712	ex F-WWYM	Port Stephens	

☐ VH-OQA	Airbus A380-841	014	ex F-WWSK	Nancy Bird Walton	
☐ VH-OQB	Airbus A380-841	015	ex F-WWSL	Hudson Fysh	
☐ VH-OQC	Airbus A380-841	022	ex F-WWSR	Paul McGinness	
☐ VH-OQD	Airbus A380-841	026	ex F-WWSX	Fergus McMaster	
☐ VH-OQE	Airbus A380-841	027	ex F-WWSY	Lawrence Hargrave	
☐ VH-OQF	Airbus A380-841	029	ex F-WWSA	Charles Kingsford Smith	
☐ VH-OQG	Airbus A380-841	047	ex F-WWAD	Charles Ulm	on order
☐ VH-OQH	Airbus A380-841	050	ex F-WWAE	Reginald Ansett	on order
☐ VH-OQI	Airbus A380-841	055	ex F-WW	David Warren	on order
☐ VH-OQJ	Airbus A380-841	062	ex F-WW	Bert Hinkler	on order

☐ VH-TJE	Boeing 737-476	24430/1820		Kookaburra
☐ VH-TJF	Boeing 737-476	24431/1863		Brolga
☐ VH-TJG	Boeing 737-476	24432/1879	ex 9M-MLE	Eagle
☐ VH-TJH	Boeing 737-476	24433/1881		Falcon
☐ VH-TJI	Boeing 737-476	24434/1912	ex 9M-MLD	Swan
☐ VH-TJJ	Boeing 737-476	24435/1959		Heron
☐ VH-TJK	Boeing 737-476	24436/1998		Ibis
☐ VH-TJL	Boeing 737-476	24437/2162		Swift
☐ VH-TJM	Boeing 737-476	24438/2171		Kestrel
☐ VH-TJO	Boeing 737-476	24440/2324		Lorikeet
☐ VH-TJR	Boeing 737-476	24443/2398		Cockatiel
☐ VH-TJS	Boeing 737-476	24444/2454		Jabiru
☐ VH-TJT	Boeing 737-476	24445/2539		Kingfisher
☐ VH-TJU	Boeing 737-476	24446/2569		Currawong
☐ VH-TJW	Boeing 737-4L7	26961/2517	ex C2-RN11	Strahan
☐ VH-TJX	Boeing 737-476	28150/2773		Sharing
☐ VH-TJY	Boeing 737-476	28151/2785		Trust

☐ VH-VXA	Boeing 737-838/W	29551/1042	ex (N979AN)	Broome
☐ VH-VXB	Boeing 737-838/W	30101/1045	ex (N980AN)	Yanani Dreaming
☐ VH-VXC	Boeing 737-838/W	30897/1049	ex (N981AN)	Gippsland
☐ VH-VXD	Boeing 737-838/W	29552/1063	ex (N982AN)	Tenterfield
☐ VH-VXE	Boeing 737-838/W	30899/1071	ex (N983AN)	Coffs Harbour
☐ VH-VXF	Boeing 737-838/W	29553/1096	ex (N984AN)	Sunshine Coast

☐ VH-VXG	Boeing 737-838/W	30901/1102	ex (N985AM)	Port Douglas	
☐ VH-VXH	Boeing 737-838/W	33478/1137	ex (N986AM)	Warmambool	
☐ VH-VXI	Boeing 737-838/W	33479/1141	ex (N987AM)	Oonadatta	
☐ VH-VXJ	Boeing 737-838/W	33480/1157	ex (N988AM)	Coober Pedy	
☐ VH-VXK	Boeing 737-838/W	33481/1160	ex (N989AM)	Katherine	
☐ VH-VXL	Boeing 737-838/W	33482/1172		Charleville	
☐ VH-VXM	Boeing 737-838/W	33483/1177	ex N6055X	Mount Hotham	
☐ VH-VXN	Boeing 737-838/W	33484/1180		Freemantle	
☐ VH-VXO	Boeing 737-838/W	33485/1183		Kakadu	
☐ VH-VXP	Boeing 737-838/W	33722/1324		Logan	
☐ VH-VXQ	Boeing 737-838/W	33723/1335		Redlands	
☐ VH-VXR	Boeing 737-838/W	33724/1340		Shepparton	
☐ VH-VXS	Boeing 737-838/W	33725/1352		St Helens	
☐ VH-VXT	Boeing 737-838/W	33760/1412	ex N1787B	Townsville	
☐ VH-VXU	Boeing 737-838/W	33761/1420		Wollongong	
☐ VH-VYA	Boeing 737-838/W	33762/1532		Narooma	
☐ VH-VYB	Boeing 737-838/W	33763/1534		Cape Otway	
☐ VH-VYC	Boeing 737-838/W	33991/1612		Arnhem Land	
☐ VH-VYD	Boeing 737-838/W	33992/1706		Eudunda	
☐ VH-VYE	Boeing 737-838/W	33993/1712		Alice Springs	
☐ VH-VYF	Boeing 737-838/W	33994/1727	ex N1784B	Evandale	
☐ VH-VYG	Boeing 737-838/W	33995/1736		Australind	
☐ VH-VYH	Boeing 737-838/W	34180/1815		Queanbeyan	
☐ VH-VYI	Boeing 737-838/W	34181/1840		Bathurst Island	
☐ VH-VYJ	Boeing 737-838/W	34182/1842	ex N1782B	Cann River	
☐ VH-VYK	Boeing 737-838/W	34183/1846	ex N1784B	Moree	
☐ VH-VYL	Boeing 737-838/W	34184/1854		Wangaratta	
☐ VH-VZA	Boeing 737-838/W	34195/2502	ex N1779B	Port Augusta	
☐ VH-VZB	Boeing 737-838/W	34196/2623	ex N1786B	Lake Macquarie	
☐ VH-VZC	Boeing 737-838/W	34197/2649		Innisfail	
☐ VH-VZD	Boeing 737-838/W	34198/2659		Geelong	
☐ VH-VZE	Boeing 737-838/W	34199/2661	ex N1786B	Bunbury	
☐ VH-OEB	Boeing 747-48E	25778/983	ex HL7416	Phillip Island	
☐ VH-OEC	Boeing 747-4H6	24836/808	ex 9M-MHN	King Island	stored VCV
☐ VH-OED	Boeing 747-4H6	25126/858	ex 9M-MHO	Kangaroo Island	stored VCV
☐ VH-OEE	Boeing 747-438ER	32909/1308	ex N747ER	Nullarbor	
☐ VH-OEF	Boeing 747-438ER	32910/1313	ex N60659	City of Sydney	
☐ VH-OEG	Boeing 747-438ER	32911/1320		Parkes	
☐ VH-OEH	Boeing 747-438ER	32912/1321	ex N5020K	Hervey Bay	
☐ VH-OEI	Boeing 747-438ER	32913/1330		Ceduna	
☐ VH-OEJ	Boeing 747-438ER	32914/1331	ex N60668	Wanula Dreaming	
☐ VH-OJA	Boeing 747-438	24354/731	ex N6046P	City of Canberra	
☐ VH-OJB	Boeing 747-438	24373/746		Mount Isa	
☐ VH-OJC	Boeing 747-438	24406/751		City of Melbourne	
☐ VH-OJD	Boeing 747-438	24481/764		City of Brisbane	
☐ VH-OJE	Boeing 747-438	24482/765		City of Adelaide	
☐ VH-OJF	Boeing 747-438	24483/781		City of Perth	
☐ VH-OJG	Boeing 747-438	24779/801	ex N6009F	City of Hobart	
☐ VH-OJH	Boeing 747-438	24806/807		City of Darwin	
☐ VH-OJI	Boeing 747-438	24887/826	ex N6009F	Longreach	
☐ VH-OJJ	Boeing 747-438	24974/835		Winton	
☐ VH-OJK	Boeing 747-438	25067/857		Newcastle	stored VCV
☐ VH-OJL	Boeing 747-438	25151/865		City of Ballarat	
☐ VH-OJM	Boeing 747-438	25245/875		GoSFord	
☐ VH-OJN	Boeing 747-438	25315/883	ex N6009F	City of Dubbo	
☐ VH-OJO	Boeing 747-438	25544/894	ex N6005C	City of Toowoomba	
☐ VH-OJP	Boeing 747-438	25545/916		City of Albury	
☐ VH-OJQ	Boeing 747-438	25546/924	ex N6005C	Manduran	
☐ VH-OJR	Boeing 747-438	25547/936	ex N6018N	City of Bathurst	
☐ VH-OJS	Boeing 747-438	25564/1230		Hamilton Island	
☐ VH-OJT	Boeing 747-438	25565/1233			
☐ VH-OJU	Boeing 747-438	25566/1239		Lord Howe Island	
☐ VH-OGA	Boeing 767-338ER	24146/231	ex N6055X	City of Whyalla	stored VCV
☐ VH-OGB	Boeing 767-338ER	24316/242	ex N6005C	City of Kalgoorlie/Boulder	
☐ VH-OGC	Boeing 767-338ER	24317/246	ex N6005C	City of Bendigo	
☐ VH-OGD	Boeing 767-338ER	24407/247	ex N6009F	City of Maitland	stored VCV
☐ VH-OGE	Boeing 767-338ER	24531/278		City of Orange	
☐ VH-OGF	Boeing 767-338ER	24853/319		City of Lismore	
☐ VH-OGG	Boeing 767-338ER	24929/343		City of Rockhampton	
☐ VH-OGH	Boeing 767-338ER	24930/344		City of Parramatta	
☐ VH-OGI	Boeing 767-338ER	25246/387		City of Port Augusta	
☐ VH-OGJ	Boeing 767-338ER	25274/396		Port Macquarie	
☐ VH-OGK	Boeing 767-338ER	25316/397	ex N6018N	City of Mackay	
☐ VH-OGL	Boeing 767-338ER	25363/402	ex N6018N	Wallabies Rugby World Cup c/s	
☐ VH-OGM	Boeing 767-338ER	25575/451		Bundaberg	
☐ VH-OGN	Boeing 767-338ER	25576/549		Partnership	
☐ VH-OGO	Boeing 767-338ER	25577/550		Unity	
☐ VH-OGP	Boeing 767-338ER	28153/615		Forbes	
☐ VH-OGQ	Boeing 767-338ER	28154/623		Birdsville	
☐ VH-OGR	Boeing 767-338ER	28724/662		City of Corowa	
☐ VH-OGS	Boeing 767-338ER	28725/665		Roma	

☐ VH-OGT	Boeing 767-338ER	29117/710		Maroochydore
☐ VH-OGU	Boeing 767-338ER	29118/713		Byron Bay
☐ VH-OGV	Boeing 767-338ER	30186/796		
☐ VH-ZXA	Boeing 767-336ER	24337/288	ex G-BNWE	
☐ VH-ZXB	Boeing 767-336ER	24338/293	ex G-BNWF	
☐ VH-ZXC	Boeing 767-336ER	24339/298	ex G-BNWG	
☐ VH-ZXD	Boeing 767-336ER	24342/363	ex G-BNWJ	
☐ VH-ZXE	Boeing 767-336ER	24343/364	ex G-BNWK	
☐ VH-ZXF	Boeing 767-336ER	25203/365	ex G-BNWL	
☐ VH-ZXG	Boeing 767-336ER	25443/419	ex G-BNWP	

QANTASLINK *(QF/QFA)* *various*

☐ VH-NXD	Boeing 717-23S	55062/5031	ex VH-VQD		
☐ VH-NXE	Boeing 717-23S	55063/5034	ex VH-VQE		
☐ VH-NXG	Boeing 717-2K9	55057/5020	ex VH-LAX		
☐ VH-NXH	Boeing 717-2K9	55055/5014	ex VH-IMD		stored ADL
☐ VH-NXI	Boeing 717-2K9	55054/5013	ex VH-IMP		
☐ VH-NXK	Boeing 717-231	55092/5077	ex VH-YQF		
☐ VH-NXL	Boeing 717-231	55093/5083	ex VH-YQG		
☐ VH-NXM	Boeing 717-231	55094/5084	ex VH-YQH		
☐ VH-NXN	Boeing 717-231	55095/5087	ex VH-YQI		
☐ VH-NXO	Boeing 717-231	55096/5093	ex VH-YQJ		
☐ VH-NXQ	Boeing 717-231	55097/5095	ex VH-YQK		
☐ VH-SBB	de Havilland DHC-8Q-311	539	ex C-FDHO		Eastern Australia
☐ VH-SBG	de Havilland DHC-8Q-315	575	ex C-GSAH		Sunstate
☐ VH-SBI	de Havilland DHC-8Q-315	605	ex C-FZKU		Sunstate
☐ VH-SBT	de Havilland DHC-8Q-315	580	ex C-FDHP		Eastern Australia
☐ VH-SBV	de Havilland DHC-8Q-315	595	ex C-GIHK		Eastern Australia
☐ VH-SBW	de Havilland DHC-8Q-315	599	ex C-GZPN		Eastern Australia
☐ VH-SCE	de Havilland DHC-8Q-315	602	ex C-GZPP		Sunstate
☐ VH-SDA	de Havilland DHC-8Q-202	482	ex C-GFQL		Eastern Australia
☐ VH-SDE	de Havilland DHC-8Q-202	453	ex N453DS		Eastern Australia
☐ VH-TQD	de Havilland DHC-8Q-315	598	ex C-GZDO		Eastern Australia
☐ VH-TQE	de Havilland DHC-8Q-315	596	ex C-GDOE		Eastern Australia
☐ VH-TQG	de Havilland DHC-8-201	430	ex C-GDNG		Eastern Australia
☐ VH-TQH	de Havilland DHC-8Q-315	597	ex C-GZDM		Eastern Australia
☐ VH-TQK	de Havilland DHC-8Q-315	600	ex C-GZPO		Eastern Australia
☐ VH-TQL	de Havilland DHC-8Q-315	603	ex C-GZPQ		Eastern Australia
☐ VH-TQM	de Havilland DHC-8Q-315	604	ex C-FZHW		Eastern Australia
☐ VH-TQS	de Havilland DHC-8-202	418	ex 9M-EKB		Eastern Australia
☐ VH-TQX	de Havilland DHC-8-202	439	ex N439SD		Eastern Australia
☐ VH-TQY	de Havilland DHC-8Q-315	552	ex C-FDHP		Eastern Australia
☐ VH-TQZ	de Havilland DHC-8Q-315	555	ex C-GDNK		Eastern Australia
☐ VH-QOA	de Havilland DHC-8-402Q	4112	ex C-FDHG	Gladstone:	Sunstate
☐ VH-QOB	de Havilland DHC-8-402Q	4116	ex C-FERF	Yeppoon	Sunstate
☐ VH-QOC	de Havilland DHC-8-402Q	4117	ex C-FFCD	Mackay	Sunstate
☐ VH-QOD	de Havilland DHC-8-402Q	4123	ex C-FFQL	Emerald	Sunstate
☐ VH-QOE	de Havilland DHC-8-402Q	4125	ex C-FFQE		Sunstate
☐ VH-QOF	de Havilland DHC-8-402Q	4128	ex C-FFQM		Sunstate
☐ VH-QOH	de Havilland DHC-8-402Q	4132	ex C-FGKH	pink colours	Sunstate
☐ VH-QOI	de Havilland DHC-8-402Q	4189	ex C-FNQL	Tamworth	Sunstate
☐ VH-QOJ	de Havilland DHC-8-402Q	4192	ex C-FNZU		Sunstate
☐ VH-QOK	de Havilland DHC-8-402Q	4215	ex C-FQXU		Sunstate
☐ VH-QOM	de Havilland DHC-8-402Q	4217	ex C-FRLL		Sunstate
☐ VH-QON	de Havilland DHC-8-402Q	4218	ex C-FRLP		Sunstate
☐ VH-QOP	de Havilland DHC-8-402Q	4238	ex C-FUOI		Sunstate
☐ VH-QOR	de Havilland DHC-8-402Q	4241	ex C-FUST		Sunstate
☐ VH-QOS	de Havilland DHC-8-402Q	4263	ex C-FXAZ		Sunstate
☐ VH-QOT	de Havilland DHC-8-402Q	4269	ex C-FXYP		Sunstate
☐ VH-QOU	de Havilland DHC-8-402Q	4275	ex C-FYGQ		Sunstate
☐ VH-QOV	de Havilland DHC-8-402Q	4277	ex C-FYIC		Sunstate
☐ VH-QOW	de Havilland DHC-8-402Q	4285	ex C-FZFT		Sunstate
☐ VH-QOX	de Havilland DHC-8-402Q	4287	ex C-FZGC		Sunstate
☐ VH-QOY	de Havilland DHC-8-402Q	4288	ex C-FZGG		Sunstate
☐ VH-FKD	Fokker F.28-0100 (Fokker 100)	11357	ex N888AU		Alliance
☐ VH-FKG	Fokker F.28-0100 (Fokker 100)	11366	ex N891US		Alliance

REGIONAL PACIFIC AIR *Horn Island, QLD (HID)*

☐ VH-RPA	Embraer EMB.120RT Brasilia	120079	ex DQ-MUM

REX – REGIONAL EXPRESS *(ZL/RXA)* *Orange, NSW/Wagga Wagga, NSW (OAG/WGA)*

☐ VH-EKD	SAAB SF.340A	340A-155	ex SE-F55
☐ VH-EKH	SAAB SF.340B	340B-369	ex SE-C69
☐ VH-EKX	SAAB SF.340B	340B-257	ex (F-GNVQ)
☐ VH-JRX	SAAB SF.340B	340B-186	ex N186CT
☐ VH-KDQ	SAAB SF.340B	340B-325	ex SE-KVO
☐ VH-KDV	SAAB SF.340B	340B-322	ex SE-KVN

☐ VH-KRX	SAAB SF.340B	340B-290	ex N361BE	
☐ VH-NRX	SAAB SF.340B	340B-291	ex N362BE	
☐ VH-OLL	SAAB SF.340B	340B-175	ex N143NC	
☐ VH-OLM	SAAB SF.340B	340B-205	ex SE-G05	
☐ VH-ORX	SAAB SF.340B	340B-293	ex N363BE	
☐ VH-PRX	SAAB SF.340B	340B-303	ex N366BE	
☐ VH-RXE	SAAB SF.340B	340B-275	ex N275CJ	
☐ VH-RXN	SAAB SF.340B	340B-270	ex N358BE	
☐ VH-RXQ	SAAB SF.340B	340B-200	ex YR-VGN	
☐ VH-RXS	SAAB SF.340B	340B-285	ex N359BE	
☐ VH-RXX	SAAB SF.340B	340B-209	ex N355BE	
☐ VH-SBA	SAAB SF.340B	340B-311	ex SE-KXA	
☐ VH-TRX	SAAB SF.340B	340B-287	ex N360BE	Kay Hull Plane
☐ VH-XRX	SAAB SF.340B	340B-179	ex N179CT	
☐ VH-YRX	SAAB SF.340B	340B-178	ex N178CT	
☐ VH-ZLA	SAAB SF.340B	340B-371	ex N371AE	
☐ VH-ZLC	SAAB SF.340B	340B-373	ex N373AE	
☐ VH-ZLF	SAAB SF.340B	340B-374	ex N374AE	
☐ VH-ZLG	SAAB SF.340B	340B-375	ex N375AE	
☐ VH-ZLH	SAAB SF.340B	340B-376	ex N376AE	
☐ VH-ZLJ	SAAB SF.340B	340B-380	ex N380AE	
☐ VH-ZLK	SAAB SF.340B	340B-381	ex N381AE	
☐ VH-ZLO	SAAB SF.340B	340B-382	ex N382AE	
☐ VH-ZLQ	SAAB SF.340B	340B-370	ex N370AM	
☐ VH-ZLR	SAAB SF.340B	340B-229	ex SE-KSK	
☐ VH-ZLS	SAAB SF.340B	340B-383	ex N383AE	
☐ VH-ZLV	SAAB SF.340B	340B-386	ex N386AE	
☐ VH-ZLW	SAAB SF.340B	340B-387	ex N387AE	
☐ VH-ZLX	SAAB SF.340B	340B-182	ex ER-SGB	
☐ VH-ZRB	SAAB SF.340B	340B-389	ex N389AE	
☐ VH-ZRC	SAAB SF.340B	340B-390	ex N390AE	
☐ VH-ZRE	SAAB SF.340B	340B-391	ex N391AE	
☐ VH-ZRH	SAAB SF.340B	340B-392	ex N392AE	
☐ VH-ZRI	SAAB SF.340B	340B-394	ex N394AE	
☐ VH-ZRJ	SAAB SF.340B	340B-396	ex N396AE	
☐ VH-ZRK	SAAB SF.340B	340B-397	ex N397AE	
☐ VH-ZRL	SAAB SF.340B	340B-398	ex N398AE	
☐ VH-ZRN	SAAB SF.340B	340B-393	ex N393AE	
☐ VH-ZRY	SAAB SF.340B	340B-401	ex N901AE	
☐ VH-ZRZ	SAAB SF.340B	340B-388	ex N388AE	

ROSSAIR CHARTER *(RFS)* *Adelaide-International, SA (ADL)*

☐ VH-NAX	Cessna 441 Conquest II	441-0106	ex VH-HXM
☐ VH-OCS	Cessna 441 Conquest II	441-0030	ex N441MM
☐ VH-XBC	Cessna 441 Conquest II	441-0297	ex N441MT
☐ VH-XMD	Cessna 441 Conquest II	441-0025	ex N441HD
☐ VH-XMJ	Cessna 441 Conquest II	441-0113	ex N27TA

ROYAL FLYING DOCTOR SERVICE

☐ VH-AMQ	Beech B200 Super King Air	BB-1813	ex VH-MVS	South Eastern
☐ VH-AMR	Beech B200 Super King Air	BB-1812	ex VH-MSB	South Eastern
☐ VH-AMS	Beech B200 Super King Air	BB-1814	ex N60914	South Eastern
☐ VH-CWO	Beech B200C Super King Air	BL-72	ex N43CE	Western Operations
☐ VH-FDA	Beech B200 Super King Air	BB-1986	ex N986KA	Queensland
☐ VH-FDB	Beech B200 Super King Air	BB-1977	ex N7317A	Queensland
☐ VH-FDC	Pilatus PC-12/45	426		Queensland
☐ VH-FDD	Beech B200 Super King Air	BB-1697	ex N40483	Queensland
☐ VH-FDE	Pilatus PC-12/45	332		Central Operations
☐ VH-FDF	Beech B200 Super King Air	BB-1696	ex N40481	Queensland
☐ VH-FDG	Beech B200 Super King Air	BB-2012	ex N60312	Queensland
☐ VH-FDI	Beech B200 Super King Air	BB-1037	ex VH-DAX	Queensland
☐ VH-FDJ	Pilatus PC-12/47	861	ex HB-FST	Central Operations
☐ VH-FDK	Pilatus PC-12/45	466	ex HB-FSZ	Central Operations
☐ VH-FDM	Pilatus PC-12/45	428		Queensland
☐ VH-FDO	Beech B200 Super King Air	BB-1056	ex VH-RFX	Queensland
☐ VH-FDP	Pilatus PC-12/45	434		Queensland
☐ VH-FDR	Beech B200 Super King Air	BB-1881	ex N36801	Queensland
☐ VH-FDS	Beech B200C Super King Air	BL-68	ex N83GA	Queensland
☐ VH-FDT	Beech B200 Super King Air	BB-1990	ex N990KA	Queensland
☐ VH-FDW	Beech B200 Super King Air	BB-1880	ex N61800	Queensland
☐ VH-FDZ	Beech B200 Super King Air	BB-1882	ex N37082	Queensland
☐ VH-FGR	Pilatus PC-12/45	438	ex HB-FRW	Central Operations
☐ VH-FGS	Pilatus PC-12/45	440	ex HB-FRX	Central Operations
☐ VH-FGT	Pilatus PC-12/45	442	ex HB-FRY	Central Operations
☐ VH-FMC	Pilatus PC-12/45	109		Central Operations
☐ VH-FMF	Pilatus PC-12/45	110		Central Operations
☐ VH-FMP	Pilatus PC-12/45	122		Central Operations
☐ VH-FMW	Pilatus PC-12/45	123		Central Operations
☐ VH-FMZ	Pilatus PC-12/45	138		Central Operations
☐ VH-HWO	Beech B200 Super King Air	BB-1641	ex N23355	Western Operations

☐ VH-IWO	Beech B200 Super King Air	BB-1639	ex N23352	Western Operations
☐ VH-KWO	Pilatus PC-12/45	363		Western Operations
☐ VH-LWO	Beech B200 Super King Air	BB-1643	ex N23356	Western Operations
☐ VH-MSH	Beech B200 Super King Air	BB-1787	ex N44857	South Eastern
☐ VH-MSM	Beech B200 Super King Air	BB-1464	ex N133LC	South Eastern
☐ VH-MSU	Beech B200C Super King Air	BL-48	ex N1860B	South Eastern
☐ VH-MSZ	Beech 200 Super King Air	BB-866	ex ZK-PBG	South Eastern
☐ VH-MVJ	Beech B200 Super King Air	BB-1842	ex N50152	South Eastern
☐ VH-MVL	Beech B200 Super King Air	BB-1333	ex N1101W	South Eastern
☐ VH-MVW	Beech B200 Super King Air	BB-1980	ex N980KA	South Eastern
☐ VH-MVX	Beech B200C Super King Air	BL-153	ex N3203R	South Eastern
☐ VH-MVY	Beech B200 Super King Air	BB-1324	ex N7087N	South Eastern
☐ VH-MWH	Beech B200 Super King Air	BB-2003	ex N32030	South Eastern
☐ VH-MWK	Beech B200C Super King Air	BL-152	ex N3202W	South Eastern
☐ VH-MWO	Pilatus PC-12/45	379		Western Operations
☐ VH-MWQ	Beech B200 Super King Air	BB-1416	ex N8254H	South Eastern
☐ VH-MWU	Beech B200 Super King Air	BB-1418	ex N131GA	South Eastern
☐ VH-MWX	Beech B200 Super King Air	BB-1424	ex N8236K	South Eastern
☐ VH-MWZ	Beech B200 Super King Air	BB-1430	ex VH-MSM	South Eastern
☐ VH-NQC	Cessna 208B Grand Caravan	208B2138		Queensland
☐ VH-NQD	Cessna 208B Grand Caravan	208B2139		Queensland
☐ VH-NWO	Pilatus PC-12/45	396	ex HB-FQQ	Western Operations
☐ VH-OWA	Pilatus PC-12/47E	1115	ex HB-FQR	Western Operations
☐ VH-OWB	Pilatus PC-12/47E	1104	ex HB-FQD	Western Operations
☐ VH-OWD	Pilatus PC-12/47E	1140	ex HB-FRN	Western Operations
☐ VH-OWG	Pilatus PC-12/47E	1155	ex HB-FSV	Western Operations
☐ VH-OWP	Pilatus PC-12/47E	1032	ex HB-FQL	Western Operations
☐ VH-OWQ	Pilatus PC-12/47E	1052	ex HB-FRF	Western Operations
☐ VH-OWR	Pilatus PC-12/47E	11082	ex HB-FSK	Western Operations
☐ VH-VWO	Pilatus PC-12/45	400	ex HB-FQR	Western Operations
☐ VH-YWO	Pilatus PC-12/45	725		Western Operations
☐ VH-ZWO	Pilatus PC-12/45	467	ex HB-FQM	Western Operations

SEAIR PACIFIC GOLD COAST — *Gold Coast, QLD (OOL)*

☐ VH-LMD	Cessna 208 Caravan I	20800217	ex 9M-FBA	Floatplane
☐ VH-LMZ	Cessna 208 Caravan I	20800173	ex LN-SEA	Floatplane
☐ VH-LYT	Cessna 208B Caravan I	208B1208	ex N1320B	
☐ VH-MBF	Britten-Norman BN-2A-8 Islander	646	ex P2-MBF	
☐ VH-MBK	Britten-Norman BN-2A Islander	158	ex P2-MBD	
☐ VH-OZH	Cessna 208 Caravan I	20800464	ex N13313	
☐ VH-SKG	Britten-Norman BN-2A-9 Islander	609	ex ZK-CRA	

SEAWING AIRWAYS — *Sydney Rose Bay, NSW (RSE)*

☐ VH-SWB	de Havilland DHC-2 Beaver	1557	ex ZK-CKD	Floatplane

SHARP AIRLINES — *Hamilton, VIC (HML)*

☐ VH-HWR	Swearingen SA.227DC Metro 23	DC-851B	ex N3025T
☐ VH-LCE	Piper PA-31-350 Navajo Chieftain	31-7305088	ex N305SP
☐ VH-SEZ	Swearingen SA.227AC Metro III	AC-637	ex ZK-RCA
☐ VH-UUN	Swearingen SA.227AC Metro III	AC-686	ex N686AV
☐ VH-UUB	Swearingen SA.227DC Metro 23	DC-894B	ex N3032F

SHINE AIR SERVICES — *Geraldtown, WA (GET)*

☐ VH-ADE	Piper PA-31-325 Navajo C/R	31-7712006	ex N62996
☐ VH-HHX	Beech 58 Baron	TH-270	ex VH-WGS
☐ VH-ITF	Piper PA-31 Navajo C	31-7812014	ex N27435
☐ VH-OMN	Piper PA-31-350 Chieftain	31-8252056	ex VH-PWM
☐ VH-PGO	Piper PA-31-350 Chieftain	31-7852109	ex VH-SFH
☐ VH-PNS	Partenavia P.68B	71	
☐ VH-SXS	Beech 58 Baron	TH-181	ex ZK-EJJ
☐ VH-SZD	Cessna 404 Titan II	404-0050	ex 5Y-BGE
☐ VH-VHT	Cessna 404 Titan II	404-0226	ex ZS-OJN
☐ VH-XSY	Beech 58 Baron	TH-425	ex ZK-TWB

SHOAL AIR — *Kununurra, WA (KNX)*

☐ VH-BFL	Gippsland GA-8 Airvan	GA8-06-107	
☐ VH-HZR	Cessna 310Q	3100468	ex N8700Q
☐ VH-KGE	Piper PA-31-350 Chieftain	31-7752114	ex N27240
☐ VH-KUZ	Gippsland GA-8 Airvan	GA8-07-110	
☐ VH-MLU	Cessna 210M Centurion	21062743	ex N6311B
☐ VH-MNN	Cessna 210L Centurion	21060746	ex ZS-MNM
☐ VH-OTB	Cessna 210L Centurion	21060067	ex ZK-FMG
☐ VH-SMP	Cessna 210L Centurion	21061544	ex N732JG
☐ VH-SUE	Cessna 310P	3100132	ex N5832M
☐ VH-UJF	Cessna 310R	3101342	ex N6215C
☐ VH-WYN	Cessna U206G Stationair	20605906	ex N6468X

SHORTSTOP AIR CHARTER — Melbourne-Essendon, VIC (MEB)

Reg	Type	C/n	Ex	Name	Notes
☐ VH-OVC	Swearingen SA.226T Merlin II	T-318	ex OE-FOW		
☐ VH-OVM	Douglas DC-3	16354/33102	ex VH-JXD	Arthur Schutt MBE	

SKIPPERS AVIATION (SY) — Perth-International, WA (PER)

Reg	Type	C/n	Ex	Name	Notes
☐ VH-FMQ	Cessna 441 Conquest II	441-0109	ex N26226		
☐ VH-LBX	Cessna 441 Conquest II	441-0091	ex VH-AZY		
☐ VH-LBY	Cessna 441 Conquest II	441-0023	ex VH-TFW		
☐ VH-LBZ	Cessna 441 Conquest II	441-0038	ex VH-HWD		
☐ VH-XFP	de Havilland DHC-8-102A	346	ex VH-TQU		
☐ VH-XFQ	de Havilland DHC-8-106	306	ex VH-TQW		
☐ VH-XFT	de Havilland DHC-8-102	52	ex ZK-NEW		
☐ VH-XFU	de Havilland DHC-8-102	151	ex ZK-NEV		
☐ VH-XFV	de Havilland DHC-8-314A	350	ex D-BMUC		
☐ VH-XFW	de Havilland DHC-8-314A	356	ex D-BKIM		
☐ VH-XFX	de Havilland DHC-8-314A	313	ex D-BHAM		
☐ VH-XFZ	de Havilland DHC-8-314A	365	ex D-BACH		
☐ VH-XUA	Embraer EMB.120ER Brasilia	120045	ex N272UE		
☐ VH-XUB	Embraer EMB.120ER Brasilia	120181	ex VH-XFW		
☐ VH-XUC	Embraer EMB.120ER Brasilia	120208	ex VH-XFV	Pelsaert Princess	
☐ VH-XUD	Embraer EMB.120ER Brasilia	120140	ex VH-XFZ	Monket Mia Flyer	
☐ VH-XUE	Embraer EMB.120ER Brasilia	120115	ex VH-XFQ		
☐ VH-XUF	Embraer EMB.120ER Brasilia	120207	ex N268UE		
☐ VH-WAI	Swearingen SA.227DC Metro 23	DC-874B	ex N3032L		
☐ VH-WAJ	Swearingen SA.227DC Metro 23	DC-876B	ex N3033U		
☐ VH-WAX	Swearingen SA.227DC Metro 23	DC-877B	ex N30337		
☐ VH-WBA	Swearingen SA.227DC Metro 23	DC-883B	ex N30042		
☐ VH-WBQ	Swearingen SA.227DC Metro 23	DC-884B	ex N30046	Laverton	

SKY AIRWORLD (SYW) — Brisbane, QLD (BNE)

Ceased operations 22/Feb/2009

SKYTRADERS — Melbourne-Tullamarine, VIC (MEL)

Reg	Type	C/n	Ex	Name	Notes
☐ VH-VHA	CASA C.212 Srs.400	474		Ginger	Wheels or skis
☐ VH-VHB	CASA C.212 Srs.400	475		Gadget	Wheels or skis
☐ VH-VHD	Airbus A319-115X	1999	ex F-GYAS		

SKYTRANS REGIONAL (NP) — Cairns, QLD (CNS)

Reg	Type	C/n	Ex	Name	Notes
☐ VH-BZK	Cessna 310R II	310R1427	ex N5161C		
☐ VH-SKJ	Cessna 404 Titan II	404-0086	ex VH-BPO		
☐ VH-SKV	Cessna 404 Titan II	404-0412	ex VH-TLE		
☐ VH-SKW	Cessna 404 Titan II	404-0042	ex VH-PNY		
☐ VH-SKZ	Cessna 404 Titan II	404-0080	ex VH-JOH		
☐ VH-SZA	Cessna 404 Titan II	404-0205	ex VH-JOA		
☐ VH-QQA	de Havilland DHC-8-102	5	ex P2-MCN		Lsd to Maroomba Air Svs
☐ VH-QQB	de Havilland DHC-8-102	4	ex VH-TQO		Lsd to Maroomba Air Svs
☐ VH-QQC	de Havilland DHC-8-102	8	ex VH-JSZ		
☐ VH-QQD	de Havilland DHC-8-102	41	ex P2-MCK		
☐ VH-QQE	de Havilland DHC-8-102	173	ex N821EX		Lsd to Aircruising
☐ VH-QQF	de Havilland DHC-8-102	14	ex P2-MCO	Cairns Taipans colours	
☐ VH-QQG	de Havilland DHC-8-102	36	ex 5W-FAA		
☐ VH-QQH	de Havilland DHC-8-102A	380	ex N982HA		
☐ VH-QQI	de Havilland DHC-8-102	67	ex VH-TQF		
☐ VH-QQJ	de Havilland DHC-8-102	392	ex N828EX		
☐ VH-SKU	Beech 200 Super King Air	BB-165	ex VH-XRF		
☐ VH-WZN	Beech 200 Super King Air	BB-963	ex RP-C367		

SKYWEST AIRLINES (XR/OZW) — Perth-International, WA (PER)

Reg	Type	C/n	Ex	Name	Notes
☐ VH-FNA	Fokker F.27 Mk.050 (Fokker 50)	20106	ex PH-EXG	City of Albany	
☐ VH-FNB	Fokker F.27 Mk.050 (Fokker 50)	20107	ex PH-EXF	Shire of Esperance	
☐ VH-FND	Fokker F.27 Mk.050 (Fokker 50)	20120	ex PH-EXB		
☐ VH-FNE	Fokker F.27 Mk.050 (Fokker 50)	20212	ex PH-PRJ		
☐ VH-FNF	Fokker F.27 Mk.050 (Fokker 50)	20200	ex PH-PRH		
☐ VH-FNH	Fokker F.27 Mk.050 (Fokker 50)	20113	ex PH-EXY	Shire of Carnarvon	
☐ VH-FNI	Fokker F.27 Mk.050 (Fokker 50)	20114	ex PH-EXZ	City of Geraldton	
☐ VH-FSL	Fokker F.27 Mk.050 (Fokker 50)	20249	ex PH-KXH		on order
☐ VH-FNC	Fokker F.28-0100 (Fokker 100)	11334	ex D-AGPO		
☐ VH-FNJ	Fokker F.28-0100 (Fokker 100)	11489	ex G-BVJA		

☐ VH-FNN	Fokker F.28-0100 (Fokker 100)	11326	ex PH-CFD	
☐ VH-FNR	Fokker F.28-0100 (Fokker 100)	11488	ex G-BVJB	
☐ VH-FNT	Fokker F.28-0100 (Fokker 100)	11461	ex B-12297	
☐ VH-FNU	Fokker F.28-0100 (Fokker 100)	11373	ex OO-TUF	
☐ VH-FNY	Fokker F.28-0100 (Fokker 100)	11484	ex N108ML	
☐ VH-FSQ	Fokker F.28-0100 (Fokker 100)	11450	ex N450FR	
☐ VH-FSW	Fokker F.28-0100 (Fokker 100)	11391	ex D-AGPR	

SLINGAIR — *Kununurra, WA (KNX)*

☐ VH-HOC	Cessna 210N Centurion II	21064689	ex N1360U	
☐ VH-NLV	Cessna 210N Centurion II	21063093	ex VH-APU	
☐ VH-NLZ	Cessna 210N Centurion II	21063769	ex VH-RZZ	
☐ VH-OCM	Cessna 210N Centurion II	21064466	ex N9300Y	
☐ VH-STB	Cessna 210M Centurion II	21062771	ex N6467B	
☐ VH-URX	Cessna 210N Centurion II	21064449	ex N6595Y	
☐ VH-BVJ	Gippsland GA-8 Airvan	GA8-07-116		
☐ VH-DER	Piper PA-31 Navajo C	31-7912110	ex N3539D	
☐ VH-HAM	Cessna 208B Caravan I	208B0296	ex N208MM	
☐ VH-IEU	Cessna 207 Skywagon	20700231	ex N69336	
☐ VH-JVO	Cessna 310R	310R0539	ex N145FB	
☐ VH-KSA	Cessna 208B Caravan I	208B0516	ex N6302B	
☐ VH-LNH	Cessna 208B Caravan I	208B0590	ex N590TA	
☐ VH-LNN	Cessna 208B Caravan I	208B0801	ex 9M-PMB	
☐ VH-LNO	Cessna 208B Caravan I	208B0925	ex N125AR	
☐ VH-MZV	Piper PA-31-350 Chieftain	31-8152092	ex N4083C	
☐ VH-NLG	Cessna U206G Stationair	U20603930	ex ZS-JGH	
☐ VH-RKD	Piper PA-31-350 Chieftain	31-8152048	ex N4076Z	
☐ VH-TWY	Cessna 310R	310R0090	ex N69336	

STRATEGIC AIRLINES — *(EF)*

☐ F-GSTR	Airbus A320-212	0436	ex N436BV	
☐ F-GSTS	Airbus A320-212	0420	ex N420BV	
☐ VH-SSA	Airbus A330-223	324	ex HB-IQR	Outback
☐ VH-YQA	Airbus A320-212	0190	ex F-OHFU	

SUNSTATE AIRLINES — *Sunstate (QF/SSQ)* — *Brisbane, QLD (BNE)*

Wholly owned by Qantas and operates scheduled services in full colours as QantasLink (q.v.)

SYDNEY SEAPLANES — *Sydney Rose Bay, NSW*

☐ VH-AAM	de Havilland DHC-2 Beaver	1492	ex VH-IMR	Floatplane
☐ VH-AQU	de Havilland DHC-2 Beaver	1544	ex VH-IDN	Floatplane
☐ VH-NOO	de Havilland DHC-2 Beaver	1535	ex VH-IDI	Floatplane
☐ VH-SXF	Cessna 208 Caravan I	20800405	ex N1122Y	Floatplane

TASAIR — *Hobart, TAS (HBT)*

☐ VH-JVD	Piper PA-31-350 Chieftain	31-7852041	ex N27523	
☐ VH-KRR	Cessna U206F Stationair 6	U20603210	ex (N8349Q)	
☐ VH-LTW	Piper PA-31-350 Chieftain	31-8152025	ex N40725	
☐ VH-MZI	Piper PA-31-350 Chieftain	31-8152131	ex N4087S	
☐ VH-SMQ	British Aerospace Jetstream 31	665	ex VH-ESW	
☐ VH-TSR	Cessna U206E Stationair	U20601650	ex N9450G	
☐ VH-TZY	Piper PA-31-350 Navajo Chieftain	31-7405166	ex N662WR	

TASFAST AIR FREIGHT — *Melbourne-Moorabin, VIC (MBW)*

☐ VH-EDV	Piper PA-31-350 Navajo Chieftain	31-7305025	ex N86568	
☐ VH-NLX	Piper PA-31 Navajo C	31-7812055	ex VH-EQX	
☐ VH-TBJ	Piper PA-31-350 Navajo Chieftain	31-7552128	ex VH-SAJ	

TASMAN CARGO AIRLINES — *Freightexpress (HJ/AXF)* — *Sydney-Kingsford Smith, NSW (SYD)*

☐ VH-DHE	Boeing 727-2J4F (FedEx 3)	22080/1598	ex N729DH	DHL Express c/s	Lsd fr BCS

TIGER AIRWAYS — *(TT)* — *Melbourne-Tullamarine, VIC (MEL)*

☐ VH-VNB	Airbus A320-232	2906	ex 9V-TAG
☐ VH-VNC	Airbus A320-232	3275	ex F-WWDE
☐ VH-VND	Airbus A320-232	3296	ex F-WWDX
☐ VH-VNF	Airbus A320-232	3332	ex F-WWBI
☐ VH-VNG	Airbus A320-232	3674	ex 9V-TAJ
☐ VH-VNH	Airbus A320-232	3734	ex F-WWDN
☐ VH-VNJ	Airbus A320-232	2982	ex 9V-TAI
☐ VH-VNK	Airbus A320-232	3986	ex 9V-TAK
☐ VH-VNO	Airbus A320-232	4053	ex 9V-TAL

TOLL PRIORITY (TFR) Brisbane, QLD (BNE)

Reg	Type	C/n	Prev	Name	Notes
☐ ZK-TLA	Boeing 737-3B7 (SF)	23383/1425	ex N508AU		Op by AWK
☐ ZK-TLC	Boeing 737-3B7 (SF)	23705/1497	ex N519AU		Op by AWK
☐ ZK-TLD	Boeing 737-3B7 (SF)	23706/1499	ex N520AU		Op by AWK
☐ VH-HPE	Swearingen SA.227DC Metro 23	DC-823B	ex N823MM		Toll c/s
☐ VH-UUO	Swearingen SA.227AC Metro III	AC-530	ex ZK-NST		
☐ VH-UZA	Swearingen SA.227AT Merlin IVC	AT-502	ex VH-UUA		
☐ VH-UZD	Swearingen SA.227AC Metro III	AC-490	ex N30693		
☐ VH-UZG	Swearingen SA.227AC Metro III	AC-553	ex N220CT		
☐ VH-UZI	Swearingen SA.227AT Expediter	AT-570	ex N570UP		
☐ VH-UZN	Swearingen SA.227DC Metro 23	DC-881B	ex N6BN		The Australian c/s
☐ VH-UZP	Swearingen SA.227AC Metro III	AC-498	ex OY-BPL	David Fell	
☐ VH-UZS	Swearingen SA.227AC Metro III	AC-517	ex VH-UUG		
☐ VH-UZW	Swearingen SA.227AC Metro III	AC-526	ex OY-GAW		Toll c/s
☐ VH-TOQ	ATR 42-300F	079	ex EI-SLB		Toll c/s
☐ VH-TOX	ATR 42-300F	024	ex EI-SLE		Toll c/s

V AUSTRALIA Brisbane-International, QLD (BNE)

Reg	Type	C/n	Name
☐ VH-VOZ	Boeing 777-3ZGER	35302/745	Didgeree Blue
☐ VH-VPD	Boeing 777-3ZGER	37938/756	
☐ VH-VPE	Boeing 777-3ZGER	37939/764	
☐ VH-VPF	Boeing 777-3ZGER	37940/801	

VINCENT AVIATION (AUSTRALIA) (BF/VIN) Darwin, NT (DAW)

Reg	Type	C/n	Prev
☐ VH-EMK	Beech 1900C-1	UC-159	ex N159GL
☐ VH-VAU	Beech 1900D	UE-90	ex ZS-PRG
☐ VH-VAZ	Beech 1900D	UE-115	ex ZS-PMD
☐ VH-VNT	Beech 1900D	UE-91	ex ZS-SEM
☐ VH-TAZ	Cessna 441 Conquest	4410005	ex N441RZ

VIRGIN BLUE AIRLINES Virgin Blue (DJ/VOZ) Brisbane-International, QLD (BNE)

Reg	Type	C/n	Prev	Name
☐ VH-VBA	Boeing 737-7Q8/W	28238/817	ex N1791B	Brizzie Lizzie
☐ VH-VBB	Boeing 737-7Q8/W	28240/832	ex N1787B	Barossa Belle
☐ VH-VBC	Boeing 737-7Q8	30638/858		Betty Blue
☐ VH-VBD	Boeing 737-7Q8/W	30707/975		Sassy Sydney
☐ VH-VBF	Boeing 737-7Q8/W	30630/1032		Mellie Melbourne
☐ VH-VBH	Boeing 737-7Q8/W	30641/1080		Spirit of Sally
☐ VH-VBI	Boeing 737-7Q8/W	30644/1107		Smurfette
☐ VH-VBJ	Boeing 737-7Q8/W	30647/1159		Perth Princess
☐ VH-VBK	Boeing 737-7Q8/W	30648/1171		Lady Victoria
☐ VH-VBL	Boeing 737-7Q8/W	30633/1220		Victoria Vixen
☐ VH-VBM	Boeing 737-76N/W	32734/1090	ex N734SH	Tassie Tigress
☐ VH-VBN	Boeing 737-76N/W	33005/1134	ex N330SF	Southern Belle
☐ VH-VBO	Boeing 737-76N/W	33418/1226		Tropical Temptress
☐ VH-VBP	Boeing 737-7BX/W	30743/922	ex N368ML	Deja Blue
☐ VH-VBQ	Boeing 737-7BX/W	30744/989	ex N369ML	La Blue Femme
☐ VH-VBR	Boeing 737-7BX/W	30745/1027	ex N370ML	Mackay Maiden
☐ VH-VBS	Boeing 737-7BX/W	30746/1085	ex N371ML	Blue Baroness
☐ VH-VBU	Boeing 737-7BK/W	30288/1322		Darwin Diva
☐ VH-VBV	Boeing 737-7BK/W	33015/1384		Moulin Blue
☐ VH-VBY	Boeing 737-7FE/W	34323/1751		Virgin-ia Blue50th titles
☐ VH-VBZ	Boeing 737-7FE/W	34322/1777		Maliblue
☐ VH-VOA	Boeing 737-8BK/W	30620/991		Blue Belle
☐ VH-VOB	Boeing 737-8BK/W	30622/1108		Matilda Blue
☐ VH-VOC	Boeing 737-8BK/W	30623/1136		Skye Blue
☐ VH-VOD	Boeing 737-8BK/W	30624/1193	ex N60656	Blue Moon
☐ VH-VOG	Boeing 737-86N/W	28644/839	ex OO-CYS	Misty Blue
☐ VH-VOH	Boeing 737-86N/W	29884/1094		Jazzy Blue
☐ VH-VOK	Boeing 737-8FE/W	33758/1359		Smoochy Maroochy
☐ VH-VOL	Boeing 737-8FE/W	33759/1364		Goldie Coast
☐ VH-VOM	Boeing 737-8FE/W	33794/1373		Little Blue Peep
☐ VH-VON	Boeing 737-8FE/W	33795/1375		Scarlett Blue
☐ VH-VOQ	Boeing 737-8FE/W	33798/1391		Peta Pan
☐ VH-VOS	Boeing 737-8FE/W	33800/1483		Kimberley Cutie
☐ VH-VOT	Boeing 737-8FE/W	33801/1501		Butterfly Blue
☐ VH-VOU	Boeing 737-8Q8/W	30665/1436		Blue Billie
☐ VH-VOV	Boeing 737-82R	30658/1325		Alluring Alice
☐ VH-VOW	Boeing 737-8Q8/W	32798/1470		Jillaroo Blue
☐ VH-VOX	Boeing 737-8BK/W	33017/1446	ex ZK-PBC	Missy Mainlander
☐ VH-VUA	Boeing 737-8FE/W	33997/1559		Bondi Baby
☐ VH-VUC	Boeing 737-8FE/W	34014/1582		Foxy Rock'sy
☐ VH-VUE	Boeing 737-8FE/W	34167/1676		Prue Blue
☐ VH-VUF	Boeing 737-8FE/W	34168/1697		Hobart Honey
☐ VH-VUG	Boeing 737-8FE/W	34438/1948		Jasmine Tasman

☐ VH-VUI	Boeing 737-8FE/W	34441/2015		Brandi Blue	
☐ VH-VUJ	Boeing 737-8FE/W	34443/2056		Suzzie Blue	
☐ VH-VUK	Boeing 737-8FE/W	36602/2353		Mackay-be Diva	
☐ VH-VUL	Boeing 737-8FE/W	36603/2356	ex N1782B	Ballina-rina Blue	
☐ VH-VUM	Boeing 737-8BK/W	29675/2414	ex N1786B	Brindabella Blue	Lsd to PBN
☐ VH-VUN	Boeing 737-8BK/W	29676/2432		Madelaide	Lsd to PBN
☐ VH-VUQ	Boeing 737-8FE/W	36605/2710	ex ZK-PBL		
☐ VH-VUR	Boeing 737-8FE/W	36606/3059	ex N1786B	Star City	
☐ VH-VUS	Boeing 737-8FE/W	36607/3082		Chitty Chitty Broome Broome	
☐ VH-VUT	Boeing 737-8FE/W	36608/3132		Yabba Dabba Blue	
☐ VH-VUU	Boeing 737-8FE/W	36609			on order
☐ VH-VUV	Boeing 737-8FE/W	37821			on order
☐ VH-VUW	Boeing 737-8FE/W	37822			on order
☐ VH-	Boeing 737-8FE/W				on order

☐ VH-ZHA	Embraer 170-100LR (170LR)	17000180	ex PT-SMX	Belle-issimo Blue
☐ VH-ZHB	Embraer 170-100LR (170LR)	17000187	ex PT-SUG	Braziliant Blue
☐ VH-ZHC	Embraer 170-100LR (170LR)	17000191	ex PT-SUR	Irresisto Blue
☐ VH-ZHD	Embraer 170-100LR (170LR)	17000227	ex PT-SFD	Cherry – Belle Blue
☐ VH-ZHE	Embraer 170-100LR (170LR)	17000247	ex PT-SFY	Bee bop a Blue
☐ VH-ZHF	Embraer 170-100LR (170LR)	17000255	ex PT-SJH	Little Miss Sunshine Coast

☐ VH-ZPA	Embraer 190-100IGW (190AR)	19000148	ex PT-SAB	Candid Canberra
☐ VH-ZPB	Embraer 190-100IGW (190AR)	19000162	ex PT-SAR	Rio de Gold Coast
☐ VH-ZPC	Embraer 190-100IGW (190AR)	19000170	ex PT-SDF	Jilla Blue
☐ VH-ZPD	Embraer 190-100IGW (190AR)	19000176	ex PT-SDL	Tickled Blue
☐ VH-ZPE	Embraer 190-100IGW (190AR)	19000187	ex PT-SDV	Bluephoria
☐ VH-ZPF	Embraer 190-100IGW (190AR)	19000193	ex PT-SGB	Maiden Brazil
☐ VH-ZPG	Embraer 190-100IGW (190AR)	19000195	ex PT-SGD	Ella E-Jet
☐ VH-ZPH	Embraer 190-100IGW (190AR)	19000199	ex PT-SGD	Hastings Highness
☐ VH-ZPI	Embraer 190-100IGW (190AR)	19000202	ex PT-SGK	Allie Albury
☐ VH-ZPJ	Embraer 190-100IGW (190AR)	19000209	ex PT-SGS	Bambino Blue
☐ VH-ZPK	Embraer 190-100IGW (190AR)	19000218	ex PT-SHB	Aussie Rob
☐ VH-ZPL	Embraer 190-100IGW (190AR)	19000220	ex PT-SHD	Samba Blue
☐ VH-ZPM	Embraer 190-100IGW (190AR)	19000262	ex PT-TLC	
☐ VH-ZPN	Embraer 190-100IGW (190AR)	19000312	ex PT-TXA	Kanga Blue
☐ VH-ZPO	Embraer 190-100IGW (190AR)	19000321	ex PT-TXJ	Portia Macquarie

WEST WING AVIATION — *Mount Isa, QLD (ISA)*

☐ VH-AAD	Pilatus PC-12/47E	1068	ex HB-FRW
☐ VH-ABP	Beech Baron 58	TH-709	ex N6771S
☐ VH-BAM	Beech Baron 58	TH-478	ex VH-FDC
☐ VH-EZN	Beech 58 Baron	TH-1222	ex N3722P
☐ VH-FBM	Cessna 310R	310R0837	ex VH-HOH
☐ VH-LAP	Beech 58 Baron	TH-646	ex 5N-ATC
☐ VH-RDZ	Cessna 402A	402A0125	ex ZK-CSX
☐ VH-SBM	Beech 200 Super King Air	BB-964	ex VH-HTU
☐ VH-TAN	Cessna 402C	402C1008	ex N1237D
☐ VH-TIA	Cessna 402B	402B0623	ex N3774C
☐ VH-VCB	Beech 200 Super King Air	BB-579	ex P2-MML
☐ VH-WZF	Britten-Norman BN-2A-21 Islander	537	ex 5Y-RAJ
☐ VH-WZI	Aero Commander 500S	1856-38	ex VH-JOG
☐ VH-WZJ	Cessna 208B Caravan I	208B1108	ex N208JJ
☐ VH-WZK	Britten-Norman BN-2A-20 Islander	421	ex VH-UBN
☐ VH-WZP	Britten-Norman BN-2B-20 Islander	2284	ex VH-ZZY
☐ VH-WZQ	Rockwell 500S Shrike Commander	1847-36	ex VH-WPX
☐ VH-WZV	Aero Commander 500U	1656-11	ex N197K
☐ VH-WZY	Cessna 208B Caravan I	208B1035	ex VH-ZGS
☐ VH-XDA	Cessna 404 Titan II	404-0408	ex VH-HOA
☐ VH-XDP	Cessna 404 Titan II	404-0845	ex ZS-PNW
☐ VH-XDU	Beech 1900D	UE-403	ex N857CA
☐ VH-XDV	Beech 200 Super King Air	BB-1100	ex N63971
☐ VH-XDW	Beech 200 Super King Air	BB-1258	ex N2748X
☐ VH-XDY	Beech 1900D	UE-396	ex N838CA

WETTENHALL AIR SERVICES — *Deniliguin, NSW (DNQ)*

☐ VH-MAB	Piper PA-39 Twin Comanche C/R	39-96	ex VH-MED
☐ VH-MAV	Rockwell 500S Shrike Commander	3280	ex N81512
☐ VH-SSL	Swearingen SA.226T Merlin	T-210	ex N173SP

VN- VIETNAM (Socialist Republic of Vietnam)

JETSTAR PACIFIC AIRLINES — *Pacific Airlines (BL/PIC)* — *Ho Chi Minh City (SGN)*

☐ VN-A189	Boeing 737-43Q	28490/2830	ex PK-GWY	
☐ VN-A190	Boeing 737-4H6	27383/2657	ex 9M-MQJ	
☐ VN-A192	Boeing 737-4Q8	26289/2486	ex OK-YGU	all white
☐ VN-A	Boeing 737-4H6	27306/2685	ex 9M-MQM	
☐ VN-A195	Airbus A320-232	0990	ex CC-CZB	

SERVICE FLIGHT CORP

☐ VN-8601	Eurocopter EC155B	6645	ex F-WQDF
☐ VN-	Eurocopter EC155B	6647	
☐ VN-8608	Aérospatiale AS.332L2 II	2348	ex F-WTNR
☐ VN-8610	Aérospatiale AS.332L2 II	2380	ex F-WQDD
☐ VN-8614	Aérospatiale AS.332L2 II	2664	ex F-OISY
☐ VN	Aérospatiale AS.332L2 II	2672	ex F-OISZ
☐ VN-8618	Eurocopter EC225LP	2730	ex F-OKEY
☐ VN-8619	Eurocopter EC225LP	2735	ex F-OKEZ

VASCO — *Vasco Air (0V/VFC)* — *Ho Chi Minh City (SGN)*

☐ VN-B206	ATR 72-212	419	ex F-WWLW
☐ VN-B594	Beech 200 Super King Air	BB-1329	ex VH-SWC

VIETNAM AIRLINES — *Vietnam Airlines (VN/HVN)* — *Hanoi-Noi Bal (HAN)*

☐ VN-B210	ATR 72-212A	678	ex F-WWET	
☐ VN-B212	ATR 72-212A	685	ex F-WWEH	Lsd to K6
☐ VN-B214	ATR 72-212A	688	ex F-WWEK	Lsd to K6
☐ VN-B216	ATR 72-212A	450	ex F-WQNF	
☐ VN-B218	ATR 72-212A	877	ex F-WWEE	
☐ VN-B219	ATR 72-212A	886	ex F-WWEP	
☐ VN-B220	ATR 72-212A	890	ex F-WWEV	
☐ VN-B221	ATR 72-212A	892	ex F-WWEX	
☐ VN-B222	ATR 72-212A	896	ex F-WWEG	
☐ VN-B225	ATR 72-212A	897	ex F-WW	
☐ VN-B	ATR 72-212A	899	ex F-WW	on order
☐ VN-B	ATR 72-212A	906	ex F-WW	on order
☐ VN-B246	ATR 72-202	523	ex G-UKTL	
☐ VN-A301	Airbus A320-214	0590	ex S7-ASA	
☐ VN-A302	Airbus A320-214	0594	ex S7-ASB	
☐ VN-A303	Airbus A320-214	0601	ex S7-ASC	
☐ VN-A304	Airbus A320-214	0605	ex S7-ASD	
☐ VN-A305	Airbus A320-214	0607	ex S7-ASE	
☐ VN-A306	Airbus A320-214	0611	ex S7-ASF	
☐ VN-A307	Airbus A320-214	0617	ex S7-ASG	
☐ VN-A308	Airbus A320-214	0619	ex S7-ASH	
☐ VN-A311	Airbus A320-214	0648	ex S7-ASI	
☐ VN-A344	Airbus A321-231	2255	ex D-AVZH	
☐ VN-A345	Airbus A321-231	2261	ex D-AVZJ	
☐ VN-A347	Airbus A321-231	2267	ex D-AVZL	
☐ VN-A348	Airbus A321-231	2303	ex D-AVZC	
☐ VN-A349	Airbus A321-231	2480	ex D-AVXC	
☐ VN-A350	Airbus A321-231	2974	ex D-AVZN	
☐ VN-A351	Airbus A321-231	3005	ex D-AVZI	Lsd to K6
☐ VN-A352	Airbus A321-231	3013	ex D-AVZW	
☐ VN-A353	Airbus A321-231	3022	ex D-AVZY	
☐ VN-A354	Airbus A321-231	3198	ex D-AVZX	
☐ VN-A356	Airbus A321-231	3315	ex D-AVZA	
☐ VN-A357	Airbus A321-231	3355	ex D-AVZB	
☐ VN-A358	Airbus A321-231	3600	ex D-AZAC	
☐ VN-A359	Airbus A321-231	3737	ex D-AZAJ	
☐ VN-A360	Airbus A321-231	3862	ex D-AZAW	
☐ VN-A361	Airbus A321-231	3964	ex D-AZAW	
☐ VN-A362	Airbus A321-231	3966	ex D-AVZC	
☐ VN-A363	Airbus A321-231	4136	ex D-AZAT	on order
☐ VN-	Airbus A321-231	4213	ex D-AVZG	on order
☐ VN-	Airbus A321-231	4277	ex	on order
☐ VN-A368	Airbus A330-322	087	ex N225LF	
☐ VN-A369	Airbus A330-223	255	ex 9M-MKU	
☐ VN-A370	Airbus A330-223	262	ex 9M-MKT	
☐ VN-A371	Airbus A330-223	275	ex HB-IQG	
☐ VN-A372	Airbus A330-223	294	ex HB-IQJ	
☐ VN-A374	Airbus A330-223	299	ex HB-IQK	
☐ VN-A375	Airbus A330-223	366	ex HB-IQP	
☐ VN-A141	Boeing 777-2Q8ER	28688/436		
☐ VN-A142	Boeing 777-2Q8ER	32701/443		
☐ VN-A143	Boeing 777-26KER	33502/450		
☐ VN-A144	Boeing 777-26KER	33503/453		
☐ VN-A145	Boeing 777-26KER	33504/491		
☐ VN-A146	Boeing 777-26KER	33505/486		
☐ VN-A147	Boeing 777-2Q8ER	27607/135	ex VP-BAS	
☐ VN-A149	Boeing 777-2Q8ER	32716/518	ex (VN-A147)	
☐ VN-A150	Boeing 777-2Q8ER	32717/541		
☐ VN-A151	Boeing 777-2Q8ER	27608/164	ex VP-BAU	

☐ VN-A502	Fokker F.28-070 (Fokker 70)	11580	ex PH-EZL
☐ VN-A504	Fokker F.28-070 (Fokker 70)	11585	ex PH-EZM

VP-A ANGUILLA (UK Dependency)

ANGUILLA AIR SERVICES — Anguilla-Wallbake (AXA)

☐ VP-AAS	Britten-Norman BN-2A-26 Islander	206	ex G-ISLA

TRANS ANGUILLA AIRLINES — Anguilla-Wallbake/St Thomas-Cyril E King, VI (AXA/STT)

☐ VP-AAA	Britten-Norman BN-2A-21 Islander	382	ex N361RA
☐ VP-AAF	Britten-Norman BN-2B-21 Islander	2024	ex N21DA

VP-C CAYMAN ISLANDS (UK Colony)

CAYMAN AIRWAYS — Cayman (KX/CAY) — Georgetown, Grand Cayman (GCM)

☐ VP-CAY	Boeing 737-3Q8	26286/2424	ex N241LF	Spirit of Recovery	
☐ VP-CKW	Boeing 737-36E	26322/2769	ex EI-CRZ		
☐ VP-CKX	Boeing 737-236 (AvAero 3)	23162/1056	ex VR-CKX		stored MZJ
☐ VP-CKY	Boeing 737-3Q8	26282/2355	ex N262KS	The Cayman Islands	
☐ VP-CKZ	Boeing 737-36E	27626/2792	ex EI-CSU		on order
☐ VP-CYB	Boeing 737-2S2C (Nordam 3)	21929/608	ex N716A	Cayman Brac	stored MZJ

ISLAND AIR (G5) — Georgetown, Grand Cayman (GCM)

☐ VP-CIN	Piper PA-31-350 Chieftain	31-8152184	ex VR-CIN

KX EXPRESS — Georgetown, Grand Cayman (GCM)

☐ VP-CXA	de Havilland DHC-6 Twin Otter 300	602	ex N602DH
☐ VP-CXB	de Havilland DHC-6 Twin Otter 300	563	ex N563DH

VP-F FALKLAND ISLANDS (UK Dependency)

BRITISH ANTARCTIC SURVEY — Penguin (BAN) — Rothera Base, Antarctica

☐ VP-FAZ	de Havilland DHC-6 Twin Otter 300	748	ex (FAP-2029)	Wheels or skis
☐ VP-FBB	de Havilland DHC-6 Twin Otter 310	783	ex C-GDKL	Wheels or skis
☐ VP-FBC	de Havilland DHC-6 Twin Otter 310	787	ex C-GDIU	Wheels or skis
☐ VP-FBL	de Havilland DHC-6 Twin Otter 300	839	ex C-GDCZ	Wheels or skis
☐ VP-FBQ	de Havilland DHC-7-110	111	ex G-BOAX	

FIGAS - FALKLAND ISLANDS GOVERNMENT AIR SERVICES — Port Stanley (PSY)

☐ VP-FBD	Britten-Norman BN-2B-26 Islander	2160	ex G-BKJK	
☐ VP-FBI	Britten-Norman BN-2B-26 Islander	2188	ex G-BLNI	dbr 19Nov06?
☐ VP-FBM	Britten-Norman BN-2B-26 Islander	2200	ex G-BLNZ	
☐ VP-FBN	Britten-Norman BN-2B-26 Islander	2216	ex G-BRFY	Fishery Patrol
☐ VP-FBO	Britten-Norman BN-2B-26 Islander	2218	ex G-BRGA	Fishery Patrol
☐ VP-FBR	Britten-Norman BN-2B-26 Islander	2252	ex G-BTLX	

VP-L BRITISH VIRGIN ISLANDS (UK Colony)

FLY BVI — Beef Island (EIS)

☐ N18AU	Cessna 404 Titan II	404-0823	ex ST-AWD
☐ N97AQ	Cessna 404 Titan II	404-0135	ex ST-AJE
☐ N6884A	Piper PA-23-250 Aztec F	27-7954105	
☐ N8438F	Cessna 401	401-0286	

VP-M MONTSERRAT (UK Colony)

AIR MONTSERRAT — Plymouth (MNI)

☐ VP-MNI	Britten-Norman BN-2A-27 Islander	0183	ex C-GLOD
☐ VP-MNT	Britten-Norman BN-2B-26 Islander	2186	
☐ VP-MON	Britten-Norman BN-2A-26 Islander	82	ex C-GCTZ

VQ-T TURKS & CAICOS ISLANDS (UK Colony)

AIR TURKS & CAICOS — Islandways (JY/TCI) — Providenciales (PLS)

☐ VQ-TBC	Embraer EMB.120ER Brasilia	120283	ex N639AS		
☐ VQ-TDA	Britten-Norman BN-2A-27 Islander	504	ex HI-704CT		
☐ VQ-TGW	de Havilland DHC-6 Twin Otter 310	414	ex N38535		
☐ VQ-TIU	Beech 200C Super King Air	BL-131	ex VH-BQR		
☐ VQ-TRS	Beech 200C Super King Air	BL-133	ex VH-BRQ		
☐ VQ-TRT	Beech 200C Super King Air	BL-125	ex VH-BRF		
☐ VQ-TVG	de Havilland DHC-6 Twin Otter 300	410	ex N974SW	Island Spirit	
☐ VQ-T	Embraer EMB.120ER Brasilia	120275	ex N503AS		

SKYKING AIRLINES — Skyking (RU/SKI) — Providenciales (PLS)

☐ VQ-TBL	Beech 1900C-1	UC-104	ex N104GL	stored TPA
☐ VQ-TEB	Beech 1900D	UE-160	ex N160EU	
☐ VQ-TGK	Beech 1900C-1	UC-128	ex N15553	stored TPA
☐ VQ-TVC	Beech 1900D	UE-222	ex N81553	stored TPA

VT- INDIA (Republic of India)

AIR INDIA — Airindia (AI/AIC) — Mumbai-Chhatrapatti Shivaji Intl (BOM)

☐ OK-YAD	Airbus A310-325	674	ex F-OIHS		Lsd fr CSA
☐ VT-AIA	Airbus A310-324	665	ex 9V-STA	Tapti	
☐ VT-AIB	Airbus A310-324	680	ex 9V-STC	Pennar	
☐ VT-EJG	Airbus A310-304	406	ex F-WWCG	Yamuna	
☐ VT-EJH	Airbus A310-304F	407	ex F-WWCH	Teesta	
☐ VT-EJI	Airbus A310-304F	413	ex F-WWCJ	Saraswati	
☐ VT-EJJ	Airbus A310-304	428	ex F-WWCR	Beas	
☐ VT-EJK	Airbus A310-304	429	ex F-WWCS	Gomati	
☐ VT-EJL	Airbus A310-304	392	ex F-WWCB	Sabarmati	
☐ VT-EQS	Airbus A310-304F	538	ex F-WWCP	Krishna	
☐ VT-EQT	Airbus A310-304F	544	ex F-WWCL	Narmada	

☐ VT-SCA	Airbus A319-112	2593	ex D-AVXL
☐ VT-SCB	Airbus A319-112	2624	ex D-AVYX
☐ VT-SCC	Airbus A319-112	2629	ex D-AVWC
☐ VT-SCD	Airbus A319-112	1668	ex C-GJTC
☐ VT-SCE	Airbus A319-112	1718	ex C-GJVS
☐ VT-SCF	Airbus A319-112	2907	ex D-AVWT
☐ VT-SCG	Airbus A319-112	3271	ex D-AVYH
☐ VT-SCH	Airbus A319-112	3288	ex D-AVWM
☐ VT-SCI	Airbus A319-112	3300	ex D-AVYN
☐ VT-SCJ	Airbus A319-112	3305	ex D-AVYO
☐ VT-SCK	Airbus A319-112	3344	ex D-AVYT
☐ VT-SCL	Airbus A319-112	3551	ex D-AVWO
☐ VT-SCM	Airbus A319-112	3620	ex D-AVYN
☐ VT-SCN	Airbus A319-112	3687	ex D-AVWE
☐ VT-SCO	Airbus A319-112	3822	ex D-AVYH
☐ VT-SCP	Airbus A319-112	3874	ex D-AVWF
☐ VT-SCQ	Airbus A319-112	3918	ex D-AVYY
☐ VT-SCR	Airbus A319-112	3970	ex D-AVYB
☐ VT-SCS	Airbus A319-112	4020	ex D-AVYH
☐ VT-SCT	Airbus A319-112	4029	ex D-AVYJ
☐ VT-SCU	Airbus A319-112	4052	ex D-AVYQ
☐ VT-SCV	Airbus A319-112	4089	ex D-AVYY
☐ VT-SCW	Airbus A319-112	4121	ex D-AVWB
☐ VT-SCX	Airbus A319-112	4164	ex D-AVYZ

☐ VT-EDC	Airbus A320-231	4201	ex		on order
☐ VT-EDD	Airbus A320-231	4212	ex F-WWDJ		on order
☐ VT-EDE	Airbus A320-231	4236	ex F-WWDE		on order
☐ VT-EDF	Airbus A320-231	4237	ex		on order
☐ VT-EPB	Airbus A320-231	0045	ex F-WWDY		
☐ VT-EPC	Airbus A320-231	0046	ex F-WWDG		
☐ VT-EPD	Airbus A320-231	0047	ex F-WWDP		
☐ VT-EPE	Airbus A320-231	0048	ex F-WWDU		
☐ VT-EPF	Airbus A320-231	0049	ex F-WWIA		
☐ VT-EPG	Airbus A320-231	0050	ex F-WWDR		
☐ VT-EPH	Airbus A320-231	0051	ex F-WWIB		
☐ VT-EPI	Airbus A320-231	0056	ex F-WWIC		
☐ VT-EPJ	Airbus A320-231	0057	ex F-WWIF	50 years titles	
☐ VT-EPK	Airbus A320-231	0058	ex F-WWID	ACT 07 c/s	
☐ VT-EPL	Airbus A320-231	0074	ex F-WWIQ		
☐ VT-EPM	Airbus A320-231	0075	ex F-WWIR	50 years titles	
☐ VT-EPO	Airbus A320-231	0080	ex F-WWIX		
☐ VT-EPP	Airbus A320-231	0089	ex F-WWDT		
☐ VT-EPQ	Airbus A320-231	0090	ex F-WWDX		

☐ VT-EPR	Airbus A320-231	0095	ex F-WWDS		
☐ VT-EPS	Airbus A320-231	0096	ex F-WWDU		
☐ VT-ESA	Airbus A320-231	0396	ex F-WWBK		
☐ VT-ESB	Airbus A320-231	0398	ex F-WWDQ		
☐ VT-ESC	Airbus A320-231	0416	ex F-WWBP		
☐ VT-ESD	Airbus A320-231	0423	ex F-WWIT		
☐ VT-ESE	Airbus A320-231	0431	ex F-WWBQ		
☐ VT-ESF	Airbus A320-231	0432	ex F-WWBS		
☐ VT-ESG	Airbus A320-231	0451	ex F-WWIN		
☐ VT-ESH	Airbus A320-231	0469	ex F-WWBD		
☐ VT-ESI	Airbus A320-231	0486	ex F-WWBH	50 years titles	
☐ VT-ESJ	Airbus A320-231	0490	ex F-WWDT	50 years titles	
☐ VT-ESK	Airbus A320-231	0492	ex F-WWBU	50 years titles	
☐ VT-ESL	Airbus A320-231	0499	ex F-WWDO		
☐ VT-EVO	Airbus A320-231	0247	ex N247RX		
☐ VT-EVP	Airbus A320-231	0257	ex N257RX		
☐ VT-EVQ	Airbus A320-231	0327	ex G-OOAC	50 years titles	
☐ VT-EVR	Airbus A320-231	0336	ex G-OOAD	50 years titles	
☐ VT-EVS	Airbus A320-231	0308	ex EC-GUR		
☐ VT-EVT	Airbus A320-231	0314	ex EC-GLT		
☐ VT-EYB	Airbus A320-231	0386	ex G-MEDD		
☐ VT-EYC	Airbus A320-231	0362	ex G-YJBM		
☐ VT-EYG	Airbus A320-231	0326	ex F-WQSM		
☐ VT-EYH	Airbus A320-231	0344	ex F-WQSO		
☐ VT-EYI	Airbus A320-231	0478	ex F-WQSN		stored BOM
☐ VT-EYJ	Airbus A320-231	0354	ex G-BVYA		
☐ VT-EYK	Airbus A320-231	0411	ex G-BVYC		
☐ VT-EYL	Airbus A320-231	0480	ex G-MEDA		
☐ VT-PPA	Airbus A321-211	3130	ex D-AVZT		
☐ VT-PPB	Airbus A321-211	3146	ex D-AVZU		
☐ VT-PPD	Airbus A321-211	3212	ex D-AVZA		
☐ VT-PPE	Airbus A321-211	3326	ex D-AVZW		
☐ VT-PPF	Airbus A321-211	3340	ex D-AVZH		
☐ VT-PPG	Airbus A321-211	3367	ex D-AVZG		
☐ VT-PPH	Airbus A321-211	3498	ex D-AVZG		
☐ VT-PPI	Airbus A321-211	3557	ex D-AVZQ		
☐ VT-PPJ	Airbus A321-211	3573	ex D-AVZC		
☐ VT-PPK	Airbus A321-211	3619	ex D-AVZF		
☐ VT-PPL	Airbus A321-211	3752	ex D-AZAM		
☐ VT-PPM	Airbus A321-211	3792	ex D-AZAR		
☐ VT-PPN	Airbus A321-211	3955	ex D-AVAU		
☐ VT-PPO	Airbus A321-211	4002	ex D-AVZB		
☐ VT-PPQ	Airbus A321-211	4009	ex D-AVZE		
☐ VT-PPT	Airbus A321-211	4078	ex D-AVZU		
☐ VT-PPU	Airbus A321-211	4096	ex D-AVZY		
☐ VT-PPV	Airbus A321-211	4138	ex D-AZAU		
☐ VT-PPW	Airbus A321-211	4155	ex D-AVZZ		
☐ VT-PPX	Airbus A321-211		ex D-		on order
☐ VT-IWA	Airbus A330-223	353	ex F-WQVY		
☐ VT-IWB	Airbus A330-223	362	ex F-WQVZ		
☐ VT-EPW	Boeing 747-337M	24159/711	ex N6018N	Shivaji	
☐ VT-ESM	Boeing 747-437	27078/987		Konark	
☐ VT-ESN	Boeing 747-437	27164/1003		Tanjore	
☐ VT-ESO	Boeing 747-437	27165/1009		Khajurao	
☐ VT-ESP	Boeing 747-437	27214/1034		Ajanta	
☐ VT-EVA	Boeing 747-437	28094/1089		Agra	
☐ VT-EVB	Boeing 747-437	28095/1093		Velha Goa	
☐ VT-AIJ	Boeing 777-222ER	26943/92	ex N790UA	Neelambam	
☐ VT-AIK	Boeing 777-222ER	28714/205	ex N205UA	Megh Malhaar	
☐ VT-AIL	Boeing 777-222ER	26935/88	ex N789UA	Kalyani	
☐ VT-AIR	Boeing 777-222	26917/8	ex N766UA	Hamsadhwani	
☐ VT-ALA	Boeing 777-237LR	36300/610	ex N6018N	Andhra Pradesh	
☐ VT-ALB	Boeing 777-237LR	36301/621	ex N5028Y	Arunachal Pradesh	
☐ VT-ALC	Boeing 777-237LR	36302/629	ex N5020K	Assam	
☐ VT-ALD	Boeing 777-237LR	36303/663	ex N5016R	Gujarat	
☐ VT-ALE	Boeing 777-237LR	36304/698		Haryana	
☐ VT-ALF	Boeing 777-237LR	36305/793		Jhardkand	
☐ VT-ALG	Boeing 777-237LR	36306/800		Kerala	
☐ VT-ALH	Boeing 777-237LR	36307/805		Maharashtra	
☐ VT-ALJ	Boeing 777-337ER	36308/643		Bihar	
☐ VT-ALK	Boeing 777-337ER	36309/652		Chattisgarh	
☐ VT-ALL	Boeing 777-337ER	36310/656		Goa	
☐ VT-ALM	Boeing 777-337ER	36311/713			
☐ VT-ALN	Boeing 777-337ER	36312/719		Jammu and Kashmir	
☐ VT-ALO	Boeing 777-337ER	36313/798		Kamataka	
☐ VT-ALP	Boeing 777-337ER	36314/804		Madhya Pradesh	
☐ VT-ALQ	Boeing 777-337ER	36315/809		Manipur	
☐ VT-ALR	Boeing 777-337ER	36316/814		Meghalaya	
☐ VT-ALS	Boeing 777-337ER	36317			

☐ VT-ALT	Boeing 777-337ER	36318		
☐ VT-ALU	Boeing 777-337ER	36319		
☐ VT-EIO	Dornier 228-201	8037	ex D-IDBG	
☐ VT-EJO	Dornier 228-201	8054	ex D-CALI	

AIR INDIA EXPRESS (AI/AXB) Mumbai-Chhatrapatti Shivaji Intl (BOM)

☐ VT-AXA	Boeing 737-86Q	30296/1647	ex N119CH	
☐ VT-AXB	Boeing 737-8BK	33023/1682	ex N323CT	
☐ VT-AXC	Boeing 737-8BK	33024/1688		dam 11Jly07
☐ VT-AXD	Boeing 737-8Q8/W	30696/1892		
☐ VT-AXE	Boeing 737-8Q8/W	29368/1910		
☐ VT-AXF	Boeing 737-8Q8/W	29369/1939	ex N1787B	
☐ VT-AXG	Boeing 737-8Q8/W	30701/1946	ex N1787B	
☐ VT-AXH	Boeing 737-8HG/W	36323/2108		
☐ VT-AXI	Boeing 737-8HG/W	36324/2132		
☐ VT-AXJ	Boeing 737-8HG/W	36325/2142		
☐ VT-AXM	Boeing 737-8HG/W	36326/2148		
☐ VT-AXN	Boeing 737-8HG/W	36327/2154		
☐ VT-AXP	Boeing 737-8HG/W	36328/2177		
☐ VT-AXQ	Boeing 737-8HG/W	36329/2258		
☐ VT-AXR	Boeing 737-8HG/W	36330/2317		
☐ VT-AXT	Boeing 737-8HG/W	36331/2324		
☐ VT-AXU	Boeing 737-8HG/W	36332/2381		
☐ VT-AXV	Boeing 737-8HG/W	36333/2481	ex N1787B	
☐ VT-AXW	Boeing 737-8HG/W	36334/2612		
☐ VT-AXX	Boeing 737-8HG/W	36335/2672		
☐ VT-AXZ	Boeing 737-8HG/W	36336/2782	ex N1786B	
☐ VT-AYA	Boeing 737-8HG/W	36337/2861	ex N6065Y	
☐ VT-AYB	Boeing 737-8HG/W	36338/2962		
☐ VT-AYC	Boeing 737-8HG/W	36339/3039	ex N1786B	

AIR INDIA REGIONAL

☐ VT-ABA	ATR 42-320	390	ex F-WQNK	
☐ VT-ABB	ATR 42-320	392	ex F-WQNL	
☐ VT-ABC	ATR 42-320	315	ex F-WQNB	
☐ VT-ABD	ATR 42-320	356	ex F-WQNF	
☐ VT-ABF	ATR 42-320	351	ex F-WQNC	
☐ VT-ABO	ATR 42-320	406	ex F-WQNE	

ALLIANCE AIR Allied (CD/LLR) Delhi-Indira Gandhi Intl (DEL)

☐ VT-EGE	Boeing 737-2A8	22281/679	ex N8291V	stored DEL
☐ VT-EGF	Boeing 737-2A8F	22282/681	ex N8292V	
☐ VT-EGG	Boeing 737-2A8F	22283/689	ex N8290V	
☐ VT-EGH	Boeing 737-2A8	22284/739		
☐ VT-EGI	Boeing 737-2A8F	22285/798		
☐ VT-EGJ	Boeing 737-2A8F	22286/799		
☐ VT-EGM	Boeing 737-2A8C	22473/747		
☐ VT-EHE	Boeing 737-2A8	22860/899	ex K-5011	Lsd to Indian AF
☐ VT-EHF	Boeing 737-2A8	22861/902		stored DEL
☐ VT-EHG	Boeing 737-2A8	22862/903		stored DEL
☐ VT-EHH	Boeing 737-2A8F	22863/907		
☐ VT-RJB	Canadair CL-600-2C10 (CRJ-700)	10217	ex D-ALTE	
☐ VT-RJC	Canadair CL-600-2C10 (CRJ-700)	10052	ex B-KBB	
☐ VT-RJD	Canadair CL-600-2C10 (CRJ-700)	10048	ex G-DUOD	
☐ VT-RJE	Canadair CL-600-2C10 (CRJ-700)	10029	ex N290RB	
☐ VT-ADC	ATR 42-320	333	ex F-WQNF	

BLUE DART AVIATION Blue Dart (BZ/BDA) Chennai (MAA)

☐ VT-BDE	Boeing 737-2A8F	21163/434	ex VT-EDR	Vision II	
☐ VT-BDG	Boeing 737-2K9F	22415/702	ex VT-SIE	Vision III	
☐ VT-BDH	Boeing 737-25C	24236/1585	ex B-2524	Vision IV	
☐ VT-BDI	Boeing 737-2T4F	23272/1093	ex B-2506	Vision V	
☐ VT-BDJ	Boeing 757-236 (SF)	24102/179	ex OO-DPI		
☐ VT-BDK	Boeing 757-236 (SF)	24267/211	ex OO-DPL		
☐ VT-BDM	Boeing 757-23N (SF)	27598/692	ex EI-LTA		
☐ VT-	Boeing 757-25CF	25898/475	ex N7273		on order

DECCAN CARGO

☐ VT-AIN	Airbus A310-324F	684	ex 9V-STD	Damodar
☐ VT-AIO	Airbus A310-324F	693	ex 9V-STE	Pamba
☐ VT-AIP	Airbus A310-324F	697	ex 9V-STF	Vaigai

FUTURA TRAVELS

☐ VT-ASH	Beech 1900D	UE-361	ex C-GSKQ

GLOBAL VECTRA HELICORP — Mumbai-Juhu

Registration	Type	c/n	Previous identity	Notes
□ VT-AZA	Bell 412SP	33188	ex 9M-SSM	
□ VT-AZC	Bell 412SP	36161	ex N45169	
□ VT-AZD	Bell 412SP	33172	ex N63385	
□ VT-AZE	Bell 412HP	36024	ex N6344X	
□ VT-AZG	Bell 412SP	33185	ex N9VH	
□ VT-AZH	Bell 412EP	36371	ex N412GV	
□ VT-AZI	Bell 412SP	33199	ex I-POPA	
□ VT-AZJ	Bell 412HP	36027	ex N412HX	
□ VT-AZK	Bell 412HP	36023	ex N175AR	
□ VT-AZL	Bell 412HP	36065	ex C-FDDI	
□ VT-AZM	Bell 412EP	36394	ex N30011	
□ VT-AZN	Bell 412EP	36397	ex C-FHWW	
□ VT-AZO	Bell 412EP	36398	ex C-FHWU	
□ VT-AZP	Bell 412EP	36407	ex N2519A	
□ VT-AZQ	Bell 412EP	36413	ex N80072	
□ VT-AZR	Bell 412EP	36415	ex N2086C	
□ VT-AZS	Bell 412EP	36416	ex N8007U	
□ VT-AZT	Bell 412EP	36422	ex N8019T	
□ VT-AZU	Eurocopter EC155B1	6759	ex F-WWOF	

GO AIR — Goair (G8/GOW) — Mumbai-Chhatrapatti Shivaji Intl (BOM)

Registration	Type	c/n	Previous identity	Notes
□ VT-WAC	Airbus A320-233	1482	ex N482TA	blue
□ VT-WAE	Airbus A320-214	3256	ex F-WWDF	
□ VT-WAF	Airbus A320-214	3306	ex F-WWIM	
□ VT-WAG	Airbus A320-214	3597	ex D-AVVE	
□ VT-WAH	Airbus A320-214	3616	ex F-WWII	
□ VT-WAI	Airbus A320-214	3798	ex F-WWBP	
□ VT-WAJ	Airbus A320-214	3827	ex F-WWIX	
□ VT-WAK	Airbus A320-214	3900	ex F-WWDU	
□ VT-WAL	Airbus A320-214	3915	ex F-WWBC	
□ VT-	Airbus A320-214		ex	on order

HELIGO CHATERS — Mumbai

Registration	Type	c/n	Previous identity
□ VT-HLB	Agusta AW139	31095	ex A6-AWD
□ VT-HLC	Agusta AW139	31106	ex A6-AWE

INDIGO AIRLINES — (6E/IGO) — Bangalore (BLR)

Registration	Type	c/n	Previous identity	Notes
□ VT-IGH	Airbus A320-232	4008	ex F-WWDZ	
□ VT-IGI	Airbus A320-232	4113	ex F-WWDV	
□ VT-IGJ	Airbus A320-232	4156	ex F-WWBM	
□ VT-IGK	Airbus A320-232	4216	ex F-WWBE	on order
□ VT-	Airbus A320-232		ex	on order
□ VT-	Airbus A320-232		ex	on order
□ VT-INA	Airbus A320-232	2844	ex F-WWIH	
□ VT-INB	Airbus A320-232	2863	ex F-WWIZ	
□ VT-INC	Airbus A320-232	2883	ex F-WWBR	
□ VT-IND	Airbus A320-232	2911	ex F-WWDG	
□ VT-INE	Airbus A320-232	2958	ex F-WWBM	
□ VT-INF	Airbus A320-232	2990	ex F-WWIO	
□ VT-INI	Airbus A320-232	3086	ex F-WWBN	
□ VT-INJ	Airbus A320-232	3159	ex F-WWDQ	
□ VT-INK	Airbus A320-232	3192	ex F-WWIT	
□ VT-INL	Airbus A320-232	3227	ex F-WWBC	
□ VT-INO	Airbus A320-232	3335	ex F-WWBJ	
□ VT-INP	Airbus A320-232	3357	ex F-WWIH	
□ VT-INQ	Airbus A320-232	3414	ex F-WWIM	
□ VT-INR	Airbus A320-232	3453	ex F-WWBF	
□ VT-INS	Airbus A320-232	3457	ex F-WWBI	
□ VT-INT	Airbus A320-232	3497	ex F-WWIM	
□ VT-INU	Airbus A320-232	3541	ex F-WWIP	
□ VT-INV	Airbus A320-232	3618	ex F-WWIJ	
□ VT-INX	Airbus A320-232	3782	ex D-AVVK	
□ VT-INY	Airbus A320-232	3863	ex F-WW	
□ VT-INZ	Airbus A320-232	3943	ex F-WWDT	

JAGSON AIRLINES — Delhi-Indira Gandhi Intl (DEL)

Registration	Type	c/n	Previous identity
□ VT-ESQ	Dornier 228-201	8006	ex A5-RGB
□ VT-ESS	Dornier 228-201	8017	ex A5-RGC
□ VT-EUM	Dornier 228-201	8096	ex D-CAAL
□ VT-JJA	Mil Mi-172	365C157	
□ VT-JJB	Mil Mi-172	365C158	

JET AIRWAYS		Jet Airways (9W/JAI)	Mumbai-Chhatrapatti Shivaji Intl (BOM)	
☐ VT-JWD	Airbus A330-243	751	ex F-WWKB	
☐ VT-JWE	Airbus A330-243	807	ex F-WWYU	
☐ VT-JWF	Airbus A330-203	825	ex F-WWKE	
☐ VT-JWG	Airbus A330-202	831	ex F-WWKL	
☐ VT-JWH	Airbus A330-202	882	ex F-WWKJ	
☐ VT-JWJ	Airbus A330-202	886	ex F-WWKS	
☐ VT-JWK	Airbus A330-202	888	ex F-WWKL	
☐ VT-JWL	Airbus A330-202	901	ex F-WWKQ	
☐ VT-JWM	Airbus A330-202	923	ex F-WWYZ	
☐ VT-JWN	Airbus A330-202	932	ex F-WWKV	
☐ VT-JWP	Airbus A330-203	947	ex F-WWKM	
☐ VT-JWQ	Airbus A330-203	956	ex F-WWYA	
☐ VT-JWR	Airbus A330-203	1056	ex F-WW	on order
☐ VT-JCA	ATR 72-212A	572	ex F-WQKD	retd?
☐ VT-JCB	ATR 72-212A	575	ex F-WQKE	
☐ VT-JCC	ATR 72-212A	593	ex F-WQKP	
☐ VT-JCD	ATR 72-212A	636	ex F-WQMC	
☐ VT-JCF	ATR 72-212A	674	ex F-WQMK	Lsd fr SFR
☐ VT-JCG	ATR 72-212A	679	ex F-WQML	Lsd fr SFR
☐ VT-JCH	ATR 72-212A	681	ex F-WQMM	Lsd fr SFR
☐ VT-JCJ	ATR 72-212A	771	ex F-WWEJ	
☐ VT-JCK	ATR 72-212A	775	ex F-WWEN	
☐ VT-JCL	ATR 72-212A	791	ex F-WWEK	
☐ VT-JCM	ATR 72-212A	793	ex F-WWEN	
☐ VT-JCN	ATR 72-212A	825	ex F-WWEN	
☐ VT-JCP	ATR 72-212A	841	ex F-WWES	
☐ VT-JCQ	ATR 72-212A	843	ex F-WWEJ	
☐ VT-JBB	Boeing 737-8HX/W	36846/2368	ex N846AG	
☐ VT-JBC	Boeing 737-8HX/W	36847/2388	ex N847AG	
☐ VT-JBD	Boeing 737-85R/W	35099/2439		
☐ VT-JBE	Boeing 737-85R/W	35106/2530	ex N1786B	
☐ VT-JBF	Boeing 737-85R/W	35082/2550	ex N1786B	
☐ VT-JBG	Boeing 737-85R/W	35083/2535	ex N1786B	
☐ VT-JBH	Boeing 737-85R/W	35289/2811	ex N1786B	
☐ VT-JBJ	Boeing 737-85R/W	36551/2974	ex N1786B	
☐ VT-JBK	Boeing 737-85R/W	36553/3074	ex N1786B	
☐ VT-JBL	Boeing 737-85R/W	35651/3000		
☐ VT-JBM	Boeing 737-85R/W	36817/3055	ex N1786B	
☐ VT-JBN	Boeing 737-85R/W	36818/3087	ex N1786B	
☐ VT-JBP	Boeing 737-85R/W	36819/3101		
☐ VT-JGA	Boeing 737-85R	30410/1228		
☐ VT-JGB	Boeing 737-75R	30411/1282	ex N1787B	
☐ VT-JGC	Boeing 737-95R	30412/1314		
☐ VT-JGD	Boeing 737-95R	33740/1350		
☐ VT-JGE	Boeing 737-83N/W	32663/1608	ex EI-DIL	
☐ VT-JGF	Boeing 737-8FH/W	29639/1643	ex EI-DIM	
☐ VT-JGG	Boeing 737-8FH/W	29668/1686	ex EI-DIN	
☐ VT-JGH	Boeing 737-83N/W	32577/973	ex EI-DKX	
☐ VT-JGJ	Boeing 737-83N/W	32578/998	ex EI-DKP	
☐ VT-JGK	Boeing 737-83N/W	32579/1002	ex EI-DKR	
☐ VT-JGL	Boeing 737-76N/W	32738/1392	ex EI-DMD	
☐ VT-JGM	Boeing 737-83N/W	32614/1201	ex EI-DME	
☐ VT-JGN	Boeing 737-83N/W	32616/1212	ex EI-DMF	
☐ VT-JGP	Boeing 737-85R/W	34798/1920		
☐ VT-JGQ	Boeing 737-85R/W	34797/2007		
☐ VT-JGR	Boeing 737-85R/W	34799/2044		
☐ VT-JGS	Boeing 737-85R/W	34800/2085		
☐ VT-JGT	Boeing 737-85R/W	34801/2125		
☐ VT-JGU	Boeing 737-85R/W	34802/2170		
☐ VT-JGV	Boeing 737-85R/W	34803/2209		
☐ VT-JGW	Boeing 737-85R/W	34804/2297		
☐ VT-JGX	Boeing 737-75R	34805/2360	ex N1781B	
☐ VT-JGY	Boeing 737-75R	34806/2404		
☐ VT-JGZ	Boeing 737-76N	35218/2342	ex N1781B	
☐ VT-JNE	Boeing 737-71Q	29043/138	ex N29879	
☐ VT-JNF	Boeing 737-71Q	29044/152	ex N29887	
☐ VT-JNG	Boeing 737-71Q	29045/169	ex N29975	
☐ VT-JNH	Boeing 737-71Q	29046/181	ex N29976	
☐ VT-JNJ	Boeing 737-85R	29038/297		
☐ VT-JNL	Boeing 737-85R	29039/326		
☐ VT-JNM	Boeing 737-85R	29040/465		
☐ VT-JNN	Boeing 737-85R	29041/489		
☐ VT-JNR	Boeing 737-85R	30403/749	ex N1781B	
☐ VT-JNS	Boeing 737-73A	28498/775	ex N498AW	
☐ VT-JNU	Boeing 737-75R	30404/835	ex N1787B	
☐ VT-JNV	Boeing 737-75R	30405/927		
☐ VT-JNW	Boeing 737-75R	30406/1016	ex N1787B	
☐ VT-JNX	Boeing 737-85R	30407/1073		

☐ VT-JNY	Boeing 737-85R	30408/1146	ex (VT-JGA)		
☐ VT-JNZ	Boeing 737-85R	30409/1185	ex (VT-JGB)		
☐ VT-	Boeing 737-75R				on order
☐ VT-	Boeing 737-75R				on order
☐ VT-	Boeing 737-8AL				on order
☐ VT-	Boeing 737-8AL				on order
☐ VT-JEA	Boeing 777-35RER	35157/627			
☐ VT-JEB	Boeing 777-35RER	35158/637			
☐ VT-JEG	Boeing 777-35RER	35163/675	ex N1785B		
☐ VT-JEH	Boeing 777-35RER	35166/678	ex N5014K		
☐ VT-JEJ	Boeing 777-35RER	35161/693			
☐ VT-JEK	Boeing 777-35RER	35165/696			

JETLITE — *Sahara (S2/RSH)* — *Delhi-Indira Gandhi Intl (DEL)*

☐ VT-JLA	Boeing 737-7Q8	30037/1449	ex EI-DZC		
☐ VT-JLB	Boeing 737-7Q8	28250/1142	ex A4O-BT		
☐ VT-SAY	Boeing 737-382	25161/2226	ex N161AN		stored DEL
☐ VT-SIE	Boeing 737-4Q8	24707/2057	ex (PK-KKW)		stored DEL
☐ VT-SIJ	Boeing 737-81Q	29049/424	ex N8253J		
☐ VT-SIK	Boeing 737-81Q	29050/444	ex N8253V		
☐ VT-SIU	Boeing 737-7K9	28090/205	ex SX-BLT		
☐ VT-SIV	Boeing 737-7K9	28091/223	ex SX-BLU		stored DEL
☐ VT-SIZ	Boeing 737-7BK	33025/1707	ex N325CT		
☐ VT-SJA	Boeing 737-7BK	33026/1715	ex N326CT		
☐ VT-SJE	Boeing 737-7Q8	30727/1005	ex S7-SEZ		
☐ VT-SJF	Boeing 737-86N	28610/449	ex EI-DIS		
☐ VT-SJG	Boeing 737-8Q8/W	30694/1863	ex N164LF		
☐ VT-SJH	Boeing 737-8Q8/W	30695/1891	ex (N201LF)		
☐ VT-SJI	Boeing 737-8K9/W	34399/2030			
☐ VT-SJJ	Boeing 737-8K9/W	34400/2053			
☐ VP-BIZ	Boeing 737-7AU/W	34477/1825	ex N746BA		on order [BBJ]
☐ VT-SAL	Canadair CL-600-2B19 (CRJ-200ER)	7224	ex N572ML		dbr?
☐ VT-SAP	Canadair CL-600-2B19 (CRJ-200ER)	7242	ex N574ML		
☐ VT-SAQ	Canadair CL-600-2B19 (CRJ-200ER)	7345	ex G-JECA		
☐ VT-SAR	Canadair CL-600-2B19 (CRJ-200ER)	7393	ex G-JECB		
☐ VT-SAS	Canadair CL-600-2B19 (CRJ-200ER)	7434	ex G-JECC		

KINGFISHER AIRLINES — *(IT/KFR)* — *Mumbai-Chhatrapatti Shivaji Intl / Bangalore (BOM/BLR)*

☐ VT-VJK	Airbus A330-223	874	ex F-WWKA		
☐ VT-VJL	Airbus A330-223	891	ex F-WWYO		
☐ VT-VJN	Airbus A330-223	927	ex F-WWKE		
☐ VT-VJO	Airbus A330-223	939	ex F-WWKK		
☐ VT-VJP	Airbus A330-223	946	ex F-WWYX		

KINGFISHER RED — *(IT/KFR)* — *Mumbai-Chhatrapatti Shivaji Intl / Bangalore (BOM/BLR)*

☐ VT-KFH	Airbus A319-131	2621	ex D-AVYM		stored DEL
☐ VT-KFI	Airbus A319-131	2634	ex D-AVWG		
☐ VT-KFJ	Airbus A319-131	2664	ex D-AVWW		
☐ VT-VJM	Airbus A319-133X	2650	ex D-AICY	Sidhartha-Leana-Tanya	VIP
☐ VT-ADR	Airbus A320-232	2922	ex F-WWDS		
☐ VT-ADU	Airbus A320-232	2874	ex F-WWBH		
☐ VT-ADV	Airbus A320-232	2366	ex F-WWDN		
☐ VT-ADW	Airbus A320-232	2376	ex F-WWBF		
☐ VT-DKR	Airbus A320-232	2731	ex F-WWBC		
☐ VT-DKS	Airbus A320-232	2747	ex F-WWBQ	Mr Citizen c/s	
☐ VT-DKT	Airbus A320-232	2753	ex F-WWDH		
☐ VT-DKU	Airbus A320-232	2676	ex F-WWIK	Mr Citizen c/s	
☐ VT-DKV	Airbus A320-232	2645	ex F-WWIC		stored BOM
☐ VT-DNZ	Airbus A320-232	3012	ex F-WWBK		
☐ VT-KFA	Airbus A320-232	2413	ex F-WWDH		
☐ VT-KFB	Airbus A320-232	2443	ex F-WWBR		
☐ VT-KFC	Airbus A320-232	2496	ex F-WWIF		
☐ VT-KFD	Airbus A320-232	2502	ex F-WWDI		damaged
☐ VT-KFE	Airbus A320-232	2522	ex F-WWDN		
☐ VT-KFF	Airbus A320-232	2531	ex F-WWIH		
☐ VT-KFG	Airbus A320-232	2576	ex F-WWBI		
☐ VT-KFK	Airbus A320-232	2670	ex F-WWDA		
☐ VT-KFL	Airbus A320-232	2817	ex F-WWDJ		
☐ VT-KFM	Airbus A320-232	2856	ex F-WWIT		
☐ VT-KFT	Airbus A320-232	3089	ex F-WWBY		
☐ VT-KFV	Airbus A320-232	3105	ex F-WWII		
☐ VT-KFX	Airbus A320-232	3270	ex F-WWBX		
☐ VT-	Airbus A320-232		ex F-WW		on order
☐ VT-	Airbus A320-232		ex F-WW		on order
☐ VT-	Airbus A320-232		ex F-WW		on order
☐ VT-	Airbus A320-232		ex F-WW		on order

☐ VT-	Airbus A320-232		ex F-WW	on order
☐ VT-KFN	Airbus A321-231	2916	ex D-AVZQ	stored BOM
☐ VT-KFP	Airbus A321-231	2919	ex D-AVZR	
☐ VT-KFQ	Airbus A321-231	2927	ex D-AVZC	
☐ VT-KFR	Airbus A321-231	2933	ex D-AVZS	
☐ VT-KFS	Airbus A321-231	3034	ex D-AVZZ	
☐ VT-KFW	Airbus A321-231	3120	ex D-AVZR	
☐ VT-KFY	Airbus A321-232	3302	ex D-AVZS	
☐ VT-KFZ	Airbus A321-231	3322	ex D-AVZU	
☐ VT-ADJ	ATR 42-500	612	ex N612VX	
☐ VT-ADK	ATR 42-500	613	ex N316VX	
☐ VT-ADN	ATR 42-500	576	ex A4O-AT	Lsd fr OMA
☐ VT-DKA	ATR 72-212A	718	ex F-WWES	
☐ VT-DKB	ATR 72-212A	720	ex F-WWEA	
☐ VT-DKD	ATR 72-212A	725	ex F-WQNG	
☐ VT-DKE	ATR 72-212A	723	ex F-WWED	
☐ VT-DKH	ATR 72-212A	739	ex F-WWET	
☐ VT-DKI	ATR 72-212A	732	ex F-WWEM	
☐ VT-DKJ	ATR 72-212A	733	ex F-WWEN	
☐ VT-DKK	ATR 72-212A	740	ex F-WWEU	
☐ VT-KAA	ATR 72-212A	699	ex F-WWEV	
☐ VT-KAB	ATR 72-212A	728	ex F-WWEI	
☐ VT-KAD	ATR 72-212A	730	ex F-WWEK	
☐ VT-KAE	ATR 72-212A	737	ex F-WWER	
☐ VT-KAF	ATR 72-212A	738	ex F-WWES	
☐ VT-KAG	ATR 72-212A	743	ex F-WWED	
☐ VT-KAH	ATR 72-212A	746	ex F-WWEG	
☐ VT-KAI	ATR 72-212A	750	ex F-WWEK	
☐ VT-KAJ	ATR 72-212A	754	ex F-WWEO	
☐ VT-KAK	ATR 72-212A	758	ex F-WWES	
☐ VT-KAL	ATR 72-212A	759	ex F-WWEV	
☐ VT-KAM	ATR 72-212A	762	ex F-WWEZ	
☐ VT-KAN	ATR 72-212A	767	ex F-WWEF	
☐ VT-KAO	ATR 72-212A	772	ex F-WWEK	
☐ VT-KAP	ATR 72-212A	776	ex F-WWEO	
☐ VT-KAQ	ATR 72-212A	777	ex F-WWEP	
☐ VT-KAR	ATR 72-212A	782	ex F-WWEX	

MDLR AIRLINES

☐ VT-MDL	Avro 146-RJ70	E1229	ex G-BUFI
☐ VT-MDM	Avro 146-RJ70	E1230	ex G-CDNB
☐ VT-MDN	Avro 146-RJ70	E1252	ex G-CDNC

NORTHEAST SHUTTLE

☐ VT-NES	Cessna 208B Caravan	208B2025	ex N23045

PARAMOUNT AIRWAYS — *(I7/PMW)* — *Coimbatore (CJB)*

☐ VT-PAB	Embraer 170-100LR (170LR)	17000005	ex PT-SZN
☐ VT-PAC	Embraer 170-100LR (170LR)	17000002	ex PT-SDH
☐ VT-PAD	Embraer 170-200SR (175LR)	17000126	ex PT-SDP
☐ VT-PAE	Embraer 170-200LR (175LR)	17000137	ex PT-SEB
☐ VT-PAF	Embraer 170-200LR (175LR)	17000147	ex PT-SEL

PAWAN HANS HELICOPTERS — *Pawan Hans (PHE)* — *Mumbai-Juhu*

☐ VT-ELD	Aérospatiale SA365N Dauphin 2	6213	
☐ VT-ELE	Aérospatiale SA365N Dauphin 2	6214	
☐ VT-ELG	Aérospatiale SA365N Dauphin 2	6217	
☐ VT-ELI	Aérospatiale SA365N Dauphin 2	6236	
☐ VT-ELJ	Aérospatiale SA365N Dauphin 2	6239	
☐ VT-ELK	Aérospatiale SA365N Dauphin 2	6245	
☐ VT-ELL	Aérospatiale SA365N Dauphin 2	6246	
☐ VT-ELM	Aérospatiale SA365N Dauphin 2	6248	
☐ VT-ELN	Aérospatiale SA365N Dauphin 2	6254	
☐ VT-ELP	Aérospatiale SA365N Dauphin 2	6260	
☐ VT-ELQ	Aérospatiale SA365N Dauphin 2	6261	
☐ VT-ELR	Aérospatiale SA365N Dauphin 2	6268	
☐ VT-ELS	Aérospatiale SA365N Dauphin 2	6273	
☐ VT-ELT	Aérospatiale SA365N Dauphin 2	6278	
☐ VT-ENW	Aérospatiale SA365N Dauphin 2	6094	
☐ VT-ENZ	Aérospatiale SA365N Dauphin 2	6163	
☐ VT-PHJ	Aérospatiale AS365N3 Dauphin 2	6628	
☐ VT-PHK	Aérospatiale AS365N3 Dauphin 2	6631	
☐ VT-PHL	Aérospatiale AS365N3 Dauphin 2	6682	
☐ VT-PHM	Aérospatiale AS365N3 Dauphin 2	6684	
☐ VT-PHO	Aérospatiale AS365N3 Dauphin 2	6734	ex F-WWOA
☐ VT-PHP	Aérospatiale AS365N3 Dauphin 2	6736	ex F-WWOU

☐ VT-PHR	Aérospatiale AS365N3 Dauphin 2	6774		
☐ VT-PHS	Aérospatiale AS365N3 Dauphin 2	6775		
☐ VT-PHA	Bell 206L-4 LongRanger IV	52019	ex N6197Y	
☐ VT-PHD	Bell 206L-4 LongRanger IV	52142	ex N64080	Op for Indian Customs
☐ VT-PHE	Bell 206L-4 LongRanger IV	52159	ex N9217Z	Op for Indian Customs
☐ VT-PHF	Mil Mi-172	356C06		
☐ VT-PHG	Mil Mi-172	356C07		
☐ VT-PHH	Bell 407	53210	ex N52263	
☐ VT-PHI	Bell 407	53212	ex N52265	
☐ VT-PHN	Bell 407	53617	ex C-FCBU	
☐ VT-PHQ	Bell 407	53689	ex C-FIAL	

SPICEJET — ***SpiceJet (SG/SEJ)*** — ***Delhi-Indira Ghandi International (DEL)***

☐ VT-SGB	Boeing 737-9GJER/W	34956/2608		Oregano	
☐ VT-SGC	Boeing 737-9GJER/W	34957/2639		Fenugreek	
☐ VT-SGE	Boeing 737-8K2/W	32693/1951	ex PH-HZR	Tamarind	
☐ VT-SGD	Boeing 737-9GJER/W	34961/2744	ex N1786B	Sesame	
☐ VT-SPE	Boeing 737-86N	28621/570	ex EI-DIT	Ginger	
☐ VT-SPF	Boeing 737-8GJ/W	34896/1861		Coriander	
☐ VT-SPH	Boeing 737-83N/W	30660/1330	ex N331TZ		
☐ VT-SPJ	Boeing 737-8GJ/W	34897/2069		Mint	
☐ VT-SPK	Boeing 737-8GJ/W	34898/2104		Fennel	
☐ VT-SPL	Boeing 737-8GJ/W	34899/2128		Cardamom	
☐ VT-SPM	Boeing 737-8GJ/W	34900/2167		Pepper	
☐ VT-SPO	Boeing 737-86N/W	35216/2321		Dill	
☐ VT-SPP	Boeing 737-86N/W	35217/2359		Rosemary	
☐ VT-SPQ	Boeing 737-8GJ/W	34903/2335		Basil	
☐ VT-SPR	Boeing 737-8GJ/W	34904/2347	ex N1782B	Thyme	
☐ VT-SPS	Boeing 737-8GJ/W	34905/2392		Mustard	
☐ VT-SPT	Boeing 737-9GJER/W	34952/2426		Clove	
☐ VT-SPU	Boeing 737-9GJER/W	34953/2466		Anise	
☐ VT-SPW	Boeing 737-86N/W	32672/1932	ex PH-HSY	Cinnamon	
☐ VT-	Boeing 737-8GJ/W				on order
☐ VT-	Boeing 737-8GJ/W				on order
☐ VT-	Boeing 737-8GJ/W				on order

STAR AVIATION

☐ VT-SMA	Embraer 170-100LR (170LR)	17000275	ex PT-TQB	on order
☐ VT-SMC	Embraer 170-100LR (170LR)	17000279	ex PT-TQF	on order

UNITED HELICHARTERS — ***Mumbai-Juhu***

☐ VT-HGA	Bell 212	30902	ex A7-HAJ	Lsd fr Gulf Helicopters
☐ VT-HGB	Bell 212	31124	ex A7-HAN	Lsd fr Gulf Helicopters
☐ VT-HGC	Bell 212	31149	ex A7-HAT	Lsd fr Gulf Helicopters
☐ VT-HGF	Bell 412EP	36206	ex A7-HBE	Lsd fr Gulf Helicopters
☐ VT-HGG	Bell 412HP	36050	ex VH-CFT	Lsd fr CHC Helicopters Intl
☐ VT-HGJ	Bell 212	35103	ex C-FAOC	Lsd fr CHC Helicopters Intl

V2- ANTIGUA (State of Antigua and Barbuda)

LIAT - THE CARIBBEAN AIRLINE — ***LIAT (LI/LIA)*** — ***Antigua-VC Bird Intl (ANU)***

☐ V2-LCY	de Havilland DHC-8-110	035	ex C-GESR		stored ANU
☐ V2-LDQ	de Havilland DHC-8-102	113	ex EI-BWX		
☐ V2-LDU	de Havilland DHC-8-103	270	ex EI-CBV		
☐ V2-LEF	de Havilland DHC-8-103	144	ex HS-SKH		
☐ V2-LES	de Havilland DHC-8-311B	412	ex C-GETI		
☐ V2-LET	de Havilland DHC-8-311B	416	ex C-GFOD		
☐ V2-LEU	de Havilland DHC-8-311	408	ex C-FWBB	Sir Frank de Lisle	
☐ V2-LFF	de Havilland DHC-8-314	410	ex N285BC		
☐ V2-LFM	de Havilland DHC-8-311A	267	ex C-GFPZ		
☐ V2-LFU	de Havilland DHC-8-311	250	ex N802SA		retd?
☐ V2-LFV	de Havilland DHC-8-311A	283	ex PH-SDR		
☐ V2-LGA	de Havilland DHC-8-311A	232	ex C-GZTX		
☐ V2-LGB	de Havilland DHC-8-311A	266	ex C-GZTB		
☐ V2-LGC	de Havilland DHC-8-311	298	ex PH-SDM		
☐ V2-LGG	de Havilland DHC-8-311A	404	ex C-FHFY		
☐ V2-LGH	de Havilland DHC-8-311	242	ex PJ-DHE		
☐ V2-LGI	de Havilland DHC-8-311A	325	ex C-FHXB		
☐ V2-LGN	de Havilland DHC-8-311	230	ex PJ-DHL		

NORMAN AVIATION — ***Antigua-VC Bird Intl (ANU)***

☐ V2-LDN	Piper PA-31-325 Navajo C/R	31-7612017	ex N99910

V3- BELIZE

MAYA ISLAND AIR — Myland (MW/MYD) — Belize City-Municipal/San Pedro (TZA/SPR)

☐ V3-HFS	Cessna 208B Caravan I	208B0579	ex N52627	for sale
☐ V3-HCD	Cessna 208B Caravan I	208B0910	ex N12522	
☐ V3-HGF	Cessna 208B Caravan I	208B0927	ex N52627	
☐ V3-HGJ	Cessna 208B Caravan I	208B0946	ex N52639	
☐ V3-HGO	Cessna 208B Caravan I	208B0995	ex N1241G	
☐ V3-HGP	Cessna 208B Caravan I	208B0998	ex N5213S	
☐ V3-HGQ	Cessna 208B Caravan I	208B0973	ex N1248G	
☐ V3-HGW	Cessna 208B Caravan I	208B1095	ex N1273Z	
☐ V3-HHA	Cessna 208B Caravan I	208B1292	ex N4117D	
☐ V3-HGE	Britten-Norman BN-2A-26 Islander	911	ex N103NE	
☐ V3-HGI	Gippsland GA-8 Airvan	GA8-01-008	ex VH-AUV	
☐ V3-HGK	Britten-Norman BN-2A-26 Islander	853	ex N271RS	

TROPIC AIR COMMUTER — Tropiser (PM/TOS) — San Pedro (SPR)

☐ V3-HFP	Cessna 208B Caravan I	208B0478	ex N1289Y	
☐ V3-HFQ	Cessna 208B Caravan I	208B0575	ex N52623	on rebuild, dam 15Oct05
☐ V3-HFV	Cessna 208B Caravan I	208B0647	ex N5268M	
☐ V3-HGV	Cessna 208B Caravan I	208B1072		
☐ V3-HGX	Cessna 208B Caravan I	208B1162	ex N5108G	
☐ V3-HIK	Cessna 208B Caravan I	208B0707	ex N23681	
☐ V3-HSS	Cessna 208B Caravan I	208B0407	ex N1116V	
☐ V3-HDT	Cessna 207A Stationair 8	20700716	ex (N9696M)	

V4- ST KITTS & NEVIS (Federation of St Christopher and Nevis)

AIR ST KITTS & NEVIS — Sea Breeze (BEZ) — Basseterre-Golden Rock (SKB)

☐ N90HL	Cessna 208B Caravan I	208B1070	ex N1271T	Freighter, op for DHL
☐ N910HL	Cessna 208B Caravan I	208B1080	ex N1268R	Freighter, op for DHL

V5- NAMIBIA (Republic of Namibia)

AIR NAMIBIA — Namibia (SW/NMB) — Windhoek-Eros/Hosea Kutako Intl (ERS)

☐ V5-NME	Airbus A340-311	051	ex D-AIMG		
☐ V5-NMF	Airbus A340-311	047	ex D-AIMF		
☐ V5-NDI	Boeing 737-528	25228/2170	ex F-GJNC		
☐ V5-TNP	Boeing 737-528	25229/2180	ex F-GJND		
☐ D-AXLF	Boeing 737-8Q8/W	28218/160	ex G-XLAB	Tinks	Lsd fr GXL

DAY AIR AVIATION — Nomad Air (NMD) — Walvis Bay (WVB)

☐ V5-FUR	Cessna 310Q	310Q0456	ex ZS-FUR
☐ V5-ODL	Cessna 208B Caravan I	208B0155	ex ZS-ODL

COMAV AVIATION — Compion (COX) — Windhoek-Eros (ERS)

☐ V5-CAR	Cessna 208B Caravan I	208B0513	ex ZS-OTU	all-white, no titles
☐ V5-NPR	Cessna 310Q	310Q0985	ex ZS-NPR	
☐ V5-SOS	Cessna 402C	402C0437	ex V5-AAS	EMS International SOS titles
☐ V5-VAN	Cessna 208B Caravan I	208B0544	ex ZS-OWC	no titles
☐ ZS-OUB	Beech 1900C	UB-20	ex V5-MNN	Khomas
☐ ZS-OUD	Beech 1900C	UB-73	ex V5-LTC	Kalahari
☐ ZS-OYA	Beech 1900D	UE-7	ex V5-COY	Kavanga

DESERT AIR — Windhoek-Eros (ERS)

☐ V5-AEM	Cessna 210L Centurion II	21061519	ex ZS-NCJ	
☐ V5-MAC	Rockwell 690B Turbo Commander	11557	ex N75WA	
☐ V5-MKR	Cessna T210N Turbo Centurion II	21063060	ex ZS-LAS	
☐ V5-MKS	Cessna T310R II	310R0583	ex N410AS	
☐ V5-SKY	Cessna T210L Turbo Centurion II	21060063	ex ZS-SKY	Sossus Air Taxi titles
☐ V5-TEM	Beech Baron 58	TH-812	ex V5-LZG	

NAMIBIA COMMERCIAL AIRWAYS — Med Rescue (MRE) — Windhoek-Eros (ERS)

☐ ZS-NAT	Britten-Norman BN-2T Turbine Islander	2158	ex 7Q-CAV	
☐ V5-NCG	Douglas DC-6B	45564/1040	ex GBM112	Batuleur

SEFOFANE AIR				Windhoek-Eros (ERS)
☐ V5-BAT	Cessna T210N Turbo Centurion II	21064543	ex ZS-MUG	
☐ V5-BUZ	Cessna T210N Turbo Centurion II	21063539	ex ZS-OXI	
☐ V5-ELE	Cessna 208B Caravan I	208B0818	ex N1289Y	
☐ V5-KUD	Cessna 210N Centurion II	21063834	ex ZS-KUD	
☐ V5-MTB	Cessna T210N Turbo Centurion II	21062933	ex ZS-MTB	
☐ V5-RNO	Cessna 208B Caravan I	208B1304	ex N41138	
☐ ZS-ELE	Cessna 208B Caravan I	208B1249	ex 9J-ELE	

WESTAIR WINGS		Westair Wings (WAA)			Windhoek-Eros (ERS)
☐ V5-AAG	Cessna 210M Centurion II	21062077	ex N9646M		tail magnetometer
☐ V5-DHL	Reims Cessna F406 Caravan II	F406-0062	ex N744C	DHL titles	
☐ V5-LWH	Cessna 310R	310R0571	ex ZS-LWH		
☐ V5-LXZ	Cessna 210M Centurion II	21063931	ex ZS-LXZ		
☐ V5-MDY	Cessna 402B	402B1353	ex D2-FFW		
☐ V5-SAC	Cessna 340A	340A0945	ex ZS-KUH		
☐ V5-WAA	Cessna 404 Titan II (RAM)	404-0210	ex N88668	Ghost Rider	
☐ V5-WAB	Cessna 310Q	310Q0727	ex N4541Q		
☐ V5-WAC	Cessna 404 Titan II	404-0616	ex ZS-KRJ		
☐ V5-WAD	Cessna 310R	310R1340	ex ZS-KEE		
☐ V5-WAE	Cessna 402C	402C0430	ex ZS-NPA		
☐ V5-WAG	Cessna 310R	310R1668	ex V5-KRK		
☐ V5-WAK	Reims Cessna F406 Caravan II	F406-0048	ex G-FLYN	DHL titles	

V6- MICRONESIA (Federated States of Micronesia)

CAROLINE ISLAND AIR				Pohnpei (PNI)
☐ V6-01FM	Britten-Norman BN-2A-27 Islander	2014	ex V6-SFM	
☐ V6-02FM	Beech 65-80 Queen Air	LC-84	ex N349N	
☐ V6-03FM	Britten-Norman BN-2A-21 Islander	660	ex VH-AUN	

V7- MARSHALL ISLANDS (Republic of the Marshall Islands)

AIRLINE OF THE MARSHALL ISLANDS		Marshall Islands (CW/MRS)		Majuro Intl (MAJ)
☐ V7-0210	de Havilland DHC-8-102	218	ex ZK-NEU	stored MAJ
☐ V7-9206	Dornier 228-212	8194	ex D-CAHD	stored MAJ
☐ V7-9207	Dornier 228-212	8201	ex D-CAHE	stored MAJ

V8- BRUNEI (Negara Brunei Darussalam)

ROYAL BRUNEI AIRLINES		Brunei (BI/RBA)		Bandar Seri Begawan (BWN)
☐ V8-RBF	Boeing 767-33AER	25530/414		
☐ V8-RBG	Boeing 767-33AER	25532/442	ex N6055X	
☐ V8-RBH	Boeing 767-33AER	25534/477	ex N6055X	
☐ V8-RBJ	Boeing 767-33AER	25533/454	ex N67AW	
☐ V8-RBK	Boeing 767-33AER	25536/504	ex N96AC	
☐ V8-RBL	Boeing 767-33AER	27189/521	ex N1794B	
☐ V8-RBP	Airbus A319-132	2023	ex D-AVWW	
☐ V8-RBR	Airbus A319-132	2032	ex D-AVYK	
☐ V8-RBS	Airbus A320-232	2135	ex F-WWIV	
☐ V8-RBT	Airbus A320-232	2139	ex F-WWDO	

XA- MEXICO (United Mexican States)

AERO BINIZA				Oaxaca (OAX)
☐ XA-UAB	Cessna 208B Caravan I	208B1017	ex XA-TVS	

AERO CALAFIA		Calafia (CFV)		Los Cabos
☐ XA-HVB	Cessna 208B Caravan I	208B1104	ex N4047W	
☐ XA-SFJ	Cessna 208B Caravan I	208B0301	ex N5538B	
☐ XA-TQW	Cessna 206H Stationair	20608072	ex N4002B	

AERO CUAHONTE		Cuahonte (CUO)		Uruapan (UPN)
☐ XA-AIR	Dornier 228-212	8236	ex F-OGVA	
☐ XA-KOC	Cessna 402C	402C0301	ex N3271M	

AERO DAVINCI INTERNACIONAL — Reynosa (REX)

	Reg	Type	c/n	Previous	Notes
☐	XA-AFL	Swearingen SA.226TC Metro II			
☐	XA-TGV	Swearingen SA.226TC Metro II	TC-350	ex N4254Y	

AEROCEDROS — Ensenada (ESE)

	Reg	Type	c/n	Previous	Notes
☐	XA-RYV	Convair 440-0	474	ex XB-CSE	
☐	XA-STJ	Cessna 402B	402B0801	ex N3792C	
☐	XA-TFY	Convair 440-0	472	ex N411GA	
☐	XA-TFZ	Convair 440-94	439	ex N44829	

Operates Convair 440s for Soc Coop Prod Pesque Pescado

AERODAN — Saltillo (SLW)

	Reg	Type	c/n	Previous	Notes
☐	XA-YYS	NAMC YS-11A	2071	ex XA-TTY	

AEROFERINCO — Playa del Carmen (PCM)

	Reg	Type	c/n	Previous	Notes
☐	XA-TFG	LET L-410UVP	851409	ex YL-PAH	Cargo stored PCM
☐	XA-TQC	LET L-410UVP	882030	ex Russ AF 2030	

AEROFUTURO — Mexico City-Toluca (TLC)

	Reg	Type	c/n	Previous	Notes
☐	XA-UGN	Swearingen SA.226TC Metro II	TC-353	ex XA-SFS	

AEROLAMSA — Playa del Carmen (PCM)

	Reg	Type	c/n	Previous	Notes
☐	XA-TYL	El Gavilan 358	003	ex TG-TDA	
☐	XA-UBD	Britten-Norman BN-2A Mk.III-2 Trislander	1044	ex YV-2523P	

AEROLINEAS CENTAURO — Centauro (CTR) — Durango (DGO)

	Reg	Type	c/n	Previous	Notes
☐	XA-JAD	Cessna U206G Stationair 6 II	U20605279		
☐	XA-NAQ	Cessna U206G Stationair 6	U20603880	ex XB-CJQ	
☐	XA-PIQ	Britten-Norman BN-2A-26 Islander	892	ex XC-DUJ	
☐	XA-RNC	Cessna TU206G Stationair 6 II	U20605747	ex XB-CGX	

AEROLINEAS REGIONALES — (RCQ) — Queretaro

	Reg	Type	c/n	Previous	Notes
☐	XA-RCB	Boeing 737-2J6C	23066	ex N306AL	

AEROMAR AIRLINES — Trans-Aeromar (VW/TAO) — Mexico City-Toluca (TLC)

	Reg	Type	c/n	Previous	Notes
☐	XA-SJJ	ATR 42-320	039	ex N71296	
☐	XA-SYH	ATR 42-320	062	ex XA-PEP	Presidente Aleman
☐	XA-TAH	ATR 42-500	471	ex F-WWLS	
☐	XA-TAI	ATR 42-500	474	ex F-WWLF	
☐	XA-TIC	ATR 42-320	058	ex F-OGNF	
☐	XA-TKJ	ATR 42-500	561	ex F-WWLW	
☐	XA-TLN	ATR 42-500	564	ex F-WWEC	
☐	XA-TPR	ATR 42-500	586	ex F-WWEA	
☐	XA-TPS	ATR 42-500	594	ex F-WWEX	
☐	XA-TRI	ATR 42-500	607	ex F-WWEA	
☐	XA-TRJ	ATR 42-500	608	ex F-WWEB	
☐	XA-UAU	ATR 42-500	462	ex I-ADLF	Edo de Veracruz
☐	XA-UAV	ATR 42-500	476	ex I-ADLG	
☐	XA-UFA	ATR 42-500	412	ex F-WQNH	

AEROMEXICO — AeroMexico (AM/AMX) — Mexico City-Benito Juarez Intl (MEX)

Member of Skyteam

	Reg	Type	c/n	Previous	Notes
☐	EI-DRD	Boeing 737-752/W	35117/2122	ex N1786B	
☐	EI-DRE	Boeing 737-752/W	35787/2111		
☐	N784XE	Boeing 737-752/W	33784/1393	ex XA-BAM	
☐	N788XA	Boeing 737-752/W	33788/1439	ex XA-GAM	
☐	N842AM	Boeing 737-752/W	32842/1814		
☐	N850AM	Boeing 737-752/W	33786/1403	ex XA-DAM	
☐	N851AM	Boeing 737-752/W	29363/1417	ex XA-EAM	
☐	N852AM	Boeing 737-752/W	33787/1421	ex XA-FAM	
☐	N853AM	Boeing 737-752/W	33791/1557	ex XA-JAM	
☐	N855AM	Boeing 737-752/W	33792/1571	ex XA-KAM	
☐	N857AM	Boeing 737-752/W	33793/1597	ex XA-LAM	
☐	N904AM	Boeing 737-752/W	28262/1565	ex N854AM	
☐	N906AM	Boeing 737-752/W	29356/1586		
☐	N908AM	Boeing 737-752/W	30038/1601		
☐	N997AM	Boeing 737-76Q/W	30283/1156	ex G-OSLH	
☐	XA-AAM	Boeing 737-752/W	33783/1381		
☐	XA-AGM	Boeing 737-752/W	35786/2098		
☐	XA-CAM	Boeing 737-752/W	33785/1398		

☐ XA-CTG	Boeing 737-752/W	35123/2374		
☐ XA-CYM	Boeing 737-752/W	35124/2456	ex N1779B	
☐ XA-GMV	Boeing 737-752/W	35118/2151		
☐ XA-GOL	Boeing 737-752/W	35785/2011		
☐ XA-HAM	Boeing 737-752/W	33789/1524		
☐ XA-MAH	Boeing 737-752/W	35122/2348		
☐ XA-NAM	Boeing 737-752/W	33790/1533	ex (XA-IAM)	
☐ XA-PAM	Boeing 737-752/W	34293/1747		
☐ XA-QAM	Boeing 737-752/W	34294/1761	ex N1786B	
☐ XA-VAM	Boeing 737-752/W	34295/1765		
☐ XA-	Boeing 737-752/W			on order
☐ XA-	Boeing 737-752/W			on order
☐ XA-	Boeing 737-752/W			on order
☐ EI-DRA	Boeing 737-852/W	35114/2037	ex N1779B	
☐ EI-DRB	Boeing 737-852/W	35115/2070		
☐ EI-DRC	Boeing 737-852/W	35116/2081		
☐ XA-JOY	Boeing 737-852/W	35121/2327	ex N1782B	
☐ XA-MIA	Boeing 737-852/W	35119/2273		
☐ XA-ZAM	Boeing 737-852/W	35120/2290	ex N1780B	
☐ XA-	Boeing 737-8CX	32360/1084	ex PR-GOK	on order
☐ XA-APB	Boeing 767-3Q8ER	27618/727	ex (XA-TMG)	
☐ XA-JBC	Boeing 767-284ER	24762/307	ex XA-RVY	
☐ XA-MAT	Boeing 767-3Y0ER	24947/351	ex N942AC	
☐ XA-OAM	Boeing 767-2B1ER	26471/511	ex C9-BAF	
☐ XA-TOJ	Boeing 767-283ER	24727/301	ex PT-TAI	
☐ N745AM	Boeing 777-2Q8ER	32718/554		
☐ N746AM	Boeing 777-2Q8ER	32719/562		
☐ N774AM	Boeing 777-2Q8ER	28689/365	ex N301LF	
☐ N776AM	Boeing 777-2Q8	28692/373	ex N181LF	
☐ XA-TPM	McDonnell-Douglas MD-87	49671/1463	ex PZ-TCG District of Para	stored MEX

AEROMEXICO CONNECT — Costera (5D/SLI) — Monterrey-Escobedo Intl/Vera Cruz (MTY/VER)

☐ XA-ALI	Embraer EMB.145LR (ERJ-145LR)	145795	ex PT-SMW	
☐ XA-BLI	Embraer EMB.145LR (ERJ-145LR)	145798	ex PT-SMY	
☐ XA-CLI	Embraer EMB.145LR (ERJ-145LR)	14500803	ex PT-SNG	
☐ XA-DLI	Embraer EMB.145LR (ERJ-145LR)	14500852	ex PT-SQU	
☐ XA-ELI	Embraer EMB.145LR (ERJ-145LR)	14500861	ex PT-SXB	
☐ XA-FLI	Embraer EMB.145MP (ERJ-145MP)	145203	ex N974RP	
☐ XA-GAC	Embraer EMB.145MP (ERJ-145MP)	145406	ex SP-LGL	
☐ XA-GLI	Embraer EMB.145MP (ERJ-145MP)	145444	ex N973RP	
☐ XA-HLI	Embraer EMB.145MP (ERJ-145MP)	145337	ex N975RP	
☐ XA-ILI	Embraer EMB.145LU (ERJ-145LU)	145564	ex D-ACIA	
☐ XA-JLI	Embraer EMB.145MP (ERJ-145MP)	145426	ex N971RP	
☐ XA-KAC	Embraer EMB.145MP (ERJ-145MP)	145322	ex N976RP	
☐ XA-KLI	Embraer EMB.145MP (ERJ-145MP)	145440	ex N972RP	
☐ XA-LLI	Embraer EMB.145ER (ERJ-145ER)	145060	ex PT-SPH	
☐ XA-MLI	Embraer EMB.145ER (ERJ-145ER)	145065	ex PT-SPI	
☐ XA-NLI	Embraer EMB.145ER (ERJ-145ER)	145083	ex PT-SPJ	
☐ XA-OLI	Embraer EMB.145ER (ERJ-145ER)	145089	ex PT-SPK	
☐ XA-PAC	Embraer EMB.145LR (ERJ-145LR)	145498	ex N824HK	
☐ XA-PLI	Embraer EMB.145ER (ERJ-145ER)	145090	ex PT-SPL	
☐ XA-QAC	Embraer EMB.145LR (ERJ-145LR)	145510	ex N825HK	
☐ XA-QLI	Embraer EMB.145LU (ERJ-145LU)	145588	ex HB-JAX	
☐ XA-RAC	Embraer EMB.145LR (ERJ-145LR)	145313	ex N830HK	
☐ XA-RLI	Embraer EMB.145LU (ERJ-145LU)	145559	ex HB-JAS	
☐ XA-SLI	Embraer EMB.145LU (ERJ-145LU)	145580	ex HB-JAW	
☐ XA-TAK	Embraer EMB.145LR (ERJ-145LR)	145475	ex N823HK	
☐ XA-TLI	Embraer EMB.145LU (ERJ-145LU)	145601	ex HB-JAY	
☐ XA-ULI	Embraer EMB.145LU (ERJ-145LU)	145570	ex HB-JAU	
☐ XA-VAC	Embraer EMB.145LR (ERJ-145LR)	145232	ex N831HK	
☐ XA-VLI	Embraer EMB.145LU (ERJ-145LU)	145574	ex HB-JAV	
☐ XA-WAC	Embraer EMB.145LR (ERJ-145LR)	145255	ex N837HK	
☐ XA-WLI	Embraer EMB.145LU (ERJ-145LU)	145434	ex HB-JAN	
☐ XA-XAC	Embraer EMB.145LR (ERJ-145LR)	145128	ex N260SK	
☐ XA-XLI	Embraer EMB.145LU (ERJ-145LU)	145456	ex HB-JAO	
☐ XA-YAC	Embraer EMB.145LR (ERJ-145LR)	145168	ex N262SK	
☐ XA-YLI	Embraer EMB.145LU (ERJ-145LU)	145400	ex HB-JAL	
☐ XA-ZAC	Embraer EMB.145LR (ERJ-145LR)	145199	ex N263SK	
☐ XA-ZLI	Embraer EMB.145LU (ERJ-145LU)	145420	ex HB-JAM	
☐ XA-AAC	Embraer 190-100LR (190LR)	19000121	ex PT-SQP	
☐ XA-BAC	Embraer 190-100LR (190LR)	19000129	ex PT-SQP	
☐ XA-CAC	Embraer 190-100LR (190LR)	19000135	ex PT-SYN	
☐ XA-EAC	Embraer 190-100LR (190LR)	19000145	ex PT-SYX	
☐ XA-FAC	Embraer 190-100LR (190LR)	19000234	ex PT-SIF	
☐ XA-IAC	Embraer 190-100LR (190LR)	19000238	ex PT-SIL	
☐ XA-JAC	Embraer 190-100LR (190LR)	19000248	ex PT-SIS	
☐ XA-	Embraer 190-100LR (190LR)		ex PT-	on order

☐ XA-	Embraer 190-100LR (190LR)		ex PT-	on order
☐ XA-	Embraer 190-100LR (190LR)		ex PT-	on order
☐ XA-	Embraer 190-100LR (190LR)		ex PT-	on order
☐ XA-	Embraer 190-100LR (190LR)		ex PT-	on order
☐ XA-	Embraer 190-100LR (190LR)		ex PT-	on order
☐ XA-	Embraer 190-100LR (190LR)		ex PT-	on order
☐ XA-	Embraer 190-100LR (190LR)		ex PT-	on order
☐ XA-TUB	SAAB SF.340B	340B-248	ex SE-KXD	

AEROMEXICO TRAVEL

☐ XA-TXC	McDonnell-Douglas MD-87	49389/1333	ex EC-GKF
☐ N583MD	McDonnell-Douglas MD-83	49659/1438	ex YV-39C
☐ N838AM	McDonnell-Douglas MD-83	49397/1331	ex N830VV

AEROMEXPRESS CARGO — *Aeromexpress (QO/MPX* — *Mexico City-Benito Juarez Intl (MEX)*

Subsidiary of Mexicana, operates services with Boeing 767-200 (SF)s leased from ABX Air as required.

AERONAVES TSM — *Saltilo (SLW)*

☐ XA-EEE	Swearingen SA.227AC Metro III	AC-503	ex N102GS
☐ XA-MIO	Swearingen SA.227AC Metro III	AC-693B	ex N446MA
☐ XA-PNG	Swearingen SA.227AC Metro III	AC-687B	ex N445MA
☐ XA-SLW	Swearingen SA.227AC Metro III	AC-628B	ex N280EM
☐ XA-TYX	Swearingen SA.227AC Metro III	AC-627B	ex N799BW
☐ XA-	Swearingen SA.227AC Metro III	AC-497	ex N98EB
☐ XA-	Swearingen SA.227AC Metro III	AC-724	ex N106GS
☐ XA-	Swearingen SA.227AC Metro III	AC-532	ex N372PH
☐ XA-ADQ	Swearingen SA.226TC Metro II	TC-409	ex C-FLNG
☐ XA-ADS	Swearingen SA.226TC Metro II	TC-404	ex C-FGPW
☐ XA-TSM	Swearingen SA.226TC Metro IIA	TC-412	ex XA-SXB
☐ XA-UFO	Swearingen SA.226TC Metro II		
☐ XA-	Swearingen SA.226TC Metro II	TC-376	ex N637PJ
☐ XA-	Swearingen SA.226TC Metro II	TC-337	ex N851LH
☐ XA-TYF	Convair 600F	101	ex N94279

AEROPACIFICO — *Aero Costa (TAA)* — *Colima (CLQ)*

☐ XA-AFT	Swearingen SA.227AC Metro III	AC-581	ex C-FAFE	Freighter
☐ XA-UAJ	Swearingen SA.227AC Metro III	AC-586	ex N911EJ	Freighter

AEROPACIFICO — *Transportes Pacifico (TFO)* — *Los Mochis (LMM)*

☐ XA-AFE	LET L-410UVP-E	902508	ex N19RZ
☐ XA-SUS	Swearingen SA.227AC Metro III	AC-430B	ex N430PF
☐ XA-UEP	British Aerospace Jetstream 31	794	ex N417UE

AEROPOSTAL — *Postal Cargo (PCG)* — *Mexico City-Benito Juarez Intl (MEX)*

☐ XA-TXS	Douglas DC-8-63CF (BAC 3)	46054/453	ex N796AL

AEROSERVICIOS MONTERREY — *Servimonte (SVM)* — *Monterrey-General Mariano Ecobedo Intl (MTY)*

☐ XA-HAC	Piper PA-31-325 Navajo C/R	31-7912088	ex N3532K

AEROTRON — *Aerotron (TRN)* — *Puerto Vallarta (PVR)*

☐ XA-ADZ	Cessna 402	402-0113	ex N772EA	
☐ XA-TNI	Cessna 208B Caravan I	208B0728		Op for Air Adventure

AEROTROPICAL — *Tropicmex (TOC)* — *Poza Rica (PAZ)*

☐ XA-UEL	Boeing 737-2H4 (AvAero 3)	22963/929	ex N91SW	stored MHV

AEROTUCAN — *Oaxaca (OAX)*

☐ XA-TDS	Cessna 208B Caravan I	208B0559	
☐ XA-UCT	Cessna 208B Caravan I	208B1093	ex N5076J

AEROUNION — *AeroUnion (6R/TNO)* — *Mexico City-Benito Juarez Intl (MEX)*

☐ XA-TUE	Airbus A300B4-203F	078	ex C-FICB	Margostored
☐ XA-TVU	Airbus A300B4-203F	074	ex G-HLAC	Nina
☐ XA-TWQ	Airbus A300B4-203F	045	ex G-HLAB	Fata [stored]

AEROVIAS CASTILLO		Aerocastillo (CLL)		Guadalajara (GDL)
☐ XA-COJ	Cessna U206G Stationair 6	U20605484	ex XB-ZIC	
☐ XA-IUL	Cessna 402C	402C0091		
☐ XA-JIO	Cessna U206G Stationair 6	U20605330		
☐ XA-JON	Cessna 402C	402C0230	ex N2718R	
☐ XA-KEB	Cessna T207A Stationair 8	20700615	ex N73705	
☐ XA-PEA	Cessna TU206G Stationair 6	U20606379	ex N7590Z	
☐ XA-POM	Cessna 421C Golden Eagle	421C0695	ex N546RP	
☐ XA-RWO	Cessna T210L Turbo Centurion II	21061474	ex N732FE	
☐ XA-SCE	Learjet 24D	24D-271	ex N4305U	

AEROVIAS MONTES AZULES		Montes Azules (MZL)		Tuxtla Gutierrez (TGZ)
☐ XA-SOG	Piper PA-31-325 Navajo C/R	31-7612056	ex XB-EGX	
☐ XA-TMQ	Cessna TU206G Stationair 6	U20604578	ex N9569E	

ASESA		Aeroespecial (SVE)		Ciudad del Carmen (CME)
☐ XA-TNF	Bell 412EP	36202	ex N4300Z	
☐ XA-TPG	Bell 412EP	36240	ex N63880	
☐ XA-TPO	Bell 412EP	36221	ex N62355	
☐ XA-TQH	Bell 412EP	36241	ex N6400Z	
☐ XA-TWD	Bell 412EP	36309	ex N24113	
☐ XA-TWE	Bell 412EP	36310	ex N2413V	
☐ XA-UAC	Bell 412EP	36323	ex N80667	
☐ XA-UAE	Bell 412EP	36325	ex N8067E	
☐ XA-UBF	Bell 412EP	36331	ex N4537J	
☐ XA-UBM	Bell 412EP	36335	ex N45391	
☐ XA-UCC	Bell 412EP	36338	ex N45378	
☐ XA-UCF	Bell 412EP	36330	ex N45371	
☐ XA-UGA	Bell 412EP	36402	ex N2077M	
☐ XA-UGY	Bell 412EP	36427	ex N5075Q	
☐ XA-UHD	Bell 412EP	36431	ex N9154R	
☐ XA-UHS	Bell 412EP	36436	ex N3128K	
☐ XA-AKY	Piper PA-31 Navajo C	31-7712061	ex N27270	
☐ XA-RTL	Aérospatiale AS365N2 Dauphin 2	6374	ex F-WYMD	
☐ XA-RUZ	Aérospatiale AS365N2 Dauphin 2	6394		

AVIACSA		Aviacsa (6A/CHP)		Tuxtla Gutierrez (TGZ)
☐ XA-SIJ	Boeing 727-276/W (Duganair 3)	22017/1564	ex VH-TBQ	stored
☐ XA-SJE	Boeing 727-276/W (Duganair 3)	21479/1357	ex VH-TBN	stored MTY
☐ XA-SLG	Boeing 727-276/W (Duganair 3)	21171/1232	ex VH-TBM	stored MEX
☐ XA-SIW	Boeing 737-2T4	22370/716	ex N139AW	
☐ XA-TTM	Boeing 737-201 (Nordam 3)	22753/865	ex N246US	
☐ XA-TTP	Boeing 737-201 (Nordam 3)	22868/963	ex N262AU	
☐ XA-TUK	Boeing 737-201 (Nordam 3)	22867/961	ex N261AU	
☐ XA-TVD	Boeing 737-201 (Nordam 3)	22758/889	ex N252AU	
☐ XA-TVL	Boeing 737-201 (Nordam 3)	22869/964	ex N263AU	
☐ XA-TVN	Boeing 737-201 (Nordam 3)	22752/845	ex N244US	
☐ XA-TWJ	Boeing 737-219 (Nordam 3)	23471/1189	ex ZK-NAU	
☐ XA-TWO	Boeing 737-219 (Nordam 3)	23475/1203	ex ZK-NAY	
☐ XA-TWV	Boeing 737-219 (Nordam 3)	23473/1197	ex ZK-NAW	
☐ XA-TXD	Boeing 737-201 (Nordam 3)	22018/651	ex N232US	
☐ XA-TXF	Boeing 737-201 (Nordam 3)	22961/984	ex N264AU	
☐ XA-TYC	Boeing 737-201 (Nordam 3)	22962/987	ex N265AU	
☐ XA-TYI	Boeing 737-201 (Nordam 3)	22757/883	ex N251AU	
☐ XA-TYO	Boeing 737-201 (Nordam 3)	22756/879	ex N249US	stored
☐ XA-UAA	Boeing 737-201 (Nordam 3)	22755/873	ex N248US	
☐ XA-UCA	Boeing 737-201 (Nordam 3)	22866/940	ex N260AU	
☐ XA-UCG	Boeing 737-201 (Nordam 3)	22445/837	ex N243US	
☐ XA-UFW	Boeing 737-301	23558/1449	ex N355US	
☐ XA-UGE	Boeing 737-301	23555/1428	ex N352US	
☐ XA-UGF	Boeing 737-301	23556/1435	ex N353US	
☐ XA-UIU	Boeing 737-247 (Nordam 3)	23186/1066	ex N238WA	
☐ XA-UIV	Boeing 737-247 (Nordam 3)	23187/1070	ex N239WA	stored MTY
☐ XA-UJB	Boeing 737-247 (Nordam 3)	23184/1061	ex N236WA	
☐ XA-UJC	Boeing 737-247 (Nordam 3)	23185/1065	ex N237WA	stored MTY

AVIONES DE SONORA		Sonorav (ADS)		Hermosillo (HMO)
☐ XA-KEA	Cessna 310R	310R1880	ex (N3223M)	
☐ XA-KOA	Cessna 340A	340A0978	ex YV-1886P	

AVOLAR AEROLINEAS		Aerovolar (V5/VLI)		Tijuana (TIJ)
☐ EI-DKV	Boeing 737-505	24272/1923	ex G-GFFC	stored
☐ EI-DNY	Boeing 737-3T0	23360/1147	ex N17309	

☐ EI-DNZ	Boeing 737-3T0	23363/1153	ex N60312	
☐ XA-UHY	Boeing 737-2C3	21016/406	ex XA-MAB	
☐ XA-UHZ	Boeing 737-201 (Nordam 3)	21816/592	ex XA-MAK	

CLICK MEXICANA — **Click Mexicana (QA/CBE)** — **Mexico City-Benito Juraex Intl (MEX)**

☐ XA-CLB	Boeing 717-2BL	55180/5132	ex N918ME		
☐ XA-CLC	Boeing 717-2BL	55169/5119	ex N905ME		
☐ XA-CLD	Boeing 717-2BL	55190/5149	ex N924ME		
☐ XA-CLE	Boeing 717-2BL	55178/5128	ex N916ME		
☐ XA-CLF	Boeing 717-2BL	55177/5127	ex N914ME		
☐ XA-CLG	Boeing 717-2BL	55167/5117	ex N903ME		
☐ N902ME	Boeing 717-2BL	55166/5116			stored MEX
☐ N906ME	Boeing 717-2BL	55170/5120			
☐ N907ME	Boeing 717-2BL	55171/5121			
☐ N913ME	Boeing 717-2BL	55176/5126			
☐ N919ME	Boeing 717-2BL	55181/5135			
☐ N920ME	Boeing 717-2BL	55182/5138			
☐ N921ME	Boeing 717-2BL	55183/5140			
☐ N926ME	Boeing 717-2BL	55192/5152			
☐ N928ME	Boeing 717-2BL	55194/5154			
☐ XA-JXT	Fokker F.28-0100 (Fokker 100)	11303	ex D-AGPF		
☐ XA-JXW	Fokker F.28-0100 (Fokker 100)	11390	ex PH-JXW	Mazatlan	
☐ XA-KXJ	Fokker F.28-0100 (Fokker 100)	11400	ex PH-KXJ	Ixtapa Zihuatanejo	
☐ XA-MQJ	Fokker F.28-0100 (Fokker 100)	11347	ex		
☐ XA-MQK	Fokker F.28-0100 (Fokker 100)	11336	ex PT-MQK		
☐ XA-MRA	Fokker F.28-0100 (Fokker 100)	11284	ex PT-MRA		
☐ XA-MRB	Fokker F.28-0100 (Fokker 100)	11285	ex PT-MRB		
☐ XA-MRG	Fokker F.28-0100 (Fokker 100)	11304	ex PT-MRG		
☐ XA-MRH	Fokker F.28-0100 (Fokker 100)	11305	ex PT-MRH		
☐ XA-SGE	Fokker F.28-0100 (Fokker 100)	11382	ex PH-JXS	Cuernavaca	
☐ XA-SGF	Fokker F.28-0100 (Fokker 100)	11384	ex PH-JXU	Puebla	
☐ XA-SHI	Fokker F.28-0100 (Fokker 100)	11309	ex PH-LMZ	Tampcio	
☐ XA-SHJ	Fokker F.28-0100 (Fokker 100)	11319	ex PH-LNB	Tuxtla Gutierrez	
☐ XA-SHK	Fokker F.28-0100 (Fokker 100)	11333	ex D-AGPN		
☐ XA-SHL	Fokker F.28-0100 (Fokker 100)	11337	ex D-AGPP		
☐ XA-TCG	Fokker F.28-0100 (Fokker 100)	11374	ex PH-JXX	Tuxpan	
☐ XA-TCH	Fokker F.28-0100 (Fokker 100)	11375	ex PH-JXR	Monclova	
☐ XA-TCM	Fokker F.28-0100 (Fokker 100)	11320	ex PT-MRC		
☐ XA-TCP	Fokker F.28-0100 (Fokker 100)	11341	ex PT-MRX		
☐ XA-TKP	Fokker F.28-0100 (Fokker 100)	11266	ex PK-JGD	San Antonio	stored VCV
☐ XA-TKR	Fokker F.28-0100 (Fokker 100)	11339	ex PK-JGH	San Luis Potosi	stored VCV

ESTAFETA CARGA AEREA — **(E7/ESF)** — **San Luis Potosi (SLP)**

☐ XA-AJA	Boeing 737-3Y0 (SF)	23747/1363	ex N331AW
☐ XA-ECA	Boeing 737-3M8 (SF)	24024/1689	ex N784DC
☐ XA-EMX	Boeing 737-375F	23707/1388	ex N336AW
☐ XA-ESA	Canadair CL-600-2B19 (CRJ-100ER)	7085	ex F-GRJC
☐ XA-GGB	Boeing 737-3M8 (SF)	24023/1675	ex N783DC
☐ XA-SPO	Canadair CL-600-2B19 (CRJ-100ER)	7088	ex F-GRJD
☐ XA-TWP	Boeing 737-229C (Nordam 3)	21738/576	ex G-BYYF

FLYMEX

☐ XA-AAS	Dornier 328-300 (328JET)	3127	ex N430Z
☐ XA-FAS	Dornier 328-300 (328JET)	3125	ex N410Z

GLOBAL AIR — **Damojh (DMJ)** — **Mexico City-Benito Juarez Intl (MEX)**

☐ XA-TWR	Boeing 737-2H4 (AvAero 3)	21812/611	ex N60SW	no titles	Lsd to VCV
☐ XA-UBB	Boeing 737-291 (Nordam 3)	21750/574	ex N988UA	no titles	
☐ XA-UMQ	Boeing 737-2Q3	24103/1565	ex N243AG		

HAWK DE MEXICO — **Hawk Mexico (HMX)** — **Mexico City/Cancun (MEX/CUN)**

☐ XA-MVD	Beech 1900D	UE-398	ex N44118

HELI CAMPECHE — **Helicampeche (HEC)** — **Campeche/Mexico City (CPE/-)**

☐ XA-AAB	Bell 412EP	36253	ex N4217U	Lsd fr OLOG
☐ XA-AAN	Bell 412EP	36254	ex N24171	Lsd fr OLOG
☐ XA-AAR	Bell 412EP	36255	ex N305AL	Lsd fr OLOG
☐ XA-HSC	Bell 412EP	36417	ex N30423	
☐ XA-HSD	Bell 412EP	36446	ex N31011	
☐ XA-HSG	Bell 412EP	36473	ex N321FB	
☐ XA-HSJ	Bell 412EP	36337	ex N45388	
☐ XA-HSK	Bell 412EP	36340	ex N45389	
☐ XA-HSL	Bell 412EP	36334	ex N45377	
☐ XA-HSM	Bell 412EP	36324	ex N8067M	
☐ XA-HSN	Bell 412EP	36488	ex N332TB	

Registration	Type	C/n	Previous identity	Notes	Remarks
☐ XA-HSO	Bell 412EP	36489	ex N331AB		
☐ XA-SMW	Bell 412HP	36038	ex SU-CAW		
☐ XA-SYL	Bell 412HP	36101	ex N87746		
☐ XA-TRC	Bell 412HP	36157	ex N389AL		
☐ XA-TTL	Bell 412HP	36065	ex D-HHZZ		
☐ XA-TXP	Bell 412EP	36311	ex N24129		
☐ XA-TXQ	Bell 412EP	36268	ex N61318		
☐ XA-TXR	Bell 412EP	36289	ex N2029N		
☐ XA-TXV	Bell 412EP	36317	ex N7020C		
☐ XA-TXZ	Bell 412EP	36314	ex N7030B		
☐ XA-TYA	Bell 412EP	36315	ex N7007Q		
☐ XA-TYQ	Bell 412SP	33210	ex 9Y-BCL		
☐ XA-UAR	Bell 412	36051	ex D-HHYY		

Registration	Type	C/n	Previous identity	Notes	Remarks
☐ XA-ADL	Bell 407	53447	ex N61201		
☐ XA-HSE	Eurocopter EC135P2+	0591	ex N135TZ		
☐ XA-HSF	Eurocopter EC135P2+	0598	ex N435AL		
☐ XA-IUR	Bell 212	30938			
☐ XA-JMB	Bell 407	53274	ex XA-TLB		
☐ XA-JOL	Bell 206B JetRanger III	786	ex N31AL		Lsd fr OLOG
☐ XA-LOC	Bell 206B JetRanger III	3284			Lsd fr OLOG
☐ XA-TPC	Bell 407	53313	ex N60664		
☐ XA-TRP	Bell 212	30869	ex N71AL		Lsd fr OLOG
☐ XA-UEB	Bell 407	53046	ex N416AL		Lsd fr OLOG

Associated with Air Logistics/Bristow Group

HELIVAN

Registration	Type	C/n	Previous identity
☐ XA-GFT	Sikorsky S-76C+	760596	ex N71154
☐ XA-MJV	Sikorsky S-76C+	760581	ex N7113J
☐ XA-RSY	Sikorsky S-76C+	760598	ex N71026
☐ XA-RYT	Sikorsky S-76C+	760582	ex N7110U

INTERJET — *(4O/INJ)* — *Toluca (TLC)*

Registration	Type	C/n	Previous identity
☐ XA-ABC	Airbus A320-214	3690	ex F-WWBE
☐ XA-ACO	Airbus A320-214	1322	ex F-WQUX
☐ XA-ALM	Airbus A320-214	1308	ex F-WQUU
☐ XA-IJA	Airbus A320-214	1244	ex F-WQUT
☐ XA-IJT	Airbus A320-214	1132	ex F-WQUR
☐ XA-INJ	Airbus A320-214	1162	ex F-WQUV
☐ XA-JCV	Airbus A320-214	3514	ex F-WWDO
☐ XA-MTY	Airbus A320-214	1179	ex XA-AIJ
☐ XA-MXM	Airbus A320-214	3286	ex F-WWDR
☐ XA-TLC	Airbus A320-214	3312	ex F-WWIP
☐ XA-UHE	Airbus A320-214	3149	ex F-WWBS
☐ XA-VAI	Airbus A320-214	3160	ex F-WWDR
☐ XA-VTA	Airbus A320-214	1259	ex XA-ITJ
☐ XA-XII	Airbus A320-214	3508	ex F-WWBU
☐ XA-ZIH	Airbus A320-214	3667	ex F-WWDZ

MAGNICHARTERS — *Grupomonterrey (GMT)* — *Monterrey-General Mariano Ecobedo Intl (MTY)*

Registration	Type	C/n	Previous identity	Notes	Remarks
☐ XA-MAA	Boeing 737-377	23655/1274	ex N812AR		
☐ XA-MAB	Boeing 737-301	23232/1169	ex N502UW		
☐ XA-MAC	Boeing 737-2C3	21014/397	ex N302AR		damaged 14Sep07
☐ XA-MAD	Boeing 737-277 (Nordam 3)	22652/831	ex N185AW	Magni titles	
☐ XA-MAE	Boeing 737-277 (Nordam 3)	22648/789	ex N181AW		
☐ XA-MAF	Boeing 737-2K9 (Nordam 3)	22505/815	ex N303AR		
☐ XA-MAI	Boeing 737-322	24537/1774	ex N368UA		

MAS AIR CARGO — *Mas Carga (MY/MAA)* — *Mexico City-Benito Juarez Intl (MEX)*

Registration	Type	C/n	Remarks
☐ N314LA	Boeing 767-316ERF	32573/848	Lsd fr LCO
☐ N420LA	Boeing 767-316ERF	34627/948	Lsd fr LCO

MAYAIR — *(MYI)* — *Mexico City-Benito Juarez Intl (MEX)*

Registration	Type	C/n	Previous identity
☐ XA-MUR	Cessna 208B Caravan I	208B0740	ex XA-TOE
☐ XA-MYI	Short SD.3-60	SH3602	ex YN-CGF

MEXICANA — *Mexicana (MX/MXA)* — *Mexico City-Benito Juarez Intl (MEX)*

Member of Oneworld

Registration	Type	C/n	Previous identity	Name
☐ XA-UBQ	Airbus A318-111	2328	ex D-AUAD	Ecuador
☐ XA-UBR	Airbus A318-111	2333	ex D-AUAE	Don Manuel
☐ XA-UBS	Airbus A318-111	2358	ex D-AUAH	Vancouver
☐ XA-UBT	Airbus A318-111	2367	ex D-AUAI	Ciudad de Mexico
☐ XA-UBU	Airbus A318-111	2377	ex D-AUAJ	San Luis Potosi
☐ XA-UBV	Airbus A318-111	2394	ex D-AUAK	Manzanillo
☐ XA-UBW	Airbus A318-111	2523	ex D-AUAA	

☐ XA-UBX	Airbus A318-111	2544	ex D-AUAB		
☐ XA-UBY	Airbus A318-111	2552	ex D-AUAC		
☐ XA-UBZ	Airbus A318-111	2575	ex D-AUAD		

☐ N62TY	Airbus A319-112	1625	ex D-AVYZ	Mexicali	
☐ N204MX	Airbus A319-112	4204	ex D-AVYG		on order
☐ N254MX	Airbus A319-112	4254	ex D-AVYm		on order
☐ N412MX	Airbus A319-112	4127	ex D-AVWD		
☐ N429MX	Airbus A319-112	1429	ex N50074	Miami	
☐ N612MX	Airbus A319-112	1612	ex EI-CXA	Merida	
☐ N618MX	Airbus A319-112	1618	ex D-AVWH	Caracas	
☐ N634MX	Airbus A319-112	1634	ex D-AVYH	Portland	
☐ N706MX	Airbus A319-112	1706	ex D-AVYQ	Sacramento	
☐ N750MX	Airbus A319-112	1750	ex D-AVYB	Vamos por Todo	
☐ N790MX	Airbus A319-112	3790	ex D-AVXL		
☐ N866MX	Airbus A319-112	1866	ex D-AVYB	Cancun	
☐ N872MX	Airbus A319-112	1872	ex D-AVYF	Villahermosa	
☐ N882MX	Airbus A319-112	1882	ex D-AVYO	Los Cabos	
☐ N925MX	Airbus A319-112	1925	ex D-AVYS	Zacatecas	
☐ XA-CMA	Airbus A319-112	2066	ex D-AVYF	Leon	
☐ XA-MXA	Airbus A319-112	2078	ex D-AVYO	Hermosillo	
☐ XA-MXG	Airbus A319-112	1630	ex C-GITT		Lsd fr ACA
☐ XA-MXH	Airbus A319-112	1673	ex C-GJTA		Lsd fr ACA
☐ XA-MXI	Airbus A319-112	1742	ex C-GJVY		Lsd fr ACA
☐ XA-MXJ	Airbus A319-112	1805	ex C-GKNW		Lsd fr ACA
☐ XA-NCA	Airbus A319-112	2126	ex D-AVWM	Saltillo	
☐ XA-UAQ	Airbus A319-112	1598	ex C-GJUK	Durango	
☐ XA-UER	Airbus A319-112	2662	ex D-AVWV		

☐ N164CG	Airbus A320-231	0164	ex 4R-ABF		on order
☐ N213MX	Airbus A320-214	3123	ex F-WWBE		
☐ N291MX	Airbus A320-231	0291	ex G-OOAA	Morelia	
☐ N292MX	Airbus A320-231	0292	ex G-OOAB	Oaxaca	
☐ N304ML	Airbus A320-231	0373	ex F-WQBD	Veracruz	
☐ N332MX	Airbus A320-231	0332	ex B-22301	Denver	
☐ N347TM	Airbus A320-231	0347	ex B-22307	San Salvador	
☐ N361DA	Airbus A320-231	0361	ex PH-FHA	Montreal	
☐ N368MX	Airbus A320-231	0368	ex F-OHMA	Oakland	
☐ N369MX	Airbus A320-231	0369	ex B-22302	Toronto	
☐ N405MX	Airbus A320-231	0405	ex EI-TLI		
☐ N406PR	Airbus A320-231	0406	ex 4R-ABB		on order
☐ N428MX	Airbus A320-231	0428	ex EI-TLG	Toluca	
☐ N971GT	Airbus A320-231	0179	ex VT-EYE		on order
☐ XA-MXF	Airbus A320-214	0566	ex TC-JLC		
☐ XA-MXK	Airbus A320-214	3304	ex F-WWIL		
☐ XA-MXL	Airbus A320-214	3374	ex F-WWDH		
☐ XA-MXR	Airbus A320-231	0252	ex F-OHME	Nueva York	
☐ XA-MXS	Airbus A320-231	0259	ex F-OHMF	Ciudad del Carmen	
☐ XA-MXT	Airbus A320-231	0260	ex F-OHMG	Monterrey	
☐ XA-MXU	Airbus A320-231	0275	ex F-OHMI	Bogota	
☐ XA-MXV	Airbus A320-231	0276	ex F-OHMJ	Cozumel	
☐ XA-MXW	Airbus A320-231	0296	ex F-OHMK	San Jose California	
☐ XA-MXX	Airbus A320-231	0320	ex F-OHML	Puerto Vallarta	
☐ XA-MXY	Airbus A320-231	0321	ex F-OHMM	Querétaro	
☐ XA-MXZ	Airbus A320-231	0353	ex F-OHMN	Chicago	
☐ XA-UAH	Airbus A320-231	0447	ex N447MX	Minatitlan	
☐ XA-UCZ	Airbus A320-231	0357	ex G-BVYB		
☐ XA-UMN	Airbus A320-231	0261	ex F-OHMH	Nuevo Laredo	

☐ XA-MXP	Airbus A330-243	966	ex F-WWYP
☐ XA-MXQ	Airbus A330-243	971	ex F-WWYU
☐ XA-MXC	Boeing 767-3P6ER	24349/244	ex N957PG
☐ XA-MXE	Boeing 767-3P6ER	23764/158	ex N964PG
☐ XA-MXN	Boeing 767-25DER	24733/261	ex SP-LOA
☐ XA-MXO	Boeing 767-25DER	24734/266	ex SP-LOB

MEXICANALINK

☐ XA-BMI	Canadair CL-600-2B19 (CRJ-200ER)	7311	ex N638BR
☐ XA-CMI	Canadair CL-600-2B19 (CRJ-200ER)	7485	ex N656BR
☐ XA-DMI	Canadair CL-600-2B19 (CRJ-200LR)	7414	ex N649BR
☐ XA-EMI	Canadair CL-600-2B19 (CRJ-200LR)	7457	ex N655BR
☐ XA-FMI	Canadair CL-600-2B19 (CRJ-200ER)	7313	ex N639BR
☐ XA-GMI	Canadair CL-600-2B19 (CRJ-200ER)	7401	ex N657BR
☐ XA-HMI	Canadair CL-600-2B19 (CRJ-200ER)	7739	ex N677SA
☐ XA-IMI	Canadair CL-600-2B19 (CRJ-200ER)	7613	ex N458CA
☐ XA-JMI	Canadair CL-600-2B19 (CRJ-200ER)	7650	ex N469SM
☐ XA-KMI	Canadair CL-600-2B19 (CRJ-200ER)	7689	ex N483CA
☐ XA-LMI	Canadair CL-600-2B19 (CRJ-200ER)	7612	ex N465SM
☐ XA-MMI	Canadair CL-600-2B19 (CRJ-200ER)	7662	ex N682SA
☐ XA-NMI	Canadair CL-600-2B19 (CRJ-200ER)	7653	ex N681SA
☐ XA-OMI	Canadair CL-600-2B19 (CRJ-200ER)	7707	ex N486CA

NOVA AIR		(M4)		Mexico City-Benito Juarez Intl (MEX)
☐ XA-OCI	Boeing 737-217 (AvAero 3)	22257/756	ex N2257	stored MEX
☐ XA-OHC	Boeing 737-291 (Nordam 3)	21640/536	ex N982UA	

REPUBLICAIR		Republicair (RBC)		Mexico City-Benito Juarez Intl (MEX)
☐ XA-RBC	Boeing 737-277 (Nordam 3)	22647/785	ex N180AW	stored MEX
☐ XA-RBD	Boeing 737-277 (Nordam 3)	22649/801	ex N182AW	

SAEMSA		Servimex (SXM)		Campeche, Tampico & Toluca (CPE/TAM/TLC)
☐ XA-SRL	Aérospatiale SA.330J Puma	1625	ex XC-CME	
☐ XA-SRN	Aérospatiale SA.330J Puma	1644	ex XC-FOI	
☐ XA-SRO	Aérospatiale SA.330J Puma	1615	ex XC-IMP	
☐ XA-SRP	Aérospatiale SA.330J Puma	1616	ex XC-OPS	
☐ XA-SRQ	Aérospatiale SA.330J Puma	1613	ex XC-SDE	
☐ XA-TFT	Aérospatiale AS365N2 Dauphin 2	6495	ex F-WQDS	
☐ XA-TFU	Aérospatiale AS365N2 Dauphin 2	6512	ex F-WQDT	
☐ XA-TFV	Aérospatiale AS365N2 Dauphin 2	6513		
☐ XA-TGS	Aérospatiale AS365N2 Dauphin 2	6515	ex F-WWOA	
☐ XA-TGY	Aérospatiale AS365N2 Dauphin 2	6516	ex F-WWOB	
☐ XA-TGZ	Aérospatiale AS365N2 Dauphin 2	6517		
☐ XA-SSB	Bell 212	30845	ex XC-DAH	
☐ XA-SSC	Bell 212	30992	ex XC-DIA	
☐ XA-SSD	Bell 212	30988	ex XC-DIF	
☐ XA-SSF	Bell 212	30987	ex XC-SER	
☐ XA-SSG	Bell 212	30939	ex XC-SET	
☐ XA-SSK	Bell 212	30924	ex XC-HFI	
☐ XA-SSL	Bell 212	35031	ex XC-HHN	
☐ XA-SRF	Cessna U206G Stationair 6	U20605823	ex XC-DOJ	
☐ XA-SRG	Cessna U206G Stationair 6	U20604684	ex XC-REX	
☐ XA-SRI	Cessna U206G Stationair 6	U20604133	ex XC-MTT	
☐ XA-SST	Cessna U206G Stationair 6	U20605820	ex XC-DOI	
☐ XA-SRK	Cessna T210M Turbo Centurion II	21062532		
☐ XA-SRW	Sikorsky S-76A	760142	ex XC-FEK	
☐ XA-SRX	Sikorsky S-76A	760094	ex XC-FES	
☐ XA-SSO	Bell 206B JetRanger	1250	ex XC-GIJ	
☐ XA-SSP	Bell 206B JetRanger III	3962	ex XC-HIB	

SAINTEX CARGO				
☐ XA-MDG	SAAB SF.340A	340A-088	ex N88XW	freighter
☐ XA-STX	SAAB SF.340A	340A-046	ex N46XJ	freighter, op for DHL

TRANSPORTES AEREOS PEGASO		Transpegaso (TPG)		Mexico City-Benito Juarez Intl (MEX)
☐ XA-EZM	MBB BK-117C-2	9051	ex D-HMBC	
☐ XA-MBB	MBB Bo.105CBS-4	S-676	ex N4573H	
☐ XA-NAT	MBB Bo.105LS-A3	2044	ex XA-TTT	
☐ XA-THI	MBB Bo.105LS-A3	2046	ex C-GERG	
☐ XA-THK	MBB BK-117B-2	7131	ex D-HBCZ	
☐ XA-THM	MBB BK-117B-2	7252	ex D-HAEC	
☐ XA-UBN	MBB BK-117C-1	7550		
☐ XA-UBO	MBB BK-117C-1	7551		
☐ XA-UBP	MBB BK-117C-1	7555		
☐ XA-UDM	Eurocopter EC135P2	0400		
☐ XA-UDN	Eurocopter EC135P2	0391		
☐ XA-UDO	Eurocopter EC135P2	0389		

VIGO JET		Mejets (MJT)		Mexico City-Benito Juarez Intl (MEX)
☐ XA-AEG	Lockheed L-188CF Electra	1147	ex HK-3706	stored PTY
☐ XA-MJE	North American NA-265 Sabre 40	282-65	ex XA-GGR	Freighter
☐ XA-UII	Boeing 727-222F (FedEx 3)	19913/672	ex N7640U	
☐ XA-UIJ	Boeing 727-222F (FedEx 3)	19911/668	ex XA-SRC	stored MEX
☐ XA-UIT	SAAB SF.340A	340A-030	ex XA-UGM	

VIVA AEROBUS		(VIV)		Monterrey-Escobedo Intl (MTY)
☐ XA-TAR	Boeing 737-301	23259/1132	ex HS-AEF	
☐ XA-UGL	Boeing 737-3B7	22958/1137	ex N385US	
☐ XA-VIA	Boeing 737-3B7	23856/1501	ex N521AU	
☐ XA-VIB	Boeing 737-3B7	23378/1339	ex HS-AAV	
☐ XA-VIF	Boeing 737-301	23552/1382	ex PK-AWV	
☐ XA-VIH	Boeing 737-301	23554/1408	ex PK-AWW	
☐ XA-VIV	Boeing 737-301	23560/1463	ex N573US	

☐ XA-VIX	Boeing 737-3B7	23312/1162	ex N390US
☐ XA-VIY	Boeing 737-3B7	22959/1140	ex N158VA

VOLARIS	(V4/VOI)	Toluca (TLC)

☐ N473TA	Airbus A319-132	1140	ex D-AVYP	Aracely	
☐ N474TA	Airbus A319-132	1159	ex D-AVWD	Aline	
☐ N501VL	Airbus A319-132	2979	ex D-AVXF	Leopoldo	
☐ N502VL	Airbus A319-132	3463	ex D-AVWL	Alejandro	
☐ N503VL	Airbus A319-132	3491	ex D-AVYU	Audrey	
☐ N504VL	Airbus A319-132	3590	ex D-AVYK	Sebastian	
☐ XA-VOA	Airbus A319-132	2771	ex D-AVWP	Alejandro	
☐ XA-VOB	Airbus A319-132	2780	ex D-AVYJ	Marco	
☐ XA-VOC	Airbus A319-132	2997	ex D-AVXK	Citlali	
☐ XA-VOD	Airbus A319-132	3045	ex D-AVWO	Diego	
☐ XA-VOE	Airbus A319-132	3069	ex D-AVWT	Francisco	
☐ XA-VOF	Airbus A319-132	3077	ex D-AVWQ	Fernando	
☐ XA-VOG	Airbus A319-132	3175	ex D-AVXI	Gabriel	
☐ XA-VOH	Airbus A319-132	3253	ex D-AVWU	Javier	
☐ XA-VOI	Airbus A319-132	2657	ex D-AVYN	Ivetta	
☐ XA-VOJ	Airbus A319-132	3279	ex D-AVYM	Jamie	
☐ XA-VOK	Airbus A319-132	3450	ex D-AVYT	Veronica	
☐ XA-VOL	Airbus A319-132	2666	ex D-AVWX	Loreta	
☐ XA-VOM	Airbus A320-233	3624	ex F-WWIM	Sara	
☐ XA-VON	Airbus A320-232	3672	ex F-WWIN	Isaac	
☐ XA-VOO	Airbus A319-132	3705	ex D-AVWK	Andres	
☐ XA-	Airbus A319-133		ex		on order

XT- BURKINA FASO (People's Democratic Republic of Burkina Faso)

AIR BURKINA	Burkina (2J/VBW)	Ouagadougou (OUA)

☐ XT-ABC	McDonnell-Douglas MD-87	49834/1714	ex I-AFRA	
☐ XT-ABD	McDonnell-Douglas MD-87	49839/1739	ex EC-EYX	
☐ XT-ABF	McDonnell-Douglas MD-83	53464/2091	ex N161BS	
☐ XT-FZP	Fokker F.28 Fellowship 4000	11185	ex PH-ZCF	Bonkougou

XU- CAMBODIA (Kingdom of Cambodia)

CAMBODIA ANGKOR AIR	(K6)	Phnom Penh-Pochentong (PNH)

☐ VN-A351	Airbus A321-231	3005	ex D-AVZI	Lsd fr HVN
☐ VN-B212	ATR 72-212A	685	ex F-WWEH	Lsd fr HVN
☐ VN-B214	ATR 72-212A	688	ex F-WWEK	Lsd fr HVN

IMTREC AVIATION	Imtrec (IMT)	Phnom Penh-Pochentong (PNH)

☐ RDPL-34148	Ilyushin Il-76T	1013409310	ex EX-76815	
☐ RDPL-34154	Ilyushin Il-76T	073411331	ex ER-IBH	based RKA
☐ RDPL-34155	Ilyushin Il-76T	073411338	ex ER-IBD	
☐ RDPL-34158	Antonov An-32	402437	ex ER-LID	Op for Laotian Army
☐ XU-315	Antonov An-12BP	2400702	ex RA-11131	

KAMPUCHEA AIRLINES	Kampuchea (E2/KMP)	Phnom Penh-Pochentong (PNH)

Suspended operations but plans to restart, 49% owned by Orient Thai Airlines

PMT AIR	Multitrade (U4/PMT)	Phnom Penh-Pochentong (PNH)

☐ XU-U4B	Boeing 737-281	20450/262	ex EX-450	
☐ XU-U4D	McDonnell-Douglas MD-83	49390/1269	ex UR-CEL	
☐ XU-U4E	McDonnell-Douglas MD-83	49395/1286	ex N9305N	stored JKT
☐ XU-U4F	Boeing 737-242 (Nordam 3)	22074/619	ex YA-GAC	
☐ XU-U4H	Boeing 727-200			

PRESIDENT AIRLINES	(TO/PSD)	Phnom Penh-Pochentong (PNH)

☐ XU-325	Antonov An-26B	12808	ex RA-26136	
☐ XU-335	Antonov An-24B	99902009	ex RA-79162	
☐ XU-881	Fokker F.27 Friendship 100	10168	ex RP-C5888	stored PNH
☐ XU-888	Fokker F.28 Fellowship 1000	11012	ex XU-001	stored PNH

ROYAL KHMER AIRLINES	Khymer Air (RK/RKH)	Phnom Penh-Pochentong (PNH)

☐ XU-RKA	Boeing 737-2H4 (AvAero 3)	22061/639	ex N63SW	Lsd to/op for BGL
☐ XU-RKB	Boeing 737-2H4 (AvAero 3)	22674/827	ex N74SW	
☐ XU-RKC	Boeing 737-2H4 (AvAero 3)	22903/905	ex (PK-RIP)	Lsd to/op for BGL
☐ XU-RKF	Boeing 727-223F (FedEx 3)	19494/661	ex 4R-SEM	

☐ XU-RKH	Boeing 737-232 (Nordam 3)	23105/1068	ex N334DL		
☐ XU-RKJ	Boeing 727-223 (Raisbeck 3)	20989/1144	ex PK-JGQ	Air Dream c/s	abandoned at HAN
☐ XU-RKK	Boeing 737-2H4	23054/969	ex PK-LYA		Lsd to IAW

ROYAL PHNOM PENH AIRWAYS — *Phnom-Penh-Air (RL/PPW)* — *Phnom Penh-Pochentong (PNH)*

☐ XU-070	AVIC 1 Y-7-100C	09706	ex B-3448	stored
☐ XU-071	AVIC 1 Y-7-100C	08708	ex B-3449	stored
☐ XU-072	AVIC 1 Y-7-100C	08705	ex B-3494	

SIEM REAP AIR INTERNATIONAL — *Siemreap Air (FT/SRH)* — *Siem Reap (REP)*

A wholly owned subsidiary of Bangkok Air and leases aircraft from parent as required – some wear joint titles

XY- MYANMAR (Union of Myanmar)

AIR BAGAN — *(W9/JAB)* — *Yangon (RGN)*

☐ XY-AGC	Fokker F.28-0100 (Fokker 100)	11327	ex G-BXWE	Lsd to MMA
☐ XY-AGD	Airbus A310-222	419	ex B-2303	
☐ XY-AGE	Airbus A310-222	320	ex B-2302	
☐ XY-AGF	Fokker F.28-0100 (Fokker 100)	11282	ex N854US	
☐ XY-AIA	ATR 72-212	422	ex F-WQNQ	
☐ XY-AIC	ATR 42-320	159	ex N34820	
☐ XY-AID	ATR 42-300	152	ex N34817	
☐ XY-AIE	ATR 72-212	458	ex F-WQNB	
☐ XY-AIH	ATR 72-212	469	ex F-OHFZ	

AIR MANDALAY — *(6T)* — *Mandalay/Yangon (MDL/RGN)*

☐ XY-AEY	ATR 72-212	393	ex F-OHFS
☐ XY-AIJ	ATR 42-320	268	ex F-OHRN

MYANMA AIRWAYS — *Unionair (UB/UBA)* — *Yangon (RGN)*

☐ XY-ADZ	Fokker F.27 Friendship 600	10574	ex PH-EXF		
☐ XY-AEQ	Fokker F.27 Friendship 400	10294	ex 5Y-BIP		stored RGN
☐ XY-AEW	Fokker F.27 Friendship 600	10352	ex CU-T1290		stored RGN
☐ XY-AEZ	ATR 72-212	475	ex F-OGUO	all-white	
☐ XY-AGA	Fokker F.28 Fellowship 4000	11232	ex PH-EZG		
☐ XY-AGB	Fokker F.28 Fellowship 4000	11184	ex YU-AOH		
☐ XY-AIB	ATR 42-320	178	ex F-WQNM		
☐ XY-AIF	ATR 72-212A	765	ex F-W		
☐ XY-AIG	ATR 72-212A	781	ex F-WWET		

MYANMAR AIRWAYS INTERNATIONAL — *Mtanmar (8M/MMA)* — *Yangon (RGN)*

☐ XY-AGC	Fokker F.28-0100 (Fokker 100)	11327	ex G-BXWE	Lsd fr JAB
☐ XY-AGG	Airbus A320-231	0114	ex S5-AAC	

YANGON AIRLINES — *(HK)* — *Yangon (RGN)*

☐ F-OIYA	ATR 72-212	479	ex F-WWEL
☐ F-OIYB	ATR 72-212	481	ex F-WWEQ

YA- AFGHANISTAN (State of Afghanistan)

ARIANA AFGHAN AIRLINES — *Ariana (FG/AFG)* — *Kabul (KBL)*

☐ TC-SGC	Airbus A310-304	519	ex VT-EVI		Fethiya KolotLsd fr SGX
☐ TC-SGI	Boeing 737-86J/W	28069/42	ex D-ABAO		
☐ YA-BAB	Airbus A300B4-203	180	ex VT-EHO		
☐ YA-BAC	Airbus A300B4-203	190	ex VT-EHQ		stored FRA
☐ YA-CAQ	Airbus A310-304	496	ex TC-JDA	Kabul	
☐ YA-CAV	Airbus A310-304ER	497	ex TC-JDB	Kandahar	
☐ YA-DAL	Antonov An-24RV	57310409	ex UR-48097		
☐ YA-DAM	Antonov An-24RV	57310404	ex YR-BMF		
☐ YA-FAM	Boeing 727-223 (Raisbeck 3)	21088/1255	ex N861AA		
☐ YA-FAN	Boeing 727-227F (FedEx 3)	21245/1202	ex 9L-LFD		
☐ YA-FAS	Boeing 727-223 (Raisbeck 3)	21388/1345	ex N876AA		
☐ YA-FAT	Boeing 727-221/W (Duganair 3)	22542/1799	ex 5N-BFY		
☐ YA-FAY	Boeing 727-228	22289/1719	ex F-GCDH		

KABUL AIR — *Kabul (KBL)*

☐ YA-KAC	Antonov An-12BP	5343204	ex ER-ACO
☐ YA-KAD	Antonov An-12BP	6343810	ex ER-ACR
☐ YA-KAN	Ilyushin Il-76TD	0043449468	ex RDPL-34146

KAM AIR — Kamgar (RQ/KMF) — Kabul (KBL)

☐ EX-736	Boeing 737-247 (Nordam 3)	23517/1261	ex N243WA	Lsd fr Eastok Avia
☐ EY-87963	Yakovlev Yak-40K	9831058	ex EP-EAK	Lsd fr TJK
☐ YA-GAD	Boeing 727-243	22702	ex	
☐ YA-KAM	Boeing 767-222	21879/49	ex N619UA	
☐ YA-KMB	Antonov An-26B	17311802	ex EK-26199	
☐ YA-KMC	Antonov An-24RV	37309008	ex Z3-AAI	
☐ YA-KMF	McDonnell-Douglas MD-82	49704/1490	ex N959U	
☐ YA-	McDonnell-Douglas MD-83	49567/1367	ex N9306T	on order

PAMIR AIR — Pamir (NR/PIR) — Kabul (KBL)

☐ YA-PIB	Boeing 737-4Y0	26077/2425	ex TC-JET	
☐ YA-PID	Boeing 737-4Y0	26085/2468	ex TC-JEV	
☐ YA-PIR	Boeing 737-232 (Nordam 3)	23077/996	ex N305DL	
☐ EX-311	Boeing 737-268	21276/468	ex EX-080	Lsd fr IKA
☐ EY-538	Boeing 737-4Y0	23980/1667	ex N239DT	

SAFI AIRWAYS — Kabul (KBL)

☐ YA-AQS	Boeing 767-2J6ER	23745/156	ex B-2554
☐ YA-HSB	Boeing 737-3J6	23303/1237	ex B-2532
☐ YA-SFL	Boeing 737-3J6	23302/1224	ex B-2531
☐ YA-TTB	Airbus A340-311	015	ex F-WBSR

YI- IRAQ (Republic of Iraq)

AZMAR AIRLINES

☐ C5-JDZ	Douglas DC-9-31	48145/1042	ex N925VJ
☐ C5-LPS	Douglas DC-9-31	48146/1044	ex N926VJ

IRAQI AIRWAYS — Iraqi (IA/IAW) — Baghdad-Al Muthana/Intl (BGW/SDA)

☐ YI-APW	Boeing 737-2B7 (Nordam 3)	22885/966	ex 9L-LEG	Lsd fr/op by TBN
☐ YI-APY	Boeing 737-201 (Nordam 3)	22274/682	ex J2-KCM	Lsd fr/op by TBN
☐ YI-APZ	Boeing 737-201 (Nordam 3)	22354/736	ex JY-JRA	
☐ YI-AQA	Canadair CL-600-2D24 (CRJ-900NG)	15189	ex C-FULE	
☐ YI-AQB	Canadair CL-600-2D24 (CRJ-900NG)	15202	ex C-FWPF	
☐ YI-AQC	Canadair CL-600-2D24 (CRJ-900NG)	15213	ex C-FWZH	
☐ YI-AQD	Canadair CL-600-2D24 (CRJ-900NG)	15220	ex C-FYED	
☐ YI-AQK	Boeing 737-7BD/W	33935/2315	ex N331AT	
☐ YI-AQL	Boeing 737-7BD/W	35789/2201	ex N317AT	
☐ YI-AQO	Boeing 737-322	24673/1920	ex N398UA	
☐ SE-RJA	Boeing 737-4Q8	26302/2620	ex EI-CXM	
☐ XU-RKK	Boeing 737-2H4	23054/969	ex PK-LYA	Lsd fr RKH
☐ 9L-LEL	Boeing 727-247 (FedEx 3)	21483/1350	ex N831WA	Lsd fr/op by TBN

KURDISTAN AIRWAYS — Erbil /Beirut (EBL/BEY)

Leases Boeing 737-200 aircraft from Dolphin Air as required

YJ- VANUATU (Republic of Vanuatu)

AIR VANUATU — Air Van (NF/AVN) — Port Vila (VLI)

☐ YJ-AV1	Boeing 737-8Q8/W	30734/2477	ex N1779B	Spirit of Vanuatu
☐ YJ-AV3	Britten-Norman BN-2A-21 Islander	483	ex F-OCXP	
☐ YJ-AV4	Harbin Y-12 II	028	ex B-958L	
☐ YJ-AV5	Harbin Y-12 II	029	ex B-978L	
☐ YJ-AV6	Harbin Y-12 II	032	ex B-979L	
☐ YJ-AV72	ATR 72-212A	876	ex F-WWED	
☐ YJ-RV8	de Havilland DHC-6 Twin Otter 300	703	ex F-ODGL	
☐ YJ-RV10	de Havilland DHC-6 Twin Otter 300	679	ex OY-SLI	Melanesian Princess
☐ YJ-RV16	Britten-Norman BN-2A-27 Islander	104	ex ZK-FLU	
☐ YJ-	Britten-Norman BN-2B-207 Islander	2172	ex JA5290	

UNITY AIRLINES — Port Vila (VLI)

☐ YJ-007	Britten-Norman BN-2B-21 Islander	2177	ex H4-WPC
☐ YJ-009	Britten-Norman BN-2A-26 Islander	65	ex V7-0009

YK- SYRIA (Syrian Arab Republic)

SHAM WINGS AIR — Damascus (DAM)

☐ SU-BOZ	McDonnell-Douglas MD-83	53192/2155	ex N192AJ		Lsd fr AMV

SYRIANAIR — Syrianair (RB/SYR) — Damascus (DAM)

☐ YK-AKA	Airbus A320-232	0886	ex F-WWDH	Ugarit	
☐ YK-AKB	Airbus A320-232	0918	ex F-WWIJ	Ebla	
☐ YK-AKC	Airbus A320-232	1032	ex F-WWDV	Afamia	
☐ YK-AKD	Airbus A320-232	1076	ex F-WWIK	Mari	
☐ YK-AKE	Airbus A320-232	1085	ex F-WWIX	Bosra	
☐ YK-AKF	Airbus A320-232	1117	ex F-WWBN	Amrit	
☐ YK-ANC	Antonov An-26	3007			Govt operated
☐ YK-AND	Antonov An-26	3008			Govt operated
☐ YK-ANE	Antonov An-26	3103			Govt operated
☐ YK-ANF	Antonov An-26	3104			Govt operated
☐ YK-ANG	Antonov An-26B	10907			Govt operated
☐ YK-ANH	Antonov An-26B	11406			Govt operated
☐ YK-AGA	Boeing 727-294	21203/1188		6 Octobre	stored DAM
☐ YK-AGB	Boeing 727-294	21204/1194		Damascus	stored DAM
☐ YK-AGC	Boeing 727-294	21205/1198		Palmyra	stored DAM
☐ YK-AGD	Boeing 727-269	22360/1670	ex 9K-AFB		stored DAM
☐ YK-AGE	Boeing 727-269	22361/1716	ex 9K-AFC		stored DAM
☐ YK-AGF	Boeing 727-269	22763/1788	ex 9K-AFD		stored DAM
☐ YK-AQA	Yakovlev Yak-40	9341932			Govt operated
☐ YK-AQB	Yakovlev Yak-40	9530443			Govt operated
☐ YK-AQD	Yakovlev Yak-40	9830158			VIP Govt operated
☐ YK-AQE	Yakovlev Yak-40K	9830258			Govt operated
☐ YK-AQF	Yakovlev Yak-40	9931859			Govt operated
☐ YK-AQG	Yakovlev Yak-40K	9941959			Govt operated
☐ YK-AHA	Boeing 747SP-94	21174/284		16 Novembre	stored DAM
☐ YK-AHB	Boeing 747SP-94	21175/290		Arab Solidarity	stored DAM
☐ YK-ANA	Antonov An-24B	87304203			
☐ YK-ATA	Ilyushin Il-76TD	093421613			Govt operated
☐ YK-ATB	Ilyushin Il-76T	093421619			Govt operated
☐ YK-ATC	Ilyushin Il-76T	0013431911			Govt operated
☐ YK-ATD	Ilyushin Il-76T	0013431915			Govt operated
☐ YK-AYA	Tupolev Tu-134B-3	63992			
☐ YK-AYB	Tupolev Tu-134B-3	63994			
☐ YK-AYE	Tupolev Tu-134B-3	66187			
☐ YK-AYF	Tupolev Tu-134B-3	63190			stored DAM

YL- LATVIA (Republic of Latvia)

AIR BALTIC — AirBaltic (BT/BTI) — Riga-Spilve (RIX)

☐ YL-BBA	Boeing 737-505	24646/2138	ex N646LS
☐ YL-BBD	Boeing 737-53S	29075/3101	ex F-GJNU
☐ YL-BBE	Boeing 737-53S	29073/3083	ex EI-DDT
☐ YL-BBF	Boeing 737-548/W	24878/1939	ex EI-CDA
☐ YL-BBG	Boeing 737-548	24919/1970	ex EI-CDB
☐ YL-BBH	Boeing 737-548	24968/1975	ex EI-CDC
☐ YL-BBI	Boeing 737-33A/W	27454/2703	ex PT-SSQ
☐ YL-BBJ	Boeing 737-36Q/W	30333/3117	ex D-ADIA
☐ YL-BBK	Boeing 737-33V/W	29332/3072	ex HA-LKR
☐ YL-BBL	Boeing 737-33V/W	29334/3089	ex HA-LKS
☐ YL-BBM	Boeing 737-522	26680/2366	ex N680MV
☐ YL-BBN	Boeing 737-522	26683/2368	ex N683MV
☐ YL-BBP	Boeing 737-522	26688/2404	ex N688MV
☐ YL-BBQ	Boeing 737-522	26691/2408	ex N691MV
☐ YL-BBR	Boeing 737-31S	29266/3092	ex G-OTDA
☐ YL-BBS	Boeing 737-31S	29267/3093	ex G-GSPN
☐ YL-BBX	Boeing 737-36Q/W	30334/3120	ex D-ADIB
☐ YL-BBY	Boeing 737-36Q/W	30335/3129	ex D-ADIC
☐ YL-BDB	Boeing 757-256/W	26251/897	ex EC-HDR
☐ YL-BDC	Boeing 757-256/W	26253/902	ex EC-HDU
☐ YL-BAE	de Havilland DHC-8-402Q	4289	ex C-FZGL
☐ YL-BAF	de Havilland DHC-8-402Q	4293	ex C-GAUI
☐ YL-BAG	de Havilland DHC-8-402Q	4296	ex C-GBJA
☐ YL-BAH	de Havilland DHC-8-402Q	4302	ex
☐ LY-BAO	Fokker F.27 Mk.050 (Fokker 50)	20189	ex YL-LAO

☐ LY-BAV	Fokker F.27 Mk.050 (Fokker 50)	20190	ex YL-BAV	
☐ LY-BAZ	Fokker F.27 Mk.050 (Fokker 50)	20153	ex YL-BAZ	
☐ YL-BAA	Fokker F.27 Mk.050 (Fokker 50)	20120	ex SE-LEB	
☐ YL-BAC	Fokker F.27 Mk.050 (Fokker 50)	20216	ex SE-LFS	
☐ YL-BAR	Fokker F.27 Mk.050 (Fokker 50)	20149	ex PH-LVL	Cesis
☐ YL-BAS	Fokker F.27 Mk.050 (Fokker 50)	20162	ex OY-KAE	Zemgale
☐ YL-BAT	Fokker F.27 Mk.050 (Fokker 50)	20163	ex OY-KAF	Riga
☐ YL-BAU	Fokker F.27 Mk.050 (Fokker 50)	20126	ex PH-AAO	
☐ YL-BAW	Fokker F.27 Mk.050 (Fokker 50)	20148	ex OY-MMS	

INVERSIJA — *Inver (INV)* — *Riga-Spilve (RIX)*

☐ YL-LAK	Ilyushin Il-76T	0003424707	ex RA-76522	Adagold titles
☐ YL-LAL	Ilyushin Il-76T	0013433984	ex RA-76755	

KS AVIA — *Sky Camel (KSA)* — *Riga-Spilve (RIX)*

☐ YL-KSA	Antonov An-74-200	36547098957	ex RA-74030
☐ YL-KSB	Antonov An-74	36547136013	ex UR-CAC

LAT CHARTER — *LatCharter (6Y/LTC)* — *Riga-Spilve (RIX)*

☐ YL-LCA	Airbus A320-211	0333	ex C-FKAJ	Lsd to ISR
☐ YL-LCD	Airbus A320-211	0359	ex C-FMSV	
☐ YL-LCY	Boeing 767-3Y0ER	/357	ex C-GGFJ	Lsd to BBA
☐ YL-LCZ	Boeing 767-3Y0ER	25000/386	ex C-GHPA	Lsd to BBR

RAF-AVIA — *Mitavia (MTL)* — *Riga-Spilve (RIX)*

☐ YL-RAA	Antonov An-26B	97311206	ex RA-26064	
☐ YL-RAB	Antonov An-26B	07310508	ex RA-26032 ACS logo	
☐ YL-RAC	Antonov An-26	07309903	ex CCCP-79169	ACS logo
☐ YL-RAD	Antonov An-26B	47313909	ex RA-26589	
☐ YL-RAE	Antonov An-26B	57314004	ex CCCP-26200	
☐ YL-RAF	Antonov An-74TK-100	36547095905	ex UR-CAE	Lsd fr CBI
☐ YL-RAG	SAAB SF.340A	340A-052	ex SE-E52	Freighter
☐ YL-RAH	SAAB SF.340A	340A-081	ex EC-IRD	Freighter

SMARTLYNX — *(6Y/ART)* — *Riga-Spilve (RIX)*

☐ YL-BBC	Airbus A320-211	0142	ex SX-BVD
☐ YL-BCB	Airbus A320-211	0726	ex EK-32007
☐ YL-LCC	Airbus A320-211	0310	ex C-FKPS
☐ YL-LCE	Airbus A320-211	0311	ex C-FKPO
☐ YL-LCF	Airbus A320-212	0446	ex N446AN

YN- NICARAGUA (Republic of Nicaragua)

AIR CHARTER CARGO — *Managua (MGA)*

☐ YN-CGA	Antonov An-32	3007	ex HP-1217AVL

Last flown in 2006 but kept in an airworthy state and available for charter

ATLANTIC AIRWAYS — *Atlantic Nicaragua (AYN)* — *Managua (MGA)*

☐ YN-CFL	LET L-410UVP-E3	871917	ex OK-SDH
☐ YN-CFM	LET L-410UVP	871916	ex OK-SDG
☐ YN-CFR	LET L-410UVP	861705	ex TG-CFD

LA COSTENA — *Lacostena* — *Managua (MGA)*

☐ YN-CFO	Cessna 208B Caravan I	208B0758	ex N5264M	
☐ YN-CGB	Cessna 208B Caravan I	208B0611	ex HP-1407APP	
☐ YN-CGI	Cessna 208B Caravan I	208B0638	ex HR-IBI	
☐ YN-CGU	Cessna 208B Caravan I	208B0607	ex HP-1400	
☐ YN-CGG	Short SD.3-60	SH3612	ex HP-1318APP	Lsd fr APP

YR- ROMANIA (Republic of Romania)

BLUE AIR — *Blue Transport (0B/JOR)* — *Bucharest-Baneasa (BBU)*

☐ YR-BAA	Boeing 737-33A	27267/2600	ex ZK-CZU	
☐ YR-BAC	Boeing 737-377	23653/1260	ex ZK-SLA	Lsd fr AWK
☐ YR-BAD	Boeing 737-4C9	25429/2215	ex EI-DGN	
☐ YR-BAE	Boeing 737-4Y0	28723/2886	ex EI-CXL	
☐ YR-BAF	Boeing 737-322F	24453/1730	ex N360UA	

☐ YR-BAG	Boeing 737-5L9	24778/1816	ex N494ST		
☐ YR-BIA	Boeing 737-8AS/W	29925/588	ex EI-CSJ		
☐ YR-BIB	Boeing 737-8AS/W	29926/722	ex EI-CSM		
☐ YR-BIC	Boeing 737-8BK/W	33019/1502	ex OY-SEM		
☐ YR-DAA	SAAB SF.340A	340A-116	ex SE-F16		
☐ YR-DAB	SAAB SF.340A	340A-137	ex SE-ISN		

CARPATAIR — *Carpatair (V3/KRP)* — *Timisoara-Giarmata (TSR)*

☐ YR-SBA	SAAB 2000	2000-038	ex HB-IZV		Lsd fr SWR
☐ YR-SBB	SAAB 2000	2000-026	ex HB-IZN		Lsd fr SWR
☐ YR-SBC	SAAB 2000	2000-039	ex HB-IZW		Lsd fr SWR
☐ YR-SBD	SAAB 2000	2000-004	ex HB-IZA		Lsd fr SWR
☐ YR-SBE	SAAB 2000	2000-041	ex HB-IZX		Lsd fr SWR
☐ YR-SBI	SAAB 2000	2000-052	ex SE-LSH		
☐ YR-SBJ	SAAB 2000	2000-018	ex HB-IZK		Lsd fr SWR
☐ YR-SBK	SAAB 2000	2000-033	ex HB-IZR		Lsd fr SWR
☐ YR-SBL	SAAB 2000	2000-013	ex SE-LOT		
☐ YR-SBM	SAAB 2000	2000-014	ex SE-014		
☐ YR-SBN	SAAB 2000	2000-044	ex SE-LSC		
☐ YR-FKA	Fokker F.28-0100 (Fokker 100)	11340	ex C-GKZC		
☐ YR-FKB	Fokker F.28-0100 (Fokker 100)	11369	ex C-GKZK		
☐ YR-KMA	Fokker F.28-070 (Fokker 70)	11564	ex HA-LMA		
☐ YR-VGP	SAAB SF.340B	340B-228	ex HB-AKO		

JETRAN INTERNATIONAL AIRWAYS — *Air Romania (MDJ)* — *Bucharest-Baneasa (BBU)*

☐ YR-MDJ	McDonnell-Douglas MD-81	48053/986	ex 3D-JET	all-white	
☐ YR-MDK	McDonnell-Douglas MD-82	49139/1090	ex N822US		Stage 4 demonstrator
☐ YR-MDL	McDonnell-Douglas MD-82	48079/1016	ex N991PG		stored BBU
☐ YR-MDR	McDonnell-Douglas MD-82	48097/1059	ex TC-MNR	all-white	
☐ YR-MDS	McDonnell-Douglas MD-82	48098/1060	ex TC-MNS		
☐ YR-MDT	McDonnell-Douglas MD-82	49570/1440	ex EC-GTO		
☐ YR-OTN	McDonnell-Douglas MD-82	49119/1070	ex YR-MDM		

MEDALLION AIR — *HBucharest-Baneasa (BBU)*

☐ YR-HBA	McDonnell-Douglas MD-82	49937/1784	ex N983JJ		

MIA AIRLINES — *Salline (JLA)* — *Bucharest-Baneasa (BBU)*

☐ YR-HRS	BAC One-Eleven 488GH (QTA 3)	259	ex G-MAAH		
☐ YR-MIA	BAC One-Eleven 492GM (QTA 3)	260	ex HR-ATS	Mirjane	

ROMAVIA — *Aeromavia (WQ/RMV)* — *Bucharest-Baneasa/Otopeni (BBU/OTP)*

☐ EX-115	Ilyushin Il-18	187009904	ex UN-75001		
☐ YR-ABB	Boeing 707-3K1C (Comtran 2)	20804/883		CarpatiRomania titles	VIP
☐ YR-BEA	British Aerospace 146 Srs.200	E2227	ex G-BVMS		
☐ YR-BEC	British Aerospace 146 Srs.200	E2062	ex G-CEVF		
☐ YR-BRE	RomBAC/BAC One-Eleven 561RC	405	ex (EI-BUQ)	Romania titles	VIP

TAROM — *Tarom (RO/ROT)* — *Bucharest-Otopeni (OTP)*

☐ YR-ATA	ATR 42-500	566	ex F-WWLF	Dunarea	
☐ YR-ATB	ATR 42-500	569	ex F-WWLH	Bistrita	
☐ YR-ATC	ATR 42-500	589	ex F-WWLR	Mures	
☐ YR-ATD	ATR 42-500	591	ex F-WWLS	Cris	
☐ YR-ATE	ATR 42-500	596	ex F-WWLY	Olt	
☐ YR-ATF	ATR 42-500	599	ex F-WWEB	Arges	
☐ YR-ATG	ATR 42-500	605	ex F-WWLG	Dambovita	
☐ YR-ATH	ATR 72-212	861	ex F-WWEH	Somes	
☐ YR-ATI	ATR 72-212	867	ex F-WWER		
☐ YR-BGA	Boeing 737-38J	27179/2524	ex N5573K	Alba Iulia	
☐ YR-BGB	Boeing 737-38J	27180/2529		Bucuresti	
☐ YR-BGD	Boeing 737-38J	27182/2663		Devaspecial c/s	
☐ YR-BGE	Boeing 737-38J	27395/2671		Timisoara	
☐ YR-BGF	Boeing 737-78J	28440/795		Brâila	
☐ YR-BGG	Boeing 737-78J	28442/827		Craiova	
☐ YR-BGH	Boeing 737-78J	28438/1394		Hunedoara	
☐ YR-BGI	Boeing 737-78J	28439/1419		Iasi	
☐ YR-BGP	Boeing 737-86J/W	37740/2638	ex D-ABKB		
☐ YR-BGR	Boeing 737-86J/W	37741/2686	ex D-ABKC		
☐ YR-BGS	Boeing 737-8GJ/W	37360/2783	ex N1787B	Siblu	on order
☐ YR-LCA	Airbus A310-325	636	ex F-WQAV	Transilvania	
☐ YR-LCB	Airbus A310-325	644	ex F-WQAX	Moldova	
☐ YR-ASA	Airbus A318-111	2931	ex D-AUAC	Aurel Vlaicu - Aviation Pioneer	

Reg	Type	C/n	Previous identity	Name/Remarks	Notes
☐ YR-ASB	Airbus A318-111	2955	ex D-AUAE	Traian Vuia - Aviation Pioneer	
☐ YR-ASC	Airbus A318-111	3220	ex D-AUAF	Henri Coanda - Aviation Pioneer	
☐ YR-ASD	Airbus A318-111	3225	ex D-AUAG		

YS- EL SALVADOR (Republic of El Salvador)

TACA INTERNATIONAL AIRLINES — Taca (TA/TAI) — San Salvador-Comalapa Intl (SAL)

Reg	Type	C/n	Previous identity	Name/Remarks	Notes
☐ N471TA	Airbus A319-132	1066	ex D-AVWE		Lsd to TPU
☐ N472TA	Airbus A319-132	1113	ex D-AVWU		Lsd to TPU
☐ N476TA	Airbus A319-132	1934	ex D-AVWH		
☐ N477TA	Airbus A319-132	1952	ex D-AVWK		
☐ N478TA	Airbus A319-132	2339	ex D-AVWG	Aviateca titles	
☐ N479TA	Airbus A319-132	2444	ex D-AVWS	Aviateca titles	
☐ N480TA	Airbus A319-132	3057	ex D-AVYV		
☐ N520TA	Airbus A319-132	3248	ex D-AVWH		
☐ N521TA	Airbus A319-132	3276	ex D-AVYK		
☐ EI-TAB	Airbus A320-233	1624	ex N485TA	Mensajero de Esperanza	
☐ EI-TAD	Airbus A320-233	1334	ex N462TA		
☐ EI-TAG	Airbus A320-233	2791	ex (N495TA)		
☐ N484TA	Airbus A320-233	1523	ex F-WWIL		stored VCV
☐ N490TA	Airbus A320-232	2282	ex F-WWBO		
☐ N491TA	Airbus A320-233	2301	ex F-WWDF		
☐ N492TA	Airbus A320-233	2434	ex F-WWDL		
☐ N493TA	Airbus A320-233	2917	ex F-WWDR		
☐ N494TA	Airbus A320-233	3042	ex F-WWDM		
☐ N495TA	Airbus A320-233	3103	ex F-WWIH		
☐ N496TA	Airbus A320-233	3113	ex F-WWIU		
☐ N497TA	Airbus A320-233	3378	ex F-WWDK		
☐ N498TA	Airbus A320-233	3418	ex F-WWIO		
☐ N499TA	Airbus A320-233	3510	ex F-WWBX		
☐ N680TA	Airbus A320-233	3538	ex F-WWIF		
☐ N681TA	Airbus A320-233	3577	ex F-WWBO		
☐ N682TA	Airbus A320-233	3581	ex F-WWDC		
☐ N	Airbus A320-233		ex F-WW		on order
☐ N564TA	Airbus A321-231	2862	ex D-AVZB		
☐ N566TA	Airbus A321-231	2553	ex D-AVZJ		
☐ N567TA	Airbus A321-231	2610	ex D-AVZM		
☐ N568TA	Airbus A321-231	2687	ex D-AVZE		
☐ N570TA	Airbus A321-231	3869	ex D-AVZO		
☐ N982TA	Embraer 190-100 (190)	19000259	ex PT-STH		
☐ N983TA	Embraer 190-100 (190)	19000265	ex PT-TLF		
☐ N984TA	Embraer 190-100 (190)	19000273	ex PT-TLN		
☐ N985TA	Embraer 190-100 (190)	19000287	ex PT-TZB		
☐	Embraer 190-100 (190)		ex PT-		on order
☐	Embraer 190-100 (190)		ex PT-		on order
☐	Embraer 190-100 (190)		ex PT-		on order

YU- SERBIA (Republic of Serbia)

AVIOGENEX — Genex (AGX) — Belgrade (BEG)

Reg	Type	C/n	Previous identity	Name/Remarks	Notes
☐ YU-ANP	Boeing 737-2K3 (Nordam 3)	23912/1401		Zadar	Lsd to JAT

JAT AIRWAYS — JAT (JU/JAT) — Belgrade (BEG)

Reg	Type	C/n	Previous identity	Name/Remarks	Notes
☐ YU-AND	Boeing 737-3H9	23329/1134		City of Krusevac	
☐ YU-ANF	Boeing 737-3H9	23330/1136			
☐ YU-ANH	Boeing 737-3H9	23415/1171	ex TC-CYO		
☐ YU-ANI	Boeing 737-3H9	23416/1175	ex Z3-AAA		
☐ YU-ANJ	Boeing 737-3H9	23714/1305	ex TC-MIO		
☐ YU-ANK	Boeing 737-3H9	23715/1310			
☐ YU-ANL	Boeing 737-3H9	23716/1321	ex Z3-ARF		
☐ YU-ANP	Boeing 737-2K3 (Nordam 3)	23912/1401			Lsd fr AGX
☐ YU-ANV	Boeing 737-3H9	24140/1524			
☐ YU-ANW	Boeing 737-3H9	24141/1526	ex TS-IED		
☐ YU-AON	Boeing 737-3Q4	24208/1490	ex N181LF		
☐ YU-AOS	Boeing 737-4D7	24551/1795	ex N429US		
☐ YU-AJK	Douglas DC-9-32	47568/689	ex Z3-ARD		
☐ YU-ALN	ATR 72-202	180	ex F-WWEP		
☐ YU-ALO	ATR 72-202	186	ex F-WWEW		
☐ YU-ALP	ATR 72-202	189	ex F-WWED	all-white	
☐ YU-ALR	ATR 72-202	357	ex G-BVTK		
☐ YU-ALS	ATR 72-202	140	ex ES-KRB		

KOSMAS AIR CARGO — Kosmas Cargo (KMG) — Belgrade (BEG)

Reg	Type	C/n	Previous	Notes
☐ YU-AMI	Ilyushin Il-76MD	0093499982	ex RA-76822	

UNITED INTERNATIONAL AIRLINES — (UIL) — Sofia (SOF)

Reg	Type	C/n	Previous	Notes
☐ YU-UIA	Antonov An-12	02348007	ex LZ-SFA	

YV- VENEZUELA (Bolivarian Republic of Venezuela)

AECA

Reg	Type	C/n	Previous	Notes
☐ YV211T	Douglas DC-3	10201	ex HK-2666X	
☐ YV214T	Douglas DC-6			

AERO CARIBE

Reg	Type	C/n	Previous	Notes
☐ YV1427	LET L-410UVP	841224	ex YV-595C	

AERO EJECUTIVOS — Venejecutiv (VEJ) — Caracas-Simon Bolivar Intl (CCS)

Reg	Type	C/n	Previous	Notes
☐ YV1434	LET L-410UVP-E	872014	ex YV-1026CP	
☐ YV1854	Douglas DC-3	6135	ex YV-500C	
☐ YV201T	Douglas DC-3	11775	ex YV-1179C	
☐ YV-426C	Douglas DC-3	4093	ex N10DC	
☐ YV-440C	Douglas DC-3	2201	ex N31PB	Caballo Viejostatus?

AERO FLY MONAGAS

Reg	Type	C/n	Previous	Notes
☐ YV1518	LET L-410UVP-E	882022	ex YV-1028CP	

AEROBOL - AEROVIAS BOLIVAR — Ciudad Bolivar (CBL)

Reg	Type	C/n	Previous	Notes
☐ YV-315C	Cessna U206G Stationair 6	U20604323	ex YV-1465P	
☐ YV-387C	Cessna U206G Stationair 6	U20605398	ex YV-1310P	
☐ YV-389C	Cessna U206G Stationair 6			
☐ YV-408C	Cessna U206G Stationair 6			
☐ YV-615C	Cessna U206G Stationair 6	U20604759	ex YV-1704P	
☐ YV-849C	Cessna U206G Stationair 6			
☐ YV-946C	Cessna U206G Stationair 6			
☐ YV-270C	Britten-Norman BN-2A-20 Islander	573	ex YV-142CP	
☐ YV-288C	Cessna 207A Stationair 8	20700708	ex YV-2143P	
☐ YV-380C	Cessna 207A Stationair 8			

AEROMED

Reg	Type	C/n	Previous	Notes
☐ YV2027	LET L-410UVP	861713	YV-1023CP	

AEROPANAMERICANO

Reg	Type	C/n	Previous	Notes
☐ YV1674	Beech 1900C-1	UC-47	ex HK-4325	
☐ YV1734	Beech 1900	UB-47	ex YV-687CP	

AEROPOSTAL — Aeropostal (VH/LAV) — Caracas-Simon Bolivar Intl (CCS)

Reg	Type	C/n	Previous	Name	Notes
☐ YV1120	Douglas DC-9-51	47705/842	ex YV-20C	El Guayanes	
☐ YV1121	Douglas DC-9-51	47719/845	ex YV-21C	El Zuliano	
☐ YV1122	Douglas DC-9-51	47703/841	ex YV-22C	El Margariteno	
☐ YV1123	Douglas DC-9-32	47727/848	ex YV-24C	El Falconiano	
☐ YV1124	Douglas DC-9-32	47721/847	ex YV-25C	El Andino	
☐ YV1126	Douglas DC-9-51	47782/893	ex YV-33C	El Venezolano	
☐ YV1127	Douglas DC-9-34CF	47752/872	ex YV-37C	El Llanero	
☐ YV135T	Douglas DC-9-51	47712/815	ex YV-35C	El Larense	
☐ YV136T	Douglas DC-9-51 (ABS 3)	47738/830	ex YV-14C		
☐ YV137T	Douglas DC-9-51 (ABS 3)	47771/883	ex YV-15C		
☐ YV138T	Douglas DC-9-51	47656/783	ex YV-42C		
☐ YV139T	Douglas DC-9-51	47695/806	ex YV-43C		
☐ YV140T	Douglas DC-9-51	47694/805	ex YV-44C		
☐ YV141T	Douglas DC-9-32	47535/610	ex YV-46C		Lsd to/op for HON
☐ YV142T	Douglas DC-9-32	45847/394	ex YV-48C		
☐ YV143T	Douglas DC-9-32	47539/637	ex YV-49C	special colours	
☐ YV148T	Douglas DC-9-51	47713/820	ex YV-10C	id not confirmed	
☐ N120DL	Boeing 767-332	23279/154			Lsd fr RYN
☐ (YV1327)	McDonnell-Douglas MD-82	49103/1083	ex YV132T		stored MIA
☐ YV130T	McDonnell-Douglas MD-83	49822/1539	ex YV-01C		stored CCS
☐ YV-40C	Boeing 727-231 (Super 27)	21632/1462	ex N54345		stored CCS

AEROSERVICIOS OK

☐ YV1752	LET L-410UVP-E	861719	ex YV-1776C

AEROSERVICIOS RANGER — Caracas-La Carlota/Lagunillas/Tumeremo (-/LGY/TMO)

☐ YV-429C	Bell 206B JetRanger III	1959	ex N9910K
☐ YV-431C	Bell 206B JetRanger III	2588	
☐ YV-433C	Bell 206B JetRanger II	2106	ex YV-330CP
☐ YV-455C	Bell 206B JetRanger	1481	ex N218AL
☐ YV-457C	Bell 206B JetRanger III	2470	ex N50056
☐ YV-571C	Bell 206B JetRanger	273	ex N59Q
☐ YV-572C	Bell 206B JetRanger	644	ex N7906J
☐ YV1204	Britten-Norman BN-2A-26 Islander	56	ex YV-920C
☐ YV1241	Britten-Norman BN-2A-26 Islander	149	ex YV-921C

AEROTECHNICA — Acarigua (AGV)

☐ YV-101C	Bell 206B JetRanger	459	ex YV-C-GAA
☐ YV-103C	Bell 206B JetRanger III	3211	
☐ YV-104C	Bell 206B JetRanger	467	ex YV-C-GAH
☐ YV-105C	Bell 206B JetRanger	889	ex YV-C-GAL
☐ YV-106C	Bell 206B JetRanger	414	ex YV-C-GAM
☐ YV-108C	Bell 206B JetRanger III	2384	
☐ YV-109C	Bell 206B JetRanger III	2402	
☐ YV-110C	Bell 206B JetRanger	1119	ex N83005
☐ YV-112C	Bell 206B JetRanger III	3213	
☐ YV-115C	Bell 206B JetRanger II	2099	ex GN-7637
☐ YV-116C	Bell 206B JetRanger II	2190	ex N103K
☐ YV-117C	Bell 206B JetRanger III	2692	
☐ YV-118C	Bell 206B JetRanger III	3409	
☐ YV-122C	Bell 206B JetRanger II	1984	
☐ YV-124C	Bell 206B JetRanger III	2215	
☐ YV-251C	Bell 206B JetRanger	1106	ex YV-T-AIN
☐ YV-254C	Bell 206B JetRanger II	2059	ex N9934K
☐ YV-320C	Bell 206B JetRanger III	2248	
☐ YV-321C	Bell 206B JetRanger III	2496	
☐ YV-322C	Bell 206B JetRanger III	3359	
☐ YV-323C	Bell 206B JetRanger	874	
☐ YV-325C	Bell 206B JetRanger II	2095	ex GN7635
☐ YV-326C	Bell 206B JetRanger	1858	
☐ YV-327C	Bell 206B JetRanger	1355	ex YV-235CP
☐ YV-328C	Bell 206B JetRanger III	3308	
☐ YV-329C	Bell 206B JetRanger III	3336	
☐ YV-333C	Bell 206B JetRanger	1699	ex YV-141CP
☐ YV-121C	Bell 206L-1 LongRanger II	45501	ex N57480
☐ YV1465	Beech 65-E90 King Air	LW-234	ex YV-118CP
☐ YV-730C	Bell 412		

ASAP CHARTER

☐ YV1404	Yakovlev Yak-40	9441137	ex YV-1100CP	VIP

ASERCA AIRLINES — Aserca (R7/OCA) — Caracas-Simon Bolivar Intl (CCS)

☐ YV116T	Douglas DC-9-31	45867/283	ex YV-705C	Virgen del Valle	wfu 2008
☐ YV117T	Douglas DC-9-31	47272/390	ex YV-707C	Virgen de la Coromato wfu?	
☐ YV119T	Douglas DC-9-31	47271/389	ex YV-710C	Virgen de Loreto	
☐ YV122T	Douglas DC-9-31	45875/365	ex YV-706C	Virgen de la Chinita	
☐ YV125T	Douglas DC-9-31	47157/322	ex YV-719C	El Ejecutivas	yellow tail c/s
☐ YV241T	Douglas DC-9-31	48118/942	ex N942AA	San Rafael	all blue c/s
☐ YV297T	Douglas DC-9-31	48155/1050	ex N941AA	Nuestra Señora de Lourdes	
☐ YV298T	Douglas DC-9-31	48147/1048	ex N940AA		dam 12Feb08
☐ YV367T	Douglas DC-9-32	47128/210	ex N614NW	Nuestra Señora del Rosario	
☐ YV368T	Douglas DC-9-32	47518/614	ex N619NW	Madre Teresa de Calcuta	
☐ YV371T	Douglas DC-9-32	47235/436	ex N617NW	San Augustin	
☐ YV372T	Douglas DC-9-32	47575/680	ex N622NW	Santa Teresa de Jesus	
☐ YV1492	Douglas DC-9-31	45864/130	ex YV-708C	Virgen de Socorro	
☐ YV1663	Douglas DC-9-31	48144/1039	ex PJ-SNK	Virgen de La Milagrosa	
☐ YV1879	Douglas DC-9-31	48139/1024	ex YV114T	Virgen del Pilar	
☐ YV1921	Douglas DC-9-31	48154/1046	ex YV111T	Cristo de Jose	
☐ YV1922	Douglas DC-9-31	48138/1021	ex YV115T	Santisima Trinidad	
☐ YV2259	Douglas DC-9-31	48120/949	ex YV243T	San Miguel Arcangel	all green c/s
☐ YV2431	Douglas DC-9-31	48119/943	ex YV242T	San Francisco de Asis	
☐ YV2433	Douglas DC-9-31	48141/1030	ex YV244T	San Cristobal	
☐ YV2434	Douglas DC-9-31	47473/598	ex YV286T	San Judas Tadeo	
☐ YV2444	Douglas DC-9-32 (ABS 3)	47282/446	ex YV248T	Espiritu Santo	white c/s
☐ YV2445	Douglas DC-9-32 (ABS 3)	47479/605	ex YV249T	Juan Pablo II	white c/s
☐ YV	Douglas DC-9-32	47129/225	ex N615NW		
☐ YV	Douglas DC-9-31	47249/297	ex N977Z		stored ROW

☐ YV	Douglas DC-9-31	47343/460	ex N979Z	stored ROW

AVIOR AIRLINES — *Avior (9V/ROI)* — *Barcelona (BLA)*

☐ YV1364	Beech 1900D	UE-270	ex YV-401C	
☐ YV1365	Beech 1900D	UE-268	ex YV-402C	
☐ YV1366	Beech 1900D	UE-279	ex YV-403C	
☐ YV1367	Beech 1900D	UE-298	ex YV-404C	
☐ YV1368	Beech 1900D	UE-304	ex YV-406C	Lsd to ATK
☐ YV1369	Beech 1900D	UE-342	ex YV-438C	
☐ YV1370	Beech 1900D	UE-343	ex YV-466C	
☐ YV1371	Beech 1900D	UE-344	ex YV-503C	
☐ YV1372	Beech 1900D	UE-331	ex YV-660C	
☐ YV1373	Beech 1900D	UE-355	ex YV-663C	
☐ YV1374	Beech 1900D	UE-356	ex YV-664C	
☐ YV1360	Boeing 737-201 (Nordam 3)	21665/534	ex YV-917C	
☐ YV1361	Boeing 737-2H4 (AvAero 3)	22286/878	ex N85SW	
☐ YV187T	Boeing 737-2H4 (AvAero 3)	22964/933	ex N92SW	
☐ YV234T	Boeing 737-2H4 (AvAero 3)	21970/613	ex YV-643C	
☐ YV340T	Boeing 737-232 (Nordam 3)	23079/1003	ex N307DL	
☐ YV342T	Boeing 737-232 (Nordam 3)	23090/1020	ex N318DL	
☐ YV343T	Boeing 737-232 (Nordam 3)	23101/1041	ex N329DL	
☐ YV399T	Boeing 737-2Y5 (Nordam 3)	24031/1523	ex N810AL	
☐ YV1182	Cessna 208B Caravan I	208B0729	ex YV-659C	dam 21Jly07
☐ YV-925C	Cessna 208B Caravan I	208B0793	ex N52627	

CARIBBEAN FLIGHTS — *Valencia Intl (VLN)*

☐ YV-912C	Douglas DC-3	14506/25951	ex CP-2255	Falcon

CHAPI AIR

☐ YV1996	Britten-Norman BN-2A-7 Islander	242	ex YV178T

CIACA AIRLINES — *Ciudad Bolivar (CBL)*

☐ YV-866CP	LET L-410UVP-E	861717	ex HK-4159	
☐ YV-978C	LET L-410UVP	810702	ex CCCP-67066	stored
☐ YV-984C	LET L-410UVP-E	831015	ex CCCP-67387	
☐ YV-1097CP	LET L-410UVP	841303	ex YV-981C	
☐ YV-1070CP	Yakovlev Yak-40	9412032	ex RA-87388	

COMERAVIA — *(CVV)* — *Cuidad Bolivar (CBL)*

☐ YV1232	LET L-410UVP	810640	ex UR-67064
☐ YV1233	LET L-410UVP	851427	ex YV-1185C
☐ YV1332	LET L-410UVP	831028	ex YV-906C
☐ YV1333	LET L-401UVP-E	861709	ex YV-1108CP
☐ YV1962	LET L-410UVP	841216	ex YV-1071C
☐ YV	Short SD.3-60	SH3713	ex G-XPSS

CONVIASA — *Conviasa (V0/VCV)* — *Caracas-Simon Bolivar Intl (CCS)*

☐ YV1005	ATR 42-320	491	ex F-WQNK		
☐ YV1008	ATR 42-320	346	ex F-WQNB		
☐ YV1009	ATR 42-320	487	ex F-WQNL		
☐ YV1010	ATR 42-300	371	ex F-WQNC		
☐ YV1850	ATR 72-201	276	ex F-WQNE		
☐ YV2314	ATR 72-200				
☐ YV2421	ATR 72-212	482	ex F-WQNB		
☐ YV2422	ATR 72-212	486	ex F-WQNA		
☐ XA-TWR	Boeing 737-2H4 (AvAero 3)	21812/611	ex N60SW	no titles	Lsd fr DMJ
☐ YV1007	Boeing 737-322	23949/1493	ex N317UA		
☐ YV2556	Boeing 737-3G7	24712/1869	ex N311AW		
☐ YV2557	Boeing 737-3G7	24633/1809	ex N306AW		
☐ YV2558	Boeing 737-232 (Nordam 3)	23096/1028	ex XA-UIZ		
☐ YV2559	Boeing 737-232 (Nordam 3)	23097/1029	ex XA-UIY		
☐ YV101T	Boeing 737-291	21747/555	ex HR-ATX		
☐ YV206T	Boeing 737-205	21184/440	ex XA-MAG		
☐ YV398T	Boeing 737-25A (Nordam 3)	23789/1392	ex OB-1799-P		
☐ YV1000	de Havilland DHC-7-102	068	ex YV-1169C		
☐ YV1003	de Havilland DHC-7-102	103	ex C-FEDO		stored
☐ YV1004	Airbus A340-211	031	ex F-WQTN		
☐ YV1115	Canadair CL-600-2C10 (CRJ-702NG)	10271	ex N628CP		
☐ YV2088	Canadair CL-600-2C10 (CRJ-702NG)	10274	ex N259CP		
☐ YV2115	Canadair CL-600-2C10 (CRJ-702NG)	10275	ex N230CP		
☐ YV	Ilyushin Il-96-300	74392302014	ex RA-96014		on order

☐ YV	Ilyushin Il-96-300	74392302011	ex RA-96017	on order

HELITEC — *Maturin (MUN)*

☐ YV171T	Swearingen SA.227AC Metro III	AC-594	ex YV-1000C	
☐ YV256T	Swearingen SA.227DC Metro III	DC-899B	ex N3217P	
☐ YV1412	Swearingen SA.227TT Merlin IIIC	TT-465	ex YV-696CP	
☐ YV-808CP	Swearingen SA.227TT Merlin 300	TT-435	ex N92RC	

ISLAND AIR EXPRESS — *Caracas-Simon Bolivar Intl (CCS)*

☐ YV-774C	Dornier 28D-2 Skyservant	4111	ex YV-764CP	
☐ YV-776C	Dornier 28D-2 Skyservant	4144	ex YV-765CP	
☐ YV-779C	Dornier 28D-2 Skyservant			

KAVOK AIRLINES — *(KVA)*

☐ YV2472	British Aerospace Jetstream 32EP	973	ex N973JX	
☐ YV2532	British Aerospace Jetstream 32EP	910	ex N910AE	

LASER — *Laser (QL/LER)* — *Caracas-Simon Bolivar Intl (CCS)*

☐ YV1240	McDonnell-Douglas MD-81	49907/1734	ex N228RF		stored CCS
☐ YV1243	McDonnell-Douglas MD-81	49908/1749	ex N908RF		stored CCS
☐ YV1382	Douglas DC-9-14	45745/32	ex YV167T	Aldebaran	
☐ YV166T	Douglas DC-9-32	45789/217	ex YV-881C		stored CCS
☐ YV167T	Douglas DC-9-32 (ABS 3)	47281/427	ex YV-1121C		stored
☐ YV231T	Douglas DC-9-32	47133/230	ex HK-4310X		
☐ YV331T	Douglas DC-9-31	48157/1054	ex N934LK		
☐ YV332T	Douglas DC-9-31	48158/1056	ex N935DS		

LINEA AEREA IAACA — *Air Barinas (KG/BNX)* — *Barinas (BNS)*

☐ YV1929	ATR 72-212	492	ex YV-1004C	

LINEA TURISTICA AEREOTUY — *Aereotuy (LD/TUY)* — *Caracas-Simon Bolivar Intl (CCS)*

☐ YV1182	Cessna 208B Caravan I	208B0720	ex YV-659C	
☐ YV1184	de Havilland DHC-7-102	30	ex YV-639C	
☐ YV1185	de Havilland DHC-7-102	5	ex YV-638C	
☐ YV1188	Cessna 208B Caravan I	208B0955	ex YV-863C	
☐ YV	ATR 42-320	110	ex LN-FAP	
☐ YV383T	ATR 42-320	206	ex LN-FAR	
☐ YV-640C	de Havilland DHC-7-102	17	ex N47RM	stored CCS

ORIENTAL

☐ YV-594C	Yakovlev Yak-40	9841159	ex CU-T1221	
☐ YV-1072C	Yakovlev Yak-40	9841059	ex CU-T1220	

PERLA AIRLINES

☐ YV	McDonnell-Douglas MD-83	49232/1178	ex N931AS	stored PMV

RAINBOW AIR — *(TZR)* — *Porlomar*

☐ EX-024	Antonov An-26B	11901	ex RA-26096	
☐ YV307T	LET L-410UVP	800407	ex CCCP-67141	
☐ YV308T	LET L-410UVP	790307	ex CCCP-67111	
☐ YV322T	LET L-410UVP	800507	ex LZ-MNO	

RUTACA — *Rutaca (RUC)* — *Ciudad Bolivar (CBL)*

☐ YV-209C	Cessna U206D Super Skywagon	U206-1338	ex N72247	
☐ YV-210C	Cessna U206G Stationair 6	U20605354		
☐ YV-214C	Cessna U206F Stationair	U20602386	ex YV-138P	
☐ YV-229C	Cessna U206G Stationair	U20603541	ex YV-1153P	
☐ YV-379C	Cessna U206G Stationair 6	U20604150	ex YV-1633P	
☐ YV-785C	Cessna U206G Stationair	U20603889	ex YV-1314P	
☐ YV-786C	Cessna U206G Stationair 6	U20605125	ex YV-1719P	
☐ YV-789C	Cessna U206G Stationair 6	U20604803		
☐ YV-793C	Cessna U206F Stationair	U20603192		

☐ YV1360	Boeing 737-2H4 (AvAero 3)	23055/970	ex YV-162T	
☐ YV1381	Boeing 737-2S3 (Nordam 3)	21774/563	ex YV-216C	Vinotinto c/s
☐ YV169T	Boeing 737-2S3 (Nordam 3)	21776/577	ex YV-1155C	
☐ YV170T	Boeing 737-2M6	21231/462	ex YV-215C	
☐ YV367T	Boeing 737-230 (Nordam 3)	22113/649	ex OB-1837-P	
☐ YV379T	Boeing 737-230 (Nordam 3)	22115/694	ex N215AG	
☐ YV380T	Boeing 737-230 (Nordam 3)	22127/745	ex N227AG	
☐ YV200T	Boeing 737-230 (Nordam 3)	22128/752	ex N128AG	

☐ YV-245C	Embraer EMB.110P1 Bandeirante	110325	ex N103TN		stored CBL
☐ YV-247C	Embraer EMB.110P1 Bandeirante	110293	ex N901A		stored CBL
☐ YV-248C	Embraer EMB.110P1 Bandeirante	110376	ex N61DA		stored CBL
☐ YV-787C	Embraer EMB.110P1 Bandeirante	110403	ex N202EB	Curacao	stored CBL
☐ YV-790C	Cessna 208B Caravan I	208B0527	ex N5283S		
☐ YV1950	Cessna 208B Caravan I	208B0555	ex YV-791C		
☐ YV1670	Cessna 208B Caravan I	208B0608	ex YV-792C		
☐ YV-794C	Cessna 208B Caravan I	208B0795	ex N5264U		

SANTA BARBARA AIRLINES — *Santa Barbara (S3/BBR)* — *Maracaibo (MAR)*

☐ YV1421	ATR 42-320	300	ex YV-1017C	La Immaculada Concepcion	
☐ YV1422	ATR 42-320	340	ex YV-1018C	Virgen de Coromoto	
☐ YV1423	ATR 42-320	360	ex YV-1015C	Virgen del Carmen	
☐ YV1424	ATR 42-320	368	ex YV-1014C	Mi Chinita	
☐ YV1449	ATR 42-300	028	ex PR-TTC		
☐ YV2314	ATR 42-300	038	ex PR-TTD	El Fatima	
☐ YV288T	Boeing 757-21B	24402/233	ex N742PA		
☐ YV304T	Boeing 757-21B	24714/262	ex N816PG		
☐ YV2242	Boeing 757-236	24119/167	ex N962PG		
☐ YV2243	Boeing 757-236	24118/163	ex N958PG		
☐ YV	Boeing 767-27GER	27048/475	ex PR-VAC		
☐ YL-LCY	Boeing 767-3Y0ER	24952/357	ex C-GGFJ		Lsd fr LTC
☐ YL-LCZ	Boeing 767-3Y0ER	25000/386	ex C-GHPA		Lsd fr LTC
☐ YV-1038C	Cessna 208B Caravan I	208B0889	ex N52677		
☐ YV-1039C	Cessna 208B Caravan I	208B0901	ex N5267K		
☐ YV-1056C	Boeing 727-2D3 (Super 27)	22269/1701	ex N969PG		
☐ YV153T	McDonnell-Douglas MD-82	49486/1317	ex N486SH		on order
☐ YV	McDonnell-Douglas MD-82	49120/1071	ex N993PG		on order

SASCA — *Porlamar*

☐ YV2211	British Aerospace Jetstream 31	645	ex SE-LGC
☐ YV186T	British Aerospace Jetstream 3103	616	ex YV-1163C
☐ YV314T	British Aerospace Jetstream 31	721	ex YV176T
☐ YV315T	British Aerospace Jetstream	697	ex N827JS
☐ YV-1126C	Cessna 208B Caravan I	208B0781	ex N5268A

SERAMI — *Cuidad Bolivar (CBL)*

☐ YV219T	Beech 1900C-1	UC-118	ex YV-1150C

SOL AMERICA — *Solamerica (ESC)* — *Caracas-Simon Bolivar Intl (CCS)*

☐ (YV1415)	Douglas DC-3	16013/32761	ex YV-911C
☐ YV1416	Britten-Norman BN-2A Mk.III-2 Trislander	1034	ex YV-872C
☐ YV2117	Dornier 28D-2 Skyservant		
☐ YV-1120C	LET L-410UVP	841329	ex YV-982C

SOLAR CARGO — *Solarcargo (OLC)* — *Valencia (VLN)*

☐ YV1402	Antonov An-26	87307207	ex CU-T1501	Lsd fr CUB
☐ YV1403	Antonov An-26	17309810	ex YV-1134C	

SUNDANCE AIR

☐ YV1544	LET L-410UVP	831032	ex YV-1114C
☐ YV2063	LET L-410UVP	831010	ex YV-1025C
☐ YV-1029C	LET L-410UVP	831027	ex PZ-TGR
☐ YV	British Aerospace Jetstream 31	909	ex N490UE

TRANACA — *Ciudad Bolivar (CBL)*

☐ YV-922CP	LET L-410UVP	851426	ex LY-ASB

TRANSAVEN (VEN) — *Caracas-Simon Bolivar Intl (CCS)*

☐ YV1417	LET L-410UVP	830939	ex YV-980C
☐ YV1463	LET L-410UVP	861714	ex YV-864C
☐ YV2082	LET L-410UVP-E	902430	ex YV-1175C
☐ YV2083	LET L-410UVP-E	892314	ex YV-1113C
☐ YV-1117C	Britten-Norman BN-2A Mk.III-1 Trislander	1007	ex HP-899PS

TRANSCARGA INTERNATIONAL AIRWAYS — *Tiaca (TIW)* — *Caracas-Simon Bolivar Intl (CCS)*

☐ YV1149	Aero Commander 500B	500B-899	ex YV-941C	ex c/n 500A-899-B
☐ YV2546	Embraer EMB.120ER Brasilia	120017	ex N125AM	

TRANSMANDU — Ciudad Bolivar (CBL)

Reg	Type	C/n	Previous		
☐ YV1019	British Aerospace Jetstream 32	911	ex N491UE		
☐ YV	British Aerospace Jetstream 32	884	ex N476UE		

TRANSPORTE AIR IGLESIAS

Reg	Type	C/n	Previous		
☐ YV1844	LET L-410UVP	831114	ex YV-953C	no titles	

TRANSVALCASA

Reg	Type	C/n	Previous		
☐ YV128T	Swearingen SA.226T Merlin II	TT-507			

TURISMO AEREO AMAZONAS

Reg	Type	C/n	Previous		
☐ YV1157	LET L-410UVP	851412	ex HH-PRT		
☐ YV1219	LET L-410UVP	851319	ex YV1147C		

VENESCAR INTERNACIONAL — Vecar (V4/VEC) — Caracas-Simon Bolivar Intl (CCS)

Reg	Type	C/n	Previous		
☐ YV2308	ATR 42-300F	061	ex YV157T	302	DHL c/s
☐ YV2309	Boeing 727-31F (FedEx 3)	20114/712	ex YV156T		DHL c/s
☐ YV154T	Boeing 727-264F (FedEx 3)	20895/1049	ex YV-907C		DHL c/s
☐ YV155T	Boeing 727-223F (FedEx 3)	20992/1187	ex YV-905C	408	DHL c/s
☐ YV	Boeing 727-227F (FedEx 3)	21996/1571	ex N781DH		

VENEZOLANA — Venezolana (VNE) — Caracas-Simon Bolivar Intl (CCS)

Reg	Type	C/n	Previous		
☐ YV260T	Boeing 737-200				
☐ YV268T	Boeing 737-232 (AvAero 3)	23099/1035	ex N327DL		
☐ YV287T	Boeing 737-217 (AvAero 3)	22728/911	ex N168WP		Lsd to CUB
☐ YV295T	Boeing 737-217 (AvAero 3)	21717/581	ex N167WP		
☐ YV296T	Boeing 737-2T5 (AvAero 3)	22024/641	ex N166WP		
☐ YV302T	Boeing 737-2T5 (AvAero 3)	23087/1013	ex N315DL		
☐ YV341T	Boeing 737-232 (Nordam 3)	23087/1019	ex N317DL		
☐ YV191T	McDonnell-Douglas MD-83	49392/1272	ex N392AP		
☐ YV179T	British Aerospace Jetstream 31	759	ex YV-1086C		
☐ YV180T	British Aerospace Jetstream 31	770	ex YV-1093C		
☐ YV-1084C	British Aerospace Jetstream 31	734	ex OB-1784-T		
☐ YV-1085C	British Aerospace Jetstream 31	729	ex OB-1785-T		
☐ YV270T	British Aerospace Jetstream 41	41097	ex N329UE		
☐ YV280T	British Aerospace Jetstream 41	41027	ex N314UE		
☐ YV283T	British Aerospace Jetstream 41	41033	ex N315UE		
☐ YV293T	British Aerospace Jetstream 41	41026	ex N313UE		
☐ YV	British Aerospace Jetstream 41	41020	ex N306UE		
☐ YV	British Aerospace Jetstream 41	41029	ex N311UE		on order
☐ YV	British Aerospace Jetstream 41	41031	ex N317UE		on order

WYNGS AVIATION

Reg	Type	C/n	Previous		
☐ YV1106	Beech 1900D	UE-241	ex YV-1152CP		
☐ YV188T	Beech 1900D	UE-294	ex YV-955CP	all-white	

Operator Unknown

Reg	Type	C/n	Previous		
☐ YV1275	Antonov An-26	07310607	ex YV-965CP		
☐ YV2263	LET L-410UVP	872016	ex YV-1003CP		

Z- ZIMBABWE (Republic of Zimbabwe)

AIR ZIMBABWE — Air Zimbabwe (UM/AZW) — Harare-International (HRE)

Reg	Type	C/n	Previous	Name	
☐ Z-WPA	Boeing 737-2N0	23677/1313	ex C9-BAG	Mbuya Nehanda	
☐ Z-WPB	Boeing 737-2N0	23678/1405		Great Zimbabwe	
☐ Z-WPC	Boeing 737-2N0	23679/1415		Matojeni	
☐ Z-WPD	British Aerospace 146 Srs.200	E2065	ex G-5-065	Jongu'e	stored
☐ Z-WPE	Boeing 767-2N0ER	24713/287		Victoria Falls	
☐ Z-WPF	Boeing 767-2N0ER	24867/333		Chimanimani	
☐ Z-WPJ	CAIC MA60	0302	ex B-874L	Nyami-Nyami	
☐ Z-WPK	CAIC MA60	0303		A'sambeni	
☐ Z-WPL	CAIC MA60	0304			

AVIENT AVIATION — Avavia (Z3/SMJ) — Harare-International (HRE)

Reg	Type	C/n	Previous		
☐ Z-ALS	Douglas DC-10-30F	46976/254	ex N372BC		
☐ Z-ALT	Douglas DC-10-30F	47818/305	ex 5X-ROY		
☐ Z-ARL	Douglas DC-10-30CF	47907/157	ex N10MB		

☐ Z-AVT	Douglas DC-10-30F	46590/266	ex N401JR	Victor Trimble	
☐ Z-BVT	McDonnell-Douglas MD-11BCF	48410/495	ex N575SH		on order
☐ Z-WTV	Ilyushin Il-76T	073410279	ex 3C-QQD		

DHL AVIATION (ZIMBABWE) — Harare-International (HRE)

☐ Z-KPS	Cessna 208B Caravan I	208B0303	ex N31SE

EXEC-AIR — Axair (LFL) — Harare-Charles Prince

☐ Z-WFP	Cessna 402A	402A0013	ex VP-WFP
☐ Z-WLW	Cessna 210M Centurion II	21061178	ex N732UE
☐ Z-WOR	Piper PA-31 Turbo Navajo	31-35	ex ZS-JWF
☐ Z-WOU	Piper PA-31 Turbo Navajo	31-118	ex ZS-SWA
☐ Z-WRB	Cessna 402B	402B0032	ex N9475P

FALCON AIR — Harare-Charles Prince

☐ Z-DDD	Reims Cessna F406 Caravan II	F406-0069	ex F-GIQD	17
☐ Z-DDE	Reims Cessna F406 Caravan II	F406-0068	ex F-GIQC	15
☐ Z-DDF	Reims Cessna F406 Caravan II	F406-0071	ex F-GIQE	16
☐ Z-DDG	Reims Cessna F406 Caravan II	F406-0067	ex F-GEUG	14
☐ Z-WKN	Cessna T207 Skywagon	20700243	ex VP-WKN	

SKY RELIEF — Harare-Charles Prince

☐ 9Q-CSR	de Havilland DHC-5 Buffalo	7	ex 5Y-SRD		Lsd fr ALS, Kenya
☐ 5Y-SRE	de Havilland DHC-5 Buffalo	9	ex Z-SRE	ICRC colours	Lsd fr ALS, Kenya

SOUTHERN CROSS AVIATION — Victoria Falls (VFA)

☐ Z-THL	Cessna U206F Stationair	U20603233	ex N8372Q
☐ Z-WFA	Cessna T207 Staionair 8	20700098	ex VP-WFA

UNITED AIR CHARTERS — Unitair (UAC) — Harare-Charles Prince

☐ Z-BWK	Cessna U206G Stationair	U20603546	ex N8794Q
☐ Z-UAC	Beech 58 Baron	TH-211	ex 9J-ADK
☐ Z-UTD	Britten-Norman BN-2A Mk.III-2 Trislander	1055	ex A2-AGY
☐ Z-WHG	Beech 95-D55 Baron	TE-761	ex VP-WHG
☐ Z-WHH	Beech 65-80 Queen Air	LD-101	ex VP-WHH
☐ Z-WHX	Britten-Norman BN-2A-7 Islander	192	ex VP-WHX
☐ Z-WKL	Cessna U206F Stationair	U20601707	ex ZS-ILV
☐ Z-WTA	Cessna U206F Stationair	U20602547	ex OO-SPX
☐ Z-WTF	Cessna 414A Chancellor	414A0062	ex G-METR
☐ Z-YHS	Cessna U206C Super Skywagon	U206-1029	ex VP-YHS

ZA- ALBANIA (Republic of Albania)

ADA AIR — Ada Air (ZY/ADE) — Tirana (TIA)

☐ ZA-ADA	Embraer EMB.110P2 Bandeirante	110303	ex F-GCMQ	DHL titles

ALBANIAN AIRLINES — Albanian (LV/LBC) — Tirana (TIA)

☐ F-GTIP	Boeing 757-28Q/W	25624/541	ex N624AG
☐ OM-ASD	Boeing 737-306	23542/1317	ex PH-BDG
☐ OM-ASE	Boeing 737-306	23545/1343	ex PH-BDK
☐ OM-ASG	Boeing 757-28A	24544/280	ex N241LF
☐ ZA-MAK	British Aerospace 146 Srs.100	E1085	ex G-CCLN
☐ ZA-MAL	British Aerospace 146 Srs.200	E2054	ex G-BZWP
☐ ZA-MEV	British Aerospace 146 Srs.300	E3197	ex VH-EWS

BELLEAIR — (LZ/LBY) — Tirana (TIA)

☐ F-ORAD	Airbus A320-233	0558	ex F-HBAE	
☐ F-ORAE	Airbus A320-233	0561	ex F-HBAD	
☐ F-ORAF	Airbus A319-132	2335	ex D-ABGD	
☐ LZ-ATR	ATR 42-300	151	ex F-WQNC	Lsd fr HMS
☐ ZA-ARD	McDonnell-Douglas MD-82	49104/1085	ex N804NK	
☐ F-ORAA	ATR 72-212A	879	ex F-WWEH	

ZK- NEW ZEALAND (Dominion of New Zealand)

AIR CHATHAMS — Chatham (CV/CVA) — Chatham Island (CHT)

☐ ZK-CIA	Beech 65-B80 Queen Air	LD-430	ex N640K	
☐ ZK-CIB	Convair 580	327A	ex C-FCIB	
☐ ZK-CIC	Swearingen SA.227AC Metro III	AC-623B	ex N623AV	Freighter Lsd to OGN

Reg	Type	C/n	Previous reg	Name	Notes
☐ ZK-CID	Convair 580F	385	ex HZ-SN11		stored PMR
☐ ZK-CIE	Convair 580	399	ex N565EA		
☐ ZK-CIF	Convair 580	381	ex N566EA		Lsd to FAJ
☐ ZK-KAI	Cessna U206G Stationair	U20603711			
☐ ZK-LYP	Britten-Norman BN-2A-27 Islander	821	ex YR-BNO		

AIR FREIGHT NZ — Auckland-Intl (AKL)

Reg	Type	C/n	Previous reg	Notes
☐ ZK-FTA	Convair 580	168	ex C-GKFP	Freighter Op for Parceline
☐ ZK-KFH	Convair 580	42	ex C-FKFL	Freighter
☐ ZK-KFJ	Convair 580	114	ex C-GKFJ	Freighter
☐ ZK-KFL	Convair 580	372	ex C-FKFL	Freighter Op for Parceline
☐ ZK-KFS	Convair 5800	277	ex C-FKFS	Freighter

AIR NAPIER — Air Napier (NPR) — Napier (NPE)

Reg	Type	C/n	Previous reg
☐ ZK-ELK	Piper PA-32-260 Cherokee Six	32-7600009	ex N8768C
☐ ZK-MSL	Piper PA-34-200T Seneca II	34-7770224	ex N5600V
☐ ZK-NPR	Piper PA-31 Turbo Navajo B	31-777	ex ZK-DOM
☐ ZK-WUG	Piper PA-34-200T Seneca II	34-7970329	ex N2891R

AIR NATIONAL — Auckland-Intl (AKL)

Reg	Type	C/n	Previous reg	Name
☐ ZK-ECN	British Aerospace Jetstream 32EP	967	ex N967JS	City of Rotorua
☐ ZK-ECO	British Aerospace 146 Srs.200	E2130	ex C-GRNX	
☐ ZK-ECP	British Aerospace Jetstream 32EP	878	ex VH-BAE	

AIR NELSON — Link (RLK) — Nelson (NSN)

Wholly owned by Air New Zealand; operates as part of Air New Zealand Link (q.v.).

AIR NEW ZEALAND — NewZealand (NZ/ANZ) — Auckland-Intl/Wellington-Intl (AKL/WLG)

Member of Star Alliance

Reg	Type	C/n	Previous reg	Name	Notes
☐ ZK-OJA	Airbus A320-232	2085	ex F-WWIN		
☐ ZK-OJB	Airbus A320-232	2090	ex F-WWBM		
☐ ZK-OJC	Airbus A320-232	2112	ex F-WWDQ		
☐ ZK-OJD	Airbus A320-232	2130	ex F-WWDK		
☐ ZK-OJE	Airbus A320-232	2148	ex F-WWIH		
☐ ZK-OJF	Airbus A320-232	2153	ex F-WWIS		
☐ ZK-OJG	Airbus A320-232	2173	ex F-WWDJ		
☐ ZK-OJH	Airbus A320-232	2257	ex F-WWDE	Star Alliance c/s	
☐ ZK-OJI	Airbus A320-232	2297	ex F-WWBU		
☐ ZK-OJM	Airbus A320-232	2533	ex F-WWIB		
☐ ZK-OJN	Airbus A320-232	2594	ex F-WWBC		
☐ ZK-OJO	Airbus A320-232	2663	ex F-WWBM	Warner special c/s	
☐ ZK-NGD	Boeing 737-3U3	28732/2966	ex N930WA		
☐ ZK-NGE	Boeing 737-3U3	28733/2969	ex N931WA		
☐ ZK-NGF	Boeing 737-3U3	28734/2974	ex N309FL		
☐ ZK-NGG	Boeing 737-319	25606/3123	ex N1795B		
☐ ZK-NGH	Boeing 737-319	25607/3126	ex N1786B		
☐ ZK-NGI	Boeing 737-319	25608/3128	ex N1786B		
☐ ZK-NGJ	Boeing 737-319	25609/3130	ex N1786B		Last 737-300 built
☐ ZK-NGK	Boeing 737-3K2	26318/2731	ex PH-TSX		
☐ ZK-NGM	Boeing 737-3K2	28085/2722	ex PH-TSY		
☐ ZK-NGO	Boeing 737-37Q	28548/2961	ex G-OAMS		
☐ ZK-NGP	Boeing 737-33A	27459/3007	ex 9H-ADH		
☐ ZK-NGR	Boeing 737-33A	27460/3021	ex 9H-ADI		on order
☐ ZK-SJB	Boeing 737-33R	28868/2881	ex PP-SFK		
☐ ZK-SJC	Boeing 737-3U3	28738/2988	ex N308FL		
☐ ZK-SJE	Boeing 737-3K2	27635/2721	ex PH-TSZ		
☐ ZK-NBT	Boeing 747-419	24855/815	ex N6018N	Kaikoura	stored AKL
☐ ZK-NBU	Boeing 747-419	25605/933		Rotorua	
☐ ZK-NBV	Boeing 747-419	26910/1180		Christchurch	
☐ ZK-NBW	Boeing 747-419	29375/1228		Wellington	
☐ ZK-SUH	Boeing 747-419	24896/855	ex N891LF	Dunedin	
☐ ZK-SUI	Boeing 747-441	24957/971	ex N821LF	Queenstown	
☐ ZK-SUJ	Boeing 747-4F6	27602/1161	ex N756PR	Auckland	
☐ ZK-NCG	Boeing 767-319ER/W	26912/509			
☐ ZK-NCI	Boeing 767-319ER/W	26913/558	ex N6009F		
☐ ZK-NCJ	Boeing 767-319ER/W	26915/574	ex N6018N		
☐ ZK-NCK	Boeing 767-319ER/W	26971/663			
☐ ZK-NCL	Boeing 767-319ER/W	28745/677			
☐ ZK-OKA	Boeing 777-219ER	29404/534			
☐ ZK-OKB	Boeing 777-219ER	34376/537			
☐ ZK-OKC	Boeing 777-219ER	34377/546			
☐ ZK-OKD	Boeing 777-219ER	29401/550			

☐ ZK-OKE	Boeing 777-219ER	32712/564		
☐ ZK-OKF	Boeing 777-219ER	34378/575		
☐ ZK-OKG	Boeing 777-219ER	29403/591		
☐ ZK-OKH	Boeing 777-219ER	34379/605		

AIR NEW ZEALAND LINK — *New Zealand (NZ/NZA)* — *Christchurch-Intl/Nelson/Hamilton (CHC/NSN/HLZ)*

☐ ZK-MCA	ATR 72-212A	597	ex F-WQKC	Mount Cook
☐ ZK-MCB	ATR 72-212A	598	ex F-WQKG	Mount Cook
☐ ZK-MCC	ATR 72-212A	714	ex F-WQMV	Mount Cook
☐ ZK-MCF	ATR 72-212A	600	ex F-WQKH	Mount Cook
☐ ZK-MCJ	ATR 72-212A	624	ex F-WQKI	Mount Cook
☐ ZK-MCO	ATR 72-212A	628	ex F-WQKJ	Mount Cook
☐ ZK-MCP	ATR 72-212A	630	ex F-WQKK	Mount Cook
☐ ZK-MCU	ATR 72-212A	632	ex F-WQKL	Mount Cook
☐ ZK-MCW	ATR 72-212A	646	ex F-WQMG	Mount Cook
☐ ZK-MCX	ATR 72-212A	687	ex F-WQMN	Mount Cook
☐ ZK-MCY	ATR 72-212A	703	ex F-WQMR	Mount Cook
☐ ZK-EAA	Beech 1900D	UE-424	ex N2335Y	Eagle
☐ ZK-EAB	Beech 1900D	UE-425	ex N2335Z	Eagle
☐ ZK-EAC	Beech 1900D	UE-426	ex N51226	Eagle
☐ ZK-EAD	Beech 1900D	UE-427	ex N50127	Eagle
☐ ZK-EAE	Beech 1900D	UE-428	ex N3188L	Eagle
☐ ZK-EAF	Beech 1900D	UE-429	ex N50069	Eagle
☐ ZK-EAG	Beech 1900D	UE-430	ex N50430	Eagle
☐ ZK-EAH	Beech 1900D	UE-431	ex N51321	Eagle
☐ ZK-EAI	Beech 1900D	UE-432	ex N5032L	Eagle
☐ ZK-EAJ	Beech 1900D	UE-433	ex N4469Q	Eagle
☐ ZK-EAK	Beech 1900D	UE-434	ex N4474P	Eagle
☐ ZK-EAL	Beech 1900D	UE-435	ex N50815	Eagle
☐ ZK-EAM	Beech 1900D	UE-436	ex N5016C	Eagle
☐ ZK-EAN	Beech 1900D	UE-437	ex N50307	Eagle
☐ ZK-EAO	Beech 1900D	UE-438	ex N4470D	Eagle
☐ ZK-EAP	Beech 1900D	UE-439	ex N50899	Eagle
☐ ZK-EAR	Beech 1900D	UE-388	ex VH-EAS	Eagle
☐ ZK-NEA	de Havilland DHC-8Q-311	611	ex C-FCPO	Air Nelson
☐ ZK-NEB	de Havilland DHC-8Q-311	615	ex C-FDRG	Air Nelson
☐ ZK-NEC	de Havilland DHC-8Q-311	616	ex C-FEDG	Air Nelson
☐ ZK-NED	de Havilland DHC-8Q-311	617	ex C-FERB	Air Nelson
☐ ZK-NEE	de Havilland DHC-8Q-311	618	ex C-FFBY	Air Nelson
☐ ZK-NEF	de Havilland DHC-8Q-311	620	ex C-FFCC	Air Nelson
☐ ZK-NEG	de Havilland DHC-8Q-311	621	ex C-FFOZ	Air Nelson
☐ ZK-NEH	de Havilland DHC-8Q-311	623	ex C-FGAI	Air Nelson
☐ ZK-NEJ	de Havilland DHC-8Q-311	625	ex C-FFPA	Air Nelson
☐ ZK-NEK	de Havilland DHC-8Q-311	629	ex C-FHPZ	Air Nelson
☐ ZK-NEM	de Havilland DHC-8Q-311	630	ex C-FHQB	Air Nelson
☐ ZK-NEO	de Havilland DHC-8Q-311	633	ex C-FIOS	Air Nelson
☐ ZK-NEP	de Havilland DHC-8Q-311	634	ex C-FIOV	Air Nelson
☐ ZK-NEQ	de Havilland DHC-8Q-311	636	ex C-FJKL	Air Nelson
☐ ZK-NER	de Havilland DHC-8Q-311	639	ex C-FJKO	Air Nelson
☐ ZK-NES	de Havilland DHC-8Q-311	641	ex C-FJKP	Air Nelson
☐ ZK-NET	de Havilland DHC-8Q-311	642	ex C-FJKQ	Air Nelson
☐ ZK-NEU	de Havilland DHC-8Q-311	647	ex C-FLTZ	Air Nelson
☐ ZK-NEW	de Havilland DHC-8Q-311	648	ex C-FLUH	Air Nelson
☐ ZK-NEZ	de Havilland DHC-8Q-311	654	ex C-FNPY	Air Nelson
☐ ZK-NFA	de Havilland DHC-8Q-311	659	ex C-FPPN	Air Nelson
☐ ZK-NFB	de Havilland DHC-8Q-311	670	ex C-FVUG	Air Nelson
☐ ZK-NFI	de Havilland DHC-8Q-311	671	ex C-FWGQ	Air Nelson

AIR SAFARIS & SERVICES — *Airsafari (SRI)* — *Lake Tekapo*

☐ ZK-FJH	Cessna P206E Super Skylane	P206-0634	ex G-BKSI
☐ ZK-NMC	GAF N24A Nomad	N24A-034	ex VH-DHP
☐ ZK-NMD	GAF N24A Nomad	N24A-060	ex VH-DHU
☐ ZK-NME	GAF N24A Nomad	N24A-122	ex 5W-FAT
☐ ZK-SAE	Gippsland GA-8 Airvan	GA8-04-055	ex VH-VFF
☐ ZK-SAF	Gippsland GA-8 Airvan	GA8-02-017	ex VH-AAP
☐ ZK-SAZ	Gippsland GA-8 Airvan	GA8-05-078	
☐ ZK-SEY	Cessna T207A Stationair 8	20700661	ex N76012
☐ ZK-SRI	Cessna 208B Caravan I	208B0636	ex N208PR

AIR WANGANUI COMMUTER — *Wanganui (WAG)*

☐ ZK-MKG	Beech 65-C90A King Air	LJ-1367	ex N111MU
☐ ZK-WTH	Piper PA-31P-350 Mojave	31P-8414003	ex N9187Y

AIR2THERE.COM — *Paraparaumu (PPQ)*

☐ ZK-MYF	Partenavia P.68B	123	ex ZK-ERA		
☐ ZK-MYH	Cessna 208B Caravan I	208B0604	ex N64BP		
☐ ZK-MYS	Piper PA-31-350 Navajo Chieftain	31-7652032	ex ZK-MCM		

AIRWORK NEW ZEALAND — *Airwork (AWK)* — *Auckland-Ardmore/ Christchurch/ Wellington (AMZ/CHC/WLG)*

☐ ZK-NQC	Boeing 737-219C (Nordam 3)	22994/928		all-white	
☐ ZK-TLA	Boeing 737-3B7 (SF)	23383/1425	ex N508AU		Op for Toll Logistics
☐ ZK-TLC	Boeing 737-3B7 (SF)	23705/1497	ex N519AU		Op for Toll Logistics
☐ ZK-TLD	Boeing 737-3B7 (SF)	23706/1499	ex N520AU		on order Op for Toll Logistics
☐ ZK-LFT	Swearingen SA.227AC Metro III	AC-582	ex ZK-PAA		EMS Op for Life Flight NZ
☐ ZK-NSS	Swearingen SA.227AC Metro III	AC-692B	ex N2707D		EMS
☐ ZK-POB	Swearingen SA.227AC Metro III	AC-606B	ex D-CABG		Op for SkyLink
☐ ZK-POE	Swearingen SA.227CC Metro 23	CC-843B	ex N30228		Op for NZ Post
☐ ZK-POF	Swearingen SA.227CC Metro 23	CC-844B	ex N30229		
☐ ZK-FOP	Piper PA-31-350 Navajo Chieftain	31-7405227	ex N888SG		EMS
☐ ZK-NAO	Fokker F.27 Friendship 500	10364	ex 9V-BFK	all-white	Op for NZ Post
☐ ZK-PAX	Fokker F.27 Friendship 500	10596	ex HB-ILJ	all-white	
☐ ZK-POH	Fokker F.27 Friendship 500	10680	ex VT-NEH	all-white	Op for NZ Post

ASPIRING AIR(OI) — *Wanaka (WKA)*

☐ ZK-EVO	Britten-Norman BN-2A-26 Islander	785	ex 5W-FAQ		
☐ ZK-EVT	Britten-Norman BN-2A-26 Islander	152	ex YJ-RV19	Lake Wanaka	

EAGLE AIRWAYS — *(EX)* — *Hamilton (HLZ)*

50% owned by Air New Zealand; operates as part of Air New Zealand Link (q.v.)

FLIGHT 2000 — *Ardmore (AMZ)*

☐ ZK-DAK	Douglas DC-3	15035/26480	ex VH-SBT	RNZAF colours	

FLIGHT CORPORATION — *Flightcorp (FCP)* — *Nelson (NSN)*

☐ ZK-SKT	Cessna U206G Stationair 6 II	U20606609	ex CP-1783		
☐ ZK-TSD	Piper PA-34-200T Seneca II	34-8070356	ex ZK-DCQ		

GREAT BARRIER AIRLINES — *(AFW)* — *Auckland-Intl (AKL)*

☐ ZK-CNS	Piper PA-32-260 Cherokee Six	32-686	ex N3766W	Stitchbird	
☐ ZK-ENZ	Piper PA-32-260 Cherokee Six	32-1117	ex ZK-DBP	Tomtit	
☐ ZK-FVD	Britten-Norman BN-2A-26 Islander	316	ex G-BJWN	Pigeon	
☐ ZK-KTR	Britten-Norman BN-2A Islander	759	ex PK-VAB		
☐ ZK-LGC	Britten-Norman BN-2A Mk.III-1 Trislander	1042	ex G-RHOP		
☐ ZK-LGR	Britten-Norman BN-2A Mk.III-1 Trislander	372	ex VH-BSP		
☐ ZK-LOU	Britten-Norman BN-2A Mk.III-1 Trislander	322	ex VH-MRJ		
☐ ZK-NSN	Piper PA-31 Turbo Navajo	31-687	ex VH-CFP	Bellbird	
☐ ZK-PLA	Partenavia P.68B	86	ex A6-ALO	Tui	
☐ ZK-RDT	Embraer EMB.820C Navajo	820127	ex PT-RDT		
☐ ZK-REA	Britten-Norman BN-2A-26 Islander	43	ex ZK-FWH	Brown Teal	Lsd to Soundsair

HELI–HARVEST — *Taupo (TUO)*

☐ ER-MHH	Mil Mi-17 (Mi-8MTV-1)	96121	ex RA-25746		Lsd fr VLN
☐ ER-MHZ	Mil Mi-17 (Mi-8MTV-1)	96078	ex RA-22503		Lsd fr VLN

HELICOPTERS (NZ) — *Nelson (NSN)*

☐ ZK-HBU	Aérospatiale AS350B2 Ecureuil	2286	ex RP-C2188
☐ ZK-HDE	Aérospatiale AS350BA Ecureuil	1491	ex N5449B
☐ ZK-HDM	Aérospatiale AS350B2 Ecureuil	2262	ex N911MV
☐ ZK-HDO	Aérospatiale AS350B2 Ecureuil	2463	ex ZK-HNZ
☐ ZK-HDQ	Aérospatiale AS350BA Ecureuil	1932	ex VH-BHX
☐ ZK-HDR	Aérospatiale AS350B2 Ecureuil	2382	ex HB-XJC
☐ ZK-HFH	Aérospatiale AS350BA Ecureuil	2132	ex VH-WCU
☐ ZK-HFK	Aérospatiale AS350B2 Ecureuil	1397	ex VH-WCD
☐ ZK-HJE	Aérospatiale AS350BA Ecureuil	1307	ex N4428V
☐ ZK-HJQ	Aérospatiale AS350D AStar III	1295	ex C-FBXE
☐ ZK-HJV	Aérospatiale AS350B2 Ecureuil	2846	ex RP-C1712
☐ ZK-HJY	Aérospatiale AS350BA Ecureuil	2005	ex JA9463
☐ ZK-HND	Aérospatiale AS350B Ecureuil	1661	ex VH-HRD
☐ ZK-HNE	Aérospatiale AS350B2 Ecureuil	2811	ex HB-XLJ
☐ ZK-HNF	Eurocopter EC130B4	4461	ex C-GECV
☐ ZK-HNK	Aérospatiale AS350B2 Ecureuil	2349	ex VH-WCS

☐ ZK-HNQ	Aérospatiale AS350BA Ecureuil	1972	ex JA9450
☐ ZK-HNX	Aérospatiale AS350BA Ecureuil	1828	ex RP-C2777
☐ ZK-IBH	Aérospatiale AS350BA Ecureuil	2469	ex JA6067
☐ ZK-IVZ	Aérospatiale AS350B2 Ecueruil	4256	
☐ ZK-HDA	Bell 412	33066	ex N626LH
☐ ZK-HDY	Bell 412EP	36099	ex A6-HGS
☐ ZK-HIU	Agusta-Bell 412	25626	ex I-BRMA
☐ ZK-HNI	Bell 412SP	33204	ex 9M-AYW
☐ ZK-HNO	Bell 212	31139	ex VH-BQH
☐ ZK-HZE	Bell 206B JetRanger	769	ex C-FTPG
☐ ZK-HNZ	Agusta AW139	31103	
☐ VH-NZE	Agusta AW139	31146	ex ZK-HUL
☐ VH-NZF	Agusta AW139	31156	

HELIPRO — ***Helipro (HPR)*** — ***Palmerston North (PMR)***

☐ ZK-HRS	Bell 206B JetRanger	877	ex JA9087
☐ ZK-HYD	Aérospatiale AS350D Ecureuil	1258	ex N36079
☐ ZK-HYE	Kawasaki/MBB BK-117A-3	1008	ex JA9615
☐ ZK-HYI	Kawasaki/MBB BK-117B-2	1011	ex JA9620
☐ ZK-HYJ	Aérospatiale AS355F1 Ecureuil 2	5280	ex VT-ERU
☐ ZK-HYN	Aérospatiale AS355F1 Ecureuil 2	5286	ex JA9588
☐ ZK-HYD	Aérospatiale AS350D Ecureuil	1186	ex N155EH
☐ ZK-HYW	Aérospatiale AS350D Ecureuil	1420	ex N5782G
☐ ZK-HYZ	Kawasaki/MBB BK-117A-3	1010	ex ZK-HRQ

JETCONNECT — ***Qantas Jetconnect (QNZ)*** — ***Auckland-Intl (AKL)***

☐ ZK-JTP	Boeing 737-476	24441/2363	ex VH-TJP
☐ ZK-JTQ	Boeing 737-476	24442/2371	ex VH-JTQ
☐ ZK-JTR	Boeing 737-476	24439/2265	ex VH-TJN
☐ ZK-JTS	Boeing 737-476	28152/2829	ex VH-TJZ
☐ ZK-ZQA	Boeing 737-838/W	34200/2989	ex VH-VZF
☐ ZK-ZQB	Boeing 737-838/W	34201/3006	ex VH-VZG
☐ ZK-ZQC	Boeing 737-838/W	34202/3048	ex VH-VZH

LAKELAND HELICOPTERS — ***Rotorua (ROT)***

☐ ZK-HCH	Bell 206B JetRanger III	2258	ex N16859
☐ ZK-HIX	Bell 206B JetRanger	869	ex VH-YDA
☐ ZK-HSP	Bell UH-1H	5352	ex N226MS
☐ ZK-HZX	Bell UH-1H	11892	ex N3061A
☐ ZK-LHL	Cessna 425 Conquest I	425-0171	ex N51CU

MILFORD SOUND FLIGHTSEEING — ***Queenstown (ZQN)***

☐ ZK-DBV	Britten-Norman BN-2A Islander	164	ex VH-EQX	
☐ ZK-MCD	Britten-Norman BN-2A-26 Islander	719	ex G-BCAG	
☐ ZK-MCE	Britten-Norman BN-2A-26 Islander	724	ex G-BCHB	
☐ ZK-MFN	Britten-Norman BN-2B-26 Islander	2168	ex N2407B	
☐ ZK-MSF	Britten-Norman BN-2A-26 Islander	2037	ex OY-PPP	
☐ ZK-TSS	Britten-Norman BN-2A-26 Islander	2043	ex RP-C693	
☐ ZK-ZQN	Britten-Norman BN-2B-26 Islander	2197	ex G-BLNW	on order

MILFORD SOUND SCENIC FLIGHTS — ***Queenstown (ZQN)***

☐ ZK-DEW	Cessna 207 Skywagon	20700161	ex VH-UBQ
☐ ZK-DRY	Cessna 207 Skywagon	20700196	ex 5W-FAL
☐ ZK-LAW	Cessna 207A Stationair 8	20700723	ex N9750M
☐ ZK-SEW	Cessna T207A Stationair 6	20700584	ex N73394
☐ ZK-SEX	Cessna T207A Stationair 6	20700609	ex N73622
☐ ZK-WET	Cessna 207A Skywagon	20700375	ex VH-SLD

MOUNT COOK AIRLINE — ***Mountcook (NM/NZM)*** — ***Christchurch-Intl (CHC)***

77% owned by Air New Zealand; operates scheduled services as Air New Zealand Link in full colours using NZ flight numbers

MOUNTAIN AIR — ***Taumarunui***

☐ ZK-DLA	Britten-Norman BN-2B-26 Islander	2131	ex VH-ISL	
☐ ZK-DOV	Cessna 206 Super Skywagon	206-0248	ex N5248U	
☐ ZK-PIW	Piper PA-23-250 Aztec E	27-7305089	ex VH-RCI	
☐ ZK-PIX	Piper PA-23-250 Aztec E	27-4738	ex N14174	
☐ ZK-PIY	Britten-Norman BN-2A-20 Islander	344	ex JA5218	
☐ ZK-PIZ	Britten-Norman BN-2B-26 Islander	2012	ex N2132M	Great Barrier Xpress titles
☐ ZK-SFK	Britten-Norman BN-2A-6 Islander	236	ex VH-CPG	

PACIFIC BLUE — Bluebird (DJ/PBN) — Christchurch Intl (CHC)

☐ VH-VUM	Boeing 737-8BK/W	29675/2414			Lsd fr VOZ
☐ VH-VUN	Boeing 737-8BK/W	29676/2432			Lsd fr VOZ
☐ ZK-PBA	Boeing 737-8FE/W	33796/1377	ex VH-VOO	Bonnie Blue	Lsd fr VOZ
☐ ZK-PBB	Boeing 737-8FE/W	33797/1389	ex VH-VOP	Whitney Sundays	Lsd fr VOZ
☐ ZK-PBD	Boeing 737-8FE/W	33996/1551	ex (VH-VOY)	Pacific Pearl	Lsd fr VOZ
☐ ZK-PBF	Boeing 737-8FE/W	33799/1462	ex VH-VOR	Tapu'itea	Lsd fr VOZ
☐ ZK-PBG	Boeing 737-8FE/W	34015/1594	ex VH-VUD		Lsd fr VOZ
☐ ZK-PBI	Boeing 737-8FE/W	34440/2003	ex VH-VUH		Lsd fr VOZ
☐ ZK-PBJ	Boeing 737-8FE/W	34013/1573	ex VH-VUB		Lsd fr VOZ
☐ ZK-PBK	Boeing 737-8FE/W	36604/2650	ex VH-VUP		Lsd fr VOZ
☐ ZK-PBM	Boeing 737-8FE/W	36601/2525	ex VH-VUO		Lsd fr VOZ

PIONAIR ADVENTURES — Queenstown (ZQN)

☐ ZK-AMY	Douglas DC-3	13506	ex VH-CAN	Lady Jane

SALT AIR — Auckland-Intl (AKL)

☐ ZK-FOO	Cessna 207 Skywagon	20700075	ex P2-SED
☐ ZK-HBC	Bell 206B JetRanger	2112	ex JA9169
☐ ZK-MJL	Cessna 208B Caravan I	208B0861	ex N861CM
☐ ZK-SAL	Cessna 207 Skywagon	20700171	ex VH-GKZ

SOUNDSAIR — Wellington (WLG)

☐ ZK-ENT	Cessna U206G Stationair	U20603667	ex N7551N	
☐ ZK-KLC	Gippsland GA-8 Airvan	GA8-03-040	ex VH-BQR	
☐ ZK-PDM	Cessna 208 Caravan I	20800240	ex N1289N	
☐ ZK-REA	Britten-Norman BN-2A-26 Islander	43	ex ZK-FWH	Lsd fr AFW
☐ ZK-SAA	Cessna 208B Caravan I	208B0862	ex N208DG	

SOUTH EAST AIR — Invercargill (IVC)

☐ ZK-DIV	Piper PA-32-260 Cherokee Six	32-7400015	ex N57306
☐ ZK-FWZ	Britten-Norman BN-2A-26 Islander	52	ex T3-ATH
☐ ZK-FXE	Britten-Norman BN-2A-26 Islander	110	ex F-OCFR
☐ ZK-JEM	Cessna A185E Skywagon	18501780	ex VH-JBM
☐ ZK-RTS	Piper PA-32-300 Cherokee Six	32-7340070	

THE HELICOPTER LINE

Queenstown/Franz Josef Glacier/Fox Glacier/Mount Cook (ZQN/WHO/FGL/MON)

☐ ZK-HKR	Aérospatiale AS350D AStar III	1234	ex N3606X
☐ ZK-HLW	Aérospatiale AS350BA Ecureuil	1524	ex JA9307
☐ ZK-HNG	Aérospatiale AS350BA Ecureuil	2409	ex JA6039
☐ ZK-HKF	Aérospatiale AS355F1 Ecureuil 2	5200	ex VH-HJK
☐ ZK-HKY	Aérospatiale AS355F1 Twin Star	5123	ex N909CH
☐ ZK-HMB	Aérospatiale AS355F1 Twin Star	5016	ex N57812
☐ ZK-HMI	Aérospatiale AS355F1 Twin Star	5029	ex N5775Y
☐ ZK-HML	Aérospatiale AS355F1 Twin Star	5032	ex N5776A
☐ ZK-HPE	Aérospatiale AS355F1 Twin Star	5229	ex N58021
☐ ZK-HPI	Aérospatiale AS355F1 Twin Star	5211	ex N5802N
☐ ZK-HPZ	Aérospatiale AS355F1 Twin Star	5107	ex N87906

VINCENT AVIATION — Wellington (WLG)

☐ ZK-JSH	British Aerospace Jetstream 31	838	ex G-IBLW
☐ ZK-VAA	Reims Cessna F406 Caravan II	F4060012	ex ZK-CII
☐ ZK-VAB	Beech 1900D	UE-302	ex ZK-JND
☐ ZK-VAC	de Havilland DHC-8-102	60	ex ZK-NEZ
☐ ZK-VAD	Cessna 402C	402C0076	ex VH-COH
☐ ZK-VAE	Beech 1900C	UC-56	ex VH-OST
☐ ZK-VAF	Reims Cessna F406 Caravan II	F406-0057	ex F-ODYZ

ZP- PARAGUAY (Republic of Paraguay)

REGIONAL PARAGUAYA — Asuncion (ASU)

☐ ZP-CAH	Boeing 737-230 (Nordam 3)	22121/720	ex N212AG	Ciudad de Ascuncion
☐ ZP-CAJ	Boeing 737-230 (Nordam 3)	22124/727	ex N214AG	Ciudad de Luque
☐ ZP-CAQ	Boeing 737-201 (Nordam 3)	20211/141	ex 3C-HAC	

TAM MERCOSUR — Paraguaya (PZ/LAP) — Asuncion (ASU)

☐ ZP-CAR	Cessna 208A Caravan I	20800033	ex PT-OGZ

Also operates services with Fokker F.28-0100 (Fokker 100) aircraft leased from parent (80% owner), TAM Brasil, as required

ZS- SOUTH AFRICA (Republic of South Africa)

AIR-TEC AFRICA — Bethlehem

☐ ZS-MWM	LET L-410UVP-E20	912613	ex 7Q-YKV		
☐ ZS-OOF	LET L-410UVP-E20	871920	ex 5H-PAJ		Op for Air Express Algeria
☐ ZS-OSE	LET L-420	922729A	ex N420Y		Op for Air Express Algeria
☐ ZS-OUE	LET L-420	012735A	ex OK-GDM		Op for Air Express Algeria
☐ ZS-OXR	LET L-410UVP	972730	ex 5H-HSA		Op for Air Express Algeria
☐ ZS-PNI	LET L-410UVP-E20	871904	ex 5Y-BSV		
☐ 5Y-BRU	LET L-410UVP-E9	912539	ex 5X-UAY		Lsd to Aero Kenya
☐ 9G-LET	LET L-410UVP-E20	871922	ex ZS-OOH		Lsd to CTQ

AIRLINK — Link (4Z/LNK) — Johannesburg-OR Tambo (JNB)

☐ ZS-ASW	Avro 146-RJ85	E2313	ex N505XJ		Lsd fr SFR
☐ ZS-ASX	Avro 146-RJ85	E2314	ex N506XJ		Lsd fr SFR
☐ ZS-ASY	Avro 146-RJ85	E2316	ex N507XJ		Lsd fr SFR
☐ ZS-ASZ	Avro 146-RJ85	E2318	ex N508XJ		Lsd fr SFR
☐ ZS-PUL	British Aerospace 146 Srs.200	E2064	ex G-JEAV		
☐ ZS-PUM	British Aerospace 146 Srs.200	E2059	ex G-JEAW		
☐ ZS-PUZ	British Aerospace 146 Srs.200	E2074	ex EI-CSL		
☐ ZS-PYM	British Aerospace 146 Srs.200	E2058	ex EI-CWA		
☐ ZS-NRE	British Aerospace Jetstream 41	41048	ex G-4-048		
☐ ZS-NRF	British Aerospace Jetstream 41	41050	ex G-4-050		
☐ ZS-NRG	British Aerospace Jetstream 41	41051	ex G-4-051		
☐ ZS-NRH	British Aerospace Jetstream 41	41054	ex G-4-054		
☐ ZS-NRI	British Aerospace Jetstream 41	41061	ex G-4-061		
☐ ZS-NRJ	British Aerospace Jetstream 41	41062	ex G-4-062		
☐ ZS-NRK	British Aerospace Jetstream 41	41065	ex G-4-065		Lsd to SZL
☐ ZS-NRL	British Aerospace Jetstream 41	41068	ex G-4-068		
☐ ZS-OEX	British Aerospace Jetstream 41	41103	ex G-4-103		
☐ ZS-OMF	British Aerospace Jetstream 41	41034	ex G-MSKJ		
☐ ZS-OMS	British Aerospace Jetstream 41	41035	ex VH-JSX		
☐ ZS-OMY	British Aerospace Jetstream 41	41036	ex VH-CCJ		
☐ ZS-OMZ	British Aerospace Jetstream 41	41037	ex VH-CCW		
☐ ZS-OTM	Embraer EMB.135LR (ERJ-135LR)	145485	ex PT-SXE		
☐ ZS-OTN	Embraer EMB.135LR (ERJ-135LR)	145491	ex PT-SXK		
☐ ZS-OUV	Embraer EMB.135LR (ERJ-135LR)	145493	ex PT-SXM		Op as Airlink Zimbabwe
☐ ZS-SJW	Embraer EMB.135LR (ERJ-135LR)	145423	ex PT-STU		
☐ ZS-SJX	Embraer EMB.135LR (ERJ-135LR)	145428	ex PT-STZ		
☐ ZS-	Embraer EMB.135LR (ERJ-135LR)	145551	ex N845RP		
☐ ZS-SNY	Embraer EMB.135LR (ERJ-135LR)	145620	ex N844RP		
☐ ZS-	Embraer EMB.135LR (ERJ-135LR)	145720	ex N838RP		
☐ ZS-SNZ	Embraer EMB.135LR (ERJ-135LR)	145725	ex N840RP		

AIRQUARIUS AVIATION — Quarius (AQU) — Lanseria (HLA)

☐ ZS-GAV	Boeing 737-2L9	22735/825	ex PK-RIR		
☐ ZS-DRF	Fokker F.28 Fellowship 4000	11239	ex 5Y-LLL	Lynne	
☐ ZS-JAV	Fokker F.28 Fellowship 4000	11161	ex N493US		Lsd to RJA
☐ ZS-JES	Fokker F.28 Fellowship 4000	11236	ex 5H-MVK		
☐ ZS-XGW	Fokker F.28 Fellowship 4000	11130	ex SE-DGN		

AWESOME FLIGHT SERVICES — Awesome (ASM) — Lanseria (HLA)

☐ ZS-JAZ	Beech 1900D	UE-6	ex VT-AVJ		
☐ ZS-OYD	Beech 1900D	UE-191	ex VH-IAR		
☐ ZS-SNO	Beech 1900D	UE-96	ex VH-NIA		

BIONIC AIR

☐ ZS-PVU	Boeing 737-2Q8C	21959/610	ex N741AS		
☐ ZS-SMO	British Aerospace 146 Srs.300	E3169	ex G-BSNS		

BRANSON AIR

☐ ZS-KIS	Boeing 737-291	22743/909	ex CC-CVG		

CHC HELICOPTERS (AFRICA) — Cape Town-International (CPT)

☐ ZS-HVJ	Sikorsky S-61N	61493	ex N9119Z		stored
☐ ZS-RDV	Sikorsky S-61N	61716	ex G-BIHH		based SSG
☐ ZS-RLK	Sikorsky S-61N	61772	ex G-BEWM		
☐ ZS-RLL	Sikorsky S-61N	61778	ex G-BFFK		
☐ ZS-RKO	Sikorsky S-76A++	760135	ex VH-LAX		

☐ ZS-RKP	Sikorsky S-76A++	760198	ex VH-LAY	Marine 2	
☐ ZS-RNG	Sikorsky S-76A++	760036	ex D2-EXJ		based BSG Lsd fr CHC Scotia
☐ ZS-RPI	Sikorsky S-76A++	760049	ex G-BHGK		based BSG Lsd fr CHC Scotia

☐ D2-EVP	Aérospatiale AS.332L2 II	2398	ex F-WQEA		Lsd to SOR
☐ ZS-KEI	Convair 580	141	ex N5822		
☐ ZS-LYL	Convair 580	39	ex N511GA		
☐ ZS-RDI	Bell 206L-3 LongRanger III	51392	ex N521EV		
☐ ZS-RGV	Bell 212	30952	ex C-FRUU		
☐ ZS-RNP	Bell 212	30893	ex C-FPKW		based Malabo
☐ ZS-RNR	Bell 212	30829	ex C-FRWL		based Malabo

A member of CHC Helicopter Corp; operates from bases in Equatorial Guinea, Namibia and Angola as well as South Africa

CIVAIR — *Civflight (CIW)* — *Cape Town-International (CPT)*

☐ ZS-FWB	Beech 95-D55 Baron	TE-726	ex 9J-FWB
☐ ZS-HGO	Bell 206B JetRanger III	2450	
☐ ZS-HVY	Bell 206B JetRanger	1471	ex N59605
☐ ZS-MUM	Beech 65-B90 King Air	LJ-408	ex N481SA
☐ ZS-RGG	MBB Bo.105C	S-52	ex N291CA
☐ ZS-RGH	Bell 206B JetRanger III	3212	ex N3898P

COMAIR — *Commercial (MN/CAW)* — *Johannesburg-OR Tambo (JNB)*

☐ ZS-NNH	Boeing 737-236	21797/653	ex PH-TSD	Kulula special colours	
☐ ZS-OAA	Boeing 737-4L7	26960/2483	ex VH-RON		
☐ ZS-OAF	Boeing 737-4S3	25116/2061	ex PP-VTL	Kulula colours	
☐ ZS-OAG	Boeing 737-4H6	27168/2435	ex JA737D	Kulula colours	
☐ ZS-OAH	Boeing 737-33A	24460/1831	ex N460TF	Kulula colours	
☐ ZS-OAI	Boeing 737-33A	24030/1654	ex N240TF	Kulula colours	
☐ ZS-OAM	Boeing 737-4S3	24164/1702	ex EI-DFE	Kulula colours	
☐ ZS-OAO	Boeing 737-4S3	24163/1700	ex EI-DFD	Kulula colours	
☐ ZS-OAP	Boeing 737-4S3	24167/1736	ex EI-DFF	Kulula colours	
☐ ZS-OAV	Boeing 737-4H6	27086/2426	ex JA737C		
☐ ZS-OKB	Boeing 737-376	23477/1225	ex VH-TAF	BAW colours	
☐ ZS-OKC	Boeing 737-376	23484/1270	ex VH-TAJ	BAW colours	
☐ ZS-OKG	Boeing 737-376	23483/1264	ex VH-TAI	BAW colours	
☐ ZS-OKH	Boeing 737-376	23479/1259	ex VH-TAH	BAW colours	
☐ ZS-OKI	Boeing 737-376	23489/1356	ex VH-TAX	BAW colours	
☐ ZS-OKJ	Boeing 737-376	23487/1306	ex VH-TAV	BAW colours	
☐ ZS-OKK	Boeing 737-376	23485/1277	ex VH-TAK	BAW colours	
☐ ZS-OLA	Boeing 737-236	23163/1058	ex G-BKYE	BAW colours	
☐ ZS-OLB	Boeing 737-236	23167/1074	ex G-BKYI	BAW colours	
☐ ZS-OTF	Boeing 737-436	25305/2147	ex G-DOCC	Kulula colours	Lsd fr SFR
☐ ZS-OTG	Boeing 737-436	25840/2197	ex G-DOCJ	BAW colours	Lsd fr SFR
☐ ZS-OTH	Boeing 737-436	25841/2222	ex G-DOCK	kulula special colours	Lsd fr SFR
☐ ZS-ZWO	Boeing 737-8K2/W	28373/51	ex PH-HZA		
☐ ZS-ZWP	Boeing 737-86N/W	28612/455	ex OK-PIK		

CTK CITYLINK

☐ ZS-CTK	SAAB SF.340A	340A-068	ex N68XJ	all-white

DHL AVIATION — *Worldstar (DHV)* — *Lanseria (HLA)*

Utilises Cessna 208B Caravans and ATR 42 operated by Solenta Aviation in full DHL colours

DODSON INTERNATIONAL CHARTER — *Pretoria-Wonderboom (PRY)*

☐ ZS-OJJ	AMI Turbo DC-3TP	16213/32961	ex N8194Q		Op for UN / Red Cross
☐ ZS-OJK	AMI Turbo DC-3TP	14165/25610	ex SAAF 6844		
☐ ZS-OJL	AMI Turbo DC-3TP	16565/33313	ex SAAF 6858		stored PRY
☐ ZS-OJM	AMI Turbo DC-3TP	14101/25546	ex N330RD	white colours	

EAST COAST AIRWAYS — *Eastway (ECT)* — *Durban-Virginia (VIR)*

☐ ZS-LAX	Beech Baron 58	TH-1268	ex G-BMGI

EGOLI AIR — *Johannesburg-Rand (QRA)*

☐ ZS-PSO	Antonov An-32B	2808	ex RA-48059

EXECUTIVE AEROSPACE — *Aerospace (EAS)* — *Johannesburg-OR Tambo (JNB)*

☐ ZS-AGB	Hawker Siddeley HS.748 Srs.2B/501	1807	ex 4R-LPV	stored JNB
☐ ZS-LSO	Hawker Siddeley HS.748 Srs.2B/FAA	1783	ex G-BMJU	
☐ ZS-NNW	Hawker Siddeley HS.748 Srs.2B/378	1785	ex G-BOHZ	stored DUR
☐ ZS-NWW	Hawker Siddeley HS.748 Srs.2B/378	1786	ex G-HDBC	stored JNB
☐ ZS-PLO	Hawker Siddeley HS.748 Srs.2B/378	1797	ex G-EMRD	
☐ ZS-TPW	Hawker Siddeley HS.748 Srs.2B/378	1784	ex (ZS-KLC)	stored JNB

EXECUTIVE TURBINE AIR CHARTER — Lanseria (HLA)

Reg	Type	C/n	Prev		Notes
☐ ZS-LFM	Beech 200 Super King Air	BB-954	ex N1839S		
☐ ZS-MES	Beech 200 Super King Air	BB-1038	ex N223MH		
☐ ZS-NTL	Beech 200 Super King Air	BB-85	ex V5-CIC		
☐ ZS-PRA	Beech B200 Super King Air	BB-1340	ex OY-GMA		Beech 1300 conversion
☐ ZS-PRC	Beech B200 Super King Air	BB-1341	ex OY-GEU		Beech 1300 conversion
☐ ZS-XGD	Beech 200 Super King Air	BB-286	ex Z-MRS		
☐ ZS-OKU	Beech 1900C-1	UC-50	ex 7Q-NXA		
☐ ZS-OLP	Beech 1900C	UB-18	ex Z-DHS		
☐ ZS-OUG	Beech 1900D	UE-14	ex VT-AVI	all-white	
☐ ZS-OYF	Beech 1900D	UE-214	ex VH-IMS		
☐ ZS-OYG	Beech 1900D	UE-230	ex 5N-BCQ	all-white	
☐ ZS-PHL	Beech 1900C-1	UC-74	ex N374UC		
☐ ZS-PJY	Beech 1900D	UE-204	ex N204GL		
☐ ZS-PKB	Beech 1900D	UE-3	ex N3YV		Lsd to TravelMax
☐ ZS-PPI	Beech 1900C	UE-179	ex N179GL		
☐ ZS-PPM	Beech 1900D	UE-150	ex N150GL	UNHS	
☐ ZS-ETA	Embraer EMB.120ER Brasilia	120277	ex N213SW		

FEDERAL AIR — Fedair (FDR) — Durban-Virginia (VIR)

Reg	Type	C/n	Prev		Notes
☐ ZS-DAT	Pilatus PC-12/45	242	ex HB-FRM		
☐ ZS-FDR	Beech 200 Super King Air	BB-1234	ex N971LE		
☐ ZS-FDL	Cessna 208B Caravan I	208B0896	ex 5Y-TWJ		
☐ ZS-KNL	Cessna 402C II	402C0646	ex N6814D		
☐ ZS-LXO	Beech Baron 58	TH-886	ex N23527		
☐ ZS-NAV	Beech 1900C	UB-62	ex VH-IYP		
☐ ZS-NVH	Cessna 208B Caravan I	208B0473	ex N1287N		
☐ ZS-OJC	Cessna 208B Caravan I	208B0593	ex N1194F		
☐ ZS-OXN	Beech 1900D	UE-83	ex N831SK	all-white	
☐ ZS-PUC	Beech 1900D	UE-84	ex N841SK		
☐ ZS-PRH	Beech 1900D	UE-316	ex N21716	all-white	
☐ ZS-PWY	Beech 1900D	UE-87	ex N87SK	all-white	
☐ 5H-FED	Cessna 208B Caravan I	208B0571	ex ZS-FED		

FUGRO AIRBORNE SURVEYS — Lanseria (HLA)

Reg	Type	C/n	Prev	Notes
☐ ZS-AIU	Cessna 404 Titan II	404-0082	ex A2-AIU	
☐ ZS-FSA	Cessna 208B Caravan I	208B0877	ex N208LW	
☐ ZS-FTA	Cessna 210N Centurion II	21063562	ex VH-JBH	
☐ ZS-KRG	Cessna 404 Titan II	404-0676	ex N6761Y	
☐ ZS-SSA	Cessna 208B Caravan I	208B0712	ex D-FLIZ	
☐ ZS-SSB	Cessna 208B Caravan I	208B0860	ex N124AA	

IMPERIAL AIR CARGO — Johannesburg-OR Tambo (JNB)

Reg	Type	C/n	Prev	Notes
☐ ZS-IAC	Boeing 727-227F (Raisbeck 3)	21247/1217	ex N73751	Lsd fr SFR
☐ ZS-SMG	Boeing 737-3Y0F	23499/1242	ex VP-BCJ	
☐ ZS-	Boeing 737-3Y0F	23500/1243	ex VP-BCN	on order

INTER-AIR — Inline (D6/ILN) — Johannesburg-OR Tambo (JNB)

Reg	Type	C/n	Prev	Notes
☐ ZS-IJI	Boeing 707-323C (Comtran 2)	19517/614	ex N29AZ	stored Pietersburg
☐ ZS-IJJ	Boeing 737-2H7C	20591/309	ex N24AZ	stored Pietersburg
☐ ZS-IJK	Boeing 727-61 (FedEx 3)	19176/290	ex 3D-ZZN	
☐ ZS-IJN	Fokker F.28 Fellowship 4000	11118	ex 3D-DAW	
☐ ZS-SIH	Boeing 737-244	22587/835		
☐ ZS-SIM	Boeing 737-244	22828/881		Lsd fr SFR
☐ 3D-ITC	Boeing 727-2F2	21260/1222	ex N103AZ	op by RFC

INTERLINK AIRLINES — Interlink (ID/ITK) — Johannesburg-OR Tambo (JNB)

Reg	Type	C/n	Prev
☐ ZS-OLC	Boeing 737-230	22119/714	ex N219AS
☐ ZS-PVF	Embraer EMB.120RT Brasilia	120261	ex EC-HFZ
☐ ZS-SIC	Boeing 737-244F	22582/805	ex OB-1806-P
☐ ZS-SIN	Boeing 737-236	21802/670	ex CC-CHS
☐ ZS-SIP	Boeing 737-230	22116/701	ex N392AS

KING AIR CHARTER — Lanseria (HLA)

Reg	Type	C/n	Prev
☐ ZS-HFG	Bell 206B JetRanger	1864	
☐ ZS-JSC	Beech B200 Super King Air	BB-1985	ex N71850
☐ ZS-LFW	Beech B200 Super King Air	BB-999	ex 9Q-CPV
☐ ZS-LRS	Beech B200C Super King Air	BL-20	ex 5Y-LRS
☐ ZS-MPC	Cessna 402C II	402C0426	ex C9-MEB
☐ ZS-NHW	Grumman G-159 Gulfstream I	141	ex N800PA
☐ ZS-OED	Beech B200 Super King Air	BB-1149	ex N200HF
☐ ZS-OOW	Beech 1900D	UE-57	ex N57YV

☐ ZS-OZE Cessna 208B Caravan I 208B0786 ex N208AH
☐ ZS-RFS Bell 206L-4 LongRanger IV 52116 ex N4252S

KULULA.COM — Johannesburg-OR Tambo (JNB)

Wholly owned low cost, no frills subsidiary of Comair who operate the aircraft

MANGO — (JE) — Johannesburg-OR Tambo (JNB)

☐ ZS-SJG Boeing 737-8BG/W 32353/711 ex N1786B Lsd fr SAA
☐ ZS-SJH Boeing 737-8BG/W 32354/725 ex PH-HZQ Lsd fr SAA
☐ ZS-SJK Boeing 737-8BG/W 32355/807 ex PH-HZT Lsd fr SAA
☐ ZS-SJL Boeing 737-8BG/W 32356/819 ex PH-HZZ Lsd fr SAA

NAC CHARTER — Slipstream (SLE) — Lanseria (HLA)

☐ ZS-NBJ Beech B200 Super King Air BB-1070 ex SE-KND
☐ ZS-OBB Beech B200 Super King Air BB-1522 ex N3272E
☐ ZS-OCI Beech 200 Super King Air BB-121 ex TR-LDX
☐ ZS-ODI Beech B200 Super King Air BB-1542 ex N202JT
☐ ZS-OUI Beech B200 Super King Air BB-688 ex 5R-MGH Catpass 250 conversion
☐ ZS-SMC Beech B200 Super King Air BB-1489 ex N1563M

☐ ZS-OMB Beech 1900D UE-81 ex N81SK all-white
☐ ZS-ORV Beech 1900D UE-42 ex N42YV all-white
☐ ZS-OSF Beech 1900D UE-35 ex N35YV
☐ ZS-PBZ Beech 1900C-1 UC-126 ex N139GA
☐ ZS-PMF Beech 1900C-1 UC-37 ex N32017
☐ ZS-SGH Beech 1900D UE-263 ex CN-RLB
☐ ZS-SHH Beech 1900D UE-36 ex N136MJ
☐ ZS-SNJ Beech 1900D UE-131 ex N131YV
☐ ZS-SNK Beech 1900D UE-132 ex N132YV

☐ ZS-HKV Aérospatiale AS350B Ecureuil 1528
☐ ZS-MKI Beech 65-C90A King Air LJ-1099 ex Z-MKI
☐ ZS-PNN Beech 95-B55 Baron TC-1794 ex A2-EAH
☐ ZS-RDR Bell 206B JetRanger III 4183 ex Z-RDR
☐ ZS-RJO Bell 407 53206
☐ ZS-RPC Bell 407 53365 ex C-GAHJ
☐ ZS-TVT Beech Baron 58 TH-1962 ex N584j

NATURELINK CHARTER — Naturelink Southafri (NRK) — Pretoria-Wonderboom (PRY)

☐ ZS-ACS Beech 200 Super King Air BB-961 ex A2-AHA
☐ ZS-KGW Beech 200 Super King Air BB-381 ex N4848M
☐ ZS-PLJ Beech B200 Super King Air BB-1401 ex VH-YDH based Kabul
☐ ZS-PLL Beech B200 Super King Air BB-1189 ex VH-KBH based Kabul

☐ ZS-OEN Embraer EMB.120RT Brasilia 120200 ex N200CD Lsd to Elysian
☐ ZS-PGY Embraer EMB.120RT Brasilia 120194 ex N269UE
☐ ZS-POE Embraer EMB.120RT Brasilia 120137 ex N137H
☐ ZS-PPF Embraer EMB.120RT Brasilia 120156 ex N156CA Op for UNHCR
☐ ZS-PSB Embraer EMB.120RT Brasilia 120196 ex N196CA based Comores Lsd to MBN
☐ ZS-PUH Embraer EMB.120RT Brasilia 120151 ex N196SW sublsd to SWX
☐ ZS-PYO Embraer EMB.120RT Brasilia 120245 ex N256CA
☐ ZS-SRW Embraer EMB.120RT Brasilia 120018 ex N95644

☐ ZS-KMN Beech 58 Baron TH-153 ex F-ODMJ
☐ ZS-OXV Cessna 208B Caravan I 208B0563 ex N330AK
☐ ZS-PCC Beech 1900C-1 UC-143 ex 9J-AFW all-white Lsd fr City Square 526
☐ ZS-PFL Cessna 208B Caravan I 208B0505 ex N880MA
☐ ZS-RWN Aérospatiale AS350BA Ecureuil 1866 ex F-GJAM

NELAIR CHARTERS & TRAVEL — Nelair (NLC) — Nelspruit (NLP)

☐ ZS-EDG Cessna U206 Super Skywagon U206-0382 ex N2182F
☐ ZS-EVB Piper PA-30 Twin Comanche 160B 30-1218 ex N8134Y
☐ ZS-IKZ Piper PA-32-300 Cherokee Six E 32-7240070 ex ZS-XAS
☐ ZS-JGW Cessna 401B 401B0106 ex N7966Q
☐ ZS-JTX Piper PA-31-350 Navajo Chieftain 31-7652059 ex N59800
☐ ZS-JZX Piper PA-34-200T Seneca II 34-7770269 ex N5911V
☐ ZS-LTL Cessna 310Q 310Q0025 ex N8925Z
☐ ZS-LVR Douglas DC-3 20176 ex N5000E
☐ ZS-MHE Piper PA-31-350 Navajo Chieftain 31-7305096 ex N74950
☐ ZS-MSO Piper PA-32-300 Cherokee Six 32-7540083 ex N33050
☐ ZS-NAO Cessna T210L Centurion II 21060092 ex N59104
☐ ZS-NKG Cessna 208 Caravan I 20800178 ex 5Y-NKG
☐ ZS-PCN Cessna U206F Stationair U20602450 ex N1080V
☐ ZS-PHI Grumman G-159 Gulfstream I 164 ex N290AS
☐ ZS-PHJ Grumman G-159 Gulfstream I 134 ex 3D-DUE
☐ ZS-PHK Grumman G-159 Gulfstream I 025 ex 3D-DLN
☐ ZS-RAN Cessna 402B 402B0439 ex ZS-XAV

NORSE AIR CHARTER — Norse Air (NRX) — Lanseria (HLA)

☐ ZS-PDO	SAAB SF.340B	340B-296	ex 9N-AHM		
☐ ZS-PDP	SAAB SF.340B	340B-289	ex B-3651		
☐ ZS-PDR	SAAB SF.340B	340B-292	ex 9N-AHK		
☐ ZS-PDS	SAAB SF.340B	340B-302	ex B-3654		Lsd to Yeti A/l
☐ ZS-PMS	SAAB SF.340A	340A-059	ex N327PX		Lsd to Nationale Regionale
☐ ZS-OLU	Beech 1900C-1	UC-116	ex 9G-KFN		
☐ ZS-PBT	Swearingen SA.227DC Metro 23	DC-820B	ex XA-SHD		
☐ ZS-PBU	Swearingen SA.227DC Metro 23	DC-826B	ex XA-SNF		
☐ ZS-PKM	Beech 200 Super King Air	BB-382	ex N92M		

1TIME AIRLINE — Next Time (1T/RNX) — Johannesburg-OR Tambo (JNB)

☐ ZS-ANX	Douglas DC-9-15	45799/69	ex (5Y-XXD)	no titles	stored JNB
☐ ZS-NNN	Douglas DC-9-32	47516/630	ex N1294L		
☐ ZS-NRA	Douglas DC-9-32	47430/609	ex G-BMAK		stored JNB
☐ ZS-NRB	Douglas DC-9-32	47468/611	ex G-BMAM	O gats	stored JNB
☐ ZS-OBK	McDonnell-Douglas MD-82	49115/1135	ex F-GPZE	kulula colours	Lsd fr SFR
☐ ZS-OPZ	McDonnell-Douglas MD-83	49617/1464	ex N831NK		Lsd fr SFR
☐ ZS-SKB	McDonnell-Douglas MD-83	49966/2047	ex G-FLTK		
☐ ZS-TRD	McDonnell-Douglas MD-82	48022/1079	ex PK-LMS	Tjooning You Straight	
☐ ZS-TRE	McDonnell-Douglas MD-82	49387/1288	ex N954AS		
☐ ZS-TRF	McDonnell-Douglas MD-82	49440/1304	ex N135NJ		
☐ ZS-TRG	McDonnell-Douglas MD-87	49830/1684	ex EC-GRN		
☐ ZS-TRH	McDonnell-Douglas MD-87	49831/1688	ex EC-GRO		
☐ ZS-TRI	McDonnell-Douglas MD-83	49707/1487	ex N315FV		
☐ ZS-SIG	Boeing 737-244	22586/829			Lsd fr SFR

PELICAN AIR SERVICES — Pelican Airways (7V/PDF) — Johannesburg-OR Tambo (JNB)

Also operates services with AMI Turbo DC-3TP and Grumman G-159 Gulfstream leased from Dodson International and Nelair as required. Associated with Ryan Blake Air Charter.

PHOEBUS APOLLO AVIATION — Phoebus (PHB) — Johannesburg-Rand (QRA)

☐ ZS-DIW	Douglas DC-3	11991	ex SAAF 6871		Pegasus
☐ ZS-PAI	Douglas C-54E	27319	ex N4989K	Atlas	
☐ S9-KAZ	Douglas DC-9-32	47368/505	ex ZS-PAK		

PROGRESS AIR — Lanseria (HLA)

☐ ZS-SDM	Swearingen SA.227AC Metro III	AC-756	ex C-FAFW		

QWILA AIR — Q-Charter (QWL) — Lanseria (HLA)

☐ ZS-NUF	Beech 200C Super King Air	BL-4	ex V5-AAL		
☐ ZS-NNZ	Beech 200C Super King Air	BL-8	ex ZS-NAX		
☐ ZS-OKL	Beech 1900D	UE-48	ex 5Y-OKL		
☐ ZS-OMC	Beech 1900D	UE-18	ex N18YV		
☐ ZS-PRE	Beech 1900C	UB-15	ex N715GL	all-white	
☐ ZS-SLG	Cessna 208B Caravan I	208B0772	ex N208LT		
☐ ZS-SLT	Cessna 208B Caravan I	208B0459	ex F-OGXK		

ROVOS AIR — Rovos (VOS) — Lanseria (HLA)

☐ ZS-ARV	Convair 340-67	228	ex CP-2237		
☐ ZS-AUA	Douglas DC-4	42934	ex PH-DDS	Flying Dutchman colours	
☐ ZS-BRV	Convair 340-67	215	ex CP-2236		
☐ ZS-CRV	Douglas DC-3	13331	ex ZS-PTG	Delaney	

RYAN BLAKE AIR — Johannesburg-Rand (QRA)

☐ ZS-OJH	Swearingen SA.227AC Metro III	AC-727	ex N100GS		stored George

SAFAIR — Cargo (FA/(SFR) — Johannesburg-OR Tambo (JNB)

☐ ZS-ASW	Avro 146-RJ85	E2313	ex N505XJ		Lsd to LNK
☐ ZS-ASX	Avro 146-RJ85	E2314	ex N506XJ		
☐ ZS-ASY	Avro 146-RJ85	E2316	ex N507XJ		Lsd to LNK
☐ ZS-ASZ	Avro 146-RJ85	E2318	ex N508XJ		Lsd to LNK
☐ ZS-OLY	Beech 1900D	UE-39	ex N39ZV		
☐ ZS-OYC	Beech 1900D	UE-117	ex VH-NTL		
☐ ZS-OYE	Beech 1900D	UE-200	ex VH-IAV		
☐ ZS-IAC	Boeing 727-227F (Raisbeck 3)	21247/1217	ex N73751		Lsd to Imperial Air Cargo
☐ ZS-PDL	Boeing 727-281F (FedEx 3)	20466/865	ex EI-LCH		

☐ ZS-GCU	Boeing 737-2V5	22531/724	ex N103AG		
☐ ZS-OTF	Boeing 737-436	25305/2147	ex G-DOCC		Lsd to CAW
☐ ZS-OTG	Boeing 737-436	25840/2197	ex G-DOCJ		Lsd to CAW
☐ ZS-OTH	Boeing 737-436	25841/2222	ex G-DOCK		Lsd to CAW
☐ ZS-SGX	Boeing 737-2T5	22396/730	ex N223AG		
☐ ZS-SID	Boeing 737-244F	22583/809		all-white	Lsd to SAA
☐ ZS-SIF	Boeing 737-244F	22585/828		Komati	Lsd to SAA
☐ ZS-SIG	Boeing 737-244	22586/820			Lsd to RNX
☐ ZS-SII	Boeing 737-244	22588/836			stored JNB
☐ ZS-SIK	Boeing 737-244	22590/854	ex 5N-YMM		
☐ ZS-SIL	Boeing 737-244	22591/859			
☐ ZS-SIM	Boeing 737-244	22828/881			Lsd to ILN
☐ ZS-SIT	Boeing 737-236	21790/599	ex V5-AND		
☐ ZS-SMH	Boeing 737-33A	23625/1283	ex N164AW		
☐ ZS-JIZ	Lockheed L-382G-35C Hercules	4695	ex F-GNMM		Op for UN/WFP
☐ ZS-ORA	Lockheed L-382G-7C Hercules	4208	ex S9-CAY		
☐ ZS-ORB	Lockheed L-382G-14C Hercules	4248	ex PK-YRW		
☐ ZS-ORC	Lockheed L-382G-23C Hercules	4388	ex S9-BOQ		
☐ ZS-RSC	Lockheed L-382G-28C Hercules	4475	ex S9-NAD		
☐ ZS-RSF	Lockheed L-382G-31C Hercules	4562	ex S9-CAI		
☐ ZS-RSG	Lockheed L-382G-31C Hercules	4565	ex S9-CAJ		
☐ ZS-RSI	Lockheed L-382G-31C Hercules	4600	ex F-GIMV		Lsd to FAB
☐ ZS-OBF	McDonnell-Douglas MD-82	48019/1001	ex F-GPZC		stored JNB
☐ ZS-OBG	McDonnell-Douglas MD-82	48020/1045	ex N823NK		stored ROW
☐ ZS-OBK	McDonnell-Douglas MD-82	49115/1135	ex F-GPZE		Lsd to RNX
☐ ZS-OPX	McDonnell-Douglas MD-83	53012/1736	ex N825NK		Lsd to RNX
☐ ZS-OPZ	McDonnell-Douglas MD-83	49617/1464	ex N831NK		Lsd to RNX

SKY ONE AIR — *Lanseria (HLA)*

☐ ZS-PWM	Fokker F.28 Fellowship 000	11045	ex PK-RJW		

SKYHAUL — *Skyhaul (HAU)* — *Johannesburg-OR Tambo (JNB)*

☐ ZS-SKG	Convair 580	025	ex EC-GDY		
☐ ZS-SKI	Convair 580	186	ex EC-GHN		
☐ ZS-SKK	Convair 580	135	ex EC-GKH		Lsd to LAC-SkyCongo
☐ ZS-SKL	Convair 580	458	ex EC-GBF		

SOLENTA AVIATION — *Lanseria (HLA)*

☐ ZS-MKE	Beech 1900D	UE-44	ex PH-ACY		Op for UN
☐ ZS-NAC	Beech 1900D	UE-28	ex N28YV		
☐ ZS-NPT	Beech 1900C-1	UC-113	ex 5Y-HAC		Op for DHL
☐ ZS-OHE	Beech 1900C-1	UC-48	ex 9J-AFJ		
☐ ZS-ODG	Beech 1900C-1	UC-158	ex N158YV		Op for DHL
☐ ZS-OYJ	Beech 1900D	UE-273	ex 5Y-NAC		
☐ ZS-OYK	Beech 1900D	UE-318	ex VH-NBN	all-white	
☐ ZS-PJL	Beech 1900C-1	UC-77	ex N77YV		
☐ ZS-PJX	Beech 1900D	UE-102	ex P2-MBX		
☐ ZS-ZED	Beech 1900D	UE-260	ex N260GL		Op for UN
☐ ZS-NIZ	Cessna 208B Caravan I	208B0353	ex 5Y-NIZ		Op for DHL
☐ ZS-SLO	Cessna 208B Caravan I	208B0485	ex F-OGXI		Op for DHL
☐ ZS-SLR	Cessna 208B Caravan I	208B0497	ex N497AC		Op for DHL
☐ ZS-TIN	Cessna 208B Caravan I	208B0261	ex 9J-DHL		Op for DHL
☐ 5Y-OBY	Cessna 208B Caravan I	208B0345	ex ZS-OBY		Op for DHL
☐ 5Y-TLC	Cessna 208B Caravan I	208B0472	ex ZS-TLC		Op for DHL
☐ TR-LII	Antonov An-26				
☐ ZS-PEA	Beech 200C Super King Air	BL-29	ex N500PH	all-white	
☐ ZS-ATR	ATR 42-300F	060	ex PH-XLC		Op for DHL
☐ ZS-LUC	ATR 42-320	032	ex PH-RAK		
☐ ZS-OVP	ATR 42-300F	088	ex F-WQNG		Op for DHL
☐ ZS-OVR	ATR 42-300F	116	ex F-WQNB		Op for DHL
☐ ZS-OVS	ATR 42-300F	075	ex F-WQNU		Op for DHL

SOUTH AFRICAN AIRWAYS — *Springbok (SA/SAA)* — *Johannesburg-OR Tambo (JNB)*

Member of Star Alliance

☐ ZS-SFD	Airbus A319-131	2268	ex D-AVWW		
☐ ZS-SFE	Airbus A319-131	2281	ex D-AVYK		
☐ ZS-SFF	Airbus A319-131	2308	ex D-AVYE		
☐ ZS-SFG	Airbus A319-131	2326	ex D-AVYT		
☐ ZS-SFH	Airbus A319-131	2355	ex D-AVWC		
☐ ZS-SFI	Airbus A319-131	2375	ex D-AVWR		
☐ ZS-SFJ	Airbus A319-131	2379	ex D-AVWU		
☐ ZS-SFK	Airbus A319-131	2418	ex D-AVYI		

Registration	Type	C/n	Previous identity	Notes	Remarks
☐ ZS-SFL	Airbus A319-131	2438	ex D-AVWP		
☐ ZS-SFM	Airbus A319-131	2469	ex D-AVYH		
☐ ZS-SFN	Airbus A319-131	2501	ex D-AVWD		
☐ ZS-SLA	Airbus A340-212	008	ex D-AIBA		
☐ ZS-SLB	Airbus A340-212	011	ex D-AIBC		
☐ ZS-SLC	Airbus A340-212	018	ex D-AIBD		
☐ ZS-SLD	Airbus A340-212	019	ex D-AIBE		
☐ ZS-SLE	Airbus A340-212	021	ex D-AIBH		
☐ ZS-SLF	Airbus A340-212	006	ex D-AIBF		
☐ ZS-SNA	Airbus A340-642	410	ex F-WWCE		
☐ ZS-SNB	Airbus A340-642	417	ex F-WWCG		
☐ ZS-SNC	Airbus A340-642	426	ex F-WWCH	Star Alliance colours	
☐ ZS-SND	Airbus A340-642	531	ex F-WWCX		
☐ ZS-SNE	Airbus A340-642	534	ex F-WWCY		
☐ ZS-SNF	Airbus A340-642	547	ex F-WWCI		
☐ ZS-SNG	Airbus A340-642	557	ex F-WWCG		
☐ ZS-SNH	Airbus A340-642	626	ex F-WWCF		
☐ ZS-SNI	Airbus A340-642	630	ex F-WWCG		
☐ ZS-SXA	Airbus A340-313E	544	ex F-WWJS		
☐ ZS-SXB	Airbus A340-313E	582	ex F-WWJT		
☐ ZS-SXC	Airbus A340-313E	590	ex F-WWJY		
☐ ZS-SXD	Airbus A340-313E	643	ex VT-JWA		
☐ ZS-SXE	Airbus A340-313E	646	ex VT-JWB		
☐ ZS-SXF	Airbus A340-313E	651	ex VT-JWC		
☐ ZS-SBA	Boeing 737-3Y0F	26070/2349	ex N700JZ		
☐ ZS-SBB	Boeing 737-3Y0F	26072/2369	ex N701JZ		
☐ ZS-SID	Boeing 737-244F	22583/809		all-white	Lsd fr SFR
☐ ZS-SIF	Boeing 737-244F	22585/828		Komati	Lsd fr SFR
☐ ZS-SJA	Boeing 737-8S3/W	29248/561			
☐ ZS-SJB	Boeing 737-8S3/W	29249/653	ex N1786B		
☐ ZS-SJC	Boeing 737-85F/W	28828/565	ex N1786B		
☐ ZS-SJD	Boeing 737-85F/W	28829/582			
☐ ZS-SJE	Boeing 737-85F/W	28830/669	ex N1786B		
☐ ZS-SJF	Boeing 737-85F/W	30006/688	ex N1787B		
☐ ZS-SJG	Boeing 737-8BG/W	32353/711	ex N1786B		
☐ ZS-SJH	Boeing 737-8BG/W	32354/725	ex PH-HZQ		
☐ ZS-SJI	Boeing 737-85F/W	30007/746	ex N1787B		
☐ ZS-SJJ	Boeing 737-85F/W	30567/761	ex N1787B		
☐ ZS-SJK	Boeing 737-8BG/W	32355/807	ex PH-HZT		
☐ ZS-SJL	Boeing 737-8BG/W	32356/819	ex PH-HZZ		
☐ ZS-SJM	Boeing 737-85F/W	30476/789	ex N788BA		
☐ ZS-SJN	Boeing 737-85F/W	30569/850	ex N1786B		
☐ ZS-SJO	Boeing 737-8BG/W	32357/918	ex PH-HZS		
☐ ZS-SJP	Boeing 737-8BG/W	32358/955	ex PH-HZU		
☐ ZS-SJR	Boeing 737-844/W	32631/1176	ex N6067U		
☐ ZS-SJS	Boeing 737-844/W	32632/1205			
☐ ZS-SJT	Boeing 737-844/W	32633/1225			
☐ ZS-SJU	Boeing 737-844/W	32634/1383			
☐ ZS-SJV	Boeing 737-844/W	32635/1407	ex N1787B	Star Alliance c/s	
☐ ZS-SAZ	Boeing 747-444	29119/1187		Montistored	
☐ ZS-SBK	Boeing 747-4F6	28959/1158	ex N1785B	The Great Northstored	
☐ ZS-SBS	Boeing 747-4F6	28960/1167	ex N60668		stored

SOUTH AFRICAN EXPRESS AIRWAYS	***Expressways (XZ/EXY)***	***Johannesburg-OR Tambo (JNB)***

Registration	Type	C/n	Previous identity	Notes	Remarks
☐ ZS-NMC	Canadair CL-600-2B19 (CRJ-200ER)	7225	ex N626BR		
☐ ZS-NMD	Canadair CL-600-2B19 (CRJ-200ER)	7233	ex N627BR		
☐ ZS-NME	Canadair CL-600-2B19 (CRJ-200ER)	7240	ex N628BR		
☐ ZS-NMF	Canadair CL-600-2B19 (CRJ-200ER)	7287	ex N634BR		
☐ ZS-NMG	Canadair CL-600-2B19 (CRJ-200ER)	7772	ex 5N-BJI		
☐ ZS-NMH	Canadair CL-600-2B19 (CRJ-200ER)	7787	ex 5N-BJK		
☐ ZS-NMI	Canadair CL-600-2B19 (CRJ-200ER)	7153	ex C-FZAN		
☐ ZS-NMJ	Canadair CL-600-2B19 (CRJ-200ER)	7161	ex C-GAUG		
☐ ZS-NMK	Canadair CL-600-2B19 (CRJ-200ER)	7198	ex C-GBMF		
☐ ZS-NML	Canadair CL-600-2B19 (CRJ-200ER)	7201	ex C-GBLX		
☐ ZS-NMM	Canadair CL-600-2B19 (CRJ-200ER)	7234	ex C-FMMT		
☐ ZS-NMN	Canadair CL-600-2B19 (CRJ-200ER)	7237	ex C-FMMX		
☐ ZS-NLT	Canadair CL-600-2C10 (CRJ-701)	10024	ex N607QX		
☐ ZS-NLV	Canadair CL-600-2C10 (CRJ-701)	10010	ex N602QX		
☐ ZS-NLW	de Havilland DHC-8-315	338	ex ZS-NLY	301	
☐ ZS-NLX	de Havilland DHC-8-315	348	ex C-GDKL	302	
☐ ZS-NLY	de Havilland DHC-8-315	352	ex ZS-NLW	303	
☐ ZS-NLZ	de Havilland DHC-8-315	354	ex C-GFRP	304	Lsd to ATC
☐ ZS-NMA	de Havilland DHC-8-315	358	ex C-GDFT	305	Lsd to ATC
☐ ZS-NMB	de Havilland DHC-8-315	368	ex C-GGIU	306	
☐ ZS-NMO	de Havilland DHC-8-402Q	4122	ex C-FFCU		
☐ ZS-NMP	de Havilland DHC-8-315B	420	ex ZS-NNJ	307	

☐ ZS-NMS	de Havilland DHC-8-402Q	4127	ex C-FFPH	

SPRINGBOK CLASSIC AIR — Spring Classic (SPB) — Johannesburg-Rand (QRA)

☐ ZS-CFC	Beech E-18S	BA-216		

STAR AIR CARGO — Johannesburg-OR Tambo (JNB)

☐ ZS-PUI	Boeing 737-2B7 (Nordam 3)	22890/986	ex 5N-BFJ	Lsd to AML
☐ ZS-SFX	Boeing 737-2B7 (Nordam 3)	22889/983	ex 5N-BFH	
☐ ZS-SHL	Boeing 737-247 (Nordam 3)	23520/1329	ex 5H-MVV	
☐ ZS-SKW	Boeing 737-219 (Nordam 3)	23474/1199	ex 9J-KDK	
☐ ZS-SMD	Boeing 737-219 (Nordam 3)	23472/1194	ex N462BC	

STARS AWAY AVIATION — (STX) — Cape Town-International (CPT)

☐ ZS-DBH	Douglas DC-9-33F (ABS 3)	47384/543	ex N931AX	
☐ ZS-DBL	Hawker Siddeley HS.748 Srs.2B/287 LFD	1737	ex VH-IMK	Freighter
☐ 9G-MKV	Hawker Siddeley HS.748 Srs.2B/287 LFD	1736	ex ZS-DBM	Freighter

TRAMON AIR — Tramon (TMX) — Lanseria (HLA)

☐ ZS-ALX	Grumman G-159 Gulfstream I	086	ex N10TB	
☐ ZS-JIS	Grumman G-159 Gulfstream I	193	ex PK-TRN	

TRAVELMAX — Lanseria (HLA)

☐ ZS-PKB	Beech 1900D	UE-3	ex N3YV	Lsd fr KUS

UTAIR SOUTH AFRICA — (UTR) — Lanseria (HLA)

☐ ZS-RUB	Mil Mi-8MTV-1	95960	ex RA-27133	
☐ ZS-RUC	Mil Mi-8MTV-1	95907	ex RA-27071	
☐ ZS-RVE	Mil Mi-8MTV-1	96264	ex RA-25809	
☐ ZS-TUT	Mil Mi-8MTV-1	95151	ex RA-25413	

VALAN INTERNATIONAL CARGO — Nalau (VLA) — Johannesburg-Rand (QRA)

☐ ZS-OWX	Antonov An-32B	2806	ex ER-AWB	all-white, no titles
☐ ZS-PEL	Antonov An-32B	3004	ex ER-AFG	all-white, no titles
☐ ZS-PHR	Antonov An-32A	2601	ex ER-AEW	on order
☐ ZS-PSO	Antonov An-32B	2808	ex RA-48059	

Reported to have ceased operations in late 2007

VSA AVIATION — Lanseria (HLA)

☐ ZS-NRN	Dornier 228-200	8021	ex OY-CHK	Op for UN
☐ ZS-OOU	Cessna 404 Titan II	404-0415	ex 9Q-CMX	Lsd to STA Mozambique
☐ ZS-OVM	Dornier 228-201	8056	ex F-GOAH	all-white

Z3- MACEDONIA (Republic of Macedonia)

AIRLIFT SERVICES

☐ Z3-AAJ	Boeing 737-33A/W	23827/1444	ex D-AHIG	

MAT MACEDONIAN AIRLINES — Makavio (IN/MAK) — Skopje (SKP)

☐ Z3-AAH	Boeing 737-529	25249/2145	ex ZS-PKU	
☐ Z3-	Canadair CL-600-2D24 (CRJ-900ER)		ex C-	on order
☐ Z3-	Canadair CL-600-2D24 (CRJ-900ER)		ex C-	

STAR AIRLINES — Skopje (SKP)

☐ Z3-CAA	Boeing 747-2U3B (SCD)	22769/562	ex N923FT	
☐ Z3-CAB	Boeing 747-256B (SF)	24071/699	ex TF-ARW	

3A- MONACO (Principality of Monaco)

HELI AIR MONACO — Heli Air (YO/MCM) — Monte Carlo Heliport (MCM)

☐ 3A-MAC	Aérospatiale AS350B Ecureuil	1673	ex HB-XBC	
☐ 3A-MAX	Aérospatiale AS350BA Ecureuil	1794	ex F-GMBN	
☐ 3A-MFC	Eurocopter EC130B4 Ecureuil	3768		
☐ 3A-MIL	Aérospatiale AS350BA Ecureuil	1709	ex F-GMBV	
☐ 3A-MJB	Aérospatiale AS350B2 Ecureuil	1988	ex F-GJCM	
☐ 3A-MPJ	Eurocopter EC130B4 Ecureuil	3662		
☐ 3A-MTP	Aérospatiale AS350B2 Ecureuil	1996	ex I-LOLO	

☐ 3A-MTT	Aérospatiale AS350B2 Ecureuil	1967	ex I-LUPJ	
☐ 3A-MCM	Aérospatiale SA365N Dauphin 2	6076	ex N9UW	
☐ 3A-MJP	Aérospatiale SA365C3 Dauphin 2	5015	ex N90049	
☐ 3A-MPG	Eurocopter EC155B1 Dauphin 2	6771		
☐ 3A-MXL	Aérospatiale AS355N Ecureuil 2	5712		

3B- MAURITIUS (Republic of Mauritius)

AIR MAURITIUS — AirMauritius (MK/MAU) — Plaisance (MRU)

☐ 3B-NAU	Airbus A340-312	076	ex F-WWJG	Pink Pigeon	
☐ 3B-NAY	Airbus A340-313X	152	ex F-WWJX	Cardinal	
☐ 3B-NBD	Airbus A340-313X	194	ex F-WWJP	Parakeet	
☐ 3B-NBE	Airbus A340-313X	268	ex F-WWJG	Paille en Queue	
☐ 3B-NBI	Airbus A340-313E	793	ex F-WWJE	Le Flamboyant	
☐ 3B-NBJ	Airbus A340-313E	800	ex F-WWJF	Le Chamarel	
☐ 3B-NBL	Airbus A330-202	1057	ex F-WWYF	Nenuphar	
☐ 3B-NBM	Airbus A330-202	883	ex F-WWKK	Trochetia	
☐ 3B-NBF	Airbus A319-112	1592	ex D-AVYX	Mon Choisy	
☐ 3B-NBG	ATR 72-212A	690	ex F-WWEM	Port Mathurin	
☐ 3B-NBH	Airbus A319-112	1936	ex D-AVWF	Blue Bay	
☐ 3B-NBK	ATR 72-212A	595	ex OY-CIO	Coin de More	Lsd fr CIM
☐ 3B-NZD	Bell 206B JetRanger III	4464			
☐ 3B-NZE	Bell 206B JetRanger III	4465			
☐ 3B-NZF	Bell 206B JetRanger III	4496	ex N8152H		

3C- EQUATORIAL GUINEA (Republic of Equatorial Guinea)

CEIBA INTERCONTINENTAL — Malabo (SSG)

☐ TC-MND	Airbus A300C4-203F	212	ex ZS-SDG	stored XCR Lsd fr MNB
☐ 3C-LLG	ATR 42-300	335	ex F-ODYE	
☐ 3C-LLH	ATR 42-300	671	ex F-WWYE	
☐ 3C-LLI	ATR 72-212A	790	ex F-WWEJ	
☐ 3C-LLM	ATR 72-212A	810	ex F-WWEX	

EUROGUINEANA DE AVIACION — EcuatoGuinea — Malabo (SSG)

Leases Airbus A321s from Spanair as required plus other aircraft when required. Part owned by Spanair.

GEASA — Geasa (GEA) — Malabo (SSG)

☐ RA-87956	Yakovlev Yak-40K	9821757	ex CCCP-87956

GENERAL WORK AVIACION — Malabo (SSG)

☐ 3C-GWA	Fokker F.28 Fellowship 4000	11240	ex HC-CDG
☐ 3C-GWB	Fokker F.28 Fellowship 4000	11156	ex 3C-LGP
☐ 3C-GWC	Fokker F.28 Fellowship 4000	11238	ex TU-TIY

GETRA — (GET) — Malabo (SSG)

☐ 3C-LLF	Fokker F.28 Fellowship 1000	11073	ex N941TD

GUINEA EQUATORIAL AIRLINES — (RGE) — Malabo (SSG)

☐ 3C-LGF	Ilyushin Il-76MD	0073479386	ex 3C-HAV

NATIONAL REGIONAL TRANSPORT — Malabo (SSG)

☐ ZS-DOA	SAAB SF.340A	340A-077	ex C-GQXD	Lsd fr AAS Leasing

STAR EQUATORIAL AIRLINES

☐ 3C-LLN	Boeing 737-260	23915/1583	ex ET-AJB

UTAGE — Utage (UTG) — Malabo (SSG)

☐ ER-AZB	Antonov An-24RV	27307507	ex RA-47690
☐ ZS-OKT	Embraer EMB.120RT Brasilia	120254	ex N261GA

3D- SWAZILAND (Kingdom of Swaziland)

AERO AFRICA — Aero Africa (RFC) — Johannesburg (JNB)

☐ 3D-AAJ	Boeing 737-222	19075/97	ex 3C-AAJ		op for BGL
☐ 3D-AVC	Boeing 727-251(FedEx 3)	21155/1169	ex 7P-LAA		VIP Lsd to MRT
☐ 3D-BGA	Boeing 737-2H4	21722/568	ex OM-ERA		Lsd to BGL
☐ 3D-ITC	Boeing 727-2F2	21260/1222	ex N103AZ		op for ILN
☐ 3D-JJM	Boeing 727-231 (Raisbeck 3)	20053/713	ex N64320		stored ELP
☐ 3D-ZZM	Boeing 737-2H7C	20590/304	ex 3C-ZZM	all-white	Lsd fr ILN

AFRICAN INTERNATIONAL AIRWAYS — Fly Cargo (AIN) — Manzini-Matsapha (MTS)

☐ 9Q-CJG	Douglas DC-8-62F (BAC 3)	46110/487	ex ZS-POL
☐ 9Q-CJH	Douglas DC-8-62F (BAC 3)	46023/407	ex 3X-GEN

EASTERN AIRWAYS — Manzini-Matsapha (MTS)

☐ 3D-AVP	LET L-410UVP	851514	ex LY-AVP

3X- GUINEA (Republic of Guinea)

AIR GUINEE EXPRESS — Future Express (2U/GIP) — Conakry (CKY)

☐ 3X-GCB	Boeing 737-2R6C	22627/779	stored PGF

EXIM TRADING

☐ 3X-GEM	Antonov An-12BK	00347005	ex ER-AXK	stored

GUINEE AIR CARGO — Conakry (CKY)

☐ 3X-GEE	Hawker Siddeley HS.748 Srs.2A	1602	ex 3D-POZ	Op Humanitarian flights

4K- AZERBAIJAN (Republic of Azerbaijan)

AZAL CARGO — Azalaviacargo (AHC) — Baku-Bina (BAK)

☐ 4K-AZ14	Ilyushin Il-76TD	1023412389	ex UK-76447	
☐ 4K-AZ15	Ilyushin Il-76TD	1033417569	ex RA-76379	
☐ 4K-AZ16	Ilyushin Il-76TD	1023412411	ex UK-76410	
☐ 4K-AZ26	Ilyushin Il-76TD	1033416525	ex UK-76844	
☐ 4K-26584	Antonov An-26B	13509	ex 26584	stored BAK

AZERBAIJAN AIRLINES — Azal (J2/AHY) — Baku-Bina (BAK)

☐ 4K-AZ01	Airbus A319-115X	2487	ex D-AVWA	Baku	Op for Govt [CJ]
☐ 4K-AZ03	Airbus A319-111	2516	ex D-AVWS	Ganja	
☐ 4K-AZ04	Airbus A319-111	2588	ex D-AVXJ		
☐ 4K-AZ05	Airbus A319-111	2788	ex D-AVYY	Gazakh	
☐ 4K-AZ54	Airbus A320-211	0331	ex 9H-ADZ		stored MLA
☐ 4K-AZ77	Airbus A320-214	2846	ex D-ABDH		
☐ 4K-AZ78	Airbus A320-214	2853	ex D-ABDI	Naftalan	
☐ 4K-AZ79	Airbus A320-214	2865	ex D-ABDJ	Oghuz	
☐ 4K-AZ52	ATR 42-500	667	ex F-WWLA	Zagatala	
☐ 4K-AZ53	ATR 42-500	689	ex F-WWLK		
☐ 4K-AZ64	ATR 72-212A	761	ex F-WWEX	Gabala	
☐ 4K-AZ65	ATR 72-212A	789	ex F-WWEH	Gusar	
☐ 4K-AZ66	ATR 72-212A	799	ex F-WWEP		
☐ 4K-AZ67	ATR 72-212A	818	ex F-WWEH	Khankandi	
☐ VP-BBR	Boeing 757-22L	29305/894	ex N6046P	Garabagh	
☐ VP-BBS	Boeing 757-22L	30834/947	ex (4K-AZ13)		
☐ 4K-AZ38	Boeing 757-256	26246/620	ex N262CT		
☐ 4K-AZ43	Boeing 757-2M6	23453/100	ex V8-RBB		
☐ 4K-AZ49	Antonov An-140-100	36525307041			stored
☐ 4K-AZ712	Tupolev Tu-134B-3	63515	ex 4K-65712		
☐ 4K-AZ713	Tupolev Tu-134B-3	63520	ex 4K-65713		
☐ 4K-AZ714	Tupolev Tu-134B-3	63527	ex 4K-65714		
☐ 4K-AZ10	Tupolev Tu-154M	98A-1013			
☐ 4K-AZ729	Tupolev Tu-154M	92A-911	ex 4K-85729		VIP
☐ 4K-AZ734	Tupolev Tu-154M	92A-916	ex 4K-85734	Shusha	
☐ 4K-AZ738	Tupolev Tu-154M	92A-921	ex 4K-85738		

IMAIR		Improtex (IK/ITX)		Baku-Bina (BAK)
☐ 4K-AZ17	Tupolev Tu-154M	85A-718	ex B-2603	
☐ 4K-85732	Tupolev Tu-154M	92A-914	ex CCCP-85732	

SILK WAY AIRLINES		Silk Line (ZP/AZQ)		Baku-Bina (BAK)
☐ 4K-AZ19	Ilyushin Il-76TD	0053460820	ex UR-76408	
☐ 4K-AZ31	Ilyushin Il-76TD	1013405184	ex RA-76426	
☐ 4K-AZ40	Ilyushin Il-76TD	1043419632		
☐ 4K-AZ41	Ilyushin Il-76TD	1093420673		
☐ 4K-AZ55	Ilyushin Il-76TD	2053420680		
☐ 4K-AZ70	Ilyushin Il-76TD	2093421717		
☐ 4K-AZ100	Ilyushin Il-76TD-90VD	2073421208		
☐ 4K-AZ101	Ilyushin Il-76TD-90VD	2083421716		
☐ 4K-AZ23	Antonov An-12BK	8345605	ex 11715	
☐ 4K-AZ808	ATR 42-500	673	ex F-WWLG	

SKY WIND		Sky Wind (AZH)		Baku-Bina (BAK)
☐ 4K-AZ32	Antonov An-12B	5343006	ex CCCP-11430	
☐ 4K-AZ37	Antonov An-12BK	00347506	ex CCCP-11938	
☐ 4K-AZ57	Antonov An-26B	9504	ex RA-26693	
☐ 4K-78129	Ilyushin Il-76MD	0083489683	ex ER-IBC	
☐ 4K-78130	Ilyushin Il-76MD	0043454611	ex UR-78130	
☐ 4K-86810	Ilyushin Il-76M	053404094	ex RA-86810	

TURANAIR		Turan (3T/URN)		Baku-Bina (BAK)
☐ 4K-474	Tupolev Tu-154B-2	81A-474	ex 4K-85474	
☐ 4K-727	Tupolev Tu-154M	86A-727	ex LZ-LCS	stored BAK

4L- GEORGIA (Republic of Georgia)

AIR SIRIN			
☐ 4L-AFL	Antonov An-26B	17310610	ex UR-AUA
☐ 4L-AFS	Antonov An-26	97308608	ex UR-AFS

AIR VICTORY			
☐ 4L-ELE	Antonov An-12BP	5342802	ex ER-ADK
☐ 4L-ROM	Antonov An-12BP	8345809	ex ER-AXL
☐ 4L-HUS	Antonov An-12BP	6343708	ex LZ-CBE
☐ 4L-IRA	Antonov An-12B	9346510	ex EX-025
☐ 4L-VAL	Antonov An-12BP	9346807	ex LZ-CBH
☐ 4L-VPI	Antonov An-12B	8345510	ex ER-ADY

AIRZENA – GEORGIAN AIRWAYS		Tamazi (A9/TGZ)			Tbilisi-Lochini (TBS)
☐ 4L-GAE	Canadair CL-600-2B19 (CRJ-200ER)	7070	ex F-GRJA	all white	
☐ 4L-GAF	Canadair CL-600-2B19 (Challenger 850)	8046	ex OY-YVI		Op for Government
☐ 4L-GAL	Canadair CL-600-2B19 (CRJ-200ER)	7076	ex F-GRJB		
☐ 4L-TGA	Boeing 737-5Q8	28055/3024	ex B-2110		
☐ 4L-TGG	Canadair CL-600-2B19 (CRJ-200ER)	7386	ex OY-MAV		
☐ 4L-TGL	Boeing 737-3B7	23859/1551	ex N524AU		Lsd to RNV
☐ 4L-TGM	Boeing 737-790/W	33012/1306	ex N647AS		
☐ 4L-TGN	Yakovlev Yak-40	9611246	ex 4L-88158		
☐ 4L-TGR	Boeing 737-59D	24694/1834	ex G-THOC	Balumi	
☐ 4L-TGT	Boeing 737-4Q8	26306/2653	ex N411LF	Tbilisi	

EUREX			
☐ 4L-KMK	Boeing 747-281F	23139/608	ex N106KZ

EUROLINE			
☐ UR-CGR	SAAB SF.340A	340A-124	ex N340JW
☐ 4L-EUR	Tupolev Tu-134A	63860	ex 4L-AAJ

GLOBAL GEORGIAN AIRWAYS		Global Georgian (GGZ)		Tbilisi-Lochini (TBS)
☐ 4L-12008	Antonov An-12BP	5343103	ex RA-11768	

SAKAVIASERVICE		Sakservice (AZG)		Tbilisi-Lochini (TBS)
☐ 4L-GLG	Antonov An-24RV	27308005	ex UR-4677	
☐ 4L-GLM	Ilyushin Il-76T	093418543	ex EX-117	

☐ 4L-GLN	Antonov An-12BK	9346704	ex EX-131	
☐ 4L-GLR	Ilyushin Il-76T	0013432955	ex UP-I7608	
☐ 4L-GLX	Ilyushin Il-76TD	0033448390	ex EW-263TH	

SKY GEORGIA — National (QB/GFG) — Tbilisi-Lochini (TBS)

☐ 4L-GNI	Ilyushin Il-76TD	0043452546	ex EX-071	
☐ 4L-GNL	Douglas DC-9-51 (ABS 3)	48134/980	ex UR-CCK	
☐ 4L-GNN	Douglas DC-9-51	47657/787	ex UR-BYL	
☐ 4L-SKY	Ilyushin Il-76TD	0053464934	ex UP-I7638	

TBILAVIAMSHENI — Tbilavia (L6/VNZ) — Tbilisi-Lochini (TBS)

☐ 4L-AAK	Yakovlev Yak-40	9531043	ex 4L-87242	Georgia titles
☐ 4L-BZG	Antonov An-24RV	47309102	ex EW-224PG	

TRANSAVIA SERVICE — Transavia Service (5I/FNV) — Kutaisi (KUT)

☐ 4L-FAS	Antonov An-72-100	36572020358	ex RA-72901	
☐ 4L-NAS	Antonov An-72	36572020362	ex EK-72902	
☐ 4L-VAS	Antonov An-12BK	7345201	ex EK-12221	

TRADE LINKS AVIATION

☐ 4L-TAS	Antonov An-24B	89901506	ex EX-004	all-white

VIP-AVIA — VIP Avia (VPV) — Tbilisi-Lochini (TBS)

☐ 4L-VIP	Yakovlev Yak-40	9320129	ex 4L-MGC	VIPop for Government

4O- MONTENEGRO (Republic of Montenegro)

MONTENEGRO AIRLINES — Motairo (YM/MGX) — Podgorica/Tivat (TGD/TIV)

☐ 4O-AOA	Embraer 190-200LR (195LR)	19000180	ex PT-SDO	
☐ 4O-AOB	Embraer 190-200LR (195LR)	19000283	ex PT-TLX	
☐ 4O-	Embraer 190-200LR (195LR)		ex PT-	on order
☐ 4O-	Embraer 190-200LR (195LR)		ex PT-	on order
☐ 4O-AOK	Fokker F.28-0100 (Fokker 100)	11272	ex YU-AOK	Sveti Petar Cetinjski
☐ 4O-AOL	Fokker F.28-0100 (Fokker 100)	11268	ex ZA-ARC	Podgorica
☐ 4O-AOM	Fokker F.28-0100 (Fokker 100)	11321	ex YU-AOM	Bar
☐ 4O-AOP	Fokker F.28-0100 (Fokker 100)	11332	ex YU-AOP	Boka
☐ 4O-AOT	Fokker F.28-0100 (Fokker 100)	11350	ex YU-AOT	

4R- SRI LANKA (Democratic Socialist Republic of Sri Lanka)

AERO LANKA AIRLINES — AeroLanka (QL/RNL) — Colombo-Bandaranayike Intl/Ratmalana (CMB/RML)

☐ 4R-	Short SC.7 Skyvan 3	SH1924	ex PK-DSU	on order
☐ 4R-SEA	Cessna 404	404-0833	ex N404AM	
☐ 4R-SER	Hawker Siddeley HS.748 Srs.2B/426	1799	ex VH-IMJ	

EXPO AIR — Expoavia (8D/EXV) — Colombo-Bandaranayike Intl/Colombo-Ratmalana (CMB/RML)

☐ 4R-EXD	Ilyushin Il-18GrM	187009802	ex YR-IMZ	Lsd fr RMV
☐ 4R-EXJ	Douglas DC-8-63CF (BAC 3)	46049/479	ex N867BX	

MIHIN LANKA — (MJ/MLR) — Colombo-Bandaranayike Intl (CMB)

☐ 4R-MLA	Fokker F.27 Friendship 500RF	10642	ex 4R-EXH	Lsd fr EXV
☐ 4R-MRA	Fokker F.27 Friendship 500RF	10631	ex A4O-FC	
☐ 4R-MRB	Airbus A320-232	0977	ex VT-ADZ	

SRILANKAN — Srilankan (UL/ALK) — Colombo-Bandaranayike Intl (CMB)

☐ 4R-ABC	Airbus A320-231	0304	ex N304RX	
☐ 4R-ABE	Airbus A320-231	0169	ex G-TICL	
☐ 4R-ABG	Airbus A320-232	2908	ex VT-ADT	
☐ 4R-ABH	Airbus A320-232	2914	ex VT-ADS	
☐ 4R-ABJ	Airbus A320-232	2564	ex VT-DKY	
☐ 4R-ALA	Airbus A330-243	303	ex F-WWYH	
☐ 4R-ALB	Airbus A330-243	306	ex F-WWYL	
☐ 4R-ALC	Airbus A330-243	311	ex F-WWYN	
☐ 4R-ALD	Airbus A330-243	313	ex F-WWYP	
☐ 4R-ADA	Airbus A340-311	032	ex F-WWJT	
☐ 4R-ADB	Airbus A340-311	033	ex F-WWJU	
☐ 4R-ADC	Airbus A340-311	034	ex F-WWJY	

☐ 4R-ADE	Airbus A340-313X	367	ex F-GTUA		
☐ 4R-ADF	Airbus A340-313X	374	ex F-GTUB		

4X- ISRAEL (State of Israel)

ARKIA ISRAELI AIRLINES — Arkia (IZ/AIZ) — Tel Aviv-Ben Gurion/Sde Dov (TLV/SDV)

☐ 4X-AHA	de Havilland DHC-7-102	60	ex 5N-BDS		
☐ 4X-AHF	de Havilland DHC-7-102	77	ex N76598		
☐ 4X-AHG	de Havilland DHC-7-102	33	ex N235SL	Metulla	
☐ 4X-AHH	de Havilland DHC-7-102	45	ex N7156J		
☐ 4X-AHJ	de Havilland DHC-7-102	50	ex G-BRYE		
☐ 4X-AHM	de Havilland DHC-7-102	73	ex 5N-SKA		stored SDV
☐ 4X-AVT	ATR 72-212A	894	ex F-WWEN		
☐ 4X-AVU	ATR 72-212A	587	ex F-WWES		
☐ 4X-AVW	ATR 72-212A	583	ex F-WWER		
☐ 4X-AVX	ATR 72-212A	656	ex F-WWEJ		
☐ 4X-AVZ	ATR 72-212A	577	ex F-WWEN		
☐ 4X-BAU	Boeing 757-3E7	30178/906	ex N1003M		
☐ 4X-BAW	Boeing 757-3E7	30179/912			
☐ 4X-EMA	Embraer 190-200LR (195LR)	19000172	ex EC-KOZ		

AYEET AVIATION — Ayeet (AYT) — Beer-Sheba (BEV)

☐ 4X-AHP	de Havilland DHC-6 Twin Otter 100	75	ex C-FCSF		
☐ 4X-AYS	Britten-Norman BN-2A-8 Islander	376	ex (G-BJWL)		

CARGO AIR LINES — CAL (5C/ICL) — Tel Aviv-Ben Gurion (TLV)

☐ 4X-ICL	Boeing 747-271C	21964/416	ex N538MC	no titles	Lsd fr GTI
☐ 4X-ICM	Boeing 747-271C	21965/438	ex N539MC	all-white	Lsd fr GTI

EL AL ISRAEL AIRLINES — ElAl (LY/ELY) — Tel Aviv-Ben Gurion (TLV)

☐ 4X-EKA	Boeing 737-858	29957/204		801 Tiberias	
☐ 4X-EKB	Boeing 737-858	29958/249		802 Eilat	
☐ 4X-EKC	Boeing 737-858	29959/314		803 Beit Shean	
☐ 4X-EKD	Boeing 737-758	29960/327		701 Ashkelon	
☐ 4X-EKE	Boeing 737-758	29961/442		702 Nazareth	
☐ 4X-EKF	Boeing 737-8HX	29638/2766		804 Kinneret	
☐ 4X-EKH	Boeing 737-88P/W	35485/2871		807 Yarden	
☐ 4X-EKI	Boeing 737-86N	28587/192	ex N802NA	812	
☐ 4X-EKJ	Boeing 737-88P/W	35486/2908	ex N1786B		
☐ 4X-EKL	Boeing 737-88P/W	35487/2941	ex N1796B		
☐ 4X-EKO	Boeing 737-86Q/W	30287/1308	ex D-ATUI		
☐ 4X-EKP	Boeing 737-8Q8/W	30639/935	ex 5W-SAO		
☐ 4X-EKS	Boeing 737-8Q8/W	36433/2702	ex N1796B		
☐ 4X-AXF	Boeing 747-258C	21594/327		405	
☐ 4X-AXK	Boeing 747-245F	22150/476	ex 9V-SQT	411 all-white	
☐ 4X-AXL	Boeing 747-2B5B (SF)	22485/513	ex 4X-ICN	412	
☐ 4X-AXM	Boeing 747-245F	22151/478	ex 9V-SQU	410 all-white	
☐ 4X-ELA	Boeing 747-458	26055/1027		201 Tel Aviv-Jaffa	
☐ 4X-ELB	Boeing 747-458	26056/1032	ex N60697	202 Haifa	
☐ 4X-ELC	Boeing 747-458	27915/1062	ex N6009F	203 Beer Sheva	
☐ 4X-ELD	Boeing 747-458	29328/1215		204 Jerusalem	
☐ 4X-ELE	Boeing 747-412	26551/1045	ex 9V-SPB		
☐ 4X-EBM	Boeing 757-258	23918/156		502	
☐ 4X-EBS	Boeing 757-258ER	24884/325		504	
☐ 4X-EBT	Boeing 757-258ER	25036/356		505	
☐ 4X-EBU	Boeing 757-258	26053/529		506	
☐ 4X-EBV	Boeing 757-258	26054/547		507	
☐ 4X-EAA	Boeing 767-258	22972/62	ex N6066Z	601	
☐ 4X-EAC	Boeing 767-258ER	22974/86	ex N6018N	603	
☐ 4X-EAD	Boeing 767-258ER	22975/89	ex N6046P	604	
☐ 4X-EAE	Boeing 767-27EER	24832/316	ex F-GHGD	605	
☐ 4X-EAF	Boeing 767-27EER	24854/326	ex F-GHGE	606	
☐ 4X-EAJ	Boeing 767-330ER	25208/381	ex N208LS	635	
☐ 4X-EAP	Boeing 767-3Y0ER	24953/405	ex TF-FIA		Lsd fr ICE
☐ 4X-EAR	Boeing 767-352ER	26262/583	ex VN-A769		
☐ 4X-ECA	Boeing 777-258ER	30831/319		101 Galillee	
☐ 4X-ECB	Boeing 777-258ER	30832/325		102 Negev	
☐ 4X-ECC	Boeing 777-258ER	30833/335		103 Hasharon	
☐ 4X-ECD	Boeing 777-258ER	33169/405		104 Carmel	
☐ 4X-ECE	Boeing 777-258ER	36083/648	ex N5017Q	105 Sderot	
☐ 4X-ECF	Boeing 777-258ER	36084/655	ex N5022E	106	

EL-ROM AIRLINES		(ELR)		Tel Aviv-Sde Dov (SDV)
☐ 4X-CCD	Piper PA-31-350 Navajo Chieftain	31-7652166	ex N62919	
☐ 4X-CCF	Piper PA-31-350 Navajo Chieftain	31-7652169	ex N62921	

ISRAIR		Israir (6H/ISR)		Tel Aviv-Ben Gurion (TLV)
☐ (4X-ABC)	Airbus A320-211	0333	ex YL-LCA	Lsd fr LTC
☐ 4X-ABD	Airbus A320-211	0384	ex YL-LCB	Lsd fr LTC
☐ 4X-ATL	ATR 42-320	089	ex F-WQCY	
☐ 4X-ATM	ATR 42-320	069	ex F-WQFS	
☐ 4X-ATN	ATR 42-320	053	ex F-WQGN	
☐ 4X-ATO	ATR 42-320	064	ex F-GPEC	

MOONAIR AVIATION		(MOO)		Tel Aviv-Sde Dov (SDV)
☐ 4X-CBY	Piper PA-23-250 Aztec E	27-7304990	ex N405PB	
☐ 4X-CCJ	Piper PA-31-350 Navajo Chieftain	31-7405140	ex G-FOEL	

SUN D'OR INTERNATIONAL AIRLINES	Echo Romeo (2R/ERO)	Tel Aviv-Ben Gurion (TLV)

Wholly owned subsidiary of El Al Israel Airlines; leases aircraft from the parent.

TAMIR AVIATION		(TMI)		Haifa (HFA)
☐ 4X-ANU	Piper PA-31 Turbo Navajo	31-616	ex N6746L	
☐ 4X-CII	British Aerospace Jetstream 32	860	ex N860AE	
☐ 4X-CIJ	British Aerospace Jetstream 32	916	ex N916AE	

5A- LIBYA (Socialist People's Libyan Arab Jamahiriya)

AFRIQIYAH AIRWAYS		Afriqiyah (8U/AAW)		Tripoli-Ben Gashir Intl (TIP)
☐ 5A-IAY	Airbus A300B4-620	354	ex TS-IAY	Lsd fr NVJ
☐ 5A-ONC	Airbus A319-111	3615	ex D-AVYM	
☐ 5A-OND	Airbus A319-111	3657	ex D-AVYS	
☐ 5A-ONI	Airbus A319-111	4004	ex D-AVYC	
☐ SU-LBG	Airbus A320-233	0743	ex 9V-VLD	Lsd fr TAS
☐ SU-LBH	Airbus A320-233	0739	ex 9V-VLC	Lsd fr TAS
☐ S5-AAA	Airbus A320-231	0043	ex SX-BAS	Lsd fr ADR
☐ 5A-ONA	Airbus A320-214	3224	ex F-WWBY	
☐ 5A-ONB	Airbus A320-214	3236	ex F-WWBI	
☐ 5A-ONF	Airbus A330-202	999	ex F-WWYV	
☐ 5A-ONG	Airbus A330-202	1024	ex F-WWYS	
☐ 5A-ONH	Airbus A330-202	1043	ex F-WWKM	
☐ 5A-ONE	Airbus A340-213	151	ex HZ-WBT4	VIPop for Govt

AIR LIBYA		Air Libya (7Q/TLR)		Tripoli-Mitiga/Benghazi (MJI/BEN)
☐ 5A-	Antonov An-140			on order
☐ 5A-	Antonov An-140			on order
☐ 5A-	Antonov An-140			on order
☐ 5A-	Antonov An-140			on order
☐ 5A-	Antonov An-140			on order
☐ EX-87664	Yakovlev Yak-40	9240825	ex CCCP-87664	Lsd fr AAP
☐ 4L-AVR	Yakovlev Yak-40	9420434	ex EX-87412	
☐ 5A-DKG	Yakovlev Yak-40	9640152	ex 4L-AVP	
☐ 5A-DKH	Yakovlev Yak-40	9631149	ex EX-88207	
☐ 5A-DKI	Yakovlev Yak-40	9331229	ex 9L-LDK	
☐ 5A-DKJ	Yakovlev Yak-40K	9720853	ex EX-88270	
☐ 5A-DKK	Yakovlev Yak-40	9420235	ex EX-87426	
☐ 5A-DKM	Yakovlev Yak-40KD	9841659	ex ST-ARK	Freighter
☐ 5A-DHN	de Havilland DHC-6 Twin Otter 300	712		
☐ 5A-DKQ	British Aerospace 146 Srs.300	E3191	ex G-JEBD	
☐ 5A-DKV	Boeing 727-2D6	22374/1711	ex 7T-VEV	
☐ 5A-DKX	Boeing 727-2D6	22765/1801	ex 7T-VEX	stored BEN
☐ 5A-DKY	Boeing 737-2D6 (Nordam 3)	22766/853	ex 7T-VEY	

AIR ONE NINE		(N6/ONR)		Tripoli-Ben Gashir Intl (TIP)
☐ ZS-GAR	Douglas DC-9-32 (ABS 3)	47132/229	ex 3D-MRO	
☐ 3D-MRL	Douglas DC-9-32	47102/198	ex S9-TGL	

Operates services for its parent, One Nine Petroleum

AL-AJNIHAH AIRWAYS *(ANH)* *Tripoli-Ben Gashir Intl (TIP)*

Operates services with Ilyushin Il-76s leased from other operators as required

ALDAWLYH AIR *Aldawlyh Air (IIG)* *Tripoli-Ben Gashir Intl/Mitiga (TIP/MJI)*

Operates cargo services with Antonov An-124 leased from Libyan Air Cargo as required

ALLEBIA AIR CARGO *Tripoli-Ben Gashir Intl (TIP)*

☐ 5A-DSH	Antonov An-72	36572020337	ex 9Q-...		

BURAQ AIR *Buraqair (UZ/BRQ)* *Tripoli-Mitiga/Benghazi (MJI/BEN)*

☐ J2-KCG	Douglas DC-10-15	48258/346	ex EX-10151		
☐ 5A-DGR	British Aerospace Jetstream 32	945	ex HL5214		
☐ 5A-DMG	Boeing 737-8GK/W	34948/2074	ex N1787B	Tripoli	
☐ 5A-DMH	Boeing 737-8GK/W	34949/2106		Benghazi	
☐ 5A-DMN	Boeing 727-228	22287/1710	ex TC-JEC		stored TIP
☐ 5A-DMO	Boeing 727-2F2	20983/1088	ex TC-JBJ		stored TIP
☐ 5A-DMP	Boeing 727-2F2	20981/1086	ex TC-JBG		stored TIP
☐ 5A-DMU	Boeing 737-2D6	21212/459	ex 7T-VEO		stored TIP
☐ 5A-DMV	Boeing 737-2D6	21286/482	ex 7T-VER		stored TIP
☐ 5A-DNA	Ilyushin Il-76TD	0023439140			
☐ 5A-MAB	Boeing 737-406	24857/1902	ex PH-BDU		

GHADAMES AIR TRANSPORT *(OG/GHT)* *Tripoli-Ben Gashir Intl (TIP)*

Operates services with British Aerospace 146s and Lockheed L1011 Tristars leased from other operators as required

GLOBAL AIR *(-/GAK)*

☐ 5A-DQA	Ilyushin Il-76TD	1003405167	ex EX-105		
☐ 5A-DQB	Ilyushin Il-86	51483208069	ex UN-86101		

KALLAT EL SAKER AIR *(KES)* *Kishinev-Chisinau / Sharjah (KIV/SHJ)*

☐ EK-85536	Tupolev Tu-154B-2	82A-536	ex CCCP-85536		Lsd fr STH
☐ XT-BRK	Lockheed L-1011-500 Tristar	293B-1243	ex OD-JOE		
☐ XT-DMK	Boeing 747-238B	21316/309	ex 3D-NEF		
☐ XT-DMS	Boeing 747-238B	20009/147	ex 3D-NED		stored
☐ XT-RAD	Lockheed L-1011-500 Tristar	193H-1246	ex OD-MIR		
☐ OD-ZEE	Lockheed L-1011-500 Tristar	293B-1239	ex SX-CVB		on order

LIBYAN AIR CARGO *Libac (LCR)* *Tripoli-Mitiga (MJI)*

☐ 5A-DOA	Antonov An-26B	12306	ex LAAF 8207		
☐ 5A-DOB	Antonov An-26B	12307	ex LAAF 8208		
☐ 5A-DOC	Antonov An-26B	12308	ex LAAF 8209		Waddan
☐ 5A-DOD	Antonov An-26B	12406	ex LAAF 8210		
☐ 5A-DOE	Antonov An-26B	13003			
☐ 5A-DOF	Antonov An-26B	13007			
☐ 5A-DOG	Antonov An-26-100	13008			
☐ 5A-DOH	Antonov An-26B	13202		no titles	
☐ 5A-DON	Antonov An-26B	13009	ex LAAF 8304		
☐ 5A-DOP	Antonov An-26B	12301	ex 5A-DNP		stored MJI
☐ 5A-DOU	Antonov An-26B-100	13201T	also reported as c/n 13202T and ex LAAF 8315		
☐ 5A-DOV	Antonov An-26B-100	13109T	ex LAAF		
☐ 5A-DOW	Antonov An-26B	11808	ex LAAF 8203		
☐ 5A-DOZ	Antonov An-26B-100		ex LAAF 8214		

☐ 5A-DKS	Ilyushin Il-76TD	1033418584	ex RA-76843		
☐ 5A-DLL	Ilyushin Il-76	0093493799			
☐ 5A-DNB	Ilyushin Il-76TD	0023437086			
☐ 5A-DNC	Ilyushin Il-76TD	0023437084			
☐ 5A-DND	Ilyushin Il-76TD	0033445299			
☐ 5A-DNE	Ilyushin Il-76T	0013432952			
☐ 5A-DNG	Ilyushin Il-76TD	0013432961			
☐ 5A-DNH	Ilyushin Il-76TD	0033446356			
☐ 5A-DNI	Ilyushin Il-76T	0013430878			stored FJR
☐ 5A-DNJ	Ilyushin Il-76T	0013430869			stored DME
☐ 5A-DNK	Ilyushin Il-76T	0013430882			
☐ 5A-DNO	Ilyushin Il-76T	0043451509	ex EX-043		
☐ 5A-DNP	Ilyushin Il-76TD	0043451516			
☐ 5A-DNQ	Ilyushin Il-76TD	0043454641			
☐ 5A-DNS	Ilyushin Il-76TD	0023439145			
☐ 5A-DNT	Ilyushin Il-76TD	0023439141			
☐ 5A-DNU	Ilyushin Il-76TD	0043454651		all-white	
☐ 5A-DNV	Ilyushin Il-76TD	0043454645			
☐ 5A-DRR	Ilyushin Il-76M	083415469			
☐ 5A-DRS	Ilyushin Il-76M	1033414474	ex RA-76367		

☐ 5A-DRT	Ilyushin Il-76TD	1003403063	ex LAAF-110		
☐ 5A-DZZ	Ilyushin Il-76M	093416501			
☐ 5A-DJQ	Lockheed L-382G-40C Hercules	4798	ex N501AK		
☐ 5A-DJR	Lockheed L-382E-15C Hercules	4302	ex RP-C99		
☐ 5A-DKL	Antonov An-124-100 Ruslan	19530502761	ex UR-82066	Susa	
☐ 5A-DKN	Antonov An-124-100 Ruslan	19530502792	ex RA-82003	Sabrata	
☐ 5A-DOM	Lockheed L-382G-62C Hercules	4992	ex N4268M		
☐ 5A-DOO	Lockheed L-382G-64C Hercules	5000	ex N4269M		
☐ 5A-DRC	Antonov An-32P	0703	ex UR-48093		Jt ops with LAAF
☐ 5A-DRD	Antonov An-32P	1306	ex UR-48004		Jt ops with LAAF
☐ 5A-DRF	Antonov An-32P	3602			Jt ops with LAAF
☐ 5A-	Antonov An-72		ex LAAF-721		
☐ 5A-	Antonov An-72		ex LAAF-722		
☐ 5A-	Antonov An-72		ex LAAF-723		
☐ 5A-	Antonov An-72		ex LAAF-724		

LIBYAN AIRLINES — *Libair (LN/LAA)* — *Tripoli-Ben Gashir Intl (TIP)*

☐ 5A-	Airbus A320-214		ex		on order
☐ 5A-	Airbus A320-214		ex		on order
☐ 5A-	Airbus A320-214		ex		on order
☐ 5A-	Airbus A320-214		ex		on order
☐ 5A-	Airbus A320-214		ex		on order
☐ 5A-LAF	ATR 42-500	691	ex F-WWLM		
☐ 5A-LAG	ATR 42-500	802	ex F-WWLU		
☐ 5A-DIB	Boeing 727-2L5	21051/1109			stored TIP
☐ 5A-DIC	Boeing 727-2L5	21052/1110			stored TIP
☐ 5A-DID	Boeing 727-2L5	21229/1213			stored TIP
☐ 5A-DIE	Boeing 727-2L5	21230/1215			stored TIP
☐ 5A-DIF	Boeing 727-2L5	21332/1257			stored TIP
☐ 5A-DIH	Boeing 727-2L5	21539/1371	ex N1253E		
☐ 5A-DII	Boeing 727-2L5	21540/1386	ex N1261E		
☐ 5A-LAA	Canadair CL-600-2D24 (CRJ-900)	15120	ex C-FPQO		
☐ 5A-LAB	Canadair CL-600-2D24 (CRJ-900)	15121	ex C-FPUM		
☐ 5A-LAC	Canadair CL-600-2D24 (CRJ-900)	15122	ex C-FPUN		
☐ 5A-LAD	Canadair CL-600-2D24NG (CRJ-900)	15214	ex C-		
☐ 5A-LAE	Canadair CL-600-2D24NG (CRJ-900)	15216	ex C-		
☐ 5A-DCT	de Havilland DHC-6 Twin Otter 300	627			
☐ 5A-DCV	de Havilland DHC-6 Twin Otter 300	637			
☐ 5A-DCX	de Havilland DHC-6 Twin Otter 300	641			
☐ 5A-DCZ	de Havilland DHC-6 Twin Otter 300	645			
☐ 5A-DDB	de Havilland DHC-6 Twin Otter 300	653			
☐ 5A-DDE	de Havilland DHC-6 Twin Otter 300	677			
☐ 5A-DHY	de Havilland DHC-6 Twin Otter 300	661	ex C-GELZ		
☐ 5A-DJG	de Havilland DHC-6 Twin Otter 300	744	ex (FAP-2029)		
☐ 5A-DJH	de Havilland DHC-6 Twin Otter 300	747			
☐ 5A-DJI	de Havilland DHC-6 Twin Otter 300	757			
☐ 5A-DJJ	de Havilland DHC-6 Twin Otter 300	769			
☐ TS-IND	Airbus A320-212	0348	ex OY-CNN		Lsd fr LBT
☐ TS-INE	Airbus A320-212	0222	ex OY-CNC		Lsd fr LBT
☐ 5A-DDQ	BAC One-Eleven 414EG (QTA 2)	158	ex C5-LKI		VIP
☐ 5A-DGC	Cessna 402C II	402C0045	ex N5800C		
☐ 5A-DHG	Cessna 402C II	402C0464	ex N8737Q		
☐ 5A-DHH	Cessna 402C II	402C0444	ex N6790F		
☐ 5A-DHZ	Swearingen SA.226AT Merlin III	T-345	ex OO-HSC		
☐ 5A-DJB	Swearingen SA.226AT Merlin III	T-388	ex OO-XSC		
☐ 5A-DLV	Fokker F.28 Fellowship 4000	11200	ex PH-EXV	Mares	stored
☐ 5A-DLW	Fokker F.28 Fellowship 4000	11194	ex PH-EXZ		
☐ 5A-DLY	Airbus A300B4-622R	601	ex TS-IAX	Al-Gordabia	
☐ 5A-DLZ	Airbus A300B4-622R	616	ex TS-IAZ	Derna	op by NVJ
☐ 5A-DTG	Fokker F.28 Fellowship 4000	11139	ex PK-MSU		
☐ 5A-DTH	Fokker F.28 Fellowship 4000	11140	ex PK-MSV		

LIBYAVIA — *Tripoli-Ben Gashir Intl (TIP)*

☐ 5A-DMX	Airbus A300C4-203F	083	ex TC-ACT	Mersin	Op by RUN

PETRO AIR

☐ 5A-AGR	de Havilland DHC-8-315	601	ex PH-AGR		

TOBRUK AIR — *Tobruk Air (7T/TQB)* — *Tripoli-Ben Gashir Intl (TIP)*

Operates cargo flights with leased Douglas DC-10-30F and Ilyushin Il-76 aircraft leased from other operators when required

5B- CYPRUS (Republic of Cyprus)

CYPRUS AIRWAYS — Cyprus (CY/CYP) — Larnaca (LCA)

	Type	c/n	Previous	Name	Remarks
☐ 5B-DAW	Airbus A320-231	0038	ex F-WWDZ	Agapinor	
☐ 5B-DBA	Airbus A320-231	0180	ex F-WWIT	Evagoras	
☐ 5B-DBB	Airbus A320-231	0256	ex F-WWBH	Akamas	
☐ 5B-DBC	Airbus A320-231	0295	ex F-WWIE	Tefkros	
☐ 5B-DBD	Airbus A320-231	0316	ex F-WWBC	Onisilos	
☐ 5B-DBO	Airbus A319-112	1729	ex D-AVWR	Nikoklis	
☐ 5B-DBP	Airbus A319-112	1768	ex D-AVWB	Chalkanor	
☐ 5B-DCF	Airbus A319-132	2718	ex N518NK	Larnaka	
☐ 5B-DBS	Airbus A330-243	505	ex F-WWKO	Ammochostos	
☐ 5B-DBT	Airbus A330-243	526	ex F-WWKY	Keryneia	

EUROCYPRIA AIRLINES — Eurocypria (UI/ECA) — Larnaca (LCA)

	Type	c/n	Previous	Name	Remarks
☐ 5B-DBR	Boeing 737-8Q8/W	30720/2235	ex N1787B	Eypos	green
☐ 5B-DBU	Boeing 737-8Q8/W	32796/1272	ex N6055X	Zephyros	pale blue
☐ 5B-DBV	Boeing 737-8Q8/W	30654/1295		Levantes	dark blue
☐ 5B-DBW	Boeing 737-8Q8/W	30671/1307	ex C-GLBW	Haistros	grey; Lsd to SWG
☐ 5B-DBX	Boeing 737-8Q8/W	33699/1309	ex C-GDBX	Gregos	white
☐ 5B-DBZ	Boeing 737-8BK/W	33030/1968		Notos	purple

5H- TANZANIA (United Republic of Tanzania)

AIR EXCEL — Tinga-Tinga (XLL) — Arusha (ARK)

	Type	c/n	Previous	Remarks
☐ 5H-AES	LET L-410UVP-E20	871811	ex 5H-PAD	
☐ 5H-AXL	Cessna 208B Caravan I	208B0401	ex D-FHEW	
☐ 5H-EMK	Cessna TU206G Turbo Stationair 8 II	U20604638	ex 5H-SDA	
☐ 5H-SMK	Cessna 208B Caravan I	208B0654	ex VT-TAP	
☐ 5H-WOW	Reims Cessna F406 Caravan II	F406-0060	ex PH-GUG	

AIR TANZANIA — Tanzania (TC/ATC) — Dar-es-Salaam (DAR)

	Type	c/n	Previous	Remarks
☐ 5H-MVZ	Boeing 737-247 (Nordam 3)	23602/1347	ex N375DL	stored JNB
☐ 5H-MWF	de Havilland DHC-8-311	474	ex G-BRYW	
☐ 5H-MWG	de Havilland DHC-8-311	462	ex G-BRYV	

AURIC AIR SERVICES — Mwanza (MWZ)

	Type	c/n	Previous	Remarks
☐ 5H-	Cessna 208B Caravan I	208B1311	ex N2123S	
☐ 5H-TWF	Cessna 208B Caravan I	208B1315	ex N21716	
☐ 5H-TWO	Piper PA-34-200T Seneca	34-8170030	ex ZS-KTK	

COASTAL AVIATION — Coastal Travel (7I/CSV) — Dar-es-Salaam (DAR)

	Type	c/n	Previous	Remarks
☐ 5H-BAD	Cessna 208B Caravan I	208B0586	ex N5QP	
☐ 5H-BAT	Cessna 208B Caravan I	208B1030	ex N12554	
☐ 5H-HOT	Cessna 208B Caravan I	208B0677	ex N1256N	
☐ 5H-JOE	Cessna 208B Caravan I	208B0570	ex N9EU	
☐ 5H-MAD	Cessna 208B Caravan I	208B0872	ex N1294K	
☐ 5H-POA	Cessna 208B Caravan I	208B0965	ex N1129Y	
☐ 5H-SUN	Cessna 208B Caravan I	208B0754	ex 5H-PAF	
☐ 5H-VIP	Cessna 208B Caravan I	208B0714	ex N208FK	
☐ 5H-CCT	Cessna TU206G Stationair 6	U20604597	ex ZS-MXV	
☐ 5H-CTL	Cessna TU206F Stationair	U20601988	ex 5H-PBF	
☐ 5H-EXC	Pilatus PC-12/45	220	ex ZS-EXC	dam, repaired?
☐ 5H-GUN	Cessna U206G Stationair 6	U20605223	ex 5H-TGT	
☐ 5H-SRP	Pilatus PC-12/45	317	ex ZS-SRP	
☐ 5H-TOY	Cessna 404 Titan II	404-0668	ex 5Y-MCK	

KILWA AIR

	Type	c/n	Previous	Remarks
☐ 5H-KLA	Britten-Norman BN-2B-21 Islander	2002	ex 5X-MHB	id not confirmed
☐ ZS-PRL	CASA 212-200	180	ex N160GA	Lsd fr KUS
☐ 5H-MLB	Cessna T210N Centurion II	21064259	ex ZS-LVC	

Current status uncertain

NORTHERN AIR — Arusha (ARK)

	Type	c/n	Previous	Remarks
☐ 5H-NAA	Cessna 208 Caravan I	20800109	ex N9628F	
☐ 5H-NAC	Cessna 208B Caravan I	208B0757	ex N1307D	
☐ 5H-SJF	Cessna 208B Caravan I	208B0950	ex N1130T	

PRECISIONAIR — *Precisionair (PW/PRF)* — *Arusha (ARK)*

Reg	Type	C/n	Previous	Notes
☐ 5H-PAA	ATR 42-320	308	ex F-WQHB	City of Arusha
☐ 5H-PAG	ATR 42-320	384	ex F-WQJO	
☐ 5H-PWA	ATR 72-212A	780	ex F-WWES	
☐ 5H-PWB	ATR 72-212A	834	ex F-WWEB	
☐ 5H-PWC	ATR 72-212A	866	ex F-WWEP	
☐ 5H-PWD	ATR 72-212A	880	ex F-WWEI	
☐ 5H-PAY	Reims Cessna 406 Caravan I	F406-0035	ex ZS-OGY	

REGIONAL AIR SERVICES — *Regional Services (REG)* — *Arusha (ARK)*

Reg	Type	C/n	Previous	Notes
☐ A6-MAR	de Havilland DHC-6 Twin Otter 300	841	ex N9045S	
☐ 5H-BMP	de Havilland DHC-7-102	80	ex 5Y-BMP	
☐ 5H-KEG	de Havilland DHC-6 Twin Otter 300	799	ex 5Y-KEG	
☐ 5H-MVJ	de Havilland DHC-6 Twin Otter 300	582	ex ZS-OVI	

SKY AVIATION TANZANIA — *Dar-es-Salaam (DAR)*

Reg	Type	C/n	Previous	Notes
☐ 5H-SKT	Piper PA-31-350 Chieftain	31-8152058	ex A2-AHP	
☐ 5H-SKX	Cessna 402B	402B-0829	ex 5Y-EAL	
☐ 5H-SKY	Piper PA-32-300 Six	32-770061	ex N3258Q	dbr?

TANZANAIR - TANZANIAN AIR SERVICES — *Dar-es-Salaam (DAR)*

Reg	Type	C/n	Previous	Notes
☐ 5H-GHL	Cessna U206F Stationair II	U20602583	ex 5H-JBJ	
☐ 5H-LDS	Cessna 310I	310I0029	ex 5Y-AJN	
☐ 5H-TZC	Reims Cessna F406 Caravan II	F406-0028	ex N7037C	
☐ 5H-TZE	Reims Cessna F406 Caravan II	F406-0046	ex OY-PED	
☐ 5H-TZT	Cessna 208B Caravan I	208B0664	ex ZS-PSR	
☐ 5H-TZU	Cessna 208B Caravan I	208B0639	ex ZS-PJJ	
☐ 5H-TZX	Beech 200 Super King Air	BB-1196	ex Z-ZLT	

TROPICAL AIR — *Zanzibar (ZNZ)*

Reg	Type	C/n	Previous	Notes
☐ 5H-OLA	Cessna 208B Caravan I	208B0384	ex 7T-VIH	
☐ 5H-TAR	Piper PA-34-200T Seneca II	34-7970038	ex 5H-MNF	
☐ 5H-TZO	Partenavia P.68B	120	ex 5H-AZO	
☐ 5H-TZY	Partenavia P.68B	149	ex 5H-AZY	

TWIN WINGS AIR — *Zanzibar (ZNZ)*

Reg	Type	C/n	Previous	Notes
☐ 5H-MAY	Cessna 404 Titan II	404-0241	ex 5Y-EDH	
☐ 5H-RAY	Cessna 404 Titan II	404-0007	ex N3935C	

ZANAIR — *Zanair (B4/TAN)* — *Zanzibar (ZNZ)*

Reg	Type	C/n	Previous	Notes
☐ 5H-LET	LET L-410UVPE-9	892226	ex 9L-LBK	
☐ 5H-ZAA	LET L-410UVP-E20	982631	ex 5H-PAE	
☐ 5H-ZAP	LET L-410UVPE-9	871824	ex 9L-LBV	
☐ 5H-ZAR	Cessna 404 Titan II	404-0835	ex 5H-AEL	
☐ 5H-ZAY	Cessna 404 Titan II	404-0207	ex N798A	
☐ 5H-ZAZ	Cessna 402C	402C0029	ex 5Y-NNM	

ZANTAS AIR SERVICE — *Dar-es-Salaam (DAR)*

Reg	Type	C/n	Previous	Notes
☐ 5H-FAT	Cessna 206H Stationair	20608168	ex 5H-CWF	
☐ 5H-TAK	Cessna 208B Caravan I	208B0891	ex N1239B	
☐ 5H-TAZ	Cessna 208B Caravan I	208B1186	ex N12998	

5N- NIGERIA (Federal Republic of Nigeria)

AERO CONTRACTORS — *Aeroline (AJ/NIG)* — *Lagos (LOS)*

Reg	Type	C/n	Previous	Notes
☐ 5N-AQK	Aérospatiale SA365N Dauphin 2	6108		Op for NNPC
☐ 5N-AQL	Aérospatiale SA365N Dauphin 2	6109		Op for NNPC
☐ 5N-BAF	Aérospatiale SA365N2 Dauphin 2	6430	ex F-WYMC	Op for NNPC
☐ 5N-BDA	Aérospatiale SA365N Dauphin 2	6077	ex 8P-PHM	
☐ 5N-BET	Aérospatiale SA365N Dauphin 2	6087	ex TJ-DEM	
☐ 5N-BGF	Aérospatiale SA365N3 Dauphin 2	6593	ex PH-SHH	
☐ 5N-BIX	Aérospatiale AS365N3 Dauphin 2	6657	ex PH-SHI	
☐ 5N-BIY	Aérospatiale AS365N3 Dauphin 2	6738	ex F-WQVR	
☐ 5N-ESO	Aérospatiale SA365N Dauphin 2	6072	ex PH-SSP	
☐ 5N-STO	Aérospatiale SA365N Dauphin 2	6106	ex PH-SSV	
☐ 5N-BIZ	Boeing 737-4B7	24558/1845	ex N436US	
☐ 5N-BJA	Boeing 737-4B7	24873/1931	ex N446US	
☐ 5N-BKQ	Boeing 737-522	26695/2423	ex VP-BSW	
☐ 5N-BKR	Boeing 737-522	26699/2485	ex VP-BSX	

☐ 5N-BLC	Boeing 737-522	26692/2421	ex VP-BSV	
☐ 5N-BLD	Boeing 737-522	26675/2345	ex VP-BSU	
☐ 5N-BLE	Boeing 737-522	26672/2343	ex VP-BSQ	
☐ 5N-BLG	Boeing 737-522	25387/2179	ex VP-BTI	on order
☐ 5N-BLH	Boeing 737-522	25383/2146	ex VP-BTG	on order
☐ 5N-BIA	de Havilland DHC-8Q-315	608	ex C-FBOA	
☐ 5N-BIB	de Havilland DHC-8Q-315	609	ex C-FCPM	
☐ 5N-BJO	de Havilland DHC-8Q-311	534	ex C-FLGJ	
☐ 5N-DAP	de Havilland DHC-8-311A	244	ex C-GCDO	
☐ 5N-AOA	Aérospatiale AS355F Ecureuil 2	5277	ex F-WZFB	Op for NNPC
☐ 5N-AOB	Aérospatiale AS355F Ecureuil 2	5278	ex F-WZFV	Op for NNPC
☐ 5N-BKG	Eurocopter EC225LP	2681		
☐ 5N-BKH	Eurocopter EC225LP	2688		
☐ 5N-BCX	Sikorsky S-76C+	760466	ex 5N-BCN	
☐ 5N-BHF	Sikorsky S-76C+	760570	ex C-GHRW	
☐ 5N-BHP	Sikorsky S-76C+	760574	ex C-GHRJ	
☐ 5N-BJC	Agusta AW139	31070	ex I-EASY	
☐ 5N-RSN	Agusta AW139	31060	ex 5N-BJB	Op for River States Govt

AFRIJET AIRLINES — *Afrijet (6F/FRJ)* — *Lagos (LOS)*

☐ 5N-BCC	Fairchild FH-227D	575	ex HK-1411	stored LOS
☐ 5N-BKO	McDonnell-Douglas MD-83	49855/1728	ex N311FV	
☐ 5N-FRJ	Fairchild F-27J	126	ex 3C-ZZE	Freighter

AIR MIDWEST — *Lagos (LOS)*

☐ 5N-PVA	Boeing 737-5H6	27354/2637	ex G-GFFH

ALLIED AIR CARGO — *Bambi (AJK)* — *Lagos (LOS)*

☐ 5N-BJN	Boeing 727-221F (FedEx 3)	22540/1796	ex 5X-TON
☐ 5N-BJX	Boeing 727-243F (Raisbeck 3)	22052/1568	ex C-FACA
☐ 5N-BMQ	Boeing 727-2Q6F (FedEx 3)	21971/1540	ex N727WF
☐ 5N-JNR	Boeing 727-217F (FedEx 3)	21056/1122	ex C-FACK
☐ 5N-RKY	Boeing 727-217F (Raisbeck 3)	21055/1117	ex C-FACR

AMBJEK AIR SERVICES — *Abuja (ABV)*

☐ 5N-BEA	LET L-410UVP-E	902435	ex OK-VDT
☐ 5N-BEB	LET L-410UVP-E	882103	ex OK-TDS

ARIK AIR — *Arik Air (W3/ARA)* — *Lagos (LOS)*

☐ 5N-MJA	Boeing 737-322	24454/1750	ex N361UA	Eddington	
☐ 5N-MJB	Boeing 737-322	24360/1692	ex N354UA	Augustine	
☐ 5N-MJC	Boeing 737-7BD/W	33932/2234	ex N320AT	Martin	
☐ 5N-MJD	Boeing 737-7BD/W	36073/2248	ex N323AT	Michael	
☐ 5N-MJE	Boeing 737-7GL/W	34761/2401	ex N737AV	McTighe	
☐ 5N-MJF	Boeing 737-7GL/W	34762/2427	ex N737BV	Queen of Angles	
☐ 5N-MJG	Boeing 737-7BD/W	33944/2576	ex N346AT		
☐ 5N-MJH	Boeing 737-7BD/W	36719/2589	ex N347AT		
☐ 5N-MJI	Boeing 737-76N/W	28640/799	ex N740AL		
☐ 5N-MJJ	Boeing 737-76N/W	28641/809	ex N741AL	City of Benin	
☐ 5N-MJK	Boeing 737-76N/W	30830/855	ex N742AL		
☐ 5N-MJN	Boeing 737-86N/W	35638/2789		Eddington	
☐ 5N-MJO	Boeing 737-86N/W	35640/2819	ex N358MT	Augustine	
☐ 5N-MJP	Boeing 737-8JE/W	38970/3030		Sultan of Sokoto	
☐ 5N-MJQ	Boeing 737-8JE/W	38971/3065		City of Calabar	
☐ 5N-	Boeing 737-8JE/W				on order
☐ 5N-	Boeing 737-8JE/W				on order
☐ 5N-	Boeing 737-8JE/W				on order
☐ 5N-JEA	Canadair CL-600-2D24 (CRJ-900ER)	15058	ex C-FHRH	Anthony	
☐ 5N-JEB	Canadair CL-600-2D24 (CRJ-900ER)	15059	ex C-FHRK	Patrick	
☐ 5N-JEC	Canadair CL-600-2D24 (CRJ-900ER)	15054	ex C-FGNB		
☐ 5N-JED	Canadair CL-600-2D24 (CRJ-900ER)	15114	ex C-FMEP	Abraham	
☐ PH-DMX	de Havilland DHC-8Q-315	574	ex EC-IFK		Lsd fr DNM
☐ PH-DMZ	de Havilland DHC-8Q-315	582	ex EC-IJP		Lsd fr DNM
☐ PH-DXA	de Havilland DHC-8Q-315	586	ex EC-IGS		Lsd fr DNM
☐ 5N-BKU	de Havilland DHC-8-402Q	4207	ex C-FPPU		
☐ 5N-BKV	de Havilland DHC-8-402Q	4219	ex C-FRSN		
☐ 5N-	de Havilland DHC-8-402Q	4262	ex C-FXAW		on order
☐ 5N-	de Havilland DHC-8-402Q		ex C-		on order
☐ 5N-	de Havilland DHC-8-402Q		ex C-		on order
☐ 5N-	de Havilland DHC-8-402Q		ex C-		on order
☐ PH-FZG	Fokker F.27 Mk.050 (Fokker 50)	20202			Lsd fr DNM
☐ PH-JXJ	Fokker F.27 Mk.050 (Fokker 50)	20232	ex PT-SLJ		Lsd fr DNM
☐ PH-KXM	Fokker F.27 Mk.050 (Fokker 50)	20252	ex PT-SLO		Lsd fr DNM

☐ PH-LMT	Fokker F.27 Mk.050 (Fokker 50)	20192	ex EC-HYJ	Lsd fr DNM
☐ CS-TFW	Airbus A340-542	910	ex F-WWTK Our Lady of Perpetual Help	
☐ CS-TFX	Airbus A340-542	912	ex F-WJKI Captin Bob Hayes, OON	

ASSOCIATED AIR CARGO — Associated (SCD) — Lagos (LOS)

☐ UR-PAS	Antonov An-12AP	2401105		op by VPB
☐ 5N-BBL	Short SD.3-60	SH3637	ex G-LEGS	
☐ 5N-BHV	Boeing 727-227F (FedEx 3)	21364/1261	ex N86426	
☐ 5N-BJX	Boeing 727-225F (FedEx 3)	20627/947	ex N361KP	
☐ 5N-BJY	Embraer EMB.120ER Brasilia	120174	ex N388JR	
☐ 5N-BJZ	Embraer EMB.120ER Brasilia	120095	ex N788JR	
☐ 5N-	Embraer EMB.120ER Brasilia	120247	ex N258CA	on order

AXIOM AIR

☐ 5N-BMA	Boeing 737-3Q4 (SF)	24209/1492	ex ZK-TLB

BELLVIEW AIRLINES — Bellview Airlines (B3/BLV) — Lagos (LOS)

☐ F-GHXK	Boeing 737-2A1	21599/514	ex N171AW	Peace	stored LOS
☐ F-GHXL	Boeing 737-2S3	21775/570	ex G-BMOR		
☐ 5N-BFM	Boeing 737-2L9	22733/812	ex N270FL	Fortitude	
☐ 5N-BFX	Boeing 737-291	23024/965	ex CC-CVH	Hope	stored LOS

BRISTOW HELICOPTERS (NIGERIA) — Bristow Helicopters (BHN) — Lagos/ Calabar/ Eket/ Port Harcourt/ Warri (LOS/CBQ/-/PHC/-)

☐ 5N-BGO	Aérospatiale AS.332L	2092	ex G-BRXU	
☐ 5N-BGP	Aérospatiale AS.332L	2046	ex G-BWMG	
☐ 5N-BKJ	Aérospatiale AS.332L	2170	ex G-PUMI	
☐ 5N-BCZ	Bell 412SP	33179	ex B-55521	
☐ 5N-BDZ	Bell 412EP	36278	ex 9Y-ALI	
☐ 5N-BFU	Bell 412EP	36318	ex N7022F	
☐ 5N-BGS	Bell 412SP	33186	ex N464AC	
☐ 5N-BHB	Bell 412EP	36273	ex XA-TTF	
☐ 5N-BHD	Bell 412EP	36354	ex N4202A	
☐ 5N-BIM	Bell 412EP	36373	ex N31195	
☐ 5N-BIO	Bell 412EP	36378	ex N106AL	
☐ 5N-BIP	Bell 412EP	36383	ex N105AL	
☐ 5N-BIR	Bell 412EP	36386	ex N107AL	
☐ 5N-BIS	Bell 412EP	36387	ex N132AL	
☐ 5N-BML	Bell 412EP	36433	ex G-OIBU	
☐ 5N-BDH	Eurocopter EC155B	6591	ex F-WQDQ	Op for Shell Nigeria
☐ 5N-BDI	Eurocopter EC155B	6602		Op for Shell Nigeria
☐ 5N-BDJ	Eurocopter EC155B	6607		Op for Shell Nigeria
☐ 5N-BDK	Eurocopter EC155B	6608		Op for Shell Nigeria
☐ 5N-BDL	Eurocopter EC155B	6610	ex F-WQDA	Op for Shell Nigeria
☐ 5N-BDM	Eurocopter EC155B	6611	ex F-WQDH	Op for Shell Nigeria
☐ 5N-BBO	Sikorsky S-76A++	760114	ex G-BVKP	
☐ 5N-BCT	Sikorsky S-76A++	760109	ex G-BZJT	
☐ 5N-BGC	Sikorsky S-76C+	760481	ex LN-ONY	
☐ 5N-BGD	Sikorsky S-76C+	760540	ex N864AL	
☐ 5N-BGE	Sikorsky S-76C+	760545	ex N20509	
☐ 5N-BIL	Sikorsky S-76C+	760591	ex N869AL	
☐ 5N-BJT	Sikorsky S-76C+	760638	ex N872AL	
☐ 5N-BJU	Sikorsky S-76C+	760640	ex N876AL	
☐ 5N-BKM	Sikorsky S-76C+	760660	ex N45083	
☐ 5N-BMD	Sikorsky S-76C+	760456	ex LN-ONZ	
☐ 5N-BMI	Sikorsky S-76C+	760732	ex G-CFPU	
☐ 5N-BLX	Sikorsky S-92A	920082	ex G-CFCA	
☐ 5N-BMN	Sikorsky S-92A	920103	ex G-CGCI	
☐ 5N-BFI	Bell 407	53550	ex N2531G	
☐ 5N-BHL	Beech 200 Super King Air	BB-387	ex G-BFOL	
☐ 5N-BJE	Aérospatiale AS365N2 Dauphin 2	6446	ex EP-HCK	
☐ 5N-	Bell 206L-4 LongRanger IV	52191	ex N178AL	

Subsidiary of Bristow Group

CAPITAL AIRLINES — Capital Shuttle (NCP) — Lagos (LOS)

☐ 5N-BLN	Embraer EMB.120RT Brasilia	120191	ex ZS-PGZ	
☐ 5N-CCE	Embraer EMB.120ER Brasilia	120120	ex N194SW	stored LOS
☐ 5N-TUE	Embraer EMB.120ER Brasilia	120109	ex N763BC	stored LOS

CAVERTON HELICOPTERS — *(CJR)* — *Lagos (LOS)*

Reg	Type	C/n	Previous	Name	Remarks
☐ 5N-BHK	Aérospatiale SA365N Dauphin 2	6128	ex CS-HFH		Lsd fr HeliPortugal
☐ 5N-BHS	Aérospatiale AS350B2 Ecureuil	1871	ex CS-HDK		Lsd fr HeliPortugal
☐ 5N-BHT	Aérospatiale AS350B2 Ecureuil	1222	ex CS-HEO		Lsd fr HeliPortugal
☐ 5N-BIK	Aérospatiale AS365N Dauphin 2	6138	ex F-GNVS		Lsd fr HeliPortugal
☐ 5N-BLJ	de Havilland DHC-6 Twin Otter 300	816	ex HB-LUB		

CHANCHANGI AIRLINES

Reg	Type	C/n	Previous	Name	Remarks
☐ 5N-BMB	Boeing 737-3J6	25079/2016	ex B-2536		
☐ 5N-BMC	Boeing 737-3Z0	25089/2027	ex B-2537		

DANA — *Dana Air (DAV)* — *Kaduna (KAD)*

Reg	Type	C/n	Previous	Name	Remarks
☐ 5N-ARP	Dornier 228-201	8013	ex (5N-AOH)		
☐ 5N-AUN	Dornier 228-201	8076	ex D-CEPT		
☐ 5N-DOB	Dornier 228-202	8026	ex N232RP		
☐ 5N-DOD	Dornier 228-202	8048	ex N235RP		for GAM, VH
☐ 5N-DOE	Dornier 228-202	8049	ex N236RP		for GAM, VH
☐ 5N-DOF	Dornier 228-202	8125	ex N245RP		for GAM, VH
☐ 5N-DOI	Dornier 228-202	8137	ex N237RP		for GAM, VH
☐ 5N-DOJ	Dornier 228-202	8138	ex N238RP		for GAM, VH
☐ 5N-DOK	Dornier 228-202	8140	ex N240RP		for GAM, VH
☐ 5N-DOL	Dornier 228-202	8145	ex N241RP		
☐ 5N-DOM	Dornier 228-202	8147	ex N242RP		for GAM, VH
☐ 5N-BCA	Piper PA-23 Aztec 250D	27-4220	ex G-AYZN		
☐ 5N-DOX	Dornier 328-110	3073	ex OE-LKF		
☐ 5N-DOY	Dornier 328-110	3089	ex OE-LKG		
☐ 5N-IEP	Dornier 328-110	3026	ex D-CDHL		
☐ 5N-SAG	Dornier 328-110	3016	ex D-CASU		

DANA AIR

Reg	Type	C/n	Previous	Name	Remarks
☐ 5N-DAL	McDonnell-Douglas MD-83	53018/1779	ex N943AS		
☐ 5N-JAI	McDonnell-Douglas MD-83	53016/1850	ex N968AS		
☐ 5N-RAM	McDonnell-Douglas MD-83	53019/1784	ex N944AS		
☐ 5N-SAI	McDonnell-Douglas MD-83	53020/1789	ex N947AS		

EAS AIR LINES — *Echoline (EXW)* — *Lagos (LOS)*

Reg	Type	C/n	Previous	Name	Remarks
☐ 5N-DOZ	Dornier 328-110	3031	ex D-CDXL		

FREEDOM AIR SERVICES — *Inter Freedom (FFF)* — *Lagos (LOS)*

Reg	Type	C/n	Previous	Name	Remarks
☐ 5N-BCY	Boeing 727-235	19461/538	ex N461RD	Hajiya Asmal	

IRS AIRLINES — *Silverbird (LVB)* — *Lagos (LOS)*

Reg	Type	C/n	Previous	Name	Remarks
☐ 5N-AKR	Boeing 727-223A (Raisbeck 3)	20984/1121	ex N843AA	Kalifa Tsitaku	
☐ 5N-BJM	Embraer EMB.145LR (ERJ-145LR)	14500984	ex PT-SKE		
☐ 5N-CEO	Fokker F.28-0100 (Fokker 100)	11295	ex N860US	Hajiya Babba	stored WOE
☐ 5N-COO	Fokker F.28-0100 (Fokker 100)	11297	ex N861US	Kalifa Junior	
☐ 5N-HIR	Fokker F.28-0100 (Fokker 100)	11498	ex G-CFBU		
☐ 5N-NCZ	Fokker F.28 Fellowship 4000	11241	ex ZS-OPS		
☐ 5N-SSZ	Fokker F.28 Fellowship 4000	11190	ex ZS-BAL		

KABO AIR — *Kabo (N2/QNK)* — *Kano (KAN)*

Reg	Type	C/n	Previous	Name	Remarks
☐ 5N-DKB	Boeing 747-251B	23548/644	ex N637US		
☐ 5N-EEE	Boeing 747-243B	19732/134	ex G-VGIN		stored MZJ
☐ 5N-JRM	Boeing 747-251B	23549/651	ex N638US		
☐ 5N-MAD	Boeing 747-251B	23547/642	ex N636US		
☐ 5N-NNN	Boeing 747-287B	21189/274	ex G-VIRG		stored CGK
☐ 5N-OOO	Boeing 747-136	20952/246	ex G-AWNP		
☐ 5N-PDP	Boeing 747-238B	20842/238	ex G-VJFK	Dr MA Dankabo Jarman Kano	
☐ 5N-PPP	Boeing 747-238B	20921/241	ex G-VLAX		
☐ 5N-RRR	Boeing 747-136	19765/109	ex G-AWNE	Alhaji Ado Bayaro, Emir of Kano	
☐ 5N-LLL	Boeing 727-224 (FedEx 3)	20654	ex N32724		stored ADD

MAXAIR

Reg	Type	C/n	Previous	Name	Remarks
☐ 5N-BMG	Boeing 747-346	23638/658	ex JA8177		
☐ 5N-DBM	Boeing 747-346	23968/693	ex JA8184		
☐ 5N-DDK	Boeing 747-346	23967/692	ex JA8183		
☐ 5N-MBB	Boeing 747-346	24018/694	ex HS-UTS		

MED-VIEW AIRLINES

☐ CS-TEB	Lockheed L-1011-500 Tristar	293A-1240	ex V2-LEO	Lsd fr MMZ
☐ CS-TFK	Boeing 757-2G5	23983/161	ex N983MQ	Lsd fr MMZ

NIGERIAN EAGLE AIRLINES (VK/VGN) Lagos (LOS)

☐ 5N-VNC	Boeing 737-33V	29338/3114	ex G-EZYN	
☐ 5N-VND	Boeing 737-33V	29337/3113	ex G-EZYM	
☐ 5N-VNE	Boeing 737-33V	29340/3121	ex G-EZYP	
☐ 5N-VNF	Boeing 737-33V	29341/3125	ex G-EZYR	
☐ 5N-VNG	Boeing 737-33V	29342/3127	ex G-EZYS	
☐ 5N-VNH	Embraer 190-100IGW (190AR)	19000210	ex PT-SGT	
☐ 5N-VNI	Embraer 190-100IGW (190AR)	19000226	ex PT-SHM	
☐ 5N-	Embraer 190-100IGW (190AR)		ex PT-	on order

OVERLAND AIRWAYS Overland (OJ/OLA) Lagos / Abuja (LOS/ABV)

☐ 5N-BCO	Beech 1900D	UE-225	ex N225GL	stored HLA
☐ 5N-BCP	Beech 1900D	UE-116	ex N116YV	
☐ 5N-BCR	ATR 42-300	031	ex F-WQNR	
☐ 5N-BCS	ATR 42-300	025	ex EC-IYE	
☐ N340SS	SAAB SF.340A	340A-022	ex SE-C22	

PAN AFRICAN AIRLINES Lagos (LOS)

☐ 5N-AMQ	Bell 206L-1 LongRanger II	45746	ex N31800
☐ 5N-AQP	Bell 206L-1 LongRanger II	45604	ex N3907E
☐ 5N-BAS	Bell 206L-1 LongRanger II	45367	ex N1076K
☐ 5N-BBN	Bell 206L-3 LongRanger III	51005	ex SU-CAD
☐ 5N-BCW	Bell 206L-3 LongRanger III	51053	ex SU-CAK
☐ 5N-BFE	Bell 206L-4 LongRanger IV	52272	ex N20796
☐ 5N-BFF	Bell 206L-4 LongRanger IV	52273	ex N2080C
☐ 5N-BFG	Bell 206L-4 LongRanger IV	52274	ex N2080W
☐ 5N-BFH	Bell 206L-4 LongRanger IV	52275	ex N2081K
☐ 5N-BFV	Bell 206L-4 LongRanger IV	52160	ex 5N-ESC
☐ 5N-BHH	Bell 206L-4 LongRanger IV	52291	ex N274AL
☐ 5N-PAA	Bell 206L-1 LongRanger II	45659	ex N39118
☐ 5N-AMW	Cessna 425 Conquest I	425-0067	ex N6844V
☐ 5N-BDD	Bell 412	33046	ex N395AL
☐ 5N-BDY	Bell 412EP	36267	ex N506AL
☐ 5N-BEM	Bell 407	53246	ex N567AL
☐ 5N-BEO	Bell 407	53190	ex N467AL
☐ 5N-BEP	Bell 407	53107	ex N427AL
☐ 5N-BES	Bell 206B JetRanger III	3216	ex N139H
☐ 5N-BIW	Cessna 208 Caravan I	20800403	ex N1316N
☐ 5N-CES	Cessna 208 Caravan I	20800249	ex N1288Y

PREMIUM AIR SHUTTLE Blue Shuttle (EMI) Lagos (LOS)

☐ 5N-BOS	Yakovlev Yak-40	9341431	ex LZ-DOA	VIP

SKYPOWER EXPRESS AIRWAYS Nigeria Express (EAN) Lagos (LOS)

☐ 5N-AXR	Embraer EMB.110P1 Bandeirante	110459	ex PT-SHM

TRANSKY AIRLINES Lagos (LOS)

☐ 5N-TSA	Boeing 737-2H4 (AvAero 3)	23110/1017	ex N104SW

WINGS AVIATION Lagos (LOS)

☐ 5N-PTL	Beech 1900D	UE-215	ex N850CA

5R- MADAGASCAR (Democratic Republic of Madagascar)

AEROMARINE Antananarivo ((TNR)

☐ F-ODQI	Piper PA-31-350 Navajo Chieftain	31-7305065	ex F-BUOI
☐ 5R-MCJ	Piper PA-23-250 Aztec C	27-3644	ex N6449Y
☐ 5R-MCR	Piper PA-31 Turbo Navajo	31-162	ex N9122Y
☐ 5R-MIK	Piper PA-23-250 Aztec B	27-2191	ex TL-ABA
☐ 5R-MKG	Beech 99	U-21	ex F-GFPE
☐ 5R-MLI	Cessna 207A Stationair 7 II	20700496	ex 5R-MVR
☐ 5R-MLJ	Cessna 310R II	310R1372	ex F-GBGB
☐ 5R-MLK	Beech 95-C55 Baron	TE-101	ex F-BOJG
☐ 5R-MLT	Cessna 310R II	310R0328	ex F-BXLT

AIR MADAGASCAR — Air Madagascar (MD/MDG) — Antananarivo (TNR)

☐ 5R-MFG	Boeing 767-383ER	25088/359	ex OY-KDM	
☐ 5R-MFJ	Boeing 767-3Y0ER	26200/450	ex N330DF	
☐ 5R-MFH	Boeing 737-3Q8	26305/2651		
☐ 5R-MFI	Boeing 737-3Q8	26301/2623	ex N319FL	
☐ 5R-MGC	de Havilland DHC-6 Twin Otter 300	328		
☐ 5R-MGD	de Havilland DHC-6 Twin Otter 300	329		
☐ 5R-MGF	de Havilland DHC-6 Twin Otter 300	482		
☐ 5R-MJE	ATR 72-212A	694	ex F-WWEQ	
☐ 5R-MJF	ATR 72-212A	698	ex F-WWEU	
☐ 5R-MJG	ATR 42-500	649	ex F-WWLG	
☐ 5R-MVT	ATR 42-320	044	ex F-WQAD	
☐ 5R-MLA	Piper PA-31-350 Chieftain	31-7952076		

MALAGASY AIRLINES — (MLG) — Antananarivo (TNR)

☐ 5R-MDB	Cessna 402B	402B0572	ex ZS-RES
☐ 5R-MHJ	Piper PA-23-250 Aztec	27-409	ex 5R-MVJ
☐ 5R-MKS	Cessna 402B	402B0014	ex 5R-MVC
☐ 5R-MLZ	Cessna TU206G Stationair 6	U20604526	ex F-BVQK
☐ 5R-MVL	Cessna 208 Caravan I	20800001	ex HB-CLD

TIKO AIR — Antananarivo (TNR)

☐ 5R-MJT	ATR 42-320	221	ex (5R-TIK)	
☐ 5R-MRM	Boeing 737-3Z9	24081/1515	ex OE-ILG	Op for Govt

Operator Unknown

☐ 5R-MJL	WSK/PZL Antonov An-28	1AJ005-14	ex ER-AJL

5T- MAURITANIA (Islamic Republic of Mauritania)

COMPAGNIE MAURITANIENNE DE TRANSPORTES – CMT — (CPM) — Nouakchott (NKC)

Operates cargo flights with Antonov aircraft leased from Aerocom and Pskovia when required

MAURITANIA AIRWAYS — (YD/MTW) — Nouakchott (NKC)

☐ TS-IMH	Airbus A320-211	0402	ex F-WWBN	Lsd fr TAR
☐ TS-	ATR 42-300		ex	Lsd fr TUI
☐ TS-IEA	Boeing 737-7L9/W	28014/766	ex OY-MRI	
☐ TS-IEB	Boeing 737-7L9/W	28015/785	ex OY-MRJ	

5V- TOGO (Togolese Republic)

AFRICAWEST CARGO — (FK/WTA) — Lome (LFW)

☐ S9-PSA	Antonov An-12BP	6344701	ex UR-TSI

ELITE AIR — Elair (EAI) — Lome (LFW)

☐ 5V-TTA	Piper PA-31-350 Navajo Chieftain	31-7405448	ex 9J-JLP
☐ 5V-TTC	Cessna 310Q	310Q0711	ex F-BUFK

5W- SAMOA (Independent State of Western Samoa)

POLYNESIAN AIRLINES — Polynesian (PH/PAO) — Apia (APW)

☐ 5W-FAV	Britten-Norman BN-2A-8 Islander	42	ex ZK-FMS	Samoa Star	stored APW
☐ 5W-FAW	de Havilland DHC-6 Twin Otter 300	827	ex C-FTLQ	Gogo	
☐ 5W-FAY	de Havilland DHC-6 Twin Otter 300	690	ex VH-UQW	Gillian	

SOUTH PACIFIC EXPRESS

☐ 5W-	Short SD.3-60	SH3693	ex N429AS

5X- UGANDA (Republic of Uganda)

AIR UGANDA — (U7/UGB)

☐ 5X-UGA	McDonnell-Douglas MD-87	49840/1745	ex EC-EYY
☐ 5X-UGB	McDonnell-Douglas MD-87	49837/1730	ex EC-EXT
☐ 5X-UGC	McDonnell-Douglas MD-87	49838/1733	ex EC-EYB
☐ 5X-UGD	Canadair CL-600-2B19 (CRJ-100ER)	7162	ex F-GRJH

EAGLE AIR		African Eagle (H7/EGU)		Entebbe (EBB)
☐ 5X-EBZ	Beech 1900C-1	UC-174	ex ZS-PIT	
☐ 5X-EIV	LET L-410UVP-E9	962632	ex 5Y-BPX	
☐ 5X-GNF	LET L-410UVP-E8	892320	ex OK-UDA	
☐ 5X-JNF	LET L-410UVP-E8	861809	ex CCCP-67596	

EAST AFRICAN AIRLINES		Crane (QU/UGX)		Entebbe (EBB)
☐ 5X-EAA	Boeing 737-291 (Nordam 3)	22741/871	ex N998UA	

RELIANCE AIR				Entebbe (EBB)
☐ 5X-ASI	Cessna 208 Caravan I	20800156	ex N9732F	

ROYAL DAISY AIRLINES				Entebbe (EBB)
☐ 5X-TEZ	Embraer EMB.120ER Brasilia	120078	ex ZS-CAE	

5Y- KENYA

ACARIZA AVIATION				Nairobi-Wilson (WIL)
☐ 5Y-FWA	Embraer EMB.110P1 Bandeirante	110195	ex ZS-OUM	
☐ 5Y-FWB	Embraer EMB.110P1 Bandeirante	110439	ex ZS-OZJ	

AD AVIATION				Nairobi-Wilson (WIL)
☐ 5Y-JMR	Beech 200C Super King Air	BL-17	ex F-GJMR	

AERO KENYA				Nairobi-Wilson (WIL)
☐ 5Y-BRU	LET L-410UVP-E9	912539	ex 5X-UAY	

AFRICAN EXPRESS AIRWAYS		Express Jet (XU/AXK)		Nairobi-Jomo Kenyatta Intl (NBO)	
☐ 5Y-AXB	Boeing 727-231	19565/603	ex 5V-TPB	Garissa	stored NBO
☐ 5Y-AXD	Douglas DC-9-32	47088/180	ex 9L-LDF		
☐ 5Y-AXE	Boeing 727-256	21611/1382	ex 9L-LDV	all-white	Lsd to Ishtar
☐ 5Y-AXF	Douglas DC-9-32	47093/237	ex 9L-LDG		
☐ 5Y-AXL	McDonnell-Douglas MD-82	49204/1179	ex I-DAWL		
☐ 5Y-AXN	McDonnell-Douglas MD-82	49207/1189	ex N461LF		
☐ 5Y-AXO	McDonnell-Douglas MD-82	49206/1188	ex N451LF		

AIRKENYA		(P2/XAK)		Nairobi-Wilson (WIL)
☐ 5Y-BGH	de Havilland DHC-6 Twin Otter 300	574	ex N4226J	
☐ 5Y-BIO	de Havilland DHC-6 Twin Otter 300	579	ex 5H-MRB	
☐ 5Y-BMJ	de Havilland DHC-7-102	83	ex N721AS	stored WIL
☐ 5Y-BPD	de Havilland DHC-7-102	32	ex 7O-ACZ	
☐ 5Y-BTZ	de Havilland DHC-8-102	203	ex VH-TNU	
☐ 5Y-PJP	de Havilland DHC-6 Twin Otter 300	424	ex ZS-LGN	

AIRWORKS KENYA				
☐ 5Y-BNH	Cessna 208B Caravan I	208B0385	ex ZS-NYS	
☐ 5Y-EGG	Cessna 208B Caravan I	208B0476	ex ZS-EGG	
☐ 5Y-NFY	Cessna 208B Caravan I	208B0294	ex ZS-NFY	
☐ 5Y-NGO	Cessna 208B Caravan I	208B0322	ex ZS-NGO	
☐ 5Y-NHB	Cessna 208B Caravan I	208B0328	ex ZS-NHB	
☐ 5Y-NKV	Cessna 208B Caravan I	208B0387	ex ZS-NKV	
☐ 5Y-NLM	Cessna 208B Caravan I	208B0375	ex ZS-NLM	
☐ 5Y-TLC	Cessna 208B Caravan I	208B0472	ex ZS-TLC	DHL colours

ALS				Nairobi-Wilson (WIL)
☐ 5Y-BVP	Beech 1900D	UE-136	ex ZS-PHM	
☐ 5Y-BVV	Beech 1900C	UB-29	ex ZS-OUC	
☐ 5Y-BVX	Beech 1900D	UE-101	ex ZS-PJG	
☐ 5Y-DHL	Beech 1900C-1	UC-100	ex N15305	Op for ICRC
☐ 5Y-LKG	Beech 1900C	UB-63	ex C-FUCB	Op for Kenya Airlink
☐ 5Y-SGL	Beech 1900C-1	UC-114	ex V5-SGL	Of for UN Humanitarian Service
☐ 5Y-BVO	de Havilland DHC-8-102	007	ex C-GFQI	
☐ 5Y-BXH	de Havilland DHC-8-102	205	ex C-FLAD	
☐ 5Y-BXI	de Havilland DHC-8-102	376	ex C-GRGQ	
☐ 5Y-PRV	de Havilland DHC-8-102	185	ex C-FGQI	
☐ 5Y-STN	de Havilland DHC-8-102	179	ex C-FCON	

☐ 5Y-BLA	Beech 200C Super King Air	BL-10	ex C-FAMB	
☐ 5Y-HAA	Cessna 208 Caravan I	20800021	ex N9349F	
☐ 5Y-MAK	Cessna 208 Caravan I	20800004	ex HB-CLI	
☐ 5Y-BVY	Embraer EMB.135LR (ERJ-135LR)	145599	ex N843RP	
☐ 5Y-BVZ	Embraer EMB.135LR (ERJ-135LR)	145661	ex N842RP	

ASTRAL AVIATION — **_Astral Cargo (8V/ACP)_** — **_Nairobi-Jomo Kenyatta Intl (NBO)_**

☐ 5Y-SAN	Douglas DC-9-34CF	47706/821	ex S9-PSR	
☐ UR-CCY	Antonov An-12B	02348106	ex RA-11124	Lsd fr VPB

BLUEBIRD AVIATION — **_Cobra (BBZ)_** — **_Nairobi -Wilson (WIL)_**

☐ 5Y-VVN	de Havilland DHC-8-102	62	ex VH-TQN	
☐ 5Y-VVP	de Havilland DHC-8-102	339	ex C-FLPP	
☐ 5Y-VVR	de Havilland DHC-8-102	204	ex VH-TQQ	
☐ 5Y-VVS	de Havilland DHC-8-102A	349	ex VH-TQT	
☐ 5Y-VVT	de Havilland DHC-8-102A	362	ex VH-TQV	
☐ 5Y-VVW	de Havilland DHC-8-402Q	4011	ex LN-RDL	
☐ 5Y-VVX	de Havilland DHC-8-402Q	4018	ex LN-RDB	
☐ 5Y-VVF	Fokker F.27 Mk.050 (Fokker 50)	20136	ex N136NM	
☐ 5Y-VVG	Fokker F.27 Mk.050 (Fokker 50)	20137	ex N137NM	
☐ 5Y-VVH	Fokker F.27 Mk.050 (Fokker 50)	20203	ex N203NM	
☐ 5Y-VVJ	Fokker F.27 Mk.050 (Fokker 50)	20133	ex D-AFFZ	
☐ 5Y-VVK	Fokker F.27 Mk.050 (Fokker 50)	20213	ex D-AFKL	
☐ 5Y-HHC	LET L-410A	720204	ex OK-DDU	
☐ 5Y-HHF	LET L-410AB	710002	ex OK-ADR	
☐ 5Y-HHL	LET L-410UVP-E9	872018	ex OK-SDA	
☐ 5Y-VVA	LET L-410UVP-E9	962633	ex OK-BDL	dam 23May04
☐ 5Y-VVB	LET L-410UVP-E9	942704	ex OK-BDG	
☐ 5Y-VVC	LET L-410UVP-E20	922728	ex ZS-NIJ	
☐ 5Y-VVE	LET L-410UVP-E20	922726	ex 5Y-YYY	
☐ 5Y-HHE	Beech 200 Super King Air	BB-547	ex ZS-NIP	

BLUE SKY AVIATION — **_Nairobi-Wilson (WIL)_**

☐ 5Y-BOD	LET L-410UVP-E20	982727	ex OK-DDF	
☐ 5Y-BSA	LET L-410UVP-E9	892323	ex OK-UDC	
☐ 5Y-BSM	LET L-410UVP-E9	871939	ex 3D-SIG	no titles

CAPITAL AIRLINES — **_Capital Delta (CPD)_** — **_Nairobi Wilson (WIL)_**

☐ 5Y-JAI	Beech 200 Super King Air	BB-557	ex OY-PAM	
☐ 5Y-SJB	Beech 200 Super King Air	BB-467	ex 5H-MUN	CatPass 250 conversion

DELTA CONNECTION — **_(Z9/DCP)_**

☐ 5Y-JAP	Boeing 737-229C	20915/401	ex 5Y-KQN	Lsd fr EAF

EAST AFRICAN AIR CHARTERS — **_Nairobi-Wilson (WIL)_**

☐ 5Y-ALY	Cessna U206F Stationair	U20602266	ex N15588U	
☐ 5Y-ART	Cessna 210L Centurion II	21059817		
☐ 5Y-BIX	Reims Cessna F406 Caravan II	F406-0055	ex N65912	
☐ 5Y-BLN	Cessna 208B Caravan I	208B0558	ex N50398	
☐ 5Y-BMH	Cessna 310R	310R0501	ex N87216	
☐ 5Y-BOX	Cessna 208B Caravan I	208B0500	ex 9M-PMV	

EAST AFRICAN EXPRESS — **_(B5/EXZ)_** — **_Nairobi-Jomo Kenyatta Intl (NBO)_**

☐ 5Y-EEE	Fokker F.28 Fellowship 4000	11229	ex 5Y-MNT	
☐ 5Y-XXA	Douglas DC-9-14 (ABS 3)	45725/19	ex N600ME	
☐ 5Y-XXB	Douglas DC-9-14 (ABS 3)	45711/4	ex N500ME	

EXECUTIVE TURBINE KENYA — **_Nairobi-Wilson (WIL)_**

☐ 5Y-BSP	Beech 1900D	UE-97	ex N97UX	
☐ 5Y-BSS	Beech 1900C-1	UC-88	ex ZS-PJA	
☐ 5Y-BTG	Beech 1900C-1	UC-96	ex ZS-PBY	
☐ 5Y-BVC	Short SD.3-60	SH3717	ex ZS-PBB	

FLY540 — **_Fly Orange (5H/FFV)_** — **_Nairobi-Jomo Kenyatta Intl (NBO)_**

☐ 5Y-BTN	Beech 1900D	UE-118	ex ZS-PPJ	
☐ 5Y-BUN	ATR 42-320	205	ex ZS-OZX	
☐ 5Y-BUT	ATR 42-320	240	ex ZS-OVL	
☐ 5Y-BUZ	de Havilland DHC-8-102	253	ex C-FOBU	
☐ 5Y-BVD	ATR 42-320	115	ex EI-SLI	

☐ 5Y-BVG	Beech 1900D	UE-62	ex N62ZV	
☐ 5Y-BXB	de Havilland DHC-8-102	213	ex N825PH	
☐ 5Y-	de Havilland DHC-8-102	114	ex C-GRGZ	
☐ 5Y-	ATR 72-212A	826	ex F-WW	on order
☐ 5X-FFD	Fokker F.27 Friendship 500CRF	10530	ex TC-MBC	
☐ 5X-FFN	Fokker F.27 Friendship 500CRF	10531	ex TC-MBD	

GLOBAL AIR CHARTERS

☐ 5Y-BSN	Beech 1900C-1	UC-69	ex OY-GML

JETLINK EXPRESS — *Ken Jet (J0/JLX)* — *Nairobi-Jomo Kenyatta Intl (NBO)*

☐ 5Y-JLA	Fokker F.28 Fellowship 4000	11093	ex 5T-CLG
☐ 5Y-JLB	Canadair CL-600-2B19 (CRJ-200)	7006	ex XA-UHB
☐ 5Y-JLC	Canadair CL-600-2B19 (CRJ-200)	7183	ex F-GPTE
☐ 5Y-JLD	Canadair CL-600-2B19 (CRJ-200)	7197	ex F-GPTF
☐ 5Y-JLE	Canadair CL-600-2B19 (CRJ-200)	7016	ex XA-UGW
☐ 5Y-JLH	Canadair CL-600-2B19 (CRJ-200)	7113	ex C-FZGN
☐ RP-C2997	British Aerospace 146 Srs.200	E2178	ex VH-NJH

KASKAZI AVIATION — *Malindi (MYD)*

☐ 5Y-BRX	Dornier 228-100	7004	ex SE-KKX
☐ 5Y-BUV	Dornier 228-201	8050	ex A6-ZYE

KENYA AIRWAYS — *Kenya (KQ/KQA)* — *Nairobi-Jomo Kenyatta Intl (NBO)*

Associate member of Skyteam

☐ 5Y-KQA	Boeing 737-3U8	28746/2863			
☐ 5Y-KQB	Boeing 737-3U8	28747/2884			
☐ 5Y-KQC	Boeing 737-3U8	29088/3034			
☐ 5Y-KQD	Boeing 737-3U8	29750/3095	ex N5573L		
☐ 5Y-KQJ	Boeing 737-248	21714/565	ex N1714T		stored NBO
☐ 5Y-KQK	Boeing 737-248	21715/579	ex N1715Z		stored NBO
☐ 5Y-KQE	Boeing 737-76N/W	30133/877			
☐ 5Y-KQF	Boeing 737-76N/W	30136/1145			
☐ 5Y-KQG	Boeing 737-7U8/W	32371/1242	ex N715BA		
☐ 5Y-KQH	Boeing 737-7U8/W	32372/1327			
☐ 5Y-KYB	Boeing 737-8AL/W	35070/2115			
☐ 5Y-KYC	Boeing 737-8AL/W	35071/2138			
☐ 5Y-KYD	Boeing 737-8Q8/W	35632/2690			
☐ 5Y-KYE	Boeing 737-8Q8/W	35286/2757	ex N1796B		
☐ 5Y-KYF	Boeing 737-8Q8/W	35637/2803			
☐ 5Y-KQP	Boeing 767-38EER	24797/328	ex N723BC		
☐ 5Y-KQQ	Boeing 767-33AER	27310/545	ex EC-IQA		
☐ 5Y-KQR	Boeing 767-3P6ER	24484/260	ex N244AV		
☐ 5Y-KQX	Boeing 767-36NER	30854/844			
☐ 5Y-KQY	Boeing 767-36NER	30841/841			
☐ 5Y-KQZ	Boeing 767-36NER	30853/837			
☐ 5Y-KYY	Boeing 767-3Q8ER	29383/747	ex N171LF		
☐ 5Y-KQS	Boeing 777-2U8ER	33683/522			
☐ 5Y-KQT	Boeing 777-2U8ER	33682/514			
☐ 5Y-KQU	Boeing 777-2U8ER	33681/479		The Pride of Africa	
☐ 5Y-KYZ	Boeing 777-2U8ER	36124/614			
☐ 5Y-KYH	Embraer 170-200LR (175LR)	17000230	ex PT-SFG		
☐ 5Y-KYJ	Embraer 170-100LR (170LR)	17000128	ex B-KXD		
☐ 5Y-	Embraer 170-200LR (175LR)		ex PT-S		on order
☐ 5Y-	Embraer 170-200LR (175LR)		ex PT-S		on order
☐ 5Y-	Embraer 170-200LR (175LR)		ex PT-S		on order

KNIGHT AVIATION — *Nairobi-Wilson (WIL)*

☐ 5Y-BPH	Embraer EMB.110P2 Bandeirante	110196	ex C9-AUG
☐ 5Y-BTX	Fokker F.27 Friendship 500F	10633	ex EI-SMF
☐ 5Y-SRJ	Fokker F.27 Friendship 500F	10372	ex N19XD

MOMBASA AIR SAFARI — *Skyrover (RRV)* — *Mombasa (MBA)*

☐ 5Y-NIK	LET L-410UVP-E9	912619	ex OK-WDW
☐ 5Y-UVP	LET L-410UVP-E9	912627	ex OK-WDY

QUEENSWAY AIR SERVICES — *Nairobi-Wilson (WIL)*

☐ 5Y-BKT	Beech 200 Super King Air	BB-258	ex ZS-NTM
☐ 5Y-BOM	Cessna 208B Caravan I	208B0605	ex ZS-NTM

SAFARI LINKS — *Nairobi-Wilson (WIL)*

☐ 5Y-BNS	Cessna 208B Caravan I	208B0394	ex N894MA	
☐ 5Y-BOP	Cessna 208B Caravan I	208B0642	ex N208GJ	
☐ 5Y-NON	Cessna 208 Caravan I	20800036	ex ZS-NON	
☐ 5Y-SLA	Cessna 208B Caravan I	208B0574	ex F-OGXY	
☐ 5Y-SLC	Cessna 208B Caravan I	208B2091	ex N2234J	
☐ 5Y-SLD	de Havilland DHC-8-102	331	ex C-FLPQ	

SKYTRAIL — *Skytrail* — *Mombasa (MBA)*

☐ 5Y-AFD	Cessna TU206B Skywagon	U206-0724	ex N3424L	
☐ 5Y-SKS	de Havilland DHC-6 Twin Otter 300	682	ex G-BGZP	
☐ 5Y-SKT	de Havilland DHC-6 Twin Otter 300	503	ex PH-STC	

SKYWAYS KENYA — *Nairobi-Wilson (WIL)*

☐ 5Y-BMB	Douglas DC-3	17108/34375	ex N2025A	stored

SOLENTA AVIATION (KENYA) — *Nairobi-Jomo Kenyatta Intl (NBO)*

☐ 5Y-OBY	Cessna 208B Caravan I	208B0345	ex ZS-OBY	DHL colours

SUPERIOR AVIATION SERVICES — *Skycargo (M7/SUK)* — *Nairobi-Wilson (WIL)*

☐ 5Y-ATH	Piper PA-23-250 Aztec E	27-7305138		
☐ 5Y-PEA	Beech 58 Baron	TH-1067	ex N60664	

748 AIR SERVICES — *Sierra Services (SVT)* — *Nairobi-Wilson (WIL)*

☐ 5Y-BSX	Hawker Siddeley HS.780 Andover C.1	Set 20	ex 9Q-COE	
☐ 5Y-SFE	Hawker Siddeley HS.780 Andover C.1	Set 6	ex 3C-JJX	
☐ 5Y-YKM	Hawker Siddeley HS.748 Srs.2B/398	1779	ex C-GDTD	
☐ 3C-KKC	Hawker Siddeley HS.780 Andover C.1	Set 18	ex NZ7625	stored Lokichoggio
☐ 5Y-HAJ	Hawker Siddeley HS.748 Srs.2B/371LFD	1776	ex SE-LIB	
☐ 5Y-BVQ	Hawker Siddeley HS.748 Srs.2B/399LFD	1778	ex SE-LIC	
☐ 5Y-JGM	de Havilland DHC-8-102A	287	ex N828PH	
☐ 5Y-IHO	de Havilland DHC-8-102	268	ex C-FOEN	

TRACKMARK CARGO — *Nairobi-Wilson (WIL)*

☐ 5Y-TAV	Cessna 208B Caravan I	208B0668	ex ZS-OIH	

TRANSWORLD SAFARIS — *Nairobi-Wilson (WIL)*

☐ 5Y-ROH	Piper PA-31-350 Chieftain	31-8152038	ex N217JP	
☐ 5Y-TWA	Beech 200 Super King Air	BB-803	ex G-WPLC	
☐ 5Y-TWC	Beech 200C Super King Air	BL-37	ex G-IFTB	Lsd fr Aerolite Investments
☐ 5Y-TWG	Cessna 208B Caravan I	208B0674	ex N1286N	
☐ 5Y-TWI	Cessna 208B Caravan I	208B0606	ex 5Y-BNA	

TRIDENT AVIATION — *Nairobi-Wilson (WIL)*

☐ 5Y-MEG	de Havilland DHC-5D Buffalo	62	ex 5V-MAG	Op for UN-WFP
☐ 5Y-OPL	de Havilland DHC-5D Buffalo	84A	ex UAE 310 (1)	Op for UN-WFP
☐ 5Y-TAJ	de Havilland DHC-5E Buffalo	108	ex C-GDOB	Op for UN-WFP
☐ 5Y-TEL	de Havilland DHC-5D Buffalo	68	ex AF-315	Op for UN-WFPdbr?
☐ 5Y-BTP	de Havilland DHC-8-102	104	ex 6Y-JMT	
☐ 5Y-BWG	de Havilland DHC-8Q-311	406	ex C-FTYU	
☐ 5Y-DAC	de Havilland DHC-8-102	251	ex C-GZAN	
☐ 5Y-EMD	de Havilland DHC-8-102	110	ex 6Y-JMZ	
☐ 5Y-ENA	de Havilland DHC-8-102	297	ex N836EX	
☐ 5Y-GRS	de Havilland DHC-8-102	355	ex SX-BIS	Echo Flight titles
☐ 5Y-MOC	de Havilland DHC-8-311	374	ex C-FDYW	
☐ 5Y-PTA	de Havilland DHC-8-315	397	ex N788BC	
☐ 5Y-	de Havilland DHC-8-102	341	ex N842EX	
☐ 5Y-	de Havilland DHC-8-102	343	ex N851EX	

TROPIC AIR — *Nairobi-Wilson (WIL)*

☐ 5Y-BRT	Cessna 208B Caravan I	208B0682	ex ZS-ELE	
☐ 5Y-BSY	Cessna 208B Caravan I	208B0907	ex N32211	

UNITED AIR LINES — *Nairobi-Wilson (WIL)*

☐ 5Y-LAV	Cessna 310R	310R0882	ex N3644G	

ZB AIR	Bosky (ZBA)		Nairobi-Wilson (WIL)

☐ 5Y-OPM	Cessna 208B Caravan I	208B0330	ex N1034S
☐ 5Y-ZBI	Cessna 208B Caravan I	208B0324	ex N1029P
☐ 5Y-ZBL	Cessna 208B Caravan I	208B0338	ex N1042Y
☐ 5Y-ZBR	Cessna 208B Caravan I	208B0446	ex N12922
☐ 5Y-ZBT	Cessna 208B Caravan I	208B1243	ex N1226X
☐ 5Y-ZBW	Cessna 208B Caravan I	208B0409	ex N1115W
☐ 5Y-ZBX	Cessna 208B Caravan I	208B1170	ex N1308N
☐ 5Y-AIS	Beech 95-D55 Baron	TE-680	
☐ 5Y-AUN	Cessna U206F Stationair	U20602531	ex N1244V
☐ 5Y-AYZ	Cessna 310R	310R0121	ex N4940J
☐ 5Y-AZS	Cessna 310R	310R0524	ex N87350
☐ 5Y-SAB	Cessna 404 Titan II	404-0675	ex N6761X
☐ 5Y-ZBK	Beech B200 Super King Air	BB-1714	ex N3214D
☐ 5Y-ZBM	Cessna U206H Stationair 6	U20608114	ex N259ME
☐ 5Y-ZBO	Cessna U206H Stationair	U20608131	ex N373ME
☐ 5Y-ZBZ	Beech 1900	5Y-	

6O- SOMALIA (Democratic Republic of Somalia)

JUBBA AIRWAYS	Jubba (6J/JUB)		Dubai/Sharjah (DXB/SHJ)
☐ 5Y-BXG	Boeing 737-247 (Nordam 3)	23519/1299	ex YA-GAE

MUDAN AIRLINES	(MDN)		Dubai (DXB)
☐ ER-46711	Antonov An-24B	99902109	ex RA-46711

STAR AFRICAN AIR	Starsom (STU)	Dubai/Sharjah (DXB/SHJ)

Operates flights with Antonov An-24 and Ilyushin Il-18 aircraft leased when required

6V- SENEGAL (Republic of Senegal)

AERO SERVICE ASF	Servo (RSG)		Dakar (DKR)
☐ 6V-AHF	Cessna 208B Caravan I	208B0634	ex N12386
☐ 6V-AHI	Cessna 402C	402C0120	ex F-OHCM

AFRIQUE CARGO SERVICES	(NFS)	Dakar (DKR)

Operated cargo flights with Antonov An-12 aircraft leased from Tiramavia as required. Current status uncertain as Tiramavia lost their AOC.

AIR SAINT LOUIS	Air Saint Louis (LOU)		Saint Louis (XLS)
☐ F-BVUN	Bell 206B JetRanger	247	ex D-HAMO
☐ 6V-AHP	Cessna 207 Skywagon	20700209	ex F-GEDM

AIR SENEGAL INTERNATIONAL	Air Senegal (V7/SNG)			Dakar (DKR)
☐ 6V-AHL	de Havilland DHC-8-315	556	ex C-GDSG	stored MST

ASECNA	(XKX)			Dakar (DKR)
☐ 6V-AFW	ATR 42-300	117	ex F-WWEN	Calibrator/Pax

TURBOT AIR CARGO	(TAC)			Dakar (DKR)
☐ UR-CAI	Antonov An-26B	7010	ex UR-26519	Lsd fr UKL
☐ UR-MDA	Antonov An-26	7108	ex Military	Lsd fr ME

6Y- JAMAICA

AIR JAMAICA	Jamaica (JM/AJM)		Kingston-Norman Manley Intl (KIN)	
☐ 6Y-JAD	Airbus A310-112	3331	ex EI-DZX	
☐ 6Y-JAF	Airbus A320-214	0624	ex N624AJ	624 The Caribbean
☐ 6Y-JAG	Airbus A320-214	0626	ex N626AJ	626 Barbados
☐ 6Y-JAI	Airbus A320-214	0628	ex N628AJ	628 Montego Bay
☐ 6Y-JMF	Airbus A320-214	1213	ex EI-DKF	632 Freedom
☐ 6Y-JMG	Airbus A320-214	1390	ex EI-DKG	634 America
☐ 6Y-JMI	Airbus A320-214	1747	ex F-WWDI	636
☐ 6Y-JMJ	Airbus A320-214	1751	ex B-6266	

☐ 6Y-JMH	Airbus A321-211	1503	ex D-AVZU	515 May Pen

INTERNATIONAL AIRLINK — Kingston-Tinson Peninsula (KTP)

☐ 6Y-JRD	Cessna U206G Stationair 6	U20604522	ex N9019M
☐ 6Y-JRF	Cessna T207A Turbo Skywagon	20700365	ex N1765U
☐ 6Y-JRG	Cessna 208B Caravan I	208B0311	ex YN-CDR

SKYLAN AIRWAYS

☐ 6Y-JIC	British Aerospace Jetstream 32EP	920	ex N920AE

TIMAIR — Montego Bay (MBJ)

☐ 6Y-JLU	Britten-Norman BN-2B-26 Islander	2170	ex 6Y-JLG
☐ 6Y-JNA	Cessna U206G Stationair	U20603837	ex N4515C
☐ 6Y-JNB	Cessna U206G Stationair	U20603615	ex N7332N
☐ 6Y-JNJ	Cessna U206G Stationair 6	U20606359	ex N2447N
☐ 6Y-JNL	Cessna U206G Stationair 6	U20605620	ex N712RS

7O- YEMEN (Republic of Yemen)

FELIX AIRWAYS — Sana'a (SAH)

☐ 7O-FAA	Canadair CL-600-2C10 (CRJ-702NG)	10267	ex C-
☐ 7O-FAB	Canadair CL-600-2C10 (CRJ-702NG)	10268	ex C-
☐ 7O-FAI	Canadair CL-600-2B19 (CRJ-200LR)	7307	ex N636BR
☐ 7O-FAJ	Canadair CL-600-2B19 (CRJ-200LR)	7308	ex N637BR

YEMENIA — Yemeni (IY/IYE) — Sana'a (SAH)

☐ 7O-ADA	Boeing 727-2N8	21842/1512	ex 4W-ACJ		Op for Govt
☐ 7O-ADD	Lockheed L-382C-86D Hercules	4827	ex 1160		Jt ops with Air Force
☐ 7O-ADE	Lockheed L-382C-86D Hercules	4825	ex 1150		Jt ops with Air Force
☐ 7O-ADF	Ilyushin Il-76TD	1033418578	ex RA-76380		Jt ops with Air Force
☐ 7O-ADG	Ilyushin Il-76TD	1023412402	ex RA-76405		Jt ops with Air Force
☐ 7O-ADH	de Havilland DHC-6 Twin Otter 310	764	ex G-GBAC		
☐ 7O-ADI	de Havilland DHC-6 Twin Otter 300	664	ex HB-LRT		Lsd fr FAT
☐ 7O-ADK	de Havilland DHC-6 Twin Otter 310	813	ex A4O-DB		
☐ 7O-ADL	Boeing 737-8Q8	30645/1129		Tarim	
☐ 7O-ADM	Boeing 737-8Q8/W	28252/1195		Shibam	
☐ 7O-ADN	Boeing 737-8Q8	30661/1186		Zabid	
☐ 7O-ADP	Airbus A330-243	625	ex F-WWYD	Sana'a	
☐ 7O-ADQ	Boeing 737-8Q8/W	30730/2399			
☐ 7O-ADR	Airbus A310-324ET	568	ex F-OGYO	Socotra	
☐ 7O-ADS	de Havilland DHC-8-102	280	ex C-FMCZ		
☐ 7O-ADT	Airbus A330-243	632	ex F-WWYH	Aden	
☐ 7O-ADU	de Havilland DHC-8-102A	327	ex C-FHLO		
☐ 7O-ADV	Airbus A310-325	702	ex F-OHPR	Seiyun	
☐ 7O-ADW	Airbus A310-325	704	ex F-OHPS	Marib	
☐ 7O-ADY	de Havilland DHC-8-103	333	ex C-FSID		
☐ 7O-YMN	Boeing 747SP-27	21786/413	ex A7-AHM		Op for Government

7Q- MALAWI (Republic of Malawi)

AIR MALAWI — Malawi (QM/AML) — Blantyre (BLZ)

☐ ZS-PUI	Boeing 737-2B7 (Nordam 3)	22890/986	ex 5N-BFJ		
☐ 7Q-YKP	Boeing 737-33A	25056/2045		Kwacha	stored JNB
☐ 7Q-YKQ	ATR 42-320	236	ex F-WWES	Shire	
☐ 7Q-YKW	Boeing 737-522	25384/2149	ex N917UA	Sapitwa	stored JNB
☐ 7Q-YKX	Boeing 737-2K9	23405/1178	ex C9-BAI		

7T- ALGERIA (Democratic & Popular Republic of Algeria)

AIR ALGERIE — Air Algerie (AH/DAH) — Algiers (ALG)

☐ 7T-VJC	Airbus A310-203	291	ex F-WZED	
☐ 7T-VJD	Airbus A310-203	293	ex F-WZEE	
☐ 7T-VJV	Airbus A330-202	644	ex F-WWKD	Tinhinan
☐ 7T-VJW	Airbus A330-202	647	ex F-WWKF	Lalla Setti
☐ 7T-VJX	Airbus A330-202	650	ex F-WWKK	Mers el Kebir
☐ 7T-VJY	Airbus A330-202	653	ex F-WWYK	Monts des Beni Chougrane
☐ 7T-VJZ	Airbus A330-202	667	ex F-WWKR	Teddis
☐ 7T-VUI	ATR 72-212A	644	ex F-OHGM	

☐ 7T-VUJ	ATR 72-212A	648	ex F-OHGN		
☐ 7T-VUK	ATR 72-212A	652	ex F-OHGO		
☐ 7T-VUL	ATR 72-212A	672	ex F-OHGP		
☐ 7T-VUM	ATR 72-212A	677	ex F-OHGQ		
☐ 7T-VUN	ATR 72-212A	684	ex F-OHGR		
☐ 7T-VVQ	ATR 72-212A	676	ex F-WWEA		
☐ 7T-VVR	ATR 72-212A	683	ex F-WWEF		
☐ 7T-	ATR 72-212A	901	ex		on order
☐ 7T-	ATR 72-212A	902	ex		on order
☐ 7T-	ATR 72-212A	903	ex		on order
☐ 7T-VEA	Boeing 727-2D6	20472/850		Tassili	
☐ 7T-VEB	Boeing 727-2D6	20473/855		Hoggar	stored ALG
☐ 7T-VEI	Boeing 727-2D6	21053/1111		Djebel Amour	stored ALG
☐ 7T-VEM	Boeing 727-2D6	21210/1204		Mont du Ksall	
☐ 7T-VEP	Boeing 727-2D6	21284/1233		Mont du Tessala	
☐ 7T-VET	Boeing 727-2D6	22372/1662		Gorges du Rhumel	
☐ 7T-VEU	Boeing 727-2D6 (Raisbeck 3)	22373/1664		Djurdjura	stored ALG
☐ 7T-VEV	Boeing 727-2D6 (Raisbeck 3)	22374/1711	ex N8292V		stored ALG
☐ 7T-VEW	Boeing 727-2D6 (Raisbeck 3)	22375/1723	ex N8295V		stored ALG
☐ 7T-VEX	Boeing 727-2D6 (Raisbeck 3)	22765/1801		Djomila	stored ALG
☐ TC-SKD	Boeing 737-4Q8	25372/2280	ex TC-JDI		Lsd fr SHY
☐ 7T-VED	Boeing 737-2D6C	20850/311			stored ALG
☐ 7T-VEF	Boeing 737-2D6	20759/332		Saoura	stored ALG
☐ 7T-VEG	Boeing 737-2D6	20884/361		Monts des Oulad Nails	stored ALG
☐ 7T-VEJ	Boeing 737-2D6	21063/407		Chrea	stored ALG
☐ 7T-VEK	Boeing 737-2D6	21064/409		Edough	stored ALG
☐ 7T-VEL	Boeing 737-2D6	21065/416		Akfadou	stored ALG
☐ 7T-VEN	Boeing 737-2D6	21211/454		La Soummam	
☐ 7T-VEQ	Boeing 737-2D6	21285/473		Le Zaccar	
☐ 7T-VES	Boeing 737-2D6C (Nordam 3)	21287/486		Le Tadmait	stored ALG
☐ 7T-VJA	Boeing 737-2T4 (Nordam 3)	22800/897	ex N4556L	Monts des Babors	
☐ 7T-VJB	Boeing 737-2T4 (Nordam 3)	22801/900	ex N4558L	Monts des Biban	
☐ 7T-VJQ	Boeing 737-6D6	30209/1115		Kasbah d'Alger	
☐ 7T-VJR	Boeing 737-6D6	30545/1131			
☐ 7T-VJS	Boeing 737-6D6	30210/1150	ex N60559		
☐ 7T-VJT	Boeing 737-6D6	30546/1152			
☐ 7T-VJU	Boeing 737-6D6	30211/1164			
☐ 7T-VJJ	Boeing 737-8D6	30202/610		Jugurtha	
☐ 7T-VJK	Boeing 737-8D6	30203/640	ex N1781B	Mansourah	
☐ 7T-VJL	Boeing 737-8D6	30204/652		Allizi	
☐ 7T-VJM	Boeing 737-8D6	30205/691			
☐ 7T-VJN	Boeing 737-8D6	30206/751		Oued Tafna	
☐ 7T-VJO	Boeing 737-8D6	30207/868	ex N1787B	Tinerkouk	
☐ 7T-VJP	Boeing 737-8D6	30208/896	ex N1787B	Mont Tahat	
☐ 7T-VKA	Boeing 737-8D6/W	34164/1748		Monts Chaboro	
☐ 7T-VKB	Boeing 737-8D6/W	34165/1768	ex N1784B	Mont de l'Assekhrem	
☐ 7T-VKC	Boeing 737-8D6/W	34166/1773			
☐ 7T-VJG	Boeing 767-3D6ER	24766/310			
☐ 7T-VJH	Boeing 767-3D6ER	24767/323			
☐ 7T-VJI	Boeing 767-3D6ER	24768/332	ex N6009F		
☐ 7T-VIG	Cessna 208B Caravan I	208B0391	ex N1122N		
☐ 7T-VII	Cessna 208B Caravan I	208B0393	ex N1123G		Lsd to DTH
☐ 7T-VIL	Cessna 208B Caravan I	208B0601	ex N1247H		
☐ 7T-VIM	Cessna 208B Caravan I	208B0602	ex N1247K		
☐ 7T-VCV	Beech A100 King Air	B-93	ex N9369Q		
☐ 7T-VHL	Lockheed L-382-51D Hercules	4886	ex N4160M		
☐ 7T-VIQ	Beech 1900D	UE-381	ex N31683		VIP
☐ 7T-VRF	Beech A100 King Air	B-147	ex N1828W		

AIR EXPRESS ALGERIA — *Algiers (ALG)*

☐ 7T-VAE	LET L-410UVP-E20	872011	ex OK-SDT	
☐ 7T-VAF	LET L-410UVP-E20	082629	ex CCCP-67698	
☐ ZS-OOF	LET L-410UVP-E20	871920	ex 5H-PAJ	
☐ ZS-OSE	LET L-420	922729A	ex N420Y	
☐ ZS-OUE	LET L-420	012735A	ex OK-GDM	Lsd fr Air-Tec Africa
☐ ZS-OXR	LET L-410UVP	972730	ex 5H-HSA	
☐ ZS-OYF	Beech 1900D	UE-214	ex VH-IMS	Lsd fr NAC

STAR AVIATION — *Algiers (ALG)*

☐ 7T-VNA	Pilatus PC-6/B2-H4 Turbo Porter	817	ex HB-FFV
☐ 7T-VNB	Beech 1900D	UE-305	ex 7T-WRF
☐ 7T-VND	de Havilland DHC-6 Twin Otter 300	502	ex HB-LRS
☐ 7T-VNE	de Havilland DHC-6 Twin Otter 300	717	ex HB-LTD

TASSILI AIRLINES		Tassili Air (SF/DTH)		Hassi Messaoud (HME)
☐ 7T-VCG	Pilatus PC-6/B2-H4 Turbo Porter	917	ex HB-FLJ	
☐ 7T-VCH	Pilatus PC-6/B2-H4 Turbo Porter	929	ex HB-FLX	
☐ 7T-VCI	Pilatus PC-6/B2-H4 Turbo Porter	933	ex HB-FLY	
☐ 7T-VCJ	Pilatus PC-6/B2-H4 Turbo Porter	934	ex HB-FLZ	
☐ 7T-VCK	Pilatus PC-6/B2-H4 Turbo Porter	930	ex HB-FMA	
☐ 7T-VII	Cessna 208B Caravan I	208B0393	ex N1123G	Lsd fr DAH
☐ 7T-VIP	Beech 1900D	UE-369	ex N30538	
☐ 7T-VCL	de Havilland DHC-8Q-402	4167	ex C-FMIT	
☐ 7T-VCM	de Havilland DHC-8Q-402	4169	ex C-FMIV	
☐ 7T-VCN	de Havilland DHC-8Q-402	4173	ex C-FMKF	
☐ 7T-VCO	de Havilland DHC-8Q-402	4178	ex C-FMTN	
☐ 7T-VCP	de Havilland DHC-8-202	661	ex C-FRIZ	
☐ 7T-VCQ	de Havilland DHC-8-202	664	ex C-FTGX	
☐ 7T-VCR	de Havilland DHC-8-202	665	ex C-FTUE	
☐ 7T-VCS	de Havilland DHC-8-202	666	ex C-FUCF	

8P- BARBADOS

TRANS ISLAND AIR 2000 — *Trans Island (TRD)* — *Bridgetown-Grantley Adams (BGI)*

Services performed by Twin Otters operated by SVG Air (J8-)

8Q- MALDIVES (Republic of Maldives)

ISLAND AVIATION SERVICES		(Q2) (986)		Male (MLE)
☐ 8Q-AMD	de Havilland DHC-8-202	429	ex C-GDKL	
☐ 8Q-IAO	de Havilland DHC-8Q-311	544	ex D-BHOQ	
☐ 8Q-IAP	de Havilland DHC-8Q-311	491	ex LN-WFE	
☐ 8Q-IAQ	de Havilland DHC-8-202	542	ex C-FIKT	
☐ 8Q-IAR	Dornier 228-212	8244	ex D-CBDX	

MALDIVIAN AIR TAXI				Male (MLE)
☐ 8Q-MAA	de Havilland DHC-6 Twin Otter 300	693	ex C-GKCS	Floatplane
☐ 8Q-MAB	de Havilland DHC-6 Twin Otter 300	287	ex C-GKBV	Floatplane
☐ 8Q-MAE	de Havilland DHC-6 Twin Otter 300	464	ex C-FPOQ	Floatplane
☐ 8Q-MAF	de Havilland DHC-6 Twin Otter 300	449	ex C-FWKQ	Floatplane
☐ 8Q-MAH	de Havilland DHC-6 Twin Otter 300	374	ex C-FMYV	Floatplane
☐ 8Q-MAI	de Havilland DHC-6 Twin Otter 300	279	ex C-GKBM	Floatplane
☐ 8Q-MAJ	de Havilland DHC-6 Twin Otter 300	837	ex C-GJDP	Floatplane
☐ 8Q-MAL	de Havilland DHC-6 Twin Otter 300	321	ex C-GBBU	Floatplane
☐ 8Q-MAM	de Havilland DHC-6 Twin Otter 300	339	ex C-GOKB	Floatplane
☐ 8Q-MAN	de Havilland DHC-6 Twin Otter 300	435	ex C-FWKZ	Floatplane
☐ 8Q-MAO	de Havilland DHC-6 Twin Otter 300	259	ex C-FKBI	Floatplane
☐ 8Q-MAP	de Havilland DHC-6 Twin Otter 300	571	ex C-FKBX	Floatplane
☐ 8Q-MAQ	de Havilland DHC-6 Twin Otter 310	611	ex C-FBKB	Floatplane
☐ 8Q-MAT	de Havilland DHC-6 Twin Otter 200	146	ex 8Q-NTA	Floatplane
☐ 8Q-MAW	de Havilland DHC-6 Twin Otter 300	722	ex C-FWKO	Floatplane
☐ 8Q-MAX	de Havilland DHC-6 Twin Otter 300	755	ex C-FWKX	Floatplane
☐ 8Q-MAZ	de Havilland DHC-6 Twin Otter 300	774	ex C-FWKU	Floatplane
☐ 8Q-MBA	de Havilland DHC-6 Twin Otter 300	691	ex D-IHAI	Floatplane
☐ 8Q-MBB	de Havilland DHC-6 Twin Otter 300	659	ex HB-LUG	Floatplane
☐ 8Q-OEQ	de Havilland DHC-6 Twin Otter 100	44	ex C-FOEQ	Floatplane
☐ 8Q-	de Havilland DHC-6 Twin Otter 400			on order
☐ 8Q-	de Havilland DHC-6 Twin Otter 400			on order

SPA AVIATION				Male (MLE)
☐ 8Q-SPA	Fairchild F-27F	110	ex 8Q-AEQ	

Commenced operations in July 2006, having previously provided handling services

TRANS MALDIVIAN AIRWAYS		Hum (TMW)		Male (MLE)
☐ 8Q-TMA	de Havilland DHC-6 Twin Otter 100	82	ex 8Q-HIA	Floatplane
☐ 8Q-TMB	de Havilland DHC-6 Twin Otter 300	587	ex C-GASV	Floatplane
☐ 8Q-TMD	de Havilland DHC-6 Twin Otter 310	530	ex 8Q-HIG	Floatplane
☐ 8Q-TME	de Havilland DHC-6 Twin Otter 300	798	ex 8Q-HIH	Floatplane
☐ 8Q-TMF	de Havilland DHC-6 Twin Otter 300	657	ex 8Q-HII	Floatplane
☐ 8Q-TMG	de Havilland DHC-6 Twin Otter 310	597	ex 8Q-HIJ	Floatplane
☐ 8Q-TMH	de Havilland DHC-6 Twin Otter 300	668	ex HK-4194X	Floatplane
☐ 8Q-TMI	de Havilland DHC-6 Twin Otter 300	754	ex N107JM	Floatplane
☐ 8Q-TMJ	de Havilland DHC-6 Twin Otter 300	781	ex N781JM	Floatplane
☐ 8Q-TMK	de Havilland DHC-6 Twin Otter 300	751	ex N710PV	Floatplane
☐ 8Q-TML	de Havilland DHC-6 Twin Otter 300	640	ex N709PV	Floatplane

☐ 8Q-TMN	de Havilland DHC-6 Twin Otter 300	700	ex TJ-OHN	Floatplane
☐ 8Q-TMO	de Havilland DHC-6 Twin Otter 300	234	ex C-FBZN	Floatplane
☐ 8Q-TMP	de Havilland DHC-6 Twin Otter 300	652	ex VH-KZN	Floatplane
☐ 8Q-TMQ	de Havilland DHC-6 Twin Otter 300	753	ex N162AY	Floatplane
☐ 8Q-TMR	de Havilland DHC-6 Twin Otter 300	270	ex N270CM	Floatplane
☐ 8Q-TMS	de Havilland DHC-6 Twin Otter 300	663	ex PK-TWH	Floatplane
☐ 8Q-TMT	de Havilland DHC-6 Twin Otter 300	454	ex C-FNBI	Floatplane
☐ 8Q-TMU	de Havilland DHC-6 Twin Otter 300	467	ex C-FOIM	Floatplane
☐ 8Q-TMV	de Havilland DHC-6 Twin Otter 300	625	ex C-FNBL	Floatplane
☐ 8Q-TMW	de Havilland DHC-6 Twin Otter 300	768	ex C-GDQM	Floatplane
☐ 8Q-ATM	ATR 42-320	194	ex N11835	
☐ 8Q-ATN	ATR 42-300	096	ex PK-VSX	

8R- GUYANA (Co-operative Republic of Guyana)

AIR SERVICES — Georgetown-Ogle (OGL)

☐ 8R-GAA	Piper PA-34-200T Seneca II	34-7870451	ex 8R-GGJ	
☐ 8R-GAS	Cessna 208B Caravan I	208B0691	ex YN-CFK	
☐ 8R-GER	Britten-Norman BN-2A-27 Islander	478	ex G-BDJX	
☐ 8R-GFI	Britten-Norman BN-2A-9 Islander	677	ex G-AZGU	
☐ 8R-GFM	Cessna U206F Stationair	U20601731	ex N9531G	
☐ 8R-GGE	Cessna U206G Stationair	U20603358	ex N8501Q	Floatplane
☐ 8R-GHB	Cessna U206G Stationair 6	U20604889	ex 8R-GPF	
☐ 8R-GHE	Britten-Norman BN-2A-6 Islander	269	ex 8R-GHB	
☐ 8R-GYA	Cessna U206G Stationair	U20603654	ex 8R-GGF	R/STOL conv

RORAIMA AIRWAYS — Roraima (ROR) — Georgetown-Ogle (OGL)

☐ 8R-GRA	Britten-Norman BN-2A-26 Islander	3006	ex N42540
☐ 8R-GRB	Britten-Norman BN-2B-26 Islander	431	ex N431V
☐ 8R-GRC	Britten-Norman BN-2B-27 Islander	2114	ex SX-DKA

TRANS GUYANA AIRWAYS — Trans Guyana (TGY) — Georgetown-Ogle (OGL)

☐ 8R-GGY	Britten-Norman BN-2A-26 Islander	470	ex N81567
☐ 8R-GHD	Britten-Norman BN-2A-27 Islander	622	ex C-GKES
☐ 8R-GHM	Britten-Norman BN-2A-27 Islander	216	ex PT-IAS
☐ 8R-GHR	Cessna 208B Caravan I	208B0519	ex PT-MEZ
☐ 8R-GHT	Cessna 208B Caravan I	208B0572	ex TI-BBG
☐ 8R-GTG	Cessna 208B Caravan I	208B0397	ex N397TA

9A- CROATIA (Republic of Croatia)

CROATIA AIRLINES — Croatia (OU/CTN) — Zagreb (ZAG)

Member of Star Alliance

☐ 9A-CTG	Airbus A319-112	0767	ex D-AVYA	Zadar	
☐ 9A-CTH	Airbus A319-112	0833	ex D-AVYJ	Zagreb	
☐ 9A-CTI	Airbus A319-112	1029	ex D-AVYC	Vukovar	
☐ 9A-CTL	Airbus A319-112	1252	ex D-AVYS	Pula	
☐ 9A-CTF	Airbus A320-212	0258	ex F-OKAI	Rijeka	
☐ 9A-CTJ	Airbus A320-214	1009	ex F-WWDN	Dubrovnik	
☐ 9A-CTK	Airbus A320-214	1237	ex F-WWIK	Split	
☐ 9A-CTM	Airbus A320-212	0671	ex C-GJUQ	Sibenik Star Alliance c/s	
☐ 9A-CQA	de Havilland DHC-8-402Q	4205	ex C-FPEL		
☐ 9A-CQB	de Havilland DHC-8-402Q	4211	ex C-FPQD		
☐ 9A-CQC	de Havilland DHC-8-402Q	4258	ex C-FWIJ		
☐ 9A-CQD	de Havilland DHC-8-402Q	4260	ex C-FWZU		
☐ 9A-CQE	de Havilland DHC-8-402Q	4300	ex		on order
☐ 9A-CQF	de Havilland DHC-8-402Q	4301	ex		on order

DUBROVNIK AIRLINE — (DBK) — Dubrovnik (DBV)

☐ 9A-CDA	McDonnell-Douglas MD-83	49602/1435	ex N491GX	Revelin
☐ 9A-CDB	McDonnell-Douglas MD-83	49986/1842	ex PK-ALG	Lovrijenac
☐ 9A-CDC	McDonnell-Douglas MD-82	49112/1068	ex PK-ALI	Minceta
☐ 9A-CDD	McDonnell-Douglas MD-82	49113/1069	ex PK-ALJ	Bokar
☐ 9A-CDE	McDonnell-Douglas MD-82	48066/1019	ex PK-ALH	Sveti Ivan

TRADE AIR — Tradeair (TDR) — Zagreb (ZAG)

☐ 9A-BTB	LET L-410UVP-E3	902506	ex LZ-KLA	
☐ 9A-BTC	LET L-410UVP-E3	902507	ex LZ-KLB	
☐ 9A-BTD	Fokker F.28-0100 (Fokker 100)	11407	ex N1424M	Op in Sun Adria colours

☐ 9A-BTE	Fokker F.28-0100 (Fokker 100)	11416	ex N1431B	Op in Sun Adria colours

9G- GHANA (Republic of Ghana)

AEROGEM AIRLINES — Aerogem (GCK) — Accra (ACC)

☐ 9G-OAL	Boeing 707-324C (Comtran 2)	19350/537	ex 9G-OLD	all-white

ANTRAK AIR GHANA — Antrak (O4/ABV) — Accra (ACC)

☐ EX-132	Boeing 737-2Q8	21687/554	ex TN-AHK	
☐ 9G-AAB	ATR 42-300	041	ex F-WQCT	
☐ 9G-ANT	ATR 42-300	086	ex ZS-ORE	retd?
☐ 9G-NAN	Douglas DC-9-51	47732/861	ex 5X-TWO	stored ACC
☐ 9G-NIN	Douglas DC-9-51	47746/864	ex 5X-TRE	stored SCC

CITYLINK — CityLink (CTQ) — Accra (ACC)

☐ 9G-CTL	SAAB SF.340A	340A-044	ex ZS-PMJ
☐ 9G-LET	LET L-410UVP-E20	871922	ex ZS-OOH

GHANA INTERNATIONAL AIRLINES — (G0/GHB) — Accra (ACC)

☐ G-STRZ	Boeing 757-258	27622/745	ex 4X-EBI	Lsd fr AEU

JOHNSONS AIR — Johnsonsair (JON) — Accra/Sharjah (ACC/SHJ)

☐ 9G-FAB	Douglas DC-8-63F (BAC 3)	46121/500	ex N786AL	
☐ 9G-LIL	Douglas DC-8-63AF (BAC 3)	46147/549	ex 9G-MKO	Lsd to RSE
☐ 9G-PEL	Douglas DC-8-62F (BAC 3)	46085/481	ex 4K-AZ29	stored RKT, Lsd fr ALG Group
☐ 9G-RAC	Douglas DC-8-63PF (BAC 3)	46093/496	ex N816AX	
☐ 9G-SIM	Douglas DC-8-63CF (BAC 3)	46061/480	ex N826AX	
☐ 9G-TOP	Douglas DC-8-63CF (BAC 3)	46151/540	ex 9G-MKN	

MERIDIAN AIRWAYS — (ACE) — Accra (ACC)

☐ TZ-MHI	Lockheed L-1011-100 Tristar	193B-1221	ex EX-35000
☐ 9G-AED	Douglas DC-8-62AF	46162/555	ex Z-ALB
☐ 9G-AXA	Douglas DC-8-63F (BAC 3)	46113/521	ex N811AX
☐ 9G-AXB	Douglas DC-8-63PF (BAC 3)	46097/503	ex N815AX
☐ 9G-AXC	Douglas DC-8-63F (BAC 3)	45999/377	ex N828AX
☐ 9G-AXD	Douglas DC-8-63F (BAC 3)	45927/327	ex N819AX
☐ 9G-AXE	Douglas DC-8-63F (BAC 3)	46041/439	ex N814AX

SOBEL AIR — Accra (ACC)

☐ 9G-AIR	Fokker F.27 Friendship 100	10266	ex SE-KZF
☐ 9G-BEL	Fokker F.27 Friendship 100	10319	ex SE-KZH
☐ 9G-SOB	Fokker F.27 Friendship 100	10287	ex (TL-ADS)

9H- MALTA (Republic of Malta)

AIR MALTA — Air Malta (KM/AMC) — Luqa (MLA)

☐ 9H-AEG	Airbus A319-112	2113	ex C-GAEG	Mdina	
☐ 9H-AEH	Airbus A319-112	2122	ex D-AVWA	Floriana	
☐ 9H-AEJ	Airbus A319-112	2186	ex D-AVWX	San Pawl il-Bahr	
☐ 9H-AEL	Airbus A319-112	2332	ex D-AVYZ	Marsaxlokk	
☐ 9H-AEM	Airbus A319-112	2382	ex D-AVWW	Birgu	
☐ 9H-AEF	Airbus A320-214	2142	ex F-WWBZ	Valletta	
☐ 9H-AEI	Airbus A320-214	2189	ex F-WWDL	Rabat – Cita Vittoria	
☐ 9H-AEK	Airbus A320-214	2291	ex F-WWBT	San Gijan	
☐ 9H-AEN	Airbus A320-214	2665	ex F-WWBN	Bormia	
☐ 9H-AEO	Airbus A320-214	2768	ex F-WWDK	Isla-Cita'Invicta	
☐ 9H-AEP	Airbus A320-214	3056	ex F-WWDV	Nadur	Lsd to ETD
☐ 9H-AEQ	Airbus A320-214	3068	ex F-WWIJ	Tarxien	
☐ 9H-AFE	Airbus A320-211	0350	ex C-FMST		Lsd to ETD

EFLY — (LEF) — Luqa (MLA)

☐ 9H-ELE	British Aerospace 146 Srs.300	E3209	ex G-JEBG

HARBOURAIR — (HES) — Grand Harbour

☐ 9H-AFA	de Havilland DHC-3 Turbo Otter	406	ex C-FHAH	Floatplane

MEDAVIA		Medavia (MDM)			Luqa (MLA)
☐ 9H-AAP	CASA C.212-200	9	ex EC-CRV		
☐ 9H-AAR	CASA C.212-200	CC15-1-161			
☐ 9H-AAS	CASA C.212-200	CC15-2-162			
☐ 9H-AET	Dornier 328-110	3117	ex D-COMM		
☐ 9H-AEW	de Havilland DHC-8-102	???	ex PH-SDH		
☐ 9H-AEY	de Havilland DHC-8-311	508	ex G-BRYX		
☐ 9H-AFD	de Havilland DHC-8Q-311A	458	ex G-BRYU		
☐ 9H-AFH	Beech 1900D	UE-372	ex PH-RAR		
☐ 9H-AFI	Beech 1900D	UE-31	ex PH-RAH		

9J- ZAMBIA (Republic of Zambia)

AIRWAVES AIRLINK		Airlimited (WLA)			Lusaka (LUN)
☐ 9J-CGC	Cessna 208B Caravan I	208B0742	ex N878C		

PROFLIGHT AIR SERVICES		Proflight-Zambia (PFZ)			Lusaka (LUN)
☐ 7Q-YMJ	Piper PA-23-250 Aztec D	27-4104	ex ZS-FTO		
☐ 9J-ABD	Cessna P206D Super Skylane	P206-0461	ex ZS-FDA		
☐ 9J-KKN	Piper PA-31-350 Chieftain	31-8052113	ex ZS-KKN		
☐ 9J-PLJ	Britten-Norman BN-2A-21 Islander	799	ex Botswana OA3		
☐ 9J-UAS	Britten-Norman BN-2A Islander	155	ex Z-UAS		
☐ 9J-WEX	Britten-Norman BN-2A Islander	619	ex Z-WEX		

ROYAL AIR CHARTERS					
☐ 9J-CID	Cessna 208B Caravan I	208B1307	ex N20527		

ZAMBEZI AIRWAYS					
☐ 9J-ZJA	Boeing 737-5Y0	26101/2544	ex N611MD	Spirit of Kafue	
☐ 9J-ZJB	Boeing 737-5Y0	26100/2538	ex N610MD	Spirit of Mosi-O-Tunya	

ZAMBIAN AIRWAYS		Zambian (Q3/MBN)			Lusaka (LUN)
☐ 9J-JOY	Boeing 737-244	22584/821	ex ZS-SIE		stored JNB

9K- KUWAIT (State of Kuwait)

GRYPHON AIRWAYS					Kuwait City (KWI)
☐ ZS-GAT	Douglas DC-9-32	47797/913	ex 3D-MRT		
☐ ZS-GAU	Douglas DC-9-32	47798/914	ex 3D-MRU		

JAZEERA AIRWAYS		Jazeera (J9/JZR)			Kuwait City (KWI)
☐ 9K-CAA	Airbus A320-214	2569	ex F-WWBF		
☐ 9K-CAB	Airbus A320-214	2584	ex F-WWDH		
☐ 9K-CAC	Airbus A320-214	2792	ex F-WWBM		
☐ 9K-CAD	Airbus A320-214	2822	ex F-WWDC		
☐ 9K-CAE	Airbus A320-214	3016	ex F-WWBQ		
☐ 9K-CAF	Airbus A320-214	3349	ex F-WWBY		
☐ 9K-CAG	Airbus A320-214	3656	ex F-WWDS		
☐ 9K-CAH	Airbus A320-214	3670	ex F-WWIF		
☐ 9K-CAI	Airbus A320-214	3919	ex F-WWBH		
☐ 9K-CAJ	Airbus A320-214	3939	ex F-WWDR		
☐ 9K-CAK	Airbus A320-214	4162	ex F-WWBS		
☐ 9K-	Airbus A320-214	4235	ex		on order
☐ 9K-	Airbus A320-214		ex		on order

KUWAIT AIRWAYS		Kuwaiti (KU/KAC)			Kuwait City (KWI)
☐ 9K-AHI	Airbus A300C4-620	344	ex PK-MAY	Al-Sabahiya	Op for Govt
☐ 9K-AMA	Airbus A300B4-605R	673	ex F-WWAQ	Failaka	
☐ 9K-AMB	Airbus A300B4-605R	694	ex F-WWAV	Burghan	
☐ 9K-AMC	Airbus A300B4-605R	699	ex F-WWAM	Wafra	
☐ 9K-AMD	Airbus A300B4-605R	719	ex F-WWAB	Wara	
☐ 9K-AME	Airbus A300B4-605R	721	ex F-WWAG	Al-Rawdhatain	
☐ 9K-ALA	Airbus A310-308	647	ex F-WWCQ	Al-Jahra	
☐ 9K-ALB	Airbus A310-308	649	ex F-WWCV	Gharnada	
☐ 9K-ALC	Airbus A310-308	663	ex JY-AGT	Kazma	
☐ 9K-ALD	Airbus A310-308	648	ex F-WWCR	Al-Salmiya	Op for Govt
☐ 9K-AKA	Airbus A320-212	0181	ex F-WWIU	Bubbyan	

☐ 9K-AKB	Airbus A320-212	0182	ex F-WWIV	Kubber	
☐ 9K-AKC	Airbus A320-212	0195	ex F-WWDP	Qurtoba	
☐ 9K-AKD	Airbus A320-212	2046	ex F-WWBG	Al-Mubarakiya	Op for Govt
☐ 9K-ANA	Airbus A340-313	089	ex F-WWJX	Warba	
☐ 9K-ANB	Airbus A340-313	090	ex F-WWJZ	Bayan	
☐ 9K-ANC	Airbus A340-313	101	ex F-WWJE	Meskan	
☐ 9K-AND	Airbus A340-313	104	ex F-WWJJ	Al-Riggah	
☐ 9K-ADE	Boeing 747-469M	27338/1046		Al-Jabariya	Op for Govt
☐ 9K-AOA	Boeing 777-269ER	28743/125		Al-Gurain	
☐ 9K-AOB	Boeing 777-269ER	28744/145		Garouh	

LOADAIR CARGO — ***Kuwait City (KWI)***

☐ 9K-DAA	Boeing 747-4HQERF	37303/1416	ex N797BA	on order
☐ 9K-DAB	Boeing 747-4HQERF	37304/1419	ex N799BA	on order

WATANIYA AIRWAYS — ***Kuwait City (KWI)***

☐ 9K-EAA	Airbus A320-214	3739	ex F-WWIG
☐ 9K-EAB	Airbus A320-214	3791	ex F-WWBF
☐ 9K-EAC	Airbus A320-214	3907	ex D-AVVA
☐ 9K-EAD	Airbus A320-214	4049	ex F-WWIM

9L- SIERRA LEONE (Republic of Sierra Leone)

AIR RUM — ***Air Rum (RUM)*** — ***Amman (AMM)***

☐ C5-GAE	Boeing 727-51 (FedEx 3)	19124/347	ex HZ-DG1		
☐ 9L-LDV	Lockheed L-1011-1 Tristar	193C-1200	ex 5Y-RUM		WFU
☐ 9L-LFB	Lockheed L-1011-1 Tristar	193P-1156	ex XU-100	Barakah	WFU

BELLVIEW AIRLINES — ***O3/ORJ*** — ***Freetown (FNA)***

Operates services with aircraft leased from Bellview Airlines (5N) as required

PEACE AIR

☐ 9Q-CQZ	LET L-410UVP	851339	ex 9L-LEM

9M- MALAYSIA (Federation of Malaysia)

AIRASIA — ***Asian express (AK/AXM)*** — ***Kuala Lumpur-Sultan Abdul Aziz Shah (KUL)***

☐ 9M-AFA	Airbus A320-214	2612	ex F-WWBV	
☐ 9M-AFB	Airbus A320-214	2633	ex F-WWDY	
☐ 9M-AFC	Airbus A320-214	2656	ex F-WWIO	Manchester United colours
☐ 9M-AFD	Airbus A320-214	2683	ex F-WWIT	
☐ 9M-AFE	Airbus A320-214	2699	ex F-WWDN	
☐ 9M-AFF	Airbus A320-214	2760	ex F-WWDT	
☐ 9M-AFG	Airbus A320-216	2816	ex F-WWIX	
☐ 9M-AFH	Airbus A320-216	2826	ex F-WWDI	
☐ 9M-AFI	Airbus A320-216	2842	ex F-WWIG	
☐ 9M-AFJ	Airbus A320-216	2881	ex F-WWBQ	
☐ 9M-AFK	Airbus A320-216	2885	ex F-WWBS	
☐ 9M-AFL	Airbus A320-216	2926	ex F-WWDX	
☐ 9M-AFM	Airbus A320-216	2944	ex F-WWIN	
☐ 9M-AFN	Airbus A320-216	2956	ex F-WWBY	
☐ 9M-AFO	Airbus A320-216	2989	ex F-WWIK	
☐ 9M-AFP	Airbus A320-216	3000	ex F-WWBC	Special 3000th c/s
☐ 9M-AFQ	Airbus A320-216	3018	ex F-WWBR	Malaysia anniversary c/s
☐ 9M-AFR	Airbus A320-216	3064	ex F-WWIC	
☐ 9M-AFS	Airbus A320-216	3117	ex F-WWBB	
☐ 9M-AFT	Airbus A320-216	3140	ex F-WWDN	
☐ 9M-AFU	Airbus A320-216	3154	ex F-WWDE	
☐ 9M-AFV	Airbus A320-216	3173	ex F-WWIO	
☐ 9M-AFW	Airbus A320-216	3404	ex F-WWBX	ATT & Williams colours
☐ 9M-AFX	Airbus A320-216	3182	ex F-WWDU	
☐ 9M-AFY	Airbus A320-216	3194	ex F-WWIV	
☐ 9M-AFZ	Airbus A320-216	3201	ex F-WWID	
☐ 9M-AHA	Airbus A320-216	3223	ex F-WWBV	
☐ 9M-AHB	Airbus A320-216	3232	ex F-WWBF	
☐ 9M-AHC	Airbus A320-216	3261	ex F-WWDN	
☐ 9M-AHD	Airbus A320-216	3291	ex F-WWDT	
☐ 9M-AHE	Airbus A320-216	3327	ex F-WWBH	
☐ 9M-AHF	Airbus A320-216	3353	ex F-WWIE	
☐ 9M-AHG	Airbus A320-216	3370	ex F-WWDF	Manchester United colours
☐ 9M-AHH	Airbus A320-216	3427	ex F-WWBB	

☐ 9M-AHI	Airbus A320-216	3448	ex F-WWIX		
☐ 9M-AHJ	Airbus A320-216	3477	ex F-WWDH		
☐ 9M-AHK	Airbus A320-216	3486	ex F-WWIH		
☐ 9M-AHL	Airbus A320-216	3521	ex F-WWDS		
☐ 9M-AHM	Airbus A320-216	3536	ex F-WWID		
☐ 9M-AHN	Airbus A320-216	3549	ex F-WWIX		
☐ 9M-AHO	Airbus A320-216	3568	ex F-WWBV		
☐ 9M-AHP	Airbus A320-216	3582	ex F-WWDE		
☐ 9M-AHQ	Airbus A320-216	3628	ex F-WWIU		
☐ 9M-AHR	Airbus A320-216	3701	ex F-WWDP		
☐ 9M-AHS	Airbus A320-216	3776	ex F-WWDX		
☐ 9M-AHT	Airbus A320-216	3997	ex F-WWDH		
☐ 9M-AHU	Airbus A320-216	4070	ex F-WWBK		
☐ 9M-AHV	Airbus A320-216	4079	ex F-WWBP		
☐ 9M-AHW	Airbus A320-216	4098	ex F-WWDJ		
☐ 9M-	Airbus A320-216		ex		on order
☐ 9M-	Airbus A320-216		ex		on order
☐ 9M-	Airbus A320-216		ex		on order
☐ 9M-	Airbus A320-216		ex		on order
☐ 9M-	Airbus A320-216		ex		on order
☐ 9M-	Airbus A320-216		ex		on order
☐ 9M-	Airbus A320-216		ex		on order
☐ 9M-	Airbus A320-216		ex		on order
☐ 9M-	Airbus A320-216		ex		on order
☐ 9M-	Airbus A320-216		ex		on order
☐ 9M-	Airbus A320-216		ex		on order
☐ 9M-	Airbus A320-216		ex		on order
☐ 9M-	Airbus A320-216		ex		on order
☐ 9M-	Airbus A320-216		ex		on order
☐ 9M-	Airbus A320-216		ex		on order
☐ 9M-	Airbus A320-216		ex		on order
☐ 9M-AEC	Boeing 737-3Y0	24677/1837	ex EI-BZJ		Lsd to AWQ

AIR ASIA X *(D7 / XAX)* *Kuala Lumpur-Sultan Abdul Aziz Shah (KUL)*

☐ 9M-XAA	Airbus A330-301	054	ex N54AN		
☐ 9M-XXA	Airbus A330-343E	952	ex F-WWKR		
☐ 9M-XXB	Airbus A330-343E	974	ex F-WWKD		
☐ 9M-XXC	Airbus A330-343E	1048	ex F-WWKI		
☐ 9M-XXD	Airbus A330-343E	1066	ex F-WWYI	Soaring Xpectations	
☐ 9M-XXE	Airbus A330-343E	1075	ex F-WWKS		on order
☐ 9M-XXF	Airbus A330-343E		ex		on order
☐ 9M-XAB	Airbus A340-313X	273	ex C-GDVW	Xcalibur	
☐ 9M-XAC	Airbus A340-313X	278	ex C-GDVZ	Xcellence	

AWAN INSPIRASI

☐ 9M-AIG	Sikorsky S-92A	920057	ex C-GOHC
☐ 9M-AIH	Sikorsky S-92A	920024	ex C-GOHA
☐ 9M-AIK	Sikorsky S-76C+	760622	ex C-GHRK
☐ 9M-AIP	Sikorsky S-76C++	760693	ex C-FRSE

BERJAYA AIR CHARTER *Berjaya (J8/BVT)* *Subang-Sultan Abdul Aziz Shah International (SZB)*

☐ 9M-TAH	de Havilland DHC-7-110	109	ex G-BRYD	
☐ 9M-TAK	de Havilland DHC-7-110	110	ex G-BOAW	
☐ 9M-TAL	de Havilland DHC-7-110	112	ex G-BOAY	
☐ 9M-TAG	ATR 72-212A	858	ex F-WWEC	
☐ 9M-	ATR 72-212A		ex F-WW	on order

FIREFLY *(7E/FFM)* *Penang (PEN)*

☐ 9M-FYA	ATR 72-212A	812	ex F-WWEB	
☐ 9M-FYB	ATR 72-212A	814	ex F-WWED	
☐ 9M-FYC	ATR 72-212A	821	ex F-WWEK	
☐ 9M-FYD	ATR 72-212A	830	ex F-WWEE	
☐ 9M-FYE	ATR 72-212A	840	ex F-WWER	
☐ 9M-FYF	ATR 72-212A	860	ex F-WWEF	
☐ 9M-FYG	ATR 72-212A	868	ex F-WWES	
☐ 9M-FYH	ATR 72-212A		ex	on order
☐ 9M-FYI	ATR 72-212A		ex	on order
☐ 9M-FYJ	ATR 72-212A		ex	on order
☐ 9M-MGI	Fokker F.27 Mk.050 (Fokker 50)	20175	ex PH-EXB	stored SZB
☐ 9M-MGK	Fokker F.27 Mk.050 (Fokker 50)	20248	ex PH-EXR	

HORNBILL SKYWAYS *Koching (KCH)*

☐ 9M-BCU	Bell 206L-4 LongRanger IV	52151	ex N337H
☐ 9M-HRM	Bell 430	49018	ex 9M-ATM

☐ 9M-HSM	Bell 206L-4 LongRanger IV	52295	ex N4204A	
☐ 9M-SGH	Bell 206B JetRanger III	4103	ex N7107Z	
☐ 9M-SGJ	Bell 206B JetRanger III	4059	ex N8129Y	
☐ 9M-WSA	Eurocopter EC135P2	0482	ex D-HECH	
☐ 9M-WSG	Eurocopter EC135P2+	0483	ex D-HECU	

LAYANG-LAYANG AEROSPACE — *Layang (LAY)* — *Miri (MYY)*

☐ 9M-LLA	Short SC.7 Skyvan 3	SH1977	ex ZS-LFG	
☐ 9M-LLB	GAF N22C Nomad	N22C-95	ex VH-SNL	
☐ 9M-LLH	Bell 206B JetRanger III	2919	ex VH-WNA	
☐ 9M-LLI	GAF N22C Nomad	N22B-69	ex VH-MSF	
☐ 9M-LLT	Bell 206B JetRanger	969	ex G-TUCH	
☐ 9M-LLU	Bolkow 105C			
☐ RA-41900	Antonov An-38-120	4160381607003		Lsd fr NPO

MALAYSIA AIRLINES — *Malaysian (MH/MAS)* — *Kuala Lumpur-Sultan Abdul Aziz Shah (KUL)*

☐ TF-ELW	Airbus A300C4-605R	755	ex D-ABFH		Lsd fm ABD
☐ 9M-MKA	Airbus A330-322	067	ex F-WWKK		
☐ 9M-MKC	Airbus A330-322	069	ex F-WWKM		
☐ 9M-MKD	Airbus A330-322	073	ex F-WWKN		
☐ 9M-MKE	Airbus A330-322	077	ex F-WWKO		
☐ 9M-MKF	Airbus A330-322	100	ex F-WWKZ		
☐ 9M-MKG	Airbus A330-322	107	ex F-WWKV		
☐ 9M-MKH	Airbus A330-322	110	ex F-WWKE		
☐ 9M-MKI	Airbus A330-322	116	ex F-WWKT		
☐ 9M-MKJ	Airbus A330-322	119	ex F-WWKJ		
☐ 9M-MKS	Airbus A330-322	143	ex C-FRAE		
☐ 9M-MKV	Airbus A330-223	296	ex EI-CZS		
☐ 9M-MKW	Airbus A330-223	300	ex EI-CZT		
☐ 9M-MKX	Airbus A330-223	290	ex EI-CZR		
☐ 9M-MLA	Boeing 737-8Q8/W	30702/1953	ex N164LF		
☐ 9M-MLB	Boeing 737-8Q8/W	30703/1964	ex N161LF		
☐ 9M-MLC	Boeing 737-8Q8/W	32690/2250	ex G-XLAO		
☐ 9M-MMA	Boeing 737-4H6	26443/2272			
☐ 9M-MMB	Boeing 737-4H6	26444/2308			
☐ 9M-MMC	Boeing 737-4H6	26453/2332			
☐ 9M-MMD	Boeing 737-4H6	26464/2340			
☐ 9M-MME	Boeing 737-4H6	26465/2362			
☐ 9M-MMF	Boeing 737-4H6	26466/2372			
☐ 9M-MMG	Boeing 737-4H6	26467/2378			
☐ 9M-MMH	Boeing 737-4H6	27084/2391			
☐ 9M-MMI	Boeing 737-4H6	27096/2395			
☐ 9M-MMJ	Boeing 737-4H6	27097/2399			
☐ 9M-MMK	Boeing 737-4H6	27083/2403			
☐ 9M-MML	Boeing 737-4H6	27085/2407			
☐ 9M-MMM	Boeing 737-4H6	27166/2410			
☐ 9M-MMN	Boeing 737-4H6	27167/2419			
☐ 9M-MMQ	Boeing 737-4H6	27087/2441			
☐ 9M-MMR	Boeing 737-4H6	26468/2445			
☐ 9M-MMS	Boeing 737-4H6	27169/2450			
☐ 9M-MMT	Boeing 737-4H6	27170/2462			
☐ 9M-MMU	Boeing 737-4H6	26447/2479	ex VT-JAV		
☐ 9M-MMV	Boeing 737-4H6	26449/2491			
☐ 9M-MMW	Boeing 737-4H6	26451/2496			
☐ 9M-MMX	Boeing 737-4H6	26452/2501			
☐ 9M-MMY	Boeing 737-4H6	26455/2507			Lsd to UBA
☐ 9M-MMZ	Boeing 737-4H6	26457/2521			
☐ 9M-MQA	Boeing 737-4H6	26458/2525			
☐ 9M-MQB	Boeing 737-4H6	26459/2530			
☐ 9M-MQC	Boeing 737-4H6	26460/2533			
☐ 9M-MQD	Boeing 737-4H6	26461/2536			
☐ 9M-MQE	Boeing 737-4H6	26462/2542			
☐ 9M-MQF	Boeing 737-4H6	26463/2560			
☐ 9M-MQG	Boeing 737-4H6	27190/2568			
☐ 9M-MQI	Boeing 737-4H6	27353/2632	ex 9H-ADJ		
☐ 9M-MQK	Boeing 737-4H6	27384/2673			
☐ 9M-MQN	Boeing 737-4H6	27673/2852	ex 9H-ADK		
☐ 9M-MQO	Boeing 737-4H6	27674/2877	ex 9H-ADL		
☐ 9M-MQP	Boeing 737-46J	28038/2794	ex N380BG		
☐ 9M-MQQ	Boeing 737-4Y0	24915/2055	ex SX-BKL		
☐ TF-AAA	Boeing 747-236B (SCD)	22442/526	ex N361FC		Lsd fr ABD
☐ TF-AAB	Boeing 747-236B (SCD)	22304/502	ex N362FC		
☐ TF-ARJ	Boeing 747-236M	23735/674	ex G-BDXN		op by ABD
☐ TF-ARN	Boeing 747-2F6B (SF)	22382/498	ex N745SA		op by ABD
☐ 9M-MPB	Boeing 747-4H6	25699/965		Shah AlamHibiscus colours	
☐ 9M-MPF	Boeing 747-4H6	27043/1017		Kota Bharu	
☐ 9M-MPH	Boeing 747-4H6	27044/1041	ex N6066B	Langkawi	

☐ 9M-MPK	Boeing 747-4H6	28427/1147		Johor Bahru
☐ 9M-MPL	Boeing 747-4H6	28428/1150		Penang
☐ 9M-MPM	Boeing 747-4H6	28435/1152		Melaka
☐ 9M-MPN	Boeing 747-4H6	28432/1247		Pangkor
☐ 9M-MPO	Boeing 747-4H6	28433/1290		Alor Setar
☐ 9M-MPP	Boeing 747-4H6	29900/1296		Putrajaya
☐ 9M-MPQ	Boeing 747-4H6	29901/1301		Kuala Lumpur
☐ 9M-MPR	Boeing 747-4H6F	28434/1371		
☐ 9M-MPS	Boeing 747-4H6F	29902/1374		
☐ 9M-MRA	Boeing 777-2H6ER	28408/64	ex N5017V	
☐ 9M-MRB	Boeing 777-2H6ER	28409/74	ex N50217	
☐ 9M-MRC	Boeing 777-2H6ER	28410/78		
☐ 9M-MRD	Boeing 777-2H6ER	28411/84		Freedom of Space c/s
☐ 9M-MRE	Boeing 777-2H6ER	28412/115		
☐ 9M-MRF	Boeing 777-2H6ER	28413/128		
☐ 9M-MRG	Boeing 777-2H6ER	28414/140		
☐ 9M-MRH	Boeing 777-2H6ER	28415/151		
☐ 9M-MRI	Boeing 777-2H6ER	28416/155		
☐ 9M-MRJ	Boeing 777-2H6ER	28417/222		
☐ 9M-MRK	Boeing 777-2H6ER	28418/231		
☐ 9M-MRL	Boeing 777-2H6ER	29065/329		
☐ 9M-MRM	Boeing 777-2H6ER	29066/336		
☐ 9M-MRN	Boeing 777-2H6ER	28419/394		
☐ 9M-MRO	Boeing 777-2H6ER	28420/404		
☐ 9M-MRP	Boeing 777-2H6ER	28421/496	ex N5016R	
☐ 9M-MRQ	Boeing 777-2H6ER	28422/498		

MASWINGS

☐ 9M-MDK	de Havilland DHC-6 Twin Otter 300	792	ex C-GESR	
☐ 9M-MDL	de Havilland DHC-6 Twin Otter 300	802	ex C-GDFT	
☐ 9M-MDM	de Havilland DHC-6 Twin Otter 300	804	ex C-GDKL	
☐ 9M-MDO	de Havilland DHC-6 Twin Otter 310	629	ex ZK-KHA	
☐ 9M-MGA	Fokker F.27 Mk.050 (Fokker 50)	20150	ex PH-EXM	
☐ 9M-MGB	Fokker F.27 Mk.050 (Fokker 50)	20156	ex PH-EXP	
☐ 9M-MGD	Fokker F.27 Mk.050 (Fokker 50)	20164	ex PH-EXL	
☐ 9M-MGE	Fokker F.27 Mk.050 (Fokker 50)	20166	ex PH-EXN	
☐ 9M-MGF	Fokker F.27 Mk.050 (Fokker 50)	20167	ex PH-EXO	
☐ 9M-MGG	Fokker F.27 Mk.050 (Fokker 50)	20170	ex PH-EXS	stored SZB
☐ 9M-MGJ	Fokker F.27 Mk.050 (Fokker 50)	20204	ex PH-EXM	stored SZB
☐ 9M-MWA	ATR 72-212A	817	ex F-WWGE	
☐ 9M-MWB	ATR 72-212A	856	ex F-WWEX	
☐ 9M-MWC	ATR 72-212A	863	ex F-WWEL	
☐ 9M-MWD	ATR 72-212A	874	ex F-WWEX	
☐ 9M-MWE	ATR 72-212A	885	ex F-WWEO	
☐ 9M-MWF	ATR 72-212A	889	ex F-WWET	
☐ 9M-MWG	ATR 72-212A	895	ex F-WWEE	
☐ 9M-MWH	ATR 72-212A	900	ex F-WW	
☐ 9M-MWI	ATR 72-212A	904	ex F-WW	on order

MHS AVIATION — *Kerteh/Miri (KTE/MYY)*

☐ 9M-SPB	Aérospatiale AS.332L2	2636	ex F-WWOO	
☐ 9M-SPC	Aérospatiale AS.332L2	2639	ex F-WWOJ	
☐ 9M-SPD	Aérospatiale AS.332L2	2646	ex F-WWOO	
☐ 9M-STS	Aérospatiale AS.332L1	2387		
☐ 9M-STV	Aérospatiale AS.332L1	2408		
☐ 9M-STW	Aérospatiale AS.332L1	2312	ex LN-OBQ	Lsd fr CHC Helicopters Intl
☐ 9M-BEG	Sikorsky S-76C+	760568	ex C-GHRY	
☐ 9M-SPP	Sikorsky S-76C+	760661	ex N45067	
☐ 9M-SPQ	Sikorsky S-76C	760662	ex N4507G	
☐ 9M-SPR	Sikorsky S-76C	760663	ex N4508G	
☐ 9M-SPS	Sikorsky S-76C+	760641	ex G-CEKP	
☐ 9M-SPT	Sikorsky S-76C+	760645	ex G-CEKR	
☐ 9M-SPV	Sikorsky S-76C+	760654	ex G-CEOR	
☐ 9M-SPW	Sikorsky S-76C+	760664	ex G-KAZD	
☐ 9M-STA	Sikorsky S-76C	760383		
☐ 9M-STB	Sikorsky S-76C	760384		
☐ 9M-STC	Sikorsky S-76C	760392		
☐ 9M-STD	Sikorsky S-76C	760397		
☐ 9M-STE	Sikorsky S-76C	760398		
☐ 9M-STF	Sikorsky S-76C	760400		
☐ 9M-STG	Sikorsky S-76C	760385	ex ZS-RTC	
☐ 9M-AVP	Sikorsky S-61N	61768	ex G-BEKJ	
☐ 9M-SNA	Aérospatiale AS365N2 Dauphin 2	6246	ex N634LH	
☐ 9M-SSV	Aérospatiale AS355F2 Ecureuil 2	5476		
☐ 9M-SSW	Aérospatiale AS355F2 Twin Star	5467	ex N467CL	

☐ 9M-SSZ	Aérospatiale AS355F2 Ecureuil 2	5292	ex 3A-MVV	
☐ 9M-STL	Beech 1900D	UE-373	ex N31110	
☐ 9M-STM	Beech 1900D	UE-374	ex N31419	

NEPTUNE AIR

☐ 9M-NEA	Boeing 737-210C (Nordam 3)	21822/605	ex PK-YGF	
☐ 9M-NEP	Boeing 727-277F (FedEx 3)	22641/1753	ex VH-VLI	

PAN-MALAYSIAN AIR TRANSPORT — *Pan Malaysia (PMA)* — *Subang-Sultan Abdul Aziz Shah International (SZB)*

☐ 9M-PIH	Short SC.7 Skyvan 3	SH1962	ex G-BFUM	

PERFECT AVIATION

☐ N854AA	Boeing 727-223F (FedEx 3)	20995/1192		

SABAH AIR — *Sabah Air (SAX)* — *Kota Kinabalu-Intl (BKI)*

☐ 9M-AUA	GAF N22B Nomad	N22B-7		
☐ 9M-AWC	Bell 206B JetRanger III	2336		
☐ 9M-AXH	Bell 206B JetRanger III	2480		
☐ 9M-AYN	Bell 206B JetRanger III	3022	ex N5738M	
☐ 9M-AZK	Bell 206L-3 LongRanger III	51484	ex N4196G	
☐ 9M-KUL	Bell 206L-4 LongRanger IV	52253	ex N9089J	
☐ 9M-SAC	Bell 206B JetRanger III	2510		

TRANSMILE AIR SERVICES — *Transmile (TH/TSE)* — *Subang-Sultan Abdul Aziz Shah Intl (SZB)*

☐ 9M-TGB	Boeing 727-2F2F/W (Duganair 3)	22998/1810	ex VH-DHF	
☐ 9M-TGF	Boeing 727-247F (FedEx 3)	21698/1474	ex N209UP	
☐ 9M-TGG	Boeing 727-247F (FedEx 3)	21699/1485	ex N207UP	
☐ 9M-TGH	Boeing 727-247F (FedEx 3)	21701/1493	ex N208UP	
☐ 9M-TGL	Boeing 727-225F (FedEx 3)	21856/1537	ex N8887Z	
☐ 9M-TGM	Boeing 727-225F (FedEx 3)	22549/1737	ex N902RF	
☐ PK-KAR	Boeing 737-209	23796/1420	ex 9M-PMZ	stored SZB as PK-KAR
☐ 9M-PML	Boeing 737-275C	21116/427	ex C-GDPW DHL colours	Freighter
☐ 9M-PMM	Boeing 737-205C	20458/278	ex RP-C2906 DHL colours	Freighter
☐ 9M-PMP	Boeing 737-248C	20220/215	ex PT-MTA	Freighter
☐ 9M-PMQ	Boeing 737-230C	20254/230	ex PT-MTB	Freighter
☐ 9M-PMA	Cessna 208B Caravan I	208B0800	ex N1278M	
☐ 9M-TGP	McDonnell-Douglas MD-11F	48444/459	ex N625FE	stored KUL
☐ 9M-TGQ	McDonnell-Douglas MD-11F	48446/463	ex N627FE	stored KUL
☐ 9M-TGR	McDonnell-Douglas MD-11F	48485/502	ex N15WF	stored KUL
☐ 9M-TGS	McDonnell-Douglas MD-11F	48486/509	ex N71WF	stored KUL

9N- NEPAL (Kingdom of Nepal)

AGNI AIR — *Kathmandu (KTM)*

☐ 9N-AHE	Dornier 228-101	7032	ex VT-EIX	
☐ 9N-AIE	Dornier 228-202K	8165	ex 9M-VAA	
☐ 9N-AIG	Dornier 228-212	8216	ex 9M-VAM	
☐ 9N-AIO	British Aerospace Jetstream 4101	41055	ex N316UE	
☐ 9N-AIP	British Aerospace Jetstream 4101	41058	ex N322UE	
☐ 9N-AIQ	British Aerospace Jetstream 4101	41064	ex N326UE	
☐ 9N-	British Aerospace Jetstream 4101	41081	ex N564HK	on order

AIR KASTHAMANDAP — *Kathmandu (KTM)*

☐ 9N-AIZ	Pacific Aerospace 750XL	154	ex ZK-JJH	
☐ 9N-AJB	Pacific Aerospace 750XL	160	ex ZK-KAZ	

BUDDHA AIR — *Buddha Air (BHA)* — *Kathmandu (KTM)*

☐ 9N-AIM	ATR 42-320	388	ex F-WQNF	
☐ 9N-AIN	ATR 42-320	403	ex F-WQNA	
☐ 9N-AIT	ATR 42-320	409	ex F-WKVF	
☐ 9N-	ATR 72-212A	666	ex F-WKVE	
☐ 9N-AEE	Beech 1900D	UE-286	ex N11194	
☐ 9N-AEK	Beech 1900D	UE-295	ex N21540	
☐ 9N-AEW	Beech 1900D	UE-328	ex N23179	
☐ 9N-AGH	Beech 1900D	UE-409	ex N4192N	
☐ 9N-AGI	Beech 1900C-1	UC-97	ex N97YV	
☐ 9N-AGL	Beech 1900C-1	UC-108	ex N15856	
☐ 9N-AHZ	Beech 1900D	UE-180	ex N862CA	

COSMIC AIR — Cosmic Air (F5/COZ) — Kathmandu/Pokhara (KTM/PKR)

☐ 9N-AEP	Dornier 228-201	8078	ex D-CBMI	stored KTM
☐ 9N-AGY	Dornier 228-100	7022	ex SE-KTM	stored KTM

GORKHA AIRLINES — (G1) — Pokhara (PKR)

☐ 9N-AHS	Dornier 228-212	8218	ex RP-C2101

NEPAL AIRLINES — Nepal (RA/RNA) — Kathmandu (KTM)

☐ 9N-ACA	Boeing 757-2F8	23850/142		Karnali
☐ 9N-ACB	Boeing 757-2F8C	23863/182	ex N5573K	Garnadi
☐ 9N-ABB	de Havilland DHC-6 Twin Otter 300	302		
☐ 9N-ABM	de Havilland DHC-6 Twin Otter 300	455	ex N302EH	stored KTM
☐ 9N-ABO	de Havilland DHC-6 Twin Otter 300	638		stored KTM
☐ 9N-ABQ	de Havilland DHC-6 Twin Otter 300	655		stored KTM
☐ 9N-ABT	de Havilland DHC-6 Twin Otter 300	812	ex C-GHHI	
☐ 9N-ABU	de Havilland DHC-6 Twin Otter 300	814	ex C-GHHY	
☐ 9N-ABX	de Havilland DHC-6 Twin Otter 300	830	ex C-GIQS	

SHANGRI-LA AIR — Kathmandu (KTM)

☐ 9N-AFX	de Havilland DHC-6 Twin Otter 310	806	ex N806AA

SHREE AIRLINES — Pokhara/Surkhet (PKR/SKH)

☐ 9N-ADD	Mil Mi-17-1 (Mi-8ATM)	59489607385	ex RA-22160	
☐ 9N-ADL	Mil Mi-17-1 (Mi-8ATM)	59489605283	ex RA-27093	stored KTM
☐ 9N-ADM	Mil Mi-8AMTV-1	95640	ex CCCP-25495	

SITA AIRLINES — Kathmandu (KTM)

☐ 9N-AHA	Dornier 228-202K	8123	ex F-ODZG
☐ 9N-AHB	Dornier 228-202K	8169	ex F-OGPI
☐ 9N-AHR	Dornier 228-202	8154	ex C-GSAU
☐ 9N-AIJ	Dornier 228-212	8239	ex 8Q-IAS
☐ 9N-AIY	Dornier 228-212	8191	ex F-ODYB

TARA AIR

☐ 9N-AGQ	Dornier 228-202K	8107	ex F-ODZF

YETI AIRLINES — (YA) — Kathmandu (KTM)

☐ 9N-AHU	British Aerospace Jetstream 41	41072	ex N555HK
☐ 9N-AHV	British Aerospace Jetstream 41	41077	ex N561HK
☐ 9N-AHW	British Aerospace Jetstream 41	41078	ex N562HK
☐ 9N-AHY	British Aerospace Jetstream 41	41066	ex N553HK
☐ 9N-AIB	British Aerospace Jetstream 41	41017	ex G-CDYH
☐ 9N-AIH	British Aerospace Jetstream 41	41085	ex N567HK
☐ 9N-AJC	British Aerospace Jetstream 41	41096	ex G-MAJM
☐ 9N-AET	de Havilland DHC-6 Twin Otter 300	619	ex C-GBQA
☐ 9N-AEV	de Havilland DHC-6 Twin Otter 300	729	ex C-FWQF
☐ 9N-AFA	de Havilland DHC-6 Twin Otter 300	665	ex VT-ERV

9Q- CONGO KINSHASA (Democratic Republic of Congo)

ADELA AIRWAYS

☐ 9Q-CEN	Antonov An-12BK	8345410	ex 11 yellow

Current status uncertain

AEROLIFT SERVICES

☐ 9Q-CJU	Antonov An-32	1408	ex D2-FED

AFRICA ONE — Kinshasa-Ndolo (NLO)

☐ 9Q-CAF	Antonov An-32	1703	ex RA-48094	Regd to Business Aviation
☐ 9Q-CFY	WSK-PZL/Antonov An-28	1AJ006-03	ex 9XR-KI	

AFRICAINE D'AVIATION — Kinshasa-Ndolo (NLO)

☐ 9Q-CAB	Antonov An-26	5605	ex RA-26179
☐ 9Q-CBD	McDonnell-Douglas MD-81	48018/995	ex N818NK
☐ 9Q-CIB	Antonov An-26	1701	ex YL-RAB

☐ 9Q-CJB	Fokker F.27 Mk.050 (Fokker 50)	20196	ex PH-LMS	
☐ 9Q-CLB	Yakovlev Yak-40	9231623	ex LZ-DOR	
☐ 9Q-	Boeing 727-231F	21986/1580	ex N54354	on order

AIR BOYOMA — Kisangani (FKI)

☐ UR-ELH	Antonov An-26B	12908	ex UR-26143	Lsd fr URG

AIR KASAI — Kinshasa-Ndolo (NLO)

☐ 9Q-CFD	Antonov An-26B	12901	ex RA-26139	
☐ 9Q-CFL	Antonov An-26B	14003	ex RA-26593	
☐ 9Q-CFM	Antonov An-26B	07310405	ex RA-26235	
☐ 9Q-CFP	Antonov An-26	07310605	ex RA-26237	
☐ 9Q-CJA	Britten-Norman BN-2A-21 Islander	898	ex I-301	
☐ 9Q-CTR	Douglas DC-3	9452	ex ZS-EDX	stored FIH
☐ 9Q-CYC	Douglas DC-3	18977	ex N9984Q	stored FIH
☐ 9Q-CYE	Douglas DC-3	19771	ex 79004	stored FIH

AIR TROPIQUES — Kinshasa-Ndolo (NLO)

☐ 9Q-CEJ	Beech 1900C	UB-74	ex ZS-ODR	
☐ 9Q-CEM	Beech 100 King Air	B-105	ex ZS-TBS	regn also reported as LET L-410UVP
☐ 9Q-CLN	Fokker F.27 Friendship 100	10152	ex ZS-OEH	
☐ 9Q-CUZ	Cessna 402B II	402B1358	ex OO-HFC	

ALAJNIHAH AIR TRANSPORT

☐ 9Q-CGV	Ilyushin Il-76TD	0033449441	ex UR-76574	Morning Star

ATO - AIR TRANSPORT OFFICE — Kinshasa-N'djili (FIH)

☐ 9Q-CTO	Lockheed L-188A Electra	1073	ex 9Q-CRM	
☐ 9Q-CVK	Hawker Siddeley HS.780 Andover E.3	Set 17	ex P4-BLL	

BRAVO AIR CONGO — (BRV)

☐ TN-AHQ	Douglas DC-9-32	48126/951	ex N481SG	
☐ 9Q-CDO	Douglas DC-9-32	48125/947	ex N481SF	stored FIH
☐ 9Q-CDT	Douglas DC-9-32	48128/964	ex N128GE	
☐ 9Q-CVT	Douglas DC-9-32	48127/961	ex N127GE	stored FIH

BUSINESS AVIATION OF CONGO — (4P) — Kinshasa-Ndolo (NLO)

☐ 9Q-CBA	Nord 262A-42	57	ex OY-IVA	

BUTEMBO — Butembo

☐ 9Q-CAX	WZK/PZL Antonov An-28	1AJ002-08	ex EX-28810	

CAA – COMPAGNIE AFRICANE D'AVIATION

☐ 9Q-CIB	McDonnell-Douglas MD-82	49394/1285	ex N94EV	

CARGAIR

☐ 9Q-CGI	Boeing 747-269M	21543/359	ex N708CK	

CETRACA AIR SERVICE

☐ 9Q-CAZ	LET L-410UVP	790205	ex UR-67169	
☐ 9Q-CKO	Antonov An-26	5210	ex ER-AFW	
☐ 9Q-CKT	Antonov An-26B	12001	ex ER-AES	
☐ 9Q-CKX	LET L-410UVP	790303	ex ER-LIB	

COMAIR

☐ 9Q-CCM	WZK/PZL Antonov An-28	1AJ010-04	ex RA-28957	non-airworthy
☐ 9Q-CKC	WZK/PZL Antonov An-28	1AJ009-18	ex RA-28952	

CO-ZA AIRWAYS — Goma (GOM)

☐ 9Q-CML	Antonov An-26	7408	ex ER-AWN	no titles

DOREN AIR CONGO — Goma (GOM)

☐ 9Q-CQZ	LET L-410UVP	851339	ex 9L-LEM	
☐ 9Q-CXZ	LET L-410UVP	841201	ex 9L-LBL	
☐ 9Q-CZA	LET L-410UVP	851524	ex OK-PDC	

EL SAM AIRLIFT

☐ 9Q-CES	Antonov An-26	97308807	ex Russian AF		

ESPACE AVIATION

☐ 9Q-CTA	Douglas DC-8-54F	45802/247	ex 3D-AFR		

ETRAM AIR WING — Kinshasa-N'djili (FIH)

☐ 4K-48136	Antonov An-32B	3103	ex CCCP-48126		
☐ D2-FDZ	Boeing 707-399C (Comtran 2)	19415/601	ex 9Q-FDZ		stored
☐ N56FA	Douglas DC-8-54F	45663/189	ex 3D-ETM		stored LAD

FILAIR — Kinshasa-N'djili (FIH)

☐ 9Q-CDN	LET L-410UVP-E	902422	ex YU-BXX		
☐ 9Q-CTR	Antonov An-24RV	77310802	ex 9L-LBQ		

HEWA BORA AIRWAYS — Allcongo (EO/ALX) — Kinshasa-N'djili (FIH)

☐ 9Q-CBW	Boeing 707-329C (Comtran 2)	20200/828	ex TL-ADJ		
☐ 9Q-CKK	Boeing 707-366C	20761/867	ex 9Q-CKB	Aisha	
☐ 9Q-CKR	Boeing 707-351C	19411/540			
☐ 9Q-CWB	Boeing 707-3B4C	20259/822	ex OD-AFD		
☐ S9-DBM	Boeing 727-22/W (Duganair 3)	18323/136	ex 3D-BOC		VIP
☐ S9-ROI	Boeing 727-30/W (Duganair 3)	18933/185	ex 3D-BOE		VIP
☐ 9Q-CHD	Boeing 727-232 (FedEx 3)	22494/1749	ex N545DA		stored FIH
☐ 9Q-CHE	Boeing 727-232 (FedEx 3)	21310/1298	ex PK-JAE		
☐ 9Q-CHF	Boeing 727-232 (FedEx 3)	22677/1785	ex N546DA		
☐ 9Q-CHG	Boeing 727-232 (FedEx 3)	21586/1488	ex PK-JGX		
☐ 9Q-CHK	Boeing 727-29F/W (Duganair 3)	19401/419	ex N712DH		
☐ 9Q-CRG	Boeing 727-30	18361/28	ex N18477	Ville de Goma	stored FIH
☐ 9Q-CRS	Boeing 727-214	19687/573	ex 5H-ARS		
☐ 9Q-CWA	Boeing 727-227	20775/998	ex N554PE	Ville de Bakavu	stored FIH
☐ S9-TOA	McDonnell-Douglas MD-82	49176/11	ex N226AA		
☐ S9-TOB	McDonnell-Douglas MD-82	49178/1122	ex N228AA		
☐ S9-TOP	Boeing 767-266ER	23178/97	ex 9Q-CJD		
☐ 9Q-CKZ	Boeing 737-293	19309/47	ex N464AC		
☐ 9Q-CHL	Douglas DC-8F-55 (QNC 2)	45820/246	ex S9-PSD		
☐ 9Q-CHM	Douglas DC-8F-55 (QNC 2)	45764/251	ex 9G-MKT		
☐ 9Q-CHC	Lockheed L-1011-500 Tristar	193H-1209	ex N767DA		stored FIH

ITAB – INTERNATIONAL TRANS AIR BUSINESS — Lubumbashi-Luano (FBM)

☐ 9Q-CAP	Nord 262A-32	35	ex F-BPNT		
☐ 9Q-CDH	Nord 262C-50P	36	ex XT-OAG		
☐ 9Q-CDP	LET L-410UVP-E	902519	ex 9L-LCL		
☐ 9Q-CJJ	Douglas DC-3	10110	ex ZS-NZA		
☐ (9Q-CON)	BAC One-Eleven 537GF	261	ex 9Q-CDY		
☐ 9Q-CSJ	BAC One-Eleven 201AC	013	ex EI-BWM	Fatima	
☐ 9Q-CVC	Hawker Siddeley HS.780 Andover C Mk.1		Set 29	ex 3C-KKT	
☐ 9Q-CYA	Britten-Norman BN-2A Islander	617	ex G-AYBB		
☐ 9Q-CYB	Hawker Siddeley HS.780 Andover C Mk.1		Set 22	ex NZ7628	

JETAIR SERVICES — Kinshasa-Ndolo /N'djili (NLO/FIH)

☐ 9Q-CCJ	Partenavia P.68B	163	ex 9Q-CEZ		
☐ 9Q-CCK	Cessna 402B	402B0304	ex TN-ACJ		

KISANGANI AIRLIFT — Kisangani (FKI)

☐ S9-DBC	Antonov An-8	OG-3410	ex 9L-LEO		status, possibly grounded?

LIGNES AERIENNES CONGOLAISES — Congolaise (LCG) — Kinshasa-Ndolo (NLO)

☐ 9Q-CSV	Boeing 737-281	20276/231	ex 4X-BAG		

Ceased operations in 2005 but believed to have recommenced limited services Aug06. Attempted partnerships with AZW and RKM in 2008 were unsuccessful. Current status unknown.

MALIFT AIR — Malila (MLC) — Kinshasa-N'djili/Khartoum (FIH/KRT)

☐ 9Q-CMD	Antonov An-32B	2210	ex RA-26221	Kevin	stored SHJ
☐ 9Q-CMK	Antonov An-24RV	47309902		Kenzo	
☐ 9Q-CMM	Britten-Norman BN-2A-21 Islander	812	ex 9U-BRV		
☐ 9Q-CMS	Antonov An-26	4206	ex 9U-BNO		non-airworthy
☐ 9Q-CPG	WSK/PZL Antonov An-28	1AJ004-12	ex CCCP-28763		Audrey

MALU AVIATION — Kinshasa-Ndolo (NLO)

☐ 9Q-CDV	Partenavia P.68B	207		
☐ 9Q-CPM	Nord 262A-32	38	ex F-BPNU	
☐ 9Q-CRA	WSK-PZL/Antonov An-28	1AJ008-08	ex RA-28922	
☐ 9Q-CSP	WSK-PZL/Antonov An-28	1AJ008-09	ex 9Q-CJF	
☐ 9Q-CSD	Short SC.7 Skyvan	SH1831	ex ZS-ORN	
☐ 9Q-	Short SC.7 Skyvan 3	SH1870	ex SE-LDK	id not confirmed

MANGO MAT AIRLINES — Goma (GOM)

☐ S9-PSK	Antonov An-12BK	8345807	ex EX-084
☐ 9Q-CVM	Antonov An-12B	8345503	ex 9U-BHO

MIDDLAND — Beni

☐ 9Q-COM	WSK-PZL/Antonov An-28	1AJ008-21	ex EX-018
☐ 9Q-CVE	Antonov An-26	5301	ex RA-26193

SERVICE AIR

☐ 9Q-	Boeing 727-2S2F	22930/1824	ex N361CW
☐ 9Q-CSV	Boeing 727-2S2F	22924/1818	ex N358PZ

SERVICE COMMUTER — Bukavu (BKY)

☐ 9Q-CFQ	WZK/PZL Antonov An-28	1AJ008-05	ex SP-FHW	non-airworthy, also a PA-23-250

SOFT TRANS AIR — Kinshasa

☐ 9Q-CYN	Antonov An-26	67304001	ex 55 blue	non-airworthy

STAG

☐ 9Q-CFB	Antonov An-26B	56312909	ex RA-26577

SUCCESS AIRLINES

☐ 9Q-CJI	Antonov An-26	6004	ex EL-AHT

SUN AIR SERVICE

☐ 9Q-CMZ	PZL/WZK Antonov An-28	1AJ-005-17	ex RA-28784

SWALA AIRLINES — Bukavu (BKY)

☐ 9Q-CXF	Short SC.7 Skyvan	SH1915	ex (5Y-)

TMK AIR COMMUTER — Goma (GOM)

☐ 9Q-CEL	de Havilland DHC-6 Twin Otter 300	719	ex N719DK

TOLAZ AVIATION GROUP

☐ 9Q-CGM	Antonov An-26B	6401	ex Ukraine AF

TRANSAIR CARGO SERVICE — Kinshasa-N'djili (FIH)

☐ 3X-GEP	Douglas DC-8-62F (BAC 3)	45921/322	ex EC-EMX
☐ 9Q-CJL	Douglas DC-8-62F (BAC 3)	45909/307	ex N802BN
☐ 9Q-CMP	Boeing 727-22C	19892/640	ex 3D-KMJ
☐ 9Q-CYS	NAMC YS-11A	2051	ex 3D-CYS

VIRUNGA AIR CHARTER — Goma (GOM)

☐ 9Q-CDD	Dornier 28D-1 Skyservant	4025	ex D-IFAQ
☐ 9Q-CTL	Partenavia P.68B	145	ex 5Y-BCG
☐ 9Q-CTN	Partenavia P.68C-TC	238-04-TC	ex OO-TZT
☐ 9Q-CTX	Dornier 128-6 Turbo Skyservant	6007	ex D-IDOQ

WALTAIR — Kinshasa-N'djili (FIH)

☐ 9Q-CPW	Hawker Siddeley HS.780 Andover C Mk.1	Set14	ex XS607	stored FIH

Believed to be grounded, status uncertain

WETRAFA AIRLIFT — Kinshasa-N'djili (FIH)

☐ 9Q-CWF	Douglas DC-9-32	47531/638	ex N15525

WIMBI DIRA AIRWAYS	Wimbi Dera (9C/WDA)		Kinshasa-N'djili (FIH)
☐ 9Q-CWD Boeing 727-231F	19562/576	ex N12305	
☐ 9Q-CWE Douglas DC-9-32 (ABS 3)	47701/822	ex N212ME	
☐ 9Q-CWG Boeing 707-323C	19587/686	ex 3D-ROK	
☐ 9Q-CWH Douglas DC-9-32 (ABS 3)	47744/837	ex N215ME	
☐ 9Q- Douglas DC-9-32	47090/190	ex ZS-NRC	
☐ S9- Douglas DC-9-34CF	47707/823	ex N787CT	

9U- BURUNDI (Republic of Burundi)

AIR BURUNDI	Air Burundi (8Y/PBU)		Bujumbura (BJM)
☐ 9U-BHG Beech 1900C-1	UC-147	ex 9U-BHD	

9V- SINGAPORE (Republic of Singapore)

AIRMARK SINGAPORE — *Singapore-Seletar (XSP)*

Lease aircraft from other operators as required

JETSTAR ASIA AIRWAYS	Jetstar (3K/JSA)		Singapore-Changi (SIN)
☐ 9V-JSA Airbus A320-232	2316	ex F-WWDR	
☐ 9V-JSB Airbus A320-232	2356	ex F-WWIQ	
☐ 9V-JSC Airbus A320-232	2395	ex F-WWIS	
☐ 9V-JSD Airbus A320-232	2401	ex F-WWIB	
☐ 9V-JSF Airbus A320-232	2453	ex VH-JQH	
☐ 9V-JSG Airbus A320-232	2457	ex VH-JQE	
☐ 9V-JSH Airbus A320-232	2604	ex VH-VQA	
☐ 9V- Airbus A320-232		ex	on order
☐ 9V- Airbus A320-232		ex	on order
☐ 9V- Airbus A320-232		ex	on order

JETT 8 AIRLINES CARGO	(JEC)		Singapore-Changi (SIN)
☐ 9V-JEB Boeing 747-281F	23350/623	ex JA8172	Shogun

SILKAIR	Silkair (MI/SLK)		Singapore-Changi (SIN)
☐ 9V-SBA Airbus A319-132	1074	ex D-AVWH	
☐ 9V-SBB Airbus A319-132	1098	ex D-AVWQ	
☐ 9V-SBC Airbus A319-132	1228	ex D-AVYL	
☐ 9V-SBD Airbus A319-132	1698	ex D-AVYE	
☐ 9V-SBE Airbus A319-132	2568	ex D-AVXA	
☐ 9V-SBF Airbus A319-132	3104	ex D-AVYI	
☐ 9V-SBG Airbus A319-132		ex D-	on order
☐ 9V-SBH Airbus A319-132		ex D-	on order
☐ 9V-SBI Airbus A319-132		ex D-	on order
☐ 9V-SBJ Airbus A319-132		ex D-	on order
☐ 9V-SLB Airbus A320-232	0899	ex F-WWDL	
☐ 9V-SLC Airbus A320-232	0969	ex F-WWBO	
☐ 9V-SLD Airbus A320-232	1422	ex F-WWBK	
☐ 9V-SLE Airbus A320-232	1561	ex F-WWBC	
☐ 9V-SLF Airbus A320-232	2058	ex F-WWBK	
☐ 9V-SLG Airbus A320-233	2252	ex F-WWBB	
☐ 9V-SLH Airbus A320-233	2517	ex F-WWIG	
☐ 9V-SLI Airbus A320-233	2775	ex F-WWDS	
☐ 9V-SLJ Airbus A320-233	3570	ex F-WWBD	
☐ 9V-SLK Airbus A320-233	3821	ex F-WWIQ	
☐ 9V-SLL Airbus A320-232	4118	ex D-AVVU	
☐ 9V-SLM Airbus A320-232	4175	ex D-AVVT	on order
☐ 9V-SLN Airbus A320-232		ex D-	on order

SINGAPORE AIRLINES	Singapore (SQ/SIA)		Singapore-Changi (SIN)

Member of Star Alliance

☐ 9V-STA Airbus A330-343E	978	ex F-WWKZ	
☐ 9V-STB Airbus A330-343E	983	ex F-WWYZ	
☐ 9V-STC Airbus A330-343E	986	ex F-WWKG	
☐ 9V-STD Airbus A330-343E	997	ex F-WWYM	
☐ 9V-STE Airbus A330-343E	1006	ex F-WWYB	
☐ 9V-STF Airbus A330-343E	1010	ex F-WWYF	
☐ 9V-STG Airbus A330-343E	1012	ex F-WWKA	
☐ 9V-STH Airbus A330-343E	1015	ex F-WWKV	
☐ 9V-STI Airbus A330-343E	1085	ex F-WWKA	on order
☐ 9V-STJ Airbus A330-343E	1098	ex F-WW	on order

	Registration	Type	c/n	Previous identity	Remarks	Status
☐	9V-STK	Airbus A330-343E	1099	ex F-WW		on order
☐	9V-STL	Airbus A330-343E	1105	ex F-WW		on order
☐	9V-STM	Airbus A330-343E	1107	ex F-WW		on order
☐	9V-	Airbus A330-343E		ex F-WW		on order
☐	9V-	Airbus A330-343E		ex F-WW		on order
☐	9V-	Airbus A330-343E		ex F-WW		on order
☐	9V-	Airbus A330-343E		ex F-WW		on order
☐	9V-	Airbus A330-343E		ex F-WW		on order
☐	9V-	Airbus A330-343E		ex F-WW		on order
☐	9V-SGA	Airbus A340-541	492	ex F-WWTP		
☐	9V-SGB	Airbus A340-541	499	ex F-WWTR		
☐	9V-SGC	Airbus A340-541	478	ex F-WWTG		
☐	9V-SGD	Airbus A340-541	560	ex F-WWTM		
☐	9V-SGE	Airbus A340-541	563	ex F-WWTU		
☐	9V-SKA	Airbus A380-841	003	ex F-WWSA		
☐	9V-SKB	Airbus A380-841	005	ex F-WWSB		
☐	9V-SKC	Airbus A380-841	006	ex F-WWSC		
☐	9V-SKD	Airbus A380-841	008	ex F-WWSE		
☐	9V-SKE	Airbus A380-841	010	ex F-WWSG		
☐	9V-SKF	Airbus A380-841	012	ex F-WWSI		
☐	9V-SKG	Airbus A380-841	019	ex F-WWSP		
☐	9V-SKH	Airbus A380-841	021	ex F-WWSQ		
☐	9V-SKI	Airbus A380-841	034	ex F-WWSC		
☐	9V-SKJ	Airbus A380-841	045	ex F-WWSG		
☐	9V-SKK	Airbus A380-841	051	ex F-WWAH		on order
☐	9V-SKL	Airbus A380-841	058	ex F-WW		on order
☐	9V-SKM	Airbus A380-841	065	ex F-WW		on order
☐	9V-SKN	Airbus A380-841	071	ex F-WW		on order
☐	9V-SMU	Boeing 747-412	27068/1000			
☐	9V-SPA	Boeing 747-412	26550/1040			
☐	9V-SPE	Boeing 747-412	26554/1070			
☐	9V-SPH	Boeing 747-412	26555/1075			
☐	9V-SPJ	Boeing 747-412	26556/1084			
☐	9V-SPM	Boeing 747-412	29950/1241			stored VCV
☐	9V-SPN	Boeing 747-412	28031/1266			stored VCV
☐	9V-SPO	Boeing 747-412	28028/1270			
☐	9V-SPP	Boeing 747-412	28029/1276		Star Alliance c/s	
☐	9V-SPQ	Boeing 747-412	28025/1289			
☐	9V-SQA	Boeing 777-212ER	28507/67			stored VCV
☐	9V-SQB	Boeing 777-212ER	28508/83			
☐	9V-SQC	Boeing 777-212ER	28509/86			
☐	9V-SQD	Boeing 777-212ER	28510/90			
☐	9V-SQE	Boeing 777-212ER	28511/122			
☐	9V-SQF	Boeing 777-212ER	28512/126			
☐	9V-SQG	Boeing 777-212ER	28518/226			
☐	9V-SQH	Boeing 777-212ER	28519/237			
☐	9V-SQI	Boeing 777-212ER	28530/390	ex N5023Q		
☐	9V-SQJ	Boeing 777-212ER	30875/406			
☐	9V-SQK	Boeing 777-212ER	33368/428			
☐	9V-SQL	Boeing 777-212ER	33370/451			
☐	9V-SQM	Boeing 777-212ER	33372/485			
☐	9V-SQN	Boeing 777-212ER	33373/487			
☐	9V-SRB	Boeing 777-212ER	28998/149			
☐	9V-SRC	Boeing 777-212ER	28999/150			
☐	9V-SRD	Boeing 777-212ER	28514/153			
☐	9V-SRE	Boeing 777-212ER	28523/239		Star Alliance c/s	
☐	9V-SRF	Boeing 777-212ER	28521/330			
☐	9V-SRG	Boeing 777-212ER	28522/337			
☐	9V-SRH	Boeing 777-212ER	30866/343			
☐	9V-SRI	Boeing 777-212ER	30867/348			
☐	9V-SRJ	Boeing 777-212ER	28527/372			
☐	9V-SRK	Boeing 777-212ER	28529/389	ex N5022E		
☐	9V-SRL	Boeing 777-212ER	32334/409			
☐	9V-SRM	Boeing 777-212ER	32320/438			
☐	9V-SRN	Boeing 777-212ER	32318/441			
☐	9V-SRO	Boeing 777-212ER	32321/447			
☐	9V-SRP	Boeing 777-212ER	33369/448			
☐	9V-SRQ	Boeing 777-212ER	33371/449			
☐	9V-SVA	Boeing 777-212ER	28524/350			
☐	9V-SVB	Boeing 777-212ER	28525/353			
☐	9V-SVC	Boeing 777-212ER	28526/355			
☐	9V-SVD	Boeing 777-212ER	30869/366			
☐	9V-SVE	Boeing 777-212ER	30870/374			
☐	9V-SVF	Boeing 777-212ER	30871/378			
☐	9V-SVG	Boeing 777-212ER	30872/398			
☐	9V-SVH	Boeing 777-212ER	28532/407	ex N5022E		
☐	9V-SVI	Boeing 777-212ER	32316/412			
☐	9V-SVJ	Boeing 777-212ER	32335/415			
☐	9V-SVK	Boeing 777-212ER	28520/419			

☐ 9V-SVL	Boeing 777-212ER	32336/422		
☐ 9V-SVM	Boeing 777-212ER	30874/430		
☐ 9V-SVN	Boeing 777-212ER	30873/431		
☐ 9V-SVO	Boeing 777-212ER	28533/471		
☐ 9V-SWA	Boeing 777-312ER	34568/586	ex N6018N	
☐ 9V-SWB	Boeing 777-312ER	33377/592		
☐ 9V-SWD	Boeing 777-312ER	34569/600		
☐ 9V-SWE	Boeing 777-312ER	34570/602		
☐ 9V-SWF	Boeing 777-312ER	34571/603		
☐ 9V-SWG	Boeing 777-312ER	34572/604		
☐ 9V-SWH	Boeing 777-312ER	34573/615		
☐ 9V-SWI	Boeing 777-312ER	34574/618		
☐ 9V-SWJ	Boeing 777-312ER	34575/623		
☐ 9V-SWK	Boeing 777-312ER	34576/644	ex N6009F	
☐ 9V-SWL	Boeing 777-312ER	34577/673		
☐ 9V-SWM	Boeing 777-312ER	34578/701		
☐ 9V-SWN	Boeing 777-312ER	34579/703		
☐ 9V-SWO	Boeing 777-312ER	34580/708		
☐ 9V-SWP	Boeing 777-312ER	34581/710		
☐ 9V-SWQ	Boeing 777-312ER	34582/716		
☐ 9V-SWR	Boeing 777-312ER	34583/722		
☐ 9V-SWS	Boeing 777-312ER	34584/729		
☐ 9V-SWT	Boeing 777-312ER	34585/759		
☐ 9V-SYA	Boeing 777-312	28515/180		
☐ 9V-SYB	Boeing 777-312	28516/184		
☐ 9V-SYC	Boeing 777-312	28517/188		
☐ 9V-SYD	Boeing 777-312	28534/192		
☐ 9V-SYE	Boeing 777-312	28531/244		Star Alliance c/s
☐ 9V-SYF	Boeing 777-312	30868/360		
☐ 9V-SYG	Boeing 777-312	28528/364		
☐ 9V-SYH	Boeing 777-312	32317/420	ex N5020K	
☐ 9V-SYI	Boeing 777-312	32327/484	ex N5028Y	
☐ 9V-SYJ	Boeing 777-312	33374/503	ex N50217	
☐ 9V-SYK	Boeing 777-312	33375/505		
☐ 9V-SYL	Boeing 777-312	33376/515		

SINGAPORE AIRLINES CARGO — *Singapore Cargo (SQ/SQC)* — *Singapore-Changi (SIN)*

☐ 9V-SFA	Boeing 747-412F	26563/1036	ex N60659	
☐ 9V-SFB	Boeing 747-412F	26561/1042		
☐ 9V-SFC	Boeing 747-412F	26560/1052		Lsd to CCA as B-2409
☐ 9V-SFD	Boeing 747-412F	26553/1069		
☐ 9V-SFF	Boeing 747-412F	28026/1105		
☐ 9V-SFG	Boeing 747-412F	26558/1173		
☐ 9V-SFJ	Boeing 747-412F	26559/1285		
☐ 9V-SFK	Boeing 747-412F	28030/1298		
☐ 9V-SFL	Boeing 747-412F	32897/1322	ex N5022E	stored VCV
☐ 9V-SFM	Boeing 747-412F	32898/1333		
☐ 9V-SFN	Boeing 747-412F	32899/1342		
☐ 9V-SFO	Boeing 747-412F	32900/1349		
☐ 9V-SFP	Boeing 747-412F	32902/1364		
☐ 9V-SFQ	Boeing 747-412F	32901/1369		

TIGER AIRWAYS — *(TR/TGW)* — *Singapore-Changi (SIN)*

☐ 9V-TAB	Airbus A320-232	2195	ex F-WWIZ	
☐ 9V-TAC	Airbus A320-232	2331	ex F-WWIF	
☐ 9V-TAD	Airbus A320-232	2340	ex F-WWIY	
☐ 9V-TAE	Airbus A320-232	2724	ex F-WWDO	
☐ 9V-TAF	Airbus A320-232	2728	ex F-WWDU	
☐ 9V-TAH	Airbus A320-232	2952	ex F-WWIV	
☐ 9V-TAM	Airbus A320-232	4181	ex F-WWIA	
☐ 9V-TAN	Airbus A320-232	4210	ex F-WWBR	on order
☐ 9V-	Airbus A320-232		ex	on order
☐ 9V-	Airbus A320-232		ex	on order
☐ 9V-	Airbus A320-232		ex	on order
☐ 9V-	Airbus A320-232		ex	on order
☐ 9V-TRA	Airbus A319-132	3757	ex D-AVXC	
☐ 9V-TRB	Airbus A319-132	3801	ex D-AVYA	

VALUAIR — *Value (VF/VLU)* — *Singapore-Changi (SIN)*

☐ 9V-VLA	Airbus A320-232	2156	ex F-WWDC
☐ 9V-VLB	Airbus A320-232	2164	ex F-WWIF

9XR- RWANDA (Rwanda Republic)

CONGO FRET ESPOIR

Reg	Type	C/n	Previous	Name	Notes
☐ 9XR-EF	LET L-410UVP				
☐ 9XR-EJ	LET L-410UVP	790216	ex 9L-LCP		stored GOM

RWANDAIR EXPRESS — Rwandair (WB/RWD) — Kigali (KGL)

Reg	Type	C/n	Previous	Name	Notes
☐ 9XR-WA	Canadair CL-600-2B19 (CRJ-200LR)	7439	ex D-ACHG		
☐ 9XR-WB	Canadair CL-600-2B19 (CRJ-200LR)	7449	ex D-ACHH		
☐ ET-AKZ	de Havilland DHC-8-202	469	ex C-GLOT		op by TNW
☐ 7Q-YKW	Boeing 737-522	25384/2149	ex N917UA	Sapitwa	Lsd fr AML

SILVERBACK CARGO FREIGHTERS — Silverback (VRB) — Kigali (KGL)

Reg	Type	C/n	Previous
☐ 9XR-SC	Douglas DC-8-62F	46068/463	ex N990CF
☐ 9XR-SD	Douglas DC-8-62F	45956/376	ex N994CF

9Y- TRINIDAD & TOBAGO (Republic of Trinidad & Tobago)

BRISTOW CARIBBEAN — Port of Spain (POS)

Reg	Type	C/n	Previous	Notes
☐ 9Y-BCO	Bell 412EP	36401	ex N8087N	
☐ 9Y-BHI	Bell 412	33032	ex N418EH	
☐ 9Y-BOB	Bell 412SP	36256	ex N368AL	
☐ 9Y-BRS	Bell 412EP	36396	ex N10269	
☐ 9Y-EVS	Bell 412SP	33212	ex XA-SBJ	Lsd fr OLOG
☐ 9Y-LNG	Bell 412	33009	ex N395AL	Lsd fr OLOG
☐ 9Y-OLG	Bell 412	33011	ex XA-TXA	Lsd fr OLOG
☐ 9Y-ONE	Bell 412EP	36421	ex N387AL	
☐ 9Y-REP	Bell 412	33065	ex XA-TUW	
☐ 9Y-SKY	Bell 412EP	36420	ex N8010C	
☐ 9Y-TJM	Bell 412SP	33169	ex PT-HUO	
☐ 9Y-TNT	Bell 412EP	36414	ex N386AL	
☐ 9Y-TSP	Bell 412SP	33169	ex XA-TAM	

CARIBBEAN AIRLINES — West Indian (BW/BWA) — Port of Spain (POS)

Reg	Type	C/n	Previous
☐ 9Y-ANU	Boeing 737-8Q8/W	28235/697	(ex 9Y-SLU)
☐ 9Y-BGI	Boeing 737-8Q8/W	28232/547	
☐ 9Y-GEO	Boeing 737-8Q8/W	28225/433	ex PH-HSX
☐ 9Y-KIN	Boeing 737-8Q8/W	28234/680	(ex 9Y-ANU)
☐ 9Y-PBM	Boeing 737-8BK/W	29635/2326	ex N810SY
☐ 9Y-POS	Boeing 737-8Q8/W	28230/506	
☐ 9Y-SLU	Boeing 737-83N/W	28246/1081	ex N317TZ
☐ 9Y-TAB	Boeing 737-8Q8/W	28233/598	
☐ 9Y-WIP	de Havilland DHC-8Q-311	538	ex C-FDII
☐ 9Y-WIT	de Havilland DHC-8Q-311	487	ex OE-LSA
☐ 9Y-WIZ	de Havilland DHC-8Q-311	557	ex C-GEMU

EVERGREEN HELICOPTERS INTERNATIONAL (TRINIDAD)

Reg	Type	C/n	Previous
☐ 9Y-DMS	Bell 212	31205	ex N827MS
☐ 9Y-DPB	Bell 212	30886	ex N16974

NATIONAL HELICOPTER SERVICES — Camden Heliport

Reg	Type	C/n	Previous
☐ 9Y-THP	MBB Bo.105CBS-4	S-758	ex N725MB
☐ 9Y-TIC	MBB Bo.105CBS-4	S-837	ex N7161N
☐ 9Y-TIW	MBB Bo.105CBS-4	S-671	ex N4573S
☐ 9Y-TJF	MBB Bo.105CBS-4	S-732	ex F-OHQZ
☐ 9Y-MCK	Sikorsky S-76C++	760745	ex N745G
☐ 9Y-NHS	Sikorsky S-76A++	760265	ex N82ES
☐ 9Y-TGW	Sikorsky S-76A	760176	
☐ 9Y-TGX	Sikorsky S-76A	760185	
☐ 9Y-TJJ	Sikorsky S-76A++	760164	ex F-GMIE
☐ 9Y-TJW	Sikorsky S-76A++	760926	ex C-GZIL

JET AND TURBOPROP AIRLINERS IN NON-AIRLINE SERVICE

Aircraft are listed in alphabetical order of manufacturer.
* Indicates a/c believed to be flown by stated operator; letters in square [ ] brackets relate to codes used.

Airbus A300

☐ F-BUAD	(B2-1C)	003	ex F-WUAD	Novaspace (Zero G trainer)
☐ YI-APX*	(B4-2C)	239	ex EK-30039	Government of Iraq
☐ 9K-AHI*	(C4-620)	344	ex PK-MAY	State of Kuwait [KAC]

Airbus A310

☐ 418*	(304)	418	ex F-WQIC	Republique Française / Armée de l'Air (call sign F-RADC) [CTM]
☐ 421*	(304)	421	ex F-ODVD	Republique Française / Armée de l'Air (call sign F-RADA) [CTM]
☐ 422*	(304)	422	ex F-ODVE	Republique Française / Armée de l'Air (call sign F-RADB) [CTM]
☐ 1021*	(304)	498	ex D-AOAA	Bundesrepublik Deutschland /op by Luftwaffe [GAF]
☐ 1022*	(304)	499	ex D-AOAB	Bundesrepublik Deutschland / op by Luftwaffe 'Theodor Heuss' [GAF]
☐ 1023*	(304F/MRT)	503	ex D-AOAC	Luftwaffe 'Kurt Schumacher' [GAF]
☐ 1024*	(304F/MRT)	434	ex D-AIDA	Luftwaffe 'Otto Lilienthal' [GAF]
☐ 1025*	(304F/MRT)	484	ex D-AIDB	Luftwaffe 'Helmut Köhl' [GAF]
☐ 1026*	(304F/MRT)	522	ex D-AIDE	Luftwaffe 'Hans Grade' [GAF]
☐ 1027*	(304F/MRTT)	523	ex D-AIDI	Luftwaffe 'August Euler' [GAF]
☐ 15001*	(304)	446	ex F-WQCQ	Canadian Armed Forces/437Sqdn [CFC] (as CC-150 Polaris '991')
☐ 15002*	(304MRT)	482	ex C-GLWD	Canadian Armed Forces/437Sqdn [CFC] (as CC-150 Polaris '992')
☐ 15003*	(304F)	425	ex C-FWDX	Canadian Armed Forces/437Sqdn [CFC] (as CC-150 Polaris '993')
☐ 15004*	(304MRTT)	444	ex F-WQCQ	Canadian Armed Forces/437Sqdn [CFC] (as CC-150 Polaris '994')
☐ 15005*	(304MRTT)	441	ex F-ZJCP	Canadian Armed Forces/437Sqdn [CFC] (as CC-150 Polaris '995')
☐ 60202*	(324)	591	ex 44-444	Royal Thai Air Force/Royal Flight (call-sign HS-TYG)
☐ AP-OOI*	(304)	473	ex A7-AAF	Pakistan Air Force
☐ A7-AFE	(308)	667	ex F-WQTO	Qatar Amiri Flight [QAF]
☐ CA-01*	(222)	372	ex 9V-STN	Belgian Defence, Aircomponent 15 W AirTpt [BAF]
☐ CA-02*	(222)	367	ex 9V-STM	Belgian Defence, Aircomponent 15 W AirTpt [BAF]
☐ EC-HLA*	(324ET)	489	ex OE-LAA	EADS-Airbus Boom Demo
☐ HZ-NSA*	(304)	431	ex P4-ABU	Arabasco Flight Operations
☐ T.22-1*	(304)	550	ex F-WEMP	Ejercito del Aire Espanol (coded 45-50)
☐ T.22-2*	(304)	551	ex F-WEMQ	Ejercito del Aire Espanol (coded 45-51)
☐ 9K-ALD*	(308)	648	ex F-WWCR	State of Kuwait [KAC]

Airbus A318

☐ A6-AAM	(112X)	1599	ex D-AIJA	Dana Executive Jets	[Elite]
☐ A6-	(112X)	4211		Al Jaber Aviation on order	[Elite]
☐ B-6186	(112X)	3333	ex D-AIMM	Asia United Business Aviation	[Elite]
☐ B-6188	(112X)	3617	ex D-AIJO	Air China Business Jets	[Elite]
☐ D-AIMM	(112X)	3886		JetAlliance	[Elite]
☐ LX-GJC	(112X)	3100	ex D-AIEA	Global Jet Luxembourg	[Elite]
☐ VP-CAH	(112X	3985		Al Jaber Aviation	[Elite]
☐ VP-CKH	(112X)	3530	ex D-AIJA	Executive Jet Aviation	[Elite]
☐ VP-CKS	(112X)	3238	ex D-AUAJ	National Air Service	[Elite]
☐ VQ-BDD	(111)	3751	ex D-AUAC	Royal Flight of Jordan	[Elite]
☐ 9H-AFL	(111)	3363	ex HB-IPQ	Comlux Aviation Malta [CLA]	[Elite]
☐ 9H-AFM	(111)	2910	ex HB-IPP	Comlux Aviation Malta [CLA]	[Elite]
☐ 9H-AFT	(111)	4169		Comlux Aviation Malta [CLA]	[Elite]

Airbus A319

☐ 0001*	(133X)	1468	ex D-AVYQ	Republica Bolivariana de Venezuela; GAT4/Esc41	[CJ]
☐ 1485*	(115X)	1485	ex F-GXFA	Republique Française / Armée de l'Air (callsign F-RBFA) [CTM]	[CJ]
☐ 1556*	(115X)	1556	ex F-GXFB	Republique Française / Armée de l'Air (callsign F-RBFB) [CTM]	[CJ]
☐ 2101*	(133X)	2263	ex D-AICY	Government of Brazil 'Santos Dumont' (VC-1A)	[CJ]
☐ 2801*	(115X)	2801	ex D-AVWU	Cesca Republica (op by Czech AF) [CEF]	[CJ]
☐ 3085	(115X)	3085	ex D-AICY	Cesca Republica (op by Czech AF) [CEF]	[CJ]
☐ A6-ESH*	(113X)	0910	ex D-AWFR	Sharjah Ruler's Flight [SHJ]	[CJ]
☐ A7-HHJ*	(133X)	1335	ex A7-ABZ	Qatar Amiri Flight 'Al Rayan' [QAF]	[CJ]
☐ B-6178	(133X)	3548		Deer Jet	[CJ]
☐ CS-TFU	(113LR)	2440	ex I-ECJA	Omni Aviacao e Tecnologia [OAV]	
☐ CS-TLU*	(133X)	1256	ex F-GSVU	Omni Aviacao e Tecnologia [OAV]	[CJ]
☐ D-ADNA*	(133X)	1053	ex D-AVYN	DaimlerChrysler Aerospace [DCS]	[CJ]
☐ D-AGAF*	(133X)	4060		German Air Force	[CJ]
☐ D-AHAD*	(115X)	3632		DaimlerChrysler Aerospace [DCS]	[CJ]
☐ D-ALEY*	(115X)	3513		DaimlerChrysler Aerospace [DCS]	[CJ]
☐ D-AVIP*	(133X)	3957		Government of Kuwait	[CJ]
☐ D-AWVM*	(133X)	3897		German Air Force	[CJ]
☐ EK-RA01	(132)	0913	ex HZ-NAS	Government of Armenia [op by RNV]	
☐ G-NMAK*	(115X)	2550	ex D-AVYH	Kharafi Group / Twinjet Leasing [TWJ]	[CJ]
☐ G-NOAH	(115X)	3826		Acropolis Aviation	[CJ]
☐ HS-TYR*	(115X)	1908	ex 60221	Thai Airways, spare Royal Flight aircraft	[CJ]
☐ MM62174*	(115X)	1157	ex D-AACI	Aeronautica Militare Italiana (Repubblica Italiana)	[CJ]
☐ MM62209*	(115X)	1795	ex D-AWOR	Aeronautica Militare Italiana (Repubblica Italiana)	[CJ]
☐ MM62243*	(115X)	2507	ex D-AVIP	Aeronautica Militare Italiana (Repubblica Italiana)	[CJ]

☐ LZ-AOA	(115X)	3139		Bulgarian Government	
☐ LZ-AOB	(115X)	3188		Bulgarian Government	
☐ M-KATE	(115X)	4151		Uralkali	[CJ]
☐ M-RBUS	(115X)	3856		Silver Arrows	[CJ]
☐ OE-LGS	(115X)	3046	ex D-AVYF	Stumpf Group / JetAlliance [CLU]	[CJ]
☐ N3618F*	(115X)	2748	ex D-AVWB	Pharmair Corp / WFBN	[CJ]
☐ OE-LGS	(115X)	3046	ex D-AVYF	Stumpf Group / JetAlliance [CLU]	[CJ]
☐ P4-ARL*	(133X)	2192	ex D-AIJO	SCM Aruba	[CJ]
☐ P4-MIS	(115X)	3133	ex D-AVXC	Sheikh Mustafa Ali Idris	[CJ]
☐ P4-VNL*	(115X)	2921	ex P4-VML	Global Jet Luxembourg	[CJ]
☐ TC-ANA*	(115X)	1002	ex TC-TCB	Turkiye Cumhuriyei (Turkish Government)	[CJ]
☐ UR-ABA	(115X)	3260	ex OE-IAC	Ukraina Aviapredpriatie / Jet Alliance	[CJ]
☐ VH-VHD*	(115LR)	1999	ex F-GYAS	CIT Aerospace	[CJ]
☐ VP-BED	(115X)	3073	ex D-AIFR	China Sonangol International [SOR]	[CJ]
☐ VP-BEX	(115X)	2706	ex D-AVIP	China Sonangol International [SOR]	[CJ]
☐ VP-BEY	(115X)	2675	ex D-AIJO	China Sonangol International [SOR]	[CJ]
☐ VP-BVA	(115X)	3542		Silver Arrows	[CJ]
☐ VP-CBN	(115X)	3243	ex D-AVHD	alf Air International	[CJ]
☐ VP-CCJ*	(133X)	2421	ex D-AVYO	Al Salaam 319	[CJ]
☐ VP-CIE*	(133X)	1589	ex D-AVYF	Bugshan Group [op by LMJ]	[CJ]
☐ VP-CVX*	(133X)	1212	ex D-AVYE	Volkswagen Group/VW Air Services [WGT]	[CJ]
☐ VT-IAH	(115X)	2837	ex D-AIMM	Reliance Industries	[CJ]
☐ VT-VJM*	(133X)	2650	ex D-AICY	UB Group [Vijay Millya] 'Sidharta, Leana, Tanya' [op by KFR]	[CJ]
☐ 4K-AZ01*	(115X)	2487	ex D-AVWA	Government of Azerbaijan, 'Baku' [Op by AHY]	[CJ]
☐ 9H-AFK	(115X)	2592	ex HB-IPO	Comlux Aviation Malta	[CJ]
☐ 9H-SNA	(115X)	3356	ex F-WBGX	Comlux Aviation Malta	[CJ]
☐ 9M-NAA	(115X)	2949	ex D-AIDR	Penerbangan Malaysia [op by RMF]	[CJ]

Airbus A320

☐ 554	(210)	3723		Oman Air Force
☐ 555	(210)	4117		Oman Air Force
☐ A4O-AA*	(232)	2566	ex F-WWDG	Oman Royal Flight [ORF]
☐ A6-DLM*	(232)	2403	ex VP-CMS	Amiri Flight
☐ A7-AAG*	(232)	0927	ex F-WWBA	Qatar Amiri Flight 'Laffan' [QAF]
☐ D-ATRA	(232)	0659	ex F-WWDB	DLR Flugbetriebe [GPL] (under conversion)
☐ F-WWBA*	(111)	0001	ex F-WWFT	EADS-Airbus (prototype, ff 22Feb87) [AIB]
☐ HZ-AJ2	(210)	3174	ex VP-BXT	Ajwa Aviation
☐ HZ-AJ3	(210)	0764	ex VP-BXS	Ajwa Aviation
☐ HZ-XY7	(210)	2132	ex VP-BBQ	National Air Service
☐ UP-A2001	(214)	3199	ex UN-A2001	Government of Kazakhstan
☐ VP-CHM	(232)	3379	ex F-WWDL	SAAD (op by National Air Service)
☐ 9K-AKD*	(212)	2046	ex F-WWBG	State of Kuwait 'Al-Mobarakiya' [KAC]

Airbus A321

☐ EP-AGB*	(231)	1202	ex F-WQSS	Islamic Republic of Iran [IRA]

Airbus A330

☐ A7-HHM*	(202)	605	ex F-WWYX	Qatar Airways Amiri Flight [QAF]
☐ A7-HJJ*	(202)	487	ex F-WWYM	Qatar Airways Amiri Flight 'Musheireb' [QAF]
☐ UP-A3001	(223)	863	ex 3B-TSL	Government of Kazakhstan
☐ VP-CAC	(202)	1053		Mid East Jet

Airbus A340

☐ A7-AAH*	(313X)	528	ex B-18851	Qatar Airways Amiri Flight [QAF]
☐ A7-HHH*	(541)	495	ex F-WWTQ	Qatar Airways Amiri Flight [QAF]
☐ A7-HHK*	(211)	026	ex F-WWJQ	Qatar Airways Amiri Flight [QAF]
☐ F-WWAI*	(311)	001		EADS-Airbus (Development aircraft, ff 25Oct91) [AIB]
☐ F-WWCA*	(642)	360	ex F-WWTA	EADS-Airbus Srs 600 prototype (ff 23Apr01) [AIB]
☐ F-RAJA*	(211)	075	ex F-HMAR	Republique Française / Armée de l'Air (also serial 75) [CTM]
☐ F-RAJB*	(211)	081	ex F-HCEL	Republique Française / Armée de l'Air (also serial 81) [CTM]
☐ HZ-124*	(213)	004	ex 'D-ACME'	Royal Saudi Air Force (conv to flying hospital)
☐ HZ-AJ1	(211)	009	ex JY-ABH	Ajwa Aviation
☐ HZ-HMS*	(213X)	204	ex V8-AC3	Royal Saudi Air Force
☐ JY-	(640)	924	ex F-WJKG	Hashemite Kingdom of Jordan [RJA]
☐ M-ABUS	(310)	955		Silver Arrows
☐ SU-GGG*	(212)	061	ex F-WWJI	Government of Arab Republic of Egypt [EGY]
☐ TS-KRT	(540)	902		Government of Tunisia
☐ VP-CCC*	(642)	779	ex F-WWCS	SAAD (op by National Air Service)
☐ V8-BKH*	(212)	046	ex V8-PJB	Sultan's Flight
☐ 7T-VPP	(540)	917		Government of Algeria

Airbus A380

☐ F-WWDD*	(841)	004		EADS-Airbus (second prototype); ff 28Oct05 for ETD [AIB]
☐ F-WWEA	(861)	009		EADS Airbus (first GP7200 powered aircraft) ff25Aug06 [AIB]
☐ F-WWOW*	(841)	001		EADS-Airbus (first prototype, ff 27 Apr 05) [AIB]
☐ F-WXXL*	(841)	002		EADS-Airbus (third protype); ff 03Nov05 for ETD [AIB]
☐ HZ-	(841)		ex F-WW	Kingdom Holding (on order)

Antonov An-26

Registration	Type	c/n	Previous	Operator
☐ D2-TAD*		4609		Government of Angola

Antonov An-148

Registration	Type	c/n	Previous	Operator
☐ UR-NTA*		0101		Antonov - prototype (ff 17Dec04)
☐ UR NTB*		0102		Antonov - second prototype (ff 19Apr05)

ATR 42

Registration	Type	c/n	Previous	Operator
☐ F-OITQ	(500)	622		Government of Tahiti
☐ TR-KJD*	(300F)	131	ex F-WWEB	Government of Gabon

ATR 72

Registration	Type	c/n	Previous	Operator
☐ F-WWEY*	(212A)	098		ATR (prototype, ff 27Oct88)

Beech 1900

Registration	Type	c/n	Previous	Operator
☐ N27NG	(D)	UE-382	ex N843CA	Northrop Grumman Systems
☐ N29NG*	(D)	UE-303	ex N11249	Northrop Grumman Systems
☐ N470MM*	(D)	UE-394	ex N41255	Schwans Shared Services
☐ N534M*	(D)	UE-333	ex N23235	Menard
☐ N535M*	(D)	UE-332		Menard
☐ N536M*	(D)	UE-334		Menard
☐ N640MW*	(C-1)	UC-1	ex N3114B	Marvin Lumber & Cedar
☐ N655MW	(D)	UE-377	ex N833CA	Marvin Lumber & Cedar
☐ 5N-MPA*	(D)	UE-149	ex N3217L	Mobil Producing Nigeria
☐ 5N-MPN*	(D)	UE-77	ex N82936	Mobil Producing Nigeria

Beriev BE-12P

Registration	c/n	Previous	Operator
☐ RA-00041*	8601004	ex 41 yellow	TANTK / Avialesoochrana 'Stoyki'
☐ RA-00049*	9601704	ex 49 yellow	TANTK / Avialesoochrana 'Ugryumy'

Boeing 707

Registration	Type	c/n	Previous	Operator
☐ 1001*	(368C)	21396/928	ex EP-NHY	Government of Islamic Republic of Iran (op by IRIAF)
☐ 1002*	(320C)		ex	Government of Islamic Republic of Iran (op by IRIAF)
☐ D2-MAN*	(321B)	20025/780	ex N707KS	Republica de Angola (Comtran 2)
☐ D2-TPR*	(3J6B)	20715/870	ex B-2404	Republica de Angola (Comtran 2)
☐ N88ZL*	(330B)	18928/457	ex N5381X	Principal Air Services / DB Air (BAC 3)
☐ N707AR*	(321B)	20029/790	ex EL-AKS	Omega Air (tanker/transport conversion)
☐ N707CA	(351B)	18586/345	ex P4-FDH	Omega Air (stored Mojave, CA)
☐ N707FR	(382B)	19740/676	ex mm62150	Omega Air
☐ N707JT*	(138B)	18740/388	ex N707XX	Jett Clipper Johnny (J Travolta) [BAC 3]
☐ N707KN	(366C)	20919/888	ex SU-AXJ	Omega Air (stored Marana, AZ)
☐ N707LG	(3M1C)	21092/899	ex A-7002	Jetran LLC
☐ TZ-TAC*	(3L6B)	21049/896	ex YR-JTX	Government of Mali (BAC 3)
☐ 5A-DAK*	(3L5C)	21228/911		Government of Libya [LAA]
☐ 9Q-CLK*	(138B)	17702/64	ex N707SK	Government of DRCBoeing 720
☐ C-FETB*	(023B)	18024/177	ex OD-AFQ	Pratt & Whitney Canada (engine testbed) [PWC]
☐ N720H*	(051B)	18384/237	ex N720GT	Honeywell International (engine testbed)
☐ N720PW*	(023B)	18021/173	ex C-FWXI	Pratt & Whitney Engine Services (engine testbed) [PWC]
☐ P4-NJR	(047B)	18453/314	ex HZ-KA4	JR Executive Aruba (stage 2) (stored Beirut)

Boeing 727

Registration	Type	c/n	Previous	Operator
☐ A9C-BA*	(2M7/W)	21824/1595	ex N740RW	Bahrain Royal Flight (Super 27 conv) [BAH]
☐ HZ-AB3*	(2U5/W)	22362/1657	ex V8-BG1	Al-Anwa Establishment (Super 27 conv) (stored Lasham)
☐ HZ-MBA*	(21)	19006/262	ex HZ-OCV	Express Camel Aviation (FedEx 3) (stored Amman)
☐ HZ-SKI*	(212/W)	21460/1340	ex P4-SKI	Precision International / ARAVCO [Super 27]
☐ J2-KBA*	(191)	19394/418	ex N727X	Presidence de la Republique de Djibouti (FedEx 3)
☐ M-FAHD	(76/W)	19254/298	ex VP-BAB	Flightec International (Super 27)
☐ N25AZ	(30)	18370/134	ex 7P-DPT	D Tokoph / Aviation Consultants
☐ N30MP*	(21)	18998/239	ex N111JL	MP Aviation (Raisbeck 3)
☐ N67JR*	(30/W)	18936/249	ex N18HH	Bank of Utah (Super 27) (stored)
☐ N169KT*	(269)	22359/1652	ex 9K-AFA	Strong Aviation / WTCo (Raisbeck 3)
☐ N289MT*	(223)	22467/1765	ex N710AA	Raytheon Company (FedEx 3) (testbed)
☐ N311AG*	(17)	20512/858	ex N767RV	Gordon P & Anne Getty (Super 27)
☐ N359PA	(230)	20789/1015	ex D-ABSI	WTCo (stored Perpignan)
☐ N400RG*	(22/W)	19149/481	ex N7085U	MBI-1 Aviation 'Al Bashaer' (Super 27)
☐ N401Z	(25C/W)	19854/628	ex N40	Federal Aviation Administration (Dugan 3) [NHK]
☐ N502MG*	(191)	19391/309	ex N502RA	Roush Racing / RD Aviation (FedEx 3)
☐ N503MG*	(191)	19392/317	ex N503RA	Roush Racing / RD Aviation (FedEx 3)
☐ N615PA*	(243)	21266/1227	ex C-GMSJ	Paradigm Air / New Jersey Devils NHL (FedEx 3)
☐ N698SS*	(223)	21369/1275	ex N864AA	Southwest Sports / Texas Rangers (Raisbeck 3)
☐ N706JP*	(35)	19835/501	ex N727HC	Petters Group Worldwide (FedEx 3)
☐ N720DC*	(77)	19253/296	ex N448DR	Aerodyne, stored damaged at West Palm Beach, FL
☐ N724CL*	(51)	19121/264	ex N299LA	Classic Limited Air / op by Clay Lacy Aviation (Raisbeck3) [CLY]
☐ N724YS*	(281/W)	21474/1378	ex N240RC	Horta LLC (Op for San Jose Sabre Cats) (Super 27)
☐ N727AH*	(21)	19261/422	ex N727PX	Classic Designs of Tampa Bay (Raisbeck 3)

☐ N727LL	(2X8/W)	22687/1784	ex N721MF	WFBN / Talos Aviation (Duganair 3)
☐ N727NK*	(212/W)	21945/1502	ex N317NE	Roush Air (Duganair 3)
☐ N727VJ*	(44/W)	19318/348	ex N44MD	N727VJ Inc (Duganair 3QWS)
☐ N800AK*	(23/W)	20045/596	ex N727WF	Peninsula Aviation (RR Tay engines)
☐ N908JE*	(31/W)	20115/735	ex N505LS	JEGE (Super 27)
☐ P4-FLY*	(22)	19148/473	ex P4-ONE	Aviation Connexions / My Personal Jets (FedEx 3)
☐ TJ-AAM*	(2R1)	21636/1414		Republc of Cameroon
☐ TY-24A	(256)	20819/1018	ex EC-CFI	Republic of Benin
☐ TZ-MBA	(2K5/W)	21853/1640	ex P4-JLI	Government of Mali
☐ VP-BAA*	(51)	19123/334	ex N727AK	Marbyia Investments (Raisbeck 3)
☐ VP-BDJ*	(23/W)	20046/605	ex VR-BDJ	DJ Aerospace / Trump Group (Duganair 3 QWS)
☐ VP-BIF	(1H2/W)	20533/869	ex N727XL	New Century Aviation-Oregon (Super 27)
☐ VP-CJN*	(76)	20371/822	ex 5X-AMM	Starling Aviation (FedEx 3)
☐ VP-CML	(2Y4/W)	22968/1815	ex HZ-HR3	Government of Afghanistan
☐ VP-CMN*	(46)	19282/495	ex VR-CMN	IDG (Cayman)
☐ VP-CZY *	(2P1/W)	21595/1406	ex N727MJ	Dunview Ltd (Super 27) [op by PJS]
☐ XT-BBE*	(14)	18990/238	ex N21UC	Government of Burkina Faso
☐ XT-BFA*	(282/W)	22430/1715	ex N727RE	Government of Burkina Faso / PetcoAir (Dugan 3/QWS)
☐ ZS-PVX*	(2N5/W)	22825/1805	ex 5N-FGN	PL Logistics Corp (Super 27)
☐ 4K-8888	(251)	22543/1700	ex 4K-AZ9	Government of Azerbaijan / SW Business Aviation (Raisbeck 3)
☐ 6V-AEF*	(2M1/W)	21091/1134	ex N40104	Government of Senegal 'Pointe de Sangomar' (Super 27)
☐ 9Q-CDC*	(30)	18934/222	ex 9Q-RDZ	Government of Democratic Republic of Congo
☐ 9Q-CMC*	(30)	18371/145	ex N134AS	Government of Congo (FedEx 3) [impounded Faro]

Boeing 737

☐ 0207*	(2N1)	21167/442	ex 0001	Republica Bolivariana de Venezuela, GAT4 / Esc41
☐ 356*	(528)	27426/2739	ex PRP-001	Fuerza Aerea del Peru, Grupo Aerea No 8 (VIP, Op for President)
☐ 921*	(58N)	28866/2929	ex N1786B	Fuerza Aérea de Chile
☐ 922*	(330QC)	23524/1272	ex D-ABXC	Fuerza Aerea de Chile
☐ 2115*	(2N3)	21165/441		Forca Aerea Brasileira
☐ 2116*	(2N3)	21166/445		Forca Aerea Brasileira
☐ 3520	(2B7)	23133/1049	ex N286AU	Fuerza Aerea Mexicana
☐ 60201*	(2Z6)	23059/980	ex 22-222	Royal Thai Air Force
☐ 85101*	(3Z8)	23152/1073		Republic of Korea Air Force
☐ 99-999*	(448)	24866/1867	ex EI-BXD	Crown Prince Maha Vajiralongkorn (call-sign HS-HRH) [Op by THA]
☐ A9C-DAA*	(268)	22050/622	ex P4-OMC	Delmun Aviation (Nordam 3)
☐ C-FFAL*	(2R8C)	21711/573	ex ZS-OWM	Xstrata Canada Corp (AvAero 3)
☐ C-FPHS*	(53A)	24970/1977	ex C-GBGL	Pacific Sky Aviation
☐ EP-AGA*	(286)	21317/483		Government of Islamic Republic of Iran
☐ HS-CMV*	(4Z6)	27906/2698	ex 55-555	Crown Prince Maha Vajiralongkorn [Op by THA]
☐ HZ-MIS*	(2K5)	22600/816	ex D-AHLH	Sheikh M Edress (Nordam 3)
☐ N35LX*	(330)	23528/1290	ex D-ABXH	Lockheed Martin Aeronautics 'CAT-Bird'
☐ N37NY*	(4Y0)	23976/1651	ex N773RA	Madison Square Garden Teams / MSG A/c Leasing
☐ N165W*	(247)	19605/57	ex N4508W	Northrop Grumman Corp
☐ N251RY	(4Y0)	25180/2201	ex EC-HBZ	US Marshals Service / WFBN
☐ N370BC*	(205)	23468/1262	ex HZ-TBA	BCM Majestic Corp
☐ N444HE	(39A/W)	23800/1409	ex N253DV	Mirage Aviation
☐ N583CC*	(291)	21069/415	ex N15255	Cavalier Sports Marketing
☐ N733PA*	(205)	23466/1236	ex N733AR	Phillips / BPX Shared Services Aviation [PDD] (Nordam 3)
☐ N736BP*	(205)	23465/1226	ex LN-SUU	Phillips / BPX Shared Services Aviation [PDD] (Nordam 3)
☐ N737DX*	(408)	24804/1851	ex TF-FIC	Transjet 3 (Phoenix Suns / Arizona Cardinals)
☐ N787WH*	(2V6)	22431/803	ex N737WH	Perpetual Motion (AvAero 3)
☐ N788LS*	(35B)	24220/1602	ex N232DZ	Las Vegas Sands / AFS Investments
☐ N789LS*	(35B)	24269/1628	ex N224DA	Las Vegas Sands / AFS Investments
☐ N902WG*	(2H6)	22620/822	ex N22620	Gary 737 (Nordam 3)
☐ RP-C4007*	(332)	25996/2488	ex RP-C2000	Government of the Philippines
☐ TP-02*	(33A)	24095/1737	ex N731XL	Fuerza Aerea Mexicana, CGTAP call-sign XC-UJB
☐ TP-03*	(322)	24361/1694	ex N355UA	Fuerza Aerea Mexicana, CGTAP call-sign XC-LJG
☐ 3520*	(2B7)	23133/1049	ex N286AU	Fuerza Aerea Mexicana, UETAAM
☐ VP-CBA*	(2W8)	22628/820	ex VP-CSA	SAMCO Aviation
☐ VP-CHK*	(2S9)	21957/618	ex N39BL	Executive Jet Aviation / Harry A Akande (AvAero 3)
☐ YR-TIB*	(3L9)	27924/2760	ex OE-ITA	Ion Tiriac Air [TIH]
☐ 4X-AOT*	(297)	21740/562	ex N70724	ELTA Electronics (research aircraft)
☐ 5R-MRM*	(3Z9)	24081/1515	ex OE-ILG	Government of Madagascar
☐ 5U-BAG*	(2N9C)	21499/513	ex (5U-MAF)	Government of Niger 'Monts Baghezan'

Boeing 737NG

☐ 01-0015*	(7DM/W)	32916/979	ex N378BJ	United States Air Force / 15ABW [C-40B]	[BBJ]
☐ 01-0040*	(7DM/W)	29971/684	ex N371BJ	United States Air Force / 1AS [C-40B]	[BBJ]
☐ 01-0041*	(7DM/W)	33080/1089	ex N374BC	United States Air Force / 1AS [C-40B]	[BBJ]
☐ 02-0042*	(7FD/W)	33500/1223	ex N237BA	United States Air Force	[BBJ]
☐ 02-0201*	(7CP/W)	30755/545	ex N752BC	United States Air Force / 201ALS / DC ANG	[BBJ]
☐ 02-0202*	(7CP/W)	30753/481	ex N754BC	United States Air Force / 201ALS / DC ANG	[BBJ]
☐ 02-0203*	(7BC/W)	33434/1211	ex N236BA	United States Air Force / 201ALS / DC ANG	[BBJ]
☐ 05-0730	(7DM/W)	34807/1908	ex N365BJ	United States Air Force / 1AS [C-40C]	[BBJ]
☐ 05-0932	(7DM/W)	34808/2008	ex N366BJ	United States Air Force / 1AS [C-40C]	[BBJ]
☐ 05-4613	(7DM/W)	34809/2141	ex N368BJ	United States Air Force [C-40C]	[BBJ]
☐ 3701*	(8AR/W)	30139/428	ex N1787B	Republic of China Air Force	
☐ 55-555	(8Z6/W)	35478/1955	ex N369BJ	Royal Thai Air Force (also HS-TYS)	
☐ A36-001*	(7DT/W)	30829/738	ex N372BJ	Royal Australian Air Force / 34Sqdn	[BBJ]
☐ A36-002*	(7DF/W)	30790/613	ex N10040	Royal Australian Air Force / 34Sqdn	[BBJ]

☐ A6-AIN*	(7Z5/W)	29268/280	ex N1786B	Amiri Flight / Royal Jet [ROJ]	[BBJ]
☐ A6-AUH*	(8EX/W)	33473/1196	ex N379BC	Amiri Flight / Royal Jet [ROJ]	[BBJ2]
☐ A6-DAS*	(7Z5/W)	29858/530		Amiri Flight / Royal Jet [ROJ]	[BBJ]
☐ A6-DFR*	(7BC/W)	30884/747	ex VP-BFE	Amiri Flight / Royal Jet [ROJ]	[BBJ]
☐ A6-HEH*	(8AJ/W)	32825/1602		Dubai Air Wing [DUB]	[BBJ2]
☐ A6-HRS*	(7E0/W)	29251/150		Dubai Air Wing [DUB]	[BBJ]
☐ A6-MRM*	(8EC/W)	32450/787	ex N1787B	Dubai Air Wing [DUB]	[BBJ2]
☐ A6-MRS*	(8E0/W)	35238/1966		Dubai Air Wing [DUB]	[BBJ2]
☐ A6-RJX*	(7AK/W)	29865/241	ex HB-IIO	Amiri Flight / Royal Jet [ROJ]	[BBJ]
☐ A6-RJY*	(7Z5/W)	29857/445	ex A6-LIW	Amiri Flight / Royal Jet [ROJ]	[BBJ]
☐ A6-RJZ*	(7Z5/W)	29269/432	ex A6-SIR	Amiri Flight / Royal Jet [ROJ]	[BBJ]
☐ A7-AAZ*	(8KB/W)	37545/2696		Qatar Amiri Flight	[BBJ2]
☐ EW-001PA*	(8EV/W)	33079/1075	ex N375BC	Government of Belarus [op by BRU]	[BBJ2]
☐ FAC001*	(74V/W)	29272/323	ex N7378P	Fuerza Aerea Colombiana	[BBJ]
☐ HL7759	(7EG/W)	35990/2107	ex N737DB	Samsung Techwin	[BBJ]
☐ HL7787	(75G/W)	36852/2475	ex N730MM	Hyundai	[BBJ]
☐ HZ-101*	(7DP/W)	32805/940	ex N372BC	Royal Saudi Air Force / Ministry of Defence & Aviation	[BBJ]
☐ HZ-102*	(8DP/W)	32451/836	ex HZ-101	Royal Saudi Air Force / Ministry of Defence & Aviation	[BBJ2]
☐ HZ-MF1*	(7FG/W)	33405/1204	ex N373JM	Saudi Ministry of Finance & Economy	[BBJ]
☐ HZ-MF2*	(7AJ/W)	33499/1217	ex N355BJ	Saudi Ministry of Finance & Economy	[BBJ]
☐ HZ-TAA*	(7P3/W)	29188/217	ex N1779B	HRH Talal bin Abdul Aziz / Arabasco Flight Operations	[BBJ]
☐ K-5012	(7HI/W)	36106/2118	ex N370BJ	Indian Air Force 'Rajdoot'	[BBJ]
☐ K-5013	(7HI/W)	36107/2325	ex N719BA	Indian Air Force	[BBJ]
☐ K-5014	(7HI/W)	36108/2425	ex N372BJ	Indian Air Force	[BBJ]
☐ LX-GVV*	(7BC/W)	30791/623	ex N191QS	Elora Air Investments / Global Jet	[BBJ]
☐ M53-01*	(7H6/W)	29274/397	ex 9M-BBJ	Royal Malaysian Air Force / Malaysian Government	[BBJ]
☐ M-URUS	(7GC/W)	34622/1785	ex P4-RUS	Silver Arrows	[BBJ]
☐ M-YBBJ*	(7HE/W)	36027/2068	ex N111NB	Silver Arrows	[BBJ]
☐ N2TS	(73Q/W)	29102/101	ex N772BC	GC Air LLC / First Virtual Aviation	[BBJ]
☐ N43PR*	(75V/W)	28581/126	ex N781TS	Town & Country Food Markets	[BBJ]
☐ N50TC*	(72T/W)	29024/131		Tracinda Corp	[BBJ]
☐ N88WR*	(79U/W)	29441/111	ex N88WZ	Sea Aviation (World Travel)	[BBJ]
☐ N90R*	(7EL/W)	32775/889	ex N376BJ	Occidental Petroleum / Swiflite Aircraft Corp	[BBJ]
☐ N108MS*	(7BC/W)	33102/1111	ex N105QS	Yona Aviation II	[BBJ]
☐ N111VM	(7GV/W)	36090/2196		Boeing Aircraft Holding Co	[BBJ]
☐ N127QS*	(7BC/W)	30327/356		Netjets	[BBJ]
☐ N129QS*	(7BC/W)	30329/384	ex N1787B	Netjets	[BBJ]
☐ N164RJ*	(7BC/W)	30328/377	ex N128QS	Bausch & Lomb 'Capt James Cook' / WFBN	[BBJ]
☐ N315TS*	(7CU/W)	30772/554	ex N1784B	Tudor-Saliba	[BBJ]
☐ N349BA*	(73Q/W)	30789/602		Flying Tiger International / CIT Group	[BBJ]
☐ N371BC	(8EF/W)	32971/996		Executive Jets	[BBJ2]
☐ N375BJ	(9HWER/W)	37546/2725		Peridot Associates	[BBJ3]
☐ N493AG	(7FY)	36493/2211	ex N1787B	CIT Group / Equipment Financing	[BBJ]
☐ N500LS*	(73T/W)	29054/143	ex N6067E	Hayes Productions (The Limited)	[BBJ]
☐ N720CH*	(7AK/W)	29866/408	ex HB-IIPN	720CH Inc	[BBJ]
☐ N720MM*	(7ET/W)	33010/1037	ex N4476S	MGM Mirage	[BBJ]
☐ N721BA	(7JR/W)	37111/2595		Wakefield Bahamas	[BBJ]
☐ N737A*	(7AX)	30181/648		ARAMCO Capital	
☐ N737AG*	(7BF/W)	30496/301	ex N180AD	Funair Corporation	[BBJ]
☐ N737CC*	(74Q/W)	29135/206	ex N60436	Mid East Jet	[BBJ]
☐ N737ER*	(7CJ/W)	30754/516	ex N61MJ	Boetti Air	[BBJ]
☐ N737GG*	(74Q/W)	29136/225	ex N1787B	Mid East Jet	[BBJ]
☐ N737GQ	(8GQ/W)	35792/2351		Pegasus Aviation Finance	
☐ N737L*	(7CG/W)	30751/401	ex N888NY	Legatum Aviation	[BBJ]
☐ N737M*	(8EQ/W)	33361/1124	ex N737SP	EIE Eagle 'Sanitra Est'	[BBJ2]
☐ N737WH*	(75T/W)	29142/167	ex N700WH	Southern Aircraft Services (Wayne Huizenga / Miami Dolphins)	[BBJ]
☐ N738A*	(7AX)	30182/690	ex N1785B	ARAMCO Capital	
☐ N739A*	(7AX)	30183/702		ARAMCO Capital	
☐ N742PB*	(73U/W)	29200/234		Chartwell Partners / op by Clay Lacy Aviation [CLY]	[BBJ]
☐ N743A*	(7AXC)	30184/925		ARAMCO Capital	
☐ N745A*	(7AXC)	30185/978		ARAMCO Capital	
☐ N800KS*	(7BC/W)	30782/586	ex N515GM	AEJ Services / op by Clay Lacy Aviation [CLY]	[BBJ]
☐ N835BA*	(7BC/W)	30572/491	ex N339BA	Boeing Co / WFBN	[BBJ]
☐ N836BA*	(7BC/W)	30756/569	ex N156QS	WFBN	[BBJ]
☐ N888AQ	(7HF/W)	35977/2047	ex VP-CLL	White Sapphire	[BBJ]
☐ N888TY*	(7AH/W)	29749/456	ex N134AR	TY Air	[BBJ]
☐ N888YF*	(7BC/W)	33036/1060	ex N110QS	AVN Air LLC / Evergreen International	[BBJ]
☐ N889NC*	(7AV/W	30070/244	ex N18NC	Newsflight II (News Corp, USA)	[BBJ]
☐ N920DS*	(75V/W)	28579/312	ex N367G	Delaware Global Operation	[BBJ]
☐ N2121	(7EI/W)	34863/1859		Shangri La Entertainment	[BBJ]
☐ N8767	(7EG/W)	32807/926	ex HL7770		[BBJ]
☐ N7600K*	(7BC/W)	32628/953	ex N102QS	SAS Institute	[BBJ]
☐ N79711*	(7BQ/W)	30547/423	ex N1787B	Dallah AVCO Flight Operations (Lsd fr GECAS)	[BBJ]
☐ OE-ILX*	(8DR/W)	32777/882	ex P4-BBJ	GlobalJet Austria	[BBJ2]
☐ PR-BBS*	(7BC/W)	32575/861	ex N182QS	Grupo Safra	[BBJ]
☐ P4-ASL	(7BH/W)	29791/336	ex P4-TBN	Arabasco	[BBJ]
☐ P4-KAZ*	(7EJ/W)	32774/853	ex N774EC	Mint Juleps Investments	[BBJ]
☐ P4-LIG	(7EJ/W)	37592/2752		Petrov Air	[BBJ]
☐ P4-NJK	(7EJ/W)	37583/2869		Itera Holdings	[BBJ]
☐ TS-IOO*	(7H3/W)	29149/348	ex N5573L	Government of Tunisia [op by TAR]	[BBJ]
☐ VP-BBJ*	(72U/W)	29273/146	ex N1011N	Picton	[BBJ]
☐ VP-BBW*	(7BJ/W)	30076/179	ex N737BF	GAMA Avn / Altitude 41	[BBJ]
☐ VP-BEL*	(74T/W)	29139/189	ex N21KR	Orient Global	[BBJ]

☐ VP-BFT	(7JB/W)	36714/2340	ex N1779B	Boeing Business Jet	[BBJ]
☐ VP-BHN*	(8AN/W)	32438/779	ex VP-BNH	Saudi Oger / Eastern Skys	[BBJ2]
☐ VP-BIZ	(7AU/W)	34477/1825	ex VT-SRS	Aircraft Guaranty Title Corp	[BBJ]
☐ VP-BJJ	(7BC/W)	30330/415	ex N888NB	Avenair Worldwide	[BBJ]
☐ VP-BNZ	(7HD/W)	35858/2029		Gazpromavia	[BBJ]
☐ VP-BRM*	(75U/W)	28976/158	ex N1786B	Dobro / Theberton USA	[BBJ]
☐ VP-BRT*	(7BC/W)	32970/988	ex N707BZ	E & R Aviation / Rostam Tariko	[BBJ]
☐ VP-BWR*	(79T/W)	29317/265	ex N1787B	Usal Ltd / Bel Air	[BBJ]
☐ VP-BYA*	(7AN/W)	29972/642		Saudi Oger / Eastern Skys	[BBJ]
☐ VP-BZL*	(8DV/W)	32915/969	ex D-ABZL	Lowa Inc / BZL (Bermuda)	[BBJ2]
☐ VP-CBB*	(8AW/W)	32806/912	ex N73721	Bugshan Group (Bosco Aviation) 'Alhalkiah'	[BBJ2]
☐ VP-CLR	(7EM/W)	34865/1865	ex N786BA	LUK Aviation	[BBJ]
☐ VP-CPA	(7AW/W)	30031/251	ex VP-CEC		[BBJ]
☐ VP-CSK	(8GG/W)	34620/1803	ex N852AK	Nafo Aviation	[BBJ2]
☐ ZS-RSA*	(7ED/W)	32627/826	ex N373BJ	Republic of South Africa / SAAF, 21Sqdn 'Inkwazi'	[BBJ]
☐ 3C-EGE*	(7FB/W)	33367/1189	ex N377JC	Government of Equatorial Guinea 'Utonde'	[BBJ]
☐ 5N-FGT*	(7N6/W)	34260/1746	ex N1781B	Federal Government of Nigeria	[BBJ]
☐ 5R-MRP*	(74U/W)	29233/197	ex N66ZB	Government of Madagascar	[BBJ]

Boeing 747

☐ 20-1101*	(47C)	24730/816	ex JA8091	Government of Japan / Japan Air Self-Defence Force
☐ 20-1102*	(47C)	24731/839	ex JA8092	Government of Japan / Japan Air Self-Defence Force
☐ 82-8000*	(2G4B)	23824/679	ex N6005C	USAF / 89AW [VC-25A]
☐ 92-9000*	(2G4B)	23825/685	ex N60659	USAF / 89AW [VC-25A]
☐ A4O-OMN*	(430)	32445/1292	ex D-ARFO	Oman Royal Flight [RS/ORF]
☐ A4O-SO*	(SP-27)	21785/405	ex N351AS	Oman Royal Flight [RS/ORF]
☐ A6-GDP*	(2B4SF)	21098/263	ex N712CK	Dubai Air Wing [DUB]
☐ A6-HRM*	(422)	26903/1171	ex N108UA	Dubai Air Wing [DUB]
☐ A6-MMM*	(422)	26906/1185	ex N109UA	Dubai Air Wing [DUB]
☐ A6-UAE*	(48EM)	28551/1131	ex V5-NMA	Amiri Flight [MO/AUH]
☐ A6-YAS*	(4F6)	28961/1174	ex N1794B	Amiri Flight [MO/AUH]
☐ A9C-HAK*	(SP-Z5)	23610/676	ex A6-ZSN	Bahrain Royal Flight [BAH]
☐ A9C-HMK*	(4P8)	33684/1324		Bahrain Royal Flight [BAH]
☐ C-FPAW	(SP-J6)	21934/467	ex N747UT	Pratt & Whitney Canada
☐ HZ-AIF*	(SP-68)	22503/529		Saudi Arabian Royal Flight [SVA]
☐ HZ-AIJ*	(SP-68)	22750/560	ex N6046P	Saudi Arabian Royal Flight [SVA]
☐ HZ-HM1	(468)	28343/1265	ex HZ-AIZ	Saudi Arabian Royal Flight [SVA]
☐ HZ-HM1A*	(3G1)	23070/592	ex N1784B	Saudi Arabian Royal Flight [SVA]
☐ HZ-HM1B*	(SP-68)	21652/329	ex HZ-HM1	Saudi Arabian Royal Flight (Mobile Hospital) [SVA]
☐ HZ-WBT7*	(4J6)	25880/926	ex N747BZ	Kingdom Establishment
☐ N747A	(SP-27)	21992/447	ex N747FU	John Fry / Ballet San Jose 'Nutcracker'
☐ N747GE*	(121)	19651/25	ex N744PA	General Electric Co (engine test-bed)
☐ N747NA*	(SP-21)	21441/306	ex N145UA	NASA (SOFIA project)
☐ N787RR*	(267B)	21966/446	ex TF-ATD	Rolls-Royce North America
☐ N905NA*	(123)	20107/86	ex N9668	NASA, Johnson Space Center (Shuttle Transporter)
☐ N911NA*	(SR-46)	20781/221	ex N747BL	NASA, Johnson Space Center (Shuttle Transporter)
☐ P4-FSH*	(SP31)	21963/441	ex A6-SMM	Ernest Angley Ministeries 'Star Triple Seven'
☐ VP-BAT*	(SP-21)	21648/367	ex VR-BAT	Worldwide A/C Holding (Bermuda)
☐ VP-BLK*	(SP-31)	21961/415	ex N992MS	Las Vegas Sands / Interface Operations
☐ VQ-BMS	(SP-21)	21649/373	ex A9C-HMH	Las Vegas Sands / Interface Operations
☐ V8-ALI*	(430)	26426/910	ex N6009F	Sultan's Flight
☐ 7O-YMN*	(SP-27)	21786/413	ex A7-AHM	People's Republic of Yemen [Op by IYE]

Boeing 757

☐ 98-0001*	(2G4)	29025/783	ex N3519L	USAF / 1stAS (VC-32A)
☐ 98-0002*	(2G4)	29026/787	ex N3519M	USAF / 1stAS (VC-32A)
☐ 99-0003*	(2G4)	29027/824		USAF / 1stAS (VC-32A)
☐ 99-0004*	(2G4/W)	29028/829		USAF / /1stAS (VC-32A)
☐ HZ-HMED*	(23A)	25495/599	ex N275AW	Saudi Arabian Royal Flight, (Flying Hospital) [SVA]
☐ N757A*	(200)	22212/1		Boeing Logistics Spares (experimental category)
☐ N757AF*	(2J4)	25155/371	ex N115FS	Vulcan Aircraft
☐ N757AG*	(256/W)	29306/920	ex EC-HIP	Funair Corp
☐ N757HW*	(225)	22194/5	ex G-JALC	Honeywell International (engine testbed)
☐ N757LL*	(23N/W)	27972/694	ex N516AT	Talos Aviation
☐ N757MA*	(24Q)	28463/739		Mid East Jet
☐ N757SS	(236)	22176/14	ex N757BJ	Dallas Stars / Texas Rangers (Op by Paradigm Air)
☐ N770BB*	(2J4/W)	25220/387	ex VP-CAU	The Yucaipa Companies
☐ N801DM	(236/W)	26240/561	ex N286CD	MLW Corp / Maverick
☐ N1757*	(23A/W)	24923/332	ex N756AF	Bank of Utah
☐ NZ7571*	(2K2)	26633/519	ex PH-TKA	Royal New Zealand Air Force
☐ NZ7572*	(2K2)	26634/545	ex PH-TKB	Royal New Zealand Air Force
☐ T-01*	(23A)	25487/470		Fuerza Aerea Argentina 'Virgen de Lujan' (stored)
☐ TP-01*	(225)	22690/151		Fuerza Aerea Mexicana, CGTAP call-sign XC-UJM
☐ UN-B5701*	(2M8ER)	23454/102	ex P4-NSN	Kazakhstan Government [op by BEC]

Boeing 767

☐ A6-JBD	(341ER)	30341/768	ex A6-EYZ	Presidential Flight
☐ A9C-HMH	(4FSER)	34205/965	ex N526BA	Bahrain Royal Flight
☐ EZ-A700	(32KER)	33968/926		Government of Turkmenistan
☐ N673BF*	(238ER)	23402/133	ex N773WD	Polaris Aviation

Reg	Type	c/n	Previous	Operator
☐ N767A*	(2AXER)	33685/903		Aramco Associated
☐ N767KS*	(24QER)	28270/629	ex N6038E	Mid East Jet
☐ N767MW*	(277)	22694/32	ex N767AT	Blue City Holdings / MLW Air / Dallas Mavericks
☐ N804MS	(3P6ER)	27255/525	ex HZ-WBT6	Interface Operations
☐ N2767*	(238ER)	23896/183	ex N772WD	Elan Express
☐ P4-MES*	(33AER)	33425/909	ex N595HA	R Ambramovich / Silver Wings [SVV]
☐ UP-B7601*	(2XER)	32954/861	ex UN-B7601	Kazakhstan Government
☐ VP-BKS*	(3P6ER)	27254/522	ex A4O-GW	Kalair (lsd fr Nisr Ltd)
☐ VP-CME	(231ER)	22567/30	ex (N515DL)	Global Jet Concept / Sheikh Mustafa MA Edrees
☐ V8-MHB*	(27GER)	25537/517	ex V8-MJB	Sultan's Flight (Operates in Royal Brunei colours)

Boeing 777

Reg	Type	c/n	Previous	Operator
☐ A6-ALN	(2ANER)	29953/252	ex VP-BRH	Presidential Flight
☐ A6-SIL	(35RER)	36353/802	ex VT-JEL	Presidential Flight
☐ N792BA	(236)	27108/17		Afrijet
☐ N777AS*	(24QER)	29271/174		Mid East Jet

Boeing 787

Reg	Type	c/n	Previous	Operator
☐ N787BA	(881)	40690/001		Boeing Corp
☐ N787EX	(881)	40691/002		Boeing Corp

British Aerospace 146

Reg	Type	c/n	Previous	Operator
☐ A6-AAB	(RJ100)	E3387	ex OH-SAN	Presidential Flight
☐ A6-LIW*	(RJ70)	E1267	ex A6-RJK	Amiri Flight / Royal Jet [ROJ]
☐ A6-RJE*	(RJ85)	E2299	ex EI-CNI	Amiri Flight / Royal Jet [ROJ]
☐ A6-RJ1	(RJ85)	E2323	ex N510XJ	Dubai Air Wing
☐ A6-RJ2	(RJ85)	E2325	ex N511XJ	Dubai Air Wing
☐ A9C-AWL	(RJ100)	E3386	ex OH-SAM	Bahrain Defence Force [BFW]
☐ A9C-BDF*	(RJ85)	E2390	ex G-6-390	Bahrain Defence Force [BFW]
☐ A9C-HWR*	(RJ85)	E2306	ex EI-CNK	Bahrain Defence Force [BFW]
☐ G-OFOA*	(100)	E1006	ex G-BKMN	Formula One Management
☐ G-OFOM*	(100)	E1144	ex N3206T	Formula One Management
☐ ZE700*	(100)	E1021	ex G-6-021	Royal Air Force 32 Sqdn
☐ ZE701*	(100)	E1029	ex G-6-029	Royal Air Force 32 Sqdn

Those listed as RJ70 / 85 or 100 were built as Avro 146-RJs

British Aerospace Jetstream 31/32

Reg	Type	c/n	Previous	Operator
☐ G-BWWW*	(3102)	614	ex G-31-614	BAE Systems (Operations)
☐ G-NFLA*	(3102)	637	ex G-BRGN	Cranfield University
☐ HS-DCA*	(3200)	960	ex HS-ASD	Thai Director of Civil Aviation
☐ N170PC	(3101)	717	ex G-31-717	N & J Aviation LLC (VIP)

British Aerospace Jetstream 41

Reg	Type	c/n	Previous	Operator
☐ N307UE	(4101)	41021	ex G-4-021	Stacy Milon t/a Milon Air
☐ N312UE	(4101)	41025	ex G-4-025	Kirland 41025 LLC
☐ N410TJ*	(4101)	41038	ex N514GP	Club Jetstream

British Aircraft Corp One-Eleven

Reg	Type	c/n	Previous	Operator
☐ HZ-ABM2	(401AK)	060	ex HZ-MAA	AMC – Aviation Management Consortium (stored Jeddah)
☐ N111JX*	(414EG)	163	ex N123H	Select Leasing / Pearl Jam Touring [QTA 3]
☐ N161NG*	(401AK)	067	ex N176BF	Northrop-Grumman (research a/c)
☐ N162W*	(401AK)	087	ex N173FE	Northrop Grumman (research a/c)
☐ N164W*	(401AK)	090	ex G-AXCK	Northrop Grumman (research a/c)
☐ N200EE*	(212AR)	083	ex N490ST	Select Leasing / Elite Express
☐ N200JX*	(203AE)	015	ex N583CQ	Select Leasing (stored Waukesha, WI)
☐ N789CF	(422EQ)	119	ex N114MX	Kori Air (stored)
☐ N999BW*	(419EP)	120	ex N87BL	Business Jet Access [QTA 3]
☐ TZ-BSB	(401AK)	086	ex YR-CJL	Government of Mali [QTA 3]
☐ XA-CMG*	(401AK)	079	ex N880P	Grupo Adelac / Coapa Air [OAP]
☐ XB-KCE*	(212AR)	183	ex XB-JSC	Aerolesen [stored after drug running]
☐ 5A-DKO*	(422EQ)	126	ex VP-BBA	Libavia (all-white)

Canadair CL-600-2B-19 (CRJ-100/200/Challenger 800/850)

Reg	Type	c/n	Previous	Operator
☐ B-4701*	(200LR)	7639	ex C-GKAK	China Maritime Service [Op by CUA]
☐ B-4702*	(200LR)	7455	ex C-GHUT	China Maritime Service [Op by CUA]
☐ C-FNRJ*	(100LR)	7002		Bombardier Inc (2nd prototype)
☐ C-FPSB		8079	ex C-FMLQ	Bombardier Aerospace
☐ C-GDTD	(850)	8067	ex G-CMBI	Flightexec
☐ C-GFIO	(200)	7526	ex N662BR	Nav Canada
☐ C-GNVC	(200)	7519	ex N660BR	Nav Canada
☐ C-GSUW	(850)	8047	ex C-FGKZ	Suncor Energy
☐ C-GWWW	(850)	8057	ex C-FHCN	Chartwright Air
☐ D-AAIJ	(850)	8065	ex C-FJRN	Imperial Jet
☐ D-AANN	(850)	8073	ex C-FOFW	ExecuJet Europe
☐ D-ATRI	(850)	8081	ex C-FQPY	DC Aviation
☐ EI-EEZ	(850)	8085		Airlink Airways
☐ G-CJMB	(850)	8055	ex N850RJ	Corporate Jet Management

☐ G-IGWT	(850)	8078	ex C-FPTI	Ocean Sky Aviation
☐ G-SHAL	(850)	8066		TAG Aviation
☐ HB-IDJ*	(100)	7136	ex VP-CRJ	TAG Aviation Service [FP/FPG]
☐ M-ANTA	(850)	8094		Tahtra Holdings
☐ M-FZMH	(850)	8068	ex C-FLOA	Execujet Middle East
☐ M-ISLA	(850)	8080	ex C-FQPV	Excellence Aviation
☐ N60GH	(200)	7274	ex N633BR	Haas CNC Racing
☐ N135BC*	(100SE)	7075	ex N877SE	DJ Burrell
☐ N155MW*	(200)	7021	ex C-FLHX	MWR Aviation / Michael Waltrip Racing
☐ N488CA	(200)	7730		Tailwind Capital
☐ N500PR*	(800)	7846	ex N846PR	Penske Jet
☐ N501LS*	(200)	7584	ex C-GJVI	Boston Enterprises LLC / The Limited Inc
☐ N502CG	(200LR)	7283	ex	SABCO Racing
☐ N529DB*	(100SE)	7152	ex N655CC	Hardwicke Properties
☐ N601LS*	(100ER)	7008	ex N501LS	Directional Visions / The Limited Inc
☐ N635BR	(200)	7295		Tailwind Capital
☐ N711WM*	(800)	7140	ex N140WC	Gaughan Flying LLC / Coast Hotels & Casinos
☐ N858TS	(200)	7508	ex G-ELNX	Aero Toy Store
☐ N75983	(200LR)	7481	ex C-FZUK	Wu Air Corporation
☐ OE-IKG	(850)	8063	ex C-FJBK	MAP Executive
☐ OE-ILI*	(850)	8048	ex C-FFVE	VistaJet
☐ OE-ILV*	(850)	8082		VistaJet
☐ OE-ILY	(850)	8076	ex C-FOYA	VistaJet
☐ OE-ILZ	(850)	8086		VistaJet
☐ OE-ISA	(850)	8043	ex C-FFHA	JetAlliance
☐ OH-SPB	(850)	8056	ex N850TS	Jetflite
☐ OY-NAD	(850)	8052	ex C-FGQS	ExecuJet Scandinavia / Amir Aviation
☐ OY-VEG	(850)	8075	ex C-FOXW	ExecuJet Europe
☐ OY-VGA	(850)	8077	ex C-FOBI	ExecuJet Europe
☐ PH-AAG	(200LR)	7763	ex N492CA	Solid Air (converted CRJ-200ER)
☐ P4-AST	(850)	8054	ex UP-C8501	Comlux KZ
☐ P4-GAZ	(100ER)	7159	ex N979CA	PremierAvia
☐ P4-GJL	(850)	8053	ex N854SA	Silver Arrows
☐ P4-VIP	(100ER)	7158	ex N855VP	PremierAvia
☐ RA-67218	(850)	8074	ex C-FOMN	Kolavia
☐ RA-67219	(850)	8090		Kolavia
☐ RA-67220	(850)	8091		Kolavia
☐ UP-C8502	(850)	8049	ex UN-C8502	Comlux CZ
☐ UP-C8503	(850)	8093	ex UN-C8503	Comlux CZ
☐ UR-ICD	(850)	8072		ISD Avia
☐ UR-RUS	(200)	7990	ex N790TS	ISD Avia
☐ VH-LEF	(850)	8060	ex C-FGTV	Linfox Aircraft Charter
☐ VP-BCC*	(200ER)	7717	ex C-GZSQ	Consolidated Contractors
☐ VP-BNH	(850)	8069	ex C-FMGW	Execujet Middle East
☐ VP-BSD	(850)	8051	ex C-GQVP	Alpha 55 Co
☐ VP-BVJ	(850)	8071	ex C-FMVS	Vacuna Jets
☐ VP-CON	(850)	8083		FTC Consulting
☐ VT-KML	(800)	7351	ex N387AA	Span Air
☐ 4L-GAF*	(850)	8046	ex OY-YVI	Georgian Airways [TGZ]
☐ 5A-UAD	(850)	8087		United Aviation
☐ 9H-AFU	(100SE)	7176	ex VP-BHX	Carre Aviation

Canadair CL-600-2C10 (RJ-700) / CL-600-2D15/24 (RJ-705/900)

☐ C-FRJX*	(900)	15991		Bombardier Inc (prototype CRJ-900, conv from CRJ-700)
☐ C-GSUA	(900)	15182		Suncor
☐ C-GSUM	(900)	15158		Suncor
☐ N1RL*	(700)	10004	ex N400MS	Indycar Aviation Services / Chase Equipment Leasing
☐ VP-BCL*	(702)	10247	ex N710TS	Global Jet Charters / Consolidated Contractors

Douglas DC-8

☐ VP-BHM*	(62)	46111/491	ex VR-BHM	Brisair Ltd
☐ 3D-FCV	(62F)	46132/535	ex 3D-FRE	Operator unknown (based South America)

Douglas DC-9

☐ N45NA*	(33F)	47410/480	ex 162753	Department of Energy, National Nuclear Security Administration
☐ N112PS*	(15RC)	47013/129	ex N557AS	Sky Way Enterprises, 'A-Liner' titles (ABS 3)
☐ N127NK	(21)	47361/488	ex (N953VV)	Bernie E Conatser
☐ N166DE*	(15RC)	47152/170	ex N66AF	US Dept of Energy (ABS 3) [Op by NRG]
☐ N229DE*	(15RC)	45826/79	ex N62AF	US Dept of Energy (ABS 3) [Op by NRG]
☐ N305PA*	(15)	45740/62	ex N911KM	Pharmair Corp
☐ N682RW*	(51)	47733/862	ex N412EA	Detroit Red Wings & Tigers / Provident Bank (ABS 3)
☐ N697BJ*	(32)	47799/918	ex N926LG	McAir Inc / Blue Jackets
☐ N880DP*	(32)	47635/754	ex N880RB	Roudball / Detroit Pistons (ABS 3)
☐ N932NA*	(33RC)	47476/569	ex 162754	NASA / Johnson Space Center, Zero G trainer
☐ N950VJ*	(31)	47564/681		Justice Prisoner & Alien Transportation System [DOJ]
☐ N8860*	(15)	45797/51	ex N8953U	Scaife Flight Operations (ABS 3)
☐ ZS-PYB	(14)	45706/61	ex N13NE	Mantuba Executive Jet / NC Aircraft

Douglas DC-10

Reg	Type	C/n	Previous	Operator	Note
N220AU*	(10)	46501/2	ex G-GCAL	Project Orbis Intl (flying hospital)	

Embraer EMB.110 Bandeirante

Reg	Type	C/n	Previous	Operator	Note
PP-EAM*	(P1A)	110498	ex PT-SBS	Governo do Estado do Amazonas	
PP-EIX*	(P1A)	110468	ex PT-SHW	Governo do Amapa	
PP-EMG*	(E)	110032	ex PT-GJV	Governo de Minas Gerais	
PP-ERN*	(P1)	110344	ex PT-FAV	Governo de Rio Grande do Norte	
PP-FFV*	(B1)	110284	ex PT-SBO	INPE Instituto Pesquisas Espacias	
PT-FRF*	(EJ)	110115	ex PT-GKK	Departamento Nac Est de Rodagem	

Embraer EMB.120 Brasilia

Reg	Type	C/n	Previous	Operator	Note
N22BD*	(ER)	120143	ex N161CA	Bill Davis Racing	
N109EM*	(ER)	120195	ex N15732	Evernham Motorsports / GEMS Aviation	
N223BD*	(ER)	120260	ex N205SW	Bill Davis Racing	
N229CR*	(ER)	120111	ex N34712	RCR Air	
N331CR*	(ER)	120121	ex PH-XLG	RCR Air	
N650CT	(ER)	120198	ex N267AS	N650CT LLC	
N651CT	(ER)	120197	ex N58733	N651CT LLC	
N652CT	(ER)	120199	ex N57734	N652CT LLC / Charter Air Transport	
N707TG*	(ER)	120182	ex N17728	Gordon Air	
N919EM*	(ER)	120160	ex N132PP	GEMS Aviation	
N16731*	(ER)	120190	ex PT-SRD	MWR Racing (Michael Waltrip Racing)	
PP-PSC*	(ER)	120213	ex F-GTSK	Embraer (corporate shuttle)	
PT-SOK	(ER)	120358		Companhia Vale do Rio Doce	

Embraer EMB.135 / EMB.140 / EMB.145/Legacy

Reg	Type	C/n	Previous	Operator	Note
209*	(135LR)	145209	ex PP-SFX	Hellenic Air Force	
484*	(135BJ)	145484	ex PP-SAD	Hellenic Air Force	[Legacy]
2520*	(145ER)	145023	ex PT-SPB	Forca Aerea Brasileira (as C-99)	
2521*	(145ER)	145020	ex PT-SPA	Forca Aerea Brasileira (as C-99)	
2522*	(145ER)	145027	ex PT-SPC	Forca Aerea Brasileira (as C-99)	
2523*	(145ER)	145028	ex PT-SPD	Forca Aerea Brasileira (as C-99)	
2524*	(145ER)	145034	ex PT-SPF	Forca Aerea Brasileira (as C-99)	
2525*	(145ER)	145038	ex PT-SPG	Forca Aerea Brasileira (as C-99)	
2526	(145ER)	145137	ex PT-SPO	Forca Aerea Brasileira (as C-99)	
2550*	(145LR)	145350	ex PT-SPP	Forca Aerea Brasileira (as VC-99B)	
2560*	(135LR)	145600	ex N846RP	Forca Aerea Brasileira (as VC-99C)	
2561*	(135LR)	145608	ex N847RP	Forca Aerea Brasileira (as VC-99C)	
2580*	(135BJ)	145412	ex N912CW	Forca Aerea Brasileira (as VC-99C)	[Legacy]
2581*	(135BJ)	145462	ex N962CW	Forca Aerea Brasileira (as VC-99C)	[Legacy]
2582*	(135BJ)	145495	ex N902LX	Forca Aerea Brasileira (as VC-99C)	[Legacy]
2583*	(135BJ)	145528	ex N908LX	Forca Aerea Brasileira (as VC-99C)	[Legacy]
2584*	(135BJ)	14500997	ex PT-SKP	Forca Aerea Brasileira (as VC-99C)	[Legacy]
2585*	(135BJ)	14501078	ex PT-SEZ	Forca Aerea Brasileira (as VC-99C)	[Legacy]
A6-AJA	(135BJ)	14501089		Al Jaber Aviation	[Legacy]
A6-AJB	(135BJ)	14501098		Al Jaber Aviation	[Legacy]
A6-DPW*	(135BJ)	14500955	ex PT-SFD	Nakheel Aviation [NKL]	[Legacy]
A6-FLL	(135BJ)	14501051		Falcon Aviation	[Legacy]
A6-FLO	(135BJ)	14501096		Falcon Aviation	[Legacy]
A6-MAZ	(135BJ)	14500978	ex A9C-MAN	Empire Aviation	[Legacy]
A6-NKL*	(135BJ)	14500944	ex PT-SCP	Nakheel Aviation [NKL]	[Legacy]
A6-NLA	(135BJ)	14501075		Prestige Jet	[Legacy]
A6-PJE	(135BJ)	14500972	ex G-MGYB	Prestige Jet	[Legacy]
A6-SSV	(135BJ)	14501041		Empire Aviation	[Legacy]
A6-SUN	(135BJ)	14501001	ex PT-SKS	Nakheel Aviation [NKL]	[Legacy]
A6-UGH	(135BJ)	14500993	ex N912LX	DAS Holdings	[Legacy]
A6-VVV	(135BJ)	14501057		Istithmar World Aviation	[Legacy]
A9C-MTC*	(135BJ)	14500975	ex (PH-CEL)	Bahrain Executive Air Service [BXA]	[Legacy]
CE-01*	(135LR)	145449	ex PT-SUU	Belgian Defence, Aircomponent 15 W AirTpt [BAF]	
CE-02*	(135LR)	145480	ex PT-SVZ	Belgian Defence, Aircomponent 15 W AirTpt [BAF]	
CE-03*	(145LR)	145526	ex PT-STR	Belgian Defence, Aircomponent 15 W AirTpt [BAF]	
CE-04*	(145LR)	145548	ex PT-SZL	Belgian Defence, Aircomponent 15 W AirTpt [BAF]	
D-ACBG	(135BJ)	14501016	ex PT-SVI	DC Aviation	[Legacy]
D-ADCN	(135BJ)	14501055		DC Aviation	[Legacy]
D-ADCP	(135BJ)	14501067		DC Aviation	[Legacy]
D-AKAT	(135BJ)	14501038	ex PT-SZH	KamAvia	[Legacy]
D-AONE*	(135BJ)	14500988	ex PT-SKD	Cirrus Aviation	[Legacy]
D-ARIF	(135BJ)	14500841	ex HB-IWX	Silver Bird	[Legacy]
D-ARTN*	(135BJ)	14500941	ex PT-SCM	DC Aviation	[Legacy]
D-ATON	(135BJ)	14501017	ex PT-SVK	DC Aviation	[Legacy]
D-ATWO*	(135BJ)	14501010	ex PK-SKZ	DC Aviation	[Legacy]
D-AVIB	(135BJ)	14501109		Vibro Air	[Legacy]
EC-IIR*	(135BJ)	145540	ex (PT-SAI)	FADESA, Op by Audeli [ADI]	[Legacy]
EC-KFQ*	(135BJ)	14500995	ex PT-SKO	Flylink Express	[Legacy]
EC-KHT*	(135BJ)	14500863	ex G-YIAN	Aerodynamics Malaga / Yianis Air	[Legacy]
FAE051	(135BJ)	14501082		Ecuador Air Force	[Legacy]
G-CFJA	(135BJ)	14501045	ex EC-KOK	TAG Aviation UK	[Legacy]
G-CJMD*	(135BJ)	14500994	ex P4-SAO	Corporate Jet Management	[Legacy]

Reg	Type	c/n	Previous	Operator	Model
☐ G-CMAF*	(135BJ)	14501011	ex PT-SVE	TAG Aviation UK	[Legacy]
☐ G-HUBY	(135BJ)	14500854	ex HB-JGS	London Executive Aviation	[Legacy]
☐ G-IRSH	(135BJ)	14501048		London Executive Aviation	[Legacy]
☐ G-OGSK	(135BJ)	14501074		TAG Aviation UK	[Legacy]
☐ G-PGRP	(135BJ)	14501102		GAMA Aviation	[Legacy]
☐ G-RHMS	(135BJ)	14501072		International Jet Club	[Legacy]
☐ G-RRAZ*	(135BJ)	14500954	ex G-RUBN	Raz Air	[Legacy]
☐ G-RUBE	(135BJ)	14501100		London Executive Aviation	[Legacy]
☐ G-SIRA*	(135BJ)	14500832	ex OE-IAS	Amsair Aircraft [Alan Sugar]	[Legacy]
☐ G-SYLJ*	(135BJ)	14500937	ex PT-SCI	TAG Aviation 'Al Mounthala'	[Legacy]
☐ G-WCCI*	(135BJ)	145505	ex G-REUB	Altarello Ltd	[Legacy]
☐ HB-JED*	(135BJ)	145644	ex PT-SAR	DiaMair / GE Lisca AG	[Legacy]
☐ HB-JEL*	(135BJ)	14500933	ex PT-SCA	Prime Air / Comlux Aviation [CLA]	[Legacy]
☐ HC-CGO	(135BJ)	14500987	ex PT-SKF	Petroecuador	[Legacy]
☐ HP-1A	(135BJ)	14501066	ex PT-SER	Government of Panama	[Legacy]
☐ K3601*	(135BJ)	14500867	ex PT-SIR	Indian Air Force 'Megadoot'	[Legacy]
☐ K3602*	(135BJ)	14500880	ex PT-SIT	Indian Air Force 'Vayudoot'	[Legacy]
☐ K3603*	(135BJ)	14500910	ex PT-SIY	Indian Air Force 'Habhdoot'	[Legacy]
☐ K3604*	(135BJ)	14500919	ex PT-SON	Indian Air Force 'Gagandoot'	[Legacy]
☐ LX-NVB*	(135BJ)	14501002	ex P4-NVB	Silver Arrows	[Legacy]
☐ LX-RLG*	(135BJ)	14500967	ex OE-IGR	Silver Arrows	[Legacy]
☐ M-AKAK	(135BJ)	14500970	ex VP-BBY	AA Kassar Sal	[Legacy]
☐ M-DSCL	(135BJ)	14500851	ex OE-ISN	Legacy Aviation	[Legacy]
☐ M-NATH	(135BJ)	14501021	ex N915LX	Club 17 SA	[Legacy]
☐ M-OLEG	(135BJ)	14500991	ex D-AAAI	Club 17 SA	[Legacy]
☐ M-YNJC*	(135BJ)	14500961	ex G-ONJC	Newjetco (Europe) Ltd	[Legacy]
☐ N6GD*	(135BJ)	14500983	ex N473MM	GNG LLC	[Legacy]
☐ N10SV*	(135BJ)	14500974	ex PT-SHD	ACM Aviation	[Legacy]
☐ N53NA*	(135BJ)	145770	ex N3005	DC-3 Entertainment 'The Lisa Mara'	[Legacy]
☐ N63AG	(135BJ)	14501061		ACM Aviation	[Legacy]
☐ N89FE	(135BJ)	14501058		FirstEnergy	[Legacy]
☐ N89LD*	(135SL)	145648	ex PT-SEI	McKee Food Transportation	
☐ N124LS*	(135BJ)	14500948	ex PT-SCT	L&G Management	[Legacy]
☐ N135SG*	(135BJ)	145706	ex PT-SAX	KIPCO-Kuwaits Projects [Op by United Aviation]	[Legacy]
☐ N135SK*	(135BJ)	14500989	ex N556JT	United Aviation	[Legacy]
☐ N135SL*	(135BJ)	145711	ex PT-SAY	KIPCO-Kuwaits Projects [Op by United Aviation] 'Dia'	[Legacy]
☐ N135SZ*	(135LR)	145728	ex N202CP	United Aviation	
☐ N226HY*	(135BJ)	14501014	ex PT-SVH	Executive Flightways	[Legacy]
☐ N227WE*	(135BJ)	14501018	ex PT-SVV	1132 Aviation	[Legacy]
☐ N325JF*	(135ER)	145499	ex PT-SXS	Intel Corp, corporate shuttle	
☐ N357TE*	(135BJ)	14501079		UMAL Group	[Legacy]
☐ N373RB*	(135BJ)	14500957	ex PT-SFF	RBGT LLC	[Legacy]
☐ N386CH*	(135ER)	145467	ex PT-SVM	Intel Corp, corporate shuttle	
☐ N451DJ*	(135BJ)	145789	ex N456MT	LP 241 LLC / DJT LLC	[Legacy]
☐ N486TM*	(135ER)	145364	ex PT-SOM	Intel Corp, corporate shuttle	
☐ N494TG*	(135BJ)	145678	ex PT-SAS	Answer Group	[Legacy]
☐ N515JT*	(135BJ)	14500950	ex PT-SCX	JT Aviation	[Legacy]
☐ N580ML*	(135BJ)	14500990	ex PT-SKK	Stone Tower Air	[Legacy]
☐ N605WG*	(135BJ)	14500980	ex PT-SHS	Wings West Aviation / Northeastern Aviation	[Legacy]
☐ N615PG*	(135BJ)	14501004	ex PT-SKV	Pacific Gas & Electric Co	[Legacy]
☐ N617WA*	(135BJ)	14500884	ex PT-SIU	Administaff Inc	[Legacy]
☐ N642AG*	(135BJ)	145642	ex PT-SAQ	Yo Pegasus / Banc of America Lsg	[Legacy]
☐ N676TC*	(135BJ)	145699	ex N691AN	Alpine Cascade Corp	[Legacy]
☐ N678RC*	(135BJ)	14501074		Financial Business Concepts	[Legacy]
☐ N702DR*	(135BJ)	14500925	ex N702CM	SCCSM Aviation / Banc of America Leasing & Capital	[Legacy]
☐ N703TS	(135BJ)	14501003	ex VP-CLI	Aero Toy Store	[Legacy]
☐ N728PH*	(135BJ)	14500985	ex PT-SKB	BHM-SCM Services / ExcelAire Services	[Legacy]
☐ N730BH*	(135BJ)	145730	ex PT-SHG	Briad Restaurant Group / Redeye II	[Legacy]
☐ N806D	(135BJ)	14501095		Dominion Resources	[Legacy]
☐ N809TD*	(135BJ)	14500809	ex N809SG	Meadow Lane Air Partners	[Legacy]
☐ N818HV	(135BJ)	14501105		HR INV LLC	[Legacy]
☐ N827TV	(135BJ)	14500971	ex N775SM	Pinnacle Aviation	[Legacy]
☐ N829RN*	(135ER)	145361	ex PT-SOP	Intel Corp, corporate shuttle	
☐ N856LS	(135BJ)	14501080		Leon Advertising	[Legacy]
☐ N888ML*	(135BJ)	14500818	ex PT-SIM	New Macau Landmark Mgmt / Legend Development Co	[Legacy]
☐ N898JS	(135BJ)	14501071		Lalit Hotels	[Legacy]
☐ N900DP*	(135BJ)	14500903	ex PT-SIW	Bus Av/Del Inc	[Legacy]
☐ N900EM*	(135BJ)	14500976	ex PT-SHI	Air by Jet Air Charter	[Legacy]
☐ N904LX*	(135BJ)	145780	ex N780SG	Flight Options [OPT]	[Legacy]
☐ N905LX*	(135BJ)	145775	ex PT-SIC	Southwest Homes [Op by OPT]	[Legacy]
☐ N909LX*	(135BJ)	14500942	ex PT-SCN	Brocade Communications Systems	[Legacy]
☐ N909TT*	(135BJ)	14501044		Transcon	[Legacy]
☐ N910LX*	(135BJ)	14500952	ex PT-SFB	Robert E Fischell / Flight Options [OPT]	[Legacy]
☐ N912JC*	(135BJ)	14501015	ex PT-SVI	Vitesse Air Services / Dalcam Inc	[Legacy]
☐ N913LX*	(135BJ)	14501007	ex PT-SKX	Fog City Stables / Flight Options [OPT]	[Legacy]
☐ N918JT	(135BJ)	14501032	ex PT-SZD	ExcelAire	[Legacy]
☐ N924AK	(135BJ)	14501034	ex PT-SZE	Talon Air	[Legacy]
☐ N925FL*	(135BJ)	14500825	ex N906LX	Flight Options [OPT]	[Legacy]
☐ N926FM*	(135ER)	145466	ex PT-SVL	Intel Corp, corporate shuttle	
☐ N939AJ*	(135BJ)	14500939	ex PT-SCK	Orfro LLC	[Legacy]
☐ N948AL*	(135ER)	145450	ex PT-SUV	Intel Corp, corporate shuttle	
☐ N966JS	(135BJ)	14500966	ex N907LX	Pebunny LLC	[Legacy]
☐ N975GR*	(135BJ)	14501069		Corporate AirSearch	[Legacy]

	Reg	Type	C/n	Previous	Operator	
☐	N983JC*	(135LR)	14500977	ex PT-SHK	St Thomas Energy Exports / Johnson Controls	
☐	N1023C*	(135LR)	145550	ex PT-SZN	Conoco Phillips / PNC Bank	
☐	OE-IBK	(135BJ)	14501110		Avcon Jet	[Legacy]
☐	OE-IBR	(135BJ)	14500960	ex P4-NRA	Global Jet	[Legacy]
☐	OE-IDB*	(135BJ)	14500999	ex PT-SKR	JetAlliance [JAG]	[Legacy]
☐	OE-IRK*	(135BJ)	14500916	ex PT-SOM	JetAlliance [JAG]	[Legacy]
☐	OK-GGG*	(135BJ)	14500986	ex PT-SKC	ABS Jets [ABP]	[Legacy]
☐	OK-JNT*	(135BJ)	14501087	ex PT-SKC	ABS Jets [ABP]	[Legacy]
☐	OK-KKG*	(135BJ)	14500873	ex PT-SIS	K&K Capital Group / Grossman Air Service	[Legacy]
☐	OK-ROM	(135BJ)	14501039	ex PT-SZI	ABS Jets	[Legacy]
☐	OK-SLN*	(135BJ)	145796	ex PT-SIF	ABS Jets [ABP]	[Legacy]
☐	OK-SUN*	(135BJ)	14500963	ex PT-SFK	ABS Legacy [ABP]	[Legacy]
☐	PK-DHK	(135BJ)	14501046		Premiair	[Legacy]
☐	PK-OME*	(135BJ)	145516	ex PT-SAG	Airfast Indonesia [AFE]	[Legacy]
☐	PK-RJG*	(135BJ)	14500969	ex PT-SFW	Premiair	[Legacy]
☐	PK-RJO	(135BJ)	14501020	ex G-FECR	Premiair	[Legacy]
☐	PK-RJW	(135BJ)	14501106		Premiair	[Legacy]
☐	PP-VVV	(135BJ)	14501099		JBS SA	[Legacy]
☐	PR-AVX	(135BJ)	14501037	ex PT-SZG	Grupo EBX	[Legacy]
☐	PR-BEB	(135BJ)	14501035	ex PT-SZF		[Legacy]
☐	PR-LTC	(135BJ)	14501091		Macbens Patrimonial	[Legacy]
☐	PR-NIO*	(135BJ)	14501012	ex PT-SVG	Compania Brasileira de Metalurgia e Mineração	[Legacy]
☐	PR-ORE*	(135BJ)	145625	ex PT-SDN	Cia Vale do Rio Doce	[Legacy]
☐	PR-RIO*	(135BJ)	145717	ex PT-SAZ	Unibanco [Legacy]	
☐	PT-SCR	(135BJ)	14500946		São Conrado Táxi Aéreo	[Legacy]
☐	PT-SKW	(135BJ)	14501006		São Conrado Táxi Aéreo	[Legacy]
☐	PT-ZJA*	(135KE)	145801		Embraer, EMB.140 prototype, conv from EMB.135, ff 27Jun00	
☐	PT-ZJB*	(145XR)	145001		Embraer, second prototype 145, ff 17Nov95	
☐	P4-AEG	(135BJ)	14501111		AEG Air	[Legacy]
☐	P4-IVM*	(135BJ)	145686	ex N686SG	Pacific Information Technology	[Legacy]
☐	P4-MIV	(135BJ)	14501031	ex PT-SZC	Rusjet	[Legacy]
☐	P4-MSG*	(135BJ)	14500913	ex N551VB	Silvershore Trading	[Legacy]
☐	P4-PAM	(135BJ)	14500982	ex G-RBRO	Petrov Air	[Legacy]
☐	P4-SIS*	(135BJ)	145586		KAB Holdings	[Legacy]
☐	P4-SVM	(135BJ)	14501060		Orex Aviation	[Legacy]
☐	P4-VVP*	(135BJ)	145549	ex PT-SAJ	Kung Fung Trading / Evolga of Moscow [Op by AOC]	[Legacy]
☐	SE-DJG	(135BJ)	14501042		European Flight Service	[Legacy]
☐	SX-CDK*	(135BJ)	14500998	ex PT-SKQ	K2 Smart Aviation	[Legacy]
☐	SX-DGM	(135BJ)	14501023	ex PT-SVY	InterJet Hellenic	[Legacy]
☐	SX-KDK	(135BJ)	14501090		K2 Smart Aviation	[Legacy]
☐	S5-ABL*	(135BJ)	14501008	ex PT-SKY	Linxair Business Aviation	[Legacy]
☐	S5-ALA	(135BJ)	14501029	ex PT-SZC	Linxair Business Aviation	[Legacy]
☐	T-501	(135BJ)	14500981	ex PT-SHT	Angola Air Force / Forca Aerea Populare de Angola	[Legacy]
☐	VH-VLT	(135BJ)	14501107		Southern Cross Jets	[Legacy]
☐	VP-BVS*	(135BJ)	14500979	ex PT-SHQ	International JetClub	[Legacy]
☐	VP-CDH	(135BJ)	14501026	ex PT-SZA	Baltic Jet AirCompany	[Legacy]
☐	VP-CFA*	(135BJ)	145637	ex PT-SAP	Samco Aviation / Sheikh Fahad Al Athel	[Legacy]
☐	VP-CHP*	(135BJ)	14500802	ex HB-JEO	Jet Aviation Business Jets	[Legacy]
☐	VP-CKP	(135BJ)	14501094		Titan Aviation	[Legacy]
☐	VP-CLL	(135BJ)	14501052		Titan Aviation	[Legacy]
☐	VP-CMK	(135BJ)	14501083		Comoro Gulf Aviation	[Legacy]
☐	VP-CNJ	(135BJ)	14501025	ex PT-SVZ	International Jetclub	
☐	VP-CUP*	(135BJ)	145555	ex HB-JEA	G5 Executivo / Pisco Overseas	[Legacy]
☐	VQ-BLU	(135BJ)	14501086		Air Mercury Ltd	[Legacy]
☐	VT-BSF*	(135BJ)	14500901	ex PT-SIX	Border Security Force	[Legacy]
☐	3C-QQH	(145EP)	145076	ex LX-LGT	Government of Equatorial Guinea	
☐	5N-BJM*	(145LR)	14500984	ex PT-SKE	Bauchi State Government, op by IRS Airlines	
☐	5N-RSG*	(135BJ)	14500891	ex PT-SIV	State Government of Rivers State	[Legacy]
☐	9K-PAA	(135BJ)	14500973	ex A6-KWT		[Legacy]

Embraer 170/175/190/195

	Reg	Type	C/n	Previous	Operator
☐	A6-ARK	(100)	19000109	ex PT-XOL	Embraer [Lineage 1000]
☐	PP-XJB*	(100SL)	17000003		Embraer, 3rd prototype, ff 25May02
☐	PP-XJC*	(100SL)	17000002		Embraer, 2nd prototype, ff 09Apr02
☐	PP-XJD*	(200SR)	17000014		Embraer, prototype 175, ff 16Jun03
☐	PP-XJE*	(100SL)	17000001	ex PP-XRJ	Embraer, prototype 170, ff 19Feb02
☐	PP-XMA*	(100LR)	19000001		Embraer, prototype 190, ff 12Mar04
☐	PP-XMC*	(100LR)	19000004		Embraer
☐	PP-XMI*	(100LR)	19000003		Embraer
☐	PP-XMJ*	(200LR)	19000005		Embraer, prototype 195, ff Dec04
☐	PP-XOL	(100)	19000109		Embraer
☐	PT-SEY*	(200LR)	17000017	ex PT-XJG	Embraer, 2nd prototype 175
☐	PT-SMC*	(100LR)	17000004	ex PP-XJF	Embraer
☐	5A-SOC	(100LR)	17000162	ex PT-SME	Sirte Oil

Fairchild F-27

	Reg	Type	C/n	Previous	Operator
☐	HC-BHD	(J)	122	ex N994	PetroEcuador

Fokker F.27 Friendship

☐ F-BYAO*	(102A)	10127	ex F-WYAO	Institut Geographique National
☐ J-752*	(200)	10281	ex AP-ATW	Pakistan Air Force (VIP)
☐ PH-FBP*	(100)	10150	ex C-3	Royal Dutch Airforce Historical Flight
☐ PH-FHF*	(100)	10105	ex VH-NLS	Fokker Heritage Flight
☐ TF-SYN*	(200)	10545	ex PH-EXC	Icelandic Coastguard / Landhelgisgaezlan [ICG]

Fokker F.28 Fellowship

☐ FAC002*	(1000)	11992	ex FAC001	Fuerza Aerea Colombiana
☐ G530*	(3000)	11125	ex PH-ZBP	Ghana Air Force
☐ M28-01*	(1000)	11088	ex FM2101	Royal Malaysian Air Force [RMF]
☐ N500WN*	(1000)	11016	ex N43AE	Wayne Newton / Desert Eagle (stored Pontiac, MI)
☐ TJ-ALG	(4000)	11227	ex N159AD	Fotso Group [RAC]
☐ 5A-DSO*	(2000)	11110	ex HB-AAS	Sirte Oil Company
☐ 5H-CCM*	(3000)	11137	ex PH-ZBS	Government of Tanzania 'Uhuru na Umoja'
☐ 5V-TAI*	(1000)	11079	ex 5V-MAB	Republique Togolaise

Fokker F.27-050 /060 (Fokker50/60)

☐ 5H-TGF*		20231	ex PH-JXG	Government of Tanzania

Fokker F.28-070 (Fokker 070)

☐ KAF308*		11557	ex PH-MXM	Kenyan Government
☐ N322K*		11521	ex PH-MKS	Ford Motor Co [FRD]
☐ N324K*		11545	ex PH-EZH	Ford Motor Co [FRD]
☐ PH-KBX*		11547		Dutch Royal Flight [op by MPH]

Fokker F.28-0100 (Fokker 100)

☐ OE-IIB		11403	ex C-GKZA	International Jet Management [IJM]
☐ OE-IIC		11406	ex C-GKZP	International Jet Management [IJM]
☐ OE-IID		11368	ex C-GKZL	International Jet Management [IJM]

Ilyushin Il-62M

☐ C5-RTG*		1356234	ex UK-86569	Republic of the Gambia
☐ ST-PRA*		2357711		The Republic of the Sudan
☐ 5A-DKT		4648414	ex 3C-QQR	Socialist People's Libyan Arab Jamahiriya 'Rayane'

Ilyushin Il-96

☐ RA-96000*	(400)	0101	ex CCCP-96000	Ilyushin OKB, prototype, ff 28Sep88
☐ RA-96001*		0103		Ilyushin OKB
☐ RA-96002	(300)	74393201001	ex CCCP-96002	Ilysuhin OKB

Ilyushin Il-114

☐ RA-54000		0101	ex CCCP-54000	Ilyushin OKB, prototype, ff 29Mar90
☐ RA-91001		1023823024		Ilyushin OKB, stored
☐ RA-91002		1033830030		Ilyushin OKB, survey aircraft (stored)
☐ RA-91003*	(LL)	1013800109		Russian Navy / Radar MMS Production Association
☐ 91005	(T)	1043800205	ex UK-91005	Ilyushin OKB, freighter prototype
☐ 91105	(100)	2063800205		Ilyushin OKB

Lockheed Hercules

☐ HZ-114*	(382C-4E)	4843	ex HZ-HM5	Saudi Arabian Royal Flight [SVA]
☐ HZ-115*	(382C-4E)	4845	ex HZ-HM6	Saudi Arabian Royal Flight [SVA]
☐ HZ-116*	(382C-26D)	4915	ex N4185M	Saudi Arabian Royal Flight [SVA]
☐ HZ-117*	(382G-63C)	4954		Saudi Arabian Royal Flight [SVA]
☐ HZ-MS 02*	(382C-32E)	4918	ex HZ-MS21	Saudi Aeromedical Evacuation (flying hospital)
☐ HZ-MS 06*	(382G-60C)	4952	ex HZ-MS6	Saudi Aeromedical Evacuation (flying hospital)
☐ HZ-MS 07*	(382C-26E)	4922	ex HZ-MS7	Saudi Aeromedical Evacuation (flying hospital)
☐ HZ-MS 08*	(382T-55E)	4986	ex HZ-MS8	Saudi Aeromedical Evacuation (flying hospital)
☐ HZ-MS 19*	(382C-93D)	4837	ex N4098M	Saudi Aeromedical Evacuation (flying hospital)

Lockheed L-1011 Tristar

☐ HZ-AB1*	(500)	193H-1247	ex JY-HKJ	Al Anwa Establishment
☐ N388LS	(500)	293A-1249	ex HZ-HM6	Las Vegas Sands Corp
☐ N389LS	(500)	193G-1250	ex HZ-HM5	Las Vegas Sands Corp
☐ VP-CGF	(500)	193Y-1195	ex VR-CGF	Jetstream Holdings / Al Anwa Establishment (stored Al-Fujirah)

McDonnell-Douglas MD-11

☐ HZ-AFAS*		48533/544	ex HZ-AFA1	ASASCO / Bin Shuaileh Group
☐ HZ-HM7*		48532/532	ex N9093P	Saudi Arabian Royal flight [SVA] (stored San Antonio, TX)

McDonnell-Douglas MD-80

☐ N168CF	(87)	49670/1453	ex N143G	Sunrider Corporation

☐ N287KB*	(87)	49768/1595	ex D-ALLJ	KEB Aircraft
☐ N789BV	(83)	49789/1642	ex	Tri-Star 1 Enterprise
☐ P4-AIR	(87)	49412/1424	ex N871DP	Sistema Corporation [op by Jet Air Group]
☐ SX-IFA*	(83)	49809/1843	ex OE-IFA	GainJet
☐ TT-ABC	(87)	49888/1692	ex N980GC	Government of Chad
☐ VP-CBH	(82)	53577/2189	ex N750AG	Palmair
☐ VP-CNI*	(87)	49767/1587	ex N721MM	Corporate Aviation Holdings
☐ VP-CTF	(87)	49777/1634	ex N807NK	SG Air Leasing

SAAB 2000

☐ N166GC*		2000-034	ex N512RH	Ginn Development / ERG Aviation III
☐ N168GC*		2000-031	ex SE-LOG	Ginn Development / ERG Aviation III
☐ N508RH*		2000-027	ex N5124	Hendrick Motorsports
☐ N509RH*		2000-030	ex N5125	Hendrick Motorsports
☐ N511RH*		2000-020	ex N5123	Hendrick Motorsports
☐ N519JG*		2000-017	ex SE-017	Joe Gibbs Racing

Sukhoi SuperJet 100 (RRJ95)

☐ RA-95001				Sukhoi Design Bureau

(Fairchild-) Swearingen SA.226TC Metro II

☐ LQ-MLV*		TC-257	ex LV-MLV	Ministero de Accion Social (EMS)
☐ PH-NLZ*		TC-277	ex N5651M	NLR-National Lucht & Ruimtevaartlaboratorium

(Fairchild-) Swearingen SA.227AC Metro III

☐ LV-WEE*		AC-516	ex N45ML	Provincia de Catamarca

Tupolev Tu-134

☐ D2-ECC*	(A)	49830		Republica de Angola (stored LAD)
☐ EK-65072*	(A-3)	49972	ex CCCP-65072	Government of Armenia
☐ EK-65975*	(A-3)	3352006	ex CCCP-65975	Government of Armenia
☐ RA-65904*	(A-3)	63953	ex CCCP-65904	Rossiya Special Flight Dept [SDM]
☐ RA-65905*	(A-3)	63965	ex CCCP-65905	Rossiya Special Flight Dept [SDM]
☐ RA-65911*	(A-3)	63972	ex CCCP-65911	Rossiya Special Flight Dept [SDM]
☐ UR-63957*	(A-3)	63957	ex 63957	Ukraine Air Force, VIP
☐ UN-65120*				Government of Kazakhstan
☐ UN-65551*	(A-3)	66212	ex CCCP-65551	Government of Kazakhstan [Op by EAK]
☐ UN-65683*	(AK)	62188	ex	Government of Kazakhstan [Op by EAK]
☐ UR-65556*	(A-3)	66372	ex 65556	Government of Ukraine [Op by UKN]

Tupolev Tu-154

☐ LZ-BTZ*	(M)	88A-781		Government of Bulgaria / Aviodetachment 28 [BGF]
☐ 101*	(M)	90A-837	ex 837	Polskie Wojska Lotnicze (Polish AF)
☐ 102*	(M)	90A-862	ex 862	Polskie Wojska Lotnicze (Polish AF)
☐ 1003*	(M)	00A-1003		SLU - Statni Letecky Utvar (op by Czech AF) [CEF] (stored)
☐ 1016*	(M)	96A-1016	ex OK-BYZ	SLU - Statni Letecky Utvar (op by Czech AF) [CEF]
☐ RA-85666*	(M)	89A-820	ex CCCP-85666	Rossiya Special Flight Dept [SDM]
☐ RA-85686*	(M)	90A-854	ex CCCP-85686	Rossiya Special Flight Dept [SDM]

Tupolev Tu-204

☐ RA-64007		1450743164007		ANTK Tupolev

Tupolev Tu-214

☐ RA-64501		14507444524001		KAPO, prototype

Tupolev Tu-234

☐ RA-64001	(300)	1450743164001	ex CCCP-64001	Tupolev Design Bureau, conv from Tu-204

Tupolev Tu-334

☐ RA-94001	(100)	01001		Tupolev OKB, prototype, ff 08Feb99
☐ RA-94005		01005		Tupolev Design Bureau, second prototype 'Aleksandr Kharlov'

VFW 614

☐ D-ADAM*		G17	ex D-BABP	DLR Flugbetriebe [GPL]

Yakovlev Yak-40

☐ 87662*		9240625	ex EP-TQG	Government of Armenia
☐ D2-EAG*		9230122	ex I-JAKO	Republica de Angola
☐ D2-MAS*		9820558	ex	Republica de Angola
☐ ER-YGD*		9830159	ex RA-87970	Government of Moldova
☐ RA-21500*	(K)	9741356	ex CCCP-21500	Baltic Finance Industrial Group [Op by RNB]

☐ RA-87221*	(K)	9831958	ex CCCP-87221	Lukoil [LUK]
☐ RA-87353*		9330231	ex CCCP-87353	Lukoil [LUK]
☐ RA-87968*		9841258	ex CCCP-87968	Rossiya Special Flight Dept [SDM]
☐ RA-87972*		9921658	ex CCCP-87972	Rossiya Special Flight Dept [SDM]
☐ RDPL-34002*		9840559		Government of Laos
☐ UN-87488*		9441638		Government of Kazakhstan
☐ UR-BWF*		0711352	ex RA-88258	PrivatBank [Op by UDN]
☐ UR-BWH*		9640951	ex RA-88238	Ukraine Regional Concern Agency
☐ UR-CAW*		9341230	ex OM-DYA	Teli Net
☐ UR-CLH				
☐ UR-FRU*		9440737	ex RA-87211	SUMY MV Frunze Science & Production Association [Op UZA]
☐ UR-LAZ				
☐ UR-MHG				
☐ UR-PVS				Mostobud
☐ UR-RTS				
☐ UR-UAS		9420835		
☐ UR-VIP				
☐ YU-AKV/71505*		9630849		Serbian Air Force (calibrator)
☐ 3C-CGE*		9821557	ex 3C-MNB	Government of Equatorial Guinea

Yakovlev Yak-42

☐ RA-42423*	(D)	4520424216606		Yakovlev Design Bureau (City Star 100 demonstrator)
☐ RA-42424*	(142)	4520421302016	ex UR-42424	Lukoil [LUK]

IATA TWO-LETTER DESIGNATORS

Code	Airline	Country
0B	Blue Air	YR
0D	Darwin Airline	HB
0V	Vasco	VN
1I	Novair	SE
1I	Pegasus Airlines	TC
1T	1Time Airline	ZS
2B	Bahrain Air	A9C
2D	Alania Airline	RA
2E	AVE.com	A6
2E	Smokey Bay Air	N
2F	Payam International Air	EP
2F	Frontier Flying Service	N
2G	Cargoitalia	I
2G	Northwest Seaplanes	N
2G	San Juan Airlines	N
2I	Star Peru	OB
2J	Air Burkina	XT
2K	Aerogal	HC
2L	Helvetic Airways	HB
2M	Moldavian Airlines	ER
2N	NAS Air	HZ
2N	Nextjet	SE
2N	Yuzmashavia	UR
2O	Island Air Service	N
2P	Puerto Rico Air Management Services	N
2P	Air Philippines	RP
2Q	Air Cargo Carriers	N
2Q	Avitrans Nordic	SE
2R	Sud d'Or International Airlines	4X
2T	Tulpar Air Service	UP
2U	Air Guinee Express	3X
2W	Welcome Air	OE
2Z	Vaso Airlines	RA
3B	Central Connect Airlines	OK
3D	Denim Air	PH
3F	Pacific Airways	N
3G	Atlant-Soyuz Airlines	RA
3H	Air Inuit	C
3K	Everts Air Cargo	N
3K	Jetstar Asia Airways	9V
3L	Intersky	OE
3M	Gulfstream International	N
3N	Air Urga	UR
3O	Peau Vava'u Air	A3
3O	Air Arabia Maroc	CN
3P	Tiara Air	P4
3R	Moskoviya	RA
3S	Air Antilles Express	F
3S	Air Guyane Express	F
3S	Aeroland Airways	SX
3T	Turanair	4K
3U	Sichuan Airlines	B
3V	TNT Airways	OO
3X	Japan Air Commuter	JA
3Y	Kartika Airlines	PK
3Z	Everts Air Alaska	N
3Z	Zoom Airways	S2
4A	Air Kiribati	T3
4B	Perimeter Aviation	C
4B	Aviastar - Tupolev	RA
4C	Click Airways	EX
4C	Aires	HK
4C	Tapo-Avia	UK
4E	Tanana Air Service	N
4G	Gazpromavia	RA
4H	United Airways	S2
4I	Izmir Airlines	TC
4K	Kenn Borek Air	C
4M	LAN Argentina	LV
4N	Air North	C
4O	Interjet	XA
4P	Viking Airlines	SE
4P	Business Aviation of Congo	9Q
4R	Hamburg International	D
4T	Belair Airlines	HB
4U	Germanwings	D
4U	Tavaj Linhas Aereas	PP
4W	Warbelow's Air	N
4Y	Airbus Transport International	F
4Y	Flight Alaska	N
4Z	Airlink	ZS
5A	Alpine Air Express	N
5B	Euro Asia International	UP
5C	Air Tahoma	N
5C	Naturair	TI
5C	Cargo Air Lines	4X
5D	Aeromexico Connect	XA
5E	SGA Airlines	HS
5F	Arctic Circle Air Service	N
5F	Best Air	TC
5G	Skyservices Airlines	C
5H	Fly540	5Y
5I	Transavia Service	4L
5J	Cebu Pacific Air	RP
5K	Hi Fly	CS
5K	Odessa Airlines	UR
5L	Aerosur	CP
5M	Murray Air	N
5M	Sibaviatrans	RA
5N	Arkhangelsk 2nd Aviation Enterprise	RA
5N	Nordavia Regional Airlines	RA
5O	Europe Airpost	F
5P	PENTA - Pena Transportes Aereos	PP
5Q	Best Air	S2
5R	Custom Air Transport	N
5R	Karthago Airlines	TS
5S	Sapair	HI
5T	Canadian North	C
5T	Transwede	SE
5U	LADE	LV
5U	Challenge Aero	UR
5V	Lviv Airlines	UR
5W	Astraeus	G
5X	UPS Airlines	N
5Y	Isles of Scilly Skybus	G
5Y	Atlas Air	N
5Z	Bismillah Airlines	S2
6A	Aviacsa	XA
6B	Tuifly Nordic	SE
6D	Pelita Air	PK
6E	Indigo Airlines	VT
6F	Ufly Airways	N
6F	Afrijet Airlines	5N
6H	Israir	4X
6I	Aviast Air	RA
6I	International Business Air	SE
6I	Euroair	SX
6J	Skynet Asia Airways	JA
6J	Jubba Airways	6O
6K	Zest Airways	RP
6M	Air Minas	PP
6N	Aerosucre	HK
6N	Nordic Airways	SE
6O	Air Satellite	C
6R	Alrosa Aviation	RA
6R	Aerounion	XA
6S	Star Air International	AP
6S	Kato Airline	LN
6T	Air Mandalay	XY
6U	Air Cargo Germany	D
6V	Axis Airways	F
6V	MRK Airlines	UR
6W	Saratov Airlines	RA
6Y	LAT Charter	YL
6Y	Smartlynx	YL
6Z	Panavia Cargo Airlines	HP
6Z	Van Air Europe	OK
6Z	Ukrainian Cargo Airways	UR
7A	Air Next	JA
7C	Jeju Air	HL
7D	Donbassaero	UR
7E	Aeroline	D
7E	Evergreen Helicopters	N

7E	Firefly	9M
7F	First Air	C
7G	British Global	G
7G	Starflyer	JA
7H	Era Aviation	N
7H	Corendon Air	TC
7I	Insel Air International	PJ
7I	Coastal Aviation	5H
7J	Tajik Air	EY
7K	Kolavia	RA
7L	Aerocaribbean	CU
7M	Air Atlantique	G
7N	Inland Aviation Services	N
7P	Batavia Air	PK
7Q	Pan Am Dominica	HI
7Q	Air Libya	5A
7R	BRA - Brasil Rodo Aereo	PP
7S	Arctic Transportation Services	N
7T	Air Glaciers	HB
7T	Trans Am	HC
7T	Wind Rose	UR
7T	Tobruk Air	5A
7U	Aviaenergo	RA
7V	Pelican Air Services	ZS
7Y	Flying Carpet Air Transport Services	OD
7Y	Mid Airlines	ST
8A	Atlas Blue	CN
8A	Arrow Panama	HP
8C	East Star Airlines	B
8C	ATI - Air Transport International	N
8D	Interavia Airlines	RA
8D	Expo Air	4R
8E	Bering Air	N
8H	Highland Airways	G
8I	Myair	I
8J	Jet4You	CN
8K	K-Mile Air	HS
8L	Lucky Airlines	B
8M	Myanmar Airways International	XY
8N	Barents Skylink	SE
8O	West Coast Air	C
8P	Pacific Coastal Airlines	C
8Q	Baker Aviation	N
8Q	Onur Air	TC
8R	SOL Lineas Aereas	LV
8R	Trip Linhas Aereas	PP
8T	Air Tindi	C
8U	Afriqiyah Airways	5A
8V	Wright Air Service	N
8V	Astral Aviation	5Y
8W	Private Wings	D
8Y	China Postal Airlines	B
8Y	Air Burundi	9U
8Z	Wizz Air Bulgaria	LZ
9D	Toumai Air Chad	TT
9H	Dutch Antilles Express	PJ
9K	Cape Air	N
9L	Colgan Air	N
9M	Central Mountain Air	C
9N	Satena	HK
9N	JP Express	JA
9O	Inter - transportes Aereos Inter	TG
9O	National Airways Cameroon	TJ
9S	Spring Airlines	B
9S	Southern Air	N
9T	Transwest Air	C
9T	ACT Airlines	TC
9U	Air Moldova	ER
9V	Avior Airlines	YV
9W	Jet Airways	VT
9X	Itali Airlines	I
A2	Cielos Airlines	OB
A3	Aegean Airlines	SX
A5	Airlinair	F
A6	Air Alps Aviation	OE
A7	Air Comet	EC
A8	Benin Golf Air	TY
A9	Airzena - Georgian Airlines	4L
AA	American Airlines	N
AB	AirBerlin	D
AC	Air Canada	C
AE	Mandarin Airlines	B
AF	Air France	F
AG	Air Contractors	EI
AH	Air Algerie	7T
AI	Air India	VT
AI	Air India Express	VT
AJ	Aero Contractors	5N
AK	Airasia	9M
AL	Trans Avia Export Cargo Airlines	EW
AL	Alsair	F
AI	Midwest Connect	N
AM	Aeromexico	XA
AO	Avianova	RA
AR	Aerolineas Argentinas	LV
AS	Alaska Airlines	N
AT	Royal Air Maroc	CN
AU	Austral Lineas Aereas	LV
AV	Avianca	HK
AW	CHC Airways	PH
AW	Dirgantara Air Service	PK
AX	American Connection	N
AY	Finnair	OH
AZ	Alitalia	I
B2	Belavia Belarussian Airlines	EW
B3	Bellview Airlines	5N
B4	Bankair	N
B4	Zanair	5H
B5	East African Express	5Y
B6	Jetblue Airways	N
B7	Uni Air	B
B8	Botir-Avia	EX
B8	Eritrean Airlines	E3
B9	Iran Air Tour Airline	EP
BA	British Airways	G
BB	Seaborne Airlines	N
BC	Skymark Airlines	JA
BD	BMI	G
BD	BMI Regional	G
BD	Servant Air	N
BE	FlyBe	G
BF	Bluebird Cargo	TF
BF	Aeroservice	TN
BF	Vincent Aviation (Australia)	VH
BG	Biman Bangladesh Airlines	S2
BH	Hawkair Aviation Service	C
BI	Royal Brunei Airlines	V8
BJ	Nouvelair	TS
BK	Okair	B
BL	Jetstar Pacific Airlines	VN
BP	Air Botswana	A2
BR	EVA Airways	B
BS	British International	G
BT	Air Baltic	YL
BV	Blu Express.com	I
BV	Blue Panorama Airlines	I
BW	Caribbean Airlines	9Y
BX	Air Busan	HL
BY	Thomsonfly.com	G
BZ	Keystone Air Service	C
BZ	Blue Dart Aviation	VT
C0	Centralwings	SP
C4	Zimex Aviation	HB
C6	Canjet	C
C7	Rico Linhas Aereas	PP
C7	Samarkand Airways	UK
C8	Cargolux Italia	I
C9	Cirrus Airlines	D
CA	Air China	B
CA	Air China Cargo	B
CB	Scotairways	G
CC	Air Atlanta	TF
CC	Macair Airlines	VH
CD	Alliance Air	VT
CF	City Airline	SE
CG	Airlines of Papua New Guinea	P2
CH	Bemidji Airlines	N
CI	China Airlines	B
CJ	BA Cityflyer	G

CK	China Cargo Airlines	B
CL	Lufthansa Cityline	D
CM	Copa Airlines	HP
CN	Grand China Airlines	B
CN	Island Nationair	P2
CO	Continental Airlines	N
CO	Continental Connection	N
CO	Continental Express	N
CO	Expressjet Airlines	N
CU	Cubana de Aviacion	CU
CV	Cargolux Airlines International	LX
CV	Air Chathams	ZK
CW	Airline of the Marshall Islands	V7
CX	Cathay Pacific Airways	B
CY	Cyprus Airways	5B
CZ	China Southern Airlines	B
D0	DHL Air	G
D2	Severstal Aircompany	RA
D3	Daallo Airlines	J2
D4	Alidaunia	I
D5	DHL Aero Expresso	HP
D6	Inter-Air	ZS
D9	Donavia	RA
DB	Brit'Air	F
DC	Golden Air	SE
DD	Nok Air	HS
DE	Condor	D
DG	South East Asian Airlines	RP
DJ	Virgin Blue Airlines	VH
DJ	Pacific Blue	ZK
DK	Thomas Cook Scandinavia	OY
DL	Delta Airlines	N
DL	Delta Connection	N
DO	Air Vallee	I
DQ	Coastal Air Transport	N
DS	Easyjet Switzerland	HB
DT	TAAG Angola Airlines	D2
DU	Hemus Air	LZ
DV	Scat Aircompany	UP
DW	Aero-Charter Ukraine	UR
DX	Danish Air Transport	OY
DY	Norwegian	LN
E3	Domodedovo Airlines	RA
E5	Samara Airlines	RA
E7	Estafeta Carga Aerea	XA
E9	Boston-Maine Airways	N
EC	Avialeasing	UK
ED	AirBlue	AP
EF	Strategic Airlines	VH
EH	Air Nippon Network	JA
EI	Aer Lingus	EI
EJ	New England Airlines	N
EK	Emirates	A6
EL	Air Nippon	JA
EM	Aero Benin	TY
EN	Air Dolomiti	I
EO	Hewa Bora Airways	9Q
EP	Iran Aseman Airlines	EP
EQ	TAME	HC
ER	Astar Air Cargo	N
ES	DHL International Aviation	A9C
ET	Ethiopian Airlines	ET
EU	United Eagle Airlines	B
EW	Eurowings	D
EX	Air Santo Domingo	HI
EY	Etihad Airways	A6
EZ	Evergreen International Airlines	N
EZ	Sun-Air of Scandinavia	OY
F3	Sky King	N
F4	Shanghai Airlines International Cargo	B
F5	Cosmic Air	9N
F7	Flybaboo	HB
F9	Frontier Airlines	N
FA	Safair	ZS
FB	Bulgaria Air	LZ
FC	Falcon Express Cargo Airlines	A6
FC	Finncomm Airlines	OH
FD	Thai Airasia	HS
FG	Ariana Afghan Airlines	YA
FI	Icelandair	TF

FJ	Air Pacific	DQ
FK	Keewatin Air	C
FK	Kivalliq Air	C
FL	Airtran Airways	N
FM	Shanghai Airlines	B
FN	Regional Air Lines	CN
FO	Airlines of Tasmania	VH
FP	Freedom Air	N
FQ	Thomas Cook Airlines Belgium	OO
FQ	Brindabella Airlines	VH
FR	Ryanair	EI
FV	Rossiya Russian Airlines	RA
FW	Ibex Airlines	JA
FX	Federal Express	N
FZ	FlyDubai	A6
G0	Ghana International Airlines	9G
G1	Gorkha Airlines	9N
G2	Avirex	TR
G3	Gol Transportes Aereos	PP
G3	Sky Express	SX
G4	Allegiant Air	N
G5	China Express Airlines	B
G5	Island Air	VP-C
G8	Go Air	VT
G9	Air Arabia	A6
GA	Garuda Indonesia	PK
GB	ABX Air	N
GD	Granstar Cargo Airlines	B
GD	Air Alpha Greenland	OY
GE	Transasia Airways	B
GF	Gulf Air	A9C
GI	Itek Air	EX
GJ	Eurofly	I
GL	Air Greenland	OY
GM	Air Slovakia	OM
GO	Kuzu Cargo Airlines	TC
GR	Aurigny Air Services	G
GS	Tianjin Airlines	B
GV	XL Airways Germany	D
GV	Grant Aviation	N
GW	Kuban Airlines	RA
GX	Pacificair	RP
GY	Tri-MG Intra-Asia Airlines	PK
GY	Gabon Airlines	TR
GZ	Air Rarotonga	E5
H2	Sky Airline	CC
H3	Harbour Air Seaplanes	C
H5	Hola Airlines	EC
H6	Hageland Aviation Services	N
H7	Eagle Air	5X
H8	Dalavia	RA
HA	Hawaiian Airlines	N
HD	Air Do	JA
HE	LGW - Luftfahrtgesellschaft Walter	D
HG	Niki	OE
HI	Papillon Grand Helicopters	N
HJ	Hellas jet	SX
HJ	Tasman Cargo Airlines	VH
HK	Four Star Air Cargo	N
HK	Yangon Airlines	XY
HM	Air Seychelles	S7
HN	Heavylift Cargo Airlines	VH
HO	Juneyao Airlines	B
HS	Direktflyg	SE
HT	Aeromost Kharkov	UR
HU	Chang An Airlines	B
HU	China Xinhua Airlines	B
HU	Hainan Airlines	B
HV	Transavia Airlines	PH
HW	North Wright Airways	C
HW	Hello	HB
HX	Hong Kong Airlines	B
HX	Trans North Aviation	N
HY	Uzbekistan Airways	UK
HZ	SAT Airlines	RA
I4	Interstate Airlines	PH
I6	Sky Eyes Aviation	HS
I7	Paramount Airways	VT
I9	Air Italy	I
IA	Iraqi Airways	YI

IB	Iberia	EC
ID	Interlink Airlines	ZS
IE	Solomons	H4
IF	Islas Airways	EC
IG	Meridiana	I
II	IBC Airways	N
IJ	Great Wall Airlines	B
IK	Imair	4K
IM	Menajet	OD
IN	MAT Macedonian Air Transport	Z3
IP	Atyrau Air Ways	UP
IQ	Augsburg Airways	D
IR	Iran Air	EP
IS	Island Airlines	N
IT	Kingfisher Airlines	VT
IT	Kingfisher Red	VT
IU	Hevi-Lift	P2
IV	Windjet	I
IW	Wings Air	PK
IY	Yemenia	7O
IZ	Arkia Israeli Airlines	4X

J0	Jetlink Express	5Y
J2	Azerbaijan Airlines	4K
J3	Northwestern Air	C
J4	Buffalo Airways	C
J4	Jordan International Air Cargo	JY
J5	Donghai Airlines	B
J5	Alaska Seaplane Service	N
J6	Cruiser Taxi Aero Brasil	PP
J7	Centre-Avia Airlines	RA
J8	Berjaya Air Charter	9M
J9	Jazeera Airways	9K
JA	BH Airlines	E9
JB	HeliJet International	C
JC	JAL Express	JA
JD	Deer Airlines	B
JE	Mango	ZS
JF	LAB Flying Service	N
JH	Fuji Dream Airlines	JA
JI	Jade Cargo International	B
JI	Eastern Caribbean Air	N
JJ	TAM Linhas Aereas	PP
JK	Spanair	EC
JL	J-Air	JA
JL	Japan Airlines	JA
JM	Air Jamaica	6Y
JP	Adria Airways	S5
JQ	Jetstar Airways	VH
JS	Air Koryo	P
JT	Lion Airlines	PK
JU	JAT Airways	YU
JV	Bearskin Airlines	C
JW	Arrow Cargo	N
JY	Air Turks & Caicos	VQ-T
JZ	Skyways Express	SE

K2	EuroLot	SP
K3	Taquan Air Service	N
K4	Kalitta Air	N
K5	Wings of Alaska	N
K6	Cambodia Angkor Air	XT
K7	Yakutia Airlines	RA
KA	Dragonair	B
KB	Druk Air	A5
KC	Air Astana	UP
KD	KD Avia	RA
KE	Korean Air	HL
KF	Blue1	OH
KG	Aerogaviota	CU
KG	Linea Aerea Iaaca	YV
KK	Atlasjet International	TC
KL	KLM Royal Dutch Airlines	PH
KM	Air Malta	9H
KN	China United Airlines	B
KN	Maroomba Airlines	VH
KO	Alaska Central Express	N
KQ	Kenya Airways	5Y
KR	Comores Aviation	D6
KR	Kitty Hawk Aircargo	N
KS	Penair	N
KU	Kuwait Airways	9K
KV	KMV Mineralnye Vody Airlines	RA
KW	Kelowna Flightcraft Air Charter	C
KX	Cayman Airways	VP-C
KY	Kunming Airlines	B
KZ	Nippon Cargo Airlines	JA

L2	Lynden Air Cargo	N
L3	DHL de Guatemala	TG
L5	CHC Helikopter Service	LN
L5	Lufttransport	LN
L6	Tbilaviamsheni	4L
LA	LAN Airlines	CC
LB	LAB Airlines	CP
LB	Lobaye Airways	TL
LC	Varig Log	PP
LD	Air Hong Kong	B
LD	Linea Turistica Aereotuy	YV
LE	Lugansk Aviation Enterprise	UR
LF	Flynordic	SE
LG	Luxair	LX
LH	Lufthansa	D
LH	Lufthansa Cargo	D
LI	LIAT - The Caribbean Airline	V2
LJ	Jin Air	HL
LL	Miami Air International	N
LM	Livingston	I
LN	Libyan Airlines	5A
LO	LOT - Polish Airlines	SP
LP	LAN Peru	OB
LS	Jet2	G
LU	LAN Express	CC
LV	Albanian Airlines	ZA
LW	Pacific Wings	N
LX	Swiss International Airlines	HB
LY	El Al Israel Airlines	4X
LZ	Belleair	ZA

M2	Mahfooz Aviation	C5
M3	North Flying	OY
M3	ABSA Cargo	PP
M4	Nova Air	XA
M5	Kenmore Air	N
M6	Amerijet International	N
M7	Marsland Aviation	ST
M7	Superior Aviation Services	5Y
M9	Motor Sich Airlines	UR
MA	Malev	HA
MB	MNG Cargo Airlines	TC
ME	Middle East Airlines	OD
MF	Xiamen Airlines	B
MG	Midex Airlines	A6
MH	Malaysia Airlines	9M
MI	Silkair	9V
MJ	Mihin Lanka	4R
MK	Air Mauritius	3B
ML	Trans Attico	ST
MM	Euro Atlantic Airways	CS
MM	SAM Colombia	HK
MN	Comair	ZS
MO	Calm Air	C
MP	Martinair	PH
MQ	American Eagle	N
MS	Egyptair	SU
MT	Thomas Cook Airlines	G
MU	China Eastern Airlines	B
MW	Maya Island Air	V3
MX	Manx2 Airlines	G
MX	Mexicana	XA
MY	Midwest Airlines Egypt	SU
MY	MAS Air Cargo	XA
MZ	Merpati Nusantara Airlines	PK

N2	Daghestan Airlines	RA
N2	Kabo Air	5N
N4	Trans Air Benin	TY
N5	Skagway Air Service	N
N6	Air One Nine	5A
N9	Nordic Solutions Air Services	LY
N9	North Coast Aviation	P2
NA	North American Airlines	N
NC	Northern Air Cargo	N
NC	Cobham Aviation Services Australia	VH

NE	Skyeurope Airline	OM
NF	Air Vanuatu	YJ
NH	ANA - All Nippon Airways	JA
NI	Portugalia Airlines	CS
NK	Spirit Airlines	N
NL	Shaheen Air International	AP
NN	Vim Airlines	RA
NO	Neos	I
NP	Skytrans Regional	VH
NQ	Air Japan	JA
NR	Pamir Air	YA
NS	Northeast Airlines	B
NT	Binter Canarias	EC
NU	Japan Transocean Air	JA
NV	Air Central	JA
NX	Air Macau	B
NY	Air Iceland	TF
NZ	Air New Zealand	ZK
NZ	Air New Zealand Link	ZK
O2	Jet Air	SP
O3	Bellview Airlines	9L
O4	Antrak Air Ghana	9G
O7	Ozjet Airlines	VH
OA	Olympic Airways	SX
OB	Boliviana de Aviacion	CP
OC	Omni - Aviacao e Tecnologia	CS
OF	Air Finland	OH
OG	One-Two Go	HS
OG	Ghadames Air Transport	5A
OI	Aspiring Air	ZK
OJ	Overland Airways	5N
OK	CSA Czech Airlines	OK
OL	OLT - Ostfriesische Lufttransport	D
OM	MIAT - Mongolian Airlines	JU
ON	Our Airline	C2
OO	Skywest Airlines	N
OQ	Chongqing Airlines	B
OR	Arkefly	PH
OS	Austrian Airlines	OE
OT	Aeropelican Air Services	VH
OU	Croatia Airlines	9A
OV	Estonian Air	ES
OV	Estonian Air Regional	ES
OX	Orient Thai Airlines	HS
OY	Omni Air International	N
OZ	Asiana Airlines	HL
P2	Airkenya	5Y
P4	Aerolineas Sosa	HR
P5	Aerorepublica Colombia	HK
P6	Transair	N
P7	Russian Sky Airlines	RA
P8	Pantanal	PP
P9	Perm Airlines	RA
PA	Florida Coastal Airlines	N
PB	Provincial Airlines	C
PC	Air Fiji	DQ
PC	Continental Airways	RA
PD	Porter Airlines	C
PF	Primera Air Scandinavia	OY
PF	Palestinian Airlines	SU-Y
PG	Bangkok Airways	HS
PH	Transavia Denmark	OY
PH	Polynesian Airlines	5W
PI	Pacific Sun	DQ
PJ	Air St Pierre	F
PK	Pakistan International Airlines	AP
PL	Southern Air Charter	C6
PL	Airstars Airways	RA
PM	Tropic Air Commuter	V3
PN	West China Airlines	B
PO	Polar Air Cargo	N
PR	Philippine Airlines	RP
PS	Ukraine International Airlines	UR
PT	Capital Cargo International Airlines	N
PT	West Air Europe	SE
PU	Pluna Lineas Aereas Uruguayas	CX
PV	Panair Lineas Aereas	EC
PV	St Barth Commuter	F
PW	Precisionair	5H
PX	Air Niugini	P2

PY	Surinam Airways	PZ
PZ	TAM Mercosur	ZP
Q2	Island Aviation Services	8Q
Q3	Zambian Airways	9J
Q5	40 Mile Air	N
Q6	Aerocondor	OB
Q8	Pacific East Asia Cargo Airlines	RP
Q8	Transair Congo	TN
QA	Click Mexicana	XA
QB	Sky Georgia	4L
QD	Air Class	CX
QE	Air Moorea	F
QF	QANTAS Airways	VH
QF	Qantaslink	VH
QH	Kyrgyzstan	EX
QI	Cimber Air	OY
QK	Air Canada Jazz	C
QL	Laser	YV
QL	Aero Lanka Airlines	4R
QM	Air Malawi	7Q
QN	Air Armenia	EK
QO	Quantum Air	EC
QQ	Alliance Airlines	VH
QR	Qatar Airways	A7
QS	Smartwings	OK
QS	Travel Service Airlines	OK
QT	Tampa Airlines	HK
QT	Regional Air	P2
QU	East African Airlines	5X
QV	Lao Airlines	RDPL
QW	Blue Wings	D
QX	Horizon Air	N
QY	European Air Transport	OO
QZ	Indonesia Airasia	PK
R0	Royal Airlines	AP
R2	Orenair	RA
R5	Jordan Aviation	JY
R6	Danu Oro Transportas	LY
R6	RACSA	TG
R7	Aserca Airlines	YV
R8	Kyrghyzstan Airlines	EX
RA	Nepal Airlines	9N
RB	Syrianair	YK
RC	Atlantic Airways	OY
RD	Ryan International Airlines	N
RE	Aer Arann	EI
RF	Florida West International Airlines	N
RG	Varig	PP
RH	Robin Hood Aviation	OE
RH	RPX Airlines	PK
RI	Mandala Airlines	PK
RJ	Royal Jordanian	JY
RK	Royal Khmer Airlines	XU
RL	Royal Phnom Penh Airways	XU
RO	Tarom	YR
RQ	Kam Air	YA
RT	Rak Airlines	A6
RU	Airbridge Cargo	RA
RU	Skyking Airlines	VQ-T
RV	Caspian Airlines	EP
RY	Royal Wings Airlines	JY
RZ	Sansa Regional	TI
S0	Slok Air International	C5
S2	Jetlite	VT
S3	Santa Barbara Airlines	YV
S4	SARA Internacional	CS
S5	Trast Aero	EX
S5	Shuttle America	N
S6	Salmon Air	N
S6	Star Air	OY
S7	S7 Airlines	RA
S8	Shovkovly Shlyah	UR
SA	South African Airways	ZS
SB	Aircalin	F
SC	Shandong Airlines	B
SD	Sudan Airways	ST
SE	XL Airways France	F
SF	Tassili Airlines	7T
SG	Spicejet	VT

Code	Airline	Reg.
SI	Sierra Pacific Airlines	N
SJ	Sriwijaya Air	PK
SK	Scandinavian Airline System	SE
SO	Superior Aviation	N
SP	SATA Air Acores	CS
SQ	Singapore Airlines	9V
SQ	Singapore Airlines Cargo	9V
SS	Corsair	F
ST	Germania	D
SU	Aeroflot Cargo	RA
SU	Aeroflot Russian Airlines	RA
SV	Saudi Arabian Airlines	HZ
SW	Air Namibia	V5
SY	Sun Country Airlines	N
SY	Skippers Aviation	VH
T0	TACA Peru	OB
T2	Nakina Outpost Camps and Air	C
T3	Eastern Airways	G
T5	Turkmenistan Airlines	EZ
T6	Tavrey Aircompany	UR
T7	Twin Jet	F
TA	TACA International Airlines	YS
TB	Jetairfly	OO
TC	Air Tanzania	5H
TE	FlyLAL	LY
TF	Malmo Aviation	SE
TG	Thai Airways	HS
TH	Transmile Air Services	9M
TI	Tolair Services	N
TI	TACA Costa Rica	TI
TK	Turkish Airlines	TC
TL	Airnorth Regional	VH
TL	Chartair	VH
TM	LAM - Linhas Aereas de Mocambique	C9
TN	Air Tahiti Nui	F
TO	Transavia France	F
TO	President Airlines	XU
TP	TAP Air Portugal	CS
TQ	Tandem-Aero	ER
TR	Tiger Airways	9V
TS	Air Transat	C
TT	Tiger Airways	VH
TU	Tunisair	TS
TV	Brussels Airlines	OO
TX	Air Caraibes	F
TX	Air Caraibes Atlantique	F
TY	Iberworld Airlines	EC
TY	Air Caledonie	F
U2	Easyjet Airlines	G
U3	Avies Air Company	ES
U4	PMT Air	XU
U5	USA 3000 Airlines	N
U6	Ural Airlines	RA
U7	Air Uganda	5X
U8	Armavia	EK
U9	Tatarstan Air	RA
UA	United Air Lines	N
UA	United Express	N
UB	Myanma Airways	XY
UC	LAN Cargo	CC
UD	Hex'Air	F
UF	Um Air	UR
UG	Sevenair	TS
UI	Eurocypria Airlines	5B
UL	Srilankan	4R
UM	Air Zimbabwe	Z
UN	Transaero Airlines	RA
UO	Hong Kong Express Airways	B
UO	Sky Shuttle Helicopters	B
UP	Bahamasair	C6
UR	Utair Express	RA
US	US Airways	N
UT	Utair Airlines	RA
UU	Air Austral	F
UV	Helisureste	EC
UW	Uni-Top Airlines	B
UX	Air Europa	EC
UY	Cameroon Airlines	TJ
UZ	Tesis	RA
UZ	Buraq Air	5A
V0	Conviasa	YV
V3	Carpatair	YR
V4	Reem Airlines	EX
V4	Volaris	XA
V4	Venescar International	YV
V5	Danube Wings	OM
V5	Avolar Aerolineas	XA
V6	VIP - Vuelos Internos Privados	HC
V6	Voyager Airlines	S2
V7	Air Senegal International	6V
V8	Air Mikisew	C
V8	Iliamna Air Taxi	N
V8	Atran - Aviatrans Cargo Airlines	RA
VC	Voyageur Airways	C
VD	Kunpeng Airlines	B
VE	Volareweb	I
VF	Valuair	9V
VG	VLM Airlines	OO
VH	Aeropostal	YV
VI	Volga-Dnepr Airlines	RA
VJ	Jatayu Air	PK
VK	Nigerian Eagle Airlines	5N
VL	VIA - Air Via	LZ
VN	Vietnam Airlines	VN
VQ	Vintage Prop and Jets	N
VR	TACV - Transportes Aereos de Cabo Verde	D4
VS	Virgin Atlantic Airways	G
VT	Air Tahiti	F
VU	Air Ivoire	TU
VV	Aerosvit Airlines	UR
VW	Aeromar Airlines	XA
VX	Virgin America	N
VY	Vueling Airlines	EC
W3	Arik Air	5N
W4	M & N Aviation	N
W5	Mahan Air	EP
W6	Wizz Air	HA
W7	Sayakhat	UP
W8	Cargojet Airways	C
W9	Air Bagan	XY
WA	KLM Cityhopper	PH
WB	Rwandair Express	9XR
WC	Islena Airlines	HR
WE	WDL Aviation	D
WE	Centurion II Air Cargo	N
WF	Wideroe's Flyveselskap	LN
WG	Sunwing Airlines	C
WI	Tradewinds Cargo	N
WJ	Air Labrador	C
WK	Edelweiss Air	HB
WL	Aeroperlas	HP
WM	Winair	PJ
WN	Southwest Airlines	N
WO	World Airways	N
WP	Island Air	N
WQ	Romavia	YR
WS	Westjet	C
WT	Wasaya Airways	C
WU	Wizz Air Ukraine	UR
WW	BMIBaby	G
WX	City Jet	EI
WY	Oman Air	A4O
X3	Tuifly	D
X7	Air Service Gabon	TR
X8	Icaro Express	HC
X9	Khors Air	UR
XA	Blue Islands	G
XC	KD Air	C
XF	Vladivostok Air	RA
XG	Clickair	EC
XK	CCM Airlines	F
XL	LAN Ecuador	HC
XM	Alitalia Express	I
XM	Australian Air Express	VH
XN	Xpress Air	PK
XP	Xtra Airways	N
XQ	Sunexpress	TC
XR	Skywest Airlines	VH
XT	Skystar Airways	HS

XU	African Express Airways	5Y
XW	Skyexpress	RA
XZ	South African Express Airways	ZS
Y2	Flyglobespan	G
Y5	Pace Airlines	N
Y8	Yangtze River Express	B
Y9	Kish Air	EP
YA	Yeti Airlines	9N
YD	Gomelavia	EW
YD	Mauritania Airways	5T
YE	Eram Air	EP
YG	South Airlines	UR
YI	Air Sunshine	N
YJ	AMC Airlines	SU
YK	KTHY Cyprus Turkish Airlines	TC
YL	Yamal Airlines	RA
YM	Montenegro Airlines	4O
YN	Air Creebec	C
YO	Heli Air Monaco	3A
YQ	Polet Aviakompania	RA
YR	Scenic Airlines	N
YS	Regional	F
YV	Mesa Airlines	N
YW	Air Nostrum	EC
YX	Midwest Airlines	N

Z3	Promech Air	N
Z3	Avient Aviation	Z
Z5	GMG Airlines	S2
Z6	Dnepr-Air	UR
Z8	Amaszonas Transportes Aereos	CP
Z9	Delta Connection	5Y
ZB	Monarch Airlines	G
ZD	Dolphin Air	A6
ZE	Arcus Air	D
ZF	Atlantic Airlines	HR
ZG	Viva Macau	B
ZH	Shenzhen Airlines	B
ZI	Aigle Azur	F
ZK	Great Lakes Airlines	N
ZL	Air Link	VH
ZL	REX - Regional Express	VH
ZM	Cityline Hungary	HA
ZN	Naysa Aerotaxis	EC
ZP	Air St Thomas	N
ZP	Silk Way Airlines	4K
ZR	Aviacon Zitotrans	RA
ZR	Air Sinai	SU
ZS	Sama Airlines	HZ
ZT	Titan Airways	G
ZV	Air Midwest	N
ZX	Air Georgian	C
ZY	Ada Air	ZA

ICAO THREE-LETTER DESIGNATORS

AAF	Aigle Azur	F
AAG	Air Atlantique	G
AAG	Atlantic Reconnaissance	G
AAL	American Airlines	N
AAP	Aerovista Airlines	EX
AAQ	Copterline	OH
AAR	Asiana Airlines	HL
AAW	Afriqiyah Airways	5A
AAY	Allegiant Air	N
ABA	Artem Avia	UR
ABD	Air Atlanta	TF
ABF	Scanwings	OH
ABG	Abakan-Avia	RA
ABJ	Abaete Linhas Aereas	PP
ABK	Alberta Citylink	C
ABL	Air Busan	HL
ABO	APSA - Aeroexpreso Bogota	HK
ABQ	AirBlue	AP
ABR	Air Contractors	EI
ABS	Transwest Air	C
ABV	Antrak Air Ghana	9G
ABW	Airbridge Cargo	RA
ABX	ABX Air	N
ABY	Air Arabia	A6
ABZ	ATA Brasil	PP
ACA	Air Canada	C
ACD	Academy Airlines	N
ACE	Meridian Airways	9G
ACI	Aircalin	F
ACL	Itali Airlines	I
ACP	Astral Aviation	5Y
ACT	Flight Line	N
ACX	Air Cargo Germany	D
ADB	Antonov Airlines	UR
ADE	Ada Air	ZA
ADI	Audeli	EC
ADO	Air Do	JA
ADR	Adria Airways	S5
ADS	Aviones de Sonora	XA
AEA	Air Europa	EC
AEB	Aero Benin	TY
AEE	Aegean Airlines	SX
AEK	Aerocon	CP
AEN	Aeroland Airways	SX
AEQ	MCA Airlines	SE
AER	Alaska Central Express	N
AEU	Astraeus	G
AEW	Aerosvit Airlines	UR
AEY	Air Italy	I
AFE	Airfast Indonesia	PK
AFG	Ariana Afghan Airlines	YA
AFL	Aeroflot Russian Airlines	RA
AFR	Air France	F
AFW	Great Barrier Airlines	ZK
AGB	Air Service Gabon	TR
AGO	Angola Air Charter	D2
AGU	Angara Airlines	RA
AGV	Air Glaciers	HB
AGX	Aviogenex	YU
AHA	Air Alpha Greenland	OY
AHC	Azal Cargo	4K
AHF	Aspen Helicopters	N
AHK	Air Hong Kong	B
AHT	HTA Helicopters	CS
AHU	ABC Air Hungary	HA
AHW	Aeromost Kharkov	UR
AHX	Amakusa Airlines	JA
AHY	Azerbaijan Airlines	4K
AIA	Avies Air Company	ES
AIC	Air India	VT
AIE	Air Inuit	C
AIN	African International Airways	3D
AIP	Alpine Air Express	N
AIQ	Thai Airasia	HS
AIT	Airest	ES
AIZ	Arkia Israeli Airlines	4X
AJI	Ameristar Air Charter	N
AJK	Allied Air Cargo	5N
AJM	Air Jamaica	6Y

AJT	Amerijet International	N
AJV	JP Express	JA
AJX	Air Japan	JA
AKF	Anikay Air	EX
AKM	Mak Air	UP
AKN	Alkan Air	C
AKY	Yak Service	RA
ALG	Air Logistics	N
ALK	Srilankan	4R
ALX	Hewa Bora Airways	9Q
ALZ	Alta Flights	C
AMA	ATMA	UP
AMC	Air Malta	9H
AMF	Ameriflight	N
AMK	Amerer Air	OE
AML	Air Malawi	7Q
AMP	Aero Transporte	OB
AMU	Air Macau	B
AMV	AMC Airlines	SU
AMW	Air Midwest	N
AMX	Aeromexico	XA
ANA	Air Nippon Airways	JA
ANA	ANA - All Nippon Airways	JA
ANE	Air Nostrum	EC
ANG	Air Niugini	P2
ANH	Al-Ajnihah Aiways	5A
ANK	Air Nippon	JA
ANO	Airnorth Regional	VH
ANQ	ADA - Aerolineas de Antioquia	HK
ANS	Andes Lineas Aereas	LV
ANT	Air North	C
ANU	Starlink Aviation	C
ANX	Canadian North	C
ANZ	Air New Zealand	ZK
AOG	Aero VIP	LV
AOH	North Coast Aviation	P2
APC	Airpac Airlines	N
APF	Amapola Flyg	SE
APO	Aeropro	C
APP	Aeroperlas	HP
APT	LAP - Lineas Aereas Petroleras	HK
APW	Arrow Cargo	N
AQU	Airquarius Aviation	ZS
ARA	Arik Air	5N
ARE	Aires	HK
ARG	Aerolineas Argentinas	LV
ARL	Airlec Air Espace	F
ARR	Air Armenia	EK
ART	Smartlynx	YL
ASA	Alaska Airlines	N
ASB	Air-Spray	C
ASE	Airstars Airways	RA
ASH	Mesa Airlines	N
ASJ	Air Satellite	C
ASM	Awesome Flight Services	ZS
ATC	Air Tanzania	5H
ATG	Aerotrans	UP
ATM	Airlines of Tasmania	VH
ATN	ATI - Air Transport International	N
ATU	Atlant Hungary	HA
AUA	Austrian Airlines	OE
AUB	Augsburg Airways	D
AUI	Ukraine International Airlines	UR
AUL	Nordavia Regional Airlines	RA
AUR	Aurigny Air Services	G
AUT	Austral Lineas Aereas	LV
AVA	Avianca	HK
AVJ	Avia Traffic Company	EX
AVN	Air Vanuatu	YJ
AVW	Aviator Airways	SX
AVX	Avirex	TR
AWC	Titan Airways	G
AWK	Airwork New Zealand	ZK
AWQ	Indonesia Airasia	PK
AWU	Aeroline	D
AWZ	Air West Cargo	ST
AXB	Air India Express	VT
AXF	Tasman Cargo Airlines	VH
AXK	African Express Airways	5Y

AXM	Airasia	9M
AXQ	Action Airlines	N
AXY	Axis Airways	F
AYN	Atlantic Airways	YN
AYT	Ayeet Aviation	4X
AYZ	Atlant-Soyuz Airlines	RA
AZA	Alitalia	I
AZE	Arcus Air	D
AZF	Air Zermatt	HB
AZG	Sakaviaservice	4L
AZH	Sky Wind	4K
AZQ	Silk Way Airlines	4K
AZS	Aviacon Zitotrans	RA
AZU	Azul	PP
AZV	Azov-Avia	UR
AZW	Air Zimbabwe	Z
AZZ	Azza Air Transport	ST
BAB	Bahrain Air	A9C
BAJ	Baker Aviation	N
BAN	British Antarctic Survey	VP-F
BAW	British Airways	G
BBC	Biman Bangladesh Airlines	S2
BBD	Bluebird Cargo	TF
BBO	Flybaboo	HB
BBR	Santa Barbara Airlines	YV
BBT	Air Bashkortostan	RA
BBZ	Bluebird Aviation	5Y
BCI	Blue Islands	G
BCS	European Air Transport	OO
BCY	City Jet	EI
BDA	Blue Dart Aviation	VT
BDI	Benair Air Service	OY
BDR	Badr Airlines	ST
BEA	Best Air	S2
BEC	Berkut State Air Company	UP
BEE	FlyBe	G
BEK	Berkut Air	UP
BER	AirBerlin	D
BET	Beta Cargo Air	PP
BEZ	Air St Kitts & Nevis	V4
BFC	Basler Airlines	N
BFF	Air Nunavut	C
BFL	Buffalo Airways	C
BGA	Airbus Transport International	F
BGH	BH Air	LZ
BGK	British Gulf Airlines	EX
BGL	Benin Golf Air	TY
BGM	Bugulma Air Enterprise	RA
BGT	Bergen Air Transport	LN
BHA	Buddha Air	9N
BHL	Bristow Helicopters	G
BHN	Bristow Helicopters (Nigeria)	5N
BHP	Belair Airlines	HB
BHR	Bighorn Airways	N
BHS	Bahamasair	C6
BID	Binair	D
BIE	Air Mediterranee	F
BIG	Big Island Air	N
BKA	Bankair	N
BKP	Bangkok Airways	HS
BLE	Blue Line	F
BLF	Blue1	OH
BLM	Blue Sky	EK
BLS	Bearskin Airlines	C
BLV	Bellview Airlines	5N
BLX	Tuifly Nordic	SE
BMI	BMI	G
BMI	BMIBaby	G
BMJ	Bemidji Airlines	N
BML	Bismillah Airlines	S2
BMM	Atlas Blue	CN
BMR	BMI Regional	G
BMY	Bimini Island Air	N
BND	Bond Offshore Helicopters	G
BNT	Bentiu Air Transport	ST
BNX	Linea Aerea Iaaca	YV
BOI	2Go	RP
BOL	TAB Cargo	CP
BON	BH Airlines	E9
BOS	Open Skies	F
BOT	Air Botswana	A2
BOV	Boliviana de Aviacion	CP
BOX	Aerologic	D
BPA	Blu Express.com	I
BPA	Blue Panorama Airlines	I
BPS	Budapest Air Services	HA
BRB	BRA - Brasil Rodo Aereo	PP
BRG	Bering Air	N
BRP	Aerobratsk	RA
BRQ	Buraq Air	5A
BRU	Belavia Belarussian Airlines	EW
BRV	Bravo Air Congo	9Q
BRZ	Samara Airlines	RA
BSK	Miami Air International	N
BSL	Air Brasil Cargo	PP
BST	Best Air	TC
BTA	Continental Express	N
BTA	Expressjet Airlines	N
BTI	Air Baltic	YL
BTR	Botir-Avia	EX
BTV	Batavia Air	PK
BUC	Bulgarian Air Charter	LZ
BUE	Orebro Aviation	SE
BUN	Bural	RA
BVT	Berjaya Air Charter	9M
BWA	Caribbean Airlines	9Y
BWG	Blue Wings	D
BXH	Bar XH Air	C
BXR	Redding Aero Enterprises	N
BYA	Berry Aviation	N
BYL	Bylina	RA
BZH	Brit'Air	F
CAI	Corendon Air	TC
CAJ	Air Caraibes Atlantique	F
CAL	China Airlines	B
CAO	Air China Cargo	B
CAT	Copenhagen Airtaxi	OY
CAV	Calm Air	C
CAW	Comair	ZS
CAY	Cayman Airways	VP-C
CBB	Cargo B Airlines	OO
CBC	Caribair	HI
CBE	Click Mexicana	XA
CBT	Catalina Flying Boats	N
CCA	Air China	B
CCE	Cairo Aviation	SU
CCG	Central Connect Airlines	OK
CCI	Capital Cargo International Airlines	N
CCM	CCM Airlines	F
CCQ	Capital City Air Carrier	N
CCY	Cherry-Air	N
CDG	Shandong Airlines	B
CDN	Canadian Helicopters	C
CDP	Aerocondor	OB
CDV	Skol Aviakompania	RA
CEB	Cebu Pacific Air	RP
CEM	Central Mongolian Airlines	JU
CES	China Eastern Airlines	B
CFA	China Flying Dragon Co	B
CFE	BA Cityflyer	G
CFG	Condor	D
CFV	Aero Calafia	XA
CFZ	Zhongfei Airlines	B
CGI	Rusair	RA
CGK	Click Airways	EX
CGL	Seagle Air	OM
CGN	Chang An Airlines	B
CGS	Geodynamica Centre	RA
CHB	West China Airlines	B
CHC	CITIC Offshore Helicopters	B
CHG	Challenge Aero	UR
CHH	Hainan Airlines	B
CHI	Cougar Helicopters	C
CHN	Channel Island Aviation	N
CHP	Aviacsa	XA
CIB	Condor Berlin	D
CID	Asia Continental Airlines	UP
CIG	Sirius Aero	RA
CII	Cityfly	I
CIM	Cimber Air	OY
CIR	Arctic Circle Air Service	N
CIU	Cielos Airlines	OB
CIW	Civair	ZS
CJA	Canjet	C
CJC	Colgan Air	N

CJR	Caverton Helicopters	5N
CJT	Cargojet Airways	C
CKK	China Cargo Airlines	B
CKM	BKS Air	EC
CKS	Kalitta Air	N
CLG	Chalair Aviation	F
CLH	Lufthansa Cityline	D
CLI	Clickair	EC
CLL	Aerovias Castillo	XA
CLW	Centralwings	SP
CLX	Cargolux Airlines International	LX
CME	Prince Edward Air	C
CMN	Cimarron Aire	N
CMP	Copa Airlines	HP
CMS	Aviation Commercial Aviation	C
CNB	Cityline Hungary	HA
CNI	Aerotaxi	CU
CNK	Sunwest Aviation	C
COA	Continental Airlines	N
COA	Continental Connection	N
COX	Comav Aviation	V5
COZ	Cosmic Air	9N
CPA	Cathay Pacific Airways	B
CPB	Corporate Express Airline	C
CPD	Capital Airlines	5Y
CPJ	Corpjet	N
CPM	Compagnie Mauritanienne de Transportes	5T
CPN	Caspian Airlines	EP
CPT	Corporate Air	N
CQH	Spring Airlines	B
CQN	Chongqing Airlines	B
CRC	Conair Aviation	C
CRF	Air Central	JA
CRG	Cargoitalia	I
CRK	Hong Kong Airlines	B
CRL	Corsair	F
CRN	Aerocaribbean	CU
CRQ	Air Creebec	C
CRT	Caribintair	HH
CSA	CSA Czech Airlines	OK
CSC	Sichuan Airlines	B
CSH	Shanghai Airlines	B
CSJ	Castle Aviation	N
CSN	China Southern Airlines	B
CSQ	IBC Airways	N
CSV	Coastal Aviation	5H
CSY	Shuangyang Aviation	B
CSZ	Shenzhen Airlines	B
CTA	Aero Charter	N
CTL	Central Air Southwest	N
CTN	Croatia Airlines	9A
CTP	Tapo-Avia	UK
CTQ	Citylink	9G
CTR	Aerolineas Centauro	XA
CTS	Center-South Airlines	RA
CTT	Custom Air Transport	N
CUA	China United Airlines	B
CUB	Cubana de Aviacion	CU
CUO	Aero Cuahonte	XA
CVA	Air Chathams	ZK
CVC	Centre-Avia Airlines	RA
CVE	Cabo Verde Express	D4
CVU	Grand Canyon Airlines	N
CVV	Comeravia	YV
CWC	Centurion II Air Cargo	N
CWY	Woodgate Executive Air Services	G
CXA	Xiamen Airlines	B
CXH	China Xinhua Airlines	B
CXI	Shan Xi Airlines	B
CXP	Xtra Airways	N
CXS	Boston-Maine Airways	N
CXT	Coastal Air Transport	N
CYP	Cyprus Airways	5B
CYZ	China Postal Airlines	B
DAE	DHL Aero Expresso	HP
DAG	Daghestan Airlines	RA
DAH	Air Algerie	7T
DAL	Delta Airlines	N
DAL	Delta Connection	N
DAO	Daallo Airlines	J2

DAP	Aerovias DAP	CC
DAT	Brussels Airlines	OO
DAV	Dana	5N
DBH	Northeast Airlines	B
DBK	Dubrovnik Airlines	9A
DCD	Air 26	D2
DCL	Transportes Aereos Don Carlos	CC
DCP	Delta Connection	5Y
DCT	Direct Flight	G
DER	Deer Airlines	B
DES	CC Helicopters	C
DHE	DAP Helicopteros	CC
DHK	DHL Air	G
DHL	Astar Air Cargo	N
DHX	DHL International Aviation	A9C
DIR	Dirgantara Air Service	PK
DKH	Juneyao Airlines	B
DKT	Business Aviation Courier	N
DLA	Air Dolomiti	I
DLH	Lufthansa	D
DMJ	Global Air	XA
DMO	Domodedovo Airlines	RA
DNL	Dutch Antilles Express	PJ
DNM	Denim Air	PH
DNU	Danu Oro Transportas	LY
DNV	Donavia	RA
DOC	Norsk Luftambulance	LN
DRK	Druk Air	A5
DRU	Alrosa Aviation	RA
DRY	Deraya Air Taxi	PK
DSM	LAN Argentina	LV
DST	Aex Air	N
DTA	TAAG Angola Airlines	D2
DTH	Tassili Airlines	7T
DTR	Danish Air Transport	OY
DVB	Don Avia	UP
DVR	Divi Divi Air	PJ
DWT	Darwin Airline	HB
DXH	East Star Airlines	B
DYL	Seair Airways	C6
EAA	Eastok Avia	A6
EAI	Elite Air	5V
EAK	Euro Asia International	UP
EAN	Skypower Express Airways	5N
EAS	Executive Aerospace	ZS
ECA	Eurocypria Airlines	5B
ECN	Euro Continental Air	EC
ECT	East Coast Airways	ZS
EDJ	Edwards Jet Centre of Montana	N
EDO	Elidolomiti	I
EDW	Edelweiss Air	HB
EEX	Avanti Air	D
EEZ	Eurofly	I
EFA	Express Freighters Australia	VH
EFG	Elifriula	I
EGN	Eagle Aviation	F
EGU	Eagle Air	5X
EIA	Evergreen International Airlines	N
EIN	Aer Lingus	EI
ELH	Elilario Italia	I
ELL	Estonian Air	ES
ELL	Estonian Air Regional	ES
ELO	EuroLot	SP
ELR	El-Rom Airlines	4X
ELY	El Al Israel Airlines	4X
EMI	Premium Air Shuttle	5N
EMT	Emetebe Taxi Aero	HC
ENI	Enimex	ES
ENJ	Enerjet	C
EPA	Donghai Airlines	B
EPS	Epps Aviation Charter	N
EQA	Elilombarda	I
EQC	Equatorial Cargo	3C
EQF	American Eagle	N
ERG	Aviaenergo	RA
ERH	Era Aviation	N
ERO	Sud d'Or International Airlines	4X
ERT	Eritrean Airlines	E3
ERV	Yer Avia	EK
ESC	Sol America	YV
ESD	Essen Air	EX

ESF	Estafeta Carga Aerea	XA
ESJ	Eastern Skyjets	A6
ESK	Skyeurope Airline	OM
ESL	Russian Sky Airlines	RA
ETC	Trans Attico	ST
ETD	Etihad Airways	A6
ETH	Ethiopian Airlines	ET
ETS	Avitrans Nordic	SE
EUP	Euroair	SX
EVA	EVA Airways	B
EWG	Eurowings	D
EWZ	East Wing	UP
EXN	Exin	SP
EXS	Jet2	G
EXT	Nightexpress	D
EXV	Expo Air	4R
EXW	EAS Air Lines	5N
EXY	South African Express Airways	ZS
EXZ	East African Express	5Y
EZA	Enzis Airways	JU
EZE	Eastern Airways	G
EZS	Easyjet Switzerland	HB
EZY	Easyjet Airlines	G
FAB	First Air	C
FAH	Farnair Hungary	HA
FAJ	Air Fiji	DQ
FAM	FAASA Aviacion	EC
FAO	Ufly Airways	N
FAT	Farnair Switzerland	HB
FCL	Florida Coastal Airlines	N
FCP	Flight Corporation	ZK
FCR	Flying Carpet Air Transport Services	OD
FDA	Fuji Dream Airlines	JA
FDD	Feeder Airlines	ST
FDE	Federico Helicopters	N
FDN	Dolphin Air	A6
FDR	Federal Air	ZS
FDX	Federal Express	N
FEI	Ernir Air	TF
FFA	Avialesookhrana Vladimir Air Enterprise	RA
FFF	Freedom Air Services	5N
FFG	Flugdienst Fehlhaber	D
FFM	Firefly	9M
FFT	Frontier Airlines	N
FFV	Fly540	5Y
FHE	Hello	HB
FHY	Freebird Airlines	TC
FIF	Air Finland	OH
FIN	Finnair	OH
FJI	Air Pacific	DQ
FKI	FLM Aviation	D
FLE	Flair Airlines	C
FLI	Atlantic Airways	OY
FLX	Flight Express	N
FNT	Flight International Aviation	N
FNV	Transavia Service	4L
FPO	Europe Airpost	F
FRE	Freedom Air	N
FRG	Freight Runners Express	N
FRJ	Afrijet Airlines	5N
FSC	Four Star Air Cargo	N
FTA	Frontier Flying Service	N
FTL	Flightline	EC
FTR	Finist'Air	F
FVS	Falcon Express Cargo Airlines	A6
FWA	Interstate Airlines	PH
FWI	Air Caraibes	F
FWL	Florida West International Airlines	N
FXI	Air Iceland	TF
FYA	Saicus Air	EC
FZB	FlyDubai	A6
GAE	Tricoastal Air	N
GAI	Moskoviya	RA
GAK	Global Air	5A
GAL	Galaxy Airlines	EX
GAO	Golden Air	SE
GAP	Air Philippines	RP
GBK	Gabon Airlines	TR
GBX	GB Airlink	N
GCK	Aerogem Airlines	9G
GCR	Tianjin Airlines	B

GDC	Grand China Airlines	B
GEA	Geasa	3C
GEC	Lufthansa Cargo	D
GEN	Gensa	PP
GET	Getra	3C
GFA	Gulf Air	A9C
GFG	Sky Georgia	4L
GFT	Gulfstream International	N
GGL	Gira Globo	D2
GGN	Air Georgian	C
GGZ	Global Georgian Airways	4L
GHB	Ghana International Airlines	9G
GHS	Gatari Air Service	PK
GHT	Ghadames Air Transport	5A
GIA	Garuda Indonesia	PK
GIP	Air Guinee Express	3X
GLA	Great Lakes Airlines	N
GLE	Goliaf Air	S9
GLG	Aerogal	HC
GLL	Air Gemini	D2
GLO	Gol Transportes Aereos	PP
GLP	Globus	RA
GLR	Central Mountain Air	C
GMI	Germania	D
GMT	Magnicharters	XA
GOA	Province of Alberta	C
GOM	Gomelavia	EW
GOR	Gorlitsa Airlines	UR
GOS	Goldfields Air Services	VH
GOT	Waltair Europe	SE
GOW	Go Air	VT
GRL	Air Greenland	OY
GRV	Ver-Avia	SX
GSC	Granstar Cargo Airlines	B
GSM	Flyglobespan	G
GSS	Global Supply Systems	G
GSW	Sky Wings	SX
GTI	Atlas Air	N
GTV	Aerogaviota	CU
GUM	Gum Air	PZ
GUM	Transportes Aereos Guatemaltecos	TG
GUN	Grant Aviation	N
GUY	Air Guyane Express	F
GWI	Germanwings	D
GWL	Great Wall Airlines	B
GWX	Stag	F
GWY	USA 3000 Airlines	N
GXL	XL Airways Germany	D
GZA	Excellent Air	D
GZD	V Grizodubova Air	RA
GZP	Gazpromavia	RA
HAD	Dragonair	B
HAG	Hageland Aviation Services	N
HAL	Hawaiian Airlines	N
HAX	Benair	LN
HBI	CHC Denmark	OY
HCW	Star1 Airlines	LY
HEC	Heli Campeche	XA
HEJ	Hellas jet	SX
HEL	Helicol	HK
HEM	CHC Helicopters (Australia)	VH
HER	Hex'Air	F
HES	Harbourair	9H
HET	TAF Helicopters	EC
HFY	Hi Fly	CS
HGD	Hangard Airlines	JU
HHA	Atlantic Airlines	HR
HHH	Helicsa Helicopteros	EC
HHI	Hamburg International	D
HHK	Sky Shuttle Helicopters	B
HIB	Helibravo Aviacao	CS
HIS	Heliswiss	HB
HIT	Heli-Italia	I
HKA	Superior Aviation	N
HKE	Hong Kong Express Airways	B
HKN	Jim Hankins Air Service	N
HKR	Hawk Air	LV
HKS	CHC Helikopter Service	LN
HLF	Tuifly	D
HLG	Helog	HB
HLR	Heli Air	LZ
HLU	Heli-Union	F

HLW	Heliworks	CC
HMA	Air Tahoma	N
HMF	Norrlandsflyg	SE
HMS	Hemus Air	LZ
HMX	Hawk de Mexico	XA
HOA	Hola Airlines	EC
HPL	Heliportugal	CS
HPR	Helipro	ZK
HSE	Helisureste	EC
HSS	Transportes Aereos del Sur	EC
HSU	Helisul	CS
HSV	Direktflyg	SE
HSW	Heliswiss Iberica	EC
HTA	Helitrans	LN
HTG	Grossmann Air Transport	OE
HVL	Heavylift International	A6
HVN	Vietnam Airlines	VN
HVY	Heavylift Cargo Airlines	VH
HWY	Highland Airways	G
HXA	China Express Airlines	B
HYD	Hydro-Quebec	C
IAR	Iliamna Air Taxi	N
IAW	Iraqi Airways	YI
IBB	Binter Canarias	EC
IBE	Iberia	EC
IBX	Ibex Airlines	JA
IBZ	International Business Air	SE
ICD	Icaro Express	HC
ICE	Icelandair	TF
ICJ	Icejet	TF
ICL	Cargo Air Lines	4X
ICV	Cargolux Italia	I
IDA	Indonesia Air Transport	PK
IGA	Sky Taxi	SP
IGO	Indigo Airlines	VT
IIG	Aldawlyh Air	5A
IKA	Itek Air	EX
ILF	Island Air Charters	N
ILN	Inter-Air	ZS
IMP	Hellenic Imperial Airways	SX
IMT	Imtrec Aviation	XU
IMX	Zimex Aviation	HB
INC	Insel Air International	PJ
INJ	Interjet	XA
INL	Intal Air	EX
INV	Inversija	YL
IOS	Isles of Scilly Skybus	G
IRA	Iran Air	EP
IRB	Iran Air Tour Airline	EP
IRC	Iran Aseman Airlines	EP
IRG	Naft Air	EP
IRK	Kish Air	EP
IRM	Mahan Air	EP
IRP	Payam International Air	EP
IRQ	Qeshm Air	EP
IRR	Tara Airlines	EP
IRU	Chabahar Air	EP
IRX	Aria Air	EP
IRY	Eram Air	EP
IRZ	Saha Airline	EP
ISA	Island Airlines	N
ISD	ISD Avia	UR
ISK	Intersky	OE
ISN	Interisland Airways	RP
ISR	Israir	4X
ISS	Meridiana	I
ISV	Islena Airlines	HR
ISW	Islas Airways	EC
ITK	Interlink Airlines	ZS
ITX	Imair	4K
IWD	Iberworld Airlines	EC
IYE	Yemenia	7O
IZA	Izhavia	RA
IZG	Zagros Airlines	EP
IZM	Izmir Airlines	TC
JAB	Air Bagan	XY
JAC	Japan Air Commuter	JA
JAE	Jade Cargo International	B
JAF	Jetairfly	OO
JAI	Jet Airways	VT
JAL	J-Air	JA
JAL	Japan Airlines	JA
JAT	JAT Airways	YU
JAV	Jordan Aviation	JY
JBA	HeliJet International	C
JBU	Jetblue Airways	N
JCI	Jordan International Air Cargo	JY
JCK	Jackson Air Services	C
JEA	Jet Air	SP
JEC	Jett 8 Airlines Cargo	9V
JET	Windjet	I
JEX	JAL Express	JA
JFU	Jet4You	CN
JJA	Jeju Air	HL
JKK	Spanair	EC
JLA	Mia Airlines	YR
JLX	Jetlink Express	5Y
JNA	Jin Air	HL
JOL	Atyrau Air Ways	UP
JON	Johnsons Air	9G
JOR	Blue Air	YR
JOS	DHL de Guatemala	TG
JSA	Jetstar Asia Airways	9V
JSI	Jet Air Group	RA
JSJ	JS Focus Air	AP
JST	Jetstar Airways	VH
JTA	Japan Transocean Air	JA
JTG	Jettime	OY
JTU	Zhetysu Avia	UP
JTY	Jatayu Air	PK
JUB	Jubba Airways	6O
JUC	Juba Air Cargo	ST
JUS	USA Jet Airlines	N
JZA	Air Canada Jazz	C
JZR	Jazeera Airways	9K
KAC	Kuwait Airways	9K
KAD	Kirovohradavia	UR
KAE	Kartika Airlines	PK
KAJ	Karthago Airlines	TS
KAL	Korean Air	HL
KAO	Kapo	RA
KAP	Cape Air	N
KAT	Kato Airline	LN
KAW	Kazair West	UP
KBA	Kenn Borek Air	C
KBR	Koral Blue	SU
KDC	KD Air	C
KEE	Keystone Air Service	C
KEN	Kenmore Air	N
KES	Kallat el Saker Air	5A
KFA	Kelowna Flightcraft Air Charter	C
KFR	Kingfisher Airlines	VT
KFR	Kingfisher Red	VT
KFS	Kalitta Charters II	N
KFS	Kalitta Flying Services	N
KGA	Kyrghyzstan Airlines	EX
KGL	Kolavia	RA
KHA	Kitty Hawk Aircargo	N
KHB	Dalavia	RA
KHH	Air Sinai	SU
KHO	Khors Air	UR
KIL	Kuban Airlines	RA
KIS	Contact Air	D
KKK	Atlasjet International	TC
KLC	KLM Cityhopper	PH
KLM	KLM Royal Dutch Airlines	PH
KMF	Kam Air	YA
KMG	Kosmas Air Cargo	YU
KMI	K-Mile Air	HS
KMV	Utair Express	RA
KMZ	Comores Aviation	D6
KNA	Kunming Airlines	B
KNE	NAS Air	HZ
KNI	KD Avia	RA
KNM	Knaapo	RA
KOP	Copters	CC
KOR	Air Koryo	P
KPA	Kunpeng Airlines	B
KPH	KVZ - Kazansky Vertoletny Zavod	RA
KQA	Kenya Airways	5Y
KRE	Aerosucre	HK

KRP	Carpatair	YR
KRT	Kokshetau Airlines	UP
KSA	KS Avia	YL
KSM	Kosmos Airlines	RA
KSP	SAEP	HK
KST	PTL Luftfahrtunternehmen	D
KTA	Kirov Avia Enterprise	RA
KTC	Kyrgyz Trans Air	EX
KTK	Katekavia	RA
KVA	Kavok Airlines	YV
KYM	Krym	UR
KYV	KTHY Cyprus Turkish Airlines	TC
KZH	Zhezhair	UP
KZR	Air Astana	UP
KZU	Kuzu Cargo Airlines	TC
LAA	Libyan Airlines	5A
LAB	LAB Flying Service	N
LAL	Air Labrador	C
LAM	LAM - Linhas Aereas de Mocambique	C9
LAN	LAN Airlines	CC
LAO	Lao Airlines	RDPL
LAP	TAM Mercosur	ZP
LAU	Lineas Aereas Sudamericanas Colombia	HK
LAV	Aeropostal	YV
LAY	Layang-layang Aerospace	9M
LBC	Albanian Airlines	ZA
LBT	Nouvelair	TS
LBY	Belleair	ZA
LCB	LC Burse	OB
LCG	Lignes Aeriennes Congolaises	9Q
LCN	Lineas Aereas Canedo	CP
LCO	LAN Cargo	CC
LCR	Libyan Air Cargo	5A
LDE	LADE	LV
LER	Laser	YV
LFL	Exec-Air	Z
LGL	Luxair	LX
LGW	LGW - Luftfahrtgesellschaft Walter	D
LHS	Lugansk Aviation Enterprise	UR
LIA	LIAT - The Caribbean Airline	V2
LID	Alidaunia	I
LIL	FlyLAL	LY
LIQ	Flygcentrum	SE
LKE	Lucky Airlines	B
LLB	LAB Airlines	CP
LLL	Lao Aviation	RDPL
LLM	Yamal Airlines	RA
LLR	Alliance Air	VT
LMY	Air Almaty	UP
LNE	LAN Ecuador	HC
LNI	Lion Airlines	PK
LNK	Airlink	ZS
LOD	Fly Logic Sweden	SE
LOF	American Connection	N
LOG	Loganair	G
LOT	LOT - Polish Airlines	SP
LOU	Air Saint Louis	6V
LPE	LAN Peru	OB
LPV	Air Alps Aviation	OE
LRA	Little Red Air Service	C
LRB	LR Airlines	OK
LRO	Alrosa Avia	RA
LRS	Sansa Regional	TI
LSE	Lassa - Lineas de Aeroservicios	CC
LSK	Aurela	LY
LSR	Alsair	F
LSY	Lindsay Aviation	N
LTC	LAT Charter	YL
LTR	Lufttransport	LN
LTS	Flight Inspections & Systems	RA
LUZ	Luzair	CS
LVB	IRS Airlines	5N
LVG	Livingston	I
LVR	Aviavilsa	LY
LXF	Lynx Air International	N
LXP	LAN Express	CC
LYC	Lynden Air Cargo	N
LYD	Lydd Air	G
LYM	Key Lime Air	N
LYN	Kyrgyzstan	EX
LYT	Apatas	LY
LZB	Bulgaria Air	LZ

LZT	Lanzarote Aircargo	EC
MAA	MAS Air Cargo	XA
MAC	Air Arabia Maroc	CN
MAH	Malev	HA
MAK	MAT Macedonian Air Transport	Z3
MAL	Morningstar Air Express	C
MAS	Malaysia Airlines	9M
MAU	Air Mauritius	3B
MAW	Mustique Airways	J8
MAX	Max Aviation	C
MBB	Air Manas	EX
MBC	Aerojet	D2
MBI	Salmon Air	N
MBM	Starjet	JY
MBN	Zambian Airways	9J
MBV	Aeriantur-M Airlines	ER
MCK	Macair Airlines	VH
MCM	Heli Air Monaco	3A
MCW	AMW Tchad	TT
MDA	Mandarin Airlines	B
MDC	Mid-Atlantic Freight	N
MDF	Swiftair Hellas	SX
MDJ	Jetran International Airways	YR
MDL	Mandala Airlines	PK
MDM	Medavia	9H
MDN	Mudan Airlines	6O
MDS	McNeely Charter Service	N
MDV	Moldavian Airlines	ER
MEA	Middle East Airlines	OD
MEM	Meridian	UR
MEP	Midwest Airlines	N
MGE	Asia Pacific Airlines	N
MGG	El Magal Aviation	ST
MGK	Mega Aircompany	UP
MGL	MIAT - Mongolian Airlines	JU
MGX	Montenegro Airlines	4O
MHS	Air Memphis	SU
MIF	Miras Air	UP
MIX	Midex Airlines	A6
MJA	Almajara Aviation	ST
MJT	Vigo Jet	XA
MKA	British Global	G
MKE	Megantara Air	PK
MKU	Island Air	N
MLA	40 Mile Air	N
MLC	Malift Air	9Q
MLD	Air Moldova	ER
MLG	Malagasy Airlines	5R
MLR	Mihin Lanka	4R
MMA	Myanmar Airways International	XY
MMZ	Euro Atlantic Airways	CS
MNA	Merpati Nusantara Airlines	PK
MNB	MNG Cargo Airlines	TC
MNG	Aero Mongolia	JU
MNJ	Menajet	OD
MNL	Miniliner	I
MON	Monarch Airlines	G
MOO	Moonair Aviation	4X
MOV	Vim Airlines	RA
MPD	Air Comet	EC
MPH	Martinair	PH
MPJ	Mapjet	OE
MPT	Miapet Avia	EK
MRA	Martinaire	N
MRE	Namibia Commercial Airways	V5
MRR	Northwest Seaplanes	N
MRR	San Juan Airlines	N
MRS	Airline of the Marshall Islands	V7
MSA	Mistral Air	I
MSC	Air Cairo	SU
MSE	Egyptair Express	SU
MSI	Motor Sich Airlines	UR
MSL	Marsland Aviation	ST
MSM	Aeromas	CX
MSQ	META - Mesquita Transportes Aero	PP
MSR	Egyptair	SU
MST	MTA Cargo	PP
MSV	Aero-Kamov	RA
MTL	RAF-Avia	YL
MTN	Mountain Air Cargo	N
MTW	Mauritania Airways	5T
MUA	Murray Air	N

MUI	Transair	N
MVD	KMV Mineralnye Vody Airlines	RA
MWA	Midwest Airlines Egypt	SU
MWT	Midwest Aviation	N
MXA	Mexicana	XA
MXE	Mocambique Expresso	C9
MXU	Maximus Air Cargo	A6
MYA	Myflug	TF
MYD	Maya Island Air	V3
MYI	Mayair	XA
MYW	Myair	I
MZL	Aerovias Montes Azules	XA
MZS	Mahfooz Aviation	C5
NAC	Northern Air Cargo	N
NAL	Northway Aviation	C
NAO	North American Airlines	N
NAX	Norwegian	LN
NAY	Naysa Aerotaxis	EC
NBE	Novosibirsk Air Enterprise	RA
NCA	Nippon Cargo Airlines	JA
NCB	North Cariboo Air	C
NCH	Phillips Air Charter	N
NCP	Capital Airlines	5N
NCS	Simpson Air Commuter Canada	C
NDC	Flynordic	SE
NDN	Transportes Aereos Cielos Andinos	OB
NEA	New England Airlines	N
NEF	Nord-Flyg	SE
NFA	North Flying	OY
NFS	Afrique Cargo Services	6V
NGK	Oriental Air Bridge	JA
NHG	NHT Linhas Aereas	PP
NIG	Aero Contractors	5N
NJS	Cobham Aviation Services Australia	VH
NKF	Barents Skylink	SE
NKS	Spirit Airlines	N
NKZ	Aerokuzbass	RA
NLC	Nelair Charters & Travel	ZS
NLF	Westair Aviation	C
NLK	Elbrus Avia	RA
NLY	Niki	OE
NMB	Air Namibia	V5
NMD	Buy Air Aviation	V5
NMI	Pacific Wings	N
NOF	Fonnafly	LN
NOK	Nok Air	HS
NOR	Bristow Norway	LN
NOS	Neos	I
NOT	Linea Aerea Costa Norte	CC
NPO	Napo Aviatrans	RA
NPR	Air Napier	ZK
NPT	West Atlantic	G
NRD	Nordic Airways	SE
NRG	Ross Aviation	N
NRK	Naturelink Charter	ZS
NRL	Nolinor Aviation	C
NRO	Aero Rent	RA
NRR	Naturair	TI
NRX	Norse Air Charter	ZS
NSE	Satena	HK
NTA	NT Air	C
NTC	Heartland Aviation	N
NTH	Hokkaido Air System	JA
NTJ	Nextjet	SE
NTV	Air Inter Ivoire	TU
NVD	Nordic Solutions Air Services	LY
NVI	Avial Aviation Co	RA
NVR	Novair	SE
NVS	Air Affaires Gabon	TR
NWL	North Wright Airways	C
NXA	Air Next	JA
NYL	Mid Airlines	ST
NZA	Air New Zealand Link	ZK
OAE	Omni Air International	N
OAL	Olympic Airways	SX
OAO	Arkhangelsk 2nd Aviation Enterprise	RA
OAV	Omni - Aviacao e Tecnologia	CS
OAW	Helvetic Airways	HB
OBS	Orbest	CS
OCA	Aserca Airlines	YV

ODS	Odessa Airlines	UR
OEA	Orient Thai Airlines	HS
OHY	Onur Air	TC
OKA	Okair	B
OKS	Slok Air International	C5
OLA	Overland Airways	5N
OLC	Solar Cargo	YV
OLS	SOL Lineas Aereas	LV
OLT	OLT - Ostfriesische Lufttransport	D
OMA	Oman Air	A4O
OMR	Minair	TL
ONE	Oceanair Linhas Aereas	PP
ONR	Air One Nine	5A
ORB	Orenair	RA
ORJ	Bellview Airlines	9L
ORZ	Zorex	EC
OST	Alania Airline	RA
OTL	South Airlines	UR
OVA	Aeronova	EC
OZJ	Ozjet Airlines	VH
OZU	Khozu Avia	UP
OZW	Skywest Airlines	VH
PAC	Polar Air Cargo	N
PAG	Perimeter Aviation	C
PAL	Philippine Airlines	RP
PAO	Polynesian Airlines	5W
PAS	Pelita Air	PK
PBN	Pacific Blue	ZK
PBU	Air Burundi	9U
PCE	Pace Airlines	N
PCG	Aeropostal	XA
PCO	Pacific Coastal Airlines	C
PCP	Aerolinea Principal Chile	CC
PDA	Podilia Avia	UR
PDF	Pelican Air Services	ZS
PDG	PDG Helicopters	G
PEA	Pan Europeenne Air Service	F
PEC	Pacific East Asia Cargo Airlines	RP
PEL	Aeropelican Air Services	VH
PEN	Penair	N
PEP	PENTA - Pena Transportes Aereos	PP
PEV	Airsea Airlines	SX
PFR	Pacificair	RP
PFZ	Proflight Air Services	9J
PGA	Portugalia Airlines	CS
PGL	Premiair Aviation Services	G
PGP	Perm Airlines	RA
PGT	Pegasus Airlines	TC
PGX	Paragon Air Express	N
PHA	Phoenix Air	N
PHB	Phoebus Apollo Aviation	ZS
PHE	Pawan Hans Helicopters	VT
PHM	PHI - Petroleum Helicopters	N
PHW	AVE.com	A6
PHY	Phoenix Avia	EK
PIA	Pakistan International Airlines	AP
PIC	Jetstar Pacific Airlines	VN
PIR	Pamir Air	YA
PIV	Sokol	RA
PKW	Sierra West Airlines	N
PLC	Police Aviation Services	G
PLJ	Platinum Air Linhas Aereas	PP
PLM	Pullmantur Air	EC
PLR	Northwestern Air	C
PLS	Aeroflot Plus	RA
PLY	Puma Air Linhas Aereas	PP
PMA	Pan-Malaysian Air Transport	9M
PMS	Planemasters	N
PMT	PMT Air	XU
PMW	Paramount Airways	VT
PNA	Universal Airlines	N
PNP	Pineapple Air	C6
PNR	Panair Lineas Aereas	EC
PNS	Penas	PK
PNW	Palestinian Airlines	SU-Y
POE	Porter Airlines	C
POT	Polet Aviakompania	RA
PPG	Phoenix Airtransport	N
PPK	Ramp 66	N
PPW	Royal Phnom Penh Airways	XU
PRF	Precisionair	5H

Code	Name	Country
PRG	Empressa Aero - Servicios Parrague	CC
PRN	Pirinair Express	EC
PRO	Propair	C
PRY	Priority Air Charter	N
PSC	Pascan Aviation	C
PSD	President Airlines	XU
PSS	Progress Aviakompania	RA
PST	Air Panama	HP
PSV	Sapair	HI
PSW	Pskovavia	RA
PTG	Privatair	D
PTI	Privatair	HB
PTK	Petropavlovsk-Kamchatsky Air Enterprise	RA
PTN	Pantanal	PP
PUA	Pluna Lineas Aereas Uruguayas	CX
PVI	Panavia Cargo Airlines	HP
PVU	Peau Vava'u Air	A3
PVV	Continental Airways	RA
PWF	Private Wings	D
PYZ	Players Air	N
QAH	Quick Airways	PH
QAT	Air Quasar	C
QCL	Air Class	CX
QFA	QANTAS Airways	VH
QFA	Qantaslink	VH
QNK	Kabo Air	5N
QNT	Qanot Sharq	UK
QNZ	Jetconnect	ZK
QTG	One-Two Go	HS
QTM	Quantum Air	EC
QTR	Qatar Airways	A7
QUE	Government of Quebec	C
QWA	Pel-Air	VH
QWL	Qwila Air	ZS
QXE	Horizon Air	N
RAC	Ryukyu Air Commuter	JA
RAD	Alada	D2
RAE	Regional	F
RAG	Regio-Air	D
RAI	Aerotur Air	UP
RAM	Royal Air Maroc	CN
RAX	Royal Air Freight	N
RBA	Royal Brunei Airlines	V8
RBC	Republicair	XA
RBW	Rainbow Jet	B
RCF	Aeroflot Cargo	RA
RCQ	Aerolineas Regionales	XA
RCT	Arctic Transportation Services	N
RDS	Rhoades International	N
REA	Aer Arann	EI
REG	Regional Air Services	5H
REK	Reem Airlines	EX
REU	Air Austral	F
REW	RAE Regional Air Express	D
REX	RAM Air Freight	N
RFC	Aero Africa	3D
RFS	Rossair Charter	VH
RGE	Star Equatorial Airlines	3C
RGL	Regional Air Lines	CN
RGN	Cygnus Air	EC
RHA	Robin Hood Aviation	OE
RHD	Bond Air Services	G
RHL	Air Archipels	F
RIT	Zest Airways	RP
RIU	Riau Airlines	PK
RJA	Royal Jordanian	JY
RKH	Royal Khmer Airlines	XU
RKM	Rak Airlines	A6
RLA	Airlinair	F
RLE	Rico Linhas Aereas	PP
RLR	Airnow	N
RLS	S-Air	RA
RLU	Rusline Air	RA
RMO	Saturn Aviakompania	RA
RMV	Romavia	YR
RMX	Air Max	LZ
RNA	Nepal Airlines	9N
RNB	Rosneft-Baltika	RA
RNG	Orange Aircraft Leasing	PH
RNL	Aero Lanka Airlines	4R

Code	Name	Country
RNV	Armavia	EK
RNX	1Time Airline	ZS
ROE	Aeroeste	CP
ROI	Avior Airlines	YV
RON	Our Airline	C2
ROR	Roraima Airways	8R
ROT	Tarom	YR
ROX	Roblex Aviation	N
RPB	Aerorepublica Colombia	HK
RPC	Aeropacsa	HC
RPH	RPX Airlines	PK
RPK	Royal Airlines	AP
RPX	HD Air	G
RRV	Mombasa Air Safari	5Y
RSB	Rubystar	EW
RSE	SNAS Aviation	HZ
RSG	Aero Service ASF	6V
RSH	Jetlite	VT
RSI	Air Sunshine	N
RSR	Aeroservice	TN
RSU	Aerosur	CP
RTM	Trans Am	HC
RUC	Rutaca	YV
RUM	Air Rum	9L
RUN	ACT Airlines	TC
RUS	Cirrus Airlines	D
RVE	Airventure	OO
RVL	Air Vallee	I
RVT	Veteran Airline	EK
RWD	Rwandair Express	9XR
RWG	C&M Airways	N
RWS	Air Whitsunday Seaplanes	VH
RXA	REX - Regional Express	VH
RYN	Ryan International Airlines	N
RYR	Ryanair	EI
RYW	Royal Wings Airlines	JY
RYZ	Ryazanavia Trans	RA
RZO	SARA Internacional	CS
RZZ	Anoka Air Charter	N
SAA	South African Airways	ZS
SAB	Sky Way Air	EX
SAH	Sayakhat	UP
SAI	Shaheen Air International	AP
SAM	SAM Colombia	HK
SAP	Avia Jaynar	UP
SAS	Scandinavian Airline System	SE
SAT	SATA Air Acores	CS
SAV	Samal Air	UP
SAX	Sabah Air	9M
SAY	Scotairways	G
SBF	SB Air	N
SBI	S7 Airlines	RA
SBM	Sky Bahamas	C6
SBU	St Barth Commuter	F
SBX	North Star Air Cargo	N
SCD	Associated Air Cargo	5N
SCE	Scenic Airlines	N
SCH	CHC Airways	PH
SCU	Air Scorpio	LZ
SCW	Malmo Aviation	SE
SCX	Sun Country Airlines	N
SDK	SADELCA	HK
SDL	Skysouth	G
SDM	Rossiya Russian Airlines	RA
SDO	Air Santo Domingo	HI
SDR	City Airline	SE
SEH	Sky Express	SX
SEE	Shaheen Air Cargo	AP
SEJ	Spicejet	VT
SEQ	Sky Eyes Aviation	HS
SEV	Serair	EC
SEY	Air Seychelles	S7
SFF	Safewing Aviation	N
SFJ	Starflyer	JA
SFN	Safiran Airlines	EP
SFR	Safair	ZS
SGB	Sky King	N
SGD	Skygate International	JY
SGS	Saskatchewan Government Northern Air Operations	C
SGX	Saga Airlines	TC
SGY	Skagway Air Service	N

SHQ	Shanghai Airlines International Cargo	B
SHU	SAT Airlines	RA
SHY	Sky Airlines	TC
SHZ	CHC Scotia Helicopters	G
SIA	Singapore Airlines	9V
SIB	Sibaviatrans	RA
SJY	Sriwijaya Air	PK
SKC	Skymaster Airlines	PP
SKI	Skyking Airlines	VQ-T
SKS	Sky Service	OO
SKT	Skystar Airways	HS
SKU	Sky Airline	CC
SKW	Skywest Airlines	N
SKX	Skyways Express	SE
SKY	Skymark Airlines	JA
SKZ	Skyway Enterprises	N
SLD	Silver Air	OK
SLE	NAC Charter	ZS
SLI	Aeromexico Connect	XA
SLK	Silkair	9V
SLM	Surinam Airways	PZ
SMC	Sabang Merauke Raya Air Charter	PK
SMH	Smithair	N
SMJ	Avient Aviation	Z
SMK	Semeyavia	UP
SMX	Alitalia Express	I
SNC	Air Cargo Carriers	N
SNG	Air Senegal International	6V
SNJ	Skynet Asia Airways	JA
SOA	Southern Air Charter	C6
SOL	Solomons	H4
SOO	Southern Air	N
SOP	Solinair	S5
SOR	Sonair	D2
SOV	Saratov Airlines	RA
SOY	Island Aviation	RP
SOZ	SAT Airlines	UP
SPA	Sierra Pacific Airlines	N
SPB	Springbok Classic Air	ZS
SPM	Air St Pierre	F
SPP	Sapphire Aviation	N
SPR	Provincial Airlines	C
SQC	Singapore Airlines Cargo	9V
SRC	Searca Colombia	HK
SRF	Transportes Aereos San Rafael	CC
SRI	Air Safaris & Services	ZK
SRK	Skywork Airlines	HB
SRO	SAEREO	HC
SRQ	South East Asian Airlines	RP
SRR	Star Air	OY
SRU	Star Peru	OB
SSC	Southern Seaplane	N
SSF	Severstal Aircompany	RA
SSG	Slovak Government Flying Service	OM
SSS	SAESA	EC
SSV	Skyservices Airlines	C
STH	South Airlines	EK
STI	Sontair	C
STP	STP Airways	S9
STT	Air St Thomas	N
STU	Star African Air	6O
STX	Stars Away Aviation	ZS
SUB	Suburban Air Freight	N
SUD	Sudan Airways	ST
SUF	Pacific Sun	DQ
SUK	Superior Aviation Services	5Y
SUM	MCHS Rossii	RA
SUS	Sun-Air of Scandinavia	OY
SUW	Interavia Airlines	RA
SVA	Saudi Arabian Airlines	HZ
SVD	SVG Air	J8
SVE	Asesa	XA
SVH	Sterling Aviation	G
SVJ	Silver Air	J2
SVK	Air Slovakia	OM
SVL	Sevastopol Avia	UR
SVM	Aeroservicios Monterrey	XA
SVR	Ural Airlines	RA
SVT	748 Air Services	5Y
SWA	Southwest Airlines	N
SWG	Sunwing Airlines	C
SWH	Adler Aviation	C
SWN	West Air Europe	SE
SWR	Swiss International Airlines	HB
SWT	Swiftair	EC
SWU	Swiss European Air Lines	HB
SWW	Shovkovly Shlyah	UR
SXM	Saemsa	XA
SXP	Sprint Air	SP
SXR	Skyexpress	RA
SXS	Sunexpress	TC
SYJ	Slate Falls Airways	C
SYL	Yakutia Airlines	RA
SYM	Sayat Air	UP
SYR	Syrianair	YK
SYW	Sky Airworld	VH
SYX	Midwest Connect	N
TAA	Aeropacifico	XA
TAC	Turbot Air Cargo	6V
TAE	TAME	HC
TAH	Air Moorea	F
TAI	TACA International Airlines	YS
TAJ	Tunisavia	TS
TAK	Tatarstan Air	RA
TAM	TAM Linhas Aereas	PP
TAN	Zanair	5H
TAO	Aeromar Airlines	XA
TAP	TAP Air Portugal	CS
TAR	Tunisair	TS
TAS	Lotus Air	SU
TAT	TACA Costa Rica	TI
TAY	TNT Airways	OO
TBM	Taban Air	EP
TBN	Teebah Airlines	J2
TBQ	Tobruk Air	5A
TCF	Shuttle America	N
TCI	Air Turks & Caicos	VQ-T
TCV	TACV - Transportes Aereos de Cabo Verde	D4
TCW	Thomas Cook Airlines Belgium	OO
TCX	Thomas Cook Airlines	G
TCY	Twin Cities Air Service	N
TDK	Transavia Denmark	OY
TDM	Tandem-Aero	ER
TDR	Trade Air	9A
TDX	Tradewinds Cargo	N
TEB	Tenir Airlines	EX
TET	Tepavia Trans Airline	ER
TFK	Transafrik International	S9
TFL	Arkefly	PH
TFO	Aeropacifico	XA
TFR	Toll Priority	VH
TFT	Thai Flying Service	HS
TGN	Trigana Air Service	PK
TGW	Tiger Airways	9V
TGY	Trans Guyana Airways	8R
TGZ	Airzena - Georgian Airlines	4L
THA	Thai Airways	HS
THE	Toumai Air Chad	TT
THK	THK - Turk Hava Kurumu	TC
THT	Air Tahiti Nui	F
THU	Thunder Airlines	C
THY	Turkish Airlines	TC
TIM	TEAM Airlines – Team Transportes Aereos	PP
TIS	Tesis	RA
TIW	Transcarga International Airways	YV
TJK	Tajik Air	EY
TJS	Tyrolean Jet Service	OE
TJT	Trast Aero	EX
TJT	Twin Jet	F
TLB	Atlantique Air Assistance	F
TLG	Investavia	UP
TLR	Air Libya	5A
TLT	Turtle Airways	DQ
TLX	Telesis Transair	N
TLY	Top-Fly	EC
TMG	Tri-MG Intra-Asia Airlines	PK
TMI	Tamir Aviation	4X
TMS	Temsco Helicopters	N
TMW	Trans Maldivian Airways	8Q
TMX	Tramon Air	ZS
TNA	Transasia Airways	B

TNB	Trans Air Benin	TY
TNL	Sky Horse Aviation	JU
TNM	Tiara Air	P4
TNO	Aerounion	XA
TNR	Tanana Air Service	N
TNT	Trans North Helicopters	C
TNV	Transnorthern Aviation	N
TNW	Trans Nation Airways	ET
TOC	Aerotropical	XA
TOK	Airlines of Papua New Guinea	P2
TOL	Tolair Services	N
TOM	Thomsonfly.com	G
TOS	Tropic Air Commuter	V3
TPA	Tampa Airlines	HK
TPC	Air Caledonie	F
TPG	Transportes Aereos Pegaso	XA
TPK	Air Horizon Afrique	TT
TPS	Tapsa Aviacion	LV
TPU	TACA Peru	OB
TRA	Transavia Airlines	PH
TRD	Trans Island Air 2000	8P
TRG	Tragsa Medios Aereos	EC
TRI	Ontario Ministry of Natural Resources Aviation Services	C
TRN	Aerotron	XA
TRS	Airtran Airways	N
TSC	Air Transat	C
TSD	TAF Linhas Aereas	PP
TSE	Transmile Air Services	9M
TSG	Transair Congo	TN
TSH	Regional 1 Airlines	C
TSK	Tomskavia	RA
TSO	Transaero Airlines	RA
TSP	Inter - transportes Aereos Inter	TG
TSU	Gulf and Caribbean Air	N
TSY	Tristar Air	SU
TTA	TTA - Sociedade de Transportes e Trabalho Aereo	C9
TTC	Transteco	D2
TTH	Tarhan Air	TC
TUA	Turkmenistan Airlines	EZ
TUI	Sevenair	TS
TUL	Tulpar Air	RA
TUM	Tyumenspecavia	RA
TUP	Aviastar - Tupolev	RA
TUR	Atur	HC
TUS	ABSA Cargo	PP
TUX	Tulpar Air Service	UP
TUY	Linea Turistica Aereotuy	YV
TVF	Transavia France	F
TVH	Tavasa	EC
TVJ	Tavaj Linhas Aereas	PP
TVL	Travel Service Hungary	HA
TVR	Tavrey Aircompany	UR
TVS	Smartwings	OK
TVS	Travel Service Airlines	OK
TWE	Transwede	SE
TWM	Transairways	C9
TWN	Avialeasing	UK
TXC	Trans Avia Export Cargo Airlines	EW
TXU	Atesa	HC
TZR	Rainbow Air	YV
UAC	United Air Charters	Z
UAE	Emirates	A6
UAK	Aviant	UR
UAL	United Air Lines	N
UAR	Aerostar	UR
UBA	Myanma Airways	XY
UCK	East Kazakhstan Region Air Enterprise	UP
UCR	Aero-Charter Ukraine	UR
UDC	Donbassaero	UR
UDN	Dnepr-Air	UR
UEA	United Eagle Airlines	B
UES	Ues Avia	UR
UFA	Ukraine Flight State Academy	UR
UGB	Air Uganda	5X
UGN	Yuzhnaya Aircompany	UP
UGP	Shar Ink	RA
UGX	East African Airlines	5X
UHS	Uvuaga	RA
UIA	Uni Air	B
UIL	United International Airlines	YU

UKL	Ukraine Air Alliance	UR
UKM	Um Air	UR
UKN	Ukraine Air Enterprise	UR
UKS	Ukrainian Cargo Airways	UR
UKU	Sverdlovsk 2nd Air Enterprise	RA
UKW	Lviv Airlines	UR
UMK	Yuzmashavia	UR
UNF	Union Flights	N
UNR	Rivne Universal Avia	UR
UNS	Uensped Paket Servisi / UPS	TC
UPL	Ukrainian Pilot School	UR
UPX	UPS Airlines	N
URG	Air Urga	UR
URJ	Star Air International	AP
URN	Turanair	4K
URP	ARP 410 Airlines	UR
URR	Aurora Airlines	S5
USA	US Airways	N
USC	Airnet Systems	N
USX	US Airways Express	N
UTA	Utair Airlines	RA
UTG	Utage	3C
UTR	Utair South Africa	ZS
UTY	Alliance Airlines	VH
UYA	Flight Alaska	N
UYC	Cameroon Airlines	TJ
UZA	Constanta Airlines	UR
UZB	Uzbekistan Airways	UK
UZS	Samarkand Airways	UK
VAA	Van Air Europe	OK
VAL	Voyageur Airways	C
VAS	Atran - Aviatrans Cargo Airlines	RA
VAT	Vision Air	EI
VAZ	Red Wings	RA
VBG	Vyborg Airlines	RA
VBW	Air Burkina	XT
VCV	Conviasa	YV
VDA	Volga-Dnepr Airlines	RA
VEA	Cargo Air	LZ
VEC	Venescar International	YV
VEJ	Aero Ejectivos	YV
VEN	Transaven	YV
VES	Vieques Air Link	N
VFC	Vasco	VN
VGN	Nigerian Eagle Airlines	5N
VGV	Vologda Air Enterprise	RA
VIK	Viking Airlines	SE
VIM	VIA - Air Via	LZ
VIN	Vincent Aviation (Australia)	VH
VIR	Virgin Atlantic Airways	G
VIS	Vision Air International	AP
VIV	Viva Aerobus	XA
VIZ	Aerovis Airlines	UR
VKG	Thomas Cook Scandinavia	OY
VLA	Valan International Cargo	ZS
VLE	Volareweb	I
VLG	Vueling Airlines	EC
VLI	Avolar Aerolineas	XA
VLK	Vladivostok Air	RA
VLM	VLM Airlines	OO
VLO	Varig Log	PP
VLU	Valuair	9V
VMM	Vuelos Mediterrano	EC
VNE	Venezolana	YV
VNZ	Tbilaviamsheni	4L
VOG	Voyager Airlines	S2
VOI	Volaris	XA
VOS	Rovos Air	ZS
VOZ	Virgin Blue Airlines	VH
VPB	Veteran Airlines	UR
VPV	Vip-Avia	4L
VRA	British International	G
VRB	Silverback Cargo Freighters	9XR
VRD	Virgin America	N
VRE	Volare Aviation Enterprise	UR
VRN	Varig	PP
VSO	Aerolineas Sosa	HR
VSO	Vaso Airlines	RA
VSV	Scat Aircompany	UP
VTA	Air Tahiti	F
VTE	Corporate Flight Management	N
VTK	Vostok Airlines	RA

VTS	Everts Air Alaska	N
VTS	Everts Air Cargo	N
VUN	Air Ivoire	TU
VUR	VIP - Vuelos Internos Privados	HC
VVA	Aviast Air	RA
VVM	Viva Macau	B
VXP	Mali Air Express	TZ
VXX	Aviaexpress Aircompany	UR
VZR	Air Loyaute	F
WAA	Westair Wings	V5
WAB	Aero Industries	N
WAE	Western Air Express	N
WAK	Wings of Alaska	N
WAM	Air Taxi & Cargo	ST
WAP	Arrow Panama	HP
WAV	Warbelow's Air	N
WBA	Finncomm Airlines	OH
WBR	Air Choice One	N
WCO	Columbia Helicopters	N
WDL	WDL Aviation	D
WEA	White Eagle General Aviation	SP
WEB	Webjet Linhas Aereas	PP
WEW	Express Air	C
WEW	West Wind Aviation	C
WFR	Alwafeer Air	HZ
WHT	White	CS
WIA	Winair	PJ
WIF	Wideroe's Flyveselskap	LN
WIG	Wiggins Airways	N
WJA	Westjet	C
WKH	Kharkov Aviation Production Association	UR
WLA	Airwaves Airlink	9J
WLB	Wings of Lebanon Aviation	OD
WLC	Welcome Air	OE
WLG	Volga Aviaexpress	RA
WLX	West Air Europe	LX
WOA	World Airways	N
WON	Wings Air	PK
WOW	Air Southwest	G
WRC	Wind Rose	UR
WRT	Wright Air Service	N
WSG	Wasaya Airways	C
WST	Western Air	C6
WTV	Western Aviators	N
WUA	Wizz Air Ukraine	UR
WVL	Wizz Air Bulgaria	LZ
WZZ	Wizz Air	HA
XAK	Airkenya	5Y
XAR	Xpress Air	PK
XKX	Asecna	6V
XLF	XL Airways France	F
XLL	Air Excel	5H
XME	Australian Air Express	VH
YZR	Yangtze River Express	B
ZAQ	Zoom Airways	S2
ZBA	ZB Air	5Y

The three-letter codes listed above are those allocated by countries that are members of ICAO [International Civil Aviation Organisation] and checked against several lists available on the internet.

Only the codes of companies listed in the main section are included here.

AIRPORT THREE-LETTER CODES

AAC Al-Arish, SU
AAH Aachen-Merzbrück, D
AAL Aalborg, OY
AAN Al Ain (A6)
AAR Aarhus-Tirstrup, OY
ABA Abakan,RA
ABD Abadan- Boigny International, EP
ABI Abilene Regional, TX
ABJ Abidjan-Felix Houphouet Boigirly, TU
ABQ Albuquerque Intl, NM
ABS Abu Simbel, SU
ABV Abuja-International, 5N
ABX Albury, NSW
ABZ Aberdeen-Dyce, G
ACA Acapulco-Gen.Alvarez International, XA
ACC Accra-Kotoka International, 9G
ACE Arrecife, Lanzarote, EC
ACH Altenrhein, HB
ACI Alderney-The Blaye, G
ACK Nantucket Memorial, MA
ACO Ascona, HB
ACS Achinsk, RA
ACT Waco Regional, TX
ACY Atlantic City Intl, NJ
ADA Adana-Sakirpasa, TC
ADB Izmir-Adnan Menderes, TC
ADD Addis Ababa-Bole International, ET
ADE Aden International, 7O
ADL Adelaide, SA
ADM Ardmore Municipal, OK
ADQ Kodiak, AK
ADS Dallas-Addison, TX
ADZ San Andres-Sesquicentenario, HK
AEH Abecher, TT
AEP Buenos Aires Aeroparque Jorge Newbery, LV
AER Sochi-Adler, RA
AES Aalesund-Vigra, LN
AET Allakaiket, AK
AEX Alexandria-International, LA
AEY Akureyri, TF
AFW Fort Worth Alliance, TX
AGA Agadir-Inezgane, CN
AGB Augsburg-Mühlhausen, D
AGC Pittsburgh-Allegheny Co, PA
AGF Agen-La Gareenne, F
AGP Malaga, EC
AGR Agra-Kheria, VT
AGV Acarigua Oswaldo Guevera Mujica, YV
AID Anderson Municipal, IN
AJA Ajaccio-Campo Dell'Oro, F
AKC Akron-Fulton International, OH
AKL Auckland International, ZK
AKN King Salmon, AK
AKT Akrotiri, 5B
AKX Aktobe/Aktyubinsk, UN
ALA Almaty, UN
ALB Albany-County, NY
ALC Alicante, EC
ALF Alta, LN
ALG Algiers-Houari Boumediene, 7T
ALW Walla Walla Regional, WA
ALY Alexandria, SU
AMA Amarillo International, TX
AMD Ahmedabad, VT
AMM Amman-Queen Alia International, JY
AMS Amsterdam-Schiphol, PH
AMZ Auckland-Ardmore, NZ
ANC Anchorage Intl, AK
ANE Angers-Marce, F
ANF Antofagasta-Cerro Moreno International, CC
ANG Angouleme / Brie-Champniers, F
ANI Aniak, AK
ANK Ankara-Etimesgut, TC
ANR Antwerp-Deurne, OO
ANU Saint Johns/VC Bird, V2
AOC Altenburg-Nobitz, D
AOG Anshun, B
AOI Ancona-Falconara, I
AOR Alor Setar, 9M
AOT Aosta-Corrado Gex, I
APA Denver-Centennial, CO
APF Naples-Municipal, FL
APS Anapolis, PP
APV Apple Valley, CA
APW Apia-Faleolo, 5W
AQJ Aqaba, JY
ARA New Iberia-Acadiana, LA
ARG Walnut Ridge, AR
ARH Arkhangelsk-Talagi, RA
ARK Arusha, 5H
ARN Stockholm-Arlanda, SE
ASB Ashgabat/Ashkhabad, EZ
ASF Astrakhan-Narimanovo, RA
ASH Nashua-Boise Field, NH
ASJ Amami O Shima, JA
ASM Asmara International, E3
ASP Alice Springs, NWT
ASU Asuncion-Silvio Pettirossi, ZP
ASW Aswan, SU
ATH Athens-Eleftherios Venizelos International, SX
ATL Atlanta-William B Hartsfield International, GA
ATW Appleton-Outagamie Co, WI
AUA Oranjestad-Reina Beatrix, P4
AUF Auxerre-Branches, F
AUH Abu Dhabi International, A6
AUR Aurillac, F
AUS Austin-Bergstrom Intl, TX
AUZ Aurora-Municipal, IL
AVB Aviano, I
AVN Avignon-Caumont, F
AVP Scranton-Wilkes Barre International, PA
AVV Avalon, VIC
AVW Marana-Regional, AZ
AWK Wake Island, V6
AWM West Memphis-Municipal, AR
AWZ Ahwaz,EP
AXA Anguilla-Wallblake, VP-A
AYK Arkalyk, UN
AYT Antalya, TC
AYU Aiyura, P2
AZI Abu Dhabi-Bateen, A6
AZP Mexico City-Atizapan, XA

BAH Bahrain International, A9C
BAK Baku-Geidar Aliev International, 4K
BAQ Barranquilla-Ernisto Cortissoz, HK
BAX Barnaul-Mikhailovka, RA
BBF Burlington, MA
BBJ Bitburg, D
BBP Bembridge, G
BBU Bucharest-Baneasa, YR
BBX Blue Bell-Wing Field, PA
BBZ Zambezi, 9J
BCN Barcelona-le Prat, EC
BCS Belle Chase, LA
BCT Boca Raton, FL
BDA Bermuda International Hamilton, VP-B
BDB Bundaberg, Qld
BDG Blanding-Municipal, UT
BDJ Banjarmasin-Syamsuddin Noor, PK
BDL Windsor Locks-Bradley International, CT
BDO Bandung-Husein Sastranegara, PK
BDQ Vadodora, VT
BDR Bridgeport-Sikorsky Memorial, CT
BDS Brindisi-Papola Casale, I
BDU Bardufoss, LN
BEB Benbecula, G
BEC Wichita-Beech Field, KS
BED Bedford-Hanscom Field, MA
BEG Belgrade International, YU
BEL Belem-Val de Caes, PP
BEN Benghazi-Benina, 5A
BEO Newcastle-Belmont, NSW
BES Brest-Guipavas, F
BET Bethel, AK
BEV Beer-Sheba-Teyman, 4X
BEW Beira, C9
BEY Beirut International, OD
BFE Bielefeld, D
BFF Scottsbluff-Western Nebraska Regional, NE
BFI Seattle-Boeing Field, WA
BFM Mobile Downtown, AL
BFN Bloemfontein-JBM Hertzog, ZS
BFP Beaver Falls, PA
BFS Belfast-International, G
BGA Bucaramanga, HK
BGF Bangui-M'Poko, TL
BGI Bridgetown-Grantley Adams International, VP-B
BGO Borgon Flesland, LN
BGR Bangor, ME
BGW Baghdad-Al Muthana, YI
BGY Bergamo-Orio al Serio, I
BHB Bar Harbor-Hancock Co, ME
BHD Belfast-City, G
BHE Blenheim, ZK
BHM Birmingham ,AL
BHQ Broken Hill, SA
BHX Birmingham International, G
BIA Bastia-Poretta, F
BIK Biak-Frans Kaiieppo, PK
BIL Billings-Logan Intl, MT
BIM Bimini International, C6
BIO Bilbao, EC
BIQ Biarritz-Parme,F
BIR Biratnagar, 9N
BJI Bemidji, MN
BJL Banjul-Yundum International, C5
BJM Bujumbura International, 9U
BJS Beijing-Metropolitan, B
BJY Belgrade-Batajnica, YU
BKA Moscow-Bykovo, RA
BKI Kota Kinabalu International, 9M
BKK Bangkok Suvarnabhumi, HS
BKO Bamako-Senou, TZ

BKV	Brooksville-Pilot Co, FL
BKY	Bukavu-Kavumu, 9Q
BLA	Barcelona-Gen Anzoategui International, YV
BLD	Boulder City, NV
BLI	Bellingham-International, WA
BLK	Blackpool, G
BLL	Billund, OY
BLQ	Bologna-Guglielmo Marconi, I
BLR	Bangalore-Hindustan, VT
BLX	Belluno, I
BLZ	Blantyre-Chileka, 7Q
BMA	Stockholm-Bromma, SE
BME	Broome, WA
BNA	Nashville International, TN
BND	Bandar Abbas, EP
BNE	Brisbane International, Qld
BNI	Benin City, TY
BNK	Ballina, NSW
BNS	Barinas, YV
BNX	Banja Luka, T9
BOD	Bordeaux-Merignac, F
BOG	Bogota-Eldorado, HK
BOH	Bournemouth International, G
BOI	Boise Air Terminal (Gowen Field), ID
BOM	Mumbai International, VT
BON	Kralendijk-Flamingo Int, Bonaire, PJ
BOO	Bodo, LN
BOS	Boston-Logan Intl, MA
BPN	Balikpapan-Sepinggan, PK
BQH	Biggin Hill, UK
BQK	Brunswick-Glynco Jetport, GA
BQN	Aguadilla-Rafael Hernandez, PR
BQS	Blagoveschensk-Ignatyevo, RA
BRE	Bremen, D
BRN	Bern-Belp, HB
BRO	Brownsville, TX
BRQ	Brno-Turany, OK
BRS	Bristol-Lulsgate, G
BRU	Brussels-National, OO
BRV	Bremerhaven, D
BRW	Barrow-Wiley Post / Will Rogers Memorial, AK
BSB	Brasilia International, PP
BSG	Bata, 3C
BSL	Basle-Mulhouse EuroAirport, HB
BSR	Basrah International, YI
BTK	Bratsk, RA
BTR	Baton Rouge, LA
BTS	Bratislava-MR Stefanik, OM
BTV	Burlington International, VT
BTZ	Bursa, TC
BUD	Budapest-Ferihegy, HA
BUF	Buffalo-Greater Buffalo International, NY
BUG	Benguela, D2
BUQ	Bulawayo, Z
BUR	Burbank-Glendale Pasadena, CA
BUS	Batumi-Chorokh, 4L
BVA	Beauvais-Tille, F
BVB	Boa Vista International, PP
BVO	Bartlesville, OK
BVX	Batesville-Municipal, AR
BWB	Barrow Island, WA
BWE	Braunschweig, D
BWI	Baltimore-Washington International, MD
BWN	Bandar Seri Begawan / Brunei International, V8
BWO	Balakovo, RA
BWS	Blaine, WA
BWU	Sydney-Bankstown, NSW
BXJ	Burundai, UN
BYG	Buffalo-Municipal, WY
BZE	Belize City-Philip SW Goldson International, V3
BZG	Bydgoszcz, SP
BZK	Bryansk, RA
BZV	Brazzaville Maya-Maya, TN
BZZ	Brize Norton, G
CAE	Columbia Metropolitan, SC
CAG	Cagliari-Elmas, I
CAI	Cairo International, SU
CAK	Akron-Canton Regional, OH
CAN	Guangzhou-Baiyun, B
CAP	Cap Haitien International, HH
CAS	Casablanca-Anfa, CN
CAY	Cayenne-Rochambeau, F-O
CBB	Cochabamba-Jorge Wilsterman, CP
CBG	Cambridge, G
CBL	Cuidad Bolivar, YV
CBQ	Calabar, 5N
CBR	Canberra, ACT
CCL	Chinchilla, Qld
CCP	Concepcion-Carriel Sur, CC
CCS	Caracas-Simon Bolivar International, YV
CCU	Calcutta-Chadra Bose International, VT
CDB	Cold Bay, AK
CDC	Cedar City-Municipal, UT
CDG	Paris-Charles de Gaulle, F
CDU	Camden, NSW
CDW	Caldwell-Essex Co, NJ
CEB	Cebu-Lahug, RP
CEE	Cherepovets, RA
CEJ	Chernigov-Shestovitsa, UR
CEK	Chelyabinsk-Balandino, RA
CEQ	Cannes-Mandelieu, F
CER	Cherbourg-Maupertun, F
CEW	Crestview-Bob Sikes, FL
CFE	Clermont-Ferrand, F
CFN	Donegal-Carrickfin, EI
CFR	Caen-Carpiquet, F
CFS	Coffs Harbour, NSW
CFU	Corfu: Kerkira-Ioannis Kapodidtrias, SX
CGH	Sao Paulo-Congonhas, PP
CGK	Jakarta-Soekarno Hatta International, PK
CGN	Cologne-Bonn, D
CGO	Zhengzhou, B
CGP	Chittagong International, S2
CGQ	Changchun, B
CGR	Campo Grande International, PP
CHA	Chattanooga, TN
CHC	Christchurch International, ZK
CHD	Chandler-Williams AFB, AZ
CHR	Chateauroux-Deols, F
CHS	Charleston Intl, SC
CHT	Chathams Island-Karewa, ZK
CIA	Rome-Ciampino, I
CIC	Chico, CA
CIH	Changzhi, B
CIX	Chiclayo-Cornel Ruiz, OB
CJB	Coimbatore-Peelamedu, VT
CJJ	Cheongju City, HL
CJN	El Cajun, CA
CJU	Cheju International, HL
CKC	Cherkassy, UR
CKG	Chongqing, B
CKY	Conakry-Gbessia, 3X
CLD	Carlsbad, CA
CLE	Cleveland-Hopkins Intl, OH
CLO	Cali-Alfonso Bonilla Aragon, HK
CLQ	Colima, XA
CLT	Charlotte-Douglas Intl, NC
CLU	Columbus-Municipal, IN
CMB	Colombo-Bandaranayike International, 4R
CMD	Cootamundra, NSW
CME	Cuidad del Carmen, XA
CMF	Chambery/Aix les Bains, F
CMH	Columbus-Port Intl, OH
CMN	Casablanca-Mohammed V, CN
CMR	Colmar-Houssen, F
CMU	Kundiawa-Chimbu, P2
CMV	Coromandel, ZK
CND	Constanta-Kogalniceanu, YR
CNF	Belo Horizonte-Neves International, PP
CNI	Shanghai, B
CNL	Sindal, OY
CNS	Cairns, Qld
CNW	Waco-James Connolly, TX
COA	Columbia, CA
COE	Coeur d'Alene, ID
CON	Concord-Municipal, NH
COO	Cotonou-Cadjehoun, TY
COR	Cordoba-Pajas Blancas, LV
COS	Colorado Springs Memorial, CO
COU	Columbia Regional, MO
CPE	Campeche-International, XA
CPH	Copenhagen-Kastrup, OY
CPQ	Campinhas-Viracopos International, PP
CPR	Casper-Natrona County International, WY
CPT	Cape Town-DF Malan International, ZS
CRD	Comodoro Rivadavia / Gen Mosconi, LV
CRE	Myrtle Beach-Grand Strand, SC
CRK	Diosdado Macapagal International, RP
CRL	Brussels-Charleroi, OO
CRU	Carriacou Island, J3
CRZ	Chardzhev, EZ
CSE	Crested Butte, CO
CSL	San Luis Obispo-O'Sullivan, CA
CSM	Clinton, OK
CSN	Carson City, NV
CSY	Cheboksary, RA
CTA	Catania-Fontanarossa, I
CTC	Catamarca, LV
CTG	Cartagena-Rafael Nunez, HK
CTM	Chetumal, XA
CTN	Cooktown, Qld
CTS	Sapporo-New Chitose, JA
CTU	Chengdu-Shuangliu, B
CUB	Columbus-Owens Field, SC
CUD	Caloundra, Qld
CUE	Cuenca, EC
CUG	Cudal, NSW
CUH	Cushing-Municipal, OK
CUM	Cumana-Antonio Jose de Sucre, YV
CUN	Cancun International, XA
CUR	Curacao-Willemstadt, YV
CUU	Chihuahua / Gen Villalobos International, XA
CUZ	Cuzco-Velaazco Astete, OB
CVF	Courchevel, F
CVG	Cincinnati-Covington International, OH
CVJ	Cuernavaca, XA
CVN	Clovis-Municipal, NM

CVQ Carnarvon, G
CVR Culver City, CA
CVT Coventry-Baginton, G
CWA Mosinee Central, WI
CWB Curitiba-Alfonso Pena, PP
CWC Chernovtsy, UR
CWF Chenault Airpark, AK
CWL Cardiff-Wales, G
CXH Vancouver-Coal Harbour, BC
CYM Chatham SPB, AK
CYS Cheyenne, WY
CZM Cozumel International, XA
CZS Cruzeiro do Sul-
Campo International, PP
CZX Changzhou, B

DAB Daytona Beach-Regional, FL
DAC Dhaka-Zia International, S2
DAL Dallas-Love Field, TX
DAM Damascus International, YK
DAR Dar-es-Salaam
International, 5H
DAY Dayton-James M Cox Intl, OH
DBO Dubbo, NSW
DBV Dubrovnik, 9A
DCA Washington-
Reagan National, DC
DCF Dominica-Cane Field, HI
DCS Doncaster-Robin Hood, G
DEL Delhi-Indira Gandhi
International, VT
DEN Denver International, CO
DET Detroit City, MI
DFW Dallas-Forth Worth Intl, TX
DGO Durango-
Guadelupe Victoria, XA
DGX St Athan, G
DHA Dhahran International, HZ
DHF Abu Dhabi-Al Dhaffra, A6
DHN Dothan, AL
DHR Den Holder/de Kooy, PH
DIJ Dijon-Longvic, F
DIL Dili-Comoro, PK
DJE Djerba-Zarziz, TS
DJJ Jayapura, PK
DJN Delta Junction-Allen AFB, AK
DKR Dakar-Yoff, 6V
DKS Dikson, RA
DLA Douala, TJ
DLC Dalian, B
DLG Dillingham-Municipal, AK
DLH Duluth-International, MN
DLU Dali City, B
DMA Davis-Monthan AFB, AZ
DMB Taraz-Zhambyl, UN
DME Moscow-Domodedovo, RA
DMK Bangkok-Don Muang, HS
DNA Okinawa-Kadena, JA
DND Dundee-Riverside Park, G
DNJ ADI Charter Services, N [c]
DNK Dnepropetrovsk-Kodaki, UR
DNQ Deniliquin, NSW
DNR Dinard-Pleurtuit, F
DNV Dannville-Vermillion County, IL
DOH Doha International, A7
DOK Donetsk, UR
DPA Chicago-du Page, IL
DPS Denpasar-Ngurah Rai, PK
DQH Douglas-Municipal, GA
DRS Dresden-Klotzsche, D
DRT Del Rio International, TX
DRW Darwin, NT
DSM Des Moines International, IA
DTM Dortmund-Wickede, D
DTN Shreveport-Downtown, LA
DTW Detroit Metropolitan, MI
DUB Dublin, EI
DUD Dunedin, ZK
DUJ DuBois-Jefferson County, PA
DUQ Duncan, BC
DUR Durban-
Louis Botha International, ZS
DUS Dusseldorf, D
DUT Dutch Harbor, AK
DVT Phoenix-Deer Valley, AZ
DXB Dubai International, A6
DYR Anadyr-Ugolny, RA
DYU Dushanbe, EY
DZN Zhezkazgan, UN

EAT Wenatchee-Pangborn, WA
EAU Eau-Claire County, WI
EBA Elba Island de Campo, I
EBB Entebbe International, 5X
EBJ Esbjerg, OY
EBL Erbil International, YI
ECN Ercan-Leskofa, 5B
EDF Anchorage-Elmendorf AFB, AK
EDI Edinburgh, G
EDM La Roche-sur-Yon, F
EFD Houston-Ellington Field, TX
EGO Belgorod, RA
EGS Eglisstadir, TF
EGV Eagle River, WI
EIN Eindhoven, PH
EIS Beef Island, VP-L
EKO Elko Municipal, NV
EKT Eskilstuna-Ekeby, SE
EKX Elizabethtown, KY
ELC Elcho Island, NT
ELM Elmira-Corning Regional, NY
ELP El Paso International, TX
ELS East London-
Ben Schoeman, ZS
EMA East Midlands-Nottingham, G
EME Emden, D
EMK Emmonak, AK
ENA Kenai Municipal, AK
ENS Twente-Enschede, PH
ENU Enugu, 5N
EOR El Dorado, YV
EPH Ephrata, WA
EPL Epinal-Mirecourt, F
EPZ Santa Teresa-
Dona Ana Co, NM
ERF Erfurt, D
ERI Erie International, CO
ERS Windhoek-Eros, V5
ESB Ankara-Esenboga, TC
ESE Ensenada, XA
ESF Alexandria-Regional, LA
ESL Elista, RA
ESS Essen-Mülheim, D
ETH Eilat-Hozman, 4X
EUG Eugene-Mahlon Sweet, OR
EVE Harstad-Norvik, LN
EVG Sveg, SE
EVN Yerevan-Zvartnots, EK
EWR Newark Liberty
International, NJ
EXT Exeter, G
EYP El Yopal, HK
EYW Key West International, FL
EZE Buenos Aires-Ezeiza, LV

FAB Farnborough, G
FAE Vagar-Faroe Island, OY
FAI Fairbanks International, AK
FAM Farmington Regional, MO
FAO Faro, CS
FAT Fresno Air Terminal, CA
FBK Fairbanks-Fort Wainwright, AK
FBM Lubumbashi-Luano, 9Q
FCM Minneapolis-Flying Cloud, MN
FCO Rome-Fiumicino, I
FDE Forde-Bringeland, LN
FDF Fort de France-
le Lamentin, F-O
FDH Friedrichshafen, D
FEW Cheyenne/Warren AFB, WY
FGI Apia-Faqali'l, 5W
FGL Fox Glacier, ZK
FIH Kinshasa-N'Djili, 9Q
FJR Fujairah International, A6
FKB Karlsruhe-Baden Baden, D
FKI Kisangani, 9Q
FLF Flensburg, D
FLG Flagstaff-Pullman Field, AZ
FLL Fort Lauderdale-
Hollywood International, FL
FLN Florianopolis-Hercilio Luz, PP
FLR Florence-Peretola, I
FLS Flinders Island, TAS
FMN Farmington-
Four Counties Regional, NM
FMO Munster / Osnabruck, D
FNA Freetown-
Lungi International, 9L
FNC Funchal-Madeira, CS
FNI Nimes-Garons, F
FNJ Pyongyang-Sunan, P
FNT Flint-Bishop Intl, MI
FOC Fuzhou, B
FOG Foggia-Gino Lisa, I
FOR Fortaleza-Pinto Martins, PP
FPO Freeport International, C6
FPR Fort Pierce / St Lucie Co, FL
FRA Frankfurt International, D
FRD Friday Harbor, WA
FRG Farmingdale-Republic Field, NY
FRJ Frejus-Saint Raphael, F
FRL Forli-Luigi Ridolfi, I
FRU Bishkek-Manas, EX
FSD Sioux Falls-Joe Foss Field, SD
FSP St Pierre et Miquelon, F-O
FTW Fort Worth-Meacham, TX
FTY Atlanta-Fulton Co, GA
FUK Fukuoka, JA
FWA Fort Wayne International, IN
FXE Fort Lauderdale Executive, FL
FZO Bristol-Filton, G

GAJ Yamaguchi, JA
GBE Gaborone-Sir Seretse
Khama International, A2
GBI Grand Bahama Island, C6
GBL Goulburn Island, NT
GCI Guernsey, G
GCJ Johannesburg-
Grand Central, ZS
GCM Georgetown-Owen Roberts
International, VP-C
GCN Grand Canyon
National Park, AZ
GCO Zhengzhou, B
GDL Guadalajara-
Costilla International, XA
GDN Gdansk, SP
GDT Grand Turk, VQ-T
GDX Magadan-Sokol, RA
GEA Noumea-Magenta, F-O
GEG Spokane International, WA
GEO Georgetown-Cheddi Jagan, 8R
GET Geraldtown, VIC
GEV Gallivare, SE
GEX Geelong, VIC
GEY Greybull-South Big Horn, WY
GHN Guanghan, B
GIB Gibraltar, G
GIG Rio de Janeiro-Galeao, PP
GIS Gisborne, ZK

GJT	Grand Junction-Walker Field, CO
GKA	Goroka, P2
GKH	Gorkha, 9N
GLA	Glasgow, G
GLE	Gainsville-Municipal, TX
GLH	Greenville, MI
GLO	Gloucester, G
GLS	Galveston-Scholes Field, TX
GLZ	Gilze-Rijen, PH
GME	Gomel-Pokalubishi, EW
GMN	Greymouth, ZK
GNB	Grenoble-St Geoirs, F
GOA	Genoa-Cristoforo Colombo, I
GOH	Godthaab-Nuuk, OY
GOI	Goa-Dabolim, VT
GOJ	Nizhny Novogorod-Streigino, RA
GOM	Goma, 9Q
GON	Groton-New London, CT
GOT	Gothenburg-Landvetter, SE
GOV	Gove-Nhulunbuy, NWT
GPT	Gulfport-Biloxi Regional, MS
GRO	Gerona-Costa Brava, EC
GRQ	Groningen-Eelde, OY
GRR	Grand Rapids-Kent County, MI
GRU	Sao Paulo-Guarulhos, PP
GRV	Grozny, RA
GRZ	Graz-Thalerhof, OE
GSE	Gothenburg-Save, SE
GSO	Greensboro-Piedmont Triad International, SC
GTR	Columbus-Golden Triangle Regional, GA
GUA	Guatemala City-La Aurora, TG
GUB	Guerrero Negro, XA
GUM	Guam-Ab Won Pat International, N
GUP	Gallup-Sen Clark Municipal, NM
GUW	Akyrau, UN
GVA	Geneva-Cointrin, HB
GVL	Gainsville, GA
GVQ	Coyhaique-Teniente Vidal, CC
GVT	Greenville-Majors Field, TX
GWO	Greenwood-le Floor, MS
GWT	Westerland-Sylt, D
GWY	Galway-Carnmore, EI
GXQ	Coyhaique-Teniente Vidal, CC
GYE	Guayaquil-Simon Bolivar, HK
GYN	Goiania-Santa Genoveva, PP
GYR	Goodyear-Litchfield, AZ
GZA	Gaza-Yasser Arafat International, SU-Y
GZM	Gozo, 9H
HAH	Moroni-Prince Said Ibrahim, D6
HAJ	Hannover, D
HAK	Haikou-Dayingshan, B
HAM	Hamburg-Fuhlsbüttel; D
HAN	Hanoi-Gialam, VN
HAO	Hamilton, OH
HAU	Haugesund, LN
HAV	Havana-Jose Marti International, CU
HBA	Hobart, TAS
HDD	Hyderabad, VT
HEL	Helsinki-Vantaa, OH
HEM	Helsinki-Malmi, OH
HER	Heraklion, SX
HEX	Santo Domingo-la Herrara, HI
HFA	Haifa U Michaeli, 4X
HGH	Hangzhou-Jianqio, B
HGL	Helgoland-Dune, D
HGR	Hagerstown, MD
HGU	Mount Hagen-Kagamuga, P2
HHN	Hahn, D
HHR	Hawthorne, CA
HID	Horn Island, Qld
HIG	Highbury, Qld
HII	Lake Havasu City-Municipal, AZ
HIK	Honolulu-Oahu Island, HI
HIR	Honiara-Henderson, H4
HKD	Hakodate, JA
HKG	Hong Kong International, B-H
HKT	Phuket International, HS
HLA	Lanseria, ZS
HLF	Hultsfred, SE
HLP	Jakarta-Halim Perdanakusuma, PK
HLT	Hamilton, VIC
HLZ	Hamilton, ZK
HME	Hassi Messaoud, 7T
HMJ	Khmelnitsky-Ruzichnaya, UR
HMO	Hermosillo-Gen Garcia International, XA
HMT	Hemet-Ryan Field, CA
HND	Tokyo-Haneda International, JA
HNL	Honolulu International, HI
HNS	Haines Municipal, AK
HOH	Hohenems-Dornbirn, OE
HOM	Homer, AK
HOT	East Hampton, NY
HOU	Houston-Hobby, TX
HRB	Harbin-Yanjiagang, B
HRE	Harare International, Z
HRG	Hurghada, SU
HRK	Kharkiv-Osnova, UR
HSH	Las Vegas-Henderson, NV
HSM	Horsham, VIC
HST	Homestead, FL
HTA	Chita-Kadala, RA
HTI	Hamilton Island, Qld
HTO	East Hampton, NY
HUF	Terre Haute-Hulman Regional, IN
HUM	Houma-Terrebonne, LA
HUV	Hudiksvall, SE
HUY	Humberside, G
HVB	Hervey Bay, Qld
HVN	New Haven-Tweed, CT
HWO	Hollywood-North Perry, FL
HYA	Hyannis-Barnstable Municipal, MA
HZB	Mervilel-Calonnel, F
IAB	Wichita-McConnell AFB, KS
IAD	Washington-Dulles International, DC
IAG	Niagara Falls-International, NY
IAH	Houston-George Bush International, TX
IBA	Ibadan, 5N
IBE	Ibague-Perales, HK
IBZ	Ibiza, EC
ICN	Seoul-Incheon, HL
ICT	Wichita-Mid Continent, KS
IEV	Kiev-Zhulyany, UR
IFJ	Isafjordur, TF
IFN	Isfahan, EP
IFO	Ivano-Frankivsk, UR
IFP	Laughlin-Bullhead Intl, AZ
IGM	Kingman, AZ
IJK	Izhevsk, RA
IKI	Iki, JA
IKT	Irkutsk, RA
ILG	Wilmington-Newcastle, DE
ILI	Iliamna, AK
ILN	Wilmington-Airborne Airpark, OH
ILR	Ilorin, 5N
IMT	Iron Mountain-Ford, MI
IND	Indianapolis International, IN
INI	Nis, YU
INN	Innsbruck-Kranebitten, OE
INT	Winston-Salem-Smith Reynolds, NC
INU	Nauru Island International, C2
INV	Inverness-Dalcross, G
IOM	Ronaldsway, M
IQQ	Iquique-Diego Aracena, CC
IQT	Iquitos-Coronel Vignetta, OB
IRK	Kirksville-Regional, MO
ISA	Mount Isa, Qld
ISB	Islamabad-Chaklala, AP
ISM	Kissimmee Municipal, FL
ISO	Kinston-Stalling Field, NC
IST	Istanbul-Ataturk, TC
ITB	Itaituba, PP
ITM	Osaka-Itami International, JA
ITO	Hilo International, HI
IVC	Invercargill, ZK
IWA	Ivanovo-Zhukovka, RA
JAA	Jalalabad, YA
JAB	Jabiru, NT
JAN	Jackson International, MS
JAV	Ilulissat-Jakobshavn, OY
JAX	Jacksonville International, FL
JDP	Paris-Heliport, F
JED	Jeddah-King Abdul Aziz International, HZ
JER	Jersey, G
JFK	New York-JFK International, NY
JGC	Grand Canyon Heliport, AZ
JHB	Johor Bahru-Sultan Ismail International, 9M
JHE	Helsingborg Heliport, SE
JHW	Jamestown-Chautauqua Co, NY
JIB	Djibouti-Ambouli, J2
JIL	Jilin, B
JJN	Jinjiang, B
JKG	Jonkoping-Axamo, SE
JNB	Johannesburg-OR Tambo International, ZS
JNU	Juneau International, AK
JST	Johnstown-Cambria County, PA
JUB	Juba, ST
JVL	Janesville-Rock County, WI
KAD	Kaduna, 5N
KAN	Kano Mallam Aminu International, 5N
KBL	Kabul-Khwaja Rawash, YA
KBP	Kiev-Borispol, UR
KCH	Koching, 9M
KDH	Kandahar, YA
KDK	Kodiak Municipal, AK
KEF	Keflavik International, TF
KEH	Kenmore Air Harbor, WA
KEJ	Kemorovo, RA
KEP	Nepalgunj, 9N
KER	Kerman, EP
KGC	Kingscote, SA
KGD	Kaliningrad-Khrabovo, RA
KGF	Qaragandy-Sary Arka, UN
KGI	Kalgoorlie, WA
KGL	Kigali-Gregoire Kayibanda, 9XR
KGO	Kirovograd-Khmelyovoye, UR
KGP	Kogalym, RA
KHH	Kaoshiung International, B
KHI	Karachi Jinnah International, AP
KHV	Khabarovsk-Novy, ra
KIH	Kish Island, EP
KIN	Kingston-Norman Manley Internatonal, 6Y
KIV	Kishinev-Chisinau, ER

KIW Kitwe-Southdowns, 9J
KIX Osaka-Kansai International, JA
KJA Krasnoyarsk-Yemelyanovo, RA
KJK Kortrijk-Wevelgem, OO
KKJ Kitakyushu-Kokura, JA
KLF Kaluga, RA
KLU Klagenfurt, OE
KMG Kunming-Wujiaba, B
KMI Miyazaki, JA
KMJ Kumamoto, JA
KMW Kostroma, RA
KNX Kununurra, WA
KOA Kailua Kona, HI
KOV Kokhshetan, UN
KOW Ganzhou, B
KRB Karumba, Qld
KRH Redhill, G
KRK Krakow International, SP
KRN Kiruna, SE
KRO Kurgan, RA
KRP Karup, OY
KRR Krasnodar-Pashkovskaya, RA
KRS Kristiansand-Kjevik, LN
KRT Khartoum-Civil, ST
KSC Kosice-Barca, OM
KSD Karlstad, SE
KSF Kassel-Calden, D
KSK Karlskoga, SE
KSM St Mary's Bethel, AK
KSN Kustanay, UN
KSZ Kotlas, RA
KTA Karratha, WA
KTE Kerteh-Petronas, 9M
KTM Kathmandu-Tribhuvan International, 9N
KTN Ketchikan International, AK
KTP Kingston-Tinson Peninsula, 6Y
KTR Katherine-Tindal, NWT
KTW Katowice-Pyrzowice, SP
KUF Samara-Kurumoch, RA
KUL Kuala Lumpur International, 9M
KUN Kaunus-Karlelava International, LY
KUT Kutaisi, 4L
KVB Skovde, SE
KVX Kirov, RA
KWE Guiyang, B
KWI Kuwait International, 9K
KXK Komsomolsk, RA
KYZ Kyzyi, RA
KZN Kazan-Bonsoglebskow, RA
KZO Kzyl-Orda, UN

LAD Luanda-4 de Fevereiro, D2
LAE Lae-Nadzab, P2
LAF Lafayette-Purdue University, IN
LAJ Lages, PP
LAL Lakeland Regional, FL
LAO Laoag International, RP
LAP La Paz Gen Leon International, XA
LAS Las Vegas-McCarran International, NV
LAW Lawton, OK
LAX Los Angeles International, CA
LBA Leeds-Bradford, G
LBB Lubbock, TX
LBD Khudzhand, EY
LBE Latrobe-Westmoreland Co, PA
LBG Paris-le Bourget, F
LBH Sydney-Palm Beach SPB, NSW
LBV Libreville-Leon M'Ba, TR
LCA Larnaca International, 5B
LCE La Ceibe-Goloson International, TG
LCH Lake Charles-Regional, LA
LCK Columbus-Rickenbacker, OH
LCY London-City, G
LDB Londrina, PP
LDE Tarbes-Ossun-Lourdes, F
LDH Lord Howe Island, NSW
LDK Lidkoping-Hovby, SE
LED St Petersburg-Pulkovo, RA
LEH le Havre-Octeville, F
LEJ Leipzig-Halle, D
LEN Leon, EC
LEQ Lands End-St Just, G
LEW Lewiston-Auburn Municipal, ME
LEY Lelystad, PH
LFT Lafayette-Regional, AL
LFW Lome-Tokoin, 5V
LGA New York-La Guardia, NY
LGB Long Beach-Daugherty Field, CA
LGG Liege-Bierset, OO
LGW London Gatwick, G
LGY Lagunillas, YV
LHD Anchorage-Lake Hood SPB, AK
LHE Lahore Allama Iqbal International, AP
LHR London-Heathrow, G
LHW Lanzhou, B
LIG Limoges-Bellegarde, F
LIL Lille-Lesquin, F
LIM Lima-Jorge Chavez International, OB
LIN Milan-Linate, I
LIS Lisbon, CS
LIT Little Rock-Adams Field, AR
LJU Ljubljana-Brnik, S5
LKE Seattle-Lake Union, WA
LKO Lucknow-Amausi, VT
LKP Lake Placid, NY
LLA Lulea-Kallax, SE
LLC Valdez, AK
LLW Lilongwe-Tilange International, 7Q
LME Le Mans-Arnage, F
LMM Los Mochis, XA
LNA West Palm Beach-Lantana Co Park, FL
LNX Smolensk, RA
LNZ Linz-Hoersching, OE
LOS Lagos-Murtala Mohammed, 5N
LPA Las Palmas-Gran Canaria, EC
LPB La Paz-El Alto, CP
LPI Linkoping-Malmen, SE
LPK Lipetsk, RA
LPL Liverpool-John Lennon International, G
LPP Lappeenranta, OH
LPY Le Puy-Loudes, F
LRD Laredo International, TX
LRE Longreach, Qld
LRH La Rochelle-Laleu, F
LRR Lar, EP
LSI Sumburgh, G
LST Launceston, TAS
LTN London-Luton, G
LTX Latacunga, HC
LUG Lugano, I
LUK Cincinatti Municipal, OH
LUN Lusaka International, 9J
LUX Luxembourg, LX
LWB Lewisburg-Greenbrier Valley, WV
LWO Lviv-Snilow, UR
LWR Leeuwarden, PH
LXA Lhasa, B
LXR Luxor, SU
LXT Latacunga, HC
LYN Lyon-Bron, F
LYP Faisalabad, AP
LYS Lyon-Satolas, F
LYT Lady Elliott Island, Qld
LYX Lydd International, G

MAA Chennai, VT
MAC Macon-Smart, GA
MAD Madrid-Barajas, EC
MAG Madang, P2
MAH Menorca-Mahon, EC
MAJ Majuro-Amata Kabua International, V7
MAN Manchester International, G
MAO Manaus-Eduardo Gomes, PP
MAR Maracaibo-La Chinita Internatonal, YV
MAW Malden, MO
MBA Mombasa-Moi International, 5Y
MBD Mmbatho International, ZS
MBH Maryborough, Qld
MBJ Montego Bay-Sangster Internatonal, 6Y
MBW Melbourne-Moorabin, VIC
MBX Maribor, S5
MCI Kansas City International, MO
MCM Monte Carlo Heliport, 3A
MCO Orlando International, FL
MCP Macapa-International, PP
MCT Muscat-Seeb International, A4O
MCW Mason City Municipal, IA
MCX Makhachkala-Uytash, RA
MCY Sunshine Coast, Qld
MDE Medellin-Olaya Herrera, HK
MDL Mandalay, XY
MDT Harrisburg International, PA
MDU Mendi, P2
MDW Chicago-Midway, IL
MEA Macae & Sao Tome, PP
MEB Melbourne-Essendon, VIC
MEL Melbourne-Tullamarine, VIC
MEM Memphis International, TN
MER Merced-Castle AFB, CA
MES Medan-Polonia, PK
MEV Minden-Douglas Co, NV
MEX Mexico City-Juarez International, XA
MFE McAllen-Miller, TX
MFM Macau International, B-M
MFN Milford Sound, ZK
MGA Managua-Sandino, YN
MGB Mount Gambier, VIC
MGL Mönchengladbach, D
MGQ Mogadishu International, 6O
MHB Auckland-Mechanics Bay, ZK
MHD Mashad-Shahid Hashemi Nejad International, EP
MHG Mannheim-Neu Ostheim, D
MHH Marsh Harnour, C6
MHP Minsk 1 International, EW
MHQ Mariehamn, OH
MHR Sacramento-Mather, CA
MHV Mojave-Kern Co, CA
MIA Miami International, FL
MID Merida, XA
MIE Newcastle, IN
MIR Monastir-Habib Bourguiba International, TS
MIU Maiduguri, 5N
MJI Mitiga, 5A
MJM Mbuji Mayi, 9Q
MJZ Mirny, RA
MKC Kansas City Downtown, MO
MKE Milwaukee-Mitchell Field, WI
MKY MacKay, Qld
MLA Malta-Luqa, 9H
MLB Melbourne-Cape Kennedy, FL
MLC McAlester-Regional, OK
MLE Male International, 8Q

MLH Basle-Mulhouse EuroAirport, F
MLU Monroe-Regional, LA
MLW Monrovia-Spriggs Payne. A8
MMK Murmansk, RA
MML Marshall-Ryan Field, MN
MMX Malmo-Sturup, SE
MNI Plymouth-WH Bramble (VP-M)
MNL Manila-Nino Aquino International, RP
MNZ Manassas, VA
MOB Mobile-Regional, AL
MOL Molde, LN
MON Mount Cook, ZK
MOR Morristown, TN
MPB Miami-Watson Island SPB, FL
MPL Montpellier-Mediterranean, F
MPM Maputo, C9
MPR McPherson, KS
MPW Marlupol, UR
MQF Magnitogorsk, RA
MQL Mildura, VIC
MQS Mustique International, J8
MQT Marquette-Sawyer, MI
MQY Smyrna, TN
MRI Anchorage-Merrill Field, AK
MRO Masterton, ZK
MRS Marseille-Marignane, F
MRU Plaisance International, 3B
MRV Mineralnye Vody, RA
MRX Morristown Nexrad, TN
MSC Mesa-Falcon Field, AZ
MSE Manston-Kent International, G
MSO Missoula Johnson-Bell Field, MT
MSP Minneapolis-St Paul International, MN
MSQ Minsk 2 International, , EW
MST Maastricht-Aachen, PH
MSU Maseru-Moshoeshoe, 7P
MSY New Orleans International, LA
MTM Metlakatla, AK
MTN Baltimore-Glenn L Martin, MD
MTS Manzini-Matsapha, 3D
MTY Monterey-Gen Escobedo International, XA
MUB Maun, A2
MUC Munich-Franz Joseph Straus, D
MUN Maturin, YV
MVA Myvatn-Rykiahlid, TF
MVD Montevideo-Carrasco International, CX
MVQ Mogilev, EW
MVY Martha's Vineyard, MA
MWO Middletown-Hook Field Memorial, OH
MWZ Mwanza, 5H
MXE Maxton, NC
MXN Morlaix-Ploujean, F
MXP Milan-Malpensa, I
MXX Mora-Siljan, SE
MYD Malindi, 5Y
MYL McCall, ID
MYR Myrtle Beach, SC
MYV Marysville-Yuba Co, CA
MYY Miri, 9M
MZJ Marana-Pinal Airpark, AZ

NAG Nagpur-Sonegaon, VT
NAL Nalchik, RA
NAN Nadi International, DQ
NAP Naples-Capodichino, I
NAS Nassau International, C6
NAY Beijing-Nan Yuan, B
NBO Nairobi-Jomo Kenyatta International, 5Y
NCE Nice-Cote d'Azur, F
NCL Newcastle, G
NDJ N'djamena, TT
NEV Nevis-Newcastle, V4
NEW New Orleans-Lakefront, LA
NFG Nefteyugansk, RA
NGO Nagoya-Chubu, JA
NGS Nagasaki, JA
NHT RAF Northolt, G
NIC Nicosia, 5B
NIM Niamey-Diori Hamani, 5U
NKC Nouakchott, 5T
NKG Nanjing, B
NKM Nagoya-Komaki AFB, JA
NLK Norfolk Island, NSW
NLO Kinshasa-N'dolo, 9Q
NLP Nelspruit, ZS
NNK Naknek, AK
NNR Connemara, EI
NOA Nowra, NSW
NOE Norden-Norddeich, D
NOU Noumea-La Tontouta, F-O
NOZ Novokuznetsk, RA
NPE Napier, ZK
NQA Millington, TN
NQN Neuquen, LV
NQY Newquay-St Mawgan, G
NRK Norrkoping, SE
NRT Tokyo-Narita International, JA
NSI Yaounde, TJ
NSK Norilsk, RA
NSN Nelson, ZK
NSO Scone, NSW
NTB Notodden, LN
NTE Nantes-Atlantique, F
NTL Newcastle-Williamstown, NSW
NTY Sun City-Pilansberg, ZS
NUE Nurenburg, D
NVA Neiva-La Marquita, HK
NVR Novgorod, RA
NWI Norwich, G
NYM Nadym, RA
NYO Nykoping-Skavsta, SE
NZC Jackonsville Cecil Field, FL

OAG Orange, NSW
OAJ Jacksonville, NC
OAK Oakland International, CA
OAX Oaxaca-Xoxocotlan, XA
OBF Oberpfaffenhofen, D
OBN Oban, G
OBO Obihiro, JA
OCF Ocala-Taylor Field, FL
ODB Cordoba-Palma del Rio, EC
ODE Odense-Beldringe, OY
ODS Odessa-Tsentralny, UR
ODW Oak Harbor, WA
OEL Orel, RA
OGG Kahului-Intl, HI
OGL Georgetown-Ogle, 8R
OGZ Vladivkavkaz-Beslan, RA
OKA Okinawa-Naha, JA
OKC Oklahoma City-Will Roger, OK
OKD Sapporo-Okadama, JA
OLB Olbia-Costa Smeralda, I
OLM Olympia, WA
OMA Omaha-Eppley Field, NE
OME Nome, AK
OMS Omsk-Severny, RA
ONT Ontario International, CA
OOL Coolangatta, Qld
OPF Opa Locka, FL
OPO Porto, CS
ORB Orebro-Bofors, SE
ORD Chicago-O'Hare Intl, IL
ORG Paramaribo-Zorg en Hoop, PZ
ORK Cork, EI
ORL Orlando-Executive, FL
ORY Paris-Orly, F
OSC Oscoda-Wurtsmith AFB, MI
OSH Oshkosh-Wittman Field, WI
OSL Oslo International, LN
OSR Ostrava-Mosnov, OK
OSS Osh, EX
OST Ostend, OO
OTP Bucharest-Otopeni Intl, YR
OTS Anacortes, WA
OTZ Kotzebue-Wien Memorial, AK
OUA Ouagadougou, XT
OUL Oulu, OH
OVB Novosibirsk-Tolmachevo, RA
OVD Castrillón-Asturias (EC)
OWD Norwood Memorial, MA
OXB Bissau Vierira Intl, J5
OXC Oxford-Waterbury, CT
OXR Oxnard, CA
OYS Mariposa-Yosemite, CA
OZH Zaporozhye-Mokraya, UR

PAC Albrook-Marcos A Gelabert Panama City, HP
PAD Paderborn-Lippstadt, D
PAE Everett-Paine Field, WA
PAP Port-au-Prince International, HH
PAQ Palmer Municipal, AK
PAZ Poza Rica, XA
PBG Plattsburgh, NY
PBH Paro, A5
PBI Palm Beach Intl, FL
PBM Paramaribo-Pengel Interntional, PZ
PCB Pondok Cabe, PK
PCL Pucalipa-Rolden, OB
PCM Playa del Carmen, XA
PDC La Verne-Bracketts Field, CA
PDK Atlanta-Peachtree, GA
PDL Ponta Delgada, CS
PDV Plovdiv, LZ
PDX Portland International, OR
PEE Perm-Bolshoe-Savino, RA
PEK Beijing-Capital, B
PEN Penang-International, 9M
PER Perth International, WA
PEZ Penza, RA
PFO Paphos International, 5B
PGA Page, AZ
PGD Punta Gorda-Charlotte Co, FL
PGF Perpignan-Rivesaltes, F
PGX Periguex-Brassillac, F
PHC Port Harcourt, 5N
PHE Port Hedland, WA
PHF Newport News, VA
PHL Philadelphia International, PA
PHS Phitsanulok-Sarit Sena, HS
PHX Phoenix-Sky Harbor Intl, AZ
PHY Phetchabun, HS
PIE St Petersburg-Clearwater Intl, FL
PIK Prestwick, G
PIR Pierre-Regional, SD
PIT Pittsburgh Intl, PA
PKC Petropavlovsk Kamchatsky-Yelizovo, RA
PKR Pokhara, 9N
PKU Pekanbaru-Simpang Tiga, PK
PKV Pskov, RA
PLB Plattsburg-Clinton Co, NY
PLH Plymouth, G
PLL Manaus-Ponta Pelada, PP
PLS Providenciales Intl, VQ-T
PLU Belo Horizonte-Pampulha, PP
PLV Poltava, UR
PLX Semipalatisnk, UN

PMB Pembina, ND
PMC Puerto Montt, CC
PMD Palmdale, CA
PMF Parma, I
PMI Palma de Mallorca, EC
PMO Palermo-Punta Raisi, I
PMR Palmerston-North, ZK
PNA Pamplona, EC
PNE Philadelphia-Northern, PA
PNH Phnom Penh-Pochentong, XU
PNI Pohnpei-Caroline Islands, V6
PNK Pontianak-Supadio, PK
PNR Pointe Noire, TN
PNS Pensacola-Regional, FL
PNX Sherman-Denison, TX
POA Porto Alegre-Canoas, PP
POC La Verne-Brackett Field, CA
POG Port Gentil, TR
POM Port Moresby, P2
POP Puerto Plata International, HI
POS Port of Spain-Piarco, 9Y
POW Portoroz, S5
POX Pontoise-Cormeilles, F
PPB Presidente Prudente, PP
PPG Pago Pago International, N
PPK Petropavlovsk, UN
PPQ Paraparaumu, ZK
PPT Papeete-Faaa, , F-O
PQQ Port Macquarie, NSW
PRA Parana, LV
PRC Prescott-
Ernest A Love Field, AZ
PRG Prague-Ruzyne, OK
PRN Pristina, YU
PRV Prerov, OK
PRY Pretoria-Wonderboom, ZS
PSA Pisa-Galileo, I
PSM Portsmouth-Pease Intl, NH
PSR Pescara, I
PSY Port Stanley, VP-F
PTA Port Alsworth, AK
PTG Pietersburg-Gateway, ZS
PTI Port Douglas, Qld
PTK Pontiac-Oakland, MI
PTN Ptterson-HPW Memorial, LA
PTP Pointe a Pitre-Le Raizet, F-O
PTY Panama City-Tocumen Intl, HP
PUF Pau-Pyrenees, F
PUG Port Agusta, SA
PUQ Punta Arenas, CC
PUU Puerto Asi, HK
PUY Pula, 9A
PVG Shanghai-Pu Dong Intl, B
PVH Porto Velho, PP
PVR Puerto Vallarta-Lic Gustavo
Dias Ordaz International, XA
PVU Provo-Municipal. UT
PWK Chicago-Pal Waukee, IL
PWM Portland Intl Jetport, ME
PWQ Pavlodar, UN
PYL Perry Island SPB, AK
PZE Penzance, G

QKC Karaj-Payam, EP
QLA Lasham, G
QPG Paya Lebar, 9V
QPI Palmira, CP
QRA Johannesburg-Rand, ZS
QRC Rancagua-
de la Independence, CC
QSC San Carlos, PP
QSM Utersen, D
QTK Rothenburg, D

RAB Rabaul, P2
RAI Praia-Mendes, D4
RAK Marrakesh-Menara, CN
RAO Ribeirao Preto, PP
RAR Rarotonga, E5
RAS Rasht, EP
RBA Rabat-Sale, CN
RBR Rio Branco-Medici, PP
RBY Ruby-Municipal, AK
RCM Richmond, Qld
RDD Redding-Municipal, CA
RDG Reading-Gen Spaatz Field, PA
RDM Redmond-Roberts Field, OR
RDU Raleigh-Durham Intl, NC
REC Recife-Guararapes, PP
REK Reykjavik, TF
REN Orenburg-Tsentralny, RA
REP Siem Reap, XU
REX Reynosa-Gen Lucio Blanco
International, XA
RFD Rockford, IL
RGN Yangon International, XY
RHE Reims Champagne, F
RHI Rhinelander-Oneida Co, WI
RHO Rhodes-Diagoras, SX
RIC Richmond-Byrd Intl, VA
RIX Riga-Skulte International, YL
RJK Rijeka, 9A
RKD Rockland-Knox County, ME
RKE Roskilde, OY
RKT Ras al Khaimah Intl, A6
RLG Rostock-Laage, D
RMA Roma, Qld
RMI Rimini, I
RML Colombo-Ratmalana, 4R
RNC McMinnville-Warren Co, OR
RNO Reno-Cannon Intl, NV
RNS Rennes-St Jacques, F
RNT Seattle-Renton, WA
ROB Monrovia Roberts Intl, A8
ROK Rockhampton, IL
ROM Rome Urbe, I
ROR Koror-Airai, T8A
ROS Rosario-Fisherton, LV
ROT Rotorua, ZK
ROV Rostov-on-Don, RA
ROW Roswell-
Industrial Air Center, NM
RPM Ngukurr, NT
RSE Sydney-Au Rose, Qld
RTM Rotterdam, PH
RTW Saratov-Tsentrainy, RA
RUH Riyadh-
King Khalid International, HZ
RUN St Denis-Gilot, F-O
RVH St Petersburg-Rzhevka, RA
RWN Rivnu, UR
RYB Rybinsk-Staroselye, RA
RZN Ryazan, RA

SAH Sana'a International, 7O
SAL San Salvador-
Comalapa International, YS
SAN San Diego-Lindbergh Intl, CA
SAT San Antonio International, TX
SAW Instanbul-Sabiha Gokcen
International, TC
SBA Santa Barbara Municipal, CA
SBD San Bernadino-Norton AFB, CA
SBH St Barthelemy, F-O
SBP San Luis Obispo, CA
SBY Salisbury-Wicomico, MD
SCC Prudhoe Bay, AK
SCH Schenectady County, NY
SCI San Cristobal-Paramilio, YV
SCK Stockton Metropolitan, CA
SCL Santiago-Merino Benitez
International, CC
SCN Saarbrucken-Ensheim, D
SCU Santiago de Cuba, CU
SCW Syktyvkov, RA
SDA Damascus- International, YK
SDF Louisville-Standiford Field, KY
SDJ Sendai, JA
SDQ Santo Domingo Intl, HI
SDU Rio de Janeiro-
Santos Dumont, PP
SDV Tel Aviv-Sde Dov, 4X
SEA Seattle-Tacoma Intl, WA
SEL Seoul-Kimpo Intl, HL
SEN Southend, G
SEZ Mahe-Seychelles Intl, S7
SFB Sanford Regional, FL
SFC St Francois, F-O
SFD San Fernando de Apure, YV
SFG St Martin-Esperance, F-O
SFJ Kangerlussuaq-
Sondre Stromfjord, OY
SFO San Francisco Intl, CA
SFS Subic Bay Intl, PR
SFT Skelleftea, SE
SGC Surgut, RA
SGD Sondeberg, OY
SGF Springfield-
Branson Regional, MO
SGH Springfield-Beckley, OH
SGL Manila-Sangley Point, RP
SGN Ho Chi Minh City-
Tansonnhat, VN
SGU St George Municipal UT
SGW Saginaw Bay, AK
SGY Skagway Municipal, AK
SGZ Songkhla, HS
SHA Shanghai-Hongqiao, B
SHE Shenyang, B
SHJ Sharjah International, A6
SHR Sheridan County, WY
SIA Xi'an-Xiguan, B
SID Sal-Amilcar Cabral Intl, D4
SIG San Juan-Isla Grande, PR
SIN Singapore-Changi, 9V
SIP Simferopol, UR
SIR Sion, HB
SIT Sitka, AK
SIX Singleton, NSW
SJC San Jose International, CA
SJJ Sarajevo-Butmir, T9
SJK Sao Jose dos Campos, PP
SJO San Jose-Juan Santamaria
International, Y3
SJU San Juan-Luis Munoz
Marin International, PR
SJY Deinajoki-Ilmajoki, OH
SKB Basseterre-Golden Rock, V4
SKD Samarkand, UK
SKE Skien-Geiteryggen, LN
SKF San Antonio-Kelly AFB, TX
SKH Surkhet, 9N
SKP Skopje, Z3
SKX Saransk, RA
SKY Sandusky, OH
SLA Salta International, LV
SLC Salt Lake City Intl, UT
SLM Salamanca Matacan, EC
SLU Castries, J6
SLW Saltillo, XA
SLY Salekhard, RA
SMA Santa Maria-Vila do Porto, CS
SMF Sacramento-Metropolitan, CA
SML Stella Maris, C6
SMN Salmon, ID
SMO Santa Monica, CA
SMX Santa Maria-Public, CA
SNA John Wayne-Orange Co, CA
SNN Shannon, EI
SNR St Nazaire-Montoir, F
SOD Sorocaba, PP

SOF Sofia-Vrazhdebna Intl, LZ
SOU Southampton International, G
SOW Show Low-Municipal, AZ
SPB St Thomas Seaplane, VI
SPI Springfield Capital, IL
SPN Saipan Island International, N
SPR San Pedro, V3
SPU Split, 9A
SPW Spencer Municipal, IA
SPZ Springdale, AR
SRG Senerang, PK
SRN Strahan, Tas
SRQ Sarasota-Bradenton Intl, FL
SRZ Santa Cruz-El Trompillo, CP
SSA Salvador-Dois de Julho, PP
SSG Malabo, 3C
SSH Sharm el Sheikh, SU
SSQ La Sarre, QU
STA Stauning, OY
STI Santiago International, HI
STL St Louis-Lambert Intl, MO
STM Santarem-Gomez Intl, PP
STN London-Stansted, G
STR Stuttgart, D
STS Santa Rosa-Sonoma, CA
STT St Thomas-Cyril E King, VI
STU Santa Cruz, V3
STW Stavropol-Shpakovskoye, RA
STX St Croix -Hamilton Airport, VI
SUA Stuart-Witham Field, FL
SUB Surabaya-Juanda, PK
SUI Sukhumi, 4L
SUS St Louis-Spirit of St Louis, MO
SUV Suva-Nausori, DQ
SVD Kingstown-ET Joshua , V8
SVG Stavanger-Sola, LN
SVH Statesville Municipal, NC
SVO Moscow-Sheremetyevo, RA
SVQ Seville-San Pablo, EC
SVU SavuSavu, DQ
SVX Yekaterinburg-Koltsovo, RA
SWA Shantou, B
SWF Newburgh-Steward-Hudson Valley International, NY
SWH Swan Hill, Vic
SXF Berlin-Schönefeld, D
SXM St Maarten-Philipsburg, PJ
SXQ Soldotna, AK
SYD Sydney-Kingsford Smith International, NSW
SYR Syracuse-Hancock Intl, NY
SYQ San Jose-Tobias Bolanos International, YS
SYX Sanya-Fenghuang, B
SYY Stornoway, G
SYZ Shiraz International, EP
SZB Subang-Sultan Abdul Aziz Shah International, 9M
SZG Salzburg, OE
SZO Shanzhou, B
SZX Shenzhen-Huangtian, B
SZZ Szczecin-Goleniow, SP

TAB Scarborough-Crown Point, 9Y
TAM Tampico-Gen Francisco Javier Mina International, XA
TAR Taranto-Grottaglie, I
TAS Tashkent-Yuzhny, UK
TAT Tatry-Poprad, OM
TBG Tabubil, P2
TBS Tbilisi-Novo Alexeyevka, 4L
TBU Tongatapu-Fua'Amotu Intl, A3
TBZ Tabriz, EP
TBW Tambov, RA
TEB Teterboro, NJ
TED Thisted, OY
TER Lajes-Terceira Island, CS
TFN Tenerife-Norte los Rodeos, EC
TFS Tenerife-Sur Reine Sofia, EC
TGD Podgorica, YU
TGR Touggourt, 7T
TGU Tegucigalpa-Toncontin Intl, HR
TGZ Tuxtla-Gutierrez, XA
THE Terresina, PP
THF Berlin-Tempelhof, D
THN Trolhattan-Vanersborg, SE
THR Teheran-Mehrabad Intl, EP
TIA Tirana-Rinas, ZA
TIF Taif, HZ
TIJ Tijuana-Rodriguez Intl, XA
TIP Tripoli International, 5A
TIS Thursday Island, Qld
TIV Tivat, YU
TJM Tyumen-Roschino, RA
TKA Talkeetna, AK
TKJ Tok, AK
TKU Turku, OH
TLC Toluca-Alfonso Lopez, XA
TLL Tallinn-Ylemiste, ES
TLR Tulare-Mefford Field, CA
TLS Toulouse-Blagnac, F
TLV Tel Aviv-Ben Gurion Intl, 4X
TMB Miami-New Tamiami, FL
TML Tamale, 9G
TMO Tumeremo, YV
TMP Tampere-Pirkkala, OH
TMS Sao Tome International, 9L
TMW Tamworth-Westdale, NSW
TNA Jinan, B
TNF Toussus-le-Noble, F
TNN Tainan, B
TNR Antananarivo, 5R
TOA Torrance, CA
TOE Tozeur-Nefta, TS
TOF Tomsk, RA
TOL Toledo-Express, OH
TOM Tombouctu, TZ
TPA Tampa International, FL
TPE Taipei-Chiang Kai Shek Intl, B
TPQ Tepic, XA
TPS Trapani, I
TRD Trondheim-Vaernes, LN
TRG Tauranga, ZK
TRN Turin-Caselle, I
TRS Trieste, I
TRW Tarawa, T3
TSA Taipei-Sung Shan, B
TSE Astana, UN
TSM Taos-Municipal, NM
TSN Tianjin, B
TSR Timisoara-Giarmata, YR
TSV Townsville, Qld
TTD Portland-Troutdale, OR
TTN Mercer-County, Trenton, NJ
TUL Tulsa International, OK
TUN Tunis-Carthage, TS
TUO Taupo, ZK
TUS Tucson International, AZ
TWB Toowomba, Qld
TWF Twin Falls, Joslin Field-Sun Valley Regional, ID
TXK Texarkana Municipal, AR
TXL Berlin-Tegel, D
TYA Tula, RA
TYF Torsby-Frylanda, SE
TYN Taiyuan-Wusu, B
TYS Knoxville-McGhee Tyson, TN
TYZ Taylor, AZ
TZA Belize-Municipal, V3

UAO Aurora-State, OR
UBS Columbus-Lowndes Co, MS
UCT Ukhta, RA
UES Waukesha, WI
UFA Ufa, RA
UIK Ust-Ilimsk, RA
UIO Quito-Mariscal Sucre, HC
UKK Ust-Kamenogorsk, UN
UKX Ust-Kut, RA
ULN Ulan Bator, JU
ULY Ulyanovsk, RA
UME Umea, SE
UNK Unalakleet Municipal, AK
UNU Juneau-Dodge Co, AK
UPG Ujang Pendang, PK
UPN Uruapan, XA
URA Uratsk, UN
URC Urumqi-Diwopou, B
URS Kursk, RA
UTN Upington, ZS
UTP Utapao, HS
UTT Umtata, ZS
UUA Bugulma, RA
UUD Ulan Ude-Mukhino, RA
UUS Yuzhno-Sakhalinsk, RA

VAI Vanimo, P2
VAR Varna International, LZ
VBS Brescia, I
VCE Venice-Marco Polo, I
VCP Sao Paulo-Viracopos, PP
VCT Victoria-Regional, TX
VCV Victorville, CA
VDM Viedma-Castello, LV
VDZ Valdez-Municipal, AK
VER Vera Cruz-Jara Intl, XA
VFA Victoria Falls, Z
VGD Vologda, RA
VGT Las Vegas-North, NV
VIE Vienna-Schwechat, OE
VIH Vichy-Rolla National, MO
VIR Durban-Virginia, ZS
VIS Visalia-Municipal, CA
VKO Moscow-Vnukovo, RA
VLC Valencia, EC
VLE Valle-J Robidoux , AZ
VLI Port Vila-Bauerfield, YJ
VLK Volgodonsk, RA
VLL Volladolid, EC
VLN Valencia International, YV
VLU Velikie Linki, RA
VNC Venice, FL
VNE Vannes-Meucon, F
VNO Vilnius International, LY
VNY Van Nuys, CA
VOG Volgograd-Gumrak, RA
VOZ Voronezh-Chertovtskye, RA
VPC Cartersville, GA
VQS Vieques, PR
VRN Verona-Villafranca, I
VSG Lugansk, UR
VTE Vientiane-Wattay, RDPL
VTG Vung Tau, VN
VVC Villavicencio-La Vanguardia, HK
VVI Santa Cruz-Viru Viru Intl, CP
VVO Vladivostock-Knevichi, RA

WAG Wanganui, ZK
WAT Waterford, EI
WAW Warsaw-Okecie, SP
WDH Windhoek-Hosea Kutako International, V5
WDR Winder-Barrow Co, GA
WFB Ketchikan Waterfront SPB, AK
WGA Wagga Wagga, NSW
WHO Franz Josef Glacier, ZK

WHP Los Angeles-Whiteman Field, CA
WIL Nairobi-Wilson, 5Y
WIR Wairoa, ZK
WKA Wanaka, ZK
WLG Wellington International, ZK
WMX Wamena, PK
WOE Woensdrecht, PH
WOW Willow, AK
WRO Wroclaw-Strachowice, SP
WST Westerly State, RI
WSY Airlie Beach-Whitsunday, Qld
WUH Wuhan, B
WVB Walvis Bay, V5
WVL Waterville-Lafleur, ME
WVN Wilhelmshaven-Mariensiel, D
WWA Wasilla, AK
WYA Whyalla, SA
WYN Wyndham, WA

XBE Bearskin Lake, ON
XCM Chatham, ON
XCR Vatry, F
XFW Hamburg-Finkenwerder, D
XIY Xi'an Xianyang, B
XLS Saint Louis, 6V
XLW Lemwerder, D
XMN Xiamen-Gaoqi, B
XPK Pukatawagan, MB
XSP Singapore-Seletar, 9V

YAG Fort Frances Municipal, QC
YAM Sault Ste Marie, ON
YAO Yaounde, TJ
YAW Halifax-Shearwater CFB, NS
YBC Baie Comeau, QC
YBL Campbell River, BC
YBW Calgary Springbank, AL
YBX Lourdes-de-Blanc Sablon, QC
YCA Courtenay, BC
YCB Cambridge Bay, NT
YCD Nanaimo-Cassidy, BC
YCE Centralia, ON
YCH Miramichi, NB
YCL Charlo, NB
YCN Cochrane-Lillabelle Lake, ON
YCR Cross Lake-Sinclair Memorial, MB
YCW Chilliwack, BC
YDF Deer Lake, NL
YDL Dease Lake, BC
YDQ Dawson Creek, BC
YDT Vancouver-Boundary Bay, BC
YDU Kasba Lake, NT
YEG Edmonton-International, AB
YEL Elliott Lake-Municipal, ON
YEV Inuvik-Mike Zubko, NT
YFB Iqaluit, NT
YFC Fredericton, NB
YFO Flin Flon, MB
YFS Fort Simpson, NT
YGG Ganges Harbour, AK
YGH Fort Good Hope, NT
YGL La Grande Riviere, QC
YGM Gimli, MB
YGR Iles de la Madelaine, QC
YGV Havre St Pierre, QC
YGX Gillam, MB
YHF Hearst, ON
YHM Hamilton, ON
YHN Homepayne, ON
YHR Chevery, QC
YHS Sechelt-Gibson, BC
YHT Haines Junction, YK
YHU Montreal-St Hubert, QC
YHY Hay River, NT
YHZ Halifax International, NS
YIB Atikokan Municipal, ON
YIP Detroit-Willow Run, MI
YJF Fort Liard, NT
YJN St Jean, QC
YKA Kamloops, BC
YKE Knee Lake, MB
YKF Kitchener-Waterloo, ON
YKL Schefferville, QC
YKS Yakutsk, RA
YKZ Toronto-Buttonville, ON
YLB Lac la Biche, AB
YLJ Meadow Lake, SK
YLL Lloydminster, AB
YLP Mingan, QC
YLQ La Tuque, QC
YLT Alert, NT
YLW Kelowna, BC
YMM Fort McMurray, AB
YMO Moosonee, ON
YMP Port McNeil, BC
YMT Chibougamau-Chapais, QC
YMX Montreal-Mirabel Intl, QC
YNA Natashquan, QC
YNC Wemindji, QC
YND Ottawa-Gatineau, QC
YNF Corner Brook, NL
YNR Arnes, MB
YOJ High Level/Footner Lake, AB
YOO Oshawa, ON
YOW Ottawa-McDonald Cartier International, QC
YPA Prince Albert, SK
YPB Port Alberni-Sproat Lake, BC
YPD Parry Sound, ON
YPE Peace River, AB
YPL Pickle Lake, ON
YPQ Peterborough
YPR Prince Rupert-Digby Island, BC
YPZ Burns Lake, BC
YQA Muskoka, ON
YQB Quebec-Jean Lesage Intl, QC
YQD The Pas, MB
YQF Red Deer, AB
YQH Watson Lake, YT
YQK Kenora, ON
YQN Nakina, ON
YQR Regina, SK
YQS St Thomas, ON
YQT Thunder Bay, ON
YQU Grande Prairie, AB
YQV Yorkton, SK
YQX Gander International, NL
YRB Resolute Bay, NT
YRJ Roberval, QC
YRL Red Lake, ON
YRO Ottawa-Rockcliffe, ON
YRP Carp, ON
YRT Rankin Inket, NU
YSB Sudbury, ON
YSE Squamish, BC
YSF Stony Rapids, SK
YSJ Saint John, NB
YSM Fort Smith, NT
YSN Salmon Arm, BC
YSQ Atlin-Spring Island, BC
YTA Pembroke, ON
YTF Alma, QC
YTH Thompson, MB
YTP Tofino SPB, BC
YTZ Toronto-City Centre, ON
YUL Montreal-Pierre Elliot Trudeau, QC
YUY Rouyn-Noranda, QC
YVA Moroni-Iconi, D6
YVC La Ronge, SK
YVG Vermillion Bay, AB
YVO Val d'Or/La Grando, QC
YVP Kuujjuaq, QC
YVQ Norman Wells, NT
YVR Vancouver International, BC
YVT Buffalo Narrows, SK
YVV Wiarton, ON
YWF Halifax-Waterfront Heliport, NS
YWG Winnipeg International, MB
YWH Victoria-Inner Harbour, BC
YWJ Deline, NT
YWK Wabush, NL
YWR White River, ON
YWS Whistler, BC
YXD Edmonton Municipal, AB
YXE Saskatoon-John D Diefenbacker, SK
YXH Medicine Hat, AB
YXJ Fort St John, BC
YXK Rimouski, QC
YXL Sioux Lookout, ON
YXS Prince George, BC
YXT Terrace, BC
YXU London, ON
YXX Abbotsford, BC
YXY Whitehorse, YT
YXZ Wawa-Hawk Junction, ON
YYB North Bay, ON
YYC Calgary-International, AB
YYD Smithers, BC
YYE Fort Nelson, BC
YYF Penticton, BC
YYG Charlottetown, PE
YYJ Victoria-International, BC
YYL Lynn Lake, MB
YYQ Churchill, MB
YYR Goose Bay, NL
YYT St Johns, NL
YYW Armstrong, ON
YYZ Toronto-Lester B Pearson International, ON
YZF Yellowknife, NT
YZH Slave Lake, AB
YZT Port Hardy, BC
YZU Whitecourt, AB
YZV Sept-Iles, QC
ZAG Zagreb-Pleso, 9A
ZAM Zamboanga Intl, RP
ZAZ Zaragoza, EC
ZFD Fond du Lac, SK
ZFM Fort McPherson, NT
ZIH Ixtapa-Zihuatenejo Intl, XA
ZJN Swan River, MB
ZNQ Ingolstadt, D
ZNZ Zanzibar-Kisuani, 5H
ZPB Sachigo Lake , ON
ZQN Queenstown-Frankston, NZ
ZQS Queen Charlotte, BC
ZRH Zurich-Kloten, HB
ZRJ Weagqmow-Round Lake, ON
ZSJ Sandy Lake, ON
ZSW Price Rupert-Seal Cove, BC
ZTH Zante-Zakinthos, SX
ZTR Zhitomyr, UR
ZUC Ignace, ON
ZUH Zhuhai-Jiuzhou, B

NATIONALITY INDEX

This index lists the world's current registration prefixes and is a guide to their location in the main part of this book.

5N-	Nigeria	589
LN-	Norway	237
A4O-	Oman	9
AP-	Pakistan	7
T8A	Palau	-
SU-Y	Palestine	483
HP-	Panama	210
P2-	Papua New Guinea	439
ZP-	Paraguay	571
OB-	Peru	399
RP-	Philippines	469
SP-	Poland	477
CS-	Portugal	112
A7-	Qatar	15
YR-	Romania	557
RA-	Russia	442
9XR-	Rwanda	618
VQ-H	St Helena	-
V4-	St Kitts Nevis	543
J6-	St Lucia	-
J8-	St Vincent & Grenadines	237
5W-	Samoa	594
T7-	San Marino	-
S9-	Sao Tome	488
HZ-	Saudi Arabia	215
6V-	Senegal	599
YU-	Serbia	559
S7-	Seychelles	487
9L-	Sierra Leone	606
9V-	Singapore	615
OM-	Slovak Republic	408
S5-	Slovenia	487
H4-	Solomon Islands	218
6O-	Somalia	599
ZS-	South Africa	572
EC-	Spain	136
4R-	Sri Lanka	583
ST-	Sudan	479
PZ-	Suriname	439
3D-	Swaziland	581
SE-	Sweden	472
HB-	Switzerland & Liechtenstein	195
YK-	Syria	556
EY-	Tajikistan	163
5H-	Tanzania	588
TT-	Tchad	500
HS-	Thailand	212
5V-	Togo	594
A3-	Tonga	9
9Y-	Trinidad & Tobago	618
TS-	Tunisia	499
TC-	Turkey	488
EZ-	Turkmenistan	164
VQ-T	Turks & Caicos Islands	535
T2-	Tuvalu	-
5X-	Uganda	594
UR-	Ukraine	506
A6-	United Arab Emirates	10
G-	United Kingdom	176
N	United States of America	247
CX-	Uruguay	116
UK-	Uzbekistan	501
YJ-	Vanuatu	555
YV-	Venezuela	560
VN-	Vietnam	532
7O-	Yemen	600
9J-	Zambia	605
Z-	Zimbabwe	565

OPERATOR INDEX

NOTES:

NOTES:

NOTES:

AIR-BRITAIN MEMBERSHIP
Join on-line at www.air-britain.co.uk

If you are not currently a member of Air-Britain, the publishers of this book, you may be interested in what we have on offer to provide for your interest in aviation.

About Air-Britain
Formed over 60 years ago, we are the world's most progressive aviation society, and exist to bring together aviation enthusiasts with every type of interest. Our members include aircraft historians, aviation writers, spotters and pilots - and those who just have a fascination with aircraft and aviation. Air-Britain is a non-profit organisation, which is independently audited, and any financial surpluses are used to provide services to the membership which currently stands at around 4,000 worldwide.

Membership of Air-Britain
Membership is open to all. A basic membership fee is charged and every member receives a copy of the quarterly house magazine, Air-Britain Aviation World, and is entitled to use all the Air-Britain specialist services and buy **Air-Britain publications at discounted prices**. A membership subscription includes the choice to add any or all of our other three magazines, News &/or Archive &/or Aeromilitaria. Air-Britain also publishes 10-20 books per annum (around 70 titles in stock at any one time). Membership runs January - December each year, but new members have a choice of options periods to get their initial subscription started.

Air-Britain Aviation World is the quarterly 48-page house magazine containing not only news of Air-Britain activities, but also a wealth of features, illustrated substantially in colour, on many different aviation subjects, contemporary and historical, contributed by our members. Now expanded to include Air-Britain Photo News.

Air-Britain News is the world aviation news monthly, containing data on aircraft registrations worldwide and news of Airlines and Airliners, Business Jets, Local Airfield News, Civil and Military Air Show Reports, and International Military Aviation News. An average 160 pages of illustrated information for the dedicated enthusiast.

Air-Britain Archive is the quarterly 48-page specialist journal of civil aviation history. Packed with the results of historical research by Air-Britain specialists into aircraft types, overseas registers and previously unpublished facts about the rich heritage of civil aviation. Averaging over 100 photographs per issue, some in colour.

Air-Britain Aeromilitaria is the quarterly 48-page unique source for meticulously researched details of military aviation history edited by the acclaimed authors of Air-Britain's military monographs featuring British, Commonwealth, European and U.S. Military aviation articles. Illustrated in colour and black & white.

Other Benefits
Additional to the above, members have exclusive access to the Air-Britain e-mail Information Exchange Service (ab-ix) where they can exchange information and solve each other's queries, and to an on-line UK airfield residents database. Other benefits include numerous Branches, use of the Specialists Information Service; Air-Britain trips; and access to black & white and colour photograph libraries. During the summer we also host our own popular FLY-IN. Each autumn, we host an Aircraft Recognition Contest.

Membership Subscription Rates - from £20 per annum.
Membership subscription rates start from as little as £20per annum (2010), and this amount provides a copy of 'Air-Britain Aviation World' quarterly as well as all the other benefits covered above. Subscriptions to include any or all of our other three magazines vary between £25 and £57 per annum (slightly higher to overseas).

Join in 2010 for two years (2010-2011) and save £5 off the total subscription

Join on-line at www.air-britain.co.uk or write to 'Air-Britain' at 1 Rose Cottages, 179 Penn Road, Hazlemere, High Wycombe, Bucks HP15 7NE, UK, or telephone/fax on 01394 450767 (+44 1394 450767) and ask for a membership pack containing the full details of subscription rates, samples of our magazines and a book list.

AIR-BRITAIN SALES

Companion publications to this AIRLINE FLEETS 2010 are also available by post-free mail order from:

Air-Britain Sales Department (Dept AF10)
41 Penshurst Road, Leigh,
Tonbridge, Kent TN11 8HL

Orders may also be placed by Answerphone/Fax 01732 835637 or by e-mail to
sales@air-britain.co.uk

For a full list of current titles and details of how to order, visit our e-commerce site at www.air-britain.co.uk Visa credit / Visa debit / Mastercard / Solo / Maestro accepted - please give full details of card number, expiry date and security code.

AIRLINE FLEETS QUICK REFERENCE - AFQR 2010

Contains 240 pages of airline fleet lists of all the major national and international carriers likely to be seen in Western Europe and in major airports world wide. The companion A5 size volume to Airline Fleets, AFQR includes types, c/ns, fleet numbers, lease data and easy-to-use tick boxes.

Price £8-95 (or £6-95 to Air-Britain members)

BUSINESS JETS & TURBOPROPS QUICK REFERENCE– BizQR 2010

Contains 160 A5-pages listing all currently active civil or military business jets and corporate airliners by country in registration/serial order. Now expanded to include Business Turboprops. Correct to January 7th 2010 and also includes US reserved registrations. *Price £8-95 (or £6-95 to Air-Britain members)*

UK/IRELAND CIVIL/MILITARY REGISTERS QUICK REFERENCE– UKQR 2010

Over 170 A5-size pages giving the regns and types of all current UK, Irish, Manx and foreign-registered aircraft based in the UK, serials and types of all current military aircraft, and lists of which aircraft are based at all of the major and many of the minor UK/Ireland civil airfields and microlight strips.

Price £8-95 (or £6-95 to Air-Britain members)

UK, IRELAND and IoM CIVIL REGISTERS 2010

The 46th annual edition of our longest-running title lists all current G-, M- and EI- allocations, plus overseas-registered aircraft based in the UK, alphabetical index by type, military-civil marks de-code, full BGA and microlight details, museum aircraft etc. At over 600 pages this is the UK civil aircraft register bible.

Publication scheduled for April/May 2010

BUSINESS JETS INTERNATIONAL 2010

The only publication that gives full production lists for all biz-jets in c/n order with details of all regns/serials carried, model numbers and fates, plus a 65,000+ index of biz-jet regns, now in its 25th edition at approaching 600 pages. *Publication scheduled for May/June 2010*

EUROPEAN REGISTERS HANDBOOK 2010

With a new dual media format and now in its 25th edition, ERH contains the current civil aircraft registers of all 45 European countries lying to the west of Russia except the UK. The c/ns and full previous identities are found on an illustrated CD which accompanies the A5 size handbook in Quick Reference style. Both formats include powered aircraft, balloons, gliders and microlights. *Publication scheduled for April 2010*

IMPORTANT NOTE - Members receive substantial discounts on prices of all the above Air-Britain publications, as shown, together with many other direct benefits. Remember to quote your Membership number when ordering.

For details of membership see previous page or visit our website at http://www.air-britain.co.uk